Chi

THE ROU

There are more than one hundred Rough Guide titles
covering destinations from Amsterdam to Zimbabwe

Forthcoming titles include
Jamaica • New Zealand • South Africa
Southwest USA

Rough Guide Reference Series
Classical Music • The Internet • Jazz • Opera • Rock Music • World Music

Rough Guide Phrasebooks
Czech • French • German • Greek • Hindi and Urdu • Indonesian • Italian •
Mandarin Chinese • Mexican Spanish • Polish • Portuguese • Russian •
Spanish • Thai • Turkish • Vietnamese

Rough Guides on the Internet
http://www.roughguides.com/
http://www.hotwired.com/rough

ROUGH GUIDE CREDITS

Text editor: Jo Mead
Series editor: Mark Ellingham
Editorial: Martin Dunford, Jonathan Buckley, Samantha Cook, Amanda Tomlin, Ann-Marie Shaw, Vivienne Heller, Paul Gray, Sarah Dallas, Chris Schüler, Helena Smith (UK); Andrew Rosenberg (US)
Production: Susanne Hillen, Andy Hilliard, Judy Pang, Link Hall, Nicola Williamson, Helen Ostick

Cartography: David Callier and Melissa Flack
Online Editors: Alan Spicer (UK); Andrew Rosenberg (US)
Finance: John Fisher, Celia Crowley, Catherine Gillespie
Marketing & Publicity: Richard Trillo, Simon Carloss, Niki Smith (UK); Jean-Marie Kelly, Jeff Kaye (US)
Administration: Tania Hummel, Mark Rogers

ACKNOWLEDGEMENTS

Special thanks to Lesley Reader, Stephen Jones, Daniel Viederman, Xiaosong Atiyah for Chinese translation, Carol Pucci for research on *Basics*, Carole Mansur for proofreading, MicroMap (Romsey, Hants), Sam Kirby and Mike Larby for additional cartography, Huw Molseed at Book Trust, Greg Ward for original Beijing and Shanghai material, Karen Sherman, Mike Sutton at Columbus Travel Insurance, SAS & Associates and PhotoOptix.

The authors would like to thank everyone at Rough Guides: Judy, Link, David, Melissa, Nicola, Andy, Susanne, and especially Jo. Additionally:

Jeremy: I would like to acknowledge the help of the following China-travellers, many of whom are owed far more than a mere mention: Jake Arnold, Brian Breslin, Gerry Burrows, Thomas Fransen, Diana Garrett, Laura Hussey, Inoue Kotaro, Anna Larsson, Louise Lim, Geoffrey O'Brian, Petra Vlasman and Micheline Tusenius. Nick, Caroline, Katie and Freddie Reynolds also deserve a big thank-you for treating me like family in Hong Kong. Finally, I would like to reserve special thanks for Que Songlian, Du Yuhua, Du Lianjie and Que Xiaomei who worked so hard to help me enjoy Shanghai for the magnificent place that it is.

David: For Peter and Shelagh Hardie for starting it all seventeen years ago; Narrell; Ferdinand Schiller; and my ol' buddy from Kalokol to Canada, Andrew Gordon. Thanks also to: Andy the Haggler; Brad and Nicole; Bundie, Mandalay and Myer; Daniel Qiang Hou and Olivia; Fabio and Simon; Fanny and Rambo; Hadji Ko Toe; Ian, Sam and Tom, co-founders of the Tiger Leaping Gorge Literary Society; Sharon Levner, Zif Bracha and Galya Levy; Loftur Vilhjalmsson; Lindsay Paul; Peng Wu, Peng Jiang and Cheng Huai Zheng; Peter and Brigitte; Stephen Poole; Jo Sielaff, Jack and Tom Li; Stan and Barbera; Xiao Luo.

Simon: In China, thanks to Wang Li, Wang Bin, Jing Wen, Lu Jin Ya and Sha Qian Fan for their friendship, help and inspiration. In London, respect to Al, Gags, Charles and Rosa.

The authors of the Rough Guide to China

After graduating from Oxford University, **Jeremy Atiyah** spent a number of years living abroad, writing and learning foreign languages, including Mandarin Chinese. His interest in China arose in 1989 when he met his future wife, who is Chinese, on the Trans-Siberian Express. He now lives in London where he works as Travel Editor for the *Independent on Sunday*.

David Leffman is an established Rough Guide author and inveterate traveller with a long history of visiting China. When not on the road he spends much of his time scuba-diving near his home in Queensland.

After working as a barman, teacher and life model in Hong Kong, **Simon Lewis** first visited China in 1993 where he began studying Mandarin Chinese. Now living in Brixton, he is a published short-story writer and is currently working on his first novel.

PUBLISHING INFORMATION

This first edition published March 1997 by Rough Guides Ltd, 1 Mercer St, London WC2H 9QJ.

Distributed by the Penguin Group:

Penguin Books Ltd, 27 Wrights Lane, London W8 5TZ
Penguin Books USA Inc., 375 Hudson Street, New York 10014, USA
Penguin Books Australia Ltd, 487 Maroondah Highway, PO Box 257, Ringwood, Victoria 3134, Australia
Penguin Books Canada Ltd, 10 Alcorn Avenue, Toronto, Ontario, Canada M4V 1E4
Penguin Books (NZ) Ltd, 182–190 Wairau Road, Auckland 10, New Zealand

Typeset in Linotron Univers and Century Old Style to an original design by Andrew Oliver.

Printed in England by Clays Ltd, St Ives PLC.

Illustrations in Part One & Part Three by Edward Briant; illustrations on p.1 and p.993 by Henry Iles.

China

THE ROUGH GUIDE

written and researched by

Jeremy Atiyah, David Leffman
and Simon Lewis

with additional contributions by

**Lesley Reader, Stephen Jones, Daniel A. Viederman,
Catharine Sanders, Chris Stewart and Rhonda Evans**

THE ROUGH GUIDES

TRAVEL GUIDES • PHRASEBOOKS • MUSIC AND REFERENCE GUIDES

 We set out to do something different when the first Rough Guide was published in 1982. Mark Ellingham, just out of university, was travelling in Greece. He brought along the popular guides of the day, but found they were all lacking in some way. They were either strong on ruins and museums but went on for pages without mentioning a beach or taverna. Or they were so conscious of the need to save money that they lost sight of Greece's cultural and historical significance. Also, none of the books told him anything about Greece's contemporary life – its politics, its culture, its people, and how they lived.

So with no job in prospect, Mark decided to write his own guidebook, one which aimed to provide practical information that was second to none, detailing the best beaches and the hottest clubs and restaurants, while also giving hard-hitting accounts of every sight, both famous and obscure, and providing up-to-the-minute information on contemporary culture. It was a guide that encouraged independent travellers to find the best of Greece, and was a great success, getting shortlisted for the Thomas Cook travel guide award,

and encouraging Mark, along with three friends, to expand the series.

The Rough Guide list grew rapidly and the letters flooded in, indicating a much broader readership than had been anticipated, but one which uniformly appreciated the Rough Guide mix of practical detail and humour, irreverence and enthusiasm. Things haven't changed. The same four friends who began the series are still the caretakers of the Rough Guide mission today: to provide the most reliable, up-to-date and entertaining information to independent-minded travellers of all ages, on all budgets.

We now publish 100 titles and have offices in London and New York. The travel guides are written and researched by a dedicated team of more than 100 authors, based in Britain, Europe, the USA and Australia. We have also created a unique series of phrasebooks to accompany the travel series, along with an acclaimed series of music guides, and a best-selling pocket guide to the Internet and World Wide Web. We also publish comprehensive travel information on our two web sites:

http://www.hotwired.com/rough
and http://www.roughguides.com/

HELP US UPDATE

We've gone to a lot of effort to ensure that this first edition of **The Rough Guide to China** is as up-to-date and accurate as possible. China is changing fast, however, and if you feel there are places we've under-rated or over-praised, or find we've missed something good or covered something which has now gone, then please write; suggestions, comments or corrections are much appreciated.

We'll credit all contributions, and send a copy of the next edition (or any other Rough Guide if you prefer) for the

best letters. Please mark letters: "Rough Guide China Update" and send to:

Rough Guides, 1 Mercer St, London WC2H 9QJ, or Rough Guides, 375 Hudson St, 9th floor, New York NY 10014.

Or send e-mail to: china@roughtravl.co.uk

Online updates about this book can be found on Rough Guides' website (see above for details)

CONTENTS

Introduction xii

• CHAPTER 7: THE YANGZI BASIN 430–495

• CHAPTER 8: FUJIAN, GUANGDONG AND HAINAN ISLAND 496–598

• CHAPTER 9: HONG KONG AND MACAU 599–657

• CHAPTER 10: GUANGXI AND GUIZHOU 658–711

• CHAPTER 11: YUNNAN 712–766

• CHAPTER 12: SICHUAN 767–821

PART THREE CONTEXTS 993

LIST OF MAPS

MAP SYMBOLS

– – –	Chapter division boundary	∴	Ruins
▬▪▬▪▬	International boundary	⌂	Cave
═══	Road	▬▬▬	Fortified wall
▬▬	Railway	▬•▬	Gate
▒▒▒	River	Ⓐ	Bus stop/station
⊥⊥⊥⊥	Canal	Ⓜ	Metro station
— —	Ferry route	✈	Airport
- - - -	Footpath	♦	Museum
🌟	Lighthouse	■	Building
�)(	Waterfall	♣	Temple or pagoda
▒▒▒	Parkland	⛩	Mosque
▲	Mountain peak	⊠	Post office
⌃⌃	Mountain range	⊞	Hospital
↘↙	Viewing point	◉	Accommodation
♦	Point of interest	▣	Restaurant

INTRODUCTION

China is not so much another country as another world. Cut off from the rest of Eurasia by the Himalayas to the south and the Siberian steppe to the north, it has grown up alone and aloof. The only foreigners it saw were visiting merchants from far-flung shores or uncivilized nomads from the wild steppe: peripheral, unimportant and unreal. Apart from a few ruling elites of Mongol and Manchu origin, who quickly became assimilated, China did not experience a significant influx of foreigners until the late nineteenth and early twentieth centuries, something which still colours the experience of today's visitors to China.

While empires, languages, nations and entire peoples in the rest of the world have risen and blossomed – then disappeared without trace – China has spent the past two millennia largely recycling itself. The ferocious dragons and lions of Chinese statuary have been produced by Chinese craftsmen, with the same essentially Chinese characteristics, for 25 centuries or more, and the script still used today reached perfection at the time of the Han dynasty, two thousand years ago. It is as though the Roman empire had survived intact into the twenty-first century, with a billion people speaking a language as old as classical Latin.

To say that the Chinese are presently enjoying better government than at any time in their recent history may not be saying much, but it is surely true. There is little sign of the Communist Party relinquishing power, or its control over the media. However, the negative stories surrounding today's China, the oppression of dissidents, the harsh treatment of criminal suspects and the imperialist behaviour towards Tibet and other minority regions, are only one part of the picture. Away from politics, the country is undergoing a huge commercial and creative upheaval. A country the size of ten Japans has entered the world market: Hong Kong-style skylines are being constructed in cities all across China, and tens of millions of people are finding jobs that earn them a spending power they have never known. The colossal historic fact of Hong Kong and Macau, the last European colonies, being returned to China in time for the new millennium, as though by celestial injunction, only adds to the sense that Chinese destiny is being restored to its rightful place at the centre of the world.

The sheer pace of change is visible in every part of Chinese life, from the economy to the still-young independent travel industry. Travellers who visited China as little as ten years ago are amazed to hear how much the place has opened up and how many more liberal trends have emerged in the wake of Deng Xiaoping's free market economics. For whatever reasons you are attracted to China – its history, art, culture, politics or simply its inaccessibility – the speed at which things are changing will ensure that your trip is a unique one.

The first thing that strikes visitors to China is the extraordinary density of population: central and eastern China do not have landscapes so much as peoplescapes. In the fertile plains, villages seem to merge into one another, while the big cities are endlessly sprawling affairs with the majority of their inhabitants living in cramped shacks or in depressingly uniform dormitory buildings. This doesn't mean that China is the same everywhere – there are many regional variations in people and language; indeed, some whole areas of the People's Republic are not populated by the "Chinese", but by so-called minority peoples, of whom there are more than two hundred distinct groups, ranging from the hill tribes of the south to the Muslims of the northwest. Nevertheless, the most enduring images of China are intrinsically Chinese ones: chopsticks, tea, slippers, massed bicycles, shadow-boxing, exotic pop music, karaoke, teeming crowds, Dickensian train stations, smoky temples, red flags and the smells of soot and frying tofu – as well as the industrial vistas you would expect from one of the world's largest economies. Away from the cities, there is the sheer joy of crossing such a vast and ancient land – from the green paddy fields and misty hilltops of the south, to the mountains of Tibet, to the scorched, epic landscapes of the old Silk Road in the northwest. And the Chinese, despite a reputation for rudeness, are generally hospitable and friendly, though in the more out-of-the-way places travellers are still considered something of an oddity.

However, it would be wrong to pretend that it is an entirely easy matter to penetrate modern China. Borders are open, visas are readily distributed and the airports are teeming with foreigners, but the standard tourist "sights" – the Great Wall, the Forbidden City, the Terracotta Army – are relatively few considering the size of the country. Indeed, historic architecture is scant to say the least, and Chinese towns and cities lack that sense of history so palpable in the great cities of Europe or the Middle East. The Communists, like all dynasties before them, simply destroyed earlier showpieces. On top of this are the frustrations of travelling in a land where few people speak English and where foreigners are regularly viewed as exotic objects of intense curiosity, or fodder for overcharging.

When planning a journey through China, bear in mind that your trip is bound to involve an element of stress and hard work. If you have lots of cities on your itinerary, try to fit in some small towns as well, which tend to be cheaper as well as more relaxing. Don't stick exclusively to the famous places and sights; often your most interesting experiences will arise in places which least expect tourists. Above all, if it's your first visit, try not to be in too much of a hurry; take your time and be selective. If your budget is tight, think about staying in just a few places and getting to know them rather than undertaking lots of expensive and exhausting journeys. Even if money is less of a problem, you might do well to forego too much travel and opt instead for higher quality restaurants and hotels. Given the inevitable frustrations of making arrangements, flexibility is essential whatever your budget.

Where to go

Inevitably, **Beijing** is on everyone's itinerary, and the Great Wall and the splendour of the Imperial City are certainly not to be missed. It's a city that's easy to be in, and enjoy, but with skyscrapers aplenty, a large foreign contingent and a wealthy and chic population, Beijing is hardly representative of the nation as a whole. You need to dig under the surface to find the more intimate, private city that exists in the twisted alleyways, the *hutongs*, to get the best out of the place which can otherwise seem vast, soulless and functional. While you're here, don't forget that Beijing offers the best food, and some of the only nightlife, in the country. It's also a good place to base yourself for a host of easy short trips. **Chengde**, just north of the capital, has some stunning imperial buildings, constructed by emperors when this was their favoured retreat for the summer, while today's city residents escape to the quiet coastal towns of **Shanhaiguan** and **Beidaihe**, which offer lush countryside, grand old fortresses and a welter of seaside kitsch.

The territory north of the Great Wall has always had a reputation for bleakness, but among the monotonous expanses and grey cityscapes of **Dongbei** (Manchuria), a few places stand out, either for their wildlife and rugged countryside, such as **Changbai Shan** in Jilin Province, or for their flavour of neighbouring foreign cultures, such as **Harbin**, capital of Heilongjiang Province, where Russian influence is visible in the skyline of onion domes and the local's taste for vodka and ice cream.

Most visitors head for the greater attractions south of the capital, along the **Yellow River Valley**, the cradle of Chinese civilization, where remnants of the dynastic age lie scattered in a unique landscape of sculptured loess terraces. The cave temples at **Datong** and **Luoyang**, are magnificent, with huge Buddhist sculptures staring out impassively across their now industrialized settings. Of the dynastic capitals, **Xi'an** is the most obvious destination, where the celebrated Terracotta Army still stands guard over the tomb of Emperor Qin Shi Huang. Other, less visited ancient towns, including sleepy **Kaifeng** in Henan, and **Qufu**, the birthplace of Confucius in Shandong, hold treasures of dynastic architecture as well as offering an intimate, human scale that is missing in the large cities. The area is also well supplied with holy mountains, some of the few places in twentieth-century China that provide an unbroken continuity with the past: grandmothers still shuffle their way up **Tai Shan**, perhaps the grandest and most imperial of the country's pilgrimage sites, to pay homage to deities as old as Chinese civilization itself; **Song Shan** in Henan sees more contemporary pilgrims, followers of kung fu, making the trek to the Shaolin Temple, where the art originated; while the inaccessibility of **Wutai Shan** in Shanxi rewards travellers with some of the best preserved religious sites in the country, as well as a lush and pretty alpine setting.

Central China forms a basin around the middle reaches of Asia's longest river, the **Yangzi**. Once the interior's single most important transport artery, several thousand kilometres are still plied by regular passenger ferries, providing one of the world's great river journeys past countless images of everyday Chinese life. Meandering upstream through the provinces of Anhui, Hubei, Hunan and Jiangxi, the shores of the two massive freshwater lakes **Poyang** and **Dongting** are heavily farmed, while a host of bustling riverside ports, including **Wuhan**, modern metropolis and former European concession, thrive on an increasing industrial and manufacturing momentum. Relics of the past range from two-thousand-year-old tombs and third-century battlefields to the Hunanese village of **Shaoshan**, Mao Zedong's birthplace. Away from the river lurk some evocative landscapes: the classically "Chinese" cloud-and-pine draped peaks of **Huang Shan** in Anhui; Hubei's **Wudang Shan**, covered in aged, esoteric Taoist temples; and the splintered cliffs and forested wilds of western Hunan's **Wulingyuan Scenic Reserve**.

Dominating China's east coast is the great port city of **Shanghai**, for years the country's main gateway to the outside world and, apart from Hong Kong, its most Westernized city. After years of stagnation Shanghai is now booming again and alongside the granite monuments of the old European-built Bund, a modern city is arising. Around Shanghai are areas offering some of China's most characteristic scenery – low-lying and wet, criss-crossed with canals and dotted with historic towns. Jiangsu Province, to the north, is home to **Suzhou** with its famous ornate gardens, while a short way to the east lies the city of **Nanjing**, crowded with relics from its tumultuous history as former capital of China. South from Shanghai, in Zhejiang Province at the terminus of the historic Grand Canal, is **Hangzhou**, one of China's greenest and most scenic cities, and a delightful place for walking in the hills around the lake, Xi Hu. Off the coast, an overnight journey by boat from Shanghai, the Buddhist island of **Putuo Shan** is rarely visited by foreign tourists, but superbly attractive, with beaches, rural walks and monasteries.

In China's southeast, comprising the coastal provinces of Fujian and Guangdong, as well as Hainan Island, you'll find all the paradoxes of any rapidly industrializing nation: incredible economic success in go-ahead Special Economic Zone cities such as Guangdong's Zhuhai and Shenzhen, back to back with chronic poverty throughout the region's rural population; and a lust for modernity and Westernization, refuted by staunch conservatism. Only a short hop from Hong Kong, the chaotic city of **Guangzhou** (Canton) and the adjacent industrial sprawl of the **Pearl River Delta** have it all to the point of absurdity: skyscrapers and temples, beggars and businessmen, nightclubs and traditional opera, fast food and the finest in classical Chinese cuisine. Guangzhou also shares a fair scattering of European architecture with other cities across the region – the Fujian island port of **Xiamen** is the nicest – built by colonial victors after the nineteenth-century Opium Wars. Elsewhere, towns such as **Chaozhou** proudly retain their traditions, seemingly little disturbed by recent history, while the Guangdong–Fujian border is home to ethnic Hakka, who live as they have done for centuries in massive fortified stone apartments. Hainan at first glance seems to have no heritage at all, just a very nice beach, but there's a little more depth to the place if you dig hard enough – most rewarding is a visit to the Li villages in the island's central highlands.

Even when the waiting is over, **Hong Kong** after the 1997 handover promises to remain one of the most talked-about places in the world. Simultaneously China's most modern city and its most conservative, there is nothing Hong Kong cannot offer in the way of tourist facilities, from fine beaches, to colonial remains to stunning cityscapes. It also contains more international food and nightlife than the rest of China put together. Watching how things pan out after the handover is likely to be one of the highlights of any China visit for some time to come. **Macau**, too, is well worth a visit, if not for its casinos then for its Baroque churches and fine Portuguese cuisine.

Aside from major tourist attractions, much of southwestern China is only just beginning to be probed by visitors, though Sichuan's **Chengdu** and Yunnan's **Kunming** remain two of China's most interesting and easy-going provincial capitals, and the entire region is, by any standards, exceptionally diverse. Guangxi and Guizhou provinces are known for their dramatic limestone scenery, the most famous of which surrounds the Li River near **Guilin** in Guangxi, while over in **Sichuan**, pilgrims flock to see the colossal Big Buddha carved into a cliffside at **Leshan**, and to ascend the holy mountain of **Emei Shan**. Yunnan, meanwhile, sets the tone for the whole area, with landscapes encompassing everything from snowbound summits and alpine lakes to steamy tropical jungles. Sichuan has a similar variety, while the damp highlands shared by Guizhou and Guangxi descend south to a hot coastline. As Yunnan and Guangxi share borders with Vietnam, Laos, and Burma, while Sichuan rubs up against Tibet, it's also not surprising to find that all four provinces have very independent histories, and are home to near-extinct wildlife and dozens of ethnic autonomous regions, whose attractions range from the fairy-tale Naxi town of **Lijiang** and Dai villages of **Xishuangbanna** in Yunnan, to the exuberant festivals and textiles of Guizhou's Miao and wooden architecture of Dong settlements in Guangxi's north.

The huge area of China referred to as the Northwest is where the people thin out and real wilderness begins. Inner Mongolia, just hours from Beijing, is already at the frontiers of Central Asia; here you can follow in the footsteps of Genghis Khan by horse-riding on the endless grasslands of the steppe. Otherwise, following the Yellow River east, the old **Silk Road** heads west out of Xi'an and you can follow it right through China and out through its western borders. Highlights en route start with the fabulous Buddhist sculptures at **Maiji Shan** and **Bingling Si** just outside **Lanzhou**, while south from Lanzhou lies the delightful rural retreat and Buddhist monastery town of **Xiahe**. Further to the west, in the northwestern part of Gansu, you'll find the terminus of the Great Wall of China, the famous last fort of **Jiayuguan**, and nearby, one of the major draws of all China, the fabulous Buddhist cave art in the sandy deserts of **Dunhuang**.

West of here lie the mountains and deserts of vast Xinjiang, where China blends into old Turkestan and where simple journeys between towns are epics of modern bus travel. The oasis cities of **Turpan** and remote **Kashgar**, with their donkey carts and bazaars, are the main attractions, though the blue waters of Tian Chi, offering alpine scenery in the midst of searing desert, are deservedly popular. Beyond Kashgar, travellers face some of the most adventurous routes of all, over the Karakoram or Torugut passes to Pakistan and Kirgyzistan respectively. **Tibet**, now open to independent travellers, still sounds the most exotic of all travel possibilities – and so in some ways it is, especially if you come across the border from Nepal or brave the long road in from Golmud in Qinghai Province.

When to go

China's **climate** is too varied for any but the vaguest generalizations: summers in most parts of the country are extremely hot and humid, which can make travel even harder work than usual, and winters are generally bitterly cold.

The **south**, however, is subtropical, with wet, humid summers (April to September), when temperatures can approach 40°C and a typhoon season on the southeast coast between July and September. Though it is often still hot enough to swim in the sea in December, the short winters, from January to March, can be surprisingly chilly.

Central China, around the Yangzi River, has brief, cold winters, with temperatures dipping below zero, and long, hot summers. Rainfall here is high all year round. Further north, the Yellow River basin marks a rough boundary in Chinese heating habits, with central heating fitted as standard in buildings north of here, helping to make northern China's harsh winters a little more tolerable. Winter temperatures in **Beijing** rarely rise above zero from December to March, and freezing winds off the Mongolian plains add a vicious windchill factor. In summer, however, temperatures can be well over 30°C. In the **far north**, Inner Mongolia and Manchuria, winters are at least clear and dry, but temperatures remain way below zero, while summers can be uncomfortably warm. The **Northwest** gets fiercely hot in summer, but without the humidity of the rest of the country, and winters are as bitter as anywhere else in northern China. **Tibet** is ideal in mid-summer, when its mountain plateaux are pleasantly warm and dry. June to September are the wettest months with winter temperatures in Lhasa frequently falling below freezing.

Overall, the best time to visit China is **spring** or **autumn** when the weather is at its most temperate: in the spring it's best to start in the south and work north or west as summer approaches; in the autumn, start in the north and work south. If you can brave the cold, winters are considerably enlivened by the preparations for Chinese New Year; but during New Year itself, travelling can be extremely difficult as offices close and much of the population is on the move.

CLIMATE CHART

Average daily temperatures (°C, max and min) and monthly rainfall (mm)

	Jan	Feb	Mar	Apr	May	June	July	Aug	Sept	Oct	Nov	Dec
Beijing												
max °C	1	4	11	21	27	31	31	30	26	20	9	3
min °C	-10	-8	-1	7	13	18	21	20	14	6	-2	-8
rainfall mm	4	5	8	17	35	78	243	141	58	16	11	3
Chongqing												
max °C	9	13	18	23	27	29	34	35	28	22	16	13
min °C	5	7	11	16	19	22	24	25	22	16	12	8
rainfall mm	15	20	38	99	142	180	142	122	150	112	48	20
Guilin												
max °C	16	17	20	25	29	31	32	32	31	27	23	19
min °C	8	10	14	19	23	25	26	26	24	19	15	12
rainfall mm	33	56	97	160	206	193	160	178	84	43	38	37
Hong Kong												
max °C	18	17	19	24	28	29	31	31	29	27	23	20
min °C	13	13	16	19	23	26	26	26	25	23	18	15
rainfall mm	33	46	74	137	292	394	381	367	257	114	43	31
Jilin												
max °C	-6	-2	6	16	23	29	31	29	24	16	5	-4
min °C	-18	-14	-6	3	10	16	21	19	11	3	-6	-15
rainfall mm	8	8	18	28	69	84	183	170	64	36	28	15
Kunming												
max °C	20	22	25	28	29	29	28	28	28	24	22	20
min °C	8	9	12	16	18	19	19	19	18	15	12	8
rainfall mm	8	18	28	41	127	132	196	198	97	51	56	15
Lhasa												
max °C	7	9	12	16	19	24	23	22	21	17	13	9
min °C	-10	-7	-2	1	5	9	9	9	7	1	-5	-9
rainfall mm	0	13	8	5	25	64	122	89	66	13	3	0
Shanghai												
max °C	8	8	13	19	25	28	32	32	28	23	17	12
min °C	1	1	4	10	15	19	23	23	19	14	7	2
rainfall mm	48	58	84	94	94	180	147	142	130	71	51	36
Ürümqi												
max °C	-11	-8	-1	16	22	26	28	27	21	10	-1	-8
min °C	-22	-19	-11	2	8	12	14	13	8	-1	-11	-13
rainfall mm	15	8	13	38	28	38	18	25	15	43	41	10
Wuhan												
max °C	8	9	14	21	26	31	34	34	29	23	17	11
min °C	1	2	6	13	18	23	26	26	21	16	9	3
rainfall mm	46	48	97	152	165	244	180	97	71	81	48	28

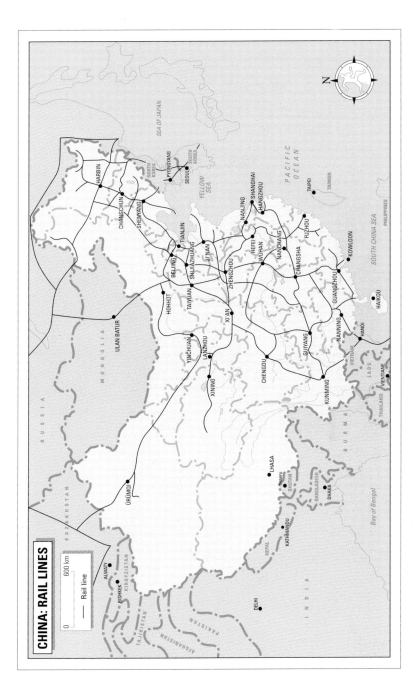

CHINA: RAIL LINES

0	600 km

—— Rail line

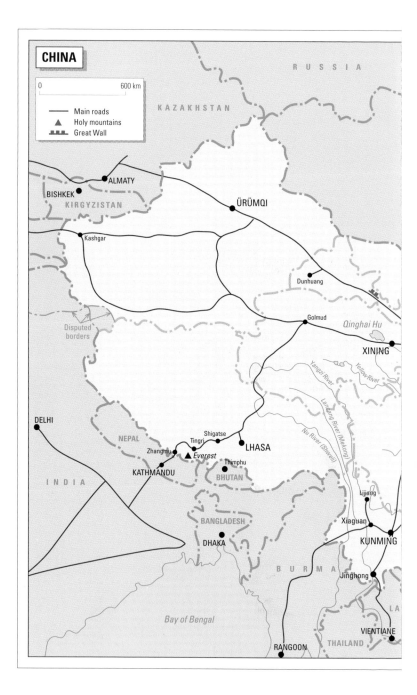

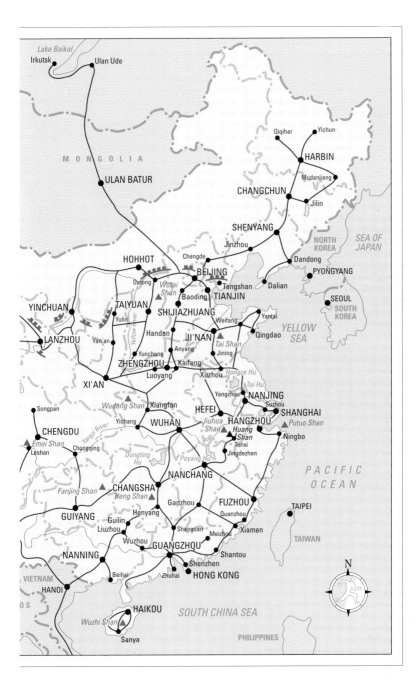

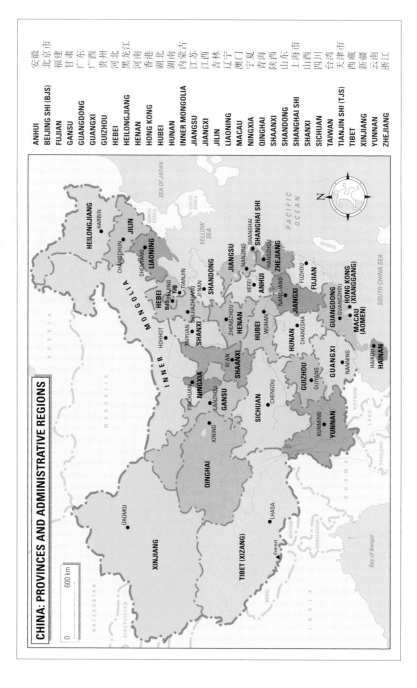

CHINA: PROVINCES AND ADMINISTRATIVE REGIONS

ANHUI	安徽
BEIJING SHI (BJS)	北京市
FUJIAN	福建
GANSU	甘肃
GUANGDONG	广东
GUANGXI	广西
GUIZHOU	贵州
HEBEI	河北
HEILONGJIANG	黑龙江
HENAN	河南
HONG KONG	香港
HUBEI	湖北
HUNAN	湖南
INNER MONGOLIA	内蒙古
JIANGSU	江苏
JIANGXI	江西
JILIN	吉林
LIAONING	辽宁
MACAU	澳门
NINGXIA	宁夏
QINGHAI	青海
SHAANXI	陕西
SHANDONG	山东
SHANGHAI SHI	上海市
SHANXI	山西
SICHUAN	四川
TAIWAN	台湾
TIANJIN SHI (TJS)	天津市
TIBET	西藏
XINJIANG	新疆
YUNNAN	云南
ZHEJIANG	浙江

PART ONE

THE

BASICS

GETTING THERE FROM BRITAIN AND IRELAND

China has several international air gateways, the most important being Beijing and Hong Kong. At least four airlines fly from London non-stop into these two cities, and to Hong Kong alone there are three or four flights daily. Additionally a whole host of other airlines offer indirect services requiring a change of plane en route. Although no other Chinese cities are served directly from the UK, it is possible to reach Shanghai, Macau, Guangzhou, Xiamen and Urumqi by air via other European or Asian cities. The non-stop flying time from London to Beijing is just ten hours, and twelve to Hong Kong.

One of *Cathay Pacific*'s daily flights to Hong Kong originates in Manchester. Otherwise, if you are using a European airline, you should be able to fly direct into the European hub from the major regional airports rather than trekking down to London first. From Ireland, there are no direct connections to China and you will need to stop over in Europe en route. For the cheapest deal this will probably involve coming to England to pick up a flight.

For details of travelling overland to China, see pp.6 and 13–15.

BUYING A TICKET

For the best **fares** you are generally advised to contact a **flight agent** first. See the box on p.5 for a list of recommended agents or check the ads in the national weekend papers, London's *Evening Standard* newspaper, *Time Out* magazine or major regional newspapers and listings magazines.

Many of the cheapest agents also advertise on the pages of Ceefax and Teletext. As a standard safety precaution, check to see whether your agent belongs to *ABTA* or *IATA*, as these will cover the cost of your refund if your agency goes bust before you get your ticket. Some agents, such as *Campus* and *STA*, specialize in discounts for **students and under-26s**, though on long-haul flights such as those to China you'll often find that the cheap fares are available to all, but that students and people under-26 benefit from fewer restrictions on their tickets.

Restrictions are a routine feature of any discounted ticket bought from a flight agent. These usually include no refund if you change your mind after buying the ticket, and you often also have to pay extra for changing the date of your flight – sometimes as much as US$100 in the case of Beijing flights. Your ticket will be of restricted duration, usually three months maximum, sometimes less. Check these restrictions carefully when looking at price quotes.

The lowest available **fares** to Beijing from London quoted by flight agents start from around £400 in low season, up to £600 in high season; to Hong Kong the range is about £450–700. You won't necessarily need a flight agent to get these fares, though – sometimes it is worth **approaching the airlines direct**. Unfancied airlines such as *Air China* and *Aeroflot* themselves offer prices which very nearly match the flight agents', and *Aeroflot*'s £440 one-year open ticket on its Shanghai flight is by far the cheapest way from Europe direct into Shanghai. Even the more upmarket airlines such as *British Airways* can be worth approaching to see if they are running any special offers or promotions – if you catch them at the right time you can enjoy the luxury of a non-stop flight at a budget price.

Airlines flying into **Hong Kong** all tend to observe the same seasons for the purpose of pricing. **Peak season** is the fortnight before Christmas, the fortnight before Chinese New Year and the whole summer, from mid-June to mid-September. **Low season** is the months of February (after Chinese New Year), May and November. To **Beijing** the peak season is summer time, though this is less predictably followed by the various airlines and seasonality does not make such a difference to price.

STOPOVERS, OPEN JAWS AND ROUND-THE-WORLD TICKETS

If you have time in hand, you might prefer to break your journey and **stop over** in one or more places on the way to China. Popular stopovers include the desert sheikhdoms of Bahrain and Dubai (with *Gulf Air* or *Emirates* respectively), Bombay or Delhi with *Air India*, Bangkok with *Thai International* and Singapore with *Singapore Airlines*. Many of the larger airlines, such as *Thai International* or *Singapore Airlines*, do not charge extra for stopover options, while others just levy a nominal fee.

Another option, considering the large distances within China, is to buy an **open-jaw ticket** which lets you fly into one city and out of another, covering the journey in between by land – for example, Hong Kong and Beijing. Most European and Southeast Asian airlines permit this, though the price you pay will be equivalent to the return price from the more expensive of the two destinations. The very cheapest discounted tickets, such as with *Aeroflot* and *Air China*, do not include such flexibilities and you'll end up paying the combined price of two single tickets,

---

AIRLINES

Aeroflot, 70 Piccadilly, London W1 (☎0171/355 2233). *Four times weekly to Beijing and once to Shanghai, all via Moscow. Can also book a weekly (expensive) connection from Moscow to Urumqi on Xinjiang Airlines.*

Air China, 41 Grosvenor Gardens, London SW1 (☎0171/630 0919, fax 630 7792). *Non-stop flights to Beijing twice weekly, with onward connections throughout China. Worth approaching direct as its prices are very low by international standards.*

Air France, 177 Piccadilly, London W1 (☎0181/742 6600). *Four times weekly to Beijing and daily to Hong Kong, via Paris.*

Alitalia, 27–28 Piccadilly, London W1 (☎0171/602 7111). *Twice weekly to Beijing and three times to Hong Kong, via Rome.*

British Airways, 156 Regent St, London W1; 146 New St, Birmingham B2; 19–21 St Mary's Gate, Market St, Manchester M1; 64 Gordon St, Glasgow G1; 32 Frederick St, Edinburgh EH2; all enquiries ☎0345/222747. *Daily non-stop to Hong Kong and twice weekly to Beijing. Off-season has some great offers, particularly on the Beijing route.*

Cathay Pacific, 52 Berkeley St, London W1 (☎0171/747 8888). *At least one direct flight daily to Hong Kong, and through its sister airline, Dragon Air, is linked to a dozen or more cities on the Chinese mainland.*

Emirates, Gloucester Park, 95 Cromwell Rd, London SW7 (☎0171/808 0033). *Daily flights to Hong Kong via Dubai. This excellent airline has some very interesting prices off-season and is worth contacting direct.*

Finnair, 14 Clifford St, London W1 (☎0171/408 1222). *Twice weekly to Beijing via Helsinki.*

Gulf Air, 10 Albemarle St, London W1 (☎0171/408 1717). *Daily flights to Hong Kong via Bahrain.*

KLM, 8 Hanover St, London W1 (☎0181/750 9000). *Twice weekly to Beijing and five times weekly to Hong Kong, via Amsterdam.*

Lufthansa, 10 Old Bond St, London W1 (☎0345/737747). *Six times weekly to Beijing, three times weekly to Shanghai and daily to Hong Kong, all via Frankfurt. The flights to Shanghai are among the very few direct from Europe.*

PIA, 45–46 Piccadilly London W1 (☎0171/7345544). *A weekly flight to Beijing via Karachi; requires an overnight stop.*

Sabena, 10 Putney Hill, London SW15 (☎0181/780 1444). *New twice-weekly flights to Macau via Brussels.*

Singapore Airlines, 143–147 Regent St, London W1 (☎0181/747 0007). *Daily flights to Beijing, Shanghai, Guangzhou, Xiamen, Hong Kong and Macau, via Singapore. A classy airline, though the route via Singapore is circuitous.*

Swissair, Swiss Centre, 1 Swiss Court, London W1 (☎0171/434 7300). *Three times weekly to Beijing and Shanghai, five times weekly to Hong Kong.*

Thai International, 41 Albemarle St, London W1 (☎0171/499 9113). *Offers a whole range of gateways to China, including Beijing, Shanghai, Hong Kong, Guangzhou and Macau, with stopovers in Bangkok.*

Uzbeki Airlines, 69 Wigmore St, London W1 (☎0171/935 4775). *Weekly connections to Beijing. Compulsory stopover in Tashkent.*

Virgin Atlantic, 14–16 Oxford St, London W1 (☎01293/747747). *Daily non-stop flights to Hong Kong. Prices slightly cheaper than British Airways or Cathay Pacific for the same or better service.*

London–Hong Kong and Beijing–London, which will come to £500–600 in low season.

A better-value option are the **Round-The-World** or **Round-Asia** tickets offered by some flight agents, which allow all kinds of stopover combinations, usually including Hong Kong. Typically, a London–Bangkok–Manila–Hong Kong–London ticket will cost less than £700. Even a Round-The-World ticket incorporating stopovers in Australia and the USA should come in well under £1000. If you have a particular list of stopovers in mind, it's well worth calling the larger flight agents for a quote.

ORGANIZED TOURS

If your time is limited, you can't face the hassles of travelling on your own, or if you have a specialist interest such as cycling or bird-watching, then an **organized tour** of China, with flights, transport and accommodation included, might be worth considering. UK-based tour operators fall into two categories: those which offer a fully cosseted holiday and talk about the "romance" of China, and those which concern themselves with the "real" China – at the earthiest end of the market, these involve rugged overland trips in spe-

FLIGHT AGENTS

Campus Travel, 52 Grosvenor Gardens, London SW1 (☎0171/730 8111); 541 Bristol Rd, Selly Oak, Birmingham B29 (☎0121/414 1848); 61 Ditchling Rd, Brighton BN1 (☎01273/570226); 39 Queen's Rd, Clifton, Bristol BS8 (☎0117/929 2494); 5 Emmanuel St, Cambridge CB1 (☎01223/324283); 53 Forest Rd, Edinburgh EH1 (☎0131/668 3303); 166 Deansgate, Manchester M3 (☎0161/833 2046); 105–106 St Aldates, Oxford OX1 (☎01865/242067). *Student/youth travel specialists and general budget agent for all ages, with branches also in YHA shops and on university campuses all over Britain.*

Council Travel, 28a Poland St, London W1 (☎0171/437 7767). *Flight agent offering student discounts.*

Inflight Travel, 92–94 York Rd, Belfast 15 (☎01232/740187 or 743341). *Long-haul flight specialist.*

IMS Travel, 21 Woodstock St, London W1 (☎0171/409 7774). *As appointed agents for Aeroflot, can issue some of the cheapest China tickets.*

Joe Walsh Tours, 8–11 Baggot St, Dublin (☎01/676 3053). *General budget fares agent.*

Nouvelles Frontières, 11 Blenheim St, London W1 (☎0171/629 7772). *As the appointed agent for Tarom (Romanian Airlines), can book cheap Beijing flights of limited availability.*

North South Travel, Moulsham Mill Centre, Parkway, Chelmsford, Essex CM2 (☎01245/492882). *Friendly, competitive travel agency, offering discounted fares worldwide – profits are used to support projects in the developing world, especially the promotion of sustainable tourism.*

STA Travel, 86 Old Brompton Rd, London SW7, 117 Euston Rd, London NW1 & 38 Store St London WC1 (☎0171/ 361 6262); 25 Queens Rd, Bristol BS8 1QE (☎0117/929 4399); 38 Sidney St, Cambridge CB2 3HX (☎01223/366966); 75 Deansgate, Manchester M3 (☎0161/834 0668); 88 Vicar Lane, Leeds LS1 (☎0113/244 9212); 36 George St, Oxford OX1 (☎01865/792800); and branches in Birmingham, Canterbury, Cardiff, Coventry, Durham, Glasgow, Loughborough, Nottingham, Warwick and Sheffield. *Worldwide specialists in low-cost flights and tours for students and under-26s; also general budget fares for all ages.*

Trailfinders, 42–50 Earls Court Rd, London W8 (☎0171/938 3366); 194 Kensington High St, London, W8 (☎0171/938 3939); 58 Deansgate, Manchester M3 (☎0161/839 6969); 254–284 Sauchiehall St, Glasgow G2 (☎0141/353 2224); 22–24 The Priory, Queensway, Birmingham B4 6BS (☎0121/236 1234); 48 Corn St, Bristol BS1 (☎0117/929 9000). *One of the best-informed and most efficient agents.*

Travel Bug, 597 Cheetham Hill Rd, Manchester M8 (☎0161/721 4000). *Large range of discounted tickets.*

Union Travel, 93 Piccadilly, London W1 (☎0171/493 4343). *Competitive airfares.*

USIT, Fountain Centre, Belfast BT1 (☎01232/324073); 10–11 Market Parade, Patrick St, Cork (☎021/270900); 33 Ferryquay St, Derry (☎01504/371888); Aston Quay, Dublin 2 (☎01/679 8833); Victoria Place, Eyre Square, Galway (☎091/565177); Central Buildings, O'Connell St, Limerick (☎061/415064); 36–37 Georges St, Waterford (☎051/72601). *Student and youth flight specialists.*

SPECIALIST TOUR OPERATORS

Asiaworld Travel ☎01932/211300. *Offers two-week "essential China" tours – Beijing, Xi'an, Guilin and Hong Kong – in conditions of considerable comfort.*

China Travel Service (CTS) ☎0171/836 9911, fax 836 3121. *An extensive range of tours including very cheap off-season hotel-and-flight packages to Beijing. This China-based operator also has offices in Hong Kong and many Chinese cities; see The Guide for addresses.*

Earthwatch ☎01865/311600. *Not a tour operator but an organization which runs environmental projects overseas. Members of the public can volunteer to join a project, paying their own transport and contributing funds. A ten-day project helping monkeys in Guangxi Province, for example, requires about £1000 to participate.*

Exodus Expeditions ☎0181/675 5550. *Offers some interesting and unusual overland itineraries in the wilds of Tibet and the Northwest. Good-value three-week tours from £1700 including flights.*

Explore Worldwide ☎01252/319448. *Three-week tours of China and her neighbours, including tours originating in Central Asia and Mongolia, as well as a Silk Road epic for under £2000.*

Imaginative Traveller ☎0181/742 8612. *An emphasis on the unusual, with cycling tours, a panda trek in Sichuan and a Kathmandu–Lhasa–Kathmandu overland trip.*

Kuoni Worldwide ☎01306/740888. *Packages China as a holiday experience; often in conjunction with side-trips to Bali or Bangkok. Seven nights Hong Kong–Shanghai–Beijing–Xi'an for £1300.*

Hayes and Jarvis ☎0181/748 5050. *Similar approach to Kuoni's, though note that their Beijing flight-and-hotel-only packages can be the cheapest around.*

Naturetrek ☎01962/733051. *Runs worldwide tours which specialize in spotting the local flora and fauna, including an annual 24-day overland trip from Chengdu to Lhasa costing around £4000.*

One Europe Travel ☎0181/566 9424. *Specializes in tailor-made Trans-Siberian train packages, with Trans-Mongolian and Trans-Central Asian rail routes also possible. All-inclusive London–Beijing price starts from £400–500.*

Regent Holidays ☎0117/921 1711. *Offers interesting Trans-Siberian packages for individual travellers in either direction and with different possible stopover permutations. The basic package Moscow–Beijing, including a one-way BA flight London–Moscow and a night in a Moscow hotel, costs around £450.*

World Expeditions ☎01628/74174. *Offers a leisurely 22-day cycling tour (13 days of actual cycling) through Guangdong Province – a good way to see real village life. £1600 excluding flights.*

---

cially modified vehicles. The advantage of the latter tours is that they sometimes penetrate parts of China inaccessible by public transport. A potentially cheaper alternative to booking your tour from home is to approach **Chinese tour operators** in China, such as *CITS* or *CTS*, though the linguistic and cultural obstacles to negotiating a fair deal with local business people are formidable – and service is likely to be poor. Generally this option is advisable only for short trips of one or two days, in out-of-the-way places (such as the Inner Mongolian grasslands). See p.35 for more details on tours in China.

Any tour including accommodation and internal travel is likely to work out more **expensive** per day than if you were travelling independently. The one important exception to this are the amazingly cheap (often less than £500) off-season **flight-and-hotel packages to Beijing** which give six or seven nights in a four-star hotel effectively for free. Don't forget, though, that quoted prices in brochures usually refer to the low-season minimum, based on two people sharing – the cost for a single traveller in high season will always work out far more expensive.

One type of package tour well worth considering is on a **Trans-Siberian train**. These are not group tours, but are booked on an individual basis, allowing travellers complete flexibility in choosing their dates of travel. Basically they provide an exciting way of beginning or ending your trip to China, and the advantage of using a tour operator to arrange the whole thing is that you will spare yourself the almighty hassle of dealing with Russian bureaucracy. The overall cost of your Trans-Siberian package – starting from £400 – will be higher than a one-way flight to China but is still very reasonable considering what you get to see en route.

GETTING THERE FROM THE USA AND CANADA

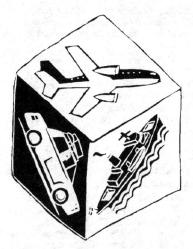

There are a number of possible routes to China from the US and Canada, with the most options being through Hong Kong. Check the ads in newspaper travel sections, and shop around. In particular, the recent influx of Hong Kong Chinese into Vancouver has prompted a surge in competition and discounted fares from Canada. Chinese-owned agencies, who deal with consolidators (wholesalers), can usually quote you a fare $200–250 lower than the airlines' discounted rates.

SHOPPING FOR TICKETS

Barring special offers, the cheapest of the airlines' published fares is usually an **Apex** ticket, although this will carry certain restrictions: you have to book – and pay – at least 21 days before departure, spend at least seven days abroad (maximum stay three months), and you tend to get penalized if you change your schedule. Some airlines also issue **Special Apex** tickets to people younger than 24, often extending the maximum stay to a year. Many airlines offer youth or student fares to **under-26s**; a passport or driving licence are sufficient proof of age, though these tickets are subject to availability and can have eccentric booking conditions.

You can normally cut costs further by going through a **specialist flight agent** – either a **con-**

solidator, who buys up blocks of tickets from the airlines and sells them at a discount, or a **discount agent**, who in addition to dealing with discounted flights may also offer special student and youth fares and a range of other travel-related services such as travel insurance, rail tickets and tours. Bear in mind, though, that penalties for changing your plans can be stiff. Remember too that these companies make their money by dealing in bulk – don't expect them to answer lots of questions.

Don't automatically assume, however, that tickets purchased through a travel specialist will be the cheapest – once you get a quote, check with the airlines and you may turn up an even better deal. Be advised also that the pool of travel companies is swimming with sharks – exercise caution and *never* deal with a company that demands cash up front or refuses to accept payment by credit card.

Regardless of where you buy your ticket, **fares** will depend on the season. Airfares from North America to China are highest from around early June to late August, and again from early December through to after Chinese New Year. All other times are considered low season. The price difference between the high and low seasons is only about $200 on a typical round-trip fare, but you'll have to make your reservations further in advance during the high season or you could end up paying more than you'd counted on.

FLIGHTS FROM THE US

Northwest is the only US carrier to fly non-stop **from the US** to mainland China. Flights to Beijing leave three days a week from Detroit. Fares are around $2000, depending on the season and the flight time is fourteen hours.

From the **East Coast**, however, China's own *China Eastern Airlines* has five non-stop flights weekly from Los Angeles (11hr) into **Beijing** with connections to **Shanghai**. Consolidators can usually quote the round-trip, midweek fare from $800 (low season) to $1000 (high season). *Asiana Airlines* and *Korean Airlines*, both Korean carriers, also make connections into Beijing and Shanghai via Seoul (16hr). This is not as convenient as flying non-stop, but stopovers in Seoul are usually available for an extra $50. Discounted fares are about the same as with *China Eastern*, but flights are more frequent and leave from more cities.

AIRLINES AND AGENTS

AIRLINES

Air Canada ☎1-800/776-3000; in Canada call ☎1-800/555-1212 for local toll-free number. *Non-stop flights from Vancouver to Hong Kong, and from Montréal and Toronto via Vancouver.*

Asiana Airlines ☎1-800/227-4262. *Daily direct to Shanghai and service five times a week to Beijing and Hong Kong via Seoul from Seattle, Los Angeles, San Francisco, Detroit, Honolulu, New York and Vancouver.*

Canadian Airlines ☎1-800/426-7000; Canada ☎1-800/665-1177. *Four non-stop flights weekly to Beijing from Vancouver and a direct service from Montréal. To Hong Kong non-stop from Vancouver and Toronto and direct from Montréal.*

Cathay Pacific ☎1-800/233-2742; in Canada call ☎1-800/555-1212 for local toll-free number. *Non-stop flights to Hong Kong from Vancouver and Los Angeles; direct flights from New York via Vancouver and Toronto via Anchorage.*

China Air ☎212/371-9899. *Five flights weekly from New York to Shanghai and Beijing. Weekly non-stop service from Vancouver. To Hong Kong from Los Angeles, San Francisco, Honolulu and Anchorage via Taipei, and from Vancouver via Los Angeles and Taipei.*

China Eastern Airlines ☎206/343-5582. *Five non-stops weekly from Los Angeles into Beijing with connections to Shanghai. Twice-weekly service from Seattle and Chicago.*

EVA Airlines ☎1-800/695-1188. *Flights to Hong Kong from New York via Seattle and Taipei and from San Francisco and Los Angeles via Taipei.*

Japan Airlines ☎1-800/525-3663. *Daily non-stop service to Tokyo from New York, Los Angeles, San Francisco, Chicago and Vancouver, with connecting service the next day to Beijing, Shanghai and Hong Kong.*

Korean Airlines ☎1-800/438-5000. *Direct to Beijing and Hong Kong via Seoul from New York, San Francisco, Los Angeles, Dallas, Chicago, Washington DC, Atlanta, Toronto and Vancouver.*

Northwest Airlines ☎1-800/447-4747. *Three non-stops weekly into Beijing and Hong Kong from Detroit, with service from other major US cities via Tokyo.*

Philippines Airlines ☎1-800/435-9725. *Flights to Beijing via Manila from San Francisco, Los Angeles and Honolulu.*

Singapore Airlines ☎1-800/742-333. *Non-stop service to Hong Kong from San Francisco; direct from Los Angeles, San Francisco and New York via Frankfurt.*

Thai International ☎1-800/426-5204; Canada ☎1-800/668-8103. *Los Angeles to Hong Kong.*

United Airlines ☎1-800/538-2929. *Daily, direct flights to Shanghai and Beijing via Tokyo from New York and Los Angeles. Non-stop service to Hong Kong from Los Amgeles and San Francisco, with direct service from New York via Tokyo or San Francisco.*

FLIGHT AGENTS

Air Brokers International, 323 Geary St, San Francisco CA 94102 (☎1-800/883-3273, e-mail airbroker@aimnet.com. *Consolidator.*

Council Travel, 205 E 42nd St, New York, NY 10017 (☎1-800/743-1823) and branches in many other US cities. *Discount travel agent, specializing in student discounts.*

Educational Travel Center, 438 N Frances St, Madison, WI 53703 (☎1-800/747-5551. *Student/youth discounts.*

Flight Centre, South Granville St, Vancouver BC (☎604/739-9539). *Discount airfares from Canada.*

Gateway Express, 3488 Columbia Center, Seattle, WA (☎206/624-3400). *Discounts on flights to Asia.*

High Adventure Travel Inc, 253 Sacramento St, Suite 600, San Francisco CA 94111 (☎1-800/428-8735, e-mail airtreks@highadv.com; world wide web site: http://www.highadv.com). *Specialist in Round-The-World and Circle-Pacific tickets.*

Last Minute Travel, 132 Brookline Ave, Boston, MA 02215 (☎1-800/LAST-MIN). *Discount airfares and hotel packages.*

Now Voyager, 74 Varick St, Suite 307, New York, NY 10013 (☎212/334-5243. *Courier flight broker.*

STA Travel, 48 East 11th St, New York, NY 10013 (☎1-800/777-0112. *Discounts for students under 25.*

Travel CUTS, 187 College St, Toronto ON M5T 1P7 (☎416/979-2406) and branches all over Canada. *Student travel organization.*

Worldtrek Travel, 111 Water St, New Haven, CT 06511 (☎1-800/243-1723). *General discount agent.*

Flying into **Hong Kong** there's a wide choice of airlines. *Singapore Airlines*, *Cathay Pacific* and *United* all fly non-stop (15hr) and *Northwest* has a direct flight from Seattle three times a week. Other airlines, such as *Japan Airlines* and *China Air*, make connections from Los Angeles or San Francisco via Tokyo, Seoul and Taipei. Round-trip fares for these flights are around $800 (low season) and $1200 (high). In addition, discounters can often find good deals from Seattle on *Canadian Airlines'* non-stop service from Vancouver – as low as $700 including the connecting flight between Seattle and Vancouver. *Asiana Airlines* via Seoul (19hr) compensates for the longer flying time by offering a very cheap fare; discount travel agents can quote this round-trip fare as low as $550.

From the **West Coast**, the best price on a direct flight to **Beijing** or **Shanghai** is on *China Air* via Anchorage. Prices range from around $1000 to $1300. It's also possible to fly into Shanghai and out of Beijing or vice versa. *Asiana Airlines* and *Korean Airlines* also make connections into Beijing and Shanghai via Seoul. Flight time via Seoul from New York is twenty hours. Discounted fares are around $1000. To **Hong Kong**, *Cathay Pacific* offers direct daily service from New York via Vancouver, while *United* has daily flights via San Francisco or Tokyo (20hr). *EVA Airlines* flies from New York through Seattle and Taipei, and *Korean* and *Asiana Airlines* fly via Seoul with a stop in Anchorage (23hr). *Singapore Airlines* offers the eastern route via Frankfurt in 21 hours. Round-trip fares range from $1000 (low season) to $1600 (high) with discounters offering fares from $800.

With time in hand you may want to travel via another Asian city which can sometimes be more cheaply reached from the US and Canada than China itself. Discount fares to **Bangkok** and **Ho Chi Minh City** range from $800 (West Coast) to $1000 (East Coast). If you're taking the Trans-Siberian Express into Beijing (see pp.10 & 13), *Aeroflot* flies non-stop to Moscow from Montréal, New York, Chicago, Los Angeles, San Francisco and Seattle. Midweek fares are $500–575 one way from East Coast cities and $600–675 from West Coast destinations.

FROM CANADA

Canadian Airlines flies non-stop from Vancouver to **Beijing** four days a week (11hr), with a mid-week round-trip ticket good for up to one year,

direct from the airline for CDN$1560. *Canadian* also offers direct service from Montréal (16hr) for around $200 more. Other options are on *Korean Airlines* which flies to Beijing three times a week from Vancouver via Seoul (CDN$1279–1429) and twice weekly from Toronto for about $200 more. The cheapest alternative from Vancouver is on *China Air's* weekly non-stop flights to **Shanghai** and Beijing for around CDN$1200.

To **Hong Kong**, *Canadian Airlines* offers daily non-stop service from Vancouver (13hr) and Toronto, and a direct service from Montréal (15hr). *Cathay Pacific* also flies daily non-stop from Vancouver and has direct flights five days a week from Toronto via Anchorage. *Air Canada* flies non-stop four to five times a week (depending on season) from Vancouver, and also offers service to Hong Kong from Montréal and Toronto via Vancouver. *China Air* makes a connection to Hong Kong from Vancouver via Los Angeles and Taipei. Round-trip fares range from CDN$1265 (low season) to $1865 (high) for Vancouver departures and from CDN$1730 to $2090 for Toronto-Montréal departures. Round-trip fares as low as CDN$825 are available through discounters on *Asiana's* daily flights from Vancouver with connections through Seattle and Seoul.

ROUND-THE-WORLD TICKETS AND COURIER FLIGHTS

Discounters such as *Air Brokers International* and *High Adventure Travel Inc* can supply **Round-the-World** and **Circle-Pacific** tickets with Beijing, Shanghai, Guangzhou and Hong Kong stopovers for $1650–2200. A good way to get familiar with routes and fares is to check out *High Adventure's* World Wide Web site which lists hundreds of possible combinations and fares (see box for details). For example, from the West Coast you can fly LA/San Francisco/Phoenix/San Diego–Tokyo–Hong Kong–Bangkok–Beijing then overland to Shanghai–LA/Seattle for $1700. From the East Coast, New York–Paris–Bombay/Delhi–Bangkok–Vientiane–Hanoi then overland to Ho Chi Minh City–Guangzhou then overland to Beijing–New York, costs $2150.

There are increasing opportunities for cheap fares on **courier** routes to China, chiefly to Hong Kong. Round-trip courier flights to Hong Kong are available for around $350, with last-minute specials as low as $150 for a flight booked within three-days of departure. For information call ☎407/582-8320 or contact *The Air Courier Association* (☎303/279-3600).

PACKAGES AND ORGANIZED TOURS

There's a wide variety of **air-hotel-sightseeing packages** available from North America, as well as three- and four-day excursions into mainland China from Hong Kong, and longer, more adventurous tours including bike trips, trekking, visits to craft villages and trips down the Yangzi River.

The travel companies associated with the airlines flying to China all offer competitive deals. *China Air Tours* has a six-night/eight-day

Beijing–Shanghai tour starting at $2100 including airfare from Vancouver and all excursions, most meals, transport within China and a visa. *United Airlines* offers an eighteen-day China and Yangzi River tour including hotels, meals, airfare, all transport and sightseeing as well as two nights in Hong Kong from $3000. Six nights in Hong Kong including airfare, transfers and a half-day sightseeing tour start at $1630 with *United Air Vacations*.

Tickets on the **Trans-Siberian Express** can be purchased from travel agencies in the US. Package tours, including overnight stays in Beijing and Moscow, are also available. *Mir Corp* offers ten-day packages starting at $475 per person for six nights on the train plus a night in Moscow.

TOUR OPERATORS

Adventures Abroad ☎1-800/665-3998, e-mail adabroad@infoserve.net. *Vancouver-based company with a good reputation for small-group tours (3-week Silk Road tour through China and Pakistan for CDN$3000).*

Asian Pacific Adventures ☎213/935-3156. *Bike trips, Yangzi River cruises, women-only tours and Hong Kong stopovers. Also offers a sixteen-day Yunnan Province ethnic tribal tour for $3680.*

Backroads ☎1-800/462-2848. *Mountain-bike tours. Their fifteen-day Guangzhou–Guilin trip covers 30–40 miles a day for $3300.*

Canadian Holidays ☎1-800/661-8881. *Air/hotel packages and sightseeing tours in conjunction with Canadian Airlines. Contact travel agents.*

Cathay Pacific Holidays ☎1-800/762-8181. *Air/hotel/sightseeing packages to Hong Kong with mainland China extensions. Also three- and four-day mini-packages into China with Dragonair from Hong Kong.*

China Air Tours ☎212/371-9899. *Air/hotel/sightseeing packages.*

Craft World Tours & **Camera World Tours** ☎716/548-2667. *Tours focusing on photography, arts and handicrafts, including a 22-day "Silk and Craft Route" tour ($4896).*

Earthwatch Expeditions ☎617/926-8200, e-mail into@earthwatch.org. *Tax-deductible volunteer research expeditions in China ("Saving China's Reefs", "Forest Monkeys of China" and a sustainable development program focusing on farms along the Yangzi) starting at around $1500.*

Mir Corp ☎1-800/424-7289. *Trans-Siberian Express tour packages starting at $475 per per-*

son. Beijing homestays from $58 per double room.

Mountain Travel Sobek ☎1-800/227-2384, e-mail info@MTSobek.com. *Travel adventure company with a 24-day China–Pakistan tour from $3400.*

Northwest World Vacations. *Offers two- and three-night Shanghai, Beijing, Xi'an accommodation and excursion packages starting at $304 (excluding flights). Contact travel agents.*

Pacific Holidays ☎1-800/355-8025. *All-inclusive package tours starting at $2350 for a seven-night Beijing, Xi'an, Shanghai tour.*

REI Adventures ☎1-800/622-2236. *Trekking and mountain-biking tours such as a 17-day Guilin bike tour of southern China for $2290.*

TBI Tours ☎1-800/223-0166. *Package tour operator with a competitive twelve-day tour including Beijing, Guilin, Guangzhou and Hong Kong from $2700. Book through travel agents.*

United Air Vacations ☎1-800/328-8181. *Two- and three-day excursions, starting at $199. Longer escorted tours also available.*

Wilderness Travel ☎1-800/368-2794, e-mail info@wildernesstravel.com. *High-quality cultural adventure tours with a 27-day China–Pakistan tour from Kashgar to Islamabad for $4595 plus airfare.*

World Expeditions ☎514/844-6364. *Canadian package tour company with departures from Montréal, Ottawa, Toronto, Vancouver, Edmonton and Calgary. The 21-day tour including Shanghai and Beijing starts at CDN$4650.*

United Air Vacations ☎1-800/328-6877. *Hong Kong city breaks.*

GETTING THERE FROM AUSTRALIA & NEW ZEALAND

The closest entry point into China from Australia and New Zealand is Hong Kong, though it's also possible to fly direct to Guangzhou, Shanghai and Beijing without having to change planes, and to elsewhere in China if you're prepared to make a stopover.

BUYING A TICKET

It's always worth shopping around and checking out agents' adverts in the weekend papers for current special deals on airfares and tours, but – especially in New Zealand – low competition means that savings are rarely substantial. **Seasons** are difficult to state exactly, as each airline has its own levels and dates. Very roughly, October and November at least are low season, with a high from June through to September, and December through until after Chinese New Year (usually February); the rest of

AIRLINES

Air China, Level 11, 115 Pitt St, Sydney (☎02/9232 7895). *At least twice a week from Sydney or Melbourne to Guangzhou, Shanghai, and Beijing.*

Air New Zealand, 5 Elizabeth St, Sydney (☎02/9223 4666); Cnr of Queen and Customs streets, Auckland (☎09/366 24240). *Brisbane to Hong Kong once a week; at least three times a week from Auckland to Beijing, Hong Kong and Shanghai.*

Ansett Australia, 501 Swanston St, Melbourne (☎03/9623 3333, reservations freecall ☎131300). *Five times a week from eastern Australia to Hong Kong.*

British Airways, 64 Castlereagh St, Sydney (☎02/9258 3300). *Daily from Australian east coast capitals to Hong Kong.*

Cathay Pacific, Level 5, 28 O'Connell St, Sydney (freecall ☎131747); Floor 11, National Bank Centre, 295–209 Queen St, Auckland (☎09/379 0861). *Daily from Australian east coast capitals to Hong Kong, Guilin and Beijing; at least once a week to Chengdu, Haikou, Hangzhou, Kunming, Nanjing, Shanghai, Xi'an and Xiamen via various transfers. Also flies at least twice weekly from Perth to Beijing, Hong Kong and Shanghai. From New Zealand, there are several flights a week from Auckland to Beijing, Guilin, Kunming, Nanjing, Shanghai and Xiamen.*

Malaysian Air, 16 Spring St, Sydney (☎02/364 3500, reservations freecall ☎132627); Floor 12, Swanson Centre, 12–26 Swanson St, Auckland (☎09/373 2741). *At least once a week from eastern Australia, Perth and Auckland to Beijing and Hong Kong, with a stopover in Kuala Lumpur.*

Garuda, 55 Hunter St, Sydney (☎02/9334 9900). *Weekly from Australian east coast capitals to Hong Kong, via a two-night stopover in Bali or Jakarta.*

Qantas, Cnr of Hunter and Philip streets, Sydney (☎02/952 9555). *From Sydney six times a week to Beijing, and daily from eastern Australia and Perth to Hong Kong.*

Royal Brunei, 9/25 Mary St, Brisbane (☎07/221 7757). *Weekly from Brisbane to Hong Kong and Beijing, with a stopover in Brunei.*

Singapore Airlines, 17–19 Bridge St, Sydney (local-call rate ☎131011). *Melbourne to Beijing three times a week, and from Sydney and Perth to Hong Kong daily.*

FLIGHT AGENTS

The following all offer competitive budget fares.

Anywhere Travel, 345 Anzac Parade, Kingsford, Sydney (☎02/9663 0411).

Brisbane Discount Travel, 260 Queen St, Brisbane (☎07/3229 9211).

Budget Travel, 16 Fort St, Auckland; other branches around the city (☎09/366 0061; toll-free ☎0800/ 808 040).

Destinations Unlimited, 3 Milford Rd, Milford, Auckland (☎09/373 4033).

Flight Centres Australia: Level 11, 33 Berry St, North Sydney (☎02/9241 2422); Bourke St, Melbourne (☎03/9650 2899); plus other branches nationwide. New Zealand: National Bank Towers, 205–225 Queen St, Auckland (☎09/209 6171); Shop 1M, National Mutual Arcade, 152 Hereford St, Christchurch (☎03/379 7145); 50–52 Willis St, Wellington (☎04/472 8101); other branches countrywide.

Northern Gateway, 22 Cavenagh St, Darwin (☎08/8941 1394).

Passport Travel, 320b Glenferrie Rd, Malvern (☎03/9824 7183).

STA Travel, Australia: 702-730 Harris St, Ultimo, Sydney (☎02/9212 1255; toll-free ☎1-800/637-444); 256 Flinders St, Melbourne (☎03/9654 7266); other offices in state capitals and major universities. New Zealand: Travellers' Centre, 10 High St, Auckland (☎09/309 0458); 233 Cuba St, Wellington (☎04/385 0561); 90 Cashel St, Christchurch (☎03/379 9098); other offices in Dunedin, Palmerston North, Hamilton and major universities.

Thomas Cook, Australia: 321 Kent St, Sydney (☎02/9248 6100); 257 Collins St, Melbourne (☎03/9650 2442); branches in other state capitals. New Zealand: Shop 250a St Luke's Square, Auckland (☎09/849 2071).

Topdeck Travel, 65 Glenfell St, Adelaide (☎08/8232 7222).

Tymtro Travel, 428 George St, Sydney (☎02/9223 2211).

SPECIALIST TOUR OPERATORS

Adventure World, 73 Walker St, North Sydney (☎02/9956 7766); 101 Great South Rd, Remuera, Auckland (☎09/524 5118, freecall ☎0800/652 954). *Massively comprehensive range of packages, from two-night city accommodation deals (A$300 and up), to extended hiking tours in Yunnan, holy mountains in eastern China, and luxury grand tours encompassing a Yangzi River cruise and all the sights of Hong Kong, Xi'an, Beijing and Shanghai (A$3000–6000). Airfares to China generally extra.*

China International Travel Service, Fifth Floor, 99 King St, Melbourne (☎03/9621 1588). *Advance bookings for transport and CITS tours within China.*

China Travel and Tour Specialists, Level 1, 141 Queen St Mall, Brisbane (☎07/3221 4599). *Ten-day to three-week tours of the main sights in Beijing, Xi'an, Guilin and Shanghai. Prices from A$1699–2700 including return flights to China and all meals, accommodation and travel within the country.*

China Travel Service, 757 George St, Sydney (☎02/9211 2633). *Bookings for all visas, plane, train and Yangzi River ferry services, and also for anything offered by CTS offices in China.*

China Unlimited, 116 Goldsmith St, Elwood, Melbourne (☎03/9531 3866). *Enthusiastic, independent-minded agent keen to seek out specialist*

packages from wildlife expeditions to bike tours. Offers an all-inclusive, 17–22-day cycle tour of southern China A$2700–4400 ex Australia.

Dawn Express, Level 10, QV1 Building, 250 St Georges Terrace, Perth (☎09/321 2121, freecall ☎008/652 121). *Pearl River Delta specialists, with seven-day tours taking in Hong Kong, Macau and Guangzhou A$1750–2412 ex Australia.*

Helen Wong, Level 18, Town Hall House, 456 Kent St, Sydney (☎02/9267 7833). *Numerous pre-arranged tours; can also tailor special-interest packages for groups of ten or more.*

San Michelle Travel, 81 York St, Sydney (☎02/9299 1111), 117 Errol St, North Melbourne (☎03/9629 4961); Cinema City Arcade, cnr Hay, Barrack and Murray streets, Perth (☎09/325 1288); country-wide freecall ☎008/222 244. *All aspects of independent travel, including arranging special-interest tours, obtaining visas and booking flights.*

Tibet Travel Centre (*Paddy Pallin Outdoor Centre*), 228 Rundle St, Adelaide (☎08/232 3155, freecall ☎008/801 119). *Scheduled departures for fully guided hiking and trekking tours from Kathmandu to Lhasa and the Everest Base Camp, and around eastern Tibet. Prices ex-Kathmandu are A$1980–4669; return airfare to Kathmandu A$1400–1700 extra.*

the year is either shoulder or low season depending on the carrier.

From eastern Australia, by far the best deal is with *Royal Brunei Airlines*, who offer low-season returns from Brisbane to Hong Kong for just A$1100 (and, even better value, A$1200 to Beijing), with high-season rates about ten percent more. Mid-range operators such as *Garuda* charge A$1200 low season/A$1600 high season to Hong Kong from east coast departure points. Upmarket carriers such as *Qantas* and *Air New Zealand* have good low-season rates – about A$1200 to Hong Kong, or A$1600 to Beijing, for instance – but their high-season fares can top A$1800/A$2100 for the same trips.

Where available, **fares from Perth** are about five percent cheaper as you're that much closer to China here. Due to lack of competition, prices

from New Zealand are relatively expensive; here you're looking at low-season minimums of NZ$1600 to Hong Kong.

ORGANIZED TOURS

There is a huge variety of **packages** on offer, which will usually work out more expensive than travelling independently, but which can save you a lot of time and hassle if your stay is a short one. However, a tour is certainly worth considering if you have a **specialist interest** such as hiking, cycling or wildlife, as you will often get taken to parts of China which are difficult to reach on your own. Seven-day **city breaks** can also be a good deal, as you'll pay well below the international-standard hotel prices by booking through a tour operator.

OVERLAND ROUTES INTO CHINA

China now has a number of land borders open to foreign travellers. When planning your route, think carefully about where you buy your Chinese visa – remember that Chinese visas must be used within three months of their date of issue, which may not be very useful if you are planning a long overland trip before arriving in China. Visas are obtainable in the capitals of virtually all European and Asian countries, though you may have to wait a few days for them to be issued (see p.16 for embassy addresses).

VIA MOSCOW

One of the classic overland routes to China is through **Russia** on the so-called **Trans-Siberian Express**. There are actually two rail lines from Moscow to Beijing: the **Trans-Manchurian** line which runs almost as far as the sea of Japan before running south through Dongbei (Manchuria) to Beijing, and the slightly more direct **Trans-Mongolian** express which cuts through Mongolia from Siberia. The Manchurian train takes about six days, the Mongolian train about five. As a one-off trip, the journey is highly recommended. The trains are relatively comfortable and clean: second-class

compartments contain four berths while first-class have two with a private shower. These days both trains tend to be full of Russian traders scurrying to and from China with vast quantities of luggage, so booking tickets can be problematic especially in summer, when you may need to plan two or three months ahead.

Booking a train ticket from Moscow to Beijing from abroad is a complex business, and to book right through from London to Beijing is a minefield – you'll need transit visas for Russia and Mongolia, and also Belarus if you plan on using the Warsaw–Moscow train. You are highly advised to use an experienced **travel agent** (some are listed in the boxes on pp.5 & 8) who can organize all tickets, visas and stopovers if required, in advance. From London, tailor-made packages typically offer a couple of nights in Moscow, with optional nights in Irkutsk or Ulan Batur as well. Prices for the trip with no stopovers can be as low as £300 one way.

VIA THE CENTRAL ASIAN REPUBLICS

Until the collapse of the Soviet Union it was almost unthinkable to travel around places like **Kazakhstan** or **Kyrgystan** on your way to China. These days, although the old land routes between China and the West are certainly reawakening, they still present bureaucratic obstacles to travellers.

The capitals of Kazakhstan and Kyrgystan – **Almaty** and **Bishkek** – are both still linked by daily trains to Moscow (3 days), though getting Russian transit visas and booking berths on these trains in advance from home is not easy – you are advised to speak to a tour operator (see the boxes on pp.6 and p.10) for the possibility of tailor-made itineraries. It is now also possible to get into Central Asia without going through Russia at all. You can get to Turkmenistan, and thence to the rest of Central Asia, either from northeastern Iran or from Azerbaijian across the Caspian Sea, though again you'll need to look closely at the visa situation of the countries you plan to cross.

Crossing into China **from Kazakhstan** is perfectly straightforward – there are very comfortable twice-weekly trains from Almaty to Urumqi, which take 35 hours and cost about US$75 for a berth in a four-berth compartment. There are also buses, which are less comfortable, but cheaper and faster (US$50; about 24hr). **From Kyrgystan**, the route is sometimes problematic – by road, the Kyrgyz capital, Bishkek, is only nine hours from Kashgar and the two cities are linked by buses in summer months. Foreigners, however, have had difficulties in trying to use these and sometimes have had to resort to expensive local tour operators to help them across.

VIA THE INDIAN SUBCONTINENT

The land route from Europe to the Indian subcontinent goes through Turkey and Iran to Pakistan and the trip is a fairly straightforward one on local buses and trains. Note that Iranian seven-day transit visas are routinely issued to Western travellers with the exception of US citizens – though visa applications may take up to two months to be processed.

The routes from the subcontinent across the mountains to China are among the toughest in Asia. The first is **from Pakistan** into Xinjiang Province over the **Karakoram Highway**, along one of the branches of the ancient Silk Road. This requires no pre-planning, except for the fact that it is open only from May to October, and closes periodically due to landslips. The Karakoram Higway actually starts at Rawalpindi (the old city outside the capital Islamabad), and in theory you can get from here to Kashgar in four days on pub-

lic buses. From Rawalpindi, first take one of the daily minibuses which run the arduous fifteen-hour trip up the Indus gorge to the village of Gilgit, where you'll have to spend a night. From Gilgit, the next destination is the border town of Sust, a five-hour journey. There are a couple of daily buses on this route. Once in Sust, immediately book your ticket to Tashkurgan in China (7hr) for the next morning – the price is 750 rupees (about US$23). See p.932 for more on crossing the Chinese border here.

The other route tourists can use from the Indian subcontinent is **from Nepal** into **Tibet**. Again this requires no pre-planning, insofar as you can simply arrive in Kathmandu and arrange everything from there, though it can work out rather expensive because foreigners may be forbidden from using the normal public buses. Basically, to cross the border, you need papers showing you have booked a **tour of Lhasa** with a legal minimum of two travellers. The tour usually entails renting a jeep, driver and guide, though some travellers find ways round this. If you are planning to continue on into other parts of China from Tibet, you must get your Chinese visa before arriving in Nepal as the "Tibet-tour visas" issued here are sometimes good for Tibet only. See p.943 for more on crossing the Nepalese border into Tibet, and remember that regulations concerning this crossing are in a constant state of flux.

From India itself there are, for political reasons, no border crossings to China, though if the situation changes, the old road through Sikkim to Tibet, north from Darjeeling, will probably be the first to reopen.

FROM VIETNAM, LAOS AND BURMA

Since the late 1980s, China has become ever more accessible from its Southeast Asian neighbours, many of whom have cultural ties to the People's Republic. **Vietnam**, which until recently was actually at war with China, now has two crossings – **Dong Dang**, 60km northeast of Hanoi, and **Lao Cai**, 150km northwest – both open daily 8.30am–5pm. Vietnamese border guards are notoriously officious, and though just about any problem can be resolved with some US dollars, things are much easier if your documents are all in order. The most costly situations arise if you have either overstayed your Vietnamese visa, or don't have it validated for the particular border crossing you're trying to use; both will set you back US$20 or more after some hard bargaining.

For Dong Dang, there are good rail and road connections from Hanoi to Lang Son, from where a minibus can take you the last 5km to the border. Once you're over, there's an afternoon train (¥40) taking five hours to cover the 170km northeast to Nanning, Guangxi's capital – see p.687 for further details. Similarly, there are daily trains from Hanoi to Lao Cai, eleven hours away in Vietnam's mountainous and undeveloped northwest, where you cross into Yunnan Province at Hekou (see p.766). An erratic train service runs from Hekou to the provincial capital, Kunming, but buses are far more reliable – the sixteen-hour journey costs about ¥90.

Crossing into China from **Laos** also lands you in Yunnan, this time at **Bian Mao Zhan** in the Xishuangbanna region. Formalities are apparently very relaxed and unlikely to cause any problems, and there's a regular supply of inter-village minibuses for the 220km from here to the regional capital, Jinghong, with a likely overnight stop in the town of Mengla along the way (see p.763). Entering China **from Burma** is an interesting possibility too, with the old **Burma Road** cutting northeast from Rangoon (Yangon) to Lashio and the crossing at Wanding in Yunnan. It isn't officially open, however, though the country's tourist situation is very volatile and it's certainly worth making enquiries when applying for your Burmese visa.

VISAS AND RED TAPE

All foreign nationals require a visa to enter the People's Republic of China. Single-entry tourist visas must generally be used within three months of issue, are usually valid for thirty days from your date of entry into China and cost the local equivalent of around US$40. The authorities increase and decrease visa durations in order to control tourist traffic, and you're more likely to be given a visa for longer than thirty days outside the summer months. Visas are available worldwide from Chinese embassies and consulates and through specialist tour operators and visa agents, although if you are planning to enter China through Hong Kong, this is probably the best place of all to buy your visa.

To apply for a **tourist visa** you have to submit an application form, one or two passport-size photographs, your passport (which must be valid for at least another six months from your planned date of entry into China) and the fee, which cannot be paid by personal cheque. You may also be asked for a copy of any air tickets and hotel bookings. You are asked on the form to give some details of your trip, such as where you are going – but you don't have to stick to this. If you apply in person, processing should take between three and five working days, but this varies from country to country.

A **business visa** is valid for three months and can be issued for multiple entries, though you'll need an official invitation from a government-recognized Chinese organization. Twelve-month **work visas** again require an invitation, plus a health certificate. **Students** intending to study for less than six months need an invitation from a college; those staying for longer also need to fill in an extra form available from embassies, and need a health certificate.

HONG KONG

Most nationalities need only a valid passport to enter Hong Kong, although the length of time you can stay varies. British citizens can currently stay for twelve months; Canadians, Australians, New Zealanders and Irish and most other European citizens can stay for three months; and Americans and South Africans for thirty days. Following the

CHINESE EMBASSIES AND CONSULATES

Australia 15 Coronation Drive, Yarralumla, ACT 2600 (☎06/273 4780).

Canada 515 St Patrick St, Ottawa, Ontario, K1N 5H3 (☎613/789 3509). *Chinese consulate offices with visa application services also in Toronto and Vancouver.*

Kazakhstan ul. Furmanova 137, Almaty (☎634966).

Kyrgystan ul. Toktogula 196, Bishkek (☎222423).

Laos Thanon Wat Nak Yai, Vientiane (☎315103).

Nepal Baluwatar, Toran Bhawan, Naxal, Kathmandu (☎412589). *Visas available only through travel agents to those travelling with a tour group, see pp.943–44.*

Pakistan Ramna 4, Diplomatic Enclave, Islamabad. *Only ten-day visas are issued from this office.*

Russia ul. Druzhby 6, Moscow (☎095/145-1543).

Thailand 57/2 Rajdapisek Rd, Bangkok (☎02/245 7032); Chiang Mai, 111 Chang Lo Rd (☎053/272197).

UK Cleveland Court, 1–3 Leinster House, London W2 (visa section is at 31 Portland Place, London W1; ☎0171/631 1430); Denison House, Denison Rd, Victoria Pk, Manchester M14 (☎0161/224 7480).

USA 2300 Connecticut Ave NW, Washington DC 20008 (☎202/328 2500 or 328 2517). *Chinese consulate offices with visa application services are in New York, Washington DC, Chicago, Houston, Los Angeles, New York and San Francisco.*

Vietnam 39 Nguyen Thi Minh Khai (☎08/829 2457), Ho Chi Minh City; Chinese Embassy Consular Section, Tran Phu, Hanoi (round the corner from the main embassy building at 46 Hoang Dieu; ☎04/823 5569).

handover in June 1997, it is expected that British citizens will eventually be given only three months' stay in Hong Kong, but it's always advisable to check the situation before travelling.

To enter the Chinese mainland fron Hong Kong you'll still need a separate Chinese visa. Chinese visas can be bought easily from most travel agencies and hotels, including all branches of the *China Travel Service* (*CTS*) or from the visa office of the Ministry of Foreign Affairs of the PRC (see p.604 for more details). You can get both one-month and three-month visas the same day for an extra fee, although normal processing takes two to three days. Multiple-entry visas also available.

VISA EXTENSIONS

Visa extensions are handled by the Foreign Affairs section of the Public Security Bureau (**PSB**), so you can apply for one in any reasonably sized town. The amount of money you'll pay for this, and the amount of hassle you'll have, varies greatly depending on where you are, your nationality and what season it is. A first extension, valid for a month, is not usually problematic to obtain. The charge for a **first extension** is ¥65 for British visitors, but usually about half this for Americans. However, you're basically at the mercy of the particular PSB office and they often decide to levy extra charges on top. In some small towns the

charge may even be waived and the process takes ten minutes; in cities it can take two working days. A **second extension** is much harder to get, though not impossible. A lot depends on the office you are dealing with and your reasons for applying. If the PSB refuses to grant an extension they may be able to point you in the direction of a private office which can. If you overstay your visa you risk a heavy fine.

CUSTOMS

You are allowed to **import** up to six hundred cigarettes, two litres of alcohol and twenty fluid ounces of perfume. It's illegal to import printed matter, tapes or videos critical of the country, but don't worry too much about this, as confiscation in practice is rare, except in sensitive areas such as Tibet. Here, some travellers have reported books specifically on Tibet being taken off them, but guidebooks to the whole of China which include Tibet are fine.

You can bring in unlimited amounts of foreign currency, but **Chinese currency** cannot be taken into or out of the country.

Export restrictions apply on items more than a hundred years old, for which you require an export form available from *Friendship Stores*. You may be asked to show receipts for any cultural relics you have; otherwise you may not be allowed to take them out of the country.

INSURANCE

Most people will find it essential to take out a good travel insurance policy. Bank and credit cards (particularly *American Express*) often have certain levels of medical or other insurance included if you use them to pay for your trip. This can be quite comprehensive, anticipating anything from lost or stolen baggage to missed connections. If you have a good "all risks" home insurance policy it may well cover your possessions against loss or theft even when overseas, and many private medical schemes also cover you when abroad – make sure you know the procedure and the helpline number.

If you plan to do some hiking, skiing or other **adventurous sport**, you'll probably have to pay an extra premium; check carefully that any insurance policy you are considering will cover you in case of an accident. Note also that very few insurers will arrange on-the-spot payments in the event of a major expense or loss; you will usually be reimbursed only after going home. In all cases of loss or **theft** of goods, you will have to contact the local **police** to have a report made out so that your insurer can process the claim. For **medical claims**, you'll need to provide supporting bills. Keep photocopies of everything you send to the insurer and note any time period within which you must lodge claims.

BRITISH AND IRISH COVER

In **Britain and Ireland**, travel insurance schemes (from around £50 for one month to China, £99 for three months) are sold by almost every travel agent or bank, and by specialist insurance companies. Policies issued by the companies listed in the box below are all good value. *Columbus* also offers a Frequent Traveller policy which gives twelve months' worldwide cover for £87.

US AND CANADIAN COVER

Before buying an insurance policy, check that you're not already covered. **Canadian provin-**

TRAVEL INSURANCE COMPANIES

BRITAIN AND IRELAND

Campus Travel ☎0171/730 8111.

Columbus Travel Insurance ☎0171/375 0011.

Endsleigh Insurance ☎0171/436 4451.

Frizzell Insurance ☎01202/292 333.

STA ☎0171/361 6262.

USIT, Belfast ☎01232/324 073; Dublin ☎01/679 8833.

USA AND CANADA

Access America ☎1-800/284-8300.

Carefree Travel Insurance ☎1-800/645-2424.

ISIS (*International Student Insurance Service* – sold by *STA Travel*) ☎1-800/777-0112.

Desjardins Travel Insurance (Canada only) ☎1-800/463-7830.

Travel Assistance International ☎1-800/821-2828.

Travel Guard ☎1-800/826-1300.

Travel Insurance Services ☎1-800/937-1387.

AUSTRALIA AND NEW ZEALAND

AFTA ☎02/9956 49800.

Cover More, in Sydney ☎02/9968 1333; elsewhere in Australia toll-free ☎1-800/251 881.

Ready Plan, Australia ☎1-800/337 462; New Zealand ☎09/379 3399.

UTAG, in Sydney ☎02/9819 6855; elsewhere in Australia toll-free ☎1-800/809 462.

cial health plans typically provide some overseas medical coverage, although they are unlikely to pick up the full tab in the event of a mishap. Students may find that their student health coverage extends during the vacations and for one term beyond the date of last enrolment. Homeowners' or renters' insurance often covers theft or loss of documents, money and valuables while overseas.

After exhausting these possibilities, you might want to contact a specialist travel insurance company; your travel agent can usually recommend one, or see the box on p.17.

Premiums for travel to China start at around $65 for a two-week trip, rising to $180 for three months. Note that most North American travel policies apply only to items lost, stolen or damaged while in the custody of an identifiable, responsible third party – hotel porter, airline, luggage consignment, etc. Even in these cases you will have to contact the local police within a certain time limit to have a complete report made out so that your insurer can process the claim.

AUSTRALIAN AND NEW ZEALAND COVER

Travel insurance is available from travel agents or direct from insurance companies (see box on p.17). Policies are broadly comparable in premium and coverage: expect to pay around A$150 for one month, A$220 for two months and A$280 for three months.

TRAVELLERS WITH DISABILITIES

There are organized tours and holidays specifically for people with disabilities, though very few organizations have regular trips to China – the contacts in the box below will be able to put you in touch with any specialists who do. If you want to be more independent, it's important to become an authority on where you must be self-reliant and where you may expect help, especially regarding transport and accommodation. Make sure you take spares of any specialist clothing or equipment, extra supplies of drugs (carried with you if you fly), and a prescription including the gener-

CONTACTS FOR TRAVELLERS WITH DISABILITIES

BRITAIN AND IRELAND

Disability Action Group, 2 Annadale Ave, Belfast BT7 3JH (☎01232/91011).

Holiday Care Service, Floor 2, Imperial Building, Victoria Rd, Horley, Surrey RH6 9HW (☎01293/774535).

Mobility International 25 rue de Manchester, 1070 Brussels, Belgium (☎032/2410 6297 or 2410 6874).

RADAR, 12 City Forum, 250 City Rd, London EC1V 8AS (☎0171/250 3222).

Tripscope, The Courtyard, Evelyn Rd, London W4 5JL (☎0181/994 9294).

USA AND CANADA

Directions Unlimited, 720 North Bedford Rd, Bedford Hills, NY 10507 (☎1-800/533-5343). *Custom tours for people with disabilities.*

Mobility International USA, PO Box 10767, Eugene, OR97440 (Voice and TDD ☎503/343-1284). *Information and referral services, access guides, tours, and exchange programs.*

Twin Peaks Press, Box 129, Vancouver, WA 98666 (☎206/694-2462 or 1-800/637-2256). *Publishes Directory of Travel Agencies for the Disabled, listing more than 370 agencies worldwide.*

AUSTRALIA AND NEW ZEALAND

ACROD, PO Box 60, Curtain, ACT (☎06/682 4333).

Barrier Free Travel, 36 Wheatley St, North Bellingen, NSW 2454 (☎066/551 733).

Disabled Persons Assembly, PO Box 10-138, The Terrace, Wellington (☎04/472 2626).

ic name – in English and Chinese characters – in case of emergency. **If there's an
association representing people with your
disability, contact them early on in the
planning process.**

Once there, you'll find that **Hong Kong** is
about the only place in China with transport,
recreation, and other services geared to disabled
travellers, all detailed in the Hong Kong Tourist
Association's excellent **free booklet**, *Hong Kong
Access Guide for Disabled Visitors*. **Macau**, too,
has some facilities, though they're more limited,
but **mainland China** is far harder to negotiate,
especially for those with restricted mobility. Some

airlines, as well as a few of the upmarket hotels
in Beijing, Shanghai and Guangzhou, have experience in assisting disabled visitors; in particular,
the *Holiday Inn* and *Hilton* chains often have
rooms designed for wheelchair users. But there's
little additional infrastructure – buses, trains and
ferries make no allowances, and streets tend to
be narrow, crowded and unevenly paved, with
only very rare lowered kerbing at downtown
crossings. The *China Disabled Person's Federation*
at 44 Beichnizi Lu, Dongchong District, Beijing
100006 (☎010/15139719) may be able to furnish
more specific information, but isn't especially
geared to helping foreign tourists.

HEALTH

**Low standards of public hygiene, stress and
overcrowded conditions are to blame for
most of the health problems that beset travellers in China. If you do get ill, medical
facilities, at least in the big cities, are
adequate, and the largest cities have high-
standard international clinics for foreigners.
For minor complaints, every town has a
pharmacy which can suggest remedies, and
doctors who can treat you with traditional
Chinese or Western techniques. You'll need
to take a phrasebook or a Chinese speaker if
you don't speak Chinese.**

BEFORE YOU GO

It's advisable to visit a doctor as early as possible
before you travel to allow time to complete any
courses of vaccinations you need. If you have any
longstanding medical conditions, or are travelling
with small children, consult your doctor and take
any necessary medicine with you. It's also wise to
get a dental check-up, and if you decide to take a
course of anti-malarial tablets, start taking them
before you go.

It's worth taking a first-aid kit with you, particularly if you will be travelling extensively outside
the cities, where the language barrier can make
getting hold of the appropriate medicines difficult. Include bandages, plasters, painkillers, oral
rehydration solution, kaolin and morphine for diarrhoea, vitamin pills, antiseptic cream and a sterile

set of hypodermics if you will be in the country for
a significant period.

VACCINATIONS

No vaccinations are required for China, except for
yellow fever if you're coming from an area where
the disease is endemic, but a hepatitis A jab is
recommended. Additional injections to consider, are
depending on where you are going and when, are
hepatitis B, meningitis and rabies – check with
your doctor. Remember also that a tetanus booster is required every ten years.

Hepatitis A is a water-borne viral infection
spread by contaminated food and water which
causes an inflammation of the liver. A significant
health hazard for travellers, symptoms are yellowing of the eyes and skin, preceded by lethar-
gy, fever and pains in the upper right abdomen.
The Havrix vaccine, which lasts for several
years, is expensive but very effective. Two injections separated by two to four weeks are
required, followed by a booster a year later. The
traditional one-shot vaccine gives protection for
three months.

The less common **hepatitis B** virus can be
passed on through unprotected sexual contact,
blood transfusions and dirty needles. The vaccine
(three injections over six months) is recommended for anyone in a high-risk category, including
those travelling extensively in rural areas or anyone likely to be in infected areas for longer than
six months.

MEDICAL RESOURCES FOR TRAVELLERS

BRITAIN AND IRELAND

British Airways Travel Clinic, 156 Regent St, London W1 (Mon–Fri 9am–4.15pm, Sat 10am–4pm; ☎0171/439 9584); branches at 101 Cheapside, London EC2 (☎0171/606 2977) and at the BA terminal in London's Victoria Station (☎0171/233 6661); plus regional clinics (call☎0171/831 5333 for details of the one nearest to you).

Hospital for Tropical Diseases, St Pancras Hospital, 4 St Pancras Way, London NW1 (☎0171/530 3454). *Operates a recorded message service on ☎0171/530 3429 which gives information on illness prevention as well as listing appropriate immunizations.*

MASTA (*Medical Advisory Service for Travellers Abroad*), London School of Hygiene and Tropical Medicine (☎0891/224100). *Operates a Travellers' Health Line 24 hours a day, 7 days a week, supplying written information tailored to your journey by return of post.*

Travel Medicine Services, PO Box 254, 16 College St, Belfast 1 (☎01232/315220).

Tropical Medical Bureau, Grafton St Medical Centre, Dublin 2 (☎01/671 9200); Dun Laoghaire Medical Centre, 5 Northumberland Ave, Dun Laoghaire, Co. Dublin (☎01/280 4996).

USA AND CANADA

Canadian Society for International Health, 170 Laurier Ave W, Suite 902, Ottawa, ON K1P 5V5 (☎613/230-2654). *Distributes a free pamphlet, "Health Information for Canadian Travellers".*

International Association for Medical Assistance to Travellers (IAMAT), 417 Center St, Lewiston, NY 14092 (☎716/754-4883) and 40 Regal Rd, Guelph, ON N1K 1B5 (☎519/836-0102). *This non-profit organization supported by donations can provide a list of English-speaking doctors, climate charts and leaflets on various diseases and inoculations.*

Travel Medicine, 351 Pleasant St, Suite 312, Northampton, MA 01060 (☎1-800/872-8633). *Sells first-aid kits, mosquito netting, water filters and other health-related travel products.*

Travelers Medical Center, 31 Washington Square, New York, NY 10011 (☎212/982-1600). *Consultation service on immunizations and treatment of diseases.*

AUSTRALIA AND NEW ZEALAND

Auckland Hospital, Park Rd, Grafton, Auckland (☎09/379 7440).

Travel Health and Vaccination Clinic, 114 Williams St, Melbourne (☎03/9670 2020).

Travellers Immunization Service, 303 Pacific Hwy, Sydney (☎02/9416 1348).

Travellers' Medical and Vaccination Centre, Level 7, 428 George St, Sydney (☎02/9221 7133); Level 3, 393 Little Bourke St, Melbourne (☎03/9602 5788); Level 6, 29 Gilbert Place, Adelaide (☎08/8212 7522); Level 6, 247 Adelaide St, Brisbane (☎07/3221 9066); 1 Mill St, Perth (☎08/9321 1977).

You should have all your shots recorded on an International Certificate of Vaccination.

GENERAL PRECAUTIONS

There's no point in being over concerned with your health while travelling in China, but it's sensible to be aware of the dangers and take sensible precautions. China is not an easy country to be in, and some visitors, particularly if they are travelling quickly or on a very tight budget, find it exhausting and stressful, thus leaving themselves vulnerable to infections. A good general tip is not to be too hard on yourself. Travel at an easy pace, and treat yourself to decent accommodation and food, at least occasionally. Take vitamin pills (you can buy them in

Hong Kong and Beijing) if you think your diet is lacking in variety.

Personal hygiene is one area you can control and it pays to be scrupulous. Wash your hands often and don't share drinks or cigarettes. When in the shower, always wear flip-flops or shower shoes, provided free at most hotels – look under the bed. The smallest cuts can become infected, so clean them thoroughly and apply an antiseptic cream, then keep them dry and covered.

Water is a potential cause of sickness as its quality varies widely across the country. In the cities tap water is chlorinated, and is at least safe to clean your teeth with; in rural areas, however, you should always boil it first. Don't take ice in drinks, or eat the ice lollies sold by street-side entrepreneurs. The Chinese boil all their drinking water scrupulously, and every hotel room is equipped with a Thermos, which the floor attendant will fill for you. Chemically treated **bottled water** is widely available from street stalls, though it tastes disgusting. If you stick to this and drink tea or carbonated drinks in restaurants, you shouldn't need to take any further precautions. However, if you're heading off the beaten track, it's well worth taking a **water purifier** with you. While boiling water for ten minutes kills most micro-organisms, it's not the most convenient method. Sterilization with iodine tablets is effective, but the resulting beverage doesn't taste very pleasant and you'll probably want to filter the water as well. (Iodine is unsafe for pregnant women, babies and people with thyroid complaints.) A range of low-cost portable water purifiers, which sterilize and filter the water, giving the most complete treatment, is now available. Made by Pre-Mac, they are available in the UK from *British Airways* Travel Clinics (see box opposite) and specialist outdoor equipment retailers (call ☎01732/460333 for details of local stockists); in Ireland through All Water Systems Ltd, Unit 12, Western Parkway Business Centre, Lr Ballymount Rd, Dublin 12 (☎01/456 4933); in the USA and Canada, contact Outbound Products (☎1-800/663-9262; in Canada ☎604/321-5464).

As for **food**, the two most important considerations are to eat at places which look busy and clean, and to stick to fresh, thoroughly cooked food. Beware of food that has been pre-cooked and kept warm for several hours. Seafood is risky as local water pollution levels are high. Fresh fruit you've peeled yourself is safe; other uncooked foods may have been washed in unclean water. The other thing to watch for is dirty **chopsticks**. The disposable chopsticks provided in most restaurants are fine but other chopsticks are often just given a quick rinse and put back on the table. If you want to be really sure, bring your own pair.

INTESTINAL TROUBLES

Diarrhoea is the most common illness to affect travellers, usually in a mild form while your stomach gets used to the unfamiliar food. Rest and rehydration is the only treatment required, and it will probably be over in a couple of days. The sudden onset of diarrhoea with stomach cramps and vomiting indicates food poisoning; again, rest up for a couple of days and the sickness

should pass. In both cases, it is important to drink lots of water and in serious cases replace lost salts with rehydration solution (ORS); this is especially important with young children. Take a few sachets with you, buy it at any pharmacy, or you can make your own by adding half a teaspoon of salt and three of sugar to a litre of cool, previously boiled water. At the same time avoid milk, greasy or spicy foods, coffee and most fruit, in favour of bland foodstuffs such as bread, rice, dumplings, noodles and soup. If symptoms persist, or if you notice blood or mucus in your stool, consult a doctor.

Dysentery is inflammation of the intestine, indicated by diarrhoea with blood or mucus and abdominal pain. There are two varieties, bacillary and amoebic. Bacillary dysentery has an acute onset with discomfort, fever and vomiting, plus severe abdominal pains with bloody, watery diarrhoea. In mild cases recovery occurs spontaneously within a week, but a serious attack will require antibiotics. Amoebic dysentery is more serious as bouts last for several weeks and often recur. The gradually appearing symptoms are marked by bloody faeces accompanied by abdominal cramps, but no vomiting or fever. If left untreated, amoebic cysts enter the bloodstream and may cause long-term problems, but a prompt course of antibiotics should restore you to health.

Giardia is distinguished by smelly burps or farts, discoloured faeces without blood or pus, and fluctuating diarrhoea. Again the disease is treatable with antibiotics under medical supervision. If you're heading for Tibet, however, where the disease is most likely to be a problem, you will not be able to get the appropriate antibiotics there, so take some *Flagyl* with you.

Typhoid and cholera are also spread by contaminated food or water, generally in localized epidemics. The varied symptoms of **typhoid** include headaches, high fever and constipation, followed by diarrhoea in the later stages. The disease is infectious and requires immediate medical treatment but it's also difficult to diagnose. The first indication of **cholera** is the sudden but painless onset of watery and unpredictable diarrhoea, later combined with vomiting, nausea and muscle cramps. The rapid dehydration caused by the diarrhoea rather than the intestinal infection itself is the main danger. However serious the vomiting and diarrhoea you can treat cholera with plenty of oral rehydration solutions, but if you can't retain enough fluids, get medical help.

Finally, if you're suffering from diarrhoea, remember that oral drugs such as anti-malarial and contraceptive pills pass through your system too quickly to be effectively absorbed.

MALARIA

Malaria is not widespread in China; it's only a problem in the south in summer and all year round in tropical areas such as Hainan Island. Even there it's not common, but you should still take precautions. The key measure is to avoid being bitten by mosquitoes which carry the disease. Though mosquitoes lurk all day in dark, humid environments like bathrooms, they are most active at dawn and dusk. At these times wear long sleeves and trousers and avoid dark colours. Use **repellent** on exposed skin. Sprays and lotions containing about forty percent DEET (diethyltoluamide) are effective and can also be used to treat clothes, but the chemical is toxic; keep it away from eyes and open wounds, and follow the manufacturer's recommendations carefully, particularly with young children. DEET has been known to cause bad dreams, nausea and dizziness. Good alternatives based on natural ingredients are *Mosi-Guard Natural* and *Gurkha* repellents.

Most hotels and guesthouses in affected areas provide **mosquito nets** but you may want to bring your own if you intend heading to any rural areas. A net which hangs from a single point is the most practical. Many nets are already impregnated with pyrethroids, but need retreating every six months; all the gear is available from travel clinics (see box on p.20) and good travel shops. Tuck the edges in well at night, sleep away from the sides and make sure the mesh is not torn. Air conditioning and fans help keep mosquitoes away, as do **mosquito coils** and knockdown **insecticide sprays**, both available in China.

If you're travelling in a high-risk area it is advisable to take **preventative tablets**, although medical opinion varies on the safety and effectiveness of the different drugs available. Mefloquine is widely regarded as the most effective since the malaria-carrying mosquito is now largely resistant to chloroquine. However, mefloquine has some unpleasant side effects such as dizzy spells, nausea and neuropsychiatric disturbances, which can persist after you've stopped taking the drug; ensure you discuss any concerns you have with your prescribing doctor. Women in

the first months of pregnancy or during lactation should avoid mefloquine and it's also important not to get pregnant for three months after taking the drug. The most common alternative is daily proguanil (Paludrine) combined with weekly chloroquine (Avloclor). Note that you need to start taking tablets at least a week before exposure, and then continue with them for four weeks after leaving a malarial region. Many doctors in Australia are now prescribing Doxycycline, a low-level antibiotic, as a malaria preventative, and it is used as standard by the Australian Army.

None of these precautions is infallible, however. **Symptoms** of the onset of malaria are recurring fevers with headaches and shivering. A blood test will confirm the diagnosis and, if caught early, treatment can be quick and effective. If you can't get to a doctor straight away, take 600mg of quinine three times a day for seven days.

OTHER MOSQUITO-BORNE AILMENTS

Mosquitoes are also responsible for transmitting **dengue fever**, whose symptoms are similar to malaria but with more severe headaches, together with aching muscles and sometimes a rash spreading from the torso over the limbs and face. There's no specific cure but most people recover after a week of rest, paracetamol and plenty of fluids; aspirin should be avoided if possible as it causes internal bleeding. A more dangerous strain called dengue haemorrhage fever primarily affects children. If you notice an unusual tendency to bleed or bruise, consult a doctor immediately.

RESPIRATORY INFECTIONS

The biggest hazard to your health in China is the host of **flu** infections that strike down a large proprtion of the population, mostly in the winter months. The problem is compounded by the overcrowded conditions, chain-smoking, pollution and widespread spitting, which rapidly spreads infection. Initial symptoms are fever, sore throat, chills and a feeling of malaise. Afterwards, severe coughing and bronchitis set in, making for some very uncomfortable nights. Initially, try drinking lots of fluids and get plenty of rest. If symptoms persist, you are advised to take an antibiotic such as *Tetracycline*, available at pharmacies or on prescription from a doctor. As with all antibiotics, it is important to complete the course, usually four tablets daily for five days.

More serious is **tuberculosis**, a respiratory disease transmitted by inhalation, and spread by coughing and spitting – so it's not hard to see why China has a high incidence. The disease becomes active when the body is weakened by fatigue, other forms of illness, or malnutrition. It strikes at the lungs and in a small number of cases can be fatal. There is no need for visitors to be overly worried about the disease, though budget travellers, who spend a lot of time on crowded trains and buses, are likely to be more at risk than other tourists. Those embarking on prolonged travel should consult their doctor about their TB-immune status – many people are immune thanks to previous, mild infections.

AIDS AND OTHER SEXUALLY TRANSMITTED DISEASES

It is doubtful that China was ever as strictly moral as the government suggests, a place where prostitution didn't exist and **sexually transmitted diseases** were a foreign problem, but it's certainly not true now. In the contemporary, more liberal climate, with an embryonic sexual revolution, STDs have become much more common. As yet, though, China has only a minor problem with **AIDS**, though there are bound to be more than the official number of two thousand cases in the country. Paranoia about the disease, and its transmission by foreigners, is rife, however, and you may find that if you turn up at a Chinese hospital the first thing they will do is test you for it. There have even been cases of hotels burning their bedsheets after foreigners have stayed in them.

The more common diseases, **gonorrhoea** and **syphilis**, identifiable by rashes around the genitals and painful discharge, are treatable with antibiotics, available from doctors. As ever, it is extremely unwise to contemplate unprotected casual sex. Local Chinese **condoms** vary in quality, but imported brands are available in big cities. If it becomes essential for you to have an injection or blood transfusion in China, try to make sure that new, sterile needles are used – to be sure, bring your own. Similarly, don't undergo acupuncture unless you are sure that the equipment is sterile.

ENVIRONMENTAL HAZARDS

Parts of China are tropical and here it can require a couple of weeks to acclimatize to the temperature and humidity, during which time you may feel listless and tire easily. Don't underestimate the strength of the sun in tropical areas such as Hainan Island, in desert regions such as Xinjiang or very high up, for example on the Tibetan plateau. **Sunburn** can be avoided by restricting your exposure to the midday sun and by liberal use of sunscreens, rarely available in China. Dark glasses help to protect your eyes and a wide-brimmed hat is a good idea. Drinking plenty of water will prevent **dehydration**, but if you do become dehydrated – signs are infrequent or irregular urination – drink a salt and sugar solution (see under "Intestinal Troubles", above). **Heat stroke** is more serious and may require hospital treatment. Indications are a high temperature, lack of sweating, a fast pulse and red skin. Reducing your body temperature with a lukewarm shower will provide initial relief. High humidity causes **heat rashes, prickly heat and fungal infections**. Prevention and cure are the same: wear loose clothes made of natural fibres, wash frequently and dry off thoroughly afterwards. Talcum powder and the use of mild antiseptic soap helps too.

At the other extreme, there are plenty of parts in China that get very **cold** indeed. If you're trekking in Tibet or visiting northern China during the winter, it is essential to be prepared. **Hypothermia**, where the overall body temperature falls, is the most serious condition, and is sometimes fatal. Symptoms are exhaustion, numbness, slurred speech and dizzy spells. To prevent the condition, wear lots of layers and a hat, and try to stay dry and out of the wind. Sugary food will help raise the body temperature but alcohol lowers it. To treat hypothermia, try to get the victim into shelter, away from wind and rain, give them hot drinks and easily digestible food, and keep them warm.

ALTITUDE SICKNESS

Several regions of China, including Tibet and areas of Xinjiang, Sichuan and Yunnan are significantly above sea level, and if you are travelling here you should be aware of the health dangers posed by **high altitudes**. In these regions, reduced air pressure means that, until you are acclimatized, the blood does not absorb oxygen efficiently. As soon as you begin ascending, your body starts to adapt and produce more red blood cells to compensate but, travelling by bus, train and especially plane, you'll ascend faster than your body can adapt. **Symptoms** of **AMS** (acute mountain sickness) are individual and unpredictable, but generally you can expect headaches, shortness of breath, aches and pains, tiredness, sleeping problems and nausea. Relaxing totally for your first two or three days at altitude and drinking copious quantities of water should help to ease the symptoms, as will a few painkillers. In Lhasa, some of the hotels even have oxygen on hand. For most people the symptoms will pass, although having acclimatized at one altitude you should still ascend slowly, no more than 300m per day. If you go up again too quickly, you can expect the symptoms to return.

On a more dangerous note, AMS can be the precursor to more serious problems, sometimes called **malignant AMS** because of its potential to kill. If the body fails to acclimatize effectively, serious lung and cerebral conditions can develop. High-altitude pulmonary oedema is characterized by severe breathing trouble, a cough and frothy white or pink sputum, while high-altitude cerebral oedema causes severe headaches, loss of balance, other neurological symptoms and even-

tually coma. Both are killers. The only treatment is rapid descent and even then survival is not assured. In Tibet, this means flying out to Kathmandu or Chengdu without delay. Medical opinion is divided about the usefulness of acetazolamide (*Diamox*) to ease the symptoms of AMS. Discuss this with your doctor before you travel.

GETTING MEDICAL HELP

Pharmacies, found in all towns, can help with minor injuries or ailments. Larger ones sometimes have a separate counter offering diagnosis and advice, though you're very unlikely to find staff who can speak anything but Chinese. The selection of reliable Asian and Western products available has improved, and it's also possible to treat yourself for minor complaints with herbal medicines. Contraceptives are widely available, as are antibiotics. You'll have to ask for what you want, so take along a phrasebook or a Chinese speaker (see "Language", p.1058, for some useful phrases). The staff will usually be able to help if you describe your symptoms.

CHINESE MEDICINE, ACUPUNCTURE AND TAI JI

The first time most visitors confront **traditional Chinese medicine** is in department stores, where among the shelves of plastic kitchenware and cheap clothes are displays of such exotica as deer horn, snake gall bladder and scorpion oil. All these are used as ingredients for medicinal preparations, along with more mundane herbs. The bizarre nature of many of the treatments used makes most visitors suspicious of their efficacy; in fact, traditional Chinese medicine, which employs a holistic style of treatment, considering the entire body rather than focusing on the complaint, can be very effective, and is these days often used in China in combination with Western medical techniques. As a general rule, Chinese medicines are very good for the relief of minor illnesses such as headaches, flu, coughs and colds. They are much less effective at treating serious illness. There are far too many herbs on offer for patients to treat themselves with any kind of likelihood of success; if you want to try these remedies, describe your symptoms to a pharmacist, or visit a traditional Chinese doctor, who will listen to your pulse and examine your tongue before writing a prescription.

Another remedy that can seem strange to foreigners is **acupuncture**, the technique of inserting needles into various precise points on the body. Each point is believed to correspond to a particular organ, so, for example, the heart can be treated through the feet. No one is quite sure how it works – perhaps through interfering with nerve pathways – but there are plenty of satisfied customers to testify to its effectiveness. It seems to work best on painful muscle and bone complaints, such as rheumatism, arthritis and back pain. If you want to be treated in this way, clinics of traditional Chinese medicine in major cities practise the technique. Make sure your acupuncturist uses sterile needles, as good ones always will.

A technique of health maintenance that you will certainly see is **tai ji**, practised in public spaces in the early morning, mostly by the elderly. Technically it's a martial art, but the slow, graceful movements involved would be of use in combat only to a real master of the art. For most, *tai ji* is used as a form of exercise, a balletic workout which is fascinating to watch, and apparently very good for you, aiding circulation, suppleness and muscle tone, as well as general health and well-being.

Large hotels usually have a **clinic** for guests offering diagnosis, advice and prescriptions – ask an English speaker from the reception desk to accompany you. Beijing, Shanghai, Guangzhou and Hong Kong have clinics specifically for foreigners where staff speak English. If you are seriously ill, head straight to a **hospital** – the local *CITS* might be able to give you useful advice in an emergency. Addresses of clinics and hospitals can be found in the "Listings" sections of major towns and cities in *The Guide*. You will be expected to pay for your treatment on the spot, but it should not be too expensive, although foreigner surcharges may well be added. Keep all medical bills and receipts so you can make an insurance claim when you get home.

INFORMATION AND MAPS

The concept of a country promoting itself by giving out tourist information for free has not yet taken hold in China. There is a very thin scattering of tourist promotion offices in foreign capitals, though even these seem only to have the function of recommending possible tour operators. A more promising source of immediate information is probably the Internet (see box overleaf).

Similarly, inside the People's Republic, there is no such thing as a tourist information office. **CITS**, the state-accredited tour operator with a special responsibility for foreigners, was originally dressed up as such, but now it is just one of a large number of competing local operators who have no function other than selling tours and tickets, and renting cars. However, it may still be worthwhile dropping in on the local branch of *CITS*, or an affiliated organization (*CYTS* or *CTS*), especially in out-of-the-way places, as it is sometimes here that you will find the only person in town who can speak English – and he or she may be delighted to have the chance to chat with a foreigner about local tourist attractions. But this is probably the exception rather than the rule. You should assume that most leaflets, brochures and maps

---

CHINESE TOURIST PROMOTION OFFICES ABROAD

Australia 19th floor, 44 Market St, Sydney, NSW 2000 (☎02/9299 4057).

France 116 Avenue des Champs-Elysees, 75008 Paris (☎1/44218282).

Germany Ilkenhanstra. 6, D–60433 Frankfurt am Main, (☎069/520135).

Japan 6F Hamamatsu Cho Building, 1-27-13 Hamamatsu Cho, Minato-Ku, Tokyo (☎81/03 3433 1461).

Singapore 1 Shenton Way, No 17-05, Ribina House, Singapore 0106 (☎65/221 8681).

Spain Gran Via 88, Grupo 2, Planta 16, 28013 Madrid (☎01/5480011).

UK 4 Glentworth St, London NW1 (☎0171/935 9787).

USA 350 Fifth Ave, Suite 6413, Empire State Building, New York, NY 10018 (☎212/760-1710 automated or 212/760-8218); 333 W Broadway Suite 201, Glendale, CA 91024 (☎818/545-7505).

from these places will not be free. Other sources of information are your own hotel staff (in upmarket places), or any local English-speakers you happen to meet. Otherwise, in certain tourist centres, restaurant proprietors have taken it upon themselves to act as the local information office, giving advice in exchange for custom.

In **Beijing** and **Shanghai** you'll find English-language magazines with bar, restaurant and other "What's On" listings, aimed mainly at the resident expatriate population. These are usually distributed free in upmarket hotels. The local English-language newspaper, the *China Daily*, also has a few listings of major cultural events forthcoming in Beijing and one or two other large cities. In **Hong Kong** and **Macau** you are beset with information on all sides. For details of listings magazines in the two territories, see the "Information" sections on pp.605 and 646.

MAPS

Street maps are available in China for almost every town and city. You can nearly always buy them in street kiosks, hotel shops and *Xinhua* bookshops, or from vendors in the vicinity of train and bus stations. The vast majority of maps are unfortunately in Chinese only, which is a pity because the maps are a mine of information showing bus routes, sights, hotels and restaurants. You'll nearly always find local bus, train and flight timetables printed on the back as well.

However, cities most commonly visited by foreign tourists do produce English-language maps for foreigners. You'll find these on sale in upmarket hotels, at the principal tourist sights, such as big museums, or in *CITS* offices. In **Beijing** and **Shanghai** you'll find various editions of such maps, issued free in smart hotels and paid for by advertising. The situation is similar in **Hong Kong** and **Macau**, where the local tourist offices provide free maps which are adequate for most visitors' needs. For very detailed street maps of Hong Kong, have a look at the *Hong Kong Island Street Map* and the *Kowloon Street Map* for sale in English-language bookshops.

Countrywide maps, which you should buy before you leave home, include the excellent 1:4,000,000 map from *GeoCenter*, which shows relief and useful sections of all neighbouring countries. If you want very high-resolution maps showing details of terrain, especially useful for cyclists and trekkers in the wilderness parts of western China, the *Operational Navigation Charts* (Series ONC) – actually designed for pilots – are worth having a look at. One of the best maps of Tibet is *Stanfords Map of South-Central Tibet; Kathmandu–Lhasa Route Map*, published by Stanfords in London (see box opposite).

MAP SUPPLIERS

BRITAIN AND IRELAND

Daunt Books, 83 Marylebone High St, W1 (☎0171/224 2295).

Easons Bookshop, 40 O'Connell St, Dublin 1 (☎01/873 3811).

John Smith and Sons, 57–61 St Vincent St, G2 (☎0141/221 7472).

National Map Centre, 22–24 Caxton St, SW1 (☎0171/222 4945).

Stanfords,* 12–14 Long Acre, WC2 (☎0171/836 1321); 52 Grosvenor Gardens, London SW1; 156 Regent St, London W1.

The Travel Bookshop, 13–15 Blenheim Crescent, London W11 (☎0171/229 5260).

*Maps by **mail or phone order** are available from *Stanfords;* ☎0171/836 1321.

USA AND CANADA

Book Passage, 51 Tamal Vista Dr, Corte Madera, CA 94925 (☎415/927-0960).

The Complete Traveler Bookstore, 199 Madison Ave, New York, NY 10016 (☎212/685-9007); 3207 Fillmore St, San Francisco, CA 92123 (☎415/923-1511).

Elliot Bay Book Company, 101 S Main St, Seattle, WA 98104 (☎206/624-6600).

Forsyth Travel Library, 9154 W 57th St, Shawnee Mission, KS 66201 (☎1-800/367-7984).

Map Link Inc, 25 E Mason St, Santa Barbara, CA 93101 (☎805/965-4402).

Open Air Books and Maps, 25 Toronto St, Toronto, ON M5R 2C1 (☎416/363-0719).

Phileas Fogg's Books & Maps, #87 Stanford Shopping Center, Palo Alto, CA 94304 (☎1-800/233-FOGG in California; ☎1-800/533-FOGG elsewhere in US).

Rand McNally,* 444 N Michigan Ave, Chicago, IL 60611 (☎312/321-1751); 150 E 52nd St, New York, NY 10022 (☎212/758-7488); 595 Market St, San Francisco, CA 94105 (☎415/777-3131); 1201 Connecticut Ave NW, Washington, DC 20003 (☎202/223-6751).

Sierra Club Bookstore, 730 Polk St, San Francisco, CA 94109 (☎415/923-5500).

Travel Books & Language Center, 4931 Cordell Ave, Bethesda, MD 20814 (☎1-800/220-2665).

Traveler's Bookstore, 22 W 52nd St, New York, NY 10019 (☎212/664-0995).

Ulysses Travel Bookshop, 4176 St-Denis, Montréal (☎514/289-0993).

World Wide Books and Maps, 1247 Granville St, Vancouver, BC V6Z 1E4 (☎604/687-3320).

* *Rand McNally* now has 24 stores across the US; call ☎1-800/333-0136 ext 2111 for the location of your nearest store, or to order maps by mail order.

AUSTRALIA AND NEW ZEALAND

Bowyangs, 372 Little Burke St, Melbourne (☎03/9670 4383).

Hema Maps, 239 George St, Brisbane (☎07/3221 4330).

The Map Shop, 16a Peel St, Adelaide (☎08/8231 2033).

Perth Map Centre, 891 Hay St, Perth (☎09/9322 5733).

Specialty Maps, 58 Albert St, Auckland (☎09/307 2217).

Travel Bookshop, 20 Bridge St, Sydney (☎02/9241 3554).

COSTS, MONEY AND BANKS

Compared to the rest of Asia, China can be an expensive place to travel. Though it's always possible to eat and move around fairly cheaply, accommodation costs can be as high as in Europe or the US, and daily expenses vary drastically, according to region. In descending order, the three main price "zones" are Hong Kong and Macau, the eastern seaboard, and the interior provinces, with some variation within these categories (for example see "Accommodation", p.36). Basically, things get cheaper the farther west you go, though costs are always relatively more expensive in popular tourist spots.

CURRENCY

Chinese currency is formally called **yuan** (¥), more colloquially known as **kuai**, and breaks down into units of ten **mao** or **jiao**, and one hun-

dred **fen** – though these latter are effectively worthless and you'll only ever be given them in official currency transactions, or see the tiny yellow and green notes folded up into little twists and used to build model dragons or boats. **Paper money** was invented in China and is still the main form of exchange, available in ¥100, ¥50, ¥20, ¥10, ¥5, and ¥1 notes, with a similar selection of mao. You occasionally come across tinny mao or fen **coins**, and rare brass ¥1 pieces.

Hong Kong's unit of currency is the Hong Kong **dollar** (HK$), divided into one hundred cents, while in **Macau** they use **pataca** (usually written M$ or ptca), in turn broken down into 100 **avos**. Both currencies are roughly equivalent to the yuan, but while Hong Kong dollars are accepted in Macau and southern China's Special Economic Zones, neither yuan or pataca are any use outside China or Macau respectively. Tourist hotels in Beijing, Shanghai and Guangzhou also sometimes accept – even insist on – payment in Hong Kong or US dollars. Hong Kong dollars are available overseas, yuan and patacas are not, though both can be obtained in Hong Kong if you're going there first, and converted back at a bank before you leave the country.

At the time of writing, the **exchange rate** was approximately ¥11 to £1, or ¥7 to US$1.

COSTS

Given the extreme regional variations, it's hard to make exact predictions of how much China costs on a daily basis. Wherever you are in **mainland China**, you should be able to keep your average daily budget for food and travel to a minimum

---

THE OLD DAYS: FEC

Yuan once came in two forms: **renminbi** ("People's Money"), in general use around the country, and **FEC**, or Foreign Exchange Certificates, which were issued only to tourists. Though both renminbi and FEC notes had the same face values and were theoretically interchangeable, in reality, FEC were worth far more as you needed them to buy **imported goods** – decent clothing, TVs, washing machines and anything else difficult to get at the time. Not surprisingly, the system was responsible for some major headaches. Although travellers benefited from a healthy black market exchange rate for FEC – furtive figures hissing "change money, change money" accosted Westerners outside many a hotel – it got to the point that accommodation, restaurants, and transport refused to accept renminbi notes from foreigners, who were nonetheless obliged to take them as change. But as China began to produce its own luxury goods, FEC lost their relevance and desirability, and were finally dropped in 1992. They are now hawked as tourist souvenirs by the same people who used to run the black market.

£10/US$15 or so by eating in cheap and mid-range restaurants, and travelling on local buses or hard train classes. What really separates the east coast (including the whole of Dongbei) from the interior provinces, however, is the cost of **accommodation**. While budget travellers can find beds in Sichuan for as little as £1/US$1.5 a night, on the east coast it's hard to find anything for less than £30/US$45. Fast or comfortable travel also comes at a premium – flights and soft-sleeper berths are double the price of a hard-sleeper train berth and at least five times as expensive as covering the same route by bus. In general, by doing everything cheaply and sticking mostly to the interior provinces you can survive on £15/US$23 a day; travel a bit more widely and in better comfort from time to time and you're looking at £30/US$45 a day; while travelling in style and visiting only key places along the east coast you're looking at daily expenses of £50/US$75 and above.

There's also a certain level of **price tiering** in China, with foreigners and Overseas Chinese paying more than locals for some services. This used to include train travel and hotels, but now mainly applies to **airfares** (though there are plans to abolish the current fifty percent foreigners' surcharge), and **entry fees** for museums and famous sites. One way around the latter is to get hold of a **Chinese Student Card**, which nets you substantial reductions at these places – they are vaguely official-looking documents, adorned with your photograph and folded into a small, red plastic wallet. You can get one officially by studying, however briefly, in China; unofficially, tour agents geared up to foreign needs can often supply them for about ¥40 and you can usually get them in the areas around backpacker hotels and restaurants. **Bargaining** is common practice throughout the land, at least in private dealings such as at markets, but isn't generally pursued with the same enthusiasm as in other Asian countries.

Costs in **Hong Kong** and **Macau** are much higher for comparable services than on the mainland, particularly for upmarket accommodation – though food and drink are again pretty reasonable and transport expenses negligible. The cheapest beds will set you back £6/US$9, while it's hard to come by a decent double room for under £60/US$90. Staying at cheap lodgings and eating simply from noodle stalls will cost you about £20/US$30 a day, up to £23/US$35 with a mid-

range restaurant meal thrown in. For more comfort and classier food, budget from £80/US$120 and up.

TRAVELLERS' CHEQUES, CASH AND CARDS

Travellers' cheques, available through banks and travel agents, are the best way to carry your funds around; their exchange rate in China is fixed and actually better than for cash, and they can be replaced if lost or stolen – keep a list of the serial numbers separate from the cheques. On the downside, in **mainland China** they can be cashed only at major branches of the *Bank of China* and tourist hotels (though very few parts of the country have neither) and the process always involves lengthy paperwork. Stick to generic brands such as *Thomas Cook* or *American Express*, as less familiar, bank-issued travellers' cheques won't be accepted in smaller places.

In case you find yourself in difficulties, it's also worth taking along a small supply of **foreign currency** such as US, Canadian or Australian dollars, or British pounds, which are more widely exchangeable. There's a low-key **black market** in China for foreign currency, but the small profits you'll make and the risks of getting ripped off or attracting police attention don't make it worthwhile. **Credit cards** are useful too, with *Visa*, *American Express*, and *Mastercard* accepted at big tourist hotels, and **cash advances** on *Visa* issued within an hour at many Chinese banks. In an **emergency**, wiring money through the *Bank of China* will definitely take weeks even in Beijing, Shanghai or Guangzhou, and rates charged at both ends make it a poor option except as a last resort. If you think it is at all possible

BANKING HOURS

Banks in major Chinese cities are sometimes open seven days a week, though foreign exchange is usually only available Monday to Friday, approximately 9am–noon & 2–5pm. All banks are closed for the first three days of the Chinese New Year (Spring Festival), with reduced hours for the following eleven days. In Hong Kong, banks are generally open Monday–Friday 9am–4.30pm, Saturday 9am–12.30pm, while in Macau they close thirty minutes earlier.

that you might have to use this route, make arrangements with your own bank before you leave home.

In **Hong Kong** and **Macau**, however, any bank or Bureau de Change will be happy to cash travellers' cheques or foreign currency notes, though rates and commissions are unpredictable (illicit interest is also often levied on credit card advances) and you always need to establish them first. Several bank ATMs in Hong Kong also have **Cirrus-Maestro** connections, which let you

draw funds from your home account – check with your bank for details. **Wiring money** to Hong Kong is no problem. Any of the major international banks here can organize a transfer from your home bank to a specific branch in Hong Kong. It will take the best part of a day, though, and you'll be charged a handling fee. International companies, such as *Western Union Money Transfer*, can also handle the transaction for you and charge a percentage of the sum transferred.

GETTING AROUND

China is huge, and unless you concentrate on a small area, you're going to spend a good deal of your time – and budget – just getting around. Fortunately, public transport is very comprehensive and reasonably priced considering the distances involved, and there's usually a choice of travel options available. You can fly to all regional capitals and many of the larger cities; the rail network extends to every province except Tibet; while if you're up to slow hours of rough riding, you can reach almost all corners of the country on local transport – which covers everything from buses to tractors. There's even a fair number of rivers still plied by passenger ferries, and a few vessels chugging between coastal ports and down to Hainan Island. Tibet is the one region where there are restrictions on independent travel (see p.946 for more details). Tours are one way of taking the pressure off travel, and in some cases are the only practical way of getting out to certain sights; they're never cheap, but can be good value.

While there are plenty of options, travel can also take some planning and patience. Bus timetables are unpredictable, with scheduled state services losing out to ad hoc private operators, while train journeys have their own peculiar pitfalls. You also want to weigh up the mental and physical rigours involved if you insist on travelling the cheapest way all the time – it's well worth covering long distances in as much comfort as possible.

TRAINS

Mainland China's first rail lines were laid in the nineteenth century, and it was popular resentment against foreign involvement in them which led directly to the successful 1911 revolution establishing the Chinese Republic. Much of the original network was destroyed during the Japanese occupation and subsequent civil war, but since its takeover in 1949, the Communist government has constantly expanded the facilities, and today China's **rail network** is vast and efficient, definitely the safest, most reliable way to travel through the country – even though getting hold of a seat can be difficult. Apart from the sheer distances covered, there are no truly great train journeys within China, however.

BUYING TICKETS

There's an incredible demand for **train tickets**, and, however you do it, you'll almost certainly need to buy one well in advance. The first thing to do is consult a **timetable**, usually on display somewhere in the ticket office, or sold from stalls around the station. These can take a little effort to decipher. You need to be able to recognize the characters for both where you are and your destination, and it helps to know the train number and how many services there are, in case your first choice isn't available. In this book, travel details at the end of each chapter give the frequency and duration of main train journeys, and the Chinese characters for most destinations are given with the town and city accounts throughout the text.

Theoretically, **tickets** are sold up to three days in advance, and stations at most big cities have **foreigners' ticket offices** which makes buying what's available fairly straightforward. Note that there's a big difference between **reserved** and **unreserved** travel. You can always, if you are desperate, go to the station and buy an unreserved hard seat ticket for the next train, but it's well worth waiting to travel for a day or two in order to book a reserved seat or berth – otherwise you'll probably have to stand for your entire journey. Have someone write down the date, destination, range of train numbers and class of travel you're after to avoid confusion. You will need to show your passport to book sleeper classes. Although it's always worth trying to get the tickets yourself, if there's no foreigners' ticket office you'll probably have to spend hours fighting with the masses to hold your place in a queue, only to find that what you want is unavailable. Usually, on popular routes and at major stations, it's far better to employ an **agent** – your hotel reception or the local *CITS*, for instance – who will have connections with station staff enabling them to buy tickets on lines which are apparently fully booked (they will usually need one or two days' notice). **Touts** who inevitably hang around busy stations are another means of getting a reservation, though it's entirely up to you to decide whether or not you can trust them.

Once you have your ticket, turn up with enough time to work out which platform your train leaves from – if you can't speak Chinese, show your ticket to station staff who will point you in the right direction. Passengers are not allowed on to the platform until the train is in and ready to leave, which means huge crowds of people with unreserved seats surging through the barriers at once. If you've been unable to buy the berth of your choice before boarding, make your way immediately to the controller's booth, usually in car 8 (all carriages are numbered on the outside), where you can sign up for beds as they become available.

CLASSES AND TRAINS

There are four train **classes**. The best is **soft berth** (*ruanwo*), an expensive option roughly the same price as flying, and generally patronized by foreigners, party officials, and successful entrepreneurs. It's a nice experience; there's a plush waiting room at the station, and on the train itself you get a wood-panelled four-berth compartment with a soft mattress, fan, optional radio, and a choice of Western- or Chinese-style toilets. There's an attendant on hand, too, and meals – though good in all classes – are more varied and taken separately from the other passengers. Basically, if you've a long way to travel and can afford it, soft berth is well worth the money and you'll arrive rested and ready to enjoy your destination.

Yingwo, **hard berth**, is about half the price of *ruanwo*, favoured by China's emerging middle class and money-conscious foreigners, and hence the most difficult to book in advance. On boarding, the carriage attendant exchanges your ticket for a metal tag, swapped back about half an hour before you arrive at your destination, whatever hour of the day or night this is. Carriages are divided into twenty sets of three-tiered bunks; if you ever have a choice in the matter, the topmost bunk is slightly cheaper, and gives you somewhere to withdraw during the day – though it's closer to the lights and radio, and cigarette smoke tends to accumulate up here. Each set of six bunks has its own vacuum flask of boiled water (topped up from the huge samovar at the end of each carriage), and you bring your own mugs and beverage. Polystyrene boxes of rice and stir-fries are wheeled around from time to time, or you can take your place in the restaurant car for the second sitting. Every carriage also has a toilet and washbasin, which fast become unsavoury; do what the locals do and carry a face towel to keep clean on long journeys. It's not a bad way to travel, though obligatory dawn-to-dusk music blaring out of the radio and a relentless investigation of yourself and possessions by fellow passengers can wear thin after a few hours. There are fairly spacious racks to stow hand **luggage** and backpacks – as always, chain it securely while you sleep.

For the really impecunious there's **hard seat** (*yingzuo*) – generally a strain on the nerves, but sometimes the only advance ticket available and bearable for short journeys. Much rarer is the more upmarket **soft seat**, only found on short-haul trains such as the express between Guangzhou and Kowloon, or the double-decker affair running from Nanning to the Vietnamese border. In hard seat, you sit on a thinly padded three-person bench with a severe upright back and barely enough room to get comfortable, let alone sleep. But at around the same price as a bus fare, it's very cheap and considerably faster, though on long journeys the discomfort can be excruciating, especially as the air is thick with cigarette smoke and every available inch of floor-space is crammed with travellers who were unable to book a seat – bear in mind that should you board a train with an unreserved ticket, you'll be standing with them. Again, you'll be the subject of intense and unabashed speculation, this time from peasants and labourers who can't afford to travel in better style. The best way to cope is to join in as best you can, whether you can speak Chinese or not; you'll probably end up playing cards, sharing food and drinking with them.

There are three **types of train** in China, and not all have the three main classes. **Express trains** do, and are that much more comfortable as a rule – they're identified by a number between 1 and 90, and you pay a small supplement to the standard fare. Trains numbered 100–350 or so are marginally cheaper, but make more stops, and have fewer berths. Anything marked 400 or above will stop whenever possible and have seats only, and should be avoided if there's any alternative.

To give you a rough idea of the equivalent **prices**, Beijing–Xi'an costs around £52/US$78 soft sleeper; £27/US$40 hard sleeper; £17/US$26 hard seat. Beijing–Turpan costs £125/US$190; £66/US$100; £40/US$60. Beijing–Shanghai is £70/US$105; £36/US$54; £22/US$33, and Beijing–Guangzhou is £85/US$130; £45/US$70; £27/US$40.

BUSES AND MINIBUSES

Despite the ever-widening net thrown by the rail lines, there are still many parts of China unreach-able by train – in which case **bus** is the cheapest (and often only) way of getting there. The huge numbers of private operators who have sprung up in the last few years means that services are increasingly frequent, even to remote places, though some cities have so many depots it can be hard to find the right departure point. The advantages of bus over train travel are that seats are cheaper and it's far less trouble to buy a ticket –

queues really don't compare. And, while you can't usually book more than a day in advance, you are also almost guaranteed a seat, albeit often a hell-ishly uncomfortable one, even if you buy the ticket minutes before departure. On the downside, bus travel is very **slow** – count on an average speed of 30km per hour, breakdowns from time to time, and stops every few minutes to pick up or set down passengers. Airhorns make the experience painfully noisy too, as drivers are obliged to announce their presence before overtaking any-thing, and earplugs are seriously recommended. There are a few new expressways, but poor sur-faces and maintenance means that country roads can be downright dangerous, as is the habit of saving fuel by coasting down hill or mountainsides in "angel gear" – neutral, with the engine off. Take some **food** along, because though buses usually pull up at inexpensive roadhouses at mealtimes, they have been known to take two drivers and plough on for a full 24 hours without stopping.

Tickets are sold at the point of departure, whether this is a proper bus station or just a kerb stop – in which case you'll pay on board. You'll do this too if you hail a bus in passing; destinations are always displayed (in Chinese characters) on the front of the vehicle. It's best to buy your ticket a day or two in advance if possible, though it's often unnecessary; hotel desks might do this for you but queues at bus stations are rarely as hor-rendous as those for the train.

The standard Chinese **long-distance bus** is fairly ramshackle, with wooden or lightly padded seats; they're never heated or air-conditioned, so dress accordingly. Legroom and ceiling height are none too bad, but you'll still feel cramped if you're more than 1.5m tall. Owing to the frequent police checks on roads in China, however, buses are sel-dom illegally overcrowded. **Luggage racks** are tiny, and you'll have to put anything bulkier than a satchel on the roof, your lap, or beside the driver. On popular routes you'll also find two more com-fortable options, although these are thirty to fifty percent more expensive than an ordinary bus. **Luxury buses** have larger, better padded seats which often recline; sometimes there's even air conditioning and video – not always a welcome addition to the noise. **Sleeper buses** have basic bunks instead of seats, and can be comfortable if a little cramped; they tend to be harder to book, however, and road travel at night is always more dangerous. Lower bunks (*xiapu*) are a bit more expensive than upper bunks (*shangpu*), but are more comfortable and have space underneath to store shoes and luggage. There are no luggage racks for upper berths.

Minibuses are common on routes of less than 100km or so, and can be immensely useful. If you've missed the only bus to where you're going, you can usually hop there in stages by minibus. All are privately run and prices vary around the country, but they typically cost a little more than the same journey by public bus.

PLANES

China has some fourteen **regional airlines** linking all major cities and many important sites, overseen by the Civil Aviation Administration of China, or **CAAC**. It's a luxury worth considering for long distances, but you'll have to offset comfort and time saved against a lamentably poor **safety record**, not to mention the **cost** – foreigners currently have to pay a hefty surcharge, making flying a little more expensive than going soft berth on a train.

Buying tickets from the local *CAAC* office, hotel desk or tour agent is seldom problematic, and there seem to be enough flights along popular routes to cope with demand. *CAAC* – both in China and abroad – can furnish you with a bilingual **timetable**, though you'll occasionally find these inaccurate. Airlines frequently, but not always, provide a **bus** to meet arrivals or take departing passengers to the airport for a small fee; as airports can be 30km or more from city centres, you need to find out well in advance if these are available. **Check-in time** for all flights is two hours before departure, and there's always a **departure tax** – currently ¥50 for internal flights.

The planes themselves vary from carrier to carrier, or sometimes destination, with older vessels palmed off on to less profitable routes – *Yunnan Airlines*, for example, is noticeably modern, and all international flights are generally of reasonable standard. Service is usually good, with soft drinks, biscuits and souvenir trinkets handed out along the way.

Foreigners currently pay a fifty percent surcharge on **airfares** which means that Beijing–Xi'an costs around £75/US$112; Beijing–Shanghai costs £85/US$128.

FERRIES

There are any number of river and sea journeys to make while in China, though **passenger ferries**

are generally on the decline as new roads are built with buses providing a faster service between points. The **Yangzi**, one of Asia's largest rivers, is navigable for thousands of kilometres between the Sichuanese port of Chongqing and coastal Shanghai, a famous journey which takes you through the spectacular Three Gorges. Another popular jaunt is the overnight spin up the **Xi River** between Guangzhou and Wuzhou, which gives easy access to famous beauty spots around Guilin. Elsewhere, while it might not always be the quickest or cheapest form of transport, a boat ride can be a refreshing change from the tribulations of train or bus travel, and it's always affordable.

Conditions on board are greatly variable, but on overnight trips there's always a choice of classes – sometimes as many as six – which can range from a bamboo mat on the floor, right through to the luxury of private cabins. Don't expect anything too impressive, however; many mainland services are cramped and overcrowded, and cabins, even in first class, are grimly functional. Toilets and food can be basic too, so plan things as best you can. On the other hand, boats in and out of Hong Kong, such as to Xiamen or Shanghai, are very clean, comfortable and spacious, and can be a pleasure to ride.

DRIVING AND CAR RENTAL

Driving a car across China is quite an appealing idea, but an experience as yet forbidden to foreigners – though bilingual road signs going up along new expressways suggest that the notion is being considered. It is possible, however, to **rent vehicles** for local use in Beijing, Shanghai, Hong Kong and Sanya, on Hainan Island. You need an international driving licence and some plastic to leave as a deposit. Special licence plates make these rental vehicles easily identifiable to Chinese police, so don't try taking them beyond the designated boundaries. Rates are about ¥300 a day plus petrol. The Chinese technically drive on the right, although in practice drivers seem to drive wherever they like – over pedestrian crossings, through red lights, even on the left. They use their horns instead of the brake, and lorries and buses plough ahead regardless while smaller vehicles get out of the way.

Elsewhere the only option is to hire a **taxi** or Chinese **jeep**. Prices are set by negotiating but you won't get anything for less than ¥400 a day, and you'll be expected to provide lunch for the driver. It's easiest to arrange this through a hotel, though some tour operators run vehicles too, which might work out better value as they often include the services of an interpreter. In Tibet, hiring a jeep with a driver is pretty much the only way to get to many destinations (see p.946).

BICYCLES

China has the highest number of **bicycles** of any country in the world, with about a quarter of the population owning one. In a land where private car ownership is beyond all but the most affluent, it's how the majority get around. Few cities have any hills, and all have **rental shops** or booths, especially around the train stations, where you can rent a set of wheels for ¥5–10 a day. You will need to leave a deposit (¥200–400) and/or some form of ID and you're fully responsible for anything that happens to the bike while it's in your care, so check brakes, tyre pressure and gearing before renting. Most rental bikes are bog-standard rattletraps, available in black or black – the really de luxe models feature bells and two working brakes. There are cheap **repair shops** all over the place should you need a tyre patched or a chain fixed up (around ¥5). Note that there's little in the way of private insurance in China, so if the bike sustains any serious damage it's up to the parties involved to sort out responsibility and payment on the spot. To **avoid theft** always use a bicycle chain or lock – they're available everywhere – and in cities, leave your vehicle in one of the ubiquitous designated **parking areas**, where it will be guarded by an attendant for a few mao.

An alternative to renting is to **buy a bike**, a sensible option if you're going to be based anywhere for a while – foreigners don't need licences, all department stores stock them (from about ¥500), and demand is so high that there should be little problem reselling the bike when you leave. The cheapest are solid, heavy, unsophisticated machines such as the famous *Flying Pigeon* brand, though multi-geared mountain-bike clones are becoming very popular – they're not always as sturdy as they look, however. You can also **take your own bike** into China with you; international airlines usually insist that the front wheel is removed, deflated, and strapped to the back, and that everything is thoroughly pack-

aged. Inside China, airlines, trains and ferries all charge to carry bikes, and the ticketing and accompanying paperwork can be baffling. Where possible, it's easier to stick to long-distance buses and stow it for free on the roof, no questions asked. Another option is to see China on a **specialized bike tour** (see pp.6, 10 or 12 for operators); though by no means cheap, these can be very good indeed. An organized bike tour could be an excellent way to start a longer stay in China.

HITCHING

Hitching around China is basically possible, and in remoter areas might save some time in reaching sights. Drivers will always charge you – usually the going bus fare – and, given the added personal risks inherent in hitching, and the fact that public transport is becoming ever-more available, it's not particularly recommended as a means of getting around.

If you must hitch, don't do it alone. The best places to try are on town and city exit roads. Get the driver's attention by waving your hand, palm down, at them. Expect to bargain for the fare, and make sure that you have your destination written down in Chinese characters.

ORGANIZED TOURS

Chinese tour operators, such as the *CITS*, can almost always organize excursions, from local city sights to river cruises and multi-day cross-country trips. While you always pay for the privilege, sometimes these tours are not bad value: travel, accommodation and food – usually plentiful and excellent – are generally included, as might be the services of an interpreter and guide. And in some cases, tours are the most practical, if not the only, way to see something really worthwhile, saving endless bother organizing local transport and accommodation.

On the downside, some operators blatantly overcharge for mediocre services, foist guides on you who can't speak local dialects or are generally unhelpful and spend three days on what could better be done in an afternoon. In general, it helps to make exhaustive enquiries about the exact nature of the tour, such as exactly what the price includes and the departure/return times, before handing any money over, though in most cases there is little you can do if promises are broken.

RECOMMENDED TOURS

Bingling Caves, *Gansu Hope International Travel Agency*, Lanzhou, Gansu (and other operators in Lanzhou). A one-day visit to the Bingling Si Buddhist cave complex outside Lanzhou. Car with driver, boat transport and entrance fee are included, giving approximately two hours at the site. ¥400–500 per person.

Birding/Wildlife Tours, *Heilongjiang Overseas Tourist Corporation*, Harbin, Dongbei. April–June only. Fifteen days return to Harbin via bird reserves at Zhalong, Beier Hu and Manzhouli; all-inclusive. ¥5000 per person. Also organizes tours to other reserves such as Wolong (Sichuan).

Dong Villages, *Wind and Rain Bridge Travel Service*, Sanjiang, Guangxi. Return to Sanjiang. Private car, driver, guide, interpreter fluent in English and local language, lunch in Dong house extra. Price negotiable as are destinations; full day from ¥500 per person.

Ice Festival, *CITS*, Harbin, Dongbei. Ten-day circuit of ice festivals in Chanchun, Harbin and Jilin in the depths of winter (Jan–Feb). Fully inclusive, but well below freezing. ¥3000 per person.

Inner Mongolian grassland tour, *Inner Mongolia Luye International Travel Company*, Hohhot (and many other operators in Hohhot). Two-day tour of the grasslands including all transport, meals, yurt accommodation, entertainment and a guide (non English-speaking). ¥250–300 per person.

Qinghai Hu, *Qinghai Jiaotong Luxingshe*, Xining, Qinghai. Two-day trip to the great lake, Qinghai Hu, plus Bird Island and Chaka Slat Lake. All-inclusive. ¥600 per person.

Steam Train Tour, *CITS*, Shengyang, Dongbei. Two-week tour of steam loco factories, workyards and museums in Beijing, Harbin and Jiamusi; also numerous rides. All-inclusive. ¥5000 per person.

Turpan, any tour operator in Turpan, Xinjiang. A one-day tour of the sights around Turpan – ancient cities, caves and underground irrigation channels. Transport only. ¥30–50 per person.

Xishuangbanna Villages, *Mengyuan Travel Service*, Jinghong, Yunnan. Three to four-day hiking through border regions. Transport connections, tents, food and English-speaking guide. ¥700 per person.

Yungang Caves, *CITS*, Datong, Shanxi. Day tour of the caves, Hanging Temple and Yingxian Wooden Pagoda – China's oldest wooden structure. Lunch, bus and an unreliable guide. ¥50 per person.

Zuo River, *CITS*, Nanning, Guangxi. Two days/one night return from Nanning; includes train connections, English-speaking guide, three-hour river trip, four big meals, hotel accommodation, one-hour Zhuang rock art tour. ¥400 per person.

CITY TRANSPORT

Most Chinese cities are spread out over areas which defeat even the most determined walker, but all have some form of **public transit system**. Hong Kong, Beijing, and Shanghai have efficient underground **metros**, while Guangzhou's is still being constructed; elsewhere the **city bus** is the transport focus. These are cheap and run from around 6am to 9pm or later, but, apart from Hong Kong's trams, are usually slow and hideously crowded. Pricier private **minibuses** often run the same routes in similar comfort but at greater speed – they're either numbered or have their destination written up at the front. If you're in a hurry or can't face another bus journey, **taxis** cruise the streets in larger towns and cities, or hang around the main transit points and hotels. They're not bad value for a group, costing about ¥10 to hire and then a set rate of ¥1–3 per kilometre. You'll also find motorized- or cycle-**rickshaws**, and **motorbike taxis** outside just about every mainland bus and train station, whose highly erratic rates are set by bargaining beforehand.

ACCOMMODATION

Accommodation in China is generally disappointing. What is lacking above all is variety – characterful old family-run institutions of the kind that can be found all over Asia and Europe simply do not exist in mainland China. Instead, the vast majority of hotels are entirely anonymous and unmemorable, comprising purpose-built blocks with standardized interiors. Hotels in China are reasonably secure places, although you would be foolish to leave money or valuables lying about in your room. If you lock valuables such as cameras inside your bag before going out you are unlikely to have problems.

Despite the lack of variety, there is a vast **range of quality** in terms of comfort and service. Newer hotels are nearly always far superior to the grim, hospital-like institutions built before the 1980s, and as for the really brand-new ones, they always enjoy a honeymoon period of enthusiastic service and stain-free carpets before poor maintenance begins to take its toll. Don't assume, however, that these differences in quality will be accurately reflected in **prices**. In fact, price in general is a very poor guide to quality, varying dramatically from region to region and town to town. Eastern China, for example, is far more expensive than western China and large cities are more expensive than small ones. Strictly speaking, hotel room prices are normally fixed, but this does not quite mean that there can never be any **bargaining** in hotels. One concession you might achieve is to reduce the foreign-

ers' surcharge (see below), or get the ten percent service charge waived. Otherwise you can sometimes persuade the receptionist to mention the existence of hitherto unsuspected cheaper rooms in another block. In most cases, however, the price is the price and bargaining will get you nowhere. Another unpredictable element is whether discriminatory **foreigners' prices** are charged or not. Some hotels have arbitrary rules stipulating that foreigners pay as much as a hundred percent extra above the locals. With polite, friendly bargaining, it is possible to reduce or eliminate such surcharges though many hotel receptionists will plead that they have no authority to bend the rules. Fortunately, the general phenomenon of foreigners' prices is now disappearing fairly rapidly, especially from the wealthier parts of China.

Another irritation for foreigners is the fact that plenty of hotels are not supposed to take them at all. Such hotels – normally the cheap ones – have not obtained the necessary documentation from the local authorities and if they are caught **housing foreigners illegally** they face substantial fines. Nothing is certain in China, however. Sometimes the receptionists themselves don't know that foreigners aren't allowed to stay, and if it is late at night, or if there is only one hotel in town, you will normally be allowed in anyway (being able to speak Chinese improves your chances as does having a Chinese student card).

FINDING A ROOM

Finding a room is mostly up to you, but if you want an easy time of it, try to avoid arriving anywhere late. Arrive after nightfall and you may find yourself in the hands of hustling rickshaw drivers who will insist on taking you to a hotel of their choice at ten times the going rate. The best situation is to arrive in broad daylight, deposit your bag at a left-luggage office at the train or bus station, then take a leisurely tour of possible accommodation options. It is considered perfectly normal to ask to see the room before deciding to take it. In some places, **touts** with hotel brochures and name cards will approach you outside stations, and you won't lose much by following them as they are paid directly by the hotels concerned, not by surcharges on your room price. Sometimes, however, touts can inadvertently waste your time by taking you to hotels which turn out not to accept foreigners.

For international-class rooms, **booking ahead** is a routine procedure and you will undoubtedly find receptionists who speak English to take your call. For any hotel below this category, however, you won't find booking easy. Hotel telephone numbers have been included in *The Guide* wherever possible but don't bet on making much headway without some spoken Chinese. The concept of booking ahead is one that does not exist in many places, although it is sometimes convenient to call – or to ask someone to call for you – to see if vacancies exist before lugging your bag across town.

CHECKING IN AND PAYING

The tiresome process of **checking in** to a hotel involves filling in a **detailed form** giving details of your name, age, date of birth, sex and address, places where you are coming from and going to, how many days you intend staying and your visa and passport numbers. Upmarket hotels have English versions of these forms, but hotels unaccustomed to foreigners usually have them in Chinese only – which explains the depression experienced by many hotel receptionists when they see a foreigner walk in the door. Filling in forms correctly is a serious business in bureaucratic China and if potential guests are unable to carry out this duty, the result is impasse. In such cases you may find yourself being waved out of sight before you have even put down your bag. On p.38 there is an example of this form in English and Chinese to help you complete it correctly.

You are nearly always asked to **pay** in advance and, in addition, leave a **deposit** against theft or damage which may amount to as much as twice the price of the room again. Don't hesitate about paying these deposits as they are always refunded; just try not to lose the receipt if you don't want to make a nuisance of yourself. If you're staying several nights, either pay the whole lot in advance, or check in again every day. You hardly ever get a **key** from reception, instead you'll get a piece of paper which you take to the appropriate floor attendant who will give you a room card and open the door for you whenever you come in. Sometimes the floor attendant will offer you the key to keep, though if you want it

you'll have to pay her another refundable deposit of ¥10–20.

TYPES OF ACCOMMODATION

In Chinese there are several different words for hotel which can be vague indicators of the status of the place. The surest indicators of upmarket pretensions are the highly modern-sounding **da jiulou** or **da jiudian** which actually translates as something like "big wine bar". The far more common term, **binguan**, is similarly used for smart new establishments, though it is also the name given to the huge government hotels built prior to the 1980s tourist boom, many of which have now been renovated; foreigners can nearly always stay in these. **Fandian** (literally "restaurant") is the least reliable term as it is used fairly indiscriminately for top-class hotels as well as humble and obscure ones. Reliably downmarket – and rarely accepting foreigners – is **zhaodaisuo**, while the humblest of all is **luguan** (sometimes translated as "inn") where you might occasionally get to stay in some very rural areas.

Whatever type of hotel you are staying in, there are two things you can rely on. One is a pair of plastic slippers under the bed that you use for walking to the bathroom, and the other is a vacuum flask of drinkable hot water that can be refilled any time by the floor attendant.

Breakfast is not normally included in the price though nearly all hotels, even fairly grotty ones, will have a restaurant where breakfast is served usually between 7–8am.

In **Hong Kong** and **Macau** the top end of the market is similar in character to the mainland, though prices are higher and service more efficient. At the bottom end of the market, however, there are a large number of privately run guesthouses and hostels. They come in all shapes and sizes and the sheer variety comes as a serious relief after the dullness of mainland hotels. Prices for double rooms in these guesthouses are generally cheaper than in hotels in most of eastern China, and very cheap dormitories are also plentiful. Hong Kong even has a selection of YHA hostels, a phenomenon as yet unknown in the rest of China. For more details see the relevant accommodation sections, pp.607 and 647.

UPMARKET HOTELS

In the larger cities – including virtually all provincial capitals – you'll find **upmarket** four- or five-

临时住宿登记表　REGISTRATION FORM FOR TEMPORARY RESIDENCE

请用正楷填写　PLEASE WRITE IN BLOCK LETTERS

英文姓
Surname

英文名
First name

性别
Sex

中文姓名
Name in Chinese

国籍
Nationality

出生日期
Date of birth

证件种类
Type of certificate

证件号码
Certificate No.

签证种类
Type of visa

签证有效期
Valid date of visa

抵店日期
Date of arrival

离店日期
Date of departure

由何处来
From

交通工具
Carrier

住何处
To

永久地址
Permanent address

停留事由
Object of stay

职业
Occupation

接待单位
Received by

房号
Room No.

star hotels, often managed by foreigners and offering all the usual international facilities, such as swimming pools, gyms and business centres. Conditions in such hotels are comparable to those anywhere in the world, though finer nuances of service will sometimes be lacking – prices for standard doubles in these places are upwards of £60/US$90 and go as high as £135/US$200. Advance booking and the use of credit cards are routine in these places.

Even if you cannot afford to stay in the upmarket hotels, they can still be pleasant places to escape from the hubbub of life in China, and nobody in China blinks at the sight of a stray foreigner roaming around the foyer of a smart hotel. As well as air conditioning and clean toilets, you'll find cafés and bars, sometimes showing satellite TV, telephone and fax facilities and seven-days-a-week money changing (though this is not always open to non-guests).

MID-RANGE HOTELS

A lot of Chinese hotels built nowadays have pretensions to being luxury hotels, without ever quite making it. Places in this **mid-range** category will generally have clean, spacious standard double rooms with attached bathroom, 24-hour hot water, TV and air conditioning, but are often suffering from dodgy plumbing, poor temperature control and insufficient lift capacity. Practically every town in China has at least one hotel of this sort. In remote places you should get a double for £10–20/US$15–30, but in any sizeable city expect to pay at least £30/US$45. Single rooms are rarely available in these establishments. Note, however, that mid-range hotels often comprise a number of wings with rooms of widely differing price, and while receptionists naturally assume that rich foreigners want the higher priced rooms, it's worth asking if anything cheaper is available. In major cities there are few new hotels being built with double rooms costing less than ¥300 (Beijing is probably the only exception here), and in quite a few cities in eastern China this can mean that it is very hard to find anything cheaper.

BUDGET HOTELS

Where you do manage to find a **budget** hotel, with doubles costing less than £10/US$15, you'll notice that the local Chinese routinely rent **beds** rather than rooms – doubling up with one or more strangers – as a means of saving money.

Foreigners are only very occasionally allowed to share rooms with Chinese people, but if there are three or four foreigners together it's often possible for them to share one big room. Otherwise, the saving grace for budget travellers is that tourist centres, including large cities such as Beijing, Shanghai and Guangzhou, tend to have one or two budget hotels with special **foreigners' dormitory** accommodation, costing around £1–5/US$1.5–7.5 per bed. Cheap hotels vary in quality from the dilapidated to the perfectly comfortable, but hot water is usually available for only limited hours in the evening and you would be advised not to leave valuables in rooms. Cheap hotels in many towns are commonly near the train station, though in the major cities such as Beijing or Shanghai you may end up far from the centre.

Another budget possibility always worth trying if you are stuck are student rooms in **universities** – more and more of them are now willing to accommodate foreign tourists. Finding a room in a university is not as hard as you might imagine given the city-like proportions of university campuses in China. Many, if not most, universities will have a building on campus variously termed something like the "Foreigners' Guesthouse" (*waibing zhaodaisuo*) or the "Foreign Experts' Building" (*waiguo zhuanjia lou*), basically designed to accommodate foreign students or teachers, though in fact any foreigner can stay in them if they have rooms free. You would be unlucky not to find some obliging English-speaking student to help you find the right block once you are inside the campus. These buildings act like simple hotels and you have to fill in all the usual forms. Expect to pay around £4–6/US$6–9 a night. Sometimes you find yourself put in to share with a resident foreign student who may be less than gracious about having you – but this happens only if the student concerned has paid for only one of the two beds in his or her room, so you needn't feel guilty about it. Although universities are cheap and friendly places to stay, the communal washing and toilet facilities can be grim, and campuses are usually located out in the suburbs.

The surest way to save money on accommodation in China, though, is to **go west**. Hotels in all of the Northwest, as well as Tibet, Sichuan and Yunnan, can be absurdly cheap with double rooms available for as little as £3/US$5.

CAMPING AND OTHER ACCOMMODATION

Camping is only really feasible in the wildernesses of western China where you are not going to wake up under the prying eyes of thousands of local villagers. In parts of Tibet, Qinghai, Xinjiang, Gansu and Inner Mongolia there are places within reach of hikers or cyclists where this is possible, though don't bother actually trying to get permission for it. This is the kind of activity which the Chinese authorities do not really have any clear idea about so if asked they will certainly answer "no". The only kind of regular, authorized camping in China is by the nomadic Mongolian and Kazakh peoples of the steppe who have their own highly sophisticated felt tents (*mengu bao*). Tourists can stay in these under certain circumstances (see p.835).

An alternative to camping are the pilgrims' inns at important monasteries and lamaseries. These are an extremely cheap, if rather primitive, form of accommodation, though vacancies disappear quickly. Foreigners are warmly welcomed in such places, and although the authorities are not particularly keen on you staying in them, you are most unlikely to be turned away if it is late in the day and you are really stuck.

ACCOMMODATION PRICE CODES

All the accommodation listed in this book has been given one of the following price codes. The rates quoted are for a **standard double room**, although there will usually be more expensive rooms available, which staff will often encourage you to take. Where a significant spread of prices is indicated (④–⑥, for example), the text will explain what extra facilities you get in the higher categories (usually an en suite bathroom).

In the cheaper hotels which have **dormitories** or which rent out individual beds in small rooms,

the price code given will represent the price of a single bed (dorms ②, rooms ⑤, for example).

It should generally be noted that in the off-season – from October to June excluding Chinese New Year – prices in tourist hotels are more flexible. Hotels either set lower prices in this season, or, at the very least, are more easily persuaded to drop their foreigners' supplements.

Note that nearly all mid-range and upmarket hotels add a service charge of between ten and fifteen percent to bills.

① less than ¥30	④ ¥100–150	⑦ ¥300–500
② ¥30–75	⑤ ¥150–200	⑧ ¥500–700
③ ¥75–100	⑥ ¥200–300	⑨ ¥700 or more

EATING AND DRINKING

The Chinese love to eat, and from market-stall buns and soup, right through to the intricate variations of regional cookery, China boasts one of the world's greatest cuisines. It's also far more complex than you might suspect from its manifestations overseas, and while food might not initially be a major reason for your trip, once here you may well find that eating becomes the highlight. However, the inability to order effectively sees many travellers missing out, and they leave desperate for a "proper meal", convinced that the bland stir-fries and dumplings served up in the cheapest canteens is all that's available. With a bit of effort you can eat well whatever your budget and ability with the language, though it can be monotonous eating solo for any length of time – meals are considered social events, and the process is accordingly geared to a group of diners sharing a variety of different dishes with their companions.

Though fresh ingredients are available from any market stall, there are very few opportunities to cook for yourself in China, and most of the time eating out is much more convenient and interesting. The **principles of Chinese cooking** are based on a desire for a healthy harmony between the qualities of different ingredients. For the Chinese, this extends right down to considering the *yin* and *yang* attributes of various dishes – for instance, whether food is "moist" or "dry" – but can also be appreciated in the use of ingredients

with contrasting textures and colour, designed to please the eye as well as the palate. Recipes and ingredients themselves, however, are generally a response to more direct requirements. The chronic poverty of China's population is reflected in the generally scant quantity of meat used, while the need to preserve precious stocks of firewood led to the invention of quick cooking techniques, such as slicing ingredients into tiny shreds and stir-frying them. The reliance on eating whatever was immediately to hand also saw a readiness to experiment with anything edible; so, though you'd hardly come across them every day, items such as bear's paw, duck's feet, shark's fin, fish lips and even jellyfish all appear in Chinese cuisine.

INGREDIENTS AND METHODS

The after-effects of Maoist policies meant that as late as the1980s the availability of good **ingredients** in China was pretty poor, leading to a miserably low standard of food served outside the highest-class hotels and restaurants. Now, in much of the country, market stalls are swamped under the weight of fresh produce, and the only problem is choosing what it is you'd like to eat and how you'd like it cooked.

Rice in various forms – grain, noodles, or as dumpling wrappers – is the staple, apart from in the north and far west of the country, where the colder climate is better suited to growing wheat and millet. **Meat** is held to be a generally invigorating substance and, ideally, forms the backbone of any meal – serving a pure meat dish is the height of hospitality. Pork is the yardstick, except in areas with a strong Muslim tradition where it's replaced with mutton or beef. **Fowl** is also considered good for you, especially in old age or convalescence, and was quite a luxury in the past (chicken was once the most expensive meat in Beijing), though today most rural people in central and southern China seem to own a couple of hens, and the countryside is littered with duck farms. **Fish** is very highly regarded and can be extraordinarily expensive, as are rarer game meats. **Dog** ("warming"), **cat** ("cooling"), and **snake** (a general panacea depending on which part you consume) are also considered delicacies in south and southwestern China, and few Chinese tourists visit these areas without trying them.

VEGETARIAN FOOD

Vegetarianism has been practised for almost two thousand years in China for both religious and philosophical reasons, and its practitioners have included historical figures such as Cao Cao, the famous Three Kingdoms warlord, and the pious sixth-century emperor Wu Di. Vegetarian cooking takes at least three recognized forms: **plain vegetable** dishes, commonly served at home or in ordinary restaurants; **imitation meat** dishes derived from Qing court cuisine, which use gluten, beancurd and potato to mimic the natural attributes of meat, fowl and fish; and **Buddhist cooking**, which avoids onions, ginger, garlic and other spices considered stimulating.

Having said all this, strict vegetarians visiting China will find their options limited. Vegetables might be considered intrinsically healthy, but the Chinese also believe that they lack any physically fortifying properties, and **vegetarian diets** are unusual except for religious reasons. There's also a stigma of poverty attached to not eating meat,

and as a foreigner no one can understand why, when you could clearly afford to gorge yourself on a regular basis, you don't want it. Although you can get vegetable dishes everywhere, be aware that cooking fat and stocks in the average dining room are of animal origins. If you really want to be sure that you are being served nothing of animal origin tell your waiter that you are a Buddhist (see "Food and Drink" box on p.46), although you won't get any garlic either.

Things are easiest in big cities such as Beijing, Shanghai, and Guangzhou, which have real **vegetarian restaurants**; elsewhere, head for the nearest **Buddhist monastery**, many of which have dining rooms open to the public at lunchtime – and even if you're not vegetarian, some serve extraordinarily good food. When ordering in these places, note that imitation meat dishes are still called by their usual name, such as West Lake fish, honey pork or roast duck.

Eggs – duck, chicken or quail – are a popular nationwide snack, often served delicately flavoured by hard-boiling in a mixture of tea, soy sauce and star anise. There's also the so-called "thousand-year" variety, preserved for a few months in ash and straw – they look gruesome, with translucent brown albumen and green yolks, but actually have a deliciously delicate, alkaline flavour. **Dairy products** serve very limited purposes in China. Goat **cheese** is eaten in parts of Yunnan, but milk and yoghurt are considered fit foods only for children and are not used in cooking.

Vegetables accompany nearly every Chinese meal, used in most cases to balance tastes and textures of meat, but also appearing as dishes in their own right. There's a wide range from water chestnuts, lettuce and radish, to "glass" noodles made out of pea starch, and **tofu**, pressed curd made from boiled soya beans – though in parts of the country the selection can be very slim. Seasonal availability is backed by a huge variety of **dried**, **salted**, and **pickled** ingredients – mushrooms, seaweed, greens, and bamboo shoots – which, along with **preserved meats and seafood**, often characterize local cooking styles. China also has an enormous assortment of regional **fruit**, great to clean the palate or fill a space between meals.

When it finally comes to **preparing and cooking** these goodies, be aware that there's far

more on offer than simply chopping everything into small pieces and stir-frying them. A huge number of **spices** are used for their health-giving properties, to mask undesirable flavours or provide a background taste. **Marinating** removes blood – repugnant to the Chinese – and tenderizes and freshens the flavour of meats; chicken and fish are often cooked whole, though they may be dismembered before serving. Several cooking methods can be used within a single dish to maximize textures or flavours, including crisping by **deep frying** in flour or a batter; **steaming**, which can highlight an ingredient's subtler flavours; **boiling and blanching**, usually to firm meat as a precursor to other cooking methods; and **slow cooking** in a rich stock.

REGIONAL COOKING

Not surprisingly, given China's scale, there are a number of distinct **regional cooking styles** divided into four major traditions. **Northern cookery** was epitomized by the imperial court and so also became known as Mandarin or Beijing cooking, though its influences are far wider than these names suggest. A solid diet of **wheat and millet** buns, noodles, pancakes and dumplings help to face severe winters, accompanied by the savoury tastes of dark soy sauce and bean paste, white cabbage, onions and garlic. The north's cooking has also been influenced by neighbours and invaders: Mongols brought their hotpots and grilled and roast meats, and Muslims a taste for mutton and chicken. Combined with exotic items imported by foreign merchants and vassal embassies visiting the court, imperial kitchens turned these rather rough ingredients and cooking styles into sophisticated marvels such as Peking duck and bird's nest soup – though most people survive on soups of winter pickles, or fried summer greens eaten with a bun.

The central coast provinces produced the **Eastern style**, whose cooking delights in seasonal fresh seafood and river fish. Winters can still be cold and summers scorchingly hot, so dried and salted ingredients feature too, pepping up a background of rice noodles and dumplings. Based around Shanghai, eastern cuisine, as opposed to daily fare, enjoys little, delicate forms and light, fresh, slightly sweet flavours, sometimes to the point of becoming precious – tiny meatballs are steamed in a rice coating and called "pearls", for example. The legendary story about a cook who boiled down a huge quantity of beansprouts to produce one bowl of soup containing the vegetable's essence also comes from this area.

China's centre and southwest are permeated by the boisterous cooking of **Sichuan**, the antithesis of the eastern style. Here, there's a heavy use of **chillis** and pungent, constructed flavours – vegetables are concealed with "fish-flavoured" sauce, and even normally bland tofu is given enough spices to lift the top off your head. Yet there are still subtleties to enjoy in a cuisine which frequently uses dried orange peel, ginger and spring onions, and the cooking methods themselves – such as dry frying and smoking – are refreshingly unusual.

Southern China is fertile and subtropical, a land of year-round plenty. When people say that southerners – specifically the **Cantonese** – will eat anything, they really mean it: fish maw, snake liver, dog and guinea pig are some of the more unusual dishes here, strange even to other Chinese; but there's also a huge consumption of fruit and vegetables, fish and shellfish. Typically, the demand is for extremely fresh ingredients, quickly cooked and only lightly seasoned, though the south is also home to that famous mainstay of Chinese restaurants overseas, sweet-and-sour sauce. The tradition of **dim sum** reached its pin-

nacle here too, where a morning meal of tiny flavoured buns, dumplings and pancakes is washed down with copious tea, satisfying the Chinese liking for a varied assortment of small dishes. Nowadays *dim sum* is eaten all over China, but southern restaurants still have the best selection (see p.50 for more details).

Hong Kong basically takes the best of Chinese cooking as its own, though heavily biased towards the southern style, while in **Macau** you'll get the chance to try the region's unique mix of Portuguese and Asian food, known as Macanese.

BREAKFAST, SNACKS AND FAST FOODS

Breakfast is not a big event by Chinese standards, more something to line the stomach for a few hours. Much of the country is content with a bowl of rice porridge or **congee**, flavoured with pickles and accompanied by a heavy, plain bun or fried bread stick. Another favourite is a plain soup with rice noodles and perhaps a little meat. Most places also have countless small, early opening **snack stalls**, usually located around markets, train and bus stations. Here you'll get things like fried or boiled *jiaozi* (a sort of ravioli), stuffed buns, grilled chicken wings, kebabs, spiced noodles, baked yams and potatoes, boiled eggs, grilled corn and countless local treats. Traditionally, these have taken the place of more familiar Western-style **fast food**, though some cities now have home-grown copies of burger bars and fried chicken joints, almost always with names and signs in English.

WESTERN AND INTERNATIONAL FOOD

There's a fair amount of **Western and international food** available in China, though supply and quality varies from place to place. Hong Kong has the best range, with some excellent restaurants covering everything from French to Vietnamese cuisine, and there are a number of hotel restaurants specializing in Western food in Guangzhou, Beijing and Shanghai. Elsewhere, areas like Yangshuo in Guangxi, which see a huge number of foreigners, and tourist accommodation in big cities, often serve "Western-style" meals, but there's often a considerable gulf between what's advertised and what actually appears – while breakfasts of eggs and toast are fairly reliable, don't put your expectations too high. Where available, your best bets for something familiar are the genuine *McDonald's*, *KFC* and *Pizza Hut* restaurants which have appeared over the last few years. Here you can be assured of products which are the same the world over.

OPENING TIMES AND PLACES TO EAT

While small noodle shops and foodstalls around train and bus stations have flexible hours, always keep an eye on **restaurant opening times**, which, outside the biggest cities, tend to be early and short. By 6am **breakfast** is usually well under way, and by 9am will have wound up. Get up late and you'll have to join the first sitting for **lunch** at 11am or so, leaving you plenty of time to work up an appetite for the **evening meal** around 5pm. An hour later you'd be lucky to get a table in some places, and by 9pm the staff will be yawning and sweeping the debris off the tables around your ankles.

Hotel dining rooms can be very flash affairs, with the most upmarket serving a range of foreign and regional Chinese food at ruinous cost, though more average establishments can often be extremely good value. Advantages include the possibility that staff may speak English, or that they might offer a **set menu** of small local dishes. **Standard restaurants** are often divided into two or three floors; the first will offer a limited choice, usually scrawled illegibly on strips of paper or a board hung on the wall. You buy chits from a cashier for what you want, which you exchange at the kitchen hatch for your food and sit down at large communal tables or benches. Upstairs will be pricier and have more formal dining arrangements, with waitress service and a written menu, while further floors (if they have them) are generally reserved for banquet parties or foreign tour groups and are unlikely to seat individuals.

The cheapest **stalls and canteens** are necessarily basic, with simple food which is often much better than you'd expect from the furnishings. Though foreigners are often given disposable chopsticks, it's probably worth buying your own set in case these aren't available – washing up often simply involves rinsing everything in a bucket of grey water on the floor and leaving it to dry on the pavement.

ORDERING AND EATING

In itself, getting fed is never difficult as everyone wants your custom. Walk past anywhere that sells cooked food and you'll be hailed by cries of *chi fan* – basically, "come and eat!" **Pointing** is all that's required at street stalls and small restaurants, where the ingredients are usually displayed out the front in buckets, bundles and cages. In bigger places you'll sometimes be escorted through to the kitchen to make your choice. One thing to watch out for here is getting the idea across when you want different items cooked together – for instance, you might end up with separate plates of nuts, meat, and vegetables when you thought you'd ordered a single dish of chicken with cashews and green peppers. Another drawback to this method is that unless you say how you want your food prepared it inevitably arrives stir-fried and you'll soon get bored unless you experiment with steamed or braised dishes. **Menus**, where available, are often more of an indication of what's on offer than a definitive list, so don't be afraid to ask for a missing favourite. English menu translations also usually omit things that the Chinese consider might be unpalatable to foreigners.

When you enter a proper restaurant you'll be quickly escorted to a chair – standing around dithering is impolite, so avoid it. In all but the cheapest places, tea, pickles and nuts immediately follow, to take the edge off your hunger while you order. The only tableware provided is a spoon, bowl, and a pair of **chopsticks**, and at this point the Chinese will ask for a flask of boiling water and a bowl to wash it all in – not usually necessary, but something of a ritual. To handle chopsticks, hold one halfway along its length like a pencil, then slide the other underneath and use them as an extension of your fingers to pick up the food – except for rice, which is shovelled in with the bowl up against your lips.

When **ordering**, unless eating a one-dish meal like Peking duck or a hotpot, try to select items with a range of tastes and textures – perhaps some seafood, meat and chicken, each cooked in a different manner; it's also usual to include a soup. In cheap places, servings of noodles or rice are huge, but as they are considered stomach fillers, quantities decline the more upmarket you go. Unless in an ornate form, rice never features at banquets – asking for it would imply that the host hadn't provided you with enough food. Dishes are generally all served at once, placed in the middle of the table for diners to share; eat fairly slowly, taking time to talk between helping yourself. With some fowl dishes you can crunch up the smaller bones, but anything else is spat out on to the tablecloth or floor, more or less discreetly depending on the establishment – watch what others are doing. Soup is generally fairly bland and is consumed last to wash the meal down, the liquid slurped from a spoon or the bowl once the noodles, vegetables or meat in it have been picked out and eaten. When you've finished your meal, rest your chopsticks together across the top of your bowl. After eating the Chinese don't hang around to talk over drinks as in the West, but get up straight away and leave.

In canteens you'll pay up front, while at restaurants you ask for the bill and pay either the waiter or at the front till. Tipping is forbidden in mainland China.

TEA

Tea was introduced into China from India around 1800 years ago, and was originally drunk for medicinal reasons. Although its health properties are still important, and some food halls sell nourishing or stimulating varieties by the bowlful, over the centuries a whole social culture has sprung up around this beverage, spawning **tea houses** which once held the same place in Chinese society that the local pub or bar does in the West. Plantations of neat rows of low bushes adorn hillsides across southern China, while the brew is enthusiastically consumed from the highlands of Tibet – where it's mixed with barley meal and butter – to every restaurant and household between Hong Kong and Beijing.

Chinese tea comes in black, red, green and flower-scented **varieties**, depending on how it's picked and processed. Some regional kinds, such as *pu'er* from Yunnan and *oolong* from the east, are highly sought after – if you like the local style, head for the nearest market and stock up. Though always drunk without milk and only very rarely with sugar, the method of **serving tea** also varies from place to place: sometimes it comes in huge mugs with a lid, elsewhere in dainty cups served from a miniature pot. When drinking in company, it's polite to top up others' cups before your own, whenever they become empty; if someone does this for you, lightly tap your first two fingers on the table to show your thanks. If you've had enough, leave your cup full, and in a restaurant take the lid off or turn it over if you want the pot refilled during the meal.

It's also worth trying some Muslim tea during your stay in China. Also known as Eight Treasures

Tea, it's available in Muslim restaurants everywhere and is sold in packets from street stalls. You'll get dried fruit, nuts, seeds, crystallized sugar and tea heaped into a cup with the remaining space filled with hot water.

ALCOHOL

The popularity of **beer** in China rivals that of tea, and, for men, is the preferred mealtime beverage (drinking alcohol in public is considered improper for Chinese women, though not for foreigners). The first brewery was set up in the northeastern port of Qingdao by the Germans in the nineteenth century, and now, though the *Tsingtao* label is widely available, just about every province produces at least one brand of four percent Pilsner. Sold in litre bottles, it's always drinkable, often pretty good, and is actually cheaper than bottled water. Draught beer is now becoming popular in Beijing.

Watch out for the term "**wine**", which doesn't usually carry the conventional meaning. China does actually have a couple of commercial vineyards producing the mediocre *Great Wall* label, more of a status symbol rather than an attempt to rival Western growers. Far better are the local pressings in Xinjiang Province, where the population of Middle Eastern descent takes its grapes seriously. More often, however, "wine" denotes **spirits**, made from rice, sorghum or millet. Serving spirits to guests is a sign of hospitality, and they're always used for toasting at banquets. Again, local homemade varieties can be quite good, while the mainstream brands – especially the expensive, nationally famous *Moutai* – are pretty vile to the Western palate. **Imported spirits**, particularly whiskies, are sold in large department stores and in tourist hotel bars, but are always very expensive.

SOFT DRINKS

Water is easily available in China, though it's best not to drink what comes out of the tap. **Boiled water** is always on hand in hotels and trains, either provided in large vacuum flasks or an urn, and you can buy **bottled spring water** at station stalls and supermarkets – read the labels and you'll see some unusual rare minerals (such as radon) listed, which you'd probably rather know weren't in there.

Canned products, usually sold unchilled, include various lemonades and colas, and the

FOOD AND DRINK

The following lists should help out where you can't make yourself understood – and, if they're written clearly, in deciphering the characters on a Chinese menu. If you know what you're after, try sifting through the staples and cooking methods to create your order, or sample one of the everyday or regional suggestions, many of which are available all over the country. Don't forget to tailor your demands to the capabilities of where you're ordering, however – a street cook with a wok isn't going to be able to whip up anything much more complicated than a basic stir-fry.

Ordering

Chopsticks	筷子	*kuàizi*
House speciality	拿手好菜	*náshǒuhǎocài*
How much is that?	多少钱?	*duōshǎo qián?*
I don't eat (meat)	我不吃(肉)	*wǒ bù chī (ròu)*
I'm Buddhist /I'm vegetarian	我是佛教徒/我只吃素	*wǒ shì fójiàotú/wǒ zhǐ chī sù*
I would like...	我想要....	*wǒ xiǎng yào...*
Local dishes	地方菜	*dìfang cài*
Menu/set menu/English menu	菜单/套菜/英文菜单	*càidān/tàocài/yīngwén càidān*
Small portion	少量	*shǎoliàng*
Spoon	勺	*sháo*
Waiter/waitress	服务员/小姐	*fúwùyuán/xiǎojiě*
Bill/cheque	买单	*mǎidān*

Drinks

Beer	啤酒	*píjiǔ*
Sweet fizzy drink	汽水	*qìshuǐ*
Coffee	咖啡	*kāfēi*
Tea	茶	*chá*
(Mineral) water	(矿泉)水	*(kuàngquán) shuǐ*
Wine	葡萄酒	*pútáojiǔ*

Staple foods

Aubergine	茄子	*qiézi*
Bamboo shoots	笋尖	*sǔnjiān*
Beans	豆	*dòu*
Bean sprouts	豆芽	*dòuyá*
Beef	牛肉	*niúròu*
Bitter gourd	葫芦	*húlu*
Black bean sauce	黑豆豉	*hēidòuchǐ*
Buns (plain)	馒头	*mántou*
Buns (filled)	包子	*bāozi*
Carrot	胡萝卜	*húluóbo*
Cashew nuts	坚果	*jiānguǒ*
Cauliflower	菜花	*càihuā*
Chicken	鸡	*jī*
Chilli	辣椒	*làjiāo*
Coriander (leaves)	香菜	*xiāngcài*
Crab	蟹	*xiè*
Dog	狗肉	*gǒuròu*
Duck	鸭	*yā*
Eel	鳝鱼	*shànyú*
Fish	鱼	*yú*
Fried dough stick	油条	*yóutiáo*
Frog	田鸡	*tiánjī*
Garlic	大蒜	*dàsuàn*

Ginger	姜	*jiāng*
Green pepper (capsicum)	青椒	*qīngjiāo*
Green vegetables	绿叶素菜	*lǜyè sùcài*
Jiaozi (ravioli)	饺子	*jiǎozi*
Lamb	羊肉	*yángròu*
Lotus root	莲心	*liánxīn*
MSG	味精	*wèijīng*
Mushrooms	磨菇	*mógū*
Noodles	面条	*miàntiáo*
Omelette	煎蛋	*jiāndàn*
Onions	洋葱	*yángcōng*
Oyster sauce	蚝油	*háoyóu*
Pancake	摊饼	*tānbǐng*
Peanut	花生	*huāshēng*
Pork	猪肉	*zhūròu*
Potato	土豆	*tǔdòu*
Prawns	虾	*xiā*
Preserved egg	皮蛋	*pídàn*
Rice, boiled	白饭	*báifàn*
Rice, fried	炒饭	*chǎofàn*
Rice porridge congee	粥	*zhōu*
Salt	盐	*yán*
Sesame oil	芝麻油	*zhīma yóu*
Sichuan pepper	四川辣椒	*sìchuān làjiāo*
Snails	蜗牛	*wōniú*
Snake	蛇肉	*shéròu*
Soup	汤	*tāng*
Star anise	茴香	*huíxiāng*
Straw mushrooms	草菇	*cǎogū*
Soy sauce	酱油	*jiàngyóu*
Sugar	糖	*táng*
Squid	鱿鱼	*yóuyú*
Tofu	豆腐	*dòufu*
Tomato	蕃茄	*fānqié*
Vinegar	醋	*cù*
Water chestnuts	马蹄	*mǎtí*
White radish	白萝卜	*báiluóbo*
Wood ear fungus	木耳	*mùěr*
Yam (sweet potato)	芋头	*yùtou*

Cooking methods

Casseroled	焙	*bèi*
Boiled	煮	*zhǔ*
Deep fried	油煎	*yóujiān*
Fried	炒	*chǎo*
Poached	白煮	*báizhǔ*
Red-cooked (stewed in soy sauce)	红烧	*hóngshāo*
Roast	烤	*kǎo*
Steamed	蒸	*zhēng*
Stir-fried	清炒	*qīngchǎo*

Everyday dishes

Braised duck with vegetables	炖鸭素菜	*dùnyā sùcài*
Cabbage rolls	卷心菜	*juǎnxīncài*
Chicken and sweetcorn soup	玉米鸡丝汤	*yùmǐ jīsī tāng*

Chicken with bamboo shoots and babycorn	笋尖嫩玉米炒鸡片	*sǔnjiān nènyùmǐ chǎojīpiàn*
Chicken with cashew nuts	坚果鸡片	*jiānguǒ jīpiàn*
Crispy aromatic duck	香酥鸭	*xiāngsūyā*
Egg flower soup with tomato	蕃茄蛋汤	*fānqié dàn tāng*
Egg fried rice	蛋炒饭	*dànchǎofàn*
Fish ball soup with white radish	萝卜鱼蛋汤	*luóbo yúdàn tāng*
Fish casserole	焙鱼	*bèiyú*
Fried shredded pork with garlic and chilli	大蒜辣椒炒肉片	*dàsuàn làjiāo chǎoròupiàn*
Hotpot	火锅	*huǒguō*
Kebab	串肉	*chuànròu*
Noodle soup	汤面	*tāngmiàn*
Pork and mustard greens	芥末肉片	*jièmò ròupiàn*
Pork and water chestnut	马蹄猪肉	*mǎtí zhūròu*
Pork and white radish pie	白萝卜肉馅饼	*báiluóbo ròuxiànbǐng*
Prawn with garlic sauce	大蒜炒虾	*dàsuàn chǎoxiā*
Roast duck	烤鸭	*kǎoyā*
Scrambled egg with pork on rice	滑蛋猪肉饭	*huádàn zhūròufàn*
Sliced pork with yellow bean sauce	黄豆肉片	*huángdòu ròupiàn*
Squid with green pepper and black bean	豆豉青椒炒鱿鱼	*dòuchǐ qīngjiāo chǎoyóuyú*
Steamed eel with black beans	豆豉蒸鳝	*dòuchǐ zhēngshàn*
Steamed rice packets wrapped in lotus leaves	荷叶蒸饭	*héyè zhēngfàn*
Stewed pork belly with vegetables	回锅肉	*huíguōròu*
Stir-fried chicken and bamboo shoots	笋尖炒鸡片	*sǔnjiān chǎojīpiàn*
Stuffed beancurd soup	豆腐汤	*dòufutāng*
Stuffed beancurd with aubergine and green pepper	茄子青椒煲	*qiézi qīngjiāobāo*
Sweet and sour spare ribs	糖醋排骨	*tángcù páigǔ*
Sweet bean paste pancakes	赤豆摊饼	*chìdòu tānbǐng*
White radish soup	白萝卜汤	*báiluóbo tāng*
Wonton soup	馄饨汤	*húntun tāng*

Vegetables and eggs

Monks' vegetarian dish	罗汉斋	*luóhànzhāi*
Aubergine with chilli and garlic sauce	大蒜辣椒炒茄子	*dàsuàn làjiāo chǎoqiézi*
Aubergine with sesame sauce	拌茄子片	*bànqiézipiàn*
Beancurd and spinach soup	菠菜豆腐汤	*bōcài dòufu tāng*
Beancurd slivers	豆腐花	*dòufuhuā*
Beans with chestnuts	马蹄豆腐	*mǎtí dòufu*
Braised mountain fungus	炖香菇	*dùnxiānggū*
Pressed beancurd with cabbage	卷心菜豆腐	*juǎnxīncài dòufu*
Egg fried with tomatoes	蕃茄炒蛋	*fānqié chǎodàn*
Fried beancurd with vegetables	豆腐素菜	*dòufu sùcài*
Fried bean sprouts	炒豆芽	*chǎodòuyá*
Spicy braised aubergine	香茄子条	*xiāngqiézitiáo*
Stir-fried bamboo shoots	炒冬笋	*chǎodōngsǔn*
Stir-fried mushrooms	炒鲜菇	*chǎoxiāngū*
Vegetable soup	素菜汤	*sùcài tāng*

Regional dishes

Northern

Aromatic fried lamb	炒羊肉	*chǎoyángròu*
Fish with ham and vegetables	火腿素菜鱼片	*huǒtuǐ sùcài yúpiàn*
Fried prawn balls	炒虾球	*chǎoxiāqiú*

Mongolian hotpot	蒙古火锅	*ménggǔ huǒguō*
Peking duck	北京烤鸭	*běijīng kǎoyā*
Red-cooked lamb	红烧羊肉	*hóngshāo yángròu*
Lion's head (pork rissoles casseroled with greens)	狮子头	*shīzitóu*
Shark's fin soup	鱼翅汤	*yúchìtāng*

Eastern

Crab soup	蟹肉汤	*xièròu tāng*
Dongpo pork casserole	东坡焙肉	*dōngpō bèiròu*
Drunken prawns (steamed in wine)	醉虾	*zuìxiā*
Five flower pork (steamed in lotus leaves)	五花肉	*wǔhuāròu*
Fried crab with eggs	蟹肉鸡蛋	*xièròu jīdàn*
Pearl balls (rice-grain-coated, steamed rissoles)	珍珠球	*zhēnzhūqiú*
Shark fin and crabmeat soup	蟹肉鱼翅汤	*xièròuyúchì tāng*
Steamed sea bass	清蒸鲈鱼	*qīngzhēnglúyú*
Stuffed green peppers	馅青椒	*xiànqīngjiāo*
West Lake fish	西湖鱼	*xīhúyú*
Yangzhou rice	扬州炒饭	*yángzhōu chǎofàn*

Sichuan and western China

Crackling-rice with pork	爆米肉片	*bàomǐ ròupiàn*
Crossing-the-bridge noodles	过桥面	*guòqiáomiàn*
Carry-pole noodles	棒棒面	*bàngbàngmiàn*
Deep-fried green beans with garlic	大蒜刀豆	*dàsuàn dāodòu*
Doubled-cooked pork	回锅肉	*huíguōròu*
Dry-fried pork shreds	油炸肉丝	*yóuzhá ròusī*
Fish-flavoured aubergine	鱼香茄子	*yúxiāng qiézi*
Gongbao chicken (with chillis and peanuts)	宫爆鸡丁	*gōngbào jīdīng*
Green pepper with spring onion and black bean sauce	豆豉青椒	*dòuchǐ qīngjiāo*
Hot and sour soup	酸辣汤	*suānlà tāng*
Hot-spiced beancurd	妈婆豆腐	*māpódòufu*
Wind-cured ham	火腿	*huǒtuǐ*
Smoked duck	熏鸭	*xūnyā*
Strange flavoured chicken (with sesame-garlic-chilli)	怪味鸡	*guàiwèijī*
Stuffed aubergine slices	馅茄子	*xiànqiézi*
Tangerine chicken	桔子鸡	*júzijī*

Southern Chinese/Cantonese

Baked crab with chilli and black beans	辣椒豆豉焙蟹	*làjiāo dòuchǐ bèixiè*
Casseroled beancurd stuffed with pork mince	豆腐煲	*dòufubāo*
Claypot rice with sweet sausage	香肠饭	*xiāngchángfàn*
Crisp-skinned pork on rice	脆皮肉饭	*cuìpíròufàn*
Fish-head casserole	焙鱼头	*bèiyútóu*
Fish steamed with ginger and spring onion	清蒸鱼	*qīngzhēngyú*
Fried chicken with yam	芋头炒鸡片	*yùtóu chǎojīpiàn*
Fried duck with pineapple and ginger	凤梨鸭	*fènglíyā*
Honey-roast pork	叉烧	*chāshāo*

Kale oyster sauce	蚝油白菜	*háoyóu báicài*
Lemon chicken	柠檬鸡	*níngméngjī*
Lichi pork	荔枝肉片	*lìzhīròupiàn*
Salt-baked chicken	盐鸡	*yánjī*
Scallops in taro patties	带子	*dàizi*
Taro "bird nest" filled with pork and vegetables	"鸟巢"	*niǎocháo*

Dim sum (Yum cha)

Barbecue pork bun	叉烧饱	*chāshāo bāo*
Chicken feet	凤爪	*fèngzhuǎ*
Crab and coriander dumpling	蟹肉虾饺	*xièròu xiājiǎo*
Custard tart	蛋挞	*dàntà*
Doughnut	炸面饼圈	*zhá miànbǐngquān*
Pork and prawn dumpling in ornate wrapping	烧麦	*shāomài*
Fried taro and mince dumpling	蕃薯糊饺	*fānshǔ húijiāo*
Lotus paste bun	莲蓉糕	*liánrónggāo*
Moon cake (sweet bean paste in flaky pastry)	月饼	*yuèbǐng*
Paper-wrapped prawns	纸包虾	*zhǐbāoxiā*
Prawn crackers	虾片	*xiāpiàn*
Prawn dumpling	虾饺	*xiājiǎo*
Prawn paste on fried toast	芝麻虾	*zhīmaxiā*
Jiaozi (steamed pork dumplings)	饺子	*jiǎozi*
Shanghai fried meat and vegetable dumpling	锅贴	*guōtiē*
Shark fin dumpling	鲨鱼鳍饺	*shāyú qíjiǎo*
Spring roll	春卷	*chūnjuǎn*
Steamed spare ribs and chilli	排骨	*páigǔ*
Stuffed rice-flour roll	肠粉	*chángfěn*
Stuffed green peppers with black bean sauce	豆豉馅青椒	*dòuchǐ xiànqīngjiāo*
Sweet sesame balls	芝麻球	*zhīma qiú*
Turnip-paste patty	萝卜糕	*luóbo gāo*

national sporting drink **Jinlibao**, an orange and honey confection which most foreigners find over sweet. **Fruit juices** can be unusual and refreshing, however, flavoured with chunks of lychee, lotus and water chestnuts. **Coffee** is grown and drunk in Yunnan and Hainan, and available as instant powder elsewhere – Hainan actually produces a nice instant blend with coconut essence. **Milk** is generally sold in pow-der form as baby food, though there seems to be some campaign in progress to promote its health qualities for invalids and the elderly, and you sometimes find cartons of UHT in supermarket fridges. Sweetened **yoghurt** drinks, available all over the country in little packs of six, are a popular treat for children, though their high sugar content won't do your teeth much good on a regular basis.

COMMUNICATIONS

China's communication system has much improved in recent years and is still being rapidly updated. International phone calls are expensive, but on the whole it's easy to phone or fax abroad, even from obscure towns, and the international mail services are reliable to or from any of the cities.

Domestic calls are nearly as good, and within the country post is very rapid. Satellite TV in English is available in the more expensive hotels. You'll find English-language newspapers only in the largest cities, with Beijing having the widest choice.

MAIL SERVICES

The Chinese **mail service** is, on the whole, fast and reliable, with letters taking less than a day to reach destinations in the same city, two or more days to other destinations in China, and up to several weeks to destinations abroad. **Overseas postal rates** are reasonable; a postcard costs ¥1.6, while a standard letter is ¥2.2–6.7 depending on the weight. Ideally you should have mail franked in front of you. **Express Mail Service** operates to most countries and to most destinations within China; the service cuts down delivery times and the letter or parcel is automatically registered.

Main **post offices** are open seven days a week, 8am–6pm; smaller offices may close for lunch or be closed at weekends. As well as at post offices, you can also post letters in green **postboxes**, though these are few and far between except in the biggest cities, or at tourist hotels, which usually have a postbox at the front desk. Envelopes can be frustratingly scarce; try the stationery sections of department stores.

To **send parcels**, turn up at the main post office with the goods you want to send and the staff will help you pack them. You can buy boxes here, or your goods will be sewn into a linen packet like a pillowcase. You pay a few yuan for the packing service, but don't try to do it yourself, the staff will only unpack everything to ensure it is packed correctly. Once packed, but before the parcel is sealed, it must be checked at the customs window in the post office. In some parts of the country, especially the south, you'll find separate parcels offices near the post office .Parcel service from China is good and reliable, but there is masses of paperwork with forms in Chinese and French (the international postal language) only. If you are sending valuable goods bought in China, put the receipt in with the parcel as it may be opened farther down the line. A one-kilogram parcel should cost around ¥50 for surface mail, ¥80 by air to Europe.

Poste restante services are available in any city. A nominal fee has to be paid to pick up mail, which will be kept for several months, and you will sometimes need to present ID when picking it up. Mail is often eccentrically filed – to cut down on misfiling, your name should be printed clearly at the top of the letter and the surname underlined, but it's still worth checking all the other pigeonholes just in case. Have letters addressed to you c/o Poste Restante, GPO, town or city, province. You can also leave a message for someone in the poste restante box, but you'll have to buy a stamp.

PHONES AND TELECOMMUNICATIONS

China's **phone system** is expanding rapidly and both international and domestic calls can be made with little fuss.

Local calls are free, and long-distance China-wide calls are fairly cheap, but **international calls** cost at least ¥20 a minute. Tourist hotels offer direct dialling abroad from your room, but will add a surcharge, and a minimum charge of between one and three minutes will be levied even if the call goes unanswered. You can also

---

PHONING CHINA FROM ABROAD

To call mainland China from abroad, dial your international access code (see below) + ☎86 (country code) + area code minus initial zero + number.

To call Hong Kong, dial your international access code + ☎852 + number, and for Macau dial your international access code + ☎853 + number.

UK ☎00   US ☎011   Canada ☎011   Australia ☎0011   New Zealand ☎00

PHONING ABROAD FROM CHINA

To call abroad from mainland China dial ☎00 + country code (see below) + area code minus initial zero + number.

From Hong Kong the international access code is ☎001 and from Macau it's ☎00.

UK ☎44   US ☎1   Canada ☎1   Australia ☎61   New Zealand ☎64

PHONING WITHIN CHINA

Everywhere in China has an area code which must be used when phoning from outside that area. Area codes are given for all telephone numbers throughout the book.

TIME DIFFERENCES

China is a single time zone, eight hours ahead of GMT, sixteen hours ahead of US Pacific Standard Time, thirteen hours ahead of US Eastern Standard Time and two hours behind Australian Eastern Standard Time.

---

make IDD calls from streetside telephone shops (usually just a man with a telephone on a table). These usually charge by the minute, but always check in advance.

International calls can be efficiently made from **telecommunications offices**, usually located next to or in the main post office and open 24 hours. You pay a deposit of ¥200 and are told to go to a particular booth. When you have finished, the charge for the call is worked out automatically and you pay at the desk. The minimum charge is for three minutes. Calls to Britain cost ¥29.5 per minute, to the US and Australia ¥26.5, and to Hong Kong ¥16.5 (though this will become cheaper after unification).

Card phones are now widely available in major cities. Cards come in units of ¥20, ¥50 and ¥100, and can be used only in the province where you buy them. They are the cheapest way to make long-distance calls as you are charged by the minute, but you will be cut off when your card value drops below the amount needed for the next minute, leaving you with a phonecard that can be used only to make calls within China.

The **business centres** you'll find off the lobby in most big hotels offer fax, telephone and telex services (as well as photocopying and typing), and you don't have to be a guest to use them.

International faxes are expensive at around ¥25 per minute, telegrams are ¥6 per word. Hotels also charge for receiving faxes, usually around ¥10 per page.

Phone and fax numbers have had new digits added to them in recent years, either at the beginning of the number or after the first digit – so if you are not getting through, you could be missing a digit. If you get stuck, check against a series of numbers for the same town and see what digits they all have in common. Beijing numbers are now eight digits long.

THE MEDIA

The Chinese news agency, **Xinhua**, is a national organization with an office in every province, a mouthpiece for the state which has a monopoly on domestic news. You can read their version of events in the *China Daily*, the only **English-language newspaper**, but it's scarce outside Beijing. The stories of economic success written in turgid prose may be numbing, but it also has a Beijing listings section and articles on uncontroversial aspects of Chinese culture. Other titles such as *Beijing Review* and *Business Beijing* are glossy publications, again very difficult to get hold of outside the capital, with articles on investment opportunities, the latest state successes, as well as interesting places to visit people. In large cities you'll find copies of imported and uncensored publications such as *Time*, *Newsweek* and the *Far Eastern Economic Review*. Try *Friendship Stores* or big tourist hotels for these.

There is the occasional item of interest on **Chinese television**, though you'd have to be quite bored to resort to it for entertainment. Travel programmes on parts of China are quite common, as are song and dance extravaganzas, the most entertaining of which feature dancers in fetishistic, tight-fitting military gear. Soap operas and historical dramas are popular, and often feature a few foreign faces. Or you can watch twenty-year-old imported American thrillers and war films. Chinese war films, in which the Japanese are shown getting mightily beaten, at least have the advantage that you don't need to speak the language to understand what's going on. There is a thirty-minute English-language broadcast every night at 10pm on China Central Television

Channel 8, showing features on aspects of Chinese life.

On the **radio** you're likely to hear the latest soft ballads, often from Taiwan or Hong Kong, or versions of Western pop songs sung in Chinese. In Beijing, *Easy FM* on 91.5 FM offers English broadcasting and mainstream Western music. *Radio Beijing* is China's overseas radio service, broadcasting the official party line in most languages. The World Service frequency varies depending on where you are in the country and what time of day it is. Try 15360 KHz, 15310 KHz, 11955 KHz, 9740 KHz or 9570 KHz.

Hong Kong has a good range of English-language newspapers including the *South China Morning Post*, the *Hong Kong Standard* and the *Eastern Express*. A number of international magazines – *Time*, *Newsweek*, *Asian Wall Street Journal* and *USA Today* – also produce Asian editions in Hong Kong. However, don't expect the free media to survive for long the changeover to Chinese control.

OPENING HOURS AND PUBLIC HOLIDAYS

The general trend in offices – airlines, travel services and the like – is for relatively early opening and closing, with long lunch hours. Typical hours are 8–11.30am and 1.30–4.30pm, with a half day on Saturday. Generalization is difficult, though, as there is no real equivalent to the Western Sunday, the universal day of rest.

Post and telecommunications offices open daily, often until late at night. **Shops**, too, nearly all open daily, keeping long, late hours, especially in big cities, and although **banks** *usually* close on Sundays – or for the whole weekend – even this is not always the case. **Tourist sights** such as parks, pagodas and temples open every day, usually 8am–5pm and without a lunch break. Most public parks open from about 6am, ready to receive the morning flood of shadow boxers. **Museums**, however, tend to have slightly more restricted hours, including lunch breaks and one closing day a week, often Monday or Tuesday. If you arrive at an out-of-the-way place that seems to be closed, however, don't despair – knocking or poking around will often turn up a drowsy doorkeeper. Conversely, you

may find other places locked and deserted when they are supposed to be open.

ADMISSION CHARGES

Virtually all tourist sights attract some kind of **admission charge**. This will often come to no more than a few yuan, but discriminatory pricing policies usually mean that foreigners are charged more than locals. Sometimes the mark-up is a matter of an extra yuan or two, other times it amounts to a hundred percent surcharge. In some extreme cases, at sites considered of international importance, such as the Forbidden City in Beijing or the Terracotta Warriors in Xi'an, foreigners may find themselves paying a hundred times or even more than the locals – up to ¥80 (US$10). Sometimes there is a special student price which you can often qualify for if you have a **student card**.

PUBLIC HOLIDAYS

There are several different kinds of holidays on the Chinese calendar when various facilities will be closed. The biggest of all, **Chinese New**

Year or Spring Festival (see below), is the only **traditional Chinese festival** marked by a holiday and it sees nearly all shops and offices closing down for three days, and a large proportion of the population off work. Even after the third day, offices such as banks may operate on restricted hours until the official end of the holiday period, eleven days later. The other traditional Chinese festivals, such as the Qingming Festival and the Mid-autumn Festival, are not marked by official holidays, though you may notice a growing tendency for businesses to operate restricted hours at these times.

There are also a number of **secular public holidays** which have been celebrated since 1949, the most important being January 1 (**New Year's Day**) and October 1 (**National Day**). Offices close on these dates, though many shops will remain open. Finally, there are a few other dates, March 8 (Women's Day), May 1 (Labour Day), June 1 (Children's Day), July 1 (Chinese Communist Party Day) and August 1 (Army Day), which are celebrated by parades and festive activities by the groups concerned, but are not general holidays. Businesses and offices tend to operate normally on these dates.

FESTIVALS

The rhythm of festivals and religious observances that marked the Chinese year was interrupted by the Cultural Revolution, and only now are old traditions beginning to re-emerge. Apart from countrywide Chinese festivals, the ethnic minorities punctuate the year with their own ritual observances and these are detailed in the appropriate chapters in The Guide. In Hong Kong all the national Chinese festivals are celebrated.

Most festivals take place on dates in the Chinese **lunar calendar**, in which the first day of the month is the time when the moon is at its thinnest, with the full moon marking the middle of the month. So, by the Gregorian calendar, such festivals are on a different day every year. Most festivals celebrate the turning of the **seasons** or propitious dates, such as the eighth day of the eighth month (eight is a lucky number in China), and are times for gift giving, family reunion and feasting. In the countryside, lanterns are lit and firecrackers (banned in the cities) are set off. It's always worth visiting **temples** on festival days, when the air is thick with incense, and people queue up to kowtow to altars and play games that bring good fortune, such as trying to hit the temple bell with thrown coins.

CHINESE NEW YEAR

New Year, or **Spring Festival**, is the biggest holiday in the Chinese calendar, two weeks of festivities marking the beginning of a new year in the lunar calendar. In Chinese astrology, each year is associated with a particular animal from a cycle of twelve; 1997 is the year of the ox, for example, and the passing into a new phase is a momentous occasion. Each year it falls on a different date in the Gregorian calendar, but it's usually in late January or early February. There's a tangible sense of excitement in the run-up to the festival, when China is perhaps at its most colourful, with shops and houses decorated with good-luck messages and stalls and shops selling paper money, drums and costumes. During the festival itself, however, is not an ideal time to be travelling the country – everything shuts down, and most of the population goes on the move, making travel impossible or extremely uncomfortable.

NATIONAL CHINESE FESTIVALS

January/February New Year. Celebrated during the first two weeks of the new lunar year. In 1998 it will begin on January 28 and in 1999 on February 15.

February Tiancang Festival. On the twentieth day of the first lunar month Chinese peasants celebrate Tiancang, or Granary Filling Day, in the hope of ensuring a good harvest later in the year.

March Guanyin's Birthday. Guanyin, the Goddess of Mercy, and probably China's most popular deity, is celebrated, most colourfully in Taoist temples, on the nineteenth day of the second lunar month.

April 4 and 5 Qing-Ming Festival. This festival (Tomb Sweeping Day) is the time to visit the graves of ancestors and burn ghost money in honour of the departed.

June/July Dragonboat Festival. On the fifth day of the fifth lunar month dragonboat races are held in memory of the poet Qu Yuan, who drowned himself in 280 BC. Some of the most famous venues for this festival in the country are Yueyang in Hunan Province, and Hong Kong. The traditional food to accompany the celebrations is *zongzi* (lotus-wrapped rice packets).

September/October Moon Festival. On the fifteenth day of the eighth month of the lunar calendar the Chinese celebrate the Moon Festival, also known as the Mid-autumn Festival, a time of family reunion that is celebrated with fireworks and lanterns. Moon cakes, biscuits with a rich filling of sugar, sesame and walnut, are eaten, and plenty of *moutai* is consumed. In Hong Kong, the cakes are stuffed with duck eggs.

September/October Double Ninth Festival. Nine is a number associated with *yang*, or male energy, and on the ninth day of the ninth lunar month such qualities as assertiveness and strength are celebrated. It's believed to be a good time for the distillation (and consumption) of spirits.

September 28 Confucius Festival. The birthday of Confucius is marked by celebrations at all Confucian temples. It's a good time to visit Qufu, in Shandong Province, when elaborate ceremonies are held in the temple there (see p.298).

December 25 Christmas. This is marked as a religious event only by the faithful, but for everyone else it's an excuse for a feast and a party.

The first day of the festival is marked by a family feast at which *jiaozi* (dumplings) are eaten, sometimes with coins hidden inside, and followed by a cacophony of **firecrackers**, supposedly to frighten demons. New Year in the cities is now a slightly more staid affair as the fireworks are banned, though enterprising stall holders sell cassette tapes of explosions as a replacement. Other ghost-scaring traditions include the pasting up of images of door gods at the threshold, and the wearing of red clothes, particularly important if the animal of your birth year is coming round again. Outside the home, New Year is publicly celebrated at **temple fairs**, which feature acrobats, drummers, and clouds of smoke as the Chinese light incense sticks to placate the gods. After two weeks, the celebrations end with the **lantern festival**, when the streets are filled with multicoloured paper lanterns, a tradition dating from the Han dynasty. Many places also have flower festivals and street processions with paper dragons and other animals parading through the town.

SOCIAL CONVENTIONS AND ETIQUETTE

Some of the culture shock which afflicts foreign visitors to China comes from false expectations, engendered through travel in other parts of Asia. The Chinese are not a "mellow" people. Profoundly irreligious, they are neither particularly spiritual nor gentle, nor are they deferential to strangers. However, the irritations sometimes experienced by foreigners – the sniggers and the unhelpful service – can almost invariably be put down to nervousness and the formidable language barrier, rather than hostility. This is not to say that at some time in your trip you will not lock yourself in your hotel room and wish never to see a Chinese face again – you probably will. But however abused you may feel, remember that foreigners are still treated far better in China than are the Chinese themselves. Indeed, communication between foreigners and locals is never a problem once you get beyond the language barrier. Visitors who speak Chinese will encounter an endless series of delighted and amazed interlocutors wherever they go, invariably asking about their age and marital status before anything else.

Even if you don't speak Chinese, you will run into enough locals eager to practise their English. If from such encounters you are subsequently invited to someone's home, a **gift** might well be expected, though people will not open it in front of you, nor will they express profuse gratitude for it. The Chinese way to express gratitude is through reciprocal actions rather than words. Indeed, elaborate protestations of thanks can be taken as an attempt to avoid obligation. If you are lucky enough to be asked out to a restaurant, you will discover that **restaurant bills** are not shared out between the guests but instead people will go to great lengths to claim the honour of paying the whole bill by themselves. Normally that honour will fall to the person perceived as the most senior, and as a foreigner dining with Chinese you should make some effort to stake your claim, though it is probable that someone else will grab the bill before you do. Attempting to pay a "share" of the bill may cause serious embarrassment.

Perhaps surprisingly, in view of the above, the main gripe of foreign travellers in China is the relentless and very widespread determination that foreigners should be **overcharged** at every opportunity. For the traveller this can become wearying and alienating. But for your own equanimity you would do well to accept overcharging to a certain degree rather than fight for your rights all across China. The sums you will be arguing about are often trivial ones. And remember that the average rickshaw driver would consider it a humiliating defeat to carry a foreigner for the same price as a local. Try to inflict that on him and you will stir up real bitterness.

Another factor that Western tourists need to note is that the Chinese have almost no concept of **privacy**. People will stare at each other from point-blank range and pluck letters or books out of others' hands for close inspection. Even toilets are built with partitions so low that you can chat with your neighbour while squatting. All leisure activities including visits to natural beauty spots or holy relics are done in large noisy groups and the desire of some Western tourists to be "left alone" is variously interpreted by locals as eccentric, arrogant or even sinister.

In a land where privacy is an unheard-of luxury, exotic foreigners inevitably become targets for **blatant curiosity**, particularly in rural areas. You may at times find people running up and jostling for a better look, exclaiming loudly to each other, *Lao Wai, Lao Wai* (literally, "old outside person"). This is not intended to be aggressive or insulting though it can give foreigners the uncomfortable feeling of being a zoo animal. One way to render yourself human again is to address the onlookers in Chinese, if you can. Otherwise, perhaps you should just be grateful that people are showing an interest in you.

Apart from staring, various other forms of behaviour perceived as anti-social in the West are considered perfectly normal in China and foreign tourists should bear this in mind before passing judgement. Take the widespread habit of **spitting**, for example, which can be observed in buses, trains, restaurants and even inside people's homes. Outside the company of urban sophisticates, it would not occur to people that there was anything disrespectful in delivering a powerful spit while in conversation with a stranger. **Smoking**, likewise, is almost universal among men and in the few places where non-smoking signs have been posted (for example, in soft-seat train compartments) the signs are rarely observed and any attempt to stop others from lighting up is met with incomprehension. As in many countries, handing out cigarettes is a basic way of establishing good-will and non-smokers should be apologetic about turning down offered cigarettes.

Although China would not normally be described as a liberal country, these days restraints on public behaviour are disappearing remarkably fast. **Skimpy clothing** in summer is quite normal in all urban areas, particularly among women (less so in the countryside), and even in potentially sensitive Muslim areas, such as the far west, many Han Chinese girls insist on wearing miniskirts and see-through blouses. Although Chinese men commonly wear short trousers and expose their midriffs in hot weather, Western men who do the same should note that the bizarre sight of hairy flesh in public – chest or legs – will instantly become the focus of giggly gossip. The generally relaxed approach to cloth-ing applies equally when visiting temples, though in **mosques** men and women alike should cover their bodies above the wrists and ankles. As for **beachwear**, bikinis and briefs are in, but nudity is yet to make its debut.

Skimpy clothing is one thing, but **scruffy** clothing is quite another. If you want to earn the respect of the Chinese – useful for things like getting served in a restaurant or checking into a hotel – you need to make some effort with your appearance. While the average Chinese peasant might reasonably be expected to have wild hair and wear dirty clothes, for a rich foreigner to do so is likely to arouse a degree of contempt. Another good way to ease your progress is to have a name or business card to flash around – even better if you can include your name in Chinese characters on it.

Hand-shaking is not a Chinese tradition, though it is now fairly common between men. Bodily contact in the form of embraces or back-slapping can be observed between same-sex friends, and these days, in cities, a boy and a girl can walk round arm-in-arm and even kiss without raising an eyebrow. **Voice level** in China seems to be pitched several decibels louder than in most other countries, though this should not necessarily be interpreted as a sign of belligerence.

POLICE, TROUBLE AND EMERGENCIES

China is basically a police state, with the State interfering with and controlling the lives of its subjects to a degree most Westerners would find it hard to tolerate – as indeed many of the Chinese do. This should not affect foreigners much, however, as the State on the whole takes a hands-off approach to visitors – they are anxious that you have a good time rather than come away with a bad impression of the country. Indeed, Chinese who commit crimes against foreigners are treated much more harshly than if their victims had been native.

The **police** (or **Public Security Bureau**) are recognizable by their green uniforms and caps, though there are a lot more around than you might at first think, as plenty are undercover. They have much wider powers than most Western police forces, including establishing the guilt of crimi-nals – trials are used only for deciding the sen-tence of the accused (though this is changing and China now has the beginnings of an independent judiciary). If the culprit is deemed to show proper remorse, this will result in a more lenient sen-tence. Laws are harsh, with execution – a bullet in the back of the head – the penalty for a wide range of serious crimes, from corruption to rape. Continuing the Confucian tradition that criminals are in part created by their upbringing, the family of the executed criminal is made to pay for the bullet that killed him.

Crime is a growth industry in fast-changing China, with official corruption and juvenile offences the worst problems. Much crime is blamed on spiritual pollution by foreign influence, the result of increasing liberalization. But serious social problems, such as mass unemployment, are as much to blame, as is the let's-get-rich atittude that has become the prevailing ideology. However, there is no need for paranoia; China is still safer to travel in than many Western countries.

THEFT AND VIOLENT CRIME

As a tourist, and therefore someone far richer than anyone else around, you are an obvious target for **thieves**. Passports and money should ideally be kept in a concealed money belt; a bum bag offers much less protection and is easy for skilled pickpockets to get into. Be wary on **buses**, the favoured haunt of pickpockets, and **trains**, particularly in hard-seat class and on overnight journeys. Take a chain and padlock to secure your luggage in the rack. On internal flights take your luggage on to the plane with you and don't trust anything valuable to the hold. **Hotel rooms** are on the whole secure, dormitories much less so. Most hotels should have a safe, but it's not unusual for things to go missing from these. It's a good idea to keep US$100 or so, separately from the rest of your cash, together with your travellers' cheques receipts, insurance policy details, and photocopies of your passport and visa. On the street, try not to be too ostentatious. Flashy jewellery and watches will attract the wrong kind of attention, and try to be discreet when taking out your cash. Not looking ostentatiously wealthy also helps if you want to avoid being ripped off by traders and taxi drivers, as does telling them you are a student – the Chinese have a great respect for education, and much more sympathy for foreign students than for tourists.

If you do have anything stolen, you'll need to get the PSB (addresses are given throughout *The Guide*) to write up a **loss report** in order to claim on your insurance. If possible take a Chinese speaker with you and be prepared to pay a small fee.

Violent crime is less of a problem, though be wary at night on dark streets. You may well see street confrontations, when huge crowds gather to watch a few protagonists push each other around, which can give the impression that China is a violent place. Mostly they are caused by the stresses and frustrations of life in overcrowded China, and usually take place where the crowds are at their most overwhelming, such as at bus stations. Though they look frightening, such fights rarely result in violence, just a lot of shouting. You may find yourself caught up in one if, say, you get in an argument with a rickshaw driver, in which case a fast exit is the best policy.

SEXUAL HARASSMENT AND ILLEGAL ACTIVITIES

Women travellers usually find incidences of **sexual harassment** much less of a problem than in other Asian countries. Chinese men are, on the whole, deferential and respectful. A much more likely complaint is being ignored, as the Chinese will generally assume that any man accompanying a woman will be doing all the talking. You may get some hassles, however, in Dongbei, where Chinese men may take you for a Russian prostitute (much embarrassment ensues when they realize their mistake) and in Muslim Xinjiang. Women on their own visiting temples, especially remote ones, definitely need to be on their guard – not obsessively paranoid, but don't assume that all monks and temple caretakers have impeccable morals. As ever, it pays to be aware of how local women are dressing and behave accordingly. Miniskirts and heels may be fine in the cosmopolitan cities, but fashions are much more conservative in the countryside.

Homosexuality is officially regarded as a foreign eccentricity and gay sexual activities are illegal. Gay Chinese men often approach foreigners, partly because they are much less likely to shop them to the police.

Since liberalization, Chinese society has seen an increase in petty crime. **Prostitution**, though still illegal and harshly punished, has made a big comeback – witness all the girls who stand by the side of major roads, soliciting for trade from passing drivers. Single Western males are likely to be approached, most commonly inside hotels. Bear in mind that AIDS is on the increase and that China is hardly Thailand – consequences may be dire if you are caught.

The Chinese are hard on **drugs**, with dealers and smugglers facing execution. However, heroin use has become fairly widespread in the south of China. A mild strain of cannabis grows wild, especially in the south, but is not much used by the Chinese; some Uighurs smoke it and, if you want to score, head for their quarter. The police pretty much turn a blind eye to foreigners with drugs, as long as no Chinese are involved. As ever, be discreet.

Visitors are not likely to be affected by **political crimes**, but foreign residents may be. Foreign teachers or students may find themselves expelled from the country for talking about politics or religion. The Chinese they talk to will be treated less leniently. In Tibet, and at sensitive border areas, censorship is taken much more seriously; photographing military installations, instances of police brutality or gulags is not a good idea.

DIRECTORY

Addresses Street numbering is so random in most Chinese cities that it's little help in finding the address. Note that floors within buildings are numbered as in the US, not as in the UK or Australia. Street level is the "First Floor", not "Ground Floor"; the next storey is the "Second Floor", not first; and so on.

Airport departure tax Currently ¥50 for internal flights, and ¥90 if you're leaving the country.

Cigarettes Most foreign brands are available for a fraction of the price they cost in the West. The cheaper, Chinese brands have some great packaging and names, but tend to be pretty rough.

Contraceptives Condoms are easy to get hold of, with imported brands available in all the big cities.

Electricity The current is 220V on the mainland and 200V in Hong Kong. Plugs come in a wide range with either two or three differently shaped prongs. Take a travel conversion plug with you, and a flashlight is also useful given the erratic power supply.

Laundry Most tourist hotels have a laundry service, though it's not usually cheap. Clothes will be returned the following day.

Left luggage Some hotels will store luggage, and there are always guarded and moderately secure luggage offices at train and bus stations (sometimes open only from dawn to dusk, however) where you can leave your possessions for a few kuai.

Photography Photography is a popular pastime among the Chinese, and all big mainland towns and cities have plenty of places to buy and process 35mm film. In Hong Kong there's likely to be at least as big a range as wherever you've come from; elsewhere, colour print stock is the most widely available. Mainland Chinese brands cost about ¥6 for 36 exposures, scarcer Western varieties are around ¥17. Processing is very variable – sometimes good, often mediocre – and costs about ¥5 per roll. Transparency film is rarely available, impossible to process in the country, and in the ¥60 price bracket. Camera batteries are beginning to be fairly easy to obtain in big city department stores. Hong Kong has every imaginable type, but it's best to bring a supply with you.

Tampons Good sanitary towels and tampons are widely available in supermarkets and department stores, and are reasonably cheap.

Things to take Unless you're a big fan of nineteenth-century literature – just about all that is available in English translation – take a few meaty books for the long train rides. Coins and stamps from your country are a good idea – they will cause much excitement and curiosity and make good small presents. Another aid to bridging the language gap is a few photos of your family and friends, even where you live. China is rarely a quiet place, and for the sake of your sanity as well as comfort, earplugs are a good idea, especially if you're contemplating long bus journeys. It's also advisable to take a set of your own chopsticks, for hygiene reasons. Also worth taking are: a universal plug adaptor and universal sink plug; a flashlight; a multi-purpose penknife; a needle and thread; and a first-aid kit (see p.19). If you'll be travelling in the sub-tropical south or at high altitudes, bring high-factor sun block and good-quality sunglasses.

Time differences China is a single time zone, eight hours ahead of GMT, sixteen hours ahead of of US Pacific Standard Time, thirteen hours ahead of US Eastern Standard Time and two hours behind Australian Eastern Standard Time.

Tipping Actually forbidden in many places on the mainland, but functions as in the West in Hong Kong.

Toilets Chinese toilets can take a lot of getting used to. Apart from the often disgusting standard of hygiene, the lack of privacy can be very off-putting – squat toilets are separated by a low, thin partition or no partition at all. Only visit toilets staffed by an attendant who you will have to pay a few jiao to before you enter. The public kind are generally too awful even to contemplate. Probably the best bet is to find a large hotel and use the toilets in the lobby. Most hotel toilets have a wastepaper basket by the side for toilet paper. Don't put paper down the loo as it blocks the primitive sewage system and staff will get irate with you.

Work and study There is much more opportunity to work or study in China than there has been in the past. Foreigners are employed in many joint-venture operations, or as teachers of English, and it's possible for students to study not just Chinese language, but subjects such as medicine, cookery and art. However, costs for foreigners living in China, thanks to strict rules on where they can live, are expensive.

Most foreign workers in China are employed as English teachers and most universities now have a few foreign teachers. Schemes to find teachers are run from Chinese embassies abroad – write to them for details. Salaries are about ¥1500 a month, more than a Chinese worker earns, but not enough to allow you to put any aside. You don't need any qualifications beyond an ability to speak English. Teachers have a workload of between ten and twenty hours a week in a college – a lot more than their Chinese counterparts have to do.

It's also worth simply turning up in Beijing and Shanghai and trawling around offices – an ability to speak Chinese is expected. Remember that foreign firms in China use the Chinese system of *guanxi* (connections) more than they would at home, and getting to know the right people is even more important here. If you want to write to companies, find out the name of the personnel manager – a letter without a name at the top won't get opened.

ESSENTIAL WORDS AND PHRASES

Below is a list of words, with their Chinese characters and pinyin, which you will need to refer to on a regular basis. Town accounts in *The Guide* have their own character and pinyin boxes giving specific details of hotels, restaurants and sights, while the language box in *Contexts*, see p.1054, gives more extensive everyday words and phrases.

Airport	机场	*jīchǎng*
Bank of China	中国银行	*zhōngguó yínháng*
Bus station	公共汽车站	*gōnggòng qìchē zhàn*
CAAC	中国民航	*zhōngguó mínháng*
CITS	中国国际旅行社	*zhōngguó guójì lǚxíngshè*
Ferry dock	码头	*mǎtóu*
Hospital	医院	*yīyuàn*
Hotel	宾馆	*bīnguǎn*
Left-luggage office	寄存处	*jìcúnchù*
Museum	博物馆	*bówùguǎn*
Post & telecommunications office	邮电局	*yóudiànjú*
PSB	公安局	*gōng'ānjú*
Restaurant	饭店	*fàndiàn*
Temple	寺院	*sìyuàn*
Ticket office	售票处	*shòupiàochù*
Toilet (men's)	(男)厕所	*(nán)cèsuǒ*
Toilet (women's)	(女)厕所	*(nǚ)cèsuǒ*
Train station	火车站	*huǒchēzhàn*

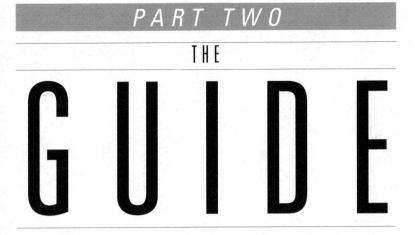

PART TWO

THE

GUIDE

CHAPTER ONE

BEIJING AND AROUND

The brash modernity of **BEIJING** (meaning Northern Capital) usually comes as a surprise. Traversed by freeways (it's the proud owner of over a hundred flyovers) and spiked with highrises, this vivid metropolis is China at its most dynamic. For the last thousand years, the drama of China's **imperial history** was played out here, with the emperor sitting enthroned at the centre of the Chinese universe, and though today the city is a very different one, it remains spiritually and politically the heart of the country. Between the swathes of concrete and glass, you'll find some of the lushest temples, and certainly the grandest remnants of the Imperial Age. Unexpectedly, some of the country's most pleasant scenic spots lie within the scope of a day trip, and, just to the north of the city, is one of China's most famous sights, the old boundary line between civilizations, the **Great Wall**.

First impressions of Beijing are of an almost inhuman vastness, conveyed by the sprawl of identical apartment buildings in which most of the city's population of twelve million are housed, and the eight-lane freeways that slice it up. It's an impression that's reinforced on closer acquaintance, from the magnificent **Forbidden City**, with its stunning wealth of treasures, the concrete desert of **Tian'anmen Square** and the gargantuan buildings of the modern executive around it, to the rank after rank of office complexes that line its mammoth roads. Outside the centre, the scale becomes more manageable, with parks, narrow alleyways and ancient sites such as the **Yonghe Gong**, **Observatory** and, most magnificent of all, the **Temple of Heaven**, offering respite from the city's oppressive orderliness. In the suburbs beyond, the two **Summer Palaces** and the **Western Hills** have been favoured retreats since imperial times.

Beijing is an invaders' city, the capital of oppressive foreign dynasties – the Manchu and the Mongols – and of a dynasty with a foreign ideology – the Communists. As such, it has assimilated a lot of outside influence, and today it is perhaps the most cosmopolitan part of China, with an international flavour appropriate to the capital of a major commercial power. Many of the new skyscrapers are funded by foreign companies, prompting cynical Beijingers to wonder why the government is so keen on getting Hong Kong back when they've been selling off the centre of the capital itself. Only in Beijing will a foreign face elicit no second glances. The city is home to a large **expat population**, housed for the most part in separate suburban ghettos with little contact with the local Chinese. Indeed, it's quite possible to spend years in Beijing eating Western food, dancing to Western music, and socializing with like-minded foreigners – hardened veterans of the expat scene compare it favourably with Hong Kong.

Beijing may appear liberal on the surface, but the government keeps an iron grip on its residents, ranging from fussy regulations – no laundry hanging from windows during the 1995 UN Women's Conference – to the brutal suppression of dissent. Yet despite its political conservatism Beijing attracts the most adventurous and progressive Chinese citizenry. The city has a well-developed **youth culture** and its campuses are regarded as such hotbeds of subversive ideas that all new students are sent for a year of "political study" (indoctrination) before they begin their courses. This facade – the front line of China's attempts to grapple with modernity – coupled with a strident reactionism, has created a city intense with contradiction. In the streets at night you'll see large groups of the older generation performing the *yangkou* (loyalty dance), Chairman

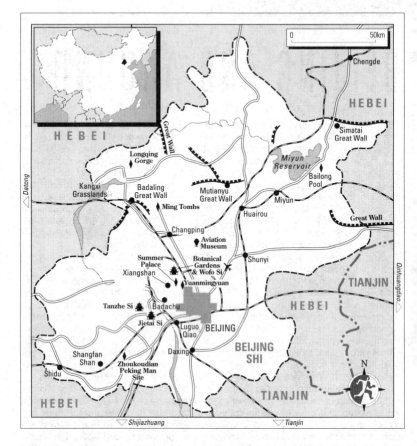

Mao's favourite dance universally learned a few decades ago, while in the discos, their kids are moshing to Nirvana. The city has seventeen branches of *McDonald's*, and they are perpetually full, but increasingly popular is a new fad known as "nostalgia cuisine" – dishes from the Cultural Revolution era – eaten in restaurants named after revolutionary slogans.

Beijing is a city that almost everyone enjoys. For new arrivals it provides a gentle introduction to the country and for travellers who've been roughing it round outback China, the creature comforts on offer are a delight. But Beijing is essentially a private city, and one whose surface, attractive though it is, is difficult to penetrate. Sometimes it seems to have the superficiality of a theme park. Certainly there is something mundane about the way tourist groups are efficiently shunted around, plugged from hotel to sight, with little contact with everyday reality. To get deeper into the city, wander the *hutongs*, the cobweb of alleys between the main streets, "fine and numerous as the hairs of a cow" (as one Chinese guidebook puts it), and check out the little antique markets, the residential shopping districts, the smaller, quirkier sights, and the parks, some of the best in China, where you'll see Beijingers performing *tai ji* and hear birdsong – just – over the hum of traffic. Take advantage, too, of the city's burgeoning nightlife and see just how far the Chinese have gone down the road of what used to be called spiritual pollution.

If the Party had any control over it, no doubt Beijing would have the best **climate** of any Chinese city; as it is, it has one of the worst. The best time to visit is in autumn, between September and October, when it's dry and clement. In winter it gets very cold, down to minus 20°C, and the mean winds that whip off the Mongolian plains feel like they're freezing your ears off. Summer (June–August) is hot, up to 30°C, and the short spring (April & May) is dry but windy.

Getting to Beijing is no problem. As the centre of China's **transport** network you'll probably wind up here sooner or later, whether you want to or not, and to avoid the capital seems wilfully perverse. On a purely practical level, it's a good place to stock up on visas for the rest of Asia, and to arrange transport out of the country – most romantically, on the Trans-Siberian or Trans-Mongolian trains. To take in its superb sights requires a week, by which time you may well be ready to move on to China proper. Beijing is a fun place, but make no mistake, it in no way typifies the rest of the nation.

Some history

It was in Tian'anmen, on October 1, 1949, that Chairman Mao Zedong hoisted the red flag to proclaim officially the **foundation of the People's Republic**. He told the crowds (the square could then hold only 500,000) that the Chinese had at last stood up, and defined liberation as the final culmination of a 150-year fight against foreign exploitation.

The claim, perhaps, was modest. Beijing's **recorded history** goes back a little over three millennia, to beginnings as a trading centre for Mongols, Koreans and local Chinese tribes. Its predominance, however, dates to the mid-thirteenth century, and the formation of **Mongol China** under Genghis and later **Kublai Khan**. It was Kublai who took control of the city in 1264, and who properly established it as a capital, replacing the earlier power centres of Luoyang and Xi'an. Marco Polo visited him here, working for a while in the city, and was clearly impressed with the level of sophistication:

> *So great a number of houses and of people, no man could tell the number... I believe there is no place in the world to which so many merchants come, and dearer things, and of greater value and more strange, come into this town from all sides than to any city in the world...*

The **wealth** came from the city's position at the start of the Silk Road and Polo described "over a thousand carts loaded with silk" arriving "almost each day", ready for the journey west out of China. And it set a precedent in terms of style and grandeur for the Khans, later known as emperors, with Kublai building himself a palace of astonishing proportions, walled on all sides and approached by great marble stairways.

With the accession of the **Ming dynasty**, who defeated the Mongols in 1368, the capital temporarily shifted to present-day Nanjing, but Yongle, the second Ming emperor, returned, building around him prototypes of the city's two greatest **monuments** – the Imperial Palace and Temple of Heaven. It was in Yongle's reign, too, that the basic **city-plan** took shape, rigidly symmetrical, extending in squares and rectangles from the palace and inner-city grid to the suburbs, much as it is today.

Subsequent, post-Ming history is dominated by the rise and eventual collapse of the Manchus – the **Qing dynasty**, northerners who ruled China from Beijing from 1644 to the beginning of the twentieth century. The capital was at its most prosperous in the first half of the eighteenth century, the period in which the Qing constructed the legendary **Summer Palace** – the world's most extraordinary royal garden, with two hundred pavilions, temples and palaces, and immense artificial lakes and hills – to the north of the city. With the central Imperial Palace, this was the focus of endowment and the symbol of Chinese wealth and power. However, in 1860, the Opium Wars brought British and French troops to the walls of the capital, and the Summer Palace was first looted and then burned by the British, more or less entirely to the ground.

While the imperial court lived apart, within what was essentially a separate walled city, conditions for the civilian population, in the capital's suburbs, were starkly different. Kang Youwei, a Cantonese visiting in 1895, described this dual world:

> *No matter where you look, the place is covered with beggars. The homeless and the old, the crippled and the sick with no one to care for them, fall dead on the roads. This happens every day. And the coaches of the great officials rumble past them continuously.*

The indifference, rooted according to Kang in officials throughout the city, spread from the top down. From 1884, using funds meant for the modernization of the nation's navy, the empress Dowager Cixi had begun building a new Summer Palace of her own. The empress's project was really the last grand gesture of **imperial architecture** and patronage – and like its model was also badly burned by foreign troops, in another outbreak of the Opium War in 1900. By this time, with successive waves of occupation by foreign troops, the empire and the imperial capital were near collapse. The **Manchus abdicated** in 1911, leaving the Northern Capital to be ruled by warlords. In 1928 it came under the military dictatorship of Chiang Kaishek's **Guomindang**, being seized by the **Japanese** in 1939, and at the end of **World War II** the city was controlled by an alliance of Guomindang troops and American marines.

The **Communists** took Beijing in January 1949, nine months before Chiang Kaishek's flight to Taiwan assured final victory. The **rebuilding of the capital**, and the erasing of symbols of the previous regimes, was an early priority. The city that Mao Zedong inherited for the Chinese people was in most ways primitive. Imperial laws had banned the building of houses higher than the official buildings and palaces, so virtually nothing was more than one storey high. The roads, although straight and uniform, were narrow and congested, and there was scarcely any industry. The new plans aimed to reverse all except the city's sense of ordered planning, with Tian'anmen Square at its heart – and initially, through the early 1950s, their inspiration was Soviet, with an emphasis on heavy industry and a series of poor-quality high-rise housing programmes.

In the zest to be free from the past and create a modern, people's capital, much of **Old Peking was destroyed**, or co-opted: the Temple of Cultivated Wisdom became a wire factory and the Temple of the God of Fire produced electric lightbulbs. In the 1940s there were eight thousand temples and monuments in the city; by the 1960s there were only around a hundred and fifty. Even the city walls and gates, relics mostly of the Ming era, were pulled down and their place taken by ring roads and avenues.

Much of the city's **contemporary planning policy** was disastrous, creating more problems than it solved. Most of the traditional courtyard houses which were seen to encourage individualism were destroyed. In their place went anonymous concrete buildings, often with inadequate sanitation and little running water. In 1969, when massive restoration was needed above ground, Mao instead launched a campaign to build a network of subterranean tunnels as shelter in case of war. Built by hand, millions of man-hours went into constructing a useless labyrinth that would be no defence against modern bombs and served only to lower the city's water table. After the destruction of all the capital's dogs in 1950, it was the turn of sparrows in 1956. A measure designed to preserve grain, its only effect was to lead to an increase in the insect population. To combat this, all the grass was pulled up, which in turn led to dust storms in the windy winter months.

Recent changes of policy have, however, had some success in terms of **environmental awareness**. The authorities have begun to do serious battle with industrial pollution, which in winter had become so acute that it blanketed the city in a pale yellow smog. Factories which can't be modernized have been closed. The city's open spaces have been revitalized with a massive tree-planting campaign. And to help with problems of overcrowding, there are ambitious plans for a series of satellite cities. Changing personal habits, however, is less easy. The city authorities' official campaign against spitting (which is reckoned to be the cause of Beijing's high rate of TB) has had minimal effect.

Orientation, arrival and information

There's no doubt that Beijing's initial culture shock owes much to the artificiality of the city's **layout**. The main streets are huge, wide and dead straight, aligned either east–west or north–south, and extend in a series of widening rectangles across the whole thirty square kilometres of the inner capital. Alongside these is the old tangled network of downtown *hutongs*, dark alleyways that twist out from the central grid.

The pivot of the ancient city was a north–south road that led from the entrance of the Forbidden City to the walls. This remains today as **Qianmen Dajie**, though the main axis has shifted to the east–west road that divides Tian'anmen Square and the Forbidden City, and which changes its name, like all major boulevards, every few kilometres along its length. It's generally referred to as **Chang'an Jie**.

Few traces of the old city remain except in the **street names**, which look bewilderingly complex but are not hard to figure out once you realize that they are compounds of a name, plus a direction – *bei, nan, xi, dong* and *zhong* (north, south, west, east and middle) – and the words for inside and outside – *nei* and *wei* – which indicate the street's position in relation to the old city walls which enclosed the centre. Central streets often also contain the word *men* (gate), which indicates that they once had a gate in the wall along their length.

The **three ring roads**, freeways arranged in concentric rectangles centring on the Forbidden City, are rapid-access corridors. The second and third, Erhuan Lu and Sanhuan Lu, are the most useful, cutting down on journey times but extending the distance travelled and therefore much liked by taxi drivers. While most of the sights are in the city centre, most of the modern buildings – hotels, restaurants, shopping centres and flashy office blocks – are along the ring roads.

You'll soon become familiar with the experience of barrelling along a freeway in a bus or a taxi while identical blocks flicker past, not knowing which direction you're travelling in, let alone where you are. To get some sense of orientation, take fast mental notes on the more obvious and imposing landmarks. The Great Hall of the People in Tian'anmen Square; the Telegraph Office on Xichang'an Jie; the seventeen-storey

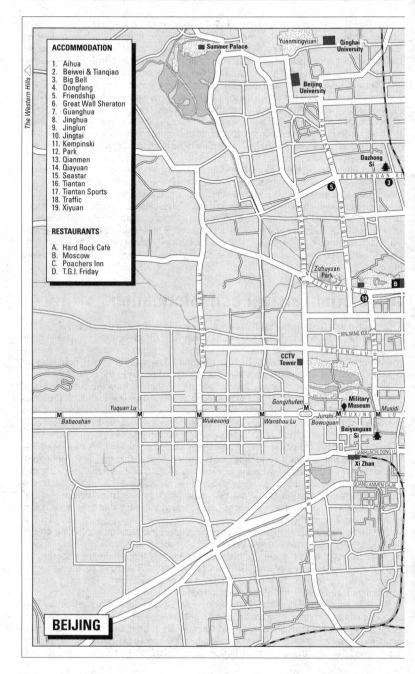

ACCOMMODATION

1. Aihua
2. Beiwei & Tianqiao
3. Big Bell
4. Dongfang
5. Friendship
6. Great Wall Sheraton
7. Guanghua
8. Jinghua
9. Jinglun
10. Jingtai
11. Kempinski
12. Park
13. Qianmen
14. Qiayuan
15. Seastar
16. Tiantan
17. Tiantan Sports
18. Traffic
19. Xiyuan

RESTAURANTS

A. Hard Rock Café
B. Moscow
C. Poachers Inn
D. T.G.I. Friday

The Western Hills

Summer Palace

Yuanmingyuan

Qinghai University

Beijing University

Dazhong Si

BEISANHUAN XI

Zizhuyuan Park

XINJIANG KOU

FUCHENG LU

CCTV Tower

Gongzhufen

Military Museum

Muxidi

Yuquan Lu

Babaoshan

Wukesong

Wanshou Lu

Junshi Bowuguan

FUXING LU

Baiyunguan Si

LIANHUACHI DONG LU

Xi Zhan

GUANG'ANMEN DAJIE

XISANHUAN ZHONG LU

BEIJING

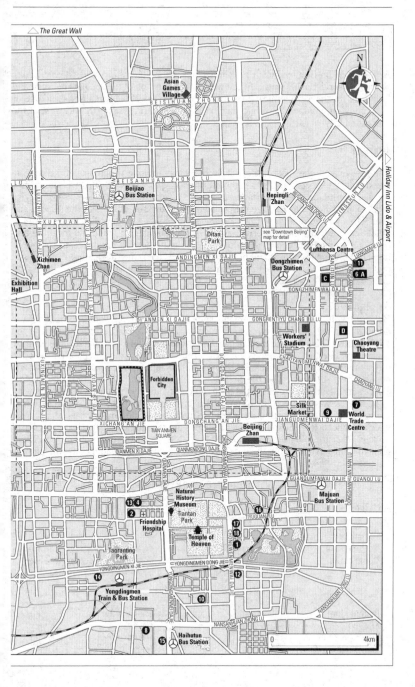

△ The Great Wall

N

△ Holiday Inn Lido & Airport

Asian Games Village

BEISIHUAN ZHONG LU

BEISANHUAN ZHONG LU

Beijiao Bus Station

Hepingli Zhan

XUEYUAN

Ditan Park

see "Downtown Beijing" map for detail

Xizhimen Zhan

ANDINGMEN XI DAJIE

Lufthansa Centre

Dongzhimen Bus Station

11
6 A

Exhibition Hall

C

DONGZHIMENWAI DAJIE

DI'ANMEN XI DAJIE

GONGRENTIYU CHANG BEI LU

Workers' Stadium

D

Chaoyang Theatre

Forbidden City

CHAOYANGMENWAI DAJIE

CHAOYANG LU

XICHANG AN JIE

DONGCHANG AN JIE

Silk Market

9

7 World Trade Centre

JIANGUOMENWAI DAJIE

TIAN'ANMEN SQUARE

Beijing Zhan

QIANMEN XI DAJIE

QIANMENDONG DAJIE

GUANGQUMENWAI DAJIE

GUANQU LU

Majuan Bus Station

Natural History Museum

13 4

2

Friendship Hospital

Tiantan Park

TIYUGUAN LU

16

17

18

Temple of Heaven

1

Taoranting Park

YONGDINGMEN XI JIE

YONGDINGMEN DONG JIE

12

14

Yongdingmen Train & Bus Station

10

NANSANHUAN ZHONG LU

8

15 Haihutun Bus Station

0   4km

Beijing Hotel on Dongchang'an Jie; and farther east on the wame road, the *Friendship Store* and World Trade Centre. At the western intersection of the second ring road and Chang'an Jie, the astronomical instruments on top of the old observatory stand out for their oddness, as does the white dagoba in Beihai Park, just north and west of the Forbidden City.

Arrival

The first experience most visitors have of China, and one which straight away confounds many expectations, is the smooth ride along the freeway, lined with hoardings and busy with Japanese cars, that leads from the airport into the city. Unless you arrive by train, it's a long way into the centre from either the bus stations or the airport, and even when you get into downtown Beijing you're still a good few kilometres from the hotels, certainly the more affordable ones. It's a good idea to hail a taxi from the centre to get you to your final destination rather than tussle with the buses, as the public transport system is confusing at first and the city layout rather alienating. Walking isn't really an option as distances are always long, exhausting at the best of times and unbearable with luggage.

By plane

Beijing Capital airport, 29km northeast of the centre, serves both international and domestic flights, and is a surprisingly small and quiet place, not the showcase you might expect. There's a branch of the *Bank of China* (24hr) on the second floor for changing money, on your left as you exit through customs, and commission rates are the same as everywhere else. Get some small change if you're planning to take any buses. The *CAAC* office on the first floor sells tickets for onward domestic flights. There's a restaurant, too, but you'd have to be very hungry to consider stopping at it.

An expressway connects the airport to the city and is one of the best and freest-flowing roads in China. Directly in front of the main exit is the **airport bus** stand, from which comfortable, though rather cramped, air-conditioned buses leave regularly. Tickets (¥12) are sold from a counter just to the left of the main doors as you exit. There are two routes, A and B, but the only way to tell which route a waiting bus will follow is

BEIJING: ARRIVAL		
Beijing	北京	*běijīng*
BUS STATIONS		
Deshengmen	德胜门公共汽车站立	*déshèngmén gōnggòngqìchē zhàn*
Dongzhimen	东直门公共汽车站立	*dōngzhímén gōnggòngqìchē zhàn*
Haihutun	海户屯公共汽车站立	*hǎihùtún gōnggòngqìchē zhàn*
TRAIN STATIONS		
Beijing Zhan	北京站	*běijīng zhàn*
Xi Zhan	西站	*xīzhàn*
Xizhimen Zhan	西直门站	*xīzhímén zhàn*
Yongdingmen Zhan	永定门	*yōngdìngmén zhàn*

to ask, by enquiring about the bus's final destination. **Route A buses** leave every fifteen minutes from 8am until the last flight arrives, and are the most useful to travellers, stopping at the *Hilton*, the Lufthansa Centre, Dongzhimen subway stop, *Swissotel*, and Chaoyangmen subway stop before terminating outside the *International Hotel*, just north of Beijing Zhan, the central train station. To get from here to the cheap hotels in the south of the city, either get a taxi or pick up a local bus at the train station (see bus routes box, p.76). There's a subway stop outside the station for other destinations in the city centre. **Route B buses** leave every hour, from 9.30am until the last flight, and make stops on the north and western sections of the third ring road, Sanhuan Lu, including the *SAS Royal Hotel*, Asian Games Village, *Friendship Hotel* and Foreign Language University, before terminating at the *Xinxing Hotel*, at the intersection of Chang'an Jie and Xisanhuan Bei Lu, close to the Gongzhufen subway stop.

Taxis from the airport into the city leave from the taxi rank just outside the main entrance, on the left; don't go with the hustlers who hang around the entrance. Make sure your taxi is registered; it should have a red sticker in the window stating the rate per kilometre and an identity card displayed in the window. Cheap yellow *miandi* taxis, which charge ¥1 per kilometre, are scarce here; you'll probably find only red cabs which charge ¥1.6 per kilometre, in which a trip to the city centre costs around ¥80.

By train

Beijing has two main **train stations**. **Beijing Zhan**, the central station, just south of Dongchang'an Jie, is where trains from destinations north and east of Beijing arrive. In the concourse outside the station, which doubles as an informal labour market, Chinese travellers squat with their luggage tied up in bundles, and many of Beijing's homeless and transient population sleep, eat, even cook, underneath huge TV screens. There are **left-luggage** lockers as well as a main luggage office here (see p.120 for details). From Beijing Zhan the only hotel within walking distance is the *International*, so most arrivals will need to head straight to the **bus terminus**, about 100m east of the station, the **subway stop** at the northwestern edge of the concourse, or to the **taxi rank**, over the road and 50m east. The waiting taxis are supervised by an official with a red armband who makes sure the queue is orderly and that drivers flip their meters on. Don't get a cab from the station concourse, as none of the drivers here will use their meters.

Travellers from the south and west of the capital will arrive at the very new west station, **Xi Zhan**, Asia's largest rail terminal at the head of the as yet incomplete Beijing–Kowloon rail line. A prestige project, the new station is ten times the size of Beijing Zhan and in the future will take more and more of the city's rail traffic. At the moment, the infrastructure needed to serve the station is not fully in place, so getting out of the area takes a little time, and its surroundings are pretty run-down. The **left-luggage office** is on the second floor and, like everything else here, it's computerized. There is a **minibus shuttle** between the two main stations, or, if you're heading south to the budget hotels, you can take bus #52 to Qianmen and get another bus from there. However, it's probably easier to take a **taxi** from the taxi rank.

Beijing does have more stations, though you are unlikely to stop at them unless you have come on a suburban train from, for example, the Great Wall at Badaling or Shidu. Beijing North, also known as **Xizhimen Zhan**, is at the northwestern edge of the second ring road, on the subway. Beijing South, or **Yongdingmen Zhan**, is in the south of the city, just inside the third ring road, a short walk from the *Qiaoyuan Hotel*, with a bus terminus outside.

By bus

The **bus system** in Beijing is extensive, but complicated, as there are many terminuses, each one serving buses from only a few destinations. **Dongzhimen**, on the northeast

MOVING ON FROM BEIJING

From Beijing you can get just about anywhere in China via the extensive air and rail system. You'd be advised to buy a ticket at least a few days in advance, though, especially in the summer or around Spring Festival. Few visitors travel long distance by **bus** as it's less comfortable than the train and takes longer, though it has the advantage that you can usually just turn up and get on as services to major cities are frequent. Buy a ticket from the ticket office in the station, or on the bus itself. Tianjin and Chengde are two destinations within easy travelling distance, where the bus and the train have about the same journey time. For details of bus stations and the points they serve, see "By bus", p.73.

By plane

Domestic **flights** should be booked at least a day in advance. The main outlet for **tickets** is the Aviation Office at 15 Xi Chang'an Jie (daily 7am–8pm; information ☎66017755, reservations ☎66013336). You can also buy tickets from a smaller *CAAC* office at 117 Dongsi Xi Dajie (daily 8am–5pm; information ☎65054415, reservations ☎64014441), and an office of *Eastern Airlines* outside the Military Museum (Mon–Sat 8am–6pm, Sun 9am–4.30pm; ☎68526333). Tickets are also available from *CITS* (see "Listings", p.121) which has offices in most large hotels. For international airline offices, see p.118.

To get to the airport, an **airport bus** runs daily 6am–5.30pm from outside the Aviation Office, and another runs from the west side of the *International Hotel* (look for the blue sign; 6am–5pm). Both buses run every thirty minutes and cost ¥12. A **taxi** to the airport will cost ¥100, and it's a good idea to book it beforehand through your hotel. The journey should take about 45 minutes. The information desk at the airport is open 24 hrs for enquiries (☎64563604).

By train

Trains depart from either **Xi Zhan**, if you're heading south or west, for example to Chengdu or Xi'an, or **Beijing Zhan**, if you're heading north or east, for example to Shanghai or Harbin.

You can buy **tickets** with an added surcharge of around ¥40 from large hotels or *CITS*, though it's not much hassle to do it yourself direct. Tickets for busy routes should be booked at least a day in advance, and can be booked up to a week ahead; take your passport along when you book tickets as they sometimes ask to see it. At Beijing Zhan, the Foreigners' Ticket Booking Office is at the back of the station, on the left side as you enter, and is signposted in English. The office is open 5.30–7.30am, 8am–noon and 1.30–5.30pm, and, for same-day and surplus next-day tickets only, 7pm–12.30am. You have

corner of the second ring road, connected by subway, is the largest bus station and handles services from Shenyang and the rest of Dongbei. **Deshengmen**, the north station serving Chengde and Datong, is 1km north of the second ring road, on the route of bus #55, which will take you to Xi'anmen Dajie, west of Beihai Park. **Haihutun**, at the intersection of the third ring road, Nansanhuan Lu, and Yongdingmenwai Dajie, is for buses from Tianjin and cities in southern Hebei. It's 1km east of the main backpacker haunt, the *Jinghua Hotel,* from which it is easier to walk than catch a bus. **Private minibuses** are more likely to terminate outside one of the two main train stations.

Information and maps

A large fold-out **map** of the city is vital. There is a wide variety available at all transport connections and from street vendors, hotels and bookshops. However, be aware that some don't mark the new train station, and most don't show the new bus routes which serve it. The best map to look out for, labelled in English and Chinese, and with bus

to complete a form, filling in the details of the train you want (numbers and times are all listed in English on the wall), then join the queue, which is not usually too bad. There is a ¥10 surcharge on all ticket prices, payable at the counter. The system at Xi Zhan is the same, and although the office is computerized, it doesn't seem any faster. The Foreigners' Ticket Booking Office is on the second floor here, on the left side as you go in.

For train information (in Chinese only) phone ☎65128931.

Trans-Siberian and Trans-Mongolian trains

The **International Train Booking Office** (Mon–Sat 8–11am & 2–4.30pm) on the west side of the *International Hotel*, 9 Jianguomenwai Dajie, is not easy to find – look for a metal door on the outside of the building. Here you can buy tickets to **Moscow** and **Ulan Batur**, even to Prague or Berlin, with the minimum of fuss. Out of season, few people make the journey, but in summer there may well not be a seat for weeks. Allow yourself a week or two for dealing with embassy bureaucracy – it's worth actually checking the **visa** situation before you buy your onward ticket. The Russians have become a lot more willing to hand out tourist visas (valid for a month and costing around US$50, more if you want it in less than seven days, with a surcharge for certain nationalities (mostly African and South American). If you buy a ticket all the way through to Prague, you'll also need a Ukrainian and Belarussian transit visa, which you can get in Moscow. These visas aren't cheap; expect to pay an extra US$40–100. Mongolia is no longer the closed territory it once was, and transit visas (valid for a week and costing US$25) are easy to get.

A bunk on the Chinese train #3 to Moscow in a second-class cabin with four beds – which is perfectly comfortable – costs ¥1806. First class is ¥2562 (four beds) or ¥3365 (two beds). The Russian train #19, which follows the same Trans–Siberian route, and the Trans–Mongolian train, are both slightly cheaper. Tickets to Ulan Batur (train #89) cost ¥730.

The easiest way to organize your journey, however, is through the **tour company** *Monkey Business*, Rm 406, Beijing Commercial Business Complex, Youanmenwai (☎63292244 ext 2532). The Business Complex is a huge building 1.5km west of the *Qiaoyuan Hotel*, with its name in English emblazoned across it. They also have an office in Hong Kong (Flat 6, 4th Floor, E Block, Chungking Mansions; ☎2731376), and have been sending travellers on these trains for years. They know everything about the route, but their prices are high and you'll pay at least an extra US$150 for the privilege of having your visas sorted out for you, getting seats next to each other on the train and being patronized by their staff of jaded ex–travellers. They can also arrange stopover tours in Mongolia en route.

routes, sights and hotels marked, is the *Beijing Tourist Communication Map*. A reasonable substitute is *Beijing: the Latest Tourist Map*. In general, the tourist maps, available in large hotels, don't go into enough detail. The free map handed out by *CITS* offices also isn't much use, but it does have good magnified sections showing the shopping areas, with many of the individual shops marked. Fully comprehensive A–Z map books are available from bookshops, but only in Chinese.

Here, as elsewhere in China, there are no actual tourist information offices but there are a number of **English-language publications** which will help you get the best out of the city. If you're staying for more than a few days, pick up a copy of the *China Daily* (¥0.8) from the *Friendship Store*, the *Foreign Language Bookstore* or the bigger hotels; it has a listings section detailing cultural events. The rest of the paper is news and propaganda written in rather turgid prose, though the headlines occasionally have an unintentional deadpan humour to them. *Beijing This Month* covers the same ground, with light features aimed at tourists. You can also pick up glossy broadsheets at the expensive hotels, and some also have copies of the annual pocketbook, *Beijing: the Official*

Guide lying around (try the *New Otani*), which contains a comprehensive listings section covering everything from angling to paintballing. You'll also find it in the *Friendship Store*, but you'll have to pay for it here (¥40). Another publication worth looking out for is *Beijing Scene*, a free, irreverent and informative newspaper written by and for expats. The listings include clubs and gigs, and the classifieds have ads for housing and jobs, as well as a cross-cultural personals column. Unfortunately it's not easy to get hold of – try the *Poachers Inn* and other expat hangouts. The best place in the city for general, practical information is the tourist office in room 218 of the *Jinghua Hotel*, which is geared up for budget travellers.

City transport

The scale of the city militates against taking bus number 11 – Chinese slang for walking – almost anywhere, and most of the main streets are so straight that going by foot soon gets tedious. The **public transport system** is extensive but somewhat over-subscribed; heaving buses carry most of the burden while the rest of the population cycle. Most visitors tire of the hassle of buses pretty quickly and take rather more taxis than they'd planned. **Cycling** is a good alternative, though, with plenty of rental outlets in the city, and traffic congestion is not too much of a problem thanks to new laws limiting the days private cars can travel inside the second ring road.

Buses

Even though every one of the city's 140 **bus and trolleybus services** runs about once a minute, you'll find getting on or off at busy times hard work (rush hours are from

---

BUS ROUTES

Bus routes are included on all good maps, with red lines detailing ordinary routes and blue lines for trolleybuses; a dot on the line indicates a stop. New routes from Xi Zhan are not included on most maps. The following are some of the most useful services:

Bus #1 and **double-decker #1** From Xi Zhan west–east along the main thoroughfare, Chang'an Jie.

Double-decker #2 From the north end of Qianmen Dajie, north to Dongdan, the Yonghe Gong and the Asian Games Village.

Bus #5 From Deshengmen, in the northwest of the city, south down the west side of the Forbidden City and Tian'anmen to Qianmen Dajie.

Bus #15 From the zoo down Xidan Dajie past Liulichang ending at the Tianqiao area just west of Yongdingmennei Dajie.

Bus #17 From Tian'anmen down Qianmen Dajie to the intersection of Yongdingmenwai Dajie and Nansanhuan Zhong Lu, 1km east of the *Jinghua Hotel*.

Bus #20 From Beijing Zhan to Yongdingmen Zhan, a short walk from the *Qiaoyuan Hotel*.

Bus #52 From Xi Zhan east to Lianhuachi Qiao, Xidan Dajie, Tian'anmen Square, then east along Chang'an Jie.

Trolleybus #103 From Beijing Zhan, north up the east side of the Forbidden City, west along Fuchengmennei Dajie, then north up Sanlihe Lu to the zoo.

Trolleybus #104 From Beijing Zhan to Hepingli train station in the north of the city, via Wangfujing.

Trolleybus #105 From the northwest corner of Tiantan Park to Xidan Dajie, then west to the zoo.

Trolleybus #106 From Yongdingmen Zhan to Tiantan Park and Chongwenmen, then up to Dongzhimennei Dajie.

Bus #332 From Beijing Zoo to Beda (University and the Summer Palace).

7–9am & 4.30–6pm). Forget about trying to see anything of the city from the window, as views tend to be limited to the backs of necks. Beijing buses are notable for their distinctive aroma, something like garlic and boiled cabbages, especially in winter when the windows are kept closed. Less aromatic are the **minibuses** which ply the same routes, are twice as expensive and a little more comfortable.

The **fare** for ordinary buses is usually a standard ¥0.5 – watch how the Chinese wrap up a one-fen coin in two two-fen notes to make a little origami package to give the conductor. In reality, rides are often free, as most passengers haven't a hope of reaching the conductor. Services generally run from 5.30am to 11pm everyday, though some are 24-hour. Buses numbered in the 200s only provide night services. There are also five comfortable **double-decker** bus services, which cost ¥2 a trip. Routes are efficiently organized and easy to understand – an important factor, since stops tend to be a good kilometre apart. You'll need to fight your way to the disembarkation point well in advance of your stop.

A word of warning – be very wary of **pickpockets** on buses. Beijing is not a particularly crime-ridden city, but the pickpockets here do target Westerners, and especially backpackers, stealing money, but more particularly passports, which can be sold for thousands of yuan.

The subway

Clean, efficient, graffiti-free and very fast, the **subway** is an appealing alternative to the bus, though again be prepared for enforced intimacies during rush hours. Mao Zedong ordered its construction in 1966, and over 20km were open within three years, but until 1977 it was reserved for the use of senior cadres only, apparently because it was too close to the underground defence network.

The subway operates from 5.30am to 11pm daily and entrances are marked by a logo of a square inside a "C" shape. **Tickets** cost ¥2 per journey; buy them from the ticket offices at the top of the stairs above the platforms. It's worth buying a few at once to save queuing every time you use the system. The tickets are undated slips of paper and an attendant at the station takes one from you before you get on to the platform. All stops

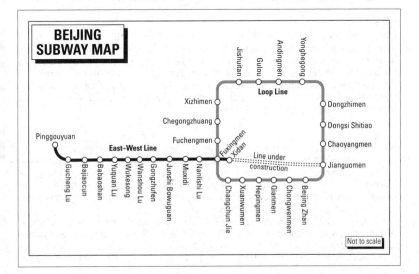

are marked in pinyin, and announced in English and Chinese over an intercom when the train pulls in, though the system is not taxing to figure out as there are only two lines.

A **loop line** runs around the city, making useful stops at Beijing Zhan, Jianguomen, (under the flyover, close to the Ancient Observatory and the *Friendship Store*), Yonghe Gong (50m north of the temple of the same name), and Qianmen, at the northern end of Qianmen Dajie. The **east–west line** runs from the western suburbs to Xidan, just west of the centre, and is more of a commuters' line, though the Military Museum is on it, and the last stop, Pingguoyuan, is where you catch buses to Xiang Shan and Badachu (see p.128). There's an interchange between the two lines at Fuxingmen station. A planned extension to the east–west line, extending it east to Jianguomen station on the loop line, should be completed in early 1997.

Taxis

In recent years, the only way to get a **taxi** in Beijing was to phone for one – now they are everywhere, the most visible symbol of recent economic progress. In particular, the distinctive yellow *miandi*, or bread loaf, so called for its boxy shape, has come to characterize modern Beijing in the same way as the red double-decker bus characterizes London.

Taxis come in all shapes and sizes, but all have a sticker in the back window which indicates the rate per kilometre. Luxury sedans are the most expensive, at ¥2 per kilometre with a minimum fare of ¥12; the *miandi* minivans are the cheapest, at ¥1 per kilometre with a minimum of ¥10; and generally, the smaller and older the car, the cheaper it is. Using a taxi after 11pm will incur a surcharge of twenty percent. Most drivers are good about using their meters; if they don't put it on, you can insist by saying *"da biao"*. It is illegal for *miandis* to carry more than four people.

Taxis can be hailed anywhere, though they are hard to find around Tian'anmen Square or during lunch hour from around noon to 1pm. One problem with *miandis* is that the drivers are picky – they like to do short journeys (for which they get paid the same as a journey of ten kilometres) or very long journeys. They will often refuse a ride if the distance is around 10km. This is especially a problem if you're staying in the cheap hotels in the south of town, as they are about 10km from the centre, so unless you're very patient you may have to resign yourself to taking a slightly more expensive cab.

Rickshaws

Cycle rickshaws should be treated with caution. Although they are good for short trips (they will travel a good couple of kilometres for ¥5), drivers can be hard to barter down and may demand more money when you get out. Make sure you both agree on the fare, and the currency you're negotiating in, before you set off. Around tourist sites the rickshaw drivers have tried to reinvent themselves as tourist attractions, now that their day-to-day role has been largely usurped by the *miandis*. Be prepared for frilly seat covers and quadrupled prices.

Bike rental

As a positive alternative to relying on public transport, it's worth **renting a bike**. Many of the cheaper hotels rent bikes on a daily basis and will negotiate weekly rates. Shops tend to be cheaper but rent only by the hour or the day (see "Listings", p.119 for rental places). Figure on a daily charge of ¥10–50 and a deposit of ¥200–500. Always test the brakes before riding off, and get the tyres pumped up. If you have any problems, there are plenty of bike repair shops on minor roads.

Chinese cycling pace is sedate, and with good reason. Chinese roads are unpredictable and at times fairly lawless, with traffic going the wrong way round roundabouts, aggressive trucks which won't get out of the way, impatient taxi drivers in the cycle lane, buses veering suddenly towards the pavement, and jaywalkers aplenty.

The **telephone code** for Beijing is ☎010

Still, riding around Beijing is less daunting than riding around many Western cities as vehicular traffic is lighter, there are **bike lanes** on all main roads and you are in the company of plenty of other cyclists, indeed several million at rush hours. Ringing your bell or shouting is rarely effective; urgent noises that would have all other road users scurrying aside in other cities hardly merit a backward glance here. At junctions cyclists cluster together then cross en masse when strength of numbers forces other traffic to give way. If you feel nervous, just dismount and walk the bike across – plenty of Chinese do.

You are supposed to park your bike at the numerous **bike parks**, where you pay ¥0.2 to the attendant, though plenty of people don't, risking a rarely enforced fine by leaving their vehicle propped up against railings or on the pavement. If you have a new bike or a mountain bike you'd be wise to get a chain as well, as theft is common. If you've been cycling around all day and just can't face the last few kilometres to your hotel, it is possible to leave your bike overnight in some of the parks, though you'll have to pay a little extra. *Miandi* taxi drivers can sometimes be persuaded to carry a bike in the back.

Car rental

The hassles and expense of **renting a car** mean it's really only an option for long-term visitors or residents. You need a special **licence** issued by the PSB, and you can't drive outside the city's limits. Rental cars are usually Volkswagens made in Shanghai, or Cherokee jeeps made in Beijing, and cost ¥250–300 a day, about the same as renting a taxi for the day. Monthly rental is ¥5,500–7,000 (see p.119 for rental companies). There are few parking facilities – you can't just pull up on the side of the road as you'll block the cycle lane, and you are allowed to drive inside the second ring road only on certain days.

Tours

Organized tours of the city and its outskirts offer a painless if expensive way of seeing all the sights quickly. *CITS* offers a wide variety of one- and two-day tour packages, which you can book from their offices or from the information desk in the *Friendship Store*. However, their tours are pricey, at least ¥300 a day. A good, cheaper option is the **hutong tour** (see p.100), a city tour that's more imaginative than most, and popular as it offers the opportunity to see a more private side of the city. The one-day tours offered by the classier hotels also tend to be expensive; better value is offered by the cheaper hotels, and you don't have to be a guest to go along. The *Jingtai* and *Tiantan* hotels offer a daily tour to the Great Wall at Badaling and the Ming Tombs for ¥60, and tours to the Summer Palace and Xiang Shan on Tuesdays, Thursdays and Saturdays for ¥50. Entrance fees are not included. Both tours leave at 8.30am; book tickets beforehand. The *Jinghua Hotel* offers good-value short evening trips to the acrobatics (¥50) and the opera (¥40) a few times a week, and day trips to Simatai Great Wall (¥80) daily in summer, once a week in the off season. Again, you must book at least a day in advance.

Accommodation

Finding **accommodation** in Beijing was once notoriously difficult and the subject of many long-winded old travellers' tales. These days it should be fairly stress-free, certainly if you have a bit of money to spend as the city is generously provided with new international-standard highrise **hotels**. However, Beijing does lack the surfeit of small,

BEIJING: ACCOMMODATION

Aihua	爱华宾馆	*àihuá bīnguǎn*
Beijing	北京饭店	*běijīng fàndiàn*
Beiwei	北纬饭店	*běiwěi fàndiàn*
Big Bell	大钟寺饭店	*dàzhōngsì fàndiàn*
Central Institute of Fine Art	中央美术学院	*zhōngyāng měishù xuéyuàn*
Chongwenmen	崇文门饭店	*chóngwénmén fàndiàn*
CVIK	赛特饭店	*sàitè fàndiàn*
Dongfang	东方饭店	*dōngfāng fàndiàn*
Friendship	友谊宾馆	*yǒuyì bīnguǎn*
Guanghua	光华饭店	*guānghuá fàndiàn*
Hademen	哈德门饭店	*hādémén fàndiàn*
Holiday Inn Downtown	金都假日饭店	*jīndūjiàrì fàndiàn*
International	国际饭店	*guójì fàndiàn*
Jinghua	京华饭店	*jīnghuá fàndiàn*
Jinglun	京伦饭店	*jīnglún fàndiàn*
Jingtai	景泰宾馆	*jǐngtài bīnguǎn*
Kempinski (Lufthansa Centre)	凯宾斯基饭店	*kǎibīnsījī fàndiàn*
Minzu	民族饭店	*mínzú fàndiàn*
New Otani	长富宫饭店	*chángfúgōng fàndiàn*
Palace	王府饭店	*wángfǔ fàndiàn*
Park	百乐酒店	*bǎilè jiǔdiàn*
Qianmen	前门饭店	*qiánmén fàndiàn*
Qiaoyuan	桥园饭店	*qiáoyuán fàndiàn*
Qinghua University	清华大学	*qīnghuá dàxué*
Qomolongma	珠穆朗玛宾馆	*zhūmùlǎngmǎ bīnguǎn*
Ritan	日坛宾馆	*rìtán bīnguǎn*
Seastar	海兴大酒店	*hǎixīng dàjiǔdiàn*
Sheraton Great Wall	长城饭店	*chángchéng fàndiàn*
Taiwan	台湾饭店	*táiwān fàndiàn*
Tiantan	天坛饭店	*tiāntán fàndiàn*
Tiantan Sports	天坛体育宾馆	*tiāntán tǐyù bīnguǎn*
Traffic	交通饭店	*jiāotōng fàndiàn*
Xiangshan	香山饭店	*xiāngshān fàndiàn*
Xiyuan	西苑饭店	*xīyuàn fàndiàn*

moderately priced hotels found in other Asian cities, and budget travellers tend to congregate at one or two large hotels offering cheap **dormitories**. Although Beijing is on the whole an expensive place, accommodation at the bottom end of the market is a bargain, and anyone who's been roughing it round China for a while will find the facilities laid on for them by sympathetic managements a welcome relief.

Central Beijing, anywhere within or just off the second ring road, is the most exciting place to stay, but budget options are predictably limited here. **Outer Beijing** places are almost all on or near the third ring road, which makes them a long way out in what is inevitably a dull area, but there are good transport connections into the centre, and these places are usually less expensive. Most of the very cheapest places are in the **south** of this outer ring, up to ten kilometres from the centre, but journeys, at least by the taxis which whizz around the ring roads, don't take too long, and additional transport costs are more than repaid by the good-value accommodation.

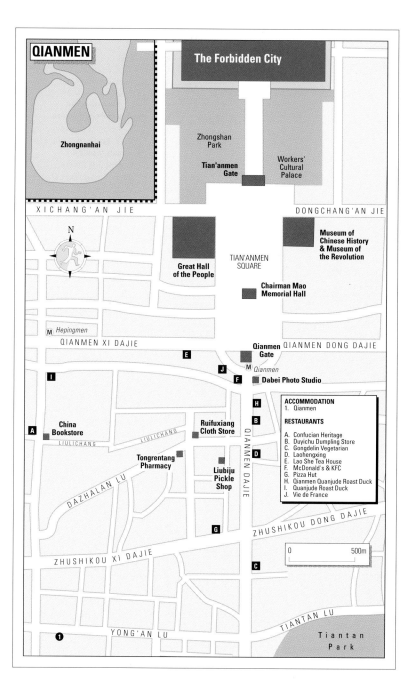

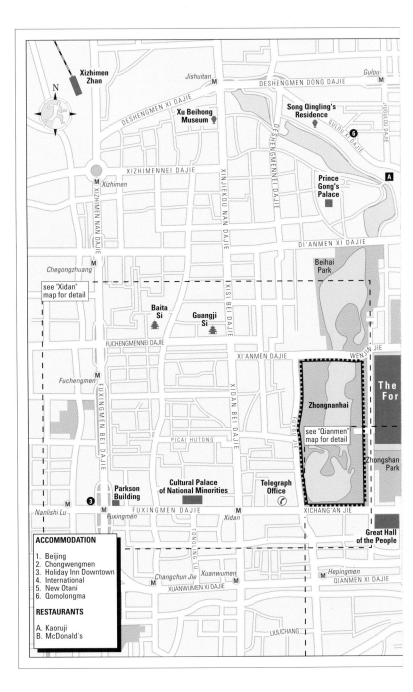

N

Xizhimen
Zhan

Jishuitan Ⓜ

DESHENGMEN DONG DAJIE

Gulou Ⓜ

DESHENGMEN XI DAJIE

Xu Beihong
Museum 🌳

Song Qingling's
Residence 🌲

GULOU XI DAJIE

Ⓜ Xizhimen

XIZHIMENNEI DAJIE

XINJIEKOU NAN DAJIE

DESHENGMENNEI DAJIE

Prince
Gong's
Palace ■

Ⓐ

JUGULOU DAJIE

XIZHIMEN NAN DAJIE

DI'ANMEN XI DAJIE

Ⓜ Chegongzhuang

Beihai
Park

see "Xidan"
map for detail

Baita
Si 🏯

Guangji
Si 🌲

XISI BEI DAJIE

WENJIN JIE

I

Ⓜ Fuchengmen

FUCHENGMENNEI DAJIE

XI'ANMEN DAJIE

XIDAN BEI DAJIE

FUYOU JIE

The
For

Zhongnanhai

see "Qianmen"
map for detail

FUXINGMEN BEI DAJIE

PICAI HUTONG

Zhongshan
Park

Ⓜ ③
Parkson
Building

Cultural Palace
of National Minorities

Telegraph
Office
Ⓒ

Nanlishi Lu Ⓜ Fuxingmen

FUXINGMEN DAJIE Ⓜ

Xidan

XICHANG'AN JIE

Great Hall
of the People

TONGLING LU

Changchun Jie

Xuanwumen
Ⓜ

Hepingmen
Ⓜ

QIANMEN XI DAJIE

XUANWUMEN XI DAJIE

LIULICHANG

ACCOMMODATION

1. Beijing
2. Chongwengmen
3. Holiday Inn Downtown
4. International
5. New Otani
6. Qomolongma

RESTAURANTS

A. Kaoruji
B. McDonald's

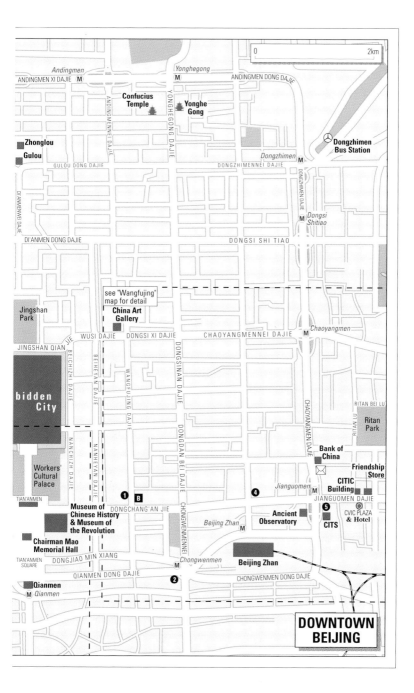

DOWNTOWN
BEIJING

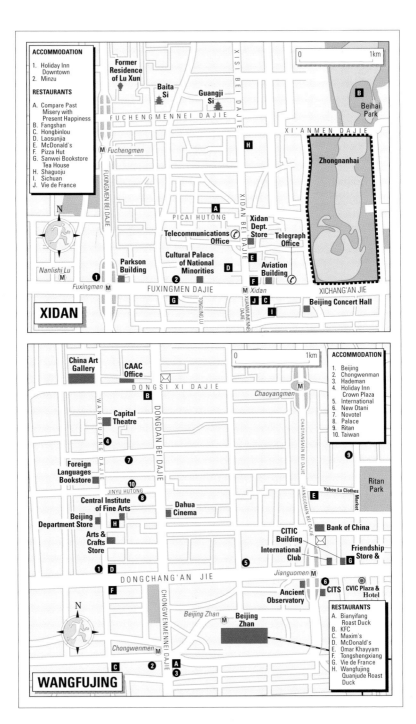

XIDAN

ACCOMMODATION
1. Holiday Inn Downtown
2. Minzu

RESTAURANTS
A. Compare Past Misery with Present Happiness
B. Fangshan
C. Hongbinlou
D. Laosunjia
E. McDonald's
F. Pizza Hut
G. Sanwei Bookstore Tea House
H. Shaguoju
I. Sichuan
J. Vie de France

Former Residence of Lu Xun
Baita Si
Guangji Si
Beihai Park
FUCHENGMENNEI DAJIE
XI'ANMEN DAJIE
Zhongnanhai
Fuchengmen
PICAI HUTONG
Xidan Dept. Store
Telecommunications Office
Telegraph Office
Parkson Building
Cultural Palace of National Minorities
Aviation Building
Nanlishi Lu
Fuxingmen
FUXINGMEN DAJIE
Xidan
XICHANG'AN JIE
Beijing Concert Hall
XISI BEI DAJIE
XIDAN BEI DAJIE
FUXINGMEN BEI DAJIE
XUANWUMEN DAJIE
TONGLING LU

WANGFUJING

ACCOMMODATION
1. Beijing
2. Chongwenman
3. Hademan
4. Holiday Inn Crown Plaza
5. International
6. New Otani
7. Novotel
8. Palace
9. Ritan
10. Taiwan

RESTAURANTS
A. Bianyifang Roast Duck
B. KFC
C. Maxim's
D. McDonald's
E. Omar Khayyam
F. Tongshengxiang
G. Vie de France
H. Wangfujing Quanjude Roast Duck

China Art Gallery
CAAC Office
DONGSI XI DAJIE
Chaoyangmen
Capital Theatre
Foreign Languages Bookstore
JINYU HUTONG
Central Institute of Fine Arts
Beijing Department Store
Arts & Crafts Store
Dahua Cinema
Ritan Park
Yabou Lu Clothes Market
CITIC Building
International Club
Bank of China
Friendship Store &
DONGCHANG'AN JIE
Jianguomen
Ancient Observatory
CITS
CVIC Plaza & Hotel
Beijing Zhan
Chongwenmen
WANGFUJING DAJIE
DONGDAN BEI DAJIE
CHONGWENMENNEI DAJIE
CHAOYANGMEN BEI DAJIE
JIANGUOMEN BEI DAJIE

Luxury and mid-range hotels

Luxury hotels in Beijing are legion – sixty at the last count and rising – too many, in fact, for business travellers and upmarket tourists to sustain, and many operate at a loss. However, even if they're well out of your budget, you can still avail yourself of their lavish facilities. If at home trying to get into the ritziest hotels wearing jeans will earn you polite abuse, here a foreign face is a passport to palatial interiors. The toilets in the lobbies of these hotels feature a uniformed attendant to wipe the seat for you, turn on the taps, and hand you warm towels with a pair of tongs when you want to dry your hands. In the lobby you will also often find free copies of the *China Daily* and a few glossy tourist broadsheets.

Central Beijing

Beijing, 33 Dongchang'an Jie (☎65137766, fax 65137703). The most central hotel, just east of Tian'anmen Square, and one of the most recognizable buildings in Beijing, this place exudes class and makes all the other luxury hotels look like yuppie upstarts. The view from the top floors of the west wing, over the Forbidden City, is superb. The cheapest rooms are US$160. ⑨.

Chongwenmen, 2 Chongwenmen Xi Dajie (☎65122211, fax 65122122). This well-located hotel, though a little cramped for space, is good-looking and good value. It's very close to the Chongwenmen subway stop on the loop line. ⑦.

CVIK Hotel, 22 Jianguomenwai Dajie (☎65123388, fax 65123542). A business-like hotel conveniently located opposite the *Friendship Store*, though on an unflattering site, tucked at the back of a car park among a cluster of office buildings. Take the loop line to the Jianguomen subway stop and walk east. ⑧.

Hademen, 2a Chongwenmenwai Dajie (☎67012244, fax 67016865). This two-star place is a little rambling, and staff speak no English, but as one of the few moderately priced, central hotels, close to the Chongwenmen subway stop, it's worth considering. ⑦.

International, 9 Jianguomenwai Dajie (☎65126688, fax 65129972). Just north of Beijing Zhan, and next to the airport bus stop, this stern-looking black building is a useful landmark, and has an International Train Ticket Booking Office for buying onward train tickets to Moscow and Ulan Batur (see p.75 for details). A standard double is US$120. If you're taking the subway, get off at the Beijing Zhan stop. ⑨.

Minzu, 51 Fuxingmen Dajie (☎66014466, fax 66014849). Well-appointed and close to some attractive parts of the city, midway between Fuxingmen and Xidan subway stops. The first-floor restaurant is good. ⑧.

New Otani, 26 Jianguomenwai Dajie (☎65125555, fax 65139810). You can get seriously pampered in this five-star modern mansion, a candidate for the most luxurious in Beijing, though the fee for the privilege, at least US$200 a night, is hefty. ⑨.

Palace, 8 Jingyu Hutong (☎65128899, fax 65129050). A discreet and fairly well-located upmarket place, if a little bland. ⑧.

Qomolongma Hotel, 149 Gulou Xi Dajie (☎64018822). This bizarre place makes a change from the predictable block-like architecture of most Beijing hotels. Housed in a temple, its halls have been crudely converted into standard mid-range Chinese hotel rooms, though the exterior is largely intact. It must once have been a very pretty, rather grand complex; today it's shabby, but its prices and the good location, well inside the northern section of the second ring road and close to some of the nicest *hutongs* in the city, make this place well worth trying. Take bus #5 from Qianmen Dajie. ⑥.

Taiwan, 5 Jinyu Hutong (☎65136688, fax 65136896). A business hotel just north of Wangfujing Dajie with an awkward-looking facade of white tile and wiggly roofs. ⑨.

Outer Beijing

Big Bell, 18 Beisanhuan Xi Lu (☎62253388). This place is a little boring in a grimy area, but not too expensive. It's not on a bus route so you'll have to take a taxi to get here. ⑥.

Friendship, 3 Baishiqiao Lu (☎68498888). Elegant and sedate four-star place which used to be a favourite among Beijing's foreign correspondents, who may still be found in the English Bar on the first floor. ⑧.

Great Wall Sheraton, 6 Dongsanhuan Bei Lu (☎65005566, fax 65001919). A very swish five-star modern compound out on the third ring road. ⑨.

Guanghua, 38 Dongsanhuan Bei Lu, (☎65018866, fax 65016516). This place is rather bland but inexpensive for its location, not too far out in the east of town. ⑦.

Holiday Inn Downtown, 98 Beilishi Lu (☎6338822, fax 68340696). An unprepossessing building slotted among the office highrises in the west of town, with all the facilities you might expect. Close to Fuxingmen subway stop. ⑨.

Jinglun (*Hotel Beijing–Toronto*), 3 Jianguomenwai Dajie (☎65002266, fax 65002022). Bland-looking from the outside, but very comfortable and plush inside. A standard double is US$110. ⑨.

Kempinski, Lufthansa Centre, 50 Liangmaqiao Lu (☎64653388). Off the third ring road, this five-star place is a little out of the way, though with a huge shopping complex attached there's no shortage of diversions on site. ⑨.

Ritan, 1 Ritan Lu (☎65125588). This small place offers a slightly more afforable alternative to the nearby lavish palaces of Jianguomenwai, but with none of their style. ⑧.

Xiyuan, 1 Sanlihe Lu (☎68313388, fax 68314577). A bland, international-standard hotel aiming for class, with a piano in the lobby. Situated opposite the zoo, so it's not in a great area, but very convenient for transport. Expensive at ¥1265 for a standard double, but it does have an excellent Korean restaurant attached. ⑨.

THE SOUTH

Aihua, 48 Tiantan Dong Lu (☎67112828). This place is worth investigating, as it's clean and quiet with staff who are anxious to please, though maybe that's just because it's new. It's on a quiet street east off Tiantan Lu – look for the huge International Tennis Centre and the street is just north of there, with the hotel about a hundred metres down on the right. Take bus #39 from Beijing Zhan. ⑥.

Beiwei and Tianqiao, 13 Xijing Lu (☎63012266, fax 63011366). This Sino-Japanese joint venture consists of two buildings, one very upmarket, one not; the inexpensive section (Beiwei) looks like a barracks compared to the battleship-like superior section (Tianqiao) next door. Bus #20 from the main station will get you to Yongdingmennei Dajie, from where the hotel is a one-kilometre walk west. ⑥–⑨.

Dongfang, 11 Wanming Lu (☎63014466). In a rather grimy location, this highrise is heavy on the marble and a bit poky, but not bad value for the standard of accommodation. ⑧.

Tiantan Sports, 10 Tiyuguan Lu (☎67013388). Full of overweight businessmen, this hotel doesn't actually feel very sporty, though the street outside is full of shops selling athletics goods. It offers a range of tours and you can rent bikes from a shop outside. Take bus #39 from Beijing Zhan. ⑥.

Park, 36 Puhuangyu Lu (☎67611615). A squat building in a dull area with a somewhat grey interior, though it's quite respectably priced for a three-star hotel. ⑦.

Qianmen, 175 Yong'an Lu (☎63016688, fax 63013883). Big, characterless hotel with its own theatre, which nightly shows a bastardized version of Beijing Opera, mostly to visiting tour groups (see p.115). ⑧.

Tiantan, 1 Tiyuguan Lu (☎67112277, fax 67116833). In a quiet area east of Tiantan Park, this is a small but comfortable place, if a little pricey at ¥740 a night. ⑨.

Traffic (*Jiaotong Fandian*), 35 Dongsi Kuiyu Nan Jie (☎67011114). Two hundred metres into a tangle of alleys accessible off Tiantan Nan Lu and Tiyuan Lu, not far from Tiantan Park. Signposts in English point the way from both main roads. The rooms here are reasonably priced, but surly staff perpetrate the most outrageous con tricks on naive foreign guests, for example, demanding an extra ¥150 "public holiday tax" during Spring Festival. Bus #39 from Beijing Zhan will get you to Tiantan Nan Lu. ⑥.

Backpacker hotels and university accommodation

Hoteliers have woken up to the potential offered by **budget travellers**, which means that if you don't mind sharing a room, you can get a bed for a cheaper price than you would pay in any other Chinese city. Different hotels move in and out of favour with the backpacking crowd, but once they move on to a new location, tour operators, cheap restaurants and student card touts quickly follow in their wake.

Another cheap option, mostly used by students studying Chinese visiting from other Chinese cities, is to stay in a **university dormitory**. These places definitely aren't hotels and you're not guaranteed a room. The language gulf can also make things hard.

Central Beijing

Fine Arts Institute, 5 Xiaowei Hutong. This university dormitory rents out some of its double rooms. It's extremely cheap and the location can't be beat, but as it's almost always booked out, it's a long shot. To get here, head north up Wangfujing Dajie, and go to the end of the second *hutong* on the right. Turn left and the compound is on your left. The dormitory is up on the eighth floor and there's also a very cheap cafeteria on the first floor. Take trolleybus #104 from Beijing Zhan to Wangfujing Dajie. ③.

Outer Beijing

Qinghua University (☎62783037). In the far north of the city, this university rents out double rooms in the foreigners' dormitory. The leafy campus is enormous and the dormitory is near the west gate, by the wall, twenty minutes' walk from the main gate. No English is spoken and there's no guarantee of a room. Take bus #331 from opposite the zoo. ③.

THE SOUTH

Jinghua, Nansanhuan Xi Lu (☎67222211). This hotel has become the centre for budget travellers, and it's certainly the best of the cheapies, thanks to astute management by the entrepreneurial Mr Su. There's cheap dormitory accommodation, either in a large room with thirty bunks or in cosy, if rather claustrophobic, six-bed basement rooms. Doubles are clean, though sometimes a little ragged, and again very good value. Staff attend mandatory English lessons and are helpful, while the tourist office in Rm 218, run by Su and John, is the best place in Beijing to go for advice and information. A number of tours are also run from here and you can rent bikes. Two backpacker restaurants vie for business in the car park outside the hotel; the furthest from the hotel entrance is the best. The hotel's most serious flaw is its location on the third ring road in a pretty grotty area, and next to a fetid canal, about 10km from central Beijing, though the management has plans to set up a hotel shuttle bus. In the meantime, take bus #17, from the terminus at the north end of Qianmen Dajie, and get off at the large roundabout at the intersection of Yongdingmenwai Dajie and Nansanhuan Zhong Lu, then walk west for a kilometre. Alternatively, take bus #14 from the terminus on Xishiku Dajie, just west of Beihai Park, to the Yangqiao Flyover at the intersection of Majiapu Dong Lu and Nansanhuan Xi Lu, which is just west of the hotel. Dorms ①, rooms ④.

Jingtai, 65 Jingtai Xi Lu (☎67224675). Although a little hard to find, the location of this hotel, in a quiet *hutong* away from the traffic, is a definite plus. From Jingtai Lu, head west along Anlelin Lu and the hotel is about 150m down the first alley on the left. Unfortunately, the unfriendly and unco-operative attitude of staff here is the main drawback to what would otherwise be a very pleasant place. Cheap prices make it quite popular with budget travellers, though some migrate to the *Jinghua* after a few days. There's a quiet restaurant inside and the hotel offers bike rental and tours to the Great Wall and other sights outside the city. There are no dorms, but double and triple rooms are good value. ④.

Qiaoyuan, Dongbinhe Lu. This hotel, near the third ring road, just west of Yongdingmen Zhan, was closed for a major renovation at the time of writing. It was once Beijing's premier backpacker hotel, loathed by thousands for its grimy decor, insouciant staff and mattresses so lumpy you'd think they were full of rocks. Now, after a change of management, it's reinventing itself as a three-star hotel, though it seems likely that when it reopens it will still offer some budget accommodation. There are a number of backpacker restaurants nearby, most notably the novel and excellent *Chapatti Connection* (see p.109). Take bus #20 or #54 from Beijing Zhan, both of them terminating at Yongdingmen Zhan. ①–⑤.

Sea Star, 166 Yondingmenwai Dajie (☎67218855). This hotel has recently opened its doors to budget travellers after a major refurbishment. Under the aegis of Mr Su of the *Jinghua*, there are windowless basement dorms and plans for an annexe in the courtyard for foreigners. The new, spacious double rooms with satellite TV are excellent value, one of the best bargains in the city, so even if you don't identify yourself with the backpacking hordes, it's worth serious consideration. It is some way out, though. Take bus #17 from the north end of Qianmen Dajie and get off at the intersection between Yongdingmenwai Dajie and Nansanhuan Zhong Lu, then walk south for about a kilometre. Dorms ③, rooms ④.

THE CITY

Beijing requires patience and planning to do it justice. Wandering aimlessly around without a destination in mind will rarely be rewarding. The place to start is **Tian'anmen Square**, geographical and psychic centre of the city, where a cluster of important sights can be seen in a day, although the **Forbidden City**, at the north end of the square, deserves a day, or even several, all to itself. The **Qianmen** area, a noisy market area south of here, is a bit more alive, and ends in style with one of the city's highlights, the **Temple of Heaven**. The giant freeway, **Chang'an Jie**, zooming east–west across the city, is a corridor of highrises with a few museums, shopping centres and even the odd ancient site worth tracking down. Scattered in the **north** of the city, a section with a more traditional and human feel, are some magnificent **parks**, **palaces and temples**, some of them in the *hutongs*. An expedition to the outskirts is amply rewarded by the **Summer Palace**, the best place to get away from it all.

Tian'anmen Square and The Forbidden City

The first stop for any visitor to Beijing is **Tian'anmen Square**. Physically at the city's centre, symbolically it's the heart of China, and the events it has witnessed have shaped the history of the People's Republic from its inception. Chairman Mao lies here in his marble **mausoleum**, with the **Great Hall of the People** to the west and the **Museum of the Chinese Revolution** to the east. Monumental architecture that's much, much older lies just to the north – the **Forbidden City of the Emperors**, now open to all.

Tian'anmen Square

Covering over forty hectares, **Tian'anmen Square** must rank as the greatest public square on earth. It's a modern creation, in a city that traditionally had no squares, as classical Chinese town planning did not allow for places where crowds could gather. Tian'anmen only came into being when imperial offices were cleared from either side of the great processional way that led south from the palace to Qianmen and the Temple of Heaven. The ancient north–south axis of the city was thus destroyed and the broad east–west thoroughfare, Chang'an Jie, that now carries millions of cyclists every day past the front of the Forbidden City, had the walls across its path removed. In the words of one of the architects: "The very map of Beijing was a reflection of the feudal society, it was meant to demonstrate the power of the emperor. We had to transform it, we had to make Beijing into the capital of socialist China." The easiest **approach** to the square is from the south, where there's a bus terminus and a subway stop. As the square is lined with railings (for crowd control) you can enter or leave only via the exits at either end or in the middle. Bicycles are not permitted, and the streets either side are one way; the street on the east side is for traffic going south, the west side for northbound traffic.

The square has been the stage for many of the epoch-making mass movements of twentieth-century China: the first calls for democracy and liberalism by the students of May 4 , 1919, demonstrating against the Treaty of Versailles; the anti-Japanese protests of December 9, 1935, demanding a war of national resistance; the eight stage-managed

BEIJING: THE CITY

Ancient Observatory	古观象台	*gǔguānxiàngtaí*
Baita Si	白塔寺	*báitǎ sì*
Baiyunguan	白云观	*báiyún guān*
Beihai Park	北海公园	*běihǎi gōngyuán*
Beijing Planetarium	北京天文馆	*běijīng tiānwénguǎn*
Beijing University	北京大学	*běijīng dàxué*
Beijing Zoo	北京动物园	*běijīng dòngwùyuán*
China Art Gallery	中国美术馆	*zhōngguó měishùguǎn*
Confucius Temple	孔庙	*kǒng miào*
Cultural Palace of the National Minorities	民族文化宫	*mínzú wénhuàgōng*
Dazhong Si	大钟寺	*dàzhōng sì*
Ditan Park	地坛公园	*dìtán gōngyuán*
Exhibition Hall	展览馆	*zhánlǎnguǎn*
Forbidden City	故宫博物院	*gùgōng bówùguǎn*
Former Residence of Lu Xun	鲁迅博物馆	*lǔxùn bówùguǎn*
Great Hall of the People	人民大会堂	*rénmín dàhuìtáng*
Gulou (Drum Tower)	鼓楼	*gǔlóu*
Guangji Si	广济寺	*guǎngjì sì*
Jingshan Park	景山公园	*jǐngshān gōngyuán*
Liulichang	琉璃场	*liúlìchǎng*
Mao Memorial Hall	毛主席纪念堂	*máozhǔxí jìniàntáng*
Military Museum	军事博物馆	*jūnshì bówùguǎn*
Museum of Chinese History	中国历史博物馆	*zhōngguó lìshí bówùguǎn*
Museum of the Chinese Revolution	中国革命博物馆	*zhōngguó gémìng bówùguǎn*
Natural History Museum	自然博物馆	*zìrán bówùguǎn*
Niu Jie	牛街	*niú jiē*
Prince Gong's Palace	恭王府	*gōngwáng fǔ*
Qianmen	前门	*qiánmén*
Qinghua University	清华大学	*qīnghuá dàxué*
Ritan Park	日坛公园	*rìtán gōngyuán*
Song Qingling's Residence	宋庆龄故居	*sòngqìnglíng gùjū*
Summer Palace	颐和园	*yíhéyuán*
Taoranting Park	陶然亭公园	*táorántíng gōngyuán*
Temple of Heaven	天坛	*tiāntán*
Tian'anmen	天安门	*tiān'ānmén*
Tian'anmen Square	天安门广场	*tiān'ānmén guángchǎng*
Tiantan Park	天坛公园	*tiāntán gōngyuán*
World Trade Centre	国际贸易中心	*guójì màoyì zhōngxīn*
Xu Beihong Museum	徐悲鸿纪念馆	*xúběihóng jìniànguǎn*
Yabao Lu Cotton Market	雅宝路	*yábǎo lù*
Yonghe Gong	雍和宫	*yōnghé gōng*
Yuanmingyuan	圆明园	*yuánmíngyuán*
Zhonglou (Bell Tower)	钟楼	*zhōnglóu*
Zhongnanhai	中南海	*zhōngnánhǎi*
Zizhuyuan Park	紫竹院公园	*zǐ zhúyuàn gōngyuán*

rallies that kicked off the Cultural Revolution in 1966, when up to a million Red Guards at a time were ferried to Beijing to be exhorted into action and then shipped out again to shake up the provinces; and the brutally repressed Qing Ming demonstration of April 1976, in memory of Zhou Enlai, that first pointed towards the eventual fall of the Gang of Four. But the square is most well known to contemporary visitors for the horrific events of 1989, when students and workers peacefully protesting for democracy were savagely suppressed (see box).

Tian'anmen Square unquestionably makes a strong impression, but this concrete plain dotted with worthy statuary and bounded by monumental buildings can seem inhuman. Together with the bloody associations it has for many visitors it often leaves people cold, especially Westerners unused to such magisterial representations of political power. For many Chinese tourists though, the square is a place of **pilgrimage**. Crowds flock to see the corpse of Chairman Mao, others quietly bow their heads before the **Monument to the Heroes**, a thirty-metre-high obelisk commemorating the victims of the revolutionary struggle. Currently, a popular place for a photo is in front of the huge digital display outside the entrance to the two museums which counts down the seconds to midnight on June 30, 1997, the date when Hong Kong reverts to Chinese control. Among the visitors you will often see monks, and the sight of robed Buddhists standing in front of the uniformed sentries outside the Great Hall of the People makes a striking juxtaposition. Others come just to hang out or to fly kites, but the atmosphere is not relaxed and a ¥5 fine for spitting and littering is rigorously enforced here. At dawn, the flag at the northern end of the square is raised in a military ceremony and lowered again at dusk, which is when most people come to see it. After dark, the square is at its most appealing and, with its sternness softened by mellow lighting, it becomes the haunt of strolling families and lovers.

The buildings

"At the centre of the centre of China lies a corpse that nobody dare remove."

Tiziano Terzani, *Behind the Forbidden Door.*

The square was not enlarged to its present size until ten years after the Communist takeover, when the Party ordained the building of ten new Soviet-style official buildings in ten months. These included the three that dominate Tian'anmen to either side – the Great Hall of the People, and the museums of Chinese History and Revolution. In 1976 a fourth was added in the centre – Mao's mausoleum, constructed (again in ten months) by an estimated million volunteers. It's an ugly building, looking like a school gym, which contravenes the principles of *fengshui* (geomancy), presumably deliberately, by interrupting the line from the palace to Qianmen and by facing north. Mao himself wanted to be cremated, and the erection of the mausoleum was apparently no more than a power ploy by his would-be successor, Hua Guofeng. In 1980 Deng Xiaoping said it should never have been built, although he wouldn't go so far as to pull it down again.

The **Chairman Mao Memorial Hall** is open every morning from 8.30am to 11.30am. After depositing your bag at the offices on the eastern side, you join the orderly queue of Chinese on the northern side. This advances surprisingly quickly, and takes just a couple of minutes to file through the chambers in silence. Mao's corpse is draped with a red flag within a crystal coffin. Mechanically raised from a freezer every morning, it looks unreal, like wax or plastic. It is said to have been embalmed with the aid of Vietnamese technicians who had recently worked on Ho Chi Minh (rumour has it that Mao's left ear fell off and had to be stitched back on). Much of the interest of a visit lies in experiencing the sense of overwhelming awe of the Chinese confronted with their former leader. The atmosphere is very reverent and any joking around will cause deep

DISSENT IN TIAN'ANMEN SQUARE

"Blood debts must be repaid in kind – the longer the delay, the greater the interest."

Lu Xun, writing after the massacre of 1926.

"Chinese history is about to turn a new page. Tian'anmen Square is ours, the people's, and we will not allow butchers to tread on it."

Wuer Kaixi, student, May 1989.

It may have been designed as a space for mass declarations of loyalty, but in this century Tian'anmen Square has as often been a venue for expressions of popular dissent; against foreign oppression at the beginning of the century, and, more recently, against its domestic form. The first mass protests occurred here on May 4, 1919, when three thousand students gathered in the square to protest at the disastrous terms of the Versailles Treaty, in which the victorious allies granted several former German concessions in China to the Japanese. The Chinese, who had sent more than a hundred thousand labourers to work in the supply lines of the British and French forces, were outraged. The protests of May 4, and the movement they spawned, marked the beginning of the painful struggle of Chinese modernization. In the turbulent years of the 1920s the inhabitants of Beijing again occupied the square, first in 1925, to protest over the massacre in Shanghai of Chinese demonstrators by British troops, then in 1926, when the public protested after the weak government's capitulation to the Japanese. Demonstrators marched on the government offices and were fired on by soldiers.

In 1976, after the death of popular premier Zhou Enlai, thousands of mourners assembled in Tian'anmen without government approval, to voice their dissatisfaction with their leaders, and again in 1978 and 1979, groups assembled here to discuss new ideas of democracy and artistic freedom, triggered by writings posted along Democracy Wall on the edge of the Forbidden City. In 1986 and 1987, people gathered again to show solidarity for the students and others protesting at the Party's refusal to allow elections.

But it was in **1989** that Tian'anmen Square became the venue for the largest expression of popular dissent in China this century, when from April to June, nearly a million protesters demonstrated against the slowness of reform, lack of freedom and widespread corruption. A giant statue, the Goddess of Liberty, a woman carrying a torch in both hands, was created by art students and set up facing Mao's portrait on Tian'anmen. The government, infuriated at being humiliated by their own people, declared martial law on May 20, and on June 4 the military moved in. The killing was indiscriminate; tanks ran over tents and machine guns strafed the avenues. No one knows how many died in the massacre – probably thousands. Hospitals were full to overflowing and there were rumours of mass graves. The truth will never be known as the official version of events is laughable. Hundreds were arrested afterwards and many are still in jail. The problems the protesters complained of have not been dealt with, and many, such as corruption, are viewed as having worsened. Any remaining moral authority the government had was destroyed. In the minds of many politically conscious Chinese, the protests in Tian'anmen Square in 1989 heralded the final stages of decline that have marked the end of so many previous dynasties.

offence. Once through the marble halls, you're herded past a splendidly wide array of tacky Chairman Mao souvenirs.

North of here, **Tian'anmen** itself, the Gate of Heavenly Peace (daily 8am–5pm; ¥30, students ¥10), is the main entrance to the Forbidden City. An image familiar across the world, Tian'anmen occupies an exalted place in Chinese iconography, appearing on banknotes, coins, stamps and indeed virtually any piece of state paper you can imagine. As such it's a prime object of pilgrimage, with many visitors milling around waiting to be photographed in front of the large portrait of Mao (one of the very few still on public display), which hangs over the central passageway. Once reserved for the sole use of the emperor, but now standing wide open, the entrance is flanked by the twin slogans "Long Live the People's Republic of China" and "Long Live the Great Union between the Peoples of the World". From the reviewing platform above, Mao delivered the liberation speech on October 1, 1949, declaring that "the Chinese people have now stood up". For an exorbitant fee you can climb up to this platform yourself where security is tight – all visitors have to leave their bags, are frisked and have to go through a metal detector, before they can ascend. Inside, the fact that most people cluster around the souvenir stall selling official certificates of their trip reflects the fact that there's not much to look at.

Taking up almost half the west side of the square is the **Great Hall of the People**. This is the venue of the National People's Congress and hundreds of black Audis with tinted windows are parked outside when it's in session. When it isn't, it's open to the public (daily 8.30–11.30am; ¥30). What you are shown is a selection, usually six, of the 29 reception rooms – each named after a province and filled with appropriate regional artefacts. The climax of the tour is the massive five-thousand-seater banqueting hall – a neat way to intimidate world leaders. When Margaret Thatcher came here in 1982, she stumbled and fell to her knees on the steps outside. This was seen in Hong Kong as a dreadful omen for the negotiations she was having on their future. Mikhail Gorbachev in 1989 couldn't even come in through the front door; the crowds of demonstrators outside meant he had to make a secret entrance through the side.

On the other side of the square, there are two **museums** housed in the same building: the Museum of Chinese History, covering the period up to 1919, and the **Museum of the Revolution** (Tues–Sun 8.30am–3.30pm; ¥5). In practice, the latter seems almost always to be closed for refits (for 12 years during the Cultural Revolution, for example) as its curators are faced with the Kafkaesque dilemma of constantly having to reinvent history according to the latest Party line. The **Museum of Chinese History** (Tues–Sun 8.30am–3.30pm; ¥5) has been recently renovated and is worth a visit, though it's intended for the education of the Chinese masses rather than foreign tourists, so there are no English captions. Without context or explanation visitors find themselves wandering the halls, divided according to dynasty, looking at the most striking or bizarre stuff, of which there is plenty – the Shang bronzes and Tang pottery are good.

For an overview of the square, head to the south gate, **Zhenyangmen** (daily 9am–4pm; ¥2), similar to Tian'anmen and 40m high, which gives a good idea of how much more impressive the square would look if Mao's mausoleum hadn't been stuck in the middle of it.

The Forbidden City

The Gugong, or Imperial Palace, is much better known by its unofficial title, the **Forbidden City**, a reference to its exclusivity. Indeed, for the five centuries of its operation, through the reigns of 24 emperors of the Ming and Qing dynasties, ordinary Chinese were forbidden from even approaching the walls of the palace. Today the complex is open to visitors daily 8.30am–4.30pm, with last admission at 3.30pm (¥55, students ¥20). You have the freedom of most of the hundred-hectare site, though not all of the buildings, which are labelled in English. If you want detailed explanation of everything you see, you can tag on to one of the numerous tour groups or buy one of the many specialist books on sale. The audio tour (¥25), available by the south gate, is also worth considering. You're provided with a cassette player and headphones and suavely talked through the complex by Roger Moore – though if you do this, it's worth retracing your steps afterwards for an untutored view. Useful **bus routes** serving the Forbidden City are #5 from Qianmen, and #54 from Beijing Zhan, or you could use #1, which passes the complex on its journey along Chang'an Jie.

Some history

After the Manchu dynasty fell in 1911, the Forbidden City began to fall into disrepair, exacerbated by heavy looting of artefacts and jewels by the Japanese in the 1930s and again by the Nationalists, prior to their flight to Taiwan, in 1949. A programme of **restoration** has been under way for decades, and today the complex is in better shape than it has been for most of this century, in the interests of over a million visitors a year. It's big enough to fill several separate visits, and its elegance on such a massive scale is extraordinary.

The complex, with its maze of eight hundred buildings and reputed nine thousand chambers, was the symbolic and literal heart of the capital, and of the empire too. From within, the **emperors**, the Sons of Heaven, issued commands with absolute authority to their millions of subjects. Very rarely did they emerge – perhaps with good reason. Their lives, right down to the fall of the Manchu in this century, were governed by an extraordinarily developed taste for luxury and excess. It is estimated that a single meal for a Qing emperor could have fed around five thousand of his impoverished peasants, a scale obviously appreciated by the last influential Manchu, the Empress Dowager Cixi, who herself would commonly order preparation of one hundred or more dishes. Sex, too, provided startling statistics, with Ming-dynasty harems numbering only just below five figures.

Although the earliest structures on the Forbidden City site began with Kublai Khan during the Mongol dynasty, the **plan** (and originals) of the Imperial Palace buildings are essentially Ming. Most date to the fifteenth century and the ambitions of the Emperor Yongle, the monarch responsible for switching the capital back to Beijing in 1403. His building programme was concentrated between 1407 and 1420, involving up to a hundred artisans and perhaps a million labourers. The halls were laid out according to geomantic theories – in accordance with the *yin* and *yang*, the balance of negative and positive – and since they stood at the exact centre of Beijing, and Beijing was considered the centre of the universe, the harmony was supreme. The palace complex constantly reiterates such references, alongside personal symbols of imperial power such as the dragon and phoenix (emperor and empress) and the crane and turtle (longevity of reign).

Entering the complex

Once through Tian'anmen, you find yourself on a long walkway, with the moated palace complex and massive Wumen gate directly ahead (this is where you buy your ticket). The two parks either side, Zhongshan and the People's Culture Park (both daily 8am–6pm) are great places to chill out away from the rigorous formality outside. The **People's Culture Park** (¥5), symbolically named in deference to the fact that only with the Communist takeover in 1949 were ordinary Chinese allowed within this central sector of their city, has a number of modern exhibition halls (sometimes worth checking) and a scattering of original fifteenth-century structures, most of them Ming or Qing ancestral temples. **Zhongshan Park** (¥1) boasts the remains of the Altar of Land and Grain, a biennial sacrificial site with harvest functions closely related to those of the Temple of Heaven (see p.93).

The **Wumen** (Meridian Gate) itself is the largest and grandest of the Forbidden City gates and was reserved for the emperor's sole use. From its vantage point, the Sons of Heaven would announce the new year's calendar to their court and in times of war inspect the army. It was customary for victorious generals returning from battle to present their prisoners here for the emperor to decide their fate. He would be flanked, on all such imperial occasions, by a guard of elephants, the gift of Burmese subjects.

Passing through the Wumen (Meridian Gate) you find yourself in a vast paved court, cut east–west by the **Jinshui He**, the Golden Water Stream, with its five marble bridges, decorated with carved torches, a symbol of masculinity. Beyond is a further ceremonial gate, the **Taihemen**, Gate of Supreme Harmony, its entrance guarded by a magisterial row of lions, and beyond this a still greater courtyard where the principle imperial audiences were held. Within this space the entire court, up to one hundred thousand people, could be accommodated. They would have made their way in through the lesser side gates – military men from the west, civilian officials from the east – and waited in total silence as the emperor ascended his throne. Then, with only the Imperial Guard remaining standing, they prostrated themselves nine times.

Inside the palace

The main **ceremonial halls** stand directly ahead, dominating the court. Raised on a three-tiered marble terrace is the first and most spectacular of the three, the **Taihedian**, Hall of Supreme Harmony. This was used for the most important state occasions, such as the emperor's coronation or birthdays and the nomination of generals at the outset of a campaign, and last saw action in an armistice ceremony in 1918. It was proposed, though not carried through, that parliament should sit here during the Republic. A marble pavement ramp, intricately carved with dragons and flanked by bronze incense burners, marks the path along which the emperor's chair was carried. His golden dragon throne stands within.

Moving on, you enter the **Zhonghedian**, Hall of Middle Harmony, another throne room, where the emperor performed ceremonies of greeting to foreigners and addressed the imperial offspring (products of several wives and numerous concubines). The hall was used, too, as a dressing room, for the major Taihedian events, and it was here that the emperor examined the seed for each year's crop.

The third of the great halls, the **Baohedian**, Preserving Harmony Hall, was used for state banquets and imperial examinations, graduates from which were appointed to positions of power in what was the first recognizably bureaucratic civil service. Its galleries, originally treasure houses, display various finds from the site, though the most spectacular, a vast block carved with dragons and clouds, stands at the rear of the hall. This is a Ming creation, reworked in the eighteenth century, and it's among the finest carvings in the palace. It's certainly the largest – a 250-tonne chunk of marble transported here from well outside the city by flooding the roads in winter to form sheets of ice.

To the north, paralleling the structure of the ceremonial halls, are the three principal palaces of the **imperial living quarters**. Again, the first chamber, the **Qiangingong**, Palace of Heavenly Purity, is the most extravagant. It was originally the imperial bedroom – its terrace is surmounted by incense burners in the form of cranes and tortoises (symbols of immortality) – though it later became a conventional state room. Beyond, echoing the Zhonghedian in the ceremonial complex, is the **Jiaotaidian**, Hall of Union, the empress's throneroom, and finally the **Kinningong**, Palace of Earthly Tranquillity, where the emperor and empress traditionally spent their wedding night. By law the emperor had to spend the first three nights of his marriage, and the first day of Chinese New Year, with his wife. This palace is a bizarre building, partitioned in two. On the left is a large sacrificial room with its vats ready to receive offerings (1300 pigs a year under the Ming). The wedding chamber is a small room, off to one side, painted entirely in red, and covered with decorative emblems symbolizing fertility and joy. It was last pressed into operation in 1922 for the child wedding of Pu Yi, the final Manchu emperor, who found it all "like a melted red wax candle" and who, disconcerted, decided that he preferred the Mind Nurture Palace and went back there.

The Mind Nurture Palace, or **Yangxindiang**, is one of a group of palaces to the west where emperors spent most of their time. Several of the palaces retain their furniture from the Manchu times, most of it eighteenth-century, and in one, the **Changchundong**, is a series of paintings illustrating the Ming novel, *The Story of the Stone*. To the east is a similarly arranged group of palaces, adapted as **museum gal-**

EUNUCHS AND CONCUBINES

For much of the **imperial period**, the Inner Court of the palace was the home of over six thousand members of the royal household, around half of this number **eunuchs**. The castrated male was introduced into the imperial court as a means of ensuring the authenticity of the emperor's offspring and as a radical solution to the problem of nepotism. In daily contact with the royals, they often rose to considerable power, but this was bought at the expense of their dreadfully low standing outside the confines of the court. Confucianism held that disfiguration of the body impaired the soul, and eunuchs were buried apart from their ancestors in special graveyards outside the city. Rather pathetically, in the hope that they would still be buried "whole", they kept and carried around their testicles in bags hung on their belts. They were usually recruited from the poorest families – attracted by the rare chance of amassing wealth other than by birth. Scarcely less numerous were the **concubines**, whose status varied from wives and consorts to basic whores. They would be delivered to the emperor's bedchamber, wrapped in yellow cloth, and carried by one of the eunuchs, since with feet bound they could hardly walk.

leries for displays of bronzes, ceramics, paintings, jewellery and Ming and Qing arts and crafts. The atmosphere here is much more initimate, and you can peer into well-appointed chambers full of elegant furniture and ornaments, including English clocks decorated with images of English gentlefolk, which look very odd among the jade trees and ornate flywhisks.

Head over to the other side of the complex to the eastern palace quarters where an extraordinary **Clock Museum** (¥5) is housed, displaying the result of one Qing emperor's collecting passion. Explosions of Baroque ornament, most are English and French, though by the entrance is a rhino-sized Chinese water clock.

Moving away from the palace chambers – and by this stage something of a respite– the Kunningmen leads out from the Inner Court to the **Imperial Garden**. There are a couple of cafés here (and toilets) amid a pleasing network of ponds, walkways and pavilions, the classic elements of a Chinese garden. At the centre is the **Qinandian**, Hall of Imperial Peace, dedicated to the Taoist god of fire, Xuan Wu. You can exit here into Jingshan Park, which provides an overview of the complex – see p.99.

South of Tian'anmen

The **Qianmen** area (see colour plates), to the south of Tian'anmen, offers a tempting antidote to the prodigious grandeurs of the Forbidden City – and a quick shift of scale. The lanes and *hutongs* here comprise a **traditional shopping quarter**, full of small, specialist stores which to a large extent remain grouped according to their particular trades. It's a part of the city to browse in, and a good place to eat, with one of the best selections of snacks available in the capital. Down Qianmen Dajie, once the Imperial Way, now a clogged road clustered with small shops, the **Museum of Natural History** contains a gruesome surprise and **Tiantan**, the ravishing Temple of Heaven, perfectly set in one of Beijing's best parks, is an example of imperial architecture at its best.

Qianmen

The entry to this quarter is marked by the imposing, fifteenth-century, double-arched **Qianmen Gate** just south of Tian'anmen Square. Before the city's walls were demolished, this sector controlled the entrance to the Inner City from the outer, suburban sector. Shops and places of entertainment were banned from the former in imperial days, and they became concentrated in the Qianmen area. The gate marks a major intersection on the public transport network: as well as a subway stop, a bus terminus here provides connections to the southern districts and tourist buses also leave from here to attractions outside the city, including the Great Wall at Badaling and Shisan Ling.

Qianmen Dajie, the quarter's biggest street, runs immediately south from the gate. Off to either side are trading streets and *hutongs*, with intriguing traditional pharmacies and herbalist shops, dozens of clothes shops, silk traders and an impressive array of sidestalls and cakeshops selling fresh food and cooked snacks. On the western side of the gate, you'll find *KFC* and *Mcdonald's*, but a better bet is the small *Vie de France* next door, where you can get coffee and a chocolate croissant for less than ¥10. Alternatively, plunge into the *hutongs* on the southeastern side of the gate, where you'll find many esoteric little greasy cafés, some of them foreign concerns, with signs in Korean or Arabic as well as Chinese. For something more ample, the famous *Qianmen Quanjude Roast Duck* is at no. 32 (see p.109 for more restaurants in this area).

Once the district was noisy with opera singers. Today the theatres have been converted to **cinemas** and the area resounds instead with film soundtracks, piped into the street, and with the bips and beeps of the computer games sold at street stalls. If this makes your thumbs twitch, **Segaworld**, with a good selection of Japanese arcade machines, is on the top floor of a building on the west side of the street, at the northern end of Qianmen Dajie, and signed from the street. Video arcades are all the rage here and, as elsewhere in China, the most popular game is a version of mah jong. For a rather sanitized taste of the district's old delights, visit the *Lao She Tea House* just west of *KFC*, which puts on nightly shows of acrobatics and opera (see p.116).

More authentic is the hustle of cramped **Dazhalan Lu**, one of the oldest and most interesting of the Qianmen lanes, opposite the *Qianmen Roast Duck* restaurant on the east side of the road, its entrance marked by a white arch. This was once a major theatre street, now it's a hectic shopping district, with mostly teashops and clothing stores occupying the genteel old buildings. Go down the first alley on the left, and one of the first shops you'll pass on the right is the *Liubiju*, a **pickle shop** that's over a century old. It looks quaint, with pickled vegetables sold out of ceramic jars, but smells awful. Back on Dazhanlan, you'll find the *Ruifuxiang*, an old **fabric shop**, a little farther down on the right – look for the storks on its facade, above the arched entrance. This is the place to get raw silk and satin, but even if you're not buying, take a look at the exhibition on the top floor of old photos of the street. On the other side of the road at no. 24 the *Tongrengtang* is a famous traditional **Chinese medicine store**, with shelves full of deer horn, bear heart capsules and the like, and a formidable array of aphrodisiacs. The shop's reputation spreads as far as Korea and Japan, and the place has a foreign exchange counter, opposite a booth holding a resident pharmacist offering on the spot diagnoses. At the end of the street, marked by a scattering of Chinese-only hotels, was the old red light district formerly containing over three hundred brothels. The street is very dead these days, though, and you're better off turning north to **Liulichang**, parallel to Dazhanlan, but not directly accessible from Qianmen Dajie. This street is famous for its **antiques and bookshops** – the originals were bulldozed in the 1950s but have now been neatly reconstructed for the benefit of visitors to make a pretty heritage street full of curio shops. The *China Bookstore* at no. 115, one of the city's best bookshops, is definitely worth a stop, and in the streets around you'll find many musical instrument shops.

The Natural History Museum and the Muslim quarter

It's a long and boring thirty-minute walk from the northern end of Qianmen Dajie down to the **Natural History Museum** (daily 8.30am–4pm; ¥10), a few blocks farther south; take bus #17 or #20. After dry halls of stuffed wildlife and plastic dinosaurs, prepare yourself for a shock on the top floor, where a ghoulish display on human anatomy has gained museum cult status among travellers with a taste for the macabre. Pickled legs, arms, brains and babies are arranged around the stars of the show, two whole corpses, a woman wearing socks, gloves and a hood, and a man with all his skin removed, leaving just the fingernails and lips. Few Westerners emerge from here unshaken, shown up by Chinese kids who seem to take it all in their stride. You can recover in the soothing surroundings of Tiantan Park (see below), whose western gate is just south of here. The only other reason to head into the rambling sprawl farther south is to find a cheap hotel, although if you're in the area, **Taoranting Park** (daily 6am–7pm; ¥0.2) on Taiping Jie, to the west, with its hills, woods and pavilions, is a pleasant little place, where you may hear old people passing the time by singing Beijing Opera.

Niu Jie (Ox Street), the city's **Muslim quarter**, is a long diversion into the ugly zone west of here. The street, a *hutong* leading off Guang'anmenwai Dajie, on the route of bus #6 from the north gate of Tiantan Park, is a cramped thoroughfare lined with offal stalls and vendors selling fried dough rings, rice cakes and *shaobang* (muffins). The white hats and the beards worn by the men are what most obviously set these Hui minority people apart from the Han Chinese – there are nearly two hundred thousand of them in the capital. The focus of the street is the **mosque** (daily 8am–5pm; ¥10) at its southern end, an attractive building colourfully decorated in Chinese style with abstract decorations and text in Chinese and Arabic over the doors. You won't get to see the handwritten copy of the Koran written in the Yuan dynasty without special permission, or be allowed into the main prayer hall, but you can inspect the courtyard, where a copper bowl used for cooking for the devotees sits near two graves of Persian imams who came here to preach in the thirteenth century.

The Temple of Heaven – Tiantan

Set in its own large and tranquil park about 2km south of Tian'anmen along Qianmen Dajie, the **Temple of Heaven** (daily 6am–6pm; ¥30, students ¥0.5), is widely regarded as the high point of Ming design. For five centuries it was at the very heart of imperial ceremony and symbolism, and its architectural unity and beauty remain for most modern visitors more appealing – and on a much more accessible scale – than the Forbidden City. There are various bus routes to Tiantan: bus #36 runs from Tian'anmen past the west and south gates, while #20 and #54 pass the west gate on their way from Beijing Zhan down to Yongdingmen, also via Tian'anmen, and bus #41 from Chongwenmen stops opposite the east gate.

The temple was begun during the reign of Emperor Yongle and completed in 1420. It was conceived as the prime meeting point of Earth and Heaven, and symbols of the two are integral to its plan. Heaven was considered round, and Earth square, thus the round temples and altars stand on square bases, while the whole park has the shape of a semicircle sitting beside a square. The intermediary between Earth and Heaven was of course the Son of Heaven, the emperor, and the temple was the site of the most important ceremony of the imperial court calendar, when the emperor prayed for the year's harvests at the winter solstice. Purified by three days of fasting, he made his way to the park on the day before the solstice, accompanied by his court in all its panoply. On arrival, he would meditate in the Imperial Vault, ritually conversing with the gods on the details of government, before spending the night in the Hall of Prayer of Good Harvests. The following day, amid exact and numerological ritual, the emperor performed sacrifices before the Throne of Heaven at the Round Altar.

It was forbidden for the commoners of old Beijing to catch a glimpse of the great annual procession to the temple and they were obliged to bolt their windows and remain, in silence, indoors. The Tiantan complex remained sacrosanct until it was thrown open to the people on the first Chinese National Day of the Republic in October

1912. Two years after this, the infamous General Yuan Shikai performed the solstice ceremonies himself, as part of his attempt to be proclaimed emperor. He died before the year was out.

The temple buildings

Although you're more likely to enter the actual park from the north or the west, to appreciate the religious ensemble it's best initially to skirt round in order to follow the ceremonial route up from the south entrance, the Zhaohen Gate. The main pathway leads straight to the **Round Altar**, consisting of three marble tiers representing Man, Earth and (at the summit) Heaven. The tiers themselves are composed of blocks in various multiples of nine, which the Chinese saw as cosmologically the most powerful odd number, representing both Heaven and Emperor. The top terrace now stands bare, but the spot at its centre, where the Throne of Heaven was placed, was considered to be the middle of the Middle Kingdom – the very centre of the earth. Various acoustic properties are claimed for the surrounding tiers, and from this point it is said that all sounds are channelled straight upwards. To the east of the fountain, which was reconstructed after fire damage in 1740, are the ruins of a group of buildings used for the preparation of sacrifices.

Directly ahead, the **Imperial Vault of Heaven** is an octagonal structure made entirely of wood, with a dramatic roof of dark blue glazed tiles. It is preceded by the so-called **Echo Wall**, said to be a perfect whispering gallery, although the unceasing cacophony of tourists trying it out makes it impossible to tell.

The principal temple building – the **Hall of Prayer for Good Harvests**, at the north end of the park – amply justifies all this build-up. It is, quite simply, a wonder. Made entirely of wood, without the aid of a single nail, the circular structure rises from another three-tiered marble terrace, to be topped by three blue-tiled roofs of harmonious proportions. Four compass-point pillars support the vault (in representation of the seasons), enclosed in turn by twelve outer pillars (for the months of the year and the watches of the day). The dazzling colours of the interior, surrounding the central dragon motif, make the pavilion seem ultra-modern; it was in fact entirely rebuilt, faithful to the Ming design, after the original was destroyed by lightning in 1889. The official explanation for this appalling omen was that it was divine punishment for a sacrilegious caterpillar which was on the point of reaching the golden ball on the hall's crest. Nonetheless, 32 court dignitaries paid with their heads.

These days, the park is a popular venue for Chinese to sit, drink tea and play, but it's also easy to find peaceful seclusion in the large areas of park away from the temple proper, which vary from semi-wilderness to formal lawns. Old men gather with their caged birds and crickets, while from dawn onwards, the park is dotted with exponents of various forms of *tai ji*, some learning swordplay in organized classes while others are lost in solitary concentration among the groves of five-hundred-year-old thuja trees.

Along Chang'an Jie

Chang'an Jie, the freeway which runs dead straight east–west across the city, changing its name four times along its length, is downtown Beijing at its most grandiose and unreal. A showcase street, it is lined with the headquarters of official and commercial power, which rub shoulders with the glitziest hotels and malls. Architectural styles are jumbled together, with international modernism, post-modern whimsy and brute Stalinism all in evidence, as well as the odd block of *hutongs*, and a couple of ancient sites looking utterly lost amid this parade of gargantuan robots. Heading west from Tian'anmen Square, the tone is mostly official, dominated by the **Communist Party Headquarters** and two **museums**, though there's a pretty good shopping district,

Xidan, where you can rub shoulders with the locals, and the pleasant **Baiyuguan Si** to chill out in. East is more glamorous, with heavy lashings of shopping, perhaps the best in China, plus flashy hotels and restaurants. In this direction, the **Observatory** provides respite from all this fun but ultimately rather exhausting consumerism. Along Chang'an Jie, you'll find most of the facilities you need: the post office, Aviation Office, central train station and plenty of banks. For a quick fix of the whole experience, take bus #1, which travels the entire length of the freeway.

West: Xichang'an Jie and beyond

The **Communist Party Headquarters**, the **Zhongnanhai**, is the first major building you pass – on the right – heading west from Tian'anmen. It's not hard to spot as armed sentries stand outside the gates, ensuring that only invited guests actually get inside. This is perhaps the most important and historic building in the country, base since 1949 of the Central Committee and the Central People's Government, and Mao and Zhou Enlai both worked here. Before the Communist takeover it was home to the Empress Dowager Cixi. In 1989, protesters camped outside hoping to petition their leaders, just as commoners with a grievance waited outside the Forbidden City centuries ago.

At the next junction, the **Beijing Telecommunications Centre** rears above you – like the buildings around Tian'anmen Square, it's another of the "ten years of liberation" construction projects, and suitably grand. Just west, the **Aviation Office**, the place to buy tickets and catch the airport bus, stands on the site of Democracy Wall, and over the road looms the **Beijing Concert Hall**, recessed a little from the street, another uninspiring construction.

Xidan (see colour plates), the street heading north from the next junction, is worth exploring, at least along its initial few blocks, though not on a Saturday when it's heaving with people. This is where the locals shop, and the area is a dense concentration of **department stores**. The choice is less esoteric, and the shopping experience less earthy, than in Qianmen. Some of the stores are underground, in basements that were once part of the city's extensive civil defence network. Perhaps of most interest to visitors are the **cafés and restaurants**: there's a *Vie de France* (the best one in Beijing, with the most seats) and a *Pizza Hut* near the junction, a *Mcdonald's* on the east side of Xidan Bei Dajie, and even a *Fast Food Beijing Duck* restaurant a little farther south. Sunk in the alleys west of here are two much more Chinese places well worth hunting down: the Muslim *Laosunjia*, and the superbly named *Compare Past Misery with Present Happiness* which specializes in honest country cooking served in an old courtyard-style house. Both are highly recommended (see "Restaurants", p.110).

Within walking distance of the Xidan junction, the **Cultural Palace of National Minorities** (Mon–Sat 9am–4.30pm, though it's often closed for trade fairs; ¥5) is an exhibition centre for the crafts and costumes of the nation's non Han Chinese. Reduced to statistics, these minorities account for only six percent of the Chinese population, but inhabit some sixty percent of the country's territory, establishing a political significance well above their numbers. The slant of the museum is, naturally enough, one of integration, with all the minority regions presented as moving from a divided feudal past to a common future. It could all be a little more imaginatively and less dogmatically displayed, though the exhibits (including brilliant-coloured ethnic clothing, jewellery and artefacts) make a strong impression, and the cases contrasting peasant and noble wear make their point. Next door, the *Minxu Hotel* has a good though pricey first-floor restaurant.

It takes persistence to continue much beyond this point, though you might be spurred on by the sight of the trio of distant **skyscrapers**, bizarre buildings which look like erect, ornamented hypodermics. The first one is the pink **Beijing Radio and TV**

Building, looking like a parody of the original, Soviet-style construction, over which it towers like a protective big sister. The others are foreign office buildings. On the way, you'll pass the **Parkson Building** on the north side of the next junction, a shopping centre for seriously rich Chinese. On the fifth floor is an exhibition hall (daily 9.30am–4.30pm; ¥15, students ¥4) with the air of an exclusive private collection, showing masterpieces from the craftwork factories across China – similar to the stuff you'll see in the *Friendship Store* but of much better quality. Though some items are a little sickly – a revolutionary meeting done in ivory, for example – the craftsmanship in evidence is astonishing.

Two kilometres west of here, another stern Soviet-style building on Fuxing Lu suits its purpose as the **Military Museum** (daily 8am–4.30pm; ¥5). It's more exciting than its name suggests and worth the trip out here – catch bus #1, which terminates close by, or the subway to Junshi Bowuguan. On entering you are confronted with giant paintings of Marx and fellow luminaries, and of a nuclear explosion, while an enormous rocket stands proud at the centre of the high main hall. With none of the problems that dog other museums of contemporary history in China – the need to tweak the displays with every shift of Party line – the museum does its job of impressing you with China's military might and achievements very well. The exhibits stake out the history of the People's Liberation Army, with heavy emphasis, inevitably, on the war against the Nationalists and the Japanese. You can also read about how the soldiers of the PLA got fired on by demonstrators in 1989, and see doctored pictures to prove it. Curiosities include, in the rear courtyard, a somewhat miscellaneous group of old aircraft – among them the shells of two American spy planes (with Nationalist markings) shot down in the 1950s.

There's little reason to continue west from here – you can visit the four-hundred-metre-high **TV Tower** on Nansanhuan Lu (daily 8am–5pm), which offers a spectacular view over the city, but it costs a steep ¥50. If you want to loop back to Qianmen from the Military Museum, bus #337 offers a useful approach. It runs past the **Baiyunguan Si**, White Cloud Temple (daily 8am–5.30pm; ¥10), just off Baiyuan Lu and signposted in English. Once the most influential Taoist centre in the country, the temple has been extensively renovated after a long spell as a military barracks and is now the location for the China Taoism Association. There are thirty resident monks, and it's become a popular place for pilgrims, with a busy, thriving feel to it, in many ways preferable to the more touristy Lamaist temple, the Yonghe Gong (see p.102). There are three monkeys depicted in relief sculptures around the temple, and it is believed to be lucky to find all three: the first is on the gate, easy to spot as it's been rubbed black, and the other two are in the first courtyard. Each hall is dedicated to a different deity, whose area of speciality is explained in English outside, with the thickest plumes of incense emerging from the hall to the gods of wealth. The eastern and western halls hold a great collection of Taoist relics, including some horrific paintings of hell with people being sawn in half and the like. An attached bookshop has only one text in English, the *Book of Changes*, but plenty of tapes and lucky charms. If you're on a bike or a very committed temple tourist, you could continue south about a kilometre from Baiyunguan to see the **Tianning Si Ta**, Heavenly Repose Pagoda, a beautiful building stranded to great effect amid heavy industrial plant, though the factories prevent you actually getting close to it.

East from Tian'anmen – Dongchang'an Jie and Jianguomen Dajie

Everything on the eastern half of Chang'an (initially called **Dongchang'an Jie**) takes its bearings from the *Beijing Hotel*, though perhaps a better marker for the abrupt transition from the political zone of Tian'anmen and around to this commercial sector is the first big billboard, opposite **Wangfujing**, Beijing's most famous shopping street. Now used for ads, for years it announced an anti-corruption conference, and policemen used to prevent foreigners from taking pictures of it.

Jianguomen Dajie, the strip beyond the second ring road, is Beijing's rich quarter, a ritzy area given much of its international flavour and distinctive atmosphere of casual wealth by a large contingent of foreigners, upmarket tourists and staff from the weird Jianguomen embassy compound. Eating and staying around here will soon sap most travellers' budgets (first-time tourists can be heard here expressing disappointment that China is as expensive as New York), but the wide variety of shopping offered – two good clothes markets, the best *Friendship Store* in China, and plazas that wouldn't look out of place in Hong Kong – will suit all pockets. The main street is about as far away from traditional China as you can get, but the **Ancient Observatory** and quiet little **Ritan Park** nearby offer less packaged experiences.

Dongchang'an Jie, Wangfujing and around

Wangfujing (see colour plates), heading north from the *Beijing Hotel* on Dongchang'an Jie, is where the capital gets down to the business of **shopping** in earnest, though it's no longer the city's premier consumer cornucopia. But it does have some good stuff, even some history, and it's short enough to stroll along its length. For a century the haunt of quality stores, before the Communist takeover it was called Morrison Street; now it's nicknamed "Mcdonald's Street" thanks to the fast-food joint on the corner – a rather stern building, this is one of the largest *Mcdonald's* in the world. On the western side of the street – the eastern has been entirely ripped up to prepare for an enormous shopping centre – are plenty of small stores selling clothes. You'll also find the *China Photo Studio* about halfway up at no. 228, which will produce passport photos as well as develop film. A medical instrument store just to the north provides some of the few real bargains you can get in China – Western suppliers come here to buy in bulk. Past it, just before the crossroads with Dong'anmen Jie, is the *Foreign Language Bookstore*, the largest in China and a priceless resource for travellers (see p.118 for more details).

On the eastern side of the street a number of **hutongs** lead into a quiet area well away from the bustle of the main street. The ten brothers of a Ming-dynasty emperor used to live here, so that he could keep a wary eye on them, and you can still see their palace at the end of Shuaifuyuan Hutong, now converted into a medical college. Continuing east through the *hutongs*, you'll reach **Dongdan Bei Dajie**, parallel to Wangfujing, which is rapidly becoming a shopping centre to rival it, full of clothing boutiques. The architectural medley on Dongchang'an Jie continues with a block of (presumably doomed) *hutongs*, followed by the chunky Women's Activity Centre, thrown up in time for the Women's Conference in 1995, past the *International Hotel* just north of Beijing Zhan, until you reach the giant concrete knot of the Jianguomen intersection, at the limit of the old walls.

Jianguomen Dajie and the Ancient Observatory

An unexpected survivor marooned amid the highrises, the **Ancient Observatory** (Wed–Sun 9am–4.30pm; ¥10) is a delightful surprise. It is tucked in the southwest corner of the Jianguomen intersection, beside the Jianguomen subway stop. The first observatory on this site was founded under the orders of Kublai Khan, the astronomers' commission being to reform the then faulty calendar. Later it came under Muslim control, as medieval Islamic science enjoyed pre-eminence, but, bizarrely, in the early seventeenth century it was placed in the hands of Jesuit Christian missionaries. The Jesuits, a small group led by one Matteo Ricci, arrived in Beijing in 1601 and astonished citizens and emperor by a series of precise astronomical forecasts. They reequipped the observatory and remained in charge through to the 1830s. Today the building is essentially a shell, and the best features of the complex are the garden, a placid retreat, and the eight Ming-dynasty astronomical instruments sitting on the roof, stunningly sculptural armillary spheres, theodolites and the like. The small **museum** attached, displaying early astronomy-influenced pottery and navigational equipment, is an added bonus.

North along Chaoyangmen Dajie, you come to the **international post office** and **Bank of China**, and south brings you to the main **CITS** office. Heading east beyond the Jianguomen intersection, the **International Club** is the first sign that you're approaching the capital's diplomatic sector. It's a restrained building, dwarfed by the CITIC building across the street, a 36-storey monolith with a speedy and efficient bank on the first floor which offers a comprehensive service to visitors. Turn left at the *International Club* up Ritan Lu and you'll hit the **Jianguomenwai Diplomatic Compound**, the first of two embassy complexes (the other is at Sanlitun, well northeast of here). It's a funny place, a giant toytown with neat buildings in ordered courtyards and frozen sentries on red and white plinths. **Ritan Park** is just one block back north from the *International Club*, a five-minute walk from Jianguomen Dajie. As with most of the capital's parks, it's not big on grass, but it's popular with embassy staff and courting couples, who make use of its numerous secluded nooks.

You'll also find two clothes markets in the area. The first of these, the **Yabao Lu Cotton Market**, lies 500m north up Ritan Lu, a long string of stalls spilling out into the surrounding streets. As well as the huge variety of clothes, the Filofaxes, sunglasses and shoes are all pretty good value – you can barter about a third off the price without too much difficulty. Traders address all big noses in Russian, and ask you how many cases you want to buy, which gives you a good idea where most of this stuff ends up.

Back on Jianguomen Dajie, beyond the CITIC building, you'll reach the **Friendship Store** (daily 9am–8.30pm), China's best. Its top floors are devoted to the usual range of goods – clothes, jewellery and paintings, but its lower floor is perhaps of more immediate and compelling use, with a carpet section, a foreign exchange (open every day), a supermarket selling plenty of foreign goodies, an information desk where you can pick up the *China Daily*, and a bookshop. Outside is a string of upmarket **coffee bars and restaurants**, the best and cheapest of which is *Vie de France*, though watch your bags here as it's a favoured hangout for thieves. On the other side of the road, the **CVIK Plaza** (daily 9am–9pm) is a more modern shopping centre with five floors of clothes and accessories. There's a coffee bar in the basement and a *Bank of China* on the first floor.

A kilometre east of the *Friendship Store*, the **Silk Market** runs north off Jianguomen Dajie. Again, it's mostly clothes, though there are a few antique stalls as well, and a couple of stalls selling ethnic clothing (try no. 42). Again, you'll need to bargain, though it's a little harder here as there are more tourists around. The underwear looks alluring, but sizes tend to be small. Good buys are silk dressing gowns, bomber jackets, ties, scarfs and jeans. Youths hang around the market, illicitly selling CD-ROM computer games and music CDs (they start at ¥20 but can be knocked down to ¥10) – they're good quality but tend to miss off the last track.

It's a long way, and you may be all shopped out by now, but dedicated consumers who continue to the **World Trade Centre**, just before the intersection with Dongsanhuan Bei Lu, about 3km east of here, are rewarded with Beijing's most exclusive mall, four shining storeys of pricey consumables. As well as boutiques there's a post office (Level B1), a *Bank of China* (Level 2), and an *American Express* office (Level 1). The restaurants here are well out of most travellers' budgets, but there's a pleasant German bar, the *Brauhaus*, which sometimes has live gigs, (see "Entertainment", p.113). The basement has a *Wellcome Supermarket* (the Hong Kong brand), which is the best stocked in the city, though it's not cheap. As well as shopping here, foreign residents advertise flats and jobs on the noticeboard.

North of Tian'anmen

The area north of Tian'anmen Square has a scattered collection of sights, many of them remnants of the imperial past, when this area was the home of princes, dukes and monks. The finest remaining palace is **Prince Gong's**, buried in Beijing's best preserved *hutongs* north of **Beihai Park**, the imperial pleasure park, while the finest temple, the **Yonghe Gong**, is in the northern outskirts of the centre. Other illustrious residents are more recent; in the northwest, the twentieth-century homes of the writer **Lu Xun** and the artist **Xu Beihong** are open as museums. For a general picture of the state of the Chinese arts, visit the **China Art Gallery** just north of Wangfujing.

Jingshan and Beihai parks

Jingshan Park (daily 8am–6pm; ¥0.3) is a natural way to round off a trip to the Forbidden City. An artificial mound, it was created by the digging of the palace moat and served as a windbreak and a barrier to malevolent spirits (believed to emanate from the north) for the imperial quarter of the city. It takes its name, meaning Coal Hill, from a coal store once sited here. Its history, most momentously, includes the suicide of the last Ming emperor, Chong Zhen, in 1644, who hanged himself here from a lotus tree after rebel troops broke into the imperial city. The spot, on the eastern side of the park, is easy to find as it is signposted everywhere (underneath signs pointing to a children's playground), though the tree that stands here is not the original.

It's the views from the top of the hill that make this park such a compelling target. They take in the whole extent of the Forbidden City, a revealing perspective, and a fair swathe of the city outside, a deal more attractive than at ground level. To the west is Beihai with its fat snake lake, in the north the Drum and Bell towers, and to the northeast the Yonghe Gong.

Beihai Park (daily 6am–8pm; ¥10, students ¥0.5), a few hundred metres west of Jingshan on the route of bus #13 from the Yonghe Gong or #5 from Qianmen, is almost half lake in extent, and it's a favourite skating spot in the frozen winter months. It was supposedly created by Kublai Khan, long before any of the Forbidden City structures were conceived, and its scale is suitably ambitious: the lake was man-made, an island being created in its midst with the excavated earth. Emperor Qianlong oversaw its landscaping into a classical garden and Mao's widow, the ill-fated Jiang Qing, was a frequent visitor here. Today its elegance is marred by funfairs and shops among the willows and red-columned galleries, though it's still a grand place to retreat from the city and recharge. Most of the buildings (daily 6am–4pm) lie on the central island, whose summit is marked by a white dagoba, built in the mid-seventeenth century to celebrate a visit by the Dalai Lama, a suitable emblem for a park which contains a curious mixture of religious buildings, storehouses for cultural relics and imperial garden architecture.

Just inside the south gate, the **Round City** encloses a courtyard which holds a jade bowl, said to have belonged to Kublai Khan. The white jade Buddha in the hall behind was a present from Burma. The **island** is accessible by a walkway from here. It's dotted with religious architecture, which you'll come across as you scramble around the rocky paths, including the **Yuego Lou**, a hall full of steles, and the giant **dagoba** sitting on top with a shrine to the demon-headed, multi-armed Lamaist deity, Yamantaka, nestling inside. An exclusive restaurant, the *Fangshan*, where decor, food and prices are imperial, sits off a painted corridor running round the base of the hill. There's a boat dock near here, where you can rent rowing **boats**, or you can get duck-shaped pedal boats from near the south gate – good ways to explore the lake and its banks. On the north side of the lake an impressive **dragon screen**, in good condition, is one of China's largest at 27m long. The Five Dragon Pavilions nearby are supposedly in the shape of a dragon's spine. Over on the other side of the lake, the gardens and rockeries here were popular with Emperor Qianlong, and it's easy to see why – even when the place is crowded at weekends, the atmosphere is tranquil.

The lake area

The area north of Beihai Park has been subject to very little modernization, and the street plan remains a tangle of alleys, centring on the two artificial **Shisha lakes**, created during the Yuan dynasty, and the port for a canal network that served the capital. The choked, grey alleys show Beijing's other, private, face: here you'll see cluttered courtyards and converted palaces, and come across small open spaces where old men sit with their birds. There are also two giant old buildings, the Bell and Drum towers, hidden away among the alleys. *CITS* has cottoned on to the appeal of this area and runs a **hutong tour** (¥160), which leaves daily at 9am and 2pm from the northern entrance of Beihai Park. More imaginative than most of their tours – visitors are biked about in rickshaws – it's very popular with tour groups (ring ☎65254262 for more information). The best way to get around by yourself is certainly by bike. Traffic is light and you're free to dive into any alley you fancy, though you're almost certain to get lost – in which case cycle around until you come to the lake, the only big landmark around. The best point of entry is the *hutong* nearest the northern entrance to Beihai Park – to get here by bus, take trolleybus #111 from Dondan Bei Dajie, or bus #13 from the Yonghe Gong.

One destination to head for is **Prince Gong's Palace** (daily 9am–4.30pm; ¥10), residence of the last Qing emperor's father and the best-kept courtyard house in the city. Follow the curving alley north from Beihai Park's north entrance – Shishaqian Hai (the lower lake) will be on your right – then take the first left, then the first right on to Qianhai Xi Jie. If you're trying to reach the palace directly by bus, you'll have to get off on Dianmen Xi Dajie and walk the same route. The attractive, leafy garden of the palace, split into discreet compounds and imaginatively landscaped, is host to irregular performances of Beijing Opera – though you'll have to time your arrival with that of the tour groups, at around 11am and 4pm to witness these. There are plenty of other **old palaces** in the area, as this was once something of an imperial pleasure ground and home to a number of high officials and distinguished eunuchs. The Palace of Tao Beile, now a school, is just west of here on Liuyin Jie. Doubling back and heading north along the lake side, you'll come to a humpback bridge at the point where the lake is thinnest. Over the bridge is the excellent *Kaorouji Restaurant* (see "Restaurants", p.111), which boasts good views over the lake. To get here from the east, it's the first *hutong* on the right walking south from the Drum Tower. Keep going along the south side of the lake and you'll find a little park about 500m farther up with a bird market in it and beyond that the ramshackle Houhai **antique market**, signposted in English, just before Deshengmennei Dajie. If you're exploring by bike you could consider a diversion out west to the Xu Beihong Museum (see p.101) from here. Back in the *hutongs*, head north along the lakeside and loop around to the east and you'll reach **Song Qingling's Residence** (daily 9am–4.30pm; ¥10), another Qing mansion, with a delicate, spacious garden. Song Qingling, the wife of Sun Yatsen, commands great respect in China and an exhibition inside details her busy life in a dry, admiring tone. From here, an alley will take you on to Gulou Xi Dajie, a major street, at the eastern end of which squats the **Gulou** or Drum Tower (daily 9am–4.30pm; ¥6), a fifteenth-century Ming creation. From this vantage point drums were beaten to mark the hours of day and night and to call imperial officials to meetings. In the gloomy interior is a small exhibition on *hutongs* and a drum you can beat for ¥10. Its twin, the **Zhonglou**, or Bell Tower (daily 9am–4.30pm; ¥6), is visible from here – at the end of a short *hutong*. Originally Ming, it was destroyed by fire and rebuilt in the eighteenth century. It still has its original bell. Both buildings are formidable structures, but a little shabby on close inspection. They stand on the city's main north–south axis – head directly south, going round Jingshan Park, and past the Forbidden City, and you'll eventually come to Qianmen Dajie, a route followed by bus #5.

The northwest

You're more likely to pass through the area northwest of Tian'anmen than stop, as it's on the way to the deservedly popular Summer Palace. The few attractions scattered around here are small scale, but make good points to break a journey farther afield.

Heading west from the south end of Beihai Park along Wenjin Dajie, you'll come to **Fuchenmennei Dajie**, just off Xidan Dajie, the area's shopping district. A couple of places along here make it worth a nose around. Bus #101 from the north exit of the Forbidden City, and #13 from the Yonghe Gong, traverse the street. The **Guangji Si**, headquarters of the China Buddhist Association, is a working Buddhist temple near its eastern end, on the north side of the road, with an important collection of painting and sculpture. There's no entrance fee and though visitors are free to look around, they are not encouraged. Farther west along the street you'll come to a temple on the north side that's been converted into a school – the spirit wall now forms one side of a public lavatory – and at no. 133 is one of China's first sex shops, with separate entrances for men and women, labelled Adam and Eve. Farther on, the massive white dagoba of the **Baita Si** (daily 9am–4pm; ¥5) becomes visible, rising over the rooftops of a labyrinth of *hutongs*; the only access is from Fuchengmennei Dajie. Shaped like an upturned bowl with an ice-cream cone on top, the 35-metre-high dagoba was built to house relics in the Yuan dynasty and designed by a Nepalese architect. The temple at its base is a little shabby, and one of the halls is now used as a doctor's surgery, but the other holds a collection of bronze *lohans*, including one with a beak, small bronze Buddhas and other, weirder Lamaist figures, together with silk and velvet priestly garments, which were unearthed from under the dagoba in 1978.

Continue west and, just before the giant intersection with Fuchengmen Bei Dajie, you'll see Xisantiao Hutong to the north, which leads to the **Former Residence of Lu Xun** (Tues–Sun 9am–4pm; ¥5), a large and extensively renovated courtyard house. Lu Xun (1881–1936) is widely accepted as the greatest modern Chinese writer, who gave up a promising career in medicine to write books with the aim, he declared, of curing thousands with his pithy, satirical stories. A hater of pomposity, he might feel a little uneasy in his house now, where the atmosphere is of uncritical admiration. His possessions have been preserved like relics, incidentally giving a good idea of what Chinese interiors looked like at the beginning of this century, and there's a photo exhibition of his life lauding his achievements. A shop in the new east wing sells busts of the great man, as well as English translations of his work. Worth picking up is *The True Story of Ah Q*, regarded as Lu Xun's greatest tale, a lively, amusing read written in the plain style he favoured as an alternative to the complex classical language of the time. Set in 1911, it's the story of a worthless peasant, epitomizing what the author saw as every character flaw of the Chinese race, who stumbles from disaster to disaster, believing each one to be a triumph. He dreams of revolution and ends up being executed, having understood nothing.

Not far from here, at 53 Xinjiekou Bei Dajie, on the route of bus #22 from Qianmen or #38 from the east end of Fuchingmennei Dajie, the **Xu Beihong Museum** (Tues–Sun 9–11am & 1–4pm; ¥3) is definitely worth the diversion. It is dedicated to a contemporary of Lu Xun who did for Chinese art what he did for literature. Son of a wandering portraitist, Xu Beihong (1895–1953) had to look after his whole family from the age of seventeen after his father died, and spent much of his early life in semi-destitution before receiving the acclaim he deserved. His extraordinary facility is well in evidence here in seven halls which display a huge collection of his work, including many of the ink paintings of horses he was most famous for, but also oil paintings in a Western style, which he produced when studying in France, and large-scale allegorical images which allude to events in China at the time. But the images it is easiest to respond to are his delightful sketches and studies, in ink and pencil, often of his son.

The northeast

The most exciting sight in the north of the city is the **Yonghe Gong**, Tibetan Lama Temple (daily 9am–4pm; ¥10), northeast of the Forbidden City and just south of the Yonghe Gong subway stop. If you see no other temple in the city, this is worth the effort – you won't see many more colourful temples, though it is a little touristy.

It was built towards the end of the seventeenth century as the residence of Prince Yin Zhen. In 1723, when the prince became the Emperor Yong Zheng and moved into the Forbidden City, the temple was retiled in imperial yellow and restricted thereafter to religious use. It became a lamasery in 1744, housing monks from Tibet and also from Inner Mongolia, over which it had a presiding role, supervising the election of the Mongolian Living Buddha, who was chosen by lot from a gold urn. After the civil war in 1949, the Yonghe Gong was declared a national monument and for thirty years was closed; remarkably it escaped the Cultural Revolution.

Visitors are free to wander through the prayer halls and gardens, though the experience is largely an aesthetic rather than a spiritual one. As well as the amazing *mandalas* hanging in side halls, there is some notable statuary. In the Third Hall the draped statues are **nandikesvras**, Buddhas having sex, which earned the lamasery its reputation as China's most illustrious sex manual – the statues were once used to educate emperor's sons. The Hall of the Wheel of Law, behind it, has a gilded bronze statue of the founder of the Yellow Hat Sect and paintings which depict his life, while the thrones next to it are for the Dalai Lamas when they used to come here to teach. In the last, grandest hall, the **Wanfu Pavilion**, an eighteen-metre-high statue of the Maitreya Buddha is made from a single trunk of sandalwood, a gift for Emperor Qianlong from the seventh Dalai Lama. The wood is Tibetan and it took three years to ship it to Beijing.

The lamasery is not just a beautiful building – and with its gardens, a refuge – but it also functions as an active **Tibetan Buddhist centre**, basically for propaganda purposes, to show China guaranteeing and respecting the religious freedom of the minorities, but it's questionable how genuine are the monks you see wandering around. This is where the puppet Panchen Lama chosen by the Chinese state was officially sworn in in 1995, the Dalai Lama's choice of soul boy, a six-year-old child having disappeared (see box, p.984).

Next to the Yonghe Gong, on the west side, is a quiet **hutong** lined with little shops selling religious tapes, incense and images, as well as one, on the corner at no. 67, that just sells stamps. This street, one of the city's oldest, has been home to scholars since the Yuan dynasty and is lined with *pailous*, decorative arches, which once graced many of Beijing's streets – they were torn down in the 1950s as a hindrance to traffic. On the right, about 100m down, the **Confucius Temple** is a rather dry place, used for decades as a museum. In the courtyard, steles record the names of those who studied here and passed the civil service exams. The last few steles are Qing, paid for by the scholars themselves as the emperor refused to fund them. The Main Hall is a dark, haphazard **museum** holding incense burners and musical instruments. At the back, a warehouse-like building holds stele texts of the thirteen Confucian classics, calligraphy which once formed the standard to be emulated by all scholars.

Returning to the Yonghe Gong and heading north, **Ditan Park** (daily 6am–9pm; ¥1) is just 100m away, more interesting as a place to wander among the trees and spot the odd *tai ji* performance than for its small **museum** (¥5) holding the emperor's sedan chair and the enormous altar at which he performed sacrifices to the earth.

Heading back to the centre from the Yonghe Gong by bus or bike you could look in at the **China Art Gallery** (Tues–Sun 9am–5pm; ¥10), at the top end of Wangfujing, on the route of bus #2 which runs north–south between Qianmen and Andingmen Dajie, or trolleybus #104, which runs between Andingmennei Dajie and Beijing Zhan. A huge and draughty building, it rarely holds less than three shows at once, though there's no permanent collection. Shows in the past have included specialist women's and minority exhibitions, even a show of socialist realist propaganda put up not to inspire renewed vigour but as a way to consider the follies of the past. Revolutionary imagery has long had its day and Chinese painting is enjoying something of a renaissance at the moment, with some very interesting work emerging from the Beijing art colleges. You can check them out in the summer, when they hold their degree shows here, and it's also a good place to meet some of the most bohemian Chinese, the art students. Check the *China Daily* for what's on.

The outskirts

The most compelling sights on the outskirts of the city are the lakeside gardens and pavilions of the **Summer Palace** – a recommended escape, summer or winter. The presence of two universities near here is not in itself of much note but they have spawned plenty of cheap **restaurants** and some of the more underground **bars**. It's generally true that all the decent **nightlife** is in the city's northern outskirts, while on the eastern edge you'll find a plethora of bars serving the city's foreign community (see "Drinking and dancing", p.112).

The Zoo, Big Bell Temple and the Summer Palaces

Beijing Zoo, (daily 7.30am–5pm; ¥10) on Xizhimenwei Dajie, marks the edge of the inner city. There's a subway stop, Xizhimen, 1km east of the zoo, and a bus terminus just south of it; bus #7, which you can catch from Fuchingmen Dajie, terminates here. Xizhimen Zhan (Beijing North train station) is north of the subway stop. The zoo itself, flanked on either side by the monumental Capital Gymnasium and Soviet-built Exhibition Centre, is hardly a great attraction. The only part worth visiting, in fact the only part of any zoo in China that's not depressing, is the panda house. You can join the queues to have your photo taken sitting astride a plastic replica, then push your way through to glimpse the living variety – kept in relatively palatial quarters and highly familiar through ritual diplomatic mating exchanges over the last decades. While the pandas lie on their backs in their luxury pad, waving their legs in the air, other animals, less cute or more endangered, slink, pace or flap around their miserable cells.

The **Exhibition Hall**, just before the zoo on Xizhimenwei, is worth a little inspection. It is the one Soviet-style building that really works in Beijing – an elegant, low-level facade with a tapering gold spire (a clear and unusual landmark in this part of the city) whose decor mixes Chinese dragons (on the doors) with the hammer and sickle (on the columns). Although now just one of many exhibition halls in the capital, it does sometimes have international shows, though it's mostly used for trade fairs. It also boasts a Russian restaurant, on a street just west of the hall, which serves surprisingly good borscht, stroganoff and black bread, but it's not cheap. Check out the crazy decor if you're just passing (see "Restaurants", p.111).

South of the zoo, by the bus station, the planetarium has hourly shows (10am–4pm; ¥10), but it's boring, and you're better off heading west to **Zizhuyuan Park**, full of bamboo and courting couples. If you're hungry and it's early evening head south to **Xinjiang Kou**, certainly one of the liveliest culinary experiences of the capital, a street full of restaurants where Beijing's population of Turkic Uighur people hang out. It's west off Sanlihe Lu, about 2km south of the zoo; trolleybus #102 from Yongdingmen, which goes up Xidan Bei Dajie, will get you near. The atmosphere, like the food, comes straight from Urumqi: men with wispy white beards and white hats usher you into their boisterous, smoky restaurants as if you're their oldest friend while doomed sheep, tied up by stalls, bleat contentedly. In summer the street is crammed and benches are put on the road, a good place to sit with a beer. Restaurants sell Uighur staples such as nan bread and spicy beef, while street stalls sell shish kebabs. Tourists don't get here much, but it's popular with foreign students, who come for the cheap food and to buy hashish, which is sold fairly openly.

The **Dazhong Si**, Great Bell Temple (Tues–Sun 8am–4.30pm; ¥5), is actually one of Beijing's most interesting little museums, though it's stuck out on Beisanhuan Lu, the north section of the third ring road, a long way from anywhere; you could visit on the way to or from the Summer Palace if you're travelling by taxi. Displayed to good effect in a converted temple, the exhibits, several hundred **bronze bells** from temples all over the country, are considerable works of art, their surfaces enlivened with relief texts in Chinese and Tibetan, abstract patterns and images of storks and dragons. The odd creature perching on their tops is called a *pulao*, a legendary creature which shrieks when attacked by a whale (the wooden poles with which the bells were struck are carved to look like whales). The smallest bell is the size of a wine cup, the largest, hanging in the back hall, is the size of a house. A Ming creation, called the **King of Bells**, at fifty tonnes it's the biggest and oldest bell in the world and reputedly can be heard up to 40km away. You can climb up to a platform above it to get a closer look at some of the 250,000 characters on its surface, and join Chinese visitors in trying to throw a coin into the small hole in the top. Its method of construction, and the history of Chinese bell-making, are explained in side halls. Tapes on sale of the bells in action are more interesting than they might appear; the shape of Chinese bells dampens vibrations, so they can be effectively used as instruments.

You'll pass **Beijing Daxue** (Beida), the capital university, on your way to the Summer Palace. Originally established and administered by the Americans at the beginning of this century, it stood on Coal Hill in Jingshan Park and was moved to its present site in 1953. Now busy with new contingents of foreign students from the West, two decades ago it was half-deserted when the Cultural Revolution saw students and teachers alike dispersed for "open schooling" or re-education. Later, in 1975–6, Beida was the power base of the radical left in their campaign against Deng Xiaoping. It's the most prestigious university in China, although recently intake has suffered as new students are put off by the compulsory year of political instruction at military camps, introduced after 1989. The technical college, Qinghua, is not far from here, to the east, though there's little point visiting the drab campus unless you want to get a room in the foreigners' dormitory (see p.83). Around the gates of both universities you'll find small, inexpensive **restaurants and bars** catering for the students.

Yuanmingyuan

Beijing's original Summer Palace, the **Yuanmingyuan** (daily 9am–6pm; ¥10), is a thirty-minute walk north of Beida, on the route of bus #375, which you catch from a terminus just north of Xizhimen subway stop, or bus #322, which leaves from a terminus outside the zoo. Built by the Qing Emperor Kangxi in the early eighteenth century, the palace, nicknamed China's Versailles by Europeans, once boasted the largest royal gardens in the world – with some two hundred pavilions and temples set around a series of lakes and natural springs. Marina Warner recreates the scene in *The Dragon Empress*:

> *Scarlet and golden halls, miradors, follies and gazebos clustered around artificial hills and lakes. Tranquil tracts of water were filled with fan tailed goldfish with telescopic eyes, and covered with lotus and lily pads; a superabundance of flowering shrubs luxuriated in the gardens; antlered deer wandered through the grounds; ornamental ducks and rare birds nestled on the lakeside.*

Today, however, there is little enough to hang your imagination upon. In 1860 the entire complex was burnt and destroyed by British and French troops, ordered by the

Earl of Elgin to make the imperial court "see reason" during the Opium Wars. The troops had previously spent twelve days looting the imperial treasures, many of which found their way to the Louvre and British Museum – their return as yet undemanded.

The park extends over 350 hectares but the only really identifiable ruins are the **Hall of Tranquillity** in the northeastern section. The stone and marble remains of fountains and columns hint at how fascinating the original must once have been, with its marriage of European Rococo decoration and Chinese motifs. Today it's a popular picnic spot, particularly among foreign residents in Beijing, who perhaps "ponder... imperial powers destroying human civilization" as a sign instructs. The government is jazzing the place up with a programme of restoration and construction, but this remains an attraction wholly eclipsed by the new Summer Palace.

The Summer Palace

Yiheyuan, usually just referred to as the **Summer Palace** (daily 8am–7pm, buildings close at 4.30pm; ¥35, students ¥2), is certainly worth the effort to seek out. Take the same buses that go to Yuanmingyuan and get off a few stops later, at the terminus. This is one of the loveliest spots in Beijing, a vast public park, two-thirds lake, where the latterday imperial court would decamp during the hottest months of the year. The site is perfect, surrounded by hills, cooled by the lake and sheltered by garden landscaping. Surviving another bout of European aggression in 1900, the impressive buildings are spread out along the lakeside and connected by a suitably majestic gallery.

There have been summer imperial pavilions at Yiheyuan since the eleventh century, although the present layout is essentially eighteenth-century, created by the Manchu Emperor Qianlong. However, the key character associated with the palace is the Empress Dowager Cixi, who ruled over the fast-disintegrating Chinese empire from 1861 until her death in 1908. Yiheyuan was very much her pleasure ground. She rebuilt the palaces in 1888 and determinedly restored them in 1902 – her ultimate flight of fancy being the construction of a magnificent marble boat from the very funds intended for the Chinese navy. Whether her misappropriations had any real effect on the empire's path is hard to determine, but it certainly speeded the decline, with China suffering heavy naval defeats during the war with Japan.

The **palaces** are built to the north of the lake, on and around Wanshou Shan(Longevity Hill) and many remain intimately linked with Cixi – anecdotes about whom are staple fare of the numerous guides. To enjoy the site, however, you need know very little. Like Beihai, the park, its lake and pavilions, form a startling visual array, like a traditional landscape painting brought to life.

Most visitors enter through the **East Gate**, where the buses stop, above which is the main palace compound, including the **Renshoudian** (Hall of Benevolence and Longevity), a majestic hall where the empress and her predecessors gave audience. It contains much of the original nineteenth-century furniture, including an imposing throne. Beyond to the right, is the **Deheyuan** (Palace of Virtue and Harmony), dominated by a three-storey **theatre**, complete with trap doors for the appearances and disappearances of the actors. Theatre was one of Cixi's main passions and she sometimes took part in performances, dressed as Guanyin, the goddess of mercy. With a neat sense of irony, the next main building, the **Yulantang** (Jade Waves Palace) on the lakeside, was for ten years the prison of the Emperor Guangxu – kept in captivity here, as a minor, while Cixi exercised his powers. Just to the west is the dowager's own principal residence, the **Leshoutang** (Hall of Joy and Longevity).

From here to the northwest corner of the lake runs the **Long Gallery**, the nine-hundred-metre covered way, painted with mythological scenes and flanked by various temples and pavilions. It is said that no pair of lovers can walk through without emerging betrothed. Near the west end of the gallery is the infamous **marble boat**, completed by Cixi with the purloined naval cash and regarded by her acolytes as a suitably witty and defiant gesture. Close by, and the tourist focus of this site, is a jetty with **rowing boats** for rent (¥10 per hour). Boating in the lake is a popular pursuit, with locals as much as foreigners, and well worth the money. You can dock again over below Longevity Hill and row out to the two **bridges** – the Jade Belt on the western side and Seventeen Arched on the east. In winter, the Chinese skate on the lake here, an equally spectacular sight, and skates are available for rent.

EATING, DRINKING AND ENTERTAINMENT

You're spoilt for choice when it comes to food in Beijing. Splurging in classy **restaurants** is a great way to spend your evenings, as prices in even the most luxurious places are very competitive and a lot more affordable than their equivalent in the West. Beijing has a great deal of entertainment options, too, and it's well worth seeking them out; remember you won't have much opportunity outside the capital. Beijing is no twenty-four-hour city like Hong Kong, but there is a promising **bar and club scene** worth sampling, if only for the strange cultural juxtapositions it throws up. If you want to check out a Chinese disco or indigenous rock band, this is the place to do it, and again, a night on the town won't break your budget. **Shopping** is another diverting pastime, with the best choice of souvenirs and consumables in the country. In particular, Beijing still has a collection of intriguing little markets offering an appealing and affordable alternative to the new giant malls.

Eating

Nowhere on the Chinese mainland has the culinary wealth of Beijing, with every style of **Chinese food** available, just about any Asian, and a smattering of world cuisines. Amongst all this abundance it's sometimes easy to forget that **Beijing** has its own culinary tradition – specialities well worth trying are **Beijing duck** (*Beijing kaoya*) and **Mongolian hotpot**. Beijing duck appears in Chinese restaurants worldwide and consists of small pieces of meat which you dip in plum sauce, then wrap with chopped onions in a pancake. It's very rich and packs a massive cholesterol count. Mongolian hotpot is healthier, a poor man's fondue, involving a large pot of boiling stock, usually heated from underneath the table, into which you dip strips of mutton, cabbage and noodles, then if you're really committed, drink the rest as soup.

There's ample opportunity to eat **Western food** in Beijing, though it generally costs a little more than Chinese. **French** food is currently fashionable with the nouveaux riches, though it's pretty mediocre and expensive. An exception is the excellent *Vie de France* chain, which has brought great French baking to Beijing at a fraction of what it costs in the West – and no praise is high enough for their coffee, about the only decent stuff in the whole country. **German** food is better, though again expensive, with a number of outlets in the more exclusive parts of town. If you really want the comforts of the familiar, try international places such as the *Hard Rock Café* – everything just like at home, including the prices. **Japanese** and **Korean** cuisine is mainly available from restaurants in upmarket hotels, though it's possible to eat both without breaking your budget, and they're well worth trying. Unusual cuisines on offer include "health-keep-

BEIJING: RESTAURANTS

Beancurd	豆花饭庄	*dòuhuā fànzhuāng*
Bianyifang Roast Duck	便宜坊烤鸭店	*biányìfáng kǎoyādiàn*
Broadway Café	百老汇	*báilǎohuì*
Compare Past Misery with Present Happiness	忆苦思甜大杂院	*yìkǔsītián dàzáyuàn*
Confucian Heritage	孔膳堂饭庄	*kǒngshàn táng fàndiàn*
Duyichu	都一处烧麦馆	*dūyīchù shāomài guǎn*
Fangshan	仿膳饭店	*fǎngshàn fàndiàn*
Gongdelin	功德林素菜馆	*gōngdélín sùcài guǎn*
Goubuli Baozi	狗不理包子铺	*gǒubùlǐ bāozi pù*
Henan	河南大饭庄	*hénán dàfànzhuāng*
Hongbinlou	鸿傧楼饭庄	*hóngbīnlóu fànzhuāng*
Kaorouji	烤肉季	*kǎoròujì*
Kaorouwan	烤肉宛饭庄	*kǎoròuwǎn fànzhuāng*
KFC	肯德基家乡鸡	*kěndéjī jiāxiāngjī*
Laosunjia	老孙家饭店	*lǎosūnjiā fànzhuāng*
Laozhengxing	老正兴饭庄	*lǎozhèngxīng fànzhuāng*
Makai	吗凯餐厅	*mákǎi cāntīng*
Maxim's	马克西姆餐厅	*mǎkèxīmǔ cāntīng*
McDonald's	麦当劳餐厅	*màidāngláo cāntīng*
Mexican Wave	墨西哥风味餐	*mòxīgē fēngwèicān*
Moscow	莫斯科餐厅	*mòsīkē cāntīng*
Omar Khayyam	味美佳餐馆	*wèiměijiā cānguǎn*
Pizza Hut	必胜客	*bìshèngkè*
Qianmen Quanjude Roast Duck	前门全聚德烤鸭店	*qiánmén quánjùdé kǎoyādiàn*
Quanjude Roast Duck	全聚德烤鸭店	*quánjùdé kǎoyādiàn*
Shaguoju	沙锅居	*shāguōjū*
Sichuan	四川酒楼	*sìchuān jiǔlóu*
Tongshengxiang	同盛祥馆	*tóngshèngxiáng guǎn*
Vie de France	大磨坊面包	*dàmòfáng miànbāo*
Wangfujing Quanjude Roast Duck	王府井全聚德烤鸭店	*wángfǔjǐng quánjùdé kǎoyādiàn*
Windows on the World	世界之窗餐厅	*shìjiè zhīchuāng cāntīng*
Xi'an	西安饭庄	*xī'ān fànzhuāng*

ing" food, a form of diet therapy originating from traditional Chinese medicine, and "nostalgia cuisine", featuring dishes from the Cultural Revolution.

Fast food comes in two forms: the Chinese version, a canteen-style serving, usually of noodles in a polystyrene packet, which you find in department stores or buy from street stalls; and Western imports such as *Pizza Hut, McDonald's* and *KFC*, which have made a considerable impact and are now greatly imitated. *McDonald's* arrived in 1992 and there are now seventeen branches, often so packed that getting served is an experience not unlike that of buying a train ticket. Prices are cheaper than in the West, but expensive by Chinese standards. **Street food**, mostly noodle dishes, is widely available, though not in the centre, where vendors are shooed away by the police. Avoid the ice cream vendors who hang around the parks as their homemade wares are often of a dubious standard.

If you want to get a picnic together, or have the facilities to try some self-catering, the capital is well stocked with **supermarkets**. The *Wellcome Supermarket* – part of the Hong Kong chain – in the basement of the World Trade Centre is the most impressive, though everything costs about fifty percent more than you would pay in Hong Kong. The supermarket on the first floor of the *Friendship Store* is not nearly as good, but it does sell butter, cheese and Western beers. For other Western ingredients, at Western prices, head out to the foreigners' ghetto of Sanlitun in the northeast of the city where you'll find a small but choice *Friendship Supermarket* at 5 Sanlitun Lu, and even a shop specializing in Italian cheeses farther south, on the other side of the street from the cluster of bars. A few hundred metres west of the the *Jinghua Hotel*, the *Asia Supermarket* is handy for snacks and for buying tea to take home.

Breakfast, snacks and fast food

Many visitors find the Chinese **breakfast** of dumplings and glutinous rice served in canteens bland and unappealing, but the classic Beijing breakfast snack sold by street vendors is definitely worth trying – vegetables wrapped in an omelette wrapped in a pancake – deftly made in thirty seconds (¥2). Most hotels offer some form of Western breakfast, with the best choice offered by the cheap backpacker restaurants – easily the best of these is the *Friendship Restaurant* in the car park of the *Jinghua Hotel* (see p.83). Alternatively, head for a branch of *Vie de France* where coffee and a croissant cost just ¥9. Every expensive hotel also has a **café**, plush and sophisticated, but not cheap – expect to spend around ¥25 for a coffee, though you can sit for as long as you like.

Baskin Robbins, Jianguomen Dajie. This quality ice cream store shares its premises with *Vie de France*, stocking all the usuals plus some fairly esoteric flavours. Open 24hrs.

Broadway Café, Jianguomen Dajie, on the west side of the *Friendship Store*. This costly café aims for New York sophistication, which is fine if you don't mind paying ¥20 for a coffee.

CVIK Building, Jianguomen Dajie. The basement canteen here, haunt of exhausted upmarket shoppers, is a good place for a snack.

Duyichu, 36 Qianmen Dajie. This restaurant has been in business for over a century, though you'd never guess from the bland modern decor, and has built up an enviable reputation for its steamed dumplings, which you can eat on the spot or take away. One of the best places in the area for a light lunch.

Fine Arts Institute, 5 Xiaowei Hutong, just off Wangfujing – see p.83 for details of how to get here. The downstairs canteen in the dormitory building, offers simple and very cheap food.

Goubuli, 155 Dianmenwai Dajie, just south of the Drum Tower. A branch of the Tianjin institution, this place sells delicious dumplings (*baozi*) for a few yuan. You can eat them here – the downstairs canteen is cheaper than upstairs – or take them home, as most of the customers do.

KFC, Qianmen Xi Dajie, just south of Qianmen Gate. Opened in 1987, this was the first Western fast-food chain to colonize China, and has long been overtaken for verve and style by its nearby competitors.

McDonald's, 31 Dongchang'an Jie; Qianmen Xi Dajie (right by the *KFC*); Xidan Bei Dajie (200m north of Fuxingmen Dajie); and branches all over the city. Few visitors successfully avoid the flagship branch on Dongchang'an Jie, at the southern end of Wangfujing, whatever they may feel about the food. This giant two-storey restaurant is one of the largest *McDonald's* in the world and a fashionable haunt for Beijing's bright young things. The other two central branches are both underground, with a nautical theme in Xidan, and surprisingly grotty toilets in Qianmen.

Pizza Hut, 33 Zhushikou Xi Jie; Jianguomen Dajie (just west of the *Friendship Store*); Xidan Bei Dajie (the southern end of the road, on the eastern side.) The Xidan branch is fearsomely busy and you may well have to queue for a seat; quietest is the one on Zhushikou.

Vie de France, Qianmen Xi Dajie (by *McDonald's*); Jianguomen Dajie (just east of the *Friendship Store*); Xichang'an Jie (on the south side of the street, just east of the intersection with Xidan Bei Dajie); basement of the Lufthansa Centre. This great little French bakery has pizza, croissant, delicious fresh cakes and the best coffee in the capital, all very reasonably priced. The most popular branch is the one beside the *Friendship Store*, where competition for seats is fierce. Watch your bags here as it's a popular place for thieves.

Restaurants

All the expensive **hotels** have several well-appointed restaurants, where the atmosphere is sedate but prices are sometimes not as high as you might expect; look out for their special offers, advertised in the city's listings magazines. Local restaurants, though, are cheaper and livelier. Expect to eat earlier than you would in Western cities; you'll need to arrive for lunch around noon and for dinner at 6pm. Few places stay open after 10pm, and most close at 9.30pm. Restaurants usually have two, sometimes more, **dining rooms**, which are priced differently – though the food comes from the same kitchen. The cheapest one is usually the open-plan area on the first floor. Restaurateurs sometimes try to usher foreigners upstairs away from the cheaper area, but you can refuse – you won't be the first. It's rarely worth phoning ahead to book a table; if you do, you will always end up in the most expensive sections. Telephone numbers have been included in the reviews below only for the more expensive and popular restaurants.

Qianmen and farther south

Beancurd, 27 Guangqumenwai Dajie. The decor may not be inspiring, but you can't fault the Sichuan-style food. Dishes are rated on the English menu according to how spicy they are. Moderately priced.

Butt's Place (*Chapatti Connection*), off Dongbinhe Lu. For the best chicken masala this side of the Himalayas, and a seedy ambience imported straight out of the backstreets of Kabul, search out this Pakistani restaurant 100m down the dingy alley on the east side of the *Qiaoyuan Hotel*. As a meeting place for Beijing's itinerant population of Central Asians – traders, students, smugglers – it's friendly and boisterous, and not the place to eat a quiet meal or stay sober.

Confucian Heritage, 3 Liulichang. Pleasantly quiet and relaxed, this small restaurant specializes in Shandong cuisine. Try a crunchy fried scorpion (¥30) for novelty value, though it really doesn't taste of much. Less exotic dishes are a lot cheaper.

Gongdelin, 158 Qianmen Nan Dajie. Well worth supporting, this odd place, the capital's only vegetarian restaurant, serves Shanghai dishes with names like "the fire is singeing the snow-capped mountains". The food is excellent – even the meat imitations – and very cheap at around ¥30 per head, a little more if you eat upstairs.

Health Food Restaurant, *Tianqiao Hotel*, 13 Xijing Lu. Recipes at this elegant if pricey place are based on traditional Chinese medicine. The staff will explain what food is good for what – eat lamb and beef for the kidneys, fruit for the skin, sour food for the liver and sweet for the lungs. Around ¥100 per head, a lot more if you choose the ginseng or snake dishes.

Laozhengxing, 46 Qianmen Dajie. This quiet place serves Shanghai cuisine, a little on the oily side for most people, but menus with pictures of the dishes on make it foreigner-friendly. Less expensive downstairs than upstairs.

Qianmen Quanjude Roast Duck, 32 Qianmen Dajie (☎67011379). "The Great Wall and Roast Duck, try both to have a luck," says a ditty by the entrance to this Beijing institution. It's professional and proficient, if obvious and touristy, though there's nothing wrong with the food. Not cheap, with lots of extra charges added to the bill – expect to pay over ¥150 per head.

Quanjude Roast Duck, 14 Qianmen Xi Dajie (☎63018833). The size of this giant eatery – seating over two thousand – has earned it its "Super Duck" moniker. Prices the same as at the Qianmen branch.

Jianguomen Dajie and around

Gyoen Teppanyaki, *Jinglun Hotel*, 3 Jianguomenwai Dajie. Beautifully presented Japanese dishes in elegant surroundings, but it's not cheap; over ¥200 per person.

Justine's, *Jianguo Hotel*, 5 Jianguomenwai Dajie. A simple and elegant diner with the best wine list in the capital. The food is mostly Western – try the lobster soup or grilled lamb. Around ¥150 per person.

Mexican Wave, Dongdaqiao Lu. This cosy bistro with a relaxed atmosphere is aimed at, and deservedly popular with, the expats from the embassy compounds nearby. The ambience is very Western, and about the only thing to remind you that you are in China is the barman's accent. The set lunch menu (¥50) changes daily, is tasty and good value, as are the many pizza options.

Omar Khayyam, Asia Pacific Building, 8 Yabao Lu (☎65139988 ext 20188). This upmarket Indian restaurant is very popular with wealthy young Chinese. The Indian manager and his staff are friendly and helpful and the fare is authentic, with *lassis* and *masala chai* on the menu as well as Indian staples such as *mutter paneer* (made with tofu) and *sag aloo*. At least ¥100 per head.

Saigon Inn, Third Floor, *Gloria Plaza Hotel*, 28 Jianguomenwai Dajie, next to the *CITS* office. This restaurant specializes in Vietnamese cuisine, and is pleasingly cheap considering its opulence. You can eat well for less than ¥150 per person, and the set lunch, at ¥50 per person, is very good value.

Sichuan Restaurant, L2, World Trade Centre, 1 Jianguomenwai Dajie. A plush place serving Sichuan cuisine. The hotpot, at ¥170 per person, is recommended.

Windows on the World, 28th and 29th floors, CITIC Building, 19 Jianguomenwai Dajie (☎65002255 ext 2828). The 28th-floor restaurant is perhaps the best place in the capital to eat Cantonese food; the 29th- does Western and Oriental dishes with an excellent seafood hotpot. The view is pretty good too. Figure on spending at least ¥100 per person.

Xidan and around

Compare Past Misery with Present Happiness, 17 Picai Hutong. Specializing in nostalgia cuisine – food from the 1960s – this restaurant sounds faddish, but in fact is one of the nicest in the capital. Honest country cooking, cheap and lots of it, is served in a small, homely-looking room decorated with 1960s memorabilia in a converted courtyard house. There's no English menu, but everything is highly recommended, if you don't mind eating under Mao's smiling countenance.

Hongbinlou, 82 Xi Chang'an Jie. It may be over 150 years old, but this Muslim restaurant could still improve its service (slow) and decor (dingy). However, the food is fine, with a wide range of popular dishes, including Beijing duck, as well as exotica such as sheep's eyes. The cheap dining hall is the first room on the right at the top of the stairs.

Laosunjia, 5 Jingjidao, Erlong Lu. A branch of the famous Xi'an restaurant, this is one of the best places in the area, and worth the effort to hunt it down. It's buried in the alleys about 200m north of Fuxingmen Dajie – head north up the first *hutong* on the west side of the *Minzu Hotel*, then take the first left, then first right and the restaurant is in front of you. The Muslim cuisine here is excellent and the house staple is *paomo* (¥12), a stew into which you break cakes of bread. Wash it down with eight treasures tea. A novelty feature is the uniformed tea man and his kettle, with a spout as long as an arm; it takes some skill to wield as the water shoots out almost horizontally, requiring him to stand some distance from the cup.

Sichuan, 51 Rongxian Hutong. Tucked in the first alley on the left as you go south down Xuanwumennei Dajie, this restaurant, dramatically housed in an old palace, serves fiery Sichuan cuisine. There's a variety of dining halls; the cheapest is at the back of the courtyard, on the right.

Wangfujing and around

Bianyifang Roast Duck, 2 Chongwenmenwai Dajie (☎67112244). The cheapest of the roast duck outlets – head through the first dining hall into the second, less pricey one, where a whole duck is only ¥80. It's always busy, so arrive early.

Fortune Garden, *Palace Hotel*, Jingyu Hutong. Stylish, upmarket Cantonese restaurant.

Maxim's, 2 Chongwenmen Xi Dajie. A branch of the famous French restaurant whose opulent interior certainly looks the part, but the food is a little mundane, and very expensive, with meals costing well over ¥200 per person.

Sawasdee, First Floor, *Novotel Hotel*, 88 Dengshikou. A well-appointed restaurant and one of the very few in the capital offering Thai food.

Tongshengxiang, Wangfujing Nan Kou. On the southeast corner of Chang'an Jie, opposite *McDonald's*, and offering a cheap lunchtime alternative. The *paomuo* here (see *Laosunjia* above) costs ¥13.

Wangfujing Quanjude Roast Duck, 13 Shuaifuyuan Hutong (☎65253310). Smaller than the others in the chain, this one earned its unfortunate nickname, the "Sick Duck", thanks to the proximity of a hospital.

The north

Fangshan, Beihai Park (☎64011879). Superbly situated on the central island in Beihai Park, there is no better place to sample imperial cuisine in Beijing. You are advised to book first, and it's expensive, around ¥200 a head.

Hard Rock Café, 8 Dongsanhuan Bei Lu. American restaurant, with a bar and a disco, the same as every other one, selling T-shirts for the stylistically challenged. A meal will set you back about ¥100. Beers ¥35.

Health Restaurant, *Xiyuan Hotel*, opposite the zoo. This upmarket place offers medicinal cuisine –more appetizing than it sounds – based on the different effect foods have on the body. Try a ginseng dish if you've got a cold, or tomato for fever, though there's no reason not to eat here if you're perfectly healthy as the food is great if expensive.

Leading Wind Grill Garden, *Xiyuan Hotel*, 1 Sanlihe Lu. A sumptuous Korean place that's not as expensive as it looks. Expect to pay around ¥150 per person. Try the *kimchi* (spicy winter vegetables) as a starter before moving on to a fish dish.

Lufthansa Centre, Beisanhuan Dong Lu. There are plenty of upmarket restaurants in this shopping complex including the *Trattoria* (☎64653388 ext 5707) for Italian food, which does free pizza delivery, or the *Brauhaus* (☎64653388 ext 5732) for German fare. Their pork and sauerkraut meal for two for ¥135 is about as cheap a meal as you'll get around here. Below, in the basement, *Sorabol* (☎64651845) specializes in Korean cuisine.

Japanese Bar, the west gate of Beijing Daxue. This tiny sushi bar is aimed at the Japanese students staying at the university, and it's about the only place offering affordable Japanese food in the capital. It's warm and welcoming, with a friendly proprietor, and an atmosphere that's rather more authentically Japanese than in the smarter restaurants in town. It's worth the trek out here: go to the west gate of Beijing Daxue, and follow the road – more of a dirt track– heading west; the restaurant is about 100m down the track, advertised by a papercut of a demon's head. The menu is in Chinese and Japanese, but there are plenty of pictures around; point at whatever looks tasty, and it shouldn't set you back more than ¥100.

Kaorouji, 37 Shichahai. In the northern *hutongs*, close to the Drum Tower, this Muslim place takes advantage of its great location on the shore of Shisha Hu, with big windows and balcony tables in summer. From the Drum Tower head south down Dianmenwai Dajie, and take the first *hutong* on the right. The restaurant is a short walk down here, just before the bridge. There's no English menu, prices are moderate and you get a sesame roll instead of rice.

Kaorouwan, 93 Fuxingmennei Dajie (☎66057707). Another Muslim place with a good selection of beef dishes. It could do with some livening up, however.

Makai, 3 Di'anmenwai Dajie. This big place serving Hunan cuisine is a little too tourist-friendly to feel very authentic. Nothing wrong with the food, though, and it's not too expensive, around ¥50 per head.

Moscow Restaurant. Beijing's only Russian restaurant is a strange place, 200m north up the first road on the west side of the Exhibition Centre by the zoo. The best thing about it is the crazed decor – the main hall is a ballroom full of knobbly columns and chandeliers, which you'll have plenty of time to appreciate as service isn't speedy. The food is authentic, though, with borscht and stroganoff on the menu. The sweetcorn soup is especially recommended. Expect to pay around ¥100 per head, and get there early as the hall is converted to a ballroom at 8pm.

Shaguoju, 60 Xisi Nan Dajie (☎66021126). New, uninspiring hotel-lobby style decor undermines this place's status as one of the capital's most venerable restaurants, famous for its pork dishes. It's fairly reasonably priced, however.

T.G.I. Friday, Dongsanhuan Lu, 300m south of the *Zhaolong Hotel*. Bland American food in an atmosphere that's a little more sedate than the *Hard Rock Café*. Expect to pay about ¥100 per person. Draught beer is ¥20.

Xi'an Restaurant, 20 Xinjiekou Nan Dajie. The decor in this large, upmarket place is a little uninspiring but the Shaanxi-style food is good.

Nightlife and entertainment

Beijing's **nightlife** and **entertainment** scene is recovering fast from the moral clamp-down following the Communist takeover, when the restrictive definitions of the state meant that "bourgeois" bars and tea houses disappeared and were replaced by an artificial emphasis on traditional Chinese culture, especially opera and formal theatre, often worthy to the point of tedium, and at its worst when dealing with revolutionary subject matter. Nowadays nobody is much interested in this sort of stuff, and modern Beijingers, who suddenly find themselves with a disposable income, living through comparatively liberal times, just want to have fun.

However, in the 1980s, the Chinese government, alarmed at the direction city youth was headed, made disco dancing illegal. The Minister of Culture berated the younger generation for its pollution by "stinking bourgeois lifestyles dedicated to nothing more than having a good time, drinking, idling and hedonism". But, such was the power of popular culture that, following widespread disobedience, this was the one political campaign that failed. It was quietly dropped in 1983 and the floodgates were allowed to open almost unopposed.

Beijing these days offers much more than the karaoke and bland hotel bars you'll find in many other Chinese cities. A trend for huge **discos** swept the city in the late 1980s, and they are still popular, packed every night with young, affluent Chinese. You'll find a disco (*disike*) in every Chinese city today, but the slickest and most proficient are here in Beijing. For foreigners, the interest probably lies in observing as much as participating, as the experience offered is an odd amalgam of Western and Chinese culture, from the music, Chinese pop with a techno back beat, to the style of dancing, a kind of regimented disco, where everyone follows the lead of a dancer on stage. The formula is always the same: a few hours of gentle dance music, followed by the slushy half-hour, when a singer comes on stage and dancers pair off, followed by a more raucous last hour or two when only the serious clubbers are left and the mood becomes much less restrained. The atmosphere is permissive but only to a point, and you'll see PSB men at the side of the dance floor peering into the dry ice to ensure that no crimes against morality take place.

The fashion for the 1990s, however, is for **bars**. Originally aimed at the city's foreign community, these have caught on in a big way and are now patronized by a cross-cultural clientele. **Music** and **performance arts**, too, show a strong Western influence, developed parallel to, and sometimes merging with, more traditional forms. Live music on offer ranges from zither and bamboo flute tunes in tea houses, to philharmonic orchestras at the Concert Hall, and beyond, to gigs by new bands such as Cobra, Beijing's all-girl grunge group. Most visitors take in at least a taste of **Beijing Opera** and the superb Chinese **acrobats** – highly recommended – both of which seem pretty timeless. In contrast, the contemporary theatrical scene is changing fast. A recent development has been a fashion for Chinese translations of Western **plays**, such as *The Mousetrap*, or homegrown dramatists experimenting with foreign forms, such as Gao Zingjian's *Bus Stop* – a kind of Chinese Theatre of the Absurd.

Cinemas these days are dedicated to feeding a seemingly insatiable appetite for kung fu movies rather than edifying the populace, although there is plenty of opportunity to catch the serious and fairly controversial movies emerging from a new wave of younger film-makers.

Drinking and dancing

Most of the **bars** are clustered around **Sanlitun**, the embassy compound in the north-east and within staggering distance of one another. It's just inside the third ring road

– take the subway to Dongzhimen, then get bus #113 east. Only a selection of the bars have been included here, just head north up Sanlitun Lu and see what catches your eye. They all offer draught beer at Western prices, and are generally much livelier than any of the hotel bars. Strategically placed around them, small cafés offer sobering blasts of coffee. You could also try your luck around the gates of **Beijing University** (Beida), where there are a few much more low-key speakeasies, hardly visible from the street, attracting a more alternative crowd, mostly students, where prices are lower than in city bars. You can get into the area on bus #375, which you catch from a terminus just north of Xizhimen subway stop, or bus #322, which leaves from a terminus outside the zoo. Other lively places for a beer are **Xinjiang Kou** (see p.103, the place to go on hot summer nights, and, of course, the backpacker restaurants – fun, if a little unadventurous. Most bars are open until around midnight, though they are at their liveliest about 10pm.

Beijing's **discos** are a long way out of the centre and the only practical way to get to them (or certainly back) is by taxi. They may not be the hippest venues on the planet but they're certainly spirited, and cheaper than a night out in a Western capital.

Bars

Brauhaus, Basement, World Trade Centre, Jianguomen Dajie. A civilized German bar – come here to read the Western papers provided or write postcards. Food is expensive, but the draught beer, at ¥20 a glass, is reasonably priced.

CD Café, Dongsanhuan Bei Lu, ten minutes' walk south of the *Great Wall Sheraton Hotel*. One of the most Chinese places, perhaps trying a bit too hard to be hip, but worth popping into. Chinese jazz musicians play here occasionally. Beers ¥15.

Howl, 100m west down the road opposite the west gate of Beida (the university). A shabby little bar usually full of students. Cheap, but very out of the way.

Jazz Ya, 18 Sanlitun Lu. This mellow place is tucked back from the road and can be hard to find; look for the yellow sign down an alley next to *Bella Coffee*.

Metro Café, 6 Gongti Xi Lu. A combination café and bar that tries for Continental style. Happy Hour, two drinks for the price of one, is Mon–Fri 5.30–8pm.

Rasput–Inn, 1 Sanlitun Lu. A Sino-Russian bar that sees some of the heaviest drinking and most intense chess-playing in the capital, especially during Happy Hour, 5–7pm.

Pig and Whistle, *Holiday Inn* Lido, Jichang Lu. An English-style pub with none of the charisma of the *Poachers Inn*.

Poachers Inn, 7 Sanlitun Lu. Deservedly, Beijing's best-known bar, this expat watering hole is more English than most pubs in England, with darts, recruiting posters and a stuffed pheasant over the bar, but it's accessible, casual and cosy. Draught beer is ¥20 a pitcher. It's very popular on Thursdays, when a jazz band plays, and on Friday and Saturday when the attached club holds a disco (and occasional gigs), where you won't hear the Village People or 2 Unlimited.

Underground Club, 1A Jianguomenwai. This small place is a mixture of restaurant, bar and disco along the lines of the *Hard Rock Café*, and is aimed at foreigners and rich young Chinese. Girls get in free except on Friday and Saturday (daily 6pm–2am; ¥30).

Waterhole, 3 Guanghua Xi Lu. Another expat pub, often full of embassy staff. Drinks are ¥20. Best at Happy Hour between 5pm and 8pm.

Discos

JJs, 74–76 Xinjiekou Bei Dajie. This cavernous club has lasers and a sci-fi theme, as well as novelties such as imported British DJs and scantily clad Russian dancing girls. Rumours of a back room where the girls reveal a lot more than their fake-tanned midriffs seem unfounded. A chic crowd bops to a mild cocktail of techno, reggae and house (daily 8pm–2am; ¥50, Sat ¥80). Take bus #22 from Qianmen.

Nasa, at the corner of Xueyuan Lu and Xitucheng Lu, just north of Sanhuan Bei Lu in Haidian district. The most alternative of Beijing's clubs and probably the most accessible to Westerners, where you can watch slim Chinese girls playing air guitar and teenagers breakdancing to Chinese rap. The haunt mostly of students and arty types, dress is black on black and music, which gets better later on, includes a healthy dose of grunge, rap and hardish techno among the pop and pap. Beers are ¥20, but no one seems to mind if you take your own (daily 8pm–2am; ¥40, Sat ¥60).

Nightman, junction of Qishen Nan Lu and Xibahe Zhong Jie, 100m south of the *SAS Royal Hotel*. This place attracts a lot of the most affluent young Chinese, and is said to be popular with the capital's very low-profile gay underground (daily 8pm–2am; ¥50, Sat ¥80).

Oriental Number One, Asian Games Village, Anding Lu. The biggest club in China, claimed to be the largest in Asia, this cavern still manages to pack out nightly, and features occasional performances by Chinese pop stars (daily 8pm–2am; ¥50, Sat ¥80).

Live music, film and cultural events

There's always a healthy variety of events taking place in the city. Check the *China Daily* or *Beijing This Month* for listings. For the best rundown of more alternative happenings, though, including gigs, try to track down a copy of *Beijing Scene*. You should see a copy in most of the bars.

Live music
The **Beijing Concert Hall** at 1 Beixinhua Jie, just off Xichang'an Jie, exists to sate the considerable appetite in the capital for **classical music**, with regular concerts by Beijing's resident orchestra, and visiting orchestras from the rest of China and overseas. For a schedule, phone ☎62047755, then dial ext 56789 when you hear a beep. For the box office, phone ☎ 66055812. Performances begin at 7.15pm every night and tickets are ¥30.

For **contemporary music**, try the *Poachers Inn* (see "Bars" above), which holds occasional gigs by local and expat rock and pop bands, as well as regular jazz, the *CD Café*, or the *Sanwei Bookstore* (see p.116). Giant gigs are held at the **Workers' Stadium**, in the northeast of the city, off Gongren Tiyuchang Bei Lu (bus #110 along Dongdaqiao), mostly featuring Chinese pop stars, though Elton John and Bjork have played here.

Film
There are plenty of **cinemas** showing Chinese films and dubbed Western films, usually action movies. Around ten Western films are picked by the government for national release every year, and shown in Beijing first; *The Lion King* and *True Lies* were the hits of 1996. Previous films to achieve state approval include *First Blood*, which introduced Chinese audiences to Rambo.

Some of the largest screens are the *Capital Cinema* at 46 Chang'an Jie, near Xidan (☎66055510), the *Dahua Cinema* at 82 Dongdan Bei Dajie (☎65127234) and the *Shengli Movie Theatre* at 55 Xisi Dong Dajie (☎66013130). Tickets cost ¥5–30. For **Western films**, in English with Chinese subtitles, try the *Holiday Inn Crowne Plaza,* 48 Wangfujing Dajie (☎65133388), whose film club has showings every Sunday at 2.30pm and Wednesday at 7.30pm (¥20). The film club *Sophia's Choice* at the Sino Japanese Youth Exchange Centre at 40 Liangmaqiao Jie (☎65004466 ext 103), in Xicheng district, near Beijing Normal University, shows Chinese films with English subtitles. There are also occasional shows, usually of French films with Chinese subtitles, at the *Salle de Cinema* (¥15) in the French Embassy at 3 Dongsan Jie in Sanlitun (☎65323531).

Opera
Beijing Opera (*Jing Xi*) is the most celebrated of the country's three hundred and fifty or so regional styles – a unique combination of song, dance, acrobatics and mime, with some similarities to Western pantomime. It is highly stylized and to the outsider can often seem obscure to the point of absurdity and ultimately tedious, since perfor-

BEIJING: ENTERTAINMENT

Beijing Concert Hall	音乐厅	*yīnyuè tīng*
Capital Theatre	首都剧场	*shǒudū jùchǎng*
Chaoyang Theatre	朝阳剧场	*cháoyáng jùchǎng*
Dahua Cinema	大华电影院	*dàhuá diànyǐngyuàn*
International Club	国际俱乐部	*guójì jùlèbù*
Lao She Tea House	老舍茶馆	*láoshě cháguǎn*
Puppet Theatre	中国木偶剧院	*zhōngguó mù'ǒu jùyuàn*
Tianqiao Tea House	天桥乐茶园	*tiānqiáolè cháyuán*
Workers' Stadium	工人体育场	*gōngrén tǐyùchǎng*
Zhengyici Theatre	正义词剧场	*zhèngyìcí jùchǎng*
Zhonghe Theatre	中和剧场	*zhōnghé jùchǎng*

mances can last up to four hours, punctuated by a succession of crashing gongs and piercing, almost discordant songs. But it's worth seeing once, and if you can acquaint yourself with the plot beforehand, there's a definite fascination. Most of the **plots** are based on historical or mythological themes – two of the the most famous titles, which any Chinese will explain to you, are "The White Snake" and "The Water Margin" – and they're rigidly symbolic. Moral absolutes begin with the costumes – red signifies loyalty; yellow, slyness; blue, cruelty; and black, evil – and with the patterns painted on faces. An interesting, if controversial, variation on the traditions, highly instructive if you know enough to work out what's going on, are operas dealing with contemporary themes – like Mao's first wife, or the struggle of women to marry as they choose.

The most accessible place to see Beijing Opera is at the *Liyuan Theatre* (☎63016688 ext 8860) on the first floor of the *Qianmen Hotel*, 175 Yong'an Lu, where nightly performances begin at 7.30pm. There's a ticket office in the front courtyard of the hotel (daily 9–11am, noon–4.45pm & 5.30–8pm). Tickets cost ¥20–80; the more expensive seats are at tables at the front where you can sip tea and nibble pastries during the performance. In season you'll need to book tickets a day or two in advance. You won't see many Chinese faces here as the opera shown, which lasts for just an hour, is a tourist-friendly bastardization, jazzed up with some martial arts and slapstick. A display board at the side of the stage gives a senseless English translation of the few lines of dialogue. Only the costumes and music are authentic. For the genuine lengthy article, try the *Zhonghe Theatre* at 5 Liangshidian Jie (☎63037083), or the *Zhengyici Theatre* at 220 Xiheyan Dajie (☎63189454); check the *China Daily* for listings.

Theatre, song and dance and puppet shows

Spoken drama was only introduced into Chinese theatres this century. The **People's Art Theatre** in Beijing became its best-known home and, before the Cultural Revolution, staged European plays which had a clear social message – Ibsen and Chekhov were among the favourites. But in 1968, Jiang Qing, Mao's third wife, declared that "spoken drama is dead". The theatre, along with most of China's cinemas, was closed down for almost a decade, with a corpus of just eight plays, deemed socially improving, continuing to be performed. Many of the principal actors, directors and writers were banished too, generally to hard rural labour. The last decade has seen a total turnabout with the People's Art Theatre reassembled in 1979, establishing its reputation with a performance of Arthur Miller's *Death of a Salesman*. Look out for them, and other companies, at the *Capital Theatre* at 22 Wangfujing Dajie (☎68313926) and the *Experimental Theatre of the Central Academy of Dramatic Arts* at 39 Dongmianhua Hutong (☎64017894).

Though a little glitzy for many foreigners' tastes, it can't be denied that the Chinese make good old-fashioned **song and dance** extravaganzas the way they don't make then any more in the West. Most evenings, you can catch one by turning the TV on, but if you want the live experience, try the *Beijing Exhibition Theatre* at 135 Xizhimenwai Dajie (☎68354455).

Chinese **puppetry** has a lineage of two thousand years and you can check it out at the *Puppet Theatre*, A1 Anhua Xi Lu (☎64254846), or free of charge at 8pm every evening at the *Jinglun Hotel* at 3 Jianguomenwai Dajie. Another ancient art, **wushu**, can be seen at the *Wuyi Diyuan Theatre* (☎64912157) where performances by martial arts masters are put on most nights (7.30–9pm). The theatre is rather out of the way at 1 Anding Lu, inside the eastern gate of the *Olympic Sports Centre* in the north of the city; take bus #108 or #328 and get off at the Xiao Guan stop.

Acrobatics

Certainly the most accessible and exciting of the traditional Chinese entertainments, **acrobatics** covers anything from gymnastics and animal tricks to magic and juggling. Professional acrobats have existed in China for two thousand years and the tradition continues at the main training school, Wu Qiao in Hebei Province, where students begin training at the age of five. The style may be vaudeville, but performances are spectacular, with truly awe-inspiring feats.

The easiest place to see a display is at the *Chaoyang Theatre* at 36 Dongsanhuan Bei Lu (☎65072421), which has a show every night (7.15–9pm; ¥30). The *Jinghua Hotel* runs a nightly tour here for ¥40, or you can arrange it with *CITS* for a commission of ¥30. The theatre fills nightly with tour groups and Chinese tourists – at the end, the Chinese rush off as if it's a fire drill, leaving the tour groups to do all the applauding. There are plenty of souvenir stalls in the lobby – buy after the show rather than in the interval, as prices go down.

Tea houses

A couple of **tea houses** have recently reappeared in the capital. You can watch a variety show of Beijing Opera, martial arts and acrobatics (¥40–130), while snacking on tea and cakes, at the *Lao She Tea House*, 3rd Floor, Dawancha Building, 3 Qianmen Xi Dajie. The same thing is available at the *Tianqiao Happy Tea House*, at 113 Tianqiao Marke (closed Mon). Both give a colourful taste of the surface aspects of Chinese culture and are popular with tour groups.

For a more authentic atmosphere, pop into the *Sanwei Bookstore* at 60 Fuxingmennei Dajie (☎66013204), opposite the *Minzu Hotel*, which is more the haunt of expats and arty Chinese, where you can hear light jazz and Chinese folk music (8.30–10pm).

Shopping

Beijing has a good reputation for **shopping**, with the widest choice of anywhere in China. **Clothes** are particularly inexpensive, and are one reason for the city's high number of Russians as smuggling them across the northern border, usually on the Trans-Siberian train, is a lucrative trade. There's also a wide choice of **antiques and handicrafts**, but don't expect to find any bargains or particularly unusual items as the markets are well picked over. Be aware that much that is passed off as antique is fake. Good souvenir buys are **art materials**, particularly brushes and blocks of ink, chops carved with a name, small **jade** items and handicraft items such as **kites**, painted snuff bottles and papercuts.

There are four main **shopping districts**: Wangfujing, popular but overrated; Xidan, whose giant department stores are of limited interest to visitors; Dongdan, which mainly sells clothes; and Qianmen, perhaps the area that most rewards idle browsing, with a few oddities among the cheap shoes and clothes stores. In addition, and especially aimed at visitors, Liulichang is a good place to get a lot of souvenir buying done quickly, or head to Jianguomenwai Dajie if it's clothes you're after. In the **markets**, you have much less guarantee of quality, but you can (and should) barter, so prices are cheaper. For general goods check the **department stores**, which sell a little of everything, and provide a good index of current Chinese taste. The *Beijing Department Store* on Wangfujing is a prime example. Of the giant **malls**, the Lufthansa Centre, on Dong Sanhuan Bei Lu is the grandest and glitziest.

Shops are open daily from 8.30am to 8pm (7pm in winter), with large shopping centres staying open till 9pm. Beijing is one Chinese city where the night markets are poor, forced out by the abundance of goods in the stores.

Antiques and curios

If you're a serious antique hunter, go to Tianjin, where the choice is more eclectic and prices cheaper (see p.141). That said, there's no shortage of **antique stores** and **markets** in the capital. Plenty of stuff is fake, and it can be hard even for experts to tell what's genuine and what's not, so just buy what looks attractive. **Carpets**, made in Xinjiang, Tibet, and Tianjin, aren't cheap, but if you're looking to spend some serious money, they're pretty good value. Antiques over one hundred years old need to be certificated before they can be exported; you can get this service at the *Friendship Store* (Mon & Fri 2–5pm). Take the object and a receipt along.

Arts and Crafts Store, 293 Wangfujing. A good if predictable selection of expensive *objets d'art*.

Beijing Curio City, Dongsanhuan Nan Lu, west of Huawei Bridge. A giant mall of over 250 stalls. Visit on a Sunday, when other antique traders come and set up in the streets around. The mall includes a section for duty-free shopping; take your passport and a ticket out of the country along and you can buy goods at the same reduced price as at the airport.

Friendship Store, Jianguomenwai Dajie. Tourist souvenirs with a wide range of prices, but generally more expensive than in the markets. Large carpet section.

Hongqiao Market and Department Store, northeast corner of Tiantan Park. The largest market, with stalls selling garden furniture, birds and fish as well as antiques. There's also plenty of opportunity to buy souvenirs, such as tea sets and packs of cards. On the other side of the road from the market is the giant *Hongqiao Department Store*. The top floor sells antiques and curios; one stall is given over solely to Cultural Revolution kitsch. The stalls share space, oddly, with a pearl and jewellery market. The second floor sells clothes and the first is the place to go for small electronic items, including such novelties as watches that speak the time in Russian when you whistle at them.

Liulichang, east of Qianmen Dajie (see p.92). This has the densest concentration of curio stores, with a great choice, particularly of art materials, though prices are steep.

Lufthansa Centre, Liangmaqiao Lu. A section in this giant mall sells expensive antiques and carpets.

Shisa Hu Antique Market, on the southern side of Shisha Hu (see p.100). A small and dusty bird and antique market.

Silk Market, Jianguomenwai Dajie (see p.98). A few stalls here sell carpets and curios.

Books

Beijing can claim a better range of **English-language literature** than anywhere else in China. If you're starting a trip of any length, stock up at the *Friendship Store, Foreign Language Bookstore* or *China Bookstore* or you'll get very sick of classic English novels after a few months. The expensive hotels all have bookstores with fairly decent collections, though at off-putting prices. Perhaps more interesting are the copies of foreign **newspapers and magazines,** such as *Time* and *Newsweek,* sold for around ¥30.

China Bookstore, 115 Liulichang (daily except Sun 8am–5pm). An enormous selection including specialist texts, dusty tomes and lavish coffee-table and art books, though no fiction in English.

The **telephone code** for Beijing is ☎010

Foreign Language Bookstore, 235 Wangfujing Dajie (daily except Sun 8am–5pm). The largest in China and invaluable, particularly if you've had enough of nineteenth-century novels. There's an information desk on the right as you go in which sells listings magazines, and on the other side of the entrance a counter sells maps, including an enormous wall map of the city (¥80), which would be great if you could get it home. Among the English books on offer, which include fiction, textbooks on Chinese medicine, and translations of Chinese classics, the *Pocket Interpreter*, produced by *Beijing Foreign Language Press*, is a good practical phrasebook, well worth picking up.

Friendship Store, Jianguomenwai Dajie. As well as a wide variety of books on all aspects of Chinese culture, the bookshop within the store sells foreign newspapers (¥40), a few days out of date. Open daily 9am–8.30pm.

Clothes

Clothes are a bargain in Beijing; witness all the Russians buying in bulk. The best place to go is Jianguomen Dajie, where the **silk** and **cotton** markets, the *Friendship Store*, and the *CVIK Plaza* offer something for every budget (see p.98).

Army Surplus Store, 188 Qianmen Dajie. A wide selection of hats and coats, plus sleeping bags and tents, are sold by the downright abusive staff here.

Mingxing Clothing Store, 133 Wangfujing Dajie. Well-made traditional Chinese women's clothing – *cheongsams* and *qipaos.*

Palace Hotel, 8 Jingyu Hutong, Wangfujing. A host of exclusive boutiques – *Harvey Nichols, Hugo Boss, Versace* – line the lobby.

PLA official factory outlet, Dongsanhuan Bei Lu, about 100m east of the *Jing Guang Centre,* not far from the *Chaoyang Theatre.* As well as military outfits, they stock a huge selection of shoes. If you're in the city in winter and you're not wearing one of their fake-fur collared, lime green, double-breasted, gold-buttoned coats, fashionwise, you're nowhere.

Ruifuxiang Store, 5 Dazhanlan (see p.92). Raw silk and cotton.

Xinqiao Fashion World, Qianmen Dong Dajie, opposite and west of *Maxim's Restaurant.* A market full of stalls selling women's clothes. This is where the locals shop.

Yuanlong Silk Corporation, 15 Yongnei Dong Jie, 200m west of the south gate of the Temple of Heaven. A good selection of silk clothes.

Listings

Airline offices *Aeroflot, Jinglun Hotel,* 3 Jianguomenwai Dajie (☎65002412); *Air France,* World Trade Centre, 1 Jianguomenwai Dajie (☎65051818); *All Nippon Airways,* Rm 1510, World Trade Centre, 1 Jianguomenwai Dajie (☎65053311); *Alitalia,* Rm 139, *Jianguo Hotel,* 5 Jianguomenwai Dajie (☎65002233 ext 139); *Austrian Airlines, Great Wall Sheraton Hotel,* 10 Donghua Bei Lu (☎65917861); *British Airways,* Rm 210, CVIK Tower, 22 Jianguomenwai Dajie (☎65124070); *CAAC,* 117 Dongsi Xi Dajie (☎64012221) or at the Aviation Office, 15 Xi Chang'an Jie (☎66016667); *Canadian Airlines,* Lufthansa Centre, Dong Sanhuan Bei Lu (☎64637901); *Dragonair,* L107, World Trade Centre, 1 Jianguomenwai Dajie (☎65054343); *Ethiopian Airlines,* World Trade Centre, 1 Jianguomenwai Dajie (☎65050314); *Finnair,* Rm 102, CVIK Tower, 22 Jianguomenwai Dajie (☎65127180 or 65127181); *Garuda Indonesia,* World Trade Centre, 1 Jianguomenwai Dajie (☎65051047); *Iran Air,* CITIC Building, 19 Jianguomenwai Dajie (☎65124940 or 65124945); *Japan Airlines, Hotel New Otani,* Changfugong Office Building, 26A Jianguomenwai (☎65130888); *Korean Air,* World Trade Centre, 1 Jianguomenwai Dajie (☎65050088); *Lufthansa,* Lufthansa Centre, Dong Sanhuan Bei Lu (☎64654488); *Malaysia Airlines,* Lot 115A/B, Level 1, West Wing Office Block, World Trade Centre, 1 Jianguomenwai Dajie (☎65052681); *LOT Polish Airlines,* World Trade Centre, 1 Jianguomenwai Dajie (☎65050136); *Pakistan Airlines,* World Trade Centre, 1 Jianguomenwai Dajie (☎65051681); *Qantas,* 1st Floor, Lufthansa Centre, Dong Sanhuan Bei Lu (☎64674794); *Swissair,* Rm 201, CVIK Tower, 22 Jianguomenwai Dajie (☎65123555); *SAS Scandinavian Airlines,* 18th Floor,

CVIK Tower, 22 Jianguomenwai Dajie (☎65120575); *Singapore Airlines*, L109, World Trade Centre, 1 Jianguomenwai Dajie (☎65052233); *Thai International*, Rm 207–209, CVIK Tower, 22 Jianguomenwai Dajie (☎65123881); *United Airlines*, 1st Floor, Lufthansa Centre, Dong Sanhuan Bei Lu (☎64631111).

American Express Rm L115, West Wing Building, World Trade Centre, 1 Jianguomenwai Dajie (Mon–Fri 9am–5pm, Sat 9am–noon) and in the lobby of the *Jinglun Hotel* at 3 Jianguomenwai Dajie (Mon–Fri 9am–5pm). *American Express* credit card and travellers' cheque holders may use the office in the World Trade Centre as an address for post restante mail, but letters are held for only sixty days.

Art galleries Apart from the official China Art Gallery (see p.102), there are a few more commercial galleries in Beijing. The most convenient is the *Wangfung Gallery* at 136 Nanchizi Dajie, just east of the Forbidden City, which has an international and progressive flavour. Or try the *Yanhuang Gallery* in the Asian Games Village at 9 Huizhong Lu, which has a permanent exhibition of Ming and Qing paintings. The work on show at the *Melodic Art Gallery*, opposite the *Friendship Store*, tends towards the insipid and eminently saleable, as does the *Art Palace* in the lobby of the *Holiday Inn Crowne Plaza* off Wangfujing. There are also a couple of commercial galleries on Sanlitun Lu, including one at no. 24 that sells Shaanxi peasant paintings.

Banks and exchange The *Commercial Bank* (Mon–Thurs 9am–noon & 1–4pm, Fri 9am–noon & 1–3pm) in the CITIC Building at 19 Jianguomenwai Dajie, next to the *Friendship Store*, offers the most comprehensive service: *Visa* cards, travellers' cheques and cash can be used to obtain yuan or US dollars. The main branch of the *Bank of China* (Mon–Fri 9am–noon & 1.30–5pm), which will advance yuan on *Visa* cards and cash travellers' cheques, is at 8 Yabuo Lu, off Chaoyangmen Dajie, just north of the main post office. Other branches are in the CVIK Plaza (Mon–Fri 9am–noon & 1–6.30pm), the World Trade Centre (Mon–Fri 9am–5pm, Sat 9am–noon) and the Lufthansa Centre (Mon–Fri 9–noon & 1–4pm), and offer the same services. A foreign exchange office (daily 9am–6.30pm) inside the entrance to the *Friendship Store* is one of the few places you can change money at the weekend at the standard rate. If you have applied for a visa and only have a photocopy of your passport, some hotels and the *Hong Kong and Shanghai Bank* in the *Jianguo Hotel* will reluctantly advance cash on travellers' cheques; most banks won't.

Bike rental The *Jinghua, Jingtai, Beiwei, Tiantan, Beiwei* and *Xiyuan* hotels all rent bikes on a daily basis and require a deposit of ¥200–500. The *Jinghua* charges ¥10 a day, but their bikes are cheap and have a tendency to fall apart; the others charge between ¥20 and ¥50 and their bikes are better. Wang Shifu, who has a stall outside the CVIK Plaza on Jianguomen Dajie (daily 8am–8pm), rents ordinary bikes for ¥20 a day (¥4 an hour) and mountain bikes for ¥40 (¥8 an hour), ¥300 deposit. Another good place is *Mike's Bike Boutique*, outside the *Sports Hotel* on Tiyuguan Lu (daily 7.30am–7pm), where ordinary bikes are ¥5 a day (¥2 an hour), and good-quality mountain bikes, possibly the best you can rent in Beijing, are ¥30 (¥5 an hour). Deposit is ¥100–500, depending on the bike. A bike repair shop at 94 Chongwenmen Dajie, near the *Chongwenmen Hotel* (7.30am–6.30pm), also has a few bikes for rent.

Business centres All the larger hotels have business centres offering fax, photocopying and sometimes courier services. For a comprehensive service, try the *Regus Centre* on the second floor of the Lufthansa Centre. For printing, design and and typesetting, try *Alphagraphics* at B142, in the west wing office tower of the World Trade Centre (☎65052907), or *Empire Quick Print* at 63 Dongdaqiao Lu (☎65929511).

Car rental *Beijing First Auto Rental Company*, 28 Xizhimen Nan Dajie (☎66053019); *CVIK Rental Service* on Level B2, CVIK Plaza (☎65123481); *Lantian Car Rental Company*, 66 Gulouwai Dajie (☎62055888).

Courier service *DHL* has a 24-hour office at 45 Xinyuan Jie (☎64662211), in Chaoyang district.

Embassies Visa departments usually open for a few hours every weekday morning (phone for exact times and to see what you'll need to take). Remember that they'll take your passport off you for as long as a week sometimes, and it's very hard to change money without it, so stock up on cash before applying for any visas. You can get passport-size photos from the *China Photo Studio* at 228 Wangfujing Jie. Some embassies require payment in US dollars; you can change travellers' cheques for these at the CITIC Building (see "Banks and exchange" above). Most embassies are either around Sanlitun in the northeast or in Jianguomenwai compound, north of and parallel to Jianguomenwai Dajie: *Australia*, 21 Dongzhimenwai Dajie (☎65322331); *Burma*, 6 Dongzhimenwai Dajie, Sanlitun (☎65321425); *Canada*, 10 Sanlitun Lu (☎65323536); *France*, 3 Dongsan Jie, Sanlitun

(☎65321331); *Germany*, 5 Dongzhimenwai Dajie, Sanlitun (☎65322161); *India*, 1 Ritan Dong Lu, Sanlitun (☎65321856); *Ireland*, 3 Ritan Dong Lu, Sanlitun (☎65322691); *Japan*, 7 Ritan Lu, Sanlitun (☎65322361); *Laos*, 11 Dongsi Jie, Sanlitun (☎65321224); *Mongolia*, 2 Xiushui Bei Jie, Jianguomenwai (☎65321203); *Pakistan*, 1 Dongzhimenwai Dajie, Sanlitun (☎65222504); *Russian Federation* (including Kazakhstan and Uzbekistan), 4 Dongzhimen Bei Zhong Jie (south off Andingmen Dong Dajie; ☎65322051); *South Korea*, 4th Floor, World Trade Centre (☎65053171); *Thailand*, 40 Guanghua Lu (☎65321708); *UK*, 11 Guanghua Lu, Jianguomenwai (☎65321708); *Ukraine*, Dong Lu Jie, Sanlitun (☎65324014); *USA*, 3 Xiushui Bei Jie, Jianguomenwai (☎65323831); *Vietnam*, 32 Guanghua Lu, Jianguomenwai (☎65321155).

Employment If you're looking for a job, try the *International Human Resources Centre* at 50 Dajue Hutong, Chegongzhuan (☎63099973) or the *Service Centre for Personnel Exchange* in the Workers' Cultural Palace, west off Nanchizi Dajie (☎65123392), or, better still, turn up and ask at the place where you want a job. Remember that employment in China (even for foreigners) is pretty much dependant on *guanxi* (connections).

English corner Sundays in Zizhuyuan Park.

Football Football is a growing sport with China determined to qualify for the World Cup by the year 2000. Beijing has the best team in China and they play on Sunday afternoons. Tickets are cheap (¥10) and you buy them at the ground on the day. They play at the massive *Workers' Stadium* in the northeast of the city, off Gongren Tiyuchang Bei Lu (bus #110 along Dongdaqiao). The Beijing team beat a visiting Arsenal squad 2–1 here in 1995, a fact brought up soon enough in any conversation between English visitors and the city's taxi drivers, but the national squad was duly trounced 3–1 by England in their run-up to Euro 96.

Hospitals and clinics Most big hotels have a resident medic. If you need a hospital, the following have foreigners' clinics where some English is spoken: *Sino Japanese Friendship Hospital* on Heping Dajie (daily 8–11.30am & 1–4.30pm; ☎64221122); *Friendship Hospital* at 95 Yongan Lu, west of Tiantan Park (☎63014411); *Beijing Hospital* at 15 Dahua Lu. For a service run by and for foreigners, try the *International Medical Centre* at S106 in the Lufthansa Centre, Dong Sanhuan Bei Lu (☎64651561), or the *Hong Kong International Clinic* on the third floor of the Swissotel Hong Kong Macao Centre, Dongsishitiao Qiao (daily 9am–9pm; ☎65012288 ext 2346). For real emergencies, the *AEA International* offers a comprehensive and expensive service at 14 Liangmahe Lu, not far from the Lufthansa Centre (clinic ☎64629112, emergency calls ☎64629100).

Left luggage There's a left-luggage office in the foreigners' waiting room at the back of the central station, Beijing Zhan, with lockers for ¥5 or ¥10 a day depending on size, though as these are almost always full, you are better off going to the main left-luggage office (daily 5am–midnight; ¥5 a day) obscurely located behind the station; come out of the exit, turn right, then right again and follow the grotty alleyway around. There is a 24-hour left-luggage office on the second floor of Xi Zhan.

Language courses You can do short courses in Chinese at Beijing Foreign Studies University on Erhuan Xi Lu, at the Bridge School in Jianguomenwai (☎64940243), which offers evening classes, or the Cultural Mission at 7 Beixiao Jie in Sanlitun (☎65323005), where most students are diplomats. Perhaps the cheapest and easiest way to study Mandarin, though, is to find a Chinese student of English – try hanging around English corner (see above) – and get them to teach you. You'll have to negotiate a fee, but they don't charge very much, maybe ¥15 an hour.

Libraries The Beijing National Library, just north of Zizhuyuan Park (Mon–Fri 8am–5pm; ☎68415566), is one of the largest in the world, with more than ten million volumes, including manuscripts from the Dunhuang Caves and a Qing-dynasty encyclopedia. The oldest texts are Shang dynasty inscriptions on bone. You'll need to join before they let you in. To take books out, you need to be resident in the city, but you can turn up and get a day pass that lets you browse around.

Martial arts You can study the martial arts, including Qigong, at the Ruyi School, 152 Yuan Ming Yuan Lu.

Pharmacies There are large pharmacies at 136 Wangfujing and 42 Dongdan Bei Dajie, or you could try the famous *Tongrentang Pharmacy* on Dazhanlan (see p.92). For imported non-prescription medicines, try *Watsons* at the *Holiday Inn Lido*, Shoudujichang Lu.

Post offices The International Post Office is on Chaoyangmen Dajie (daily 8am–7pm), just north of the intersection with Jianguomen Dajie. This is where post restante letters end up. They are supposed to be divided alphabetically, but you should rifle through them all as they are sloppily filed. If you do get a letter, you have to pay ¥1.5 for it. It's also possible to rent a PO Box here and there's a packing service for parcels and a wide variety of stamps on sale, but staff are not very helpful. There are other post offices in the World Trade Centre, on Xi Chang'an Jie, just east of the Concert Hall, and at the northern end of Xidan Dajie, all open daily from 9am to 5pm. Express mail can be sent from the Media Centre, just west of the Military Museum at 11B Fuxingmen Lu (Mon–Fri 7am–6pm).

PSB The Foreigners' Police at 85 Beichizi Dajie (Mon–Fri 8–11.30am & 1.30–5pm; ☎65255486) will extend a visa for a steep fee of ¥120. They won't give a second visa extension, but will send you to a private firm who charge ¥350 to sort it out for you.

Radio Easy FM at 91.5FM has twelve hours of Western music, mostly pap, plus news on the hour. It's a good resource for finding out about cultural events in the capital.

Swimming pool Try the Olympic-size pool in the *Asian Games Village,* Anding Lu (daily 8am–9pm; ¥50), on the route of trolleybus #108 from Chongwenmennei Dajie, which also boasts some of the city's fiercest showers.

Telecommunications There's a 24-hour telecommunications office in the Telegraph Office at 11 Xi Chang'an Jie, about 300m from the intersection with Xidan Bei Dajie. Instead of paying for your call afterwards at a desk, you have to buy a phonecard for ¥50 or ¥100, and as phonecalls abroad have a three-minute minimum charge, you are forced to buy the ¥100 cards. This annoying system also operates in the 24-hour telecom centre by the main post office on Chaoyangmen Dajie. With these cards you can also use the orange phoneboxes dotted around the city centre. The Telegraph Office runs a heavily subscribed e-mail and Internet service. Phone ☎66010757 for details.

Travel agents The *CITS* office next to the *Gloria Plaza Hotel* at 28 Jianguomenwai Dajie (daily 8.30–11.30am & 1.30–4.30pm; ☎67236820) offers expensive tours, a tour guide and interpreter service, and advance ticket booking for trains, planes and ferries (from Tianjin), with a commission of around ¥50 added. Other offices at 103 Fuxingmennei Dajie (☎66011122), in the *Beijing Hotel*, 33 Dongchang'an Jie (☎65120507) and *New Century Hotel* (☎68491426) opposite the zoo, offer tickets and tours.

Translation Services Try *Sinofile* at 137 Qianmen Xi Dajie (☎66086628) or the *Huanyu Agency* at 57 Xuanwumen Xi Dajie (☎63073203).

AROUND BEIJING

There are plenty of scenic spots and places of interest scattered in the plains and hills around the capital, and no visit would be complete without a trip to the **Great Wall**, accessible in three places within easy journey time of Beijing. In addition, the Western Hills in particular shouldn't be overlooked, and if you're in the capital for any length of time, they provide an invigorating breather from the pressures of the city. Other spots such as the excavations at **Zhoukoudian** or the **Aviation Museum** will probably be of most interest to those with a special interest, and scenic places like Shidu or the Kangxi Grasslands to long-term residents.

The Great Wall

This is a Great Wall and only a great people with a great past could have a great wall and such a great people with such a great wall will surely have a great future.

Richard M.Nixon

The most commonly told fact about the **Great Wall** – that it is the one man-made structure visible from the moon – is perhaps the most impressive. But other statistics are close rivals. The wall was begun in the fifth century BC, continued until the sixteenth century and stretches some 6000km across China. Today's surviving sections, placed end to end, would link New York with Los Angeles, and if the bricks used to build it

AROUND BEIJING

Aviation Museum	航空博物馆	*hángkōng bówùguǎn*
Badachu	八大处	*bādàchù*
Badaling	八大岭	*bādàlíng*
Biyun Si	碧云寺	*bìyún sì*
Botanical Gardens	植物园	*zhíwùyuán*
Great Wall	长城	*chángchéng*
Jietai Si	戒台寺	*jiètái sì*
Kangxi Grasslands	慷西草原	*kāngxī cǎoyuán*
Longqing Gorge	龙庆峡	*lóngqìng xiá*
Lugou Qiao	卢沟桥	*lúgōuqiáo*
Miyun Reservoir	密云水库	*mìyún shuǐkù*
Mutianyu	慕田峪	*mùtiányù*
Shidu	十渡	*shídù*
Shisan Ling	十三陵	*shísān líng*
Simatai	四马台	*sìmǎtái*
Tanzhe Si	潭柘寺	*tánzhé sì*
Western Hills	西山	*xīshān*
Wofo Si	卧佛寺	*wòfósì*
Xiangshan Park	香山公园	*xiāngshān gōngyuán*
Zhoukoudian	周口店	*zhōukǒudiàn*

were made into a single wall 5m high and 1m thick, it would more than encircle the earth. Even at ground level, and along the small, most-visited section at Badaling, constantly overrun by Chinese and foreign tourists, Wan Li Changcheng (The Long Wall of Ten Thousand Li), is clearly the PRC's most spectacular sight.

The Chinese have walled their cities since earliest times and during the Warring States period, around the fifth century BC, simply extended the practice to separate rival territories. The Great Wall's **origins** lie in these fractured lines of fortifications and in the vision of **Qin Shi Huang**, who, unifying the empire in the third century BC, joined and extended the sections to form one continuous defence against barbarians. Under subsequent dynasties – the Han, Wei, Qi and Sui – the wall was maintained and, in response to shifting regional threats, grew and changed course. It did lose importance for a while, with Tang borders extending well to the north, then shrinking back under the Song, but with the emergence of the Ming it again became a priority, and military technicians worked on its reconstruction right through the fourteenth to the sixteenth century.

For much of it's history, the wall was hated. Qin Shi Huang's wall, particularly, was a symbol of brutal tyranny – he wasted the country's wealth and worked thousands to death in building it. It is estimated that he mobilized nearly a million people to construct it, but other dynasties surpassed even that figure. Many of the labourers were criminals, but in the Sui dynasty, when there weren't enough men left for the massive project, widows were pressed into service. A Song-dynasty poem expresses a common sentiment:

The wall is so tall because it is stuffed with the bones of soldiers,
The wall is so deep because it is watered with the soldiers' blood.

The irony, of course, is that the seven-metre-high, seven-metre-thick wall, with its 25,000 battlements, did not work. Successive invasions crossed its defences (Genghis Khan is supposed to have merely bribed the sentries), and it was in any case of little use against the sea powers of Japan and later Europe. But the wall did have significant functions. It allowed the swift passage through the empire of both troops and goods – there is room for five horses abreast most of the way – and, perhaps as important, it restricted the movement of the nomadic peoples in the distant, non-Han minority regions.

During the Qing dynasty, the Manchus let the wall fall into disrepair as it had proved no obstacle to their invasion. Slowly the wall crumbled away, useful only as a source of building material. Now, though, the Great Wall, as Nixon might have added, is great business. At the restored sections, **Badaling**, and to a lesser extent, **Mutianyu**, the wall is daily besieged by masses of visitors. It's possible to escape the crowds at **Simatai**, as yet untouched by development – though get there quickly. Other places to see the wall are at Shanhaiguan (see p.146), Zhangye (see p.872) and Jiayuguan (see p.876).

Badaling

The best-known section of the wall, and the one most people see, is at **BADALING** (daily 8am–4pm; ¥30, students ¥15), 70km northwest of Beijing. It was the first section to be restored, in 1957, and opened up to tourists. Here the wall is 6m wide with regular watchtowers dating from the Ming dynasty. It follows the highest contours of a steep range of hills, forming a formidable defence, and this section was never attacked directly but taken by sweeping around from the side.

It's the easiest part of the wall to get to but it's also the most packaged, and to get the best out of it you need to escape the paths along which visitors are herded. A giant tourist circus greets you at the entrance, including a plethora of restaurants, rank after rank of souvenir stalls, a bank and post office. On the wall, flanked with guardrails and metal bins and accompanied by hordes of other tourists, it's hard to feel that there's anything genuine about the experience. Indeed, the wall itself is hardly original here, being a modern reconstruction on the ancient foundations. From the entrance you can walk along the wall to the north (left) or south (right). Few people get very far, which gives you a chance to lose the crowds and, generally, things get better the farther you go.

If you head south, which most people do, you'll come to a cable car (¥60), after about 2km, which will take you down to a car park, and a zoo full of sad, mad bears. Keep going past the cable car and you'll reach an unreconstructed section that in parts is quite hard to climb around. Eventually the wall peters out, and from here a complex route – basically just keep heading southeast – will take you through the scrub to Qinglongqiao West station, from where there are infrequent trains back to Beijing. If you're going to try this, bring a sleeping bag and be prepared to spend the night sleeping rough as you may well get stranded.

Head north from the main entrance and you'll shake off the crowds fairly quickly. After about a kilometre you come to the end of the reconstructed section, and from here you can climb down on to the old wall and keep going. It's on this ruined section that you get a much better impression of the wall's real, more frightening character – a lonely road plodding on and on through a silent landscape. If you've come here with sleeping bags intending to stay the night – only really feasible in the summer months – this is the section to head for, but look out for the guards as dusk falls, as they'll order you off.

Practicalities

All the more expensive Beijing hotels and a few of the cheaper ones, as well as *CITS,* run **tours** to Badaling, with prices that are often absurd. If you come with a tour you'll arrive in the early afternoon, when it's at its busiest, spend an hour or two, then return, which really gives you little time for anything except the most cursory of jaunts, a few photo opportunities, and the purchase of an "I climbed the Great Wall" T–shirt. It's just as easy, and cheaper, to travel under your own steam, and with more time at your disposal you can make for the more deserted sections. By far the easiest way to get here is by tourist **bus** (¥6) from the terminus at Qianmen; look for a bus with a green number 1 on the side. Buses run daily 6–10am, departing every twenty minutes, and the journey takes about two hours. These government-run buses are reliable and were started in response to complaints about the private minibuses who run the same route. A few still do, but they are not recommended – you may well find yourself having to stump up more cash en route or be dumped along the way.

You can also get here by **train**, though it's a bit more hassle. There are two train stations within walking distance of Badaling, Badaling itself and Qinglongqiao West (the closest). From Yongdingmen Zhan in the city, train #527 leaves every morning at 9.40am and arrives at Qinglongqiao West, on the line from Beijing to Hohhot, at 12.30pm. From here you are about 1km distant from the wall. You can also get to Qinglongqiao West on local trains from Xizhimen Zhan, near Xizhimen subway stop. From the station, walk north through the scrub to the unrestored section (there is a path, but it's difficult to follow), then head west along the wall towards the entrance and the crowds. You should get away with not paying, though the authorities are wising up to this and security guards may intercept you and ask to see your ticket.

Getting back to Beijing shouldn't be a problem, as buses run until about 6pm. Tourist bus #1 goes from here to Shisan Ling (see p.125), then returns to the city.

Mutianyu

Mutianyu Great Wall (daily 8am–4pm; ¥10), 90km northeast of the city, is more appealing to most travellers than Badaling as it's somewhat less developed. A two-kilometre section of the wall, well endowed with guard towers, built in 1368 and renovated in 1983, it passes along a ridge through some lush, undulating hills. From the entrance, steep steps lead up to the wall; most people turn left, which leads to the cable car (¥30, students ¥15) for an effortless trip down again. Turn right and you can walk along the wall for about 1km until you come to a barrier – unlike at Badaling, you can't get on to the unreconstructed sections. The atmospheric *Mutianyu Great Wall Guesthouse* (☎010/69626867; ④), situated in a reconstructed watchtower 500m before this barrier, is a good place for a quiet break.

To get to Mutianyu, **minibuses** leave from the street just south of the Great Hall of the People off Tian'anmen Square every morning (¥10) and include four photo stops along the way. You can buy tickets, and check on departure times, the day before from a ticket booth on the pavement. Otherwise there are minibuses from Dongzhimen bus station early every morning. Getting there on regular buses won't save you any money, and involves several changes. Returning to the city shouldn't be a hassle provided you don't leave it too late, as plenty of minibuses wait in the car park to take people back to Beijing. If you can't find a minibus back to Beijing, get one to Huairou, from where you can get a regular bus back to the capital – the last bus back from Huairou leaves at 6.30pm.

Simatai

Simatai (daily 8am–4pm; ¥16), 110km northeast of the city, is the most unspoilt section of the Great Wall around Beijing, and, as it snakes across purple hills that resemble crumpled velvet from afar, with blue mountains in the distance, it's easily the most beautiful. Uncrowded, peaceful and semi-ruined, it fulfils the expectations of most visitors more than the other sections.

At the entrance, merely a booth in a car park, there is only a handful of souvenir stalls, and none near the wall itself, though a cable car is under construction, so no doubt Simatai's underdeveloped status will not last long. The only vendors around are local villagers. Make it understood from the outset that you are not interested in what they have to sell, otherwise it is quite likely that some poor kid with two cans of soft drink and a few postcards will follow you all afternoon.

Most of this section is unrenovated, dating back to the Ming dynasty, and sporting a few late innovations such as spaces for cannon, with its inner walls at right angles to the outer wall to thwart invaders who have already breached the first defence. From the small car park, a winding path takes you up to the wall and regularly spaced watchtowers allow you to measure your progress uphill along the ridge. The walk over the ruins is not an easy one, and gets increasingly precipitous after about the tenth watchtower, with sheer drops and steep angles. The views are sublime, though. After about the fourteenth tower (2hr), the wall peters out and the climb becomes quite dangerous, and there's no point going any farther.

Practicalities

At present the **tour** that runs from the *Jinghua Hotel* is the only easy way to get here. It runs irregularly, once a week in the off season, daily in the summer. Minibuses leave at 8.30am, and you have to buy a ticket (¥80) from the office in room 218 a day or two beforehand. The journey takes about three hours. You can get here by yourself but it's a lot of hassle, even if you speak Chinese, and it will take even longer. Get a bus to Miyun from the car park of the Workers' Stadium, near Dongsishitiao subway stop, then take another bus to Machang or Tanghe Bridge from where you'll have to try to find a taxi. Alternatively, you can take a train from Beijing North station to Gubeikou, then get a taxi. Be aware that you may end up paying a hefty price as unscrupulous taxi drivers know they are your only way to get back before nightfall. No doubt there will be Chinese tours running out here soon. A rented **taxi** will cost about ¥300, there and back including a wait. Take a packed lunch as there's only one stall in the car park selling snacks.

The Ming Tombs and around

Thirteen of the sixteen Ming-dynasty emperors were entombed in and around the Shisan Ling Valley, 40km northwest of Beijing. Two of these **Ming Tombs** (daily 8.30am–4.30pm; ¥30, students ¥15), Chang Ling and Ding Ling, were restored in the 1950s and the latter was also excavated, yielding up various treasures to the capital's museums. They are very much on the tour circuit, conveniently placed on the way to Badaling. However, the fame of the tombs is overstated in relation to the actual interest of the sites, and unless you've a strong archeological interest, this isn't a trip worth making for its own sake. If you want to come, the easiest way to get here is to take green tourist bus #1 from Qianmen (¥8) or from Badaling (¥2). On public transport, take bus #345 from Deshengmen to Changping, then bus #314 to the tombs. Buses drop you at a car park just before Ding Ling, where you buy your ticket.

The third Ming emperor, **Yongle**, who shifted the capital back from Nanjing to Beijing, chose this site for its landscape and it's undeniably the loveliest around the capital. Its scenic appeal has also caught the eye of Beijing's tourist planners, and the area is currently under development as a "tourist park" with hotels, amusement centres and even a golf course. Fortunately, at present only the two principal tombs have had much notice taken of them – the other eleven stand neglected and very beautiful amid former gardens, with grass and weeds breaking through their tiled roofs and marble foundations. They make a nice place to picnic if you just feel like a break from the city and its more tangible succession of sights. To get the most out of the place, plan to spend a day here and hike around the smaller tombs farther into the hills rather than sticking to the tourist route between Ding Ling and the car park. You'll need a **map** to do this and you'll find one on the back of some Beijing city maps, or you can buy one at the site.

The approach to the Ming Tombs, the seven-kilometre **Spirit Way**, is Shisan Ling's most exciting feature. This commences with the Dahongmen (Great Red Gate), a triple-entranced triumphal arch, through the central opening of which only the emperor's dead body could be carried. Beyond, the road is lined to either side with colossal stone statues of animals and men. Startlingly larger than life, the statues all date from the fif-teenth century and are among the best surviving examples of Ming sculpture. The sequence begins with groups of animals, real and mythological, including the qilin, a reptilian-like beast with deer's horns and a cow's tail, and the horned, feline xiechi. The avenue then changes alignment slightly and you are met by the first, stern human fig-ures of military mandarins. The precise significance of the statues is unclear, although it is assumed they were intended to serve the emperors in their next life.

Animal statuary reappears at the entrances to several of the tombs, though the struc-tures themselves are something of an anti-climax. **Chang Ling**, Yongle's tomb and the earliest at the site, stands at the end of the avenue. There are plans to excavate it, an exciting scheme since it is contemporary with some of the finest building of the Imperial Palace in the capital. At present the enduring impression is mainly one of scale: vast courtyards and hall buildings approached by terraced white marble. Its main feature is the Hall of Eminent Flowers, supported by huge columns of single tree trunks which it is said were imported all the way from Yunnan along frozen roads, slip-pery with ice.

The main focus of the tour, however, is **Ding Ling**, the underground tomb-palace of the Emperor Wanli. Wanli ascended the throne in 1573 at the age of ten and reigned for almost half a century. He began building his tomb when he was 22, in line with com-mon Ming practice, and hosted a grand party within on its completion. The mausoleum was opened in 1956 and found to be substantially intact, revealing the emperor's coffin, flanked by those of two of his empresses, and floors covered with the remains of scores of trunks containing imperial robes, gold and silver, and even the imperial cookbooks. Some of the treasures are displayed in the tomb, a huge musty vault, undecorated but impressive for its scale, and others have been replaced by replicas. It's a cautionary sight of useless wealth accumulation, as pointed out by the tour guides.

Miyun, Longqing Gorge and the Aviation Museum

The town of **MIYUN** lies some 65km northeast of Beijing, at the foot of the long range of hills along which the Great Wall threads its way. Buses run here from Dongzhimen bus station in the city. The area's claim to fame is the reservoir built in the flat, wide val-leys behind the town. Supplying over half the capital's water, it's a huge lake, scattered with islets and bays, backed by mountains and the deep blue of the Beijing sky. The reservoir has become a favourite destination for Beijing families, who flock out here at weekends to go swimming, fishing, boating and walking. Joining them is half the fun; however, if you're here for a little solitude, it's easy enough to wander off on your own. Behind the reservoir, in the hills, you'll find rock pools big enough to swim in, streams, trees, flowers and a rushing river – and on the hill tops there are outposts of the Great Wall, still in ruins.

Longqing Gorge is another reservoir and local recreation spot, 90km northwest of the capital, and accessible by bus from Beijiao Market bus station, or on train #575, which leaves Xizhimen Zhan at 8.30am, arriving two and a half hours later. The main attraction here is the **ice festival**, similar to the one in Harbin, held in late January and February, sometimes into March. The ice sculptures, with coloured lights inside for a gloriously tacky psychedelic effect, look great at night; unfortunately, the few hotel rooms here are expensive. Not too far from here, the **Kangxi Grasslands**, accessible by train from Beijing North station or by minibus from the gorge, is an established summer resort, where you can go horseriding.

Finally, for something different, the **Aviation Museum** (daily 8.30am–5.30pm; ¥40, students ¥20), stuck out in the sticks 60km north of the city, is a fascinating place, though, as it takes a long time to get here, it's probably only worth it for real enthusiasts. Take bus #345 from Deshengmen bus station, close to the subway stop, and tell the conductor where you want to go. After about ninety minutes, you'll need to get off, cross the freeway, and get bus #912 for the last few kilometres. The enormous museum has a decidedly military feel, with over three hundred aircraft displayed in a giant hangar and on a concourse, from the copy of the Wright brothers' plane flown by Feng Ru in 1909, to helicopter gunships used in the Gulf War. As well as plenty of fighters, many that saw action in the Korean War, the bomber that dropped China's first atom bomb is here, as is Mao's personal plane and the plane that scattered Zhou Enlai's ashes, which is covered with wreaths and tributes.

South and west of Beijing

The Western Hills are not far out of the city but, with swathes of wooded parkland dotted with temples, they feel a lot farther – except on weekends when the crowds are dense. The places of note south of Beijing are Zhoukoudian, where Peking Man was discovered, and on the way there or back you could make a quick stop at the Luguo Qiao. Shidu, farther south, a stretch of countryside far from the capital, is popular with local tourists.

The Western Hills

Like the Summer Palace, the **Western Hills**, 20km west of the city, are a place to escape urban life for a while, though more of a rugged experience. Because of its relative coolness at the height of summer, the area has been long favoured as a restful retreat by religious men and intellectuals, as well as politicians in this century – Mao lived here briefly, and the Politburo retreated here in 1989. West of the Summer Palace, and north from Pinguoyuan, the last subway stop, it takes about an hour and a half to get here by public transport from the city. The hills are divided into three parks, the closest of which is the Botanical Gardens, directly west of the Summer Palace. Two kilometres farther west, Xiangshan is the largest and most impressive park, but Badachu, south of here, a collection of temples strung out along a hillside, is just as pretty. A day gives you ample time to explore each of the three areas, if your legs are willing.

The **Botanical Gardens** (daily 8am–5pm; ¥1) are accessible by bus #333 from the Summer Palace (see p.105). Two thousand varieties of trees and plants are arranged in formal gardens which are pretty in the summer, though the terrain is flat and the landscaping is not as original as in the older parks. The main path leads after 1km to the **Wofo Si** (daily 8am–4.30pm; ¥1), whose main hall houses a huge reclining Buddha, over 5m in length and cast in copper. With two giant feet protruding from the end of his painted robe, and a pudgy, baby face, calm in repose, he looks rather cute, although he is not actually sleeping but dying, about to enter nirvana. Huge shoes, presented as offerings, are on display around the hall. Behind the temple is a bamboo garden, from which paths wind off into the hills. One heads northwest to a pretty cherry valley, just under 1km away, where Cao Xueqiao is supposed to have written *The Dream of Red Mansions*.

Deservedly the most popular is **Xiangshan Park** (daily 7am–6pm; ¥2), whose main, eastern entrance is 2km west of the Botanical Gardens. Bus #333 continues to here, or you can approach from the south; go to the Pinguoyuan subway stop and walk left out of the station about 500m to the crossroads to pick up bus #318. Both buses terminate by the main east gate. The park is a carefully landscaped range dominated by Incense Burner Peak in the western corner. It's at its best in the autumn (before the sharp November frosts), when the leaves turn red in a massive profusion of colour. At weekends the park is busy, but it's too big to be swamped and it's always a good place for a hike and a picnic. Close to the main entrance, the **Xiangshan Hotel** (☎62591166; ⑦), one of the city's most innovative buildings, comes as an unexpected sight. Designed by Bei Yuming, who also designed the pyramid at the Louvre in Paris, the light and airy building is somewhere between a temple and an airport lounge, and a great location to escape the smoke for a weekend. Northeast from here, the **Zhao Miao** (Temple of Brilliance), one of the few temples in the area that escaped vandalism by Western troops in 1860 and 1900, was built by Qianlong in 1780 in Tibetan style, designed to make visiting Lamas feel at home. From here, follow the path west up to the Peak (1hr) from where, on clear days, there are magnificent views down towards the Summer Palace and as far as distant Beijing. You can hire a horse to take you down again for ¥20, the same price as the cable car (¥20). Both drop you on the northern side of the hill, by the north entrance, a short walk from the superb **Biyun Si** (Azure Clouds Temple), just outside the park gate. A striking building, it's dominated by a north Indian-style dagoba and topped by extraordinary conical stupas. Inside, rather bizarrely, a tomb holds the hat and clothes of Sun Yatsen – his body was held here for a while before being moved in 1924. The giant main hall is now a maze of corridors lined with *arhats*, five hundred in all, and it's a magical place. The benignly smiling golden figures are all different – some have two heads or sit on animals, one is even pulling his face off – and you may see monks moving among them and bowing to each.

Badachu, or the Eight Great Sights (daily 8am–5pm; ¥2), is a forested hill 10km south of Xiangshan Park and accessible on bus #311 from Pingguoyuan subway stop, (it's only ¥10 in a taxi from here), or bus #347 from the zoo. Along the path that snakes around the hill are eight **temples**, fairly small affairs, but quite attractive on weekdays, when they're not busy. The new pagoda at the base of the path holds a Buddha tooth, which once sat in the second temple. The third, a nunnery, is the most pleasant, with a tea house in the courtyard. There's a statue of the rarely depicted thunder deity inside, boggle-eyed and grimacing. As well as the inevitable cable car, it's also possible to slide down the hill on a metal track.

The Tanzhe Si and Jietai Si

Due west of Beijing, two temples sit in the wooded country outside the industrial zone that rings the city. Getting to and from the area by public transport is a hassle, though you can get close without too much difficulty – bus #307 from Qianmen goes to the Hetan terminal, from where you'll need to find an unnumbered bus to the Tanzhe Si. From here a taxi to the Jietai Si should be around ¥20, but there's no transport back from here. Unless you've got private transport, or are willing to shell out for a taxi for the day (about ¥150 from Pinguoyuan subway stop), the temples are hardly worth the effort it takes to get around.

Forty kilometres west of the city, the **Tanzhe Si** (daily 8am–6pm; ¥10) occupies the most beautiful and serene temple site anywhere near the city. It's the largest, too, and one of the oldest, first recorded in the third century as housing a thriving community of monks. Wandering through the complex, past terraces of stupas, you reach an enormous central courtyard, with an ancient towering gingko that's over a thousand years old (christened the "King of Trees" by Emperor Qianlong), at its heart. Across the courtyard, a second, smaller tree is known as "The Emperor's Wife" and is supposed to produce a new branch every time a new emperor is born. From here you can take in the other temple buildings, on different levels up the hillside, or look round the lush bamboo gardens, whose plants are supposed to cure all manner of ailments. The spiky zhe (Cudrania) trees near the entrance apparently "reinforce the essence of the kidney and control spontaneous seminal emission".

Twelve kilometres back along the road to Beijing, in complete contrast to the Tanzhe Si, the **Jietai Si** (daily 8am–6pm; ¥20, students ¥10) sits on a hillside looking more like a fortress than a temple, surrounded by forbiddingly tall, red walls. It's famous for its venerable pines, eccentric-looking trees growing in odd directions. Indeed, one, leaning out at an angle of about thirty degrees, is pushing over a pagoda on the terrace beneath it. In the main hall is an enormous Liao-dynasty platform of white marble, 3m high and intricately carved with figures – monks, monsters (beaked and winged) and saints – at which novice monks were ordained. Another, smaller hall, holds a beautiful wooden altar that swarms with dragons in relief.

Zhoukoudian and around

Fifty kilometres south of Beijing is **ZHOUKOUDIAN** village, terminus of bus #914, which leaves from a station on Beiwei Lu, just south of the *Beiwei Hotel*. The main attraction is an excavation site (daily 9am–4pm; ¥20) in the limestone hills to the south of town (¥10 by meterless taxi from the bus station). This is where the first relic – a single tooth – of **Peking Man** who lived here between 500,000 and 230,000 years ago, was uncovered in 1921. Excavations began in earnest after archeologists realized they had found a new genus, a link between neanderthal and modern man, and they christened it *homo erectus Pekinensis*. Excavations gradually revealed the remains of over forty individuals, as well as tools and ornaments and parts of animals too. The top of a skull was found in 1929 but lost again during the chaos of the Anti-Japanese War. As well as wandering around the site – a nice walk but not exactly revealing – you can visit the **museum**, which displays just enough to ignite the imagination. The first room contains the archeologists' digging tools, contrasting with Peking Man's flint tools, shown later on together with his bone needles and ornaments. No weapons were found – it seems Peking Man lived on nuts and tubers and only occasionally hunted. He was pretty short, with three quarters of the brain capacity of modern man. Copious explanations in English, diagrams and paintings, make up for the fragmentary nature of the objects shown – tools and fragments of bone. Much more dramatic are the remains of animals, fearsome beasts now extinct, found at the site, which are accompanied by models or paintings of what they would have looked like. As well as the teeth of a sabre-toothed tiger, there's the whole skeleton of a huge panther-like creature, and the skull of a deer-like animal with bony plates on its head and thick antlers with a two- metre spread. The last bus back to the city is around dusk.

The **Luguo Qiao**, Reed Moat Bridge (daily 8am–6pm; ¥4), is on the route of bus #339 from the Liuli flyover in the city; ask the conductor to tell you when to get off. It's not really worth a special visit, but it can be combined with a trip to Zhoukoudian if you are in a taxi. Built in 1192, with 250 grey marble balustrades emblazoned with carved lions, each of which wears a different expression, this bridge was described in the writings of Marco Polo, earning it its alternative name, Marco Polo Bridge. Today, substantially preserved, including the elephants holding it up at either end, it's still remarkable, although the area around is pretty shabby and the river has dried up, leaving a dusty expanse used as a practice ground by the capital's driving schools.

WANPING, on the river bank by the bridge, is a small country village, and the site of the first shot fired in the war between China and Japan in 1937, prompted by the illegal Japanese occupation of a rail junction nearby. After that it was only a short step to a full-scale assault on Beijing. The Anti-Japanese War is commemorated by a **museum** (Tues–Sun 8am–5pm; ¥5) in the village, whose declared message of international friendship seems at odds with its gruesome dioramas of executions and medical experiments, and photos of dead babies.

Shidu

Shidu is a scenic strip along the Juma River, 100km southwest of Beijing. You can get a bus here from Lianhuachi bus station, or a train from Yongdingmen Zhan. The area earned its name, which means "ten ferries", from the ten zigzags the river makes as it flows through the karst rocks along a fifteen-kilometre valley. Nicknamed Beijing's Guilin, its lush foliage, craggy peaks and clear water make it a popular day trip destination for local Chinese. If you're unlucky and get bad weather, the rain and mist produce views like a splashed ink landscape painting. The area along the riverbank is in places quite developed, with photographers and fruit vendors, but drift downstream in a boat or hike off into the hills and you should get some uninterrupted quality time with nature. You arrive by both bus and train at the tenth zigzag; you can rent boats at the ninth (¥10 per hour), and there's a popular bathing spot at the sixth.

travel details

Trains

Beijing Zhan to: Baotou (daily, 14hr); Beidaihe (3 daily, 7hr); Changchun (daily, 18hr); Chengde (4 daily, 4hr 30min); Dalian (2 daily, 20hr); Dandong (daily, 20hr); Datong (2 daily, 7hr); Fuzhou (daily, 40hr); Hangzhou (daily, 25hr); Harbin (daily, 22hr); Hohhot (2 daily, 12hr); Ji'nan (3 daily, 9hr); Nanjing (daily, 21hr); Qingdao (daily, 19hr); Shanhaiguan (3 daily, 8hr); Shanghai (2 daily, 20hr); Shenyang (3 daily, 12hr); Tai'an (2 daily, 10hr); Tianjin (6 daily, 2–3hr); Yantai (daily, 20hr).

Xi Zhan to: Changsha (daily, 24hr); Chengdu (2 daily, 35hr); Chongqing (2 daily, 40hr); Guangzhou (3 daily, 35hr); Guiyang (daily, 35hr); Lanzhou (daily, 35hr); Luoyang (daily, 14hr); Kunming (daily, 60hr); Nanchang (daily, 25hr); Nanning (daily, 40hr); Shijiazhuang (daily, 4hr); Taiyuan (daily, 12hr); Ulan Batur (Mongolia; weekly, 90hr); Urumqi (daily, 80hr); Xi'an (5 daily, 18hr); Yuncheng (daily, 20hr); Yichang (daily, 27hr); Zhanjiang (daily, 40hr); Zhengzhou (2 daily, 12hr).

As well as the above, there are weekly services from Xi Zhan to Moscow and Ulan Batur; see pp.74–75 for details.

Buses

There is little point travelling to destinations far from Beijing by bus; the journey takes longer than the train and is far less comfortable. The following destinations are within bearable travelling distance. Services are frequent, usually hourly during the day, with a few evening buses travellling at night.

Deshengmen bus station to: Chengde (5hr); Datong (10hr).

Dongzhimen bus station to: Shenyang (18hr).

Haihutun bus station to: Shijiazhuang (10hr); Tianjin (3hr).

Majuan bus station to: Beidaihe (9hr); Shanhaiguan (9hr).

Planes

Beijing to: Anqing (2 weekly; 2hrs); Baotou (2 weekly; 1hr 30min); Beihai (2 weekly; 4hr 15min); Changchun (3–5 daily; 1hr 45min); Changsha (3 daily; 2hr); Chaoyang (4 daily; 1hr 20min); Chengdu (7 daily; 2hr 30min); Chifeng (3 weekly; 3hr); Chongqing (2–4 daily; 2hr 40min); Dalian (4–7 daily; 1hr 20min); Fuzhou (2 daily; 2hr 50min); Guangzhou (7 daily; 3hr); Guilin (2 daily; 3hr); Guiyang (2 daily; 4hr 45min); Haikou (4 daily; 3hr 45min); Hailar (weekly; 2hr 20min); Hangzhou (5 daily; 1hr 50min); Harbin (5 daily; 2hr); Hefei (1–3 daily; 1hr 30min); Hohhot (2–3 daily; 1hr 10min); Hong Kong (4 daily; 3hr); Huangyan (4 weekly; 2hr 40min); Jilin (2 weekly; 1hr 50min); Ji'nan (daily; 1hr); Jinzhou (3 weekly; 1hr 20min); Kunming (3 daily; 3hr 30min); Lanzhou (2 daily; 2hr 20min); Lianyungang (2 weekly; 1hr 30min); Liuzhou (2 weekly; 2hr 45min); Luoyang (weekly; 1hr 40min); Mudanjiang (daily; 1hr 50min); Nanchang (daily; 2hr); Nanjing (5 daily; 1hr 45min); Nanning (3 daily; 3hr 30min); Nantong (3 weekly; 2hr 30min); Nanyang (2 weekly; 1hr 30min); Ningbo (1–2 daily; 2hr 20min); Qingdao (2–4 daily; 1hr 15min); Qiqihar (2 weekly; 2hr); Quzhou (weekly; 2hr 30min); Sanya (daily; 5hr 20min); Shanghai (14 daily; 1hr 50min); Shantou (2–3 daily; 3hr); Shenyang (5 daily; 1hr); Shenzhen (7 daily; 3hr

10min); Taiyuan (daily; 1hr 10min); Tianjin (daily; 30min); Tongliao (2 weekly; 1hr 45min); Wenzhou (2–5 daily; 2hr 20min); Wuhan (5 daily; 2hr); Wulanhot (2 weekly; 3hr 20min); Xiamen (4 daily; 2hr 50min); Xi'an (4 daily; 1hr 30min); Xiangfan (3 weekly; 2hr); Xilinhot (2 weekly; 1hr 40min); Xining (2 weekly; 2hr 30min); Yangon (weekly; 5hr); Yanji (1–3 daily; 2hr); Yantai (3 daily; 1hr); Yinchuan (daily; 2hr); Yiwu (3 weekly; 2hr); Zhangjiajie (2 weekly; 3hr); Zhanjiang (daily; 3hr 30min); Zhengzhou (3 daily; 1hr 20min); Zhuhai (3hr 30min).

CHAPTER TWO

HEBEI AND TIANJIN

Hebei is a somewhat anonymous province, split into two distinct geographical areas, with two great cities, Beijing and Tianjin, at its heart, but administratively outside its borders. In the south, a landscape of flatlands is spotted with heavy industry and mining towns – China at its least glamorous – home to the majority of the province's sixty million inhabitants. Most travellers pass through here, on their way to or from the capital, but few stop. The bleak, sparsely populated tableland rising from the Bohai Gulf, in the north of the province, however, has more promise. For most of its history this marked China's northern frontier, and was the setting for numerous battles with invading forces; both the Mongols and the Manchus swept through here. The mark of this bloody history remains in the form of the **Great Wall**, winding across its lonely ridges.

The first wall was built in the fourth century AD, along the Hebei–Shanxi border, an attempt by the small state of Zhongshan to fortify its borders against its aggressive neighbours.Two centuries later, Qin Shi Huang's Wall of Ten Thousand Li (see p.121) skirted the northern borders of the province. The parts of the wall still visible today, though, are the remains of the much later, and more extensive, Ming-dynasty wall, begun in the fourteenth century as a deterrent against the Mongols. You can see the wall at **Shanhaiguan**, the point where it meets the sea, today a relaxing little fortress town only a day's journey from Beijing. While you're there, don't miss the strange resort of **Beidaihe**, just to the south, as appealing to foreign travellers for its garish atmosphere and its history as the holiday home of the Party elite as for its many beaches. Well north of the wall, the town of **Chengde** is the province's most diverting attraction, an imperial base set amidst the wild terrain of the Hachin Mongols, and conceived on a grand scale by the eighteenth-century emperor Kangxi, with monuments and temples to match. All three towns are popular spots with domestic tourists, particularly Beijingers snatching a weekend away from the capital's bustle and stress, and part of the interest of going is in seeing the Chinese at their most carefree. Though the Chinese like their holiday spots the way they like their restaurants, *rehao* – hot and noisy, it's easy to beat the crowds and

ACCOMMODATION PRICE CODES

All the accommodation in this book has been graded according to the following price codes, which represent the cheapest double room available to foreigners. Most places have a range of rooms, however, and staff will usually offer you the more expensive ones – it's always worth asking if they have anything cheaper. Where the text refers specifically to dorm beds, the price code represents the price per bed. See p.40 for more details.

① less than ¥30	④ ¥100–150	⑦ ¥300–500
② ¥30–75	⑤ ¥150–200	⑧ ¥500–700
③ ¥75–100	⑥ ¥200–300	⑨ ¥700 or more

find some great scenery, and each town makes a rewarding visit even if you are just returning to the capital afterwards.

Tianjin, an industrial giant, has outgrown its role as the region's capital to become a separate municipality. An ex-concession town with a distinctly Western stamp, it's worth a day trip from Beijing to see its unique streetscapes, a striking medley of nineteenth-century European architecture and Chinese modernism. Hebei's new capital, **Shijiazhuang**, in the south, is a major rail junction, but a rather dull town, though you may well find yourself passing through, in which case it's worth checking out the few historical sites scattered in the countryside around.

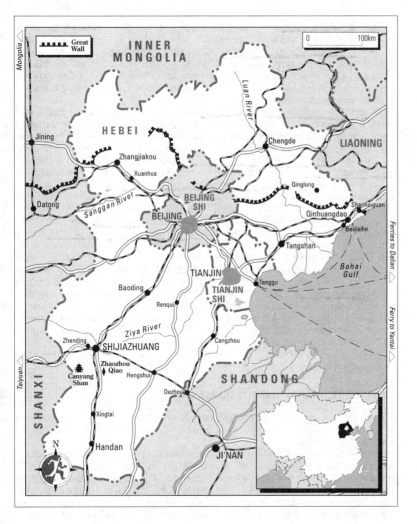

Tianjin

And there were sections of the city where different foreigners lived – Japanese, White Russians, Americans and Germans – but never together, and all with their own separate habits, some dirty, some clean. And they had houses of all shapes and colours, one painted in pink, another with rooms that jutted out at every angle like the backs and fronts of Victorian dresses, others with roofs like pointed hats and wood carvings painted white to look like ivory.

Amy Tan *The Joy Luck Club*

China's third largest city, the commercial centre of **TIANJIN** 80km east of Beijing, is by Chinese standards a dynamic, modern city, but for visitors its most attractive feature is its legacy of **colonial buildings** reflecting an assortment of foreign styles. Overshadowed by the capital and little visited by tourists, Tianjin has architecture and shopping opportunities, especially for antiques, that make it worth a day trip from Beijing, less than two hours away by train. A longer trip will prove expensive as there is no budget accommodation in the city.

An important **port** since the Ming dynasty, when goods destined for the capital were stored here, Tianjin caught the attention of the seafaring Western powers in the nineteenth century, who used a minor infringement – the boarding of an English ship by Chinese troops – as an excuse to declare war. With well-armed gunboats, they were assured of victory, and the Treaty of Tianjin, signed in 1856, gave the Europeans the right to establish concessionary bases on the mainland from where they could conduct trade and sell opium.

These separate **concessions**, along the banks of the Hai River, were self-contained European fantasy worlds: the French built elegant chateaux and towers, while the Germans constructed red-tiled Bavarian villas. The Chinese were discouraged from intruding, except for servants, who were given pass cards. Tensions between the indigenous population and the foreigners exploded in the **Tianjin Incident** of 1870, when a Chinese mob attacked a French-run orphanage, and killed the nuns and priests, in the belief that the Chinese orphans were being kidnapped for later consumption. Twenty Chinese were beheaded as a result, and the prefect of the city was banished. A centre for secretive anti-foreign movements, the city had its genteel peace interrupted again by the Boxer Rebellion in 1900 (see *Contexts*, p.1001), after which the foreigners levelled the walls around the old Chinese city to enable them to keep an eye on its residents.

Today port activity has moved to Tanggu, 50km east, and Tianjin is given over to industry and commerce. In 1976 the region suffered a devastating earthquake, centred on the town of Tangshan, 80km north, which reduced the town to rubble in seconds. Over a quarter of a million people died and Tianjin was briefly closed to foreigners while parts of the city were rebuilt.

Orientation, arrival and city transport

Though it's a massive place, the part of Tianjin of interest to visitors, the dense network of ex-concession streets south and west of the central train station, south of the Hai River, is fairly compact.

Tianjin's large international **airport**, 15km east of the city, is served by regular shuttle buses, terminating outside the *CAAC* office on Heping Lu. A taxi should cost around ¥30. If you arrive by **ferry**, you'll find yourself in the port of Tanggu, a dull and very expensive appendage of the city. Buses to take you the 50km into the city centre congregate around the passenger ferry terminal. The train is quicker, taking just under an hour, but Tanggu South station is inconveniently situated about 2km west of the ferry terminal.

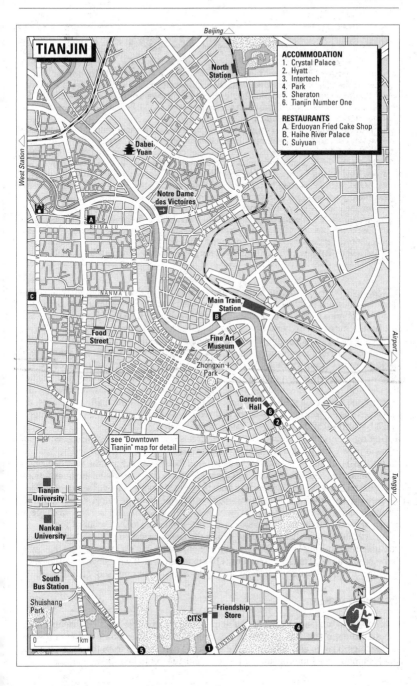

TIANJIN

ACCOMMODATION
1. Crystal Palace
2. Hyatt
3. Intertech
4. Park
5. Sheraton
6. Tianjin Number One

RESTAURANTS
A. Erduoyan Fried Cake Shop
B. Haihe River Palace
C. Suiyuan

Beijing

North Station

West Station

Dabei Yuan

Notre Dame des Victoires

BEIMA LU

NANMA LU

Main Train Station

Fine Art Museum

Food Street

Zhongxin Park

CHANGJIANG DAO

Gordon Hall

see "Downtown Tianjin" map for detail

Airport

Tanggu

Tianjin University

Nankai University

South Bus Station

Shuishang Park

DUIXIANGTAI LU

CITS

Friendship Store

BINSHUI DAO

0   1km

N

FERRIES FROM TANGGU

Tianjin's port, at **Tanggu**, 50km east, has an **international ferry** service. A ferry to **Kobe,** in Japan (48hr), leaves Tanggu every Monday; another goes to **Inchon,** in South Korea (28hr), leaving every five days. Domestic ferries serve **Dalian** every other day and **Yantai** about six times a month. Tickets can be bought from Tianjin or Beijing *CITS* for a small surcharge, or from the ferry booking office at 1 Pukou Dao (☎3399573), a small street west off Taierzhuang Lu in Tianjin.

Frequent **minibuses** to Tanggu run from outside Tianjin main station. Public **buses** leave from the South bus station at the northeastern edge of Shuishang Park, or you can catch the #151 which leaves from a small street opposite the main station; go over the bridge to the west, turn left, then take the second right and walk about 100m down the street. Two **trains** to Tanggu leave from the main station early every morning, taking just under an hour. Tanggu has two train stations, of which the South station, the second that the train calls at, is closest to the ferry terminal.

Tanggu itself is very expensive. The cheapest **place to stay** is the *International Seamen's Club* (⑥), just north of the passenger terminal. As domestic ferries leave in the afternoon, it is possible to travel here from Beijing and make a same-day connection. The international ferries all leave in the morning, however, and as you need to check in two hours before departure time, a night in expensive Tianjin or Tanggu is unavoidable.

The city's huge, new **main train station** is well run and well organized, and conveniently located just north of the Hai River; the town centre is a few kilometres south (take bus #24). There are two other stations in town, North, which you are likely to arrive at if you have come from northeast China, and West which is on the main line between Beijing and destinations farther south. Trains terminating in Tianjin may call at one of the other stations before reaching the main station. The most stylish way to arrive is on the double-decker express train which leaves Beijing early every morning, and takes under two hours (30min quicker than regular trains). It's bright orange and brazenly modern, and the platform staff at Tianjin station salute it as it comes in. Public **buses** from Beijing also arrive at the main train station, as do most of the private ones – the highway between the two cities has cut journey times down to three hours. Arriving from the port at Tanggu, you'll be dropped at the South bus station near Shuishang Park.

Getting around the central-grid patterned streets is made difficult by the absence of any signs in pinyin, but there are plenty of distinctive landmarks. Downtown and the old concession areas are just small enough to explore on foot, fortunately, as the **bus** network is both complicated and overcrowded. Bus maps are widely available around the train stations. Some useful buses are #24, which runs from the West station, into town, then doubles back on itself and terminates at the main station; #1 which runs from the North station into town, terminating at Zhongxin Park, the northern tip of the downtown area; and #50 which meanders into town from the main train station and takes you close to the Catholic Church.

An alternative to the fiendish bus system is the L-shaped **subway** line (¥2 per journey), running from Nanjing Lu to the West train station, although it's a little far from the sights to be of much use. **Taxis** are plentiful (¥10 minimum, which will be sufficient for most journeys around town), and **bicycles** are readily available for rent (see "Listings", p.141).

Accommodation

Tianjin is a rotten place to stay if you're travelling on a budget, with **no cheap hotels** on offer, though you may be able to talk your way into a dormitory at one of the two universities, Tianjin and Nankai, in the south of town (bus #8 from the main train station), though it's a time-consuming process, and one not to be relied upon.

The **telephone code** for Tianjin is ☎022

A cluster of expensive hotels is located in the south of the city, in a grimy area, though next to a couple of parks. Bus #4 from the centre will get you within walking distance. The hotels within the city centre are a better option for a short stay.

Hotels

Crystal Palace, Youyi Lu (☎8356888, fax 8350591). This Sino-American joint venture sits next to a lake in Yanyuan Park, and looks a little like a luxury cruiser, with the same sort of facilities and a price tag to match. ⑨.

Friendship, 94 Nanjing Lu (☎3117878). A modern and somewhat banal building oposite the earthquake memorial south of the town centre. ⑦.

Guomin, corner of Heping Lu and Yingkou Dao. This small place has an appealing faded elegance – the building dates back to 1923. It's relatively cheap and well located right in the centre of town. From the main station, take bus #4 to Heping Lu and then walk east for ten minutes. Rooms at the front have wrought-iron balconies. ⑤.

Huizhong, 2 Huizhong Lu (☎7110086). Tucked away in an alley off Heping Lu – look for an arch with the hotel's name on it, in English, on the southern side of the street. The staff at this cheerful place giggle uncontrollably when faced with a foreigner. ⑦.

Hyatt, Jiefang Bei Lu (☎3318888, fax 3310021). A four-star modernist mansion overlooking the Hai River. ⑧.

Intertech, 23 Youyi Lu (☎8358888). Not living up to its sci-fi moniker, this place is a standard, unexciting business hotel in the far south of the city, but cheap by Tianjin standards. ⑦.

Park, Leyuan Lu (☎8309818, fax 8302042). The least expensive of the southern hotels, this place is quiet and appealing, but some distance from anything exciting. ⑦.

Sheraton, Zijinshan Lu (☎3343388, fax 3358740). Inconveniently located in the south of town, but next to the pleasant Yanyuan Park. ⑧.

Tianjin Number One, Jiefang Bei Lu (☎3310707, fax 3313341). A rather nice, rambling old colonial building, but cowed by the *Hyatt* down the road. ⑦.

The City

Tianjin is a good place to go **shopping**, particularly for antiques and handicrafts, but there are few actual sights, and it's the city's streetscapes, an assemblage of nineteenth- and early twentieth-century foreign architecture, mostly European, juxtaposed with the concrete and glass monoliths of wealthy contemporary China, which are its most engrossing attraction. The old city was strictly demarcated into national zones, and each section of the city centre has retained a hint of its old flavour. The area northwest of the main train station, on the west side of the Hai River, was the old Chinese city. Running from west to east along the north bank of the river were the Austrian, Italian, Russian and Belgian concessions, though most of the old buildings here have been destroyed. Unmistakable are the chateaux of the French concession, which now make up the downtown district just south of the river, and the haughty mansions the British built east of here. Farther east, but still south of the river, the architecture of an otherwise unremarkable district has a sprinkling of stern German buildings.

Downtown Tianjin

The majority of Tianjin's colonial buildings are clustered in the grid of streets on the southern side of the river. Coming from the main train station, Liberation Bridge, built by the French in 1903, leads south to an area given an oddly Continental feel by the pastel colours and wrought-iron scrollwork balconies of the French concession, which is

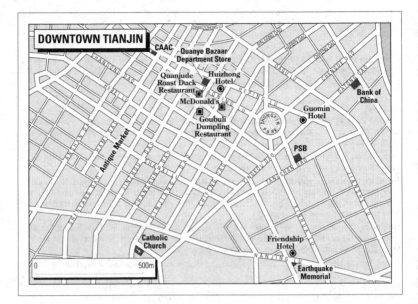

at its most appealing around the glorified roundabout known as **Zhongxin Park**. On
the corner of Jiefang Bei Lu and Harbin Dao, the **Fine Art Museum** (daily 8am–4pm;
¥5), a slightly pompous old building, has a broad collection of paintings, kites, Chinese
New Year prints and *ni ren*, literally "mud men", clay figurines which became a popular local craft in the nineteenth century. Their greatest exponent was a skilled carica-
turist called Zhang who made copies of opera stars and other notables; some of his
work is on display; unfortunately none of his depictions of Tianjin's foreigners, which
got him into trouble with the authorities, is here.

Zhongxin Park marks the northern boundary of the main **shopping district**, an area
bounded by Dagu Lu, Jinzhou Dao and Chifeng Dao; Heping Lu and Binjiang Dao are
the two busiest streets. Though stuffed with intrepid shoppers (at least as fashionably
dressed as a Beijing crowd), the narrow streets have a pleasingly laid-back feel, as traffic is light, and Binjiang Dao itself is pedestrianized. The **Quanye Bazaar Department
Store**, a nine-storey turquoise steel fortress on the corner of Changchun Dao and
Heping Lu, has an enormous selection of goods, and although a huge number of staff
is the norm in Chinese department stores, this could be the only store in China that
uses real people rather than mannequins to model the clothes. A wider range of cheap-
er clothes is available from a massive **street market** that stretches the length of
Binjiang Dao. If you're in the area at lunchtime, there are plenty of places for a snack;
McDonald's and *KFC* are right on Binjiang Dao along with more traditional places (see
"Eating and drinking", p.141).

Just west of here is a shopping district of a very different character, the **antique
market**, a great attraction even if you have no intention of buying. The alleys are lined
with dark, poky shops, pavement vendors with their wares spread out in front of them
on yellowed newspapers and stallholders waving jade and teapots in the faces of
passers by. Centred on Shenyang Jie, but spilling over into side alleys, the market is
open daily but expands and contracts according to the time of year; small in winter, big

TIANJIN

Tianjin	天津	*tiānjīn*

ACCOMMODATION

Crystal Palace	水晶宫饭店	*shuǐjīnggōng fàndiàn*
Friendship	友谊宾馆	*yǒuyì bīnguǎn*
Guomin	国民大酒店	*guómín dàjiǔdiàn*
Hyatt	凯悦饭店	*kǎiyuè fàndiàn*
Intertech	科技咨询大厦	*kējì zīxún dàshà*
Nankai University	南开大学	*nánkāi dàxué*
Park	乐园宾馆	*yùyuán bīnguǎn*
Sheraton	喜来登大酒店	*xǐláidēng dàjiǔdiàn*
Tianjin Number One	天津第一饭店	*tiānjīn dìyī fàndiàn*
Tianjin University	天津大学	*tiānjīn dàxué*

THE CITY

Ancient Culture St	古文化街	*gǔwénhuà jiē*
Antique Market	旧货市场	*jiùhuò shìchǎng*
Catholic Church	西开教堂	*xīkāi jiàotán*
Dabei Yuan	大悲院	*dàbēiyuàn*
Earthquake Memorial	抗震纪念碑	*kàngzhèn jìniànbēi*
Fine Art Museum	艺术博物馆	*yìshù bówùguǎn*
Mosque	清真寺	*qīngzhēn sì*
Notre Dame des Victoires	望海楼教堂	*wànghǎilóu jiàotáng*
Quanye Bazaar	劝业场	*quànyè chǎng*
Zhongxin Park	中心公园	*zhōngxīn gōngyuán*

RESTAURANTS

Erduoyan Fried Cake Shop	耳朵眼炸糕店	*ěrduōyǎn zhágāndiàn*
Goubuli Stuffed Dumpling Restaurant	狗不理包子铺	*gǒubúlǐ bāozipù*
Haihe River Palace	海河皇宫	*hǎihé huánggōng*
Quanjude Roast Duck	全聚德烤鸭店	*quánjùdé kǎoyādiàn*
Suiyuan	随园酒家	*suíyuán jiǔjiā*

AROUND TIANJIN

Tanggu	塘沽	*tánggū*
International Seamen's Club	国际海员俱乐部	*guójì hǎiyuán jùlèbù*

in the summer, and it's at its largest on Sundays, swelled by Beijingers here for the weekend. The market is generally cheaper than any in the capital, though the shop-keepers know the value of everything they are selling and you will have to look hard for a bargain. Bartering is mandatory, and be aware that some of the stuff is fake. The variety of goods on display is astonishing: among the standard jade jewellery, ceramic teapots, fans and perfume bottles are Russian army watches, opium pipes, snuff boxes, ornate playing cards, old photographs, pornographic paintings, and rimless "Fu Manchu" sunglasses. Look out for the stalls selling picture postcards of revolutionary dramas depicting synchronized ballet dancers performing graceful mid-air leaps with hand grenades, and the shop specializing in Mao alarm clocks, which have a picture of eager red guards on the face; the second hand is a girl waving the Little Red Book.

At the end of Binjiang Lu, about 500m south of the market, the **Catholic Church** (Sun only), which has an odd facade of horizontal brown and orange brick stripes topped with three green domes, is one of the most distinctive buildings in the city, and a useful landmark. The diffuse zone of unremarkable buildings east of here, around Nanjing Lu, is notable only for the **Earthquake Memorial** opposite the *Friendship Hotel*. A hollow pyramid more tasteful than most Chinese public statuary, it commemorates the people who died in the Tangshan earthquake of 1976. Heading northeast back towards the river, you pass more nineteenth-century architecture – the most notable is **Gordon Hall** on Dagu Lu, just west of the *Astor Hotel*, a fortress-like building that used to house the British administrative offices.

North of the centre

The main sight in the northern part of the city is the **Dabei Yuan** (daily 8am–4pm; ¥4), on a narrow alleyway off Zhongshan Lu. Tianjin's major centre for Buddhist worship, it's easy to find as the alleys all around are crammed with stalls selling a colourful mix of religious knick-knacks: incense, tapes of devotional music, mirror-glass shrines, and ceramic Buddhas with flashing lights in their eyes. Outside the first hall, built in the 1940s, the devout wrap their arms around a large bronze incense burner before lighting incense sticks and kowtowing. In the smaller, rear buildings, seventeenth-century structures extensively restored after the Tangshan earthquake, you'll see the temple's jovial resident monks, standing chatting and giving each other haircuts. A hall in the west of the complex displays small antique wood and bronze Buddhist figurines. Large bronze vessels full of water stand outside the buildings, a fire precaution that has been in use for centuries.

The tall, dark cathedral, **Notre Dame des Victoires** (Shengmu Desheng Tang), stands over Shizilin Dajie, just south of here, on the north bank of the river. Built in 1904, it's the third to stand on this site; the first was destroyed in the massacre of 1870, a year after it was built, and the second was burnt down in 1900 in the Boxer Rebellion. Its dark stone and the rigorous formality of its lines give it an austere presence, in contrast to the Catholic Church farther south. The cathedral is open to the public only on Sunday, when a morning service is held.

The more prosaic **Ancient Culture Street**, a short walk southwest of here after crossing the bridge by the cathedral, runs off the southern side of Beima Lu, its entrance marked by a colourful arch. Like Liulichang in Beijing, this is a recreation of a Chinese street from the last century, minus beggars and filth and plus neon "OK Karaoke" signs, designed as a tourist shopping mall. It's all false, but with carved balconies and columns decorating the facade of red and green wooden shops topped with curling, tiled roofs, it's undeniably pretty. The shops sell pricey antiques and souvenirs, and there's an especially large range of different teapots. Reality intrudes at the southern end of the street as you face a rash of of white skyscrapers.

More genuine streets lie west of here, in the old city, a rectangular block bounded by the four horse (*ma*) streets – Beima, Nanma, Dongma and Xima. The area is characterized by quiet, grey courtyards off intimate alleyways and it's a good place to wander, an essentially private quarter of small shops and houses, appealing for its human scale in a city with so much grand public architecture. The excellent **Erduoyan Fried Cake Shop** (see "Eating and drinking" below) is located here and there are plenty of small noodle and dumpling places around. The **mosque**, farther west, off Dafeng Lu, is a fine example of Chinese Muslim architecture, with some striking wood carvings of floral designs in the eaves and around the windows. It's an active place of worship and you're free to wander around, but not to enter the buildings.

Eating and drinking

Food Street, off Nanmenwai Dajie. A cheerful, two-storey mall, this is the best place to eat in Tianjin. With fifty or so restaurants on each level, there's something to suit all budgets and tastes. Upstairs try the *Zhejiang Restaurant* for Zhejiang cuisine; *Suzhou Deyuelou* for Jiangsu food, and *Penglaichun* for Shandong dishes. There are two reasonably priced Sichuan restaurants, *Emei* and *Gujing*, downstairs and a good but expensive Japanese restaurant, *Kobe*. In between the restaurants are stalls and shops selling cakes, biscuits, dried fruit, nuts, chocolates, and dead ducks.

Goubuli Stuffed Dumpling Restaurant, 77 Shandong Lu. Handy if you're shopping around Binjiang Dao – look for the man in a chef's hat who stands outside. A famous Tianjin restaurant, the place is small and low-key, and the dumplings are delicious and cheap. The name, which means "dogs won't touch it", is thought to be a reference either to the ugliness of the original proprietor or to the low-class status of dumplings.

Quanjude Roast Duck, Heping Lu. A branch of the famous Beijing restaurant. Duck and all the trimmings for two should come to around ¥200.

Erduoyan Fried Cake Shop, Beima Lu. A century-old institution that specializes in rice powder cakes fried in sesame oil.

Haihe River Palace. This upmarket restaurant built in classical Chinese style on a pontoon on the Haihe River, just east of Liberation Bridge, south of the train station, specializes in Cantonese food.

Suiyuan, Huanghe Dao. A good selection of Shandong-style dishes for around ¥50 per head.

Listings

Airlines The main *CAAC* office is at 242 Heping Lu (Mon–Sat 8am–5pm; ☎7305888). The airport bus service runs from outside here. There's an *Air China* office (Mon–Fri 8.30–11.30am & 1.30–4.30pm) just west of the *Friendship Hotel* on Nanjing Lu. Domestic tickets are sold downstairs (☎3301543), international upstairs (☎3393497).

Banks and exchange The main office of the *Bank of China* is in a grand colonial edifice at 80 Jiefang Bei Lu (Mon–Fri 8am–noon & 2–4pm).

Bike rental Bikes can be rented from a huge bike park (daily 8am–7pm) outside the main train station. It can be hard to find as it's hidden underground; a ramp on the west side of the station concourse leads up and then down into the park. Bikes are ¥10 a day with a ¥100 deposit.

Bookshops The *Foreign Language Bookstore* is at 130 Chifeng Dao.

Buses Privately run buses from Tianjin to Beijing leave from outside Tianjin main station throughout the day.

Post office In a building on the east side of the train station (Mon–Fri 8am–7pm).

PSB For police and visa extensions go to 30 Tangshan Dao.

Shopping As well as for the clothes and antique markets in the centre of the city, Tianjin is renowned for its handmade rugs and carpets. While they're not cheap, they are of good quality, featuring bright, complex, abstract patterns, and are best bought directly from the factories in the suburbs of the city; try *Factory Number Five* at 57 Chifeng Lu, Heping District (ring for current transport arrangements ☎3390501). *Ni ren* figurines (see p.138) continue to be made by the Zhang family, though these days output is more standardized. You can buy the colourful fifteen-centimetre-high figures at the *Zhang Art Store* on Guwenhua Jie (again, call for transport details ☎2355248). Tianjin is also noted for its kites and New Year posters – bright, woodblock prints of domestic subjects, pasted up for good luck at Chinese New Year – made and sold at the *Yangliuqing Picture Studio* on Sanhe Dao. *Tianjin Arts and Crafts Factory* at 503 Huanghe Jie and the *Tianjin Special Handicrafts Factory* at 16 Liuwei Lu both sell handicrafts, as do a number of the stores on Ancient Culture Street (see p.140). The *Tianjin Cultural Relics Company*, fairly central at 161 Liaoning Lu (☎7300308), has a wide selection of antique jade, embroidery, calligraphy, and carvings. You can buy the same things from the *Friendship Store*, at 21 Youyi Lu, whose supermarket contains some really priceless commodities for anyone who's been in China for any length of time: Guinness, peanut butter, Marmite and Worcester sauce.

Telephones The 24-hr telecommunications office is in the same building as the post office.

Trains The majority of trains leave from the main station. A few trains to the northeast leave only from the North station, and some trains to southern destinations, such as Shanghai, that don't originate in Tianjin, call only at the West station. To avoid the queues when buying train tickets from the main station, try the soft-sleeper ticket office; go up the escalator,turn left towards the soft-sleeper waiting room, and the discreet office is on your left.

Travel agents A generally unhelpful branch of *CITS* is at 22 Youyi Lu (☎8358501), opposite the *Friendship Store*. They won't part with much information but they will book train and boat tickets for onward travel (☎8350822).

Beidaihe and around

BEIDAIHE is bizarre. A seaside resort on the Bohai Gulf, 300km east of Beijing, it was originally patronized by European diplomats, missionaries and businessmen around the turn of the century, who must have chosen it out of homesickness. Its coastline – rocky, sparsely vegetated, erratically punctuated by beaches – is reminiscent of the Mediterranean. They built villas and bungalows here, and reclined on verandahs sipping cocktails after indulging in the new bathing fad. After the Communist takeover, the village became a pleasure resort for Party bigwigs, reaching its height of popularity in the 1970s when seaside trips were no longer seen as decadent and revisionist. Strict rules ordered where individuals could bathe, according to their rank: West Beach was reserved for foreigners after they were let in in 1979, with guards posted to chase off Chinese voyeurs interested in glimpsing their daringly bourgeois swimming costumes. The Middle Beach, demarcated by rope barriers, was reserved for Party officials, with a sandy cove – the best spot – set out for the higher ranks. Dark swimsuits were compulsory, to avoid the illusion of nudity.

These days the barriers have gone, along with the inhibitions of the urban Chinese (bikinis are fashionable now) and the contemporary town is a fascinating mix of the austerely communist and the gaudy kitsch of any busy seaside resort. On the hill behind the beach, on leafy streets guarded by discreet soldiers, sit the villas of the Party elite. It's rumoured that every Politburo member once had a residence here, and probably many still do. All around are huge, chunky buildings, often with absurd decorative touches – Roman columns, fake totem poles, Greek porticos – grafted on to their ponderous facades. These are work-unit hotels and sanatoriums for heroes of the people, factory workers, soldiers and the like, when they are granted the privilege of a seaside holiday. On the beach, stirring revolutionary statues of lantern-jawed workers and their wives and children stand among the throngs of bathers, while on the beachfront behind them stalls sell Day-Glo swimsuits and sculptures of chickens made of shells and raffia.

Though you still see serious men in uniforms and sunglasses licking lollipops, and black Audis with tinted windows (the Party cadre car) cruising the waterfront, these days most of Beidaihe's visitors are ordinary, fun-loving tourists, usually well-heeled Beijingers. In season, when the temperature is steady around the mid-20s Centigrade and the water warm, it's noisy and crowded, and a fun place to spend a day or two. Everyone is here to enjoy themselves, and it's a real pleasure simply to see the Chinese looking so relaxed.

The Town and beaches

The streets along the seafront are the liveliest – most buildings are either restaurants, with crabs and prawns bobbing about in buckets outside, or shops selling bikinis, inflatables, snorkels and souvenirs. Moving away from the sea, up the hill, the tree-lined streets are much quieter and many of the buildings are guesthouses.

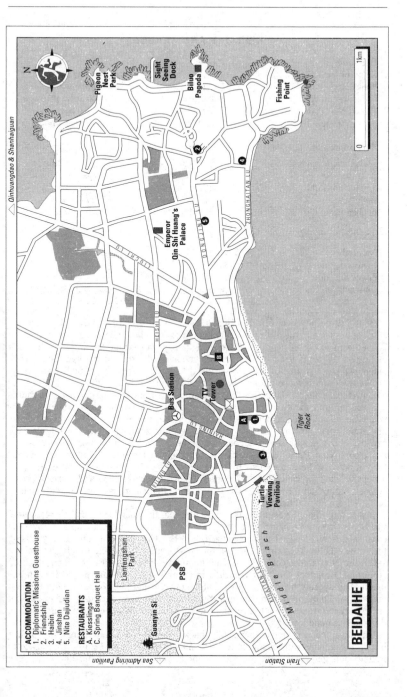

BEIDAIHE

ACCOMMODATION
1. Diplomatic Missions Guesthouse
2. Friendship
3. Haibin
4. Jinshan
5. Nite Dajiudian

RESTAURANTS
A. Kiesslings
C. Spring Banquet Hall

Pigeon Nest Park
Sight Seeing Dock
Biluo Pagoda
Fishing Point
Emperor Qin Shi Huang's Palace
HONGHAITAN LU
HEISHI LU
Bus Station
TV Tower
Tiger Rock
Turtle Viewing Pavilion
Middle Beach
HAITAN LU
Lianfengshan Park
PSB
Guanyin Si

Qinhuangdao & Shanhaiguan
Sea Admiring Pavilion
Train Station

1km
0

BEIDAIHE AND AROUND

Beidaihe	北戴河	*běidàihé*
Emperor Qin Shi Huang's Palace	秦皇宫	*qínhuáng gōng*
Kiesslings	起士林餐厅	*qǐshìlín cāntīng*
Lianfengshan Park	联峰山公园	*liánfēngshān gōngyuán*
Pigeon Nest Park	鸽子窝公园	*gēziwō gōngyuán*
Spring Banquet Hall	宴春楼饭庄	*yànchūnlóu fànzhuāng*

ACCOMMODATION

Diplomatic Missions Guesthouse	外交人员宾馆	*wàijiāo rényuán bīnguǎn*
Friendship Hotel	友谊宾馆	*yǒuyì bīnguǎn*
Haibin Hotel	海滨饭店	*hǎibīn fàndiàn*
Jinshan Hotel	金山宾馆	*jīnshān bīnguǎn*

AROUND BEIDAIHE

Nandaihe	南戴河	*nándàihé*
Qinhuangdao	秦皇岛	*qínhuángdǎo*
Friendship Hotel	国际海员俱乐部	*guójìhǎiyuán jùlèbù*
Qinhuangdao Hotel	秦皇岛宾馆	*qínhuángdǎo bīnguǎn*

Of the three beaches, **Middle Beach**, really many small beaches with rocky outcrops in between, is the most convenient and most popular. The promenade at the back is lined with soft drink vendors, photo stalls, hoopla games, and bathing huts that look like moon dwellings from a 1950s science fiction movie. You can get your photograph taken on top of a stuffed tiger or in a cardboard speedboat, or dressed up like an emperor. **West Beach** is more of the same, but a little quieter. East of the resort (bus #3 or #4), stretching fifteen kilometres to Qinhuangdao, is **East Beach**, popular with cadres and sanatorium patients for its more sedate atmosphere. The beach is long enough for you to be able to find a spot where you can be alone, though most of the muddy shoreline is not very attractive. The slope of the beach is gradual, and at low tide its wide expanse is dotted with seaweed collectors in rubber boots. At the beach's western tip is **Pigeon Nest Park,** a twenty-metre-high rocky outcrop named after the seagulls fond of perching here, obviously by someone who wasn't hot on bird identification. It's a popular spot for watching the sunrise. Mao sat here in 1954 and wrote a poem, "Ripples sifting sand/Beidaihe," which loses something in translation. To get here take bus #21 from Zhonghaitan Lu.

Just before Pigeon Nest Park, the bus stops near the dock for Beidaihe's **sight-seeing boats**. In season, boats leave regularly during the day and chug up and down the coast, which isn't really that spectacular (2hr; ¥15). The highlight of the trip is passing the strange **Biluo Pagoda**, a hotel on the coast south of the dock, which resembles a seven-storey concrete conch shell. One kilometre directly west of the boat dock on Heishi Lu, **Emperor Qin Shi Huang's Palace** (Tues–Sun 8am–5pm; ¥15) is an imitation Qing-dynasty building with exhibits, dioramas and photos concerning the first emperor of China, who made an inspection tour of the area during his reign. It's not really very informative, but the reconstructed throne room, complete with dressed up dummies, is good if tacky.

On the far western side of town, 500m back from the beach, **Lianfengshan Park**, a hill of dense pines with picturesque pavilions and odd little caves, is a good place to wander and get away from the crowds for a while. On top of the hill is the **Sea**

Admiring Pavilion which has good views of the coast. There are also a couple of unexciting historical sites and the quiet temple, **Guanyin Si**.

Practicalities

Beidaihe **train station** is inconveniently located 15km north of the town; bus #5 will take you from here into the centre. If you arrive at night (likely if you're coming from Beijing), there will be private minibuses and taxis waiting, but you'll have to barter hard to get a decent price of less than ¥50. If you intend stopping at both Beidaihe and Shanhaiguan, 35km to the east along the coast, it might be better to go to Shanhaiguan first (two stops farther down the line, but check, as some trains don't stop there), where the station is close to the hotels. Buses #3 and #4 (¥2), and minibuses (¥5) run throughout the day to Beidaihe from Shanhaiguan, passing through the port of Qinhuangdao and terminating at Beidaihe's **bus station**; it's a fifteen-minute downhill walk from here to Middle Beach. Taxis around town cost ¥10, but Beidaihe is small enough to get around easily on foot. **CITS** is located in the *Haibin Hotel* and will arrange onward train tickets and tours to the nearby nature reserve.

Accommodation, eating and drinking

Few of Beidaihe's 159 **hotels** are open to foreigners. One of the best options is the *Diplomatic Missions Guesthouse* (☎0335/4041807; dorms ③, rooms ⑧), at 1 Baosan Lu, on a quiet street ten minutes' walk north of Middle Beach. It's a stylish complex of thirteen villas set among gardens of cypress and pine, with a karaoke bar, a nightclub, a gym and a good outside restaurant where barbecues are held in the summer. It's also one of the few places in China where you can get a game of tennis. Other good options include the *Haibin* (☎0335/4041373; ⑤), well located right next to the beach, but a little bland and characterless; and the *Jinshan* on Zhonghaitan Lu (☎0335/4041678; ⑦), a three-star complex with pool, right out of the way in a quiet cove by the sea. The *Friendship Hotel* (☎0335/4041945; ⑥) to the north of here, on the route of bus #21, has over five hundred rooms, a huge restaurant and a recreation centre, but is awkwardly located, far from anything of interest. The *Nite Dajiudian* on Dongjing Lu (look for the sign in pinyin; ②) looks expensive, but has reasonably priced dorms.

Beidaihe is noted for its crab, cuttlefish and scallops – try one of the innumerable small and cheapish **seafood** places on Haining Lu, where you order by pointing to the tastiest looking thing scuttling or slithering around the bucket, or *Kiesslings*, on Dongjing Lu near the *Diplomatic Missions Guesthouse*. Originally Austrian, this restaurant has been serving the foreign community for most of this century, and still has a few Western dishes on its reasonably priced menu – Western diners are even issued with knifes and forks. It's an ideal place for breakfast, offering good pastries and bread. The *Haibin Hotel* also has a good, mid-range restaurant, and the *Spring Banquet Hall* on Zhonghaitan Lu, a short walk from Middle Beach, does excellent cuttlefish.

Around Beidaihe

Fifteen kilometres west along the coast, **NANDAIHE** is a new tourist resort constructed to take advantage of Beidaihe's popularity. It's the same sort of thing, but more regimented and artificial, with 3km of beach and a few parks and viewpoints. The main attraction here is **Golden Beach** to the west, where you can go "sand sliding" down the steep sand dunes on a rented sledge – great fun provided you remember to keep your elbows in the air. Foreigners can stay at the expensive *Nandaihe Beach House* resort complex (☎0335/442807; ⑦), but on the whole Nandaihe has less atmosphere

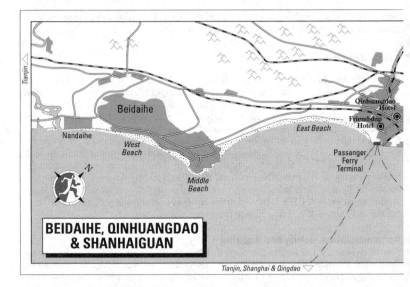

Tianjin ◁

Beidaihe

Nandaihe

West Beach

Middle Beach

East Beach

Qinhuangdao Hotel

Friendship Hotel

Passanger Ferry Terminal

BEIDAIHE, QINHUANGDAO & SHANHAIGUAN

Tianjin, Shanghai & Qingdao ▽

than Beidaihe and is best visited as a day trip; frequent minibuses leave from the Beidaihe bus station.

The countryside around Beidaihe has been designated as a **nature reserve** and is a stopping-off point for Siberian and red-crowned cranes migrating to Dongbei in May. Ask at *CITS* in Beidaihe or Qinhuangdao for details of the best places to see them and tour prices.

Qinhuangdao

The only reason to visit **QINHUANGDAO**, an industrial city and charmless modern port, 15km east of Beidaihe, is to make arrangements to leave – the **ferry terminal** here operates passenger services to Dalian, Shanghai, Tianjin, and Qingdao. Tickets for same-day travel can be bought from *CITS* at 8 Wenhua Bei Jie (☎0335/335974) or from the ferry terminal itself.

If you get stuck in the city overnight, try the *Friendship Hotel* (⑤) near the harbour, or the *Qinhuangdao Hotel* (☎0335/332443; ⑥) on Yiengbin Jie. **Buses** and minibuses can be caught around the train station and passenger ferry terminal. The thirty-minute trip to Shanhaiguan or Beidaihe costs ¥5.

Shanhaiguan and beyond

SHANHAIGUAN, "The Pass Between the Mountains and the Sea", a town at the northern tip of the Bohai Gulf, was originally built as a fortress in the Ming dynasty, to defend the eastern end of the **Great Wall**. The wall crosses the Yanshan Mountains to the north, forms the east wall of the town and meets the sea a few kilometres to the south. It's a sleepy, dusty little place of low buildings and quiet streets, still arranged along its original plan of straight boulevards following the compass points, intersected with a web of alleys. Dominating the town is a fortified gatehouse in the east wall, which

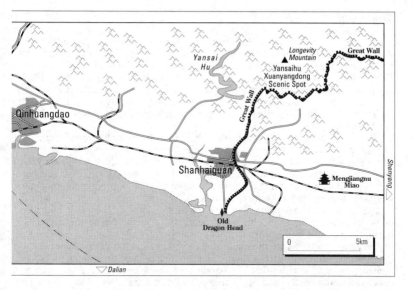

for centuries was the entrance to the Middle Kingdom from the barbarian lands beyond. Far from being a solitary castle, Shanhaiguan originally formed the centre of a network of defences, and smaller forts, now nothing but ruins, existed to the north, south and east, and beacon towers were dotted around the mountains.

Shanhaiguan is a popular tourist destination with the Chinese, but doesn't seem to be much on the traveller circuit, which is odd, as it's well worth a visit. The town, small enough to walk around, is peaceful and pretty and has two good hotels, and the surrounding countryside contains some fine sturdy fortifications and remnants of the wall. Even buying a train ticket out is pretty stress-free. The best thing to do here is to rent a bike and spend a few days exploring.

SHANHAIGUAN AND BEYOND

Shanhaiguan	山海关	*shānhǎiguān*
Dongfang Hotel	东方宾馆	*dōngfāng bīnguǎn*
First Pass Under Heaven	天下第一关	*tiānxiàdìyìguān*
Great Wall Museum	长城博物馆	*chángchéng bówùguǎn*
Jingshan Hotel	京山宾馆	*jīngshān bīnguǎn*
North Street Hotel	北街招待所	*běijiē zhāodàisuǒ*

BEYOND SHANHAIGUAN

Jiao Shan	角山	*jiǎo shān*
Lao Long Tou	老龙头	*lǎolóngtóu*
Longevity Mountain	长寿山	*chángshòu shān*
Mengjiangnu Miao	孟姜女庙	*mèngjiāngnǚ miào*
Yangsai Hu	燕塞湖	*yànsài hú*

The Town

The biggest building in town, the **First Pass Under Heaven**, a gate in the Great Wall, makes the surrounding structures look puny in comparison. An arch topped by a two-storey tower, it must have looked even more formidable when it was built in 1381, with a wooden drawbridge over a moat 18m wide, and three outer walls for added defensive strength. Its name is emblazoned in red above the archway, calligraphy attributed to Xiao Xian, a Ming-dynasty scholar who lived in the town. The arch remained China's northernmost entrance until 1644, when it was breached by the Manchus.

These days, the gate (daily 8am–6pm; ¥10) is overrun by hordes of marauding tourists, and is at its best in the early morning before most of them arrive. A steep set of steps leads up from Dong Dajie to the impressively thick wall, nearly 30m wide. The tower on top, a two-storey, ten-metre-high building with arrow slits regularly spaced along its walls, is now a **museum** (¥2), appropriately containing weapons, armour and costumes, as well as pictures of the nobility so formally dressed they look like puppets. You can stroll a little way along the wall in both directions; an enterprising man with a telescope stands at the far northern end, and through it you can watch other tourists on the Great Wall at Jiaoshan several kilometres to the north, where the wall zigzags and dips along vertiginous peaks before disappearing over the horizon. There's plenty of tourist tat for sale at the wall's base, including decorated chopsticks, hologram medallions and jade curios, while in a courtyard to the northern side, a statue of Xu Da, the first general to rule the fort, frowns sternly down on the scene.

Follow the city wall south from the gate, past CITS, and you come to the **Great Wall Museum** (daily 7.30am–6pm; ¥3, ¥5 for the annexe). This modern imitation Qing building has eight halls, showing the history of the region in chronological order from Neolithic times. Though there are no English captions, the exhibits themselves are fascinating and well displayed. As well as the tools used to build the wall, there's a display of the vicious weaponry used to defend and attack it, including mock-ups of siege machines and broadswords that look too big to carry, let alone wield. The last three rooms contain dioramas, plans and photographs of local historic buildings. The last room, with a large-scale model of the local area as it looked in Ming times, gives a clear idea of the extent of the area's defences, with many small outposts and fortifications in the district around. With models of the area's historic buildings and pictures of them on the wall, it's much better than any CITS map or glossy brochure and should inspire a few bike rides. The annexe outside the museum contains a rather strange exhibition of photographs of tribal people's body decorations, with enough scarification, branding, piercing and tattooing to satisfy the curiosity of any modern primitive.

Practicalities

Whether you arrive at the **train** or **bus station**, both outside the walls, south and east respectively, you will be greeted by an eager mob of drivers. Public buses don't go inside the city walls, but a motor-rickshaw to any destination in town should cost ¥5, and a taxi ¥10. **Local buses** from Qinhuangdao and Beidaihe farther west along the coast don't use the bus station, but collect and deposit passengers just outside the southern gate of the city. Frequent tourist minibuses, which you can catch from any major road, ply the same route, linking Qinhuangdao and Beidaihe. **CITS** is just south of the First Pass Under Heaven, but there never seems to be anyone there. However, buying tickets at the train station is straightforward, so you'll have little need of them

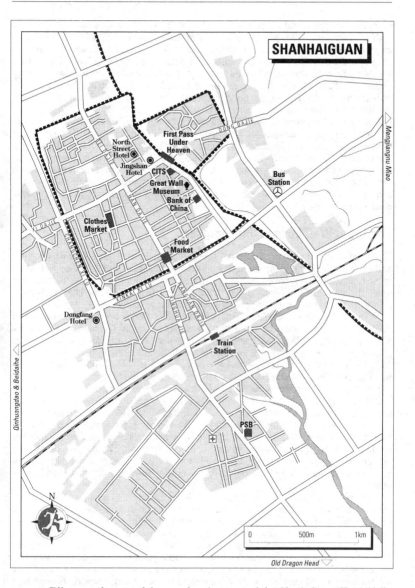

anyway. **Bikes** can be rented from a shop just east of the *North Street Hotel* (daily 8am–5.30pm; ¥10 a day).

Shanhaiguan has two great **hotels**, ideally located next to the First Pass Under Heaven. The *North Street Hotel*, at 2 Mujia Hutong (dorms ①, rooms ④), feels like a temple: stone lions guard the impressive gates, and inside, rooms lead off cloisters around a courtyard and garden. It's small, friendly and the rooms are large, though staff are perhaps a little too laid-back. The *Jingshan Hotel* (☎0335/5051130; ④) nearby on Dong Dajie is palatial, built to imitate a Qing mansion, with high ceilings, decorative friezes, curling roofs and red-brick walls and balconies. Rooms with TV and fan are off a series of small courtyards. If you can't get into either of these, try the *Dongfang* (☎0335/5051376; ⑦) with singles and doubles, on Xinkai Lu, outside the city's south wall. It's new and adequate, but not a patch on the other two, and it's a long way from the interesting part of town.

Don't expect gourmet fare in Shanhaiguan, although the *Jingshan Hotel* does have a good mid-range **restaurant** attached. The portions are more than generous (seafood especially good), and the manager makes a fuss of Westerners. Xi Dajie, the street west of Shanhaiguan's main crossroads, is full of small, cheap family-run restaurants whose owners encourage you to come inside as you walk past. They are all much the same, notable only for the bizarre English on their menus, though the matronly owner of the restaurant at no. 12 is very friendly and can also help you with accommodation if you're stuck.

The Great Wall beyond Shanhaiguan

You'll see plenty of tourist **minibuses** grouped around the major crossroads in town and at the station, all serving the sights outside Shanhaiguan. Public **buses** also travel these routes, but if you have the time you're best off travelling by **bike**, as the roads are quiet, the surrounding countryside is strikingly attractive and there are any number of pretty places off the beaten track where you can escape the crowds.

Follow the remains of the Great Wall south and after 4km you'll reach **Lao Long Tou** (Old Dragon Head), the point at which the wall hits the coast. The name comes from a large stone dragon's head that used to look out to sea here. A miniature fortress with a two-storey temple in the centre, reconstructed in 1981, stands right at the end of the wall. It's an impressive building, and the beaches either side of the wall are popular bathing spots. Bus #24 goes here from Xinghua Jie, near the train station.

Six and a half kilometres northeast of town is the **Mengjiangnu Miao**, dedicated to a legendary woman whose husband was press-ganged into one of the Great Wall construction squads. He died from exhaustion, and she set out to search for his body to give him a decent burial. She wept as she walked along the wall, and so great was her grief, it is said, that the wall crumbled in sympathy, revealing the bones of her husband and many others who had died in its construction. The temple is small and elegant, with good views of the mountains and the sea. Statues of the lady herself and her attendants sit looking rather prissy inside. Take bus #23 from outside the south gate.

A couple of kilometres to the north of Shanhaiguan, it's possible to hike along the remains of the Great Wall, though it has disappeared in many places. You'll pass the ruins of two forts – stone foundations and earthen humps – along the way. About 10km north is a reconstructed section known as **Jiao Shan**, which lies on the route of the #25 bus. This section, accessible by cable car or a steep path, winds over some dramatic scenery into the Yunshan Mountains, and you can lose the crowds within thirty minutes in either direction along the top of the wall. A few kilometres east of here are a trio of passes in the wall, and a beacon tower that's still in good condition.

Tourist leaflets compare **Yangsai Hu**, in the mountains directly north of Shanhaiguan, to Guilin, but in contrast, the place is still quiet and unspoilt. **Longevity Mountain**, to the east of the lake, is a hill of rugged stones, many of which have been carved with the character *shou* (longevity). There's also a pool here – a good place for a quiet swim. Bus #25 from the south gate will get you into the area.

Chengde

CHENGDE, a small country town 250km northeast of Beijing, sits in a river basin on the west bank of the Wulie River, surrounded by the Yunshan mountain range. It's a quiet, unimportant place, rather bland in appearance, but on its outskirts are remnants from its glory days as the summer retreat of the Manchu emperors – these include some of the most magnificent examples of **imperial architecture** in China. A string of gorgeous temples stands in the cabbage fields around town, and a palace-and-park complex (known as the mountain resort) covers an area nearly as large as the town itself. In recent years it has once more become a summer haven, filling up at weekends with Beijingers escaping the hassles of the capital.

Some history

Originally called Rehe, the town was discovered by the Qing-dynasty emperor **Kangxi** at the end of the seventeenth century, while marching his troops to the Mulan hunting

	CHENGDE	
Chengde	承德	*chéngdé*
ACCOMMODATION		
Chengde Binguan	承德宾馆	*chéngdé bīnguǎn*
Chengde Dasha	承德大厦	*chéngdé dàshà*
Huilong	会龙大厦	*huìlóng dàshà*
Mongolian Yurts Holiday Inn	蒙古包渡假村	*mónggǔbāo dùjiàcūn*
Shanzhuan	山庄宾馆	*shānzhuāng bīnguǎn*
Xinhua	新华饭店	*xīnhuá fàndiàn*
Yunshan	云山饭店	*yúnshān fàndiàn*
Yiwanglou	倚望楼宾馆	*yǐwànglóu bīnguǎn*
THE MOUNTAIN RESORT AND THE TEMPLES		
Anyuan Miao	安远庙	*ānyuǎn miào*
Arhat Hill	罗汉山	*luóhàn shān*
Frog Crag	蛤蟆石	*hámá shí*
Mountain resort	避暑山庄	*bìshǔ shānzhuāng*
Palace	正宫	*zhènggōng*
Pule Si	普乐寺	*pǔlè sì*
Puning Si	普宁寺	*pǔníng sì*
Puren Si	溥仁寺	*pǔrén sì*
Putuozongcheng Miao	普陀宗乘之庙	*pǔtuózōngchéng zhī miào*
Shuxiang Si	殊像寺	*shūxiàng sì*
Sledgehammer Rock	棒锤山	*bàngzhōng shān*
Xumifushouzhi Miao	须弥辐寿之庙	*xūmífúshòu zhī miào*
RESTAURANTS		
Fangyuan	芳园居	*fāngyuán jū*
Songhezhai	松鹤斋大酒楼	*sōnghèzhāi dàjiǔlóu*
Taoyuan	桃园大酒楼	*táoyuán dàjiǔlóu*
Yueminglou	月明楼酒家	*yuèmínglóu jiǔjiā*

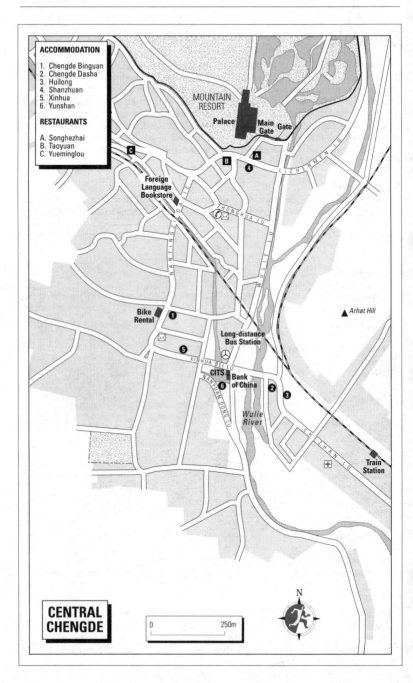

ACCOMMODATION

1. Chengde Binguan
2. Chengde Dasha
3. Huilong
4. Shanzhuan
5. Xinhua
6. Yunshan

RESTAURANTS

A. Songhezhai
B. Taoyuan
C. Yueminglou

MOUNTAIN RESORT

Palace

Main Gate

Gate

LIZHENMEN LU

Foreign Language Bookstore

ZHONGHUA LU

NANYINGZI DAJIE

WULIE LU

Arhat Hill

Bike Rental

Long-distance Bus Station

XINHUA BEI LU

CITS

Bank of China

NANYUAN DONG LU

Wulie River

CHEZHAN LU

Train Station

CENTRAL CHENGDE

0   250m

N

range to the north. He was attracted to the cool summer climate and the rugged land-scape, and built small lodges here from where he could indulge in a fantasy Manchu lifestyle, hunting and hiking like his northern ancestors. The building programme expanded when it became diplomatically useful to spend time north of Beijing, to forge closer links with the troublesome Mongol tribes. Kangxi, perhaps the ablest and most enlightened of his dynasty, was known more for his economy – "The people are the foundation of the kingdom, if they have enough then the kingdom is rich"– than for such displays of imperial grandeur. Chengde, however, was a thoroughly pragmatic creation, devised as an effective means of defending the empire by overawing Mongol princes with splendid audiences, hunting parties and impressive military manoeuvres. He firmly resisted all petitions to have the Great Wall repaired, as an unnecessary bur-den on the people, and as a poor means of control, too, no doubt, as it had imposed no obstacle to the founders of his dynasty only a few years before.

Construction of the first **palaces** started in 1703; by 1711 there were 36 palaces, tem-ples, monasteries and pagodas set in a great walled park with ornamental pools and islands dotted with beautiful pavilions and linked by bridges. Craftsmen from all parts of China were gathered to work on the project, with Kangxi's grandson, Qianlong (1736–1796), adding another 36 imperial buildings during his reign, which was consid-ered to be the heyday of Chengde.

In 1786, the **Panchen Lama** was summoned from Tibet by Qianlong for the emper-or's birthday celebrations. This was an adroit political move to impress the followers of Lamaist Buddhism with the devotion and good intentions of the Dragon Throne. The Buddhists included a number of minority groups who were prominent thorns in the emperor's side, such as Tibetans, Mongols, Torguts, Eleuths, Djungars and Kalmucks. Some accounts (notably not the Chinese) tell how Qianlong invited the Panchen Lama to sit with him on the Dragon Throne, which was taken to Chengde for the summer sea-son. He was certainly feted with honours and bestowed with costly gifts and titles, but the greatest impression on him and his followers must have been made by the **replica of the Potala** and of his own palace, constructed at Chengde to make him feel at home – a munificent gesture, and one that would not have been lost on the Lamaists. However, the Panchen Lama's visit ended questionably when he succumbed to small-pox, or possibly poison, in Beijing and his coffin was returned to Tibet with a stupen-dous funeral cortege.

The first **British Embassy** to China, under Lord Macartney, also visited Qianlong's court. Having suffered the indignity of sailing up the river to Beijing in a ship whose sails were painted with characters reading, "Tribute bearers from the vassal king of England", they had been somewhat disgruntled to discover that the emperor had decamped to Chengde for the summer. However, they made the 150-kilometre journey – in impractical European carriages – arriving at Chengde in September 1793. They were well received by the emperor, despite McCartney's refusal to kowtow – the humil-iating ceremony of kneeling and knocking your head on the ground – and in spite of Qianlong's disappointment with their gifts, supplied by the opportunist East India Company. Qianlong, at the height of Manchu power, was able to hold out against the British demands, refusing to grant any of the treaties requested and remarking, in reply to a request for trade: "We posses all things. I set no value on objects strange or inge-nious, and have no use for your country's manufactures." His letter to the British monarch concluded, magnificently, "O king, Tremblingly Obey and Show No Negligence!"

Chengde gradually lost its imperial popularity when the place came to be seen as unlucky after emperors Jiaqing and Xianfeng died here in 1820 and 1860 respectively. The buildings were left empty and neglected for most of the twentieth century, but largely escaped the ravages of the Cultural Revolution. Restoration, in the interests of tourism, began in the 1980s and is still ongoing.

Arrival, getting around and accommodation

The train journey from Beijing to Chengde takes four and a half hours, travelling through verdant, rolling countryside and past the Great Wall before arriving at the **train station** in the south of town. Travelling from Beijing by bus is slightly quicker as the route is more direct. Buses terminate at the long-distance **bus station** just off Wulie Lu in the centre of town. Hotel touts wait in ambush at both stations, and can be useful if you already have a hotel in mind, as you won't be charged for the ride there. Onward train tickets can be booked from **CITS** at 6 Nanyuan Lu (☎2026827), near the *Yunshan Hotel*, or from any of the hotels, for a surcharge of around ¥10.

Getting around Chengde by public transport isn't easy, as **buses** are infrequent and are always crammed. Buses #2 and #3, which go from the train station to the mountain resort, and bus #6, from the resort to the Puning Si, are the most useful. **Taxis** are exasperatingly uncommon, and the drivers are unwilling to use their meters. The standard charge is ¥10, which has to be negotiated. At peak hours during the summer season (June–Sept), the main streets are so congested that it's quicker to walk. The town itself is just about small enough to cover on foot, but the best way to get around is by **bicycle**, which you can rent from a shop (daily 8.30am–5pm; ¥10 a day) opposite the *Chengde Guesthouse*.

If your time is limited, a minibus **tour** is worth considering as a way to cram in all the sights. English-speaking tours can be arranged through *CITS* or through the larger hotels; expect to pay around ¥50 for a day. Chinese tours, which leave sporadically from outside the train station, are slightly cheaper. A one-day organized tour, to the resort in the morning and the biggest temples in the afternoon, is something of a trial of endurance, however, and they do tend to overlook the less spectacular temples, which is a shame, as these are the quietest. Probably the best way to see everything in a short time, without going down with temple fatigue, is to take a minibus or a bike around the temples one day and explore the mountain resort the next. If you're travelling in a group you can rent a taxi or a minibus for around ¥150 a day (barter hard) and make up your own itinerary.

There are also longer tours on offer, stretching to four and five days and taking in a section of the Great Wall at Jinshanling, 113km southwest, and the Eastern Tombs in Zunhua County 150km east, so expect to spend a lot of time on a bus.

The **telephone code** for Chengde is ☎0314

Accommodation

Chengde has a good selection of hotels in the town itself, with a couple of expensive places inside the mountain resort.

Chengde Binguan, 33 Nanyingzi Dajie (☎2023157, fax 2021341). A little threadbare, but friendly. There are two buildings, front and back, of which the front is the more pleasant. The restaurant is mediocre, but the lobby, with abstract art on the walls, ambient lighting and cosy armchairs, is a pleasant surprise. It's the best value in town if you can persuade them to give you one of their cheap doubles, which they would rather not tell you about. ④–⑦.

Chengde Dasha, Chezhan Lu (☎2088808, fax 2024319). This fifteen-storey block is convenient for the station, but in an uninteresting area of town. ⑦–⑨.

Huilong, Chezhan Lu (☎2025369, fax 232404). Opposite the *Chengde Dasha*, and the better of the two. Twelve storeys high, with a grand lobby, but the rooms are rather small and merely adequate. ⑥–⑧.

Mongolian Yurts Holiday Inn (☎2022710). Inside the mountain resort, on the eastern side and convenient for the temples. It's a sort of Genghis Khan holiday camp where you stay in luxury, family-sized yurts (felt tents), each with TV, fan and carpet. ⑨.

Shanzhuan, 127 Lizhengmen Lu (☎2023501). This well-located, grand (if slightly intimidating) complex, with big rooms and high ceilings and a cavernous, gleaming lobby, is good value if you get one of the large, comfortable rooms in the main building. If they put you round the back, in the ugly new building that looks like a factory, be prepared for noise pollution and a view of a building site. Buses #2 or #3 from the station will get you here. ④.

Xinhua, 4 Xinhua Bei Lu (☎2023724). Simple, standard, cheapish accommodation, in a rather ugly building that's showing its age. However, it has a good restaurant specializing in Shandong food. Bus #7 gets you here. ⑤.

Yunshan, 6 Nanyuan Dong Lu (☎2026171, fax 2024551). This modern block is the most luxurious place to stay in town, and is popular with tour groups. The second-floor restaurant is good and surprisingly inexpensive. Bus #9 from the train station passes the door, or it's a ten-minute walk. ⑧.

Yiwanglou (☎2023528). Inside the mountain resort, just to the left of the front entrance, this is a new, well-run, three-star hotel in a pleasing imitation Qing-style building. ⑨.

The Town

The **town** itself is nothing special, the majority of its one-million-strong population living in a semi-rural suburban sprawl to the south of the centre. Despite a rash of recent highrise construction, Chengde is still fairly small-scale with distant mountains and fields visible from the town centre. However, the surrounding buildings, parks and lakes attract hundreds of thousands of visitors a year and, on summer weekends especially, the town is packed with tourists and its main arterial road, Nanyingzi Dajie, is clogged with traffic.

The **mountain resort**, a landscaped imperial park with a fabulous palace complex, lies to the north of the town, while farther north and to the east, on the other side of the river, stand Chengde's eight imposing **temples**.

The mountain resort

The resort (daily 5.30am–6pm, ¥20 combined ticket for the park and the palace), surrounded by a ten-kilometre wall, occupies the northern third of the town's area and is larger than the Summer Palace in Beijing. This is where, in the summer months, the Qing emperors lived, feasted, hunted, and occasionally dealt with affairs of state. The **palace buildings** just inside the front entrance are unusual for imperial China as they are low, wooden and unpainted; simple, but elegant, in contrast to the opulence and grandeur of Beijing's palaces. It's said that Emperor Kangxi wanted the complex to mimic a Manchurian village, to show his disdain for fame and wealth, though with 120 rooms and several thousand servants he wasn't exactly roughing it. The same principle of idealized naturalness governed the design of the **park**. With its twisting paths and streams, rockeries and hills, it's a fantasy recreation of rough northern terrain and southern Chinese beauty spots that the emperors would have seen on their tours of inspection. The whole is an attempt to combine water, buildings and plants in graceful harmony. Lord Macartney, visiting in 1793, noted its similarity to the "soft beauties" of an English manor park of the Romantic style.

The main gate is in the south wall, off Lizhengmen Dajie, but it's also possible to enter about halfway up on the eastern side. Covering the whole park and its buildings takes at least a day, and an early start is recommended. It's at its nicest in the early morning anyway, when a vegetable market sets up just outside the front gate, and old people practise *tai ji* or play Go by the palace. The park is simply too big to get overcrowded, and if you head north beyond the lakes, you're likely to find yourself alone.

THE PALACE

The **palace quarter**, just inside the mountain resort to the west of the main gate, is built on a slope, facing south, and consists of four groups of dark wooden buildings

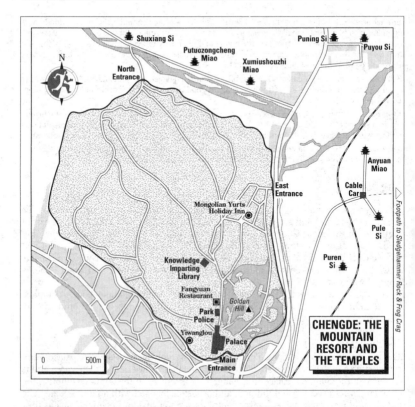

Labels on map:
Shuxiang Si
Putuozongcheng Miao
Xumiushouzhi Miao
Puning Si
Puyou Si
N
North Entrance
Anyuan Miao
East Entrance
Cable Car
Mongolian Yurts Holiday Inn
Pule Si
Knowledge Imparting Library
Puren Si
Fangyuan Restaurant
Golden Hill
Park Police
Yiwanglou
Palace
Main Entrance
0   500m
Footpath to Sledgehammer Rock & Frog Crag

CHENGDE: THE MOUNTAIN RESORT AND THE TEMPLES

spread over an area of 100,000 square metres. The first, southernmost group, the **Front Palace**, where the emperors lived and worked, is the most interesting, as many of the rooms have been restored to their full Qing elegance, decked out with graceful furniture and ornaments. Even the everyday objects are impressive: brushes and inkstones on desks, ornate fly whisks on the arms of chairs, little jade trees on shelves. Other rooms house displays of ceramics, books, and exotic martial art weaponry. The Qing emperors were fine calligraphers, and examples of their work appear throughout the palace.

There are twenty-six buildings in this group, arranged south to north in nine successive compounds which correspond to the nine levels of heaven. The main gate, or **Lizhengmen**, leads into the **Outer Wumen**, where high-ranking officials waited for a single peal of a large bell, indicating that the emperor was ready to receive them. Next is the **Inner Wumen**, where the emperor would watch his officers practise their archery. Directly behind, the **Hall of Frugality and Sincerity** is a dark, well-appointed room made of cedar wood, imported at great expense from south of the Yangzi by Qianlong, who had none of his grandfather Kangxi's scruples about conspicuous consumption. The hall has nine bays and is topped with a curved roof. Patterns on the walls include symbols of longevity and good luck. The **Four Knowledge Study Room**, behind, was where the emperor did his ordinary work, changed his clothes and rested. A vertical scroll on the wall outlines the four knowledges required of a gentleman, as written in the Chinese classics: he must be aware of what is small, obvious, soft and strong. It's more spartanly furnished, a little more intimate and less imposing than the other rooms.

The main building in the **Rear Palace** is the **Hall of Refreshing Mists and Waves**, the living quarters of the imperial family, where Emperor Xianfeng signed the humiliating Beijing Treaty in the 1850s, giving away more of China's sovereignty and territory after her defeat in the Second Opium War. The **Western Apartments** are where the notorious Cixi, better known as the **Dowager Empress**, lived when she was one of Xianfeng's concubines. A door connects the apartments to the hall, and it was through here that she eavesdropped on the dying emperor's last words of advice to his ministers, intelligence she used to help to force herself into power. The courtyard of the Rear Palace has a good **souvenir shop**, inside an old Buddhist tower which you reach by climbing a staircase by the rockery.

The other two complexes are much smaller. The **Pine and Crane Residence**, a group of buildings parallel to the front gate, is a more subdued version of the Front Palace, home to the emperor's mother and his concubines. In the **Myriad Valleys of Rustling Pine Trees**, to the north of here, Emperor Kangxi read books and granted audiences, and Qianlong studied as a child. The group of structures southwest of the main palace is the **Ahgesuo**, where during the Manchurian rule, male descendants of the royal family studied; lessons began at 5am and finished at noon. A boy was expected to speak Manchu at six, Chinese at twelve, be competent with a bow by the age of fourteen, and married at sixteen.

THE LAKES, PLAINS AND HILLS
The best way to get around the **lake area** of the mountain resort – a network of pavilions, bridges, lakes and waterways – is to rent a rowing boat (¥8 an hour). Much of the architecture here is a direct copy of southern Chinese buildings. In the east, the **Golden Hill**, a cluster of buildings grouped on a small island, is notable for a hall and tower modelled after the Golden Hill Monastery in Zhenjiang, Jiangsu Province. The **Island of Midnight and Murmuring Streams**, roughly in the centre of the lake, holds a three-courtyard compound which was used by Kangxi and Qianlong as a retreat, while the compound of halls, towers and pavilions on the **Ruyi Island**, the largest, was where Kangxi dealt with affairs of state before the palace was completed.

Just beyond the lake area, on the western side of the park, is the Wenjinge, or **Knowledge Imparting Library**, surrounded by rockeries and pools for fire protection. The grey-tiled building seems to have two storeys from the outside; in fact there are three – a central section is windowless to protect the books from the sun. A fine collection is housed here, including *The Four Treasures*, a 36,304-volume Qing-dynasty encyclopedia, but you can't go inside.

A vast expanse of **grassland** extends from the north of the lake area to the foothills of the mountains, comprising Wanshun Wan (the Garden of Ten Thousand Trees) and Shima Da (the Horse Testing Ground). Genuine Qing-dynasty **yurts** sit here, the largest an audience hall where Qianlong received visiting dignitaries from ethnic minorities.

The hilly area in the northwest of the park has a number of rocky valleys, gorges and gullies with a few tastefully placed lodges and pagodas. The deer who used to graze here and were wiped out by imperial hunting expeditions have recently been reintroduced.

The outer temples and beyond
Originally there were twelve temples in the foothills of the mountains around Chengde, but two have been destroyed and another two are dilapidated. They are built in the architectural styles of different ethnic nationalities, so that wandering among them is

rather like being in a religious theme park. This is not far from the original intention, as they were constructed by Kangxi and Qianlong less to express religious sentiment than as a way of showing off imperial magnificence, and also to make envoys from anywhere in the empire feel more at home. Though varying in design, all the temples share Lamaist features – Qianlong found it politically expedient to promote Tibetan and Mongolian Lamaism as a way of keeping these troublesome minorities in line.

The **temples** (May–Sept 8am–6.30pm; Oct–April 8am–5pm) are now in varying states of repair, after being left untended for decades. A lot has recently been done to restore their glory in the interests of tourism, though they are still a little shabby round the edges. The restoration is being paid for by the high entrance fees charged in the large temples. The best way to see them is to rent a **bicycle** as the roads outside the town are quiet, it's hard to get lost and you can dodge the tour groups. You can see the northern cluster in the morning, returning to town for lunch, as it's impossible to cross the river to the eastern temples from outside town. In the afternoon, head for the Pule Si, then up to Sledgehammer Rock by cable car. The Anyuan and Puren temples are small and peaceful, and good places to chill out with a book before you head back to town (see p.154 for details of tours).

THE NORTHERN TEMPLES

Just beyond the northern border of the mountain resort, these five temples were once part of a string of nine. The **Puning Si** (Temple of Universal Peace; ¥20), is a must, if only for the statue of Avalokiteshvara, or Guanyin, the Goddess of Mercy, the largest wooden statue in the world. It's the only working temple in Chengde, with shaven-headed Mongolian monks manning the altars and trinket stalls, though the atmosphere is not very spiritual; it's always clamorous with day-trippers, some of whom seem to take outrageous liberties, judging by the sign that says "No shooting birds in the temple area". There are rumours that the monks you see are really paid government employees working for the tourist industry, though the vehemence with which they defend their prayer mats and gongs from romping children suggests otherwise.

The temple was built in 1755 to commemorate the Qing government's victory over Mongolian rebels at Junggar in northwest China, and is based on the oldest Tibetan temple, the Samye. Like traditional Tibetan buildings, it lies on the slope of a mountain facing south, though the layout of the front is typically Han, with a gate hall, stele pavilions, a bell and a drum tower, a Hall of Heavenly Kings, and the Mahavira Hall. The statue of a fat, grinning monk holding a bag in the Hall of Heavenly Kings is **Qi Ci**, a tenth-century character with a jovial disposition who is believed to be a reincarnation of the Buddha. Four gaudy *devarajas* (guardian demons) glare down at you with bulging eyeballs from niches in the walls. In the West Hall are statues of Buddha Manjusri, Avalokiteshvara and Samantabhadra. In the East Hall, the central statue, flanked by *arhats*, depicts **Ji Gong**, a Song-dynasty monk who was nicknamed Crazy Ji for eating meat and being almost always drunk, but who was much respected for his kindness to the poor.

The rear section of the temple, separated from the front by a wall, comprises 27 Tibetan-style rooms laid out symmetrically, with the Mahayana Hall in the centre. Some of the buildings are solid, with false doors, suggesting that the original architects were more concerned with appearances than function. The hall itself is dominated by the awe-inspiring, 23-metre-high wooden **statue of Avalokiteshvara**. She has forty-two arms with an eye in the centre of each palm, and three eyes on her face which symbolize her ability to see into the past, the present and the future. The hall has two raised entrances and once you've been suitably towered over from ground level it's worth looking at the statue from these higher viewpoints as they reveal new details, such as the eye sunk in her belly button, and the little Buddha sat meditating on top of her head.

On the thirteenth day of the first lunar month (in January), the monks observe the ritual of "**catching the ghost**". A ghost made of dough is placed on an iron rack while monks dressed in white dance around it, then divide it into pieces and burn it. The ritual is thought to be in honour of a ninth-century Tibetan Buddhist, Lhalung Oaldor, who assassinated a king who had ordered the destruction of Tibetan Buddhist temples, books, and priests. The wily monk entered the palace on a white horse painted black, dressed in a white coat with a black lining. After killing the king, he washed the horse and turned the coat inside out, thus evading capture from the guards who did not recognize him.

The **Xumifushouzhi Miao** (Temple of Sumeru Happiness and Longevity; ¥2), southwest of Puning Si, is at present being restored and much of it is closed to the public; the parts that are open are not in a good state of repair. The temple was built in 1780 for the ill-fated sixth Panchen Lama (see p.153) when he came to Beijing to pay his respects to the emperor. Built in Mongolian style, its most notable feature is the Hall of Loftiness and Solemnity. Eight sinuous gold dragons, each weighing over a thousand kilograms, usually sit on the roof, but during the restoration work the dragons are being stored in a courtyard, and the enterprising workmen charge visitors ¥5 to look at them.

The magnificent **Putuozongcheng Miao** (Temple of Potaraka Doctrine; ¥20), was built in 1771 and is based on the Potala Palace in Lhasa. Covering 220,000 square metres, it's the largest temple in Chengde, with sixty groups of halls, pagodas and terraces. The grand red terrace forms a Tibetan-style facade screening a Chinese-style interior, although many of the windows on the terrace are fake, and some of the whitewashed buildings around the base are merely filled-in shapes. Inside, the West Hall is notable for holding a rather comical copper statue of the Propitious Heavenly Mother, a fearsome woman wearing a necklace of skulls and riding side-saddle on a mule. According to legend, she vowed to defeat the evil demon Raksaka, so she first lulled him into a false sense of security – by marrying him and bearing him two sons – then swallowed the moon and in the darkness crept up on him and turned him into a mule. The two dancing figures at her feet are her sons; their ugly features betray their paternity. The Hall of all Laws Falling into One, at the back, is worth a visit for the quality of the decorative religious furniture on display. Other halls hold displays of Chinese pottery and ceramics and Tibetan religious artefacts, an exhibition slanted to portray the gorier side of Tibetan religion and including a drum made from two children's skulls. The roof of the temple has a good view over the surrounding countryside.

The **Shuxiang Si** (Temple of Manjusri; ¥3), a short walk west, is Han in style, simple and unspectacular and, for that reason, quiet. Built in 1744, it consists of towers and pavilions set in somewhat overgrown gardens and rockeries, and is a loose copy of a temple in the Wutai Mountains in Shanxi. The statue of Manjusri, the Wenshu Buddha, in the main hall, apparently looks suspiciously like Qianlong himself.

THE EASTERN TEMPLES

These three temples are easily accessible off a quiet road that passes through dusty, rambling settlements, 3–4km from the town centre. From Lizhengmen Lu, cross over to the east bank of the river and head north.

The **Puren Si** (Temple of Universal Benevolence; ¥2), is the first one you'll reach and the oldest in the complex. Although architecturally unimpressive, it contains some interesting sculpture. It was built in 1713 by Kangxi, as a sign of respect to the visiting Mongolian nobility, come to congratulate the emperor on the occasion of his sixtieth birthday. The temple is a four courtyard compound built in the Han style, with a gate and three halls arranged on a central axis, and a drum and bell tower. The Hall of Generous Shade of the Cloud, the main building, has some Ming-style gilded lacquer statues of Sakyamuni and his disciples. The best thing in the temple is the collection of wooden **arhats** in a side hall, though most are fairly generic, rather stiff-looking figures. Still, the almost life-size image of an old man, whose lined face seems to radiate benevolence, being carried on a young disciple's back, is an unusually quirky statue.

The **Pule Si** (Temple of Universal Happiness; ¥20), farther north, was built in 1766 by Qianlong as a place for Mongol envoys to worship, and its style is an odd mix of Han and Lamaist elements. The Lamaist back section, a triple-tiered terrace and hall, with a flamboyantly conical roof and lively, curved surfaces, steals the show from the more sober, squarer Han architecture at the front. The ceiling of the back hall is a wood and gold confection to rival the Temple of Heaven in Beijing. Glowing at its centre is a mandala of Samvara, a Tantric deity, in the form of a cross. The altar beneath holds a Buddha of Happiness, a life-size copper image of sexual congress. More cosmic sex is depicted in two beautiful mandalas hanging outside. In the courtyard, prayer flags flutter while prayer wheels sit empty and unturned. Just north of the temple is the path that leads to Sledgehammer Rock, and the cable car (see below).

The **Anyuan Miao** (Temple of Appeasing the Borders; ¥2), the most northerly of the group, was built in 1762 for a troop of Mongolian soldiers who were moved to Chengde by Qianlong. It's not spectacular and it's not in great shape – the courtyard is overgrown and the side halls are falling down – and the attendants seem to regard the few tourists as an annoying interruption in their day's relaxation. It's a good quiet place to stop if you're cycling, with sunflowers emerging from cracks in the flagstones and swaying against the background of crumbling red walls. The main building of the temple, the Hall of Saving All Souls, has a black-glazed tile roof and houses an ominous gilded figure of Ksitigarbha, the Buddha of the underworld, with nine heads and thirty-four arms, who looks quite sinister in the hall's murky, cobwebbed gloom.

SLEDGEHAMMER ROCK AND BEYOND

Of the scenic areas around Chengde the one that inspires the most curiosity is **Sledgehammer Rock** (¥10), a phallic protuberance on top of a hill that dominates the eastern horizon of the town. It's a couple of kilometres on foot from the Pule Si or there's a cable car (15min; ¥20 return) offering impressive views. Thinner at the base than at the top, the towering column of rock is over 20m high, and skirted by stalls selling little metal copies and Sledgehammer Rock T-shirts. According to legend, the rock is a huge dragon's needle put there to plug a hole in the peak which was letting the sea through the sea.

On the south side of the rock, at the base of a cliff, is **Frog Crag**, a stone that vaguely resembles a sitting frog. It's not very exciting, but the two-kilometre walk here is pleasant. Other rocky highlights within walking distance are **Arhat Hill**, on the eastern side of the river, supposed to look like a reclining Buddha, and **Monk's Headgear Peak**, 4km south of town, the highest point in the area and best reached by bike – head south down Chezhan Lu.

Eating, drinking and nightlife

Chengde is located in Hebei's most fertile area, which mainly produces maize and sorghum, but also yields excellent local chestnuts, mushrooms and apricots. This fresh produce, plus the culinary legacy of the imperial cooks, means it is possible to eat very well here. The town is also noted for its **wild game**, particularly deer, hare and pheasant, and its medicinal **juice drinks**: almond juice is said to be good for asthma; date and jujube juice for the stomach; and jinlianhua juice for a sore throat. Date and almond are the sweetest and most palatable. Local **cakes**, such as the glutinous Feng family cakes, once an imperial delicacy but now a casual snack, can be found in the stalls on Yuhua Lu and Qingfeng Jie. Rose cakes, a sweet, crisp pastry cake and a particular favourite of Qianlong, are sold in Chengde's department stores.

Restaurants

There are a few good budget **restaurants** on Lizhengmen Lu, opposite the main entrance to the mountain resort, which are lively on summer evenings, when rickety tables are put on the pavement outside. A meal for two should be about ¥50 and plenty of diners stay on drinking well into the evening.

Fangyuan, inside the mountain resort. Imperial cuisine in an attractive environment, with exotica such as Pingquan frozen rabbit.

Songhezhai, Lizhengmen Dajie. Cheap, local food, with good dumplings.

Taoyuan, Lizhengmen Dajie. The decor of this large modern hall isn't inspiring, but the food is simple and inexpensive.

Xinhua, Xinhua Bei Lu. The restaurant of the *Xinhua Hotel* has a good reputation for Shandong cooking, particularly pheasant and hare dishes. Around ¥50 per person.

Yueminglou, Lizhengmen Dajie. Local food, with expensive game dishes a speciality.

Nightlife

Chengde is at its liveliest on Friday and Saturday summer nights, when the weekenders are here, though the *Yiyuan Nightclub*, just west of the *Shanzhuan Hotel,* caters strictly for wealthy tourists.The main shopping drag, Nanyingzi Dajie, is a good place to come in the evening when a **night market** stretches all the way down it. Many of the vendors sell antiques and knick-knacks which are generally cheaper than in either Beijing or Tianjin. You'll have to bargain hard and don't expect everything to be genuine.

Shijiazhuang and the monasteries

Five hours by train southwest from Beijing, but at least five years behind in progress, the capital of Hebei, **SHIJIAZHUANG**, is a major rail junction that you may find yourself passing through if you're heading south to the Yellow River. At the beginning of the century Shijiazhuang was hardly more than a village, but the building of the rail line made it an important junction town, and by the 1920s it had a population of ten thousand. Having industrialized rapidly, it's now an unglamorous, sprawling place that seems uncomfortable about its provincialism. A distinctive feature of its rather grey

---

SHIJIAZHUANG AND THE MONASTERIES

Shijiazhuang	石家庄	*shíjiāzhuāng*
Hebei Grand Hotel	河北市宾馆	*héběi shì bīnguǎn*
Hebei Museum	河北省博物馆	*héběishěng bówùguǎn*
Hebei Teachers' University	河北师范大学	*héběi shīfàndàxué*
Martyrs' Memorial	烈士陵园	*lièshì língyuán*
Railway Hotel	铁道大厦	*tiědào dàshà*
Zhongjing Hotel	中京大酒店	*zhōngjīng dàjiǔdiàn*
Zongyi Restaurant	综艺大酒店	*zōngyì dàjiǔdiàn*

THE MONASTERIES

Cangyan Shan Si	苍岩山 寺	*cāngyánshān sì*
Longxing Si	隆兴寺	*lóngxīng sì*
Zhaozhou Qiao	赵州桥	*zhàozhōu qiáo*
Zhengding	正定	*zhèngdìng*

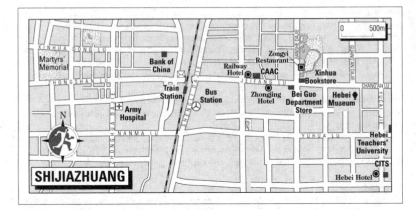

streets are large billboards with political slogans, in English as well as Chinese, such as "Build economy up by millions of people all of one mind." Home to China's largest pharmaceutical factory, it's known as a centre for medicine and is reputedly a good place to study traditional Chinese medicine.

For tourists, the grave of Canadian surgeon, Norman Bethune, and the city museum are worth a look, but the best sights are all out of town. The main reason to stop over in Shijiazhuang is to pick up a connection to Zhengding's **Longxing Si**, the **Cangyan Shan Si** and **Zhaozhou Qiao**. All are accessible by tourist minibuses which leave in the mornings from a park about 100m northeast of the train station.

The City

Downtown Shijiazhuang is laid out on a grid with long axial roads, which change their names several times along their course, running north–south and east–west. The main street running east–west across town, just north of the train station and served by the #5 bus, is one of the most interesting. Five blocks west of the station along a section called Zhongshan Lu, you'll find the **Martyrs' Memorial** (daily 6am–5pm), an ordered, sober-looking park, containing the graves of the only two foreigners to be honoured as heroes of the Revolution. On the west side of the park, the grave of **Dr Norman Bethune**, a Canadian doctor, is marked by an ornate sarcophagus, a photo exhibition, and a statue, identical to one standing in Bethune Square, Montréal. Bethune (1890–1939), whose remains were moved here from Canada at the request of the Chinese government in 1953, was a brilliant, idealistic surgeon, who came to China to help the Communists in the fight against the Japanese after working on the Republican side in the Spanish Civil War. He was present at most of the major battles of the era, and became a close confidant of Mao when the Red Army was holed up in Yan'an after the Long March, so impressing him with his devotion to his work that Mao later exhorted the Chinese to "learn selflessness from Dr Bethune". One of the most well-known foreigners in China, Bethune is one reason why most Chinese are well disposed towards Canadians. **Dr Dwarkanath Kotnis** (1900–1942), is given identical treatment on the east side of the park. Dr Kotnis, one of five Indian doctors who came to China in the 1930s, stayed in the country for nearly a decade, joining the Communist Party just before his death. Both doctors are celebrated in a small **museum** at the back of the park; items on display include the exercise books in which they practised writing in Chinese and the crude surgical implements they had to work with.

The large number of photographs include pictures of Bethune operating by torchlight and in conference with Mao.

East of the station, the road becomes Jiefang Lu, the city's commercial sector, with a few department stores, the largest of which, the ostentatious five-storey **Bei Guo Department Store**, at the intersection with Bei Dajie, is the biggest in Hebei, and the pride of local residents, who express regret that it isn't even taller. It's over-staffed and full of window shoppers, and is probably the city's premier tourist attraction. There's nothing special, though, about the household goods and clothes on display.

Two blocks farther east is the unexpectedly above-average **Hebei Museum** (daily 8.30–11.30am & 2.30–4.30pm; ¥10). The downstairs rooms hold dull temporary exhi-bitions of local products, but the two rooms upstairs display a fascinating hotchpotch of historic artefacts. The first hall includes a complete mammoth skull and tusk, a miniature terracotta army unearthed in a nearby tomb and a jade burial suit. The sec-ond hall, concerned with modern history, has displays of weaponry, photographs of battlefields, and a model village with a network of tunnels underneath illustrating how the Red Army hid from their enemies.

It's not an obvious tourist destination, but *CITS* arranges tours to the showpiece **Bethune Army Hospital**, just west of the train station, one of the best-equipped and most advanced in China. Similarly, there are *CITS* group tours to the **Military Academy** outside town, where you'll be introduced to some happy, smiling soldiers by your attentive chaperone, and see some fit, well-adjusted cadets practising their drill. What happens when you are not around is another question, as this is where counter-revolutionary students from Beijing are sent for refresher courses in ideological cor-rectness. Prices for these tours vary depending on numbers, but at least four tourists are needed – expect to pay around ¥200.

Practicalities

Shijiazhuang **airport**, 45km northeast of the city, is served by an airport bus which takes you to the *CAAC* office on Bei Dajie. The large **train station** is conveniently located in the middle of town, and its concourse is the arrival and departure point for minibuses to Beijing. The **long-distance bus station** stands a block south of the train station, on the eastern side. Getting around town by bus is straightforward; buses #5 and #6, which run east and west across town, are the most useful. **Taxis** around town have a ¥10 minimum charge.

Accommodation

Hebei, 23 Yucai Jie (☎0311/6015961). Shijiazhuang's biggest and best hotel, this eight-storey block in the quiet eastern side of town dominates the surrounding low buildings. The hotel has two restaurants, a nightclub, a karaoke lounge, and they can book train tickets for you. ⑦.

Hebei Teachers' University, Yuhua Lu. The foreign teachers' dormitory is a cheap and friendly place to stay offering well-maintained double rooms. Go through the main gate, take the first left and the building is on the right, signposted in English. There are plenty of small restaurants and street stalls around the university. Take bus #6 from the train station. ③.

Railway, 69 Jiefang Lu (☎0311/6074581). A central three-star hotel with a good restaurant. An office in the lobby will book plane and train tickets for you given three days' notice. ⑤.

Zhongjing, 20 Jiefang Lu (☎0311/6032551). This stylish, low-key place has helpful staff and a good location on the main thoroughfare. ⑦.

Listings

Airlines *CAAC* (☎0311/606884) is at 5 Bei Dajie. You can also buy tickets from an office next to the Hualian Commercial Building opposite the train station.

Banks and exchange The *Bank of China* is at 136 Xinhua Dong Lu (Mon–Fri 8.30am–noon & 2–4.30pm).

Bike rental Bikes can be rented from a stall on the east side of the train station concourse, opposite the Hualian Commercial Building, at the back of a large bike park (daily 8am–8pm; ¥5 a day, deposit ¥50).

Bookshops The *Xinhua Bookstore* at 13 Jiefang Lu sells English-language classic novels on the second floor.

Post office On Gongli Jie, opposite the west side of the train station (daily 7am–9pm). There's a 24hr telephone office in the same building.

Trains The advance booking office for train tickets is on 47 Zhongshan Lu (daily 8am–noon & 2–5pm), though buying tickets from the large station itself should not be too stressful. The soft-seat waiting room, behind the station – come out of the entrance, turn right, then right again– with fishponds and an aviary, is glorious. Several hotels in town will also book train tickets for you.

Travel agents The unusually helpful *CITS* office, 22 Yucai Jie (☎0311/5815102), is on the seventh floor of the building opposite the *Hebei Hotel*. Staff speak English and can give you information about the whole province.

Zhengding and Longxing Si

Though it has since slipped into rural obscurity, the small town of **ZHENGDING**, 15km northeast of Shijiazhuang, was an important county town and religious centre until the eighteenth century. The finest remnant of its mystic past is the **Longxing Si** (daily 8am–5pm; ¥20), on the eastern outskirts of the town, a large complex, said to be the oldest monastery in China. Its halls now serve as a **museum** (the monks disappeared after the Communist takeover), holding a few excellent and varied examples of large-scale Buddhist sculpture. Outstanding are a richly embellished bronze statue of four Buddhas on a lotus throne, supporting four smaller Buddhas, who in turn support four more, and a colourful wooden image, awash with rococo curves, of Guanyin, Goddess of Mercy, sitting in a grotto. A hall on the west side is filled with a huge wooden machine described as a "movable bookshelf". Reminiscent of a mill, it's a giant spinning wheel whose revolving sides would once have held written sutras. The finest artefact is at the centre of the Main Hall (Da Bei Ge), a 22-metre-high bronze image of multi-armed Guanyin, a rare and magnificent example of Song-dynasty craftsmanship, nearly a thousand years old.

All that remains of the town's many temples are four **pagodas** dotted around the town. Entrance to each is just a few yuan and you can climb to at least the second storey of each; the attendants rent out flashlights as it's very dark inside. The forty-metre-high brick **Lingxiao Pagoda**, originally built in the Tang dynasty but renovated in the Ming, stands a kilometre to the west of the monastery. You can climb to the fourth floor on the inside, then continue to the top on an external wooden staircase that winds around a wooden pillar supporting the pagoda's iron tip. One block southwest of here, the simple, chunky **Xumi Pagoda** is unusually austere and geometrical in design. It was built in 540 AD and though it has been renovated often since, its original form has been retained and the pagoda now provides an insight into typical Tang architecture. A belfry outside the pagoda contains a three-metre-tall Tang-dynasty bronze bell. The **Chengling Pagoda**, a fifteen-minute walk south, is thin, knobbly with ornament and topped with an elaborate iron spike and was built to honour Yixuan, a ninth-century Buddhist monk who lived in a former monastery on this site. He was a highly original teacher – famous for shouting at and hitting his pupils to surprise them – and was one of the founders of the style of Buddhism which came to be known as Zen in Japan. Today, the pagoda is a popular site with Japanese tourists and pilgrims. Finally, the **Hua Pagoda**, a short walk south of here, is a rare Jin-dynasty structure – China has only a handful of similar buildings. Its finest feature is the fourth-storey section, just under the tip, which swarms with carvings of elephants, Buddhas, and whales. The lower half of the pagoda is in pretty bad shape.

Minibuses from Shijiazhuang to Zhengding terminate right opposite the Longxing Monastery. Walking from here, around the pagodas and back to the bus stop should take about two hours.

Cangyan Shan Si and Zhaozhou Qiao

Thirty kilometres southwest of the city, **Cangyan Shan Si** (daily 8am–5pm), conceived in the Sui dynasty and rebuilt by the Qing, is an elegant monastic complex made beautiful by its dramatic site. Hundreds of feet up, on the steep rocky side of a mountain, the monastery perches on top of a bridge spanning a cleft in the almost vertical face of Cangyan Shan. The two main buildings are Sui in design, with colourful double roofs and attached gardens and are reached by a pleasant two-hour walk along a twisting cliff path.

In the summer, **minibuses** run daily from Shijiazhuang to the monastery (2hr 30min). Out of season you'll have to make your own way here. Take a bus from the long-distance bus station in Shijiazhuang to Gingxing County, then hire a motor-rickshaw to take you the last ten kilometres. In winter, the path up to the monastery is sometimes impassable due to snow.

Zhaozhou Qiao, 40km southeast of Shijiazhuang, just outside the town of Zhaoxiang, is a simple, elegant bridge that will impress architects and engineers. Built at the beginning of the seventh century, its builder, Li Chun, had to reconcile several conflicting problems. The bridge had to be flat enough for the chariots of the imperial army to pass over it, yet not so low that it would be destroyed by the frequent floods. Strong enough to withstand the military and trading convoys, the bridge also had to rest on soft river banks. The result of Li's deliberations was a single flattened arch, spanning over 36 metres with a rise of just seven metres. It's still in use, one of the undoubted masterpieces of Chinese architecture, and the model for dozens of northern Chinese stone bridges.

travel details

Trains

Beidaihe to: Beijing (3 daily; 7hr); Qinhuangdao (3 daily; 30min); Shanhaiguan (3 daily; 1hr); Shenyang (daily; 5hr); Tianjin (3 daily; 6hr).

Chengde to: to Beijing (4 daily; 4hr 30min); Dandong (daily; 30hr); Shenyang (2 daily; 7hr); Tianjin (2 daily; 5hr).

Qinhuangdao to: Beidaihe (3 daily; 30min); Beijing (3 daily; 7hr 30min); Shanhaiguan (3 daily; 30min); Shenyang (daily; 5hr 30min); Tianjin (3 daily; 6hr 30min).

Shanhaiguan to: Beidaihe (3 daily; 1hr); Beijing (3 daily; 8hr); Qinhuangdao (3 daily; 30min); Shenyang (daily; 6h); Tianjin (3 daily; 7hr).

Shijiazhuang to: Beijing (4 daily; 4hr 30min); Ji'nan (4 daily; 4hr); Taiyuan (2 daily; 8hr); Tianjin (4 daily; 7hr); Zhengzhou (2 daily; 8hr).

Tianjin to: Beidaihe (3 daily; 6hr); Beijing (6 daily; 2–3hr, includes 3 express services); Chengde (2 daily; 5hr) Guangzhou (daily; 38hr); Jilin (3 daily; 20hr); Qinhuangdao (3 daily; 6hr 30min); Shanghai (daily; 22hr); Shanhaiguan (3 daily; 7hr); Shijiazhuang (4 daily; 7hr); Xi'an (daily; 22hr).

Buses

While long distances by bus have little to recommend them (they are much slower than the train and very uncomfortable), there are bearable road routes linking towns in Hebei with Tianjin and Beijing. Services are frequent, usually hourly during the day.

Beidaihe to: Beijing (9hr); Qinhuangdao (30min); Shanhaiguan (30min); Tianjin (3hr 30min).

Chengde to: Beijing (3hr); Tianjin (4hr).

Qinhuangdao to: Beidaihe (30min); Beijing (9hr 30min); Shanhaiguan (30min); Tianjin (4hr).

Shanhaiguan to: Beidaihe (1hr); Beijing (10hr); Qinhuangdao (30min); Tianjin (4hr 30min).

Shijiazhuang to: Beijing (8hr).

Tianjin to: Beidaihe (2hr 30min); Beijing (4hr); Chengde (4hr); Qinhuangdao (3hr); Shanhaiguan (3hr 30min).

Ferries

Qinhuangdao to: Dalian (3 weekly; 17hr); Qingdao (2 weekly; 12hr); Tianjin (2 weekly; 18hr); Shanghai (weekly; 28hr).

Tianjin to: to Dalian (every other day; 20hr); Inchon (South Korea; every 5 days; 28hr); Kobe (Japan; weekly; 48hr); Qinhuangdao (2 weekly; 18hr); Yantai (6 times monthly; 24hr).

Planes

Qinhuangdao to: Dalian (4 weekly; 40min); Guangzhou (2 weekly; 3hr 30min); Harbin (2 weekly; 5hr); Shanghai (2 weekly; 2hr 10min); Shenyang (4 weekly; 1hr 20min); Shijiazhuang (5 weekly; 2hr); Taiyuan (weekly; 1hr 20min).

Shijiazhuang to: Changsha (weekly; 2hr 10min); Chengdu (4 weekly; 2hr 20min); Chongqing (2 weekly; 4hr); Guangzhou (1–3 daily; 2hr 25min); Haikou (weekly; 5hr); Hohhot (daily; 1hr 10min); Qinhuangdao (5 weekly; 1hr); Shanghai (daily; 2hr); Shenyang (4 weekly; 1hr 50min); Shenzhen (2 weekly; 3hr 20min); Taiyuan (3 weekly; 1hr); Wenzhou (2 weekly; 2hr 50min); Wuhan (weekly; 3hr 20min); Xi'an (3 weekly; 2hr); Zhengzhou (weekly; 1hr).

Tianjin to: Beijing (daily; 30min); Chengdu (2 weekly; 3hr 50min); Dalian (2 weekly; 1hr 30min); Fuzhou (2 weekly; 2hr 30min); Guangzhou (2 daily; 3hr); Haikou (3 weekly; 3hr 45min); Harbin (2 weekly; 2hr); Hong Kong (daily; 3hr 15min); Huangshan (weekly; 2hr 15min); Kunming (2 weekly; 3hr); Nanjing (2 weekly; 2hr); Shanghai (2 daily; 1hr 40min); Shantou (2 weekly; 2hr 45min); Shenyang (4 weekly; 2hr); Shenzhen (daily; 3hr); Taiyuan (4 weekly; 1hr 30min); Urumqi (2 weekly; 4hr 20min); Wenzhou (6 weekly; 2hr 30min); Wuhan (2 weekly; 2hr); Xiamen (4 weekly; 2hr 30min); Xi'an (2 weekly; 1hr 45min).

CHAPTER THREE

DONGBEI

H ome to the most extreme factions in Chinese politics and distinguished by a landscape of industrial sprawl and monotonous expanse, coupled with a harsh climate, **Dongbei**, or more evocatively Manchuria, feels at once hardline and uncompromising. China's northernmost arm, a vast expanse of plains, forest and mountain ranges, covers three provinces, **Liaoning**, **Jilin** and **Heilongjiang**, and borders Siberia and North Korea. The region has never impressed with its hospitality: "Although it is uncertain where God created paradise," wrote a French priest when he was here in 1846, "we can be sure he chose some other place than this." However, with immense swathes of fertile fields and huge resources of **mineral wealth**, Dongbei is metaphorically a treasure house, and this cold, unwelcoming territory has been fiercely contested for much of its history. Today the region is an industrial heartland, producing over a third of the country's heavy machinery, half its coal and oil and most of its military equipment. Economically, Dongbei is perhaps the most important region of China, and with four thousand kilometres of sensitive border territory, it's strategically one of the most vulnerable. Not many tourists get up here as there's not much to see and travel is arduous. It feels a long way from China proper, and has much in common with its neighbours; country people live Korean or Manchu lifestyles and its cities are tinted with Russian grey.

Dongbei's colourful side is its history, the remains of which can be seen in the southern city of **Shenyang**, in the imperial palace and tombs built by the local Manchu warlords who once conquered the whole of China, and in the northern city of **Harbin** whose architecture identifies it as an outpost of imperial Russia in the last century. It's hard to find much to recommend about the industrial cities in-between – **Jilin** and **Changchun** are best avoided, while **Dalian**, a thriving port, is pleasant but with few sights. More interesting is the countryside around them, at its most dramatic around the lake of Tian Chi, in the mountainous **Changbai Shan Nature Reserve** near the Korean border, at the **Zhalong Nature Reserve** and around **Jingbo Hu** farther north. The sub-Siberian wilderness north of here will reward hardy souls with virgin forests and rugged mountains – and very primitive conditions.

Dongbei's **climate** is one of extreme opposites. In summer it is hot, and in winter it is very, very cold, with temperatures as low as minus thirty degrees, and howling Siberian gales. But if you can stand the cold, a trip in late January has the added attractions of **ice festivals** in Jilin and Harbin, as well as winter sports. As for **transport**, there's an efficient rail system between the cities, but roads throughout the region are terrible; don't take a bus unless you have to.

Owing to the area's political sensitivity and conservatism, foreigners bear the full brunt of bureaucracy, and **regulations** concerning what you can do and where you can go are strictly enforced. Practically, this means that getting a visa extension in the northeast involves proving you are not a spy or a smuggler, and shelling out for officially approved accommodation. **Hotel prices** for foreigners in Dongbei's cities are so outrageously high – you'll rarely find a room for less than ¥300 a night – that anyone travelling on a tight budget is advised to avoid the region altogether.

With all these difficulties, it's no wonder that tourists are an unusual sight and that a Western face is automatically assumed to belong to a Russian smuggler. Visitors do

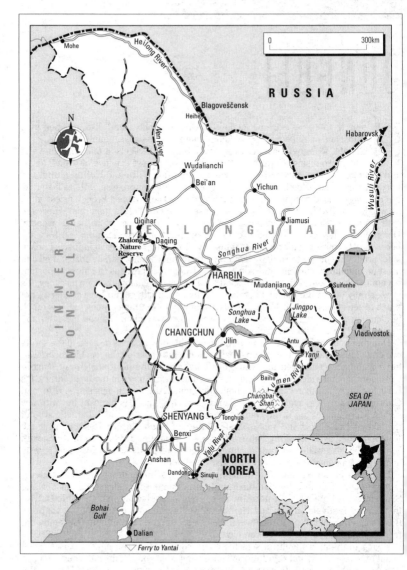

tend to come for specific reasons: steam buffs will find plenty of trains to get excited about, and keen hunters, hikers and bird-watchers will all find places to indulge their passions. Ask at *CITS* for details of their special interest tours to the region, and see *Basics*, p.35 for more information.

One tour you won't get out of *CITS* is a trip to one of the many "reform through labour" **prison camps**, clustered here in the far north (and also in Xinjiang). Between eight and fourteen million Chinese are believed to be held in such camps across China,

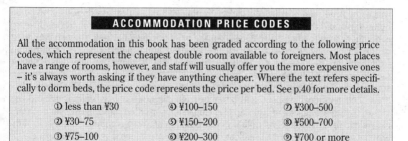

many of whom have never had a trial; an estimated ten percent are dissidents. The goods produced in the camps have a significant effect on the national economy and often end up abroad.

Some history

The history of Manchuria proper begins with **Nurhaci**, a tribal leader who in the sixteenth century united the warring tribes of the northeast against the corrupt central rule of Ming-dynasty Liaoning. He introduced an alphabet based on the Mongol script, administered Manchu law and, by 1625, had created a firm and relatively autonomous government that was in constant confrontation with the Chinese. His successor, Dorgun, the regent of his grandson, Shunchih, went a stage further and with the help of the defeated Ming general, Wu Sankuei, marched on Beijing, proclaiming the **Qing dynasty** in 1644 and becoming the first of a long line of Manchu emperors.

Keen to establish the Qing over the whole of China, the first **Manchu emperors** – Shunchih, Kangxi and Qianlong – did their best to assimilate Chinese customs and ideas. They were, however, even more determined to protect their homeland, and so the whole of the northeast was closed to the rest of China. This way they could guard their monopoly on the valuable ginseng trade, and keep the Chinese from ploughing up their land and desecrating the graves of their ancestors. But it was a policy that could not last for ever, and the eighteenth century saw increasing migration into Manchuria. By 1878, the laws had been rescinded and the Chinese were moving into the region by the million, escaping the flood-ravaged plains of the south for the fertile land of the northeast.

All this time, Manchuria was being coveted by its neighbours. The **Sino–Japanese War** of 1894 left the Japanese occupying the Liaodong Peninsula in the south of Liaoning Province, and the only way the Chinese could regain it was by turning to **Russia**, also hungry for influence in the area. The deal was that the Russians be allowed to build a rail line linking Vladivostok to the main body of Russia, an arrangement which in fact led to a gradual and, eventually, complete occupation of Manchuria by the imperial Russian armies. This was a bloody affair, marked by atrocities and brutal reprisals, and followed in 1904 by a Japanese declaration of war in an attempt to usurp the Russians' privileges for themselves. Japan's designs on Manchuria didn't end there; their population had almost doubled in the last sixty years, and this, coupled with a disastrous economic situation at home and an extreme militaristic regime, led to their invasion of the region in 1932, establishing the puppet state of **Manchukuo**. This regime was characterized by instances of horrific and violent oppression – not least the secret germ warfare research centre in Pingfang where experiments were conducted on live human subjects. Rice was reserved for the Japanese and it was a crime for the locals to eat it.

It was only with the establishment of a united front between the **Communists** and the **Guomindang** that Manchuria was finally rid of the Japanese, in 1945, although it was some time (and in spite of a vicious campaign against the Communists backed by both Russia and the USA) before Mao finally took control of the region. Recent history is dominated by relations with Russia. In the brief romance between the two countries in the 1950s, Soviet experts helped the Chinese build factories and workshops in exchange for the region's agricultural products. The efficient, well-designed **Soviet factories**, such as the plant that produces the Liberation Truck in Changchun, remain some of the best in the area. In the 1960s relations worsened, the Soviets withdrew their technical support, and bitter **border disputes** began, notably around the Ussuri, where hundreds of Russian and Chinese troops died fighting over an insignificant island in the world's first military confrontation between communist states. In addition, an extensive network of nuclear shelters was constructed in northeastern cities. Following the collapse of the Soviet Union, military build-up around the border areas and state paranoia have lessened, and the shelters have been turned into underground shopping centres. Russian faces can again be seen on the streets, often not as tourists or foreign advisers but **traders**, legal and otherwise, buying up consumer goods to take over the border now that Russia's own manufacturing industry has almost collapsed.

Shenyang

Capital of Liaoning Province, **SHENYANG** is the major industrial city of the northeast, a trade centre, rail junction and home to any number of factories that have been laid open to the public as examples of Chinese endeavour. A sprawling city of seven million people, Shenyang is gritty and austere, though a few temples and tombs set uneasily in the harsh concrete cityscape bear witness to its historical importance.

Though well-known in China as an important power base for the more radical hardline factions in Chinese politics – Mao's nephew, Yuanxin, was deputy party secretary here until he was thrown in jail in 1976 – Shenyang's real heyday was in the early seventeenth century. The city (then known as Mukden) was declared first **capital** of the expanding **Manchu empire** by Nurhaci. He died in 1626, as work on his palace was

SHENYANG		
Shenyang	沈阳	*shěnyáng*
East Tomb	东陵	*dōng líng*
Imperial Palace	沈阳故宫	*shěnyáng gùgōng*
Liaoning Provincial Museum	辽宁省博物馆	*liáoníngshěng bówùguǎn*
North Pagoda	北塔	*běitǎ*
North Tomb	北陵	*běi líng*
Pagoda of Buddhist Ashes	舍利塔	*shèlìtǎ*
Zhongshan Square	中山广场	*zhōngshān guǎng chǎng*
ACCOMMODATION		
Friendship	友谊宾馆	*yǒuyì bīnguǎn*
Huasha	华厦宾馆	*huáshà fàndiàn*
Liaoning Binguan	辽宁宾馆	*liáoning bīnguǎn*
Liaoning Dasha	辽宁大厦	*liáoning dàshà*
Phoenix	凤凰饭店	*fènghuáng fàndiàn*
Zhongxing	中兴宾馆	*zhōngxīng bīnguǎn*

just beginning, and was succeeded by his eighth son, Abahai, who consolidated and extended Manchu influence across northern China. When the Manchus, having defeated the resident Ming, moved to Beijing in 1644, and established the Qing dynasty, Shenyang became a secondary power centre of steadily declining importance. The city began to take on its modern, industrial role with the arrival of the Russians in the nineteenth century, who made it the centre of their rail building programme. Years later, the puppets of the Japanese state also set up shop here, exploiting the resources of the surrounding region and building an industrial infrastructure whose profits and products were sent home to Japan. There's no getting away from the fact that the contemporary city is grim and its architecture is the last word in socialist overstatement. Twelve hours by train from Beijing, it's best visited as a brief stop on a trip farther north.

The City

Shenyang has some great examples of uncompromising Soviet-style building and you may well find yourself staying in one. The giant **Mao statue** in Zhongshan Square at the city's centre, erected in 1969, is by far the most distinctive landmark, its base lined with strident, blocky peasants, Daqing oilmen, PLA soldiers and students, though the Little Red Books they were waving have mostly been chipped off. Above them, the monolithic Mao stands wrapped in an overcoat, a bald superman, whose raised hand makes him look as if he's directing the traffic which swarms around him. Head in the direction he's facing and you'll hit the city's shopping district, centred around Zhongshan Lu, Zhonghua Lu and Taiyuan Jie, which abounds with department stores. South of here, the Nan River marks the southern boundary of the downtown area.

Contemporary Shenyang, though, is frankly boring. More rewarding are the Manchu structures on its outskirts, and best of these is the **Imperial Palace** (daily 8.30am–5.30pm; ¥15), begun in 1626, a miniature replica of Beijing's Forbidden City, located at the centre of the old city in the east of town (trolley bus #13 from the South station). The complex divides into three sections: the first, the Cong Zhen Dian, is a low, wooden-fronted hall where the emperor first proclaimed the Qing dynasty and which was used by ministers to discuss state affairs. Beyond here, in the second courtyard, stands the Phoenix Tower, most formal of the ceremonial halls, and the Qing Ning Lo, which served as bedrooms for the emperor and his concubines. Passing through to the eastern section of the complex is the Da Zheng Dian, a squat, octagonal, wooden structure in vivid red and lacquered gold, with two pillars cut with writhing golden dragons in high relief. Here the emperor Shunchih was crowned before seizing Beijing – and the empire – in 1644. Just in front stand ten square pavilions, the Shi Wang, once used as offices by the chieftains of the Eight Banners (districts) of the Empire, and now housing a collection of bizarrely shaped swords and pikes.

From here, bus #213 will get you to the **North Tomb** (daily 8am–6pm; ¥10) in Beiling Park, or take bus #220 or trolleybus #6 direct from the South station. Abahai is buried here, and though it was his father who was the real pioneering imperialist, Abahai certainly got the best tomb. The well-preserved complex, constructed in 1643, is entered through a gate to the south, either side of which are pavilions; the easternmost was for visiting emperors to wash and refresh themselves, the westernmost for sacrifices of pigs and sheep. A drive flanked with statues of camels, elephants, horses and lions leads to the Long En Hall, which contains an altar for offerings and the spirit tablets of the emperor and his wife. Their tree-covered burial mounds are at the rear, where you'll also see a fine dragon screen.

The more restrained **East Tomb** (daily 8am–6pm; ¥10), built in 1629 as the last resting place of Nurhaci, is set among conifers in Dongling Park in the east of the city,

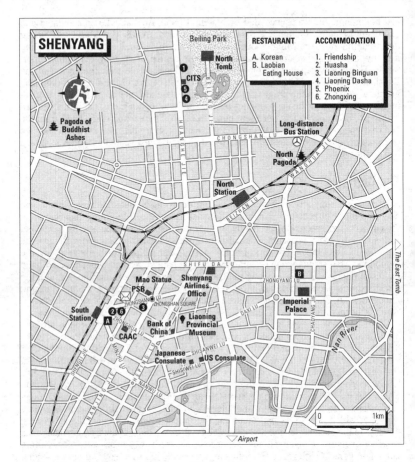

reached by bus #18 from its stop one block north and one block east of the Imperial Palace. The tomb is less monumental in layout and shows more signs of age, but it's still an impressive structure, with fortified walls and a three-storey tower.

Shenyang's other sights are hardly worth tracking down unless you have time to spare or are in the area. There were formerly four pagodas and four temples at the limits of the city, one on each side. The only one that remains in a reasonable state is the **North Pagoda** (¥5), just to the south of the long-distance bus station, which contains a "sky and earth Buddha", an image of twin Buddhas rarely seen in Chinese temples. Also in the north of the city is the **Pagoda of Buddhist Ashes** (¥5), a thirteen-storey, fifty-metre-high hollow brick pagoda constructed in the Liao dynasty, around nine hundred years ago. It's in good shape, though stained from pollution, and from the top you can get good views of the city. On display are relics that were found when the pagoda was restored, including a fine, gold-plated, copper Buddha. Bus #205 from the South station will get you near; get off when you see the river and walk over the bridge. The **Liaoning Provincial Museum** (Tues–Sun 8–11.30am &

1–4.30pm; ¥8), in the heart of the downtown area, may be a little dusty, and they really should clean the windows, but it's one of the largest museums in the northeast. The three thousand or so exhibits include embroidery, painting, copperware, pottery and porcelain. Perhaps most interesting are the fragments of polished bone inscribed with characters and used for divination, which are some of the earliest extant examples of written Chinese.

Practicalities

Shenyang **airport**, the busiest in the northeast with flights to Irkutsk and daily domestic connections to all major Chinese cities, is 20km south of the city and linked to the *CAAC* office in the centre by an airport bus.

Five rail lines converge on Shenyang's two main **stations**. You'll arrive at the **South station**, the larger and more central one, if you've come from Beijing or farther south. It's convenient for the cheapest hotel, the grotty *Huasha*, just over the road (see below). The newer **North station**, serving destinations to the north of Shenyang, is well out of the centre; take trolleybus #5 from here to Zhongshan Square and the South station. The **long-distance bus station** is in the northeast of town. To get into the centre from here, walk east to Wanghua Jie and get bus #325, which terminates at the South station.

Shenyang is very spread out and trying to walk anywhere is frustrating. **Taxis** are widely available, congregating around the stations, where the drivers can be intimidating en masse. Their meters are purely decorative, and the standard charge for foreigners is ¥20. Fortunately, the **bus** system is extensive and not too crowded. Bus maps can be bought outside the stations.

Accommodation

Several **hotels**, mostly serving tour groups and gangs of businessmen, are clustered around Beiling Park, near the North Tomb, well out of the centre. It's a quiet area, with few shops around, served by trolleybus #6 from the South station and bus #220, which passes the west side of the North station. The hotels in the city centre are more convenient, though downtown Shenyang is no beauty spot.

Friendship, 1 Huanghe Bei Dajie (☎024/6801122, fax 6800132). A Party hang-out with frowning, Stalinist villas, out by Beiling Park. Guests and staff to match. ⑨.

Huasha, 3 Zhongshan Lu (☎024/7833423). This shabby building opposite the South station looks like it's about to fall down. Inside the rooms are large, but ragged round the edges, and the bathrooms show their age. The cheapest place in town. ⑥.

Liaoning Binguan, Zhongshan Lu (☎024/7829166). Opposite the Mao statue, an incongruously refined, chic building, with art-nouveau curves and decorative flourishes, built by the Japanese in 1927. This is the nicest place to stay in Shenyang. ⑧–⑨.

Liaoning Dasha, 1 Huanghe Dajie (☎024/6865501). A bulky, no-frills building, with good service and spacious, if rather bare, rooms. North of the centre, by Beiling Park. ⑧.

Phoenix, 109 Huanghe Nan Dajie (☎024/6846501). Plush place, near the *Liaoning Dasha*, offering a gym, sauna, coffee bar, beauty parlour and a good Western-style pastry shop. They can book transport for guests and there's a twenty percent discount if you have a student card. ⑨.

Zhongxing, 86 Taiyuan Bei Jie (☎024/3838188, fax 8804096). Just east of the South station, near the street market – look for the distinctive red pyramid top. This airy modernist mansion, characterless but with friendly staff, is one of the more reasonably priced places in the centre. ⑦.

Eating and drinking

The better hotels have **restaurants**, but they're nothing special, and the cheaper hotels' food halls are definitely to be avoided. For cheap meals, you're best off around the South train station: the *Korean Restaurant* (with a sign in English), directly oppo-site the station entrance on Shengli Lu, does spiced, cold noodles (nicer than they sound) for a few yuan, *KFC* is just around the corner on Zhonghua Lu, and there's an excellent noodle place a few doors farther down. About 100m north of the *Huasha Hotel* on Zhongshan Lu, check out the *Haolilai Cake Shop*, which sells lurid but tasty cream cakes. More upmarket, the *Laobian Eating House*, at 6 Zhongyang Lu, is noted for its dumplings, and if you really want to splash out, try the *Hong Kong Delicious Food City*, 284 Qingnian Lu (☎3896188), a new joint venture, and probably Shenyang's most de luxe restaurant, with gold-plated tables and prices to match.

Listings

Airlines *CAAC* is at 117 Zhonghua Lu. Plane tickets can also be bought from an office on the sec-ond floor of the South station, from hotels or from *CITS*.

Banks and exchange *Bank of China*, 75 Heping Bei Dajie (Mon–Fri 8am–12.30pm & 2–4.30pm).

Consulates The Japanese, North Korean and US consulates are all in the same road, Shisiwei Lu, in the south of the city. The Russian consulate is in the *Phoenix Hotel*, 109 Huanghe Nan Dajie, by Beiling Park. Theoretically, you can get a Russian visa here, but don't bank on it.

PSB The PSB is on Zhongshan Lu, by the Mao statue (Mon–Fri 8am–5pm).

Post office and telecommunications Shenyang's main post office is at 32 Zhongshan Lu (Mon–Fri 8am–6pm), and there's a 24hr telecom service inside.

Trains Trains to southern destinations usually leave from the South station and to northern desti-nations from the North station. Both stations have an upstairs ticket booth where you can buy tick-ets for trains the next day, which saves struggling through the riots at the main windows below. Tickets for trains leaving from the North station can be bought from the South station, and vice versa. Make sure you check which station your train leaves from when you buy a ticket.

Travel agents The *CITS* office at 113 Nan Huanghe Lu (☎024/6809383, fax 6808772), in the same compound as the *Phoenix Hotel*, is the central branch for Liaoning Province, and it's the place to come if you want to go on an organized tour of the northeast. Possibilities include an ice and snow tour of the Changbai Shan Reserve, a steam locomotive tour, a whizz around the Inner Mongolian grasslands, or a tour that includes a slice of North Korea. Expect to pay at least ¥5000. They can also get soft-sleeper train tickets given four days' notice, and you can get city maps in English here too.

Dalian

DALIAN, at the southern tip of the Liaodong Peninsula, is clean, modern and rich – and very expensive. It's one of China's most cosmopolitan cities, partly because it has changed hands so often; as the only **ice-free port** in the region it was eagerly sought by the foreign powers who held sway over China in the nineteenth century. The Japanese gained the city in 1895, only to lose it a few years later to the Russians, who saw it as an alternative to ice-bound Vladivostok. In 1905, after decisively defeating the Russian navy, the Japanese wrested it back and remained in control for long enough to complete the construction of the port facilities. After World War II, the Soviet Union occupied the city for ten years, finally withdrawing when Sino-Soviet relations improved. Today Dalian is busier than ever, the funnel for Dongbei's enormous natur-al and mineral wealth and an industrial producer in its own right, specializing in petro-chemicals and shipbuilding. The city is booming as fast as any in China and, though the foreign devils are still here, they're now invited. Dalian has been designated a Special Economic Zone, one of China's "open door" cities with regulations designed to attract overseas investment. The Japanese have a particularly strong presence, and at the uni-versity more students learn Japanese than English.

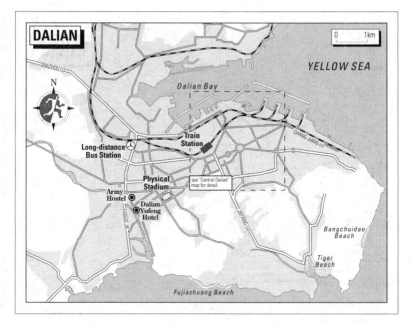

There are no sights as such and little to interest foreign visitors, but it's popular with indigenous tourists who come here for the scenic spots and **beaches** outside the city, to recover their health in beach sanatoriums and to stuff themselves on seafood. The city is also known for soccer, which explains the large sculptures of footballs you'll see around – Dalian's team is second only to Beijing. The city holds two **festivals**: the Locust Flower Festival in spring is the time to visit the city's parks, and the International Fashion Festival around September 10 sees fashion models parading in the streets. Basically, though, it's more a place to do business, and spending any time here will soon drain a modest budget.

The City

Nicknamed the Hong Kong of the north, Dalian shares that city's brash self-confidence and sense of urgency. The skyline is an angular jumble of new skyscrapers and cranes, and the locals are more modern, better dressed and wealthier than their counterparts in the north. Indeed, living expenses here are higher than in Beijing and conspicuous mobile phone use is rife.

The hub of Dalian is **Zhongshan Square** (really a circle) and its spokes are the most interesting streets in the city. Japanese and Russian buildings, German cars, girls in miniskirts and Western dance music blaring from the shops give the area an international flavour. The main **shopping** streets are Shanghai Lu and Tianjin Jie, where you'll find designer-label clothes and shoes, as well as stalls selling a wide range of pop music, Chinese and Western. The *English Language Bookstore*, at 178 Tianjin Jie, has novels in English on the second floor and intriguingly contains a political section that staff refuse to let foreigners go near. There are two *Friendship Stores*,

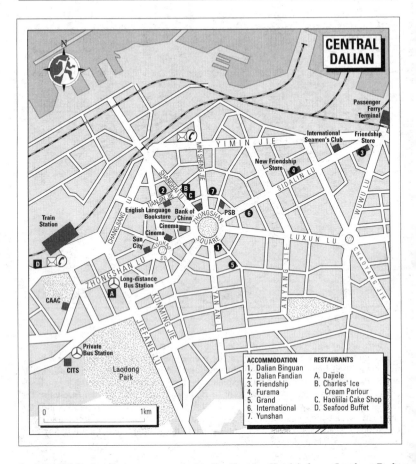

both on Sidalin Lu; the newer one, next to the *Furama Hotel,* is huge. Laodong Park, in the south of the city on the route of bus #102, has a good **night market** centring on Jiefang Lu (daily 5–9.30pm).

The **beaches,** Dalian's main attraction, are some way south of the city centre. The best way to get to them is to take the double-decker bus (the only one in Dalian) from the main station, which visits them and then returns to the station. It runs until 8pm. Otherwise a taxi will cost between ¥30 and ¥70, depending on which beach you go to. Heading around the coast from east to west, the first beach (missed out on the bus route) is Bangchuidao, which is reserved for cadres and foreign VIPs. As a Westerner you may be able to get in here, but ordinary Chinese are not allowed. Highly developed Tiger Beach, next, is the bus's first stop. It's more of a fun park with a designated beach zone. The funfair, which includes a waterborne dodgem ride, has an ¥18 entrance charge, which doesn't include any rides. The unexciting aquarium (daily 8am–9pm) is an extra ¥10. On summer evenings the area is lit up with colourful lanterns, and is thronged with people.

Nicer is Fujiazhuang Beach, a little less developed and more secluded, sheltered from the wind in a rocky bay. If you want privacy, you can charter a speedboat to one of the islands in the bay, and arrange to be picked up later – you'll have to barter hard to get a decent price of less than ¥100 for this. The beach has the usual complement of kitsch stalls and hawkers, as well as tents on the sand which you can rent by the hour. At the back of the beach are plenty of good, open-air seafood restaurants; expect to pay around ¥80 for a meal for two.

Practicalities

A taxi to or from the **airport**, 10km northeast of the city, should be ¥25, or there's a regular airport bus (¥10) to and from the *CAAC* office. The main **train station** (there are three in total), long-distance **bus stations** and passenger **ferry terminal** are all fairly central, and as the city centre is compact, the minimum ¥10 fare in a taxi will get you to most places. The beaches rimming the southern edge of the peninsula are about 5km out and easily accessible by bus.

Accommodation

Dalian is very expensive, and if you're travelling on a tight budget you don't want to be stuck here for even a night. If you are, the *Army Hostel* (☎0411/4306130; dorms ①, rooms ②) may let you in. It's 50m beyond the *Dalian Yufeng Hotel*, on the same side of the road, and has blue double doors with the *bin guan* characters above them. The place is owned by the army, who these days are trying to supplement their budget by running profit-making enterprises, which seems to be why they can accept foreigners. No one speaks English, but it's clean, ordered, and the downstairs restaurant is surprisingly good. If you have no luck here, you can try to wheedle your way into a Chinese hotel – if you can speak Chinese, have a Chinese friend with you, or a friendly taxi driver, or a student card, or all of the above, you may manage it. Another possible option is to sleep in the passenger ferry terminal if you have a ferry ticket, or if you can get past the attendant. You could also try the university, near the terminus of bus #202 from the station, or join the sleeping bodies at the back of the cinemas near Zhongshan Square, which show films all night.

HOTELS
Dalian Binguan, 4 Zhongshan Square (☎0411/2633111, fax 2634363). A stylish old building, built by the Japanese in 1927, who also constructed the *Bank of China* across the way. The grandeur is worth it if you can afford it, at nearly ¥1000 a night. ⑨
Dalian Fandian, 6 Shanghai Lu (☎0411/2633171, fax 2804197). A good central location, with its own restaurant, coffee shop and business centre. ⑧–⑨.

DALIAN		
Dalian	大连	*dàlián*
Army Hostel	军人俱乐部	*jūnrén jùlèbù*
Dalian Binguan	大连宾馆	*dàlián bīnguǎn*
Dalian Fandian	大连饭店	*dàlián fàndiàn*
Furama Hotel	富丽华大酒店	*fùlìhuá dàjiǔdiàn*
Friendship Hotel	友谊饭店	*yǒuyì fàndiàn*
Grand Hotel	博览大酒店	*bólǎn dàjiǔdiàn*
International Hotel	国际酒店	*guójì jiǔdiàn*
Yunshan Hotel	云山宾馆	*yúnshān bīnguǎn*

Dalian Yufeng, 199 Chenren Jie, Shahekou District (☎0411/4300808). Very out of the way, 5km west of the centre, but it's a nice, small place. Bus #15 from the eastern side of Zhongshan Square will get you near – stay on until the terminus, then it's a five-minute walk south. ⑦.

Furama, 60 Renmin Lu (☎0411/2630888, fax 2804455). Not particularly well-located, but this place has every imaginable facility, a lobby like a football pitch and palatial rooms. Standard doubles start at US$200. ⑨.

Friendship, 3rd Floor, 137 Sidalin Lu (☎0411/2634127). The best bargain in town, above the *Friendship Store*. Nobody speaks English and the place isn't very efficiently run, but the rooms are nice enough. ⑥.

Grand, 1 Jiefang Jie (☎0411/2806161, fax 2806980). A good location with all the amenities, but modern, bland and soulless. ⑨.

International, 9 Sidalin Lu (☎0411/2638238, fax 2630008). Modern monolith with everything the harried business traveller could want. ⑨.

Yunshan, off Zhongshan Square (☎0411/2818180). Well-located in a quiet square, and with friendly staff. ⑦–⑨.

Eating, drinking and entertainment

Dalian is full of **restaurants** and **fast food** places, especially around Tianjin Jie, where you'll also find cheap food stalls. For **seafood** head down to the beaches, try the pricey hotel restaurants, or go to the *Seafood Buffet Restaurant* near the train station, next to the post office, where you can eat as much as you like for ¥35. A good bet for breakfast is the *Dajiele Restaurant* by the long-distance bus station, which is best between 7.30 and 8.30am, when you can choose anything on the breakfast buffet table for ¥10. There's also the *Charles Ice Cream Parlour* on Shanghai Lu – ¥4 for a scoop and ¥5 for a coffee – a good place to hang out and write letters and there's a no-smoking policy. At 15 Shanghai Lu you'll find a branch of the *Haolilai Cake Shop*.

For **nightlife**, the foreign crowd hangs out at *Sun City* on Youhao Square, a club that plays Western dance music that's not too far out of date. It's open till 2am and girls get in free, but it's ¥100 for men. The *Galaxy Nightclub* on Tiger Beach is also open till two, and is popular with Chinese students, but has the same discriminatory door policy. The *International Seamen's Club* on Sidalin Lu has disco nights and occasionally shows plays or operas. There are **cinemas** at 2 Zhongshan Lu and on Youhao Square (10pm–5am; ¥20 for an all-night ticket). You can also check out Dalian's **football** team which plays most Sundays at the Physical Stadium in the southwest of the city (¥10 a ticket), on the route of bus #2 from the western end of Zhongshan Lu.

Listings

Airlines *CAAC*, 143 Zhongshan Lu (Mon–Sat 8am–5pm; ☎0411/6641792). The new *Friendship Store*, Sidalin Lu, also has an airline booking office.

Banks and exchange The *Bank of China* is at 9 Zhongshan Square (Mon–Fri 8am–noon & 2–4.30pm). Outside office hours you can change money and travellers' cheques at the *Dalian Binguan* opposite. The new *Friendship Store* on Sidalin Lu also has a money exchange.

Buses There are two long-distance bus stations: one at the terminus of bus #201 from the train station, the other on Zhongshan Lu. Buses leave between 5am and 9am and tickets can be bought the night before to avoid queues. A private bus company also runs services from opposite the *CITS* building. They are cheaper, but their vehicles are smaller and older.

Ferries A ferry service runs to Shanghai, Yantai and Qingdao (see travel details, p.195). It's cheaper than the train, and the ferry to Qingdao and Yantai is faster than by rail. Tickets can be bought in advance from the passenger ferry terminal on Yimin Jie in the northeast of the city. *CITS* will only book first- and second- class tickets, but third class is comfortable enough and worth considering.

PSB Centrally located right on Zhongshan Square.

Post office and telecommunications The post office (Mon–Sat 8am–6pm) is next to the main train station and there's a 24hr telecommunications office next door.

Travel agents The *CITS* office on the fourth floor at 1 Changtong Jie (☎0411/3687868, fax 3637631) will book tickets for onward travel.

Trains At the main train station, window #12 is reserved for foreigners to buy tickets.

Dandong

An obscure port tucked away in the corner of Liaoning Province at the confluence of the Yalu River and the Yellow Sea, **DANDONG**'s interest to travellers lies in its proximity to North Korea – the Korean city of Sinuiju lies on the other side of the Yalu River – and its convenience as a departure point for the Changbai Shan Nature Reserve (see p.184).

The place is a tourist centre, but Westerners are a rare sight. South Koreans come here to look across at their northern neighbour, and it's the first stop on the North Korean tourist trail through China. The Chinese come here just to see the border of their country. A strong **Korean** influence can be felt in the city; restaurants serve Korean food and the distinctive Korean script can be seen outside shops. When the Chinese entered the Korean War, Dandong was bombed by the Americans, who attempted to destroy the original Yalu River Bridge. The war, or at least the Chinese version of events, is recorded in the city's amazing **Museum to Commemorate the Defeat of American Aggression**. This little city may soon have its day as it's the planned entrance into China for an ambitious new highway and undersea tunnel network that will allow trains to travel from Beijing, through Korea, to Tokyo.

DANDONG		
Dandong	丹东	*dāndōng*
Fishing Village Restaurant	多海鱼村	*duōhǎi yúcūn*
Jinhe Hotel	金和大酒店	*jīnhé dàjiǔdiàn*
Mudanfeng Hotel	牡丹峰酒店	*mǔdānfēng jiǔdiàn*
Museum to Commemorate US Aggression	抗美援朝纪念馆	*kàngměiyuáncháo jìniànguǎn*
Yalu River Guesthouse	鸭绿江大厦	*yālùjiāng dàshà*

The City

Dandong is small enough to feel human in scale, and the main streets are uncrowded, clean and prosperous. The most intriguing diversion is the presence of North Korea just over the water, and vendors by the bridges sell North Korean stamps, with slogans in English such as "The Great Leader Kim Il Sum Designs the National Flag", and pictures of the great man receiving accolades from adoring multi-racial children on the occasion of his eightieth birthday. North Korean TV, which you can pick up on hotel sets, seems to consist of a string of programmes dedicated to reporting the superhuman achievements of the country's leaders.

The nearest you can get without a visa is halfway across the river on the **Old Yalu Bridge** (¥10) in the south of town, next to the new bridge. The Koreans have dismantled their half but the Chinese have left theirs as a memorial – it's covered with pockmarks left by American machine-gun strafing. You can also take a **boat trip** down the

river; boats (¥5) leave from a pier by the new bridge when full from 9.30am onwards and there are also speedboats for charter (¥30). The boats skim the boundary line, halfway across the river, and photography is prohibited, but there's nothing compromising to see, just fishermen, trains and the odd flag – most of Sinuiju is hidden behind an artificial embankment. You can do your bit for international relations by waving back at the pedestrians.

The riverside by the bridges is the most scenic area, full of promenading tourists, particularly in the early evening. Nearby is **Yalu River Park** where you can pose for photos by a stranded MiG fighter. **Culture Square**, at the western end of the riverside promenade, is the local hang-out in the evening, with kids riding around in buggies and young guys playing hacky sack and kick badminton. Westerners are a source of great curiosity, and you're bound to get a game.

Don't miss the **Museum to Commemorate US Aggression** (Tues–Sun 8.30am–5pm; ¥30) in a compound in the northwest of the city, close to the Korean War Memorial, an inscribed square column. You can get here on bus #4 or #5 from the station; get off by the sports stadium and walk north for five minutes. This new, gleaming museum, aimed perhaps at North Korean tourists, has eight exhibition halls on the **Korean War**, full of maps, plans, dioramas, machine guns, hand grenades, gory photographs and sculptures of lantern-jawed Chinese and Korean soldiers. Hall five is a trench simulation. In hall seven an impressive revolving panorama shows Korean and Chinese soldiers hammering American aggressors. Next door is a display of North

Korean folk art, including dolls and distinctive children's shoes. The final hall is a memorial to individual Chinese soldiers, sanctified national heroes, whose photographs are printed next to descriptions of their deeds. Everything is labelled in Korean and Chinese; the only English in evidence is on Chinese propaganda which was dropped behind the American lines, in which worried wives wonder what their husbands are fighting for, and on the United Nations official declaration of war, in the first hall, which is the only written record in the entire museum of the trifling historical detail that the North Koreans kicked off the war by invading the South. A couple of MiGs and some Red Army tanks sit in a compound to the side of the museum.

Practicalities

Arriving at Dandong **train station**, or at the **long-distance bus station** just to the north, puts you right in the centre of town, close to the least expensive hotels and about 1km north of the Yalu River. You'll be met by touts who work for **hotels** that don't take foreigners, though they're not always aware of this. The most convenient place to stay is the *Mudanfeng* at 3 Liu Jin Jie (☎0415/2132196; ⑥), right next to the train station. It's clean and ordered, though the staff could try a bit harder. The downstairs restaurant is good if you can ignore the tacky decor. A good alternative is the friendly *Jinhe* (☎0415/2132771; ⑤), well located next to the Yalu Bridge, with a view of the river and North Korea. It's fifteen minutes' walk south from the train station. The most luxurious place in town, the *Yalu River Guesthouse* at 87 Jiu Wei Lu (☎0415/2125901; ⑧), is a Sino–Japanese hotel, with its own swimming pool. Head due north from the station and you'll see the turning on the right; the hotel is a few hundred metres down the road.

Most facilities, including the **Bank of China** and **post and telecommunications offices** are on Qi Jin Jie, the main road running east from the station. You can also change money at the *Yalu River Guesthouse*. **Food** in Dandong is surprisingly good, with freshwater fish and Korean dishes the local speciality. Try *Duohai Yucun (Fishing Village Restaurant)* just west of the Yalu Bridge, where you choose your fish from a selection of cooked dishes at the back, and it's then served with glutinous rice, soup, bread and dumplings. A feast for two is a bargain at ¥40–50. The *Sun Dining Hall* opposite the train station is a great experience – hot and boisterous with excellent food. You'll also find a number of small Korean restaurants on Liu Jie, Qi Jie and Ba Jin Jie.

If you're planning to head off to the **Changbai Shan Nature Reserve**, you'll need to spend the night in Dandong and then get the 6.30am **bus to Tonghua**, a bumpy ten hours away. Buy a ticket the night before from the efficient booking office at the bus station. Train tickets can be booked through the helpful **CITS** on the second floor of the *Mudanfeng Hotel* (☎0415/2120187), next to the train station. They also run a ten-day **tour** which takes in Sinuiju, Pyongyang and Mount Kumgang in North Korea – going on such rigidly organized tours is the only way you'll ever get into the country, but they aren't cheap; figure on spending at least ¥6000. *CITS* will help you sort out your visa, but they need at least two weeks' notice.

Into Jilin Province: Changchun and Jilin

Dull and industrial and with outrageously pricey hotels, the cities of Jilin Province are probably best avoided. You may find yourself stopping over, however, en route to the much more diverting Changbai Shan Nature Reserve, a swathe of mountain and forest which rewards the struggle it takes to get there with some breathtaking scenery.

CHANGCHUN AND JILIN

Changchun	长春	*chángchūn*
Changbaishan Hotel	长白山宾馆	*chángbáishān bīnguǎn*
Changchun Hotel	长春宾馆	*chángchūn bīnguǎn*
Industrial University	工业大学	*gōngyè dàxué*
Jixiang Hotel	吉香宾馆	*jíxiāng bīnguǎn*
Puppet Emperor's Palace	伪皇宫	*wěihuánggōng*
Jilin	吉林	*jílín*
Beishan Park	北山公园	*běishān gōngyuán*
Dongguan Hotel	东关宾馆	*dōngguān bīnguǎn*
Jiangnan Park	江南公园	*jiāngnán gōngyuán*
Jilin Hotel	吉林宾馆	*jílín bīnguǎn*
Silver River Hotel	银河大厦	*yínhé dàshà*
Songhua Hu	松花湖	*sōnghuāhú*
Yinhua Hotel	银花宾馆	*yínhuā dàshà*

Changchun

CHANGCHUN is an industrial city based on coal, petroleum and iron. The Number One Automobile Factory, which once produced the Red Flag Automobile, the now defunct cadre car with a wooden interior, still produces the **Liberation Truck**, seen all over the country. Its design has hardly changed since the factory was set up by the Russians in the 1950s, and neither, you feel, has the city, grubby, bland and full of severe buildings. At least it's well laid out, with wide, straight boulevards built by the Japanese when it was the capital of the puppet state of Manchukuo during the 1930s. There's no real reason to stay here and as hotel prices are high, it's best avoided, or used merely as a transit point.

Apart from the vast car factory, which you won't get into unless you arrange a tour with *CITS*, the only attraction worth noting is the **Puppet Emperor's Palace** (daily 8am–4pm; ¥20), in the east of the city on the route of bus #10 from the train station, where the last Chinese emperor, Puyi, was established as a powerless figurehead by the Japanese. In 1912, at the age of eight, Puyi ascended to the imperial throne in Beijing, at the behest of the dying Dowager Cixi. Although forced to abdicate by the Republican government in the same year, he retained his royal privileges, continuing to reside as a living anachronism in the Forbidden City. Outside, the new republic was coming to terms with democracy and the twentieth century and Puyi's life, circumscribed by court ritual, seems a fantasy in comparison. In 1924, he was expelled by Nationalists uneasy at what he represented, but the Japanese protected him and eventually found a use for him here in Changchun as a figure who lent a symbolic legitimacy to their rule. After the war he was re-educated by the Communists and lived the last years of his life as a gardener. His story was the subject of a lavish film, *The Last Emperor*, by the Italian director, Bertolucci, and watching the film is probably more engrossing than visiting this palace. Like its former occupant, it's really just a shadow of Chinese imperial splendour, a poor miniature of Beijing's Forbidden City, with two badly maintained courtyards and a garden, though the exhibition hall telling the story of Puyi's life is interesting.

Practicalities

A bus from the airport, 10km northwest of town, drops you outside the *CAAC* office, close to the train station. The **train** and **bus** stations are in the north of town, with frequent connections to the rest of the northeast. Jilin is two hours away by bus or train and Harbin four hours by train. From the station head due south down Sidalin Lu for 2km to the centre of the city, Renmin Square.

The cheapest **hotel** is the *Jixiang* on Jiefang Da Lu (☎0431/5620610; ⑥). Head 1km south from Renmin Square and the road leads off to the west. The *Changbaishan* at 12 Xinmin Lu (☎0431/5648624; ⑨), south then west from Renmin Square, is large and characterless, but has a good restaurant and coffee lounge, and the *Changchun*, at 10 Xinhua Lu (☎0431/8921619; ⑨) northwest of Renmin Square, is more pleasant all round, but really none of these hotels justifies its prices. For simple, good-value accommodation, try the Industrial University just west of Gongnong Square. Head south down Sidalin Lu, the main street south from the station, for 4km, then turn west on to Ziyou Lu, and the square is 1km farther.

The *Bank of China* (Mon–Fri 8am–noon & 1–5pm) and *CITS* (☎0431/882401, fax 882419) are both behind the *Changbaishan Hotel*, although *CYTS*, at 49 Sidalin Lu, is more willing to dispense practical information. *CAAC* is at 2 Liaoning Lu.

Jilin and around

JILIN city is split in two by the Songhua River with the downtown area spread along its northern shore. The only things worth noting about Jilin, and then only marginally, are its parks. Largest is **Beishan Park**, in the west of town on the route of bus #7 from the station, which has some impressive working Buddhist temples (¥5, plus additional charges of a few yuan for other buildings). Best is the **Sky King Temple**, with its gangs of fortune-tellers outside reading ripples in water held in metal bowls. Next door to the park entrance is a **kung fu school**, one of the best in Dongbei, offering a three-month intensive course for ¥300 – ask nicely and they'll give you a demonstration of the use of some of the exotic weapons that hang on the wall. They have recently diversified and now also run a ladies' weight loss programme. Outside, vendors sell tasty roast baby duck on skewers. **Jiangnan Park**, in the south of the city on the route of buses #30 and #3 from the station, is worth a look in winter, if you can stand the cold, when it hosts the city's **ice festival**.

Practicalities

Bus #38 goes to and from the **airport** in the northwest of town to the fairly central train and bus station the northern bank of the river, including the *Dongguan* at 2 Jiang Wan Lu (☎0432/454272; ⑥), by the bridge, which is cavernous and frayed, but its large rooms are some of the cheapest you'll find. Another cheaper option is the uninspiring and draughty *Jilin* at 38 Jiangnian Dajie (☎0432/661541; dorms ⑨, rooms ⑦), just south of the river on the east side of the main north–south road. Perhaps the best bet is the *Yinhua* on Jiangnian Dajie (☎0432/661406; ⑥), 1km north of the *Jilin*. It's shoddy-looking, but has a friendly atmosphere. The most luxurious place in town, with its own dance hall, is the *Silver River* to the west at 175 Songjiang Lu (☎0432/241780; ⑦). It's also convenient, with the *Bank of China* just next door. If you're headed for Changbai Shan, it might be worth inquiring at the *CITS* office (☎0432/454272), just east of the *Dongguan Hotel,* about weather and the latest transport situation. They will no doubt tell you about the expensive tours and flights they run to the area (see p.185 for details).

Next to the *Dongguan Hotel* on Songjiang Lu are a couple of pleasant mid-range **restaurants**, where you can sit on balconies outside and watch the street. Classier food can be found at the *Big Restaurant*, 61 Guang Hua Lu.

Songhua Hu

Twenty kilometres east of Jilin is **Songhua Hu**, a popular local beauty spot. The deep lake is very attractive, set in a large forested park and surrounded by hills. A taxi here should cost about ¥40, and there are rowing boats for rent for ¥5 an hour. In 1992 an off-duty soldier reported being attacked by a dragon while boating here – it's a risk you'll just have to take. Unlike most Chinese scenic attractions, Songhua Hu seems big enough to absorb the impact of all its visitors, and even on weekends it's possible to escape to some quiet, peaceful spot.

At the lake's southern end is the huge **Songhua Dam**, a source of great local pride. Although in recent years the Songhua River's level has dropped by half – a result of extensive tree felling in its catchment area – the river floods every year, and at least a couple of the dam's four sluice gates have to be opened. With ruthless Chinese pragmatism, cities in Dongbei have been graded in order of importance in the event that the annual floods ever become uncontrollable. Jilin, as it has a hydro-electric power station, is judged to be more important than Harbin, so if the river does ever flood disastrously, all four sluice gates will be opened, Jilin will be spared, and Harbin will drown.

Changbai Shan Nature Reserve

The Changbai mountains run northeast to southwest along the Chinese/Korean border for about a thousand kilometres. The highest peak, Baitou Shan, at 2744m, is the tallest mountain on the eastern side of the continent, and with its long, harsh winters and humid summers, this is the only mountain range in east Asia to possess alpine tundra. The huge lake, **Tian Chi**, high in the Changbai mountains, is one of the highlights of Dongbei, and the area around, the **Changbai Shan Nature Reserve**, with jagged peaks emerging from swathes of lush pine forest, is beautiful and wild. This is remote, backwater China, difficult to get to even with the recent growth of a tourist infrastructure to shuttle people from the nearby cities to the lake and back again. Heading a little off the tourist track into the wilderness is the way to get the most out of the area, though you'll need to come well prepared.

The **nature reserve** centres on the magnificent waters of Tian Chi, at the summit of Changbai Shan, and covers over eighty thousand hectares of luxuriant forest. Established in 1961, most of the reserve lies between 500 and 1100 metres above sea level. At the base of the range, the land is dense, with huge Korean pine trees, which can grow up to 50m tall, and mixed broadleaf forest. The rare Manchurian fir is also found here. Higher altitudes are home to the Changbai Scotch pine, recognizable by its yellow bark, and the Japanese yew. As the climate becomes colder and damper higher up, the spruces and firs get hardier before giving way to a layer of sub-alpine grassland with colourful alpine plants and tundra. Animal species on the reserve include the leopard, lynx, black bear and **Siberian tiger**, all now protected, though decades of trapping have made them a rarity. Notable bird species include the golden-rumped

| **Changbai Shan** | 长白山 | *chángbáishān* |

swallow, orioles and the ornamental red crossbill. The area is rich in medicinal plants, too, and since the eleventh century has been a focus of scientific research. The Chinese regard the region as the best place in the country for **ginseng** and deer antlers, both prized in traditional remedies, and, recently, the reserve's rare lichens have been investigated as a treatment for cancer.

Visitors, mostly domestic tourists, South Koreans and Japanese, come here in great numbers and a tourist village has grown up, with the result that the scenery is somewhat marred by litter, souvenir stalls and hawkers. Not all visitors are here for the scenery; plenty come to search for herbs, and many of the Japanese are here to catch butterflies (to keep) and ants (to eat). When the day-trippers have left, though, it's peaceful, and there is plenty of opportunity to hike around far from the crowds.

Mountain practicalities

Changbai Shan is a place that rewards detailed exploration. Head any distance from the obvious paths and you're quickly swallowed up in the wilderness. Settlements are few and far between, though, and the only roads are dirt tracks, so don't wander too far unless you know what you're doing. The **weather** in the region is not kind and can change very suddenly. In summer, torrential rain is common, mist makes it impossible to see far and the buildings at the summit often lose their electricity supply. However, a trip is really only practical in the summer months as winter temperatures can drop very low and snow makes the roads in and out completely impassable.

If you're planning to stay any length of time, good preparation and the right equipment are essential. Bring insect repellent, tiger balm (for bites), walking boots, waterproof clothing and a sweater. You'll also need a flashlight, a good sleeping bag and all-weather gear if you're planning to camp. Before going it's wise to get a weather report, which you can do by phoning Dandong ☎121 if you speak Chinese, otherwise talk to a branch of *CITS*. The only time when there is any public transport is between June and September and you should generally be all right at this time, but don't make a trip if the rains are heavy, as the roads may flood and trap you on the mountain. At other times of the year, you'll have to rent a jeep.

Into the reserve

Changbai Shan is a long way from anywhere, and getting here is not easy. **Access** has improved in the interests of tourism, but the roads are still rough. However, you can travel in by **train** as far as Baihe (see below), a village at the base of the mountain. Services are infrequent, but are uncrowded and relatively comfortable.

The simplest way in is to **fly**. A biplane leaves Jilin every morning, arriving at Tian Chi an hour later. You have till 4pm to look around, and then it's back on the plane for the return trip. Tickets (¥1500) can be bought through Jilin *CITS* (see p.183). Three-day **minibus tours** (¥295) also go from Jilin – again, *CITS* will give you details. The journey takes about ten hours, unfortunately giving you only a day in the reserve.

By **public transport**, you can approach from Dandong, Jilin or Changchun. **From Dandong**, a bus leaves daily for Tonghua at 6.30am (11hr). The bus zigzags through rural China along roads that are little better than dirt tracks, a rough but engrossing ride. **From Jilin**, trains run to Tonghua (8hr). **TONGHUA** is a dump, so as soon as you arrive buy a ticket for the train to Baihe (¥70 hard sleeper; 8hr); there are two daily at 9am and 9pm. The station is being rebuilt and at the moment the ticket office is a hole in a wall down a back alley. If you're coming **from Changchun**, get a train south to Antu (10hr), then catch a morning bus on to Baihe, five hours away.

GINSENG

Changbai **ginseng** is regarded as the finest in China. It has been collected as a medicinal plant for millennia, and the first Chinese pharmacopoeia written in the first century, records its ability to nourish the five internal organs, sharpen intelligence, strengthen *yin* (female energy) and invigorate *yang* (male energy). It generally grows in the shade of the Korean pine, and it is said that a plant of real medicinal value takes fifty years to mature. Changbai ginseng hunters work in summer, when the plant can be spotted by its red seeds. One way to find it is to listen for the call of the Bangchui sparrow, which becomes hoarse after eating ginseng seeds.

It's quite conceivable to search for weeks and not find a single root, which has given rise to a host of **superstitions**. Hunters have even disappeared, causing rumours that the roots are guarded by snakes and tigers. Legend has it that if a hunter should dream of a laughing, white-bearded man or a group of dancing fairies he must get up, remain silent, and walk off into the forest. His colleagues, following him, must not speak to him, and he will lead them to a root.

When a ginseng root is found, a stick is planted in the ground and a red cloth tied to it. Traditionally, the cloth stops the ginseng child –the spirit of the root– from escaping. The plants lie horizontally, with their roots growing upwards in the topsoil. Digging one out is a complex, nail-biting operation, as if any of the delicate roots are damaged, the value of the whole is severely diminished. Roots are valued not just by weight, but by how closely the root system resembles a human body, with a head and four limbs. If you find a wild root, you're rich, as Changbai ginseng sells for ¥1000 a gram. Artificially reared ginseng is worth a fraction of this.

Baihe

The village of **BAIHE** is the farthest into Changbai you can get by train; from here on, it's buses, dirt roads and dusty villages. Baihe is a friendly little place, and village life carries on regardless of the tourists. The *Yanleyuan Restaurant*, opposite the train station, is good and not only do they serve local specialities such as mushrooms and rare fungus, but the restaurant owner is a one-man tourist office; he can get tickets for onward travel, arrange accommodation and sort out transport around the reserve. If you do not plan staying on the mountain, you can leave your bags at the restaurant.

There's a small **hotel** in Baihe (③), five minutes' walk from the station; turn right out of the station and then left. A more interesting alternative, however, is to ask around the little family restaurants by the station. Many of them have rooms at the back where you can stay for as little as ¥10 per person. These rooms have *kangs* – a raised wooden platform constructed over a pipe that leads from the oven in the kitchen – a characteristic of cold northern China. During the day the platform is used as a dining area, and at night mattresses are rolled out and it becomes a bed. The platform is always on the west side of the room, the side where the ancestors are worshipped, and it's the most honoured place to sleep. These rooms can get very hot at night, full of dry, stuffy air, but in winter the warmth is essential. If you do stay in one of these places, the locals appreciate it if you keep as low a profile as possible, as the PSB disapproves.

The bus trip from Baihe on to Tian Chi takes two hours (¥35), and regular tourist buses run up and down the mountain during the summer months. The train is the best way back out of the Changbai Shan region, although there is an unreliable bus service from Baihe which supposedly leaves every morning at 6.30am going to Jilin (¥41; 10hr) and then on to Changchun (¥49; 12hr).

Tian Chi and around

A deep volcanic crater lake 5km across, surrounded by angular peaks, with waterfalls gushing around it and blue, snow-capped mountains in the distance, **Tian Chi** (Heaven Pool) is dramatic and beautiful. At the reserve entrance, foreigners have to pay an outrageous ¥120; Chinese and student-card holders pay ¥15. The bus drops you off in a car park higher up, from where a road leads to the lake; the walk up the main path takes about an hour. There's a longer western path branching off from the car park, which is more scenic but more dangerous with jagged rocks everywhere. Jeep taxis to the lake are ¥100. There's a pretty waterfall 500m off to the east from the car park. Just south of the car park, a bathhouse offers hot spring baths for ¥40 per person. Once you've seen the lake, and walked round it, tracks leading off into the mountain offer the chance of further exploration.

The last buses return to Baihe around 4pm. If you want to stay at the mountain, head south from the car park, back the way the bus has come from. The official hotel for foreigners is the *Dujuanshan* (⑦), where the standard of accommodation is pretty good considering the location, and rooms have electric blankets. If they are booked up, the sympathetic staff will help you get a room in one of the Chinese hotels farther down the road (③). Technically, these places are not allowed to take non-Chinese, but as the PSB doesn't get up here much, they can be persuaded to waive the rules if you're persistent, charming or soaked through. The hotels don't always have heating, hot water or constant electricity. Camping is possible, though again it's against the rules; pick somewhere secluded. Food up here is dull and expensive; your best bet is the restaurant and shop in the *Dujuanshan*.

Harbin and beyond

The last major conurbation before you hit the sub-Siberian wilderness and its scattering of oil and mining towns, **HARBIN** is the capital of Heilongjiang Province and probably the northernmost location that's of interest to visitors. It's worth a visit for its **winter ice festival** alone, but it's also one of the few northern cities with a distinctive character, the result of colonialism and co-operation with nearby Russia. The city was a small fishing village on the Songhua River – the name means "where the fishing nets are dried" – until world history intervened. In 1896 the Russians obtained a contract to build a rail line from Vladivostok, through Harbin to Dalian, and the town's population swelled. More Russians arrived in 1917, White Russian refugees fleeing the Bolsheviks, and many stayed on for the rest of their lives. In 1932, the city was briefly captured by the Japanese forces invading Manchuria, then in 1945 it fell again to the Russian army, who held it for a year before

---

HARBIN'S FESTIVALS

In compensation for the cruel winter weather, the annual **Ice Lantern Festival**, centred on Zhaolin Park, is held from January 5 to February 5. The park becomes a fairytale landscape with magnificent sculptures and sometimes entire buildings, complete with stairways, arches and bridges, made of ice, carved with chainsaws and picks, and often with coloured lights inside them to heighten the psychedelic effect. Highlights of past festivals have included detailed replicas of St Paul's Cathedral and life-size Chinese temples, though these days cartoon characters outnumber more traditional Chinese subject matter. During the festival, plenty of other cultural events take place and its end is marked by a firework display.

In summer, Harbin hosts a classical and traditional **music festival** from the middle to the end of July, during which orchestras and groups play in the city's eight theatres.

HARBIN AND BEYOND

Harbin	哈尔滨	*hāěrbīn*

ACCOMMODATION

Beiyuan	北苑饭店	*běiyuàn fàndiàn*
Double Crane	双鹤饭店	*shuānghè fàndiàn*
Guochai	果菜大厦	*guócài dàshà*
International	国际饭店	*guójì fàndiàn*
Liangmao	粮贸饭店	*liángmào fàndiàn*
Longyun	龙运宾馆	*lóngyùn bīnguǎn*
Modern	马达尔宾馆	*mǎdáěr bīnguǎn*
Swan	天鹅饭店	*tiāné fàndiàn*
Tianzhu	天竹宾馆	*tiānzhú bīnguǎn*

THE CITY

Childrens' Park	儿童公园	*értóng gōngyuán*
Culture Park	文化公园	*wénhuà gōngyuán*
Flood Control Monument	防洪纪念碑	*fánghóng jìniànbēi*
Germ Warfare Base	日本细菌室	*rìběn xìjūnshǐ*
Provincial Museum	省博物馆	*shěng bówùguǎn*
Stalin Park	斯大林公园	*sīdàlín gōngyuán*
Sun Island	太阳岛公园	*tai'yángdǎo gōngyuán*

RESTAURANTS

Beilashun	北来顺饭店	*běiláishùn fàndiàn*
Futailu	福泰楼饭店	*fútàilóu fàndiàn*
Harharle	哈哈乐饭店	*hāhālè fàndiàn*
Huamei	华梅西餐厅	*huáměi xīcāntīng*
Jinxiu Hotpot City	锦标火锅城	*jǐn biāo huǒ guōchéng*

Stalin and Chiang Kaishek finally came to an agreement. The city reverted to the Chinese, though when they withdrew, the Russians took with them most of the city's industrial plant. Things haven't been totally peaceful since – Harbin was the scene of fierce factional fighting during the Cultural Revolution, and when relations with the Soviet Union deteriorated, the inhabitants looked anxiously north as fierce border skirmishes took place.

The city used to be nicknamed "**Little Moscow**" and though much of the old architecture has been torn down and replaced with sterile blocks and skyscrapers, the town still looks a little like the last threadbare outpost of imperial Russia. Leafy boulevards are lined with European-style buildings painted pastel shades, and bulbous onion domes dot the skyline. It's possible to eat in Russian restaurants and the locals have picked up on some of their neighbour's customs; as well as developing a taste for ice cream, Harbin's residents have a reputation as the hardest drinkers in China.

During the summer the **climate** is quite pleasant, but in winter the temperature can plummet to well below minus 30°C. Local people wear so many layers they look like waddling bears and milk is sold as solid bricks.

Attractions beyond here are limited, and journeys are arduous and long. Ornithologists will be interested in the Zhalong Nature Reserve, home of the rare red-crowned crane, and a few Chinese tourists get up to Wudalianchi, an isolated health spa. Further overland travel is limited by border restrictions – it's very hard to get the necessary paperwork for a trip north into Russia – and the inhospitable mountainous terrain to the west, which prevents an easy journey out of Dongbei into Inner Mongolia. Unless you get on the weekly Trans-Siberian train in Harbin, northern Dongbei is basically a dead end.

Orientation, arrival and accommodation

Downtown Harbin, the most interesting part for visitors, is laid out on the southern bank of the Songhua River, with the liveliest streets between here and the train station. The urban sprawl farther south is best avoided.

Harbin **airport** is 50km southwest of the town, and served by an airport bus (¥10) which drops you outside the *CAAC* office. From the central **train station**, a clutch of cheap hotels is a short walk away, or you could head north to the somewhat less seedy and hectic central streets. The **long-distance bus station** is on Songhuajiang Jie, near the train station.

The most useful **city bus** is #103, which runs between Zhongshan Lu and Zhaolin Park. **Taxis** around the city are ¥10, unless the meter's "broken", in which case it's at least ¥20 – the drivers can be aggressive bargainers. Travelling around the city takes a long time as the streets are very congested. In an effort to control the problem, the authorities have introduced a range of new traffic rules and one-way systems which simply bewilder the local drivers. In summer there are small boats (¥10) across the Songhua, or you can take the ferry (¥2).

> The **telephone code** for Harbin is ☎0451

Accommodation

Harbin is one of the less expensive cities of the northeast for accommodation. The choice of **hotels** is better and the prices almost reasonable, although expect heavy surcharges during the ice festival. A cluster of hotels sits around the train station, but although the location is convenient, the area is noisy, dirty and crowded, and the hotels in town are a much better option if you're staying for any length of time.

Beiyuan (☎3643146). Directly in front of the station, this seedy dive is strangely popular with budget travellers, who are herded on to the grotty fifth floor. Otherwise, it's full of Russians. Rooms are threadbare, staff are insolent and untrustworthy and it's not even that cheap. There's a fur shop, a useless branch of *CITS*, a bookshop and a sprinkling of prostitutes in the lobby. ⑦.

Double Crane, 118 Minsheng Lu (☎2603677). The flashest place in town, charging US$150 for a double room, but that does include an American breakfast. ⑨.

Guochai, 42 Beima Lu (☎8307877). Easily the best of the cheaper places. It's a small hotel, the rooms are clean, new and light and with satellite TV, the staff are nice, the location is quiet, if a bit far out, and the second-floor restaurant is excellent. Don't get your hair cut in the first-floor salon though. To get here, turn left out of the train station and walk to the roundabout, then get bus #107 or #109 down Jingyang Jie. If you're travelling on your own, staff can often be persuaded to give you a room for half the price. ⑤.

International, 124 Dazhi Jie (☎3641441, fax 3625651). A good location but it's a dingy, crumbling building with a depressing atmosphere. Staff walk around in dirty uniforms listlessly swatting flies. Bus #11 goes here from the station. ⑥.

Liangmao, 11 Beima Lu (☎8326503). Directly opposite the *Guochai*, this is another good place to stay, but not quite as good as its neighbour. ⑥.

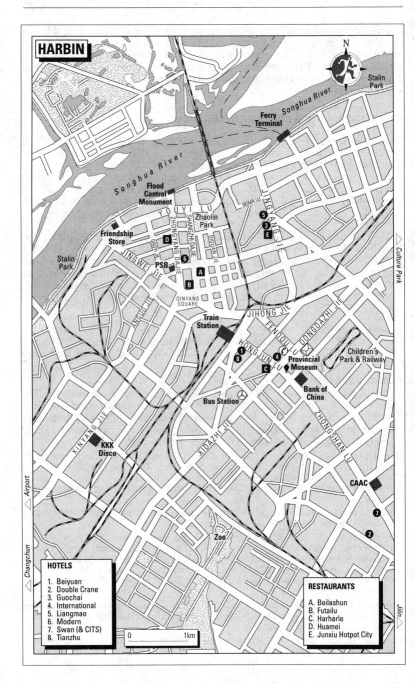

HARBIN

N

Stalin Park

Songhua River

Ferry Terminal

Songhua River

Flood Control Monument

YOUYI LU

Zhaolin Park

BEIMA LU

JINGYANG JIE

5
3
E

Friendship Store

ZHONGYANG DAJIE

SHANGZHI DAJIE

D

DIDUANJIE

Stalin Park

JINGWEI JIE

PSB

6
B
A

QINYANG SQUARE

JIHONG JIE

DONGDAZHI JIE

Train Station

HONG JUN JIE

FENDOU LU

Children's Park & Railway

1
8

4

Provincial Museum

ANSHUN JIE

C

Bus Station

Bank of China

ZHONGSHAN LU

XINYANG JIE

KKK Disco

XIDAZHI JIE

CAAC

7

2

Zoo

Airport ◁

Changchun ◁

Jilin ◁

Culture Park ▷

HOTELS

1. Beiyuan
2. Double Crane
3. Guochai
4. International
5. Liangmao
6. Modern
7. Swan (& CITS)
8. Tianzhu

0   1km

RESTAURANTS

A. Beilashun
B. Futailu
C. Harharle
D. Huamei
E. Junxiu Hotpot City

Longyun (☎3634528). A clean and modern place on the right and behind the *Beiyuan* as you exit the station. Rooms are good value if you have a student card, as there's a thirty percent discount. ⑤.

Modern, 89 Zhong Yong Lu (☎6615846, fax 4614997). The name is a misnomer, as it was actually built in 1906 and is Harbin's oldest hotel. An elegant building on one of the city's busiest streets, it's got a lot of character, with European- and Russian-style restaurants and 160 rooms. The staff are helpful and speak English. ⑨.

Swan, 73 Zhongshan Lu (☎2300201). A bright, white modern building, inconvenient for anything except the airport. *CITS* and *CAAC* are nearby. ⑧.

Tianzhu (☎3643725). Just to the right of the station, this is the most pleasant hotel in the area, a thin nineteen-storey building that hasn't yet started to fall apart. ⑤.

The City

Harbin is more a recreational centre than a cultural mecca, a good place to shop and explore the streets. The place to head for is the **downtown area**, a triangle outlined by Diduan Jie and Jingwei Jie, where there are plenty of brand-name clothes stores, fur shops and department stores. The smaller streets and alleys around here are the best places to see the city's Russian architecture with its decaying stucco facades and elegant balconies. There's an extensive market selling women's clothes off Xinyang Square, while the best large department stores are on Diduan Lu and Zhongyang Lu. Jingjang Jie has a busy **night market** and, among the row after row of plastic combs, toothbrushes and *"Roobek"* and *"Channel"* T-shirts, are a few interesting stalls selling traditional Chinese medicines and good tea. If you're lucky you may see men skilfully making crickets out of grass or mythological figures out of coloured flour paste.

Another district to wander in is along the **riverbank**, starting from the **Flood Control Monument** at the bottom of Zhongyang Dajie. Built in 1958, it commemorates the many thousands who have died in the Songhua floods, most recently in the 1930s and 1950s, and is a notable piece of revolutionary realism, in granite tinged with submarine green, standing on one of the miles of Communist-built dykes which protect the land from this notoriously unpredictable stretch of river. The square here is a popular hang-out for locals, as is **Stalin Park**, a strip of land running east along the river, particularly lively on weekends. People come here to wash their clothes, meet and chat, and even bathe in the river – not a good idea, as mercury levels in the water are so high fish can no longer survive in it. Others cluster around palm-readers and storytellers, who relate old Chinese folk legends. Private entrepreneurs have set up bingo games, a new pastime which seems to be something of a local craze. A bingo card costs ¥1 and it's a good chance to practise your Chinese numbers, though don't play to win as even if you do you'll probably only end up with a tacky plastic clock. Street vendors sell ginseng, probably smuggled in from Siberia, and in small alleys off to the south a semi-legal trade in smuggled puppies goes on, a result of the new fashion for dog ownership among the Chinese middle classes. The puppies are adorable, white, fluffy and very stoned, as they're doped up for the journey across the border and often do not survive. Just south of here **Zhaolin Park**, unremarkable in summer, is host to the spectacular winter Ice Festival (see box, p.187).

In winter, the **Songhua River** freezes solid and you can rent skates or walk across – the ice is so thick it will support a fully loaded bus or lorry and it gets used as a road. In summer, ferries will take you across to the northern bank and the resort and sanatorium village of **Sun Island** (daily, 6am–5pm; ¥10), an enormous park and leisure complex with lakes for boating, swimming pools, an arms museum and fairground rides. It's unpleasantly busy on summer weekends, and getting around takes a lot of walking – it's probably of more interest to residents and Chinese tourists.

Culture Park (daily 8am–8pm; ¥1) in the east of the city, is a similar thing, but can be fun, boasting Waterworld, a large swimming complex (¥10), miniature railways, fairground rides and a rollercoaster (¥15 a ride). The Children's Park (¥2) in the centre of town has a two-kilometre miniature railway seating ninety passengers and staffed by children, who could teach their adult counterparts on the China railways a few lessons about service and efficiency. The railway has two stations, Beijing and Moscow.

Not far from here, Harbin's Provincial Museum (Tues–Sun 9.30am–5.30pm; ¥8), opposite the *International Hotel,* has a dull permanent collection of dusty relics, but its temporary, politically motivated exhibitions can be worth checking out for comic relief. In 1995, for example, it held a sex exhibition, designed "so that the sexual revolution of the West can never happen here", with pictures of pin-ups and gay pride marches with prurient captions. At the Zoo (daily 8am–5pm; ¥10) in the south of the city, on the route of bus #81 from Xidazhi Jie, you can see the rare Manchurian tiger – only about thirty are left in the wild. The tigers have bred successfully here, saving them from extinction, though being kept in a Chinese zoo is not much of a life.

Eating, drinking and nightlife

Influenced by Russian cuisine, local cooking is characterized by a heavy use of garlic and a lot of potato. Expensive regional specialities include bear paw and deer muzzle, available in the upmarket hotels. Staying away from the delicacies, however, food in Harbin is good value.

For nightlife, try the *KKK* disco at 502 Qinyang Lu (daily 7pm–2am; ¥10, Sat & Sun ¥20). As it's fairly cheap, this is the favoured hang-out of Harbin's trendy young crowd, as opposed to all the other city hotspots, such as the *CAAC* nightclub, at 107 Zhongshan Lu, which tend to attract rich businessmen.

Restaurants

Beilashun, 113 Shangzhi Jie. Hotpots with a Muslim twist.

Futailu, 19 Xi Shisandou. Chinese food, specializing in Beijing duck, which is cheaper here than in the capital.

Harharle, 52 Hongjun Jie. A cheap and cheerful canteen serving Chinese fast food.

Huamei, 142 Zhongyang Jie. Harbin's only Russian restaurant, so the food is fairly Western and eaten with knives and forks. It's a little pricey – expect to pay at least ¥80 per person – but the food is good, especially the stroganoff, and makes a change. Those who can afford it can indulge themselves on caviar.

Jinxiu Hotpot City, 294 Jinyang Jie. Choose from a wide range of raw dishes and throw them into the hotpot in the middle of the table. The food is great and you do the cooking. It gets very hot when busy, and extremely chaotic, with waitresses dashing around putting out fires.

Listings

Airlines *CAAC* is at 87 Zhongshan Lu (☎2632337). *Shanghai Airlines,* at 224 Zhongshan Lu (☎2637953), sells tickets at half price to anyone with a student card on certain flights to Beijing and Shanghai in the summer months. If you're leaving the city by plane, allow plenty of time to get to the airport through the almost gridlocked city streets. An airport bus runs from outside the *CAAC* office – don't go with the taxi drivers who hang around outside as you'll certainly be ripped off.

Banks and exchange The *Bank of China* is on Hongjun Jie (Mon–Fri 8am–5pm). The office for travellers cheques' and credit-card advances is just round the corner.

Bookshops *Foreign Language Bookstore,* 23 Jinwei Jie.

Ferry A ferry service operates in the summer months to Jiamusi (27hr), a town 200km farther east. The ferry terminal is towards the eastern end of Stalin Park.

PSB Zhongyang Dajie (Mon–Fri 8–11am & 2–5pm).

Post office The main post office is at 51 Jianshe Jie (Mon–Sat 8am–6pm).

Telephones There's a 24hr telecom office on Fendou Lu.

Theatre "Errenzhuan" is a form of local drama performed by two actors. Ask at *CITS* for details of public performances, held irregularly in the tourist hotels.

Travel agents *CITS*, who can arrange tickets for onward travel, is in the grounds of the *Swan Hotel* at 73 Zhongshan Lu (☎2621655). More convenient and probably more useful is the *Heilongjiang Overseas Tourist Corporation* at 124 Dazhi Lu (☎3633613, fax 3621088), next to the *International Hotel*. Both organizations can arrange tours to areas farther north, including specialist hunting, fishing, skiing and bird-watching tours.

Around Harbin

Harbin's most notorious and macabre attraction is outside the city proper, about 30km away, in the tiny village of **PINGFANG**, near the terminus of bus #338 which you can catch at the train station. This was the home of a secret Japanese research establishment during World War II and is now open to the public as a grisly **museum** (daily 8–11.30am & 1–5pm; ¥15). Here prisoners of war were injected with deadly viruses, dissected alive and frozen or heated slowly until they died. Over four thousand people were murdered in the name of scientific research. After the war, the Japanese tried to hide all evidence of the base, and its existence only came to light through the efforts of Japanese investigative journalists. It was also discovered that, as with scientists in

DONGBEI'S MINORITY COMMUNITIES

After forcing minority communities to embrace official communist culture during the 1950s and 1960s, the Chinese government now takes a more enlightened, if somewhat patronizing approach to the minority nations of the north. The **Manchu** people, spread across Inner Mongolia and Dongbei, are the most numerous and assimilated. Having lived so long among the Han they are now almost identical, though they tend to be slightly taller and men have more facial hair. They are noted for an elaborate system of etiquette and will never eat dog, unlike their Korean neighbours who love it. The "three strange things" that the southern Chinese say are found in the northeast are all Manchu habits: paper windows pasted outside their wooden frame, babies carried by their mothers in handbags and women smoking in public.

In the inhospitable northern margins of Dongbei live small communities such as the **Hezhen**, one of the smallest minority nations in China with an estimated 1400 members, who inhabit the region where the Songhua, Heliong and Ussuri rivers converge and who are known to the Chinese as the fish tribe. Their culture and livelihood centre around fishing, and they are the only people in the world to make clothes out of fish skin. The fish is gutted, descaled, then dried and tanned and the skins sewn together to make light, waterproof coats, shoes and gloves. More numerous are the **Daur**, 120,000 of whom live along the Nenjiang River. They are fairly seamlessly assimilated these days, but still retain distinctive marriage and funerary traditions, and have a reputation for being superb at hockey, a form of which they have played since the sixth century.

However, perhaps the most distinctive minority are the **Oroqen**, a tribe of nomadic hunters living in patrilineal clan communes called *wulileng* in the northern sub-Siberian wilderness. Although they have recently begun living a more settled existence, their main livelihood still comes from deer hunting, while household items, tools and canoes are made by Oroqen women from birch bark. Clothes are fashioned from deer hide, and include a striking hat made of a roe deer head, complete with antlers and leather patches for eyes, that is used as a disguise in hunting.

defeated Nazi Germany, the Americans gave the Japanese scientists immunity from prosecution in return for their research findings.

Jingbo Hu (Mirror Lake) is an attractive spot, 150km east of Harbin, one of Heilongjiang's prettiest places. At 45km long, set deep among forested hills, it's a good place to go fishing, boating and hiking, or just to sit and eat fruit, as many of the Chinese visitors seem to do. There's a rash of development concentrated at the northern end, which most people stick to, and mile after mile of virgin countryside beyond.

To get here, take a train to Mudanjiang (4hr) and then a tourist bus (3hr) to the lake itself. It's possible to stay in Mudanjiang at the *Mudanjiang Hotel* (⑤) or on the north side of the lake at the *Jingbo Villa* (⑤). There are plenty of Chinese-only guesthouses around that are a lot cheaper, but you'll need to do some persuading to convince them to take you.

Qiqihar and the Zhalong Nature Reserve

About six hours' train journey west of Harbin, **QIQIHAR** is Heilongjiang Province's second city, one of the oldest cities of the northeast and a thriving industrial centre. Shopping and eating are good here, but the main reason to come is to visit the **Zhalong Nature Reserve**, 30km outside town. This flat, marshy plain abounds in shallow reedy lakes and serves as the summer breeding ground of thousands of species of birds, including white storks, whooper swans, spoonbills, white ibis, and, the star attractions, nine of the world's fifteen species of **cranes**. Most spectacular of these is the endangered red-crowned crane, a lanky black and white bird, over a metre tall, with a scarlet bald patch. It has always been treasured in the East as a paradigm of elegance – the Japanese call it the Marsh God – and it's a popular symbol of longevity, as birds can live as long as sixty years. The birds mate for life and the female only lays one or two eggs each season, which the male stands guard over. A vociferous defender of their young, cranes have been known to stab eagles to death with their sharp beaks. The best time to visit is from April to June, when the migrants have just arrived.

There are two **trains** daily from Harbin to Qiqihar. **Buses** to the reserve (1hr 15min) leave from Qiqihar's bus station, 1km south down the road from the train station, on the left. Splendid though the birds are, it can be difficult to fill the time you're obliged to spend in Qiqihar by the bus timetable and a better bet might be to take one of the flat-bottomed boat tours run by *CITS*, which leave from the reserve entrance. Walking around the reserve, while not forbidden, is not encouraged by the keepers or the murderous swarms of mosquitoes – come prepared. Binoculars are a good idea, too. Dedicated ornithologists might like to spend a few days here, but for most people, an afternoon crouched in the reedbeds is quite enough.

There's a basic **hotel** at the reserve (④), and two more opulent **hotels** for foreigners in Qiqihar itself, the *Beifang* (⑦) and the *Hubin* (⑦), both on the route of trolleybus #15 from the train station. *CITS*, who can book a tour for you, is in the *Hubin Hotel*.

The far north: Wudalianchi

Seven hours north of Harbin, the train reaches the town of Bei'an, a transit point to the village of **Wudalianchi** and the volcanoes beyond – take one of the regular buses and minibuses which congregate around the train station. The name refers to the "five great linking pools" which curl around the foot of the biggest volcano, Laohei Shan (Old Black Hill). Wudalianchi is best known for its mineral waters (a bit like drinking soda water from a rusty bucket, but not unpleasant) and several springs around the village feed a bathing pool and a number of individual outdoor baths. A clinic and several sanatoriums service a flow of people in search of relief from skin disorders, blood problems and baldness.

INTO SIBERIA

From northern Heilongjiang, there are a number of crossing points **into Siberia**, of which **Heihe**, a large border town that sees a lot of traffic with the Russian town of Blagoveshchensk, is the best option. From Harbin, take a train to Bei'an (8hr), then a bus on to to Heihe (10hr) – Russia is a few strides and a mountain of paperwork away. A bus connection also exists between Suifenhe (4hr from Harbin) and Vladivostok. In practice, however, these routes are fraught with difficulties; there is no tourist infrastructure, distances are long and conditions primitive. The biggest problem with crossing from Dongbei into Siberia is getting a **visa**, which you will have to sort out in Beijing, although you may get one in Shenyang if you're lucky. To get a two-week tourist visa, all your hotel accommodation in Russia must be booked in advance, and prices are steep; expect to pay at least US\$50 a night. A few travellers, through connections, have managed to get hold of business visas, which last a month and give you more flexibility. It is possible to get a tourist visa extended when in Russia, but this is a Herculean task. By far the simplest way to get into Russia from Dongbei is to hop on the **Trans-Siberian train** to Moscow which passes through Harbin every Friday morning, though again you'll need to get your visa sorted out in Beijing (see p.75 for details of the train).

Cheap rooms are available at the tatty *Wudalianchi Hotel* (④), where a good restaurant serves locally caught fish and also hires out jeeps which will take you to the volcano. Laohei Shan last erupted in 1719, making it China's youngest fire mountain. Around its base spreads a plain of fantastically contorted lava and pumice stone. It's only 300m high and the climb takes twenty minutes, the path emerging from the tree line to give daunting views of the lava plain, dotted with lesser sleeping volcanoes and fields of wheat and barley. It's a long way to go for a cure, but there can be few more remote and quiet places in which to recuperate.

travel details

Trains

Changchun to: Antu (daily; 10hr); Dandong (daily; 11hr); Harbin (4 daily; 4hr); Jilin (6 daily; 2hr); Shenyang (4 daily; 5hr); Tongliao (daily; 7hr).

Dalian to: Beijing (2 daily; 20hr); Harbin (2 daily; 15hr); Shenyang (4 daily; 5hr).

Dandong to: Changchun (daily; 8hr); Shenyang (2 daily, 7hr).

Harbin to: Bei'an (2 daily; 7hr); Beijing (daily; 18hr); Changchun (4 daily, 4hr); Hailar, Inner Mongolia (daily; 12hr); Jilin (4 daily; 2hr); Moscow (weekly; 6 days); Qiqihar (2 daily; 4hr); Shenyang (2 daily; 9hr); Yichun (2 daily; 6hr).

Jilin to: Changchun (6 daily, 2hr); Harbin (4 daily, 2hr); Tonghua (daily; 8hr).

Shenyang to: Beijing (3 daily; 12hr); Changchun (4 daily; 5hr); Dalian (4 daily; 5hr); Dandong (daily; 6hr); Harbin (4 daily; 9hr); Jilin (4 daily; 7hr); Tianjin (5 daily; 12hr).

Buses

Bus connections are comprehensive, but buses are not recommended except for short journeys as roads, particularly around Changbai Shan and in the far north, are appalling.

Ferries

Dalian to: Yantai (daily; 8hr); Tianjin (3 weekly; 20hr); Shanghai (2 weekly; 40hr); Qingdao (alternate days; 30hr); Guangzhou (2 monthly; 5 days).

Harbin to: Jiamusi (daily in summer; 18hr).

Planes

DOMESTIC

Changchun to: Beijing (3 daily; 1hr 45min); Chengdu (4 weekly; 4hr 15min); Chongqing (weekly; 5hr 30min); Dalian (2 daily; 2hr); Fuzhou (2 weekly; 3hr); Guangzhou (daily; 4hr 20min); Haikou

(2 weekly; 5hr 20min); Hangzhou (weekly; 2hr 40min); Hefei (2 weekly; 5hr 30min); Hong Kong (weekly; 4hr 20min); Ji'nan (2 weekly; 4hr); Kunming (2 weekly; 6hr); Nanjing (weekly; 2hr 20min); Qingdao (2 weekly; 4hr); Shanghai (daily; 2hr 45min); Shenyang (daily; 1hr 30min); Shenzhen (daily; 4hr 50min); Wenzhou (2 weekly; 3hr); Wuhan (2 weekly; 3hr 10min); Xiamen (4 weekly; 3hr 50min); Yantai (2 weekly; 1hr 40min).

Dalian to: Beijing (6 daily; 1hr 20min); Changchun (2 daily; 2hr); Changsha (weekly; 3hr); Chaoyang (2 weekly; 1hr 30min); Chengdu (3 weekly; 3hr 40min); Chongqing (weekly; 4hr 50min); Fuzhou (2 weekly; 2hr 40min); Guangzhou (daily; 3hr 30min); Guilin (2 weekly; 4hr 20min); Hangzhou (2 weekly; 2hr); Harbin (2 daily; 1hr 30min); Hefei (2 weekly; 4hr); Hong Kong (4 weekly; 3hr 30min); Ji'nan (4 weekly; 1hr 50min); Kunming (2 weekly; 5hr 40min); Luoyang (weekly; 2hr); Nanjing (3 weekly; 1hr 30min); Ningbo (3 weekly; 2hr); Qingdao (6 weekly; 1hr 20min); Qinhuangdao (4 weekly; 1hr 10min); Qiqihar (2 weekly; 3hr 45min); Shanghai (2 daily; 1hr 45min); Shenyang (2 daily; 1hr 20min); Shenzhen (daily; 4hr 40min); Taiyuan (2 weekly; 3hr 20min); Tianjin (2 weekly; 1hr 30min); Urumqi (weekly; 6hr 30min); Wenzhou (3 weekly; 2hr 15min); Wuhan (3 weekly; 2hr 20min); Xiamen (4 weekly; 4hr); Xi'an (weekly; 2hr 20min).

Harbin to: Beijing (5 daily; 2hr); Changsha (2 weekly; 3hr 50min); Chaoyang (4 weekly; 3hr 30min); Chengdu (daily; 5hr); Chongqing (3 weekly; 5hr 15min); Dalian (2 daily; 1hr 40min); Fuzhou (2 weekly; 3hr); Guangzhou (2 daily; 4hr 10min); Haikou (4 weekly; 6hr 45min); Hangzhou (3 weekly; 5hr 10min); Hong Kong (2 weekly; 4hr); Jiamusi (3 weekly; 1hr 20min); Ji'nan (4 weekly; 2hr); Kunming (weekly; 6hr); Lanzhou (weekly; 5hr); Nanjing (weekly; 2hr 40min); Ningbo (2 weekly; 4hr 45min); Qingdao (6 weekly; 2hr); Qinhuangdao (2 weekly; 5hr); Shanghai (2 daily; 3hr); Shenyang (2 daily; 1hr 40min); Shenzhen (daily; 6hr); Urumqi (weekly; 7hr); Wenzhou (6 weekly; 3hr 30min);

Wuhan (6 weekly; 3hr 30min); Xiamen (4 weekly; 5hr); Xi'an (2 weekly; 4hr 50min); Yantai (daily; 2hr); Zhengzhou (5 weekly; 2hr 40min).

Jilin to: Beijing (2 weekly; 1hr 50min); Guangzhou (2 weekly; 6hr); Shanghai (2 weekly; 2hr 30min).

Qiqihar to: Beijing (2 weekly; 2hr); Dalian (2 weekly; 3hr 45min); Guangzhou (weekly; 6hr 10min); Shanghai (2 weekly; 3hr 10min); Shenyang (2 weekly; 2hr).

Shenyang to: Beijing (5 daily; 1hr); Changchun (daily; 3hr 40min); Changsha (6 weekly; 3hr 30min); Chaoyang (2 weekly; 1hr 15min); Chengdu (daily; 6hr 40min); Chongqing (4 weekly; 3hr 30min); Dalian (2 daily; 1hr 20min); Fuzhou (3 weekly; 3hr 20min); Guangzhou (2 daily; 3hr 50min); Hangzhou (4 weekly; 2hr 30min); Harbin (2 daily; 1hr 10min); Hefei (weekly; 2hr 30min); Hong Kong (4 weekly; 4hr); Ji'nan (3 weekly; 2hr); Kunming (daily; 5hr 20min); Lanzhou (4 weekly; 4hr 20min); Nanjing (5 weekly; 2hr); Nanning (4 weekly; 5hr 45min); Ningbo (3 weekly; 2hr 30min); Qingdao (6 weekly; 1hr 20min); Qinhuangdao (4 weekly; 1hr 15min); Qiqihar (2 weekly; 2hr); Shanghai (daily; 5hr 20min); Shenzhen (daily; 5hr 20min); Shijiazhuang (4 weekly; 1hr 50min); Taiyuan (2 weekly; 4hr 15min); Tianjin (4 weekly; 1hr 30min); Urumqi (2 weekly; 6hr 50min); Wenzhou (5 weekly; 2hr 45min); Wuhan (8 weekly; 2hr 50min); Xiamen (5 weekly; 4hr 40min); Xi'an (daily; 2hr 40min); Yantai (weekly; 1hr 20min); Zhengzhou (7 weekly; 2hr); Zhuhai (2 weekly; 5hr 30min).

INTERNATIONAL

Dalian to: Fukuoka (2 weekly; 3hr 30min); Osaka (2 weekly; 3hr 50min); Seoul (4 weekly; 2hr 10min); Tokyo (3 weekly; 4hr).

Harbin to: Khabarovsk (2 weekly; 1hr).

Shenyang to: Irkutsk (2 weekly; 3hr 40min); Seoul (3 weekly; 2hr 40min).

CHAPTER FOUR

THE YELLOW RIVER

T he central Chinese provinces of **Shanxi**, **Shaanxi**, **Henan** and **Shandong** are linked and dominated by the **Yellow River** (Huang He), which has played a vital role in their history, geography and fortunes. The river is often likened to a dragon, a reference not just to its sinuous course, but also to its uncontrollable nature, and its behaviour, by turns benign and malevolent. It provides much-needed irrigation to an area otherwise arid and inhospitable, but as its popular nickname, "China's Sorrow", hints, its floods and changes of course have repeatedly caused devastation, and for centuries helped keep the delta region in Shandong one of the poorest areas in the nation.

The river's modern name is a reference to the vast quantities of yellow silt – **loess** – it carries, which has clogged and confused its course throughout history, and which has largely determined the region's geography. Loess is a soft soil, prone to vertical fissuring, and in Shanxi and northern Shaanxi it has created one of China's most distinctive landscapes, plains scarred with deep, winding crevasses, in a restricted palette of browns. In southern Shaanxi and Henan, closer to the river, the landscape is flat as a pancake and about the same colour. It may look barren, but where irrigation has been implemented the loess becomes **rich and fertile**, easily tillable with the simplest of tools. It was in this soil, on the Yellow River's flood plain, that Chinese civilization first took root.

Sites of **Neolithic habitation** along the river are common, but the first major conurbation appeared around three thousand years ago, heralding the establishment of the Shang dynasty. For the next few millennia, every Chinese dynasty had its capital somewhere in the area and most of the major cities, from Datong in the north, capital of the Northern Wei, to Kaifeng in the east, capital of the Song, have spent some time as the centre of the Chinese universe, however briefly. With the collapse of imperial China the area sunk into provincialism, and it was not until late this century that it again came to prominence. The old capitals have today found new leases of life as industrial and commercial centres, and thus present two sides to the visitor, a static history, preserved in the interests of tourism, and a rapidly changing, and sometimes harsh, modernity. It is the remnants of **dynastic history** that provide the most compelling reason to visit, but the region also has much to offer in the way of scenery, with more than its fair share of holy mountains.

Shanxi Province is the poor relation of the set, relatively underdeveloped and with the least agreeable climate – temperatures hit minus 15°C in winter – and geography, a swathe of mountain plateau. But it does have some great attractions, most notably the stunning **Yungang cave temples**, and one of the most beautiful – and inaccessible – holy mountains, **Wutai Shan**. Dotted around the small towns along the single rail line leading south to the Yellow River plain, you'll find quirky temples and villages that seem stuck in the last century. In contrast, wealthy **Xi'an**, capital of low-lying, fertile Shaanxi Province, has as many temples, museums and tombs as the rest of the province put together, with the **Terracotta Army** deservedly ranking as one of China's premier sights. It's also the home of a substantial Muslim minority, whose cuisine is well worth sampling. Within easy travelling distance of here, following the Yellow River east, are two more holy mountains, **Hua Shan** and **Song Shan** (home of the legendary Shaolin monks), and the city of **Luoyang** in Henan, with the superb **Longmen cave temples**

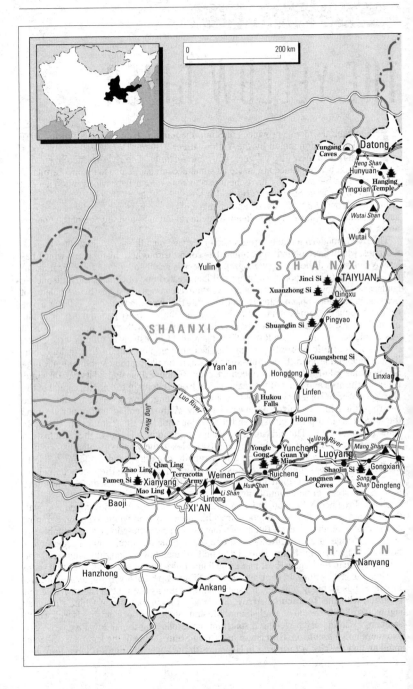

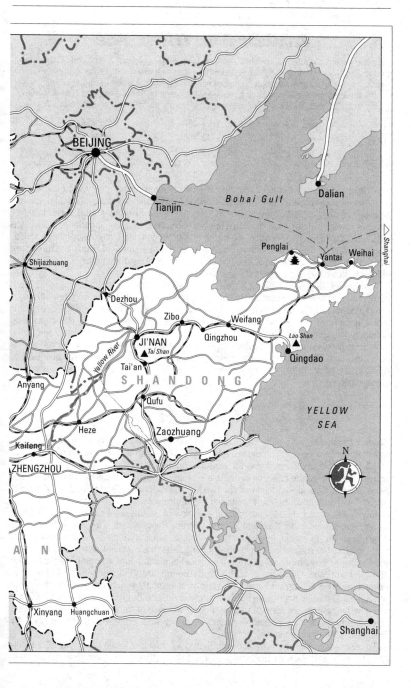

and **Baima Si** just outside. Continuing east brings you to the little-visited but appealing town of **Kaifeng**, a mellow place that provides a refreshing change of scale. A diversion to **Anyang**, capital of the Shang dynasty, or to the **Linxian Canal**, a reminder of China's modern history, is possible from here. Farther east lies Shandong, a province with less of a distinctive identity, but home to more small and intriguing places – **Qufu**, the birthplace of Confucius, with its giant temple and mansion, **Tai Shan**, the most popular holy mountain in the area, and the bizarre city of **Qingdao**, a replica of a Bavarian village built by the Germans in the last century.

With generally good rail links, a well-developed tourist industry and an agreeable climate outside the winter months, **travel** in the region presents few difficulties, although the rail network in Shanxi and northern Shaanxi is noticeably sparse and their cities are still a decade or so behind their richer southern neighbours. Sadly, the capricious nature of the river makes river travel impossible in the region. Most towns and cities now have hotels offering accommodation catering for a wide range of budgets, with a few travellers' dormitories in the most popular destinations. The best-value hotels, though, are in small towns, such as Kaifeng, Qufu and Tai'an, which are anxious to attract visitors.

SHANXI

Shanxi Province, with an average height of 1000m above sea level, is one huge mountain plateau. Strategically important, bounded to the north by the Great Wall and to the south by the Yellow River, it was for centuries a bastion territory against the northern tribes. Today its significance is economic – nearly a third of China's coal reserves are to be found in Shanxi – and around the two key towns, **Datong** and the capital **Taiyuan**, major development of the mining industry is under way.

Physically, Shanxi is dominated by the proximity of the Gobi desert, and wind and water have shifted sand, dust and silt right across the province. The land is farmed, as it has been for millennia, by slicing the hills into steps, creating a plain of ribbed hills that look like the realisation of a cubist painting. The dwellings in this terrain often have mud walls, or are simply caves cut into vertical embankments, seemingly a part of the strange landscape. Great tracts of this land, though, are untillable, due to soil erosion caused by tree felling, and the uncertainty of rainfall, which has left much of the province fearsomely barren, an endless range of dusty hills cracked by fissures. Efforts are now being made to arrest erosion and the advance of the desert, including a huge tree-planting campaign. Sometimes you'll even see wandering dunes held in place by immense nets of woven straw.

Tourist workers in the province call Shanxi a "museum above the ground", a reference to the many **ancient buildings** that dot the region, some from dynasties almost unrepresented elsewhere in China, such as the Song and the Tang. In the same breath they call neighbouring Shaanxi a "museum under the ground", an unfair comment no doubt engendered by that province's much greater popularity as a tourist destination. Shanxi's unpopularity, despite its rich crop of historical buildings, can be put down to the grimness of its cities, dominated by the coal industry, and the relative inaccessibility of most of the province's fine constructions. Visitors usually restrict themselves to the main attraction, the **Yungang cave temples** at Datong, seven hours from Beijing, which are easily taken in en route to Hohhot in Inner Mongolia, or Xi'an farther south. Anyone who has time to explore the province further, however, is richly rewarded at **Wutai Shan**, a holy mountain in the northeast on the border with Hebei, that has only recently been fully opened to foreigners. Its combination of ancient temples, breathtaking mountain scenery and remoteness – it's an eight-hour bus ride from Taiyuan, the nearest city – make it one of the best mountain sites in the country, as it's not yet swamped by tourism. Taiyuan itself is hardly worth a stop, with only the Song buildings of the **Jinci Si** deserving a mention. But farther south, all within a bus ride of the towns spread along the rail line between Taiyuan and Xi'an, are obscure little places, well off the predictable China trails, full of memorable sights. Particularly fine are the superb temples stuck out in the middle of nowhere, such as the **Shuanglin Si** outside Taiyuan, with its amazing sculptures, and the striking murals of the **Yongle Gong** at Ruicheng. At **Pingyao**, again requiring some effort to reach, the whole town seems stuck in a time warp, its alleys lined with charming Qing-dynasty architecture. Once you venture far off the main arterial rail line, travel becomes hard work, as roads, and bus connections, are not good. Another worthwhile diversion, though, is to the banks of the Yellow River, which runs down the western margin of the province. It is here, at **Hukou Falls**, that the river presents its fiercest aspect, which so impressed the Chinese that they put a picture of the torrent on the back of their fifty-yuan bills.

CAVE HOUSES

A common sight among the stern folds and fissures of the dry loess plain of northern Shanxi (and neighbouring Shaanxi) are **cave dwellings**. Hollowed into the sides of hills terraced for agriculture, they house over eighty million Chinese people. A traditional form of dwelling in use for nearly two thousand years, caves are eminently practical: they are cheap, easy to make and and long lasting. In fact, a number of intact caves in Hejin, on the banks of the Yellow River, in the west of the province, are said to date back to the Tang dynasty. In a region where flat land has to be laboriously hacked out of the hillside and villagers need to maximize the amount of tillable earth, caves are economical and don't take up land that could be cultivated. Naturally insulated, they are warm in winter and cool in summer.

The **facade** of the cave is usually a wooden frame on a brick base. Most of the upper part consists of a wooden lattice, designs of which are sometimes very intricate, faced with white paper, which lets in plenty of light, but preserves the occupants' privacy. Tiled eaves above protect the facade from rain damage. Inside, the **single-arched chamber** is usually split into a bedroom at the back and a living area in front, furnished with a *kang* (stove) whose flue leads under the bed to heat it, then outside to the terraced field that is the roof. Sometimes the first visible indication of a distant village is a set of smoke columns rising from the crops.

Such is the popularity of cave homes that prosperous cave dwellers often prefer to build themselves a new courtyard and another cave rather than move into a house. Indeed, in the suburbs of towns and cities of northern Shaanxi, new **concrete apartment buildings** are built in imitation of caves, with three windowless sides and an arched central door. It is not uncommon even to see soil spread over the roofs of these apartments with vegetables grown on top.

Datong and around

Don't be put off by first impressions of contemporary **DATONG**, the second largest city in Shanxi Province, situated in the far north, near the border with Inner Mongolia. Amid the blasted landscape of modern industrial China – coalmines, power stations and a huge locomotive factory – are some marvellous ancient sites, remnants of the city's glory days as the capital city of two non-Han Chinese dynasties.

The Turkic Toba people took advantage of the internal strife afflicting central and southern China to establish their own dynasty, the **Northern Wei** (386–534), taking Datong as their capital in 398 AD, by which time they had conquered the whole of the north. Though the period was one of strife and warfare, and the Wei never fully consolidated their hold on power, the Northern Wei, who became fervent Buddhists, made some notable cultural achievements, the finest of which was a magnificent series of **cave temples** at Yungang, just west of the city, still one of the most impressive sights in northern China. Over the course of almost a century, more than fifty caves were completed, containing over fifty thousand statues, before the capital was moved south to Luoyang (see p.256), where construction began on the similar Longmen Caves.

A second period of greatness came with the arrival of the Mongol **Liao dynasty**, also Buddhists, who made Datong their capital in 907. They were assimilated into the Jin in 1125, but not before leaving a small legacy of statuary and some fine temple architecture, notably in the **Huayan** and **Shanhua temples** in town, and a **wooden pagoda**, the oldest in China, in the nearby town of Yingxian. Datong remained important to later Chinese dynasties for its strategic position just inside the Great Wall, south of Inner Mongolia, and the tall city walls date from the early Ming dynasty. Though most visitors today are attracted by the Buddhist sites, Datong is also the closest city to **Heng Shan**, one of the five holy mountains of Taoism, whose most spectacular building, the almost unbelievable **Hanging Temple**, is firmly on the tour agenda.

DATONG AND AROUND

Datong	大同	*dàtóng*
Datong Binguan	大同宾	*dàtóng bīnguǎn*
Hongqi Restaurant	红旗大酒家	*hóngqí dàjiǔjiā*
Huayan Restaurant	华严饭店	*huáyán fàndiàn*
Huayan Si	华严寺	*huáyán sì*
Nine Dragon Screen	九龙壁	*jiǔlóng bì*
Shanhua Si	善化寺	*shànhuà sì*
Tielu Fandian	铁路饭店	*tiělù fàndiàn*
Yungang Binguan	云冈宾馆	*yúngāng bīnguǎn*
AROUND DATONG		
Yungang Caves	云冈石窟	*yúngāng shíkū*
Yingxian	应县	*yīngxiàn*
Jingcheng Binguan	金城宾馆	*jīnchéng bīnguǎn*
Yingxian Wooden Pagoda	应县木塔	*yīngxiàn mùtǎ*
Hunyuan	浑源	*húnyuán*
Hanging Temple	悬空寺	*xuánkōng sì*
Heng Shan	恒山	*héngshān*
Hengshan Binguan	恒山宾馆	*héngshān bīnguǎn*

Datong now produces a third of all China's **coal**, enough to fuel the two power stations on the city's outskirts, one of which supplies electricity for Beijing, the other for the whole of Shanxi Province. Coal dominates the modern city – it sits in the donkey carts and lorries that judder up and down the main roads, it stains the buildings black and it swirls in the air you breath, making Datong one of the most polluted cities in China. Once you have seen the caves and temples, there's no reason to stay around and a day or two here is enough. The city is well connected by rail, and by travelling on the evening sleeper trains, Datong can be seen as a day trip from Beijing (7hr), or as a stop-off en route between Beijing and Xi'an.

Orientation, arrival, city transport and accommodation

Downtown Datong, bounded by square walls, is split by Da Bei Jie and Da Xi Jie, two dead straight streets on north–south and east–west axes, which intersect at the heart of the city, just north of the old Bell Tower. The tourist sights are all within walking distance of the crossroads, while the tourist hotels are considerably farther south.

Datong's **train station** is in the city's northern outskirts, at the end of Da Bei Jie, far from any of the sights and even farther from the hotels. A major railhead at the intersection of a line to Xi'an and the line between Beijing and Baotou, this is the first stop in China for trains from Mongolia, and it makes a harsh, disorientating introduction to the country for passengers stepping off the train from Ulan Batur. Grimy and cavernous, the station is usually thronged with passengers, many of them peasants migrating in search of construction work, their possessions tied up in grain sacks. Hotel touts wave signs at the crush of arriving passengers emerging from the platform gates on the station's west side. They mostly represent places which won't accept foreigners, though often they'll tell you they do. More usefully, you may be grabbed by a representative of the helpful **station CITS office**, at first indistinguishable from the pushy touts and taxi drivers. If he misses you, the office, inside the station on the west side, is a recommended first stop, a good place to get your bearings and meet other travellers and, unusually, to receive advice and information.

Long-distance buses terminate just south of the train station on Xinjian Bei Lu. The airport, south of town, did not have commercial flights at the time of writing, but a rudimentary service should be up and running soon.

The train station is the origin of Datong's clutch of **bus routes**. Annoyingly, no single bus travels the length of the city's north–south axis, along which most places of interest to visitors are located. Bus #4 will get you from the station to the main crossroads, where it turns west, past the Huayan Si, before terminating just outside the old city walls. To get from the crossroads to the southern hotels, take bus #17 from its terminus on the east side of Da Nan Jie. To get to these hotels direct from the train station, take bus #15, which travels south down Xinjian Nan Lu, then turns east on to Yingbin Xi Lu. A few meterless **taxis** cruise the streets; the fare for any destination within the city should be ¥10. **Walking** around the city is tiring, as it's quite spread out – over 10km from the station to the hotels – and roads are tediously straight. Keep to the main streets after dark; at night Datong is not always a friendly city.

Accommodation

Only three **hotels** in Datong accept foreigners, but if they are full, *CITS* at the train station can arrange accommodation in one of the city's many Chinese-only hotels.

Your best bets are both in the south of the city, a long way from the centre. The *Yungang Binguan* at 21 Yingbin Dong Lu (☎0352/521601; ⑦) is the most comfortable, and there's a foreign exchange, a post office and a coffee shop on the premises. Its pleasant rooms have satellite TV – a consideration in a town that shuts down at dusk – and there's a *CITS*-run dormitory (①) with three-bed rooms on the third floor of a separate, rather grotty, building on the eastern side of the hotel concourse. The adequate *Datong Binguan* (☎0352/232476; ⑤) is farther west on Yingbin Xi Lu. The only other official option, the *Tielu Fandian* (②–⑤), a tall tower on the left as you exit the train station, doesn't actually seem to like the idea of taking foreigners much.

The City

The yellow earthen **ramparts** that once bounded the old city are still quite impressive, though they have been heavily cut into and demolished in places as modern Datong has expanded. The best stretches are in the east of the city. Inside the walls, the few treasures that remain of Datong's considerably more prestigious past are off sombre streets lined with utilitarian buildings and walls painted with propaganda slogans. Outside the centre, the streets, along which Mao-suited men ride donkey carts brimming with coal, have a gritty, Dickensian feel which those who don't have to live here might just find appealing.

Downtown

Just south of the crossroads of Da Xi Jie and Da Bei Jie, at the heart of the city, Datong's three-storey **Drum Tower** dates back to the Ming dynasty. You can't go inside but it makes a useful landmark. A little way east from the crossroads, on the south side of Da Dong Jie, the **Nine Dragon Screen** (daily 8am–6.30pm; ¥5) stands in a courtyard a few metres back from the road, looking a little out of place without the palace it once stood in front of, which was destroyed by fire in the fifteenth century. Originally it would have stood directly in front of the entrance, an unpassable obstacle to evil spirits which, it was thought, could only travel in straight lines. The raised relief of nine sinuous dragons depicted in separate glazed tiles along its 45-metre surface, rising from the waves and cavorting among suns, is lively and colourful. Underneath, the dragons and other animals, real and imaginary, are depicted in a separate, much smaller relief. A long, narrow pool in front of the screen is meant to reflect the dragons and give the illusion of movement when you look into its rippling surface.

About a kilometre west of here, the **Huayan Si** (daily 8am–5pm; ¥5) is reached by an alley leading south off Da Xi Jie; look for the temple's roofs, visible above the surrounding low shops. Originally a large temple in the Liao and Jin dynasties, the remaining buildings, mostly Qing, are now split into two complexes. The **Upper Temple**, the first one you come to, is a little shabby, but with some interesting details, and it seems to be at least semi-working, with the odd monk wandering around. Look for the unusual roof decoration on the first building – elephants carrying pagodas on their backs – and the small handmade shrines that have been placed in the temple courtyard by modern worshippers. The huge twelfth-century **Main Hall** is still impressive despite being cobwebbed with scaffolding while it is restored. Set on a four-metre-high platform, the hall is one of the largest Buddhist halls in China, and unusual for facing east – it was originally built by a sect which worshipped the sun. The design at the end of the roof ridge curves inwards like a horn, a rare design peculiar to the region. Inside, five Ming Buddhas, made of stucco or wood and painted gold, sit on elaborate painted thrones, attended by twenty life-size guardians, some of whom look Indian in appearance, gently inclined as if listening attentively. Qing-dynasty frescoes on the walls, depicting Buddha's attainment of nirvana, and nearly one thousand roof panels depicting flowers, Sanskrit letters and dragons, are currently being repainted in their original gaudy hues. Turn right out of the entrance to this complex and you come to the **Lower Temple**, notable for its rugged-looking hall, a rare Liao-dynasty construction from 1038, according to an inscription on a roof beam. Inside, a varied collection of 31 stucco Buddhas and Bodhisattvas, with elegantly carved drapery and delicate features, also

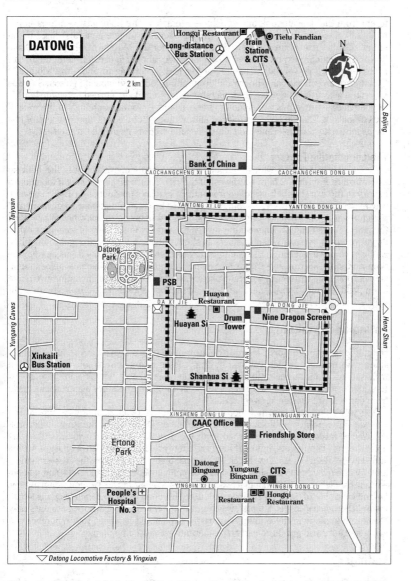

DATONG

0   2 km

N

◁ Taiyuan

◁ Yungang Caves

▷ Beijing

▷ Heng Shan

Hongqi Restaurant

Long-distance Bus Station

Train Station & CITS

Tielu Fandian

Bank of China

CAOCHANGCHENG XI LU   CAOCHANGCHENG DONG LU

YANTONG XI LU   YANTONG DONG LU

XINJIAN BEILU

Datong Park

DA BEI JIE

PSB

DA XI JIE

Huayan Restaurant

DA DONG JIE

Huayan Si   Drum Tower   Nine Dragon Screen

XINJIAN NAN LU

XIAO NAN JIE

Xinkaili Bus Station

Shanhua Si

XINSHENG DONG LU   NANGUAN XI JIE

CAAC Office

NANGUAN NAN JIE

Friendship Store

Ertong Park

Datong Binguan   Yungang Binguan   CITS

YINGBIN XI LU   YINGBIN DONG LU

People's Hospital No. 3

Hongqi Restaurant Restaurant

▽ Datong Locomotive Factory & Yingxian

Liao, sit gathering dust in the gloom. The walls are lined with bookcases for holding scriptures, made to look like little houses.

In the south of town, just inside the old city wall off Nanguan Nan Jie, the **Shanhua Si** (daily 8am–5pm; ¥12) is a Ming restoration of a Jin building, though a temple has stood here since the Tang dynasty. The two halls, with little decoration, thick russet walls and huge, chunky wooden brackets in the eaves, have a solid presence very different from the delicate look of later Chinese temples. The Jin-dynasty **statues** in the main hall, five Buddhas in the centre with 24 *lokapalas* (divine generals) lined up on either side, are exceptionally finely detailed. Look for the Mother of Ghosts, a matronly woman of benign expression, with a small green, impish figure with long teeth, carrying a child on its shoulder, standing at her feet. According to myth, the Mother of Ghosts was an evil woman who ate children until Buddha kidnapped her son. She was so racked with grief that when Buddha returned the child she agreed to devote her life to good deeds; the imp is a depiction of her evil side. A wooden building, in the west of the complex, is Tang in style, with three storeys and a double roof, and impressive just for its longevity – an inscription on a beam inside records its construction in 1154.

The Locomotive Factory

An attraction in keeping with the character of the contemporary city is the **Datong Locomotive Factory**, 2.5km southwest of the city. This was the last steam locomotive factory in the world until it switched from steam to diesel production in 1988. The only way to get in is to take the *CITS* tour, which has to be arranged at least a few hours but preferably a day in advance, and costs ¥250, divided between the number of people in the party. Tours run only on weekdays when the factory is open – it is sometimes shut down for short periods when business is slack. After a talk from the guide in stilted English, you're led through the giant plant, impressive for its scale – it has nearly nine thousand staff, all working with a horrifying lack of safety provisions – before being shown round the **museum**, which displays six steam locomotives, including two made in England and one from Japan. The climax of the tour is a short **ride in a steam train** which was made here in 1987.

Eating and drinking

Datong is far enough north for **mutton hotpot** to figure heavily in the local cuisine, along with potatoes, which you can buy, processed into a starchy jelly and seasoned with sauces, from street stalls. Other typically northern dishes available are *zongyi* (glutinous rice dumplings) and *yuanxiao* (sweet dumplings). Rather bland snacks made from oatmeal are on sale at street stalls.

You won't find any gourmet food in Datong, but you can sample local fare at the *Huayan Restaurant*, one block east of the temple on Da Xi Jie, or the grandly decorated *Hongqi Restaurant* over the road from the *Yungang Binguan*, which is about as upmarket as Datong gets, but staff here are snooty and there are extra charges for tea and service. Better is the tiny, much less formal place next door on the western side – look for the fairy lights outside. Cheap and comfortable, with small tables and a handwritten English menu, it's popular with travellers staying in the *Yungang's* dormitory. On the west side of the train station concourse, a second branch of the *Hongqi* is worth trying, though try to get a table away from the private rooms, whose residents may break into karaoke in the evening. A meal for two should be about ¥50. Wherever you eat, make sure you get there early – restaurants are closed by 9pm.

Listings

Airlines The *CAAC* office (☎0352/523357) is on Nanguan Nan Jie, with another office in the *Yungang Binguan*.

Banks and exchange The *Bank of China* (weekdays 8am–noon & 2.30–5pm) is on Caochangcheng Jie, just north of the crossroads with Caochangcheng Xi Lu, on the route of bus #14 from the station, or you can change money at the *Yungang Binguan*.

Buses Buses for local towns, including Yingxian and Hunyuan, leave from the bus station on Xinjian Bei Lu about 1km from the train station. Xinkaili bus station, in the west of town, is the place to catch buses to the Yungang Caves. Technically, foreigners are not allowed to travel on local buses; however, this rule is not rigorously enforced except on buses to Wutai Shan, which must be accredited by *CITS* before they are allowed to carry you. Enquire at *CITS* at the station for further information.

Hospital People's Hospital No. 3 is in the south of the city on Yingbin Xi Lu, just west of the crossroads with Xinjian Nan Lu.

Left luggage There's a left-lugagge office outside the train station on the western side of the concourse.

Post and telecommunications The large Russian-looking stately building on Xinjian Nan Lu, just south of Da Xi Jie, houses both the post office (Mon–Fri 8am–5pm), and a 24-hour telecom office.

PSB The police station (Mon–Sat 8.30–noon & 2.30–6pm) is on Xinjian Bei Lu, 200m north of the post office.

Shopping There's a small *Friendship Store* at 17 Nanguan Nan Jie.

Trains A comfortable waiting room, featuring armchairs and TV, at the back of the station, opposite the front door, is guarded by a stern lady who tells you when your train arrives.The privilege costs ¥5 for two hours. *CITS* buys most foreigners' tickets for them, but there's no reason why you can't leap into the fray at the booking office and try it for yourself.

Travel agents The main *CITS* office (daily 6.30am–6pm; ☎0352/5024176), on the eastern side of the concourse of the *Yungang Binguan,* deals with tour groups and provides guides. The more useful train station *CITS* office (daily 6.30am–6pm; ☎0352/2024536 ext 24886), inside the station itself, is particularly helpful and worth a visit for information on the city and the area. Their tours of the major sights are also worth considering (see below), and they'll book same-day train tickets for a ¥40 charge.

Around Datong

The sights outside the city are far more diverting than those within. Apart from the glorious **Yungang Caves**, the ancient buildings dotted around in nearby country towns are worth checking out, if you have time to spare. Roads in the area are not good (and often blocked in winter, when transport times can be as much as doubled), but at least journeys are enlivened by great views: the lunar emptiness of the fissured landscape is broken only occasionally by villages whose mud walls make them look like they have grown out of the raw brown earth. Some of the villages in the area still have their beacon towers, left over from the time when this really was a wild frontier.

To help explore the area around the city, pick up a **map** of Datong from outside the bus station, as this includes maps of Hunyuan and Yingxian, together with bus timetables on the back. Getting around by yourself is trying and time-consuming, and the daily *CITS* **tour**, a painless way to get round the major sights in a day, saves a lot of hassle. The tour, which goes to the Yungang Caves and, depending on the weather, the **Hanging Temple** or the **Yingxian Wooden Pagoda**, leaves daily at 9am and returns in the evening and will pick up and drop off at your hotel. Costs vary depending on numbers, but the usual price is ¥40–80 per person, including lunch and an inaccurate English-speaking guide. Buy tickets from the *CITS* office in the Datong train station (see "Listings" above). During the tour, the minibus also stops briefly in a village of squat, mud-walled houses and cave dwellings.

The Yungang Caves

Just 45 minutes by bus from Datong, the monumental **Yungang Caves** (daily 9am–5pm; ¥25), a set of Buddhist grottoes carved into the side of a sandstone cliff, 16km west of the city, are a must. Access is straightforward: take **bus** #2 from the train station or bus #17 from Yingbin Xi Lu, to the Xinkaili bus station in the west of the city; bus #3 from here terminates at the caves.

The artistry on show is unsurpassed in China, and just the labour is impressive: the caves took forty thousand workmen nearly a century to complete. Construction began in 453 AD, when Datong was the capital of the Wei dynasty, and petered out around 525, after the centre of power moved to Luoyang. China's first **stone statues**, the soft, rounded modelling of the sandstone Datong figures have more in common with the terracotta carvings of the Mogao Caves near Dunhuang in Gansu (see p.883), begun a few years earlier, than with the sharp, more linear features of Luoyang's later limestone work (see p.262). In style and design the caves are influenced by similar Indian structures, and they may also have been inspired by earlier cave art in Afghanistan. Certainly many of the craftsmen who worked on the project came from India and Central Asia, and there is much **foreign influence** in the carvings: Greek motifs (tridents and acanthus leaves), Persian symbols (lions and weapons), and bearded figures, even images of the Indian deities Shiva and Vishnu, are incorporated among the more common dragons and phoenixes of Chinese origin. In addition, a number of the seated Buddhas have sharp, almost Caucasian noses.

The caves were made by first hollowing out a section at the top of the cliff, then digging into the rock, down to the ground and out, which leaves two holes, one above the other. Their present condition is misleading as originally the cave entrances would have been covered with wooden facades and the sculptures would have been faced with plaster and brightly painted. The larger sculptures are pitted with regular holes which would once have held wooden supports on which the plaster face was built. Over the centuries, some of the caves have inevitably suffered from weathering, though there seems to have been little vandalism, certainly less than at Luoyang.

The **caves** are arranged in three clusters, east, central and west, and numbered east to west from 1–51. If it's spectacle you're after, just wander at will, but to get an idea of the changes of style and the accumulation of influences, you need to move between the various groups. The earliest group are caves 16–20, followed by 7, 8, 9 and 10, then 5, 6 and 11 – the last to be completed before the court moved to Luoyang. Then followed 4, 13, 14 and 15 with the caves at the eastern end, 1, 2 and 3, and cave 21 in the west, carved last. Caves 22–50 are smaller and less interesting.

THE EASTERN CAVES

The **late caves**, 1–4, are slightly set apart from, and less spectacular than, the others. **Caves 1 and 2** are constructed around a single square central pillar, elaborately carved in imitation of a wooden stupa but now heavily eroded, around which devotees perambulated. **Cave 3**, 25m deep, is the largest in Yungang; an almost undecorated cavern, it may once have been used as a lecture hall. The three statues at the west end, a ten-metre-high Buddha and his two attendants, are skilfully carved and in good condition. The rounded fleshiness of their faces, with double chins and thick, sensuous lips, hints at their late construction as they are characteristic of Tang-dynasty images. **Cave 4**, which again has a central pillar, carved with images of Buddha, has a well-preserved, cross-legged Maitreya Buddha on the west wall.

THE CENTRAL CAVES

The most spectacular caves are numbers 5–13, dense with **monumental sculpture**. Being suddenly confronted and dwarfed by a huge, seventeen-metre-high Buddha as you walk into **cave 5**, with his gold face shining softly in the half light, is an awesome, humbling experience. His otherworldly appearance is helped by blue hair and ruby red lips. Other Buddhas of all sizes, a heavenly gallery, are massed in niches which honeycomb the grotto's gently curving walls, and two Bodhisattvas stand attentive at his side.

Cave 6, though very different, is just as arresting. A wooden facade built in 1652 leads into a high, square chamber dominated by a thick central pillar carved with Buddhas and Bodhisattvas in deep relief, surrounded by flying Buddhist angels and musicians. The vertical grotto walls are alive with images, including reliefs depicting incidents from the **life of the Buddha** at just above head height, which were designed to form a narrative when read walking clockwise around the chamber. Easy-to-identify scenes at the beginning include the birth of the Buddha from his mother's armpit, and Buddha's father carrying the young infant on an elephant. The young prince's meeting with a fortune-teller – here an emaciated man with a sharp goatee, who (the story goes) predicted he would become an ascetic if confronted by disease, death and old age – is shown on the north side of the pillar. In an attempt to thwart this destiny, his father kept him in the palace all through his youth. Buddha's first trip out of the palace, which is depicted as a schematic, square Chinese building, is shown on the east wall of the cave, as is his meeting with the grim realities of life, in this case a cripple with two crutches.

Caves 7 and 8 are a pair, both square, with two chambers, and connected by an arch lined with angels and topped with what looks like a sunflower. The figures here, such as the six celestial worshippers above the central arch, are more Chinese in style than their predecessors in caves 16–20, perhaps indicating the presence of craftsmen from Gansu, which the Wei conquered in 439 AD. Two figures on either side of the entrance to **cave 8** are some of the best carved and certainly the most blatantly foreign in the complex: a five-headed, six-armed Shiva sits on a bird on the left as you enter, while on the right, a three-headed Vishnu sits on a bull. These Indian figures have distinctly Chinese features, however, and the bird, a garuda in Hindu mythology, is identical to the Chinese phoenix.

The columns and lintels at the entrances of **caves 9, 10 and 12** are awash with sculptural detail in faded pastel colours: Buddhas, dancers, musicians, animals, flowers, angels and abstract, decorative flourishes (which bear a resemblance to Persian art). Parts of **cave 9** are carved with imitation brackets to make the interior resemble a wooden building. The tapering columns at the entrance to cave 12 are covered with tiny Buddhas, but look out for the cluster of musicians with strange-looking instruments depicted behind them.

The outstretched right arm of the fifteen-metre-high Buddha inside **cave 13** had to be propped up for stability so his sculptors ingeniously carved the supporting pillar on his knee into a four-armed mini-Buddha. The badly eroded sculptures of **caves 14 and 15** are stylistically some way between the massive figures of the early western caves and the smaller reliefs of the central caves.

THE WESTERN CAVES

Compared to the images in the central caves, the figures in these, the **earliest caves** (nos. 16–20), are simpler and bolder, and though they are perhaps more crudely carved, they are at least as striking. The **giant Buddhas**, with round faces, sharp noses, deep eyes and thin lips, are said to be the representations of five emperors. Constructed between 453 and 462, under the supervision of the monk Tan Hao, all are in the same pattern of an enlarged niche containing a massive Buddha flanked by Bodhisattvas. The Buddha in **cave 16**, whose bottom half has disintegrated, has a knotted belt high on his chest, Korean style. The Buddhas were carved from the top down, and when the sculptors of the Buddha in **cave 17** reached ground level they needed to dig down to fit his feet in. The same problem was solved in **cave 18** by giving the Buddha shortened legs. Despite his stumpy limbs, this is still one of the finest sculptures in the complex, in which charming details, including the rows of tiny Bodhisattvas carved into his robe, are set off by strong sweeping forms, such as the simplified planes of his face. The fourteen-metre-high Buddha in **cave 20**, sitting open to the elements in a niche that once would have been protected by a wooden canopy, is probably the most famous, and certainly the most photographed. The figure is characteristic of Northern Wei art, with the folds of his garments expressed by an ordered pattern, and his physiognomy and features formed by simple curves and straight lines. His huge ears almost touch his shoulders.

The small caves 20–50, the least spectacular of the set, are not much visited, but the ceiling of **cave 50** is worth a look for its flying elephants, which also appear in cave 48, and in caves 50 and 51 there are sculptures of acrobats.

Yingxian Pagoda

At the centre of the small town of **YINGXIAN**, 60km south of Datong, the stately **Yingxian Pagoda** (daily 8am–5pm; ¥15), built in 1056 in the Liao dynasty, is the oldest wooden building in China, a masterful piece of structural engineering that looks solid enough to stand here for another millennium. The pagoda is nearly 70m high, octagonal in plan, with nine storeys, though only six layers of eaves on the outside. The first storey is taller than the rest with extended eaves held up by columns forming a cloister around a mud and straw wall. Everything from here up is made of wood. The original pagoda was constructed without a single metal nail, though there are plenty in the floors now, which are new. You can climb up as far as the fourth storey, and it's definitely worth going inside as this is where the almost unornamented structure is at its most impressive. The ceilings and walls of the spacious internal halls are networks of beams held together with huge, intricate **wooden brackets**, called *dougongs*, of which there are nearly sixty different kinds. Interlocking, with their ends carved into curves and layered one on top of another, these give the pagoda a burly, muscular appearance, and as structural supports they perform their function brilliantly – the building has survived seven earthquakes.

Originally each storey had a statue inside, but now only one remains, an eleven-metre-tall **Buddha**. During a recent renovation a cache of treasures was found buried underneath the pagoda, including Buddhist sutras printed by woodblocks dating back to the Liao dynasty.

Local **buses** to Yingxian from Datong take two hours and leave from the long-distance bus station. Yingxian bus station, where you will be dropped, is on the western section of the town's main east–west road, about 1km southwest of the pagoda. You can stay the night in Yingxian at the *Jincheng Binguan* (②), about 2km south of the pagoda on the main north–south road. From Yingxian it is possible to get a connection to Hunyuan for Heng Shan and the Hanging Temple, about 50km away, without returning to Datong. Buses leave every hour until 4pm, also the time of the last bus back to Datong.

Heng Shan and the Hanging Temple

Heng Shan, a 250-kilometre-long range curling east to west around northern Shanxi Province, comprises one of the five holy Taoist mountains in China, whose history as a religious centre stretches back more than two thousand years. Plenty of emperors have put in an appearance here to climb the highest peak, Xuanwu (2000m), a trend begun by the very first emperor, Qin Shi Huang. Contemporary pilgrims usually set out from **HUNYUAN**, 75km southeast of Datong, a small country town with some appealing Ming street architecture, 12km north of Tainfengling Peak. You can catch a tourist bus from the town to the base of the mountain, from where a path leads up to the summit, passing a number of small temples on the way. **Buses** run to Hunyuan from the Datong long-distance bus station, terminating just opposite the *Hengshan Binguan* (②). The last bus back from Hunyuan to Datong is at 3.30pm.

Seventy kilometres southeast of Datong and 5km south of Hunyuan, the **Hanging Temple** (Xuankong Si; daily 9am–5pm; ¥20), is Heng Shan's most impressive building. A temple clinging perilously halfway up the side of a sheer cliff face (its name literally translates as Temple Suspended in the Void), it is propped up on long wooden stilts anchored to ledges. There has been a temple on this site since the Northern Wei, though the present structure is mostly Qing. Periodically, the temple buildings were destroyed by the flooding of the Heng River at the base of the cliff (now no longer there, thanks to a dam farther upstream), and at each successive rebuilding, the temple was built higher and higher. At its best from a distance, when its dramatic, gravity-defying location can best be appreciated, the temple reveals itself as a bit of a tourist trap as you get closer, and from the inside it looks carelessly restored. Tall, narrow stairs and plank walkways connect the six halls – natural caves and ledges with wooden facades – in which, very unusually, shrines exist to all three of China's main religions, Confucianism, Buddhism and Taoism, all of whose major figures are represented in nearly eighty statues in the complex, made from bronze, iron and stone. In the Three Religions Hall, at the top of the complex, statues of Confucius, Buddha and Lao Zi are seated happily together. From Hunyuan there are plenty of tourist minibuses around to take you here.

Taiyuan

Midway on the rail line between the more appealing destinations of Datong and Xi'an, and the most convenient starting point for a trip to the temples of Wutai Shan (see p.219), **TAIYUAN**, an industrial powerhouse and the capital of Shanxi Province, sees more visitors passing through than stopping. Certainly there is little to hang around

TAIYUAN AND AROUND

Taiyuan	太原	*tàiyuán*

ACCOMMODATION

Bingzhou	并州饭店	*bìngzhōu fàndiàn*
Dianxing	电信大酒店	*diànxìn dàjiǔdiàn*
Guo Fang Ke	国防科工办招待所	*guófángkē kōngbàn zhāodàisuǒ*
Shanxi Grand	山西大酒店	*shānxī dàjiǔdiàn*
Yingze	迎泽宾馆	*yíngzé bīnguǎn*
Yunshan	云山宾馆	*yúnshān bīnguǎn*

THE CITY

Chongshan Si	崇善寺	*chóngshàn sì*
City Museum	省博物馆	*shěng bówùguǎn*
Confucius Temple Museum	文庙博物馆	*wénmiào bówùguǎn*
Shuangta Si	双塔寺	*shuāngtǎ sì*
Wuyi Square	五一广场	*wǔyī guángchǎng*
Yingze Park	迎泽公园	*yíngzé gōngyuán*

RESTAURANTS

Chuanniu Hotpot City	川妞火锅城	*chuānniū huǒguōchéng*
Shipin Jie	食品街	*shípǐn jiē*
Yingze	迎泽酒家	*yíngzé jiǔjiā*

AROUND TAIYUAN

Jinci Si	晋祠寺	*jìncí sì*
Pingyao	平遥	*píngyáo*
Shuanglin Si	双林寺	*shuānglín sì*
Tianlong Shan	天龙山	*tiānlóng sì*
Xuanzhong Si	玄中寺	*xuánzhōng sì*

The **telephone code** for Taiyuan is ☎0351

for; the modern city is known only for coal, and there are scant remains of its long and turbulent history. It's not unpleasant, though, with good hotels and restaurants on the showcase street, Yingze Dajie. If you are breaking your journey here to head for Wutai, there is also a scattering of ancient buildings outside town worth a diversion.

A city never far from shifting frontiers, Taiyuan, or Jinyang as it was originally called, sits in a valley next to the Fen River in the invasion corridor between the barbarian lands to the north and the Chinese heartland around the Yellow River to the south. As a result it has suffered even more than most Chinese cities from invaders and the strife that accompanies the dynastic collapse. The Mongolian Huns invaded first in 200 BC, ousted when the Tobas, a nomadic Turkish people, swept south in the fourth century and established the Northern Wei dynasty. During the Tang dynasty, the city enjoyed a brief period of prosperity as an important frontier town on the edges of Han Chinese control and the barbarian lands, before becoming one of the major battlefields during the Five Dynasties (907–979), a period of strife following the Tang's collapse. In 976 the expanding Song dynasty razed the city to the ground.

In this century, the city was the site of one of the worst massacres of the Boxer Rebellion (see *Contexts*, p.1001), when all the city's foreign missionaries and their families were killed on the orders of the provincial governor. This wasn't enough, though, to put off the English, French and Russians, who over the next two decades stepped up their exploitation of the city's mineral reserves begun at the end of the eighteenth century. A habit of playing host to warlike leaders continued when Taiyuan was governed by Yan Xishan between 1912 and 1949. One of the Guomindang's fiercest warlords, he treated the city as a private empire. According to Carl Crow's contemporary *Handbook for China*, Xishan's city was a reform-minded place, well-known for the suppression of opium and its anti-foot-binding movement. His rule did not stop the city's gradual development by foreign powers, however, and extensive coal mines were constructed by the Japanese in 1940. Industrialization began in earnest after the Communist takeover and today it is the factories that dominate, relentlessly processing the region's coal and mineral deposits.

Orientation, arrival, city transport and accommodation

Although it's a sprawling place, Taiyuan is easy to get around as the majority of places of interest are on or near **Yingze Dajie**, the city's main thoroughfare. The street runs east–west across town, passing the south side of Wuyi Square, the heart of the city, and most sights, hotels and restaurants are within walking distance.

Taiyuan's new **airport** is 15km southeast of the city. Local officials are so proud of it that a model of the modernist building sits in Yingze Park in the city centre. The **train station**, on the line between Beijing and Xi'an, is likewise the focus of local pride, judging by the number of camera stalls lined up outside catering to those who want to get their photograph taken in front of it. As Chinese stations go, it's a pleasant one: clean, new and efficient, though with the usual chaos of buses and stalls outside. It's conveniently located at the eastern end of Yingze Dajie, from where bus #10 runs the full length of the thoroughfare. The **long-distance bus station** is just west of the train station, also on Yingze Dajie.

Most city **bus routes** begin from a terminal at the northeastern corner of Wuyi Square. Bus #28, which heads west down Yingze Dajie, then turns left on to Xinjian Nan Lu, may be of use. There are also five **tram** routes, which mostly travel north–south. Tram #2, which begins from a terminus on the west side of Jianshe Nan Lu, just north of the train station, travels west to Wuyi Square, then turns north up Wuyi Lu. **Taxis** are cheap, with a ¥6 minimum fare, and plentiful. The ride to the airport costs ¥25.

Accommodation

Most hotels are located along Yingze Dajie; the western end is less interesting and farther from the sights, while the eastern end, near the train station, is livelier but noisier.

Bingzhou, 32 Yingze Dajie (☎4042111). With a good location opposite Wuyi Square, this is one of the best mid-range options. The cheapest rooms are in a claustrophobic basement, and it's worth paying a little more for one of the spacious rooms upstairs. ②–⑥.

Dianxing (☎4033865). This cramped and poky little place on an alley parallel to Yingze Dajie, behind the telecom office, is badly managed but cheap. ④.

Guo Fang Ke, 12 Yingze Dajie (☎4041711). A Chinese-style place with intrusive and frankly curious staff. Basic, noisy, but convenient and very cheap, with dorms. ①–④.

Shanxi Grand, 5 Xinjian Nan Lu (☎4043901). The plushest place in town, where tour groups end up, but it's a little far west. Oddly decorated in a mish-mash of styles, but very comfortable. ⑨.

Yingze Binguan, 189 Yingze Dajie (☎4043211). This stylish hotel consists of two buildings: the western wing is the upmarket section, with excellent facilities; the eastern wing is more down to earth and affordable. Single rooms are good value here. ⑦–⑧.

Yunshan, 99 Yingze Dajie (☎4041351). A pleasant and agreeably low-key place that features doormen with ridiculously tall hats. ⑧.

The City

China's largest stainless steel sculpture, an image of three noble workers with improbably angular physiognomies, stands outside Taiyuan train station, and sets the tone for the main city street, **Yingze Dajie**, beyond. New and gleaming, somewhere between a boulevard and a freeway, it has eight lanes and a metal barrier down the middle to prevent you walking across anywhere except at the pedestrian crossing point just east of Wuyi Square and at traffic intersections. Outside the centre, Taiyuan is a dull industrial sprawl, but along Yingze Dajie the city tries its best to live up to its status as provincial capital, with a sprinkling of neon, flashy new buildings and some garish statuary.

About 1km west of the train station, down Yingze Dajie, past numerous hotels and restaurants, you'll find **Wuyi Square**, a concrete plaza marked by a terrible sculpture of a man playing a flute, a deer and a woman with pneumatic breasts, that is lit up in sickly green at night. Just west of here, the **City Museum** (daily 8am–5pm; ¥10) is housed in a grand Ming temple complex, the Chunyanggong, that has seen better days. The charming complex of small, multi-storey buildings accessible by steep stairways off small courtyards, once a place to offer sacrifices to the Taoist deity Lu Dongbin, seems ill-suited to its present function of housing a motley collection of stuffed birds and animals. There's even a couple of desiccated human specimens pickled in formaldehyde, whose internal organs are kept in separate cases. Best are the rooms at the back, which contain some fine examples of Buddhist statuary in bronze and stone, some of which is Sui in origin, though mostly Ming or Qing. Many of the statues have donations of paper money stuffed into the cracks between the panes of glass in their display cases, suggesting a popular resurgence of the building's original function. The many images of warriors and of Guan Yu, god of war, hint at the martial preoccupations of the city's previous inhabitants.

A second section of the museum, housed in the **Confucius Temple** (daily 8am–5pm; ¥10) east of here off Jianshe Bei Lu, comprises mostly displays of photographs and relics concerning Shanxi's modern history, as well as a few Shang bronzes and a large collection of Buddhist sutras. However, the attractive Ming buildings are more engrossing than the exhibits themselves.

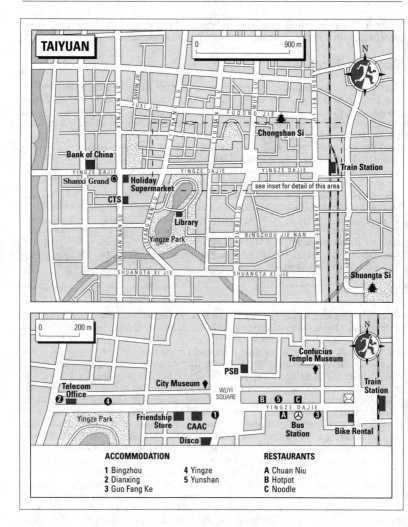

TAIYUAN

0   900 m

N

SHIPIN JIE

XINJIAN LU

FUXI JIE

JIEFANG LU

LUGUAN

FUDONG JIE

WUYI LU

JIAN SHE BEI LU

Chongshan Si

Bank of China

YINGZE DAJIE   YINGZE DAJIE   YINGZE DAJIE   **Train Station**

Shanxi Grand ◉ **Holiday
Supermarket**   see inset for detail of this area

CTS ■

JIEFANG NAN LU

Library

XINJIAN NAN LU

Yingze Park

BINGZHOU BEI LU

BINGZHOU JIE NAN

JIANSHE NAN LU

SHUANGTA BEI LU

SHUANGTA XI JIE   SHUANGTA XI JIE   **Shuangta Si**

0   200 m

N

**Confucius
Temple Museum**

PSB ♦

City Museum ♦

WUYI
SQUARE

**Train
Station**

**Telecom
Office**

2 ●   ● 4

B ⑤ C

YINGZE DAJIE
✉

Yingze Park   **Friendship
Store** **CAAC**   A ⊘ 3

① ●

**Bus
Station**   **Bike Rental**

Disco ■

ACCOMMODATION		RESTAURANTS
1 Bingzhou 4 Yingze		A Chuan Niu
2 Dianxing 5 Yunshan		B Hotpot
3 Guo Fang Ke		C Noodle

Northeast of Wuyi Square, reached along alleys that grow shabbier the farther you go, the **Chongshan Si** (Temple of Veneration of Benevolence) is worth the fifteen-minute walk – look for the fortune-tellers who congregate outside. Though there is nothing extraordinary about the architecture, the main hall is well maintained and full of the paraphernalia of worship: offerings, painted sheets hanging from the pillars and prayer mats stitched together out of discarded packaging, a genuine contemporary folk art. The temple also contains a display of scrolls and books – sutras printed in the Song, Yuan and Ming dynasties, some in Tibetan, and a number of woodcut illustrations. Directly south of the temple, with an entrance at its southern end, the monastery complex that it was once attached to has been converted into workshops and warehouses. You can poke around, but most of the buildings are fairly dilapidated.

The focus for a wander around sparse **Yingze Park** is provided by a Ming-dynasty library (daily 8am–5pm; ¥10) south of the park entrance on Yingze Dajie. You can't go inside, but there is some nice eave decoration, including images of pandas. A tour of the city's ancient buildings is completed with a look at the two fifty-metre-tall pagodas of the **Shuangta Si** (Twin Pagoda Temple), south of the train station off Shuangta Bei Lu. These were built by a monk called Fu Deng in the Ming dynasty, under the orders of the emperor, and today have become a symbol of the city. You can climb their thirteen storeys for a panoramic view of Taiyuan.

Eating, drinking and nightlife

Yingze Dajie has a good smattering of **restaurants**, many catering for tourists, and if you're staying along here it shouldn't be hard to find some decent food within short walking distance of your hotel. In particular, there are two great **hotpot** places, *Chuanniu Hotpot City* at 16 Yingze Dajie, just west of the train station on the southern side of the road, that looks more expensive than it is, and another on the north side a little farther west. They are both easy to find – just look for the steamed-up windows – and a meal for two at either should come to no more than ¥50. The **noodle restaurant**, at 73 Yingze Dajie, is very popular and unusual for serving no rice. Food comes in deep bowls, and last to arrive is a bowl of noodles which you add to the remains of your other dishes. The cheapest food on Yingze Dajie can be had at no. 27. Best of the **hotel restaurants** is the first-floor place in the west wing of the *Yingze Binguan*, which is not too expensive (about ¥50 per person). The atmosphere is unintimidating and there are small tables and friendly, attentive staff.

Parallel to Jiefang Lu, north of Yingze Dajie, **Shipin Jie** is packed full of restaurants, and very busy in the evening. There's everything here, from cheap, fast-food style noodle shops to quiet, upmarket places, as well as stalls selling nuts and fruit, and karaoke bars and hairdressers. Pick the busiest place to eat at as it's a good sign of its quality.

For **nightlife**, try the *Chinatown Disco* (daily 8–12pm; ¥30) at 49 Bingzhou Bei Lu, not far from the intersection with Yingze Dajie. Don't let the unfortunate spelling mistake on the sign ("pisco") put you off, as this huge place is surprisingly slick for a provincial city, with Western DJs and an impressive interior including a laser, a giant bat and a spacecraft hanging from the ceiling. The high entrance charge means the clientele is more chic than bohemian, and generally too cool to pay much overt attention to foreigners on the dance floor.

Listings

Airlines *CAAC* is at 38 Yingze Dajie (Mon–Sat 8am–8pm; ☎4042903).

Banks and exchange The *Bank of China* is at 67 Yingze Dajie (Mon–Fri 8am–noon & 2.30–6pm, Sat 8.30–noon).

Bike rental Bikes can be rented from a stall (daily 8am–8pm) at the eastern end of Yingze Dajie, opposite the station, for ¥3 a day.

Buses Buses to nearby towns, including Pingyao, leave from outside the train station; the long- distance bus station is off Yingze Dajie on the southern side.

Cinema Kung fu violence and mayhem are available at the cinema at 20 Yingze Dajie (¥5).

Post office The white building opposite the train station on the northern side of Yingze Dajie houses an impressively modern and efficient post office (daily 8am–8pm). There's a smaller branch at 215 Yingze Dajie (daily 8am–6pm).

PSB The PSB office is at the northeastern corner of Wuyi Square.

Shopping The *Friendship Store* at 45 Yingze Dajie has the usual selection of jade handcrafts and art materials. For a less predictable, though still pricey selection of souvenirs, try the *Arts and Crafts Store* at 54 Yingze Dajie, or the *Antique Store* at 15 Jiefang Lu. If you feel the need for imported chocolate biscuits, the *Holiday Supermarket,* selling upmarket foodstuffs, is on Xinjian Nan Lu just south of the intersection with Yingze Dajie.

Telephones The telecom office, open 24hr, is at 213 Yingze Dajie, on the corner of Liugang Lu.

Trains There's a booking office on the south side of the station, but there are no windows for foreigners. However, the crowds aren't too bad, and heavy police presence and cattle bars ensures disciplined queuing.

Travel agents A friendly office of *CTS* (daily 8am–noon & 2–5pm, ☎4049270), at 8 Xinjian Nan Lu, offers information and will book tickets.

Around Taiyuan

There are some notable attractions in the flat countryside around Taiyuan. Definitely worth a diversion are the little town of **Pingyao**, a relic from the Qing dynasty, and the **Shuanglin Si** nearby, full of breathtaking sculpture, which together make a more interesting day trip than the better-known, but very touristy, **Jinci Si**. To the west, **Tianlong Shan**'s Buddhist grottoes deserve investigation if you're not heading to the caves near Datong or the Longmen site at Luoyang.

Jinci Si, Tianlong Shan and Xuanzhong Si

From Taiyuan, bus #8 from the terminal east of Wuyi Square will take you the 25km to the **Jinci Si** (daily 8am–5pm; ¥15). First impressions don't augur well – after a juddering ride through a stark industrial zone, the bus drops you at the park outside the temple, a charmless fair of souvenir stalls and ragged camels. Although this large temple complex, by a river at the base of a mountain, contains some exceptional architecture, perhaps the finest Song-dynasty buildings in the country, neglect, and its extensive development as a tourist resource, means it is not as impressive as it could be. A temple has been on the site since the Northern Wei and today's buildings are a diverse collection from various dynasties.

The open space just inside the gate was once used as a theatre, with the richly ornamented Ming stage, the **Water Mirror Platform**, at its centre. Beyond here, a small river channelled across the complex, now ruined with litter, must have been one of its most pleasant features. Over the bridge behind the stage, four Song-dynasty **iron figures** of warriors stand on a platform, apparently guardians of the river, but looking furious. Inscriptions on their chests record their dates of construction, though parts have been replaced since. The **Hall of Offerings** beyond and, behind that, the **Hall of the Holy Mother** were originally constructed in the Jin dynasty as places to worship the mother of Prince Shuyu, who founded the dynasty and was attributed with magical powers. They were rebuilt in the Song and today are two of the largest buildings from that dynasty still extant. The **Yijiang Si** (Hall of the Holy Mother), one of the earliest wooden halls in China, is the highlight of the complex, its facade a mix of decorative flourishes and the sturdily functional, with wooden dragons curling around the eight pillars that support the ridge of its upward-curving roof. The hall's interior is equally impressive, with some fine, delicate-looking Song-dynasty female figures, posed naturalistically, some with broomsticks, jugs and seals, attendants to a central image of a gracious-looking Holy Mother. Turn right out of the hall and you come to a smaller temple, a Ming tower, and a hot spring, as well as an infuriatingly tacky waxwork show. The buildings beyond are hardly interesting in themselves, though one has been converted into an art gallery. Among the buildings to the right of the Hall of the Holy Mother, a Tang-dynasty stele records the visit of Emperor Tai Zong in 647 AD.

Tianlong Shan

Forty kilometres south of Taiyuan, **Tianlong Shan** is host to a small cluster of Buddhist cave temples (daily 8.30am–4.30pm; ¥15). The caves on its eastern and western sides were carved between 534 and 907 AD, from the Eastern Wei to the Tang dynasties. Much less impressive than anything at Datong or Luoyang, the cave sculptures are badly weathered, though the large exposed Buddha in Cave 9, bare-chested and sitting regally as if on a chair, is a fine image, distinctive for his chubby face and bulging eyes. The eastern caves are protected by a Ming-dynasty wooden facade built across the cliff face. To get here, take **bus #30** from the northeast corner of Wuyi Square to **Qingxu**, then hire a motor-rickshaw for the last 3km.

The **Xuanzhong Si**, 70km southwest of Taiyuan, is famous as one of the birthplaces of Zen Buddhism – the priests Daochuo and Shandao, two of its founders, taught here – and has a history stretching back over 1500 years, though most of the present buildings, built on tiers up the side of a hill, are Ming and Qing. A thriving place of worship, today it's a popular pilgrimage spot for the Japanese, some of whom come to hear the contemporary masters preach. Tourist **minibuses** run direct from outside the train station in Taiyuan (¥15), or you can take a **bus** from the bus station to **Jiaocheng**, a town 4km northeast of the temple, and hire a motor-rickshaw from there.

Pingyao and the Shuanglin Si

The small town of **PINGYAO**, 100km south of Taiyuan, and the Shuanglin Si nearby, two of the most impressive yet least visited places in the area, are certainly worth making an effort to get to. Don't let the grotty train station at Pingyao, with its pushy rickshaw drivers, put you off, this really is an extraordinary place. A town has stood here since the Zhou dynasty (about 770 BC), but it reached its height in the Ming, when it was a prosperous banking centre, one of the first in China. Its wealthy residents constructed luxurious mansions and square walls around the city to defend them. In this century, the town slid rapidly into provincial obscurity, which has kept it largely unmodernized, and it's one of the few places in this part of China that has retained more than a token segment of the infrastructure and buildings of its nineteenth-century glory. Nearby, the **Shuanglin Si** has a hoard of wood and terracotta sculptures, some lifelike, some ghostly, some comical, which are unparalleled in the region.

The Town

Pingyao's narrow streets, lined with elegant **Qing architecture** – no neon, no white tile, no cars – are a revelation. Few buildings are higher than two storeys and many are over a hundred years old. Most are small shops much more interesting for their architecture than their wares, with ornate wood and painted glass lanterns hanging outside, faded paintings on their eaves, and intricate wooden lattice work holding paper rather than glass across the windows. This kind of street is what Liulichang, the fake antique street in Beijing, is a copy of. Zhang Yimou filmed the hauntingly beautiful *Raise the Red Lantern* here, in which the rigid, ordered design of the town's Qing architecture is used as a visual complement to the stifling formality that rules the life of the main character, the fourth wife of a wealthy man.

The **plan** of the city is very simple. Square walls, each 1.5km long, enclose four main streets arranged along the compass points (which don't quite meet in the centre – Nan Dajie, South Street, is a little to the east), a typical design that the Chinese compare to the markings on a tortoise shell. In between the main streets, a lattice of even narrower alleyways links courtyards which are well worth poking around in.

From the train station, outside the walls, head due south, straight down the unremarkable muddy street opposite. About 300m on, the first major left turn leads into a busy market street. Keep walking east and you come to the west gate of the old town walls; a map of the town's simple layout is printed on the wall here. Just inside the arch of the gate are steps leading up to the Ming **city walls** (daily; ¥8), 12m high, and crenellated with a watchtower along every 50m of their 6km length. You can walk all the way around them in two hours, and get a good view into some of the many courtyards inside the walls (and at an army training base outside them, where you can watch recruits practising drill and throwing fake hand grenades). At the southeast corner of the wall, the Kuixing Tower, a tall fortified pagoda with a tiled, upturned roof, is a rather flippant-looking building in comparison to the martial solidity of the battlements.

It's possible to climb the **Bell Tower**, on Nan Dajie, a charming little building, if you can find anyone to unlock the door; the shopkeepers nearby are eager to help, but have no idea who has the key. The eave decoration, which includes colourful reliefs of fish and portly merchants, is very fine. At the eastern end of Dong Dajie, you can look around the **Risshengchang** (daily 9am–5pm), a bank established in 1824, the first in the country and one of the first places in the world where cheques were used.

Practicalities

Buses to Pingyao leave from outside Taiyuan train station, and the trip along good roads takes only two and a half hours. Regular **trains** also leave Taiyuan every morning – Pingyao is one of the first stations on the line to Xi'an – but you'll have to join the long queue for a ticket. The train, which takes a circuitous route, takes about the same time as the bus. Buses terminate outside the train station in the north of town, which is also where you can catch a minibus back to Taiyuan. En route to Xi'an, you can break your journey in Pingyao for the day and then pick up one of the two evening trains that pass through on their way south. The ticket office at the tiny Pingyao station opens thirty minutes before the train's arrival. Luggage can be left behind the counter at the station shop.

The Shuanglin Si

The **Shuanglin Si**, which holds an extraordinary collection of Buddhist sculpture, is 7km southwest of Pingyao in a stretch of quiet countryside, accessible only by rickshaw (you'll find them outside the train station in Pingyao). Extensive haggling is required to get a decent price (¥30 there and back, including an hour's wait, is not unreasonable). Originally built in the Northern Wei, the present buildings, ten halls arranged around three courtyards, are Ming and Qing. Protected by high walls and a gate, the complex looks more like a fortress from outside. Once inside, the fine architecture pales beside the contents of the halls, a treasury of coloured terracotta and wood **sculptures**, over two thousand in all, dating from the Song to the Qing dynasties. The statues are arranged in tableaux, with backgrounds of swirling water or clouds, turning the dusty wooden halls into rich grottoes. Some of the figures are in bad shape but most still have a good deal of their original paint, although it has lost its gaudy edge. The halls are usually kept padlocked, either for the protection of the figures or simply because visitors are uncommon, and you will be shown around them one by one by an earnest caretaker who will tell you all about the figures, whether or not you understand his breathless Chinese.

The horsemen dotted in vertical relief around the **Wushung Hall**, the first on the right, illustrate scenes from the life of Guan Yu, the god of war, but the figures in most of the halls are depictions of Buddha or saints and guardians. The *arhats* in the **second hall**, though they are unpainted, are eerily lifelike, somewhat sinister in the gloom with their bulging foreheads, long tapering fingernails and eyes of black glass that follow you round the room. In the **third hall**, the walls are lined with elegant twenty-centimetre-high Bodhisattvas, like so many roosting birds, ranked on shelves carved to represent the levels of existence (demons on the bottom, clouds and angels at the top), who incline towards a set of larger Buddha figures at the centre. In the **fourth hall**, look out for the monsters hanging above the Buddhas, and in the **fifth**, for a superb figure of many-armed Guanyin.

Wutai Shan

One of China's four Buddhist mountains, the five flat peaks of **Wutai Shan** – the name means Five-terrace Mountain – rise around 3000m above sea level in the northeast corner of Shanxi Province, near the border with Hebei. An isolated spot, it rewards the long bus ride it takes to get here with fresh air, superb alpine scenery, some of the best temple architecture in China and, with monks, fortune-tellers, and pilgrims outnumbering tourists, a peaceful, spiritual tone.

One of the earliest sites where Buddhism took hold in China, Wutai Shan has been a religious centre at least since the reign of Emperor Ming Di (58–75 AD), when, according to legend, an Indian monk arrived at the mountain and had a vision in which he met the **Manjusri Buddha**. Each Buddhist mountain is dedicated to a particular Bodhisattva, and Wutai Shan became dedicated to Manjusri (also known as the Wenchu Buddha), god of wisdom, who is depicted riding a lion and carrying a sword to cleave ignorance and a manuscript (to represent a sutra). By the time of the Northern Wei, Wutai Shan was a prosperous Buddhist centre, important enough to be depicted on a mural at the Dunhuang Caves in Gansu. The mountain reached its height of popularity in the Tang dynasty, when there were over two hundred temples scattered around its peaks, in which monks devoted themselves to the study of the Avatamsaka sutra, which contained references to "a pure and fresh mountain in the northeast" where Manjusri once resided, thought to be Wutai Shan. The number of temples declined in the late Tang, when Buddhism was persecuted, but the mountain enjoyed a second upsurge of

	WUTAI SHAN	
Wutai Shan	五台山	*wǔtáishān*
Bishan Si	碧山寺	*bìshān sì*
Foguang Si	佛光寺	*fóguāng sì*
Jinge Si	金阁寺	*jīngé sì*
Longquan Si	龙泉寺	*lóngquán sì*
Luohou Si	罗侯寺	*luóhóu sì*
Nanchan Si	南禅寺	*nánchán sì*
Nanshan Si	南山寺	*nánshān sì*
Pusa Ding	菩萨顶	*púsà dǐng*
Shuxiang Si	数象寺	*shùxiàng sì*
Tayuan Si	塔院寺	*tǎyuàn sì*
Wanfo Hall	万佛阁	*wànfó gé*
Xiantong Si	显通寺	*xiǎntōng sì*
Zhenhai Si	镇海寺	*zhènhǎi sì*
Taihuai	台怀	*táihuái*
Qixiange Guesthouse	七相阁宾馆	*qīxiànggé bīnguǎn*
Youyi Binguan	友谊宾馆	*yǒuyí bīnguǎn*
Yunfeng Binguan	云峰宾馆	*yúnfēng bīnguǎn*

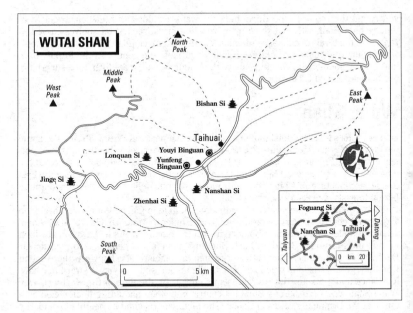

popularity in the Ming dynasty, when it found imperial favour; Emperor Kangxi was a frequent visitor. The Manjusri Buddha is particularly important in Tibetan and Mongolian Buddhism, and Wutai Shan became an important pilgrimage place for Lamaists. In the fifteenth century, the founder of the Tibetan Yellow Hat sect, which emphasizes austerity and rigour over the more indulgent, less doctrinaire, earlier Red Hat sect, came to the area to preach.

The mountain's inaccessibility has always given it a degree of protection during purges, and many of the temples survived the Cultural Revolution intact. Most of the forty temples remaining today are in the monastic village of **Taihuai**, which sits in a depression surrounded by the five holy peaks. Highlights are the ninth-century **revolving library** of the Tayuan Si and the two **Tang-dynasty halls** in the Foguan and Nanchan temples, two of the four extant Tang buildings left in China. All the temples today are working, and shaven-headed monks in orange and brown robes conducting esoteric ceremonies or perambulating around the stupas are a common sight.

Wutai Shan practicalities

Wutai Shan's remote alpine location means a **winter** trip is likely to be unfeasible and certain to be uncomfortable; even in **spring**, be prepared for temperatures well below freezing and transport times that can double due to treacherous roads. The area has only recently been opened up, and although you now no longer need a special permit and there are tourist minibuses plying the route, it's still a long and bumpy trip across winding mountain passes. You can approach Taihuai from either Datong or Taiyuan. Cheap local **buses** ply both routes, but the more expensive tourist buses (¥30) are worth the extra price as they sometimes stop at temples along the route which are far from Taihuai. The bus trip **from Datong** (see p.202) takes nine hours and travels south over some of the highest ground, passing close to the northern peak and Wanghai Si; in winter this road is usually impassable. The police at Datong, concerned about safety, make a fuss about foreigners travelling on local buses (which you can catch from Datong long-distance bus station) and may insist that you take one of the tourist minibuses which leave early on summer mornings (June to August) from outside the station. Ask advice from Datong *CITS* before you leave. Easier is the trip **from Taiyuan** (see p.211), 240km to the southwest, which also takes nine hours, but travels up the lower, southern approach road – it's a smoother ride, which passes close to the remote and superb Nanchan and Foguang temples. The least painful trip is from the town of **Shinjiu**, which lies on the train line between Datong and Taiyuan, from where buses take six hours, travelling up the southern route.

On the mountain itself, be prepared for unpredictable **weather** and take plenty of supplies – only the most basic items are available in Taihuai, and they're expensive. Climbing the peaks should present few difficulties as there are paths everywhere, but do allow plenty of time for journeys as the paths are hard to find in the dark and the temperature drops sharply at sundown.

Taihuai and around

An unusual and attractive little place, **TAIHUAI** is a strip of tourist facilities and temples set along the west bank of a river, surrounded by green hills which rise to the blue mountains on the horizon. Gently curling grey roofs, decorative double eaves, and pagodas are so thick on the ground that it's hard to tell where one temple ends and another begins. The streets are busy with stallholders hectoring passing tourists, clusters of slow-moving monks, wandering pilgrims and fortune-tellers sitting at the roadside.

The village temples

Reached via a stone staircase of 108 steps (the number of beads on a Buddhist rosary), the **Pusa Ding**, a Ming and Qing complex in which emperors Kangxi and Qianlong once stayed, sits on a hill in the centre of Taihuai, an ideal vantage point from which to survey the town and plan a jaunt around it. The fifty-metre-high, Tibetan-style pagoda of the **Tayuan Si**, a short walk south of here, is Taihuai's most distinctive feature, and used as a symbol of the village. Its bulbous, whitewashed peak, sitting on a large square base, rises high above the grey roofs, and the chimes of the 250 bells hung from its bronze top can be heard across the town when the wind is strong. The largest of many such bottle-shaped pagodas on Wutai Shan, it testifies to the importance of the mountain to Tibetan and Mongolian Lamaism, which is also represented by the tall wooden poles with bronze caps standing inside many of the temple's entrances. Behind the pagoda, a Ming-dynasty, two-storey library was built to house a bizarre and beautiful revolving wooden **bookcase**, much older than the rest of the complex and still in use today. A hexagonal tower, the bookcase rises through the first-floor ceiling into the library's second storey and is topped by a conical roof; it turns around a narrow base painted to resemble a lotus flower. Thirty-three layers of shelves, split into cubbyholes and painted with decorative designs, hold volumes of sutras, in Tibetan and Mongolian as well as Chinese, including a Ming sutra written in blood, and others whose ink is made of crushed precious stones.

The **Xiantong Si**, behind the Tayuan Si, is said to date back to the Eastern Han (52 AD), although the present complex is Ming and Qing. Among the four hundred rooms is a hall made entirely of bronze, complete with brackets and hinges in imitation of fine timberwork. Its walls and doors are covered with animal and flower designs on the outside and rank upon rank of tiny Buddhas on the inside with an elegant bronze Manjusri Buddha sitting on a human-faced lion. In the central courtyard stand two bronze pagodas, whose intricate decoration includes figures riding fish and horses through the sea as well as lines of Bodhisattvas. The temple is also known for the delicacy of its brickwork, which can be seen at its best in the Hall of Immeasurable Splendour, whose eaves are built in imitation of wooden brackets.

Just east of the Tayuan Si, the **Luohou Si**, a Ming-dynasty reconstruction of a Tang temple, is notable for a round wooden altar in the main hall with a wave design at its base supporting a large wooden lotus with movable petals. A mechanism underneath opens the petals to reveal four Buddhas sitting inside the flower.

Continuing south of here, you come to the **Wanfo Hall**, once a part of the Tayuan Si, which contains a huge number of Buddhist statues. Outside it sit two Tibetan-style stone pagodas. Farther south, the **Shuxiang Si** is the largest in Wutai Shan, a Qing restoration of a Tang building, notable for a bronze Manjusri Buddha flanked by five hundred *lohans*.

Practicalities

Buses arrive in the centre of Taihuai, a short walk west from the *Qixiange Guesthouse* (dorms ②, rooms ⑥), where foreign tour groups are billeted. A complex of single-storey grey buildings with upturning eaves, it's supposed to resemble a monastery, though there's nothing monastic about the carpeted rooms with armchairs and TV. Other, much simpler hotels in town may be persuaded to take foreigners; it helps to wave a student card. The *Youyi Binguan* (⑤) and the *Yunfeng Binguan* (⑤), which has a *CITS* office, are the other designated hotels for foreigners. They are comfortable, typically Chinese-style places 1.5km and 2km south of town respectively. Many of the pilgrims stay in the temples themselves, most of which have rudimentary facilities for guests, and this may also be possible for foreigners.

Food around Wutai is almost universally expensive and mediocre. The throng of street stalls are not very hygienic and it's best to stick to the dining halls of the above hotels.

Into the mountains

Few of the local tourists get very far out of Taihuai; it's certainly worth the effort, however, as not just the temples, but the views and the scenery, are gorgeous. The following are all within an easy day's hike from Taihuai.

The **Nanshan Si** sits in a leafy spot halfway up the Yangbai Mountain 5km south of Taihuai. It's approached by a wide stone staircase, its entrance marked by a huge screen wall of cream-coloured brick. More decorated brickwork inside, including fake brackets and images of deities in flowing robes, is the temple's most distinctive feature. Eighteen Ming images of *lohans* in the main hall are unusually lifelike and expressive; one gaunt figure is sleeping with his head propped up on one knee, his skin sagging over his fleshless bones. Two kilometres southwest of here, the **Zhenhai Si**, sitting in a beautiful leafy spot at an altitude of 1600m just off the road, seems an odd place to build a temple celebrating the prevention of floods, although legend has it that Manjusri tamed the water of the spring that now trickles past the place. During the Qing dynasty a monk called Zhang Jia, reputed to be the living Buddha, lived here; he is commemorated with a small pagoda south of the temple.

The **Longquan Si** is on the west side of the river, 5km southwest of Taihuai, just off the main road, and easily accessible by bus from town. Its highlight is the decorated marble entranceway at the top of 108 steps, whose surface is densely packed with images of dragons, phoenixes and foliage buried in a mass of abstract pattern. The rest of the temple seems sedate in comparison, though the Puji Pagoda inside is a similar confection – a fat stupa carved with guardians, topped with a fake wooden top and guarded by an elaborate railing. Both structures are fairly late, dating from the beginning of the twentieth century.

The **Bishan Si**, 2km north of the town, was originally used as a reception house for monks and *upasaka* (lay Buddhists). The Ming building holds many Qing sculptures, including a white jade Buddha donated by Burmese devotees.

The far temples and the peaks

Too far to reach on foot, the following temples and peaks are all served by minibuses which assemble at Taihuai bus station, or run direct from the larger hotels. Preserved from vandalism by their inaccessibilty, the temple complexes include some of the oldest buildings in the country.

The **Jinge Si** is 15km southwest of Taihuai, and worth the trip for an impressive seventeen-metre-tall Guanyin inside, the largest statue at Wutai Shan. Some of the original Tang structure remains in the inscribed base of the pillars.

The superb Nanchan Si and Foguang Si require a considerable diversion to reach. The **Nanchan Si** is about 50km south of Taihuai, a little way off the road from Taiyuan, near the town of **Wutaixian**. Tour buses sometimes stop here on their way into Taihuai, otherwise you can catch a bus to Wutaixian, then get a motor-rickshaw. The temple's small main hall, built in 782, is the oldest wooden hall in China, a perfectly proportioned building whose columns and walls slope gently inwards, the sturdiness given by its thick, carved, wooden bracket nicely offset by the slight curves of its wide, flaring roof. Two inward-curving peaks sit at the ends of the roof ridge – all features characteristic of very early Chinese architecture. The hall of the Jin-dynasty **Yanqing Si**, accessible by a short path behind the Nanchan Si, is somewhat dilapidated but notable for quirky architectural detail, particularly the carved demons' heads which sit atop the two columns on either side of its main entrance.

The **Foguang Si**, 25km west of Taihuai, is a complex of over a hundred buildings, mostly late, but including Wutai Shan's second Tang-dynasty hall, built in 857, whose eaves are impressive for the size and complexity of their interlocking *dougongs*. The walls inside the hall are decorated with lively Tang and Song paintings of Buddhist scenes; most of the images are of saintly figures sitting sedately, but a few ferocious demons are shown, dragging emaciated bodies behind them.

The five flat **peaks** around Taihuai, north, south, east, west and middle, are all approximately 15km away and considerably higher than Taihuai at 3000m above sea level. On the summit of each sits a small temple, and pilgrims endeavour to visit each one, a time-consuming process even with help of minibuses which go some way up each mountain. In the past, the truly devout took up to two years to reach all the temples on foot, but today, most visitors make do with looking at the silhouette of the summit temples through the telescopes of entrepreneurs in town. Set off in any direction out of town for a rewarding walk, although the South Peak is regarded as the most beautiful, its slopes described in a Ming poem as "bedecked with flowers like a coloured silk blanket".

South of Taiyuan

The small towns spaced between the cities of Taiyuan and Xi'an, north of the Yellow River, are largely ignored by foreign travellers, though there are some interesting places tucked away here, which should attract anyone who wants to break their journey with a little exploration off the beaten track. **Linfen**, about 150km south of Taiyuan, is popular with domestic tourists who come here in order to pick up a connection to **Hukou Falls**, regarded by the Chinese as one of their premier beauty spots. The less-visited **Guangsheng Si**, not far from here, is another possible excursion, and its magnificent glazed pagoda makes up for the hassle of getting there. Farther south, the town of Yuncheng is an access point for the **Guan Yu Miao**, a fine late temple popular with the Taiwanese, and for the town of **Ruicheng** and the nearby **Yongle Gong**, a Taoist temple with some excellent murals, from where Xi'an is only a four-hour bus ride away.

SOUTH OF TAIYUAN		
Hongdong	洪洞	*hóngdòng*
Guangsheng Si	广胜寺	*guǎngshèng sì*
Susan Prison	苏三囚牢	*sūsān qiúláo*
Jixian	吉县	*jíxiàn*
Linfen	临纷	*língfēn*
Pingyang Hotel	平阳宾馆	*píngyáng bīnguǎn*
Ruicheng	芮城	*ruìchéng*
Ruicheng Binguan	芮城宾馆	*ruìchéng bīnguǎn*
Yongle Gong	永乐宫	*yǒnglè gōng*
Yuncheng	运城	*yùnchéng*
Guan Yu Miao	解州关帝庙	*jiězhōu guāndìmiào*
Huanghe Hotel	黄河大厦	*huánghé dàshà*
Yuncheng Grand Hotel	运成大酒店	*yùnchéng dàjiǔdiàn*

Linfen and around

A provincial town, **LINFEN** is not unpleasant, though there's no point in hanging around. The town is just big and prosperous enough to have taxis (¥5 minimum fare), which aren't plentiful; they congregate around the train station, in the west of town. The bus station, for connections to Hongdong and Hukou Falls, is on the other side of town.

Accommodation is available at the *Pingyang Hotel* at 6 Jiefang Nan Lu (☎0357/214844; ①–⑤), which has many different faces, with rooms ranging from very basic to plush. The dining hall of the hotel, which serves reasonable food, is getting on for the size of an aircraft hangar, with round tables big enough to park a car on.

Hongdong and the Guangsheng Si

The village of **HONGDONG** lies 20km northeast of Linfen, about an hour's bus ride away. The reason to come is to pick up a connection to the Guangsheng Si, but while you're passing through, you might be interested in the **Susan Prison** (daily 8am–5pm; ¥13), 1km west of the bus station. China's earliest surviving prison, this Ming-dynasty squat black and white brick building consists of cloisters off which the cells, surprisingly spacious with curved ceilings, compare favourably to a cheap Chinese hotel room. They now hold displays of torture instruments and grisly dioramas demonstrating their use. The stele in the back courtyard contains a list of inmates.

From Hongdong bus station you'll need to charter a taxi to get the extra 15km to the **Guangsheng Si** (¥50 there and back with an hour's wait is reasonable), which sits on a hill top in a rural area dotted with small kilns for brickmaking. You're likely to have the place almost to yourself, with just a couple of monks, who look after the temple, and a few locals, who man the obligatory souvenir stall, around. The complex is in three parts, the Upper Temple, Lower Temple, and Temple of the God of Water, most of it dating back to the early fourteenth century, when the complex, established in the Eastern Han (25–22 AD), was rebuilt after a fire. The buildings, with roof ridge decorations which turn inwards, (a characteristic of early temple architecture) and chunky wooden brackets atop sturdy walls, have a blocky, barn-like feel. As you walk in you are confronted by the literally dazzling **Feihong Ta** (Flying Rainbow Pagoda), built in 1527 and covered with glazed tiles of green, blue and yellow which glisten in the sunlight. Each of the thirteen storeys is so heavily decorated with glazed figures – guardians, lions, birds, mythical animals, even people riding dragons – that not much of the wall is left visible. Inside the first room steps lead up into the pagoda behind the large Buddha figure. You can climb to the ninth storey, but it isn't easy, or safe, as it's pitch black inside, and the unusual staircase consists of a series of perilous ledges winding round the edge of a vertical shaft.

The **Lower Temple** behind, built in 1309, contains three Buddhas, their thrones finely carved, with lions and elephants depicted around them. The eave decoration, which includes images of fish and birds, is impressively detailed. Beside it, separated by a wall, the **Temple to the God of Water** contains graphic and lively murals painted in 1324, some still in good condition. Their realism and attention to detail make them invaluable to scholars, particularly the rare depiction on the south wall of ten actors on a temple stage, which provides an insight into the nature of ancient drama. The actors are in ritual dress, and some are playing instruments, while a girl peeks at them from behind the stage curtain. On the upper part of the east wall, a painting shows what the temple looked like in the Yuan dynasty.

Hukou Falls

Poetically described by *CITS* as "giant dragons fighting in a river", **Hukou Falls**, 150km west of Linfen, is the Yellow River at its most impressively turbulent. At Jinshan Gorge the four-hundred-metre-wide river is suddenly forced into a twenty-metre gap and tumbles down a cliff, where the fierce torrent squirts spray high into the air; the hiss of the water can be heard 2km away, which is what gives it the name "hukou", meaning kettle spout. It's best in the summer when the river level is highest. A popular spot with the Chinese, travellers give it mixed reports. The falls are undoubtedly magnificent, but it's a long way to go, and, with souvenir stalls aplenty, is not exactly a wilderness experience.

To get here, take a long-distance bus to Jixian County from Yuncheng or Linfen, from where a minibus will take you the remaining 30km, or catch a tourist minibus (summer only) from outside Linfen or Yuncheng train stations. Jixian County is about 150km from Linfen and Yan'an (see p.254), slightly farther from Yuncheng. Buses take between four and six hours, so unless you charter a taxi (¥800 there and back from Linfen) you will have to stay the night; the *Hukou Guesthouse* (②–④) is new and quite adequate.

Yuncheng and the Guan Yu Miao

YUNCHENG, about 100km south of Linfen, is the last major town before Xi'an on the train line south from Datong. It's another possible base from which to visit the Hukou Falls and also the starting point for bus trips west and south to the Guan Yu Miao, Ruicheng and the Yongle Gong (see below). The **train station**, with a statue of Guan Yu outside glaring at the townspeople, is in the northwest of town, at the north end of Zhan Nan Lu, while the **bus station** is a little farther south on the western side of the same road. Walk east from the station concourse to the end of Zhan Dong Lu and you'll come to the *Huanghe Hotel* (☎0359/2023135; dorms ②, rooms ④–⑥), a friendly place with a wide range of rooms and a decent restaurant. Tour groups end up at the *Yuncheng Grand Hotel* (☎0359/220508; ⑥), which has a small *CITS* office.

About 20km west of Yuncheng, the **Guan Yu Miao** (daily 9am–3pm; ¥13), the finest temple to the god of war in China, sits in the small country town of **JIEZHOU**, accessible by bus #11 from the station. Contemporary Jiezhou doesn't look like much. The bus drops you in a muddy square lined with a few stalls and pool tables, which makes the massive temple complex on its western side look quite out of proportion. However, this was the birthplace of **Guan Yu** (also called Guan Di), a general of the Three Kingdoms period (220–280 AD; see box, p.432). Something of a Chinese King Arthur, Guan Yu was a popular folk hero who, like many Chinese historical figures who became the stuff of legend, was later deified. As god of war, his temple (founded in 589

AD, though the present structure is eighteenth century), is appropriately robust, looking from the outside more like a castle, with high battlements and thick wooden doors. Among the images on the wooden arch at the entrance is a victorious jouster gleefully carrying off the loser's head. The martial theme is carried into the interior, with much smiting of enemies going on in the superb Qing-dynasty friezes and stone carvings in the eaves and on the pillars of the three halls. Guan Yu is very popular in Taiwan and many Taiwanese come here in winter for the **temple fair** held between October 18 and 28.

Ruicheng and the Yongle Gong

The bus journey from Yuncheng to **RUICHENG**, 80km south, a village just north of the Yellow River, is an engrossing if hair-raising trip across the Zhongtiao Mountains, an ochre landscape of utter desolation. Occasionally the bus stops at some lonely peak and, astonishingly, people get off – it seems incredible that anyone could live here. Though the sense of travelling through a wilderness leaves when you pull into Ruicheng, you are still very much in an isolated and backward part of China, and foreigners attract a lot of attention: courteous strangers may offer you their seat on a bus or canteen owners insist that your meal is on the house. The bus pulls in just east of the crossroads of Ruicheng's four streets, not far from the *Ruicheng Binguan* (③) on the north side of the west road.

The **Yongle Gong**, Palace of Eternal Joy (daily 9am–4pm; ¥20), is a major Taoist temple, 4km south of the village, most notable for its excellent wall paintings. Its name derives from the position it once held in the village of Yongle, farther south on the banks of the Yellow River. It was moved brick by brick, in 1959 when the dam at Sanmenxia was built and Yongle disappeared beneath the water. There are three halls, three sides of which are covered in vivid **murals**. In the **first hall**, the three major gods of Taoism, sitting on thrones, are surrounded by the pantheon of minor deities, looking like emperors surrounded by courtiers. Each figure is over 2m tall, brightly painted and concisely outlined, but although great attention is paid to an exact rendering of the details of facial expression and costume, the images have no depth. The figures, four deep, are flat, like staggered rows of playing cards. Some have the faces of monsters, others have beards which reach almost to their waists in which every hair is painted, and one man has six eyes. In the **second hall**, elegant, robed figures disport themselves in finely observed walled courtyards and temple complexes set among misty, mountainous landscapes. These are images from the life of **Lu Dongbin**, one of the eight Taoist immortals who was born at Yongle, and are arranged in panels like a comic strip. The murals in the **third hall**, showing the life of a Taoist priest, are unfortunately damaged and little remains visible.

ON TO XI'AN

From Ruicheng there are **buses to Xi'an** every morning between 6.30 and 9.30am. The journey takes four hours, travelling through a sparse but impressive loess plain dotted with villages of the same brown hue as the landscape, whose only decorative touch is the odd stone bird perched on top of old slate roofs. After two hours the bus passes Hua Shan (see p.252), where you can break your journey if you feel energetic. If you miss the bus to Xi'an, get one instead to **Fengling Du**, an unappealing country town two hours west of Ruicheng on the rail line. A **train to Xi'an** stops here every evening at 9.30pm, and there are occasional, though irregular, buses too.

SHAANXI AND HENAN

The provinces of **Shaanxi** and **Henan** are both remarkable for the depth and breadth of their history. The region itself is dusty, harsh and unwelcoming, with a climate of extremes; in winter, strong winds bring yellow dust storms, while summer is hot and officially the rainy season. But, thanks to the Yellow River, this was the cradle of Chinese history, and for millennia the centre of power for a string of dynasties, the remains of whose capital cities are strung out along the southern stretch of the plain.

Traces of Neolithic settlements are thick along the river – the homes of farmers, fishermen and excellent potters – but there was no large-scale building until the time of the Shang dynasty (1600 –1066 BC), who also left behind written records. For the

THE YELLOW RIVER

The **Yellow River** flows for six thousand kilometres through nine provinces, from the Tibetan plateau in the west, through Inner Mongolia, turning abruptly south into Shanxi and then east through the flood plains of Shaanxi, Henan and Shandong to the Bohai Gulf. The upriver section provides much-needed irrigation and power (see p.842); but in the latter half of its journey it causes as much strife as it alleviates.

The problem is the vast quantity of **silt** the river carries along its twisted length – 1.6 billion tonnes a year – whose choking nature has confused its course throughout history. Sometimes the river has flowed into the sea near Beijing, at others into the lower Yangzi valley, and its unpredictable swings have always brought chaos. From 1194–1887 there were fifty major Yellow River **floods**, with three hundred thousand people killed in 1642 alone. In 1855, the river's mouth moved from the north to the south of the Shandong peninsula, a distance of more than 350km, a shift which can partly be blamed on corrupt officials, who embezzled funds intended for flood control. A disastrous flood in 1933 was followed in 1937 by another this time man-made tragedy when **Chiang Kaishek** used the river as a weapon against the advancing Japanese, breaching the dykes to cut the rail line. A delay of a few weeks was gained at the cost of hundreds of thousands of Chinese lives.

Dykes have been built since ancient times, and today in some eastern sections the river bottom is higher than the surrounding fields, often by as much as five metres. Dyke builders are heroes around the Yellow River, and every Chinese knows the story of Yu the Great, the legendary figure responsible for battling the capricious waters. It is said that he mobilized thousands of people to dredge the riverbed and dig diversionary canals after a terrible flood in 297 BC. The work took thirteen years, and during that period Yu never went home.

Attempts to enhance the river's potential for creation rather than destruction began very early, at least by the eighth century BC, when the first **irrigation canals** were cut. In the fifth century BC the Zheng Guo Canal irrigation system stretched an impressive 150km and is still in use today. But the largest scheme was the building of the 1800-kilometre **Grand Canal** in the sixth century, which connected the Yellow and the Yangzi rivers and was used to carry grain to the north. It was built using locks to control water level, an innovation that did not appear in the West for another four hundred years. Today **river control** continues on a massive scale. To stop flooding, the riverbed is dredged, diversion channels cut and reservoirs constructed on the river's tributaries. Land around the river has been forested to help prevent erosion and so keep the river's silt level down.

For most of its course, the river meanders across a flat flood plain with a horizon sharp as a knife blade. Two good places to see it are at the **Viewing Point in Kaifeng** or from the **Yellow River Park** outside Zhengzhou. To see the river in a more tempestuous mood, take a diversion to **Hukou Falls** (see p.225), farther north on the border between Shaanxi and Shanxi provinces.

next three thousand years this small strip of the Yellow River basin saw the development of the Chinese state and civilization – a development constantly threatened by tribes from the north and by the perils of the river itself, but steady nonetheless. The Zhou dynasty, masters of north China from about 1000 BC, established a capital near Xi'an, moving on to Luoyang after this had been sacked. After them came the great emperor Qin Shi Huang, who by 221 BC had established a dominion which stretched from the Great Wall in the north to regions far south of the Yellow River. The next dynasty, the Han, also had their capital near Xi'an. This was a period in which the establishment of the **Silk Road** through Central Asia to Syria, and the rich trade with the West which followed, greatly strengthened the Yellow River area. Other influences came down the road too, most importantly **Buddhism**. At Xi'an, magnificent capital of the Tang dynasty (618–907), there were over a hundred temples alone, and five of the ten main schools of Buddhism in China originated here. It was under the Tang that the cities of the Yellow River basin appeared to reach the zenith of their prosperity and power, but with hindsight it is clear that the economic balance had long been shifting to the south. The **Grand Canal**, completed in 608, linking the Yangzi and the Yellow rivers, strengthened the Yangzi basin's position as China's food bowl and the main source of the empire's finances. Kaifeng, which became the Song capital in 960, was the last on the Yellow River: in 1127 a further wave of invasions forced the imperial court to retreat to the south.

Of these ancient capitals, none is more impressive today than thriving **Xi'an**, the capital of Shaanxi Province, which is perhaps the most cosmopolitan city you will find in China outside the eastern seaboard, but which still retains copious evidence of former glories, most spectacularly the tomb guards of Qin Shi Huang, the renowned **Terracotta Army**, but also in a host of temples and museums. The whole area is crowded with buildings which reflect the development of Chinese Buddhism from its earliest days; one of the finest is the Baima Si in **Luoyang**, a city farther east thought by the ancient Chinese to be the centre of the universe. The temple is still today a Buddhist centre, and the last resting place of monks who carried sutras back along the road from India. The **Longmen Caves**, just outside the city, are among the most impressive works of art in China, but also rewarding are excursions in the area around, where two holy mountains, **Hua Shan** and **Song Shan**, one Buddhist, one Taoist, offer a welcome diversion from the monumentality of the cities. **Zhengzhou**, farther east, the capital of Henan, has little to offer beyond comfort, but the town of **Kaifeng**, the Song-dynasty capital farther east, is a pretty and quiet little place, though scant remains of its past thanks to its proximity to the treacherous Yellow River. The city of **Anyang**, just north of here, remains a backwater with an impressive archeological heritage – you can inspect what little remains of the Shang dynasty in the museum here. If you've had enough of the relics of ancient cultures, check out **Yan'an** in high northern Shaanxi, the isolated base high in the loess plateau to which the Long March led Mao in 1937. Or for an impressive achievement of the 1960s visit the **Red Flag Canal** at Linxian in northern Henan.

Xi'an

Modern **XI'AN** is a manufacturing town of five million inhabitants and the capital of Shaanxi Province, holding a key position in the fertile plain between the high loess plateau of the north and the Qingling Mountains to the south. It's one of the more pleasant of Chinese cities, more prosperous than any other city in inland China except Chengdu, with streets full of Japanese cars, stores flooded with consumables, and stylish locals in the new discos. It's certainly far richer than the surrounding area, a fact suggested by the large numbers of rural migrants who hang around at informal labour

XI'AN

Xi'an	西安	*xī'ān*

ACCOMMODATION

Bell Tower	钟楼饭店	*zhōnglóu fàndiàn*
Dynasty	秦都酒店	*qíndū jiǔdiàn*
Flats of Renmin Hotel	人民大厦公寓	*rénmín dàshà gōngyù*
Golden Dragon	金龙大酒店	*jīnlóng dàjiǔdiàn*
Hyatt	凯悦饭店	*kǎiyuè fàndiàn*
Jiefang	解放饭店	*jiěfàng fàndiàn*
New World	古都大酒店	*gǔdū dàjiǔdiàn*
Renmin	人民大厦	*rénmín dàshà*
Royal	皇城宾馆	*huángchéng bīnguǎn*
Victory	胜利饭店	*shènglì fàndiàn*
Wuyi	五一饭店	*wǔyī fàndiàn*
Xi'an	西安宾馆	*xī'ān bīnguǎn*
Xijiang	西江饭店	*xījiāng fàndiàn*
Xijing	西京饭店	*xījīng fàndiàn*
Zhiyan	止园饭店	*zhǐyuán fàndiàn*

THE CITY

Baxian Gong	八仙宫	*bāxiān gōng*
Bell Tower	钟楼	*zhōnglóu*
Big Goose Pagoda	大雁塔	*dàyàn tǎ*
Dacien Si	大慈恩寺	*dàcíēn sì*
Daxingshan Si	大兴善寺	*dàxīngshàn sì*
Drum Tower	鼓楼	*gǔlóu*
Great Mosque	大清真寺	*dàqīngzhēn sì*
Shaanxi Historical Museum	陕西历史博物馆	*shǎnxī lìshǐ bówùguǎn*
Shaanxi Provincial Museum	陕西省博物馆	*shǎnxī shěng bówùguǎn*
Small Goose Pagoda	小雁塔	*xiǎoyàn tǎ*
Tang Dynasty Arts Museum	唐代艺术馆	*tángdài yìshùguǎn*

RESTAURANTS AND NIGHTLIFE

Baohua Jiujia	宝华酒家	*bǎohuá jiǔjiā*
Bob and Betty's	宝之碧	*bǎozhī bì*
Coffee Bar	茗芦咖啡房	*mínglú kāfēfáng*
Didi's Disco	帝者迪斯科	*dìzhě dísīkē*
Dongya Fandian	东亚饭店	*dōngyà fàndiàn*
Laosunjia	老孙家	*laǒsūnjiā*
Sichuan Fandian	四川饭店	*sìchuān fàndiàn*
Singapore Food Court	新洲风味美食厅	*xīnzhōu fēngwèi měishítīng*
Twenty One Disco	龙都二十一世纪迪斯科	*lóngdū èrshíyīshíjì díshìkē*
Wuyi Fandian	五一饭店	*wǔyī fàndiàn*
Xi'an	西安饭店	*xī'ān fàndiàn*
Xianghelou Roast Duck	祥和楼烤鸭店	*xiánghélóu kǎoyādiàn*

markets near the city gates, and which becomes starkly obvious if you take a bus ride into the plains outside the city. The city is also a primer in Chinese history, as between 1000 BC and 1000 AD it served as the **imperial capital** for eleven dynasties. You'll find a wealth of important sites and relics hereabouts: Neolithic Banpo, the Terracotta Army of the Qin emperor, the Han and Tang imperial tombs (see pp.245–252), and in the city itself, the **Goose Pagodas** of the Tang, the **Bell and Drum towers** and **Ming city walls**, as well as two excellent **museums** holding a treasury of relics from the most glamorous parts of Chinese history. Despite the drawbacks of **pollution** (many of the locals walk around with white face masks on) and congestion, common to all rapidly industrializing Chinese cities, Xi'an is very popular with **foreign residents**, and many come here to study, as the colleges are regarded as some of the best places to learn Chinese.

Some history

This area has been the site of some of the oldest cities in the world's oldest civilization. Its history begins in the Bronze Age, three thousand years ago, when the western Zhou dynasty, known for their skilled bronzework, built their capital at **Fenghao**, a few miles west. Nearby, one of their chariot burials has been excavated. When Fenghao was sacked by northwestern tribes, the Zhou moved downriver to **Luoyang** and, as their empire continued to disintegrate into warring chiefdoms, the nearby Qin kingdom expanded. In 221 BC the larger-than-life Qin Shi Huang (see p.248) united the Chinese in a single empire, the Qin, with its capital at **Xianyang**, just north of Xi'an. The underground **Terracotta Army**, intended to guard his tomb, are this tyrant's inadvertant gift to today's tourist prosperity.

His successors, the Han, also based here, ruled from 206 BC to 220 AD. Near contemporaries of Imperial Rome, they ruled an empire of comparable size and power. Here in Xi'an was the start of the Silk Road (see box, p.826), along which, among many other things, Chinese silk was carried to dress Roman senators and their wives at the court of Augustus. There was also a brisk trade with south and west Asia; Han China was an outward-looking empire. The emperors built themselves a new, splendid and cosmopolitan capital a few miles northwest of Xi'an which they called **Chang'an** – Eternal Peace. Its size reflected the power of their empire, and records say that its walls were 17km round with twelve great gates. When their dynasty fell, Chang'an was destroyed. Their tombs remain, though, including Emperor Wudi's mound at **Mao Ling**.

It was not until 589 that the Sui dynasty reunited the warring kingdoms into a new empire, but their dynasty hardly lasted longer than the time it took to build a new capital near Xi'an called **Da Xingcheng** – Great Prosperity. The Tang, who replaced them in 618, took over their capital, overlaying it with their own buildings. This city was in its day the capital of a great empire and one of the biggest conurbations in the world, with more than a million people housed in a **magnificent city** whose plan was so rational that it was taken as the model for the building of many other Chinese cities and for the Japanese capital, Nara, in 710. The huge rectangle enclosed by walls nearly 10km long was divided by further walls into 108 districts, crisscrossed by a grid plan of streets. These walled-in quarters had no communication with each other except by a single gate which led to the main street; the gates were closed at sunset and reopened at dawn. Only top officials were allowed doors giving directly on to the street. The preoccupation with order and compartmentalizing society became even more apparent in the Imperial City, enclosed by more walls, and the palace, further enclosed, inside that.

The Tang period was a **golden age** for the arts, and ceramics, calligraphy, painting and poetry all reached new heights. You can get some idea of the quality from the Tang horses and camels in Xi'an's Shaanxi History Museum, the Classics of Filial Piety in the Forest of Steles, the wall paintings in the Tang tombs and the relics buried as offerings to the Buddha's fingerbone in the Famen Si. The Roman glassware found here testifies to the flourishing trade along the Silk Road at the time, as do the many foreign coins in the museum. The open society was reflected in its religious tolerance – not only was this a great period for Buddhism, with monks at the Jianfu Si busy translating the sutras the adventurous monk Xuan Zong had brought back from India, but the city's Great Mosque dates from the Tang, and one of the steles in the Provincial Museum bears witness to the founding of a chapel by Nestorian Christians.

After the fall of the Tang, Xi'an went into a long **decline**. It was never again the imperial capital, though the Ming emperor Hong Wu rebuilt the city as a gift for his son; today's great walls and gates date from this time. Occasionally, though, the city did continue to provide a footnote to history. When the Empress Dowager Cixi had to flee Beijing after the Boxer Rebellion, she set up her court here for two years. In 1911, dur-

The **telephone code** for Xi'an is ☎029

ing the uprising against the Manchu Qing dynasty, the Manchu quarter in Xi'an was destroyed and the Manchus massacred. And in 1936, Chiang Kaishek was arrested at Huaqing Hot Springs nearby in what became known as the Xi'an Incident (see p. 246).

Orientation, arrival and city transport

Xi'an is easy to get around as the layout of today's city closely follows the ordered grid map of the ancient one, with straight, wide streets running along the compass directions. The **centre** is bounded by square city walls, with a bell tower marking the crossroads of the four main streets, Bei Dajie, Nan Dajie, Dong Dajie and Xi Dajie – north, south, east and west streets. Another major street runs south from the train station, where it's called Jiefang Lu, across the city, crosses Dong Dajie where it changes its name to Heping Lu, then to Yanta Lu outside the walls and continues all the way to the Big Goose Pagoda in the **southern outskirts**, where many of the city's sights are. The only exception to the grid plan of the central streets is the Muslim quarter, northeast of the Bell Tower, around whose unmarked winding alleys it is easy (though not unpleasurable) to get lost.

The **modern city**, extending far beyond the confines of the walls, in general adheres to the same ordered pattern, with two large highways forming ring roads, the innermost of which goes around the outside of the city walls.

Arrival

The arrivals gate at **Xi'an airport**, outside the town of Xianyang, 40km northwest of the city, is thronged with taxi drivers, who should charge ¥80 for a ride into town, but you're better off getting the **airport bus** (¥15; buy tickets from an office on the right of the main airport entrance as you exit), as unscrupulous taxi drivers sometimes double their prices en route. The bus journey takes an hour and leaves you outside the *CAAC* office on Laodong Lu, where again you should be wary of taxi drivers. Don't take a taxi from inside the compound, as unlicensed drivers often ambush disorientated visitors – hail one from the street.

The busy **train station**, in the northeast corner of town, just outside the city walls, is a major terminus on a west–east line which splits just east of the city; one branch going north to Beijing, the other east to Shanghai. City buses leave from the north end of Jiefang Lu, just south of the station, and taxis congregate on the western side of the concourse outside. If you arrive from Beijing you will probably be met by one of the girls from *Mum's* or *Dad's*, the two restaurants outside the *Flats of Renmin Hotel*, the main backpacker haunt, who will fight for the privilege of escorting you to the *Flats*. They'll also probably pay for the taxi. The girls are friendly and trustworthy and their altruism is sound business; they want you to eat at their restaurant, though they are not pushy about it. Even if you don't intend to stay at the *Flats*, accepting a ride to one of the restaurants is not a bad idea, as they are comfortable places to get your bearings, as well as have breakfast, and the English-speaking owners are helpful and knowledgeable, certainly more so than *CITS*.

Buses supposedly arrive in Xi'an at either the bus station just south of the train station or at the terminus at the southwest corner of the city walls, but in practice where you arrive depends a lot on the bus company, the direction you approach from and the whim of the driver. As most buses arrive at night, and you are as likely to find yourself standing at the side of a main road somewhere as in the terminus, it's best to have a destination in mind and hail a taxi.

City transport

The largest concentration of city **buses** is found outside the train station at the northern end of Jiefang Lu. There are other clusters just outside the South Gate, and at the southern end of Yanta Lu, just north of the Big Goose Pagoda.

The city also has five **trolleybus** lines, which all run east–west across the city; most useful is trolleybus #101, which runs south from a terminus outside the station, down Jiefang Lu, then turns west on to Dong Dajie, runs past the Bell Tower, and continues through the west gate on to Fenghao Lu, coming close to the *CAAC* office.

Plentiful red **taxis** cruise the streets and can be hailed anywhere. Most destinations within the city come inside the ¥10 minimum rate. Note that a rule obliges you to pay an extra ¥2.5 on top of what the meter says – a sign on the dashboard explains this, but as it's only in Chinese, foreigners often think they're being ripped off.

As the streets are wide and flat, **cycling** is a good way to get around Xi'an. All the major streets have **cycle lanes**, controlled at major intersections by officials with flags. There are, however, few bike parks, and most people run the risk of a rarely enforced ¥10 fine by leaving their bikes padlocked to railings. Make sure you have a good security chain, especially if your bike is anything other than a downbeat Flying Pigeon. For rental places, see p.242.

The yellow city **maps** available everywhere are generally reliable and hold a lot of information, but are useless in the Muslim quarter, and their restaurant listings should be trusted about as much as the cure for cancer advertised across the top.

USEFUL BUS ROUTES

#3 Train station–Bell Tower–Nan Dajie–Chang'an Lu.

#41 Train station–Heping Lu–Big Goose Pagoda.

#215 South Gate–Chang'an Lu.

#501 Huangcheng Xi Lu, 200m east of the *Flats of Renmin Hotel*–Nan Dajie–Big Goose Pagoda.

#601 Big Goose Pagoda–Dong Dajie–Bell Tower–Bei Dajie.

Accommodation

The seriously cheap accommodation is chiefly outside the walls. If your budget will stretch to it, it's much more convenient and atmospheric to stay inside the walls, in the thick of things.

Inside the walls

Bell Tower (☎7279200, fax 7218970). Opposite the southwest corner of the Bell Tower, right in the centre of town, this Holiday Inn-run hotel has a great location and is very comfortable. ⑧.

Hyatt, Dong Dajie (☎7231234, fax 7216799). Just by the intersection with Heping Lu, this plush steel and concrete fortress full of amenities is the most luxurious place in Xi'an, and is where most tour groups end up. Prices start at US$120. ⑨.

Jiefang, 321 Jiefang Lu (☎7278946, fax 7212617). As it's outside the train station, this hotel is especially convenient for a short stay, with a good range of services including a *CITS* office, bike rental and tours on offer. Staff are on the ball and it's reasonably priced. ⑤.

Royal, 334 Dong Dajie (☎7235311, fax 7235887). This Japanese joint venture is well located and de luxe. Rooms from US$90. ⑨.

New World, 48 Lianhu Lu (☎7216868, fax 7219754). The grand entrance leads to a lobby that's a bare plain of marble with an air of spare elegance. Quite luxurious with a price tag to match, but in rather a grey part of town. ⑧.

Renmin, 319 Dongxin Jie (☎7212538, fax 7218152). The bulbous facade of this quirky building, built in the 1950s to house Russian advisers, looks vaguely eastern European. The inside has been renovated and now looks like everywhere else, but this must have been a great place to stay in the early 1980s, when it was a cheap backpacker hotel. ⑦.

Wuyi, 351 Dong Dajie (☎7213824). In a superb location tucked behind a dumpling shop in the centre of town, this little hotel has character and is good value, as well as housing an excellent restaurant. Deservedly popular and often full. Take trolleybus #101 from the station. ⑤.

Zhiyan, Qingnian Lu (☎7210701). Go down the driveway of this complex and turn left for building no.6 which is the hotel. A car park full of Toyota jeeps and black cars with tinted windows flying red flags on the bonnet indicates the semi-official character of this cadre hang-out. Just asking for a room in the steel lobby full of Party members takes some nerve. ⑦.

Xijiang, 124 Xiyi Jie (☎7214806). This Chinese hotel is very cheap and well located, though it's an obscure little place that's hard to find. Head down the alley by the street number, into the courtyard, and the hotel is the unsignposted building at the back. Dorms ①, rooms ②.

Xijing, 241 Xi Dajie (☎7210255). Chintzy decor and big glossy pictures in the lobby set the tone for this fussy-looking mid-range Chinese hotel that sees few foreigners. No English spoken. ⑥.

Outside the walls

Dynasty, 55 Huancheng Xi Lu (☎7212718, fax 7212728). This four-star hotel, whose most striking feature is a bronze judge glaring at guests in the lobby, is aimed mainly at homesick Chinese businessmen, with luxurious karaoke rooms in the style of different regions – including a northern farmhouse, complete with fake *kang*. ⑨.

Flats of Renmin Hotel, 9 Fenghe Lu (☎6252352).This is where most backpackers end up. There's nothing particular to recommend about the institutional architecture or lacklustre staff, but rooms are spacious and cheap and *Mum's* and *Dad's*, the two restaurants opposite (see "Restaurants", p.241), which offer laundry, bike rental and information (as well as pretty good food) are a big plus. A little far out in an uninteresting area, the *Flats* are six stops west on bus #9 from the train station – look for the hotel's name in English on a pink sign on the west side of Xinhuo Lu; the hotel is 200m west down the next side road, over the rail line. If you're getting a taxi, make sure the driver doesn't take you to the *Renmin Hotel* in the centre of town. Dorms ②. Rooms ④.

Golden Dragon, 34 Caotan Bei Lu (☎6253371). Located far away from anything interesting, this place is shabby and small with antiquated bathrooms. It keeps changing its prices and is only really worth considering if the sporadically available cheap dorms reappear. ⑤.

Victory, Heping Lu (☎7893040). Just outside the South Gate in the city wall, this budget place is better located than the *Flats of Renmin Hotel*, and prettier, but staff are appallingly slack and uncooperative, and guests have been known to migrate to the *Flats* after a few days. The hotel offers bike rental and daily tours. Take bus #14 or #41 from the station. Dorms ②, rooms ③.

Xi'an, 36 Chang'an Lu (☎5261351, fax 5261796). A large, comfortable place with a huge brown lobby, but a little too far south to be convenient. ⑧.

The City

Xi'an successfully integrates its architectural heritage with the modern city, its imposing walls and ancient geometric street plan, centring on the Bell Tower, giving it a distinct identity missing in the sprawl of most Chinese cities. Downtown Xi'an, inside the walls, is just about compact enough to get around on foot, with enough sights to fill a busy day. And it is here that the city's new prosperity is most in evidence, in the variety and prices of goods in the shops on **Dong Dajie**, the main shopping street, where you'll also find the best hotels and restaurants, and in the number of cars that choke it during rush hours. **Nan Dajie** to the south, is another shopping district at the end of which you will find the **Provincial Museum**, which holds a massive collection of steles, next to the **city walls**, more imposing remnants of imperial China. Contrast is provided by the **Muslim quarter** off Xi Dajie, which preserves a different side of old China in its labyrinth of alleys centring on the **Great Mosque**.

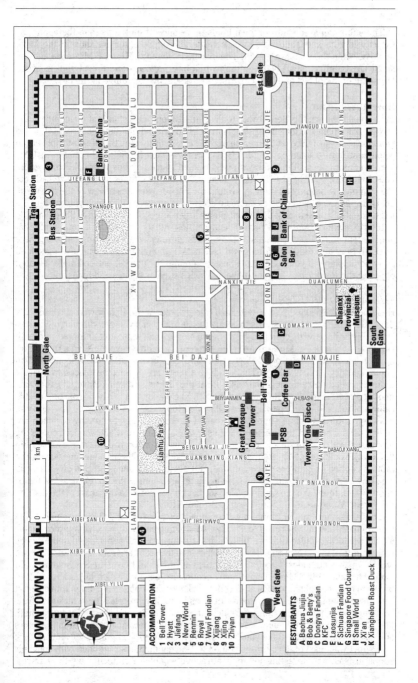

DOWNTOWN XI'AN

N

0   1 km

ACCOMMODATION
1 Bell Tower
2 Hyatt
3 Jiefang
4 New World
5 Renmin
6 Royal
7 Wuyi Fandian
8 Xijiang
9 Xijing
10 Zhiyen

RESTAURANTS
A Baohua Jiujia
B Bob & Betty's
C Dongya Fandian
D KFC
E Laosunjia
F Sichuan Fandian
G Singapore Food Court
H Small World
J Xi'an
K Xianghelou Roast Duck

West Gate

XIBEI YI LU
XIBEI ER LU
XIBEI SAN LU
BAYI JIE
QINGNIAN LU
LIANHU LU
DAMAISHI JIE

Lianhu Park

XIAOPIYUAN
DAPIYUAN

LIXIN JIE
BEI DAJIE
ERFU JIE

North Gate

BEI DAJIE

XINN JIE

Bell Tower

XIYANG SHI JIE
BEIYUANMEN
Great Mosque
Drum Tower

PSB

Twenty One Disco
NANYUANMEN

BEIGUANGJI JIE
GUANGMING XIANG
HONGYING JIE
XI DAJIE
DABAOJI XIANG
HONGGUANG JIE

Coffee Bar
ZHUBASHI
NAN DAJIE

LUOMASHI

Shaanxi
Provincial
Museum

South Gate
DUANLUMEN

NANXIN JIE
DONG DAJIE
XIXIN JIE
XI YI LU

Salon
Bar

DONGXIAN MEN

XIAMALING
HEPING LU

Bank of China

DONG DAJIE
DONGYI LU
DONGXIN JIE
DONG ER LU
DONG SAN LU
DONG SI LU
DONG WU LU

JIANGUO LU

East Gate

JIEFANG LU
JIEFANG LU
JIEFANG LU

Bank of China
DONG LU
DONGBA LU
DONGQI LU
XI QI LU
XI BA LU

SHANGDE LU
SHANGDE LU

XI WU LU

Train Station

Bus Station

The suburban area south of town holds more ancient buildings than the centre, as the city in Han and Tang times was considerably more extensive than in the Ming dynasty, when the walls were built. The excellent **Shaanxi History Museum** and the small **Daxingshan Si** sit between the two **Goose pagodas** and their temples, which are some of the oldest and certainly the most distinctive buildings in the city.

Downtown Xi'an

In the heart of town the **Bell Tower** (daily 9am–5.30pm; ¥10) stands at the centre of the crossroads where the four main streets meet. The original building, built in 1384, stood two blocks west of here, at the centre of the Tang-dynasty city; the present triple-eaved wooden structure standing on a brick platform was built in 1582 and restored in 1739. You can enter only via the subway on Bei Dajie, in which you buy your ticket and where you must leave your bags (¥2). Inside is an exhibition of chimes and a bronze bell (not the original). A balcony all the way around the outside provides a view of the city's traffic. **Dong Dajie**, east of here, is the main downtown street, along which you can buy the latest jeans or trainers, pick up a pizza, post a letter or get film developed. Shops include a good *Friendship Store* and name-brand clothes outlets as well as a couple of giant department stores (see "Shopping", p.239). Restaurants worth checking out along here are *Laosunjia* and the *Xi'an Restaurant* (see p.241), though there are plenty of fast-food and noodle places if you just want to snack. Pop into the market entered under an arch opposite the *Royal Hotel*, full of captive delicacies such as snakes and toads.

THE MUSLIM QUARTER

Head north off Xi Dajie, a street of small traders west of the Bell Tower, and suddenly the scale of the streets constricts to create the intimacy of a village, with narrow, unsurfaced alleys lined with cramped brown, two-storey buildings, half-timbered and with verandahs. This is the **Muslim quarter**, for centuries the centre for Xi'an's Hui minority who today number around thirty thousand, a people said to be descended from eighth-century Arab soldiers. The winding streets are rewarding places to wander around; a good entry point is Damaishi Jie at the district's western extremity, the main market street, marked at the intersection with Xi Dajie by a green arch sporting Arabic calligraphy. Walk north up this street – it's often too packed even to cycle up – and you pass poky little dumpling shops with rows of street stalls in front, many of which are selling offal. Look out for the sheep skulls – when you buy one the vendor scoops the brains out with a chopstick and wraps them up in paper for you. More palatable, and definitely worth sampling, are the sweets, some stamped with good luck messages, the mutton cooked on skewers while you wait, and the nuts and seeds heaped on plates outside tiny, dark shops. Head east of here at a junction about 200m up the street, walk for about 700m, then take the winding alley south and you come to the heart of the district, the **Great Mosque** (daily 8am–noon & 2–6pm; ¥15).

The largest mosque in China, it was originally established in 742, then rebuilt in the Qing dynasty and heavily restored. An east–west facing complex, which integrates Arabic features into a familiar Chinese design, it's a calm place, unpenetrated by the hectic atmosphere of the streets outside. On either side of the stone arch at the entrance are two **steles** by two of the most famous calligraphers in China, Mi Fei, of the Song dynasty and Dong Qichang of the Ming. The attractive courtyard beyond, which holds a minaret in the form of an octagonal pagoda at its centre, is lined with wooden buildings with abstract eave decorations – the usual figurative designs being inappropriate for a mosque. Freestanding steles hold inscriptions in Chinese, Persian and Arabic. The **main prayer hall**, just beyond the two fountains, has a turquoise roof and some fine carvings on the doors and eaves; you can enter (take your shoes off) when it's not being used for prayers.

A short walk east of here brings you on to Beiyuanmen, a street lined with souvenir shops at least as interesting for their attractive wooden architecture as their wares.

Head south and you come to the **Drum Tower** (daily 8.30am–5.30pm; ¥10), which marks the limit of the Muslim quarter. It's a triple-eaved wooden building atop a fifty-metre-long arch straddling the road. You enter up steps on the western side, though there's not much to see when you're up there, as the building no longer holds the drum which used to be banged at dusk, a complement to the bell in the Bell Tower which heralded the dawn.

THE SHAANXI PROVINCIAL MUSEUM

Heading south from the Bell Tower along Nan Dajie, a street of department stores and offices, you come to the huge **South Gate**, an arch in the wall topped with a triple-eaved wooden building, not open to the public. Turning east on to Shuyuanmen, a cobbled street of souvenir shops dressed up to look like Qing buildings, walk for 500m alongside the wall to reach the **Shaanxi Provincial Museum** (daily 8.30am–5.30pm; ¥30, students ¥10), a converted Confucian temple. Most of the exhibits are **steles**, from the Han to the Qing dynasties, which you don't need to understand Chinese to find fascinating; many are marked with maps and drawings.

An annexe on the west side holds an exhibition of small stone **Buddhist images**, a wealth of which have been discovered in Shaanxi. Exhibited chronologically, the sculptures demonstrate the way the physiology of Buddha images changed over the centuries. The first, from 420 AD, are of plump, Indian-style Buddhas; later images become much more Han-looking, as Buddhism developed Chinese characteristics and absorbed the influence of Confucianism and Taoism. The Sui and Tang figures are particularly good.

The rest of the museum collection consists of six halls containing over a thousand **steles**. The first hall contains the twelve Confucian classics, texts outlining the Confucian philosophy – carved onto 114 stone tablets, a massive project ordered by the Tang emperor Wenzong in 837 as a way of ensuring the texts were never lost or corrupted by copyists' errors. Like most of the steles in the museum, these are set in a stone wall or secured in a steel frame. The second hall includes the **Daqing Nestorian tablet**, on the left as you go in, recognizable by a cross on the top, which records the arrival of a Nestorian priest in Chang'an in 781 and gives a rudimentary description of Christian doctrine. Condemned as a heresy in the West for its central doctrine of the dual nature of Christ, both human and divine, and for refusal to deify the virgin mother, Nestorianism spread to Turkey and the East as its priests fled persecution. It was the first Christian doctrine to appear in China. In the third hall, one stele is inscribed with a **map of Chang'an** at the height of its splendour, when the walls were extensive enough to include the Big Goose Pagoda within their perimeter. Rubbings are often being made in the fourth hall, where the most carved drawings are housed; thin paper is pasted over a stele and a powdered ink applied with a flat stone wrapped in cloth. Among the steles is an image called the "God of Literature Pointing the Dipper", with the eight characters which outline the Confucian virtues – regulate the heart, cultivate the self, overcome selfishness and return propriety – cleverly made into the image of a jaunty figure. To point the dipper meant to come first in the exams on Confucian texts which controlled entry to the civil service. Other tablets hold lively line drawings of local scenic spots. At the back of the hall, a stele records the harsh recriminations taken by the Qing government against a village which massacred foreign missionaries in 1903. The other three halls contain mainly texts, but notable is a stele inscribed with the large character "Hu", meaning tiger, written in a dynamic single stroke by the Qing calligrapher, Ma Dezhao.

THE CITY WALLS

Xi'an's **walls**, built in 1370 and recently restored, are the most distinctive feature of the modern city, largely intact and imposing enough to act as a physical barrier between the city centre and the suburbs, as there are few roads which cross them;

traffic often has to circle around the outside for some distance before it can gain entry. Forming a rectangle whose sides total 12km in length, they were originally built of rammed earth on the foundation of the walls of the Tang-dynasty imperial city. The walls, which took their modern form in 1568, when they were faced with brick, are 12m high, with a width of 18m at the base and capped with crenellations, a watch-tower at each corner and a fortress-like gate in the centre of each side. Originally the city would have been further defended with a moat and drawbridges, but today the area around the walls is a thin strip of parkland, created after a major restoration in 1983. You can climb the walls (daily 8am–6pm; ¥6) from the inside at steps 200m east of the South Gate and at the West Gate. Unrestored sections, mostly in the north and west, mean you can't walk all the way around; you can get farthest if you ascend at the West Gate and walk south, descending when you come to the road, then climbing back up at the south entrance. Locals sometimes use the wall as a nifty shortcut if traffic is bad, and there's nothing to stop you riding a bike along the top, though it will cost you an extra ¥2.

The Small Goose Pagoda and the Daxingshan Si

The Xiaoyan Ta, or **Small Goose Pagoda** (daily 8am–6pm; ¥10), is southwest of the South Gate on Youyi Lu. From the train station, take bus #3 or #14 and get off at the cross-roads with Chang'an Lu. A 45-metre-tall, delicate construction, founded in the Tang dynasty in 707 to store sutras brought back from India, the pagoda sits in what remains of the Jianfu Si. Two of the pagoda's original fifteen storeys were damaged in an earth-quake, leaving a rather abrupt jagged top to the roof, to which you can ascend for an extra ¥10 for a view of the city. A shop at the back of the complex sells Shaanxi folk arts.

Just south of here on Xingshan Xijie, in Xinfeng Park, accessible down a narrow mar-ket street, the small **Daxingshan Si** (daily 8am–6pm; ¥1) is usually overlooked by vis-itors, but is worth a visit. Destroyed in the Tang persecution of Buddhism, today's small, low buildings are mainly Qing and Ming. It's the only working Buddhist temple in Xi'an, and monks in baggy orange trousers will write your name on a prayer sheet in the main hall for a donation.

Shaanxi History Museum

The **Shaanxi History Museum** (daily 9am–5.30pm, last entrance 4.30pm; ¥38, students ¥15; bags and cameras must be left outside) is an impressive modern building opened in 1992, on the route of buses #5 and #14 from the station, and within walking distance of the Daxingshan Si and the Big Goose Pagoda. The exhibition halls are spacious, well laid out, and have English captions, displaying to full advantage a magnificent collection of over three thousand relics, one of the city's major highlights.

The **lower floor**, which contains a general survey of the development of civilization until the Shang dynasty, holds mostly arrowheads and simple ornaments – most impressive is a superb set of Western Zhou and Shang **bronze vessels** covered in geo-metric designs suggestive of animal shapes, used for storing and cooking ritual food. A small **upstairs section** displays relics from the Han to the Northern Zhou; notable are the Han ceramic funerary objects, particularly the model houses.

Back on the lower floor, two **side halls** hold themed exhibitions, the western one of bronzes and ceramics, in which the best-looking artefacts are Tang. Large numbers of ceramic **funerary objects** include superbly expressive and rather vicious-looking camels, guardians, dancers, courtiers and warriors, glazed and unglazed. There's even an ostrich and a rhinoceros, gifts from foreign ambassadors. The eastern hall holds a display of Tang **gold and silver**, mainly finely wrought images of dragons and tiny, delicate flowers and birds, and an exhibition of Tang costume and ornament. The hall's introduction states that Tang women led "brisk and liberated lives", though it's hard to imagine how when you see the **wigs** arranged to show their complex, gravity-defying hair-dos, with names like "frightened swan coil", and the tall, thin wooden soles on their **shoes**.

The Dacien Si, Big Goose Pagoda and Tang Dynasty Arts Museum

The **Dacien Si**, Temple of Grace (daily 8am–5pm; ¥9), in the far south of town, 4km from the city wall on the route of bus #41 from the station, is the largest temple in Xi'an, though when it was established in 647 it was much larger, with nearly two thousand rooms, and a resident population of over three hundred monks. The original was destroyed in 907 and the present buildings are Qing, as are the garishly repainted figures of *lohans* in the main hall. Other rooms hold shops and exhibitions of paintings. All around the temple you'll see rubbings from a Qing stele in the Xingjiao Si of images of the Tang-dynasty monk **Xuan Zang**, the temple's most famous resident, who spent fifteen years collecting Sanskrit sutras in India before translating them here into 1335 volumes. He is shown with the largest bamboo-frame backpack you're likely to see on your travels.

At his request, the Dayan Ta, or **Big Goose Pagoda** (daily 8am–5pm; ¥25, students ¥10), was built at the centre of the temple as a fireproof store for his precious sutras. No one seems to know where the name "Goose" comes from – perhaps from the tale in which Xuan Zang and Monkey, heroes of the popular classic *Xi Yu Ji* (*Journey to the West*), are saved by a goose when they get lost in the desert. More impressive than its little brother, the Big Goose Pagoda, in comparison, is sturdy and angular, square in plan, and over 60m tall. It has been restored and added to many times, though the current design is not far from the original. On the first floor is an exhibition of different pagoda styles, and, at either side of the south entrance, stone tablets hold calligraphy by two Tang emperors, surrounded by bas relief dragons and flying angels, also Tang, as is a fine carving of Buddha and his disciples sitting in a Chinese building over the lintel of the west door. The pagoda has seven storeys, each with large windows (out of which visitors throw money for luck). The view from the north windows is the most impressive, for the rigorous geometry of the streets below, though it's hard to believe that when built the temple was at least 3km inside the Tang city, a great beauty spot dotted with pavilions and praised by poets.

A short walk east of here, the **Tang Dynasty Arts Museum** (daily 8am–5pm; ¥6) is not as good as it could be, considering the wealth of relics from this age, regarded as the high point of Chinese arts, but it does contain some excellent pieces, mostly pottery horses and camels and tri-coloured glazed figures, including among the usual range of warriors and courtiers a couple of stuffy-looking bureaucrats in elaborate costumes. The exhibits are dated but have no English captions.

The Baxian Gong

The **Baxian Gong** (also known as Baxian An), at the centre of a shabby area outside the East Gate, is the only Taoist temple in Xi'an, home to around a hundred monks and nuns. Containing an interesting collection of steles, including pictures of local scenic areas and copies of complex ancient medical diagrams of the human body, the temple is the setting for a popular religious festival on the first and fifteenth day of every lunar month. However, it is probably of most interest to visitors for the **antique market** that takes place outside every Wednesday and Sunday (see "Shopping" below).

Shopping

Xi'an is an excellent place to pick up **souvenirs and antiques**, which are generally cheaper and more varied than in Beijing, though prices have to be bartered down and the standard of goods, especially from tourist shops, is sometimes shoddy. Be aware that many of the antiques sold are fake.

Xi'an is something of an art centre and the **paintings** available here are much more varied in style than those you see elsewhere, and strong competition means you can pick them up quite cheaply if you're prepared to bargain – a good, large painting can be had for less than ¥100. As well as the line and wash paintings of legendary figures, flowers and animals that you see everywhere, look for bright, simple folk paintings, usually of country scenes. A traditional Shaanxi art form, appealing for their decorative, flat design and lush colours, these images were popular in the 1970s in China for their idealistic, upbeat portrayal of peasant life, and many villagers, especially from the town of Huxian, 20km south of Xi'an, have made a career of producing them. A good selection of these is sold in a shop just behind the Small Goose Pagoda, in the temple compound, and outside the Banpo Museum (see p.245), together with bright folk art paper cuts and flour figures. There are a number of painting shops on Beiyuanmen, north of the Drum Tower; try no. 144. For rubbings from steles, much cheaper than paintings and quite striking, try the Big Goose Pagoda and the Provincial Museum.

Beiyuanmen is also the place to go for small **souvenirs**, engraved chopsticks, teapots, chiming balls and the like. Another strip of tourist shops lies along the pedestrianized Shuyuanmen, a cobbled street just east of the South Gate where an attempt has been made to prettify the shops by making them look like Qing-dynasty buildings. Clusters of stalls and vendors swarm around all the tourist sights, and are often a nuisance, though the stalls around the Great Mosque are worth checking out – you'll see Muslim shabaria knives among the Mao watches and other tourist knick-knacks. Some stalls sell small figures of terracotta soldiers in a mesh basket; you can bargain them down to just a few yuan, but the figures aren't fired properly, and will leave your hands black whenever you touch them. For better quality, buy them from the *Friendship Store*, on the corner of Nanxin Jie and Dong Dajie, which sells the usual jade, ink slabs and brushes, but is also well stocked with clothes, and you can get film developed on the first floor. For a personalized souvenir, try the seal engraver at 22 Heping Lu.

There is a touristy antique shop at 14 Nanxin Jie, but the best place to go for **antiques** is the market outside the Baxian An, held every Wednesday and Sunday, more of a local affair than a tourist bonanza, so prices are cheaper. Many vendors are villagers from the outlying regions who look as if they are clearing out their attic. You can find much more unusual items here than you will see in the stores, such as books and magazines dating from the Cultural Revolution containing rabid anti–Western propaganda, Qing vases, opium pipes, even rusty guns.

A wide range of expensive **clothes** are sold on Dong Dajie, with a good selection of name-brand stores. For cheaper stuff try the street market in the first alley on the right as you go down Dong Dajie from the Bell Tower. Head right to the bottom of the alley, past the stores selling fake DKNY bomber jackets and the like, and on the west side you'll find a shop which sells practical, hard-wearing clothes, such as hooded sweatshirts. The *Xi'an Department Store*, opposite the *Wuyi Hotel* on Dong Dajie, and the *Guangren Department Store*, just east of the Bell Tower, sell a wide variety of household goods, sports equipment and stationery. There's a **night market** on the eastern section of Dongxin Jie, with a lively atmosphere, but little to buy that's of interest to visitors – it's mostly plastic kitchenware.

Eating, drinking and nightlife

It's possible to eat very well in Xi'an; as well as the good selection of **restaurants** in the centre of town, excellent **street food**, such as *hele* (buckwheat noodles) and *mianpi* (flat noodles made of refined wheat dough), is available from numerous stalls. Try the **Muslim quarter**, particularly Damaishi Jie (see p.236) or the **night market** on the eastern end of Dongxin Jie. **Muslim cuisine**, featuring delicious mutton and beef dishes, is widely available in restaurants, and it's generally true that a restaurant with Arabic above the door can be relied on to be more sanitary than most. The popularity of Xi'an with budget travellers means that there are a couple of **backpacker cafés**, some open only in the season, offering the familiar attractions of banana pancakes, beer late into the night, and fake student cards.

Xi'an's large student population and general prosperity make it more exciting at night than most Chinese cities, and there are a couple of good **discos and bars**.

Restaurants

Baohua Jiujia, Lianhu Lu. Just west of the *New World Hotel*, this is a popular local place, though it does have an English menu, to suit all tastes and budgets. Try the braised pork, or the fish with chrysanthemum if money is no object. The side rooms are more pleasant than the narrow front hall.

Bob and Betty's, Dong Dajie, opposite the *Royal Hotel*. A fast-food place popular with young locals that sells rather bland pizza and apple pie. Sit upstairs for a view over the street.

Dad's Home Cooking, Fenghe Lu. Opposite the *Flats of Renmin Hotel*, and in fierce competition with *Mum's* next door. A backpacker haunt, with the usual sweet and sour pork, chocolate pancakes, and chips; try the apple dipped in caramel. The owner of this friendly place, Lily, is a mine of information. Check the restaurant's book for travellers' news and tips. They also offer cheap bike rental and laundry.

Dongya Fandian, 46 Luoma Shi. A large, expensive Shanghai restaurant founded in 1916 that serves Wuxi and Suzhou cuisine, but it's a little uninspiring, with an English menu that doesn't give you many options.

KFC, Nan Dajie, just south of the Bell Tower. A vast place, so big it always seems empty.

Laosunjia, 364 Dong Dajie. This Muslim restaurant, where foreigners are escorted upstairs to the third floor, is highly recommended. Most of the customers eat the house speciality, *paomo*, meat stew (¥15). First you are given two cakes of bread, which you break into little pieces with your fingers and drop into a bowl – a time-consuming process, but it gets you hungry. Then the bowl, marked with a numbered clothes peg, is taken to the kitchen and piled with shredded meat, noodles and sauces. The beef and oxtail here is also very good. Wash your food down with eight treasure tea, a mixture of tea, nuts, fruit and crystallized sugar.

Mum's Home Cooking, Fenghe Lu, opposite the *Flats of Renmin Hotel*. An imitator of *Dad's* offering all the same services. Again, staff are friendly, English-speaking and clued up about what travellers want.

Sichuan Fandian, 151 Jiefang Lu. This place is tucked away above an unpromising-looking canteen; the stairs are on the north side. Excellent food and very popular, though they tone down the spices for foreigners.

Singapore Food Court, 237 Dong Dajie. The only notable thing about this Asian fast-food place is that it is open 24 hours.

Small World Restaurant, Heping Lu, near the South Gate. Closed at the time of writing, this place offers backpacker food to the residents of the *Victory Hotel* (summer only).

Wuyi Fandian, 351 Dong Dajie. Offers steamed buns and dumplings which you buy on the street, then take inside to the canteen. The third floor of the hotel upstairs has a restaurant with a more sedate atmosphere specializing in Jiangsui and Anhui cuisine.

Xi'an Restaurant, Dong Dajie. A Xi'an institution, this huge place has four dining floors (the second floor is the best). The good tables have a view over Dong Dajie. Somewhat lacking in atmosphere, it's not cheap, with a meal for two costing at least ¥100.

Xianghelou Roast Duck, 365 Dong Dajie. The entrance to this second-floor place is on the west side of an alleyway just off Dong Dajie. Specializes in Beijing duck and is good value at ¥80 for a set meal for two.

Bars and discos

Chaplins Bar on the first floor of the *Bell Tower Hotel* is a pleasant place for a quiet drink – features include a full-size snooker table and barmen in bowties with drinks at Western prices. The snug *Salon Bar* just east of the *Royal Hotel*, slightly tucked back from the road on a side street, is run by English-speaking Chinese and has a very

Western look. A beer is ¥20. The 24-hour *Coffee Bar* at 6 Nan Dajie is cosy, warm and very expensive – the cheapest cup is ¥18 – and though it looks flash it doesn't sell real coffee, only instant; you're better off sticking to the tea. In the daytime, Xi'an's rich business set meet here, while a few trendy young things come here in the evening before and after the discos.

Tuesday is the most popular night to go out, when girls get in free to all the **discos**. Foreigners who enter are likely to attract a lot of attention at first, and can live out all their *Saturday Night Fever* fantasies on the dance floor, but if you just want to watch you'll be left alone. A favourite with foreign students is *Didi's* on Huangcheng Xi Lu (daily 8pm–midnight; ¥20), where foreigners get in free, presumably because they are exotic and buy drinks (¥15 for a beer). It's a relatively small place and fairly alternative – the music is a mix of hip hop, dance, rap and slushy love songs from a live singer. Things are a lot livelier after 10.30pm, when the music gets faster and only the serious clubbers are left. *Twenty One* on Nanyuanmen (daily 8pm–midnight; ¥20) is a bigger, glitzier place where sound technicians wear silver macs and a giant spaceship in the ceiling disgorges free tickets to the club every Saturday to the sound of the *Star Wars* theme tune.

Listings

Airlines *CAAC* is on the southeast corner of the crossroads with Fenghao Lu (Mon–Sat 8.30am–9pm; ☎4264026). The airport bus leaves from the bus stop outside every thirty minutes between 5am and 6pm daily.

Bike rental Bike rental costs ¥5 a day, with a deposit of up to ¥400. You can rent a Flying Pigeon from the *Flats of Renmin Hotel*, the *Jiefang Hotel* and the *Victory Hotel*. *Mum's* and *Dad's* restaurants also have a few bikes for rent.

Banks and exchange Branches of the *Bank of China* (Mon–Fri 9am–5pm, Sat 9am–3pm) are at 318 Dong Dajie and 233 Jiefang Lu.

Bookshops The *Foreign Language Bookstore* at 347 Dong Dajie has little in English except Agatha Christie novels. For books on Xi'an try the Shaanxi Historical Museum or the shop behind the Small Goose Pagoda. Most are expensive, with more glossy pictures than text, but there are a couple of reasonably priced, well-illustrated paperbacks on sale.

Buses The most central and largest bus station is just south of the train station on the west side of Jiefang Lu; destinations served include Hua Shan, Yan'an, Ruicheng and Luoyang. Another station just outside the southwest corner of the city on Huancheng Nanlu has a regular service to destinations south and west of the city.

Cinema You can watch Bruce Willis speaking Mandarin at the picture houses at 379 Xi Dajie and 352 Bei Dajie, where they show the occasional dubbed foreign action movie, a change from all the homegrown action movies.

Hospital The Provincial Hospital is on Youyi Xi Lu, just west of the intersection with Lingyuan Lu.

PSB 138 Xi Dajie (Mon–Sat 8am–noon & 3–5pm).

Post office There is a post office opposite the *Hyatt* at 161 Dong Dajie (Mon–Fri 9am–7pm), and another opposite the *New World Hotel* on Lianhu Lu (Mon–Fri 9am–noon & 2–5pm).

Telephones A 24hr telephone service is available in the same building as the post office on 161 Dong Dajie.

Trains There is a Foreigners' Booking Office on the second floor of the train station booking hall (daily 10.30am–12.30pm & 2.30–4.30pm), but it's of limited use – staff ask you where you want to go and when, then write it in Chinese and tell you which of the other windows you should queue up at actually to buy the ticket. The Advance Ticket Booking Office on Lianhu Lu, marked in English on some maps, often won't sell tickets to foreigners. You can also buy tickets from the backpacker restaurants and *CITS* in the *Jiefang Hotel*.

Travel agents The main office of *CITS* is at 32 Chang'an Lu (Mon–Fri 8am–noon & 2–6pm; ☎5262066, fax 5261558), but the friendly pair who staff the small *CITS* office (daily 8am–9pm; ☎7431023) at the back of the *Jiefang Hotel* are more approachable, and sell tickets for onward travel by train and plane, for the airport bus and for Yangzi River cruises.

Around Xi'an

You could spend days on excursions around Xi'an; look at any tourist map and the area is dense with attractions. Most people see at least the justifiably famous **Terracotta Army**, **Banpo Museum** and the **Imperial Tombs**. Other recommended attractions off the tour group itinerary are the **Famen Si**, with a superb museum attached, which is a little too remote for most visitors, and **Hua Shan**, the holy mountain (see p.252).

The easiest way to see the sights around Xi'an is to take one of the many **tours** on offer. There are two routes: the popular **eastern route** covers the Huaqing Pool, the Terracotta Army, Qin Shi Huang's tomb and the Banpo Museum; the **western route**, going to the Imperial Tombs and the Famen Si, is less popular as more travelling is involved, and it's more expensive (it's also hard to find anyone running it off season). **Chinese tour buses** run by private operators leave from outside the train station every morning; get there early as most of the buses have left by 9am. Look for the ticket booths, with boards outside showing the route and the price – these are located outside the bus station and on the east side of Jiefang Lu. Tours should cost about ¥30 per person. Tour operators on the western route often skip the remote Famen Temple despite advertising it on their signs.

More trustworthy are the tours that operate out of the **hotels**. The *Flats of Renmin Hotel* runs a tour for ¥25, leaving daily at 8.30am and visiting all the eastern sights except the overrated Huaqing Pool; no lunch or guide is included. The *Victory Hotel* offers the same route for ¥50, with a guide included, and it also sends a minibus along the western route in summer. **CITS tours** (¥50) covering both routes, with the Huaqing Pool included on the eastern route, leave every morning at 8am from the *Jiefang Hotel*; buy tickets the day before to check the tour is running and to ensure a seat.

Chartering a **taxi** for the day will require some nifty negotiating to get a price below ¥300. It's possible to take **local buses** (detailed below) to all the sights, and this is certainly a convenient way to get to the eastern attractions, though you won't be able to go round them all in one day. Last buses back to the city are around dusk. Getting to the western sights by local bus is very time-consuming.

AROUND XI'AN

Banpo Museum	半坡博物馆	*bànpō bówùguǎn*
Famen Si	法门寺	*fǎmén sì*
Huaqing Pool	华清池	*huáqīng chí*
Hua Shan	华山	*huáshān*
Huashan Binguan	华山宾馆	*huáshān bīnguǎn*
Huayan Si	华严寺	*huáyán sì*
Mao Ling	茂陵	*màolíng*
Princess Yong Tai's Tomb	永泰墓	*yǒngtài mù*
Qian Ling	乾陵	*qiánlíng*
Qin Shi Huang's Tomb	秦始皇陵	*qínshǐhuáng líng*
Terracotta Army	兵马俑	*bīngmǎyǒng*
Xianyang	咸阳	*xiányáng*
Xianyang Museum	咸阳博物馆	*xiányáng bówùguǎn*
Xingjiao Si	兴教寺	*xìngjiào sì*
Xingji Si	香积寺	*xiāngjī sì*
Zhao Ling	昭陵	*zhāolíng*

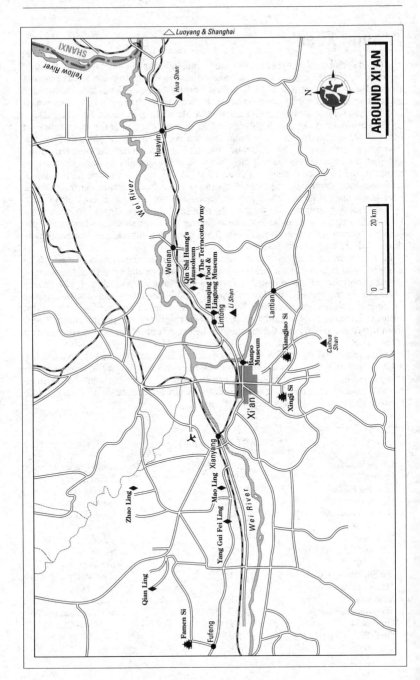

AROUND XI'AN

Luoyang & Shanghai

SHANXI

Yellow River

Hua Shan

Wei River

Huayin

Weinan

Qin Shi Huang's
Mausoleum

The Terracotta Army

Huaqing Pool &
Lingtong Museum

Lintong

Li Shan

Lantian

Xiangjiao Si

Cuihua Shan

Banpo
Museum

Xi'an

Xingji Si

Xianyang

Mao Ling

Yang Gui Fei Ling

Zhao Ling

Wei River

Qian Ling

Famen Si

Fufeng

N

20 km

0

Banpo Museum

The **Banpo Museum**, on the eastern outskirts of the city, 8km from the station, is the first stop on most eastern tours. If you want to arrive independently, take trolleybus #105, which leaves from a terminus on Bei Dajie, 300m north of the Bell Tower, and get off at the second stop after you cross the river – it's about an hour's ride. The ticket office at the museum actually sells two **tickets**, one for the museum (daily 9am–5.30pm; ¥15, students ¥5), and one for the model village (daily 9am–5.30pm; ¥40, students ¥15) which is a waste of time. If you don't specify otherwise, they'll sell you both tickets. The site gets mixed reviews; it's not visually spectacular, so some imagination is required to bring it alive.

The Banpo Museum is the excavated site of a **Neolithic village**, discovered in 1953, that was occupied between around 4500 BC and 3750 BC. It's the biggest and best-preserved site so far found of Yangshao culture, and is named after the village near the eastern bend of the Yellow River where the first relics of this culture were found. A history written around 300 BC states that the Yangshao people "knew their mothers but not their fathers. Living together with the deer they tilled the earth and wove cloth and between themselves there was no strife." This, and the fact that the women's graves have more objects in them than the men's, has led to the Chinese contention that the society was **matriarchal**, and the somewhat questionable claim that theirs was "a primitive communist society", as tourist literature states. From bone hooks and stone tools unearthed it is more securely known that they farmed, fished and kept domestic animals.

You can walk around the covered excavation site, a lunar landscape of pits, craters and humps, on raised walkways, but it can be hard to relate these to the buildings and objects described on the signs in whimsical English. The village is divided into three areas; the first is a **residential section** bounded by a surrounding trench for defence, which includes the remains of 46 houses, round or pyramid-shaped and constructed half underground around a central firepit with walls of wood faced with mud and straw. Around the houses are pits, used for storage, and the remains of pens which would have held domestic animals. A larger, central building was used as a communal hall.

North of here was a **burial ground**, around which are exhibitions of skeletons and funerary objects, mostly ceramic bowls and jade or bone ornaments. One grave, of a young girl, buried in an earthenware jar, contained 76 objects, including jade earrings and stone balls. Other ceramics found at the site, which were made in **six kilns** here, are displayed in the **museum wing**, They are surprisingly sophisticated, made by hand of red clay and decorated with schematic images of fish, deer and heads, or with abstract patterns, sometimes with marks on the rim which appear to be a form of writing. Also in the museum you can see barbed fish hooks with weights, stone tools, spindles and bone needles.

A compound of huts ouside the museum, the **Culture Village**, is a crude attempt to reconstruct the original village – a Neolithic theme park entered through the nether regions of an enormous fibreglass woman. Little attempt is made at authenticity beyond trying to cover the fire extinguishers with leaves.

Huaqing Pool and the Lintong Museum

Huaqing Pool (daily 8am–7pm; ¥30, students ¥16) is at the foot of Li Shan, 30km east of Xi'an on the road to the Terracotta Army (take bus #306 or #307 from west of the train station). Its springs, with mineral-rich water emerging at a constant and agreeable 43°C, have been attracting people for nearly 2500 years, including many emperors. Qin Shi Huang had a residence here, as did the Han emperors, but its present form, a complex of **bathing houses and pools**, was created in the Tang dynasty. The first Tang emperor, Tai Zong, had a palace here, but it was under his successor, Xuan Zong, who spent much of the winter here in the company of his favourite concubine, Yang Guifei, that the complex reached its height of popularity as an imperial pleasure resort.

The story of **Xuan Zong and Yang Guifei** is one of the great Chinese tragic romances, the equivalent to the Western Antony and Cleopatra, and often depicted in art and drama, most famously in an epic by the great Tang poet, Bai Juyi. Xuan Zong took a fancy to Yang Guifei, originally the concubine of his son, when he was over sixty, and she was no spring chicken (indeed, contemporary accounts describe her as somewhat portly). They fell in love, but his infatuation with her, which led to his neglect of affairs of state, was seen as harmful to the empire by his officials, and in part led to the rebellion of the disgruntled General An Lushan. As An Lushun and his troops approached the capital, the emperor's guards refused to take arms against the invaders unless he order the execution of Yang Guifei; in despair, she hanged herself.

Today **Huaqing** is a complex of classical buildings, a little less romantic than it sounds. The buildings are nothing special and the site is always thronged with day-trippers. The old **imperial bathhouses**, at the back of the complex, must once have looked impressive, but today they just resemble half-ruined, drained swimming pools. The largest is Lotus Pool, over a hundred metres square, reserved for the use of Xuan Zong; a little smaller is Crabapple Pool, reserved for concubine Yang. As well as the pools there are a few halls, now housing souvenir shops, and a small **museum**, where fragments of Qin and Tang architectural detail, roof tiles and decorated bricks, hint at past magnificence. A **marble boat**, at the edge of Jiulong Pond, on the left as you enter, was constructed in 1956. The **Huaqing Hot Spring Bathhouse** behind it offers you the chance to **bathe** in the waters; for a steep ¥60 you are shut in a room that looks like a mid-range hotel room (complete with a photo of a glossy tropical paradise on the wall and little plastic bottles of shampoo) with a bath and a shower. Better is the **public bathhouse** at the front of the complex, on the left as you go in, where you can bathe in a communal pool for ¥15; you'll need to take your own towel and soap.

Tours can spend as long as two hours here, much more time than the place really warrants. Fortunately, the **Lintong Museum** (daily 8am–5.30pm; ¥20) nearby provides a rewarding diversion; turn right out of the Huaqing Pool complex, then run a gauntlet

---

THE XI'AN INCIDENT

Huaqing Pool's modern claim to fame is as the setting for the **Xi'an Incident** in 1936, when **Chiang Kaishek** was arrested by his own troops and forced to sign an alliance with the Communists. The story is a little more complicated than this. As Japanese troops continued to advance into China, Chiang insisted on pursuing his policy of national unification – meaning the destruction of the Communists before all else. In December 1936 he flew to Xi'an to overlook another extermination campaign. The area was under the control of **Marshall Zhang Xueliang** and his Manchurian troops. Although GMD supporters they, like many others, had grown weary of Chiang's policies, a disillusionment fuelled by the failure to make any real impression on the Red Army and by the fact that the Manchurian homeland was now occupied by the Japanese. In secret meetings with Communist leaders, Zhang had been convinced of their genuine anti-Japanese sentiments, and so, on the morning of December 12, Nationalist troops stormed Chiang's headquarters at the foot of Li Shan, capturing most of the headquarters staff. The great leader himself was eventually caught halfway up the slope in a house at the back of the complex, behind the pools. Still in his pyjamas and without his false teeth, he had bolted from his bed at the sound of gunfire. A neo-Grecian pavilion on the lower slopes of the mountain marks the spot. Chiang was forced to pay a heavy ransom but was otherwise unharmed, his captors allowing him to remain in control of China provided that he allied with the Communists against the Japanese.

of souvenir sellers for 150m and you'll see the museum on your right. Though small and relatively expensive (and one of the few places in China with staff who can spot a fake student card), it's worth it for a varied collection that includes silver chopsticks and scissors, a bronze jar decorated with human faces, a crossbow and numerous Han funerary objects, including ceramic figures of horses, dogs, ducks and pigs. The best exhibit, a **Tang reliquary** unearthed nearby is in the second of the three rooms. Inside a stone stupa about a metre high, decorated with images of everyday life, was found a silver coffin with a steep sloping roof, fussily ornamented with silver spirals, strings of pearls and gold images of monks on the side. Inside this, a gold coffin a few inches long held a tiny glass jar with a handful of dust at the bottom. These delicate relics, and the dust, optimistically labelled "ashes of the Buddha", though crudely exhibited in what look like perspex lunchboxes, are more interesting than anything at Huaqing Pool.

The Terracotta Army and Tomb of Qin Shi Huang

The Terracotta Army (Bingma Yong) – probably the highlight of a trip to Xi'an – and the Tomb of Qin Shi Huang which it guards, are 28km east of Xi'an, just beyond Huaqing Pool. Plenty of tours come here, giving you two hours at the army and twenty minutes at the tomb, but it's easy enough to get here by yourself; take **bus** #306 or #307 from the car park on the east side of Xi'an train station; the journey, on minor roads, through villages, takes an hour. Slightly more expensive, but a little quicker, are the **minibuses** which leave from right outside the station and take the direct highway. The buses run only to the site of the Terracotta Army; if you want to see the tomb you'll have to walk from there.

The Terracotta Army

No records exist of the **Terracotta Army** (daily 8am–6pm; ¥60, students ¥20) which was set to guard Qin Shi Huang's tomb, and it was discovered by peasants sinking a well in 1974. Three rectangular vaults were found, built of earth with brick floors and timber supports. Today, hangars have been built over the excavated site so that the ranks of soldiers, designed never to be seen, but now one of the most popular tourist attractions in China, can be viewed in situ.

Vault 1 is the largest, and about a fifth of the area has been excavated, revealing over a thousand **figures** (out of an estimated 8000) ranked in battle formation. Facing you as you enter the hangar, this is one of the most memorable sights in China; you can inspect the static soldiers at closer range via raised walkways. Originally the troops carried real bows, swords, spears and crossbows, over ten thousand of which have been found. The metal weapons, made of sophisticated alloys, were still sharp when discovered, and the arrowheads contained lead to make them poisonous. Averaging 1.8m in height, the figures are hollow from the thighs up; head and hands were modelled separately and attached to the mass-produced bodies. Each soldier has different features and expressions and wears marks of rank; some believe that each is a portrait of a real member of the ancient Imperial Guard. Their hair is tied in buns and they are wearing knee-length battle tunics; the figures on the outside originally wore leather armour, now decayed. Traces of pigment show that their dress was once bright yellow, purple and green, though it's grey now. A central group of terracotta horses are all that remain of a set of chariots. These wore harnesses with brass fittings and have been identified as a breed from Gansu and Xinjiang. Each has six teeth, an indication that they are in their prime.

Vault 2 is a smaller, L-shaped area, containing four groups – crossbowmen, charioteers, cavalry and infantry – who display more variety of posture and uniform than the figures in the main vault, though a large number of smashed and broken figures make the scene look more like the aftermath of a battle than the preparation for one. Four exceptional figures found here are exhibited at the side: a kneeling archer, a cavalry-man leading a horse, an officer with a stylish goatee and the magnificent figure of a general, 2m tall, wearing engraved armour and a cap with two tails. Also on show are some of the weapons found at the site, including a huge bronze battleaxe.

The much smaller **vault 3**, where 68 figures and a chariot have been found, seems to have been battle headquarters. Armed with ceremonial *shu*, a short bronze mace with a triangular head, the figures are not in battle formation but form a guard of honour. Animal bones found here provide evidence of ritual sacrifices, which a real army would have performed before going into battle. A photo exhibition gives some idea of how the figures would have been painted.

At the side of vault 2 is a small **museum** where one of the two magnificent **bronze chariots**, found in 1982 near Qin Shi Huang's tomb, is displayed. It's about half actual size, with four horses and a driver, and decorated with dragon, phoenix and cloud designs, with a curved canopy and a gold and silver harness. Behind the driver is a large compartment featuring a silver door latch and windows that open and close. The whole has been made with astonishing attention to detail; even the driver's knuckles, nails and fingerprints are shown. Another museum holds small artefacts found around the area, including a skull with an arrowhead still embedded in it, and a few kneeling pottery attendants, the only female figures depicted.

QIN SHI HUANG

Though only thirteen when he ascended to the throne of the western state of Qin in 246 BC, within 25 years **Qin Shi Huang** had manged to subjugate all the quarrelsome eastern states, thus becoming the first emperor of a **unified China**. "As a silkworm devours a mulberry leaf, so Qin swallowed up the kingdoms of the Empire," as the first-century BC historian Sima Qian put it. During his eleven years as the sole monarch of the Chinese world, Qin Shi Huang set out to transform it, hoping to create an empire that his descendents would continue to rule for "ten thousand years". His reign was marked by centralized rule, and often **ruthless tyranny**. As well as standardizing weights and measures, even the width of cart wheels, and ordering a unified script to be used, the First Emperor decreed that all books, except those on the history of the Qin and on such practical matters as agriculture, be destroyed, along with the scholars who produced them. It was only thanks to a few Confucian scholars, who hid their books away, that any literature from before this period has survived. Qin Shi Huang himself favoured the strict philosophy of "legalism", a system of thought which taught that human nature was intrinsically bad, and must be reined in by the draconian laws of the state.

As well as overseeing the construction of roads linking all parts of the empire, mainly to aid military operations, Qin Shi Huang began the **construction of the Great Wall**, a project which perhaps more than any of his harsh laws and high taxes turned the populace, drummed into constructing it, against him. Ambitious to the end, Qin Shi Huang died on a journey to the east coast seeking the legendary island of the immortals and the secret drug of longevity they held. His entourage concealed his death, easy to do as he lived in total seclusion from his subjects, and installed an easily manipulated prince on the throne. The empire soon disintegrated into civil war and within a few years of his death, Qin Shi Huang's capital had been destroyed, his palace burnt and his tomb ransacked. It is possible that Qin Shi Huang, seen as an archetypal tyrant, has been harshly judged by history, as the story of his reign was written in the Han dynasty, when an eastern people whom he subjugated became ascendant. They are unlikely to have been enamoured of him, and the fact that the Terracotta Army faces east, the direction that Qin Shi Huang thought threats to his empire would come from, indicates the animosity that existed. The outstanding artistry of the terracotta figures has revised the accepted view of the Qin dynasty as a time of unremitting philistinism and his reign has been reassessed in the twentieth century. Mao Zedong, it is said, was an admirer of his predecessor in revolution.

The complex around the Terracotta Army is a tourist circus, with a souvenir city of industrial proportions; the most popular goods are postcards and slides, as you are not allowed to take pictures inside the halls (though you can get away with it if you pretend not to speak English or Chinese). They also sell miniature terracotta figures, fur coats and folk crafts. The food is diabolical and it's best to eat before you go. The shops inside the halls sell souvenirs of slightly better quality, including full-size terracotta figures (¥36,000). A bemused looking peasant sits signing postcards in the shop at Vault 2, supposedly Yang Zhi Fa, the man who discovered it all in 1974.

The Tomb of Qin Shi Huang

The **Tomb of Qin Shi Huang** (daily 8am–5pm; ¥8) is now no more than an artificial hill, nearly 2km west of the Terracotta Army. The burial mound was originally at the southern end of an inner sanctuary with walls 2.5km long, itself the centre of an outer city stretching for 6km, none of which remains. There's not much to see here; you can walk up stone steps to the top of the hill, hassled at every step by souvenir sellers, where you have a view of fields scraped bare for agriculture. According to accounts by Sima Qian in his *Historical Records*, written a century after the entombment, 700,000 labourers took 36 years to create an imperial city below ground, a complex full of wonders: the heavens were depicted on the ceiling of the central chamber with pearls and the geographical divisions of the earth were delineated on a floor of bronze, with the seas and rivers represented by pools of mercury and made to flow with machinery. Automatic crossbows were set to protect the many gold and silver relics. Abnormally high quantities of mercury have recently been found in the surrounding soil, suggesting that at least parts of the account can be trusted. Secrecy was maintained, as usual, by killing most of the workmen. The tomb has yet to be excavated; digs in the surrounding area have revealed the inner and outer walls, ten gates and four watchtowers.

North and west of the city

Except for the museum at **Xianyang**, the tombs, temples and museums in the north and west of Xi'an are a little far out to be visited conveniently. Trying to get around yourself is a hassle, as **local buses** are slow, routes complex and the country roads which pass through a stark loess plain, where coloured paper fluttering from the odd grave provides the only bright touches in the brown landscape, aren't good. At least it's easy to get back into Xi'an – just stand by a road and wave down a minibus. **Tours** start early and get back late, with the sights thinly spread out in a long day of travelling, but the museums are stimulating and it's good to get the feel of the tombs from which so many museum treasures come, even though most are little more than great earth mounds. The farthest, most obscure sight, the **Famen Si**, is also the most rewarding.

Xianyang

Most travellers who see anything of **XIANYANG**, a nondescript city eclipsed by Xi'an 60km southeast, usually do so only from the window of the *CAAC* bus, as this is the site of Xi'an's airport. A good highway connects Xi'an and Xianyang, so the bus journey from Xi'an takes only about ninety minutes.

Today the city is a pale shadow of its southern neighbour, but a couple of millennia ago, this was the centre of China, the site of the **capital of China's first dynasty**, the Qin. Little evidence remains of the era, however, except a flat plain in the east of the city that was once the site of Qin Shi Huang's palace. Relics found on the site, mostly unspectacular architectural details of most interest to archeologists – roof tiles, water pipes, bricks and so on, are in the city **museum** (daily 8am–5.30pm; ¥12) on Zhongshan Lu, a converted Confucian temple. From the Xianyang bus station the museum is about 2km away: turn left on to Xilan Lu, then immediately left on to Shengli Anoing Lu, which turns into Zhongshan Lu when it crosses Leyu Lu – the museum is on Zhongshan Lu, on the left. Star of the collection is a miniature terracotta army unearthed from a tomb, probably of a high official, 20km away, a lot less sinister than the original as each of the nearly three thousand terracotta figures is about 50cm high. The mass-produced figures are of two types, cavalry and infantry, some of which have heavy armour and a cap; others have light armour and a bun hairstyle. Some also still have traces of their original bright paint scheme, which show that the designs on their shields varied widely. The warriors are fairly crude, but the horses are well done.

The adequate *Qindu Fandian* (④) is on Xilan Lu, on the right as you exit the bus station, though there's little reason to stay in the city.

The Imperial Tombs

Mao Ling (daily 8am–5pm), 40km west of Xi'an, is the largest of more than twenty **Han tombs** in the area, the resting place of the fifth Han emperor Wu Di (157–87 BC). It's a great green mound against the hills, which took more than fifty years to construct and contains, among many treasures, a full **jade burial suit** – jade was believed to protect the corpse from decay and therefore enhanced the possibilities of longevity of the soul. A dozen smaller tombs nearby belong to the emperor's court and include those of his favourite concubine and his generals, including the brilliant strategist Huo Qubing who fought several campaigns against the northern tribes (the Huns) and died at the age of 24. A small **museum** displays some impressive relics, including many massive stone sculptures of animals which once lined the tombs' spirit ways, simplified figures which look appealingly quirky; look for the frogs and a cow, and the horse trampling a demonic-looking Hun with its hooves, a macabre subject made to look almost comical.

Qian Ling (daily 8am–5pm) is 80km northwest of Xi'an, and usually second in a tour after Mao Ling. To get here under your own steam, take a long-distance bus to **Qianxian**, then hire a rickshaw. This hill tomb, on the slopes of Liang Shan, is where **Emperor Gao Zong** and his empress **Wu Zetian** were buried in the seventh century. Wu's rise to power, in a society which generally regarded women as little better than slaves, is extraordinary. Originally the concubine of Gao Zong's father, she emerged from her mourning to win the affections of the son, bear him sons in turn, and eventually marry him. As her husband ailed, her power over the administration grew until she was strong enough, at his death, to usurp the throne. Seven years later she was declared empress in her own right, and ruled until her death in 705 AD. In later years her reign became notorious for intrigue and bloodshed, but that may be the result of historical bias, as a woman in the position of supreme power (her title was "Emperor", there being no female equivalent for so exalted a position) offended every rule of China's increasingly ossified society. The criticism ranged from the historian who described her as a whore for taking male lovers (while any male emperor would be expected to number his concubines in the hundreds), to the decapitation of the stone mourners along the Imperial Way leading to her tomb, the political vandalism of unknown later generations.

The **Imperial Way** is lined with carved stone figures of men and flying horses, and by two groups of now headless mourners – guest princes and envoys from tribute states, some with their names on their backs. The tall **stele** on the left praises Gao Zong; opposite is the uninscribed Wordless Stele, erected by the empress to mark the supreme power which no words could express.

In the southeast section are seventeen **lesser tombs**; the five excavated since 1960 include the tomb of Prince Zhang Huai, second son of Gao Zong, forced to commit suicide by his mother. You walk down into a vault frescoed with army and processional scenes, a lovely tiger with a perm in the dip on either side. One fresco

shows the court's welcome to visiting foreigners, with a hooknosed Westerner depicted. There are also vivid frescoes of polo playing and, in the museum outside, some
Tang pottery horses.

Princess Yong Tai's tomb is the finest here – she was the emperor's granddaughter, who died at the age of seventeen. Niches in the wall hold funeral offerings
and the vaulted roof still has traces of painted patterns. The passage walls leading
down into the tomb are covered with murals of animals and guards of honour. The
court ladies are still clear, elegant and charming after 1300 years, displaying Tang
hairstyles and dress. At the bottom is the great tomb in black stone, lightly carved
with human and animal shapes. Some 1300 gold, silver and pottery objects were
found here and are now in Xi'an's museum. At the mouth of the tomb is the traditional
stone tablet into which the life story of the princess is carved – according to this,
she died in childbirth, but some records claim that she was murdered by her grand-
mother, the Empress Wu. The **Shun mausoleum** of Wu Zetian's own mother is
small, but it's worth a look for the two unusually splendid granite figures which guard
it, a lion 3m high and an even bigger unicorn.

At **Zhao Ling**, east of Qian Ling, 70km northwest of Xi'an, nineteen **Tang tombs**
include that of Emperor Tai Zong. Begun in 636 AD this took thirteen years to complete. Tai Zong introduced the practice of building his tomb into the hillside instead of
as a tumulus on an open plain. From the main tomb, built into the slope of Jiuzou, a
great cemetery fans out southeast and southwest, which includes 167 lesser tombs of
the imperial family, generals and officials. A small **museum** displays stone carvings,
murals and pottery figures from the smaller tombs.

The Famen Si

One of the most extraordinary places in the area, the **Famen Si**, 120km west of Xi'an,
home of the fingerbone of the Buddha, and the nearby **museum** containing an unsurpassed collection of Tang-dynasty relics, are worth the long trip it takes to get here. If
you're lucky, you might find a tour bus to take you, otherwise, take the hourly bus to
Fufeng, a small country town of white-tile buildings and cave houses, from Xi'an's long-
distance bus station (4hr). From Fufeng bus station take a minibus to the temple
(20min). If you want to return to Xi'an via one of the Imperial Tombs above, you'll need
to stay the night in Fufeng to get an early start the next morning. Your only option is
the frugal *Fufeng Hotel* (④) on the main street.

In 147 AD, King Asoka of India, to atone, it is said, for his warlike life, distributed
precious **Buddhist relics** (*sarira*) to Buddhist colonies throughout Asia. One of the
earliest places of Buddhist worship in China, the Famen Si was built to house his gift
of a **finger**, in the form of three separate bones. The temple enjoyed great fame in the
Tang dynasty, when Emperor Tuo Bayu began the practice of having the bones temporarily removed and taken to the court at Chang'an at the head of a procession,
repeated every thirty years. The procession to bear the finger to Emperor Tai Zong in
873 was reputed to be over 100km long. After the emperor had paid his respect to the
Buddha, the fingerbones were closed back up in a vault underneath the temple stupa,
together with a lavish collection of offerings, with each emperor attempting to outdo
the last in pious generosity. After the fall of the Tang, the crypt was forgotten about
and the story of the Buddha's finger was dismissed as a legend until 1981, when the
stupa collapsed, revealing the crypt beneath, full of the most astonishing array of Tang
precious objects, and at the back, concealed in box after box of gold, silver, crystal and
jade, the legendary finger of the Buddha.

Today the temple (daily 8am–6pm; ¥3) is a popular place of pilgrimage. The stupa has
been rebuilt with a large **vault** (¥5) underneath, around the original crypt, with a shrine
holding the finger at its centre. A praying monk is always in attendance, sitting in front

of the finger, next to the safe in which it is kept at night. Indeed, the temple's monks are taking no chances and the only entrance to the vault is protected by a huge metal door of the kind usually seen in a bank. You can see into the original crypt, the largest of its kind ever discovered in China (21m long), though there's not much to see in there now. Much better is the **museum** (daily 8am–5pm; ¥30, students ¥12), west of the temple, housing the well-preserved Tang relics found in the crypt, and certainly one of the best small museums in China. Exhibits are divided into sections according to their material, with copious explanations in English. On the lower floor, the **gold and silver** is breathtaking for the quality of its workmanship; especially notable are a silver incense burner with an internal gyroscope to keep it upright, a silver tea basket, the earliest physical evidence of tea-drinking in China, and a gold figure of an elephant-headed man. Some unusual items on display are twenty **glass plates and bottles**, some Persian, with Arabic designs, some from the Roman Empire, including a bottle made in the fifth century. Glassware, imported along the Silk Road, was more highly valued than gold at the time. Also in the crypt were a thousand volumes of Buddhist sutras, pictures of which are shown, and 27,000 **coins**, the most unusual of which, made of tortoiseshell, are on display here. An annexe holds the remains of the silk sheets all the relics were wrapped up in, together with an exhibition on its method of manufacture. At the centre of the main room is a gilded **silver coffin** which held one of the fingerbones, itself inside a copper model of a stupa, inside a marble pagoda. Prominent upstairs is a gold and silver monk's staff which would ironically have been used for begging alms, but the main display here is of the **caskets** the other two fingerbones were found in – finely made boxes of diminishing size, of silver, sandalwood, gold and crystal, which sat inside each other, while the fingerbones themselves were in tiny jade coffins.

South of the city

In the wooded hilly country south of Xi'an are a number of important **temples** which could make the focal points for a day's excursion. No tours go here, but most of the temples are accessible on **bus #215**, which leaves from just outside the South Gate. Ride right to the last stop, then take a rickshaw to the temples; you'll have to negotiate a return trip.

The temples
The **Xingjiao Si**, 24km southeast of the city on a hillside by the Fan River, was founded in 669 AD to house the ashes of the travelling monk Xuan Zang (see p.239), whose remains are underneath a square stupa at the centre of the temple. The two smaller stupas either side mark the tombs of two of his disciples. Beside the stupa a pavilion holds a charming and commonly reproduced stone carving of Xuan Zang looking cheery despite being laden down under a pack. Little remains of the **Huayan Si**, on the way to the Xingjiao Si, except two small brick pagodas, one of which holds the remains of the monk Dushun, one of the founders of Zen Buddhism. The **Xingji Si**, 5km west of here, has a ten-storey pagoda which covers the ashes of Shandao, founder of the Jingtu sect.

Hua Shan

The five peaks of **Hua Shan**, 120km east of Xi'an, are supposed to look like a five-petalled flower, hence the name, Flowery Mountain. Originally it was known as Xiyue, Western Mountain, because it is the westernmost of the five mountains which have been sacred to Taoism for over two thousand years. It's always been a popular place for pilgrimage, though these days people puffing up the steep, narrow paths or enjoying the dramatic views from the peaks are more likely to be tourists.

There's a Chinese saying, "There is one path and one path only to the summit of Hua Shan", meaning that sometimes the hard way is the only way. This **path** begins at Yuquan Si (Jade Fountain Temple), dedicated to the tenth-century monk Xiyi who lived here as a recluse, then passes under the rail line and crisscrosses a river flowing down a rocky gulley. Every few hundred yards a wayside refreshment place offers stone seats, a burner, tea, soft drinks, maps and souvenirs – the higher you go, the more attractive the knobbly walking sticks on sale seem. In summer you'll be swept along in a stream of Chinese, mostly youngish couples, dressed in their fashionable, but often highly impractical holiday finest, including high-heeled shoes.

The deceptively easy climb up the gullies, known as the Eighteen Bends, in fact winds for about two hours before reaching the flight of narrow stone steps which ascend to the first summit, **North Peak**. The mountain was formerly dotted with temples and there are still half a dozen. Many people turn back at this point, although you can continue to Middle Peak next, then East, West and South peaks, which make up an eight-hour circuit trail.

Though the summits are not that high, the gaunt rocky peaks, twisted pines and rugged slopes certainly look like genuine mountain scenes as they swim in and out of the mist trails. The going is rough in places, but chain handrails have been attached to the rock at difficult points, such as the evocatively named Thousand Feet Precipice and Green Dragon Ridge, where the path narrows to a ledge along a cliff face. Some people arrive in the evening and climb by moonlight in order to see the sun rise over the Sea of Clouds from Middle or East Peak.

Practicalities

As Hua Shan is a stop on the rail line to Luoyang (see p.256) you can take in the mountain en route between the two cities, or as an excursion from Xi'an or on the way to Xi'an from Ruicheng in Shanxi (see p.226). A couple of direct **trains** from Xi'an leave every morning, with one in the evening (2hr 30min), or you can take one of the more frequent trains to **Menyuan** station, from where minibuses cover the remaining 20km to Hua Shan. **Buses** to the mountain, from Xi'an long-distance bus station, take three or four hours depending on the weather.

From the **train station** at Hua Shan village, buses go to the trailhead for ¥1, or it's a twenty-minute walk; head south to the bottom of the road, turn right on to the main road, and take the next road on the right to the trailhead. The **bus station** is a little closer, on the main road itself. Ascent and descent in a single day are possible, on a day trip from Xi'an – the last bus back is at 8pm, the last train a little earlier. However, if you're planning to stay the night, there are several options. The most pleasant **hotel** in the village, the *Hua Shan Binguan* (☎0913/661836; ②–⑥), at the base of the mountain, on the main road, just west off the trailhead turn-off, is a good prospect after a long day's walk. Rooms at the back, with views of the mountain, are the best. There are also rough-looking hotels about every 5km along the circuit route, where a bed should cost about ¥20, but you'll have to bargain. Don't expect light or heat at these places, and if you plan to stay the night on the mountain it's a good idea to take your own sleeping bag. These places are at least easy to find and hotel touts waylay travellers along the route. There's a more upmarket place on top of the East Peak, the unimaginatively named *East Peak Guesthouse* (⑦), catering to the sun watchers.

The nicest thing to be said about the **food** in the village and on the mountain is that it's palatable. It's also more expensive the higher you go, so best stick to the restaurant at the *Huashan Binguan* if you're on a tight budget, or stock up before you go. If you plan to climb at night, take some warm clothes and a flashlight with spare batteries.

Yan'an

The town of **YAN'AN**, set deep in the bleakly attractive dry loess hills of northern Shaanxi, has very little in common with the other cities of this province. Geographically and temperamentally it belongs with the high industrial cities of Shanxi rather than the ancient capitals of the Yellow River plain; however, the only easy way to get here is on the train or bus from Xi'an, 250km to the south. The town is a quiet backwater, and walking its dour streets it's hard to imagine that, as the headquarters of the Communist Party in the 1930s and early 1940s, this was once one of China's most popular tourist spots, a major revolutionary pilgrimage site second only to Mao's birthplace at Shaoshan (see p.470). In the changed political climate, with enthusiasm for the Party waning (and no longer compulsory), it's now hardly different from any other northern town, rarely visited except by groups of PLA soldiers and the odd ideologue.

There's nothing spectacular about the sights, unless the fact that Mao and Co were once here is enough to inspire awe by itself, but some insight into China's modern history is given not just by the **Revolutionary Museum**, but by the town centre, built during the tourist boom, an example of utilitarian 1950s and 1960s **architecture**, and by the slopes around, which are full of traditional Shaanxi **cave houses**. There is something perversely attractive in the town's grimness, which, together with the beauty of the surrounding countryside, makes it worth a day trip from Xi'an.

YAN'AN		
Yan'an	延安	*yán'ān*
Former Revolutionary Headquarters	革命旧址	*géming jiùzhǐ*
Revolutionary Museum	革命纪念馆	*géming jìniànguǎn*
Yan'an Binguan	延安宾馆	*yán'ān bīnguǎn*
Yan'an Pagoda	延安塔	*yán'ān tǎ*

The Town

After the ride here through the ribbed loess hills, one of China's most glorious landscapes, arrival is a disappointment as Yan'an presents a Stalinist frown to the visitor. Arranged in a Y-shape around the confluence of the east and west branches of the Yan River, the town is a narrow strip of brutalist breeze block architecture, about 7km long, hemmed in by steep hills. Ironically, the centre conforms to Cold War clichés of communist austerity, with streets lined with identical apartment buildings of crumbling grey concrete, plagued by frequent electricity cuts and water shortages. The town's margins are much more attractive, as the dour buildings give way to caves, and windowless houses built to look like caves, on the slopes around.

In the northeast corner of town, the **Revolutionary Museum** (daily 8am–5pm; ¥8), has something of the aura of a shrine, and a sculpture depicting revolutionary struggle inside, opposite the entrance, has offerings of money in front of it. The huge halls hold a massive collection of artefacts; curatorial policy seems to be that anything that was in the town between the years of 1935 and 1949 is now worth exhibiting. Relics include deflated footballs, sewing machines, rusty mugs and hundreds of guns and hand grenades. There is a stuffed white horse that is said to have once carried Mao, and translations of books by Lenin, Stalin and Trotsky in Chinese. There are no English labels, and the things of most interest to non-Chinese speakers are probably the propaganda pictures which include wood and paper cuts of Red Army soldiers helping peasants in the fields. The walls of the halls are covered with photographs taken at the time, and sinologists can amuse themselves by trying to match the portraits of awkwardly posed, youthful, fresh-faced figures, identically dressed in Mao suits, to the octogenarian leaders of late twentieth-century China.

The **Former Revolutionary Headquarters** (daily 8am–5pm: ¥10) is just around the corner from the museum, but can be hard to find – turn immediately left as you leave the museum compound and walk 200m down a small path that seems to lead into a village. The headquarters, a compound of low buildings, is on the right, marked by a faded signpost. It's a remarkably low-key approach to what was not long ago one of the most visited tourist spots in the country, the place where Mao, Zhou Enlai and Zhu De among others, lived and worked. More worthwhile than the museum, the simple, low buildings of white plaster over straw, mud and brick, typical of traditional local architecture, are elegant structures, with wooden lattice windows faced with paper, sometimes incorporating the Communist star into their design. The complex has a rather monastic feel. The arched rooms, with cups sitting on the table and bedding still on the beds, as if their inhabitants will soon return, have the simplicity of monks' cells, and the main hall, an unadorned timber building with wooden benches lined up in rows before a platform, is reminiscent of a prayer hall. Occasionally the place is host to groups of PLA soldiers, who start their tour by marching into the courtyard, unfolding collapsible chairs, and listening to a lecture, but most of the time the compound is deserted. There isn't even a souvenir stall, though the attendants do sell a single book in Chinese with plenty of photos from the period (¥10).

Standing on a hill in the southeast corner of town, on the east bank of the river, the Ming-dynasty **Yan'an Pagoda** (daily 8am–5pm; ¥10) is sometimes used as a symbol of the Communist Party. The route here is circuitous, as you have to double back a long way on the leg of the "Y" to find a bridge to cross the river. It's an extra ¥3 to ascend the nine flights of narrow stairs. High above the town, the pagoda commands an impressive view of its angular planes and the ragged hills, pocked with caves, beyond.

THE COMMUNISTS IN YAN'AN

The arrival of the Communists in October 1935 marked the end of the **Long March**, an astonishing and now semi-mythical journey in which eighty thousand men, women and children of the Red Army fled their mountain bases in Jiangxi Province to escape encirclement and annihilation at the hands of the Nationalists and in a year marched 9500km across some of the world's most inhospitable terrain (see box, p.492).

When Mao finally arrived in Yan'an there were only about five thousand still with him, but here they met up with northern Communists who had already established a soviet and gradually stragglers, and those who had been sent on missions to other parts, arrived to swell their numbers. The **Yan'an soviet** came to control a vast tract of the surrounding country, with its own economy and banknotes to back the new political system. Soldiers in China usually lived parasitically off the peasants unfortunate enough to be in their way; but Mao's troops, trained to see themselves as defenders of the people, were under orders to be polite and courteous and pay for their supplies. Mao said victory would only be achieved "with guns and millet", that is, by co-opting peasants to the cause, and in the following years the Communists instigated land reform and organized peasants into co-operatives, while conducting a campaign of guerrilla warfare against the Japanese. **Mao** wrote some of his most important essays here, including much that was later included in the Little Red Book. As well as most of the major political personalities of Communist China, a number of distinguished foreigners came here too, including Edgar Snow, whose book *Red Star Over China* includes descriptions of life in Yan'an, and Norman Bethune, the Canadian surgeon who died in the service of the Red Army (see p.162).

Outside, tourists can pose for photographs dressed up in the blue and grey military uniforms of the first Communist soldiers, complete with red armband and wooden gun.

From the hill it's possible to see other revolutionary sites dotted around town – look for the red flags – but they're mainly bridges and the sites of buildings since disappeared. A more diverting excursion can be had outside the town, tramping round the surrounding hills and cave villages.

Practicalities

Yan'an lies on a branch rail line that begins in Xi'an and winds around the mountainous terrain of northern Shaanxi, a stark, beautiful landscape of raw earth with few touches of colour, just the the odd red flag flying above villages. It's a view which you'll have plenty of time to appreciate as the ponderous **steam train** takes ten hours to get here. The **train station** is in the far south of town, a long way from anything interesting. Bus #1 goes from the station, up the east fork of Yan'an's Y-shape; bus #2 travels up the west fork, past the *Yan'an Binguan* and the museum. A few taxis, with a ¥10 minimum fare, also cruise the streets. Long-distance **buses**, which take just as long as the train but are less comfortable, arrive at the **bus station**, about 1km east of the town centre. A service from Linfen in Shanxi and Yulin in the north, close to the border with Inner Mongolia, also arrives here.

Accommodation is available at the *Yan'an Binguan* on Yan'an Lu (☎2113122; ③–⑥), in the centre of town just south of the river's fork, whose uncompromising facade belies a cosy interior. It's on the river's western bank, a short walk south of the bridge. A little persuasion may be required to get the receptionist to admit to the existence of the cheap rooms clearly marked on the board behind her. Other hotels around town may take foreigners; business has been bad of late. There's a fairly useless branch of *CITS* in the courtyard of the *Yan'an Binguan*, on the right as you go in. Forget about shopping or nightlife, even **eating** out presents problems if you want anything more sophisticated than a bowl of noodles. Your best bet is probably the **restaurant** in the *Yan'an Binguan*.

There are two daily **steam trains** to Xi'an, one in the morning, one in the evening. Hard sleeper tickets are sold only from the first window of the station ticket office (daily 6–7am, 3.30–5pm & 8–9.30pm). Big noses attract an inordinate amount of attention in the cavernous train waiting room, and station police, anxious to prevent a disturbance, have been known to guard foreigners, shooing away the curious but friendly locals. There are long-distance **buses** to destinations in Inner Mongolia (a rough ride), and one bus daily to Hukou Falls (see p.225), a ten-hour trip.

Luoyang and around

LUOYANG, in the middle reaches of the Yellow River valley, has two sides. There is industrial Luoyang – established in the 1950s, drab and of little interest except in April when visitors flock to see the peony blossom – and there is the ancient "City of Nine Capitals", occupied from Neolithic times through to 937 AD and now relegated to a few sites on the fringe of the modern city. Though ancient Luoyang holds an important place in Chinese history, with many finds in the museum to prove it, there is little to be seen on the ground of the once glorious palaces and temples, and the city bears a resemblance to other provincial cities such as Zhengzhou and Shijiazhuang. Beyond the city limits, though, you can still see the **Longmen Caves**, whose Buddhist carvings provide one of the most important artistic sites in China, and the venerable Baima and Guanlin **temples**. The city also makes a good base for an exploration of **Song Shan**, the holy mountain, and the **Shaolin Si**, home of martial arts.

LUOYANG AND AROUND

Luoyang	洛阳	*luòyáng*
Arts and Crafts Building	工艺美术楼	*gōngyì měishùlóu*
Luoyang Museum	洛阳博物馆	*luòyáng bówùguǎn*
Wancheng Park	王成公园	*wángchéng gōngyuán*

ACCOMMODATION

Aviation	航空大厦	*hángkōng dàshà*
Friendship	友谊宾馆	*yǒuyì bīnguǎn*
Luoyang Lushe	洛阳旅社	*luòyáng lǔshè*
Luoyang Ying Binguan	洛阳迎宾馆	*luòyáng yíng bīnguǎn*
Peony	牡丹大酒店	*mǔdān dàjiǔdiàn*
Tianxiang	天香旅社	*tiānxiāng lǔshè*
Xuangong	旋宫大厦	*xuángōng dàshà*

RESTAURANTS

HM	弘棉大酒店	*hóngmián dàjiǔdiàn*
Guangzhou	广州酒家	*guǎngzhōu jiǔjiā*
Luoyang	洛阳酒店	*luòyáng jiǔdiàn*

AROUND LUOYANG

Baima Si	白马寺	*báimǎ sì*
Cloud Reaching Pagoda	齐云塔	*qíyún tǎ*
Guanlin Miao	关林庙	*guānlín miào*
Longmen Caves	龙门石窟	*lóngmén shíkū*

Some history

Much of Luoyang's history was revealed only by the rebuilding of the city in the 1950s and by the terracing and irrigation work in the surrounding countryside, which brought to light some sixty sites and a thousand tombs. By 5000 BC this area was already heavily populated – the Neolithic site discovered to the west of Luoyang in 1921, at **Yangshao**, proved to be just one of a whole series of sites along the Yellow River plain. Luoyang's site is a fine strategic one, guarded on three sides by hills and cut across by four rivers. Bronze Age Shang-dynasty remains have been found here, but the first real development seems to have been a walled city built by the Zhou around 1000 BC. When their rulers were forced to retreat from Xi'an in 771 BC, this became their capital – tradition claims that Confucius studied here and that Lao Zi was keeper of the archives. Under the Qin emperor and his early Han successors, Xi'an regained its title but later Han emperors (between 25 and 220 AD) were once again obliged to withdraw to **Luoyang**, building their city east of the Baima Si.

Luoyang's trade and communications with the West along the **Silk Road** grew rapidly: Buddhism was introduced here in 68 AD; the Imperial College was founded with thirty thousand students and a great library; Cai Lun invented paper; and Zhang Hen, the imperial astronomer, invented the armillary sphere, demonstrating that the Chinese knew the movement of the heavens long before the West.

For a time, in the turbulent years after the fall of the Han, Luoyang remained the **capital of a series of dynasties** and the centre of Chinese culture. Here the poet Zuo Si wrote a series of poems, *The Three Capitals*, which were so popular that people copying them caused a paper famine.

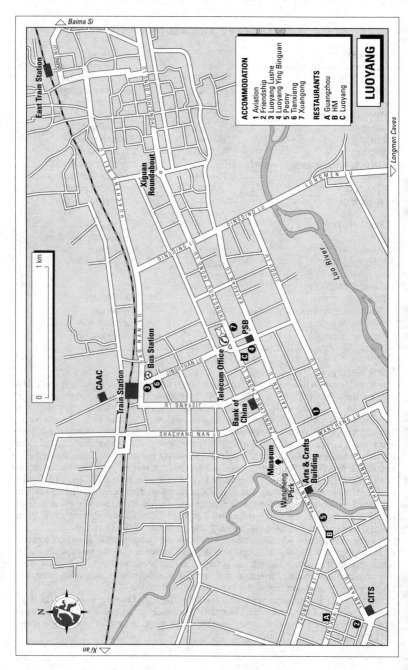

LUOYANG

ACCOMMODATION
1 Aviation
2 Friendship
3 Luoyang Lushe
4 Luoyang Ying Binguan
5 Peony
6 Tianxiang
7 Xuangong

RESTAURANTS
A Guangzhou
B HM
C Luoyang

The **telephone code** for Luoyang is ☎0379

When the northern **Toba Wei** invaders decided to move their capital from Datong into the Chinese heartland, Luoyang was the site they chose, probably because it was believed to be the centre of the world. In 493, at the command of Emperor Xiao Wendi, they moved almost overnight to Luoyang and constructed a new capital. In thirty years it had grown to a city of half a million people, with markets selling goods from all over Asia and with more than 1400 Buddhist temples. The great carvings at **Longmen** were begun in this period. In 543, at the command of another Wei emperor and even more suddenly than it had been taken up, Luoyang was again **abandoned** and its people forced to move to **Yeh**. An account written thirteen years later described the city walls collapsed and overgrown with artemisia, the streets full of thorn trees, and millet planted between the ceremonial towers of the ruined palace.

Luoyang lay in ruins once more for seventy years until under the **Sui dynasty** it was rebuilt west of the Wei ruins on a grid pattern spreading across both banks of the Luo River. Two million men were conscripted for the work and the new city rapidly became the most important market centre in China, a magnet for foreign traders, with a population of a million, three separate major markets within the walls, over three thousand shops and stalls and around four hundred inns for merchants. To feed the crowds, grain was brought up the Grand Canal from the Yangzi basin and stored in enormous barns: the Hanjia granary, discovered in 1971 west of the old city, held 250,000 tonnes and was proof against damp, mildew, rats and insects. Emperor Yang Di also brought three thousand musicians to live at court and surrounded himself with scholars, scientists and engineers.

Under the **Tang**, Luoyang was only the secondary capital. It's said that in 800 AD Empress Wu Zetian, enraged that the **peonies**, alone among flowers, disobeyed her command to bloom in the snow, banished them from her capital at Chang'an. Many were transplanted to Luoyang where they flourished, and have since become one of the city's most celebrated attractions, the subject of countless poems and cultivation notes. Several times drought forced the court to follow the peonies to Luoyang, where the empress commissioned some of the most important carvings at Longmen.

With the decline of the Tang, Luoyang finally lost its importance for good; the capital moved to **Kaifeng** and gradually the whole balance of the nation shifted south. Luoyang never recovered, and by 1920 there was only a run-down settlement of some twenty thousand people here. The first Five Year Plan earmarked the city for **industrial development**, and its new incarnation has not looked back since. Growth has been rapid ever since the early 1950s, helped by a position astride the east–west rail line and the southern spur to Yichang. Once again Luoyang is a thriving metropolis, if a lot less attractive and more polluted than the city of old.

Orientation, arrival and city transport

Luoyang is spread east–west between the Luo River and the rail line, with the old city in the east, the more modern conurbation of factories and residential blocks in the west. Zhongzhou Zhong Lu is the main thoroughfare, crossing the length of the city. A T–junction is formed at the centre of town where this street meets the main road heading south from the train station, Jinguyuan Lu.

Luoyang **airport**, 20km north of town, is tiny and served by a bus which drops you off at the *CAAC* office behind the train station. The **train station** itself is a busy junction on the line between Xi'an and Zhengzhou, and it's a centre of operations for most visitors as the **bus station** is opposite, tours to the sights leave from the concourse, and the budget hotels are nearby. However, it's situated in the town's northern extremity, a long walk to anywhere exciting or to the prettier parts of town.

The station is the place to pick up most city **bus** connections, with another clutch of routes beginning from the Xiguan roundabout in the east of the city, too far out to be handy for much, although you can get to the Baima Si from here. From the train station, trolleybus #102 and bus #2 go south down Jinguyuan Lu, turning west along Zhongzhou Zhong Lu at the central T–junction; bus #5 from the station takes the eastern fork, passing the Xiguan roundabout. **Taxis**, which can be hailed on the streets, are plentiful, with a ¥5 basic rate.

Accommodation

Basing yourself around the train station is not the bad idea it usually turns out to be in most Chinese cities, as in Luoyang most of the attractions are outside the city anyway, and at least here you're conveniently located for all the transport connections. But if you're staying any length of time, and can afford it, stay in town; it's less noisy and cleaner.

Aviation, junction of Fanglin Lu and Kaixuan Xi Lu (☎3944668). Staff at this nine-storey place wear the most stylish uniforms of any Luoyang hotel, and guests – plenty of pilots and air hostesses – are pretty chic too. The lobby, appropriately, looks like an airport lounge. It's a shame it's in such a shabby area. Take bus #8 from the train station and get off on Wancheng Lu. ⑥.

Friendship, 6 Xiyuan Lu (☎4912780). This pleasant red-brick building with a chocolate-coloured lobby is stylish and rather elegant but perhaps a little far west to be convenient. If you arrive at night you'll see the sleeping staff stretched out across the reception desk in their natty uniforms. ⑦.

Luoyang Lushe (☎338622). A tall white tower opposite the train station with its name on the roof, this is the best budget option. Although it's big, basic and in a noisy place, it's clean inside and staff are pleasant. Try to get a room at the back, out of earshot of the chiming station clock. The cosy four-bed dormitories are a bargain. Dorms ①, rooms ②.

Luoyang Ying Binguan, 6 Renmin Xi Lu (☎335414). A well-located new place, one of the best mid-range options, with its own air ticket office. ⑥.

Peony, 15 Zhongzhou Zhong Lu (☎4913699, fax 4913668). The most upmarket place in town, charging up to ¥1000 for the most luxurious rooms. All mod cons provided and there's a *CITS* office and a good, though expensive, restaurant. ⑧–⑨.

Tianxiang, Jinguyuan Lu (☎337846). Just around the corner from the train station, this seedy place has creaky beds, no carpets, and it's not even that cheap. ④.

Xuangong, 275 Zhongzhou Zhong Lu (☎3931940). Well-located in the thick of things, this is a comfortable hotel with a good restaurant attached; you can't miss it at night when the front door is lit up by neon arches. ⑦.

The City

There's nothing much to detain you in Luoyang itself; but if you've got time between trips to the attractions outside town, there are a few nice restaurants, a museum and the old city to poke around in.

The main downtown area is around the T-junction where Jinguyuan Lu meets Zhongzhou Zhong Lu. Here you'll find the *Department Store*, six storeys of shopping with a café in the basement, next door to the *Xuangong Hotel*. Head west down tree-lined Zhongzhou Zhong Lu for a kilometre, or take bus #9, #2, or trolleybus #102, and you come to **Wancheng Park** (daily 8am–6pm; ¥4), at its best in April when it's full of **peonies**. Luoyang's peonies have been intensively cultivated and collected so that the city now boasts over 150 varieties, which have found their way on to every available patch or scrap of ground – a splendid sight. The peony motif is also everywhere in the city, from trellises to rubbish bins.

Out of season, Wancheng is just another park, with a melancholy zoo, and the river dries up and smells in winter. However, **excavations** undertaken in the park have revealed much of the Zhou capital of 771 BC including walls, palaces, temples and a marketplace, though none of this can be seen by the public. Across the suspension bridge in the northwest corner of the park there are also two **Han tombs**, closed at the time of writing, apparently with some good early murals. Otherwise, almost all that has been left of the ancient cities has been gathered into the **museum** (Tues–Sun 8am–noon & 2–5.30pm; ¥12), just east of the park. There are five halls arranged chronologically, which at first, with no English captions and a surfeit of the bronze vessels that seem to characterize all provincial museum collections, look uninspiring, but get much better as you go on. Look in Hall 2 for the **Shang bronzes** and an endearing **jade tiger** from the Zhou; Hall 4 has some Indian-influenced **Wei statuary**, as well as a model farm from a Han tomb with a sow and her row of piglets; and in Hall 5 you'll find some comical **Tang polychrome figures**, including camels and a travelling merchant keeling over under the weight of his pack. Upstairs is an excellent new hall, in which well-presented relics, copiously captioned in English, are grouped by category – bronze, silver and jade – rather than by dynasty, an unusual system that here works very well, allowing direct comparisons across the centuries. As usual, the Tang wins hands down in the **pottery** section with their expressive camels and a hooknosed, pointy-chinned foreigner, and in **gold and silver**, where their ornate decorative objects show the influence of Persian and Roman styles. There are some strange little animal sculptures in the jade section which belong to the Xia and Shang, and in the **bronze** section, particularly extensive as the area around Luoyang entered the Bronze Age before the rest of China, a horse's harness from a Shang chariot.

Turn off the glossy main boulevards and you'll find the rutted streets lined with piles of rubble and stacks of identical brown apartment buildings, a marked contrast that illustrates how rapid and uneven the city's development has been. Head east from the train station along Dao Nan Lu and you pass a huge wholesale produce market selling apples, oranges and nuts, which enlivens a gritty street whose other main feature seems to be coke factories. South of here, and east of Xiguan roundabout, the alleyways of the **old city** are a rewarding area to browse around, preferably by bicycle as it's fairly spread out. The best alleys are those south of Zhongzhou Dong Lu, where whitewashed, half-timbered buildings house small family shops whose wares include seals (engraved with your name while you wait), tea and art materials. There's a **pagoda** in the far south of this area, sunk deep in the web of alleys; it's marked on all the Chinese maps of the area and it's fun trying to find it, though don't be disappointed if you fail, as it's not very exciting.

Eating and drinking

There are a few dim, poky **noodle places** around the train station – the best is the one just on the left as you come out of the *Tianxiang Hotel*, a backpacker restaurant in embryo whose staff are trying hard to learn English. Also opposite the station you'll find plenty of snacks – oranges, apples and nuts – sold from wooden stalls that set up every evening, near the long line of shoe shiners. The city's scattering of **restaurants** is worth sampling though.

HM, Zhongzhou Zhong Lu. A new place opposite the intersection with Zhongzhou Xi Lu and highly recommended though it's not cheap, around ¥50 per person. There's an intimate atmosphere, small tables and an English menu is provided. A good range of dishes is on offer, but the highlight for homesick palates must be the soufflé and the delicious banana rolls.

Guangzhou, Jinghua Lu. Out of the way but worth the trip, with an English sign so it's easy to spot. Don't walk into the grotty canteen on the lower floor, the real restaurant, serving Cantonese food, is upstairs. It's boisterous and lively, full of diners playing the game that involves shouting numbers at each other – the one who shouts loudest isn't necessarily the winner, though it's easy to come away with that impression. No English is spoken and there's no English menu, but the staff are friendly (and curious). They'll do half portions for half price, so if there's only one or two of you, you can still have four or five dishes, which should come to less than ¥100.

Luoyang, Zhongzhou Zhong Lu, near the intersection with Jinguyuan Lu. A quiet place , especially if you get one of the snug booths at the side, where you can eat cheap, basic dishes with "terilized choslicks".

Xuangong, Zhongzhou Zhong Lu, next to the *Xuangong Hotel*. Though they only have big tables for serving large groups, this place has a friendly atmosphere and staff are eager to please. They even give you a form after your meal asking you to rate your dining experience and suggest how it could have been improved. The English menu offers standard dishes at reasonable prices. Arrive early as this place is very popular.

Listings

Airlines The main *CAAC* office is on Dao Bei Lu (8am–6pm; ☎3335301), 200m west of the station. You can also buy air tickets from the *CITS* office in the *Peony Hotel* and a *CAAC* office in the *Luoyang Ying Binguan*.

Banks and exchange The *Bank of China* is tucked slightly back from the street at 268 Yan'an Lu (Mon–Fri 8am–5pm, Sat 8am–noon). The much more high profile *Industrial Bank*, at the corner of Zhongzhou Xi Lu and Zhongzhou Zhong Lu (Mon–Sat 8am–5pm), will only change cash.

Bike rental A woman outside the *Luoyang Lushe,* opposite the station, has a few bicycles for rent for ¥5 a day (8am–6pm).

Bookshops The *Xinhua Bookshop*, next door to the *Xuangong Hotel* on the western side of Zhongzhou Zhong Lu, has a few novels in English and a good selection of art books.

Buses Luoyang's long-distance bus station is next to the train station on the eastern side of Jinguyuan Lu. Tickets can be bought from the office (daily 8am–5pm) or on the bus itself. Minibuses to local tourist destinations leave from the concourse outside the train station, but be wary of unscrupulous private operators.

Post office The post office is tucked on the north side of Zhongzhou Zhong Lu, near the junction with Jinguyuan Lu (Mon–Sat 8am–6pm).

PSB 1 Kaixuan Xi Lu (Mon–Sat 8am–noon & 2–6pm), with gory pictures of traffic accidents displayed outside.

Shopping Locally made tricolour ceramics (copies of Tang sculptures) are on sale at the *Arts and Crafts Building* at 90 Yan'an Lu. For domestic goods try the *Department Store* next to the *Xuangong Hotel* on Zhongzhou Zhong Lu.

Telephones There's a 24hr telecom building around the corner from the post office, on Jinguyuan Lu.

Travel agents The new *CITS* office, not open at the time of writing, is on the second floor of a white building behind the new hotel being constructed on the corner of Nanchang and Xiyuan Lu. It's not easy to find. Another more accessible office is in the *Peony Hotel* (daily 8am–6.30pm; ☎4913699). They can arrange day tours to sites in the area and will buy train tickets.

Around Luoyang

The **Longmen Caves** and the **Guanlin Miao** and **Baima Si** can all be visited in a packed single day's excursion from Luoyang by **public transport**, if you don't have the time to explore a little more leisurely. Additionally, the Baima Si is on the way to **Song Shan** and the **Shaolin Si** (see p.267), and tours usually stop here on the way back. If you're travelling independently to Song Shan, it makes sense to break the four-hour trip at the temple. All the sights are also served by private **tourist minibuses** which run from outside the station. If you have limited time, the Buddhist carvings at Longmen are the place to head first: however little you know about Buddhism or about sculpture you cannot help but be impressed by the scale and complexity of the work here and by the extraordinary contrast between the power of the giant figures and the intricate delicacy of the miniatures.

The Longmen Caves

You can get to the **Longmen Caves** (daily 8am–6pm), situated 8km south of town, on bus #81, which leaves from a terminus at the north end of Jinguyuan Lu; there's also a stop en route just west of the *Xuangong Hotel*. Bus #60 goes to the caves from a stop outside the *Friendship Hotel*, and bus #53 from Xiguan roundabout. At the ticket office they will try to sell you two **tickets**, one for the caves themselves (¥25) and another for a tacky display of dioramas at the end (¥10), which isn't worth it. The caves are very busy in the summer, overrun with tourists posing for photos in the lotus position in the empty niches and clambering over the sculptures. The best times to visit are in the early morning, at lunchtime or in the evening.

The **caves** are shallow recesses in the cliffs south of Luoyang where the Yi River cuts through a cleft called the Dragon Gate. Legend has it that this was formed when the Great Yu, Tamer of Floods, split the mountain to release an imprisoned dragon which was causing havoc. Man has since added 1350 caves, 750 niches and 40 pagodas containing 97,306 statues carved out of the sheer **limestone cliffs** bordering the river. From a distance the multi-veined cliffs, decked with green cypresses, look like a vast slab of gorgonzola cheese, and close up the different rocks provide some spectacular effects, giving an extra dimension of expressiveness to the figures. Most of the carvings, which stretch over some 800m, are on the west bank.

The **Toba Wei** began the work in 495 AD, when they moved their capital to Luoyang from Datong, where they had carved the Yungang Caves (see p.207). At Longmen they adapted their art to the different requirements of a harder, limestone surface. Three sets of caves, **Guyang**, **Bingyang** and **Lianhua**, date from this early period. Work continued for five hundred years and reached a second peak under the **Tang**, particularly under Empress Wu Zetian, a devoted adherent of Buddhism. The carvings were commissioned by emperors, the imperial family, other wealthy families wanting to buy good fortune, generals hoping for victory and religious groups. You can see a clear progression from the early style brought from Datong, of simple, rounded, formally modelled holy figures, to the complex and elaborate, but more linear, Tang carvings, which include women and court characters. In general the Buddhas are simple, but the sculptors were able to let their imagination go and show off their mastery with the attendant figures and the decorative flourishes around the edge of the caves. You can also see traces of vandalism and looting (lots of missing heads and hands) which began with the anti-Buddhist movement in the ninth century, continuing through souvenir-hunting Westerners in the nineteenth and twentieth centuries and finally (surprisingly muted) attacks by Red Guards during the Cultural Revolution.

Starting from the entrance at the northern end and moving south down the group, the following are the largest and most important carvings. They are not labelled in English but stand out due to their size. The three **Bingyang** caves are early; the central one, commissioned by Emperor Xuan Wu to honour his parents, has an inscription recording that 802,336 men worked from 500 to 523 AD to complete it. The eleven statues of Buddha inside show northern characteristics – long features, thin faces, splayed fishtail robes – and traces of Greek influence. The side caves, completed under the Tang, are more natural and voluptuous, carved in high relief. **Wanfo** (Cave of Ten Thousand Buddhas), just south of here, was built in 680 by Gao Zong and his empress Wu Zetian, and has fifteen thousand Buddhas carved in tiny niches, each one different and the smallest less than 2cm high. **Lianhua** (Lotus Flower Cave) is another early one, dating from 527, and named after the beautifully carved lotus in its roof. **Fengxian** (Ancestor Worshipping Cave) is the largest and most splendid of all. Made in 672 for Empress Wu Zetian, it has an overwhelming seated figure of Vairocana Buddha, 17m high with two-metre-long ears. On his left a Bodhisattva wears a crown and pearls and a divine general grinds a malevolent spirit under foot. This is the highest development of Tang carving and worth studying carefully. **Medical Prescription Cave**, built in 575, details several hundred cures for everything from madness to the common cold. **Guiyang** is the earliest of all, begun in 495. Here you can still see traces of the vivid paintwork which originally gave life to these carvings. There's a central Buddha and nineteen of the "Twenty Pieces" which are important examples of ancient calligraphy.

From the end of the west bank you can cross the bridge to the east bank, for a good view of the caves peppering the opposite bank like rabbit warrens. Up the hill is the **Tomb of Bai Juyi**, the famous Tang poet, who spent his last years in Luoyang as the Retired Scholar of the Fragrant Hill.

The Guanlin Miao

Buses to the Longmen Caves pass through the town of **GUANLIN**, 7km south of the city and the temple here makes a convenient stop on the way to or from the caves. From Luoyang, don't get off at the main stop in the centre of town, but go to the next stop along, at the end of the red crenellated wall on the east side of the road. The temple is at the end of Guanlin Nan Lu, which leads east off from the main road, by this bus stop.

The quiet, pretty temple (daily 8am–5pm; ¥10) is dedicated to **Guan Yu**, a hero of the Three Kingdoms period (see box, p.432) and loyal general of Liu Bei, King of Shu. He was defeated and executed by the King of Wu who sent his head to Cao Cao, King of Wei, hoping in this way to divert on to the Wei any revenge that might be coming. Cao Cao neatly sidestepped this grisly game of pass the parcel by burying the head with honour in a tomb behind the temple.

Despite its military theme, this temple is strikingly beautiful; the elegant Ming buildings are highly carved and richly decorated. Especially fine are the carved stone lionesses lining the path to the Main Hall. Each has a different expression and a different cub, some riding on their mother's back, some hiding coyly behind her paws. In the first hall, look carefully at the eaves for rather comical images of Guan Yu fighting – he's the one on the red horse – and leading an army engaged in sacking a city engulfed by carved wooden flames. Inside stands a seven-metre-high statue of the general, resplendent in technicolour ceremonial robes with a curtain of beads hanging from his hat. More images of the general are in the second and third halls, whose decoration includes frescoes of warriors jousting and men playing Go. In side halls are exhibitions of art and some fine carved tombstones and massive stone animals – the sheep are excellent, the lions almost unrecognizable. It's a quiet place, well restored and brilliantly coloured against the grey and green background of stone and the many twisted cypresses.

The Baima Si

You can get to the **Baima Si** (White Horse Temple), 12km east of Luoyang, on bus #56 from the Xiguan roundabout or on a minibus from outside the station. It's on the way to Song Shan and the Shaolin Si, but this leafy place, attractive for its ancient buildings and devotional atmosphere, is the most pleasant temple in the area, worth investigating in its own right on a day trip from Luoyang.

Founded in 68 AD, the Baima Si has some claim to be the first Buddhist temple in China. Legend says that the Emperor Mingdi of the Eastern Han dreamed of a golden figure with the sun and moon behind its head. Two monks sent to search for the origin of the dream reached India and returned riding white horses with two Indian monks in tow, and a bundle of sutras. This temple was built to honour them.

Its layout bears out the legend as there are two stone horses, one on either side of the entrance, and the tombs of the two monks, earthen mounds ringed by round stone walls, lie in the first courtyard. Once inside the temple, out of earshot of the highway and the pushy souvenir sellers with their glazed pottery, this is a placid place, its silence only pricked by the sound of gongs or the tapping of stonemasons carving out a stele. Beyond the Hall of Celestial Guardians, the **Main Hall** holds a statue of Sakyamuni flanked by the figures of Manjusri and Samantabhadra. Near the Great Altar is an ancient bell weighing over a tonne; in the days when there were over ten thousand Tang monks here it was struck in time with the chanting. The inscription reads: "The sound of the Bell resounds in Buddha's temple causing the ghosts in Hell to tremble with fear." Behind the Main Hall is the Cool Terrace where, it is said, the original sutras were translated. Offerings of fruit on the altars, multi-coloured cloths hanging from the ceilings, and lighted candles in bowls floating in basins of water, as well as the heady gusts of incense issuing from the burners in the courtyards, indicate that, unlike other temples in the area, this is the genuine article. This is also suggested by the presence of flocks of finches in the well-maintained gardens at the side of the halls – real temples, with their population of pacifists, are a haven to birdlife.

Home to a thriving community of monks, including a few Westerners, the Baima Si is primarily a place of worship rather than a tourist attraction, and over-inquisitive visitors are tactfully but firmly pointed in the right direction. The monks' daily midday perambulation around the Great Altar may have a timeless look to it, but contemporary life intrudes here in more than just the presence of tourists; the abbot has a TV in his quarters to remain in touch with the political swings of an unsympathetic regime, and all the monks must carry red identity cards, a bit like a student card.

Southwest of the temple, in a separate compound where the monks live, is the **Ciyou Ta** (Cloud Reaching Pagoda), built in the tenth century and restored several times since. Visitors are not allowed to enter but this doesn't stop the tacky park (¥10), in between the temple and the quarters, from putting a large picture of the pagoda outside its ticket office as a lure to unsuspecting visitors.

Song Shan

The seventy peaks of the **Song Shan** range stretch over 64km across Dengfeng County, midway between Luoyang and Zhengzhou. When the Zhou ruler Ping moved his capital to Luoyang in 771 BC, it was known as Zhong Yue, Central Peak – being at the axis of the five **sacred Taoist mountains**, with Hua Shan to the west, Tai Shan to the east, Heng Shan to the south and another Heng Shan to the north. The mountains, thickly clad with trees, rise from narrow, steep-sided rocky valleys and appear impressively precipitous, though with the highest peak, Junji, at just 1500m, they're not actually very lofty. When the summits emerge from a swirling sea of cloud, though, and the slopes are clad in their brilliant autumn colours, they can certainly look the part.

You can visit Song Shan on a **day trip** from either **Luoyang or Zhengzhou**. Tours leave from outside both cities' train stations early every morning and take in at least the **Shaolin Si** (see p.267) and the **Zhongyue Miao** (see p.268), though you won't see much of the mountain itself. Tours from Luoyang usually take in the Baima Si (see p.264) on the way back too. From **Dengfeng**, a town at the centre of the range, there is plenty to occupy two or three days' walking, with numerous paths meandering around the valleys, passing temples, pagodas and guard towers, and some wonderful views. Unlike at other holy mountains, there is no single set path, and as the slopes are not steep and the undergrowth is sparse you can set out in any direction you like. The

SONG SHAN		
Song Shan	嵩山	*sōngshān*
Observatory	观星台	*guānxīng tái*
Shaolin Si	少林寺	*shàolín sì*
Songyang Academy	嵩阳书院	*sōngyáng shūyuàn*
Songyue Temple Pagoda	嵩岳寺塔	*sōngyuè sì tǎ*
Zhongyue Miao	中岳庙	*zhōngyuè miào*
Dengfeng	登封	*dēngfēng*
Songshan Binguan	嵩山宾馆	*sōngshān bīnguǎn*

sights are far from one another so you won't be able to do more than one or two a day to count on getting back to Dengfeng before nightfall. **Maps** of the area are included on the back of maps of Zhengzhou (see p.269), or can be bought from Dengfeng hotels.

Dengfeng and around

The ideal base for exploring the area is **DENGFENG**, a little town stretched along a valley at the heart of the Song Shan range, 13km from Shaolin and 4km from the Zhongyue Miao. There's nothing much here; it's basically one main street, unusual for having the name and function of every shop written neatly in English under the Chinese characters. The *Dengfeng Legendary Kungfu Weapon Shop* sells curvy swords, pointed sticks, throwing stars and the like, cheaper than those at the Shaolin Si.

Dengfeng is not on the rail line. **Buses** from Luoyang and Zhengzhou both take about three hours and arrive at the bus station at the western end of the main street, from where there are local buses to the temples. The only **hotel** foreigners can stay in is the simple but clean *Songshan Binguan* (☎2872755; ②), 1km east of the bus station, slightly recessed from the road.

The Songyang Academy, Songyue Pagoda and Gaocheng Observatory

Three kilometres north of Dengfeng and a good focus for a walk, the **Songyang Academy** consists of a couple of lecture halls, a library and a memorial hall, founded in 484 AD, which was one of the great centres of learning under the Song. In the courtyard are two enormous

---

SHAOLIN KUNG FU

Kung fu was first developed at the Shaolin Si as a form of gymnastics to counterbalance the immobility of meditation. The monks studied the movement of animals and copied them – the way snakes crawled, tigers leapt and mantises danced. As the temple was isolated in fairly lawless territory, it was often prey to bandits, and gradually the monks turned their exercises into a form of **self-defence**.

The monks owed their strength to rigorous **discipline**. From childhood, monks trained five hours a day, every day. To strengthen their hands, they thrust them into sacks of beans, over and over; when they were older, into bags of sand. To strengthen their fists, monks punched a thousand sheets of paper glued to a wall; over the years the paper wore out and the young monks punched brick. To strengthen their legs, they ran around the courtyard with bags of sand tied to their knees, and to strengthen their heads, they hit them with bricks. In the Hall of Wen Shu in the temple, the depressions in the stone floor are caused by monks standing in the same place and practising their stance kicks, year after year.

Only after twenty years of such exercises could someone consider themselves a fully fledged Shaolin monk, by which time they were able to perform **incredible feats**, examples of which you can see illustrated in the murals at the temple and in photographs of contemporary *wushu* masters on sale in the souvenir shops. Apart from such commonplaces as breaking concrete slabs with their fists and iron bars with their heads, the Shaolin monks of old could balance on one finger, take a sledgehammer blow to the chest, and hang from a tree by the neck. Contemporary *wushu* masters are as proficient. Just as impressive to watch, though, are the **katas**, a series of movements of balletic grace incorporating kicks and punches, in which the art's origins in animal movements can be clearly seen. Most striking are the exercises called "Drunken Monkey", performed with a pole, and "Praying Mantis", performed almost entirely on one leg.

However, the monks were not just fighters and their art was also intended as a technique to reach the goal of inner peace, with monks spending as many hours **meditating and praying** as practising. They obeyed a moral code, which included the stricture that only fighting in self-defence was acceptable, and killing your opponent was to be avoided

cypresses said to be three thousand years old, as well as a stele from the Tang dynasty. Many famous scholars from history lectured here, including Sima Guang and Cheng Hao. The path beyond climbs to Junji Peak or branches off to the **Songyue Temple Pagoda**, 5km north of Dengfeng. Built at the beginning of the sixth century by the Northern Wei, this 45-metre structure is the oldest pagoda in China, rare for having twelve sides.

Just within a day's walk of Dengfeng, the **Gaocheng Observatory** is 7km southeast of the town. Built in 1279 and designed by Gui Shou Jing to calculate the solstices, it's a fascinating, sculptural-looking building, an almost pyramidical tower with a long straight wall marked with measurements, running along the ground behind it, which would originally have been used to calculate the solstices.

Shaolin Si

Venerable and deadly monks are today in pretty short short supply at the **Shaolin Si** (daily 8am–6pm; ¥33), the famous home of **kung fu** (*wushu*), and you're more likely to meet tour groups of the voluble and doddery. However, this tourist black spot is still interesting as the prime pilgrimage site of the cult of kung fu that has swept contemporary China. From Zhengzhou or Luoyang it's easy to get here as tourist **minibuses** (¥10) leave regularly, covering the trip in about three hours from both directions.

The approach to the temple, through bleak, mountainous countryside, does nothing to prepare you for the crowds of visitors when you arrive, swarming along the kilometre-long road, jammed with food stalls and souvenir shops, that leads from the car park to the temple itself. Most of the shops are full of weapons, everything from throw-

if possible. These rules became a little more flexible over the centuries as emperors and peasants alike sought their help in battles, and the Shaolin monks became legendary figures for their interventions on the side of righteousness. Well-known Chinese tales include the story of the monk who fought a thousand enemies with a stick while pretending to be drunk, and the tale of the cook who kept a horde at bay with a poker at the temple gates while the other monks continued their meditations undisturbed.

The monks were at the height of their power in the Tang dynasty, though they were still a force to be reckoned with in the Ming, when **weapons** were added to their discipline. The monks did not put up much of a fight in the Cultural Revolution, though, when Red Guards sacked the temple and arrested many of them; others escaped to become peasants. Though their art lived on abroad in **judo, karate and kendo**, all of which acknowledge Shaolin kung fu as their original form, the teaching of kung fu in China was **banned** for many years until the 1980s, when, partly as a result of the enormously popular film *Shaolin Temple*, there was a **resurgence of the art**. The old masters were allowed to teach again and the government realized that the temple was better exploited as a tourist resource than left to rot.

Evidence of the **popularity of kung fu** in China today can be seen not just at the tourist circus of the Shaolin Si, but in any cinema, where **kung fu films**, often concerning the exploits of Shaolin monks, make up a large proportion of the entertainment on offer. Many young Chinese today want to study kung fu, and to meet demand numerous **schools** have opened around the temple. Few of them want to be monks, though – the dream of many is to be a movie star. It's possible to study at the Shaolin Si itself, but such a distinction does not come cheap; one day of training costs ¥300, the price for a month at most schools. Though they are undoubtedly skilled fighters, the present residents of the temple cannot be called genuine Shaolin monks as the religious, spiritual side of their discipline is absent. Indeed, the present abbot of the monastery has a reputation for aggression which seems entirely at odds with the Shaolin way. Genuine Shaolin monks do still exist, however, but they keep a low profile; the last place you will find one is in the Shaolin Si.

ing stars to cattle prods, or tracksuits. Unfortunately, you can't buy the blue tracksuit tops you see worn by the students from the fourteen *wushu* schools in the area, which say "Shaolin Monastery" in English and Chinese on the back. You'll forget any plans to steal one when you see them practising at the side of the road, kicking and punching straw-filled dummies. However, if you don't see any kung fu kicking taking place, there's plenty of evidence of it around in the broken and splintered bark of many of the trees. In September the place is particularly busy, filling up with martial arts enthusiasts from all over the world, who come to attend the international **Wushu Festival**.

The original Shaolin Si was built in 495 AD. Shortly after, according to tradition, **Boddhidarma**, an Indian monk credited with the founding of Zen Buddhism, came to live here, after visiting the emperor in Nanjing, then crossing the Yangzi on a reed. At Shaolin he sat motionless for nine years facing a wall in a state of illumination (the mystic knowledge of the Nothingness of Everything). A tablet in the temple shows him crossing the Yangzi. However, very little remains today of the temple's long history, as it has been burnt down on many occasions. The last time was in 1928, when the warlord Shi Yousan ordered its destruction, so the present complex is fairly newly restored and gaudily repainted, with most of the halls now housing souvenir shops. A few shaven-headed kids wander around and man the shops, and will demonstrate their flexibility for a foreign coin.

The first courtyard of the temple holds **steles**, one of which celebrates, in English, the recent visit of American kung fu masters. The **murals** in two of the halls at the back are one of the few things here that are genuine, and they are delightful, though the monks depicted look more comic than frightening. The pictures in the **White Robe Hall**, an illustration of the Rescue of Emperor Tai Zong by Thirteen Monks, are Qing depictions of typical kung fu moves. In the **Thousand Buddha Hall** is a well-known Ming-dynasty mural of five hundred *arhats*.

Your ticket also gets you into all the other attractions in the area, such as the cinema showing educational films and a hall of modern *arhats*. Most worthwhile is the **Forest of Dagobas**, 200m farther up the hill from the temple, where there are hundreds of stone memorials erected between the ninth and the nineteenth centuries. Up to 10m tall, and with a stepped, recessed top, each one commemorates an individual monk and is inscribed with the names of his disciples. The golden stone structures look particularly impressive against the purple mountain when snow is on the ground, or when the students from the temple are practising here in their orange robes (one of their exercises involves fighting while balanced halfway up the almost vertical sides of the dagobas).

Beyond here the mountain can be ascended by cable car or stone steps, but there is not much to see except the **cave** where Boddhidarma supposedly passed his nine-year vigil. You can save yourself some effort by paying a few yuan to look at it from the road through a high-powered telescope.

Zhongyue Miao

The **Zhongyue Miao** (daily 8am–6pm; ¥4), 4km east of Dengfeng on the route of bus #68, is a huge Taoist temple founded as long ago as 220 BC, and subsequently rebuilt and considerably extended by the Han emperor, Wu Di. It was rebuilt again in the Ming, then again in 1986, when damage caused by Japanese bombs was repaired. Don't be put off by the stuffed tigers and fairground games at the gate, inside it's an attractive place, its broad open spaces and brilliantly coloured buildings standing out against the grey and green of the mountain behind. Though it's a bit shabby in places, this is a working Taoist monastery, staffed by friendly monks in characteristic blue robes, their long hair tied tightly on the top of the head, sticking through a topless blue hat. They live and worship at the rear of the temple, in old barn-like buildings, while the front is given over to stallholders.

A series of gateways, courtyards and pavilions lead to the **Main Hall** where the emperor made sacrifices to the mountain. The Junji Gate, just before the hall, has two great sentries, nearly 4m high, brightly painted and flourishing their weapons. The courtyard houses gnarled old cypresses, some of them approaching the age of the temple itself, and there are four great iron statues dating from the Song on the eastern side. The Main Hall itself has 45 separate compartments with red walls and orange tiles, and a well-preserved relief carving of dragons on the terrace steps. The **Bedroom Palace** behind is unusual for having a shrine that shows a deity lying in bed. Other deities, whose blue skin, spiky red hair and eyebrows to their knees make them look to Western eyes like punks or superheroes, sit in a long line in halls on either side. Contemporary worshippers tend to gravitate to the back of the complex, where you may see people burning what look like little origami hats in the iron burners here, or practising Qigong, exercises centring around control of the breath.

If you go right to the back of the complex, past the monks' quarters on the right, you come to the temple's back exit, where you are charged ¥2 for the privilege of walking 200m up stone steps to a little **pagoda** on a hill behind the temple. From here **paths** take you through pine woods to the craggy peaks of the mountain, a worthwhile afternoon's excursion and a rare chance for solitude; the only other person you are likely to see is the odd shepherd.

Zhengzhou and around

Close to the south bank of the Yellow River, **ZHENGZHOU** lies almost midway between Luoyang in the west and Kaifeng to the east. The walled town that existed here 3500 years ago was probably an early capital of the Shang dynasty. Excavations have revealed

ZHENGZHOU AND AROUND

Zhengzhou	郑州	*zhèngzhōu*
Chenghuang Miao	城隍庙	*chénghuáng miào*
Erqi Pagoda	二七塔	*èrqī tǎ*
ACCOMMODATION		
Asia	亚细亚大酒店	*yàxìyà dàjiǔdiàn*
Erqi	二七宾馆	*èrqī bīnguǎn*
Greenland	格林兰大酒店	*gélínlán dàjiǔdiàn*
Henan	河南宾馆	*hénán bīnguǎn*
Holiday Inn	中州宾馆	*zhōngzhōu bīnguǎn*
International	国际饭店	*guójì fàndiàn*
Zhengzhou	郑州饭店	*zhèngzhōu fàndiàn*
Zhongyuan	中原大厦	*zhōngyuán dàshà*
RESTAURANTS		
Caolaowu	曹老五泡馍馆	*cáolǎowǔ pàomóguǎn*
Muslim	穆斯林饭店	*mùsīlín fànzhuāng*
Shaolin	少林饭店	*shàolín fàndiàn*
AROUND ZHENGZHOU		
Gongxian	巩县	*gǒngxiàn*
Gongxian Grottoes	巩县石窟寺	*gǒngxiàn shí kū sì*
Gongyishi Binguan	巩义市宾馆	*gǒngyìshì bīnguǎn*
Song Tombs	宋陵	*sòng líng*
Yellow River Park	黄河公园	*huánghé gōngyuán*

The **telephone code** for Zhengzhou is ☎0371

bronze foundries, bone-carving workshops and sacrificial altars, though there is little evidence of any history above ground except a stretch of the old city walls. Nowadays Zhengzhou is the capital of Henan Province, though this owes nothing to its past and everything to a position astride the meeting of the north–south (Beijing to Guangzhou) and west–east (Xi'an to Shanghai) rail lines. As probably the most important **rail junction** in China, it has a population of over three million and the industry to match.

Zhengzhou is an archetypal post-1949 boom town, making up in vitality what it lacks in beauty. The modern city is basically a business and transport centre, with no major tourist sights, but at least there's a good range of hotels and restaurants, fortunate as the place is difficult to avoid if you are travelling in central China. From here, Kaifeng and Luoyang are easily accessible, and you can take bus trips to Song Shan (see p.265).

Orientation, arrival, city transport and accommodation

The Erqi Pagoda stands at the heart of the modern city, a roundabout east of the station from which the main roads radiate off. The old city, cut through by the ruins of the old walls, is in the southeast of town.

Zhengzhou **airport** is 3km east of the city and a taxi into the centre should cost ¥15. The **train station**, in the southwestern corner of the city, is fronted by a bustling square dominated by a huge screen that entertains waiting passengers with TV programmes, mostly American, such as compilations of amusing home videos. Contrasted with the scene below – food stalls, migrant workers, families camping out with their luggage – it gives the whole area something of a surreal atmosphere. Most travellers who don't intend spending a lot of time in the city probably won't stray far beyond this area as the cheap hotels, post and telecom offices and **long-distance bus station** are all located around here. It's not grotty but it is noisy. Some buses from western towns including Luoyang arrive at the small **western bus station** in the suburbs of the city; from where bus #24 will get you to the train station.

There are two clusters of **city bus** termini, one just north of the train station, one just south, on either side of the square outside. Bus #2, from the southern side, goes to the Erqi Pagoda, then up Erqi Lu; bus #10, from the northern side, goes up Renmin Lu, then Huayan Lu. **Taxis** are plentiful, and have a ¥6 minimum rate, but they are not allowed to enter the square in front of the station; you can hail them everywhere else. Most have CB radios, so if you understand Chinese you can hear them telling their mates about you. **Maps**, with details of bus routes, are available outside the train station, but these don't have any English on them. Maps with English labels are available from the *International Hotel*.

Accommodation

Zhengzhou has a good range of accommodation to suit all price ranges. If you are just here for a night to pick up a transport connection, the **hotels** around the **train station** are adequate – the area is convenient and clean, but noisy. Otherwise head into town, or up to **Jinshui Lu** if you're not on a tight budget.

Asia, 165 Jiefang Lu (☎6968866, fax 6969877). This efficient hotel, well located by the Erqi Pagoda, is very comfortable and looks more expensive than it is. ⑦.

Erqi, Jiefang Xi Lu (☎6968801). The best budget option, well located if spartan. You can get here on bus #2 from the train station. Dorms ②, rooms ③.

Greenland, 93 Datong Lu (☎6968888). This noisy place gives the impression of trying hard, but it's very worn around the edges with an arctic atmosphere. ⑥.

Henan, 26 Jinshui Lu (☎3945522). Opposite Renmin Park, but very out of the way on the route of bus #2 from the station. ④–⑤.

Holiday Inn (*Zhongzhou Binguan*), 115 Jinshui Lu (☎5950055, fax 5990770). A lobby of cream-coloured marble gives the hotel a palatial look. All mod cons imaginable and prices ranging from US$90 to US$550. ⑨.

International, 114 Jinshui Lu. (☎0086371, fax 5950161). Slick, sleek and modernist with en suite everything. ⑧.

Zhengzhou, 8 Xinglong Jie (☎6966172). On the left as you leave the station. A huge building, rather bare looking, with staff who require persuasion to allow you the privilege of staying in one of their cheap rooms. Dorms ①, rooms ④.

Zhongyuan (☎6966172). This multi-storey warren directly opposite the train station has a very small front door set among the shops selling fruit and bags. There's an enormous stack of budget rooms with an eccentric atmosphere and a wide variety of prices. Huge, cheap doubles come complete with fly swat and spittoon and it's possible to get a single room for as little as ¥20, though it may have a lift shaft passing through it. Dorms ①, rooms ②.

The City

Today Zhengzhou is an almost entirely modern city, rebuilt virtually from scratch after suffering heavily in the war against Japan. Its main streets have the slick look of prosperous Chinese cities, but there is still a little catching up to do – some of the citizens, still dressed in Mao suits, don't look entirely comfortable with the new China, and plenty of the streets, including some small, useful roads in the centre, are narrow, muddy tracks that regularly get blocked by cars. Although there are plenty of modern facilities, the town's few old sights are neglected. Droves of foreigners come here to do business, but no one expects them to go sightseeing.

At the hub of downtown Zhengzhou the **Erqi Pagoda** (daily 8am–5pm; ¥5) is a seven-storey structure built to commemorate those who were killed in a Communist-led strike of rail workers in 1923 that was put down with great savagery by the warlord Wu Pei Fu. As the exhibition of photos inside is badly maintained and has no English captions, the pagoda is best thought of as a landmark. The streets that lead off it are modern, store-lined boulevards, the largest and most interesting being **Erqi Lu** and **Renmin Lu**, which lead north to the east–west **Jinshui Lu**, the most exclusive district. East of the huge and complex roundabout at the junction of Jinshui Lu and Renmin Lu (and a host of smaller streets) is a string of classy restaurants and hotels. Just on the west side of the roundabout, a statue of Mao, whose view of the gleaming, foreign-owned luxury monoliths on the east side is fortunately obscured by a flyover, stands outside the old city museum, now closed. Most taxi drivers will bring you here if you ask to go to the museum and don't specify where it is. The **new museum**, a giant glass pyramid which apparently has a good collection of Shang-dynasty relics, is at the end of Jing Qi Lu, and is due to open in 1997.

The **old city** to the east is cut through by the **Shang city walls**, rough earthen ramparts 10m high, originally built over two thousand years ago, though frequently repaired since. They were made by constructing a wooden frame, filling it with earth, pounding it down, then removing the frame, a technique that is still used in domestic architecture. There is a path along the top, and you can walk for about 3km along the south and east sections; the west section has been largely destroyed by development. The south section is open to the street, and you can scramble up anywhere. You have to descend to cross Nan Dajie, then walk through an alleyway to pick up the path again, and repeat the process at Shangcheng Lu. Planted with trees, the walls are now used by the locals as a short cut and a park, and in the early evening the path is full of courting couples, kids who slide down the steep sides on metal trays, and old men who hang their cagebirds from the trees and sit around fires cooking sweet potatoes. Some peo-

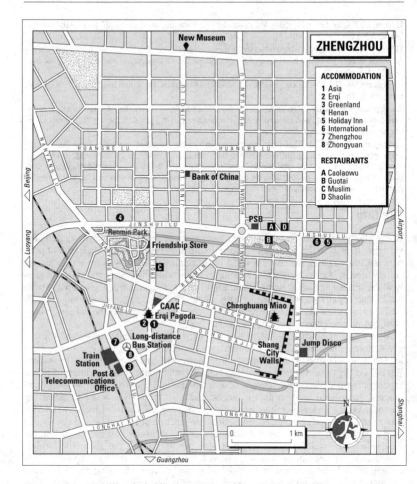

ZHENGZHOU

ACCOMMODATION
1 Asia
2 Erqi
3 Greenland
4 Henan
5 Holiday Inn
6 International
7 Zhengzhou
8 Zhongyuan

RESTAURANTS
A Caolaowu
B Guotai
C Muslim
D Shaolin

ple grow vegetables at the wall's base, others throw their rubbish here. Indeed, the charm of the wall comes from the way it has been incorporated by the inhabitants – it doesn't seem to occur to anyone to treat the walls as a historical monument.

A short walk from the eastern wall, on the north side of Shangcheng Lu, the **Chenghuang Miao** (Temple of the City God; daily 8am–4.30pm; ¥6) is worth a look around. The attendants regard visitors as an interruption in their day's knitting and usually keep the doors closed; you have to shout through the gap to gain admittance. Though the temple has the look of an abandoned warehouse (which it probably is), with tumbled trees and odd boxes lying around and, outrageously, a toilet built right next to the Main Hall, it retains a glimmer of its past glory in the roof decoration. Well-observed images of birds decorate the eaves of the first hall, underneath roof sculptures of dragons and phoenixes. The East Hall now contains a small art gallery; upstairs is one of those exhibitions of African body art that the Chinese seem so fascinated by. The interior of the Main Hall is modern, with a mural on three walls whose style owes much to 1950s socialist realism. In the centre a sculpture of a stern-looking Chenghuang, magisterial defender of city folk, in a judge's costume, sits flanked by two attendants.

Eating, drinking and entertainment

Around the train station there are plenty of small **dumpling canteens**, all much the same, and enormous numbers of shops selling travellers' nibbles – walnuts, oranges and dates – which testify to the great number of people passing through here every day. The *Greenland Hotel*, by the station, has a revolving restaurant on the twenty-eighth floor – go for the view rather than the food, though, and don't trust anything it says in the English menu.

The best food in town is available from the dense concentration of stylish restaurants on Jinshui Lu. Though they look a little intimidating on the outside, prices aren't as expensive as you might expect, due to fierce competition, and a meal for two should be around ¥100 in most. The *Guotai* and *Shaolin* are both good, and the *Caolaowu*, which serves Muslim cuisine, is a little cheaper than the others, and worth checking out at lunchtime for the buffet. The *Muslim Restaurant* on Erqi Lu is a little more upmarket, at around ¥50 per person. For something unusual try the tofu in toffee.

For a fun night out try the *Jump Disco* (daily 8pm–midnight; ¥30), in the southeast of town on the corner of Dong Dajie and Chengdong Lu. The facade, a relief collage of the Arc de Triomphe, the Eiffel Tower and a good sprinkling of neon, sets the tone nicely. The music is a mix of Chinese ballads with a techno back beat, the sort of 1980s pop you thought you'd never hear again, and, of course, the Village People. A mostly student crowd that never seems quite big enough does its best to fill the huge interior with enthusiastic bopping. Dancing big noses can expect to be the star attraction.

Listings

Airlines The main *CAAC* office (Mon–Sat 8am–6pm; ☎6964789) is on the east side of Erqi Lu, just north of the intersection with Renmin Lu. You can also buy tickets from a small office next to the main post office (Mon–Sat 8am–10pm) and from most hotels.

Banks and exchange The *Bank of China* (Mon–Fri 8am–noon & 2–5.30pm) is on Jing Qi Lu. The *International Hotel* will also change travellers' cheques and don't ask you if you are staying at the hotel.

Bike rental A stall next to the *Zhengzhou Hotel*, outside the train station, has bikes for rent for ¥8 a day. Deposit is ¥100.

Bookshops The *Foreign Language Bookstore* is just west of the Erqi Pagoda on Jiefang Lu.

Buses Zhengzhou's long-distance bus station, opposite the train station, has a computerized ticket office (daily 7am–6pm), which seems to cut down on queues, though the waiting room is the usual dirty hall full of anxious humanity on plastic chairs. Tours to Song Shan leave every morning between 8 and 10am from a compound on the south side of the station concourse.

PSB The PSB for visa extensions is at 10 Jinshui Lu (Mon–Fri 8am–11pm). For other matters, there's an office appropriately situated next to the *999 Hotel* at 108 Erqi Lu.

Post office The main post office is next to the station on the south side (Mon–Fri 8am–6.30pm).

Shopping The *Friendship Store* is on Erqi Lu, at the north end of Renmin Park. There are also a few pricey antique stores at the eastern end of Jinshui Lu.

Telephones There's a 24-hr telecom office next door to the main post office.

Trains The train station has a huge two-storey booking office that can be confusing, with over thirty windows to choose from. You can also buy tickets from an advance booking office (Mon–Fri 8am–noon & 1.30–3.30pm) at 131 Erqi Lu.

Travel agents The *CITS* office (Mon–Sat 8am–5pm) is situated in the *International Hotel*.

Around Zhengzhou

The most diverting attractions in the area are covered under Song Shan (see p.265), but a couple of locations within an easy bus ride of the capital deserve a mention. You'd have to be very interested in cave temples to make it to Gongxian, but the shabby Yellow River Park at least provides the opportunity of seeing the river if you haven't already caught sight of it through a bus or train window.

Gongxian and around

The town of **GONGXIAN**, midway between Luoyang and Zhengzhou, on the rail line to Shanghai, is an unremarkable place, though it could be used as a base to explore Song Shan if you can't get a room in Dengfeng. If you do wind up here, there are some Song-dynasty tombs and a few Buddhist cave temples to visit outside the town.

Foreigners are supposed **to stay** at the *Gongyishi Binguan* (④), a dull building with a fancy entranceway, on the main street north and west of the train station, but you may get into a much cheaper Chinese hotel. **Hotpot stalls** set up every evening in the square outside the *Bank of China*, at the main crossroads in the centre of town. The few **taxis** in town congregate outside the train station; hard bargaining is needed to charter one for an afternoon, and you'll get a huge audience while you do so.

The **tombs**, spread over a thirty-kilometre area southeast of the town, have the same layout as the Tang tombs near Xi'an, though the Song emperors had very different funerary practices from their predecessors. In particular, each emperor's tomb was built for him by his successor and had to be completed within seven months of the emperor's death. Not surprisingly, the results are considerably less grandiloquent than the tombs which earlier emperors had spent their own lifetimes preparing. There are seven tombs, each with a spirit way in varying states of repair that include figures of lions, sheep and elephants. To get to them you will have to charter a **taxi** from Gongxian, though tour buses on their way from Zhengzhou to Song Shan sometimes stop here briefly. Look out for the tombs if you're travelling between Luoyang and Zhengzhou by bus.

Eight kilometres north of Gongxian are a set of five **Buddhist grottoes** (daily 8am–6pm; ¥10) from the Northern Wei dynasty. The carving is cruder than at Longmen, the figures are sturdier and blockier, but there is a lot of variety, with musicians, dancers and imperial processions, even a couple of figures with rabbit and monkey heads, among the seated Buddhas. The caves have a central pillar around which worshippers perambulated. Few people get here and this is not a big tourist sight, though the man who looks after the place has a few books for sale. Behind the caves is a village, and beyond that the dramatic rugged landscape of stepped loess hills is a rewarding place to get lost for an afternoon.

The Yellow River Park

Twenty-eight kilometres north of the city at the terminus of bus #16, which leaves from Minggong Lu just outside the train station, the **Yellow River Park** (daily 8am–6pm; ¥10) is really a stretch of typical Chinese countryside, incorporating villages and allotments, that you have to pay to get into because it has a view of the Yellow River. There's a pretty hill, Mang Shan, but none of the sights listed on the map you can buy at the entrance – dilapidated temples and statues, including a huge image of Yu the Great – is worth it. You can spend an afternoon here walking around the hills at the back of the park, or riding – there are plenty of men hiring out horses, and an escorted trot around the hills for an hour or two should cost about ¥20. From the hilltops you have a good view over the river and the plain of mud either side of it, flat and devoid of incident except for the electricity pylons crossing it. It's hard to imagine that in 1937, when

Chiang Kaishek breached the dykes 8km from the city to prevent the Japanese capturing the rail line, the Yellow River flooded this great plain, leaving over a million dead and countless more homeless.

Anyang and around

The city of **ANYANG**, 200km north of Zhengzhou, is the site of the Shang-dynasty capital and one of the most important archeological sites in China. As the ancient city lies under the ground, however, and the contemporary one is too small for a glamorous downtown and too big to have much character, it hardly justifies a stop unless you have a special interest or want to break a trip to or from Beijing. Most of the town is south of the Huan River, but the ancient sites, the **Yinxu Ruins** and the **Yuan Forest** are just north of it, in a grey industrial zone.

Jiefang Lu and **Honqi Lu** are the liveliest districts of the modern city, with a night and weekend market on Honqi Lu. The most rewarding excursion you can take in central Anyang is a wander around the **old city**, the area around the Bell Tower at the south end of Honqi Lu, with dusty, unpaved streets and alleyways mostly too narrow for cars or lorries, but full of people and carts. From the streets you see only the long, whitewashed walls of the compounds with their tiled roofs. Direct entrance to the courtyards from the street is blocked by further walls, a traditional defence against evil spirits. Inside the old city, southwest of the Bell Tower, you'll find the **Wenfeng Pagoda** (daily 8am–5pm; ¥3), built in 925 AD and unusually shaped; it gets larger towards the top, ending with a dagoba-shaped peak atop a flat roof. Southeast of the Bell Tower, the **Gaoge Miao** (daily 8am–4.30pm; ¥10), built in 1451, is an attractive building with stone carvings of dragons and lions around its entrance, well suited to its present purpose as a gallery displaying the work of local artists. On show are paper cuts, calligraphy and masks, and many of the local calligraphers use the Shang script.

ANYANG AND AROUND

Anyang	安阳	*ānyáng*
Anyang Hotel	安阳宾馆	*ānyáng bīnguǎn*
Gaoge Miao	府城隍庙	*fǔchénghuáng miào*
Tomb of Yuan Shikai	袁世恺墓	*yuánshìkǎimù*
Wenfeng Pagoda	文峰塔	*wénfēng tǎ*
Yinxu Ruins	殷墟博物院	*yīnxū bówùyuàn*
Zhuquan Hotel	珠泉宾馆	*zhūquán bīnguǎn*
Linxian	林县	*línxiàn*
Linxian Red Flag Canal	林县红旗运河	*línxiàn hóngqí yùn hé*

The ancient sites

The **Yinxu Ruins** (daily 8am–5.30pm; ¥10) are all that is left of ancient Anyang, a city which vanished into the dusty fields so long ago that its very existence had been forgotten. The historian Sima Qian, writing in the first century BC, mentioned the ruins of an early city on the banks of the Huan River, but this and its ruling houses were thought to be mere legend until, in 1899, quantities of oracle bones were found. Later, in the 1920s and 1930s, excavations proved beyond doubt that this had been the capital of a historical dynasty, the Shang, which flourished from 1711 to 1066 BC, and which is known today for its large decorated bronze vessels, which you can see in most large Chinese museums.

To visit the ruins, take bus #5 from the train station and get off at the first stop on Tiexi Lu. Then walk back up the road to Angang Lu, head west for 100m, cross the rail line and follow the track northwest for about a kilometre. At the site, a rough stretch of wasteland, there's little to see as the more obviously impressive relics are now in the Beijing History Museum. The excavations uncovered the city of Yin, with royal tombs containing horses, chariots, and sacrificial victims; houses and workshops with tools; splendid bronze vessels, one inscribed with the name of the royal consort Fu Hao and still bearing soot marks from the fire; jade and pottery of fine design; and most importantly of all – tens of thousand of **oracle bones**, which are the only relics still on display here, in two imitation Yin buildings, held up by thin columns and topped with thatched roofs. Peasants had been digging up these chunks of bone covered with markings and selling them as dragon bones for use in medicine before they were recognized as script and excavations started. The bones were used in divination – the priest or shaman applied heated sticks to them and interpreted the cracks which appeared– and they provide all sorts of useful information about hunting, war, the harvest and sacrifices as this was scratched on to the bone afterwards. The bones were also used for keeping records and reveal a great deal about the complicated organization of the Shang city, the names of its rulers, the titles and functions of its officials and the collection and spending of tribute money. The bones are displayed with a translation into modern Chinese, and the characters used are recognizably the more pictorial ancestors of those used today.

There are some more Shang exhibits in the small, crusty museum in the **Yuan Forest** (daily 8am–5.30pm; ¥3) also in the north of the city, on the route of bus #8 which you can catch outside Renmin Park. Bus #2, from the station, will get you to the bridge over Shengli Lu, from which it's a short walk. You would probably have to be an expert, though, to get excited about the displays of pottery fragments and yellowing photographs. The best exhibit is a bronze horse's bridle. Behind the museum a grassy mound with a stone wall around its base is the **Tomb of Yuan Shikai**, a Qing warlord whose brief moment of glory was in 1915 when he declared himself emperor after taking over from Sun Yatsen as president of the Republic. He died shortly afterwards.

Practicalities

Anyang's **bus and train stations** are at the western end of Jiefang Lu, the town's main east–west thoroughfare, at the terminus of a clutch of bus routes. Bus #3 goes east along the street's length to Renmin Park, while bus #2 goes east, then turns north up Honqi Lu, the main north–south road.

Both buses will get you to the *Anyang Hotel* (☎0372/422244; ④), on Jiefang Lu just east of the crossroads with Zhangde Lu, comfortable if not pretty. A cheaper alternative is the *Zhuquan* (☎0372/5923612; ④), farther east on Jiefang Lu. The *Jindi Hotel* (☎0372/5925994; ②), just south of the station, offers dorms only. You can **rent bikes** from a stall outside the hotel for ¥3 a day. For food, try the **night market** on Honqi Lu or the **restaurant** at the *Anyang Hotel*.

Linxian and the Red Flag Canal

For anyone who has had more than enough pagodas to be going on with, the side trip from Anyang to the **Red Flag Canal**, in the Taihuang Mountains in the far northwest of Henan Province, makes an unusual diversion. Like Yan'an in the north of Shaanxi, it is one of the holy sites of Communism and, like Yan'an, fascinating not just in itself but for the glimpse it gives of more ideological times.

While most of the province lives under the threat of devastating floods, this area's problem has been severe drought. The acute water shortage allied to stony, infertile hills condemns the local peasants to a hard life, labouring to scrape a living from the mountain dust. The ambitious plan to irrigate the area by taking water from the Zhang River in Shanxi, begun in 1960, was a flagship project of Mao's new, self-reliant China. It took more than twelve years to complete, and is undoubtedly a triumph of the human spirit, one of those massive engineering feats the Chinese have always excelled at, from the Great Wall onward. All the work was done by volunteers with picks and panniers – to complete one section, men even abseiled down the mountain to hack away at over- hangs. Chinese pamphlets for visitors proudly state the figures: over 1000km of chan- nel dug, 1250 hills blasted into, 143 tunnels excavated, thousands of acres of barren land made fertile. They don't mention that over 130 people died during construction, or the criticisms of the canal made by Liu Shaoshi, who believed the same effect could have been achieved by laying a single irrigation pipe.

At one time a visit to the canal was almost obligatory for young cadres and students; key political figures and VIPs from other countries were also brought up here in lim- ousines to scramble up the hillside, admire the work and have their picture taken along- side local dignitaries. Few come here now, those that do freely admitting that such a venture, built on the optimism and spirit of volunteers, would not be possible in con- temporary China. Now the heroic slogans beside the canal have faded, and the provinces it passes through have begun squabbling over water rights. Visitors today are given **tours** that begin at the Youth Tunnel, where the water arrives in the valley through the ridge of a mountain. You then climb up to follow the course of the canal clinging to the hillside high above the valley where you can see it winding endlessly across spurs running down from the mountain ridges – an impressive sight. The rest of the tour takes in a dam and one of the main aqueducts, with names redolent of the 1960s such as Hero Branch Canal and Seizing Bumper Harvest Aqueduct.

Every morning one **bus** leaves Anyang bus station for **LINXIAN**, 70km west and the jumping-off point for the canal; it drops you off in Linxian town centre. Alternatively, you can go by slow **train** along a branch line, though the station is a forty-minute bus ride from the centre of town. From Linxian you can negotiate a jeep tour to the canal– the drivers will find you quickly enough – for about ¥100.

Kaifeng

Located on the alluvial plains in the middle reaches of the Yellow River, 70km east of Zhengzhou, **KAIFENG** is an ancient capital with a history stretching back over three thousand years. But its situation, repeatedly exposed to northern invaders and to flood- ing from the unpredictable Yellow River just to the north, has left few relics to conjure any past glory. However, unlike other ancient capitals in the area, the city hasn't grown into an industrial monster, and remains pleasingly compact, with all its sights in a fair- ly small area within the walls. It's been spruced up a lot recently, and today Kaifeng is a thriving town, not at all the sleepy place you might expect, with a big campaign cur- rently underway to attract tourists. On the downside this means tourist resources, theme parks and the like, are being constructed, which together with a mass influx of visitors may destroy the charm of the place, but on the plus side the PSB takes a relaxed attitude towards foreign visitors and you can stay wherever you like in any number of good, cheap hotels, and get a visa extension with little hassle. A great night market, a sprinkling of sights – some pretty temples and pagodas – and a calm atmos- phere make this a worthwhile place to spend a few days, especially if you've grown weary of the scale and pace of most Chinese cities.

The city's heyday came under the Northern Song dynasty between 960 and 1127 AD. First heard of as a Shang town around 1000 BC, it served as the capital of several early kingdoms and minor dynasties, but under the Song the city became the political, eco-

KAIFENG

Kaifeng	开封	*kāifēng*

ACCOMMODATION

Bianjing	汴京饭店	*biànjīng fàndiàn*
Dajintai	大金台旅馆	*dàjīntái lǚguǎn*
Dongjing	东京大饭店	*dōngjīng dàfàndiàn*
Kaifeng	开封宾馆	*kāifēng bīnguǎn*
Song Capital	宋都饭店	*sòngdū fàndiàn*
Yingbin Fandian	迎宾饭店	*yíngbīn fàndiàn*

THE TOWN

Fan Pagoda	繁塔	*fán tǎ*
Iron Pagoda Park	铁塔公园	*tiětǎ gōngyuán*
Kaifeng Museum	开封博物馆	*kāifēng bówùguǎn*
Memorial Temple to Lord Bao	包公祠	*bāogōng cí*
Number One Restaurant	第一大饭店	*dìyī dàfàndiàn*
Shanshangan Guild Hall	陕山甘会馆	*shǎnshān gānhuìguǎn*
Xiangguo Si	相国寺	*xiàngguó sì*
Yanqing Si	延庆观	*yánqìng guān*
Yellow River Park	黄河公园	*huánghé gōngyuán*
Yu Terrace	古吹台	*gǔchuī tái*
Yuwangtai Park	禹王台公园	*yǔwángtái gōngyuán*

nomic and cultural centre of the empire. A famous five-metre-long horizontal scroll by Zhang Azheduan, *Riverside Scene at the Qingming Festival*, now in the Forbidden City in Beijing, unrolls to show views of the city at this time, teeming with life, crammed with people, boats, carts and animals. It was a great age for painting, calligraphy, philosophy and poetry, and Kaifeng bcame famous for the quality of its textiles and embroidery and for its production of ceramics and printed books. It was also the home of the first mechanical clock in history, Su Song's astronomical clock tower of 1092, which worked by the transmission of energy from a huge water wheel. This Golden Age ended suddenly in 1127 when Jurchen invaders overran the city, looting palaces and temples and putting everything else to the torch. The emperor and his court were led away as prisoners. Just one royal prince escaped to the south, to set up a new capital out of harm's reach at Hangzhou beyond the Yangzi, but Kaifeng itself never recovered. Nor did much survive. What did has been damaged or destroyed by repeated flooding since – between 1194 and 1887 there were over fifty severe incidents including one fearful occasion when the dykes were breached during a siege and at least three hundred thousand people are said to have died.

Orientation, arrival and city transport

Central Kaifeng, bounded by walls roughly 3km long at each side, is fairly small, and most places of interest are within walking distance of one another. **Zhongshan Lu** is the main north–south thoroughfare, while **Sihou Jie**, which changes its name to Gulou Jie at the centre and Mujiaqiao Jie in the east, is the main east–west road. The town's heart is the **crossroads** of Sihou Jie and Shudian Jie, where the night market sets up. The town is crisscrossed by canals, once part of a network that connected it to Hangzhou and Yangzhou in ancient times; these are useful for orientation. The

The **telephone code** for Kaifeng is ☎0378

train station, on the line between Xi'an and Shanghai, is in a grotty area outside the walls, about 2km south of the centre. The main **long-distance bus station** is next to the train station and there's a smaller bus station, for buses to or from western destinations, notably Zhengzhou, on Yingbin Lu, just inside the walls.

Most of the city's **bus routes** begin outside the train station. Bus #1 goes from here north up Yingbin Lu, then along Zhongshan Lu, skirts Panjia Hu and continues to the north section of the wall, terminating on Beimen Lu at a second, small bus terminus. To get to the centre from the station, take bus #4, which runs up Yingbin Lu, then traverses the length of the town along Sihou Jie. Bus #3 is also useful, travelling north up the street that begins as Wolong Jie then changes its name to Beixing then Beimen Jie. For a relatively small place, there are a lot of **taxis** cruising the streets, evidence of recent prosperity. **Cycling** is an ideal way to get around as the streets are wide and flat, but the only rental bike is outside the *CITS* office in the far south of town, so unless you're staying nearby it's a long walk back to your hotel once you've returned the bike.

Maps of the city are available from bookshops or from *CITS*. Take the sights of interest listed on maps with a pinch of salt as no distinction is made between ancient buildings and tacky modern "tourist resources", such as dreadful waxwork shows.

Accommodation

Uniquely, you are allowed to stay anywhere in Kaifeng, which means that despite its small size, there is a wealth of **good, cheap hotels** to choose from, some more used to seeing foreigners than others. In Chinese hotels you pay for a bed, not a room, which often works in favour of lone travellers as the hotels are generally reluctant to put a Chinese in a room with foreigners, so you'll usually get a room to yourself. Rather than paying by the night, you leave a deposit, usually ¥100, when you register, and pay or are paid the difference when you leave. Be prepared for Chinese conventions of communal living – you may wake up to find the *xiaojie* sweeping under your bed. For those who value their privacy, or want to shower alone, there are a few more upmarket tourist hotels which aren't at all bad.

Bianjing, corner of Dong Dajie and Beixing Jie (☎5958811). Go into the large compound and the reception is the first building on the left. The map of the world on the wall here sets the tone for this rambling place; all the clocks show the wrong time and South America is falling off. But it's central and clean. Take bus #3 from the station. ②.

Dajintai, Gulou Dajie. Not easy to find, this hotel is in an unmarked courtyard off the street, about 50m west of the Dazhong Cinema, on the route of bus #4. Reception is the building immediately on the right as you enter the courtyard. The location is excellent, right in the centre of things but quiet, and while conditions are basic – no carpets or showers and sporadic hot water – you can't complain about the prices. Dorms ①, rooms ②.

Dongjing, 14 Yingbin Lu (☎331482, fax 556661). This compound of buildings set in a park just inside the walls to the south of the city, on the shore of Bao Hu, looks like a health sanatorium. Its quiet, low-key and comfortable, with a good range of services including a post office. You can get here on bus #1 or #9 from the station. It's a short walk from the west bus station. ⑦.

Kaifeng, 64 Ziyou Lu (☎555589). This central, two-star hotel in a large, attractive compound off the street is where most tour groups end up. It's comfortable without being ostentatious and surprisingly inexpensive. Take bus #9 from the station. ④.

Song Capital (☎5957744). Just outside the walls on the south side of Mujiaqiao Jie, on the route of bus #9 from the station, this spacious hotel is not very well located and facilities are fairly basic. ②.

Yingbin Fandian, Yingbin Lu (☎3931943). Just north of the *Dongjing*, to which this brown, institutional-looking building is a budget alternative. Friendly staff are game for long negotiations over the price. ①–②.

The Town

The town walls, tamped earth ramparts, have been heavily destroyed and there's no path along them, but they are a useful landmark and a boundary line that serves to divide the city into a downtown and a suburban section. Inside the walls, Kaifeng is quite an attractive place, with a sprinkling of good-looking buildings close to each other along streets that have a more human scale and are freer of traffic than most Chinese towns.

Inside the walls

Shudian Jie is a pretty street at the centre of town, lined with two-storey Qing buildings with fancy balconies. Finest is the building on the corner at the intersection with Gulou Jie – inside it's an ordinary dumpling shop, but the architectural detail outside, particularly the stone reliefs at the base, are very fine. Come here in the evening to see this sedate street transformed into a busy **night market**, when brightly lit stalls selling mostly underwear, cosmetics and plastic kitchenware line its length. You may find the odd trinket worth bartering for, especially if you collect novelty lighters, but it's really a place to wander in your best clothes, which is what most of the locals do. The stalls on Gulou Jie sell books with lurid covers, some of which sport curious English titles, such as *She Married a Foreigner*. Of most interest, though, are the **food stalls** that set up around the crossroads, huge numbers of them, where for a few yuan you can get food to make the back of the legs quiver (see p.283).

An alley, Xufu Jie, too thin to be marked on some maps, leads west off the northern end of Shudian Jie to the **Shanshanguan Guild Hall** (daily 8am–4.30pm; ¥6), which is worth the effort needed to find it, as it's a superb example of Qing-dynasty architecture at its most lavish. It was established by merchants of Shanxi, Shaanxi and Gansu provinces to provide cheap accommodation and a social centre for visiting merchants. In 1985 it was part of the school next door, now it's being pushed as a tourist site and undergoing restoration. With a spirit wall, drum and bell tower, and Main Hall flanked by smaller side halls, it has the structure of a flashy, ostentatious temple. The wood carvings on the eaves are excellent, including lively and rather wry scenes from the life of a travelling merchant, lots of portly figures playing instruments, sitting in boats or riding horses; look for the man being dragged along the ground by his horse on the

---

KAIFENG'S JEWS

The origins of Kaifeng's **Jewish community** are something of a mystery. A Song-dynasty stele now in the town museum records that they arrived here in the Zhou dynasty, nearly three thousand years ago, though this seems doubtful. It's more likely their ancestors came here from central Asia around 1000 AD, when trade links between the two areas were strong, a supposition given some weight by the characteristics they share with Persian Jews, such as their use of 27 rather than 22 letters of the Hebrew alphabet. The community was never large, but it seems to have flourished until the nineteenth century, when perhaps as a result of disastrous floods, including one in 1850 which destroyed the synagogue, the Kaifeng Jews almost completely died out. The synagogue, which stood at the corner of Pingdeng Jie and Beixing Jie, on the site of what is now a hospital, was never rebuilt, and no trace of it remains today. A number of families in Kaifeng trace their lineage back to the Jews, and, following the atmosphere of greater religious tolerance in contemporary China, have begun practising again. You can see a few relics from the synagogue in Kaifeng Museum, including three steles that once stood outside it, but most, such as a Torah in Chinese now in the British Museum, are in collections abroad.

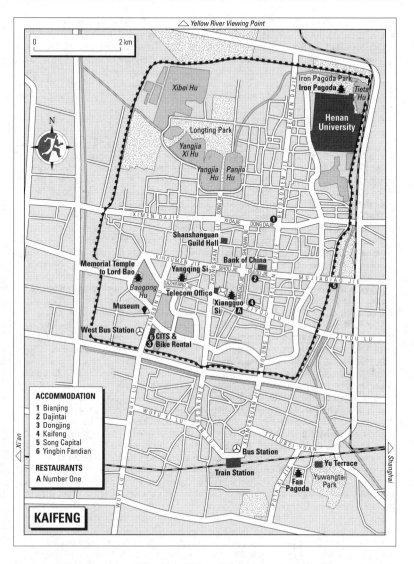

KAIFENG

ACCOMMODATION
1 Bianjing
2 Dajintai
3 Dongjing
4 Kaifeng
5 Song Capital
6 Yingbin Fandian

RESTAURANTS
A Number One

Eastern Hall. In the eaves of the Main Hall, gold bats (a symbol of luck) sport beneath accurate images of animals and birds frolicking among bunches of grapes. Inside is a model of the modern town next to one of the Song city, and in a side hall is the usual exhibition of tribal body art.

Head back on to Shudian Jie and walk south, past the crossroads, and you'll come to Madao Jie, signposted, in English, as "The Street of Insurance Service for Preventing Disaster" – bizarrely, it's full of clothing boutiques. At the bottom of this street, turn right and you'll come to the **Xiangguo Si** (daily 8am–6pm; ¥10), which was originally built in 555 AD, though the present structure dates back to 1766. The simple layout of the three buildings is pleasing, though the front courtyard now holds an amusement park. Things get better the farther in you go. At the back of the Main Hall is a colourful, modern frieze of *arhats*, and the Daxiong Baodian (Great Treasure House) has a good early Song bronze Buddha. In an unusual octagonal hall at the back you'll see a magnificent four-sided Guanyin carved in gingko wood and covered in gold leaf, about 3m high.

A kilometre west, along Ziyou Lu, is the **Yanqing Si** (daily 8am–5.30pm; ¥6), whose rather odd, knobbly central building, the **Pavilion of the Jade Emperor**, is all that remains of a larger complex built at the end of the thirteenth century. The outside of this octagonal structure of turquoise tiles and carved brick is overlayed with ornate decorative touches, such as imitation *dougong* (wooden brackets); inside, a bronze image of the Jade Emperor sits in a room that is by contrast strikingly austere. The rest of the complex at first looks just as old, though the images of kangaroos among the animals decorating the eaves give a clue to its recent construction.

The temple is within walking distance of **Baogong Hu**, one of the large bodies of water inside Kaifeng whose undisturbed space helps give the town its laid-back feel. On a promontory on the western side, and looking very attractive from a distance, the **Memorial Temple to Lord Bao** (daily 8am–6pm; ¥8) is a modern imitation of a Song building holding an exhibition of the life of this legendary figure who was Governor of Kaifeng during the Northern Song. Judging from the articles exhibited, including modern copies of ancient guillotines, and the scenes from his life depicted in paintings on the walls, Lord Bao was a harsh but fair judge, who must have had some difficulty getting through doors if he really wore a hat and shoes like the ones on display.

The **Kaifeng Museum**, a substantial mansion on the south side of the lake, was closed for repairs at the time of writing. Apparently it holds steles recording the history of Kaifeng's Jewish community that used to stand outside the synagogue.

A second large body of water, **Yangjia Hu**, in the northeastern corner of town, which was originally part of the imperial park, is today at the centre of a large programme of tourist construction, including an amusement park based on the Song-dynasty scroll painting of the city. You can walk along a raised path to **Longting Park** (daily 6am–6pm; ¥2), but it's all a bit bland around here. One new attraction that isn't actually that bad is **Song Jie**, the northern section of Zhongshan Lu, on the site of the Song-dynasty Imperial Palace. This is a street of tourist shops built to look like Song buildings, and is entered through an arch at the southern end. The shops look impressive from a distance but they're pretty shabbily made, especially the Fan Tower, an entertainments centre at the northern end, which is marked as a major attraction on tourist maps. The shops sell antiques and curios, including **New Year pictures** from Zhuxian township nearby, which has been producing them for eight hundred years, and there are two good art shops on the eastern side. In the winter, when most of the tourists have gone, many of the shops change over to the sale of household goods.

From the northern end of Song Jie, bus #1 goes to the far northeast corner of the rough square formed by the city walls, to **Iron Pagoda Park** (daily 8am–6pm; ¥20), just north of Henan University, and only accessible off Beimen Dajie. At the centre of this leafy park you'll find the **Iron Pagoda** which gives it its name, a striking Northern Song construction so called because its surface of glazed tiles give the building the russet tones of rusted iron. It has thirteen storeys and its base, like all early buildings in Kaifeng, is buried beneath a couple of metres of silt deposited during floods. Most of the tiles hold relief images, usually of the Buddha, but also of Buddhist angels, animals and abstract patterns. You can climb up the inside, via a gloomy spiral staircase, for an extra ¥5.

Outside the walls

Two kilometres south of town, about 1km east of the train station, you'll find the pleasant **Yuwangtai Park**; bus #14 will get you close, otherwise it's a long and dusty walk through the most rundown part of town. It's main feature is the **Yu Terrace** (daily 8am–6pm; ¥3), an earthen mound now thought to have been a music terrace, that was once the haunt of Tang poets. The park, dotted with pavilions and commemorative steles, is pleasant in summer when the many flower gardens are in bloom.

Not far from here, its top visible from the park, the **Fan Pagoda** (Po Ta), is not in a park as maps say, but sits between a car repair yard and a set of courtyards in a suburbia of labyrinthine alleys. The only approach is from the western side. The fact that the local inhabitants tie their washing lines to the wall around the base and peel sweetcorn in the courtyard adds to the charm of the place. Built in 997 AD and the oldest standing building in Kaifeng, this dumpy hexagonal brick pagoda was once 80m tall and had nine storeys; three remain today, and you can ascend for a view of rooftops and factories. The carved bricks on the outside are good, though the bottom few layers are new after vandalism in the Cultural Revolution.

From a bus station on the west side of Beimen Dajie, opposite the entrance to the Iron Pagoda Park, it's worth catching bus #6 to the **Yellow River Viewing Point**, 11km north of town, especially if you haven't seen the river before. From the pavilion here you can look out on to a plain of silt that stretches to the horizon, across whose dramatic emptiness, the syrupy river meanders. Beside the pavilion is an iron ox which once stood in a now submerged temple. It's a cuddly-looking beast with a horn on its head, making it look like a rhino sitting on its hind legs. An inscription on the back reveals its original function – a charm to ward off floods.

Eating, drinking and nightlife

The best place to eat is the **night market** on Shudian Jie (see p.280), where the food as well as the ambience is much better than in the few sit-down canteens. You'll find not just the usual staples such as *jiaozi*, made in front of you, and skewers of mutton cooked by Uigur pedlars, but a local delicacy consisting of **hot liquid jelly**, into which nuts, berries, flowers and fruit are poured. You can spot jelly stalls by the huge bronze kettle they all have with a spout in the form of a dragon's head. Another delicious sweet on sale here is slices of banana covered with pancake mix then deep-fried.

On the south side of Gulou Jie are a couple of **fast-food places** frequented by the town's trendier set who probably come here to be conspicuous in the glare of the lighting rather than for the food. The **restaurant** in the *Kaifeng Hotel* is pretty good, and opposite the hotel, a little farther west on Ziyou Lu, the *Number One Restaurant* is fairly inexpensive with reasonable food, but the decor, with chickens trussed up just inside the door and empty aquariums, could be improved.

Evening **entertainment** prospects, aside from the night market, are poor. Try the *Dazhong Cinema* at the eastern end of Gulou Jie, or the *Menghua Dancehall*, on the south side of Dong Dajie, which is very popular with the students, though they only play slow numbers – the only repetitive beats you'll hear are from the music stalls around Sihou Jie. You could try hanging around the university south of the Iron Pagoda Park, hoping something bohemian happens, but it's a long shot.

Listings

Banks and exchange The *Bank of China* is on the north side of Gulou Jie (Mon–Fri 8am–noon & 2–4pm).

Bike rental You can rent a bike from a small shop outside the *CITS* office on Yingbin Lu (daily 8am–11pm). Pretty good bikes for ¥5 a day.

Bookshops The *Xinhua Bookstore* on the east side of Shudian Jie, not far from the intersection with Xi Dajie, has a grand total of four English books, but they do sell good maps.

Buses The long-distance bus stations are pretty seedy-looking, and big noses will attract a lot of attention. Both Anyang and Zhengzhou are within comfortable travelling times. The west station sells tickets to destinations west of the city such as Luoyang and Xi'an, the main station farther south serves all other destinations. You can buy tickets from the booking offices (daily 7am–6pm) or on the bus itself.

Post and telecommunications There's a large, efficient post office on Ziyou Lu (Mon–Fri 8am–noon & 2.30–6pm), with a 24-hour telecom office next door.

PSB The main police station is on Dazhifang Jie, but the section that deals with visas is at 16 Sihou Jie, where the staff are so laid-back they're almost hip; a visa extension can take ten minutes, and you may even get a free cup of tea into the bargain.

Shopping Kaifeng is a good place to pick up art materials, one of the best buys in China. Apart from the shops on Song Jie, there's a good, cheap art shop on the corner of Sihou Jie, not far from the intersection with Shudian Jie. For souvenirs, try Song Jie.

Trains The train station is small and not too hard to figure out. You can also buy tickets at an advance booking office at 70 Sihou Jie (Mon–Fri 8.30am–12.30pm & 2.30–4.30pm).

Travel agents Staff in the *CITS* office at 14 Yingbin Lu (☎3980084) are very friendly and like to practise their language skills. They offer one- and two-day tours, sell train tickets and have a free map in English that looks good but is pretty inaccurate.

SHANDONG

Shandong Province, a fertile plain through which the Yellow River completes its journey, is shaped like an eagle launching itself into the sky – an appropriate image for a province beginning to assert itself after a fraught and stagnant past. For centuries Shandong languished as one of the poorest regions of China, over-populated and at the mercy of the Yellow River, whose course has continually shifted, its delta swinging over time from the Bohai Gulf in the north to the Yellow Sea in the south, bringing chaos with every move.

However, the fertility of the flood plain means that human settlements have existed here for over six thousand years, with **Neolithic remains** found at two sites, Dawenkou and Longshan. Relics such as wheel-made pottery and carved jade indicate a surprisingly highly developed agricultural society. In the Warring States Period (720–221 BC) Shandong included the states of Qi and Lu, and the province is well endowed with **ancient tombs and temples**, the best of which are to be found on **Tai Shan**, China's holiest Taoist mountain near the centre of the province, and its most spectacular tourist site. A second major religious site is at **Qufu**, home of the province's most illustrious son, **Confucius**. Although he was ignored during his lifetime, the esteem in which he was held by later generations, and the power of his descendants, who were regarded as almost equal in status to the emperor, are graphically illustrated in the little town by the magnificence of the temple and the mansion in which his clan, the Kong, lived.

Shandong's modern history, though, is dominated by **foreign influence** and its ramifications. In 1897 the Germans arrived, occupying the port of **Qingdao** in the south of the province. They made themselves at home and today the city's streetscapes, which look transplanted from Bavaria, presiding over the best beaches in northern China, make it one of the finest-looking of all Chinese cities. The province's ugly contemporary capital, **Ji'nan**, soon followed, and German influence spread as they built a rail system across the province. Their legacy is still visible in the Teutonic forms of many of Shandong's train stations. At the beginning of this century, resentment at foreign interference, exacerbated by floods and an influx of refugees from the south, combined to make Shandong the setting for the **Boxer Rebellion** (see *Contexts*, p.1001).

Behind Qingdao's German facade is evidence of a new side to Shandong, and a sprawling mass of factories testifies to the rapid pace of modernization and industrialization. Qingdao is the main industrial town, with Ji'nan second, and most trade is done through the port of **Yantai**. The new **Shengli oilfield**, in the northeast, is China's second largest, and as large oil reserves in the Bohai sea bed have only just begun to be exploited, a massive economic resurgence seems on the cards. After a slow start, Shandong's **tourist industry** also seems to be kicking off, and a tourist infrastructure now exists in most large places. Although the rail network is sparse, travelling around the province is made much easier by new highways which connect the major cities. One welcome feature of the province is the relative laxity of the rules on where foreigners are allowed to stay, and budget travellers will find the main sites, Tai Shan and Qufu, agreeably inexpensive. Another bonus is the friendliness of the people, who are proud of their reputation for hospitality, a tradition that goes right back to Confucius, who declared in *The Analects*, "Is it not a great pleasure to have guests coming from afar?"

Ji'nan

The capital of Shandong and a busy industrial city with three million inhabitants, **JI'NAN** is the province's major transit point and communication centre, and anyone travelling in the area is bound to visit at some point. It's possible to kill a day here, but as the tourist sights are unspectacular and the hotel situation is poor, the city is best thought of as a stopoff on the way to or from Qufu and Tai'an, a few hours south.

Though you'd never guess it, the city has an illustrious past. It stands on the site of one of China's oldest **settlements**, and pottery unearthed nearby has been dated to

JI'NAN		
Ji'nan	济南	*jì'nán*
ACCOMMODATION		
Aviation	航空大厦	*hángkōng dàshà*
Guidu	贵都大酒店	*guìdū dàjiǔdiàn*
Ji'nan	济南 天酒店	*jì'nán tiānjiǔdiàn*
Minghu	明湖大酒店	*mínghú dàjiǔdiàn*
Pearl	珍珠大酒店	*zhēngzhū dàjiǔdiàn*
Qilu	齐鲁宾馆	*qílǔ bīnguǎn*
Shungeng	舜耕山庄	*shùngēng shānzhuāng*
THE CITY		
Black Tiger Spring	黑虎泉	*hēihǔ quán*
Daming Hu	大明湖	*dàmíng hú*
Ji'nan Park	五龙潭公园	*wǔlóngtán gōngyuán*
Shandong Provincial Museum	山东省博物馆	*shāndōng shěng bówùguǎn*
Thousand Buddha Mountain	千佛山	*qiānfóshān*
RESTAURANTS		
Huiquan	汇泉饭店	*huìquán fàndiàn*
Ji'nan People's Market	人民商场	*Jì'nán rénmín shāngchǎng*
Ji'nan Roast Duck	济南烤鸭店	*Jì'nán kǎoyādiàn*
Oriental Gourmet	东方美食城	*dōngfāng měishíchéng*

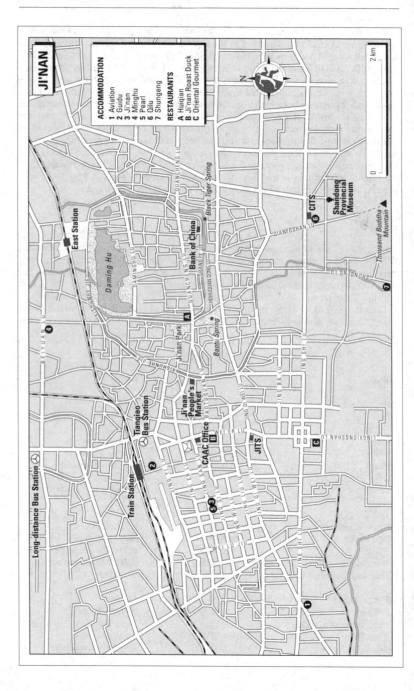

The **telephone code** for Ji'nan is ☎0531

over four thousand years ago. The present town dates from the fourth century AD when Ji'nan was a military outpost and trading centre. The town expanded during the Ming dynasty, when the city walls were built – they no longer stand but you can see where they were on any map by the moats that once surrounded them. Present development dates back to 1898, when the Germans obtained the right to build the Shandong rail lines. Track was laid from Qingdao, another German concession town, and the line completed in 1904. The city was opened up to foreign trade in 1906, and industrialized rapidly under the Germans, English and Japanese.

Ji'nan is famous in China for its **natural springs**, which are actually pretty dull. Once impressive sights, giving the town a reputation for cleanliness and health, these days they are little more than muddy pools. Describing the Qing city, the poet Li Fenggao wrote: "Waterlilies on four sides, willows on three, half the city is a mountain, half is a lake" – so it wasn't always ugly. Some of the nineteenth-century German and Japanese architecture remains, but Ji'nan's buildings aren't pretty. The fashion for facing buildings with white bathroom-style tiling seems to have reached its zenith here, and to Western eyes the city looks like an enormous complex of public conveniences. The most interesting places are all outside the centre, and the most rewarding way to spend any time in the city is to stroll through the **parks** with their attractive lakes, or slog your way up **Thousand Buddha Mountain** in the south.

Orientation, arrival, city transport and accommodation

Ji'nan is a sprawling city. The biggest shopping streets are located just south of the huge lake, Daming Hu, but the most interesting streets are the ordered blocks west of here, south of the train station. Most of the attractions are in the southern suburbs.

Ji'nan's **airport**, with international connections to Japan, South Korea and Hong Kong, is 40km east of the city, and served by an airport bus which drops you outside the *CAAC* office. Taxis into the city cost ¥150. The large and noisy main **train station**, at the junction of the north–south line between Beijing and Shanghai, and a line that goes east to Yantai and Qingdao, is in the northwest of town; the **long-distance bus station** is even farther out of the way, directly north of the station.

Most of the **city's bus routes** begin from the train station; bus #3 is the most useful, heading east into town along Quancheng Lu. The mob of **taxi drivers** at the station are some of the most aggressive in China – as ever, don't let yourself get hussled into a cab, it's better to walk some distance away and hail one yourself. Yellow taxis are cheap with a ¥5 basic fare, which will just about get you around the city centre.

Accommodation

Ji'nan's **hotel** situation is awful, unless you have a big budget. Most of the hotels that are allowed to take foreigners are inconveniently located and pricey. You won't find a room for less than ¥150, which is the same price as a taxi to Tai'an, a much nicer place altogether.

Aviation, 408 Jing Shi Lu (☎7964446). This is the cheapest place in Ji'nan, but it really is depressing, with sneering staff, tatty rooms, a terrible restaurant and an atmosphere of perpetual gloom. It's also a long way out, on the route of bus #6 from the station or trolleybus #101 from the centre. ⑤.

Guidu, 1 Shengping Lu (☎6900888, fax 6900099). An expensive ten-storey place, very close to the train station. ⑧.

Ji'nan, 240 Jing San Lu (☎7938981). A better bet than the *Aviation* if you're travelling on a tight budget, though it's still no bargain. However, at least this solid, characterless place has a good location. ⑤–⑥.

Minghu, 398 Beiyuan Lu (☎5956688, fax 5951634). A 22-storey three-star hotel, reasonably priced for Ji'nan. On the route of bus #33, which you can catch on Wei Er Lu, just south of the train station. ⑥.

Pearl, 164 Jing San Lu(☎7932888, fax 7932688). Three-star monolith, quite convenient for the train station. ⑧.

Qilu, 8 Qianfoshan Lu (☎2966888, fax 2967676). The plushest place in Ji'nan, located in the south of the city. ⑨.

Shungeng, Shungeng Lu (☎2951818, fax 2955288). This place in the far south of the city, near the Thousand Buddha Mountain, is the nicest-looking hotel, an attempt to combine modernist and classical Chinese forms. ⑧.

The City

Ji'nan is frustratingly spread out and there's no real downtown shopping district. However, the centre of town is easily identifiable on maps as a rectangular area south of Daming Hu bounded by streams and fed by springs which, bafflingly, are regarded as the city's main attraction – a case of historical precedent overriding reality. The **springs** have always been synonymous with Ji'nan and acquired their romantic names around the tenth and eleventh centuries, when they were compared by poets to pearls arising from the earth and tigers springing from their lairs. Now, like the rest of the city, they are somewhat uninspiring: half of them don't even seem to exist any more, or are slyly assisted with hoses; pollution and droughts seem to have caused the drying up. The most famous is **Black Tiger Spring** on Heihuquan Dong Lu, which rises from a subterranean cave and emerges through tiger-headed spouts. The stone pools here are a popular bathing spot.

There are a few sights in Ji'nan worth checking out while you're waiting for connections. The park (daily 6am–6pm; ¥5) around **Daming Hu**, on the route of bus #11 from the train station, is quite pleasant, containing some quaint gardens, pavilions and bridges, and the lake is edged with willow trees and sprinkled with water lilies. On an island in the centre the **Li Xia Pavilion** holds portraits of the Tang poet Du Fu and the calligrapher Li Yong; they were supposed to have met here. To the south is the **Memorial Hall** to Xin Qiji, a famous Song poet who was banished for his political views and his poems criticizing the monarch for failing to resist the Jin invasion from the north. The pleasant and restrained building has a couple of courtyards and exhibition halls displaying calligraphy.

Ji'nan Park (6am–6pm; ¥5), south of here on the route of bus #3 from the train station, is nice enough, though little remains of its three springs, which were mentioned in the *Spring and Autumn Annals*, government texts of 694 BC. **Luoyuan Pavilion** on the north side was originally constructed in the Song dynasty, and is inscribed with a couplet by Zhao Mengfu, a thirteenth-century artist, which reads:

"Clouds and mist in wet vapours, glory unfixed; the sound of the waves thunders in the Lake of Great Brightness."

In the east of the park, next to the trickle that is Gushing from the Ground Spring, is the **Hall to Commemorate Li Qingzhao**, one of China's most famous woman poets, born in 1084 in Ji'nan. The modern hall contains portraits, extracts from her work, and poems and paintings by well-known contemporary artists.

The other scenic spot worth a trip is **Thousand Buddha Mountain** (daily 8am–6pm; ¥5), to the south of the city, on the route of bus #31 which leaves from a terminus in the northeast corner of Daming Park; the journey is about 5km. The mountainside is leafy and tracked with winding paths, the main one lined with painted opera masks. Most of the original statues that once dotted the slopes, free-standing images of Buddhas and Bodhisattvas, were destroyed by Red Guards, but new ones are being added, largely paid for by donations from overseas Chinese. The new statues, though, tend not to have the simplicity and purity of the old. It's quite a climb to the summit (2hr), but the sculptures, and the view, get better the higher you go. Behind the **Xingguo Si** near the top are some superb sixth-century Buddhist carvings. The temple courtyard contains a sculpture of the mythical Emperor Shun, supposed to have reigned around 2000 BC, who, legend has it, ploughed the soil in Ji'nan, as well as inventing the writing brush.

Near the mountain, and accessible on the same bus, is the **Shandong Provincial Museum** (daily 8am–5pm; ¥11), which contains a number of fine Buddhist carvings as well as exhibits from the excavations at Longshan and Dawenkou, two nearby Neolithic sites noted for the delicate black pottery unearthed there. The remains date back to 5000–2000 BC and consist mostly of pottery and stone and shell farming implements. The society is judged to have been agricultural, settled and fairly sophisticated, practising ancestor worship. Also on display is China's earliest extant **book**, found at a Han tomb nearby. Preceding the invention of paper, the book was written with brush and ink on thin strips of bamboo which were then sewn together. It includes a full calendar for the year 134 BC, and a number of military and philosophical texts, including Sun Bin's *Art of War*. Though these exhibits are historically very important, it does take a degree of imagination to find them impressive in themselves.

Eating and drinking

For cheap food, try the stalls around the train station. If you want to eat out in style, the *Ji'nan Roast Duck Restaurant*, at 10 Wei Er Lu, is glitzy though not cheap at ¥100 per person, but the roast duck, cooked Beijing-style, is excellent. The *Oriental Gourmet Restaurant* at 188 Yingxiongshan Lu is also pricey, serving Shandong speciality dishes, such as carp and scorpion. The same dishes are available at a lower price, at the *Huiquan Restaurant* at 22 Baotuquan Lu. The *Ji'nan People's Market* (see "Listings" below) is well stocked with flash restaurants and fast-food places.

Listings

Airlines The main *CAAC* office is at 348 Jing Er Wei Lu (☎7933191); *Shandong Airlines* is at the bottom of Thousand Buddha Mountain on Wenhua Xilu (☎6936777) and *China Eastern Airlines* at 408 Jing Shi Lu (☎7964445). They all sell the same tickets.

Bookshops The *Foreign Language Bookstore* is on Quancheng Lu, opposite the Baihua building, but the second-floor bookshop at 269 Daguanyuan has a slightly better selection.

Buses Ji'nan's main long-distance bus station has services to Beijing and Qingdao. To travel to Tai'an or Qufu, both within easy travelling distance, go to the Tianqiao bus station by the train station. Minibuses to these destinations also leave from in front of the train station. You can buy tickets from the office or on the bus.

Banks and exchange The *Bank of China* is at 10 Shangye Jie (Mon–Fri 8.30am–noon & 2–4.30pm).

Post and telecommunications Ji'nan's main post office is on Wei Er Lu at the intersection with Jing Er Lu (Mon–Sat 8am–6pm) and there's a 24-hour telecom office inside.

Shopping The most impressive department store is the *Ji'nan People's Market*, an enormous shopping mall on Baotuquan Lu. There's also an arts and crafts store on 88 Jing Shi Lu.

Travel agents *CITS* is at 88 Jing Shi Lu (☎2965858), in a building behind the *Qilu Hotel*. It mainly deals with tour groups, but Lu Xinsheng in the European Department is very helpful. *JITS* at 117

Jin Qi Wei Lu (☎6912804), a rival outfit, is smaller and more useful to individual travellers. Both offices will book train tickets if given a day's warning.

Trains There are two big stations in Ji'nan. Most trains call at the main station, but a few trains serving destinations east of Ji'nan originate and depart from the eastern one.

Tai'an and Tai Shan

Tai Shan is not just a mountain, it's a god. Lying 100km south of Ji'nan, it's the easternmost and holiest of China's five holy Taoist mountains (the other four being Hua Shan, the two Heng Shans and Song Shan), and has been worshipped by the Chinese for longer than recorded history. It is justifiably famed for its scenery and the ancient buildings strung out along its slopes. Once host to emperors and the devout, it's now Shandong's biggest tourist attraction. The walk up is sometimes tacky, often engrossing, occasionally beautiful – and always very hard work.

The town of **Tai'an** lies at the base of the mountain, and for centuries has prospered from the busy traffic of pilgrims coming to pay their respects to the mountain. You'll quickly become aware just how popular the pilgrimage is – on certain holy days ten thousand people might be making their way to the peak, and year round the town sees over half a million visitors.

TAI'AN AND TAI SHAN		
Tai'an	泰安	*tài'ān*
Puzhao Si	普照寺	*pǔzhào sì*
Tai Miao	岱庙	*dài miào*
ACCOMMODATION		
Longtan Binguan	龙潭宾馆	*lóngtán bīnguǎn*
Overseas Chinese Hotel	华侨大厦	*huáqiáo dàshà*
Taishan Binguan	泰山宾馆	*tài shān bīnguǎn*
Waimao Dasha	外贸大厦	*wàimào dàshà*
Tai Shan	泰山	*tàishān*
Bixia Si	碧霞祠	*bìxiá cí*
Black Dragon Pool	黑龙潭	*hēilóng tán*
Cable Car	索道站	*suǒdào zhàn*
Dou Mu Convent	斗母宫	*dòumǔ gōng*
Five Pines Pavilion	五松亭	*wǔsōng tíng*
Hongmen Gong	红门宫	*hóngmén gōng*
Nantianmen	南天门	*nántiān mén*
Pavilion of the Teapot Sky	壶天阁	*hútiān gé*
Sheng Xian Fang	升仙房	*shēngxiān fáng*
Stone Sutra Ravine	泾石谷	*jīngshí gǔ*
Sun Viewing Point	日观峰	*rìguān fēng*
Tower of Myriad Spirits	万仙楼	*wànxiān lóu*
Wangmu Chi	王母池	*wángmǔ chí*
Yitianmen	一天门	*yītiān mén*
Yuhuang Si	玉皇顶	*yùhuáng dǐng*
Yunbu Qiao	云步桥	*yúnbù qiáo*
Zhongtianmen	中天门	*zhōngtiān mén*
Zhongtianmen Hotel	中天门宾馆	*zhōngtiānmén bīnguǎn*

Tai'an

TAI'AN is unremarkable, but it's not unpleasant. There's a small-town atmosphere, with buildings that are not too grand and the streets not too wide. It's just small enough to cover on foot, though few people pay it much attention; the town is overshadowed, literally, by the great mountain just to the north.

Dongyue Dajie is the largest street, running east–west across town, with Qingnian Lu, the main **shopping street**, leading off it. Hongmen Lu leads north to the trail head, flanked by a string of souvenir shops selling gnarled walking sticks made from tree roots, and shoes. Just south of Daizhong Dajie, in the north, are some busy **market streets** selling medicinal herbs which grow on the mountain, such as ginseng, the tuber of the multiflower knotweed, and Asian puccoon, along with strange vegetables, bonsai trees and potted plants.

Tai Miao

Tai'an's main sight is the **Tai Miao** (Tai Shan Temple; daily 7.30am–6pm; ¥6), the traditional starting point for the procession up Tai'an, where emperors made sacrifices and offerings to the mountain. It's a magnificent structure, with yellow-tiled roofs, red walls and towering old trees, one of the largest temples in the country and one of the most celebrated. Though it appears an ordered whole, the temple complex is really a blend of buildings from different belief systems, with veneration of the mountain as the only constant factor. The Main Hall, **Tiankuangdian** (the Hall of the Celestial Gift), is matched in size only by halls in the Forbidden City and at Qufu. The hall's construction started as early as the Qin dynasty (221–206 BC), though construction and renovation have gone on ever since, particularly during the Tang and Song dynasties. It was completed in 1009 and restored in 1956, and is now in an excellent state of preservation. Inside is a huge **mural** fully covering three of the walls. This Song-dynasty masterpiece depicts the God of Tai Shan on an inspection tour and hunting expedition. It's really a

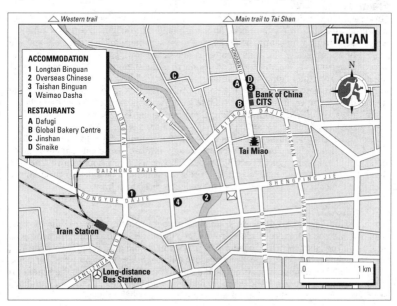

massive ego trip as the painting was produced to celebrate the deification of the mountain by Emperor Zhen Zong, who also built the temple, and there is a strong resemblance between the God of the Mountain in the painting and Zhen Zong himself. The fresco itself is not in good shape, but some of its original glory remains and you can still see most of the figures of the painting's cast of thousands, each rendered with painstaking attention to the details of facial expression and gesture. There is also a statue of the God of Tai Shan, enthroned in a niche and dressed in flowing robes, holding the oblong tablet which is the insignia of his authority. The five sacrificial vessels laid before him bear the symbols of the five peaks.

Today the courtyards and the temple gardens are used as an open-air **museum for steles**. It's an impressive collection, covering a timespan of over two thousand years. The oldest, inside the Dongyuzuo Hall, celebrates the visit of Emperor Qin and his son in the third century BC. Many of the great calligraphical masters are represented, and for aesthetically inclined Chinese this place is unmissable. Calligraphy is an art of great subtlety and refinement, but even the untrained Western eye can find something to appreciate here. Charcoal rubbings of the steles can be bought from the mercifully discreet souvenir shops inside the temple complex. The courtyard also contains ancient cypresses, gingkos and acacias, including five cypresses supposedly planted by the Han emperor Wu Di.

The other temple halls are also used as **museums**. One houses a collection of early sacrificial vessels and some exquisite Tang pottery, while another is given over to the Chinese art of cutting and polishing tree roots. The art lies not in what is done to the root, but in its selection; the roots are picked for their abstract beauty and figurative connotations.

In a side courtyard at the back of the complex is the Temple of Yanxi, a Taoist resident on the mountain, linked with the mountain cult of the Tang dynasty. A separate Taoist hall at the rear is devoted to the Wife of the Mountain, a deity who seems somewhat of an afterthought, appearing much later than her spouse.

Practicalities

On arrival at the **train station**, on the line south from Ji'nan to Shanghai, or at the **long-distance bus station** south of here on Sanlizhuang Lu, you'll be greeted by a mob of eager taxi drivers, who cannot be persuaded to go anywhere for less than ¥10 and will generally ask at least ¥30. An alternative is one of the town's four **bus routes**, all of which leave from, or stop at, a terminus just north of the station. Bus #3 is the most useful, looping from the beginning of the main Tai Shan trail head to the train station and north again to the beginning of the western trail route. Bus #2 goes from the south to the north of the town, from Hongmen Lu to Dongyue Dajie, while buses #1 and #4 traverse the east–west axis, both travelling along Shengping Jie.

The **post office** is on Dongyue Dajie (Mon–Fri 8am–6pm), near the junction with Qingnian Lu, and the **Bank of China** is located on Hongmen Lu (Mon–Fri 8am–noon & 2–4.30pm), near the *Taishan Binguan,* though you can also change money in the hotel. A helpful branch of **CITS** (☎0538/8223259) is just a few doors down from the hotel. However, it's not easy to find as there's no nameplate outside; go through the arch into the courtyard and *CITS* is in the building directly in front.

ACCOMMODATION

Uniquely, the Tai'an PSB does not seem to care where you stay. If your budget is really tight, try some of the grotty places round the **station**. They don't have English signs, so look for the characters for *binguan* (see p.61). You should get a room for around ¥50, less for a dorm, but don't expect anyone to speak English, and be prepared for some odd looks in the communal washrooms. It's worth considering staying at the **hotels on the mountain**, if you can stand slogging up there with your gear, as the surroundings are more pleasant and the price not unreasonable. See p.297 for details.

The best place to stay in Tai'an, for travellers of all budgets, is the *Taishan Binguan* (☎0538/8224678; dorms ②, rooms ⑦), a five-storey place conveniently located at the beginning of the main Tai Shan trail on Hongmen Lu, whose three-bed dormitories are excellent value. The hotel has a good restaurant, and most of the services you could want, including the *Bank of China*, *CITS* and souvenir shops, are nearby. Another option, the *Waimao Dasha* (☎0538/8222288; ④) is a gaunt fifteen-storey building on Dongyue Dajie that looks disturbingly flimsy from the inside, with spacious but ragged doubles. It's only worth it if you get a top-storey room with a view of the mountain. Stay on the wrong side and you'll see a melancholy expanse of block after block of identical buildings. The restaurant here is really bad.

For rock-bottom, no-frills accommodation, try the *Longtan Binguan* (dorms ②, rooms ③), on the corner of Longtan Lu and Dongyue Dajie. At the other end of the scale, the four-star *Overseas Chinese Hotel* (☎0538/8228112; ⑧) on Dongyue Dajie is the most exclusive place to stay in town, gleaming like a tiara but with as much character as a plastic cup. It's nineteen storeys high, with a gym, sauna and swimming pool.

EATING AND DRINKING

A speciality of **Tai'an cuisine** is red-scaled **carp** from pools on the mountain, which is fried while it's still alive. Other dishes from the mountain include chicken stewed with siliquose pelvetia (a kind of fungus only found within 2m of the ancient pine trees around the Nine Dragon Hill), coral herbs and hill lilac. The best **restaurants** are in the *Taishan Binguan* and *Overseas Chinese Hotel*, which serve Western dishes as well as the local specialities. The *Overseas Chinese Hotel* even has an Italian restaurant (among fifteen others), but you're better off sticking to the first-floor Chinese restaurant, which is more reasonably priced.

There are some other good places to eat along Hongmen Lu, including the *Sinaike Restaurant*, a cheap diner which serves generous portions, and the *Dafugui Restaurant* over the road, a classy place with classy prices. For seafood try the colourfully decorated *Jinshan Restaurant* in the north of town. Stock up on picnic staples for the ascent of the mountain at the *Global Bakery Centre* at 7 Hongmen Lu.

TOURS

Apart from trips up the mountain, which you'd be better off doing under your own steam, *CITS* runs two **tours** that are worth considering. The **Buyang Village Tour** is a chance to visit a real, dusty, ramshackle Chinese village and get a taste of rural life. You can go fishing with the locals or try your hand at making dumplings, and if you're really interested you can stay the night at a farmer's house. You'll need to get a group of at least five together and the tour costs ¥40 per person per day plus ¥26 for the guide and interpreter. It's another ¥40 to stay the night, plus ¥30 for dinner.

Another tour (¥40 per person) is by taxi to the **Puzhao Si** to see a venerable old Taoist monk, a Qi Gong master who can apparently swallow needles and thread them with his tongue. Don't expect a performing clown – he only does his stuff when he feels like it. This tour gets mixed reactions and some visitors have reported feeling intrusive.

Tai Shan

More so than any other holy mountain, **Tai Shan** was the haunt of emperors, and owes its obvious glories – the temples and pavilions along its route – to the patronage of the imperial court. From its summit, a succession of **emperors** surveyed their empires, made sacrifices and paid tribute. Sometimes their retinues stretched right from the top to the bottom of the mountain – eight kilometres of pomp and ostentatious wealth. In 219 BC, Emperor Qin Shi Huang had **roads** built all over the mountain so that he could ride here in his carriage under escort of the royal guards when he was performing the

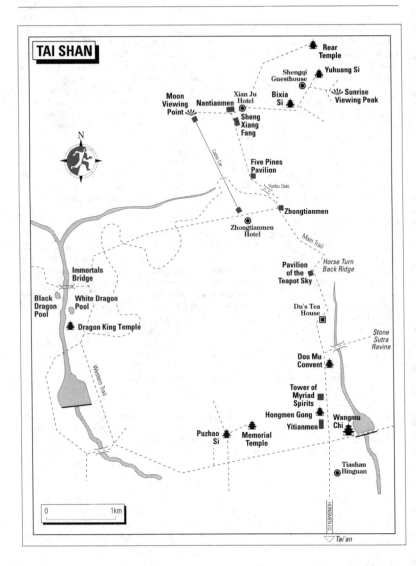

TAI SHAN

Rear Temple

Yuhuang Si

Shengqi Guesthouse

Sunrise Viewing Peak

Moon Viewing Point

Nantianmen

Xian Ju Hotel

Bixia Si

Sheng Xiang Fang

Cable Car

Five Pines Pavilion

Yunbu Qiao

Zhongtianmen

Zhongtianmen Hotel

Main Trail

Horse Turn Back Ridge

Pavilion of the Teapot Sky

Immortals Bridge

Black Dragon Pool

White Dragon Pool

Du's Tea House

Dragon King Temple

Stone Sutra Ravine

Western Trail

Dou Mu Convent

Tower of Myriad Spirits

Hongmen Gong

Wangmu Chi

Yitianmen

Puzhao Si

Memorial Temple

Tiashan Binguan

HONGMEN LU

0   1km

N

Tai'an

grand ceremonies of *feng* (sacrifices to heaven) and *chan* (offerings to earth). Participating in such ceremonies was seen as the greatest possible honour a court official could be granted. When the historiographer Sima Tan discovered he could not accompany the emperor to the summit he was said to be so distressed he was still weeping over it on his deathbed. Various titles were offered to the mountain by emperors keen to bask in reflected glory. In 725, the mountain was granted the title of King Equal to the Sky, and in 1101, it was promoted to Emperor. As well as funding the temples, emperors had their visits and thoughts recorded for posterity on steles here, and men of letters carved poems and tributes to the mountain on any available rockface. The path up the mountain is like a huge open-air museum of religion and rule spanning the whole length of Chinese history.

It's also a giant **tourist attraction**. The twentieth century's contribution to the mountain's illustrious architectural history has been its mutation into a religious theme park, and the path is now thronged with a constant procession of tourists. There are photo booths, souvenir stalls, soft drinks vendors and tea houses. You can get your name inscribed on a medal, get your photograph taken and buy fungus and ginseng from vendors squatting on walls. Halfway up there's a **bus station** and **cable car**. Despite this, Tai Shan still retains an atmosphere of grandeur; the buildings and the mountain are magnificent enough to survive their trivialization.

It is surprising, though, how many among the hordes of tourists are genuine **pilgrims**. Taoism, after a long period of Communist proscription, is again alive and flourishing and you're more than likely to see a bearded Taoist monk or ancient Shandong peasant woman shuffling up by inches with bound feet. Women come specifically to pray to **Bixia Yuan Jun**, the Princess of the Rosy Clouds, a Taoist deity believed to be able to help childless women conceive. As well as its central position in the official imperial religion, Tai Shan plays an important role in the **folk beliefs** of the Shandong peasantry. In villages in the area, the first stone in the foundations of a house is inscribed with the name of the mountain as a protection against it falling down, and blind alleys have a Tai Shan stone to deter evil spirits. Tradition has it that anyone who has climbed Tai Shan will live to be a hundred.

The other figures you will see are the streams of **porters**, balancing enormous weights on their shoulder poles, moving swiftly up the mountain and then galloping down again for a fresh load. They carry supplies and building materials for the hotels, restaurants and temples at the top. It's a traditional job, handed down from father to son, and well paid, but the job takes its toll and most workers past their thirties have distorted backs. It's impossible not to admire their stamina; they may make three trips a day, six days a week.

For ordinary mortals, once is quite tiring enough. There are 5500 narrow steps, each of which you'll learn to hate. The trip down is even more wearying on the legs, and though it's possible to go up and down by foot in one day, the next will probably find you in bed for the duration. If you're seriously fit you might like to take part in the annual **Tai Shan Race**, held in early September (check with *CITS* for dates) which has a prize for the best foreigner competing.

Mountain practicalities

Tai Shan is 1545m high, and it's about 8km from the base to the top. There are two main **paths** up the mountain: the grand historical central route, and a quieter, more scenic western route. They converge at **Zhongtianmen**, the midway point. Most walkers ascend by the main route and descend by the western. The walk up takes about four or five hours, half that if you rush it, and the trip down – almost as punishing on the legs – takes two to three hours.

It is also possible to take a **bus** (¥9) or **taxi** (¥100) to Zhongtianmen. The truly sedentary can then complete the journey by **cable car** (¥35 return, ¥20 one-way). You can also go up with a *CITS* tour (¥80), or catch one of the **minibuses** which leave from the train station in Tai'an each morning (around ¥15).

Whatever the **weather** is in Tai'an, it's usually freezing at the top of the mountain and always unpredictable. The average **temperature** at the summit is 18°C in summer, dropping to minus 9°C in winter. You should take warm clothing and a waterproof and wear walking shoes, though indomitable Chinese tourists ascend dressed in T-shirts, plimsolls and high heels. It's a good idea to take your own **food** as well, as the fare you can get on the mountain is unappealing and gets more expensive the higher you go.

If you want to see the sunrise, you can stay at the **guesthouses** on the mountain, or risk climbing at night – take a flashlight and warm clothes. There are now plans afoot to have the path lit with floodlights.

The ascent

The **ascent** begins from **Daizhong Fang**, a stone arch just to the north of the **Tai Miao** in Tai'an. Just up from the arch and on the right is the **Wangmu Chi** (Heavenly Queen Pool), a small and rather cute-looking nunnery, from where you can see the whimsically named Hornless Dragon Pool and Combing and Washing River. In the main hall of the nunnery is a statue of Xiwang Mu, Queen Mother of the West, the major female deity in Taoism.

YITIANMEN TO ZHONGTIANMEN

About 500m up is the official start of the path at **Yitianmen** (First Heavenly Gate). This is followed by a Ming arch, said to mark the spot where Confucius began his climb, and the **Hongmen Gong** (Red Gate Palace), where emperors used to change into sensible clothes for the ascent, and where you buy your ¥15 ticket. Built in 1626, Hongmen Gong is the first of a series of temples dedicated to the Princess of the Rosy Clouds. It got its name from the two red rocks to the northwest which together resemble an arch.

There are plenty of buildings to distract you around here. Just to the north is the Tower of Myriad Spirits, and just below that the Tomb of the White Mule is said to be where the mule that carried the Tang emperor Xuan up and down the mountain finally dropped dead, exhausted. Xuan made the mule a posthumous general and at least it got a decent burial. The next group of buildings is the former **Dou Mu Convent**, a hall for Taoist nuns. Its date of founding is uncertain but it was reconstructed in 1542. Today there are three halls, a drum tower, a bell tower and a locust tree outside supposed to look like a reclining dragon. Like all the temple buildings on the mountain, the walls are painted with a blood-red wash, here interspersed with small grey bricks.

A kilometre north of here, off to the east of the main path, is the **Stone Sutra Ravine** where the text of the Buddhist Diamond Sutra has been carved on the rockface. This is one of the most prized of Tai Shan's many calligraphic works, and makes a worthwhile diversion from the main path as it's set in a charming, quiet spot. It's unsignposted, but the path is wide and well trodden.

Back on the main path, don't miss **Du's Tea House**, built on the spot where General Cheng Yao Jing Tang planted four pines over a thousand years ago, three of which are still alive. The tea house and everything in it was built out of polished tree roots, which makes the interior look a fairyland – the "girl tea" is excellent.

After a tunnel of cypress trees, and the **Pavilion of the Teapot Sky** (so called because the peaks all around supposedly give the illusion of standing in a teapot.) you see a sheer cliff rising in front of you, called **Horse Turn Back Ridge**. This is where Emperor Zhen Zong had to dismount because his horse refused to go any farther. Not far above is **Zhongtianmen** (Halfway Gate to Heaven) marking the midpoint of the climb. There are some good views here, though the cable car will be the most welcome sight if you're flagging. The pleasant *Zhongtianmen Hotel* (☎0538/8227874; dorms ②, rooms ⑦) is situated here and there's also a collection of rather dull restaurants.

ZHONGTIANMEN TO THE TOP

The path is thankfully level for a while after this. The next sight is **Yunbu Qiao** (Step Over the Clouds Bridge), after which you arrive at **Five Pines Pavilion**, where the first Qin Emperor took shelter from a storm under a group of pines. The grateful emperor then promoted the lucky pine trees to ministers of the fifth grade. From here you can see the lesser peaks of Tai Shan: the Mountain of Symmetrical Pines, the Flying Dragon Crag and Hovering Phoenix Ridge.

Farther up you pass under **Sheng Xian Fang** (the Archway to Immortality) which, according to mountain myth, assures your longevity. Here Li Bai, the Tang poet, wrote: "In a long breath by the heavenly gate, the fresh wind comes from a thousand miles away", though by this point most climbers are long past being able to appreciate poetry, let alone compose it.

The **final section** of the climb is the hardest, as the stone stairs are steep and narrow, climbing almost vertically between two walls of rocks. Each step, often through thick white mist, towards Nantianmen standing black against the sky at the top, calls for great effort, and pairs of fit young men offer rides on homemade sedan chairs to the exhausted.

On reaching the top you enter Tian Jie (Heaven Street), and the Tai Shan theme park, where you can buy an "I climbed Tai Shan" tie-dyed T-shirt or a plastic necklace, slurp a pot noodle and get your picture taken dressed as an emperor. There are a couple of **restaurants** here, **hotels** and a few **shops**. This thriving little tourist village on the top of a mountain represents a triumph of the profit motive over the elements; the weather is really not hospitable up here in the clouds, often it's so misty you can hardly see from one souvenir stall to the next. In the middle of the street is Elephant Trunk Peak, which, it is planned, will become the terminal station of a funicular railway. If you want to stay the night, the best option is the three-star *Shenqi Guesthouse* (⑦) above the Bixia Ci (see below). There's a pricey restaurant, and an alarm bell that warns you when to get up for the sunrise. At no. 2 Tian Jie is the grotty *Xian Ju Hotel* (☎0538/8226877; dorms ②, rooms ⑥).

The **Bixia Si** (Temple of the Princess of the Rosy Clouds), on the southern slopes of the summit, is the final destination for most of the bona fide pilgrims, and offerings are made to a bronze statue of the princess in the main hall. It's a working temple, not a tourist trap, and its guardians enforce strict rules about where the merely curious are allowed to wander. It's a splendid building, the whole place tiled with iron to resist wind damage, and all the decorations are metal, too. The bells hanging from the eaves, the mythological animals on the roof, and even the two steles outside are bronze. From 1759 until the fall of the Qing, the emperor would send an official here on the eighteenth day of the fourth lunar month each year to make an offering. Just below is a small shrine to Confucius, at the place where he was supposed to have commented, "the world is small".

At the **Yuhuang Si** (Jade Emperor Temple), you have truly arrived at the highest point of the mountain and a rock with the characters for "supreme summit" carved on it stands within the courtyard. In Chinese popular religion, which mixes Taoism and Confucianism with much earlier beliefs, the Jade Emperor is the supreme ruler of heaven, depicted in an imperial hat with bead curtains hanging down his face. Outside the temple is the **Wordless Monument**, thought to have been erected by Emperor Wu, over two thousand years ago. The story goes that Wu wanted to have an inscription engraved that would do justice to his merits. None of the drafts he commissioned came up to scratch, however, so he left the stele blank, leaving everything to the imagination of posterity.

Southeast of here is the peak for **watching the sunrise**, where thousands of visitors gather every morning before dawn. It was here that the Song emperor performed the *feng* ceremony, building an altar and making sacrifices to heaven, in 1008. On a clear day you can see 200km to the coast, and at night you can see the lights of Ji'nan. "From the pinnacle," the Tang poet Du Fu said, "all eight corners under the sky are in view." From the summit there are numerous trails to fancifully named scenic spots – Fairy Bridge, Celestial Candle Peak, and the like. If the weather is good, it's a great place for aimless wandering.

The descent

The best way to descend is down the **western trail**, which is longer, quieter and has some impressive views. It starts at Zhongtianmen, loops round and joins the main trail back at the base of the mountain. Midway is the **Black Dragon Pool**, a dark, brooding pond, home of the Tai Shan speciality dish, red-scaled carp, once so precious that the fish was used as tribute to the court. Near the bottom, the **Puzhao Si** (Temple of Universal Clarity), at the end of a path leading north off the main track, is a pretty complex of mostly Qing buildings, though there has been a temple on this site for over 1500 years.

Qufu and around

QUFU, a dusty rural town in the south of Shandong, easily accessible by bus or train from Tai'an, 100km north, and Ji'nan, 180km away, is quiet and pretty with an agreeably sluggish feel, but of great historical and cultural importance. **Confucius** was born here around 551 BC, taught here – largely unappreciated– for much of his life, and was buried just outside the town, in what became a sacred burial ground for his clan, the **Kong**. All around the town, despite a flurry of destructive zeal during the Cultural Revolution, is architectural evidence of the esteem in which he was held by successive dynasties and most monumentally by the Ming, who were responsible for the two dominant sights, huge buildings whose scale seems more suited to Beijing, the **Confucius (or Kong) Mansion** and the **Confucius Temple**.

Qufu is a great hassle-free place to stop over for a few days, with plenty to see concentrated in a small area. It's small enough to walk everywhere, along unpolluted streets with little traffic – there are even trees full of singing birds and benches to sit on. Around the end of September, on Confucius's birthdate in the lunar calendar, the pace of the town picks up when a **festival** is held here and reconstructions of many of the original rituals are performed at the temple.

QUFU AND AROUND		
Qufu	曲阜	*qūfù*
Bell Tower	钟楼	*zhōnglóu*
Confucian Forest	孔林	*kǒnglín*
Confucius Temple	孔庙	*kǒngmiào*
Drum Tower	鼓楼	*gǔlóu*
Yanhui Temple	颜庙	*yánmiào*
Zhou Miao	周公庙	*zhōugōng miào*
ACCOMMODATION		
Confucius Mansion	孔府	*kǒng fǔ*
Dongfang	东方宾馆	*dōngfāng bīnguǎn*
Gold Mansion	金府宾馆	*jīnfǔ bīnguǎn*
Queli	阙里宾舍	*quèlǐ bīnshè*
Yingshi Binguan	影视宾馆	*yǐngshì bīnguǎn*

The Town

Orientation is easy, as the centre of town lies at the crossroads of Gulou Dajie and Zhonglou Jie, just east of the temple and mansion. There's not much reason to leave this area except to visit the **Confucian Forest** in the northern suburbs. The centre is a Confucius theme park, with a mass of shopping opportunities clustered between the sights. Everything here is packed tight enough together to make using public transport unnecessary.

Confucius Mansion

The First Family Under Heaven – the descendants of Confucius – lived continuously at the **Confucius Mansion** (daily 8am–4.30pm; ¥25) in the centre of town, accessible off Queli Jie, for over 2500 years, spanning 77 generations. Intricate and convoluted, there is something decidedly eccentric about this complex of twisting alleyways and over 450 rooms (most of them sixteenth century).

The opulence and size of the mansion testifies to the power and wealth of the **Kong clan** and their head, the Yansheng Duke (see box, p.302). Built on a north–south axis, it is loosely divided into living quarters, an administrative area and a garden. In the east is a temple and ancestral hall, while the western wing includes the reception rooms for important guests and the rooms where the rites were learned.

CONFUCIANISM

Confucius lived in poverty, largely ignored, all his life. A minor official in the Lu state court, he failed in his ambition to achieve real power, and began to travel from state to state, trying to convince rulers to accept his code of morals. His ideas were widely disseminated only after his death, when his students collected his teachings together in *The Analects*.

Confucianism is a philosophy; it was never intended as a religion, though that is how it was spread. Confucius taught gentlemanly conduct, ethics and the principles of government. He believed individuals and states should be placid, moderate and law-abiding, and should avoid extremes and excess. The state should serve the people, gathering the virtuous to it, and rulers should be well educated, humane and behave with courtesy, diligence, good faith and kindness. Peasants should be good peasants, rulers should be good rulers, and everyone should be happy with their position in society. Altruism was of fundamental importance: "Do not impose on others what you yourself do not desire." Confucius was a child of his time and his ideas reflected the opinions and ideals of the ruling class of a static, feudal society. His ideal form of government was **benevolent despotism**; the correct structure of society and the family, he believed, was a rigid hierarchy.

Confucian ethics were adopted by rulers as a suitable system to keep the population in line, and the cult of Confucius began in earnest immediately after his death in 479 BC. Confucianism has since had an enormous impact on Chinese culture and his stress on education formed the basis of the **civil service exams** right up until the twentieth century. When the **Communists** came to power they saw Confucianism as an archaic, feudal system and an anti-Confucius campaign was instigated with much Confucian culture being destroyed in the Cultural Revolution. Now, however, it is making something of a **comeback**. Conservatives, perhaps frightened by the pace of change, the growing generation gap, and the new materialism of China, are calling for a return to Confucian values of respect and selflessness, just as their nervous counterparts in the West preach a return to family values. Confucian social morality – obey authority, regard family as the seat of morality and emphasize the mutual benefits of friendship – is sometimes hailed as one of the main causes of the success of East Asian economies, just as Protestantism provided the ideological complement to the growth of the industrialized West.

Most of the Confucian buildings in Qufu have been recently renovated, but this is strictly in the interests of **tourism**, not worship. Though the values may be returned to, Confucianism as a religious force was thought to have died; and yet the ability of Chinese traditions to survive modernization and suppression always surprises observers. A social survey recently revealed that students in two private schools in Guizhou are once more memorizing the Confucian classics.

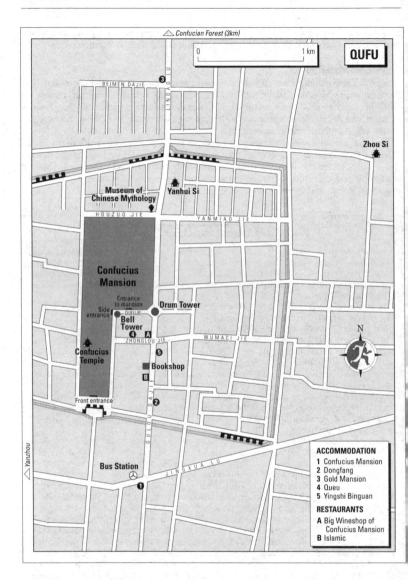

△ Confucian Forest (3km)

QUFU

0   1 km

BEIMEN DAJIE ❸

LINDAO LU

Zhou Si

Museum of
Chinese Mythology
Yanhui Si

HOUZUO JIE

YANMIAO JIE

**Confucius
Mansion**

Entrance
to mansion

Side   QUELIJIE
entrance

Drum Tower

**Bell
Tower** ❹ Ⓐ

ZHONGLOU JIE   WUMACI JIE

N

**Confucius
Temple**

❺

GULOU DAJIE

■ **Bookshop**

Ⓑ

Front entrance

❷

Bus Station

JINGXUA LU

❶

△ Yanzhou

ACCOMMODATION
1 Confucius Mansion
2 Dongfang
3 Gold Mansion
4 Queu
5 Yingshi Binguan

RESTAURANTS
A Big Wineshop of
   Confucius Mansion
B Islamic

    Inside the complex lies a central courtyard lined with long, narrow buildings, which were once administrative offices; now they hold a few trinket shops. The one English book they all sell is worth a look for its colour reproductions of portraits of the fancily dressed Yansheng dukes through the centuries. The **Gate of Double Glory** to the north was opened only on ceremonial occasions or when the emperor dropped in. To its east and west are old **administrative departments**, modelled after the six ministries of the imperial government, and an odd list by any contemporary standard: the

Department of Rites was in charge of ancestor worship; the Department of Seals concerned with jurisdiction and edicts; then followed Music, Letters and Archives, Rent Collection and Sacrificial Fields. Beyond the Gate of Double Glory, the **Great Hall** was where the Yansheng duke sat on a wooden chair covered with a tiger skin and administered the family and proclaimed edicts. The flags and arrow tokens hanging on the walls are symbols of authority. Signs next to them reading "Make way!" were used to clear the roads of ordinary people when the duke left the mansion.

The next hall was where the duke held examinations in music and rites, and beyond it lies the **Hall of Withdrawal**, where he took tea. The hall contains two sedan chairs; the green one was for trips outside the mansion, the red one for domestic use.

THE RESIDENTIAL APARTMENTS

The **residential apartments** of the mansion are to the north, accessible through gates, which would once have been heavily guarded; no one could enter of their own accord under pain of death. Tiger-tail cudgels, goose-winged pitchforks and golden-headed jade clubs used to hang here to drive the message home. Even the water carrier was not permitted, and emptied the water into a stone trough outside that runs through the apartment walls. On a screen inside the gates is a painting of a tan, an imaginary animal shown eating treasures and greedily eyeing the sun. Feudal officials often had this picture painted in their homes as a warning against avarice.

The first hall is the seven-bay **Reception Hall**, where relatives were received, banquets held and marriage and funeral ceremonies conducted. The central eastern room contains a set of furniture made from tree roots, presented to the mansion by Emperor Qianlong. On the table is an original imperial decree. In the eastern room, check out the dinner service; it contains 404 pieces, including plates shaped like fish and deer, for consumption of the appropriate animals. Banquets for honoured guests could stretch to 196 courses.

Past the outbuildings and through a small gate, you reach the **Front Main Building**, an impressive two-storey structure in which are displayed paintings and clothes. The eastern central room was the home of Madame Tao, wife of Kong Lingyi the 76th duke. Their daughter, Kong Demao, lived in the far eastern room, while Kong Lingyi's concubine, Wang, originally one of Tao's handmaids, lived in the inner western room. It doesn't sound like an arrangement designed for domestic bliss; indeed, whenever the duke was away, Madame Tao used to beat Wang with a whip she kept for the purpose. When Wang produced a male heir, Tao poisoned her. A second concubine, Feng, was kept prisoner in her rooms by Tao until she died.

The duke himself lived in the **rear building**, which has been left as it was when the last duke fled to Taiwan. Behind that is the garden where, every evening, flocks of **crows** come to roost noisily. Crows are usually thought to be inauspicious in China, but here they are welcome, said to be the crow soldiers of Confucius, who protected him from danger on his travels. To the southeast of the inner east wing is a four-storey building called the **Tower of Refuge**, a planned retreat in the event of an uprising or invasion. The first floor was equipped with a movable hanging ladder, and a trap could be set in the floor. Once inside, the refugees could live for weeks on dried food stores.

THE TEMPLE

In the east of the complex you'll find the family temple, the Ancestral Hall and residential quarters for less important family members. The **temple** is dedicated to the memory of Yu, wife of the 72nd duke, and daughter of Emperor Qianlong. The princess had a mole on her face which, it was predicted, would bring disaster unless she married into a family more illustrious than either the nobility or the highest of officials. The Kongs were the only clan to fulfil the criteria, but technically the daughter of the Manchu emperor was not allowed to marry a Han Chinese. This inconvenience was got around

THE YANSHENG DUKE AND THE KONG FAMILY

The status of the **Yansheng Duke** – Confucius's direct male descendant – rose throughout imperial history as emperors granted him increasing **privileges and hereditary titles**. Emperor Liu Bang (256–195 BC) named the ninth-generation descendant Lord of Sacrifices, and in 739 AD the duke also became Lord of Literary Excellence. Under the Five Dynasties (907–960 AD) he was the equivalent of a fifth grade official, under the Yuan dynasty he rose to grade three, and by the early Ming he ranked as a grade one official, second in status only to the prime minister. Towards the end of the imperial age, under the Qing dynasty, he enjoyed the unique privilege of being permitted to ride a horse inside the Forbidden City and walk along the Imperial Way inside the palace. Emperors presented the duke with large areas of sacrificial fields (so called because the income from the fields was used to pay for sacrificial ceremonies), as well as exempting him from taxes.

As a family the Kongs remained close-knit, practising a **severe interpretation of Confucian ethics**. For example, any young family member who offended an elder was fined two taels of silver and battered twenty times with a bamboo club. Strict rules governed who could go where within the house, and when a fire broke out in the living quarters in the last century it raged for three days as only twelve of the five hundred hereditary servants were allowed to go into the area to put it out. Women get a hard time under Confucianism, and a female family member was expected to obey her father, her husband and her son. When one of the male Kongs, Wenxun, died just before the date of his wedding, his distraught fiancee hanged herself and the family erected a stone tablet in her honour. One elderly Kong general, after defeat on the battlefield, cut his throat for the sake of his dignity. When the news reached the mansion, his son hanged himself as an expression of filial piety. After discovering the body, his wife hanged herself out of female virtue. On hearing this, the emperor bestowed the family with a board, inscribed "A family of faithfulness and filiality".

The Kong family enjoyed the good life right up until the beginning of this century. **Decline** set in rapidly with the downfall of imperial rule, and in the 1920s the family was so poor that when wine was required for entertaining a guest, the servants bought it out of their own pocket, as a favour to their masters. In 1940, the last of the line, **Kong Decheng**, fled to Taiwan during the Japanese invasion, breaking the tradition of millennia. He is still alive, as is his sister, **Kong Demao**, whose book *The House of Confucius*, available in *Foreign Language Bookstores*, is a fascinating account of life lived inside this strange family chained to the past. Half of Qufu now claims descent from the Kongs, who are so numerous there is an entire local telephone directory dedicated to the letter K.

by first having the daughter adopted by the family of the Grand Secretary Yu, and then marrying her to the duke as Yu's daughter. Her dowry included twenty villages and several thousand trunks of clothing.

Confucius Temple

The **Confucius Temple** (daily 8am–5pm; ¥24) ranks with Beijing's Forbidden City and the summer resort of Chengde as one of the three great classical architectural complexes in China. It's certainly big: there are 466 rooms, and it's over a kilometre long, laid out in the design of an imperial palace, with nine courtyards on a north–south axis. It wasn't always so grand, first established as a three-room temple in 478 BC, containing a few of Confucius's lowly possessions: some hats, a zither and a carriage. In 539, Emperor Jing Di had the complex renovated, starting a trend, and from then on, emperors keen to show their veneration for the sage – and ostentatiously to display their piety to posterity – renovated and expanded the complex for over two thousand years. Most of the present structure is Ming and Qing.

Though there is an entrance on Queli Lu, just west of the mansion, the temple's main approach is in the southern section of the temple wall, and this is a better place to enter if you want an ordered impression of the complex.

Through the gate, flanked by horned creatures squatting on lotus flowers, first views are of clusters of wiry cypresses and monolithic steles, some sitting on the backs of carved *bixi*, stoic-looking turtle-like creatures, in an overgrown courtyard. A succession of gates leads into a courtyard holding the magnificent **Kui Wen Pavilion,** a three-storey wooden building constructed in 1018 with a design unique in Chinese classical architecture – a triple-layered roof with curving eaves and four layers of crossbeams. It was renovated in 1504 and has since withstood an earthquake undamaged, an event recorded on a tablet on the terrace. To the east and west the two pavilions are abstention lodges where visiting emperors would fast and bathe before taking part in sacrificial ceremonies.

The **thirteen stele pavilions,** in the courtyard beyond, are worth checking out and contain 53 tablets presented by emperors to commemorate their visits, repairs and gifts of land to the Kong family. The earliest are Tang and the latest are from the Republican period. Continuing north, you come to five gates leading off in different directions. The eastern ones lead to the hall where sacrifices were offered to Confucius's ancestors, the western to the halls where his parents were worshipped, while the central Gate of Great Achievements leads to a large pavilion, the **Apricot Altar.** Tradition has it that Confucius taught here after travelling the country in search of a ruler willing to implement his ideas. The cyprus just inside the gate was supposed to have been planted by Confucius himself and its state of health is supposed to reflect the fortunes of the Kongs.

The **Hall of Great Achievements,** behind the altar, is the temple's grandest building, and its most striking feature is 28 **stone pillars** carved with bas relief dragons, dating from around 1500. Each pillar has nine gorgeous dragons, coiling around clouds and pearls towards the roof. There is nothing comparable in the Forbidden City in Beijing, and when emperors came to visit, the columns were covered with yellow silk to prevent imperial jealousy. Originally the temple was solely dedicated to the worship of Confucius, but in 72 AD, Emperor Liu Zhuang offered sacrifices to his 72 disciples, too. Five hundred years later, Zhen Guan of the Tang dynasty issued an edict decreeing that 22 eminent Confucians should also be worshipped. Emperors of later dynasties (not wishing to be outdone) added more, until by this century there were 172 "eminent worthies".

Behind the main hall is the inner hall for the worship of Confucius's wife, **Qi Guan,** who also, it seems, merited deification through association. The phoenixes painted on its columns and ceiling are symbols of female power, in the same way as the dragon symbolizes masculinity.

Beyond is the **Hall of the Relics of the Sage,** where 120 carved stone plates made in the sixteenth century from Song paintings depict scenes from Confucius's life. They begin with Confucius's mother praying for a son, and end with his disciples mourning at his grave. The workmanship is excellent but the light in the room is dim and you'll have to squint.

The **eastern axis** of the temple is entered here, through the Gate of the Succession of the Sage next to the Hall of Great Achievements. Here is the **Hall of Poetry and Rites** where Confucius was supposed to have taught his son, Kong Li, to learn poetry from the *Book of Odes* in order to express himself, and ritual from The *Book of Rites* in order to strengthen his character.

A solitary wall in the courtyard is the famous **Lu Wall,** where Kong Fu, a ninth-generation descendant of Confucius, hid the sage's books when Qin Shi Huang, the first emperor (see p.248), persecuted the followers of Confucius and burned all his books. Several decades later, Liu Yu, prince of Lu and son of the Emperor Jing Di, ordered

Confucius's dwelling to be demolished in order to build an extension to his palace, whereupon the books were found, which led to a schism between those who followed the reconstructed version of his last books, and those who followed the teachings in the rediscovered originals.

The **western section** is entered through the Gate of He Who Heralds the Sage, by the Hall of Great Achievements. A paved path leads to a high brick terrace on which stands the five-bay, green-tiled Hall of Silks and Metals and the Hall of He Who Heralds the Sage, built to venerate Confucius's father, Shu Lianghe. He was originally a minor military official who attained posthumous nobility through his son. Behind is, predictably, the Hall of the Wife of He Who Heralds the Sage, dedicated to Confucius's mother.

In the east wall of the temple, near the Lu Wall, an unobtrusive gate leads, legend has it, to the site of **Confucius's home**, sandwiched between the spectacular temple and the magnificent mansion, a tiny square of land, just big enough to have held a couple of poky little rooms.

The rest of town

Not far to the east of the gate of the Confucius Mansion is the Ming **Drum Tower**, which forms a pair with the **Bell Tower** on Queli Lu. The drum was struck to mark sunset, the bell to mark sunrise, and at major sacrificial ceremonies they would be sounded simultaneously. You can't go inside either.

Half a kilometre to the northeast of the Confucius Temple is a smaller complex dedicated to **Yanhui**, regarded as Confucius's greatest disciple and sometimes called "The Sage Returned". A temple has been here since the Han dynasty, though the present structure is Ming. It's attractive, quieter than the Confucius Temple, and contains some impressive architectural details, such as the dragon pillars on the main hall, and a dragon head embedded in the roof. The eastern building now contains a display of locally excavated Neolithic and Zhou pottery.

In the northeast of the town is the **Zhou Miao**, dedicated to a Zhou-dynasty duke. The main hall contains a statue of the duke, together with his son Bo Qin and Bo Qin's servant. Legend has it that Bo Qin was a rasher man than his father, and the duke, worried that his son would not act sensibly in state matters, inscribed a pithy maxim from his own political experience on a slate and directed the servant to carry it on his back. Whenever Bo Qin was about to do something foolish, the ever-present servant would turn his back and Bo Qin, after reading his father's warning, would check himself. The open terrace before the hall, where sacrifices were made to the duke, contains a striking stone incense burner carved with coiling dragons.

Qufu's contemporary attractions don't compare with its historical wealth. The **Museum of Chinese Mythology** (daily 8am–5pm; ¥30), behind the mansion on Houzuo Jie, provides ten minutes of comic relief with its tacky fairground-style show of mechanical dioramas operated by listless guides. One room, the Chinese idea of hell, is quite amusing, with lots of plastic skulls and fake gore. "Heaven" is a room full of half-naked shop-window dummies.

The Confucian Forest

The **Confucian Forest** (daily 7am–6pm; ¥6) is in the suburbs 3km north of the town centre, and you can get here by cycle-rickshaw (¥5). On the way, look out for stone-masons chiselling away at sculptures – dragons, lions, eagles, women in bikinis – at the side of the road. The forest is the **burial ground of the Kongs** and, like the temple, it expanded over the centuries from something simple and austere to a grand complex, in this case centring around a single grave – the tomb of Confucius. In the Song dynasty, the place was planted with trees and in 1331 a wall was built around it. Pavilions and halls were added in the Ming dynasty and large-scale reconstructions made in 1730 when

Yong Zhen constructed some impressive memorial archways. Confucian disciples collected exotic trees to plant here, and there are now over a hundred thousand different varieties. Today it's an atmospheric place, full of ancient trees, sculptures half concealed in thick undergrowth, tombstones standing aslant in groves of trees and wandering paths dappled with sunlight. This is a real, wild forest, with real wild animals and, be warned, real wild oriental insects with nasty stings. A great place to spend an afternoon, it's one of the few famous scenic spots in China that it's possible to appreciate unaccompanied by crowds. Just inside the entrance you can rent a bike for ¥5 and this is the best way to get around; at 200 hectares, it's really too large to explore on foot.

Running east from the chunky main gate the imperial carriageway leads to a gateway and an arched stone bridge, beyond which is the spot where Confucius and his son are buried. The Hall of Deliberation, just north of the bridge, was where visitors put on ritual dress before performing sacrifices. An avenue, first of chop carvers and souvenir stalls, then of carved stone animals, leads to the Hall of Sacrifices, and behind that to a small grassy mound – the **grave**. Just to the west of the tomb a hut, looking like a potting shed, was where Confucius's disciples each spent three years watching over the grave. Confucius's son is buried just north of here. His unflattering epitaph reads: "He died before his father without making any noteworthy achievements."

According to legend, before his death Confucius told his disciples to bury him at this spot because the *fengshui* (the Chinese geomantic system whereby propitious sites for buildings are discovered) was good. His disciples objected, as there was no river nearby. Confucius told them that a river would be dug in the future. After the first Qin emperor, Qin Shi Huang, unified China, he launched an anti-Confucian campaign, burning books and scholars, and tried to sabotage the grave by ordering a river to be dug through the cemetery, thus inadvertently perfecting it.

Practicalities

Qufu doesn't have a **train station**; when the suggestion was brought up it was vetoed by the Kongs who thought it would disturb the sage's grave. Trains stop at **Yanzhou**, 16km west, on the Beijing–Shanghai line and regular buses run between the two towns, arriving in Qufu at the **bus station** to the south. This is also where long-distance buses pull in, after rattling across flat fertile land where aubergines, beans and potatoes are farmed.

Local transport is by **cycle-rickshaw** in which the passenger is slung low in the front, giving an uninterrupted dog's-eye view of the street. A ride anywhere in town should cost ¥5 or less. The drivers are, on the whole, honest and friendly – maybe it's the Confucian influence. There are also horse-drawn gypsy-style carts, strictly for tourists, so not cheap. A few **taxis** wait around the bus station, but no local buses go along any useful tourist routes.

From Qufu it's not easy to get to anywhere in the area except by rickety bus. If you want to travel by train, go to Ji'nan, four hours away by bus, which avoids the problem of connecting with trains at Yanzhou, which will almost certainly arrive full.

ACCOMMODATION

Qufu has plenty of good, inexpensive **hotels**. The following are the most conveniently located.

Confucius Mansion, Jingxua Lu (☎0537/4411783). Opposite the bus station at the bottom of Gulou Dajie. With a laid-back atmosphere and friendly staff, this place is popular with budget travellers. ④.

Dongfang, 31 Gulou Dajie (☎0537/4412794). This clean, modern place is good value, with pleasant, if rather small, rooms. ④.

Gold Mansion, 1 Beimen Dajie (☎0537/4413469, fax 4413209). A luxury joint venture hotel a little way out of the centre. It's not as nice as the *Queli*, but is very popular with Overseas Chinese. ⑦.

Queli, 1 Queli Jie (☎0537/4411300, fax 4412022). If you can afford it, stay in this impressive modern building, one of the few Chinese luxury hotels which harmonizes with, rather than dominates, its surroundings. Located right next to the Confucius Temple and the Mansion. ⑦.

Yingshi Binguan, 18 Gulou Dajie (☎0537/4412422). This place is perfectly acceptable, though not quite as good value as the *Dongfang*. ⑤.

SHOPPING

There are plenty of touristy **shops** in the centre of town, and there's a **night market** on Wumaci Dajie. Worth checking out are the chops (which they will carve with your name in a couple of minutes), rubbings taken from the steles in the temple and pistachio carvings, a local craft. The Confucian connection has been exploited to the hilt with Confucius fans, Confucius beer, Confucius sweets and something called the Confucius Treasure Box which includes an acorn from the Confucian Forest and sand from the great sage's grave – basically a box of very expensive and lovingly packaged dirt. Getting back to basics, the **Kui Wen Bookstore** at 23 Gulou Dajie, sells English translations of the classic Confucian texts. There's also a charming traditional **Chinese medicine store** on Zhonglou Jie, near the *Queli Hotel*. Look for the herbs drying on the pavement. Get your scorpion essence – a local product, advertised as a general tonic – in the department stores on Wumaci Jie.

EATING, DRINKING AND NIGHTLIFE

Local specialities include fragrant rice and **scorpions**, boiled in salt and soaked in oil. The Kong family also developed its own cuisine, featuring dishes such as Going to the Court with the Son (pigeon served with duck) and Gold and Silver Fish (a white and a yellow fish together). It's possible to sample this refined cuisine at the *Queli Hotel*, which does a special **Confucian Mansion Banquet** for groups, at around ¥200 per head.

For simpler fare, there are a few **restaurants** on Gulou Dajie but none is great. The *Islamic Restaurant* on Gulou Dajie, with an English sign, is good for a change; try the beef dishes. *The Big Wineshop of Confucius Mansion,* also signposted in English, near the *Queli Hotel*, is good but a little pricey at around ¥80 for a blow-out meal. It's very popular with well-heeled visitors, and conditions in the small, elegant room can get quite cramped. At night, Wumaci Dajie fills up with open-air **food stalls**, offering tasty-looking hotpots and stews. The food's not bad and the atmosphere is lively, though make sure you know the price before you order anything.

For **nightlife**, you'll have to make do with the nightclub – karaoke and expensive drinks – on the corner of Gulou Dajie and Zhonglou Jie.

Qingdao and around

The port city of **QINGDAO** in the east of Shandong Province makes a remarkable first impression. Emerging from the train station and walking north with your eyes fixed on the skyline you could almost believe you had got off at the wrong continent; it's like stepping into a replica of a nineteenth-century Bavarian village, nestling on the Bohai Gulf. With its Teutonic shapes and angles – red roofs, cobbled streets, intricate iron balconies – this area, the old **German Concession**, provokes an eerie sense of dislocation. The marriage of German architecture and contemporary China has created bizarre juxtapositions, with oriental stone lions sitting in discreet European gardens and buildings with grand, pompous facades now used as little shops and laundries.

Qingdao's distinctive Teutonic stamp dates back to 1897, a legacy of **Kaiser Wilhelm's** industrious attempts to extend a German sphere of influence in the East. The kaiser's annexation of Qingdao, along with the surrounding Jiazhou peninsula, was

QINGDAO AND AROUND

Qingdao	青岛	qīngdǎo

ACCOMMODATION

Badaguan	八大关宾馆	bādàguān bīnguǎn
Friendship	友谊宾馆	yǒuyì bīnguǎn
Jinchuan	金川宾馆	jīnchuān bīnguǎn
Jingshan	晶山宾馆	jīngshān bīnguǎn
Haiqing	海青宾馆	hǎiqīng bīnguǎn
Huiquan Dynasty	汇泉王朝大酒店	huìquán wángcháo dàjiǔdiàn
Qingdao	青岛饭店	qīngdǎo bīnguǎn
Railway	铁道大厦	tiědào dàshà
Xinhao Hill	信号山迎宾馆	xìnhàoshān yíngbīnguǎn

THE CITY

Brewery	青岛啤酒厂	qīngdǎo píjiǔ chǎng
Catholic Church	天主教堂	tiānzhǔ jiàotáng
Huilange Pavilion	回澜阁	huílán gé
Lu Xun Park	鲁迅公园	lǔxùn gōngyuán
Museum of Marine Products	海产博物馆	hǎichǎn bówùguǎn
Passenger ferry terminal	港客运站	gǎng kèyùnzhàn
Qingdao Museum	青岛市博物馆	qīngdǎo shì bówùguǎn
Qingdaoshan Park	青岛山公园	qīngdǎoshān gōngyuán
Xiaoqingdao Isle	小青岛	xiǎo qīngdǎo
Xiaoyushun Park	小鱼山公园	xiǎoyúshān gōngyuán
Xinhaoshan Park	信号山公园	xìnhàoshān gōngyuán
Zhanqiao Pier	栈桥	zhàn qiáo
Zhongshan Park	中山公园	zhōngshān gōngyuán

RESTAURANTS AND ENTERTAINMENT

Chunhelou	春和楼饭店	chūnhélóu fàndiàn
International Seamen's Club	国际海员俱乐部	guójì hǎiyuán jùlèbù
Nanhai	南海饭店	nánhǎi fàndiàn

justified in terms typical of the European actions of the time. It was prompted by concern for "safety", following the murder of two German missionaries by the **Boxer movement** (see p.1001). The kaiser raised the incident to an international crisis, making a near-hysterical speech (which coined the phrase "yellow peril") demanding action from the feeble Manchu government. He got his concession, the Chinese ceding the territory for 99 years, along with the right to build the Shandong rail lines. Qingdao had previously been an insignificant fishing village, but the German choice was carefully calculated, the ubiquitous Baron von Richtofen having carried out a survey and found it ideal for a deep-water naval base. The town was split into a European, a Chinese and a business section, with a garrison of two thousand soldiers to protect its independence. A brewery was built in 1903, the rail line to Ji'nan (another concession town) was completed in 1904, and the town prospered. It was to remain German until 1914 when the **Japanese**, anxious to acquire a foothold in China, and emboldened by the support of their British allies, bombarded Qingdao. The town was taken on November 7 and five

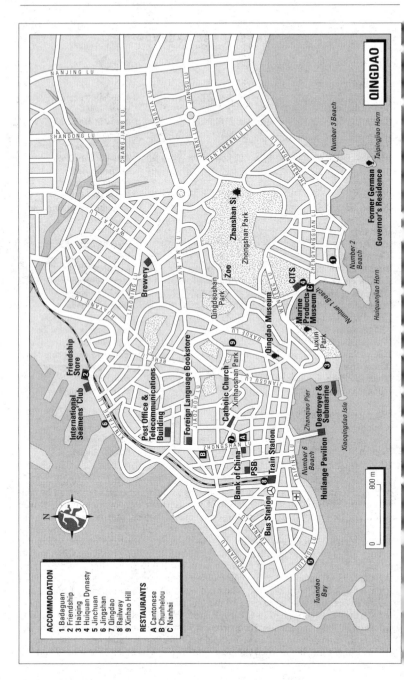

QINGDAO

NANJING LU

SHANDONG LU

TAN ANSANLU LU

JIANGSU LU

CHANGJIANG LU

NINGXIA LU

JIANXI LU

Number 3 Beach

Taipingjiao Horn

Former German
Governor's Residence

Zhanshan Si

Zhongshan Park

Zoo

ZHENYANGGUAN LU

Number 2
Beach

Huiquanjiao Horn

Qingdaoshan
Park

Brewery

Number 1 Beach

Marine
Products
Museum

CITS

LIAONING LU

YAN'AN LU

WENDENG LU

Luxun
Park

Qingdao Museum

DAXUE LU

Friendship
Store

Foreign Language Bookstore

Catholic Church

Xinhaoshan Park

Post Office &
Telecommunications
Building

JIAZHOU LU

JIANGSU LU

Destroyer &
Submarine

International
Seamen's Club

Zhanqiao Pier

Xiaoqingdao Isle

Bank of China

ZHONGSHAN LU

PSB

Train Station

Number 6 Beach

Huilange Pavilion

Bus Station

TAIPING LU

SICHUAN LU

GUANGZHOU LU

Tuandao Bay

0   800 m

N

ACCOMMODATION
1 Badaguan
2 Friendship
3 Haiqing
4 Huiquan Dynasty
5 Jinchuan
6 Jingshan
7 Qingdao
8 Railway
9 Xinhao Hill

RESTAURANTS
A Cantonese
B Chunhelou
C Nanhai

The **telephone code** for Qingdao is ☎0532

thousand prisoners were carted off to Japan. In the Treaty of Versailles, the city was ceded to Japan, which infuriated the Chinese, and led to demonstrations in Beijing – the beginning of the May Fourth Movement (see *Contexts*, p.1002). The port was eventually returned to China in 1922.

Modern Qingdao is still a very important **port**, China's fourth largest, and behind the old town is an area with a very different character, a sprawling industrial **metropolis** of highrises and factories. One of China's first "open door" cities, with an excellent geographical position and transport facilities, Qingdao has a rapidly growing industrial base. Perhaps most importantly, at least from a visitor's point of view, it continues to produce the world-renowned **Tsingtao Beer** (Tsingtao is the old spelling of Qingdao) which owes its crisp, clean flavour to the purity of the spring water from Laoshan, an attractive mountain area east of the city, with which it is brewed.

Despite its size, the parts of the city you'd actually want to visit are all within manageable walking distance, and the atmosphere at the waterfront is more small-town pleasure zone than anonymous metropolis, thanks mainly to the white sand **beaches** dotted along the shoreline, the best in northern China. Though the authorities seem more interested in constructing new skyscrapers and beach hotels than in restoring old buildings, the speedy development has not yet impinged upon the area's charm. It's a relaxed and hedonistic place, with an atmosphere that's mellower than in most Chinese cities – even the pace at which people walk is slower. The season runs from June to September, though many visitors come in late April and early May, when the cherry trees are blooming in Zhongshan Park. Fans of the local brew may be interested in the annual **Beer Festival** (August 12–26).

Orientation, arrival and city transport

The old concession area and the beachfront are easy to get to know and get around. Zhongshan Lu, running north–south is the modern, glitzy shopping district and the heart of the concession district; on the east–west axis, Taiping and Laiyang Lu follow the coastline.

The large city **airport**, 30km north of the city, is served by a regular *CAAC* bus which drops passengers on Zhongshan Lu. Arriving in Qingdao by **train** is the easiest option. The station, which is on a single line that splits, one fork leading to Ji'nan, the other to Yantai, is a grand German edifice at the heart of the old town, within walking distance of the beach and the seafront hotels. The **long-distance bus station** is just behind and to the west of the train station, and a new expressway has now cut the journeytime from Ji'nan to seven hours. The **passenger ferry terminal**, with services from Dalian and Shanghai, is in the grotty north of town, with a few cheap hotels nearby. To get to the **seafront** from here, take bus #21 south, get off halfway down Sichuan Lu, opposite Xiaogang Port, walk east to the end of Zhongshan Lu and catch a #6. Or go to the last stop of the #21 route, walk south down to Guizhou Lu and catch bus #25 east. Get off just after Huilange Pavilion, before it turns up Daxue Lu. As this is pretty involved, it's a lot easier just to get a cab if you are arriving with luggage.

Bus #6 is a useful one to know about. It goes from the top of Zhongshan Lu down towards the train station, then heads east along the seafront, gets close to Number 1 beach and terminates near the entrance to Zhongshan Park. Private **minibuses** also run on most bus routes. They're more common, faster, but a little more expensive. **Taxis** to most destinations within the city are ¥7, and the drivers are good about using their meters.

FERRIES FROM QINGDAO

Ferries from Qingdao to **Dalian and Shanghai** run every four days and save considerably on the comparative train journey in both cost (there's no foreigners' mark-up) and comfort. Journey times are roughly the same as for the train (26 hours to Dalian, 27 hours to Shanghai).

Tickets can be bought in advance from the passenger ferry terminal close to the *Friendship Store* on Xinjiang Lu. There are five classes (special, first, second, third and fourth), with severe gradations in price as you move down the scale. Third class is about the same level of comfort as hard sleeper on a train and is probably best unless you're particularly loaded or skint. Third class on the ferry to Dalian costs around ¥100; the Shanghai ferry is a little more expensive.

Accommodation

Finding a room in Qingdao is easy if you don't mind paying for luxury, as there are plenty of top-class international **hotels**, well located on the seafront. If you're travelling on a budget, your choices are much more limited, and you'll probably end up some way from the picturesque parts of town. Qingdao is probably the most expensive city in Shandong, though outside the season hotel rooms can be cheaper and it's worth bargaining.

Badaguan, 19 Shanhaiguan Lu (☎3872168). A quiet place just above Number 2 beach. The hotel also operates a series of expensive, renovated stone villas around town – ask for details at reception. ⑦–⑨.

Friendship, Xinjiang Lu (☎2828165). This hotel is a long way out in the same building as the *Friendship Store*, next to the passenger ferry terminal. The building is bare and ragged, but the pleasant rooms are a bargain and popular with budget travellers. It's also notable for having a helpful, English-speaking manager. Try to avoid the fourth floor as there's a nightclub here which blasts out old Euro pop till two in the morning. Dorms ②, rooms ⑤.

Jinchuan, 15 Guizhou Lu (☎2862028). A bland concrete building with bland rooms, but near the seafront. ⑥.

Jingshan, Xiaogang Er Lu (☎2827954). In the same area as the *Friendship Hotel*, five minutes' walk southwest from the ferry terminal, this place is big, bright and shiny – the tallest building around – but blighted by its unattractive location. ⑥.

Haiqing, Laiyang Lu (☎2877760). Small, snug and comfortable, with friendly staff and in a good location, this is an excellent place to stay. Rooms at the back have balconies. ⑥.

Huiquan Dynasty, 9 Nanhai Lu (☎2873366) A well-located four-star hotel. Doubles start at US$115. ⑨.

Qingdao, 53 Zhongshan Lu (☎2879068). A grand, glitzy tower bang in the middle of town, offering substantial reductions with a Chinese student card. ⑧.

Railway, 2 Tai'an Lu (☎2869963). Right next door to the train station, this spartan place is noisy but clean. It's very popular, as it's the cheapest hotel in the beachfront area, and is often booked out. Dorms ②, rooms ⑤.

Xinhao Hill, 26 Longshan Lu (☎2866209). Beautiful old German mansion nestling among the trees in Xinhaoshan Park. Rooms start at US$85. ⑨.

The City

Qingdao has plenty of diversions to offer, but the main thing to do here is stroll. The **waterfront** is a place to see and be seen, with the same indolent, flirtatious atmosphere common to beach resorts the world over, while the faster-paced downtown streets are the haunt of the well-heeled inhabitants and have a definite cosmopolitan feel.

Unusually for a city outside Beijing, there's even evidence of the new Chinese youth culture: buskers work the crowds on the esplanade, beach bums recline elegantly on the sands and skateboarders weave down the hills. As well as the **beaches** and **old German town**, some very pleasant **parks** are an added bonus, ensuring that Qingdao is easily one of the most charismatic of Chinese cities.

The German Concession and the brewery

Zhongshan Lu is the main shopping drag, awash with shoe shops and designer clothing stores. At its northern end, up a steep cobbled street, is the fine **Catholic Church**, a German relic, whose distinctive double spires can be seen from all over the city. Services are held here on Sunday mornings, which seems to be the only time you can get inside. The streets east of here, some cobbled, and many lined with pink buildings with black iron balconies overlooking the street, are a good place to wander and take in the flavour of the old German town.

The **Qingdao Museum** on Daxue Lu (Tues–Sun 8am–5pm; ¥15) is worth a diversion. This beautiful building, constructed in 1931, was originally a welfare institute, the headquarters of the benign but sinister-sounding *Red Swastika Association*. There's a collection of paintings from the Yuan through to Qing dynasties, and an archeological section in the courtyard which contains four large standing **Buddhas** dating to 500–527 AD. They are slim, striking figures with bulbous, smiling heads, one hand pointing upward to heaven, the other down to the earth. The heads were cut off in 1928 by the Japanese, and taken away to museums in Japan. They've now been restored to their rightful shoulders and you can hardly see the join. The museum staff seem proudest, however, of a souvenir collected by Qingdao sailors during the 1985 Chinese expedition to the South Pole – a simple lump of rock – which sits proudly in a specially constructed pavilion in the courtyard.

Fans of **Tsingtao Beer** can take a trip into the industrial zone to see the **brewery**. It's on the route of bus #25 and easy enough to spot, but the only way to get inside is to take a tour with *CITS* (see p.314). Free samples are available, including an unusual dark brown stout, but you'll have to sit through a lot of statistics first.

The beaches and the waterfront

Qingdao's **beaches**, with fine white sand, are active from very early in the morning, when *tai ji* exponents and beachcombers turn out, to well into the evening, when holidaymakers come for the bars and cafés on the beach and esplanade or just to sit and look out to sea. **Number 1 beach**, off Laiyang Lu, flanked by skyscrapers on one side, red-tiled roofs on the other, is the biggest (580m long) and best. In season it's a lively, crowded place, swarming with ice-cream vendors, trinket stalls selling carved shells and a rash of photographers. Fortunately, unlike Beidaihe, the other northern beach resort (see p.142), it doesn't feel overloaded with "Kiss me Quick" style kitsch. The whole place is very organized, with odd, beachball-shaped changing huts, shower facilities, multi-coloured beach umbrellas, and designated swimming areas marked out with buoys and protected by shark nets. The water, however, is like Chinese soup – murky and warm, with unidentifiable things floating in it, so swimming is not recommended. Sit down and you're not likely to remain alone for long as there are plenty of people around who want to practise their English.

If Number 1 beach feels too crowded, head east to the more sheltered and quieter **number 2 and 3 beaches**. These are more sedate, and popular with the older, sanatorium-dwelling crowd. For the liveliest social scene, head to the illogically named **Number 6 beach**, at the bottom of Zhongshan Lu.

Above the beaches is the **esplanade**, stretching from the western end of the peninsula all the way to Number 1 beach. Hopeful fishermen with rods line the stretch around Tuandao Bay. Farther east from Tuandao Bay, you come to **Zhanqiao Pier**, the symbol of the city. At its end sits the octagonal **Huilange Pavilion**, where small craft exhibitions are held. The stretch above Number 6 beach has numerous little stalls selling gaudy swimsuits and cheap souvenirs. This area really comes alive in the evening, when it becomes a crowded thoroughfare: couples stroll arm in arm and young men show off by diving from the pier. Two large **screens** on Taiping Lu show Chinese opera and films and a part of the wide pavement is given over to an open-air cinema. It's a great place to wander, though the view out to sea has been compromised; enterprising Chinese advertisers have even found a way to use the ocean as a hoarding and neon characters sit on stilts stuck into the sea bed some way out from the shore.

East of the pier, a decommissioned **submarine** and a **destroyer** sit in the water, looking rather out of place. You are required to leave any cameras at the ticket booth (¥5 for each vessel), which seems a little over-sensitive as both exhibits are virtually antiques. The destroyer is small and rusting, with a display of fearsome weaponry. The submarine is much more interesting and well worth a look, certainly if you've never been in one before. The series of narrow, dark rooms arrayed with masses of chunky old valves, dials, levers and knobs, many of them bearing Russian markings, rewards a detailed examination. You descend in the torpedo launch room, go through the sailors' quarters, hardly larger than a cupboard though they still found room for their flasks of tea, and ascend from the engine room. There are no guides or attendants inside, and travellers who have tried it report that taking a camera in is easy.

Next to the sub, a sandbank leads to **Xiaoqingdao Isle** (¥3). There's a pleasant little park here, a few cafés with good views, and a surprisingly lascivious statue of a sea nymph playing a violin. A white beacon stands at the highest point.

Around the bend is **Lu Xun Park** (daily 6am–7pm; ¥2), a good approach to Number 1 beach. It has green pine trees and cypresses, little winding paths, pavilions, benches and tables, full of couples indulging in what must be the well-heeled Chinese tourists' favourite hobby, photographing your spouse. Inside the park is the **Museum of Marine Products** (daily 7.45am–6pm; ¥15), consisting of two buildings, an aquarium shaped like a castle and a two-storey exhibition hall, with a seal pool in between. Founded in 1932, it's billed as the best aquarium in China, though to Western eyes it's pretty unexciting – lots of exotic marine life swimming about in tanks make it look like the average Chinese restaurant.

The farther east you go, the grander and more exclusive the buildings get. Past the *Huiquan Dynasty Hotel* is the **Badaguan area**, a health resort of sanatoriums and classy guesthouses set among trees. A pretty place with a suburban feel, each street is lined with a different tree or flower – there are peach blossoms on Shaoguan Lu, crab apple on Ningwuguan Lu, and crab myrtle on Zhengyangguan Lu – and unlike most of the old gardens in Qingdao, the ones here are well looked after. At the eastern end of Number 2 beach stands the former German Governor's Residence, a grand castle looking out to sea.

Zhongshan Park and around

Qingdao's **parks**, dotted above the waterfront and serving as a buffer zone between the interesting parts of the city, the waterfront, and the boring industrial bits, are among the best in China. The largest is **Zhongshan Park** (daily 6am–6pm; ¥5), on the side of Taiping Hill which covers 800 square kilometres. Within its boundaries sits the Buddhist **Zhanshan Si**, the zoo, a couple of theme parks, a tea house and the TV Tower, looking as if it's just landed from outer space. A cable car runs from near the entrance to the top of the hill. It's a good place to lose the crowds and hike around, but as it's so enormous you'll need a whole day to explore it thoroughly. The park is famed for its **cherry trees**, which turn the park into a pink forest when they're in bloom in late April and early May. Thousands of visitors come just to see the spectacle.

Just west of Zhongshan Park, **Qingdaoshan Park** (daily 6am–6pm; ¥3) contains the small **Jingshan Fort**. Farther west, near the museum, the steep but very pleasant **Xinhaoshan Park** holds the *Xinhao Hill Hotel*, a grand old mansion which is worth a photograph even if you can't afford to stay here. The highest point of the park, reached by tortuous winding paths, is a good place to get an overview of the city. **Xiaoyushun Park**, on the top of a hill by the side of Huiquan Bay, is styled like a classical Chinese garden. The main three-storey, octagonal structure at the summit is the **Lanchaoge Pavilion**, traditionally used for watching the tide.

Eating, drinking and nightlife

Qingdao has plenty of **restaurants** to choose from. The speciality is, unsurprisingly, seafood; mussels and crabs here are particularly good, and not expensive. There are plenty of small **seafood places** along Laiyang Lu, particularly around the *Haiqing Hotel*. They're all small, noisy and busy, but competition means that standards are high, and the food is reasonably cheap, but beware of overcharging. The expensive **hotels** also have restaurants, and although they're pricey, the food is very good and the setting is often palatial. The first-floor restaurant in the *Huiquan Hotel* is one of the best. If you're staying by the ferry terminal, you would be better off heading south to eat, as the only sanitary restaurant in the area is the *Friendship Restaurant*, next to the *Friendship Hotel*, where the food is average but pricey and the service is terrible.

Pick of the seafront places is the *Nanhai*, 14 Nanhai Lu, opposite the *Huiquan Dynasty Hotel*. The food is excellent, though the portions are a little small, and the beer comes in real pint mugs. Expect to pay about ¥60 per person. On and around Zhongshan Lu, try the *Chunhelou* at 146 Zhongshan Lu, a quiet little place with discreet service, small tables and ambient lighting which gives it quite a Continental feel. The food is very good, and portions are more than generous – the spicy chicken is highly recommended. Just off the main drag, the *Cantonese Restaurant*, Qufu Lu, has good *dim sum* and seafood. There's a *KFC* at 53 Zhongshan Lu.

Nightlife is not as exciting here as might be expected. A lot of Chinese visitors end up in karaoke bars or expensive hotel nightclubs which aren't so appealing to foreigners. The best place to be in the early evening is around Zhanqiao Pier, where everyone goes for a stroll after eating. There's a good American-style **bar** here, shaped like a boat, at the back of Number 6 beach. Later in the evening, try the *International Seamen's Club* by the passenger ferry terminal, where there's a **disco** till 2am, or the small **nightclub** on the fourth floor of the *Friendship Hotel*.

Listings

Airlines There's a *CAAC* office inside the passenger ferry terminal. *China Eastern Airlines* operates out of the *Yellow Sea Hotel* at 75 Yan'an Yi Lu. It is also possible to book plane tickets in the *Huiqian Dynasty Hotel*.

Banks and exchange The main *Bank of China* at 62 Zhongshan Lu (Mon–Fri 8am–noon & 2–5.30pm) doesn't change travellers' cheques. A separate office directly opposite the front of the Catholic Church, with the same hours, deals with money drawn against credit cards and travellers' cheques.

Bookshops The *Foreign Language Bookstore* on Zhongshan Lu, near the intersection with Jiaozhou Lu, stocks all the usual dusty old novels.

Buses Qingdao's shambolic long-distance bus station is just west of the train station. Yantai is the only interesting destination within easy reach by bus. You buy tickets on the bus.

PSB The PSB is at 29 Hubei Lu (Mon–Sat 8am–noon & 2–7pm), not far from the train station.

Post and telecommunications The main post office and telecom building is at the northern end of Zhongshan Lu (Mon–Sat 8am–6pm).

Shopping There's an antiques store at 40 Zhongshan Lu and a large *Arts and Crafts Centre* at the northern end of the road. The *Friendship Store* is by the ferry terminal, but it's disappointing.

Travel agents *CITS* is in a separate building at the back of the *Huiquan Dynasty Hotel*, on Nanhai Lu (☎2870695). As usual, it caters more for groups than independent travellers, running a "health tour" which includes acupuncture, massage, qigong and sunbathing, but you can also arrange a brewery tour here (at least ¥150 per head, with a minimum of four people required).

Laoshan

The **Laoshan** area, 400 square kilometres of rugged scenery along the coast 40km to the east of Qingdao, is easily accessible from the city. **Minibuses** (¥10) leave frequently from outside the train station, dropping you off at the foot of Lao Shan itself, or you can catch a **boat** from the local ferry wharf, at the bottom of a narrow side street off Laiyang Lu, close to the northern end of Zhongshan Lu. Boats leave irregularly, cost ¥20, and drop you off by the Taiqing Gong. There are minibuses and boats back to Qingdao from both these locations, or you can hail a minibus from any of the three roads inside the area. Minibuses travel between each of the temples and the mountain, so it is not hard to travel from one of the popular scenic spots to another. Maps of the area are included on all city maps, and it's a good idea to get one before you set out.

Lao Shan itself (1133m) is one of China's famous peaks, appearing in Chinese mythology as the home of the Immortals. In the Tang dynasty there were 72 Taoist temples in the area; now time, neglect and the Cultural Revolution have reduced them to ruins. It's a good place to hike around – the whole area is dotted with caves, springs and waterfalls amid striking scenery – and with a bit of effort, it's possible to lose the crowds and trinket stalls. Wherever you go in the Laoshan area you will see large, distinctive, oddly shaped granite **stones** named after an often tenuous resemblance to an animal or person. They're interesting forms but you need to use a lot of imagination, or a lot of *Tsingtao Red*, to get the allusion. **Jiushui Valley**, to the northeast of the mountain, is the origin of **Laoshan mineral water**, which gives Tsingtao beer its taste; it's one of the few Chinese bottled mineral waters that doesn't taste of swimming pools. Writers have been inspired by the scenery for centuries, and have left noble graffiti of **poems and sage reflections** cut into rocks all round the area. *Strange Stories at Liao's House* by the Qing-dynasty author, Pu Songling, was written here.

On a clear day, the **coastal road route** from Qingdao is spectacular, winding somewhat precariously along cliff tops. On the way you'll pass the **Stone Old Man**, a ten-metre-high rock standing in the sea, not far from the beach. Legend has it that long ago a beautiful local girl, Mudan, was kidnapped by Longwang, the King of the East Sea. Her distraught father stood so long looking out to sea for his missing daughter that he eventually turned to stone.

Around the mountain

Within Laoshan itself there are three **roads**, each route taking in some magnificent views. The southern road takes you past the Taiqing Gong, Mingxia Cave and Longtan Waterfall. The eastern route goes to Taiping Gong and the middle road going southeast takes you to a village at the foot of Lao Shan. From the village, a pathway of stone steps, constructed a century ago by the enterprising German Laoshan company to cater for their compatriots, weakness for alpine clambering, runs all the way to the summit and then back down a different route on the other side.The **path** climbs past gullies and woods, streams and pools, and the ascent takes about two hours. There's a temple halfway up, where you can fortify yourself with fruit and tea for the final haul. At the summit, a ruined temple now houses a meteorological station. The view inspires superlatives, and gets even better as you descend by the alternative route, which takes you back to the village,

Other scenic spots have a religious connection. On Naloyan Shan, 2km northeast of Lao Shan, is a cave in which the Naloyan Buddha was said to have meditated, and on the coast just north of here the Baiyun Cave was once the home of a famous monk, Tian Baiyun. Ever since, it has been seen as an auspicious place to meditate. Mingxia Cave, 3km farther south down the coast on the slopes of Kunyu Shan, was written about by a famous Taoist, Qiu Changchun. Inside the cave are stones which reflect the rays of the morning sun, and the flat area outside is a good vantage point to watch the sunset.

Well worth a visit is the **Taiqing Gong**, a temple to the south of Lao Shan, by the coast, and close to the boat dock. It's the oldest and grandest of Laoshan's temples, consisting of three halls set amid attractive scenery. Outside the first hall are two camellias about which Pu Songling wrote a story. It's a photogenic, leafy place, containing some rare flowers and trees, including Hanbai paleo-cypresses, planted in the Han dynasty, and Tangyu elms dating back to the Tang. There are nine temples nearby, which, though smaller, are quiet, peaceful places.

Yantai and around

The city of **YANTAI**, on the Yellow Sea in northern Shandong, 235km northeast of Qingdao, is a somewhat battered-looking seaside town, with a burgeoning port and a tourist industry based around its average beaches. It's Qingdao's poor relation, the same sort of thing without the glamour and style, and the best reason to visit is to check out the **temple of Penglai**, 70km west of the city, or to pick up a transport connection; **ferries** leave to Tianjin, Shanghai and Dalian in the northeast, and **Weihai**, where you can catch a ferry to South Korea, is a bus ride away.

Yantai means "smoke mound" due to the ancient practice of lighting wolf-dung fires on the headland to warn of imminent Japanese invasion, or (more likely) approaching pirates. Prior to 1949, it was a fishing port called Chefoo, and its recent history, like that of Qingdao, is closely bound up with European adventurism. In 1862, Chefoo was made a **British treaty port** as a prize of the Opium War. Thirty years later the **Germans** arrived, wishing to extend their influence on the peninsula. After World War I it was the turn of the **Americans**, who used the port as a summer station for their entire Asian fleet, then the **Japanese**, who set up a trading establishment here. However, all this foreign influence has not left a distinctive architectural mark, there has never been a foreign concession, and though you will see the odd incongruous nineteenth-century grand European building, most of the town is of much more recent origin, a product of the rapid industrialization that has taken place since 1949. The **port** has been expanded and Yantai is now a Shandong industrial

YANTAI		
Yantai	烟台	*yāntái*
Number 1 Bathing Beach	第一海水浴场	*dìyī hǎishuǐ yùchǎng*
Number 2 Bathing Beach	第二海水浴场	*dìèr hǎishuǐ yùchǎng*
Yantai Museum	烟台博物馆	*yāntái bówùguǎn*
Yantaishan Park	烟台山公园	*yāntáishān gōngyuán*
ACCOMMODATION		
Golden Shell	金贝大酒店	*jīnbèi dàjiǔdiàn*
International Trade Hotel	国贸大厦	*guómào dàshà*
Yuhuangding	毓璜顶宾馆	*yùhuángdǐng bīnguǎn*
Zhifu	芝罘宾馆	*zhīfú bīnguǎn*

heavyweight. In the early years of this century, the main exports were beancake, vermicelli, groundnuts and silks, and a hundred thousand coolies a year, bound for Siberia. Now the area produces and exports large amounts of apples, peanuts, fish and shrimp, as well as wooden clocks. It's also known for its more than passable **wine**, produced in vineyards set up by Singaporean Chinese in 1893, who learned their skills from French soldiers stationed here.

The City

Plenty of foreigners come to Yantai on the ships that call in at the huge port in the north of town. Mostly Russian sailors, few of them get much farther than the *International Seamen's Club* opposite the train station, whose bar is probably the city's most popular attraction, or the well-stocked *Friendship Store* just around the corner from here, where you can stock up on local wine and brandy. They're not missing much as there's nothing spirited about the rest of the city, although the museum is worth checking out, but for the building more than the exhibits.

Wandering the **seafront** is the most pleasant way to spend any time here. A large, modern fishing fleet is based in Yantai and fishermen can be seen repairing their nets (and drinking and playing cards) around the headland at the eastern end of town. Optimistic anglers line the promenade. **Yantaishan Park** (¥2) stands at the western end of the seafront, marking the eastern edge of the port area. This steep hill, latticed with twisting paths, is where the locals used to keep an eye out for pirates. It has a modern beacon (¥5) which offers an impressive overview of the port from the top. There are also a few pavilions, a couple of former European consulates and an old Japanese military camp. The city's two **beaches** are both east of here, but they're not great – littered, windy and hemmed in by unattractive buildings. Number 2 beach, the furthest, is the best, though the water is very polluted. Binhai Lu, along the waterfront, has a number of small seafood restaurants.

The one site you shouldn't miss is the **Yantai Museum** (daily 8am–5pm; ¥12) on Nan Dajie housed in the largest and most beautiful of the city's old guild halls, set up for the use of merchants and shipowners. The entrance hall is startling, decorated with an ensemble of over a hundred stone and wood carvings. The beams are in the shape of a woman lying on her side nursing a baby and beneath the eaves are Arab figures playing musical instruments. Other panels to the north show scenes from the *Romance of the Three Kingdoms* (see p.432), the story of the Eight Immortals who Crossed the Sea, and the story of the second-century General Su Wu, condemned to look after sheep for nineteen years as a punishment for refusing to go over to the Huns.

The main building here is the **Temple to the Goddess of the Sea**. This goddess started out as a real person, the sister of four brothers who were fishermen. It is said that she fell into a deep trance while her brothers were out on a long fishing trip. Her parents, fearing that she was dead, woke her, whereupon she told them that she had dreamed of her brothers caught in a violent storm. Later, the youngest brother returned and reported that the others had been drowned. He had been saved by a woman who had appeared in the sky and towed his boat to safety. Generations of sailors in trouble at sea reported being guided to safety by the vision of a woman. Under the Ming and Qing she became an official deity, and temples in her honour proliferated along the coast. The temple itself is in the style of imperial buildings of the Song dynasty. It was brought from Fujian by ship in 1864 – a unique and beautiful example of southern architecture in northern China, with its double roof, sweeping horns to the eaves, fancifully ornamented with mythical figures in wood, stone and glazed ceramics. Below are stone columns, their deep relief dragon motif carvings among the finest to be seen in China. The whole temple complex is set in a little garden with pools and a stage (the goddess is said to have been fond of plays). The muse-

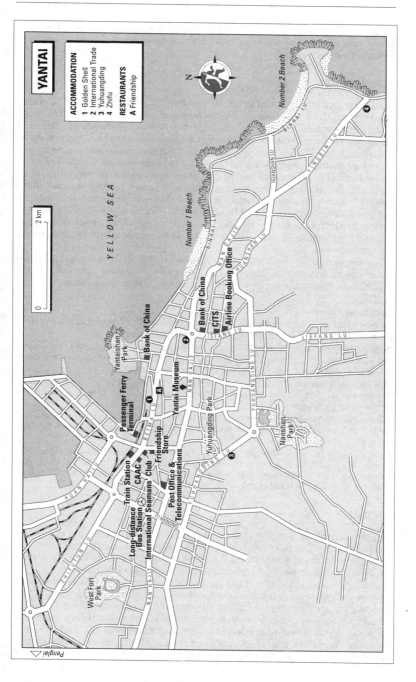

YANTAI

ACCOMMODATION
1 Golden Shell
2 International Trade
3 Yuhuangding
4 Zhifu

RESTAURANTS
A Friendship

N

0   2 km

YELLOW SEA

Yantaishan Park

Bank of China

Passenger Ferry Terminal

Bank of China

CITS

Airline Booking Office

JIEFANG LU

JIEFANG LU

Number 1 Beach

BINHAI LU

Number 2 Beach

BINHAI LU

HUANSHAN LU

NAN DAJIE

HUANSHAN LU

YINGBIN LU

Yantai Museum

NAN DAJIE

Yuhuangding Park

YUHUANGDING LU

Nanshan Park

Friendship Store

CAAC

Train Station

International Seamans' Club

Long-distance Bus Station

Post Office & Telecommunications

Yuhuangding Park

YUHUANGDING LU

BEIMA LU

BEIMA LU

HUAN HAI LU

NAN DAJIE

ANTUN LU

West Port Park

Penglai

um in the side galleries houses a number of Stone Age cooking pots, axes and arrow heads, believed to be six thousand years old, and some fine seventeenth- and eighteenth-century porcelain.

Practicalities

Yantai's **airport** is 15km south of the city and taxis into the centre should be around ¥50. Ferries arrive at the **passenger ferry terminal** in the northwest of town, which is packed in summer with peasants beginning their annual migration to Manchuria for the harvest. The **train station** near here is at the terminus of two lines, one to Qingdao and one to Ji'nan. The bus from Qingdao rockets along an expressway and terminates at the **long-distance bus station** on Qing Nian Lu, southwest of the train station

Bus #2 is the most useful around the city, travelling east from the train station along Nan Dajie, the main street, then turning south down Jiefang Lu. Both the **post office** (Mon–Fri 8am–6pm) and the **Bank of China** (Mon–Fri 8am–noon & 2–5pm, Sat 8am–noon) are on its route. The **CITS** office at 181B Jiefang Lu (☎0535/6234144) sells ferry and train tickets. You can also get ferry tickets from a booking office in the passenger ferry terminal. The *CAAC* office (Mon–Sat 8am–5pm) is opposite the train station on Beima Lu.

The two best **restaurants** in town are the *Golden Shell Hotel* on Beima Lu (try the seafood stew) and, east of here, the more expensive *Friendship Restaurant*. Small, rather casual restaurants on the seafront offer shrimp, crab and fish dishes.

Accommodation

Yantai's **hotel** situation is not good. The city is popular with Chinese tourists and there are many small guesthouses, but they are not open to foreigners.

Golden Shell, 172 Beima Lu (☎0535/6226150). This small and comfortable place, ten minutes' walk from the station, is probably the cheapest you'll find, and if you're travelling alone staff can be persuaded to give you a double room for half price if you grovel nicely. ⑤.

International Trade Hotel, 303 Nan Dajie (☎0535/6217888). A striking new 28-storey highrise towering over the town centre that looks more expensive than it is. It has all the usual flash amenities, including a bowling hall. ⑦.

Yuhuangding, Yuhuangding Xi Lu (☎0535/6244401). This low-key place is a little out of way. Take bus #3 from the station and get off at the southern end of Yuhuangding and walk north for a kilometre. ⑦.

Zhifu, 1 Yingbin Lu (☎0535/6888288). Reposing in a quiet suburban area 8km out of town, this highrise is a good place to get away from it all and the beach is just ten minutes' walk away. However, buses are too infrequent to bother with and it's a 45-minute hike into town. The hotel restaurant is good, which is just as well, as you won't find another one in the vicinity. ⑦.

Penglai

Penglai, a temple on a hill top 70km west of the city, is worth a day trip as it's more exciting than anything in Yantai. Tourist **minibuses** leave irregularly from outside the station, or you can get a local bus to Penglai town from the long-distance bus station. The temple is 3km beyond the town, but there are plenty of minibuses.

Over a thousand years old and in a good state of repair, the temple, whose military features such as crenellated walls make it look more like a castle, is a strikingly attractive complex brooding over the cliff face, dominated by a lighthouse-like tower. There are six main buildings, extensively restored and added to. The Main Hall contains a fine gilt Sea Goddess, behind whose dais is a spectacular mural of sea and cloud dragons disporting themselves. You can swim or catch crabs in the sea, which is a little cleaner here than in Yantai, while you wait for the return bus.

The temple is famous for the **Penglai mirage**, which locals claim appears every few decades. Accounts vary widely, from a low-lying sea mist to an island in the sky, complete with people, trees and vehicles. The phenomenon lasts about forty minutes, and if you're not lucky enough to witness it you can watch it on TV in a room set aside for the purpose inside the temple.

Weihai

The port of **WEIHAI**, 60km east of Yantai, has nothing to recommend it to tourists, but it's an important transit point. A twice-weekly passenger **ferry** leaves from here for Inchon in **South Korea**. Tickets (the cheapest are US$110) can be booked at Weihai *CITS* at 27 Heping Lu (☎0896/5225850), Yantai *CITS* (see p.318) or from the business centre at the *Wehaiwei Dasha* (☎0896/5232542; ⑨) on Kunming Lu, the main road leading to the port. Cheaper **accommodation** is offered at the *Weihai Dajiudian* (☎0896/5233888; ④), on a small street one block north of Kunming Lu, which has a very plush seafood restaurant. The **Bank of China**, where you can change travellers' cheques, is a few minutes farther west along Kunming Lu from the *Weihaiwei Dasha*. Weihai's **long-distance bus station** is about ten minutes south of the *Bank of China*, or 25 minutes' walk from the port. There's a sleeper bus to Beijing every afternoon at 2pm (¥140), and frequent services to Yantai and Qingdao.

travel details

Trains

Anyang to: Beijing (11 daily; 7hr); Linxian (1 daily; 2hr); Shijiazhuang (3 daily; 5hr); Zhengzhou (12 daily; 3hr).

Datong to: Baotou (2 daily; 8hr); Beijing (4 daily; 7hr); Hohhot (24 daily; 5hr); Lanzhou (daily; 25hr); Linfen (daily; 12hr); Taiyuan (6 daily; 7hr); Xi'an (daily; 20hr).

Hua Shan to: Xi'an (4 daily; 3hr); Yuncheng (2 daily; 5hr).

Ji'nan to: Beijing (4 daily; 9hr); Qingdao (6 daily; 6hr); Shanghai (daily, 14hr); Tai'an (4 daily; 1hr); Yantai (4 daily; 8hr); Yanzhou, for Qufu (daily; 3hr).

Kaifeng to: Shanghai (6 daily; 12hr); Xi'an (daily; 5hr); Zhengzhou (3 daily; 2hr).

Linfen to: Taiyuan (1 daily; 5hr); Xi'an (2 daily; 9hr); Yuncheng (3 daily; 4hr).

Luoyang to: Beijing (daily; 14hr); Shanghai (3 daily; 20hr); Xi'an (4 daily; 6 hr); Zhengzhou (6 daily; 2 hr).

Qingdao to: Beijing (2 daily; 19hr); Ji'nan (5 daily; 6hr); Shenyang (daily; 25hr); Tianjin (2 daily, 17hr); Yantai (3 daily; 5hr).

Tai'an to: Beijing (daily; 10hr); Ji'nan (4 daily; 1hr); Yanzhou, for Qufu (5 daily; 2hr).

Taiyuan to: Beijing (4 daily; 13hr); Datong (5 daily; 7hr); Linfen (daily, 7hr); Pingyao (4 daily; 3hr); Shijiazhuang (6 daily; 6hr); Xi'an (4 daily; 14hr); Yuncheng (daily; 9hr); Zhengzhou (2 daily; 13hr).

Xi'an to: Baoji (11 daily; 4hr); Beijing (5 daily; 18hr); Datong (2 daily; 22hr); Guangzhou (2 daily; 40hr); Hua Shan (4 daily; 3hr); Lanzhou (8 daily; 12hr); Linfen (2 daily; 6hr); Luoyang (14 daily; 6hr); Taiyuan (5 daily; 12hr); Shanghai (5 daily; 24hr); Urumqi (daily; 60hr); Xining (4 daily; 16hr); Yuncheng (3 daily; 10hr); Yan'an (2 daily; 10hr); Zhengzhou (14 daily; 10hr).

Yantai to: Beijing (daily; 20hr); Ji'nan (3 daily; 8hr); Qingdao (6 daily; 5hr).

Yuncheng to: Linfen (3 daily; 4hr); Taiyuan (1 daily; 9hr); Xi'an (2 daily; 4hr).

Zhengzhou to: Anyang (4 daily; 3hr); Beijing (2 daily; 12hr); Guangzhou (2 daily; 35hr); Luoyang (8 daily; 2hr); Shanghai (3 daily; 14hr); Taiyuan (3 daily; 12hr); Xi'an (5 daily; 10hr).

Buses

With so many services operating in the region, bus frequencies have not been included. To most of the following destinations buses leave at least hourly during the day, with a few buses leaving in the evening and travelling through the night.

Anyang to: Kaifeng (4hr); Linxian (3hr); Zhengzhou (4hr).

Datong to: Wutai Shan (summer-only service; 9hr); Taiyuan (10hr).

Dengfeng to: Gongxian (2hr); Luoyang (3hr); Zhengzhou (3hr).

Gongxian to: Dengfeng (2hr); Luoyang (3hr); Zhengzhou (3hr).

Ji'nan to: Beijing (10hr); Qingdao (7hr); Qufu (5hr); Tai'an (3hr).

Kaifeng to: Anyang (4hr); Zhengzhou (2hr).

Linfen to: Taiyuan (8hr); Yuncheng (5hr).

Luoyang to: Anyang (4hr); Dengfeng (3hr); Gongxian (3hr); Ruicheng (4hr); Xi'an (10hr); Yuncheng (6hr); Zhengzhou (3hr).

Qufu to: Qingdao (10hr); Ji'nan (5hr); Tai'an (2hr).

Tai'an to: Ji'nan (3hr); Qufu (2hr).

Taiyuan to: Datong (10hr); Shijiazhuang (9hr); Wutai Shan (summer-only service; 9hr); Yuncheng (12hr); Zhengzhou (15hr).

Xi'an to: Hua Shan (3hr); Luoyang (10hr); Ruicheng (4hr); Yan'an (10hr); Yuncheng (6hr); Zhengzhou (7hr).

Yantai to: Qingdao (4hr); Weihai (3hr).

Yuncheng to: Linfen (5hr); Xi'an (8hr); Taiyuan (12hr); Ruicheng (4hr).

Zhengzhou to: Anyang (4hr); Dengfeng (3hr); Gongxian (3hr); Luoyang (3hr).

Ferries

Qingdao to: Dalian (every 4 days; 26hr); Shanghai (every 4 days; 27hr); Inchon (South Korea; weekly; 25hr).

Weihai to: Inchon (South Korea; 2 weekly; 24hr).

Yantai to: Dalian (3 weekly; 10hr); Shanghai (2 weekly; 35hr); Tianjin (daily; 7hr).

Planes

DOMESTIC

Ji'nan to: Beijing (1–2 daily; 1hr); Changchun (2 weekly; 4hr); Chengdu (6 weekly; 2hr); Chongqing (2 weekly; 1hr 40min); Dalian (4 weekly; 1hr 50min); Fuzhou (3 weekly; 2hr); Guangzhou (1–3 daily; 3hr); Haikou (2 weekly; 4hr 50min); Harbin (4 weekly; 2hr); Hong Kong (3 weekly; 2hr 30min); Kunming (4 weekly; 3hr); Nanjing (2 weekly; 1hr 30min); Qingdao (2 weekly; 1hr); Shanghai (2–3 daily; 1hr 40min); Shenyang (3 weekly; 1hr 40min); Shenzhen (4 weekly; 2hr 45min); Urumqi (3 weekly; 6hr); Wenzhou (2 weekly; 2hr); Wuhan (4 weekly; 1hr 30min); Xiamen (4 weekly; 2hr);

Xi'an (4 weekly; 1hr 50min); Yantai (2 weekly; 1hr).

Luoyang to: Beijing (weekly; 1hr 40min); Chengdu (2 weekly; 1hr 40min); Dalian (weekly; 1hr 45min); Guangzhou (5 weekly; 2hr 45min); Hong Kong (weekly; 2hr 20min); Shenyang (weekly; 2hr 20min); Shenzhen (weekly; 2hr 15min); Xiamen (weekly; 2hr 10min).

Qingdao to: Beijing (2–3 daily; 1hr 15min); Changchun (2 weekly; 3hr 40min); Changsha (4 weekly; 2hr); Chengdu (2 weekly; 2hr 45min); Chongqing (2 weekly; 2hr 40min); Dalian (6 weekly; 1hr); Fuzhou (4 weekly; 2hr); Guangzhou (1–3 daily; 3hr); Guilin (2 weekly; 2hr 50min); Haikou (weekly; 3hr 30min); Hangzhou (2 weekly; 1hr 20min); Harbin (6 weekly; 2hr); Hefei (2 weekly; 2hr 10min); Hong Kong (daily; 3hr 15min); Ji'nan (2 weekly; 1hr 10min); Kunming (1 weekly; 3hr); Lanzhou (2 weekly; 2hr 20min); Nanjing (5 weekly; 1hr 30min); Ningbo (2 weekly; 1hr 50min); Shanghai (2–4 daily; 1hr 15min); Shenyang (daily; 3hr); Shenzhen (6 weekly; 3hr 10min); Urumqi (weekly; 6hr 30min); Wenzhou (2 weekly; 2hr); Wuhan (4 weekly; 2hr); Xiamen (5 weekly; 4hr 20min); Xi'an (2 weekly; 2hr 20min); Zhengzhou (3 weekly; 2hr).

Taiyuan to: Beijing (daily; 1hr 10min); Changsha (2 weekly; 2hr); Chengdu (5 weekly; 2hr 20min); Chongqing (2 weekly; 4hr 30min); Dalian (2 weekly; 3hr 30min); Fuzhou (weekly; 4hr 20min); Guangzhou (weekly; 3hr); Haikou (2 weekly; 4hr 30min); Hangzhou (weekly; 2hr 20min); Hong Kong (weekly; 2hr 45min); Nanjing (2 weekly; 2hr); Qinhuangdao (weekly; 1hr 20min); Shanghai (7 weekly; 2hr); Shenyang (2 weekly; 4hr); Shenzhen (2 weekly; 3hr 15min); Shijiazhuang (3 weekly; 1hr); Tianjin (4 weekly; 1hr 30min); Wenzhou (weekly; 4hr 15min); Wuhan (2 weekly; 3hr 30min); Xiamen (weekly; 4hr 30min); Xi'an (2 weekly; 2hr 30min); Zhengzhou (2 weekly; 1hr 10min).

Xi'an to: Baotou (2 weekly; 2hr 10min); Beijing (4 daily; 1hr 30min); Changsha (daily; 1hr 50min); Chengdu (2 daily; 1hr 15min); Chongqing (2 daily; 2hr); Dalian (weekly; 2hr); Fuzhou (daily; 2hr); Guangzhou (2 daily; 2hr 30min); Guilin (2 daily; 2hr); Haikou (daily; 3hr); Hangzhou (4 weekly; 1hr); Harbin (2 weekly; 4hr 45min); Hong Kong (4 weekly; 2hr 30min); Ji'nan (4 weekly; 1hr 30min); Kunming (daily; 2hr 15min); Lanzhou (1–2 daily; 1hr 10min); Nanjing (5 weekly; 2hr); Ningbo (weekly; 2hr 40min); Qingdao (2 weekly; 2hr 10min); Shanghai (2–4 daily; 1hr 40min);

Shenyang (daily; 2hr 20min); Shenzhen (daily; 2hr 20min); Shijiazhuang (3 weekly; 2hr); Taiyuan (3 weekly; 1hr 30min); Tianjin (2 weekly; 2hr); Urumqi (1–3 daily; 3hr 20min); Wenzhou (4 weekly; 2hr 30min); Wuhan (1–3 daily; 2hr 20min); Xiamen (daily; 3hr); Xining (3 weekly; 2hr), Yantai (3 weekly; 2hr).

Yantai to: Beijing (2–4 daily; 1hr); Changchun (2 weekly; 1hr 40min); Chengdu (3 weekly; 4hr); Guangzhou (5 weekly; 2hr 25min); Haikou (2 weekly; 4hr 15min); Harbin (1–3 daily; 1hr 30min); Ji'nan (2 weekly; 1hr 10min); Nanjing (2 weekly; 1hr 45min); Shanghai (4 weekly; 1hr 30min); Shenyang (weekly; 1hr); Shenzhen (6 weekly; 3hr 30min); Wenzhou (2 weekly; 2hr); Wuhan (4 weekly; 1hr 50min); Xiamen (weekly; 4hr 30min); Xi'an (3 weekly; 2hr 10min); Zhengzhou (2 weekly; 4hr 15min).

Zhengzhou to: Beijing (2 daily; 1hr 20min); Changsha (2 weekly; 3hr 10min); Chengdu (5 weekly; 1hr 45min); Chongqing (2 weekly; 1hr 50min); Fuzhou (3 weekly; 1hr 40min); Guangzhou (3–4 daily; 2hr 20min); Haikou (5 weekly; 4hr 45min); Harbin (5 weekly; 2hr 20min); Hong Kong (4 weekly; 2hr 20min); Kunming (5 weekly; 2hr 30min); Lanzhou (weekly; 2hr 10min); Nanjing (daily; 1hr 50min); Qingdao (3 weekly; 2hr); Shanghai (1–3 daily; 1hr 20min); Shenyang (0–2 daily; 1hr 50min); Shenzhen (2 daily; 2hr 20min); Shijiazhuang (weekly; 1hr); Taiyuan (2 weekly; 1hr 20min); Urumqi (3 weekly; 4hr 20min); Wenzhou (6 weekly; 1hr 50min); Wuhan (5 weekly; 1hr 30min); Xiamen (daily; 2hr); Yantai (2 weekly; 4hr 20min).

Planes

INTERNATIONAL

Qingdao to: Osaka (2 weekly; 3hr 30min); Seoul (5 weekly; 2hr 30min).

Xi'an to: Nagoya (daily; 6hr).

CHAPTER FIVE

SHANGHAI

After forty years of stagnation, the great metropolis of **SHANGHAI** is currently undergoing one of the fastest economic expansions that the world has ever seen. While shops overflow and the skyline fills with cranes, Shanghai now seems certain, some time in the twenty-first century, to recapture its position as East Asia's leading business city, a status it last held before World War II. And yet, for all the modernization in terms of infrastructure, lifestyle and availability of consumer goods, Shanghai in the late 1990s is still a city inextricably linked with its **colonial past**.

Shanghai is still mainly known in the West for its infamous role as the base of **European imperialism** in mainland China – its decadence, illicit pleasures, racism, appalling social inequalities and mafia syndicates. The intervening fifty years have almost been forgotten, as though the period, from when the Communists arrived and the foreigners moved out, was an era in which nothing happened. To some extent this perception is actually true: for most of the Communist period, the central government in Beijing has deliberately been running Shanghai down, siphoning off its surplus to other parts of the country, to the point where the city came to resemble a living museum, frozen in time since the 1940s.

Yet the Shanghainese never lost their ability to make waves for themselves and, in recent years, China's central government has come to be dominated by individuals from the Shanghai area, who look with favour on the rebuilding of their old metropolis. In the early 1990s the decision was made to push Shanghai once again to the forefront of China's drive for **modernization**, and an explosion of **economic activity** has been unleashed. City planners are already busy, creating a subway network, colossal high-ways, flyovers and bridges, shopping malls, hotel complexes and the beginnings of a "New Bund" – the Special Economic Zone across the river in Pudong, already crowned by one of Asia's tallest buildings, the **Oriental Pearl TV Tower**. With by far the most highly skilled labour force in the country, the long-suppressed Shanghai ability to combine style and sophistication with a sharp sense for business is once again riding high.

Not that the old Shanghai is set to disappear overnight. The city still, in large parts, resembles a 1920s vision of the future; a grimy metropolis of monolithic pseudo-classical facades, threaded with overhead cables and walkways, bursting with the noise of rattling trolleybuses and choked by vast crowds of purposefully scurrying pedestrians. Unlike other major Chinese cities, Shanghai has only very recently been subjected to large-scale rebuilding. Most of the urban area was partitioned between foreign powers until 1949, and their former embassies, banks and official residences still give large areas of Shanghai an early-century European flavour which the odd Soviet-inspired government building cannot overshadow. It is still possible to make out the boundaries of what used to be the foreign concessions, with the bewildering tangle of overhanging alleyways of the old Chinese city at its heart. Only along the Huangpu waterfront, amid the solid grandeur of the **Bund**, is there some sense of space – and here you feel the past more strongly than ever, its outward forms, shabby and battered, still very much a working part of the city. It is an intriguing irony that relics of hated foreign imperialism such as the Bund are now proudly protected by the Shanghainese as city monuments.

Inevitably, many of the social ills that the Communists were supposed to have eliminated after 1949 are making a comeback as well. Unemployment, drug abuse and pros-

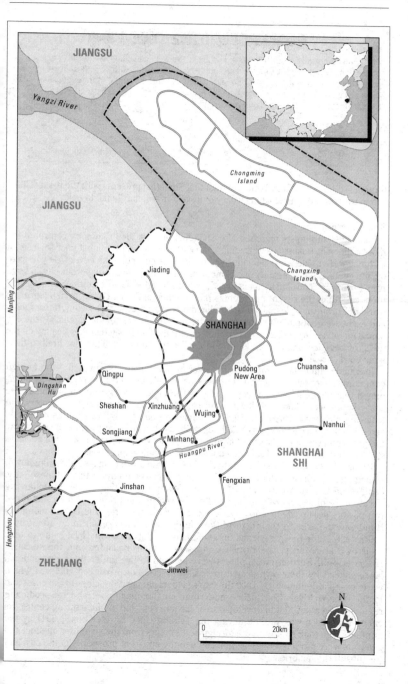

JIANGSU

Yangzi River

JIANGSU

Chongming
Island

Changxing
Island

Jiading

SHANGHAI

Pudong
New Area

Chuansha

Qingpu

Nanjing

Dingshan
Hu

Sheshan

Xinzhuang

Wujing

Songjiang

Minhang

Nanhui

Huangpu River

SHANGHAI
SHI

Jinshan

Fengxian

Hangzhou

ZHEJIANG

Jinwei

N

0   20km

ACCOMMODATION PRICE CODES

All the accommodation in this book has been graded according to the following price codes, which represent the cheapest double room available to foreigners. Most places have a range of rooms, however, and staff will usually offer you the more expensive ones – it's always worth asking if they have anything cheaper. Where the text refers specifically to dorm beds, the price code represents the price per bed. See p.40 for more details.

① less than ¥30	④ ¥100–150	⑦ ¥300–500
② ¥30–75	⑤ ¥150–200	⑧ ¥500–700
③ ¥75–100	⑥ ¥200–300	⑨ ¥700 or more

titution are rife. But the dynamic contrast that Shanghai presents with the rest of China is one that even the most China-weary of travellers will hardly fail to enjoy.

Some history

When the Communists marched into Shanghai in May 1949 they took control of the most important business and trading centre in Asia, an international port where vast fortunes were made while millions lived in absolute poverty. Whichever side you were on, life in Shanghai was rarely one of moderation. China's most prosperous city, in large part European- and American-financed, it introduced Asia to electric light, boasted more cars than the rest of the country put together, and created for its rich citizens a world of European-style mansions, tree-lined boulevards, chic café society, horse racing and exclusive gentlemen's clubs. Alongside, and equally part of the legend, lay the city famed for adventure, organized crime and prostitution, of bloated bodies floating on the tides, of beggars, starving children and coolies, of hungry millions in thrall to their daily bowl of rice.

Inevitably, after the Communist takeover, the bright lights dimmed – the foreign community may have expected "business as usual", but the new regime was determined that Shanghai should play its role in the radical reconstruction of China. The worst slums were knocked down to be replaced by apartments, the gangsters and singsong girls were taken away for "re-education", and foreign capital was ruthlessly taxed if not confiscated outright (although Chiang Kaishek did manage to spirit away the gold reserves of the *Bank of China* to Taiwan, leaving the city broke). For 35 years Western influences were discouraged and often forcibly suppressed.

Before the **Opium Wars**, Shanghai had been little more than a small fishing town, walled against pirate raids (this original town survives today as the "Chinese" city, centred on the Yu Yuan). After the Opium Wars, the British moved in under the Treaty of Nanking in 1842, to be rapidly followed by the French in 1847, and these two powers set up the first **foreign concessions** in the city – the British along the Bund and the area to the north of the Chinese city; the French in an area to the southwest. Later the Americans, in 1863, and the Japanese, in 1895, came to tack their own areas on to the British Concession which expanded into the so-called **International Settlement**. Traders were allowed to live under their own national laws, policed by their own armed forces, in a series of privileged enclaves which were leased indefinitely. By 1900 the city's favourable position, close to the coast and to the Yangzi River (the main trade route to the major silk and tea-producing regions), had allowed it to develop into a sizeable port and manufacturing centre. Its cheap workforce was swollen during the Taiping Uprising (see box, p.391) by the numbers who took shelter in the foreign settlements from the slaughter outside, and peasants were attracted in their thousands to the apparent prosperity of the city, and the jobs in the factories.

Here China's first urban proletariat emerged, and the squalid living conditions, outbreaks of unemployment and glaring abuses of Chinese labour by foreign investors made Shanghai a natural breeding ground for **revolutionary politics**. The Chinese Communist Party was founded in the city in 1921, only to be driven underground by the notorious massacre of hundreds of strikers in 1927. Even since 1949, the city has remained a centre of radicalism – Mao, stifled by Beijing bureaucracy, launched his Cultural Revolution here in 1966. Certain Red Guards even proclaimed a Shanghai Commune, before the whole affair descended into wanton destruction and petty vindictiveness. After Mao's death Shanghai was the last stronghold of the Gang of Four in their struggle for the succession, though their planned coup never materialized. Today, many key modernizing officials in the central government are from the Shanghai area, including President Jiang Zemin, and finance minister Zhu Rongji, both former mayors of the city.

As well as an important power-base for the ruling party, Shanghai has always been by far the most **fashion-conscious** and **outward-looking** city in China. The Shanghainese are renowned for their quick wit and entrepreneurial skills – a high proportion of the overseas Chinese successful in business elsewhere in the world originally emigrated from this area – and their dialect is all but incomprehensible to other Chinese. Even during the Cultural Revolution, Western excesses like curled hair and holding hands in public survived in Shanghai, and it has always been easier for visitors to communicate with the locals here than anywhere else in the country, because of the excellent level of English spoken and the familiarity with foreigners. The city's relative wealth has also allowed a greater interest in **leisure** activities and **nightlife**, with a wide variety of public entertainment on offer as well as new privately run bars. Not only does Shanghai remain the nation's premier industrial base, it is also the major consumer centre, and the variety and quality of goods in the shops attract people from all over China.

Some problems remain, however, and above all Shanghai continues to suffer acute **overcrowding**. Although the housing stock has soared in recent years, even official statistics give the average inhabitant living space little larger than a double bed, and in practice this often means three generations of a family sleeping in one room. Everywhere you look, there are too many people, and the resultant stress frequently results in outbreaks of bad temper and sometimes public brawling. As a centre of huge oil refineries, chemical and metallurgical plants, Shanghai is also afflicted by air **pollution** in the form of sulphurous clouds pouring from the factory chimneys. About four million tons of untreated industrial and domestic waste flow daily into the Huangpu River, the city's main source of drinking water, while the Suzhou Creek is black and foul-smelling. Finally, the **unemployment** rate is noticeably higher than that of other major cities. The problem of outsiders without Shanghai residence papers (and hence without accommodation) pouring into the city under the lure of fantastic riches has the potential to lead to serious social unrest. Today, though nominally closed to internal migration, and despite the one-child policy and three hundred thousand abortions annually, Shanghai continues to grow – to the point where a population of over twelve million makes it one of the largest (and most congested) cities in the world.

Orientation, arrival and city transport

Shanghai is a surprisingly compact place, considering its enormous population, and although its layout is less obviously geometrical than that of Beijing, it's not hard to find your way around the various quarters on foot – though you'll certainly need buses or taxis for crossing from one quarter to the next. The area of most interest to visitors is bordered to the east by the **Huangpu River** (which flows from south to north), and to the north by the **Suzhou Creek** (which flows from west to east). A good place to get your bearings is at the southwestern corner of the junction of these two rivers, at the

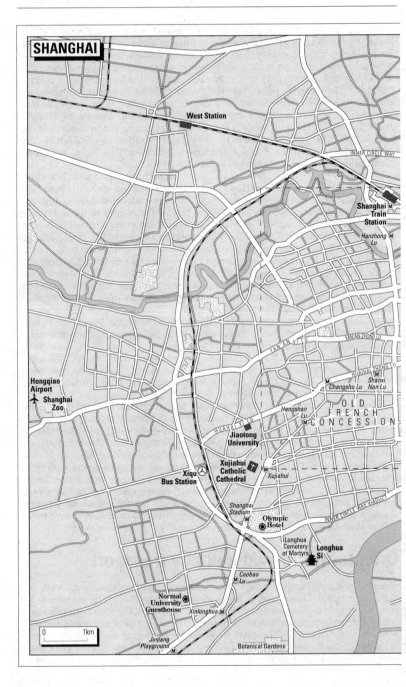

SHANGHAI

West Station

INNER CIRCLE WAY

Shanghai
Train
Station M

Hanzhong M
Lu

YAN'AN XI LU

YAN'AN ZHONG LU

HUAIHAI ZHONG LU

Changshu Lu M *Shanxi
Nan Lu*

O L D
F R E N C H
C O N C E S S I O N

*Hengshan
Lu* M

Hongqiao
Airport
Shanghai
Zoo

HUAIHAI XI LU

Jiaotong
University

Xujiahui
Catholic
Cathedral M
Xujiahui

Xiqu
Bus Station

*Shanghai
Stadium* M
Olympic
Hotel

INNER CIRCLE WAY VIADUCT

Longhua
Cemetery
of Martyrs Longhua
Si

Caobao M
Lu

Normal
University
Guesthouse
Xinlonghua M

Jinjiang
Playground M   Botanical Gardens

0   1km

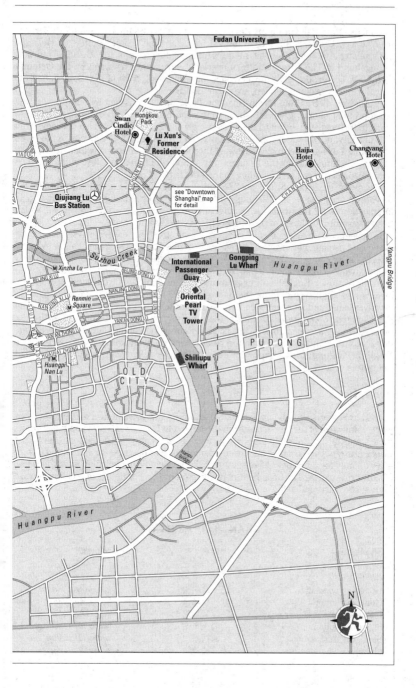

entrance of the small **Huangpu Park**. To the north, across the iron **Waibaidu Bridge** over Suzhou Creek, is the area of the old Japanese Concession. South from Huangpu Park, along the western bank of the Huangpu River, runs the **Bund** – officially Zhongshan Lu. The **Bund** is in turn overlooked from the east bank by the **Oriental Pearl TV Tower**, the city's most conspicuous landmark. A lot of hotels, including the only dormitory accommodation, are in the Bund area.

A hundred metres south from Huangpu Park, the Bund is met by **Nanjing Lu**, the city's premier shopping street, which runs west, past the northern edge of **Renmin Park** in the centre of the city. Like all east–west routes Nanjing Lu takes its name from that of a city; north–south roads are named after provinces. A few blocks to the south of Nanjing Lu is another major east-west thoroughfare, **Yan'an Lu**, which, to the east, leads into a tunnel under the Huangpu River. South of here, just west of the Bund, is the oval-shaped area corresponding to the **Old City**.

The most important of the north–south axes is **Xizang Lu**, cutting through the downtown area just west of Renmin Park. Heading south, Xizang Lu runs down to an intersection with **Huaihai Lu**, Shanghai's other main shopping boulevard, which heads west into the heart of the **old French Concession**.

In Shanghai, as in many other Chinese cities, long streets are divided into sections for the purpose of naming. For example Yan'an "East" Street (Yan'an Dong Lu), Yan'an "Middle" Street (Yan'an Zhong Lu) and Yan'an "West" Street (Yan'an Xi Lu). This convention is very useful when looking for an **address**. North and south are *bei* and *nan* respectively.

Various glossy English-language **maps** are available, with clear information on streets and sights – including the *Shanghai Official Tourist Map* which is paid for by advertising and is issued free in hotels. Additionally, bus routes can be found on the *Shanghai Communications Map*, though this map has street names in Chinese only. All maps are available in the large hotels or bookshops, or from street vendors. A vital source of information about current events in the city is the free **English-language newspaper** for expatriates, *Shanghai Talk*, available in upmarket hotels.

Arrival

Arrival in Shanghai can be an exhausting affair. By **air** you'll arrive at **Hongqiao airport**, 15km west of the city. A taxi from the airport to Huaihai Lu costs about ¥30 on the meter, and to the Bund about ¥45; alternatively you can ride the airport **bus** to the *China Eastern Airlines* office on Yan'an Lu, more or less opposite the Exhibition Centre – very handy for a number of five-star hotels in the vicinity, but still 3km from the Bund. The bus ride can take up to an hour depending on traffic. For details of booking onward flights, see "Listings", p.352).

SHANGHAI: ARRIVAL		
Shanghai	上海	*shànghǎi*
ARRIVAL		
Gongping Lu wharf	公平路码头	*gōngpínglù mǎtóu*
Hongqiao airport	虹桥机场	*hóngqiáo jīchǎng*
International passenger quay	国际客运站	*guójì kèyùnzhàn*
Shanghai station	上海火车站	*shànghǎi huǒchēzhàn*
Shanghai West station	上海西站	*shànghǎi xīzhàn*
Shiliupu wharf	十六浦码头	*shíliùpǔ mǎtóu*

The main **train** station – **Shanghai station** – is to the north of Suzhou Creek. Its vast concrete forecourt is a seething mass of encamped peasants at all hours, and it's not a particularly safe place to hang around at night. City buses are not an easy way to get out of the station area; fortunately, however, the single line of Shanghai's new underground metro network begins and ends here, which is very convenient if your hotel happens to be near a station on the line. Much the best bet otherwise is to take a taxi which shouldn't cost more than ¥15–20. There's an official taxi rank outside the station and there is no trouble with drivers hustling foreigners. Another station in the remote northwest of town, **Shanghai West station**, is the terminus for a few long-distance trains, such as the train from Inner Mongolia. This is linked to the metro and taxi rank at the main station by bus #106.

Hardly any tourists arrive in Shanghai by **bus**, and one good reason to avoid trying to do this is that you are likely to be dropped somewhere in the remote outskirts of the

---

MOVING ON FROM SHANGHAI

The soft seat waiting room in the main **train station** (enter from the forecourt, near the eastern end; there's an English sign) has an office that sells same-day tickets only, hard seat as well as soft. Alternatively, the *Longmen Hotel*, a couple of minutes west of the station square, has a foreigners' ticket office (daily 7am–5.30pm & 6–9pm) in the lobby which sells tickets for same-day or next-day travel – mainly seats to Nanjing and Hangzhou, though it does also sell sleepers to a few important destinations such as Beijing or Guangzhou. To book further in advance (up to six days) you can buy tickets (with a mark-up) from *CTS* in the *Pacific Hotel* on Nanjing Xi Lu, or from the *CITS* office at 2 Jinling Dong Lu (both daily 8.30–11.30am & 1–4.45pm).

Tourists rarely travel by **bus** into or out of Shanghai, though for a few destinations buses might offer a convenient way to leave the city, because they are cheaper than trains and it is easy to get a seat. In the western part of the train station square several private operators offer tickets, up to a day in advance, for Hangzhou, Wenzhou and other destinations in Zhejiang Province, and the Qiujiang Lu bus station, just west of Henan Bei Lu, is useful for nearby towns in Jiangsu. For a few destinations outside the city (see p.345), but inside the Shanghai Municipality, services leave from the **Xiqu bus station** (bus #113 from the train station) or a nameless bus stop on Shaanxi Nan Lu, outside the Wenhua Guangchang, just south of Fuxing Lu. For these buses, you pay on board.

Leaving by boat also deserves serious consideration, with tickets cheaper and travelling conditions sometimes better than the trains. You can buy tickets from any travel service for an added fee, or go to the **boat ticket office** (daily 7–11.30am & 12.30–6pm) at the corner of Jinling Dong Lu and the Bund, which sells every kind of boat ticket out of Shanghai. The office has no English sign, but the entrance is opposite the *CITS* booking office. The downstairs windows sell tickets for the coastal routes. There are no surcharges for foreigners except on the Putuo Shan route, and therefore prices are fairly low. Sample first-class fares include Dalian ¥256, Qingdao ¥206, Ningbo ¥117, Putuo Shan ¥132, Wenzhou ¥176 and Mawei (for Fuzhou) ¥320. If you want to travel as cheaply and can put up with crowds and discomfort, note that the lowest class fares for even the most expensive destinations are less than ¥70. For **Putuo Shan** there are also special ticket windows belonging to private operators – for details, see Putuo Shan (p.422). **Yangzi River** boat tickets are sold upstairs, with a fifty percent surcharge for foreigners without Chinese student cards. Fares (before surcharge) include: Nanjing ¥23–120, Wuhan ¥57–301 and Chongqing ¥138–737. Finally, if you go right through the upstairs hall and beyond, there are a couple of offices (daily 8.30am–noon & 1–4.30pm) for tickets to **Japan** and **Hong Kong** respectively. For Japan there are connections to Yokohama, Osaka (the most frequent) and Nagasaki (the nearest and cheapest). At the time of writing, the Osaka boat cost around US$230. The frequency of all these boats varies seasonally, but there are usually several departures weekly. The conditions are pretty luxurious, with boats equipped with swimming pools, restaurants, discos and clean, comfortable berths.

city. Some services use the **bus station** on Qiujiang Lu, just west of Henan Bei Lu, and a few private buses terminate at the train station itself, but generally speaking it's pot luck where you end up.

Probably the nicest way to arrive in Shanghai is by **boat**, whether from Hong Kong, Japan, or the towns along the coast or inland up the Yangzi. The Yangzi ferries and coastal boats to and from Ningbo, Wenzhou and Putuo Shan sail south right past the Bund to the **Shiliupu wharf**, linked by bus #55 to the northern end of the Bund. Coastal boats to and from Qingdao, Dalian and Fuzhou use the **Gongping Lu wharf** which is only about twenty minutes' walk to the northeast of the Bund, or a short ride on bus #135, while boats from Hong Kong or Japan dock at the **International passenger quay**, about five minutes' walk east from the *Pujiang Hotel*.

City transport

The new **Shanghai metro** currently comprises a single line, though several more are planned. The line runs from the main train station in the north, down through the centre of town, with a stop at Renmin Park, and then turns west along Huaihai Lu. All tickets, irrespective of distance, cost ¥2, and are bought from a ticket window. There are no travel passes for tourists, though you can buy as many tickets as you want in advance to save time on queuing.

Local **buses** run everywhere, but suffer from two serious defects – they are unbelievably crowded, especially during the early morning and late evening rush hours, and they are extremely slow owing to the grotesque traffic congestion in the city. They run from around 4am to 10.30pm. **Bus maps** mark the widely separated stops with a small dot. **Fares** vary but are never more than a few jiao; buy your ticket from the conductor on the bus.

Taxis are fairly easy to get hold of and, if you're not on a very tight budget, they are often the most comfortable way to get around – fares usually come to between ¥20 and ¥35 for rides within the city. The smaller taxis are marginally cheaper. The only kind of hassle you're likely to suffer is from drivers who take you on unnecessarily long routes, but if you sit in the front seat and hold a map on your lap they will usually be persuaded to behave themselves. However, very late at night, conventions change – meters are switched off and you may have to negotiate the fare.

To cross the Huangpu River over to the Pudong the cheapest way is to take the very frequent **ferry** from the central part of the Bund opposite the end of Jinling Dong Lu.

USEFUL SHANGHAI BUS ROUTES

NORTH–SOUTH

#18 (trolley) From Hongkou Park, across the Suzhou Creek and along Xizang Lu.

#41 Passes Tianmu Xi Lu, in front of the train station and goes down through the French Concession to Longhua Park.

#64 From the train station, along Beijing Lu, then close to the Shiliupu wharf on the south of the Bund.

#65 From the top to the bottom of Zhongshan Lu (the Bund), terminating in the south at the Nanpu Bridge.

EAST–WEST

#19 (trolley) From near Gongping Lu wharf in the east, passing near the *Pujiang Hotel* and roughly following the course of the Suzhou Creek to the Jade Buddha Temple just before the terminus.

#20 From Jiaojiang Lu (just off the Bund) along Nanjing Lu, past Jing'an Si, then on to Zhongshan Park.

#42 From Guangxi Lu just off the Bund, then along Huaihai Lu in the French Concession.

#135 From Yangpu Bridge via the Bund to the eastern end of Huaihai Dong Lu.

The **telephone code** for Shanghai is ☎021

Buy a plastic token for ¥0.4 – the ride takes about ten minutes and gives you an interesting feel of how crowded these waterways are.

For anyone brave enough to give it a try, Shanghai is taking its first steps into the **car rental** market. At the airport, *Angel Car Rental* will fix you up with a temporary licence (a translation of your foreign licence) and rent you a car on the spot for ¥320 per day. Bear in mind, however, that Shanghai's traffic is slow-moving at the best of times, and you may not be allowed to drive your car beyond the city limits.

Accommodation

Accommodation in Shanghai is plentiful, and in places highly stylish, but prices are generally higher than elsewhere in China. The **grand old-world hotels** that form so integral a part of Shanghai's history cost at least US$100 per room these days, though a short stay in, for example, the famous *Peace Hotel* will certainly give you a memorable flavour of how Shanghai used to be. Even if you're not a resident, however, there's nothing to stop you strolling in to admire some of the finest art-deco interiors in the world. Meanwhile, **brand-new skyscraper hotels** are going up all the time; there's a *Sheraton* and a *Hilton*, as well as large numbers of top-class hotels out in the western part of town. All the luxury hotels charge an additional ten percent service charge, though during the off-season (in winter) some good discounts are offered. Prices are often quoted in US dollars, though you can always pay in yuan.

There is only one really **budget option** in the whole city, the *Pujiang*, which not surprisingly fills up rapidly in peak season; most other vaguely cheap places are located far out in the suburbs.

The Bund and around

Metropole, 180 Jiangxi Lu (☎63213030, fax 63217365). Just off the Bund and dating from 1931, this is one of the more affordable of the "old" hotels. A great lobby, but the rooms are plain. ⑦.

New Asia, 422 Tian Tong Lu (☎63242210, fax 63269529). Located to the north of Suzhou Creek, a couple of blocks west of the *Shanghai Mansions*, this is good value for its location. ⑦.

Peace, junction of the Bund and Nanjing Dong Lu (☎63216888, fax 63290300). Formerly the *Cathay Hotel*, the most famous hotel in Shanghai, occupies both sides of the road and is home to the *Jazz Bar* (see "Entertainment", p.349). Well worth a visit to see the art-deco interiors of the lobby. Despite its high prices, however, the service in this hotel is definitely not five-star standard. Doubles start at US$130, de luxe suites with original decor from US$380. ⑨.

Pujiang, 15 Huangpu Lu (☎63246388, fax 63065147). Located across the Waibaidu Bridge north of the Bund and slightly to the east, opposite the blue Russian Consulate building. Formerly the *Astor Hotel*, and dating back to the middle of the last century, it's a nice, stylish old place with wooden floors and high ceilings. This is the only place offering budget dormitory accommodation in the whole city. Conditions are not at all bad, each dormitory having an adjoining bathroom and toilet, as well as communal shower rooms on another floor. Dorms ②, rooms ⑦.

Tung Feng, 3 Zhongshan Dong Lu (☎63218060, fax 63210261). Good location right on the Bund, and one of the original Shanghai hotels. The lobby these days looks like a market, but there are some great suites with original decorations as well as plainer doubles. ⑦–⑨.

Seagull, 60 Huangpu Lu (☎63251500, fax 63241263). On the north bank of the Suzhou Creek, just east of the blue Russian Consulate, this is a smart, modern Chinese hotel. ⑧.

Shanghai Mansions, 20 Suzhou Bei Lu (☎63246260, fax 63065147). This is the huge ugly lump of a building on the north bank of the Suzhou Creek, visible from the north end of the Bund. Originally a residential block built in the 1930s, it now offers excellent rooms, larger than the *Peace* and with superb views along the length of the Bund. Its most illustrious resident was Jiang Qing (wife of Mao

SHANGHAI: ACCOMMODATION

Changyang	长阳饭店	*chángyáng fàndiàn*
Garden	花园酒店	*huāyuán jiǔdiàn*
Haijia	海佳饭店	*hǎijiā fàndiàn*
Jinjiang	锦江饭店	*jǐnjiāng fàndiàn*
Metropole	新城饭店	*xīnchéng fàndiàn*
New Asia	新亚大酒店	*xīnyà dàjiǔdiàn*
Normal University Guesthouse	师范大学外宾搂	*shīfàn dàxué wàibīnlóu*
Pacific	金门大酒店	*jīnmén dàjiǔdiàn*
Park	国际饭店	*guójì fàndiàn*
Peace	和平饭店	*hépíng fàndiàn*
Portman Shangrila	波特曼香格里拉酒几	*bōtèmàn xiānggélǐlājiǔdiàn*
Pujiang	浦江饭店	*pǔjiāng fàndiàn*
Seagull	海鸥饭店	*hǎi'ōu fàndiàn*
Shanghai Conservatory Guesthouse	音乐学院招待所	*yīnyuèxuéyuàn zhāodàisuǒ*
Shanghai Mansions	上海大厦	*shànghǎi dàshà*
Swan Cindic	天鹅信谊宾馆	*tiānéxìnyì bīnguǎn*
Tung Feng	东风饭店	*dōngfēng fàndiàn*

Zedong) who issued a decree during the Cultural Revolution banning barges and sampans from travelling up the Huangpu or Suzhou while she was asleep. If you're not staying here, you can appreciate the views by taking the lift to the eighteenth floor. Doubles start at US$110. ⑨.

Western Shanghai: Nanjing Xi Lu and the old French Concession

Garden, 58 Maoming Lu (☎64151111, fax 64151234). Japanese-managed and probably the best hotel in Shanghai, constructed around what used to be the French Club, in the French Concession. Doubles from US$200. ⑨.

Jinjiang, 59 Maoming Lu (☎62582582, fax 64725588). A vast place in the French Concession, with many wings, and one of the best hotels in the city. Richard Nixon stayed here on his famous visit in 1972. Doubles from US$100. ⑨.

Pacific, 104 Nanjing Xi Lu (☎63276226, fax 63999620). Another historic place, virtually in the centre of the city, with an extremely grand entrance and lobby. ⑧.

Park, 170 Nanjing Xi Lu (☎63275225 ext 110, fax 63276958). Very central, right opposite Renmin Park; for many years this was the tallest building in Shanghai. Although the hotel dates back to the 1930s, the interiors have been modernized. Doubles from ¥870. ⑨.

Portman Shangrila, 1376 Nanjing Xi Lu (☎62798888, fax 62798999). Part of the luxury *Shanghai Centre* complex, which includes restaurants, airline offices and extremely expensive bars. Doubles from US$250, with discounts off season. ⑨.

Shanghai Conservatory Guesthouse, 20 Fen Yang Lu (☎64372577). Off Huaihai Lu, close to Changshu metro station, this is a pleasant and very cheap place to stay, right inside the grounds of the college, surrounded by music students. Unfortunately it's nearly always full. Doubles with or without showers. ④–⑥.

Outer Shanghai

Changyang, 1800 Changyang Lu (☎65434890). Far away to the northeast of town, but this is an excellent modern place with very reasonably priced doubles. Bus #22 running from just north of Suzhou Creek passes very close; get off at Linqing Lu bus stop. ⑥.

Haijia, 1001 Jiangpu Lu (☎65411440). Remote location in the northeast of town but one of the cheapest in the city, and currently under renovation. To get here take bus #310 from the train station to Jiangpu Lu bus stop; bus #22 from just north of Waibaidu Bridge also passes. ⑥.

Normal University Guesthouse (☎64701860, fax 64369249). Far away in the southwest of the city, this is a quiet and reasonably priced place to stay, offering nice doubles. To reach it, take the metro to Shangtiguan station, then take bus #43 to the terminus. ⑥.

Swan Cindic, 111 Jiang Wan Lu (☎63255255 ext 2104, fax 63248002). A very smart place in a pleasant area away from the centre near Hongkou Park. ⑦.

The City

Although most parts of Shanghai that you are likely to visit lie to the west of the **Huangpu River** and its classic colonial riverfront, the **Bund**, by far the most easily recognizable landmark in the city is the rocket-like **Oriental Pearl TV Tower** on the east side, in the **Pudong Special Economic Zone**. The best way to check out both banks of the Huangpu River and their sights is to take the splendid **Huangpu River Tour** (see p.338).

Nanjing Lu, reputedly the busiest shopping street in China, runs through the heart of downtown Shanghai headed at its eastern end by the famous **Peace Hotel** and leading west to **Renmin Park**, which today houses Shanghai's **Museum**. Shanghai's other main sights lie about 1.5km south of Nanjing Lu in the **Old City**, the longest continuously inhabited part of the city, with a fully restored classical Chinese garden, the **Yu Yuan**, neighbouring bazaars and the traditional **Huxinting Tea House** at its heart. To the southwest of here lies the marvellous **old French Concession**, with its cosmopolitan cooking traditions, European-style housing and revolutionary relics.

Farther out from the centre remains a scattering of sights. North of the Suzhou Creek is the interesting **Hongkou Park**, with its monuments to the great twentieth-century writer, Lu Xun. Finally, in the far west are two of Shanghai's most important surviving religious sites, the **Longhua Si** and the **Yufo Si**.

The Bund and the Huangpu River

A combination of Liverpool and 1920s Manhattan, the most impressive street in Shanghai has always been the **Bund**, since 1949 known officially as Zhongshan Lu. During Shanghai's riotous heyday it was not only the city's financial centre but also a hectic working harbour where anything from tiny sailing junks to ocean-going freighters unloaded under the watch of British – and later American and Japanese – warships. Everything arrived here, from silk and tea to heavy industrial machinery, and amidst it all were the wealthy foreigners disembarking to pick their way to one of the grand hotels through crowds of beggars, hawkers, black marketeers, shoeshine boys and overladen coolies. Named after an old Anglo-Indian term, *bunding* (the embanking of a muddy foreshore), the Bund was in every sense old Shanghai's commercial heart, with the river on one side, the offices of the leading banks and trading houses on the other. In recent years, the Bund has taken on an entirely new aspect, with the construction, just across the river, of the dramatically conspicuous Oriental Pearl TV Tower.

The northern end of the Bund starts from the confluence of the Huangpu and the Suzhou Creek, by **Waibaidu Bridge**, and runs south for 1.5km to Jinling Dong Lu, formerly Rue du Consulat. At the outbreak of the Sino-Japanese War in 1937 the Waibaidu Bridge formed a no-man's-land between the Japanese-occupied areas north of Suzhou Creek and the International Settlement – it was guarded at each end by Japanese and

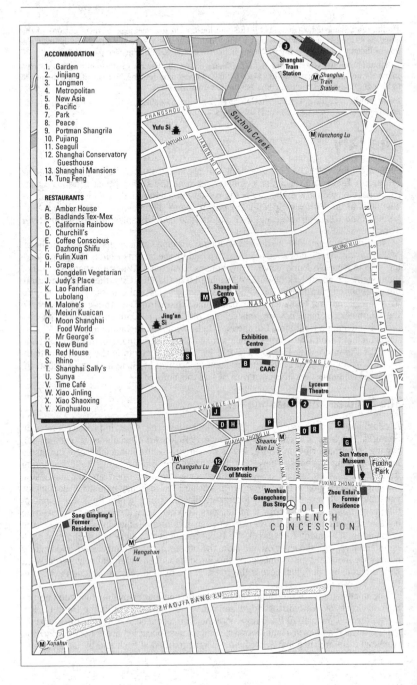

ACCOMMODATION

1. Garden
2. Jinjiang
3. Longmen
4. Metropolitan
5. New Asia
6. Pacific
7. Park
8. Peace
9. Portman Shangrila
10. Pujiang
11. Seagull
12. Shanghai Conservatory Guesthouse
13. Shanghai Mansions
14. Tung Feng

RESTAURANTS

A. Amber House
B. Badlands Tex-Mex
C. California Rainbow
D. Churchill's
E. Coffee Conscious
F. Dazhong Shifu
G. Fulin Xuan
H. Grape
I. Gongdelin Vegetarian
J. Judy's Place
K. Lao Fandian
L. Lubolang
M. Malone's
N. Meixin Kuaican
O. Moon Shanghai Food World
P. Mr George's
Q. New Bund
R. Red House
S. Rhino
T. Shanghai Sally's
U. Sunya
V. Time Café
W. Xiao Jinling
X. Xiao Shaoxing
Y. Xinghualou

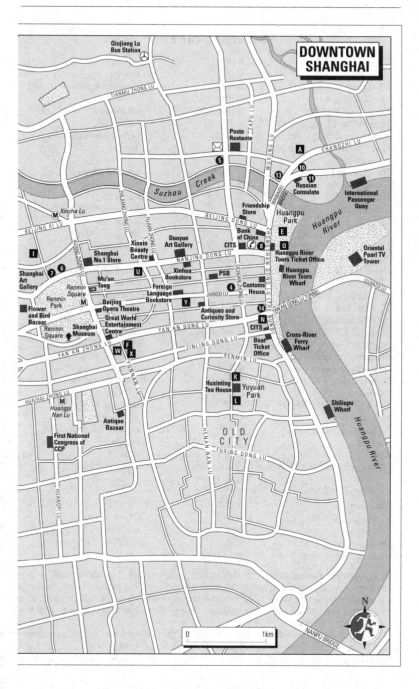

DOWNTOWN SHANGHAI

Qiujiang Lu Bus Station

TIANMU ZHONG LU

ZHEJIANG ZHONG LU

FUJIAN ZHONG LU

ZAPU LU

Poste Restante

5

A

CHANGZHI LU

Suzhou Creek

13

10

11

Russian Consulate

WAIBAIDU BRIDGE

International Passenger Quay

M Xinzha Lu

BEIJING XI LU

BEIJING DONG LU

Friendship Store

E

Huangpu Park

Huangpu River

I

Duoyun Art Gallery

NANJING DONG LU

Bank of China

CITS

8

Q

Huangpu River Tours Ticket Office

Shanghai Art Gallery

7 **6**

Xinxin Beauty Centre

Xinhua Bookstore

PSB

SICHUAN ZHONG LU

ZHONGSHAN DONG LU

Oriental Pearl TV Tower

Shanghai No.1 Store

Mu'en Tang

Foreign Language Bookstore

JIANGXI LU

4

Customs House

Huangpu River Tours Wharf

HUAQIULU

XIANG ZHONG LU

Renmin Park

M

Beijing Opera Theatre

Y

Antiques and Curiosity Store

14

YAN AN DONG LU TUNNEL

Flower and Bird Bazaar

Renmin Square

Great World Entertainment Centre

YAN AN DONG LU

N

CITS

Cross-River Ferry Wharf

Shanghai Museum

Renmin Square

F

JINLING DONG LU

Boat Ticket Office

YAN AN ZHONG

W

X

YUNNAN LU

RENMIN LU

HUAIHAI ZHONG LU

M

Huangpi Nan Lu

Huxinting Tea House

K

Yuyuan Park

Shiliupu Wharf

L

Huangpu River

Antique Bazaar

First National Congress of CCP

HUANGPI LU

HENAN NAN LU

O L D C I T Y

FUXING DONG LU

0   1km

N

NANPU BRIDGE

SHANGHAI: THE CITY

Bund	外滩	*wàitān*
Botanical Gardens	植物园	*zhíwùyuán*
Chenghuang Miao	城皇庙	*chénghuángmiào*
Customs House	海关楼	*hǎiguān lóu*
Dongtai Lu Market	东台路市场	*dōngtái lù shìchǎng*
First National Congress of CCP	一大会址	*yīdàhuìzhǐ*
Flower and Bird Bazaar	花鸟市场	*huāniǎo shìchǎng*
Great World Entertainment Centre	大世界	*dàshìjiè*
Hongkou Park	红口公园	*hóngkǒu gōngyuán*
Huangpu River	黄浦江	*huángpǔ jiāng*
Huxinting	湖心亭	*húxīntíng*
Longhua Park	龙华公园	*lónghuá gōngyuán*
Longhua Si	龙华寺	*lónghuá sì*
Lu Xun Memorial Hall	鲁迅纪念馆	*lǔxùn jìniànguǎn*
Lu Xun's Former Residence	鲁迅故居	*lǔxùn gùjū*
Mu'en Tang	沐恩堂	*mù'ēn táng*
Oriental Pearl TV Tower	东方明珠广播电视塔	*dōngfāngmíngzhū guǎngbōdiànshìtái*
Pudong New Area	浦东新区	*pǔdōng xīnqū*
Renmin Park	人民公园	*rénmín gōngyuán*
Renmin Square	人民广场	*rénmín guǎngchǎng*
Shanghai Art Museum	美术展览馆	*měishù zhǎnlǎnguǎn*
Shanghai Centre	上海商城	*shànghǎi shāngchéng*
Shanghai Exhibition Centre	上海展览中心	*shànghǎi zhǎnlǎnzhōngxīn*
Shanghai Museum	上海博物馆	*shànghǎi bówùguǎn*
Song Qingling's Former Residence	宋庆龄故居	*sòngqìnglíng gùjū*
Sun Yatsen Former Residence	孙中山故居	*sūnzhōng shān gùjū*
Waibaidu Bridge	外白渡桥	*wàibáidù qiáo*
Xujiahui Cathedral	徐家汇天主教堂	*xújiāhuì tiānzhǔjiàotáng*
Yu Yuan	玉园	*yùyuán*
Yufo Si	玉佛寺	*yùfó sì*
Zhou Enlai's Former Residence	周恩来故居	*zhōu'ēn lái gùjū*

OUTSIDE THE CITY

Dianshan Hu	淀山湖	*diànshān hú*
Grand View Garden	大观园	*dàguān yuán*
She Shan	蛇山	*shéshān*
Songjiang	松江	*sōngjiāng*

British sentries. Today, though most shipping docks farther downstream, the waterways are still well-used thoroughfares, and the Bund itself is a popular place for locals to stroll after dinner or to exercise in the early morning, while tourists from all over China patrol the waterfront taking photos of each other against the backdrop of the Oriental Pearl TV Tower.

The first building south of the bridge was one of the cornerstones of British interests in old Shanghai, the former **British Consulate**, once ostentatiously guarded by magnificent Sikh soldiers. Perhaps it is a sign of the times that although the British are long gone, the blue building just to the northeast of here across the Suzhou Creek still retains its original function as the **Russian Consulate**.

Right on the corner of the two waterways, **Huangpu Park** was another British creation, the British Public Gardens, established on a patch of land created by chance when mud and silt gathered around a wrecked ship. Here too there were Sikh troops, ready to enforce the rules which forbade dogs or Chinese from entering (unless they were servants accompanying their employer). After protests the regulations were relaxed to admit "well-dressed" Chinese, who had to apply for a special entry permit. These days the park (daily 5am–9pm; free) contains a stone monument to the "Heroes of the People", and is also a popular spot for citizens practising *tai ji* early in the morning; but it's best simply for the promenade which commands the junction of the two rivers.

Walking down the Bund you'll pass a succession of grandiose neoclassical edifices, once built to house the great foreign enterprises. Jardine Matheson, founded by **William Jardine** – the man who did more than any other individual to precipitate the Opium Wars and open Shanghai up to foreign trade – was the first foreign concern to buy land in Shanghai and their base, just north of the *Peace Hotel*, is now occupied by the **China Textiles Export Corporation**.

Just south of here, straddling the eastern end of Nanjing Lu, is one of the most famous hotels in China, the **Peace Hotel**, formerly the *Cathay Hotel*. The main building (on the north side of Nanjing Lu) is a relic of another great trading house, **Sassoon's**, and was originally known as Sassoon House. Like Jardine's, the Sassoon business empire was built on opium trading, but by the early years of this century the family fortune had mostly been sunk into Shanghai real estate, including the *Cathay*, which was the place to be seen in prewar Shanghai. It offered guests a private plumbing system fed by a spring on the outskirts of town, marble baths with silver taps and vitreous china lavatories imported from Britain. Noel Coward is supposed to have been staying here when he completed *Private Lives*. Sassoon lived long enough to see his hotel virtually destroyed by the Japanese, but also long enough to get most of his money away to the Bahamas. The *Peace Hotel* today still caters to the rich, but it's well worth a visit for the **bar** with its legendary jazz band (see p.349), and for a walk around the lobby and upper floors to take in the faded art-deco elegance. The smaller wing on the south side of Nanjing Lu was originally the *Palace Hotel*, built around 1906; its first floor now holds the Western-style *Peace Café*, much used as a city-centre rendezvous.

Carrying on down the Bund, the **Customs House** is one of the few buildings to have retained its original function, though its distinctive clock tower has been adapted to chime *The East is Red* at six o'clock every morning and evening. You can step into the downstairs lobby for a peek at some faded mosaics of maritime motifs on the ceiling. Right next to this, and also with an easily recognizable domed roofline, the former headquarters of the **Hong Kong and Shanghai Bank** (built in 1921) is one of the most imposing of all the Bund facades. After 1949 it was taken over and turned into the local Shanghai government headquarters, until 1995 when they relocated to a site off Renmin Park in the centre of the city. This has opened the way for negotiations leading to the probable reoccupation of the building by its original owners.

At the corner of the Bund and Yan'an Dong Lu you'll come to the **Tung Feng Hotel**, which until 1949 was home to a bastion of white male chauvinism, the *Shanghai Club*. Like the *Peace* much of the interior remains intact and there's still a strong feel here of the Shanghai of the 1920s and 1930s. The lobby in particular, with its cream pillars, black and white tiled floor, sweeping staircase and panelled lift, is reminiscent of another age, despite the recent introduction of an untidy clutter of shops and snack bars. The club's showpiece, the 33-metre mahogany Long Bar, where the wealthiest of the city's merchants and their European guests propped themselves at cocktail hour, is unfortunately no more.

The Huangpu River Tour

One highlight of a visit to Shanghai, and the easiest way to view the edifices of the Bund, is to take a **Huangpu River Tour**. The Huangpu is still a vital resource for Shanghai, and the sixty-kilometre round-trip down to its confluence with the Yangzi and back will introduce you to the vast amount of shipping which still uses the port. One third of all China's trade passes through here and you'll also be able to inspect all the paraphernalia of the shipping industry, from sampans and rusty old Panamanian-registered freighters to sparkling Chinese navy vessels. On the way up the river, you'll also get an idea of the colossal construction that is taking place on the eastern shore, before you reach the mouth of the Yangzi River itself, where the wind kicks in and it feels like you're almost in open sea. The Huangpu is also Shanghai's chief source of drinking water, although its thick brownish waters contain large quantities of untreated waste, including sewage and high levels of mercury and phenol. At least it no longer serves as a burial ground – in the 1930s Chinese too poor to pay for the burial of relatives would launch the bodies into the river in boxes decked in paper flowers.

The river **tours**, which last 3hr 30min, leave from the waterfront close to Huangpu Park. You can book tickets at a small kiosk (daily 8am–1.30pm) on the pavement, riverside, just north from the *Peace Hotel*. There are daily departures at 9am and at 2pm, and in summer at 7pm. Given that there are sometimes several boats leaving at each of these times you should check your booking carefully. **Three classes** are available: third class (¥45) gives you crowds of local tourists, a hard seat and a great deal of noise; second class (¥60) entitles you to a plastic table outside with endless tea and sweets; and first class (¥80) has a lounge furnished with great overstuffed armchairs, and usually provides entertainment in the form of a Chinese juggling act. In foggy or windy weather, the tours do not run (for information call ☎63744461).

The East Bank of the Huangpu – Pudong New Area

Before 1990 the city of Shanghai did not really extend to the eastern bank of the Huangpu River at all. In that year, however, fifteen years after China's economic reforms had first started, it was finally decided to grant the status of Special Economic Zone (SEZ) to **Pudong**, a large area of mainly agricultural land across the river. This decision, more than any other, is now fuelling Shanghai's rocket-like economic advance into the next century.

With widespread confidence that Pudong will eventually be one of the major business centres of Asia, and perhaps of the world, US$40 billion of investment has already been pumped into the area. The recently completed city ring road connects the western and eastern banks of the Huangpu River for the first time, with the help of two of the largest **cable bridges** in the world, Yangpu to the north and Nanpu to the south, while Yan'an Dong Lu in the centre of the city has been extended east via a tunnel into the heart of Pudong. The skyline is a sea of cranes and already a number of skyscrapers are in place. The idea is to create a city of the twenty-first century to match, or preferably excel, the largely foreign-inspired city of the twentieth. This "New Bund" is rising under the gaze of the 457-metre-high **Oriental Pearl TV Tower** (daily 8am–9pm; ¥50), and ascending the tower to admire the fabulous, giddying views has become a mandatory pilgrimage for all visitors to Shanghai, despite the high entrance fee. At the top of the tower are souvenir stands, while down below on the first floor there's a resident jazz band, a café and a display of other great world cities.

Getting to Pudong is still not entirely straightforward by public transport. The simplest way is to catch a **taxi** through the Yan'an Lu tunnel; otherwise, make enquiries about the minibus services which should be starting soon from the area around the south side of Renmin Square. For a more picturesque trip, catch the cross-river **ferry** from the Bund opposite the eastern end of Jinling Lu, then walk north past construction sites for about twenty minutes.

Nanjing Lu and around

Stretching west from the Bund through the heart of Shanghai lie the main commercial streets of the city, among them the premier shopping street, **Nanjing Lu**, with its two major parallel arteries, **Beijing Lu** and **Yan'an Lu**. In the days of the foreign concessions, Nanjing Lu was described as a cross between Broadway and Oxford Street, and even after 1949, Nanjing Lu remained a centre for theatre and cinema as well as one of the most crowded shopping streets in the world.

Nanjing Dong Lu

On its eastern stretch, Nanjing Dong Lu, garish neon lights and expensive window displays of foreign and luxury goods are as prominent as they have ever been and if any street in mainland China resembles downtown Hong Kong shopping areas, this is it. Take a stroll among the crowds before things close up in late evening (9–10pm), to check out the mass of fast-food outlets, fashion boutiques, cinemas, hotels and particularly the huge **department stores**. Off the circular overhead walkway at the junction between Nanjing and Xizang Lu, just northeast of Renmin Park, is the grandest of them all, the venerable *Shanghai No.1 Store* (formerly *The Sun Department Store*). This, the largest store in the country, is visited by a hundred thousand Chinese each day, many of whom are country folk visiting Shanghai for the first time. Another feature of Nanjing Lu is the **beauty salons**, where customers are beautified in shop windows for the entertainment of the public on the pavement outside. One of the most famous of these is the *Xin Xin Beauty Centre*, just west of Fujian Lu, which employs no fewer than eighty stylists and masseurs.

Renmin Park and Renmin Square

Immediately west of the junction with Xizang Lu – where Nanjing Dong Lu becomes Nanjing Xi Lu – lies **Renmin Park** and a newly remodelled **Renmin Square** to the south. This whole area was originally the site of the Shanghai racecourse, later converted into a sports arena by Chiang Kaishek who decided it was unwise to pander to the Chinese passion for gambling. During the war the stadium served as a holding camp for prisoners and as a temporary mortuary. Afterwards most of it was levelled, and while the north part was landscaped with grass and trees to become the surprisingly intimate and secluded Renmin Park, the rest was paved to form a dusty concrete parade ground for enormous political rallies. This former area of paving has now been turned over to green grass, fountains and pigeons, while what used to be the bomb shelters beneath have become some of the city's premier **shopping malls**. The views from Renmin Square are novel, offering an unexpected panoramic vista of the developing city, but more importantly, the city's brand-new, showpiece **Shanghai Museum** (daily 9am–5pm) is located here. This should definitely not be missed – from the outside alone the museum is one of the most impressive new buildings in the city, and inside, the presentation, labelling (in English as well as Chinese) and lighting are first class. The museum's collections of **scrolls**, **ceramics** and **bronzes** are particularly outstanding.

From Renmin Park, a small detour south down Xizang Lu will bring you to the **Mu'en Tang** (Baptized with Mercy Church), a couple of blocks down on the left. Visiting a church in Shanghai is an extraordinary experience, and Mu'en is the closest to the heart of the city. Athough the service is in Chinese only, visitors are more than welcome and you'll be given a seat in the balcony overlooking the packed congregation – a whole cross-section of Shanghai society ranging from cross old Communists to young women in silver mini-skirts. There are services on Tuesday and Friday evenings as well as at various times on Sunday (check the board outside). By contrast, a block farther south on the junction with Yan'an Lu stands the neon-lit **Great World Entertainment Centre** (see p.351).

Nanjing Xi Lu

On the western section of Nanjing Lu, Nanjing Xi Lu, opposite Renmin Park, stand the historic **Pacific** and **Park hotels**. The *Park Hotel*, for many years the tallest building in Shanghai, once had a reputation for superb food and for its dances, when the roof would be rolled back to allow guests to dance under the stars. Latterly, Mao Zedong always stayed here when he was in Shanghai. Today, however, it has been stripped of most of its old-world charm. The *Pacific* by contrast, a few metres to the east of the *Park*, is still well worth having a look at, both for its mighty and ostentatious façade and for the fabulous plaster reliefs in the lobby. A few minutes west of Renmin Park along Nanjing Xi Lu is the **Shanghai Art Museum** (daily 9–11am & 1–4pm; ¥10), housing a fairly extensive though dry collection of highly traditional contemporary Chinese art on three floors. Much more exciting, on a small lane called Jiangyin Lu just to the south of here and parallel to the main road, is Shanghai's permanent **Flower and Bird Bazaar**. This is a superbly picturesque little corner, with locals daily crowding the alley looking to buy puppies, kittens, goldfish, cagebirds, crickets and other insects, as well as a whole host of plants.

The western end of Nanjing Xi Lu was known to "Shanghailanders" (the Europeans who made their homes here) as Bubbling Well Road, after a spring which used to gush at the far end of the street. In those days, as today, it was one of the smartest addresses in the city, leading off into the tree-lined streets where Westerners' mock-tudor mansions and immaculate lawns sheltered behind high walls. Now it's the location of a number of luxury hotels, including the **Shanghai Centre**, an ultra-modern complex of luxury shops, restaurants and residential flats centred around the *Portman Shangrila Hotel*. Also at this end of Nanjing Lu, a few hundred metres west of the *Shanghai Centre*, is **Jing'an Si** (daily 8am–5.30pm; ¥2), a small though active temple nestling beside the tiny Jing'an Park and awkwardly surrounded by highrises. Its apparent obscurity belies its past as the richest Buddhist foundation in the city, headed by legendary abbot, Khi Vehdu, who combined his abbotly duties with the lifestyle of a gangster. The abbot and his seven concubines were shadowed wherever they went by White Russian bodyguards, each carrying what appeared to be an ordinary leather briefcase but which was in fact lined with bulletproof steel to be used as a shield in case of attack.

A block due south of the *Shanghai Centre* on Yan'an Lu is a memorial of a different era, from the wedding-cake school of architecture – the gigantic, Stalinist **Shanghai Exhibition Centre**, worth seeing for its colossal ornate entrance, decorated with columns patterned with red stars and capped by a gilded, star-topped spire. Constructed by the Russians in 1954, it was originally known as the *Palace of Sino-Soviet Friendship* and housed a permanent exhibition of industrial produce from the Shanghai area – proof of the advances achieved after 1949. In recent years it has become more of a vast and rather vulgar shopping mall selling everything from lacquer furniture through jewellery and silks to trinkets and souvenirs, all at well above the going rate.

The Old City

The **Old City** never formed part of the International Settlement and was known by the foreigners who lived in Shanghai, somewhat contemptuously, as the **Chinese City**. Based on the original **walled city** of Shanghai which dated back to the eleventh century, the area was reserved in the nineteenth and early twentieth centuries as a ghetto for vast numbers of Chinese who lived packed in conditions of appalling squalor, while the foreigners carved out their living space all around them. Today it still covers an oval-shaped area of about four square kilometres, circumscribed by Renmin Lu (to the north) and Zhonghua Lu (to the south) and coming to within a couple of hundred metres of the southern Bund on its northeastern side. In modern times it has been slashed down the middle by the main north–south artery, Henan

Lu. The easiest approach from Nanjing Dong Lu is to walk due south along Henan Lu or Sichuan Lu.

Tree-lined ring roads had already replaced the original walls and moats as early as 1912, and sanitation has obviously improved vastly since the last century, but to cross the boundaries into the Old City is still to enter a different world. The twisting alleyways are a haven of free enterprise, bursting with makeshift markets of fish, vegetables, cheap trinkets, clothing and the appetizing smells of cooking food. Two of Shanghai's **antique markets** are also located in or near the Old City. Ironically, for a tourist entering this area, the feeling is indeed a little like entering a Chinatown in a Western city.

The centre of activity today is an area known locally as **Chenghuang Miao** (after a local temple) surrounding the two most famous and crowded tourist sights in the whole city, the Yu Yuan and the Huxinting Tea House, both located right in the middle of a new, touristy bazaar which caters to the rapidly swelling numbers of local Chinese tourists who pour into the area. "Antiques", scrolls and various kitschy souvenirs feature prominently, and there are also lots of good places to eat *dian xin*, Shanghai *dim sum* (see "Restaurants", p.345). The **Yu Yuan** (Jade Garden; daily 8.30am–4.30pm; ¥15) is a classical Chinese garden of pools, walkways, bridges and rockeries, originally created in the sixteenth century by a high official in the imperial court, in honour of his father. Despite fluctuating fortunes, the garden has surprisingly survived the passage of the centuries. It was spared from its greatest crisis – the Cultural Revolution – apparently because the anti-imperialist "Little Sword Society" had used it as their headquarters in 1853 during the Taiping Uprising. Garden connoisseurs today will appreciate the whitewashed walls topped by undulating dragons made of tiles, and the huge, craggy and indented rock in front of the Yuhua Tang (Hall of Jade Magnificence). The Yu Yuan is not more impressive than the gardens of nearby Suzhou (see p.357), but given that it pre-dates the relics of the International Settlement by some three centuries, the Shanghainese are understandably proud of it.

After visiting the garden, you can step into the delightful **Huxinting** (Heart of Lake Pavilion; downstairs daily 5.30–noon, 1.30–5pm & 6.30–9.30pm; upstairs daily 8.30am–5pm & 6–11pm), where practically every visitor who has ever been to Shanghai, including the Queen of England, has dropped in for tea. The tea house is reached across a zigzag bridge spanning a small ornamental lake, just across from the entrance to Yu Yuan. In the downstairs section, you buy a ticket for ¥10 and can then enjoy endless refills while watching the elderly locals, who sit for hours amid the wood panelling, dozing to the traditional music of a venerable Chinese orchestra. Upstairs, during the daytime, it costs ¥25, but you get air conditioning and quails' eggs with your tea, while in the evening (¥55), the waitresses perform traditional tea ceremonies wearing *qipao*, the long tight silk dresses with high slits up the sides. Whenever you come though, the tea is excellent and the china used is the dark and distinctive Yixing ware (see p.374).

If you're in Chenghuang Miao early on Sunday morning (8–11am is the best time though trade continues to mid-afternoon) you can visit a great **Sunday market** on Fuyu Lu, the small street running east to west along the northern edge of Yu Yuan. The market has a very raw, entrepreneurial feel about it; all sorts of curios and antiques – some real, some not – ranging from jade trinkets to Little Red Books can be found here, though you'll have to bargain fiercely if you want to buy.

Just outside the Old City in a small alley called **Dongtai Lu** leading west off Xizang Nan Lu, is the largest **permanent antique market** in Shanghai (daily 10am–4pm), and possibly in all China. Even if you're not interested in buying, this is a fascinating area to walk around. The range is vast, covering every era of Chinese history, from old Buddhas, coins, vases and teapots, to Mah Jong sets, renovated furniture and Cultural Revolution badges. Some of the antiques are clearly fakes, but many of the traders are serious, respectable people with reputations to defend.

The old French Concession

Established in the mid-nineteenth century, the **French Concession** (sometimes referred to as Frenchtown), lay to the south and west of the International Settlement, abutting the Chinese City. Despite its name, it was never particularly French: before 1949, in fact, it was for the most part a relatively low-rent district inhabited by White Russians, who, for all their claims to wealth and titles back home, were looked down on by other Westerners as latecomers, obliged to take jobs which should have been left to the Chinese. Fascinatingly, however, certain French characteristics have lingered here, in the local chic, and in a taste for bread and sweet cakes – exemplified in **Huaihai Lu** the main street running through the heart of the area. Not as crowded as Nanjing Lu, Huaihai Lu is considerably more upmarket, particularly in the area around Maoming Lu and Shaanxi Lu, where fashion boutiques, extremely expensive department stores and excellent cake shops abound. The two plushest hotels in town, the *Garden* and the *Jinjiang* are on Maoming Lu just north of Huaihai Lu.

Frenchtown was also notorious for its lawlessness and the ease with which police and officials could be bribed, in contrast to the relatively staid, well-governed areas dominated by the British. This made it ideal territory for gangsters, including the king of all Shanghai mobsters, Du Yuesheng (more commonly known as Big-eared Du). For similar reasons, **political activists** also operated in this sector – the first meeting of the Chinese Communist Party took place here in 1921, and both Zhou Enlai and Sun Yatsen, the first provisional President of the Republic of China after the overthrow of the Qing dynasty, lived here. The preserved former homes of these two in particular (see below) are worth visiting simply because, better than anywhere else in modern Shanghai, they give a sense of how the Westerners, and the Westernized, used to live.

Moving west into the French Concession, the **First National Congress of the Chinese Communist Party** (Tues–Sun 8–11am & 1–4pm, closed Thurs am; ¥3) is the first preserved 1920s relic that you'll come across, just off Huaihai Lu, at the junction of Xingye Lu and Huangpi Nan Lu. The official story of this house is that on July 23, 1921, thirteen representatives of the Communist cells which had developed all over China, including its most famous junior participant Mao Zedong, met here to discuss the formation of a national party. The meeting was discovered by a French police agent (it was illegal to hold political meetings in the French Concession) and on July 30 the delegates fled to Zhejiang Province, where they resumed their talks in a boat on the lake Nan Hu. Quite how much of this really happened is unclear, but it seems probable that there were in fact more delegates than the record remembers – the missing names would have been expunged according to subsequent political circumstances. The site today, preserved in its original condition since 1949, contains a little exhibition hall downstairs with English labels, detailing instances of the kinds of oppressions that inspired the Communist movement in the first place.

A few hundred metres west of here, beyond the gigantic north–south flyover and very close to **Fuxing Park**, is Sinan Lu, where two of the heroes of modern China lived. Just north of Fuxing Lu is the **Sun Yatsen Museum** (Mon–Fri 9am–4pm, Sun 9–11am & 1.30–4pm; ¥4), with its large British-style lawn in the back garden, screened by mature trees and high walls. This is where Sun Yatsen lived for six years and inside the house you can see his books, a gramophone, fireplaces and verandahs – all fantastically disorienting in 1990s Shanghai. Sun's widow Song Qingling (see below) also stayed in the house until 1937. The other place to visit on Sinan Lu (just south of Fuxing Lu) is **Zhou Enlai's Former Residence** (Mon 1.15–4pm, Tues & Wed 8.30am–11 & 1.15–4pm, Thurs 1.15–4pm, Fri–Sun 8.30am–11 & 1.15–4pm; ¥4). This delightful house has a terrace at the back with rattan chairs and polished wooden floors and its garden, with hedges and ivy-covered walls could easily be a part of 1930s suburban London.

Finally, a good deal farther west, on Huaihai Xi Lu, about twenty minutes' walk northwest from the Hengshan Lu metro station, is **Song Qingling's Former Residence** (daily 9–11am & 1–4.30pm; ¥8), who lived here on and off from 1948 until her death in 1981. As the wife of Sun Yatsen, Song Qingling was part of a bizarre family coterie – her sister Song Meiling was married to Chiang Kaishek and her brother, known as "T.V. Soong", was finance minister to Chiang. Song Qingling herself was to remain loyal to China throughout her life, latterly as one of the honorary "Presidents" of the People's Republic, while Meiling – now reviled in the People's Republic – is still alive today, having made her permanent home in New York City. Once again the house is a charming step back into a residential Shanghai of the past, and although this time the furnishings – including her official limousines parked in the garage – are largely post-1949, there is some lovely wood panelling and lacquerwork inside the house.

Western Shanghai

In the west of the city, sights thin out considerably, and you'll certainly need some form of motorized transport. The main sights include two **temples**, the rambling old Longhua Si to the southwest, and Yufo Si, with its superb statuary, to the northwest. Due west from the city, there is less to see; if you follow Nanjing Lu beyond Jing'an Si, it merges into Yan'an Lu, which, in turn (beyond the city ring road), eventually turns into Hongqiao Lu, the road that leads to the airport. Shortly before the airport it passes **Shanghai Zoo** (daily 6am–4.30pm; ¥20), a massive affair with over two thousand animals and birds caged in conditions which, while not entirely wholesome, are considerably better than in most Chinese zoos. The star attraction, inevitably, is a giant panda. Next door, at 2409 Hongqiao Lu, stands the mansion which was once the Sassoons' home. It has served since as a Japanese naval HQ, a casino and as the private villa of the Gang of Four, but now suffers the relative ignominy of being rented out as offices. Bus #57 from the western end of Nanjing Lu will bring you out here.

The southwest

The **southwestern** limits of the city offer a few points of interest. First is the **Xujiahui Catholic Cathedral**, one of many places of public worship which have received a new lease of life in recent years. Built in 1906, it was closed for more than ten years during the Cultural Revolution, reopening in 1979. The congregations are remarkable for their size and enthusiasm, especially during the early Sunday morning services and at Christmas or Easter. If you're up in time, take a metro train to Xujiahui station, a short walk from the cathedral.

About a kilometre to the southeast of Xujiahui (and a short walk south of the terminus of bus #41) is Longhua Park, now officially named the **Longhua Cemetery of Martyrs** (daily 7am–8pm; free) to commemorate those who died fighting for the cause of Chinese Communism in the decades leading up to the final victory of 1949. In particular it remembers those workers, activists and students massacred in Shanghai by Chiang Kaishek in the 1920s – the site of the cemetery is said to have been the main execution ground. The area contains an exhibition hall and large numbers of commemorative stones, each bearing a photo and a name. The fresh flowers brought here daily testify to the power that the memories of these events still hold.

Just along from the Martyrs' Cemetery is one of Shanghai's main religious sites, the **Longhua Si** (daily 8am–5pm; ¥9), with its associated seventeen-hundred-year-old pagoda. The pagoda itself is an octagonal structure, about 40m high, its seven brick storeys embellished with wooden balconies and red lacquer pillars. What you see today has been restored after a long period of neglect – apart from anything else it was used by the Red Guards as a convenient structure to plaster with banners. The temple is slightly later in date than the pagoda (345 AD) and is now the most active Buddhist site in the city, with large numbers of new monks being trained. Although it has also seen reconstruction, it is regarded as a prime specimen of Southern Song architecture. On the right as you enter there's a bell tower, where you can strike the bell for ¥10, apparently to ease your worries, and you might be in need of this after running the gauntlet of beggars around the entrance. In the street outside are one or two excellent vegetarian noodle-and-steamed-dumpling shops.

An extra kilometre south (bus #56 down the main road, Longwu Lu, just to the east of the Longhua Si site) will bring you to the **Shanghai Botanical Gardens** (daily 7.30am–4pm; ¥6). Among the more than nine thousand plants on view are two pomegranate trees said to have been planted in the eighteenth century during the reign of Emperor Qianlong, and still bearing fruit despite their antiquity. Take a look as well at the orchid chamber, with more than a hundred different varieties on show.

The northwest

Just south of the Suzhou Creek, **northwestern** Shanghai boasts the second of the city's most important religious sites, the **Yufo Si** (Temple of the Jade Buddha; daily 8am–4.30pm; ¥12), a monastery built in 1882 to enshrine two magnificent statues which had been brought from Burma. Each of these Buddhas is carved from a single piece of white jade: the larger statue, a reclining figure, is displayed downstairs, while the smaller, but far more exquisite, sitting statue is housed in a room upstairs as part of an extensive collection of Buddhist sutras and paintings. Although the temple was closed from 1949 until 1980, it is now large and active, despite its suffocating location surrounded by highrises. A hundred or so monks are in residence, dividing their time between training novices to repopulate monasteries reopening throughout China, and keeping an eye on tourists (photos are not allowed). The temple is on Anyuan Lu, just south of the intersection of Changzhou Lu and Jiangning Lu. Bus #112 from Renmin Square passes here, as does #24 from Huaihai Lu (along Shaanxi Lu); alternatively you can walk from the train station in about 25 minutes.

North of Suzhou Creek

North across the Waibaidu Bridge from the Bund, you enter an area which, before the War, was the Japanese quarter of the International Settlement, and which since 1949 has been largely taken over by housing developments. The obvious interest lies in the **Hongkou Park** area (also known as Hongkou Park), with its monuments to the political novelist **Lu Xun**, although the whole district is a lively and architecturally interesting residential quarter.

Hongkou Park (daily 6am–8pm; ¥1) is one of the best places for seeing the daily work-out session of *tai ji* and other sports undertaken by the Shanghai masses between 6 and 8am in the morning. It's also notable for housing the grandiose and rather pompous **Tomb of Lu Xun**, complete with a seated statue and an inscription in Mao's calligraphy, which was erected here in 1956 to commemorate the fact that Lu Xun had spent the last ten years of his life in this part of Shanghai. Also in the park, to the right of the main entrance, is the **Lu Xun Memorial Hall** (daily 9–11am & 1.30–4pm; ¥4). The exhibits include original correspondence, including letters and photographs from George Bernard Shaw, though unfortunately for foreign tourists the notes are in Chinese only.

A block east of the park on Shanyin Lu (lane 132, house 9), you can also visit **Lu Xun's Former Residence** (daily 9–11am, 1.30–4.30pm; ¥3). It's definitely worthwhile going out of your way to see this place, especially if you have already visited the former

LU XUN

The man known by the literary pseudonym **Lu Xun** (his real name was Chou Shujian) was born in 1881 in the small city of Shaoxing. His origins were humble, but he would eventually come to be revered as the greatest of twentieth-century Chinese authors. Writing in a plainer, more comprehensible prose-style than any Chinese writer before him – and considered by the Communists as a paragon of Socialist Realism – he sought to understand and portray the lives of the poor and downtrodden elements of Chinese society.

He had not always intended to write. His first chosen career had been as a **doctor** of medicine, which he studied in Japan, under the impression that medicine would be the salvation of humanity. Later however, horrified at the intractable social problems that beset China, he turned to writing, and published his *Madman's Diary*, modelled on the work of Gogol, in 1918. This Western-style short story, the first ever written in Chinese, was in reality a scathing satire of Confucian society. Three years later Lu Xun then published his most famous short story, **The True Story of Ah Q**, which features a foolish, Panglossian illiterate whose only remedy against the numerous evils which befall him, is to rationalize them into spiritual victories – once again, the logic of Confucianism. Lu Xun's writings soon earned him anger and threats from the ruling Guomindang, and in 1926 he fled his home in Beijing, to seek **sanctuary** in the International Settlement of Shanghai. The last ten years of his life he spent living in the then Japanese quarter of the city where he worked to support the Communist cause. The fact that he refused actually to join the Party did not stop the Communists from subsequently adopting him as a posthumous icon. He died in 1936.

residences of Zhou Enlai and Sun Yatsen in the French Quarter (see p.342). Lu Xun's house offers a fascinating glimpse into typical Japanese housing of the period – a good deal smaller than the European, but still surprisingly comfortable with balconies overlooked by palm trees.

Outside the city

Shanghai Shi (Shanghai Municipality) covers a huge area of approximately two thousand square kilometres, comprising ten counties and extending far beyond the limits of the city itself. To the north it includes three **islands** in the Yangzi River delta, the largest of which, Chongming Island, is nearly 100km long. To the northwest and southwest are the provinces of Jiangsu and Zhejiang respectively, while to the east the municipality abuts the East China Sea. Surprisingly, very little of this area is ever visited by foreign tourists, though there are a couple of interesting sights.

The most obvious of these is **She Shan** (She Hill), about 30km southwest of the city. The hill only rises about 100m, but such is the flatness of the surrounding land that it is visible for miles around – and it is unexpectedly crowned by a huge and thoroughly impressive **basilica**, a rare legacy of the missionary work undertaken by Europeans in the last century. The hill has been under the ownership of a Catholic community since the 1850s, though the present church was not built until 1925. Services take place only on Christian festivals; nevertheless, it is a pleasant walk up the hill at any time of year (or you can take the newly built cable car if you prefer), past bamboo groves and the occasional ancient pagoda. Most of the peasants in this area are fervent **Catholics** and highly welcoming towards any Westerners they come across. Also on the hill is a meteorological station and an old observatory, which contains a small exhibition room displaying an ancient earthquake-detecting device – a dragon with steel balls in its mouth which is so firmly set in the ground that only movement of the earth itself, from the vibrations of distant earthquakes, can cause the balls to drop out. The more balls drop, the more serious is the earthquake.

To reach She Shan, take a bus from the Wenhua Guangchang bus stop, or the Xiqu bus station (see p.329). If there are no direct buses, you can catch any bus to **Songjiang** and get off a few stops before the terminus – you'll have to ask. You'll then need to take a motor-rickshaw the remaining distance to She Shan (¥10).

Another twenty or so kilometres to the west of here, in Qingpu County, is **Dianshan Hu** and the **Grand View Garden**. For local tourists, the area around the southeastern shore of Dianshan Hu is being turned into a real holiday resort, with opportunities for boating, swimming, fishing and even golf. The Grand View Garden is unashamedly intended for tourists, having been modelled on the famous garden from the eighteenth-century Chinese novel, *Dream of the Red Chamber*. To get here, take a bus to Qingpu, and then change for the short ride to the lake.

Eating, drinking and entertainment

As with so many other aspects of life, Shanghai is on China's cutting edge where leisure activities are concerned. Despite the fact that most Shanghainese have never been to a theatre or restaurant in their lives, there is now a sufficiently large class of people for whom dining out and evening entertainments are a serious option. **Restaurants** in particular have improved enormously in recent years, in terms of quality and quantity. Simply getting a table is no longer a cut-throat business, nor is it confined to narrow opening hours. The sheer variety of food on offer is a reflection both of the openness

SHANGHAI: RESTAURANTS

Amber House	琥珀房子	*hǔpò fángzi*
Dazhong Shifu	大众食府	*dàzhòng shífǔ*
Deda Xicanshe	德大西餐社	*dédà xīcānshè*
Fulin Xuan	福临轩	*fúlín xuān*
Gongdelin	功德林素食馆	*gōngdélín sùshíguǎn*
Grape	葡萄园	*pútáoyuán*
Huanghe Lu	黄河路	*huánghé lù*
Hubin Mei Shilou	湖滨美食楼	*húbīn měishílóu*
Lao Fandian	老饭店	*lǎo fàndiàn*
Lubolang	绿波廊餐厅	*lǜbōláng cāntīng*
Meixin Kuaican	美心快餐	*měixīn kuàicān*
Moon Shanghai Food World	月上海美食世界	*yuèshànghǎi měishíshìjiè*
Moon Shanghai Blue Village Food City	蓝村美食城	*láncūn měishíchéng*
Red House	红房子	*hóng fángzi*
Rhino	福德餐厅	*fúdé cāntīng*
Shashi Xiaochi Shijie	沙市小吃世界	*shāshì xiǎochī shìjiè*
Sichuan	四川饭店	*sìchuān fàndiàn*
Sunya	新雅饭店	*xīnyǎ fàndiàn*
Xiao Jinling	小金陵	*xiǎo jīnlíng*
Xiao Shaoxing	小绍兴	*xiǎo shàoxīng*
Xinghualou	杏花楼	*xìnghuālóu*
Yunnan Lu	云南路	*yúnnán lù*
Zapu Lu	乍浦路	*zàpǔ lù*

of the city, and of the presence of an increasing expatriate population. There has been a similar explosion in the diversity of other types of evening entertainment, which range from **English pubs** to **Beijing Opera** and from **discos** to **classical music**.

Restaurants and snack food

The traditions of Shanghai's cosmopolitan past are still dimly apparent in the city's **restaurants**. Many of the old establishments have continued to thrive and although the original wood-panelled dining rooms are succumbing to modernization year by year, the growth of private enterprise ensures that the choice of venues is now wider than ever. **Prices** are generally very reasonable by international standards – even in the more upmarket places, standard dishes shouldn't cost more than a few US dollars each, while the expensive hotel restaurants often have excellent deals on set meals at lunch time. Cheap **snack food** can be bought from almost any part of the city at any time of the night or day, and **Western fast-food** outlets, such as *McDonald's* and *KFC*, are dotted along the main thoroughfares. Almost all hotels have respectable restaurants, many of which serve **dim sum** at breakfast and lunch.

There is an excellent diversity of food in the city, with most Chinese regional cuisines represented, and even a range of foreign cuisine now available including Indian, Japanese and European. Compared to, for example, Sichuan or Cantonese cuisine, **Shanghai cuisine** is not particularly well-known or popular among foreigners; nevertheless, there are still some interesting dishes, especially if you enjoy exotic seafood. Fish and shrimps are considered basic to any half-decent meal, and if possible eels and crab will appear as well. In season – between October and December – you may get the chance to try *dazha* crab, the most expensive and supposedly the most delicious. Most cooking is done with added ginger, sugar and Shaoxing wine, but without heavy spicing. Unlike many other Chinese, the Shanghainese are famous for their sweet tooth, which is indulged by over 1800 **coffee and pastry shops** – a tradition which dates back to the period of the International Settlement – selling more than two thousand tonnes of pastries and confectionery each week.

One general **warning** about restaurant dining in Shanghai is the need to establish with absolute clarity – in advance – the prices of the dishes you are ordering. Shanghai restaurateurs are notoriously unscrupulous when it comes to billing foreign tourists.

The Bund, Nanjing Dong Lu and around

The highlight of this area is the presence of a number of **specialist food streets**. In order of proximity to the top end of Nanjing Lu, the first of these is **Shanghai Shashi Xiaochi Shijie**, a small lane leading south off Nanjing Dong Lu, just west of Jiangxi Lu. It contains a number of cheap restaurants, good for hotpots, or for snacks such as the small, fine steamed dumplings (*xiao longbao*) that are a speciality of the Shanghai area. North of the Suzhou Creek, and just a few minutes' walk west of the *Pujiang Hotel* is **Zapu Lu** – at night it is entirely neon-lit and easily recognizable. There are large numbers of restaurants along here, many of them serving good food, but foreigners need to be very careful not to be over-charged. **Yunnan Lu** is perhaps the most interesting of the food streets, with a number of speciality restaurants, and a huge crowd of outdoor stalls selling snacks at night; it leads south from Nanjing Lu a block to the east of Renmin Park. Finally **Huanghe Lu**, due north of Renmin Park – and in particular the section north of Beijing Lu – contains another large concentration of restaurants.

Amber House, corner of Changtai Lu and Minghang Lu. Just a few minutes from the *Pujiang Hotel*, this is colourfully painted inside and out and doubles as a cheap bar and restaurant. Small, crowded and fun, foreigners are welcome.

California Rainbow, Beijing Dong Lu. On the third floor of the *Friendship Store* building, there's also another branch on Huaihai Lu. Good for coffee and American breakfasts.

Coffee Conscious, on the Bund, riverside, immediately south of Huangpu Park. This place serves excellent but expensive Western breakfasts and snacks.

Dazhong Shifu, Yunnan Lu (east side), a couple of hundred metres up from Jinjiang Lu. The place to come for typical local snacks of the dumpling variety, *xiao long bao* and *bai ye bao* (white-leaf dumpling), as well as fried noodles and noodle soups.

Deda Xicanshe, Sichuan Lu, just south of Nanjing Dong Lu. A traditional coffee bar, famous for chocolate buns and the like. Also serves Western and Japanese-style meals.

Gongdelin Vegetarian, Huanghe Lu. A short walk north of Nanjing Xi Lu, this is probably the best vegetarian restaurant in town – everything is made of vegetables and tofu but designed to look like fish and meat.

Meixin Kuaican, on the Bund, just south of Yan'an Dong Lu. Excellent value Hong Kong fast-food outlet, with plastic models of the dishes displayed at the counter. Order by pointing.

New Bund, on the Bund, riverside, just south of Huangpu Park. Fairly exclusive, tourist-orientated place with good hotpots.

Sichuan, 457 Nanjing Dong Lu. Good, relatively inexpensive Sichuan cooking, though not quite as spicy as the real thing.

Sunya (Xinya), Nanjing Dong Lu (south side), immediately west of Zhejiang Lu. One of the oldest most famous restaurants in town, serving excellent if pricey Cantonese cuisine. Great *dim sum* for breakfast.

Xiao Jinling, Yunnan Lu (west side), a few minutes north from Jinjiang Lu. Inexpensive and packed with locals. Try the excellent salted duck (*yanshui ya*).

Xiao Shaoxing Yunnan Lu, immediately north of Jinjiang Lu. Famous in Shanghai for its "white cut chicken" (*bai qie ji*).

Xinghualou, Fuzhou Lu, a couple of blocks west of Henan Lu. Another long-established Cantonese restaurant, but less expensive than the *Sunya*.

The French Concession and western Shanghai

This is the area where most expatriates eat and correspondingly where prices begin to move towards international levels. The compensation is that you'll find menus are almost certainly in English, and English will often be spoken too. For travellers tired of Chinese food, **international cuisine** is most likely to be available in this area – eat-all you-can **buffets**, for example, are offered by some of the large hotels, of which the *Hilton*'s is generally reckoned to be the best, though the *Portman Shangrila* buffet is much cheaper. **Fast food** and **snacks**, although not as abundant as farther east, are nevertheless plentiful enough along Huaihai Lu. At the junction of Nanjing Xi Lu and Shaanxi Lu is the so-called **Food Theatre** which is, in fact, a mall of immaculately clean fast-food outlets.

California Rainbow, Huaihai Lu, just west of Sinan Lu. Good coffees and American breakfasts.

Ch Euros, in the *Olympic Hotel*, very close to the Tiyuguan metro station. Serving excellent German food at less than German prices.

Churchill's, Xinle Lu. From Huaihai Lu, walk north up Xiangyang Lu and take the first left. British restaurant and pub, serving full roast beef meals, steak and kidney pudding, fish and chips. Price and a little absurd.

Badlands Tex-Mex, Yan'an Lu, right opposite the Shanghai Exhibition Centre. Good and cheap all you-can-eat buffet of Mexican food.

Friendship, inside the Shanghai Exhibition Centre. Chinese cuisine, slightly orientated to Western tastes; popular among expatriates

Fulin Xuan, Sinan Lu, just south of Huaihai Lu. Reputed to offer the best *dim sum* in town, run by Macau Chinese.

Grape (Putaoyuan), Xinle Lu, a few minutes east of *Churchill's*. English-speaking Chinese restaurant, good service, great food.

Kotobuki, Huaihai Lu (south side), between Shaanxi Lu and Maoming Lu. Japanese-owned and one of the best cake and pastry shops in the area. The chocolate eclairs are excellent.

Moon Shanghai Food World, Huaihai Lu, just east of Maoming Lu. Down an obscure alley with the restaurant name written in blue neon above the entrance, you'll find some excellent Chinese dishes from an interesting menu, including specialities such as tofu with freshwater crab and Beggar's Chicken. Another branch, the *Moon Shanghai Blue Village Food City* on nearby Sinan Lu specializes in Korean-style hotpot.

Mr George's, Huaihai Lu (north side), just west of Shaanxi Lu. Cheap Japanese fast-food outlet with dishes cast in plastic and displayed in the window.

Red House, Huaihai Lu, just east of Maoming Lu. Traditional European-style restaurant more notable for its history than its food – it dates back to the pre-Communist era, when it was known as *Chez Louis.*

Rhino (Fude Canting),Yan'an Lu, a short walk west of the Shanghai Exhibition Centre. Easily recognizable by the rhino head hanging above the front door. Superb marinated chicken wings.

Tandoor, *Jinjiang Hotel*, New South Building. First-class but relatively expensive Indian food, from ¥150–200 per head (much cheaper at lunchtime).

Time Café, Huaihai Lu, just east of Chengdu Lu. A second floor establishment offering a Western ambiance, steaks, salads and milkshakes. Every table has a telephone and there's live music after 9.30pm. Minimum charge of ¥45.

Tony Roma's, *Shanghai Centre*, next to the *Portman Shangrila*. Probably the most American place in China, famous for spare-ribs and BBQ sauce.

The Old City

The Yu Yuan area has traditionally been an excellent place for snack eating – *xiao-long bao* and the like, eaten in unpretentious snack-bar style surroundings. Although the quality is generally excellent and prices very low, the drawback is the long lines which form at peak hours. Try to come to these places mid-morning or mid-afternoon, outside the main eating times of 11.30am–1.30pm, and after 5.30pm. There are a number of snack bars in the alleys around the Yu Yuan, though the *Lubolang* immediately west of the Huxingting Tea House is perhaps the best, with a large variety of dumplings and noodles. Very close to the Yu Yuan entrance is the *Hubin Mei Shilou*, which serves a delicious sweet bean *changsheng zhou (*long-life soup). The *Lao Fandian* (Old Restaurant), just north of the Yu Yuan on Fuyou Lu, is one of the most famous restaurants in town serving local Shanghai food, though prices are slightly inflated.

Nightlife

Shanghai probably has more **nightlife** than any other Chinese city apart from Beijing, which is of course not saying terribly much. There are now Western-style **bars** opening late, nearly all of which serve food, and some of which have room for dancing, but although you'll meet a few Chinese people in all of the places listed below, most of them are heavily expat and slightly male-orientated. There is a full range of drinks available in Shanghai bars, though beer is usually bottled rather than draught and prices are on the high side; reckon on ¥25–40 per drink in most places, which is a lot more than what you'll pay in many restaurants. If it's Chinese rock that you are after, **live music** can certainly be found though don't bet on the quality. For up-to-date information about current events, and also news about the latest bars that are opening up, check the "What's on" section of the expat newspaper *Shanghai Talk* (see p.328).

Bars

Amber House, corner of Changtai Lu and Minghang Lu near the *Pujiang Hotel*. Serves beer at much cheaper prices than the other places listed here.

Peace Hotel Jazz Bar, junction of the Bund and Nanjing Dong Lu. A dark and cavernous pub inside the *Peace Hotel*, legendary for its eight-piece dance band whose members played here in the

1930s, suffered persecution during the Cultural Revolution, then re-emerged in the twilight of their years to fame and fortune. Recently, those of the surviving originals have been celebrating their newfound stardom by embarking on all-China and even world tours. Their younger successors now play stately instrumental versions of Fats Domino and Elvis Presley standards rather than the old Thirties swing, while portly tourists swirl to the nostalgic rhythms and sip cocktails amid the original 1930s decor. The bar is in the North Building of the *Peace Hotel* (not to be confused with the *Peace Café* in the South Building, which has its own rival and inferior band on some evenings). Cover charge ¥42. Open 8pm–1.30am

New York, New York, Huqiu Lu, just north of the eastern end of Beijing Lu, behind the *Friendship Store*. Popular bar crowded with Chinese as well as young expats. The cover charge of ¥70, plus a mandatory ¥10 to look after your bag, gets you one beer.

Judy's Place, entrance on Changle Lu, 20m east of Fumin Lu (between Yan'an Lu and Huaihai Lu). German draught beer, food and dancing in a small crowded space. Open most of the night, frequented by expats and Chinese.

Long Bar, *Shanghai Centre*, Nanjing Xi Lu. Sedate and extremely expensive, catering mainly to expats, but often has live jazz music – check *Shanghai Talk* for details.

Malone's, Tongren Lu, just west of the *Shanghai Centre*. Part of a Canadian chain, containing lots of TV screens showing current international sports action; sometimes has live music.

Jurassic Park, Maoming Lu, near the *Jinjiang Tower Hotel*. Caters mostly to Hong Kong and Taiwan Chinese. Worth seeing for the dinosaur decor alone – the urinals are tyrannosaurus mouths. Expensive drinks.

Manhattan's, opposite the *Hilton Hotel*, on Huashan Lu. A small rowdy place open twenty-four hours a day – the liveliest (and only) place to be at 5am.

Shanghai Sally's, corner of Sinan Lu and Xiangshan Lu opposite Sun Yatsen's former residence (south of Huaihai Lu). A British-Antipodean-flavoured place, with lots of beer, darts and pool tables. A nice mix of expats and locals.

Entertainment

Shanghai has always had a moderately healthy **cultural scene**, with cinemas showing foreign and Chinese films, and theatres featuring opera, dance, drama, acrobatics and puppets. To find out what's on and where, look out for the weekly "Around Shanghai" section of the *China Daily*, or read the "What's on" section of *Shanghai Talk*. Otherwise ask *CITS* to check the listings in a local newspaper for you. For many events it's worth either booking at the relevant venue in advance (try to have your requirements written out in Chinese) or getting *CITS* to do it for you (for a fee), although you may be lucky just turning up on the night.

The most important venue is the huge, new multi-purpose theatre (☎62798600) in the *Shanghai Centre* on Nanjing Xi Lu which hosts concerts, ballet, opera and acrobatics of international standard. For **Beijing Opera**, there's an additional venue on Fuzhou Lu (south side) just opposite Renmin Park, while the nightly **acrobatics** performances have recently moved to what used to be the Lyceum Theatre, home of that mainstay of colonial life, the British Amateur Dramatic Society, located just opposite the *Jinjiang Hotel* on the corner of Changle Lu and Maoming Lu. The nightly acrobatics show by the famous Shanghai Acrobatics Troupe is a superb spectacle: in Western terms it's more of a circus, including tumbling, juggling, clowning, magic and animal acts. Some of these skills – sword swallowing, fire eating and the amazing balancing acts – were developed as long ago as the Han dynasty, others have taken on a more trashy look featuring motorbikes, spectacular costumes and even a giant panda driving a car. Tickets (¥60 per show) can be bought on the same day from a window outside the theatre, and performances usually take place at 7.30pm.

There are plenty of **cinemas** in Shanghai, some of them dating back to the pre-1949 days, though all foreign films are dubbed into Chinese. For those interested in English language films, *Malone's* bar (see p.350) has a weekly film night on Wednesdays, and the British Council also shows films from time to time.

Of the venues where you can hear **classical music**, one of the most pleasant has to be the **Shanghai Conservatory of Music** at 20 Fenyang Lu, south of Huaihai Lu, quite near Changshu Lu metro station. Established in 1927 as a college for talented young musicians, it continues to train many of the infant prodigies who appear from China at regular intervals. There are performances here every Sunday evening at around 7pm. To find the ticket office, go in through the main entrance and turn immediately right, until you come to a noticeboard; the office is on the third floor of the building opposite here. It's best to book a day or two in advance to be sure of a seat. Tickets are incredibly cheap – just a few yuan (Chinese speakers can call ☎64370137 ext 2166 to make enquiries). Other theatres for classical music include the **Shanghai Concert Hall** at 523 Yan'an Dong Lu, and the **Jinjiang Hotel Auditorium**.

For a little taste of everything, the **Great World Entertainment Centre** is unbeatable. Standing in neon-lit splendour at 1 Xizang Zhong Lu, next to Renmin Park on the corner of Guangdong Lu, it began life in the 1920s as an even bigger complex of buildings putting on every conceivable kind of entertainment. It now consists of four floors with two auditoriums on each, surrounding a central well with an open-air stage. Staircases fly off in all directions; supposedly one used to have a dummy doorway at the top, through which ruined gamblers could step to their deaths as the climax to an unsuccessful evening. Peripheral amusements include dodgems, a Hall of Mirrors, snooker, bowling and video games, but in addition there are simultaneous performances of Beijing Opera, a large-scale puppet theatre, at least one movie, talent shows, gyrating pop singers and discos, while the main stage features non-stop acrobatics, clowning and comedy. You can wander at will from one room to another, walking to the front for example to examine the opera orchestra at close range and then leaving when the plot gets too complicated. There is a single ticket giving admission to the whole complex; the last ticket is sold at 8.30pm.

Shopping

Although Shanghai cannot yet hope to compete with places such as Hong Kong where **shopping** is concerned – mainly because imported goods are a lot more expensive here – the city's old mercantile and consumerist traditions are reviving fast and there are now goods worth picking up. A good place to start is **antiques**. The two antique markets at **Dongtai Lu** and **Fuyou Lu** in the Old City area (see p.341) are the best places for simply browsing, though if you don't like the risks associated with bargaining you might be better off visiting the city's government antique stores, the largest of which, the **Shanghai Antique and Curio Store** at 218–226 Guangdong Lu, has a large array of modern arts and crafts as well as some large antiques. There's also a much better-value private store, **G. E. Tang Antique and Curio Shop**, with its head office at 85 Dongtai Lu, which sells extremely attractive restored Chinese furniture and other larger pieces. For Chinese **art**, pay a visit to the **Duoyun Art Gallery**, on Nanjing Dong Lu just west of Shanxi Lu. Some superb scrolls (watercolours and calligraphy) are on sale here, as well as art books and all the equipment for producing traditional Chinese art.

Another area where Shanghai has pretensions to compete with Hong Kong is in **clothing**. Some of the low-price (but good quality) Hong Kong own-brand chain stores such as *Giordano* have a presence in the city, though large-sized Westerners may have difficulty finding clothes which fit. **Silk products**, particularly traditional Chinese ladies' wear, are cheap and for these you might try department stores such as the monumental but basic *No. 1 Store* at the junction of Nanjing Lu and Xizang Lu, or – much more upmarket – the very swish Huaihai Lu department stores, *Shanghai Paris Printemps* at the junction with Shaanxi Lu and the Japanese-run *Huating-Istan Department Store* just east of Chengdu Lu.

Finally, the *Friendship Store* (daily 9am–10pm) at 40 Beijing Lu, close to the *Peace Hotel*, is always worth a visit given its wide range of goods.The first floor is full of food, Chinese medicines, leather goods and consumer durables, while the second and third floors contain arts, handicrafts and clothing, as well as every type of silk. It's a fun place to browse but don't expect any bargains.

Listings

Airlines *China Eastern Airlines* (domestic ☎62475953; international ☎62472255) is at 204 Yan'an Xi Lu. The following airlines, most of which operate out of Shanghai, also have offices in the city: *Aeroflot, East Lake Hotel*, Donghu Lu (☎64711665); *Air France*, Hongqiao airport (☎62558817); *All Nippon Airways*, 2nd floor, East Wing, I (☎62797000); *Canadian*, 6th floor, New Jinjiang Tower (☎624153091); *Dragon Airlines*, Rm 202, East Wing, *Shanghai Centre* (☎62798093); *Japan Airlines*, 2nd floor, Ruijin Building, 205 Maoming Lu (☎64723000); *Korean Air*, Rm 104–5, *Hotel Equatorial*, 105 Yan'an Xi Lu (☎62481777); *Lufthansa, Hilton Hotel*, 250 Huashan Lu (☎62481100); *Northwest*, Rm 207, East Wing, *Shanghai Centre* (☎62798088); *Singapore Airlines*, Rm 208, East Wing, *Shanghai Centre* (☎62798000); *United Airlines*, Rm 204, West Wing, *Shanghai Centre* (☎62798009).

American Express Rm 206, Retail Plaza, *Shanghai Centre*, 1376 Nanjing Xi Lu (Mon–Fri 9am–5pm, Sat 9am–noon; ☎62798082).

Banks and exchange Travellers' cheques can be exchanged at most hotels and at all branches of the *Bank of China*, the head office of which is at 23 Zhongshan Lu (The Bund; Mon–Fri 9am–noon & 1.30–4.30pm, Sat 9am–noon).

Bike rental Only residents are allowed to ride bikes in Shanghai's crowded streets. If you have a bike you won't be stopped, but there is nowhere for visitors to rent them.

Bookshops The *Xinhua Bookstore* at 345 Nanjing Dong Lu has the best selection of foreign material and English translations of Chinese classics. The *Foreign Language Bookstore*, 390 Fuzhou Lu, is also worth trying, and has a selection of specialist translated Chinese literature around the corner at 201 Shandong Zhong Lu. Western paperbacks and periodicals can be found at all major hotels and at the *Friendship Store*.

British Council 5B Qihua Tower, 1375 Huaihai Zhong Lu (☎64714849). Sometimes has film evenings. Call for details.

Consulates *Australian*, 17 Fuxing Xi Lu (☎64334604); *French*, 21A Qihua Mansion, 1375 Huaihai Zhong Lu (☎64377414); *German*, 151 Yongfu Lu (☎64336951); *Indian*, 2200 Nanjing Xi Lu (☎62758885); *Japanese*, 1517 Huaihai Zhong Lu (☎64336639); *New Zealand*, 15th floor, Qihua Mansion, 1375 Huaihai Lu (☎64332230); *Russian*, 20 Huangpu Lu (☎63242682); *UK*, 5B Qihua Mansion, 1375 Huaihai Zhong Lu (☎64330508); *USA*, 1469 Huaihai Zhong Lu (☎64336880).

Football Shanghai were the champions of China in 1996. During the football season (winter) you might try seeing a game at the Shanghai Tiyuguan, by the Tiyuguan metro station. Enquire at *CITS* or *CTS* for details.

Hospitals A number of the city's hospitals have special areas for foreigners, including the Huadong Hospital at 121 Yan'an Xi Lu (☎62483180). In the event of a serious emergency, call *International SOS Assistance* ☎62484344, at 2004 Nanjing Xi Lu.

Post office There are several major offices in the city, including ones at 1761 Sichuan Lu, 359 Tiantong Lu, and 276 Bei Suzhou Lu. Poste restante arrives at the Bei Suzhou Lu office, beside the Suzhou Creek near *Shanghai Mansions* – each separate item is recorded on a little slip of cardboard in a display case near the entrance. The very efficient parcels office has a separate entrance in the same building. Most hotels, including the *Pujiang*, also accept and hold mail.

PSB 210 Hankou Lu, near the corner of Henan Zhong Lu. For visa extensions go to 222 Hankou Lu.

Telephones International calls are most easily and cheaply made with phone cards that can be bought and used in hotels. Otherwise they can be made from the telegraph office next door to the North Building of the *Peace Hotel*, where there is a special foreigners' section with a large, full-time staff to deal with every request.

Travel agents *CITS* has a helpful office next door to the North Building of the *Peace Hotel* on Nanjing Dong Lu (Mon–Sat 8.30–11.30am & 1–4.45pm; ☎63217200), providing travel and entertainment tickets, for roughly ¥30 commission per ticket. There's another branch just off the Bund at 2 Jinling Dong Lu (Mon–Sat 8.30–11.30am & 1–4.45pm), opposite the boat ticket office. Most if not all hotels have travel agencies offering the same services.

travel details

Trains

Shanghai station to: Beijing (4 daily; 19hr); Changsha (daily; 25hr); Changzhou (10 daily; 3hr); Chengdu (daily; 50hr); Chongqing (daily; 50hr); Guangzhou (daily; 31hr); Fuzhou (daily; 26hr); Hangzhou (5 daily; 3hr); Harbin (daily; 33hr); Hefei (daily; 12hr); Kunming (daily; 60hr); Lanzhou (daily; 36hr); Lianyungang (daily;17hr); Nanchang (16hr); Nanjing (10 daily; 4hr); Nanning (19hr); Ningbo (7hr); Qingdao (26hr); Shaoxing (4hr); Shenyang (24hr); Suzhou (10 daily; 90min); Tianjin (17hr); Urumqi (daily; 76hr); Wuxi (10 daily; 3hr); Xiamen (daily; 28hr); Xi'an (daily; 23hr); Xining (daily; 46hr); Xuzhou (5 daily; 11hr); Zhenjiang (10 daily; 4hr).

Shanghai West station to: Baotou (daily; 43hr); Hohhot (daily; 40hr).

Buses

There is little point travelling to destinations far from Shanghai by bus; the journey takes longer than the train and is far less comfortable. The following destinations are within bearable travelling distance.

Shanghai to: Hangzhou (frequent; 5hr); Lianyungang (daily; 15hr); Shaoxing (several daily; 6hr); Suzhou (frequent; 2hr); Wuxi (several daily; 3hr); Wenzhou (daily; 17hr); Yangzhou (daily; 6hr).

Ferries

Shanghai to: Chongqing (daily; 6 days); Dalian (48hr); Fuzhou/Mawei (3 weekly, 36hr); Hong Kong (2 weekly; 60hr); Japan (Osaka, Nagasaki, Yokohama; seasonal, several weekly; 36hr);

Nanjing (6 weekly; 16hr); Ningbo (daily; 12hr, some catamarans 4hr); Putuo Shan (daily ferry; 12hr, some catamarans 4hr); Qingdao (26hr); Wenzhou (every two days; 24hr); Wuhan (4 daily; 56hr).

Planes

DOMESTIC

Shanghai to: Baotou (twice weekly; 2hr 50min); Beijing (14 daily; 1hr 50min); Changchun (daily; 2hr 45min); Chengdu (5 daily; 2hr 45min); Chongqing (2 daily; 2hr 30min); Dalian (twice daily; 1hr 30min); Fuzhou (5 daily; 1hr 30 min); Guangzhou (9 daily; 2hr); Guilin (twice daily; 2hr 20min); Haikou (2-4 daily; 3hr); Hangzhou (daily; 25min); Harbin (2 daily; 2hr 40min); Hohhot (twice weekly; 2hr 20min); Hong Kong (8 daily; 2hr 10min); Huangshan (weekly; 1hr); Kunming (daily; 3hr); Lanzhou (daily; 3hr); Nanjing (daily; 40min); Nanning (daily; 3hr); Ningbo (daily; 40min); Qingdao (5 daily; 1hr 20min); Shenzhen (6 daily; 2hr); Taiyuan (2 weekly; 2hr); Tianjin (daily; 1hr 30min); Urumqi (5 weekly; 5hr); Wenzhou (3-5 daily; 1hr); Wuhan (4-6 daily; 1hr); Wuyishan (twice weekly; 1hr 10min); Xiamen (7 daily; 1hr 30min); Xi'an (twice daily; 2hr 15min).

INTERNATIONAL

Shanghai to: Bangkok (2 weekly; 6hr); Frankfurt (3 weekly; 10hr); Los Angeles (3 weekly; 11hr); Madrid (twice weekly; 10hr); Nagasaki (twice weekly; 2hr 15min); New York (twice weekly; 14hr); Paris (2 weekly; 10hr); San Francisco (3 weekly; 12hr) Singapore (3 weekly; 7hr); Tokyo (2 daily; 3hr).

CHAPTER SIX

JIANGSU AND ZHEJIANG

C hina's original heartland may have been the dusty Yellow River basin, but it was the greenness and fertility of the **Yangzi River estuary** which drew the Chinese south and provided them with the wealth and power needed to sustain a huge empire. The provinces of **Jiangsu** and **Zhejiang**, which today flank the metropolitan area of Shanghai to the north and south, have been playing a vital part in the cultural and economic development of China for the last two thousand years. No tour of eastern China would be complete without stopovers in some of their classic destinations.

Historically, the story begins in the sixth century BC when the area was part of the state of Wu and had already developed its own distinct culture. The flat terrain, the large crop yield and the superb communications offered by coastal ports and navigable waterways enabled the principal towns of the area to develop quickly into important **trading centres**. These presented an irresistible target for the expanding Chinese empire under the Qin dynasty, and in 223 BC the region was annexed, immediately developing into one of the economic centres of the empire. After the end of the Han dynasty in the third century AD, several regimes established short-lived capitals in southern cities, but the real boost for southern China came when the Sui (589–618 AD) extended the **Grand Canal** to link the Yangzi with the Yellow River and ultimately to allow trade to flow freely between here and the northern capitals. With this, China's centre of gravity took a decisive shift south. Under later dynasties, Hangzhou and then Nanjing became the greatest cities in China.

Visiting the region, you find yourself in a world of **water**. The whole area is intensively drained, canalized, irrigated and farmed, and the rivers, canals and lakes which web the plain give it much of its character. The traditional way to travel here was by **boat**, and today ferries continue to ply the Yangzi, while the major sea ports – Shanghai, Ningbo, Wenzhou – are also linked by coastal passenger services. There are even still a few local services inland, such as those between Suzhou, Wuxi and Hangzhou, along the **canals** in among silk farms and tea plantations.

The powerful commercial cities of the waterways have long acted as counterweights to the bureaucratic tendencies of Beijing, and both **Hangzhou** and **Nanjing** have

---

ACCOMMODATION PRICE CODES

All the accommodation in this book has been graded according to the following price codes, which represent the cheapest double room available to foreigners. Most places have a range of rooms, however, and staff will usually offer you the more expensive ones – it's always worth asking if they have anything cheaper. Where the text refers specifically to dorm beds, the price code represents the price per bed. See p.40 for more details.

① less than ¥30	④ ¥100–150	⑦ ¥300–500
② ¥30–75	⑤ ¥150–200	⑧ ¥500–700
③ ¥75–100	⑥ ¥200–300	⑨ ¥700 or more

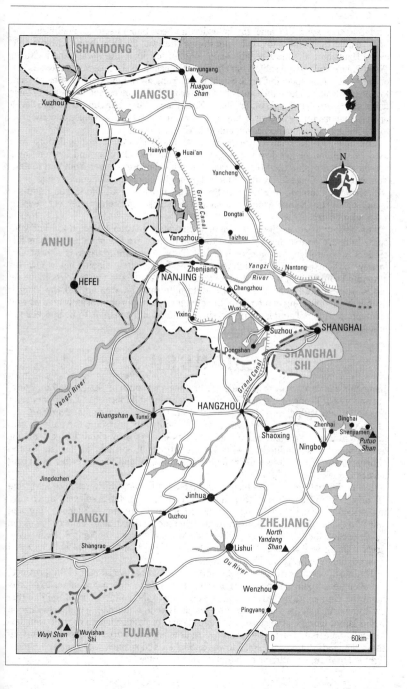

served as the capital of China, the latter having been Sun Yatsen's capital during the brief years of the Chinese Republic after the overthrow of the Qing dynasty. Marco Polo called Hangzhou "the most beautiful and magnificent city in the world", and its Xi Hu (West Lake), still recognizable from classic scroll paintings, is deservedly rated as one of the most scenic spots in China. **Suzhou** and **Yangzhou**, too, should not be missed, for the bustle of life along the canals that crisscross their centres, and the peace of their famous **gardens**. These and other cities – **Zhenjiang**, **Wuxi**, **Ningbo** – have also developed as manufacturing centres, enjoying the boom which has put Jiangsu and Zhejiang to the forefront of economic development in China.

The downside to relative prosperity in China is chronic over-population. Well over 120 million people live in Jiangsu, Shanghai and Zhejiang and it sometimes seems when crossing the area by train that it has been built over from end to end. You will be hard-pressed to find much that might be classed as countryside here, with the exceptions of the charming **Shaoxing**, and, above all, the sacred Buddhist island of **Putuo Shan**, which has superb beaches and monasteries set deep in wooded hillsides.

For visitors, perhaps the most important point is that most foreign tourists who come here are on expensive package tours and there are few facilities, such as foreigners' dormitories, for independent travellers. **Accommodation** is almost uniformly on the expensive side, with the cheapest hotels rarely dipping below ¥150 for a double room – often university accommodation is the only budget possibility. As far as **seasons** are concerned, you should note that the area around the Yangzi, despite being low-lying and far from the northern plains, is unpleasantly cold as well as damp in winter. The terrain needs summer rains and sunshine to be appreciated in its finest greenery.

JIANGSU

Jiangsu is a long, narrow province hugging the coast south of Shandong. Low-lying, flat and wet, it is one of the most fertile and long-inhabited areas of China, dense in population and with plenty of sights of interest. The provincial capital, **Nanjing**, one of the great historical cities of China, was until only fifty years ago the nation's capital. **Suzhou** and **Yangzhou** are ancient cities famous throughout China for their gardens and silk production, while **Wuxi** attracts thousands of tourists to the shores of **Tai Hu** for its scenery, fruit trees and fish, and for the caves of **Yixing** across the lake.

The traditional route across Jiangsu is the **Grand Canal**, which was once navigable all the way from Hangzhou in Zhejiang Province to Beijing, and is still very much alive in the sections which flow through southern Jiangsu. In addition to Suzhou, Yangzhou and Wuxi, **Zhenjiang** and **Changzhou** are two more classic trading centres full of the bustle of canal life. The province's other great water highway – the **Yangzi River** – connects Nanjing with the seaport of Shanghai, ensuring that trade from both east and west continues to bring wealth to the region.

The northwest has traditionally been the poor and backward part of the province, but even here **Xuzhou** is now a major rail junction with modern coal mines to supplement the fame of its early Han origins. A rail link – the continuation of the line that eventually runs all the way across Asia and Europe to Rotterdam – connects Xuzhou with **Lianyungang** on the coast. The central parts of Jiangsu have a coast too shallow for anchorage, but ideal for salt panning, traditionally the source of its income. Among these flat lands dotted with small towns and lakes, and seamed with canals, the highlight is **Huai'an**, the attractive birthplace of Zhou Enlai.

THE GRAND CANAL

The **Grand Canal** (Da Yunhe) ranks alongside the Great Wall of China as the country's greatest engineering achievement. For centuries, the 1800-kilometre waterway, the longest canal on earth, has played a key role in the nation's trade and in the lives of the millions of people in the towns along its banks. The first sections were dug about 400 BC, probably for military purposes, but the historic task of linking the Yellow and the Yangzi rivers was not achieved until the early seventh century AD under the Sui emperor Yang Di, when as many as six million men may have been pressed into service for its construction.

The original function of the canal was to join the fertile rice-producing areas of the Yangzi with the more heavily populated but barren lands of the north, and to alleviate the effects of regular crop failures and famine. Following its completion, however, the canal became a vital element in the expansion of **trade** under the Tang and Song, benefiting the south as much as the north. Slowly the centre of political power drifted south – by 800 AD the Yangzi basin was taking over from the Yellow River as the chief source of the empire's finances, a transformation that would bring an end to the long domination of the old northern capitals, and lead to Hangzhou and Nanjing becoming China's most populous and powerful cities. A Japanese monk, Ennin, who travelled in China from 836 to 847 AD, described the traffic on the water then, and in places he might find similar scenes today:

> *Two water buffalo were tied to more than 40 boats, with two or three of the latter joined to form a single raft and with these connected in line by hawsers. Since it was difficult to hear from head to stern there was great shouting back and forth... Boats of the salt bureau passed laden with salt, three or four or five boats bound side by side and in line, following one another for several tens of li. This unexpected sight is not easy to describe ...*

By the twelfth century, the provinces of Jiangsu and Zhejiang had become the economic and political heart of China. The Song dynasty moved south and established a capital at **Hangzhou** and the Ming emperors subsequently based themselves in **Nanjing**. During this period, and for centuries afterwards, the canal was constantly maintained and the banks regularly built up. A Western traveller, Robert Morrison, journeying as late as 1816 from Tianjin all the way down to the Yangzi, described the sophisticated and frequent locks and noted that in places the banks were so high and the country around so low that from the boat it was possible to look down on roofs and treetops.

Not until early in the twentieth century did the canal seriously start falling into **disuse**. Contributing factors included the frequent flooding of the Yellow River, the growth of coastal shipping and the coming of the rail lines. Unused, much of the canal rapidly silted up. But since the 1950s its value has once more been recognized, and renovation undertaken. The stretch **south of the Yangzi**, running from Zhenjiang through Changzhou, Wuxi and Suzhou (and on to Hangzhou in Zhejiang Province), is now navigable all year round, at least by flat-bottomed barges and the cruisers built for the tourist trade. Although most local **passenger boat services** along the canal have been dropped, the surviving services from Hangzhou to Suzhou or Wuxi will probably give you enough of a taste. It's fascinating rather than beautiful – as well as the frenetic loading and unloading of barges, you'll see serious pollution and heavy industry. **North of the Yangzi**, the canal is seasonably navigable virtually up to Jiangsu's northern border with Shandong, and major works are going on to allow bulk carriers access to the coal-producing city of Xuzhou. Beyond here, towards the Yellow River, the canal remains sadly impassable.

Suzhou and around

Famous for its gardens and its silk, the ancient and moated city of **SUZHOU**, just ninety minutes from Shanghai by train, lies at the point where the rail line meets the Grand Canal, about 30km to the east of Tai Hu (see p.368). The town itself is built on a net-

SUZHOU AND AROUND

Suzhou	宝带桥	*sūzhōu*
	灵岩山	

ACCOMMODATION

Huayuan	花苑饭店	*huāyuàn fàndiàn*
Lexiang	乐乡饭店	*lèxiāng fàndiàn*
Nanlin	南林饭店	*nánlín fàndiàn*
Nanyuan	南园宾馆	*nányuán bīnguǎn*
Shenjiang	申江大酒店	*shēnjiāng dàjiǔdiàn*
Suzhou	苏州饭店	*sūzhōu fàndiàn*
Suzhou Medical School Guesthouse	苏州医学院招待所	*sūzhōu yīxuéyuàn zhāodàisuǒ*
Waimao	外贸宾馆	*wàimào bīnguǎn*
Wuzhou	五州大饭店	*wǔzhōu dàjiǔdiàn*
Yingfeng	迎枫饭店	*yíngfēng fàndiàn*
Youyi	友谊宾馆	*yǒuyì bīnguǎn*

THE CITY

Beisi Ta	北寺塔	*běisì tǎ*
Canglang Ting	沧浪亭	*cānglàng tíng*
Feng Qiao	枫桥	*fēng qiáo*
Hanshan Si	寒山寺	*hánshān sì*
Huqiu Shan	虎丘山	*hǔqiū shān*
Liu Yuan	留园	*liú yuán*
Museum of Opera and Theatre	戏曲博物馆	*xìqǔ bówùguǎn*
Pan Men	盘门	*pánmén*
Ruiguang Ta	瑞光塔	*ruìguāng tǎ*
Shizi Lin	狮子林	*shīzi lín*
Shuang Ta	双塔	*shuāng tǎ*
Wangshi Yuan	网师园	*wǎngshī yuán*
Wumen Qiao	吴门桥	*wúmén qiáo*
Xi Yuan	西园	*xīyuán*
Xuanmiao Guan	玄妙观	*xuánmiào guān*
Yi Yuan	怡园	*yíyuán*
Zhuozheng Yuan	拙政园	*zhuózhèng yuán*

RESTAURANTS

Bali Island Restaurant	岜厘岛大酒店	*bālǐdǎo dàjiǔdiàn*
Gongdelin	功德林素食馆	*gōngdélín sùshíguǎn*
Songhelou Caiguan	松鹤楼	*sōnghèlóu*
Xibu Pijiu Niupa Cheng	西部啤酒牛扒城	*xībùpíjiǔniúpáchéng*

AROUND SUZHOU

Baodai Qiao	宝带桥	*bǎodài qiáo*
Lingyan Shan	灵岩山	*língyán shān*
Tianping Shan	天平山	*tiānpíng shān*
Tongli	同里	*tónglǐ*

work of interlocking canals whose waters feed the series of renowned **classical gardens** which are Suzhou's pride and glory. Crisscrossed with water and dotted with greenery, the city retains traces of its original character, though these days Suzhou's chief claim to fame – from the locals' point of view – is as home to "Little Singapore", an entire industrial city being built on the outskirts by Singaporean investment.

He Lu, semi-mythical ruler of the Kingdom of Wu, is said to have founded Suzhou in 600 BC as his capital, but it was the arrival of the **Grand Canal** over a thousand years later which marked the beginning of the prosperity of the city. The **silk trade**, too, was established early here, flourishing under the Tang and thoroughly booming when the whole imperial court moved south under the Song. To this day, silk remains one of Suzhou's sources of income.

With the imperial capital close by at Hangzhou, Suzhou attracted an overspill of scholars, officials and merchants, bringing wealth and patronage with them. In the late thirteenth century, Marco Polo reported "six thousand bridges, clever merchants, cunning men of all crafts, very wise men called Sages and great natural physicians". When the first Ming emperor founded his capital at Nanjing, the city continued to enjoy a privileged position within the orbit of the court and to flourish as a centre for the production and weaving of silk. In this period, the business was transformed by the gathering of the workforce into great sheds in a manner not seen in the West until the coming of the Industrial Revolution three centuries later.

Until recently, Suzhou's good fortune had been to avoid the ravages of history, despite suffering brief periods of occupation by the Taipings in the 1860s and by the Japanese during World War II. The city walls, however, which even in 1925 were still an effective defence against rampaging warlords, were almost entirely demolished after 1949, and the parts of the old city that still survive – moats, gates, canals, bridges, old streets and houses – are disappearing fast. Soon there may be little more than the famous gardens themselves to provide testimony to the city's past.

Orientation, arrival and accommodation

The historic town lies within a rectangular moat formed by canals. The city's clear grid of streets and waterways makes Suzhou a relatively easy place in which to get your bearings. **Renmin Lu**, the main street, bulldozes south through the centre from the **train station** which is just to the north of the moat. Most facilities for the traveller are located on or near Renmin Lu, including the **post office**, the **Bank of China** and the **PSB**. The traditional commercial centre of the city lies around **Guanqian Jie**, halfway down Renmin Lu, an area of cramped, animated streets thronged with small shops, tea houses and restaurants. A newer, smarter shopping area has also developed outside the northwestern part of the moat around **Shi Lu**, while the area of town due west of the moat is the modern, ugly **Xincheng**.

Nearly all travellers arrive by **train**, Suzhou being on the main Shanghai–Nanjing rail line and served by frequent trains to and from both cities. Buses #1 and #20 take you into town from just east of the train station. Some private **minibuses** also use the train station square as their terminus, for example services to and from Wuxi and points on Tai Hu.

The **Nanmen bus station**, which has hourly connections with Shanghai, is at the southern end of Renmin Lu; take bus #1 into the centre. Very near the Nanmen bus station is the **passenger dock** for canal boats to and from Hangzhou. One other bus station travellers might use is the **Xianshi bus station** in the far south of the town, one

The **telephone code** for Suzhou is ☎0512

large block south of the moat (city bus #1 also passes here). This is the base for buses to and from local towns such as Tongli.

There is no airport at Suzhou (the nearest is at Shanghai, accessible in about an hour by taxi), though there is a *CAAC* office for bookings (see "Listings", p.367).

Accommodation

The main **hotel** area, and the heaviest concentration of gardens and historic buildings, is in the south, around **Shiquan Jie**. Unfortunately for budget travellers, Suzhou is geared heavily towards the needs of tour groups and cheap accommodation is hard to come by.

Huayuan, Suzhan Lu (☎7275510). Dilapidated and mosquito-infested, this place nevertheless offers the cheapest accommodation in town for foreign tourists. It's about fifteen minutes' walk north of the train station. To reach it, turn right as you emerge from the station, then right again through a tunnel under the rail line. Follow the road to the T-junction, and the hotel is on your right, on the corner (no English sign). Grotty doubles with or without bath. ②–④.

Lexiang, Dajin Xiang (☎5222890, fax 5244165). A good, friendly, central hotel, on the third lane south of Guanqian Jie, running east off Renmin Lu, which has some three- or four-bed rooms which can work out pretty cheap if you bring enough friends to fill them. There's an English sign advertising "Bike Rent" at the top of the lane. ⑤.

Nanlin, Shiquan Jie (☎5194641, fax 5191028). A big garden-style affair right opposite the *Nanyuan* with a superbly immaculate lobby. The new wing has luxury rooms, while the old wing still offers reasonably priced doubles and triples. ⑥–⑨.

Nanyuan, Shiquan Jie (☎5227661, fax 5238806). Smart place offering all facilities. ⑦.

Shenjiang, Liuyuan Lu (☎5331266, fax 7232930). Out in the west of the city, beyond the moat (take bus #7 from the train station). Standard new accommodation. ⑥.

Suzhou, Shiquan Jie (☎5204646, fax 5205191). A huge place, and the best established of the upmarket hotels. ⑧.

Suzhou Medical School Guesthouse, Renmin Lu (east side), south of Shiquan Lu. It is sometimes possible to get into the very cheap rooms here, though you'll probably need some Chinese to manage it. ②.

Waimao, Renmin Lu (☎7531762). Very convenient for train travellers – cross the bridge opposite the station and the hotel is the first place on your left. A much nicer alternative to the nearby *Huayuan*. ⑥.

Wuzhou, Shi Lu (☎5332313, fax 5336015). Around the corner from the *Shenjiang*, just south of the Guangji Bridge (bus #7 from the train station). Handy for the Shi Lu shopping area. ⑦.

Yingfeng, Wuya Chang (☎5300907). Just off Shiquan Jie – take the small lane opposite the *Suzhou*, cross the bridge and it's on the right. A new, friendly and good-value hotel, one of the cheapest in this area. ⑥.

Youyi (*Friendship Hotel*), Zhuhui Lu (☎5205218, fax 5206221). A block south of Shiquan Jie, this is large and friendly with good-value rooms. ⑥–⑦.

The City

Among the Chinese, Suzhou is one of the most highly favoured tourist destinations in the country, and the city is packed with visitors from far and wide. This can make for a festive atmosphere, but it also means that you are rarely able to appreciate the **gardens** in the peace for which they were designed. Seasons make surprisingly little difference as the gardens can be appreciated at any time of year, although springtime brings blossom and brighter colours.

Suzhou is one of the more enjoyable cities in China for simply roaming without special purpose. Wherever you go you'll come across pagodas, temples, lively shopping districts and hectic canal traffic. Distances are too large to rely purely on walking, but **cycling** is an excellent alternative as the terrain is pretty flat (see p.367 for rental details).

SUZHOU'S GARDENS

Gardens, above all, are what Suzhou is all about. Elsewhere in China you'll find grounds – as at the mountain resort of Chengde or the Summer Palace outside Beijing – laid out on a grand scale, but here they're tiny in comparison, and far closer to the true essence of a Chinese garden – "infinite riches in a little room".

Chinese gardens do not set out to imitate or to improve upon a slice of nature, they are a serious art form where, as with painting, sculpture and poetry, the aim is to produce for contemplation the **balance, harmony, proportion and variety** which the Chinese seek in life. The garden designer works with rock, water, buildings, trees and vegetation in subtly different combinations. Nothing could be further from the intention than to look natural, which is why many Western eyes find them hard to accept or enjoy.

Gardens have been laid out in Suzhou since the Song dynasty, a thousand years ago, and in their Ming and Qing heyday it is said that there were two hundred of them here. Some half-dozen major gardens have now been restored, as well as a number of smaller ones. They were built by wealthy scholars and merchants, often in small areas behind high compound walls. The designers used little pavilions and terraces to suggest a larger scale, undulating covered walkways and galleries to give a downward view, and intricate interlocking groups of rock and bamboo to hint at, and half conceal, what lies beyond. **Effects** depended on glimpses through delicate lattices, tile-patterned openings, moon gates or reflections in water; cunning perspectives which either suggested a whole landscape, or borrowed outside features (such as external walls of neighbouring buildings) as part of the design in order to create an illusion of distance. **Essential features** of the Suzhou gardens were considered to include white pine trees, odd-shaped rocks from Tai Hu and stone tablets over the entrances; the whole was completed by animals. There are still fish and turtles in some ponds today.

Differences in style among the various gardens arise basically from the mix and balance of the ingredients – some are three-parts water, others are mazes of contorted rock, others mainly inward-looking, featuring pavilions full of strange furniture. And remember that almost everything you see has some symbolic significance – the pine tree and the crane for long life, mandarin ducks for married bliss, for example.

It is possible to overdo the gardens; the mannered and artificial combination of nature, art and architecture may seem cluttered and pedantic, and the brief flourish of spring blossom apart, they can appear colourless and muted. If possible, choose a day with blue sky and a hint of cloud – the gardens need contrast, light and shade, clear shadow and bold reflection – and don't feel you need to see them all. The gardens all **open daily**, from around 8am to 4.30–5pm and entrance fees vary from ¥5 to ¥20.

Within the moat

Moving south down Renmin Lu from the train station, the first place you pass, looming up unmistakably, is the **Beisi Ta** (North Temple Pagoda; daily 8am–5.30pm; ¥6 for the garden, ¥4 to climb the tower). First built in the third century AD, and rebuilt in 1582, the Beisi Ta retains only nine of its original eleven storeys, but it is still, at 76m, the highest Chinese pagoda south of the Yangzi. Climbing it gives an excellent view over some of Suzhou's more conspicuous features – the Shuang Ta, the Xuanmiao Guan, and in the far southwest corner, the Ruiguang Ta. There's also a very pleasant tea house on the site.

Virtually opposite the Beisi Ta, also on Renmin Lu, is the **Suzhou Silk Museum** (daily 9am–6pm; ¥4), one of China's better-presented museums, clearly marked in English throughout. Starting from the legendary inventor of silk, the concubine of the equally legendary Emperor Huang Di, it traces the history of silk production and its use from 4000 BC to the present day, and includes a collection of reproductions of early silk patterns, as well as actual fragments. The section on the science of sericulture is particularly fascinating, as is the display of early weaving machines.

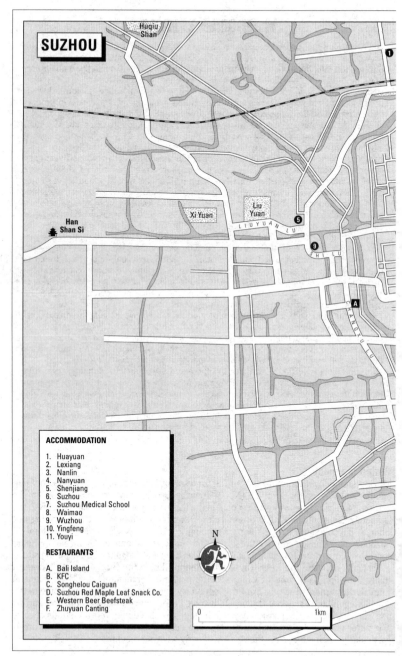

SUZHOU

Huqiu Shan

Han Shan Si

Xi Yuan

Liu Yuan

LIUYUAN LU

SHI LU

CHANGXU LU

ACCOMMODATION

1. Huayuan
2. Lexiang
3. Nanlin
4. Nanyuan
5. Shenjiang
6. Suzhou
7. Suzhou Medical School
8. Waimao
9. Wuzhou
10. Yingfeng
11. Youyi

RESTAURANTS

A. Bali Island
B. KFC
C. Songhelou Caiguan
D. Suzhou Red Maple Leaf Snack Co.
E. Western Beer Beefsteak
F. Zhuyuan Canting

N

0   1km

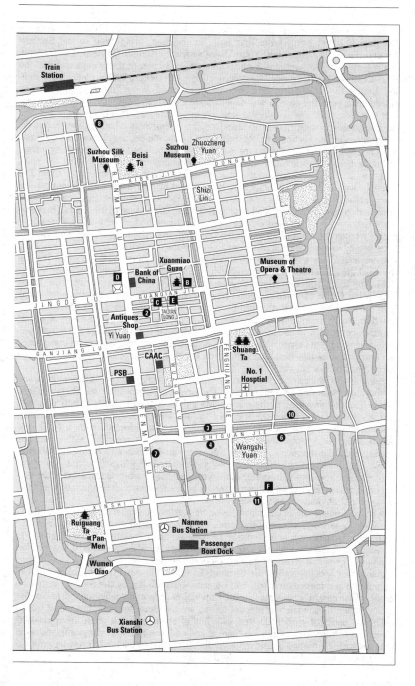

Train Station

8

Suzhou Silk Museum

Beisi Ta

Suzhou Museum

Zhuozheng Yuan

DONGBEI JIE

XIBEI JIE

RENMIN

Shizi Lin

Xuanmiao Guan

Bank of China

D

B

C E

GUANQIAN JIE

JINGDE LU

2

TAIJIANLONG

Museum of Opera & Theatre

Antiques Shop

Yi Yuan

GANJIANG LU

CAAC

PSB

WUQUE LU

FENGHUANG JIE

Shuang Ta

No. 1 Hosptial

SHIZI JIE

RENMIN LU

3

SHIQUAN JIE

4

7

Wangshi Yuan

10

6

F

ZHUHUI LU

11

XINSHI LU

Ruiguang Ta

Pan-Men

Nanmen Bus Station

Passenger Boat Dock

Wumen Qiao

Xianshi Bus Station

Turning east immediately south of Beisi Ta, along Xibei Jie (which shortly becomes Dongbei Jie) and beyond the first large intersection, brings you to the **Suzhou Museum** and the **Zhuozheng Yuan** (Humble Administrator's Garden). The museum (daily 8am–4pm; ¥5) contains a rather obscure collection of dusty ceramics with no English labels, but the garden next door (daily 8am–4.30pm; ¥20) is compulsory visiting. Built at the time of the Ming by an imperial censor, Wang Xianchen, who had just resigned his post, the garden was thus named by its creator as an ironic lament on the fact that he could now administer nothing but gardening. Much the largest of the Suzhou gardens, covering four hectares, the Zhuozheng Yuan is based on water and set out in three linked sections: the eastern part (inside the entrance) consists of a small lotus pond and pavilions; the centre is largely water, with two small islands connected by zigzag bridges; while the western part has unusually open green spaces.

A couple of minutes south of the Zhuozheng Yuan is another garden, the **Shizi Lin** (Lion Grove Garden). The monk who laid this out in 1342 named it in honour of his teacher who lived on Lion Rock Mountain, and the rocks of which it largely consists are supposed to resemble lions in all shapes and sizes. Once chosen, these strange water-worn rocks were submerged for decades in Tai Hu to be further eroded. Part of the rockery takes the form of a convoluted labyrinth, from the top of which you emerge occasionally to gaze down at the water reflecting the green trees and grey stone. Qing emperors Qianlong and Kangxi were said to be so enamoured of these rockeries that they had the garden at the Yuanmingyuan Palace in Beijing modelled on them.

Moving south from here, down into the very heart of the city, you arrive at the Taoist **Xuanmiao Guan** (Temple of Mystery), just north of Guanqian Jie. Founded originally in the third century AD, this has been destroyed, rebuilt, burnt down and put back together many times during its history. The complex consists basically of a vast entrance court with, at its far end, a hall of Taoist deities. For centuries the temple was the scene of a great bazaar where travelling showmen, acrobats and actors entertained the crowds. Nowadays it's still an attractive, lively place, full of gossiping old men and surrounded by market stalls.

A ten-minute walk due east of Guanqian Jie, along narrow lanes, is the unusual and memorable **Museum of Opera and Theatre** (daily 8am–4pm) on Zhongzhangjia Xiang. The building itself is the star – a Ming-dynasty theatre made of latticed wood, with the stage raised up on the second floor of a large pavilion (beneath a spiralling wooden dome), with an open-air "pit", and galleries to all sides. Although it's still used occasionally for demonstration performances, the rooms are filled with costumes, masks, musical instruments, and even a full-sized model orchestra, complete with cups of tea. There are no English captions, but you can trace the history from a century of photographs; look for the interlude in the years of lavish costumes and spectacular productions, when the disgruntled company can be seen performing revolutionary operas, dressed in drab denim, in a vast steelworks.

A few minutes south of Guanqian Jie, on the northwest corner of the Renmin Lu and Ganjiang Lu junction, is one of the lesser gardens, **Yi Yuan**, the Garden of Harmony. Late Qing-dynasty, and hence considerably newer than the others, it is supposed to encompass all the key features of a garden (see box, p.361). Unusually, it also has formal flower beds and arrangements of coloured pebbles.

Altogether less stylized is the **Shuang Ta** (Twin Pagodas), several blocks east of Renmin Lu and immediately south of Ganjiang Lu. Built during the Song dynasty by a group of successful candidates in the imperial examinations who wanted to honour their teacher, these matching slender towers are too flimsy to climb, but sprout from a delightful patch of garden. Dotted with bits of statuary like a scene from classical Greece, it features a gardener's cottage at one end, teeming with chrysanthemums in pots and lovingly tended bonsai trees. At the other end is a tea house crowded with old men fanning themselves against the heat in summer.

A kilometre or so farther south of here, just beyond Shiquan Jie, are two more gardens. The **Canglang Ting** (Dark Blue Wave Pavilion), at the corner of Renmin Lu and Zhuhui Lu, approached through a ceremonial marble archway, is the oldest of the major surviving gardens, originally built in the Song dynasty, around 1044 AD. There is no enclosing wall on the northern side and the garden was supposed to "borrow" features from outside, which then became integral parts of the overall effect. Inside the garden, the central mound is designed to look like a forested hill. In the south of the garden (away from the entrance) stands the curious Five Hundred Sage Temple lined with stone tablets recording the names and achievements of great statesmen, heroes and poets of Suzhou.

The nearby **Wangshi Yuan** (Master of the Nets Garden), on Shiquan Jie, is a short walk west from the *Suzhou Hotel* and down a narrow alleyway on the left. This tiny and intimate garden was started in 1140, but later abandoned and not restored to its present layout until 1770. Considered by garden connoisseurs to be the finest of them all, it now has rather more visitors than it can cope with. With an attractive central lake, minuscule connecting halls and pavilions with pocket-handkerchief courtyards and carved wooden doors, the garden's main features are its delicate latticework and fretted windows through which you can catch a series of glimpses – a glimmer of bamboo, dark interiors, water and a miniature rockery framed in the three windows of a study. It is said to be best seen on moonlit nights, when from the Moon-watching Pavilion the moon can be seen three times over – in the sky, in the water and in a mirror (serious garden connoisseurs should enquire at *CITS* for the possibility of visiting the garden after normal closing hours).

Finally, in the far southwestern corner of the moated area, stands **Pan Men** (Pan Gate) and a stretch of the original city wall. The best approach to this area is from the south, via **Wumen Qiao**, a delightful high-arched bridge with steps built into it and a great vantage point for watching the canal traffic (bus #7 from the train station passes the southern edge of the moat). Walking north from the bridge brings you to Pan Men, where you can climb up and walk east along the city wall. From the top of the wall itself you'll have good views of the barges, the ramshackle houses, stone bridges, willow trees and cobbled streets, and more specifically, to the northeast, of the dramatic **Ruiguang Ta**, a thousand-year-old pagoda, now almost a ruin.

West of the moated city

If you're relying on public transport, the gateway to sites west of the moated city is the bus interchange at the busy **Shi Lu** shopping area (buses #2 and #7 from the train station; bus #5 from Jingde Lu downtown). Otherwise the following sites can all be reached by bicycle.

There are two elegant gardens not far to the west of Shi Lu, both on bus routes #5 and #11. The **Liu Yuan** (Garden to Linger In) was originally built during Ming times, but destroyed by the Japanese and restored in 1953. Its four scenic areas, and their buildings, are connected by a seven-hundred-metre-long winding corridor which assiduously follows the changing landscapes. Among the attractions is the largest of all the Tai Hu rocks, a single lump weighing around five thousand kilos and known as the **Cloud-crowned Peak**.

Just a couple of hundred metres to the west of here is the **Xi Yuan**, more temple than garden, its great sweeps of yellow-ochred walls contrasting richly with the charcoal-grey roof tiles and the red woodwork. The main hall of the temple here has a striking ceiling, and a wing to one side contains ranks of impressively sculpted *arhats*. It's a pleasant spot, despite the droves of tourists, with giant carp and soft-shelled turtles cruising in the pond.

Due north of these gardens rises **Huqiu Shan** (Tiger Hill), the legendary site of the tomb of a king of Wu, guarded by a mythical white tiger. There are terraces laid out with shrubs and trees, a tea house, and everywhere rocks and pools each with their own name and hoary legend. They include the **Thousand Men Rock**, where the men who built the tomb were supposedly executed to keep its whereabouts secret, and the **Sword Pond** which is said to conceal the treasures of the king's tomb – including three thousand swords. At the summit stands Suzhou's very own leaning tower, the **Yunyan Ta** or Cloud Rock Pagoda. Octagonal, with seven brick storeys, it needs constant attention to prevent it from toppling altogether and during one such operation, in 1965, workmen found a box containing tenth-century Buddhist sutras wrapped in silk. Archeologists suspect that one reason for the subsidence of the tower is the presence of underground passages, which may hold the secrets of the legendary tomb.

Huqiu Shan is at the terminus of bus #5; from the bus stop follow the crowds through the souvenir stands to the hill. If you're coming by bike, one fascinating (albeit boneshaking) option is the direct route, following the cobbled towpaths lining the small Shantang canal, past the splendour of the former merchants' houses with their imposing facades and watergates.

Hanshan Si (Cold Mountain Temple) also lies in the suburbs, about 5km west of town. Take bus #6 from Shi Lu to the stop by the temple, then walk straight ahead, past the temple wall, until you reach the canal. Here you'll see the superb arched bridge **Feng Qiao**, and the main entrance to the temple is to your right (you can also sometimes get here along the canals, on a tour boat from Pan Men). Dating from around 500 AD, the temple is particularly famous in both China and Japan because the celebrated Tang poet Zhang Ji wrote a poem about it which is inscribed on a stone stele inside:

> *Moonset; through the freezing air the caw of a crow;*
> *By Feng Qiao, breaking my rest, the fishing lamps glow;*
> *To me as I lie in my boat the dark hour brings*
> *The plangent repeated sound as the temple bell rings*
> *At Han Shan beyond Suzhou.*

At new year, Han Shan is crammed with Japanese visitors who come to hear the midnight bell. So wealthy has the temple now become through donations, that large-scale additions – including new halls and pagodas – are currently being built to the east of the original site.

Eating and drinking

Suzhou's cooking is justly renowned, and the area around Guanqian Jie is a good place to look for food. The *Songhelou Caiguan*, on the south side of Guanqian Jie, a couple of hundred metres east of Renmin Lu, is the most famous **restaurant** in town – it claims to be old enough to have served Emperor Qianlong. The menu is elaborate and long on fish (crab, eel and squirrel fish among them), and it's an interesting if not cheap place to dine. A short walk farther east brings you to a small alley, leading south, called Taijian Long, where a number of traditional Chinese restaurants are located, including the excellent *Gongdelin* which serves vegetarian dishes only.

Back on Guanqian Jie, just east of Taijian Long, is the *Xibu Pijiu Niupa Cheng*, signposted in English as "Western Beer Beefsteak", and dressed up as an outpost of the American Wild West, but there's a menu in English and it's good value. Farther east still, just beyond the Xuanmiao Guan, is a branch of *KFC* (there's another branch on Shi Lu just to the west of the moat). Fast food of an oriental variety can also be found at the *Suzhou Red Maple Leaf Snack Co Ltd* (signposted in English) on the west side of Renmin Lu, a couple of minutes north of Guanqian Jie – order by pointing to the pictures. Down in the southeast of town, opposite the *Youyi Hotel,* is a good place for cheap, quick Chinese dishes, the *Zhuyuan Canting.*

If you want a complete change of atmosphere, try the Indonesian *Bali Island Restaurant* – a highly unusual find in China – with bright lights, immaculate decor and an interesting menu in English. It's on Changxu Lu, parallel to the western border of the moat, a few hundred metres south of Shi Lu.

Listings

Airlines The main *CAAC* reservations and ticketing office is at 120 Renmin Lu, a few minutes' walk south of Gangjiang Lu (☎5222788; daily 8–11.30am & 1–5.15pm). The nearest airport is in Shanghai.

Banks and exchange The *Bank of China* head office (Mon–Fri 8am–4.30pm & Sat 8am–12.30pm) is on Renmin Lu right in the centre of town, just north of Guanqian Jie. You can change travellers' cheques in any of the upmarket hotels if you are a guest.

Bike rental There are one or two obscure bike rental shops dotted around, including one at the *Huayuan Hotel* and another on the corner of Renmin Lu and Dajin Xiang, near the *Lexiang Hotel*. You might also try enquiring around the train station.

Boats Connecting Suzhou and Hangzhou, there is one service daily in both directions, taking around thirteen hours. The incoming boat arrives in the early morning, and the outward boat leaves at 5.30pm – tickets range from ¥20 (hard seat) to ¥200 for a private cabin. There is a bar and karaoke on board. Buy tickets at the dock at the southern end of Renmin Lu.

Hospital The No. 1 Hospital is in the east of town, at the junction of Fenghuang Jie and Shizi Jie.

Post office Suzhou's main post office is at the corner of Renmin Lu and Jingde Lu.

PSB On Renmin Lu, at the junction with the small lane Dashitou Xiang.

Tours If you're in a hurry, a one-day tour can be an excellent way to get round all the main sights – minibuses depart from the train station square around 8am, and cost ¥15 exclusive of admission charges. Tours specially geared for foreign tourists in air-conditioned buses can be booked at *CITS* (or other travel services) for around ¥260, which includes lunch and all admission fees.

Trains Tickets are sold from the office at the eastern end of the train station square, where the windows for soft seats are clearly marked in English. For trains in the direction of Nanjing, queue downstairs, and for Shanghai, upstairs; buy tickets one day in advance.

Travel agents Nearly all hotels have their own travel agencies. Otherwise *CITS* is in a wing of the *Suzhou Hotel* on Shiquan Jie (daily 9am–4pm; ☎5211054).

Around Suzhou

In the immediate vicinity of the city, there are a number of places which make easy day or half-day trips by bike or local bus. A short bike ride **south** of the city, out along the canals to the main section of the Grand Canal where it heads off towards Hangzhou, is **Baodai Qiao**, a 53-arched Tang-dynasty bridge. It's not wildly exciting, but with traffic now re-routed over a newer crossing, it does make a tranquil spot to sit and contemplate the boats and the local anglers. To reach it, cross the southern border of the moat at Renmin Lu, then at the first major intersection south of here, turn left (east) and head straight for 2–3km, until the next major junction, where you turn right along a canal. Farther south of the bridge, 23km from Suzhou, is the little town of **TONGLI**, a superb example of a town built on water – every house backs on to canals, there are 49 stone bridges and nearly all movement takes place by boat. You can reach Tongli by minibus from the Xianshi bus station, south of the moat, for a few yuan.

There's more of interest to the **west**, towards Tai Hu. Fifteen and eighteen kilometres respectively from Suzhou, **Lingyan Shan** and **Tianping Shan** lie close to each other in the low hills, and together make a good day's outing on a bicycle, following Sufugong Lu away from the southwestern corner of the moat. At Lingyun Shan (Divine Cliff Hill) you climb stone steps past a bell tower to reach a walled enclosure with a temple hall, a seven-storey pagoda and a well. Tianping Shan (Sky Level Hill), 3km beyond, was already a well-known beauty spot under the Song. Wooded paths meander up to the summit past pavilions and small gardens, the hillside is cut with streams and dotted with strange rock formations, and in autumn the maples which cover the slope seem to blaze. There are also tremendous views from both hills.

Tai Hu and beyond

One of the four largest freshwater lakes in China, constantly replenished by heavy rains, **Tai Hu** is liberally sprinkled with islands and surrounded by wooded hills. With an average depth of just two metres, it's a natural reservoir of relatively unpolluted water, where fish are bred, and lotus and water-chestnut grown in ideal conditions on the islands. Other plant and wildlife is rich too and the shores are clad with tea plantations and orchards of loquat, pear, peach, apricot and plum, particularly on the western

TAI HU AND BEYOND		
Tai Hu	太湖	*tàihú*
Dong Shan	东山	*dōngshān*
Zijin An	紫金庵	*zǐjīnān*
Mei Yuan	梅园	*méiyuán*
Taihu Hotel	太湖饭店	*tàihú fàndiàn*
Xi Shan	西山	*xīshān*
Donghe	东河	*dōnghé*
Yuantou Zhu	鼋头渚	*yuántóu zhǔ*
Hubin Hotel	湖宾饭店	*húbīn fàndiàn*
Wuxi	无锡	*wúxī*
Miaoguang Pagoda	妙光塔	*miàoguāng tǎ*
Xihui Park	锡惠公园	*xīhuì gōngyuán*
ACCOMMODATION		
Jinhua	锦华大饭店	*jǐnhuá dàfàndiàn*
Milido	美丽都	*měilìdū*
Qinggongye University Foreign Experts Hotel	轻工业大学专家楼	*qīnggōngyè dàxué zhuānjiālóu*
Taishan	泰山饭店	*tàishān fàndiàn*
Tianma	天马大酒店	*tiānmǎ dàjiǔdiàn*
Wuxi Grand	无锡大饭店	*wúxī dàfàndiàn*
Xinglong	兴隆大酒店	*xīnglóng dàjiǔdiàn*
Changzhou	常州	*chángzhōu*
Dingshu (Dingshan)	丁蜀 (丁山)	*dīngshǔ (dīngshān)*
Yixing County	宜兴县	*yíxīng xiàn*
Yixing Town	宜兴市	*yíxīng shì*
Beisite Guoji	贝斯特国际大酒店	*bèisītèguójì dàjiǔdiàn*
Huating Hotel	华亭大酒店	*huátíng dàjiǔdiàn*
Yixing Hotel	宜兴宾馆	*yíxīng bīnguǎn*
AROUND YIXING		
Linggu Caves	灵谷洞	*línggǔ dòng*
Shanjuan Caves	善卷洞	*shànjuǎn dòng*
Zhanggong Caves	张公洞	*zhānggōng dòng*

side among the caves and potteries of **Yixing County**. The southeastern shore of the lake, particularly the charming rural areas of **Dong Shan** and **Xi Shan**, are most easily visited from Suzhou, but the most famous and popular Tai Hu scenic area, **Yuantou Zhu**, is best visited from the town of **Wuxi**, set in a landscape of water, fertile plains and low hills some 40km to the northwest of Suzhou. Finally, away from the lake – but still dominated by water and water transport – lies the traditional canal city of **Changzhou**, just 30km north of Wuxi along the Nanjing rail line.

Dong Shan and Xi Shan

Some 35km from Suzhou, and within easy reach of the city, lie two green fingers of land projecting into Tai Hu, known as **Dong Shan** (East Hill) and **Xi Shan** (West Hill) respectively. There is some illusion here, for although Dong Shan is a genuine peninsula, Xi Shan is actually an island, joined to the mainland via an artificial causeway. This area of Tai Hu is entirely rural with small villages of friendly people, green hillsides, fragrant fruit orchards and hardly a trace of industry. One possible long day trip from Suzhou is to ride out to Dong Shan by minibus, cross to Xi Shan by boat, then return home. From the west side of the train station square in Suzhou there are frequent private **minibuses** to Dong Shan and to Donghe (on Xi Shan); city bus #20 also goes to Dong Shan. Minibuses to Dong Shan arrive at a T-junction, the point where the approach road meets the circuit road that runs right around the hill. To get around Dong Shan, you usually have to rely on **motor-rickshaws** (which will seek you out when you arrive). Expect to pay ¥30–40, including waiting time for any stopovers, for the trip round the hill.

The pier for **ferries** (*lugang matou*) to Xi Shan is about 12km round from the T-junction, in either direction; take the road south (left) for the chance to visit the ancient **Zijin An** (Purple Gold Nunnery; daily 8am–5pm; ¥4), on the way. The nunnery is notable for its ancient statuary and its location in a beautiful, secluded wood surrounded by sweet-smelling orange groves.

From the ferry pier there are twice-daily crossings to the nearby island of Xi Shan (May–Oct 9am & 2pm). On Xi Shan you can take a motor-rickshaw to **Donghe**, the small settlement on the island, and then pick up a return bus to Suzhou. The last bus is around 7pm.

Wuxi

The town of **WUXI**, the regional centre close by the northern shore of the lake, is not particularly attractive, but it's the most convenient place to base yourself for a visit to the main Tai Hu beauty spots. The tin mines which brought in the earliest settlers 2500 years ago were already exhausted under the Han (Wuxi means "Without Tin"), and it was the construction of the Grand Canal centuries later which brought importance to local trade and industry, as it did for so many other canal towns. The result here is something of a hotchpotch as far as tourists are concerned, with Wuxi surpassed as a lakeside city by Hangzhou, and as a canal town with traditional gardens by Suzhou. Local Chinese come here in droves to sample the lakeside scenery, but foreign travellers will not miss too much if they pass it by.

The old city of Wuxi is roughly oval-shaped, and surrounded by a ring of canals. The main branch of the Grand Canal runs outside this ring (but well inside the modern city) about 1km to the southwest. Inside the canal ring, the ring road, Jiefang Lu, is cut from north to south by Zhongshan Lu, and from east to west by Renmin Lu. The junction of Renmin Lu and Zhongshan Lu forms the approximate centre of downtown Wuxi, a busy, throbbing area of shops and restaurants.

One place in town to pass a few hours amid trees and small paths is **Xihui Park** (daily 7am–7pm; ¥2; bus #2 through town from the train station), west of the centre, off

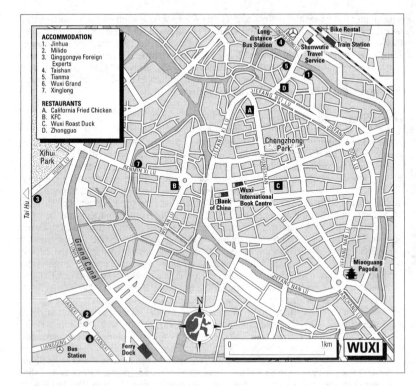

ACCOMMODATION
1. Jinhua
2. Milido
3. Qinggongye Foreign Experts
4. Taishan
5. Tianma
6. Wuxi Grand
7. Xinglong

RESTAURANTS
A. California Fried Chicken
B. KFC
C. Wuxi Roast Duck
D. Zhongguo

Xihui Lu. The path from the main entrance on Huihe Lu leads directly up to the Dragon Light Pagoda on top of **Xi Shan**; more interesting, though, is the **cable car** (¥15) whose long, slow trajectory links with another peak on neighbouring **Hui Shan**. The cable-car ride is definitely worth the panoramic views over to Tai Hu on a clear day, though you'll need a good head for heights. On the way, you'll pass over a small lake surrounded by a group of tiled pavilions and paved stairways which look like the curving ribs of some mammoth skeleton. Here are the remains of the 1500-year-old **Huishan Si** alongside the **Jichang Yuan** (Carefree Garden). Hui Shan itself is the source of a special black clay used for the ugly painted figurines sold all over Wuxi, and which have been made here since at least the Ming dynasty.

Finally, the banks of the **Grand Canal** provide one or two sights. Right at the southern tip of the Jiefang Lu ring road is the tenth-century **Miaoguang Pagoda**, of the Nanchan Buddhist Temple; it's worth climbing up for the views. About 1km south of here, along Nanchang Lu, you'll come to Qingming Bridge, the best-preserved ancient stone arch bridge in Wuxi.

Practicalities

All trains running between Shanghai and Nanjing stop at Wuxi **train station**, which is outside the canal ring to the northeast. Bus #11 goes right across town from here. When purchasing **onward tickets** from the station, foreigners should queue up at window no. 2 where service will be a little quicker. On the northwest side of the station square are a couple of useful facilities. The *Shenwutie Travel Service*, in a kiosk, offers all-day bus **tours** to Tai Hu (¥20) as well as day tours of the caves in Yixing County (see p.373) for ¥30, which is excellent value. There's also a **bike rental** shop (daily 6am–8pm; bikes ¥2 per hour) – there's no English sign, but it's in front of a row of buildings facing the local city bus station, immediately northwest of the train station.

The main **long-distance bus station** is a couple of minutes' walk to the west of the train station, and is served by buses from most nearby cities including Shanghai, Nanjing and a number of remoter destinations such as Yangzhou and Wenzhou. Diametrically on the other side of the city from here, across the Liangxi Bridge over the Grand Canal, is a smaller bus station from where there are frequent connections with Suzhou and Yixing. Bus #20 and frequent minibuses cross the city from here on their way to the train station.

You may even arrive by **boat** at the ferry dock on the Grand Canal, a few hundred metres south of the Liangxi Bridge (bus #1 goes through town from here to the train station, via Jiefang Xi Lu). There's a daily service to and from Hangzhou; boats take approximately thirteen hours, departing early evening and arriving early morning at both ends. For a bed in a four-bed berth, there is a special foreigners' rate of ¥175.

There are a few reasonable **restaurants** on Zhongshan Lu, just south of Renmin Lu; among them, the *Wuxi Roast Duck Restaurant* has an English menu. For snacks, try the *Wangxingji Wonton Restaurant*, at the train station, famous in these parts for its "three-fresh" wonton soup as well as steamed buns stuffed with crab. Also close to the train station – across the bridge and a couple of blocks south on the left – is the interesting *Zhongguo Restaurant* which serves Jiangsu food, including a tasty cold dish of crispy eel. A little to the west of the canal ring, on Wu'ai Lu just south of Renmin Lu, there's a *KFC*. For more fast food you can visit the local branch of California Fried Chicken at the northern end of Zhongshan Lu.

ACCOMMODATION

Accommodation in Wuxi is relatively expensive unless you can get into the university rooms. Staying in the city is convenient, but for similar rates you can also stay right by the lakeside (see p.373).

Jinhua, Dongliangxi Lu (☎0510/2720612, fax 2711092). From the train station, cross the bridge, then turn left along the canal bank. This is a friendly place and about the best value of a mediocre bunch. ⑥.

Milido, Liangxi Lu (☎0510/6765665, fax 6701668). A couple of hundred metres west of the Liangxi Bridge over the Grand Canal. This hotel is part of the *Holiday Inn* group, and has standards and prices to match. ⑨.

Qinggongye University Foreign Experts Hotel, Huihe Lu (☎0510/6761034). From the train station, take bus #2. Get off at the second stop (*Qingshanwan*) after the big bridge over the Grand Canal. Cross the road and walk a few metres farther on until you see the English sign. By far the cheapest rooms in town, with clean and very comfortable singles and doubles. It helps to get a room here if you can speak a bit of Chinese. ⑤.

Taishan, Tonghui Dong Lu (☎0510/2303888 ext 7). The most convenient hotel for the train station and surprisingly one of the cheaper ones in town. Walk towards the bridge, but turn right along Tonghui Lu before you cross. The hotel is the huge block on the left (doubles and triples). ⑥.

Tianma, Xiliangxi Lu (☎0510/2727988, fax 2727878). From the train station, head across the bridge directly in front, then walk right a short way along the canal bank. A reasonable place, which also contains a large travel service. ⑦.

Wuxi Grand, Liangqing Lu (☎0510/6706789, fax 2700991). Opposite, and in direct competition with, the *Milido*. The rooms here may be slightly larger than those of its rival, but the service is less efficient. ⑨.

Xinglong, Renmin Xi Lu (☎0510/2713213, fax 2719219). Just to the west of the Jiefang Lu ring road, this is a standard modern Chinese hotel, offering singles and doubles. ⑦.

Mei Yuan and Yuantou Zhu

The shores of Tai Hu closest to Wuxi, fringed with gardens, woods, pagodas and water-side hotels, boast two particularly charming parks, **Mei Yuan** and **Yuantou Zhu**, where you can spend half a day rambling. There are two possible arrival areas, either on the shore due west from town (Mei Yuan), or, slightly farther away, on the northern end of a peninsula extending into the lake (Yuantou Zhu). Bus #1 to Yuantou Zhu and #2 to Mei Yuan both run through town from the train station square, otherwise it's a pleasant hour's bicycle ride following Liangxi Lu west out of town to Mei Yuan. The two areas are linked by boat and a circular trip from town taking in both of them is perhaps the best way to go.

On the slopes of a small hill, looking down through the woods to the spread of fish-ponds fringing the lake, **Mei Yuan** (Plum Garden; daily 8am–5pm; ¥2) is a delightful introduction to the lakeside area. Originally established in 1912, the park now offers a springtime sea of blossom from four thousand plum trees, best appreciated from the pagoda at the highest point. In autumn you can enjoy the heady scent of osmanthus blossom, used to flavour the local delicacy, honeyed plums. From just south of Mei Yuan there are small boats to and from Yuantou Zhu; there may also be, by the time you read this, a bus service linking the two scenic spots via a new causeway.

Yuantou Zhu (Turtle Head Isle; daily 8am–5pm; ¥25) is the principal Tai Hu pleasure spot and is certainly a relaxing place to stroll around for a few hours. The area, basical-ly a huge park, covering the northwestern end of the peninsula in the lake (which bears little obvious resemblance to a turtle's head), is capped by a small lighthouse at the west-ern tip, and scattered with tea houses and pavilions, former summerhouses of the wealthy. Apart from the lake, the greenery and the atmosphere, there's nothing of over-

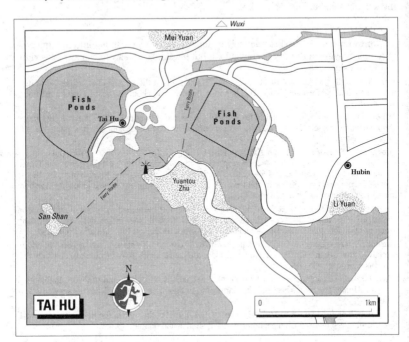

riding interest, and the best policy is to buy a map at the entrance (near the #1 bus terminus) and wander at will. Beside the Yuantou Zhu entrance is the Tai Hu Space Centre, a bizarre theme park that is unlikely to appeal much to foreign tourists.

From a pier on Yuantou Zhu, a little north of the lighthouse, a ferry (¥3) shuttles tourists regularly to and from the tiny former bandits' lair of San Shan (Three Hills Island), comprising a central knob of land, linked by causeways to minuscule outcrops on either side. Neat paths lead up to a tea house, pavilion and pagoda giving views of tree-clad islands, winding inlets, fishing boats under sail and – if you are lucky enough to catch a sunny day – blue waters.

From another pier, on the northern edge of Yuantou Zhu (facing the mainland), you can catch small, fast boats to the Mei Yuan area, near the #2 bus terminus. Buy your ticket from the kiosk (¥6), not on the boat. You arrive at an obscure pier apparently in the middle of nowhere – walk straight ahead, cross a small bridge, then walk along a canal with an entertainment park on the other side, and you'll emerge more or less opposite Mei Yuan.

There's one more very popular garden a couple of stops before the #1 bus terminus which you could visit on the way to or from Yuantou Zhu. Right on the lakeshore and in front of the *Hubin Hotel*, Li Yuan is heavily embellished with artificial bridges and pagodas, and is nothing like as attractive as Mei Yuan, despite its vantage point right on the waterfront.

Accommodation

Although most people stay in Wuxi, the hotels out near the lake offer great opportunities for enjoying some peace and quiet, particularly after the rush of day-trippers has subsided. Twenty minutes' walk south of the #2 bus terminus, the *Taihu Hotel* (☎0512/6767901; ⑥) stands among the fish ponds just south of Mei Yuan. It's a great, secluded (if remote) place to stay, surrounded by flame trees, with birdsong and green fireflies in the gardens. More convenient, situated close to the Li Yuan on the #1 bus route, shortly before Yuantou Zhu, is the *Hubin Hotel* (☎0512/6701888; ⑦), a highrise building catering mainly for tour groups and offering motel-style accommodation.

Yixing County

Yixing County lies on the western shores of Tai Hu about 60km from Wuxi. It's a mild, fertile plain crisscrossed by canals with a smattering of small lakes that make it ideal for the cultivation of tea and bamboo. The most important and traditional of all the local products, however, is the pottery from the small town of Dingshu. The other main attractions of the area are the underground caves which have formed, hollowed out of the karst hills in a skein running southwest from Yixing Town. The whole area can be visited on a hectic day trip from Wuxi (see p.369), though you might choose to spend a night in Yixing, perhaps en route from Wuxi to Nanjing.

Although there's precious little to see in YIXING TOWN itself, you'll almost certainly have to pay it a visit, as it's the regional transport and accommodation centre. There's no train station, so all travellers arrive by bus, either at the Sheng (Provincial) bus station, or at the smaller Xian (County) bus station, both of which are in the far northwest of town. Frequent minibuses (¥3) in and out of the stations make the connection with Dingshu to the south (see below).

If you're looking for accommodation in Yixing, walk east along Taige Lu from either station, in the direction of the tall *Bank of China* building, the top of which is clearly visible. About fifteen minutes' walk along here is the *Beisite Guoji Hotel* (⑥) offering large, smart doubles. Alternatively, turn south across the bridge (before reaching the *Beisite Guoji*) down the main street, Renmin Lu. A little way down here, on

Jiefang Lu to the left, is the *Huating Hotel* (☎0510/7911888; ⑥) which has similarly upmarket rooms. Finally, virtually in the centre of the city, farther south down Renmin Lu and on the left through an imposing archway, is the best place in town, the *Yixing Hotel* (☎0510/7916888, fax 7900767; ⑦). Just inside the archway here are a couple of **travel services** which will book tours for you and rent cars with drivers.

Dingshu

If you're interested in pottery, or if you simply want to buy a Chinese tea set, head for **DINGSHU** (often referred to nowadays as **Dingshan**), a thirty-minute **minibus** ride from Yixing. There may be nothing to see here beyond pots and ceramic artefacts, but it's fascinating to find the products of the **pottery factories** literally crammed into every nook and cranny. Ceramic lampposts line the road into town, pottery shards crunch under your feet on the main street and the walls of buildings are embedded with broken tiles. It's worth taking a short stroll around just to see the scale of production, and also to visit the Pottery Exhibition Centre.

It is an incredible fact that this obscure town has been producing pots since the beginning of recorded history. Primitive unglazed pots have been found here which date back to the Shang and Zhou periods, some three thousand years ago. Since the Han dynasty at least, around 200 BC, this has been the most renowned site for glazed wares in China – Dingshu can take a lot of the credit for our use of the word "china" to mean ceramics. In terms of wealth, Dingshu had its heyday under the Ming from the fourteenth century, but manufacturing is still going strong today. A sandy local clay is used to produce the **purple sand pottery**, a dull brown unglazed ware, heavy in iron, whose properties of retaining the colour, fragrance and flavour of tea make for incomparable teapots. If you buy one, don't wash it between brews – eventually it'll become so thoroughly imbued that you'll never need to add tea leaves again. All along Dingshu's main street you'll find stalls and pavement displays with tea sets on offer at very low prices. If you are interested in **buying a tea set**, there are certain points to bear in mind. Check that the lid fits properly and that there is a clear sound when the pot is tapped. Also feel the texture. A rough texture does not indicate poor quality – in fact pots should be rough, especially on the inside.

Dingshu is also where replacement **roof tiles** and ornaments are manufactured for use in the vast work of reconstructing China's temples. The enormous pots decorated with writhing dragons are extremely fine, as are the round, heavy, blue-glazed tables found in so many Chinese gardens. In the **Pottery Exhibition Centre** you can see both artistic pieces – from delicate Song-dynasty teapots to flamboyant modern lamps – as well as lavatory bowls and sparkplug insulators.

The Yixing Caves

South and west of Yixing Town and Dingshu are delightful hills, woods, tea plantations and, below ground, several collections of **karst caves**. All the caves can be reached by buses from Yixing Town – you'll have to ask around both bus stations – and are often connected to each other by further private minibuses, so it's easy to spend a pleasant day trundling independently around the area. Alternatively, you can join a group tour, either from Yixing or from Wuxi. Sturdy shoes and some form of waterproof protection against dripping stalactites are a good idea. The caves are all open daily and charge varying entrance fees up to ¥20.

The nearest set of caves, **Zhanggong**, is just forty minutes on the bus from Yixing, and only ten minutes from Dingshu. It consists of 72 separate caves, connected on two levels by over 1500 steps; you actually climb a hill, but on the inside. Although the stalactites, stalagmites and other rock formations are all named for their resemblance to exotic beasts or everyday objects, you'll need a powerful imagination to work out which is which. The real highlight is the **Hall of the Sea Dragon King** where the rock soars upwards in strange contortions and emerges on to the green hillside far above – look up and you'll see an eerie patch of swirling, dripping mist.

A farther fifteen minutes on the bus south of the Zhanggong Caves takes you through tea plantations to the most recently discovered group, the **Linggu Caves**, which feature an underground waterfall. This series of large interlinked caverns has yet to be fully explored, though ancient human remains have been found here along with Tang inscriptions.

The third group, **Shanjuan**, is the most impressive and popular cave site, located 25km southwest (an hour on the bus) from Yixing. The caves are set on three interconnecting levels, the most interesting being the **Water Cave**, at the bottom, from where a boat then takes you to the exit through subterranean passages, while the boatman picks out highlights with his flashlight. Out on ground level, beyond the exit, is a small temple and a number of souvenir and snack shops.

Changzhou

CHANGZHOU, just thirty minutes by train and an easy day trip from Wuxi, is yet another of the towns taking advantage of the dual axis of the Grand Canal and the Shanghai–Nanjing rail line. Like its neighbours, it has reaped economic benefits from convenient transport links, but in Changzhou new-found wealth (mainly from textiles) has not yet meant the wholesale destruction of the ancient city centre. Indeed, the central area, riddled with small waterways running off the main canal, still contains a few temples, narrow alleys, street markets and tiny stone bridges. Changzhou sees very few foreign tourists, but you could pleasantly spend a few hours wandering the town centre.

As with many of the canal towns, the old city of Changzhou is heart-shaped and ringed by canals; at the centre of the heart, **Dong Dajie** and **Nan Dajie** are the two main streets, where you are most likely to find places to eat. This area, inside the innermost ring of the canal network, is the most interesting – as well as busy wharves, there are shops everywhere selling the locally produced silks and fabrics and Changzhou's own traditional painted wooden **combs**, available in every conceivable shape and size.

You're most likely to arrive in Changzhou by **train**, though by **bus** there are direct links with places like Yixing which are not on the rail line. The **train station** is in the northeast of town, just outside the canal ring, at the eastern end of Xinfeng Jie. The principal long-distance **bus station** is just a short distance to the southwest from here, along the same street.

Zhenjiang

If not the most beautiful of cities, **ZHENJIANG** does offer some excellent vistas of the Yangzi River from its three famous **hills** and is worth a stopover either as a day trip from Nanjing or, more realistically, as an overnight stop en route between Shanghai or Suzhou and Nanjing.

For over two thousand years, Zhenjiang has provided a safe harbour and a strong defensive position at the junction of two of the world's greatest trade routes, the **Yangzi River** and the **Grand Canal**. Protected on three sides by low hills, the focus of this outward-looking city remains very much set on the mighty river and across it towards Yangzhou on the northern bank. During the Three Kings period, a Wu ruler built a walled city on this site as his capital; it grew rapidly, boosted over the centuries by the southern branch of the Grand Canal, and by proximity to the Ming capital at Nanjing. Marco Polo remarked on the richness of the local **silks** and gold fabrics and these are

ZHENJIANG

Zhenjiang	镇江	*zhènjiāng*
Beigu Shan	北固山	*běigù shān*
Jiao Shan	焦山	*jiāo shān*
Jin Shan	金山	*jīn shān*

ACCOMMODATION AND RESTAURANTS

Dahuangjia	大皇家酒店	*dàhuángjiā jiǔdiàn*
Dantuxian	丹徒县招待所	*dāntúxiàn zhāodàisuǒ*
Jingkou	京口饭店	*jīngkǒu fàndiàn*
Xijiao	西郊宾馆	*xījiāo bīnguǎn*
Yanchun Jiulou	宴春酒楼	*yànchūn jiǔlóu*
Zhenjiang Binguan	镇江宾馆	*zhènjiāng bīnguǎn*
Zhenjiang Dajiudian	镇江大酒店	*zhènjiāng dàjiǔdiàn*

still renowned, as are, less romantically, Zhenjiang vinegar and pickles. After the Opium Wars the British and French were granted **concessions** here and some intriguing traces of these remain today around the site of the former British Consulate. Now on the main Shanghai–Nanjing rail line, and still an important Yangzi anchorage, Zhenjiang's prosperity remains assured, with yet more expansion on the way as a giant new harbour terminal complex nears completion.

The City

Although sheer size means that walking is rarely a practical way of getting around Zhenjiang, it is a relatively easy place to get your bearings. Across the north flows the Yangzi; in the south, the rail line forms another barrier; and down through the middle, meandering approximately north–south across the city centre, is the Grand Canal. The modern downtown area centres on **Dashi Kou**, the junction of Zhongshan Lu and Jiefang Lu, a couple of kilometres east of the train station, and one kilometre south of the Yangzi. The old city, and the three hills, are all close up to the riverbank, and can be reached by city buses #2 and #4.

The oldest part of the city, due north of the train station and just south of the river, around Daxi Lu and Boxian Lu, is a fascinating area for a stroll, with ancient architecture, dozens of small shops and tiny alleys running off in all directions. West along Daxi Lu is the extraordinary red brick of the former **British Consulate** – part British colonial, part Qing-dynasty – now housing the local **museum** (daily 9am–4.30pm; ¥2). It's definitely worth dropping in, for the building if not for the museum contents. Built in the 1890s, the creaky staircases, wooden floorboards, and balconies offering views over the river are delightfully reminiscent of another era. A few minutes farther south from here brings you to another bizarrely improbable facade, the **Dahuangjia Hotel**, formerly the *Royal Hotel* – take a look at the opulent 1920s lobby, even if you're not planning to stay. Daxi Lu is on the bus #2 route from the train station via Dashi Kou.

Jin Shan Si, a temple scenically located in its own **Jin Shan Park** (daily 8am–8pm; ¥10) in the far northwest of the city at the terminus of bus #2, is a popular riverside spot. At one time a small island in the Yangzi, Jin Shan has silted up over the years to create a low-lying peninsula, with a series of rectangular fishponds overlooked by a small hill. The temple buildings wrap themselves dramatically around this hill behind a series of heavy yellow-ochre walls. Twisting stairways lead past them to the **Cishou Pagoda**,

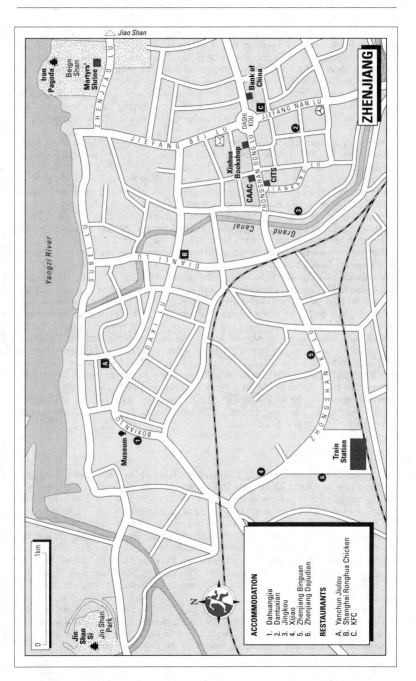

ZHENJIANG

Jiao Shan

Iron Pagoda
Beigu Shan
Martyrs' Shrine

Bank of China

C

JIEFANG NAN LU

DASHI KOU

2

JIEFANG BEI LU

ZHENJIAO LU

Xinhua Bookshop

CAAC

ZHONGSHAN DONG LU

CITS

JIANKANG LU

3

Grand Canal

Yangzi River

SUBEI LU

DIANLI LU

B

DAXI LU

A

BOXIAN LU

Museum

1

ZHONGSHAN XI LU

5

Train Station

4

6

Jin Shan Si

Jin Shan Park

1km

0

N

ACCOMMODATION
1. Dahuangjia
2. Dantuxian
3. Jingkou
4. Xijiao
5. Zhenjiang Binguan
6. Zhenjiang Dajiudian

RESTAURANTS
A. Yanchun Jiulou
B. Shanghai Ronghua Chicken
C. KFC

renovated in 1900 at great expense to celebrate the Dowager Empress Cixi's sixty-fifth birthday. From the top of this seven-tiered octagonal tower you get a superb view down to the jumbled temple roofs, and across the ponds to the river. The temple itself, with a 1500-year history and a former complement of three thousand monks, has recently been restored to something of its former glory and is packed with the usual unselfconscious mix of tourists and worshippers. From a canal in the park you can catch an imitation dragon boat (¥10) around the corner to the **First Spring Under Heaven** at the edge of a small lake. The spring itself is of no special interest, but it's nice to get out on the water.

The other sights are to the northeast of town. The first of these, **Beigu Shan** (daily 7.30am–5pm; ¥5), on the route of bus #4, is a refreshing hill top, named 1400 years ago by an enthusiastic emperor as the "Best Hill in the World above a River". From the entrance, climb the stairs on the right, then turn left along the rampart. You'll come to the lightning-damaged remains of the nine-hundred-year-old **Iron Pagoda** and, on top of the hill, the exquisite **Lingyun Ting** (Soaring Clouds Pavilion), where you can sit in the shade and enjoy the commanding views over the river. Immediately south of Beigu Shan, on the hill across the road, is the modern **Martyrs' Shrine** for victims of the wars which brought communism to China.

Farther east, a few more stops along the bus #4 route, is the most interesting place in Zhenjiang, **Jiao Shan** (daily 7.30am–5pm; ¥7), still a genuine island, some 5km downstream from the city centre. From the terminus of bus #4, walk a little farther east to the ticket kiosk and small jetty where half-hourly boats take tourists out to the island (the boat ride is included in the entrance ticket). A cable car now under construction should also be ready by the time you read this. The island, verdant and rural, lush with bamboo and pine, is a great place for just roaming around. For an overall view, climb up to the **Xijiang Lou**, a viewing tower commanding a glorious stretch of the river and city beyond. Below are the remains of gun batteries used in turn against the British in 1842, the Japanese when they invaded in World War II, and the British again, when *HMS Amethyst* got trapped in the river during the Communist takeover in 1949. Close to the jetty, there's a cluster of halls and pavilions among which **Dinghui Si**, with six hundred trees in its forecourt, stands out for its elaborate carved and painted interiors and fine gilt Buddha. An hour or two should be enough to see everything on Jiao Shan.

Practicalities

The train ride between Zhenjiang and Shanghai takes about three hours; Nanjing is less than one hour west. Zhenjiang's **train station**, on Zhongshan Lu, is in the southwest of the city. From here, buses #2 and #4 run to Dashi Kou and then head north, while buses #10 and #12 run to Dashi Kou and turn south. Points of arrival by **bus** are harder to predict: some buses stop very close to the train station, others at the bus station on Jiefang Nan Lu, 500m south of Dashi Kou. If you plan on **leaving** Zhenjiang by bus, there are frequent minibuses to Nanjing from the train station square, and from the Jiefang Nan Lu bus station there are buses to Nanjing, Huai'an, Yangzhou and Lianyungang. The bus journey to and from **Yangzhou** is an experience not to be missed, with the bus climbing aboard a flat-bottomed barge to make the Yangzi crossing.

Most facilities are in the Dashi Kou area, including the **Bank of China** (Mon–Fri 8–11.30am & 1.30–4pm), just to the east on Zhongshan Lu, and the **post office** immediately to the north on Jiefang Bei Lu. *CITS* (☎0511/5231806) is at the corner of Zhongshan Dong Lu and Jiankang Lu, quite near the *Jingkou Hotel*.

Accommodation

Hotel accommodation is not cheap in Zhenjiang, though there is one very interesting option in the old city by the river, the *Dahuangjia*, which is something of a tourist sight in itself.

Dahuangjia (*Royal Hotel*), Boxian Lu (☎0511/5285486). Situated in the old city, on the #2 bus route from the train station; get off immediately after you see the red-brick former British Consulate. The hotel is a highly unexpected anachronism, with columns and statues on the outside, and a lobby from the 1920s. Its main boast, surprisingly in the People's Republic, is that Chiang Kaishek once stayed here. The actual rooms are nothing special, but it's still a great place to spend a night. ⑥.

Dantuxian, Shuilusi Xiang (☎0511/5011666). On a small lane a little south of Dashi Kou, this friendly place is signposted in English from the main road, and offers pretty cheap singles, doubles and triples. Convenient for the bus station on Jiefang Lu. ⑨.

Jingkou, Binhe Lu (☎0511/5238988). Centrally located down a small lane running south from Zhongshan Lu, immediately east of the Grand Canal. From the train station it's a thirty-minute walk, or a few yuan in a rickshaw; walk right through to the back for the reception. You'll find a very wide range of rooms here, from some of the cheapest in town to the most expensive. ④–⑨.

Xijiao, Zhongshan Xi Lu. Two minutes west of the train station square and just across the road, but apart from its proximity to the station, not a good bet given its grotty conditions. ⑤.

Zhenjiang Dajiudian, Zhongshan Xi Lu (☎0511/5235290). A smart, modern place, conveniently located right in the train station square – to the left as you emerge from the station. ⑥.

Zhenjiang Binguan, Zhongshan Xi Lu (☎0511/5233888 ext 511). About ten minutes' walk east of the station square, this is one of the most upmarket places in the city. There are also a couple of travel agents based in the lobby. ⑧.

Eating and drinking

Among the locals, the most famous **restaurant** in town is the *Yanchun Jiulou*, on an alley just north of Daxi Lu, a short way east of the former British Consulate. Specialities here include little appetizers of cold dishes brought round on a trolley – salads, stuffed buns and diced rectangles of pork which have been tenderized so that they literally melt in the mouth. This area of the old town also contains numerous noodle and dumpling shops. For fast food (Chinese style), try the exceedingly popular *Shanghai Ronghua Chicken* at the junction of Daxi Lu and Dianli Lu, or the the more mundane *KFC* just south of Dashi Kou.

Yangzhou

Straddling the Grand Canal north of the Yangzi, an hour by bus north of Zhenjiang and a couple of hours from Nanjing, **YANGZHOU** is a leafy and relaxing city. Today its proud boast is of having produced the nation's leader – President Jiang Zemin – but its origins go back to around 500 BC when the Wu rulers had channels dug here which were later incorporated into the Grand Canal. Thanks to its position at the junctions of the Yangzi, the Grand Canal and the Huaihe River, Yangzhou rapidly developed into a prosperous city, aided by a monopoly of the lucrative **salt trade**. Under the Tang and later, many foreign merchants, including a community from Persia, lived and traded here, leaving behind a twelfth-century **mosque** and a much-quoted (though wholly unsubstantiated) tale that Marco Polo governed the city for three years. It was a city renowned too for its culture, its storytellers and oral traditions, with stories being handed down through the generations. As such, it frequently attracted the **imperial court** and its entourage, as well as artists and officials moving here in retirement, who endowed temples, created enclosed gardens and patronized local arts.

YANGZHOU

Yangzhou	扬州	*yángzhōu*
Daming Si	大明寺	*dàmíng sì*
Ge Yuan	个园	*gèyuán*
He Yuan	何园	*héyuán*
Shi Kefa Memorial	史可法纪念馆	*shǐkěfǎ jìniànguǎn*
Shi Ta	石塔	*shítǎ*
Shouxi Hu	瘦西湖	*shòuxī hú*
Tomb of Puhaddin	普哈丁墓	*pǔhādīng mù*
Wenfeng Ta	文峰塔	*wénfēng tǎ*
Wuting Qiao	五亭桥	*wǔtíng qiáo*
Xianhe Mosque	仙鹤寺	*xiānhè sì*

ACCOMMODATION AND RESTAURANTS

Dongyuan	东园饭店	*dōngyuán fàndiàn*
Fuchun Tea House	富春茶社	*fùchūn cháshè*
Qionghua	琼花大厦	*qiónghuā dàshà*
Shita	石塔宾馆	*shítǎ bīnguǎn*
Xiyuan	西园饭店	*xīyuán fàndiàn*
Yangzhou Binguan	扬州宾馆	*yángzhōu bīnguǎn*
Yangzhou Dajiudian	扬州大酒店	*yángzhōu dàjiǔdiàn*

Despite the industrial belt which now stretches round the south and east of the city, there's still a faint sense of a cosmopolitan, cultured past here, evident in the **gardens**, in the Islamic relics and in the layout of roads, waterways and bridges in the city centre.

The City

Downtown Yangzhou is cut through the middle from north to south by Guoqing Lu, which, to the south, turns into Dujiang Lu; south of the canal this eventually leads to the main bus station. Running from east to west across Guoqing Lu are two or three of the main shopping streets (all confusingly with different names to the west and to the east of the main road). The western and eastern extents of the area are delineated by Huaihai Lu and Taizhou Lu respectively. Gardens and temples are scattered thinly throughout the city, though there is a concentration of sights around the canal to the north and north-west, where you'll find the two huge parks, **Shouxi Hu** and **Daming Si**. Much of the town can be explored on foot, though you'll need city buses for trips right across town.

Starting from the centre and moving north, the first of the gardens is a classical rock and water Chinese composition, the **Ge Yuan** (daily 8am–6pm; ¥2) which can be entered from Yanfu Dong Lu, a few minutes' walk east of Guoqing Lu (or from Dongguan Lu to the south). Despite being relatively free of visitors, however, the Ge Yuan, with its ponderously styled pavilions and landscaped rockery supposedly suggesting the four seasons, is in a state of some neglect and less attractive than the He Yuan farther south (see below).

A rather more promising line of exploration is to cross the canal immediately north of Ge Yuan and walk a few minutes west from the top of Guoqing Lu, as far as the **Museum** (daily 8–11am & 2–5pm; ¥3), overlooking the canal near the *Xiyuan Hotel*. A delightful group of assorted old pavilions set in large grounds, this is one of the more interesting of China's provincial museums, featuring a thousand-year-old wooden boat recovered from the Grand Canal, as well as an extraordinary funeral suit made of five hundred pieces of jade, which dates back to the Han dynasty. Right next to the museum, to the east, in grounds full of flowers and plum trees, is the **Shi Kefa Memorial** (daily 8–11am & 2.30–5pm; ¥2), a temple devoted to the memory of the local hero, Shi Kefa, who in the last days of the Ming dynasty gave his life resisting the advancing Qing armies. The victorious Qing subsequently raised this memorial to him in recognition of his courage. West from the museum is a strip along the canal now gearing up to become a tourist centre, with "traditional" architecture and souvenir shops, while in front, right on the canal itself, stands a small jetty from where tour group boats run up to Shouxi Hu and Daming Si (see below).

Moving to the **west** of the central area, you'll find the main surviving testament to the presence of Persian traders in the city in the Middle Ages, the **Xianhe (Crane) Mosque**, just north of Ganquan Lu, on the small turning to the east of Wenhe Lu. Small and austere, its main feature is one wall covered entirely with Arabic script. You may have to sign your name in the book before being admitted here.

The streets in this western quarter conceal several more sights, a seemingly haphazard selection of survivors from different eras of history, scattered thinly in among the traffic and the modern shopping streets. One is the **Shi Ta**, a diminutive Tang-dynasty stone pagoda standing in the shade of a thousand-year-old gingko tree, on Shita Lu just west of Huaihai Lu. Right in the middle of the junction between Shita Lu and Wenhe Lu you'll come across the round Ming-dynasty **Wenchang Pavilion**, resembling a mini Temple of Heaven, and one block north, there's the thirteenth-century **Si Wang Ting** (Four View Pavilion), a three-storeyed octagonal pavilion.

For more evidence of the early Muslim presence in Yangzhou, take a look to the **east** of the centre, just past the canal on Jiefang Nan Lu. From the west bank of the canal, or from the Jiefang Bridge, just to the north, you'll see a wooded hill and a complex of dilapidated buildings. This rather sad, dusty relic from the most cosmopolitan era of China's history is actually the **Garden Tomb of Puhaddin** (or Bulhanding), a descendant of the Prophet Mohammed, who came to China in the thirteenth century, spent ten years in Yangzhou and adopted the city as his home, to the extent that he insisted on being buried here after his death. At the time of writing, the memorial was closed for repairs, but will reopen.

There are a couple more attractions in the **south** of the city, though again rather randomly scattered. A short way north of the canal, in an old, quiet part of town, is the exquisite **He Yuan** (daily 8am–6pm; ¥5). Designed in the nineteenth century, this tiny garden uses trees, shrubs and a raised walkway to give an ingenious illusion of variety and depth – it's a beautiful, picturesque little place for a stroll on a sunny morning. The He Yuan also contains a couple of charming tea houses.

Finally, in the far south of the city, on Wenfeng Lu, is the conspicuous seven-storey **Wengfeng Ta** (daily 7.30am–5.30pm; ¥2), standing by a bend in the Grand Canal in a small plot crammed with hollyhocks. Built in 1582, it was intended to bring luck to local candidates in the imperial examinations, though its main interest now is as a vantage point over the intense activity on the water. Walk up alongside the canal and wharves for a closer view of the heavy river traffic and the small family boats queuing in vast jams to be laden with anything from grain and bottled drinks to gravel and truck tyres. There is no longer any bus connection to the pagoda (despite what maps say), so you'll either have a rather ugly thirty-minute walk southwest from the long-distance bus station, or you can take a rickshaw.

Shouxi Hu and Daming Si

Out on the northwest edge of town are Yangzhou's two main sights, a lake and a temple, both of which were part of Emperor Qianlong's regular tourist itinerary in the eighteenth century. It makes sense to visit Shouxi Hu and Daming Si in conjunction; if you enter

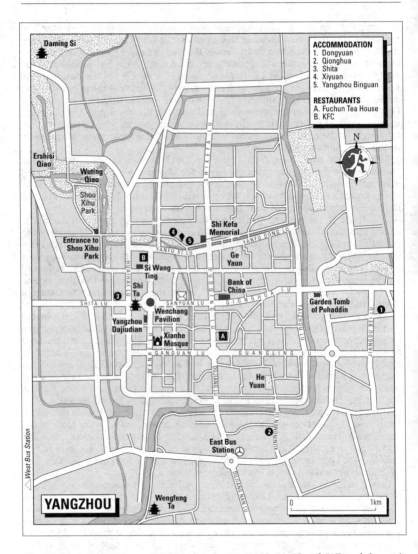

ACCOMMODATION
1. Dongyuan
2. Qionghua
3. Shita
4. Xiyuan
5. Yangzhou Binguan

RESTAURANTS
A. Fuchun Tea House
B. KFC

Daming Si

Ershisi Qiao

Wuting Qiao

Shou Xihu Park

Entrance to Shou Xihu Park

Shi Kefa Memorial

Si Wang Ting

Ge Yaun

Shi Ta

Bank of China

Wenchang Pavilion

Garden Tomb of Puhaddin

Yangzhou Dajiudian

Xianhe Mosque

He Yuan

West Bus Station

East Bus Station

Wengfeng Ta

YANGZHOU

0   1km

Shouxi Hu at the southern end (near bus routes #1, #3, #4, #5 and #15) and then exit through the northern end, you're halfway to Daming Si. You can pick up bus #5 from here for the remaining distance, or take a rickshaw. The other way to get around both sights is by **tourist boat** – south of the Shouxi Hu the canal runs east to Qianlong's old imperial barge landing-place, in front of what is now the *Xiyuan Hotel*. In recent years a new jetty has been built here so that tourists can travel by mock dragon boats, complete with plush yellow furnishings and cushions, through the Shouxi Hu and right up as far as Daming Si. The high prices make this only really practicable for large groups, however – reckon on several hundred yuan to rent a twenty-person boat for a couple of hours.

The **Shouxi Hu**, which winds, snake-like, through an elongated park area, literally translates as "Thin West Lake" – so named to recall the original "fat" West Lake at Hangzhou. In some respects it's a typical Chinese park, full of water and melancholy weeping willows, though it does also contain an array of interesting structures, follies in the romantic sense. A plain white **Dagoba**, modelled after the dagoba in Beihai in Beijing; the **Chui Tai** (Happiness Terrace) whose three moon gates each frame a different scene; and in particular the much-photographed **Wuting Qiao** (Five Pavilion Bridge), an eighteenth-century construction with massive triple-arched and yellow-tiled roofs. If you walk about fifteen minutes west from the Wuting Qiao, along the north bank of the lake, you'll also come to another bridge, the spectacular **Ershisi Qiao** whose single hump is so high and rounded as to form a virtual circle through which boats could pass.

A kilometre or so north of Shouxi Hu, in the far northwest of town, and well worth an hour of your time, **Daming Si** (Temple of Great Light; daily 8.30am–5.30pm; ¥6) occupies a huge area on top of a hill. The temple, originally built in the fifth century, is experiencing a boom – much of what you see today has in fact been reconstructed after damage during the Taiping Uprising (see box, p.391), while the temple's centrepiece, a **Memorial Hall** to honour the Chinese monk, Jian Zhen, who is credited with having introduced *ritso* Buddhism to Japan, was only built in 1973. A profound scholar of the eighth century, Jian Zhen was invited to teach in Japan only to find that on five successive occasions storms and misfortune drove him back to Chinese waters. Finally, on his sixth attempt, at the age of 66, he made it to Japan and sensibly decided against trying the return trip. He is still much revered in Japan, and a nine-storey Japanese-funded **pagoda** has just been built here to replace an original Song-dynasty structure that was razed by fire. Some way north of the temple itself, there are parks and gardens laid out in 1751 around a natural spring, the so-called **Fifth Spring under Heaven**. You can sample the spring waters, and the local tea, from a cool, breezy tea house overlooking the water, where plump goldfish and carp glide past.

Practicalities

Since Yangzhou is not served by rail, you are almost certain to arrive either at the main **East bus station** on Dujiang Nan Lu in the south of the city, or at the remote **West bus station**, connected to the main bus station by bus #8. Generally speaking, the very frequent buses to and from Zhenjiang and Nanjing use the West station, while longer-distance buses, including long-distance sleepers, use the East station. The nearest **train station** is at Zhenjiang, though it's usually possible to book train tickets in Yangzhou at the main bus station and at the (now disused) canal ferry terminal on the northern bank of the canal, north of the bus station. The nearest airport is at Nanjing – tickets can be booked at major hotels.

Eating is a pleasure in Yangzhou if you know where to look. The best-known restaurant in town is the *Fuchun Tea House*, down a small alley called Dexingqiao running east off Guoqing Lu – there's a big sign suspended over the alley entrance. A plate of ten different kinds of dumpling here costs just ¥15; other specialities include *doufu gansi* (dried shreds of tofu) and *qingshao xiaren* (fried shrimps). The restaurant in the *Qionghua Hotel* is also worth trying and there are plenty of noodles and dumplings on offer in the area around Ganquan Lu. *KFC* is located near the northern end of Wenhe Lu. For cakes and pastries head for *Maxim's Pastry Shop* on Guoqing Lu (west side), a short way north of Sanyuan Lu.

Accommodation

Dongyuan, Jiangdu Bei Lu (☎0514/7233003). Slightly remote, out in the east of the city, but bus #12 stops right outside. The quiet, decent-quality rooms are reasonably priced. ④.

Qionghua, Pifang Lu (☎0514/7811321). On the corner with Xuningmen Lu. The only place within walking distance (about 20min) from the bus station. Fairly smart, but has good-value singles and doubles. ⑥.

Shita, Shita Lu (☎0514/7344467 ext 81021). Just west of Huaihai Lu, the *Shita* offers very smart and comfortable rooms; on bus routes #7 and #13 from the bus station. ⑦.

Xiyuan, Fengle Shang Jie (☎0514/7344888, fax 7233870). In large grounds located just north of the museum on Yanfu Xi Lu, this hotel has a wide range of rooms and is very convenient for the sights. Various travel agents have their offices here. ⑥.

Yangzhou Binguan, Fengle Shang Jie (☎0514/7342611, fax 7343599). An upmarket, highrise tower located in the north of the city, next to the museum. ⑦.

Yangzhou Dajiudian, Wenhe Lu (☎0514/7344011 ext 2288). Part of a department store complex, just south of Wenchang Pavilion. It's slightly dreary, but comfortable enough. ⑨.

Nanjing and around

NANJING, formerly known in the West as Nanking, is one of China's greatest cities. Its very name, "Southern Capital", stands as a direct foil to the "Northern Capital" of Beijing, and the city is still considered the rightful capital of China by many overseas Chinese, particularly those from Taiwan. Today, it's a wealthy, prosperous city, benefitting both from its proximity to Shanghai, and from its gateway position on the **Yangzi River**, which stretches away west deep into China's interior. Although it has become rather an expensive place to visit, Nanjing now offers an (almost) cosmopolitan range of facilities for the tourist, as well as a wealth of historic sites.

Occupying a strategic site on the south bank of the Yangzi River in a beautiful setting of lakes, river, wooded hills and mountain defences, Nanjing has had an important role from the earliest times, though not until 600 BC were there the beginnings of a walled city. By the time the Han empire broke up in 220 AD, Nanjing was the capital of half a dozen local dynasties, and when the Sui reunited China in 589, the building of the **Grand Canal** began considerably to increase the city's economic importance. It became renowned for its forges, foundries and weaving, especially for the veined **brocade** made in noble houses and monasteries. During the Tang and Song periods, Nanjing rivalled nearby Hangzhou as the wealthiest city in the country, until in 1368 the first emperor of the Ming dynasty decided to establish it as the **capital** of all China.

For centuries thereafter, although Nanjing's claims to be the capital would be usurped by the heavily northern-based Qing dynasty, anti-authoritarian movements always associated themselves with movements to restore the old capital. For eleven years, in the mid-nineteenth century, the **Taiping rebels** (see box, p.391) set up the capital of their **Heavenly Kingdom** at Nanjing. The siege and final recapture of the city by the foreign-backed Qing armies in 1864 was one of the saddest and most dramatic events in China's history. After the Opium War, the **Treaty of Nanking** which ceded Hong Kong to Britain was signed here in 1841, and Nanjing itself also suffered the indignity of being a treaty port. Following the overthrow of the Qing dynasty in 1911, however, the city flowered again and became the provisional capital of the new Republic of China, with Sun Yatsen as its first president. Sun Yatsen's mausoleum, **Zhongshan Ling**, on the edge of modern Nanjing, is one of the Chinese people's great centres of pilgrimage.

In 1937, the name of Nanjing became synonymous with one of the worst atrocities of World War II, after the so-called **Rape of Nanking**, in which invading Japanese soldiers butchered an estimated three hundred thousand civilians. Subsequently, Chiang Kaishek's government escaped the Japanese advance by moving west to Chongqing, though after Japan's surrender and Chiang's return, Nanjing briefly resumed its status as the official capital of China. Just four years later, however, in 1949, the victorious Communists decided to abandon Nanjing as capital altogether, choosing instead the ancient – and highly conservative – city of Beijing in which to base the country's first "modern" government.

NANJING

Nanjing	南京	*nánjīng*

ACCOMMODATION

Central	中心大酒店	*zhōngxīn dàjiǔdiàn*
Daqiao	大桥饭店	*dàqiáo fàndiàn*
Hongqiao	虹桥饭店	*hóngqiáo fàndiàn*
Jinling	金陵饭店	*jīnlíng fàndiàn*
Mandarin Chamber	悦华大酒店	*yuèhuá dàjiǔdiàn*
Nanjing	南京饭店	*nánjīng fàndiàn*
Nanjing University Foreign Students' Residence	南京大学外国留学生宿舍	*nánjīngdàxué wàiguóliúxuéshēng sùshè*
Normal University (Nanshan Hotel)	师范大学南山宾馆	*shīfàn dàxué nánshān bīnguǎn*
Shuangmenlou	双门楼宾馆	*shuāngménlóu bīnguǎn*
Xihuamen	西华门饭店	*xīhuámén fàndiàn*
Xinli	信力酒店	*xìnlì jiǔdiàn*
Xuanwu	玄武饭店	*xuánwǔ fàndiàn*
Zhongshan	中山大厦	*zhōngshān dàshà*

THE CITY

Bailuzhou	白鹭洲	*báilùzhōu*
Chaotiangong	朝天宫	*cháotiāngōng*
Dujiang Jinianbei	渡江纪念碑	*dùjiāng jìniànbēi*
Fuzi Miao	夫子庙	*fūzǐ miào*
Gugong Park	故宫	*gùgōng*
Gulou	鼓楼	*gǔlóu*
Linggu Si	灵谷寺	*línggǔ sì*
Meiyuan Xincun	梅园新村	*méiyuán xīncūn*
Memorial to Nanjing Massacre	南京大屠杀纪念馆	*nánjīngdàtúshā jìniànguǎn*
Ming Xiaoling	明孝陵	*mingxiàolíng*
Mochou Hu Park	莫愁湖公园	*mòchóuhú gōngyuán*
Nanjing Museum	南京博物馆	*nánjīng bówùguǎn*
Qinhuai River	秦淮河	*qínhuáihé*
Shixiang Lu	石象路	*shíxiàng lù*
Taiping Heavenly Kingdom History Museum	太平天国历史博物馆	*tàipíngtiānguólìshǐ bówùguǎn*
Tianchaogong	天朝宫	*tiāncháogōng*
Xinjiekou	新街口	*xīnjiēkǒu*
Xuanwu Hu Park	玄武湖公园	*xuánwǔhú gōngyuán*
Yangzi River Bridge	长江大桥	*chángjiāng dàqiáo*
Yuhuatai Park	雨花台公园	*yǔhuātái gōngyuán*
Zhonghua Men	中华门	*zhōnghuá mén*
Zhongshan Ling	中山陵	*zhōngshān líng*
Zhongshan Men	中山门	*zhōngshān mén*
Zhongyang Men	中央门	*zhōngyāng mén*
Zijin Shan	紫金山	*zǐjīn shān*

RESTAURANTS

Ali Wanzhuang	阿里万壮饭店	*ālǐwànzhuāng fàndiàn*
Jiangsu	江苏饭店	*jiāngsū fàndiàn*
Lao Zhengxing	老正兴菜馆	*lǎozhèngxīng càiguǎn*
Liaolizhuhu	料理竹虎	*liàolǐzhúhǔ*

Nowadays, despite its fall in status, the city remains an important rail junction – a great 1960s bridge carries the Beijing–Shanghai line over the Yangzi – and a major river port for large ships. The capital of Jiangsu Province with a population of over four million, Nanjing's broad tree-lined boulevards and balconied houses within Ming walls and gates, make it one of the most attractive of the major Chinese cities.

Orientation, arrival and city transport

The city's broken and meandering Ming walls are still a useful means of orientation, and the main streets run across town between gates in the city wall. The big gate in the north, now marked by a huge traffic circle, is **Zhongyang Men**. To the northeast of here, outside the city wall, is the **train station**, while inside the wall, running due south from Zhongyang Men, the city's main street (called Zhongyang Lu, then Zhongshan Lu, then Zhongshan Nan Lu), runs for 10km before emerging through the southern wall at **Zhonghua Men**. Moving from north to south, this street passes two of the major intersections of the city, the first where it is crossed by Beijing Lu, in the area of **Gulou**, and then at **Xinjiekou** from where Zhongshan Dong Lu runs east to **Zhongshan Men**, the major gate in the eastern wall. South of Xinjiekou (a kilometre or two before Zhonghua Men) is another important commercial and tourist centre, growing in fashion, called **Fuzi Miao**.

Outside the city wall, many of the historic sites are on **Zijin Shan** to the east, while fringing it to the northwest is the **Yangzi River**, crossed by the Yangzi River Bridge.

Arrival and city transport

Nanjing airport is to the southeast of the city, not far beyond the city walls, and is connected to the city by frequent *CAAC* buses which terminate at their main office on Ruijin Lu. From here, bus #4 makes direct connections with Xinjiekou.

From the **main train station**, bus #1 travels south through the city, via Gulou, Xinjiekou and Fuzi Miao. There is also a faint chance of your train terminating at the small **West train station** outside the city walls and near the Yangzi River; from here bus #16 goes to Gulou and Xinjiekou.

Buses are notoriously inconsistent in where they choose to drop you. The largest long-distance bus station is in the north, at **Zhongyang Men**, though there are several others, including the much more central **Hanfu Jie bus station** (on a small road north of Zhongshan Dong Lu).

The other possibility is to arrive by **boat** on the Yangzi River at one of the docks on Jiangbian Lu. The Yangzi River boats connect Nanjing with Shanghai (17hr to the east), and with Wuhan and distant Chongqing to the west (see p.805 for more details). From Jiangbian Lu, bus #10 goes all the way to Zhongyang Men and the train station; otherwise ride just one stop (or walk) to the West train station and catch bus #16 into town.

Although **taxis** are a very cheap and easy way to get around Nanjing, you may want to use the **city buses** as well. These make reasonably convenient connections, but are absurdly crowded at rush hours, even by Chinese standards. A good **map** showing bus routes is pretty much indispensable, and an English-language version can be bought at most large hotels and some tourist sights.

Accommodation

Hotels in Nanjing are almost uniformly on the expensive side, and a large proportion of them seem to be almost identical in terms of facilities and cost. If you're willing to

The **telephone code** for Nanjing is ☎025

pay in excess of ¥300, you'll have a good choice of which area you would like to stay in. For cheap accommodation, however, the only options are the two universities which house foreign students.

Hotels

Central, Zhongshan Lu, west side (☎4400888, fax 4414194). Just five minutes' walk north of Xinjiekou, this is one of the most luxurious places in town. ⑨.

Daqiao, Daqiao Nan Lu (☎8801544). Southeast of the junction with Jianning Lu, in the northwest of the city, and just over 1km east of the Yangzi River ferry terminal. A friendly place offering single and double rooms; take bus #10 from the train station or Zhongyang Men. ⑦.

Hongqiao, Zhongshan Bei Lu (☎3400888, fax 3420756). Two kilometres northwest of Gulou, and just north of Xinmofan Malu; bus #13 from the train station. A pleasant hotel, used to foreigners, and with very comfortable doubles. ⑦.

Jinling, Hanzhong Lu (☎4455888 ext 4114, fax 4704141). A few steps west of Xinjiekou, this is the city's premier hotel, with doubles starting from ¥1000. ⑨.

Mandarin Chamber, Gongyuan Xi Jie (☎2202555, fax 2201876). A great place to stay in a great location, right in the heart of lively Fuzi Miao, situated on a small lane facing the southern end of Taiping Lu. ⑧.

Nanjing, Zhongshan Bei Lu (☎3411888). Right opposite the *Hongqiao*, this is a slightly old-fashioned hotel set in large secluded gardens. ⑦.

Shuangmenlou, Huju Lu (☎8805961 ext 280). Located at the northern end of Huju Lu, just south of Zhongshan Lu, in the northwest of the city. Not a bad place, it offers some of the cheapest rooms in Nanjing in the as yet unrenovated wing, and is surrounded by large gardens. ⑥.

Xihuamen, Zhongshan Dong Lu, south side (☎4596221 ext 2888). About 2km east of Xinjiekou (just west of a small canal). Quite an attractive place set in gardens, and relatively cheap with perfectly decent rooms. ⑥.

Xinli, Jianning Lu (☎5504688 ext 281). Immediately north from the main long-distance bus station at Zhongyang Men. It's remote from the centre of town, but has surprisingly good-value rooms. ⑥.

Xuanwu, Zhongyang Lu (☎3303888, fax 3302234). Two kilometres due south of Zhongyang Men, just north of Hunan Lu. A huge place with good views over Xuanwu Hu Park, this place has pretentions to being a luxury hotel and almost makes it. ⑧.

Zhongshan, corner of Zhongshan Lu and Zhujiang Lu (☎3361888 ext 0008, fax 3304185). Very centrally located, exactly between Gulou and Xinjiekou. There's a disco and an airline office on the premises. ⑦.

University rooms

Nanjing Normal University (Nanshan Hotel), Ninghai Lu, a short walk west of Nanjing University (see below). Take bus #13 to Beijing Lu, walk south down Shanghai Lu, then cut west down one of the small alleys to Ninghai Lu. Walk into the university campus through the imposing gate and straight ahead to the grassy oval, then bear left up a slope. *Nanshan Hotel* (actually student accommodation) is at the top. You can take either a single bed or a two-bed room with shower. If you can get a bed here, it's a very pleasant, relaxing place to stay. Beds ②, rooms ③.

Nanjing University (Foreign Students' Residence), Shanghai Lu (☎3304651 ext 3589). Take bus #13 from the train station to Beijing Lu, then it's a short walk south; you'll see the highrise building on your left and the entrance is on a small lane. Two-bed rooms with or without attached bath, or singles beds are rented out. Beds ②–③, rooms ③–⑤.

The City

The city is huge and a thorough visit of all its sights would take several days. The **downtown** area comprises three main focal points and offers good shopping and dining as well as a few fascinating relics of the city's turbulent pre-1949 history. The **north** of the city takes in the enormous **Xuanwu Hu Park** and the **Yangzi River** area, while to the **west** are a number of smaller parks, including the **Chaotian Palace** and the

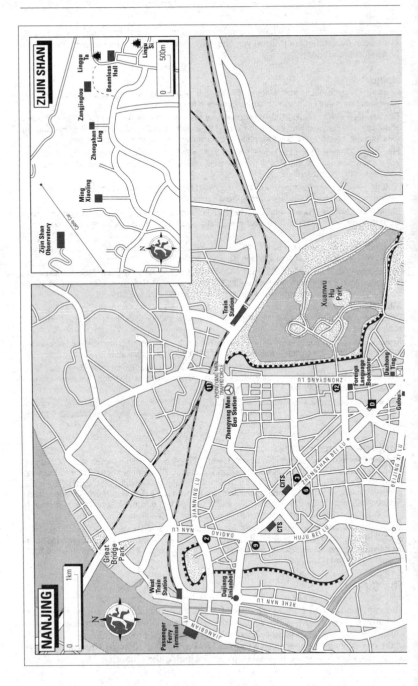

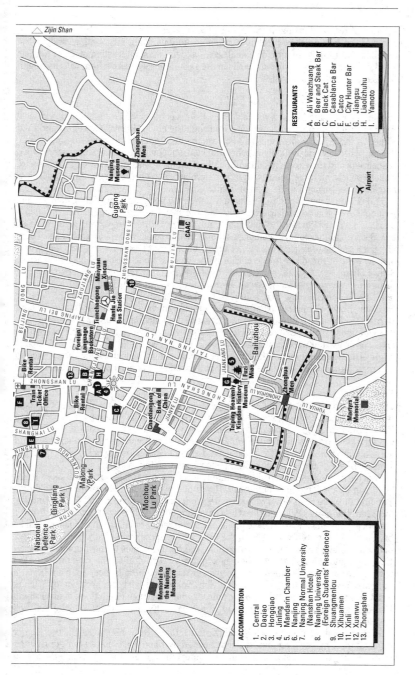

RESTAURANTS

A. Ali Wanzhuang
B. Beer and Steak Bar
C. Black Cat
D. Casablanca Bar
E. Catco
F. City Hunter Bar
G. Jiangsu
H. Liaolizhuhu
I. Yamoto

ACCOMMODATION

1. Central
2. Daqiao
3. Hongqiao
4. Jinling
5. Mandarin Chamber
6. Nanjing
7. Nanjing Normal University (Nanshan Hotel)
8. Nanjing University (Foreign Students' Residence)
9. Shuangmenlou
10. Xihuamen
11. Xinli
12. Xuanwu
13. Zhongshan

Memorial to the Victims of the Nanjing Massacre. The **east** and the **south** contain some of the best-preserved relics of Nanjing's mighty Ming **city wall**, as well as the excellent **Nanjing Museum**. The final area – and the most interesting of all for tourists – is the green hill beyond the city walls to the east of the city, **Zijin Shan**, with its wealth of historical and cultural relics.

Downtown

Nanjing is not a city blessed with a single obvious centre, rather it has a series of local centres stretching north to south down through the city – **Gulou**, **Xinjiekou** and **Fuzi Miao**. Of these Xinjiekou and Fuzi Miao are the most interesting areas for simply wandering, with historic buildings, pedestrianized shopping streets, canals, some good restaurants and the excellent Museum of the Taiping Uprising. It's a long six-kilometre walk to take in all three centres, though a number of bus routes, including #1, #16, #26 and #33, pass through or near all of them.

The **Gulou** area, around the junction between Zhongyang Lu, Zhongshan Lu and Beijing Lu, is the administrative centre in the heart of old Nanjing. When Nanjing became a Treaty Port in the mid-nineteenth century, the foreign consulates were all based here, though today it comprises mostly traffic jams overlooked by offices. There are just a couple of relics from earlier times, both rather lost in the bustle. One, immediately west of the main traffic circle, is the six-hundred-year-old Gulou itself (daily 8am–4.30pm; ¥1), a small, solid **drum tower** on a grassy mound in the road, entered through a traditional-style gateway. Historically, a drum used to call the watch from here seven times a day, and sound warnings at times of danger; now the interior exhibits shows of amateur paintings. The other sight by Gulou is the **Dazhong Ting** (Great Bell Pavilion), immediately northeast of the junction, sitting in a well-kept garden and housing an enormous fourteenth-century bell. A ghastly legend has it that the emperor ordered it to be cast in an alloy of iron, silver and gold fused by the blood of a virgin. The two daughters of the city's blacksmith threw themselves into the furnace so that their father could obey the emperor and escape the penalty of death.

XINJIEKOU

Two kilometres due south of Gulou along Zhongshan Lu lies the main commercial centre of Nanjing, **Xinjiekou**, centred on a huge traffic circle adorned by a statue of Sun Yatsen. As the geographical centre of the city, you are certain to pass through here, whether for shopping, dining or simply catching buses. Teeming with banks, hotels and department stores, the traffic circle itself does not contain any specific sights but the streets are lively and quite major sights lie within walking distance.

Shortly to the east, about fifteen minutes' walk from Xinjiekou, and a short block north, on Changjiang Lu (running into Hanfu Jie), are a couple of fascinating buildings. The first of these is an otherwise obscure government building at 292 Changjiang Lu, the **Tianchaogong** (Palace of the Heavenly Kingdom; daily 8am–4.30pm; ¥8). From a historical point of view, this is one of the most interesting buildings in China – originally built over six hundred years ago in the early Ming, and subsequently used as the seat of the provincial governor, it was seized in 1853 by the armies of the Taiping Heavenly Kingdom, and converted into their headquarters. Later, after the overthrow of the Qing, it became the Guomindang Government's Presidential Palace. So, from here, in the early decades of this century, first Sun Yatsen and later the arch-enemy Chiang Kaishek governed China. Visiting the palace today, you'll see exhibitions of the Taiping Uprising and of the life and times of Sun Yatsen. Even the hated Chiang Kaishek appears in a few photos.

A short walk east is the **Meiyuan Xincun** (daily 8am–4.30pm; ¥10), the former office of the Chinese Communist Party, headed by Zhou Enlai, based here during the time of the Guomindang government. Unfortunately all the explanations are in

Chinese, though there are one or two fascinating photos, including a little-known snap of Chiang Kaishek and Mao Zedong standing chatting together.

In the other direction from Xinjiekou – about 1km to the southwest – on Jianye Lu (bus route #4 from Fuzi Miao), is the former Ming palace, the **Chaotiangong**, now containing the **Municipal Museum** (daily 9–11am & noon–4.30pm; ¥20 including the court rites show). The large square which houses the palace, bounded by a high vermilion wall on one side and a gateway protected by tigers on the other, is supposedly the site of the ancient Ye Cheng (Foundry City), built in the fifth century BC. The palace was subsequently built here in 1384 by the Ming, and used for audiences with the emperor – hence the name Chaotian, meaning Worshipping Heaven. Later it became a seat of learning and a temple to Confucius, before becoming a tiny museum, which contains a few excellent bronzes. In the palace square, there is additionally a display of **Ming-dynasty court rites** (daily 11.15am–noon), showing the emperor's entrance surrounded by courtiers, eunuchs, guards and dancing girls. It's touristy and amusing rather than seriously educational, but quite an elaborate show.

FUZI MIAO

Another 2km farther south of Xinjiekou is the **Fuzi Miao** (Temple of Confucius) area, which begins south of Jiankang Lu, around the bottom end of Taiping Lu, and contains pedestrian walkways, shops, tourist kitsch, interesting little restaurants and an attractive waterfront area, from where you can pick up canal leisure boats (¥10) that trundle south to Zhonghua Men. The central **Temple of Confucius** itself, which resembles a Disney Confucian theme park inside, complete with mannequins in fancy dress, is hardly worth bothering about, but across the canal in front of the temple, and a short walk southeast, brings you to a small park, **Bailuzhou** (Egret Isle). This ancient corner of the city remained the Chinese quarter after the arrival of the Manchu Qing dynasty in the seventeenth century, and it is still full of traditional houses.

Ten minutes' walk west of the Temple of Confucius, on the small Zhanyuan Lu, just east of Zhonghua Lu, is the **Taiping Heavenly Kingdom History Museum** (daily 6am–6pm; ¥10). The sad but fascinating story of the Taiping Uprising (see box), which

---

THE TAIPING UPRISING

One of the consequences of the weakness of the Qing dynasty in the nineteenth century was the extraordinary **Taiping Uprising**, an event which would lead to the slaughter of millions, and which has been described as the most colossal civil war in the history of the world. The Taipings were led by **Hong Xiuquan**, failed civil service candidate and Christian evangelist, who, following a fever, declared himself to be the younger brother of Jesus Christ. In 1851, he assembled twenty thousand armed followers at **Jintian village**, near Guiping in Guangxi Province, and established the **Taiping Tianguo**, or Kingdom of Heavenly Peace. This militia then routed the local Manchu forces, and by the following year were sweeping up through Hunan into central China. They **captured Nanjing** in 1853, but though the kingdom survived another eleven years, this was its last achievement. Poorly planned expeditions failed to take Beijing or win over western China, and Hong's leadership – originally based on the enfranchisement of the peasantry and the outlawing of opium, alcohol and sexual discrimination – devolved into paranoia and fanaticism. After a gigantic struggle, **Qing forces** finally managed to unseat the Taipings when Western governments sent in assistance, most notably in the person of Queen Victoria's personal favourite, Charles "Chinese" Gordon. Despite the ultimately disastous **failure of the rebellion**, the whole episode is seen – despite its overtly Christian message – as a precursor to the arrival of communism in China. Indeed, in its fanatical rejection of Confucianism and the incredible damage it wrought on buildings and sites of historic value, it finds curious echoes in Mao Zedong's Cultural Revolution.

culminated in the occupation of Nanjing by rebels from 1853 to 1864, is told here in pictures and relics, with English captions. The building itself was the residence of one of the rebel generals during the uprising.

The north

The northern part of Nanjing covers a huge area, bordering the Yangzi River to the northwest and the rail line to the northeast. To the east of Zhongyang Lu and south of the train station, the enormous **Xuanwu Hu Park** is unspectacular except perhaps as a chance to mingle with the locals who come here en masse to relax at weekends. Formerly a resort for the imperial family, it became a park in 1911 and comprises mostly water, with hills on three sides and the city wall skirting the western shore. The lake is 5km long and contains several small **islands** linked by causeways and bridges, with restaurants, tea houses, pavilions, rowing boats, paddle boats with awnings, places to swim, an open-air theatre and a zoo. The most scenic of the islands is **Yingzhou** in a part of the inner lake covered with lily pads and surrounded by fantastical trees with trunks shaped like corkscrews. The most convenient point to enter the park is through Xuanwu Gate, on Zhongyang Lu about 1km north of Gulou (bus #1).

The far northwest of town in the area of the **Yangzi River** offers a modicum of interest. The streets around the **West train station** (bus #16 from Gulou and Xinjiekou) and the port, just beyond the city wall, are quite atmospheric and a good place to wander, with their crumbling alleys and smelly fish markets. Marking the junction between Rehe Lu and Zhongshan Bei Lu, the huge stone monument, **Dujiang Jinianbei**, was erected in memory of the crossing of the river from the north and the capture of Nanjing by the Communists in 1949. If you're in this area you should definitely take a look at the 1.5-kilometre-long double-decker bridge over the Yangzi, still a source of great pride to the Chinese who built it under their own steam after the Russians pulled out in 1960. Before the bridge was built, trains and road vehicles took an hour and a half to ferry across the river. For a great view of the bridge and the banks of the Yangzi, head for **Great Bridge Park** (daily 8am–4.30pm) on the eastern bank; you can ride in an elevator up to a raised platform above the upper (road) deck of the bridge, for ¥2. To reach Great Bridge Park, take bus #15 from Zhongyangmen or Gulou.

The west

The west and southwest of the city have a few scattered sights to offer. An impressive bastion of the city wall is located at the so-called **Stone City** towering high above the small Qinhuai River, which runs a little way to the east of the Yangzi. This is part of the original city wall, around two thousand years old. Although it was constantly strengthened and eventually became part of the Ming defences, the original structure, of red rock in places, is still plainly visible along a three-hundred-metre section of the wall. You can see it from bus #18 which runs outside the walls between Xinjiekou and the West train station.

Inside the wall in this area is a sprinkling of small parks. Hard by the wall itself, the **National Defence Park** contains specimens of military hardware, while immediately to the east of here, across Huju Lu (just west of the Normal University) is the very pleasant little **Qingliang Shan**, where Song emperors once kept residence for the torrid summer months. The tiny **Malong Park**, another short walk south of here, is often full of old musicians who gather to sing opera and play traditional instruments.

Farther south, but just outside the walls, lies the entrance to **Mochou Hu Park**, which gives the feel of being almost in open country. An open-air stage juts out into the lake here, with a substantial tea house behind. A clutch of pavilions and walkways includes the **Square Pavilion**, with a statue of the legendary maiden, Mochou, after whom the lake is named: her name means "sorrow free" because her sweet singing

NANJING'S CITY WALLS

Nanjing was walled as long as 2500 years ago and traces of the original red stone wall can still be seen at Stone City in the west of the city. The present **city wall**, however, is basically the work of the first Ming emperor, who extended and strengthened the earlier walls in 1369–73. Built of brick and over 32km long, his wall followed the contours of the country, skirting Xuanwu Hu in the north, fringing Xijin Shan in the east, and tracing the Qinhuai River to the west and south, which doubled as a moat. The wall was mainly paid for by rich families resettled here by the emperor: one third of it was "donated" by a single native of Wuxiang in Zhejiang Province. Its construction employed two hundred thousand conscripts, who ensured that the bricks were all the same size and specification, each one bearing the names of the workman and overseer. They were held together, to an average height of twelve metres and a thickness of seven, by a mixture of lime and glutinous rice paste.

could soothe away all unhappiness. You can drop in on Mochou Hu Park (bus #7 from Fuzi Miao) on the way to or from the **Memorial to the Nanjing Massacre** (daily 8am–5pm; ¥10), also served by bus #7. A visit to this grim, gravelly garden, with its displays of bones and short pictographic account (in English) of the butchery, is both an education and a way for visitors to show respect to the incredible sufferings endured by the Chinese people at the hands of the Japanese during World War II. Hearteningly, the last room is devoted to reconciliation between the Chinese and Japanese peoples with displays of contrite letters written by Japanese schoolchildren.

The east

Out of the centre on Zhongshan Dong Lu, about 3km east of Xinjiekou (buses #5 and #9 from Xinjiekou; #20 from Gulou) is the huge **Nanjing Museum** (Tues–Sun 9–11.45am & 1.30–4.40pm; ¥10), one of the best provincial museums in China, especially in terms of clarity of explanations – nearly everything is labelled in English. Its highlights include some superb examples of heavy cast bronzes, dating from as early as the Western Zhou (1100–771 BC). The jade and lacquerwork sections are also well worth seeing.

The spectacular facade a few hundred metres west of the museum – in the direction of Xinjiekou – belongs to **Gugong Park** (daily 8am–5pm; ¥1), the site of the former imperial palace of the Ming dynasty. Clearly this was once a colossal structure, perhaps something on the scale of the Forbidden City in Beijing, but today, once through the entrance it's little short of a wasteland, with only a small exhibition hall at the back displaying a model of the original palace.

A short walk east of the museum is **Zhongshan Men**, the easternmost gate of the ancient city walls. You can climb up to the top of the wall here, and walk along a little way to the north before the structure crumbles into a lake. It's surprisingly spacious and peaceful on the top and there are excellent views.

The south

Another excellent place to see wall-associated fortifications is at **Zhonghua Men** in the far south, now bereft of its wall and isolated in the middle of a traffic island, just inside the river moat on the bus #16 route from Xinjiekou and Gulou. This colossal gate actually comprises four gates, one inside another, and its enclosures were designed to hold three thousand men in case of enemy attack, making it one of the biggest of its kind in China. Today you can walk through the central archway and climb up two levels, passing arched recesses which are used for displays and snack stalls and are beautifully cool in summer. Up above, there's a tremendous view of the gates with the city spread out beyond.

The road south, across the Qinhuai River, between Zhonghua Men and Yuhuatai Park, is an interesting stretch. It has two-storey wooden-fronted houses, many with balconies above, while below are small shops and workshops. The all-purpose trees lining the pavement provide shade as well as room to hang birdcages, pot plants and laundry. Not far beyond, the road reaches a small hill, now a park known as **Yuhuatai**. In legend it was here that a fifth-century Buddhist monk delivered sermons so moving that flowers rained down from the sky upon him. You still see Chinese tourists grubbing around here for the multi-coloured stones called *Yuhuashi* (Rain Flower Pebbles), associated with the legend. Sadly, however, the hill also has other very much less pleasant connotations. After 1927 it was used as an execution ground, and vast numbers of people are said to have been murdered here by the Guomindang. The spot is now marked by a **Martyrs' Memorial**, a colossal composite of nine thirty-metre-high figures, well worth seeing as a prime example of gigantic Chinese Socialist Realism. The park itself is pleasantly laid out on a slope thickly forested with pine trees, where you can witness locals giving their cagebirds an airing in the cool of the morning, while they gossip and play cards underneath.

Zijin Shan

Not far outside the Zhongshan Gate to the east is **Zijin Shan** (Purple Gold Mountain) named after the colour of its rocks. Traditionally, the area has been a cool and shady spot to escape the furnace heat of Nanjing's summer, with beautiful fragrant woods and stretches of long grass, but here also are the three most visited sites in Nanjing. Of these, the centrepiece, right in the middle of the hill, is **Zhongshan Ling**, the magnificent mausoleum of China's first president, Sun Yatsen. To the east of Zhongshan Ling is the **Linggu Si** temple complex, and to the west are the ancient **Ming Xiaoling**, tombs of the Ming emperors who ruled China from Nanjing.

Visiting the three main sites on Zijin Shan can easily take a full day, though access to and from the hill is not difficult. Large numbers of private **minibuses** run along Zhongshan Dong Lu on the way to Zijin Shan; most terminate at Zhongshan Ling (¥3) but some go via one of the other two sites. Bus #9 goes to Zhongshan Ling via Linggu Si. Perhaps the best way to visit all three is to catch a bus from town to either Ming Xiaoling or Linggu Si, and then walk to the other two sites – this enables you to avoid backtracking. Alternatively, you can **cycle** round the whole area (see p.397 for rental details) and although this involves negotiating some uphill slopes, it's a very pleasant and convenient way to see Zijin Shan. Various half-day **bus tours** are also available from town; ask at any travel service or upmarket hotel.

Finally, if you're interested in an overview of the whole mountain, you can ride a **cable car** to the peak from a station about 1km east of Taiping Men, the gate by the southern end of Xuanwu Park.

LINGGU SI

Starting from the eastern side of the hill, farthest from the city, the first, if least interesting sight on Zijin Shan is the collection of buildings around **Linggu Si** (daily 8am–5pm; ¥5 entry to the whole site). If you arrive here by bus, the main building in front of you is the so-called **Beamless Hall**. Completed in 1381, and much restored since, it's unusual for its large size, but particularly for its self-supporting brick arch construction with five columns instead of a central beam. The hall was used to store Buddhist sutras before the Taiping rebels made it a fortress; now it's an exhibition hall. A couple of minutes' walk from the Beamless Hall is the Linggu Si itself, a very much smaller, and much restored, version of its original self, but still a thoroughly active temple attended by monks in yellow robes. North of the hall stands a small pavilion surrounded by beautiful cypresses and pines, and north of this again is the **Linggu Ta**, an octagonal, nine-storey, sixty-metre-high pagoda, dating back to the 1930s and built, rather extraordinarily, as a monument to the Guomindang members killed in the fighting against insurgent Communists in 1926–27. It's well worth climbing up for the views over the surrounding countryside.

Although the Linggu buildings and Zhongshan Ling are connected by a shuttle bus (¥1), there's also a delightful and fairly clear footpath through the wood between the two, leading northwest from the Linggu buildings. On the way, you'll pass one or two more buildings, including the Zangjinglou (Buddhist Library) at the top of a grand stairway, which now houses the rather dull **Sun Yatsen Museum** – a collection of pictures with explanations in Chinese only.

ZHONGSHAN LING

Dr Sun Yatsen, the first president of post-imperial China and the only hero revered by Chinese jointly on both sides of the Taiwan Straits, is, if anything, growing in status as China gropes towards a post-communist future and closer relations with Taiwan. This is reflected in the incredible pulling power of the former leader's mausoleum, the **Zhongshan Ling** (daily 7.30am–5.30pm; ¥12; compulsory bag deposit) which, with its famous marble stairway soaring up the green hillside, is one of the most popular sites for Chinese tourists in the entire country. Walking up the steps (or riding a sedan chair for ¥50) is something that every tourist to Nanjing has to do once, if nothing else for the great views back down the stairs and across the misty, rolling hills to the south.

An imposing structure of white granite and deep blue tiles (the nationalist colours), set off by the dark green pine trees, the mausoleum was completed in 1929, four years after Sun Yatsen's death. From the large bronze statue at the bottom, 392 marble steps lead up to the Memorial Hall, dominated by a five-metre-tall seated white marble figure of the great man. Beyond the marble figure is the burial chamber with another marble effigy lying on the stone coffin, from where, according to unsubstantiated rumours, the bones were removed to Taiwan by fleeing Guomindang leaders in 1949. The Guomindang ideals – Nationalism, Democracy and People's Livelihood – are carved above the entrance to the burial chamber in gold on black marble.

MING XIAOLING

A thirty-five-minute walk along the road west from Zhongshan Ling brings you to the **Ming Xiaoling** (daily 8am–5.30pm; ¥5, also covers the Shixiang Lu, see below), the burial place of Zhu Yuan Zhang, founder of the Ming dynasty and the only one of its fourteen emperors to be buried at Nanjing (his thirteen successors are all buried in Beijing).

So colossal was the task of moving earth and erecting the stone walls that it took two years and a hundred thousand soldiers and conscripts to complete the tomb in 1383. Although originally far larger than the Ming tombs near Beijing, its halls and pavilions, and 22-kilometre-long enclosing vermilion wall, were mostly destroyed by the Taipings. Today what remains is a walled collection of beautiful trees, stone bridges and dilapidated gates leading to the lonely wooded mound at the back containing the (unexcavated) burial site of the emperor and his wife as well as the fifty courtiers and maids of honour who were buried alive to keep them company.

The Ming Xiaoling actually comprises two parts, the tomb itself and the approach to the tomb, known as Shandao (Sacred Way) or, more commonly, **Shixiang Lu** (Stone Statue Road) – which leads in a crooked line to the tomb as a means of deterring evil spirits, which can only travel in straight lines. It is perhaps unfortunate that most people visit the tomb first and the approach afterwards, simply because the road from Zhongshan Ling arrives immediately outside the tomb entrance. To reach the Sacred Way, from the tomb entrance (with the tomb behind you), follow the road right and then round to the left for about fifteen minutes. Shixiang Lu is lined with twelve charming pairs of stone animals – including lions, elephants and camels – and four pairs of officials, each statue being carved from a single block of stone. The pairs of animals here are grouped together on a central grass verge, with the road passing either side, while the officials stand among the trees farther off; it's a strange and magical place to walk through.

Finally, one more sight 2 or 3km to the north of the Ming Xiaoling, is the **Zijin Shan Observatory**, built in 1929 high on one of the three peaks where the Taipings formerly had a stronghold. For fresh air and spectacular views you might try to find a minibus heading this way.

Eating, drinking and entertainment

While not quite on a par with neighbouring Shanghai, Nanjing offers a much wider range of places to eat and drink than most provincial capitals. The presence of a heavy contingent of foreign students in the city, as well as a growing population of expatriate and home-grown business people, ensures a scattering of highly Westernized restaurants and bars, which are not always that expensive. There are, in particular, a number of places around the Nanjing University Foreign Students' Residence that cater to Western palates. Otherwise Xinjiekou and Fuzi Miao (where you'll also find the inevitable *KFC* and *McDonald's*) are generally good districts to browse for restaurants. For standard Chinese snacks – noodles, *jiaozi* and *wonton* soup – promising areas include Ninghai Lu, just north from the main entrance of the Normal University, and also the area immediately south of Xinjiekou.

Restaurants

Ali Wanzhuang, Changjiang Lu. Immediately south of the *Central Hotel*, this is a good-value Chinese restaurant serving standard dishes right in the centre of town (no English menu, though).

Beer and Steak Bar, Zhongshan Lu, just north of Changjiang Lu. Not terribly attractive from its street entrance, but if you go upstairs you'll find cheap steak meals, as well as Chinese dishes, on an English menu.

Black Cat, along a small alley north from Hanzhong Lu, just west of the western end of Changjiang Lu, near Xinjiekou. You can get a superb meal of steak, chips and as much salad as you can eat here for just ¥30.

Catco, across Shanghai Lu from the Nanjing University residence. Candle-lit, with an extremely Western ambiance, and serving remarkably good pizzas and salads. Another branch of the *Black Cat* company.

Danube, Changjiang Lu. Virtually next door to the *Ali Wanzhuang* Chinese restaurant, and actually in the back of the *Central Hotel*. Serves European-flavoured fast food in a fairly exclusive atmosphere.

Jiangsu, Jiankang Lu, just east of Zhonghua Lu in Fuzi Miao. One of the most upmarket places to try local food – pressed, salted duck is a speciality.

Lao Zhengxing, Gongyuan Jie. A traditional, lively place with interesting local dishes, two minutes southeast of the Temple of Confucius, backing on to the river.

Liaolizhuhu Japanese, Zhongshan Lu. A Japanese restaurant with Chinese waitresses in kimonos; not totally plush but not particularly expensive either.

Yamoto, off Shanghai Lu. Situated a couple of minutes east of the Nanjing University residence. Very civilized, with an inexpensive menu featuring Japanese, Korean and Western snacks and dishes. It also does great French toast – reckon on ¥15–20 for an excellent breakfast. *Henry's*, close by, below the *Grouse* pub, has a very similar menu.

Bars, discos and other entertainment

There are some remarkably Western **bars** in Nanjing, complete with draught beer and pub games such as darts and pool. The clientele in the places mentioned below is usually a mixture of Chinese and foreigners, and they can be excellent places to meet well-to-do locals. You'll find the bars are generally busy throughout the week, though dancing is usually reserved for Friday and Saturday nights. Generally nightlife in the city is fairly expensive – watch out for minimum charges in some of the bars.

Ten-pin bowling is the latest craze to have hit Nanjing. Try the *Jashide Bowling Alley* on Hanzhong Lu, opposite and slightly to the west of the *Jinling Hotel*, on the top floor of a two-storey building. It costs ¥30 a game in the evening (¥20 during the day).

Casablanca Bar, Zhongshan Bei Lu, a little way north from Gulou. Popular with young foreign students at weekends.

Casablanca Disco, *Xuanwu Hotel*, Zongyang Lu. Not always entirely atmospheric, but it often admits foreigners free while local Chinese have to pay.

City Hunter, Beijing Xi Lu, on the south side facing the Drum Tower. Huge and cavernous, with a fireplace and dartboard, this is an almost unbelievably Western bar, mainly frequented by Chinese. Drinks are pricey, but it's well worth a visit.

Grouse Pub, off Shanghai Lu, almost opposite Nanjing University Foreign Students' Residence. Usually packed with Westerners and inexpensive, but can be claustrophobic.

Manhattan's, southern end of Yanling Xiang, a small lane leading south from Zhongshan Dong Lu, a few blocks east of Xinjiekou (all taxi drivers seem to know the English name). A bar/disco with a mainly Chinese clientele, which is allegedly frequented by gangsters and prostitutes as well as Western students.

Red Lips Nightclub (Hongchun Yezonghui), eastern end of Zhujiang Lu. For something different, try this popular place, featuring KTV, a disco and, in the basement, shooting with real guns and ammunition for fun. Expensive.

Zhongshan Hotel, Zhongshan Lu, at the junction with Zhujiang Lu. Every Friday night Western students are admitted free of charge to its disco – as a result it packs out and can be a good place to meet people. Without a student card you pay ¥10.

Listings

Airlines The main *CAAC* reservations and ticketing office is at 52 Ruijin Lu (daily 8am–noon & 1.30–5.30pm; ☎4499378) in the southeast of town. *China Eastern Airlines* head office is at 34 Taiping Nan Lu (daily 8.30am–12.30pm & 1.30–6pm; ☎4400102). Smaller offices of both airlines are dotted all over town; there's a very convenient one in the *Zhongshan Hotel* (daily 8am–8pm; ☎3361888).

Banks and exchange The *Bank of China* head office (Mon–Fri 8am–4.30pm, Sat 8am–12.30pm) is a few hundred metres due south of Xinjiekou on Zhongshan Nan Lu. You can change travellers' cheques in any of the smaller branches, as well as at upmarket hotels if you are a guest.

Bike rental A fast diminishing option in Nanjing, unfortunately. There are two very small central places (both 8am–8.30pm; ¥1 per hour, ¥200 deposit), one on Zhongshan Lu (west side) just north of the intersection with Changjiang Lu and the other, also on Zhongshan Lu, immediately south of the Gulou intersection.

Bookshops There's a very large foreign language bookstore near Xuanwu Hu Park, on Zhongyang Lu, just south of Hunan Lu, and a smaller one on Zhongshan Dong Lu (north side) a short way east of the Xinjiekou intersection.

Buses The most convenient station to use when departing from Nanjing is the Hanfu Jie station east of Xinjiekou. Nearby destinations that cannot be reached by train include Yixing, Huai'an and Yangzhou. You can only buy tickets for same-day departures.

Hospitals The most central hospital is the Gulou Hospital, on Zhongshan Lu just south of the Gulou intersection.

Post office Nanjing's main post office (daily 8am–6pm) is at 2 Zhongyang Lu, immediately north of Gulou. There's also a post office at 19 Zhongshan Lu, just north of Xinjiekou.

Telecommunications IDD calls and fax services are available at the main post office, though it's usually more convenient to buy phone cards in the upmarket hotels and use their telephones.

Trains Buying train tickets out of Nanjing is a very time-consuming business. You can either join the long queues at the station itself or at the ticket office on Zhongshan Lu (west side) just south of Gulou (daily 8am–noon & 1.30–5pm); there are no special foreigners' windows. Otherwise use a travel agent.

Travel agents Nearly all hotels have their own travel agencies. In addition, *CITS* is at 202 Zhongshan Bei Lu (daily 9am–4pm; ☎3421125, fax 3421960), a couple of kilometres northwest of Gulou. *CTS*, whose staff speak good English, is nearby at 309 Zhongshan Bei Lu (daily 8am–noon & 1.30–5.30pm; ☎8801502, fax 8801533). Both services can supply train, boat and plane tickets, and also organize local tours.

Northern Jiangsu

There's considerably less of interest once you get away from the historic canal towns in the south of Jiangsu Province. Although the canal north of the Yangzi is – in season – navigable all the way to the borders of Shandong, and occasionally even as far as the Yellow River, and there are now ambitious plans to dredge deep enough to allow large vessels access at least as far as the major rail junction and heavily industrialized mining city of **Xuzhou** in northwestern Jiangsu, the only thing people are likely to be transporting in this area is coal. There is no tourist traffic along here, and frankly not a great deal to see. For the most part, the country is flat and wet, ideal for **salt panning** but little else. Of the towns in the area, none positively demands attention, though tiny, rural **Huai'an**, birthplace of Zhou Enlai, is an attractive old place, while **Lianyungang**, strangely isolated on the northern coast, offers a mixture of sea atmosphere, hill temples and 1930s architecture, from the time when completion of the rail line from Zhengzhou brought wealth and trade to the port.

NORTHERN JIANGSU		
Huai'an	淮安	*huáiān*
Liu E's Former Residence	刘鹗故居	*liúè gùjū*
Wu Cheng'en's Former Residence	吴承恩故居	*wúchéngēn gùjū*
Xiao Hu	肖湖	*xiāohú*
Zhou Enlai's Former Residence	周恩来故居	*zhōuēnlái gùjū*
Zhou Enlai Memorial	周恩来纪念馆	*zhōuēnlái jìniànguǎn*
ACCOMMODATION		
Chuzhou	楚州宾馆	*chǔzhōu bīnguǎn*
Huai'an Binguan	淮安宾馆	*huáiān bīnguǎn*
Huai'an Dajiudian	淮安大酒店	*huáiān dàjiǔdiàn*
Taoliyuan	桃李园大酒店	*táolǐyuán dàjiǔdiàn*
Lianyungang	连云港	*liányúngǎng*
Huaguo Shan	花果山	*huāguǒshān*
Kanping Hotel	康平双厦	*kāngpíngshuāngshà*
Lianyun	连云	*liányún*
Longhe Guangchang	龙河广场	*lónghé guǎngchǎng*
Xinpu	新浦	*xīnpǔ*
Yuntai Hotel	运泰饭店	*yùntài fàndiàn*
Xuzhou	徐洲	*xúzhōu*

Huai'an

HUAI'AN was already settled five thousand years ago, and has been a walled town for 1600 years, but these days it's famous throughout China as the birthplace of the much-loved Premier Zhou Enlai – people still come here to visit Zhou's preserved old home, as well as pay respects to the huge, specially constructed memorial in his honour. Apart from this, Huai'an is a quiet, attractive town of parks and lakes with a large amount of old housing, located in a fertile and agriculturally productive part of Jiangsu.

Huai'an is one of those pleasant places where you can get around entirely on foot, and orientation is unproblematic. The main street, Zhenhuai Lu, cuts from east to west across the middle of the city, with the **bus station** at the far eastern end (there is no train station). Exactly in the middle of town, on Zhenhuai Lu, is **Drum Tower Square**, with the town's other important commercial street, Nanmen Dajie, leading south from here. The older part of town lies to the north and northwest of Drum Tower Square, with streets crammed full of little shops, restaurants, fortune-tellers and interesting architecture.

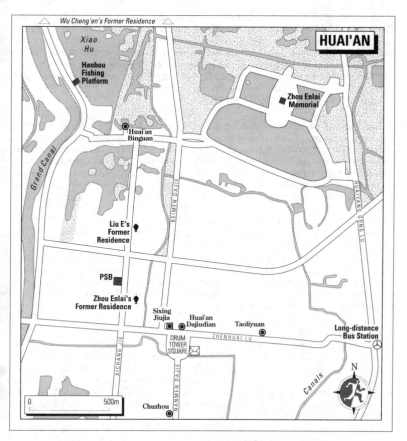

Zhou Enlai's Former Residence (daily 8am–4.30pm; ¥2) is the main attraction in the centre of town. From the Drum Tower walk a few minutes west, then take an alley to the north – there is a sign to the residence (if you reach Xichang Jie you have come too far). The attractive house of black brick and heavy roof tiles where Zhou was born in 1898 has been lovingly restored to its original splendour, and considering the several courtyards within the walls, and the separate rooms for Zhou's stepmother and nanny, the family were obviously well-off. As well as some interesting old wooden furniture, the house contains a small photo exhibition documenting Zhou's life, and also that of his wife, Deng Yingchao, who occupies a similarly high place in the Chinese people's affections.

Continuing north another ten minutes from Zhou Enlai's residence, up the main Xichang Jie, brings you to another former residence, this time of a local intellectual **Liu E**, who died in 1909, and is known in China for his achievements both as a scientist and novelist. The former occupant may be obscure, but his house is a delightful place and some afternoons you'll find traditional storytelling performances going on in the courtyards, the spoken word accompanied by a small drum. Here, amid the bamboos and goldfish ponds, you can catch an insight into the very peaceful, cultured world of old China.

The far **west** of Huai'an is delineated along its entire length by the **Grand Canal**. There's a good walk here up to the northwest, then around a small lake, Xiao Hu to the north, and back to the main road Beimen Jie, lasting about two hours in all, which will take you through areas almost wholly untouched by modern life; start walking north along the canal from the area just west of the *Huai'an Binguan*. Along the waterway you'll be able to watch the bustle of canal life with barges manoeuvring for position and people loading and unloading by hand. Shortly, **Xiao Hu** will appear to your right, and a stone gateway by the lake is the sign that you've reached **Hanhou Fishing Platform**, an attractive walking area by the lakeside amid trees and long grass. Back on the road, and farther north from here, a right turn just where the canal begins bending round to the west takes you into an interesting old area of stone-tiled houses. If you walk approximately northeast through here along country lanes – you'll need to ask the locals for help – you'll reach the **Former Residence of Wu Cheng'en** (daily 8am–4.30pm; ¥2) the sixteenth-century author of the famous classic *Journey to the West*. It's another charming old house of black brick, with colonnaded walkways and clumps of bamboo in the courtyards. From here, head east along more country lanes, through allotments and vegetable patches, before coming out on the main north–south road, Beimen Jie, where you can catch a rickshaw back into town for ¥3.

The **Zhou Enlai Memorial** (daily 8am–5pm; ¥7) stands to the northeast of the centre of town. There are two possible entrances, one twenty minutes due north of the bus station along Huaiyang Gong Lu, and the other just east off Beimen Jie, about 1km north of the Drum Tower. The park, and the memorial itself, built on a small lake, seems to have been modelled on a certain presidential memorial in Washington DC – the seated statue of Zhou is remarkably similar to that of Abraham Lincoln. The craftsmanship and quality of stone, however, are sadly inferior.

Practicalities

There are a few **accommodation** options in town. Fifteen minutes' walk west of the bus station along Zhenhuai Lu, you'll find the *Taoliyuan Hotel* (③) on the right, with comfortable air-conditioned doubles, but no English sign. A little farther west, opposite the Drum Tower marking the town centre, is the basic *Huai'an Dajiudian* (②). Farther afield, down Nanmen Dajie, the attractive *Chuzhou Hotel* (②–⑤) has a range of nice double rooms, while there's more upmarket accommodation at the *Huai'an Binguan* (⑥) in the north of town on Xichang Jie.

The main **Bank of China** (Mon–Fri 8–11.30am & 1.30–5pm) is not particularly central, away to the south along Nanmen Dajie, about thirty minutes' walk from the Drum

Tower, but the **post office** is right in the centre. There are a few places to **eat** around the Drum Tower; try the friendly *Sixing Jiujia* just west of the square, on the north side of the main road. There's no English sign here but you'll see the big red letters in the windows. A huge bowl of *pingchao dofu* – tofu with delicious black pepper and coriander – will cost you just a few yuan. Otherwise, the restaurant in the *Taoliyuan Hotel* is not bad.

Lianyungang

In the extreme northeastern corner of the province, on the Yellow Sea coast, **LIANYUNGANG** is very much out on a limb from the traveller's point of view. It's a working port rather than a tourist attraction, though the surroundings – a fine harbour with mountains behind – and the 1920s and 1930s architecture do at least offer something to look at. Its great boast these days is of being the **terminus of the Longhai rail line**, a line which reaches west through Xi'an to northwest China, beyond into central Asia, and eventually all the way to another seaport at the opposite end of the Eurasian land mass – the Dutch port city of Rotterdam.

Lianyungang Municipality actually covers a vast area, stretching from the new port, pushed up against the sea by hills and known as **Lianyun**, to the heart of the original city some 20km inland, known as **Xinpu**. Xinpu is where most travellers are likely to arrive, either at the **Xinpu train station** or at the **new bus station**, both of which are inconveniently located far to the north of town. Bus #8 connects both stations with **Lao Zhan** (the old station) in the downtown area, on Jiefang Lu. Walking out from Lao Zhan, turn right, then take the first left heading south down Tongguan Lu. About ten minutes down here you'll come to the *Kanping Hotel* (☎0518/5511888; ⑥) which is one of the few **hotels** accepting foreigners and by far the nicest, offering both single and double rooms. Otherwise, try the obscurely located *Yuntai Hotel* (⑤), in the far east of Xinpu on Hailian Lu, east of the vast double traffic circle, Longhe Guangchang, which offers grotty doubles. You'll find various town amenities along **Longhe Guangchang**, including the **Bank of China** at its northwestern end, just west of a little canal. This street is also the departure point for many private buses and minibuses, especially the fast and frequent service to Nanjing.

Apart from the tree-lined streets of Xinpu themselves, which have quite a pleasant antiquated feel, there's really only one tourist sight to speak of, **Huaguo Shan** (Flower and Fruit Hill; daily 7am–8pm; ¥18), 30km from town in the Yuntai hills, which not only sports some delightful scenery, but also gets a mention near the beginning of the classic Chinese novel, *Journey to the West*. If you come early in the morning you can easily spend the whole day climbing footpaths over the hill – there are towers, pavilions, temples and some highly rural scenes of village life on the way. The highlight is the Tang-dynasty **Sanyuan Daoist Temple**, high up on the hillside, which has three grand halls, one shaded by two thousand-year-old gingko trees.

The hill is about twenty minutes in a taxi from town (¥30 each way), though there are also occasional buses here from Lao Zhan in Xinpu.

ZHEJIANG

ZHEJIANG, one of the smallest provinces but also one of the wealthiest, is made up of two quite different areas. The northern part shares its climate, geography, history and the Grand Canal with Jiangsu – the land here is highly cultivated, fertile and netted with waterways, hot in summer but cold in winter. The south, however, mountainous and sparsely populated in the interior, thriving and semi-tropical on the coast, has much more in common with Fujian Province. Even the dialect spoken in the area around Wenzhou has many similarities to Fujianese.

Recent excavations have shown, contrary to expectations, that the Yangzi delta had Neolithic settlements every bit as old as those in the Yellow River valley. At Hemudu on the Shaoxing–Ningbo plain, settled farmers were growing cultivated rice and building solid, precisely structured two-storey houses as long as seven thousand years ago, when rhinoceros and elephant still roamed the land. For millennia thereafter, the region remained prosperous but provincial, politically in the shadow of the more populous Yellow River basin in northern China. The eventual economic shift to the south slowly worked to the region's advantage, however. The Grand Canal was built, and finally, in the twelfth century AD, the imperial court of the Song moved south and set up capital in Hangzhou. For over two centuries, northern Zhejiang enjoyed a spell of unprecedented power which ended only when the capital moved back to Beijing.

The whole province has an attractive, prosperous air, but most of the tourist destinations are in the north. **Hangzhou**, the terminus of the Grand Canal, once a great capital and still a centre for silk, tea and papermaking, is one of the greenest, most attractive cities in China, with a famous lake, former resort of emperors. Nearby **Shaoxing**, a charming small town threaded by canals, offers the chance to tour its beautiful surroundings by boat, while **Ningbo**, although long superseded by Shanghai as an industrial port, is beginning to be seriously infected by the economic boom of the coast. The Buddhist island of **Putuo Shan**, offshore from Ningbo, has huge tourist potential and, with more temples than cars, it is as fresh, green and tranquil as eastern China ever gets. Finally, in the south of the province, you might consider a visit to the rather isolated and individual town of **Wenzhou**, a former treaty port, now generating a mini-economic boom all of its own.

Hangzhou

HANGZHOU, capital of the province and southern terminus of the Grand Canal, lies in the north of Zhejiang at the head of Hangzhou Bay. The canal has been the instrument of the city's wealth and fortunes, establishing it for over a thousand years as a place of great wealth and culture. Apart from the fact that Yu the Great, tamer of floods, is said to have moored his boats here, however, Hangzhou has little in the way of a legendary past or ancient history for the simple reason that the present site, on the east shore of **Xi Hu** (West Lake), was originally under water. Xi Hu itself started life as a wide shallow inlet off the bay, and it is said that Emperor Qin Shihuang sailed in from the sea and moored his boats on what is now the northwestern shore of the lake. Only around the fourth century AD did river currents and tides begin to throw up a barrier of silt which eventually resulted in the formation of the lake.

However, the city rapidly made up for its slow start. The first great impetus came from the building of the **Grand Canal** at the end of the sixth century and Hangzhou developed with spectacular speed as the centre for trade between north and south, the Yellow and Yangzi river basins. Under the **Tang dynasty** it was a rich and thriving city, but its location between lake and river made it vulnerable to the fierce equinox tides in Hangzhou Bay. When Tang-dynasty governors were building locks and dykes to control the waters round Hangzhou, a contemporary writer, describing the beginning of a sea wall in 910 AD, explained that "archers were stationed on the shore to shoot down the waves while a poem was recited to propitiate the King of Dragons and Government of the Waters; the waves immediately left the wall and broke on the opposite bank so the work could go on." The problem of **floods** – and the search for remedies – was to recur down the centuries.

During the **Song dynasty**, Hangzhou received its second great impetus when the encroachment of the Tartars from the north destroyed the northern capital of Kaifeng and sent remnants of the imperial family fleeing south in search of a new base. The result of this upheaval was that from 1138 until 1279 Hangzhou became the **imperial**

HANGZHOU

Hangzhou	杭州	*hángzhōu*

ACCOMMODATION

Hangzhou University	杭州大学	*hángzhōu dàxué*
Huabei	华北饭店	*huáběi fàndiàn*
Huaqiao	华侨饭店	*huáqiáo fàndiàn*
Jinyazhuang	金雅庄大饭店	*jīnyǎzhuāng dàfàndiàn*
Shangrila	香格里拉饭店	*xiānggélǐlā fàndiàn*
Taipingyang	太平洋大酒店	*tàipíngyáng dàjiǔdiàn*
Xi Hu	西湖饭店	*xīhú fàndiàn*
Xinqiao	新桥饭店	*xīnqiáo fàndiàn*
Youzheng	邮政大厦	*yóuzhèng dàshà*
Zhejiang	浙江宾馆	*zhèjiāng bīnguǎn*
Zhonghua	中华饭店	*zhōnghuá fàndiàn*

THE CITY

Bai Di	白堤	*báidī*
Baoshu Ta	保淑塔	*bǎoshūtǎ*
Feilai Feng	飞来峰	*fēiláifēng*
Gu Shan	孤山	*gūshān*
Jinci Si	净慈寺	*jìncí sì*
Huanglong Dong Park	黄龙洞公园	*huánglóngdòng gōngyuán*
Hupaomeng Quan	虎跑梦泉	*hǔpáomèng quán*
Lingyin Si	灵隐寺	*língyǐn sì*
Liuhe Pagoda	六和塔	*liùhé tǎ*
Longjing	龙井	*lóngjǐng*
Nine Creeks and Eighteen Gullies Road	酒溪十八涧	*jiǔxīshíbājiàn*
Santanyinyue	三潭印月	*sāntányìnyuè*
Su Di	苏堤	*sūdī*
Xi Hu	西湖	*xīhú*
Xiaoying Island	小瀛洲	*xiǎoyíngzhōu*
Xiling Seal Engravers' Society	西泠印社	*xīlíngyìnshè*
Yuefei Mu	岳飞墓	*yuèfēimù*
Zhejiang Museum	浙江博物馆	*zhèjiāng bówùguǎn*
Zhongshan Park	中山公园	*zhōngshān gōngyuán*

RESTAURANTS

Bafangyuan	八方缘	*bāfāngyuán*
Jingyuan Jiujia	镜苑酒家	*jìngyuán jiǔjiā*
Kuiyuan Guan	奎元馆	*kuíyuán guǎn*
Louwailou	楼外楼	*lóuwàilóu*
Zhiweiguan	知味观	*zhīwèiguān*

capital. There was an explosion in the silk and brocade industry, and indeed in all the trades that waited upon the court and their wealthy friends. When Marco Polo wrote of Hangzhou towards the end of the thirteenth century, he spoke of "the City of Heaven, the most beautiful and magnificent in the world. It has ten principal market places, always with an abundance of victuals, roebuck, stags, harts, hares, partridge, pheasants, quails, hens and ducks, geese... all sorts of vegetables and fruits... huge pears weighing ten pounds apiece. Each day a vast quantity of fish is brought from the ocean. There is also an abundance of lake fish." So glorious was the reputation of the city that it rapidly grew overcrowded. On to its sandbank Hangzhou was soon cramming over a million people, a population as large as that of Chang'an (Xi'an) under the Tang, but in a quarter of the space – tall wooden buildings up to five storeys high were crowded into narrow streets, creating a ghastly fire hazard.

After the Southern Song dynasty was finally overthrown by the Mongols in 1279, Hangzhou ceased to be a capital city, but it remained an important centre of commerce and a place of luxury, with **parks and gardens** outside the ramparts and hundreds of boats on the lake. In later years, the Ming rulers repaired the city walls and deepened the Grand Canal so that large ships could go all the way from Hangzhou to Beijing. Two great Qing emperors, Kangxi and Qianlong, frequented the city and built villas, temples and gardens by the lake. Although the city was largely destroyed by the **Taiping Uprising** (1861–63), it recovered surprisingly quickly, and the **foreign concessions** which were established towards the end of the century – followed by the building of rail lines from Shanghai and Ningbo – stimulated the growth of new industries alongside the traditional silk and brocade manufacturers.

Since 1949 the city has grown to attain a population of around one million, much the same as under the Song. As is often the case in China, the modern city is not of much interest in itself, but Xi Hu and its shores still offer wonderful Chinese vistas of trees, hills, grass, old causeways over the lake, pavilions and pagodas – all within a walk of the city centre. Today Hangzhou is one of China's busiest resorts, particularly at weekends when the city is packed with trippers escaping from the concrete jungle of Shanghai. This has pushed up hotel prices, but it also brings advantages: there are plenty of restaurants, the natural environment is being protected and the bulk of the Taiping destruction on the lakeside has been repaired (the temples rebuilt and the gardens replanted). Most of the places to visit are on the lake or immediately around its shores, and can be visited on foot or bicycle; for those attractions farther afield city buses are very convenient.

Orientation, arrival and accommodation

Hangzhou is a city of two halves. To the east and north is **downtown** Hangzhou, with its shops and tourist facilities, while to the west and south is the **lake** offering greenery and scenic spots. In fact, the lake shouldn't be regarded as being on the edge of the city – more realistically, its eastern shore marks the centre, and even the relatively remote western shore is now being developed for upmarket tourist accommodation.

The main east–west street, Jiefang Lu, runs from the **train station** in the east to the lake, with major north–south streets crossing it, including Zhongshan Lu, and, closer to the lake, Yan'an Lu. The area around the **Jiefang Lu–Yan'an Lu intersection** (including the lake front and the small streets just to the north) is the commercial centre of town where you can shop, stay, eat and catch buses round the lake.

On the outskirts of the city, the **Qiantong River**, Hangzhou's gateway to the sea, flows well to the south and west, while the **Grand Canal** runs across to meet it from the north – many travellers to Hangzhou never see either of them.

Arrival

Hangzhou's **airport** is 15km from town, and connected by *CAAC* bus to the main booking office on Tiyuchang Lu, just east of Hushu Lu.

The **train station** is not a particularly charming place to arrive. To reach the lake from here on foot takes about forty minutes; walk straight ahead out of the station and keep bearing right until you hit Jiefang Lu heading due west. Otherwise, take bus #7 direct to the lake or #151 or #152 as far as Yan'an Lu. Frequent private **buses** also use the train station square, connecting with nearby cities such as Suzhou, Shanghai and Wenzhou.

The main **long-distance bus station** is in the north of town, on Hushu Nan Lu, just north of Huancheng Lu; bus #151 through town to and from the train station passes here. Most long-distance buses use this station, except for those from Shaoxing and Ningbo which use the remote **East bus station** in the northeast of town, which is connected by bus #502 to the long-distance bus station and #503 to the train station. To reach town from here go to the long-distance bus station first, then head south on #151.

Since the Grand Canal has been so important for Hangzhou, it would seem appropriate to arrive here by **boat** – and there are still daily passenger services connecting Hangzhou with Suzhou and Wuxi, both arriving in the morning and leaving in the early evening. The dock is on the Grand Canal in the far northeast of town and bus #305 into town passes very near here. For tickets and more detailed information on the canal boats, consult a travel service (see "Listings", p.412).

Accommodation

There are some excellent **hotels** in Hangzhou, particularly those around the lake, but there is an extreme shortage of budget accommodation. The only cheaper options are in the universities. If the Hangzhou University listed below is full, you could try the Zhejiang University not far to the southwest (bus #16 from the lakeside).

Hangzhou University, Tianmushan Lu. Located at the northern end of Hangda Lu, in the north of town (bus #11 or #153 from the train station). There are two options here. Slightly to the east of the main university entrance is the *Foreign Experts' Hotel*, which has double rooms of hotel standard. Much cheaper, however, is the *Foreign Students' Dormitory*; go inside the main gate, turn right, then walk straight ahead for about five minutes. There are sometimes a few spare beds or even entire double rooms, with communal showers, available. Beds ②, rooms ②–⑤.

Huabei, Beishan Lu (☎7980486 ext 3803). A big old place on a slope overlooking the far northwestern corner of the lake, and offering doubles and triples. Considering the leafy location, it's one of the better deals, though rooms are slightly fusty. Bus #7 from the train station. ⑥.

Huaqiao (*Overseas Hotel*), Hubin Lu (☎7074401, fax 7074978). On the lake front near the western end of Changsheng Lu, this is a delightful place in a great location. ⑧–⑨.

Jinyazhuang, Jiefang Lu (☎7048724). Located at the very eastern end of Jiefang Lu, a few minutes' walk north of the *Youzheng*. Considering the inconvenient position, the only advantage of this place is that its rooms are among the cheapest around – but staff sometimes try to charge foreigners a fifty percent surcharge. ④–⑤.

Shangrila, Beishan Lu (☎7077951, fax 7073545). Total air-conditioned luxury in beautiful, secluded grounds, overhung by trees, on the northern shore of the lake. ⑨.

Taipingyang (*Pacific Hotel*), Pinghai Lu (☎7077666, fax 7063638). Just east of Yan'an Lu and fairly anonymous, but clean and comfortable. ⑦.

Xi Hu, Hubin Lu (☎7066933). Perfectly located on the lake front, but not a particularly good bet for foreigners, who are surcharged ¥50 for slightly ropy rooms. Take bus #7 from the train station. ⑥–⑦.

Xinqiao, Jiefang Lu (☎7076688, fax 7071428). An absolutely central location, on the corner with Yan'an Lu, and one of the plushest of the town-based hotels. ⑦–⑧.

Youzheng (*Hangzhou Post Mansion*), Huancheng Dong Lu (☎7800568, fax 7813329). Exiting from the train station, turn right and walk straight ahead (north) for fifteen minutes, passing under an overpass; the hotel is on the left. Conveniently located for those arriving very late, and with excellent new rooms. ⑥.

Zhejiang, Longjing Lu (☎7977988 or 7971904). Remote, but peaceful and rural, down to the southwest of the lake, amid tea plantations (see p.410). Take bus #27 from Pinghai Lu. ⑦.

Zhonghua, Youdian Lu (☎7027094, fax 7067096). Very central, between the lake front and Yan'an Lu, this is about the best deal in town with nice new single and double rooms. ⑥.

The City

The municipality of Hangzhou is unusual by the standards of Chinese cities in that it encompasses large areas of greenery which might normally be classified as countryside. This is mainly thanks to the lake Xi Hu itself – so central and dominant a role has the lake played in the city's history that even today a trip right round the shores of the lake does not feel like an excursion out of the city, despite the fact that the built-up area lies almost entirely to the east and north of the lake.

Within the lake are various **islands** and causeways, while the shores are home to endless **parks**, which include Hangzhou's most famous individual sights, ranging from the extravagant and historic **Yuefei Mu** (Temple and Tomb of Yuefei) to the

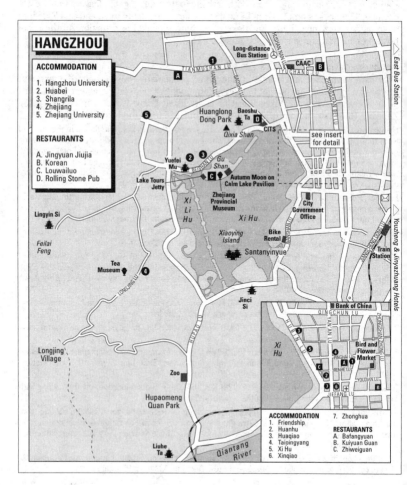

HANGZHOU

ACCOMMODATION
1. Hangzhou University
2. Huabei
3. Shangrila
4. Zhejiang
5. Zhejiang University

RESTAURANTS
A. Jingyuan Jiujia
B. Korean
C. Louwailuo
D. Rolling Stone Pub

ACCOMMODATION
1. Friendship
2. Huanhu
3. Huaqiao
4. Taipingyang
5. Xi Hu
6. Xinqiao
7. Zhonghua

RESTAURANTS
A. Bafangyuan
B. Kuiyuan Guan
C. Zhiweiguan

ancient hillside Buddhist carvings of **Feilai Feng** and its associated temple, the **Lingyin Si**, one of China's largest and most renowned. Farther afield, beautiful tea plantations nestle around the village of **Longjing** and the bizarre former home of the disgraced leader **Lin Biao**, while south down to the **Qiantang River** are excellent walking opportunities.

Xi Hu

A voyage on this lake offers more refreshment and pleasure than any other experience on earth...

Marco Polo

Xi Hu forms a series of landscape designs with rock, trees, grass and lakeside buildings all reflected in the water and backed by luxuriant wooded hills. On a sunny day the colours are brilliant, but even with grey skies and choppy waters, the famous lake views are delicate, soothing and tranquil; for the Chinese they are also laden with literary and historic associations. Although the crowds are sometimes distracting, the area is so large that it is possible to find places to escape the hubbub. The lake itself stretches just over 3km from north to south and just under 3km from east to west, though the surrounding parks and associated sights spread far beyond this.

As early as the Tang dynasty, work was taking place to control the waters of the lake with dykes and locks, and the two **causeways** which now cross sections of the lake, Bai Di across the north and Su Di across the west, originated in these ancient embankments. Mainly used by pedestrians and cyclists, the causeways offer instant escape from the noise and smog of the built-up area to the east. Strolling the causeways at any time of day or night, surrounded by clean, fresh water and flowering lilies, is a real pleasure and a favourite pursuit of all romantic Chinese couples.

The northern **Bai Di** causeway is the shorter and more popular of the two, about 1.5km in length. Starting in the northwest of the lake near the *Shangrila Hotel*, it runs along the outer edge of Gu Shan (Solitary Island) before crossing back to the northeastern shore, enclosing a small strip known as Beili Hu (North Inner Lake). The little island of **Gu Shan** in the middle of the Bai Di causeway is one of Hangzhou's highlights, a great place to relax under a shady tree. Sprinkled with pavilions, pagodas and other buildings, this tiny area was originally landscaped under the Tang, but the present style dates from the Qing, when Emperor Qianlong built himself a palace here, surrounded by the immaculately green and quiet **Zhongshan Park**. Part of the palace itself, facing south into the centre of the lake, is now the **Zhejiang Provincial Museum** (Tues–Sun 8.30am–4.15pm; ¥10), a huge place with clear English captions throughout and a number of different wings. The main building in front of the entrance houses historical relics, including some superb bronzes from the eleventh to the eighth century BC. Another hall centres on coin collections and has specimens of the world's first banknotes, dating to the Northern Song; you'll get an appreciation of the deep conservatism of Chinese society from its coinage, which remained fundamentally unchanged for two thousand years from the Han to the Qing dynasties.

The curious **Xiling Seal Engravers' Society**, founded in 1904, occupies the western side of the hill, next to the museum. Its tiny park encloses a pavilion with a pleasant blend of steps, carved stone tablets and nearby a small early Buddhist stupa; drop in here and you can often see the engravers at work. On the southeastern side of the hill by the water is another of Qianlong's buildings, the **Autumn Moon on a Calm Lake Pavilion**, which is the perfect place to watch the full moon. It's a tea house now, very popular after sunset and full of swooning honeymooners.

From the causeway just east of Gu Shan you can rent paddle boats which are fun in the cool of the evening (¥10 per hour, ¥100 deposit). The low stone bridge, **Duan Qiao**

(Broken Bridge), at the far eastern end of the causeway, gets its name because winter snow melts first on the hump of the bridge, creating the illusion of a gap.

The second, longer causeway, **Su Di**, named after the Song-dynasty poet-official Su Dong Po, who was governor of Hangzhou, starts from the southwest corner of the lake and runs its full length along the west side to the northern shore close to Yuefei Mu. Consisting of embankments planted with banana trees, weeping willows and plum trees, linked by six stone-arch bridges, the causeway encloses a narrow stretch of water, **Xili Hu** (West Inner Lake), in the south of which, on a promontory, is the small Song-dynasty **Huagang Park**. Today the park contains a pond full of enormous fish and there are also wonderful stretches of grass and exotic trees under which to relax.

One of the pleasantest elements of a visit to Hangzhou is a **boat trip** on the water offering a chance to visit the islands, the largest of which is **Xiaoying Island**. This roughly circular embankment was built up in 1607 and bridges link across from north to south and east to west so that the whole thing seems like a wheel with four spokes and a central hub just large enough for a pavilion, doubling as a shop and a restaurant. Obscure mythologies surround the island, and at its southern edge are three "flags" in the water, actually stone pagodas. These are said to control the evil spirits lurking in the deepest spots of the lake, and are known as the **Santanyinyue** (Three Flags Reflecting the Moon).

The small canopied boats which are poled around the lake can be picked up at various points including the jetty on Gu Shan, near the museum, and on Hubin Lu. The boat owners charge a fixed fee per hour, which is posted at the jetties, but watch out for tourist rip-offs. For a cheaper, but less intimate ride, go to the jetty in front of the Yuefei Mu on the northern shore (see below) from where there are regular departures for the islands and the Three Flags for ¥16. A round trip back to the jetty via some of the islands and the Three Flags, in a fancy dragon boat, takes just over an hour.

The lake shore

Most of Hangzhou's sights are on or near the lake shore. An ideal way to get between them is by **bike**, otherwise you can use the local buses or simply walk. It's possible to walk round the entire circumference in one day, but you wouldn't have time to stop at all the sights en route.

Starting from the northeast of the lake on Beishan Lu, and moving anti-clockwise, the first sight looming up on the hillside to your right is the seven-storey **Baoshu Ta** on Baoshi Shan. The pagoda is not original – it's a 1933 reconstruction of a Song-dynasty tower – but it's a nice place to walk to along hillside tracks. From Beishan Lu a small lane leads up behind some buildings to the pagoda. Tracks continue beyond and you can climb right up to **Qixia Shan** (Mountain where Clouds Linger) above the lake. There's a delightful walk along the ridge, passing **Chuyang** (Sunrise Terrace) which is traditionally the spot for watching the spring sun rise over the lake, Gu Shan and the northern shore. If you continue west, you'll eventually reach some steep stone stairs which will bring you back down to the road, close to the Yuefei Mu at the northeast end of the lake.

The **Yuefei Mu** (Temple and Tomb of Yuefei; daily 7.30am–6pm; ¥8) is one of Hangzhou's big draws. The twelfth-century Song general, Yuefei is considered a hero in modern China thanks to his unquestioning patriotism. Having emerged victorious from a war against barbarian invaders from the north, he was falsely charged with treachery by a jealous prime minister, found guilty and executed at the age of 39. However, twenty years after his execution, the next emperor annulled all charges against him and had him reburied here with full honours, thus guaranteeing his name to posterity. Walk through the temple to reach the tomb itself – a tiny bridge over water, a small double row of stone men and animals, steles, a mound with old pine trees and four cast-iron statues of the villains, kneeling in shame with their hands behind their backs. On the front wall of the tomb the calligraphy reads, "Be loyal to your country." At the site, there's also an interesting exhibition hall with photos showing the decidedly unpatriotic damage done here during the Cultural Revolution.

Immediately west of Yuefei's Tomb is a lane leading away from the lake and north into the hills behind. Thirty minutes' walk along here eventually leads to the **Huanglong Dong Park** (Yellow Dragon Cave Park; daily 8am–7pm; ¥4) to the north of Qixia Shan. The park can also be approached from the roads to the north of here, south of Hangzhou University. The main area of the park is charmingly secretive, sunk down between sharply rising hills with a pond, some tea houses, a shrine to the Chinese writer Yue Lao, and a pavilion with musicians performing traditional music – you can even choose a tune if you like, for ¥10.

Feilai Feng and Lingyin Si

Three kilometres west, away from the lake (bus #7 from Yuefei Mu to its terminus) are Hangzhou's most famous sights, scattered around **Feilai Feng** (daily 7am–4.30pm; ¥10). The hill's bizarre name – meaning "The Hill that Flew Here" – derives from the Indian Buddhist devotee who, upon arrival in Hangzhou, thought he recognized the hill from one back home in India, and asked when it had flown here. Near the entrance is the **Ligong Pagoda**, constructed for Hui Li, the original founder of the hill's Buddhist temple. If you turn left shortly after entering the site, you'll come to a surprisingly impressive group of fake rock carvings of giant Buddhas. To the right of the entrance is a snack bar and beautiful views over the neighbouring tea plantations rolling up the hill.

The main feature of Feilai Feng, other than the crowds of tourists, is the hundreds of **Buddhist sculptures** carved into its limestone rocks. These date from between the tenth and fourteenth centuries and are the most important examples of their type to be found south of the Yangzi. Today you'll see the little Buddhas and other figurines dotted about everywhere, moss-covered and laughing out of the foliage. It's possible to follow trails right up to the top of the hill if you want to escape the tourist hubbub.

Deep inside the Feilai Feng tourist area you'll eventually arrive at **Lingyin Si** (daily 7am–4.30pm; ¥10; entrance only from within the Feilai Feng site), one of the biggest temple complexes in China. Founded in 326 AD by the Indian monk, Hui Li, who is buried nearby, it was the largest and most important monastery in Hangzhou and once had three thousand monks, nine towers, eighteen pavilions and 75 halls and rooms. It has been restored at least sixteen times and was so badly riddled with woodworm in the 1940s that the main crossbeams collapsed on to the statues. In 1956, however, a replica was produced of the eighteen-metre-high Tang-statue of Sakyamuni, carved from 24 pieces of camphorwood. In Lingyin Si the old frequently brushes against the new – the **Hall of the Heavenly King** contains four large and highly painted Guardians of the Four Directions made in the 1930s, while the Guardian of the Buddhist Law and Order, who shields the Maitreya, was carved from a single piece of wood eight hundred years ago. The complex was said to be among those protected by Zhou Enlai during the Cultural Revolution, and today it is an attractive working temple with daily services.

Longjing and around

Down in the southwestern quarter of the lake, in the direction of the village of **Longjing**, the dominant theme is **tea production**. Gleaming green tea bushes sweep up and down the land and old ladies pester tourists into buying fresh tea leaves. Access to the area is by bus #27 from the centre of town at Pinghai Lu. If you get off more or less opposite the *Zhejiang Hotel*, then walk southwest along a small lane just to the north of, and parallel to, the main road, you'll come to the **Tea Museum** (daily 8.30am–4.30pm; ¥7). This is a new, very smart place with lots of captions in English and well worth a visit. It traces the history of tea, from its early medicinal uses through to the etiquette of tea drinking and its close relationship with Buddhism. You'll find displays on different varieties of tea, techniques of growing, the development of special teaware, and finally, reconstructed tea-drinking rooms, in various ethnic styles, such as Tibetan and Yunnanese.

The nearby **Zhejiang Hotel** houses one of China's oddest attractions, connected with the hotel's most famous former resident, the disgraced **Marshal Lin Biao**, formerly Mao Zedong's anointed number two, who in 1972 mysteriously died with his family in an alleged plane crash over Mongolia, while attempting to defect to the Soviet Union. Somebody with a sense of humour has decided to capitalize on Lin Biao's sinister reputation by setting up a rather absurd **chamber of horrors** (¥10) of monsters, skeletons and other ghouls in the once secret underground rooms to which Lin had access. On a more serious note, you can also visit the rooms above ground where he lived and worked with his family – your guide will dwell on Lin's cowardice and paranoia, pointing out the padded lamp shades, which could do no injury if dislodged from above, and the one-way windows. To find a guide (Chinese–speaking only), enquire at the reception beside the driveway into the hotel. One of the bored security guards there will usually show you round.

The village of **LONGJING** ("Dragon Well"), with tea terraces rising on all sides behind the houses, is famous as the origin of **Longjing Tea**, perhaps the finest variety of green tea produced in China. It's interesting to stroll around here and, depending on the season, you'll see leaves in different stages of processing – being cut, sorted, or drying. You'll be pestered to buy when you get off the bus, but have a good look around first as there is a very complex grading system and a huge range in quality and price. The **Dragon Well** itself is at the end of the village – a group of buildings around a spring, got up in a rather touristy fashion.

South of the lake

The area to the south and southwest of Xi Hu, down to the Qiantang River, is full of trees and gentle slopes. Of all the parks in this area, perhaps the nicest is the **Hupaomeng Quan** (Tiger Running Dream Spring; daily 7.30am–7pm; ¥5). Buses #308 and #315 both run here from the city centre, down the eastern shore of the lake. The spring here – according to legend, originally located with the help of two tigers – is said to produce the purest water around, and the only water that serious connoisseurs would use for brewing the best Longjing teas. For centuries, this has been a popular site for hermits to settle and is now a large forested area dotted with tea houses, shrines and pavilions.

A few more stops south on bus #308 takes you to the thousand-year-old **Liuhe Pagoda**, occupying a spectacular site overlooking the Qiantang River, a short way west of the rail bridge. A huge, impressive structure of wood and brick, hung with 104 large iron bells on its upturned eaves, the tower was originally built to ward off the spirit responsible for the heavy tides which caused so much flooding before the dykes were constructed. Now, ironically, it's the most popular vantage point from which to view the dramatic tidal bores during the autumn equinox.

Twenty minutes' walk upriver west from the pagoda, at the #2 bus terminus, a lane known as **Nine Creeks and Eighteen Gullies** runs off at right angles to the river and up to Longjing. This is a delightful narrow way, great for a bike ride or a half-day stroll, following the banks of a stream and meandering through paddy fields and tea terraces with the hills rising in swelling ranks on either side. Halfway along the road, a restaurant straddles the stream where it widens into a serene lagoon. It's an exquisite spot with a tiny pavilion nestling into the woody slope above, and it serves excellent tea and food. From here, you continue north up a bumpy rock and cobbled track, constantly crisscrossed by streams with neat stepping stones, to Longjing.

Finally, back by the southern shore of Xi Hu, is another temple, **Jinci Si**. Although nowhere near as active and busy as Lingyin Si – it remains slightly derelict, with restoration not yet complete – it does house an impressively large Buddha. Across the road from the temple, furthermore, is an intriguing toy village, built by monks around an artificial pond, displaying China's four holy Buddhist mountains (Putuo Shan, Emei Shan, Wutai Shan and Jiuhua Shan) in miniature. Buses #308 and #315 to and from town run past.

Eating and drinking

As a busy resort for local tourists Hangzhou has plenty of good places to eat, though there is nothing like the cosmopolitan range of either Shanghai or Nanjing. *KFC* has a couple of branches in Hangzhou, one on Renhe Lu in town, and the other next to Yuefei's Tomb on the north shore of the lake. Bars, as such, are almost non-existent, though there is one option, the *Rolling Stone Pub*.

Restaurants and bars

Bafangyuan, Pinghai Lu. In the middle of town, a little east of Yan'an Lu, this is a popular, clean and efficient Taiwanese-owned snack bar serving teas, coffees, desserts, hotpots and full set meals.

Jingyuan Jiujia, Tianmushan Lu. A couple of minutes due west of Hangzhou University main gate; you'll recognize it from the lanterns outside. As well as being convenient for the university accommodation, this tiny, friendly place also has a huge menu in English.

Korean Restaurant, Zhongshan Bei Lu. Quite a smart restaurant, at the corner with Tiyuchang Lu, offering good Korean dishes.

Kuiyuan Guan, Jiefang Lu. A very interesting place, just west of Zhongshan Zhong Lu (second floor; go through the entrance with Chinese lanterns hanging outside), which specializes in every kind of noodle dish.

Lingyin Si Vegetarian, Lingyin Si. If you're at the temple at lunchtime, try out the excellent vegetarian restaurant here; full meals come to around ¥50 per person.

Louwailou, Gu Shan Island. The best-known restaurant in Hangzhou, on the southern shore of Gu Shan Island, very near the museum. It's not an expensive place to eat and specialities include dongpo pork, fish shred soup and beggar's chicken (a whole chicken cooked inside a ball of mud, which is broken and removed at your table). Standard dishes are ¥30–40.

Rolling Stone Pub, off Baoshu Lu. Located on an alley just west off Baoshu Lu, near its southern end. A neon sign marks this scruffy bar which serves very cheap beers and is a hang-out for foreign students from Hangzhou University.

Zhiweiguan, Renhe Lu. One of the nicest places in town for lunch, on the lake front, at the corner of Hubin Lu. In a very urbane atmosphere, with piped classical music, you can eat assorted *dian xin* (local equivalent to *dim sum*) by the plate for around ¥20, including *xiao longbao* (small, fine stuffed dumplings) and *mao erduo* (fried, crunchy stuffed dumplings). The *hundun tang* (wonton soup) and *jiu miao* (fried chives) are also good. Order and pay at the small window on the left as you enter; collect your food yourself at the back.

Listings

Airlines The main *CAAC* reservations and ticketing office is at 160 Tiyuchang Lu in the north of town (daily 8.15am–8pm; ☎5154259 domestic flights, ☎5152575). *CAAC* buses to the airport leave here approximately 2hr 30min before each flight's departure.

Banks and exchange The *Bank of China* head office is at 140 Yan'an Bei Lu (Mon–Fri 8am–4.30pm & Sat 8am–12.30pm), immediately north of Qingchun Lu. You can change travellers' cheques in any of the smaller branches as well, and at upmarket hotels if you're a guest.

Bike rental Unfortunately rather difficult to find in Hangzhou. There is one very small place, (8am–8.30pm; ¥1 per hour, ¥200 deposit) obscurely located on Nanshan Lu (lakeside) towards the southern end of the eastern shore of Xi Hu. You might also try enquiring around the train station.

Buses For Shanghai, Suzhou or Wenzhou there are private buses from the train station square; otherwise go to the main long-distance bus station on Hushu Nan Lu. For Ningbo or Shaoxing use the East bus station.

Hospitals The most central is the Shengzhong Hospital, on Youdian Lu three blocks east of the lake.

Post office The main post office is just north of the train station on Huancheng Dong Lu.

PSB For visa extensions, enquire at the City Government office in the centre of town, on the southwest corner of the junction between Jiefang Lu and Yan'an Lu.

Telephones IDD calls are most easily made with phone cards from hotels.

Trains The train station contains a very convenient soft seat ticket office for foreigners (Mon–Sat 8–11.30am & 1–4.30pm) on the left as you approach the station. For hard seats or hard sleepers, queue inside the station at window #1.

Travel agents Nearly all hotels have their own travel agencies. Otherwise, *CITS* is on the north shore of the lake, near the junction of Beishan Lu and Baoshu Lu (daily 9am–4pm; ☎5152888, fax 5156667).

Shaoxing and around

Located south of Hangzhou Bay in the midst of a flat plain crisscrossed by waterways and surrounded by low hills, **SHAOXING** is one of the oldest cities in Zhejiang, having established itself as a regional centre in the fifth century BC. During the intervening centuries – especially under the Song, when the imperial court was based in neighbouring Hangzhou – Shaoxing remained a flourishing city, though the lack of direct access to the sea has always kept it out of the front line of events.

For the visitor, Shaoxing is a quieter and more intimate version of Suzhou, combining some attractive little sights with great opportunities for boating round classic Chinese countryside. It's a small city that seems to have played a disproportionately

SHAOXING AND AROUND		
Shaoxing	绍兴	*shàoxīng*
Bazi Qiao	八子桥	*bāzǐqiáo*
Fushan Park	府山公园	*fǔshān gōngyuán*
Lu Xun's Former Residence	鲁迅故居	*lǔxùn gùjū*
Lu Xun Memorial Hall	鲁迅纪念馆	*lǔxùn jìniànguǎn*
Qingteng Shuwu	青藤书屋	*qīngténg shūwū*
Qiu Jin's Former Residence	秋瑾故居	*qiūjǐn gùjū*
Sanwei Shuwu	三味书屋	*sānwèi shūwū*
Yingtian Pagoda	应天塔	*yìngtiān tǎ*
ACCOMMODATION		
Jiaoyundasha Luguan	交运大厦旅馆	*jiāoyùn dàshàlǚguǎn*
Jinyu	金鱼宾馆	*jīnyú bīnguǎn*
Shaoxing Dasha	绍兴大厦	*shàoxīng dàshà*
Shaoxing Fandian	绍兴饭店	*shàoxīng fàndiàn*
AROUND SHAOXING		
Dong Hu	东湖	*dōnghú*
Lanting	兰亭	*lántíng*
Yu Miao	禹庙	*yúmiào*

large role in Chinese legend and culture – some of China's more colourful characters came from here, including the mythical tamer of floods Yu the Great, the wife-murdering Ming painter Xin Wei, the female revolutionary hero Qiu Jin, and the great twentieth-century writer Lu Xun, all of whom have left their mark on the city. Shaoxing is also known throughout China for its sweet yellow **rice wine**, a favourite of so many Chinese recipe books worldwide. Although sometimes recommended as a day trip from Hangzhou, a single day is definitely not enough to do justice to the town and its surroundings. And, if any added incentive is needed, hotel accommodation in Shaoxing is cheap.

The City

Although Shaoxing's immediate centre comprises a standard shopping street, elsewhere there are running streams, black-tiled whitewashed houses, narrow lanes divided by water and alleys paved with stone slabs, which can easily be explored by bicycle. **Fushan Park** (daily 7am–8pm) in the west of town, south of the *Shaoxing Hotel*, is as good a place as any to get your orientation. There's a large temple here near the entrance, a number of small pavilions as you climb the hill, and from the top you can see out over the town's canals and bridges. The main entrance to the park is on Fushanhen Jie, a small street running west from the north–south thoroughfare, Jiefang Lu.

Along Jiefang Lu are a number of famous people's former residences. A hundred metres south of the turning to the park is the beautifully tranquil **Qingteng Shuwu** (Green Vine Study; daily 8am–4.30pm; ¥1), a perfect little sixteenth-century whitewashed house on a small alley, Qianguan Xiang, west off the main road. The serenity of the place belies the fact that it was once the home of an eccentric painter and dramatist called Xu Wei (1521–93), who among other violent acts in his life is notorious for having murdered his wife.

Another 500m south down Jiefang Lu from here the **Yingtian Pagoda** (daily 8am–5pm; ¥1) crowns a low hill, Tu Shan. Part of a temple founded by the Song, burnt down by the Taiping rebels and subsequently rebuilt, the pagoda repays the stiff climb with splendid views over the canals of the town. The black roof tiles, visible a block to the south, belong to the former residence of the early radical woman activist, **Qiu Jin**, situated on a small lane, Hechang Tang. Born here in 1875, Qiu Jin went to study in Japan, before returning to China to work as a teacher and join Sun Yatsen's clandestine revolutionary party. After working as editor of several revolutionary papers in Shanghai, and taking part in a series of abortive coups, she was captured and executed in Hangzhou in 1907 by Qing forces. The **house** (daily 8.30am–4pm; ¥0.5) is full of background material on her life, and although there's no explanation in English, the photographs and paintings convey some of the atmosphere of the time. It's a reflection of the ideological changes that have taken place in China in recent years that Qiu Jin's house today is a neglected and forlorn place.

Heading east off Jiefang Lu, down Luxun Lu, are several sights associated with the writer **Lu Xun** (see box, p.345). His childhood and early youth were spent in Shaoxing, and local characters populate his books. Thanks to the fact that the city has been relatively sheltered from violent change, many of the scenes from his writings are still recognizable today. The first one you'll come to is the **Lu Xun Memorial Hall** (daily 8am–4.30pm; ¥6), though for foreigners there's little of interest here as the exhibition lacks English captions. A few minutes farther east, however, beyond the plain **Lu Xun Library**, you'll find **Lu Xun's Former Residence** which has now been converted into a **Folk Museum** (daily 8am–4.30pm; ¥1). Drop in here for a wander through the writer's old rooms and for a stroll in his garden. Having seen the high, secretive outer walls of so many compounds, it makes a change to get a look at the spacious interior and numerous rooms inside a traditional house. Immediately

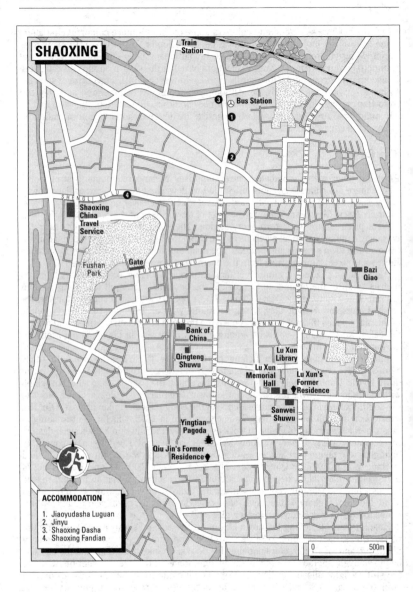

SHAOXING

Train
Station

❸ Bus Station
❶

❷

SHENGLI XI LU   ❹   SHENGLI ZHONG LU

Shaoxing
China
Travel
Service

Gate

Fushan
Park

FUSHANHEN LU

Bazi
Qiao

RENMIN XI LU   RENMIN ZHONG LU

Bank of
China

Qingteng
Shuwu

Lu Xun
Library

Lu Xun
Memorial
Hall

Lu Xun's
Former
Residence

Sanwei
Shuwu

Yingtian
Pagoda

Qiu Jin's Former
Residence

N

ACCOMMODATION

1. Jiaoyudasha Luguan
2. Jinyu
3. Shaoxing Dasha
4. Shaoxing Fandian

0   500m

across the road from the museum is the **Sanwei Shuwu** (Three Flavour Study; daily 8am–5pm; free), the small school where Lu Xun was taught as a young boy. There is just one room to see, and on a small desk to the right is a smooth stone and a bowl of water, which, in former times, were the only available tools for calligraphy students too poor to buy ink and paper. Visitors today are supposed to write their names in water on the stone for luck.

One further sight definitely worth seeking out in Shaoxing predates Lu Xun by several hundred years. Lying a couple of hundred metres to the north of the Lu Xun buildings, in the east of the town – in the heart of one of Shaoxing's most picturesque and traditional neighbourhoods – is the most famous of all the town's old bridges, **Bazi Qiao** (Character Eight Bridge). Having acquired its name because the bridge looks like the Chinese character for the number eight, this thirteenth-century piece of engineering is still very much in use. To find it, head a couple of blocks north from Renmin Lu, up Zhongxing Zhong Lu. The small alley called Baziqiao Zhi Jie, leading to the bridge, runs east off here.

Practicalities

Shaoxing's **train station** is in the far north of town – the rail line that comes through here is a spur running between Hangzhou (1hr from Shaoxing) and Ningbo (about 3hr away). Buying tickets from here is a relatively stress-free enterprise, and foreigners should queue at window #2.

Jiefang Lu begins one block to the east of the station and at its northern end is the long-distance **bus station**, about fifteen minutes' walk from the train station. From the train station, buses #1, #2, #3 and #4 all run past the bus station, while #2 and #4 continue on to the southern end of Jiefang Lu. For **bike rental** there's a shop right outside the *Jinyu Hotel* on Jiefang Lu.

The main **Bank of China** is on Renmin Xi Lu (daily 7.30am–5pm), while the very friendly and English-speaking staff of **Shaoxing CTS**, 360 Fushan Lu (☎0575/5155888), a few minutes west of the *Shaoxing Hotel,* can arrange tours of the surrounding area as well as book onward travel connections.

Shaoxing is unusually liberal concerning its **accommodation** policy for foreigners, and there appear to be no restrictions on where you can stay. There are a few options clustered round the northern end of Jiefang Lu. Immediately south of the bus station, the *Jiaoyundasha Luguan* (②) is far from salubrious, but does have very cheap doubles without bath. Across Jiefang Lu, opposite the bus station, is the *Shaoxing Dasha* (④), with reasonable air-conditioned doubles. Five minutes south of the bus station, the *Jinyu* (④–⑤) is easily the best of the bunch with semi-luxurious singles and doubles. Finally, the most upmarket hotel in town is the *Shaoxing Fandian* on Shengli Lu (☎0575/5155888; ⑥–⑦), a couple of hundred metres west of Jiefang Lu – take bus #3 from the train station. This is a huge and charming place in grounds so large that you can travel around them by boat.

You'll find a few **restaurants** around the northern half of Jiefang Lu, including a *KFC*. The restaurant in the *Jinyu Hotel* is quite good, though the menu is in Chinese only. Dried freshwater fish is a great speciality in Shaoxing, as is the **yellow rice wine** which they claim to have been making round here for over two thousand years. It's made from locally grown glutinous rice and (most importantly) water from Jian Hu, a substantial lake to the southwest. These days the wine is more commonly used for cooking than drinking. To try it, your best bet is to order *Shaoxing ji* (Shaoxing chicken – cooked in the wine) for dinner.

Around Shaoxing

Beyond Shaoxing, but still easily accessible from town, **Dong Hu** (East Lake; daily 7.30am–5.30pm; ¥5) is an attractive thirty-minute ride away at the terminus of the #1 bus route. Despite appearances, the lake is not a natural one. In the seventh century the Sui rulers quarried the hard green rock east of Shaoxing for building, and when the hill streams were dammed, the quarry became a lake, to which, for picturesque effect, a causeway was added during the Qing. The lake is highly photogenic, with the massive cliff edge of the quarry leaning over its whole length, the colours and contortions of the rock face reflected in the water. Once inside the site, you can rent a little boat (three people maximum; ¥24) to take you around the various caves, nooks and crannies in the cliff face. You can also be dropped on the opposite shore from where a flight of steps leads up to a path running to the cliff top, offering superb views over the surrounding paddy fields. The last bus back to Shaoxing leaves around 5.30pm.

There's also plenty of water transport around the area. You can take a **boat** back to Shaoxing instead of returning on the bus (1hr), or continue on to Yu Ling (below), threading through the network of waterways. This is a great trip (1hr 20min; ¥60 per boat) on long, slim, flat-bottomed boats with a curved awning where you can sit in the shade as you glide past the paddy fields, the peace broken only by the occasional goose or duck. In the stern, the boatman steers with a paddle and propels the boat with his bare feet on the loom of the long oar.

Yu Ling itself (Tomb of Yu; daily 7.30am–6pm; ¥6) is tucked into the hillside, a heaped-up chaos of temple buildings in a beautiful setting of trees, mossy rocks and mountains. Legendary founder of the Xia dynasty, around 2000 BC, Yu earned his title "Tamer of Floods" by tossing great rocks around and dealing with the underwater dragons who caused so many disasters. It took him eight years to control a great flood in the Lower Yangzi, after which he settled, and died, here. The first temple was probably built around the sixth century AD, while the actual tomb, which seems to pre-date the temple, may be Han dynasty. The temple today, most recently restored in the 1930s, contains a large painted figure of Yu and scores of inscribed tablets. Outside the temple, the tall, roughly shaped tombstone is sheltered by an elegant open pavilion. The vigorous worshipping you'll see inside the temple shows what a revered figure Yu still is in modern China. **Bus** #2 links Yu Ling to Shaoxing.

Another wonderfully rural excursion from Shaoxing is out to **Lanting**, the Orchid Pavilion (daily 8am–6pm; ¥4), 15km southwest of Shaoxing, where the fourth-century poet and calligrapher, Wang Xishi, held a party with forty friends and allegedly composed the *Orchid Pavilion Anthology*. Today Lanting is considered a shrine, a place of real resonance for all Chinese serious about calligraphy and poetry. There's also some classic Chinese countryside around here with paddy fields and green hills on all sides, while inside the Lanting site you'll find geese, bamboos, lakes and tea houses as well as small exhibition halls. Lanting is on the #3 bus route from Jiefang Lu (45 min), but you'll have to ask locals where to get off.

Ningbo and beyond

The rail spur from Hangzhou through Shaoxing ends at **NINGBO** (Calm Waves), an important coastal and ocean-going port in the northeast corner of the province. Despite being a port, the city is actually set some 20km inland, at the point where the Yuyao and Yong rivers meet to flow down to the ocean together. All around you'll see flat watery plain and paddy fields, and, along the heavily broken and indented shoreline, the signs of local salt-panning and fishing industries. Ningbo today would hardly be worth a special journey, except that it is a vital staging post for the trip to the nearby island of **Putuo Shan**. If you're passing through, however, there are one or two features of interest, in the relics of the treaty port, and also in the old quarter around the historic Tianyige Library.

Ningbo possesses a short but eventful history. Under the Tang in the seventh century, a complicated system of locks and canals was first installed, to make the shallow tidal rivers here navigable, and at the end of the twelfth century a breakwater was built to protect the port. From that time onwards, **trade** with Japan and Korea began to develop massively, with silk being shipped out in exchange for gold and,

NINGBO AND BEYOND

Ningbo	宁波	*níngbō*
Dongmen Kou	东门口	*dōngmén kǒu*
Jiangsha Bridge	江厦桥	*jiāngshà qiáo*
Tianfeng Pagoda	天封塔	*tiānfēng tǎ*
Tianyige Library	天一阁图书馆	*tiānyīgé túshūguǎn*
Xinjiang Bridge	新江桥	*xīnjiāng qiáo*
Yue Hu	月湖	*yuè hú*
Zhongshan Park	中山公园	*zhōngshān gōngyuán*

ACCOMMODATION

Dongya	东亚饭店	*dōngyà fàndiàn*
Huaqiao	华桥饭店	*huáqiáo fàndiàn*
Jinlong	金龙饭店	*jīnlóng fàndiàn*
Manao	玛瑙宾馆	*mǎnǎo bīnguǎn*
Tianyi	天一大酒店	*tiānyī dàjiǔdiàn*
Zhuangyuan Lou	状元楼宾馆	*zhuàngyuán lóu bīnguǎn*

BEYOND NINGBO

Ayuwang Si	阿育王寺	*ā yù wáng sì*
Baoguo Si	保国寺	*bǎoguó sì*
Tiantong Si	天童寺	*tiāntóng sì*

under the Ming, Ningbo became China's most important port. There was early European influence too. By the sixteenth century the Portuguese were using the harbour, building a warehouse downstream and helping to fight the pirates, while in the eighteenth century the East India Company began pressing to set up shop. Eventually, in 1843, after the Opium War, Ningbo became a **treaty port** with a British Consulate.

The town was swept briefly into the Taiping Uprising in 1861, but thereafter lost ground to Shanghai very rapidly. Only since 1949 has it begun to expand once more, and the river has been dredged, passenger terminals and cargo docks built, bridges completed and facilities generally expanded to handle the output of the local food-processing and canning industries. However, despite the fact that Ningbo today is considered one of the boom areas of China, it still wears a rather dilapidated, provincial air.

The City

Downtown Ningbo is divided in three by the confluence of its two rivers. Connecting the western part of town, the area of the original walled city, with the northern part, the former foreign concession, is the **Xinjiang Bridge** (bus #1 from the train station), and this is the best place to start soaking up a bit of atmosphere. Just south of the bridge, on its west side, is an interesting dried fish market, while on the northern bank, you'll find fishing boats, sailors and all the trappings of a busy harbour. Also on this side, east of the bridge, a few of the elaborate porticos and verandahs of the old **treaty port** still survive, flanked by impromptu waterside fish markets.

South of the Xinjiang Bridge is the big junction of **Dongmen Kou**, where the main commercial street, **Zhongshan Lu**, cuts across from east to west. The eastern section, across the **Jiangsha Bridge**, is a developing upmarket shopping area, but it's the west-

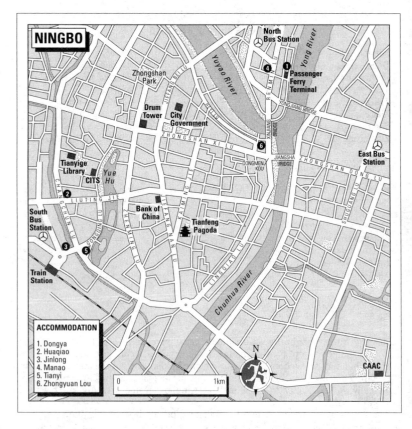

ern stretch that's the heart of the modern city, a broad avenue lined with modern buildings housing Ningbo's big department stores. About 1km west of Dongmen Kou, Zhenming Lu, a street full of half-timbered houses and arched trees leads north past the **Drum Tower** to **Zhongshan Park**, a small open space which teems with martial arts enthusiasts in the early mornings.

South, in the opposite direction off Zhongshan Lu, it's worth taking a walk down Kaiming Jie, which is crowded with little shops and stalls, and has some of the better places to eat local seafood. About 1km down here, near the junction with Jiefang Lu, you'll find the fourteenth-century **Tianfeng Pagoda**, which you can climb for views.

The most interesting and oldest part of town, however, is an area to the southwest around **Yue Hu** (Moon Lake); take bus #7 from just south of the Xinjiang Bridge, or it's twenty minutes' walk east of the train station. Little more than a large version of a village pond, the lake has an enclosed area for swimming and the usual crowd of people doing their washing on the stone steps. But between the walkway along the western shore and the main north–south road, Changchun Lu, to the west, is a maze of narrow alleys leading to **Tianyige Library** (daily 8am–5pm; ¥3). Built in 1516 and said to be the oldest surviving library building in China, it was founded by Ming official Fan Qin, whose collection went back to the eleventh century and included woodblock and handwritten copies of the Confucian classics, rare local histories and lists of the candidates successful in imperial examinations. Nowadays you can visit the library's garden and outhouses, some of which contain small displays of old books and tablets. It's quite a charming place and the buildings, their bamboo groves, pool and rockery still preserve an atmosphere of seclusion, contemplation and study.

Practicalities

Ningbo's **train station** is in the southwest of the city. Minibuses and bus #1 run from here through the town centre, north over Xinjiang Bridge and close to the North bus station and the ferry terminal. Bus #10 also connects the station to the centre of the city, via the eastern part of town. The **South bus station**, for services to Wenzhou, is just next to the train station, while the **North bus station** a few blocks north of the Xinjiang Bridge, serves Shaoxing, and the **East bus station** at the corner of Shuguang Lu and Ningbo Lu, east across the river, operates suburban services to the temples and pagodas outside town.

The **ferry terminal**, for boats to and from Putuo Shan and Shanghai, is in the northern part of town, north of the Xinjiang Bridge, on Waima Lu (frequent minibuses and bus #1 to and from the train station via the town centre). If approaching by bus, get off just north of Xinjiang Bridge, just after passing beneath an overpass, then walk for a couple of minutes northeast. The main **ticket office** here (daily 6.30am–12.15pm & 1–6pm) sells tickets for the daily departures to Putuo Shan and Shanghai, and for some irregular services to Suzhou. For both principal destinations there are fast, comfortable boats, usually in the morning, and slow, crowded boats in the afternoon or evening. The fast, early-morning trips involve a sixty-minute bus journey to Zhenhai Dock, where you board the boat. Slow boats depart from just behind the ticket office. The exact schedule changes seasonally (for more details on Putuo Shan boats, see p.422).

Most of the city's facilities are in the town centre right at the Dongmen Kou junction, including the main **post office** and a branch of the **Bank of China**. The main *Bank of China* office (Mon–Fri 7.30–11am & 1–4.15pm) is on Jiefang Lu, just south of Liuting Lu. For **visa extensions**, enquire at the City Government headquarters east off Jiefang Bei Lu. If you need a **travel service** to help with tickets, enquire at any upmarket hotel or *CITS* which is located on a small lane, Yanyue Lu (Mon–Sat 8am–4.30pm; ☎0574/7312850), between Yue Hu and the Tianyige Library.

Food in Ningbo is dominated by **fish** and fresh **seafood**, and Kaiming Jie is one of the best places to look, as are the streets south of the ferry terminal. The restaurant in the *Jinlong Hotel* serves stupendous crab. For fast food, there's a *KFC* on Zhongshan Lu, east of the Jiangsha Bridge.

Accommodation

There are two **hotel** areas to consider in Ningbo, one near the train station, and one near the ferry terminal. Take your pick according to which is most convenient.

Dongya (*East Asia Hotel*), Zhongma Lu (☎0574/7356224, fax 7353529). Right near the ferry terminal in a characterful old part of town, this is a pleasant place to stay, though the staff try to surcharge foreigners. Friendly persuasion can get round this. From the train station, take bus #1 and get off at the second stop (*lunchuan matou*) after Xinjiang Bridge. Walk a little farther north, and take the first alley on the right (east). ⑤.

Huaqiao, Liuting Jie (☎0574/7293175, fax 7294790). Within walking distance of the station, on the junction of Changchun Lu, and just a few minutes due north of the *Tianyi*. The hotel has unjustified pretensions to being the smartest place in town, and the cheaper rooms are only sometimes available. ⑤–⑧.

Jinlong (*Golden Dragon*), Gongqing Lu (☎0574/7318888 ext 7114, fax 7312288). An excellent place to stay, right opposite the train station. ⑦.

Manao, Renmin Lu (☎0574/7353330). Right across the road from the #1 bus stop at *lunchuan matou*, offering smart rooms and a handy location for the ferry terminal. ⑥.

Tianyi, Gongqing Lu (☎0574/7316595 ext 40). Situated on the corner with Changchun Lu, about five minutes' walk from the train station – take the main road leading northeast out of the station square and across a canal. If you're in a group, you might be able to talk yourselves into the five-bed dorms. There are also doubles and triples available and there's a boat ticketing office in the lobby. Dorms ②, rooms ⑤.

Zhuangyuan Lou, Heyi Lu (☎0574/7368991). Central location, just north of Zhongshan Lu and very near Dongmen Kou. You can recognize it from the lanterns hanging outside. Reasonable doubles with air-conditioning and private bath. ⑤.

Beyond Ningbo

There are numerous temples and pagodas to be visited in the countryside around Ningbo. Perhaps the most interesting is **Baoguo Si**, some 15km northwest of town. Bus #332 runs evey thirty minutes from just north of Xinjiang Bridge, out into a landscape of endless green paddy fields broken only occasionally by villages with their obligatory duckponds. After about forty minutes you reach the temple, nestling into a hill which rises from emerald green at its base to a deep green, darkly forested summit. The temple itself is one of the oldest wooden buildings in China, built in 1013 and restored under the Qing, but left bare so that its structure can be clearly seen. The entire hall is constructed without nails, relying on its interlocking structure to stay upright. Beyond, continue up the steps to a pavilion – the view of the temple is half-concealed by trees from here, but there's a fine vista of the flat lands beyond the ridge, with ribbons of water threading through the paddies into the distance.

Southeast of the city are a couple more sites which can be combined into a single excursion, either using public transport from the East bus station, or with a car rented from a travel service. **Ayuwang Si**, the temple of King Asoka, is about 20km east of town, on the slopes of Tai Ba Shan. Built in the fifth century, it's notable for its miniature stupa which allegedly contains a bone of Sakyamuni. The architecture is rightly renowned too – a spectacular blend of orange tile and dark red wood against the green of the hill, with cool grey steps and a refreshingly shadowy interior. Bus #82 runs out here from near the ferry terminal.

A few kilometres farther on from Ayuwang Si, the Children of Heaven Temple – **Tiantong Si** – is a splendid collection of buildings in the forest. Founded in the third century AD, this is one of the largest monasteries in China, with 963 halls and many important Buddhist works of art. At the centre of it all there's a very large, very fat Buddha with an enormous smile. You may also see a crowd of Japanese visitors – the Japanese monk Dogen came here to study in 1223 and on his return home founded the Sotoshi sect which now has some eight million adherents in Japan.

Putuo Shan

Lurking a few hours by boat north of Ningbo and south of Shanghai, the tiny island of **Putuo Shan** is one of the four Chinese mountains sacred to Buddhism, and undoubtedly one of the most charming places in the whole of eastern China. Quiet and serene, with no cars, no department stores, only endless vistas of blue sea, sandy beaches and green hills dotted with ancient monasteries, it's an ideal place to escape and to recuperate from the traffic and dirt of the big cities. Divided by a narrow channel from the much larger Zhoushan Island, and just twelve square kilometres in area, rising at one end to a peak of 300m, the whole island is effectively a giant park with endless opportunities for walking. Although seasonal bursts of local tourists at times threaten the serenity (chiefly at weekends and in summer), there is certainly scope to avoid them.

Putuo Shan – the centre of the **cult of Guanyin**, Goddess of Mercy – has been attracting Buddhist pilgrims from all over northeast Asia for at least a thousand years, and there are many legends to account for the island's status. According to one, the goddess attained enlightenment here; another tells how a Japanese monk travelling home with an image of the goddess took shelter from a storm here and was so enchanted by the island's beauty that he stayed, building a shrine on the spot. Over the years, more than a hundred monasteries and shrines were built, with magnificent halls and gardens to match. At one time there were four thousand monks squeezed onto the island, and even as late as 1949 the Buddhist community numbered around two thousand. Until that date indeed, secular structures were not permitted on the island, and nobody lived here who was not a monk.

Although there was a great deal of destruction on Putuo Shan during the Cultural Revolution, many treasures survived – some are now in the Zhejiang Provincial Museum in Hangzhou, others remain in situ. Restoration continues steadily, and from only 29 monks in the late 1960s there are now several hundred. Three principal monasteries survive – **Puji** the oldest and most central, **Fayu** on the southern slopes and **Huiji** at the summit. There are also large numbers of lesser temples and monuments. You'll notice when touring Putuo Shan that the crowds of Chinese tourists carry identical yellow cotton bags which are stamped with symbols of Guanyin at each temple, sometimes in exchange for donations. With the old superstitions on the rise again, many people come specifically to ask the goddess for favours, often to do with producing children or grandchildren.

PUTUO SHAN

Putuo Shan	普陀山	*pǔtuóshān*
Chaoyang Dong	潮阳洞	*cháoyáng dòng*
Chaoyin Dong	潮音洞	*cháoyīn dòng*
Dasheng An	大乘庵	*dàshèng ān*
Duobao Pagoda	多宝塔	*duōbǎo tǎ*
Fanyin Dong	梵音洞	*fányīn dòng*
Fayu Si	法雨寺	*fǎyǔ sì*
Foding Shan	佛顶山	*fódǐng shān*
Huiji Si	慧济寺	*huìjì sì*
Puji Si	普济寺	*pǔjì sì*

ACCOMMODATION

Haijun Zhaodaisuo	海军招待所	*hǎijūn zhāodàisuǒ*
Putuo Shan Zhuang	普陀山庄宾馆	*pǔtuóshānzhuāng bīnguǎn*
Ronglai Yuan	融来院	*rónglái yuàn*
Sanshengtang	三圣堂饭店	*sānshèngtáng fàndiàn*
Xilai Xiao Zhuang	息来小庄宾馆	*xīlái xiǎozhuāng bīnguǎn*
Xilai Yuan	息来院饭店	*xīláiyuàn fàndiàn*
Xilin	锡麟饭店	*xīlín fàndiàn*

BOATS TO AND FROM PUTUO SHAN

The only way in or out of Putuo Shan is by **boat**. Several ferries connect the island with **Ningbo** every day (4–5hr), and there is one boat from **Shanghai** every other day (11hr). Second class on the overnight Shanghai boat gives a tolerably comfortable three- or four-bed cabin with a washbasin and costs ¥120. At weekends and holidays there are also fast catamarans to and from Shanghai, run by the *Shanghai Free Flying Transport and Yacht Company*, that take just four hours, two hours of which are spent in a bus, and cost around ¥200 in the cheapest seats. These tickets can be bought from a special window downstairs in the boat ticket office at Jinling Dong Lu in Shanghai (see p.329). For tickets for departures from Putuo Shan, go to the jetty office (daily 8–11.30am & 2–4pm).

You can also travel to or from Putuo Shan via **Shenjiamen**, on the neighbouring island of Zhoushan, linked by at least seven boats per day (30min). Shenjiamen is in itself an interesting place to spend a few hours, and from here you can get frequent bus connections to Ningbo crossing on the vehicle ferry. Alternatively, thirty minutes from Shenjiamen by bus is the port of **Dinghai**, from where overnight ferries connect with Shanghai when there is no direct boat from Putuo Shan.

Around the island

The island is long and thin, with the ferry arrival point in the south, and the main "town" – a tiny collection of hotels, shops and restaurants – about 1km to the north. The town comprises a recognizable central square around three ponds, dotted with trees and faced to the north by the island's principal temple, Puji Si. There are only a few roads, travelled by a handful of minibuses which connect the port with Puji Si and other sights farther north.

All of the three main temples on the island are in extremely good condition, recently renovated, with warm yellow-ochre walls offsetting the deep green of the mature trees in their forecourts. This is particularly true of **Puji Si** (daily 7.30am–6pm; ¥4) right in the centre of the island, built in 1080 and enlarged by successive dynasties. It stands among magnificent camphor trees with a statue bridge and an elegantly tall pagoda with an enormous iron bell.

South of here, the **Duobao Pagoda**, just to the east of the square ponds, was built in 1334 and is five storeys tall with Buddhist inscriptions on all four sides. Twenty minutes' walk farther south down on the southeastern corner of the island, the cave **Chaoyin Dong** is remarkable for the din of its crashing waves, thought to resemble the call of Buddha (and hence a popular spot for monks to commit suicide in earlier days).

The two temples in the northern half of the island make a pleasant half-day outing from the minibus stop just southeast of the central square. **Huiji Si** stands near the top of **Foding Shan**, and the summit provides some spectacular views of the sea and the surrounding islands. The temple itself, although not as old as Puji – mainly built during the nineteenth century – occupies a beautiful site just to the northwest of the summit surrounded by green tea plantations. Its halls stand in a flattened area between hoary trees and bamboo groves, with the greens, reds, blues and gold of their enamelled tiles gleaming magnificently in the sunshine. There's also a vegetarian restaurant here.

You can then walk down along a marked path leading south towards the third major temple, Fayu Si – the whole walk takes about an hour. Shortly after setting off, you'll see a secondary track branching away to the left towards the **Ancient Buddha Cave**, a delightfully secluded spot by a sandy beach on the northeastern coast of the island; give yourself a couple of hours to get there and back, though. Back on the main path, the steep steps bring you to the **Xiangyun Pavilion** where you can rest and drink tea with the friendly monks.

Thirty minutes farther on you'll reach the **Fayu Si** (daily 7.30am–5.30pm; ¥4), another superb collection of halls amid huge green trees, built up in levels against the slope

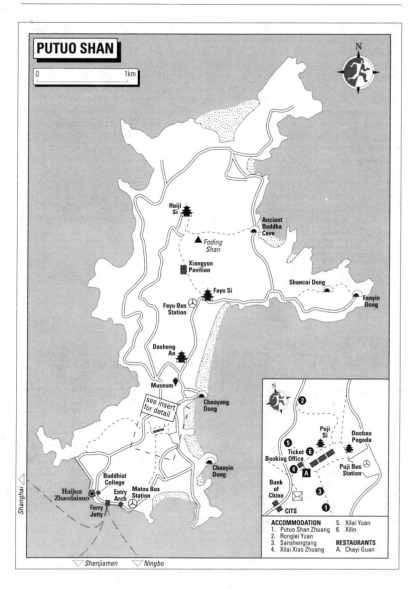

with the mountain behind and the sea just in front. As with all the temples, it's a delightful place to sit in peaceful contemplation. The **Daxiong Hall** has just been brilliantly restored, and the **Dayuan Hall** has a unique beamless arched roof and a dome, around the inside of which squirm nine carved wooden dragons. This hall is said to have originally stood in Nanjing, being moved here by Emperor Kangxi in 1689. Its great statue of **Guanyin**, flanked by monks and nuns, is the focal point of the goddess's birthday celebrations in early April, when thousands of pilgrims and sightseers crowd on to the island for chanting and ceremonies which last all evening. Bus services from directly outside the temple link it to Puji and to the ferry jetty. There are also occasional minibuses heading out along the promontory immediately east of Fayu Si to **Fanyin Dong**, a cave in the rocky cliff with a small shrine actually straddling a ravine. From here, you can follow a path up through beautiful scenery in a northwesterly direction to another cave, the **Shancai Dong**. Walking around anywhere on the promontory is a pleasure given the absence of crowds and the difficulty of getting seriously lost.

Along the east coast of the island, the road between Fayu Si and Puji Si makes another delightful walk, offering views over golden sandy beaches on one side, and green hills on the other, dotted by occasional temples. One kilometre south of Fayu Si is the **Dasheng An** (daily 8am–5.30pm; ¥1), a nunnery notable for the reclining Buddha downstairs in the main hall, and the thousands of tiny seated Buddhas upstairs. Just south of here, the rather forlorn **museum** offers a little collection of cultural artefacts from the island's history. A couple of minutes farther on, on the small headland between two long beaches, is **Chaoyang Dong**. Just inside this little cave there's a tea house and a seating area overlooking the sea, while from the top of headland itself you'll get great views.

Practicalities

All visitors arrive at the **ferry jetty** in the far south of the island and are required to pay a ¥20 fee to enter the island. Most hotels are located in the town at the centre of the island and you can get here either by following the road heading west or the one heading east from the jetty (20min). The westerly road is slightly shorter and takes you past most of the modern buildings and town facilities on the island, including the **Bank of China** (daily 7.30–11am & 1–4.15pm) and **CITS** directly opposite. A little farther north, up a small lane to the left just before the *Xilei Xiaozhuang Hotel* is the **post office**, while in the central square, at the northwestern corner, you'll find a **ticket booking office** where you can book domestic flights from Ningbo or Shanghai. The alternative eastern route from the jetty takes you through a ceremonial arch symbolizing the entrance to the mountain and then on to a path that cuts away to the left a few minutes later. For those with heavy luggage, there's a small bus station in this direction, a couple of minutes after the arch, with **minibuses** running to Puji Si every few minutes. Buses also run from here to Fayu Si and Foding Shan.

Eating and drinking is not likely to be the highlight of your trip to Putuo Shan, but there are a few options, mostly in the hotels. The lane running northeast away from Puji Si also has a string of rather dingy-looking eating houses which specialize in **seafood**, but also have standard dishes and noodles. For a more upmarket eating experience in very pleasant surroundings, try the *Chayi Guan*, in the central square, southwest from Puji Si. As well as excellent tea here, you can get *dian xin* (Shanghainese *dim sum*) for breakfast or lunch, and full meals in the evening.

Accommodation

There are several delightful **hotels** on Putuo Shan, including a number of converted monasteries, but be warned that in the peak summer months, and especially during the weekend stampede out of Shanghai, you may face a trek around town before you find an empty room. Another option is to stay in a private house – although this is standard practice for Chinese tourists on Putuo Shan, it's technically illegal for foreigners, so use your discretion.

Haijun Zhaodaisuo (☎0580/6091204). This is the nearest place to the jetty, but by no means the nicest hotel around. However, if you're stuck there are a lot of beds here and it's fairly cheap and set in pleasant gardens. Walk along the west route to town from the jetty and you'll pass it after about five minutes, on the left, just as the main road branches north. There's no English sign, just go in through the big gate on the road. ⑤–⑥.

Putuo Shan Zhuang (☎0580/6091666, fax 6091667). A beautiful and extremely comfortable option just south of the *Sanshengtang*; probably the best on the island. ⑦.

Ronglei Yuan (☎0580/6091262). A great place to stay – you feel like you are walking into an ancient monastery overhung by giant trees. Walk past Puji Si to its eastern end, through an arch, then turn left (north) up the first alley. The alley first bends slightly to the right, then seriously to the left (the hotel is actually directly behind Puji Si). This is the only hotel on the island that rents out individual beds in dorms. Dorms ②, rooms ⑥.

Sanshengtang (☎0580/6091277). On the eastern route from the jetty to town, this is just a couple of minutes due south of the centre. Quite an attractive place, in temple-style, but they have an annoying habit of attempting to surcharge foreigners by fifty percent. ⑤–⑥.

Xilai Xiao Zhuang (☎0580/6091644 ext 55, fax 6091023). A very comfortable hotel, though not a terribly attractive building. You'll pass it at the northern end of the west route just before reaching the centre of town. ⑦.

Xilai Yuan (☎0580/6091119 ext 3568). One of a number of former monasteries converted into hotels, this is well located at the end of a tiny lane immediately west of Puji Si. There are some good cheap rooms here too (two-bed and four-bed). ④–⑥.

Xilin (☎0580/6091303). A great location right on the central square, to the west of Puji Si, with an entrance that makes it look like a temple. Foreigners are usually surcharged here, though. ⑥.

Wenzhou

Tucked away on the southeastern coast of Zhejiang Province, away from any rail link and with no important historical associations, **WENZHOU** appears at first glance to be an obscure provincial backwater. However, its location on the sea is crucial. The inhabitants of southern Zhejiang, along with Fujian to the south – hemmed in on the coast by the mountainous interior – have for centuries looked out to the sea, rather than to the mainland, for their livelihood. Shipping, fishing and trading have been the mainstay of

WENZHOU		
Wenzhou	温洲	*wēnzhōu*
Christian Church	基督教堂	*jīdūjiàotáng*
Jiangxin Park	江心孤屿	*jiāngxīn gūyǔ*
North Yandang Mountain	北雁荡山	*běiyàndàng shān*
Ou River	瓯江	*ōujiāng*
ACCOMMODATION		
Dong'ou	东瓯大厦	*dōngōu dàshà*
Guoji Haiyuan Julebu	国际海员俱乐部	*guójìhǎiyuán jùlèbù*
Huaqiao	华侨饭店	*huáqiáo fàndiàn*
Hubin	湖宾饭店	*húbīn fàndiàn*
Jiaoyu Guesthouse	教育招待所	*jiàoyù zhāodàisuǒ*
Mochi	墨池饭店	*mòchí fàndiàn*
Wenzhou	温洲大酒店	*wēnzhōu dàjiǔdiàn*
Xi'ou	西瓯饭店	*xīōu fàndiàn*
RESTAURANTS		
Awailou	阿外楼餐馆	*āwàilóu cānguǎn*
Wenzhou	温洲酒家	*wēnzhōu jiǔjiā*

the economy, while politically the tendency has been to ignore the rest of China altogether, a tendency that can still be seen today both in the notoriously eccentric local dialect and in the free-market economy gone wild. Smuggling and the pirating of brand-named products have always been popular sidelines down here, and now, with the city being granted the status of Special Economic Zone, local entrepreneurial skills have made this a boom town like no other in China – flights in and out of the city are booked solid for weeks in advance.

Quite apart from the difficulty of getting here, the effect of this economic maelstrom on **tourism** is questionable. Although Wenzhou has plenty of hotels, its attractions are mainly confined to **Jiangxin Park** in the middle of the Ou River, a moderately interesting waterfront, and a surprisingly well-preserved old city, dating to the days when the city was a prosperous **foreign treaty port**, from the 1870s onwards.

The old town centre corresponds roughly to the area facing on to the broad **Ou River** to the north, bounded by the two important shopping streets, Xinhe Lu and Jiefang Lu, to the west and east respectively. To the south, the area is bordered approximately by Renmin Lu, although you'll see that the bulldozers and architects of the modern city are encroaching steadily over this line. At the time of writing, the city as

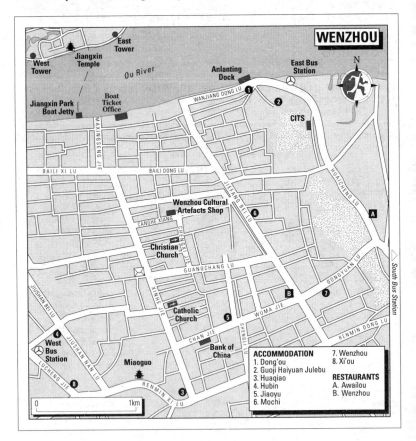

WENZHOU

ACCOMMODATION
1. Dong'ou
2. Guoji Haiyuan Julebu
3. Huaqiao
4. Hubin
5. Jiaoyu
6. Mochi
7. Wenzhou
8. Xi'ou

RESTAURANTS
A. Awailou
B. Wenzhou

far north as the main shopping street, the pedestrianized **Wuma Jie**, was being virtually rebuilt. Farther towards the river, though, life is still much as it has always been, with some unexpected old stone facades above the shop entrances.

There are also a few specific sights worth searching out. Right in the middle of the old town area, on Canghe Xiang, is the **Wenzhou Cultural Artefacts Shop**, where all kinds of art-related objects (including brushes, paints, scrolls and some antiques) are on sale in an interesting old building. Just south of here, suddenly looming up on Chengxi Jie, is an incongruous **Christian Church**, a gothic building of black brick dating back to 1778, originally built by a British missionary. Many residents of the surrounding streets here are fervent Christians and if you enquire they'll gladly show you into their church, though it's nothing special inside. A few minutes south, on Zhouzhaisi Xiang running east from Xinhe Jie, is the rather larger but less attractive **Catholic Church**, dating to 1888 during the treaty port era.

One rather more typically Chinese sight is the **Miaoguo**, on Renmin Xi Lu, on the southern side of Songtai Hill. Originally constructed in the Tang dynasty, over a thousand years ago, this temple has been rebuilt many times, most recently in 1984.

The major tourist sight of Wenzhou, however, is **Jiangxin Park**, an island located a few minutes offshore in the Ou River to the north of town. The island – where no cars are allowed – contains a number of pavilions, towers and gardens, and is well worth two or three hours for a stroll or a picnic, among the huge old trees. The most notable features of the island's skyline are its two **towers**; of these the one to the east is old and decrepit, but the western one has been fully restored. To reach the island, go to the jetty at the northern end of Maxingseng Jie from where boats run every few minutes (daily 8am–4pm; ¥5 combined boat ride and island entrance fee). Returning from the island, you pay another ¥3 when you disembark townside.

Outside Wenzhou, there is some superb mountain scenery, with the **North Yandang Mountain**, an area of soaring cliffs and stunning verdant slopes, lying some 80km to the northeast of town, in Leqing County. Although very few Western tourists have been to this area, it is easily accessible by bus from Wenzhou's West bus station and accommodation is available here.

Practicalities

Given the absence of a rail link, and the difficulty of obtaining seats on flights, Wenzhou is overrun by **long-distance bus connections**. There are three major bus stations – the West, East and South stations, all of which lie within thirty minutes' walk of the old town centre. Although in theory Shanghai buses use the West station, Ningbo buses the East station (actually located in the north of town) and Fuzhou buses the South Station, in practice there is such hot competition between operators that when **buying tickets**, you might as well just go to the nearest station. You'll find ticket kiosks in and outside the stations, with people trying to grab your custom. Buses seem to run to almost everywhere in China including such far-flung places as Beijing and Shenzhen (both 48hr).

The **airport** is 25km away to the east of town and there's a *CAAC* bus which drops passengers at the main **booking office** remotely located in the southeast of town on Minhang Lu (8am–4pm ☎0577/8333197). Bus #5 runs from here along Renmin Lu, the southern perimeter of the central area, where a number of hotels are located.

The other possibility is to arrive by **ferry** from Shanghai, in which case you'll find yourself at Anlanting dock in the northeastern part of town, on the Ou River. Bus #4 (running west along Wangjiang Dong Lu) takes you south along Jiefang Lu. The ferry **ticket office** is located on a small alley just to the east off the northern end of Maxingseng Jie (daily 8–11.30am & 1.30–4.30pm). There are departures every other day and tickets range from ¥245 (special class) through ¥176 (first class) to ¥45, though be warned that this is no luxury cruise – even first class is very functional and the lower classes can be hellish. Despite the proud ferry-route map on the wall of the office, all boat routes other than that to Shanghai are now defunct.

Wenzhou's **Bank of China** is on Chan Jie (Mon–Fri 8–11.45am &1.30–4.45pm) while the main **post office** (daily 8am–6pm) is off Xinhe Jie.

Away from the hotels, there are a number of **restaurants** worth trying out and their specialities are, unsurprisingly, **seafood** dishes. One of the liveliest and most popular places is the *Wenzhou Restaurant* at the junction of Wuma Jie and Jiefang Lu. Low-budget dishes are served on the first floor; go upstairs for smarter service. The *Awailou Restaurant* on Huaicheng Lu in the east of town is another good place with some interesting seafood items on the menu.

Accommodation

There's plenty of accommodation in Wenzhou, some of it surprisingly cheap, though you may have some trekking to do as it is fairly widely scattered round the town.

Dong'ou, Wangjiang Lu (☎0577/8227901). This is the tall building right on the waterfront opposite the docking point for the Shanghai ferries. Slightly shabby singles and doubles. ⑤.

Guoji Haiyuan Julebu (*International Sailors' Club*; ☎0577/8226906). Up on a hill overlooking the river; take the small alley running south from the east side of the *Dong'ou Hotel* and follow it up and around. Despite the name, it's not only for sailors and has great views, although it's a slightly faded, forlorn place to stay, and not cheap. ⑥.

Huaqiao (*Overseas Hotel*), Xinhe Jie (☎0577/8222406, fax 8229656). Located at the southern end of Xinhe Jie, near Renmin Xi Lu, in a busy commercial area, this is one of Wenzhou's best-established and biggest hotels. ⑥.

Hubin, Youyongqiao Lu (☎0577/8227961, fax 8210600). A couple of minutes' walk east from the West bus station. Comfortable and upmarket. ⑦.

Jiaoyu Guesthouse, Chan Jie (☎0577/8227890). Excellently situated in the centre of town, just west of Wuma Jie. Good-value rooms, doubles and triples, all with 24-hour hot water and air-conditioning. ③–④.

Mochi, Jiefang Lu (☎0577/8292929 ext 3188). In the heart of the old town, a couple of blocks north of Guangchang Lu, this place has a grotty lobby, but the rooms are tolerable, and very cheap. ②.

Wenzhou, Gongyuan Lu (☎0577/8235991, fax 82221333). To the east of Jiefang Lu – one of the bigger, smarter hotels, with standard facilities. ⑥.

Xi'ou, Lucheng Lu (☎0577/8247011). A few minutes' walk south from the West bus station, with fairly plain singles and doubles. ⑥.

travel details

Trains

Hangzhou to: Beijing (daily; 22hr); Guangzhou (daily; 33hr); Ningbo (6 daily; 4hr); Nanchang (daily; 13hr); Nanjing (3 daily; 7hr); Shanghai (8 daily; 3hr); Shaoxing (6 daily; 1hr 30min); Suzhou (daily; 4hr); Wuxi (daily; 5hr).

Lianyungang to: Nanjing (daily; 13 hr); Shanghai (daily; 17hr); Xuzhou (7 daily; 6hr).

Nanjing to: Beijing (5 daily; 16hr); Changzhou (10 daily; 3hr); Chengdu (daily; 45hr); Fuzhou (daily; 26hr); Hangzhou (3 daily; 7hr); Lianyungang (daily; 13 hr); Suzhou (10 daily; 4hr); Shanghai (10 daily; 5hr); Wuhu (daily; 4hr); Wuxi (10 daily; 3hr); Xi'an

(daily; 20hr); Xuzhou (6 daily; 5hr); Zhenjiang (10 daily; 1hr).

Ningbo to: Hangzhou (6 daily; 4hr); Shanghai (2 daily; 7hr); Shaoxing (6 daily; 3hr).

Shaoxing to: Hangzhou (6 daily; 1hr 30min); Ningbo (6 daily; 3hr); Shanghai (2 daily; 4hr).

Suzhou to: Changzhou (10 daily; 2hr); Hangzhou (daily; 4hr); Nanjing (10 daily; 4hr); Shanghai (10 daily; 1hr); Wuxi (10 daily; 1hr); Zhenjiang (10 daily; 4hr).

Wuxi to: Changzhou (10 daily; 1hr); Hangzhou (daily; 5hr); Nanjing (10 daily; 3hr); Shanghai (10 daily; 2hr); Suzhou (10 daily; 1hr); Zhenjiang (10 daily; 2hr).

Xuzhou to: Beijing (6 daily; 11hr); Shanghai (5 daily; 10hr); Qufu (daily; 5hr); Ji'nan (5 daily; 7hr); Kaifeng (4 daily; 5hr); Lianyungang (7 daily; 6hr); Nanjing (6 daily; 5hr); Zhengzhou (12 daily; 6hr).

Zhenjiang to: Changzhou (10 daily; 1hr 30min); Nanjing (10 daily; 1hr); Shanghai (10 daily; 4hr); Suzhou (10 daily; 4hr); Wuxi (10 daily; 2hr).

Buses

Vast numbers of bus companies operate throughout the Jiangsu–Zhejiang region and beyond, so it is not possible to give an exact indication of bus frequencies.

Hangzhou to: Huang Shan (5hr); Lianyungang (15hr); Nanjing (6hr); Ningbo (4hr); Shanghai (3hr); Shaoxing (1hr); Suzhou (4hr); Wenzhou (12hr); Wuxi (5hr); Yangzhou (7hr).

Huai'an to: Lianyungang (3hr); Nanjing (5hr); Yangzhou (5hr); Zhenjiang (6hr).

Lianyungang to: Hangzhou (15hr); Huai'an (3hr); Nanjing (8hr); Qingdao (8hr); Shanghai (14hr); Zhenjiang (9hr).

Nanjing (*Hanfu Jie station*) to: Hangzhou (6hr); Huai'an (5hr); Huang Shan (5hr); Lianyungang (8hr); Ningbo (10hr); Qingdao (18hr); Wuhan (24hr); Yangzhou (3hr); Yixing (5hr).

(*Zhongyangmen station*) to: Beijing (40hr); Shanghai (7hr); Suzhou (5hr); Wenzhou (17hr); Wuxi (4hr); Zhenjiang (1hr).

Ningbo (*South station*) to: Wenzhou (9hr).

(*North station*) to: Hangzhou (4hr); Nanjing (10hr); Shaoxing (3hr).

Shaoxing to: Hangzhou (1hr); Ningbo (3hr).

Suzhou (*Nanmen station*) to: Dingshan (3hr); Hangzhou (4hr); Nanjing (5hr); Shanghai (2hr); Wuxi (1hr); Yangzhou (5hr); Yixing (3hr); Wenzhou (12hr).

Wenzhou to: Fuzhou (10hr); Guangzhou (42hr); Hangzhou (12hr); Nanjing (17hr); Ningbo (9hr); Shanghai (15hr); Suzhou (12hr); Wuxi (16hr); Xiamen (17hr).

Wuxi (*South station*) to: Hangzhou (5hr); Suzhou (1hr); Yixing (2hr).

(*North station*) to: Nanjing (4hr); Shanghai (2hr); Wenzhou (16hr); Yangzhou (4hr).

Yangzhou (*East station*) to: Hangzhou (7hr); Huai'an (5hr); Shanghai (6hr); Suzhou (5hr); Wuxi (4hr). (*West station*) to: Nanjing (3hr); Zhenjiang (1hr 30min).

Yixing to: Nanjing (5hr); Wuxi (2hr); Zhenjiang (4hr).

Zhenjiang to: Huai'an (6hr); Lianyungang (9hr); Nanjing (1hr); Yangzhou (1hr 30min); Yixing (4hr).

Ferries

Hangzhou to: Suzhou (daily; 14hr); Wuxi (daily, 15hr).

Nanjing to: Chongqing (3 daily; 5 days); Shanghai (7 daily; 14hr); Wuhan (7 daily; 2 days).

Putuo Shan to: Ningbo (4 daily; 4hr); Shanghai (every other day;10hr; plus a catamaran at weekends; 4hr).

Ningbo to: Putuo Shan (4 daily; 4hr); Shanghai (4 daily; 9hr).

Suzhou to: Hangzhou (daily;14hr).

Wenzhou to: Shanghai (every other day; 22hr).

Wuxi to: Hangzhou (daily; 15hr).

Planes

Hangzhou to: Beijing (4 daily, 2hr); Fuzhou (daily; 1hr 15min); Guangzhou (4–6 daily; 2hr); Guilin (3 weekly; 2hr); Nanjing (3 weekly; 50min); Shanghai (daily; 25min); Shenzhen (daily; 2hr); Wenzhou (2 daily; 1hr); Xiamen (2 daily; 1hr 20min); Xi'an (4 weekly; 2hr 20min).

Lianyungang to: Beijing (2 weekly; 1hr 35min); Guangzhou (4 weekly; 2hr 20min); Nanjing (3 weekly; 1hr).

Nanjing to: Beijing (7 daily; 1hr 50min); Chengdu (daily; 2hr 25min); Fuzhou (daily; 1hr 50min); Guangzhou (4 daily; 1hr 55min); Guilin (2 weekly; 2hr); Hangzhou (3 weekly; 50min); Lianyungang (3 weekly; 1hr); Ningbo (3 weekly; 1hr); Shanghai (daily; 45min); Shenzhen (daily; 2hr 15min); Wenzhou (daily; 1hr 20min); Xiamen (daily; 1hr 45min); Xi'an (5 weekly; 2hr 10min).

Ningbo to: Beijing (2 daily; 2hr); Guangzhou (daily; 2hr); Nanjing (3 weekly; 1hr); Shanghai (daily; 40min); Wenzhou (3 weekly; 50min).

Wenzhou to: Beijing (2 daily, 2hr 30min); Guangzhou (3 daily; 2hr); Hangzhou (daily; 1hr 5min); Nanjing (daily; 1hr 20min); Ningbo (3 weekly; 50min); Shanghai (4 daily; 1hr 5min); Shenzhen (daily; 1hr 55min); Xi'an (5 weekly; 2hr 30min).

CHAPTER SEVEN

THE YANGZI BASIN

aving raced out of Sichuan through the narrow Three Gorges, the Yangzi widens, slows down, and loops through its flatter, low-lying middle reaches, fed and swelled by countless streams and lesser rivers which drain off the highlands surrounding the four provinces of the Yangzi basin – **Anhui**, **Hubei**, **Hunan** and **Jiangxi**. As one of the key routes for trade and transport throughout Chinese history, the river (known in China as the **Changjiang**) has turned the region into a centre of development and habitation since the earliest times. In the thirteenth century, Marco Polo was overawed by the "innumerable cities and towns along its banks, and the amount of shipping it carries, and the bulk of merchandise that merchants transport by it"; and while surrounding paddy fields have formed the backbone of central China's grain and rice production since the Ming era, a network of modern hydro-electric dams currently under construction in the middle reaches are the first stage towards building a local industrial economy to rival that of the east coast.

As such a large, vital and influential feature, visitors tend to gravitate towards the Yangzi, undertaking lengthy **cruises** between Sichuan and Shanghai, and sightseeing along the shores of China's two largest freshwater lakes: **Dongting**, which both separates and twins Hunan and Hubei, and **Poyang**, in northern Jiangxi, famed for porcelain produced at nearby **Jingdezhen**. Riverside towns are also interesting working ports and many, such as **Wuhu** in Anhui, are historical centres of commerce where it's still possible to see traditional river industries – fish farming, grain, rice and bamboo transportation – existing alongside newer ventures in manufacturing. Strangely enough, while all four regional capitals are located near water, only **Wuhan**, in Hubei, is actually on the Yangzi itself, a privileged position which has turned the city into central China's liveliest urban conglomeration. By contrast, the other provincial capitals – **Changsha** in Hunan, Anhui's **Hefei**, and Jiangxi's **Nanchang** – seem somewhat dishevelled, though all are more interesting than they might at first appear, with a scattering of worthwhile sites and museums to visit.

The region's long settlement has left a good deal of **history** in its wake, though most relics which have survived the basin's many upheavals are footnotes to China's past rather than part of a coherent narrative. While some items – **bronzework** from Hubei's

---

ACCOMMODATION PRICE CODES

All the accommodation in this book has been graded according to the following price codes, which represent the cheapest double room available to foreigners. Most places have a range of rooms, however, and staff will usually offer you the more expensive ones – it's always worth asking if they have anything cheaper. Where the text refers specifically to dorm beds, the price code represents the price per bed. See p.40 for more details.

① less than ¥30	④ ¥100–150	⑦ ¥300–500
② ¥30–75	⑤ ¥150–200	⑧ ¥500–700
③ ¥75–100	⑥ ¥200–300	⑨ ¥700 or more

Warring States period, and **Han tombs** near Changsha – might seem rather dustily academic, Ming-dynasty **architecture** scattered across Anhui and Jiangxi is still very much in use, and everywhere you seem to stumble over sites from the epic of the **Three Kingdoms** – making the tale almost essential background reading (see box, p.432). The Yangzi basin can also fairly claim to be the **cradle of modern China**: Mao Zedong was born in Hunan Province; Changsha, Wuhan and Nanchang are all closely associated with Communist Party history; while the mountainous border between Hunan and Jiangxi was both a Red refuge during right-wing purges in the late 1920s and the starting point for the subsequent Long March to Shaanxi.

Those able to pull themselves away from the river will find some marvellous **hiking** through forested peaks around the regional fringes, the pick of which are undoubtedly at **Huang Shan** in southern Anhui, and **Zhangjiajie** in Hunan's far west. Pilgrims have a wide choice of Buddhist and Taoist **holy mountains** to scale on seemingly unending stone-flagged staircases, and less dedicated souls can find eagle views at the mountain resort town of **Lu Shan** in Jiangxi.

Flood-prone as it is, deciding **when to visit** the Yangzi basin is vital if you plan to abandon river transport and head off across the plains. In theory, **getting around** isn't a problem, with **rail** lines from all over China crossing the region, and a comprehensive

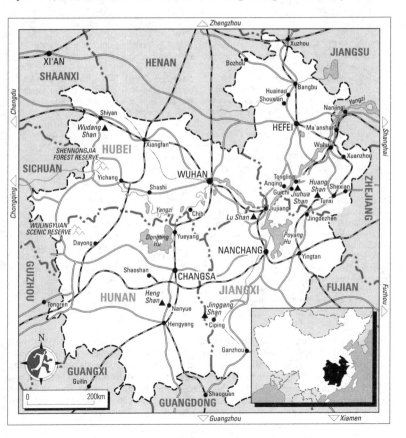

THE THREE KINGDOMS (*SANGUO*)

"The empire, long divided, must unite; long united, must divide. Thus it has ever been."

So, rather cynically, begins one of China's best known stories, the fourteenth-century historical novel, **Romance of the Three Kingdoms**. Though well-founded in fact, the *Three Kingdoms* is – like King Arthur – essentially the stuff of legend. Opening in 168 AD, the tale recounts the decline of the Han empire, how China was split into three states by competing warlords, and the subsequent (shortlived) reunification of the country in 280 AD under a new dynasty. Covering 120 chapters and a cast of thousands, the story touches heavily on the Yangzi basin, which, as a buffer zone between the three kingdoms, formed the backdrop for many major battles and key events. Some surviving sites are covered both in this chapter and elsewhere in *The Guide*.

The main action began in 189 AD. At this point, the two protagonists were the villainous **Cao Cao** and the pathetic but virtuous **Liu Bei**, whose character defects were compensated for by the strength of his spirited oath brothers **Zhang Fei** and **Guan Yu** – the latter eventually becoming enshrined in the Chinese pantheon as the red-faced god of war. Having put down the rebellious Yellow Turbans in the name of the emperor, both Cao and Liu felt their position threatened by the other; Cao was regent to the emperor **Xian**, but Liu had a remote blood tie to the throne. Fighting against each other now, though both claiming to support the emperor's wishes, Cao was defeated in Hubei at the **Battle of the Red Cliffs** (208 AD) after Liu engaged the aid of the wily adviser **Zhuge Liang**, who boosted Liu's heavily outnumbered forces by enlisting the help of a third warlord, **Sun Quan**.

Consolidating their positions, each of the three formed a private kingdom: Cao Cao retreated north to the Yellow River basin where he established the state of **Wei** around the ailing imperial court; Sun Quan set up **Wu** farther south along the lower Yangzi; while Liu Bei built a power base in the riverlands of Sichuan, the state of **Shu**. Jostling for position, the alliance between Shu and Wu fell apart when Sun Quan asked Guan Yu, Liu Bei's oath brother, to betray Liu. Guan refused and was assassinated by Sun in 220 AD. At this point Cao Cao died, and his ambitious son, **Cao Pi**, forced the emperor to abdicate and announced himself head of a new dynasty. Fearing retaliation from the state of Shu after Guan Yu's murder, Sun Quan decided to support Cao Pi's claims, while over in Shu, Liu Bei also declared his right to rule.

Against Zhuge Liang's advice, Liu marched against Wu to avenge Guan Yu's death but his troops mutinied, killing Liu's other blood brother, Zhang Fei. Defeated, Liu fled to **Baidicheng** in the Yangzi Gorges and died of shame. With him out of the way, Cao Pi attacked his own ally, Sun Quan, who was forced to renew his uncomfortable alliance with Shu – now governed by Zhuge Liang – to keep the invaders out of his kingdom. By 229 AD, however, things were stable enough for Sun Quan to declare himself as a rival emperor, leaving Zhuge to die fighting against the armies of Wei five years later. Wei was unable to pursue the advantage, as a coup against Cao Pi started a period of civil war in the north, ending around 249 AD when the **Sima clan** emerged victorious. Sun Quan died soon afterwards, while Shu abandoned all claim to the empire. Wei's Sima clan founded a new dynasty, the **Jin**, in 265 AD, finally overpowering Wu and uniting China in 280 AD.

bus network linking cities to the remotest of corners. Autumn is probably the most pleasant time of year, though even winters are generally mild, but the summer (June to August) is best avoided, with humidity and near-constant rains making the region resemble a tropical Netherlands without the dykes. In 1954, **flooding** along the Yangzi killed three million people, while in July 1995, some two thousand perished in Hunan and Jiangxi – cities were isolated, millions of hectares of crops destroyed, local dams collapsed and communications all but wiped out.

ANHUI

Despite government hopes that it will one day become a wealthy corridor between the coast and interior, **Anhui** largely lives up to its tradition as eastern China's poorest province. Its history initially belies this with remains showing that the region was inhabited almost a million years ago by the proto-human *homo erectus*, while more recently, Shang copper mines in southern Anhui fuelled China's Bronze Age. The province later became well known for its artistic refinements, from decorative Han tombs through to Song-dynasty porcelain and Ming architecture.

All this, however, has been a struggle against Anhui's unfriendly geography. Arid and eroded, the north China plains extend into its upper third as far as the **Huai River**, and while the south is warmer and wetter, allowing for tea and tobacco cultivation, the fertile wooded hills soon climb to rugged mountains, and not much in the way of food can be grown there. But it is the **Yangzi** itself that ensures Anhui's poverty by regularly inundating the province's low-lying centre, which would otherwise produce a significant amount of crops. Further, the lack of any bridges across the river creates a very physical division, separating the province's mountainous south from its more settled regions. Despite recent work, such as the highway between Hefei and Wuhan, major rail and road links still skirt the province, isolating Anhui's economy and leaving it set to enter the next century as an obstacle, and not a pathway, to travelling inland.

For the visitor, this is not all bad news. While neither the northern regions nor the provincial capital, **Hefei**, have much beyond their history, there are compensations for Anhui's lack of development **south of the Yangzi**. Here, superlative mountain landscapes at **Huang Shan** and the collection of Buddhist temples at **Jiuhua Shan** have been pulling in droves of sightseers for centuries, and there's a strong cultural tradition stamped on the area with a substantial amount of antique rural architecture surviving intact around **Tunxi**. Relatively low pollution levels have also aided the **Yangzi river dolphin** and **Chinese alligator**, two of the world's most endangered animals, whose tiny populations receive some protection in riverside reserves.

Flooding aside – and there's a near guarantee of this affecting bus travel during the summer months – the main problem with finding your way around Anhui is that many towns have a range of aliases, and can be differently labelled on maps and timetables. There are two main **rail lines**: one follows the river from Nanjing to **Wuhu**, Anhui's major port and a stop for Yangzi ferries, with a spur continuing west along the bank to the manufacturing town of **Tongling**; the other runs the length of the province, connecting southern Anhui with centrally placed Hefei and lines north to Xi'an and Beijing.

Hefei and the north

Nestled in the very heart of the province but generally overlooked in the rush to cross the Yangzi and reach Huang Shan, Anhui's capital, **HEFEI**, gets very few chance visitors. An unimportant backwater until 1949, when rail links to the rest of China saw the city develop a modest industrial base, the sole points of interest are a couple of **Three Kingdoms sites** and an unusually thorough **museum**. However, it's a comfortable place, untouched by the ugly building mania sweeping the rest of the country and dignified by a number of important science and technology colleges. Heading north, both **Shouxian** – just about feasible as a day trip from the capital – and **Bozhou** are historic towns, perhaps worth a day's scrutiny on the long haul in or out of the province.

HEFEI AND THE NORTH

Hefei	合肥	*héféi*
Leisure Ford Park	逍遥津公园	*xiāoyáo jīn gōng yuán*
Luogang airport	骆岗机场	*luògǎng jīchǎng*
Mingjiao Si	明教寺	*míngjiāo sì*
Provincial Museum	省博物馆	*shěng bówùguǎn*
Three Kingdoms	三国	*sān guó*
ACCOMMODATION		
Anhui	安徽饭店	*ānhuī fàndiàn*
Changjiang	长江宾馆	*chángjiāng bīnguǎn*
Overseas Chinese Hotel	华侨饭店	*huáqiáo fàndiàn*
Xinya Dajiundian	新亚大酒店	*xīnyà dàjiǔdiàn*
NORTHERN ANHUI		
Bangbu	蚌埠	*bàngbù*
Bozhou	亳州	*bózhōu*
Cao Family Tombs	曹氏家族墓	*cáo shì jiāzú mù*
Huainan	淮南	*huáinán*
Shouxian	寿县	*shòuxiàn*
Bao'en Monastery	报恩寺	*bàoén sì*

The City

Ringed by canals and parkland which soon give way to paddy fields, downtown Hefei resembles a suburban high street more than a provincial capital. Nothing is too far away to reach on foot, although the main roads are travelled by frequent **buses** – including claustrophobic double-deckers – and a few **taxis** prowl the centre.

The well-presented **Provincial Museum** on Mengcheng Lu (Mon–Fri 8.30–10.40am & 2–4pm, Sat & Sun 8.30–11.40am & 2–5pm; ¥10) provides sound evidence for Anhui's quiet contributions to Chinese culture. A cast of the **homo erectus** brain case from Taodian in the south of the province is proudly displayed in an oversized glass case (along with a walk-through plaster cave), while splinters of more immediate history emerge in a few Stone Age items and an exceptionally worked Shang bronze urn decorated with tiger and dragon motifs. Also interesting are the carved blocks taken from **Han-dynasty mausoleums** – Chinese speakers might be able to decipher the comments about the **Cao family** (of *Three Kingdoms* fame) incized into the bricks of their Bozhou tomb by construction labourers. Farther on, there's a special exhibition of the so-called "**Four Scholastic Treasures**": high quality inks and heavy carved ink stones of Tang ancestry, weasel-hair writing brushes and modern multicoloured papers for which the province is famed. Make sure you press on to the last hall, where there are photographs, scale models and some life-size reconstructions of impressive Ming **Huizhou architecture** from the Tunxi area comprising domestic buildings and monumentally carved stone memorial arches.

First built in the Tang dynasty, the current **Mingjiao Si** on Huai He Lu (¥2) is a sixteenth-century temple, restored in 1991 after Cultural Revolutionaries had left their mark. Fortress-like walls front the unpretentious halls, a peach garden and a quiet **vegetarian restaurant** hidden to one side, while there are some older relics to hunt out. The temple occupies the site of a *Three Kingdoms* platform where the northern leader

Cao Cao drilled his crossbowers during the winter of 216–217 AD and later defended the city against the kingdom of Wu's forces. Earlier, his general Zhang Liao had routed Wu's armies at the bloody battle of **Xiaoyao Jin** (Leisure Ford) – the site is now a **park** directly north of the temple – where Sun Quan, the leader of Wu, had to flee on horseback by leaping the bridgeless canal. A **well** in the temple's main courtyard reputedly dates from this time, and definitely looks ancient; a worn stone ring set close to the ground, deeply scored by centuries of ropes being dragged over the rim.

Practicalities

Luogang airport is about 7km due south of the city, connected by an airport bus to the *East China Airways* office at 246 Jinzhai Lu (Mon–Fri 8.30am–5pm & Sat–Sun 9am–5pm; ☎0551/2822357). The new **train station** is 3km northeast of the centre at the northeastern end of Shengli Lu, while the old station and a group of country **bus and minibus depots** are huddled together closer in along the same road, which continues over a couple of junctions and a canal before linking up with **Changjiang Lu**. This thoroughfare stretches west right through the centre, with all essential services in its vicinity: a **department store**; a huge **Bank of China** (foreign exchange Mon–Fri 8.30am–4.30pm) where you can watch suitcases full of money changing hands over the counter; a selection of English and Chinese classics in the *Xinhua* **bookstore** near the junction of Changjiang Lu and Fuyang Lu; and a helpful and fluently bilingual **CITS/CTS** at Jiuzhou Mansions, Jinzhai Lu (Mon–Fri 8.30–11.30am & 2–5pm; ☎0551/2651522, fax 2654308).

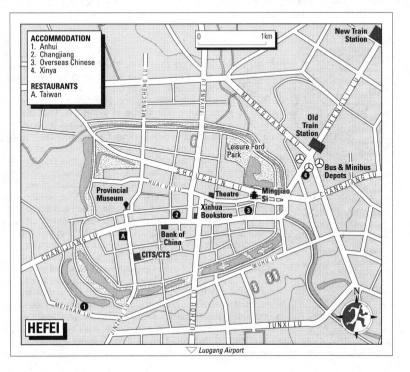

ACCOMMODATION
1. Anhui
2. Changjiang
3. Overseas Chinese
4. Xinya

RESTAURANTS
A. Taiwan

New Train Station

Old Train Station

Bus & Minibus Depots

Leisure Ford Park

Provincial Museum

Theatre

Mingjiao Si

Xinhua Bookstore

Bank of China

CITS/CTS

HEFEI

▽ Luogang Airport

Accommodation

Hefei's wealth of **hotel** beds is countered by generally upmarket prices, although persistence may get you into one of the budget **hostels** around the train and long-distance bus stations.

Anhui, 18 Meishan Lu (☎0551/3631818). An expensive, quiet retreat, nicely sited in parkland just southwest of the centre. ⑧.

Changjiang Binguan, Changjiang Lu (☎0551/2656441). A faded grey building with cheap dorms, but they're difficult for foreigners to get into. ②.

Overseas Chinese Hotel, 98 Changjiang Lu (☎0551/2652221, fax 2642861). Overpriced, but clean and with decent facilities. Cheaper doubles and triples in the old wing, while the newer rooms include a light breakfast in the room price. ⑤–⑨.

Xinya Dajiudian, near the old train station on Shengli Lu (☎0551/2621112). A very upmarket modern business hotel with a good shop, restaurant and IDD telephones. ⑥–⑧.

Eating, drinking and entertainment

Hefei's hotel **restaurants** have decent menus, and there are plenty of reasonable places to fill up on braised vegetables and anonymous fish and meat dishes along Changjiang Lu and Jinzhai Lu. On the latter, the *Taiwan Restaurant* is one of the neater places to dine in town. There's no English menu, but staff are pleasant and serve up Cantonese-style cooking. For lighter meals, try the snack houses near the long-distance bus stations on Shengli Lu. In season you can also buy lychees and peaches from street hawkers around town.

For an evening out, Hefei has something of a reputation for **stage productions** – there are at least two indigenous opera styles and a local acrobatic troupe – and there's a **theatre** just west of Mingjiao Si on Huai He Lu. Consult the ticket office, local papers or *CITS* for performance information.

Northern Anhui

Cynics say that northern Anhui's high points are the roads, which run on flood-proof embankments a few metres above the plains. Certainly, about the only geographic feature is the **Huai River**, smaller and less temperamental than the Yangzi and the setting for the region's main city, **BANGBU**, whose attractive name (it means Oyster Port) belies a rather drab industrial and grain centre. The **battle of Huai Hai** took place nearby in 1948, when a million Guomindang and PLA combatants fought a decisive encounter in which the guerrilla-trained Communists overran Chiang Kaishek's less flexible forces. A demoralized GMD surrendered in Beijing in January the next year, and though war resumed when the two sides couldn't agree on terms, after this it was largely a mopping-up operation by the Communists against GMD bastions.

All this is mainly background for what you'll see along the way, but a couple of northern towns do make interesting overnight stops. From the coal-mining centre of **HUAINAN**, about 100km north of Hefei and connected by daily train and bus services, you can pick up local buses for the thirty-minute ride to **SHOUXIAN**, whose cross-shaped Song-dynasty street plan is the best surviving example of its kind in China. There's also one minibus daily, direct from Hefei, returning the following morning. A regional capital as far back as the Warring States period (241 BC), Shouxian consists of a small country seat surrounded by over 6km of dykes and massive **stone walls** which can be climbed above the east gate for town views. Though few buildings are of great age, none is new, and wandering the tiny back lanes you frequently come across well-preserved wooden lintels and bronze detailing on doors. **Bao'en Monastery** on the western main road, however, *is* old – Ming-dynasty – as are the bee-infested tower outside and the incredibly rickety row of **shops** opposite, complete with buckled walls, undulating, mildewed tiles and warped timbers. There's a small **hotel** in town (②) should you need to spend the night.

Larger than Shouxian, **BOZHOU** lies in Anhui's northwestern corner on the main route between Hefei and Zhengzhou in Henan. This is the home town of the *Three Kingdoms*, arch villain, **Cao Cao**; though despised in much of China – "Speak of Cao Cao" is the literal Chinese equivalent of "Speak of the Devil" – he and his sons were nonetheless respectably good poets. In Bouzhou you can visit the **Cao Family Tombs** and travel the narrow underground tunnel used by their soldiers. The city has also long been a major source of **traditional medicines**, and the **Hua Theatre**, a well-preserved seventeenth-century building with elaborate stone and wood decorations, is named after a Han-dynasty doctor. Bozhou also boasts several large markets selling medicinal herbs and dried products. For **accommodation**, there's the *Gujing Dajiudian* on Qiaoling Lu (☎05681/521274; ⑤), about ten minutes south of the bus station, and the better-value *Bozhou Binguan*, more centrally located on Banjie Lu (②–④).

Wuhu and the Yangzi River towns

Powering up the Yangzi from Nanjing into eastern Anhui you immediately pass **MA'ANSHAN**, an industrial nightmare notable only for being where the itinerant romantic Tang poet **Li Bai** drowned in 762 AD after drunkenly falling out of a boat while trying to touch the moon's reflection. Far better is **WUHU**, a brisk market and trading crossroads set on the Yangzi's south bank at its confluence with the Qingyi River. Formerly a treaty port, this was as far upstream as steamers could navigate, and the shipyards were kept busy turning out smaller rafts capable of carrying coastal wares farther along the Yangzi and its tributaries. In return, the steamers loaded up with provincial goods bound for Shanghai or the oceans beyond. Wuhu's wharves still handle a substantial amount of cargo, and you'll see boats heading for Nanjing or Shanghai piled high with bamboo or weighed down with rice, but much modern traffic is carried away by rail and the city's focus is increasingly towards textiles and other light industries. One of these produces **wrought-iron pictures** – possibly China's most pointless handicraft – an artistic technique said to have resulted from an argument between a painter and a blacksmith in the seventeenth century.

For visitors, Wuhu's importance is as a staging post for the trip to Huang Shan in the south of the province, besides being a regular stop for **Yangzi cruise boats**. Traffic from Hefei is ferried across the river here, and it's also where the rail line from

---

WUHU AND THE YANGZI RIVER TOWNS

Yangzi River	长江	*cháng jiāng*
Anqing	安庆	*ānqìng*
Guichi	贵池	*guìchí*
Ma'anshan	马鞍山	*mǎ ānshān*
Tongling	铜陵	*tónglíng*
Wusong Shan Binguan	五松山宾馆	*wǔsōng shān bīnguǎn*
Yangzi river dolphin	白鲫	*báijì*
Wuhu	庑湖	*wǔhú*
Jing Hu	镜湖	*jìng hú*
Yangzi ferry terminal	码头	*mǎtóu*
Zheshan Park	锗山公园	*zhěshān gōngyuán*
Zhongjiang Pagoda	中江塔	*zhōngjiāng tǎ*
Xuanzhou	宣州	*xuān zhōu*
Chinese Alligator Breeding Centre	扬子鳄养殖场	*yángzǐ'è yǎngzhíyángchǎng*

Shanghai links with north–south services. A waterfront walk is the obvious way to pass the time between connections. Wuhu's **train station** is in the ugly northeastern quarter of town, facing the **bus station** across a huge empty field. Bus #4 runs from here down Dazhai Lu past hilly **Zheshan Park** on the right, where you can get off and clamber up to a semi-ruinous three-storey pagoda which has great views over the town. Bus #4 terminates at the **Yangzi ferry terminal**, about 1km north of where the rivers meet at the five-storey **Zhongjiang** (Mid-river) **Pagoda**, best seen in the evening light against a backdrop of ships and the broad sweep of the Yangzi. Not far from here, through the leafy, narrow streets of the old town centre, is **Jing Hu** (Mirror Lake), which is little more than an overgrown pond and small pavilion. Of the **hotels**, the *Tieshan Binguan*, 3 Gengxin Lu (☎0553/334736; ⑤) is nicely located on the west side of Zheshan Park, or you can try for a budget room at the train station's hostel (②).

Xuanzhou

Chinese speakers interested in wildlife should make the trip to **XUANZHOU**, two hours by bus to the southeast of Wuhu across low hills patterned by tea plantations (confusingly, you pass another Wuhu, the county town, halfway there). Xuanzhou itself is an untidy but incredibly friendly place (foreigners are a great novelty), well known for producing much sought-after writing paper, and also as the site of a **Chinese alligator breeding centre**, which has obtained a number of these two-metre-long reptiles for research purposes. Getting out to the centre, which is several kilometres south of town, can be impossible after rain – you're likely to find the road under water and locals paddling between their houses in wooden tubs – otherwise, negotiate with the minibus drivers at the crossroads near the bus station. It's worth the effort because these timid alligators are shockingly rare; until successes in a worldwide breeding project co-ordinated by the US Bronx Zoo boosted their population in 1996, there were only about twenty left.

For **accommodation**, food, and information in Xuanzhou, there's a hostel to the left of the **bus station** on the Wuhu road, or the much more upmarket *Xuanzhou Binguan* (☎0553/315350; ⑤) – turn right out of the bus station, left at the crossroads and it's on the right. If you can't speak Chinese, try asking *CITS* at Tunxi or Hefei to phone ahead and arrange a visit for you.

Tongling, Guichi and Anqing

Connected by train to Wuhu, **TONGLING** marks the halfway point in the Yangzi's journey across the province, and is another place of interest to naturalists – this time for its associations with the light grey **Yangzi river dolphin** (*baiji*), whose story is much the same as Xuanzhou's alligators. Once common as far west as Sichuan, the *baiji*'s steady decline to just three hundred individuals seems directly linked to the growth of river industries, traffic and net fishing since the 1950s, and they are now confined to downstream of Yichang in Hubei, by the Gezhouba dam. Tongling, meanwhile, has taken the dolphin to heart, and a two-kilometre artificial channel has been created as a reserve and study centre near town. There's even a **Baiji beer** with the dolphin's Latin name, *lipotes vexillifer*, stamped on the bottle top. For a closer look, the *Wusong Shan Binguan* at 55 Yi'an Lu in the north of town (☎05612/235243; ⑤) provides beds, and the nearby *CITS* at 45 Yi'an Lu (☎05612/231168) can arrange tours to the reserve.

Continuing upstream towards the border with Jiangxi and Hubei, **GUICHI** is the next stop for river traffic, and also the place to disembark for buses to Jiuhua Shan (see p.444), clearly visible off to the south. Not much farther on is the northern bank town of **ANQING**, the last likely port of call within Anhui and a **Taiping rebel** stronghold during the late 1840s. Beyond here the boat takes half a day to reach Jiujiang and Lake Poyang in Jiangxi Province (see p.484).

Southern Anhui: Huang Shan

There is an old saying that once you've ascended the heights of **Huang Shan**, the Yellow Peak Range, you will never want to climb another mountain. Certainly the experience is quite staggeringly scenic with spiralling pinnacles emerging from thick bamboo forests, above which rock faces dotted with ancient, contorted pine trees growing from narrow ledges disappear into the swirling mists. Sometimes these views seem instantly familiar, for Huang Shan's landscape has left an indelible impression on Chinese art, and painters are still a common sight on the paths, huddled in padded jackets and sheltering their work from the incipient drizzle beneath umbrellas – the more serious of them spend months at a time up here.

As an ancient pilgrimage site trodden by emperors and Communist leaders alike, Huang Shan is regarded as sacred in China, and it's the ambition of every Chinese to conquer it at least once in their lifetime. Consequently, don't expect to climb alone – there are droves of visitors, and formerly muddy tracks have been tidied up into neat paved paths embellished with stairs, railings and even a cable-car link to the top. All this easy access can make the experience feel like visiting a huge amusement park, but then you'll turn a corner and come face to face with a huge, smooth monolith topped by a single tree, or be confronted with views of a remote square of forest growing isolated on a rocky platform. Nature is never far away from reasserting itself here.

SOUTHERN ANHUI: HUANG SHAN		
Huang Shan	黄山	*huáng shān*
Banshan Si	半山寺	*bànshān sì*
Beginning-to-Believe Peak	始信峰	*shǐxìn fēng*
Beihai Hotel	北海宾馆	*běihǎi bīnguǎn*
Far-flying Rock	飞来石	*fēi lái shí*
Jiyu Bei	鲫鱼背	*jìyú bèi*
Tiandu Feng	天都峰	*tiāndū fēng*
White Goose Peak	白鹅峰	*báié fēng*
Xihai Hotel	西海宾馆	*xīhǎi bīnguǎn*
Yuping Lou	玉屏楼	*yùpíng lóu*
Shexian	歙县	*shèxiàn*
Tangyue archway	堂说牌坊	*tángyuè páifáng*
Tangkou	汤口	*tāngkǒu*
Hot springs	温泉	*wēnquán*
Huangshan Binguan	黄山宾馆	*huángshān bīnguǎn*
Taoyuan Binguan	桃源宾馆	*táoyuán bīnguǎn*
Wenquan Dajiudian	温泉大酒店	*wēnquán dàjiǔdiàn*
Xiaoyao Binguan	逍遥宾馆	*xiāoyáo bīnguǎn*
Tunxi	屯溪	*túnxī*
Cheng Dawei's House	程大位居	*chéng dàwèi jū*
Cheng Family House	程氏三宅	*chéngshì sānzhái*
Jiangnan Dajiudian	江南大酒店	*jiāngnán dàjiǔdiàn*
Tunxi Binguan	屯溪宾馆	*túnxī bīnguǎn*
Yindu Dajiudian	银都大酒店	*yíndū dàjiǔdiàn*
Xidi	西递	*xīdì*
Yixian	黟县	*yīxiàn*

Mountain practicalities

Transport pours into the Huang Shan region from all over eastern China. There are direct buses from Shanghai, Hangzhou and Nanjing, as well as Wuhu and other places within Anhui. Much of this, and all rail traffic, passes through **Tunxi** (also known as Huang Shan Shi), with regular shuttle buses connecting the train and bus stations here with the gateway village of **Tangkou**, 50km away in the mountain's foothills. Some long-distance buses, however, go directly to Tangkou; be aware that these might refer to Tangkou (and not Tunxi) as "Huang Shan" on their timetables.

You'll need to spend two or three days on the mountain to allow for an easy-going ascent and circuit of the peaks. With enough time, villages around Tunxi are well worth extending your stay to explore. At a pinch, you could see a substantial part of Huang Shan in a single day, but this would still mean two nights in the area. There's plenty of **accommodation** and **food** available in Tunxi, Tangkou and on the mountain itself, but you'll need to come prepared for steep paths, clouds, rain and winter snow – all an essential part of the experience. Hiring guides and porters is something of an extravagance, as paths are easy to follow and accommodation in Tangkou will store surplus gear; just bring a day-pack, strong shoes and something warm for the top.

Tunxi and around

Most foreigners don't see anything of **TUNXI** beyond the train or bus stations, allowing themselves to be whisked away on arrival by the horde of waiting Huang Shan-bound minibuses. But if you've the slightest interest in Chinese architecture, or wonder what it would be like to step back several hundred years, then the town and its environs are worth checking out. Anhui's poverty and isolation have played a large part in preserving a liberal sprinkling of seventeenth-century monuments and homes in the Tunxi area, including entire villages at **Shexian** and **Yixian**.

The Town

If you don't have time to visit other examples, there are a few old buildings worth checking out in Tunxi itself. South off Huang Shan Dong Lu – you'll need a map to find them – are the remains of two homes belonging to the Ming-dynasty **Cheng family**, which are classic examples of the indigenous **Huizhou** style. Neither building is well marked and the more easterly house – that of the mathematician Cheng Dawei – is in a sorry state of repair, but their plan, of two floors of galleried rooms based around a courtyard, proved so popular that it became the benchmark of urban domestic architecture in central and eastern China.

Better still, head down to Tunxi's historic, flagstoned **main street**, reached by pushing on into the maze of narrow market streets at the Xin'an Lu intersection. Here, a kilometre of immaculately restored **Ming shops** running parallel to the **Xin'an River** are still open for business, selling local teas, medicinal herbs and all manner of artistic materials and "antiques" – inkstones, brushes, Mao badges, jade hairpins and carved wooden panels prised off old buildings. You'll also see characteristic **horse head gables** rising above the rooflines in steps. These originated as fire baffles between adjoining houses, stopping the spread of flames from building to building, but around Tunxi (and adjoining regions of Zhejiang and Jiangxi, for that matter) they've become somewhat decorative affairs.

Practicalities

Tunxi's **train station** is at the end of Jingyuan Bei Lu at the northern city limits; the **bus station** is a couple of hundred metres east along Guoliao Gong Lu. **Maps** on sale in the vicinity show a couple of city bus routes, but at the time of writing these were non-existent – the centre is a twenty-minute walk away to the southwest down Huang

Shan Dong Lu, at the intersection with Xin'an Lu. Most **places to stay** are located around the arrival points, including the small, friendly and unnervingly quiet *Yindu Dajiudian* across the rubble around the bus station (③–⑥), and the more upmarket *Jiangnan Dajiudian* (☎0559/2511186; ④) on the roundabout outside the train station. *Tunxi Binguan* (☎0559/2512585; dorms ③, rooms ⑥), in the centre near the Huang Shan Dong Lu–Xin'an Lu intersection, is a modest, reasonably priced place, though they sometimes refuse foreigners.

There's also a **Bank of China** down here for foreign exchange (Mon–Fri 8.30am–5pm), and a **post office** up towards the train station on Jingyuan Bei Lu. For local advice, an English-speaking branch of the *CTS* is just a couple of doors along at 12 Jingyuan Bei Lu (Mon–Fri 8.30am–noon & 1.30–5pm, with variable hours at the weekend; ☎0559/2115832, fax 2114040) – renting a private car for the day will set you back ¥500.

Shexian and Yixian

Two other cultural centres can be reached by regular **buses** from Tunxi. Anhui owes a good deal to the town of **SHEXIAN**, about 25km east on the Hangzhou road, once a regional capital and important trading centre on the Xin'an River – the name "Anhui" is a telescoping of Anqing and Huizhou, Shexian's former name. The region blossomed in the seventeenth century after local salt merchants got rich and started raising buildings to celebrate their wealth. The province's opera styles were formalized here, and the town became famous for *hui* stone ink slabs and fine-grained *she* ink sticks, the latter still considered China's best. Aside from the dozens of traditional homes, complete with their ornamental gardens, there are a number of contemporary stone **memorial gates** built by the merchants in showy competition with one another. The finest is the intricately carved **Xuguo archway** in the centre of Shexian, but buses also run out a few kilometres to the northwest, where the **Tangyue archway** forms a rather strange spectacle of six ornamental gates standing isolated in a row in a field.

The finest collection of Huizhou homes are found near **YIXIAN** at **XIDI village**, 60km due west of Tunxi, constituting a virtual museum of some 120 perfectly maintained eighteenth-century houses set along a riverbank, most of which – like the **Lufu Mansion** – are still inhabited. The local dialect is suitably dated, and there are endless examples of wonderfully carved gilded wooden screens and panels, as well as thin line paintings on front walls showing pairs of animals or "double happiness" characters. Mirrors placed above the three-tiered door lintels reflect bad luck or reveal a person's true character – a useful tool for judging the nature of strangers.

Tangkou and the hot springs

It takes a couple of hours by bus from Tunxi to reach **TANGKOU**, a small hamlet at the base of Huang Shan where roads from Wuhu, Tunxi and Jiuhua Shan meet above the **Taohua gully**. This is where most Huang Shan transport terminates, and is the cheapest place to look for lodgings – though the **hot springs area** (see below), a farther 3km uphill, has alternative accommodation, and marks the mountain trail head.

Tunxi **minibuses** collect and drop off at the central bridge, while the long-distance **bus** stop (there is no station proper) is about 1km upstream at Huang Shan's official entrance. For **accommodation**, get out at the bridge and take the steps down to the river, walk downstream through a mass of food and souvenir stalls, and you'll find the gloomy facade of the *Xiaoyao Binguan* (Free and Unfettered Hotel; ☎0559/5562571; ②–⑥). Facilities and staff are fine, however, and there's hot water in the evenings. For a much cheaper deal, the *Xiwei Fandian* is the green and white building on the corner to the right of the *Xiaoyao*, with unadorned dorm beds (①) and an English-speaking owner. There are also a couple of moderately priced places to stay (②) up towards the mountain entrance on the left side of the road, but the rooms are minute.

Food is good but noticeably expensive. The cheapest places to grab a filling noodle or *baozi* breakfast are at tables under the bridge. Try the hotels for something more substantial: the *Xiwei*'s bilingual menu offers arresting delights such as squirrel hotpot and scrambled mountain frog, and their soya-braised platter of local bamboo shoots and fungi is excellent. You can also pick up umbrellas, walking sticks and **mountain maps** – some more decorative than useful – from various hawkers and stalls around Tangkou.

The hot springs

Minibuses regularly potter uphill during the day from Tangkou's long-distance bus stop to the bridge at the **hot springs** area, where a **thermal bathhouse** – a great place to unkink trail-weary muscles – and a handful of hotels are perched above a picturesque gorge and waterfall. Huang Shan's two **hiking trails** diverge here: stay on the minibus if you're heading up the road to the eastern route or cable car (a farther 8km); for the longer western track, get out here and follow the signposts (in English) for fifteen minutes to the beginning of the trail at **Merciful Light Temple**.

Accommodation prospects include the smart *Taoyuan Binguan* (Peach Blossom Hotel; ☎0559/5562666, fax 5562888; ⑧), which looks across the bridge to its newly restored, red-roofed rival, the *Huangshan Binguan* (☎0559/5562202; ⑤–⑥). Down in the gorge is another freshly decorated effort, the *Wenquan Dajiudian* (☎0559/5562196; ⑦). There's also a basic **hostel** attached to the bathhouse offering dorm beds (①–②).

Huang Shan hikes

The Huang Shan range barely rises above 1870m, but as you struggle up either of the staircases it can begin to feel very high indeed. As compensation, the scenery is better the more difficult the path you choose. Certainly, there's little to see from the overcrowded gondola during the twenty-minute **cable car** ascent; it's also expensive (¥70 each way), queues can be monumental, and unless you really lack time or energy there are better options. The easiest of these is the seven-kilometre **eastern route**, which follows the cable car's path and can reasonably be climbed in around three hours. The exceptional landscapes on the fifteen-kilometre **western route** are accompanied by over six hours of exhausting legwork and it's in no way shameful to save this for the descent.

The Huang Shan **entry fee**, payable at the start of the trails or the cable-car ticket office, is ¥85, or ¥60 if you can wring a concession. Once at the top, there's a range of accommodation and a half-day of relatively easy hiking around the peaks. Alternatively, you

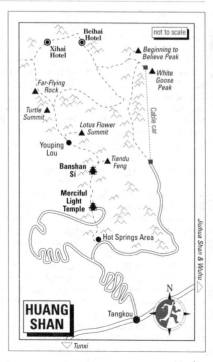

HUANG SHAN

could simply take the cable car up, spend a few hours touring the lookouts, and return down the eastern steps in the mid-afternoon.

The eastern route and peak circuit

Huang Shan's **eastern route** follows a forested gully and the canopy above blocks any views of the mountain until you emerge on to the viewing platform next to where the cable car docks. The path divides here for a three-hour **circuit around the peaks**, and most people head north (anticlockwise) to where a side track leads out to **Beginning-to-Believe Peak** (Shixin Feng). A cluster of rocky spires makes a wonderful perch to gaze down from off the heights to lowland woods and rivers, with white-rumped swifts and pine and rock silhouettes moving in and out of shifting silver clouds. Tour groups concentrate on the higher levels, so the lower stairs are more peaceful.

The next stop is round at the shiny new *Beihai Hotel* (☎0559/5562555; cabin beds ①, rooms ⑤–⑧), where crowds congregate each morning to watch the **sunrise** over the "northern sea" of clouds, one of the most stirring sights on the mountain. Views are still good even without the dawn, and the area tends to be crowded all day with tourists and food stalls. Another thirty minutes brings you to the luxurious *Xihai Hotel* (☎0559/5562132; ⑧), the perfect spot to sip drinks on the terrace and watch, in its turn, the sun setting over the "western cloud sea". Below is a huge complex of **bamboo cabins** painted bright orange, and with a little persuasion, you might get a mildewed **dorm bed** here (②), but facilities are basic indeed.

Continuing through some thick pine forests, the lonely tower of Felai Shi, the **Far-flying Rock**, makes another fine place to watch the sunset, and looks across at cascades dropping off lesser peaks into infinity. Beyond here, the path undulates along the cliff edge to where the western route branches off to the right. In the opposite direction the main track returns to the *Beihai*, while there's a minor footpath past the **transmitter tower** and back to the cable car.

The western route

From the Merciful Light Temple at the hot springs, over two thousand rough-stoned steps lead up to the terrace of **Banshan Si**, the misleadingly named Midway Monastery. This is where things start to get interesting as you continue up an increasingly steep and narrow gorge, its sides overgrown with witch hazel, azaleas and wild plum. The rocks are huge, their weirdly contorted figures lending some credence to the usual gamut of bizarre names, and the broken hillside is riddled with caves. In one – the **House of Clouds** – you can scramble up a flight of teetering steps and clamber over an enormous boulder to emerge, squeezing out of a fissure, 30m higher up the path. Alternatively, a steep, hour-long detour from Banshan – definitely not a climb for those nervous of heights – follows steps cut into the cliffs up to **Tiandu Feng** (Heavenly City Peak), where **Jiyu Bei** (Kingfish Ridge), a narrow, ten-metre-long path extending over a precipice towards distant pinnacles surrounded by clouds, provides Huang Shan's most spectacular views.

Back on the main track, **Yuping Lou**, the beautifully positioned Jade Screen Pavilion, is the true halfway house at around three hours into the journey and an elevation of 1680 metres. The vegetation thins out here, exchanged for a scene of bare rocks with only the occasional solitary tree, one of which, the **Welcoming Pine**, is instantly recognizable, having been immortalized in countless pictures. The steps wind on up to a pass between **Peacock and Lotus Flower summits**, where more strange rocks – including the Turtle, Snake, and Fantastic Fish – jut out of the mist. By now you're up around the main peaks. Dropping down into a valley you pass through a narrow cave where, according to legend, a kindly spider helped the first Ming emperor, **Zhu Yuanzhang**, to elude his enemies by spinning a web over the cave entrance after he had hidden inside. From here, it's about a thirty-minute walk anticlockwise around the peaks past a transmitter tower to the eastern route and cable-car terminus on **White Goose Peak**.

Jiuhua Shan

As an alternative to Huang Shan, **Jiuhua Shan** has many advantages: it's lower, with a summit a little over 1300m, the walking is considerably easier, the landscape less severe and there's plenty of interest beyond just the scenery. A place of worship for fifteen hundred years, this has been one of China's **four sacred Buddhist mountains** ever since the Korean monk **Jin Qiaojue** (believed to be the reincarnation of the Bodhisattva Dizang, whose doctrines he preached) died here in a secluded cave in 794 AD. Today there are over sixty temples – some built back in the seventh century – containing a broad collection of sculptures, religious texts and early calligraphy. There are also plenty of visitors, but their bustle hardly lessens the atmosphere of genuine devotion evident in the often austere halls with their wisps of incense smoke and distant chanting.

JIUHUA SHAN		
Jiuhua Shan	九华山	*jiǔhuá shān*
Baisui Gong	百岁宫	*bǎisuì gōng*
Huacheng Si	化城寺	*huàchéng sì*
Julong Dajiudian	聚笼大酒店	*jùlóng dàjiǔdiàn*
Longquan Binguan	龙泉饭店	*lóng quán fàndiàn*
Tiantai Zhending	天台正顶	*tiāntái zhèngdǐng*
Xiao Tiantai	小天台	*xiǎo tiāntái*
Zhiyuan Si	执园寺	*zhǐyuàn sì dàjiǔdiàn*
Qingyang	青阳	*qīngyáng*

To Qingyang and Jiuhua Shan village

Jiuhua Shan is about 60km northwest of Tangkou as the crow flies, and there are two **buses** daily each way, a six-hour journey through flood-prone countryside, involving a ferry trip across the **Taiping reservoir**. Some transport coming from Wuhu, Guichi and beyond will drop you about 25km short at **QINGYANG**, from where mountain minibuses leave throughout the day; if you get stuck here there's a good **hotel** (②) attached to Qingyang's bus station. The twisting Jiuhua Shan road passes villages scattered through the moist green of rice fields and bamboo forests, white-walled houses built of bricks interlocked in a "herringbone" pattern, topped by distinctive back sloping roofs facing into the prevailing weather.

The roads ends at **JIUHUA SHAN** village, where you'll find all of the mountain's accommodation, and the most famous temples, grouped around a couple of cobbled streets and squares.

The temples

Virtually the first building inside Jiuhua Shan village gates, **Zhiyuan Si** (Tend the Land Monastery) is also the most imposing, a Qing monument built with smooth, vertical walls, upcurving eaves and yellow-tiled roof nestled right up against a cliff. Despite a sizable exterior, the numerous little halls are cramped and stuffed with sculptures, including a fanged, bearded and hooknosed thunder god bursting out of its protective glass cabinet just inside the gate. Head for the main hall, in which a magnificently gilded **Buddhist trinity** sits solemnly on separate lotus flowers, blue hair dulled by incense smoke, and ringed by *arhats*. This makes quite a setting for the annual **temple fair**, held in Dizang's honour on the last day of the seventh lunar month, when the hall is packed with worshippers, monks and tourists. Make sure you look behind the altar, where Guanyin statuettes ascend right to the lofty wooden roof beams.

After Zhiyuan Si, hike up the staircase behind to **Baisui Gong** (Hundred Year Palace Temple), where there are some good views over the village from outside the elderly stone walls. The interior is far from weatherproof, with clouds drifting in and out of the main hall as monks go about their devotions, and contains the mummy of the Ming priest, **Wu Xia**, best known for compiling the **Huayan sutras** in gold dust mixed with his own blood. His tiny body is displayed seated in prayer, grotesquely covered in a thick, smooth skin of gold leaf.

Back below in the centre of Jiuhua Shan village, **Huacheng Si** (Transforming Monastery) is the mountain's oldest surviving temple, in part possibly dating right back to the Tang, though it's undergoing major renovations. The sagging stone entrance is set at the back of a large cobbled square whose centrepiece is a deep pond inhabited by some gargantuan goldfish. Inside, Huacheng's low-ceilinged, broad main hall looks set to become very garish, but hopefully the new work won't obscure some beautifully carved roof brackets and the highly accomplished "**Nine Dragons**" panel, finished early on in the Ming dynasty. The hall doubles as a **museum** at present, with paintings depicting the life of Jin Qiaojue from his sea crossing to China (accompanied only by a faithful hound) to his death at the age of ninety, and the discovery of his miraculously preserved corpse three years later. Seldom displayed, the museum's collection of **religious writings** includes a set of Sanskrit sutras written on palm leaf scrolls, and the complete Nirvana Sutra donated by the Ming emperor Shenzong.

Between the Heavenly Platforms

A few minutes beyond Huacheng Si brings you to a short staircase leading to **Xiao Tiantai** (Small Heavenly Platform), whose entrance-hall atrium contains some gruesomely entertaining, life-sized sculptures of **Buddhist hell**. These are so graphic that it's hard not to feel that the artists enjoyed their task of depicting sinners being skewered, pummelled, strangled, boiled and bisected by demons, while the virtuous look down, doubtless exceedingly thankful for their salvation. Climbing a steep flight of steps to the left of the temple brings you out on to Xiao Tiantai itself, where a tottering five-storey pagoda is being restored to its original condition.

It's about a ten-minute walk from Xiao Tiantai to **Pheonix Pine**, a twisted tree marking the start of the two-hour ascent to the platform at the top of Jiuhua Shan – there's also a **cable car** (¥16 each way) which will take you to just below the peak. The walk is pretty, and the **sunrise** seen from the terrace at **Tiantai Zhengding** (Upper Heavenly Platform) inspired the Tang man of letters, **Li Bai**, to bestow Jiuhua Shan (Nine Flower Peaks) with its name, having seen the major pinnacles rising up out of clouds like lotus buds.

Jiuhua Shan practicalities

There's a ¥35 **entry fee** payable at Jiuhua Shan village gates – the ticket kiosk and **bus stop** are immediately on the left as you enter. A host of market stalls here sell everything from food to ornamental knives and bamboo roots carved into faces. You can also pick up a waterproof **map** and umbrella for the frequently sodden weather.

You'll be grabbed on arrival and offered all manner of **accommodation**. The most upmarket facilities belong to the snobbish *Julong Dajiudian* (☎0566/5011368; ⑥–⑧) to the right of the village gates behind a grotesquely illuminated fountain, although rooms are damp. Directly opposite, Zhiyuan Si has extremely bare beds (①) designed for itinerant monks, though these are sometimes available to tourists. Just up the main street and on the left you'll find a neat **hostel** offering double rooms (②) at the top of a very grubby driveway and staircase. The toilets are rudimentary, but otherwise it's a good deal. Carrying on up the road, the clean *Longquan Binguan* (☎0566/5011412; ②–③) is on a corner on the right.

HUBEI

HUBEI is Han China's agricultural and geographic centre, mild in climate and well-watered. Until 280 BC this was the independent state of **Chu**, whose sophisticated bronzeworking skills continue to astound archeologists, but for the last half millennia the province's eastern bulk, defined by the low-lying **Jianghan plain** and spliced by waterways draining into the Yangzi and Han rivers, has become an intensely cultivated maze of rice fields, so rich that (according to tradition) they alone are enough to supply the national need. More recently, Hubei's central location and mass of transport links by rail, road and river into neighbouring regions saw the province becoming the first in the interior to be heavily industrialized. With the completion of the colossal **Three Gorges hydro-electric dam** early next century, car manufacturing, already up and running with the help of foreign investment, and long-established iron and steel plants, will provide a huge source of income for central China.

As the "Gateway to Nine Provinces", skirted by mountains and midway along the Yangzi between Shanghai and Chongqing, Hubei has always been of great strategic importance, and somewhere that seditious ideas could easily spread to the rest of the country. The central regions upriver from the capital, **Wuhan**, feature prominently in the lore of the *Three Kingdoms* (see box, p.432), with the ports of **Yichang**, **Shashi**, **Jiangling** and **Chibi** retaining their period associations, while Wuhan itself thrives on industry and river trade, and played a key role in modern China's revolutions. In the west, the ranges which border Sichuan contain the holy peak of **Wundang Shan**, alive with Taoist temples and martial arts lore, and the remote and little-visited **Shennongjia forest park**, said to be inhabited by China's yeti.

Wuhan

One way or the other, almost anyone travelling through central China has to pass through **WUHAN**, Hubei's energetic capital, most likely cruising in along the Yangzi from Sichuan or Shanghai, or rattling in by rail. In truth, transport links are the sole reason for spending any time in the city. Although there's enough to keep you entertained in the way of sights and food between train or ferry connections, it can't honestly be claimed that Wuhan, despite its size and obvious importance to the region, contains much in the way of essential viewing.

The name is a portmanteau label for the original triple settlements of **Wuchang**, **Hankou**, and **Hanyang**, still separate and facing each other across the junction of the Han and Yangzi rivers, but now given some sense of unity by three great interconnecting bridges. At first glance, the city's character is shaped by the volume of traffic and Hankou's former role as a foreign concession, which contributed to an extraordinary mix of **architectural styles** ranging from (reconstructed) Qing through to nine-

The **telephone code** for Wuhan is ☎027

WUHAN

Wuhan	武汉	*wǔhàn*
Hankou	汉口	*hànkǒu*
Hanyang	汉阳	*hànyáng*
Wuchang	武昌	*wǔchāng*

ARRIVAL

| Tianhe airport | 天河飞机场 | *tiānhé fēijīchǎng* |
| Yangzi ferry terminal | 武汉港客运沾 | *wǔhàn gǎng kè yùnzhàn* |

ACCOMMODATION

Dadongmen	大东门饭店	*dàdōngmén fàndiàn*
Jianghan	江汉饭店	*jiānghàn fàndiàn*
Linjiang	临江饭店	*línjiāng fàndiàn*
Lunchuan Gongsi Zhaodaisuo	轮船公司招待所	*lúnchuān gōngsī zhāodaìsuǒ*
Shengli	胜利饭店	*shènglì fàndiàn*
Xuangong	璇宫饭店	*xuángōng fàndiàn*
Yangtze	长江大酒店	*chángjiāng dàjiǔdiàn*

THE CITY

Botanical Gardens	植物园	*zhíwù yuán*
Central Peasant Movement Institute	中央农民运动研究所	*zhōngyāng nóngmín yùndòng yánjiūsuǒ*
Dong Hu	东湖	*dōng hú*
Flood Control Monument	防洪纪念碑	*fáng hóng jì niàn bēi*
Great Changjiang Bridge	长江大桥	*chángjiāng dàqiáo*
Gui Shan	龟山	*guī shān*
Guiyuan Si	归元寺	*guīyuán sì*
Hong Ge	红阁	*hóng gé*
Hubei Provincial Museum	湖北省博物馆	*húběi shěng bówùguǎn*
Jiu Nudun	九女墩	*jiǔ nǔdūn*
Mao's Villa	毛泽东别墅	*máo zí dōng bié shù*
Moshan	磨山	*móshān*
New Changjiang Bridge	长江公路桥	*chángjiāng gōnglù qiáo*
She Shan	蛇山	*shé shān*
Workers' Cultural Palace	文化宫	*wénhuà gōng*
Wuhan Department Store	武汉商店	*wǔhàn shāngdiàn*
Wuhan University	武汉大学	*wǔhàn dàxué*
Yellow Crane Tower	黄鹤塔	*huánghè tǎ*
Yue Hu	月湖	*yuè hú*
Zhongshan Park	中山公园	*zhòngshān gōngyuán*

RESTAURANTS AND ENTERTAINMENT

Da Zhonghua	大中华	*dà zhōnghuá*
Dehua	德华	*déhuá*
Lao Tongcheng	老通成	*lǎo tōngchéng*
Wuhan Acrobatic Hall	武汉杂技厅	*wǔhàn zhá jì tīng*
Xiao Taoyuan	小桃园	*xiǎo táoyuán*

teenth- century European classic and stolid Communist efforts. The docks and river-side promenades further lend the place the atmosphere of any waterside city, and there are some historic sites, including the **Guiyan Si** and a fine **Provincial Museum**, plus a handful of monuments linked with the **1911 revolution**. As the main beneficiary of profits from river trade and Hubei's postwar industrial development, however, Wuhan's real function is as an enthusiastically busy shopping and social centre, with many stores open late to meet demand. On the minus side, the city has a well-deserved reputation as one of China's three summer "furnaces": between May and September you'll find the streets melting and the gasping population surviving on a diet of watermelon and ice lollies.

Orientation, arrival and city transport

At over 10km across, Wuhan is very large, and with a choice of transit points spread all over the place – each of the three districts has a separate train and long-distance bus station – it's important to know where you're arriving before you get here. Most people stay on the northern bank of the Yangzi in **Hankou**, which, as the city's trade and business centre, contains most of the services and accommodation. South across the smaller Han River is lightly industrial **Hanyang**, while **Wuchang** recedes southeast of the Yangzi into semi-rural suburbs and parkland.

The new **Tianhe airport** lies 30km to the north of the city along a good road, with a **bus link** from here to both the airline office in Hankou's *Great Wall Hotel* on Hangkong Lu, and Hankou's **train station**. This is Wuhan's main rail terminus, set on the northern edge of Hankou along Fazhan Dadao, but many services also call in at Wuchang's station, right across town on Zhongshan Lu.

It's a similar story with **long-distance buses**. The major depots are on Jiefang Dadao in downtown Hankou, on Hanyang Dadao in Hanyang and near Wuchang's train station on Zhongshan Lu. Buses from all three depart for rural Hunan and beyond. The **Yangzi ferry terminal** sits on Yanjiang Dadao in Hankou – current timetables and ticket offices are within, and you'll probably have to change boats here if you're travelling the entire 2500km between Shanghai and Chongqing.

City transport

Wuhan is too large to consider walking everywhere, though the overloaded **bus and trolleybus** system seldom seems to be much quicker, and stops can be widely spaced. But services are at least regular and cheap – it only costs ¥1 between Wuchang and Hankou stations – crawling out to almost every corner of the city between around 6am

---

YANGZI RIVER CRUISES FROM WUHAN

Ferries depart Wuhan daily for Yichang and Chongqing upstream, and also downriver through Anhui Province (see p.437–38) to Nanjing and Shanghai. As foreigners are apt to be charged up to fifty percent more than the published fares, the following costs should be used as a guide only, although you can negotiate reductions with student cards. Prices are for foreigners travelling on standard ferries for private cabins, followed by the three levels of shared berth accommodation. Consult "The Yangzi River" section (p.805) for general information about types of vessels and classes available.
Fares and journey times from Wuhan:

Chongqing ¥790/330/235/185 (5 days) **Shanghai** ¥510/215/155/120 (3 days)
Nanjing ¥350/135/105/85 (48hr) **Yichang** ¥255/105/75/60 (36hr)

and 10pm. **Taxis**, found around transit points and hotels, tend to be an expensive option because of the distances involved, and cost ¥10 just to hire. For short hops, haggle with **motorbike** and **motor-rickshaw** drivers who prowl the bus and train depots. **Bicycles** are difficult to rent and not overly used, partly because of Wuhan's size, but also because of traffic regulations banning them from being ridden across the bridges. During daylight hours, there are **passenger ferries** across the Yangzi from Wuchang to Hankou or Hanyang; trips cost ¥1 and take about thirty minutes.

Maps of Wuhan showing transport routes can be picked up at bus and train stations, but shop around first as they seem to be either painfully detailed or almost abstract. City maps **in English** are sold by some foreign-language bookshops (see "Listings", p.456).

Accommodation

Almost all of Wuhan's **hotel** accommodation is upmarket. In addition to those listed below, there are **hostels** attached to Wuchang and Hankou train stations, but they are reluctant to take foreigners.

Hankou

Jianghan, 245 Shengli Jie (☎2811600, fax 2814342). Wuhan's best, a totally renovated French colonial mansion, with porphyry floors and wooden panelling through the lobby, relatively luxurious rooms and mostly bilingual staff. Polite enquiries often get non-guests the use of banking, mail and telephone facilities. Singles, doubles and suites. ⑧.

Linjiang, 1 Tianjin Lu (☎2832377). Nice mid-range rooms behind a sombre colonial facade. Central but quiet. ⑤.

Lunchuan Gongsi Zhaodaisuo, off Jiefang Gongyuan Lu. Take bus #509 from Hankou train station along Jainshe Dadao, or #24 to Jiefang Park from Zhongshan Dadao. A nostalgic experience for old hands – hostile reception staff and everything broken, but rooms are all right for the price. Doubles with or without private facilities. ①–②.

Shengli (*Victory Hotel*), 11 Siwei Lu (☎2838641, fax 2832604). Modern, five-storey block with much the same facilities as the nearby *Jianghan*, but none of the panache. ⑦.

Xieli, Tianjin Lu (☎2803903). Too new to be tarnished yet; nice staff and very central. ⑤.

Xuangong, 57 Jianghan Yi Lu (☎2810365, fax 2816942). Gloomy but atmospheric 1920s concession building with comfortable, barracks-like singles and doubles. ⑦–⑧.

Yangtze, 1131 Jiefang Dadao (☎5862828, fax 5854110). The latest hotel in the vicinity, whose *Chu Palace Restaurant* is currently the talk of the town. Located on a horrendously busy intersection, but otherwise good, with gym, bar and business facilities which non-guests may be allowed to use. Singles, doubles and suites. ⑦.

Wuchang

Dadongmen, Zhongshan Lu, on the intersection with Wuluo Lu. Buses #507 and #10 from Hankou run past the door and it's near Wuchang's train and bus stations. The staff seem none too delight-

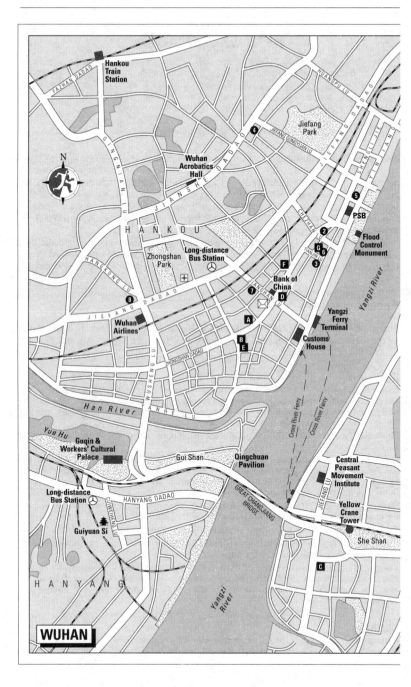

Hankou Train Station

Jiefang Park

JIEFANG GONGYUAN LU

4

Wuhan Acrobatics Hall

FAZHAN DADAO

QINGNIAN LU

JIANSHE DADAO

HUANGPU LU

JIEFANG DADAO

SHENGLI JIE

YINTIAN

HANKOU

5

PSB

CHEZHAN

2

Flood Control Monument

Zhongshan Park

Long-distance Bus Station

HANKONG LU

JIANGHAN DADAO

JIEFANG DADAO

G 6

3

F

Bank of China

7

D

Yangzi River

8

Wuhan Airlines

A

Yangzi Ferry Terminal

B
E

ZHONGSHAN DADAO

WUSHENG LU

Customs House

Han River

HANHE LU

Cross River Ferry

Cross River Ferry

Yue Hu

Guqin & Workers' Cultural Palace

Gui Shan

Qingchuan Pavilion

Central Peasant Movement Institute

Long-distance Bus Station

HANYANG DADAO

CUIWEIHENG LU

Guiyuan Si

GREAT CHANG-JIANG BRIDGE

JIEFANG LU

Yellow Crane Tower

She Shan

C

HANYANG

Yangzi River

WUHAN

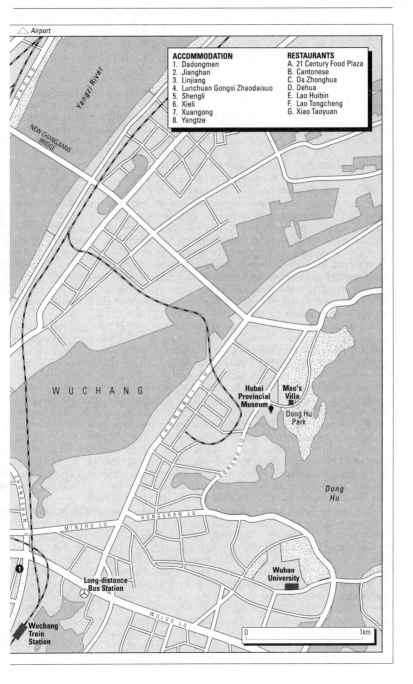

△ Airport

Yangzi River

NEW CHANGJIANG BRIDGE

DADAO

ACCOMMODATION
1. Dadongmen
2. Jianghan
3. Linjiang
4. Lunchuan Gongsi Zhaodaisuo
5. Shengli
6. Xieli
7. Xuangong
8. Yangtze

RESTAURANTS
A. 21 Century Food Plaza
B. Cantonese
C. Da Zhonghua
D. Dehua
E. Lao Huibin
F. Lao Tongcheng
G. Xiao Taoyuan

WUCHANG

HONGBEI LU

Hubei
Provincial
Museum

Mao's
Villa

Dong Hu
Park

DONGHU LU

HONGSHAN LU

Dong
Hu

HONGSHAN LU

MINZHU LU

Long-distance
Bus Station

Wuhan
University

WULUO LU

Wuchang
Train
Station

0   1km

ed at the occasional overseas guest, but they'll give you a bed, either in cheap, grubby singles or slightly better doubles, if one is available. Avoid rooms facing out on to the noisy main road. ⑨.

Hankou

Now the largest of Wuhan's districts, **Hankou** was once no more than a minor fishing harbour on the northern banks of the Yangzi. But deals struck at the end of the Second Opium War saw it opened to the world as a **treaty port** in 1861, and the colonial powers lost no time in building a grandiose concession. A violent history followed. Owing to its exclusive foreign connections, central Hankou was almost levelled during the nationwide **1911 uprisings** against the Qing, and later, rail workers leading the Communist-inspired 1923 strike were massacred in Hankou by the Nationalist warlord **Wu Beifu**. In 1937 the Guomindang, evicted from Nanjing by the Japanese, briefly established a national government in town before being forced farther west, and thirty years later Hankou again saw fighting between the PLA and various movements opposed to the Cultural Revolution and its Red Guards.

Today, bursting with traffic and crowds, but with no tourist sights as such, Hankou is a place to walk, shop, spend money and watch modern Chinese doing the same. This all happens in the area sandwiched between **Yanjiang Dadao**, along the banks of the Yangzi, and **Jiefeng Dadao**, parallel and about 1km to the northwest. Between the two runs Hankou's main thoroughfare, **Zhongshan Dadao**, a surprisingly narrow five-kilometre stretch of old and modern buildings densely packed with stores, restaurants and people. **Buses** #101 and #24, and **trolleybuses** #2 and #5, are handy for ranging along its length.

For a broad taste of the city, start on the southwestern end of Jiefang Dadao near the crossroads with Qingnian Lu (which runs 5km north to the station) at **Zhongshan Park**, once the colonial racecourse and now housing a small zoo and a collection of rare trees. Across the road, **Wuhan Department Store** is the city's most fashionable shopping centre, stacked with the latest in imported clothing and home appliances. Tellingly, many labels are in English, and only big spenders can afford to do more than look at the collection of blenders, microwaves and (given the climate) cruelly expensive air-conditioners. Past here, any street heading south will lead you to the more modern end of Zhongshan Dadao. Turn left and a kilometre or two of window shopping brings you to the crossroads with Jianghan Lu. This was the centre of the former foreign concession, and there are plenty of grand old buildings restored after the 1911 riots. The **Bank of China** is one of the best, an imposing Victorian-style edifice with a high panelled ceiling, Corinthian columns and chandeliers, while Jianghan Lu's **Huakong Grocery** presents a strange clash of century-old European decor – black and white floor tiles and glass counters – with Chinese confections on sale inside.

Wandering northeast through the back lanes from here brings you to the **old train station** on Chezhan Lu, whose derelict gothic shell is surrounded by a slightly seedy mass of shops and stalls, one of the liveliest areas of town in the evening if you're looking for inexpensive food. Alternatively, heading south from Zhongshan Dadao, you'll emerge somewhere on Yanjiang Dadao between the old **Customs House** and **Yangzi ferry terminal** on your right – the latter vaguely resembling the Sydney Opera House – and the **1954 Flood Control Monument** up on the left in Binjiang Park, a tall obelisk embellished with Mao's portrait and some very unpatriotic graffiti. It's a good spot to admire Wuhan's two trans-Yangzi links: upstream, the **Great Changjiang Bridge** between Hanyang and Wuchang was built as recently as 1957, before which all traffic – rail included – had to be ferried across the 1500-metre-wide river; downstream is the recently completed **New Changjiang Bridge** over into northern Wuchang, whose two-kilometre span is partially supported by a spray of suspension cables.

Hanyang

From Hankou, you can cross over the Han River into **Hanyang** (bus #45 from the Flood Monument or Zhongshan Dadao, or trolleybus #1 from Zhongshan Dadao), Wuhan's smallest district. Settled as far back as 600 AD, Hanyang remained insignificant until the late nineteenth century when the far-sighted viceroy, **Zhang Zhidong**, built the country's first large-scale iron and steel foundry as part of the "Self-strengthening Movement" – a last-ditch effort to modernize China during the twilight years of the Qing dynasty. Hanyang remains Wuhan's principal manufacturing sector, the streets dotted with factories producing "gourmet powder" (monosodium glutamate) and *Parrot* tape cassettes, but there are also a couple of worthwhile sights hidden away here.

The highway from Hankou crosses the Han Bridge and runs south to a huge roundabout, where the east road, out to the Changjiang Bridge, is flanked by **Gui Shan** (Tortoise Hill). Here the mythical hero Yu quelled the great floods four thousand years ago, and there's a splendid view out over the river from the upper level of the tatty Qing-style **Qingchuan Pavilion**. In the opposite direction are gardens surrounding **Yue Hu** (Moon Lake), where **Guqin** (the Ancient Lute Platform) was the haunt of legendary strummer **Yu Boya**. He is said to have played over the grave of his friend Zhong Ziqi and then smashed his instrument because the one person able to appreciate his music was dead. There's a bright but lifeless pavilion in his honour (¥1), and infrequent musical gatherings at the adjacent **Workers' Cultural Palace**, where the band performs traditional tunes to a slumbering, elderly audience.

Guiyan Si, the Temple of Original Tranquillity (daily 8.30am-5pm; ¥2), is a busy Buddhist monastery a couple of streets south of Guqin on Cuiweiheng Lu, behind Hanyang's long-distance bus station. There's a pervading sense of schoolroom authority in the plain, cavernous interior halls, with statues protected behind dusty glass cases and temple paraphernalia bundled away and tied up with cotton. The monastery's **scripture collection** – which includes a complete seven-thousand volume set of the rare Longcan Sutra – has made Guiyan famous in Buddhist circles, but visitors are more likely to be impressed by the several hundred individually styled saintly statues in the **Arhat Hall**, and the **statue of Sakyamuni** in the main hall, carved from a single block of white jade, a gift from Burma in 1935. Outside, there's an excellent **vegetarian restaurant** in the far from tranquil temple grounds, and an incense burner permanently ringed with visitors trying to get coins to stick to the (partially magnetized) surface.

Wuchang

Wuchang, on the right bank of the Yangzi, is historically the most important of the three districts. The walled capital of Wu during the *Three Kingdoms* period, Tang rulers later made the city a major port which, under the Mongols, became the administrative centre of a vast region covering present-day Hunan, Hubei, Guangdong and Guangxi provinces. Until 1911, however, the city had sidestepped the mainstream of Chinese history, but on October 10 that year a **bomb** exploded prematurely at the headquarters of a revolutionary group planning to protest against the politics behind the construction of the Hankou–Chongqing rail line. The police moved in and a pitched battle ensued, starting the nationwide rebellion which toppled the Qing dynasty and saw the formation of a republican government under **Sun Yatsen** in Nanjing the following year.

Still a provincial bureaucratic hub, Wuchang has few shops, none of Hankou's European architecture, and a good part of its outskirts are taken up by residential suburbs and by **Dong Hu** (East Lake), a natural expanse of greenery and water created by the silting up of a huge lake through which the Yangzi once flowed. A fine escape in itself from the bustle of Hankou, the park has a number of monuments around it including the nearby **Provincial Museum**, with other historic sites to stop off at along the way. To get to Wuchang, **buses** #503 and #45 run from central Hankou, or trans-Yangzi **ferries** cross between the southern end of Hankou's Yanjiang Dadao to Wuchang's **city bus terminus**, below and just north of the Great Changjiang Bridge.

Yellow Crane Tower and revolutionary relics

Once over the river, the bridge road becomes Wuluo Lu, almost immediately kinking around **She Shan** (Snake Hill). This and the whole riverbank are overlooked by the **Yellow Crane Tower**, no less magnificent for being an entirely modern Qing-style reproduction sited 1km from where the original third-century construction burned to a cinder in 1884. Over 50m tall, with five yellow-tiled levels stacked above each other and supported by scores of auspiciously red wooden columns, the tower has been the subject of countless poems and tales throughout the ages. One tells of a Taoist Immortal who paid his bills at a nearby inn by drawing a picture of a crane on the wall, which would fly down at intervals and entertain the guests. A few years later the Immortal returned and flew off on his creation, and the landlord, who doubtless could afford it by then, built a pavilion in his honour. Climb the internal staircases to the top floor and see Wuhan and the Yangzi at their best.

On the southern slopes of She Shan, **Hong Ge** (Red House) was the headquarters of the 1911 uprising, and a bronze **statue of Sun Yatsen** stands in the courtyard, though at the time he was abroad raising funds. About 1km north, near the river on Jiefang Lu, the **Central Peasant Movement Institute** (8.30am–noon & 2–5pm; ¥3) is where **Mao Zedong** is said to have trained eight hundred peasants during 1926–27. This is virtually abandoned nowadays, and inside there are only various bits of dusty furniture left over from Mao's time. As far as Wuhan is concerned, the Chairman is probably better known for his unlikely hour-long swim down the Yangzi on July 16, 1966, when, aided by currents, he allegedly covered 15km.

Hubei Provincial Museum

Bus #14 from Wuchang's riverside city bus terminus runs east to the main entrance to Dong Hu Park in about thirty minutes. At the stop before there's a signpost to the right for **Mao's Villa** (8.30am–5pm; ¥20), the house where he stayed when visiting the city. Strangely, there's no indication of the infinitely better **Hubei Provincial Museum** (daily 8.30am–noon & 2–5pm; ¥10), before the villa on the same road. Souvenir stalls outside the museum sell antiques and Cultural Revolution mementoes, and students from the nearby Wuhan University often hang around on Sundays, hoping to act as unpaid guides for foreigners.

There's a well laid-out section on the top floor about Hubei's general history, including folklore, remains of the Stone Age "Changyang Man" from southern Hubei, the Opium War and revolutionary events, most of which can be followed easily enough through old banknotes and photographs. But the real reason to spend a morning browsing here is to see the seven thousand items unearthed in 1978 from the nearby 2400-year-old **tomb of the Marquis Yi**, which are carefully arranged in cases downstairs. Particularly impressive are the set of **64 bronze bells** found in the waterlogged tomb with the wooden frame from which they once hung in rows; although many Chinese museums have similar examples, this is the largest set ever discovered. Clapperless (they are played with hand-held rods) and weighing between a couple of kilos and a quarter of a tonne, each bell can produce two notes depending on where it is struck. The knowledge of metals and casting required to achieve this initially boggled modern researchers, who took five years to make duplicates. Over a hundred other musical instruments are also on show, including stone chimes, drums, flutes and zithers, along with spearheads and a very weird brazen crane totem sprouting antlers – an inscription suggests that this was the Marquis's steed in the afterlife. The **museum shop** sells recordings of period tunes played on the bells.

Around Dong Hu

Up the road from the museum and laid out as a park in 1949 (take bus #14 as above), **Dong Hu** occupies some 73 square kilometres of winding lakeshore and green open spaces, somewhere to relax in relative peace among picnicking families and courting couples. Walking along the shore from the entrance with the water on your right, you pass a series of **pavilions and gardens** whose evocative names – Billow Listening House and Poem Reciting Hall, for example – compensate for their scruffy modern construction. Farther on, **Jiu Nudun** (Nine Heroines Tomb) is the resting place of nine women who fought in the Taiping Army during the great rebellion of 1851–64. From here, a five-kilometre-long **causeway** – covered by bus #54 – crosses to a mid-lake pavilion (where you can have lunch) and over to the far shore at **Moshan**.

Alternatively, you can catch a **boat** from near the park entrance to Moshan, where there's another restaurant in the *Bibo Hotel*, just north of the **Botanical Gardens**. These are a not entirely successful attempt to recreate a "traditional" garden, being over-elaborate and addicted to pot plants, which are ranged in rows, stands and piles. Further around the shore, there's a weekend **market**. From Moshan, bus #36 will take you round the southern shore and back to the Changjiang Bridge terminus past **Wuhan University** on Luojia Hill, whose intriguing campus, built in 1913 in pagoda-style, was the setting for a fierce battle in 1967 between anti-revolutionary forces and the PLA.

Eating, drinking and entertainment

Hubei cooking is characterized by its slow-steamed or braised dishes flavoured with light sauces, and, along the Yangzi at least, the use of **fish and shellfish**. You've really mastered chopsticks when you can eat a plate of shrimps the way they're served here – unshelled, which requires peeling them with your teeth. Wuhan itself excels in good food, and local dishes include: "flower" *shaomai*, where the dumpling corners are drawn up into five little pockets and filled with different-coloured stuffings; hot and dry noodles, flavoured with a sesame-paste sauce; *laotongcheng*, bean-paste omelettes; and medicinal soups made by the long and gentle stewing of fried chicken with seasonings. There are so many **fish dishes** that restaurants specialize in them – most famous are Wuchang fish and Brown-sauce fish, both braised in distinctive stocks. Banquet dishes, which are sometimes available on restaurant menus, include one of eastern China's gastronomic pinnacles, **dongpo pork**, a fat square of belly pork served meltingly soft after being steamed for hours in soy sauce.

For something a bit cheaper, try the backstreets through the old concession area of Hankou around Zhongshan Dadao and Jianghan Lu, where you'll find a gathering of nondescript, good-value restaurants and **food stalls**. The train stations at Hankou and Wuchang also have some surprisingly good budget places, serving mostly vegetable and fish dishes. In addition, Zhongshan Dadao in Hankou is peppered with *Fried Chicken* outlets, offering reasonable fast food.

As for entertainment, there's a knot of **cinemas** in Hankou around Jianghan Lu and Zhongshan Dadao. Wuhan is well known for its **acrobats**, who sadly seem to be anywhere but in town. Performances occur infrequently at the **Wuhan acrobatic hall** on Jianshe Dadao, Hankou (used as a rollerskating disco when the acrobats are off touring), and also in Hankou at the **Wuhan acrobatic troupe**'s headquarters on Yanjiang Dadao; ticket offices are in the vicinity. Details of these and other travelling shows are published in the Chinese paper *Wuhan Wenbao*, or try asking at a hotel reception.

Restaurants

21 Century Food Plaza on Qianjin 4 Lu, off Zhongshan Dadao, Hankou. A rather more unusual fast-food place with a full range of "Asian" dishes – Thai, Indonesian, Indian.

Cantonese Restaurant, Zhongshan Dadao, Hankou. This is a huge place with an Arabic sign currently being built about halfway along Zhongshan Dadao – possibly a resurrected version of *Dong Lai Shun*, one of Wuhan's old Muslim restaurants. Worth trying for roast lamb and poultry, and other southern dishes.

Da Zhonghua, Pengliuyang Lu, Wuchang. Four-storey establishment, long known for its classic and innovative ways with fish – try the red berry sauce. Dumplings and local soups on the first floor, general dining room on the third, tea house on top.

Dehua, Sanmin Lu (south of Zhongshan Dadao–Jianghan Lu intersection), Hankou. Beijing-style restaurant, with good range of *shaomai* and other dumplings as well as more expensive banquet dishes like braised abalone and shark fin soup.

Lao Huibin, near corner of Mingquan Lu/Qianjin Lu, Hankou. Recently relocated, this is a treat, one of the city's longest running and most renowned restaurants, offering everything from famous Hubei dishes down to dumplings and snacks.

Lao Tongcheng, Zhongshan Dadao, Hankou. Unbelievably busy canteen-style dumpling house, renowned for its *doupi* (beanpaste rolls). "Three flavoured" are considered best, stuffed with a mixture of tongue, heart and bamboo shoots, but there are also shrimp and chicken fillings for those not addicted to offal.

Sun Generation, under the *Brother Fai* shopping centre on the corner of Zhongshan Dadao and Qianjin 5 Lu, Hankou. The nearest thing in town to a fast-food burger bar.

Vegetarian Restaurant, Guiyan Si, Hanyang. Sound, if not unusual, cooking. Open for lunch only.

Xiao Taoyuan, Shengli Jie, Hankou. Restorative soups are the speciality of the house here, usually made with slow-cooked chicken flavoured with various spices.

Listings

Airlines *Hubei International Airlines*, 4 Jianghan Nan Lu, Hankou (Mon–Sat 9am–5pm; ☎5862607); *Wuhan Airlines*, Qiangnian Lu, Hankou (daily 8am–8pm; ☎5831320). The main airline booking office is in the *Great Wall Hotel* on Hangkong Lu and see travel agents, below.

Banks and exchange *Bank of China*, Zhongshan Dadao, Hankou (Mon–Sat 8.30am–4.30pm, Sun 9am–noon). Some larger hotels have foreign exchange facilities, and might allow you to change travellers' cheques even if you're not staying there.

Bookshops There's a huge bookstore with some English titles – including abridged texts of Chinese classics such as *Dream of Red Mansions* – near the Jianghan Lu junction on Zhongshan Dadao, Hankou. Stalls on Hangkong Lu also have the odd foreign-language item, including city maps, and the post office here stocks the *China Daily*.

Buses Wuhan's biggest and busiest long-distance bus station is on Jiefang Dadao in Hankou, handling departures to destinations all over China. Those in Wuchang and Hanyang are more limited, but with additional useful services south at least as far as Nanchang and Changsha. Sleeper and standard buses leave from all stations and, with so much traffic, there's seldom any problem getting a seat wherever you're heading.

Ferries The Yangzi ferry terminal is on Yanjiang Dadao, Hankou; booking office open daily 9am–noon & 2–5pm; ☎2839546. Bigger hotels can also make reservations. For prices and departures from Wuhan to Shanghai and Chongqing, see the "Yangzi River Cruises" box, p.448.

Hospitals These are everywhere – the *Tongji*, west of the Jiefang Dadao–Qingnian Lu crossroads in Hankou, is considered Wuhan's best. Another good one is the hospital atttached to the *Hubei Traditional Medicine College*, just north of She Shan, Wuchang.

Left luggage There are lockers at the bus and train stations.

Markets Coin and stamp collectors congregate outside the post office on Hangkong Lu, Hankou. There's a good live produce market below street level on Zhongshan Lu, Wuchang (across from the *Dadongmen Hotel*), and countless stalls in the side streets of Hankou's old concession area, north of Zhongshan Dadao.

Pharmacies In addition to smaller places elsewhere, Hankou's Hangkong Lu has a string of pharmacies stocking traditional and modern medicines next door to the Tongji Medical University.

PSB Yanjiang Dadao, Hankou (☎5866666).

Post offices The main offices are on Zhongshan Dadao and at the junction of Hangkong Lu and Qingnian Lu, Hankou (daily 8am–6pm). There is no GPO as such, so don't expect to be able to locate mail labelled "GPO Wuhan" – ensure you use the street name and "Hankou", or it could end up anywhere in the city.

Telephones International telephones are available at both of the main post offices in Hankou. Upmarket hotels have their own facilities, and may allow non-residents to use them.

Shopping Downtown Hankou seethes with shopping opportunities, but most items are household goods no different from those sold all over the world. For "antiques", try *Wuhan Historical Relics Store* at the southwestern end of Zhongshan Dadao, and the shop and stalls attached to the Provincial Museum over in Wuchang. Back in Hankou, the *Friendship Store* on Baocheng Lu is poorly stocked and conspicuously deserted, while shops nearby sell the latest karaoke systems and Japanese motorbikes.

Trains Wuhan's two main stations are at Hankou and Wuchang. Though some services pass through both, Hankou is seen as the city's main station; generally, use Hankou for northern destinations and Wuchang if you're heading south. The huge amount of rail traffic passing through town means that you've a better than normal chance of securing a berth if you try at least two days in advance; there's a special sleeper reservation booth inside the Hankou terminal, while foreigners should use window #14 when booking in Wuchang. You can only buy onward tickets at the station the service departs from.

Travel agents For what it's worth, *CITS* is in Hankou at 1365 Zhongshan Dadao (Mon–Fri 8.30–11am & 2–5pm; ☎5782306), but seems to know nothing about either Wuhan or Hubei, and can only speak Mandarin or Russian. For airline bookings, try *CHOTC*, opposite the *Xuangong Hotel* on Jianghan Yi Lu, Hankou (Mon–Fri 8.30–11am & 2–4.30pm; ☎2842335).

On up the Yangzi

It takes around 36 hours to navigate the bland plains upstream between Wuhan and **Yichang**, from where the exciting journey through the Yangzi Gorges and on to Chongqing in Sichuan begins. Towns on the way can be seen at a distance from the deck of the cruise boats, though to reach them you'll probably have to skip the river and go cross-country from Wuhan.

ON UP THE YANGZI		
Chibi	赤壁	*chìbì*
Jingzhou	荆州	*jīngzhōu*
Puqi	蒲圻	*púqí*
Shashi	沙市	*shāshì*
Yichang	宜昌	*yíchāng*
Taohualing Binguan	桃花岭宾馆	*táohuālíng bīnguǎn*

Chibi, Shashi and Jingzhou

The first place of any significance along the river lies about 80km southwest of Wuhan at **Chibi**. It's not a regular cruise stop, so to get here you'll generally need to take a train to **PUQI**, a town on the rail line about two-thirds of the way between Wuhan and Yueyang in Hunan, from where it's a ninety-minute local bus ride.

Clearly visible from the river, **CHIBI** (Red Cliffs) is little more than a large village, but its history touches on one of the most important battles of the *Three Kingdoms* period, making for an interesting half-day walk from the high street bus stop. It was here in 208 AD that the northern armies of Wei, led by Cao Cao, descended on the combined southern forces of Liu Bei and Sun Quan. Though heavily outnumbered, the southerners had brought two remarkable strategists along – **Zhuge Liang** and **Pang Tong** – who took full advantage of Cao's foolish decision to launch a naval assault across the river. Misled by Pang Tong's spies, Cao chained his ships together on the north bank whilst preparing for the attack, and Zhuge Liang – using Taoist magic – created an unseasonal southeasterly wind and sent a flotilla of burning hulks across the Yangzi, completely incinerating Cao's armada and permanently imprinting the colour of flames on the cliffs. The rock face on the southern bank just outside town is carved with the two characters for "*chibi*", supposedly by the triumphant Wu general, **Zhou Yu**.

A flight of steps on the right near the bus stop leads to the whitewashed **Feng Chu Temple** on Jingluan Hill, where Pang Tong studied military strategy and so conceived the plan that defeated Cao. The path continues up to a stele and the small **Yinjiang Pavilion**, a former guard post which still commands broad views of the terraced paddy fields below. Back on the high street, bearing left brings you to **Nanping Shan**, where two stone lions up on the hill flank the entrance to **Wuhou Palace** and **Baifeng Terrace**. Four statues here commemorate Zhuge Liang and Liu Bei, along with Liu Bei's oath brothers, Guan Yu and Zhang Fei (see box, p.432). Spears, arrowheads and pottery shards in a gloomy museum nearby offer proof that the legends have a historical basis.

The other main sights on the way to Yichang are at **SHASHI** and adjacent **JINGZHOU**, which lie on the north bank of the Yangzi about 120km from Chibi. River boats might call in to Shashi, from where it's possible to catch a bus to its sister town which, as **Jiangling**, was the birthplace of the poet Qu Yuan and centre of his beloved state of Chu. It later featured in *Three Kingdom's* mythology, when Guan Yu commanded Shu's eastern defences here and built the city walls. These are still standing, and even older are the **mummified remains** of a Han noble on display in the local museum.

Yichang

While there's little more to **YICHANG** than its transit terminals and the streets in between, the town was an important commercial centre under the Han, and became a treaty port last century. Fading somewhat during the early twentieth century, the blossoming of Yangzi tourism and northwestern Hubei's car manufacturing industry, as well as the building of the **Gezhouba dam** upstream (soon to be overshadowed by the Three Gorges project, see p.459), has seen an optimistic renaissance replacing the once decrepit atmosphere. That said, there's little of interest in the newly rebuilt city centre – glaring and shadeless in summer – but animated evening scenery along the river compensates, with water traffic moored up, nightclub barges throbbing to karaoke efforts, and crowds gorging themselves on hotpots and shellfish at nearby street restaurants, or just sitting on the banks cooling off with ice creams.

The town stretches along the northern river bank for around 5km directly below the Gezhouba dam, with **buses and trains** pulling in near each other on Dongshan Dadao. Due south of the train station, itself atop a huge flight of stairs, buses #3 and #4 run for a kilometre down **Yunji Lu** through the town centre to Yanjiang Dadao and the river, then turn left for another couple of kilometres to the **ferry terminal** and booking office. Daily departure times in both directions are chalked up on a blackboard here, but because the journey into Sichuan through the Three Gorges takes five days against

THE THREE GORGES DAM

Through the centuries, the **Yangzi**'s unruly nature has been a source of trauma for local people, and conquering the river's tendency to flood extravagantly once a decade has become a symbol of limitless power in China. So far this has only been achieved in legend, when the mythical Shang emperor Yu quelled twelve capricious water dragons. However, by 2009 the river may finally come under human control. After almost a century of planning (the idea was first mooted by Sun Yatsen), the **Three Gorges Dam**, currently under construction at **Sandouping**, about 30km upstream from Yichang, will be the largest of its kind in the world, the 185-metre-high wall creating an artificial lake extending back for over 550km through the Three Gorges to Chongqing. Though investment has been promoted through the dam's hydro-electric potential – its eventual output will provide ten percent of all China's power needs – it's the dam's flood-controlling capabilities which Premier **Li Peng** (himself a hydro-electric engineer) is using to counter mounting protests against the project, which many see as inviting disaster on all fronts. It is a financial monster – eventual costs are estimated at around ¥120 billion and rising – and environmental concerns have prompted the US to advise its companies not to become involved, while increased water levels of up to 115 metres through the Three Gorges will submerge countless communities, require the relocation of millions of people, and doubtless lessen the scenic spectacle. It doesn't bear thinking about what would happen should the completed dam wall ever give way, but protesters also point out that the project will probably do little to relieve flooding – which occurs along tributaries as much as the Yangzi itself – and say it would be more effective and cheaper to build a string of lesser dams.

the current from Yichang to Chongqing, instead of three coming the other way, most people start this trip upstream – see pp.805–809. Bus and train departures from Yichang head up into Hubei's northwest, east to Wuhan and south into Hunan.

For **accommodation**, the *Taohualing Binguan* (*Peach Blossom Hotel*), off Yunji Lu (☎0717/442244, fax 445701; ⑤–⑧) has the best rooms in town in its new wing and damp, overpriced doubles in the old. It also contains a good **restaurant**, a branch of *CITS*, international phones, post office and banking facilities. For budget travellers, rooms at the *Xiazhou* on Yiling Lu (☎0717/448089; ⑤), which crosses Yunji Lu near the station, are slightly cheaper and certainly no worse. Or you could try arguing your way into a bed at the **hostel** (②) across from the bus station. There's a **post office** (daily 8am–6pm) at the junction of Yunji Lu and Yiling Lu, and another *CITS* agent – good for cruise bookings if nothing else – at 27 Yunji Lu (daily 8.30–11am & 2–5pm; ☎0717/445175).

Northwestern Hubei

Much of northwestern Hubei, which butts up against Henan, Shaanxi and Sichuan, is covered by mountain ranges and steeped in legends centred around **Wudang Shan**, the Military Mountain, known for its Taoist temples and *wushu* fighting style. Despite being out of the way, a relatively easy ascent coupled with the mountain's scenery really make the journey worthwhile, though the surrounding region has recently become central China's **car manufacturing capital**, and whole valleys, virtually uninhabited a decade ago and still remote except for their rail links to Yichang and Wuhan, now lie under the fumes from factories producing indigenous Volkswagens and Citroëns. Overseas visitors are rare, though occasionally you'll encounter bemused foreign experts, here to start up new businesses or to help in upgrading old ones.

NORTHWESTERN HUBEI

Shennongjia Forest Reserve	神农架林区	*shénnóng jià línqū*
Shiyan	十堰	*shíyàn*
Wudang Shan Town	武当山市镇	*wǔdāngshān shìzhèn*
Wudang Shan	武当山	*wǔdāngshān*
Feisheng Rock	飞升岩	*fēishēng yán*
Huangjing Hall	皇经堂	*huángjīng táng*
Huanglong Dong	黄龙洞	*huánglóng dòng*
Jindian Gong	金殿宫	*jīndiàn gōng*
Nanyan Gong	南岩宫	*nányán gōng*
Taihe	太和宫	*tàihé gōng*
Zixiao Gong	紫霄宫	*zǐxiāo gōng*
Xiangfan	襄樊	*xiāngfán*
Railway Grand Hotel	铁路大酒店	*tiělù dàjiǔdiàn*

To Wudang Shan

The road up Wudang Shan starts at **Wudang Shan Town**, reached either from **Shiyan**, 30km to the west, or **Xiangfan**, 120km east. Trains to Shiyan run from Wuhan and Yichang via Xiangfan (see below), or you can bus it from Yichang to Shiyan past the **Shennongjia Forest Reserve**. Traversed in the early twentieth century by the botanist **E. H. Wilson**, who discovered several new plant species for Kew Botanical Gardens in London, this is a wild region not yet much affected by tourism, though there is accommodation and food available at the reserve entrance some 30km east of the main road. The highlight is **Da Shennongjia**, the highest peak in central China at an impressive 3053m, coupled with intriguing rumours of the **Chinese apeman**, whose existence (though captured specimens have so far proved to be stump-tailed monkeys) seems far from impossible in this mountain stronghold of ancient, primitive plants.

Xiangfan

XIANGFAN, a friendly city about eight hours from both Yichang and Wuhan, is the northwest's administrative capital, with a history reaching back to the Zhou dynasty (1066–221 BC). It was at the nearby hill resort of **Longzhong** that the *Three Kingdoms'* warlord, Liu Bei, first sought the advice of the reclusive genius **Zhuge Liang** in his struggles against Cao Cao. Dismissed from Longzhong three times without meeting Zhuge, Liu's patience finally gained him an interview, and in the "Reply at Longzhong", Zhuge outlined the philosophy which was to enable Liu to defeat Cao's superior forces. Zhuge subsequently left Longzhong to join Liu's war effort as his chief adviser, and later became **Kongming**, governor of the state of Shu. One later relic is Xiangfan's Ming-dynasty **city wall** – you can take a round trip on bus #13 or #14 from the train station and over the Han River, where some sections have recently been restored with construction blocks.

None of this necessitates a stop here, but lack of transport connections may see you spending a night in town. **Buses** arrive in Xiangfan along Zhongyuan Lu; turn left (east) out of the depot and the **train station** is a two-minute walk away at the end of the road on Qianjin Lu. For a **place to stay** try the tower opposite the station which houses the very comfortable *Railway Grand Hotel* (☎0710/220043, fax 221774; ⑦). More modest rooms are available at the guesthouse set back off the pavement a short way south down Qianjin Lu (②–③). The whole area is thick with inexpensive **restaurants** and mobile food stalls, while *Orgies Fast Food*, in the southeast of town on Changzheng Lu, is worth a visit for the name and its very palatable burgers.

Moving on, there are several morning **trains** for the three-hour run to Shiyan, and an afternoon service which actually stops at Wudang Shan Town (the only train to do so). Alternatively, **buses** leave in the morning for Shiyan via Wudang Shan Town (roughly five hours) from both the depot and outside the train station.

Shiyan and Wudang Shan Town

There's nothing of interest behind **SHIYAN**'s ugly industrial facade, and it's best to hop straight on one of the frequent minibuses to Wudang Shan departing from opposite the train station or inside the long-distance bus forecourt. The sixty-minute journey to the mountain (¥7) takes you through a mess of satellite towns smeared along what was previously a pretty river valley; trucks shuttle back and forth between factories and trains, trays stacked with black, clean chassis.

There's seldom any need to stay in two-street **WUDANG SHAN TOWN** itself – though there's at least one hostel and a couple of hotels here – as minibuses sporting red and white Tao symbols hang around arrival points at least until early evening for the thirty-kilometre run up the ridges to the mountain's trail head. Hawkers proffer bilingual **maps**, and there's a stop among souvenir stalls at the **park gates** just outside town to pay the mountain entrance fee (¥13). The drivers waste no time on the road, tearing past dry fields lower down before the slopes become too extreme to be cultivated, and wild vegetation clutters up the roadside. You'll see ranks of young martial arts students training with swords outside temples along the way. The road terminates on the upper reaches of the range in a "village square" formed by a cluster of **hotels**, gift shops and bars. The best-value beds are in the large block right at the end, where there are clean doubles (③) and sometimes dormitory space (①). All of the accommodation places have somewhere **to eat** on the premises, and there are a couple of scruffy canteens here too.

On Wudang Shan

Peaking at its 1600-metre **Tianzhu summit**, Wudang Shan's 72 pinnacles, have, since Tang times, been liberally covered in Taoist **temples**. Those which survived a wave of thirteenth-century revolts were restored following proclamations for the development of religion under the Ming emperor **Cheng Zi** in 1413 – the work took three hundred thousand labourers ten years to complete – and the recent lifting of restrictions is seeing another bloom of religious fervour on the mountains, with many of the temples emerging fabulously decorated and busy after decades of neglect.

In China at least, Wudang Shan is also famous for its **martial arts**, which command as much respect as those of Henan's Shaolin Si (see p.267). It's said that the Song-dynasty monk Zhang Sanfeng developed Wudang boxing after watching a fight between a snake and a magpie, which revealed to him the essence of *neijia*, an internal force used – in typical Taoist manner – to control action with inaction. Fighting skills would also have come in handy considering the vast number of **outlaws** who've inhabited these mountains over the centuries. The Ming peasant leader **Li Zicheng** massed his forces and rose in rebellion from his stronghold here, and there's a tablet recording the suppression of the Red Turbans on the mountain by Qing troops in 1856. More recently, the Communist **Third Front Army** found sanctuary in 1931, after their march from Hong Lake in southern Hubei.

On a more peaceful note, Wudang Shan is also famed as the retreat of Emperor **Zhen Wu**, a Taoist mystic, who cultivated his longevity on Tianzhu during the fifteenth century. A hundred years later, Wudang's valuable plants attracted the attention of pharmacologist **Li Shizhen**, who included four hundred local species among the 1800 listed in his *Materia Medica*, still a source work on the medicinal use of Chinese herbs.

Zixiao Gong and Nanyan Gong

About 1km downhill from the road head – you'll have seen it in passing – is **Zixiao Gong** (Purple Cloud Palace), an impressively huge early Ming temple complex whose pattern of successively higher platforms appears to mimic the structure of the hills above and which is fast becoming the mountain's most important single monastery. You can walk through the gates and up the broad stone staircase to the main hall, whose exterior is lightened by the graceful sweep of its tiled roof. Inside is a crowd of dusty statues, and a particularly fine ceiling formed from interlocking wooden beams, spiralling up to a flat grid sunk with an octagonal panel, richly decorated in red, blue and gold. Quite apart from this, the whole place is pleasantly active with monks, tourists and the occasional mendicant traveller.

In a completely different league, a track from the hotel area leads, almost immediately, to **Nanyan Gong** (Nanyan Palace), perched fortress-like on a precipice. The buildings are necessarily austere, carved as they are out of the cliff face, but the main sight here is **Dragon Head Rock**, a two-metre-long slab sculpted with swirls and scales which projects straight out over the void. Countless people lost their lives trying to walk to the end with a stick of incense before it was roped off. Carry on past the temple to **Feisheng Rock** for far safer views of the scenery.

Tianzhu

It takes around two hours to walk from the square to the top of Tianzhu along a comfortably paved path (a waterproof or umbrella may come in handy as protection against Wudang Shan's famously changeable weather). One way to keep your mind off the flights of steps is by watching out for **birdlife** in the forest – the boisterous red-billed magpies, with graceful blue tails, are the easiest to spot. The path divides halfway along at **Huanglong Dong** (Yellow Dragon Cave) to form an eventual circuit via the peak; continue straight ahead for the least taxing walk and superb views through the canopy towards Tianzhu's apparently unscalable vertical cliffs. Above, the cloud-swept summit is crowned with the Ming-dynasty Golden Palace Temple, **Jindian Gong**, and, having climbed the staircase to the terrace, you take a breather and admire the spectacular scenery (clearest in the morning), looking down from the top of the world, with sharp crags dropping away through wispy clouds into the forest below. **Taihe**, the temple below the summit, is impressive not just for its age, but also for the atmosphere of grand decay enclosed by the thick green tiles and red walls of **Huangjing Hall**. Monks stand around the cramped stone courtyards or pray in the richly decorated, peeling rooms squeezed inside. For a further ¥10 you can ascend the unbelievably steep **Jiulendeng** (Staircase of Nine Turns) to the Golden Palace itself, a temple shrine decorated with a gilded bronze roof embellished with cranes and deer, whose tiny interior is filled by a statue of armour-clad Zhen Wu sitting behind a desk in judgement.

HUNAN

For many travellers, their experience of **Hunan** is a pastiche of the tourist image of rural China – a view of endless muddy tracts or intensely farmed paddy fields rolling past the train window, green or gold depending on the season. But the bland countryside, or rather the lot of the peasants farming it, has greatly affected the country's recent history. Hunan's most famous peasant son, **Mao Zedong**, saw the crushing poverty inflicted on local farmers by landlords and a corrupt government, and was incensed by the brutality with which any protests against the system were suppressed.

Though he is no longer accorded his former god-like status, monuments to Mao litter the landscape around the provincial capital **Changsha**, which, as somewhere to break an overlong train journey, is a convenient base for exploring the scenes of his youth. By contrast, the relaxed, history-laden town of **Yueyang** in northern Hunan, where the Yangzi meanders past **Dongting Hu**, China's second largest lake, offers more genteel attractions. Both Hunan and Hubei – literally "south of the lake" and "north of the lake" respectively – take their names from this vast expanse of water, which is intricately tied to the origins of **dragon-boat racing**. Farther afield, there's a pleasant group of mountain temples a day's journey south of Changsha at **Heng Shan**, and some inspiringly rugged landscapes to tramp through far to the west at **Wulingyuan Scenic Reserve**.

Changsha and around

There's little evidence to show that the site of **CHANGSHA**, Hunan's tidy, nondescript capital, has been inhabited for three thousand years, but it has long been an important river town and, prior to Qin invasions in 280 BC, was the southern capital of the kingdom of **Chu**. Caught in the crossfire of the nineteenth-century peasant rebellions which swept through central China, most of what was left of the old city was torched in the 1940s by the Guomindang, who were trying to dislodge Japanese resistance, and the rest was largely cleared in recent modernizations. While ancient sites and objects occasionally surface nearby – such as Shang-era bronze wine jars, and the magnificently preserved contents of three **Han burial mounds** – their presence is swamped by more contemporary structures: busy clover-leaf intersections, grey concrete facades and electronic billboards advertising cigarettes with the help of a famous cartoon beagle.

Primarily, though, Changsha is known for its links with **Mao**. He arrived here from his native village in 1911, aged eighteen and eager to be educated, at a time of considerable social tension. **Rice riots** in the city had followed two severe **famines** in 1906 and 1910, when, deprived of land rights, Hunanese peasants had starved in their thousands. More directly, the overthrow of the Manchu dynasty coincided with his arrival, and, as nationwide power struggles erupted, Mao dropped out of school to spend six months as a private in the local militia, returning to the classroom in 1913 where he remained until completing his studies. During his residence, Changsha became a breeding ground for secret political societies and intellectuals, and by 1918 there was a real movement for Hunan to become a self-governing, independent state. For a time, this idea even found favour with the powerful local warlord **Zhao Hendi**, though he eventually violently turned on the students and workers who supported him. Mao, by now a teacher, was singled out and fled to Beijing, where he was soon to co-found the Chinese Communist Party. He later returned to the city and spent much of the 1920s organizing peasant uprisings in rural Hunan.

Mao was by no means the only young Hunanese profoundly affected by these events, and a number of his contemporaries later surfaced in the Communist government: **Liu Shaoqi**, Mao's deputy until he became a victim of the Cultural Revolution; four Politburo members under Deng Xiaoping, including the former CCP chief, **Hu Yaobang**; and **Hua Guofeng**, Mao's lookalike and briefly empowered successor. Today, Changsha's few formal attractions are dominated by the Chairman's presence, though there are also a couple of parks to wander around, and a fascinating **Provincial Museum**. The only real day trip from Changsha is out to Mao's birthplace at **Shaoshan**, 90km to the southwest, a very pleasant excursion made easier by well-organized public transport.

CHANGSHA AND AROUND

Changsha	长沙	*chángshā*

ACCOMMODATION

Binhua	宾华宾馆	*bīnhuá bīnguǎn*
Chuyun	楚云饭店	*chǔyún fàndiàn*
Civil Aviation	民大酒店	*mín dàjiǔdiàn*
Cygnet	小天鹅大酒店	*xiǎo tiāné dàjiǔdiàn*
Lotus	芙蓉宾馆	*fúróng bīnguǎn*
Louyuan	陋园宾馆	*lòuyuán bīnguǎn*

THE CITY

Aiwan Pavilion	爱晚楼	*àiwǎn lóu*
First Teachers' Training School	第一师范	*dìyī shīfàn*
Hunan Provincial Museum	湖南省博物馆	*húnán shěng bówùguǎn*
Martyrs' Park	烈士公园	*liè shì gōngyuán*
Orange Island	桔子洲	*júzi zhōu*
Qingshui Tang	清水潭	*qīngshuǐ tán*
Wangxiang Pavilion	望乡楼	*wàngxiāng lóu*
Xiang River	湘江	*xiāng jiāng*
Yuelu Academy	岳麓书院	*yuèlù shū yuàn*
Yuelu Shan	岳麓山	*yuèlù shān*

RESTAURANTS

Fire Palace	火宫饭店	*huǒgōng fàndiàn*
Xiao Xiang	小乡	*xiǎo xiāng*

AROUND CHANGSHA

Shaoshan	韶山	*sháoshān*
Dripping Water Cave	滴水洞	*dī shuǐ dòng*
Mao Ancestral Temple	毛氏宗祠	*máo shì zōng cí*
Mao Zedong Exhibition Hall	毛泽东纪念馆	*máo zédōng jìniàn guǎn*
Mao's Family Home	毛泽东故居	*máo zédōng gù jū*

ACCOMMODATION

Hongri Fandian	红日饭店	*hóngrì fàndiàn*
Shaoshan Binguan	韶山宾馆	*sháoshān bīnguǎn*
Shaoshan Fandian	韶山饭店	*sháoshān fàndiàn*

Orientation, arrival, city transport and accommodation

The bulk of Changsha is spread east of the **Xiang River**, and the city's name – literally "long sand" – derives from a narrow midstream bar, now called **Orange Island**. The river itself is spanned by the lengthy Xiangjiang Bridge, which links the city to the west bank suburbs, **Yuelu Academy** and parkland. **Wuyi Lu** is Changsha's main drag and forms a very unfocused downtown district, divided into eastern (Dong Lu), middle (Zhong Lu), and western (Xi Lu) sections as it runs broad and straight for 4km between the train station and river.

The **telephone code** for Changsha is ☎0731

The airport is 15km east of town, connected to the airline offices on Wuyi Lu by a **shuttle bus** (¥20), but you're more likely to find yourself elbowing through chaotic throngs at the **long-distance bus station**, or standing in the square outside the rather more placid **train station**, both within a stone's throw of each other at the end of Wuyi Dong Lu. Long-distance buses arriving after the bus station closes at 6pm, however, sometimes pull up across the river in the western suburbs, and you might have to wait there until the city transport revs up after daybreak – take a taxi or bus #12 across the bridge and down Wuyi Lu.

City transport

As the city is large and the sights are spread out, you'll certainly need to use the **public transport system** at some time or other. The reasonably comprehensive **bus and trolleybus** network runs between about 6am and 9pm, but because of Changsha's scale and congested roads, you should allow plenty of time to get anywhere, and expect to have to change buses to reach your destination. Almost all services originate at, or at least stop at, the train station square. Chinese **maps** of the city, with the **bus routes** ambiguously marked, are easily picked up from street vendors outside the train station, which is also a good place to hail a **taxi**. These cost around ¥8 to hire; you then pay for distance covered in ¥1.60 increments. At present, **bicycles** seem almost impossible to rent – *CITS* or your hotel reception might be able to find you one.

Accommodation

Due to tight controls, **hotels** in Changsha able to accept foreigners are, without exception, fairly expensive. With plenty of time to spare, it might be worth leaving your bags in a locker somewhere and politely asking the *CITS* if they know of any cheaper options for you to chase up on foot, though they don't seem very attuned to the situation. All of the following have restaurants, with the best Hunanese fare at the *Lotus* and *Cygnet*.

Binhua, Bayi Lu. Take bus #1 from outside the train station, or it's a short walk from the bus station. This is a busy Chinese hotel which occasionally lets foreigners stay in its three-bed dorms, although staff are none too welcoming. ②.

Chuyun, Xiaoyuan Lu, opposite the train station (☎2299080). Generally the city's cheapest and most convenient rooms, though last reports spoke of renovations. Consider yourself very lucky to get a dorm bed here, otherwise there's a range of single and double rooms. Dorms ①, rooms ④–⑤.

Civil Aviation, 5 Wuyi Lu (☎2290888, fax 2298014). Close to the bus and train stations, this is a well-run and recently refurbished *CAAC* operation, full of scheduling victims. Decent doubles. ⑤–⑦.

Cygnet, 26 Wuyi Zhong Lu (☎4410400, fax 4423698). This huge multi-storey complex (bus #12 from the train station), designed to lure international business folk, has a cabaret nightclub, swimming pool and gym. ⑦.

Lotus, 8 Wuyi Dong Lu (☎4401888, fax 4445175). A rambling, early 1980s-style hotel, once upmarket but now showing distinct signs of wear. Bus #12 from train station. ⑥.

Louyuan, Xiangchun Zhong Lu (☎4421258, fax 4437409). Not central – you'll need to take a taxi here (¥12) – but rooms are airy and tidy and reasonable value. ⑥.

The City

Much of Changsha is functional, with little to absorb between the sights, but people are noticeably friendly and it's not unusual to acquire a guide while walking around. Wrinkled **betel nut** pods (*bin lang*) are sold by scissor-wielding vendors around the centre – chewing these boiled slices of areca palm seed is mildly stimulating, but as the

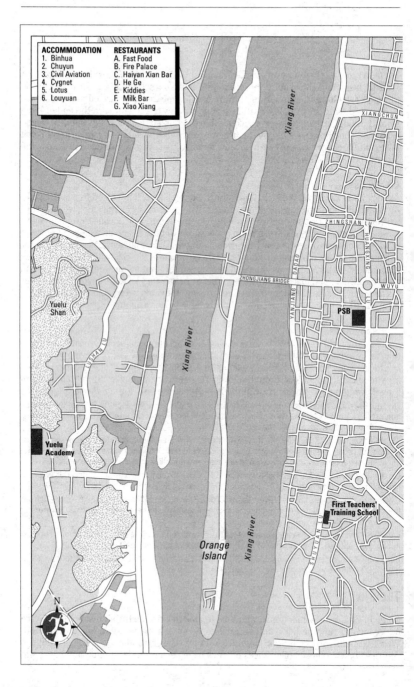

ACCOMMODATION
1. Binhua
2. Chuyun
3. Civil Aviation
4. Cygnet
5. Lotus
6. Louyuan

RESTAURANTS
A. Fast Food
B. Fire Palace
C. Haiyan Xian Bar
D. He Ge
E. Kiddies
F. Milk Bar
G. Xiao Xiang

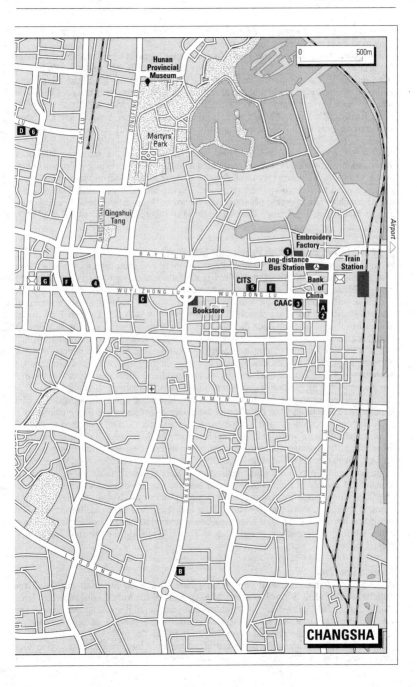

CHANGSHA

palms are native to the tropics it's unclear how the habit arrived in Changsha, nor does it seem to be in vogue elsewhere in the province.

Qingshui Tang (Clearwater Pool), Mao's former home in Changsha and the site of the first local Communist Party offices, is on Bayi Lu (daily 8.30am–5pm; ¥5; bus #1 stops outside). A white marble statue of Mao greets you at the gate, and the garden walls are covered with stone tablets carved with his epigrams. Near the pool itself is a scruffy vegetable patch and the reconstructed room in which Mao and his second wife, **Yang Kaihui** (daughter of Mao's stoical and influential teacher, Yang Chang Qi), lived after moving here from Beijing following their marriage in 1921. There's also a display of peasant tools – a grindstone, thresher, carrypole and baskets – and a short history of Chinese agriculture. A few minutes' walk farther on is the monumental **Local Museum**, brightly tiled in red and containing a low-key but interesting collection of historical artefacts, including clay tomb figurines – look for the bearded horseman – and a cannon used for defending the city against Taiping incursions in 1852. These pieces lead through to a depressing photographic record of Guomindang atrocities and eulogies to Mao, Zhou Enlai, and others. The three red flags here are those of the Party, the PLA, and the nation.

Memorial Park and Hunan Provincial Museum

From Qingshui Tang, follow Qingshuitang Lu north and then turn east into a street with a proliferation of **street cafés** and food stalls extending towards the southern gates of **Martyrs' Park**. Though it's crowded at weekends, plenty of shade and lakes complete with ornamental gardens, bridges and pagodas make the park a beautiful place to stroll. But the main reason to head up this way is to visit **Hunan Provincial Museum** (Tues–Sun 9am–noon & 2.30–5pm; ¥30), whose unmarked entrance lies off Dongfeng Lu in the park's northwestern corner (buses #3 and #103 stop outside).

The museum is one of Changsha's high points and not to be missed despite the stiff entrance fee, though it's dedicated to just one subject: the Han-era tomb of **Xin Zui**, the **Marquess of Dai**. Xin Zui died around 160 BC, and her subterranean tomb was one of three discovered in 1972 during construction work at **Mawangdui**, about 4km northeast (the others contained her husband and son). Rammed walls of clay and charcoal kept out any damp, and the body's excellent state of preservation was ensured by a triple wooden sarcophagus and wrappings of linen and silk. So well-protected was it that modern pathologists were able to establish that the Marquess was suffering from tuberculosis, gall stones, arteriosclerosis and bilharzia before she died – incredibly enough, given this list of ailments – aged fifty. The coffins are on view in an upper room, while access to the mummy (after sealing your dusty shoes in plastic bags) is through a basement display of richly embroidered silks, lacquered bowls and musical instruments, wooden tomb figures and other funerary offerings. Not on display, but also found in the tomb, was a complete text of the Taoist classic *I Ching* written on silk. The Marquess herself lies in a fluid-filled tank below several inches of perspex, a gruesome white fabric doll decently covered from chin to thigh, with her internal organs displayed in jars.

Around the river

A couple of kilometres south of the Xiangjiang Bridge on Shuyuan Lu, the **First Teachers' Training School** is where Mao completed his formal education and later taught during the 1920s – take bus #102 from the junction of Wuyi Xi Lu and Huangxing Lu. Historical associations aside, there's nothing to see and the school is, in fact, a reconstruction after the original burned down in the 1930s.

More interesting, and containing just about the only buildings in town more than thirty years old, is the midstream **Orange Island** (Jiezi Zhou) served by bus #16 hourly from either end of the bridge. One of the most attractive parts of Changsha, thickly cultivated and planted with mandarin trees, the island was settled by the local **European community** as a safeguard against mob violence after the famine-induced riots of 1906 had wrecked the city (the whole of Hunan had been opened up to foreign traders in 1904). Many of their former homes are still standing, though one-time mansions are now partitioned into family apartments. Legend has it that Mao used to swim regularly to shore from the southern tip of the island, a feat he repeated on his sixty-fifth birthday as one of his famous river crossings.

Over on the west side of the river, **Yuelu Shan** is a famous beauty spot, and a breezy hill-top refuge from Changsha's humid summer streets. Take bus #12 to the west bank terminus, where there's a busy **clothes market**, then pick up a #5 south to the large Mao statue in the square outside Changsha's university, the **Yuelu Academy**. Paths flanked by food and souvenir stalls lead from here to the park gates (¥2), then meander uphill for forty minutes or so through pleasant woodland to **Wangxiang Pavilion** and views over the city. On the way, the unremarkable **Aiwan Pavilion** has poetic associations. Besides being one of Mao's youthful haunts (there's a tablet here bearing his calligraphy), the name "Aiwan", meaning "loving dusk", derives from a verse by the soulful Tang poet Du Fu:

A stony path winds far up cool hills
Towards cottages hidden deep amongst white clouds
Loving the maple trees at dusk I stop my cart
To sit and watch the frosted leaves
Redder than February flowers.

Eating, drinking and entertainment

Hunanese food shares Sichuan's predilection for copious amounts of chillies – Mao himself claimed that it was the fiery food which made locals so red – but it doesn't seem to have evolved into an individual cooking style. Nonetheless, there are some pungent **regional specialities** to try: *dongan* chicken, where the shredded, poached meat is seasoned with a vinegar-soy dressing; *gualiang fen*, a gelatinous mass of cold, shaved rice noodles covered in a spicy sauce; *chou dofu* (literally "stinking tofu"), a fermented beancurd dish which actually tastes good; and a mass of different snacks – preserved eggs, pickles, buns and glutinous rice dumplings – which form the regular restaurant fare in town. The province is also known for its air-cured and **chilli-smoked meat** dishes, though these more usually appear in family cooking. There is a huge number of open-air restaurants and **food stalls** outside the south entrance to Martyrs' Park, serving everything from eels to hotpots, as well as a string of "hole in the wall" options in the side street around the corner from *Kiddies* restaurant (see below).

Entertainment options are limited to the newly opened *Haiyuan Xian* (Coastline) bar on Wuyi Zhong Lu – which does get in some decent DJs and live bands at weekends – flat discos at the more expensive hotels, and little else.

Restaurants

Fast Food, Chezhan Lu, opposite the train station – look for the sign in English. Long canteen serving light meals, soup, and everyday *baozi* and *jiaozi* by the plateful.

Fire Palace, junction of Laoding Lu and Shaoshan Lu; take bus #7 from outside the train station. Red and gold exterior, bright and clean inside, and the best place in town for both Hunanese snacks (lower floor) and Hunanese blow-outs (top floor).

He Ge, Xiangchun Lu, near the *Luoyuan Hotel*. Slightly upmarket tea room with communal, solid stone benches, known for its range of small dishes, including tasty rice noodles and spiced beef soup.

Kiddies Restaurant, Wuyi Dong Lu. Greasy diner serving warm burgers, clammy rice dishes, hideous coffee and Carpenters. music.

Milk Bar, near the northwest corner of Wuyi Zhong Lu and Furong Lu. A tiny counter selling cartons of flavoured UHT milk, New Zealand butter and soft processed cheese.

Xiao Xiang, Wuyi Zhong Lu. Comfortable, very good formal restaurant with a moderately priced menu, window seats for people-watching and nicely presented food.

Listings

Airlines There's a *CAAC* booking desk at the *Civil Aviation Hotel*, 5 Wuyi Dong Lu (daily 8am–5.30pm; ☎2290888 ext 233, fax 2298014).

Banks and exchange *Bank of China*, near the train station on Wuyi Dong Lu (Mon–Sat 8am–noon & 2.30–5.30pm). Hotels such as the *Lotus* and *Cygnet* also change travellers' cheques, and might not mind whether you're staying or not.

Bookshops The bookstore on Wuyi Zhong Lu, just past the junction with Shaoshan Lu, has a good art section including books on painting techniques, but slim pickings in English. The *Lotus Hotel* shop sometimes has foreign paperbacks.

Buses The ticket office at the bus station opens daily around 6am and closes by 5.30pm; the station is locked after 6pm.

Hospital Changsha Number 2 Medical College, Renmin Lu (☎5550400 or 5550511).

Left luggage Aside from offices at the train and bus stations, both *CAAC* and *CITS* might be persuaded to look after your bags for a short while.

PSB The Foreign Affairs Department is on Huangxing Lu (Mon–Fri 8.30am–5pm; ☎4413851).

Post offices There are two major branches: one on Wuyi Zhong Lu near the junction with Cai'er Lu; and the more convenient office – with parcel post and international phones – in the train station square. Both are open daily 8am–8pm, though some services seem to be unavailable at the weekends and during lunchtime.

Shopping As you'll appreciate after visiting the Provincial Museum, Changsha has long had a reputation for silk embroidery, and there's a factory on Bayi Lu whose shop sells pieces of varying quality – from ¥50 for a souvenir handkerchief, to ¥900 or more for a top-notch, towel-sized animal design. The two department stores near the bus and train stations also sell embroideries, plus anything else you'll need for daily existence.

Telephones International calls can be made from large hotels and the post office in the train station square.

Trains Window #6 for foreigners, #23 and #24 for tickets to Shaoshan. The staff are pretty helpful here (daily 8.15am–noon & 2.30–5.45pm).

Travel agents The friendly *CITS* office is in the grounds of the *Lotus Hotel* on Wuyi Dong Lu (daily 8am–5pm; ☎4433355 or 2224855). Very polite staff, but basically it's a booking office for domestic and international flights, rather than a source of more general information.

Shaoshan

Mao Zedong's birthplace, the hamlet of **SHAOSHAN**, lies 90km to the southwest of Changsha, a fine day trip from the capital through the mild Hunanese countryside. Once a pilgrimage site overflowing with thousands of visitors, today there are rarely more than a few hundred souls between the sights, attesting to the battering which the Great Helmsman's reputation has suffered since his death in 1976. The best way to get here is on the **daily train** from Changsha, which leaves at 6.30am for the three-hour journey (¥5 each way; leaves Shaoshan around 3.30pm). Alternatively, **tour buses** leave from the square outside the train station ticket office at 6am (guided day tour ¥55 return). There are also daily long-distance buses from Changsha, but these usually involve a change of vehicle in the manufacturing port of Xiangtan.

Shaoshan is, in fact, two settlements: a knot of hotels and services which have sprung up around the rail head and long-distance bus depot, and **Shaoshan Dong**, the village itself, some 6km distant. Patriotic jingles and a large portrait of Mao greet **arrivals** at the train station, as do **minibuses** heading up to the village (¥1). Unless you're planning to stay overnight or are hungry – in which case there's a cheap **hotel** (②) and several **restaurants** ahead and round to the right near the bus depot – you should hop straight on board the first minibus. The first place to disembark is just before the village proper outside **Mao's Family Home**, a compound of bare adobe buildings next to a lotus-filled pond, where Mao was born on December 26, 1893. Here he led a thoroughly normal childhood, one of four children in a relatively wealthy peasant household which comfortably survived the terrible famines in Hunan during the first decade of the twentieth century. Though a rebellious youth, it was not until he moved to Changsha in his late teens that he became politicized. The home is neatly preserved, with a few pieces of period furniture and the odd photograph completing the spartan furnishings.

Just up the road is the huge **village square**, where, next to a bronze statue of an elderly Mao and a swarm of souvenir stalls selling the tackiest of trinkets emblazoned with his portrait, is the **Mao Zedong Exhibition Hall** (daily 8.30am-5pm; ¥5). Opened in 1967 at the height of the Cultural Revolution, this museum originally had two identical exhibitions to cope with the swarms of idolatrous Red Guards, but now the single surviving wing easily accommodates the trickle of Party faithful. Photos and knick-knacks chart Mao's career, though today there's a great distinction between Mao the revolutionary – still often regarded as a hero – and the character who inflicted the Great Leap Forward and Cultural Revolution on his country. The exhibition reflects this: noticeable omissions include the Little Red Book, and just about any mention of the years between 1957 and his funeral in 1976. An additional ¥5 gains admission to a collection of "things left behind by Mao Zedong" – prescription lenses, writing brushes, possibly *the* prototype "Mao" cap and jacket, and various other everyday items. Next door to the museum is the former **Mao Ancestral Temple**, now a memorial to the leader's early work among the peasants here.

When you've had enough nostalgia, head off into the countryside for a stroll, or catch a minibus up to **Shaoshan peak** for a look at the local landscape – not really typical, given the amount of tourist revenue, but a nice scene of healthy fields and bamboo thickets. Another option is to bus over to Dishui Dong, **Dripping Water Cave**, where Mao meditated for a few days in 1966 on the harsh works of writer **Lu Xun**, after a major disagreement had erupted between himself and Lin Biao over the course of the Cultural Revolution. There are also a few restaurants and **places to stay** in Shaoshan village around the square, including the inexpensive *Hongri Fandian* near the Mao Ancestral Temple, offering simple beds (①); the *Shaoshan Fandian* in the square itself, with a jumble of indifferent rooms around an ornamental pool (☎682309; ④); and the pricey but pleasant *Shaoshan Binguan* (☎682127; ⑤–⑧) hidden away behind the statue.

Heng Shan

Some 120km south of Changsha, the **Heng Shan region** is one of China's most holy sites. Spread over 80km or so, the ranges form scores of low peaks dressed in woodland with a smattering of **Buddhist and Taoist temples**, some of which were established over 1300 years ago. A favourite with scholars and artists, it's somewhere to relax and admire the scenery – frosted in winter, golden in autumn and often green and misty year-round – either tackling the easy walks between shrines on foot, or resorting to local transport to ascend the heights.

HENG SHAN

Heng Shan	蘅山	*héng shān*
Danxia Si	丹霞寺	*dānxiá sì*
Huangting Si	黄庭寺	*huángtíng sì*
Shangfeng Si	上封寺	*shàngfēng sì*
Water Curtain Cave	水濂洞	*shuǐ lián dòng*
Xuandu Si	玄都寺	*xuándū sì*
Zhurong Palace	祝融殿	*zhùróng diàn*
Zushi Gong	祖师宫	*zǔshī gōng*
Hengyang	衡阳	*héng yáng*
Nanyue	南岳	*nányuè*
Nanyue Damiao	南岳大庙	*nányuèdàmiào*
Zhusheng Si	祝圣寺	*zhùshèng sì*

Confusingly, it's **Nanyue**, and not the nearby town of Hengshan, that marks the start-ing point up into the hills. Early morning **buses** from Changsha or Shaoshan take around five hours to reach Nanyue via Xiangtan, where you might have to change both bus and stations (the two are next door to each other). Coming up from the south by road or rail from Shaoguan in Guangdong Province, or Guilin in Guangxi, the nearest city is **HENGYANG**, where minibuses to Nanyue leave for the hour-long trip from the depot on Jiefang Lu – bus #1 connects Hengyang's nightmarishly busy **train station** with this depot, which is across the river. Alternatively, leave the train farther on at **Hengshan Town**, where regular minibuses cover the ten-kilometre trip west to Nanyue.

Nanyue

Banners strung across the highway welcome visitors to **NANYUE** (South Mountain), a small but expanding village of old flagstoned streets and new hotels set around Nanyue Damiao and Zhusheng Si, the two largest and most architecturally impressive temple complexes in the area. The Changsha–Hengyang highway runs along the east-ern side of the village, with the **bus station** at its southern (Hengyang) end, where map sellers, rickshaw drivers and hotel touts descend on new arrivals. There's fairly inexpensive **accommodation** a few doors along above a hairdresser and restaurant, offering secure, plain doubles with bathroom (②); otherwise, try the more upmarket *Xiufeng Binguan* (☎0734/666111; ④–⑤), opposite the ornamental **stone archway** which forms the "entrance" to the village proper. **Places to eat** are plentiful, and you'll be beckoned over to establishments as you pass – asking prices are high, however, so fix them when ordering.

From the highway, look for the small humpbacked bridge across which streets lead through the old village centre to **Nanyue Damiao** (Grand Nanyue Temple; ¥6). There's been a place of worship at this site at least since 725 AD – some say that it was sanctified in Qin times – but the older buildings succumbed to fire long ago and were replaced last century by a small version of Beijing's Imperial Palace. It's a lively place, freshly painted, echoing with bells and thick with smoke from incense and detonating firecrackers – there are actually furnaces in the courtyards to accommodate the huge quantities offered up by the crowds. Seventy-two pillars representing the peaks of the Heng Shan range support the massive wooden crossbeams of the **main hall**'s double-staged roof, and gilt phoenixes loom above scores of kneeling worshippers paying homage to Taoist and Buddhist deities. Other halls in the surrounding gardens are far more humble, but sport detailed carvings along their eaves and exterior alcoves.

Far quieter, with fewer tourists and more monks in evidence, is the monastery, **Zhusheng Si**, a short walk left out of the temple gates. A purely Buddhist site originating around the same time as Nanyue, the entire monastery was reconstructed for the anticipated visit of **Emperor Kangxi** in 1705 – the name translates as "Imperial Blessings" – but he never showed up. The smaller scale and lack of pretension here contrast with Nanyue's extravagances, though there's a series of five hundred engravings of Buddhist *arhats* set into the wall of the rear hall, and a fine multi-faced and many-handed likeness of **Guanyin** to seek out among the charming courtyards. Just beyond Zhusheng Si you can take a stroll to **Water Curtain Cave**, a pretty cascade named after the home of the legendary Monkey King.

In the hills

There's a good day's walking to be had between Nanyue and **Zhurong Gong**, a hall perched 15km from town on Heng Shan's 1290m apex. Even major temples along the way are small and unassuming, requiring little time to investigate, and tracks are easy, so between six and eight hours should be enough for a return hike along the most direct route – though you'd need at least ten hours to see everything on the mountain. **Minibuses** also run between Nanyue and Shangfeng Si, below the summit, in under an hour (¥10). **Food stalls** lurk at strategic points, so there's no need to carry much beyond something to keep out any seasonally inclement weather at the top.

Take the main road through Nanyue to the park gates behind Nanyue Damiao, where the **admission fee** (¥19) covers entry to all temples and includes a bilingual **map** of the mountain. The first two hours are spent passing occasional groups of descending tourists and black-clad Taoist mendicants, as the road weaves past rivers and patches of farmland before reaching the temple-like **Martyrs' Memorial Hall**, built to commemorate those killed during the 1911 revolution. Entering pine forests shortly after, **Xuandu Si** (Profound Capital Monastery) marks the halfway point – it's also known as the Midway Temple – and is Hunan's Taoist centre, founded around 700 AD. Even so, an occasional Buddhist saint graces side shrines, but the best feature is the unusually domed ceiling in the second hall, watched over by a statue of Lao Zi holding a pill of immortality.

The rest of the ascent is past a handful of functioning, day-to-day temples with monks and nuns wandering around the gardens – **Danxia Si** and **Zushi Gong** are larger than most – before arrival outside **Shangfeng Si**'s red timber halls, which mark the minibus terminus. Overpriced **hotels** here cater for those hoping to catch the dawn from the **sunrise-watching terrace**, a short walk away below a radio tower. On a cloudy day, it's more worthwhile pushing on a further twenty minutes to the summit, where **Zhurong Gong**, a tiny temple built almost entirely of heavy stone blocks and blackened inside from incense smoke, looks very atmospheric as it emerges from the mist. For the descent, there's always the bus, or an alternative track from Xuandu Si which takes in Lingzhi spring, the Mirror Grinding Terrace and the bulky Nantai Monastery, before winding back to town past the quiet halls of **Huangting Si**, another sizeable Taoist shrine.

Yueyang and Dongting Hu

Yueyang, a major riverside city and stop on the Beijing–Guangzhou rail line, lies 120km north of Changsha on the eastern shores of **Dongting Hu**, the second largest freshwater lake in the land. Fed by four principal rivers and itself draining into the Yangzi,

YUEYANG AND DONGTING HU

Yueyang	岳阳	*yuèyáng*
Chenglingji	城陵矶	*chénglíngjī*
Cishi Pagoda	慈氏塔	*císhì tǎ*
Miluo River	汨罗江	*mìluó jiāng*
Tomb of Lu Su	鲁肃墓	*lǔ sù mù*
Yueyang docks	岳阳楼客运站	*yuèyáng lóu kèyùn zhàn*
Yueyang Tower	岳阳楼	*yuèyáng lóu*

ACCOMMODATION

Xuelian	雪莲宾馆	*xuělián bīnguǎn*
Yueyang Binguan	岳阳宾馆	*yuèyáng bīnguǎn*
Yueyanglou Binguan	岳阳楼宾馆	*yuèyánglóu bīnguǎn*
Yunmeng	云梦宾馆	*yúnmèng bīnguǎn*

Dongting Hu	洞庭湖	*dòngtíng hú*
Dongting Nature Reserve	洞庭自然保护区	*dòngtíng zìrán bǎohùqū*
Junshan Island	君山岛	*jūnshān dǎo*
Lotus Lake	莲湖	*lián hú*
Nanyuepo docks	南岳码头	*nányuè mǎ tóu*

Dongting's shallow spread surrounds **Junshan Dao**, an island famed for its tea, tortoises and bamboo, while regional history encompasses the origins of **dragon-boat racing** and some two-thousand-year-old sites – even if existing monuments are more recent.

Yueyang

Extolled by poets from Du Fu to Mao Zedong and always an important trading centre, **YUEYANG** was opened to foreigners as a treaty port in 1898 but never figured large in China's history. Despite accelerating tourism and a new city springing up in the background, Yueyang's older lakeside quarter still retains the atmosphere and disinterested hospitality of a small town. The main street, **Baling Lu**, runs for 5km, bare, broad and numbingly straight from Yueyang's newest, eastern fringes right up to **Nanyuepo docks** on the lake shore. Here it's crossed by Dongting Lu, with the old part of town, most of the accommodation, and all the sights close to this junction, including the unusual and impressive **Yueyang Tower** and a network of rambling stone alleys. The best time to be in town is for the **dragon-boat festival** (see box), though beds will be in short supply. It's also worth asking at your hotel about possible evening **opera performances**; spectacular, if less formal than Beijing's.

The Yueyang Tower

Frequently packed with Chinese tourists, the **Yueyang Tower** on Dongting Bei Lu (¥20) is an obvious place to start any city tour. Rising from walled ramparts overlooking the lake, the site originally housed a platform used by general **Lu Su** to review his troops during the third century (see below). A tower was first built in 716, but the current edifice is of early Qing design, and was fully restored in 1983. Twenty metres tall, made of timber and held together without a single nail, three upward-curving, yellow-glazed roofs are supported by four huge blood-red pillars of nanmu wood. Twenty-four more hold the lower-floor eaves, and the upper storey rests on another twelve. Screens and crossbeams are decorated with animal carvings, and the tower makes a striking

DRAGON BOATS

The former state of **Chu**, which encompassed northern Hunan, was under siege in 278 BC from the first stirrings of the ambitious Qin armies, who were later to bring all of China under their thumb. At the time, Dongting was the haunt of the exiled poet **Qu Yuan**, a victim of palace politics but nonetheless a great patriot of Chu. Hearing of the imminent invasion, Qu picked up a heavy stone and drowned himself in the nearby **Miluo River** rather than see the state he loved conquered. Distraught locals raced to save him in their boats, but were too late. They returned later to scatter **zongzi** (packets of meat and sticky rice wrapped up in reeds and lotus leaves) into the river as an offering to Qu Yuan's spirit.

The **dragon-boat festival** held throughout China on the fifth day of the fifth lunar month (June or July) commemorates the rowers' hopeless rush – though many historians trace the tradition of food offerings and annual boat races to long before Qu's time. At any rate, it's a festive rather than mournful occasion, with huge quantities of steamed *zongzi* eaten and keen competition between local dragon-boat teams, who can be seen practising in their narrow, powerful crafts months before the event, to the steady boom of a pacing drum. It's a lively spectator sport, with crowds cheering their rowers along, and you need to be up early to get the most from the ceremonies – such as the dedication of the dragon-headed prows – as the race itself lasts only a few minutes. The event is still held on the Miluo River south of Yueyang, and in 1995 the first **International Dragon-boat Competition** took place here, with boats from various countries extending the proceedings. Contact either the *CITS* or your hotel for transport details.

and brilliant spectacle. From the top you can look down on grand views of the lake, which quickly whips up into a stormy sea scene at the first breath of wind. Flanking the tower are two lesser pavilions: **Xianmei Ting** (Heavenly Plum Flower) – named after the design delicately etched on to a Ming stone tablet within – and **Sancui Ting** (Thrice Drunk). This recalls the antics of **Yu Dongbin**, who regularly visited the pavilion to down a wine gourd or two; there's a comic painting of this inside, warts and all, and an overflowing votive box. One of the Taoist Eight Immortals, he's also credited with populating Dongting Hu with shoals of silvery fish by tossing woodshavings into the water.

Xiao Qiao, the wife of another historic general, lies buried at the northern end of the surrounding gardens, the grassy mound honoured by a tablet bearing the calligraphy of the renowned Song-dynasty poet, **Su Dongpo**. Buildings here house a **gallery** – check out the highly original paintings based on Guizhou batik designs – and a **waxworks** full of historical characters associated with the area.

The Old Town

The few surviving backstreets in the old town make a fascinating, if brief, stroll. About 300m down the road opposite the southern entrance to the Yueyang Tower (past the *Yueyanglou Binguan*), stands the modern reconstruction of the **Tomb of Lu Su**, a *Three Kingdoms* general who commanded a garrison here until his death in 217 AD. Lu is best known for his diplomacy in uniting the armies of his native Wu and those of Shu against the overwhelming forces of Wei, who were subsequently defeated in 208 AD at the Battle of the Red Cliffs (see p.432).

Near the Nanyuepo docks down at the Dongting Bei Lu–Bailong Lu junction, the **indoor market** is the best place to see lake fauna – turtles, frogs, crayfish, eels and countless types of fish – and there's also a busy huddle of snake vendors manipulating peevish cobras with heavy gloves. Stalls outside are stacked with plates of rigid squid, piles of wood-ear fungus, pulses and other dried produce. Carry on down narrow Dongting Nan Lu, crammed with food and clothes barrows, and you'll soon see the crumbling stone **Cishi Pagoda** surrounded by old houses on your right, so weighed down by vegetation that it resembles a terraced garden tower. It was built in 1242 to evict flood-inducing lake spirits, but Dongting remained famous for its seasonally variable water levels until the 1980s, when dykes greatly reduced the fluctuations.

Practicalities

The **bus and train stations** are on opposite sides of a huge, multi-level roundabout far down Baling Lu. The **city bus** network is being revised, but bus #22 should run from the train station to the lake and then north along Dongting Bei Lu – pick up a current **map** on arrival. Most **Yangzi ferries** stop 17km north of the city at **Chenglingji**, where bus #1 connects with the train station; a few pull into the **Yueyang docks** just past the Yueyang Tower on Dongting Bei Lu. Leaving, don't try to book a long-distance sleeper train from Yueyang; go first to Changsha or Wuhan and look for a service originating there.

There's a **post office** way down Baling Lu towards the bus and train stations (daily 8am–6pm), but for postal services and **foreign exchange**, you're better off trying one of the larger hotels. The English-speaking **CITS** (daily 9–11.30am & 2–5pm) is inside the grounds of the *Yunmeng Hotel* and can arrange tours to lakeside sights. All the hotels have **restaurants** with menus based around lake produce, and there are plenty of others along Dongting Bei Lu.

Accommodation

Xuelian, Dongting Bei Lu (☎0730/225677), opposite the Yueyang Tower and docks. Look out for the Tibetan script outside and the loose live wiring in the showers. Otherwise it's an excellent-value, friendly, family-run guesthouse offering beds in tidy doubles. ③.

Yueyang Binguan, Dongting Bei Lu (☎0730/223011). The town's top tourist accommodation, and snobbish with it. Facilities include a downstairs canteen for the masses, a mail and foreign exchange counter and a densely stocked gift shop. Comfortable, overpriced singles, doubles and triples. ⑤.

Yueyanglou Binguan (*Yueyang Tower Hotel*), in the side street opposite the southern entrance to the Yueyang Tower (☎0730/253188). Clean doubles in a newish apartment building. ④–⑦.

Yunmeng, 25 Chengdong Lu (☎0730/221115). Ordinary, often damp, rooms in a slightly downbeat concrete complex (Chengdong Lu runs south off Baling Lu around 1km west of the Dongting Lu intersection). ⑥.

The lake and Junshan Island

Dongting Hu covers a crescent-shaped area of 2500 square kilometres southwest of Yueyang, fringed with reeds and lotus ponds and surrounded by villages farming rich cane and paddy fields. Many locals also earn a livelihood from fishing, and right up until the 1970s, the lake was a common haunt of the **Yangzi river dolphin** (see p.438), but these are seldom, if ever, seen here nowadays. Clearly visible from the top of the Yueyang Tower, **Junshan Island** is steeped in apocryphal legends and makes an entertaining excursion from Yueyang. Between July and September, when lilies are in flower and migrant waterfowl swarm into the region, scenery hunters and twitchers should contact the Yueyang *CITS* to arrange a day tour out to **Lotus Lake** and **Dongting Nature Reserve**, both some distance away on the western shore.

Junshan Island

Junshan Island (Monarch's Island), in effect an isolated city park, lies a thirty-minute boat ride from Yueyang across the lake's placid brown waters (it's not worth the trip in bad weather). **Ferries** depart four times daily 7.30am–3.30pm from both the Yueyang docks – follow the alley downhill to the water immediately north of the tower – and the Nanyuepo docks at the western end of Baling Lu (¥10 each way). Last boat back is at 4.30pm. Private **speedboats** make regular crossings too, but you'll have to negotiate fares with the touts.

Once a Taoist retreat, the island covers an area of barely more than one square kilometre, consisting of a score of gently undulating rises planted with tea bushes, bamboo groves and assorted trees. It costs ¥30 per person to land (students half price), and winding paths lead up from the concrete jetty to cultivated terraces planted with the region's famous **silver needle tea**, *yinhao maojian*. These precious tips look like pale green twists; pour boiling water over them, inhale the musty vapour and watch them bob up and down in the glass. Supposed to impart longevity, this highly valued brew used to be paid in tribute to the emperor and its production remains the chief livelihood of the island's two hundred inhabitants. Even today it's incredibly expensive and is sold in Yueyang at around ¥5 a teaspoon. Another endemic plant is **speckled bamboo**, which, according to legend, was stained by the tears of Emperor **Shun**'s two widows on learning of his death in 2500 BC. They wasted away from grief and are buried here next to a bamboo grove, beneath a suspiciously modern tomb and stone tablet. **Golden tortoises** also inhabit the island (some of the tea houses near the docks keep a few scruffy specimens to show tourists), mice are everywhere and reedbeds on the northern shore twitter with **birdlife**: finches, egrets, ducks and other wildfowl. The island has its own vast quantities of carefully contrived legends and **The Bell Which Flew Here** is always a favourite, looking distinctly foolish wedged halfway up a tree. The twelfth-century rebel **Yang Yao** is supposed to have used the bell to summon meetings in his cave.

Wulingyuan Scenic Reserve

Hidden away in the northwestern extremities of Hunan, **Wulingyuan Scenic Reserve** protects a mystical landscape of sandstone shelves and fragmented limestone towers, with practically every horizontal surface hidden under a primeval, sub-tropical green mantle. Often misted in low cloud and scored by countless streams, sixty percent of the park still has its original vegetation. Among the 550-odd tree species (twice Europe's total) are rare dove trees, gingkos, and **dawn redwoods** – believed extinct until 1948 and identified by their stringy bark and feathery leaves fringed in red. The **wildlife** list is impressive too, including civets, giant salamanders, monkeys and gamebirds, and the reserve has been given *UNESCO* World Heritage listing. Consequently, Wulingyuan is remarkable in China for its total **fire ban** (smoking included), frequent litter bins and a generous number of flagged, erosion-resistant paths. The region is also home to several

WULINGYUAN SCENIC RESERVE

Wulingyuan Scenic Reserve	武陵源风景区	*wǔlíngyuán fēngjǐngqū*
Bewitching Terrace	迷魂台	*mí hún tái*
Black Dragon village	黑龙寨	*hēilóng zhài*
Huangshi village	黄石寨	*huángshí zhài*
Suoxi village	索溪峪镇	*suǒxīyù zhèn*
Baofeng Hu	宝峰湖	*bǎofēng hú*
Huanglong Cave	黄龙洞	*huánglóng dòng*
Immortals' Bridge	仙人桥	*xiānrén qiáo*
Shentangwan	神堂湾	*shéntángwān*
Ten-li Corridor	十里画廊	*shí lǐ huà láng*
Tianzi Shan	天子峰	*tiānzǐ fēng*
Zhangjiajie	张家界	*zhāngjiājiè*
Qingyan Shan Binguan	青岩山宾馆	*qīng yán shān bīnguǎn*
Zhangjiajie Binguan	张家界宾馆	*zhāngjiājiè bīnguǎn*

million ethnic **Tujia**, said by some to be the last descendants of western China's mysterious prehistoric Ba Kingdom. Apart from some remote mountain areas, however, much of their tradition has been lost over the last millennia through close contact with the Han.

Wulingyuan covers 370 square kilometres, and most people base themselves on the southern boundaries at the village of **Zhangjiajie**, where there's certainly enough to keep you occupied for a few days. With more time, it's possible to organize extended walks north to **Tianzi Mountain**, or east to the **Suoxi Valley**. There are villages and stalls along the way supplying accommodation and food, but take water and snacks on long journeys. You'll need comfortable walking shoes and the right seasonal dress; it's humid in summer, cold from late autumn and often covered in light snow early on in the year.

Dayong, Zhangjuajie and around

DAYONG is the regional hub, 33km south of Zhangjiajie village but often labelled "Zhangjiajie" on timetables and maps, and it's a twelve-hour slog across the province from Changsha to get here **by bus**, through the river city of **Changde**. Dayong's **train station**, a farther 9km south, serves a minor line between Guangxi and Henan, with access from Changsha via a connection in **Huaihua**. Some Chinese tourists also combine a trip to Wulingyuan with one to **Fanjing Shan**, over the border in Guizhou (see p.705 for connecting routes). **Minibuses** prowl Dayong's arrival points for the sixty-minute journey to Zhangjiajie (¥10), meeting all trains and delivering customers to various hotels in Zhangjiajie.

ZHANGJIAJIE is simply a couple of streets in the valley at the reserve entrance, overflowing with **map** and souvenir retailers, pricey restaurants (meat dishes are particularly expensive), a **post office** and **places to stay**. The best value of these is the **hostel** (②) built on two levels around a tiny courtyard at the Dayong end of the main road (look for a sign advertising a service centre and massage). Another cheap option is the *Qingyan Shan Binguan* (②) at the end of the road leading along a stream off to the left, but rooms here tend to be literally dripping with moisture. Closer to the gates, the *Zhangjiajie Binguan* (☎07483/712718; ③–⑦) is more expensive, but quite nice, with smart doubles in the new wing, and clean but damp rooms in the older section, arranged around an ornamental pond. Cheaper dorms exist but are inevitably "full". *CITS* has its offices here too, and is fairly helpful with general hiking advice, and can arrange **whitewater rafting** day tours (¥250 per person) in the Suoxi Valley.

Zhangjiajie trails

A closely packed forest of tall, eroded karst pinnacles splintering away from a high plateau, Zhangjiajie's scenery is awesomely poetic – even Chinese tour groups are often hushed by the spectacle. The road through the village leads downhill to the **reserve entrance** (¥46, no concessions), past a throng of Tujia selling medicinal flora and cheap plastic ponchos. There are also **bicycles** – of dubious value for many of the tracks – and sedan chairs for rent. The left path here follows a four-hour circuit along a short valley up to **Huangshi village**, on the edge of a minor, island-like plateau surrounded by views of the area, while the right path has several options. The shortest of these (again, around 4hr) runs along **Golden Whip Stream**, branching off to the right and back to base through a particularly dense stand of crags below two facing outcrops known as the **Yearning Couple** (engraved tablets along the path identify many other formations). Alternatively, bearing left after a couple of kilometres – consult a map – takes you up past **Bewitching Terrace** into the **Shadao Valley**. From here, basic trails continue through magnificent scenery around the western edge of the plateau to **Black Dragon village**, then circuit back to the park gates. This is a lengthy day's walk, and you won't see many other tourists along the way.

Suoxi Valley and Tianzi Shan

With much the same facilities as Zhangjiajie, **SUOXI village** makes a good base for exploring the east and north of the reserve. Ten kilometres as the crow flies from Zhangjiajie but the better part of a day on foot; it's also possible to get between the two (and probably from Dayong) by local bus. Set in the **Suoxi Valley**, the attractions include groups of rhesus monkeys and relatively open riverine gorges where it's possible to **cruise** – or even go whitewater rafting – between the peaks. Around the two-kilometre-long **Baofeng Hu**, a lake accessed by a ladder-like staircase from the valley floor, there's a chance of encountering golden pheasants, tragopans (a splendidly coloured, grouse-like bird), and **giant salamanders**. Considered a great delicacy, these secretive, red-blotched monsters reach two metres in length and are sometimes seen in the early mornings around Baofeng's shore. There's also **Huanglong Dong** (Yellow Dragon Cave), a few kilometres east of Souxi, a mass of garishly lit limestone caverns linked by a subterranean river, and **Hundred Battle Valley**, where the Song-dynasty Tujia king, Xiang, fought imperial forces.

The **Tianzi Shan** region, which basically covers the north of the park, is named after an isolated 1250-metre-high peak, and contains most of Wulingyuan's caves. It's probably best visited from Suoxi village, where there's a possible circuit of 30km setting off along the **Ten-li Corridor**. High points include the mass of lookouts surrounding **Shentangwan**, a valley thick with needle-like rocks where Xiang is said to have committed suicide after his eventual defeat, and **Immortals' Bridge**, next to the peak itself, an unfenced, narrow strip of rock bridging a deep valley. Instead of returning to Souxi, it's feasible to continue past the mountain to **TIANZI SHAN village**, spend the night in the guesthouse there, and then either hike south to Zhangjiajie, or leave Wulingyuan by catching a bus first to Songzhi (45km) and then on to Dayong (another 60km).

JIANGXI

Stretched between the Yangzi in the north and a mountainous border with Guangdong in the south, **Jiangxi Province** has always been a bit of a backwater. Though it was patchily inhabited for some four thousand years, the first major influx of settlers came as late as the Han dynasty, when its interior offered sanctuary for those dislodged by warfare. The northern half benefited most from these migrants, who began to farm the great plain around China's largest freshwater lake, **Poyang Hu**. A network of rivers covering the province drains into Poyang, and when the construction of the Grand Canal created a route through Yangzhou and the lower Yangzi in the seventh century, Jiangxi's capital, **Nanchang**, became a key point on the great north–south link of inland waterways. Then the region enjoyed a long period of quiet prosperity, until coastal shipping and the opening up of treaty ports took business away in the 1840s. The next century saw a complete reversal of Jiangxi's fortunes: the population halved as millions fled competing warlords and, during the 1920s and 1930s, protracted fighting between the Guomindang and Communist forces were concentrated in the southern **Jinggang Shan** ranges, which eventually led to an evicted Red Army starting on their **Long March** across China.

Despite the troubles, things picked up quickly after the Communist takeover, and a badly battered Nanchang licked its scars and reinvented itself as a revolutionary city and centre of modern heavy industry. More traditionally, access provided by Poyang and the Yangzi tributaries benefit the hilly areas to the east, where **Jingdezhen** retains its title as China's porcelain capital. North of the lake, **Jiujiang** is a key Yangzi port on the doorsteps of Anhui and Hubei, while the nearby mountain area of **Lu Shan** offers a pleasant reminder of Jiangxi's better days, having long been a summer retreat for Chinese literati and colonial servants.

Nanchang

Hemmed in by hills, **NANCHANG** (Southern Prosperity) sits on Jiangxi's major river, the **Gan Jiang**, some 70km south of where it flows into Poyang Hu. Built on trade, today Nanchang has the rail link with Shanghai and Changsha to thank for its character; unfortunately, this mostly reflects its steel and chemical industries and a hasty, incomplete reconstruction since the 1950s. An initially dirty and noisy place afflicted by the usual stifling summer temperatures, first impressions are slightly moderated by the handful of older monuments gradually being resurrected, and the sheer enthusiasm with which locals have grasped free-market principles, crowding every alley with stalls.

Provincial capital or not, Nanchang saw little action until the twentieth century, when the city was occupied by the Guomindang army in December 1926. At the time, the military was still an amalgam of Nationalist and Communist forces, but when Chiang Kaishek broke his marriage of convenience with the Communists the following year, any left-wing elements were expelled from the Party. On August 1, 1927, **Zhou Enlai** and **Zhu De**, two Communist GMD officers with a sizeable army under their command, mutinied in Nanchang and took control of the city with thirty thousand troops. It was a shortlived victory, and they were soon forced to flee into Jiangxi's mountainous south, but the day is celebrated as the foundation of the **People's Liberation**

NANCHANG		
Nanchang	南昌	*nánchāng*
Xiangtan airport	香檀飞机场	*xiāngtán fēijīchǎng*
ACCOMMODATION		
Jiangxi Binguan	江西宾馆	*jiāngxī bīnguǎn*
Jiangxi Fandian	江西饭店	*jiāngxī fàndiàn*
Poyang	鄱阳大酒店	*póyáng dàjiǔdiàn*
Xiangshan	象山宾馆	*xiàngshān bīnguǎn*
THE CITY		
August 1 Monument	八一纪念塔	*bāyī jìniàntǎ*
August 1 Uprising Museum	八一纪念馆	*bāyī jìniànguǎn*
Ba Dashan Ren Studio	八大山人纪念馆	*bādàshānrén jìniànguǎn*
Bayi Park	八一公园	*bāyī gōngyuán*
Provincial Museum	省博物馆	*shěng bówùguǎn*
Qingyun Pu	青云谱	*qīngyún pǔ*
Renmin Square	人民广场	*rénmín guǎngchǎng*
Shengjin Ta	绳金塔	*shéngjīn tǎ*
Taxia Si	塔下寺	*tǎ xià sì*
Tengwang Pavilion	滕王阁	*téngwáng gé*
Youmin Si	佑民寺	*yòumín sì*
RESTAURANTS		
Great Eastern	大东饭店	*dàdōng fàndiàn*
Huadu Dajiudian	华都大酒店	*huádū dàjiǔdiàn*
Lao Di Fang	老地方	*lǎo dìfāng*

Army and the red PLA flag still bears the Chinese characters "8" and "1" (*bayi*) for the month and day – as do several of Nanchang's streets and public spaces.

Orientation, arrival, and accommodation

Nanchang sprawls away from the east bank of the Gan River into industrial complexes and wasteland, but the centre is a fairly compact couple of square kilometres between the river and **Bayi Dadao**, which runs north through the heart of the city from the huge **Fushan roundabout** and past **Renmin Square**, becoming **Yangming Lu** as it turns east over the Bayi Bridge.

Xiangtan airport is 28km south, and you'll need to take a taxi into town (¥35), but other transit points are more central. Nanchang's **train station** is 500m east of the Fushan roundabout at the end of Zhanqian Lu. The main building is derelict and looks like the victim of a successful rocket attack, while the ticket office and makeshift departure halls are hidden away to either side. Some buses from Lu Shan, Jinggang Shan and farther afield terminate here, but the main **long-distance bus station**, with user-friendly timetables and helpful staff, is 1km away on Bayi Dadao. The **ferry port** lies just south of the Bayi Bridge, handling daily services to towns around Poyang Hu and less frequent traffic south along the Gan River. **Taxis** and motor-rickshaws wait around downtown arrival points, while **city bus** #2 runs from the train station along Bayi Dadao, and then makes a circuit of the central area, either passing or coming close to all the hotels.

Accommodation

Jiangxi Binguan, 78 Bayi Dadao (☎0791/6221131). A classic 1950s Communist facade at odds with its modern wood and marble lobby and very capitalist shopping mall selling duty-free motorbikes and strings of pearls. There's definitely nothing else like this in town. Singles, doubles and suites. Bus #2 from the train or bus stations. ⑧.

Jiangxi Fandian, 76 Bayi Dadao (☎0791/6212123). Not to be confused with its namesake, this is an indifferent Chinese hotel whose staff need to do some spring cleaning. Doubles with and without private facilities, but the cheaper rooms are usually full. Bus #2 from train or bus stations. ②–④.

Nanchang, on the Fushan roundabout (☎0791/6219698). Close to the train and bus stations, this fairly drab building has some decent doubles and very plain dorms. ①–④.

Poyang, Jinggang Shan Dadao. This is on the south exit of Fushan roundabout, within 500m of both train and bus stations. A dingy exterior, but smart inside and well placed for transport connections. ④.

Xiangshan, Xiangshan Bei Lu. Mild insistence is needed to secure a bed for a reasonable price in this uninspiring, if tidy, complex. Bus #5 goes from the train station to the door via Zhanqian Lu and Xiangshan Lu. Dorms ②, rooms ④.

The City

Despite a few antiques rising from the rubble, history has made Nanchang something of a modern period piece, its architecture mostly reflecting the Civil War years and later Soviet-inspired industrialization. Much of this, such as the overbearing **Exhibition Hall** and the much finer *Jiangxi Binguan*, is concentrated around **Renmin Square**, an enormous open space impressive only for its size and a pair of giant television screens on which weekend football matches are broadcast at high volume. At the southern end is the white **August 1 Monument**, and also the **Provincial Museum** (closed at the time of writing), with a large collection of Jingdezhen ceramics.

Nanchang's bustling shopping districts are due west of Renmin Square along **Ruzi Lu** and **Zhongshan Lu**, but to continue a tour of the city, head up Bayi Dadao and then left down Minde Lu. Not far along and set back off the street is **Youmin Si**, a Buddhist

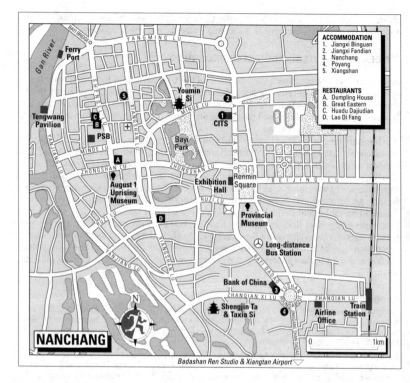

ACCOMMODATION
1. Jiangxi Binguan
2. Jiangxi Fandian
3. Nanchang
4. Poyang
5. Xiangshan

RESTAURANTS
A. Dumpling House
B. Great Eastern
C. Huadu Dajiudian
D. Lao Di Fang

NANCHANG

Badashan Ren Studio & Xiangtan Airport

temple dating back to 503 AD, which (perhaps because of the city's revolutionary associations) Nanchang's Red Guards seem to have been especially diligent in wrecking during the 1960s. It's encouraging, however, to see it active again despite piles of bricks and a forest of scaffolding obscuring the entrance. Beyond is an ancient tree and courtyard leading up to some splendid gate guardians and Buddha statues inside the main hall. Opposite the temple, **Bayi Park**, while not ravishingly attractive, does at least offer some greenery after the dusty colours of the city streets.

Tengwang Pavilion and the August 1 Uprising Museum

A kilometre or so west of Youmin Si on riverfront Yanjiang Lu is Nanchang's **ferry port** and, overlooking it, the mighty **Tengwang Pavilion** (daily 8am–late; ¥15). There have been 26 multi-storeyed towers built on this site since the first was raised over a thousand years ago in memory of a Tang prince, and the current "Song-style" building was only completed in 1989. It's impressive to look at, nonetheless, a huge structure isolated by a square of flat, grey paving and a monumental stone base, each floor lightened by a broadly flared roof supported by interlocking wooden beams. Disappointingly, the six-storeyed interior is rather a let-down – a host of gift shops and a **natural history museum** downstairs consisting of abysmally mounted lake fauna – and the upper level balconies offer sweeping views of a very drab cityscape. However, it is worth catching the lift to the top floor at weekends, when a tiny indoor **theatre** hosts traditional dances and music sessions, and with luck, there may even be a performance of local opera.

From the pavilion, head south along Yanjiang Lu, turn left into Zhongshan Lu and it's a five-minute walk to the **August 1 Uprising Museum** (daily 8am–5.30pm; ¥3). Formerly a hotel, this was occupied by the embryonic PLA as their 1927 General Headquarters. Gloomy nowadays, its three floors are stuffed with period furniture, weapons – notably a plaster cast of Zhu De's *Mauser* carbine – and maps labelled in Chinese.

Southern Nanchang

West of the Fushan roundabout off Zhanqian Lu (bus #5), the gates to the partially restored **Taxia Si** are frequently locked, barring entry to **Shengjin Ta**, perhaps because a legend says that the city will fall if the seven-storey pagoda is ever destroyed. The warning is still taken fairly seriously, despite the fact that Shengjin has been knocked down several times, the last time being in the early eighteenth century. At any rate, the pagoda itself is only of moderate interest, but the looking-glass logic needed to find the entrance will see you thoroughly exploring the neighbourhood, which is a pleasure. Nanchang was once famous for its **tea houses**, most of which have long gone, but a few down-to-earth, open-fronted establishments, patronized exclusively by gregarious old men watching the world go by, linger on in this market quarter – as do some equally archaic barber shops.

For an easy reprieve from the city, head well south of the centre to the suburb of **Qingyun Pu** and the tomb and studio of the early Qing painter **Zhu Da**, also known by his Buddhist name, **Ba Dashan Ren**. A descendant of the Ming imperial house, Zhu Da was a wandering Buddhist monk who came to live in the former Meixian temple in 1661. He is said to have painted in a frenzy, often while drunk, and his pictures certainly show great spontaneity. Catch bus #3 down Jinggang Shan Dadao from the Fushan roundabout to Qingyun, then walk southwest for fifteen minutes down Qingyun Lu (over the rail line) to where his tomb and the small **museum** (Tues–Sun 8.30am-4pm; ¥3) sit surrounded by water. There are a number of originals displayed inside, and some good reproductions on sale.

Eating and drinking

Nanchang's hotels all have reasonable **restaurants**, otherwise there are plenty of options along Minde Lu and Shengli Lu. Dishes are fairly uncomplicated; everywhere serves lightly sauced fresh fish, crayfish, frogs and vegetables, with more established places offering local specialities such as five-flower pork (steamed slices flavoured with five-spice powder) and three-cup, soy-braised chicken. Evening quick-fry wok **stalls**, with the menu in buckets and trays, are set up along several streets parallel with the river and north of Zhongshan Lu. Those on Xiangshan Bei Lu are particularly good.

Great Eastern (*Dadong*), Shengli Lu. A cheap and uncomplicated canteen.

Dumpling House, Shengli Lu, a few doors up from the intersection with Zhongshan Lu. New and clean. You order from the range of plastic cards behind the cashier, or point to whatever others are eating. Soup, buns and light meals from around ¥3 a serving.

Huadu Dajiudian, Shengli Lu. Mid-range, rather bare restaurant, specializing in river food plucked straight from the tank.

Lao Di Fang, Xiangshan Nan Lu. A bright, airy and very popular place serving tea and dumplings on the lower floor and the full range of local options upstairs.

Listings

Airlines CAAC/*China Eastern* main office is at 36 Zhanqian Lu (daily 9am-6pm ☎0791/6223656).

Bank and exchange The *Bank of China* is on the Fushan roundabout at the intersection of Bayi Dadao and Zhanqian Lu (foreign exchange Mon–Fri 9–11.30am & 2–5pm). The bank at the *Jiangxi Binguan* is open only to guests.

Bookshops There's a bookstore with a few foreign-language titles near the Exhibition Hall, Renmin Square.

Buses Nanchang's bus station looks huge and crowded, but the ticket office is user-friendly and there's no problem in getting seats on services to all main towns in Jiangxi and central China.

Ferries There are seasonally variable departures from Nanchang to hamlets right around Poyang Hu. During the bird-watching season cruise boats also run to the Hou Niao Baohu reserve (see "Jiujiang and Lu Shan" below).

Hospital First City Hospital, Xiangshan Lu.

PSB In the large government office building on Minde Lu.

Post and telecommunications Mail services and telephones are available at the main post office on Bayi Dadao, just south of Renmin Square (Mon–Sat 8am–8pm & Sun 8am–7pm).

Shopping *Nanchang Department Store*, the city's largest and best stocked department store, is west of Renmin Square along Zhongshan Lu, Nanchang's fashion quarter. *Arts and Crafts of Nanchang*, near the Youmin Si on Minde Lu, sells local artistic trinkets such as writing brushes, painted plates and Jingdezhen porcelain. More of the same, and *wushu* swords, are available from the antiques store near the August 1 Uprising Museum on Shengli Lu.

Trains There are daily departures from Nanchang towards Shanghai, Wuhan and Changsha, and the city also lies on the soon-to-be-completed Kowloon–Beijing line. Currently, it's pretty difficult to get anything better than a hard seat, however. Try *CITS* or window #9 at the train station.

Travel agents *CITS* is on the southern side of the courtyard behind the *Jiangxi Binguan* (daily 8.30–11.30am & 2–5pm; ☎0791/6221131 ext 372; fax 6224844). English and German speakers on hand Mon–Fri only.

Jiujiang and Lu Shan

Set on the Yangzi some 150km north of Nanchang, **Jiujiang** had its heyday last century as a treaty port, and now serves mostly as a jumping-off point for tourists exchanging the torrid lowland summers for nearby cool hills at **Lu Shan**. Buses from Nanchang run directly to both Jiujiang and Lu Shan, but if time is no problem, try travelling **by water** across Poyang itself – there are ferries from Nanchang right up to the northern tip of the lake at **Hukou** (see p.488), about an hour's drive east of Jiujiang, and also to **Xingzi**, on the southeastern side of Lu Shan, from where you can pick up public buses onwards. On the way, you might consider stopping 70km north of Nanchang where the Gan River enters Poyang at the hamlet of **Wucheng**. Between November and March the adjacent **Hou Niao Baohu** bird reserve attracts 160 varieties of wintering wildfowl, notably mandarin ducks, storks and a flock of two thousand rare **Siberian cranes**. Additional tour boats operate from Nanchang in season, and the reserve is also accessible by bus and boat via **Yongxiu**, a town on the Nanchang–Jiujiang highway.

Jiujiang

JIUJIANG (Nine Rivers) is well named, being built on the south bank of the Yangzi just west of where Poyang Hu disgorges itself in a generous maze of streams. Small, but always an important staging post for river traffic, the town grew wealthy during the Ming dynasty through trade in Jingdezhen's porcelain, which was distributed all over China from here. Largely destroyed during the Taiping Uprising, Jiujiang was rebuilt as a treaty port in the 1860s and today seems to be enjoying a low-scale renaissance, with the docks and adjacent streets busy from dawn to dusk.

The west side of town between the Yangzi and **Gantang Hu** is the most interesting area, a collection of narrow streets packed with small stores selling bright summer clothing, porcelain, and homemade hardware utensils. Completely occuping a tiny islet in the lake is **Yanshui Pavilion** (¥5), one of the most picturesque spots in Jiujiang. The Tang poet-official **Li Bai** was responsible for the causeway as well as the much restored moon-shaped sluice gate, and the tastefully proportioned Ming pavilion is now a peaceful **museum** adorned with statues to Li's memory. A ten-minute walk southeast of here down Yuling Lu leads to the red walls and flower beds surrounding the **Nengren Si** (¥2), whose battered five-storey pagoda rises over three plain halls, the largest of which is barely big enough to contain a looming, blue-haired Buddha statue.

Much more garish, the **Xunyang Tower** (daily 9am–late; ¥10) is an "antique" wine-house facing the Yangzi on Binjiang Lu, about 1.5km east of the ferry port. Built in 1986 to replace a previous Tang-dynasty structure, it was the setting – in literature – for a scene in *Outlaws of the Marsh*, China's equivalent to the Robin Hood legend, where the rebel leader **Song Jiang** impudently composed some revolutionary verses after downing too much wine. Wooden decor and open views from the upstairs **bar and tearoom** are the biggest attraction, and those familiar with *Outlaws* can check the heroic porcelain figurines of "Nine-dragons" Shi Jin, Song Jiang and others in the lobby. Just east again is another elderly pagoda, with fine views of the river once you've climbed the seven flights of wobbly wooden stairs.

JIUJIANG AND LU SHAN

Jiujiang	九江	*jiǔjiāng*
Bailu Binguan	白鹿宾馆	*báilù bīnguǎn*
Dongfeng Fandian	东风饭店	*dōngfēng fàndiàn*
Gantang Hu	甘棠湖	*gāntáng hú*
Nengren Si	能仁寺	*néngrén sì*
Xunyang Tower	寻阳塔	*xún yáng tǎ*
Yanshui Pavilion	烟水亭	*yānshuǐ tíng*
Lu Shan	庐山	*lúshān*
Botanical Garden	植物园	*zhíwù yuán*
Five Immortals' Peak	五仙人山	*wǔ xiānrén shān*
Lulin Hu	芦林湖	*lúlín hú*
People's Hall	人民剧院	*rénmín jùyuàn*
Ruqin Hu	如琴湖	*rúqín hú*
San Diequan	三叠泉	*sān dié quán*
Xianren Dong	仙人洞	*xiānrén dòng*
Guling	牯岭	*gǔlíng*
Guling	牯岭饭店	*gǔlíng fàndiàn*
Lulin	芦林饭店	*lúlín fàndiàn*
Lushan Binguan	庐山宾馆	*lúshān bīnguǎn*
Lushan Dasha	庐山大厦	*lúshān dàshà*
Lushan Fandian	庐山饭店	*lúshān fàndiàn*
Lushan Villas	庐山别墅	*lúshān bié shù*
Meilu Villa	美庐别墅	*měilú biéshù*
Hukou	湖口	*húkǒu*
Wucheng	误成鸟保护区	*wùchéng niǎo bǎo hù qū*
Xingzi	星子	*xīngzǐ*

Practicalities

Close together on the west side of town are the **Yangzi ferry port** (ticket office daily 8.30–11am & 2.30–5pm) on Binjiang Lu, and the **train station** at the end of Dazhong Lu, served by **minibuses** from Lu Shan and Nanchang throughout the day. Bus #4 and Xunyang Lu run east of here for 2km, past an English-speaking **CITS** office (north side of the road, look for the sign and they're on the sixth floor; Mon–Sat 8.30am–noon & 1–5pm; ☎0792/8239535) and a **Bank of China** (Mon–Fri 8.30–11am & 1.30–5pm), to Jiujiang's **long-distance bus station** lurking in the town's drab eastern quarter.

Most of the **accommodation** is also on Xunyang Lu. The *Bailu Binguan*, at no. 33 (☎0792/8224404; ④–⑤) is a flashy place patronized by well-heeled tour groups; watch out for the karaoke restaurant and forty percent price hikes during the summer tourist season. A little farther west, the *Dongfeng Fandian* (dorms ③; rooms ②) is shabby but much better value, the staff are nice and there's a good **restaurant** on the second floor.

Summer evenings are too close to spend indoors – especially during the frequent power cuts – and everyone heads down Xunyang Lu to window-shop and eat at one of the **pavement cafés** on Gantang's north shore, admiring views of Lu Shan and gorging on fish and crayfish hotpots, sautéed frogs and piles of freshwater snails.

Lu Shan

Lu Shan's cluster of wooded hills rises to a sudden 1474m from the level shores of Poyang Hu, and have been praised since ancient times by poets and travellers for their beauty and pleasant summer climate. Once covered in temples, in the mid-nineteenth century Lu Shan became a resort area for wealthy Chinese and European expatriates, who were carried up in sedan chairs. **Chiang Kaishek** built a summer residence and training school for Guomindang officials up here in the 1930s, and, unlike most of the temples, these have been preserved, as have the sites of more recent meetings of the Communist Central Committee. Rambling rather than climbing country, nowadays the place is overrun with teenagers, cadres and tour parties who pack out the restaurants and troop along the paths to enjoy the clean air. The former mansions have been converted to hotels and sanatoriums for their benefit. Crowds can reach plague proportions between spring and autumn, when the lowlands are hot and the landscape is blooming, so winter – though very cold – can be the best season to visit. It's a pleasant place at any time, and a weekend's walking is enough for a good sample of mountain scenery.

Guling

The thirty-kilometre trip from Jiujiang takes two hours on the sharply twisting road, with sparkling views back over the great lake and its junction with the Yangzi. There's a pause at the top gates for passengers to pay an **entry fee** (¥30), then it's a short way to **GULING** township in Lu Shan's northeastern corner, whose handful of quaintly cobbled streets, stone villas and bungalows harps back to the colonial era. The one sight in town is the very European **Meilu Villa** on Hexi Lu, former residence of Chiang Kaishek and of interest simply because it is one of the few exhibitions in China to so much as mention the Generalissimo. Other than this there are some nice views around the centre of Guling's mosaic of red roof tiles and grey buildings nestled among the fir trees.

The **bus** drops you at the arrival stop on He Dong Lu immediately after emerging from a tunnel into town (though minibuses from Jiujiang might terminate anywhere). Fifty metres downhill on the right is a pedestrian mall leading through to **Jiexin Garden** and Guling Lu. Most essential services are either in the mall or on Guling Lu: souvenir shops selling **maps**, a post office, *Bank of China* (though larger hotels are a better bet for exchanging travellers' cheques) and a **market** selling vegetables, bananas, peaches and lychees.

There are plenty of **restaurants** in Guling, mostly good value despite the numbers of tourists, and some post their menus and prices outside. At the junction of the mall and He Dong Lu, the inexpensive *Fenghua* serves dumpling breakfasts and simple meals during the rest of the day. More upmarket options include a Sichuanese place diagonally opposite, and a cheapish, uninspired Cantonese diner across from the park on Guling Lu. For local flavours – mountain fungus and fish – try the stalls and open restaurants around the market, or the *Wurong Canting*, above a teashop in the mall.

Leaving Lu Shan is fairly simple, though due to the one-way road system in Guling, departing buses and their **ticket offices** are on Guling Lu, separate from the arrival points. It's essential to book tickets the day before departure. Regular buses head to Jiujiang, Nanchang and beyond; if you can't find direct services, go first to Jiujiang for Wuhan for roads east, and Nanchang for southern or westerly destinations.

ACCOMMODATION

Summers are warm, damp and very busy, so it's a good idea to arrive early on in the day to make sure of a room. Winters see fewer tourists but are cold enough for snow, so check out what the heating arrangements are before taking a room.

Guling, 104 He Donglu (☎0792/8282435). The two wings face each other across the road about 100m downhill from the bus stop. The older, cheaper section has perfectly decent dorm beds and doubles, while the rooms in the newer building are much smarter. Dorms ①, rooms ②–⑥.

Lulin, Lulin Hu (☎0792/8282424). Very quiet, self-contained retreat, offering triples and doubles, south of Lulin Hu, a lake about 7km from Guling – minibuses heading out to the lake can drop you off. ⑤–⑦.

Lushan Binguan, 446 Hexi Lu (☎0792/8282843), Ten minutes farther on past the *Guling*, this is a heavy stone mansion with slightly ordinary cheaper rooms, good value suites and a fine restaurant. ⑤–⑦.

Lushan Dasha, 506 Hexi Lu (☎0792/8282178). A regimental exterior betrays this hotel as the former Guomindang Officers' Training Centre, but the rooms are well furnished and comfortable. ⑤.

Lushan Fandian, Guling Lu (☎0792/8285430). One of a string of places near the bus ticket booths that might be persuaded to take foreigners; clean and basic. Dorms ①, rooms ③.

Lushan Villas (☎0792/8282525). Nice quiet location off Hexi Lu in a group of recently renovated cottage villas named after different historic figures. Two excellent restaurants on site. ⑤.

Into the hills

Covering some 300 square kilometres, Lu Shan's highlands form an elliptical platform tilted over to the southwest, comprising a central region of lakes surrounded by pine-clad hills, with superb rocks, waterfalls and views along the vertical edges of the plateau. Freelance minibuses cruise Guling Lu and usually charge a flat fee of ¥10 per person to any site in Lu Shan, while tour buses cover a variety of places on day trips from the long-distance bus arrival stop.

For an easy walk out from town (3hr round trip), follow the road downhill to the southwest from Guling Lu and the Jiexin Garden to the far end of **Ruqin Hu**, where you can pick up the **Floral Path**. This gives impressive views of the Jinxui Valley as it winds along Lu Shan's western cliff edge past **Xianren Dong**, the Immortal's Cave, once inhabited by an ephemeral Taoist monk and still an active shrine, complete with a slowly dripping spring.

The most spectacular scenery is found on Lu Shan's southern fringes, around 10km from Guling at **Hanpokou**. A full exploration makes a fair day's hike, and even hardened walkers will probably take advantage of transport into the area. About an hour's stroll down Hexi Lu and then left takes you past the **People's Hall**, site of two Central Committee meetings and now an unpleasantly crowded Communist Party museum

(8am–5pm; ¥3), to **Lulin Hu**, a nice lakeside area with its attractive Dragon Pools and elderly Three Treasure trees over to the west. Hanpokou, however, lies another good hour to the east past China's only sub-alpine **botanical garden**, and is the finest spot in Lu Shan to watch the sunrise – though should you miss it, there are also good views of the hills descending to Poyang Hu. A walking track continues around the ridges to **Five Immortals' Peak** and up to **San Diequan** (Three Waterfalls), a hard ninety minutes' work (if you ignore the recently completed **monorail**), but well worth the effort on a fine day. Admittedly, these are a rare commodity on Lu Shan, whose peaks are frequently obscured by mist – the local brew is suitably known as "Cloud Fog Tea".

The Northeast and Jingdezhen

From Nanchang, road and rail lines head northeast towards **Jingdezhen** and on into Anhui Province. Skirting Poyang's eastern shore, they pass through the copper-mining town of **YINGTAN**, 180km from Nanchang, locally famed for the nearby Taoist retreat of **Longhu Shan** (Dragon-Tiger Mountain). The five-hour journey from Jiujiang across to Jingdezhen is also interesting, as the road crosses Poyang Hu at the point where the lake empties into the Yangzi. Queues here for the vehicular ferry across to **HUKOU** can be slow progress, but once on the eastern side you'll see the Qing pagoda and halls of **Shizhong Shan Gong**. Built right on the lake, the temple's name – Stone Bell Mountain – derives from the sound of waves pounding against the rocks below during storms.

THE NORTHEAST AND JINGDEZHEN		
Jingdezhen	景德镇	*jǐngdézhèn*
Jingdezhen Binguan	景德镇宾馆	*jǐngdézhèn bīnguǎn*
Jingdezhen Fandian	景德镇饭店	*jǐngdézhèn fàndiàn*
Longzhu Ge	龙珠阁	*lóngzhū gé*
Museum of Ceramic History	古陶瓷博览区	*gǔtáocí bólǎnqū*
Yingtan	鹰潭	*yīngtán*
Longhu Shan	龙虎山	*lónghǔ shān*
Poyang Hu	鄱阳湖	*póyáng hú*

Jingdezhen

Northeast of Nanchang – 200km as the crow flies – between Poyang Hu and the Anhui border, **JINGDEZHEN** was producing pottery at least two thousand years ago, and, despite half-hearted attempts to introduce new industries, pottery remains the city's chief source of income. This is entirely due to local geography and national politics. Jingdezhen lies in a river valley rich not only in clay suitable for firing but also in the feldspar needed to turn it into **porcelain**. When the Ming rulers developed a taste for fine ceramics in the fourteenth century, Jingdezhen's location was conveniently close to the original court at Nanjing. An **imperial kiln** was built in 1369, and its wares became so highly regarded – "as white as jade, as thin as paper, as bright as a mirror, as tuneful as a bell" – that Jingdezhen retained official favour even after the Ming court shifted to Beijing fifty years later.

As demand grew, workshops experimented with new **glazes** and a classic range of decorative styles emerged: *qinghua*, blue and white; *jihong*, rainbow; *doucai*, a blue and white overglaze; and *fencai*, multi-coloured *famille rose*. The first examples reached

Europe in the seventeenth century, and became so popular that our very word for China clay – kaolin – derives from its source at **Gaoling**, near Jingdezhen. Factories began to specialize in **export ware** shaped and decorated in European-approved forms, which reached the outside world via the booming Canton markets – the famous **Nanking Cargo**, comprising 150,000 pieces salvaged from the 1752 wreck of the Dutch vessel *Geldermalsen* and auctioned in 1986, was one such shipment. Foreign sales on this scale petered out after European ceramic technologies improved at the end of the eighteenth century, but Jingdezhen survived by sacrificing its earlier spirit of innovation for a more production-line mentality. After a low point early on in the twentieth century, the industry is once more on the move, and today Jingdezhen's scores of private and state-owned kilns employ some fifty thousand people.

The Town
Surrounded by paddy fields and tea terraces, Jingdezhen is a thoroughly scruffy city whose leafy streets can't obscure the effects of severe pollution caused by the numerous porcelain factories dotted throughout the centre. The town is concentrated on the east bank of the **Changjiang** (not the actual Yangzi, but a lesser river of the same name). **Zhushan Lu** runs away from the river for a kilometre through the city centre to where roads converge at a small, grassless park, notable for its daytime croquet sessions and the sociable crowds that gather for a chat and a stroll every evening.

The only available vistas of Jingdezhen are from the three-storey **Longzhu Ge** (Dragon Pearl Pavilion), overlooking the river on Jiang Dong Lu. This is a pleasant construction in wood and orange tile along the lines of Hunan's Yueyang Tower (see p.474). From the top, the town's smoggy horizon is liberally pierced by smokestacks of varying sizes, which fire up by late afternoon.

But porcelain, not views, is the reason Jingdezhen figures on tourist itineraries, and the town is geared towards selling. **Shops** around Zhushan Lu and adjoining streets are the best place to browse for a quick souvenir among an incredible amount of brightly coloured tack, from metre-high vases and ugly moulded statuettes of Buddhist and historical figures, down to porcelain pandas for the mantelpiece. The **night market**, which fills the park end of Zhushan Lu and Xincun Xi Lu with snack stalls and private sellers hawking factory rejects and the occasional older piece, is the place to pick up bargain-priced crockery, some of which is quite good. Serious buyers after bulk purchases should head over the river and catch bus #4 north to the city limits, where there's a kilometre of shops overflowing with stacks of giant urns, statues and teapots – it's a surreal sight, as are the Chinese visitors buying by the cartload.

THE MUSEUM OF CERAMIC HISTORY
To experience the manufacturing side of things, either try to join a *CITS* **factory tour**, or visit the **Museum of Ceramic History** (daily 9am–5pm; ¥6 entry for each building). Normally the museum is a bit quiet, but if a big tour party is expected, the workshops get fired up and it's much more entertaining. The museum is out of town on the west side of the river – take bus #3 from Zhushan Lu to its terminus just past the Xingfeng Lu long-distance bus station, then cross over Cidu Dadao (Porcelain Capital Avenue) and under the ornamental arch opposite. A fifteen-minute walk through fields leads to a surprising collection of antique buildings divided into two sections. A **Ming mansion** houses the museum proper, and its ornate crossbeams, walled gardens and gilt eave screens tend to distract attention away from the small **ceramics display** inside the main hall. Pieces here start with thousand-year-old kiln fragments, and work through the early Ming's classic simplicity to the overwrought, multi-coloured extravagances of the late nineteenth century. Next door, another walled garden conceals a Qing porcelain **workshop**, complete with a Confucian temple and working pottery,

where the entire process of throwing, moulding and glazing takes place. Out the back is a rickety two-storey **kiln**, packed with all sizes of the unglazed yellow pottery sleeves commonly seen outside local field kilns – these shield each piece of porcelain from damage in case one explodes during the firing process.

Practicalities

The **train station** is 1.5km from Jingdezhen's centre, down past the *Bank of China* on Tongzhan Lu – trolleybuses #1 and #3 head up to central Zhushan Lu from here. The **long-distance bus station** is 3km southwest across the river on Xingfeng Lu, connected to Zhushan Lu by bus #3 and trolleybus #2. Long-distance buses which don't terminate in Jingdezhen might drop passengers off northwest of town at the end of the #4 bus route; take this for five stops down Cidu Dadao, then catch the #1 over the bridge and along Zhushan Lu.

Jingdezhen's **accommodation** prospects are sadly dire. The grimy dormitories at the *Wenyuan Grand Hotel* (①), next to the train station on Tongzhan Lu are at least cheap. The same cannot be said of the rat-infested *Jingdezhen Fandian* (⑥), across from the park on the corner of Zhushan Lu and Lianshi Bei Lu – ignore the two-star rating plaque in the lobby. Unfortunately for those on a tight budget, the one place offering good value is the very upmarket *Jingdezhen Binguan* (☎0798/225010, fax 226416; ⑦), nicely located 1km due north of the centre along Lianshi Bei Lu in **Lianhuata Park**, with a *CITS* office in the building out front.

Eating is limited to a selection of **restaurants** and food stalls along Lianshi Bei Lu offering hotpots and stir fries, and the *Jingdezhen Binguan*'s good regional menu.

Southern Jiangxi

When Zhou Enlai and Zhu De were driven out of Nanchang after their abortive uprising, they fled to the **Jinggang Shan** ranges, 300km southwest in the mountainous border with Hunan. Here they met up with Mao, whose peasant revolt in Hunan had also failed, and the remnants of the two armies joined to form the first real PLA divisions. Their initial base was near the country town of **Ciping**, and, though they declared a

SOUTHERN JIANGXI		
Ciping	茨坪	*cípíng*
Former Revolutionary Headquarters	革命旧居群	*gémìng jiùjūqún*
Jinggang Shan Binguan	井岗山宾馆	*jǐnggāng shān bīnguǎn*
Jinggang Shan Fandian	井岗山饭店	*jǐnggāng shān fàndiàn*
Martyrs' Tomb	革命烈士纪念堂	*gé mìngliè shì jì niàn táng*
Revolutionary Museum	井岗山博物馆	*jǐnggāng shān bówùguǎn*
AROUND CIPING		
Wulong Tan	五龙潭	*wǔlóng tán*
Wuzhi Feng	五指峰	*wǔ zhǐfēng*
Ganzhou	赣州	*gànzhōu*
Bajing Park	八境公园	*bājìng gōngyuán*
Ji'an	吉安	*jí ān*
Jinggang Shan	井岗山	*jǐnggāng shān*

Chinese Soviet Republic in 1931 at the Fujian border town of **Ruijin**, Ciping was where the Communists stayed until forced out by the Guomindang in 1934.

Once isolated and difficult to reach, new roads have made Jinggang Shan reasonably accessible, though it doesn't seem to be attracting a great number of casual tourists – probably because it is so far from anywhere else. This makes it a pleasant proposition, especially after dealing with the crowds at Lu Shan, as there is some splendid forest scenery and a few hiking trails.

Ciping and around

Jinggang Shan is an eight-hour bus trip from Nanchang via the ancient river town of **JI'AN**, whose **Yunzhang Ge** (Cloud Sect Pavilion) is built out on a wooded midstream island, clearly visible south of the main bridge. From here the road runs southwest, past paddy fields and attractive houses with upswept eaves and whitewashed walls, until woodland and clouds begin to close in at the foot of the tortuous trail up into the ranges.

Also known as Jinggang Shan Shi, **CIPING** is, at least in scale, nothing more than a village. Completely destroyed by artillery bombardments during the 1930s, it was rebuilt after the Communist takeover as one enormous revolutionary relic, though recent greening projects have lightened the heavily heroic architecture and monuments, giving the place a dated rural charm. The main streets form a two-kilometre elliptical circuit, the lower half of which is taken up with a lake surrounded by grassy gardens – much appreciated by straying cattle – and a tiny amusement park, complete with a real MiG-style fighter plane to play on.

Ciping's austere historical monuments can be breezed through fairly quickly, as it's the surrounding hills which better recreate a feeling of how the Communist guerrillas might have lived. Five minutes west of the bus station at the top end of town is the squat, angular **Martyrs' Tomb**, positioned at the top of a broad flight of stairs and facing the mountains that the fighters it commemorates died defending. Farther round at the **Revolutionary Museum** (8am–4pm; ¥4), signs ban smoking, spitting and laughter, and the exhibition consists almost entirely of maps showing battle sites and troop movements up until 1930 – after this the Communists suffered some heavy defeats. Paintings of a smiling Mao preaching to peasant armies face cases of the spears, flintlocks and mortars which initially comprised the Communist arsenal, perhaps suggesting that righteousness will prevail against all odds. On a more mundane level, a group of mud-brick rooms across the park at the **Former Revolutionary Headquarters** (8am–4pm; ¥4) gives an idea of what Ciping might have originally looked like, and, as the site of where Mao and Zhu De co-ordinated their guerrilla activities and the start of the Long March, is the town's biggest attraction as far as visiting cadres are concerned.

Practicalities

Ciping's **bus station** is on the northeastern side of the circuit, served by buses from Nanchang and Hengyang (see p.472) in Hunan Province, from where there are decent transport links into southern and central China.

About 100m downhill from the bus staion, on the left past a gauntlet of **restaurants**, the *Jinggang Shan Fandian* (dorms ②, rooms ②–⑤) is a comfy Chinese hotel whose seemingly limitless wings and floors contain a huge number of beds, including three-bed dorms with private facilities. Farther along, just past the Former Revolutionary Headquarters, is a large *Bank of China* only too happy to change travellers' cheques (Mon–Fri 9–11.30am & 2–5pm).

Alternatively, from the bus station take the first street down the hill on the right through Ciping's **tourist market**, a collection of white-tiled shops selling local teas,

---

THE LONG MARCH

In 1927, Chiang Kaishek, the new leader of the right-wing Nationalist Guomindang government, began an obsessive war against the six-year-old Chinese Communist Party, using a union dispute in Shanghai as an excuse to massacre their leadership. In response, the Communists went underground, setting up half a dozen remote rural bases or soviets across central China. The most important of these were the **Fourth Front army** in northern Sichuan, under the leadership of **Zhang Guotao**; the **Hunan soviet**, controlled by the talented and irrepressible peasant general **He Long**; and the main **Jiangxi soviet** in the Jianggan Mountains, led by Mao and **Zhu De**, the Communist Commander-in-Chief.

Initially poorly armed, the Jiangxi soviet successfully fought off Guomindang attempts to oust them, acquiring better weapons in the process and swelling their ranks with disaffected peasantry and defectors from the Nationalist cause. But they over-estimated their position and, abandoning Mao's previously successful guerrilla tactics in 1933, were drawn into several disastrous pitched battles. Chiang, ignoring Japanese incursions into Manchuria in his eagerness to defeat the Communists, blockaded the mountains with a steadily tightening ring of bunkers and barbed wire, systematically clearing areas of guerrillas with artillery bombardments. Hemmed in and facing eventual defeat, the **First Front army**, comprising some eighty thousand Red soldiers, decided to break through the blockade in October 1934 and head west to team up with the Hunan soviet – the beginning of the **Long March**.

Technically a retreat, the Long March was highly disciplined. Covering a punishing average of 30km a day, the Communists moved after dark whenever possible so that the enemy would find it difficult to know their exact position – even so, they faced daily skirmishes. One thing in their favour was that many putative Guomindang divisions were, in fact, armies belonging to local warlords who owed only a token allegiance to Chiang Kaishek and had no particular reason to fight the Communists once it became clear that the Red Army was crossing, not invading, their territory. But after severe losses incurred during a battle at the **Xiang River** near Guilin in Guangxi, the Communists found their progress north impeded by massive Guomindang forces determined to prevent their joining up with the Hunan soviet, and they were obliged to continue west to Guizhou where they took the town of **Zunyi** in January 1935. With their power structure in disarray and with no obvious options left to them, an emergency meeting of the Party hierarchy was called. This was the **Zunyi Conference**, from which **Mao** emerged as the undisputed **leader of the Chinese Communist Party** with a mandate to "go north to fight the Japanese" by linking up with Zhang Guotao's Fourth Front army in Sichuan. During the following months they circled through Yunnan and

---

cloud ear fungus and bamboo roots carved into faces. Straight through the market is the *Jinggang Shan Binguan* (☎0791/22272; ⑨), favoured by visiting officials but otherwise a bit dreary and grey. The **CITS** office here (no apparently fixed opening times; ☎0791/222504) might be able to arrange a local tour with an English-speaking guide, or offer some explanation for the inadequate **maps** of walking trails available from the bus station and outside the museum.

Around Ciping

Having waded through the terribly serious displays in town, it's nice to escape from Ciping into Jinggang Shan's surprisingly wild **countryside**. Some of the peaks provide glorious views of the sunrise, or more frequent mists, and there are colourful plants, natural groves of pine and bamboo, deep green temperate cloud forests, and hosts of butterflies and birds. *CITS* can arrange a jeep and driver, and infrequent minibuses leave from the station when full. One problem with walking anywhere is that maps of

Guizhou, trying to shake off the Guomindang, routing twenty regiments of the Guangxi provincial army at the **Loushan Pass** in the process, then suddenly moved up into Sichuan to cross the Jinsha River and, in one of the most celebrated and heroic episodes of the march, took the **Luding Bridge** across the Dadu River (see p.818). They now had to negotiate **Daxue Shan** (Great Snowy Mountains) where hundreds died from exhaustion, exposure and altitude sickness before the survivors met up on the far side with the Fourth Front army.

The meeting between these two major branches of the Red Army was tense, with **Mao** and **Zhang Guotao** quarrelling over supreme military command. Mao, with Party backing, wanted to start resistance against the Japanese, but Zhang, who felt that his better-equipped forces and higher education gave him superiority, wanted to found a Communist state in Sichuan's far west. Zhang eventually capitulated, and both he and Mao took control of separate columns in order to cross the last natural barrier they had to face, the **Aba Grasslands** in northern Sichuan. But here, while Mao was bogged down with swamps, hostile nomads and dwindling food reserves, Zhang suddenly retreated with his column to **Garzê**, where he set up an independent government. Mao and what remained of the First Front managed to struggle through southern Gansu, where they suffered further losses through Muslim supporters of the Guomindang, finally arriving in Communist-held **Yan'an**, Shaanxi Province, in October 1935. While the mountains here were soon to become a Communist stronghold, only a quarter of those who started from Jiangxi twelve months before had completed the 9500-kilometre journey. Zhang was soon harried out of western Sichuan by Chiang's forces, however, and after meeting up with He Long, he battled his way through to Shaanxi to add another twenty thousand followers to the Communist ranks. Here he made peace with Mao in October 1936, but later defected to the Guomindang.

Though he eventually wrote many a romantic poem about the Long March, Mao summed it up accurately immediately afterwards, admitting that in terms of losses and the Red Army's **failure** to hold their original positions against the Nationalists, the Guomindang had won. Yet in a more lasting sense, the march was an incredible success, uniting the Party structure under Mao and defining the Communists' aims, while creating a **legend** which changed the Communists' popular image from simply another rebel group opposing central authority into one of a determined, honest and patriotic movement. After Zunyi, Mao turned the march into a deliberate propaganda mission to spread the Communist faith among the peasantry, opening up prisons in captured Guomindang towns and promoting tolerance and co-operation with minority groups (though not always successfully). As Mao said, "*Without the Long March, how could the broad masses have learned so quickly about the existence of the great truth which the Red Army embodies?*"

the footpaths are pretty vague, and locals can be shy of foreigners, running off should you stop to ask directions.

Relatively easy to find and also one of the nicest areas for its own sake, **Wulong Tan** (Five Dragon Pools) is about 8km north along the road from the Martyrs' Tomb. A footpath follows from the road head past where some poetically pretty waterfalls drop into the pools (of which there are actually eight) between a score of pine-covered peaks. The same distance south is **Jinggang Shan** itself, also known as **Wuzhi Feng**, apex of the mountains at 1586m. Follow the road out of town past the *Bank of China*, then turn right and take the concrete "driveway" uphill past company housing and on to a dirt road. About ten minutes later this forks; go left down to the bridge, cross over and carry on past a huge quarry, where machinery turns boulders into gravel, and on to a **tunnel** leading into the hillside. Ignore the tunnel and follow the steps above up through a small patch of forest full of ginger, ferns and moss-covered trees, to more stairs ascending to Wuzhi Feng's sharp and lightly wooded summit. The last bit of the track is slippery and not overly used, giving a rare opportunity to be on your own, musing on how the Communists must have found things and watching the trees and waterfalls below sliding in and out of the clouds. Examine the bushes and you'll find that some extraordinary insects congregate up here: multi-coloured crickets, scarabs with orange antennae and huge, bushy caterpillars.

Ganzhou and beyond

Six hours south of Jinggang Shan, **GANZHOU** lies on the tropical side of the mountain ranges and is very different from the north of the province. A small port city on the Zhang River, Ganzhou is due to rise in importance as a stop on the future Kowloon–Beijing rail link, and for now makes an interesting few hours' break in your journey. The **long-distance bus station** is down at the southeastern corner of town on Bayi Si Dadao. Pick up a map here, then catch bus #1 to the **clock tower** in the old, northern riverside quarter. From here, it's a ten-minute walk through narrow alleyways to **Bajing Park**, where a **temple** overlooks the river and reconstructions of the old city walls stretch for 5km along the banks. Heading back towards the bus station in a more or less direct line, you'll see the decaying colonial buildings along the wharves – Ganzhou was probably a treaty port – and an unsuspected, unrestored, century-old residential district, with remarkable walled mansions, a couple of tiny nunneries, and a pagoda. Back at the station, buses run east to **Yong'an** in Fujian Province, and south to **Shaoguan** and **Guangzhou** in Guangdong Province.

travel details

Trains

Changsha to: Guangzhou (5 daily; 15hr); Guiyang (5 daily; 17hr); Hengyang (5 daily; 3hr); Nanchang (5 daily; 9hr); Shaoshan (daily; 3hr); Wuhan (5 daily; 5hr); Yueyang (4 daily; 2hr).

Dayong to: Huaihua (for connections to Guiyang or Changsha; daily; 5hr); Jishou (for buses to Tongren; daily; 3hr); Yichang (daily; 6hr).

Hefei to: Beijing (daily; 20hr); Huainan (daily; 3hr); Nanjing (daily; 6hr); Shanghai (daily; 12hr); Tunxi (daily; 15hr); Wuhu (daily; 5hr).

Jiujiang to: Nanchang (4 daily; 3–5hr); Shanghai (2 daily; 20hr).

Nanchang to: Beijing (4 daily; 30hr); Changsha (2 daily; 11hr); Guangzhou (4 daily; 22hr); Jiujiang (4 daily; 3–5hr); Shanghai (2 daily; 15hr); Wuhan (4 daily; 9hr).

Tunxi to: Hefei (daily; 15hr); Nanjing (daily;12hr); Shanghai (2 daily; 15hr); Wuhu (daily; 8hr).

Wuhan to: Changsha (8 daily; 5hr); Nanchang (4 daily; 9hr); Shiyan (3 daily; 14hr); Xiangfan (3 daily; 8hr); Yichang (5 daily; 8hr); Yueyang (6 daily; 4hr); Zhengzhou (8 daily; 9hr).

Wuhu to: Hefei (daily; 5hr); Nanjing (daily; 4hr); Shanghai (daily;12hr); Tunxi (daily; 6hr).

Xiangfan to: Shiyan (3 daily; 5hr); Wuhan (3 daily; 8hr); Yichang (4 daily; 4hr).

Yichang to: Wuhan (5 daily; 8hr); Xiangfan (4 daily; 4hr).

Yueyang to: Changsha (6 daily; 2hr); Wuhan (6 daily; 4hr).

Buses

Changsha to: Dayong (14hr); Heng Shan (4–5hr); Jiujiang (20hr); Nanchang (10hr); Wuhan (13hr); Yueyang (5hr).

Hefei to: Huainan (4hr); Nanchang (20hr); Nanjing (6hr); Wuhan (12hr); Tunxi (10hr); Wuhu (5hr).

Jingdezhen to: Jiujiang (5hr); Nanchang (8hr); Poyang (2hr); Tunxi (5hr).

Jinggang Shan to: Ji'an (3hr); Ganzhou (6hr); Hengyang (6hr); Nanchang (8hr).

Jiujiang to: Changsha (20hr); Jingdezhen (5hr); Lu Shan (2hr); Nanchang (3hr 30min); Wuhan (16hr).

Lu Shan to: Jiujiang (2hr); Nanchang (3hr 30min).

Nanchang to: Changsha (10hr); Hefei (20hr); Jingdezhen (8hr); Jinggang Shan (8hr); Jiujiang (3hr 30min); Lu Shan (3hr 30min); Wuhan (12hr).

Tunxi to: Hefei (10hr); Huang Shan (2hr); Jingdezhen (5hr); Jiuhua Shan (8hr); Nanjing (10hr); Shanghai (12hr); Shexian (1hr); Wuhu (6hr); Yixian (2hr 30min).

Wuhan to: Changsha (13hr); Hefei (12hr); Jiujiang (16hr); Nanchang (12hr); Yichang (10hr).

Wuhu to: Hefei (5hr); Jiuhua Shan (8hr); Nanjing (4hr); Tunxi (6hr); Tongling (2hr 40min); Xuanzhou (2hr).

Xiangfan to: Wudang Shan (7hr); Yichang (6hr).

Yichang to: Shennongjia (6hr); Wuhan (10hr); Xiangfan (6hr).

Ferries

Jiujiang to: Guichi (for Jiuhua Shan and Huang Shan; daily; 12hr); Nanjing (daily; 24hr); Shanghai (daily; 48hr); Wuhan (8 daily; 12hr).

Nanchang to: Hou Niao Baohu Bird Reserve (Nov–March only, irregular schedule; 2–5hr); Poyang (for Jingdezhen; daily; 5–10hr).

Wuhan to: Chongqing (daily; 5 days); Nanjing (daily; 48hr); Shanghai (daily; 3 days); Wuhu (daily; 30hr).

Yichang to: Chongqing (daily; 2–3 days); Wuhan (daily; 22hr).

Planes

Changsha to: Beijing (3 daily; 1hr 40min); Guangzhou (daily; 4hr); Hefei (3 weekly; 5hr); Shanghai (daily; 2hr); Wuhan (2 weekly; 2hr 30min).

Hefei to: Beijing (5 weekly; 1hr 30min); Changsha (3 weekly; 5hr); Guangzhou (daily; 2hr); Shanghai (daily; 40min); Tunxi (daily; 1hr); Wuhan (daily; 1hr).

Nanchang to: Beijing (2–3 daily; 2hr); Guangzhou (1–2 daily; 1hr 20min); Shanghai (daily; 1hr).

Tunxi (Huang Shan) to: Beijing (5 weekly; 2hr); Guangzhou (9 weekly; 1hr 40min); Hefei (daily; 1hr); Shanghai (6 weekly; 50min); Wuhan (daily; 1hr).

Wuhan to: Beijing (4 daily; 1hr 40min); Changsha (2 weekly; 2hr 30min); Guangzhou (7 daily; 1hr 15min); Hefei (daily; 1hr); Shanghai (4 daily; 1hr); Tunxi (daily; 1hr).

CHAPTER EIGHT

FUJIAN, GUANGDONG AND HAINAN ISLAND

Theres something very self-contained about the provinces of **Fujian**, **Guangdong** and **Hainan Island**, which occupy 1200km or so of China's convoluted southern seaboard. Though occasionally taking centre stage in the country's history, the provinces share a sense of being generally isolated from mainstream events by the mountain ranges which surround Fujian and Guangdong, physically cutting off the rest of the empire. Forced to look seawards, the coastal regions have a long history of contact with the outside world, continually importing – or being forced to endure – foreign influences and styles. This is where Islam entered China and porcelain left it; where the mid-nineteenth-century theatricals of the Opium Wars, colonialism, the Taiping Uprising and the mass overseas exodus of southern Chinese were played out; and where today you'll find China's most modern, Westernized cities. Conversely, the interior mountains enclose some of the country's wildest, remotest corners, with parts which were literally in the Stone Age within living memory.

Possibly because its specific attractions are thinly spread and somewhat out of the way, the region receives scant attention from visitors. Huge numbers do pass through Guangdong in transit between the mainland and Hong Kong and Macau, but only because they have to, and few look beyond the overpowering capital, **Guangzhou**. Yet while the other two regional capitals – **Fuzhou** in Fujian, and Hainan's **Haikou** – to some extent share Guangzhou's modern veneer, all three also hide temples and antique architecture that have somehow escaped developers, while other cities and towns have managed to preserve their old, character-laden ambiance intact. The pick of these are the Fujian port of **Xiamen**, its streets almost frozen in time since the turn of the century, and **Chaozhou** in eastern Guangdong, a staunchly conservative place consciously preserving its traditions in the face of the modern world.

Indeed, a sense of local tradition and of being "different" from the rest of the country pervades the whole region, though, aside from people being more assertive and

---

ACCOMMODATION PRICE CODES

All the accommodation in this book has been graded according to the following price codes, which represent the cheapest double room available to foreigners. Most places have a range of rooms, however, and staff will usually offer you the more expensive ones – it's always worth asking if they have anything cheaper. Where the text refers specifically to dorm beds, the price code represents the price per bed. See p.40 for more details.

① less than ¥30	④ ¥100–150	⑦ ¥300–500
② ¥30–75	⑤ ¥150–200	⑧ ¥500–700
③ ¥75–100	⑥ ¥200–300	⑨ ¥700 or more

open – in habits sometimes regarded by reserved northerners as uncouth – this feeling is rarely expressed in any tangible way. **Language** is one difference you might notice, however; the main dialects here are Cantonese and Minnan, whose rhythms, even if you can't speak a word of Chinese, are recognizably removed from Mandarin. Specific **ethnic groups** are rarely obvious, though they include the **Hakka**, a widely spread Han sub-group whose mountainous Guangdong–Fujian heartland is dotted with fortress-like mansions; the Muslim **Hui**, who form large communities in Guangzhou, coastal Hainan and in **Quanzhou** in Fujian; and the **Li**, Hainan's animistic, original inhabitants.

While a quick look around much of the region's coastal areas leaves a gloomy impression of uncontrolled development, much of this is actually contained within various **Special Economic Zones**, specifically created in the mid-1980s as a focus for heavy investment and industrialization. Beyond their boundaries lurk some respectably wild – and also nicely tamed – corners where you can settle back and enjoy the scenery. Over in western Guangdong, the city of **Zhaoqing** sits beside some pleasant lakes and hills, while the **Wuyi Shan** range in northeastern Fujian contains the region's lushest, most picturesque mountain forests. Way down south, the country's best **beaches** have encouraged the tourist industry to hype Hainan as "China's Hawaii", and there's also a limited amount of hiking to try through the island's interior highlands.

While the region is generally seen as somewhere that has to be ploughed through on the way to better places, anyone wanting to stop off and explore will find plentiful local and long-distance **transport** from ferries to trains, though **accommodation** can be expensive and suffers additional seasonal price hikes in Guangzhou. The **weather** is nicest in spring and autumn, as summer storms from June to August bring daily doses of heavy humidity, thunder and afternoon downpours on the coast, while the higher reaches of the Guangdong–Fujian border can get very cold in winter.

FUJIAN

FUJIAN, on China's southeastern coast, is well off the beaten track for most Western travellers, which is a pity because the province possesses not only a wild mountainous interior, but also a string of old ports, including, in the city of **Xiamen**, China's most attractive and interesting coastal city. From Hong Kong the well-trodden routes head directly west towards Guilin, or north to Shanghai, but Xiamen would make an excellent introduction to mainland China – boats from Hong Kong come here, as does a spur of China's rail network.

Culturally and geographically, the province splits into distinct halves. One is made up of large, historical seaports and lush, semi-tropical coastal stretches, where the sun shines warmly and trees blossom even in January. The other is a rugged, mountainous and largely inaccessible interior, freezing cold in winter, home to around 140 different local dialects and with a history of poverty and backwardness – it is said that when the Red Army finally arrived in the 1960s they found communities unaware that the Qing dynasty had been overthrown. However, while inland Fujian knew very little of China, contacts between the coastal area and the outside world had been flourishing for centuries. In the Tang dynasty, the port of **Quanzhou**, considered on a par with Alexandria as the most international port in the world, teemed with Arab traders, some of whose descendants still live in the area today. So much wealth was brought into the ports here that a population explosion led to mass emigration, and large parts of the Malayan Peninsula, the Philippines and Taiwan were colonized by Fujianese. In the early eighteenth century this exodus of able-bodied citizens became so drastic that the imperial court in distant Beijing tried, ineffectually, to ban it.

Today little seems to have changed. The interior of Fujian remains largely unvisited and unknown, with the exception of the scenic **Wuyi Shan** area in the northwest of the province. The coast, however, is booming, with colossal investment pouring in both from Hong Kong and, in particular, from neighbouring **Taiwan**, many of whose citizens originate from the province and speak the same dialect, Minnan Hua. The cities of **Fuzhou** and **Xiamen** are among the wealthiest in the country, particularly Xiamen, whose clean beaches, charming, immaculate streets and shopping arcades perhaps bear the face of Chinese cities to come. The proximity of Taiwan to Xiamen accounts not only for the rapid economic development and the proliferation of first-class tourist facilities, but also for the occasional outbreak of tension, such as during the 1996 Taiwanese presidential election when the mainland authorities suddenly decided to hold large-scale military exercises just off the Taiwanese coast, as a gentle reminder to the Taiwanese people not to vote for separatist candidates.

Fuzhou

Capital of Fujian Province, and a venerable city with over a thousand years of history behind it, **FUZHOU** has few historical relics and little colour. As an important regional centre, however, and the major coastal city between Hong Kong and Shanghai, it is

FUZHOU

Fuzhou	福州	*fúzhōu*

ARRIVAL

Chating bus station	茶亭汽车站	*chátíng qìchēzhàn*
Mawei boat terminal	马尾码头	*mǎwěi mǎtóu*

THE CITY

Bai Ta	白塔	*báitǎ*
Fuzhou Provincial Museum	福建省博物馆	*fújiànshěng bówùguǎn*
Hualin Si	华林寺	*huálín sì*
Lin Zexu Memorial Hall	林则徐纪念馆	*línzéxú jìniànguǎn*
Mao Statue	毛塑像	*máo sùxiàng*
Min River	闽江	*mǐn jiāng*
Wenquan Park	温泉公园	*wēnquán gōngyuán*
Wuyi Square	五一广场	*wǔyī guǎngchǎng*
Wu Shan	乌山	*wūshān*
Wu Ta	乌塔	*wūtǎ*
Xi Hu Park	西湖公园	*xīhú gōngyuán*
Yu Shan	于山	*yúshān*
Zuohai Park	左海公园	*zuǒhǎi gōngyuán*

ACCOMMODATION AND RESTAURANTS

Huafu	华福宾馆	*huáfú bīnguǎn*
Hualin	华林宾馆	*huálín bīnguǎn*
Huaqiao	华侨大厦	*huáqiáo dàshà*
Jiangbin	江宾大酒店	*jiāngbīn dàjiǔdiàn*
Lekepaomo Tea House	乐客泡沫红茶店	*lèkè pàomò hóngchádiàn*
Nangong	南公大酒店	*nángōng dàjiǔdiàn*
Nanyang	南洋饭店	*nányáng fàndiàn*
Success Link International	成功国际大酒店	*chénggōngguójì dàjiǔdiàn*
Taiwan	台湾	*táiwān fàndiàn*
Wenquan	温泉大饭店	*wēnquán dàfàndiàn*
Yushan	于山宾馆	*yúshān bīnguǎn*

by no means a bad place for a stopover, with a few sights to offer including a large number of giant, ancient **banyan trees**, with thick, twisted trunks and aerial roots.

Fuzhou was in its day an important trading centre, visited by Marco Polo during the Yuan dynasty. In the fifteenth century, Fuzhou shipbuilders earned themselves the distinction of having built the world's largest ocean-going ship, the *Baochuan*, sailed by the famous Chinese navigator Zheng He, who used it to travel all around Asia and Africa. One thing Polo noted when he was here was the high-profile presence of Mongol armies to suppress any potential uprisings, and, by coincidence, the city is no less well defended today, forming the heart of Fujian's military opposition to Taiwan. Much like Xiamen farther south, it was the postwar tension between the Nationalists and the Red Army that contributed to Fuzhou's decline after the arrival of the Communists. Today, the proximity of Taiwan is contributing to the enormity of the city's economic boom.

MOVING ON FROM FUZHOU

Outward-bound **train** tickets are sold at the ticket office to the west of the station (the left as you face it). There's a special window for foreigners upstairs (daily 8.30am–noon & 1.30–5pm) which generally sells only soft sleepers, but which can sometimes be persuaded to part with a hard sleeper. If you're travelling along the coast, however, for example to Wenzhou to the north, or Quanzhou to the south, you're better off going by **bus**; even for Xiamen the bus is far quicker than the train.

    Boat services in and out of Fuzhou's port, Mawei, change seasonally, though the only certain service is that to Shanghai which runs about six times a month each way and takes around 36 hours; tickets cost ¥70–203. Services to Wenzhou and Putuo Shan run irregularly in summer. You can buy tickets in downtown Fuzhou at the boat office towards the southern end of Wuyi Lu, on the west side of the street (daily 8–11.30am & 2.30–5pm; ☎0591/3268880).

Orientation, arrival and accommodation

The **Min River**, which roughly delineates the southern border of Fuzhou, flows east–west through the city. The main north–south axis, called Wusi Lu in the north and Wuyi Lu farther south, cuts right through the city, intersecting with Dong Jie, and farther south with Gutian Lu, marking the centre of the city at **Wuyi Square**. The main shopping areas are **Bayiqi Lu** (parallel with Wuyi Lu), the area around Gutian Lu, and one more much farther south, almost at the river on Rongcheng Gujie.

    The **train station** is in the far northeast of town; bus #51 runs straight down Wusi/Wuyi Lu to the Min River from here, while bus #20 runs down Bayiqi Lu. There are a number of **bus stations** around town, including the North station a few minutes' walk south of the train station, and the South station at the junction of Guohuo Lu and Wuyi Lu. It's hard, however, to be certain where you'll be dropped, as both stations are served by buses from just about everywhere in neighbouring provinces. There is also a smaller bus station on Guangda Lu, just north of Guohuo Lu – Chating bus station – which serves local destinations around Fuzhou.

    If you're arriving in Fuzhou by coastal boat you'll be dropped at the **Mawei boat terminal** several kilometres to the southeast of the city. This is connected to town by local trains and, more conveniently, by bus #37 to the Chating bus station, as well as some minibuses from Wuyi Square. The **airport** is a fairly short distance to the south of the city, and buses run to and from the *CAAC* office (8am–5.30pm; ☎0591/3345988) on Wuyi Lu, a few minutes north of Guohuo Lu. Travelling out to the airport, pick up the bus from inside the courtyard of the *Fujian Civil Aviation Hotel*, next door to the *CAAC* office. For booking **tours** (useful for Wuyi Shan), approach *CITS* on Wusi Lu (☎0591/7552052), just north of the *Huaqiao Hotel*.

Accommodation

Huafu, Wusi Lu (☎0591/7857898 ext 866, fax 7853078). Right opposite the *Wenquan Hotel* (bus #5 from the train station). An older-style hotel, pleasant and quiet in large gardens with tennis courts. ⑦.

Hualin, Hualin Lu (☎0591/7841680). In the north of town, on the route of buses #5 and #20 from the train station and North bus station, this is quite a smart place with comfortable doubles and triples. ⑤.

Huaqiao (*Overseas*), Wusi Lu (☎0591/7557603, fax 7550648). Conveniently located just south of Hudong Lu on the way into the centre from the train station. A branch of *CTS* is based here. ⑥.

Jiangbin, Taijiang Lu (☎0591/3268701, fax 3268834). In the south of the city, overlooking the Min River and the old foreign concession area. An interesting location offering singles, doubles and riverfront views. ⑥.

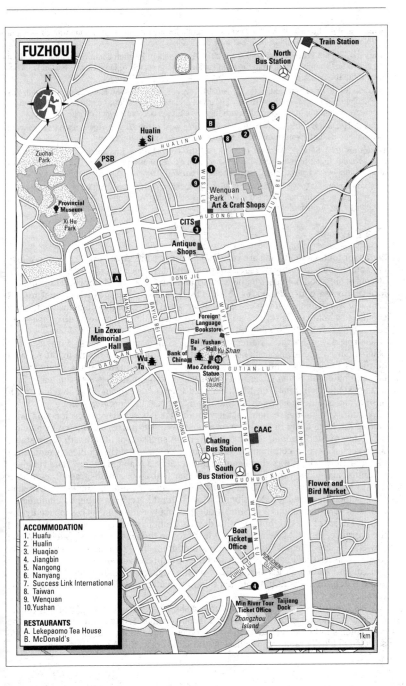

FUZHOU

N

Train Station

North Bus Station

Zuohai Park

Hualin Si

PSB

HUALIN LU

Provincial Museum

Xi Hu Park

B

Wenquan Park Art & Craft Shops

7
1
9

WUSI LU

LIUYI BEILU

HUDONG LU

CITS
3

Antique Shops

DONG JIE

A

MAIHOU JIE

BAYIOU BEILU

WUYI LU

Foreign Language Bookstore

Lin Zexu Memorial Hall

SAN LU

DAOS

Wu Ta

Bai Ta

Yushan Hall

Yu Shan

Bank of China

Mao Zedong Statue

WUYI SQUARE

GUTIAN LU

BAYIOU ZHONG LU

GUANGDA LU

WUYI ZHONG LU

LIUYI ZHONG LU

CAAC

Chating Bus Station

South Bus Station

5

GUOHUO XI LU

Flower and Bird Market

WUYI NAN LU

Boat Ticket Office

TUHUA LU

AUNCHENG LU

Min River Tour Ticket Office

Taijiang Dock

Zhongzhou Island

0   1km

ACCOMMODATION
1. Huafu
2. Hualin
3. Huaqiao
4. Jiangbin
5. Nangong
6. Nanyang
7. Success Link International
8. Taiwan
9. Wenquan
10. Yushan

RESTAURANTS
A. Lekepaomo Tea House
B. McDonald's

Nangong, Wuyi Lu (☎0591/3311369 ext 222). Right opposite the South bus station with singles and doubles all with air-con and 24-hour hot water. ④.

Nanyang, Hualin Lu (☎0591/7579699 ext 231). A convenient location about ten minutes south of the North bus station (20min from the train station), on the corner of Liuyi Lu and Hualin Lu. Very good-value rooms. ③.

Success Link International, Wusi Lu (☎0591/7822888, fax 7821888). Hong Kong-managed, this immaculate place, just south of Hualin Lu, gives a classy impression, but the rooms are not as expensive as you might imagine, although there is a fifteen percent service charge. ⑦.

Taiwan, Hualin Lu (☎0591/7840570). A few minutes west of the *Hualin*. Again, a smart place with pleasant rooms, but Western tourists are usually charged extra here. ⑤.

Wenquan (*Hot Spring*), Wusi Lu (☎0591/7851818, fax 7835150). Just south of the *Success Link International*, this is the smartest place in town, with a cavernous interior full of Pierre Cardin shops and the like. Service is excellent. Doubles start from ¥770. ⑨.

Yushan, Gutian Lu (☎0591/3351668 ext 201). The location of this place can't be beaten, bang in the centre, right up on the southern slope of the hill, overlooking Wuyi Square. It's a bit faded but good value, offering both singles and doubles. ⑥.

The City

Sights for tourists in Fuzhou are very thin on the ground. Apart from a few minor tow-ers and temples, the only two areas of town with any special character are a couple of streets of old wooden houses in the west around the **Lin Zexu Memorial Hall**, and the former **foreign concession** area south of the Min River. The **Min River boat tour** is also well worth joining, if you can catch a day when it runs. Other than that, you could spend a few hours to visit **Gu Shan**, a hill 9km outside the city, dotted with temples and relics, but crowded to bursting with day-trippers.

A stroll down the wide, rather anonymous main boulevard, **Wusi Lu**, has a few points of interest. Moving from north to south, the first place you come to, off Wusi Lu on the east side, and a little north of Hudong Lu, is **Wenquan Park**, a shady area of bamboo huts with rattan tables and chairs where you can take snacks and tea. A little farther south of the park on the main road there's a string of small **art and craft shops**, and another a little way farther down, just past the *Huaqiao Hotel*.

A long, two-kilometre haul farther south (take bus #51), to the junction with Gutian Lu, brings you to the huge expanse of **Wuyi Square**, dominated by a colos-sal statue of Mao Zedong looking out over the square from the north. This statue was erected here to commemorate the Ninth Congress of the Chinese Communist Party in 1969, which was significant in that it ratified Maoism as the "state religion" of China, and named the mysterious Lin Biao (subsequently disgraced) as official heir to Mao's throne. Just behind Mao's statue, the large modern building is Yushan Hall, sometimes used for exhibitions, while behind here, accessible by climbing up to the west of the hall, is **Yu Shan** (Jade Hill; daily 8am–6pm; ¥4), supposedly the cultural heart of the city, but its sights don't amount to much. As you walk up beyond the entrance, the first lane on your left leads to the thousand-year-old **Bai Ta** (White Tower), beside a temple and a small exhibition of the contents of a Song-dynasty tomb excavated in Fuzhou, which includes the preserved bodies of a man and a woman and some silk garments. Back on the main path leading up the hill again, you'll reach the summit in about ten minutes, scattered with big old trees, and giv-ing views over the city.

West from Yu Shan, across Bayiqi Lu, is a slightly more interesting neighbourhood, marked by another small hill, Wu Shan. From Wushan Lu, take the first lane on the right, then another small lane to the left and you'll find the **Wu Ta** (Black Tower), con-structed of black granite, dating back to the same era as the White Tower and containing some attractive statuary. You can climb up the seven floors to the top for great views over the surrounding area, and the tiny temple immediately next door.

North from Wu Shan, you'll soon reach the east–west Daoshan Lu. The most interesting and characterful old street in Fuzhou, lined with trees and wooden houses, and fringed by tiny alleys, runs north from here, initially called Aomen Lu, and shortly becoming Nanhou Lu. On Aomen Lu, west side, you'll find the **Lin Zexu Memorial Hall** (daily 8am–5pm; ¥2), a quiet, attractive couple of halls and courtyards with funereal statues of animals and big trees. Lin Zexu (1785–1850) is fondly remembered as the patriotic and upright Qing-dynasty official who did more than any other individual to fight against the importation of opium by foreigners from Hong Kong in the early part of the nineteenth century, having thousands of chests of the drug destroyed and even writing persuasive and intelligent letters to Queen Victoria on the subject.

The northwest of the city is dominated by **Xi Hu Park** (daily 7am–9pm; ¥1) and the adjoining **Zuohai Park** – basically a funfair – farther north. Xi Hu itself is an artificial lake, originally formed by excavations some seventeen hundred years ago. Today you can go boating or stroll with the masses here. Also within the grounds are a zoo and the **Fuzhou Provincial Museum** (Tues–Sun 8am–4.30pm; ¥3), which has a fairly interesting historical collection, including a 3500-year-old coffin-boat removed from a Wuyi Shan cave. You can reach the south entrance to Xi Hu on buses #1 and #2, both of which come up from the southern end of Bayiqi Lu.

Finally, if you're walking back from Xi Hu Park to the northern part of Wusi Lu, along Hualin Lu, you'll pass the obscure **Hualin Si**, a Tang-dynasty temple located in a grassy garden, which has recently undergone extensive restoration (bus #20 from Bayiqi Lu runs past).

The south

The southern part of the city, down towards the river, contains another dusting of sights. Awkwardly located just east off Liuyi Lu, the north–south express road to the east of Wusi/Wuyi Lu, is the **flower and bird market** (bus #8 from Gutian Lu), packed at weekends with people buying cagebirds and puppies. Farther south, right by the river, several pedestrianized streets are crammed with shoppers, especially the small streets between the southern ends of Bayiqi Lu and Wuyi Lu, and Rongcheng Gujie just east of Wuyi Lu. Right on the riverfront itself, facing the southern end of Wuyi Lu, you'll find the kiosk (8.30am–4.30pm; ☎0591/3277388) selling advance tickets for the **Min River boat tour**. This is a great trip, similar to the better-known Shanghai Huangpu River tours, in which the boat proceeds slowly to the mouth of the river and back again, offering views of barges, freighters and all the paraphernalia of river life. The tour lasts from 7.30am to 5pm and costs ¥18 but runs only when there is sufficient demand – most probable during the summer and at weekends. The tours leave from the Taijiang dock, just below the kiosk.

The area **south** of the river, including the small mid-river island Zhongzhou (reached from Jiefang Bridge), is worth a wander if you're in the vicinity. The **former foreign concession** was based here and you can still see some of the old banks, consulates, residences and churches. A random stroll along the south bank and the neighbouring streets will uncover any number of buildings in the colonial style with verandahs and shuttered windows. Bus #1 coming down Bayiqi Lu from Xi Hu Park crosses to the south bank.

Gu Shan

Fuzhou's most highly touted tourist attraction is **Gu Shan** (Drum Mountain), about 9km east of the city. To get here catch one of the regular buses from the Chating bus station (¥3), or a minibus from Wuyi Square (¥10). It's an attractive 45-minute journey through forested hills with sweeping views as the road starts climbing. The Gu Shan area offers walks through the woods as well as scattered sights, including the thousand-year-old (but heavily restored) Yongquan Si which gets phenomenally crowded at weekends. One way to escape the crowds is to climb the 2500 stone steps behind the temple to the wooded summit of Gu Shan.

Eating and drinking

Places to eat are thinly scattered around the city, and you may well end up eating in your **hotel**. As far as upmarket dining is concerned, the eat-all-you-can buffet in the lobby of the *Wenquan Hotel* is good value, while foreign food can be sampled at the reasonable Japanese restaurant on the second floor of the *Changcheng Hotel* just north of Yu Shan on Wuyi Lu.

For **snacks**, the Wenquan Park area, on Wusi Lu, just north of Hudong Lu, is a pleasant place to sit and eat outdoors, and a couple of minutes south of here, on the other side of Wusi Lu, there's a branch of *California Fried Chicken*. Fuzhou also has a number of branches of *McDonald's*, including one in the far north at the junction of Wusi Lu and Hualing Lu, and another in the far south on Taijiang Lu. Finally, the *Lekepaomo Tea House*, on Yangqiao Dong Lu in the northeast of town, an immaculately clean place (under Taiwanese management), serves hundreds of different kinds of tea, milkshakes and fruit juices, as well as food in the evening.

Wuyi Shan

Far away in the northeast of the province, close to the Fujian–Jiangxi border, is the **Wuyi Shan** scenic district, containing some of the most unspoilt and picturesque scenery in southern China. It's the only inland part of Fujian regularly visited by tourists and consists of two principal parts, the **Jiuqu River** which meanders at the feet of the mountains, and the **Thirty-six Peaks** that rise up from the river, mostly to its north. With peaks protruding from low-lying mists, the scenery is classic Chinese scroll-painting material, and the reserve, dotted with small, attractive villages, can be a tremendous place to relax for a few days, offering clean mountain air and leisurely

WUYI SHAN		
Wuyi Shan Scenic District	武夷山风景区	*wǔyíshān fēngjǐngqū*
Chishi	赤石	*chìshí*
Chongyang Stream	崇阳溪	*chóngyáng xī*
Dawang Feng	大王峰	*dàwáng fēng*
Jiuqu River	九曲溪	*jiǔqū xī*
Shuilian Cave	水帘洞	*shuǐlián dòng*
Tianyou Feng	天游峰	*tiānyóu fēng*
Wuyigong	武夷宫	*wǔyígōng*
Wuyishan Shi	武夷山市	*wǔyíshān shì*
Yingzui Yan	鹰嘴岩	*yīngzuǐ yán*
ACCOMMODATION		
Jiuqu	酒曲宾馆	*jiǔqū bīnguǎn*
Wuyi Shan Manting Villa	武夷山 幔亭山房	*wǔyíshān màntíngshānfáng*
Wuyishan Shi Work Hotel	武夷山市劳动宾馆	*wǔyíshānshì láodòng bīnguǎn*

walks through scenery of lush green vegetation, deep red sandstone mountains, soaring cliff faces, rock pools, waterfalls and caves. Despite the remoteness, Wuyi is surprisingly full of local tourists in high summer, so a visit off-season might be preferable, when you'll also see the mountain tops cloaked with snow. With foreign tourists relatively rare in Wuyi, you should bear in mind that they are regarded as fair game for some serious overcharging. Wuyi is best visited en route between Fuzhou and Xiamen, given that the circuitous rail link between the two cities passes very close to here.

The sixty-square-kilometre site is bordered by the **Jiuqu** (Nine Twist) **River** to the south, which runs its crooked course for some 8km between Xingcun village to the west, and the main village in the area, **WUYIGONG** to the east – where it joins the **Chongyang Stream** running from north to south and bordering the area to the east. Wuyigong, which contains the bus stop and some hotels, lies in the cleft between the junction of these two waterways.

The traditional, and still the best, way to appreciate the Wuyi Shan area is to take a leisurely two-hour bamboo-raft trip along its main artery, the Jiuqu River. The rafts leave daily between 7.30am and 2pm all year round, and you can pick one up from more or less anywhere on the river. From the first crook in the meandering river right up to the ninth, you'll have stupendous views all the way. The odd boat-shaped coffins in caves you can glimpse above the fourth crook, are said to be four thousand years old. The fee currently being charged for a six-passenger boat along all nine twists is around ¥60 per person, though you'll need to have your own group.

There are a series of trails heading north into the mountains from the main trailhead area behind the *Jiuqu Hotel* (about halfway between Xingcun and Wuyigong).

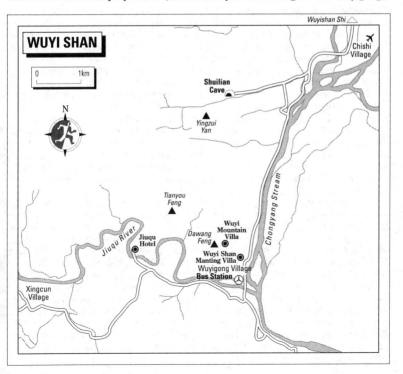

Foreigners are charged a very steep ¥50 for entering the trails here, though it is possible to avoid this charge by walking a little downstream and looking for a path cut into the rock. The **mountains** look quite large and imposing, but in fact are relatively easy to climb. The summit of **Tianyou Feng** (Heavenly Tour Peak) is no more than a thirty-minute clamber away from the *Jiuqu Hotel*. The best time to get up here is early morning, when you can catch the sunrise and watch the early-morning mists clear to reveal a good view of the nine crooks in the Jiuqu River. There are a number of tiny pavilions and tea gardens on the lower slopes should you need sustenance on the way up. Another peak well worth the ascent is **Dawang Feng** (King of Peaks) at the easternmost end of the river, north of Wuyigong, more of a gentle walk than a climb (2hr). If you have time, try to get to the **Shuilian Cave**, about 6km north of the river; you can walk along easy trails or take a minibus from the *Jiuqu Hotel* area or from Wuyigong. In summer months a large waterfall cascades down a cliff of red sandstone, into which a tea house has been cut. You can sit in the tea house and sip the locally grown tea – one of the best varieties in China – while the waterfall literally crashes beside you (watch out for a heavy charge at the entrance to the cave, though). The walk between the cave and river passes tea plantations, more tea houses and all kinds of little sights, including **Yingzui Yan** (Eagle Beak Hill), whose point of interest is the walkways leading to a set of caves where, during the Taiping Uprising, local bigwigs fled to escape persecution.

Practicalities

The cheapest possible way to get to Wuyi is from Fuzhou on the daily Nanchang **train** as far as the town of Shaowu; then catch a bus to Wuyi Shan. If you're coming from outside Fujian Province, the nearest train station is at Shangrao in Jiangxi, on the Hangzhou–Nanchang rail line. The frequent **buses** connecting Shaowu train station and Wuyi Shan – running through extremely scenic terrain – take up to two hours, while buses from Shangrao take up to four hours. Some buses may take you direct to Wuyigong, but most will deposit you at **WUYISHAN SHI** (the main local town, 15km north of the scenic area), in which case you will need a further minibus to Wuyigong.

For a more comfortable approach, enquire at Fuzhou *CITS* (see p.500) for special tour buses heading directly from Fuzhou to Wuyigong. It's also worth enquiring at long-distance bus stations to see whether direct services have recently commenced. The alternative is to fly into the recently constructed **Wuyi airport** – there are direct connections with Fuzhou (¥380 each way; three flights weekly), Xiamen and Shanghai. The airport is at the village of Chishi, a few kilometres to the northeast of the scenic area and to the south of Wuyishan Shi. Minibuses and cycle-rickshaws will be on hand to take you to Wuyigong and the Jiuqu River area.

As far as **accommodation** goes, the *Jiuqu Hotel* (③) is perhaps the most scenically located and cheapest hotel, on the north bank of the river, at the head of many walking trails into the hills. Cycle-rickshaws and minibuses run between here and the village of Wuyigong. Alternatively, you can stay at the luxury hotels in Wuyigong itself, where the *Wuyi Shan Manting Villa* (⑦), just north of the village, has a branch of *CITS* and a Western-style nightclub complex with bar, dance hall and plush restaurant. The *Wuyi Mountain Villa* (⑦) nearby is even smarter, with a marvellous location, resting hard under the Dawang Feng and built round a Suzhou-style ornamental garden. You can also ask around for cheaper hotels here in Wuyigong. You may end up spending a night in Wuyishan Shi, in which case the *Wuyishan Shi Work Hotel* (⑥) has comfortable doubles.

Foodwise, it's the local Shilin frogs which make **Wuyi cuisine** special. Along with other popular dishes such as bamboo shoots and fungus, they're served almost everywhere. If you want to get out of the hotel restaurants and eat with the locals, there are takeaway stalls in the villages.

Quanzhou and around

> *I tell you that for one shipload of pepper which may go to Alexandria or to other places, to be carried into Christian lands, there come more than one hundred of them to this port.*

Thus wrote Marco Polo when he visited **QUANZHOU**, then called Zaytoun (from the Arabic word for olive, symbol of peace and prosperity), in the late thirteenth century. At this time, Quanzhou was a great port, one of the two largest in the world, exploiting its deep natural harbour and strategic position in relation to the islands of Taiwan, the Philippines and the rest of Southeast Asia. It also became a uniquely cosmopolitan city by Chinese standards, with tens of thousands of Arabs and Persians settling here, some of them to make colossal fortunes. It is thought that the Arabs of Quanzhou were responsible for introducing to the West the Chinese inventions of the compass, gunpowder and printing. The Song and Yuan dynasties saw the peak of Quanzhou's fortunes, however. With the advent of the Ming, the city began to suffer from the effects of overcrowding and a decaying harbour, and an enormous exodus began, with citizens seeking new homes in Southeast Asia. According to Chinese government statistics, there are more than two million Quanzhounese living abroad today – which compares to just half a million remaining in the entire municipal area.

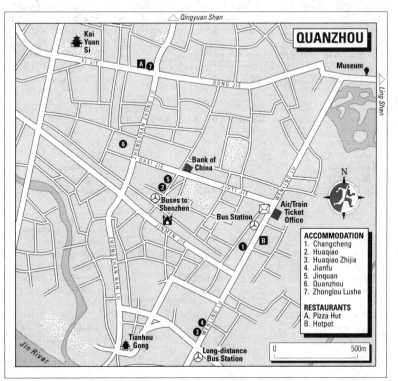

Perhaps because of these depredations of history, Quanzhou today is a shadow of its former self, with only a few meagre reminders of its glorious past. It's not really worth more than an overnight visit, perhaps as a stopover between Fuzhou and Xiamen.

The Town

Quanzhou is a small town, located entirely on the northeast bank of the Jin River, and the majority of its sights can be reached on foot; a bicycle, however, is ideal, if you can rent one from your hotel. The two major north–south streets are Zhongshan Lu (to the west) and Wenling Lu (to the east). The town centre falls mainly between these two, with the oldest part of town to the west, and up along the northern section of Zhongshan Lu where you'll find attractive arcaded streets, lined with trees and packed with shops and cyclists.

Of Quanzhou's historical remains, by far the most impressive is the **Kai Yuan Si**, (bus #2 from the long-distance bus station), in the northwest of town on Xi Jie, a huge, restful temple dotted with magnificent trees, dating back to 686 AD, though it has been repeatedly extended and rebuilt since then. In the thirteenth century, for example, the two five-storey stone pagodas were added, and the whole temple was later rebuilt under the Ming dynasty after it had been destroyed by fire.

Formerly known as the Lotus Flower Temple and home to around a thousand monks, the Kai Yuan was originally built, legend has it, after the owner of a small mulberry grove on this site was visited in a dream by a Buddhist monk who asked him to erect a place of worship on his land. "Only if my mulberry trees bear lotus flowers," replied the owner dismissively – whereupon the lotus flowers duly appeared. In memory of this, an ancient mulberry in the temple courtyard bears the sign "Mulberry Lotus Tree". The temple is highly regarded architecturally, not least for its details which include a hundred stone columns supporting the roof of the main hall, most of which are carved with delicate musicians holding instruments or sacrificial objects. The pagodas, too, are carved on each of their eight sides, with two images of the

QUANZHOU AND AROUND		
Quanzhou	泉州	*quánzhōu*
Kai Yuan Si	开元寺	*kāiyuán sì*
Laojun Yan	老君岩	*lǎojūnyán*
Ling Shan	灵山	*língshān*
Qingyuan Shan	清源山	*qīngyuán shān*
ACCOMMODATION		
Changcheng	长城宾馆	*chángchéng bīnguǎn*
Huaqiao Zhijia	华侨之家	*huáqiáo zhījiā*
Jianfu	建福大厦	*jiànfú dàshà*
Jinquan	金泉酒店	*jīnquán jiǔdiàn*
Quanzhou	泉州酒店	*quánzhōu jiǔdiàn*
Zhonglou Lushe	钟楼旅社	*zhōnglóu lǚshè*
AROUND QUANZHOU		
Anping Bridge	安平桥	*ānpíng qiáo*
Luoyang Bridge	洛阳桥	*luòyáng qiáo*
Shishi	石狮	*shíshī*
Sisters-in-law Tower	姑嫂塔	*gūsǎo tǎ*

Buddha, and inside, one of them has forty ancient Buddhist stories inscribed on its walls. The temple grounds hold a special exhibition hall, whose exhibits number among them a wooden sailing vessel said to be from the twelfth or thirteenth century – Quanzhou's one and only reminder of its magnificent trading past and, in its design, a fine example of just how far advanced Chinese shipbuilders were compared to their counterparts in Europe. The vessel was found in 1974 (a series of photos detail the stages of the excavation), still with the herbs and spices it had been carrying preserved in its hold. Also in the museum are a number of Arab tombstones, those of merchants and sailors who were based here during Quanzhou's golden years.

Further evidence of the Arab presence is the granite-built **Mosque** (daily 8am–5pm; ¥2) on Xinmen Lu, exactly halfway between Zhongshan Lu and Wenling Lu. Getting on for a thousand years old, and last renovated in 1313, this ranks as one of the three oldest mosques in China, and is perhaps unique in eastern China for being purely Middle Eastern in design. It is now supposedly a nationally protected monument, sporting a gate tower said to be an exact copy of a Damascus original, but the building is in a sadly ruinous condition with only a few traces of Arabic calligraphy and designs still visible on the stonework. A dingy exhibition hall in the back, however, has quite a detailed and interesting account of the Arab presence in Quanzhou, with an English translation.

There are a few more sights on the fringes of town. Of these, perhaps the most famous is the huge **Qingyuan Shan** scenic area, 3km to the north, which is scattered with small peaks, pavilions and temples. The hill gives good views over Quanzhou, though most people come out here for the huge stone **Laojun Yan**, a Song-dynasty sculpture of Laozi which is said to aid longevity if you climb on to its back and rub noses. You can walk up to Qingyuan Shan in about an hour by following Zhongshan Lu due north; otherwise take a motor-rickshaw or taxi for about ¥20. The hill is too steep to cycle up.

Slightly easier to reach, to the east of the town centre, on Donghu Jie (follow Wenling Lu to the northern end, then turn right), is **Ling Shan** with its sacred graves, another relic of Islam. Either take bus #7 or you can bike here in about twenty minutes (avoid walking, it's not a pleasant route along the main road). You may need to ask passers-by for some help, but the entrance to the hill can be seen to the south of the road – when you glimpse a stone archway, take the alley leading towards it. Once inside, you cross a canal where local women wash clothes, then enter a peaceful semi-forested area. The graves at the back, which have been recently restored, supposedly include those of two of Mohammed's disciples, sent to China in the seventh century to do missionary work. Another feature of the site is the **Fengdong Shi** (Rock that Moves in the Wind), a huge boulder so balanced that it wobbles when you push it.

Practicalities

The only way to arrive in Quanzhou is by bus. The **long-distance bus station** is down in the newer, southeastern part of town, just east of Wenling Lu. From here there are frequent minibus connections with Xiamen (¥20) and Fuzhou (¥40), as well as long-distance buses for practically anywhere in southern China, from Ningbo and Hangzhou in the north, to Guangzhou and Shenzhen in the south. Luxury sleeper buses for Shenzhen and Guangzhou also depart from a spot just south of the *Jinquan Hotel*, where there is a ticket kiosk. For booking **train** or **plane tickets** out of Fuzhou or Xiamen, try one of the several ticket offices on Wenling Lu south of Jiayi Lu.

When it comes to **eating and drinking**, the big surprise downtown, on Xi Jie just west of Zhongshan Lu, is the presence of a *Pizza Hut*, which is especially welcome for those with a craving for salad. North from here, up Zhongshan Lu, there's a whole series of cheap noodle stalls. Otherwise try the hotels – the *Quanzhou* has a Western-style restaurant, the *Jinquan* has a coffee bar in the lobby, and the *Jianfu* has an excellent *dim sum* restaurant on the fifth floor where you can go for breakfast or lunch. On

Wenling Lu, there's an attractive restaurant – big, bright and full of young people – specializing in hotpot, with pictures to help you order.

Accommodation

Changcheng, Wenling Lu (☎0595/2287938 ext 4008). Very standard conditions but in a good, lively location, a few hundred metres north of the bus station. ⑥.

Huaqiao Zhijia, Wenling Lu (☎0595/2283559). At the southern end of Wenling Lu, within a few minutes' walk of the bus station. Standard, fairly smart rooms. ⑤.

Jianfu, Wenling Lu (☎0595/2283511). Immediately north of the *Huaqiao Zhijia* and a notch smarter. ⑥.

Jinquan (*Golden Fountain*), Baiyuan Lu (☎0595/2285078, fax 2284388). Situated on a small road leading south from Daxi Jie, in the centre, this is the upmarket wing of the *Huaqiao Hotel*. ⑤–⑦.

Quanzhou, Zhuangfu Xiang (☎0595/2289958). Semi-luxurious establishment on a small lane right in the centre of town, just west of Zhongshan Lu. ⑦.

Zhonglou Lushe, Xi Jie. About the cheapest place in town, in a lively, central area at the junction with Zhongshan Lu. Doubles come with or without bath. ②–④.

Around Quanzhou

In the vicinity of the city, there are some more attractions, accessible by local bus or bicycle. Closest is the eight-hundred-metre **Luoyang Bridge**, about 10km east of Quanzhou. Built in the eleventh century, this Song-dynasty masterpiece can easily be reached on one of the many minibuses heading for the small town of Luoyang. Slightly farther away to the south, and also on the route of local minibuses, is the town of **SHISHI** (Stone Lion), from where you can pick up a ride for the 5km to the beautiful **Sisters-in-law Tower** overlooking the sea, another Song-dynasty monument. Finally, some 30km to the south of Quanzhou, just outside the town of Anhai, the spectacular two-kilometre-long pedestrian **Anping Bridge**, built of granite, actually crosses a section of sea. The bridge is over eight hundred years old. For minibuses to all the above destinations, try the small bus station on Wenling Lu, just south of Jiuyi Jie, as well as the long-distance bus station.

Xiamen

XIAMEN, traditionally known in the West as **Amoy**, is one of China's most tourist-friendly cities. Located until the mid-1950s on an offshore island, it is now joined to the mainland by a five-kilometre-long causeway, and its streets and buildings, attractive shopping arcades and bustling seafront have a nineteenth-century European flavour. Smaller and much prettier than the provincial capital Fuzhou, and with a lot more to see, it is in addition the cleanest and, perhaps, most tastefully renovated city you'll see anywhere in the country, giving it the feel of a holiday resort, despite the occasional seedy, fishy backstreet redolent of old Macau. Compounding the resort atmosphere is the wonderful little island of **Gulangyu**, a ten-minute ferry ride to the southwest, the old colonial home of Europeans and Japanese whose decaying mansions still line the island's traffic-free streets. Gulangyu has some great hotels and staying on the island is highly recommended.

As is the case with many of China's ports, Xiamen has a relatively short but interesting history. It was founded in the mid-fourteenth century and grew in stature under the Ming dynasty, becoming a **thriving port** by the seventeenth century, influenced by a steady and rather secretive succession of Portuguese, Spanish and Dutch fortune-

XIAMEN

Xiamen	厦门	*xiàmén*
Bailu Dong	白鹿洞	*báilù dòng*
Huli Shan Pao Ttai	胡里山炮台	*húlǐ shān pàotái*
Huxiyan	虎溪岩	*hǔxī yán*
Jinmen	金门	*jīnmén*
Nanputuo Si	南普陀寺	*nánpǔtuó sì*
Overseas Chinese Museum	华侨博物馆	*huáqiáo bówùguǎn*
Wanshi Botanical Gardens	万石植物馆	*wànshí zhíwùguǎn*
Xiamen University	厦门大学	*xiàmén dàxué*

Gulangyu	鼓浪屿	*gǔlàngyǔ*
Shuzhuang Garden	菽庄花园	*shūzhuāng huāyuán*
Statue of Koxinga	郑成功塑像	*zhèngchénggōng sùxiàng*
Sunlight Rock	日光岩	*báiguāngyán*
Koxinga Memorial Hall	郑成功纪念馆	*zhèngchénggōng jìniànguǎn*

Jimei School Village	集美学校村	*jíměi xuéxiàocūn*
Ao Park	鳌园	*áoyuán*
Chen Jiageng (Tan Kahkee)	陈嘉庚	*chén jiāgēng*

ACCOMMODATION

Aihua	爱华宾馆	*àihuá bīnguǎn*
Donghai	东海大厦酒店	*dōnghǎi dàshàjiǔdiàn*
Gulangyu Guesthouse	鼓浪屿宾馆	*gǔlàngyǔ bīnguǎn*
Heping	和平酒店	*hépíng jiǔdiàn*
Holiday Inn	假日皇冠海景大酒店	*jiàrì huángguān hǎijǐng dàjiǔdiàn*
Lujiang	鹭江宾馆	*lùjiāng bīnguǎn*
Luzhou	绿洲酒店	*lùzhōu jiǔdiàn*
Traffic Company Guesthouse	交通公园招待所	*jiāotōng gōngyuán zhāodàisuǒ*
Xiamen Guesthouse	厦门宾馆	*xiàmén bīnguǎn*
Xiamen Plaza	东南亚大酒店	*dōngnányà dàjiǔdiàn*
Xiaxi	厦溪旅社	*xiàxī lǚshè*
Xinqiao	新桥酒店	*xīnqiáo jiǔdiàn*

RESTAURANTS

Haoke Lai	豪客来中西餐亭	*háokèlái zhōngxī cāntīng*
Huangzehe Huashengtang Dian	黄则和花生汤店	*huángzéhé huāshēng tāngdiàn*

hunters. When invading Manchu armies poured down from the north in the seventeenth century, driving out the Ming, Xiamen became a centre of resistance for the old regime. The pirate and self-styled **Prince Koxinga**, heavily romanticized by later writers, led the resistance before being driven out to set up his last stronghold in Taiwan where he eventually died, before Taiwan too was captured by the Manchus.

A couple of hundred years later the **British** arrived, increasing trade and establishing their nerve centre on the nearby island of Gulangyu; the manoeuvre was formalized with the Treaty of Nanjing in 1842. By the turn of the century, Xiamen, with its off-shore foreigners, had become a relatively prosperous community, supported partly by a steady turnover in trade and by the trickle of wealth back from the city's emigrants, who over the centuries had continued to swell in numbers. This happy state of affairs continued until the **Japanese invasion** at the beginning of World War II.

The end of the war did not bring with it a return to the good old days, however. The **arrival of the Communists** in 1949, and the final escape to Taiwan by Chiang Kaishek with the remains of his Nationalist armies, saw total chaos around Xiamen, with thousands of people streaming to escape the Communist advance in boats across the straits. In the following years the threat of war was constant, as mainland armies manoeuvred in preparation for the final assault on Taiwan, and more immediately, on the smaller islands of Jinmen and Mazu (known to the West as Quemoy and Matsu) which lie only just off the mainland, within sight of Xiamen.

Today the wheel of history has come full circle. Although Jinmen and Mazu are still in the hands of the Nationalists, the threat of conflict with Taiwan has been replaced by the promise of colossal economic advantage. In the early 1980s Xiamen was declared one of China's first **Special Economic Zones** and, like Shenzhen on the border with Hong Kong, the city has entered a period of unprecedented boom.

Orientation, arrival and accommodation

The island on which Xiamen stands is located inside a large inlet on the southeastern coast of Fujian. The built-up area occupies the western part of the island, which faces the mainland, while the eastern part faces on to the Nationalist island of Jinmen. The areas of most interest are the **old town** in the far southwest, and the islet of **Gulangyu** just offshore. The remainder of the city is the Special Economic Zone, which stretches away to the east and the north, and to the causeway back to the mainland. There's little to detain you here, though the small town of **Jimei**, on the mainland just beyond the causeway, has the attraction of its **School Village**. The main north–south road, passing through the centre of the old town, is Siming Lu, which is crossed from east to west by Zhongshan Lu, the main shopping street. Zhongshan Lu emerges on the seafront by the *Lujiang Hotel*.

Xiamen's **train station** is about 4km inland from the seafront, and connected to the centre of town by Xiahe Lu running west; many buses from the station run down here, including #1 and #3. Xiamen's main **long-distance bus station** is about 2km northeast of the centre, on Hubin Lu. Buses #3 and #10 both run past here on their way to the *Lujiang Hotel*. The most central arrival point, the **passenger ferry terminal**, is fifteen minutes' walk south along the seafront from the *Lujiang Hotel*, and served by boats from Hong Kong. Twelve kilometres to the north of town, the **airport** is connected to town by bus #17 which runs to and from the small Siming bus station on Siming Bei Lu, just south of Xiahe Lu.

Accommodation

There's a good range of pleasant accommodation in Xiamen, ranging from the surprisingly cheap to the luxurious. Some of the nicest hotels are on **Gulangyu Islet**, although you'll have to carry your own luggage here as there are no buses or taxis. The wonderful peace and quiet of the island more than compensate for this, however.

DOWNTOWN XIAMEN

Donghai (*East Ocean*), Zhongshan Lu (☎0592/2021111, fax 2033264). One block east of the *Lujiang*. An excellent location and nice rooms, both singles and doubles. ⑦.

Heping (*Peace Hotel*), Tongwen Lu (☎0592/2024495 ext 2100). Right inside the port area, across the rail line from the actual dock. Nothing fancy, but convenient if you're arriving by boat at some ungodly hour. ⑤.

Holiday Inn, Zhenhai Lu (☎0592/2023333, fax 2036666). At the junction with Siming Nan Lu, this has all the usual international facilities. Doubles from ¥1200. ⑨.

Lujiang, Zhongshan Lu (☎0592/2022922, fax 2024644). Occupying a prime site on the seafront, at the western end of Zhongshan Lu and right in the centre of things, this is the ideal place to stay for views over Gulangyu Islet. Singles and doubles on offer. ⑦.

Traffic Company Guesthouse, Siming Bei Lu. Just opposite the small bus station a little south of Xiahe Lu, there's a garage-like entrance with the reception on the right. It may not look like a hotel, but it's a homely, friendly place that has some quite acceptable doubles with private bathroom. ③.

Xiamen Guesthouse, Huyuan Lu (☎0592/2024941). Built up a hillside and overhung by lots of trees, this is an attractive and secluded place to stay, without being too remote. Bus route #1 from the train station comes this way. If you pay in US dollars you get a discount. ⑥.

Xiamen Plaza, Xiahe Lu (☎0592/5058888 ext 1063, fax 5058877). Convenient for the train station, but quite far from the town's tourist attractions. Offers complete luxury with all the facilities. Rooms from ¥900. ⑨.

Xiaxi, Xiaxi Lu (☎0592/2024859). The established backpacker haunt situated north of Zhongshan Lu on a small lane a few minutes east of Siming Lu. There's a range of double rooms with and without bath as well as cheap three- and four-bed dorms. Foreigners are charged a small supplement. Dorms ②, rooms ②–④.

Xinqiao, Xinqiao Lu (☎0592/2038883, fax 2038765). A nice hotel at the junction of Zhongshan Lu, mainly frequented by business people. ⑦.

GULANGYU ISLAND

Aihua (☎0592/2063515). A few minutes beyond the *Luzhou*. Carry on past until you reach the first crossroads, then take a left and follow the road around to the left. There are signs to the hotel here; it's next door to a church and immaculately clean inside. ⑥.

Gulangyu Guesthouse, Huangyan Lu (☎0592/2063856). Fifteen minutes' walk from the jetty, though you need to cut southwest through a maze of streets to get here. The hotel is next to a sports ground and to the east of Sunlight Rock, an excellent place to stay and a tourist attraction in itself. There are some inexpensive plain rooms, but the rooms in the historic middle block are worth shelling out for. ⑤–⑧.

Luzhou (*Oasis*), Longtou Lu (☎0592/2065391). Just one minute's walk from the jetty. After disembarking, turn to the right and take the first street on the left – the hotel faces a green lawn. Altogether, a great and convenient place to stay. ⑥.

The City

The main pleasure in Xiamen, apart from visiting Gulangyu Islet, is simply walking the streets of the old city. Starting from the Siming and Zhongshan Lu intersection, you'll be amazed at the juxtaposition of turn-of-the-century facades and clean orderly streets, pavements and shops. At the western end of Zhongshan Lu, where the **seafront** opens up, you'll see the island of Gulangyu right in front, across the water. Just south of Zhongshan Lu, on the waterfront, is a kiosk organizing boat trips, the most fascinating of which circumnavigates the Nationalist island of Jinmen (Sat & Sun; ¥80 per person) – for good views of the Guomindang front line, bring binoculars.

Southeast and east from the town centre there's a thin scattering of tourist sights. On Siming Nan Lu, about 2km south of Zhongshan Lu, you'll find the **Overseas Chinese Museum** (daily 9am–4.30pm; ¥6), accessible on buses #1 and #2. This houses collections presented by the huge Fujianese diaspora around the world, including pottery

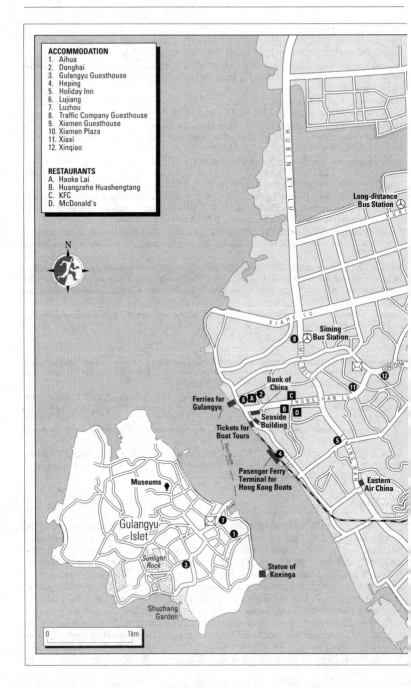

ACCOMMODATION
1. Aihua
2. Donghai
3. Gulangyu Guesthouse
4. Heping
5. Holiday Inn
6. Lujiang
7. Luzhou
8. Traffic Company Guesthouse
9. Xiamen Guesthouse
10. Xiamen Plaza
11. Xiaxi
12. Xinqiao

RESTAURANTS
A. Haoke Lai
B. Huangzehe Huashengtang
C. KFC
D. McDonald's

Long-distance Bus Station

HUBIN XI LU

N

XIAHE LU

Siming Bus Station

Bank of China

Ferries for Gulangyu

ZHONGSHAN LU

Seaside Building

Tickets for Boat Tours

Ferry Route

Museums

Gulangyu Islet

Sunlight Rock

Shuzhang Garden

Pasenger Ferry Terminal for Hong Kong Boats

Statue of Koxinga

Eastern Air China

RONGYUAN

0   1km

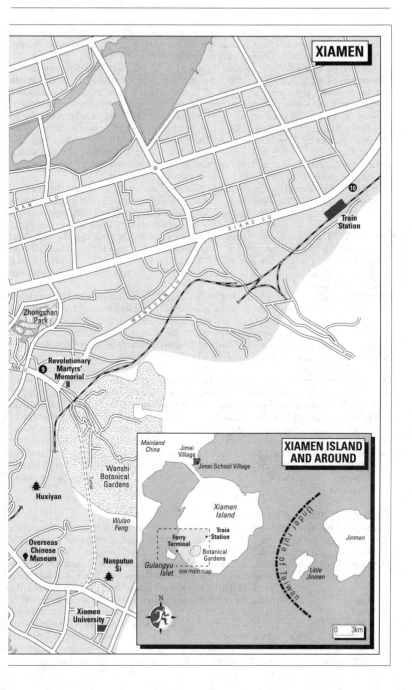

and some exceptional bronzes going back as far as the Shang dynasty, three thousand years ago. On the ground floor is an interesting display of paintings, photographs and relics depicting the life of Chinese people abroad over the centuries.

Another kilometre farther southeast (bus #1 to *Xiada*, Xiamen University) is the **Nanputuo Si** (daily 8am–5pm; ¥10), a temple built over a thousand years ago on the southern slopes of Wulao Shan. This is one of China's most impressive Buddhist temples, its roofs a gaudy jumble of flying dragons, human figures and multi-coloured flowers, and containing among its collection of treasures a set of tablets carved by resistance fighters at the time of the early Qing, recording Manchu atrocities. Inside the main hall, behind the Maitreya Buddha, is a statue of Wei Tuo, the deity responsible for Buddhist doctrine, who holds a stick pointing to the ground – a sign which means the monastery is a rich one and can provide board and lodging for itinerants. The temple today is very active and has a vegetarian restaurant.

Immediately south of Nanputuo stands **Xiamen University**. From here you can cut through to Daxue Lu, the coastal road, which runs past attractive sandy beaches. A kilometre or so southwest brings you to **Huli Shan Pao Tai** (Huli Mountain Cannon Platform), at the terminus of bus #2. This nineteenth-century hunk of German heavy artillery had a range of 10,000 metres and was used during the Qing dynasty to fend off foreign imperialists. You can rent binoculars here to look across to the Nationalist-held island of **Jinmen**, which lies less than 20km to the west. Until 1984, because of the close proximity of Taiwan, this whole area was out of bounds, and the beaches were under a dusk-till-dawn curfew.

In the opposite direction from Nanputuo, a lengthy hike (at least two hours) takes you from inside the temple grounds, up and over the forested Wulao Shan behind the temple. Climbing up the hill is a bit of a struggle and the path is far from clear, but it's easy enough to find your way down the other side from the summit. Eventually you'll arrive at the back entrance of the **Wanshi Botanical Gardens** (daily 8am–6pm; ¥9) where a stock of four thousand varieties of plant life includes a redwood tree brought here by President Nixon on his official visit to China. Alternatively, from Nanputuo, you can walk under the hill to the gardens, through a tunnel whose southern entrance is a few minutes north towards town up Siming Lu, and along a small road to the right.

From the botanical gardens, the north (main) gate comes out on a rail line, close to the Revolutionary Martyrs' Memorial, about 1.5km west of the town centre, near the #1 bus route. Southwest of here, along the rail line, is the **Huxiyan** (Tiger Stream Rock) on your right, built up high on a rocky hillside. If you climb up you'll find a great little temple nestling here amid a pile of huge boulders, and you can actually slip through a cave to one side and climb rock-hewn steps to the top of the largest boulder. A second small temple, called **Bailu Dong** (White Deer Cave), commands spectacular views over the town and the sea.

Gulangyu Island

Gulangyu Islet was Xiamen's foreign concession until World War II, and architecturally it remains more or less intact from that time. In summer and at weekends the island is rather packed and accommodation can be hard to find but, with neither cars nor bicycles, the atmosphere is always restful and exploring the island can easily fill up a day or more of your time – in fact it is the nicest place in Xiamen to base yourself (see "Accommodation", p.513). The boat for the island departs from the small pier opposite the *Lujiang Hotel*. On the way out to the island, the lower deck is free (the upper deck is ¥0.5) and on the way back the lower and upper decks cost ¥0.5/0.8 respectively. Boats run from early morning to midnight and the short ride gives you delightful views over the waterways.

Initially, Gulangyu's narrow tangle of streets can be a confusing place to find your way around, but the small size of the island (less than two square kilometres) means this is not really a problem. The **island centre** (basically a couple of small shopping streets with a bank, a post office, a few restaurants and shops) is a couple of minutes' walk to your right as you disembark from the ferry. The various sights are scattered around the island and any stroll through the streets will uncover plenty of architectural attractions, overhung with flowers and blossom at all times of the year. It's not possible to walk a complete circumference of the island as a section to the northwest is off-limits to tourists.

If you head southeast from the jetty (left as you disembark), you'll pass a number of grand old buildings, including the former British and German consulates. The road continues on to a park containing the island's most easterly headland, an enormous rock topped by the gigantic granite **Statue of Koxinga**, dressed in grand military attire and staring meaningfully out towards Taiwan, the island he once heroically recaptured from foreign colonialists. Shortly beyond the park, the road heads west towards the middle of the island, bringing you to a sports ground, with the **Gulangyu Guesthouse** facing on to it. This is a superb old place with magnificent trees and grand colonial mansions and worth strolling around even if you're not staying here. Inside the middle building the original 1920s decor and furniture are intact, with dark wooden panelling, a billiard hall and a terrace with rattan chairs. President Nixon stayed here on his 1972 trip and it's still the haunt of Chinese VIPs. You can have a peep inside, though for security reasons you might be chased away if you're not a guest.

Due south, on the southern shore, is the **Shuzhuang Garden** (daily 7am–8pm; ¥5), which is full of flowers and has some delightful shady areas for taking tea right by the sea, as well as a music saloon. Running west from the park the clean, sandy beach is very tempting for swimming when it's not too packed out. The beach is overlooked to the north by the **Sunlight Rock** (daily 8.30am–5pm; ¥10), the highest point on the island (93m) and something of a magnet for the large numbers of local tourists who make the easy climb up to the platform for the views right over the entire island. At the foot of the rock (and covered by the same entrance ticket) is the **Koxinga Memorial Hall**, which contains various relics including Koxinga's own jade belt and bits of his "imperial" robe; unfortunately there are no English captions.

Jimei School Village

Some 15km north of Xiamen proper, across the bridge, on the mainland, is the **Jimei School Village**, a site of huge significance for the local Chinese and the Fujianese in particular, as a model of what Overseas Chinese patriots are capable of when they return their money to the motherland. **Chen Jiageng**, or **Tan Kahkee** as he is known in the local dialect (1874–1961), is Fujian's most famous "returnee". Having earned his millions in Malaya, he started endowing educational institutions in the Xiamen area after the establishment of the Republic in 1911, and continued to do so for the next fifty years. As well as Xiamen University itself, Tan Kahkee's most enduring legacy is here at Jimei, where what must be the smartest high school in the country is set in a beautiful park on the seafront. You can reach Jimei by bus either from the small bus station on Siming Lu just south of Xiahe Lu (buses run every 30min and take 30–60min depending on traffic) or from outside the train station. From the Jimei bus stop you can hire a cycle-rickshaw to take you around the whole site for about ¥40, otherwise it's a pleasant two-hour walk.

From the main gate to the village (very close to the Jimei bus stop), the sights are about twenty minutes' walk east. The enormous **Jimei High School** itself, a grand Chinese-Gothic arrangement of patterned bricks and fancy windows, is the huge building facing on to the lake. Past the front of the school, bear left through a small park containing Tan Kahkee's statue and across a street at the northern end you'll see his **former residence**. The wing on the left contains a fairly interesting photographic record of his life, his business achievements and his patriotism, with captions in English. The ideological complications of a communist state accepting money from a millionaire capitalist are not addressed. A short walk farther east from the residence is the celebrated **Ao Park**, projecting right into the sea, and entered through a corridor lined with a series of stone engravings telling the stories of China's mythic ancient history.

Eating and drinking

The local **food** is one of Xiamen's assets, with plenty of fresh fish and seafood, particularly oysters, crabs and prawns, and a liberal use of **peanuts**. A good place to try the town's peanut snacks is the *Huangzehe Huashengtang Dian* (*Sweet Peanut Shop*) on Zhongshan Lu, south side, a few minutes west of Siming Lu. Sweet peanut soup is served with everything, and there are also excellent steamed buns stuffed with peanut. In the same area, next to the back door of the *Lujiang Hotel*, is *Haoke Lai*, which serves excellent value set-meals in "Western" style including soup, salad, bread, wine and sizzling steaks for only ¥25. Inside the *Lujiang* itself, you can have excellent *dim sum* breakfasts or lunches on the lower floor, with the items brought round on trolleys; while upstairs there's a very pleasant rooftop restaurant/café overlooking the sea. The *Holiday Inn* serves an evening buffet dinner which is relatively inexpensive, if unexciting, at ¥125 per head. For a vegetarian lunch, try the restaurant at the Nanputuo Si.

Listings

Airlines The main *Eastern Air China* booking office is at 311–15 Siming Nan Lu (☎0592/2028936), while *Air China* is in the Huguang Dasha building, on Hubin Dong Lu (☎0592/5084376). Various other airlines also fly in and out of Xiamen airport: the Hong Kong-based *Dragon Air* is located on the first floor of the Haibin Dasha (Seaside Building) just south of the western end of Zhongshan Lu (☎0592/2025389), while *Philippine Airlines*, which operates regular flights to nearby Manila, is at 837 Xiahe Lu (☎0592/5094551).

Banks and exchange The *Bank of China* head office is on Zhongshan Lu a few metres from the seafront (Mon–Fri 8am–4.30pm & Sat 8am–12.30pm).

Boats To buy tickets to Hong Kong, head into the port area (ignore the barrier) and continue south until you see buildings on your right across the rail tracks. The office here is open 8–11.15am and 2–5pm (☎0592/2022517). Boats sail four times weekly and the eighteen-hour trip costs ¥342–672 (the cheapest bed class costs ¥400) in immaculately clean and comfortable surroundings.

Post office Xiamen's main post office, where IDD telephone calls can also be made, is on Xinhua Lu, south of the junction with Siming Dong Lu.

Trains Buying tickets is not too problematic – foreigners should queue at window #2 (8.10am–noon, 1.40–6.10pm & 7.20–9.30pm) – though train services in and out of Xiamen are circuitous and slow, especially to Fuzhou.

Travel agents For what it's worth, the *CITS* head office is on the fifteenth floor of the Zhenxing Dasha building, on Hubin Bei Lu (☎0592/5051822). Branch offices are scattered around as well, including one near the *Bank of China* building on Zhongshan Lu.

GUANGDONG

Halfway along **Guangdong**'s 800km coastline, rivers from all over the province and beyond disgorge themselves into the South China Sea through the tropically fertile **Pearl River Delta**, one of China's most densely cultivated areas. Perched right at the delta's northern apex and adjacent to Hong Kong and the Portuguese enclave at Macau, the provincial capital, **Guangzhou**, provides many travellers with their first taste of mainland China. Unfortunately, uninspiring signs of rapid and thorough industrialization prompt most visitors to flee not just Guangzhou but the entire province on the first available transport. Resist the temptation: once you've found your bearings, Guangzhou's world-famous **food** merits a stop, as does a rich assortment of museums and monuments, and the action surrounding one of China's best produce **markets**. The Pearl River Delta itself has a few patches of green and a wealth of history to pick up in passing, but the major targets are the cities of **Shenzhen** and **Zhuhai**, modern, purpose-built economic buffer zones at the crossings into Hong Kong and Macau.

Farther afield, the rest of the province is far more picturesque, with a mass of sights from Buddhist temples to Stone-Age relics to slow you down around **Shaoguan**, up north by the Hunan and Jiangxi borders. Over in the east near the border with Fujian, the former colonial treaty port of **Shantou** is the springboard for journeying up through some beautiful countryside to the ancient towns of **Chaozhou** and **Meizhou**. Travelling west into Guangxi Province, **Zhaoqing** sports well-touristed but impressive formalized lake and hill landscapes, while those heading towards Hainan need to aim for the disjointed, bland ferry port of **Zhanjiang**, down in Guangdong's southwestern extremities.

Guangdong has a generous quantity of rail and road traffic, and **getting around** is none too difficult, though securing anything better than a hard seat on a train can be well-nigh impossible. **Rail lines** run north through Shaoguan and up into Hunan and central China, east to Meizhou, and west through Zhaoqing to Zhanjiang and Guangxi. As an alternative, **river travel** is something of a highlight of the province, as this is one of the last regions in China where public ferries are still in regular use. The best-known service runs up the Xi River from Guangzhou to Wuzhou in Guangxi Province, but others worth trying include an excellent excursion from the northern town of **Qingyuan** to some riverside temples, and the trip down the **Han River** from remote northeastern Guangdong to Chaozhou. For the truly adventurous, there's even the seasonal thrill of **white-water rafting** on a wild section of river northwest of Shaoguan. As for the **climate**, summers can be sweltering across the province, while winter temperatures get decidedly nippy up in the northern ranges, though it's more likely to be miserably wet than to snow, except around the highest mountain peaks.

Guangzhou

GUANGZHOU, once known to the Western world as **Canton**, leaves many visitors with the unfavourable impression that China dwells in relentless chaos and that the city is simply a bad caricature of Hong Kong. Guangzhou is indeed very much modern China pushed to the limits: the traffic and pollution are horrendous, bridges and crumbling flyovers which seemed ludicrously over-ambitious when built in the mid-1980s now groan under the weight of vehicles and shelter the homeless during wet weather, and the city seems not so much to be booming as blowing apart at the seams. Buffeted by the crowds, travellers tend to stay only long enough to tackle a couple of temples and museums before organizing a ticket out, hoping that the rest of the country will prove less overwhelming.

If you can master the initial shock, however, Guangzhou is a city you can learn to enjoy. Compared with Beijing's bureaucratic aloofness or the image-conscious populace of Shanghai, the city's inhabitants seem immediately upfront, and pleasantly indifferent to foreign faces after two thousand years of direct contact with the Western world. They're also obsessively garrulous, turning **eating** and **business** – the city's two famous pastimes – into social occasions, and filling streets, restaurants and buildings with the alternately guttural and musical sounds of **Yuehua**, the rhythmic Cantonese language. Guangzhou has also traditionally been the first place where foreign influences have seeped into the country, often through returning Overseas Chinese, and this is where to watch for the latest fashions and to see how China will interpret alien styles. The sounds of Hong Kong rap and Canto-pop, Wham! (seemingly immortalized by their 1985 tour) and Michael Jackson blare out of the nightclubs here, not karaoke and Chinese folk tunes, and trendy youths in leather and

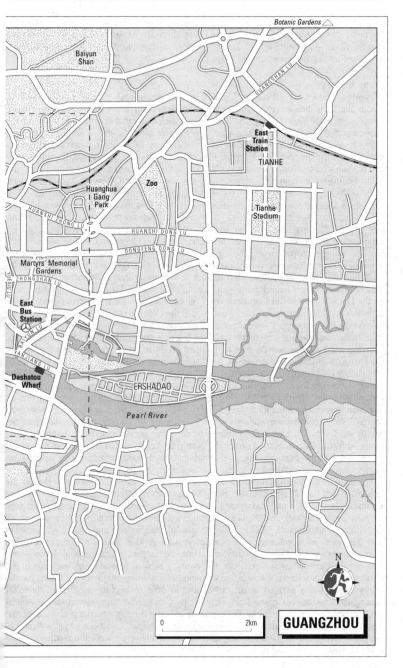

Botanic Gardens

Baiyun
Shan

GUANGSHAN LU

East
Train
Station

TIANHE

Zoo

Huanghua
Gang
Park

HUANSHI ZHONG LU

Tianhe
Stadium

HUANSHI DONG LU

DONGFENG DONG LU

Martyrs Memorial
Gardens

ZHONGSHAN LU

East
Bus
Station

BAIYUN LU

YUEXIU LU

YANJIANG LU

Dashatou
Wharf

ERSHADAO

Pearl River

N

0   2km

GUANGZHOU

blue-tinted, wraparound sunglasses ride Japanese Harley-Davidson clones. Although the city lacks any great sights, you can easily ditch its Western veneer by wandering into the maze of flagstoned back lanes, in search of monuments and busy markets hidden away from casual observers.

Some history

Legend tells how Guangzhou was founded by **Five Immortals** riding five rams, each of whom planted a sheaf of grain symbolizing that the inhabitants would never know famine. It was nicknamed **Yang Cheng**, the Ram City, in their honour, and ornamental stone lions outside public buildings here often sprout goat horns. Myths aside, an administrative city called **Panyu** had sprung up here by the third century BC, when a rogue Qin commander founded the independent **Nanyue Kingdom** and made it his capital. Even then, the city probably had ties with foreign lands; road building in central Guangzhou during the 1970s uncovered remains of a gigantic Qin–Han era **shipyard**. How far its mariners ventured isn't clear, but an embassy representing the Roman emperor "Ah Tun" (possibly Antoninus Pius) reached Guangzhou around 160AD, and from Song times vessels travelled along the "Maritime Silk Road" to Middle Eastern ports, later introducing **Islam** into China and exporting porcelain to Arab colonies in distant Kenya and Zanzibar. By 1405 Guangzhou's population of foreign merchants and Overseas Chinese was so large that the Ming emperor Yongle founded a special quarter for them, and when imperial xenophobia later closed the rest of China to outsiders, Guangzhou became the country's main link with the world. Restricted though it was, this contact with other nations ultimately proved to be Guangzhou's – and China's – undoing. From the eighteenth century, the **British East India Company** used the city as a base from which to purchase silk, ceramics and tea, but soon became frustrated at the Chinese refusal to accept trade goods instead of cash in return. To even accounts, the company began to illegally import **opium** from India, long used as a medicine in China but now encouraged as a recreational drug. Demand and addiction soared, making colossal profits for the British and members of the **Co Hong**, their Chinese distributors, but badly denting the country's economy; no taxes were being paid and trade was rapidly depleting Chinese stocks of silver. In 1839 the Qing government sent the famously incorruptible Commissioner **Lin Zexu** to Guangzhou with a mandate to stop the drug traffic. Having blockaded the foreigners into their quarters on Shamian Island, Lin demanded the handover of all opium stocks and publicly destroyed them. Britain declared war, and, with a navy partly funded by the opium-trading Jardine-Matheson Company, forced the Chinese to cede five ports (including Guangzhou and Hong Kong) to British control under the **Nanking Treaty** of 1842. For the next seventy years Guangzhou's populace laboured to support the demands of impossibly wealthy foreigners and their middlemen, a status quo backed by British arms.

Unsurprisingly, Guangzhou became a revolutionary cauldron. It was here during the late 1840s that the Christian fanatic, Hong Xiuquan, formulated his anti-Manchu **Taiping Uprising** (see p.391), and sixty years later the city hosted a slightly premature attempt by **Sun Yatsen** to kick out China's Qing rulers. Guangzhou even briefly became Sun's Guomindang capital in the 1920s, while a youthful Mao Zedong and Zhou Enlai flitted in and out between mobilizing rural peasant groups. At this time the Guomindang and Communists were working together, and a substantial part of Guangzhou's leftist youth was enrolled in militias and sent into the country against troublesome warlords in the **Eastern and Northern Expeditions**. Having effectively unified central China for the government, many arrived in the north just in time to become victims of the 1927 **Shanghai Massacre**, Chiang Kaishek's bloody Communist suppression (see p.343). A Red uprising in Guangzhou that December failed, and the city's working class, once the best organized in the country, was left totally demoralized. Controlled by the Japanese during the war and the Guomindang afterwards, in 1949 they were too apathetic to liberate themselves and had to wait for the PLA to do it for them.

Few people would today describe Guangzhou's population as apathetic, at least when it comes to business acumen, though the city has again become a place of fabulous wealth and bitter poverty. A superficially high standard of living is undercut by the constant influx of China's increasingly mobile rural community, who frequently end up involved in ruinous speculation and petty crime. Street life here is visibly tougher than elsewhere in China and daily expenses are noticeably higher. Vast amounts of cash do indeed flow into (and out of) the city, particularly during the bi-annual **Trade Fair**, but this creates more inflation than jobs and the profits tend to be concentrated in volatile commercial capital. On the other hand, government incentives and the mainland's cheap labour costs compared with Hong Kong have seen accelerating domestic and foreign investment in southern China, and Guangzhou – while remaining fairly unaffected itself – is now profiting again from its position at the core of the Pearl River Delta's industrial and manufacturing sprawl.

Orientation, arrival and city transport

For a city of four million people, Guangzhou is compact and easy to navigate. It was originally divided up into an inner heart, enclosed by walls and sectioned into old and new quarters, with the surrounding district outside. The walls came down in the 1920s, but it is this area, bounded south by the Pearl River and north by **Huanshi Lu**, and cut by four arterial roads – **Zhongshan** and **Dongfeng** running east–west and **Jiefang** and **Renmin** running north–south – that constitutes downtown Guangzhou today. The longer streets are divided up into north, south, east, west and central sections, with the exception of Zhongshan Lu, whose segments are numbered.

North of Dongfeng Lu, tall buildings and wide boulevards are dwarfed by the city's two major parks, **Yuexiu** and **Liuhua**. South, between Dongfeng Lu and the river, the main roads are noticeably narrower, with flyovers taking the traffic, and it's here that you'll find most of the city's historical monuments. Down on the southwestern **waterfront** is Guangzhou's busiest corner, with the net of tiny streets north of **Liuersan Lu** forming a particularly crowded and compelling **market district**, and **Shamian Island**, the quiet nineteenth-century foreigners' quarter, lying across a canal. Over on the other side of the Pearl River from here is **Honan**, while east across the city, **Tianhe** is a vividly contrasting example of a suburban community.

Arrival

Baiyun, Guangzhou's international airport, is 6km and a ¥30 taxi ride north of the city centre – there's no airport bus. Arriving on the local train from Shenzhen (or from the eastern provinces through Meizhou once the line is completed in 1998) lands you at the new and giant **East train station**, out in the suburb of Tianhe. A taxi to the centre will cost ¥20–30. Bus #272 runs between here and the equally imposing **North train station**, 5km west at the northern end of Renmin Lu. Definitely the most daunting place to arrive in town, this is where express trains from Kowloon and services from all over the rest of China terminate, and the vast **square** outside perpetually seethes with passengers, hawkers and hustlers. **Buses** into town leave from the western side of the square: #5 and #31 will take you down to the waterfront near Shamian Island, and #30 and #272 head east along Huanshi Lu.

Five minutes' walk west of here is Guangzhou's main **long-distance bus station**, with the **Liuhua depot** opposite handling short-range traffic, mostly from northern and western Guangdong. A variety of services from central and western China also use

The **telephone code** for Guangzhou is ☎020

the **East bus station** on Baiyun Lu or the **West bus station** on Huangsha Lu – neither is far out, but taxis are your best bet for reaching accommodation.

Boats from Macau, Hong Kong and Haikou put in at **Zhoutouzui wharf**, across the Pearl River in Honan. After customs formalities (there's a bank here too) you exit into the eager arms of taxi and minibus drivers who will try to negotiate ridiculous fares; find a vehicle with a meter and insist on its use. A short walk straight out of Zhoutouzui's gates brings you to **Gongye Lu**, where you can pick up bus #31 heading north across Renmin Bridge, past Shamian Island and up Renmin Lu to the North train station. With little luggage, it's an easy thirty minutes on foot from the wharf to Shamian. Vessels from Wuzhou and Zhaoqing dock at **Dashatou wharf**, on Yanjiang Lu in southeastern Guangzhou. The most useful buses from here are #7 up to the North train station and #57 to Liuersan Lu.

City transport and maps

Getting around Guangzhou isn't difficult, though the city is a bit too big to walk everywhere – it's about 5km from the river to the North train station. **Bicycles** are not ideal because of the heavy traffic conditions, but there are plenty of guarded parking zones and a few rental stalls – see "Listings", p.545. **Bus and trolleybus services** are less congested than in other Chinese cities and painfully slow, but very cheap; a few yuan will take you right across the city. Note, however, that many of Guangzhou's bus routes are being

---

GUANGZHOU: ARRIVAL AND ACCOMMODATION

Guangzhou	广州	*guǎngzhōu*
ARRIVAL		
Baiyun airport	白云机场	*báiyún jīchǎng*
Dashatou wharf	大沙头客运站	*dàshātóu kèyùn zhàn*
East train station	东方火车站	*dōngfāng huǒchē*
Liuhua bus depot	流花客运站	*liúhuā chē kèyùn zhàn*
North train station	北方火车站	*běifāng huǒchēzhàn*
Zhoutouzui wharf	州头嘴码头	*zhōutóuzuǐ mǎtóu*
ACCOMMODATION		
Aiqun	爱群大酒店	*àiqún dàjiǔdiàn*
Beijing	北京大酒店	*běijīng dàjiǔdiàn*
China	中国大酒店	*zhōngguó dàjiǔdiàn*
Dongfang	东方宾馆	*dōngfāng bīnguǎn*
Equatorial	贵都酒店	*guìdū jiǔdiàn*
Friendship	友谊宾馆	*yǒuyì bīnguǎn*
Fulihua	富丽华宾馆	*fùlìhuá bīnguǎn*
Garden	花园酒店	*huāyuán jiǔdiàn*
Guangdong Binguan	广东宾馆	*guǎngdōng bīnguǎn*
Guangzhou Youth Hostel	广州青年招待所	*guǎngzhōu qīngnián zhāodàisuǒ*
Liuhua	流花宾馆	*liúhuā bīnguǎn*
Shamian	沙面宾馆	*shāmiàn bīnguǎn*
Shengli	胜利宾馆	*shènglì bīnguǎn*
White Swan	白天鹅宾馆	*báitiāné bīnguǎn*
Xinhua	新华大酒店	*xīnhuá dàjiǔdiàn*

renumbered, so pick up a recent **bus map** from hawkers at arrival points to confirm current destinations before boarding. To make proper use of the legion of private **minibuses** you need good language skills, as routes are so complicated that often the Chinese themselves hardly know where they're going. Still, wave a map at the driver or shout the name of your destination and you'll probably get there, and a mistake will cost you only ¥2 or so.

Taxis are plentiful and can be hailed in the street. They tend to cruise around hotels and points of arrival. Fares start at about ¥10 plus ¥2 per kilometre, but larger vehicles charge more – all should have meters. Few drivers give any trouble, though the city's complex traffic flows can sometimes make it seem that you're heading in the wrong direction.

It's worth checking on the progress of Guangzhou's long-awaited **metro**, advancing spasmodically but due to open in the immediate future. The two lines will run from the airport straight through the city, and from the East train station down towards Shamian Island, intersecting near the Zhongshan Lu–Jiefang Lu crossroads.

Guangzhou is notable for its quantity of street signs in English, with large bilingual **maps**, randomly distributed around the main streets, which indicate restaurants, hotels and museums. Portable versions of varying detail and quality are sold for ¥2–5 by hawkers at the train and bus stations, and at numerous bookshops, hotels and stalls around the city. Out of a huge choice, one of the best is the orange bilingual *Guangzhou Tourist Map* (although several have this title). It lacks bus routes but is consequently very clear and detailed, with the city on one side and its environs on the other.

Accommodation

With Guangzhou long exposed to business travellers, it's unfortunate but not surprising to find that room prices here reflect the idea that all foreigners can afford the going rate in their own country. Real budget accommodation is almost non-existent – even Hong Kong has a better range – so resign yourself to this and plan your finances accordingly. Prices rise during the three-week Trade Fair each April and October, when beds can also be in short supply, and tend to be lower in winter, when fewer tourists are about. Almost every hotel has some sort of travel booking service and smarter places have their own banks, post offices, restaurants and shops. They're also likely to accept various international credit cards.

For anything more than an overnight stop, **Shamian Island** is the best place to hole up, whatever your budget. It's a pleasant spot, with well-tended parks and plenty of good places to eat. More practical, especially for onward transport, is the general area around the **North train station** in the north of town, and there's also a cluster of fairly upmarket venues a couple of kilometres east of here along **Huanshi Dong Lu**.

Shamian Island

Bank of China, Shamian Dajie (☎8885913). A strange place to have a hotel, but it's newly opened and eager for foreign business. Pretty straightforward furnishings and service, in keeping with its reasonable price. ⑥.

Guangzhou Youth Hostel (*Guangzhou Qingnian Zhaodaisuo*), Shamian 4 Jie (☎8884298, fax 8884979). Across from the *White Swan* and one of Guangzhou's cheapest options – there's usually a waiting list for spare beds, which are distributed at noon. The lobby bar serves beer and coffee, and there are left-luggage facilities and an unreliable rail booking service. The single and double rooms are cramped and damp, but the three-bed dorms are much better. Dorms ③, rooms ⑤.

Shamian, Shamian Nan Jie (☎8912288). Rooms are small and most are windowless, but otherwise this is a very snug and comfortable option, just around the corner from the youth hostel. There's a travel service in Room 3211 (Mon–Fri 9am–5pm). ⑥.

Shengli, corner of Shamian 4 Jie and Shamian 2 Jie (☎8862622). A good-value upmarket choice. Formerly the *Victoria* in colonial days, it's now locally known as the *Victory* and has expanded into two separate buildings. ⑦–⑧.

MOVING ON FROM GUANGZHOU

Leaving Guangzhou can be the hardest part of your stay here. The city might have one of China's most comprehensive travel networks, but it's also the most overloaded, and buying tickets – especially for the train – can be a nightmare. Despite the unpredictable service fees involved, paying a **hotel ticket agent** often cuts out so much bother that it's money well spent. Most, however, deal only with major destinations like Shanghai, Beijing, Hong Kong, Guilin and Xi'an, so there are times when you'll have to do everything yourself.

Plane

Guangzhou is connected by air to all major cities in China, and several in Southeast Asia and Australia – though the provincial carrier, *Southeast China Airlines*, has one of the country's worst safety records. *CAAC* is just east of the train station and their well-organized ticket office upstairs is open 7am–7pm, with counters #2 and #3 reserved for foreigners and Overseas Chinese. Hotel travel desks can also reconfirm tickets. There is no airport bus, so catch a taxi to arrive at the airport at least two hours before your flight is due to leave.

Train

Leaving Guangzhou by train can be difficult, as demand on all routes is very high. In theory, tickets become available three days before departure, but sleepers sell out immediately, as do even hard seats on popular lines. For **hard seats only** from either of Guangzhou's stations, there's a small advance purchase office on Baiyun Lu, north of the Dashatou wharf. Queues can sometimes be daunting, but the whole business is computerized and the staff are polite.

The **North train station** (bus #5 or #31 from the south of the city) handles the comfortable, non-stop **express to Kowloon** (¥200), and all other destinations except those along the Meizhou and local Shenzhen lines. The Kowloon terminal is at the extreme eastern end of the building. Baggage over 20kg attracts an excess charge, but unless you arrive hopelessly encumbered with suitcases, nobody bothers to weigh anything. Just west of here is an anonymous doorway which leads upstairs to the efficient **advance booking office** (daily 5.30–9pm). It mainly deals with Kowloon tickets, but try here first for all other destinations, whatever class of comfort you're after.

Otherwise, take a deep breath and head to the western side of the station, where you'll see a large grey barrier fence surrounding the **public ticket office**. Just before you reach it there are a few windows in the station wall which sell seats for the short trips to Zhaoqing and Foshan. Entry into the main ticket hall is through guarded gateways in the fence which are closed off from time to time at the whim of the police. Once inside, destinations are labelled in Chinese above or beside each booth: usually, windows #5–12 are for the line to Changsha; #13 for Nanning and Chengdu; #17–20 for Beijing; #21 and #24 for Kunming; #23 for Shanghai; and #25 and #26 for Guilin. Staff can be positively hostile and the queues horrendous, with the police sometimes keeping order with whips. If all else fails, **ticket touts** often approach foreigners. Some are con artists and you'll obviously need to use your discretion, but they can work wonders – though you never really know until the train pulls out whether your ticket is real.

White Swan (*Baitian Binguan*), Shamian Nan Jie (☎8886968, fax 8861188). Once Guangzhou's most famous place to stay, this lavish, government-funded hotel is probably still the most prestigious. There's a waterfall in the lobby, river views, an on-site bakery and countless services – some reserved for the use of guests alone. ⑨.

Around the waterfront

Aiqun, Yanjiang Lu (☎8866668 ext 20, fax 8883519). Slightly gloomy (or possibly atmospheric) 1950s monumental mansion block with good river views. Fair-value doubles and singles. ⑦.

The **East train station** (bus #272 from outside the North train station) handles departures for Shenzhen and Meizhou, and an increasing amount of traffic north through to Wuhan in Hubei Province. Still under construction, the ticket office is on the second floor and the departure lounge is on the fourth.

Bus

Leaving Guangzhou by bus is the cheapest of all exit options, and more comfortable than the average hard-seat experience if you have any distance to travel. The **long-distance bus station** on Huanshi Xi Lu is always full of people, but tickets are relatively easy to get and there are at least daily departures to everywhere in Guangdong, and as far afield as Guilin (Guangxi), Hankou/Wuhan (Hubei), and Fuzhou (Fujian). Nearby, private **luxury buses** leave daily from in front of the *CITS/CAAC* offices on the far side of the train station for various destinations, notably Haikou, Beihai and Nanning. Though up to fifty percent more costly than a normal bus, they have air conditioning and better seats with considerably more legroom. For ordinary transport to Jiangxi or Hunan, it's also worth trying the **East bus station** on Baiyun Lu, north of Dashatou wharf. Most hotels should take bookings for the express bus service to Hong Kong via Shenzhen.

Opposite the long-distance bus station, **Liuhua station** concentrates just on Guangdong destinations, with plenty of traffic leaving for the Pearl River Delta and towards Shantou and Shaoguan, though there are also regular departures to Haikou (Hainan) via Zhanjiang. For **Foshan**, minibuses leave hourly from the Foshan depot at the western end of Zhongshan Lu – trolleybus #104 from Renmin Lu terminates nearby.

Boat

Taking the ferry **up the Xi River to Wuzhou** in Guangxi Province is a popular way to cover the first leg of the journey to Guilin and Yangshuo. Boats leave daily from **Dashatou wharf** at the eastern end of Yanjiang Lu (bus #7 from the North train station, or #57 from Liuersan Lu), and, depending on whether they're fast or slow, take 5–12 hours to reach Wuzhou, where Guilin buses await (see p.676). There are also daily ferries from Dashatou to **Zhaoqing** (p.574). The ticket office at the wharf is open daily 7–11am, 11.30am–5.15pm and 5.45–8pm.

For **Macau, Hong Kong** and **Haikou** (Hainan Island), make your way down to **Zhoutouzui wharf** on the south bank of the Pearl River – bus #31 from the North train station down Renmin Lu takes you to Gongye Lu, a five-minute walk away. The ticket office is inside the terminal on the left (daily 7–11am & 1–5pm), and sells tickets several days in advance of all departures. There are slow boats with various classes of berth – all pretty reasonable – every evening to Hong Kong (from ¥200) and Macau (from ¥100), and every morning to Haikou (from ¥300), as well as an afternoon fast catamaran to Hong Kong (¥250).

With plenty of time, it's also possible to reach some of the Pearl River Delta towns by ferry, with daily departures from the wharf across from the Customs House on Yanjiang Lu to Lianhua Shan, Lanshi (for Foshan) and east towards Dongguan.

Beijing, Xihao Er Lu (☎8884988). Absolutely typical inner-city Chinese hotel – smart lobby, slightly tarnished rooms, huge restaurant and, of course, a karaoke hall. ⑥.

Binjiang, Yanjiang Lu (☎3834110). Across the road and just west of the Dashatou wharf. Inexpensive, friendly and perfect for late arrivals and early departures along the river. ③.

Fulihua, Changdi Lu (☎8863288, fax 8863388). Part of the *Furama* international business hotel group. ⑦.

Xinhua, corner of Renmin Lu and Yanjiang Lu (☎8882688, fax 8868809). Another classic urban hotel. It can be noisy, but it's tidy and well-priced for the location. Triples, doubles and singles. ⑥.

The train station area and the north

Airways, Huanshi Dong Lu. Part of the *China Southern Airways* office, just east of the station. Rooms here are reserved for people "between flights", but if they have space they'll usually let you stay. Dorms ④, rooms ⑤.

China, Liuhua Lu (☎6666888, fax 6677014 or 6677288). Five-star labyrinth of red marble corridors, shopping malls and places to eat. You almost need a map to get around and have to pay in foreign currency, but rooms are luxurious. ⑨.

Dongfang, Liuhua Lu (☎6662946, fax 6662775). Constantly being renovated and literally in the *China*'s shadow, this is another self-contained maze with a ridiculous quantity of restaurants housed in dull 1950s buildings around a nice garden. ⑨.

Equatorial, Renmin Bei Lu (☎6672888, fax 6672582). Part of an Asian chain of hotels, it's modern and decent enough, though not comparable with others in this price bracket. ⑦.

Friendship, Renmin Bei Lu (☎6679898, fax 6678653). Nothing exceptional, but fairly quiet and inexpensive, given its busy location near to the Trade Fair halls. Rarely gives its cheaper rooms to foreigners. Triples, doubles and singles available. ⑤.

Garden, Huanshi Dong Lu (☎3338989, fax 3350467). The city's most opulent accommodation, this private-enterprise version of the *White Swan* (there's even another waterfall) is its superior in every respect except the setting. ⑨.

Guangdong Binguan, Jiefang Bei Lu (☎3332950, fax 3332911). A huge complex of square concrete wings, Sinicized with green tiling and flared eaves and best known for its twenty different dining rooms. Quite comfortable, but fading around the edges. ⑦.

Guangdong International, Huanshi Dong Lu (☎3311888, fax 2033565 or 20331349). Extremely smart attempt to outdo the nearby *Garden*. It doesn't succeed, but it's first-rate all the same. ⑧–⑨.

Liuhua, Huanshi Xi Lu (☎6668800, fax 6667828). South of the train station and once one of the city's budget venues, now raising its standards in a half-hearted way. There's a range of rooms, but the cheaper ones are frequently not that good. ⑤.

Train station hostel, upstairs in the main building, diagonally opposite the soft-sleeper waiting room. Simple comforts and pretty unfriendly reception staff, but very cheap if they'll take you. ②.

The City

Depending on your mood, Guangzhou can be compulsively energetic or disturbingly chaotic – either way, not somewhere to come for peace and relaxation. Commerce is its lifeblood, a religion inspiring everybody from train station pickpockets to company directors and, with this in mind, it's one of the most vibrant cities in China. At times there doesn't seem to be enough room for all the wheeling and dealing: markets completely block alleyways, and the need to set up shop wherever there's space has caused some strange bedfellows – where else would you find a store selling mining drills and laser theodolites sandwiched between a florist and a nightclub? Yet there's another, more community-orientated side to the city, rarely farther away than the nearest alley. With a fair sense of direction, the best way to get to grips with Guangzhou is to make your way around on foot, taking every available back lane. It can be a real surprise after the main streets to come across older residential districts with their flagstones, tiny collectors' markets, laundry strung on lines between buildings, and homes screened away behind wooden doors with heavy swing gates.

Downtown Guangzhou

The Jiefang Lu–Zhongshan Lu crossroads form the crux of downtown Guangzhou's mix of old and new roads, alleys and buildings, the hyperactive heart of the city's small businesses. There are few obviously quiet corners, and everything is rather grubby, too, though here and there you'll see newly painted facades, with litter kept down by an army of streetsweepers. The numerous sights revolve around some excellent **temples** and fairly dry historic **monuments**, mostly concentrated between Jiefang Lu and Renmin Lu, with the rest scattered farther east or west. **Buses** through the area are in turmoil at present, as large sections of road are unpredictably closed off during construction of Guangzhou's metro, but general services are included below, and #5 from either end of Jiefang Lu stops conveniently near the Zhongshan Lu crossroads.

HUA TA AND LIURONG SI

Guangzhou's most perfectly maintained religious building is the 57-metre-high **Hua Ta**, the Flower Pagoda, which rises inside the temple grounds of Liurong Si on Liurong Lu (daily 8.30am–5pm; ¥4), a five-minute walk northwest from the Zhongshan Lu–Jiefang Lu intersection. A pagoda first sprang up here in 537 AD, built to enshrine holy relics brought from India by Emperor Liang Wu's uncle, Tan Yu, though today's tower is a restored eleventh-century elaboration, its wooden eaves adorned with carvings of lions, insects and birds. The main gate ticket allows you to climb Hua Ta's seventeen storeys, of which nine have balconies and eight are blind. The interior stairway

GUANGZHOU: THE CITY		
Baiyun Shan	白云山	*báiyún shān*
Chen Jia	陈家寺	*chén jiā sì*
Dafo Si	大佛寺	*dàfó sì*
Ershadao	二沙岛	*èrshā dǎo*
Guangxiao Si	光孝寺	*guāngxiào sì*
Haizhuang Park	海幢公园	*hǎizhuàng gōngyuán*
Honan	河南	*hénán*
Hua Ta	花塔	*huā tǎ*
Huaisheng Mosque	怀圣清真寺	*huáishèng qīngzhēn sì*
Hualin Si	华林寺	*huálín sì*
Huanghua Gang Park	黄花岗公园	*huánghuā gǎng gōngyuán*
Islamic Cemetery	清真古墓	*qīngzhēn gǔmù*
Liuhua Park	流花公园	*liúhuā gōngyuán*
Liurong Si	六榕寺	*liùróng sì*
Martyrs' Memorial Gardens	烈士陵园	*lièshì língyuán*
Mausoleum to the 72 Martyrs	七十二烈士墓	*qīshíèr lièshìmù*
Municipal Museum	广州博物馆	*guǎngzhōu bówùguǎn*
Nanyue Tomb	西汉南越王墓	*xīhàn nányuèwáng mù*
Orchid Garden	兰圃	*lán pǔ*
Peasant Movement Training Institute	农民运动讲习所	*nóngmín yùndòng jiǎngxí suǒ*
Qingping Market	清平市场	*qīngpíng shìchǎng*
Sanyuan Li	三元里	*sānyuán lǐ*
Shamian Island	沙面岛	*shāmiàn dǎo*
South China Botanical Gardens	华南植物园	*huánán zhíwùyuán*
Sun Yatsen Memorial Hall	中山纪念堂	*zhōngshān jìniàn táng*
Tianhe Sports Stadium	天河体育中心	*tiānhé tǐyù zhōngxīn*
Trade Fair Hall	体育馆	*tǐyùguǎn*
Wuxian Guan	五仙观	*wǔxiān guān*
Yuexiu Park	越秀公园	*yuèxiù gōngyuán*

is not spiral, but a series of flights between floors, and you have to exit on to each balcony and circle ninety degrees to the right to ascend the next, lower-ceilinged level – watch your head. Landing niches are full of golden Buddhas in various poses, and at the top is a gigantic bronze pillar covered with over a thousand reliefs of meditating figures rising up through the roof, solid enough to support the five-tonne begging bowl and pearl that you can see from ground level.

Liurong Si's compact temple buildings are of mild interest, especially the modern caricatures of sixteen *arhats* in the main hall. Originally called Bao Zhuang Si, the temple's name was changed to Liurong (Six Banyans) in 1100, after a visit by the dissident poet-governor **Su Dongpo** (see p.789). Inspired by some beautiful trees then growing in the temple grounds – sadly, long dead – Su contributed the huge characters for "Liu Rong" inscribed on the two stone steles just inside the gates, and there's a contemporary carved portrait of him here, too, casually attired in clogs and bamboo hat.

GUANGXIAO SI

The narrow lane along Liurong Si's northern boundary leads west through a street market on to Haizhu Bei Lu. Turn south and then west again for the entrance to **Guangxiao Si** (daily 8am–5pm; ¥5), the oldest of Guangzhou's Buddhist temples – bus #31 also stops nearby on Renmin Lu. In 113 BC this was the residence of **Zhao Jiande**, last of the Nanyue kings, becoming a place of worship only when the 85-year-old Gandharan (Kashmiri) monk **Tanmo Yeshe** built the first hall in 401 AD. The temple was later visited by Buddhist luminaries such as the sixth-century monk Zhiyao Sanzang, who planted the fig trees still here today, and the Indian founder of Chan (Zen) Buddhism, **Bodhidharma**.

Though none of the original buildings survives, the grounds feel peaceful and spacious, due more to their well-ordered design rather than actual size. To the right of the entrance is the oldest surviving structure in Guangzhou, a mushroom-shaped pillar from 826 said to be inscribed with an "awful curse" – against whom isn't clear. Around the gardens are pavilions concealing wells and engraved tablets from various periods, while three buildings at the back house some imposing Buddha images; the westerly one is unusually reclining, while a more ordinary trinity fills the central hall. Under one of the older trees is a statue of **Hui Neng**, a Guangdong monk who became the sixth Chan patriarch in 676 after bettering the vague preachings of the incumbent abbot. Over to the west is a courtyard containing the lower three storeys of a three-metre-high **iron pagoda**, cast in 963; its twin is hidden away in the temple warehouses. You might want to look for it, as the grounds are a nice place to wander around, and there's a **vegetarian restaurant** on the eastern side doling out simple set meals for ¥2 at midday.

HUAISHENG MOSQUE AND WUXIAN GUAN

About a kilometre south of Guangxiao Si, Haizhu Lu is crossed by Guangta Lu, and turning east along it almost immediately brings you to the walls surrounding **Huaisheng Mosque** and its grey, conical tower, **Guangta**. This is probably the world's oldest minaret outside Mecca and something of a stylistic fossil for Islamicists, said by some to have been built by Abu Waqas in the seventh century (see p.537). It's also the only surviving part of the original mosque, as the rest was restored during the Ming dynasty. Both buildings are closed to non-Muslims, but there is little to see inside except a few prayer mats and whitewashed walls. During the fifteenth century, Huaisheng's environs were known as **Fanfang**, the foreigners' quarter; today there is a smattering of halal canteens and restaurants in the vicinity.

A ten-minute walk south from the mosque is Huifu Xi Lu, where you'll find the well-concealed entrance of **Wuxian Guan**, the Five Immortals' Temple (9am–noon &

1.30–5pm; ¥2). Dating from 1377, the original wooden building is nonfunctional and dusty, but some obviously ancient statues pop up around the place: weathered guardian lions flank the way in, and there are some stylized Ming sculptures out the back, looking like giant chess pieces. The Five Immortals – three men and two women – are depicted too, riding their goatly steeds as they descend through the clouds to found Guangzhou. More impressive, however, is a fourteenth-century **bell tower** behind the temple, in which hangs a colossal three-metre-high, five-tonne bronze bell, silent since receiving the blame for a plague which broke out shortly after its installation in 1378. It has been called the "Forbidden Bell" ever since.

DAFO SI AND THE PROVINCIAL MUSEUM

One kilometre east from Wuxian Guan along Huifu Dong Lu is **Dafo Si**, the Big Buddha Temple (daily 8am–5pm; free). Like Wuxian Guan, this is cunningly hidden up a cul-de-sac on the north side of the road, but look for the bulbous golden statue of Maitreya at the gates. Professional beggars at the door put on quite a show if they see you coming, but sit around chatting amiably and sharing cigarettes when they think nobody is watching. Otherwise, this little temple's recently tiled hall isn't very engrossing.

Of more interest is the usually deserted **Provincial Museum** (daily 9am–5pm; ¥10), set back in a square behind a full-sized steel dragon-boat sculpture, farther east on Yuexiu Lu. Bus #3 from Huifu Xi Lu passes the door, as does #70 from east of Renmin Bridge on Yanjiang Lu. There's a weird mix of subjects here, the first floor showcasing Guangzhou's industries with photos, washing machines and stuffed toys. Head upstairs and there's a **natural history museum**, incorporating cases of rarities and an innovative walk-through "jungle" with spotlit creatures hidden in the undergrowth. A Yangzi River dolphin looks more like a badly stuffed sofa, but the English captions convey an unexpected appeal for conservation in a country which usually puts development ahead of all other considerations. Other rooms house exquisitely fine art objects, including superb porcelain, finely carved jade and Ming household ornaments. The lack of visitors and explanatory notes somewhat deadens it all, but it's remarkable to see such a high standard of exhibits.

REVOLUTIONARY MONUMENTS

Thanks to the subsequent career of its dean, Mao Zedong, Guangzhou's **Peasant Movement Training Institute** (daily 9am–4pm; ¥2) is the city's most frequented revolutionary site. You'll find it some 1.5km east of Jiefang Lu on Zhongshan Lu, and one block north of the Provincial Museum (bus #70 from Renmin Bridge terminates just around the corner on Yuexiu Lu). It still looks like the Confucian Academy it was for six hundred years, before **Peng Pai**, a "rich peasant" from Guangdong, established the Institute in 1924 with Guomindang permission and 38 students. Courses were brief, but included lectures by Sun Yatsen followed by a practical session of organizing in the country. The school lasted just over two years, with Mao, Zhou Enlai and Peng Pai taking the final classes in August 1926, eight months before the Communist and Guomindang alliance violently ended in Shanghai. A quick turn through the grounds gives a good idea of the students' spartan regime and, in the Chinese labels, a dose of sycophantic Maoist stories linked to the little stone bridge, the canteen and his carefully austere room. More poignant are the photographs of alumni who failed to survive the years following the Shanghai Massacre and the subsequent **1927 Communist Uprising** in Guangzhou.

The scene of the latter event lies farther east along Zhongshan Lu at the **Martyrs' Memorial Gardens** (daily 8am–7pm; ¥3). It was near here, on December 11, 1927, that a pathetically small and ill-equipped Communist force under **Zhang Teilai** managed to

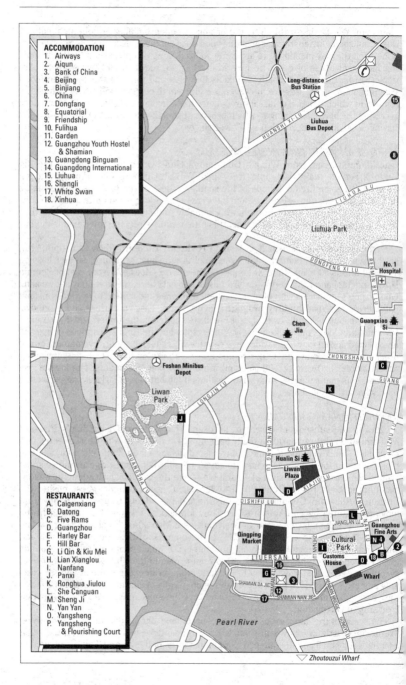

ACCOMMODATION
1. Airways
2. Aiqun
3. Bank of China
4. Beijing
5. Binjiang
6. China
7. Dongfang
8. Equatorial
9. Friendship
10. Fulihua
11. Garden
12. Guangzhou Youth Hostel
   & Shamian
13. Guangdong Binguan
14. Guangdong International
15. Liuhua
16. Shengli
17. White Swan
18. Xinhua

RESTAURANTS
A. Caigenxiang
B. Datong
C. Five Rams
D. Guangzhou
E. Harley Bar
F. Hill Bar
G. Li Qin & Kiu Mei
H. Lian Xianglou
I. Nanfang
J. Panxi
K. Ronghua Jiulou
L. She Canguan
M. Sheng Ji
N. Yan Yan
O. Yangsheng
P. Yangsheng
   & Flourishing Court

Long-distance
Bus Station

Liuhua
Bus Depot

Liuhua Park

HUANSHI XI LU

LIUHUA LU

DONGFENG XI LU

RENMIN BEI LU

No. 1
Hospital

Chen
Jia

Guangxiao
Si

ZHONGSHAN LU

GUANG

Foshan Minibus
Depot

Liwan
Park

LONGJIN LU

WENCHANG LU

CHANGSHOU LU

Hualin Si

Liwan
Plaza

XIAJIU LU

HAIZHU LU

HUANGSHA LU

DISHIFU LU

JIANGLAN LU

Guangzhou
Fine Arts

Qingping
Market

Cultural
Park

Customs
House

LIUERSAN LU

ZHENNAN LU

RENMIN NAN LU

Wharf

SHAMIAN DA JIE

SHAMIAN NAN JIE

RENMIN BRIDGE

GONGYU

Pearl River

▽ *Zhoutouzui Wharf*

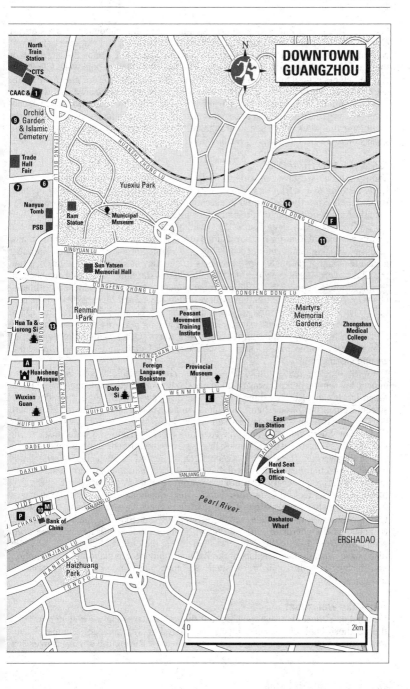

DOWNTOWN GUANGZHOU

N

North Train Station

CITS

CAAC & ①

⑨ Orchid Garden & Islamic Cemetery

Trade Hall Fair

⑦ ⑥

Nanyue Tomb

PSB

Ram Statue

Municipal Museum

Yuexiu Park

HUANSHI ZHONG LU

HUANSHI DONG LU

⑭

Ⓕ

⑪

JIEFANG BEI LU

QINGYUAN LU

Sun Yatsen Memorial Hall

DONGFENG ZHONG LU

DONGFENG DONG LU

YUEXIU LU

Renmin Park

Peasant Movement Training Institute

Martyrs' Memorial Gardens

Zhongshan Medical College

Hua Ta & Liurong Si ⑬

LIURONG LU

ZHONGSHAN LU

Foreign Language Bookstore

Provincial Museum

Ⓐ Huaisheng Mosque

TA LU

JIEFANG ZHONG LU

Dafo Si

WENMING LU

Ⓔ

YUEXIU LU

Wuxian Guan

HUIFU DONG LU

HUIFU XI LU

BEIJING LU

East Bus Station

DADE LU

DAXIN LU

BAXUN LU

Hard Seat Ticket Office

⑤

YANJIANG LU

Pearl River

YIDE LU

Ⓜ

CHANGDI

YANJIANG LU

Ⓟ

⑩

Bank of China

Dashatou Wharf

ERSHADAO

BINJIANG LU

NANHUA LU

Haizhuang Park

TONGFU LU

0   2km

take the Guangzhou Police Headquarters, announcing the foundation of the **Canton Commune**. A "soviet" was appointed, industries nationalized, and workers were given control of production, but expected support never materialized, and on the afternoon of the second day Guomindang forces moved in. Five thousand people were killed outright or later executed for complicity. Today, the memorial gardens are one of the cleanest, quietest spots in the city. There's a small lake, some trees and a lawn, and the paths are lined with flowers, while on the western side is a small **museum** with English captions (¥1), worth a trot through to see how chaotic the Guomindang were in those days. Out along the paths you'll see a strange rifle-like monument to the events and the grassy mound where the insurgents lie buried.

CHEN JIA AND HUALIN SI

Zhongshan Lu's western arm cuts through a new, relatively tidy district before eventually heading over a tributary of the Pearl River and out of the city towards Foshan. About 2.5km from the Jiefang Lu intersection you pass under a pedestrian walkway; take the lane heading north here and follow the English signs to **Chen Jia**, the Chen Family Temple (daily 9am–5pm; ¥10) – trolleybus #104 struggles up here from the middle reaches of Renmin Lu. For an idea of the immense fortunes enjoyed by South China's late-Qing clans you need only spend an hour here, surrounded by the most garish tiles and gorgeously carved screens that money could buy in the 1890s, when the Chens were one of the wealthiest families in the kingdom. Originally an ancestral temple, then a school, the buildings now contain period decor and a continually changing "popular arts" exhibition, with very fine Yao, Li and Miao textiles in the rear hall. Have a good look at the extraordinary brick reliefs under the eaves. One of the first, on the right as you enter, features an opera being performed to what looks like a drunken horse, squirming on the floor with mirth. Other cameos feature stories from China's "noble bandit" saga, *Outlaws of the Marsh*, and some of the sights around Guangzhou.

Two kilometres due south of Chen Jia lies **Hualin Si** (daily 8am–5pm; free), an interesting temple tucked away in the maze of alleyways between Changshou Lu and Xiajiu Lu. It's most fun getting there by weaving your way through the older backstreets from either Zhongshan Lu or Liuersan Lu, but quicker to take the alley north next to the *Guangzhou* restaurant on Xiajiu Lu. Bus #31 comes as close as the Changshou Lu–Renmin Lu junction. There's a carefully contrived **jade market** outside Hualin's entrance, worth a quick browse even though most pieces are expensive and probably fake. The temple forecourt stands behind an auspiciously red-painted gateway, with the main hall immediately to the right. Founded as a modest nunnery by the Brahman prince **Bodhidharma** in 527, Hualin is doubly sacred as the first place that he set foot on Chinese soil and is also known as **Xila Chudi** (First Arrival from the West). Bodhidharma's Chan teachings really caught on in the the seventeenth century and the temple was hugely expanded in 1654, the main hall's interior reshaped as the character *tian* – a box with a cross in it – with five hundred *arhat* sculptures ranged along the aisles. Trashed during the Cultural Revolution, the sculptures have recently been replaced, the halls are undergoing elaborate redecoration, and during festivals you'll be crushed, deafened and blinded by the crowds and incense smoke.

Along the waterfront

Guangzhou's most vigorous quarter, and the most interesting for idle strolls, abuts the northern bank of the Pearl River. This, together with adjacent Shamian Island, forms the oldest and most congested part of the city. During the **spring flower fes-**

tival, a southern Chinese tradition originating in Guangzhou, the backstreets here are almost impassable, crammed to capacity with crowds buying blooms of every colour and shape for good luck in the coming year. To get into the area, take bus #5 from the train station square to **Yanjiang Lu**, the waterfront's main boulevard. The eastern stretch here is a favourite spot with older residents who come down in the early morning to practise *tai ji*, and during the summer its stone benches, breezy location, ice-cream vendors and shady trees make it popular with anyone looking for relief from the humidity.

Walk west from the bottom of Renmin Lu towards Shamian Island, past the old **Customs House** and a tight grouping of colonial buildings – worth observing from a distance for their unlikely roof gardens – and bear right under the complicated overpass associated with Renmin Bridge to **Liuersan Lu**. The name means "6 2 3 Road", referring to June 23, 1925, when a demonstration of over a hundred thousand Chinese, demanding among other things the return of Shamian Island to Chinese sovereignty, was fired on by British and French troops. Fifty-two people were killed, and hundreds seriously wounded. Heading east along Liuersan you'll come to the southern entrance of the **Cultural Park** (daily 6am–late; ¥2), where gangs of children queue for their turn on arcade games and fairground rides, and theatre and sound stages host weekend performances of anything from local rock to opera. Alternatively, continue west past a host of home industries, canteens, utensil and clothing stores, and you'll find yourself under a pedestrian overpass crossing to Shamian, at the mouth of **Qingping Market**. This is huge, extending far into the backstreets along Qingping Lu and Heping Lu, each intersecting east–west road forming a natural dividing line for the sale of different goods. One of China's most exotically exciting markets, it can be a taxing one, too, if you're at all squeamish. Though there are friendly English signs, and trade in rarer animals such as pangolins has been prohibited as a concession to foreign eyes (the occasional Tibetan does hang around the entrance proffering tiger paws), the Cantonese demand for fresh ingredients is met by slaughtering chickens – or fish, deer, turtles, owls, cats and dogs – on the spot. The section nearest Liuersan Lu sells dried medicines and herbs, the next fresh vegetables, and the third is given over to livestock, bird and fish stalls. Farther up are pets (insects and songbirds), pottery and bonsai trees, while to the east there's a smaller market and a lively collection of restaurants, bars and al fresco stalls in the evening.

Shamian Island

It's only a short hop across Liuersan Lu on to **Shamian Island**, but the pace changes instantly, and Guangzhou's busiest quarter is exchanged for its most genteel. A tear-shaped sandbank about 1km long and 500m wide, Shamian was leased to European powers as an Opium War trophy, the French getting 44 acres and the British the rest. Having doubled the island's size through land reclamation, the colonials recreated their own backyards, planting trees (now massive) and throwing up solid, Victorian-style buildings which housed all the trappings of life at home. Grand villas, churches and tennis courts once excluded the Chinese, shutting them out by means of huge iron gates on the bridges which were secured every night, leaving the Europeans in self-imposed isolation from the bustle of Guangzhou across the water.

Shamian retains something of that atmosphere today, a quiet bolt-hole for many long-term travellers in the city. There's restricted traffic flow, and the well-tended architecture, greenery and general peace make it a refreshing place to visit, even if you're not staying or sampling the restaurants and bars. There's also a good **park** on the **Shamian Nan Jie** esplanade, and two **cannons**, cast in nearby Foshan during the Opium Wars, facing out across the river behind the tennis court.

The Pearl River and Ershadao

Oily grey and second only to the Yangzi in importance as an industrial channel, the Pearl River (Zhu Jiang) forms one of China's busiest waterways, continually active with ferries and barges loaded down with coal and stone. Its name comes from a legend about a monk named Jiahu who lost a glowing pearl in its waters, and although it shone on the riverbed night after night, nobody was ever able to recover it.

Cruises (¥15) depart daily at 3.30pm from the ticket office and wharf roughly opposite the Customs House on Yanjiang Lu, spending ninety minutes on the return trip east to **Ershadao** (Two-sand Island). Along the way are fine views of Shamian Island and Guangzhou's busy waterfront, and the homes of the city's former boat dwellers. For centuries, thousands of "outcasts" lived and worked on the Pearl River, forbidden to settle ashore or marry anyone who lived on land, or even to take the Imperial Examinations. After the Communist takeover they were resettled into a purpose-built estate of apartment buildings on Ershadao, which goes under the name of New Riverside Village.

Between April and October there's also a **night cruise** (¥50) from the same wharf, currently departing at 7.45pm; it's popular with the Cantonese, so buy a ticket by the early afternoon. To the accompaniment of tea and cakes, nuts and plums – included in the price – you can sit back and watch the lights of the city slip slowly past your table, or savour the delights of the on-board karaoke. It all lasts about two hours, taking you past the *White Swan Hotel* and then back under Renmin Bridge, past Haizhu Bridge and down to the grand Guangzhou suspension bridge at the far end of Ershadao, from where on a clear moonless night you can see the lights of international freighters riding at anchor far downstream in **Huangpu**. This was the site of a **Military Academy** during the 1920s where Mao studied under Chiang Kaishek, his future arch enemy and leader of the Guomindang.

South of the river: Honan

Most Chinese cities are a collection of old villages, nowhere more obvious than in Guangzhou's south-bank suburb of **Honan**. The city's notorious red-light district before 1949, crawling with opium dens, brothels and gambling houses, today it's a striking example of what can be done when a little money is blended with civic co-operation and a dash of idealism. Bordering on such a contemporary, high-paced city, this relaxed little enclave was specially chosen as a model for **Hu Yaobang**'s 1984 "Civic Spirit" campaign and, though his guiding principles have long been purged (even if steles engraved with them lurk on every corner), he made Honan one of the nicest places to live in Guangzhou.

From the north bank it's easiest to reach Honan by simply walking over Renmin Bridge. From farther afield catch bus #31 from the North train station or along Renmin Lu. Once across the bridge, the main road continuing south is Gongye Lu, while **Binjiang Lu** runs east along the river, a local lovers' lane. Immediately behind Binjiang Lu are **Nanhua Lu** and **Tongfu Lu**, side streets which best illustrate the ideals of this little socialist utopia. There are kindergartens and old folks' clubs on nearly every block, bicycles must be wheeled and the street committees keep the flagstones surgically clean. Yet aside from their heavy wooden doors, the houses seem austere, little more than dormitories with a TV, mahjong table and perhaps a little shrine to the god of wealth. Here the pleasures of life – gardens, songbirds and culture – are kept out in the open, where everybody can enjoy them.

With all this in mind, don't miss **Haizhuang Park**, sandwiched between Nanhua Lu and Tongfu Lu, about ten minutes' walk from Renmin Bridge. A public space of pretty gardens, old trees and a children's playground, buildings here have recently been returned to their original purpose as **Qian Chu Si**, once Guangzhou's largest

Buddhist monastery. It's a bit of a shambles at present, but monks are back in residence and restorations are underway to spruce up the broad south hall with its fine statuary and interlocked wooden beam roof, so typical of south China's early Qing temple buildings.

The north: the Islamic Cemetery and Orchid Garden

Cut by a modern urban backdrop of expressways, hotels and office towers, the area surrounding Guangzhou's North train station above Dongfeng Lu has the best of the city's parks and museums – something for both fine and wet weather. Most of the attractions here are in the vicinity of Jiefang Lu or Renmin Lu, which are covered along their lengths by buses #5 and #31 respectively.

Despite the frenetic atmosphere outside the train station, there are two oases of peace and quiet in the immediate vicinity, invaluable after a long session of queuing for tickets. East of the station and on the south side of Huanshi Lu, look for a bus compound whose gateposts sport little green minarets and Arabic script; walk through to the lane behind, and you're among the bamboo stands of Guangzhou's **Islamic Cemetery**. The cylindrical stone graves are all aligned roughly northwest towards Mecca, and on the right is a walled courtyard built around the tomb of **Abu Waqas**, a seventh-century missionary who brought Islam to China. The details are a little sketchy, however, as Abu Waqas supposedly died around 629, three years before Mohammed, and the Quran wasn't collated for another generation afterwards. The courtyard's wooden gates are usually locked, but you can peer through at the brightly coloured atrium within, a nice blend of Islamic and Chinese design.

For pure pleasure, however, it's hard to beat Guangzhou's delightful **Orchid Garden**, just next door (daily 8am–5pm; ¥8, entry includes tea in the central pavilion). Though fairly small, there are far more than just orchids here, including ponds surrounded by tropical ferns and lilies, winding stone paths, palms and giant figs with drooping aerial roots and pink-flowering azaleas. Apart from the filtered traffic noise, it's hard to believe that the city lies just outside.

SANYUAN LI

For a return to earth after the Orchid Garden, continue east to the Huanshi Lu–Jiefang Lu crossroads and walk north for a kilometre, before turning west along Guanghua Lu. You're now above the North train station in **Sanyuan Li**, a rough and ready district whose back lanes are home to a mass of migrant workers including Uigurs from northwestern China. This was where the **Sanyuan Li Anti-British Movement** formed in 1841 after the British stormed into the area during the First Opium War. Following months of abuse from the invaders, local workers and peasants rose under the farmer **Wei Shaoguang** and attacked the British camp, killing over two hundred soldiers with the simple farm tools and ceremonial weapons now on display at the **temple museum** about 250m along on the south side of Guanghua Lu (daily 9–11.30am & 2–4pm; ¥2). Though the tale might appear to be the unlikely later invention of Maoist propaganda, reflected in the museum's turgid captions, historians have few doubts about its authenticity and the British were sufficiently irked at the time to destroy the original temple, site of the first engagement. The current building dates from 1860.

YUEXIU PARK

A huge part of the city's northeastern end is taken up by **Yuexiu Park** (daily 7am–7pm; ¥2), which, encompassing over ninety hectares of sports courts, historic monuments, tea houses and shady groves, is China's biggest spread of urban greenery. There are some bilingual signposts in the park and entrances at every point of the compass. The front gate is on Jiefang Bei Lu, a ten-minute walk southeast of the Orchid Garden; bus #5 stops outside.

To the north of the porcelain dragons here is **Beixiu Hu**, where you can rent dinghies and pedal boats, stroll around the rockeries, and see what's on display in the exhibition hall, full of terrific flower displays in spring. Paths heading south from the entrance converge in about fifteen minutes at **Zhenhai Lou**, the "Gate Tower Facing the Sea", a wood and rendered brick building which once formed part of the Ming city walls. Today it houses the **Municipal Museum** (Tues–Sun 9am–4pm; ¥5), three floors of illuminating exhibits covering over two thousand years of local history and guarded by some nineteenth-century cannons tumbled about in the courtyard (two made by the German company, Krupp). The museum starts with the Neolithic age, working up through successive dynasties to the Opium Wars and the eve of the 1911 Revolution, with almost everything substantiated by local archeological and historical evidence. There are Stone-Age pottery fragments, ivory from Africa found in a Han-dynasty tomb, fifth-century coins from Persia and a copy of *Good Words for the World*, the Christian tract which converted the Taiping leader, Hong Xiuquan. A statue of Lin Zexu and original letters from him to the Qing emperor documenting his disposal of the British opium stocks always draws big crowds of tongue-clicking Chinese. Of esoteric interest is a still-functioning water clock from 1316, and a grossly pretentious eighteenth-century brass timepiece, inlaid with coloured glass and garnets. Your ticket includes a cup of tea on the top floor, where you can gaze south across Guangzhou's sprawl.

Due west of the museum, on the far side of a small lake, is the rather banal but much photographed **Five Rams Statue**, commemorating the myth of Guangzhou's foundation. Far more entertaining is the *Journey to the West* **theme park** off to the northeast (¥20), a forty-minute dollop of gloriously tacky mechanics and papier-mâché models of characters and scenes from this ever-popular Buddhist fairy tale – kids scream at the demons and skeletons looming in grottoes; adults just laugh. Far more stately is the very European-looking **Memorial Tower to Sun Yatsen** five minutes' walk south of the museum, built of huge sandstone blocks on top of a well-wooded hill. All through the park, but here in particular, you'll see incense and votive candles at the base of trees and rocks. Yuexiu Park was once a burial ground, where many Cantonese families had their ancestors interred.

Walk down the stone steps from here and you'll end up on **Qingquan Lu**, Yuexiu's southern boundary. Directly across the road on an abnormally pristine green lawn is the **Sun Yatsen Memorial Hall** (8am–6pm; ¥5), a respectful tribute to the man regarded by Guomindang and Communists alike as the father of modern China. Built in 1931 on the spot where Sun took the presidential oath, the large rotunda and blue-tiled roof was modelled on Beijing's Temple of Heaven. Inside it's an unadorned auditorium with seating for two thousand people and a photographic record of Sun's life captioned in Chinese.

THE NANYUE TOMB

Five hundred metres north of Yuexiu Park's Jiefang Bei Lu entrance is the looming red sandstone facade of the **Nanyue Tomb**, housing a two-thousand-year-old site discovered in 1983 during foundation digging for a residential estate (9.30am–5.30pm, last admission 4.45pm; ¥15). The museum really deserves a couple of hours of your time, and the ticket price entitles you to watch a video in good English and tour the mass of exhibits, though it's an extra ¥5 to enter the tomb itself. Bus #5 passes the museum.

The **Nanyue Kingdom** was founded by **Zhao Tuo**, a Qin general from Hebei Province who was ordered down here in 214 BC to subjugate China's unruly southern tribes. Following the collapse of the Qin empire, Zhao, backed by half a million troops, declared himself head of an independent state. Having replaced the Qin, the new Han rulers grudgingly acknowledged his position and even granted him the title of "Emperor Wu" during his 67-year reign. But by the time of his grandson **Zhao Mo**, whose tomb this is, the empire was in decline, and, within a century, the Han had sacked his capital and reclaimed the territory for central China. Remains of the Nanyue palace were excavated south of Guangzhou in the early twentieth century, a layer of ashes confirming the account of its destruction given by Sima Qian, the Han-dynasty historian.

Zhao Mo made a better job of his tomb than running his kingdom, and excavators found it stacked with gold and priceless trinkets – all on view in the museum – including a burial suit made out of over a thousand tiny jade tiles, and the ash-like remains of slaves and concubines immured with him. It's all fascinating and expertly presented, particularly worthwhile if you plan to visit contemporary grave sites in Changsha or Xi'an. Incidentally, Zhao Tuo's tomb still awaits discovery, though rumours of its fabulous treasures had eager excavators turning Guangzhou inside out as long ago as the *Three Kingdoms* period (220–280 AD).

THE TRADE FAIR HALL AND LINHUA PARK

On the eastern side of Renmin Lu, 500m south of the train station, is Guangzhou's massive **Trade Fair Hall** (bus #31), venue for the biannual Chinese Export Commodities Fair (April & October). First held in 1957 to encourage Western investments, today it's used as more of a showcase for Chinese tractors, plastic buckets and cheap clothing, though business dealings continue behind the scenes. Outside of fair times, the building becomes the "Foreign Trade Centre Store", full of lounge suites, imported jeans and perfume, and a motley collection of Chinese souvenirs.

Liuhua Park, another kilometre south on the west side of Renmin Lu (bus #31 again; daily 7am–7pm; ¥2), is a large expanse of lakes, purpose-built in 1958 and pleasantly bland during the week – weekends are hellishly crowded. Liuhua means "Floating Flowers", a name said to date back to the Han period when palace maids tossed petals into a nearby stream while dressing their hair.

The eastern suburbs

Hemmed in on all other flanks by rivers and hills, Guangzhou inevitably expands east to accommodate its ever-growing population. You'll find yourself out this way if you have to use the **East train station** in the suburb of **Tianhe**, and there are a couple of things to see in the area. Out along Xianlie Lu, which heads northeast off Huanshi Dong Lu about 5km from the North train station, **Huanghua Gang Park** (daily 8am–5pm; ¥2) holds reminders of Sun Yatsen's abortive **Canton Uprising** against the Qing government in April 1911. The empire was already crumbling, and this failed coup was one of many enacted across the country in the months before events in Sichuan and Hubei finally demolished the dynasty. In 1918 a **Mausoleum to the 72 Martyrs** killed in Guangzhou was built at Huanghua Gang, a very peculiar monument designed to reflect the nationalities of numerous donors who had contributed to its construction – Buddhist iconography rubbing shoulders with a Statue of Liberty and Egyptian obelisk.

Of more general appeal is **Guangzhou Zoo**, about a kilometre farther out along Xianlie Lu (9am–4pm; ¥10; take bus #6 from Dongfeng Lu, one block east of the Sun Yatsen Memorial Hall). This is the third largest in the country, with the animals kept in relatively decent conditions – though far below what you'll probably consider pleasant. Among the rarities are clouded leopards, several species of wildfowl and, of course, pandas.

Surrounding the train station 2km due east of the zoo is Tianhe, a monument to the dreary bureaucratic urban planning which includes people as an afterthought. The showpiece here is the huge **sports stadium** built for the 1987 National Games, but the surrounding residential blocks are horribly anonymous, and there are no other public facilities – the total antithesis of Honan.

Baiyun Shan and the Botanical Gardens

Two places are close enough to central Guangzhou to reach on city buses, but open enough to leave all the city's noise and bustle behind. Just 6km north of downtown, **Baiyun Shan** (White Cloud Mountain) was once covered with numerous monasteries, and though these have gone, its heavily reforested slopes offer lush panoramas out over Guangzhou and the delta region. A **park** (¥5) encloses almost thirty square kilometres, and it's a good three-hour walk from the entrance off Luhu Lu to **Moxing Ling** (Star-touching Summit), past strategically placed tea houses and pavilions offering views and refreshments. There's also a cable car (¥20) from the entrance as far as the **Cheng Precipice**, a ledge roughly halfway to the top which earned its name when the Qin-dynasty minister **Cheng Ki** was ordered here by his emperor to find a herb of immortality. Having found the plant, Cheng nibbled a leaf only to see the remainder vanish; full of remorse, he flung himself off the mountain but was caught by a stork and taken to heaven. Sunset views from the precipice are spectacular. Baiyun Shan's entrance is a thirty-minute ride on bus #24 from the south side of Renmin Park, immediately northeast of the Jiefang Lu–Zhongshan Lu crossroads.

Harder to reach but requiring far less energy to enjoy, the **South China Botanical Gardens** (Huanan Zhiwu Yuan; 8am–4.30pm; ¥5) are 15km out to the northeast of the city. Catch bus #56 from east of the mosque on Guangta Lu to its terminus, and then #28 to the gardens – the total journey should take around an hour. You're sure to find something of interest among the three thousand native and introduced species here. One of the nicest parts is near the entrance, where a thin lake looks nicely tropical, surrounded by palms and bamboos. Farther in there are individual groves of protected and relict species – look out for gingkos, and the rare red-fringed leaves of the **Dawn Redwood** (*metasequoia*) – with an area at the back given over to **medicinal plants**.

Eating, drinking and nightlife

Guangzhou has its own **opera style**, superficially similar to Beijing's, but more rustic. It doesn't get much of an airing any more, though you might see travelling amateur groups performing in the parks at the weekends. The Cultural Park on Liuersan Lu has a proper stage, and hotel staff can usually translate announcements of forthcoming events in local newspapers for you.

GUANGZHOU: RESTAURANTS

Caigenxiang	菜根香	*càigēnxiāng*
Datong	大同大酒家	*dàtóng jiǔjiā*
Five Rams Muslim Resaurant	五羊回民饭店	*wǔyáng huímín fàndiàn*
Guangzhou	广州酒家	*guǎngzhōu jiǔjiā*
Li Qin	利群饮食店	*lìqún yǐnshídiàn*
Nanfang	南方	*nánfāng*
Ronghua Jiulou	荣华酒楼	*rónghuá jiǔlóu*
She Canguan	蛇餐馆	*shé cānguǎn*

Nowadays, **eating out** is the main preoccupation. Cantonese youngsters also flock to the **cinema** to see Hong Kong kung fu epics or Western action films, both usually subtitled in English and Chinese, while there are also discos/karaoke sessions at many of the tourist hotels. Guangzhou also has, for China, an unusually high number of **nightclubs**, though these are very rarely patronized by foreigners and can be slightly intimidating. You can't miss the screaming eagle over the door to the *Harley Bar* on Yuexiu Lu across from the Provincial Museum, which gets going after dark, the music selections orientated towards Western pop. Harder to find is the *One Love Bar* at the far eastern end of Dongfeng Dong Lu, universally regarded as a den of iniquity.

For a more Western atmosphere, there are numerous "beer cellars" along Shamian Island's northern waterfront, parallel with Liuersan Lu. They look authentic enough, and their imported beer is real and expensive (around ¥20 a bottle). Over in the north, a couple of similar clubs across from the entrance to Liuhua Park on Renmin Lu get variable reports, but it's worth seeking out the *Hill Bar*, opposite the *Garden Hotel* on Huanshi Dong Lu, the favoured haunt of Guangzhou's large and jaded expat community. Foreign beer, spirits and very passable "pub meals" are on hand throughout the day, and the place is usually packed after 9pm on Fridays and Saturdays. The customers here can be a useful source of information about other nocturnal hotspots.

Restaurants and food stalls

Guangzhou's restaurants, the best to be found in a province famed for its cuisine, are in themselves justification to spend a few days in the city, and it would be a real shame to leave without having eaten in one of the more elaborate or famous places. While you can stuff your face from dawn to dusk, you'll need to pace yourself to stay fit for sight-seeing (unless you're planning to walk everywhere between meals). Breakfast here can be anything from a quick bowl of noodles to an hour-long linger over *dim sum*, and lunch, though sometimes fussed over by the Chinese, is best kept light and quick. **Dinner** is the main session, worth setting time and money aside to enjoy in style.

If you're worried about what you might be served, there are any number of Western fast-food outlets throughout the city, and all the big tourist **hotels** have restaurants offering everything from *dim sum* through to Western meals and full-blown Chinese banquets. Hotels are also worth checking for special sittings: afternoon tea at the *China* (4–6pm; ¥45 per person), or bottomless coffee/buffet breakfasts at the *White Swan* before 11am (¥16/¥80) for instance, the latter featuring the best riverside views in Guangzhou. But it's better to eat out and most of the big restaurants have English menus if you ask for them. The cooking is more adventurous and not necessarily loaded with exotic ingredients, and there's nothing to match the experience of tucking into a Cantonese spread while being surrounded by an enthusiastic horde of Chinese diners.

You'll find the highest concentration of **restaurants** spread through the waterfront district either side of the southern end of Renmin Lu, with plenty of others in the down-town area. Unfortunately, the sociable Cantonese fashion of entertaining (and impressing) family or wealthy clients with food has caused restaurant **prices** to soar as the population demands ever more lavish preparations. After a ten percent **service charge** is added, expect to pay at least ¥50 a person for a good three-course meal; ¥100 each would allow you to try some house specialities.

You can, of course, eat for a fraction of this cost day or night at the city's numerous **food stalls**. Those in the southwestern corner around Liuersan Lu and the Cultural Park are particularly good, with a choice of dishes including meat and chicken dumplings, prawn balls, egg and rice snacks and battered chicken legs. Small cafés serve good meat and vegetable dishes for a couple of yuan each, and evening markets deal in frogs, turtles and snails, quickly cooked to your order. Be sure and try a selection of **cakes and buns** – Liuersan Lu has several shops – and the fresh tropical **fruits** sold from stalls along

COOKING IN GUANGDONG: THE CANTONESE STYLE

Guangdong cooking is one of China's four major regional styles and, despite northern critics decrying it as too uncomplicated to warrant the term "cuisine", it's unmatched in the clarity of its flavours, its artistic presentation and the attention paid to the ingredients' natural characteristics. The style itself can be subdivided into **Cantonese**, emanating from the Pearl River Delta region; **Chaozhou**, from the city of the same name in the far east of Guangdong; and **Hakka**, from the northeastern border with Fujian, named after the Han subgroup with whom it originated. Though certain Chaozhou and Hakka recipes have been incorporated into the main body of Guangdong cooking – sweet and sour pork with fruit, and salt-baked chicken, for instance – it's Cantonese food which has come to epitomize its principles. With the majority of Chinese emigrants leaving through Guangzhou, it's also the most familiar to overseas visitors, though peruse a menu here and you'll soon realize that most dishes served abroad as "Cantonese" would be unrecognizable to a local resident.

Spoiled by good soil and a year-round growing season, the Cantonese demand absolutely **fresh ingredients** whether cooking at home or dining out. To prove the quality of their product, restaurants keep their ingredients alive and kicking in cages, tanks or buckets at the front of the restaurant for diners to select themselves. Westerners can be repulsed by the collection of live dogs, chickens, palm civets (protected) and snakes outside some Guangdong establishments, and even other Chinese comment that the Cantonese will eat anything with legs that isn't a piece of furniture, and anything with wings that isn't an aeroplane. The cooking itself concentrates on the natural aspects of the food, designed to keep **textures** distinct and **flavours** as close to the original as possible, using a minimum amount of mild and complimentary seasonings to prevent dishes from being bland. **Fast stir-frying** in a wok is the best known of these procedures, but **roasting** and **slow-simmering** in soy sauce and wine are also used as appropriate to tease out the essential characteristics of the food.

No full meal is really complete without a simple plate of rich green and slightly bitter **choisam**, Chinese rape, blanched and lightly dressed with oyster sauce. Also famous is **fish and seafood**, often simply steamed with ginger and spring onions, and nobody cooks **fowl** better than the Cantonese, always juicy and flavoursome whether served crisp-skinned and roasted or fragrantly casseroled. Guangzhou's citizens are also compulsive snackers, and outside canteens you'll see roast meats, such as strips of *cha shao* pork, waiting to be cut up and served with rice for a light lunch, or burners stacked with **claypots**, a one-person dish of steamed rice typically served in the cooking vessel with vegetables and slices of sweet *lap cheung* sausage. **Cake shops** selling heavy Chinese pastries and filled buns are found everywhere across the region. Some items like **custard tartlets** are derived from foreign sources, while roast pork buns and flaky-skinned **mooncakes** stuffed with sweet lotus seed paste are of domestic origin.

Perhaps it's this delight in little delicacies which led to the Chinese tradition of **dim sum** really blossoming in Guangdong, where it's known as **yum cha**. Here it has become an elaborate form of breakfast most popular on Sundays, when entire households pack out restaurants. *Yum cha* basically means "with tea", and the term *dim sum* is derived from a Chinese proverb suggesting that you should "order dishes by inclination", both summing up the procedure. Packed inside bamboo steamers or displayed on plates, little dishes of fried, boiled and steamed snacks are wheeled around the restaurant on trolleys, which you stop for inspection as they pass your table. On being seated you're given a pot of tea which is constantly topped up, and a card which is marked for each dish you select and later surrendered to the cashier. Try rice porridge congee (here called *juk*), spring rolls, buns, cakes and plates of thinly sliced roast meats, and small servings of restaurant dishes like spareribs, mince-stuffed capsicum, or squid with black beans. Save most room, however, for the myriad types of little fried and steamed **dumplings** which are the hallmark of a *dim sum* meal, such as *har gau*, juicy minced prawns wrapped in transparent rice-flour skins, and *shao mai*, a generic name for a host of delicately flavoured, open-topped packets.

Yangjiang Lu; local lychees are so good that the emperors once had them shipped direct to Beijing. Guangzhou is also known for its **ice cream**, with some of the best sold in cones on the first floor of the *Fu Cheng* restaurant, at the south end of Renmin Lu.

Some canteens open as early as 5am and *dim sum* is usually served 7–10am, later on Sundays or if the restuarant has a particularly good reputation. Lunch is on offer 11am–2pm, and dinner 5–10pm, though most people eat early rather than late.

DOWNTOWN

Caigenxiang, 167 Zhongshan Lu. Strict vegetarian restaurant (there's even a large Buddha statue in the lobby), with low prices. It's extremely good – the gluten and beancurd "roast pork" is perfect from the taste to the texture – though the meat imitations are not as fine as the "fish" or pure vegetable dishes.

Five Rams, southeast corner of the Renmin Lu–Zhongshan Lu crossroads. The city's biggest Muslim restaurant, with the menu touting some strange items such as T-bone steaks, satays and Portuguese chicken. Also good local-style hotpots, roast duck, lemon chicken and spicy lamb, with a cheaper canteen downstairs. Always fills up by late afternoon. Inexpensive to moderately priced.

Guangzhou, corner of Wenchang Nan Lu and Xiajiu Lu (☎8862285). The oldest, busiest and most famous restaurant in the city, with entrance calligraphy by the Qing emperor Kangxi and a neon roof sign flashing "Food in Canton". The menu is massive and worth saving up for, and you won't find better fragrant oil chicken or crisp-skinned pork anywhere. There are three floors, prices increasing with each level.

Lian Xianglou, 67 Dishifu Lu. Comfortable, mid-range place skilled at preparing duck fried with lotus flowers.

Panxi, Liwan Park (☎8815955). Situated on the western edge of the city, take bus #71 from the western end of Liuersan Lu, or #74 from Dongfeng Xi Lu. A tea house of poor repute in the 1940s, now serving the finest *dim sum* selection in the city, and some delicious afternoon fare such as hibiscus crab slices.

Ronghua Jiulou, Longjin Dong Lu. One of several typical low-range Cantonese restaurants in this street, with a cheap dumpling house on the first floor. No English menu, but they try hard to help out.

THE WATERFRONT, SHAMIAN ISLAND AND SOUTH OF THE RIVER

Datong, 63 Yanjiang Xi Lu (☎8888447). This nine-storeyed riverview restaurant is the best place in Guangzhou to enjoy a noisy, crowded *dim sum* session; they also pride themselves on their roast suckling pig. Window seats are in high demand, so arrive very early.

Flourishing Court, Changdi Lu. The most reasonably priced of the street's upmarket seafood restaurants, though specialities like shark's fin soup are still hideously expensive. The one English menu may take staff some time to locate. Fried scallops in taro, steamed river fish with black beans, and roast meats are all good.

Kiu Mei, Shamian Island, near the *Shengli Hotel*. There are various sections here: a suave, always busy restuarant on the main street with excellent fish and unexciting stir-fries, and a lower-profile claypot and game hall around the corner. Mid-range prices.

Li Qin, Shamian Island, next to Kiu Mei. Cheap diner catering to Western budget travellers with tables spilling out on to the pavement. Particularly good spareribs in black bean sauce, and – if you've an asbestos mouth – large green chillis stuffed with pork.

Nanfang, Zhe Nan Lu, north off Liuersan Lu. Look for the long red frontage covered with gold characters, and tanks in the window. Ever popular mid-range fish restaurant, divided into a noisy cheaper canteen and (slightly) calmer dining room.

Nanyuan, 142 Qianjin Lu, south of the river (☎8448380). Possibly the best restaurant in Guangzhou; cheapish *dim sum* until about 10am, then it transforms into an upmarket establishment. Superb stewed Chaozhou-style goose, Maotai chicken and fish with pine nuts. Bus #35 from Haizhu Square on Yanjiang Zhong Lu.

She Canguan, 43 Jianglan Lu. Guangzhou's famous snake restaurant, serving a range of dishes from different parts of the serpentine anatomy. Come in a group and try a selection, but it's probably worth avoiding the tourists' highlight of having the snake peeled alive at the table.

Sheng Ji, Changdi Lu, opposite the main *Bank of China* building. The most extravagant seafood restaurant in town, with a Japanese sashimi chef downstairs and imported rarities like moray eels and maori wrasse in the huge front tank. If you can't afford the prices here, smaller places nearby have less pretentious fishy dishes.

Yangsheng, southern end of Renmin Lu, and opposite the lesser *Bank of China* on Changdi Lu. Two in a chain of tea houses, easily identifiable by their open frontages revealing smart, dark decor and huge brass urns of medicinal brews sold by the bowlful. The name means "Health Preserving", and the buffet-style food is clean and fresh – try steamed bitter gourd stuffed with mince, or sauteed tofu.

Yan Yan, Xihao Er Lu. Long-running favourite for reasonably priced regional fare, including some nice treats such as shrimp balls simmered with straw mushrooms, and chicken with cloud ear fungus. Throughout the day they also sell a broad range of take-away *dim sum* dumplings outside.

Shopping

Guangzhou's **shopping** ethos is very much towards the practical side of things, but while it might not be the best place in the country to pick up a bargain piece of art, it's fun to join the masses and see what they're buying. **Liwan Plaza** is a spanking new shopping complex, about a kilometre north of Shamian Island between Changshou Lu and Xiajiu Lu on the southwest side of town, no different really from others across the city. But the streets around here are interesting, full of stalls and markets selling cheapish clothes and household items, with a couple of places specializing in stylish-looking but very cheap watches. Over to the east, **Beijing Lu** is in the trendier side of town, with all kinds of department stores lined up between the river and Zhongshan Lu. If you can't find what you want in either of these places, try the **Nanfang Department Store** on Liuersan Lu, across from the Cultural Park, for everything from clothing to toiletries.

For functional memorabilia, the streets running east off the southern end of Renmin Lu might give you some ideas. Yide Lu has several huge wholesale warehouses stocking **dried foods** and **toys** – action figures from Chinese legends, rockets and all things that rattle and buzz. Other shops in the area deal in home decorations, such as colourful tiling or jigsawed decorative wooden dragons and phoenixes, and at New Year you can buy those red and gold good luck posters put up outside businesses and homes.

For out-and-out tourist souvenirs, head first to the *White Swan Hotel* on Shamian Island. Their ethnic batiks and clothing, carved wooden screens and jade monstrosities are well worth a look, if only to make you realize what a good deal you're getting when you buy elsewhere – such as the shops in the vicinity of the *Shamian Island Hostel*, just outside on Shamian 4 Jie. *Guangzhou Fine Arts* on Changdi Lu has a relatively small selection of authenticated antiques, jade, lacquerwork, scrolls, chops and cloisonné artefacts, identical to what you'll find in the *Yue Hua* stores in Hong Kong, but half the price. Finally, the *Antiques and Handicrafts Market*, in an alleyway north off Liuersan Lu down towards the Cultural Park (look for an English sign), often has some interesting curios, from Little Red Books to fossils and "old" trinkets and coins.

Listings

Airlines *CAAC/China Southern Airlines*, 181 Huanshi Dong Lu, two doors east of the North train station (☎6662969 or 6661803; unlikely to be English speakers available). *Garuda* (Mon–Fri 9am–12.30pm & 1.30–5pm, Sat 9am–12.30pm; ☎3325424, fax 3325481); *Singapore Airlines* (Mon–Fri 9am–noon & 1–5pm, Sat 9am–noon); and *Thai International* (Mon–Fri 9am–5pm, Sat 9am–12.30pm) all have offices at the *Garden Hotel*, Huanshi Dong Lu.

Banks and exchange The two major branches of the *Bank of China* are in the south of the city on Changdi Lu and on Shamian Dadao, Shamian Island (both open for currency exchange Mon–Fri 9–11.30am & 1.30–5pm). Counters at the *Liuhua*, *China* and *Garden* hotels will also change currency for non-residents; the *White Swan* will not.

Bike rental If your hotel can't provide anything, there's a good place opposite the *Guangzhou Youth Hostel* on Shamian Island with rates from ¥10 a day.

Bookshops The *Foreign Language Bookstore*, Beijing Lu, has an unexciting range of English literature, magazines and translated Chinese classics. Hotels are better: the *White Swan* has a good but expensive selection of everything, from potboilers to coffee-table works and contemporary Chinese fiction paperbacks; or try the random assortment at the far cheaper *Dongfang*, and the *China* or *Garden* for international papers and news magazines.

Cinemas The *Nanguan* and *Yonghan* on Beijing Lu show a range of imported and domestic celluloid each week. The latest Hong Kong blockbusters are shown at the screen next to the *Yan Yan* restaurant on Xihao Er Lu. Seats cost ¥10–20.

Consulates and embassies *Japanese Consulate General*, *Garden Hotel*, Huanshi Dong Lu (Mon–Fri 9am–12.30pm & 2–5.30pm); *Polish Embassy*, Shamian Dadao, western end of Shamian Island (Mon–Fri 9am–noon & 2–4pm); *US Consulate General*, Shamian Nan Jie, Shamian Island (visa department Tues–Fri 8.30–11am only); *US Consulate General Information Office*, *Garden Hotel*, Huanshi Dong Lu (Mon–Fri 8.30am–12.30pm & 1.30–5.30pm).

English corner There are probably several of these in Guangzhou: one is held at 9am on Sundays in the grounds of the library on Zhongshan Lu, next door to the former Peasant Movement Training Institute.

Interpreters The major hotels can organize interpreters for around ¥250 per day – you're also expected to cover all additional incidental costs such as meals and transport.

Hospitals and health centres The main hospital catering to foreigners is the City No.1 Hospital on Renmin Bei Lu (☎3333090); the Zhongshan Medical College at 58 Zhongshan Er Lu (☎8778223) is also recommended. Guangzhou's largest traditional medicine institute is the Herbal College in the Sanyuan Li district, north of the train station (☎6661912). For vaccinations, try the *International Traveller Health Centre* on Shamian Dadao, central Shamian Island (Mon–Fri 8–11.30am & 2–4pm).

Pharmacies *Jian Min*, Beijing Lu, at the crossroads just north of the *Foreign Language Bookstore*, is full of prescription drugs and traditional medicines in modern, comfortably ordinary surroundings. Similar and equally helpful is *Youbing Yi Yao*, opposite and just north of the Cultural Park entrance on Renmin Lu. The smaller *Cai Zhi Lin*, near the *Yan Yan* restaurant on Xihao Er Lu, stays open daily until 9pm.

PSB "Section of Aliens' Administration of Guangzhou Municipal PSB", Jiefang Bei Lu (Mon–Fri 8–11.30am & 2.30–5pm, Sat 8–11.30am; ☎3331060). This is the place to go for all police dealings, from visa extensions to reporting theft.

Post and telecommunications Guangzhou's GPO (daily 7am–7pm), with IDD telephones, parcel post and post restante is on the western side of the square outside the North train station. For stamps, letters and more phones, there's another large branch on Zhongshan Lu, about 200m east of Renmin Lu (daily 8am–5pm); and for mailing large overseas parcels only there's a depot on Liuersan Lu (daily 8am–5pm), across from the Cultural Park entrance. Shamian Island's post office counter is open 8am–5pm for stamps, envelopes and deliveries. Just about all hotels catering to foreigners also have postal services and international call facilities – and most will let non-guests use them – though there are surprisingly few public phone booths around the city.

Travel agents Generally, hotel travel desks (particularly at the *Garden* and *China* hotels) are the best places for individuals to get information, arrange organized tours and make transport reservations. The computerized office outside the *White Swan* is good solely for confirming plane tickets and booking transport to Beijing, Shanghai and Hong Kong. *CITS* has a huge office immediately east of the North train station square on Huanshi Dong Lu (☎6666271, fax 6678048), but their attitude is summed up by the lengthy list on their door outlining all the things that they can't do for you. They are definitely not there to help individual travellers, so don't waste time visiting them for anything except major tour bookings.

The Pearl River Delta

The **Pearl River Delta** initially seems entirely a product of the modern age, dominated by industrial complexes and the glossy, high-profile cities of **Shenzhen**, east on the crossing to Hong Kong, and westerly **Zhuhai**, on the Macau border. Back in the 1980s these were marvels of Deng Xiaoping's reforms, rigidly contained **Special Economic Zones** whose officially sanctioned free-market activities were anathema to Communist ideologies. Their incredible success inspired an invasion of the delta by foreign and domestic companies, obscuring an economic history dating back to the time of Song engineers who constructed irrigation canals through the delta's **five counties** – Nanhai, Panyu, Shunde, Dongguan and Zhongshan. From the Ming dynasty, local crafts and surplus food were exported across Guangdong, artisans flourished and funded elaborate guild temples, while gentlemen of leisure built gardens in which to wander and write poetry.

Today, it's all too easy to hop on high-speed transport and cut through the delta in a couple of hours, seeing little more than the unattractive urban mantle which surrounds the highways. But spend a little longer on your journey or dip into the region on short trips from Guangzhou, and there's a good deal to discover about China here, especially in the way that everything looks hastily built and temporary – development is clearly happening too fast for any unified planning. The past survives too. Don't miss the splendid **Ancestral Temple** at **Foshan**, or **Lianhua Shan**, an intriguingly landscaped

---

THE PEARL RIVER DELTA

Cuiheng	翠亨村	*cùihēng cūn*
Sun Yatsen's Residence	孙中山故居	*sūn zhōngshān gùjū*
Dongguan	东莞	*dōng guǎn*
Keyuan	可园	*kěyuán*
Duyuan	杜阮	*dù ruǎn*
Foshan	佛山	*fóshān*
Ancestral Temple	祖庙	*zǔmiào*
Lianhua Market	莲花市场	*lián huā shìchǎng*
ACCOMMODATION		
Overseas Chinese	华侨大厦	*huáqiáo dàshà*
Pearl River	珠江大酒店	*zhūjiāng dàjiǔdiàn*
Rotating Palace	旋宫酒店	*xuángōng jiǔdiàn*
Humen	虎门	*hǔmén*
Jiangmen	江门	*jiāngmén*
Nancun	南村	*nán cūn*
Yuying Shanfang	余英山房	*yúyīng shāngfáng*
Panyu	番禺	*pānyú*
Lianhua Shan	莲花山	*liánhuā shān*
Shajiao	沙角	*shājiǎo*
Lin Zexu Park	林则徐公园	*līn zéxú gōngyuán*
Shenzhen	深圳	*shēnzhèn*
Folk Culture Village	民俗文化村	*mínsú wénhuàcūn*
Litchi Park	荔枝公园	*lìzhī gōngyuán*

ancient quarry. Historians can also visit **Humen**, where the destruction of British opium in 1839 ignited the first Opium War, and **Cuiheng**, home village of China's revered revolutionary elder statesman, **Sun Yatsen**.

The delta has China's highest density of expressways, covered by an equal abundance of short-range minibuses connecting every town, whose habit of constantly accelerating and decelerating tests the strongest of stomachs. Less convenient, if more comfortable, are the limited number of ferries and, along the east side of the delta, the train line linking Guangzhou and Hong Kong.

East to Shenzhen: Dongguan and Humen

It's 175km from Guangzhou to Shenzhen, an easy trip either along the coastal **Guangshen Expressway** from the Liuhua or long-distance bus stations, or farther inland on the slow **local train** from Guangzhou's East station (the Kowloon Express passes through without stopping). An hour out of Guangzhou on the expressway, **DONGGUAN** is the administrative seat of the delta's most productive county, its factories churning out textiles, electronic components and **pirated computer software** – an industry which, controlled as it is by the military, Beijing has had limited success in suppressing despite US threats of major trade sanctions. You might have to stop here to change buses for Humen, and could take the time to have a look at **Keyuan** (8am–4pm; ¥4), once one of Guangdong's "Four Famous Gardens". Walk north from

Shekou	蛇口	*shékǒu*
Splendid China	锦绣中华	*jǐnxiù zhōnghuá*
ACCOMMODATION		
Airlines	航空大酒店	*hángkōng dàjiǔdiàn*
Dongnan	东南大酒店	*dōngnán dàjiǔdiàn*
Dragon	港龙大酒店	*gǎnglóng dàjiǔdiàn*
Far East	远东酒店	*yuǎndōng jiǔdiàn*
Landmark	深圳富苑酒店	*shēnzhèn fùyuàn jiǔdiàn*
Nanyang	南洋大酒店	*nányáng dàjiǔdiàn*
Shunde	顺德	*shùndé*
Qinghui Yuan	清晖园	*qīnghuì yuán*
Yuan Lin	园林宾馆	*yuánlín bīnguǎn*
Xinhui	薪会	*xīnhuì*
Little Birds' Paradise	小鸟天堂	*xiǎoniǎo tiāntáng*
Xiqiao	西樵	*xīqiáo*
Zhongshan	中山	*zhōngshān*
Zhuhai	珠海	*zhūhǎi*
Gongbei	拱北	*gǒngběi*
Jida	吉大	*jídà*
Xiangzhou	香州	*xiāngzhōu*
ACCOMMODATION		
Zhuhai Holiday Village	珠海度假村	*zhūhǎi dùjiàcūn*
Lianhua Dasha	莲花大厦	*liánhuā dàshà*
Jiuzhou Binguen	九州宾馆	*jiǔzhōu bīnguǎn*
Yuehai Jiudian	粤海酒店	*yuèhǎi jiǔdiàn*

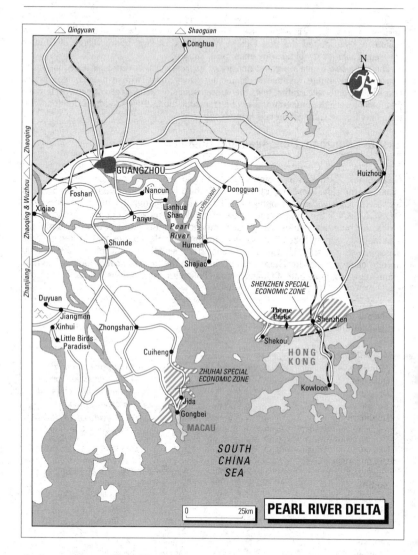

the **bus station** up Wantai Dadao for 250m, turn west along Keyuan Nan Lu, and it's about 1km away across the river. Laid out for the Qing minister, **Zhang Jingxiu**, Keyuan puts its very limited space to superb use, cramming an unlikely number of passages, rooms, pavilions and devious staircases inside its walls, all built in distinctive, pale blue bricks. There are a few flowerbeds and trees, but Keyuan's most striking aspect is the way it shuts out the rest of the city at ground level – though Dongguan's motorways are only too obvious from the upper storey of the main **Yaoshi Pavilion**.

Humen and Shajiao

Minibuses from Dongguang's Wantai Dadao can take you 25km southwest to **HUMEN** (pronounced "Fumen" locally), a place famous for its role in the nineteenth-century **Opium Wars**. Other transport drops you 5km short on the Guangshen Expressway, where shuttle buses wait to carry you into town. Humen is Dongguan's port, and there's also a **daily ferry** here from the Customs House wharf on Yanjiang Lu in Guangzhou, which docks 4km south of Humen's centre at **SHAJIAO**.

In 1839, after a six-week siege of the "Foreign Factories" in Guangzhou, the British finally handed over a whopping 1200 tonnes of **opium** to **Lin Zexu**, the virtuous Qing official charged by the government to rid the country of the imported drug. Lin brought it all to Humen, mixed it with quicklime, and dumped it in two 45-metre pits on the beach at Shajiao; after three weeks the remains were flushed out to sea. Incensed, the British massacred the Chinese garrisons at Humen and on nearby **Weiyun Island**, and attacked Guangzhou. Lin got the blame and was exiled to the harsh frontier province of Xinjiang, only to be replaced by the abysmally incompetent **Yi Shan**, a nephew of the emperor, later a signatory to the humiliating Treaty of Nanking.

These events are recounted in Chinese documents and heroic sculptures at the **Lin Zexu Park Museum** on Jiefang Lu (daily 9am–4pm; ¥5), a twenty-minute walk between the skyscrapers northwest of Humen's bus station. It's more rewarding, however, to catch a minibus to Shajiao where the opium pits remain, along with a fortress, **Shajio Paotai** (daily 9am–5pm; ¥8). The whole place is thick with poinsettias, banyans and butterflies, all making for a nice couple of hours on the beach.

Shenzhen

If **SHENZHEN** had been around in classical times, poets would doubtless have compared its gleaming downtown towers to mountain peaks, each rising higher than the other. Incredibly, in 1979 this metropolis was a simple rural hamlet and train station on the Hong Kong border called **Baoan**, with the first office foundations yet to be dug in its alluvial plains. Within six years, delegations from all over China were pouring in to learn how to remodel their own businesses, cities and provinces on Shenzhen's incentives-based economy. By 1990 the city had four harbours and its manufacturing industries alone were turning over two billion US dollars a year, necessitating the construction of a nuclear power station to deal with local energy needs. Shenzhen may not have been the cause of capitalism in the People's Republic, but it was a glorious piece of propaganda for those who promoted its virtues, and almost two decades later the city remains a model for how the rest of the country would look if it too had been built from scratch with generous foreign investment.

The City

Although Shenzhen is all very impressive, after a quick sniff around there's little reason to stay any longer than it takes to organize your next move into or out of the mainland. For a good glimpse of the city's shoppers, tourists, beggars and businessmen, spend an hour strolling along Renmin Lu, which runs northeast from the train station and **Lo Wu border crossing** through the centre. The **International Trade Centre** is a three-storey block on the corner of Jiabin Lu, full of people browsing through stocks of upmarket Chinese watches and perfume. Push on over Jiefang Lu and you're in the tangle of narrow lanes which formed **the old town of Baoan**, now a downmarket selection of stalls selling cheap clothes, shoes and gadgets. There's a historic monument of sorts here in a squat, blue-roofed diner on Qingyuan Lu – China's original *McDonald's* restaurant.

For a shot of culture, walk or catch bus #4 for 1.5km west from the centre along Shennan Zhong Lu to the **museum** (Tues–Fri 9am–4pm; ¥5), on the south side of **Litchi Park**. Photos and models chart Shenzhen's meteoric rise, the park has a nice lake and there's a very modern **opera house** here too, worth checking out for occasional performances of Chinese theatre. More reliably, hop on bus #204 from Jianshe Lu for the thirty-minute ride west to Shenzhen's three very professional **theme parks**, next to each other on the Guangshen Expressway (daily 8am–5.30pm; ¥90–110 for each park with various joint entry discounts) – look for a miniaturized Golden Gate Bridge spanning the road. Among limitless souvenir stalls, **Splendid China** and **Window on the World** are a collection of scale models of famous monuments such as the Great Wall and Eiffel Tower, while the **Folk Culture Village** is an enjoyably touristy introduction to the nation's ethnic groups – there are yurts, pavilions, huts, archways, rock paintings, and mechanical goats, with colourful troupes performing different national dances every thirty minutes.

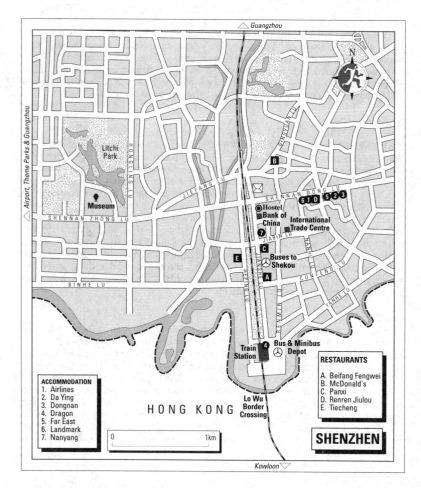

SHENZHEN

Practicalities

A five-kilometre-wide semicircle immediately north of the Hong Kong border, Shenzhen is evenly bisected by the **rail line** which descends straight down Jianshe Lu and over the crossing, with the downtown area occupying the two square kilometres east of the rail line, and between Jiefang Lu and the border.

Shenzhen's **international airport** is 20km west, with a shuttle bus (¥15) operating between here and the *Airlines Hotel* on Shennan Dong Lu. The **port** lies 15km west at **Shekou**, where ferries from Macau, Zhuhai and Hong Kong pull in throughout the day, and is served thrice hourly by the #204 bus to Jianshe Lu. Shenzen's **train station** is in a vast square, right on the Hong Kong border at the southern end of Jianshe Lu, with the **ticket office** upstairs. The last train to Guangzhou East station is at 7.15pm. You'll also wind up here if you caught the MTR to the Hong Kong side and walked across into Shenzhen, or arrived by **minibus** from elsewhere in the delta. **Long-distance buses**, however, arrive a couple of kilometres to the northeast on Dongmen Lu, and the #1 bus from here runs south through the centre to the train station square. Taxis and minibuses roam all arrival points, and the city has an enviably efficient bus service. There are **banks** at the airport, ferry terminal and some hotels, with Jianshe Lu's suitably oversized *Bank of China* open Monday to Friday 9am–5pm.

The cheapest places to **eat** are in the streets immediately north of Jiefang Lu, where Chinese canteens can fill you up with good dumplings, soups and stir-fries for around ¥15 per person. There are dozens of smarter options all through the centre, such as inexpensive casseroles at *Renren Jiulou*, east of the *Airlines Hotel* on Shennan Dong Lu; mantis shrimps, stonefish and other seafood at the *Panxi*, on the corner of Jianshe Lu and Jiabin Lu; fine northern cooking and an ornate red and gold exterior at the *Beifang Fengwei*, farther down Jianshe Lu; and moderately priced snake, cat and wildfowl delights at the *Tiecheng*, west of the tracks on Heping Lu. The **hotels** have good restaurants, too, along with karaoke bars, interpreters and postal services.

Moving on, the Hong Kong border is open daily 7am–9pm. It's uncertain how the former colony's return to China will affect Shenzhen's border crossing, though if Beijing keeps its promise of "One Country, Two Systems", it's likely that the physical barrier and other restrictions will stay in place for the time being. Larger hotels such as the *Airlines, Dragon, Far East* and *Landmark* can all make transport reservations.

ACCOMMODATION

Airlines, Shennan Dong Lu (☎0755/2237999, fax 2237866). Ordinary rooms, with just enough space to be comfortable. Good seafood restaurant and expensive coffee shop. The *CAAC* office here can book all flights. ⑥.

Da Ying, Shennan Dong Lu (☎0755/2258104 ext 3201). Grubby and needs a facelift, but the staff are friendly, there are triples, doubles and singles available and it's certainly cheap for Shenzhen. ⑤.

Dongnan, Shennan Dong Lu (☎0755/2288688, fax 2291103). A reasonably priced, low-frills hotel with the usual complement of places to eat and drink. ⑤.

Dragon, at the train station, Jianshe Lu (☎0755/2329228, fax 2334585). Rooms are smartly furnished, but a little small, probably to accommodate the huge Cantonese restaurant (good *dim sum*). ⑦.

Far East, Shennan Dong Lu (☎0755/2205369, fax 2200239). Well-organized business venue advertising its rooms, billiard hall, Sichuanese restaurant and dance hall as "environmentally friendly". ⑦.

Hostel, Jianshe Lu. Just north of the *Bank of China*, this is a neat little place, but they're not sure if foreigners are allowed to stay – try anyway. Doubles and singles on offer. ④.

Landmark, Nanhu Lu, corner of Shennan Dong Lu (☎0755/2172288, fax 2290473). Rightly claims to be the best hotel in Shenzhen, a beautifully furnished neo-colonial interior, with "Banquet Halls", instead of restaurants. ⑨.

Nanyang, Jianshe Lu (☎0755/2224968, fax 2238927). Tidy, decent-sized rooms, all with balcony views of Shenzhen's skyline. ⑥.

The western delta: Foshan

Due to the fact that it isn't in a direct line between Hong Kong and Guangzhou, and because the land is fragmented by streams, inlets and canals, the **western side of the Pearl River Delta** is less completely developed than its counterpart across the river, and there are more nooks and crannies to explore. There's no single expressway covering the 155km between Guangzhou and Zhuhai, rather a mesh of roads which you can follow more or less directly south between sights. Buses to **Shunde**, **Jiangmen** and **Zhuhai** leave from the Liuhua and long-distance bus stations in Guangzhou (see the accounts below for further transport details).

Twenty-five kilometres southwest of Guangzhou and today virtually a satelite suburb of the city, historically **FOSHAN** (Buddha's Hill) is very much a town in its own right, with a recorded history dating back to 628 AD when the town won its name after the excavation of three statues, earlier enshrined and forgotten by a wandering monk. Along with the nearby village of **Shiwan**, Foshan became famous for its ceramics, silk, metalwork and woodcarving – a reputation it still enjoys – and the splendour of its **temples**, two of which survive on **Zumiao Lu**, a kilometre-long street shaded by office buildings and set in the heart of what was once the old town centre. Towards the northern end is **Renshou Si** (Benevolent Longevity Temple), a former Ming monastery whose southern wing, graced by a short seven-storey pagoda, is still consecrated. The rest has been cleaned out and turned into the **Foshan Folk Arts Studio**, a good place to look for souvenir papier-mâché masks, chops, **paper cuts** – which you can watch being cut by hand – and superb multicoloured screenprints based on papercut designs. At New Year, the side halls are also full of giant dragons, fish and phoenixes constructed from wire and coloured crepe paper for festival celebrations.

Foshan's architectural masterpiece, however, is Zu Miao, the **Ancestral Temple** (daily 8.30am–4.30pm; ¥10), down at the southern end of Zumiao Lu. Founded in 1080 as a metallurgist's guild temple, the complex was progressively expanded until the mid-Qing, and today its buildings comprise a museum of classic temple architecture. Ahead and to the left of the entrance is an elevated garden fronted by some locally made Opium War **cannons** – sadly for the Chinese, poor casting techniques and a lack of rifling made these innacurate and liable to explode. Nearby stand some magnificent glazed **roof tile** assemblies of frolicking lions and characters from local tales, all made in Shiwan for temple restorations in the 1830s. Walk through the gate here and the temple's **main hall** is on the left, its interior completely filled by massive, minutely carved wooden screens, oversized guardian gods leaning threateningly out from the walls, metal armour, weapons and incense burners. Less ostentatious is the wooden roof, ingeniously constructed from mortice and tenon joints. At the back stands a three-tonne **statue of Beidi**, God of the North, who in local lore controlled low-lying Guangdong's flood-prone waters – hence this shrine to snare his good will. At Foshan, he became even more popular when his presence apparently prevented the Ming rebel Huang Xiaoyang from capturing the city.

Opposite the hall are a pond and some elaborate masonry forming the **Lingying archway**, the only one of its kind outside Shexian in Anhui Province (see p.441). Foshan is considered the birthplace of **Cantonese Opera**, and past the archway you'll find the highly decorative **Wanfu stage**, built in 1685 for autumnal opera performances given to thank the Divine Emperor for his bountiful harvests.

Lianhua Market and beyond

A short walk northeast of the temple along Lianhua Lu, **Lianhua Market** is also worth a look, if only to confirm that Qingping in Guangzhou is not unique – at least by local standards. Around the area are some once grand old houses, now very tatty and doubtless due for demolition, and the open-fronted shops along Lianhua Lu look nicely dated and sell an eclectic assortment of wares: wooden cake moulds, padded silk jackets and glossy new porcelain statuettes.

On from Foshan, a popular weekend watering hole for local residents is **Xiqiao Shan**, just 12km southwest. The seventy-odd peaks rise to about 300m, pitted with crags and waterfalls, and exude a calm beauty which makes this a good place to unwind from city tensions. Paths start from **XIQIAO** township at the northern foot of the hills. Either catch a bus from Foshan, or get there direct from the Foshan departure points in Guangzhou. Farther afield, there's ample transport from Foshan down to Jiangmen and Zhuhai, and less frequent services north to Qingyuan and west to Zhaoqing.

Practicalities

There are hourly minibuses from Guangzhou to Foshan from the bus station at the western end of Zhongshan Lu, and several daily from the Liuhua bus station on Huanshi Xi Lu. On arrival, Fenjiang Bei Lu forms the western boundary of the old town, running south for about 2km from the **train station**, over a canal, past the efficient **long-distance bus station** and through to where the highrises, which constitute Foshan's business centre, cluster around a broad roundabout. **Minibuses** deposit you either outside the train station, or just east of the roundabout on Jianxin Lu. From the latter, walk 50m east and you're at the bottom end of Zumiao Lu, five minutes from the Ancestral Temple. To reach Zumiao Lu from the stations, head down Fenjiang Bei Lu for about 700m, then east along tree-lined Qinren Lu. A couple of minutes brings you to the *Bank of China* (Mon–Fri 9–11.30am & 1–5pm), with Lianhua Lu and the market straight ahead, and Zumiao Lu running south.

Foshan's **accommodation** prospects include the tidy and quiet *Artkins Hotel* next to the long-distance bus station (☎0757/2230000; ⑤); the swish *Overseas Chinese Hotel* (☎0757/2223828, fax 2227702; ⑦) across from Renshou Si on Zumiao Lu; and the rather more average *Pearl River Hotel* (☎0757/2287512, fax 2292263; ⑥) and *Rotating Palace Hotel* (☎/fax 0757/2285622; ⑦), opposite each other at the north end of Zumiao Lu. All have **restaurants** and bars, with some cheaper snack stalls up around the bus and train stations.

Lianhua Shan and Yuyin Shanfang

A couple of attractive sights surround the town of **PANYU**, about 50km east of Foshan. It's roughly the same distance by road from Guangzhou, where transport leaves from the city's **Panyu bus station**, south of the river off Gongye Lu. There's also a morning **ferry** to Lianhua Shan from the Customs House wharf on Yanjiang Lu.

Overlooking the Pearl River 15km east of Panyu, **Lianhua Shan** (8am–4pm; ¥10) is an odd phenomenon, a mountain quarried as long ago as the Han dynasty for its red stone, used in the tomb of the Nanyue king, Zhao Mo. After mining it in such a way as to leave a suspiciously deliberate arrangement of crags, pillars and caves, Ming officials planted the whole thing with trees and turned it into a pleasure garden laid with lotus pools, stone paths and pavilions. A fifty-metre-high pagoda was built in 1612, and the Qing emperor Kangxi added a fortress to defend the river. Still a popular excursion from Guangzhou, it's a lovely spot to while away a few hours, though frequently crowded. The comfortable *Lianhua Mountain Villa* (④) at the top has a good **restaurant**, or you can follow the current barbecue craze by buying ingredients in Guangzhou and cooking them on the hotplates provided around the park.

A twenty-kilometre drive north of Panyu is **NANCUN** village and **Yuying Shanfang**, Yu's Dim Mountain Retreat (8am–5pm; ¥5). This was founded in the Qing dynasty by the successful Imperial Examination candidate, **Wu Yantian**, who spent a fortune hiring the biggest names in contemporary landscape gardening and created an artificial mountain, a lake, bamboo clumps, calligraphy walls and an octagonal pavilion. Here Wu sat listening to flocks of cagebirds, and the muted tones of stringed *zheng* and *pipa*, played upstairs in the ladies quarters' (now a tea house). The music has gone, and the former ancestral temple has been converted into a dance hall for wedding receptions, but the gardens remain as a nicely nostalgic tribute to a more refined time.

Shunde

Another Qing garden is one reason to pause in the county town of **SHUNDE** (also known as Daliang Zhen), 50km south of Guangzhou on the most direct route to Zhuhai. The other highlight is the *Qinghui Yuan Restaurant*, revered by the gastronomically inclined as the epitome of classic **Cantonese cooking**. Both are in the grounds of the extraordinarily good-value *Qinghui Yuan Binguan* on Qing Lu (☎0765/2222394, fax 2222515; ④), a twenty-minute walk north from the Jianhai Nan Lu **bus station** – exit the station and follow the canal up to the bridge, turn right along the main road (Huanshan Lu), which soon bears left as Qing Lu. It costs ¥4 to enter the garden, whose osmanthus, mulberry bushes and bamboo are beautifully arranged around square fish ponds, with some of the old buildings now simply refurbished as hotel accommodation. The **restaurant** (7–9am, 11am–2pm & 5–7pm) is fairly expensive and has no set menu, but the dishes are superb, with mild, fresh flavours which have to be taken slowly to be properly appreciated. If the *Qinghui's* hotel is full, try the *Yuan Lin* (☎0765/2222811 or 2225293; ⑤) just north on Qing Lu, a good hotel in itself, but lacking the garden.

After eating, you can walk off your meal in the streets behind the gardens, where the old town centre forms a miniature version of Guangzhou's back lanes, with flagstones, hectic markets and a few century-old houses. The canals are interesting, too, still used by small family-operated barges, each with its own guard dog, kitchen and sleeping quarters.

Jiangmen and around

Halfway between Guangzhou and Zhuhai but slightly off to the west, **JIANGMEN** was formerly a pleasant town on the busy Jiangmen River, birthplace of the Ming poet **Chen Baisha**, and later dressed in cobbled streets and rows of nineteenth-century European-style mansions. Sadly, these have all but vanished, and the city has well and truly sold its soul to the ugliest side of urban development, retaining only its reputation for gymnastic excellence. You'll pass through if you're on the bus between Foshan and Zhuhai; keep your eyes peeled along the way for an English banner across the highway bizarrely proclaiming South China's "Furniture Castle" – a fifteen-kilometre stretch of wholesale warehouses displaying chairs, beds and tables of every possible shape, style and colour along the roadside.

While Jiangmen itself holds little appeal, the surrounding countryside might inspire you to stop off long enough to pick up a local minibus from beside the bus station on Jianshe Lu. There are a few very dilapidated Ming villages in the vicinity, some sporting two-storey towers built early this century by returning Overseas Chinese to parade their riches. About 15km southwest, via the town of **XINHUI**, flocks of cranes and waterfowl roost in the huge sprawl of a five-hundred-year-old fig tree in the middle of the Tianma River, known locally as Xiaoniao Tiantang, the **Little Birds' Paradise**. There are walkways around the tree, and paddle boats for rent. **DUYUAN**, 10km west of Jiangmen, sits at the bottom of **Guifeng Shan**, a nicely formalized mountain offering a day's pleasant hiking between temples, trees and waterfalls on the way up to the windswept **Chishi Crag**.

Zhongshan County: Cuiheng and Sun Yatsen

Almost every settlement in China has a park or road named **Zhongshan**, a tribute to the county which produced the remarkable **Dr Sun Yatsen**, China's first Republican president. There's no need to visit the characterless Zhongshan County Town itself, 100km from Guangzhou, but 30km east of here on the coastal road to Zhuhai is the good doctor's home village of **CUIHENG**, now the site of a **memorial garden** (daily 8.30am–5pm; ¥5) celebrating his life and achievements. Transport from Zhongshan town and from Zhuhai (35km south) sets you down right outside, where there are also a few cheap **places to eat** and buy ice creams.

Along with a banyan tree supposedly brought back from Hawaii and planted by Sun, the grounds incorporate a comprehensive museum of photographs, relics (including the original Nationalist flag) and biographical accounts in English emphasizing the successful aspects of Sun Yatsen's career. There's also the solid, Portuguese-style family home where he lived between 1892 and 1895, "studying, treating patients and discussing national affairs with his friends". Out the back of Sun's home are some rather more typical period buildings belonging to the peasant and landlord classes, restored and furnished with wooden tables and authentic silk tapestries – the main difference between Cuiheng's rich and poor seems to have been the quality and quantity of their possessions. **Moving on**, public transport heads in both directions along the highway until at least 6pm.

SUN YATSEN

Born in 1866, **Sun Yatsen** grew up during a period when China laboured under the humiliation of colonial occupation, a situation justly blamed on the increasingly feeble Manchu (Qing) court. Having spent three years in Hawaii during the 1880s, Sun studied medicine in Guangzhou and Hong Kong, and inspired by that other famous Guangdong revolutionary, Hong Xiuquan (see p.391), he began to involve himself in covert anti-Manchu activities. Back in Hawaii in 1894, he abandoned his previous notions of reforming the imperial system and founded the **Revive China Society** to "Expel the Manchus, restore China to the people and create a federal government." The following year he incited an uprising in Guangzhou under **Lu Haodong**, notable for being the first time that the green Nationalist flag painted with a white, twelve-pointed sun (still used in Taiwan) was flown. But the uprising was quashed, Lu Haodong captured and executed, and Sun fled overseas.

Orbiting between Hong Kong, Japan, Europe and the US, Sun spent the next fifteen years raising money to fund revolts in southern China, and in 1907 his new Alliance Society announced its famous **Three Principles of the People** – Nationalism, Democracy and Livelihood. He was in Colorado when the Manchus finally fell in October 1911, and on returning to China he was made provisional president of the Republic of China on January 1, 1912, but was forced to resign in February in favour of the powerful warlord, **Yuan Shikai**. Yuan established a Republican Party, while Sun's supporters rallied to the Nationalist People's Party – **Guomindang** – led by **Song Jiaoren**. Song was assassinated by Yuan's henchmen following Guomindang successes in the 1913 parliamentary elections, and Sun again fled to Japan. Annulling parliament, Yuan tried to set himself up as emperor but couldn't even control military factions within his own party, who plunged the north into civil war on his death in 1916. Sun, meanwhile, returned to his native Guangdong and established an independent Guomindang government, determined to unite the country eventually. Though unsuccessful, he died in 1925 greatly respected by both the Guomindang and the four-year-old Communist Party for his lifelong efforts to enfranchize the masses.

Zhuhai

ZHUHAI is an umbrella name for the Special Economic Zone encompassing three separate townships immediately north of the Portuguese colony of **Macau** (Aomen): **Gongbei** on the border itself, and **Jida** and **Xiangzhou**, the port and residential districts, 5–10km farther up along the coast. Though full of new offices, immensely wide roads and tasty economic incentives, Zhuhai really hasn't taken off yet, though the whole zone is completely surrounded by an electrified fence to stop smuggling, and you'll need your passport to get through the checkpoints on the way in. The coastline hereabouts is pretty enough on a warm day, but there are no true beaches and, even more so than Shenzhen, the border is the only real reason to be here.

The **ferry port** and ticket office is at **JIDA**, with continual services to Shenzhen 7.50am–6pm, and a half-dozen or so daily departures each to Hong Kong and Macau. Bus #4 runs between here and Gongbei (6.30am–9.30pm) or you can hail a taxi. If you want to

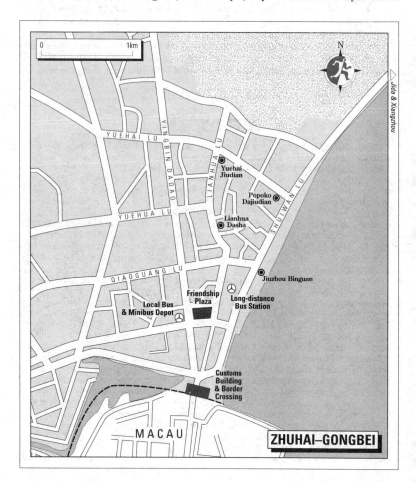

ZHUHAI–GONGBEI

stay nearby, the sole option is 500m up the road at the five-star **Zhuhai Holiday Village** (☎0756/3332038, fax 3332036; ⑨), whose apartments and villas are spread around large grounds overlooking the sea. **GONGBEI** itself has the atmosphere of a new seaside resort town, and is small enough to walk around in an hour. All **minibuses and buses** wind up at one of the three depots within spitting distance of the border crossing. The most interesting area to investigate is immediately north of the crossing along Lianhua Lu, where there's a big produce market under the **Friendship Plaza** near the corner with Youyi Lu and a night market in the stretch north of Qiaoguang Lu selling souvenirs. For **accommodation**, try the *Lianhua Dasha* on Lianhua Lu (④), a cool, clean and fairly quiet budget hotel in Gongbei's market district; the large and good-value *Popoko Dajiudian* on Yuehai Lu (☎0756/8886628, fax 8889992; ⑤); *Jiuzhou Binguan* overlooking the sea on Shuiwan Lu (☎0756/8886851, fax 8885254; ⑥), whose ragged decor is offset by negotiable discounts and set meals included in the room price; and the very upmarket *Yuehai Jiudian* (*Guangdong Hotel*) on Yuehai Dong Lu (☎0756/8888128, fax 8885063; ⑨), whose exterior glass lift offers ear-popping views out over Macau. Of the numerous **places to eat**, a canteen opposite the *Lianhua Dasha* on Lianhua Lu serves excellent **Hakka chicken**, baked in salt and displayed outside wrapped in paper, while the *Huang Tao* restaurant, upstairs at the Friendship Plaza, serves Zhuhai's best *dim sum* every morning.

Moving on, the Macau border is open 7am–9pm, while the bus stations have regular departures for destinations through the delta to Guangzhou.

Shaoguan and around

Up in Guangdong's hilly northern reaches, **SHAOGUAN** lies on the watershed between the Pearl River Valley and the Yangzi basin, guarding the main route through which peoples, armies and culture flowed between central China and the south – there are even remains of the physical road, broad and paved, up near the Jiangxi border. Its strategic position was noted by the nineteenth-century Wesleyan Church, who found the town a useful base for their missions in northern Guangdong, but it also made Shaoguan the target of Japanese saturation bombing during the 1930s, which robbed the town of much extant heritage. Since the 1950s, textile mills and steelworks have ensured a moderate prosperity, if not a pretty skyline, but there's plenty to do in the immediate area. Domestic tourists flock in to visit the Buddhist shrine of **Nanhua Si**, climb **Danxia Shan**, the local formalized sacred mountain, and to go **white-water rafting** down the Wu River. Relics of regional history span prehistoric finds at **Shizi Yan** and a Taiping Uprising site. Shaoguan is also a jumping-off point for a backwoods trip west into Guangxi Province through ethnic Yao and Zhuang territories.

North to Shaoguan

Trains from Guangzhou take a decently brief four hours to cover the 200km to **Shaoguan** up in the north of the province – not an impossible length of time to spend in hard seat. The advantage in heading this way slowly by bus, however, is that it gives you an opportunity to visit **Qingyuan**, a smallish, busy back-road market town on the **Bei River** about 80km north of the capital. Surrounded by countryside thick with rice fields and mudbrick villages, Qingyuan itself is ringed by unprepossessing suburbs given over to grimy manufacturing complexes and poorly built housing estates, though the centre of town is none too bad, if overpoweringly crowded by narrow streets and hordes of pedestrians. Its attraction lies in its position as a departure point for day trips 20km upstream to the poetically isolated, elderly temple complexes of **Feilai and Feixia**, which can be reached only by catching the twice-daily public ferry to Feixia, or by hiring a private boat.

Qingyuan and the temples

Set on the north bank of the Bei River, **QINGYUAN**'s slightly disjointed axes are formed by Beimen Jie, which runs south from the **main bus station** for 500m to Shifeng Zhong Lu which cuts across it at right angles, then continues as Nanmen Jie for another 200m through the central markets and on to the river. Facing the water at the bottom of Nanmen Jie, turn left (east), the **ferry ticket office and docks** for transport to the temples is well concealed down a flight of steps about 50m along on the right – look for the blue plastic gate. There are two scheduled services daily at 7.30am and 8am to **Feixia** (¥25), and one at 12.50pm to **Jiankou** (¥40), a port upstream beyond the temples. On weekends at least, you can also hire **private boats** (about ¥40 per person return) from the dockside to Feixia and Feilai which leave when they have enough people to cover their costs – it's a popular day trip with locals, so if you get here fairly early you shouldn't have to wait too long. The problem with the public ferry is that you'll probably have to miss Feilai as,while there's no problem getting dropped off here, there's no guarantee of being able to find return or onward transport afterwards. Private boats, though more expensive, give you plenty of time to look around both temples. **Moving on** from Qingyuan, there's only one bus a day right through to Shaoguan, and you'll definitely need to buy tickets for this the day before you travel.

For **accommodation**, Qingyuan's bus station hostel (①) is reluctant to take foreigners. The best place to try is about 100m down Beimen Jie at the *Fengyuan Binguan* (look for the English sign; ⑤), a standard Chinese guesthouse set in a quiet courtyard; or, if they're full, the noisier, more expensive *Overseas Chinese Hotel* (⑤) farther along on the corner of Nanmen Jie. Both hotels have formal **restaurants**, with good Cantonese meals available at the *Bubuquan*, opposite the bus station, or in numerous canteens along the main streets. There's also a popular place with outside tables specializing in fish down on the corner of Nanmen Jie and the riverfront.

FEILAI AND FEIXIA

In winter, the Bei River is broad but very shallow and the boats oscillate from bank to bank along the navigable channels. For the first hour or so it's a placid journey past a few brick pagodas, bamboo stands screening off villages and wallowing water buffalo being herded by children. Hills rise up on the right, and then the river bends sharply east into a gorge and past the steps outside the ancient gates of **Feilai Gusi** (¥6), a charmingly positioned Buddhist temple whose ancestry can be traced back 1400 years. Wedged into the steep slopes at the base of Tiger-quelling Hill, the current cramped halls date from the Ming dynasty, and though in a generally poor state of repair manage to look extremely dignified, something that a facelift is gradually enhancing. You'll only need about forty minutes to have a look at the lively ridge tiles and climb up through the thin pine forest to where a modern pavilion offers pretty views of the gorge scenery. If you have time to spare before your boat heads on, the temple gates are a good place to sit and watch the tame cormorants sunbathing on the prows of their owners' tiny sampans, or you can bargain for freshwater mussels and carp with the local women – you'll have a chance to get these cooked for you at Feixia.

Some 3km farther upstream from Feilai at the far end of the gorge, **Feixia Gusi** (¥10) is far more recent and much more extensive in the scale and scope of its buildings. Founded in 1863 and expanded fifty years later during the twilight of the Qing, two entirely self-sufficient Taoist monasteries were built up in the hills in the Feixia and Cangxia grottoes, with hermitages, pavilions and academies adorning the 8km of interlinking, flagstoned paths in between. Chinese visitors initially ignore all this, however, and head straight for the huge collection of **al fresco restaurant shacks** on the riverbank, where they buy and organize the preparation of river food with the numerous, eager wok-wielding cooks – a nice way to have lunch.

SHAOGUAN AND AROUND

Shaoguan	韶关	*sháoguān*
Danxia Shan	丹霞山	*dānxiá shān*
Nanhua Si	南华寺	*nánhuá sì*
Qujiang	曲江	*qǔjiāng*
Renhua	仁化	*rénhuà*
Shizi Yan	狮子岩	*shīzi yán*
Lechang	乐昌	*lèchāng*
Liannan	连南	*liánnán*
Lianzhou	连州	*liánzhōu*
Pingshi	坪石	*píngshí*
Jinji Ling	金鸡岭	*jīnjī lǐng*
Nine Torrents and Eighteen Shoals	九泷十八滩漂流	*jiǔlóng shíbātān piāoliú*
Sanpai	三排	*sānpái*
Qingyuan	清远	*qīngyuǎn*
Feilai Gusi	飞来古寺	*fēilái gǔsì*
Feixia Gusi	飞霞古寺	*fēixiá gǔsì*
Fengyuan Binguan	风苑宾馆	*fēngyuàn bīnguǎn*

Once you've eaten, a couple of hours is plenty of time to have a look around. A broad and not very demanding set of steps runs up from the river front through a pleasant woodland where, after twenty minutes or so, you pass the minute Jinxia and Ligong temples, cross an ornamental bridge, and encounter **Feixia** itself. Hefty surrounding walls and passages connecting halls and courtyards, all built of stone, lend Feixia the atmosphere of a medieval European castle. There's nothing monumental to see – one of the rooms has been turned into a **museum** of holy relics, and you might catch a weekend performance of **traditional temple music** played on bells, gongs and zithers – but the gloom, low ceilings and staircases running off in all directions make it an interesting place to explore. Walk up through the monastery and take any of the tracks heading uphill, which in another ten minutes or so lead to the short **Changtian Pagoda** perched right on the top of the ridges, decorated with mouldings picked out in pastel colours, with views down over Feixia and the treetops. Another small temple next door offers food, drink and basic accommodation (②).

Five minutes' walk east along the main track from Feixia brings you to the similar but smaller complex of **Cangxia**. Restorations began here in 1994, but Cangxia remains in a semi-ruinous state and is apparently uninhabited, though monks hounded out during the 1960s are back in attendance, and many of the statues and shrines are smudged with incense soot. Look for the garden with its fragrant white magnolia tree, an unusual, life-sized statue of Sun Wu Kong, the Monkey God, and some wonderful **frescoes** – an immortal crossing the sea on a fish, storm dragons and two golden pheasants.

Shaoguan

Shaoguan's downtown area fills a south-pointing **peninsula** shaped by the **Zhen River** on the east side and the **Wu River** on the west, which merge at the peninsula's southern tip to form the Bei River. The main street, Fengdu Lu, runs vertically through the centre to leafy Zhongshan Park, crossed by Fengcai Lu at the north end of town, and Jiefang Lu in the south. While there's plenty of activity in the clothing and trinket **markets** which fill the side streets off Fengdu Lu, most of the town is functional and modern, and Shaoguan's sole sight is **Fengcai Ta**, a 1930s reconstruction of the old eastern city gate tower, up along Fengcai Lu – something to note in passing rather than seek out.

Neither **arrival point** is actually on the peninsula, but they're not far away. Immediately to the east, the **train station** is in a huge square overlooking the Zhen River, linked to Jiefang Lu by the Qujiang Bridge, while the quiet **long-distance bus station** is a ten-minute walk over the Wu River on Gongye Dong Lu, which crosses on to the middle of the peninsula via the Wujiang Bridge. **Motor-rickshaws** are the local taxi service, with **minibuses** out to nearby attractions leaving from the vicinity of the train station. Hotels in town can also organize **tours**, or there's the Chinese-speaking *CITS* upstairs at 126 Jiefang Lu, diagonally across from the *Fengdu Yuan Dajiudian*.

Accommodation prospects include *Shaotie Dasha* (③), on the northern side of the train station square, shambolic and undergoing massive rebuilding work; the more upmarket *Post Office Hotel* (⑥) directly opposite, whose karaoke bar makes it a noisy, if more comfortable, option; the good value *Fengdu Yuan Dajiudian* (☎0751/8882888, fax 8881690; ⑤), immediately across the river next to the Qujiang Bridge on Jiefang Lu; and the less animated and dusty *Shaohua Binguan* (☎0751/8881870, fax 8881998; ⑥), farther west down Jiefang Lu near the *Bank of China* (Mon–Fri 9–11.30am & 1–5pm). This branch is a bit baffled by travellers' cheques, but will usually change them.

Shaoguan's **restaurants** are very good indeed and, compared with Guangzhou, offer excellent value. For well-presented, low-key dishes, such as barbecued spare ribs and stir-fries, try the mid-range place next to the *Fengdu Yuan Binguan*. A fine *dim sum* range is served before 10am on weekends upstairs at the *Shaoguan Jiulou*, near the pedestrian overpass on the corner of Jiefang Lu and Xunfeng Lu, while the second floor of the *Dongjiang Fandian* on Fengdu Lu has the best evening meals in town – a whole steamed chicken, pigeon soup, stuffed beancurd casserole and blanched greens costs just ¥80. Nowhere has English menus, but staff are helpful and patient.

Moving on, there's the usual trouble with obtaining train tickets. This is the main line north out of Guangdong and, despite a continuous stream of trains passing through, it's perpetually overcrowded, as is the train station itself. Long-distance buses – heading north into Jiangxi and Hunan, east to Meizhou, south to Guangzhou and west to Lianshan – tend to leave very early on in the day, with the exception of luxury buses to Guangzhou, which depart in the late afternoon from outside the train station.

Nanhua Si, Danxia Shan and Shizi Yan

The huge and picturesque **Nanhua Si** (¥5), the Southern Flower Temple, lies 25km southeast of Shaoguan beyond the town of **Qujiang**, easily reached on minibuses from Shaoguan's train station square – they run whenever full for about ¥10 per person. Founded in 502 AD by the Indian monk Zhiyao Sanzang, the temple became famous through the activities of its sixth patriarch, **Huineng**, who sat in meditation here for 36 years before suddenly reaching enlightenment upon hearing the Diamond Sutra. His successors spread his doctrine of Nanzong Chanfo, or **Chan Buddhism**, throughout China from where it filtered into Japan as **Zen**. Consequently, Nanhua Si is revered by Zen Buddhists throughout the world. The seven halls are gorgeously decorated and in excellent order, but, chock-full of holy relics as they are, it's a bit of an effort to get around them all without your enthusiasm waning. Look for the **bell tower**, in the atrium on the far side of the first hall, whose massive bronze bell was cast in 1167; the room beyond houses a riot of *arhats* and Bodhisattvas cavorting with sea monsters in a sea of papier mâché. Pick of the sculptures here are those of **Ji Gong**, the Song beggar-monk with a tatty pandanus leaf fan who became a sort of Robin Hood to China's poor, and an unidentified fat priest waddling on improbable stilts at the back. A collection of fine **wooden sculptures** and a seventh-century cast-iron statue of a levitating spirit grace another room, dedicated to Guanyin, while in the back of the final hall is a **model of Huineng** – which some maintain was cast from his corpse – who sits

Southwest USA
THE ROUGH GUIDE
Greg Ward

India
THE ROUGH GUIDE
David Abram, Devdan Sen,
Harriet Sharkey and Gareth John Williams

China
THE ROUGH GUIDE

Vietnam
THE ROUGH GUIDE
Jan Dodd and Mark Lewis

Peru
THE ROUGH GUIDE
Dilwyn Jenkins

Paris
THE ROUGH GUIDE
Kate Baillie and Tim Salmon

Spain
THE ROUGH GUIDE
Mark Ellingham and John Fisher

Norway
THE ROUGH GUIDE
Jules Brown and Phil Lee

London
THE ROUGH GUIDE
Rob Humphreys

Mallorca
& Menorca
THE ROUGH GUIDE
Phil Lee

Indonesian
A ROUGH GUIDE
PHRASEBOOK

French
A ROUGH GUIDE
PHRASEBOOK

Mandarin
Chinese
A ROUGH GUIDE
PHRASEBOOK

Hindi & Urdu
A ROUGH GUIDE
PHRASEBOOK

Thai
A ROUGH GUIDE
PHRASEBOOK

The Internet
AND WORLD WIDE WEB
THE ROUGH GUIDE 2.0
Angus J. Kennedy from Internet

Jazz
THE ROUGH GUIDE

World Music
THE ROUGH GUIDE

Opera
THE ROUGH GUIDE
Matthew Boyden

Rock
THE ROUGH GUIDE
THE DEFINITIVE GUIDE TO 1000 ARTISTS
AND BANDS FROM THEN...TO NOW

100% Reliable

* illustrated are some of our latest publications   www.roughguides.com

Stay in touch with us!

ROUGH*NEWS* is Rough Guides' free newsletter.
In three issues a year we give you news, travel
issues, music reviews, readers' letters and the
latest dispatches from authors on the road.

I would like to receive ROUGH*NEWS*: please put me on your free mailing list.

NAME . . . .

ADDRESS . . . .

Please clip or photocopy and send to: Rough Guides, 1 Mercer Street, London WC2H 9QJ, England
or Rough Guides, 375 Hudson Street, New York, NY 10014, USA.

Travel the world
HIV *Safe*

Travel *Safe*

HIV, the virus that causes AIDS, is worldwide.

You're probably aware of the dangers of getting it from unprotected sex, but there are many other risks when travelling.

Wherever you're visiting it makes sense to take precautions. Try to avoid any medical or dental treatment, but if it's necessary, make sure the equipment is sterilised. Likewise, if you really need to have a blood transfusion, always ask for screened blood.

Make sure your travelling companions are aware of the risks and the necessary precautions. In fact, you should take your own sterile medical pack, available from larger high street pharmacies.

Remember, ear and body piercing, acupuncture and even tattoos could be risky, because they all involve puncturing the skin. And although you might not normally consider any of these things now, after a few drinks - you never know.

Of course, the things that are dangerous at home are just as dangerous when you travel. So don't inject drugs or share works.

Avoid casual sex and always use a good quality condom when having sex with a new partner (and each time you have sex with them).

And it's not just a gay disease' either. In fact, worldwide, it's most commonly transmitted through sex between men and women.

For information in the UK:

Ring for the TravelSafe leaflet on the Health Literature Line freephone 0800 555 777, or pick one up at a doctor's surgery or pharmacy.

Further advice on HIV and AIDS: National AIDS Helpline: 0800 567 123. (Cannot be reached from abroad).

The Terrence Higgins Trust Helpline (12 noon–10pm) provides advice and counselling on HIV/AIDS issues: 0171 242 1010.

MASTA Travellers Health Line: 0891 224 100.

Travel *Safe*

Travel the world HIV *Safe*

with pendulous earlobes and sunken eyes, staring at a bhodi tree. There's a good **veg-etarian restaurant** over on the east side of the temple grounds, and the gift shop sells *tiancha*, a special liquorice-flavoured tea made by Nanhua's nuns.

DANXIA SHAN

The region's other main holy site is **Danxia Shan**, a holy peak featuring temples, restaurants and unusually vivid red sandstone cliffs, some 50km northeast of Shaoguan near the town of **RENHUA**. Local buses from Shaoguan's train station square run periodically through the day to Renhua (¥8), from where, for a couple of yuan, you can pick up minibuses for the nine-kilometre run to the mountain's entrance. At weekends there are also minibus day tours from Shaoguan. With about 12km of paths up the various summits, however, it's worth considering staying overnight on Danxia at one of the hotels here and joining Chinese tourists who come to catch the sunrise from the pavilion at the mountain's apex, **Changlao**. There's also accommodation at Renhua, should you miss the last bus back to Shaoguan in the late afternoon.

SHIZI YAN

Of more esoteric interest, excavations around **Shizi Yan** (Lion Crag; daily 9am–4pm; ¥6), some 18km south of Shaoguan, uncovered two ancient human sites, one perhaps 120,000 years old, the other a mere four thousand. Unless you can hook up with a tour, the easiest way to get here from Shaoguan is to catch a bus from the edge of the train station square near the Qujiang Bridge to Qujiang town (also known as **Maba**; last bus back to Shaoguan around 6pm; ¥3), and then either hire a cycle-rickshaw (¥20) or simply walk the final 3km – head west along Fuqian Zhong Lu, then turn south down Jiangshe Nan Lu, over a corroded metal footbridge, and follow the rutted main road off into the country. Once clear of the town you'll see Shizi Yan not far off, a short limestone hill projecting out of the ground like a tooth. The entrance is marked by a stone archway on the roadside. The crag turns out to be hollow and surrounded by "caveman" statues, and a Chinese-speaking guide takes you through the small caverns and explains how human remains were first found by the Guomindang when they were caching silver here during the 1930s. More comprehensive investigations twenty years later uncovered animal and human bones in quantities, suggesting that the cave was regularly occupied by *homo erectus* (here nicknamed Maba Man), our immediate ancestors. A further ¥3 gets you into the **museum** back near the main gate, where there's a second-floor exhibition of stone axes, arrowheads, pottery and other artefacts unearthed from more recent Neolithic burials found in the surrounding fields in 1977. Unfortunately, labelling is scanty and in Chinese only.

West into Guangxi

Though the main transport routes run north and south from Shaoguan, if you're looking for an unusual way into Guangxi Province, consider heading west through the mountainous strongholds of Guangdong's **Yao** and **Zhuang** population, a corner of the province virtually untouched by tourism. An early-morning bus leaves Shaoguan's long-distance station daily and takes about five hours to cover the 185km to **LIANZHOU**, itself a Han town ever since being established by Emperor Wudi in 111 BC. There's an ancient **hexagonal pagoda** here whose base is of Song vintage, and it may well be possible to take a **ferry down the Lian River**, which flows southeast for 70km, through the Huangchuang Gorges to **Yangshan**. Yangshan is on the back road between Qingyuan and Shaoguan, connected to both by a daily bus in either direction. Another 15km southwest from Lianzhou is **LIANNAN**, from where you can catch minibuses 10km out to **Sanpai**, a predominantly Yao village, and 35km beyond Liannan you'll find **LIANSHAN**, surrounded by Yao and Zhuang hamlets. Continuing through to Guangxi, the road from Lianshan runs a farther 100km over the mountains to **Liantang**, a small town on the main road between Yangshuo and Wuzhou.

Pingshi and rafting the Nine Torrents

In 1986, after many attempts and much loss of life, the Chinese Academy of Sciences finally succeeded in shooting the entire length of the Yangzi River on rubber rafts, thereby sparking nationwide interest in the sport and a new tourist industry at **PINGSHI**, a small, functional town 100km northwest of Shaoguan on the Wu River. Though not part of the Yangzi system, the 103-kilometre flow between Pingshi and southerly **Lechang** – not entirely fancifully described as comprising "**Nine Torrents and Eighteen Shoals**" – is perfectly suited to recreational rafting, and there's even a month-long **rafting festival** in Lechang each July. During the summer, Chinese tour groups from all over the country come to ride these rapids, and you can either organize a round trip with tour agents in Shaoguan, or go to Pingshi and make all arrangements there. There's at least one bus daily from Shaoguan to Pingshi (5hr; ¥20), or several trains can get you there in about three hours. The **rafting ticket office** (daily 9–11am & 1.30–5pm; ¥250 per person) is opposite Pingshi's train station, and if there are no tickets left here for the next day, try the *CITS* at the nearby *Jingling Binguan* (③–⑤). The older wing of this hotel is a bit tatty but pleasant, while in the newer building you get your own shower.

Ideally, give yourself the best part of a day in Pingshi and climb **Jinji Ling**, Golden Rooster Ridge, which sits 1km to the north. While it peaks at a modest 350m, the rock formations and vegetation here are fabulous, especially the vertical tower of **Yizi Ling**. Previews of the forthcoming rapids can be had from the rather more accessible, flatter humps at Yizi's base, where a handful of modern pavilions and a statue reveal that during the 1850s this was the training grounds for **Hong Xuanjiao**, a female comander of the Taiping army.

DOWNSTREAM TO LECHANG

At 9am you gather at the ticket office to be fitted with a life jacket and then board your vessel, an inflatable, heavyweight rubber dinghy seating nine or ten people – these are motorized, but the trip is still pretty exciting. As you speed downstream past a gamut of strangely contorted crags, keep your eyes peeled for holes worn deep into the rocks on either side of the river, where pilots of the less manoeuvrable wooden boats, which regularly used to haul cargo and passengers along this stretch, tried to gain a purchase for their bamboo poles. Back in the Tang dynasty, one of these crafts carried **Han Yu**, the disgraced prime minister of Emperor Xuanzong, into distant exile at Chaozhou, and there's a **temple** on the right bank to commemorate his sad trek.

There are other natural and historic sites along the way which the raft might stop at for a while, and sometimes **mishaps** do occur (boats even occasionally hit rocks and sink), but it generally takes about seven hours to reach **LECHANG**. At this point you could rush to catch a late-afternoon or night train onwards, but there are several guesthouses, highly regarded local snails for gourmets to sample, and several buses and trains the next morning heading south to Shaoguan and Guangzhou, or north into Hunan.

Eastern Guangdong

All in one go, it's an arduous six-hundred-kilometre journey east from Guangzhou to Xiamen in Fujian Province, but there's a wealth of intrinsically interesting territory on the way, well worth breaking your trip to explore. Only three hours away, **Huizhou**'s watery parkland makes it an excellent weekend bolthole from Guangzhou's chaos, while over near the Fujian border, the seedy splendour of the former treaty port of **Shantou** is just an hour from **Chaozhou**, famed for its own cooking style and splendid

EASTERN GUANGDONG

Chaozhou	潮州	*cháozhōu*
Chaozhou Binguan	潮州宾馆	*cháozhōu bīnguǎn*
Chaozhou Dajiudian	潮州大酒店	*cháozhōu dàjiǔdiàn*
Chaozhou Jiudian	潮州酒店	*cháozhōu jiǔdiàn*
Hanwen Gong	韩文公	*hánwén gōng*
Kaiyuan Si	开元寺	*kāiyuán sì*
Taiwan Binguan	台湾宾馆	*táiwān bīnguǎn*
Xihu Park	西湖公园	*xīhú gōngyuán*
Huizhou	惠州	*huìzhōu*
Dongjiang Jiudian	东江酒店	*dōngjiāng jiǔdiàn*
Huizhou Binguan	惠州宾馆	*huìzhōu bīnguǎn*
Xi Hu	西湖	*xīhú*
Xihu Binguan	西湖宾馆	*xīhú bīnguǎn*
Meizhou	梅州	*méizhōu*
Dongshan Bridge	东山桥	*dōngshān qiáo*
Meijiang Bridge	梅江桥	*méijiāng qiáo*
Qianfo Si ta	千佛寺塔	*qiānfósì tǎ*
Renjinglu	人境庐	*rénjìnglú*
Wenhua Park	文化公园	*wénhuà gōngyuán*

ACCOMMODATION

Huaqiao Dasha	华侨大厦	*huáqiáo dàshà*
Jiangnan Dasha	江南大厦	*jiāngnán dàshà*
Wangjiang Dajiudian	望江大酒店	*wàngjiāng dàjiǔdiàn*

AROUND MEIZHOU

Dadong	大东	*dàdōng*
Dapu	大埔	*dàpǔ*
Guyie	古野	*gǔyě*
Lingguang Si	灵光寺	*língguāng sì*
Sanhe	三河	*sānhé*
Songkou	松口	*sōngkǒu*
Yinna Shan	阴那山	*yīnnà shān*
Shantou	汕头	*shàntóu*
Guangchang Matou terminal	广场码头	*guǎngchǎng mǎtóu*
Mayu Dao	妈屿岛	*māyǔ dǎo*
Jiaoshi	觉石	*jiàoshí*
Shanjiao Ferry	汕觉客运轮渡	*shànjiào kèyùn lúndù*
Tianhou Gong	天后宫	*tiānhòu gōng*
Zhongshan Park	中山公园	*zhōngshān gōngyuán*

ACCOMMODATION AND RESTAURANTS

Hai Pa Wang	海霸王	*hǎibà wáng*
Hualian Jiudian	华联酒店	*huálián jiǔdiàn*
Huaqiao Dasha	华侨大厦	*huáqiáo dàshà*
Nanhai Yucun Jiulou	南海渔酒楼	*nánhǎiyú jiǔlóu*
Xinhua Binguan	新华宾馆	*xīnhuá bīnguǎn*

Ming-era architecture. With enough time, you could spend a few days farther north in the hilly country around **Meizhou**, investigating ethnic **Hakka culture** in its heartland. An advantage to visiting Meizhou first is that by travelling in this direction you can take the **Han River ferry** down to Chaozhou, a wonderful way to arrive at this historic town. The **coastal highway** runs via Huizhou to Shantou and on into Fujian, while the **rail line** from Guangzhou's East train station bends northeast from Huizhou and terminates at Meizhou. By 1998 this will join up with track in Fujian to create an eastern link between Guangzhou and Beijing.

Note that the only **banks** in the region able to convert travellers' cheques are in Huizhou and Shantou, so ensure you have enough cash if you venture beyond their boundaries.

Huizhou and Xi Hu

HUIZHOU, 160km from Guangzhou, is a place of water, caught between five lakes and the confluence of the Dong and Xizhi rivers. It was settled over two thousand years ago and later became capital of the Southern Han court. What saves Huizhou from being just another small, run-of-the-mill Chinese town is the genteel scenery surrounding the two-square-kilometre **Xi Hu** (West Lake). First laid out as a park by Song-dynasty engineers and the subject of poets and artists ever since, the lake is a pleasant place to spend a day or a few hours strolling around the constructed landscapes and watching crowds of locals do the same.

Huizhou isn't a large place, and Xi Hu covers about the same area as the centre of town. There are several **entrances** open from 6am until after dark (¥3), but the main one is next to the *Huizhou Binguan* on Huangcheng Lu. The path here crosses the lake over a five-hundred-metre causeway, whose two sections are joined by a small humpbacked bridge made of white marble. It was built in 1096 by a monk named **Xigu** and funded by the Sichuanese poet-official **Su Dongpo**, then Huizhou's governor and composer of a famous verse extolling the beauty of the full moon seen from this spot. On the far shore there's a thirteen-storey brick pagoda from 1618, whose wobbly wooden stairs can be climbed for fine views north and south across the waters. Next door is a noble statue of Su Dongpo, with an adjacent museum displaying a battered inkstone said to have belonged to this ubiquitous man of letters. The main path heads off across the lake again from here, this time via a zigzagging bridge and a series of strategically placed islets, thick with bamboo groves, to the northern shore forecourt of **Yuan Miao**, an old Taoist nunnery. It's a bizarre place, fully functioning but somewhat in need of repairs, with an improbable number of tiny rooms and atriums decorated with Taoist symbols and auspicious carvings of bats, tigers and cranes. Off to one side is the inevitable shrine to the Buddhist deity Guanyin and a pit full of live tortoises, while in the far hall acolytes and nuns dance and sing themselves into a religious frenzy. Walking back down Huangcheng Lu from here, there are a few more islands linked to the footpath, the favoured haunt of weekend street performers who keep crowds entertained with theatre and martial arts displays.

Practicalities

Huizhou's town centre sits immediately below a kink in the five-hundred-metre-wide Dong River, a proportionately thin strip of land hemmed in by the smaller Xizhi River to the east, and Xi Hu to the west. The **train** pulls in about 3km west, from where you'll need to catch a taxi into the centre. Huizhou's **long-distance bus station** is on a roundabout 1km south of the lake on Eling Bei Lu, which runs north, away from the roundabout, to Huangcheng Lu, which in turn follows Xi Hu's eastern shore. Take any of the small side streets east off Huangcheng Lu and you'll end up on parallel Shuimen Lu, Huizhou's functional shopping precinct.

For inexpensive **accommodation**, stick around the bus station, where numerous noisy hostels offer basic facilities (②), but, particularly if you're here for a break from Guangzhou, it's better to splash out for a nicer room near the lake. Best is the *Huizhou Binguan*, right on Xi Hu's eastern shore on Huangcheng Lu (☎0752/2232333, fax 2231439; ⑦), a very comfortable affair with spacious doubles. If they're full, try the more ordinary but good-value *Dongjiang Jiudian* (☎0752/2233848; ④), farther up Huangcheng Lu, or the *Xihu Binguan* (☎0752/2228111, fax 2228332; ⑦), a stuffy Hong Kong-owned option near the Yuan Miao nunnery on the lake's north shore. For **food**, there are canteens near the bus station and inexpensive restaurants along Huangcheng Lu and Shuicheng Lu. Try the hotels for more upmarket Cantonese meals – the *Huizhou Binguan* might even be able to rustle up an English menu – or the moderately priced Sichuanese place just up past the *Dongjiang*.

The hotels can also **change money**, and there's a huge *Bank of China* (Mon–Fri 9am–noon & 1.30–5pm) five minutes' walk east of the bus station roundabout along Eling Dong Lu. **Moving on**, you can book train tickets through the *Huizhou Binguan*'s travel service (daily 8am–8pm), and there should be little trouble getting a seat on the numerous daily buses heading on to Shantou, Guangzhou and Shenzhen.

Shantou

The bus journey between Huizhou and Shantou is somewhat surreal. As undulating hills and plains float by in the background, you pass kilometre after kilometre of unbroken, appallingly anonymous housing, built one block deep like a film set, and Qing-era estates of grey rectangular buildings packed as closely as possible into stark grids. The dreary modern flats are so similar they can be distinguished only by their inhumane addresses – A10, E5 – painted on their fronts. Still, the highway is good and stops are few, making for fast and furious driving, and it's not unusual to cover the 300km in a respectable six hours.

SHANTOU sits in a well-protected marine harbour at the mouth of the stunted Rong River, where eastern Guangdong's major waterway, the **Han River**, disgorges into the South China Sea through a complex estuary. This strategic access to the south's mountainous interior, not to mention a useful position between Guangzhou and Xiamen in Fujian, was overlooked until Shantou was first opened to foreigners in 1858 following the post-Opium War **Tianjin Treaty**. The mainly British entrepreneurs who moved in called the town **Swatow** after the local pronounciation. They followed the Han River upstream to establish Church missions, built a city in grand colonial style and, by 1900, had turned Shantou from a fishing village into a major trading port. It remained so for half a century, but the Communist takeover saw the city's interests gradually shifting towards light industries, which were greatly expanded after Shantou's 1980 elevation to one of Guangdong's Special Economic Zones. Today the old waterfront district is somewhat neglected, as a new, modern business city of over a million inhabitants expands steadily east. While incredibly crowded and noisy, the crumbling old quarter, a few nice traditional buildings and a couple of quick trips across the harbour make Shantou a bearable place to pause before continuing east into Fujian, or north to Chaozhou.

The City

Overall, Shantou is a huge, sprawling city, but everything of interest is in the western end, a stubby, three-kilometre-broad thumb of land bounded south by the harbour and farther west and north by various trailing outflows descending from the Han River estuary. One

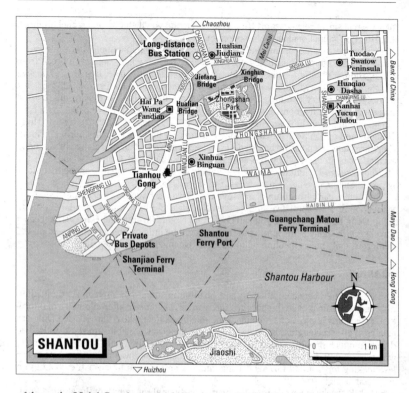

of these, the **Meixi Canal**, surrounds **Zhongshan Park** (¥2) on the northern side of the "thumb", a twenty-minute walk from the long-distance bus station – take Xinghua Lu east over the Xinghua Bridge, then follow the footpath south along the canal. The nicest place in Shantou to start the day in relative calm among ballroom dancers and martial arts experts training with swords, there's a small outdoor **theatre** on the eastern side (where Chaozhou opera gets an airing most weekends) and plenty of trees and water.

Five minutes southwest of the park along Minzu Lu you'll find yourself on a large **roundabout**. Anping Lu continues down into Shantou's seedy old colonial quarter from here, but first turn east along Shengping Lu and seek out **Tianhou Gong**. Built in 1879 and beautifully restored during the 1980s, it's possibly the smallest temple you'll see anywhere. Partitioned in two, the main courtyard can barely contain ten people, but the statues and decorations are extraordinarily opulent, with guardian spirits hand-painted on the wooden doors, beams carved into dragons and animals, and roof tiles showing scenes from the lives of the red-faced warrior Guan Yu, and a local heroine and her tiger. A similar building a few minutes farther east along Waima Lu sports two large rooftop dragons facing off across a glass "pearl".

Back at the roundabout, Anping Lu runs southwest for over a kilometre towards the waterfront between some incredible, mouldering **colonial facades** (once the city's pride) and block upon block of three-storeyed town houses and warehouses, all with elaborate, decaying plaster decor and fluted columns flanking windows and doorways. Though decidedly downmarket and not a little claustrophobic – many of the buildings look as if they're about to keel over on top of you – it's easy to spend a couple of absorbing hours poking around. When you've had enough, press on farther down to Xidi Lu, which crosses Anping and runs southeast for 200m or so to the **Shanjiao Ferry** (6am–at least 6pm; ¥2). This carries you south across the harbour in about ten minutes, landing at **Jiaoshi**, an airy headland covered in paths where you could spend half a day wandering among granite boulders and low trees. Better yet is the trip out to **Mayu Dao**, a small island an hour's ferry ride east on the daily 9.30am service from the **Guangchang Matou** terminal over on Haibin Lu (best reached by taxi). Small enough to walk around in about forty minutes, the island is sacred to the Heavenly Empress, protector of fisherfolk, and there's a well-maintained **temple** to her here, always full of worshippers. This aside, the eastern side of the island has a nice sandy beach and an overpriced **hotel** (⑥) with a fine restaurant. The boat back to the mainland leaves at 2pm.

Practicalities

Arriving by bus from Huizhou, you cross the harbour on a vehicular ferry and enter straight into the southwestern corner of Shantou's old quarter, where a mass of **private buses** terminates on Xidi Lu. The main **long-distance bus station**, however, is 3km northeast on the #11 bus route, just over the Meixi Canal at the junction of Chaoshan Lu, Xinghua Lu and Huoche Lu. Chaoshan Lu heads north out of town towards Chaozhou; Xinghua Lu runs east across the Xinghua Bridge into Jinsha Lu and the newer parts of the city, covered by bus #4; while Huoche Lu heads southwest over the Jiefang and Huilan bridges onto Minzu Lu, and back down into Shantou's old quarter. **Minibuses from Chaozhou** might drop off a couple of kilometres farther north again on Chaoshan Lu, from where bus #7 will take you down to the main long-distance terminal. Shantou's other arrival point is the **ferry port**, with twice-weekly services from Hong Kong docking east of the centre on Haibin Lu, from where you'll need to hail one of Shantou's plentiful **taxis** to get to a hotel. Watch out for pickpockets on local buses.

The *Huaqiao Dasha* has a **bank**, but its services are generally reserved for guests only. The huge *Bank of China* on Jinsha Lu is 5km east (foreign exchange Mon–Fri 9am–5pm) – take bus #4 along Jinsha Lu until it turns north, then walk the last 200m. **Moving on**, minibuses make the hour-long run up to Chaozhou throughout the day from around the main bus station, where there are also regular departures as far as Xiamen, Shenzhen, Meizhou and Guangzhou. Although purportedly open daily 8am–5pm, the dockside **Hong Kong ferry ticket office** is often locked up, but the *Huaqiao Dasha* has a booking service.

Shantou's **cooking style** is derived from Chaozhou's distinctive cuisine (for more of which see p.571), and the city has a good reputation for fish and dumplings. Cheap stalls and canteens fill the old quarter's back lanes, while the two best **restaurants** are the *Nanhai Yucun Jiulou*, beside the *Huaqiao Dasha* on Changping Lu, and *Hai Pa Wang Fandian*, in an unmissable warehouse-like building by the Huilan Bridge, where Huoche Lu becomes Minzu Lu. Both specialize in authentic Chaozhou dishes, and *Hai Pa Wang* has a buffet 11am–2pm (¥43 per person), where you're let loose to cook unlimited piles of fresh vegetables, meats, seafood and local dumplings on individual hotplates – quite a treat.

ACCOMMODATION

Hualian Jiudian, Xinghua Lu (☎0754/8228389). Opposite the long-distance bus station, a completely forgettable standard Chinese affair, usefully positioned on city bus routes. ⑤.

Huaqiao Dasha, Shanzhang Lu (☎0754/8629888, fax 8252223). Shanzhang Lu runs south off Jinsha Lu, about 1.5km east of the main long-distance bus station – take a taxi from arrival points. This is Shantou's main tourist hotel, a maze of tarnished decor with various restaurants, shops and facilities. Some cheaper beds in three-bed rooms might be available if you persevere. ⑥.

Tuodao Binguan/Swatow Peninsula, Jinsha Lu (☎0754/8231261). The cheapest place in town willing to take foreigners, with clean and spartan doubles. It's a two-kilometre ride on bus #4 from the main bus station. ④.

Xinhua Binguan, corner of Minquan Lu and Waima Lu. The cheaper rooms here are a bit run-down, but the hotel is nicely positioned a ten-minute stroll east of Minzu Lu and the edge of the old centre. Take a taxi from arrival points. ⑤.

Chaozhou

Just 40km north of Shantou on the banks of the Han River, **CHAOZHOU** is one of Guangdong's most culturally significant towns, yet manages to be overlooked by tourist itineraries and government projects alike – principally through having had its limelight stolen last century by its noisy southern sister. In response, Chaozhou has become staunchly traditional, proudly preserving the architecture, superstitions and local character which Shantou, a recent, foreign creation, never had, making it an infinitely nicer place to spend some time.

Founded back in mythology, by the Ming dynasty Chaozhou had reached its zenith as a place of culture and refinement, and the originals of many of the town's monuments date back to this time. A spate of tragedies followed, however. After an anti-Manchu uprising in 1656, only Chaozhou's monks and their temples were spared the imperial wrath and it's said that the ashes of the hundred thousand slaughtered citi-

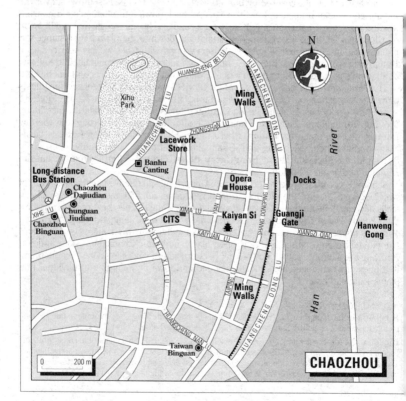

zens formed several fair-sized hills. The town managed to recover somehow, but was brought down in the nineteenth century by famine and the Opium Wars, which culminated in Shantou's foundation. Half a million desperately impoverished locals fled Chaozhou and eastern Guangdong through the new port, many of them **emigrating** to European colonies all over Southeast Asia, where their descendants comprise a large proportion of Chinese communities in Thailand, Malaysia, Singapore and Indonesia. Humiliatingly, Shantou's rising importance saw Chaozhou placed under its administration until becoming an independent municipality in 1983, and there's still real rivalry between the two.

For the visitor, Chaozhou is a splendid place. Among some of the most active and comfortably scaled street life in southern China, there are some fine historic **monuments** to tour, excellent shopping for local **handicrafts**, and a nostalgically dated small-town ambiance to soak up. Chinese speakers might also note that Chaozhou's **language** is related to Fujian's *minnan* dialect, radically different from both Mandarin and Cantonese, though both of these are widely understood.

Orientation, arrival and accommodation

Laid out on the western bank of the Han River, Chaozhou comprises an oval, 1.5-kilometre-long **old town centre**, enclosed by Huangcheng Lu, which, divided into north, south, east and west sections, follows the line of the **Ming-dynasty stone walls**. A stretch of these still face the river on the centre's eastern side, while Chaozhou's modest modern fringe spreads west of Huangcheng Lu. The old town's main thoroughfares are Taiping Lu, orientated north–south, crossed by shorter Zhongshan Lu, Xima Lu, and Kaiyuan Lu, which all run east from Huangcheng Lu, through arched gates in the walls, and out to the river.

Chaozhou is well suited to pedestrians, with transit points and accommodation all located near the old town. The best way to arrive is **by boat** down the Han River from the Meizhou region, as this lands you atmospherically on the docks immediately outside the town walls, from where you can hire a cycle-rickshaw – the only vehicle able to negotiate the narrow lanes – to carry you in pre-Communist style through the gateway and markets. Less romantically, the **long-distance bus station** and most of the accommodation is in Chaozhou's newer quarters, 1km west on Xihe Lu.

Places to stay include the touristy, decent-value *Chaozhou Binguan* (☎0768/2261168, fax 2264298; ⑥) across from the bus station; the slightly gloomy, cavernous *Chaozhou Dajiudian* (☎0768/2202128; ④), on the same side and 100m east of the bus station on Xihe Lu; *Chaozhou Jiudian* (☎0768/2261211; ④), a plain place with nervous, friendly staff opposite the *Chaozhou Dajiudian* on Xihe Lu; and the *Taiwan Binguan* (☎0768/2261881; ⑤), a smart business hotel 1km away on the south side of town at 35 Huangcheng Nan Lu. Neither the hotels or Xihe Lu's *Bank of China* seem able to cash travellers' cheques, so stock up with money before you arrive.

MOVING ON FROM CHAOZHOU

Moving on, there are daily buses to Meizhou, Guangzhou and Shenzhen, and minibuses for Shantou cruise Xihe Lu from dawn to dusk, and also meet Han River ferry arrivals. Nobody seems to know the details of the **ferry timetable**, though final destinations are set by the seasonal river level. During the winter there's supposed to be a daily service upstream as as far as **Guyie** (12hr), while after the summer rains you can get as far as **Sanhe** (15hr) or even **Songkou** (20hr), all of which are a minibus ride from Meizhou – see p.573 for more details of the trip. Chaozhou's hotels might be able to help with bookings, or try *CITS* at 171 Xima Lu (Mon–Sat 9–11.30am & 1.30–5pm; ☎0768/2224349).

The Town

Chaozhou's old centre has none of Shantou's decrepitude. Instead you'll find an endlessly engaging warren of narrow flagstoned lanes packed with a well-maintained mixture of colonial and traditional buildings. In the quieter residential back lanes, look for old buildings, Ming-dynasty stone archways, and century-old family mansions, protected from the outside world by thick walls and heavy wooden doors, and guarded by mouldings of gods and good luck symbols. Out on the main streets, motorbikes and cycle-rickshaws weave among the shoppers, who are forced off the pavement and into the roads by the piles of goods stacked up outside stores. Walking through the throngs can be a bit frustrating, and evening is often a better time for a laid-back wander. It's also worth heading up to the spacious and shady hills of **Xihu Park**, actually just north of the old town across a "moat" on Huangcheng Bei Lu, where there's an ornamental pagoda and some unrestored sections of the town walls.

If you bother with only one sight in Chaozhou, make it **Kaiyuan Si** (daily 8am–6pm; ¥1) at the eastern end of Kaiyuan Lu. A lively Buddhist temple founded in 738 AD, three sets of solid wooden doors open into courtyards planted with figs and red-flowered phoenix trees, where a pair of Tang-era **stone pillars**, topped with lotus buds, symbolically support the sky. The various halls are pleasantly proportioned, with sweeping, low-tiled roofs with brightly coloured lions, fish and dragons sporting along ridges. Off to the west side is a **Guanyin pavilion** with a dozen or more statues of this popular Bodhisattva in all her forms. Another room on the east side is full of bearded Taoist saints holding a *yin-yang* wheel, while the interior of the **main hall** boasts a very intricate vaulted wooden ceiling and huge brocade banners almost obscuring a golden Buddhist trinity.

About 100m east past the temple down Kaiyuan Lu you run up against the **old town walls**. Seven metres high and almost as thick, these were only ever breached twice in Chaozhou's history, and over 1.5km still stand in good condition, though sometimes obscured by warehouses and homes built up against them. Kaiyuan Lu runs under the **Guangji Gate**, where there's a set of steps up to a rickety guard tower and a walking track along the top of the wall. Pass through the gate and you're standing by the river next to the five-hundred-metre-wide **Xiangzi Qiao**, a bridge whose piles were sunk in the twelfth century. Until the 1950s the central section was spanned by a row of wooden punts, now replaced by an ordinary concrete construction, closed to heavy traffic and popular with hawkers selling cheap clothes. Crossing over, you can see the shrub-covered shell of the tall **Fenghuang Pagoda**, a couple of kilometres downstream, while on the far bank a short street bears left to the gate of **Hanwen Gong** (¥2), a temple complex built in 999 in memory of the official **Han Yu**, a Confucian scholar who had denounced Buddha as a barbarian and cleared the river of troublesome crocodiles a century earlier. A flight of broad, steep granite stairs leads up to three terraces, each with a hall. The top one has numerous ancient stone proclamation tablets and a painted statue of Han Yu.

Adherence to the past has made Chaozhou a centre for **traditional arts and crafts**, and a great place to buy souvenirs. For something a bit unusual, the **hardware market**, just inside the Guangji Gate along Shangdong Ping Lu, has razor-sharp cleavers, kitchenware and old-style brass door rings. **Temple trinkets**, from banners to brass bells, ceramic statues and massive iron incense burners, are sold at numerous stores in the vicinity of Kaiyuan Si on Kaiyuan Lu, also a good area to find ceramic **tea sets** and **silk embroideries**. The best place to buy **lacework** is at the large store on the corner of Zhongshan Lu and Huangcheng Lu, opposite Xihu Park. While not dirt cheap, prices for all these things are very reasonable and the quality is high.

Eating, drinking and entertainment

Chaozhou's cooking style is becoming ever more popular in China, though thanks to last century's emigrants from the region, it has long been unconsciously appreciated overseas. Seafood is a major feature, while local roast goose, flavoured here with sour plum, rivals a good Beijing duck. Chaozhou dishes often contain sweet, scented flavours, going to the extent of cooking with fruit – this is where sweet-and-sour pork with lychees originated. Hotel restaurants all serve authentic Chaozhou food, and, on a good day, the *Chaozhou Dajiudian*'s is the best. One of the nicest spots to tuck into a meal, however, is immediately south of Xihu Park on Huangcheng Bei Lu, where several restaurants overlook the greenery and water. *Banhu Canting* is good, and serves a portion of cold chopped goose and green vegetables for about ¥45 (enough for two) but everywhere along here looks pretty wholesome. As always, check prices before ordering. Ordinary snacks and light Chinese dishes can be had all around the town: there's a good **ice-cream shop** in between the restaurants on Huangcheng Bei Lu, and you can buy very fresh **milk**, warm from the cow or goat, from the farmer who tethers his animals around the park gates in the afternoons – bring your own bottle.

The local **tea** is called *gongfu cha*, and Chaozhou's residents go through the rituals of its consumption on the slightest pretext – if nobody offers you a cup, most soft drinks shops serve it at a couple of yuan a session. First, the distinctive tiny pot and cups arrive on a deep ceramic tray with a grid on top for drainage; the pot is stuffed to the brim with the large, coarse leaves, filled with boiling water, and immediately emptied – not into the cups, but the tray. Then the pot is topped up and left to steep for a moment before the cups are filled with a rapid movement which delivers an equal strength brew to all. For all this effort you have a thimbleful of bitter tea, which has to be swiftly downed before it goes cold, more of a social activity than a source of refreshment.

For **entertainment**, try and track down a performance of *Chaoju*, the indigenous **opera style**. There's actually an old **opera house** on Yian Lu, parallel with Taiping Lu and one block west, though this has been converted into a cinema, sometimes screening videotaped opera performances. Your best bet now for live action are the infrequent shows in Xihu Park, most likely during festivals. *Chaoju* is quite listenable, with little of the warlike clanging and falsetto singing of Beijing's theatre. The plots, if you can follow them, tend to involve witty cautionary tales about lax sexual morality.

Meizhou and the Hakka

Right in the foothills of the Fujian border, 200km north of Chaozhou by road and 6–8 hours by train from Guangzhou, **MEIZHOU** has three claims to fame: a nationally respected football team; the province's best middle school outside Guangzhou; and the original home of a huge number of Overseas Chinese, whose descendants have begun to pump an enormous quantity of money back into the region. Sometimes still called by its old title, **Meixian** (both names mean "Plum City"), the town and surrounding countryside are home to the **Hakka**, a Han sub-group known to locals as *Kejia* (Outsiders) and to nineteenth-century Europeans as "China's Gypsies". Originating in the Yangzi basin during the third century and dislodged ever southward by war and revolution, today the Hakka form large communities in Hong Kong, Hainan Island and along the Fujian–Guangdong border. They managed to retain their original languages and customs by remaining aloof from their neighbours in the lands which they settled, a habit which caused resentment and led to their villages being well defended. Hakka houses in the Meizhou area are **fortress-like mansions** built of solid stone, the largest of which are three storeys high, circular and contain scores of families. While not a pretty town, Meizhou is a fine place to get a feel for the region's background and, if you can't make it out to remoter areas, a nearby mountain temple makes a good excuse for a quick trip into the countryside.

The Town

Surrounded by hills, Meizhou is a lightly industrial town producing handbags and clothing, set in the fertile bowl of a prehistoric lake bed through which flows the convoluted **Mei River**. The scruffy centre is a two-square-kilometre spread on the north bank, connected to the neat, newer southern suburbs by the **Meijiang** and **Dongshan bridges**. As in Chaozhou, almost everything is within walking distance or the range of cycle-rickshaws.

Meizhou's social focus and main shopping district surrounds the open **square** at the junction of various main roads immediately north of the **Meijiang Bridge**. The colonial-style shopfronts on Lingfeng Lu, which runs west along the riverfront, are mildly interesting, but the tone is set by a huge billboard at the entrance to **Wenhua Park**, advertising the next **football match** at the stadium here. You'll certainly know when a game is on: the entire town has the day off to watch and descends on the park, with merrymaking kept in order by police. At other times the park isn't up to much, though at night a number of small ancestor temples here look very atmospheric, lit by tapers and coloured lamps.

For more local culture, head northeast off the square up Shaofeng Lu, and then follow the lanes and Chinese signs five minutes east to some scummy ponds outside **Renjinglu**, former home of Meizhou's nineteenth-century poet and diplomat, **Huang Zunxian**. The building is the most ornate of several around the ponds, the others being classically austere **Hakka town houses**, with high central gateways and square-sided walls and windows. Of more obvious appeal and definitely worth a visit is **Qianfo Sita** (the Thousand Buddha Temple Pagoda) which overlooks Meizhou 1km east of the Meijiang Bridge. Take Jiangbian Lu east along the river for 700m to the Dongshan Bridge, follow Dongshan Dadao north for another 100m, then bear right over the rail lines and uphill to the gates. On the right here, the **temple kitchen** serves incredibly good **vegetarian meals** daily at noon, including imitation meat dishes which are virtually indistinguishable from the real thing. There's no menu; just take what they give you and pay by putting a donation in the box on the wall. A little way farther up the hill, both the original temple and pagoda were demolished in 1995 in order to be totally rebuilt (with funding from a Thai expatriate), with an attention to detail which has to be seen to be believed. The stonework is particularly accomplished, the temple pillars carved in deep relief with heroes and coiling dragons, while the base of the pagoda has finely executed scenes from Buddha's life.

Practicalities

Meizhou's main **bus station** is at the junction of Meishi Lu and Meizhou Dadao, which runs 1km east to the square at Wenhua Park and the Meijiang Bridge. There's also a **bus station for Shenzhen and Guangzhou** 50m east of the square off Shaofeng Lu, while Meijiang Dadao heads over the Meijiang Bridge and 7km south to the small shed which currently serves as Meizhou's **train station**. You'll need to be quick to grab a **taxi** on arrival. These are generally minibuses which hold about eight people.

For **somewhere to stay**, there's an uninspiring **hostel** opposite the bus station on Meishi Lu (②). Better prospects include comfortable beds at the quiet *Jiangnan Dasha* (☎0753/2248489, fax 2249964; ③), 500m south of the Meijiang Bridge on the corner of

DOWN THE HAN RIVER

The **ferry ride** down the Han Jiang to Chaozhou is not to be missed – as long as you can find the boat. When the water level is high enough you can catch it at **Songkou**, 54km northeast of Meizhou, and **Sanhe**, 80km east of Meizhou and 20km from Dapu. During the winter it leaves from **Guyie**, also 80km east of Meizhou, but farther downstream. The hotels in Meizhou might be able to advise you on the best starting point, but the **timetables** are a complete mystery – departures will definitely be early, though, so wherever you decide to catch the ferry, you need to spend the night before in the relevant town and ask there; they all have basic hotels. From Guyie, at least, the boat leaves at around 8am in March, and the six-hour trip to Chaozhou costs ¥75 per person for the sole private cabin, and ¥30 for a bench downstairs with everyone else. Food is simple, filling and about ¥15 extra, depending on how much you want.

One of the best things about this trip is that it's a local service, not a tourist boat, and there are plenty of stops at riverside villages along the way to pick up passengers. The first part is especially good, as the river runs through a fairly narrow valley past clumps of bamboo and local pagodas and temples built facing out over the water. After the halfway town of **Liuhuang**, recognizable from the church spire and trees rising above the stone wharf, the scenery opens up but the river channels become narrower, forcing the coal barges with which you share the river into long convoys as they snake along their way. The grand finale is actually arriving at Chaozhou, underneath the five-hundred-year-old city walls, see p.568.

Meijiang Dadao and Jiangnan Lu; and luxury accommodation at the *Huaqiao Dasha* (☎0753/2232388, fax 2210008; ⑤) and *Wangjiang Dajiudian* (☎0753/2220988, fax 2220918; ⑦), two Hong Kong-owned concerns opposite each other just east of the Meijiang Bridge on Jiangbian Lu.

Make sure you **eat** at Qianfo Sita (see above), and also try the **Hakka specialities** sold at stalls and diners around the park, including juicy salt-baked chicken, wrapped in greaseproof paper; little doughy rissoles made with shredded cabbage; and quick-fried cubes of beancurd, stuffed with pork and served in a gluey, rich sauce. Try the hotel restaurants for more upmarket local treats (chicken cooked with ginger and wine, for instance) or there's an excellent place on Dongshan Dadao, about 100m north of the Dongshan Bridge on the right, over another, smaller stream – look for the windows covered in opaque plastic film. **Hakka wine** is pretty nice by Chinese standards, similar to a sweet sherry and often served warm with ginger.

Moving on, there are two trains daily to Guangzhou (hotels can obtain tickets); early-morning buses daily to Guangzhou, Chaozhou, Shantou and Xiamen (Fujian) from the main bus station; and more comfortable direct buses to Shenzhen and Guangzhou from the Shaofeng Lu depot. **Minibuses to Dapu** leave about twice an hour from along Binfang Dadao, the southern continuation of Dongshan Bridge, from where you can also find minibuses to **Songkou** and **Guyie** if you're planning to catch the **Han River ferry** downstream to Chaozhou.

Around Meizhou

One good day trip from Meizhou is 50km east to **Yinna Shan**, sanctified by the elderly temple of **Lingguang Si**. You need to start early, as, unless your hotel can organize you a private jeep and driver (¥300), getting there and back is time-consuming. Take a minibus from the roundabout immediately south of the Dongshan Bridge to either **Sanxiang** or **Yanyang**, two villages in lush rice-growing country on Yinna Shan's eastern side, then hire a tractor for the 7km or so to the walking track leading up to the temple (30min). Last minibuses back are in the mid-afternoon.

Lingguang Si was founded in 861, though the present buildings are restored Qing. There are two thousand-year-old trees either side of the gate (a third died 300 years ago), and an extremely unusual wooden spiral ceiling in the main hall, the only other example being in a temple on Wudang Shan in Hubei Province.

Dapu and beyond

To learn more about the Hakka you need to head out to settlements north and east of Meizhou, surrounded in summer by some very attractive countryside. The small, dishevelled town of **DAPU**, two hours thirty minutes and 100km east via the Han River ferry stop at **Sanhe**, is a good place to start. A fraction of the size of Meizhou, the town shares the same river valley setting and an unexciting centre, but the fringes are very interesting. In the fields just outside, next to a modern sports stadium (another gift from an expatriate investing in his homeland), there's a huge square-sided **weiwu**, a three-storeyed Hakka house, with walls as solid as any castle's. The residents, amazed to see a foreign face, will come out to chat if you walk over for a look. Elsewhere are some very nicely constructed low-set family compounds, whose walls enclose several temple-like halls, all with decorated roofs, and at least two small but traditionally circular homesteads.

The **bus station** is on the northern edge at the corner of Renmin Lu and Hu Shan Lu, which runs south right through Dapu, terminating below steps ascending to the tidy parkland of **Hu Shan** (Tiger Hill). There's **accommodation** at a relatively garish hotel (③) in a courtyard about halfway down Hu Shan Lu on the eastern side, and plain beds (①) in the peeling hostel 50m west down Yanhua Lu on the right. If you're heading for the Han River ferry, there are dawn minibuses to Sanhe and Guyie, which might get you there before departure – see box above.

The largest, most highly regarded Hakka mansion anywhere in China, however, is a farther 40km east of Dapu at **DADONG village**, right on the Fujian border – take the morning minibus from Dapu, stay the night at Dadong's guesthouse, and return the next day. The building, a completely circular stone structure, 20m high with enough apartments for a thousand people, is featured on the standard ¥1 stamp.

Western Guangdong

While not an unpleasant area, there's very little to delay your passage across western Guangdong en route to Guangxi or Hainan Island. Buses aside, there are two modes of travel: the daily **ferry** along a 250-kilometre stretch of the **Xi River**, between Guangzhou and Wuzhou in Guangxi, popular with those heading to Guilin or Yangshuo; while the rail line is the quickest way to cover the 450km between the capital and **Zhanjiang**, where boats to Hainan depart. Either way, consider stopping off for a day or two at **Zhaoqing**, a pleasant resort town whose famous scenery has been a tourist attraction for over a thousand years.

Zhaoqing and Dinghu Shan

Road, rail and river converge 110km west of Guangzhou at **ZHAOQING**, founded as a Qin garrison town to plug a gap in the line of a low mountain range. The first Europeans settled here as early as the sixteenth century, when the Jesuit priest **Matteo Ricci** used Taoist and Buddhist parallels to make his Christian teachings palatable, but since the tenth century Zhaoqing has been better known for the limestone hills comprising the adjacent **Qixing Yan**, the Seven Star Crags. Swathed in mists and surrounded by lakes, they lack the scale of Guilin's peaks, but make for a very enjoyable day's wander, as do the surprisingly thick forests at **Dinghu Shan**, just a short local bus ride away from town.

Set on the north bank of the Xi River, Zhaoqing is squashed between the river and the northerly lakes bordering Qixing Yan Park. Jianshe Lu runs right across town east to west in numbered sections, and **Tianning Lu**, orientated north–south, lies between Qixing's boundaries and the river. Their crossroads marks Zhaoqing's downtown area. There's actually quite a bit to see in the town itself, though the sights are widely scattered and not of great individual importance. Zhaoqing's **inkstones** are some of the finest in China, and there's a factory here which turns out the basic models sold as tourist souvenirs across the land. Far better are those at the *Guangdong Antique Store*, opposite the *Huguang Hotel*, which has its own artisans, some beautifully carved inkstones and low prices.

Overlooking the river, **Chongxi Ta** (¥2) is a Ming pagoda at the eastern end of Jiangbin Lu, a road which runs parallel with Jianshe Lu along the riverfront. Recently restored and looking much like Guangzhou's Liurong Ta, at 57.5m this is the highest pagoda in the province. The view from the top takes in sampans, cargo boats and red cliffs across the river topped by two more pagodas of similar vintage and in poorer condition, covered in scaffolding. A few aged buildings lurk in the backstreets west of here behind Jiangbin Lu, including **Da Chen Miao** on Yuejiang Lu, a dusty, four-hundred-year-old Confucian academy of stone and beam construction, but Zhaoqing's most interesting quarter is a thirty-minute walk away on the far side of Tianning Lu, where Chengzong Lu and Jianshe Wu Lu run west through the site of the original town. There's a tight knot of early twentieth-century lanes, shops and homes here – all typically busy and noisy – and traces of the ancient city walls in the two low ridges running across Chengzong Lu.

WESTERN GUANGDONG

Zhanjiang	湛江	*zhànjiāng*
Chikan	赤坎	*chìkǎn*
Xiashan	霞山	*xiáshān*
ACCOMMODATION		
Cuiyuan Binguan	翠园宾馆	*cuìyuán bīnguǎn*
Overseas Chinese Hotel	华侨宾馆	*huáqiáo bīnguǎn*
Youyi Binguan	友谊宾馆	*yǒuyì bīnguǎn*
Zhaoqing	肇庆	*zhàoqìng*
Chongxi Ta	崇禧塔	*chóngxi tǎ*
Dinghu Shan	鼎湖山	*dǐnghú shān*
Qixing Yan Park	七星岩公园	*qīxīngyán gōngyuán*
ACCOMMODATION		
Duanzhou Dajiudian	端州大酒店	*duānzhōu dàjiǔdiàn*
Huaqiao Dasha	华侨大厦	*huáqiáo dàshà*
Huata Jiudian	花塔酒店	*huātǎ jiǔdiàn*
Huguang	湖光酒店	*húguāng jiǔdiàn*

Arranged in the shape of the Big Dipper and said to be fallen stars, the seven peaks which make up **Qixing Yan Park** (8am–5pm; ¥20) are 2km north of town on the far side of **Xin Hu** (Mars Lake). To get here, go to the top end of Tianning Lu and cross over busy Duanzhou Lu to the paved area on the lakeshore, from where a **causeway** continues north across Xin Hu. Towards the opposite shore it forks but either route leads to the park gates. The crags themselves are quite modestly scaled, named after objects they imaginatively resemble – **Chaunchu** (Toad), **Tianzhu** (Heavenly Pillar), **Shizang** (Stone Hand) – and an interlocking network of arched bridges, pathways, graffiti-embellished caves and willows all make for a pleasantly romantic three-hour stroll. Pedal boats (¥25 per hour) and **boat tours** (around ¥15 a person) are also available from the Duanzhou Lu side of the lake if you want to enjoy the scenery from the water.

Practicalities

Zhaoqing's **train station** is 5km away to the northwest of town beyond Xin Hu. The **long-distance bus station** is on Danzhou Lu, 100m east of the northern end of Tianning Lu, while the **ferry port** lies on the southeastern side of town at the junction of Jiangbin Lu and Gongnong Lu, near Chongxi Ta. **Taxis** can be hailed all around town, but otherwise there isn't much in the way of public transport; Zhaoqing is, anyway, somewhere to get about on foot.

The town has abundant **accommodation**, but it's expensive. Reasonable-value options include the damp, waterside *Huguang* (☎0758/2227377; ⑤) at the start of the Xin Hu causeway; the *Huaqiao Dasha* (☎0758/2232952; ⑦) and *Duanzhou Dajiudian* (☎0758/2232281; ⑦), big, well-maintained places next to each other at the north end of Tianning Lu; and the dreary *Huata Jiudian* (☎0758/2232427; ④) in Gongnong Lu, a street parallel with Tianning Lu, but 500m east. The *Duanzhou* has a **bank** (Mon–Fri 9am–noon & 1–5pm) where non-residents can cash travellers' cheques.

Stalls all through the centre sell **snacks**, the *Huata Jiudian* has good Sunday *dim sum* and canteens by the lake on Danzhou Lu display caged exotica like turtles, civet, snake, dog and cat. There's also *Tao Zhen*, a **Muslim restaurant** on Chezong Lu, just west of its crossroads with Tianning Lu, specializing in roast duck and chicken – cheap, very popular and very good.

Moving on, there are buses to Qingyuan, Shaoguan, Zhanjiang and just about everywhere between Guilin and Guangzhou. Trains go to Nanning, Zhanjiang, Guangzhou and through to Shenzhen. The **ferry ticket office** (daily 8–11.30am & 2–5pm) is on the corner of Gongnong Lu and Jiangbin Lu near Chongxi Ta, with daily departures to Wuzhou and Guangzhou.

Dinghu Shan

Twenty kilometres east of Zhaoqing is **Dinghu Shan**, a mountain range whose streams and thick forests support such a variety of native plants that the region has been incorporated into the *UNESCO* biosphere programme. The few kilometres open to the public get crowded at the weekends, but at other times Dingu Shan makes an excellent half-day out – particularly in summer, when the mountain is cooler than Zhaoqing – with well-formed paths giving access to a waterfall, temple and plenty of trees.

The #15 bus (¥5) leaves Zhaoqing twice an hour from the bus station near the Xin Hu causeway on Duanzhou Lu, terminating at the edge of the forest. A road runs in past souvenir stalls to where a row of cages gives you an idea of the range of plants and animals found here, including rare white-eared pheasants and stately fish-tail palms. Beyond here the walking track starts, dividing either to follow a stream or to climb a flight of stairs to **Qingyun Si**, a large temple with a fine **vegetarian restaurant** open at lunchtime, a three-hundred-year-old **camelia tree** with white flowers, and abysmal restorations which have decked the exterior in green bathroom tiles. The track along the stream takes you in ten minutes to a thirty-metre-high **waterfall**, whose plunge pool has been excavated and turned into a swimming hole. A lesser-used track continues up the side of the falls and eventually up to a vehicle road, which you can follow across to the temple. The round trip takes about two hours, and the last bus back to Zhaoqing leaves at 5pm.

Zhanjiang

The only reason to make the long haul to **ZHANJIANG**, 400km from Guangzhou on the province's southwestern coastline, is to catch the ferry running the 100km to Hainan Island. Otherwise the town, though a major port, is entirely without interest. The French obtained a lease here in 1898, and today they've been joined by US and British prospectors, who since 1975 have poured capital and labour into Zhanjiang as they scour sites in the South China Sea for **oil**. Signs of Western money are everywhere – especially in the huge docking facilities designed to accommodate large tankers, and a heliport to ferry workers out to the rigs – but the town remains a grey, dull place, with everyone still waiting for the first major strikes.

Zhanjiang is curiously split into two equal but well-separated halves. There's no need to visit northerly **Chikan** unless your bus terminates here, in which case catch the #11 city bus to the port area at **Xiashan**, 10km south along straight and empty Renmin Lu, where there's another long-distance bus station and Zhaoqing's train station. Much of Xiashan was built by the French, and there are some fairly grand blocks here along with conspicuously broad, tree-lined avenues, but nothing is particularly attractive. The **Hainan ferry and ticket office** (daily 9am–5pm) are right at the very end of Renmin Lu, from where two daily passenger ferries can whisk you over to Hainan's capital, Haikou, in just three hours (¥100).

Practicalities

Xiashan is a two-kilometre-wide grid of streets, with Renmin Lu and Jiefang Lu the main axes. The **train station** is right at the western end of Jiefang Lu, where taxis await new arrivals, and the **bus station** proper is in the southwest of town on Gongnong Lu, which runs diagonally up to the intersection of Jiefang Lu and Renmin Lu.

The best of the **accommodation** is at the informal *Youyi Binguan* (☎0759/2286622; ⑤), at the Renmin Lu–Jiefang Lu crossroads; the slightly more upmarket *Overseas Chinese Hotel* (☎0759/2281966, fax 2281347; ⑥); and the friendly *Cuiyuan Binguan* (☎0759/2286633; ⑤) on Minzhi Lu. The *Overseas Chinese* has a **travel service** able to book train and ferry tickets, though non-residents may politely have to persuade the English-speaking staff to help. There's also a **Bank of China** around the corner from the *Overseas Chinese* in Hongwu Lu (Mon–Fri 9–11.30am & 1.30–5pm), where travellers' cheques transactions take ages. The hotel **restaurants** are all good, with several independent places and cake shops along Minzhi Lu and the surrounding streets.

Unless you're heading to Haikou, arranging to **leave Zhanjiang** can be tiresome. There are trains to Zhaoqing, Nanning and Guangzhou, though the station ticket office is chaotic and you should try to organize things through the *Overseas Chinese Hotel*. Buses run to the same destinations, and to Haikou, from the long-distance bus station, but these are unpredictable (again, the *Overseas Chinese* can book seats on sleeper services) while private buses meet train arrivals for trips to Guangzhou and, if the timetables coincide with ferry departures, to Haikou.

HAINAN ISLAND

Rising out of the South China Sea between Guangdong and Vietnam, **Hainan Island** marks the southernmost undisputed limit of Chinese authority, an intriguing, three hundred-kilometre-broad mix of beaches, mountain scenery, history, myth and – most of all – the effects of exploitation. Today a province in its own right, Hainan was historically the "Tail of the Dragon", an enigmatic full stop to the Han empire inhabited by unspeakably backward races, only surfacing into popular consciousness when it could be of use. Han settlements were established around the coast in 200 AD, but for millennia Hainan was only seen fit to be a place of exile. Later, even Western powers largely ignored the island, though noting its strategic position between China and their concerns in the rest of Southeast Asia. So complete was Hainan's isolation that, as recently as the 1930s, ethnic **Li**, who first settled here over two thousand years ago, still lived a hunter-gatherer existence in the interior highlands.

Modern Hainan is no primitive paradise, however. After two years of naval bombardments, the Japanese occupied the island in 1939, and by the end of the war had executed a full third of Hainan's male population in retaliation for raids on their forces by Chinese guerrillas. It was closed to general access throughout the **Vietnam War** –

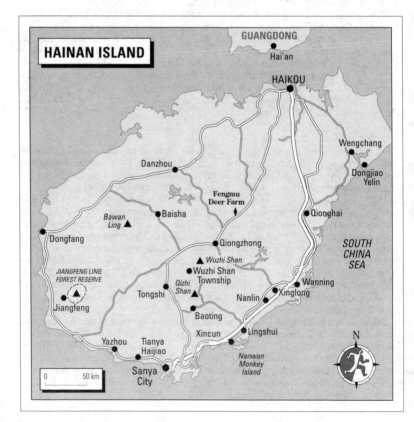

when the US briefly considered invading after a B-52 was shot down during the "Rolling Thunder" operation – and in the 1980s by China's own conflict with Vietnam. Hainan's current status as a Special Economic Zone seems simply to have been a licence for a succession of governments to strip brutally its natural resources and abandon the inhabitants to fend for themselves. It would be harder to imagine a worse example of **economic mismanagement**: there might be skyscrapers and modern factories around the cities, but you'll also see country people so poor that they live in lean-tos made of mud and straw, which have to be rebuilt after each wet season. Some of these are locals, others are recent migrants from the mainland, drawn by the official promotion of Hainan as an easy place to get rich. With no experience of garnering a living in a tropical climate, they blindly experiment with different crops – rubber, mango, coconuts and coffee, in the hope that a market will emerge. Forestry used to be a mainstay but now there is no forest left, with the exception of ragged remnants clinging to the very tips of Hainan's mountains. **Tourism** seems to be the sole reliable source of income, and everyone is desperate to be involved. Persistent marketing has made Hainan the place that all Chinese want to come for a holiday, but investment has been wildly over-optimistic, with numerous hotels and entertainment complexes around the place standing empty, unfinished or never used.

Yet despite all this, Hainan as a whole remains one of China's most unexplored corners. For foreign and domestic tourists alike, the most obvious reason to come here is to flop down on the warm, sandy **beaches** near the southern city of **Sanya**, and, as a rest cure after months on the mainland, it's a very good one. Initially there doesn't seem much more to get excited about. **Haikou**, Hainan's capital, bears evidence of brief colonial occupation, but its primary importance is as a transit point between the island and mainland, while Han towns along the **east coast** have only slightly more character and scenic appeal. Spend a little time and effort elsewhere, however, and things start to get much more interesting: the highlands are the place to start looking for **Li culture** – not least around the town of **Tongshi** – and the mountainous southwest hides some virtually unvisited **nature reserves**, where what's left of Hainan's indigenous flora and fauna hangs by a thread. There are even a handful of underwater sites off the southern coast, the only place in provincial China where those with the necessary qualifications can go **scuba diving**.

Getting to Hainan is straightforward, with daily flights from all over the country to Haikou and Sanya, and regular ferries from Hong Kong, Guangzhou, Zhanjiang and Beihai. Once here, **getting around** is easy: there's a paved road around the island, while another down through the centre has been joined by a first-rate highway between Haikou and Sanya, with myriad smaller roads and tracks connecting these arteries to interior villages. Hainan has an unbelievably prolific quantity of **local transport**, too, the legacy of an illicit manoeuvre by the local government during the mid-1980s which saw a quarter of a million vehicles of all shapes and sizes imported on to the island. Consequently, almost every road is covered on at least a daily basis. High-speed buses link Haikou and Sanya in just three hours, while you can easily hop around the rest of the island by bus and minibus. Sanya is also one of only three cities in China where you can **rent a car** and drive around on your own, though this is not a cheap option. Indeed, its financial plight, and the fact that everyone on the island is hungry to make money, means that Hainan is noticeably more **expensive** than the adjacent mainland – even Chinese tourists grumble about being constantly overcharged.

Hainan's extremely hot and humid **wet season** lasts from June to October. It's better to visit between December and April, when the climate is generally dry and tropically moderate, sunny days peaking around 25°C on the southern coast. Note that many towns here have different local and Chinese names. As the latter occur more frequently on maps and bus timetables, Chinese names are used below in the main text and character boxes, with local names indicated in brackets.

Haikou and the east coast

HAIKOU is Hainan's steamy capital, set at the north of the island and separated from Guangdong Province by the 30-kilometre-wide Qiongzhou Channel. Business centre, main port and first stop for newly arrived holiday-makers and hopeful migrants alike, Haikou has all the atmosphere of a modern, typical Southeast Asian city. There's a smattering of French colonial architecture, a few parks and monuments, gleaming new highrises, broad streets choked with traffic and pedestrians, and the all-pervading spirit of wilfully glib commerce. An indication of the ethos driving Haikou is that nobody seems to be a local: officials, businessmen and tourists are all from the mainland, while Li, Miao and Hakka flock from southern Hainan to hawk trinkets, as do the Muslim Hui who run the money-changing businesses – all drawn by the opportunities that the city represents. Energetic yet strangely soulless, Haikou feels a little more spacious and friendly than the average provincial capital, but, while by no means a bad place to spend a day in transit, nobody would pretend there is much to see or do here. Moving on, if you can resist heading straight to Sanya to work on your tan, spend a couple of days hopping down between the towns along Hainan's **east coast**. This is the part of Hainan longest under Han dominion, and it's a good way to get the feel of the island.

Orientation, arrival, city transport and accommodation

Haikou appears fairly spread out on maps, but the downtown area forms a relatively compact block between waterfront Changti Dadao and the **airport**, about 2km south off Jichang Lu. The centre is marked by a busy mess of wide one-way traffic flows and

---

MOVING ON FROM HAIKOU

Flying is the easiest way out of Haikou, with the city connected to Sanya and two dozen mainland locations between Urumqi and Hong Kong. **Ferries** leave Haikou's New Port about every hour to Hai'an, at Guangdong's southernmost tip (90min; buses meet ferries for the 150km run to Zhanjiang); three times daily to Zhanjiang (3hr); and several times a week to Guangzhou and Hong Kong (25hr). There are also three daily services to Beihai, in Guangxi, from Xiuying wharf (11hr). Ticket offices at the ports open daily 9am–4pm, and there's usually no trouble in getting a seat for the next service. Various levels of comfort, from bench seats to beds, are available on the longer hauls, and it's definitely worth paying for a cabin rather than spending the trip surrounded by seasick hordes watching non-stop kung fu flicks. Your accommodation will be able make bookings for boats and planes if you give them at least a day's notice, or see "Listings", p.584, for airline and tour operator details.

The practicalities of getting out by **bus** depend on where you're heading. Most roads lead to **Sanya**, with several services a day from the long-distance bus station, and most hotels will be able to book you on to **luxury buses** which speed down the highway in real comfort. These also leave from a depot about 200m east of Haikou Park on the south side of Haifu Dadao. For anywhere else, first try the long-distance bus station, which has daily departures to all of Hainan's larger settlements, and also through services (ferry fare included) to the mainland cities of Liuzhou, Beihai and Nanning in Guangxi, and to Guangzhou, Hai'an and Zhanjiang in Guangdong. More local destinations are covered by **minibuses** from depots on the relevant sides of town. To reach these, take bus #6 from Changti Dadao 5km out to the **western depot**, and bus #9 from near Haikou Park to the **eastern depot**, 2km along Haifu Dadao.

pedestrian overpasses surrounding **Haikou Park**, with the most interesting shopping districts in the northerly **old colonial quarter** along Jiefang Lu and Boai Bei Lu. The **New Port** is north off Changti Dadao on Xingang Lu, where ferries from Guangdong and Hong Kong pull in; those from Beihai in Guangxi use the **Xiuying wharf**, 5km farther east along Binhai Dadao. Whichever you end up at, high-speed and regular buses to Sanya will be waiting, thus avoiding the need to stay in Haikou. Arriving by road from elsewhere on the island, the official **long-distance bus station** is centrally positioned south of Haikou Park on Daying Houlu, with short-range **minibuses** dropping off all over the city's outskirts.

The crowded central roads don't make Haikou's **city bus service** a very good way of getting around, except to reach remote transit points (bus #3 runs east from the Xiuying wharf area right to the western end of Changti Dadao, while #7 runs from the airport through the centre to the New Port. **Taxis** are much faster and so absurdly plentiful that you have only to pause by the kerb for one to pull up instantly. They cost about ¥10 to hire, and a trip right across the city shouldn't be much more than twice this.

HAIKOU AND THE EAST COAST

Haikou	海口	hǎikǒu

ARRIVAL

Eastern minibus depot	海口东站	hǎikǒu dōngzhàn
New Port	海口新港	hǎikǒu xīngǎng
Western minibus depot	海口西站	hǎikǒu xīzhàn
Xiuying wharf	秀英港	xiùyīng gǎng

ACCOMMODATION AND RESTAURANTS

Erge Zui Fandian	二哥醉饭店	èrgēzuì fàndiàn
Friendship	友谊大酒店	yǒuyì dàjiǔdiàn
Haikou	海口宾馆	hǎikǒu bīnguǎn
Nanhai	南海酒店	nánhǎi jiǔdiàn
Overseas Chinese	华侨大厦	huáqiáo dàshà
Post and Telecommunications	邮电大厦	yóudiàn dàshà
Wuzhi Shan	五指山酒店	wǔzhǐshān jiǔdiàn

THE CITY

Hai Rui Mu	海瑞墓	hǎiruì mù
Wugong Ci	五公祠	wǔgōng cí

THE EAST COAST

Lingshui	陵水	língshuǐ
Nanwan Monkey Island	南湾猴岛	nánwānhóu dǎo
Nanlin	南林	nánlín
Qionghai	琼海	qiónghǎi
Wanning	万宁	wànníng
Dongshan Ling	东山岭	dōngshān lǐng
Wenchang	文昌	wénchāng
Dongjiao Yelin	东郊椰林	dōngjiāo yēlín
Xinglong	兴隆	xīnglóng

The **telephone code** for Haikou is ☎0898

Larger cabs are more expensive to hire and their rate per kilometre is higher, while all vehicles are charged an extra ¥3 or so to enter a port area.

There's a staggering lack of information about the island in Haikou, with tour agents only geared to getting you to Sanya as fast as possible. If you plan to explore Hainan's backwaters, there's a good **map of the island** (naturally called *Map of Hainan*) worth getting hold of from hawkers or kiosks. It includes spreads of Haikou, Sanya and Tongshi, and a detailed road map of the island with even minor sights marked in English.

Accommodation

The city's accommodation is all pretty central, most of it near the long-distance bus station in the streets east of Haikou Park. In summer, you'll want air conditioning, and room rates are always worth bargaining over. The biggest places have their own banks (guests only), postal and phone services, shops and restaurants.

Friendship, corner of Jiefang Lu and Datong Lu, about 700m due north of the park (☎6225566). Decent, standard Chinese hotel, with mildly tatty rooms and service. ⑤.

Hainan Guanbo Dianshi Zhaodaisuo, Daying Houlu. Very cheap and basic guesthouse which probably won't let you stay – look for the faded English writing and try anyway. Beds ②.

Haikou, Daying Houlu (☎5350221, fax 5350232). Very popular, hugely expensive, multi-starred monster with all facilities. ⑧.

Huaiyuan, corner of Daying Xi Lu and Daying Houlu, immediately south of Haikou Park (☎6773385). The lobby is an old Portuguese building, though the rooms out the back are of more conventional motel style. Quiet after the karaoke closes down. ⑥.

Nanhai, Jichang Dong Lu (☎6778015). Best bargain in town, and consequently full up most of the time. Clean, threadbare doubles with or without air conditioning. ③–⑤.

Overseas Chinese, Datong Lu (☎6773289, fax 6772094). A three-star business centre and good value considering local prices. Doubles and triples. ⑥.

Post and telecommunications, Nanbao Lu (☎6778227, fax 6778200). Hidden away in the backstreets. The lobby is depressingly dusty and dingy, but rooms are not bad value. ⑤.

Wuzhi Shan, Jichang Dong Lu (☎5355101). Moderately priced hotel with no frills. ⑥.

The City

More than anything, Haikou is a truly tropical city, complete with palm-lined streets, something particularly striking if you've just arrived from a miserable northern Chinese winter. Noisy but laid-back, it's also pleasantly shabby, despite the amount of money spent on modernizing the centre – even in upmarket areas, you only have to walk down the side streets to find the usual Chinese jumble of fast-food stalls and hawkers, small trestle tables spread with cheap crockery, clothes and household goods. The **old quarter**, boxed in by Boai Bei Lu, Jiefang Lu and Datong Lu, is the best area to stroll through with its grid of century-old colonial architecture, here partially restored and functioning as stores and businesses. It's especially good in the evening when the streets are brightly lit and bursting with people out shopping, eating and socializing.

Haikou has just two formal sights, either of which will fill you in on Hainan's position in Han Chinese history. About 5km west of the downtown area, a park and stone sculptures of lions and guards surround **Hai Rui Mu**, tomb of the virtuous Ming-dynasty official Hai Rui (daily 9am–4pm; ¥3). Take bus #2 from Longhua Lu to the Hai Rui Mu stop on Haixiu Dadao, and it's about 500m south off Shugang Dadao. Hai Rui's honesty, which earned him exile during his lifetime, caused a furore in the 1960s when historian **Wu Han** wrote a play called *The Dismissal of Hai Rui*, a parody of events sur-

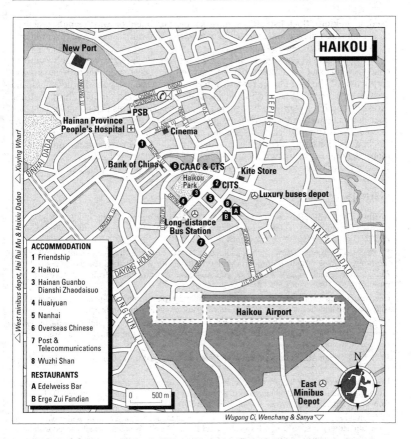

ACCOMMODATION
1 Friendship
2 Haikou
3 Hainan Guanbo Dianshi Zhaodaisuo
4 Huaiyuan
5 Nanhai
6 Overseas Chinese
7 Post & Telecommunications
8 Wuzhi Shan

RESTAURANTS
A Edelweiss Bar
B Erge Zui Fandian

Wugong Ci, Wenchang & Sanya

rounding the treatment of Marshall **Peng Dehui**, who had criticized Mao's Great Leap Forward. The play's supression and the subsequent arrest of Wu Han, who happened to be a friend of Deng Xiaoping, are generally considered to be the opening events of the Cultural Revolution.

On the other side of town is **Wugong Ci**, the Five Officials' Memorial Temple, 2.5km southeast of the centre along Haifu Dadao (daily 8.30am–5pm; ¥5; bus #9). This brightly decorated complex was built during the late Qing to honour Li Deyu, Li Gang, Li Guang, Hu Chuan and Zhao Ding, Tang men of letters who, yet again, were banished here after rashly criticizing their government. There's also a hall in the grounds commemorating Hainan's most famous exile, the rather better-known Song-dynasty poet **Su Dongpo**, who spent his later years near **Danzhou**, in the island's northwest.

Eating and drinking

There's some good eating to be had in Haikou, although, perhaps because this is essentially a mainland Chinese colony, restaurant dishes are not as exotic as you might hope for. The quantity and variety of ingredients on display at market stalls and outside diners are certainly promising: green, unhusked coconuts (sold as a drink, but seldom used in cooking); thick fish steaks, mussels, eels, crab and prawns; mangoes, pineapples, bananas, watermelons, guavas, plums, star fruit and jak fruit; and, everywhere, piles of seasonal green vegetables.

The upper end of Longhua Lu is a good place to find **cheap snacks** such as grilled chicken wings and local "pizza" made from fried rice crust sprinkled with carrots and spring onion. The best **cheap restaurants** are around the junction with Jiefang Lu and west down Changti Dadao, with some fine seafood places and a variety of **hotpot stalls**. Closer to the hotels and the bus station, Jichang Dong Lu also has some good-value open-air canteens and formal restaurants, such as *Erge Zui Fandian*, about 150m east of the *Nanhai Hotel*, which cooks seafood to your specifications, and also specializes in chicken and fish casseroles. Aside from these, try the **hotel restaurants and bars** for more elaborate fare, though menus are expensive. The trendy *Edelweiss Bar*, also in Jichang Dong Lu, has the best coffee in town, served in plunger mugs.

Listings

Airlines The *CAAC* office is next to the *Overseas Chinese Hotel* on Datong Lu (daily 8am–10pm; ☎6781735 or 6706281). There's also a branch of *China Southern Airlines* (daily 8am–5.30pm; ☎5350221 or 6777019) at the *Haikou Hotel*.

Banks and exchange Your accommodation may be able to help with money-changing, otherwise the *Bank of China* is at 10 Datong Lu (Mon–Fri 8am–6pm). White-hatted Hui women outside the *Haikou Hotel* openly change foreign currency, apparently with police permission, and give good rates.

Cinema There's a popular screen and entertainment complex on Jiefang Lu, and an open-air effort with concrete benches and palm trees in Haikou Park on the Daying Houlu side.

Hospital Hainan Provincial People's Hospital, Longhua Lu (☎6225933). In addition, reflexology and massage practitioners set up in the afternoons at the bottom end of Datong Lu, across from the *Overseas Chinese Hotel*.

PSB The Foreign Affairs Department is on Changti Dadao, just west of the junction with Longhua Lu.

Post and telecommunications The main post office, parcel post service and IDD phones are in the north of the city on Deshengsha Lu, parallel and immediately south of Changti Dadao (daily 8am–6pm). Most hotels have their own postal and IDD services too.

Shopping Pearls are a good thing to buy while on Hainan, but Sanya is a much better place to find a bargain. Hotel gift shops can sell you strings of them, as well as coconut shells carved with faces, coral branches stained fluorescent colours and mounted in glass cases, and seashells, some carved with cameos. Whole shark skins – like sandpaper – dried jellyfish and other maritime curiosities in the shops along Jiefang Lu are worth a look, and there's a good kite store on the north side of Haifu Dadao, about 200m east of Haikou Park, with a beautiful collection of handmade silk dragons, butterflies and birds.

Travel agents Hotels have tour desks, but neither they, the *CTS*, next to the *Overseas Chinese Hotel* on Datong Lu (daily 9am–5pm; ☎6719603 or 6795297), nor the *CITS*, around the corner from the *Haikou Hotel* on Haifu Dadao (daily 7.30am–11.30pm; ☎5354314 or 5358463), are really much use for anything other than transport bookings.

The east coast

Most east coast communities comprise small settlements of ethnic subgroups such as the Hakka, who were shuffled off the mainland by various turmoils, or returning Overseas Chinese deliberately settled here by the government, and many live by fishing, cash crop farming or pearl cultivation. Nowhere takes more than half a day to look round, with **Lingshui**, a hamlet with a long history, unexpected Communist connections and a nearby wildlife reserve, the pick of the bunch. It's best to travel on a flexible schedule, ready to stay put or move on as the situation demands. Everywhere has accommodation and places to eat, and **minibuses** are the best way to get around, with shuttle services running between towns from sunrise until after dark. Bear in mind that there are **no banks** capable of foreign currency transactions along the way, so carry enough cash to last until Sanya.

Wenchang, Qionghai, Wanning and around

WENCHANG, a decent-sized county town 70km southeast of Haikou, is known to the Chinese as the birthplace of the sisters **Song Qingling** and **Song Meiling**, respective wives to Sun Yatsen and Chiang Kaishek. Built up as a commercial centre last century by the French, it has now rather gone to seed. The **main bus station** is on the northern outskirts. From here walk downhill into town along Wenxin Lu and you'll quickly pass the reasonably priced *Yunshan Binguan* (③) and *Xiange Binguan* (③) on the left, before coming to an acute kink in the road over a **canal** with well-constructed stone embankments. Cross over and turn left, and some 500m straight ahead is the **new town** and a far more modern bridge, where you can catch minibuses out to the coastal village of **Qinglan** (20min). Take the ferry here across a small inlet, and it's another brief ride to **Dongjiao Yelin**, Hainan's first **coconut plantation**. Acres of beachfront have been planted with trees, making a nice backdrop, and, though the area is becoming developed in a haphazard way, with a handful of hotels under construction, it's a nice place to laze for a few hours.

Back in Wenchang and across the modern bridge, the road leads uphill to the outskirts of town and another minibus depot, where you can catch a ride 60km farther south to the city of **QIONGHAI** (Jiaji), where China's **first Communist cell** was formed in 1924. There's little to see, but it's a busy place, unusually tidy and with a healthy glut of markets specializing in locally made cane furniture. Qionghai's most famous resident is **Huang Sixiang**, a female guerrilla leader on Hainan during the Japanese occupation. The main road through town is Dongfeng Lu, offering air-conditioned rooms at the *Guangxing Binguan* (④), and plenty of places to eat in the streets around the heroic revolutionary sculpture which marks the town centre – try the two-storey *Meixiang Canting*.

The next stop, another 50km south, is **WANNING** (Wancheng), an unexciting town from where motorbike taxis with sidecars can take you 3km southeast to coastal vistas at **Dongshan Ling** (East Mountain Ridge), a formation of strangely sculpted and delicately balanced rocks, traced with paths and steps linking strategically placed pavilions and drink vendors. Continuing south along the highway from town, it's about 20km to **XINGLONG**, a dusty little village of interest for its **Tropical Agricultural Research Station**, set up by expatriate Chinese from Vietnam, Malaysia and Indonesia and famed for its coffee, as well as the nearby **hot springs** resort, 3km from town. The cheapest beds in the area are in Xinglong itself, while the Research Station and hot springs are expensive (cheapest deals around ⑥). If you fancy something wilder, try heading 15km south again to **NANLIN** village, which lies just northwest of a small but protected area of **native forests**, with some good hiking potential through the low hills.

Lingshui

Ninety minutes south of Wanning, **LINGSHUI** (Lingcheng) has been around for a long time. They were forging iron tools and making pottery here as far back as the Han dynasty, while uncovered silver tomb ornaments point to the town being an important commercial centre by the Ming dynasty. Somewhere that Li and Han seem to have always easily coexisted, Lingshui played a part in modern history when, having shifted south from Qionghai, China's **first Communist government** convened here in 1928, just months after Chiang Kaishek's bloody clampdown in Shanghai. The cell was still functioning when the Japanese stormed Hainan in February 1939, and its members retreated into the hills to wage guerrilla war on the invaders with the help of the local

Li population. The Communists never forgot this, and once in power granted the district nominal self-rule as **Lingshui Li Autonomous County**. For more on the Li, see box on p.593.

Today, Lingshui's dozen or so narrow streets are set back off the highway where it bends sharply past town near the bus station. Around town you'll see remains of a **Qing-dynasty monastery**, the interior still decorated with original frescoes, but now used to store video game machines; a **Communist Museum** in another building of similar vintage (there's a cannon outside); several fifty-year-old shops with what look like their original fittings; and one recent innovation, a **karaoke lottery lounge**, easily identifiable by the mass of ticket sellers and waste stubs scattered outside. Wander off to Lingshui's fringes and you could be stepping back a century ago with lanes twisting into the countryside between walls of low-family compounds, houses sporting decorative columns topped with lotus bud motifs, and courtyards thickly planted with slender **areca palms**, often with conical buckets strapped around the trunks. These catch falling **betel nuts** (*binlang*), a crop cultivated as a stimulant by the Li since at least Ming times. Women are the biggest users, but just about everyone in Lingshui seems to have stained their lips and teeth from chewing slices of the palm seed, wrapped inside a heart-shaped pepper vine leaf.

Lingshui's main **bus station**, on a bend in the highway, is where most minibuses from Wanning drop off and where Sanya- and Haikou-bound vehicles depart. If you're arriving from the south, you might also end up at the **minibus depot** about 1km down the road on the Sanya side of town. This is where you'll also find onward **transport to Xincun**. For **accommodation**, try the rooms at the *Jincheng Binguan* (③) or the dorm-style doubles at the *Yeyun Yuleting Zhaodaisuo* (②), near each other on the highway just north of the bus station – look for the adjacent *Bank of China* (which is unable to change travellers' cheques). The best places to **eat** are around here too. There's a popular and good-value restaurant directly opposite the bus station ticket office, and numerous bustling **tea houses** along the highway and backstreets.

Xincun and Nanwan Monkey Island

About 10km south of Lingshui, **XINCUN** is a small market town with a large Hakka population – you'll see plenty of black-clad Hakka women with broad hats and gold and jade jewellery. **Ferries** ply from here across to **Nanwan Monkey Island** (Nanwan Hou Dao), which is actually a peninsula, but there's no landward access. The **research station** based here studies local groups of macaques, small, bronze-haired monkeys with pale eyelids and red backsides, and there's a **visitors' centre** where you can feed them. Check that the island is open before heading out here, however, as access is periodically denied due to "monkey illnesses".

Minibuses from Lingshui leave you on Xincun's main street, and having pushed your way between market stalls and down to the water, you'll be grabbed by sampan owners to negotiate the cost of the ten-minute ride over to Nanwan; ¥5 per person is a decent price for the return trip, though locals pay far less. The inlet here is crammed with Hakka houseboats, all linked by boardwalks, with posts and nets marking their **pearl farms**, a major source of income for the town. On landing on the island, tractors can take you up to the visitors' centre for a small fee, or it's a thirty-minute walk along a well-maintained road – a good option, as you'll almost certainly get your best views of completely wild monkeys along the way. Those that hang out at the visitors' centre itself (¥5) are technically wild too, but seeing them here can be an awful experience, mainly because Chinese tourists like to intimidate them with big sticks and thrash any monkey they can catch, and the animals have become understandably hostile as a result. Buy peanuts at the gate if you want to feed them, but you'll be mobbed if you show any food and it's much better just to walk through the grounds and climb the hillside for views of family troupes crashing around in the treetops.

Sanya and the southern coast

Across the island from Haikou on Hainan's central southern coast (320km direct down the expressway), **SANYA** is, sooner or later, the destination of every visitor to the island. Though relics at the westerly town of **Yazhou** prove that the area has been settled for close on a thousand years, **Sanya city** itself is entirely modern, maintained as a scruffy tourist centre, fishing port and **naval base** for monitoring events (and staking China's claims) in the South China Sea. What pulls in the crowds are the surrounding sights, especially easterly **Dadonghai beach**, one of the few places in China where you can unwind in public. The Chinese also flock to associated legendary landmarks atop the **Luhuitou Peninsula** and west at **Tianya Haijiao**, while foreigners generally find the day trip out to a couple of tiny inhabited **coral islands** off Dadonghai more interesting.

Farther afield, the coastal arc between Sanya and the western industrial port of **Dongfang** sees few visitors. While Dongfang alone doesn't really justify a trip, it's emphatically worth getting as far as **Jianfeng Ling**, the most accessible surviving fragment of Hainan's indigenous mountain rainforest. If this doesn't appeal, there's plenty of transport north from Sanya to the Li stronghold of Tongshi, and on into the central highlands.

SANYA AND THE SOUTHERN COAST		
Sanya	三亚	*sānyà*
Dadonghai	大东海	*dàdōnghǎi*
Luhuitou Peninsula	鹿回头	*lùhuítóu*
ACCOMMODATION		
Green Island	绿岛饭店	*lǜdǎo fàndiàn*
Nanxiang	南乡饭店	*nánxiāng fàndiàn*
Sanya	三亚宾馆	*sānyà bīnguǎn*
Xiang Yuan	香苑宾馆	*xiāngyuàn bīnguǎn*
Zhaoqing	肇庆饭店	*zhàoqìng fàndiàn*
AROUND SANYA		
Dongfang	东方	*dōngfāng*
Jiangfeng	尖峰	*jiān fēng*
Jiangfeng Ling Forest Reserve	尖峰岭热带 原始森林自然保护区	*jiānfēnglíng rèdài yuánshǐsēnlín zìrán bǎohùqū*
Tianya Haijiao	天涯海角	*tiānyáhǎijiǎo*
Yazhou	崖州	*yázhōu*

Orientation, arrival and accommodation

The Sanya area comprises three distinct sections: Sanya city, Dadonghai and the Luhuitou Peninsula. **Sanya city** occupies a three-kilometre-long peninsula bounded west by the Beibu Gulf and east by the Sanya River. Aligned north–south, **Jiefang Lu** is the main road through town, forking at its southern end to run briefly southwest to the cargo wharves as Jiangang Lu, and east to form busy **Gangmen Lu**. This extends 4km out to **Dadonghai**, a kilometre-long spread of hotels, restaurants and shops backing on to Dadonghai beach, beyond which are the start of routes to Haikou and

> The **telephone code** for Sanya is ☎0899

Tongshi. Accessible either by boat from Sanya or by road from Dadonghai, the **Luhuitou Peninsula** is a huge granite headland rising immediately south of the city, separated from the cargo wharves by the harbour.

Arriving by air, Phoenix airport is about 15km to the north, and, as there is no airport bus, you'll need to catch a taxi into the city (¥20). Coming in by road, Sanya's main **long-distance bus station** is at the northern end of Jiefang Lu, while luxury buses from Haikou and minibuses from Tongshi and Lingshui pull up farther south, at various points between here and the Jiefang Lu–Gangmen Lu intersection. All first pass through Dadonghai, so if you're planning to stay there, ask to be set down en route. **Getting around**, there's the usual overload of taxi cabs and some motorcycle-and-sidecar assemblies as well as **public buses** – #2 and #4 run three times an hour from 6am until well after dark between the long-distance bus station and Dadonghai. You can also **rent cars** and bicycles (see "Listings", p.590 for details).

Accommodation

Sanya's accommodation is plentiful but pricey. Bargaining can often get substantial reductions on advertised rates, however, so politely put up a struggle when you check in. The two main areas are in Sanya itself and at Dadonghai, connected by buses #4 and #2.

Green Island, Jiefang Lu, Sanya (☎8268330). Friendly, mid-range place by local standards, with popular bar and restaurant. Triples, doubles and singles available. ⑦.

Hawaii, Dadonghai (☎8212210). Unimaginative tower block on the highway, but pretty relaxed and organized. ⑦.

Jinling Villa, Dadonghai. The only way to find this bargain-priced but under-the-counter guesthouse is to make enquiries at the *Roamland Garden Restaurant*. Very clean, neat doubles with shared bathrooms. ④.

Luhuitou, Luhuitou Peninsula (☎8212202). Take a taxi or motorbike from Dadonghai as this place is somewhat isolated. Set in large, rambling grounds with a coral rubble beach to lie on, it's a bit run-down, but you can get some very reasonable prices if you haggle. The self-contained units sleep two, three or five. ⑤.

Nanxiang, Xinjiang Lu, Sanya (☎8261094, fax 8277130). Brand-new, upmarket venture at the southern end of town, with helpful management and good facilities for the price. ⑦.

Sanya, Jiefang Lu, Sanya (☎8274703). Elderly and sombre, but reasonably maintained, offering triples, doubles and singles. ⑤.

South China, Dadonghai (☎8214998, fax 8212018). Comfortable, international-standard beachfront resort with all imaginable facilities, including pool, gym and Western and Oriental restaurants. ⑨.

Xiang Yuan, Jiefang Lu, Sanya (☎8273302). Inexpensive, but a bit of a walk to anywhere except the long-distance bus station, though local bus #2 passes by the door. Staff speak a little English. Triples, doubles and singles. ⑤.

Zhaoqing, Jiefang Lu, Sanya (☎8274135). Clean, simple rooms, with 24-hour hot water and air conditioning. ⑤.

The City

Sanya city is a classic port, busy, noisy and grubby, complete with neatly uniformed navy recruits scooting around on bicycles. There are several places to soak up the atmosphere and, for sheer sleaziness, you can't beat the **wharf area** along Jiangang Lu, where dubious characters, scantily clad women and an air of lazy indifference fill the untidy tea houses and back alleys. The **fishing docks** at the western end of Xinan Lu have a powerful

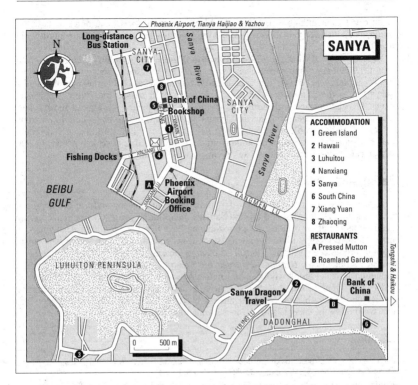

△ Phoenix Airport, Tianya Haijiao & Yazhou

SANYA

Long-distance Bus Station

SANYA CITY

Sanya River

Bank of China
Bookshop

SANYA CITY

Sanya River

Fishing Docks

XINJIANG LU

BEIBU GULF

Phoenix Airport Booking Office

GANGMEN LU

Tongshi & Haikou △

ACCOMMODATION
1 Green Island
2 Hawaii
3 Luhuitou
4 Nanxiang
5 Sanya
6 South China
7 Xiang Yuan
8 Zhaoqing
RESTAURANTS
A Pressed Mutton
B Roamland Garden

LUHUITON PENINSULA

Sanya Dragon Travel

Bank of China

DADONGHAI

0   500 m

mix of stench and activity as trawlers unload their catches to be auctioned off and ferried away on the back of cycle-rickshaws. It's worth a visit with a camera, despite having to wade ankle-deep through the mess – gumboots are sold at the gates.

At night, Sanya's **main market**, held in streets parallel and east of southern Jiefang Lu, is an interesting place to snack on local seafood and shop around the open-fronted stores, many so full that their wares overflow on to tables set up outside. You can buy boiled sweets by the kilo, hardware from coconut graters to giant cleavers and woks, and expensive imported toiletries, cigarettes and spirits smuggled in through Vietnam. There are also a couple of tea warehouses stocked with tea from all over the country, locally grown Xinglong coffee beans, and sachets of instant coffee flavoured with coconut.

Dadonghai and the Luhuitou Peninsula

Only 150m from the main road, occasionally crowded and seasonally blistering hot, **Dadonghai** has pretty well everything you could ask for in a tropical beach. Three kilometres long, there are palm trees, white sands (picked over and swept clean every day), and warm, blue water – a fair reward for making the journey to Hainan. A beachside bar and kiosks renting out jet skis, catamarans and rubber rings complete the scene, but on the whole the Chinese appear strangely bemused by beach life, as if they know it should be fun but are unsure of sure how to go about enjoying themselves. Swimming out farther than waist-deep water is sure to draw disbelieving looks from holidaying mainlanders, who seem uncomfortably self-concious in swimwear and hardly dare get their ankles wet. While it's all very relaxed for China, don't mellow too much, as unattended valuables will vanish, and women going topless, or any nudity, will lead to arrests.

Unless you're staying there, the **Luhuitou Peninsula** shouldn't take up much of your time. A ferry crosses from Sanya's wharf area to Luhuitou's shore (¥1), or you can catch a motorcycle combi from outside the *Hawaii Hotel* at Dadonghai over the peninsula's top to the *Luhuitou Hotel* (¥6). This latter road passes the summit entrance, where ¥15 gains access to a ponderous granite statue depicting a Li legend about a deer transforming into a beautiful girl as it turned to face a young hunter – Luhuitou means "Deer Turns its Head". From here the road slaloms downhill through barren scrub, past half-completed, abandoned holiday units, to the *Luhuitou Hotel* and nearby beach, whose rough coral composition can't compete with Dadonghai's sand.

Eating and drinking

The best places to try local **seafood** without bankrupting yourself are the al fresco night stalls at Dadonghai and around Sanya's main market, where you choose moray eel, reef fish, crab or cockles from buckets and have them cooked in front of you – fix prices first. Dadonghai has the cheapest sit-down restaurants, with some very clean, open-fronted places offering basically the same food as the stalls but in more comfort and at higher prices. *Roamland Garden* here also has coffee, bilingual menus and a Sichuanese owner/cook who speaks English and seems to have his finger on Sanya's pulse. The popular *Pressed Mutton Restaurant*, down near Sanya's wharves on Jiangang Lu, is good too, with wooden floors and sea breezes. For a real blow-out, big spenders can try the hotels, especially the *Green Island* and *Hawaii*.

Listings

Airlines Phoenix airport booking office is at the junction of Gangmen Lu and Jiefang Lu, Sanya, (Mon–Sat 9am–noon & 1.30–5pm; ☎8278221 or 8277409).

Banks and exchange The main *Bank of China*, Jiefang Lu, Sanya (Mon–Fri 8am–noon & 2.30–6pm), is excruciatingly understaffed and slow. There's also a Dadonghai branch, but it has been known to refuse to cash travellers' cheques. Hui women, their heads wrapped in towels, hang about the Jiefang Lu-Gangmen Lu junction if you want to change foreign currency.

Bookshops The bookstore on Jiefang Lu has a selection of maps and a few paperbacks in English.

Buses Minibuses from Jiefang Lu reach as far as Tongshi, Yazhou and Lingshui, while long-distance buses head east to Haikou and coastal destinations, west to Yazhou and Dongfang, and north to Tongshi. Luxury buses to Haikou are best organized through your accommodation, travel agents or from the departure point outside the Phoenix airport booking office.

Post office Sanya's GPO is on Xinjiang Lu, Sanya (daily 7.30am–7.30pm).

Scuba diving Low visibility and maximum depths between 10m and 30m don't make Hainan the most exciting location, but it can be good fun and there's always the novelty of having dived in China. The three areas are at Yalong Bay, east of Sanya (best for its moderate coral growth, variety of fish and lobster); Tianya Haijiao, over to the west (good for molluscs, but extremely shallow); and the coral islands, also west (the deepest sites). Staff are NAUI/PADI qualified, rental gear is fine and you need to have your C-card with you. Two shore dives cost ¥380, two boat dives ¥550. For bookings, see "Travel agents" below.

Shopping Sanya is an excellent place to pick up pearls, white, pink, yellow or black. The best buys are from local hawkers on Dadonghai beach, who sell strings of "rejects" for ¥50 or less with hard bargaining. Most of these pearls are perfectly genuine, just not of good enough quality, shape or size for commercial jewellery. If in doubt, scratch the surface – flaking indicates a thinly coated plastic bead.

Travel agents Upmarket hotels have their own travel desks, or try *Sanya Dragon Travel*, down past the *Hawaii Hotel* on Luling Lu, Dadonghai (8.30am–5pm; ☎8213526, fax 8213799). They speak some

English, and can arrange car rental if you've got a licence (¥350 per day, plus credit card deposit); scuba diving; mountain bike rental (¥20 a day); coral island or fishing trips; airport transfers and bookings; and day tours to Tongshi.

Around Sanya

Of the many coral islets south of Sanya, two – **Xidao** and **Dongdao**, the West and East islands – are deemed of no military significance, and can make an enjoyable trip in good weather. You're really doing this for the ninety-minute journey, which takes in some beautiful views of the coastline and mountains rising to the north, and the sight of long lines of grey destroyers powering west to patrol China's maritime boundaries. Once on the islands, the inhabitants, who live in houses built from coral blocks, are not particularly friendly, the beaches are mediocre and there's little to do except try out the local seafood and sit around waiting for the boat home. An academic attraction is that the islands mark the southernmost limit of China's unquestioned political authority – though there are ongoing attempts to stretch this as far as the **Spratly Islands** (see box below).

If you can speak Mandarin, boat owners might approach you on Dadonghai beach and offer their services. You can usually negotiate the cost down to ¥100 or less a head for a four-person boat, and pilots seem strangely willing to accept payment after the trip. Booking through an agent costs about twenty percent more, cash upfront. Either way, pack a bottle of drinking water, a sunscreen, hat and sunglasses, as there's scant shade on the islands and the boats are open-topped. The whole excursion lasts from about 8.30am to 5.30pm.

Tianya Haijiao and Yazhou

Any westbound bus, or a minibus from the upper reaches of Jiefang Lu in Sanya, can cart you 20km out of the city to **Tianya Haijiao**, a long beach strewn with curiously shaped boulders, whose name roughly translates as the "End of the Earth". This isn't as fanciful as it sounds, as for Hainan's scholarly political exiles this was just about as far as you could possibly be from life's pinnacle at the imperial court. The modern world has unfortunately descended very heavily on the area, however, and a new township with expensive accommodation and restaurants, ever-escalating entry fees to the beach itself and overly persistent hawkers make for an irritating experience. Chinese come in their thousands to have their photographs taken next to rocks inscribed with big red characters marking them as the "Sweetheart Stones", or "Limit of the Sky, Edge of the Sea".

THE SPRATLY ISLANDS

Chinese maps of China always show a looped extension of the southern borders reaching 1500km down through the South China Sea to within spitting distance of Borneo, enclosing a host of reefs and minute islands. These sit over what might be major **oil and gas reserves**, and are consequently claimed by every nation in the region – China, Malaysia, the Philippines, Taiwan and Vietnam all have garrisons posted on different atolls. Occupied by Japan during the 1940s but unclaimed after World War II, the **Spratly Islands** are perhaps the most contentious group. Vietnam and China have both declared ownership since the 1970s, coming to blows in 1988 when the Chinese navy sank two Vietnamese gunboats. Then the Philippines stepped in in 1995, destroying Chinese territorial markers erected over the most westerly reefs and capturing a nearby Chinese trawler. While there are unlikely to be any real disputes before guaranteed oil reserves are found, it's unsettling to know that the US oil company *Exxon* is sure enough of results to be investing in the region already.

Another 15km west of here on local transport, past a luxurious golf course, is **YAZHOU**, formerly one of Hainan's biggest towns but now more of a bottleneck for through traffic. It's chiefly known as the place where the thirteenth-century weaver **Huang Daopo** fled from her native Shanghai to escape an arranged marriage. After forty years living with the coastal Li, she returned to northern China in 1295 and introduced their superior textile techniques to the mainland. Get out when you see the reconstructed **Ming city gate**, and walk through it to a tiny **Taoist temple museum**, which includes traditional Li clothing and a Muslim Hui headstone and mosque oil lamp. The Hui have been on Hainan for several centuries and the countryside hereabouts is peppered with their distinctive cyclindrical graves. There's also a big mosque just north of Sanya. Walk back on to the main road and continue a kilometre or so west out of town, and you'll find a four-hundred-year-old, seven-storey brick **pagoda** leaning at a rakish angle next to a school – one of the few genuinely old structures on the island. The last direct transport back to Sanya leaves in the late afternoon.

West to Jiangfeng and Dongfang

There are departures until after midday from Sanya's long-distance bus station for the 165km run to the western port of **Dongfang**, up the coast beyond Yazhou, though you can also travel there in stages by minibus until later on in the day. This side of the island is incredibly poor and undeveloped compared with the east, partly because it's too far out of the way to benefit from tourism, also because the main sources of income here are various forms of **mining**, an industry that sees little financial returns for local communities.

The real reason to head out this way is to spend a day at **Jiangfeng Ling Forest Reserve**, a small indication of what the whole of southwestern Hainan looked like less than thirty years ago. Head first for **JIANGFENG** township, which lies at the base of the distinctively peaked Jiangfeng range some 10km east of the coastal road, about 115km from Sanya. Dongfang-bound transport can drop you at the turning, from where you can walk or wait for the next passing vehicle to pick you up. A dusty little hollow where pigs and dogs roam the streets between the market, Jiangfeng has two tea houses and around a hundred homes. The sole **guesthouse** (②) is a friendly place with a fine **restaurant** (try the chicken with locally grown cashew nuts), functioning plumbing and electric power.

The reserve itself is in the mountains 18km beyond Jiangfeng, reached daily by a single scheduled minibus (¥10), although it's possible to hire one (¥70 up, ¥50 down). **Jiangfeng Ling** – the mountain range itself – was agressively logged until 1992, when a *UNESCO* survey found 400 types of butterfly and 1700 plant species up here and persuaded the Chinese government to establish the reserve, leaving a sharp-edged forested crown above bare lowland slopes. Though commercial timber stands have since been planted, locals have been left without a livelihood for the time being, a problem slightly eased by aid packages from the *Asian Development Bank*. The dirt road to the summit ends on the forest's edge at a group of stores, a small restaurant, a botanical research station, and a little-frequented **hotel** (④), whose staff will be most surprised to see you. A tiled gateway marks the reserve entrance about 100m back up the road, from where partially paved paths lead off uphill for an hour-long circuit walk taking in some massive trees, vines, orchids, ferns, birds, butterflies and beautiful views from the 1056-metre ridge. After dark, armed with a flashlight and some caution, it's a good place to look for small mammals and reptiles.

Dongfang

Four hours from Sanya, **DONGFANG** (Basuo) is an industrial port with unfortunate associations. During the 1940s, the Japanese took Dongfang as their Hainan headquarters, developing mining operations inland, building the goods rail line which still runs between here and Sanya, and executing thousands of Li who are buried in a mass grave on a nearby hill. Arms smuggling and a large floating population of Vietnamese, Malay and Filipino "merchants" have given the town something of a wild reputation today, with tales of gun battles and banditry surrounding freelance gold mines in the area. However, though it's friendly enough, Dongfang itself is definitely dull. Should you end up here, there's one grey, overly long main street, a few places to eat and the best-value **hotel** is next to the bus station (②). Plenty of onward traffic covers the roads back to Sanya or northeast to Haikou via Danzhou.

Tongshi and the highlands

Occupying the island's central core, **Hainan's highlands** get scant attention from visitors, despite evidence of long association with **Li and Miao** peoples. Just 100km north of Sanya, **Tongshi**'s quiet pace and large concentration of Li make it the favoured place to start delving into the region, while farther out, **Baisha** and **Qiongzhong** are less obvious alternatives, though shot through with scenic and historic appeal. Tongshi and Qiongzhong lie on the main inland route between Haikou and Sanya, while Baisha is more remotely positioned on a less-frequented road in Hainan's central west.

LI AND MIAO

Hainan's million-strong **Li** population take their name after the big topknot or *li* which men once wore. Archeological finds and traditions shared with other southwestern Chinese peoples point to their arriving on Hainan from Guangxi about 200 BC, when they occupied the coast and displaced the aboriginal inhabitants. Driven inland themselves by later Han arrivals, the Li finally settled Hainan's central highlands (though a few remained on the coast) and spent the next two thousand years as rice farmers and hunters, living in villages with distinctive tunnel-shaped houses, evolving their own shamanistic religion, and using poisoned arrows to bring down game. **Li women** have long been known for their **weaving** skills, and the fact that, until very recently, many had their faces heavily **tattooed** with geometric patterns. This was partly so that the ancestors would recognize them after death, but also to make them undesirable to raiding parties of slavers from the coast, or rival **clans**. The latter form five major groups –Ha, Qi, Yun, Meifu and Cai – and they have never coexisted very well, quarrelling to this day over territorial boundaries and only really united in their dislike of external rulers. Though actively supporting Communist guerrillas against the Japanese, the Li have no great affection for the Han as a whole, and there were fourteen major rebellions against their presence on the island during the Qing era alone. Superficially assimilated into modern China, the Li would probably revolt again if they felt they could get away with it.

The Li are, however, pretty friendly towards outside visitors, and though traditional life has all but vanished over the last half-century, there are still a few special events to watch out for. Best is the **March 3 Festival** (held on the third day of the third lunar month), the most auspicious time of the year in which to choose a partner, while in more remote corners of the highlands, **funerals** are traditionally celebrated with gunfire and three days of hard drinking by male participants.

Touted as Hainan's second "native minority" by the tourist literature, **Miao** are in fact comparatively recent arrivals, forcibly recruited from Guizhou Province as **mercenaries** to put down an eighteenth-century Li uprising. But when the money ran out the Miao stopped fighting and settled in the western highlands, where today they form a fifty-thousand-strong community. Though they now apparently intermarry with the Li, the US adventurer, Leonard Clark, who traversed the highlands in 1937, reported them as living apart in the remotest of valleys.

TONGSHI AND THE HIGHLANDS

Tongshi	通什	*tōngshí*
Baoting	保亭	*bǎotíng*
Qizhi Shan	七指山	*qīzhǐ shān*
Wuzhi Shan	五指山	*wǔzhǐ shān*
Baisha	白沙	*báishā*
Qiongzhong	琼中	*qióngzhōng*
Fengmu Deer Farm	枫木养鹿场	*fēngmù yánglùchǎng*

Tongshi and around

Two hours north of Sanya, **TONGSHI** (Tongza) was voted China's most liveable modern town in 1995, and it deserves the accolade. Pocket-sized and surrounded by pretty countryside, a lack of heavy traffic or industry make it a pleasantly unpolluted spot to hang out for a day or two. Before 1987, Tongshi was also capital of Hainan's autonomous Li government, until it blew a billion-yuan road grant by importing luxury goods from Hong Kong and Vietnam, and building the literally palatial offices, now **Qiongzhou University**, on the hill above town. When Beijing caught up with what was going on they sacked the government and put the region under their direct control, a move which, while entirely justified, was greatly resented by the Li. The town has a well-presented **museum** and there's the possibility of making local contacts in Tongshi itself, while energetic hikers might want to go scrambling up nearby **Qizhi Shan** and **Wuzhi Shan**, whose summits are both steeped in local lore.

The Town

Reached via a street running uphill just past the bus station, the recently opened **Nationality Museum** (8am–5pm; ¥5) affords views across town to the aptly named **Nipple Mountain**, 5km away to the west, while the collection itself is excellent and English-speaking guides are available for ¥10. **Historical exhibits** include prehistoric stone tools and a bronze drum decorated with sun and frog motifs, similar to those associated with Guangxi's Zhuang; Ming manuscripts about island life; Qing wine vessels with octopus and frog mouldings; and details of the various modern conflicts culminating in the last pocket of Guomindang resistance being overcome in 1950. There's a fine array of artefacts and photos illustrating Hainan's **cultural heritage**, too – Li looms and textiles, traditional weapons and housing, speckled pottery from Dongfang, and pictures of major festivals. The museum is also near to the **university**, if you fancy a closer look at its absurdly ostentatious green-tiled architecture.

Back across the river, the town centre is a far less pretentious handful of streets and modern concrete-and-tile buildings which you can tour in around thirty minutes. **Henan Lu** runs west along the waterfront from the bridge, popular in summer with its outdoor restaurants and cool breezes, though it sometimes gets flooded by the river after heavy rain. One block back, Tongshi's **public square** is a sociable place to hang out after dark and meet people, full of tables serviced by drink and snack vendors, crowds watching open-air table-tennis tournaments and queuing for the cinema. Nearby, on Jiefang Lu, there's a chance to see dark-dressed Miao and the occasional older Li women with tattoos at the early-morning produce **market** where wares include sweet, milky-white spirit sold in plastic jerrycans, deer and dog meat, and also **rat**, split open like a French roll and grilled.

You can see more of the Li by catching a minibus 2km south to the tacky displays at **Fanmao Mountain Fortress Village**, but there's more to be said for just heading off into the countryside on foot. From the north side of the bridge, follow Hebei Xi Lu west along the river for 150m to a grossly patronizing **statue** of grinning Li, Miao and Han characters standing arm in arm. The crack in the middle is where somebody deliberately drove a truck into it a week after its unveiling. Take the road uphill from here and keep going as far as you want to, through vivid green fields and increasingly poor villages, ultimately built of mud and straw and surrounded by split bamboo pickets to keep livestock in. Among these you'll see more substantial barns with traditional tunnel shapes and carved wooden doors.

Practicalities

Set at the base of low hills, Tongshi's tiny centre sits on the southern bank of a horseshoe bend in the generally unimpressive **Nansheng River**. The main road comes up from the coast as **Haiyu Lu**, bypasses the centre, crosses over the river, turns sharply left past the **bus station**, and bends off north through the island towards Qiongzhong and Haikou. The cheapest **accommodation** is the sparkling clean hostel immediately on the south side of the bridge (②), with more spacious, equally well-maintained rooms at the *Tourist Guest House* (☎622688; ④) on the north side of the river and east down Hebei Dong Lu – look for the blue-and-white horse symbol. The restaurant opposite the bus station does good **dim sum** breakfasts, while Henan Lu's **restaurants** offer mixed menus of fish, fowl and vegetables; fix prices first as they always overcharge. There are plenty of places selling cakes and snacks in the centre, too, along with a *Bank of China* on Jiefang Lu (Mon–Fri 8am–5pm) which usually gives no trouble cashing travellers' cheques.

Leaving, scheduled buses head to Sanya, Baoting, Wuzhi Shan, Baisha, Qiongzhong and Haikou, with Sanya minibuses constantly circling the town. They leave only when full, so never get into an empty vehicle unless you want a long wait.

Wuzhi Shan and Qizhi Shan

Several Li myths explain the formation of **Wuzhi Shan** (Five-finger Mountain) whose 1867m summit rises 30km northeast of Tongshi at Hainan's apex. In one tale the mountain's five peaks are the fossilized fingers of a dying clan chieftain, while another holds that they represent the Li's five most powerful gods. Either way, Wuzhi Shan was once a holy site drawing thousands of people to animist festivals. Though the mountain is rarely a place of pilgrimage for the Li today, remoter villages in this part of Hainan maintain the old religion, raising archways over their gates which are occasionally embellished with bull or chicken heads. It's still possible to climb the mountain – take a bus from Tongshi to **WUZHI SHAN** township, then local transport to the *Wuzhi Shan Binguan* (④). From here it's a steep and slippery three-hour scramble to the peak, initially through jungly scrub, then pine forests. Although it's often clouded over, the summit offers further contorted pines, begonias and views.

Qizhi Shan (Seven-finger Mountain), representing seven lesser Li immortals being vanquished by Wuzhi's five, lies about 40km by road southeast of Tongshi via **BAOTING** (Baocheng). A somnulent little hollow, Baoting is another good place to wander aimlessly off into the countryside from, and you can get to the base of the mountain by catching available transport 10km east to **Shiling**, and thence 11km north to **Ba Cun**. The climb is said to be shorter than that at Wuzhi Shan, but march harder.

Baisha and Qiongzhong

The sixty-kilometre journey from Tongshi north to **Baisha**, along a turning off the main road, takes in some splendid views as the road weaves up Hainan's denuded central ranges. Passing a couple of abandoned, ruinous blockhouses which were the headquarters of Hainan's Communist forces during the Japanese occupation, the bus eventually reaches a ridge from where on a clear day you can see the remarkable peaks of **Hong Mo Shan**, the Red Mist Mountains, away to the northeast. Thirty minutes later you rumble into **BAISHA**, an unattractive sugar town with a large but not obvious Li population and two **places to stay** – the cheap and grubby *Baisha Lushe* (②), and a neater, pricier guesthouse near the bridge (④). At one end of a high, fertile valley covered in patchy remnant forests and various plantations, Baisha's surroundings make very appealing walking country, however, overlooked by the broodingly romantic **Bawang Ling** mountain range, 20km away to the west, whose jungles are home to Hainan's last **black gibbons**. The animals were remorselessly hunted for their long forearm bones, which were turned into chopsticks valued for their rumoured ability to turn black if dipped in poisoned food. Now only an estimated nineteen survive.

The road from Tongshi to **QIONGZHONG** (Yinggen) bears east around the base of Wuzhi Shan, with viewing platforms along the roadside to take in the spectacle of **Baihua Waterfall** tumbling off the peak, a spot said to be inhabited by several Li goddesses. Qiongzhong itself is an intensely busy, thoroughly scruffy three-street market centre, with no shortage of places to eat and good-value **accommodation** in the white-tiled transport building downhill from the bus station (②) – look for the circular bus symbol on the roof. About 25km northeast along the Haikou road, the entrance to **Fengmu Deer Farm** (daily 9am–4pm; ¥2) is marked by an unmissable stylized concrete deer and a reception centre hoping to tap interest in another rare beast, the **Hainan deer**. On the shores of a small reservoir, the farm was established as a breeding centre in 1964 after the Hainan deer became extinct in the wild, and has since reintroduced populations to reserves in the west of the island. There's a small paddock at the back, where visitors can stroke the animals and be deafened by their shrill whistles. There's plenty of passing traffic throughout the day in both directions along the main road.

travel details

Trains

Fuzhou to: Beijing (daily; 33hr); Guangzhou (daily; 36hr); Nanchang (daily; 14hr); Shanghai (daily; 26hr); Xiamen (daily; 16hr).

Guangzhou to: Beijing (4 daily; 33hr); Changsha (9 daily; 14hr); Chengdu (daily; 50hr); Foshan (8 daily; 45min); Guilin (2 daily; 18hr); Guiyang (2 daily; 40hr); Huizhou (2 daily; 3hr); Kowloon (4 daily; 2hr); Kunming (2 daily; 60hr); Meizhou (daily; 7hr); Nanchang (4 daily; 17hr); Nanning (daily; 18hr); Shanghai (2 daily; 33hr); Shaoguan (12 daily; 5hr); Shenzhen (hourly; 2hr); Zhaoqing (daily; 2hr).

Huizhou to: Guangzhou (2 daily; 3hr); Meizhou (2 daily; 5hr).

Meizhou to: Guangzhou (2 daily; 8hr); Huizhou (2 daily; 5hr).

Shaoguan to: Changsha (5 daily; 10hr); Guangzhou (12 daily; 5hr); Hengyang (3 daily; 5hr).

Shenzhen to: Changsha (2 daily; 15hr); Guangzhou (hourly; 2hr); Kowloon (50mins); Shaoguan (3 daily; 6hr).

Xiamen to: Fuzhou (daily; 16hr); Hangzhou (daily; 29hr); Nanjing (daily; 30hr); Shanghai (daily; 29hr).

Buses

Chaozhou to: Guangzhou (14hr); Huizhou (10hr); Meizhou (8hr); Shantou (1hr); Shenzhen (15hr).

Fuzhou to: Guangzhou (22hr); Ningbo (20hr); Quanzhou (4hr); Shenzhen (22hr); Wenzhou (11hr); Xiamen (7hr).

Guangzhou to: Beihai (24hr); Changsha (20hr); Chaozhou (16hr); Dongguan (1hr); Foshan (1hr); Fuzhou (30hr); Ganzhou (14hr); Guilin (24hr); Haikou (20hr); Huizhou (5hr); Jiangmen (3hr); Meizhou (12hr); Nanning (30hr); Panyu (1hr); Qingyuan (3hr); Shantou (15hr); Shaoguan (9hr); Shenzhen (3hr); Shunde (1hr 30min); Xiamen (30hr); Zhangjiang (13hr); Zhaoqing (3hr); Zhuhai (4hr).

Haikou to: Guangzhou (20hr); Lingshui (6hr); Qionghai (3hr 30min); Qiongzhong (5hr); Sanya (3-7hr); Shenzhen (20hr); Tongshi (5hr); Wanning (5hr); Wenchang (2hr); Zhanjiang (7hr).

Huizhou to: Chaozhou (11hr); Guangzhou (5hr); Meizhou (10hr); Shantou (10hr); Shenzhen (4hr).

Meizhou to: Chaozhou (8hr); Dapu (4hr); Guangzhou (12hr); Shaoguan (12hr); Shantou (9hr); Shenzhen (12hr).

Quanzhou to: Fuzhou (4hr); Xiamen (2hr).

Qingyuan to: Guangzhou (5hr); Shaoguan (8hr); Zhaoqing (5hr).

Sanya to: Baisha (4hr); (Baoting (90min); Dongfang (4hr); Haikou (3-7hr); Lingshui (2hr); Qionghai (4hr 30min); Qiongzhong (4hr); Tongshi (2hr); Wanning (3hr); Wenchang (6hr); Yazhou (1hr).

Shantou to: Chaozhou (1hr); Guangzhou (15hr); Huizhou (10hr); Meizhou (9hr); Shaoguan (12hr); Shenzhen (14hr).

Shaoguan to: Ganzhou (Jiangxi Province, 6hr); Guangzhou (10hr); Meizhou (12hr); Pingshi (4hr); Qingyuan (8hr); Shantou (12hr).

Shenzhen to: Dongguan (2hr); Guangzhou (3hr); Hong Kong (2hr).

Xiamen to: Fuzhou (7hr); Guangzhou (20hr); Shenzhen (20hr); Wenzhou (18hr).

Zhanjiang to: Guangzhou (13hr); Zhaoqing (10hr).

Zhaoqing to: Guangzhou (3hr); Qingyuan (5hr); Zhanjiang (10hr).

Zhuhai to: Cuiheng (1hr); Foshan (4hr); Guangzhou (4hr); Jiangmen (2hr); Shunde (2hr 30min).

Ferries

Chaozhou to: Guyie (for Dapu or Meizhou; daily; 11hr).

Fuzhou (Mawei) to: Shanghai (6 monthly; 36hr).

Guangzhou to: Haikou (daily; 30hr); Hong Kong (2 daily; 4–14hr); Lianhua (daily; 2–8hr); Macau (daily; 7hr); Shajiao (daily; 4hr); Shanghai (weekly; 60–100hr); Wuzhou (daily; 12–18hr); Xiamen (weekly; 24hr); Zhaoqing (daily; 4hr).

Haikou to: Beihai (3 daily; 11hr); Guangzhou (twice weekly; 25hr); Hai'an (hourly; 90min); Hong Kong (twice weekly; 25hr); Zhanjiang (2 daily; 3hr).

Shantou to: Hong Kong (weekly; 14hr); Xiamen (weekly; 20hr).

Shenzhen to: Hong Kong (7 daily; 45min); Macau (daily; 2hr); Zhuhai (30 daily; 1hr).

Xiamen to: Hong Kong (4 weekly; 17hr).

Zhanjiang to: Haikou (2 daily; 3hr).

Zhaoqing to: Guangzhou (daily; 4hr); Wuzhou (daily; 8hr).

Zhuhai to: Hong Kong (8 daily; 1hr); Macau (5 daily; 20min); Shenzhen (30 daily; 1hr).

Planes

DOMESTIC

Fuzhou to: Beijing (2 daily; 3hr); Guangzhou (2 daily; 1hr 30min); Hong Kong (3 daily; 1hr 30min); Shanghai (3 daily; 1hr 10min); Wuyi Shan (3 weekly; 40min); Xiamen (2 daily; 35min).

Guangzhou to: Beihai (2 daily; 50min); Beijing (9 daily; 2hr 45min); Changsha (2 daily; 1hr); Changzhou (daily; 2hr); Chengdu (5 daily; 1hr 45min); Chongqing (7 daily; 1hr 30min); Dalian (daily; 3hr); Fuzhou (2 daily; 1hr); Guilin (4 daily; 40min); Guiyang (3 daily; 1hr 15min); Haikou (9 daily; 50min); Hangzhou (3 daily; 1hr 30min); Harbin (2 daily; 4hr); Hefei (daily; 1hr 30min); Hohhot (2 weekly; 5hr); Hong Kong (5 daily; 30min); Kunming (3 daily; 2hr); Lanzhou (daily; 3hr); Meizhou (daily; 30min); Nanchang (2 daily; 1hr); Nanjing (5 daily; 2hr); Nanning (4 daily; 50min); Qingdao (2 daily; 2hr 30min); Sanya (2 daily; 1hr 10min); Shanghai (11 daily; 2hr); Shantou (4 daily; 40min); Taiyuan (daily; 2hr); Tianjin (daily; 2hr 30min); Urumqi (2 daily; 5hr); Wuhan (6 daily; 1hr 20min); Xiamen (2 daily; 1hr); Xi'an (3 daily; 2hr); Zhengzhou (4 daily; 1hr).

Haikou to: Beijing (4 daily; 3hr); Changsha (daily; 2hr); Chengdu (7 weekly; 2hr); Guangzhou (9 daily; 1hr); Guilin (4 weekly; 1hr 20min); Kunming (daily;1hr 20min); Nanjing (5 weekly; 2hr 40 min); Shanghai (2 daily; 2hr); Shenzhen (2 daily; 50min); Urumqi (weekly; 8hr); Wuhan (daily; 2hr); Xi'an (4 weekly; 4hr); Zhanjiang (daily; 30min).

Sanya to: Beijing (5 weekly; 5hr); Guangzhou (2 daily; 1hr); Shanghai (5 weekly; 2hr 30min); Shenzhen (daily; 1hr 15min).

Shenzhen to: Beihai (daily; 1hr 30min); Beijing (6 daily; 3hr); Changsha (2 daily; 1hr); Chengdu (2 daily; 2hr 20min); Chongqing (3 daily; 2hr 20min); Fuzhou (daily; 1hr 10min); Guilin (daily; 50min); Guiyang (5 weekly; 1hr 20min); Haikou (3 daily; 50min); Hangzhou (daily; 1hr 40min); Harbin (daily; 5hr); Hefei (3 weekly; 2hr); Kunming (2 daily; 2hr

40min); Meizhou (3 weekly; 45min); Nanchang (2 daily; 1hr); Nanjing (daily; 1hr 50min); Sanya (daily; 1hr); Shanghai (5 daily; 2hr); Shantou (daily; 40min); Wuhan (4 daily; 1hr 30min); Xiamen (daily; 1hr); Xi'an (daily; 2hr).

Wuyi Shan to: Fuzhou (3 weekly; 40min), Shanghai (2 weekly; 1hr); Shantou (weekly; 1hr 20min); Wuyi Shan (5 weekly; 40min).

Xiamen to: Beijing (3 daily; 2hr 30min); Fuzhou (daily; 30 min); Guangzhou (3–5 daily; 50min); Shanghai (7 daily; 1hr 10min); Shenzhen (2 daily; 1hr 10min); Wuyi Shan (5 weekly; 40min).

INTERNATIONAL

Guangzhou to: Bangkok (3 weekly; 3hr); Ho Chi Min City (2 weekly; 5hr); Jakarta (2 weekly; 5hr 30min); Kuala Lumpur (4 weekly; 3hr 30min); Manila (weekly; 4hr); Melbourne (weekly; 10hr); Penang (3 weekly; 5hr); Singapore (2 weekly; 4hr); Surabaya (2 weekly; 6hr); Sydney (weekly; 10hr); Vientiane (weekly; 3hr).

Shenzhen to: Bangkok (3 weekly; 3hr); Jakarta (weekly; 3hr); Singapore (weekly; 4hr);

Xiamen to: Manila (4 weekly; 3hr); Singapore (daily; 4hr 10min);

CHAPTER NINE

HONG KONG AND MACAU

The long-awaited handover of **Asia's last two European colonies**, Hong Kong in 1997 and Macau in 1999, is one of the great historic dramas of our time. Nothing could better illustrate the rising power of East Asia and the eclipse of Europe at the dawn of the new millennium, than the unique spectacle of sovereignty over Hong Kong being voluntarily surrendered, under the terms of a 99-year-old treaty, to what is now the government of the People's Republic of China. Travellers to this region of China in the months and years after July 1, 1997 will be witnessing history in the making.

The **handover** has of course been a long time in coming. In the half century since the end of World War II, the status of these two pockets of land, clinging to the underside of China like tiny offspring, has become anachronistic to a degree that we almost overlook. Some thirty or forty years after the vast bulk of the world's colonies reverted to self-rule, the citizens of Hong Kong, for example – one of the richest, most self-confident cities in Asia – have remained subjects of a **governor** appointed without consultation by the British prime minister. That this anomalous situation has lasted, can mainly be attributed to the fact that the government of mainland China over the past fifty years has been so eminently bad by comparison. In Hong Kong, in particular, apart from demonstrations and some acts of violence at the height of the Cultural Revolution when the whole of China was in uproar, life has been one long ride to **economic success**, and the city is now perceived by virtually all of China as a model for future development.

This is not to say that Hong Kong and Macau are not thoroughly **Chinese**, of course, and very largely Cantonese. Not only is the population of the two territories 97 percent Chinese, but the overwhelming majority of the people speak only Chinese, eat only Chinese food, pray in Chinese temples and enjoy close cultural and blood relations with

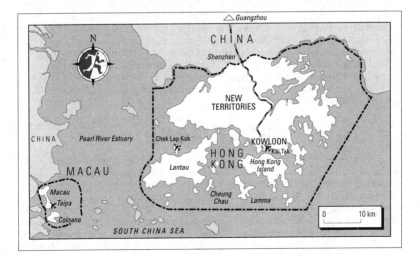

their Cantonese cousins on the mainland. Indeed, it is hard to overstate the symbolic importance of the handover from the point of view of the Chinese people in general – sealing the final end of the era of foreign domination, with the return of the last piece of occupied soil to the motherland just at the start of what many expect to be "China's century". Worrying questions, such as whether the Two Systems/One Nation policy dreamed of by Deng Xiaoping is worth the paper it is printed on, or whether life for the people of Hong Kong and Macau after 1997 can really be "business as usual", have become mere subplots, submerged in the misty-eyed reflections on the nation's glorious future. The fact that protest, repression and violence in the former colonies may be just around the corner will not dampen the millennial celebrations in Beijing.

Amid the uncertainty, however, it can only be assumed that in certain crucial ways life will continue as normal in both territories, even if the familiar old European names ("Victoria" Peak and "Queen's" Road, to name but a couple) are slowly replaced by Chinese versions. **Hong Kong** will continue to offer the densest concentration and greatest variety of **shops and shopping malls** of any place on earth, and the superb vistas of sea and island, luxuriantly green mountains and futuristic cityscapes will remain. What is even more certain is that the superb **culinary standards** of the region will be maintained, even if the range of ethnic restaurants and bars – from Nepali snackbars to British pubs – may suffer in the long term. The excellent infrastructure, including the brand **new airport** at Chek Lap Kok and the state-of-the-art underground trains, the ultra-helpful tourist advice offices and all the conveniences of a fully international city, make this an extremely soft entry indeed into the Chinese world.

While Hong Kong is a place to do business, **Macau** is known in the region as a Chinese playground, a haven for **gambling** and other sins, a mini Las Vegas of the East. But unlike Hong Kong, it will continue to bear the marks of its colonial past long after the handover, in its **Portuguese architecture**, old churches and (almost) Mediterranean seafront promenade. It can even boast its own indigenous population, the Macanese, a tiny mixed-blood minority, whose origins in the colony date back centuries and who are often bilingual in Portuguese and Cantonese. The cheap Portuguese wine and **Macanese cooking** – an extremely felicitous marriage of Chinese and Mediterranean influences – are further reminders of colonial heritage, as is the faintly Latin lifestyle, altogether less hectic and mellower than in other parts of southern China. South of the main city, on the tiny islands of Taipa and Coloane, are beaches and quiet fishing villages where you can eat fish and drink Portuguese rum in total peace.

Visitors to this part of southern China can expect to spend more **money** here than in other parts of the country, though not necessarily as much as you might expect considering the often huge differential in terms of quality of service compared to the mainland. **Public transport** in both Hong Kong and Macau is still incredibly cheap. Travellers on a tight budget who stay in dormitory accommodation can certainly get by on US$15 a day, though at the other end of the market in hotels, resturants and shops, prices quickly rise to international levels.

HONG KONG

In its multi-faceted role as a repository of traditional Chinese culture, the last jewel in the crown of the British Empire and the front-line state of the Pacific Rim economic explosion, **HONG KONG** is East Asia's most extraordinary city. Certain facts speak volumes: the territory's per capita GNP, for example, has doubled in a decade, overtaking that of the old imperial power in the process. With a population of just six million, the territory is currently the largest trading partner of the People's Republic of China, a country of over one billion people. The view of sky-scrapered Hong Kong Island, across the harbour from Kowloon, is replacing Manhattan as the most stunning urban panorama on earth. And, with a relatively free press and a sophisticated, well-informed public, the 1997 sovereignty handover to the still nominally Communist government in Beijing is an event unprecedented in modern history.

The territory of Hong Kong comprises an irregularly shaped peninsula abutting the Pearl River Delta to the west, and a number of offshore islands, which cover in total over a thousand square kilometres. The bulk of this area, namely the land in the north of the peninsula as well as most of the islands, is in fact rural and is known as the **New Territories** – this was the land leased to Britain for 99 years in 1898. The southern part of the peninsula, known as **Kowloon**, and the island immediately south of here, **Hong Kong Island**, the principal urban areas of Hong Kong, were in theory leased to Britain in perpetuity, though the British government in 1984 saw no alternative but to agree to hand back the entire territory as one piece. From midnight on June 30, 1997 the whole territory will become a **Special Administrative Region** (SAR) of China.

The island of Hong Kong offers not only traces of the **old colony** – from villages with English names to ancient trams trundling along the shore – but also superb **modern architecture** and bizarre cityscapes of towering buildings teetering up impossible slopes, as well as unexpected opportunities for **hiking** and even bathing on the delightful **beaches** of its southern shore. Kowloon, though, and in particular its southernmost tip, **Tsimshatsui**, is where the majority of tourists end up staying. This is not only the budget accommodation centre of Hong Kong, but also the most cosmopolitan area of perhaps any Chinese city, with a substantial population of immigrants from the Indian subcontinent. And as the territory's principal tourist trap, it boasts more shops offering a greater variety of goods per square kilometre than anywhere in the world (not necessarily at reasonable prices, though). North of Tsimshatsui, Kowloon stretches away into the New Territories, an area of so-called **New Towns** as well as ancient villages, secluded beaches and rural tranquillity. In addition, there are the **offshore islands**, which are well worth a visit for their fish restaurants, scenery and, if nothing else, for the experience of chugging about on the **inter-island ferries**. The islands of **Lamma** and **Lantau**, in particular, offer an extraordinarily rural and traffic-free contrast to the hubbub of downtown Hong Kong.

Some visitors dislike the speed, the extreme materialism and the obsession with shopping and brand names in Hong Kong. As in many a Western city, the locals are reserved towards strangers and, with its perennial massive engineering projects, downtown is certainly not a place to recover from a headache. On the other hand, it's hard not to enjoy the sheer energy of its streetlife and, given the uncertainties over the long-term development of the city, it may well be that now is the time to appreciate Hong Kong as perhaps never again.

Some history

While the Chinese may argue, with justification, that Hong Kong is Chinese territory, the development of the city only began with the **arrival of the British** in Guangzhou in the eighteenth century.

The **Portuguese** had already been based at Macau, on the other side of the Pearl River Delta, since the mid-sixteenth century and as Britain's sea power grew, so its merchants, too, began casting envious eyes over the Portuguese trade in tea and silk. The initial difficulty was to persuade the Chinese authorities that there was any reason to want to deal with them, though a few traders did manage to get permission to set up their warehouses in Guangzhou – a remote southern outpost, from the perspective of Beijing – and slowly trade began to grow. In 1757 a local Guangzhou merchants' guild called the **Co Hong** won the exclusive rights to sell Chinese products to foreign traders, who were now permitted to live in Guangzhou for about six months each year.

In the meantime, it had not escaped the attention of the foreigners that the trade was one-way only, and they soon began thinking up possible products the Chinese might want to buy in exchange. It did not take long to find one – **opium** from India. In 1773 the first British shipload of opium arrived and an explosion of demand for the drug quickly followed, despite an edict from Beijing banning the trade in 1796. Co Hong, which received commission on everything bought or sold, had no qualms about distributing opium to its fellow citizens and before long the balance of trade had been reversed very much in favour of the British.

The scene for the famous **Opium Wars** was now set. Alarmed at the outflow of silver and at the rising incidence of drug addiction among his population, the emperor appointed Lin Zexu as Commissioner of Guangzhou to destroy the opium trade. Lin, later hailed by the Chinese Communists as a patriot and hero, forced the British in Guangzhou to surrender their opium, before ceremonially burning it. Such an affront to British dignity could not be tolerated, however, and in 1840 a naval expeditionary force was dispatched from London to sort the matter out once and for all. After a year of gunboat diplomacy – blockading ports and seizing assets up and down the Chinese coast – the expeditionary force finally achieved one of their main objectives, through the **Treaty of Nanking** (1842), namely the ceding to Britain "in perpetuity" of a small offshore island. The island was called Hong Kong. This was followed eighteen years later, after more blockades and a forced march on Beijing, by the **Treaty of Peking** which granted Britain the Kowloon peninsula too. Finally, in 1898, as the Qing dynasty was entering its terminal phase, Britain secured a 99-year lease on an additional one thousand square kilometres of land to the north of Kowloon, which would be known as the New Territories.

The twentieth century has seen Hong Kong grow from a seedy merchants' colony to a huge international city, but progress has not always been smooth. The drug trade was voluntarily dropped in 1907 as the Hong Kong merchants began to make the transfer from pure trade to manufacturing. Up until World War II, Hong Kong prospered as the growing threat of both civil war and Japanese aggression in mainland China increasingly began to drive money south into the apparently safe confines of the British colony. This confidence appeared glaringly misplaced in 1941 when **Japanese forces** seized Hong Kong along with the rest of eastern China, though after the Japanese defeat in 1945, Hong Kong once again began attracting money from the mainland which was in the process of falling to the Communists. Many of Hong Kong's biggest tycoons today are people who escaped from mainland China, particularly from Shanghai, in 1949.

Since the beginning of the **Communist era**, Hong Kong has led a precarious existence, quietly making money while taking care not to antagonize Beijing. Had China wished to do so, it could have rendered the existence of Hong Kong unviable at any moment, by a naval blockade, by cutting off water supplies, by a military invasion – or by simply opening its border and inviting the Chinese masses to stream across in search of wealth. That it has never wholeheartedly pursued any of these options, even at the height of the Cultural Revolution, is an indication of the huge **financial benefits** that Hong Kong brings to mainland China in the form of its international trade links, direct investment and technology transfers.

For the last twenty years, the spectre of **1997** has begun to loom large in people's minds. Although it might seem odd that an "unequal treaty" imposed on the ailing Qing dynasty by Queen Victoria's government should still be recognized in the late twentieth century, it has suited both parties to honour it. Britain can offload six million subjects that it does not want and China can finally evict the foreign "barbarians" from its soil. Mrs Thatcher's **goodwill agreement** voluntarily to hand over the entire territory, including Hong Kong Island and Kowloon, might have been expected to yield more

---

Hong Kong phone numbers have no area codes. From outside the territory, dial the normal international access code + ☎852 (country code) + the number. However, **from Macau** you need only dial ☎01 + the number.

solid Chinese concessions on the future rights and freedoms of the citizens of Hong Kong, or at the very least to promote good relations between London and Beijing. However, disputes over the meanings of the 1984 treaty have led to even worse relations than before. Indeed, with Beijing setting up an administration of "yes" men, and the likelihood that the free media will not long survive the sovereignty transfer, it now appears that Britain's concessions have achieved precisely nothing for Hong Kong. Futile attempts by Governor **Chris Patten** to introduce democracy at the last minute may be well-meaning but they only serve to throw into relief the neglect of the interests of the people of Hong Kong by previous British administrations.

After 1997

Possible new **entry requirements** to Hong Kong after the 1997 handover are not likely to trouble casual tourists in the immediate future. Just as Hong Kong citizens will retain their right to visa-free travel to most countries of the world, so most foreigners will be allowed to enter Hong Kong without prior permission. The only likely change will be to the allowed length of stay. Prior to the handover, British nationals could stay for a full twelve months on arrival and many other nationalities for three months. For up-to-date information, contact your local HKTA office.

Hong Kong will continue to have its own separate currency after 1997, the **Hong Kong dollar**, which is pegged at between $7.50 and $8 to the US dollar. Coincidentally, one Hong Kong dollar is almost exactly equal to one Chinese yuan, though yuan and Hong Kong dollars cannot be used interchangeably in either territory. In this chapter, the symbol $ refers to Hong Kong dollars throughout unless stated.

Orientation, arrival and information

Orientation for new arrivals in the main urban areas is relatively easy: if you are "**Hong Kong-side**" – on the northern shore of Hong Kong Island – **Victoria Harbour** lies to your north, while to your south the land slopes upwards steeply to the **Peak**. The heart of this built-up area on Hong Kong Island is known, rather mundanely, as **Central**. Just across the harbour, in the area known as **Tsimshatsui**, you are "**Kowloon-side**", and here all you really need to recognize is the colossal north–south artery, **Nathan Road**, full of shops and budget hotels, that leads down to the harbour, and to the phenomenal view south over Hong Kong Island. Two more useful points for orientation on both sides of Victoria Harbour are the **Star Ferry terminals** where the popular cross-harbour ferries dock, in Tsimshatsui (a short walk west of the south end of Nathan Road) and in Central.

Arrival

Public transport is so convenient and efficient that even first-time arrivals are unlikely to face any particular problems in reaching their destination within the city – apart from the difficulty of communicating with taxi drivers. All signs are written in English and Chinese and distances from the main international arrival points are short, though traffic is often heavy.

By plane

Hong Kong's new airport at **Chek Lap Kok** is due to come into operation in early 1998. Although a good deal farther out from the downtown areas than the existing Kai Tak airport, high-speed, state-of-the-art rail and road links are being constructed simultaneously so that by the time the airport opens, trains will whisk passengers to and from Central in as little as twenty minutes. In the meantime, the old **Kai Tak** continues to

MOVING ON: ROUTES INTO MAINLAND CHINA

To enter China, you'll need a **visa** – 1997 will not make any difference to these regulations, and visas will still be easily obtainable in Hong Kong. Any travel agency and most hotels, even the cheapest hostels, offer this service, though if you want to queue you can do it yourself slightly more cheaply by going to the visa office of the Ministry of Foreign Affairs of the PRC, 5th Floor, Lower Block, China Resources Bldg, 26 Harbour Rd, Wanchai (Mon–Fri 9am–12.20pm & 2–5pm, Sat 9am–12.20pm; ☎2827 9569). The fee varies according to whether you want a single-entry or double-entry, one-month or three-month visa, and whether you want fast (same-day) processing or the normal two to three days. Most people pay around $200, though same-day visas can cost up to $400. It's now possible to make brief trips to Shenzhen without a visa, depending on your nationality, but you should check with the Ministry of Foreign Affairs (above) before attempting to do this.

The simplest route into China is by **direct train to Guangzhou**. There are several trains daily, the trip takes around three hours and costs $250; tickets are obtainable in advance from *CTS* or *CITS* (see "Listings", p.643), or on the same day from the Hung Hom Railway Station. From July 1997 there should be also direct trains running to Beijing and other Chinese cities. As a cheaper alternative, ride the KCR up to Lo Wu, cross into Shenzhen on foot and pick up one of the hourly trains to Guangzhou from there – tickets can be easily purchased in Hong Kong dollars and cost about $100.

The other land route is by **bus**. *Citybus*, Rm 28, Lower Ground Floor, China Hong Kong City, 33 Canton Rd, Tsimshatsui (☎2736 3888), runs frequent services to Shenzhen and Guangzhou; the Guangzhou run takes about 3hrs 30mins and costs $170.

By **boat**, you can travel to several Chinese cities, all from the China Hong Kong ferry terminal in Tsimshatsui, where tickets can be bought in advance from a branch of *CTS*. There is a daily overnight ferry service to **Guangzhou** as well as a daily three-hour jet-cat; both cost about the same as the train. Frequent local departures to nearby destinations such as **Shenzhen**, **Shekou** and **Zhuhai** are also available. Finally, there are less frequent long-distance departures for **Xiamen**, **Shanghai**, **Wuzhou** (on the way to Guilin) and **Haikou** (Hainan Island). These long-distance ferries are generally clean and comfortable and represent the most stress-free way of approaching mainland China for the first time. Ticket prices vary according to class but are not expensive – Shanghai starts from $920, Xiamen from $450 and Haikou from just $288.

Finally, you can **fly** from Hong Kong into virtually all major Chinese cities either on *CAAC* or, to a more restricted number, on the Hong Kong-based *Dragonair*. Note that many of *CAAC*'s flights are technically "charter flights", which means that tickets are non-refundable. There is little if any discounting on flights into China from Hong Kong, though consult travel agencies for possible deals (see "Listings", p.643). When leaving Hong Kong by air, note that there is an **airport tax** of $50 which is not always included in the price of tickets bought in Hong Kong. The tax must be paid in cash when you check in.

serve as Hong Kong's only international airport, despite being officially saturated and dangerously located in the heart of a built-up area, just 5km from Tsimshatsui. At least the central location makes for an exciting approach with planes virtually skimming the rooftops as they come down to land.

By far the best way into town from Kai Tak is on one of the **airport buses**, clearly signposted from the terminal halls; just remember that no change is given on any of Hong Kong's buses. There are several routes, all of which stop at major hotels on the way, running daily between about 7am and midnight. Bus #A1 ($12) runs down through Tsimshatsui, along Nathan Road to the Star Ferry terminal; #A2 ($17) and #A20 ($17) cross to Hong Kong Island, running through Wanchai and Central, with #A2 running on to the Macau ferry terminal; #A3 ($17) goes to Causeway Bay. **Taxis** are a much less expensive way of reaching town from the airport than in most international cities; the ride to the cheap hotel area in Tsimshatsui will only cost about $50, and around double that to reach Hong Kong Island via the cross-harbour tunnel. Don't automatically expect the taxi drivers to speak better English here than in mainland China; they'll usually understand the names of major hotels, districts and streets, but it may help to show them a map if you're heading for a particularly obscure location.

By train and bus

The main land route into Hong Kong is by **train**. After the sovereignty handover, it is hoped that direct trains will be connecting Hong Kong with Beijing and other cities all over China. In the meantime, the only direct trains run from Guangzhou and use **Hung Hom Railway Station**, otherwise known as Kowloon Station, a couple of kilometres to the northeast of Tsimshatsui (for purchasing tickets from Hong Kong to Guangzhou, see box below). Buses #8, #8A and #5C run from the station to Nathan Road and the Star Ferry terminal; #104 and #105 connect with Wanchai and Central; #102 and #112 connect with Causeway Bay. If you're not using the convenient and direct Guangzhou train, a cheaper alternative is to cross the border by foot from Shenzhen (which is accessible from Guangzhou by train or bus, see p.549). The Hong Kong side of the border is directly adjacent to Lo Wu KCR station, from where regular KCR trains ($27) take fifty minutes to run to Kowloon Station.

By **bus** there are now regular daily services from Guangzhou and Shenzhen operated by *Citybus* (see box); these take about one hour longer than the direct train and arrive in downtown Tsimshatsui.

By ferry

Arriving by sea is a great way to approach Hong Kong for the first time. There are two important long-distance ferry terminals, one for Macau ferries and one for ferries from other Chinese ports. The **Macau ferry terminal** is in the Shun Tak Centre, on Hong Kong Island, from where the Sheung Wan MTR station is directly accessible (for details on travel to and from Macau, see p.645). The **China Hong Kong ferry terminal**, where ferries from Shanghai, Xiamen, Guangzhou, Shekou and Zhuhai (and a few from Macau) dock, is in the west of Tsimshatsui, just ten minutes' walk from Nathan Road.

Information and maps

The **Hong Kong Tourist Association** (HKTA) issues more leaflets, pamphlets, brochures and maps than the whole of the rest of China put together – and you don't have to pay for them. They have an office in the airport (daily 8am–10pm), whose staff walk round trying to find new arrivals even before you find them. In downtown Hong Kong, there are two more offices, for personal callers only, one in Tsimshatsui at the Star Ferry terminal (Mon–Fri 8am–6pm, Sat & Sun 9am–5pm) and one in the basement of Jardine House, the building with porthole windows in Central, just south of the Star Ferry terminal on Hong Kong Island (Mon–Fri 9am–6pm, Sat 9am–1pm). The offices are staffed by helpful, trained English speakers and there's also an HKTA multilingual **telephone service** (Mon–Fri 8am–6pm, Sat & Sun 9am–5pm; ☎2807 6177).

HKTA **maps**, and the maps in this book, should be enough for most purposes though more detailed versions such as the *Hong Kong Island Street Map* and the *Kowloon Street Map*, which include all bus routes, can be bought from English- language bookstores (see "Listings", p.642). HKTA **listings magazines** include the useful *Hong Kong This Week*, and the *Official Hong Kong Guide* which covers all events for the current month. Among the unofficial listings magazines, the trendy *HK Magazine* and *BC Magazine* are both free and available in hotels and restaurants.

City transport

Hong Kong's public transport system has been designed to serve virtually the entire population. The consequence is that it is efficient, fast, comfortable, extremely extensive and relatively cheap.

Trains and trams

The **MTR** (Mass Transit Railway) is Hong Kong's underground train system, and it has three lines. The Island Line (marked blue on maps) runs along the north shore of Hong Kong Island, from Sheung Wan in the west to Chai Wan in the east, taking in important stops such as Central, Wanchai and Causeway Bay. The Tsuen Wan Line (red) runs from Central, under the harbour, through Tsimshatsui, and then northwest to the new town of Tsuen Wan. Finally, the Kwun Tong Line (green) connects with the Tsuen Wan Line at Mongkok in Kowloon, and then runs east in a circular direction, eventually coming back down south under the harbour to join the Island Line at Quarry Bay (see colour insert for a route plan). A new MTR line is also under construction, which will run from Central to the new airport at Chek Lap Kok. With exact change you can buy single-journey **tickets** ($4–11) from easy-to-understand dispensing machines in the stations, or Common Stored Value Tickets in $70, $100 or $200 denominations, which electronically deduct your fare each time you use the ticket. Feed your ticket into the turnstyle to enter and exit the platform area.

The MTR is not to be confused with the **KCR** (Kowloon–Canton Railway) which is Hong Kong's main overground train line, running from Kowloon station in East Tsimshatsui, north through the New Territories to the border with China at Lo Wu. Apart from the direct trains running through to Guangzhou, there are frequent local trains running between Kowloon and Lo Wu, though note that you are not allowed to travel beyond the penultimate station of Sheung Shui, unless you have documentation for crossing into China. There is an interchange between the KCR and MTR at Kowloon Tong station. A third transport system, the **LRT** (Light Rail Transit) runs between towns in the western New Territories, though tourists rarely use it.

Trams

For such a modern, hi-tech city it may seem odd that Hong Kong still has these ancient vehicles clanking around its streets. Nevertheless, **trams** are as popular as ever, and are a great way for visitors to tour along the north shore of Hong Kong Island. The trams run between Kennedy Town in the west and Shau Kei Wan in the east, via Central, Wanchai and Causeway Bay (some going via Happy Valley; check the front of the tram). You board the tram at the back, and drop the money in the driver's box ($1.20; no change given) when you get off. If you can get a seat upstairs the views of street life along the way are excellent.

The so-called **Peak Tram** is, in fact, not a tram but a (historic) funicular railway and an essential trip for all visitors to Hong Kong (see p.619).

Buses, taxis and cars

The double-decker **buses** that run around town are not fast (being subject to frequent traffic snarl-ups) but are comfortable enough, especially now that air-conditioned vehicles are being introduced, and they are essential for many destinations, such as the south of Hong Kong Island, and parts of the New Territories, not served by trains. You pay as you board and exact change is required; the amount is

A FEW IMPORTANT BUS ROUTES	
FROM CENTRAL:	**FROM TSIMSHATSUI STAR FERRY:**
#6 and #6A to Stanley via Repulse Bay	#8, #8A and #5C to Hung Hom station
#15 to the Peak	#1K to Mongkok
#70 to Aberdeen	#6A to Song Dynasty Village
#90 to Ocean Park	#1, #1A, #2, #6, #7 and #9 to Temple Street Night Market

often posted up on the timetables at bus stops. HKTA issues useful up-to-date information on bus routes, including the approximate length of journeys and cost. The **main bus terminal** in Central is at Exchange Square, a few minutes' walk west of the Star Ferry terminal, though some buses also start from right outside the ferry terminal. In Tsimshatsui, Kowloon, the main bus terminal is right in front of the Star Ferry terminal.

As well as the big buses, there are also ubiquitous cream-coloured **minibuses** that can be stopped anywhere on the street, though these often have the destination written in Chinese only. They cost a little more than regular buses, and you usually pay the driver as you disembark; change can be given.

Taxis in Hong Kong are not expensive, though they can be hard to get hold of in busy areas and at rush hours. Note that there is a $10 toll to be paid on any trips through the cross-harbour tunnel between Kowloon and Hong Kong, and drivers often double this to $20 on the grounds that they have to get back again. Do not assume that taxi drivers all speak English and be prepared to show the driver the name of your destination written down in Chinese.

Car rental is theoretically possible, though highly inadvisable in Hong Kong. Taxis are far cheaper and more convenient.

Ferries

One of the most enjoyable things to do in Hong Kong is to ride the humble **Star Ferry** between Kowloon and Hong Kong Island. The views of the island are superb, particularly at dusk when the lights begin to twinkle through the humidity and the spray. You'll also get a feel for the frenetic pace of life on Hong Kong's waterways with ferries, junks, hydrofoils and larger ships looming up from all directions. You can ride upper deck ($1.80) or lower deck ($1.50) on the ferry, though in many ways the views from the lower deck are better, where you are only just above water level and in the thick of it all. Ferries run every few minutes between Tsimshatsui and Central (a 7-minute ride; daily 6.30am–11.30pm), and between Tsimshatsui and Wanchai. There are also similarly cheap and fun ferry crossings between Hung Hom and Central, and between Jordan Road (in Kowloon) and Central.

In addition, a large array of other boats run between Hong Kong and the outlying islands, most of which use the piers immediately north of Exchange Square; see p.631 for details.

Accommodation

Hong Kong boasts a quite colossal range of **hotels and guesthouses**, particularly in the Tsimshatsui area of Kowloon, and you will never fail to find a room if you are prepared to do some traipsing around. At the upper end of the market, you'll find some of the best hotels in the world, such as the legendary *Peninsula*, which is a tourist sight

---

ACCOMMODATION PRICE CODES

All the accommodation in this book has been graded according to price codes, which represent the cheapest double room available. Accommodation in Hong Kong has been given codes from the categories below. Where the text refers specifically to dorm beds, the price code represents the price per bed.

① under $30	④ $100–150	⑦ $300–500
② $30–75	⑤ $150–200	⑧ $500–700
③ $75–100	⑥ $200–300	⑨ over $700

---

in its own right. At the lower end, most of the options are squeezed into one or two giant blocks on Nathan Road, principally the **Chungking Mansions** and the somewhat more salubrious **Mirador Mansion**. Many of the guesthouses in these buildings have recently been renovated and most are perfectly clean inside (with TV and air conditioning), in spite of what you might think from the appallingly dirty stairwells in the Chungking Mansions. Always check the room to see its size (many rooms are minuscule), whether the shower is separate, whether it has a window and whether you have to pay extra for the use of air conditioning.

Even budget accommodation is not that cheap, however – you'll be lucky to find a room for less than $200, and only if you are willing to sleep in shared **dormitory accommodation** at one of the crowded travellers' hostels will you get down as low as $50 a night for a bed. One of the cheapest options is to stay at one of Hong Kong's seven official **youth hostels**, all of which offer excellent conditions and very reasonable dormitory accommodation at around $50 with an IYHF membership card ($75 without). The most popular of these hostels is the *Mount Davis Youth Hostel* on Hong Kong Island (see below); there are four more hostels in the New Territories and two on Lantau Island. The charm of the hostels lies in their fabulously rural locations, but the drawback is getting to them in the first place – advance booking, especially at weekends, is essential to avoid wasted journeys. For detailed information on all of them, pick up the free *Member's Handbook* from the head office at Room 225, Block 19, Shek Kip Mei Estate, Sham Shui Po, Kowloon (☎2788 1638, fax 2788 3105).

Kowloon

Most of the accommodation listed below is within fifteen minutes' walk of the Tsimshatsui Star Ferry terminal – conveniently central, though very touristy. For a less claustrophobic atmosphere you might choose to stay slightly farther out. Places listed represent a fraction of the total on offer, and it is always worth having a look at several options to get a feel of what suits you.

Baccarat Hotel, 11th Floor, Windsor Building, 29–31 Chatham Rd, Tsimshatsui (☎2366 5922, fax 2723 5398). This building in the eastern part of Tsimshatsui, just south of Hart Avenue, contains several hotels, generally of the upmarket variety, although they appear to be ordinary guesthouses from the outside. The *Baccarat* has a range of comfortable rooms, some of which are really large and bright. ⑦.

Hakkas Guesthouse, Flat L, 3rd Floor, New Lucky House, 300 Nathan Rd, Jordan (☎2770 1470). One of a number of guesthouses in this building, slightly to the north of the main tourist area, at the junction with Jordan Road, by the Jordan MTR station. Offers a whole range of oddly-shaped doubles, triples and quads, all with private bath. ⑥.

Holiday Inn Golden Mile, 50 Nathan Rd, Tsimshatsui (☎2369 3111, fax 2369 8016). A few steps from the Tsimshatsui MTR, this hotel offers the usual excellent facilities from this international chain, including a roof-top swimming pool. Doubles start at $1900. ⑨.

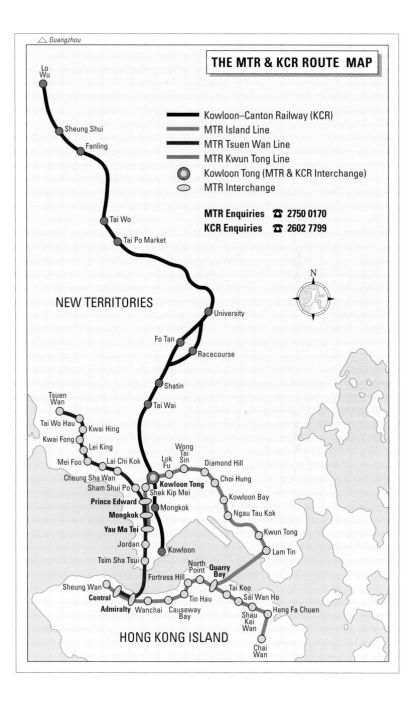

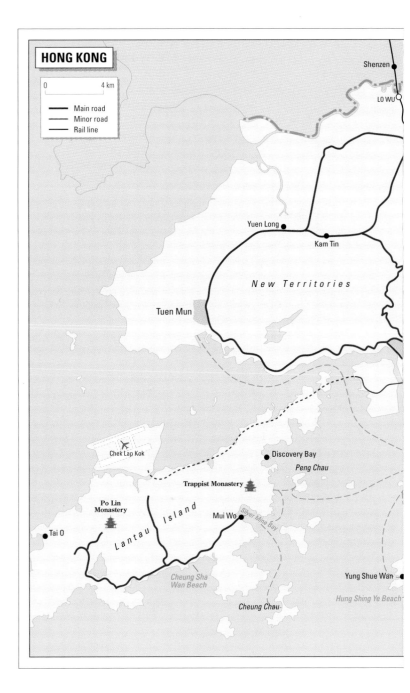

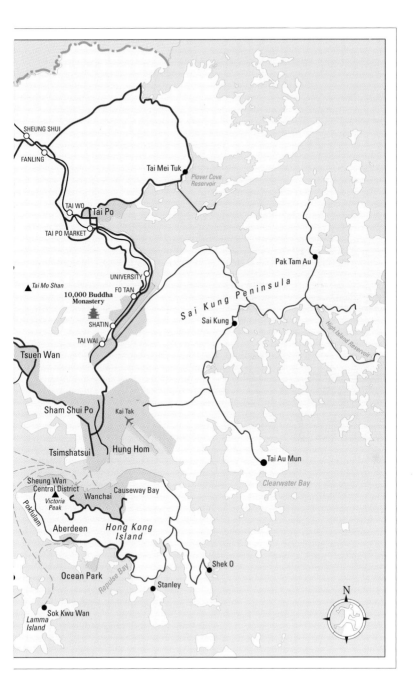

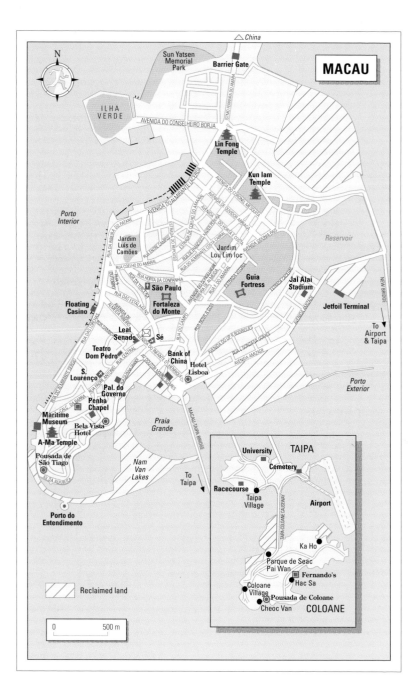

King's Hotel, 473–473A Nathan Rd, Yau Ma Tei (☎2780 1281, fax 2782 1833). Immediately south of the Yaumatei MTR. More than a guesthouse – it occupies the whole building – the *King's* is probably the cheapest "real" hotel in town. Single and double rooms. ⑦.

Lee Garden Guesthouse, Block D, 8th Floor, 34–36 Cameron Rd, Tsimshatsui (☎2367 2284). Under the same ownership as the *Star Guesthouse* (below), and with the same pleasant conditions, though this place also offers triple rooms. ⑥.

Peninsula, Salisbury Rd, Tsimshatsui (☎2366 6251, fax 2722 4170). One of the classiest hotels in the world, which has been overlooking the harbour and Hong Kong Island for nearly seventy years. If you want to be picked up at the airport by a green Rolls Royce, make a booking here. If not, at least pop in for afternoon tea (see p.625). Rooms start at $2500. ⑨.

STB Hostel, 2nd Floor, Great Eastern Mansion, 255–261 Reclamation St, Mongkok (☎2710 9199). On the corner of Reclamation and Dundas streets, a few minutes northwest of Yaumatei MTR station. This hostel is pleasantly located out of Tsimshatsui, but the dormitories (salubrious three-and-four-bed rooms with attached shower) aren't cheap. Dorms ⑤, rooms ⑦.

"The Salisbury" YMCA, 41 Salisbury Rd, Tsimshatsui (☎2369 2211, fax 2739 9315). The location could not be better, right next door to the *Peninsula* and with views over the harbour and Hong Kong Island. There's a very wholesome atmosphere here, though it's slightly sterile compared to the Chungking Mansions. Open to both men and women and all rooms attract a ten percent service charge. Four-bed dorms with attached shower are also available, but cannot be reserved in advance. Dorms ⑤, rooms ⑨.

Rich Shekel Guesthouse, 5th Floor, James Lee Mansion, 33–35 Carnavon Rd, Tsimshatsui (☎2369 6535). Pleasant, air-conditioned doubles with attached showers. ⑦.

Star Guesthouse, Flat B, 6th Floor, 21 Cameron Rd, Tsimshatsui (☎2723 8951). Very clean and friendly, with good English spoken. The rooms with windows and own bath are bright but slightly pricey for what they are; the cheaper rooms have shared bath. ⑥.

Victoria Hostel, Middle Floor, 33 Hankow Rd, Tsimshatsui (☎2376 0621, fax 2376 2609). Just west of Nathan Road. If you can cope with his brusqueness and rigid rule-keeping, the Sri Lankan owner of this hostel is honest, very helpful and understanding of budget travellers' needs. He also personally cooks superb low-cost meals for guests. Dorm beds decrease in price the more days you commit yourself to staying. Dorms ②–③, rooms ⑥–⑦.

Chungking Mansions

Occupying one of the prime sites towards the southern end of Nathan Road, the Chungking Mansions is an ugly monster of a building, as deep and wide as it is tall, looking just about fit for demolition. The arcades on the lowest two floors are an exotic warren of tiny shops and restaurants mostly patronized by residents from the Indian subcontinent, while the remaining sixteen floors are crammed with budget guesthouses. Above the second floor, the building is divided into five blocks, lettered A to E, each served by two tiny lifts which can carry only a few people at a time. The lifts for blocks A and B in particular, which contain the largest concentration of guesthouses, are often attended by long queues. If you decide to use the stairs instead, be warned that the stairways are dark, damp and dirty. Overall, the guesthouses in the Chungking Mansions are pleasant and cheap, and the atmosphere is a very characterful Sino-Indian mixture, but bear in mind that the whole building is not only claustrophobic, with its endless dingy stairwells and gloomy interiors, but also something of a fire-hazard. The guesthouses listed below are just a handful of the total.

Carlton Guesthouse, Flat 7, 15th Floor, B Block (☎2721 0720). Good English spoken and spotlessly clean, refurbished rooms on offer. ⑥.

Chungking House, 4th & 5th floors, A Block (☎2366 5362, fax 2721 3570). The most upmarket place in the whole building, just like a proper hotel, with carpets and even bath tubs. ⑦.

Dragon Garden, Flat 1, 5th Floor, D Block (☎2311 6641). Reasonably sized, inexpensive rooms ⑤.

Fortunate Guesthouse, Flat 2, 11th Floor, A Block (☎2366 5900). Passable English spoken here and the rooms are a quite decent size. Doubles, triples and quads. ⑥.

Garden Guesthouse, Flat 5, 16th Floor, B & C Block (☎2368 0981). This place is actually accessible from both blocks, though the main entrance is from C Block. It's a bright, airy place with good views. ⑥.

Kowloon Guesthouse, Flat 7, 10th Floor, B Block (☎2369 9802). A big, well-run place with some very cheap windowless, bathless singles, as well as pleasant doubles. You pay extra for your air conditioning here, approximately $2 per hour. ⑥.

New Asia Guesthouse, Flat 7, 8th Floor, A Block (☎2724 0426). Rather gloomy but very cheap, offering singles and doubles. ⑤.

New Shanghai, Flat 3, 8th Floor, D Block (☎2723 0965). All types of room on offer, with and without bath, at good prices. ⑤.

New World Hostel, 6th Floor, A Block (☎2723 6352). As far as Hong Kong dormitories go, this one is bearable, with air conditioning and a TV. Dorms ②.

Park Guesthouse, Flat 1, 15th Floor, A Block (☎2368 1689, fax 2366 7936). Run by an intelligent, friendly woman with excellent English, this is a very good place to stay. Rooms have fridges and baths, and some even have a view of the sea. ⑤–⑥.

Payless Guesthouse, Flat 2, 7th Floor, A Block (☎2723 0148). Quite friendly with English spoken. Has clean, tiny doubles with bath. ⑥.

Tom's Guesthouse, Flat 5, 8th Floor, A Block (☎2722 4956, fax 2366 6706). Under very friendly management, the double and triple rooms here are reasonably bright and very good value. *Tom's* has another branch at Flat 1, 16th Floor, C Block (☎2722 6035), where the rooms are positively salubrious. ⑤ & ⑥ respectively.

Travellers' Hostel, 16th Floor, A Block (☎2368 7710). A time-worn, shabby retreat for backpackers offering six-bed dorms with or without air conditioning. There's a useful budget travel agency next door and you should ask for "John-the-book" if you want to buy or trade any books here. Dorms ②.

Mirador Mansion

This is the big block at 54–64 Nathan Road, on the east side, in between Carnarvon Road and Mody Road, right next to the Tsimshatsui MTR station. Dotted about in among the residential apartments are large numbers of guesthouses. The advantage of Mirador over the Chungking Mansions is that the stairwells and corridors are a lot cleaner, brighter and quieter, and there is no queue for the lifts.

Garden Hostel, Flat F4, 3rd Floor (☎2311 1183). A scruffy but friendly travellers' hangout, with washing machines, lockers and even a patio garden. Mixed and women-only dorms; beds get cheaper if you pay by the week. Dorms ②.

Kowloon Hotel, Flat E1, 13th Floor (☎2311 2523, fax 2368 5241). Offers a range of immaculately clean singles and doubles. ⑥.

Lily Garden Guesthouse, Flat A9, 3rd Floor (☎2366 2575, fax 2312 7681). One of a number of guesthouses under the same ownership in the Mirador. Room prices here are comparatively low and conditions good, with cheap singles as well as doubles. ⑥.

Man Hing Lung, Flat F2, 14th Floor (☎2722 0678, fax 2311 6669). Run by a helpful, friendly man with good English, this is a clean and newly furbished place, offering singles and doubles. ⑦.

Man Lee Tak Guesthouse, Flat A1, 6th Floor (☎2739 2717, fax 2724 2772). Another spotlessly clean option. ⑥–⑦.

New Garden Hostel, Flat D1, 13th Floor (☎2311 2523). Next door to, and under the same ownership as, the *Kowloon Hotel*, this has one of the cleanest dormitories in Hong Kong, with windows and a balcony. Dorms ②.

Hong Kong Island

Accommodation on the island is nearly all of the upmarket variety, with just one budget option, the delightful *Mount Davis Youth Hostel*. The *Noble Hostel* in Causeway Bay is another relative bargain.

Fu Lai Villa, 5th Floor, Phoenix Apartments, Lee Garden Rd, Causeway Bay (☎2577 0648). Like all the other hotels in this building, this is actually a "love-hotel" in which rooms can be rented by couples for the hour. Tourists who want to rent for the whole night are very welcome, however, and the atmosphere is perfectly respectable. Rooms have big baths, round beds and soft lighting, and are relatively cheap. ⑦.

Grand Hyatt, 1 Harbour Rd, Wanchai (☎2588 1234, fax 2802 0677). Right next to Central Plaza, easily recognizable as Hong Kong's tallest building. The sumptuous lobby needs to be seen to be believed. Regarded by people in the know as the best place in town. Doubles from $2600. ⑨.

Harbour View International House, 4 Harbour Rd, Wanchai (☎2802 0111, fax 2802 9063). Very close to the Wanchai ferry terminal, and next door to the Arts Centre, this is an excellent place to stay with good-value rooms starting at the bottom of this category. ⑨.

Mandarin Oriental, 5 Connaught Rd, Central (☎2522 0111, fax 2810 6190). Old-timers say it's no longer quite the place it was, but for sheer luxury in the very heart of Hong Kong you can hardly do better. ⑨.

Mount Davis Youth Hostel (Ma Wui Hall), Mt Davis Path, Mt Davis (☎2817 5715). If you're sick and tired of the hustle of Tsimshatsui, this is the perfect escape. Perched on the top of a mountain, it has superb views over the harbour and the atmosphere is unbelievably peaceful. The only catch is that getting here is a major expedition. From Exchange Square outside the Star Ferry terminal, catch bus #5B (Mon–Sat 7–10.25am & 4.25–8pm only) to its terminus at Felix Villas. Alternatively you can take bus #47 or #77, but you'll have to ask people where to get off. From the Felix Villas bus stop, walk back a few metres the way you came, and you'll see Mt Davis Path branching off up the hill. You can walk up here to the hostel – but it's a long hot walk of at least thirty minutes. The sensible alternative if you have luggage is to get off the bus in Kennedy Town and catch a taxi from there ($30 plus $5 per item of luggage). Conditions in the hostel are excellent, though all guests are expected to carry out one small cleaning task daily. YHA members pay less. Dorms ②, doubles ⑤.

Noble Hostel, Flat A3, 17th Floor, Great George Building, 27 Paterson St, Causeway Bay (☎2576 6148, fax 2577 0847) A great place to stay, right in the middle of Causeway Bay, one of the most attractive eating and shopping areas in Hong Kong. Rooms are immaculately clean and good sizes, and are available as singles, doubles, triples and quads. Airport bus #A3 stops on Gloucester Road just around the corner. ⑦.

Park Lane, 310 Gloucester Rd, Causeway Bay (☎2890 3355, fax 2576 7853). Near to Victoria Park, the *Park* is conveniently sited for the shopping and eating delights of Causeway Bay. ⑨.

YWCA Garden View International House, 1 Macdonnell Rd, Central (☎2877 3737, fax 2845 6263). Just off Garden View Road, south of the Zoological and Botanical Gardens. Bus #12A from Admiralty MTR runs past. Very salubrious, and the cheapest place in this area of Central – but not as cheap as its name might suggest. ⑧.

The New Territories and Outer Islands

The point of staying in these outer regions is to escape into rural tranquillity where the hubbub is less and prices cheaper. Be warned, though, that at weekends these places are likely to double in price, and may be booked solid anyway. Advance planning is always necessary.

Six of Hong Kong's seven official **youth hostels** are here, two on Lantau Island, and four in the New Territories (see p.608). Don't imagine, however, that you can use them as a base for exploring the rest of Hong Kong – they are far too remote and you are even advised to take your own food with you.

Concierto Inn, Hung Shing Ye Beach, Lamma Island (☎2982 1688, fax 2836 3311). A great rural location by an isolated beach, with a delightful terraced restaurant (see p.632). ⑦.

Bradbury Lodge, Tai Mei Tuk, Tai Po, New Territories (☎2662 5123). Of all the hostels this is about the easiest to get to. Take the KCR train to Tai Po, then bus #75K to Tai Mei Tuk terminal. Walk south a few minutes with the sea on your right. Lots of boating, walking and cycling opportunities right by the scenic Plover Cove Reservoir (see p.629). Dorms ②.

Lamma Vacation, Main St, Yung Shue Wan, Lamma Island (☎2982 0427). A few minutes' walk from the ferry pier, with Chungking Mansions-sized rooms offering a very cheap way of staying on the island. ④.

Man Lai Wah, Yung Shue Wan, Lamma Island (☎2982 0220). Right in front of the ferry pier where ferries from Hong Kong dock. Has pleasant doubles with private baths. ⑦.

Mui Wo Inn, Silvermine Bay, Mui Wo, Lantau Island (☎2984 8295). A few minutes farther round the bay from the *Silvermine Beach* (below) when approaching from the ferry pier. It's a small place with a range of rooms, some with seafront views and balconies. ⑦.

Pak Sha O Hostel, Pak Sha O, Hoi Ha Rd, Sai Kung, New Territories (☎2328 2327). Take bus #94 from Sai Kung (see p.630). Get off at Ko Tong, walk 100m farther on and take Hoi Ha Road on the left – from here it's a forty-minute walk. Great for access to Hong Kong's cleanest, most secluded beaches. Dorms ②.

S. G. Davis Hostel, Ngong Ping, Lantau Island (☎2985 5610). From Mui Wo (see p.633) take bus #2 to the Ngong Ping terminal and follow the paved footpath south, away from the Tian Tan Buddha and past the public toilets. It's a ten-minute walk and well signposted. This is a great base for hill walking on Lantau, and you can eat at the nearby Po Lin Monastery. It's cold on winter nights, though – bring a sleeping bag. Dorms ②.

Silvermine Beach Hotel, Silvermine Bay, Mui Wo, Lantau Island (☎2984 8295, fax 2984 1907). Superbly located right on the beachfront, a few minutes' walk from the Mui Wo ferry pier. The rooms here are comfortable, quiet and good value. ⑨.

Hong Kong Island

As the oldest colonized part of Hong Kong, its administrative and business centre, and site of some of the most expensive real estate in the world, **Hong Kong Island** is naturally the heart of the whole territory. Despite its tiny size, just 15km from east to west and 11km from north to south at the widest points, and despite the phenomenal density of development on its northern shore, the island offers a surprising range of **mountain walks** and attractive **beaches** as well as all the attractions of a great city.

On the northern shore of Hong Kong Island, overlooking **Victoria Harbour** and Kowloon on the mainland opposite, are the major financial and commercial quarters of **Central** and **Wanchai**, which in the last two decades have sprouted several of Asia's tallest and most interesting skyscrapers. To the east is **Causeway Bay**, an upmarket shopping and entertainment area, while to the west is **Kennedy Town**, one of the most traditionally Chinese parts of the city, where streets are lined with shops selling dried fish and ancient Chinese medicines. A cliche it certainly is, but whether it be a smoky temple squatting among skyscrapers, or *Chanel*-dressed shoppers jammed into a smelly fish market, the built-up areas of Hong Kong are a fascinating blend of East and West.

The verdant, beach-lined southern shore of the island, on the other hand, is more notable for its small towns and villages, including **Aberdeen**, its harbour brimming with traditional barrel-shaped fishing boats (junks) as well as Hong Kong's famous floating restaurants. Finally, the centre of the island rises steeply to a series of wooded peaks. Of these, the most famous, **Victoria Peak**, immediately south of Central district and accessible on the one-hundred-year-old **Peak Tram**, commands superb views of the city and the harbour below.

Central

The area known as **Central** takes in the core of the old city. It extends out from the Star Ferry terminal a few hundred metres in all directions, east to the Admiralty MTR, west to the Central Market and south, up the hill, to the Zoological and Botanical Gardens. Starting from the Star Ferry terminal, the first things you'll see as you emerge are a number of ancient hand-pulled rickshaws and their runners who pre-date the time when the last licences were issued and who interestingly may yet survive to see the arrival of the Communists. Now they are just there for the tourists, so if you take photos expect to pay for them.

The busy streets of Central are not ideal for walking. Moving inland from the shore, the main west–east roads are Connaught Road, Des Voeux Road and Queen's Road respectively, though pedestrians are better off concentrating on the extensive system of **elevated walkways**. To reach this system from the Star Ferry terminal, climb the slightly grotty stairs to the west (the right as you come out). Ahead, on the seafront, you see the newly built **ferry piers for the outlying islands**, and beyond them a vast ongoing reclamation project to win yet more precious real estate from the steadily shrinking harbour. If you take the walkway left opposite the ferry piers, and follow it inland, you'll pass right between **Jardine House** (the tall building full of portholes) on your left and **Exchange Square** on your right. Jardine House contains a branch of the HKTA in its basement, while Exchange Square is home to the three gloriously opulent marble-and-tinted-glass towers which house the Hong Kong Stock Exchange. The Exchange Square bus station is located underneath the square. A further branch of the elevated walkway runs northwest from here, parallel with the shore and along the northern edge of Connaught Road, past Exchange Square and all the way to Sheung Wan MTR; follow this for some great views over the harbour. Otherwise continue across Connaught Road into the heart of an extremely upmarket shopping area, around Des Voeux Road.

Easily recognizable from the tramlines that run up and down here, **Des Voeux Road** used to mark Hong Kong's seafront before the days of reclamation, hence the name of the single smartest shopping mall in the area, the **Landmark**, on the corner with Pedder Street. Of all the shops around here, one definitely worth a visit is **Shanghai Tang**, across Pedder Street from the Landmark, for kitschy Mao memorabilia and superb designer garments recalling traditional Chinese wear.

The stretch of Des Voeux Road running west from the Landmark is connected by a series of lanes running south to the parallel Queen's Road. Two of these, Li Yuen Street East and Li Yuen Street West, are **markets**, packed out with clothes and fabrics stalls. About 300m from the Landmark, you'll reach the **Central Market** – worth dropping in on during the morning business for some incredible photo opportunities of poultry, fish and meat being hacked about on a huge scale. Just southwest of Central Market, leading uphill from Queen's Road Central, is **Graham Street**, one of the great canvas-covered fruit and vegetable markets which still manage to survive and flourish in downtown Hong Kong. Also leading uphill from Queens Road, immediately south of Central Market, is the fantastic **Hillside Escalator Link**, basically a giant series of escalators which runs 800m straight up the hill as far as Conduit Road in the quiet, very expensive residential area known as **Mid-Levels**. During the morning rush hour when people are on their way to work, the escalators run downwards only; from 10am to 11pm they run up. It's well worth riding up to the top, if for nothing else, to appreciate this quite unique piece of urban public transport.

In the opposite direction from the Landmark, east along Des Voeux Road, you'll find **Statue Square** on your left towards the shore. This is an oddly redundant empty space of land, divided from east to west in the middle by Chater Road, which was the heart of the late-nineteenth-century colony. Today it is principally used as a picnic area by the city's hundreds of Filippina maids on Sundays, their weekly day off. The ninety-year-old domed, granite building to the east of the square, dwarfed and overlooked by the gigantic modern buildings immediately to the south, has, in the last years of Hong Kong's colonial period, been the home of the Legislative Council, the territory's parliament – hence its name, the **Legco Building**. Marooned as the last colonial structure surviving in Central, the Legco Building is likely to seem more irrelevant than ever after 1997.

Seawards, the north of Statue Square contains the **Cenotaph** war memorial, now the rallying point for meetings every year on June 4 to mark the anniversary of the 1989 Tian'anmen Square killings. Again, whether these meetings will continue to take place

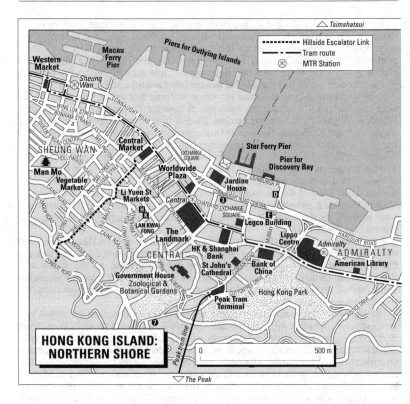

Legend:
- -------- Hillside Escalator Link
- —— - Tram route
- ⊛ MTR Station

Piers for Outlying Islands
Western Market
Macau Ferry Pier
△ Tsimshatsui
Sheung Wan ⊛
WING LOK STREET
BONHAM STRAND
CONNAUGHT ROAD CENTRAL
QUEEN'S ROAD CENTRAL
SHEUNG WAN
HOLLYWOOD ROAD
Man Mo
Vegetable Market
CAINE ROAD
Central Market
WELLINGTON
Li Yuen St Markets
EXCHANGE SQUARE
Worldwide Plaza
Central ⊛
Star Ferry Pier
Pier for Discovery Bay
EDINBURGH PL
Jardine House
CHATER RD EXCHANGE
❸
D
Legco Building
E
Lippo Centre
LAN KWAI FONG
The Landmark
CAINE ROAD
MOSQUE STREET
CONDUIT ROAD
CENTRAL
HK & Shanghai Bank
St John's Cathedral
Bank of China
Admiralty ⊛
ADMIRALTY
HARCOURT ROAD
American Library
Government House
Zoological & Botanical Gardens
Hong Kong Park
COTTON TREE DRIVE
Peak Tram Terminal
JUSTICE DRIVE
❼
Peak tram line

HONG KONG ISLAND: NORTHERN SHORE

0 _____ 500 m

▽ The Peak

after the arrival in the territory of the People's Liberation Army is open to question. An underground walkway connects the square to the Star Ferry concourse to the north.

Immediately south of Statue Square is the magnificently hi-tech **Hong Kong Bank** building, designed by Norman Foster and reputedly the most expensive building ever constructed. At ground level you can see that the whole building is supported on groups of giant pillars and it's possible to walk right under the bank and come out on the other side – a necessity stipulated by the old *fengshui* belief that the centre of power on the island, Government House, which lies directly to the north of the bank, should be accessible in a straight line by foot from the main point of arrival on the island, the Star Ferry. From under the bank the building's insides are transparent, and you can look up, through the colossal glass atrium, into the heart of the building.

East, a couple of hundred metres down the road from the Hong Kong and Shanghai Bank, is the three-hundred-metre blue-glass **Bank of China**, the tallest building in Central. As though under instructions from Beijing, the designers of this bank had no hesitation in by-passing all the normal *fengshui* sensitivities, and this knife-like structure is accordingly feared and disliked in Hong Kong. For more attractive, and less offensive, skyscraper wizardry, walk along the elevated walkways, or ride the tram, another 200m or 300m east down Queensway into the area known as **Admiralty**. The most striking building here is the bulging **Lippo Centre**, a general office building which you'll pass to the north before the Admiralty MTR station.

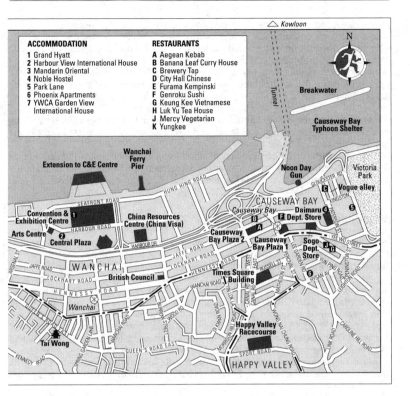

South of Queen's Road

South of Queen's Road the land begins to slope seriously upwards and walking can become extremely laborious in hot weather. Head south up D'Aguilar Street (just west of Pedder Street) from Queen's Road, and you'll enter the **Lan Kwai Fong** area, the main focus for eating and particularly drinking in Central. Lan Kwai Fong itself is actually an L-shaped lane jammed with overflowing bars that branches southeast off D'Aguilar Street, though several of the neighbouring lanes and small streets boast an interesting range of snack bars and restaurants. The most interesting of these for visitors is the **Luk Yu Tea House** on Stanley Street (just west of D'Aguilar Street), a delightfully traditional Chinese tea house (see "Eating, drinking and nightlife", p.636).

In a general southerly direction from Lan Kwai Fong – a short but steep walk along Glenealy Street and under the flyover – are the **Hong Kong Zoological and Botanical Gardens** (daily 7am–7pm; free), originally opened in 1864 and still a pleasant refuge from the hubbub of Central, though the caged birds and animals are nothing spectacular. The gardens are cut down the middle by Albany Street, but an underground walkway connects the two halves. To get here direct from the Star Ferry terminal area, catch buses #3 or #12 heading east along Connaught Road.

North of the gardens, just across Upper Albert Road, **Government House** has been the official residence of Hong Kong governors since 1855, and is not open to the public. A few hundred metres to the east, and rather more impressive than the nearby gardens, is **Hong Kong Park** (daily 7am–11pm; free). From the eastern exit of the

Botanical Gardens you can walk to the park in about ten minutes along Garden Road. There's also an entrance just to the east of the Peak Tram terminal (see p.620). Otherwise, the main entrance to the park is from the north, on Supreme Court Road; follow signs from Admiralty MTR station. The highlight here is the excellent **aviary** which, if you are at all interested in birds, is well worth a visit. Walk around the raised walkways inside the superbly recreated natural environment, and you'll find yourself surrounded by rare birds swooping about, nesting and breeding. At the south (highest) end of the park, there is also a *tai ji* court, while in the north is the **Museum of Teaware** (daily except Wed, 10am–5pm; free), housed in Hong Kong's oldest surviving colonial building, constructed 1844–46, and today incongruously located right in the shade of the *Bank of China* tower.

One other relic of the earliest days of Hong Kong's colonial past is the Anglican **St John's Cathedral**, a little farther north down Garden Road from the Peak Tram terminal. Dating back to the late 1840s, the church is now located in a hillside grove of trees in the lee of skyscrapers.

Wanchai and Causeway Bay

Stretching away east of Central, the built-up area on the north shore runs for at least 6km and comprises a number of localized centres, of which the two most visited by tourists for nightlife, dining and shopping are **Wanchai** and **Causeway Bay**. The street layout of both districts is similar to Central, with a number of east–west streets running parallel to the shore. The main street, **Hennessy Road**, is a continuation of Queensway from Central, and carries the tramlines right through the whole area (apart from where they temporarily divert south to Johnston Road). Immediately north of Hennessy Road, and parallel with it, is Lockhart Road, while farther north still is the principal east–west highway, **Gloucester Road**, a continuation of Connaught Road. South of Causeway Bay the low-lying area known as **Happy Valley** is home to Hong Kong's racecourse.

MTR trains and trams connect Central with both Wanchai and Causeway Bay, as do numerous buses, including #2 and #11. Wanchai is additionally accessible by ferry from Tsimshatsui.

Wanchai

In the 1950s and 1960s **Wanchai** was known throughout east Asia as a thriving red-light district, catering in particular to the needs of US soldiers on leave from Korea and Vietnam. Hong Kong's most famous fictional character, Suzy Wong, a prostitute from Richard Mason's novel, *The World of Suzy Wong*, resided and worked here. Nowadays, however, the soldiers have gone and Wanchai is every bit as gentrified as the rest of Hong Kong, though the **restaurants and bars** are still certainly worth a visit.

In the far west of the area, just north of Gloucester Road on the corner of Fenwick Street and Harbour Road, is the **Hong Kong Arts Centre** (ten minutes' walk from Wanchai MTR), which is worth dropping in on for its art galleries, films and other cultural events. You can pick up a free copy here of the monthly magazine *Artslink*, which has a detailed diary and reviews of what's happening on the art scene in Hong Kong. There's also an arts café here.

Immediately to the east of the Arts Centre stands a vast new set of gleaming modern buildings that have changed the face of Wanchai beyond all recognition. The **Hong Kong Convention and Exhibition Centre** on the seafront is probably the biggest and best of its kind in Asia. When there are no events going on, you can visit the centre's extraordinary interior, which includes the largest glass wall in the world, extending up five storeys. The most expensive hotel in Hong Kong, the *Grand Hyatt*, is also located here, while in the harbour in front of the Centre, yet more land reclamation has recently taken place and an ultra-modern extension is currently under construction.

Immediately inland, across Harbour Road, soars the tallest edifice in Hong Kong, the 78-storey **Central Plaza**, the golden, glowing cladding of which is visible from far away to the north in Kowloon. You can reach Central Plaza and the Exhibition Centre by walking along raised walkways from Wanchai MTR station, or from the ferry terminal immediately in front.

In contrast to these hi-tech marvels near the seafront, inland Wanchai is a solidly functional area packed with residential highrises and shopping streets with just a scattering of curiosities. On Queen's Road East, south of the tramlines on Johnston Road, is the little **Tai Wong Temple**, built into a hillside. This old brick building, smoke-blackened and hung with ancient draperies, was once a shrine by the sea; now, rather sadly, it has been marooned far inland by reclamation. There's a tiny flower and bird market opposite the temple, on Tai Wong Road West. A couple of hundred metres east of the Tai Wong Temple, you'll pass the quaint, whitewashed and unexpectedly ancient **Wanchai Post Office**, built in 1912 and only closed finally in 1992. In honour of its longevity, it has now been turned into an environmental resource centre (Mon–Sat 10am–5pm, closed Wed pm) providing information on Hong Kong's ecological situation. A short walk from here, along Stone Nullah Lane running south from Queen's Road East, is the **Pak Tai Temple**, where you can see craftsmen making fantastic little burial offerings out of bamboo and paper, including cars, houses and aeroplanes.

Causeway Bay

Causeway Bay derives its name from the fact that it used to be a bay, until reclamation in the 1950s. Now it is thoroughly earth-based, a colourful, upmarket district packed with shops and restaurants centred around the area between the eastern end of Lockhart Road and the western edge of Victoria Park. Trams run just to the south of here along Yee Wo Street, a continuation of Hennessy Road from Wanchai. Causeway Bay has an MTR station and is also the point of arrival of the original **cross-harbour tunnel** which carries vehicle traffic over from Kowloon. Airport bus #A3 arrives here through the tunnel.

The main interest in Causeway Bay is definitely shopping and consumption. Within a couple of minutes of the MTR station you'll find a number of ultra-modern **Japanese department stores**, including *Sogo* and *Daimaru*, while slightly to the north is **Vogue Alley**, a lane to the east of and parallel with north–south Paterson Street, which is, as its name suggests, a highly commercial gathering of fashion boutiques. South of Yee Wo Street the atmosphere is slightly more downmarket, but just as busy, particularly around Jardine's Bazaar and Jardine's Crescent, two alleys almost immediately south of Causeway Bay MTR.

Specific tourist sights are thin on the ground here, though you might stroll up to the shore, in front of the *Excelsior Hotel* on Gloucester Road, to see the **Noon Day Gun** – immortalized in Noel Coward's song *Mad Dogs and Englishmen* – which is fired off with a loud report every day at noon. The Noon Day Gun overlooks the Causeway Bay Typhoon Shelter which is always jammed full of small boats.

The eastern part of Causeway Bay is dominated by **Victoria Park**, a surprisingly extensive patch of green grass by Hong Kong's standards, which contains a swimming pool and other sports facilities. Down at the southeastern corner of the park, right by the Tin Hau MTR, is the two-hundred-year-old **Tin Hau Temple**, a rather dark, gloomy place surrounded unhappily by highrises. Tin Hau is the name given locally to the Goddess of the Sea, and her temples can be found throughout Hong Kong, normally in prominent positions by the shore where they were frequented by fishermen and sailors. The fact that temples such as this one have now been submerged in development is a reflection of priorities in modern Hong Kong. You can also reach this Tin Hau Temple on any tram heading for North Point; get off immediately after passing Victoria Park on your left.

One last sight in the hills to the south of Causeway Bay is the **Aw Boon Haw Gardens**, otherwise known as the Tiger Balm Gardens (daily 9.30am–4pm; free). This bizarre landscaped garden was built in the 1930s by a Hong Kong millionaire, Mr Aw Boon Haw, who had made his fortune out of **Tiger Balm**, a pain-killing ointment still widely available and sold in tiny red tins. Weird painted rockeries, statues of animals in suits, caves, a pagoda and, above all, a statue of Mr Aw Boon Haw himself make up the picture, all leered over as ever by soaring residential apartment buildings. It's interesting as an insight into what a genuinely Chinese Disney theme park would be like. Bus #11 from Central or from Yee Wo Road in Causeway Bay pass the park.

Happy Valley

The low-lying area, extending inland from the shore south of Wanchai and Causeway Bay and known as Happy Valley, really means only one thing for the people of Hong Kong: horse-racing, or more precisely, gambling. The **Happy Valley Racecourse**, which dates back to 1846, was for most of Hong Kong's history the only one in the territory, until a second course was built at Shatin in the New Territories. Hong Kong is gripped by serious gambling fever during the racing season, which runs from September until June, with two meetings weekly at Happy Valley. If you're interested in witnessing the madness, entrance to the public enclosure is just $10. Otherwise, enquire at HKTA about their "Come Horse-racing Tour" ($490), which includes transportation to and from the track, entry to the Members' Enclosure and a buffet meal at the official Jockey Club – and tips on how to pick a winner. Happy Valley can be reached from Central or Causeway Bay on a spur of the tramline, or on bus #1 from Central.

Western District

West of Central lies a district rather older and more exotic in character than other parts of Hong Kong. An almost entirely Chinese-inhabited area, its crowded residential streets and traditional shops form a characterful contrast to Central, though today the traditional nature of the area is under threat with the imminent completion of the **Western Harbour Crossing**, the second cross-harbour road tunnel from Kowloon. Sheung Wan is the largest sub-zone within this area and like Central it comprises straight east–west roads near the shore, and increasingly meandering roads up the hill away from the harbour. Kennedy Town in the far west is squeezed up against the shore by sharply rising hills and served by tramlines which extend from Central along Des Voeux Road, Connaught Road West, Des Voeux Road West, and finally Kennedy Town Praya.

Sheung Wan, immediately adjacent to Central, spreads south up the hill from the seafront at the modern Shun Tak Centre which houses the Macau ferry terminal (for details of travel to Macau, see p.646) and the Sheung Wan MTR station, for the time being still the last stop on this line. You can reach the Shun Tak Centre by a pleasant fifteen-minute walk along the elevated walkway from Exchange Square in Central, though you'll get more flavour of the district by following the tramlines along Des Voeux Road, west from Central Market (see p.613). A number of interesting lanes extend south from this stretch of Des Voeux Road, such as Wing Sing Street which specializes in preserved eggs, and Man Wa Street very near the Sheung Wan MTR where Chinese character chops (name stamps) are carved from stone or wood. Another couple of minutes along Des Voeux Road from here, brings you to the back end of **Western Market** (daily 10am–7pm), a delightful brick Edwardian building on the outside, and since 1991 no longer a stinking market but a mall full of small kitschy kiosks and fabric shops.

A short walk south, up the hill from the harbour, is **Bonham Strand**, which specializes in Chinese medicinal products and herbs. This is a fascinating area for poking around, with shop windows displaying items such as snakes (alive and dead), snake-bile wine, birds' nests, antlers and crushed pearls, as well as large quantities of expensive ginseng root. You'll find medicinal shops scattered along an east–west line extending from Bonham Strand to the small **Ko Shing Street** – the heart of the trade – which is adjacent to, and just south of, Des Voeux Road West. This section of Des Voeux Road boasts another long line of extremely exotic shops specializing in every kind of dried food, including sea slugs, starfish, shark fins, snakes and flattened ducks.

A short but stiff walk up from Bonham Strand leads to the scenically located **Hollywood Road**, running west from Wyndham Street in Central (immediately south of Lan Kwai Fong; see p.615) as far as the small Hollywood Park in Sheung Wan, where it runs into Queen's Road West. Bus #26 takes a circular route from Des Voeux Road in Central to the western end of Hollywood Road, then east again along the whole length of the road. The big interest here is the array of **antique and curio shops**, and you can pick up all sorts of oddities here, from tiny embroidered women's shoes to traditional coffins. These culminate on the small alley, Upper Lascar Row, commonly known as **Cat Street**, which is immediately north of the western end of Hollywood Road and due south of the Sheung Wan MTR. Here you'll find wall-to-wall curiosity stalls with coins, ornaments, jewellery and chop seals all on sale. There's even an air-conditioned mall, the Cat Street Galleries, offering serious antiques in more salubrious surroundings.

Another attraction in the Cat Street area is **Ladder Street**, which runs north–south across Hollywood Road and is, almost literally, as steep as a ladder. This is a relic from the nineteenth century when a number of such stepped streets existed to help sedan-chair carriers get their loads up the steep hillsides. On Hollywood Road adjacent to Ladder Street, the 150-year-old **Man Mo Temple** (daily 7am–5pm) is notable for its great hanging coils of incense suspended from the ceiling. The two figures on the main altar are the Taoist gods of Literature (Man) and the Martial Arts (Mo). Located as it is in a deeply traditional area, this is one of the most atmospheric small temples to visit in Hong Kong.

You'll find three more small temples a few minutes southwest of Hollywood Road on **Tai Ping Shan Street**, which you can reach by climbing a little way south up Ladder Street and taking the second lane on the right. This was one of the first areas of Chinese settlement in Hong Kong and the temples are still very much part of the fabric of the neighbourhood.

Kennedy Town, oddly named after an early governor of the colony, is the farthest west point of the built-up area on the northern shore and was for many years a busy town of crumbling old streets facing an old harbour jammed with green and red painted barges. There are still traces of character in Kennedy Town – fish markets and junks – though large-scale reclamation has recently started in the harbour. The final terminus of the tramline from Central is here.

The Peak

The uppermost levels of the 550-metre hill that towers over Central and Victoria harbour have always been arrogantly known as **the Peak** and, until recent years, the area was quintessentially colonial with upper-class expats in expensive houses literally lording it over the vast mass of the population who had the misfortune to live down at lower, more pestilential levels. The story of the colonization of what was originally a barren, treeless rock is an extraordinary one. Before 1859, when the first path up to the Peak was carved out, it was barely possible to get up here at all, let alone put houses on it. And yet within twenty years, a number of summer homes had been built for a wealthy minority of British merchants, who sought out the higher levels as a way of escaping the heat and malaria of the seafront in summer. Incredible though it is to imagine now, everything – from human beings to building materials – was carried laboriously up the hill by coolies.

The idea of building a rail link to the top of the Peak was originally scoffed at when first proposed, because the gradients were considered impossibly steep. In 1888, however, this all changed with the successful opening of a **funicular railway** known as the Peak Tram, which allowed speedy and regular connections to the harbour. What had been a barren rock began to be transformed with the planting of trees as well as the construction of a regular summer village. By 1924, when the first road to the Peak was built, permanent homes had begun to appear, though Chinese were still not allowed to set up home on the hill until relatively recently. Now, anyone can live here who can afford it – and these days that usually means Chinese tycoons. Aside from its exclusive residential area, the Peak is still a cool, peaceful retreat from the rigours of downtown and a vantage point offering some extraordinary panoramic views over the city and harbour below.

Ascending the Peak

Ascending the Peak is half the fun, assuming you plan to ride the **Peak Tram**. The track is incredibly steep and at times you'll feel that you are practically lying on your back in your seat as the tram climbs the 373 vertical metres to its terminus. The journey takes about eight minutes and there are actually some intermediate stations on the way, in Mid-Levels, though tourists are not likely to bother with these.

To find the Peak Tram terminal in Central, the easiest solution is to catch the free shuttle bus (Mon–Sat 10am–8pm, Sun 10am–9pm) from outside the Star Ferry terminal. On foot it's not a particularly convenient place to get to – it's on Garden Road a little way south of St John's Cathedral (see p.616). The Peak Tram itself (daily 7am–midnight; $14 single, $21 return) runs every fifteen minutes and you can also use the shuttle bus back to the Star Ferry afterwards, provided you still have your Peak Tram ticket.

If you have an irrational fear of funicular railways, you can catch **bus** #15 or #15B to the Peak from the Star Ferry area – the views are just as good, but it takes a lot longer. Fitness fanatics can **walk** up if they wish, though for most people walking down is a more realistic option. See below for routes.

On and around the Peak

The Peak Tram drops you right below the brand-new **Peak Galleries**, a shopping mall full of souvenir shops and pricey bars and cafés with spectacular views – even the local *Mcdonald's* has a terrace commanding a vast panorama. Virtually opposite here is the historic **Peak Café**, a traditional place with rattan chairs and fans that has now been somewhat modernized, but still has a great outdoor terrace where you should definitely enjoy at least one cold beer (see "Eating, drinking and nightlife", p.636).

From the Peak Tram terminal area, you'll see three roads leading off to the west and north. Of these, the middle one, Mount Austin Road, leads up to the very top of the Peak where you'll find the Victoria Peak Garden, formerly the site of the Governor's residence. The other two roads, however, which form a circuit around the Peak taking about an hour on foot, actually make a far more attractive walk. Harlech Road (leading due west) is a delightfully shady, rural stroll through trees with a picnic area en route. After half an hour the road runs into Lugard Road, which heads back towards the terminal around the northern rim of the Peak, giving magnificent views over Central and Kowloon.

An excellent way to **get down** from the Peak is to walk, along one of a number of possible routes, the simplest being to follow the sign pointing to Hatton Road, from opposite the picnic area on Harlech Road. The **walk** is along a very clear path all the way through trees, eventually emerging in Mid-Levels, after about 45 minutes, near the junction between Kotewall Road and Conduit Road. Catch bus #13 from Kotewall Road to Central, or you can walk east for about 1km along Conduit Road until you reach the top end of the Hillside Escalator Link (see p.613) which will also take you into Central. Another route down is to take a road leading from Harlech Road, not far from the Peak Tram, signposted to **Pokfulam Reservoir**, a very pleasant spot in the hills. Beyond the reservoir, heading downhill, you'll eventually come out on Pokfulam Road, from where there are plentiful buses to Central.

Hong Kong Island: the southern and eastern shores

On its south side, Hong Kong Island straggles into the sea in a series of dangling peninsulas and inlets. The atmosphere is far quieter here than on the north shore, and you'll find not only separate towns such as **Aberdeen** and **Stanley** with a flavour of their own, but also remarkably good beaches such as that at **Repulse Bay**, and much farther east, at the remote little outpost of **Shek O**. Especially if you're travelling with children you should consider a visit to **Ocean Park**, a huge adventure theme park, just beyond Aberdeen. Buses are plentiful to all destinations on the southern shore, and Aberdeen is linked to Central by a tunnel under the Peak. Nowhere is more than an hour from Central.

Aberdeen

Aberdeen is the largest separate town on Hong Kong Island, with a population of around sixty thousand, a dwindling minority of whom still live on **sampans and junks** in the narrow harbour that lies between the main island and the offshore island of Ap Lei Chau. The boat people who live here are following a tradition that certainly preceded the arrival of the British in Hong Kong, though, sadly, it now seems that their ancient way of life is facing extinction, if plans to fill in Aberdeen Harbour are implemented. In the meantime, a time-honoured and highly enjoyable tourist activity in Aberdeen is to take a tour around the harbour on one of the surviving sampans.

You won't get lost in Aberdeen. From the bus stop just head in the direction of the shore and cross over the main road using the footbridge, where women will be waiting to solicit your custom for a **sampan tour**. Either do a deal with one of these private entrepreneurs, or walk along the ornamental park by the waterfront until you reach a sign advertising "Water Tours" ($50 per head for a thirty-minute ride, irrespective of the number of travellers). The trip offers great photo opportunities of the old houseboats jammed together, complete with dogs, drying laundry and outdoor kitchens, as well as endless rags, nets and old tyres. Along the way you'll also pass boat yards and the three **floating restaurants**, which are especially spectacular when lit up at night (though they are really better for admiring from the outside than for eating in; see "Eating, drinking and nightlife", p.636).

To reach Aberdeen, catch **bus** #7 or #70 from Central, or #72 from Causeway Bay (30min). There's also a **boat** connection between here and nearby Lamma Island (see p.632).

Ocean Park

Ocean Park, a gigantic theme and adventure park (daily 10am–6pm; $130, children $65, one child free for every adult), covers an entire peninsula to the east of Aberdeen. The price of the ticket is all-inclusive, and once you're inside all rides and shows are free. You could easily spend the best part of a day here and at weekends in summer you may find yourself frustrated by queues at the popular attractions, so make sure you arrive early in order to enjoy yourself at a relaxed pace. The park is divided into a number of sections joined together by wacky transportation facilities: from the Lowland section, which is devoted to the wonders of nature – and includes some superb life-size dinosaur models – there's a 1.5-kilometre **cable car ride** to the Headland section at the tip of the peninsula. This is the area where you'll find one of the fastest and longest **roller coasters** in the world, as well as an **aquarium** where you can view **sharks** nose-to-nose through glass, and the so-called Ocean Theatre, where trained **dolphins and whales** perform. There's also a new feature, the **Atoll Reef**, a huge coral reef aquarium, containing over five thousand fish. From the Headland you can then ride an enormous escalator down to **Middle Kingdom**, actually a separate park though covered by the same ticket, which aims to recreate five thousand years of Chinese history through architecture, crafts, theatre and opera. All in all it's great value for an extraordinary amount of entertainment.

A special bus service runs from Admiralty MTR to Ocean Park every thirty minutes from 8.40am to 3.40pm Monday to Saturday, and every fifteen minutes from 9am to 3.30pm on Sundays and holidays (the all-inclusive ticket covering the return bus ride and the park entrance fee is $152, children $76, with one child is free for each adult). If you prefer local buses, the #6 minibus runs from the Star Ferry to Ocean Park (Mon–Sat); otherwise take bus #70 or #90 from Central, or #73 from Causeway Bay, and get off immediately after the Aberdeen Tunnel and follow the signs. On Sundays, buses #90 and #73 stop right by the park.

Deep Water Bay, Repulse Bay and beyond

Two bays with names ringing of adventure on the high seas, **Deep Water Bay** and **Repulse Bay**, line the coast east of Ocean Park. Despite stories you may have heard about polluted water around Hong Kong, the beaches in both bays are immaculately clean and the water can really be quite inviting at times, though in summer everything gets very crowded. Of all the bays around here, Repulse Bay is the most popular, partly because it contains a number of shops and restaurants, but also because of its Tin Hau Temple which has a longevity bridge, the crossing of which is said to add three days to your life. The backdrop to Repulse Bay is slightly bizarre with an enormous, garish tower silhouetted against verdant hills, but the very wide, deep beach is the finest in the area. South of Repulse Bay you'll find **Middle Bay** and **South Bay**, fifteen and thirty minutes farther along the coast. These offer more secluded but narrower beaches.

You can reach Repulse Bay on **buses** #6, #61 or #260 from Central. Between Aberdeen (to the west) and Stanley (to the east) there are frequent buses that pass all of the bays mentioned above.

Stanley

Straddling the neck of Hong Kong's most southerly peninsula, **Stanley** is a moderately attractive residential village, of which perhaps the main draw is the number of pubs and restaurants catering to expatriates. It's a tiny place – walk downhill from the bus stop and you'll soon find **Stanley Market** (selling a mish-mash of cheap clothes and tourist souvenirs), while a little way to the north of here is **Stanley Beach**, which, although not suitable for swimming, has a little row of great seafront restaurants. If you continue walking north, beyond the restaurants, you'll come to a two-hundred-year-old **Tin Hau Temple** which for some reason has a large tiger skin hanging on one wall. In the opposite direction, south down the peninsula along Wong Ma Kok Road, it's about a ten-minute walk to the fairly pleasant St Stephen's Beach, accessible by steps down to the right immediately after a playing field. Beyond here is **Stanley Cemetery**, containing the graves of many of those killed fighting the Japanese in World War II, and also the top-security Stanley Prison. The southern part of the peninsula is a closed military zone. Stanley is accessible on **buses** #6 and #260 from Central, or #73 from Aberdeen or Repulse Bay.

Shek O

In the far east of the island, **Shek O** is Hong Kong's most remote settlement and incredibly it really does give the feeling of being "undiscovered", if such a thing is possible in Hong Kong. There's a strong surf beating on the wide, white **beach** which has a shady area of vine trellises at one end for barbecues and, during the week, is more or less deserted. Come for sunbathing and lunch at one of the cheap local restaurants.

You can't miss the beach – it's just a few minutes' walk east from the bus stop, beyond a small roundabout. For a small detour through the village, however, stop at the excellent Thai restaurant with outdoor tables and chairs that you see on your left just before the roundabout. If you take the small lane left running right through the restaurant area, you'll pass first the local temple and then, somewhat improbably, a Scottish art gallery (☎ 2809 2866) full of contemporary art from Scotland.

Reaching Shek O in the first place is one of the best things about it. First you need to get to **Shau Kei Wan** on the northeastern shore of Hong Kong Island, either by tram or MTR. From the bus terminal outside the MTR station, catch bus #9 to Shek O, a great journey over hills (30min) during which you'll be able to spot first the sparkling waters of the Tai Tam Reservoir, then Stanley (far to the southwest) and finally Shek O itself, appearing down below like a Mediterranean village on the shore.

Kowloon

A four-kilometre strip of the mainland grabbed by the British in 1860, to add to their offshore island, **Kowloon** was part of the territory ceded to Britain "in perpetuity" and was accordingly developed with gusto and confidence. With the help of land reclamation and the diminishing significance of the border between Kowloon and the New Territories at Boundary Street, Kowloon has over the years just about managed to accommodate the vast numbers of people who have squeezed into it. Today, areas such as Mongkok, jammed with soaring tenements, are thought to be the most densely populated urban areas in the world.

While Hong Kong Island has mountains and beaches to palliate the effects of urban claustrophobia, Kowloon has just more shops, more restaurants and more hotels. It's hard to imagine that such an unmitigatedly built-up, crowded and commercial place as this could possibly have any cachet among the travelling public – and yet it does. One of the reasons is that this is the best place for viewing Hong Kong Island. The **view** across the harbour to the island, wall-to-wall with skyscrapers, is one of the most unforgettable city panoramas you'll see anywhere, especially at night. This, and its ritzy neon-lit streets full of hotels and restaurants in the couple of square kilometres at the tip of the peninsula that make up **Tsimshatsui** are enough to keep drawing in the crowds. Another attraction of Tsimshatsui is the presence of a very visible community of immigrants from the Indian subcontinent. Their great stronghold is the **Chungking Mansions**, which, as well as being a **budget accommodation** haven, is a superbly atmospheric shopping arcade where the great cultures of Asia mingle in a haze of spices and incense.

North, into **Yaumatei** and **Mongkok**, you'll find less touristy districts teeming with local life, while farther north still, beyond Boundary Street – technically just outside Kowloon – is a scattering of sights including one of Hong Kong's busiest temples, the **Wong Tai Sin**, and the historical theme park, the **Sung Dynasty Village**.

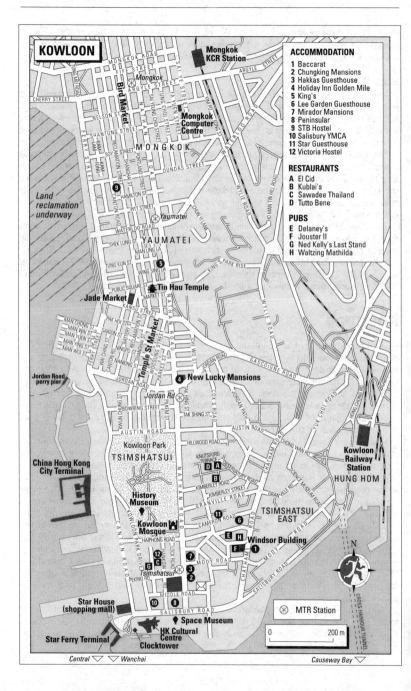

KOWLOON

Mongkok KCR Station

Mongkok

Bird Market

Mongkok Computer Centre

MONGKOK

Land reclamation underway

Yaumatei

YAUMATEI

Tin Hau Temple

Jade Market

Temple St Market

Jordan Road ferry pier

New Lucky Mansions

Jordan Rd

China Hong Kong City Terminal

Kowloon Park

TSIMSHATSUI

History Museum

Kowloon Mosque

Kowloon Railway Station

HUNG HOM

TSIMSHATSUI EAST

Windsor Building

Star House (shopping mall)

Star Ferry Terminal

Space Museum

HK Cultural Centre Clocktower

Simshatsui

ACCOMMODATION
1 Baccarat
2 Chungking Mansions
3 Hakkas Guesthouse
4 Holiday Inn Golden Mile
5 King's
6 Lee Garden Guesthouse
7 Mirador Mansions
8 Peninsular
9 STB Hostel
10 Salisbury YMCA
11 Star Guesthouse
12 Victoria Hostel

RESTAURANTS
A El Cid
B Kublai's
C Sawadee Thailand
D Tutto Bene

PUBS
E Delaney's
F Jouster II
G Ned Kelly's Last Stand
H Waltzing Mathilda

⊛ MTR Station

0   200 m

N

CROSS HARBOUR TUNNEL

Central ▽   ▽ Wanchai

Causeway Bay ▽

Tsimshatsui and beyond

The tourist heart of Hong Kong, **Tsimshatsui**, is an easy place to find your way around. The **Star Ferry terminal**, for ferries to Hong Kong Island, is right on the southwestern tip of the peninsula. East of here, along the southern shore, facing Hong Kong Island, are a number of hi-tech, modern museums and galleries built on reclaimed land, while the main road just to the north of these is **Salisbury Road**, dominated by the magnificently traditional **Peninsula Hotel**. Running south to north right through the middle of Tsimshatsui, and on through the rest of Kowloon, is Hong Kong's most famous street, **Nathan Road**, jammed with shops and shoppers at all hours of the day and night. All the streets immediately to the east and west of here are likewise chock-a-block with small traders.

Given the brash speed of change in this area, it's almost a miracle to find anything more than a few years old here. Nevertheless, there are a handful of relics surviving from earlier times, one of these being the **Clock Tower**, about 100m east of the Star Ferry terminal. The tower is the only remaining piece of the original Kowloon Railway Station which was demolished in 1978. The seafront **promenade** runs east from here, giving fantastic views over Hong Kong Island, particular popular at night when people come to stroll, sit, roller skate and fish.

Between the western section of the promenade and Salisbury Road to the north, is a series of buildings which cynics might regard as Tsimshatsui's desperate attempt to acquire a more cultured image. The distinctive winged, ski-slope roofline of the **Hong Kong Cultural Centre**, which occupies the former site of the Kowloon Railway Station, is unmissable. Inside there are concert halls, theatres and galleries including, in an adjacent wing, the **Museum of Art** (Mon–Wed, Fri & Sat 10am–6pm, Sun 1–6pm; $10) which is definitely worth a visit. As well as calligraphy, scrolls and an intriguing selection of paintings covering the history of Hong Kong, the museum houses an excellent Chinese antiquities section which has far more informative English labels than comparable museums in China. For information on events in the Cultural Centre, pop into the foyer for an up-to-date brochure.

Immediately to the east of the Cultural Centre, the domed **Hong Kong Space Museum** (Mon & Wed–Fri 1–9pm, Sat & Sun 10am–9pm; $10) houses some highly user-friendly exhibition halls on astronomy and space exploration. The highlight here, however, is the planetarium, known as the **Space Theatre**, which presents pretty amazing wide-screen space shows for an additional fee ($26, concessions $13; call ☎2734 2722 for show times).

Salisbury Road, running east–west immediately north of the Cultural Centre, is patrolled by Rolls Royces, many of them belonging to the chauffeur-driven fleet of the **Peninsula Hotel**. Before reclamation pushed the shore a couple of hundred metres south, the *Peninsula* commanded a view directly across the harbour to the island. By way of compensation for having lost its view, however, the *Peninsula* became the first building in Kowloon to exceed the old twenty-storey height limit imposed on development, with its new wing towering up at the back. Needless to say, rooms are pricey, but it's worth dropping by for lunch or afternoon tea in the foyer if you are not feeling too scruffy.

Immediately east of the *Peninsula*, running north from Salisbury Road, is the neon-lit **Nathan Road** which dominates the commercial heart of Kowloon. While by no means a beautiful street, it's one you'll find yourself drawn to again and again for Hong Kong's most concentrated collection of electronics shops, tailors, jewellery stores and fashion boutiques. The variety of goods on offer is staggering, but the southern section of Nathan Road, known as the Golden Mile for its commercial potential, is by no means a cheap place to shop these days (for more details, see "Shopping", p.640). One of the least salubrious but most exotic corners of Nathan Road is the gigantic **Chungking Mansions** (see "Accommodation", p.609), a couple of hundred metres north of the junction with Salisbury Road. The shopping arcades here on the two lowest floors are a steaming jungle of ethnic shops, curry houses and dark corners which seem to stretch away into the impenetrable heart of the building, making an interesting contrast with the antiseptic air-conditioned shopping malls that fill the rest of Hong Kong.

A few hundred metres north of Chungking Mansions, **Kowloon Park** (daily 6am–midnight) is marked at its southeastern corner by the white-domed **Kowloon Mosque** which caters to the substantial Muslim population of the area – tourists are not allowed in without special permission (call ☎2724 0095). The park itself provides welcome green respite from the unremitting concrete of Tsimshatsui, though strangely you can't see it from the street and have to climb steps up from Nathan Road. There's also an indoor heated Olympic-sized swimming pool complex in the grounds, which unfortunately is open only in July and August. Another feature of the park is Hong Kong's **Museum of History** (Mon–Thurs & Sat 10am–6pm, Sun 1–6pm; $10) which contains a predictably hi-tech and well-presented display of relics, including a mock-up of an entire nineteenth-century street.

A few blocks to the east of Nathan Road, beyond Chatham Road, the area known as **Tsimshatsui East** is built on entirely reclaimed land and comprises exclusive hotels and shopping malls. From the Star Ferry terminal an excellent walk follows the seafront promenade east and then north past this area as far as **Hung Hom**, the site of the Kowloon–Canton Railway Station.

Yaumatei and Mongkok

In some ways, the part of Kowloon north of the tourist ghetto of Tsimshatsui is more rewarding to walk around, with more authentic Chinese neighbourhoods and interesting markets. **Yaumatei**, whose name, meaning "Place of Sesame Plants", rather belies its present appearance, is jammed with highrise tenements and busy streets. The area begins north of Jordan Road and most of the interest lies in the streets to the west of Nathan Road. You can walk up here from Tsimshatsui in about twenty minutes, otherwise take the MTR or, if you're coming from Central, take the cross-harbour ferry to the Jordan Road Ferry pier.

Temple Street, running north off Jordan Road a couple of blocks west of Nathan Road, becomes a fun-packed **night market** after around 7pm every day. As well as buying cheap clothing, watches and souvenirs, you can get your fortune told here, eat some great seafood from street stalls, and sometimes listen in on impromptu performances of Chinese opera. A minute or two to the north of here, is the local **Tin Hau Temple**, just off Nathan Road, tucked away between Public Square Street and Market Street, a couple of minutes south of Jordan MTR. Surrounded by urban hubbub, this old little temple devoted to the sea, with its banyan trees and beggars, looks slightly forlorn these days. A couple of minutes east of the Tin Hau Temple, just under the Kansu Street flyover, the **Jade Market** (daily 10am–3.30pm) has hundreds of stalls offering an amazing variety of items from souvenir trinkets to family heirlooms – it's another good place for a browse.

Another market, a few hundred metres north of here, in the direction of Mongkok MTR, is the delightful **Bird Market** (daily 10am–6pm), on a small lane called Hong Lok Street between Shanghai Street and Portland Street. As well as the hundreds of birds on sale here, along with their intricately designed bamboo cages, you can also pick up singing crickets of prodigious size. This place gives a real glimpse into a traditional area of Chinese life which is spiritually a thousand miles from Tsimshatsui.

Finally, to the east of Nathan Road, at the corner of Nelson Street and Fa Yuen Street, is a specialist market of a rather different flavour, the **Mongkok Computer Centre**, where some incredible bargain software can be picked up on CD, though be warned that much of this is pirated and, strictly speaking, illegal – exercise caution when importing such material into your own country.

Outer Kowloon

A few hundred metres north of Mongkok and you reach **Boundary Street**, which marks the border between Kowloon and the New Territories, though these days this distinction is pretty meaningless. By far the busiest tourist attraction in this area is well to the northeast at **Wong Tai Sin Temple** (daily 7am–5.30pm; free but small donation requested), a huge, thriving place packed with more worshippers than any other temple in Hong Kong. Big, bright and colourful, it's interesting as a glimpse into the practices of modern, popular Chinese religion: vigorous kneeling, incense-burning and the noisy rattling of joss sticks in canisters, as well as the presentation of food and drink to the Taoist deities. Large numbers of English-speaking fortune-tellers have stands to the right of the entrance and charge $200 for palm reading, about half that for a face-reading. The temple can be reached directly from the Wong Tai Sin MTR station.

Northwest from Mongkok, in the opposite direction from Wong Tai Sin, are a couple of places worth a visit. The **Lei Cheng Uk Museum** (daily 10am–1pm & 2–6pm, closed Sun am; free) a branch of the main Museum of History in Kowloon Park, has been constructed over a two-thousand-year-old Han-dynasty tomb which was discovered by workmen in 1955. By far the oldest structure discovered in Hong Kong, the tomb offers some rare proof of the ancient presence of the Chinese in the area. What is really interesting, however, is to compare photos of the site from the 1950s (paddyfields and green hills) with the highrises that surround the area today. You can reach the museum from Chang Shan Wan MTR; take exit A2, walk for five minutes along Tonkin Street and the museum is on your left.

Carrying on a couple more MTR stops from here, to Mei Foo station, brings you to the **Sung Dynasty Village** (daily 10am–8.30pm; $120, children $65), a "living" museum from the Song dynasty (960–1279 AD) with villagers in period costume, working on traditional handicrafts and arts. You can even buy their wares with Song-dynasty "money", available from the local moneychanger. There's street theatre, restaurants, a wax museum and mock historic architecture, which is all quite pleasant and educational, but it's best avoided if you're allergic to tourist kitsch. If you're not coming by MTR (the station is a few minutes' walk from the village), you can ride bus #6A from the Tsimshatsui Star Ferry terminal, or bus #105 from Central via the cross-harbour tunnel, direct to the entrance.

The New Territories

Many people fly in and out of Hong Kong without even realizing that the territory comprises anything more than the city itself. The mistake is an unfortunate one, for it is in the **New Territories** that some of the most scenic and traditionally Chinese areas of Hong Kong can be found. Comprising some 750 square kilometres of land abutting the southern part of China's Guangdong Province, the New Territories come complete with country roads, water buffalo, old villages, valleys and mountains – as well as booming New Towns which now house upwards of three million people.

It's the country areas that hold most appeal, and there is a whole series of designated **country parks**, including the amazingly unspoilt **Sai Kung Peninsula** to the east, offering excellent hiking trails and secluded beaches. For serious extended hikes, the **MacLehose Trail** extends right across the peninsula and beyond. Some of the towns are also interesting in their own right, either as ordinary residential districts, or as gateways to relics from the past such as Shatin's **Ten Thousand Buddha Monastery**, or the **walled villages** near Kam Tin.

Getting around the New Territories is simplicity itself – frequent buses connect all towns, while the MTR reaches as far as Tsuen Wan and the KCR runs north through

Shatin, the Chinese University and Tai Po. There are also a number of boats from Central, including the fast hoverferries that connect with Tuen Mun in only thirty minutes. Tuen Mun is the terminus of the LRT rail line that runs north to Yuen Long. You can get a flavour of the New Territories in just one day's independent exploration, or it's worth considering a **HKTA tour** ($335, children $285). These run every day except Sunday, take six hours and include lunch. Covering such a large distance, this is probably one of their best tours in terms of convenience and value.

By **public transport**, a satisfying do-it-yourself tour can be made in a few hours along the following route, starting from Jordan Road Ferry pier in Kowloon (accessible by ferry from Central, or bus #8 from Tsimshatsui): take bus #60X to Tuen Mun bus terminal, then from here ride the LTR north to its terminus at Yuen Long. From Yuen Long, take bus #76K to Sheung Shui bus terminal in the north. Finally ride the KCR train south back to Kowloon.

The west

Tsuen Wan in the west of the New Territories is one of Hong Kong's **New Towns** – a satellite town, built from scratch in the last 25 years to absorb some of the overflow from Hong Kong's burgeoning population. With getting on for a million inhabitants, Tsuen Wan now has all the amenities of a large city in its own right, and is easily reached from downtown Hong Kong by MTR or by hoverferries from Central. If you are interested in seeing a New Town, this is the perfect place to start.

One really attractive sight virtually in the middle of Tsuen Wan is the **Sam Tung Uk Museum** (daily except Tues 9am–4pm; free), which is essentially a restored two-hundred-year-old walled village of a type typical of this part of southern China. The village was founded in 1786 by a Hakka clan named Chan, who continued to live here, incredibly, until the 1970s. Now the houses have been restored with their original furnishings, and there are various exhibitions on aspects of the lives of the Hakka people. You can reach the museum by following signs out of Tsuen Wan MTR station – it's about a five-minute walk.

A couple of blocks south of the MTR station (in the direction of the shore), on Shiu Wo Street, minibus #81 runs up to the nearby Lo Wai Village, where the **Yuen Yuen Institute** is located. This is a large temple complex dedicated to the three main religions practised in Hong Kong – Buddhism, Taoism and Confucianism – and its main structure is a copy of the Temple of Heaven in Beijing. Its chief attractions, however, are the beautiful hillside location and an excellent vegetarian restaurant.

Moving on from Tsuen Wan, you can either catch buses #60M and #68M from the bus terminal opposite the MTR to **Tuen Mun** – another huge New Town whose main boast is that it holds Hong Kong's largest shopping mall – or, from an overpass just north of the MTR, catch bus #51 north to Kam Tin. The ride to Kam Tin is a spectacular one, running right past Hong Kong's highest peak, **Tai Mo Shan**, which at 957m is nearly twice the height of Victoria Peak on Hong Kong Island. If you want to climb up to the top of the mountain, there's a bus stop on a pass right under the peak – get off here and follow a signposted path up to the top. The excellent **MacLehose Trail** runs right through here and this is as good a place as any to join it. For detailed information on the trail, which in all runs 100km across the New Territories from Tuen Mun in the west to the Sai Kung Peninsula in the east, contact the HKTA (see p.605) or the Country Parks Authority on the 12th Floor, 393 Canton Rd, Tsimshatsui, Kowloon (Mon–Fri 9am–5pm, Sat 9–noon; ☎2733 2132).

Kam Tin

This small town is famous in Hong Kong as the site of **Kat Hing Wai**, one of Hong Kong's last inhabited **walled villages**. Dating back to the late seventeenth century when a clan named Tang settled here, the village ($1 donation) still comprises a moat, thick six-metre-high walls and guard towers. Inside the walls, there's a wide lane running down the middle of the village, with tiny alleys leading off it. A few souvenir sellers and old Hakka ladies in traditional hats pester visitors with cameras for more donations, but the atmosphere is as different from Hong Kong as you can possibly imagine. To get here, get off bus #51 in Kam Tin, walk a few minutes farther west (the same direction as the bus) and it's on your left, visible from the main road.

North: the KCR route

There is a whole series of possible outings to be made from the stops dotted along the **Kowloon–Canton Railway** as it wends its way north from Kowloon to the border with mainland China. As well as booming New Towns, you can still find traces of Hakka communities, the women dressed in conspicuous baggy trousers and heavy fringed hats. If you're on a day trip, visits to the New Towns of **Shatin** and **Sheung Shui** might be all you have time for, though if you're really keen on getting out into some countryside, the excellent walks around **Plover Cove Country Park** will need a day in themselves.

Shatin

The first important stop is at the booming New Town of **Shatin**, best known to Hong Kongers as the site of the territory's second **racecourse**, which is packed with fanatical gamblers on race days during the season (for details on the HKTA horse-racing tour, see "Happy Valley", p.618). For tourists, however, the main attraction of Shatin is the forty-year-old **Ten Thousand Buddhas Monastery**, which is probably the single most interesting temple in the whole of the New Territories, if not in all Hong Kong. To reach it from the KCR station, follow the signs saying "buses", and exit the station on the side facing the green hilly area; it's a few minutes' walk north along the road from here. The first you'll see of the temple is a giant new escalator (daily 9am–5pm) stretching up the hill. If you feel like some exercise, however, or if the escalator is closed, there's a delightful fifteen-minute stepped walk through dense forest up to the back door of the temple, starting just to the right of the escalator area.

The "Ten Thousand Buddhas" – actually more like thirteen thousand – are stacked on shelves filling the inside walls of the main temple hall, surrounding the central Buddha. The terrace outside, which commands some great views over Shatin, also contains a quite bizarre array of giant statues, including an elephant and a dragon. Overall the mixture of jungle, panoramic views and colourful statuary makes this an excellent spot. You can also follow a path farther up the mountain to another terrace containing some smaller temples.

Tai Po and the Plover Cove Country Park

Tai Po, a few KCR stops north of Shatin, is not in itself an enormously exciting place but it does offer opportunities for escaping into some serious countryside. To reach **Plover Cove Country Park**, take bus #75K from outside Tai Po Market KCR station to its terminus at the small village of **Tai Mei Tuk**, right by the Plover Cove Reservoir. The signposted circular walk around the park takes about an hour. Alternatively, you can stroll, or ride a rented bike ($40 per day from rental shops in Tai Mei Tuk) along the road to **Bride's Pool**, an attractive picnic site beside pools and waterfalls, or follow on foot the five-kilometre **Pat Sin Leng Nature Trail**, a highly scenic, if slightly circuitous, route from Tai Mei Tuk to the pool. The pool area is very crowded at weekends, but during the week it can be pretty quiet. For more details about the many walks in this area, contact the HKTA.

Sheung Shui

Unless you're planning to cross the border into mainland China, **Sheung Shui** is as far as you can get on the KCR – in fact, it lies just 3km south of the border. There are no special tourist sights as such, but of all the towns in the New Territories, this is one of those least affected by modern development, and casual exploration in the Shek Wu Hui area just outside the KCR station will reward you with some great old markets full of haggling Hakka women. Sheung Shui is also linked by bus #77K to Yuen Long and Kam Tin in the west of the region.

The east

The eastern part of the New Territories, around **Clearwater Bay** and the **Sai Kung Peninsula**, is the last word on secluded beaches and walks in Hong Kong, though at weekends even these can begin to fill up. The best way to appreciate the seclusion is to come during the week and bring a picnic – you'll need to put aside a whole day to visit either place. The starting point for buses into both areas is Choi Hung MTR station

Clearwater Bay

The forty-minute ride on bus #91 from Choi Hung MTR to Clearwater Bay already gives an idea of the delightful combination of green hills and sea that awaits you. Around the terminus at **Tai Au Mun**, overlooking Clearwater Bay, are a couple of excellent, clean **beaches**, and to the south is the start of a good three-to-four-hour walk around the bay. First, follow the road south along the cliff top, as far as the Clearwater Bay Golf and Country Club (the only way visitors can use the tennis, swimming and golf facilities of this luxury club is to join HKTA's "Sports and Recreation Tour" which costs $380 plus pay-as-you-play charges). From here, follow signposts on to the wonderfully located **Tin Hau Temple** in **Joss House Bay**. There is thought to have been a temple to the Taoist goddess of the sea here for nearly a thousand years and although today's temple dates back only to its last restoration in 1962, there is a venerable feel about the place. As one of Hong Kong's few Tin Hau temples actually still commanding the sea, it's of immense significance, and on the 23rd day of the third lunar month each year (Tin Hau's birthday) a colossal seaborne celebration takes place on fishing boats in the bay.

Heading back, you can take another path leading from the Golf and Country Club down to **Sheung Lau Wan**, a small village on the western shore of the peninsula. From here it's possible to catch an irregular boat back to Sai Wan Ho on Hong Kong Island, or else you can continue on a circular route around the headland back to the Clearwater Bay bus terminal.

Sai Kung Peninsula

Some way to the north of Clearwater Bay, the irregularly shaped Sai Kung Peninsula, jagged with headlands, bluffs and tiny offshore islands, is the least developed area in the whole of Hong Kong, and a haven for hikers and beach lovers.

The only sizeable town in the area, **Sai Kung Town**, accessible on bus #92 from Choi Hung MTR, lies slightly to the south of the peninsula but is nevertheless the jumping-off point for explorations of Sai Kung. It's now being developed fairly fast, though still retains the pleasant features of a fishing town, with a promenade packed with seafood restaurants. Small boats also run from the quayside to the various islands, the nearest and most popular of which is **Kiu Tsui Chau**, boasting a beach and a short hike to its highest point.

The highlights of Sai Kung, however, are the **country parks** that cover the penin-sula with virgin forest and grassland leading to perfect sandy beaches. Although it is possible to see something of these on a day trip, the only way really to appreciate them is to bring a tent or consider staying at the youth hostel on Sai Kung (see "Accommodation", p.612). Access to the parks is by bus #94 from Sai Kung Town and #96R (Sundays only) from Choi Hung MTR, which pass through **Pak Tam Chung** on their way to Wong Shek pier in the north of the peninsula. Buses depart hourly, on the hour. Don't come to Pak Tam Chung expecting a town – all you'll find is a **visitors' centre** (daily except Tues 9.30am–4.30pm; ☎2792 7365), which supplies hikers with vital information about the trails.

Of the many possible hikes, the MacLehose Trail, liberally dotted with campsites, heads east from here, circumventing the **High Island Reservoir** before heading west into the rest of the New Territories. If you want to follow the trail just a part of the way, the **beaches** at Long Ke, south of the reservoir, and Tai Long, to the northeast, are Hong Kong's finest, though to walk out to them and back from Pak Tam Chung takes several hours. The last bus back from Pak Tam Chung is at 7.30pm.

The Outlying Islands

Officially part of the New Territories, the **outlying islands** of Hong Kong are havens of escape for weary visitors after the urban hubbub of Tsimshatsui has become too claustrophobic. Covering twenty percent of the land area of the territory but containing just two percent of the population, the islands offer a delightful mix of seascape, rural calm and quiet old fishing villages, almost entirely free of motor vehicles, except for a few taxis and buses on Lantau Island. The islands are conveniently connected to Central by plentiful **ferries** and other boats, but for the time being development has been relatively restrained. Whether this will continue to be the case after the comple-

---

FERRIES TO THE ISLANDS

The following is a selection of the most useful island ferry services. Schedules differ slightly on Saturdays and Sundays:

To Cheung Chau

From Central (pier 7) – first boat out 6.25am, last boat back 11.30pm (at least hourly; 1hr). There are also five hover-ferries daily from pier 6.

To Sok Kwu Wan, Lamma Island

From Central (pier 6) – first boat out 8am, last boat back 10pm (7 daily; 50min).

From Aberdeen – first boat out 6.50am, last boat back 7.15pm (6–8 daily; 30min).

To Yung Shue Wan, Lamma Island

From Central (pier 6) – first boat out 6.45am, last boat back 10.35pm (at least hourly; 40min).

To Discovery Bay, Lantau Island (hoverferries)

From Central (the pier east of the Star Ferry) – 24-hour departures (at least every 30min between 6.50am and 12.30am; 30min).

To Mui Wo (Silvermine Bay), Lantau Island

From Central (pier 7) – first boat out 7am, last boat back 11.10pm (at least hourly; 1hr). Early and late sailings go via Peng Chau. There are also four hoverferries daily from pier 6, all via Peng Chau.

From Peng Chau – first boat out 5.40am, last boat back midnight (6 daily; 25min).

To Peng Chau

From Central (pier 7) – first boat out 7am, last boat back 11.30pm (hourly; 50min).

tion of the new **Chek Lap Kok airport** on the northern shore of the largest and emptiest island, Lantau, remains to be seen.

Although most tourists come on day trips, there is some **accommodation** on the islands (see p.611), and **restaurants** of the fishy variety are also numerous.

Lamma

Lamma is the closest island to Hong Kong Island, lying just to the southwest of Aberdeen, and conspicuous for the giant chimneys protruding from its power station on the western shore. The tiny population of less than ten thousand chiefly comprises Western expatriates who have come here in search of a more laid-back existence. Despite the power station and the island's quarrying industry, the air is clean, there are lots of cheap, interesting restaurants, no cars and you can walk across green hills to sandy beaches.

There are two possible points of **arrival** on Lamma, either by ferry from Central to Yung Shue Wan, or to Sok Kwu Wan either from Central or from Aberdeen. By far the nicest way to appreciate the island is to take a boat to either Yung Shue Wan or Sok Kwu Wan, then walk to the other and catch the boat back from there.

Yung Shue Wan is a pretty little tree-shaded village, with one or two hotels and a clustering of small grocery stores, bars and cheap eating places catering for both Chinese and Western palates. There's a very relaxed feel to the place in the evening when people sit out under the banyan trees. To walk to Sok Kwu Wan from here (1hr), follow the easy-to-find cement path that branches away from the shore shortly before the Tin Hau Temple. You'll soon find yourself walking amid butterflies, long grass and trees. After about fifteen minutes you'll arrive at **Hung Shing Yeh Beach**, a beautiful place if you stick to its northern half; stray a few metres to the south, though, and you'll rapidly find your horizon filling up with power station. There's a smart restaurant and hotel here (the *Concierto Inn*, see p.611), where you can sit on the outdoor terrace and enjoy a drink. On from the beach, the path climbs quite sharply up to a little summit with a pavilion commanding views over the island. Continue on for another thirty minutes or so and you'll reach **Sok Kwu Wan**, which basically comprises a row of seafood restaurants with terraces built out over the water. The food is excellent and the banquets are noisy and fun. Many people simply get the ferry over to Sok Kwu Wan in the evening for dinner, though make sure you don't miss the last boat back at 10pm, because there's nowhere to stay here – your only option would be to hire a sampan back to Aberdeen.

Cheung Chau

Another great little island where you can spend a couple of hours strolling around and then have dinner is **Cheung Chau**, just south of Lantau and an hour from Hong Kong by ferry. Despite its minuscule size of just 2.5 square kilometres, Cheung Chau is nevertheless the most crowded of all the outer islands, with a population of some twenty thousand. Historically the island is one of the oldest settled parts of Hong Kong, being notorious as a base for pirates who enjoyed waylaying the ships that ran between Guangzhou and the Portuguese enclave of Macau. Today, it still gives the impression of being an economically independent little unit, with the narrow strip between its two headlands jam-packed with tiny shops, markets and seafront restaurants. As well as romantic dinners and late-night ferry rides home, the island offers attractive **walks** around the old but thriving fishing ports and views of traditional junk building. It also has some interesting temples, the most important being the two-hundred-year-old **Pak Tai Temple**, a few hundred metres northwest of the ferry pier, along the interesting Pak She Street, lined with old herbalists and shops selling religious trinkets. Fishermen come to the temple to pray for protection, and beside the statue of Pak Tai, the god of the sea, is an ancient iron sword, discovered by fishermen and supposedly symbolizing good luck. For a few days in late April or early May the temple is the site of one of Hong Kong's liveliest and most spectacular festivals, the so-called **Tai Chiu (Bun) Festival**.

The main beach on the island, the excellent but crowded **Tung Wan Beach**, is due west of the ferry pier. Windsurfers are available for rent on the beach just south of here.

The southern headland of Cheung Chau contains more walking possibilities. If you catch a small sampan from the ferry pier across the bay to the small pier of **Sai Wan** – a five-minute ride – you can then follow marked trails to the nearby **Tin Hau Temple** and then the **Cheung Po Tsai Cave**, named after Cheung Chau's most famous pirate who used the cave as a hide-out in the early part of the nineteenth century. Legend aside, however, the cave is nothing special. The walk back from the cave area to the main ferry pier is an attractive one that takes about an hour.

Lantau

It comes as something of a surprise that **Lantau Island** is actually twice as big as Hong Kong Island – and given that only a few thousand people live here, there is clearly considerable scope for getting off the beaten track. With wild countryside, monasteries, old fishing villages and seriously secluded beaches, Lantau is the ultimate fast escape from downtown Hong Kong. The only cause for worry is the northern shore, where Hong Kong's vast new airport and associated infrastructure projects are nearing completion. Flight paths will not cross the island, however, and it does seem that much of Lantau's tranquillity will not be fatally disturbed.

Serious hikers might want to take advantage of the seventy-kilometre **Lantau Trail**, which links up the popular scenic spots on the island and is dotted along its length by campsites and youth hostels; for detailed information on this, pay a call to the Country Parks Authority in Kowloon (see p.628). Even if you intend doing only a short hike or a quick whip round the main sights, try to set aside a full day for Lantau, or plan to pay two or more visits, as the sights are scattered. The main point of arrival for visitors to Lantau Island is **Mui Wo**, otherwise known as **Silvermine Bay**, about one hour from Central. Some of the Mui Wo boats stop at the small island of Peng Chau en route. There are also a few ferries daily which connect Mui Wo with Cheung Chau.

The other point of arrival is **Discovery Bay**, a residential area connected by frequent high-speed ferries from Central that run throughout the day. The Discovery Bay pier is a few steps to the east of the Star Ferry terminal.

From Mui Wo to Discovery Bay

Mui Wo itself is not much to speak of, and having disembarked at the ferry pier, most people head straight for the bus station right outside. There are, however, some excellent walks that can be made directly from Mui Wo, one of which, the trail to Discovery Bay (2hr 30min), is reasonably straightforward. From the pier you need to head northwest towards the attractive, curving, sandy bay you'll see from the ferry as it approaches. Keep following the bay around to the end of the beach until you reach a small river flowing down from the hills. Take the path left from here, immediately after the river. The path climbs up through virtual jungle, heading in a generally easterly direction for about ninety minutes, until you reach the **Trappist Haven Monastery**. There's not much to see here apart from rushing streams, hills and trees, though you can buy milk and cookies from the local dairy run by the monks. The normal access to the monastery, if not on foot, is by an infrequent boat service from nearby Peng Chau Island to the pier about fifteen minutes walk below the monastery. Continuing from the monastery to **Discovery Bay**, follow the road down towards the pier and a little way down on your left you'll see a flat-topped, derelict building; the path begins immediately opposite here. After an hour, walking north with the sea on your left, you'll arrive at a beach, a shanty town and then Discovery Bay itself, which with its condominiums, shopping malls, kids and ubiquitous golf buggies will leave you wondering whether you've stepped through a time warp. This is the main settlement on the island, almost exclusively inhabited by expatriate families. From Discovery Bay you can either catch a ferry back to Mui Wo, or direct to Central.

Western Lantau

The road west from Mui Wo passes along the southern shore which is where Lantau's best beaches are located. **Cheung Sha Beach**, with a couple of cafés and a hotel, is the nicest and buses #2, #4 and #5 all pass by here.

Beyond the beaches, there are a couple more interesting sights in the western part of the island that can also be reached by direct bus from Mui Wo. The first of these is the **Po Lin Monastery** (daily 10am–4pm; free) which is by far the largest temple in the whole territory of Hong Kong. Located high up on the Ngong Ping Plateau, this is not an ancient site, indeed it was only established in 1928. Nevertheless, it is very much a living, breathing temple and busloads of locals arrive here by the hour, in particular to pay their respects to the new bronze **Tian Tan Buddha**, the largest seated bronze outdoor Buddha in the world, and to eat in the huge vegetarian **restaurant** (noon–5pm; meal tickets $60 from the ticket office outside). The Po Lin Monastery, referred to in bus schedules as Ngong Ping, is reached by bus #2 from Mui Wo, and it's a spectacular forty-minute ride through the hills. The last bus back to Mui Wo leaves at 7.30pm (7.10pm Sun).

Right on the far northwestern shore of Lantau is the fascinating little fishing village of **Tai O**. This remote place, constructed over the shore and a tiny offshore island, clings to the old ways almost as hard as the rest of Hong Kong seeks new ones. The village boasts an ancient rope-pulled ferry, wooden houses built on stilts, caged pigs and crumbling old temples on the island. You can reach it by bus #41 from Mui Wo (last bus back 10.15pm) and also by the relatively infrequent bus #21 from the Po Lin Monastery.

Eating, drinking and nightlife

As one of the great culinary capitals of the world, Hong Kong can boast not only a superb native cuisine – **Cantonese** – but also perhaps the widest range of **international restaurants** of any city outside Europe or North America. This is due in part to the cosmopolitan nature of the population, but perhaps more importantly, to the incredible seriousness attached to dining by the local Chinese.

As well as the joys of **dim sum** – another Hong Kong speciality – the city offers the full gamut of Chinese restaurants from Beijing to Shanghai to Sichuan (and many smaller localities). It also offers excellent **curry houses** from the Indian subcontinent, surprisingly cheap **Japanese** sushi bars, **British** pub-style food and endless cheap outlets of the noodle-and-dumpling variety which are often the best value for money of all. You'll also find the local Chinese **fast-food** chains, *Café de Coral* and *Maxim's*, alongside *McDonald's*, *Pizza Hut* and *KFC*. The choice is endless, and all budgets are catered for. Travellers arriving after a long stint in mainland China are in for the gastronomic blow-out of their lives. The places listed below are a mere fraction of the total, with an emphasis on the less expensive end of the market. Serious gourmets should consult HKTA's *Dining and Entertainment Guide*.

Hong Kong sometimes seems to have more **nightlife** than the rest of China put together, though a lot of it – particularly where heavy drinking and riotous behaviour is concerned – is expatriate rather than Chinese. In the **pubs** and **bars** you'll sometimes find **live music and dancing**.

BREAKFASTS AND CAFÉS

All the bigger hotels serve expensive buffet breakfasts. For cheaper, traditional Western breakfasts head for any of the cafés listed (all open throughout the day), although *dim sum* with tea is a more authentic way to start the morning (see "Restaurants" below).

Delifrance, Worldwide Plaza, Central. French café-chain with baguette sandwiches, croissants and other pastries along with coffees and juices.

Kiku Express, in the basement of Jardine House, the tower with porthole windows on Connaught Rd, Central. All kinds of breakfasts, from big English fry-ups to bowls of noodles.

Kona Coffee Specialists, on a small lane branching north off Cameron Rd, just east of Nathan Rd, Tsimshatsui. Offering a range of coffees and croissants, this is a good place for breakfast, as is the busy Chinese place opposite that specializes in sweet breads and tea.

Mad Dogs, D'Aguilar St, a few metres south of Stanley St, Central (with another branch at 32 Nathan Rd, Tsimshatsui). An Edwardian-style British pub with all-day breakfasts as well as beer and pub food.

Mall Café, *YMCA*, 41 Salisbury Rd. Large, excellent breakfasts – Western or Chinese – in a relaxing atmosphere.

Oliver's Super Sandwiches, 28 Hankow Rd, Tsimshatsui. Popular chain offering excellent sandwiches, salads, baked potatoes, fried breakfasts and fresh juices.

Restaurants

Eating is an enormously large part of life in Hong Kong and restaurant dining in particular is a sociable, family affair. The authentic Chinese restaurants are large, noisy places where dining takes place under bright lights – not as discreet as the candle-lit ambiances so beloved in the West but much more fun. Don't be intimidated by the speed with which you will be rushed to your seat: service is brisk but generally courteous. Menus in all but the cheapest restaurants are in English as well as Chinese. In the very cheap noodle-and-dumpling shops, order by pointing at other people's dishes.

The busiest, brightest restaurants of all are often those serving **dim sum** for breakfast or lunch – snack-sized portions of savoury dumplings, rolls and buns served in bamboo baskets or small plates from trolleys which are pushed around the restaurant. In these places you simply request items from passing trolleys and a card on your table will be marked with the item. Keep picking things up until you are full and the bill will rarely come to $100 per head, and often far less.

The largest restaurant area in Hong Kong Island is probably **Causeway Bay**, bordering on to neighbouring **Wanchai**, though the streets around D'Aguilar Street in **Central**, just a couple of minutes' walk south from the MTR, are particularly popular with young people and yuppie expatriates. This area is usually known as **Lan Kwai Fong**, after the small lane branching off D'Aguilar Street to the east, which is chock-a-block with bars and restaurants. South of Central, **Stanley** and **Aberdeen** are all popular spots for tourists on dining excursions.

In Kowloon, the choice of eateries is hardly less than on the island, though watch out for the possibility of tourist rip-offs in the Chinese restaurants in the **Tsimshatsui** area, such as heavy charges on unasked-for side-dishes. For Indian food the best-value places are secreted away in the recesses of the Chungking Mansions.

Opening hours are long, to accommodate the long working day, and you'll have no trouble getting served late. Don't worry too much about **tipping** either. Expensive restaurants will add on their own service charge, usually ten percent, while in cheaper places it's customary just to leave the small change. Generally

prices are comparable to those in the West: a full dinner without drinks is unlikely to cost less than $100 per head, and that figure can climb to $500 or more in the plushest venues.

Aberdeen

Jumbo Floating Restaurant, Aberdeen Harbour (☎2553 9111). One of three broadly similar restaurants in the harbour; the lights of this floating edifice shining on the water are one of Hong Kong's night-time landmarks. Shuttle boats carry customers to and from the quayside. The actual food rather pales beside the venue, but it's a great experience.

Central

Ashoka, 57–59 Wyndham St. South of the Lan Kwai Fong area, this is an excellent, well-established Indian restaurant, one of a number on Wyndham Street and Hollywood Road.

Beirut, Winner Building, 26–39 D'Aguilar St. Stylish, with a plush ambiance, and serving excellent if expensive Lebanese food; main dishes around $140 each.

City Hall Chinese Restaurant, 2nd Floor, City Hall Low Block, a short walk east of the Star Ferry pier. A good place for the classic *dim sum* experience with enormous halls, bright lights and crowds. Avoid the midday rush – come for breakfast around 10am.

Fat Heung Lam, 94 Wellington St. A Cantonese-style vegetarian restaurant of excellent quality, where prices are reasonable.

Furama Kempinski, 1 Connaught Rd, Central. For a splash-out, the multinational dinner buffet in this revolving restaurant in the heart of Hong Kong is hard to beat.

Luk Yu Tea House, 26 Stanley St, just west of D'Aguilar St. A living museum with spitoons, sixty-year-old furniture and geriatric waiters, this is possibly the most atmospheric restaurant in Hong Kong. Tea and *dim sum* as well as full meals are available, though the prices are somewhat tourist-inflated.

Man Wah, 25th Floor, *Mandarin Oriental Hotel*, 5 Connaught Rd Central (☎2522 0111). If there's anything that the chefs here can't cook, you shouldn't bother eating it. Superb Cantonese food at connoisseurs' prices.

Noodles Restaurant, 36 Stanley St. From D'Aguilar St, walk west until you pass the *Eat Eat Wonton* restaurant – the noodle restaurant is next door. There's no English here but you can get cheap bowls of shrimp wonton or noodles for a fraction of the price of any of the smarter restaurants in the area. Order by pointing at other people's dishes.

Peak Café, 121 Peak Rd (☎2849 7868). For years this has been *the* place to dine on the Peak, and although the traditional colonial-style fittings have now been somewhat jazzified, views from the terrace are incomparable, and the food, with an Asian-Indian slant, is reasonable value; reckon on around $200 per head for a full meal.

Tokio Joe, 16 Lan Kwai Fong. Relatively cheap *sushi* and *sashimi* served to a young crowd.

Yungkee, 32–40 Wellington St, on the corner with D'Aguilar St. An enormous place with bright lights, scurrying staff and seating for a thousand, this is one of Hong Kong's institutions. Roast meats are a speciality. Highly recommended.

Shek O

Shek O Chinese Thai Seafood, Shek O. On the way from the main bus stop to the seafront. Laid-back atmosphere with outdoor tables under a trellis. The food here is excellent. The perfect place for lunch if you are on a day trip to Shek O.

Stanley

The following are located next to each other along the quiet Stanley Main Street, and have views over the seafront.

King of Pasta. Excellent Italian pizzas and pasta dishes at around $80 each, prepared by a genuine Italian chef.

Lord Stanley's Bar and Bistro. Part English pub, part European-style bistro; the food on offer here ranges from steaks to fish and chips.

Stanley Oriental. A very pleasant, fairly upmarket place serving all manner of Asian dishes, from Indian to Chinese.

Tsimshatsui

Ah Yee Leng Tong, *Imperial Hotel,* 32–34 Nathan Rd, Tsimshatsui. Old-style rosewood furniture and a focus on healthy, traditional, Chinese foods – including special soups for males and females – provide a novel, inexpensive experience in this fast-growing cheap restaurant chain.

Au Trou Normand, 6 Carnarvon Rd. A fine place to escape the hustle of Hong Kong if you want to imagine yourself in rural France for a night. For a good dinner with wine reckon on $200–300 per head.

El Cid, 14 Knutsford Terrace (☎2312 1898). Just along from *Tutto Bene* (see below), this is Hong Kong's finest tapas bar and Spanish restaurant.

Felix, 28th Floor, *Peninsular Hotel* (☎2366 6251). This possibly ranks as Hong Kong's most exclusive restaurant: the incredible views of Hong Kong Island in themselves warrant a visit here. The food is Eurasian and understandably expensive.

Fung Lum, Polly Commercial Building, 21–23 Prat Ave. Excellent spicy Sichuan dishes.

Jade Garden Chinese, BCC Bank Building, 25–31 Carnarvon Rd. A good place for straightforward, inexpensive Chinese food.

Java Rijstafel, 38 Hankow Rd. A tiny, friendly place serving interesting, filling Indonesian dishes. The *rijstafel* itself is an excellent buffet comprising many small dishes – try it.

Kublai's, 55 Kimberly Rd (☎2722 0733). A little north of the main Tsimshatsui scene, this new-style Mongolian hotpot restaurant allows you to cook your own meal. Take a bowl, fill it with your own selection of raw ingredients (every kind of meat, fish, vegetable, herb, spice, sauce and oil is available), then hand it over to be stir-fried. At only $50 for the set lunch – including the chance to refill your bowl once – this is excellent value.

Manna Korean Restaurant, Basement, 83b Nathan Rd. An inexpensive place to grill your *bulgogi* (Korean-style barbecue) and fill up on spicy noodles.

Peking Restaurant, 227 Nathan Rd, Jordan MTR. Just north of the main Tsimshatsui area. One of the best places for Beijing duck in Hong Kong.

Peninsula Hotel Lobby, *Peninsula Hotel.* The small set lunch here comes to only $165 plus ten percent service, which, considering the venue, makes this an excellent option if you can get a table.

Sawadee Thailand Restaurant, 6 Ichang St (☎2376 3299). This is the small road running west off Hankow Road, a block north of Peking Road. First-class Thai food in a friendly, relaxed environment.

Tutto Bene, 7 Knutsford Terrace (☎2316 2116). Located on a small lane just north of Kimberly Road and little known to tourists, this is a popular expatriate hangout. Superb Italian food in a pleasant atmosphere with tables spread out on the pavement.

EATING IN CHUNGKING MANSIONS

Everest, 3rd Floor, D Block. Interesting Nepali-Indian food served in the form of cheap set meals.

Gujurati Mess, 4th Floor, B Block. The cheapest deal around, with eat-all-you-can helpings of rice, plus dahl and curry from an incredible $12.

Italy-France-Japan Food Plaza, Basement. To find this place, walk through the entrance from Nathan Road signposted "Fashion Food Square" and then through a cosmetics shop. Open 24-hours a day, this collection of fast-food stalls offers some great budget meals, including *dim sum* (1.30am–4pm).

Taj Mahal Mess, 3rd Floor, B Block. Excellent Indian food and good value if you avoid the relatively expensive drinks.

Shang Palace Basement 1, *Shangri-la Hotel*, 64 Mody Rd (☎2721 2111). A great upmarket dining experience with very interesting Cantonese food and truly grand interior decor.

Yoshinoya, Cameron Rd, just east of Nathan Rd, opposite *McDonald's*. A good alternative to the burger bar, this Japanese fast-food restaurant offers big bowls of rice and chicken.

Wanchai and Causeway Bay

Aegean Kebab, 453 Lockhart Rd, a short walk west of Percival St, Causeway Bay. Cheap and interesting array of grilled meats, offal, seafood and vegetables on offer, as well as fresh salads and Greek snacks.

Baan Thai, 4th Floor, Causeway Bay Plaza 1, 489 Hennessy Rd, Causeway Bay. Excellent, authentic Thai food served in upmarket surroundings.

Banana Leaf Curry House, 440 Jaffe Rd, just west of Canal Rd, Causeway Bay. One of a number of branches of this highly popular Malaysian-style restaurant, offering great mild curries full of cream and coconut.

Fook Lam Moon, 35–45 Johnston Rd, Wanchai (☎2866 0663). Reputedly one of the best places in Hong Kong to eat Cantonese food. Expensive.

Genroku Sushi Company, Jaffe Rd, just west of Percival St, Causeway Bay (another branch in Wellington St, Central). Efficient chain of restaurants offering one of the cheapest ways to eat Japanese food. Either take away by ticking items on a form, or sit inside picking up dishes from a conveyor belt. Portions of any sushi are just $14 each.

Harry Ramsden's, Wu Chung House, Queen's Rd East, near Spring Garden Lane, Wanchai. An improbable but highly successful incarnation of Britain's favourite fish 'n' chip shop and restaurant in Hong Kong.

Jade Garden, 1st Floor, Hennessy Centre, 500 Hennessy Rd, Wanchai. Friendly, easily negotiable *dim sum* restaurant.

Keung Kee Vietnamese, Jardine's Bazaar, Causeway Bay. A couple of minutes south of the *Mercy Vegetarian*. Lots of outdoor tables, cheap and popular.

Mercy Vegetarian, 29 Jardine's Bazaar, immediately south of the Causeway Bay MTR. Interesting and cheap vegetarian food, with set lunches from just $32. Tofu prominent.

Pak Lok, 25 Hysan Ave, Causeway Bay (☎2576 8886). Specializes in Chiu Chow food. The menu in this upmarket restaurant is large and exotic and very popular among discerning locals.

Roy's at the New China Max, 11th Floor, Times Square, 1 Matheson St, Causeway Bay. A highly stylish venue offering a huge, imaginative range of great Asian-American food.

Szechuan Lau, 466 Lockhart Rd, Causeway Bay. A classy, atmospheric restaurant where you can try any of the standard, spicy Sichuan specialities, and some of the more exotic ones as well.

Tai Hing Roast Shop, Jardine's Bazaar, Causeway Bay. Succulent roast meats – duck, chicken and pork – served with rice at very cheap prices.

Vegi Food Kitchen, Cleveland St, Causeway Bay. On a small street a couple of blocks east of Paterson St at its northern end. The sign informing customers not to "bring meat of any kind into this restaurant" says it all. Classy, strictly vegetarian Chinese food.

W's Entrecote, 13th Floor, Times Square, 1 Matheson St, Causeway Bay. For meat aficionados, this is the perfect place, with variations on steak, chips and salad the only thing on the menu.

Bars, pubs and clubs

The most concentrated collection of bars is in the **Lan Kwai Fong** area on Hong Kong Island. A stroll along Lan Kwai Fong Lane, and neighbouring streets, will take you past any number of possibilities for late-night carousing, with drinkers spilling out on to the street. **Wanchai** is another busy area after dark, though not so convenient for browsing as the various locations are more thinly scattered. **Tsimshatsui** is not generally known for its nightlife, though in fact there is something of a scene here, too, catering for both travellers and expats. Hart Avenue and Prat Avenue, west from Chatham

Road South, are the best places to look for a drink, with several alternatives very close together. For up-to-the-minute listings consult the latest issue of *BC Magazine* or other listings publications.

Some venues charge an entrance fee on certain nights (generally Fridays and Saturdays), which ranges from around $50 to as much as $200 in the flashest clubs. In the early evening, on the other hand, a lot of places run **happy hours** – some lasting several hours – serving two drinks for the price of one. Opening times often extend well into the small hours. **Live music**, and sometimes even **raves**, can be found if you look hard, though they are unlikely to match what you're used to back home. For details, consult *BC Magazine*. The **gay scene**, while hardly prominent, is at least more active than in other Chinese cities, given that laws on homosexuality are somewhat more liberal here than on the mainland.

Hong Kong Island

BB's, 114–120 Lockhart Rd, Wanchai. A wine bar boasting the widest range of bottled beers in Hong Kong.

Brewery Tap, Paterson St, northern end, Causeway Bay. Upmarket British-style pub serving traditional roast beef, warm ales and the like.

Carnegie's, 53–55 Lockhart Rd, Wanchai. Raucous and reliably fun with dancing on the tables almost a formality after midnight. Regularly features local bands.

Club 64, 12–14 Wing Wah Lane, Central. Just west off D'Aguilar Street, opposite the entrance to Lan Kwai Fong. Whether this provocatively named bar will survive 1997 is unclear (64 refers to June 4th, the date of the massacre in Tian'anmen Square), but in the meantime it has an exciting, lively atmosphere with a mixed Chinese and expat clientele.

Hardy's Folk Club, 35 D'Aguilar St, Central. Cheap beer, acoustic guitars and singalongs.

Jazz Club, 2nd Floor, Californian Entertainment Bldg, 34–36 D'Aguilar St, Central. Live jazz is performed here on Friday and Saturday nights, though it's predictably expensive, up to $100 for bigger jazz names.

The Jump, 7th Floor, Causeway Bay Plaza 2, 463 Lockhart Rd, Causeway Bay. Ritzy, American bar which is packed at weekends and has some dancing late at nights.

Mad Dogs, 1 D'Aguilar St, Central. A few metres south of Stanley St (with another branch at 32 Nathan Rd). Always packed out with expats who can get fairly riotous by the late evening. Occasionally has live bands.

Pettycoat Lane, Tu Wo Lane, next to the escalator (on Cochrane St), just south of Hollywood Rd, Central/Sheung Wan. Obscurely located gay bar.

Post '97, 9 Lan Kwai Fong, Central. A disco downstairs and a vaguely arty, bohemian atmosphere in the bar upstairs with a strong gay presence on Friday nights.

Ridgeways, 81–85 Lockhart Rd, Wanchai. Pool tables and other home-from-home pub accessories.

The Smugglers Inn, Stanley Main Rd, Stanley. As English as you can get, with darts and other pub games as well as pub-grub such as steak and kidney pies.

Kowloon

Bahama Mama's, 4–5 Knutsford Terrace (just north of Kimberly Rd). A good atmosphere with a vibrant mix of nationalities, and plenty of space for pavement drinking.

Delaney's 3–7A Prat Ave. A rather upmarket Irish pub with draught beers, including Guinness; features Irish folk music most nights. There's an unusually timed happy hour starting at 1am.

Jouster II, 19–23 Hart Ave. A good mix of Chinese and expats, interesting decor and very cheap drinks before 9pm.

Ned Kelly's Last Stand, 11A Ashley Rd. Very popular with both travellers and expats. Features a nightly performance from an excellent ragtime jazz band.

Waltzing Mathilda, Hart Ave, just west of Chatham Rd South. Popular and unpretentious bar.

Shopping

Visitors are still coming to Hong Kong to go **shopping** despite the fact that the cost of living in the territory has risen above that of most other countries in the world. The famed **electronic goods** of Nathan Road, for example, are by no means cheap any more and when you consider the high possibility of some form of rip-off, you are probably best advised to buy your cameras and other gadgets at home. What is special about Hong Kong, however, is the enormous range of goods on offer – and all in such a tiny area of land. And some things are indeed cheap, particularly **clothes**, **footwear** and **pirated goods** made in the People's Republic, though you'll invariably find that the farther you are from touristy Tsimshatsui, the cheaper your shopping becomes. Shops stay open late and are open daily. In Tsimshatsui and Causeway Bay, the main two shopping areas, general hours are 10am–10pm; in Central it's 10am–7pm. For more detailed shopping listings, consult the HKTA shopping guide.

Antiques, arts and crafts

You will certainly not find any antiques bargains in Hong Kong but you may find it pleasanter making your purchase here than in aggressive mainland China. The main area for antiques is Hollywood Road (see p.619) in Central, where there is a whole series of small outlets. There are also a number of department stores specializing in goods from China, including *China Products*, 19–31 Yee Wo St, Causeway Bay, and *Chinese Arts and Crafts*, Star House, Salisbury Rd, Tsimshatsui. The jade market in Mongkok is another good place to look for Chinese crafts (see p.626). Some more specific stores include:

Banyan Tree, 214–218 Prince's Building, Chater Rd, Central (also 257 Ocean Terminal, Canton Rd, Tsimshatsui). Antique and reproduction furniture.

Chinese Arts and Crafts Bazaar, Level II, New World Shopping Centre Mall, 18–24 Salisbury Rd, Tsimshatsui. A wide range of traditional craft products.

Creative Hands, Shop 34, Western Market, 323 Des Voeux Rd, Sheung Wan. Paintings, watercolours and prints.

Shanghai Tang, Pedder Building, Pedder St, Central. Superb designer goods – mainly clothes – recalling traditional Chinese wear. Also smaller items such as Mao and Deng memorabilia.

Clothes

These can be good value in Hong Kong, particularly the local fashion brand names such as *Gordiano* and *Bossini*, which have branches all over the city. Big-name designer clothes can also be found with remarkable ease, and you'll notice that prices here, while hardly cheap, are about 25 percent lower than they would be in the country of origin – thanks to the absence of duty and value added tax. Another interesting and potentially very cheap way to buy clothes (including designer clothes without the labels) is from **factory outlets**; consult the HKTA brochure, *Factory Outlets*, for addresses. Some of these discount clothes are also sold from shops along Granville Road in Tsimshatsui.

Tailor-made clothes are a traditional speciality of the Hong Kong tourist trade and wherever you go in Tsimshatsui you'll be accosted by Indian tailors offering this service. Although prices are relatively low here, have a long chat with your tailor before spending any money. Several fittings, over several days, are really essential if you want a good product. You'll need to pay about fifty percent of the price as deposit. The best-established tailor in town is probably *Sam's Tailors*, at 94 Nathan Road, Tsimshatsui.

Computers

Both hardware and software can work out very cheap in Hong Kong, though if you are buying hardware check that it is compatible with your country's electrical mains voltage, and make sure you get the right kind of warranty. Without an international warranty you won't be able to have your computer repaired or replaced once you have left Hong Kong. **Pirated computer software** is also big business, though these days it's very discreet. As with all pirated goods the risk is yours. You pay very little but it may not work and you may even have difficulty importing it into your own country.

Asia Computer Plaza, Lower Ground Floor, Silvercord, 30 Canton Rd, Tsimshatsui (also 2nd Floor, Star House, Salisbury Rd, Tsimshatsui). Relatively mainstream but good-quality computer malls. No pirated goods.

Golden Shopping Arcade, 156 Fuk Wah St, Sham Shui Po, Kowloon. Lots of cheap computer goods, including pirated ware.

Mongkok Computer Centre, at the corner of Nelson St and Fa Yuen St, Mongkok. One of the best places for pirated CDs.

Department stores

You probably never intended to while away your time in China walking around department stores but it must be said that Hong Kong's air-conditioned stores, which usually feature cafés and small restaurants, are some of the nicest anywhere.

Daimaru, Household Square, Kingston St, Causeway Bay, and Fashion Square, Paterson St, Causeway Bay. Japanese-owned stores; the first houses a Japanese supermarket.

Lane Crawford, 70 Queen's Rd, Central (and other branches). Hong Kong's oldest Western-style department store.

Mitzukoshi, Hennessy Centre, 500 Hennessy Rd, Causeway Bay. If you've never been to Japan, try this place at least. Possibly the smartest of all the Causeway Bay stores.

Sogo, East Point Centre, 555 Hennessy Rd, Causeway Bay. Another of the Japanese contingent. Immaculately presented goods over ten floors.

Wing On, 26 Des Voeux Rd, Central (and other branches). Another long-established store. Standard goods rather than luxuries.

Listings

Airlines *Air India*, Rm 4205–07, 42nd Floor, Gloucester Tower, Central (☎2522 1176); *British Airways*, 30th Floor, Alexandra House, 7 Des Voeux Rd, Central (☎2868 0303); *Cathay Pacific*, Swire House, Chater Rd, Central (☎2747 1888); *Dragonair*, 22nd Floor, Devon House, Taikoo Place, 979 King's Rd, Quarry Bay (☎2590 1328); *JAL*, 20th Floor, Gloucester Tower, Pedder St, Central (☎2523 0081); *KLM*, Rm 2201–03, World Trade Centre, 280 Gloucester Rd, Causeway Bay (☎2808 2111); *Korean Air*, 11th Floor, 2 South Seas Centre, 75 Mody Rd, Tsimshatsui East (☎2733 7111); *Malaysia Airlines*, Rm 1306, Prince's Bldg, Chater Rd, Central (☎2521 8181); *Qantas*, Rm 1443, Swire House, Chater Rd, Central (☎2842 1438); *Singapore Airlines*, Ground Floor, Alexandra House, 7 Des Voeux Rd, Central (☎2520 2233); *Thai International*, Shop 122–124, Worldwide Plaza, Pedder St, Central (☎2525 7051); *United Airlines*, 29th Floor, Gloucester Tower, Central (☎2810 4888).

American Express, Ground Floor, New World Tower, 16–18 Queen's Rd, Central (Mon–Fri 9am–5.30pm, Sat 9am–noon; ☎2844 8668).

Banks and exchange Banks generally open Mon–Fri 9am–4.30pm, Sat 9am–12.30pm, though there is quite a hefty commission on travellers' cheques in many banks; among the banks which don't charge commission are the *Hang Seng* and the *Wing On*. The licensed moneychangers, on the other hand, which open all hours including Sundays, may not charge commission but sometimes give very poor rates. Especially avoid moneychangers with windows looking on to Nathan Road, and always ask around before changing money as there are huge variations in rates.

Bookshops For such a cosmopolitan city, Hong Kong should be ashamed of its thin supply of foreign-language bookshops. The *Swindon Book Company* has what is probably the largest English-language bookstore at 13–15 Lock Rd, Tsimshatsui; it has another branch at the Star Ferry concourse, Tsimshatsui. The *Government Publications Centre*, at Lower Block, Ground Floor, 66 Queensway, Admiralty, has Hong Kong maps, and all kinds of books on local politics and the local environment. For foreign magazines and popular novels you're probably best off visiting one of the many branches of *Bookazine*, for example the one in the basement of Jardine House, Central. Otherwise, department stores usually have small book sections.

Cinema All the main English-language films find their way to Hong Kong soon after release, and they are usually shown in original-language versions with Chinese subtitles. Conversely, most of the Chinese-language films are shown with English subtitles – all those kung fu movies are suddenly brought to life. The major cinemas include *United Artists* at One Pacific Place, 88 Queensway, Central, and also at Times Square, Causeway Bay. For alternative or art films, including Chinese, try the Hong Kong Arts Centre at 2 Harbour Rd, Wanchai (☎2582 0200).

Embassies and consulates *Australia*, 23rd Floor, Harbour Centre, 25 Harbour Rd, Wanchai (☎2827 8881); *Britain* No consulate pre-July 1997; for assistance, contact Hong Kong Immigration Department, 7 Gloucester Rd, Wanchai (☎2829 3000); *Canada*, 12th Floor, 1 Exchange Square, Central (☎2810 4321); *China*, 5th Floor, China Resources Bldg, Lower Block, 26 Harbour Rd, Wanchai (☎2827 1881); *India*, 16th Floor, United Centre, 95 Queensway, Central (☎2528 4028); *Japan*, 24th Floor, Bank of America Tower, 12 Harcourt Rd, Admiralty (☎2522 1184); *Korea*, 5th Floor, Far East Financial Centre, 16 Harcourt Rd, Central (☎2527 2724); *Malaysia*, 23rd Floor, Malaysia Building, 50 Gloucester Rd, Wanchai (☎2527 0921); *New Zealand*, Rm 3414, Jardine House, Connaught Rd, Central (☎2525 5044); *Philippines*, 22nd Floor, Wah Kwong Regent Centre, 88 Queen's Rd, Central (☎2866 8738); *Taiwan*, 4th Floor, East Tower, Lippo Centre, 89 Queensway, Admiralty (☎2525 8315); *Thailand*, 8th Floor, Fairmont House, 8 Cotton Tree Drive, Central (☎2521 6481); *USA*, 26 Garden Rd, Central (☎2523 9011); *Vietnam*, 15th Floor, Great Smart Tower, 230 Wanchai Rd, Wanchai (☎22591 4510).

Festivals Festivals specific to Hong Kong include the *Tin Hau* festival, in late April or May, in honour of the Goddess of Fishermen. Large seaborne festivities take place, most notably at Joss House Bay on Sai Kung Peninsula (see p.630). Another is the *Tai Chiu* festival (known in English as the Bun Festival) held on Cheung Chau Island during May. The *Tuen Ng* (Dragon-boat) festival takes place in early June, with races in various places around the territory in long, narrow boats. Other Chinese festivals, such as New Year and Mid-Autumn, are celebrated in Hong Kong with as much, if not more, gusto than on the mainland.

Hospitals Government hospitals have 24-hour casualty wards, where treatment is free. These include the Princess Margaret Hospital, Lai King Hill Rd, Lai Chi Kok, Kowloon (☎2310 3111) and the Queen Mary Hospital, Pokfulam Rd, Hong Kong Island (☎2819 2111). For an ambulance dial ☎999.

Laundry There is a cheap laundry service on the ground floor of the Golden Crown Court on Nathan Rd (one block north of the Mirador Mansion) – use the red entrance; you'll see a sign at the end of the corridor. Same-day service for three kilos of clothes costs $30. Mirador Mansion, 13th Floor, has a similar place called *Posh Wash*.

Left luggage Kai Tak airport has a left-luggage office (daily 6.30am–1am). There are also coin-operated lockers in the Hong Kong China international ferry terminal in Tsimshatsui.

Library The main English-language library is in the City Hall High Block, Edinburgh Place, Central (Mon–Thurs 10am–7pm, Fri 10am–9pm, Sat 10am–5pm, Sun 10am–1pm). The British Council, 255 Hennessy Rd, Wanchai, also has a library with a selection of UK newspapers (Mon–Fri 9.30am–8.30pm, Sat 10am–5pm, closed Wed am; ☎2879 5145). There's also the American Library at 1st Floor, United Centre, 95 Queen's Rd, Admiralty (Mon–Fri 10am–6pm).

Lost property All enquiries on ☎2860 2000.

Police Crime hotline ☎2527 7177. For general police enquiries call ☎2860 2000.

Post office The general post office is at 2 Connaught Place, Central (Mon–Fri 8am–6pm, Sat 8am–2pm), just west of the Star Ferry and north of Jardine House (the tower with porthole windows). Post restante mail is delivered here, unless specifically addressed to "Kowloon". The Kowloon main post office is at 405 Nathan Rd near Yaumatei MTR, which also has an excellent packing department where you can buy boxes, string and tape to pack any stuff you want to send home.

Sport For horse-racing, see "Happy Valley", p.618. Every Easter, Hong Kong is host to an international Rugby Sevens tournament (information from Hong Kong Rugby Football Union, ☎2504 8300). The following activities are also available in the territory: sailing (information from the Hong Kong Yachting Association (☎2504 8160); windsurfing (try the *Windsurf Centre* on Kwun Yam Wan beach, Cheung Chau, for rentals and instruction); martial arts (*tai ji* takes place in all public parks; for more general information, call the HK Chinese Martial Arts Association ☎2394 4803); marathon-running (the Hong Kong marathon takes place in January; to enter, call the HK Amateur Athletic Association (☎2504 8215).

Swimming pools One of the most conveniently located public pools is in Kowloon Park on Nathan Rd, Tsimshatsui (summer only 6.30–11.30am & 1–10pm; adults $17). Another is in Victoria Park, Causeway Bay (summer only daily 7–11.15am & 1–9.45pm; adults $17).

Telephones All local calls are free and you can use any phones in hotel lobbies and restaurants for no charge. For IDD calls, use a payphone or go to a Hong Kong Telecom office; there's one at 10 Middle Rd, Tsimshatsui (24hr), and also at Unit 102A, 1 Exchange Square, Central (24hr). For directory enquiries in English dial ☎1081.

Thomas Cook Travellers' cheques service available at 18th Floor, Vicwood Plaza, 199 Des Voeux Rd, Central (Mon–Fri 9am–5.30pm, Sat 9am–1pm) or Mirador Mansion Arcade, Nathan Rd, Tsimshatsui (daily; 8am–10pm, ☎2366 9687).

Tours HKTA runs a series of interesting theme-tours, such as the "Sports and Recreation Tour" (see "Clearwater Bay", p.630) and the "Come Horse-racing Tour" (see "Happy Valley", p.618). These tours are fun, but are really for those in a hurry and with plenty of money. Consult HKTA's brochures for details. Other operators offering numerous tour opportunities – the harbour, New Territories, Kowloon – are advertised in brochures available around the Star Ferry ticket windows.

Travel agents Tsimshatsui is full of budget travel agents including *Shoestring Travel Ltd*, Flat A, 4th Floor, Alpha House, 27–33 Nathan Rd (☎2723 2306, fax 2721 2085) and *Hong Kong Student Travel Ltd*, Rm 1021, 10th Floor, Star House, Salisbury Rd (☎2730 3269), next to the Kowloon-side Star Ferry. The cheaper hostels often have useful up-to-date information and contacts for budget travel as well. For train tickets, tours, flights and visas to mainland China, try the Chinese state travel agency, *CITS*, Rm 1213–15, 13th Floor, Tower A, New Mandarin Plaza, 14 Science Museum Rd, Tsimshatsui East (☎2732 5878, fax 2721 7204), or alternatively, the more friendly *CTS* whose main office is on the 4th Floor, CTS House, 78–83 Connaught Rd, Central.

MACAU

Sixty kilometres west across the Pearl River estuary from Hong Kong lies the tiny Portuguese enclave of **MACAU**. A mere sliver of mainland and a couple of islands covering just eighteen square kilometres in total, the territory is geographically and economically a midget compared to its booming cousin across the water, and the transfer of sovereignty back to China, scheduled for 1999, has none of the drama or controversy surrounding that of Hong Kong. Despite this, however, and the fact that Macau, like Hong Kong, is largely populated by Cantonese-speaking Chinese, the territory has always had an atmosphere distinct not only from Hong Kong but from other parts of southern China. With outdoor cafés, charming Portuguese place names, public squares, the odd palm tree and numerous Portuguese restaurants, there is a definite whiff of southern Europe in the air.

However, by the millions of gambling fanatics living in nearby Hong Kong (and increasingly Shenzhen and Guangzhou as well), Macau, with its liberal gambling laws, is seen as little more than one giant **casino**. It is largely as a spin-off from the colossal gambling trade that money is being pumped in, allowing large-scale construction to take off, including that of Macau's own **airport**, recently opened on the island of Taipa. New highrise hotels, highways and bridges are appearing and even the Hong Kong speciality of land reclamation has begun in earnest.

Nevertheless, temptations for non-gamblers remain. With a colonial past predating that of Hong Kong by nearly three hundred years, Macau's **historic buildings** – from old fortresses, to Baroque churches, to faded mansion houses – are still plentiful, while the crumbling backstreets around the port are reminiscent of Hong Kong as it might have been fifty years ago. Finally, the two islands of **Taipa** and **Coloane**, now being linked to the peninsular by bridges and land reclamation, contain pockets of total tranquillity with fine **beaches** and restaurants.

Considering that costs are a good deal lower here than in Hong Kong, and the ease of travel between Guangzhou, Hong Kong and Macau, it's a great pity not to drop in on the territory if you are in the region. A day trip from Hong Kong is possible (tens of thousands do it every weekend), though you need a couple of nights really to do the place justice.

The Macau **currency** is the pataca (abbreviated as "ptca" in this book; also sometimes seen as "M$"), which is worth fractionally less than the HK dollar, and is very nearly equivalent to the Chinese yuan. HK dollars (but not yuan) are freely accepted as currency in Macau and a lot of visitors from Hong Kong don't bother changing money at all. Like the Hong Kong dollar, the pataca is set to continue its status as a separate currency for the foreseeable future.

Visa regulations are not set to change either, certainly not before 1999, and probably not even after then. Citizens of Britain, Ireland, Australia, NZ, Canada, USA and most European countries are automatically granted permission to stay twenty days on arrival. If in doubt (before 1999), approach the nearest Portuguese consulate. In Hong Kong there's one at 10th Floor, Two Exchange Square, Connaught Place, Central (☎2523 1338).

Some history

For over a thousand years all **trade** between China and the West had been carried out by land along the Silk Road through Central Asia, but in the fifteenth century the growth in European seafaring, pioneered by the **Portuguese**, finally led to the demise of the land route. Henceforth, sea trade and control of sea ports were what the European powers looked for in Asia.

Having gained toeholds in India (Goa) and the Malay Peninsula (Malacca) in the early sixteenth century, the Portuguese finally managed to persuade local Chinese officials, in 1557, to rent them a strategically well-placed peninsula at the mouth of the Pearl River Delta with fine natural harbours, known as **Macao** (Aomen). With their important trade links with Japan, as well as with India and Malaya, the Portuguese soon found themselves in the delightful position of being sole agents for merchants across a whole swathe of east Asia. Given that the Chinese were forbidden from going abroad to trade themselves, and that other foreigners were not permitted to enter Chinese ports, their trade boomed and Macau grew immensely wealthy. With the traders came **Christianity**, and among the luxurious homes and churches built during Macau's brief half-century of prosperity was the Basilica of St Paul, a great church whose facade can still be seen today.

By the beginning of the seventeenth century, however, Macau's fortunes were already on the wane, and a slow decline, which has continued almost ever since, set in. A combination of setbacks for the Portuguese, including defeats in war against the Spanish back home, the loss of trading relations with both Japan and China, and the rise of the Dutch as a trading power, saw Macau almost wiped off the map by mid-century.

Macau phone numbers have no area codes. From outside the territory, dial the normal international access code + ☎853 (country code) + the number. To **call Hong Kong from Macau** dial ☎01 + the number

In the eighteenth century, fortunes looked up somewhat, as more and more non-Portuguese European traders came looking for opportunities to prise open the locked door of China. For these people, Macau seemed a tempting base from which to operate, and eventually they were permitted to settle and build homes in the colony. The British had greater ambitions than to remain for ever as guests in someone else's colony and when they finally seized their own piece of the shore to the east in 1841, Macau's status – as a backwater – was definitively settled. Despite the introduction of **licensed gambling** in the 1850s, as a desperate means of securing some kind of income, virtually all trade was lost to **Hong Kong**.

Over the last century, Macau's population has increased massively to over half a million as repeated waves of **immigrants** have flooded the territory, whether fleeing Japanese invaders or Chinese Communists, but, unlike in Hong Kong, this growth has not been accompanied by the same spectacular economic development. Indeed, in 1974, with the end of the fascist dictatorship in Portugal, the Portuguese attempted to unilaterally hand Macau back to China; the offer was refused. Only after the 1984 agreement with Britain over the future of Hong Kong did China agree to negotiate the formal return of Macau as well. In **1999**, the last year of the millennium, the final piece of Asian soil still in European hands will be surrendered.

When they depart, however, the Portuguese will leave one rather low-profile legacy – the **Macanese**, offspring of mixed Chinese-Portuguese parentage, many of whom are entirely rooted in the fundamentally Chinese world of Macau, but still maintain Portuguese traditions and speak Portuguese. Having lived for possibly centuries in southern China, the Macanese are in Macau to stay.

Orientation, arrival, information and getting around

Macau comprises three distinct parts: the **peninsula**, which is linked by bridge to the island of **Taipa**, which is in turn linked by bridge to a second island, **Coloane**. The peninsula of Macau, where the original old city was located and where most of the historic sights still are (as well as the city amenities), is entirely developed right up to the border with China in the north, though the islands, Coloane in particular, contain some quiet rural patches.

The peninsula is not large and it's possible to get around much of it on foot, though you'll need buses for the longer stretches. Macau's jetfoil terminal, for boats to and from Hong Kong, is in the southeast of the peninsula. The most important road, **Avenida Almeida Ribeiro**, cuts across from east to west, taking in the *Hotel Lisboa*, one of Macau's most famous landmarks, and exits on its western end near to the **Floating Casino** and the docking point for ferries from Guangzhou. The western part of Almeida Ribeiro is also the budget hotel area.

Arrival

In Macau, all boats from **Hong Kong**, and some infrequent boats from **Taiwan**, use the same terminal, usually referred to on bus schedules and maps as the **jetfoil terminal** (Nova Terminal in Portuguese), in the southeast of town by Avenida da Amizada. This is connected to the *Hotel Lisboa* and the budget hotel area on Almeida Ribeiro by buses #3, #3A and #10.

If you're arriving from **Guangzhou** by ferry, you'll disembark at the Floating Casino which is diametrically on the opposite side of the peninsula. From here you can easily walk to Avenida Almeida Ribeiro.

For those arriving at the new **airport** on Taipa Island, the airport bus #AP1 goes to the *Hotel Lisboa* and the jetfoil pier, while if you've walked across the border, in the far

GETTING TO MACAU AND GETTING AWAY

Access to and from Macau is chiefly by **boat** from Hong Kong. Large numbers of competing vessels make the one-hour journey between Macau and Hong Kong's Shun Tak Centre daily, including jetfoils (marginally the fastest at 55 minutes, and the most frequent, even running through the night), jumbocats (the roomiest) and high-speed ferries (roomy and cheap, but infrequent and much slower than the others). There are also bumpy hoverferries, which depart from the China Hong Kong City ferry terminal in Tsimshatsui. **Tickets** vary slightly in price according to type of boat, time and class of travel; reckon on paying HK$100–120 each way, though about half that for the high-speed ferry (ticket prices all include a government departure tax). Unless you're planning to travel at peak times, such as weekends, it is not normally necessary to book in advance, though you can do so if you wish. In Macau, advance tickets are available from the *Hotel Lisboa* office (Mon–Sat 9.30am–11.30pm, Sun 9.30am–7.30pm), and other outlets. Otherwise, for travel in either direction, simply show up at the pier, purchase a ticket for the next sailing, clear passport control and board.

Guangzhou is the other important city linked to Macau by boat. Tickets (100–120ptca depending on class) for outward-bound Guangzhou ferries, which leave daily at 8pm from beside the Floating Casino, can be bought from the *Yuet Tung Shipping Co* (daily 8am–noon & 2–5.30pm) at the same pier. The boat arrives in Guangzhou the next morning at 7.30am, the same time as the daily inbound ferry arrives in Macau.

By **air**, you can fly to and from Beijing, Shanghai, Taipei, Kuala Lumpur and Singapore and a quickly increasing list of other Chinese cities. The first direct airlink between Beijing and Taipei has been established by the fledgling *Air Macau* through the new Macau airport – the planes touch down in Macau, and change their flight-numbers (to satisfy the Beijing authorities) but through passengers do not need to disembark before the planes continue on their way.

By land, you can either **walk** across the border (daily 7am–9pm) at the Barrier Gate, into the Zhuhai SEZ, or try to catch one of the new **bus** services direct to Guangzhou; tickets for the buses are available at the *Kee Kwan Motors* by the Floating Casino.

north of the peninsular, from Zhuhai in China, you can ride bus #5 from there to Almeida Ribeiro. There are now also a couple of direct **buses** from Guangzhou right into Macau; these deposit passengers near the Floating Casino.

Information

The **Macau Tourist Information Bureau** (MTIB) is a helpful organization well worth your time. They provide various leaflets on Macau's fortresses, parks, churches and outlying islands as well as a good city **map**, and a free monthly **newspaper** called *Macau Travel Talk* which contains listings of all current happenings in the cultural world of the territory.

You can find MTIB even before you leave Hong Kong, in the Macau ferry terminal, Rm 3704, Shun Tak Centre (Mon–Fri 9am–1pm & 2–6pm, Sat 9am–1pm; ☎2540 8180). Otherwise drop by their friendly Visitor Information Centre (daily 9am–6pm, ☎555 424) on arrival in the jetfoil terminal, or their main office at Largo do Senado 9 (Mon–Fri 9am–1pm & 3–6pm, Sat 9am–12.30pm; ☎315 566).

Getting around

Being such a tiny place, you'll have little difficulty getting around Macau. Many, if not all, places can be reached on foot. And if you get tired, try the cheap **taxis**, bearing in mind that trips to Taipa or Coloane will attract a surcharge of 5ptca and 10ptca respectively on top of the meter reading. Otherwise, hop on to one of the many **buses** – some important bus interchanges include the jetfoil terminal (referred to as Nova Terminal), the *Hotel Lisboa*, Almeida Ribeiro, Barra (near the A Ma Temple), Praça Ponte e Horta (by the Floating Casino), the Barrier Gate (referred to as Porto do Cerco) and the islands Taipa and Coloane. As in Hong Kong, change is not given on buses but fares are low. There are two main bus companies, and some useful routes include:

#1A from the jetfoil terminal to Barra.

#3 and #3A from the jetfoil terminal to *Hotel Lisboa* and Almeida Ribeiro.

#5 from Barra to Almeida Ribeiro to the Barrier Gate.

#21, #21A, #26, #26A from Almeida Ribeiro to Taipa Village and Coloane.

#28B from the jetfoil terminal to *Hotel Lisboa* and *Bela Vista Hotel*.

Finally, **cycling** is a possibility, on the islands at least, though note that you are not allowed to cycle over the causeway from the mainland to Taipa. For details on rental, see p.654).

Accommodation

Accommodation is a good deal cheaper in Macau than in Hong Kong. For the same money that would get you a tiny box in Chungking Mansions, you can find quite a spacious room with private shower and a window here. At the bottom end, furthermore, there are one or two ancient **Chinese hostels** of a type that probably don't exist anywhere else in the Chinese world, though foreigners are not always particularly welcome at the cheaper places. Conversely, at the top end are a couple of the most delightful **hotels** in Asia.

Be warned, however, that at weekends **prices** shoot up everywhere and you are advised to come during the week if you can. Other times to avoid if possible are Chinese holidays, the Macau Grand Prix (third weekend in November) and generally the summer season, which is more expensive than the winter.

The densest concentration of hotels occurs around the western end of Almeida Ribeiro, spreading out from the inner harbour, though one or two places can be also be found in remote, tranquil places such as the island of Coloane. Note that addresses are written with the number after the name of the street.

Western Macau

East Asia, Rua da Madeira 1A (☎922 433, fax 922 430). A couple of blocks north from the western end of Almeida Ribeiro. One of Macau's oldest hotels, and a very smart, comfortable place, with great views from some of the upstairs windows. Friendly staff and very good value. ⑤–⑦.

Grand, Almeida Ribeiro 146 (☎921 111, fax 922 397). At the western end of Macau's main thoroughfare, a standard but fairly upmarket hotel. ⑥.

London, Praça de Ponte e Horta 4 (☎937 761). A nice place offering single, double and triple rooms. ⑥.

ACCOMMODATION PRICE CODES

All the accommodation in this book has been graded according to price codes, which represent the cheapest double room available. Accommodation in Macau has been given codes from the categories below. Where the text refers specifically to dorm beds, the price code represents the price per bed.

① under 30ptca	④ 100–150ptca	⑦ 300–500ptca
② 30–75ptca	⑤ 150–200ptca	⑧ 500–700ptca
③ 75–100ptca	⑥ 200–300ptca	⑨ over 700ptca

San Va Hospedaria, Rua Felicidade 7 (☎573 701), just south of Almeida Ribeiro. A classic old Macau hostel – primitive and a fire-trap, but high on atmosphere, perfectly clean and very cheap. ②.

Sunsun, Praça de Ponte e Horta 14–16 (☎939 393, fax 938 822). Brand-new and immaculate, with an anonymity reminiscent of new hotels on the mainland, but not expensive. ⑦.

Tai Fat, Rua da Caldeira 43–45 (☎933 908). A good, clean place; some of the attached bathrooms even have bathtubs instead of the standard showers. ⑥.

Vila Capital, Rua Constantino Brito 3 (☎920 154). A block north from the far western end of Almeida Ribeiro. A clean and decent place. ⑥.

Vila Kuan Heng, Rua Ponte e Horta 4 (☎573 629). Located at the eastern end of Praça Ponte e Horta, a square just south of the Floating Casino. Very nice rooms, clean and bright. Singles, doubles and triples available. ⑥.

Vila Universal, Rua Felicidade 73 (☎573 247). South of Almeida Ribeiro, this is a fairly large place, very clean and comfortable with spacious rooms. Highly recommended. ⑥–⑦.

Vo Peng Hospedaria, 2nd Floor, Rua da Caldeira 37 (☎573 598). Again, just south of Almeida Ribeiro. Basic but clean. ⑤.

Vong Kong Hospedaria, Rua das Lorchas 45. On the seafront road, opposite the Floating Casino, this place offers a glimpse into the lost world of sailor life on the South China seas. Dingy and dirty, with ancient furniture and wooden partitions, but it certainly has atmosphere. ②.

Southern and eastern Macau

Bela Vista, Rua do Comendador 8 (☎965 333, fax 965 588). With cream-painted stuccoed columns and verandahs commanding sea views, this newly renovated colonial masterpiece in the south of the peninsula is now one of the finest hotels in the world – try and drop by for a peep into the lobby if you aren't staying. From Avenida da República on the shore you'll see it perched on the hillside. Very expensive, though, with rooms starting from 1800ptca. ⑨.

Central, Almeida Ribeiro 26–28 (☎373 838). A highly popular and very central hotel. Good value for its location. ⑦.

Lisboa, Avenida da Amizade (☎577 666, fax 567 193, Hong Kong reservations ☎2546 6944). This is the bizarre orange-coloured, cylindrical building you pass on the way into town from the ferry, Macau's major architectural landmark. As well as Macau's most popular casino, the *Lisboa* also houses a shopping arcade and numerous restaurants. ⑨.

Metropole, Rua da Praia Grande 63 (☎388 166, fax 330 890). A few hundred metres west of the *Lisboa*, well located and smartly fitted out. ⑦–⑧.

Pousada de São Tiago, Avenida da República (☎378 111, fax 552 170). Constructed from an old fortress on the southern tip of the peninsula, with walled stairways lined by gushing streams, huge stone archways and delightfully furnished rooms, this place is if anything even more enchanting than the *Bela Vista* and quite a bit cheaper. ⑨.

Coloane

Pousada de Coloane, Praia de Cheoc Van (☎328 143, fax 328 251). Great scenery, if somewhat remote, situated by Cheoc Van Beach on the far south shore of the island of Coloane. All rooms have balconies overlooking the beach and if you want a relaxing holiday experience this is the place for it. ⑨.

Macau Peninsula

The town of Macau started down in the south of the peninsula, around the bay-front road known as the **Praia Grande**, and grew out from there. Unfortunately, these days a stroll on the seafront is not what it was, with the bay now being enclosed and reclamation work underway. More rewarding is the main road that cuts the Praia from east to west, called **Avenida do Infante d'Henrique** to the east and **Avenida de Almeida Ribeiro** to the west. At the eastern end of the road rises the extraordinarily garish *Lisboa Hotel*, though most of the interest lies in the section west of the Praia, particu-

---

GAMBLING

The eight official Macau **casinos**, although numerous and always packed, have none of the glamour of casinos in places such as Las Vegas or Monte Carlo. You are free to enter any casino at any time of the day or night, dressed in any attire, with the only restriction being that you should be eighteen years of age, and your cameras should be deposited at the entrance. Once inside, another restriction you should note is that there is a **minimum bet** of 50ptca on nearly all games.

The four-storey casino in the *Hotel Lisboa* is the largest and probably the most interesting for a visit. For information on how to play the various games, ask MTIB for a leaflet, or buy their more detailed *A-O-A Macau Gambling Guide*. Be warned, however: signs in tiny print at the entrances to the casinos politely suggest that punters should engage in betting for fun only, and not as a means of making money. Revenues from the gambling trade in Macau are thought to approach half a billion US dollars annually.

---

larly in the beautiful **Largo do Senado** (Senate Square) which marks the downtown area and bears the unmistakeable influence of southern Europe, not only in its architecture, but also in its role as a place for people to stroll, sit and chat in open air.

At the northern end of Largo do Senado, away from the main road, is the beautiful seventeenth-century Baroque church, **São Domingos**, while to the south, facing the square from across the main road, stands the **Leal Senado** (Mon–Sat 1–7pm; free), generally considered the finest Portuguese building in the city. If you step into the interior courtyard here you'll see wonderful blue and white Portuguese tiles around the walls, while up the staircase from the courtyard, you reach first a formal garden and then the richly decorated **senate chamber** itself. In the late sixteenth century this hall used to be packed out with the entire citizenry of the colony, who gathered to debate issues of importance. The senate's title *leal* (loyal) was earned during the period when Spain occupied the Portuguese throne and Macau became the final stronghold of loyalists to the true king. Today the senate chamber is still used by the municipal government of Macau, though it's hardly the democratic chamber of old. Adjacent to the chamber is the wood-carved **public library**, whose collection includes a repository of many fifteenth- and sixteenth-century books which you can still see on the shelves.

A couple of hundred metres west from Largo do Senado, Almeida Ribeiro emerges on to the so-called **Inner Harbour**, which overlooks, and is sheltered by, the mainland just across the water. Ferries to Guangzhou still use this harbour, though its main interest for many visitors is the **Floating Casino**, an ugly wooden contraption on the water, teeming with gamblers at all hours. Some of the streets immediately inland from here, especially those just north of Almeida Ribeiro, are worth poking around. Streets such as Rua Felicidade, parallel with Almeida Ribeiro, have shaken off their former seediness and are now full of friendly restaurants and small hotels. South from the Floating Casino, the seafront road, Rua das Lorchas, is lined by old arcades and characterful shops.

São Paulo and around

A few hundred metres north of Largo do Senado is Macau's most famous landmark, the church of **São Paulo**, once hailed as the greatest Christian monument in east Asia, but today surviving as no more than a facade. Originally constructed at the beginning of the seventeenth century, it dominated the city for two hundred years until its untimely destruction by fire in 1835. Fortuitously, however, the facade, which did not collapse, was always considered the highlight of the building – richly carved and laden with statuary, the cracked stone still presents an imposing sight from the bottom of the stone steps leading up from the Rua de São Paulo.

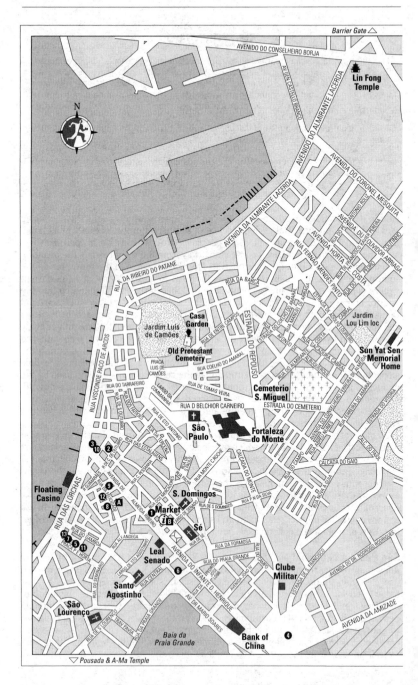

Barrier Gate △

AVENIDO DO CONSELHEIRO BORJA

Lin Fong Temple

AVENIDO DO ALMIRANTE LACERDA

AV. GEN CASTILLO BRANCO

AVENIDA DO CORONEL MESQUITA

AVENIDA DU OUVIDOR ARRIAGA

AVENIDA DA ALMIRANTE LACERDA

AVENIDA HORTA

RUA FERNAO MENDES PINTO

RUA DA BARCA

RUA DA RIBEIRO DO PATANE

RUA DE ENTRE CAMPOS

Casa Garden

Jardim Luis de Camões

ESTRADA DO REPOUSO

Jardim Lou Lim Ioc

Old Protestant Cemetery

RUA COELHO DO AMARAL

PRACA LUIS DE CAMÕES

Sun Yat Sen Memorial Home

RUA VISCONDE PACO DE ARCOS

RUA DO TARRAFEIRO

RUA DE TOMAS VIERA

LARGO DA COMPANHIA

RUA D BELCHIOR CARNEIRO

Cemeterio S. Miguel

ESTRADA DO CEMETERIO

RUA DE STO ANTONIO

São Paulo

Fortaleza do Monte

RUA DAS ESTALAGENS

CALCADA DO MONTE

CALCADA DO GAIO

RUA DE 5 DE OUTUBRO

❸ ❿ ❷

❾

Floating Casino

RUA DAS LORCHAS

❶❷ ❽ Ⓐ

S. Domingos

Market ❶

ⒿⒷ

Sé

❶❸ ❼❺ ❺ ⓫

RUA DO GAMBOA

Leal Senado

AVENIDA DO INFANTE D. HENRIQUE

RUA DA FORMOSA

Clube Militar

Santo Agostinho

RUA CENTRAL

❻

São Lourenço

Baia da Praia Grande

Bank of China

❹

AVENIDA DA AMIZADE

▽ Pousada & A-Ma Temple

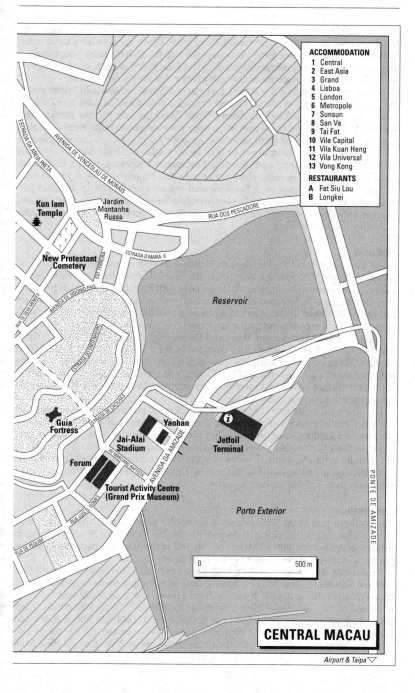

ACCOMMODATION
1 Central
2 East Asia
3 Grand
4 Lisboa
5 London
6 Metropole
7 Sunsun
8 San Va
9 Tai Fat
10 Vila Capital
11 Vila Kuan Heng
12 Vila Universal
13 Vong Kong

RESTAURANTS
A Fat Siu Lou
B Longkei

CENTRAL MACAU

Airport & Taipa ▽

Immediately east of São Paulo looms another early seventeenth-century monument, the **Fortaleza do Monte** (daily 9am–5.30pm; free). Climb up and take a stroll round the old ramparts for some great views over the city. It's an impressive pile, though it was only once used in a military function, to repel the Dutch in 1622, when it succeeded in blowing up the Dutch magazine with a lucky shot from a cannon ball.

Negotiating the roads a few hundred metres northwest of São Paulo brings you to perhaps the nicest part of Macau, around **Praça Luís de Camões** (also accessible on buses #19 and #23 from Almeida Ribeiro). North, facing the square, is the **Jardim Luís de Camões**, a delightful shady park full of large trees and popular with locals. The park was built in honour of the great sixteenth-century Portuguese poet, Luís de Camões, who is thought to have been banished here for part of his life. Immediately east of the square, though, is the real gem, the **Old Protestant Cemetery**, where all the non-Catholic traders, visitors, sailors and adventurers who happened to die in Macau were buried. The gravestones have all been restored and are quite legible. In this quiet garden, under the shade of trees, the last testaments to these mainly British, American and German individuals, who died far from home in the early part of the last century, make incredibly poignant reading.

The east

About 1km northeast of the Fortaleza do Monte, is another area worth walking around (buses #12 and #22 run up here from the *Hotel Lisboa* along the Avenida do Conselheiro Ferreira de Almeida). At the junction with Estrada de Adolfo Loureiro, the first site you'll reach, screened off behind a high wall, is the scenic **Jardim Lou Lim Ioc** (daily 6am–10pm; 1ptca), a formal, Chinese garden full of bamboos, pavilions, birds in cages and old men playing mah jong. A couple of minutes around the corner from here you'll find the **Sun Yatsen Memorial Home** (Mon & Wed–Fri 10am–1pm, Sat & Sun 3–5pm; free) at the junction of Avenida de Sidonia Pais and the Rua de Silva Mendes. There isn't that much to see – basically it's an attractive, rambling old mansion scattered about with mementoes of Sun Yatsen, who spent some time living in Macau in the years before he turned to revolutionary activities. Drop by to see the turn-of-the-century interior decor if nothing else.

The sharp hill to the east of here is Macau's highest, and its summit is crowned by the seventeenth-century **Guia Fortress**, the dominant feature of which is a charming whitewashed lighthouse, added in the last century and reputed to be the oldest anywhere on the Chinese coast. You can take a leisurely hike along a path up to the fort in about an hour for some superb views over the whole peninsula, including, on a clear day, a glimpse of Lantau Island far to the east. There's a tourist information centre and café (daily 9am–5.30pm) up here as well.

The north

The northern part of the peninsula up to the border with China is largely residential, though it has a couple of points of interest. It's possible to walk the 3km from Almeida Ribeiro to the border, but the streets at this end of town are not particularly atmospheric, so it makes sense to resort to the local buses.

On Avenida do Coronel Mesquita, cutting the peninsula from east to west about 2km north of Almeida Ribeiro, is the enchanting **Kun Iam Temple** (daily 7am–6pm), accessible on buses #12 and #28C from the *Hotel Lisboa*. The complex of temples here, dedicated to the Goddess of Mercy, is around four hundred years old, but the most interesting fact associated with the place is that here, in 1844, the United States and China signed their first treaty of trade and co-operation – you can still see the granite table they used to sign it on. Inside the complex, shaded by banyan trees, are a number of small shrines, with the main temple hall approached via a flight of steps. Around the central statue of Kun Iam herself, to the rear, are a crowd of statues representing the eighteen wise men of China, among whom, curiously, is Marco Polo (on the far left), depicted with a curly beard and moustache. The worshippers you'll see here shaking bamboo sticks in cylinders are trying to find out their fortunes.

From the Kun Iam Temple you can catch bus #28C direct to the **Portas do Cerco**, or Barrier Gate, the nineteenth-century stuccoed archway gate marking the border with China. These days unfortunately the old gate itself is redundant – people actually cross the border through a customs and immigration complex to one side. This does at least mean that you can examine the monument from close quarters as it is no longer a restricted area. A short walk to the west of the gate is **Sun Yatsen Memorial Park**, which gives interesting views over Zhuhai in the People's Republic, immediately across a small canal. Buses #3 or #10 will get you back to Almeida Ribeiro from the gate.

The south

The small but hilly tongue of land south of Almeida Ribeiro is a highly interesting place to stroll, with colonial mansions and their gardens looming up round every corner. The best way to start exploring this area is to walk up the steep Rua Central leading south from Almeida Ribeiro just east of Largo do Senado. After five minutes you can detour off on a small road to your right, which contains the pastel-coloured early nineteenth-century church of **Santo Agostinho**. Back along Rua Central again will lead you to another attractive church of the same era, the cream and white **São Lourenço**, standing amid palm trees.

Continuing several hundred metres farther south you'll reach the seafront on the southwestern side of the peninsula. As you face the sea, the celebrated **A Ma Temple** is immediately to your right. Situated underneath Barra Hill overlooking the Inner Harbour, this temple may be as old as six hundred years in parts, and certainly predates the arrival of the Portuguese on the peninsula. Dedicated to the goddess A Ma, whose identity blurs from Queen of Heaven into Goddess of the Sea (and who seems to be the same as Tin Hau in Hong Kong), the temple is an attractive jumble of altars and little outhouses among the rocks.

Immediately across the road from here, on the seafront, stands the twentieth century's votive offering to the sea, the **Maritime Museum** (daily except Tues 10am–5pm; 8ptca, Sun 4ptca). This is an excellently presented, modern museum, covering old explorers, seafaring techniques, equipment, models and boats. For an additional charge, you can even join a boat tour (daily 10.30am, 11.30am, 3.30pm & 4.40pm; 15ptca) on one of the junks moored just outside the museum. This gives you a chance to sail around the Inner Harbour, hearing details of the lives of local fishermen in English.

A short walk south along the shore from the museum brings you to the very tip of the peninsula, which is today marked by the *Pousada de São Tiago*, an incredible hotel built into the remains of the seventeenth-century Portuguese fortress, the **Fortaleza de Barra**. Enter the front door and you find yourself walking up a stone tunnel running with water – it's well worth climbing up to the *Pousada*'s verandah café for a drink overlooking the sea. Continuing the walk around the southern headland, and back to the north again, you'll pass another superb hotel high up on your left, the gleaming white *Bela Vista*, the finest colonial-style hotel in the territory and a beautiful throwback to another age. The road north from here up to the Praia Grande, near the *Hotel Lisboa*, takes about another ten minutes on foot. The wonderful pink building on your left shortly before the *Praia Grande* is the nineteenth-century **Palácio do Governo**, which unfortunately is not open to visitors.

The islands

Macau's two islands, **Taipa** and **Coloane**, are just dots of land which traditionally supported a few small fishing villages, though now, with the opening of the new airport on Taipa and a second bridge from the mainland, that old tranquillity may be on the way out. Indeed, Taipa is fast acquiring the characteristics of a city suburb. In the meantime, however, life seems to remain relatively quiet, particularly on Coloane, and the two islands are well worth a visit, either by bus or by rented bicycle.

Buses #11 and #33 go to Taipa Village from Almeida Ribeiro, while buses #21, #21A, #26 and #26A go to both Taipa and Coloane. Bus #14 additionally joins Taipa with Coloane.

Taipa

Until the eighteenth century **Taipa** used to be two islands separated by a channel, the silting up of which subsequently caused the two to merge into one. In an interesting repetition of history, the same fate is now befalling Taipa and Coloane, except that this time it is not siltation which is the culprit, but land reclamation – the two islands are being deliberately fused into one, to make space for new development.

Although Taipa's northern shore is hardly worth a stop now that it is being subsumed into the general Macau conurbation, **Taipa Village** on the southern shore, with its old colonial promenade, makes a pleasant stop for an extended lunch. There isn't much more than a few streets to the modern village, where the buses stop, though there are some great restaurants (see p.655) along the central north–south alley Rua do Cunha, and, to the west – the right as you face the shore – a couple of temples in the vicinity of a quiet old square. Next to the Pak Tai Temple there's also a bike rental outlet where you can rent bikes for 12ptca an hour, if you want to continue your exploration of Coloane (below) under your own steam.

The real interest lies a few minutes' walk to the east of Taipa Village, at the old waterfront area. Here, as though frozen in time, remains a superb old colonial promenade, the **Avenida da Praia**, complete with its original houses, public benches and street lamps. Great, faded mansions with verandahs overlook the water which has now receded almost out of sight and been replaced by thick shrubbery. One of the mansions, the **Taipa House Museum** (Tues–Sun 9.30am–1pm & 3–5.30pm; free) is open to the public and reveals details of turn-of-the-century domestic life for the resident bourgeoisie. The residents of these houses were Macanese families, highly religious, well-to-do but not enormously wealthy. Unsurprisingly, the furniture is a Eurasian hybrid, combining features such as saint statuettes with Chinese dragon motifs on the sofas.

Coloane

Coloane is considerably bigger than Taipa and, although it has no outstanding attractions, it's a pleasant place to spend a few hours. The buses all stop at the roundabout in **Coloane Village** on the western shore, overlooking mainland China just across the water. There's no beach, just mud, in which you'll see old men fishing with nets. To the north of the village are a few junk-building sheds, while the street leading south from the village roundabout, one block back from the shore, contains a couple of interesting old shops and the unexpected yellow and white **St Xavier Chapel** where a relic of the saint's arm bone is venerated. A couple of hundred metres beyond this is the **Tam Kong Temple**, housing a metre-long whale bone carved into the shape of a ship.

On the north side of the village roundabout there's a small shop where you can rent bicycles for 12ptca an hour. Cycling is a good way to travel the 3km farther round to **Hac Sa Beach** on the eastern shore (otherwise take bus #14, #26 or #26A), perhaps dropping in on **Cheoc Van Beach** to the south on the way as well. The beach at Hac

Sa, though, tree-lined and stretching far off round the bay, is without doubt the best in Macau, despite the black colour of its sand, and has good facilities including showers and toilets as well as some fine nearby restaurants (see p.656). There's also a sports and swimming pool complex here (daily 9am–9pm).

Eating, drinking and nightlife

Despite comparison with the overwhelming variety on offer in Hong Kong, there is nevertheless plenty of good food to be had in Macau, with a particular emphasis on **Macanese food**, the territory's native cuisine, a fascinating blend of Portuguese and Asian elements. The Portuguese elements include fresh bread, cheap imported wine and coffee, as well as an array of dishes ranging from *caldo verde* (vegetable soup) to *bacalao* (dried salted cod). Macau's most interesting Portuguese colonial dish is **African chicken**, a concoction of Goan and east African influences, comprising chicken grilled with peppers and spices. Straightforward **Cantonese restaurants**, often serving *dim sum* for breakfast and lunch, are also plentiful, though you'll find wine on the menus even here. Alongside the local dumplings and noodles, Macau's numerous snack bars often offer fresh-milk products such as fruit milkshakes and milk puddings, unusual for China. Don't rely on restaurants here opening as late as in Hong Kong; you might not get a meal served much after 10pm. Costs, however, are nearly always lower, with bills even in smart venues usually not exceeding 150–200ptca per head.

Bars and **nightlife** are pretty sparse in Macau, as most of the drinking is done in restaurants. There are nevertheless one or two options listed below.

Restaurants and cafés

Alfonso III, Rua Central 11. Genuine and excellent Portuguese food in a Portuguese environment, though the waiters speak English. Centrally located, not far from Largo do Senado.

Ali's Curry House, Avenida da República 4. Interesting Indian food, served in a quiet seafront area with outdoor tables below the *Bela Vista* hotel, a ten-minute walk south from the Praia Grande.

Bela Vista Hotel, Rua Comendador Kou Ho Neng (☎965 333). It's hard to imagine a finer place for dinner than the verandah of this classic colonial-style hotel. Excellent Portuguese food is served and the prices are not as high as you would expect – 300ptca per head maximum. Advance booking essential.

Café Sang Lei, on a small alley, parallel with Rua do Pedro Jose Lobo, in the area between the northern section of Praia Grande and Avenida do Infante Henrique. One of a couple of cafés here with lots of outdoor tables where you can get coffee, beers and snacks during the day.

La Casa Macanese, Rua de São Lourenço. A couple of hundred metres south up the hill from Almeida Ribeiro (follow the continuation of Rua Central). Interesting Macanese dishes including African chicken in an unpretentious environment.

Fat Siu Lou, Rua da Felicidade 64. A very popular, traditional old restaurant in an area busy with cafés and restaurants.

Leitoria I Son, Largo do Senado 7. Virtually next door to *Long Kei*, this is an excellent milk bar offering milk with everything – fruit, chocolate, eggs, ice creams, puddings and breakfasts.

Long Kei, Largo do Senado 7B. A one-hundred-year-old traditional but inexpensive Cantonese restaurant, on the left side as you face the square from Almeida Ribeiro. *Dim sum* available.

Pele Restaurant, Rua de São Tiago da Barra 25. A short walk south of the Maritime Museum and offering excellent Macanese dishes in a friendly atmosphere.

Restaurante Safari, Patio do Coto Velo 14. Very close to the Leal Senado, this restaurant offers excellent cheap meals, ranging from European breakfasts to spicy steaks and fried noodles.

TAIPA

Leong Un, Rua da Cunha (northern end). One of a large number of restaurants down this alley, this is an Italian place with inexpensive pizzas and pastas.

Galo, Rua da Cunha 47. Low-priced, basically international menu.

Restaurante Panda, Rua Direita Carlos Eugenio 4–8. On a tiny alley leading east from the southern end of Rua da Cunha. Great Portuguese place, with outdoor tables in good weather.

COLOANE

Nga Tim Café, Coloane Village. A small, very friendly cheap place ideal for lunch, right opposite the Chapel of St Francis Xavier.

Alem Mar, Coloane Village. A rather upmarket Cantonese restaurant immediately north of the main roundabout.

Fernando's, Hac Sa Beach (☎328 264). Not far from the bus stop. With its beach front, live guitars, tables-under-the-trellis atmosphere, this place cannot be bettered for getting away from it all. Add on great Portuguese food and you've got one of the best restaurants in the territory. You might need a taxi to get home, though – reckon on 50ptca for the ride back to the peninsula. Advance booking recommended.

Bars and nightlife

Billabong Bar, Beco do Goncalo 2C. Walk south up Rua Central from Almeida Ribeiro and take the first lane on your right to find this plain Aussie-style bar with an emphasis on cheap beer drunk in large quantities.

Talkers, Rua de Pedro Coutinho 104. A little south of Avenida do Coronel Mesquita, just west of the Kun Iam Temple, are several bars and pubs that make up most of Macau's nightlife. *Talkers* tends to get very busy very late.

Crazy Paris Show, Mona Lisa Hall, *Hotel Lisboa*, Avenida da Amizade (☎377 666). Something of a Macau institution now, this vaguely naughty cabaret-style show of scantily clad dancing girls can be seen nightly at 8pm and 9.30pm (also 11pm Sat; 250ptca).

Listings

Airlines The airline situation in Macau is likely to develop fast, though as yet airline representation in the territory is thin. *Air Macau* is at Avenida da Praia Grande 639 (☎396 6888). For other airlines operating from Macau, including *Singapore Airlines*, *Malaysia Airlines* and *EVA Airways* (of Taiwan), call the airport flight enquiries (☎785 448) or contact a travel agency.

Banks and exchange Banks generally open all day from 9am until 4 or 4.30pm, but close by lunchtime on Saturdays. There are also licensed moneychangers which exchange travellers' cheques (and which open seven days a week), including a 24-hr one in the basement of the *Hotel Lisboa*, and one near the bottom of the steps leading up to São Paulo.

Bookshops Don't bother looking for English-language books here – go to Hong Kong.

Bike rental For details of bike rental possibilities on Taipa and Coloane see p.654.

Festivals The normal Chinese holidays are celebrated in Macau, plus some Catholic festivals introduced from Portugal, such as the procession of Our Lady of Fatima from São Domingos church annually on May 13.

Hospitals There's an emergency department at the government hospital on Estrada Visconde São Januário (☎577 199; English spoken).

Police The main police station is at Avenida Dr Rodrigo Rodrigues (☎573 333). In an emergency call ☎999.

Post office Macau's General Post Office is in Largo do Leal Senado, on the east side (Mon–Fri 9am–1pm & 3–5.30pm, Sat 9am–12.30pm); post restante is delivered here. Small red booths all over the territory also dispense stamps from machines.

Telephones Local calls are free from private phones, 1ptca from payphones. Cardphones work with *CTM* cards, issued by the *Macau State Telecommunication Company,* on sale in hotels or in the telephone office (Mon–Sat 8am–midnight, Sun 9am–midnight) behind the GPO in Largo do Senado Leal, where you can also make direct calls. For calls to Hong Kong, dial ☎01 followed by the eight-digit number.

Travel agencies *CTS*, Rua de Nagasaki (☎705 506) can sort out China visas and tickets, as can most other tour operators.

travel details

Trains

Hong Kong to: Guangzhou (4 daily; 3hr); Lo Wu (KCR line, for Shenzhen; frequent; 50min).

Buses

Hong Kong to: Guangzhou (frequent; 3hr); Shenzhen (frequent; 1hr).

Macau to: Guangzhou (several daily; 6hr).

Boats

Hong Kong to: Guangzhou (2 daily; jetcat 3hr, ferry 9hr); Haikou (weekly; 18hr); Macau (frequent; 1hr); Shanghai (weekly; 60hr); Shekou (8 daily; 45min); Shenzhen airport (6 daily; 1hr); Wuzhou (daily; 10hr); Xiamen (4 weekly; 20hr); Zhuhai (6 daily; 1hr 10min).

Macau to: Guangzhou (daily; 9hr); Hong Kong (frequent; 1hr); Shekou (daily; 1hr 30min).

Planes

Hong Kong to: Beijing (several daily; 2hr 45min); Chengdu (daily; 2hr 30min); Fuzhou (3 daily; 1hr 5min); Guangzhou (several daily; 30min); Guilin (daily; 1hr); Haikou (daily; 50min); Hangzhou (daily; 2hr); Kunming (daily; 2hr); Lanzhou (weekly; 4hr 30min); Nanjing (daily; 2hr); Ningbo (daily; 2hr); Qingdao (5 weekly; 3hr 10min); Shanghai (4 daily; 2hr); Shengyang (4 weekly; 3hr 30min); Tianjin (daily; 2hr 50min); Wuhan (daily; 1hr 30min); Xiamen (2 daily; 1hr); Xi'an (daily; 2hr 30min).

Macau to: Bangkok (4 weekly; 3hr); Beijing (daily; 1hr 54min); Brussels (2 weekly; 12hr); Kuala Lumpur (3 weekly; 5hr); Lisbon (2 weekly; 13hr); Seoul (6 weekly; 3hr); Shanghai (daily; 2hr); Singapore (2 weekly; 6hr); Taipei (8 daily; 1hr 30min); Xiamen (daily; 1hr).

CHAPTER TEN

GUANGXI AND GUIZHOU

C hina's subtropical central southwest, comprising **Guangxi** and **Guizhou**, manages to include one of China's most intensely visited areas while remaining largely unknown as a whole. This is entirely due to the countryside's picturesque limestone hills which, though a tourist phenomenon today, have in the past made communications virtually impossible and have created some of provincial China's worst agricultural land. So poor that they were hardly worth the trouble of invading, local tribes were left pretty much to their own devices, and the region evolved into a stronghold for **ethnic groups**. Some kept their nominal identity but more or less integrated with the Chinese, while others thoroughly resisted assimilation by occupying isolated highlands, and even today retain many of their cultural traditions. A very long way from the flow of things, the region generally remained in obscurity until the **Taiping Uprising** exploded in central Guangxi in 1850, marking the start of a century of devastation caused by warlords and famine. Harrison E. Salisbury's *The Long March* describes how Red Army soldiers passing through rural Guizhou in the 1930s found people working naked in the fields and an economy based on opium. The Communist takeover saw the minority groups enfranchized by the formation of several **autonomous prefectures**, but industry and infrastructure still remain underdeveloped and few of the cities – including **Guiyang** and **Nanning**, the provincial capitals – have much to offer except transport to more interesting locations.

Small wonder, then, that most visitors are drawn to the **landscape**, epitomized by the tall karst (weathered limestone) towers rising out of the plains around the city of **Guilin** in northeastern Guangxi, instantly familiar to Chinese and Westerners alike through centuries of eulogistic poetry, paintings and photographs. So famous has this become, and in all fairness quite justifiably, that it totally overshadows the rest of the region, so that in remote areas you can still feel like a pioneer, seeing parts of the country little known either in China or the outside world. Most rewarding is the chance of close contact with ethnic groups, particularly the **Miao**, **Dong** and **Zhuang**, whose culture is apparent not only in their daily lives but also in traces of their prehistoric past.

ACCOMMODATION PRICE CODES

All the accommodation in this book has been graded according to the following price codes, which represent the cheapest double room available to foreigners. Most places have a range of rooms, however, and staff will usually offer you the more expensive ones – it's always worth asking if they have anything cheaper. Where the text refers specifically to dorm beds, the price code represents the price per bed. See p.40 for more details.

① less than ¥30	④ ¥100–150	⑦ ¥300–500
② ¥30–75	⑤ ¥150–200	⑧ ¥500–700
③ ¥75–100	⑥ ¥200–300	⑨ ¥700 or more

There's also further terrain to explore encompassing beaches, moist mountain forests and some of the country's largest waterfalls and limestone caverns.

While **travel** out to all this can be time-consuming, a reasonable quantity of buses and trains (the latter inevitably crowded) means that remoteness is not the barrier it once was. **Language** is another matter, as many rural people understand neither Mandarin nor Cantonese; since 1995 the government has, unusually, approved the use of local dialects alongside Mandarin in schools to encourage literacy. But in any case, locals rarely expect to communicate easily with foreigners, and you'll find that hand signals and patience will go a long way. With a geography which includes the South China Sea and some respectable mountains, **weather** is fairly localized, though you should expect warm, wet summers and cool winters. The region also occasionally experiences severe spring flooding.

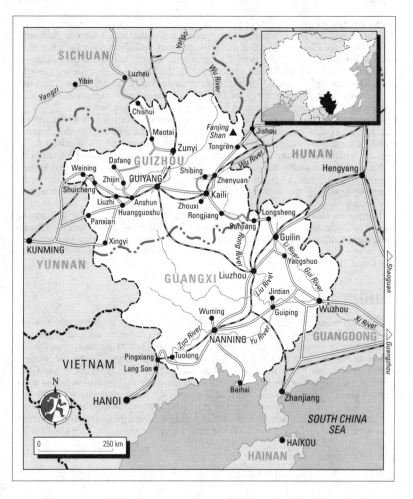

GUANGXI

Lush and green most of the year round, **Guangxi** unfolds south from the highlands it shares with Guizhou to a tropical coast and border abutting Vietnam. The pick of the postcard-perfect limestone and paddy-field landscape is concentrated around the north-eastern city of **Guilin**, which, long famous and easily accessible from Hong Kong and Guangzhou, has become a massive tourist draw. Not everyone likes the city itself, but most visitors find the scenery accompanying a trip along the **Li River** to the budget-travellers' haven of **Yangshuo** quite unforgettable, and ample compensation for the high prices and irritating commercial hype you might have to endure.

The one drawback to all this is that Guilin has become a hard act to follow, and, despite some equally rich material, the rest of Guangxi seems to have given up trying. Since 1958 the province has not been a province at all but the **Guangxi Zhuang Autonomous Region**, heartland of China's thirteen million-strong **Zhuang** nationality. They constitute about a third of the regional population and, although thoroughly assimilated into Chinese life today, there's enough archeological evidence to link them with a Bronze-Age culture spread throughout Southeast Asia, including a fantastic series of prehistoric **rock friezes** surviving along the **Zuo River** near the open **border with Vietnam**. Other areas, such as the northeastern hills around **Sanjiang**, are home to less-integrated groups, such as the **Dong**, whose more actively traditional way of life makes for a fascinating trip, hopping between villages on public buses.

The attraction of Guangxi's cities is more ephemeral, as their characters are vanishing along with traces of their colonial heritage. **Liuzhou** is at the heart of Guangxi's rail network, while plenty of people pass through easterly **Wuzhou**, terminus for the journey up the Xi River from Guangzhou. Far fewer manage to reach the south and the tropically languid capital, **Nanning**, or the coastal port of **Beihai**. Those who do, cross a central region whose history touches on the origins of the **Taiping Uprising**, nineteenth-century China's most widespread rebellion against the rotting Qing empire.

Despite its subtropical latitude, Guangxi's **weather** can be deceptive – it actually snows in Guilin about once every ten years. Another thing of note is that the **Zhuang language**, instead of using *pinyin*, follows its own method of rendering Chinese characters into Roman text. This accounts for the novel spellings you'll encounter on street signs and elsewhere – "Minzu Dadao", for example, becomes "Minzcuzdadau".

Guilin

GUILIN (Osmanthus Forest) is perhaps China's worst tourist trap, dependent on visitors for its income and flaunting an expensive service industry tailored to the well-heeled tour groups that are for ever passing through. The city has some good points: plenty of English is spoken and booking agents are everywhere; there's the lovely **Li River cruise**, one of the most worthwhile "things to do" in China; and, while Guilin itself is no scenic marvel, the surrounding landscape is as beautiful today as it has always been. On the downside, locals unable to tap the tourist dollar have to suffer spiralling living costs, and most independent travellers detest the mercenary attitude of Guilin's all too worldly inhabitants – avoid letting students guide you around, unless you want to end up footing the bill at the most expensive restaurant they can find. If it

The **telephone code** for Guilin is ☎0773

GUILIN

| Guilin | 桂林 | *guìlín* |

ACCOMMODATION

Hidden Hill	隐山饭店	*yǐnshān fàndiàn*
Holiday Inn	桂林宾馆	*guìlín bīnguǎn*
Jingui	京桂宾馆	*jīngùi bīnguǎn*
Lijiang	漓江饭店	*líjiāng fàndiàn*
Osmanthus	丹桂大酒店	*dāngùi dàjiǔdiàn*
Sheraton	文华大酒店	*wénhuá dàjiǔdiàn*
Taihe	泰和饭店	*tàihé fàndiàn*

THE CITY

Camel Hill	骆驼山	*luòtuóshān*
Diecai Shan	叠彩山	*diécǎi shān*
Duxiu Feng	独秀峰	*dúxiù fēng*
Elephant Trunk Hill	象鼻山	*xiàngbí shān*
Fubo Shan	伏波山	*fúbō shān*
Huanzhu Dong	还珠洞	*huánzhū dòng*
Li River	漓江	*lí jiāng*
Old South Gate	旧南门	*jiùnán mén*
Reed Flute Cave	芦笛岩	*lúdí yán*
Rong Hu	榕湖	*róng hú*
Seven Star Cavern	七星洞	*qīxīng dòng*
Seven Star Park	七星公园	*qīxīng gōngyuán*
Shan Hu	杉湖	*shān hú*
Stone Forest	石林	*shílín*
Ta Shan	塔山	*tǎ shān*
Xi Shan Park	西山公园	*xíshān gōngyuán*
Yueya Shan	月牙山	*yuèyá shān*

RESTAURANTS

| Jiulong | 九龙 | *jiǔ lóng* |
| Longfeng | 龙凤 | *lóng fēng* |

all gets to you, abandon Guilin's pace and high prices for the more mellow village of **Yangshuo**, just ninety minutes away to the south.

The capital of Guangxi from the Ming dynasty until 1914, Guilin only started to play any significant role in history after losing that rank to Nanning. Sun Yatsen planned the Nationalists' "Northern Expedition" here in 1925; the Long Marchers were soundly trounced by Guomindang factions outside the city nine years later; and the war with Japan saw over a million refugees hiding out in Guilin, increasing the population tenfold. Wartime bombing spared the city's natural monuments but turned the centre into a shabby provincial shell, neatened up during the late 1980s by well-planned but unimaginative high-density reconstruction. Today, a generous sprinkling of sweet-scented osmanthus trees through the central streets somewhat lightens the grey architecture and heavy pedestrian and motor traffic, but it's the famous hills and accompanying legends which are Guilin's focus of interest, not the city itself.

Orientation, arrival and accommodation

Central Guilin is laid out on the western bank of the south-flowing **Li River**, though its suburbs are steadily expanding in all directions. Various peaks are scattered around the centre, but tall buildings render them mostly invisible from ground level and of little use for orientation. Parallel with the river and about 500m west, **Zhongshan Lu** is the main street, running north for 4km or so from the **train station** (where minibuses from Yangshuo terminate) past a knot of accommodation and services, the **long-distance bus station** and on through the centre. The main roads which cross it are **Nanhuan Lu**, **Ronghu Lu** and adjoining **Shanhu Lu**, and **Jiefang Lu**, all of which stretch for at least 1km west across town from **Binjiang Lu**, the riverside promenade. Guilin's busy **airport** is 14km south of the city, connected to the *CAAC* office on Shanghai Lu by **airport bus** (¥5) and taxi (about ¥50).

Some of Guilin's sights are close enough to walk to, others can be easily reached on public buses, **taxis** (a fixed ¥10–12 fare within the city limits), and **bicycles** – see "Listings", p.668, for rental shops.

Accommodation

Budget **accommodation** is not Guilin's strong point. Although many hostels display friendly welcoming signs in English, none is actually allowed to accept foreigners – staff are apologetic, but powerless in the face of official instructions. If you are staying in town, perhaps use it as an enforced opportunity to try one of China's plusher places. All the following are central; the more expensive also have post and banking facilities, and international telephones.

Hidden Hill, Zhongshan Nan Lu (☎3833540). Just north of the train station; you can get here on bus #2 or #3. This is about the bottom line for foreigners in Guilin and rooms are correspondingly furnished. ③–⑤.

Holiday Inn, 14 Ronghu Nan Lu; (☎2823950, fax 2822101). Nicely positioned near what's left of the older parts of town. Take bus #2 north along Zhongshan Lu from the train or bus station. ⑨.

Jingui, 103 Zhongshan Nan Lu (☎3834328). Old and not especially flash hotel, but rooms are cheap. On the route of buses #2 and #3. ③–⑤.

Lijiang, 1 Shanhu Bei Lu (☎2822881, fax 2822891). A vaguely tatty atmosphere, though rooms are large and comfortable and some have good views of the city and hills. Take bus #3 north along Zhongshan Lu. ⑧.

MOVING ON

Minibuses to Yangshuo leave the train station forecourt through the day whenever full, otherwise, **moving on from Guilin** can require some planning. Despite the huge number of people trying to get out at any one time, trains don't originate here, and being located at least twenty hours down the track from departure points has made Guilin a notoriously difficult place to buy a rail ticket from. While hotels take bookings, and there's even a **foreigners' ticket office** (usually open 8am–5pm) at the station, berths are quickly snapped up and you'll need to start enquiries at least three days in advance. Hard seats are another matter, but as the lengthy trips to Changsha, Guangzhou, Shanghai or Kunming would be a wretched experience without something better, you'd be well advised to either **fly** out of Guilin, or, if you have the time, do the journey in stages by **bus**. There are at least daily services all over the province and beyond from here, and options include heading north to Sanjiang and Guizhou Province (pp.672–676); to Guangzhou (either direct or via Wuzhou and the Xi River ferry, see p.676); or to the holy peaks at Heng Shan in Hunan.

Osmanthus, 451 Zhongshan Nan Lu (☎3834300, fax 3835316). The choice of many Chinese conference groups, rooms are variable, though grounds and facilities are pleasant. On the route of buses #2 and #3. ⑤.

Sheraton, 9 Binjiang Nan Lu (☎4843388). Definitely one of the nicest hotels in town, overlooking the river and across to Seven Star Park. Take bus route #2. ⑧.

Taihe, 427 Zhongshan Nan Lu (☎3834801, 3835504). Standard, informal place just north of the bus station, and again on the route of buses #2 and #3. ④.

The City

Before starting a tour of Guilin's hills, head 2km north of the train station to where Zhongshan Lu cuts between **Rong Hu** (Banyan Lake) and **Shan Hu** (Fir Lake), named after the trees which once grew here. The lakes originally formed the moat that surrounded the Tang city walls. Today, the ring of walls has long gone – their last trace survives in **Gunan**, the old South Gate, just west near the *CITS* office on Ronghu Lu – and the area surrounding the moat has been landscaped and planted with willow, peach and kumquat trees. For an overall **view of the city**, wander east to the *Lijiang Hotel* on Shanhu Bei Lu, and take the lift to the thirteenth floor. From here you look south to riverside **Elephant Trunk Hill**, said to be the body of a sick imperial baggage elephant who was cared for by locals and turned to stone rather than rejoin the emperor's army.

Guilin's three most central peaks are within a twenty-minute walk north of here, close to the river. Two kilometres up along Binjiang Lu is **Fubo Shan**, a hill where the giant **Jie Die** fought a demon which was descending on Guilin with a vanguard of deadly animals. The demon was vanquished and the city never troubled by evil spirits again. At its foot is **Huanzhu Dong** (Returned Pearl Cave), named after the story of a guilt-stricken fisherman who returned a sleeping dragon's stolen treasure. Climb to Fubo's summit and you pass three hundred Buddha images, carved into the rock during the Tang and Song dynasties.

A further ten minutes' walk north brings you to riverside **Diecai Shan** (Folded Brocade Hill), its limestone seams eroded into a series of small peaks, supposedly resembling a pile of interlaced fabric. The same distance west of Fubo is **Duxiu Feng**, also known as Solitary Beauty Peak, which stands within the grounds of the mansion of **Zhu Shouqian**, Guilin's fourteenth-century ruler and grandson of the emperor Hongwu. Apart from the gate, there's little of the original left; the present building once served as Sun Yatsen's office and is now the home of the Guangxi Teachers' College. Three hundred and six steps lead to the top of the peak, where views once again make the climb worthwhile.

Seven Star Park

Don't leave Guilin without seeing Qixing Gongyuan, the **Seven Star Park** (¥15), a wonderful place to spend a day exploring half a dozen major caves and seven great peaks arranged in the shape of the Great Bear (Big Dipper) constellation. The main **entrance** lies east over the river, and bus #13 from Zhongshan Lu stops outside. On the way in you cross over a nicely restored Song-dynasty covered bridge, complete with palisades and tiled roof. The left-hand mass as you enter the park is **Putuo**, named after Zhejiang's famous Buddhist mountain and topped by peaks representing the Great Bear's four northern stars, Tianshi, Tianxuan, Tianji and Tianquan. There's a choice of routes here: the left track leads down past a pavilion to the **Stone Forest** and the 22-storey-high **Putuo Si**, a temple behind which is a cave where the Bodhisattva Suddhana Kumara reputedly preached; the right leads to a chain of caves culminating at the huge **Seven Star Cavern**. Over 1km long, 40m wide and almost 30m tall, it was originally a channel cut by a subterranean river (indeed, lower reaches are still flood-

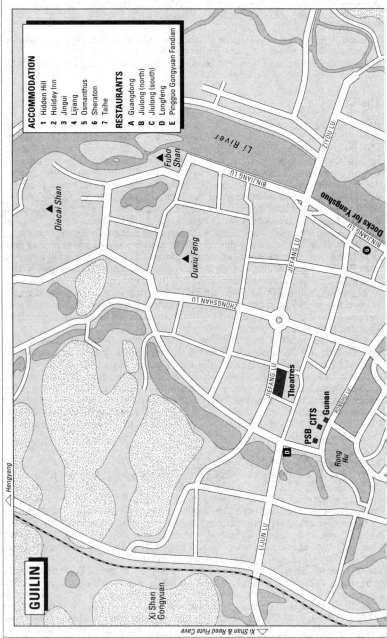

GUILIN

ACCOMMODATION
1 Hidden Hill
2 Holiday Inn
3 Jingui
4 Lijiang
5 Osmanthus
6 Sheraton
7 Taihe

RESTAURANTS
A Guangdong
B Jiulong (north)
C Jiulong (south)
D Longfeng
E Pingguo Gongyuan Fandian

Li River

Diecai Shan

Fubo Shan

Duxiu Feng

ZHONGSHAN LU

BINJIANG LU

ZIYOU LU

JIEFANG LU

Docks for Yangshuo

Theatres

PSB

CITS

Gunan

RONGSHU LU

Rong Hu

Xi Shan Gongyuan

LIJUN LU

Hengyang

Xi Shan & Reed Flute Cave

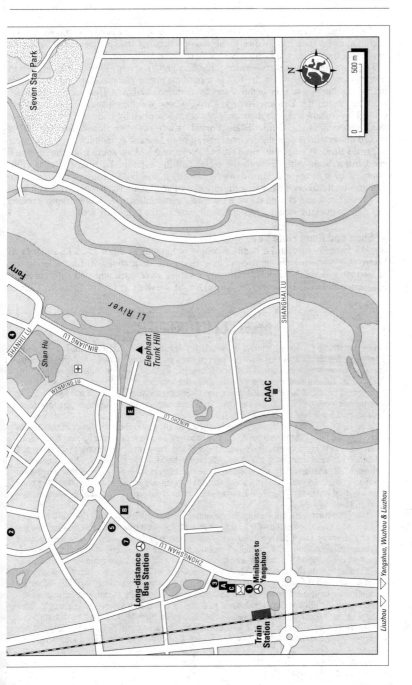

Seven Star Park

Ferry

Shan Hu

Li River

BINJIANG LU

SHANHU LU

WENMING LU

Elephant Trunk Hill

MINZHU LU

SHANGHAI LU

CAAC

N

500 m

0

E

B

5

7

2

4

Long-distance Bus Station

ZHONGSHAN LU

3

A

C

1

Minibuses to Yangshuo

Train Station

Liuzhou ▷ ▷ Yangshuo, Wuzhou & Liuzhou

ed), and while access is restricted, what you can see is impressive enough. As always, each contorted rock has its own name; one particularly imaginative one is "Magpies Spreading their Wings to Form a Bridge Across the Milky Way".

The remaining three stars – Yuleng, Kaiyang and Yaoguang – are atop **Yueya Shan** in the south of the park. At the foot is a pavilion where you can stop and buy drinks before climbing up to ever better views from various lookouts. Descending on the far side, you reach the **Dragon Refuge Cave**, whose walls are patterned with "scales" caused by erosion and with thousands of poems inscribed by visitors. There's more of this farther on at the **Guilin Stele Forest**, where over two thousand stone tablets record dissertations on subjects from literature to Marxist economics.

Lutuo Shan (Camel Hill) rises east of Yueya, and looking south from the top you'll see **Chuan Shan** (the Hill with the Hole) and the adjacent **Ta Shan** (Pagoda Hill), crowned by a hexagonal Ming-dynasty pagoda. It was built to imprison a centipede demon which had been harassing the city's populace, after a worthy cockerel who lived on Chuan Shan had chased it into a cave on the mountain. The people swiftly erected this demon-quelling structure, permanently sealing the centipede inside.

Xi Shan and Reed Flute Cave

Bus #3 from Zhongshan Lu heads a couple of kilometres down Lijun Lu towards **Xi Shan**, the Western Hills, an area of long Buddhist associations. Xi Shan's peaks are named after Buddhist deities, and many grottoes were once adorned with carvings, long since defaced. However, the **Xiqinglin Si** survives as one of southern China's

---

THE LI RIVER CRUISE

The **Li River** (Li Jiang) meanders south for 85km between **Guilin and Yangshuo** through the finest scenery that this part of the country can provide, and the **six-hour cruise** from the docks above Elephant Trunk Hill is, for some, the highlight of their trip to China. Others find the cost extortionate, the journey too long, and, with some two thousand people a day in peak season, the river overcrowded. If any of this seems likely to bother you, the Li can be explored in a cheaper and more leisurely manner from Yangshuo itself (see p.671).

You can book cruises through hotels, the *CITS* or, more cheaply, direct at the **docks** on Binjiang Lu. Cruise boats leave daily at 8am, and the ¥400 price tag to Yangshuo (¥360 one-way) gets you a comfortable seat, decent food, running commentary in Chinese and a bus from Yangshuo back to Guilin. Alternatively, ¥100 buys you a two-hour excursion down to **Zhujiang** which, while missing the most impressive peaks, presents a beautiful scene in autumn, with the banks coloured red by maple trees. In winter, the river runs so low that boats for Yangshuo have to start from Zhujiang anyway, and passengers are taken there by bus.

The cruise is a generally tranquil experience despite the legend that the spirit of every sailor who ever drowned on the Li River rocks boats as they navigate the rougher shoals. Along the way you'll pass **cormorant fishermen** (see box, p.669) poling their almost submerged bamboo rafts, buffaloes wallowing in the fields and, of course, scores of grotesquely shaped hills with exotic names. About a third of the way down is **Wanfu Shi** (Yearning for Husband Rock). The story goes that while sailing downriver a family ran out of rice and moored on an island so that the husband could look for help. When he failed to return, his wife picked up her baby and eventually found him fossilized on a hill top; mourning for him, she turned to stone too. The atmosphere ends abruptly after docking at Yangshuo, when several hundred stallholders descend on passengers and desperately try to push their faked coins and glass animals before the Guilin buses arrive. Yangshuo has a far better side, but you'll need to stay overnight to appreciate it.

major Buddhist halls, filled with hundreds of exquisitely executed statues ranging from ten centimetres to over two metres in height. There's also a **regional museum** in the park (daily 9am–noon & 2.30–5pm; free), which manages to animate a massive collection of ethnic clothing by using mannequins to depict key festival events – staff in the gift shop downstairs might offer to translate for you.

The #3 bus terminates another 6km north along the Peach Blossom River outside **Reed Flute Cave** (daily 8.30–11am & 12.30–3.30pm; ¥40), a huge warren eaten into the south side of **Guangming Shan** in one of the most extraordinary examples of limestone erosion in the country. The entry fee is high, and the coloured lighting is at once overpowering and crude, but the size and variety of the rock formations are genuinely spectacular, even if you don't know that you're looking at "Rosy Dawn in a Lion Forest" or "Waterfall Splashing Down from a High Valley". You're meant to follow one of the tours which run every twenty minutes, but you can always linger inside and pick up a later group if you want to spend more time. The cave was developed as a tourist site only in the 1950s, before which it provided a safe refuge from banditry and Japanese bombs.

Eating, drinking and entertainment

Guilin's **restaurants** are famous for serving exotic dishes, and though pangolins, palm civets and rare birds are seldom displayed caged outside restaurants any more (in case the sight disturbs foreign guests), they are, sadly, often available. Fortunately, you can eat very well here without devouring endangered species. Food is generally of good quality though prices can be very steep – at least ¥50 per person in a proper restaurant – and it's essential to check them before ordering. Plenty of **dumpling stalls** and cheaper places to eat surround the bus and train stations on Zhongshan Lu, serving simple, pungently spiced dishes. Most larger establishments have English menus and almost all hotels have their own restaurants.

Restaurants

Jingui Binguan, 103 Zhongshan Nan Lu. Downmarket hotel with an excellent fish restaurant. Prices are very reasonable.

Jiulong, Zhongshan Lu. By the bridge opposite the *Osmanthus* hotel, this is a good-value, multi-storey place with mid-range prices. The main restaurant is downstairs; *dim sum* and bar upstairs.

Jiulong, Zhongshan Lu, north of the post office. Hard-sell waitresses lug you off the street into this grubby café (and the nearby *Guangdong*) offering cheap rice dishes and stir-fries. Somewhere to sit down while waiting for a bus.

Longfeng, Lijun Lu. A fairly expensive restaurant whose house speciality is *gui yu*, a Li River fish simply steamed or fried whole.

Pingguo Gongyuan Fandian, Minzhu Lu, near Elephant Trunk Hill. Small, good and, at around ¥70 a head for a simple meal, very expensive. Specializes in plainly cooked eight-piece chicken, snake and fish. No English menu.

Entertainment

A tradition of **opera and ballad singing** in Guilin goes back several hundred years, though performances of these have been supplanted by "minority displays" laid on for tour groups by thirteen of the region's ethnic groups. There's actually nothing wrong with these for their own sake, though visiting Chinese audiences seem to pay scant attention and you'll probably want to avoid occasional specials such as horse fighting – not an edifying spectator sport. There are several **theatres** along Jiefang Xi Lu and the surrounding streets, busiest Friday through to Sunday nights; tickets for the hour-long performances are sold at the doors (¥40–50).

Listings

Airlines *CAAC*, Shanghai Lu (daily 9am–5pm; ☎3824007).

Banks and exchange The main *Bank of China* is on Shanhu Bei Lu, with a sub-branch south of the long-distance bus station on Zhongshan Lu also able to change currency and travellers' cheques (both branches Mon–Fri 9–11.30am & 1.30–5pm). Larger hotels, such as the *Holiday Inn*, *Sheraton* and *Hidden Hill*, generally allow non-residents to use their services too.

Bike rental There are plenty of rental shops advertising their services along Zhongshan Lu, or ask at your hotel reception; going rates are ¥10–20 a day.

Bookshops The bookstore on Zhongshan Lu, just south of the crossroads with Ronghu Lu, has a big selection of English classics and translations of modern Chinese novels.

Hospital Renmin Hospital, off Wenming Lu, is the best place to head if you get sick and your accommodation can't help out.

Pharmacies There's a good pharmacy at the southeastern corner of the Jiefang Lu–Zhongshan Lu intersection.

PSB Sanduo Lu, west off Zhongshan Lu, just north of Rong Hu.

Post office On Zhongshan Lu, just north of the station (daily 8am–8pm). Mail services and poste restante downstairs.

Shopping Zhongshan Lu is lined from top to bottom with uninspiring junk souvenirs and well-stocked department stores, but check out some of the English names – where else in the world would you find a "Multiplex Changing Figure Ironing Shop"?

Telephones Upstairs in the main post office on Zhongshan Lu.

Travel agents Hotel tour desks can help with plane, bus and boat tickets, or try the big, multilingual *CITS* at 14 Ronghu Bei Lu (daily 7.30am–noon, 1–6pm & 7–9pm; ☎2827254).

Yangshuo and around

Nestled 70km south of Guilin in the thick of China's most spectacular karst scenery, **YANGSHUO**, meaning Bright Moon, rose to prominence during the mid-1980s, when visitors on Li River cruises from Guilin realized that beyond simply spending an hour here buying souvenirs, the village made an excellent place to settle down and get on intimate terms with the river and its peaks. Yangshuo has grown a bit since then, but remains essentially the same, and as Guilin has orientated itself more and more towards big-spending tour groups, so independent travellers – an increasing number of them Chinese – have made Yangshuo their haven instead. It's an ideal spot to cocoon

YANGSHUO AND AROUND		
Yangshuo	阳朔	*yángshuò*
Green Lotus Peak	碧莲峰	*bìlián fēng*
Moon Hill	月亮山	*yuè liàng shān*
Yangshuo Park	阳朔公园	*yángshuò gōngyuán*
AROUND YANGSHUO		
Black Buddha Caves	黑佛洞	*hēifó dòng*
Black Dragon Caves	黑龙洞	*hēilóng dòng*
Langshi	浪石	*làngshí*
Xingping	兴坪	*xīngpíng*
Yangdi	杨堤	*yángdī*

ruffled nerves: hills surround everything, village lanes swarm with market activity and there are restaurants and accommodation everywhere. You can rent a bike and spend a day zipping between hamlets, scale the peaks, study calligraphy or *tai ji* or just relax in the village park.

The village

Not surprisingly for somewhere which was a simple country marketplace before the tourists arrived, Yangshuo has little to see, but it's still a nice place to be. Nor do you have to go far to find a hill to climb, as the village is completely hemmed in by them. West off Die Cui Lu is **Yangshuo Park**, a pleasant place in summer with its colourful formal garden and breezy vantages of town from pavilions lodged on the main rise. Squeezed between the highway and the river directly opposite is **Green Lotus Peak**, the largest in the immediate area, which can be climbed from a footpath along the bank. Otherwise, just walk upstream from Yangshuo for a kilometre or two and take your pick of the rough paths which scale many other slopes to summits covered in tangled undergrowth and sharp, eroded rocks.

The presence of tourists hasn't altered the daily routine of local villagers who spend hours inspecting and buying wares in the **produce market**. There's a particularly good selection of fruit, nuts and fungus laid out on sheets in the street here, including fresh straw and needle mushrooms, and "arrowheads" which look like miniature buffalo horns but contain a kernel similar to a Brazil nut. It's an interesting place to hang out, but foreigners tend to save their money for the shops down at the river end of Xi Jie, one of the best places in China to pick up a bargain **souvenir**. There are things from all over the country: Little Red Books in English, stylish and ridiculously cheap jackets and T-shirts made here (to order, if needed) from Anshun batiks or silk, modern and traditional paintings turned out by art students in Guilin, chops, and heaps of elaborately carved wooden screen panels, printing blocks and grotesque theatre masks. Coins and jade are invariably fake. As always in China, buy because you like something, not because it looks valuable – under layers of carefully applied grime most articles are "new antiques". Vigorous, friendly bargaining is essential.

Those who find themselves spending weeks in Yangshuo linger not for the sights or shopping but because the village offers a window into the more esoteric side of Chinese culture. Normally the domain of specialists, for around ¥15–20 a session you can take **courses** in martial arts, painting, calligraphy, languages, cooking, massage and many other subjects. Cafés (see "Practicalities" below) have the current information, or try the following: *Buckland Foreign Language School*, at the river end of Xi Jie (where they also frequently need help teaching English); *Susannah's Café*, also on Xi Jie, is the best

---

CORMORANT FISHING

When you've had enough scenery for one day, do something unusual and spend an evening watching **cormorant fishing** (book through cafés; ¥20 for a 90-minute trip). This involves heading out in a punt at dusk, closely following a tiny wooden fishing boat or bamboo raft from which a group of cormorants fish for their owner. Despite being turned into a tourist activity at Yangshuo, people still make their living from this age-old practice throughout central and southern China, raising young birds to dive into the water and swim back to the boat with full beaks. The birds are prevented from swallowing by rings or ties around their necks, but it's usual practice for the fisherman to slacken these off and let them eat every seventh fish – apparently, the cormorants refuse to work otherwise.

place to ask about martial arts; and *Yangshuo Culture and Arts Institute*, on the highway (☎0773/8822981, fax 8822904), which offers just about everything.

Practicalities

Most people arrive in Yangshuo by bus, having sped south down the new expressway from Guilin between stalls selling bamboo furniture and seasonal gluts of pomelos, plums and peaches. The highway bends in from the west to the **bus station**, passes east along the edge of town in about 500m, then kinks off due south en route to Moon Hill, Liuzhou and Wuzhou. Yangshuo's two main streets run north off the highway to the **Li River**; **Die Cui Lu** extends from the bus station through the village centre to the **docks**, while east and parallel with Die Cui Lu is **Xi Jie**, pleasantly cobbled and lined with old wooden shops down near the waterfront. **Moving on**, minibuses to Guilin cruise around the bus station all day long, from where there are also daily long-distance departures to Guangzhou, Liuzhou, Nanning and Wuzhou.

There's an unusual quantity of **information** to be had in Yangshuo. The hotels have information desks, and the helpful *CITS/CAAC* office is located at the highway end of Die Cui Lu (daily 8.30am–noon & 2.30–5.30pm; ☎0773/8822256). However, many people make all arrangements and bookings by shopping around Yangshuo's ubiquitous **cafés**. Specifically geared to Western travellers, these act as meeting places to swap the latest news – some have noticeboards, others leave journals out for you to write in and read – and all offer deals on everything that it's possible to do during your stay here. Hotels, cafés and the *CITS* also book **taxis to Guilin airport** and all long-distance transport, including hovercraft and ferries from Wuzhou and, with at least three days' warning, can obtain **train tickets** from Guilin.

For other services, the **bank** is on the waterfront between Xi Jie and Die Cui Lu (foreign currency transactions daily 9am–noon & 1–5pm); the **post office** (daily 8am–5pm; parcel and post restante services available) is over on the highway; while you'll find IDD **telephones** all around Yangshuo and in the bigger hotels. Should you get sick, there's a **foreigners' clinic** next to the *Xilang Hill Hotel* on Die Cui Lu, and also a **Hospital of Traditional Chinese Medicine** on Xi Jie.

Accommodation

You tend to get what you pay for in Yangshuo, and there's little to separate **hotels** within similar price brackets; everywhere offers laundry services and most have restaurants. Room rates drop during the winter low season, when you might want to check the availability of heating and hot water.

Golden Leaves, on the highway across from the bus station (☎0773/8822860). All rooms are heated and have bathrooms, staff are friendly and facilities are reasonable. Dorms ③, rooms ④.

Good Companion Holiday Inn, on the highway near the bus station. Clean, nondescript dorms and double rooms. ①–③.

Jinlong, Die Cui Lu (☎0773/8822674). The best of the mid-range options with very obliging and informed staff. ③.

Si Hai, river end of Xi Jie. Popular for its simple budget rooms and all-day hot water. The higher-category rooms have private bathrooms and heating. ①–③.

Xilang Hill, Die Cui Lu (☎0773/8822312). A very decent place usually booked out by Chinese groups. ③–⑤.

Yangshuo Youth Hostel, on the highway across from the bus station (☎0773/8822347). Basic, cheap and cheerful option. Dorms ①, rooms ②.

Zhu Yang, east on the highway, below Green Lotus Peak (☎0773/8821601). An upmarket place by local standards, with 24hr hot water and jacuzzis in the more expensive rooms. Dorms ①, rooms ②–⑥.

Eating, drinking and nightlife

As domestic tourism has discovered Yangshuo, so the first **karaoke bar** has appeared, the *Mingcheng Nightclub* on Die Cui Lu, haunt of hustlers and honeymooners. The **cinema** on Xi Jie is busy every night, as are countless private video screens easily located by the high-volume, scream-and-thud soundtracks emanating from within.

Otherwise, you'll probably while away the evenings drinking *Guilin* beer and eating Mexican and Chinese food with other foreigners in the cafés. Most cafés open early in the morning for Western breakfasts and coffee, and generally serve decent meals; everyone finds their own favourites, and the following recommendations should be treated as a starting point. There are also plenty of **Chinese canteens** and **food stalls** selling noodle soups and buns around the market and upper Xi Jie, with good Chinese meals served in most **hotel restaurants**.

RESTAURANTS

Green Lotus Peak Winehouse, corner of the highway and Xi Jie. Most upmarket of Yangshuo's restaurants, with fine Chinese and edible Western food.

MC Blues Bar, corner of highway and Xi Jie. Beyond cocktails and burritos there are some eye-opening treats like snake, snails and bamboo rats. They also do a fine vegetarian hotpot.

Lisa's, Xi Jie. Current pick of the backpacker joints down this way, along with the nearby *Minnie Mao's*. Perennially popular for cheap food and comfortable atmosphere.

Paris Café, highway end of Xi Jie. Westernized Chinese food ranging from good (Beijing duck and twice-cooked pork) to poor (most of their fish dishes). The street tables are popular in summer.

Serena's, on the highway near the post office. Cosy and friendly, with fine food and useful information on the Sanjiang and Longsheng regions.

Around Yangshuo

Getting to see the countryside around Yangshuo is no problem, as the land between the hills is flat and perfect for **bicycles** – there's a **rental shop** on Xi Jie across from the *Paris Café* (¥5 a day, plus deposit). Various people offer excellent and inexpensive **guided bike tours** too, allowing close contact with villages and locals through an interpreter. **Motor-rickshaws** also cruise around, destinations listed on their windshields in Chinese, but are relatively expensive and the drivers don't speak English. Most of the sights are near main roads, however, so you can always catch a long-distance bus heading in the right direction and get off where you want – a fair amount of traffic means that getting back or farther on shouldn't be a problem as long as you don't leave things too late.

In summer, a popular way to see the **river** is by renting an **inner tube** from one of the cafés and simply drifting around. **Boats** for more furnished excursions leave all year round from piers either side of Green Lotus Peak, where touts sell tickets every morning – just keep repeating your destination until you find the right vessel. While it's not such a good idea to travel the whole way to Guilin from Yangshuo along the river – an ultimately tedious twelve-hour journey upstream – there are plenty of shorter trips to make, and the prices here are a fraction of the cost you'd pay from the city. The thickest, most contorted collection of peaks lies between Yangshuo and the neighbouring villages of **Yangdi** and **Langshi**, about a third of the way to Guilin; people have managed to wrangle this as a six-hour round trip (returning by bus) for as little as ¥25 per person in winter, though in the summer peak season ¥60 would be more usual. **Xingping**, just a couple of hours upstream, is another good target, close enough to pedal back from after you've taken your bike up there by boat; as is **Fuli**, a pretty little village with a Wednesday market an hour's ride downstream from Yangshuo on the east bank.

Moon Hill

There's nothing to stop you simply picking a hill or village in the distance and heading out there, but for a specific target it's hard to beat the twenty-kilometre round trip out to **Moon Hill**. This lies on the highway southwest of town as it twists between the sudden peaks – some of these are negotiable for a fair height before becoming too sheer to climb. A **rifle range** about 3km from Yangshuo welcomes you to "shoot a gun in this beautiful place it makes you in madness happy", but far more interesting are the **Black Buddha New Water Caves**, accessed down a 500-metre easterly track just short of Moon Hill. Discovered only in 1991, aside from the usual rock forms there's an underground river, fossils and bats. Another 3km along the same track are the equally imposing **Black Dragon Caves**, where you take a boat, then have to wade and stagger through the largest regional caverns yet discovered to a fifteen-metre subterranean waterfall and swimming holes inhabited by blind fish. Both sets of caves cost about ¥40 for a three- or four-hour flashlight tour; come prepared to get wet.

Moon Hill itself (¥3) requires forty minutes of effort to ascend a stone staircase rising through bamboo and brambles to the summit. A beautiful sight, the hill is named after a crescent-shaped hole that pierces the peak. Views from the top are breathtaking, with the whole of the Li River valley spread out before you, fields cut into uneven chequers by rice and vegetable plots.

Longsheng, Sanjiang and on to Guizhou

A hundred kilometres northwest of Guilin the road winds steeply through some of the finest stands of mountain bamboo you're ever likely to see, and enters the southern limit of a fascinating ethnic **autonomous region**. With a superbly rich landscape as a backdrop, it's simple to hop on local transport from the county towns of **Longsheng** and **Sanjiang** and head off to tour the predominantly **Dong** villages, experiencing first-hand life in a corner of rural China that seemingly remains little affected by the modern world. Day trips abound, but, with five days or so to spare, you can push right through the mountainous Dong heartlands northwest of Sanjiang into Guizhou Province, a fabulous journey which takes you to the area around **Kaili**, similarly central to the Miao people.

Longsheng and beyond

LONGSHENG sits on the torrential **Rongshui River**, known for the tiny quantities of alluvial **gold** found in its tributaries which still entice the occasional Chinese dreamer up into the hills with shovels and pans. It's also a clandestine marketplace for those interestingly shaped rocks which end up in miniature gardens and bonsai pots throughout the land. Judging by the number of weekend pavement stalls, nobody really cares that trade in these is, ridiculously, illegal.

The town itself is unattractive, but it makes a convenient base. Turn right out of the bus station and it's a short walk to the comforting "English Spoken" sign outside the *Riverside Hotel* (②), a cheap, friendly place run by an English teacher. Past here you reach a **bridge** across to the centre and numerous places to eat, while 5km in the opposite direction along the Sanjiang road is a well-advertised "typical" **Dong village**, really just a tower and bridge built recently for tourists in the Dong style.

The best idea, though, is to explore the rest of the county, scattered with farming communities. An hour to the southeast is **LONGJI** village, where there are two basic wooden **guesthouses** and the most extraordinarily extreme **rice terracing** that exists in China: whole ranges of hills, steep-sided and closely packed, have been carved over centuries of backbreaking effort to resemble the literal form of a contour map. **Huaping Primeval Forest** is another beauty spot, a couple of hours to the southwest of Longsheng via the village of **SANMEN**. North is some genuine Dong architecture at **PINGSI**, on the way through to the remote **Nanshan** area, domain of the pastoral **Yao**. Some Yao still hunt for a living, and more aspiring locals in town depict them as rustic savages, happy to own just a gun and a knife. There are at least daily minibuses from Longsheng to Longji, Sanmen and Pingsi, but check at the *Riverside Hotel* for their exact frequencies.

Sanjiang and around

Two-and-a-half hours west of Longsheng the bus crosses a high stone bridge over the Rongshui and clatters into the main street at **SANJIANG**, the desperately untidy capital of **Sanjiang Dong Autonomous County**. Sanjiang's main attraction is the Dong themselves. Already you'll have passed their villages along the roadside, and in the marketplaces here you'll come across these neat, indigo-clad people, renowned for their unique wooden houses, towers and bridges which dot the countryside hereabouts. It's well worth lingering out in the country around Sanjiang, moving short distances between villages with the help of minibuses and converted tractors known

LONGSHENG, SANJIANG AND ON TO GUIZHOU		
Baxie	八协	*bāxié*
Chankou	产口	*chǎnkǒu*
Chengyang	程阳	*chéngyáng*
Congjiang	丛江	*cóng jiāng*
Diping	地坪	*dìpíng*
Dudong	独峒	*dúdòng*
Fulu	富禄	*fúlù*
Heli	和里	*hélǐ*
Hualian	华联	*huálián*
Liping	黎平	*lí píng*
Longji	龙脊	*lóngjǐ*
Huaping Primeval Forest	花坪原始森林	*huāpíng yuánshǐ sēnlín*
Longsheng	龙胜	*lóngshèng*
Mapang	马胖	*mǎpàng*
Mengjiang	孟江	*mèngjiāng*
Nanshan	南山	*nánshān*
Pingsi	平寺	*píngsì*
Rongjiang	榕江	*róng jiāng*
Sanjiang	三江	*sānjiāng*
Baihuo Zhaodaisuo	百货招待所	*bǎihuò zhāodàisuǒ*
Sanjiang Government Guesthouse	三江人民政府招待所	*sānjiāng rénmín zhèngfǔ zhāodàisuǒ*
Wind and Rain Bridge Travel Service	风雨桥旅行社	*fēng yǔ qiáo lǚ xíngshè*
Sanmen	三门	*sānmén*
Tongle	同乐	*tónglè*
Zhaoxing	肇兴	*zhào xīng*

locally as "Dong taxis". There's a scattering of simple hostels and places to eat, and locals will sometimes offer accommodation and food – hotpots, **oil tea** and home-made spirits – though it's polite to offer payment in these circumstances. **Language** can be problematic, as almost nobody speaks *putonghua*; people are, however, generally very friendly.

In Sanjiang itself, the cheapest **place to stay** is just across from the bus station at the *Baihuo Zhaodaisuo* (①), above the department store, or follow the road up the hill behind the bus station for the *Sanjiang Government Guesthouse*, whose self-contained doubles and good **restaurant** make it a fine alternative (②–③). Just at the foot of the hill is the *Wind and Rain Bridge Travel Service* (☎0772/8613369, fax 8612896), a particularly helpful and conscientious source of **information** as the manager, Daniel Hou, is fluent in both English and the Dong dialect. They'll also be glad to advise on local transport for travelling right on up to Kaili in Guizhou Province; otherwise give serious thought to their ¥500 full-day tour of just about every important village in the vicinity.

Chengyang

Eighteen kilometres north of Sanjiang is **CHENGYANG**. Buses heading up to **Linqi** pass through, making a stop at the end of the **Chengyang wind and rain bridge**. There are many of these bridges, or *fengyu qiao*, in the region, but Chengyang's is the finest and most elaborate of them all. Raised in 1916, five solid stone piers support an equal number of graceful pavilions linked by covered walkways, entirely built from pegged cedar – the Dong proudly point out that not one nail was used in the bridge's construction. Cool and airy in summer, and protected from downpours, *fengyu qiao* are perfect places to sit around and gossip, though they once served a religious purpose, too, and other examples have little shrines grimed with incense smoke in their halfway alcoves. The shrine on Chengyang's is vacant as the bridge is a protected cultural relic and no fire is allowed.

Buses back to Sanjiang pass by until mid-afternoon, but the village is an ideal place to spend a bit longer investigating **Dong crafts**. The *Chengyang National Hostel* (dorms and rooms ②), a traditional wooden building with simple facilities and nice staff, will gladly put you up for the night. Women hawk pieces of embroidery, cotton blankets boldly patterned in black and white, and the curiously shiny blue-black Dong jackets, dyed indigo and varnished in egg-white as a protection against mosquitoes. The village is a pretty collection of two- and three-storeyed **wooden houses** set around a green lagoon. The main beams are often contorted and the rest of the building follows suit.

The Dong are not great believers in stone or concrete, as traditional wooden houses can more easily be extended or even shifted as necessary. Fire is a major concern, though, and throughout the year each family takes turns to guard the village from this hazard. At the centre of Chengyang is a **drum tower** which, like the wind and rain bridges, are synonymous with the Dong. These multi-storeyed wooden pagodas were once lookout posts when the country was at war, the drums inside beaten to rouse the village; today people gather here for meetings and entertainment. Wander out to the fields and you'll see creaky black **waterwheels** wonderfully made from plaited bamboo, somehow patiently managing to supply the irrigation canals despite dribbling out most of their water in the process.

Mapang and the Meng River region

Feasible as a day trip from Sanjiang, **MAPANG** lies some 30km north of town via **Bajiang**, and features a huge drum tower with an unusually broad rectangular base. The most interesting corner of this land, however, lies northwest across the mountains from Bajiang along the **Meng River**, which ultimately runs down from the north to Chankou on the Sanjiang road (see below). The bus from Sanjiang to **Dudong** crosses these ranges, emerging 33km away above a deep valley containing the tiny, dark-roofed village of **ZHUOLONG**, where Deng Xiaoping rested up during the Long March. There are two drum towers here, but press on a couple of kilometres north to **BAXIE**, whose bright green and yellow bridge was built in 1980 (purists might notice a few nails in the decking). The cobbled village square in front of Baxie's drum tower also has a small stage carved with monkeys and lions for festival performances. The oldest surviving bridge, built in 1861, is in the next village north, **HUALIAN**, after which comes a unique two-tier example at the village of **BATUAN**, with one lane for people and one for animals. This bridge still has its shrine, a cupboard with a bearded god on a stone slab, and, at the far end, a path leads along the riverbank to where tall trees shade a small new temple.

After a night in Dudong, take the **Tongle** bus back past all these places as far as **MENGJIANG**, an interesting village only a few kilometres south of Zhuolong. Mengjiang is half Miao, half Dong, each community settled on opposite banks of the river. After generations of fighting over land, their leaders became reconciled in the 1940s, and together built the traditionally designed **Nationality Union Bridge** across the divide. Today it's hard to distinguish between the two peoples, as both dress similarly – women wearing heavy metal earrings or a piece of white cord through the lobe – though the only drum tower is on the Dong side. It's a great place to wander between the large houses and out into the fields, and tractors can be hired for the run down to **TONGLE**. Here you'll find a store, hostel and an early-morning minibus for the ninety-minute ride back to Sanjiang.

Into Guizhou: Sanjiang to Kaili

While the roads west of Sanjiang hardly swarm with tourists, an increasing trickle of travellers rave about the countryside and the people they have encountered in the 200km between here and the Miao stronghold of **Kaili** in Guizhou Province. A daily bus runs from Sanjiang to the border hamlet of **Fulu**, with a variety of short-range transport options from here to the town of **Rongjiang**, from where there's regular scheduled traffic up to Kaili. As with villages around Sanjiang, accommodation is in a scattering of basic hostels along the way. Though distances between places are not huge, some villages are connected only on a daily basis; miss the bus and you'll have to stay overnight. Three days is a likely minimum for the trip, though five would be more realistic and it is, anyway, not a journey to be hurried.

About 20km west from Sanjiang, the area around **HELI** sports a semi-ruined, white-washed **Buddhist monastery** next to three wind and rain bridges, and a further two drum towers in a nearby village – another possible day trip from town. A farther 10km brings you to the junction with the road from Dudong and Tongle at the town of **CHANKOU**, a smattering of modern concrete-and-tile buildings with a huge **banyan tree**, social focus for villages right across tropical Asia, and a lovely stretch of unpolluted river.

Four hours west of Chankou is the Guangxi–Guizhou border hamlet of **FULU**, known for its **firecracker festival** on the third day of the third lunar month. You can catch a **boat** west from here to **Congjiang** along the **Duliu River** (6–8hr; ¥6) – indeed, you may have to if heavy rain has washed the roads out – or cross the border and continue north to **DIPING**, which sports a good Dong bridge and two drum towers. The best of these, however, lie an hour or so beyond at **ZHAOXING**, a wonderful place with a small hotel and **five drum towers**, each built by separate clans. Three hours more brings you to **CONGJIANG**, a relatively large town on the Duliu River; and a farther six hours beyond is **RONGJIANG**. There's a hostel here, a good Sunday market where you can watch local villagers bargaining the last mao out of a deal, and an elaborate, triple-towered wind-and-rain bridge, nicely maintained. Northeast is **LIPING** (150km), famous as the place where the Long Marchers made up their minds to storm Zunyi, or you can continue a farther six hours northwest from Rongjiang to Kaili. For more about Kaili and the Miao, see p.697–703.

Wuzhou

WUZHOU, 220km southeast of Guilin, is an increasingly modern, prosperous trading city and river port, its fragmentary colonial architecture a reminder of foreign influence during the late nineteenth century when British steamers puffed down the **Xi River** to Guangzhou and Hong Kong. Today these have been replaced with faster domestic ferries and hovercraft, but the river remains a major transport artery – so much so that Wuzhou has never been linked to the national rail network – and most foreign visitors still arrive or depart along it. Lured by the prospects of Guilin, Yangshuo or Guangzhou, few leave time between connections to have a look around, but Wuzhou is an interesting place; eminently Chinese, comfortably sized and a fine introduction to the interior of the People's Republic.

The City

The city occupies high ground either side of the **Gui River** at the point where it descends from the north into the much larger Xi River. Once you've got your bearings, you can comfortably walk around all of Wuzhou in a day, and the backstreets make for a particularly atmospheric stroll.

There's a small **shipyard** putting together wooden sampans and motorized junks laid out on the mudflats on the eastern edge of town, but daily life in Wuzhou is best experienced at its many **markets**, the largest of which fills the streets north of Xijiang Yi Lu. It's all here: dried and fresh food by the sackful or slab, goldfish and songbirds of all descriptions, an army of cobblers, key cutters and watch repairmen, pots of ancient-looking bonsai, and a few half-hearted "antique" stalls that nobody seems to take seriously. On Sunday mornings the crowds are medieval in their intensity, though everything is unusually clean and organized, and prices clearly marked – even if they turn out to be merely a starting point in negotiations.

From the market area, head up Nanhuan Lu and turn right until you come to the Zhongshan Lu junction, where a shady fig tree overhangs a tiny triangle of green, a meeting point for the city's domino and chess players. Ten minutes north is **Zhongshan Park**, a leafy hill top covered in well-established, relaxing ornamental gardens. There's a funfair at the entrance, including a pedal-powered elevated monorail running between gaps in the trees, and steps ascending past ponds and flowerbeds to the well-preserved 1928 exterior of the **Sun Yatsen Memorial Hall**. Carry on through to the park's north gates and you'll find, almost directly opposite, an alleyway winding around the hill to **Xiji Si**, the Western Bamboo Temple, whose yellow, fortress-like walls and green-tiled roof stand proudly above the city. Restored in the 1980s and run by a handful of nuns who go about their devotions with quiet enthusiasm, the necessarily cramped halls are steeply stacked up the slope, and contain wooden Buddhist statues and a decent **vegetarian restaurant**, open for an hour or two around noon.

Wuzhou Snake Farm

One of the world's largest **snake farms** is about 1.5km northeast of downtown Wuzhou along **Shigu Lu**, and if you're curious to know why the southern Chinese eat, pickle and milk these creatures so enthusiastically, it's open every day to visitors 9am–4pm (¥4). After being shown a video of the hapless reptiles goaded into action against collectors, there's a rather better tour round the cages to meet some of the charismatic inmates – banded kraits, cobras, leaf-nosed vipers – all fanged but handled with shocking abandon by the English-speaking tour guide. The non-venomous common rat snake is said to taste the best, while the preparation of a really fine anti-arthritic **snake wine** requires a tree snake, rat snake and cobra to be steeped in rice spirits for a year; the shop sells various by-products. It's probably best to visit in summer, when the farm is up to its half-million capacity, as during the winter stocks can get low and the inhabitants are very sluggish.

Practicalities

Wuzhou occupies the Xi River's north bank, the city centre bounded to the west by the **Gui River**, which descends from the north into the Xi, and to the north by the heights of Zhongshan Park. The main streets are **Xi Jiang Lu**, which follows the river; **Nanhuan Lu** and **Fumin Lu**, which together run east for 1.5km through the centre

---

WUZHOU

Wuzhou	梧州	*wúzhōu*
Guijiang Bridge	桂江一桥	*guìjiāng yīqiáo*
Hebin Park	河滨公园	*hébīn gōngyuán*
Hovercraft dock	汽垫船港	*qìdiàn chuán gǎng*
Wuzhou Snake Farm	梧州蛇仓	*wúzhōu shécāng*
Xi Jiang ferry	西江渡船	*xījiāng dùchuán*
Xijin Si	西禁寺	*xījìn sì*
Zhongshan Park	中山公园	*zhōngshān gōngyuán*
ACCOMMODATION		
Beishan	北山饭店	*běishān fànfdiàn*
Erqing Zonghe Da Lou	二轻综合大楼	*èrqīng zōnghé dàlóu*
Hebin	河滨饭店	*hébīn fàndiàn*
Wuzhou	梧州大酒店	*wúzhōu dàjiǔdiàn*
Yuanjiang	鸳江酒店	*yuānjiāng jiǔdiàn*

from the **Guijiang Bridge**; and **Zhongshan Lu**, which runs 1km north between Xi Jiang Lu and the Nanhuan Lu–Fumin Lu intersection.

The **hovercraft from Hong Kong** arrives on alternate days below **Hebin Park**, west of the centre over the Guijiang Bridge, and departs at 8am the following morning. The two **Xi River ferry docks** are down on Xijiang Lu, 500m apart, with daily departures downstream to Guangzhou and also west towards Guiping, Liuzhou and Nanning (destinations in this direction are affected by the seasonal river level). **Tickets** for ferries and the hovercraft can be bought at the docks or from agencies nearby, and most accommodation can make bookings too, for a fee. Wuzhou's overflowing **long-distance bus station** is at the junction of Xijiang Lu and Zhongshan Lu, handling traffic to Yangshuo and Guilin, Guiping, Nanning and Guangzhou. **Taxis and cycle-rickshaws** haunt arrival points and bus #3 runs from the long-distance bus station up Zhongshan Lu, turns west down Nanhuan Lu and over the Guijiang Bridge past the northern end of Hebin Park.

The *Wuzhou Hotel*'s **bank** handles foreign transactions Monday–Friday 9–11.30am and 1–5pm, as does the *Bank of China* on Danan Lu, which runs west off Zhongshan Lu and parallel with Nanhuan Lu and Xijiang Lu. The **post office**, with IDD telephones, is on Nanhuan Lu itself (main counter daily 8am–9pm, but customs inspections for parcels only function 9am–5.30pm). There are **pharmacies** and an acupuncture clinic (with an English sign) along Dazhong Lu, which runs north off Nanhuan Lu from opposite the post office; the **People's General Hostpital** (Renmin Yiyuan) is just west of Zhongshan Park on Jianshe Lu.

Accommodation

Beishan, 12 Beihuan Lu (☎0774/2822151 or 2822241, fax 2826202). Flustered staff and an excellent restaurant front this comfortably average mid-range hotel, the destination of most tour groups. Small, self-contained double rooms. ⑤.

Erqing Zhonghe Da Luo, Dazhong Lu. The sign for this welcoming, basic hostel is in Chinese characters only. ②.

Hebin, Daxue Lu (☎0774/3823410). Smart but reasonably priced affair overlooking the river near the hovercraft terminal. There's a highly recommended seafood restaurant here, and two-, three- and four-bed rooms are on offer. Bus #3 stops outside. ②.

Wuzhou, Xijiang Er Lu (☎0774/2822193 or 2827135). The city's best-appointed hotel, with its own *Bank of China* for visiting business folk. The restaurant is good but, along with their lobby coffee shop, very expensive. Bus #3 terminates outside. ④.

Yuanjiang, 11 Xijiang Yi Lu (☎0774/2824918 or 2828422). Threadbare, minimally maintained hotel awaiting refurbishment. There's a reasonable dining hall, and the mercenary manageress speaks good English. On the route of bus #6 west along Xijiang Yi Lu. Dorms ②, rooms ③.

Eating and drinking

Wuzhou deals entirely in **Cantonese food**, with plenty of fresh fish and vegetables, and cake shops selling custard tarts and roast pork buns. There are cheap places to eat serving dumplings, noodle soups and small pots all through the centre; in addition to the following, check hotel listings for more restaurants. The best place for **dim sum** overlooks the river on Xijiang Yi Lu opposite the *Yuanjiang Hotel* – the perfect place to spend a Sunday morning with relaxing views, hectic company, a wonderful choice of snacks and hospitable staff.

Café Canadian, due north of the post office on Dazhong Lu. A tiny cake shop with real bread, croissants, meringues, chocolate-dipped biscuits and percolated coffee. Unbelievable.

Dajing Jiujia, Nanhuan Lu, across from the post office. A cheap canteen with a moderately priced upstairs restaurant serving "smorgasbord" lunchtime hotpots and a Cantonese menu.

Xinguangwei Fandian, Fumin Lu, just east of the Zhongshan Lu intersection. Noodle and cake shop on the ground floor, and a good morning *dim sum* hall and restaurant on the second floor.

Xinlong Men, Fumin Lu. Very smart, popular place to dine, and prices are lower than the decor suggests.

Xiji Si (Western Bamboo Temple), Zhongshan Park. An inexpensive vegetarian restaurant with a limited English menu, strict enough not to even imitate meat dishes: plenty of undisguised mushrooms, bamboo shoots and tofu.

Guiping, Jintian and Liuzhou

Most visitors make use of the Xi River only between Wuzhou and Guangzhou, though this is in fact just a tiny section of a waterway which, under various names, cuts west right across central Guangxi and well into Yunnan. Approaching **Guiping**, 200km west of Wuzhou, it runs faster and deeper, dividing into the Qian River which heads north as the Liu River to rail junctions at **Liuzhou**, while the Yu River branches down towards **Nanning**. Though variable water levels and increasing siltation have seen roads replacing river transport along much of its length, ferries are a fine way to see the area. Otherwise you can get into the region less romantically, but much faster, by bus from Wuzhou or train from Guilin or Nanning.

The countryside here doesn't look too badly off today, but during the 1840s southwest China was destitute, wracked by famine and the raising of new taxes to pay off indemnities levied by Britain following the Opium War. Rebellion flared across the region, channelled by anti-dynastic societies such as the **Tiandi Hui** (Heaven and Earth Society, later known as *Sanho* or Triads), which led a prolonged revolt in the Guangxi–Hunan border regions from 1847. Nothing, however, touched on the scale of the subsequent **Taiping Uprising**, a movement which started at the village of **Jintian** near Guiping, and ultimately involved millions of participants and saw the foundation of a rebel capital at Nanjing, in Jiangsu Province (see p.384). More recently, a moral famine during the 1960s saw the region involved in one of the more shocking episodes of China's recent history – see the "Cultural cannibalism" box, p.680.

Guiping and Jintian

Though set at the junction of two major rivers, **GUIPING** is slightly disappointing; just an ordinary small Chinese town, a thirteen-hour ferry cruise west from Wuzhou, with a little industry and a lot of agriculture. Typically, a long flight of stairs scales the bank from the Xi River dock to the **ferry ticket office** for Nanning, Wuzhou and Guangzhou; Liuzhou traffic leaves from the Qianjiang dock in the north of town. Coming out of the ferry terminal, head west for twenty minutes down **Dacheng Lu** to Guiping's centre. Here you'll find the town's **accommodation**: the big and functional *Guiping Zhaodaisuo* (④), and cleaner *Guiping Binguan* (④). Farther west again is the **bus station**, with connections to Jintian, Liuzhou and Wuzhou.

GUIPING, JINTIAN AND LUIZHOU		
Guiping	桂平	*guìpíng*
Jintian	金田	*jīntián*
Taiping Museum	太平博物馆	*tàipíng bówùguǎn*
Liuzhou	柳州	*liǔzhōu*
Liujiang Zhaodaisuo	柳江招待所	*liǔjiāng zhāodàisuǒ*
Liusi Park	柳寺公园	*liǔsì gōngyuán*
Liuzhou Fandian	柳州饭店	*liǔzhōu fàndiàn*

CULTURAL CANNIBALISM

The apparently insignificant town of **Wuxuan**, a five-hour boat ride from Guiping, is one of the poorest, most purely rural corners of southern China. It hardly seems credible that in the summer of 1968 – while students were demonstrating in Paris and the anti-war movement was at its height in Washington DC – in Wuxuan they were **eating people**. The revolting details are documented in a secret but thorough report compiled by the county government in 1987, which listed the "different forms of eating human flesh"; taboos were eroded by degrees until students ate their teachers and human flesh was being cheerfully served at banquets with wine. When news of the events reached Beijing, the army was swiftly sent in to remove Wuxuan's Red Guard factions and the **ritual cannibalism** ceased – but only after five hundred people had already been eaten. The report listed by name 27 local Party cadres who had been expelled from the Party for cannibalism, as well as a large number of peasant members, only a small proportion of whom were ever jailed. Most of the participants live and prosper in Wuxuan today.

The Chinese government has never publicly admitted that these grotesque events ever occurred, and the details first reached the outside world through the investigative efforts of the dissident writer Zheng Yi. They've since been corroborated in the book *From Cannibalism to Karaoke* by British journalist John Gittings, who visited Wuxuan in 1995 and spoke to witnesses. It's impossible to justify such madness, though these events were certainly part of the wider political conflicts which tore China apart during the Cultural Revolution, and which saw (according to the official minimum estimate) ninety thousand people killed in Guangxi alone. But, so far as is known, only in Wuxuan did this lead to the killing and eating of "class enemies". Certainly there was a tradition, in poorer parts of China, of eating people during times of famine, and so-called "revenge cannibalism" was also noted by the philosopher Menicius in the fourth century BC. Whatever the answer, an open investigation of the crimes is unlikely during the lifetime of the current regime.

The Chinese come to Guiping to see **Xi Shan**, a typical formalized sacred mountain right on the western outskirts. Far tamer than the country's great holy peaks, Xi Shan is a comfortable introduction to the Chinese obsession with landscaping natural phenomena to turn them into places of pilgrimage and weekend excursions. There are the usual temples and tea houses, neatly paved paths leading off into a forest of mambarillas and gingkoes, and a summit with hazy views of the two rivers snaking across a watery flatland to join at Guiping. **Tea** aficionados should sample the famous *Xi Shan* brand; rumour has it that temple-bought leaves are superior to anything you'll find in Guiping's markets.

Jintian

For Taiping enthusiasts, Guiping is simply a stop on the way to **JINTIAN**, about 25km and an hour by bus to the north. On arrival, get off at Jintian's south gate, then head through the stone arch and down the long road leading west. A quiet walk once you've escaped the main road, the track crosses the fertile irrigated plain towards distant blue mountains, passing clusters of mud-brick farmhouses and village ponds. After about 4km you come to a small wooded hill and the site of the former **Taiping headquarters**. A recent reconstruction of this fort houses a small **museum** with erratic opening hours (¥3), where a few period documents, rather jolly paintings and some old weapons glorify the revolutionary zeal of Taiping leader **Hong Xiuquan** and his generals. Just north is a circular grassy bank beneath the trees, marking all that remains of the original fort. As is so often the case in China, it's the effort of travel and the site associations, rather than tangible relics, which justify the journey. The last bus back to Guiping passes Jintian between 5pm and 7pm.

Liuzhou and around

Rail lines, roads and rivers from all over Guangxi and beyond converge on **LIUZHOU**, a city with morbid connotations in the Chinese mind, as its local cedar wood was once much prized for coffins. An untidy, manufacturing conglomeration between Guilin and Nanning, it doesn't have much to keep you unless you have to change transport, though the surrounding bald hills theoretically harbour settlements of ethnic Yao, Miao and others. In practice, however, these communities are well integrated into the majority Zhuang–Han populace, and it's only during festivals (dates and places can be obtained from the *CITS* in Liuzhou) that you'll see much beyond the everyday rural scenes common to all of southwestern China.

In earlier times Liuzhou itself was a posting for disgraced court officials such as **Liu Zongyuan**, who was transferred here as governor in 815 AD. His poetry, expressing the hard lot of working people, has recently become popular again, and the city's only real sight is the **temple** built in his honour in **Liusi Park**, due east of Liuzhou Square. The park is very peaceful and has some impressively large trees. Paths wind around a deep pond to Liu's tomb, a grander version of the circular cairns littering the fields out of town, and the temple itself, where there's a stone rubbing of his portrait and explanations of his various good deeds as governor.

Practicalities

The city is split in two by the **Liu River**, with all traffic arriving on the south side of the river. **Ferries** dock below the most easterly of Liuzhou's three bridges; **trains** arrive 2km away at the end of Fei'e Lu on the city's western outskirts; while **buses** terminate in between off the southern end of Longcheng Lu. Rickshaws and taxis await at all arrival points. At the junction of Longcheng Lu and Fei'e Lu you'll find a post office and clean **accommodation** at the *Yufeng Dasha* (⑤), whose good **restaurant** offers the usual Sunday *yum cha* selection. There are also plenty of cheap places to eat around the bus and train stations. Longcheng Lu continues north, crossing the river by the middle bridge and running past cheaper beds at the *Liujiang Zhaodaisuo* (①–④), on the corner of Gongyuan Lu, and up to spacious **Liuzhou Square**, abode of two mighty dragon sculptures – buses #4, #10 and #11 go this way, or it's about a twenty-minute walk. Northeast of here at the end of Youyi Lu you'll find a *CITS* office (☎0772/2825669 or 2822637) and more rooms at the *Liuzhou Fandian* (④).

Nanning and beyond

Founded during the Yuan dynasty, **NANNING** was only a medium-sized market town until European traders opened a river route from Wuzhou in the early twentieth century, starting a period of rapid growth which saw the city supplanting Guilin as the provincial capital. Largely untouched by the civil war and Japanese invasion, it became a centre of supply and command during the **Vietnam War**, when the Nanning–Hanoi rail line was used to transport arms shipments via the border town of Pingxiang, 160km away. Nanning saw particularly vicious street fighting after these weapons were looted by rival Red Guard factions during the Cultural Revolution. The military returned for a decade when China and Vietnam came to blows in 1979, but with the resumption of cross-border traffic in the 1990s the city looks set to capitalize on future trade agreements with its neighbour.

The **telephone code** for Nanning is ☎0771

NANNING AND BEYOND

Nanning	南宁	*nánníng*

ACCOMMODATION

Airways	民航饭店	*mínháng fàndiàn*
Majestic	明园酒店	*míngyuán jiǔdiàn*
Nanning	南宁宾馆	*nánníng bīnguǎn*
Yongjiang	邕江宾馆	*yōngjiāng bīnguǎn*

THE CITY

Renmin Park	人民公园	*rénmín gōngyuán*
Nanhu Park	南湖公园	*nánhú gōngyuán*
Provincial Museum	省博物馆	*shěng bówùguǎn*

RESTAURANTS

Muslim Restaurant	回人饭店	*húirén fàndiàn*
Nanhu Park Fish Restaurant	南湖公园海鲜饭几	*nánhú gōngyuán hǎixiān fàndiàn*

BEYOND NANNING

Beihai	北海	*běihǎi*
Beihai Binguan	北海宾馆	*běihǎi bīnguǎn*
Haiyun Binguan	海运宾馆	*hǎiyùn bīnguǎn*
Hua Shan	花山	*huā shān*
Panlong	攀龙	*pānlóng*
Longrui Nature Reserve	陇瑞自然保护区	*lóngruì zìrán bǎohùqū*
Pingxiang	凭祥	*píngxiáng*
Tuolong	驮龙	*tuólóng*
Ningming	宁明	*níngmíng*
Yiling	伊岭	*yīlíng*

Aside from a certain boom-town atmosphere and the occasional signs of hasty construction, there's little evidence of this history, but the **open border with Vietnam** means that Nanning is the first – or final – taste of China for an increasing number of independent travellers. While not somewhere to get wildly enthusiastic about, the city at least has plenty of good food, a **museum** strong on regional archeology, placid parks and a nearby cave and mountain for day trips. Heading farther south, there's regular transport to the Vietnamese border past the **Zuo River**, where cliffs were vividly marked two millennia ago by the ancestors of the Zhuang people. There are equally good connections southeast to **Beihai**, former colonial port and back door to Hainan Island.

Orientation, arrival, city transport and accommodation

Well over 5km across, with its downtown area concentrated on the northern bank of the **Yong River**, **Nanning** is a blandly user-friendly city, its streets dusty, hot and planted with exotic trees. The bulk of the city's accommodation and attractions are in the vicinity of **Chaoyang Lu**, Nanning's main thoroughfare, which runs for 2km due north through the city centre from a complicated riverside traffic intersection associated with the **Yongjiang Bridge**. Roughly parallel with Chaoyang Lu but somewhat shorter, easterly **Xinmin Lu** cuts through the more modern part of town, linked to Chaoyang Lu by, amongst others, **Minzhu Lu**, **Minsheng Lu** and **Minzu Dadao**.

Train and **long-distance bus stations** are within 100m of each other at Chaoyang Lu's northern end, where you'll also end up if you caught the *CAAC* bus (¥10) from the **airport**, 35km southwest of Nanning – taking a taxi costs around ¥100. In the city itself, a **taxi** trip shouldn't cost more than ¥15, and Chaoyang Lu is covered along its length by **city buses** #2 and #6.

Accommodation

Airways, Chaoyang Lu, between the bus and train station. Looks a little dingy but in fact is comfortable and ruthlessly clean. All rooms have their own showers and toilets, and the attached restaurant is very reasonable. ②.

Hostels There are at least two rock-bottom lodgings opposite the train station at the top end of Chaoyang Lu, both well looked after and busy. Triples, doubles and dorm beds on offer. ③.

Majestic, 38 Xinmin Lu (☎2830808, fax 2830811); bus #7 from the train station. Part of a chain of exclusive hotels owned by an Overseas Chinese management: immaculate, self-contained, seamlessly run and with more places to eat than the rest of town combined. ⑧.

Milky Way, 84 Chaoyang Lu (☎2828223). Good-value mid-range hotel, with polite staff. ⑤.

Nanning, Minsheng Lu (☎2824720); bus #8 from the train station. A huge, anonymous concrete and glass box capable of swallowing thousands of Chinese tourists and conference delegates; staff seem as lost as the guests. ⑦.

Yongjiang, 41 Jiangbin Dong Lu (☎2808123, fax 2800535). Just off the southern end of Chaoyang Lu, this luxurious hotel on the river has a musical lobby fountain, coloured mood lighting everywhere and six restaurants. The cheaper rooms in the old wing are fairly worn. ⑤–⑧.

The City

To get the feel of Nanning's bustle, try wandering around the crowded markets and narrow lanes either west or southeast of Chaoyang Lu among the last remnants of the city's colonial architecture. Along with clothes, chickens, ducks, turtles and frogs, there's a mouthwatering variety of perfumed **tropical fruit**, and the city has some of China's best **longan** (a bit like a spherical lychee). **Chaoyang Lu** itself is mostly modern, full of late-opening department stores colourfully lit up with fairy lights at night, and with bus shelters creatively modelled along Dong architectural lines. At the station end is a small creek which unfortunately smells like an open sewer, but there's a nicer spot halfway along at the corner of Renmin Dong Lu, where there's a **minibus rank** for countryside excursions, and a small patch of green used by *tai ji* enthusiasts in the morning.

DAY TRIPS FROM THE CITY

A number of places around Nanning can be visited as day or overnight trips. *CITS* organizes tours, and there's regular transport from the long-distance bus station and minibus rank at the Chaoyang Lu–Renmin Dong Lu junction. **Yiling Dong**, a cavern 25km to the northwest, near the village of **YILING**, is the closest, worth seeing if you're keen on caves. Over 1km long, it's not as spectacular as Guilin's but is every bit as garishly lit. On a different tack, **Daming Shan**, a 1200-metre peak covered in cliffs, primeval vegetation and, usually, thick cloud, is a superb place to stretch your legs. It's about 100km due north of Nanning via the town of **WUMING**, where you'll probably need to stay the night. Wuming also has some hot spas, though these have been funnelled into uninspiring concrete pools.

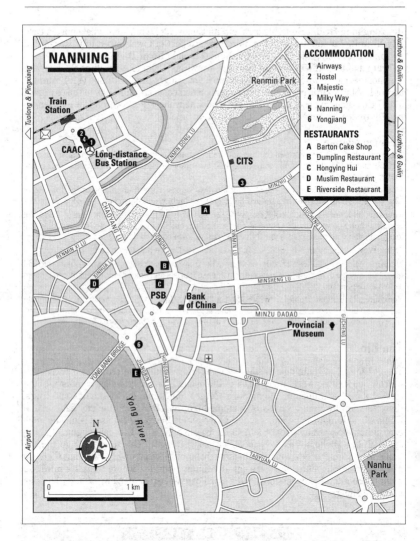

Tuolong & Pingxiang

Liuzhou & Guilin

Liuzhou & Guilin

Airport

NANNING

Renmin Park

Train Station

CAAC

Long-distance Bus Station

CITS

ACCOMMODATION
1 Airways
2 Hostel
3 Majestic
4 Milky Way
5 Nanning
6 Yongjiang

RESTAURANTS
A Barton Cake Shop
B Dumpling Restaurant
C Hongying Hui
D Muslim Restaurant
E Riverside Restaurant

PSB

Bank of China

Provincial Museum

Nanhu Park

Yong River

N

0   1 km

Better still is **Renmin Park**, a couple of square kilometres of lawns, gardens and water about a twenty-minute walk east of the train station on Renmin Dong Lu. Stone causeways zigzag across the lake between islets inhabited by willows and chess players. The paths are lined with jackfruit trees and the hills planted with tall cedars, while the tropical plants garden has a medicinal herb plot and a carefully constructed jungle of giant "elephant-ear" taro, bird nest ferns and cycads. A few kilometres southwest at the #2 bus terminus, **Nanhu Park** is worth a look during the annual fifth-month **dragon-boat festivals** (usually early June), when a quarter of a million people turn up to watch this colourful and thoroughly joyful event. At other times the park is simply a peaceful retreat, a huge, broad stretch of canal crossed by a white humpbacked bridge.

The Provincial Museum

Essential viewing for anyone heading southwest to the Zuo River, the **Provincial Museum** on Minzu Dadao (bus #6 from Chaoyang Lu; daily 8.30–11.30am & 2.30–5pm; ¥2) provides an insight into the enigmatic **Dongson culture**. Sophisticated metal-workers, the Dongson flourished over two thousand years ago in the Guangxi–Yunnan–Vietnam border area, and their works were ultimately traded as far afield as Burma and Indonesia. The characteristic Dongson artefact is a narrow-waisted **bronze drum**, and scores have been excavated across the region. Cast by a complicated double-mould process, they are finely chased with lively designs of birds, mythical animals, cattle, dancers and stars. Those from Guangxi often incorporate small human and **frog** figurines sitting on the rim (suitably for a drum, frogs are associated with the thunder god in Zhuang mythology) and are noted for their large size, a feature caused by competition between ruling families. Exactly how they originated is not known but, according to a Ming historian, the drums became a symbol of power: "*Those who possess bronze drums are chieftains, and the masses obey them; those who have two or three drums can style themselves king.*" Drums were cast locally right up until the late Qing period and their ceremonial use survives among remote groups of Zhao, Yi, Miao and Yao in China, and on the eastern Indonesian island of Alor.

The museum has about a dozen well-preserved Han-dynasty examples standing up to a metre high, excavated 120km east of the capital near Guixian and, along with a wooden coffin, closer in at Yongning. Other things to absorb are copies of the Zuo River paintings and the endless cases of more modern **ethnic clothing**, musical instruments, theatre masks and puppets. The museum grounds are nice, too, with bamboo and palms growing between full-sized wooden buildings in regional architectural styles: a Zhuang rural theatre, Dong bridge and Miao houses, which are all put to good use by Nanning's various communities during festivals.

Eating and drinking

In addition to the following places to eat, just about every downtown corner has somewhere to **snack**, whether serving steamers of small, soft *baozi*, hotpots, cakes or a seasonal choice of fresh fruit. At night, **Zhongshan Lu** is the most popular place for **street stalls** serving quick-fried shrimps, grilled chicken wings, steamed packets of lotus-wrapped *zongzi* with deliciously unusual fillings (a mix of pork, beans and sometimes shredded coconut), dog hotpot and plates of juicy snails.

The hotels also have **restaurants**, but for something a little different, try the riverside effort, 100m down from the Yongjiang Bridge on the north bank. Stairs lead down to waterfront hotpot tables under an open-sided awning with night views of the bridge. Meals are expensive considering the simple arrangements, but it's a nice place just to sit over a pot of tea and a plate of fruit. For **yum cha** and light Chinese meals, there's an excellent place two minutes east of the *Nanning Hotel* on Gonghe Lu. What look like temple gates front this large, busy and friendly establishment, where you can choose from a wide range of dumplings, spiced noodles, cold meats and soups. Everything is on display, so just point if you can't ask.

Barton, Minzhu Lu. Extremely popular bread shop where you'll have to join the afternoon crowds pushing to buy fresh rolls, breadsticks and buns. The adjacent restaurant has set meals for ¥40 per person.

Hongying Hui, Minsheng Lu. Roughly opposite the *Nanning Hotel*, this is the best in a group of inexpensive restaurants here serving Cantonese stir-fries, roast duck and chicken. They also have tasty fish casseroles and rice claypots at lunchtime.

Muslim, Xinhua Lu. Barely furnished and often virtually empty, but the food is fine (though meat is sometimes gristly) and very cheap – try the red-cooked lamb.

Nanhu Park Fish Restaurant, on the south bank of Nanhu Park. Long famous, the food makes up for the concrete decor and rickety plastic tables. As always with fish restaurants, fix prices first.

Listings

Airlines *CAAC*, 82 Chaoyang Lu (daily 8–11.30am & 2.30–5.30pm; ☎2814159).

Banks and exchange *Bank of China*, Minzu Dadao (foreign exchange Mon–Fri 8–11.30am & 2.30–5.30pm). Flasher hotels will cash travellers' cheques for their guests.

Buses There are daily services to all major towns in Guangxi, and also direct services to Guangzhou and Kunming – sleeper buses also run some of the longer routes. Luxury affairs to Guangzhou leave from outside the train station in the late afternoons; buy tickets for these at the stalls opposite.

Hospital The City First Hospital (Shiyi Yiyuan) is southeast of the centre along Qixing Lu.

PSB On the roundabout at the south end of Chaoyang Lu. Foreign Affairs Department (Mon–Fri 9am–noon & 2–5pm).

Pharmacies There's a large pharmacy on Chaoyang Lu next to the bus station.

Post and telephones The main post office is at the train station (8am–6pm).

Shopping The *Nanning Antique Store*, next to the museum, has a very touristy selection of batiks, teapots, chops, paintings and jade, on two floors. If you're heading up towards a northern winter, there's an army surplus store on Gucheng Lu selling heavy coats, blankets and truncheons.

Trains Window #6 is for foreigners, with the main line heading up into central and western China via Liuzhou. Sleeper tickets are usually easy enough to obtain as long as you give the usual three days' notice, but you may well find the staff failing to book you a berth for your entire journey – this isn't deliberate obstruction; they simply are unable to reserve them on certain services beyond Changsha and Guiyang. Heading southwest to the Zuo River and the Vietnamese border, there's seldom any trouble getting a soft seat on the sole daily double-decker train to Pingxiang.

Travel agents *CITS*, 40 Xinmin Lu (daily 8am–noon & 3–5.30pm; ☎2816197, fax 2804105 or 2801041). Reserved, but helpful if prompted, the staff speak good English, arrange local tours and Zuo River trips and – with a week's notice – can obtain Vietnamese visas for the Pingxiang crossing (¥400).

On to Vietnam: the Zuo River and Pingxiang

The **Vietnamese border** crossing lies about 170km southwest of Nanning, a smooth five-hour ride on the daily early-morning double-decker train to **Pingxiang** – coming the other way, the train returns to Nanning in the early afternoon. The border aside, it's worth heading down this way to catch a boat along the **Zuo River** to **Panlong** village, an area with superb karst scenery, prehistoric **rock paintings** and a remote nature reserve. There are no roads to Panlong, and the only access is by boat from **TUO-LONG** (Ningming station), a horrible place about an hour short of Pingxiang. Theoretically, Chinese speakers could go to Tuolong and negotiate a vessel there, but as this might leave you stranded in Tuolong for the night it's much better to take Nanning's *CITS* two-day **tour**. While seemingly expensive at ¥400 per person, this includes all transport, meals, accommodation and an English-speaking guide – far better value than the similarly priced Li River cruise from Guilin.

Along the Zuo

It's a placid ninety-minute journey upstream along the Zuo from Tuolong to Panlong – buffalo wallow in the shallows, people fish from wooden rafts and tend family plots, and the banks are thick with bamboo and spindly branched kapok trees, flowering red in

April. Mountains spring up after a while, flat-faced and sheer by the river, and it's here you'll see the the first painted figures, red, stick-like markings, though most are very faded or smeared with age. **PANLONG** comprises a fun group of large wooden **hotel** buildings, loosely based on traditional ethnic designs, offering good meals and three-and four-bed rooms as well as doubles (③). From the hotel, a rough path leads up to the **Longrui Nature Reserve** in the hills above. An incredible place whose rough tracks see almost no visitors, Lungrui's densely vegetated peaks are squeezed together to form an isolated, elevated valley inhabited by China's last four hundred **white leaf monkeys**, and is well worth setting a day aside for.

The most extensive series of **rock paintings** are another forty minutes upstream at **Hua Shan**, a steep cliff overhanging the river. Nobody has worked out a definitive interpretation, or even how they were painted in such inaccessible positions, but Hua Shan's 1900 sharply posed figures have been dated to two thousand years ago and include drummers and dancers, dogs and cattle, a dragon-boat race, men with arms bent upwards, a "king" with a sword, and just two women, long-haired and pregnant. The designs are similar to those decorating the Dongson drums and there's little doubt that they were produced by the same culture, currently identified with the Zhuang people. A few Bronze-Age weapons have also been found here.

Into Vietnam

PINGXIANG is a bustling border town with plenty of food and expensive accommodation, and frequent minibuses out to the **two crossings** 15km away, only one of which is for Westerners (*youyi guan*). Get out of the minibus at the obvious junction, where motorbike-taxis are waiting to carry you the last kilometre or so to customs. Assuming you have a valid visa for this crossing, entering Vietnam shouldn't be too complicated, though the border guards examine all documents minutely. The Vietnamese town on the far side is **Dong Dang**, where there's further transport 5km south to the town of **Lang Son**, the rail head for Hanoi.

Beihai

BEIHAI, a pleasant town situated on the **Beibu Gulf** on the south coast of Guangxi, was adopted from neighbouring Guangdong Province in 1954 so that Guangxi would have a viable seaport. It got going in the late nineteenth century when the British signed the **Yantai Trading Agreement** with the Qing court, and grew swiftly as Europeans set up schools, churches, offices and banks. A tiring half-day bus journey from Nanning or an overnight ride on the **ferry from Hainan Island**, Beihai's importance as a trading centre for the southwest is now being realized, and the city is expanding again.

While the only reason to visit Beihai is in transit to Hainan, there's no problem filling in time between connections. The older part of town is along the seafront and on **Zhongshan Lu**, where mouldering colonial buildings add to the sleepily tropical atmosphere. It's best in the morning when the fresh catches arrive, and there's a fabulous **fish market** here selling every type and part of sea life imaginable. Hop on a #2 bus heading west down **Haijiao Lu** from the end of Zhongshan Lu and you end up a couple of kilometres away at the **harbour**, packed with scores of wooden-hulled junks, motorized and sailless, but otherwise traditionally designed. Most of the vessels here belong to the community of thirteen thousand refugee "**boat people**" living in the adjacent UN-sponsored village. They were victims of an attempt by the Vietnamese authorities to remove ethnic Chinese from their territory, a major cause of the 1979 war between China and Vietnam. China's reciprocal group are the **Jing**, ethnic Vietnamese who settled islands off Beihai in the sixteenth century.

Practicalities

A hugely sprawling grid of right-angled streets, Beihai is so positioned on a broad peninsula that the main seafront, unexpectedly enough given its location on China's southern coast, is to the north of town. The centre is marked by a **roundabout** at the intersection of north–south orientated **Sichuan Lu**, and **Beibuwan Lu**, which crosses it at right angles. **Arrival points** are widely spread across the city from here: the **ferry port** is 2km west along the seafront on Haijiao Lu, connected to the roundabout by a #2 bus; while the **long-distance bus station** is 1.5km east of the roundabout on Beibuwan Lu (bus #7).

For **accommodation**, try the upmarket and fairly modern *Hualian Binguan* (☎0779/2024467; ⑥), about 100m west of the roundabout on Beibuwan Lu; the rather more atmospheric colonial-style *Beihai Binguan* (☎0779/2020131; ⑤–⑧), a short walk west of the bus station; or the more down-to-earth *Haiyun Binguan* (②–④), on Sichuan Lu just north of the roundabout on the west side of the road. There are **places to eat** either at the hotels or nearby, and some cheap, hole-in-the-wall **seafood** restaurants beside the ferry terminal.

GUIZHOU

A traditional saying describes **Guizhou** as a land where there are "no three days without rain, no three kilometres without a mountain, and no three coins in any pocket". Superficially this is accurate. Despite a generally mild climate and growing industrial output, Guizhou has the highest rainfall in China and a poverty ensured by over eighty percent of its land being covered in untillable mountains or leached limestone soils. Perhaps this is why tourists scorn the province, but it is, in fact, a spectacular and fascinating place, largely because of its undesirable reputation.

Chinese influence was established here around 100 BC, when farms and garrisoned towns spread along the relatively accessible and fertile **Wu River**, a tributary of the Yangzi which settlers followed down from southern Sichuan. Beyond the river valley, however, the Han encountered fierce opposition from the indigenous peoples they were displacing, and the empire eventually contented itself less with occupying the province than with extracting a nominal tribute from local chieftains. Full subjugation came as late as the Qing era, after war and population growth in central China saw waves of immigrants flooding into Guizhou's northeast. The tribes rose in rebellion but were overwhelmed, and finally retreated into remote mountain areas. Consisting of about thirty nationalities and forming a quarter of Guizhou's population, they remain there today as farmers and woodworkers: principally the **Miao** and **Dong** in the eastern highlands; the **Bouyei**, a Thai people, in the humid south; and the **Yi** and Muslim **Hui** over on western Guizhou's high, cool plateaus. Generally welcoming to outsiders, they indulge in a huge number of **festivals**, some of which attract tens of thousands of participants and are worth any effort to experience. There is also an accomplished artistic tradition to investigate, notably some unusual architecture and exquisite **textiles**, one of which, the **Anshun batik**, is rapidly becoming a trendy fashion statement in southern China.

Poor though it is, Guizhou's countryside nonetheless hides some wonderful **scenery**. Even the innocuous provincial capital, **Guiyang**, has some good parks and beauty spots, and its central location makes it a comfortable base from which to plan a thorough exploration of the province. Just a couple of hours away to the west, **Anshun** marks the starting point for easy excursions out to the mighty **Huangguoshu waterfall** and **Zhijin Caves**, and, rather more distant, the lake of **Caohai Hu** on the Yunnanese border, a paradise for ornithologists and others seeking China's wilder corners. Elsewhere, the north of the province is steeped in Long March lore surrounding the historic city of **Zunyi**, while those on a cultural quest will relish the villages, traditions and festivals of the **Miao and Dong Autonomous Region**, reached through the easterly town of **Kaili**. Finally, away on the northeastern border with Hunan, is the town of **Tongren** and Guizhou's own holy mountain, **Fanjing Shan**, whose cripplingly tiring stone staircases rise into an impressively undeveloped nature reserve for the endangered golden monkey.

Guiyang and around

GUIYANG lies on a rare patch of flat ground right in the middle of the province it governs, encircled by a range of hills which stopped the city expanding several years ago. Established as a capital during the Ming dynasty, Guiyang received little attention until the early 1950s, when the new Communist government repaid minority groups for their tacit help during the civil war by filling the centre with heavy monuments and expanding the provincial rail line to make the city a hub for western China. This encouraged investment, though wealth seems to have come recently and unexpectedly, accelerating Guiyang from a quiet conglomerate of tumbledown town houses to an uneven spread of building sites sprouting twentieth-century highrises, with little in the way of an intermediate phase. The result may not be one of China's most beautiful cities, but Guiyang is at least intriguing – it's almost impossible to predict whether the next corner will bring you to a Communist hall, a new shopping centre, or an ancient block of wobbly-roofed houses surrounded by market stalls.

Most visitors simply spend one night here en route to Anshun and the Huangguoshu Falls, but anyone planning to range farther afield in the province could do worse than seek out Guiyang's unusually informative *CITS* office (see p.694 for details), and spend a couple of hours browsing through the **Provincial Museum**'s

GUIYANG AND AROUND		
Guiyang	贵阳	*guìyáng*
ACCOMMODATION		
Guizhou Park	贵州公园饭店	*guìzhōu gōngyuán fàndiàn*
Gymnasium	体育宾馆	*tǐyù bīnguǎn*
Jinqiao	金桥饭店	*jīnqiáo fàndiàn*
Jinzhu	金筑大酒店	*jīnzhù dàjiǔdiàn*
Tongda	通达饭店	*tōngdá fàndiàn*
THE CITY		
Qianming Si	黔明寺	*qiánmíng sì*
Jiaxiu Lou	甲秀楼	*jiǎxiù lóu*
Provincial Museum	省博物馆	*shěng bówùguǎn*
Qianling Shan	黔灵山	*qiánglíng shān*
Hongfu Si	弘福寺	*hōngfú sì*
RESTAURANTS		
Guiyang Fandian	贵阳饭店	*guìyáng fàndiàn*
Jue Yuan Vegetarian Restaurant	觉园素餐馆	*jué yuán sù cài guǎn*

collection. There's also a scattering of **temples and pavilions** and several spacious **parks** set within easy distance of the centre.

Orientation, arrival, city transport and accommodation

Central Guiyang is a concentrated couple of square kilometres around the narrow **Nanming River**, with the downtown area focused along **Zhonghua Lu**, orientated north–south through the city.

Leizhuang **airport** is 35km distant, and arrivals are loaded on to a bus and ferried from here to the *CAAC* offices on **Zunyi Lu**; this runs southwest off Zhonghua Lu, over the river, and terminates 1km from the centre at the **train station**. Outside is a square brimming with shifty-looking hawkers selling anything from snacks and **maps** to pieces of mummified monkey. You'll also find the occasional **taxi** (¥15 will get you anywhere within the city limits), and a crowd of **buses** here. For central Guiyang hop on bus #1 or #2 from outside the *Tongda Hotel* on the right of the station, which both follow a circular tour of the city.

On the far side of the square is Guiyang's **alternative long-distance bus station**, whose services include departures to Kaili and day trips to Huangguoshu. The **main long-distance bus station** is on the #1 and #2 bus route on the western side of the city, where Yan'an Xi Lu meets Zhaoshan Lu. Official services seem to have been upstaged by freelance operators who have turned the forecourt into a circus of manoeuvring vehicles.

Accommodation

Guizhou Park, 66 Beijing Lu (☎6822888 or 6823888, fax 6824397). Sleek and overpriced three-star highrise at the north end of town, with surprisingly mediocre restaurants. On the route of buses #1 and #2. ⑦–⑧.

Gymnasium, corner of Jiefang and Zunyi Lu (☎5821777 ext 3112). Just 500m from the train station, the hotel is on the left side of the entrance to the sports ground. Welcoming and spacious, but definitely tatty. ④.

Jinqiao, 34 Ruijin Zhong Lu (☎5825310). A bulging, peeling 1959 exterior immediately sets this hotel apart from the more modern buildings nearby, though it's in a comfortable state of repair inside, with a good restaurant and helpful staff. Take bus #2 from the train station or #1 from the long-distance bus stations. There are carpeted four-bed dorms with shared bathrooms as well as double rooms. Dorms ②, rooms ③.

Jinzhu, 2 Yan'an Dong Lu (☎/fax 6825888). Downtown international-style effort, with several good Chinese restaurants, gift shops, and the only easy place in town to change money. Bus #17 from the train station goes past and #3 from the bus station terminates almost opposite. ⑥–⑧.

Tongda, Zunyi Lu (☎5820567, fax 5820566). Right next to the train station, this brand-new 23-storey "business" hotel has a disco and revolving restaurant decorated with Renaissance nudes. The rooms are a little small and ordinary, but everything works. Rooms are priced according to the view. ⑤–⑦.

The City and around

Though Guiyang is well suited to pedestrians, it's easy to tour the city by bus, getting off from time to time to explore various sights. Bus #1 runs from the train station north through the city along Zunyi Lu and Zhonghua Lu, turning west along Beijing Lu and back to the train station down Ruijin Lu, while bus #2 does the same route in reverse. You'd need a good half-day to see everything, though the bus itself completes the circuit in under an hour.

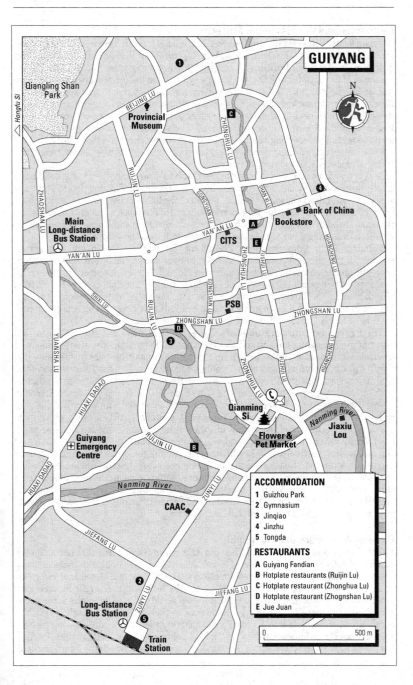

GUIYANG

Qianling Shan Park

◁ Hongfu Si

Provincial Museum

Main Long-distance Bus Station

CITS

Bank of China Bookstore

PSB

Qianming Si

Jiaxiu Lou

Flower & Pet Market

Guiyang Emergency Centre

CAAC

Long-distance Bus Station

Train Station

N

BEIJING LU
ZHAOSHAN LU
ZHONGHUA LU
RUIJIN LU
GONGYUAN LU
YAN'AN LU
YAN'AN LU
SHIXI LU
RUIJIN LU
GONGYUAN LU
ZHONGHUA LU
FUSHUI LU
SHAN XI LU
HUANCHENG LU
ZHONGSHAN LU
ZHONGSHAN LU
ZHONGHUA LU
FUSHUI LU
HUANCHENG LU
YUANSHA LU
HUAXI DADAO
RUIJIN LU
ZUNYI LU
Nanming River
Nanming River
HUAXI DADAO
JIEFANG LU
ZUNYI LU
JIEFANG LU
ZUNYI LU

ACCOMMODATION
1 Guizhou Park
2 Gymnasium
3 Jinqiao
4 Jinzhu
5 Tongda

RESTAURANTS
A Guiyang Fandian
B Hotplate restaurants (Ruijin Lu)
C Hotplate restaurant (Zhonghua Lu)
D Hotplate restaurant (Zhognshan Lu)
E Jue Juan

0   500 m

Downtown and the Provincial Museum

Guiyang's most interesting quarter lies immediately north of the Nanming River, around where Zunyi Lu and Zhonghua Lu meet at the enormous **Post and Telecommunications building**. A bit grubby today, thirty years ago this would have been one of the grander buildings in town, a symbol that the formerly isolated province had at last been connected to the outside world. Across the road, Guiyang's lively **flower and pet market** sets up in an alleyway among a knot of old houses leading down to the river, selling an extraordinary mix of puppies, salamanders, terrapins and bug-eyed goldfish to the young and curious. The street runs on past groups of older men thoughtfully inspecting rows of songbirds in wicker cages to **Qianming Si**, where a few monks practise their devotions among some peaceful Ming-dynasty courts and halls – a pleasant spot to linger over a cup of tea.

A short walk east of here along the river, **Jiaxiu Lou** is another Ming building, a small, three-storeyed pavilion reached over the Bridge of Floating Jade. The most attractive example of Guiyang's original architecture (others lurk around the city, awaiting probable demolition), the pavilion was built in 1587 to inspire students taking imperial examinations. Though it has been carefully restored and houses some antique scrolls, and carvings, garbage in the river tends to lessen the spectacle.

Running north from the river, **Zhonghua Lu** is Guiyang's major commercial precinct, a frenetically crowded area of department stores and shops selling clothes, domestic appliances, sound systems and more. Initially narrow, it opens up at the crossroads with Zhongshan Lu, then carries on up to the city's formal centre, **Da Shizi**, a roundabout at the intersection with Yan'an Lu. Yan'an Lu cuts through Guiyang's busiest **market area**, though you'll need to head off down the side streets to appreciate this – Shanxi Lu is locally renowned for its snack stalls.

The **Provincial Museum** (officially Tues–Sun 9–11.30am & 1–4pm; ¥8) lies 1km north of the Zhonghua Lu–Yan'an Lu intersection on Beijing Lu. The front looks like a truck depot, but once you've woken up the surprised staff upstairs in the left wing, they'll unlock everything and escort you around. Even if you can't understand their commentary, the dusty collection of **Miao and Bouyei** artefacts is enough to sharpen your interest in the rest of the province. There are costumes brightly embroidered in primary colours on black, and complex headpieces decorated with silver bells, leaves, and animal and dragon embossing. The **Dong**, southeastern Guizhou's other main minority, are represented by models of their distinctive dark wooden houses, multi-level drum towers and covered bridges. Scattered round the walls are photos of Guizhou's many **festivals**, with key items, such as a dragon-boat prow hung with duck carcasses, drums and *lusheng* gourd pipes, arranged nearby. At the end is a brief effort to flesh out the province's fragmentary **history**, with one room devoted to a Han-era stone sarcophagus and brocade wrappings, while another displays a fifty-thousand-year-old skull fragment found near Anshun and a strange Shang bronze model of a tortoise being ridden by a big-nosed, tall-hatted figure.

Qianling Shan Park and Hongfu Si

About 1km west of the Provincial Museum, **Qianling Shan Park** (¥1) is a delightful handful of hills right on the edge of town, thickly forested enough to harbour some colourful birdlife and noisy groups of monkeys. There's a popular **funfair** at the gates, and a large **lake** with paddle boats to rent, but the highlight is **Hongfu Si**, an important Buddhist monastery. Check out the infra-red aerial photo of the paths at the gates, then follow the steps for the thirty-minute walk to the very top of Qiangling Hill. You come out of the woods into a courtyard containing the ornamental, four-metre-high **Fahua Pagoda** and a screen showing Buddha being washed at birth by nine dragons. On the right is a **bell tower** with a five-hundred-year-old bell, which the guardian monk might invite you to strike. The missing chunk was removed during the Cultural Revolution, when the temple was completely destroyed. Now it's the headquarters for Guizhou's Buddhist Association, being rebuilt to hold a comprehensive collection of Buddhist texts. There are some older sculptures among the glossy paintwork of recent restorations, including a 32-armed Guanyin, each palm displaying an eye, facing a rather benevolent-looking King of Hell. There's a tea house too, and a good **vegetarian restaurant** open at lunchtime.

Eating and drinking

Except for its predilection for dog meat, Guizhou's cuisine goes unnoticed in China, but the capital has some good places to eat, nonetheless. Nondescript **restaurants** on Zhonghua Zhong Lu and intersecting streets all serve staples such as hot-spiced chicken, pork, vegetables and dumplings through the day.

Summer street stalls sell thin **crepes**, which you stuff from a selection of pickled and fresh vegetables to resemble an uncooked spring roll – they sound bland, but make a nice change from fried food. The **"volcano" hotplate** is more fun: thin sections of meat or vegetables are cooked against a hollow iron cone with the top snipped off fixed over a heat source (charcoal versions spit sparks like the real thing, gas ones are less impressive). These are offered at several restaurants, the most central of which is on the south side of Zhongshan Xi Lu, just east of the Ruijin Zhong Lu intersection.

Guiyang's **hotpots**, a winter favourite but always available, consist of a table centred round a bubbling pot of chicken stock, in which you cook your own food after buying individual plates of vegetables or various meats. Shan Xi Lu, which runs north off the eastern end of Yan'an Lu, has the best hotpot stalls; there are slightly more formal affairs overlooking the Nanming River by the bridge on Ruijin Nan Lu. **Dog** is another winter dish, usually stir-fried, soya-braised, or part of a hotpot. If you're worried about being served this delicacy by accident, say *"wo buchi gourou"* (I don't eat dog).

Restaurants

Guiyang Fandian, southeast corner of the Zhonghua Lu–Yan'an Lu roundabout. A huge state-operated affair and nothing extraordinary, but the food isn't bad at all – reasonably priced and tasty.

Hongfu Si. Excellent vegetarian temple restaurant in Qianling Shan Park; open daily for lunch only.

Jinqiao Fandian, 34 Ruijin Zhong Lu. Second-floor hotel restaurant serving local food at cheap prices. It's usually packed with tour groups, but is willing to serve single foreigners.

Jinzhu Dajiudian, 2 Yan'an Dong Lu. Good, upmarket hotel fare specializing in regional Chinese food, mostly Beijing and Cantonese.

Jue Yuan, 51 Fushui Bei Lu. Another vegetarian restaurant in the town centre – the food is simple and filling.

CANINE CUISINE

Dog meat is widely appreciated not only in Guizhou, Guangxi and Guangdong, but also in nearby culturally connected countries such as Indonesia and Vietnam. Possibly the habit originated in China and was spread through Southeast Asia by tribal migrations. Wherever the practice began, the meat is universally considered to be warming in cold weather and an aid to male virility. As a regional speciality, Chinese tourists to Guizhou generally make a point of trying a dog dish, but for Westerners, eating dog can be a touchy subject. Some find it almost akin to cannibalism, while others are discouraged by the way restaurants display bisected hindquarters in the window, or soaking in a bucket of water on the floor.

Listings

Airlines *CAAC*, 170 Zunyi Lu (daily 8.30am–5.30pm; ☎5823000).

Banks and exchange The main *Bank of China* is on the southeastern side of the Yan'an Lu–Zhonghua Lu roundabout (foreign exchange Mon–Fri 9–11.30am & 1.30–5pm), but it often makes a fuss over travellers' cheques. There's an easier exchange service at the *Jinzhu Hotel*.

Bookshops The *Foreign Language Bookstore* on Yan'an Dong Lu, despite the name, has little in English beyond dictionaries and technical manuals.

Buses A quiet ticket office hides behind the temple-like exterior of the long-distance bus station at the junction of Yan'an Xi Lu and Zhaoshan Lu, with direct departures at least as far as Zunyi, Chongqing, Nanning, Kunming, Anshun and Kaili. Alternatively, you can get to Zunyi, Kaili and Anshun on services departing from the west side of the train station square – just find the ranks of buses and shout your destination – where early-morning minibuses also leave for day trips to the Huangguoshu Falls area.

Hospital Guiyang Emergency Centre (Guiyang Shi Jijiu Zhan) is on Huaxi Dadao on Guiyang's western side.

PSB The foreign affairs department is in the city centre on Zhongshan Xi Lu.

Post office Guiyang's Post and Telecommunications building is at the southern end of Zhonghua Nan Lu (daily 8.30am–5pm), handling all mail, parcels and post restante. For letters only, there's a sub-branch on the northeast corner of the Yan'an Lu–Zhonghua Lu roundabout.

Shopping Check out the art store with brushes, chops, ink stones and paintings on Gongyuan Bei Lu, an old street running north off Zhongshan Xi Lu. For ethnic ware – Anshun batiks, Miao clothing and silver – try the Hongfu Si gift shop in Qiangling Shan Park.

Telephones Housed with the post office in the grand building on Zhonghua Nan Lu. There are also telephones in the sub post office (see above).

Trains Routes out of Guiyang head east into central China and beyond via Kaili; north to Zunyi and Chongqing; west to Kunming via Anshun and Lupanshui; and south to Liuzhou and other destinations in Guangxi. The timetables at the station are difficult to follow, but the staff are helpful. Foreigners have to buy all sleeper tickets after 8.30am at the first-class waiting room upstairs.

Travel agents *CITS* is at 20 Yan'an Zhong Lu (Mon–Sat 8.30–11am & 1–5pm; ☎5825873 or 5861909; fax 5823095). An exceptionally helpful office with youthful, polylingual staff who will happily sit down with you and a cup of tea and discuss any aspect of the province. They can also make ticket and tour bookings.

Zunyi and the north

Northern Guizhou is mountainous and undeveloped, the two main attractions being the historic city of **Zunyi** and an only recently accessible pocket of natural forest and waterfalls around the town of **Chishui**. Zunyi is on the main road and rail routes between Guiyang and Chongqing in Sichuan, while Chishui lies off the beaten track, right up along the Sichuanese border in the northwestern corner of the province.

Zunyi and around

Some 170km north of Guiyang, **ZUNYI** is high and refreshingly cool in summer, a pleasant city despite visible industrialization, and site of one of the most important events in China's modern history. The Communist army arrived here on their **Long March** in January 1935, in disarray after months on the run and having suffered two defeats in their attempts to join up with sympathetic forces in Hunan. Having taken the city by surprise, the leadership convened the **Zunyi Conference**, a decision which was to alter the entire purpose of the March and see Mao Zedong emerge as political head of the Communist Party. Previously, the Party had been led by Russian Comintern advisers, who modelled their strategies on urban-based uprisings among the proletariat. Mao felt that China's revolution could only succeed by mobilizing the peasantry, and that the Communist forces should base themselves in the countryside to do this. His opinions carried the day, saving the Red Army from certain annihilation at the hands of the Guomindang and, though its conquest still lay fifteen years away, marking the Communists' first step towards Beijing. (For more on the Long March, see p.492.)

The City

The obvious first place to head for is the **Site of the Zunyi Conference** (daily 8.30am–5pm; ¥10), an attractive and rather ornate European-style house over the river on Ziyin Lu. There's a powerful feeling that this is where history was made, though there's little to see beyond a tour of the rooms – including the leaders' quarters and, of course, the Conference Hall – all of which have been restored to their 1930s condition and filled with period furniture. For more in the way of information, head a short way back east to the nineteenth-century **French Catholic Church**, now a **Long March Museum** (daily 8.30am–5pm; ¥3). Photos and maps illustrate the Communist peregrinations through Guizhou; they actually circled around to the north and captured the city again shortly after leaving it, completely disorganizing local Guomindang militias. One thing discreetly absent is any mention of the actual manoeuvrings behind Mao's appropriation of the political scene, and doubtless there never will be. For a last taste of Red history, cross back over the river and up into **Fenghuang Shan Park**, where the **Monument to the Red Army Martyrs** rises to the west, a reminder that of the eighty thousand soldiers who started the Long March, only twenty thousand arrived at the Communists' final base in Shaanxi. However, it's grand rather than maudlin, with four huge red sandstone busts (vaguely resembling Lenin) supporting a floating, circular wall and a pillar topped with the Communist hammer and sickle.

Practicalities

Zunyi is set on the slopes below **Fenghuang Shan** (Phoenix Hill), with the centre concentrated along the **Xiang River**, which winds along the western side of the hill. The **bus and train stations** are on **Beijing Lu**, about 2.5km northeast of the centre off **Zhonghua Lu**, which runs down into town, turns north as Zhongshan Lu, then crosses west over the river to the main revolutionary sites.

ZUNYI AND THE NORTH		
Zunyi	遵义	*zūnyì*
Long March Museum	长征博物馆	*chángzhēng bówùguǎn*
Monument to the Red Army Martyrs	红军烈士纪念坤	*hóngjūn lièshì jìniànbēi*
Site of the Zunyi Conference	遵义会议址	*zūnyì huìyì zhǐ*
ACCOMMODATION		
Beijing Lu Luguan	北京路旅馆	*běijīnglù lǚguǎn*
Xiangshan Binguan	香山宾馆	*xiāng shān bīnguǎn*
Zunyi Binguan	遵义宾馆	*zūnyì bīnguǎn*
BEYOND ZUNYI		
Chishui	赤水	*chì shuǐ*
Shizhangdong Falls	十丈洞瀑布	*shízhàngdòng pùbù*
Maotai	茅台	*máotái*
Sidonggou	四洞沟	*sìdònggōu*
Yang Can Mu	杨粲墓	*yángcàn mù*

Very basic **accommodation** (which might not accept foreigners) is offered at the *Beijing Lu Luguan* and *Qianbei Luguan*, opposite each other near the bus and train stations on Beijing Lu. It's better to hop on a minibus into town, where there should be no trouble getting a comfortable room at either the conveniently placed *Zunyi Binguan* (☎0852/222911; ③–⑤), at the junction of Xima Lu and Shilong Lu, or the *Xiangshan Binguan* (☎0852/225754; ⑤–⑦), slightly south on Wanli Lu. If you're looking for somewhere cheaper, there's a clean hostel just up the street leading due east from the bridge, though again, they'll probably wave you away. Hotels can provide **meals**, as can the *Zunyi Binguan*, overlooking the river on the west side of the bridge.

Yang Can Mu

Zunyi has a much longer history than the city's monuments admit. Twenty-five kilometres south of town in the village of **HUANGFENZUI** is **Yang Can Mu**, the immaculately preserved resting place of the Song-dynasty official **Yang Can** and his wife. The Yang family ruled this region for over four hundred years, with Can holding the hereditary position of deputy defence minister until his death around 1250. The sandstone tomb is decorated with some superb relief carvings of both mythical and real beasts, plants and guardian figures – check out the character emerging from between the dragon gate at the mouth of the tomb chamber.

Minibuses run out here from the city centre (¥5); ask at the *Xiangshan Binguan*'s reception desk for details.

On to Sichuan: Chishui and Maotai

The rail line continues smoothly north of Zunyi into Sichuan, but there's also a roundabout route out of the province by road, taking in Guizhou's second most impressive waterfalls. On the Sichuanese border some 250–350km from Zunyi, depending on the route you take, the town of **CHISHUI** is bang in the middle of a fabulous area of subtropical **forests** harbouring monkeys and groves of three-metre-high tree ferns. Two patches are accessible: the best is 40km due south of Chishui where the Fengxi River steps out at the **Shizhangdong Falls**, similar to the more famous Huangguoshu (see p.708) except for the refreshing lack of tourists. Closer to town, about 15km to the southwest, **Sidonggou** is simply a good place to explore the vegetation along well-formed paths, though there's an impressive twin waterfall here, too. As ever, things are at their best after rain in late summer.

There are two routes to Chishui from Zunyi, either of which means at least a good eight hours or more on daily buses. The shorter one initially follows the rail line north to **Tongzi** (where the Red Army cut through the Luoshan Pass and down to Zunyi) and then bends northwest to Chishui via the similarly named town of **Xishui**. The other circles west via the small town of **MAOTAI**, set in a valley along the Chishui River. Nobody seems to know exactly how long spirits have been produced here, but the town's **sorghum distillery** has made the *Moutai* brand a household word across China, and the white porcelain bottle with its red diagonal stripe is essential at any banquet. While it certainly numbs your nervous system in a slow, creeping manner which takes you unawares, Westerners tend to be of the opinion that it's pretty indistinguishable from the contents of a cigarette lighter.

As the area has only recently been opened to tourism, once again it's best to check practical details with Guiyang's *CITS*, though there's definitely **accommodation** in Chishui and, at least during the summer tourist season, regular minibuses run out to the sights. **Moving on**, daily buses run from Chishui to the Yangzi River port of **Luzhou** in **Sichuan** (about 120km). If the water level is high enough it's possible to pick up a **ferry** from here along the river, otherwise Luzhou is connected by road to Chongqing and Zigong (see pp.798 and 795).

Eastern Guizhou

The journey from Guiyang into **eastern Guizhou** passes through a quintessentially Asian landscape of high rolling hills cut by waterfalls and rice terraces. After a couple of hours the Bouyei stonework begins to fade out and you start to see women working in the fields, babies strapped to their backs under brightly quilted pads, and their long braided hair coiled into buns secured by fluorescent plastic combs. They are Miao, and the scene marks the border of the **Miao and Dong Autonomous Prefecture**, an intrinsically beautiful area and arguably the best place in China to meet ethnic peoples on their own terms. Miao villages around the district capital, **Kaili**, are particularly noted for their hundred or more annual **festivals**. The bigger events attract busloads of tourists, but are such exuberant social occasions that there's no sign of their cultural integrity being compromised. Beyond Kaili, adventurous visitors can head southeast on public buses to the mountainous border with Guangxi Province, where **Dong** hamlets sport their unique drum towers and bridges, or push on northeast through the pretty countryside surrounding **Zhenyuan** and the **Wuyang River** to **Tongren**, jumping-off point for the demanding hike up to cloud forests atop **Fanjing Shan**.

Even if you don't plan anything so energetic, the region is still enjoyable on a day-to-day basis, the attractive home of a friendly people who take pride in their traditions. They are, however, almost impossible to understand: modern schooling has come late to the region and while younger villagers might speak Mandarin, the older generation know only a few baffling phrases in addition to their own languages. **Travelling around**, you'll find that minibuses cover more destinations and leave more frequently than long-distance buses, but to reach remoter corners you'll probably have to aim for the nearest main-road settlement and take pot luck with tractor taxis or whatever else is available.

Kaili and the Miao

Surrounded by scores of villages and some lush countryside, **KAILI**, five hours or so from Guiyang, is a rural, easy-going focus for China's 7.5 million **Miao**, though migrations and forced resettlements since the Tang dynasty have spread their population from Sichuan right down to Hainan Island. They were formerly treated as slaves by the Han, and many of their popular heroes were rebel leaders, such as **Zhang Xiumei**, who seeded almost twenty years of insurrection against the Qing in the late nineteenth century before finally being defeated outside Kaili. His suppression left Guizhou in the desperately poor state witnessed by the Red Army sixty years later, when, understandably sympathetic with the Communist cause, the Miao were rewarded for their help by being given their autonomy. The Cultural Revolution set things back, but since the late 1980s the area has received government assistance in schooling, medical services and transport, and today there's no doubt that Miao culture is flourishing.

The Town

A small town well suited to pedestrians, Kaili is orientated around the **Beijing Lu–Zhaoshan Lu** (spelt "Shaoshan" on road signs) crossroads. Split by the crossroads into east and west sections, Beijing Lu has most of Kaili's shops and businesses, while Zhaoshan Lu extends a short way north into the older residential end of town, and south past more shops into the countryside.

To get your bearings, head up from the crossroads to the northern end of Zhaoshan Lu, turn east along **Ximen Jie**, and then follow a footpath north through the back-

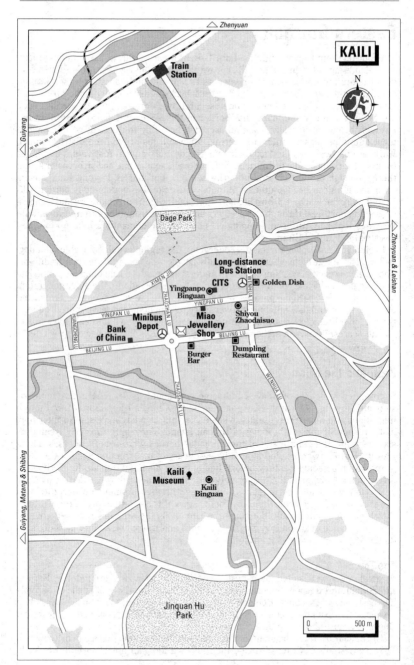

streets to **Dage Park**, a shady hill top inhabited by old men who gather to smoke and decorate the trees with their caged songbirds. There's also a **pagoda** to climb, its wooden interior home to a mix of Buddhist and Taoist statues. From here, you can see the town spreading out on to an unusually level valley (*kaili* is a Miao word roughly translating as "prepared fields"), while **Xianglu Shan** (Incense-burner Mountain) is the flat tableland rising off to the northwest, an important landmark for exploration farther afield.

Back down on Ximen Jie, head west for 500m and you'll end up at a busy **produce market** filling Huancheng Lu, active daily but packed on Sunday mornings with Miao, Yao and Dong in town to sell their wares. They also visit stalls near the Zhaoshan Lu–Beijing Lu crossroads where you may be able to pick up items of clothing and jewellery. There are also **shops** selling Miao crafts around the entrance to the *Yingpanpo Binguan* east off Zhaoshan Lu on **Yingpan Dong Lu**. They open irregularly, but some of their stock is very good – nicely embroidered jackets and full head-pieces in alloy, not silver.

Fifteen minutes south of the crossroads at the end of Zhaoshan Lu, **Kaili Museum** (¥8) is a disappointingly lifeless array of photographs, costumes and artefacts, housed in an apparently derelict building hidden behind a wall near the *Kaili Binguan* – make enough noise and the caretaker will appear with a bunch of keys. It's probably more interesting to carry on walking for another thirty minutes south of here to **Jinquan Hu Park**, where the conical wooden **Gulou drum tower** is a full-sized Dong construction painted in blue and white (for more on these, see p.675). Built for tourists in 1985 and stuck way out here, it's fascinating nonetheless, assembled without nails and sometimes serving as a meeting place for locals.

Practicalities

Most of the accommodation and places to eat are in the vicinity of the main crossroads, along with a **Bank of China** (foreign exchange Mon–Fri 8.30–11am & 1–5pm), and a **post office**. The **minibus depot** is here too, with regular shuttles to destinations as far away as Guiyang. Buses pull in a kilometre east at the **long-distance bus station** on Wenhua Bei Lu. The **train station** is about 3km by road to the north of town, and rickshaws and a minibus usually meet arrivals.

Comfortable **accommodation** is provided by the *Kaili Binguan* (☎0855/224301 or 224302; ⑤), a smart, motel-like affair 1.5km to the south of the crossroads – go to the southern end of Zhaoshan Lu, turn east, then take the first turning south and it's on your left. More convenient is the *Yingpanpo Binguan* (☎0855/223163; dorms ②, rooms ④), near the centre off Yingpan Dong Lu. The two wings are dusty but sound, and the adjacent karaoke hall is offset by a good **restaurant** and tolerant staff. Also on Yingpan Dong Lu, the bizarrely named *Shiyou Zhaodaisuo* (Crude Oil Hostel; dorms ①, rooms ②), a busy block of tiny rooms just around the corner from the bus station, is Kaili's real budget option.

The town has some good **places to eat**. For **snacks**, cake stalls around the main crossroads sell various goodies, including wafers of sweetened rice flour resembling a very dry halva. Stalls outside the bus station whip up **hotpots** and quick meals, while there's a good **dumpling house** on the south side of Beijing Dong Lu. Hole-in-the-wall joints opposite the *Yingpanpo Binguan* are the cheapest places to eat indoors (don't order any chilli dishes unless you have a cast-iron stomach), with slightly more accomplished fare across the road from the bus station at the *Golden Dish*. There's even an attempt at a Western **burger bar**, diagonally opposite the post office on Beijing Lu, serving tiny meat patties inside a giant bun.

Kaili's **CITS**, just inside the gates at the *Yingpanpo Binguan* (daily 8.30–11.30am & 2.30-6pm; ☎0855/222547 or 222506), has helpful staff who speak English, know the latest about festivals, and stock invaluable bilingual **maps** of Kaili and its environs. They're also very flexible, available as **guides** for anything from an afternoon to a fortnight (though their knowledge of local dialects is patchy), organizing **river trips** along the Wuyang River between Zhenyuan and Shibing (see p.704) and **private tours** out to nearby villages by car at around ¥400 a day. With polite prompting they'll also provide **public transport details** to budget travellers trying to do the same thing on their own.

Around Kaili

The biggest problem around Kaili is deciding where to go. There are at least twenty **Miao villages** within a couple of hours' drive of town, many of which are worth visiting depending on your specific interests. **Festivals**, of course, make the choice much easier – most take place in early spring, early summer and late autumn, when there's little to do in the fields and plenty of food to share. Totally full-on events, the bigger ones attract around fifty thousand people for four days or more of buffalo fights, dances, singing matches and horse or boat races. Others may have special displays of drum dancing, wrestling and pole climbing. Participants mostly dress in traditional, multi-coloured finery, and the action often crosses over to the spectators – foreigners are rare treats, so don't expect to be able to sit quietly on the sidelines.

If planning a trip to coincide with particular events, be careful of **dates**, as Chinese information constantly confuses lunar and Gregorian calendars – "9 February", for instance, almost invariably means "the ninth day of the second lunar month". As Miao communities tend to be self-reliant, different villages have their own festivals, or can hold the same festival on different dates, further muddling matters. The biggest events of the year are the various **Lusheng festivals**, held just about everywhere in the region and named after a long-piped gourd instrument which accompanies Miao dances; **Sisters' Meal**, the traditional time for girls to choose a partner; and the **Dragon-boat races**, held on the same day, but for a different reason, as others in China.

Though some Miao villages are interesting in themselves, outside of the festival season people will be working in the fields and smaller places may appear completely deserted. *CITS* tours aside, all the villages below are connected by at least daily bus or minibus services from Kaili, and also make fine stopovers on the way into the Rongjiang or Zhenyuan regions. Return transport can leave quite early, however, so be prepared to negotiate accommodation or hitch back if you leave things too late.

MIAO COSTUME

Separate Miao communities such as Long-horned Miao, Big Flower Miao and Black Miao are initially distinguished less by their individual customs than by their ornamentation, and perhaps this is the reason that **traditional dress** has become so distinctive. Decoration is an important aspect of life, and Miao are famous for their astonishingly detailed **embroideries**, all the more impressive for generally being stitched freehand, without patterns. Young girls start practising with sashes and dress sleeves at an early age, and the more accomplished their work, the higher their social standing. Dresses for public events such as weddings are so intricate that they take years to complete, and often become treasured heirlooms. Stylized designs of plants, animals and people are arranged into geometric patterns, with dragons a popular symbol, as are transformation motifs, such as butterflies.

Many of these themes recur in Miao **silverwork**, the most elaborate pieces again being made for wedding assemblages. Women appear at some festivals weighed down with coil necklaces, spiral earrings and huge headpieces, all of which are embossed or shaped into flowers, bells and beasts.

KAILI AND THE MIAO

Kaili	凯里	*kǎilǐ*
Dage Park	大阁公园	*dàgé gōngyuán*
Gulou drum tower	恫族鼓楼	*dòngzú gǔlóu*
Incense-burner Mountain	香炉山	*xiānglú shān*
Jinquan Hu Park	金泉湖公园	*jīnquánhú gōngyuán*
Kaili Museum	州民族博物馆	*zhōu mínzú bówùguǎn*

ACCOMMODATION

Kaili Binguan	凯里宾馆	*kǎilǐ bīnguǎn*
Yingpanpo Binguan	营盘坡宾馆	*yíngpānpō bīnguǎn*
Shiyou Zhaodaisuo	石油招待所	*shíyóu zhāodàisuǒ*

MIAO VILLAGES

Chong An	重安	*chóngān*
Fanjing Shan	梵净山	*fànjìng shān*
Heiwan	黑湾	*hēiwān*
Jiankou	剑口	*jiànkǒu*
Jinding Si	金顶寺	*jīndǐng sì*
Fanpai	反排	*fǎnpái*
Huangping	黄平	*huángpíng*
Feiyun Dong	飞云洞	*fēiyún dòng*
Langde	郎德	*lángdé*
Leishan	雷山	*léishān*
Leigong	雷公山	*léigōngshān*
Matang	麻塘	*mátáng*
Qingman	青曼	*qīngmàn*
Shibing	施秉	*shībǐng*
Renmin Binguan	人民宾馆	*rénmín bīnguǎn*
Yuntai Shan	云台山	*yúntái shān*
Shidong	施洞	*shīdòng*
Taijiang	台江	*táijiāng*
Wenchang Ge		
Tongren	铜仁	*tóngrén*
Jinjiang Binguan	锦江宾馆	*jǐnjiāng bīnguǎn*
Xijiang	西江	*xījiāng*
Zhenyuan	镇远	*zhènyuǎn*
Qinglong Dong	青龙洞	*qīnglóng dòng*
Wuyang River	舞阳河	*wǔyáng hé*
Zhouxi	舟溪	*zhōu xī*

Matang and the Gejia

MATANG is a small village 20km northwest of Kaili, home of the **Gejia**, a Miao subgroup renowned for their artistry. To get here, find a vehicle heading up to **Shibing**; the track to Matang heads off across the paddy fields from below square-topped **Xianglu Shan**, the mountain where the rebel leader Zhang Xiumei met his end at the hands of imperial troops in 1873 – there's a big festival here each August. It's a two-hundred-metre walk from the main road to the village, a completely traditional place

AROUND KAILI & ZHENYUAN

which has nonetheless become used to tourists, and you'll be mobbed on arrival by old women selling jewellery, batik and **embroidery**. Some of these pieces are very fine, others less so, and bargaining is essential. With luck, you'll also be offered a tour of the village, invited round a home, fed – pickled vegetables and hotpot, with some homemade firewater to wash things down – and asked if you'd like to see some antique wedding garments or have a young woman don full festival regalia for your camera. All this will cost, but it's offered in good humour and well worth the price if you've missed the festival season and don't have the time to travel farther afield. To move onwards from Matang, return to the main road and flag down a passing vehicle.

The Gejia are a very small group found only between Matang and Shibing, but at least two other communities are also worth visiting: **CHONG AN**, a beautiful riverside village about 50km north of Matang with the *Shiujianna* ("Susannah") guesthouse (②) and a highly recommended **market** held every fifth day; and **HUANGPING**, a large town 20km north again, known for its skilled **silversmiths** and the nearby **Feiyun Dong**, a pretty Taoist temple on the Shibing road.

To Qingman, Leishan and Guangxi

One simple trip from Kaili is out to **ZHOUXI**, an untidy but interesting collection of traditional homes and bunker-style concrete buildings about 20km southwest of Kaili on the Danzhai road, where you might see people soaking sheets in wooden vats of indigo dye. There's also a fine Sunday market where you can pick up local silk work, and a particularly big **Lusheng festival** at the end of the Spring Festival celebrations in February. Nearby **QINGMAN** village has a reputation for producing the best *lusheng* players.

A broader option, which could ultimately see you ending up 200km from Kaili over the border in Guangxi Province, starts 25km southeast of town at **LANGDE**, a big collection of traditional wooden houses, cobbles, mud and chickens surrounded by flat fields. Due east of here along a side road is **XIJIANG**, also known as the "Thousand Miao Village" and reckoned to be the largest Miao settlement in existence. Another 20km south down the main road from Langde is **LEISHAN**, a famous tea-growing region, with some superb hiking away to the east at the remote **Leigong Shan Nature Reserve** – you'll need *CITS* help to reach this.

Four hours southeast of Leishan are the fringes of a remote land of steep mountain terraces and dark wooden villages dominated by elaborately shaped towers and bridges: **Dong country**. You can see the main features in a couple of days, but with time it's very rewarding to push right through to the other side of their territory at **Sanjiang** in Guangxi Province. You'll need some patience and durability to do this, however, as roads and accommodation are basic, and bus services limited. Your first target is the town of **Rongjiang**, 100km southeast of Leishan and connected to Kaili by a direct daily bus: for more about the Dong, their architecture, and details of the trip, see pp.672–676.

Taijing and Shidong

TAIJIANG town lies 55km northeast of Kaili on the Zhenyuan road, where the **Qingshui River** becomes the setting of the biggest regional **Dragon-boat festival** in late June or early July. Typically at odds with Han traditions, this celebrates the slaying of a ferocious black dragon by a local fisherman, not the memory of Qu Yuan's suicide in 280 BC (see p.475). Taijiang also hosts a major **Sisters' Meal festival** in April/May, and is yet another good place to shop for embroideries and visit the market. On the hills behind town is the particularly beautiful **Wenchang Ge**, a recently restored Qing temple, and from here you can drop down past old wooden town houses and follow a stream into the terraced fields beyond. There's a good **restaurant** and **hostel** in Taijiang if you want to stay longer.

High in the mountains, 30km east of Taijing, the ancient village of **FANPAI** is said to be well worth visiting for its terraced fields and unusual dances, though transport out here is erratic. Easier to reach, **SHIDONG** is an unremarkable farming town another 30km north along the Zhenyuan road, which shares its festivals with Taijiang. There's plenty of attractive countryside to admire, and it might be possible to rent one of the graceful wooden boats used on the river here just to pole around between villages.

Zhenyuan and the Wuyang River

ZHENYUAN was founded as long ago as two thousand years, though today's town, occupying a constricted valley 100km northeast of Kaili on the **Wuyang River**, sprang up in the Ming dynasty to guard the trade route through to central China. It's a splendid place, with narrow streets and tall, old stone houses piled together beside an aquamarine stretch of water along which you can cruise upstream through a string of wild, verdant gorges which lie between here and the westerly town of **Shibing**.

The town itself is not much more than two streets on either side of the river. **Minibuses**, **boats** and the Guiyang–Changsha **train** arrive on the south bank near to several cheap places to **stay and eat**. Cross over the **bridge** and there's a very variable restaurant on the corner, a hostel (①) with tiny rooms and big beds up the stone flight of stairs straight ahead, and, five minutes along to the left, the **long-distance bus station**. Turn right at the bridge, however, and you can wander down to another crossing – a multiple-arch, solid stone span at least a century old – leading to **Qinglong Dong**, a strange sixteenth-century temple whose separate Taoist, Buddhist and Confucian halls appear to grow out of a cliff face overlooking Zhenyuan. The main shrine, Black

Dragon Cave, is dripping wet and scattered with idols, while a mess of vines forms a delightful curtain between the overhang and pavilions, and there are some nice views along the river of rickety sampans, children swimming and (in early June) dragon-boat rehearsals. It's also interesting to spend an hour climbing up the ridges north of town to **Feiyunyan Ge**, not so much for this temple but because on the way there's a cave inhabited by an old woman who solves people's troubles by invoking a weirdly shaped rock draped in red cloth.

To catch a **cruise boat to Shibing**, look for the *CTS* office just upstream from the main bridge on the south bank. The five-hour, one-way excursion costs about ¥140 per person, though there are shorter trips possible along the **Tiexi stream**. You may get a better deal off freelance touts in the vicinity, though there doesn't seem to be much ordinary river traffic around as locals travel by bus nowadays. Kaili's *CITS* can also organize this trip in advance for you (see p.699).

Shibing

Somewhere between a small town and large village, **SHIBING**, the terminus of the river cruise, is set in a wide, humid valley 45km west of Zhenyuan and 100km by road north of Kaili. Shibing's ramshackle wooden shacks, grey concrete mansions and small-town atmosphere are only of mild interest, but aside from the river there are hiking trails to negotiate up the wild sides of **Yuntai Shan**, a forested, isolated peak off to the north.

Buses usually set down parallel with the river somewhere along the main road, where you also hail onward traffic. The only **accommodation** in town willing to take foreigners is the *Renmin Binguan* (③) – find the side street running south from the *Agricultural Bank*, with its golden sheaf logo, on the main road, and it's about 50m down on the left. It's a clean, almost modern place, with a hard-to-find branch of the *CITS* upstairs in the block opposite the lobby entrance.

Tongren and Fanjing Shan

The only settlement of any size in far northeastern Guizhou, **TONGREN** is a small, lightly industrial city only a stone's throw from the Hunanese border. It was formerly known simply as a source of mercury, but in 1981 a nature reserve was formalized at nearby **Fanjing Shan**, a Buddhist mountain long recognized for the extraordinary diversity of its plants and wildlife, and there's been a steady flow of Chinese visitors since access improved in the early 1990s. You need to be fit, but Fanjing Shan is well worth the climb; the scenery is magnificent and there's always the chance of seeing **golden monkeys**, one of China's prettiest endangered species.

Tongren is curiously isolated, and it takes the best part of a day to travel here from Zhenyuan. The Guiyang–Changsha rail line comes as close as the town of **Yuping**, 70km south, from where there are plenty of buses. Alternatively, you could travel the entire way by road from Zhenyuan, a six-hour operation involving a further change of vehicles at **Sanhui**. Hardy tourists follow up the trip to Fanjing Shan by visiting **Zhangjiajie**, over the border in Hunan (p.478). To do this, take the morning bus from Tongren to **Jishou**, from where you can catch a train on to **Dayong**, Zhangjiajie's rail head. Door-to-door it takes about eleven hours, with splendid views back off the hills into Guizhou and some interesting houses with upswept "swallow-tail" eaves along the way.

The Town

Situated on the south bank of the **Jin River**, the centre of Tongren is small and shambolic, half demolished and half rebuilt. Walk west along the river and you'll soon pass a small hill with a stone staircase leading to what might well be China's only official **Nuo temple**. Nuo is an ancient animistic religion, now watered down by Buddhist and Taoist influences but retaining something of its original form in open-air **theatre**, still held at festivals in villages around Tongren. Performing stylized fights to rhythmic drumming, dancers don grotesquely shaped **masks**, each of which is individually named and has a spirit that the wearer is constantly in danger of being overwhelmed by, unless it is propitiated with a sprinkle of chicken's blood. The number of masks owned by a troupe increases their reputation. The temple has over a hundred arranged in two halls, along with local batiks, a very tacky "Nuo" shrine, and other trappings of the religion.

Tongren's two **bus stations** are close to each other on **Jinjiang Bei Lu**, which follows the northern bank of the river. Local transport, including minibuses to Fanjing Shan, tends to use the westerly depot, set at the edge of town on a roundabout, while long-distance buses pull up 500m east of here. Both are near **bridges** across to the town centre where a five-minute wander around will uncover a **department store**, a bookshop with **map** vendors outside, and a *Bank of China* easily made nervous by travellers' cheques. **Accommodation** is all along Jinjiang Bei Lu: there's a very decent guesthouse up a side street between the stations (②); the apparently upmarket, but actually filthy *Jinjiang Binguan* (⑤), about 200m east of the long-distance bus station; and a similarly priced but better effort farther east again. All have **restaurants** in keeping with their standards, and the westerly bus depot is completely surrounded by cheap canteens and market stalls.

Fanjing Shan

It's a 75-kilometre journey by road from Tongren to **Fanjing Shan**, and you'll need to leave at first light if you want to make any sort of impression on the mountain on the first day. The summit rises to 2500m, and you should allow for one day up, one day on the top, and one day to return. The mountain is only an option for seasoned walkers, as Fanjing Shan has over seven thousand stairs, long sections of which are narrow, steep, and in a bad state of repair, and the ascent takes five hours. There's sufficient **accommodation** and **food** along the whole route, so copy the Chinese, who carry only a jar of tea with them. Summers are humid down low, but cold wind and fog often tears across the upper levels, and winters are freezing – take some warm clothing.

From Tongren, minibuses go to **JIANKOU** (2hr), a single-street town with some uppity urchins, from where jeeps and smaller minibuses bounce along the 25-kilometre dirt track leading up the valley to the mountain. Prices, speed and eventual destination of this latter stage vary according to the vehicle and disposition of the driver; ¥15 should carry you as far as the **park gates** (¥4) at **Heiwan**, a collection of basic shops, restaurants and accommodation. In 1995, the **golden monkey breeding station** here celebrated its first birth only two years after being established – a notable success with an animal whose wild population numbers only a few hundred individuals. Around 170 live on Fanjing Shan's upper reaches and it's easy to recognize their slight build, big lips, tiny nose and, in males, vivid orange-gold fur, should you be lucky enough to spot one.

A bright red earth road runs 7km from Heiwan to within thirty minutes' walk of the dreaded staircase. There's very infrequent transport along here, but it's an enjoyable walk through lowland forests of bamboo and flowering trees, clouds of butterflies and a near-vertical waterfall. At the end is **Dahe** – two tearooms where porters lounge, hoping to carry you up in a bamboo litter, a souvenir shop selling walking sticks and **maps**, and a bridge over the stream – and then you're on the lower stairs, in every respect the worst on the mountain. It's a long ninety minutes to where the steps begin following less extreme ridges, through thinner woodland and a dwarf bamboo understorey. This continues pretty well all the way, past a halfway meal shack (they'll let you sleep here if need be) to heath country, basic lodgings and restaurant at **Jinding Si**, the Golden Summit Monastery. Strangely, this tiny stone temple is nowhere near the summit, which is up another five hundred stairs to the right past some intriguingly piled rock formations. The general practice is to overnight around the temple and then climb up to watch the sunrise, but there's also a good day's hiking out to minor peaks.

Western Guizhou

Western Guizhou extends for 350km of ever more mountainous country between Guiyang and the border with neighbouring Yunnan Province. About a third of the way along on the rail line and main highway west is the Bouyei town of **Anshun** and adjacent **Huangguoshu Falls**, Guizhou's biggest natural tourist attraction and a magnet for busloads of tourists on day trips from the capital. Both the town and the falls area really deserve a longer look than this, however, as do less touted landscapes between here and the Yunnanese border. Heading in this direction, bus and trains can take you to northwesterly **Liupanshui** town, springboard for a detour through Yi, Hui and Miao settlements to a remote wildfowl sanctuary at **Caohai Hu**; the highway follows a more southerly road into Yunnan through the Yi border town of **Panxian**; while a lesser route snakes southwest from Anshun to further scenic attractions at **Xingyi**. All three of these routes ultimately lead to Kunming, Yunnan's capital.

Anshun and around

ANSHUN is an attractive country town 100km from Guiyang, established as a garrisoned outpost in Ming times to keep an eye on the empire's unruly fringes. Later a stage for merchants treading the difficult roads between central China and Yunnan, it became a centre for distributing **opium** between the 1880s and the Communist takeover, but today the emphasis is on subsistence farming, textiles and tourism, with the town acting as a base for tours to the nearby **Longgong Caves** and **Huangguoshu Falls**.

Anshun is centred around two main streets, Zhonghua Lu and Tashan Lu, and overlooked by the white **Xixiu Shan Pagoda**, a short Ming-dynasty affair currently isolated by a sea of roadworks. The maze of twisting alleys off from here are lined with dark wooden houses and packed with scenes typical of healthy rural commerce: horses hauling cartloads of coal, market crowds bargaining over bags of ducks and neat piles of fresh cabbages, shops selling cheap clothes and every imaginable plastic

---

ANSHUN BATIK

Anshun is particularly famous for its **batik** work, a tradition said to have originated over two thousand years ago when wax from a convenient beehive dribbled unnoticed over some linen awaiting dyeing. People were amazed at the resulting patterns and started creating them deliberately. In its pure form, molten wax is first applied with a copper "knife" on white cloth, most often in spirals and curves said to represent buffalo horns or liquorice plants, and in geometric designs. The cloth is simply dyed once in **indigo**, then boiled to fix the colour and remove the wax, leaving bold white patterns on a dark blue background.

Though batik is practised throughout southwestern China by Miao, Yao, and Bai people, it was Guizhou's Bouyei who cornered the commercial ethnic textile market after Anshun's **batik factory** opened in 1953. A bold venture at the time, today their products are in demand across the country, with modern multi-coloured, mass-produced designs supplementing older monochrome patterns. A dozen **shops** outside the factory on Nanhua Lu sell banners and wall hangings in various styles. Few are strictly "traditional" designs, but many have a local feel: blue monochrome portraits of Bouyei girls in bridal finery, or banners depicting stylized figures and animals from Bouyei myths. Prices are low, but bargaining is quite acceptable.

household utensil. For a specific target, try to find **Wen Miao**, a six-hundred-year-old Confucian academy with a finely restored, carved stone gateway, hidden away at the top end of town.

New arrivals are likely to find themselves 2–3km southeast of all this, either where the road from Guiyang crosses Zhonghua Lu at the **long-distance bus station**, or 500m farther south at the huge, echoing **train station**. Long-distance departures from either are best booked a day in advance, and if you have trouble try either the *CITS* at the *Minzu Binguan*, or the **CYTS**, near the station at 2 Nanhua Lu (Mon–Sat 9–11.30am & 2–5pm; ☎0853/227286, fax 227286) – they speak very little English, but do their best to help.

Accommodation is straightforward with only two places at present willing to take foreigners. The *Xixiu Shan Binguan* on Nanhua Lu (☎0853/224230; ②–④), is a hopelessly disorganized, but friendly, hotel with an inexpensive restaurant, threadbare rooms and shared bathrooms, while the more upmarket *Minzu Binguan*, on Tashan Dong Lu (☎0853/222621; ⑤–⑦), is aimed at visiting business folk. Their Muslim restaurant varies between good and dreadful, while the pick of cheaper **places to eat** are down near the bus station – staff here try to drag potential customers in off the street. **Dog** is always offered (though it's not obligatory), and the best in this line is available at *Gouzhenpeng*, a small establishment whose English sign invites you to "lunch of dog of China" – head south down Zhonghua Lu to the long-distance bus station, and the restaurant is diagonally opposite on the Guiyang road.

WESTERN GUIZHOU

Anshun	安顺	*ānshùn*
Xixiu Shan Pagoda	西秀山塔	*xīxiùshān tǎ*
Wen Miao	文庙	*wén miào*
Xixiu Shan Binguan	西秀山宾馆	*xīxiùshān bīnguǎn*
Minzu Binguan	民族宾馆	*mínzú bīnguǎn*
Batik factory	蜡染总厂	*làrǎn zǒngchǎng*
BEYOND ANSHUN		
Longgong Caves	龙宫	*lóng gōng*
Huangguoshu Falls	黄果树瀑布	*huángguǒshù pùbù*
Huangguoshu Binguan	黄果树宾馆	*huángguǒshù bīnguǎn*
THE FAR WEST		
Dafang	大方	*dà fāng*
Hundred Li Azalea Forest	百里杜鹃林带	*bǎilǐ dùjuān líndài*
Liupanshui	六盘水	*liù pán shuǐ*
Liuzhi	六枝	*liù zhī*
Panxian	盘县	*pán xiàn*
Shuicheng	水城	*shuǐ chén*
Weining	威宁	*wēi níng*
Caohai Hu	草海湖	*cǎohǎi hú*
Xingyi	兴义	*xīng yì*
Maling Canyon	马陵峡谷	*mǎlíng xiágǔ*
Panjiang Binguan	盘江宾馆	*pánjiāng bīnguǎn*
Zhijin	织金	*zhījīn*
Zhijin Caves	织金洞	*zhījīn dōng*

Longgong and Huangguoshu

The 150-kilometre round trip from Anshun out to **Longgong Caves** and **Huangguoshu Falls** is also a good opportunity to take a look at rural Guizhou. A **minibus day tour** combining the two is the easiest way to travel, and indeed the only transport option for visiting the caves. Minibuses leave from the train stations in both Guiyang and Anshun daily at around 7am. If just Huangguoshu is enough and you want to linger in the area, aim for **Huangguoshu township** at the top of the falls, which can be reached on direct minibuses from Guiyang and Anshun, or long-distance buses heading to Yunnan can drop you off on the highway nearby.

While the land around Anshun is relatively flat, the province's brittle limestone hills are never far away, and the limited spaces in between are intensely farmed by blue-skirted **Bouyei** busy planting rice or using buffalo to plough the muddy flats. Closely related to Guangxi's Zhuang nationality (see p.660), the Bouyei number 2.5 million and range throughout southwestern Guizhou, though this is their heartland. Brick kilns – so common elsewhere in rural China – are conspicuously absent from this region, as there simply isn't enough spare clay to waste on making building blocks. Instead, angular homes are skilfully constructed from stone and roofed in slate, with villages occupying wooded outcrops surrounded by neatly tended terraces.

LONGGONG CAVES

About an hour from Anshun you arrive at **Longgong Caves** (various fees totalling about ¥30), where you embark on a tin boat and drift off into the caverns. All around are creepers, shrubs and bright blossomed trees starkly positioned on rocky outcrops, many of which have been named and draped with flashing neon lights. The ride culminates at a huge revolving plastic mermaid, which lewdly sprays water from cunningly placed nozzles; beyond this there's a brief trip on foot through another cave where a trail of rock steps returns you to the start. You get over an hour in all at the caves, and there should be time to enjoy more thick vegetation and some curious rock formations on the way, before ambling back down to the bus through bamboo groves and tea stalls.

HUANGGUOSHU FALLS

After Longgong, it's a further thirty minutes to **Huangguoshu Falls** (the Yellow Fruit Tree Falls; ¥15), some 70km from Anshun on the main highway heading west to the border at Panxian. At sixty-eight metres high this may not quite rank as China's highest cataract, but in full flood after summer rains it's certainly the most spectacular, and probably the loudest – on a good day the thunder rolls way off into the distance.

The falls road loops off the highway, passing the damp but upmarket *Huangguoshu Binguan* (☎0853/225243; ④), curving around past the falls' entrance and downhill to tiny **HUANGGUOSHU** township, before bending over a bridge and back on to the highway. Just before the bridge is *Tianxing Zhoudaisuo* (①), a quiet hostel with dorm and double beds. **Minibuses** set down at the falls' entrance, where you can also pick up freelance services back to Guiyang and Anshun throughout the day. If you're continuing west to Xingyi and Kunming, catch a minibus from here 7km west to **Guanling** and look for connections there.

Despite the overcrowded paths, photo booths and insistent Bouyei trying to press their badly made trinkets on you, the falls remain a powerful sight. A staircase descends through subtropical shrubberies to the blue-green river below the falls, and the most imposing view of Huangguoshu is off to the left where the full weight of its eighty-one-metre span drops into the **Rhino Pool** – expect a good soaking from the spray. At times of low water levels it's possible to wade across here; otherwise head back to the wire **suspension bridge** downstream before ascending to the hundred-metre-long, windowed **tunnel** running behind the water curtain (¥5). Trails on the far side weave round to the hillside facing the falls for a different, far less crowded, perspective and a short walk up to the township (see below). Alternatively, downstream past the suspension bridge there's a little-used path and a **funicular railway** to the *Huangguoshu Binguan* in town.

Huangguoshu is a beautiful area, and it's difficult to do it justice in the few hours that a tour allows. When the fields are green in summer, just head straight off cross-country for a stroll among the Bouyei architecture, including stone barns, houses and tombs. For a dip, take your swimming gear a couple of kilometres upstream to **Doupotang**, a wide cascade where the river bed fragments into house-sized boulders. **Tianxing Jing** is a much gentler spot about 5km downstream with some spiky karst islands, more weird and wonderful caves on the east bank and the pretty Silver Chain Falls.

The far west

Anshun sits on the threshold of western Guizhou, with a relatively easy circuit back to Guiyang past China's most extensive cave system and a seasonal flower phenomenon, or a range of wilder routes and sights for those tackling the long journey into Yunnan Province. Either way, you'll need to be flexible as lines of communication are often restricted to narrow passes twisting between peaks and, after rain, buses are frequently unable to negotiate the minor roads out to the sights, even if nearby towns can be reached.

Zhijin and around
Three buses a day make the five-hour haul north from Anshun to **ZHIJIN**, an ancient township offering simple hostel accommodation (①) – though there are future plans for a fully-fledged guesthouse – and tours out to the subterranean splendours of **Zhijin Dong**, a ten-kilometre string of limestone caverns naturally hollowed out of hills to the northeast of town. You're issued with a hard hat on entry, then you follow the paths into the caves' awesomely scaled interior (one chamber is 173m wide, and several top 100m in height), crowded with some of the most bulky, spectacularly shaped rock formations imaginable, and probably unique in China for their total absence of coloured lighting.

You can continue directly to Guiyang from Zhijin on daily buses, but between May and July the **Hundred Li Azalea Forest** (Baili Dujuan Lindai) makes an attractive extension to the trip. Sited northeast of **DAFANG** town, a belt of red, pink and white flowers spreads for 50km over the hills between the villages of **Pudi** and **Jinpo**. Dafang is probably the best place to look for accommodation, and there are further buses from here to both Guiyang and Zunyi – check details with the *CITS* in Guiyang or Anshun.

Panxian and Xingyi
The main road into Yunnan runs due west of Anshun to the Yi-dominated border town of **PANXIAN**, southern limit of the Liupanshui district (see below). A less direct alternative leads down through the **Xingyi region** at Guizhou's southwestern extremities. The scene of sporadic fighting between the Guomindang and locally organized guerrillas before the PLA took control of the south in 1951, the regional centre is about 250km from Anshun at **XINGYI**, a small but aspiring city surrounded by a magnificent range of sharp limestone peaks. The *Panjiang Binguan* on Panjiang Xi Lu (②) is a reasonable place to stay, and Xingyi makes a good spot to break the 24-hour bus journey to Kunming and go hiking in the hills, investigate nearby Bouyei and Miao villages, or get a minibus heading a couple of kilometres northeast to **Maling Canyon**, a tortuous, fifteen-kilometre river gorge complete with forests, deep cliffs and hazardous waterfalls.

Liupanshui and Caohai Hu

The coal-mining **Liupanshui district** – named after the three regional centres of Liuzhi, Panxian, and Shuicheng – begins at **LIUZHI**, an hour west of Anshun on the Guiyang–Kunming rail line. Liuzhi is a dismal place, though the surrounding area harbours villages of **Long-horned Miao**. Women of this particular group wear the strangest of headpieces, resembling bolsters made from plaited hair bound around wooden "buffalo horns" (for more on the Miao, see p.700). The land beyond Liuzhi forms a tumultuous karst barrier of jagged mountains and fathomless valleys. Buses can't handle the road after rain and it's better to rely on the train, which masterfully cuts through everything via a string of tunnels and long sweeps of clouded track teetering over the abyss.

Two hours from Liuzhi the train rocks in to **SHUICHENG**, an industrial mess of note as the jumping-off point for wildlife enthusiasts heading up to the waters of **Caohai Hu**. From the station, cross the tracks and go down to the main road, turn left and walk about 400m to a well-disguised hostel and **bus station**, where there are early-morning departures for the eight-hour run northwest to **Weining**, close to the lake. Shuicheng itself is a couple of kilometres from the train station, which can be covered in a cycle-rickshaw for about ¥5. In town, there's a steel foundry, numerous places to eat, and rooms at the crumbling *Zhongshan Fandian* (③) on Zhongshan Xi Lu.

WEINING is a small pastoral town with basic amenities set on an infertile plateau 2000m above sea level, freezing in winter and parched in summer. The hardy local communities of Han, Hui, Yi and Miao survive by farming sheep and maize. Covering an area of thirty square kilometres, **Caohai Hu** (Grass Sea Lake) **Nature Reserve** is immediately south, best reached on foot from Weining. In spring and autumn flocks of migratory waterfowl descend in their thousands; **black-necked cranes** are the most famous of these visitors, though recently the tree-dwelling **mandarin duck** has been seen. This ornate bird was once endemic to China, but deforestation has meant that the populations introduced to Europe now outnumber their wild brethren at home. **Moving on** from Weining, you'll have to head back to Shuicheng for the train, though it's also possible to catch buses direct from Weining to **Zhaotong** and **Qujing** in Yunnan, for connections to Xichang (Sichuan) and Kunming respectively.

travel details

Trains

Anshun to: Guiyang (3 daily; 2hr); Kunming (daily; 18hr); Shuicheng (daily; 3hr).

Beihai to: Nanning (4 daily; 5hr).

Guilin to: Changsha (daily; 10hr); Guangzhou (2 daily; 20hr); Guiyang (daily; 12hr); Kunming (daily; 30hr); Liuzhou (3 daily; 5hr); Nanning (daily; 12hr).

Guiyang to: Anshun (3 daily; 2hr); Beijing (2 daily; 55hr); Changsha (daily; 16hr); Chengdu (daily; 18hr); Chongqing (daily; 10hr); Guangzhou (4 daily; 30hr); Kaili (5 daily; 4hr); Kunming (daily; 12hr); Liuzhou (daily; 10hr); Shanghai (daily; 45hr); Shuicheng (daily; 5hr); Zhenyuan (daily; 7hr); Zunyi (2 daily; 5hr).

Kaili to: Guangzhou (daily; 27hr); Guiyang (5 daily; 4hr); Liuzhou (daily; 10hr).

Liuzhou to: Changsha (daily; 15hr); Guilin (3 daily; 5hr); Guiyang (daily; 10hr); Nanning (daily; 7hr).

Nanning to: Beihai (4 daily; 3hr); Guangzhou (daily; 36hr); Guilin (daily; 10hr); Liuzhou (3 daily; 5hr); Pingxiang (daily; 4hr).

Buses

Anshun to: Guiyang (2–3hr); Xingyi (8hr); Zhijin (5hr).

Beihai to: Nanning (7hr); Wuzhou (10hr).

Guilin to: Guangzhou (22hr); Hengyang (15hr); Liuzhou (5hr); Longsheng (3hr 30min); Nanning (12hr); Sanjiang (6hr); Wuzhou (9hr); Yangshuo (1hr 30min).

Guiyang to: Anshun (2–3 hr); Huangguoshu (4hr); Kaili (5hr); Kunming (at least 24hr); Tongren (10hr); Xingyi (12hr).

Kaili to: Guiyang (5hr); Rongjiang (6hr); Shibing (3hr); Zhenyuan (3hr).

Liuzhou to: Guilin (5hr); Nanning (10hr); Wuzhou (14hr).

Nanning to: Beihai (8hr); Guangzhou (23hr); Guilin (12hr); Kunming (36hr); Liuzhou (12hr); Wuzhou (12hr); Yangshuo (10hr 30min).

Wuzhou to: Beihai (10hr); Guangzhou (15hr); Guilin (9hr); Liuzhou (10hr); Nanning (12hr); Yangshuo (8hr).

Yangshuo to: Guilin (1hr 30min); Liuzhou (5hr); Nanning (10hr 30min); Wuzhou (8hr).

Ferries

Beihai to: Haikou (at least daily; 10hr).

Liuzhou (dependent on water level) to: Guiping (daily; 11hr); Wuzhou (daily; 24hr).

Nanning (depending on water level) to: Guangzhou (alternate days; 46hr); Guiping (alternate days; 15hr); Wuzhou (alternate days; 30hr).

Wuzhou to: Guangzhou (daily; 12hr); Guiping (daily; 13hr); Hong Kong (alternate days, 7hr).

Planes

Guiyang to: Beijing (daily; 2hr 40min); Changsha (4 weekly; 1hr); Chengdu (daily; 1hr); Guangzhou (2 daily; 1hr); Guilin (5 weekly; 1hr 10min); Kunming (5 weekly; 1hr 20min); Nanning (3 weekly; 1hr 20min); Shanghai (daily; 2hr); Wuhan (3 weekly; 1hr 25min).

Guilin to: Beijing (11 weekly; 2hr 15min); Changsha (3 weekly; 1hr 20min); Chengdu (6 weekly; 1hr 20min); Guangzhou (at least 2 daily; 45min); Guiyang (5 weekly; 1hr 10min); Haikou (4 weekly; 1hr); Kunming (6 weekly; 1hr 20min); Shanghai (3 daily; 2hr); Shenzhen (daily; 50min); Xi'an (2 daily; 1hr 30min).

Nanning to: Beijing (7 weekly; 3hr); Guangzhou (2 daily; 50min); Guiyang (3 weekly; 1hr 20min); Haikou (2 weekly; 50min); Hanoi (Vietnam; weekly, 1hr); Kunming (5 weekly; 1hr); Shanghai (5 weekly; 2hr 15min).

CHAPTER ELEVEN

YUNNAN

Yunnan has always stood apart from the rest of China, set high on the empire's "barbarous and pestilential" southwestern frontiers and shielded from the rest of the nation by the unruly, mountainous provinces of Sichuan and Guizhou. Within this single province, unmatched in the complexity and scope of its history, landscape and peoples, you'll find a mix of geography, climates and nationalities which elsewhere on Earth take entire continents to express. This diversity makes Yunnan as difficult a place for the modern traveller to come to grips with as it was for

successive dynasties to govern, and however long you spend here, it's rare to feel that you've done more than obtain the most superficial of impressions.

The northeast of the province is fairly flat and productive, seat of the attractive capital, **Kunming**, whose mild climate earned Yunnan its name, meaning literally "South of the Clouds". Increasingly touristed, it's nonetheless a charming area, with enjoyable day trips to nearby scenic marvels. West of Kunming, the Yunnan plateau rises to serrated, snowbound peaks surrounding the ancient historic towns of **Dali** and **Lijiang**, while farther over, on the central **border with Burma**, is subtropical **Dehong**, a busy trading region and unlikely Chinese holiday destination. Yunnan's deep south comprises the tropical forests and paddy fields of **Xishuangbanna**, a botanic, zoological and ethnic cornucopia abutting Burma and Laos, as well as some historically rich but little-visited sites down near **Vietnam**, only recently accessible after a decade of war.

Moving amongst this blur of border markets, mountains, jungles, lakes, temples, modern political intrigue and remains of vanished kingdoms are 28 recognized **ethnic groups**, the greatest number in any single province. Providing a quarter of the population and a prime reason to visit Yunnan in themselves, the indigenous list includes Dai and Bai, Wa, Lahu, Hani, Jingpo, Nu, Naxi and Lisu, plus a host shared with other provinces or adjoining nations. Though much of what you'll initially glean of their cultures is put on for tourists, anyone with even a couple of days to spare in Xishuangbanna or Lijiang can begin to flesh out this image. With more time you can look for shyer, remoter groups leading lives less influenced by the twentieth century.

Yunnan's sheer scale makes travel very time-consuming, and – whatever your usual preferences – it's tempting to **fly** occasionally. Fortunately *Yunnan Air* is one of China's better airlines, and a good excuse to avoid retracing a back-wrenching, four-day bus journey. The state of country **buses and roads** often leaves much to be desired, but they are at least plentiful and it's an undeniable achievement that some routes exist at all. Make sure you travel at least briefly along the famous **Burma Road** between Kunming and the western border, built with incredible determination during the 1930s. There's a limited **rail network** inside Yunnan – an irregular service through the southeast to the Vietnamese border, and a soon-to-be-completed line to Xiaguan, near Dali – though Kunming is well linked to the rest of the country via Sichuan and Guizhou. The **weather** is generally moderate throughout the year, though northern Yunnan has cold winters and heavy snow up around the Tibetan border, while the south is always warm, with a torrential summer wet season.

One factor confusing travel in the border regions is the oscillating open status of various areas, although, technically, almost all of the province is accessible to foreigners. The causes for closures vary from dangerous roads to reported outbreaks of plague, but it's often due to the army looking for illegal cross-border traffic in cars, timber, gems and **opiates**. Most of the world's heroin originates in Burma and is funnelled through China to overseas markets, often with the help of local authorities. Officially

---

ACCOMMODATION PRICE CODES

All the accommodation in this book has been graded according to the following price codes, which represent the cheapest double room available to foreigners. Most places have a range of rooms, however, and staff will usually offer you the more expensive ones – it's always worth asking if they have anything cheaper. Where the text refers specifically to dorm beds, the price code represents the price per bed. See p.40 for more details.

① less than ¥30	④ ¥100–150	⑦ ¥300–500
② ¥30–75	⑤ ¥150–200	⑧ ¥500–700
③ ¥75–100	⑥ ¥200–300	⑨ ¥700 or more

the Yunnanese government is tough on the drug trade, executing traffickers, forcibly rehabilitating addicts and, since 1992, intercepting over four tonnes of heroin – twice the quantity netted by Thai officials during the same period. All this means that, open or not, there are military **checkpoints** on many rural roads, where you'll have to show passports and may be asked for obscure documents such as International Health Certificates. It pays to be polite, but things are always easier if you avoid appearing fluent in Chinese.

Some history

Yunnan has been inhabited for a very long time indeed, with evidence reaching back through galleries of Stone-Age rock art to two 1.5-million-year-old teeth found near the northern town of Yuanmou. Records of civilization, however, are far more recent. According to the Han historian Sima Qian, the Chinese warrior prince **Zhuang Qiao** founded the pastoral **Dian Kingdom** in eastern Yunnan during the third century BC, though it's probable that he simply became chief of an existing nation. The Dian were a slave society, who vividly recorded their daily life and ceremonies involving human sacrifice in sometimes gruesome **bronze models** unearthed from contemporary tombs. The kingdom was acknowleged by China in 109 AD, its ruler receiving military aid and a golden seal from the emperor **Wu Di**, who hoped to control the Southern Silk Road through to India. But the Chinese army came poorly prepared for their task and never accomplished it, and the collapse of the Han empire in 204 was followed by the dissolution of Dian into private statelets which were absorbed during the eighth century by the emerging **Nanzhao Kingdom**, based around Dali.

Politically and culturally, the Nanzhao and its successors managed to dominate large parts of Southeast Asia before succumbing in the thirteenth century to the armies of **Kublai Khan**. Directly controlled by China for the first time, for a while Yunnan simply served as a remote dustbin for political troublemakers, thereby escaping the population explosions, wars and migrations that plagued central China. But the Mongol invasion had also introduced a large **Muslim population** to the province, who, angered by their deteriorating status under the Chinese, staged a **rebellion** in 1856, storming Kunming and briefly managing to establish an independent state at Dali. Millions died in the rebellion's suppression, and a wasted Yunnan was left to local bandits and private armies for the following half-century.

Strangely, it was the **Japanese invasion** during the 1930s which sparked a resurgence of the province's fortunes. Blockaded into southwestern China, the Nationalist **Guomindang government** initiated great programmes of rail and road building through the region, though they never really controlled Yunnan. Moreover, their cruel treatment of minority groups made the Red Army's cause all the more attractive when civil war resumed in 1945. Liberation came smoothly, and it's a reflection of Yunnan's generally tolerant atmosphere that reform here was apparently accomplished with very little bloodshed, the landlords losing their power and fading into obscurity rather than being bludgeoned out of the way. But the **Communists'** good intentions of coexistence with minorities, better hospitals, schools and communications were badly stalled during the Cultural Revolution and then, in the 1980s, by the war with Vietnam, and it's only now that Yunnan is finally benefiting from its association with Beijing. Never agriculturally rich – only a tenth of the land is considered arable – the province looks to mineral resources, tourism and its potential as a future conduit between China and the much discussed, but as yet unformed, trading bloc of **Vietnam, Laos, Thailand and Burma**. Though political snags have slowed its formation, should these countries ever form an unrestricted economic alliance, the amount of trade passing through Yunnan would be immense – a resurrection of the old Silk Road – and highways, rail and air services have already been laid for the day the borders open freely.

KUNMING AND THE NORTH

Northern Yunnan contains elements of everything that draws visitors to this corner of China. The major city is **Kunming**, the comfortable, fair-weather provincial capital, while to the northwest the land rises inexorably towards the Tibetan plateau, with an ethnically diverse population centred around the ancient towns of **Dali** and **Lijiang**. Press on in this direction and you'll find back doors into Tibet and Sichuan through the remote lands around **Zhongdian** and **Lugu Lake**. Southwest of Dali is the historic city of **Baoshan** and the **Dehong region**, a warm, subtropical pocket full of shady traders and ludicrous antics revolving around the Burmese border markets at **Ruili** and **Wanding**.

The north also enjoys the best of Yunnan's **transportation**. Flight paths radiate out from Kunming to the rest of the province and well beyond, while there's soon to be an easy train ride west to **Xiaguan**, Dali's rail head. Here starts the most interesting stretch of the **Burma Road**, sometimes good, often very rough. International relations permitting, you could theoretically follow it from Kunming right down to Mandalay, though Westerners can currently only get as far as Wanding on the Chinese border. Elsewhere, minor roads can be very slow going, and some patience and flexibility are essential.

Kunming and around

Basking 2000m above sea level in the warm, fertile heart of the Yunnan plateau, **KUNMING** does its best to live up to its English title as the City of Eternal Spring. However, until recently it was considered a savage frontier settlement, and authorities began to realize the city's promise only when people exiled here during the Cultural Revolution refused offers to return home to eastern China, preferring Kunming's more relaxed life, better climate and friendlier inhabitants.

At first glance a fairly ordinary blend of broad, monochrome main roads and public buildings, there's an air of satisfied well-being in the crowded restaurants, bustling streets and markets supplying year-round fresh produce. The people, too, are mellow enough to mix typically Chinese garrulousness with introspective pleasures, such as quietly greeting the day with a stiff hit of Yunnanese tobacco from fat, brass-bound bamboo pipes. There are other novelties – streets of old wooden houses with balconies and shutters, clean pavements enforced since 1987 by on-the-spot fines, and a low-profile but sizeable gay community – all emphasizing that Kunming's two million or so residents enjoy a quality of life well above that of most urban Chinese.

Historically the domain of Yunnan's earliest inhabitants and first civilization, Kunming long profited from its position on the caravan roads through to Burma and Europe and was visited in the thirteenth century by Marco Polo, who found the locals of **Yachi** (Duck Pond Town) using cowries for cash and enjoying their meat raw. Little of the city's wealth survived the 1855 Muslim rebellion, when almost all Buddhist sites in the capital were razed. In 1911 the **Kunming–Haiphong rail line** was completed, built by the French so that they could tap Yunnan's mineral resources for their colonies in Indo-China, but laying the seeds of a valuable future route into Vietnam. Twenty-five years later, **war with Japan** brought a flock of wealthy east-coast refugees to the city, whose money helped to establish Kunming as a solid industrial and manufacturing base for the wartime government in Chongqing. The allies provided essential support for

---

The **telephone code** for Kunming is ☎0871

729

this, importing materials along the Burma Road from British-held Burma, and, when that was lost to the Japanese, through the volunteer US-piloted **Flying Tigers**. The city consolidated its position as a supply depot during the Vietnam War and subsequent border clashes, though the **Cultural Revolution** hit hard. The mayor and others were tortured to death, and buildings that missed the attentions of nineteenth-century vandals perished at the hands of the Red Guards. Survivals include a couple of temples, the long-established **university** and a **Minorities' Institute** set up in the 1950s to promote mutual understanding among Yunnan's multi-faceted population.

The mid-1980s brought snowballing tourism and foreign investment. Neighbouring nations such as Thailand trace their ancestries back to Yunnan and have proved particularly willing to channel funds into the capital, and the city has become ever more developed and accessible as a result. Though not packed with historical monuments, and even as its outward appearance changes, Kunming remains a thoroughly enjoyable place to experience the bustle and daily activity of a healthy Chinese city. It has good food, warm summers and tolerably cool, bright winters, and it's just a short hop to temples and landscapes surrounding the sizeable lake, **Dian Chi**, and the celebrated **Stone Forest**.

Orientation, arrival, city transport and accommodation

Kunming has few natural landmarks to help guide you around, but fortunately its layout is uncomplicated. The city hangs off two main thoroughfares. Scruffy and grey, **Beijing Lu** forms the north–south axis, passing just east of the centre as it runs for 5km between the city's two train stations, while **Dongfeng Lu** crosses it halfway along, divided into east (**Dongfeng Dong Lu**) and west (**Dongfeng Xi Lu**) sections as it cuts right through the business centre and Kunming's older western quarters. The far end runs out of the city as **Renmin Xi Lu**, which formed the first stage of the Burma Road. Most of the city's accommodation lies along Dongfeng Dong Lu and the southern half of Beijing Lu, while the majority of specific sights are north and west of the centre around Dongfeng Xi Lu and **Cuihu Park**. Circling most of this is the city's first highway ring road, **Huacheng Lu**, though others are planned for the near future.

Arrival and city transport

Kunming's continually busy **airport** is out in the southeastern suburbs, with the international and domestic terminal buildings next to each other. In the square outside you'll find a **CAAC bus** which runs about six times daily to Dongfeng Dong Lu for a couple of yuan. There are also slightly more expensive **public minibuses** to various places around the centre – not an option if you have much luggage – and squadrons of **taxis** charging ¥20–30 for a ride into town. Another cheap way to reach Dongfeng Dong Lu is on the **#52 bus**. Walk directly across the square and turn right – the bus leaves from the stop on the first corner and, because this is the terminus, things should be easier if you have big luggage or a pack.

The main **long-distance bus and train stations** are 500m apart at the seedy southern end of Beijing Lu, their forecourts thick with characters hawking rank-smelling goat skins dyed to resemble tiger and leopard pelts. From here, bus #23 runs right up to the **North train station** past hotels and the Dongfeng Lu intersection, where you should alight and head east for further accommodation prospects. You'll end up at the North train station only in the unlikely event that you're arriving by rail on the notoriously fickle service from Vietnam. There's also the **Western bus station** on Renmin Xi Lu, of most use for excursions around Kunming, though a few long-distance services also operate from here.

MOVING ON

The **airport bus** (and city bus #52) leaves from outside the airline offices near the *Kunming Fandian* on Dongfeng Dong Lu (not the *Yunnan Air* headquarters in town) every other hour 5.30am–6pm. The journey (¥2) takes about thirty minutes and it's recommended that you get to the airport with two hours to spare. As well as flights to all major centres in the country, there are regular services to Vietnam, Burma, Singapore and Thailand (see "Travel Details" at the end of the chapter). *Yunnan Air* is very helpful and organized, and can also book you on other airlines.

At the **train station**, windows #17 and #18 at the ticket office are for foreigners (daily 8.30am–noon & 2–5pm). Trains run from here **north to Chengdu** – try breaking your journey at Xichang in southern Sichuan (see p.794) – and **east through Guizhou** via Liupanshui and Anshun (pp.706–710) into the rest of the country. Both lines are heavily over-booked, though agents can often wrangle berths. Hard seats are sold three days in advance and sleeper tickets the day before departure. Note that, if operating, the **service to Hekou** on the Vietnamese border leaves from the North train station, and you have to buy tickets there – take bus #23 heading up Beijing Lu.

The **long-distance bus station** ticket office is computerized and staff are helpful, with **sleeper buses** to Dali, Jinghong and Hekou, but finding the right vehicle out the back can be a protracted business. Keep a tight hold on your luggage, as nearly everybody seems to get something pinched either at the station or in transit. You can also catch long-distance buses to various destinations such as Dali from the **Western bus station** on Renmin Xi Lu (take bus #5 from Dongfeng Xi Lu) and, more conveniently, from the west side of the **main train station square** underneath the big giraffe. Services from these latter two tend to be cheaper (if often less comfortable) than those from the main depot.

Leaving China overland through Vietnam and Laos is also possible, through the respective crossings at Hekou in southeastern Yunnan (p.766) or Bian Mao Zhan in Xishuangbanna (p.762). At the time of writing, foreigners entering Burma had to fly in to Rangoon – no overland entry was allowed – and had to change US$300 for their stay. See p.724 for consulate and visa details.

Kunming is not too large to walk around, and **bicycles** are readily rented from several of the hotels (see "Accommodation" below). Otherwise there are plenty of **taxis** and **public buses** cruising the main streets, and you can stay up to date with the ever-changing routes by picking up a bus **map** from street sellers.

Accommodation

Camellia Binguan, Dongfeng Dong Lu (☎3163000 or 3162918, fax 3147033). Pleasant three-winged affair and a budget travellers' favourite. Cheaper rooms have shared, powerful showers, and there's a foreign exchange counter, expensive bar and restaurant, ticket booking service, luggage storage and bike rental. Dorms ②, rooms ④.

Chuncheng Fandian, Dongfeng Xi Lu, near the junction with Zhengyi Lu (☎3163962). Downmarket but comfortable, offering basic doubles through to suites, and well positioned for the more interesting western parts of town. Bus #2 from the train station stops nearby. ②–⑤.

Cuihu Binguan, Cuihu Nan Lu (☎5158888, fax 5153286). Long-established and highly regarded hotel in pleasant surroundings north of the centre. The drab exterior actually hides very plush furnishings. Airport transfers, all major credit cards accepted and an excellent restaurant. ⑧.

Golden Dragon (*Jinlong Fandian*), Beijing Lu (☎3133015, fax 3131082). Four-star comforts aimed at the upmarket business traveller, but recent renovations haven't been completely successful in dispelling a tired atmosphere. ⑧.

Holiday Inn, Dongfeng Dong Lu (☎3165888, fax 3135189). Kunming's lap of luxury featuring a string quartet in the lobby, and a coffee shop serving extortionately priced Western breakfasts to clean-clad visitors. ⑧.

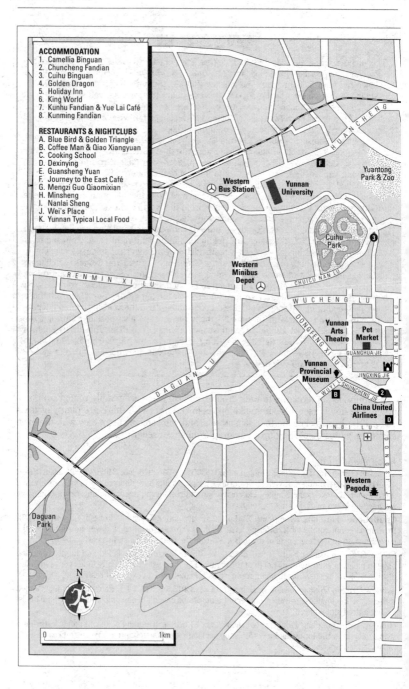

ACCOMMODATION
1. Camellia Binguan
2. Chuncheng Fandian
3. Cuihu Binguan
4. Golden Dragon
5. Holiday Inn
6. King World
7. Kunhu Fandian & Yue Lai Café
8. Kunming Fandian

RESTAURANTS & NIGHTCLUBS
A. Blue Bird & Golden Triangle
B. Coffee Man & Qiao Xiangyuan
C. Cooking School
D. Dexinying
E. Guansheng Yuan
F. Journey to the East Café
G. Mengzi Guo Qiaomixian
H. Minsheng
I. Nanlai Sheng
J. Wei's Place
K. Yunnan Typical Local Food

Western Bus Station

Yunnan University

Yuantong Park & Zoo

Cuihu Park

Western Minibus Depot

RENMIN XI LU

CHUICU NAN LU

WUCHENG LU

DONGFENG XI LU

Yunnan Arts Theatre

Pet Market

ZHENGYI LU

GUANGHUA JIE

Yunnan Provincial Museum

JINGXING JIE

WUYI LU

SHUINCHENG JIE

DAGUAN LU

B

Chuncheng Fandian

China United Airlines

D

JINBI LU

BEIJING LU

Western Pagoda

Daguan Park

N

0   1km

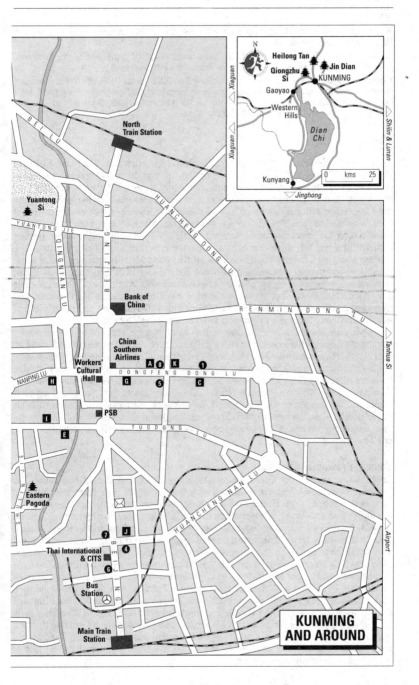

KUNMING
AND AROUND

King World (*Jinhua Dajiudian*), Beijing Lu (☎3138888, fax 3131910). Smart, executive-style hotel, full of Thai business people. ⑧.

Kunhu Fandian, Beijing Lu (☎3133737). Basic, clean, noisy and convenient for the travellers' cafés, bus and train stations, but staff are indifferent. Dorms ①, rooms ③.

Kunming Fandian, Dongfeng Dong Lu (☎3162063 or 3162172, fax 3163784). Wade through a gauntlet of minority saleswomen and blind masseurs hanging around the entrance and you'll find a big hotel with good services and food, also offering bikes for rent. It's not cheap, though – the less expensive rooms are in the older south wing. ⑥–⑧.

The City

Kunming's public focus is the huge square outside the grandiose **Workers' Cultural Hall** at the Beijing Lu–Dongfeng Lu intersection, alive in the mornings with regimented crowds warming up on hip pivots and shuttlecock games. Later on in the day it's a prime place to consult a fortune-teller, or receive a shoulder and back massage from the hard-fingered practitioners who pounce on passers by. The city's true centre is west of here outside the modern *Kunming Department Store* at the **Dongfeng Dong Lu–Zhengyi Lu crossroads**, an uncontrollably crowded shopping precinct packed with clothing and hi-fi stores. An area of importance to Kunming's Hui population, the southwestern back lanes around **Shuncheng Jie** form a **Muslim quarter**, full of wind-dried beef and mutton carcasses, pitta bread and raisin sellers, and huge woks full of roasting coffee beans being earnestly stirred with shovels. Hidden behind market stalls one block north along Zhengyi Lu, at the corner of **Jingxing Jie**, is a very dilapidated **mosque**, its curled eaves, tiles and woodwork little different from any other place of worship in China, though it's reputedly several hundred years old.

Jingxing Jie itself leads in to one of the more bizarre corners of the city, with Kunming's huge **pet market** convening daily in the street connecting it with the parallel, northerly, **Guanghua Jie**. This is no run-of-the-mill mix of kittens and grotesque goldfish: rare, multicoloured songbirds twitter and squawk in the wings, while furtive hawkers display geckos, monkey-like lorises and other endangered oddities illegally "liberated" from Xishuangbanna's forests. There are plants here, too, and up near Guanghua Jie the street divides around a small park, surrounded by **antique and curio** booths – somewhere to find dirt-cheap coins and Cultural Revolution mementoes, bamboo pipes and prayer rugs – from where backstreets continue through to the city's northwest.

Yunnan Provincial Museum

About 500m west of the centre along Dongfeng Xi Lu and the #5 bus route, the **Yunnan Provincial Museum** (Mon–Thurs 9am–5pm, Fri 9am–2pm; last entry an hour before the museum closes; ¥10) definitely has its moments, though the collection of clothes and simpering photographs near the entrance fails to shed much light on most of Yunnan's cultural groups. Far better are the **Dian bronzes** on the second floor, dating back more than two thousand years to the Warring States period and excavated from tombs on the shores of Dian Chi, south of Kunming. The largest pieces include an ornamental plate of a tiger attacking an ox and a **coffin** in the shape of a bamboo house, but lids from **storage drums** used to hold cowries are the most impressive, decorated with dioramas of figurines fighting, sacrificing oxen and men and, rather more peacefully, posing with their families and farmyard animals outside their homes. A replica of the Chinese imperial **gold seal** given to the Dian king early on in the second century implies that his aristocratic slave society at least had the tacit approval of the Han emperor. Upstairs again is a **prehistoric museum** with enjoyably awful plaster models and casts of locally found trilobites, armoured fishes, bits of dinosaurs and early human remains.

KUNMING AND AROUND

Kunming	昆明	*kūnmíng*

ACCOMMODATION

Camelia	茶花宾馆	*cháhuā bīnguǎn*
Chuncheng	春城饭店	*chūnchéng fàndiàn*
Cuihu	翠湖宾馆	*cuìhú bīnguǎn*
Golden Dragon	金龙饭店	*jīnlóng fàndiàn*
Holiday Inn	假日酒店	*jiǎrì jiǔdiàn*
King World	金华大酒店	*jīnhuá dàjiǔdiàn*
Kunhu	昆湖饭店	*kūnhú fàndiàn*
Kunming	昆明饭店	*kūnmíng fàndiàn*

THE CITY

Cuihu Park	翠湖公园	*cuìhú gōngyuán*
Daguan Park	大观公园	*dàguān gōngyuán*
Eastern Pagoda	东寺塔	*dōngsì tǎ*
Mosque	清真寺	*qīngzhēn sì*
Pet market	宠物市场	*chǒngwù shìchǎng*
Western Pagoda	西寺塔	*xīsì tǎ*
Yuantong Si	圆通寺	*yuántōng sì*
Yunnan Provincial Museum	云南省博物馆	*yúnnán shěng bówùguǎn*
Zoo	动物园	*dòngwù yuán*

RESTAURANTS

Guansheng Yuan	冠生园	*guànshēng yuán*
Minsheng	民生饭店	*mínshēng fàndiàn*

AROUND KUNMING

Dian Chi	滇池	*diān chí*
Dragon Gate Grotto	龙门村	*lóngmén cūn*
Heilong Tan	黑龙潭	*hēilóng tán*
Jin Dian	金殿	*jīndiàn*
Kunyang	昆阳	*kūn yáng*
Lunan	路南	*lùnán*
Qiongzhu Si	筇竹寺	*qióngzhú sì*
Tanhua Si	昙华寺	*tánhuá sì*
Stone Forest	石林	*shílín*
Stone Forest Hotel	石林宾馆	*shílín bīnguǎn*
Western Hills	西山	*xīshān*
Yunlin Hotel	云林宾馆	*yúnlín bīnguǎn*

Cuihu Park, Yuantong Si and the Zoo

A twenty-minute walk west from the museum along Dongfeng Xi Lu (bus #5 again) brings you to **Xiaoximen**, one of Kunming's older shopping districts. Rickety balconies and carvings of phoenixes and flowers on century-old wooden buildings up along Wucheng Lu and Cuihu Nan Lu provide visitors with a glimpse of a vanishing era, but local residents find the houses unhygienic fire-traps, and plans are afoot to modernize them. North off Cuihu Nan Lu, **Cuihu Park** (on the #2 bus route from the southern end of Beijing Lu) is at least half lake, a good place to join thousands of others exercising, sipping tea and listening to storytellers, feeding wintering flocks of gulls or just milling over the maze of bridges. The park is also right next to the **Yunnan University** campus, and it's a favourite haunt for students eager to practise their English conversation.

East from Cuihu Park along Yuantong Jie is **Yuantong Si** (daily 7.30am–7pm; ¥10), northern Yunnan's major Buddhist temple and an active place of pilgrimage. Mostly of Ming and Qing vintage, there's an air of neglect in the peeling paint and plaster, though the temple is busy and cheerful enough, with gardens of bright pot plants just inside the entrance. A bridge over the central pond crosses through an octagonal pavilion to the threshold of the **main hall**, where two huge central pillars wrapped in colourful, dynamically sculpted **dragons** support the ornate wooden ceiling. Faded frescoes on the back wall were painted in the thirteenth century, while a new annexe out the back houses a graceful white marble sculpture of Sakyamuni recently donated by the Thai king. Cooks in the **vegetarian restaurant** over in the western rooms work wonders at lunchtime.

The temple sits on the southern slope of the large **Yuantong Park**, though to reach this you have to go out and follow the main roads east and around to the north. Kunming's **Zoo** (daily 8am–5pm; ¥10) is up here, too, with the entrance at the corner of Yuantong Jie and Qingnian Lu on the #4 bus route. It's not the worst in China, offering nice vignettes of children stroking and feeding the deer, along with views of the city from a hill top planted with crab apple groves.

Southern Kunming

Jinbi Lu runs roughly parallel to and south of Dongfeng Lu and the centre through a pleasantly leafy residential district, reached on bus #3 from Beijing Lu. Two large Tang-dynasty **pagodas** rise in the vicinity, each a solid thirteen storeys of whitewashed brick crowned with four jolly iron cockerels. South down Dongsi Jie, a busy market street choked with bicycle traffic, the entrance to the **Western Pagoda** is along a narrow lane on the right. A few jiao gain you admission to the tiny surrounding courtyard where sociable idlers while away sunny afternoons playing cards and sipping tea in the peaceful, ramshackle surroundings. The **Eastern Pagoda** is a more tattered duplicate standing by the roadside a few minutes' walk away on Shulin Jie. The temples associated with both pagodas are not open to the public.

For a total change of atmosphere, ride bus #4 from Dongfeng Lu to its terminus at **Daguan Park** (7am–8pm; ¥5) on Kunming's southwestern limits. Originally laid out by the energetic seventeenth-century Qing emperor Kangxi, it has been modified over the years to include a noisy funfair, photographers, snack stalls and souvenir emporiums, and is a favourite haunt of Kunming's youth. Among shady walks and pools, Daguan's focal point is the **Daguan Pavilion**, a square, three-storeyed affair built to better Kangxi's enjoyment of the distant **Western Hills** and now a storehouse of calligraphy extolling the area's charms. The most famous poem here is a 118-character verse, carved into the gateposts by the Qing scholar Sun Ran, reputed to be the longest set of rhyming couplets in China. The park is set on Daguan Stream, which flows south into **Dian Chi** (see p.726), and there are frequent hour-long cruises down the grubby black waterway, lined with willows, to points along Dian's northern shore.

Eating, drinking and entertainment

Eating out is the main pleasure after dark in Kunming, with the city's **nightlife** concentrating on cinemas and karaoke clubs, although some hotel bars daringly open until midnight. The southern end of Beijing Lu is Kunming's nocturnal underbelly, with a disproportionate number of unattached women hanging around outside tiny, dingy **clubs**. A better choice is the nightclub associated with the *Qiaoxiang Yuan* restaurant

---

YUNNANESE FOOD

The **Yunnanese cooking** style broadly splits into three regions. In the **north**, a cold, pastoral lifestyle produces dried meats, vegetables and – very unusually for China – dairy products, infused with a Muslim cuisine, a vestige of the thirteenth-century Mongolian invasion. Typical dishes include wind-cured ham (*yuntui* or *huotui*), sweetened, steamed and served with slices of bread; toasted cheese and dried yoghurt wafers (*rubing* and *rushan*); the local version of crisp-skinned duck (*shaoya*), flavoured by painting it with honey and roasting over a pine-needle fire; and *shaguoyu*, a tasty fish casserole.

Southeastern Yunnan produces the most recognizably "Chinese" food. From here comes *qiguoji*, chicken flavoured with medicinal herbs and stewed inside a specially shaped earthenware steamer; and **crossing-the-bridge noodles** (*guoqiao mixian*), probably the most famous dish in the province. A sort of individualized hotpot, the curious name comes from a tale about a Qing scholar who retired every day to a lakeside pavilion to compose poetry. His wife, an understanding soul, used to cook him lunch, but the food always cooled as she carried it from their home over the bridge to where he studied – until she hit on the idea of keeping the heat in with a layer of oil on top of his soup. It's best sampled in Kunming, where numerous places serve a huge bowl of oily, scalding chicken stock with a platter of noodles, shredded meats and vegetables, which you add along with chilli powder and spices to taste.

Not surprisingly, Yunnan's **southwestern borders** are strongly influenced by Burmese cooking methods, particularly in the use of such un-Chinese ingredients as coconut, palm sugar, cloves and turmeric. Here you'll find a vast range of soups and stews displayed in aluminium pots outside fast-turnover restaurants, roughly recognizable as **curries**, and oddities such as purple rice-flour pancakes sold at street markets. As most of these aren't generally available outside the area, however, their description and a glossary of local names appears in the relevant section. The southwest also produces good **coffee** and red *puer cha*, Yunnan's best **tea**, both widely appreciated across the province.

---

near the museum in Wuyi Lu, though along with the *Blue Bird* and *Golden Triangle* on Dongfeng Dong Lu, it's usually fairly limp.

The city has several **operatic troupes** and indigenous entertainments which include *huadeng*, a lantern dance. Indoor performances are sadly infrequent, but there are often informal shows at the weekend in Cuihu Park. Keep an eye on local newspapers (or ask at your hotel) for similar activities at the *Yunnan Arts Theatre* on Dongfeng Xi Lu and *Dianju Theatre* on Dongsi Lu, near the pagodas.

Restaurants and cafés

Kunming is stacked with Yunnanese specialities and more ordinary Chinese fare, though there's also a smattering of places serving Western dishes. Back lanes running north off **Dongfeng Xi Lu** or **Jinbi Lu** have the best stalls and cheap restaurants where you can battle with the locals over grilled cheese, hotpots, fried snacks rolled in chilli powder, loaves of excellent soda bread stuffed with meat and spring onions, and rich duck and chicken casseroles. **Hotels** have the most refined surroundings, while city restaurants tend to focus their efforts on the food, so don't be discouraged by the outward appearance of some venues. Kunming's **Muslim** quarter has endless rows of cheap diners with glazed ducks and fresh ingredients piled up outside; mutton stews are popular in winter. There's also a small canteen opposite the *Dongfeng Department Store* on Dongfeng Xi Lu selling cakes and *laomien* – Muslim "pulled noodles" – in soup.

Almost everywhere serves **coffee**, and a number of cakeshop-cafés have sprung up over the years, swinging in and out of fashion with Kunming's expat community. For **breakfast**, Jinbi Lu has a particularly fine selection of eating halls serving early-morning bowls of rice noodle soups with fried batter sticks and unusual, orange-coloured sweet *baozi*. There's also the *Nanlai Sheng Coffee and Bread House* here, a tiny place selling Chinese-style pastries and coffee.

Coffee Man, Wuyi Lu, around the corner from the museum. Fairly decent coffee and burgers served in cosy, clean surroundings. Open daily 11am–1am.

Cooking School, Dongfeng Dong Lu, opposite the *Camellia Binguan*. Probably the best of a handful of local efforts serving inexpensive, fairly ordinary Chinese meals. The food isn't bad, but the service is, and foreigners have to pay in advance for noticeably small portions.

Dexinying, Nantong Jie. The most famous place in the city to tuck into a bowl of crossing-the-bridge noodles. There's a very basic mess hall downstairs and a slightly smarter restaurant above offering Yunnanese cooking.

Guansheng Yuan, Jinbi Lu. Upstairs restaurant open at mealtimes only. Despite its name ("Cantonese style"), there's a fine local spread including taro and pork casserole, soups, crispy-skinned and steamed chicken, and delicious fish and game dishes. Basic decor, limited English menu and very reasonable prices.

Journey to the East, off Huancheng Lu west of the university. This is a fine book exchange-cum-coffee house frequented by students.

Mengzi Guo Qiaomixian, Dongfeng Dong Lu, west of the *Holiday Inn*. An early-closing Yunnanese restaurant serving superb local dishes – it's a jam-packed riot at lunchtime.

Minsheng, Huoguo Lu. The best place in town to eat in a thoroughly Chinese atmosphere. This is a cheap, grubby, noisy canteen that looks like a Ming-dynasty food court, with various businesses selling everything from *baozi* to full-blown meals under one roof.

Qiao Xiangyuan, Wuyi Lu, near the museum. A restaurant-bar wrapped in stars and stripes and "beer beer beer" detailing. Mid-priced hotpots, Chinese food of varying quality and full-bore karaoke after dark.

Vegetarian restaurant The restaurant at the Yuantong Si seems to be an independent venture, with waitresses, beer and very good food. Open at lunchtime, there's an English menu offering "sweet and sour spareribs" (bamboo shoots, celery, and fried beancurd skin), "fish" (deep fried mashed potato served in a rich garlic and vinegar sauce) and other gastronomic puzzles.

Wei's Place, Huacheng Nan Lu. Tiny bamboo-decor café popular with foreign residents for its low prices, music, library and unusual Chinese food, including river moss with coriander and Hakka beancurd, as well as sandwiches, eggs and coffee.

Yue Lai and **City Gentlemen's Café**, Beijing Lu, near the *Kunhu Fandian*. Two crowded backpacker hangouts offering beer, approximately Western food, bike rental, "tourist consultancies" and earwax removers.

Yunnan Typical Local Food, corner of Dongfeng Dong Lu and Baita Lu. Cheap, unadorned restaurant with unaccountably hostile staff, English menu and simple fare that actually does live up to the restaurant's name – including very good steampot chicken with various healthy additives.

Listings

Airlines *China Southern*, Beijing Lu (daily 8.30am–noon & 2–7pm), down from the *Bank of China*; *China United*, next door to *Chuncheng Fandian* on Dongfeng Xi Lu (daily 8.30am–noon & 2.30–6pm; ☎3166207 or 3134514); *Thai*, next door to the *King World Hotel*, Beijing Lu (Mon–Fri 9am–noon & 1–5pm; ☎3133315 or 3133139, fax 3167354); *Yunnan*, Tuodong Lu (daily 8.30am–7.30pm; ☎3164270).

Banks and exchange The *Bank of China* is at the corner of Beijing Lu–Renmin Dong Lu (Mon–Fri 9–11.45am & 2.30–5.30pm). Some hotels also have foreign exchange counters with identical rates.

Bookshops The *Foreign Language Bookstore* on Qingnian Lu has the usual Victorian potboilers and a good selection in English on Yunnan, translations of Chinese literature, coffee-table works and bilingual maps.

Cinema Kunming's main screen is on the south side of the Dongfeng Lu–Zhengyi Lu intersection.

Consulates *Burma* (Myanmar), Wing 3, Floor 3, *Camellia Binguan*, Dongfeng Dong Lu (Mon–Fri 8.30am–noon & 1–4.30pm, closed during frequent Burmese public holidays; ☎3176609; 28-day tourist visa issued in 24 hours, ¥85); *Laos*, Wing 3, Floor 2, *Camellia Binguan*, Dongfeng Dong Lu (Mon–Fri 8.30–11.30am & 2.30–4.30pm; ☎3176623, fax 3178556; seven-day, non-extendable transit visas, US$28); *Thailand*, Floor 3, in an annexe next to the *King World Hotel* on Beijing Lu (Mon–Fri 8.30am–noon & 2–5.30pm; visa department open until noon only; sixty-day visas, ¥110). Vietnamese visas for the Hekou–Lao Cai crossing are available in China only through consulates in Hong Kong and Beijing.

Left luggage Offices at both train and bus stations, open dawn to evening.

Hospital There's a small Western–Chinese medicine clinic on Beijing Lu opposite the GPO; for serious attention try the Yunnan First People's Hospital on Jinbi Lu.

PSB The Foreign Affairs Department is on Beijing Lu (daily 8–11am & 2.30–5.30pm; ☎3166191). They speak good English and are helpful for visa extensions, though their information on the open status of various places in Yunnan can be at odds with the local authorities.

Post office The GPO is on the southern stretch of Beijing Lu (daily 8am–8pm). Post restante can also be addressed to the *Kunhu, Camellia* and larger hotels with their own postal desks.

Shopping The *Kunming Antique Store* on Qingnian Lu is worth ten minutes for its collection of wooden panels prised off Qing-dynasty homes, silver hairpins and bracelets and some nice ink-stones. For local flavour, there are tacky paintings and minorities products hawked outside the *Holiday Inn* and *Kunming* hotels, and more "authentic" bamboo pipes and home-grown tobacco sold in backstreet markets. Yunnan also has a reputation as a source of **rare medicines**, though prices in Kunming for many of these are grossly inflated – if you're curious, check out the handful of shops south of the Beijing Lu GPO for caterpillar fungus, dragon's blood and other weird items.

Telephones The larger hotels have international phone facilities, as does the GPO. Card phones are the latest thing to hit town, but the cards (available from hotel desks and some kiosks around the city) often falter halfway through calls.

Travel agents The main *CITS* is reputed to be at 1–8 Wuyi Lu (☎3138888 ext 3104 & 3105, fax 3148988), but takes some finding. There are branches near the *Kunming Fandian* on Dongfeng Dong Lu and next to the *King World Hotel* on Beijing Lu (Mon–Sat 9am–noon & 1–5pm), where some English is spoken. They can generally organize private tours around the city and to Shilin, Dali and Xishuangbanna, and obtain train and plane (but not long-distance bus) tickets. *CYTS* is at the *Kunhu Fandian*, worth trying for tickets if you're staying there, but otherwise often unfriendly. The *Camellia Binguan*'s private service is recommended for independent travellers. Other hotels also have tour agents offering bus tours, and can book passage on most transport. *Mengyuan International*, 139 Shulin Lu (☎3187259) arranges hiking trips in Xishuangbanna through their main office in Jinghong.

Around Kunming

Kunming might be short on specific sights, but the surrounding countryside has enough to keep you occupied for a good few days, shuttling around on public transport or private tours out from the capital. Extraordinary sculptures make the westerly **Qiongzhu Si** the pick of local holy sites, while immediately south of Kunming is **Dian Chi**, a spectacular 270-square-kilometre spread of deep blue water peppered with the rectangular sails of fishing junks. You can boat across to the lakeside towns, but Dian's colourful sprawl is best absorbed from the nearby heights of Xi Shan, the **Western Hills**. Further afield, **Shilin**, the spectacular Stone Forest, is one of the highlights of Yunnan's tourist trail.

Heilong Tan, Jin Dian and Tanhua Si

Three pleasant temple parks are easily visited from Kunming on public buses. Ten kilo-metres north on bus #9 from the North train station, **Heilong Tan** (Black Dragon Pool; 8am–6pm; ¥5) is set in a garden of ancient trees, full of plum blossoms in spring. The two Ming temple buildings are modest Taoist affairs dedicated to the Heavenly Emperor and other deities, while the pool itself is said to be inhabited by a dragon forced by the Immortal, Lu Dongbin, to provide a permanent source of water for the local people. It should also be haunted by a patriotic Ming scholar who zealously drowned himself and his family as a gesture of defiance in the face of invading Qing armies; his tomb stands nearby.

The same distance to the northeast on bus #10 from the North train station, the **Jin Dian** (Golden Temple; 8am–5pm; ¥5) has a convoluted history. Built in 1602 as a copy of the Taihe Hall atop Wudang Shan in Hubei Province (see p.461), the original temple was shifted to a monastery on Jizu Shan near Dali 35 years later, and the current double-eaved structure was founded by the Qing rebel general Wu Sangui in 1671. Again associated with the mystical Lu Dongbin, who apparently instigated its construction, the temple is supported on a marble base and the lattices, beams and statues in the main hall are made entirely of that thoroughly Yunnanese metal, **bronze**, and house two magical swords used by Taoist warriors. The gardens here are full of fragrant camellias and weekend picnickers, and a tower on the hill behind encloses a large Ming bell from Kunming's demolished southern gates.

Tanhua Si (¥3) is 4km east of the city at the base of the Jinma Hills, over the creek and about 1km north of where the #4 bus from Renmin Dong Lu terminates. There's little to see in the heavily restored Ming Buddhist temple, but the **ornamental gardens** are exquisite, with narrow paths winding around groves of exotic trees, bamboos, peonies and azaleas. "Tanhua" is a type of magnolia which grew here in profusion before the temple was built, though now just one slender, broad-leafed tree survives in a small courtyard next to the scripture hall.

Qiongzhu Si

A fantastic array of over-the-top sculptures makes up for the effort needed to reach **Qiongzhu Si**, the Bamboo Temple, which faces Kunming from hills 10km to the west. Irregular **minibuses** run from the Western bus station on Renmin Xi Lu, at the end of the #5 bus route, and more reliable services from a depot just up from the Provincial Museum on the corner of Dongfeng Xi Lu and Longjing Jie. A dignified building with black and red woodwork standing on Yuan-dynasty foundations, the temple has been restored continually through the ages and, late in the nineteenth century, the eminent Sichuanese sculptor **Li Guangxiu** and his five assistants were engaged to embellish the main halls with five hundred clay statues of *arhats*. This they accomplished with inspired gusto, spending ten years creating the comical and grotesquely distorted crew of monks, goblins, scribes, emperors and beggars which crowd the interior – some sit rapt with holy contemplation, others smirk, roar with hysterical mirth or snarl grimly as they ride a foaming sea alive with sea monsters. Unfortunately it all proved too satirical for Li's conservative contemporaries and this was his final commission, though it's hard to see how he could possibly have bettered this work in originality. While you're here, there's also a fourteenth-century **stone tablet** to seek out in the main hall recording dealings between imperial China and Yunnan in Mongolian and Chinese script, and there are courtyards shaded with bamboo and loquat trees, where you can quietly sip tea.

Dian Chi and the Western Hills

Kunming has always owed much of its easy living to the well-watered farmland surrounding **Dian Chi** (Dian Lake), which stretches for 50km south from the city. A road circuits the shore, and you could spend a couple of days hopping around, starting from Kunming's Western bus station, though the workers' sanatoriums and recently industrialized lakeside hamlets are not greatly appealing. One place to aim for is southerly **KUNYANG**, birthplace of China's only famous navigator, the Ming-dynasty Muslim eunuch **Zheng He**. A hill outside Kunyang has been set aside as a **park** (Zheng He Gongyuan) to his memory, complete with a temple museum and the mausoleum of Zheng's pilgrim father, **Hadji Ma**.

Far better, however, are the views of the lake from the top of Xi Shan, the well-wooded **Western Hills**, which rise to 2500m over the shore, 16km southwest of Kunming. The easiest way to get here is on bus #6 from Dongfeng Xi Lu to its terminus at the township of **GAOYAO** (last bus back to Kunming around 6pm), from where you can either slog up to the summit 8km south in about three hours, pausing for breath and refreshment in temples along the way, or catch a minibus up.

The first of the temples is **Huating Si**, originally designed as a country retreat for Gao Zhishen, Kunming's eleventh-century ruler, in the form of a pavilion surrounded by gardens and a small pond. Developed as a Buddhist temple from the fourteenth century, it was destroyed in 1857 and rebuilt in the 1920s. Today, there are some fine **statues** – especially the two gate guardians inside the entrance hall – and a moderately priced **Yunnanese restaurant**, a handy place to break your journey. Winding on through groves of ancient trees you next reach the halfway **Taihua Si**, a monastery set up by the roving Chan (Zen) sect monk **Xuan Jian** in 1306. Best known for its carelessly arranged **botanical gardens**, there's a massive gingko tree near the entrance claimed to be almost as old as the temple itself. A couple more kilometres bring you to the Taoist complex of **Sanqing Ge**, another former royal villa set on the Western Hills' highest peak. The nine halls are stacked up the slopes in a fine display of Tao style and Qing architecture, each one dedicated to a particular patriarch.

Less than a kilometre beyond Sanqing Ge the path runs into the **Dragon Gate Grotto**, a series of chambers and narrow tunnels through the hillside which took the late eighteenth-century monk **Wu Laiqing** and his successors over seventy years to excavate, and which were designed to replace a dangerous set of wooden stairs morticed into the cliffs. It's incredible that anyone could conceive of such a project, far less complete it with enough flair to incorporate the sculptures of Guanyin and the gods of study and righteousness which decorate niches along the way. At the end is **Grand Dragon Gate**, (Dalong Men), a precarious balcony offering magnificent views as it overhangs the wide expanse of Dian Chi.

Shilin: the Stone Forest

Yunnan's premier natural wonder is **Shilin**, the **Stone Forest**, an exposed bed of limestone spires weathered and split into intriguing clusters, 130km east of Kunming. There are many such "forests" in Yunnan, but here the black, house-sized rocks are embellished with trees and vines, steps, paths and pavilions, and Shilin possibly qualifies as China's most heavily commercialized natural theme park. An enjoyable day trip if you can accept the fairground atmosphere and crowds dutifully tagging behind their cosmetically perfect tour guides, it takes about an hour to cover slowly the main circuit through the pinnacles to **Sword Peak Pond**, an ornamental pool surrounded by particularly sharp ridges which you can climb along a narrow track leading right up across the top of the forest. This is the most frequented part of the park, with large red characters incised into famous rocks and ethnic **Sani**, a Yi subgroup, in unnaturally clean dresses strategically placed for photographers, but paths heading out towards the perimeter are far quieter and lead out to smaller, separate stone groupings in the fields beyond. You can see a bit more by staying the night, as Shilin is surrounded by Sani villages. Wednesday is **market day** in the town of **Lunan**, a thirty-minute ride on the back of a motorbike-taxi from outside the park gates, where Sani sell their wares and sport embroidered costumes.

Transport to Shilin is not a problem. A comfortable option are the **day tours** run by hotels and agents in Kunming from ¥40 upwards, but there are also much cheaper early-morning **buses** from both the main long-distance bus station and Western bus station (last buses back from Shilin leave about 3pm), and **minibuses** from the corner of Huancheng Nan Lu, next to the *King World Hotel* (both about ¥15). The journey takes around three hours and ends at a mess of Chinese hostels and stalls at the park gates selling poor souvenir embroideries and excellent, reasonably priced **food** – roast duck, pheasant, pigeon or fish.

Entry costs ¥33 (though getting in for free has to be the worst-kept secret in the country), after which you cross the bridge and bear left up the hill for 50m to the basic hostel (①) in the square. Continue round the lake and you'll find the ageing but comfortable *Stone Forest Hotel* (☎0871/7711405; ⑤) and the more modern *Shilin Summer Palace Hotel* (☎0871/7711888; ⑥) either side of steps which lead directly down into the forest itself. Keep going around the lake and uphill for the better-value *Yunlin Hotel* (☎0871/7711409; ⑤), which offers singles, doubles and triples. All of the places to stay have decent **restaurants**, and the hotels host infrequent evenings of **Sani dancing**, surprisingly enthusiastic, spontaneous events which counter the tacky image portrayed by hawkers at the park.

Northwestern Yunnan

Vigorously uplifted over the last fifty million years as the Indian subcontinent buckled up against China, **northwestern Yunnan** is a geologically unsettled region of thin pasture, alpine lakes and shattered peaks painted crisply in blue, white and grey. Twelve hours from Kunming on the southern tip of **Er Hai Lake**, **Xiaguan** is the regional access point, the start of roads north towards Tibet and Sichuan past the Bai town of **Dali**. Though Dali is well adapted to the needs of Western backpackers and appears firmly on the beaten track, the lake and mountains make a splendid backdrop, and a wilder China is not too distant.

A few hours beyond Dali is the former Naxi kingdom of **Lijiang**. The Naxi are still resident, though the old town and surrounding villages were seriously damaged in the terrible 1996 earthquake. Here hikers can organize themselves for a two-day trek through **Tiger Leaping Gorge**, where a youthful Yangzi cuts through the deepest chasm on Earth. East is **Lugu Hu**, lakeside home to the matrilineal Mosuo, while north again is the Tibetan town of **Zhongdian**, beginning of an illicit trip to Lhasa. Given that a few peaks here reach above 5000m, the northwest's **weather** is surprisingly mild – summer through to early winter is fairly warm and wet, with the likelihood of snow between late November and March increasing as you move north.

To Xiaguan: Chuxiong and the Burma Road

The first 390km of the **Burma Road** runs west of Kunming to Xiaguan through a succession of valleys and mountain ranges which would well repay a few days' exploration. But for most, the lure of Dali is too great, an all-too-easy trip from Kunming on a direct bus or, once the line opens in late 1997, by train via Xiaguan – a project which has taken sixty years to complete.

If the leisurely approach suits you, the midpoint town of **CHUXIONG** makes a good base, inhabited since the Zhou dynasty (700 BC) and now home to a substantial Yi population who celebrate their **Torch Festival** on the 24th day of the sixth lunar month with a fair and night-time revelries. The markets here are known for their silver jewellery, there are a few nearby parks and temples – most notably 20km away at **Zixi Shan**, a wooded mountain dedicated to Buddhism since the twelfth century – and, for historians and paleontologists, some interesting associations. In 1975 a huge Zhou mausoleum was discovered on Chuxiong's southern outskirts at **Wanjiaba**, containing farm tools and five of the oldest **bronze drums** yet discovered in Asia, now in Kunming's Provincial Museum (for more on bronze drum cultures, see p.685). Separate sites surrounding the town of **LUFENG**, 80km east, closer to Kunming, have yielded dinosaur bones and fragments of *ramapithecus* and *sivapithecus* fossils, possible hominid prototypes. For **accommodation** in Chuxiong, try the *Chuxiong Binguan* on Xinshi Jie (②–④) or the *Zixi Luguan* (dorms ①, rooms ③) on central Zhong Da Lu, both with first-rate restauarants.

Xiaguan

Also confusingly known as Dali Shi, **XIAGUAN** lies on the southern shore of Er Hai Lake, and is very much a transport hub. The centre is **Jianshe Dong Lu**, a 500-metre-long street between Tai'an Lu in the east and Renmin Lu in the west. The **train station** is a couple of kilometres east on Dianyuan Lu along the #5 and #6 bus routes. Long-distance buses stop at a number of depots along Jianshe Dong Lu, though the **main bus station** is down towards Renmin Lu on the south side of the road. There's a cheap and basic **hotel** (②) here, with the upmarket *Xiaguan Fandian* (☎8072/2125859; ⑤–⑧), favoured by tour groups and with a *CITS* desk, about 100m east, and the mid-range *Xiaguan Binguan* (④) on the Jianshe Dong Lu–Renmin Lu corner. Markets and cheap places to eat fill the backstreets, and if you've got time to kill, go for a stroll in **Erhai Gongyuan**, a green, hilly park a couple of kilometres northeast of the centre on the lakeshore.

Minibuses to Dali (¥7) leave every hour during the day from the upper reaches of Renmin Lu – wave them down as they cruise around. It might also be possible to catch a **boat** to Dali and other lakeside settlements from the Xiaguan docks along the Xi Er River in the north of town, though there are no regular timetables. The main bus station has daily departures west to **Baoshan**, northeast to Jizu Shan and Lugu Hu via **Binchuan**, and, for the hardened traveller only, a nerve-shattering 72-hour run south to **Jinghong** in Xishuangbanna (see p.754).

THE BURMA ROAD

Trade routes through northern Yunnan into **Burma** and beyond were established over two thousand years ago by merchants carrying goods between the Han empire and Rome along the Southern Silk Road. Travelled by Marco Polo on one of his errands for the Mongol court, it became known as the Tribute Road following China's successful eighteenth-century annexation of eastern Burma, but later fell into disuse as the Qing court stagnated and cut off ties with the outside world. When Japan invaded China during the 1930s they drove the Guomindang government to Sichuan, isolating them from their eastern economic and industrial power base. Turning west for help, the Guomindang found the **British**, who then held Burma and were none too keen to see China's resources in Japanese hands. In fact, there had been plans for a link through to Burma for forty years, and a road had already been built from Kunming to Xiaguan. Britain agreed to help extend this into a 1100-kilometre-long supply line connecting **Kunming** with the Burmese rail head at **Lashio**.

This was to become the **Burma Road**, swiftly completed by three hundred thousand labourers in 1938, an incredible feat considering the basic tools available and the number of mountains along the way. After the Japanese stormed French Indochina in 1940 and halted rail traffic between Vietnam and Kunming, the road became China's only line of communication with the allies, though it was always a tenuous one, frequently cut by landslides and summer monsoons. Lashio fell a year later, however, and the road became redundant once more, remaining so after the war ended through Burma's self-imposed isolation and the chaos of the Cultural Revolution. Now partially sealed and open again as the Yunnan–Burma Highway, the 910-kilometre Chinese stretch between Kunming and the border crossing at **Wanding** remains – like the Great Wall – a triumph of stolid persistence over unfavourable logistics.

Dali

No more than an hour's bus ride north of Xiaguan, **DALI** draws in swarms of foreigners seeking an escape from the realities of China, coddling them with English signs advertising beer gardens, massages, language courses, day trips and Western food. It might sound grim, but the visitors are partially absorbed by the indigenous **Bai** and Han population, while Dali itself and the surrounding villages are both pretty and interesting, full of old houses, friendly people and itinerant pedlars from the hills. To the east lies the great **Er Hai Lake**, while the invitingly green valleys and clouded peaks of the fifty-kilometre-long **Cang Shan range** rear up behind town, the perfect setting for a few days' walking or relaxation.

And there's much more to Dali than the picturesque tourist haven it has become. Favouring its profitable location on the Silk Road, an aspiring eighth-century Yunnanese prince named **Piluoge** assassinated his rivals and established the **Nanzhao Kingdom** here, a realm later expanded to include much of modern Burma, Thailand and Vietnam. In 937, the Bai warlord **Duan Siping** toppled the Nanzhao and set up a smaller **Dali Kingdom**, which survived until Kublai Khan and his Mongolian hordes

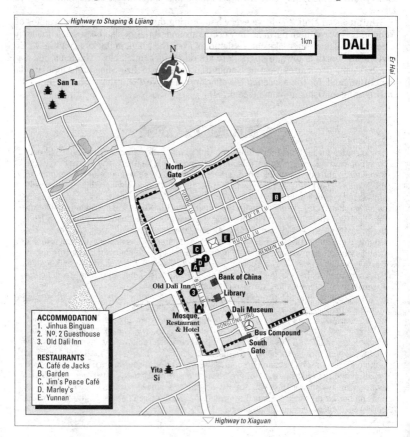

descended in 1252, subduing the Bai and imposing Chinese rule. Little changed until 1856 when, inspired by the Taipings, **Du Wenxiu** led the **Muslim Uprising** against the Qing empire to Dali, and again declared the town capital of an independent state. But in 1873 the Qing government brutally crushed the rebellion with the wholesale massacre of Yunnan's Muslim population; Du Wenxiu was killed and Dali was devastated, never to recover its former political position.

Today some Muslims and Han remain, but the majority of Dali's two-million-strong regional population are still Bai. If you can, visit during the **Spring Fair**, held from the fifteenth day of the third lunar month (April or May). Originally a Buddhist festival, the event has grown into five hectic days of horse trading, wrestling, racing, dancing and singing, attracting thousands of people from all over the region to camp at the fairground just west of town. You'll probably have to follow suit, as beds in Dali will be in short supply.

Orientation, arrival and getting around

Covering only about four square kilometres, much of Dali is contained by the remains of its Ming-dynasty walls. These aside, an earthquake destroyed the town in 1925, but it was rebuilt in its former style. Cobbled and planted with cherry trees, the main axis of its grid-like street plan is **Fuxing Lu**, which runs between the old north and south gates. **Bo'ai Lu** runs parallel and to the west, while the centre hinges around **Huguo Lu**, cutting across both at right angles.

Long-distance buses pull into a compound just inside the south gates on Fuxing Lu, where there's also a **ticket office** and a large bronze statue of a soldier with a sign stating "This Area Under Martial Law" tacked on to the base. **Xiaguan minibuses** congregate about 50m north on the corner of Honglong Jing, a side street, while other local minibuses are more likely to drop you off either on Bo'ai Lu or on the highway, which skirts the western side of town.

You don't need them for Dali itself, but **bicycles** for trips out to nearby sites can be rented from the hotels and foreigners' cafés for about ¥10 per day, plus deposit. The *Old Dali Inn* has a good range of bikes with gears. Always check the rental policy and condition of the bike, as you are fully responsible for any damage or loss.

Accommodation

Low-pressure touts meet the buses, hoping to escort arrivals to accommodation. In winter, you definitely want to check hot water availability, as it's generally restricted. Toilets everywhere are fairly basic.

Jinhua Binguan, corner of Fuxing Lu and Huguo Lu (☎0872/2673343, fax 2673846). Dali's upmarket setting, right in the town centre and complete with an art gallery and cold tiling. Dorms ①, rooms ⑥.

Mosque, Bo'ai Lu. You can't miss the minarets at the corners of this interesting variation on local options. There's a decent Muslim restaurant here, too, though rooms are rather spartan. Dorms ①, rooms ④.

No. 2 Guesthouse, western end of Huguo Lu. Very mixed reports about staff attitude and basic conditions, but some people swear by it. Dorms ①, rooms ②–④.

Old Dali Inn (also known as "No. 5"), Bo'ai Lu (☎0872/2670382). Best of the lot, a courtyard surrounded by two tiers of dusty wooden "traditional Bai" rooms. The staff are friendly, there are powerful showers and a good Chinese restaurant. Dorms ①, rooms ②–⑤.

The Town

Dali is small enough to walk around in a morning, though you might well be slowed down by the crowds during the main **market** every Thursday. Most places of specific interest are along Fuxing Lu, but the narrow stone side streets are good for a purposeless wander. Get your bearings from on top of Dali's old **south gate**, where you can study Xiaguan, Er Hai Lake, the town and mountains from the comfort of a tea house. Dali's antique **pagodas** stand as landmarks above the roof lines, **Yita Si** due west, and the trinity of **San Ta** a few kilometres north.

The **Dali Museum** (Tues–Sun 9am–5pm; ¥1) is opposite the bus compound, just 50m or so inside the gate. Built for the Qing governor and appropriated as Du Wenxiu's "Forbidden City" during his insurrection, the museum takes the form of a small Chinese palace with stone lions guarding the gate and cannons in the courtyard. Historic relics include a strange bronze model of two circling dragons, jaws clenched around what might be a tree, a few Buddhist figurines from the Nanzhao period, and some lively statues of an orchestra and serving maids from a Ming noblewoman's tomb – a nice addition to the usual cases of snarling gods and warrior busts. With the mountains behind, the gardens outside are very peaceful, planted with lantana and bougainvillea.

Moving north up Fuxing Lu, young and old socialize in the square outside the **library**, playing dominoes or video arcade games according to their interests. A few doors down is the *Bank of China* (foreign exchange Mon–Fri 9–11.30am & 2–5pm), with Dali's **international telephone counter** at the **post office** (daily 8am–8pm), a little farther along at the Huguo Lu crossroads. Huguo Lu's western arm forms the core of the budget travellers' world, a knot of **cafés**, cheap tailors, bilingual **travel agents** happy to book you on tours or long-distance buses, and massage clinics advertising their services with couplets like "Painful In, Happy Out". It's also the best place to purchase Bai jewellery, beautifully embroidered baby carriers and attractive tie-dyed batiks from villagers – asking prices are usually ludicrously high, dropping swiftly once bargaining commences. Don't show any interest unless you really want to buy, or you'll be mercilessly hounded.

Aside from the **north gate** (which can also be climbed), Dali's northern end has a busy **artisans' quarter** along the upper reaches of Bo'ai Lu and Fuxing Lu. Here carpenters and masons turn out the heavy and uncomfortable-looking tables and chairs inlaid with streaky grey **Dali marble** that lurk in Chinese emporiums around the world. Mined up in the hills, smaller pieces of marble are worked into all sorts of souvenirs – rolling pins, miniature pagodas, chopping boards – which you can buy from shops and stalls in town.

Eating and drinking

Sweet buns and noodle soups constitute a typical Dali breakfast and are sold by street stalls and cheap restaurants around the centre. Snacks include pickled vegetables wrapped in a fine pancake, and brittle "fans" of dried yoghurt often fried and crumbled over other dishes – much nicer than they sound. Two **specialities** are based on fish from Er Hai Lake: *shaguoyu*, where the fish is fried, then simmered with dried vegetables in a pork stock, and *youdeyu*, a casserole of small oily sprats and tofu.

Dali's **cafés** serve a hotchpotch of Sinicized Western dishes, and are good places to meet other foreigners and get in touch with the latest martial art, language or painting courses. They swing in and out of favour, so it's difficult to make recommendations, but the ones listed below are good starting points. Check the accommodation listings for **hotel restaurants**.

Café de Jacks, Bo'ai Lu. Popular after dark for its bar and Chinese version of curries, pizzas and salads.

Jim's Peace Café, Huguo Lu. A long-termers' hangout serving a fine yak stew.

Garden Restaurant (*Xinghua Jiudian*), eastern end of Yu'er Lu. Despite a monastic austerity in the stone floors and well-used wooden furniture, this is the best place in town for an inexpensive, accomplished and tasty Chinese meal.

Marley's, Huguo Lu. Known for its chocolate cake, Marley's also organizes "Bai banquets" on Sunday night if they can get the numbers; book before 6pm.

Yunnan Restaurant, eastern end of Huguo Lu. A tidy and refined place to eat spinach lasagne as well as more traditional specialities. Good masseur upstairs.

Around Dali

Plentiful public **minibuses** shuttle between Xiaguan and the villages along Er Hai's western shore. These can be flagged down on the highway immediately west of Dali, and are a cheaper and more flexible way to get around than the **tours** offered by agents – though the latter are convenient and reasonable value. Alternatively, you could rent a bike (see p.731).

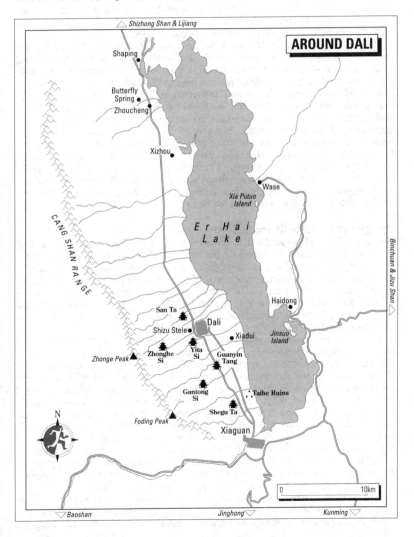

The pagodas and southern sites

Built when the region was a major Buddhist centre, Dali's distinctively tall and elegant pagodas are still standing after a millennium of wars and earthquakes. Just west of Dali's southern gate is the solitary **Yita Si**, a tenth-century tower and Ming temple surrounded by ancient trees and virtually abandoned. Better presented is **San Ta**, the **Three Pagodas**, a twenty-minute walk north of town in the grounds of the now vanished Chongsheng Monastery (8am–5pm; ¥6). Built around 850, the square-based **Qianxun tower** stands 69m high, some hundred years older than the two smaller octagonal pagodas behind. All were raised using the "earth-stacking" method – an immense rampart was built around each pagoda as it grew layer by layer, and then removed. As the structures are sealed, San Ta really looks best at a distance – the entrance fee gives you access only to souvenir stalls and a hall at the back containing religious relics discovered during renovations in the 1970s.

With the exception of **Du Wenxiu's Tomb**, a stone sarcophagus 4km southeast at the lakeside village of **Xiadui**, most historic sites **south of Dali** lie along the highway to Xiaguan. **Guanyin Tang** is about 5km away, a temple complex famed for an unusually square and heavily ornamented pavilion raised to Guanyin, the Goddess of Mercy, who routed Dali's enemies during the Han dynasty. Walk west of Guanyin Tang into the hills and it's about an hour's climb to **Gantong Si**, once Dali's most celebrated Buddhist monastery but now reduced to two partially restored halls. Back on the highway about halfway to Xiaguan, two ill-defined ridges on the plain below Foding Peak are all that remain of the Nanzhao city of **Taihe**, though a modern pavilion here houses the contemporary **Nanzhao Stele**, recounting eighth-century dealings between the Nanzhao and Tang courts. Finally, look for the forty-metre-high **Shegu Ta** (Snake-bone Pagoda) at **Yangping village**, almost in Xiaguan's northern suburbs, a Ming pagoda commemorating the fatal battle between a young hero and a menacing serpent demon, both of whom are buried below.

Zhonghe and north to Shizhong Shan

Due **west** of Dali, **Zhonghe Peak** is one of the tallest in the Cang Shan range, its four-thousand-metre summit often snow-capped until June. For a partial ascent, start at the small bridge on the highway just north of town and walk through the graveyards to the **Shizu Stele**, a four-metre-high inscribed tablet planted in 1304 to record Kublai Khan's conquest of Yunnan half a century earlier. The fairly easy path winds up through the pine trees from here up to **Zhonghe Si** (2hr), where you can enjoy a cup of tea with the Buddhist monks and admire the stupendous view of the lake and the mountains beyond.

There are some interesting **villages** along the lake **north** of Dali. About 20km up the highway, motor-rickshaws wait to carry passengers the couple of kilometres east to **XIZHOU**, a military base during the Nanzhao Kingdom and later a wealthy agricultural town known for the Bai mansions raised by leading families. Ninety of these compounds survive, based on wings of rooms arranged around a courtyard and decorated with "pulled" eaves and wall paintings. North again is **ZHOUCHENG**, known for its tie-dyeing, and beyond here is the **Butterfly Spring**, a small pond which supposedly becomes the haunt of clouds of rare butterflies when an overhanging acacia flowers in early summer, though there's little to see otherwise. Overlooking the very top of the lake about 30km from Dali, **SHAPING** is definitely worth a visit for its incredible **Monday market**, when what seems like the entire regional population of peasants, labourers, con-men and artisans crowds on to the small hill behind town to trade in everything imaginable from livestock to hardware and bags of hemp.

With a couple of days to spare, head out to the forested slopes of **Shizhong Shan**, 140km northwest of Dali via the towns of Diannan and Shaxi, where there's accommodation. A handful of temples and grottoes dating back to the Nanzhao Kingdom

NORTHWESTERN YUNNAN

Chuxiong	楚雄	*chǔxióng*
Chuxiong Binguan	楚雄宾馆	*chǔxióng bīnguǎn*
Dali	大理	*dàlǐ*
Dali Museum	大理博物馆	*dàlǐ bówùguǎn*

AROUND DALI

Butterfly Spring	湖蝶泉	*húdié quán*
Du Wenxiu's Tomb	杜文秀之墓	*dù wénxiù zhī mù*
Er Hai Lake	洱海	*érhǎi*
Gantong Si	甘通寺	*gāntōng sì*
Guanyin Tang	观音堂	*guānyīng táng*
Jizu Shan	鸡足山	*jīzú shān*
San Ta	三塔寺	*sāntǎ sì*
Shaping	沙坪	*shāpíng*
Shegu Ta	蛇骨塔	*shégǔ tǎ*
Shizhong Shan	石钟山	*shízhōng shān*
Taihe	太河	*tài hé*
Wase	挖色	*wāsè*
Xizhou	喜洲	*xǐzhōu*
Yita Si	一塔寺	*yītǎ sì*
Zhoucheng	周城	*zhōuchéng*

Lijiang	丽江	*lìjiāng*
Black Dragon Pool Park	黑龙潭公园	*hēilóng tán gōngyuán*
Dongba Cultural Research Institute	东巴文化研究室	*dōngbā wénhuà yánjiūshì*
Five Phoenix Hall	五凤楼	*wǔfēng lóu*
Lion Hill	狮子山	*shīzī shān*
Mu Clan Garden	木家院	*mù jiā yuán*

ACCOMMODATION

Grand Lijiang	丽江大酒店	*lìjiāng dàjiǔdiàn*
Red Sun	红太阳酒店	*hóng tàiyán jiǔdiàn*
Yu Quan	玉泉饭店	*yù quán fàndiàn*
Yunshan	云杉饭店	*yúnshān fàndiàn*

AROUND LIJIANG

Baisha	白沙	*báishā*
Jinjiang	金江	*jīnjiāng*
Lugu Hu	泸沽湖	*lúgǔ hú*
Meili Xue Shan	梅里雪山	*méilǐ xuě shān*
Ninglang	宁蒗	*nínglàng*
Qiaotou	桥头	*qiáo tóu*
Shigu	石鼓	*shígǔ*
Tiger Leaping Gorge	虎跳峡	*hǔtiào xiá*
Weixi	维西	*wéi xī*
Yongsheng	永胜	*yǒng shèng*
Yuhu	玉湖村	*yùhú cūn*
Yulong	玉龙	*yùlóng*
Yufeng Si	玉峰寺	*yùfēng sì*
Zhongdian	中甸	*zhōngdiàn*
Xiaguan	下关	*xiàguān*
Xiaguan Binguan	下关宾馆	*xiàguān bīnguǎn*
Xiaguan Fandian	下关饭店	*xiàguān fàndiàn*

are ranged up the slopes, connected by a thousand-step staircase, full of very out of the ordinary sculptures and frescoes. Some of these are graphically sexual, others show emissaries from India and the Middle East, and everyday scenes from the Nanzhao court.

Er Hai Lake and Jizu Shan

Heading east out of Dali's north gate, an hour's walk brings you to the shores of forty-kilometre-long **Er Hai Lake**, so called because it's shaped like an ear ("*er*"). The thing to do here is arrange a **fishing trip** or excursion out to the islets and villages around the east shore (¥25–50), most easily done through an agent in Dali, though Chinese speakers can try going down first thing in the morning and bargaining directly with boat owners.

A pleasant day out, there's really nothing to do on the lake beyond watching clouds constantly forming and dissipating over Cang Shan. Directly across from Dali, uninhabited **Jinsuo Island** was the summer retreat for Nanzhao royalty, while more northerly **Xia Putuo Island** is a tiny rock completely occupied by a decrepit temple and equally withered guardian who stumbles out after payment. The far shore settlements of **HAIDONG** and **WASE** are full of fishing gear. You can stay the night in Wase at the government guesthouse (②) and catch the Saturday morning market, certainly less touristed than Shaping's.

From Wase there are minibuses 30km south to Xiaguan, and also 60km southwest to **BINCHUAN**, from where it's a short hop to **SHAZHI** at the foot of **Jizu Shan** (Chicken Foot Mountain), one of western China's holiest peaks after the legendary monk **Jiaye** brought Buddhism from India to China and fought here with the wicked Chickenfoot King. By the seventh century both Buddhist and Taoist pilgrims were coming in their thousands to honour his memory. In its heyday, a hundred or more monasteries graced Jizu's heights, including the original Golden Temple transported here from Kunming, though by 1980 all but half a dozen had decayed. Things are now picking up again, and everyone who visits the mountain enthuses about the scenery, **Zhusheng Si**, and the ninth-century **Lengyan Pagoda** and accompanying **Jinding Si**, a temple splendidly positioned on a cliff edge at the summit. The track to the peak takes about half a day, with food and basic lodgings at Shazhi, Zhusheng, and Jinding.

Lijiang and around

Five hours north of Dali through numerous Bai and Yi hamlets, the bus makes its final descent from the ridges to a plain dominated by the inspiringly spiky and ice-bound massif of **Yulong Xue Shan**, the Jade Dragon Snow Mountain. Nestled to the south-east among green fields and dwindling pine forests is **LIJIANG**, capital of the old **Naxi Kingdom** and everything that China really should be, but so rarely is. Miraculously surviving political turmoils and now given state protection, much of the old town was built over two centuries ago, and it's worth the journey here just to lose yourself for a day among the fairy-tale maze of winding lanes and clean streams, wooden wineshops, weeping willows and rustic stone bridges. Then there are the **Naxi** themselves, descended from a race of Tibetan nomads who settled the Lijiang valley before the tenth century – "Naxi" means "Black People", from the colour of the tents in which they once lived. Until recently a matriarchal society, they brought with them what are still considered some of the sturdiest horses in China, and a shamanistic religion known as **Dongba**. A blend of Tibetan Bon, animism and Taoist tendencies, Dongba's scriptures were written with unique pictograms and its pantheistic **murals** still decorate village temples around Lijiang.

THE 1996 EARTHQUAKE

During research for this guide in February 1996, northwestern Yunnan was hit by a **Force 7 earthquake** centred 60km north of Lijiang. Villages were levelled, three hundred people killed outright, tens of thousands injured and two thirds of the regional population were left homeless. Despite Dayan being reopened to tourists within a month, it was estimated that ¥290 million was needed just to restore its streets and houses to their original style, and the total cost of repairs throughout the county runs into billions. As the guide went to press the condition of specific sites in the area was unknown.

Lijiang and the Naxi were the subject of an exhaustive account back in the 1930s by the eccentric botanist-anthropologist **Joseph Rock**, who lived in the region for twenty years. His book, *The Ancient Nakhi Kingdom of Southwest China*, is well worth dipping into before you leave home (it consists of two massive volumes). Also set in Lijiang and only slightly less monumental, the 1990s British television documentary *Beyond the Clouds* provides insights about the general concerns of modern China's rural population, rather than being a comprehensive account of local culture.

The Town

Orientated north–south, **Xinde Lu** is Lijiang's three-kilometre-long main street. Just about everything west of this line was built during the 1950s in the drabbest Soviet manner imaginable, but east, behind **Lion Hill**'s radio mast, is where you'll find the old town, known locally as **Dayan**. It's not easy to navigate around these backstreets, but as there are few particular sights this hardly matters. While you wander, try to peek in around the solid wooden gates of **Naxi houses**. These substantial two-storey homes are built around a central paved courtyard, eaves and screens carved with mythological figures and fish, representing good luck. Family houses are very important to the Naxi – Lijiang was formerly organized into clans – and many people spend a large part of their income maintaining and improving them.

Turning east off Xinde Lu at a large junction about halfway along its length, you'll find yourself at the top end of a square. From here, **Xinhua Lu** and **Xianfeng Lu** both run due south through the maze, more or less directly, to **Sifang**, Dayan's main marketplace. Though it is more and more geared up to the tourists who come to buy embroidery and wooden carvings of hawks and cockerels, cheap **restaurants** around the square make it a fine place to stop and watch for older people wearing traditional dark tunics and capes patterned in cream and blue, representing the cosmos. South and east are more markets, streams and cobbles, while to the west there are are views of Dayan's tiled roofs from **Lion Hill**, and the **Mu Clan Garden**, named after Lijiang's hereditary rulers during the Ming dynasty.

When you've had enough of strolling the old streets, head up to **Black Dragon Pool Park** (Heilongtan Gongyuan; daily 7am–late evening; ¥6) on Dayan's northern outskirts. Less contrived than the average public space in China, the sizeable pool is also known as **Yuquan** (Jade Spring), after the clear, pale green water which wells up from the base of surrounding hills. With Jade Dragon Mountain behind, the elegant mid-pool **Deyue Pavilion** is Lijiang's most photographed scene – take advantage of the park's late opening hours and share the sunset view with courting couples and hosts of unseen frogs.

A path runs around the shore between a spread of trees and buildings, passing first the cluster of compounds which comprise the **Dongba Cultural Research Institute**. The word "dongba" relates to the shamans themselves, about thirty of whom are still

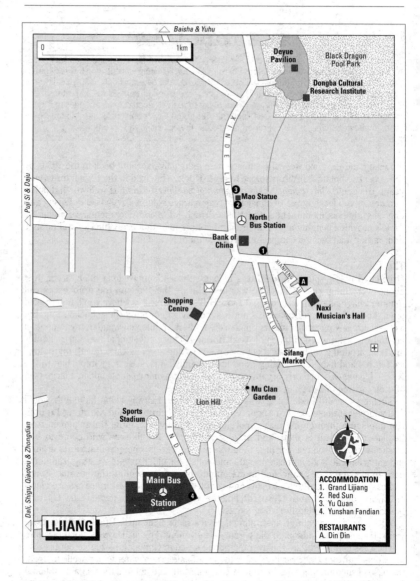

alive and kept busy here translating twenty thousand rolls of the old Naxi scriptures, *dongba-jings*, for posterity. Farther around is a low wooden hall and kiosk where the **Naxi Orchestra** holds afternoon sessions three times a week, and almost at the top end of the pool is a group of halls imported in the 1970s from the site of what was once Lijiang's major temple, **Fuguo Si**. The best of these is Wufeng Lou, the **Five Phoenix Hall**, a grand Ming-dynasty palace with a triple roof and interior walls embellished with reproductions of Baisha's temple murals (see p.740).

THE NAXI ORCHESTRA

While in Lijiang, make sure you catch the incredible **Naxi Orchestra**, so perfectly fitting the mood of the old town that it's hard to imagine them existing anywhere else. Using antique instruments, the performers are the last musicians in China playing Song tunes derived from the Taoist *Dong Jin* scriptures. The tradition apparently arrived in Lijiang with Kublai Khan, who donated half his court orchestra to the town after the Naxi chieftain helped his army cross the Yangzi, and it remained in vogue here long after being forgotten in the rest of the country. Banned from performing for many years, the orchestra regrouped after the Cultural Revolution under the guidance of **Xuan Ke**, though the deaths of many older musicians have reduced their repertoire from over 60 to just 23 pieces.

Invited to Britain for eight concerts in 1995 – a visit that the Chinese government allowed but declined to fund – the orchestra now plays almost daily in Lijiang. Performances take place every other night at 8pm in their well-marked hall on Xianfeng Lu, and at 2.30pm Monday, Wednesday and Friday in Black Dragon Pool Park. The music is haunting, and it's worth the ¥20 entrance fee just to listen to Xuan Ke's commentary (he speaks excellent English) and watch the elderly musicians, each apparently off in their own private world as they strum, warble and hammer on their instruments.

Practicalities

The **main bus station** is one of many grey concrete blocks at Lijiang's southern end. A fifteen-minute walk uphill along Xinde Lu takes you past a shopping centre and the **post office** to the town's major intersection. Head east here and you're on your way into Dayan, while Xinde Lu continues north past the *Bank of China*, the small **North bus station** and a statue of Chaiman Mao, ultimately taking you towards Black Dragon Pool Park. Rickshaws hang around the bus stations, but walking and cycling are the main means of getting around – try the pool hall a few doors up from the main bus station if your hotel can't rent you a bike. There is some overlap but, as a rule of thumb, buses **leaving Lijiang** for northern destinations such as Tiger Leaping Gorge and Zhongdian depart from the North bus station, while other directions are covered from the main depot.

All of Lijiang's **accommodation** is in the new town. Options include the *Yunshan Fandian* (☎08891/2124711; ①–③) at the main bus station, with "colourful TV in all rooms"; the *Red Sun Hotel* (*Hong Taiyan Jiudian*; ☎08891/2121018; ①–③) next to Mao's statue, whose clean dormitories overlooking the mountains, and hot showers, are a budget traveller's dream; the neat *CITS*-run *Yu Quan Hotel* on Mao's far side (dorms ①, rooms ③); and the flashest place in the county, the *Grand Lijiang Hotel* (☎08891/2128888; ⑧), just off the main road on the way into Dayan.

Lijiang's **restaurants** enjoy a good standard of cooking, though food is rarely remarkable. Local treats are limited to *baba*, a rather stodgy deep-fried flour patty stuffed with meat or vegetables, and the ill-defined "eight dish banquet" selection. **Hotels** all have accomplished kitchens, and there are several canteens near Mao's statue, but the old town's **inns** around Sifang marketplace are a better setting for rice pots, pork stews and dried ham dishes. Some have gone to the trouble of translating their names into English, such as "Welcome to Flourish Snack" and "Playroom of Magnificent Electron". On the way to Sifang, evening **hotpot** stalls set up along Xinhua Lu, while there are several large **tourist restaurants** on Xianfeng Lu: *Din Din* is currently popular with Chinese and foreigners alike for its broad range of cooking styles and low prices. In winter, keep an eye open in the markets for the best **walnuts** in Yunnan, and bright orange **persimmons** growing on big, leafless trees around town – these have to be eaten very ripe and are definitely an acquired taste.

Puji, Baisha and beyond

Rich pickings surround Lijiang, with numerous **temples** and villages on the lower slopes of Yulong Shan well within bicycle range. Single women should be on their guard when visiting the more remote temples, as the recent behaviour of some of the caretakers has been less than exemplary.

The monastery of **Puji Si** is the closest to Lijiang, and though it's difficult to find and not of great importance, in summer the journey there takes you through a valley brimming with wild flowers of all descriptions. Head west from the Mao Statue for about 1.5km, then turn left; snake around for a further couple of kilometres on a dirt track and you'll reach **PUJI village**. Ask here for a safe place to leave your bicycle and walk up the hill for thirty minutes or so to where an eccentric caretaker will open the monastery up for you. Inside it's new (like other temples in the area, Puji was destroyed during the Cultural Revolution) and completely deserted.

More ambitious is a trip to the village of **BAISHA**, about 10km north of Lijiang. From the top of Xinde Lu, take the road left just before Black Dragon Pool Park and follow it for a couple of kilometres until you reach a big reservoir. Keep straight on up the main road for 8km and then take a substantial track left across the fields. Baisha is an attractive place, planted with willows and home to the renowned **Doctor Ho** who lives at the north end and will doubtless detect your presence, inviting you in to drink one of his cure-all herb teas and make a donation. Prise yourself away and make for the alleyway leading up from the school to **Liuli Dian**, a temple housing the most wonderful Ming-dynasty **murals** whose strange mix of Taoist, Tibetan and Buddhist influences was the work of local Dongbas.

It takes around an hour to reach Baisha by bike, and another ten minutes of pedalling north brings you to **YULONG village**. Nearby is **Beiyue Si**, a temple whose eighth-century origins predate the arrival of the Naxi in Lijiang, though it's been managed by descendants of the first Naxi landowners for almost a thousand years and is dedicated to one of their gods, **Sanduo**. There's a mighty statue of him inside, faced by the cringing, life-sized image of a peasant, a feudal tableau restored in 1987 after a visitation by the Red Guards. Farther north again is another village, and here a steep path leads up from the main road to **Yufeng Si**, the Jade Peak Temple (30min). It's not of great interest in itself, but there's an ancient, intertwined **camellia tree** in the top hall representing matrimonial harmony, and in spring the flower-filled courtyard with its mosaic floor is a nice spot for peaceful contemplation.

Two kilometres along the main road beyond Yufeng is **Yuhu**, the Jade Lake village where Joseph Rock based himself in the 1920s and 1930s. His house, "Nguluko", still stands and a steadily dwindling number of locals can remember him. Alternatively, Yufeng Si sits in the foothills of Yulong Shan itself, and higher up are the villages of **Yi** herders and woodcutters, whose women wear oversized black bonnets and three-coloured skirts. The 5596-metre mountain is too difficult to climb without proper equipment, but there are endless possibilities for careful wandering around the trails across the lower slopes.

Beyond Lijiang: Shigu and Weixi

Buses head in all directions from Lijiang: south back to Dali; west to the dead-end town of **Weixi**; north past **Tiger Leaping Gorge** to **Zhongdian** near the Tibetan frontier; and east to **Lugu Hu** and Sichuan. While the latter journey has become a popular alternative route between the provinces, note that the Tibetan border is notorious for closing without warning, and you shouldn't count on being able to reach Lhasa this way.

Seventy kilometres west of Lijiang, **SHIGU** (Stone Drum) is a small place named after a tablet raised here by one of the Mu clan to mark the incorporation of the town into Lijiang's boundaries. Broad and not too rough, the **Yangzi River** makes its first major bend here, deflected sharply to the northeast towards Tiger Leaping Gorge, having flowed uninterrupted in a thousand-kilometre arc from its source away on the Tibet–Qinghai border. The Red Army chose this point to ford the Yangzi during the Long March in April 1936, breaking through Nationalist lines under the guidance of the spirited Communist general He Long. There's a small **guesthouse** (①) in Shigu, and it's a pretty area to spend a spring day walking around.

For the adventurous, buses run 100km northwest beyond Shigu through a beautiful, little-explored area which still lacks any tourist infrastructure. The road follows the Yangzi to the halfway town of **Jiudian**, and then bears west past the slopes of **Hengduan Shan** and **Xinzhu Botanical Garden** – basically just a protected natural hillside boasting over three hundred species of trees, some of which are estimated to be a thousand years old. **WEIXI** town marks the end of the road, of interest for nearby villages inhabited by the **Pumi**, a Tibetan race forming one of China's smallest nationalities.

Tiger Leaping Gorge

About 100km north of Lijiang, the Yangzi River's upper reaches, the Jinsha Jiang, channel dramatically through **Tiger Leaping Gorge** (Hutiao Xia), a gorge so narrow in places that legend has it a tiger once escaped pursuit by leaping across. The drama is heightened by this being the world's deepest canyon, set at an altitude of 2500 metres with the line of ash grey mountains forming its southern wall rising for a further 3km above the rapids. Statistics aside, what makes the **two-day hike through the gorge** so compelling is that for once you are doing this entirely for its own sake: there are no temples to see, the villages along the way are quaint but minute, and the gorge's pastoral residents have long since stripped the land of trees and shrubs.

The forty-kilometre-long trail runs between westerly **Qiaotou**, on the Lijiang–Zhongdian road, and **Daju** in the east, both connected by daily services to Lijiang's North bus station. Hostel **accommodation and meals** are easily available at the end points and along the way, though you need to bring snacks, a solid pair of boots, flashlight and a first-aid kit. Winter days are often warm enough to hike in a T-shirt and shorts, but nights are cold throughout the year.

It's best not to walk alone – most locals are friendly, if baffled by your presence, but there have been several **muggings** in recent times. Impoverished gorge communities have been polarized by tourism as everybody tries to profit from this new source of income. This has led to paths being deliberately obscured and some people having a very difficult time while others find helpful guides who steer them through the pitfalls. Try and pick up the homemade **maps** floating around in Lijiang, as these provide some protection against misdirection. **Landslides** are a more serious hazard and killed a party of seven hikers in 1994 – do not attempt the walk in bad weather.

QIAOTOU TO DAJU

All things considered, the hike is superb. The dawn bus from Lijiang arrives about three hours later in the small township of **QIAOTOU**, where English signs pick out a canteen (a good place to fill up) and lodgings on the roadside. If you're ending your hike here, there are at least two buses a day **to Zhongdian**, another three hours north, and the same number back to Lijiang. Cross over the bridge, turn right and hand over ¥10 to pass through the gate at the start of the trail. Mountains rise to the left as you follow a vehicle track through open country for the next hour or so, then the path narrows at a concrete tiger statue and bends east into the gorge. The stretch between here and the halfway point is the best; the gorge is tight and steep, the Yangzi fast and rough, and the path narrow and potentially dangerous. Mining operations in the early stages don't help, undercutting the cliffs above the track, and the remains of two major landslides need some care to negotiate safely. Eight hours after leaving Qiaotou should see you at the open valley surrounding the tiny village of **WALNUT GROVE**, where two rival establishments provide good meals, beer and warm beds. The westerly one faces into the gorge and is a favourite for its front porch, where you can sit after dark and watch an amazing number of satellites zipping through the clear night skies.

Next morning it's only about two hours' walk before the mountains suddenly pull away at the gorge's eastern mouth, and you find yourself winding downhill with settlements and paths spread all over the plateau beyond. The main track circles around a huge bowl-shaped depression, and then seems to carry on down to the river. Leave it here and clamber up the slope above to a moderately sized village. Bear right through here and out into the fields and, ignoring any tracks crossing at right angles, keep going east for an hour more through a smaller group of stone houses, and you should be standing above the river again, overlooking a pagoda on the far bank. A sandy track cuts down to a **ferry** (¥10) and once across it's an easy hour's walk south to the dusty little jumble of stone-walled houses at **DAJU**. There are several restaurants and two simple guesthouses here, along with alpine scenery and outlying villages to explore. The **bus to Lijiang** leaves Daju around 2pm and takes an uncomfortable four hours, cutting through patches of primeval forests and finally skirting the base of Yulong Shan.

Zhongdian

Six hours and 200km northwest of Lijiang, **ZHONGDIAN** is a potential springboard **into Tibet or Sichuan**, though neither route is officially open. An uncharismatic town set on a wide plateau, there's a heavy police presence and a good number of Tibetans wandering around – a fine setting for being an anonymous bystander. The **bus station** is on the main road running north, with a **post office** next door. Walk east from here until you come to a T-junction. The **PSB** and *Chocolate Café* are a few minutes' walk north, with the *Bank of China* and Zhongdian's best **accommodation** at the *Tibet Hotel* (☎08895/222448, fax 222296; ①–④) in the opposite direction. In addition to food, the café provides information and **jeep rental** for trips north to **Meilu Xue Shan**, Yunnan's 6740-metre apex, and claims to be able to arrange travel permits from here to Lhasa and Chengdu with the PSB. An hour's walk from town (take the main road north, turn left at the fork, and then right soon afterwards and keep going), the **Jietang Songlin Monastery** will keep you busy for a day. Destroyed during the 1960s, it is now reactivated and there are four hundred monks in residence.

From Zhongdian, it's an extremely rough and unpredictably long 300km northeast to **Litang** in **Sichuan**, followed by the best part of a day's travel from Litang to Kangding (see p.820). The route northwest to the Tibetan border town of **Deden** is theoretically easier – this is the main Yunnan–Tibet highway after all – but the PSB will have to approve your presence before any vehicle will have you on board. Beyond Deden the road follows the dramatic upper reaches of the Lancang River to Markam, and then turns west towards Lhasa.

Lugu Hu and Jinjiang

An easier route into Sichuan from Yunnan heads 200km due east from Lijiang over the border to **Jinjiang**, the rail head for **Dukou** on the Kunming–Chengdu line. It's about a ten-hour trip — twelve coming the other way — and you're unlikely to forget the early stages of the journey, as the road traverses an almost sheer 1200-metre cliff on the way to the Yangzi crossing and the town of **YONGSHENG**, where the bus will probably stop for lunch. From here you could spend several days detouring 300km north on public transport to **NINGLANG** and thence to **Lugu Hu**, a remote lake whose partially forested shores are inhabited by groups of **Norzu** and **Mosuo**. A branch of Yi, the Norzu were **slave owners**, and well into the 1950s would raid surrounding lowlands for captives. These were dragged off into the mountains and condemned to live in abject misery while their masters had the power of life and death over them (more of the story is told in Alan Winnington's *Slaves of the Cool Mountains*). For their part, the Mosuo are a Naxi subgroup, still retaining the **matrilineal traditions** lost in Lijiang, such as *axia* marriage, sealed without a specific ceremony and freely broken by either party. Children are automatically adopted by the mother – men have no descendants or property rights. It takes a full day to get from Lijiang to Ninglang, and another half-day from here to the lakeshore **LUGU township**, where there's basic accommodation.

If you don't detour to Lugu, it takes about five hours to reach Jinjiang from Yongsheng, with most of the trip spent above the edges of broad irrigated valleys. Dukou's barren hills and grim industrial mess appear first, with **JINJIANG** – also known as **Panzhihua** – not far beyond. The bus stops right outside the station and, as Jinjiang is not somewhere you'd choose to stay for long, try and get on one of the evening trains. It's very hard to find anything better than hard seat for the fifteen-hour journey, however, so consider a comfort stop along the way at **Xichang** (see p.794). There's a **hostel** (②) opposite the train station if you get stuck, and a daybreak bus back to Lijiang.

Baoshan and Dehong

Southwest of Xiaguan, the latter 500km of China's section of the Burma Road continues relentlessly through **Baoshan Prefecture** and into the **Dehong Bai–Jingpo Autonomous Region**, cut by the deep watershed gorges of Southeast Asia's mighty **Mekong** and **Salween rivers** (Lancang Jiang and Nu Jiang respectively). It's spectacular country, almost entirely covered by tightly pinched extensions of the **Gaoligong Mountains**, whose dark monsoonal forests are believably inhabited by leopards and tigers, and the road for ever wobbles across high ridges or descends towards the green fields of rice and sugar cane which occupy the broad valleys in between. Settlements have large populations of **Dai**, **Burmese**, **Jingpo** and others, and until recently mainstream China never had a great presence here. Even after Kublai Khan invaded and left his relatives to govern from inside walled towns, the region was basketed into the "Department of Pacification and Mollification" and largely left to the pleasure of local *satraps* or **Saubwas**, hereditary landowners. They were deposed in the 1950s, but it's still often unclear whether rules and regulations originate in Beijing or with the nearest officer in charge – some of the goings-on along the Burmese border seem very unofficial indeed.

The Burma Road itself links the towns of **Baoshan**, **Mangshi** and the border crossing at **Wanding**, from where it's only an hour west to weird wonders at **Ruili**, more of a circus than a city. There's also a rougher back road between Baoshan and Ruili, taking in the tectonically unstable **Tengchong** region and some very dense jungle. Whichever way you travel, roads tend to disintegrate during the subtropically humid **wet season** between May and October, when airports at Baoshan and Mangshi may provide the only access.

Baoshan and around

Six hours from Xiaguan along 120km of bumpy, hand-cobbled highway, **BAOSHAN** certainly has its share of history. The region was settled long before Emperor Wudi's troops oversaw the paving of stretches of the Southern Silk Road nearby in 109 AD, and the famous third-century Sichuanese minister **Zhuge Liang** apparently reached Baoshan in one of his invasive "expeditions" across southwestern China. Kublai Khan fought a massive battle with the Burmese king **Narathihapade** outside the town in 1277, won by the khan after his archers managed to stampede Burmese elephants back through their own lines. Twenty years later the women and slaves of Marco Polo's "Vochan" (today's Baoshan) supported a tattooed, gold-toothed aristocracy — tooth-capping is still practised

BAOSHAN AND DEHONG

Baoshan	保山	*bǎoshān*
Taibao Shan Park	太保山公园	*tàibǎoshān gōngyuán*
Wenbi Pagoda	文笔塔	*wénbǐ tǎ*
Wuhou Si	武候寺	*wǔhòu sì*
Yu Huang Si	玉皇寺	*yùhuáng sì*
ACCOMMODATION		
Baoshan	保山饭店	*bǎoshān fàndiàn*
Yindou	银都大酒店	*yíndoū dàjiǔdiàn*
Yongchang	永昌宾馆	*yǒngchāng bīnguǎn*
AROUND BAOSHAN		
Banqiao	板桥	*bǎnqiáo*
Jihong Bridge	霁虹桥	*jìhóng qiáo*
Shuizhai	水寨	*shuǐzhài*
Wofo Si	卧佛寺	*wòfó sì*
Heshun Xiang	和顺乡	*héshùn xiāng*
Longlong	弄弄	*lònglòng*
Manbang	曼棒	*mànbàng*
Mangshi	芒市	*mángshì*
Mazhan	马站	*mǎzhàn*
Huo Shan Kou	火山口	*huǒ shān kǒu*
Rehai	热海	*rèhǎi*
Ruili	瑞丽	*ruìlì*
Mingrui	明瑞宾馆	*míngruì bīnguǎn*
Nanya	南亚宾馆	*nányà bīnguǎn*
Ruili	瑞丽宾馆	*ruìlì bīnguǎn*
Yongchang	永昌大酒店	*yǒngchāng dàjiǔdiàn*
AROUND RUILI		
Denghannong Si	召尚弄寺	*zhàoshàng nòngsì*
Jiexiang	姐相	*jiěxiàng*
Jinya Ta	金鸭塔	*jīnyā tǎ*
Nongdao Xiang	弄岛乡	*nòngdǎo xiāng*
Tengchong	腾冲	*téngchōng*
Laifeng Shan Park	来风山公园	*láifēng shān gōngyuán*
Si Lushe	四旅社	*sì lǚshè*
Tengchong Binguan	腾冲宾馆	*téngchōng bīnguǎn*
Wanding	畹町	*wǎndīng*
Wanding Binguan	畹町宾馆	*wǎndīng bīnguǎn*
Wanding Forest Park	畹町国家森林公园	*wǎndīng kuójiā sēnlín gōngyuán*
Yufeng Dasha	裕丰大厦	*yùfēng dàshà*
Zhonghe	中和	*zhōng hé*
Daying Shan	打应山	*dáyīng shān*

both here and in Xishuangbanna today. Baoshan was again in the front line in the 1940s, when a quarter of a million Chinese troops fought to keep the Japanese from invading through Burma, and remains garrisoned today, with young army recruits in poorly fitting green fatigues drilling around the parks and parade grounds.

The Town and around

Baoshan's centre is boxed in by **Huancheng Lu**, whose north, south, east and west sections follow the square lines of the now demolished Ming city walls. Ennobled as a city in 1983, Baoshan is nonetheless very much a provincial town, and its grubby, half-modernized streets are full of activity. In the Burma Road's heyday the shops stocked Western goods siphoned off from supply convoys heading through to Kunming, and even now they seem abnormally well provisioned with locally grown "World Number One Arabica" coffee, tins and bottles of imported luxuries, smart suits and shoes. Rural produce gets an airing in the **main marketplace** on Qingzhen Jie, a good place for a browse among Baoshan's older buildings, but it's not especially exciting. A nicer spot to spend a few hours among pine trees, butterflies and twittering birds is **Taibao Shan Park**, about 1.5km west of the centre at the end of Baoxiu Lu. Near the entrance is **Yu Huang Si**, a Ming Taoist temple whose slanted pillars support a small octagonal dome. It's no longer a place of worship, now filled with photos and maps describing local engagements with the Japanese forces, but you'll have to remove your shoes to visit the five alabaster Buddhas in the tiny nunnery next door.

The path climbs farther up to pavilions offering views over town and the surrounding Baoshan Plain, until it reaches **Wuhou Si** on the flattened, wooded summit. Wuhou Si commemorates the *Three Kingdoms* leader Zhuge Liang (see p.432), whose huge bearded statue sits between his ministers Wang Kang and Lu Kai. Behind the hall are some respectably large trees, and fragments of stone tablets recording imperial proclamations. On the far side of Taibao Shan is the thirteen-storey **Wenbi Pagoda** – blocked off and surrounded by graves – and **Yiluo Chi**, an uninteresting walled pond below the steps leading up to Baoshan's **Teacher Training College**. If you're looking for conversation, students and the couple of overseas teachers quartered here are often glad to talk to foreigners.

Practicalities

The **main bus station** (ticket office daily 8am–9pm) is on the corner of Huancheng Dong Lu and Baoxiu Lu, which runs due west straight through the city. About 500m along it's crossed by Zhengyang Lu, where there's a **Bank of China** (Mon–Fri 9–11.30am & 2–5pm), department store, and a tiny, well-concealed **airline office**. Gradually narrowing in its final kilometre, Baoxiu Lu is further crossed by Qingzhen Jie and Huancheng Xi Lu before ending at a staircase leading up to Taibao Shan Park.

Most **accommodation and food** options are also along Baoxiu Lu. Surrounded by dumpling, soup and noodle stalls, the bus station itself has a cheap **hostel** (①) attached. East and across the road are comfortable beds and awful plumbing at the *Sunshine Hotel* (①–②), while 50m west, the nondescript *Baoshan Fandian* (①–②) is a similar set-up and has its own bus ticket office. More upmarket are the *Yindou Dajiudian* (④), right next to the bank, and the *Yongchang Binguan* (②–④), in a courtyard on the south side of Baoxiu Lu just over Zhengyang Lu. Not counting the hotels, there are a dozen or more **restaurants** turning out decent stir-fries and casseroles between the bus station and the park, with the yellow-tiled Muslim place on the corner of Qingzhen Jie the best of the bunch – look for the Arabic script.

Moving on, there are direct daily buses to all destinations east and west including Kunming, Tengchong and Ruili, and also a lengthy southern link with Jinghong in Xishuangbanna – see p.753 before undertaking this journey.

Around Baoshan

Two more historical snippets lie near the town of **BANQIAO**, thirty minutes by bus from Baoshan on the Xiaguan road. About 7km northwest of Banqiao, **Wofo Si** (Reclining Buddha Temple) is a split-level cave at the foot of Yunyan Shan, named after a graceful fifteen-metre marble statue said to date from the Tang dynasty. Fifteen kilometres northeast of Banqiao is **SHUIZHAI township**; an hour's walk short of here the heavy-duty, five-hundred-year-old chains of the **Jihong Bridge** (Jihong Qiao) cross the **Mekong River**. There are infrequent minibuses to both sites from Baoshan, or you could try taking any bus to Banqiao and looking for local transport from there.

Tengchong and the back road to Ruili

The ghost of the former Southern Silk Road runs west of Baoshan, and the bus is initially slowed by police roadblocks and crowded village markets, then by steep hairpin bends as it skirts the seemingly impenetrable undergrowth of the **Gaoligong Shan Nature Reserve**. Two valleys along the way are fertilized by the early stirrings of the Salween and **Shweli** rivers (the latter a tributary of the Irrawaddy), both of which ultimately empty into the sea several thousand kilometres away in southern Burma.

Seven hours from Baoshan the bus trundles to a halt at **TENGCHONG**, an untidily dusty or muddy town depending on the season. A Han-dynasty settlement which first grew wealthy on Silk Road trade, Tengchong has a high incidence of **earthquakes**, which have left it bereft of large historic monuments or tall buildings, but business still flourishes and there are some unusual geological sights nearby. The **bus station** is in the eastern outskirts along Huancheng Dong Lu. For the centre, continue south past shops selling bamboo furniture and pipes, and then bear west down either Guanghua Lu or parallel Yingjiang Lu to where Tengchong's high street, **Fengshan Lu**, cuts across them at right angles. A farther kilometre south down Fengshan Lu takes you past a post office and bank (only useful as a landmark) to the junction with **Fangshou Lu**, the main road west out of town towards Ruili. Cycle-rickshaws wait at the station, though a walk right across town takes only thirty minutes.

Tengchong's premier market is the **Frontier Trade Bazaar**, held every morning along western Guanghua Lu. With most business revolving around imported household luxuries, things are not quite as romantic as they sound, but there's also a **jewellery and gem market** on Fengshan Lu, and both should whet your appetite for better affairs in Ruili. For a stroll, follow Guang Xiang for twenty minutes to its end at **Laifeng Shan Park**, several dozen square kilometres of hilly woodland immediately southwest of Tengchong. Full of family activity at weekends, paths meander out to the pretty **Dieshui He waterfall** and **Laifeng Si**, a monastery-turned-museum whose pleasantly restored Qing halls house exhibits expounding Tengchong's history.

For **accommodation**, try the rambling, simply furnished *Si Lushe* (①), hidden in a courtyard on the southern side of Yingjiang Lu, near where it meets Fengshan Lu. If this doesn't appeal, walk to the western end of Fengshan Lu, cross straight over Fangshou Lu and follow Guang Xiang – the continuation of Fengshan Lu – uphill. Take the first turning left and the quiet *Tengchong Binguan* (☎0875/5121044; dorms ①, rooms ③) is about 100m farther on. Their cheapest rooms are bare, but they can arrange **tours** into the countryside, and the **restaurant** provides small set meals for the princely sum of ¥4. Other general places to eat lurk along Yingjiang Lu and Guanghua Lu, where evening stalls also sell charcoal-grilled chicken and fish. There's a tiny **Burmese bar** at the entrance to *Si Lushe*, marked with an equally small English sign and patronized by people claiming to be diamond merchants – you'll make friends here if you can hold your rum.

Around Tengchong

Five kilometres west of town along Fangshou Lu, **HESHUN XIANG** is a Qing-style village whose splendid memorial gateways, ornamental gardens and thousand or more houses are tightly packed within a whitewashed brick wall. It is trumpeted for the achievements of its former residents, many of whom have led profitable lives after emigrating overseas and have since ploughed money back into the village's upkeep, and you could easily spend half a day here with a camera. In particular, look for **Yuanlong Tan**, a delightful pond surrounded by pavilions and a creaky water mill.

Geological shuffles over the last fifty million years have opened up a couple of hotspots around Tengchong, though unless the *Tengchong Binguan* has a tour going they take a little effort to reach from the bus station. Some 11km southwest along the Ruili Road at **Rehai** ("Hot Sea"), the scalding **Liuhuang** and **Dagungguo** pools steam and bubble away, contained by incongruously neat stone paving and ornamental borders. Volcano hunters should head 10km northwest to **Zhonghe** village and the slopes of 2614-metre-high **Daying Shan**, or 30km north to **Huo Shan Kou**, a large crater near the town of **Mazhan**. These two are the largest of many surrounding cones, dormant but covered in lava rubble from previous eruptions.

On to Ruili

The quickest way from Tengchong to Ruili is by taking the southeasterly road via Mangshi and Wanding (below), but there's also a direct road running west, towards and then along the Burmese border, a five-hour trip on a good day. This begins smoothly, cruising through a river valley where the scenery becomes less and less "Chinese" as the bus passes Dai villages with rounded wats, red-leaved poinsettias and huge, shady fig trees. Progress becomes less predictable after a lunch stop and more officious police checks near **Yingjiang**, where the road turns south to cross the ranges above Ruili. You may well get a close look at the forests here – one downhill stretch is notorious for the house-sized boulders which crash down from the slopes above to block the road completely, causing extended delays as labourers hammer and blast away at the obstructions. If this happens, go for a walk along the road, as there's birdlife hiding in patches of vegetation and villages along the way which have seen few foreigners.

Mangshi

South of Baoshan the Burma Road makes a grand descent into the Salween River valley on the five-hour journey to **MANGSHI**, Dehong's pocket-sized administrative capital and the site of its airport. Surrounded by Dai and Jingpo villages and usually marked on maps as **Luxi**, the Mangshi region has a reputation for excellent pineapples and silverwork, though the town itself has only enough to occupy a couple of hours between connections. Hot and grey, the highway runs through as **Tuan Jie Dajie**, its eastern end marked by a large roundabout and its western end by a narrow, black canal. Just over this canal, **Yueyi Lu** points north into a jumble of quieter, older streets filled with markets and a fair complement of **Buddhist temples** raised on wooden piles in the ornate Dai style, many of them being restored.

The **airport** is about 7km south off the highway, where taxis and minibuses to Mangshi, Ruili and Wanding meet incoming flights. Most Mangshi vehicles will set down at the eastern end of Tuan Jie Dajie, either on the roundabout outside the **airline office** (daily 8.30–11.30am & 1.30–5pm; the bus to the airport leaves 2hr before each flight) or about 100m west at the cluster of depots where **long-distance buses and minibuses** stop. The airline office has a clean and simple **hotel** attached (②), or there are the basic guest rooms of the *Dele Wineshop* (dorms ①, rooms ②), halfway between the roundabout and the canal, and the smart *Dehong Binguan* (③), nicely located in large grounds at the top of Yueyi Lu. The *Dehong* has a good **restaurant**, and there are countless shacks serving buns and shapeless curries in almost every back lane through the town.

Wanding and around

Two hours south of Mangshi the road crosses the Shweli River (Long Jiang) and then finally slaloms down the slopes of a narrow valley to where the shallow Wanding Stream separates Chinese **WANDING** from **Jiugu village** over in Burma. Opened in 1938 as the Burma Road's purpose-built border crossing, Wanding was immediately attacked by villagers who suspected that this customs post was connected with Guomindang units who were then busy trying to exterminate Mangshi's Jingpo hill tribes. The tension hasn't lasted, but, although hundreds of trucks a day passed through during the war, Wanding has never amounted to much – possibly because, aware of its showpiece status as China's official point of entry into Burma, authorities deter the illicit backroom dealings which make neighbouring Ruili such an attractive proposition for traders.

Not that Wanding is uninteresting. The **Wanding Bridge crossing** is a marvel, decked in customs houses, smartly uniformed military, barriers, barbed wire, flags and signs everywhere prohibiting unauthorized passage. The bridge itself – though ridiculously short – is a sturdy concrete arch, and there's even a prominent red line painted across the road on the Chinese side. But it's all a sham. Walk 100m downstream and you'll find people rolling up their trousers and wading across a ford almost within sight of patrolling soldiers, while farther on some enterprising soul has even set up a rubber raft to punt customers over to the far bank. Naturally everyone knows what's happening, but this arrangement spares authorities and locals (for whom the border is more or less open anyway) endless official bother.

Unfortunately, **foreigners wanting to cross** will find the situation very different. At the time of writing, Westerners could enter Burma only by flying to Rangoon (see "Kunming", p.717 for more details), and though some have quietly snuck across from Wanding for an hour or two, bear in mind that you'll be very conspicuous and that there's little to see in Jiugu apart from a large wat on the hill above.

Practicalities

Wanding stretches thinly for 1.5km along the north bank of the Wanding Stream and Minzhu Jie, both of which run west towards Ruili, with Guofang Jie descending from the hills at Minzhu's eastern end to the border checkpoint and Wanding Bridge. There's no **bus station** as such, but local transport and vehicles shuttling between Mangshi and Ruili stop around the Minzhu Jie–Guofang Jie intersection. Here you'll also find a couple of fairly wholesome **restaurants**, with a **bank** (Mon–Fri 8.30–11.30am & 2–5pm) and **post office** (daily 8am–8pm) nearby on Minzhu Jie. **Accommodation** prospects are limited to the cavernous but clean *Yufeng Dasha* on the northeast corner of the intersection (dorms ①, rooms ②), and the surprisingly good *Wanding Binguan* (②–④) uphill off Minzhu Jie on Yingbin Lu. Despite the border, the backstreet **markets** along Wanding Stream are unenthusiastic affairs. Street hawkers sell herbs and roots and you can pick up presentation packs of **Burmese coins** from a little shop near the bridge.

Around Wanding: the Forest Park and the Jingpo

One of the best ways to get a good look at Burma from the Chinese side is to spend an hour in **Wanding Forest Park** – walk uphill along Guofang Jie, take the first lane on the left and follow it upwards to the park gates. A few minutes more bring you to an amusement area, where a dirt footpath leads into scrub and pine plantations behind the dodgems, eventually ending up at a newly completed **temple**, bare inside except for prayer cushions and a large alabaster Buddha. The front entrance looks down across the border at undulating green hills and the red earth continuation of the Burma Road heading south of the crossing towards Lashio.

There are a number of **Jingpo villages** around Wanding. The *Wanding Binguan* sometimes organizes tours, otherwise look for minibuses at the intersection in town. Fifteen kilometres west via **Manbang** township, **LONGLONG** comes alive for the **Munao festival** on the last day of the lunar new year (usually some time in February), when hundreds of Jingpo take part in an ancient dance said to have been handed down to their ancestors by the children of the sun god. Always considered a primitive spirit-worshipping race by the Han government, and so poor that in the early twentieth century they were forced to grow opium as a cash crop (hence the Guomindang campaign against them), the Jingpo live a relatively secluded existence in the Dehong highlands, and their settlements around Wanding are some of the most accessible.

Ruili and around

Yunnan's most westerly town, **RUILI** is barely an hour by road from the sober formalities and politely quiet cross-border sneaking at Wanding, but infinitely distant in spirit. Once the capital of the Mengmao Dai Kingdom but now an absurdly ostentatious boom town, Ruili revels in the commercial possibilities of its proximity to Burma – 5km south over the Shweli – with such a heavy flow of primarily illegal traffic pouring over the dozens of crossing points to **Mu Se**, its Burmese counterpart, that locals quip "feed a chicken in China and you get an egg in Burma". It's a two-way trade, however, and Ruili is the main conduit for Burmese heroin entering China, reflected in the town's high incidence of addicts and AIDS patients, all of them intravenous drug users. Burmese, Pakistani and Bangladeshi nationals wander around in sarongs and thongs, clocks are generally set to Rangoon time, markets display foreign trade goods and most Chinese in town seem to be tourists, attracted by the chance to pick up some cut-price trinkets and the decadent thrill of night-long karaoke sessions. Ruili's **karaoke craze** is so intense that there are not enough clubs for the howling hordes of late-night revellers, so scores of entrepreneurs set up videos, microphones and amplifiers out in the streets, blocking pavements and making the town audible kilometres away. While all this might sound like something to avoid, here at the fringes of the Chinese empire Ruili is a surreal treat. If the town's nightlife appals you, the **markets** are fascinating, and many foreign traders speak good English and make interesting company.

The markets

Washed red and blue at night in the glare of competing neon signs, by day Ruili's broad pavements and drab construction pin it down as a typical modern Chinese town. Fortunately, the markets and people are anything but typical, and the predominantly **Burmese stallholders** in Xingshi Jie can sell you everything from haberdashery and precious stones to birds, cigars, Thai whisky and Western-brand toiletries. Dai girls from both sides of the border unevenly powder their faces with yellow talc, youths politely ask whether you'd like to part with your watch and street sellers skilfully assemble little pellets of stimulating *pan* – slices of boiled **betel nut** dabbed in ash paste and wrapped in pepper-vine leaf – which stains lips red and teeth black.

The Burmese are very approachable, and some are refugees of a sort, as upheavals in Rangoon in 1991 saw Muslims slipping over the border to enjoy China's relatively tolerant attitudes on religious freedom. Many pedal their wares at the **jade and gem**

market in an alley off Xingshi Jie, where Chinese dealers come to stock up on ruinously expensive wafers of deep green jade. You'll need hard currency (prices are given in US dollars) but most of the rubies, amethysts, blue quartz "sapphires", moonstones and garnets on show are flawed and poorly cut. The art of buying is a protracted process here, with dealers producing their better stones only for properly appreciative customers. For the newcomer, it's safer just to watch the furtive huddles of serious merchants, or negotiate souvenir prices for coloured pieces of sparkling Russian glass "jewels", chunks of polished substandard jade and heavy brass rings. When you've filled your pockets, Dai and Jingpo haunt Ruili's huge **produce market**, ten minutes' walk past the post office off the west end of Xingshi Lu. What you can't find here isn't worth eating, and the piles of deer meat and wildcat pelts, limes, palm sugar blocks (*jaggery*), coconuts, curry pastes and pickles make the market a far cry from the standard Chinese effort.

Practicalities

Ruili's kilometre-long main street is **Nanmao Jie**, which runs west from a roundabout tree past the *Bank of China* (foreign exchange Mon–Fri 9–11.30am & 2.30–4.30pm), a **minibus depot** for transport into the immediate area, and the **long-distance bus station**, ending at a T-junction with Renmin Lu. Turn north here and there's a **post office** (daily 8am–6pm) 50m away on the corner of Xingshi Jie, along which is Ruili's major market. Cross over the broad junction here and continue up Jianshe Lu for *Ruili Travel Service* (Mon–Sat 7.30–11.30am & 3–6.30pm) next to the *Ruili Hotel*. They don't speak English, but can organize air tickets, and there's an **airport bus** from here to Mangshi every morning – book the day before. **Leaving**, there are minibuses every hour to Wanding, and at least daily buses to everywhere along the highway between here and Kunming.

ACCOMMODATION

Lucheng, behind the Nanmao Jie minibus depot (☎0692/4146988). Quite smart but overpriced standard Chinese hotel. Triples and doubles. ⑤.

Mingrui, western end of Nanmao Jie. It doesn't look too promising at first, with peeling decor, a basement disco and second-floor karaoke, but this place actually has the best budget rooms in Ruili. Also rents out bicycles. ②.

Nanya, southern end of Renmin Lu. Simple hostel in a quieter part of town. Dorms ①, rooms ③.

Ruili, corner of Jianshe Lu and Xinjian Lu (☎0692/4141463 or 4141269). Nice grounds with a palm garden, fair-value rooms – all have shared toilets – and a good restaurant. Scruffy dorms ①, rooms ④.

Yongchang, Renmin Lu, near the corner with Nanmao Jie. A relaxed, clean place, almost always full with Burmese merchants. Rarely available dorm beds ②, rooms ④.

EATING AND DRINKING

The mobile **stalls** around the market on Xingshi Jie serve fine grilled meats, hotpots, soups and buns, and you'll also come across some Burmese delicacies. Try *moongsee joh*, a sandwich made from purple glutinous rice pancakes heated over a grill until they puff up, and spread with sugar and peanut powder. Another similar confection involves bamboo tubes stuffed with pleasantly bland, sweetened rice jelly.

Hotel restaurants all have good Chinese fare, but since you're here, try the *Lucky Restaurant*'s first-rate **Burmese food**, hidden away at the eastern end of the Xingshe Jie market. It doesn't look much, but this Muslim family café can produce a platter of a half-dozen small pots of tasty pickles, curry and dhal for about ¥8, and also sells plain cakes and tea. If you can't find English speakers to help, try ordering from the box below.

BURMESE GLOSSARY			
Hello (polite)	*Min galaba jinbaya*	Fish soup with	*Moh hin gha*
Thank you	*Jayzu tinbadé*	banana stem	
I'd like to eat	*Htamin saa gyinbadé*	and noodles	
Beef	*Amé*	Milk	*Nwa nou*
Chicken	*Je*	Noodles	*Kaukswe*
Curry	*Hin, tha*	Pickled vegetables	*Lapatoh*
Cold drink	*A-ay*	Rice	*Htamin*
Dhal (split pea soup)	*Pey hin*	Sour sauce	*Achin*
Fish	*Nga*	Tea	*La pay-ee*

Around Ruili

Villages and Buddhist monuments dot the plains around Ruili, easy enough to explore either by renting a bicycle from the *Mingrui Binguan*, or by minibus from the Nanmao Jie depot – just keep repeating the name of your destination and you'll be shepherded to the right vehicle. *Ruili Travel Service* can also organize private transport for the day, but it tends to be expensive. Most of the destinations below are only of mild interest in themselves, really just excuses to get out into Ruili's often beautiful countryside. For more about the Dai, see the Xishuangbanna section (p.752).

A few sights lie within walking distance. About 5km east along the Mangshi road is the two-hundred-year-old **Jiele Jin Ta**, a group of seventeen portly **Dai pagodas** painted gold and said to house several of Buddha's bones. Nearby are some open-air hot springs where you can wash away various ailments. The same distance south takes you past the less expansive **Jinya Ta** (Golden Duck Pagoda) to the busy **bridge over the Shweli River** into Burma, though apart from the volume of traffic, there's little to see.

Heading west along the road from Jinya Ta, another 5km brings you to a small bridge with the region's largest Buddhist temple, the nicely decorated **Hansha Si**, just off to the north. Ten kilometres beyond Hansha Si is the town of **JIEXIANG** and the splendid Tang-era **Leizhuang Xiang**, where the low square hall of a nunnery is dominated by a huge central pagoda and four corner towers, all in white. Another fine temple with typical Dai touches, such as "fiery" wooden eave decorations, **Denghannong Si**, is farther west again, and though the current halls were built only during the Qing dynasty, the site is said to mark where Buddha once stopped to preach. Beyond Denghannong, about 25km in all from Ruili, **NONGDAO XIANG** is a nice place to spend the evening chatting to locals. There's a hostel (②) next to the post office, and the town is surrounded by Dai communities.

SOUTHERN YUNNAN

Even more so than northern Yunnan, which at least backs on to other Chinese territories, southern Yunnan's culture and history are products of adjoining countries. **Transport** into the south has always been a problem for any external power seeking to control the area. Even the regional rivers – historically so important for interprovincial communications in central China – here run out of the country into Laos and Vietnam, and long-promised highways were only completed in the 1990s. Most visitors find their attention fully taken up by the ethnically and environmentally diverse southwestern corner of **Xishuangbanna**, but there should soon be unrestricted access to the southeastern reaches **between Kunming and Vietnam**, though the border here (and the crossing into Laos from Xishuangbanna) has been open to independent travellers for some time. In early 1996, exactly where you could go was subject to negotiations; the Kunming PSB was adamant that, though the routes themselves were open for transit purposes, the regions surrounding the Vietnam border and the road into Xishuangbanna from northwestern Yunnan were off-limits to foreigners. Typically, those Westerners who didn't bother asking for permission found local officials completely indifferent to their presence, and roamed about unimpeded. Still, it's best to be aware of the possibility of being turned around or fined if you wander too far off-track.

Xishuangbanna

A lush tropical spread of virgin rainforests, plantations and paddy fields nestled 750km southwest of Kunming along the Burmese and Laotian borders, **Xishuangbanna** has little in common with the rest of provincial China. Despite recent resettlement projects to affirm Han authority, thirteen of Yunnan's ethnic groups still constitute a sizeable majority of Xishuangbanna's 500,000 population. Foremost are the **Dai**, northern cousins to the Thais, whose distinctive temples, bulbous pagodas and saffron-robed clergy are a common sight down on the plains, particularly around **Jinghong**, Xishuangbanna's sleepy capital. The region's remaining nineteen thousand square kilometres of hills and jungle are split between the administrative townships of **Mengla** in the east and **Menghai** in the west, peppered with villages of Hani, Bulang, Jinuo, Wa and Lahu; remoter tribes are still animistic, and all have distinctive dress and customs. Cultural tourism aside, there are a number of exciting and only marginally developed

wildlife reserves inhabited by elephants and other rare beasts, plenty of hiking trails, and China's **open border with Laos** to explore.

Historically, there was already a Dai state in Xishuangbanna two thousand years ago, important enough to send ambassadors to the Han court in 69 AD. Subsequently incorporated into the Nanzhao and Dali kingdoms, a brief period of full independence ended with the Mongols' thirteenth-century conquest of Yunnan. For ease of administration, the Mongols governed Xishuangbanna through Dai chieftains whom they raised in status to **Pianling**, hereditary rulers, and the region was later divided into **twelve rice-growing districts** or *sipsawng pa na*, phonetically rendered as "Xishuangbanna" in Chinese. The Pianling wielded enormous power over their fiefdoms, suppressing other minorities and treating people, land and resources as their personal property. This virtual slave system survived well into the twentieth century, when Xishuangbanna came under the thumb of the tyrannical Han warlord, **Ke Shexun**.

Not surprisingly, the **Communists** found Xishuangbanna's populace extremely sceptical of their attempts at reconciliation after taking control of the region in 1950, an attitude eventually softened by the altruistic persistence of medical and educational teams sent by Beijing. But trust evaporated in the violence of the **Cultural Revolution**, and the current atmosphere of tolerance and cultural freedom is undercut by resentment at what verges on colonial assimilation. More contentious aspects of religion have been banned, forests are logged to the detriment of semi-nomadic hunter groups – who then have to settle down and plant rice – and many ethnic people feel that the government would really like them to behave like Han Chinese, just dressing in colourful clothing to attract the tourists. On the other side of the coin, administrators are the first to admit the "terrible mistakes" of the past, and feel that they are now developing the area as sensitively as possible given its special needs.

Xishuangbanna's emphatically tropical **weather** divides into just two main seasons: a drier stretch between November and May, when warm days, cool nights and dense morning mists are the norm, after which high heat and torrential daily rains settle in for the June–October **wet season**. Given the climate, you'll need to take more than usual care of any cuts and abrasions, and to guard against mosquitoes (see "Health" in *Basics*, p.22). The only busy time of the year is mid-April, when thousands of tourists flood to Jinghong for the Dai **Water-splashing Festival**, and hotels and flights will be booked solid for a week beforehand. Once there, **getting around** Xishuangbanna is easy enough, with a handful of well-maintained roads connecting Jinghong with outlying districts. **Place names** can be confusing, though, as the words *Meng-*, designating a small town, or *Man-*, a village, prefix nearly every destination.

Into Xishuangbanna

From Kunming, it takes barely an hour to reach Xishuangbanna on the thrice-daily Jinghong flight. Coming by road is not such a bad option either, with sleeper buses making the twenty-four hour incarceration as comfortable as possible, but watch that your luggage doesn't disappear while you slumber – chain bags securely or rest your legs over them.

Far more interesting is the overland route **from Xiaguan or Baoshan** in Yunnan's northwest, though it's a tough three-day trip. The five-hunded-kilometre road is so poor that it can be quicker to travel via Kunming – which is what the PSB will tell you to do if you ask about access – but you'll certainly penetrate China's untouristed backwaters, zigzagging across cold, thinly inhabited mountain folds between the Nu and Lancang river systems. About a third of the way into the journey is the city of **Lincang**, from where it's worth detouring 150km west towards the Burmese border at **CANGYUAN**. A trading centre supplying everything from motorbikes to betel nut and mushrooms, Cangyang is surrounded by attractive villages whose population are mostly **Wa**.

Though Buddhism was introduced at some point from Burma, several remote **rock painting sites** associated with earlier religious rituals survive in the Awa Mountains northeast of the city. In the distant past the Wa were also headhunters, more recently known for their sacred drums, passion for smoking and festivals involving the frenzied dismemberment of bulls – though such things are rare events today.

The road divides at Lincang, the eastern branch crossing the Mekong and proceeding to Jinghong via **Simao**, briefly a French concession and formerly the site of Xishuangbanna's airport. The western branch heads to **LANCANG**, where the *Lancang Guesthouse* (②) and *Guizhou Restaurant* supply beds, food and English information on the surrounding **Lahu Autonomous County**. Hunters of legendary skill whose name loosely implies "Tiger-eaters", the **Lahu** probably originated in the Dali area, perhaps driven into this southern refuge by the Mongols. Though around Lancang the Lahu are pastoralists and superficially resemble neighbouring Dai, traditionally both men and women hunt, shave their heads and wear turbans. As at Cangyuan, the main reason to pause in the area is to spend a day or two looking at nearby villages.

Alternatively, try basing yourself 40km southwest of Lancang at **MENGLIAN** township, where there's a busy market every fifth day patronized by **Hani** wearing porcupine quills and colourful beetles in their hair. From here you can hitch tractor rides out to more Wa settlements, such as **Fu'ai**, 28km northwest. From Lancang, it takes a further day to reach Jinghong, descending into Xishuangbanna through the westerly town of Menghai (see p.764).

Jinghong

JINGHONG, Xishuangbanna's tiny and wonderfully relaxed "Dawn Capital", first became a seat of power under the Dai warlord **Bazhen**, who drove the Bulang and Hani tribes off these fertile central flatlands and founded the independent kingdom of Cheli in 1180. It has been maintained as an administrative centre ever since. There was a brief period of excitement in the late nineteenth century when a battalion of British soldiers marched in during a foray from Burma, but they soon decided that Jinghong was too remote to be worth the effort of defending. An attempt to forge a highway through Xishuangbanna into Burma during the 1950s (only recently completed) saw Jinghong built up in the grey edifices of the contemporary Han style. Now much weathered, these make a suitably colonial backdrop for Dai women in bright sarongs and straw hats meandering along the gently simmering, palm-lined streets.

For the most part, the city is simply an undemanding place to spend a couple of days adjusting to Xishuangbanna's climate and investigating Dai culture. Aside from energetic excesses during the water-splashing festivities, you'll find the pace of life is set by the tropical heat – even bicycle traffic is light, and nobody bothers rushing anywhere. Once you've tried the local food and poked around the temples and villages which encroach on the suburbs, there's plenty of transport into the rest of the region.

Orientation, arrival and city transport

Jinghong sits on the southwestern bank of the **Lancang River**, which later winds downstream through Laos and Thailand as the Mekong. The city centre is marked by an ornamental fountain set where **Jinghong Lu**'s four arms radiate north (*bei*), south (*nan*), east (*dong*), and west (*xi*). A kilometre up along Jinghong Bei Lu is the **Lancang Bridge** and the top of **Galan Lu**, which runs south from here between Jinghong Bei Lu and the river.

The **telephone code** for Jinghong is ☎0691

The **airport** lies about 10km southwest of the city, a ¥3 minibus ride into the centre. There are two **long-distance bus stations**: the main one on Jinghong Bei Lu handles the Kunming and eastern Xishuangbanna traffic, while the depot 500m south on Minzu Lu concentrates on western destinations. Jinghong is too small for a public bus service – nothing is more than a twenty-minute walk from the centre – but if you need to be driven anywhere there are plenty of motor-rickshaws for hire, whose battered drivers seem to sustain a huge amount of late-night physical abuse from irate customers. Watch out for pickpockets at the post office and stations.

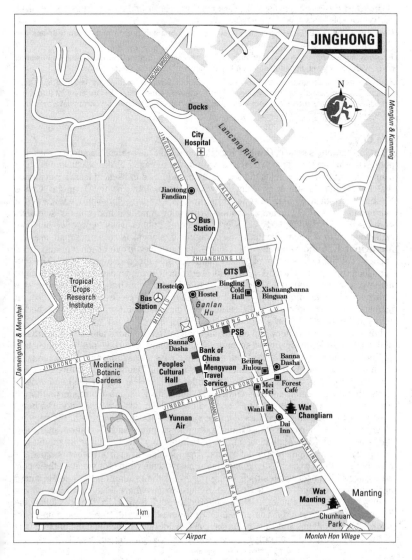

Accommodation

All but the smallest lodgings have restaurants, and can make tour bookings with the *CITS* or their own services. In addition to the hotels, there are two basic **hostels** (①), on either side of Jinghong Bei Lu up around Ganlan Hu Park, offering threadbare triples and doubles.

Banna Dasha, south end of Galan Lu (☎2132026). Not to be confused with its namesake or the *Xishuangbanna Binguan*, this is a typically drab Chinese hotel with a sauna, a "Western Restaurant" selling Chinese food and fried eggs, and tidy triples and doubles. ⑤.

Banna Dasha, corner of Jinghong Xi Lu and Jinghong Nan Lu (☎2125100 or 2122049). Big, modern, comfortable block of double rooms and suites. ⑥.

Dai Inn, Manting Lu. Simple comforts in spotless bamboo stilt houses with separate toilets and showers, run by a resident Dai family. ②.

Jiaotong Fandian, next to the Jinghong Bei Lu bus station. Better than the average bus station hotel, with decently equipped doubles and dusty dorms. Dorms ①, rooms ③.

Xishuangbanna Binguan (also known as the *Banna Binguan*), Galan Lu (☎2123679). Large grounds and a pleasantly faded air perfectly suit Jinghong's atmosphere. Dorms are a bit dingy, but the triple and double rooms are very clean and comfortable. All rooms and dorms have their own bathrooms. Dorms ①, rooms ②–④.

The City

Right in Jinghong's centre, **Ganlan Hu** (Peacock Lake) is a small, flagstoned park and pond used for early-morning exercises, with a row of caged birds, beasts and reptiles from Xishaungbanna's jungles hidden off to one side. Sad in itself, at least it's evidence that these animals still survive in the wild. More uplifting is the **Tropical Crops Research Institute**, 1.5km west down Jinghong Xi Lu (daily 8am–5pm), a few acres of palms and vines nicely arranged around a thin lake. Among other projects, scientists here have spent the last forty years cross-breeding rubber trees to produce one specially suited to Xishuangbanna's steep highland slopes. Across the road are the **Medicinal Botanic Gardens** (daily 8am–5pm), a quiet grove of gingers and small shrubs growing in the gloom of closely planted, unidentified rainforest trees. The gardens lead through to a large **Traditional Medicine Clinic**, whose friendly staff might invite you in for a cup of tea and impromptu *qigong* demonstration – one doctor specializes in plugging himself into a wall socket and passing electrical currents through patients' bodies. Shops outside the gardens on Jinghong Xi Lu sell locally made herbal remedies such as **"dragon's blood"** (see p.761 for more details).

For some more greenery and an introduction to Dai life, head about 3km southeast of the centre to **Manting**, once a separate village but now absorbed into Jinghong's lazy spread. On the way here down Manting Lu, you'll pass a brisk morning market outside the temple school of **Wat Changliarn**. Traditionally, all Dai boys spend three years at such institutions getting a grounding in Buddhism and learning to read and write – skills therefore denied to Dai women. Manting itself is mostly modern, though Neolithic pottery has been dug up here and a few older, two-storey wooden Dai houses still lurk in the wings (you'll see entire villages of these elsewhere in the region). Near the end of the road is **Wat Manting**, Jinghong's main **Buddhist monastery** and the largest in all Xishuangbanna, a huge but simply furnished affair being rebuilt in a grand style with donations from Thailand. Dai temples differ from others across the land both in their general shape and the almost exclusive use of wood in their construction, which necessitates their being raised off the ground on low piles to guard against termites and rot. Also unlike Buddhists anywhere else in China, whose Mahayana (Greater Vehicle) teachings filtered through from India, the Dais follow the **Theravada** (Hinayana, or Lesser Vehicle) school of thought, a sect common to Sri Lanka, Thailand, Laos and Burma. As the Dai consider feet to be the most unclean part of the body, remember to **remove your shoes** before entering any temple.

THE LANCANG RIVER AND NEW YEAR FESTIVITIES

Despite its potential as a great river highway, the **Lancang River** has never seen much traffic and today the docks in the north of town at the junction of Galan Lu and Jinghong Bei Lu are moribund. Though Jinghong's tour operators daydream about the possibility of cruises into Laos, if regional politics would allow it, the only vessels you're likely to see are rare barges running down to the tiny Thai port of Chiangkhong, and a bi-weekly workers' ferry to the hydro-electric plant 20km upstream – neither of which will carry foreigners.

Where the river does come into its own, however, is during the highlights of the **Dai New Year celebrations** (also held in Dai communities all over Xishuangbanna) of which the famous **Water-splashing Festival** is just a part. Once set by the unpredictable Dai calendar, but now reliably fixed by the Han authorities for 13–16 April, the first day sees a **dragon-boat race** on the river, held in honour of a good-natured dragon spirit who helped a local hero outwit an evil king. On the second day everybody in Jinghong gets a good soaking as water-splashing hysteria grips the town, and basinfuls are enthusiastically hurled over friends and strangers alike to wash away bad luck and, hopefully, encourage a good wet season. The third-day finale includes **Diu Bao** (Throwing Pouches) games, where prospective couples fling small, triangular beanbags at each other to indicate their affection, and there's a mammoth **firework display**, when hundreds of bamboo tubes stuffed with gunpowder and good luck gifts are rocketed out over the river. Nightly carousing and dancing takes place in the parks and public spaces: look out for the **Peacock dance**, a beautifully fluid performance said to imitate the movements of the bird, bringer of good fortune in Dai lore; and the **Elephant-drum dance**, named after the instrument used to thump out the rhythm.

Next to Wat Manting is the rather more secular **Chunhuan Park** (daily 8am–5pm; ¥6), where the royal slaves were formerly kept. Official tour groups are shown water-splashing highlights here on a daily basis, and you can cross over one of the Lancang River's tiny tributaries to inspect full-scale copies of Jingzhen's Bajiao Ting (see p.764) and a generalized Dai pagoda. Corners of the park are very pleasant, but sideshows along the main paths include what has to be the most barbaric sight in the whole country – target practice using a crossbow and a live chicken. On a lighter note, following the path past the entrance to Chunhuan Park brings you to **Manloh Hon village**, which gets its water through the efforts of a large bamboo waterwheel, beyond which is a ferry across the Lancang to paddy fields, villages and banana groves.

Eating, drinking and entertainment

Jinghong is the best place in Xishuangbanna to try **authentic Dai cooking**, either in restaurants or on the street. **Rice** in various guises is the staple, usually just plain boiled, but it's also served mixed with coconut and pineapple. There's also a glutinous variety wrapped in banana leaves, rammed into a bamboo tube and grilled, and a prized purple strain is used as the basis of pancakes, stuffed with sugar and chopped nuts. Formal menus often feature meat or fish courses flavoured with sour bamboo shoots or lemon grass, while oddities like **fried moss** and **dried banana wafers** appear as side dishes. For something more simple, there's an abundance of year-round fresh **tropical fruit** sold around town – try jackfruit, physically weighty and heavily scented – and sit-down stalls sell pans of chunky curries, actually quite bland and difficult to tell apart. Claypot casseroles and huge bowls of noodle soup are a popular import from the north, and there are always the **hotel restaurants** for more ordinary Chinese food. The area around the night market on Jinghong Nan Lu has a host of small, low-cost canteens specializing in stewed and simmered dishes, and there's a bigger, perpetually full affair just around the corner in Jingde Lu. As usual, **tourist**

XISHUANGBANNA

Xishuangbanna	西双版纳	*xīshuāngbǎnnà*
Bulangshan	布朗山	*bùlǎng shān*
Cangyuan	沧原	*cāngyuán*
Daluo	打洛	*dǎluò*
Damenglong	大勐龙	*dàměnglóng*
Manguanglong Si	曼光龙寺	*mànguānglóng sì*
Manfeilong Bei Ta	曼飞龙笋塔	*mànfēilóng sǔntǎ*
Hei Ta	黑塔	*hēi tǎ*
Gelanghe	格朗和	*gélǎnghé*
Jinuoluoke	基诺	*jīnuò*
Jinghong	景洪	*jǐnghóng*
Banna Dasha	版纳大厦	*bǎnnà dàshà*
Jiaotong Fandian	交通饭店	*jiāotōng fàndiàn*
Xishuangbanna Binguan	西双版纳宾馆	*xīshuāngbǎnnà bīnguǎn*
THE CITY		
Chunhuan Park	春欢公园	*chūnhuān gōngyuán*
Manting	曼听	*màntīng*
Medicinal Botanic Gardens	药用植物园	*yàoyòng zhíwùyuán*
Tropical Crops Research Institute	热带作物科学研究所	*rèdàizuòwù kēxué yánjiūsuǒ*
Wat Manting	曼听佛寺	*màntīng fósì*
RESTAURANTS		
Beijing Jiulou	杯京酒楼	*bēijīng jiǔlóu*
Wanli	婉丽餐厅	*wǎnlì cāntīng*
Jingzhen	景真	*jǐngzhēn*
Baijiao Ting	八角亭	*bājiǎo tíng*
Lancang	澜沧	*láncāng*
Mannanan	曼那因	*mànnànān*
Sancha He Wildlife Reserve	三岔河自然保护区	*sānchàhé zìrán bǎohùqū*
Manting	曼听	*màntīng*
Menghai	勐海	*měnghǎi*
Menghan	勐罕	*měnghǎn*
Menghun	勐混	*měnghùn*
Mengla	勐腊	*měnglà*
Bronze Spire Pagoda	青铜尖顶塔	*qīngtóng jiāndǐng tǎ*
Menglian	勐阿	*měng ā*
Menglun	勐仑	*měnglún*
Tropical Botanic Plant Garden	热带植物园	*rèdài zhíwù yuán*
Mengyang	勐养	*měngyǎng*
Mengzhe	勐遮	*měngzhē*
Manlei Fo Si	曼类佛寺	*mànlěi fósì*
Mo Han	边贸站	*biān mào zhàn*
Shangyong	尚勇	*shàngyǒng*
Yaoqu	瑶区	*yáoqū*
Bupan Aerial Walkway	补蚌望天树空中索道	*bǔbàng wàngtiānshù kōng zhōngsuǒdào*

cafés are expensive, but good places to pick up local information, and have become the haunt of some unusual characters.

Entertainment is unpredictable. Sometimes people just seem to assemble spontaneously in the streets after dark and go through dance routines, at other times tour groups can trigger performances at the **People's Cultural Hall** between Jinghong Nan Lu and Minhang Lu. Outside the hall is a huge open space where you can mix with the general public rollerskating, playing pool and stuffing their faces at the **night market** every evening after 7pm.

RESTAURANTS

Beijing Jiulou, Jingde Dong Lu. Smart, upper-range Chinese restaurant offering crispy fried spareribs, crackling rice and roast duck.

Bingling Cold Hall, Galan Lu. Across from the *Xishuangbanna Binguan*, this is just an ordinary cold drinks and snacks bar, but popular with the Burmese from the souvenir markets around the corner in Zhuanghong Lu.

Forest Café, just down the easterly side street off the southern end of Galan Lu. This newly opened place is run by an English-speaking pair from Hunan. Good coffee, fast Chinese food and cold beer.

Mei Mei, northern end of Manting Lu. Tiny, Aini-run café currently a favourite with long-term visitors to Xishuangbanna for its generous portions of local staples.

Wanli, Manting Lu. The best of Jinghong's authentic Dai restaurants, which are all southeast of the centre on Manting Lu. There's an English menu offering excellent treats such as pineapple rice and coconut and lemon-grass chicken. The nearby *White Elephant* and *Peacock* also come recommended, but more for nightly Dai dancing than their food.

Listings

Airlines *Yunnan Air*, corner of Jingde Xi Lu and Minhang Lu (Mon–Sat 8–11.50am & 3–6pm. Their airport bus is unreliable; better to catch any minibus heading south down Minhang Lu.

Banks and exchange The *Bank of China* on Jinghong Nan Lu is open for foreign exchange Mon–Fri 8–11.30am & 3–6pm. The *Xishuangbanna Binguan* and other larger hotels will cash travellers' cheques outside these hours.

Bike rental The *Xishuangbanna Binguan* has a cluster of good bikes for rent at ¥10 per day, plus whatever they decide is a reasonable deposit.

Hospital The City Hospital (Shi Yiyuan) is at the top end of Galan Lu, and there's a clinic and pharmacy attached to the *Xishuangbanna Binguan*.

Laundry There's an expensive and unreliable service next to the *Banna Dasha* at the southern end of Galan Lu.

Massage White-robed practitioners set up along central Galan Lu in the evening.

Post office Corner of Jinghong Bei Lu and Jinghong Xi Lu (daily 8am–6pm). Parcels, post restante and international telephones.

PSB Jinghong Dong Lu, across from Ganlan Hu Park (Mon–Fri 7–11.30am & 3–5.30pm; ☎2130366). Visa extensions and contradictory information about the region.

Shopping Zhuanghong Lu, a thin street between Galan Lu and Jinghong Bei Lu, has a very regulated arts and crafts market run for the most part by Burmese selling gems, jade, colourful curios and heavy wooden carvings of elephants. The City Produce Market is at the western end of Jingde Lu, near the *Yunnan Air* offices, where there's a massive range of food and clothing.

Tour agents *CITS*, opposite the *Xishuangbanna Binguan* on Galan Zhong Lu (☎2124479 or 2123708), and most other agents in Jinghong offer much the same range of day trips for ¥100–200 to: Daluo on the Burmese border; the Botanic Gardens at Menglun; Mandian waterfall; the Menglong region; the Sunday market at Menghun; and (very rarely) Sancha He Wildlife Reserve. For something different, *Mengyuan Travel Service*, up the flight of steps next to the *Bank of China* on Jinghong Nan Lu (☎2125214, fax 2123310), organizes three to four-day guided treks in the forests and hills of Menglong and Menglun districts, covering 10–15km per day through Bulang, Lahu, Ake and Hani territory. ¥700 gets you an English-speaking guide and includes all food, transport and accommodation.

Exploring Xishuangbanna

Flowing down from the northwest, the Lancang River neatly cuts Xishuangbanna into two regions on either side of Jinghong. **East** there's a choice of roads through highland forests or more cultivated flatlands to the astoundingly good botanic gardens at **Menglun**, down beyond which lies **Mengla**, only newly opened to foreigners, and the **Laotian border**. Head **west** and your options are split between the **Damenglong** and **Menghai** regions – linked by a three-day hiking trail – with a more varied bag of ethnic groups and a firmly closed crossing into Burma. There are direct public buses and tours to most destinations from Jinghong's two bus stations, but once in an area the mass of short-range minibuses is far more convenient, with tractors picking up where these won't go. Cycling around is another possibility in the lowlands, though Xishuangbanna's hill roads are steep, twisted and long.

With the exception of Mengla, most main centres can be visited on day trips from Jinghong, but you won't see more than the superficial highlights unless you stop overnight. The towns are seldom attractive or interesting in themselves, and you'll need to get out to surrounding villages, temples and countryside to experience Xishuangbanna's exciting side. Be prepared for basic accommodation and generally bland, if plentiful, food. Many people are friendly and some villagers may offer meals and a bed for the night, but elsewhere locals are wary of strangers, let alone foreigners – don't force your presence while looking around.

East to Menglun: the northern route

The road to Menglun, 80km east of Jinghong, divides shortly after crossing the Lancang Bridge on the outskirts of town. The **northern route** initially follows the road to Kunming, winding up through forested hills for 35km before levelling out at **MENGYANG**, a market and transport stop surrounded by a host of **Huayao** villages. The Huayao (Flower Belt) form one of three Dai subgroups, though they differ greatly from the lowland "Water Dai", who scorn them for their over-elaborate costumes and the fact that they are not Buddhists. Though you'll see plenty at Mengyang – the women wear turbans draped with thin silver chains – the village considered most typical is about 10km farther north along the main road at **MANNANAN**, where there might be limited accommodation.

On a completely different tack, a farther 18km beyond Mannanan (still on the Kunming road) is the **Sancha He Wildlife Reserve**, a fantastically dense chunk of rainforest based around the Sancha Stream. Transport heading north from Mengyang to Dadugang, Puwen or Kunming can drop you at the large stone sign which marks the reserve entrance. Entry is ¥10, and construction work suggests that the simple eating and sleeping arrangements (①) are going upmarket – not that the reserve gets many visitors. You might well feel safer with a **guide** (¥20, but they can't speak English), as a family of seven **wild elephants** is the attraction here, frequently seen at dawn from creaky wooden riverside hides. The jungle gets more interesting the farther in you go along the heavily overgrown, partially paved trails, and you're sure to encounter elephantine footprints, along with brightly coloured birds, butterflies and snakes. **Minibuses** heading in both directions along the Kunming road pass the reserve entrance until well into the afternoon.

The latter 45km of the northern route to Menglun misses all this, however, diverging east off the Kunming road between Mengyang and Mannanan. Twenty kilometres along is **JINUOLUOKE township** (Jinuo Shan), home to the independently minded **Jinuo**, who received official recognition of their ethnicity (and hence aid packages) as recently as 1979. An enigmatic group who some say are descended from the remnants of Zhuge Liang's third-century expedition to Yunnan, the Jinuo once lived by hunting and slash-and-burn farming, but now grow tea as a cash crop. They never got on well with external rulers, describing their highlands homeland as *Youle* (Hidden from the Han), and were almost annihilated by Ke Shexun and the Dai ruling caste after they poisoned a government tax collector in 1942. Numbering about twenty thousand today, Jinuo women wear a distinctive white-peaked hood, and both sexes pierce their ears and formerly practised tattooing. Jinuoluoke is not the most welcoming of places, but there's a guesthouse (①) which might let you stay, and a fair amount of through traffic for the final 25km run to Menglun.

The southern route to Menglun

Because of the time it takes to climb the range to Mengyang, most buses between Jinghong and Menglun follow the **southern road**. This begins across the Lancang Bridge following the Lancang River valley downstream for 30km between endless neat rows of rubber trees to **MENGHAN** and the famously fertile **Ganlanba** (Olive-shaped Flatland). This is one of Xishuangbanna's three major agricultural areas won by force of arms over the centuries and now vitally important to the Dai (the other two are west at Damenglong and Menghai). You'll see plenty of farming hamlets in the vicinity sporting traditional wooden houses completely covered by huge roofs, raised on stilts off the moist earth. Menghan itself is pleasantly surrounded by paddy fields and low hills bordering the flatland and is a good place to stop over. The *Bamboo House* (①) offers simple rooms and Dai food, and a stack of information about day walks in the area. A couple of kilometres east, at **MANTING**, there's the excellent **Manting Fo Si** (Manting Buddhist Temple) and **Da Duta** (Grand Single Pagoda), both fine reconstructions of twelfth-century buildings destroyed during the 1960s. East, paths lead off from Manting along and across the river to more pagodas and villages, somewhere to spend a couple of days of easy exploration.

Menglun

Routes from Jinghong meet at **MENGLUN**, a dusty couple of streets overlooking the broad flow of the **Luosuo River**. There's no bus station so vehicles pull up wherever convenient on the main road, usually among the restaurants and stores on the eastern side of town. Take the side street downhill through the all-day market, and within a couple of minutes you'll find yourself by a large pedestrian **suspension bridge** over the river. Here you pay ¥20 to cross into Menglun's superb **Tropical Botanic Gardens**, founded in 1959 by the visionary botanist and chemist **Cai Xi Tau** who, having carved the gardens out of the jungle, started investigating the lives and medicinal qualities of Xishuangbanna's many little-known plant species. One of his pet projects involved the effects of resin from the **Dragon's Blood Tree**, which looks like a thin-stemmed yucca with spiky leaves, used as a wound-healing agent in Chinese medicine. It was believed extinct in China since the Tang dynasty (supplies were formerly imported from Cambodia), but Cai Xi located a wild population in Xishuangbanna in 1972 and transplanted some to the gardens, which now produce bottles of the powdered medicine. Once you've crossed the bridge and followed through the bamboo corridor, bear left uphill and you'll come to the research institute buildings, outside which is a little pond. Cai Xi's ashes were interred under the Dragon's Blood Tree here, while sap from the huge *jianshe feng hao* nearby was used for poison arrowheads. You could spend a good half-day in the gardens, as there's masses more to see, from rainforest species to a thousand-year-old cycad and groves of palms, vines and shrubs. Look for the unlikely sight of Chinese visitors seranading the undistinguished-looking "Singing Plant", which is supposed to nod in time to music.

Right at the back of the gardens past the pretty lily pond you'll find a **guesthouse** (②), easily Menglun's premier place to stay and eat. A dreary alternative is the *Post and Telecommunications Garden Hotel* (②) with an English sign, back up on the main road.

You'll need to tramp back on to the main road to catch onward transport, though beyond the garden guesthouse is an exit on to the Mengla road, where you can flag down buses heading southeast.

Mengla

Having been a patchy affair so far, the jungle really sets in for the hundred-kilometre trip from Menglun to Mengla (4hr). The first part is slow-going uphill, then the bus suddenly turns along a ridge giving early-morning passengers an incredible view (best in winter) back down on to a "cloud sea" over the treetops below. Farther on are rock outcrops and small roadside settlements carved out of the forest, and though once over the mountains the trees begin to give way to rubber plantations and cultivated land, it's all pretty impressive. This is the largest of Xishuangbanna's five wildlife reserves, fairly untouched tracts which the government has set aside to be protected from development, and full of the plants you'll have seen at the Botanic Gardens up the road.

Doubtless anything would inevitably be a disappointment after this, but **MENGLA** seems a deliberately ugly town, grey and tumultuous. It was once famous for Qingtong Jianding Ta, the **Bronze Spire Pagoda**, originally founded in antiquity by two fervent Burmese monks as a shrine for three of Buddha's bones and hairs. With a spire donated by heaven, the pagoda's presence brought lasting peace to the land, though it eventually fell into disrepair and had to be rebuilt in 1759, when Jinghong's Dai ruler contributed thirty thousand silver pieces to cover the pagoda and temple columns in bronze. What happened next is a bit of a mystery, as Mengla was closed to foreign eyes for almost thirty years after the Cultural Revolution, but nobody in town today will own up to the pagoda's existence. Even so, there are plenty of monks floating around the streets, and a smaller temple pagoda on the hill to the west.

There's a proper **bus station** (buses head back to Menglun throughout the day) with an attached white-tiled **hotel** (②) in Mengla's main street at the northeast end of town. If you get no joy here, turn back up the road and there's another place on the outskirts of town. Walk south and the road forks, with the right-hand branch heading after 1km to the centre past various cheap noodle shops and **restaurants**, and the left-hand bearing through the **market** quarter and due north out of town. **Plainclothes police** are everywhere – even among the Uigur running the main-street kebab stalls – as this is the last major town before the Laos border, 60km away to the southeast.

Around Mengla: to Yaoqu and Laos

An afternoon bus runs from Mengla to the small town of **YAOQU** (returning the following morning), 40km or so north along the beautiful farmland and forest scenery flanking the **Nanla He**. Yaoqu is a road head for remote highland villages, with two **hostels** (①) and all sorts of people turning up to trade, including Yao, dressed in dark blue jackets and turbans, and possibly Kumu, one of Xishuangbanna's officially unrecognized nationalities. Not far off the road, just over halfway to Yaoqu, is the **Bupan aerial walkway**, a very insecure-looking metal "sky bridge" running across the forest canopy; some construction in the area might be future accommodation.

Heading south **towards Laos**, it takes about ninety minutes on a minibus from Mengla's main street to reach **MO HAN** township (also known as **Bian Mao Zhan**, literally "Frontier Trade Station"), 6km from the **border crossing**. **SHANGYONG**, the last place before Mo Han, is a centre for Xishuangbanna's isolated **Miao** population, more closely allied here with their Hmong relatives in Laos than with other Miao groups in China. The Hmong made the mistake of supporting US forces during the Vietnam War and were savagely repressed in its aftermath, many fleeing into China from their native regions in northern Vietnam and, after the Vietnamese army swarmed into the country in 1975, Laos.

INTO LAOS

Laos has been open to independent travellers since the late 1980s and the few who have been in rave about the country, though no English is spoken and the north is desperately poor. Seven-day, non-extendable **transit visas** are available from the Lao Consulate in Kunming – see Kunming "Listings", p.724.

On the opposite side of the border from Mo Han is the Lao village of **Ban Boten**, where there's nowhere to stay or change your Chinese currency for Laotian kip, though yuan seem acceptable. The nearest banks and beds are a ¥10 truck ride away at the town of **Louang Namtha**, from where you can hitch out to the early-morning markets at **Muong Sing** to see locals in full tribal regalia. There's also transport from Louang Namtha to **Nung Kie** via Muong Tai, and thence by boat down the Mekong to **Louangphrabang** – you can also come the whole way from the border by road. Louangphrabang was Laos's Buddhist centre and royal capital until the military took over in 1975, and there are caves and dozens of sumptuously decorated temples dating back to the eighteenth century here, as well as the former Royal Palace, now a museum. Louangphrabang also has good road and air connections to the present capital, **Vientiane**.

There's basic **accommodation** at Mo Han, and transport to the very relaxed customs post where it's rumoured that, should you have forgotten to get one in advance, Lao visas can be bought for a small consideration.

West: Damenglong and the trail to Bulangshan

Several buses a day make the seventy-kilometre run from Jinghong's Minzu Lu depot southwest to **DAMENGLONG** (or "Menglong" as it's often marked on maps), one of the many western Xishuangbanna towns worth visiting for its **Sunday market**. It's also an area rich in Buddhism, and just about every village along the way has its own temple and pagoda. One worth closer inspection is **Manguanglong Si** near **Gasa** (15km from Jinghong), a monastery with a wonderful dragon stairway. The most impressive and famous structure in the region is **Manfeilong Bei Ta** (White Bamboo Shoot Pagoda), set up on a hill a thirty-minute walk north of Damenglong. First built in the thirteenth century and now brightly adorned with fragments of evil-repelling mirrors and silver paint, it's a regular place of pilgrimage for Burmese monks, who come to meditate and to worship two footprints left by Sakyamuni in an alcove at the base. The pagoda's unusual name derives from the nine-spired design, which vaguely resembles an emerging cluster of bamboo tips. On a separate rise closer to town, Damenglong's other renowned Buddhist monument is the disappointingly shoddy **Hei Ta** (Black Pagoda), though it looks good from a distance.

While there are plenty of cheap places to eat in Damenglong, the terrible **guesthouse** (①) doesn't make the town an appealing overnight stop. What might convince you to stay, however, is the three-day **hiking trail** which follows 40km of local paths northwest along the Nana He and its tributaries to **Bulangshan** township, through an otherwise inaccessible region of forests and farmland. The route isn't marked as such, and you'll almost certainly need to ask for directions along the way (few locals speak Chinese, let alone English, but you can get the idea across). Food and camping gear will come in handy too, though it is possible to negotiate meals and accommodation in the villages.

Start by taking any available transport 15km south from Damenglong to **Manguanghan**. Carry on along the road for about 1km, then look for a tractor track to the right leading shortly to **Guanmin**, a riverside Hani settlement. Another 5km takes you past a **thermal spring** to the Bulang village of **Manpo**, beyond which the track becomes a walking path only. In the next 20km you'll pass **Nuna** village before crossing the river and proceeding to **Song'er** (both of which are inhabited by Lahu), then cross back over and re-enter Hani territory at Bangnawan and **Weidong**. Here the track improves again for the final 10km to the trail head at **BULANGSHAN**, mountainous headquarters of the dark-clad **Bulang** nationality. There's formal accommodation at Bulangshan (①), and at least one bus a day 50km north to **Menghun**, on the Menghai–Daluo road (see below).

Menghai and the Hani

MENGHAI is western Xishuangbanna's principal town, centrally placed on the highland plains 55km from Jinghong. The usual scruffy assemblage of kilometre-long high street and back lanes, Menghai was once a **Hani** (Aini) settlement until, as elsewhere, they were defeated in battle by the Dai and withdrew into the surrounding hills. They remain there today as Xishuangbanna's second largest ethnic group and long-time cultivators of Xishuangbanna's **pu'er tea**, the red, slightly musty brew esteemed from Hong Kong to Tibet for its fat-reducing and generally invigorating properties. There's a tea-processing factory in Menghai which Jinghong's *CITS* can arrange a tour around, but otherwise the place is best seen as a stop on the way towards outlying Dai and Hani regions.

The **bus station** is at the eastern end of town, with the **post office**, **bank**, canteens and the *Banna Hotel* (②), offering basic doubles, grouped around the central crossroads. The **minibus depot** for western destinations is on the far outskirts, along with slightly more comfortable rooms in the white-tiled **hotel** (③) opposite.

Beyond Menghai to the Burmese border

The main routes beyond Menghai head southwest down to **Daluo and the Burmese border**, or northwest out of Xishuangbanna towards the Lancang region (see p.754). The most celebrated Buddhist sights around Menghai are within an hour's drive along this latter road, including **Baijiao Ting** (Octagonal Pavilion), 20km away at **JINGZHEN**, and **Manlei Fo Si** (Manlei Buddha Temple), 5km farther on at **MENGZHE**. Though inferior copies of older buildings, Baijiao Ting is an interestingly bizarre structure built in the eighteenth century to quell an angry horde of wasps, and both have important collections of Buddhist manuscripts written on fan palm fibre. There's plenty of **minibus** transport to Mengzhe throughout the day.

One of the best places to come to grips with the Hani is at **GELANGHE** township, 30km southeast of Menghai, where there's hostel accommodation (①). In fact, many of the people here are Dai and **Ake**, a long-haired Hani subgroup spread as far afield as Menglian and Simao. In common with other Hani, unmarried women have elaborate head ornaments while wives wear cloth caps decorated with silver beads and coins. An excellent walk leads up into the hills above Gelanghe past a lake and plenty of traditional wooden Ake villages, but people are very shy.

Somewhere to catch locals unawares is 25km out along the Daluo road at tiny **MENGHUN**, whose **Sunday market**, starting at daybreak and continuing until noon, does a good job of lowering ethnic barriers. It's best to stay in Menghun the night before as this way you'll have left before the mid-morning tour buses from Jinghong descend, although you'll have to decide which of Menghun's two atrocious guesthouses (①) deserves your custom – one is in the main street (look for the English sign), the other 75m on the left down the road leading south into the fields. However, the market is easily worth a night's discomfort: Hani women arrive under their staggering silver-beaded headdresses; Bulang shuffle around with their heavy earrings and wide Napoleonic-style turbans; groups of Dai ladies buy rolls of homemade paper and sarongs; silver belt and bracelet hawkers hassle foreigners with outrageous prices; and here and there are remote hill dwellers in nondescript clothing, carrying hundred-year-old rifles. Take a look around Menghun itself too, as there's a dilapidated nineteenth-century **monastery** with a pavilion built in the style of Jingzhen's octagonal effort, and a **pagoda** hidden in the bamboo groves on the hills behind town. Another temple down on the flats to the south is linked to a legend that the stream here changed course at the bidding of Sakyamuni.

Beyond Menghun, the fifty-kilometre-long road takes you past the turning south to Bulangshan (see p.764) and through a stretch of forest inhabited by an as-yet unnamed nomadic group who speak an unintelligible language and were only "discovered" in the late 1980s. At the end of the bitumen is the town of **DALUO** (two buses daily between here and Menghai), set just in from the Burmese border. Here there's a multi-trunked, giant **fig tree** whose descending mass of aerial roots form a "forest", and the daily **border trade market** is timed for the arrival of Chinese package tours between 11am and 1pm. Chinese nationals can also get a two-hour visa for Burma, ostensibly to shop for jade; in fact, many are really going over to catch transvestite stage shows held for their benefit – check out the photos in the windows of Jinghong's processing labs.

Southeastern Yunnan

Southeastern Yunnan, the region between Kunming and Vietnam, was off-limits until the early 1990s due to the effects of the Sino-Vietnamese War, and, despite the officially open border crossing, foreign access since then has been limited. The two PSB-approved methods of travelling the 350km between Kunming and the border town of **Hekou** are either on the unreliable **train**, or the daily **long-distance bus** service, neither of which are supposed to leave during the journey (see Kunming's "Moving On" box, p.717). But it's likely that the area will free up considerably in the immediate future, and there are already those who have spent some time down here, so the following is an outline of places to head for.

There are few stations on the rail line, so travelling by road is the best option if you want to have a look around. About 70km from Kunming is **Fuxian Hu**, a lake which rivals its northwestern sister, Dian Chi, in scale and beautiful scenery. At the northern end is the county capital, **CHENGJIANG**, whose Confucian temple, **Wenmiao Si**, dates back to 1571 and was used by Guangdong Province's Zhongshan University as its campus during the Japanese occupation. Another 70km south is **TONGHAI**, set on the far smaller **Qilu Hu** and best known for its silversmiths and the four thousand **Mongolians** living 15km away at the western-shore settlement of **Xinmeng**, descendants of an army garrison left behind by Kublai Khan.

Eighty kilometres beyond Tonghai is **JIANSHUI**, known throughout Yunnan for its uniquely shaped earthenware steamers whose inverted funnel design allows chicken

SOUTHEASTERN YUNNAN		
Chengjiang	澄江	*chéngjiāng*
Fuxian Hu	抚仙湖	*fúxiān hú*
Hekou	河口	*hékǒu*
Jianshui	建水	*jiànshuǐ*
Kaiyuan	开远	*kāiyuǎn*
Malipo	麻栗坡	*málìpō*
Tonghai	通海	*tōnghǎi*
Xinmeng	薪门	*xīnméng*
Yanzi Dong	燕子洞	*yànzī dòng*

to poach delicately in its own juices. The Ming-dynasty **Chaoyang Ta**, the former eastern gate tower in the city walls, is said to be worth a look, but more popular are **Yanzi Dong**, the Swallows' Caves, 40km east in the karst formations along the Lu River valley. Named after the thousands of birds who nest here in summer, Yanzi Dong has been a Chinese tourist attraction for centuries, now featuring walkways, underground restaurants and a subterranean river.

Jianshui is about 50km west of **KAIYUAN**, a major stop on the Kunming–Hekou rail line. With time to spare, there's an interesting two-hundred-kilometre side trip by road southeast of Kaiyuan via the city of Wenshan to **MALIPO**, a small town which authorities may not want you to visit owing to its proximity to a remote section of the Vietnamese border. A number of ethnic groups inhabit the region, and there's a collection of **rock paintings** on a cliff about 1km west of town near the Chaoyang River, apparently connected with local Zhuang mythology (for more on which, see p.687).

From Kaiyuan, it's 150km due south by train or bus to **HEKOU**, the crossing into Vietnam. Rail tracks are laid on both sides, but the connecting bridge was destroyed in 1979 and you have to walk across. The customs guards here are very picky, so make sure that your visa is squeaky clean; it "costs" a $US1 note at each of the three departments who take it in turns to inspect your passport, luggage and health – the Vietnamese attitude to foreign capital makes the Chinese commercial mind seem positively sluggish. Once over, take time to look around the town of **Lao Cai**, where there's a huge cross-border market in endangered birds, reptiles and mammals to supply Chinese palates.

travel details

Trains

Kunming to: Anshun (2 daily; 14hr); Beijing (daily; 60hr); Chengdu (2 daily; 24hr); Hekou (often suspended; 14hr); Guangzhou (2 daily; 60hr); Guilin (2 daily; 25hr); Guiyang (5 daily; 12hr); Kaiyuan (often suspended; 8hr); Liupanshui (2 daily; 8hr); Shanghai (daily; 60hr); Xichang (2 daily; 12hr).

Ruili (26hr); Shilin (3hr); Simao (19hr); Wanding (25hr); Xiaguan (11hr); Xichang (24hr); Xingyi (13hr).

Xiaguan to: Baoshan (7hr); Binchuan (2hr); Dali (1hr) Jinghong (72hr); Kunming (11hr); Lijiang (6hr); Lincang (12hr); Lancang (48hr); Ruili (14hr); Tengchong (14hr); Wanding (12hr); Zhongdian (11hr).

Buses

Baoshan to: Jinghong (72hr); Kunming (18hr); Lancang (48hr); Mangshi (4hr); Lincang (12hr); Ruili (8hr); Tengchong (7hr); Wanding (7hr); Xiaguan (7hr).

Dali to: Lijiang (5hr); Shaping (1hr); Xiaguan (1hr); Xizhou (30min); Zhoucheng (45min).

Jinghong to: Baoshan (72hr); Daluo (5hr); Damenglong (2hr); Kunming (24hr); Lancang (12hr); Lincang (48hr); Menghai (2hr); Menghun (3hr); Mengla (7hr); Menglun (3hr); Xiaguan (72hr).

Kunming to: Anshun (24hr); Baoshan (18hr); Chengdu (36hr); Dali (12hr); Jinghong (24hr); Guiyang (72hr); Hekou (18hr) Kaiyuan (10hr); Mangshi (22hr); Nanning (72hr); Panxian (12hr);

Planes

Baoshan to: Kunming (3 weekly; 30min).

Jinghong to: Kunming (3 daily; 55min).

Kunming to: Bangkok (Thailand; daily; 1hr); Baoshan (3 weekly; 30min); Beijing (3 daily; 2hr 35min); Chengdu (3 daily; 1hr 5min); Chongqing (1–3 daily; 50min); Guangzhou (3 daily; 1hr 20min); Guilin (6 weekly; 1hr 30min); Guiyang (5 weekly; 1hr 10min); Hong Kong (daily; 2hr 45min); Mangshi (2 daily; 45min); Rangoon (Burma; weekly; 2hr 15min); Shanghai (3 daily; 2hr 30min); Singapore (2 weekly; 3hr 40min); Vientiane (Laos; weekly; 2hr 20min); Xi'an (7 weekly; 1hr 40min).

CHAPTER TWELVE

SICHUAN

SICHUAN stretches for over a thousand kilometres across China's southwest, the country's largest province and, from food to politics, one of the most radical. Ringed by mountains which proverbially made the journey here "harder than the road to heaven", Sichuan has always played the renegade, determinedly different from the rest of China and inaccessible enough both to ignore central authority and to provide a haven for those fleeing it. Yet the province itself is far from unified, physically divided into two very different halves: a densely populated eastern plain, and a mountainous west, emphatically remote.

In the east, peaks surround the fertile **Red Basin**, home to most of Sichuan's 110 million residents and one of the country's most densely settled areas. This is Han China's "rice bowl", where a subtropical climate and rich soil conspire to produce endless green fields turning out three harvests a year, a bounty envied by the rest of China and one which has created an air of easy affluence apparent in **Chengdu**, Sichuan's capital. Elsewhere you'll find that the influence of Buddhism is literally part of the landscape: at **Leshan** where, for foreigners at least, a giant Buddha sculpted into riverside cliffs provides one of the most evocative images of China; and farther east at **Dazu**, where a marvellous procession of stone carvings have miraculously escaped desecration. There's also the opportunity of joining pilgrims on **Emei Shan** in a hike up the holy mountain's forested slopes, or of journeying **down the Yangzi** from **Chongqing**, Sichuan's industrial centre and terminus of one of the world's great river journeys.

In contrast, the western half of Sichuan is dominated by densely buckled ranges overflowing from the heights of Tibet; a wild, thinly populated land of snow-capped peaks, where yaks roam the treeline and roads negotiate hair-raising gradients as they cross ridges or follow deep river valleys. To the north, the mountains briefly level out on to the high-altitude **Aba Grasslands**, while south the ranges run lower but no less severe, cloaked in the impenetrable greenery of cloud forests. Occupied but never tamed by Han China, and often excruciatingly difficult to traverse, the west's biggest appeal is its very inaccessibility. Nearest to Chengdu, at **Wolong Nature Reserve**, there's a chance to see giant pandas in the wild, while travelling north takes you through ethnic Hui and Qiang heartlands to the vivid blue lakes and beautiful mountain scenery at **Jiuzhai Gou** and **Huanglong**. Due west are the very fringes of Tibet,

---

ACCOMMODATION PRICE CODES

All the accommodation in this book has been graded according to the following price codes, which represent the cheapest double room available to foreigners. Most places have a range of rooms, however, and staff will usually offer you the more expensive ones – it's always worth asking if they have anything cheaper. Where the text refers specifically to dorm beds, the price code represents the price per bed. See p.40 for more details.

① less than ¥30	④ ¥100–150	⑦ ¥300–500
② ¥30–75	⑤ ¥150–200	⑧ ¥500–700
③ ¥75–100	⑥ ¥200–300	⑨ ¥700 or more

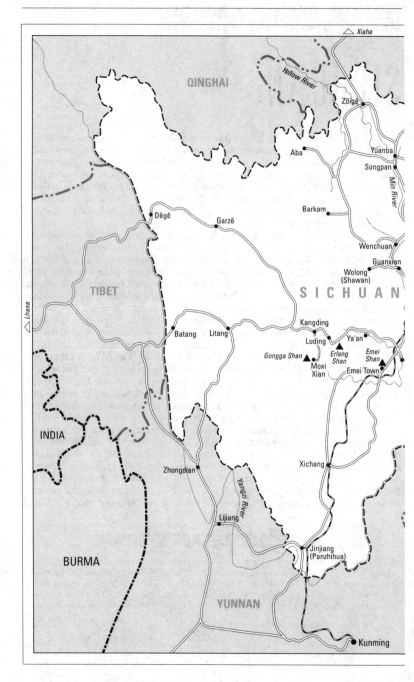

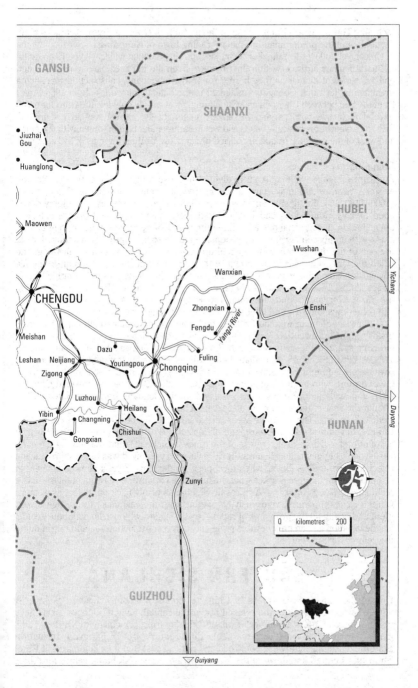

including **Hailou Gou Glacier** lying in the foothills of **Gongga Shan**, Sichuan's highest peak, and the predominantly Tibetan trading town of **Kangding**.

Unless you follow the Yangzi or fly in, just entering Sichuan will leave you in no doubt of the difficulties of **travel** within the province. Even the rail lines have to pass through endless series of tunnels as they bore through the mountains; construction was such a monumental task that Chengdu was linked to the national network only in 1956. Apart from the line between Chengdu and Chongqing, most people only use the **train** for travel beyond Sichuan's borders, and **buses** are generally the easiest way to get around. Sichuan's **weather** is basically warm and wet in summer and cold in winter, with the north and west of the province frequently buried under snow for three months of the year.

Some history

Prehistoric Sichuan was apparently divided into two kingdoms, the eastern **Ba** and western **Shu**, which may have amalgamated at some point during Shang times (1600–1100 BC). Shang sites suggest the Ba-Shu was a slave society with highly developed metalworking skills and bizarre aesthetics; among gold and bronze artefacts unearthed from sacrificial pits at Sanxingdui, near Chengdu, was a metre-wide bronze mask with an obscene grin and eyes popping out on stalks. Agricultural innovations at the end of the third century BC opened up eastern Sichuan to intensive farming, and when the Qin armies made the province their first conquest, they found an economic power base which financed their unification of China in 221 BC – as did Genghis Khan's forces almost 1500 years later. In between, the province rejected external rule during the *Three Kingdoms* period, becoming the state of *Shu* – a name by which Sichuan is still sometimes known – and later twice provided refuge for deposed emperors.

Otherwise, Sichuan was too far from the mainstream to play much part in China's history, until the twentieth century when government interference in Sichuan's rail industry sparked the nationwide rebellions of 1911 which toppled the Qing empire. This wasn't to Sichuan's immediate benefit, however, as for the next quarter-century rival warlords fought for control of the province. Briefly unified under the **Nationalist government**, who made Chongqing their capital after the Japanese invaded China in 1937, nominally independent states persisted within Sichuan's borders as late as 1955: "When the rest of the country is at peace, Sichuan is the last to be brought to heel", went the saying. The province went on to suffer some of the worst effects of the Cultural Revolution – **Jung Chang**'s autobiography, *Wild Swans*, gives a vivid first-hand account of the vicious arbitrariness of the times in Sichuan – and was left, by the early 1970s, poor, hungry and agriculturally devastated. Typically, it was the first province to reject the revolution's ideals, when local party leader Zhao Ziyang allowed farmers to sell produce on the free market, spearheading the nationwide reforms of fellow native Sichuanese, **Deng Xiaoping**. As a result, Sichuan is firmly back on its feet as western China's richest province, vigorously competing with the east coast for foreign investment and facing all the problems of rapid growth: runaway industrial pollution, ecological devastation and an unbelievable scale of urban reconstruction reaching right out to the remotest rural centres.

EASTERN SICHUAN

One of the most pleasant areas of China to explore randomly, Eastern Sichuan is focused around **Chengdu**, the relaxed provincial capital. Famed not least for its fiery cuisine, the city offers a number of worthwhile day trips, principally to **Xindu**'s Tang-dynasty monastery, and the remarkable third-century BC **Dujiangyan Irrigation Scheme**. Heading southwest, both road and rail run past Buddhist landmarks at **Emei Shan** and **Leshan** and down to the Yunnanese border via **Xichang**, centre for ethnic

Yi and China's beleaguered space programme, and **Jinjiang** (Panzhihua), springboard for a trip into Yunnan's backwaters. Southeast of the capital is a little-explored region backing on to Guizhou Province, based around the historic towns of **Zigong** and **Yibin**, whose highlights include picturesque bamboo forests, and traces of an obscure, long-vanished society. East of Chengdu, there are further Buddhist sites surround the country town of **Dazu**, and beyond, Sichuan's largest city, **Chongqing**, marks the start the **journey down the Yangzi** to Yichang and Wuhan in Hubei, with ferries exiting the province through a dramatic series of gorges.

Chengdu and around

Virtually in the middle of Sichuan, **CHENGDU** is a city with two faces: a rapidly modernizing provincial capital whose streets sport blue-glassed skyscrapers, Japanese four-wheel-drives and fluorescent-coloured bicycles, coupled with narrow back lanes where old men play cards in noisy tea houses and pot plants crowd the wooden porches of traditional, half-timbered homes. Whether you're an old hand or arriving through the air link with Tibet for your first taste of Han China, you'll find Chengdu a far from typical metropolis – it's one of the country's most mellow cities, intrinsically interesting and built on a very human scale.

Settled for over 2400 years and once ringed by almost 20km of battlements and gates, Chengdu was styled **Brocade City** in Han times, when the urban elite were buried in elegantly decorated tombs, and its silk travelled west along the caravan routes as far as imperial Rome. Later a refuge for Emperor Xuan Zong after his army mutinied over his infatuation with the beautiful concubine Yang Guifei, the city became a **printing** centre, producing the world's first paper money. Sacked by the invading Mongols in 1271, Chengdu recovered soon enough to impress Marco Polo with its busy artisans and handsome bridges, and has since survived similar cycles of war and restoration to become, once again, a major industrial and business centre. There's a **university** founded in the 1920s, an important **School of Chinese Medicine**, a bustling economy and a strong cultural tradition enjoyed by a million and a half people.

Few key sites have survived this chequered history, though there's a sprinkling of monuments and temples worth a few days' browsing. Nonetheless, with its embryonic nightlife, a couple of trips out to nearby scenery and historical remains, and one of China's most outstanding cuisines to spike your taste buds on, at the very least Chengdu offers a comfortable base to organize travel into the rest of Sichuan, or to recuperate afterwards.

Orientation, arrival, city transport and accommodation

Around 4km across, Chengdu's roughly circular downtown area contains a warped grid of streets enclosed on three sides by the sluggish, canal-like Fu and **Jin** rivers, themselves surrounded by an ever-increasing number of ring roads. Broad and lined with plane trees, **Renmin Lu** is the main thoroughfare, divided into north, middle and south sections. It runs from the **train station** on the northern edge of town, through the city centre and down past a knot of hotels before crossing the Jin River and heading out to the goods station and routes to the airport. The centre itself is marked by a large, rectangular traffic flow around the grounds of the city's ponderous **Exhibition Hall**, from where **Renmin Dong Lu** heads east to Chengdu's entertainment and shopping precincts, while **Renmin Xi Lu** points west towards **Renmin Park**.

The **telephone code** for Chengdu is ☎028

Arrival

Shambolic **Shuangliu airport** is 16km southwest of town, a twenty-minute ride on the shuttle bus to the *China Southwest Airlines* office on Renmin Nan Lu (approximately twice an hour, 4.30am–6.30pm; ¥3); alternatively, a taxi costs around ¥30. Four kilometres north of the city centre, the **train station** is dwarfed by a square and roundabout out front, packed with jostling crowds of passengers, beggars and hawkers. The **city bus terminus** is off this square to the west down a short street, from where bus #16 runs the length of Renmin Lu, and trolleybus #1 terminates near the *Jiaotong Hotel*.

Otherwise, you'll be arriving at one of Chengdu's **long-distance bus stations**, set on opposite sides of the city. About 4km out to the northwest, you'll find yourself at **Ximen bus station** if in transit from northern Sichuan, though some services from Leshan and Emei Shan also terminate here. Bus #4 runs from Ximen southeast across town, through the centre, then out down Dongfeng Lu. Coming from anywhere else, you'll wind up at **Xinnanmen bus station**, on the south bank of the Jin River about 1.5km southeast of the centre, next to the *Jiaotong Hotel*. From here, trolleybus #1 runs around – not through – the centre and up to the train station, and taxis wait in the street along the river.

City transport

Chengdu's extensive **bus and trolleybus** network covers every area of the city, if not every street, between approximately 6am and 10pm. Fares start at ¥0.5, though pricing seems somewhat arbitrary; stops are marked by roadside signs bearing the route number and destinations. As Chengdu's transit system is being currently overhauled, however, check routes below with a current **bus map**, on sale from stalls and hawk-

---

MOVING ON FROM CHENGDU

Chengdu is roughly halfway along the Xi'an–Kunming **rail line**, and also connected to routes into Guizhou and central China through easterly Chongqing. The congested **ticket office** is on the eastern side of the train station square, with window #29 reserved for foreigners. For advance bookings (hard seat only) up to three days ahead, there are booths at Ximen and Xinnanmen bus stations, and a ticket office on Dong Yujie (daily 8am–noon & 1.30–5.30pm). For travellers leaving **by bus**, services from Ximen station concentrate on northern and western destinations, while those from Xinnanmen head south and east. **Flying out**, Chengdu is connected to a handful of cities throughout China, but most appealingly to **Lhasa** in Tibet (see below). There is seldom trouble reserving bus or plane tickets if you plan ahead, though train tickets can be problematic – travel agents (see p.785) can book all transport for you if you have any difficulties.

Getting to Tibet is simple, if expensive, to arrange. Any airline office will sell you your plane ticket and a "permit" (which you never set eyes on) for next-day travel for ¥2300. However, Chengdu doesn't make a good place to start **overland** for Tibet. First enquiries must be made at the Chengdu PSB, and failing help there, *CITS*, though the visa to enter Tibet by road is virtually impossible to obtain: the "official" price is variously quoted at anywhere between ¥450 and US$200, it will takes weeks to arrange, and you'll have to provide a detailed itinerary of your movements and stick to it. Even with official permission, travel beyond Kanding (see p.820) is an uphill struggle – trucks won't take you (they risk crippling fines), buses are reluctant to let you on and local police will have the final say about letting you cross their territory. Overcome the odds, and at minimum you're looking at a two-week journey from Chengdu to Lhasa, for which you'll need copious warm clothing, food and a good deal of luck.

ers through the city. Private **minibuses** ply the same routes as the buses with the route number displayed up front. They charge ¥2 a trip but will pick up and set down at any point.

Taxis are to hand outside the bus and train stations, and bigger hotels. Cabs cost ¥7.50–10 to hire, with additional charges for the distance covered – a trip right across town shouldn't cost more than ¥15. Drivers often want to negotiate a price rather than use the meter, but you'll be overcharged this way; you should also watch out for being driven round in circles. **Motor-rickshaws** are another option on offer around the stations, and for short hops might work out cheaper than a taxi depending on your bargaining skills. **Cycling**, you'll find well-regulated bicycle lanes and guarded parking throughout Chengdu, but few places to rent from (see "Listings", p.784). Even pedestrians are catered to, with flag-wielding wardens ensuring fair play at crossings and traffic lights equipped with countdown timers so you know if it's worth risking a dash across the road.

A note on **security**: if you wander around late at night, stick to well-lit roads. While Chengdu's crime rate isn't bad, considering that you can buy a mind-boggling array of weapons from stun guns to hunting knives from stalls at the bus stations, midnight muggings occasionally occur down backstreets and along the Jin River – if threatened, don't resist.

Accommodation

Most of Chengdu's tourist accommodation lies along Renmin Lu, especially in the vicinity of the Jin River; bus #16 stops near these hotels. All but the cheapest include some sort of light breakfast in the room price, while some have banking, IDD, postal facilities and tour booking services on the premises.

Chengdu Grand, 29 Renmin Bei Lu (☎3333888, fax 3336818). Well-placed for the station, but otherwise a bit too low-key for the price tag. ⑧.

Hei Kafei (*Black Coffee*), Binjiang Lu. Famously sleazy former air-raid shelter whose maze of mildewed, low-ceilinged corridors conceals a bar complete with anonymous cubicles lit by coloured twenty-watt bulbs. Airless, three-bed cells with straw mattresses and unwelcome wildlife complete the very basic amenities. Take the #16 bus down Renmin Nan Lu. ①.

Jiaotong (*Traffic*), 77 Jinjiang Lu (☎5551017, fax 5582777). Simply one of the best-value hotels in China, and Chengdu's budget mainstay. Facilities include spotless doubles and three-bed dorms with TV and shared or private bathroom, a cheap left-luggage office and a message board outside advertising travelling companions and used gear. Trolleybus #1 terminates nearby. ②–③.

Jinhe, 18 Jinhe Lu (☎6642888, fax 6632037). Multi-storey tower near Renmin Park with accommodation ranging from comfortable but tiny "economy rooms" with shared bathroom, up to upmarket suites. ④–⑧.

Jinjiang, 180 Renmin Nan Lu (☎5582222). Uninspiring Soviet-style building with red carpets and cream wallpaper. Recent renovations have raised prices ridiculously high, though rooms are decent enough. ⑧.

Minshan, 55 Renmin Nan Lu (☎5583333, fax 5582154). Chengdu's top business venue, whose comfortable but fairly ordinary rooms are a bit of a letdown after the acres of granite tiling and string quartet in the lobby. There are several good restaurants offering Chinese and Western food here, but you need to be smartly dressed. ⑨.

Xizang (*Tibet*), 10 Renmin Bei Lu (☎3333988, fax 3333526). Apparently sponsored by the Tibetan government and set up to lure you into Tibet. Doubles are reasonable value but the best feature is the painfully artificial weekend "Tibetan-style" stage show at the Red Palace Dancehall Restaurant here. ⑦–⑧.

Yuanding, Shi Shi Xiang (☎6636522). Not an easy place to find, but nicely sited in an older part of town south of Renmin Park. It's a bit tatty, but the double rooms are perfectly acceptable; also has threadbare three-person dorms. Dorms ①, rooms ②.

The City

Cool in winter and hot in summer, Chengdu is a cheerful city, full of activity and simply a nice place to be. Girls in colourful dresses window-shop arm-in-arm, streets and parks are full of flowers – especially during the **spring flower festival** – while market stalls groan under the weight of seasonal fruit. Everywhere else, **buildings** are going up and coming down, demolitions carefully carried out brick by brick using muscle and sledgehammer. Much of this new work is a result of the government trying to involve central and western China in the economic boom sweeping the eastern provinces. Isolated as it is, Chengdu seems to have attracted a disproportionate amount of investment compared with some of the more central provincial capitals. Locals put this down to their good, aggressive business sense, cynics to Chengdu being Deng Xiaoping's home city. Whatever the reason, the shops are well stocked with imported goods, while more traditional enterprises still flourish in the backstreets, which can make reaching the city's scattered sights more interesting than the sights themselves.

Downtown Chengdu and Wenshu Si

Chengdu's geographic centre is firmly marked by a massive white statue of **Chairman Mao** – ignored on all street maps – who smiles benevolently over traffic congestion as he faces south, his back to the Exhibition Hall. East of here, Renmin Dong Lu runs east into **Dongfeng Lu** and **Dong Dajie**, through the heart of the city's shopping precinct. Running between the two is **Chunxi Lu**, a prestigious shopping street where you'll find a good few older, traditional establishments; nothing is really eye-catching, but there's a certain dated ambiance which is becoming rare as the city is steadily modernized. South from Chunxi Lu, a quiet string of walled alleys runs down behind leafy Hongxing Lu towards the river, where wooden gateways lead into the courtyards of century-old homes.

About 1.5km north of Mao's statue on the route of bus #16, the entrance to **Wenshu Si** (¥1), also known as the Hollow Wood Temple, lies east off Renmin Zhong Lu down Wenshu Yuan Jie, a narrow lane crammed with stalls selling paper money, incense and nasty porcelain Buddha statues. Dedicated to Wenshu, God of Wisdom, and the headquarters of Sichuan's Chan (Zen) Buddhist sect, the temple is the busiest in town, perpetually full of sightseers and locals posturing to shrines and showing their children how to do likewise.

TEA HOUSES

The Sichuanese have a reputation for being particularly garrulous, best seen at one of Chengdu's many **tea houses** (*chadian*), where the elderly and idle can spend whole days chatting, playing chess, Go – all the rage at the moment – or cards. Crowds surround good games; elsewhere people lounge in open-backed bamboo chairs smoking cheroots, chewing melon seeds and arguing with their neighbours, while a sharp-eyed waiter moves around filling up cups from a broken-spouted teapot. Though it's a nationwide institution, Chengdu has always been famous for its tea houses. Traditionally these were working clubs, where people met to finalize deals, hold meetings and relax after work listening to storytellers or watching acting troupes perform. They suffered badly during the Cultural Revolution, when such activities were labelled as bourgeois, and while they've recovered in recent times, much of the "men only" atmosphere of the older establishments is disappearing along with the backstreets and buildings that housed them. Today, most tea houses are in parks, temple grounds and theatres, and you'll find them open to anyone, foreigners included; somewhere to socialize for the price of a perpetually full cup of tea.

Founded in the seventh century, and last rebuilt around 1700, Wenshu's five halls sport beautifully sweeping tiled roofs, carved eaves and painted ceilings enclosing statues of Maitreya and Guanyin, all bathed in incense smoke. The third hall contains a row of gilt *arhats* under glass – look for the one whose eyebrows droop on to his chest – while the next houses a wonderful painting of a strange dog-like creature behind a smiling Buddha. The monastery also has a famous collection of **sutras**, some written in blood, stored away in the last hall. Outside in the gardens, shady rows of pine and gingko trees surround a noisy **tea house**, jam-packed with Chinese clamouring for refreshment, and a fine **vegetarian restaurant** whose food is prepared by monk chefs – an excellent reason to visit Wenshu at lunchtime.

Renmin Park and western Chengdu

Ten minutes' walk west of the Exhibition Centre on Jinhe Lu, **Renmin Park** (¥0.5) is typical of Chengdu's open spaces. Reached from the station on trolleybus #4, it's best in the early morning as *tai ji* and *wushu* enthusiasts compete for space with groups of ballroom dancers circling to piped music, and old men hang up their caged songbirds and sit down for a game of cards or a chat. Inside the main entrance you'll see the **Monument to the Martyrs**, a tall obelisk dedicated to those killed in the 1911 revolutions which ended the Qing empire. Up at the northern end of the park, there's a children's **funfair**, including a wonderfully tacky string of tunnels lined with disintegrating, life-sized papier-mâché models of world leaders. Farther round, a low wall protects a pleasant **ornamental garden**, surrounded by flowers, green lawns (elsewhere trampled to dust) and artificial rock formations. At the southern end of the park, there's a small **lake** where you can rent pedal boats and squeak across the waters (¥1), while the nearby tea house gets going by mid-morning. The south exit leads straight into a lively produce market and narrow lanes containing older homes with pole-frame balconies.

TO QINGYANG GONG

The road continues due west past Renmin Park for 2km or so, first as Tonghuimen Jie and then Shierqiao Jie, where you'll find the Sichuan Medical College and attached **Traditional Medicine Institute** across from the #4 trolleybus terminus. Foreigners are allowed to study here, and some classes are held in English – contact any travel agent (see p.785) to arrange a visit. Just past the college, Qingyang Gong is a ten-minute walk south along Yihuan Lu, or flag down bus #42 which terminates opposite the temple.

Alternatively, coming from Renmin Park you could turn off Tonghuimen Jie down **Xichengbian Jie**, an extraordinary street being rebuilt in the Qing style. It's wonderful to look at, though probably nowhere in China was ever quite this perfect and the result is like a Chinese version of a Western "Chinatown"; once up and running it will doubtless be somewhere to head for expensive restaurants and karaoke bars. At the southern end of the street you can either turn left and follow the road to Qingyang, or follow the ornamental bridge across the Jin River to **Baihuatan Park** (¥1), famous for its pretty **flower gardens** decorated with gnarled bonsai, orchids and an ancient **gingko tree**, said to date back to Tang times. Rather incongruously, there's also a dinosaur theme park, whose entrance is graced by a life-sized brass band of mechanical pandas.

Sited in the **Cultural Park** – itself worth a visit around the lunar new year when it becomes the focus for Chengdu's flower festival – **Qingyang Gong**, the Green Goat Temple (¥2), is dedicated to Taoism's mythical proponent, Laozi. Subjected since Tang times to the usual cycle of desecrations and restorations, the exterior of the main **Three Purities Hall** is decorated with brightly coloured animals and dragons, while two coin-spattered **bronze goats** in the entrance are fenced off from marauding hands after being worn smooth by the caresses of luck-seekers. The right-hand "goat" is somewhat odd, being the simultaneous incarnation of all twelve zodiacal animals. Inside, plaster

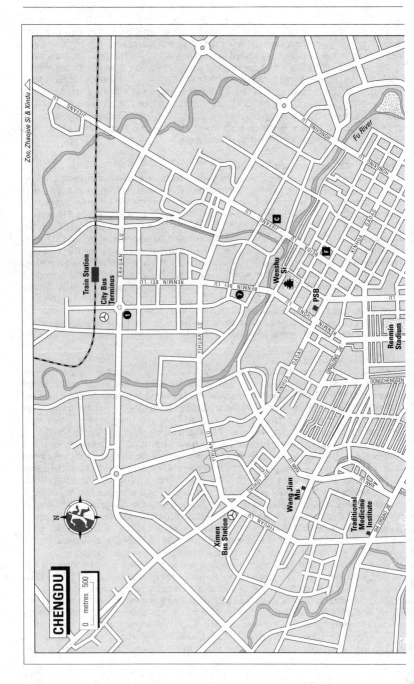

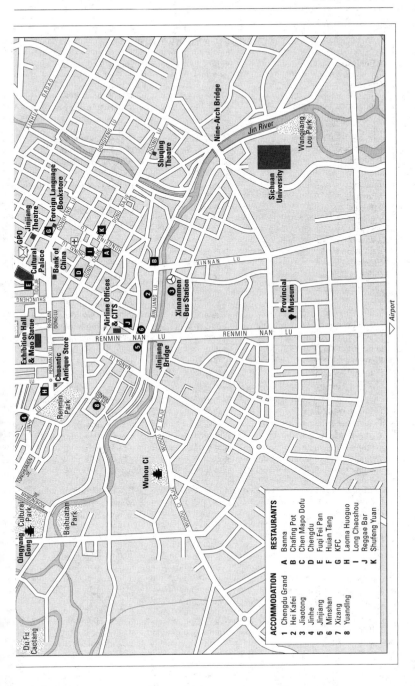

ACCOMMODATION
1 Chengdu Grand
2 Hei Kafei
3 Jiaotong
4 Jinhe
5 Jinjiang
6 Minshan
7 Xizang
8 Yuanding

RESTAURANTS
A Banna
B Chafing Pot
C Chen Mapo Dofu
D Chengdu
E Fuqi Fei Pan
F Huian Tang
G KFC
H Laoma Huoguo
I Long Chaoshou
J Reggae Bar
K Shufeng Yuan

CHENGDU AND AROUND

Chengdu 成都 *chéngdū*

ARRIVAL

Ximen bus station	西门车站	*xīmén chēzhàn*
Xinnanmen bus station	新南门车站	*xīnnánmén qìchē zhàn*

ACCOMMODATION

Black Coffee (Hei Kafei)	黑咖啡饭店	*hēi kāfēi fàndiàn*
Chengdu Grand	成都大酒店	*chéngdū dàjiǔdiàn*
Jiaotong	交通饭店	*jiāotōng fàndiàn*
Jinhe	金河大酒店	*jīnhédàjiǔdiàn*
Jinjiang	锦江宾馆	*jǐnjiāng bīnguǎn*
Minshan	岷山饭店	*mínshān fàndiàn*
Tibet (Xizang)	西藏饭店	*xīzàng fàndiàn*
Yuanding	园丁饭店	*yuándīng fàndiàn*

THE CITY

Baihuatan Park	百花潭公园	*bǎihuātán gōngyuán*
Chengdu Zoo	成都动物园	*chéngdū dòngwùyuán*
Cultural Palace	文化宫	*wénhuà gōng*
Jinjiang Theatre	锦江剧场	*jǐnjiāng jùchǎng*
Du Fu's (Caotang)	杜甫草堂	*dùfǔ cǎotáng*
Exhibition Hall	省展览馆	*shěng zhǎnlǎnguǎn*
Panda Research Centre Museum	大熊猫博物馆	*dàxióngmāo bówùguǎn*
Provincial Museum	省博物馆	*shěng bówùguǎn*
Qingyang Gong	青羊宫	*qīngyáng gōng*
Renmin Park	人民公园	*rénmín gōngyuán*
Renmin Stadium	人民体育场	*rénmín tǐyùchǎng*
Shuqing Theatre	蜀清剧场	*shǔqīng jùchǎng*
Sichuan University Museum	四川大学博物馆	*sìchuān dàxué bówùguǎn*
Tomb of Wang Jian	王建墓	*wángjiàn mù*
Traditional Medicine Institute	中医附院	*zhòngyī fùyuàn*
Wangjiang Lou Park	望江楼公园	*wàngjiānglóu gōngyuán*
Wenshu Monastery	文殊院	*wénshū yuàn*
Wuhou Ci	武侯祠	*wǔhóu cí*
Zhaojue Si	照觉寺	*zhàojué sì*

RESTAURANTS

Banna	版纳酒家	*bǎnnà jiǔ jiā*
Chengdu	成都餐厅	*chéngdū cāntīng*
Chen Mapo Tofu	陈麻婆豆腐	*chén mápó dòufu*
Fuqi Fei Pan	夫妻肥盘	*fūqī féipán*
Shufeng Yuan	蜀风园	*shǔfēng yuán*

AROUND CHENGDU

Guanxian	灌县	*guànxiàn*
Dujiangyan Irrigation Scheme	都江堰	*dūjiāngyàn*
Qingcheng Shan	青城山	*qīngchéng shān*
Shangqing Gong Si	上青宫寺	*shàngqīnggōng sì*
Xindu	新都	*xīndū*
Baoguang Si	宝光寺	*bǎoguāng sì*

saints lining the walls are overlooked by the golden bulks of the Three Purities themselves, representing the three levels of Taoist heaven. Behind them is a spirited carved panel of the Purities riding their assigned beasts: a crane, a tiger and a nine-headed lion. For active entertainment, head around the back of the final hall, where you'll see those after a blessing stumbling with eyes shut and arms outstretched towards a large good luck symbol painted on the bricks, hoping to make contact; onlookers laugh at their efforts before trying themselves.

DU FU CAOTANG

The line of minibuses pulled up outside **Du Fu Caotang** (Du Fu's Thatched Cottage; 9am–5pm; ¥15), located in parkland a couple of kilometres west of Qingyang on Chengdu's fringes, attests to the respect the Chinese hold for the Tang-dynasty poet **Du Fu**. Born in 712 AD and an unlucky aspirant to the civil service, Du Fu struggled for years to obtain a minor position at the imperial court in Chang'an, succeeding only after one of his sons had died of starvation and just as a civil war was breaking out. Forced to leave the capital, he arrived in Chengdu around 759 and, as war swept the country, holed up in a simple grass-roofed dwelling outside the city's west wall. Here he wrote some 240 of his 1400 surviving poems; direct, moving pieces about daily life, human suffering, and his longing for his home in Henan. Later forced to move on again, he spent the rest of his days wandering central China "like a lonely gull between the sea and the sky", dying on a boat in Hunan in 770.

This temple park was founded three centuries after his death. Rebuilt and enlarged over the years, it now includes a **main hall** with a statue of Du Fu, and a **museum** wing with some marvellous early woodblock and hand-written versions of his poems. The gardens themselves are nice, there's the inevitable tea house, and a silly thatched pavilion meant to resemble the poet's hut.

WUHOU CI AND WANG JIAN MU

Historians may find two other sites in western Chengdu worth a look, though neither is otherwise a very inspiring place. **Wuhou Ci**, south of the Jin River on Wuhou Ci Dajie (bus #1 from Renmin Nan Lu terminates nearby), is a much-restored Tang-dynasty structure dedicated to **Zhuge Liang**, the virtuous, Machiavellian strategist of *Three Kingdoms* fame (see p.432). As **Kongming**, he became the first prime minister of the independent state of Shu (Sichuan) around 212 AD. The rather gloomy **temple** (¥2) houses his statue, the **Three Wonder Tablet** of 809 AD – so called because it is considered perfect in text, calligraphy and carving – recording his achievements, and the tomb of emperor and founder of the state of Shu, **Liu Bei**, who lies buried here alongside his two wives.

Over in the north of town off Xian Lu and the #42 bus route, **Wang Jian Mu** (Tues–Sun 9am–5.30pm; ¥1) is a cleaned but otherwise unrestored tomb commemorating one of the rulers of Shu during the chaotic Five Dynasties period (907–60 AD). Unfortunately, there's not really much to see, just a small display of tomb relics, a statue of Wang Jian himself, and the tomb chamber where twelve carved muscular gods support the coffin platform, while the walls are decorated in relief with musicians and dancers.

The Provincial Museum

Some 2km south of Mao's statue and over the Jinjiang Bridge on Renmin Nan Lu, the dusty **Provincial Museum** (Tues–Fri 9am–noon & 2–5pm; ¥2), on the route of bus #16, is worth an hour's browse. English captions are few, but a map in the left-hand hall detailing Sichuan's archeological sites leaves no doubt as to Chengdu's historic importance. Local finds go right back to Shang **Ba-Shu** relics, and exhibits include a four-metre-long wooden **hanging coffin** found in a cliffside cave above the Yangzi, and casts of the extraordinary **masks** found in the Sanxingdui **sacrificial pits**. Later bronzework is represented by cases of spearheads and swords, but there is also a fine set of fourteen clapperless **bells** from the Warring States period, contemporary with those found at Wuhan in Hubei (see p.454). Over in the right wing, a statue of the third-century BC engineer **Li Bing**, discovered in 1974 face-down in the bed of his irrigation project at Dujiyangyan, stands at the far end like a giant chess piece. The rest of the room is taken up with rubbings of **Han tomb reliefs**, panels alive with wavy, elongated figures in rural and court settings depicting scenes from the deceased's life – one has a savage-toothed camel and its handlers – and similarly animated **pottery** figurines including portly animal sculptures and an ugly model of a storyteller banging a drum.

Sichuan University and Wangjiang Lou Park

Away on Chengdu's southeastern extremity, **Sichuan University** merits a visit if only for its own museum and the nearby **Wangjiang Lou Park** – though there's also the possibility of meeting and talking with students. Bus #35 runs along the north bank of the Jin River to the **Nine-arch Bridge**, where Tibetans sit on the pavement selling tiger paws and dried monkey carcasses; cross over and walk east along the south bank for ten minutes to the university gates. Inside, an avenue leads down to a neatly planted garden, with the building to your right housing the excellent **University Museum** (9am–noon & 2.30–5pm; ¥10, concessions ¥5). Downstairs are more Han tomb reliefs and the fragmentary remains of some beautifully proportioned Tang **Buddhist statues**, while upstairs houses some worthy, if dry, **ethnology** exhibits, including Qiang, Yi and Miao textiles, and a room devoted to Tibetan religious artefacts – silverwork, paintings and a human thigh-bone flute. Better is a separate display of local items, including swathes of Chengdu's famous **brocades**, some made into wedding costumes and coverings for an elaborate Qing bridal sedan. At the back of the upper floor a model tearoom has cups laid out at tables in front of a **shadow-puppet theatre**, once the province of roving puppeteers but now, sadly, a virtually extinct art form. The walls are covered with the puppets – jointed heroes, villains and mythical beasts, snipped and pierced like paper-cuts out of flat pieces of leather.

Just beyond the university gates, **Wangjiang Lou** (River-viewing Pavilion; 9am–5pm; ¥1) sits in a small park hugging the river bank. A Ming-dynasty building, this is said to be the spot where the Tang poetess **Xue Tao** lived and used the local well water to wash and dye a special kind of red paper, still available today. Three buildings are given over to displays of scrollwork and bonsai, while outside, river breezes stir the hundred or so varieties of **bamboo** which flank the paths.

Chengdu Zoo and Zhaojue Si

Over in the city's northeastern suburbs, **Chengdu Zoo** and the adjoining **Zhaojue Si** make a good half-day excursion. Bus #302 runs from just east of the train station on Erhuan Lu to the zoo gates in about fifteen minutes, or you could cycle there in about the same time.

The **zoo** (daily 8am–6pm; ¥2.50), despite nice bamboo gardens and the fuss made over its **pandas**, of which there are both the giant and the smaller red species, is probably best skipped. The animals sit lethargic and fleabitten behind bars while the public throw ice-cream sticks and rubbish at them to try and get a reaction. To be fair, the zoo has successfully bred the giant panda, a rare feat, and the **birds** here – cranes, peacocks, waterfowl and even parrots – are all in good condition, but the atmosphere isn't particularly uplifting. For more about pandas, there's a museum at the **Panda Research Centre**, some 18km north of town; it's not generally open to the public, but some travel agents can arrange a visit (see "Listings", p.785).

Next door to the zoo is the far more worthy **Zhaojue Si** (¥1), whose temple grounds house a dozen halls and over two hundred monks from a blend of Buddhist sects. Founded in Tang times, enlarged under the Qing, comprehensively wrecked during the Cultural Revolution, and now restored, the splendid **main hall** is set on a raised foundation and dominated inside by three gigantic, blue-haired, gilt Buddhas who sit gazing over a sea of brightly-coloured patchwork prayer cushions, while orange and red dragon banners droop from the ceiling. The rest of the complex repays a wander, with the surrounding courtyards hiding small, smoky shrines dedicated to various pudgy deities, while monks chant and strike bells in the background. There's also a **vegetarian restaurant** (closes mid-afternoon) and tearoom near the gates. The **last bus** back to Chengdu leaves at 6.15pm.

Eating, drinking and entertainment

Once you've seen the sights, **eating out** is one of the best reasons to prolong a stay in Chengdu. Fiery and pungent, you won't forget your first taste of genuine Sichuanese food, and the city has the province's best **restaurants**, from formal affairs down to cheap backstreet kitchens and snack stalls.

Eating aside, it's also worth spending an afternoon at the **theatre**, soaking up at least the atmosphere, if not the plots, of one of China's main **opera** styles, and you'll also find a limited **nightlife** beginning to emerge. For something different, head up to the modern **Renmin Stadium** on Renmin Zhong Lu, where you'll find **football matches** scheduled for most weekend afternoons. Tickets (¥10–50) are sold from the office outside on the morning of the match, but they sell out fast – get in early. Newspapers and tour agents might have details of these and other offerings such as travelling troupes performing in parks or tea houses. If all else fails, you could head down to the Jinjiang bridges to try target practice; ¥1 buys ten pots with an air rifle at balloons strung over the water.

Restaurants

You could spend months experimenting with food in Chengdu. The downtown area must have one of the world's highest densities of **restaurants**, most looking like greasy-spoon canteens, but hung with dark brown, crispy fried ducks and spicy local dishes. Out **in the streets**, Muslims grill chilli- and coriander-coated kebabs over open coals, peddlers trundle around selling steamed buns, noodles and spicy tofu and, at night, the kerbsides are thick with al fresco **hotpot stalls**. The lower part of Hongxing Lu has the best in pavement hotpots, which set up around dusk. Ingredients are largely vegetarian – lotus root, potato slices, white radish, "dry" tofu, boiled quail's eggs – negotiate the price per skewer beforehand (around ¥0.1 each), and count on a small service charge. Formal hotpot restaurants, where you'll pay considerably more, include *The Chafing Pot*, on the corner of Hongxing and Binjiang roads, and *Laoma Huoguo*, on Yi Yujie, near Renmin Park, which also has live woodwind music evenings. See "Accommodation" listings, p.773, for **hotel restaurants**.

Banna, southwest corner of Hongxing Lu and Dong Dajie. Yunnanese restaurant specializing in Dai food, with wooden elephants at the door and private tables screened with bamboo inside. Best is the pineapple rice and chicken coconut curry; you'd be excused for avoiding the "crispy-fried newborn dog (whole or half)".

Chen Mapo Dofu, Jiefang Lu, just north of the Fuhe bridge. There are several restaurants with this name in Chengdu, but this high-ceilinged, bare canteen is supposed to be the original home of Grandma Chen's beancurd. ¥4 buys a bowl of tofu glowing with minced meat, chilli oil and wild pepper sauce, plus rice, tea and a thin soup to wash it down.

Chengdu, 134 Shandong Dajie, a westerly extension of Dong Dajie. Reasonably priced and one of the best places to try classic Sichuanese dishes, or a filling ¥20 "sampler" of local snacks: sweet and

"AROMATIC HEAT": SICHUAN COOKING

If your experience of **Sichuan food** outside China has been a stir-fry drowned in red food colouring and tabasco, then you're in for a shock the first time you sit down to eat in Chengdu. As unique as the province that produced it, the Sichuan style is one of China's four main regional cuisines and, surprisingly, one of the most subtle – once you grasp the principles behind the use of the far-from-subtle ingredients. You'll also find a range of regional dishes outside the orthodoxy of the classic Sichuanese style, many of which have become popular in other parts of China.

The most glaringly obvious ingredient in Sichuanese cooking, often before even tasting a dish, is **chilli**, glistening under a layer of bright red oil. Locals explain its use as a result of climate – chillis are warming in winter and cooling in summer and, according to Chinese medicine, dispel "wet" illnesses brought about by damp or humid conditions. Unfortunately for novices, they can also be the biggest hurdle to enjoying the food, as, even by Asian standards, the Sichuanese can heap a phenomenal amount on any one dish. But chillis don't simply blast the tastebuds, they stimulate them as well, and, once conditioned, you'll find flavours much more complex than they might appear at the initial, eye-watering, mouthful.

Often present in the same dish, Sichuan cuisine's two most definitive tastes are the "**manifold flavour**" – a blend of hot, salty, sweet and sour – and **aromatic heat** (*mala*), characterized by the use of spring onions and **wild pepper** (Sichuan pepper), with its slightly soapy perfume and lip-tingling side-effects. Typical dishes include **hot and sour soup, tangerine chicken** – cooked with the slivered, dried peel of local fruit – and **mapo dofu**, beancurd and minced pork swamped in a *mala* sauce. Mapo dofu also illustrates another feature of Sichuan food, where flavour is more important than the main ingredient. The same is true of the classic "**fish-flavoured sauce**" (made from vinegar, soy sauce, sugar, ginger and sesame oil), which can be served over vegetables or meat to provide a "fish" dish out of season. Similarly, in **strange-flavoured chicken** – cold chicken shreds served with a dressing of sesame paste, vinegar, chilli oil, wild pepper, spring onion, ginger and garlic – the meat becomes a simple vehicle for the sauce.

Here, too, as in the rest of the country, **texture** plays an important role in food, but where the Cantonese try for variety, and in Shandong they favour the soft and smooth, the Sichuanese often concentrate on a **chewy, dry** effect, the result of prolonged cooking. While this may sound unappealing, with dishes such as **dry-fried pork shreds**, which arrives at the table dark and slightly oily, the effort of chewing seems to enhance the rich flavour of the meat.

Several famous dishes that originated in Sichuan otherwise have little in common with the above examples. For instance, **double-cooked pork**, where a plain piece of meat is boiled, sliced thinly and then stir-fried with green chillis, is a straightforward meal invented by salt miners in eastern Sichuan. **Smoked duck** – especially a version using camphor wood shavings – is a chilli-free banquet dish, aromatic and acrid. A more common favourite is **crackling rice**, where a meat soup is poured over a sizzling bed of deep-fried rice crusts.

Eating in Sichuan is not always a gastronomic experience, and much of everyday food is similar to what you'd eat elsewhere in China, though often given a Sichuanese twist. Anywhere should be able to cook up **gongbao pork**, the local version of stir-fried pork and peanuts; spiced and oily **dandan mien** (carry-pole noodles); dumplings served with chilli and garlic relish; and braised aubergine (eggplant) with chillis. Perhaps the most striking adaptation to local taste is the **hotpot** (*huoguo*) which, though found all over China in one form or another, has really been taken to heart by the Sichuanese. At its best eaten informally at street restaurants, hotpot here consists of skewers of meat, boiled eggs or vegetables, cooked by you at the table in a bubbling pot of chicken stock liberally laced with chillis and cardamom pods. You then season the cooked food in oil spiced with msg, salt and chilli powder. The effect is powerful, and during a cold winter in Chengdu you may well find that hotpots fast become your favourite food.

savoury dumplings, small crispy-fried fish and marinated squid. Try the outside tables, set around a goldfish pool, and get in early, before debris from other diners litters the floor.

Fuqi Fei Pan, Tidu Lu, directly north of Renmin Dong Lu. The name of this inexpensive restaurant, roughly "Husband and Wife's Choice Slices", refers to a snack made of paper-thin beef slices in a sauce of celery, garlic shoots and spring onions; an excellent winter dish.

Huian Tang, Beida Lu, south of the Fuhe bridge. Medicinal restaurant where you state your ailment and they serve up a suitable dish.

KFC, Dongfeng Lu. Fitting quite nicely into the modern end of town, and a haven for scorched palates. Prices moderate.

Long Chaoshou, Chunxi Lu. A renowned dumpling house, this chaotic, canteen-style place is jammed full at lunchtime with a face-stuffing clientele making the most of the selection of local snacks for ¥5–20 a plateful.

"Number 80". Literally almost a hole-in-the-wall, this nameless restaurant in the lane immediately north of Wenshu Si serves everyday food – ¥10 buys enough rice, tea, spiced beancurd and pork with green beans for two.

Shufeng Yuan, 153 Dong Dajie, on the northeast corner of the crossroads with Hongxing Lu. Expensive Sichuan cuisine, but well worth it, with traditional-style rooms arranged around a courtyard.

Xiangzhai Tang (Wenshu Si restaurant, see p.775). Superb and inexpensive vegetarian restaurant whose English menu includes obvious vegetable dishes, as well as duck (beancurd skins), fish (potato or taro) and roast pork (gluten).

Opera and theatre

Over two hundred years old and immensely popular in Chengdu, the **Sichuan Opera** derived from local religious and folk festival perfomances blended with Beijing and Guangzhou styles. There are five forms: **gaoqiang**, with high-pitched singing; **kunqu**, **huqin** and **tanxi**, featuring flute, violin, and zither accompaniment respectively; and **denxi**, lantern-play. The main differences between Sichuan and Beijing operas involve the themes – far more rustic here, based on everyday events and local legends – and the **language**, which is not impossible for outsiders to appreciate. All local pieces are performed in Sichuanese, a distinctively rhythmic dialect well suited to theatre, which allows for puns – the Sichuanese are renowned for their sense of humour and clever word-play – and also affects the pace of the music, closely linked as it is to speeches. The music itself is noticeably cruder than in the Beijing Opera, with a relatively basic orchestra featuring harsh-pitched oboes and heavy use of the drum, a reflection of the Sichuan Opera's humble origins.

There's an **opera school** in Chengdu, and students often appear in minor roles. Performances are held daily around the city, though the best actors and biggest crowds appear on Sundays. Don't expect Beijing-style glamour, however; shows are far lower-key and even large venues tend towards a tea-house atmosphere, with the audience obviously relaxed and enjoying the acting. Programmes last for the whole afternoon, consisting of at least three short pieces or episodes from longer sagas, often interspersed with non-operatic skits such as **qingyin** ballad singing or **jinqianban** "castanet" dances.

Places to see opera include the small tea-house theatre at the back of the **Cultural Palace** on Tidu Jie, a very casual affair, full of octogenarians crunching sunflower seeds, slurping the complimentary tea, and occasionally breaking off from gossiping to applaud the actors' finer points. More professional efforts take place at the **Jinjiang Theatre** on Xinglong Jie, and the **Shuqing Theatre** way down Dong Dajie on Zidong Lu. For the cheapest **tickets** (¥2.50–20, depending on seat and venue) go direct to the theatre box offices – the daily fare is chalked up outside. Alternatively, ¥50 to a travel agent (see "Listings" below) buys a **guide** to accompany you, translate, explain plots and get you in backstage beforehand to see the actors preparing. These tours are often well worth it, but check the guide's English and where the performance is before paying, and never buy from wandering touts – you don't want to end up in a tea-house theatre, fun though they are, for this price.

Bars and discos

Chengdu's **after-dark entertainment** is chiefly limited to **karaoke** venues at the hotels, though for a little variety on this theme you could try the bland *Barbyson Bar* on Binjiang Lu. Slightly better, and somewhere you'll meet younger Chinese, are the discos: *JJ* near Renmin Park, *UA* in Renmin Park, and *MTown* on Renmin Nan Lu. These get going after dark, charge a moderate entry fee and are not places where foreigners often turn up. More off-beat, by any standards, is the *Reggae Bar* just up the lane from the *Minshan Hotel*, where you'll find the bar propped up by locals, foreigners and Tibetans. There's a huge mural of Bob Marley weirdly set off by the UV-lighting, and interesting musical selections by a French-Chinese DJ. Although it's free to get in, beer (*San Miguel* only) is expensive and things can get rough at the weekends.

Listings

Airlines Airline offices are grouped together just north of the *Minshan Hotel* on Renmin Nan Lu: *China Southwest Airlines*, Renmin Nan Lu (☎6665911); *Dragonair* at *CITS*, 65 Renmin Nan Lu (☎6658731, 6672970 or 6663794); *Sichuan Airlines*, 11 Renmin Nan Lu (☎6752083, 6647196 or 6667461).

Banks and exchange The *Bank of China* is on Renmin Dong Lu (☎6662646). Foreign exchange and credit card transactions Mon–Fri 9–11.30am & 2–5.30pm. Main hotels also have foreign exchange counters, though some allow only guests to use them.

Bike rental Bikes can be rented from a booth in the courtyard of the *Jiaotong Hotel* (¥10 per day plus ¥200 deposit).

Bookshops The cheapest places are the stalls behind Mao's statue, though there's little in English beyond Victorian-era novels. The *Sichuan Foreign Language Bookstore* on Dongfeng Lu has similar stock, in addition to translations of Chinese classics and a small collection of pulp paperbacks.

Cinema The most central screens are at the Cultural Palace and opposite the telecommunications office on Renmin Dong Lu; posters and blackboards outside display the price (¥5–10), time and content – usually Chinese or Western (dubbed) action pics.

Consulates *US* 4 Lingshiguan Lu, Section 4, Renmin Nan Lu, about 1km south of the Provincial Museum on the same side of the road (☎5589642).

English Corner Sunday evenings on the corner of Renmin Nan Lu and Binjiang Lu, by the Jinjiang bridge.

Hospitals People's No.1 Hospital and Chengdu Municipal Chinese Medicine Research Institute, Chunxi Lu (☎6667223); Sichuan Hospital, Yihuan Xi Lu (☎5551312 or 5551255).

Left luggage The train station and Ximen and Xinnanmen bus stations all have left-luggage facilities if you can produce an onward ticket. Some hotels can also look after excess gear while you're off in the wilds. Prices range from a flat rate of ¥4 to ¥1 per day.

Massage Some hotels have masseurs for around ¥80 an hour; cheaper operators set up outside the *Minshan Hotel* in the evenings, or cruise the tourist restaurants along the Jin River.

PSB Foreigners after visas or reporting problems are directed to the compound opposite the police headquarters on Xinhua Dadao (Mon–Fri 8.30am–5.30pm; ☎6626577). Visiting in person, you'll find someone who can speak English, but it might be best to seek linguistic help from your hotel if you need to phone.

Post office An unmistakeable colonial-style grey brick building on the corner of Xinglong Jie (daily 8am–6pm). Poste restante ends up in a cardboard box kept at the EMS counter.

Shopping Hours are 8.30am–5.30pm or later. Fruit and vegetable stalls can be found outside Xinnanmen bus station (good value), the *Minshan Hotel* (expensive), and throughout the city centre. There's a busy night market in Chunxi Lu until about 11pm – worth a look to watch the crowds of new middle class buying plastic trinkets, books and CDs. *Friendship Plaza*, cnr Dong Dajie and Chunxi Lu, is currently Chengdu's biggest, best-equipped shopping centre, selling everything from toothpaste to home gym kits, where the underpressed staff watch table tennis championships on wide-screen TVs. More interesting, however, is the bustle down at the four-storey *Chengdu Department Store* (cnr of Renmin Nan Lu and Dongyu Jie), which sells food, cameras, chess sets, teapots and everyday items – you can hardly get in here over the bicycles parked outside. For antiques and souvenirs try the *Chuantic Antique Store*, cnr Dongchenggen Lu and Renmin Xi Lu (9am–5pm). Prices are fairly high, but at least items here are genuine, certified with a wax seal if over a century old: chops from ¥80 (name carving ¥20 extra), snuff bottles, jewellery and porcelain. For dubiously antique coins, Cultural Revolution icons and brocades, try the night market stalls outside the *Minshan Hotel* in Renmin Nan Lu. Shops in nearby side streets stock scrolls, wooden masks and carvings. Stamp and coin collectors also set up daily outside the post office along Xinglong Jie. You'll find several competing army surplus stores at the Xinnanmen bus station, and across from the Wenshu Si on Renmin Zhong Lu. For camera supplies and reasonable-quality, one-hour print processing, try the stores on Chunxi Lu.

Telephones Orange-capped public booths accepting phonecards are located all round the centre. The telecommunications office on Renmin Dong Lu, just east of Mao's statue, has a row of cardphones outside and is open daily 8am–6pm for long-distance and IDD calls; alternatively, try the larger hotels.

Toilets Public toilets cost a couple of jiao and are marked around the city by blue "WC" signs.

Travel agents A number of independent travel agents can help out with advice on local sights, obtain train and bus tickets, and take bookings for tours into the rest of Sichuan. The best of these are *John's Tours*, at the *Jiaotong Hotel* (8.30am–5pm; ☎5542595), and *Tray Lee*, next door at Xinnanmen bus station (8am–6pm; ☎5543510, fax 5554250), who also cover less obvious themes such as the Traditional Medicine Institute, the Panda Research Centre, and birdwatching and natural history tours. Many of the larger hotels also have their own travel services. Staff at *CITS*, just north of the *Minshan Hotel* at 65 Renmin Nan Lu (daily 8.30am–5.30pm; ☎6658731), speak good English and charge a ¥20 service fee for obtaining all transport tickets, but their tours are hideously expensive. Expect to pay around ¥6500 for car and driver only (accommodation and food extra) to Jiuzhai Gou (6 days); ¥1100 for Wolong (3 days); and ¥6500 for Hailou Gou Glacier (7 days). English-speaking guides are about ¥100 per day extra (you'll also have to pay for their bed and board).

Around Chengdu

The countryside around Chengdu offers a couple of interesting day trips through pretty fields dotted with busy peasants and languid water buffalo, but it's perhaps not surprising that visitors, lured or sated by grander prospects at Leshan and Emei Shan, tend to give them a miss. Even so, those not yet overdosed on temples will find **Xindu** and its Buddhist monastery worth a look, while sites surrounding the town of **Guanxian** – a possible first stop on the journey north to Wolong or Jiuzhai Gou – include an impressive, two-thousand-year-old irrigation scheme and a wooded mountain park, peppered with shrines.

Xindu and Baoguang Si

A forty-minute bus ride some 18km north of Chengdu (buses every 30min from the train station forecourt; ¥2), the market town of **XINDU** lies knee-deep in summertime vegetables and stalls selling locally made and highly coloured basketware, but what really draws the crowds is the **Baoguang Si** (Monastery of Divine Light). A large and still influential complex from the Tang dynasty, these days it's something of a tourist black spot but all the more lively for it, and its treasures include a **stone tablet** from 540 AD cut with the figures of a thousand Buddhas, an unusually wide range of Ming- and Qing-era **paintings** and calligraphy, and some tiny, jewel-like gardens that hide away in secluded corners. Look, too, for the thirteen-storey **Sheli Pagoda** whose upper storeys are slightly tilted off the perpendicular and, in the gloomy **Arhat Hall**, a set of five hundred comical and eerie statues sculpted in 1851. These all represent Buddhist saints but for two, which depict the emperors Kangxi and Qianlong, adorned in beards, boots and capes. For lunch, try the airy and cheap **vegetarian restaurant** in the monastery compound.

Guanxian and beyond

GUANXIAN, some 60km northwest of Chengdu from Ximen bus station (last bus back leaves Guangxian around 5pm; ¥8), is a dull town in itself, but there's enough to hold you in the vicinity for at least a day. On arrival, turn left out of the bus station down the main street and left again across the bridge to Lidui Park, which encloses the original heart of the remarkable third-century BC **Dujiangyan Irrigation Scheme**. This was set up in 256 BC to harness the **Min River**, then a notoriously capricious tributary of the Yangzi, by the provincial governor, **Li Bing**. Li designed a three-part engineering project based around a central dam which split the Min into an inner flow for irrigation and an outer channel for flood control. A spillway directed the flood water, regulated the outflow and allowed the silt to be dredged, while an opening carved through the hillside controlled the flow of oncoming water. Work was continued by Li Bing's son, and the scheme has been maintained and developed ever since, so that the present system of dams, reservoirs and pumping stations irrigates some 3.2 million hectares. A stone statue of Li Bing dated to 168 AD graces **Fulong Guan**, a faded wooden temple in Lidui Park with a rickety upper storey and magical animal carvings on the curved tile roof. For the finest view of the dam, make your way to **Erwang Miao**, the Two Kings Temple, across a gaudily coloured, galleried footbridge and along a slender street banked with precariously overhanging houses. Left up a series of crumbling steps and along the river takes you to the temple, commandingly positioned in steep tiers. Posthumously dedicated to Li Bing and his son, who are remembered by statues in the two main halls, this is nicely unspoiled and holds a wedge of tree trunk said to be four thousand years old. Back in Guanxian, the *Dujiangyan Binguan* on Jianshe Lu (②) is a reasonable option if you need **accommodation**.

Minibuses run through the day from Guanxian to **Qingcheng Shan**, the Azure City Mountain, 15km away – you can also get here direct from Chengdu on early-morning services from Ximen and Xinnanmen bus stations. Once the quietest spot under heaven, but now a popular weekend getaway, complete with a funfair with grotesque animal slide, Qingcheng still makes a good alternative if you haven't the time or energy for the higher, more distant Emei Shan (see below). Entrance costs ¥7, and the summit, topped by the Taoist monastery **Shangqing Si** (where you can sleep in a spartan dormitory; ①), is a six-kilometre walk up tree-covered slopes scattered with pavilions, bridges and temples, the best of which is **Tianshi Dong** (Grotto of the Heavenly Teacher), about halfway up, whose main hall is decorated with Ming-dynasty panels.

Leaving Guanxian, there are at least daily services passing through to Wolong and Jiuzhai Gou. While Wolong is only three to four hours away, however, getting a seat on the notoriously crowded Jiuzhai Gou bus may be impossible, in which case it's better to return to Chengdu and start your journey direct from there.

Emei Shan, Leshan and Xichang

Some 150km southwest of Chengdu lies the edge of the Red Basin and the foothills of the mountain ranges which sprawl south and west into Tibet and Yunnan. Fast-flowing rivers from all over central Sichuan converge here at **Leshan**, where over a thousand years ago sculptors created a **giant Buddha** overlooking the waters, one of the world's most imposing religious monuments. An hour away, **Emei Shan** rises to over 3000m, its forested slopes rich in scenery and temples. As Sichuan's two most famous sights, easy access has made them somewhat overtouristed, but they are well worth the effort and, at Emei at least, it's possible to dodge the crowds. Most people combine the two as part of a round trip from Chengdu, but they could also form the first part of an extended circuit out to western Sichuan, or a stopover on your way down south to Yunnan. If you're heading this way, there are a couple of other spots in the far south perhaps worth your time, of which the most interesting is the ethnic centre of **Xichang**. A horde of interconnecting buses and minibuses is the easiest way to get around the region, though Emei and Xichang are also serviced by the Chengdu–Kunming rail line.

Emei Shan

Emei Shan has been a place of pilgrimage for over 1800 years, and by the sixth century it had become one of the country's four sacred Buddhist mountains. The Bodhisattva **Samantabhadra** once preached here – you'll find images of the elephant that carried him at many of Emei's shrines – and these hallowed slopes once held 150 **temples** and monasteries. Around thirty survive today, offering food and simple refuge to pilgrims and hikers alike. Religious considerations aside, Emei is also one of China's most pristine natural regions, reflected in its poetic name: Emei means "eyebrows of beauty", since the Chinese say that from a distance the two main peaks – there are three in all – resemble the delicate eyebrows of a young woman. It's a wonderful place to explore, its slopes scored by numerous hiking trails set against a background of rich **animal and plant life**. The landscape changes markedly with the seasons: most people come in the **summer**, when the vegetation is a dense, lush green and the weather still warm but a welcome escape from higher temperatures on the surrounding plains. **Autumn** brings brilliant colours and a cooler climate, and a hardy few still make the ascent in **winter**, when the crowds have gone, the light is clear and the snow lends grandeur.

Ideally, plan to spend three or four days walking the lower slopes, allowing a better chance of picking a fine day for the assault on the top and, perhaps, the mountain's actual apex, **Wanfoding** (Ten Thousand Buddha Peak), which rises to 3099m. It's only really worth climbing this high if the weather's good – for a richer bag of views, temples, streams and vegetation, everything, in fact, but the satisfaction of reaching the summit, you won't be disappointed with the lower paths.

Access to the area is through **Emei Town**, some 150km southwest of Chengdu. The mountain's **trail head** is a short minibus ride away at **Baoguo Si**, and dedicated pilgrims can start a stern three-day round trip from here. Those with less time can omit the first few kilometres by taking a further bus from Baoguo Si to alternative starting points near either **Qingyin Ge** for the southern route (8km from Baoguo Si) or **Wannian Si** for the shorter northern route (12km). Leaving early enough, you could make it to the top in one day from either of these via **Xixiang Chi** (Elephant Washing Pool) and **Jinding** – the first peak – descending the next morning. If you're really pushed, you could get up and down in a single day by catching the minibus between Baoguo Si and **Jieyin Hall**, located an easy walk, or an effortless **cable car** ride, from Jinding, but this way you're unlikely to see much of what makes Emei Shan such a special place.

Practicalities

Shoes need to be comfortable and have a reasonable grip for the slippery mountain paths. Don't forget **warm clothing** for the top, which is around 15°C cooler than the plains and so liable to be below freezing between October and April. You'll also want some protection against the near certainty of **rain**; an umbrella is ideal. A **walking stick** is handy for easing the pressure on thigh muscles during descent, and ornamental, but effective, ones are for sale along the way for a few yuan. One thing you don't want to take is a heavy backpack – store spare gear at the lower monasteries and hotels, or in Chengdu if you're contemplating a round trip.

Temples always charge a small **entry fee**, while **accommodation** varies considerably in comfort and cost, from around ¥5 for a straw mattress in a large dormitory (not often available to foreigners) to ¥45 or more for a bed in a double room. Reception offices are

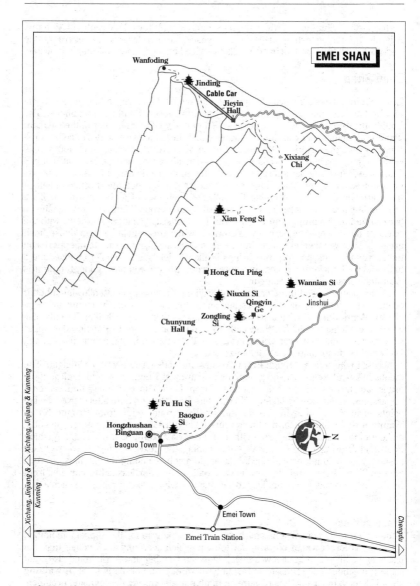

at the temple gates; you'll need to haggle to get a good deal and, to be sure of a bed, start looking for lodgings by mid-afternoon. There's unlikely to be running water and there may be no electricity either (though some monasteries even have electric blankets), so carry a flashlight for nocturnal visits to the toilet. Temple restaurants are the best places to **eat** – vegetarian dinners cost ¥6–20 – and stalls along the way can keep you topped up with bottled drinks, snacks and hot food, such as rice gruel, garlic soup and noodles.

Meishan and Emei Town

Some 60km from Chengdu, both rail and road pass **MEISHAN**, where Ming and Qing pavilions at **Sansu Ci** (the Three Su's Ancestral Hall; 8.30am–5pm; ¥3) honour this renowned local family of Song-dynasty artists. Best known is **Su Dongpo**, who reached the pinnacle of literary aspirations by securing a post at court, only to lose it and be exiled first to Hubei and then Hainan Island. Undaunted, he remained an influential poet during his lifetime, and is still known today for his atmospheric verses, his theses expounding his views on painting and, strangely, a pork banquet dish named in his honour. There isn't much to see unless you admire calligraphy, of which there's plenty, but the grounds are very pleasant.

Farther on, bustling, untidy **EMEI TOWN** lies about 7km from Baoguo Si and the foot of the mountain. Trains pull into the **train station** 3.5km away, while **buses** from Chengdu and Leshan terminate either in Emei's main street depot or at Baoguo Si, with minibuses constantly shuttling between the train station, town and Baoguo during daylight hours.

Baoguo Si and around

The road from Emei Town runs west to insubstantial **BAOGUO**, where it passes through an ornamental gateway and continues for one long, straight kilometre before fizzling out at a T-junction. About 150m north of this is **Baoguo Si**, a large and busy Song-era temple, rebuilt and enlarged during the seventeenth century. Four main halls rise one behind the other up the slope, decorated with carved doorways which open into courtyards containing bonsai and flower displays. The porcelain Buddha in the **Sutra Hall** is eye-catching, with its red-lined black garments covered with tiny golden icons, and it's said that the huge Ming-dynasty **bell** here, encrusted with characters, can be heard 15km away. The temple is often awash with guided tours, however, so it's worth the short walk to quieter **Fu Hu Si** (Taming Tiger Temple) where you can also stay. Set in a thick forest of nanmu trees, it's a comfortable place to rest up, with seemingly limitless **accommodation** on hand. Here you'll find the **Huayan Pagoda**, fourteen storeys but only 7m tall, cast of bronze in the sixteenth century and engraved with 4700 images of Buddha.

Baoguo Town is simply a string of tacky hotels flanking the road, where you'll also find the *Teddy Bear Café*, which has a menu in English, average food and an English-speaking proprietor. The most upmarket **place to stay**, with a bank and booking office, is the *Hongzhushan Binguan* (☎08426/525888, fax 525666; ③–⑧), 100m south of the T-junction. The road past Baoguo Si ends at the *Forestry Hotel*, a drab affair with languid staff and fairly basic rooms (dorms ①, rooms ④). Both hotels have **restaurants**, and there are plenty more scattered between. You can, of course, also stay and eat at Baoguo Si itself. **Moving on**, morning minibuses leave from outside Baoguo Si to drop-off points for Qingyin Ge and Wannian Si, or direct to Jinding or Leshan. There are also regular **long-distance buses** from Emei Town's main street depot to Leshan and Chengdu, and at least daily services west to Ya'an. If you're planning to catch the **train** on from Emei, either the *Teddy Bear Café* or the *Hongzhushan Hotel* will know the current timetables.

Routes to the summit

From Baoguo Si and Fu Hu Si, **the path** up the mountain takes you past some minor sights to **Chunyang Hall**, where you can spend the night and take in some panoramic views of the summit. From here the track leads past **Zhongling Si** (Mid-peak Temple) and through another dense copse of nanmu trees to the charming **Qingyin Ge** (Clear Sound Pavilion), at the hub of two rivers and several paths. You can follow the quicker northern route to the top by pressing on for a few kilometres to Wannian

---

MOUNTAIN FLORA

Of Emei Shan's three thousand or so plant species, over a hundred are endemic to either the mountain or China. The **red nanmu tree**, thin and tall, is one of these, and another is the **dove tree**, which has hard spherical fruit, thin pale leaves and a white, two-petalled flower said to resemble a perching dove. Most remarkable, though, is the stately **gingko** – *yin xing*, the silver apricot — found worldwide in prehistoric times. Once extinct in the wild, botanic lore has it that the gingko was unintentionally saved from oblivion by its popularity as an ornamental tree in monastery gardens, where it was possibly grown for the medicinal qualities of its mildly poisonous fruit, said to curb desire. From these it has reintroduced itself and is now found in a semi-wild state in China's central southwest. Chengdu is planted with gingko's, and they cluster around temples here at Emei Shan. The leaves are a distinctive lobed crescent, similar to but much larger than those of a maidenhair fern, from which the gingko's alias derives.

The gingko is not the only mountain plant to have benefited from cultivation. Most of Europe's ornamental **roses** are hybrids derived from wild Chinese stock two hundred years ago, and in summer you'll still find bushes of their small pink and white ancestors blooming on Emei's lower slopes. The region is also famous for its **tea**, with an excellent jasmine-scented variety on offer at Baoguo or Emei Town for around ¥50 per kilo. In addition, the mountain provides a huge range of fungi and **medicinal herbs**, which you'll see for sale all over the place: make sure you know what you're buying and how to use it though, as some – such as the scarlet and black beans on display in glass jars outside Baoguo Si – are extremely poisonous.

Si (see below), or take the southern route up to **Niuxin Si**, the Ox Heart Monastery, home of the mountain's famous **bearded frogs** – at least, the males are bearded, females make do with stripes. Climbing higher, the path passes **Hong Chu Ping**, the Ancient Trees Terrace, where you can also stop for the night, before reaching the conifer forest surrounding further accommodation at **Xian Feng Si** (Fairy Peaks Monastery). From here it's a couple of hours to where the trail joins the north route near **Xixiang Chi** (see below).

Most people, however, take **the bus** from Baoguo direct to **Jinshui**, drop-off point for Emei's northern route. Not far along the path is Emei's oldest temple, **Wannian Si** (Myriad Years Monastery), established in the fourth century and rebuilt by the Tang emperor Xi Zong around 880. The temple is famous for the contents of the dumpy hall in front, whose bare whitewashed bricks and thousands of tiny iron Buddhas surround a stunning **sculpture of Samantabhadra**, riding a gilt lotus flower astride a great six-tusked white elephant, whose feet rest in four lotus blossoms. This huge bronze statue was part of a tenth-century project to develop the mountain for Buddhism, and was brought from Chengdu in pieces. Wannian is also one of the best monasteries to spend the night at; **accommodation** is frugal, but the food is excellent and you should find that the atmosphere makes up for any discomfort. Evenings are alive to the sound of frogs croaking – like guitars, say the Chinese – and later the drone of the monks' chants and the sing-song of their bells reverberate through the halls.

A steady three hours from Wannian through thick mists and groves of bamboo and pine and you should be mounting the last slippery steps to **Xixiang Chi**, a pool where the elephant carrying Samantabhadra stopped for a dip on his way up the mountain. Finely set on a hill top, a nearby **temple** is not as imposing as Wannian but has a wide view, surrounded by groves of age-old trees and rhododendron bushes. It's about four hours on to the top from here, but if you plan to stay the night you'll find that the temple's position at the meeting of the ways makes for crowds – get in early to be sure of a bed.

Beyond here the path gets easier, but you'll have to endure gangs of aggressive **monkeys** who threaten you for food with teeth bared. Strangely, they seem able to distinguish between locals, whom they ignore, and tourists whom they plague. Showing empty hands and calling their bluff by striding on seems to work, daunting though their response can be and you'll probably feel safer with a stick in your hand at this point. The path continues through thick woods to **Jieyin Hall**, where the road from Baoguo Si, which has snaked its way round the back of the mountain, ends at a **cable car** connection to the summit, and the area is thick with minibus tour parties fired up for their one-day crack at the peak. It's also somewhere to find a lift off the mountain on your way down, if you've run out of time or steam. **Hostels** around Jieyin look good, but have a reputation for rudeness once they've got your money.

Whether you take the cable car (20min; ¥24 up, ¥18 down) or spend the next couple of hours hoofing it past an accelerating concentration of stalls, **Jinding**, the Golden Summit (3077m), is the next stop and, for most, the main reason to be up here at all. The name of this somewhat austere temple, set in a terraced complex near the cliff edge, derives from its former shiny bronze roof, replaced in 1989 with bright yellow tiles. You can **stay the night** in the temple (and rent a padded jacket to take the edge off the cold), and then get up at dawn and join the swarms huddling on the terrace in the hope of catching the **sunrise**, which is marvellous on a good day, as it lights up the sea of clouds below the peak. In the afternoon, these clouds sometimes catch rainbow-like rings known as **Buddha's Halo**, which surround and move with your shadow, while in clear conditions it's said you can even make out **Gongga Shan** (see p.819), over 150km to the west. On a bad day, Jinding is wrapped in wet, cold clouds, with the huge broadcasting mast looming above the temple complex the only scenery. In these conditions you certainly won't be tempted to plod on for a final hour up to **Wanfoding** (Ten Thousand Buddha Summit), the true top of the mountain.

Leshan

Set beside the wide convergence of the Qingyi, Min and Dadu rivers, 180km from Chengdu and about 20km from Emei Shan, **LESHAN** is a 1300-year-old market town in the throes of major reconstructions. These have reduced the outer edges to rubble, while the centre glistens with sleek paving and tall new offices, streets adorned with banners urging people to "Control Population Growth, Raise Population Quality". Surprisingly, then, it's a nice spot to spend an evening drinking tea and snacking at stalls along the river, before taking the morning ferry across to the incredible **Dafo**, who looks out over the water and past the town from his deep niche in the cliffs.

Leshan's multiple-named main street runs south from the bus stations into the triangular town centre past the huge **Minjiang Bridge**, a *Bank of China* and a bizarre crocodile-and-maiden statue. Here Binjiang Lu splits southwest off along the riverfront and down to the **ferry terminals**. Stay on the main road to reach the newest shopping centres at the crossroads with Dong Dajie. Turn right here for the **post office** and, farther on along Yutang Jie, the older quarter of town, which has some inexpensive **places to eat** along the narrow lanes.

Leshan has no rail link, and arriving by road will land you at one of the **bus stations** along Shengshui Jie, about 1km north of the centre. **Moving on**, there are buses to Chengdu and Emei Town through the day, and less plentiful traffic to Chongqing, Xichang and Ya'an. After the June rains have raised the river levels high enough, it's also possible to reach **Chongqing by ferry** via **Yibin** (see p.795) from the dock on Binjiang Lu.

EMEI SHAN AND LESHAN

Emei Shan	峨眉山	éméi shān
Baoguo Si	报国寺	bàoguó sì
Fu Hu Si	伏虎寺	fúhǔ sì
Hongzhushan Binguan	红珠山宾馆	hóngzhūshān bīnguǎn
Jieyin Hall	接引殿	jiēyǐn diàn
Jinding	金顶	jīndǐng
Meishan	眉山	méi shān
Niuxin Si	牛心寺	niúxīn sì
Qingyin Ge	清音阁	qīngyīn gé
Wannian Si	万年寺	wànnián sì
Xian Feng Si	仙峰寺	xiānfēng sì
Xixiang Chi	洗象池	xǐxiàng chí
Leshan	乐山	lèshān
Great Buddha	大佛	dàfó
Lingyun Shan	凌云山	língyún shān
Wuyou Si	乌优寺	wǔyōu sì
ACCOMMODATION		
Dongfeng	东风饭店	dōngfēng fàndiàn
Educational Research Centre	教育研究 所	jiàoyù yánjiūsuǒ
Jiazhou	嘉州宾馆	jiāzhōu bīnguǎn
Jiurifeng Binguan	就日峰宾馆	jiùrìfēng bīnguǎn
Nanlou Binguan	南楼宾馆	nánlóu bīnguǎn
Xichang	西昌	xīchāng
Jiaotong Gongyu	交通公寓	jiāotōng gōngyù
Liangshan Binguan	凉山宾馆	liángshān bīnguǎn
Space Flight Centre	航天发射中心	hángtiān fāshè zhòngxīn

Accommodation

Dongfeng, Shangtu Qiao Jie, across from the bank (☎0833/234560). A scruffy and worn hotel only worth the effort if elsewhere is full. The no-frills dorms are very hard to get in to. Dorms ①, rooms ③.

Educational Research Centre, behind the country bus station (☎0833/234257). Touts hang around the bus stations looking for customers for this place which offers clean, basic dorms with varying numbers of beds and better doubles with TV. Dorms ①, rooms ②–④.

Jiazhou, 19 Baita Jie (☎0833/239888, fax 233233). A smart complex usually full of foreign tour groups. There's a good, pricey restaurant with river views, a sauna, airline office, shops and money-changing facilities for guests. ⑤–⑧.

Post and Communications Hotel, Yutang Jie (☎0833/235450). Tucked away in a courtyard behind the post office; the exterior is grotty but the rooms are fairly comfy, and there's a respectable restaurant. ③–⑥.

Dafo

Enormous and impassive, **Dafo** (the Great Buddha) peers out from under half-lidded eyes, uncaring of the sightseers swarming round his head, clambering over his toes and nearly capsizing their boats in their eagerness to photograph his bulk. Touted as the world's largest Buddhist sculpture at 71m tall, one thing the statistics can't convey is the feeling of seeing this squat icon, comfortably seated with his hands resting on his knees, growing as the ferry nears and first appreciating the effort of hand carving it from the surrounding red sandstone cliffs, which took over ninety years.

Work on Dafo was started by the monk **Haitong** in 713, who felt that the image would protect boats navigating the rough waters below **Lingyun Hill**. After Haitong blinded himself to convince the government to hand over funds, the project was continued by the monks **Zangchou** and **Weigao**, who designed the Buddha's robes and hair to shed water and incorporated an internal drainage system to reduce weathering. Once construction started, **temples** sprang up above the Buddha at **Lingyun Shan** and on adjacent **Wuyou Shan**, and today you can spend a good five hours walking between the sights. **Ferries** (¥7) leave Leshan jetty to Lingyun and Wuyou from about 8am until mid-afternoon (last ferries back around 6pm). Most people start at Wuyou, the route described below, but you'll encounter tour parties going either way. You're charged **admission fees** at various stages; all told, these amount to around ¥30.

WUYOU SI TO THE BUDDHA

Crossing from Leshan jetty to Wuyou Shan, cruise boats turn in mid-stream so that both sides get a look at Dafo from beneath – the best view by far – and the vessel tilts alarmingly as people rush to the railings. Two much smaller **guardians** flank the main statue and, as you approach the Wuyou jetty, you'll see countless smaller sculptures, most nearly weathered to oblivion, as well as graffiti carved into the cliffs.

Once ashore, a steep staircase leads up to **Wuyou Si**, a warm pink-walled monastery founded in 742 AD, with a good **vegetarian restaurant** right on top of the hill. The monastery **decorations** are particularly good – look for the splendid gate guardians as you enter, the animated scenes from *Journey to the West* on the second hall (Xuan Zang being carried off by demons, Monkey leaping to the rescue) and the grotesque *arhat* sculptures inside.

Moving on, the path drops down through woodland to the water's edge, where a sturdy covered bridge links Wuyou with **Lingyun Shan**. Wuyou was a peninsula until some two thousand years ago, when the ubiquitous Li Bing created this channel to moderate annual floods. Turn left on the far side and up more stairs to a spanking **new temple** complex, with some more excellent views and over-the-top statues, or continue along the main path to the courtyard around the top of the **Great Buddha** himself. Elbowing your way through the throngs assembling for photos, you'll find yourself up against railings level with Dafo's ear, where you can watch lines descending the slippery **Staircase of Nine Turns** to his feet. In the vicinity of the courtyard there's **accommodation** at the clean, damp *Nanlou Binguan* (☎0833/233811; ②–④), various tearooms and restaurants, a **museum** housing statues of Haitong and his successors, and the thirteen-storey, whitewashed **Lingbao Pagoda** out the back. The *Jiurifeng Binguan* (☎0833/230827; ③–⑦) below has further **beds**, but the rooms are very ordinary.

Heading back to Leshan, the main path descends from the Buddha to the road running along the east bank of the Min River parallel with town. On the way down have a good look at where the three rivers meet – despite Dafo's protection, there are still some vicious currents as brown and black waters mingle over low-lying shoals. Once at the bottom and through the gates, you can catch a ferry back to Leshan's jetty or tout around the **buses** for a lift back to town.

On to Yunnan: the far south

The 22-hour train journey from Emei Town down through **southern Sichuan** to Kunming is famous not for the scenery itself, splendid though it is, but for the fact that you rarely catch a glimpse of it. Estimates vary, but there are over **two hundred tunnels** along the way, some lasting seconds, others several minutes, and you'll soon get fed up trying to get a long look at the peaks and gorges passing the window.

THE YI

Spread through the mountains of southwestern China, the **Yi** form the region's largest minority group, with a population of around five million. Their shamanistic religion, language and unique, wavy script indicate that they probably originated in northwestern China. Until the 1940s they were farmers with a matriarchal **slave society** divided into a landowning "Black" caste, and subordinate tenants and labourers who comprised a "White" caste. Today such divisions are gone and the majority of Yi live and work in urban centres, but shamanism is certainly still practised and there's a chance of at least a superficial view of the old ways during occasional **festivals**. These can be riotous occasions with heavy drinking sessions, bullfights and wrestling matches interspersed with music and archery displays. Traditionally everyone dressed up, though today this is largely left to the women who don finely embroidered jackets and sometimes twist their hair into bizarre horned shapes, the married women wearing black turbans. Best is the **torch festival** at the end of the sixth lunar month, commemorating both an ancient victory over a heavenly insect plague, and the wife of Tang-dynasty chieftain Deng Shan, who starved to death rather than marry the warlord who had incinerated her husband. The Yi also hold their new year early, in the tenth lunar month.

Some seven hours from Emei is **XICHANG**, of interest partly as a centre for ethnic **Yi** and also as the site of China's **Long March Space Programme**, which launches communications satellites with varying degrees of success in competition with *NASA* and Europe's *Ariane* project. Only slightly geared up to Chinese tour groups who come to visit the Space Flight Centre and photograph the natives, Xichang is an ordinary kind of place, with the Yi not much in evidence except on big market days. For more on the Yi, there's a **museum** at **Qionghai Hu**, a large lake 5km to the south of town where exhibits range from festival clothing to household items, and books written in the Yi language. Your accommodation should be able to arrange tours of the **Space Flight Centre**, if they're running, though they don't always accept foreigners and last reports were that the site was closed after two Long March rockets crash-landed on nearby settlements in 1995 and 1996, possibly killing several thousand people. Xichang's **places to stay** include the basic *Jiaotong Gongyu* (①) and the slightly better *Liangshan Binguan* (②–④), both near the **bus station** on Shengli Lu. Take your pick of the food stalls nearby.

Back on the train, five hours beyond Xichang is **Jinjiang** (Panzhihua), rail head for the ugly industrial city of **Dukou**. Stay on board and it's a farther ten hours or so to Kunming, but you could also catch a bus west from Jinjiang into Yunnan's far north – see p.742.

Zigong and Yibin

Surrounding the confluence of the Yangzi and Min rivers 250km southeast of Chengdu, where Sichuan, Yunnan and Guizhou provinces meet, the **Zigong and Yibin districts** receive scant attention from foreigners, though there are some intriguing attractions. Zhuhai, the **Bamboo Sea**, is beginning to pull in a steady stream of Chinese visitors, as are some esoteric historical relics including dinosaurs, salt mines and hanging coffins.

Forming a seventy-kilometre-broad triangle, the main towns in the area are **Zigong**, **Yibin** and **Luzhou**. The latter two are on the Yangzi River between Leshan and Chongqing, and are therefore accessible by ferry from either after the June rains raise the river level high enough to be navigable. A more reliable way into the region is by

train via the sugar city of **Neijiang**, which lies halfway along the Chengdu–Chongqing line and is just a short bus ride from Zigong, though a slow rail line also snakes down through Zigong to Yibin. Coming from Leshan, bus or the ferry to Yibin are your options. An interesting way out of the region is by catching a bus southeast from Luzhou to **Chishui** in Guizhou Province – see p.696.

Zigong

ZIGONG, a thriving industrial centre, is best known in China as an important source of **salt**, tapped for thousands of years from deep artesian basins. Predictably, the third-century engineer Li Bing is credited with the first strikes, and a century later the Sichuanese were sinking three-hundred-metre-deep boreholes using bamboo fibre cables attached to massive stone bits. Later innovations saw the development of more effective two-piece percussion drills, and by the 1600s, bamboo buckets were used to draw brine from wells bored a kilometre or more beneath Zigong, hundreds of years before European technology (which borrowed Chinese techniques) could reach this deep. **Natural gas**, a byproduct of drilling, was used from the second century to power the furnaces extracting the salt from the brine. The lavish Qing-era buildings of the former salt merchants' guildhall in the town centre are now an absorbing **Salt Museum** (8.30–11.30am & 2–5pm; ¥5), full of photos and mining relics, though the captions are all in Chinese.

The town is also worth a stopover for its excellent **Dinosaur Museum** (9–11.30am & 1.30–5pm; ¥10), built 15km north at **Dashanpu** over the site of excavations carried out during the 1980s with the help of the British Museum. There's a **hotel** in Zigong just off Tanmulin Jie (dorms ②, rooms ④), and frequent buses out to the museum, where in addition to the near-perfect skeletal remains of a dozen Jurassic titans, some bones have been left partially excavated *in situ*, looking very spooky as they emerge from the earth.

Yibin and around

Balanced on the border with Yunnan, the port city of **YIBIN** is unexceptional in itself (although the central *Zhudian Zhaodaisuo* (②) is recommended if you have to stay), but 50km to the southeast via **Changning**, reached by bus from near Yibin's train station, is the extraordinary **Bamboo Sea**, which covers over forty square kilometres of mountain slopes with feathery green tufts. Foreigners on the bus are turned in at the park gates to cough up the ¥10 entrance fee, from where the road follows through to **accommodation** prospects at the *Jiaotong Binguan* (dorms ①–②, rooms ③–⑤). Paths lead from here into the forest, an unusual walk given such a large expanse of just the one type of plant. It's surprisingly dark, with the tall, slender trunks reaching up 10m or more. For the best views of the "sea", however, climb the hills above to a scattering of **temples**, from where the bowed tips of bamboo ripple in waves as breezes sweep the

ZIGONG AND YIBIN		
Gongxian	珙县	*gǒngxiàn*
Hanging coffins	悬棺	*xuánguān*
Yibin	宜宾	*yíbīn*
Bamboo Sea	竹海	*zhúhǎi*
Zigong	自贡	*zìgòng*
Dinosaur Museum	恐龙博物馆	*kǒnglóng bówùguǎn*
Salt Museum	盐业历史博物馆	*yányè lìshǐ bówùguǎn*

slopes. The best of the shrines is the Buddhist–Taoist **Feiyun Dong**, which contains some really grotesque Ming-dynasty sculptures.

The Bo and burials

Around thirty Bo **hanging coffins**, dated to over four hundred years old, decorate cliffs lining the Dengjia River near the town of **GONGXIAN**, 50km south of Yibin and connected by daily buses. The **Bo people** themselves are a bit of an enigma, having vanished during the sixteenth century, routed by imperial forces after their leader rashly declared himself emperor during a rebellion against the local governor. Often portrayed as a degenerate aboriginal race skulking along the river basins and stirring up trouble among the populace, their cliff burials show a well-developed artistic culture – the sites contain engraved and carved artefacts, and frescoes depicting everyday activities – while the location of the coffins, arranged high up in the open on wooden galleries, is believed to have aided the return of spirits to the sky. How the coffins were actually positioned is unknown, though presumably the process involved some sort of scaffolding. There are no organized tours to the coffins, so you will have to travel independently to Gongxian and ask for directions there. Alternatively, the hotel in Zigong may be able to help.

Dazu

About 180km east of Chengdu and 90km west of Chongqing, the celebrated **cliff sculptures** of **Dazu** lie amid beautiful lush countryside of green rolling hills cut with gentle terraces. One translation of Dazu is "Big Foot", referring to a story of Buddha leaving a footprint on rocks nearby, though perhaps this is just a way of saying that the sculptures here were divinely inspired. They are certainly extraordinary, comprising some fifty thousand images carved into niches, caves and overhangs in the sides of **Bei Shan** (North Hill) and **Baoding Shan** (Precious Summit Hill), with lesser examples scattered around the outlying countryside. Begun in 892, work on them continued for over four hundred years, and they have since avoided the ravages of weather through an ingenious internal drainage system, and the attentions of foreign looters and native vandals by isolation and decree respectively. Some of the sculptures are small, others huge, many are brightly painted and form comic-strip-like narratives, their characters portraying religious, moral and historical tales. While most are set fairly deeply into the rock faces, all can be viewed by natural light and are connected by walkways and paths.

Dazu Town, Bei Shan and Baoding Shan

The base for exploring the sculptures is **DAZU TOWN**, 200km from Chengdu and 100km from Chongqing. A pleasant, nondescript place with a centre only a few hundred metres across, Dazu is set along the mild Laixi River immediately south of Bei Shan, whose carvings can be reached on foot via Bei Jie, with most of the town spread along the north side of the river. Baoding Shan is 16km off to the east, connected to Dazu by frequent minibuses through the day (¥2; last one back leaves Baoding Shan around 5pm).

Dazu's main **bus station** is by the bridge on the south bank, a six-hour haul from Chongqing, or a very uncomfortable ten hours from Chengdu's Xiannanmen station. In slightly less time, you can also take the train from either city to **Youtingpou**, and a local bus for the thirty-kilometre trip from there. **Accommodation** is expensive and limited (as far as foreigners are concerned) to the recently rebuilt *Dazu Binguan* (③–④) and the similar *Beishan Binguan* (④), both left out of the bus station, over the bridge and down on the right. Student ID holders may be able to negotiate a thirty percent discount, and the high prices mean that they are very unlikely to be full. For **food**, try the hotels or the dozen or so restaurants along the main streets.

Bei Shan

A couple of kilometres' walk north from Dazu's main street brings you to a flight of steps leading up to the area's earliest carvings, begun in the ninth century, at **Bei Shan** (daily 8am–5pm; ¥20), and constituting 264 decorated recesses cut into the hillside and joined by a path. The work was started by General **Wei Junjing**, who is suitably remembered by a piece carved in his honour by a defeated Shu warlord. Other sculptures were funded by donations, some military, some given by monks and nuns whose names are recorded in inscriptions or appear on the arrangements themselves.

There's plenty to see here, but, for the utterly overwhelmed, **cave 245** (they are all numbered) is outstanding, with over six hundred figures and some nice details of contemporary Tang life, including ornaments, dress and musical instruments. Just north of here, though, the finest detail and craftsmanship are displayed in some **Song-dynasty** carvings. **Cave 113** has an elegant **Guanyin Gazing at the Moon's Reflection**, and in **cave 125** the Bodhisattva appears again with a rosary, looking more like a shy debutante than a girl renouncing the world. The **largest cave, 136**, depicts Sakyamuni flanked by the feature-filled figures of twenty Bodhisattvas, among them Manjusri riding a blue roaring lion, and Samantabhadra sitting calmly in a lotus position on a sturdy elephant.

Baoding Shan

Exciting, comic and realistic by turns, the sculptures at **Baoding Shan** (daily 8am–5pm; ¥40) comprise the best of Dazu's art, funded by subscriptions collected between 1179 and 1245 by **Zhao Zhifeng**, a dedicated local monk. Because he alone organized the work over such a long period there's little repetition of the stories, all taken from Buddhist scriptures, and the ten thousand images divide into two clear groupings. **Xiaofowan** is the earliest, carved into stone-walled grottoes supported by pillars and beams, but most people concentrate on the later and more impressive **Dafowan**, whose 31 sculpted niches are more naturally incorporated into the inner side of a horseshoe curve of hills overlooking a narrow valley. Here, as at Bei Shan, there's a chance to get eye to eye with some quite incredible and illuminating detail. **Fierce Tiger Descending a Mountain** greets you with superb elan, and leads to another striking group, the **Six Ways of Transmigration**, in which a brightly coloured Atlas holds a great segmented disc, representing one of the six courses of predestination. The path leads from here to **niche 5**, where there's a gigantic representation of Vairocana, Manjusri and Samantabhadra, the last holding out a stone pagoda said to weigh half a tonne. No less imposing is niche 8, the **Dabei Pavilion**, where the figure of a thousand-armed Guanyin is the largest ever carved in China. Each hand is different, fanning out in glowing gold like peacock feathers. Impressive in a different way are the thirty-metre-high **reclining Buddha** in niche 11, and niche 15, **Requital of Parent's Kindness**. Here, seven Buddhas represent the stages of a man's life – praying for a son, conception, birth, feeding and washing the baby, arranging a marriage – right through to old age. By contrast, the next but one along shows **Buddha Requiting his Parents' Kindness**, with figures recalling his goodness to his parents while on the left heretics slander him as unfilial. Niche 20 houses the memorable **Eighteen Layers of Hell**, a Chamber-of-Horrors scene interspersed with delicate and amusing comic-strip cameos such as the **Hen Wife** and the **Drunkard and his Mother**. Near the exit, **niche 30** returns to a naturalistic theme, showing ten buffaloes with their herder, both a symbol of meditation and a tranquil picture of pastoral life.

Chongqing and around

Centred around a crowded, comma-shaped peninsula at the junction of the Yangzi and Jialing rivers, **CHONGQING** is Sichuan's powerhouse, the province's largest city both in scale and population, and an industrial centre thriving on nearby mineral wealth. It's also a busy **port**, whose location, 2400km upstream from Shanghai at the meeting point between eastern river traffic and overland trade routes with Tibet and Burma, has given it a commercial importance long coveted by foreign and Chinese powers. It oozes the atmosphere of a typical waterfront city, dirty, seedy and not particularly attractive, but bursting with life.

Able to trace its history right back into legend, Chongqing was capital of the state of Ba when the mythical king **Yu**, tamer of floods, found a consort here. It was formerly known as Yuzhou, and the current name, meaning "Double Celebration", was bestowed by former resident **Zhaodun** on his becoming emperor in 1189. The city has a long tradition as a place of defiance against hostile powers, despite being ceded as a **treaty port** to Britain and Japan in the nineteenth century. In 1242 near **Hechuan**, some 60km to the north, Song forces held Mongol invaders at bay for 36 years during the longest continuous campaign on Chinese soil, and it was to Chongqing that the Nationalist Guomindang government withdrew in 1937, having been driven out of Nanjing by the Japanese. An influx of refugees and heavy bombing raids against the undefended wartime capital did little to raise morale, as the beleaguered Nationalists became more preoccupied with a propaganda war against the Communists than defeating the invaders. After the Japanese surrender in 1945 and the resumption of civil war following the failure of US-brokered talks in the city between Mao and Chiang Kaishek, Chongqing remained one of the last Guomindang bastions, falling to Communist forces in November 1949. Rebuilding itself from the rubble, Chongqing is booming today: over two million people rub elbows on the peninsula, with five times that number in the surrounding suburbs, and there seems to be no end to the expanding wave of apartment buildings and industrial developments spreading away from the river.

Built on and surrounded by steep-sided hills, the **Mountain City** has, in many respects, little initial appeal. Faster paced and noticeably less friendly than Chengdu, coal and grime seem to coat everything, and even in sunshine the city is hazed with dust. Nor does the climate help. Pollution is often compounded with winter fogs, and nowhere does Sichuan's summer humidity feel more oppressive than on the peninsula's narrow streets, although it's markedly fresher in the several hilltop **parks** scattered through the city. There's next to nothing in the way of buildings to show Chongqing's age either, though some **revolutionary sites** where the Communists negotiated with the ailing Guomindang survive, as do **prisons** where Reds and subversives were kept and tortured. All things considered, then, it's more rewarding simply to wander around the city streets – dirt and all, there's plenty of character – and concentrate on Chongqing's excellent opportunities for arranging **Yangzi river cruises**, and trips west to Yibin (see p.794) and the Buddhist grottoes at **Dazu** (see p.796).

Orientation, arrival, city transport and accommodation

Much of what Chongqing has to offer lies on the four-kilometre-long peninsula of the city proper, which sprawls below the grassy parks atop **Pipa Shan** and **Eling Shan**. The **city centre** and most of Chongqing's accommodation prospects are grouped around **Victory Monument** in the eastern Jiefangbei commercial district. Several pri-

---

The **telephone code** for Chongqing is ☎0811

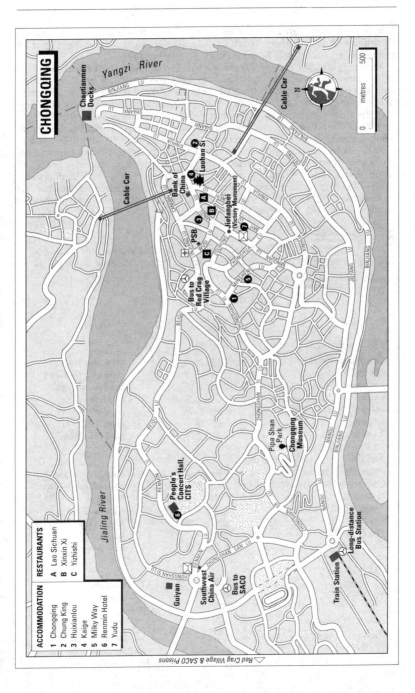

CHONGQING

Yangzi River

Jialing River

Chaotianmen Docks

Cable Car

Cable Car

Bank of China

Luohan Si ②

④

Jiefangbei (Victory Monument)

A

B

③ PSB

C

⑦

Bus to Red Crag Village

① ⑤

Pipa Shan Park

Chongqing Museum

People's Concert Hall, CITS ⑥

Guiyan

Southwest China Air

Bus to SACO

Train Station

Long-distance Bus Station

Red Crag Village & SACO Prisons

N

0   metres   500

ACCOMMODATION
1 Chongqing
2 Chung King
3 Huixianlou
4 Kaige
5 Milky Way
6 Renmin Hotel
7 Yudu

RESTAURANTS
A Lao Sichuan
B Xinxin Xi
C Yizhishi

BINJIANG LU

SHAANXI

SHAANXI

CANGBAI LU

PHOENIX

PHOENIX

ZHONGHUA LU

MINSHENG LU

LINJIANG

CANGBAI LU

BEIQU

BEIQU

RENMIN

RENMIN

ZHONGSHAN SI LU

ZHONGSHAN SAN LU

ZHONGSHAN

NANQU

NANQU

HONGSHAN

JIEFANG

BINJIANG LU

vate buses **from Dazu** and elsewhere also have their terminuses here, and the **Chaotianmen docks**, where Yangzi ferries pull in, are right at the eastern tip of the peninsula, just a short walk from the centre (or take bus #103).

Most people arrive, however, at the western end of town. The airport shuttle bus (¥10) transports passengers the 30km from the **airport** to *China Southwest Airlines* building on Zhongshan San Lu (from where buses #104 and #105 run along Renmin Lu to the Jiefangbei terminus on Linjiang Lu). The main **long-distance bus and train stations** are southwest of the centre, near river level. From here, either flag down bus #102 from the roundabout to Chaotianmen docks, or cross the road and catch the **funicular railway** up to Zhongshan Er Lu, where trolleybus #405 runs to Jiefangbei.

At ¥1 or less for a ride within the peninsula, **buses** are the easiest way to get around if you want to give your legs a break from the serpentine stone staircases linking different levels of town. Because of the hills, **bicycles** are a rare sight. If at all possible, avoid Chongqing's piratical **taxis**, or establish the fare first and make sure you have the exact change. The peninsula is so small that it shouldn't cost much more than the cab's standing charge (¥9–12) to reach anywhere central.

Accommodation

There's a shortage of budget and mid-range accommodation for foreigners in Chongqing, and beware of a ten to fifteen percent service charge at the larger places.

CHONGQING AND AROUND		
Chongqing	重庆	*chóngqìng*
ACCOMMODATION		
Chongqing Guesthouse	重庆宾馆	*chóngqìng bīnguǎn*
Chung King	重庆饭店	*chóngqìng fàndiàn*
Huixianlou	会仙楼宾馆	*huìxiānlóu bīnguǎn*
Kaige	凯歌招待所	*kǎigē zhāodàisuǒ*
Milky Way	银河大酒店	*yínhé dàjiǔdiàn*
Renmin	人民宾馆	*rénmín bīnguǎn*
Yudu	愉都大酒店	*yùdū zhāodàisuǒ*
THE CITY		
Chaotianmen docks	朝天门码头	*cháo tiānmén mǎtóu*
Chongqing Museum	重庆市博物馆	*chóngqìngshì bówùguǎn*
Luohan Si	罗汉寺	*luóhàn sì*
People's Concert Hall	人民大礼堂	*rénmín dà lǐtáng*
Pipa Shan Park	枇杷山公园	*pípáshān gōngyuán*
Red Crag Village	红岩村	*hóngyán cūn*
SACO prisons	中美合作所	*zhōngměi hézuòsuǒ*
RESTAURANTS		
Lao Sichuan	老四川	*lǎo sìchuān*
Yizhishi	颐之时	*yízhīshí*
AROUND CHONGQING		
Nanshan Gongyuan	南山公园	*nánshān gōngyuán*
Northern Hot Springs	北温泉	*běi wēnquán*

Most **hotels** are located near the eastern Jiefangbei commercial district and all but the *Kaige* have international phones, booking agents and money-changing counters for guests.

Chongqing, 235 Minsheng Lu (☎3845888, fax 3830643). Overpriced but comfortable enough business venue, with full facilities and two good restaurants specializing in banquets and "sizzling hot" Western food. ⑧.

Chung King, 41–43 Xinhua Lu (☎3849301, fax 3843085). Interesting 1930s building housing a Hong Kong-run hotel. The rooms and the Sichuanese restaurant are good. ⑤–⑥.

Huixianlou, 186 Minzu Lu (☎3845101, fax 3844234). Very central with moderately surly staff, tatty furnishings and just about the only cheapish beds in Chongqing – seven-bed dorms with shared bathrooms. Dorms ②, rooms ⑥.

Kaige, 10 Luohan Si Jie. A Chinese hostel directly outside Luohan Si. The simple three- and four-bed dorms are cheap, but police seem to be cracking down and they won't always take foreigners. ①–②.

Milky Way, 49 Datong Lu (☎3808585, fax 3812080). Chongqing's best international-style lodgings, plush, smart and organized. ⑦–⑧.

Renmin, 173 Renmin Lu (☎3851421). This hotel is in the wings of the grandiose People's Concert Hall; buses #103, #104 and #105 pass the door. Despite its setting and popularity with Chinese tour groups, rooms and service are sadly average. ⑧.

Yudu, 168 Bayi Lu (☎3835212, fax 3830343). Rooms here offer reasonable comforts and value, and the restaurant delivers fine Guangdong meals, but the hotel's best feature is the view from the circular "Nine Heavens Hall" on the top floor. Some three-bed dorms on offer. Dorms ④, rooms ⑦.

The City

Chongqing's steep slopes, back alleys and bicycle-free streets immediately set the city apart from others in China, though things have changed from the heady 1890s when **George Morrison**, an Australian journalist who later became an adviser to the mendacious warlord Yuan Shikai, described an enormously rich port with mighty walls, temples, pagodas and great public buildings – seemingly financed by the surrounding fields of **opium poppies**. The wealth is still here, and even the basic, congested street plan seems unaltered, but the opium trade, buildings and walls were mostly destroyed by Japanese bombs during the last war, or have since fallen victim to relentless expansion. Today Chongqing is best characterized by inner-city development and urban sprawl.

Jiefangbei and Luohan Si

Jiefangbei, the **Victory Monument**, marks the city's commercial heart, though you'd expect something better than this drab concrete clock tower to celebrate the Communists' hard-won struggle to liberate the city from seventy years of colonial and right-wing occupation. The surrounding crossroads becomes a **pedestrian area** at weekends, packed with noisy, well-dressed crowds investigating the latest imports piled high at the several department stores, watching pop videos on the two huge TV screens hung up outside and blithely disregarding the signs asking them not to litter. The backstreets are busy, too; narrow pavements congested with bright, cheap clothing stalls, the air spiked with nitric acid fumes from dozens of squinting **jewellers**, who sit hunched over their workbenches fixing baubles with oxyacetylene torches. The main **market** here is around Bayi Lu, where you'll find buckets of frogs, cages of snakes – which vendors laughingly invite you to handle – and huge, fragrant bags of dried spices and fungi.

Moving northeast along Minzu Lu takes you past **Luohan Si** (¥2), set down an alleyway but given away by the incense and paper money sellers hanging around the gates. Beyond the unusual entrance, lined by weathered rock carvings, the best feature of this tiny, century-old temple is the **arhat hall**, where you're guided anti-clockwise by a rope handrail through a maze of five hundred brightly painted, life-sized statues of Buddhist saints. All the figures are distinctive, some with grotesquely contorted features, one with five eyes and another reaching elongated arms heaven-wards. Outside stands an isolated statue of a drunkard and there's a spartan **vegetarian restaurant**, open to the public for lunch.

Across the road and around the corner from the temple, along Cangbai Lu is the **cable-car** station from where you can ride high across the river to northern Chongqing (¥1) – there's another cable-car route to the southern suburbs from Xinhua Lu. Views from either take in river traffic, trucks collecting landfill in low-season mud, and distant hills merely faint grey silhouettes behind the haze. However, the machinery tends to break down in the rain.

Chaotianmen docks

Chongqing's main appeal is as the terminus for the three-day **Yangzi river cruises** which head downstream through the **Three Gorges** to Yichang and Wuhan (see p.458 & p.446). The **Chaotianmen docks** are a five-minute walk downhill from Luohan Si along Xinhua Lu, and the main activity here focuses on the loading and unloading of vessels moored out in the centre of the river. Heavily laden porters carry bundles of goods on carrypoles across seemingly random walkways laid out over the sticky sea-sonal mudflats between the boats and shore – a route you may well be taking, perhaps at night, if you take the ferry from here during winter.

Xinhua Lu ends at a stone wharf above the river, where there's a bus terminal, a **left-luggage depot**, the official **ticket office** and a number of **independent agents**, some of whom can speak English – follow the signs if nobody grabs your arm. It's probably best to arrange things a few days in advance, but outside the autumn tourist season you should be able to find tickets for next day travel. Because of Chongqing's rather vague docking arrangements, ask for the **dock number** when buying tickets, and try to locate it during daylight.

Ferries leave daily between 6am and 8am, and this allows you to sidestep the city's expensive accommodation and **sleep on board** the night before departure; go down with your luggage after 8pm and pay the purser. Note that the charge for this is set by your ticket class and the purser's private whim, and not by the ticket agents – their guesses are generally way off, and expectations of an unrealistically cheap night often lead to arguments on board.

CRUISE FARES FROM CHONGQING

Competition between agents, along with surcharges and the fact that foreigners are charged between thirty and fifty percent more than the posted fares, means that the following per-person prices for travel from Chongqing should be used as a guide only (see pp.806–7 for more details). For the best deals, take along a Chinese student card and shop around.

Yichang 2-berth cabin ¥535; 8-berth ¥225; 16-berth ¥160; 24-berth ¥125.

Wuhan 2-berth cabin ¥790; 8-berth ¥330; 16-berth ¥235; 24-berth ¥185.

It's possible to book fares all the way through to **Shanghai**, too, but this usually involves a change of vessel at Wuhan: 2-berth cabin ¥1200; 8-berth ¥610; 16-berth ¥420; 24-berth ¥275.

Luxury cruises to Wuhan start at around ¥1275. There's also a daily **hydrofoil** from Chaotianmen to **Wanxian** at 10am (¥196; 7hr), and, after the summer rains deepen the flow, a regular ferry link upstream to **Leshan** (see p.791).

Pipa Shan and the west end

A ten-minute ride on the #405 trolleybus west of Jiefangbei down Zhongshan Yi Lu lands you outside the gates of **Pipa Shan Park** (¥1), from where a short walk uphill leads to a pavilion perched on the airy, grassy peak. At 220m this is the highest spot in Chongqing – below, the city labours under a haze of smog and the chink of countless construction hammers drifts up in the breeze, but at night, pollution is invisible, and the hills and river are picked out by streetlamps and industrial spotlighting. Halfway down the south side, the quiet **Chongqing Museum** (daily 9am–5.30pm; ¥3) has a leaden collection of paintings and porcelain, two dynamic, dragon-draped **warrior busts** from Ya'an, a **hanging coffin** akin to those still pinioned on to cliffs near Yibin (see p.796), and a few interesting Ba-Shu pieces including bronzes and **sword blades** finely etched with animals and some undeciphered hieroglyphics. There's also a small **natural history** wing next door (¥1.50), whose pride and joy are casts of Sichuanese **dinosaur fossils**, including a nest of eggs and the skeleton of a Yangchuanosaurus, a lightweight allosaur, mostly unearthed during the 1980s at Zigong (p.795).

Other west end sights are things to take in passing, rather than making a special trip for, though it's hardly possible to miss the green-tiled roof and monumental dimensions of the **People's Concert Hall** if you're in the vicinity on Renmin Lu. Built in the 1950s along the lines of Beijing's Temple of Heaven, this lavish construction seats four thousand opera-goers in the circular rotunda, while the *Renmin Hotel* occupies three adjoining wings. Things look best at a distance as, once you've negotiated the staircase in front, the paintwork is peeling and the hall's vast interior is bland rather than awe-inspiring. Nearby, one **revolutionary monument** hidden away to the northwest along Zhongshan Si Lu is at least historically significant, if otherwise ordinary. **Guiyan** (Osmanthus Garden) is the house where Mao stayed while in town between August 12 and October 10, 1945, toasting the victory over Japan and negotiating the **Double Tenth Treaty** with Chiang Kaishek – the famous "words on paper" which established a short-lived truce between the Red Army and Guomindang (see below).

Red Crag Village and the SACO prisons

About 4km from the centre through the western riverside suburbs, **Red Crag Village** (8.30am–5pm; ¥6), is where China's wartime government, an uneasy alliance between Chiang Kaishek's Nationalist and Mao's Communist parties, set up in 1938 – wisely remote from the Japanese bombing raids concentrated around the peninsula. Mao visited here with **US Ambassador Patrick Hurley** in August 1945 to negotiate a role for the Communists in a postwar government, but Chiang's insistence that the Red Army should disband led to nothing but a lukewarm agreement on political freedom, which was almost immediately wrecked by the US assisting Guomindang troop deployment in Communist-strong areas. To get here, take **bus** #104 downhill from the roundabout on Beiqu Lu to Hongyan terminus.

For the Chinese, Hongyan today is synonymous with two great twentieth-century figures, Mao and future premier **Zhou Enlai**, who spent much of the war here as secretary of the regional Communist Party (there's no mention of Chiang Kaishek). Nervous-looking cadres assemble to have their photos taken in front of the Chairman's bronze statue which overlooks Chongqing from the forecourt. For others, however, the pleasant few acres of hilly parkland surrounding the site are likely to prove more appealing than the restored government buildings and photo collections which make up the bulk of the exhibition.

The events surrounding Hongyan ultimately led to the renewal of civil war in 1946 and the Guomindang defeat three years later. Chongqing was one of their last stands, and when it fell, the Communists found the grim **SACO prisons** (8.30am–5pm; ¥4) at the foot of Gele Hill on the city's northwestern limits; take bus #217 from Liziba Lu, near the *China Southwest Airlines* office. Now called the **US-Chiang Kaishek Criminal Acts Exhibition Hall**, this is where political prisoners were tortured under the baleful eye of the Guomindang's "hatchet man", **General Dai Li**. *SACO* refers to the Sino-American Co-operation Organization of 1937, which had inadvertently provided the prison's funding. Photographs and instruments of torture from the war years make the prison a dismal place to visit, and the museum's run-down condition suggests that nobody really wants to remember those days when China was divided.

Eating and drinking

As in Chengdu, Chongqing's centre is alive with canteens and food stalls, and at meal times, already busy side streets and markets become obstacle courses of plastic chairs, low tables and wok-wielding cooks. For classic Sichuanese food, try one of the **hotel restaurants** (see "Accommodation", p.801). Local tastes lean towards small-dish assemblies in which fish figure strongly alongside chicken, duck and offal. Chongqing is also said to be where Sichuan's **hotpot** originated, and residents are certainly dedicated, tucking into them even during the sweltering summers. A variation here is that the raw ingredients arrive on plates, not skewers, so the pots are divided up into compartments to prevent mixing. Night tables along Wuyi Lu are popular, but you'll need to stay alert not to get ripped off here, even after fixing prices per plate (and for beer). There are also a few inexpensive indoor hotpot restaurants along leafy Wusi Lu, including one opposite the police station – look for the panda mural.

Lao Sichuan, Wuyi Lu. A good, long-established place, typical of many smaller restaurants around the area, offering both classic courses and side dishes such as preserved eggs, dry-fried beef, chilli-braised frogs and eels, and green beans with garlic.

Luohan Si, Luohan Si Jie. Temple restaurant with filling vegetable dishes at ¥3–5 a portion. Try the spiced tofu and fried noodles.

Xinxin Xi, Minzu Lu. Relatively expensive, but with an extensive Sichuanese menu.

Yizhishi, Zourong Lu. A stylish place for a full-on meal upstairs, or a downstairs dumpling lunch, cheap and excellent – best in this line are the steamed or "potsticker" *jiaozi* with chilli sauce for ¥3.50 a basket. There are also glutinous rice balls, vegetables and cold braised meats.

Listings

Airlines *China Southwest Airlines*, Zhongshan San Lu (daily 8.30–11.30am & 2.30–5.30pm; ☎3862643 or 3862970).

Banks and exchange *Bank of China*, 104 Minzu Lu (☎3844816). Foreign exchange Mon–Fri 8.30–11.30am & 2.30–5pm. Hotels have exchange facilities for guests.

Bookshops The *Foreign Language Bookstore* near the post office on Minzu Lu has a wide selection of the usual nineteenth-century titles, with an art section in the back used mostly as a reference library by students.

Buses Chongqing's brand-new bus station is excellent and there should be no problems organizing tickets out to Chengdu, Leshan, Yibin, Dazu or beyond. Private services also run to these destinations, with depots and ticket offices grouped in the vicinity of the Victory Monument at either end of Qingnian Lu, and southwest off Xinhua Lu.

Cinema There are two central places on Zuorong Lu and Zhonghua Lu, showing Chinese action extravaganzas.

Hospital Chongqing Traditional Medical College and Second Hospital, Linjiang Lu.

Post office The main branch on Minzu Lu is as helpful as possible, but language problems make collecting mail very difficult. Overseas post sometimes winds up at the small branch office at the Zhongshan San Lu–Renmin Lu roundabout, near the *China Southwest Airlines* building.

PSB The foreign affairs department is at 48 Wusi Lu, a narrow side road round the corner from the main police building on Linjiang Lu (☎3847017). Staff speak English, but can be intimidating.

Shopping The *Chongqing Art Store* on Minsheng Lu is an alternative to the hotel shops for paintings and stone carvings. The subterranean *Friendship Store* on Wuyi Lu has low prices, imported chocolate and a range of Chinese spirits.

Telephones There are international booths at the main post office; staff don't speak English, though, so it may be easier to use hotel facilities.

Trains At least daily departures to Chengdu, Yibin, Beijing, Guangzhou and Guiyang. Booth #17 willingly sells foreigners' tickets, though things can be slowed by the queues. Chinese student cards are accepted with a smirk.

Travel agents All train, bus, boat and plane tickets can be arranged direct yourself, or through the *CTS/CITS*, inside the *Renmin Hotel* grounds, 175 Renmin Lu (daily 8.30–11.30am & 2.30–5.30pm; ☎3850598 or 3851306). They speak good English here, but are pretty disorganized and not of much use for general information.

Around Chongqing

With a day to spare in Chongqing, there are a couple of places an hour or so away by bus which make a pleasant alternative to the city's rather downbeat attractions. Twenty kilometres to the south, **Nanshan Gongyuan** (South Mountain Park) offers enjoyable hill walks and the dark, cool **Laojun Cave**, once frequented by the philosopher **Laotzi**. A few kilometres farther out is **Nan Wenquan**, the Southern Hot Springs, set among more green hills, pine woods and bamboo groves, with a stalactite cave and indoor and outdoor spas fed by underground water at 38°C. There's some confusion at the moment over **bus routes** to the area; check first either at your hotel reception or *CITS*.

If you're serious about splashing around in thermals, then the Northern Hot Springs, **Bei Wenquan**, are a bigger, better-organized option, 30km north of Chongqing on the lower slopes of **Jinyun Shan**. Bus #252 takes over an hour to run from Minquan Lu near the Victory Monument to its terminus 3km from the springs (¥5); local minibuses cover the remainder between about 9am and 3pm. First used as a spa in 423 AD, you can swim in three enormous spring-fed pools, and then take a boat along the river for lunch. The surrounding parkland has some early Qing Buddhist shrines dedicated to Guanyin, and paths lead up the mountain through forest to **Jinyun Temple** and the peak.

The Yangzi River

Sichuan means "Four Rivers", and of these the most important is the **Yangzi**, once virtually the only route into the province and today, plied by barges and ferries, still a major link between Sichuan and eastern China. The Yangzi's Chinese name – **Chang Jiang**, the Long River – is appropriate. Its source rises in the mountains above Tibet, receiving seven hundred tributaries as it sweeps 6400km across the country to spill its muddy waters into the East China Sea, making it the third longest flow in the world. Sometimes known simply as the Da Jiang, or Great River, different stretches have different names. Jinsha Jiang (River of Golden Sands) refers to the waters above Chongqing where gold was once panned, while the name applied by foreigners to the river as a whole, Yangzi, derives from a ford near Yangzhou in Jiangsu Province. Defining the border with Tibet and Yunnan, it skirts Sichuan's western ranges before running up to Chongqing, from where it first becomes navigable year-round to all vessels as it continues east towards Shanghai and the coast.

Although people have travelled up and down the Yangzi for over a thousand years, it was not, until recently, an easy route – though preferable to traversing Sichuan's difficult, bandit-ridden mountains. The river's most dangerous stretch was the **Three Gorges**, 200km of wind-driven rapids between Baidicheng and Yichang in Hubei

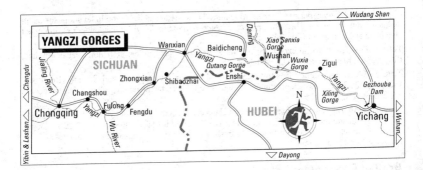

Province, formed around seventy million years ago when a huge inland lake forced a drainage channel between two limestone mountains, carving out a series of vertical cliffs and sharp hairpin bends which constricted and accelerated the Yangzi's flow. Well into the twentieth century, nobody could negotiate this vicious stretch of river alone; steamers couldn't pass at all, and small boats had to be hauled literally inch by inch through the rapids by teams of **trackers**, in a journey that could take several weeks, if the boat even made it at all.

With the last of the rocks and reefs blasted away in the 1950s, today the **ferry journey** provides a respite from thrashing around on trains and buses, as well as the chance to cruise through some spectacular scenery, steeped in history and legend. Few bother with the full six days between Chongqing and Shanghai, nor is this necessary unless you enjoy river travel for its own sake. The best of the scenery – the Three Gorges themselves – is covered in the two-day cruise between Chongqing and the Hubei port of **Yichang**, though it's only a further day from Yichang to **Wuhan** if you can handle the extra time on a Chinese boat. Many of the towns along the river are also accessible by **road** from Chongqing, so you can also shorten the river trip by picking up the ferry along the way.

Practicalities

The journey to Yichang and Wuhan is covered by two types of vessels, local **ferries** and **tour boats**. Most tourists plump for the crowded and noisy ferries as these are cheaper and easier to arrange. Few people make full use of them, however, and stay on board all the way to their destination. If you have the time, it's easy enough to get off and spend an extra day or two examining towns along the way. Historic associations aside, many of these will be submerged in the next decade after the **Three Gorges Dam** is completed (see box, p.459).

Whether you're buying **ferry tickets** through an agent or direct from the ticket office, foreigners are charged up to fifty percent more than the posted fares (though student cards bring the price down a little) and there's a surcharge for each day spent on the river – **prices** from Chongqing to Yichang and Wuhan are given on p.802. Officially, there's nothing actually called "first class", though tour operators have tired of trying to explain this to baffled foreigners, and sometimes refer to this category. By whatever name, the **options** boil down to private cabins, shared berths and mats on the floor. Comfortable but small, **cabins** are the most expensive level, with double/twin beds, private amenities, lounge, deck and dining room shielding you from the more squalid aspects of the boat. **Shared berths** come with between 8 and 24 bunks in three prices; the higher range includes a washbasin and padded, rather than rattan, mattress. It's very unusual for foreigners to be able to buy anything cheaper. If you are, pick up a bamboo mat and get in early to claim some floor space – long before the boat pulls out, the stairwells, decks and toilets are awash with bodies, sacks and phlegm.

THE YANGZI RIVER

Yangzi River	长江	cháng jiāng
Baidicheng	白帝城	báidìchéng
Fengdu	丰都	fēngdū
Fulong	伏龙	fúlóng
Three Gorges	三峡	sānxiá
Wanxian	万县	wànxiàn
Wushan	巫山	wūshān
Xiao Sanxia	小三峡	xiǎo sānxiá
Zhongxian	中县	zhōngxiàn

Not all ferries pull in at all ports, and some stay longer than others. If you're boarding anywhere except the endpoints, vessels are unlikely to arrive precisely on time, so get to the dock early and be patient; once aboard, make haste for the purser's office on the mid-deck, where available beds are distributed. As for **facilities**, with all but cabin class, the toilets fast become vile, and **meals** (buy tickets from the mid-deck office) are cheap, basic and only available for a short time at 7am, 10am and 6pm. Bring plenty of snacks, and perhaps a variety of pickled vegetables to add to your food.

Alternatively, you could travel in style on a **tour boat**, including the *Kunlun*, formerly Chairman Mao's private transport. These resemble floating hotels, with glassed-in observation decks, games rooms and real restaurants. At least double the cost of a cabin on local services, they're usually booked out by tour parties, though *CITS* and some of Chongqing's private operators can often get you on at short notice outside the August–November peak season.

Chongqing to Yichang

The first day on the river covers the 250-odd kilometres between Chongqing and the mouth of the Three Gorges at Wanxian. The first place of importance along the way is the ancient Ba city of **FULONG** at the mouth of the Wu River, long a stopover for river traffic heading south into Guizhou Province. Beyond here, the great **Baihe ridge** sits plum in midstream, bearing on its side a set of carvings centuries old that are thought to have served as water-level marks – though these days they're only visible if the flow is running particularly low. **FENGDU** comes next, glowered over by Ming Shan, the mountainous abode of **Tianzi**, King of the Dead. Temples and shrines liberally cover the heights, all crammed full of colourful demon statues – well worth a look if the boat stops for long enough.

Unfortunately, most vessels don't pull in, and it's the same story downstream at **ZHONGXIAN**, a town famous for its fermented bean curd and, rather more venerably, the **Hall of Four Virtuous Men** where the poet Bai Juyi is commemorated. Nearby, however, you'll certainly get a good look at **Shibaozhai** (Stone Treasure Stronghold), a lumbering rock buttress on the north bank. Thirty metres high, the bright red **Lanruo Dian** (Orchid-like Temple) is built into its side, with circular "portholes" on each level instead of more conventional windows. It's said that there was once a tiny hole in the temple's granary wall, through which poured just enough rice to feed the monks; greedily, they tried to enlarge it, and the frugal supply stopped forever – a Chinese version of the goose with the golden eggs.

Most ferries pull in overnight at **WANXIAN**, an old trading city clinging fortress-like to the hillside at "the gateway to eastern Sichuan", with steps leading up through slits in the enormous walls. Late-afternoon arrival means there's time to get off the boat and stroll around the main street market, where visiting Chinese enthusiastically bargain for Wanxian's most famous produce – bamboo and rattan cane, woven into steamers, furniture and brightly coloured baskets. Wanxian is also on a main road, with **buses** running west to Chongqing (though not via other river towns) and southeast to **Enshi** in Hubei, from where there are further services down to the Hunanese town of **Dayong** (see p.478).

The Three Gorges

Boats time their departure from Wanxian to reach the mouth of the Three Gorges at dawn. The gorges themselves begin at **BAIDICHENG**, a town closely associated with events of the *Three Kingdoms* (see box, p.432) – it was here that **Liu Bei** died of despair after failing to avenge his sworn brother Guan Yu in the war against Wu. Both of them, and the remaining two "Four Musketeers" of the legend, Zhuge Liang and Zhang Fei, are commemorated by statues in the **Baidi Temple**. It also has eight sandalwood chairs, supposedly used by the leaders of the mid-nineteenth century Taiping Uprising.

The first of the gorges, eight-kilometre-long **Qutang**, is an impressive sight, its angry waters described by the Song poet Su Dongpo as "like a thousand seas poured into one cup". The vertical cliffs are pocked by **Meng Liang's staircase**, square holes chiselled into the rock as far as the platform halfway up, where legend has it that the Song general **Yang Jiye** was killed by traitors. When his bodyguard climbed the cliff to recover the headless corpse, he was deceived by a monk whom he later up-ended and hung by the feet from the cliff face. Other man-made features include wooden scaffolds supporting four **hanging coffins**, similar to those at Gongxian near Yibin (see p.796).

WUSHAN marks a possible detour north up the minor, but very impressive, **Xiao Sanxia** (Three Little Gorges) lining the **Daning River**. Local vessels from Wushan take two days to cover the 33-kilometre stretch of the Daning up to Dachang and back, passing the spectacular **Dragon Gate Gorge**, another hanging coffin and remains of a Qin-era path cut into the cliffs. Back on the Yangzi, Wushan is also the start of the second set of gorges, **Wuxia**, 45km of fantastic precipices where the goddess **Yao Ji** and her eleven sisters quelled some unruly river dragons and then turned themselves into mountains, thoughtfully positioned to help guide ships downriver. Nearby, a rock inscription attributed to the *Three Kingdoms* strategist Zhuge Liang proclaims: "Wuxia's peaks rise higher and higher" – ambiguous words that nonetheless so frightened an enemy general that on reading them he turned tail and fled with his army.

Farther downstream, **ZIGUI** town was the birthplace of the poet **Qu Yuan**, whose suicide a couple of millennia ago is commemorated throughout China by dragon-boat races, and it's also where **Xiling**, the longest gorge, begins. The Xiling stretch was always the most dangerous: Westerners passing through last century described the shoals as forming weirs across the river, the boat fended away from threatening rocks by trackers armed with iron-shod bamboo poles, as it rocked through into the sunless, narrow chasm. The scenery hasn't changed a great deal since then, but the rocks, rapids and trackers have gone and the boat passes with relative ease, sailing on to a number of smaller gorges, some with splendid names – Sword and Book, Ox Liver and Horse Lung – suggested by the rock formations. Another of these, Huang Mao Xia, the **Yellow Cat Gorge**, marks the future site of the monstrous Three Gorges Dam, due for completion around 2008. Past here are the sheer cliffs and shifting currents of **Nanjin Pass**, and after that the broad gentle plain above **Gezhouba**, an enormous complex of dams, power plants, locks and floodgates. The boat squeezes through the lock, which can take some time, to dock in **Yichang**. Aside from continuing downriver from here to Wuhan, there are buses from Yichang to **Wudang Shan** in Hubei's mountainous north – details of this, Yichang and river travel between here and Nanjing are covered in Chapter Seven (see pp.437–462).

WESTERN SICHUAN

Very much on the fringes of modern China despite development and resettlement projects, **Sichuan's western half**, extending north to Gansu and west to Tibet, is in every respect an exciting place to travel. The countryside couldn't be farther from the mild Chengdu plains, with the western highlands forming some of China's most imposing scenery – dense forests, dripping with moisture, snowbound gullies and passes, and unforgettable views of mountain ranges rising up against crisp blue skies. Larger towns contain Han populations but you'll find Qiang, **Hui** and, most noticeably, **Tibetans** living among them and in the hills. The area has a strong sense of history, too, with monuments to the Communists' **Long March** during the 1930s still dotting the map.

It's a remote but certainly not undisturbed region, with endless convoys of blue logging trucks hogging the road, decorated with Tao symbols and bulging with freshly cut timber. Western Sichuan also hides some fabulously rare **wildlife**. Only a few hours from Chengdu at **Wolong Nature Reserve**, birders can spot white- and blue-eared pheasants and the unbelievably coloured, grouse-like Temminck's tragopan. Above 2000m, there are scattered groups of golden monkeys, near-mythical snow leopards and, between April and October when conditions for tracking them are optimum, **giant pandas**. In truth, these animals are so rare that your chances of seeing them are very slim – which is, in itself, an excellent reason to try.

Travel in western Sichuan has always been an endurance test, even dangerous. Traditionally, traders between China and Tibet managed to cross the mountains only by using wooden galleries hammered into sheer cliffs, and even today you'll see deep gorges spanned by no more than a spindly bridge or terrifyingly basic passenger-operated sling-and-pulley arrangement – probably as you sit on the roadside waiting for your bus to be repaired. Vehicles suffer terribly, shedding tyres and bits of chassis as they battle gradients, appalling roads, oncoming traffic and landslides. Don't count on arriving at your destination in the same bus you started in, travel lightly, carry enough **cash** to see you through – there are few banks – and regard the journey times given below as a bare minimum. As for the **seasons**, the area looks fantastic in spring and autumn, with rain most likely between May and October. Once the winter snows have set in, you'll need plenty of warm clothing and an infinitely flexible timetable.

It's worth noting that Huanglong and the Aba Grasslands, together with several roads through mountain passes in the region, rise to well over 3000m, and you might experience **altitude sickness** which manifests itself as shortness of breath, headaches, nausea, and disorientation. Symptoms usually subside after a day or two, but get back to a lower altitude as soon as possible if you have any trouble breathing (see p.23 for more details on this).

Routes west

There are basically two routes into western Sichuan from Chengdu, and you'll leave first thing in the morning whichever you take. **Heading north** on buses from Ximen station gives you the option of either visiting **Wolong Nature Reserve**, or taking the long road up to the town of **Songpan**. From here you can explore the local hills on horseback before continuing on to the scenery at **Huanglong Si** and **Jiuzhai Gou**; or bus through the **Aba Grasslands** right up into Gansu Province (p.870). Jiuzhai Gou is also accessible by bus from **Guangyuan**, a station on the Chengdu–Xi'an line; however, travellers attempting this little-used option report grillings by local police and demands for FEC notes, years after their abolition.

Heading west, buses leave daily from Xinnanmen station via Ya'an and up over the ranges to the historic town of **Luding**, where you can detour to take in **Hailuo Gou**

Glacier, then on to **Kangding**, a former outpost on the trade route to Tibet. Coming **from the Emei Shan region**, there are early morning buses to Ya'an via Meishan. You can buy tickets for Chinese minibus tours to Wolong, Jiuzhai Gou, Luding, Kanding and Hailuo Gou from booths outside Chengdu train station. Tour operators in Chengdu can also arrange jeeps with English-speaking guides for ¥600–1000 per day to anywhere in the region (see Chengdu "Listings", p.784).

Wolong

Covering a respectable two thousand square kilometres of high-altitude forests 140km northwest of Chengdu in the Qionglai Shan range, **Wolong Nature Reserve** was established in 1975 as the first region specifically protecting the **giant panda**. You can spend days or even weeks among the belts of rhododendron, pine and bamboo thickets which cover the gorges and hillsides here and, even if you don't see much in the way of wildlife, it's worth the trip to savour one of China's true wilderness areas. In 1980, the government set up a panda study programme at Wolong in association with the **World Wide Fund for Nature**; a breeding centre followed in 1983, which today allows those unable to spend time tracking the elusive beasts at least to see them, caged but surrounded by their natural habitat.

While research here using radio tracking has greatly expanded knowledge of the panda's lifestyle and needs, Wolong has had its setbacks. Most serious was a **bamboo flowering** in 1980 (see box, p.810) during which over a hundred pandas – ten percent of the entire wild population – may have starved to death. There has also been trouble with Tibetan and Qiang communities who were forcibly resettled from inside the reserve in the 1980s, and who have refused to move into new housing on poorer agricultural land elsewhere.

PANDAS AND RESERVES

Two animals share the name panda: the raccoon-sized **red panda**, still relatively common in Sichuan, and the unrelated and better-known **giant panda**, black-eyed symbol of endangered species worldwide. Panda is a Nepalese word, originally applied in the West to the red panda; the Chinese call the giant panda *da xiongmao* meaning big bear-cat.

News of giant pandas first reached Europe in the nineteenth century through the untiring French zoologist and traveller, **Père Armand David**, who came across a skin in China in 1869. They are decidedly odd creatures, bearlike and endowed with a carnivore's teeth and a digestive tract poorly adapted to their largely vegetarian diet. Though once widespread in southwestern China, they've probably never been very common, and today their endangered status is a result of human encroachment combined with the vagaries of their preferred food – **fountain bamboo** – which periodically flowers and dies off over huge areas, leaving the animals to make do with lesser shrubs and carrion, or starve. Half of Sichuan's panda habitat was lost to logging between 1974 and 1989, which, coupled with the results of a bamboo flowering during the 1980s, has reduced the total wild population to a thousand animals, with seventy at Wolong and the remainder scattered through twelve other **reserves** in Sichuan, Yunnan and Guizhou.

To their credit, the Chinese government has taken the giant panda's plight to heart, setting up successful **breeding programmes** at Chengdu and Wolong and arresting anyone found harming pandas. The most serious problems in the past have been that reserves were isolated from each other, leading to inbreeding, and were just too small to prevent the effects of the bamboo's cyclic lifestyle, though the formation of fourteen new interconnected reserves in 1995 should relieve the situation.

WOLONG		
Wolong Nature Reserve	卧龙自然保护区	*wòlóng zìrán bǎohùqū*
Shawan	沙湾	*shāwān*
Yinchang Gou	银厂沟	*yínchǎng gōu*
Yingxiong Gou	英雄沟	*yīngxióng gōu*

Practicalities

Wolong is about five hours by **bus** from Chengdu (¥56), and three to four from Guanxian (see p.786); there's no entry fee at present, though this may change as the reserve attracts more visitors. Once inside the highland valley which forms the bulk of the reserve, the road follows the **Pitiao River** for 40km to **SHAWAN**, a small cluster of buildings at the park's centre. Assuming you've packed some wet-weather gear, well-soled shoes and energy food for hiking, the **park headquarters** here provides all you'll need: **maps** of walking trails, a **museum** displaying preserved local flora and fauna and a hostel offering **meals** and simple cabin **accommodation** (dorm ②, rooms ④).

The park headquarters might also be able to help out with lifts through the reserve and advice on promising places to start looking for wildlife. **Hiking trails** head from Shawan along the river and its offshoots, 5km downstream to the **breeding centre**, or there are considerably longer treks upstream along meagre paths through **Yingxiong Gou** (Hero Gully) or **Yinchang Gou** (Silver Mine Gully) – the latter starts some 10km from Shawan and hence is the least visited.

To Jiuzhai Gou: an epic journey

Not something to be contemplated by anyone who demands the least of comforts, the trip north from Chengdu to **Songpan** and beyond to either **Gansu** Province or **Jiuzhai Gou Scenic Reserve** nevertheless offers plenty of rewards, including glimpses of minority groups, grasslands, alpine forests and lakes, and the fact that even completing your journey can itself be something of an achievement. Roads are affected by summer rains, when landslides are more frequent, and winter snows, both of which can leave you stranded or forced into long detours. A day-long drama to Songpan at the best of times, you should allow at least three days to reach Jiuzhai Gou, and probably a week to reach Xiahe in Gansu. Considering the effort involved in getting there coupled with a hefty entrance fee, those heading to Jiuzhai Gou will also want to spend at least three days on site, and need to take its status as a "Scenic Reserve" literally. While there's good **hiking**, and inaccessible corners are very wild indeed, the sealed roads and dolled-up Tibetan villages can initially be something of an anticlimax – it's scenery, and not a wilderness experience, which is provided here.

Chengdu to Songpan

An hour north of Chengdu, the mountains rise up, forcing the road into a deep gully alongside the fast-flowing Min River. At **WENCHUAN**, a small town where the bus pauses for lunch, there's a miniature hydro-electric dam and three bridges arranged in a triangle formation over the shallow flow. Strips of the old town walls still stand above the bus station, while up on the hills you'll see the distinctive rectangular split stone houses and forty-metre-high watchtowers of the **Qiang**, a once-nomadic group who now tend the apple and walnut groves lining the roadside. A close look at the houses reveals flat roofs covered in earth for winter insulation, their eaves hung with long bunches of drying corn cobs. The Qiang themselves are easily identifiable: most rural Sichuanese wear white headscarves – in mourning, they say, for the popular *Three Kingdoms* minister Zhuge Liang – but the Qiang, who were persecuted by Zhuge, generally wear black turbans instead, while the women dress in broad, embroidered jackets with split skirts. July brings a glut of fruit to local markets, but the valley is at its best in May, when the orchards are in bloom. Wenchuan also marks where the road forks 250km northwest to the towns of **Barkam** and **Zöigê** in the Aba Grasslands (see p.814), used as an alternative, but very roundabout, bad-weather route to Songpan.

Back on the main Songpan road, circumstances might see you making a stopover some 50km farther on at **MAOWEN**, whose simple main street contains a Tibetan stupa and several Hui Muslim restaurants, recognizable by Arabic script over their doorways or paintings of an idealized Mecca on the walls, which serve breakfasts of congee and buns. In fact, the town is better known as a Qiang stronghold, though there's little evidence of this. Should you get delayed here, the **hotel** at the bus depot has cheap dormitory beds (①), or you might be allowed to sleep aboard the bus.

North of Maowen the landscape is sombre at times; felled logs cut far upstream wash ashore or tumble in the current, while the steep slopes, long stripped of timber, are notoriously unstable despite some attempts at reafforestation and terracing. **Landslides** aside, the bus can also be held up, literally, by farmers needing help in towing their bogged tractors. Closer to Songpan, there's a sudden rash of new timber and stone houses built in an attractively loose interpretation of the local style, red-tiled roofs proudly topped by satellite dishes.

Songpan

The early-evening arrival in **SONGPAN**, 220km north of Chengdu, is followed by a stampede into the bus station to snap up beds at the **bus station hotel**, which offers dorm beds with hot showers at certain times of the day only (①). Should you fail to get a room here, walk through the bus station and turn right into the dirt main street. Two alternative **hotels**, the *Songpan* and *Songzhou*, are diagonally opposite each other about 50m through the tunnel under the **North Gate**. Facilities are much the same at either: fairly clean four-bed dorms (①) and double rooms (③), thick blankets in winter, erratic hot water and no showers. Their **restaurants** serve meals as good as any in town, and main-street stalls sell noodle soups and highly spiced **yak jerky**.

Songpan was founded as a Qing garrison town straddling the Min River, and three of its massive stone gateways still stand. From up on top of the North Gate, the town's dark-tiled rooftops look rather gloomy, though over in the northeastern quarter the bright colours of the **mosque** are an exception (Songpan has a substantial Muslim Hui population). It's not a large town, and dogs, chickens and horses roam the kilometre-long main street, which runs down to the **South Gate** past the ramshackle wooden fronts of cheap **restaurants** dishing out noodles and tasteless bowls of soup, and past shops selling Qiang and Tibetan clothes, ornate knives, horsetail switches, fox pelts, decorated ram skulls and jewellery. Tibetan couples wander around shopping, men sloppily dressed in capes and felt hats, women wearing silver bracelets, red scarves and chunky amber necklaces. About a third of the way down there's a **crossroads** and several department stores stocked with essentials; turn left for the **East Gate**, now pretty well worn, and out of town. Farther along the main street, the narrow Min River is spanned by the open-sided cloister of an attractive **all-weather bridge**, whose roof, corners drawn out into long points, is embellished with painted dragon, bear and flower carvings.

The reason most people stop in Songpan is to spend a few days **horse trekking** through the hills. You'll be met by guides at the bus station offering their trekking ser-

TO JIUZHAI GOU

Aba	阿坝	*ābà*
Aba Autonomous Prefecture	阿坝自治州	*ābà zìzhìzhōu*
Barkam	马尔康	*mǎěrkāng*
Huanglong	黄龙	*huánglóng*
Maowen	茂汶	*màowèn*
Songpan	松潘	*sōngpān*
Wenchuan	汶川	*wènchuān*
Yuanba	元坝	*yuánbà*
Zöigê	诺尔盖	*nuòěrgài*
Jiuzhai Gou	九寨沟	*jiǔzhàigōu*
Nuorilang	诺日朗	*nuòrìlǎng*
Primeval Forest	原始森林	*yuánshǐ sēnlín*
Rize	日则	*rìzé*
Shuzheng	树正	*shùzhēng*
Zechawa	则查洼	*zécháwā*
ACCOMMODATION		
Guanliju Zhaodaisuo	管理局招待所	*guǎnlǐjú zhāodàisuǒ*
Jiuzhaigou Hotel	九寨沟白河宾馆	*jiǔzhàigōu báihé bīnguǎn*
Nuorilang Zhaodaisuo	诺日朗招待所	*nuòrìlǎng zhāodàisuǒ*
Shuzheng Zhaodaisuo	树正招待所	*shùzhēng zhāodàisuǒ*
Yangdong Hotel	羊峒招待所	*yángdòng zhāodàisuǒ*

vices, and although the horses are unevenly tempered, the experience, taking in out-of-the-way lakes and gorges, is certainly worth the money. Accommodation is in tents and the guides are attentive. Expect to pay around ¥50 per person per day, which includes everything except fees to enter the reserve (around ¥70 extra); padded jackets are available for winter nights.

Moving on from Songpan, don't be too discouraged by poor weather, as this is often localized. When the roads are open, there are up to three buses weekly northwest to the Aba Grasslands town of Zöigê, en route to Gansu, and daily buses to Jiuzhai Gou. In summer only, there's also erratic transport to Huanglong, though it's possible to get off the Jiuzhai Gou bus at Yuanba (see p.814) and look for onward transport to Huanglong from there.

The Aba Grasslands, Zöigê and on to Gansu

Songpan sits just east of the vast, marshy **Aba Autonomous Prefecture**, which sprawls over the Sichuan, Gansu and Qinghai borders. Resting at around 3500m and draining directly into the convoluted headwaters of the Yellow River, the **Aba Grasslands** are the domain of the strongly independent-minded **Goloks**, a nomadic group of herders. The region enjoys a certain infamy in China for the losses the Red Army sustained here during their Long March, at the mercy of Golok snipers and the waterlogged, shelterless terrain, but it's also a **Bonpo** stronghold (see box above) and something of a corridor between Sichuan and Gansu Province.

The most direct route across the region is by road through the grasslands' northern-most edge at **ZÖIGÊ**, 150km northeast of Songpan. The town is a drab collection of buildings enlivened during the June/July **horse races** when horsemen set up tents out-

---

BON

Scattered through Sichuan's northwestern reaches, the **Bonpo** represent the last adherents to Tibet's native religion, **Bon**, before it fused with Buddhist ideas to form Lamaism. A shamanist faith founded by **Gcen-rabs**, one of eighteen saints sent to clear the kingdom of demons, Bon lost influence in Tibet after 755 AD, when the Tibetan royalty began to favour the more spiritual doctrines of Buddhism. As Yellow-hat Sect Lamaism developed and became the dominant faith, the Bonpo were forced out to the borders of Tibet, where the religion survives today.

Though to outsiders Bon is superficially similar to Lamaism – so much so that it's often considered a sub-sect – the two religions are, in many respects, directly opposed. Bonpo circuit their stupas anti-clockwise, use black where Lamas would use white, and still have rituals reflecting **animal sacrifice**. Because of this last feature, both the Chinese government and Lamas tend to view Bon as a barbaric, backward belief, and Bonpo are often not keen to be approached or identified as such. Bon monasteries survive at Huanglong and several towns in the central Aba Grasslands.

---

side the town and show off their riding skills to the crowds. Markets here occasionally display **medicinal oddities**, such as deer musk, the lung- and kidney-strengthening orange caterpillar fungus, and a cough medicine derived from fritillary bulbs, but Zöigê can also be an intimidating place. Dreadlocked, knife-wielding Goloks ride motorcycles down the main street, and people trying to hitch from here to Xiahe have been threatened after turning down the outrageous prices asked by truck drivers. There are several **places to stay** – the *Liangju Binguan* (①) is recommended – and two **bus stations** with up to three buses a week south to Songpan, and 180km north to **Hezuo** in Gansu, a couple of hours short of Xiahe (see p.870).

Otherwise, to see more of the region you'll have to detour west from either Wenchuan or Songpan. About 150km northwest of Wenchuan off the Wenchuan–Zöigê road, the regional capital, **Barkam**, sports the **Baisha Monastery**, with its splendid Sutra Hall, while 200km due west of Songpan, the simple **Gemo Temple** sits near the town of Aba on the Qinghai border. You'll find only basic accommodation and food along the way, and irregular buses whose drivers may be reluctant to let you on board, but, especially if you're discouraged by Juizhai Gou's hype, the area is at least refreshingly uncommercialized.

Yuanba and Huanglong

Some 50km north of Songpan, the remarkably ostentatious statue of a soldier at **YUANBA**, arms raised heavenwards astride a massive gold-tiled pedestal, marks both the passage of the Red Army through here in 1935 during the Long March and, more or less, the turning east to **Huanglong Reserve** (¥50). Small, intimate and relatively untouristed, Huanglong (Yellow Dragon) lacks the grandeur of Jiuzhai Gou, but is still beautiful. Set in a forested fold of hills, the Fu River pools into a series of turquoise **lakes** patterned by encrusted formations said to resemble dragon scales. **Temples** here were associated with the Bon religion, though the one survivor, **Huanglong Si**, is today little more than the focus of a rather secular festival (derived from the Bon calendar) in the middle of the sixth lunar month, when you'll find the park busy with equal quantities of locals and tourists.

Huanglong's **entrance gates** are 25km from Yuanba, surrounded by a couple of basic **guesthouses** (dorms ①, rooms ②), a restaurant, and stalls selling drinks, biscuits and **maps**. From here, a nine-kilometre track climbs up the valley past the pick of the scenery: ruins of the Tang-dynasty **Arhat Hall** and **Midway Temple**, several

waterfalls (including Xishen Dong's curtain cave and the yellow limestone ridges at Golden Dragon-back Cascade) and the mountains reflected in Huanglong's nine major lakes. A slow couple of hours' walk brings you up to 3500m above sea level and the end of the track at **Huanglong Si** itself. Inside the simple hall is a statue of the mythical monk Huanglong who, according to legend, brought Buddhism here in ancient times.

Jiuzhai Gou

Deep in the heart of the 4500-metre-high, perpetually snow-clad Min Shan Range, **Jiuzhai Gou Scenic Reserve** encloses one of provincial China's most spectacular landscapes. It was settled centuries ago by ethnic Tibetans, whose fenced villages gave Jiuzhai Gou (Nine Stockades' Gully) its name, and legend has it that the goddess **Semo** accidentally smashed her mirror here, the shards forming the hundred or so impossibly vivid blue **lakes** which descend the valley in a series of broad steps. The park was created back in 1978 and, beneath a veneer of intense tourism, traditional life continues – yaks are still herded, prayer wheels turn in the streams, and shrines adorned with prayer flags protect unstable cliffs against further slips. **Wildlife** abounds, too, and the authorities seem keen to keep it that way, with garbage bins at popular spots and signs at the park gates warning against "shooting or hitting animals". Beneficiaries of this policy include shy rarities such as giant pandas and the obscure, bison-like **takin**. More obviously, the lakes swarm with fish and birds including waterfowl, kingfishers, shrikes, wagtails, hoopoes and pheasants.

Jiuzhai Gou's **layout** is simple. The valleys form a north-orientated Y-shape, with the entrance gates at southern **Jiuzhai Gou town**. The most convenient base is in the centre of the park at **Nuorilang**, a township some 14km south of the entrance below **Semo Shan**, where roads head off 18km or so to **Long Lake** or the **Primeval Forest**. Either option takes in some fine scenery, with a couple of villages along the way offering further basic accommodation. For the more adventurous, gullies and forests head up into the hills, and camping is certainly an option, though not officially sanctioned – mainly because of the risk of forest fires.

While walking is the best way of seeing Jiuzhai Gou, **jeeps** (with drivers) can be rented at the gates from about ¥100 an hour, or you can sometimes negotiate cheaper lifts with locals inside the reserve. **Supplies** – snacks, drinks and films – are expensive, and **meals** on offer at accommodation and a few simple township canteens palatable but on the small side, so bring essentials with you from Songpan or Chengdu. **Warm clothing** is a must throughout the year with daytime temperatures ranging from 16°C in July to minus 4°C in January, though it can be surprisingly hot in the valleys at midday. Don't leave marked trails without good orienteering skills, a **first-aid kit** and adequate supplies.

Accommodation

All places to stay in the reserve have some sort of restaurant either on site or nearby. Few have anything but a basin to wash in. There are also very frugal hostels at Zechawa and Rize settlements, along the Long Lake and Primeval Forest roads respectively.

AT THE PARK GATES

Guanliju Zhaodaisuo. Clean, cabin-style rooms downhill behind the park administration office. The only drawback is that the staff seem convinced that it's someone else's job to register you. Dorms ①, rooms ②.

Jiuzhaigou Binguan. Comfortable and the longest standing of the newer hotels, about 3km back along the approach road to Jiuzhai Gou. ⑤.

Yangdong Zhaodaisuo. Very basic dorm facilities just down the road from the park entrance. ①.

INSIDE THE PARK

Heye Zhai, Heye. Brightly painted, newly constructed stone and wood "chalet" run by a local family. Decent food and strangely warm rooms. ③.

Minzu Lushe, Shuzheng. Not much more than somewhere to sleep. ①.

Nuorilang Zhaodaisuo, Nuorilang. Whitewashed, barracks-like buildings with very communal toilets; rooms are clean and basic. The park entrance fee includes one night's lodgings here and tour parties sometimes get a whole goat barbecued for them. ②–⑤.

Shuzheng Zhaodaisuo, Shuzheng. Multi-level concrete construction with neon decorations and a karaoke bar, often block-booked by tour groups. ③.

The scenic reserve

After the journey along the 105-kilometre Songpan–Jiuzhai Gou road with its fine mountain scenery, yaks grazing in alpine meadows, and conifers and sharp-edged ranges covered in snow, arrival at **JIUZHAI GOU** township is a huge disappointment – the surrounding hills have been clear-logged to provide materials for an ugly sprinkling of expensive concrete and tile hotels. Nor is there much joy at the **park gates**, where you're obliged to cough up the monstrous **entry fee** (¥158, which includes one night's accommodation at Nuorilang, see "Accommodation" above). The **bus depot** is just back off the main road, and you should buy your return tickets well in advance, before you go into the park, to be sure of a seat out on the daily service back to Songpan and Chengdu. There are kiosks selling **maps** and snacks at the gates, vehicles touting for business and, between May and October, a very irregular **minibus link** to Nuorilang, the Primeval Forest and Long Lake.

In fact, it's worth covering the four-hour hike from the park gates to Nuorilang **on foot**. The road follows a stream uphill through groves of pine, soon passing the gateway to **Zaru Temple** on the left, a wooden structure with cliffs rising behind. Farther along is Heye village, where the stream drains out of a marshy tract known as **Reed Lake**. This in turn is fed by the more substantial **Shuzheng lakes**, one of the largest, and with **Dege Shan** rising behind, most impressive, group in the reserve, particularly in autumn when red stands of **maple** contrast brilliantly with the waterfalls, pine and mountain scenery. Just over halfway along, where the twenty-metre **Shuzheng Falls** squeeze between the road and a wooded island, **Shuzheng village** is a good place to stop and play tourist. Tibetan men offer photo sessions on horseback, women and girls sell knives, jewellery and ethnic clothing, and a group of "typical" Tibetan dwellings sits on the lakeshore, the cabins crowded by a water-powered millstone and a decorative but empty **prayer wheel** – it should contain ten thousand written prayers which are "spoken" when tumbled around inside the rotating drum. Head about 500m up the road towards **Rhinoceros Lake**, however, and there's another wheel emblazoned with a *savastika*, and a lack of tourists suggesting that it's not for show.

NUORILANG, THE PRIMEVAL FOREST AND LONG LAKE

Another 4km from Rhinocerous Lake, **NUORILANG** consists simply of a hotel, a restaurant, two stores and Jiuzhai Gou's most famous cascades, the **Nuorilang Falls**. Often dry in the late afternoon as water is redirected for other purposes, in full flow they look best from the road, framed by trees as water forks down over the strange, yellow crystalline rock faces.

The road forks east and west at Nuorilang, either direction offering a full day's return hike (around 36km). Heading east takes you to the **Primeval Forest** via **Pearl Beach Falls**, where a whole hillside has calcified into an ankle-deep cascade ending in a ten-metre waterfall similar to Nuorilang's, and **Panda-Arrow Bamboo Lake**, a shallow affair whose optimistic name has long been out of date in such a heavily grazed valley. There's another, rather mysterious reference to pandas at the halfway point of **Rize village**. The settlement consists of a road maintainence depot, a very under-used hostel, and a large, firmly locked hall whose dusty entrance is capped by the legend "**Panda Hospital**". As residents are apt to deny the building's very existence, it's unclear whether the facilities are for unlucky hikers or injured beasts. The scenery slacks off for a while after Rize, as the road climbs through a pass to **Grass Lake** and then follows the left-hand stream into the **Primeval Forest**, a dense and very atmospheric belt of conifers. A discreetly placed tent here would allow a full day exploring the area.

The slightly longer road from Nuorilang to **Long Lake** is, on the whole, less interesting and so less frequented by tour buses. Not far along is **Zechawa village** and a small Tibetan-run hostel and store. After here there's little to see until near the end at the stunning **Five-coloured Lake** which, for sheer intensity, if not scale, is unequalled in the park. Superlatives continue at the road's end, where the mundanely named **Long Lake** is both exactly that and, at 3103m, Jiuzhai Gou's highest body of water.

The far west: Chengdu to Tibet

The main road **west of Chengdu** still follows an ancient **trade route** between China and Tibet. Porters, weighed down with compressed blocks of tea, once made the three-week journey over the mountains from Ya'an to the town of Kangding, where their loads were exchanged for Tibetan wool. The first **Europeans** through here were French Catholic organizations in the 1850s, who spread Christianity among the Tibetan, Yi and Qiang populace. Many of their **churches** survive today, though by the late 1920s political instabilities had forced the foreigners away. As early as 1893, when Tibet independently established its borders and formed trade links with Britain at the **Sikkim Convention**, China's claims to rule Tibet – which it had nominally done since the Mongol invasions some six hundred years earlier – were being seriously undermined. Further unsanctioned talks between the two nations in 1904 caused the Chinese government to send troops into the east of the country, destroying monasteries and evicting the Dalai Lama. The Qing empire fell soon afterwards, however, and Lhasa regained the disputed territory. In 1929 the Nationalists tried once again to establish Chinese control by creating **Xikang Province**. Stretching from Ya'an through to within 200km of Lhasa, Xikang's presence on paper did little to alter the real situation. Divided itself, China was unable to counter rival claims from Tibet or control its own unruly forces in the province. With a capital moving ever east from Batang to Kangding and finally Ya'an, Xikang remained effectively independent for

THE FAR WEST		
Batang	巴塘	*bātáng*
Dêgê	德格	*dégé*
Garzê	甘孜	*gānzī*
Kangding	康定	*kāngdìng*
Anjue Si	安觉寺	*anju és ì*
Jiaotong	交通饭店	*jiāotōng fàndiàn*
Kangding Guesthouse	康定宾馆	*kāngdìng bīnguǎn*
Paoma Shan	跑马山	*pǎomǎ shān*
Luding	泸定	*lùdìng*
Moxi Xiang	磨西乡	*móxī xiāng*
Gonga Shan	贡嘎山	*gōng shān*
Hailuogou Glacier Park	海螺沟公园	*hǎiluógōu gōngyuán*
Ya'an	雅安	*yǎān*

over two decades, surviving until five years after the border issue was made redundant by China's annexation of Tibet in 1950.

With luck, the journey from Chengdu's Xinnanmen bus station to Kangding now takes just fourteen hours (¥60). While continuing **overland to Tibet** is not really feasible for foreigners at present (see below and the box "Moving on from Chengdu", p.772), it's certainly worth the effort to reach the **Hailuo Gou Glacier** in the foothills of the mighty **Gongga Shan**. En route there's a tangible monument to the efforts of the Long March at **Luding**, and the monasteries, people and frontier atmosphere of **Kangding** itself.

As **access** into the region is through a difficult mountain pass, the road is frequently closed in winter; if it's open, progress will be very slow, and supplies on the far side severely limited. After dry spells, winds can sometimes whip up clouds of dust along the valleys, ruining the views and muting colours. **Distances and times** can be confusing – Ya'an, for instance, is halfway between Chengdu and Kangding as the crow flies, but barely a third of the way as far as journey time is concerned – and downhill return legs can be considerably quicker than outward travel uphill. Prices for the same stretches can also vary from bus to bus, so fares quoted may contradict each other.

Ya'an and the Erlang Pass

First stop on the journey west is the town of **YA'AN**, which sits on the banks of the Qingyi River below Erlang Shan, five hours by bus from Chengdu across the flat Red Basin. Originally a garrisoned staging post on the trail to Tibet, and briefly the capital of Xikang before its dissolution in 1955, today Ya'an has ambition. The approach road tunnels through a hillside and on to an empty plain, where an isolated colonnade of tall street lights, the first stage of a massive urban expansion project, flank the highway into town. Whether coming from Chengdu or the Emei Shan–Leshan region, the bus will stop in Ya'an until after midday, as the narrow road up over the **Erlang Pass** is open to traffic only for twelve hours at a time in each direction.

Almost continuous maintenance on the pass means that the journey over can be lively, with work crews tackling the impossible task of stabilizing loose cliffs and widening the road. Because of the pass opening times, vehicles tend to form **convoys** which snake up through the cool green gorges along the river, the near-suicidal drivers engaged in a constant overtaking game. Where the road emerges into the open, the summer hillsides are dotted with purple, pink and white **rhododendron** blooms. The road then begins to turn endlessly back on itself and there's usually a brief stop at one of the small roadside canteens to hose down various overheated bits of the engine with ice-cold water supplied for the purpose. As the bus climbs higher, vegetation recedes to a few gullies and boulders covered with lichen or moss, and at the small shrine marking the **top of the pass** the bus is buffeted by headwinds and you're suddenly confronted with an amazing vista. On the far side, the road drops down through tenuous forestry plantations to **Luding**, while out over distant green and gold fields rises one of the best views there is of the snow-capped massif of Gongga Shan, lit by the afternoon sun.

Luding

For travellers heading towards Hailuo Gou Glacier, the scruffy, two-street market town of **LUDING** marks a half-day hiatus between buses, with plenty of time to soak up some history at the **Luding Bridge**, one of the great icons of the Long March. In May 1935, the Red Army reached Anshunchang on the southern side of the Dadu River but were unable to cross the rapids there. Pressured by enemy troops, they decided to head upstream to where a nominal Guomindang force, baulking at destroying the only crossing for hundreds of kilometres, had pulled the decking off the Luding suspension bridge, but left the chains intact. On a forced march, the Communists covered the 100km to Luding in an incredible two days, where 22 **heroes** braved heavy fire to climb hand-over-hand across the chains and take Guomindang emplacements on the west bank. Official accounts say that only three men were killed.

Though substantial by local standards, the bridge is simply a series of thirteen heavy-gauge chains spanned by planks which look as if they might have been pirated from a packing crate. The Dadu flows roughly below, while temple-style gates and ornaments at either end lend the bridge an almost religious aspect. On the near side is a ticket office (¥1) and a gold-lettered tablet detailing the events of May 29, 1935, while a pavilion on the far side houses a **museum** with period photos.

There's precious little to see in the town itself, though it's full of nondescript places to **eat** and so busy in spring that an overflow of produce from stalls has to be laid out on sheets in the narrow main street. For **accommodation**, try the *Yagudu Hotel* and **restaurant** (③), where they don't speak a word of English, despite a scattering of signs, or there's a choice of cheaper rooms, such as the polite *Comfortable Inn* (①–②), to the right of the bus station. **Moving on**, there are at least daily buses to Kangding (2–3hr; ¥10), Moxi Xiang (for Hailuo Gou; 3–4hr; ¥7) and Chengdu (12hr; ¥50.50).

Moxi Xiang and the Hailuo Gou Glacier

Tracks etched along the cliffs between Luding and Moxi Xiang are barely wide enough for the two-way traffic that uses them, and frequent, heart-stopping encounters with logging trucks tend to focus your attention on the **scenery** far below: two timber mills, people pole-net fishing in the river, deep gorges spanned by vestigial footbridges, and Qiang wandering around their stone villages, black robes set off by violent pink sashes.

Surrounded by fields of barley and maize, the upper-valley village of **MOXI XIANG** comprises a single street of closely stacked dark wooden shops selling karaoke ghettoblasters and other modern necessities. Just left off the street, there's a small **Catholic Church** built in the 1920s, whose blue and yellow bell tower overlooks a European, box-like main building, its eaves pinched as a concession to local aesthetics. After the action at Luding, Mao and the Red Army rested up in Moxi Xiang before heading off on a 56-kilometre trek north to Xiaojin over **Jiajin Shan**, through the "land of everlasting snow". Hundreds died of exposure and altitude sickness, and Mao himself was stretcher-ridden. Few visitors today attempt anything so strenuous, most using the town simply as a base camp for the trip to **Hailuo Gou Glacier**. The bus pulls in at a pleasant **guesthouse** (①), a creaking wooden structure with views down the valley from the upper rooms, though the toilets out back are a bit distant if they put you on the top floor. Glacier practicalities can be arranged either here or at one of the two **restaurants** up the road. Heading back to Luding, the bus leaves around 6 or 7am.

Gongga Shan and the Hailuo Gou Glacier

The highest point in western China, and only 1300m lower than Everest, **Gongga Shan**, known locally as Minya Konka, rises to 7556m behind Moxi Xiang, a stunning sight on the rare mornings when the near constant cloud cover and haze of wind-driven snow above the peak suddenly clear. Hailuo Gou Glacier is the lowest of four descending the mountain, carving out **Conch Gully** as it extends right down to the treeline, some 13km from Moxi inside **Hailuo Gou Glacier Park** (¥60). Though the terrain and the three-thousand-metre altitude make for slow and steady hiking, it's possible to slog up the valley to the glacier in a single day, though the unexpectedly thick forests and alpine scenery, not to mention the glacier itself – a tongue of blue-white ice scattered with boulders and black gravel – are spellbinding, and at least three days is recommended for the trip there and back. Basic **meals and accommodation** are available along the way, or you can pitch a tent at one of the three **campsites**.

Guides can be hired in Moxi Xiang from ¥50 per day, though with well-marked trails through the park they're not really necessary in warmer months – your entry fee into the park anyway includes a guide from the last camp to the glacier itself. You should take some energy food, good footwear and warm, padded clothing whatever the time of the year. Just up the road from Moxi, a cluster of stalls surrounds the **park gates**. The **first camp** is just 1km farther on and there are **hot springs**, hostel accommodation and kiosks both here and 5km up the valley at the **second camp**, where rhododendron bushes finally give way to forest proper. You could easily forget about the glacier for a while and spend a day exploring here, though it's only another 5km to the trail head at **camp three**, a relatively substantial affair with orange, four-person "chalet" dorms (②) offering basic protection from the elements. Here you pick up your guide for the last 2km from the camp to the **viewing platform** and out along the glacier itself, which takes several hours to explore properly.

Kangding and beyond

Even before you arrive in town, it's not hard to see why **KANGDING**, 60km west of Luding, is portrayed as one of the wildest settlements in China, nor why the government had such a tough time controlling the region until the 1950s. The walls of **Daxue Shan** (Great Snowy Mountain) rise immediately behind the town and, whatever the maps might say, this is where Tibet really begins. Carelessly laid out along the rough, fast-flowing **Zhepuo River** at the bottom of a steep valley dotted with monasteries and bulbous white *chortens* (Tibetan pagodas), Kangding is immediately arresting, still very much a nexus between cultures. As the administrative capital of the **Ganzi Tibetan Region**, the town is thick with government staff, while recently arrived Hui rub shoulders with monks and rough-looking **Khampas**, Tibetan "cowboys", here to buy supplies.

Though tea is no longer the prime currency, **trade** is still Kangding's lifeblood, and the central streets bustle with activity. On the south bank, there's a produce market in the rickety alleys near the **mosque**'s blue gate, shops selling Persian rugs, religious attire and finely ornamented knives, as well as **markets** grouped around the public square on the far bank, with wares piled high on collapsible beds being scrutinized by Tibetans sporting straw hats and heavy turquoise jewellery. Over the second bridge, **Anjue Si** is a quietly busy collection of courtyards and shrines over on the north bank – monks here are tolerant but not overjoyed at tourists wandering around.

Practicalities

From the upper slopes of **Paoma Shan**, where there are a couple of temples and a **horse-race festival** in the middle of the fourth lunar month, Kangding is a mosaic of orange and black rooftops packed either side of the east–west orientated Zhepuo River. The **bus station** is on the eastern side of town – turn right and follow the street for a couple of minutes past several **canteens** to the river. This is the south bank; a high street and an associated network of back lanes run west through town on either side of the flow, linked by three bridges.

The cheapest **place to stay** is the filthy bus station hostel (①). Better options are the blue-glassed *Kangding Guesthouse* (☎0836/23137; ①–③), behind Anjue Si on the north bank, and the friendly *Traffic Hotel* (☎0836/22254 or 22638; ①–②) offering simple dorms and doubles, about 500m west along the south side, just where the road bends sharply left. For **food** there are a couple of **cake shops**, and plenty of street corners staffed by white-capped Hui where you can fill up on *mantou* or a bowl of *laomien* (pulled noodles) and coriander soup. The best **breakfast** is eaten early with the locals at market stalls: Tibetan **butter tea**, noodle soup, *shaomai* and fried dough coils spiced with mince and wild pepper. After dark, there are even a couple of **nightclubs** to try out; the dingy one near the bus station is where the locals go.

Kangding to Tibet

Two routes head west from Kangding over the mountains to where the Jinsha River, the upper reaches of the Yangzi, marks China's border with Tibet. The fact that they link up on the far side and press right **through to Lhasa** is currently an academic one for foreigners. Rules come and go, but at the time of writing, trying to travel beyond Kangding without the (practically unobtainable) relevant paperwork from the Chengdu PSB was a guarantee of being pulled off the bus at the first stop, grilled by police and booted back the way you came. Political considerations aside, authorities are not simply being obstructive. These are some of the world's most dangerous roads, high, riven by gorges and permanently snowbound, and the Chinese government is not keen to extend the list of tourists killed in bus crashes along the way. What might make it worth the risk is that the journey takes you within sight of the world's highest unclimbed mountain ranges, and even those hardened by stints in the Himalayas have reported the scenery as staggeringly beautiful.

Permits are most frequently given for less impressive stretches to towns within Sichuan. On the southern route, destinations include **Litang**, where another seldom-open road heads south to **Zhongdian** in Yunnan (p.742), and the border town of **Batang**, once a headquarters for various Christian missions and capital of Xikang. The settlements of **Garzê** and **Dêgê**, on the longer northern route, both sport impressive monasteries; Garzê itself, a valley town surrounded by chessboard fields and mountains, is also where the Communist leader **Zhang Guotao** formed a short-lived splinter government after differences between himself and Mao erupted during the Long March in 1935.

travel details

Trains

Chengdu to: Beijing (daily; 36hr); Chongqing (3 daily; 12hr); Dazu (daily; 7hr); Emei (daily; 3hr); Guangzhou (daily; 49hr); Guiyang (daily; 18hr); Kunming (daily; 24hr); Shanghai (daily; 48hr); Xi'an (daily; 16hr).

Chongqing to: Beijing (daily; 38hr); Chengdu (3 daily; 12hr); Guangzhou (daily, 46hr); Guiyang (daily; 12hr); Neijiang (daily; 6hr); Wuhan (daily; 24hr); Yibin (daily, 10hr).

Emei to: Chengdu (daily; 3hr); Kunming (daily; 22hr); Xichang (daily; 5hr).

Emei to: Chengdu (5hr); Leshan (90min); Xichang (10hr); Ya'an (3hr).

Leshan to: Chengdu (5hr); Chongqing (11hr); Emei (90min); Xichang (10hr).

Ferries

Chongqing to: Leshan (2 weekly June–Jan only; 2 days); Wanxian (daily; 12hr); Wuhan (daily; 3 days); Yichang (daily; 36hr).

Leshan to: Leshan (2 weekly June–Jan only; 36hr); Yibin (2 weekly June–Jan only; 24hr).

Buses

Chengdu (Ximen bus station) to: Emei (5hr); Jiuzhai Gou (36hr); Leshan (5hr); Shawan/Wolong (5hr); Songpan (12hr).

Chengdu (Xinnanmen bus station): Chongqing (12hr); Emei (5hr); Kangding (14hr); Leshan (5hrs); Luding (12hr); Meishan (3hr).

Chongqing to: Chengdu (12hr); Dazu (7hr); Neijiang (6hr); Yibin (10hr); Zigong (8hr).

Planes

Chengdu to: Beijing (12 daily; 2hr); Chongqing (9 daily; 45min); Guangzhou (10 daily; 2hr); Kunming (5 daily; 90min); Lhasa (2 daily; 1hr 50min); Shanghai (2 daily; 2hr 15min).

Chongqing to: Beijing (2 daily; 2hr); Chengdu (9 daily; 45min); Guangzhou (5 daily; 90min); Shanghai (2 daily; 2hr).

CHAPTER THIRTEEN

THE NORTHWEST

R eaching across in a giant arc from the fringes of eastern Siberia to the borders of Turkic Central Asia, the provinces of **Inner Mongolia**, **Ningxia**, **Gansu**, **Qinghai** and **Xinjiang** account for an entire third of China's land area. Compressing so vast a region into a single chapter of a guidebook may seem something of a travesty – but at least it is based on a perception that originates from China itself, namely that these territories lie largely beyond the Great Wall. To ancient Chinese thinking the whole region is remote, subject to extremes of weather and pop- ulated by non-Chinese-speaking "barbarians" who are, quite literally, the peoples from beyond the pale – *zai wai ren*. It is here, thinly scattered through the vast areas of steppe and grassland, desert and mountain plateau, that the bulk of China's **ethnic minorities** still live. Out of deference to these, Inner Mongolia, Ningxia and Xinjiang are officially not provinces at all, but so-called **Autonomous Regions**, for the Mongol, Hui and Uigur peoples respectively.

However, a **Chinese presence** in the area is not new. Imperial armies were already in control of virtually the whole northwest region by the time of the Han dynasty two thousand years ago and since then Gansu, Ningxia and the eastern part of Qinghai have become Chinese almost to the core. The uncultivatable plains of Inner Mongolia have been intimately bound up with China since Genghis Khan created his great empire in the early thirteenth century, and even Xinjiang – although it has repeatedly broken free – has always found itself drawn back into the Chinese sphere.

Today the relatively unrestricted use of **local languages** and **local religions** in all these areas can be taken as a sign of China's desire to **nurture patriotism** in the minority peoples, and regain some of the sympathy lost during the disastrous repres- sions both under communism and in previous eras. Furthermore, in economic terms, there is a clear transfer of wealth, in the form of industrial and agricultural aid, from the richer areas of eastern China to the poorer, outer fringes of the country. On the other hand, the degree of actual autonomy in the "autonomous" regions is strictly controlled, and relations between Han China and these more remote corners of the empire remain fractious in places. **Dissent** on the part of the Uigurs of Xinjiang, for example, has shown itself as recently as the large-scale city riots in Kashgar in the 1990s.

Tourism in these areas has boomed in the last few years. Travellers, above all, are drawn by the **Silk Road**, a series of historic towns strung out across the desert, run- ning from Xi'an in Shaanxi Province, through Ningxia, Gansu and Xinjiang, and even- tually on into Central Asia. The Northwest also offers possibilities for enjoying the last great remaining **wildernesses** of China – the grasslands, mountains, lakes and deserts of the interior – far from the teeming population centres of the east. For this, there is perhaps no place better to start than **Inner Mongolia**'s famous **grasslands** on which Genghis Khan trained his cavalry and where nomads on horseback still live today. As well as visiting the supposed **tomb of Genghis Khan**, outside Dongsheng, it's also possible, in places, to catch a glimpse of the Mongols' ancient and unique way of life, packaged for tourists to a greater or lesser degree depending on how far off the beat- en track you are willing to travel. You can sleep in a nomad's circular felt tent (yurt), sample the unusual Mongol food and ride a horse across the grasslands, all within half a day's train journey from Beijing.

The other great natural feature of Inner Mongolia is the Yellow River, which detours north into the region from tiny, rural **Ningxia**. Here, at the resort of **Shapotou** by the banks of the life-giving river, you can witness the spectacle of a mighty river running between the sand dunes of a bare desert. Rarely visited by foreign tourists, Ningxia also offers quiet, attractive cities and a variety of scenery ranging from terraced, abundantly fertile hillsides in the south to pure desert in the north. Extending west from here is **Gansu**, the historic periphery of ancient China. This rugged terrain of high mountains and deserts is spliced from east to west by the **Hexi Corridor**, a narrow path through the mountains, historically the only road from China to the West, and still marked along its length by the Great Wall – terminating magnificently at the fortress of **Jiayuguan** – and a string of Silk Road towns culminating in **Dunhuang**, with its fabulous Buddhist cave art.

South of the Hexi Corridor rise the mountains which extend all the way to the plains of northern India. The ancient borderland between the mountains and China proper is **Qinghai**, perhaps the least-explored province in the whole of the Northwest, which offers mountains, monasteries, the colossal lake of **Qinghai Hu** and, above all, the **road to Tibet**, along one of the highest mountain routes in the world. Originating in this province, too, are the Yellow and Yangzi rivers, the main transport arteries of China throughout recorded history.

Finally, guarding the westernmost passes of the empire, is **Xinjiang**, where China ends and another world – once known in the West as Chinese Turkestan – begins. Culturally and geographically a part of Central Asia, this vast, remote region is a land where Turkic Uigurs outnumber the Han Chinese, where mosques replace temples, lamb kebabs replace steamed dumplings, and where travellers must cross searing deserts and snowy mountain ranges in their search for Silk Road relics. Highlights of Xinjiang include the desert resort town of **Turpan** and, in the far west, fabled **Kashgar**, a city which until recently few Westerners had ever reached.

Travel in the Northwest can still be hard going, with enormous distances and an extremely harsh continental climate to contend with. **Winter** is particularly severe, with average temperatures as low as minus 15°C or 20°C in Inner Mongolia, Qinghai and Xinjiang. Conversely, in **summer**, Turpan in eastern Xinjiang is China's hottest city. Despite the wild, rugged terrain and the great distances, however, facilities for tourists have developed considerably in recent years. In nearly all towns, there are now **hotels and restaurants** catering for a range of budgets – in general, the price of accommodation is a good deal cheaper here than in eastern China. Where rail lines have not been built, nearly everywhere is accessible by bus, and quite a few towns by plane as well. Finally there is now the possibility of onward travel to or from China's Asian neighbours – the Republic of Mongolia, Kazakhstan, Kirgyzistan and Pakistan can all be reached by road or rail from the provinces covered in this chapter (though remember that visas are generally required for all of these countries and you may need to acquire these in Beijing or elsewhere before setting out).

ACCOMMODATION PRICE CODES

All the accommodation in this book has been graded according to the following price codes, which represent the cheapest double room available to foreigners. Most places have a range of rooms, however, and staff will usually offer you the more expensive ones – it's always worth asking if they have anything cheaper. Where the text refers specifically to dorm beds, the price code represents the price per bed. See p.40 for more details.

① less than ¥30	④ ¥100–150	⑦ ¥300–500
② ¥30–75	⑤ ¥150–200	⑧ ¥500–700
③ ¥75–100	⑥ ¥200–300	⑨ ¥700 or more

INNER MONGOLIA

Mongolia is an almost total mystery to the outside world, its very name being synonymous with remoteness. For hundreds of years, landlocked between the two Asian giants Russia and China, it seems to have been frozen in time, doomed to eternal obscurity, trapped in a hopeless physical environment of fleeting summers and interminable, bitter winters. And yet, seven hundred years ago the people of this benighted land suddenly burst out of their frontiers and for a century subjugated and terrorized virtually the entire Eurasian continent.

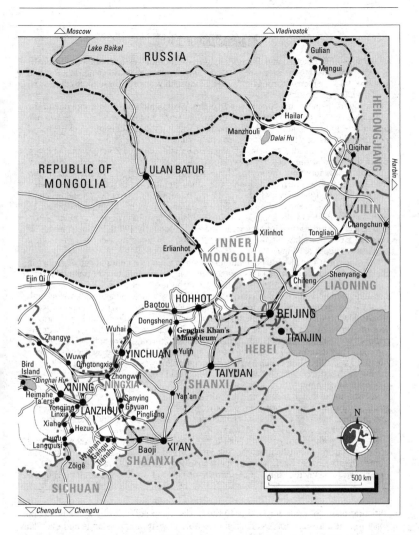

Visitors to the **Autonomous Region of Inner Mongolia** will not necessarily find many signs of this today, and if you come here expecting to find something reminiscent of Genghis Khan you are likely to be disappointed. The modern-day heirs of the Mongol hordes are not only placid – quietly going about their business of shepherding, herding horses and entertaining tourists – but they are anyway vastly outnumbered by the Han Chinese even in their own autonomous region (by seventeen million to two million). In addition, this is, and always has been, a sensitive border area and there are still restrictions on the movements of tourists here, despite the demise of the Soviet Union.

Nevertheless, there are still traces of the "real" Mongolia out there, in terms of both landscape and people. Dotting the region are enormous areas of **grassland**, gently

THE SILK ROAD

The passes of Karakoram and Torugut, linking China with western Asia – and ultimately with the whole of the western world – have only in recent years re-opened to a thin and tentative trickle of cross-border traffic. Yet a thousand years ago these were crucial and well-trodden trade routes.

The foundations for this famous **road to the West**, which was to become one of the most important arteries of **trade and culture** in world history, were laid over two millennia ago. In the second century BC nothing was known in China of the existence of people and lands beyond its borders, except by rumour. In 139 BC, the imperial court at Chang'an (Xi'an) decided to despatch an emissary, a man called Zhang Qiang, to investigate the world to the west and to seek possible allies in the constant struggle against nomadic marauders from the north. Zhang set out with a party of a hundred men; thirteen years later he returned, with only two other members of his original expedition – and no alliances. But the news he brought nevertheless set Emperor Wu Di and his court aflame, including tales of Central Asia, Persia and even the Mediterranean world. Further **expeditions** were soon despatched, initially to purchase horses for military purposes, and from these beginnings trade soon developed. By 100 BC a dozen immense caravans a year were heading west into the desert. Jade, porcelain, lacquerware and silk began flowing out of China.

The **silkworm** had already been domesticated in China for hundreds of years, but in the West the means by which this exotic material was manufactured remained a total mystery – people believed it was combed from the leaves of trees. The Chinese took great pains to protect their monopoly, punishing any attempt to export silkworms with death. It was only many centuries later that sericulture finally began to spread west, when silkworm larvae were smuggled out of China in hollow walking sticks by Nestorian monks. The first time the **Romans** saw silk, snaking in the wind from the banners of their Parthian enemies, it filled them with terror and resulted in a humiliating rout. They determined to acquire it for themselves, and soon Roman society became obsessed with the fabric which by the first century AD was coming west in such large quantities that the corresponding outflow of gold had begun to threaten the stability of the Roman economy.

Silk was not all that passed along the route. From China came oranges, peaches, pears, roses, chrysanthemums, cast iron, gunpowder, the crossbow, the wheelbarrow, paper and printing, and from the West came cucumbers, figs, chives, sesame, walnuts, grapes (and winemaking), wool, linen and ivory.

The entire **route**, from eastern China to the Mediterranean, was incredibly long and arduous. Starting from Chang'an, the Silk Road curved northwest through Gansu to the Yumen Pass, where it split. Leaving the protection of the Great Wall, travellers could follow one of two routes across the terrible deserts of Lop Nor and Taklamakan, braving the

undulating plains of grass stretching to the horizon and still used by nomadic peoples as pastureland for their horses. Tourists are able to visit the grasslands and even stay with the Mongols in their yurts, though the only simple way to do this is by **organized tour** out of the regional capital **Hohhot** – an experience rather short on authenticity. If you don't find what you are looking for in the Hohhot area, however, don't forget that there is a whole vast swathe of Mongolia stretching up through northeastern China that remains virtually untouched by Western tourists. If you are sufficiently determined, it *is* possible to see something of the grasslands and their Mongol inhabitants on your own, especially in the areas around **Xilinhot** and **Hailar**. Finally, Inner Mongolia offers overland connections with China's two northern neighbours, the Republic of Mongolia (Outer Mongolia) and Russia, through the border towns of **Erlianhot** and **Manzhouli** respectively.

attacks from marauding bandits, to Kashgar. The **southern route** ran through Dunhuang, Lop Nor, Miran, Niya, Khotan and Yarkand; the **northern route** through Hami, Turpan, Kuqa and Aqsu. The **oases** which were staging posts and watering holes along the route inevitably prospered, becoming important and wealthy cities in their own right and garrisons were maintained in them, to protect the caravans. When Chinese domination periodically declined, many of these cities turned themselves into self-sufficient city states, or **khanates**. Today, many of these once powerful cities are now buried in the sands.

High in the Pamirs beyond Kashgar, the merchants traded their goods with the middlemen who carried them beyond the frontiers of China, either south to Kashmir, Bactria, Afghanistan and India, or north to Ferghana, Tashkent and Samarkand. Then, laden with western gold, the Chinese merchants would turn back down the mountains for the three-thousand-kilometre journey home.

As well as goods, the Silk Road carried new ideas in **art and religion**. Nestorian Christianity and Manichaeism trickled east across the mountains, but by far the most influential force was **Buddhism**. The first Buddhist missionaries appeared during the first century AD, crossing the High Pamirs from India, and their creed gained rapid acceptance among the nomads and oasis dwellers of what is now western China. All along the road, monasteries, chapels, stupas and grottoes proliferated, often sponsored by wealthy traders. By the fourth century, Buddhism had become the official religion of much of northern China and by the eighth it was accepted throughout the empire.

The remains of this early flowering of **Buddhist art** along the road are one of the great attractions of the Northwest for modern-day travellers. Naturally, history has taken its toll – zealous Muslims, Western archeologists, Red Guards and the forces of nature have all played a destructive part – but some sites have miraculously survived intact, above all the cave art at **Mogao** outside Dunhuang.

The Silk Road continued to flourish for centuries, reaching its zenith under the Tang (618–907 AD) and bringing immense wealth to the Chinese nobility and merchants. But it remained a slow, dangerous and expensive transport route. Predatory tribes to the north and south harried the caravans despite garrisons and military escorts. Occasionally entire regions broke free of Chinese control, requiring years to be "re-pacified". The route was physically arduous too, taking at least **five months** from Chang'an to Kashgar, and whole caravans could be lost in the deserts or in the high mountain passes.

There was a brief final flowering of the trade in the thirteenth century, to which **Marco Polo** famously bore witness, when the whole Silk Road came temporarily under Mongol rule. But by now the writing was clearly on the wall for the overland routes. With the arrival of sericulture in Europe and the opening of sea routes between China and the West, the Silk Road had had its day. The road and its cities were slowly abandoned to the wind and the blowing sands.

Some history

Genghis Khan (1162–1227) was born, ominously enough, with a clot of blood in his hand. Under his leadership, the **Mongols** erupted from their homeland to ravage the whole of Asia, butchering millions, razing cities and laying waste all the land from China to eastern Europe. It was his proud boast that his destruction of cities was so complete that he could ride across their ruins by night without the least fear of his horse stumbling.

Before Genghis exploded on to the scene, the nomadic Mongols had long been a thorn in the side of the settled, city-dwelling Chinese. Construction of the **Great Wall** had been undertaken to keep these two fundamentally opposed societies apart. But it was always fortunate for the Chinese that the early nomadic tribes of Mongolia fought as much among themselves as they did against outsiders. Genghis Khan's achievement was to weld together the warring nomads into a fighting force the equal of which the world had never seen. Becoming Khan of Khans in 1206, he also introduced the *Yasak*, the first **code of laws** the Mongols had known – few details of its Draconian tenets survive today (though it was inscribed on iron tablets at Genghis's death) but Tamerlane, at Samarkand, and Baber the Great Mogul in India, were both later to use it as the basis for their authority.

The secret of Genghis Khan's success lay in **skilful cavalry tactics**, acquired from long practice in the saddle on the wide open Mongolian plains. Frequently his armies would rout forces ten or twenty times their size. Each of his warriors would have three or four horses and nothing more. Food was taken from the surrounding country, the troops slept in the open, meat was cooked by being placed under the saddle; and when the going got tough they would slit a vein in the horse's neck and drink the blood while still on the move. There was no supply problem, no camp followers, no excess baggage.

KUBLAI KHAN

In Xanadu did Kublai Khan a stately pleasure dome decree...

Immortalized not only in the poetry of Samuel Coleridge but also in the memoirs of Marco Polo, **Kublai Khan** (1215–1294) – known to the Chinese as Yuan Shizu – is the only emperor in all of China's long history popularly known by name to the outside world. And little wonder. As well as mastering the subtle statecraft required to govern China as a foreigner, this grandson of Genghis Khan commanded an **empire** that encompassed the whole of China, central Asia, southern Russia and Persia, a larger area of land than perhaps anyone in history has ever ruled over, before or since. And yet this king of kings had been born into a nomadic tribe which had never shown the slightest interest in political life, and who, until shortly before his birth, were almost entirely illiterate.

From the beginning, Kublai Khan had shown an unusual talent for politics and government. He managed to get himself elected **Khan of the Mongols** in 1260, after the death of his brother, despite considerable opposition from the so-called "steppe aristocracy" who feared his disdain for traditional Mongolian skills. He never learned to read or write Chinese, yet after audaciously establishing himself as **Emperor of China**, proclaiming the Yuan dynasty in 1271, he soon saw the value of surrounding himself with advisers steeped in Confucianism. This was what enabled him to set up one hundred thousand Mongols in power over perhaps two hundred million Chinese. As well as **reunifying China** after centuries of division under the Song, Kublai Khan's contributions include establishing **paper money** as the standard medium of exchange, and fostering the **development of religion**, Lamaist Buddhism in particular. Above all, under his rule China experienced a brief – and uncharacteristic – period of cosmopolitanism which saw not only foreigners such as Marco Polo promoted to high positions of responsibility, but also a final flowering of the old Silk Road trade, as well as large numbers of Arab and Persian traders settling in seaports around Quanzhou in southeastern China.

Ironically, however, it was his admiration for the culture, arts, religion and sophisticated bureaucracy of China – as documented so enthusiastically by Marco Polo – that aroused bitter hostility from his own people, the Mongols, who despised what they saw as a betrayal of the ways of Genghis Khan. Kublai Khan was troubled by skirmishing nomads along the Great Wall no less than any of his more authentically Chinese predecessors, and it was this **loss of contact with its Mongol roots** that ensured that the Yuan dynasty could not long survive the death of its founder. The great palace of **Xanadu** (in Inner Mongolia, near the modern city of Duolun), where Kublai Khan kept his legendary summer residence, was abandoned to fall into ruin. Today virtually nothing of the site remains.

The onslaught that the Mongols unleashed on China in 1211 was on a massive scale. The Great Wall proved no obstacle to Genghis Khan, and with his two hundred thousand men he cut a swathe across northwest China towards Beijing. It was not all plain sailing, however – so great was the destruction wrought in northern China that **famine and plague** broke out, afflicting the invader as much as the invaded.

Genghis Khan himself died in 1227, before the **capture of Beijing** had been completed. His body was carried back to Mongolia by a funeral cortege of ten thousand, who murdered every man and beast within ten miles of the road so that news of the Great Khan's death could not be reported before his sons and viceroys had been gathered from the farthest corners of his dominions. The whereabouts of his **tomb** is uncertain, though according to one of the best-known stories his ashes are in a mausoleum near Dongsheng, south of Baotou.

In the years after Genghis Khan's death, the fate of both China and of distant Europe teetered together on the brink. Having conquered all of Russia, the Mongol forces were poised in 1241 to make the relatively short final push across Europe to the Atlantic, when a message came from deep inside Asia that the invasion was to be cancelled. The decision to spare western Europe cleared the way for the **final conquest of China** instead, and by 1276 the Mongols had established their own dynasty, the **Yuan dynasty**. It was the first time the Chinese had come under foreign rule.

The Yuan is still an era about which Chinese historians can find little good to say, though the boundaries of the empire were expanded considerably, to include Yunnan and Tibet for the first time. The magnificent zenith of the dynasty was achieved under **Kublai Khan**, as documented in Marco Polo's *Travels* (see box, p.828). Ironically, however, the Mongols were able to sustain their power only by becoming thoroughly Chinese, and abandoning the traditional nomadic Mongol way of life. Kublai Khan and his court soon forgot the warrior skills of their forefathers, and in 1368, less than a hundred years later, the Yuan, a shadow of their former selves, were **driven out of China** by the Ming. The Mongols returned to Mongolia, and reverted to their former ways, hunting, fighting among themselves and occasionally skirmishing with the Chinese down by the Wall. Astonishingly, history had come full circle.

Thereafter, Mongolian history moves gradually downhill, though right into the eighteenth century they maintained at least nominal control over many of the lands to the south and west originally won by Genghis Khan. These included **Tibet**, from where **Lamaist Buddhism** was imported to become the dominant religion in Mongolia. The few Tibetan-style monasteries in Mongolia that survive are an important testimony of this. Over the years, as well, came **settlers** from other parts of Asia: there is now a sizeable Muslim minority, and under the Qing many Chinese settlers moved to Inner Mongolia, escaping overpopulation and famine at home, a trend that has continued under the Communists. The incoming settlers tried ploughing up the grassland with **disastrous ecological results** – wind and water swept the soil away – and the Mongols withdrew to the hills. Only recently has a serious programme of land stabilization and reclamation been established.

Sandwiched between two imperial powers, **Mongolia's independence** was constantly threatened. The Russians set up a protectorate over the north, while the rest came effectively under the control of China. In the 1930s, Japan occupied much of eastern Inner Mongolia as part of Manchuguo, and the Chinese Communists also maintained a strong presence. In 1945 Stalin persuaded Chiang Kaishek to recognize the independence of **Outer Mongolia** under Soviet protection as part of the Sino-Soviet anti-Japanese treaty, effectively sealing the fate of what then became the Mongolian People's Republic. In 1947, **Inner Mongolia** was designated the first Autonomous Region of the People's Republic of China.

Hohhot and around

There has been a town at **HOHHOT** (known as Huhehaote to the Chinese) since the time of the Ming dynasty four hundred years ago, though it did not become the capital of Inner Mongolia until 1952. Until relatively modern times, it was a small town centred on a number of **Buddhist temples**. The temples are still here – but Hohhot is now a major city. Nevertheless, it's a relatively green and leafy place in summer and the city is an interesting mix of the old and the new. As well as the shiny new banks and department stores downtown, there's an extensive area in the south of the town with old, narrow streets built of black bricks and heavy roof tiles. These days Hohhot is largely a Han city, though there is also a Hui and a Mongol presence; it's worthwhile tracking down the **Mongol** areas, not least to try some of their interesting **food**. The other reason for visiting Hohhot is its proximity to some of the famous Mongolian **grasslands** which lie within a hundred-kilometre radius of the city.

Orientation, arrival and accommodation

Hohhot is a fairly easy place to find your way around, and although distances are large, the terrain is flat, making it a very good place for cycling. The heart of the modern commercial city, including most hotels, lies in the blocks to the south of the train and bus stations, while the old city and its interesting temples are in the southwest of town, south of the central Renmin Park.

The **airport** is 35km east of the city and the airport bus drops arriving passengers at the *CAAC* office on Xilinguole Lu (see "Listings", p.834). Hohhot's **train** and **bus** stations are next to each other in the north of the city, at the top end of the north–south axis Xilinguole Lu. Travellers arriving by train, in particular, are often subjected to furious and persistent harassment from the moment they disembark, by travel agents trying to sell them grassland tours. The only practical way to escape the melee is to get into a **taxi**. There is a flat fare of ¥10 which applies to all rides within the city.

Accommodation

Bayi, Chezhan Dong Lu (☎0471/6956688 ext 3263). A small but quite salubrious place offering doubles with bath. Turn left as you come out of the train station, and walk for ten minutes up the road. ④.

Hohhot, Yingbin Bei Lu (☎0471/6962200). An old-fashioned place with unspectacular rooms, not terribly welcoming to foreigners. Turn left out of the station, walk a few minutes and take the first turning on the right – it's about a fifteen-minute walk. ⑥.

Inner Mongolia, Wulanchabu Lu (☎0471/6964233 ext 8330). Nice double rooms 1km southeast of the *Xincheng*; it's also possible to get into the back of the hotel via a short cut from the grounds of the *Xincheng*. ⑦.

Tongda, Chezhan Dong Lu (☎0471/6968731). Very convenient for the train station – it's straight across the road, and a little to the left as you come out. All rooms are clean with private bath – doubles and three- and four-bedded dorms. If you have a student card, you may get a fifty percent discount. The only drawback about this place are the predatory travel agents, most of whom have offices in the hotel. Dorms ②, rooms ④.

Xincheng, Hulunbei'er Lu (☎0471/6963322). In the east of the city, this is by far the best option for budget accommodation and offers 24-hour hot water. The hotel is set in large grounds, which even have sheep grazing in them. There's no convenient bus here, though it takes only about five minutes in a taxi from the train or bus station. Dorms ②, rooms ④–⑨.

Yunzhong, Zhongshan Xi Lu (☎0471/6968822). An upmarket place right behind the Nationalities Market offering double and triple rooms. Student discount available. To find the reception, walk from the main street under the bridge that connects the two parts of the Nationalities Market. Bus #1 from the train station goes right past here. ⑥.

Zhaojun, corner of Xilinguole and Xinhua Dajie (☎0471/6962211). In the centre of town, diagonally facing Xinhua Square. Probably the most upmarket place in town, despite a slightly unprepossessing exterior. ⑧.

The City

The focus of the city is **Xinhua Square**, at the junction of Xilinguole Lu and the east–west axis Xinhua Dajie; early in the morning the square becomes an exercise ground for hundreds of people. A few blocks to the east of here is the newest shopping street in town, Xincheng Lu (New City Street), while the busiest shopping area is on Zhongshan Lu, south of Xinhua Lu, around the **Nationalities Market**, a huge department store. Just to the south, **Renmin Park** is a fairly standard arrangement of lakes, causeways and pavilions, home to the city zoo.

There is just one historic building marooned in the new city, away to the east on Xincheng Xi Jie. This is the **Jiangjun Yashu** (daily 8am–4.30pm; ¥5). It was actually the government office of a prominent Qing-dynasty general, even though it looks like a temple. Now it's a tiny museum with some bizarre modern Buddhist art in the right wing, and some curious Qing office furniture at the back.

More centrally located, the **Inner Mongolia Museum** (daily 9am–4pm; ¥8) on the corner of Xinhua Dajie and Hulunbei'er Lu – a few minutes' walk from the *Xincheng Hotel* – is well worth a visit. In the downstairs exhibition, there's a large display of ethnic Mongolian items, such as costumes, saddles, long leather coats and cummerbunds, as well as hunting and sporting implements, including some very European-looking hockey sticks and balls. There's also a fascinating paleontology display, with complete fossils of a woolly rhinoceros and a sizeable dinosaur. Upstairs are interesting maps and objects detailing the exploits of Genghis Khan, and the huge Mongol empire of the thirteenth century.

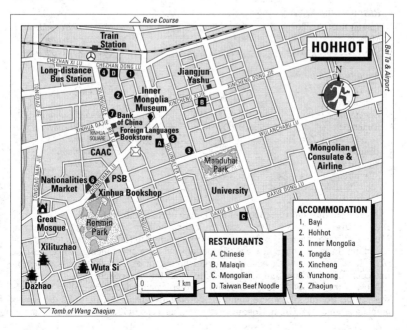

HOHHOT AND AROUND

Hohhot	呼和浩特	*hūhéhàote*

ACCOMMODATION

Bayi	八一宾馆	*bāyī bīnguǎn*
Hohhot	呼和浩特宾馆	*hūhéhàotè bīnguǎn*
Inner Mongolia	内蒙古饭店	*nèi ménggǔ fàndiàn*
Tongda	通达饭店	*tōngdá fàndiàn*
Xincheng	新城宾馆	*xīnchéng bīnguǎn*
Yunzhong	云中大酒店	*yúnzhōng dàjiǔdiàn*
Zhaojun	昭君大酒店	*zhāojūn dàjiǔdiàn*

THE CITY

Dazhao	大召	*dàzhào*
Great Mosque	清真大寺	*qīngzhēn dàsì*
Inner Mongolia Museum	内蒙古博物馆	*nèi ménggǔ bówùguǎn*
Jiangjun Yashu	将军衙署	*jiāngjūn yáshǔ*
Mongolian Consulate	蒙古共和国领事馆	*ménggǔ gònghéguó*
		lǐngshìguǎn
Nationalities Market	民族商场	*mínzú shāngchǎng*
Renmin Park	人民公园	*rénmín gōngyuán*
Xilituzhao	席里图召	*xílítú zhào*
Xinhua Square	新华广场	*xīnhuá guǎngchǎng*
Wuta Si	五塔寺	*wǔtǎ sì*

RESTAURANTS

Taiwan Beef Noodle	台湾牛肉面	*táiwān niúròumiàn*
Malaqin	马拉沁饭店	*mǎlāqìn fàndiàn*
Daxue Lu Shangchang	大学路商场	*dàxué lù shāngchǎng*

AROUND HOHHOT

Bai Ta	百塔	*bǎi tǎ*
Erlianhot	二连浩特	*èrliánhàotè*
Gegentala	格根塔拉草原	*gégēntǎlā cǎoyuán*
Huitengxile	辉腾锡勒草原	*huīténgxīlè cǎoyuán*
Tomb of Wang Zhaojun	昭君墓	*zhāojūnmù*
Ulan Batur	乌兰巴托	*wūlán bātuō*
Wusutu Zhao	乌素图召	*wūsùtú zhào*
Xilamuren	希拉穆仁草原	*xīlāmùrén cǎoyuán*

Away from the centre, a couple of kilometres north of the train station, is a gigantic **race course**, apparently the biggest in China, built in the shape of two circular Mongolian yurts, adjacent and connected to each other, to form the elongated shape of a stadium. In the evening, displays of Mongolian singing and dancing sometimes take place here (try enquiring at the upmarket hotels, or at *CTS* for details of performances). Take #13 bus from the centre of town for the race course.

Most of the historic buildings of Hohhot are crowded into the interesting old south-western part of the city, where you can enjoyably spend the best part of a day simply ambling around. The **Great Mosque**, at the southern end of Zhongshan Lu, is an attractive old building bearing traces of Chinese and Arabic style, constructed of black brick and accompanied by a Chinese-style minaret with a pagoda roof. Some of the Hui people who worship here are extremely friendly and they will probably be delighted if you look round their mosque (though ask first). The streets around the mosque comprise the Muslim area of town, and you'll see a lot of old men here with wispy beards and skull caps.

Walking south from the mosque for about fifteen minutes along the main road, you'll come to a couple of Buddhist temples. The biggest of these is the **Dazhao** (daily 8am–5pm; ¥5), down a side street west of the main road. Originally constructed in 1579 and recently renovated, the Dazhao is an excellent example of its type. In the late seventeenth century, the temple was dedicated to the famous Qing emperor Kangxi – a gold tablet with the words "Long Live the Emperor" was set before the silver statue of Sakyamuni and in the main hall murals depicting the visit of the Emperor Kangxi can still be seen.

Just a few minutes from Dazhao, over on the other side of the main road, is the **Xilituzhao** (daily 8am–5pm; ¥3), another temple of similar scale and layout to the Dazhao, and dating from the same era. Since 1735 this has been the official residence of the Living Buddha, who is in charge of Buddhist affairs in the city.

Farther east, via an interesting walk along winding, narrow alleys, you'll come to the most attractive piece of architecture in the city, known as the **Wuta Si** (Five Towers Temple; daily 8am–5pm; ¥2). Built in 1727, in pure Indian style, this composite of five pagodas originally belonged to the Ci Deng Temple, which no longer exists. It's relatively small, but its walls are engraved with no fewer than 1563 Buddhas, all in slightly different postures. Currently stored inside the pagoda building is a rare, antique Mongolian cosmological map which marks precisely the position of hundreds of stars.

Eating and drinking

There is plenty of standard Chinese food in Hohhot. The hotel restaurant of the *Xincheng* is good and cheap; for a livelier atmosphere, however, there are two very popular Chinese restaurants right opposite the hotel entrance. In the vicinity of the train station, try the *Taiwan Beef Noodle Restaurant* – which has an English menu – a little to the east of the *Tongda Hotel*. At the Nationalities Market, there's a fast-food café in the left wing (as you face the bridge) where you can get passable hamburgers and fries.

The highlight of eating in Hohhot, however, is the chance to eat **Mongolian food**, which is by no means as dreadful as reports would have it. Mongolian **hotpot** or *shuan yangrou* is a perfectly respectable dinner that even the Chinese enjoy. It's similar to Korean food, in that you cook it yourself; piles of thinly sliced mutton, ordered by the *jin* (half kilo), are cooked by being dropped into a cauldron of boiling water at the table, then quickly removed and dipped into a spicy sauce. Tofu, glass-noodles, cabbage and mushrooms are common accompaniments which all go into the pot too. Many restaurants in Hohhot serve *shuan yangrou* – try the *Malaqin Restaurant* on Xincheng Xi Jie, a few blocks east of Hulunbei'er Lu. Dinner here with plenty of beer shouldn't cost more than ¥30 per head.

For an even more exotic meal, however, with the focus on Mongolian dairy products, head for the Mongolian quarter in the southeast of town. Bus #4 comes down here – get off at Daxue Lu just south of the university. During term time, this area is packed with students and restaurants stay open late. Any restaurant with Mongolian letters above the door is worth trying; one in particular is just 200m down the small street leading south from beside the Daxue Lu Shangchang (University Street Market). For an excellent breakfast or lunch, order a large bowl of milk tea, with sugar, and *chaomi* (buckwheat), *huangyou* (butter), *nailao* (hard white cheese), *naipi* (a sweetish, biscuit-like substance formed from the skin of boiled milk). Toss everything into the tea, and eat it with chopsticks – it's surprisingly delicious. To make this into a substantial meal, try *mengu baozi* and *xianbing* – dough stuffed with ground mutton, steamed or fried respectively.

Listings

Airlines *CAAC*, Xilinguole Lu, just south of Xinhua Square (7.30–1.30am & 2.30–6.30pm; ☎0471/6964103). *MIAT* (the airline of the Republic of Mongolia; ☎0471/4953250), in the east of the city next to the Mongolian Consulate and near to the *Neimenggu Jiancai Xuexiao* (Inner Mongolia Construction Materials College). To reach the *MIAT* office, take a taxi or ride a #2 bus east to *nong-wei* bus stop, then walk a little farther east, and a couple of blocks south.

Banks and exchange The easiest place to change money, including travellers' cheques, is inside the *Zhaojun Hotel*. It offers the same rates as the bank, and it operates at weekends. The head office of the *Bank of China* is actually across the road from the hotel.

Bike rental You can rent bikes cheaply (¥1 per hour) from a place right outside the *Xincheng Hotel*, immediately to the north of the entrance.

Bookshops There is a *Foreign Language Bookstore* on Xilinguole Lu, across the road from Xinhua Square. There is also a branch of *Xinhua Bookstore* on Zhongshan Lu, across the road from (and a couple of minutes to the south of) the Nationalities Market.

Consulate The Consulate of the Republic of Mongolia (Mon, Tues & Thurs 8.30am–noon; ☎0471/4953250) is in the east of the city, next to the *MIAT* office. Visas are now fairly easy to obtain, though they cost US$50 and may take some time to be issued. A letter of invitation is usually asked for, though these are not always scrupulously checked for authenticity.

Post office The main office, where you can also make IDD calls, is on the south side of Zhongshan Lu, just east of Xilinguole Lu.

PSB In the government building to the south of the junction between Zhongshan Lu and Xilinguole Lu.

Travel agents There are numerous travel agents in town, many of whom will find you before you find them. They nearly all have English-speaking employees, and deal in grassland tours as well as booking train tickets. *CTS*, in the back building, 3rd floor of the *Inner Mongolia Hotel* (☎0471/6964233 ext 8936), has some pleasant, approachable staff. The *Tongda Hotel* is also full of travel services.

Around Hohhot

There are a few more sights scattered around the outer suburbs of Hohhot, some of which can be reached on city buses. The **Tomb of Wang Zhaojun**, about 8km to the south of Hohhot, is the burial site of a Tang-dynasty princess sent from Chengdu to cement Han-Mongol relations by marrying the king of Mongolia. It isn't a spectacular

---

MOVING ON FROM HOHHOT

There are daily bus services from Hohhot to **Erlianhot** (see box, p.836) and **Xilinhot** (see p.837), but note that although station staff may sell you tickets to these destinations, you will not be allowed on to the bus if you look like a Westerner and do not have a travel permit. Either go to the PSB to apply for a permit, or, in the case of Erlianhot, you'd do better to catch the daily (slow) train at 6.40am. No permit is required if you travel by train.

To **Baotou**, there are buses running every thirty minutes; you can find them on the main street outside the station, attended by people with loud-hailers. There is also one daily (early-morning) bus to **Dongsheng** for Genghis Khan's Mausoleum (see p.842). In addition, two sleeper buses leave Hohhot in late afternoon, bound for **Tianjin** and **Beijing**, respectively – these buses work out far cheaper than the trains and it is also a lot easier to buy tickets.

Leaving Hohhot by **train**, it's best to seek the help of a travel agent (see "Listings" above). You'll pay a small commission and you'll need to give them at least 36 hours' notice for a hard sleeper – but if you queue up at the station by yourself you may not get any reservation at all. Hohhot is linked by train to **Lanzhou** to the west, **Beijing** to the east and **Hailar** (a sixty-hour direct journey via Beijing) to the northeast. There are also trains to **Ulan Batur** in the Republic of Mongolia (see box, p.836).

sight — a huge mound raised from the plain and planted with gardens in the centre of which is a modern pavilion — but it is a romantic story with important implications for modern Chinese politics (the harmonious marrying of the Han with the minority peoples). In the rose garden, amongst pergolas festooned with gourds, is a tiny museum devoted to Zhaojun. It contains some of her clothes, including a tiny pair of shoes, jewels, books and a number of steles. You can reach the tomb by the #14 bus, or by cycling due south along the main road from the Great Mosque in the west of town.

Another site that can be reached by city bus is the **Wusutu Zhao** complex, the only temple in Mongolia to have been designed and built solely by Mongolians. It has buildings in Mongolian, Tibetan and Han styles and lies 12km northwest of Hohhot, south of the Daqing Mountain and in attractive countryside at the terminus of the #23 bus from Xilinguole Lu. Slightly farther out is one more site that you can reach only by hired car or by a long bicycle ride: the **Bai Ta** (White Pagoda), about 17km east of the city, is an attractive, 55-metre-high wood and brick construction, erected as long ago as the tenth century and covered in interesting carvings of coiling dragons, birds and flowers on the lower parts of the tower. You can reach it by following Xincheng Xi Jie east out of the city; a possible stopoff on the way to the airport.

The grasslands

Mongolia is not all one giant grassland, but there are three areas in the vicinity of Hohhot which are certainly large enough to give the illusion of endlessness. These are **Xilamuren** (80km north of Hohhot), **Gegentala** (150km north) and **Huitengxile** (120km west). It is hard to differentiate among them, save that Xilamuren is probably the most visited and Gegentela the least visited. Xilamuren is the only grassland that can feasibly be visited independently (see below). Bear in mind that your grassland experience in the immediate area of the regional capital is likely to be a rather packaged affair and you may find yourself surrounded by crowds of rowdy tourists from other parts of East Asia. A visit to a grassland in another, remoter part of the region (such as Xilinhot or Hailar (see p.837 and p.838) may well give you a more authentic flavour of Mongolia.

The most convenient way to visit the grasslands is to take one of the semi-notorious **Grassland Tours**. An interesting fact about the tours is that Western tourists hardly ever enjoy them, whereas tourists from East Asia almost always love them. If you accept the idea that you are going to the grasslands primarily to participate in a bizarre social experience, then you should get more out of it. A two-day tour (with one night in a yurt) is definitely enough – in a group of six or seven people, this should come to between ¥250 and ¥350 each. If you're travelling alone, some travel services (such as the *Inner Mongolia Luye International Travel Company* based in the *Tongda Hotel*, Room 424; ☎0471/6968613), can tack you on to existing groups. Bear in mind that if you choose this option, you may find yourself sleeping crushed into a small yurt with six Japanese girls who don't speak your language.

The tours always follow a very similar pattern. You are based at a **yurt site**, which comprises a number of yurts, plus a dining hall, kitchen and very primitive toilets. The larger yurt sites, at Xilamuren, are as big as small villages. Transport, meals and accommodation are all included in the price, as are various unconvincing "Mongolian entertainments" – wrestling and spectacular horse-riding in particular – and visits to typical Mongol families in traditional dress. Of these only the food is consistently good. During the evening banquet your Mongolian hosts bring round to every table silver bowls of local *baijiu* (a clear and nauseatingly powerful vodka-like spirit), which you are more or less forced to drink. The banquet is followed by a fairly degenerate evening of drinking, dancing and singing.

Despite the communal nature of the tours, however, it is perfectly possible to escape from your group if you wish to do so. You can hire your own horse, or just walk off over the horizon into an endless expanse of grass. If your stay happens to coincide with a bright moon, you could be in for the most haunting experience of your life.

THE ROAD TO OUTER MONGOLIA

The Republic of Mongolia, otherwise known as **Outer Mongolia**, is now open to foreign tourists travelling independently. It is possible to get your **visa** in Hohhot (see "Listings", p.834) or in Beijing, and these are likely to become even easier to obtain since the final departure of the old Communists from power in Ulan Batur in July 1996.

There are various ways into the country from China. From both Beijing and Hohhot you can either fly, or take a direct train, to Ulan Batur. **From Beijing** *CAAC* and *MIAT* both fly twice weekly to Ulan Batur; tickets cost US$150–200 one way, while the direct train, which takes about 36 hours, costs US$100 (special "foreigners' price"). Alternatively, you can do the journey by stages, which works out a lot cheaper and is perhaps more interesting. The first stage is to get to the border at **Erlianhot**. From Beijing you can get there by taking the Hohhot train as far as Jining (10hr; ¥75), then changing to the Erlianhot train (8hr; ¥42). **From Hohhot,** *MIAT* flies twice weekly to Ulan Batur for US$130. By train, there are relatively expensive direct services to Ulan Batur; otherwise take the direct daily service to the border at Erlianhot (12hr). The bus from Hohhot to Erlianhot takes only eight hours, but tourists must have a permit to travel on it (apply at the PSB).

ERLIANHOT is a curious border town in the middle of nowhere, which caters to Mongolian nomads and shepherds coming to town to do their shopping. It's also a famous centre for wool production. Twice a week its train station briefly fills with foreigners as the Trans-Mongolian Express comes through on its way to or from Moscow – there's even a disco and a bar here for their entertainment. There is some very cheap accommodation available in town. Eat all you can here, because the food in Outer Mongolia is notoriously poor.

Crossing the border is still something of a palaver if you are not on a through-train. Assuming you arrive in Erlianhot in the evening you'll certainly have to spend one night here. In the morning there's one local bus that does the seven-kilometre trip across to the Mongolian town of **Zamen Uud**, though you may wait hours for it to leave, and it'll cost you an absurd US$15. From there to Ulan Batur it's an eighteen-hour train journey which costs about US$5.

Travelling independently to the Xilamuren grassland can work out a good deal cheaper than taking a tour. Store your luggage at your hotel in Hohhot, and catch a bus from the long-distance bus station to the small settlement of **Zhaohe** (twice daily, 2–3hr; ¥8), adjacent to the grassland. When you get off you will be accosted by people offering to take you to their yurts – try to negotiate an all-inclusive daily rate of about ¥50 per person, for food and accommodation, before you accept any offer. Bring a bottle of *baijiu* as a gift to smooth relations. You are not exactly in the wilderness here, but you can wander off into the grass and soon find it.

The Northeast

The colossal area of land that comprises Inner Mongolia to the east and north of Hohhot is scarcely visited by tourists. As an area populated by nomadic sheep-herders since the beginning of time, its attractions lie not in historic towns, but in the wilderness. The terrain is hilly and the farther north you go the wetter it gets and the more trees there are. The grass on the **eastern grasslands** is accordingly longer and more lush, though for only a brief period each year. People are few and far between, the land outside the towns only occasionally punctuated by the sight of **muchang jia** – pastureland homes – comprising groups of yurts in the grass, surrounded by herds of sheep, cattle or horses. Visiting *muchang jia* is an exclusively summer activity; during the long winters, temperatures can dip to an appalling minus 50˚C.

THE NORTHEAST		
Chifeng	赤蜂	*chìfēng*
Dalai Hu	达赉湖	*dálài hú*
Hulunbuir Grasslands	呼伦贝尔草原	*hūlúnbèi'ěr cǎoyuán*
Hailar	海拉尔	*hǎilāěr*
Manzhouli	满洲里	*mǎnzhōulǐ*
Muchang jia	牧场家	*mùchǎng jiā*
Tongliao	通辽	*tōngliáo*
Xilinhot	锡林浩特	*xīlínhàotè*

For travellers the area is not an easy one to explore, given the paucity of **transport** connections. The only rail lines are in the far north, offering access to **Hailar** and **Manzhouli** on the Russian border and, given that the local authorities are none too keen on foreign travellers crossing the region by bus, flying is sometimes the only option.

Xilinhot

XILINHOT, 500km northeast of Hohhot and 600km north of Beijing, is probably the most visited town in the whole area, though it is by no means straightforward to get here. The joy of a place like this is that you are already in the **grasslands** – they begin at the edge of town.

Even here, there are *CITS*-approved grassland sites, and travel services will compete for the honour of escorting you there. **Tours** from Xilinhot are likely to be cheaper and more tranquil than those operating from Hohhot. Considering, however, that you are so close to the grasslands here, it is quite feasible if you speak a little Chinese to do a **private deal** with somebody – a travel-service employee, a hotel-worker or a taxi-driver – to take you out to any *muchang jia* with which they have acquaintance. This needn't cost much: reckon on about ¥2 per kilometre. Given that you are going to stay with a family, it is essential to take a present with you; a bottle of the local *baijiu* is best. You will still be expected to pay for the pleasure of staying with the family, but the terms are likely to be friendlier. Try to arrange some all-inclusive daily rate which includes all meals and drinks, but don't be too aggressive about it; ¥50 per day is a good rate.

The main difficulty with Xilinhot is getting there in the first place. There is a daily **bus** from Hohhot (14hr), but you will be barred from getting on it without a travel permit – apply to the Hohhot PSB. The alternatives are either to take a train to Erlianhot (see p.934), and then try to get a bus from there; or simply to **fly** directly from Hohhot (or Beijing). The flights from Hohhot leave on Tuesday and Saturday and cost ¥520.

In Xilinhot, **accommodation** is available at the upmarket *Baima* (⑤) or, just behind the bus station, at the *Xilinhot* (③).

Hailar and the northeast frontier

In the far north of Inner Mongolia, **HAILAR**, with both rail connections and an airport, is the main transport hub of the region, and a centre for grassland visits. It is also one of the remotest places in China, requiring a full sixty hours by train from the provincial capital Hohhot – one of the epic train journeys of China and, for train enthusiasts, itself a possible reason for going to Hailar.

The route from Hohhot first passes east through Datong to Beijing, and then moves north back into Inner Mongolia, passing the towns of **Chifeng** and **Tongliao** – both of which are surrounded by their own grasslands which can also be visited. From here the train drifts east into Jilin Province (Dongbei). Much later the train cuts back into Inner Mongolia at Zhalantun from where it travels northwest to Hailar. On the last day, the train passes through hilly, grassy pastures, mist-hung rivers and cool, wooded valleys. For hour after hour there's barely a sign of life.

The town of Hailar itself is of minimal interest, a small, light industrial and agricultural place on the banks of the Heilongjiang (Amur) River with a small Muslim population as well as the usual Mongol/Han mix. There are a number of Muslim and Chinese restaurants, and a market which specializes in fresh river fish, edible fungi and vegetables of prodigious quality. In addition, the town has a couple of shops selling a variety of Mongol handicrafts – saddles, rugs, pots, pipes, knives and very fine leather riding boots.

The main reason for coming here is to see the North Mongolian **Hulunbuir Grasslands**, an apparently limitless rolling land of plains and low grassy mountains, traced by slow rivers teeming with fish. Hundreds of thousands of sheep, cattle and horses graze this inexhaustible pasture, spread over hundreds of miles. In summer they graze the higher pastures and in winter they come down to the lowlands, still often deep in snow. Transport in the area is mostly by camel and pony.

As elsewhere in Inner Mongolia, there are the *CITS*-approved villages of Mongol herders, who earn part of their income from occasional groups of tourists, mostly from Japan. Just as at Xilinhot (see p.837), you can either join an official **grassland tour** with *CITS*, or try to strike off independently; one advantage of the grassland tours in this area, however, is that they are not attended by hordes of people. The grass on the Hulunbuir Grasslands is also special – not only is it scattered with a variety of flowers and huge fungi, but, as you soon discover, it is also alive with little black toads, grasshoppers, birds and insects. It is just about impossible to avoid stepping on the toads. By the same token the insects find it impossible to avoid stepping on you – **mosquito repellent** is essential.

A day trip to eat a traditional mutton banquet on the grassland, for a group of four people, costs in the region of ¥120 each. If you want to spend a night on the grasslands as well, reckon on around ¥200.

Beyond Hailar

A few hours to the west of Hailar is **MANZHOULI** on the border with Russia. There is a daily train here from Hailar, and the Trans-Siberian train from Beijing to Moscow also passes through once a week in each direction. The town has important steam locomotive yards, which you can visit, and not far to the south of town is the great lake **Dalai Hu** (Hulun Nur in Mongolian), a shallow expanse of water set in marshy grazing country where flocks of swans, geese, cranes and other migratory birds come to nest. The grasslands in this region are said to be the greenest in all Mongolia.

North of Hailar is a true wilderness, the final frontier of China. Here are some of the last great areas of untouched primeval forest in the country, a natural habitat for the wolf and the much-threatened Manchurian tiger. There is a rail line that meanders up as far north as Mangui, above the 52nd parallel, but before attempting to visit this area you should check with the Hailar PSB.

Baotou and beyond

Just three hours to the west of Hohhot by train or bus lies Inner Mongolia's biggest city, **BAOTOU**. Its primary significance is as the chief iron- and steel-producing centre in China: if you're arriving at night from the direction of Yinchuan, your first glimpse of the city is likely to be of satanic fires burning in the great blast furnaces. The sky over the western half of Baotou is a more or less permanent yellow, orange and purple colour. For visitors, there can be something magnificent about ugliness on such a scale, but otherwise, apart from a few minor sights, including **Wudangzhao**, an attractive Tibetan-style monastery outside the town, the city does not have a huge amount to offer. One further site of considerable romantic interest, if nothing else – **Genghis Khan's Mausoleum** – lies well to the south of Baotou near the town of Dongsheng.

The City

Baotou is a colossal city stretching for miles in all directions. It comprises three main areas: Donghe, the oldest part of town, to the east, and Qingshan and Kundulun to the west. Qingshan is a nondescript shopping and residential area, while Kundulun includes the iron and steel works on its western edge. The three parts of the city are well connected by frequent buses and minibuses which take thirty to forty minutes to travel between the Donghe and Kundulun districts. They cost ¥2.5, and you can stop them anywhere on the street.

The only area in the whole city that could be described as remotely attractive is **Donghe** north of Renmin Park, where the tangled old streets are quite interesting to wander around. You can see a lot of old mud-brick houses here, each opening on to fascinating little courtyards full of plants and bicycles. **Kundulun**, however, is mainly interesting as a monument to town-planning gone wrong – the streets and squares are wide and bleak beyond belief. Even the "sights" – the **Iron and Steel Works** and the **Steam Locomotive Museum** – are not especially easy or cheap to visit. The museum is located in a particularly remote area, 25km out to the northwest. You may be able to visit it by yourself in a taxi, but make enquiries first; *CITS* in the *Baotou Hotel* can arrange a day trip to the two sites, with a car and a guide, at ¥350 for a car (maximum three passengers), which is quite reasonable.

Practicalities

The **airport** is just a couple of kilometres south of the Donghe train station, and a twenty-minute taxi ride from hotels in this part of town. The **CAAC** office (☎0472/4172266 ext 4258) is now based at the *Donghe Hotel*, in the back building, on the right as you walk in.

There are two major **train stations**, one in Kundulun (*Baotou Zhan*) and one in Donghe (*Baotou Dong Zhan*) – all through-trains, including express trains from Beijing and Lanzhou, stop at both stations, so be sure to get off at the right one. The **bus station** is right opposite the train station; tickets for Hohhot should be bought on the bus, but for Dongsheng (every 30min), you should buy your ticket inside the bus station.

CITS is in Room 331 of the *Baotou Hotel*, no. 4 building (☎0472/5154615). The staff here are very friendly and eager to help and have some excellent English speakers to hand. The **PSB** (for visas) is also in the *Baotou* on the first floor.

If you want to change travellers' cheques, you will have to go to the main office of the **Bank of China** in Kundulun, on the main road just east of A'erding Square. The *Bank of China*'s branches in Donghe can change cash only. The main **post office** is in Kundulun near the *Bank of China*, but there's also a branch in Donghe.

Accommodation, eating and drinking

Of the two ends of town, **Donghe** is the more pleasant and convenient place **to stay**. From the train station, walk north straight up the main road – the large white tower about ten minutes up on the left is the *Beiyang* (*North Pacific*,☎0472/4175656; dorms ①, rooms ③), which has quite decent double rooms with bath as well as three-bed dorms. About another fifteen minutes farther on, also on the left, is the old-fashioned but quite pleasant *Donghe* (☎0472/4172266; ②–⑤).

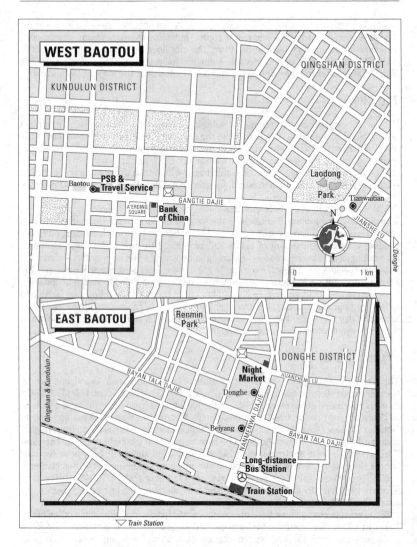

WEST BAOTOU

QINGSHAN DISTRICT

KUNDULUN DISTRICT

Baotou · PSB & Travel Service

A'ERDING SQUARE

GANGTIE DAJIE

Bank of China

Laodong Park

Tianwaitian

JIANSHE LU

Donghe

N

0   1 km

EAST BAOTOU

Renmin Park

Qingshan & Kundulun

DONGHE DISTRICT

BAYAN TALA DAJIE

Night Market

HUANCHENG LU

Donghe

MAMENWAI DAJIE

Beiyang

BAYAN TALA DAJIE

Long-distance Bus Station

Train Station

▽ *Train Station*

If you want to stay in **Kundulun**, be warned that the hotels in this part of town are a long way from the station. If you get stuck, there's the *A'erding Fandian* (no English sign; dorms ①, rooms ②), just outside the station on the right, which will accept foreigners if pressed. Bus #1 from the station will take you into the centre. A good bet here is the *Baotou* (☎0472/5156655; ③–⑥), on the main east–west road Gangtie Dajie, a few hundred metres west of A'erding Square. It's tolerably comfortable, central and home to the city's PSB and *CITS* offices. The one splendidly upmarket hotel in town, with swimming pool and fitness centre, is the *Tianwaitian* (☎0472/3137766 ext 99; ⑧) on the southern end of Hudemulin Dajie in Qingshan district.

BAOTOU AND BEYOND		
Baotou	包头	*bāotóu*
Donghe	东河	*dōnghé*
Iron and Steel Works	钢铁公司	*gāngtiě gōngsī*
Kundulun	昆都仑	*kūndūlún*
Qingshan	青山	*qīngshān*
Steam Locomotive Museum	蒸汽火车博物馆	*zhēngqìhuǒchē bówùguǎn*
ACCOMMODATION		
A'erding	阿尔丁饭店	*āěrdīng fàndiàn*
Baotou	包头宾馆	*bāotóu bīnguǎn*
Beiyang	北洋饭店	*běiyáng fàndiàn*
Donghe	东河宾馆	*dōnghé bīnguǎn*
Tianwaitian	天外天大酒店	*tiānwàitiān dàjiǔdiàn*
BEYOND BAOTOU		
Wudangzhao	五当召	*wǔdāng zhào*
Yellow River	黄河	*huánghé*
Dongsheng	东胜	*dōngshèng*
Genghis Khan's Mausoleum	成吉思汗陵园	*chéngjísīhàn língyuán*

The *Donghe Hotel* has a **restaurant**, which is a cheap if rather lonely experience. Otherwise, there's a small and friendly **night market** a short way to the north (turn left out of the hotel). There's also a night market near the Donghe train station should you get caught down here.

Wudangzhao and the Yellow River

The one definite attraction of the Baotou area, **Wudangzhao** (daily 8am–6pm; ¥10), is located about 70km northeast of the city. This is the best-preserved Lamaist monastery still functioning in Inner Mongolia, and is one of the results of the Mongolian conquest of Tibet in the thirteenth century. For centuries afterwards, the roads between Tibet and Mongolia were worn by countless pilgrims and wandering monks, bringing Lamaist Buddhism to Mongolia. This particular monastery, of the Yellow Sect, was established in 1749 and at its height housed twelve hundred lamas; seven generations of Living Buddhas were based here, the ashes of whom are kept in one of the halls. Today, however, the few remaining monks are greatly outnumbered by local tourists from Baotou and sadly their main duties now seem to involve hanging around at the hall entrances to check tourists' tickets.

Set in a pretty, narrow valley scattered with pine trees, the monastery is nevertheless an attractive place. You can hike off into the surrounding hills and, if you're keen, you should be able to stay in the pilgrims' hostel in the monastery as well. To get to Wudangzhao, catch the daily **minibus** from outside the Donghe train station in Baotou at around 8am. Otherwise, take **bus #7** from the east side of the station square (the right as you exit the station) to the terminus at Shiguai. The monastery is another 25km – if you arrive early enough there are one or two minibuses that go from here. If there are no minibuses, take a taxi from Shiguai for about ¥30. Returning to Baotou is fairly easy as there are various minibuses and other tour vehicles plying the route, up to around 5pm.

The other main sight in the Baotou area is the **Yellow River**. It's worth going to have a look at, to ruminate on its historical significance if nothing else. Right on the northern edge of the great northerly loop of the Yellow River, the whole area from Baotou to Hohhot was never automatically considered a part of China. In fact, the Chinese often built their Great Walls far to the south of here, leaving the area enclosed by the loop – known as the Ordos – to remain the dominion of the nomad. It was a simple dilemma: the Yellow River seemed like the logical northern limit of China, but the Ordos, to the south of the river, was part of the steppe and desert of Central Asia. The Qing eventually decided matters once and for all not only by seizing control of the Ordos, but also by moving north of the river into the heart of Mongolia. Today, the whole Yellow River region from Yinchuan in Ningxia Province, up to Baotou and across to Hohhot, is thoroughly irrigated and productive land – without the river, it would be pure desert. You can take a stroll along the northern bank of the Yellow River by taking **bus** #18 from in front of Donghe train station for about 6km to the new bridge. The river here is nearly a mile wide, shallow, sluggish and chocolate brown.

Genghis Khan's Mausoleum

The first thing to be said about **Genghis Khan's Mausoleum** is that it's not what it's cracked up to be: it probably isn't the tomb of Genghis Khan, and it isn't a particularly attractive place anyway. Its chief interest lies in the chance to see the modern cult of Genghis Khan in practice, for whatever the truth about the location of his burial place, the popular view among Mongolians, both in China and in the Republic of Mongolia, is that this is a holy site.

The main part of the mausoleum is formed by three connecting halls, shaped like Mongolian yurts. In the middle of the main hall is a five-metre-high marble **statue** of the Khan. There are several altars, with incense sticks burning, offerings of flowers and bottles of liquor, as though to a god. The corridors connecting the halls are adorned with bizarre murals supposedly depicting the life of the Khan – but note the ladies in Western dress (1890s style). Special **sacrificial ceremonies** take place four times a year on certain days of the lunar calendar – the fifteenth day of the third lunar month, the fifteenth day of the fifth lunar month, the twelfth day of the ninth month and the third day of the tenth month. On these occasions, Mongolian monks lead solemn rituals which involve piling up cooked sheep before the statue of the Khan. The ceremonies are attended not only by local people, but by pilgrims from the Republic of Mongolia itself.

Although it is true that Genghis Khan died in northern China, it is unlikely that the great man is indeed buried here. His funeral cortege may have passed through this region on its way back to Mongolia, but the story that the wheels of his funeral cart got stuck in the mud here resulting in his burial on the spot is almost certainly apocryphal. At best, scholars believe, the site contains a few relics – perhaps weapons – of Genghis Khan. The real tomb is thought to be on the slopes of Burkhan Khaldun, in the Hentei Mountains, not far to the east of Ulan Batur in Outer Mongolia. The reason why it came to be so strongly believed that the Khan was buried here in China, appears to be that the tribe who were charged with guarding the real sepulchre later drifted down across the Yellow River to the Ordos – but continued to claim the honour of being the official guardians of the tomb.

The alleged relics here have a murky political history. Several times they have been removed, and later returned, the most recent occasion being during World War II, when the Japanese tried to kidnap them. Apparently the Japanese had plans to set up a puppet Mongol state, centred around a Genghis Khan shrine. They even drew up plans for an elaborate mausoleum to house them – plans which were then commandeered by the Chinese Communists who, having safely returned the relics from a hiding place in

Qinghai, built the mausoleum for themselves in 1955 as a means of currying favour with the Mongolian people.

Practicalities

The mausoleum (daily; ¥25) is located in a tiny village in the Ordos, on a small road leading south into Shaanxi Province. To reach it from Baotou or Hohhot, take a bus first to **DONGSHENG**. From Baotou there are frequent buses that take about three hours; from Hohhot it takes five to six hours. It would be possible, if you left Baotou very early in the morning, to reach the mausoleum and make it back the same evening. The last bus from Dongsheng to Baotou leaves at about 8pm. Dongsheng is also accessible from Yinchuan in Ningxia, via Wuhai. On the way to Dongsheng, you'll pass spectacular areas of sand dune as well as grassland.

From Dongsheng to the mausoleum it takes a further two hours by bus or minibus (¥9), and there are only a few departures a day; if you leave for the mausoleum much after lunch, you may have to spend the night there. To return to Dongsheng from the mausoleum, simply stand in the road and flag down passing minibuses. There are also buses heading south, connecting the mausoleum with **Yulin** in Shaanxi Province.

If you need a bed, you can stay either in Dongsheng or at the mausoleum itself. The best place **to stay in Dongsheng** is right by the bus station. Come out of the station, turn right, then immediately right again into a cul-de-sac. On the right at the back is a pleasant hotel (②) with "Room Dep" written in English above the door, offering double rooms with bath. In the square outside here is a **night market** where you can get your dinner. A few minutes farther down the main street, away from the bus station, is the upmarket *Dongsheng Dajiudian* (☎0477/327333; ⑥). Carry on past here, then turn right, and you'll come to the *Waimiao* (②), about 200m down on the left. This hotel has doubles with bath and also a rather elegant restaurant. There are also rooms (③) **at the mausoleum** itself, or you can stay in a very fake yurt on concrete for ¥36 per person. Either way, there is no shower. However, you will find plenty of food available around the mausoleum and in the adjacent village on the main road.

NINGXIA

Ningxia Autonomous Hui Region is the smallest of China's provinces. Covering just 66,000 square kilometres, it squeezes in beside its giant neighbours, Inner Mongolia to the north and Gansu to the west, like a small appendage. Until recent times, its very existence as a separate zone has remained an open question. Having first appeared on the map in 1928, the region was then temporarily subsumed by Gansu in the 1950s – before finally reappearing again in 1958. It appears that the authorities of the People's Republic could not make up their minds whether the Muslim **Hui minority** was substantial enough to deserve its own autonomous region, in the same way as the Uigurs and the Mongols. Historically, the area has never been a secure one for the Chinese; almost every dynasty built its section of **Great Wall** through here and, in the nineteenth century, the Hui people played an active part in the Muslim rebellions, which were subsequently put down with such ferocity by the Qing authorities.

Today, the Hui make up about thirty percent of the tiny four million population, the remainder comprising mainly Han. As with all the autonomous regions of the Northwest, the central government has steadily encouraged **Han immigration** – or colonization – as a way of tying the area to the Chinese nation. The situation of the Hui people, however, is not comparable with that of China's other minorities, such as the disaffected Uigurs or Tibetans. Having originally arrived in China over a thousand years ago as descendants of Middle Eastern traders, they have in fact long since adapted to the Han culture. They are still **Muslims** in faith and in culture, but the vast majority of them speak Chinese as their mother tongue and, at present, there is little concept of a Hui nation floating round the backstreets of Yinchuan. Quite apart from that, most Hui people do not live in Ningxia at all, but are scattered around neighbouring regions.

Geographically, the area is dominated by the **Yellow River**. Apart from the hilly, green and extremely beautiful area in the south, Ningxia would be a barren, uninhabitable desert without its life-giving river. Unsurprisingly, the science of **irrigation** is at its most advanced here. As long as two thousand years ago, the great founding emperor of China, Qin Shihuang, sent a hundred thousand men here to dig irrigation channels. To those ancient systems of irrigation, which are still very much in use, have now been added ambitious reafforestation and desert reclamation projects. Some of these can be visited, particularly around the city of **Zhongwei.** Other sights include the regional capital **Yinchuan**, which makes a pleasant stopover, and one relic from an obscure northern branch of the Silk Road, the delightful **Xumi Shan Grottoes**, located well away from the Yellow River in the southern hills.

Despite a certain degree of industrialization since the Communists came to power, and the opening of the Lanzhou to Baotou rail link in 1958, Ningxia remains very much a rural area. For visitors, the rural scenes are very much the charm of the place, but this province is one of the poorest parts of the country.

Yinchuan and around

The capital of Ningxia, **YINCHUAN** is a pleasant, leafy place that has prospered from the proximity of the Yellow River since earliest times. Although it does not possess outstanding tourist interest, it is certainly possible to spend two or three enjoyable days visiting the city and its surroundings. Try, in particular, to reach the city's most interesting sight, the mysterious Xixia Wangling, or Mausoleums of the Western Xia, some 20km outside the city.

Orientation, arrival and accommodation

Yinchuan is another of China's vast spread-out cities, with its main bus and train stations at opposite ends, around 12km apart. The train station and the airport (which is right behind the station) are in the western part of town, known as **Xincheng** (New City), while the bus station is in the east – **Laocheng** (Old City). The new city is beginning to develop in size and does now contain a few hotels; the old city, however, bisected from east to west by its main street, **Jiefang Jie**, is undoubtedly the centre of things and is probably the best place to stay.

Yinchuan's **airport** is easily accessible, just 3km west of Xincheng. Airport buses connect with the *CAAC* office on Minzu Jie, a little north of Jiefang Jie. Long-distance **buses** from Xian, Lanzhou and Baotou via Linhe, use the Nanmen bus station in the south of Laocheng. The **train station** is located in the remote end of Xincheng, far to the west of town, serving Lanzhou in the west, and Beijing (via Inner Mongolia) in the east. Bus #1 and private minibuses run from the train station (the stop is in the left part of the station square as you come out) into Xincheng and on to the bus station in Laocheng. Most of the hotels lie in the vicinity of this route – in Xincheng you should get off at Tiedong Lu, while in Laocheng you can get off along Jiefang Jie.

Accommodation

Accommodation in Yinchuan can be amazingly tight in midsummer: Chinese tourists flock here and you may end up doing a lot of traipsing around to find a place. Fortunately, however, there are plenty of options in both Xincheng and Laocheng.

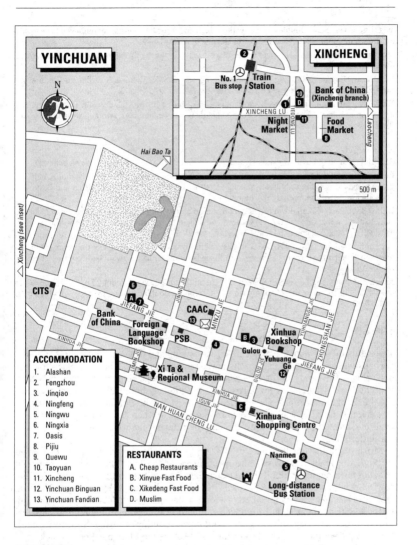

YINCHUAN

XINCHENG

ACCOMMODATION

1. Alashan
2. Fengzhou
3. Jinqiao
4. Ningfeng
5. Ningwu
6. Ningxia
7. Oasis
8. Pijiu
9. Quewu
10. Taoyuan
11. Xincheng
12. Yinchuan Binguan
13. Yinchuan Fandian

RESTAURANTS

A. Cheap Restaurants
B. Xinyue Fast Food
C. Xikedeng Fast Food
D. Muslim

LAOCHENG

Jinqiao, Jiefang Jie (☎0951/626431 ext 337). Just west of the Drum Tower. A smart place with relatively good-value doubles and three-bed dorms. Dorms ②, rooms ④.

Ningfeng, Jiefang Jie (☎0951/627162). At the junction with Minzu Jie. Brand-new and one of the most upmarket places in town. ⑦.

Ningwu, Nanmen Square. Conveniently located in the southwest of the square just outside the bus station, offering doubles with bath, as well as cheaper dorm rooms. Dorms ①, rooms ②.

Ningxia, Gongyuan Jie (☎0951/545131). A very smart place just north of Jiefang Lu. ⑤–⑦.

Oasis, Jiefang Jie (☎0951/546351). In the western part of Laocheng, just west of Limin Jie. Clean, conveniently located and surrounded by restaurants, this is the hotel where most foreign travellers stay (English spoken). Doubles with or without bath and three-bed dorms, although you have to pay for the whole room if you're on your own. Dorms ②, rooms ③–⑤.

Quewu, Nanmen Square. New and quite smart, located in the northeast of the square. Good-value doubles with bath. ③.

Yinchuan Binguan, Yuhuang Ge Jie (☎0951/622531 ext 35). Just south of Jiefang Jie, offering rather old-fashioned doubles and three-bed dorms. Dorms ②, rooms ⑤.

Yinchuan Fandian, Jiefang Jie, a short walk east of Jining Jie (☎0951/623053). Relatively cheap for the area, it has a whole range of rooms including singles, doubles with and without bath and three-bed dorms. Dorms ②, rooms ②–⑤.

XINCHENG

Alashan, Xincheng Lu just west of Tiedong Lu, (☎0951/366733). A rather run-down place. ④.

Fengzhou, north side of the train station square (turn right as you leave the station). With no English sign, this is the only hotel walkable from the station. It's extremely cheap and basic and does not always accept foreigners. Communal bathroom only. ②.

Pijiu (*Beer Hotel*). South down the first intersection east of Tiedong Lu if you are coming from the station, along a market street. A very cheap and simple place not used to foreigners, where a few words of Chinese will come in handy for getting a bed. ②.

Taoyuan, Tiedong Lu (☎0951/368470). Just north of Xincheng Lu. Probably the smartest of the hotels in Xincheng; all rooms, doubles and three-bed dorms, have private bathrooms. Dorms ②, rooms ④,

Xincheng, Xincheng Lu (☎0951/366010). Right on the corner with Tiedong Lu, this is one of the only hotels in the area that does not charge foreigners double. Amazingly cheap doubles with bath. ②.

The City

The sights of Yinchuan are all located in Laocheng and can easily be visited on foot – perhaps with the help of cycle-rickshaws – in a single day. The best place to start exploring is the centre of the city, based around the eastern part of Jiefang Jie which is dominated by a couple of well-restored, traditionally tiered Chinese towers guarding the chief intersections. Coming from the west, the first of these is **Gulou** (Drum Tower) at Gulou Jie, while the second, one block farther east, is the four-hundred-year-old **Yuhuang Ge** (Yuhuang Pavilion), at Yuhuang Jie, which also contains a tiny exhibition room.

Moving south from this part of Jiefang Jie towards the train station takes you through the main **downtown shopping area** of the city. The actual commercial heart of town centres around the massive new *Xinhua Shopping Centre* on Gulou Jie, worth seeing as an example of how fast China has developed, even in little Ningxia. Opposite is a giant, air-conditioned fast-food restaurant (see p.848) with troops of uniformed staff working round the clock mopping the floor, to the sound of classical music. From here it is about another kilometre southeast to the **Nanmen** (South Gate) at the southern end of Zhongshan Jie near the bus station, where a mock-up of the front gate of the Forbidden City in Beijing has been erected, complete with Mao Zedong's portrait and tiered seating for dignitaries. Fifteen minutes' walk southwest of Nanmen is the **Mosque**. Originally built in 1915, it was rebuilt in 1981 after years of damage and neglect during the Cultural Revolution. The mosque is in the Arabian style with green domes and minarets, which sets it apart from the purely Chinese style of flying eaves and pagoda-style minarets of many mosques farther east.

Moving to the eastern half of Laocheng you'll find a couple more sights. On Jinning Jie, a few blocks south of Jiefang Jie, is the small **Regional Museum** and **Xi Ta**, both together on the same site (daily 8am–5pm; ¥20). The most interesting section of the museum is to the right as you enter, where there are some splendidly preserved Han

YINCHUAN AND AROUND

Yinchuan	银川	yínchuān

ACCOMMODATION

Alashan	阿拉善饭店	ālāshàn fàndiàn
Fengzhou	风洲招待所	fēngzhōu zhāodàisuǒ
Jinqiao	金桥宾馆	jīnqiáo bīnguǎn
Ningfeng	宁丰宾馆	níngfēng bīnguǎn
Ningwu	宁武饭店	níngwǔ fàndiàn
Ningxia	宁夏宾馆	níngxià bīnguǎn
Oasis	绿洲饭店	lǜzhōu fàndiàn
Pijiu	啤酒饭店	píjiǔ fàndiàn
Quewu	雀舞宾馆	quèwǔ bīnguǎn
Taoyuan	桃园宾馆	táoyuán bīnguǎn
Yinchuan Binguan	银川宾馆	yínchuān bīnguǎn
Yinchuan Fandian	银川饭店	yínchuān fàndiàn
Xincheng	新城饭店	xīnchéng fàndiàn

THE CITY

Gulou	鼓楼	gǔlóu
Hai Bao Ta	海宝塔	hǎibǎo tǎ
Laocheng	老城	lǎochéng
Nanmen	南门	nánmén
Regional Museum	宁夏博物馆	níngxià bówùguǎn
Xi Ta	西塔	xītǎ
Xincheng	新城	xīnchéng
Xinhua Shopping Centre	新华购物中心	xīnhuágòuwù zhōngxīn
Yuhuang Ge	玉皇阁	yùhuáng gé

RESTAURANTS

Xikedeng Fast Food	喜可登快餐厅	xǐkědēng kuàicāntīng
Xinyue Fast Food	新月快餐厅	xīnyuè kuàicāntīng

AROUND YINCHUAN

108 Dagobas	一百零八塔	yìbǎilíngbā tǎ
Baisikou Shuang Ta	拜寺口双塔	bàisìkǒu shuāngtǎ
Gunzhong Pass	滚钟口	gǔnzhōng kǒu
Helan Shan	贺兰山	hèlán shān
Qingtongxia	青铜峡	qīngtóngxiá
Sha Hu	沙湖	shāhú
Xixia Wangling	西夏王陵	xīxià wánglíng
Zhenbeibu	镇北堡	zhènběibǔ

relics, including ancient Chinese characters engraved on stone tablets, figurines and glazed pots. There are also some attractive coloured figures, some on horseback, from the Western Zhou, though perhaps the most interesting item is a bronze drinking vessel of Graeco-Roman origins, imported along the Silk-Road two thousand years ago and recently discovered in Ningxia. Out in the grounds of the museum once again, you'll see the Xi Ta, a classic Chinese pagoda and a place of worship for Buddhists, which was built during the time of the Western Xia, around 1050. You can climb the 65-metre tower right to the top for excellent views.

Look north up Jinning Jie from Jiefang Jie and you'll see another tower peering up from the horizon in the distance directly ahead – this is the 1500-year-old **Hai Bao Ta**, otherwise known as the North Pagoda. Brick-built, 54 metres high and of an unusual, angular shape, with protruding ledges and niches at every level, the Hai Bao Pagoda is architecturally by far the most interesting structure in Yinchuan and well worth a visit. Walking there from Jiefang Jie takes forty minutes; otherwise you can take a cycle-rickshaw.

Eating and drinking

In Xincheng, there's a small **night market** that sets up on the south side of the intersection between Xincheng Jie and Tiedong Jie (near the hotels), where you can get spicy grilled lamb kebabs and bowls of yogurt. Walking east from this intersection, and taking the first right, takes you into a larger market street where you can buy food during the day and night. Otherwise, try the Muslim restaurant next door to the *Taoyuan Hotel* on Tiedong Lu. You can get standard Chinese fare here (though there is no English menu).

Rather better eating takes place in Laocheng. Just north of Nanmen, and to the west along Liqun Jie, is a good **outdoor eating area**. Round the corner, on Gulou Lu, the giant, air-conditioned **fast-food Muslim restaurant**, the *Xikedeng Fast Food*, is worth a visit for the cleanliness and the classical music. As well as Chinese food, it offers cakes, coffee, even hamburgers and fries. The food is not brilliant, but at least there's a good range and it's easy to order – just point. A filling dinner won't cost more than ¥20. Inside the air-conditioned *Xinhua Shopping Centre* opposite, there's an area of tables and chairs where you can sit and sip a Coke.

On Jiefang Jie you'll find restaurants in all the hotels and quite a few more besides. One excellent example is the *Xinyue Fast Food*, serving delicacies in a very urbane atmosphere right next door to the *Jinqiao Hotel* just east of the drum tower. Still on Jiefang Jie, though much farther east, there are lots of small Hui restaurants, immediately to the east of the *Oasis Hotel,* serving big bowls of noodles and cheap snacks.

Listings

Airline *CAAC*, Minzu Jie (Mon–Sat, 8am–noon & 2.30–6pm; ☎0951/622063).

Banks and exchange The main *Bank of China* building is in the western part of Laocheng, on Jiefang Jie (Mon–Sat 9am–noon & 2.30–6.30pm). There is also a branch in Xincheng, on Xincheng Lu a few hundred metres east of Tiedong Lu.

Bike rental The *Oasis Hotel* has a few bicycles for rent.

Bookshops There are a couple of stores where you can sometimes pick up English-language novels as well as local maps. The *Foreign Language Bookstore* is at the corner of Jiefang Jie and Jining Jie; the *Xinhua Bookstore* is more conveniently central, between the Drum Tower and Yuhuang Pavilion on Jiefang Jie.

Post office The main post office is at the junction of Jiefang and Minzu Jie, and long-distance calls can be made from here too.

Trains Buying outward-bound tickets can be done directly from the station, but you are unlikely to get more than a hard seat. If you want a sleeper, your hotel will almost certainly be able to arrange it for you, with around ¥30 commission, as long as you give at least 36 hours' notice. Otherwise try a travel agent.

Travel agents The *China Travel Service of Ningxia* (☎0951/544485) is located at 150 Jiefang Jie, at Ximen in the western end of Laocheng. *Ningxia CITS* (☎0951/543720) is also here at the same address. Enquire at these for tours of areas outside the city.

Around Yinchuan

Outside the city, there are a few interesting spots that can comfortably be visited as day trips from Yinchuan. The best of these are the **Xixia Wangling** (Mausoleums of the Western Xia) about 20km west of the new city. Dotted around on the plain at the foot of the eastern slopes of the Helan Shan, these giant earth tumuli stand as monuments to the kings of the Western Xia, whose kingdom was based at Yinchuan from 1038 to 1227 and saw the reign of twelve kings. Today the site is spectacular and atmospheric, with towering piles of brown earth, slowly and silently disintegrating, punctuating the view for miles around. The cheapest way to reach the site is to take **bus** #17 which goes right through both Laocheng and Xincheng. Ride to the end stop, and take a taxi or motor-rickshaw for the last 10km – a return trip from the bus stop to the mausoleums should cost ¥30–50.

The **Helan Shan** also have other sites of interest. The **Gunzhong Pass**, about 25km west of Xincheng, is a pleasant summer-resort area, with attractive, historic buildings and plenty of opportunities for hiking around the hills and admiring the views. Six or seven kilometres north of here are the **Baisikou Shuang Ta**, a couple of twelve-metre-high pagodas guarding another pass, a few more kilometres to the east of which is the village of **Zhenbeibu**, where the film *Red Sorghum*, directed by Zhang Yimou, was shot. The film depicts village life in northwest China during the period leading up to World War II – in part a rural idyll, in part a brute struggle to survive. The scenes of dry, dusty hillsides alternating with the lush fields of sorghum are a fair record of how Ningxia still looks today. A tour of these three places in the Helan Mountains costs around ¥180–200 in a rented car or small minivan which you can pick up in the street, or rent from a travel agent (see "Listings" above).

Farther away from town, about 57km north of Yinchuan, is the beautiful **Sha Hu** (Sand Lake). This is a developing summer resort par excellence, with swimming, sand-dunes, rafting and beautiful scenery. As yet few Western tourists have visited this place, though it is an easy ninety-minute minibus ride from Nanmen; accommodation is available at Sha Hu.

Finally, about 80km south of Yinchuan, are the **108 Dagobas**. These dagobas – Buddhist stupas of the type found in Tibetan monasteries – stand in a strange triangular pattern on a slope on the west bank of the Yellow River in Qingtongxia County. The white, bell-shaped dagobas are arranged in twelve rows, tapering from nineteen in the bottom row to a single one at the top. They are thought to have been put there in the fourteenth century during the Yuan dynasty, though their exact meaning is not known. To visit the dagobas, catch the 7.30am slow train to Qingtongxia from Yinchuan; it takes a couple of hours. From Qingtongxia you can catch a motor-rickshaw to the dagobas for about ¥30, or hike. Check the time of the one returning train from Qingtongxia to Yinchuan that passes through in early evening.

Zhongwei and Shapotou

A small country town, **ZHONGWEI** is 160km and a few hours by bus to the southeast of Yinchuan near the Yellow River. Historically, the old, walled city of Zhongwei was said to have had no north gate – simply because there was nothing more to the north of here. The city is still in a potentially awkward location, between the fickle **Yellow River** to the south and the sandy Tenger Desert to the north, but today Zhongwei is surrounded by a rich belt of irrigated fields and the desert is kept at bay through reafforestation projects. The river outside the town, at **Shapotou**, is a splendid sight and should definitely be visited if you are in the area.

Zhongwei is based around a simple crossroads, with a traditional Gulou (Drum Tower) at the centre. It's small enough to walk everywhere, although there are cycle-

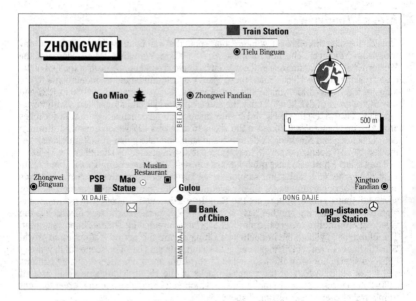

rickshaws to ferry you around. The town has one intriguing sight, the **Gao Miao** (daily 8am–6pm; ¥3), a quite extraordinary temple catering for any number of different religions, including Buddhism, Confucianism, Taoism and even Christianity. Originally built in the early fifteenth century, and rebuilt many times, the temple is now a magnificent jumble of buildings and styles. From the front entrance you can see dragon heads, columns, stairways and rooftops spiralling up in all directions; altogether there are over 250 temple rooms, towers and pavilions. Inside, you need a pretty expert eye to distinguish the saints of the various religions – they all look very much alike. To reach the Gao Miao, walk a few minutes north from the crossroads, and take a left turn down a small lane opposite the *Zhongwei Fandian*.

Practicalities

Zhongwei is on the main Lanzhou–Beijing (via Inner Mongolia) rail line and all trains stop here. Branch lines also serve Wuwei in Gansu Province and Baoji in Shaanxi Province. Zhongwei's **train station** is just off the north arm of the crossroads and the **bus station** is on the east road, with connections to Guyuan farther south and Wuwei in Gansu Province. Buses to and from Yinchuan run frequently, but stop at around 3pm.

If you're arriving in Zhongwei by train, you'll find **accommodation** right outside the station at the *Tielu Binguan* (*Railway Hotel*; ②). It's a nice, clean and friendly place, offering double rooms with bath. From the train station, it's a short walk into town – turn right as you exit the station, and then take the first left on to Bei Dajie into the centre. Along here, you'll pass the pleasant *Zhongwei Fandian* (②) on the left, more or less opposite the entrance to the Gao Miao. The most upmarket hotel in town is the *Zhongwei Binguan* (☎0953/712941; ③), ten minutes' walk west from the centre along the Xi Dajie. East from the centre, on Dong Dajie near the bus station, is the *Xingtuo Fandian* (dorms ①, rooms ②). It does not have a permit to take foreigners, but they will anyway – turn right as you come out of the station and walk for a couple of minutes. It's not as nice as the other budget hotels, and is slightly remote.

There are lots of cheap **noodle shops** along Bei Dajie near the Gao Miao, and opposite the *Zhongwei Fandian*. You'll also find quite a good **Muslim restaurant** almost immediately to the northwest of Gulou in the centre – dinner here with beer will cost less than ¥20 per head. For a slightly smarter ambiance (but still not expensive) try the restaurant in the *Zhongwei Hotel*.

Shapotou

Sixteen kilometres west of Zhongwei, **SHAPOTOU** is a kind of tourist resort by the banks of the Yellow River. Most people come on a day trip, but you can easily spend an enjoyable night or two here. The main pleasure of the place is in the contrast between the leafy, shady banks of the river itself, and the harsh desert that lies just beyond. There's also some dramatic sand dune scenery, and the spectacle of sandy desert actually in the process of being reclaimed: the **Shapotou Desert Research Centre** has been based here for forty years, working on ways to conquer the desert sands, and some of the fruits of their labour can be seen en route to the resort. Travelling either by bus or train between Zhongwei and Shapotou, you'll see the chequerboard grid of straw thatch implanted to hold the sands in place. Into this painfully constructed grid, trees are then planted. It's a slow process, but so far several thousand hectares have already been treated in this way, and all the trees you see along the way are the results of this work.

Arriving at the **train station**, facing the river, turn right and walk a few hundred metres along the road to the entry point to the tourist resort, marked by a couple of kiosks. Stepping through the gate (¥6), you'll find yourself on the top of a gigantic dune from where you can look down on to the research institute, surrounded by an entire plain of reclaimed greenery. Reaching the resort area from here is easy – simply slide down the dune (the reverse journey can be done by a kind of ski lift; ¥5). It's quite a charming place, with shady trees, cafés and outdoor restaurants. There are also activities such as camel-riding and, more unusually, **sheepskin rafting**. These traditional rafts comprise sewn-up sheep skins, pumped full of air like footballs with legs, and tied together. You'll see a lot of these rafts in various stages of production and maintenance.

A few minutes downstream, is the *Shapo Shanzhuang* (☎0953/781481; ③), a delightful **hotel** in a very cool and pleasant location, with gardens full of trees and vine trellises. It has nice doubles with bath and you can wake in the morning with the muffled roar of the Yellow River soothing your ears.

The journey from Zhongwei to Shapotou takes thirty to forty minutes, either by **minibus** from the bus station, or by the daily slow **train** that leaves Zhongwei at around 11.30am. This train actually originates at Yinchuan at 7.30am – so you could even come to Shapotou as a day trip from there. The return train passes through Shapotou at 5.40pm.

ZHONGWEI AND SHAPOTOU

Zhongwei	中卫	*zhōngwèi*
Gao Miao	高庙	*gāomiào*
Tielu Binguan	铁路宾馆	*tiělù bīnguǎn*
Xingtuo Fandian	兴拓饭店	*xìngtuò fàndiàn*
Zhongwei Binguan	中卫宾馆	*zhōngwèi bīnguǎn*
Zhongwei Fandian	中卫饭店	*zhōngwèi fàndiàn*
Shapotou	沙坡头	*shāpōtóu*
Desert Research Centre	沙漠研究所	*shāmò yánjiūsuǒ*
Shapo Shanzhuang	沙坡山庄	*shāpō shānzhuāng*

Southern Ningxia

Located in the remote, impoverished southern part of Ningxia, the town of **Guyuan** has seen very little tourist traffic. Only in 1995 did it finally join the rail network, with the opening of the Zhongwei–Baoji line, and it remains to be seen how much of an impact this will make. There is one point of interest in the area, the Buddhist grottoes at **Xumi Shan** – a major relic of the Silk Road, curiously marooned far to the north of the main route from Lanzhou to Xi'an. Apart from this, travellers can enjoy some lovely countryside, especially if you're coming up from Tianshui or Pingliang in Gansu Province to the south. The hills along this road have been terraced for centuries; every inch of land in the entire vast landscape is under cultivation, with terraces laddering up the slopes and flowing round every tiny hillock and gully in fantastic swirls of colour. The high pass on the border with Gansu, **Liupan Shan** (which you cross on the way to or from Tianshui) is also famous for another reason. It was a crucial point at one of the last stages of Mao Zedong's Long March to escape pursuing Guomindang forces in the 1930s. A commemorative stone marks the spot.

Guyuan

GUYUAN is a useful place to base yourself for a visit to the Xumi Shan Grottoes, but itself is of no special interest – in fact tourists are so rare here that you are likely to be mobbed wherever you go. Although trains now pass through Guyuan on their way between Zhongwei and Baoji in Shaanxi Province, the **train station** is inconveniently located several kilometres from town. It's easier to rely on long-distance **buses**: to the east, buses connect Guyuan with Xi'an and Luoyang; west, there are buses from Lanzhou, Tianshui and Pingliang in Gansu. The great Taoist temple Kongtang Shan (see p.858) at Pingliang is only two hours from Guyuan, another possible day trip. There are also frequent connections to Zhongwei and Yinchuan.

Accommodation is available at the *Jiaotong Fandian* (*Traffic Hotel*; ③), which is actually built into the front of the bus station. It's an excellent place, with nice, spacious double rooms and, depending on your bargaining skills, you may be able to get a room for half the official foreigners' price. The only snag is the bus station bell that rings loudly to announce every departure from around 6am. Turning right out of the bus station, a couple of minutes' walk brings you to the very primitive *Yongxiang Fandian* (dorms ①, rooms ②).

The **restaurant** of the *Jiaotong Fandian* – just round the corner from the hotel down a side street – is pleasant enough. Otherwise, the street in front of the bus station becomes quite a lively **night market** in the evening, with kebabs, noodles, and *hundun* soup all available. There's some excellent fruit including melons and peaches here in summer too.

SOUTHERN NINGXIA		
Liupan Shan	六盘山	*liùpánshān*
Sanying	三营	*sānyíng*
Xumi Shan	须弥山	*xūmíshān*
Guyuan	固原	*gùyuán*
Jiaotong Fandian	交通饭店	*jiāotōng fàndiàn*
Yongxiang Fandian	永祥饭店	*yǒngxiáng fàndiàn*

Guyuan's **post office** is a short walk from the bus station: turn right out of the station and continue past the *Yongxiang Fandian* to the first intersection, then turn right. Continue walking and it's on the right just past the traffic circle. For the **Bank of China**, walk left from the bus station for a few minutes, and you'll see it on the right.

The Xumi Shan Grottoes

The **Xumi Shan Grottoes** (daily; ¥20) are located approximately 50km north of Guyuan and 350km south of Yinchuan. Over one hundred caves have been carved out from the cliff faces on five adjoining hillsides here, and a large number of statues survive, primarily from the Northern Wei, Sui and Tang dynasties. As is usually the case with Buddhist cave sites, the natural backdrop is beautiful and secluded; at Xumi Shan, the grottoes occupy a huge site of rusty red sandstone cliffs and shining green tree-covered slopes commanding panoramic views. The site takes at least two hours to walk all round.

After entering the cliffs area, bear left first for cave no. 5 and the **Dafo Lou**, a statue of a giant twenty-metre-high Maitreya Buddha facing due east. Originally this Buddha used to be inside a protective wall, but the wall has long since fallen away. Head back to the entrance again and you'll see the five hillocks lined up along an approximate east–west axis, each with one key sight and a cluster of caves. After the Dafo Lou, the second major sight you come to is **Zisun Gong** (Descendants' Palace), followed by **Yuanguang Si**, a modern temple. From here you have to cross a bridge and bear left, to reach **Xiangguo Si**, centred around the magnificent cave no. 51 with its five-metre high Buddhas all seated around a central pillar. Returning to the bridge, walk underneath it, and up the dry river bed towards the cliff, to reach **Taohua Dong** (Peach Blossom Cave).

The caves make an enjoyable and easy day trip from Guyuan. At the grottoes' car park, there's a kiosk where you can buy **drinks and snacks**. There's also a basic **hotel** in the unlikely event that you might need to stay the night. The cheapest way to reach Xumi Shan is first to take a public **bus** (or train) to the small town of **SANYING**. Frequent buses and minibuses (hourly; ¥3) run back and forth between the Guyuan bus station and Sanying all day until early evening. It's also possible to stay in Sanying if you wish, at the very respectable, new and cheap *Dianli Fandian* (③). From Sanying to the caves, you'll have to rent a motor-rickshaw, which takes about thirty minutes. For a return trip to the caves (and at least a two-hour wait while you look around), you should pay about ¥30.

On the way to the caves from Sanying, you'll be driving through one of the remotest corners of rural China. At the height of summer, you can see the golden wheat being cut by hand, then spread out over the road to dry before being tossed to separate the chaff.

GANSU

Gansu may be wild and remote by Chinese standards, but it's a province of enormous historical interest. The **Mogao Caves** at **Dunhuang** in the far west house the finest examples of Buddhist art in all China, and further Silk Road sights are scattered right along the length of the province, ranging from the country's largest reclining Buddha at **Zhangye** to the stunning Buddhist caves at **Bingling Si** and **Maiji Shan**. The Great Wall, snaking its way west, comes to a symbolic end at the great Ming fortress at **Jiayuguan**, and, in the south of the province, right on the edge of the Tibetan plateau, is the fascinating Labrang Monastery at the Tibetan town of **Xiahe**.

Traditionally, the Chinese have regarded this province as marking the outer limit of China. During the Han dynasty (206 BC–220 AD), the first serious effort was made to expand into the western deserts, primarily as a means to ensure control over the Silk

Road trade. Prefectures were established and, although Gansu did not officially become a Chinese province until the Mongolian Yuan dynasty (1279–1368), it is unquestionably a part of the Chinese heartland. At various stages over the last two thousand years in fact, Chinese control has extended well beyond here into Xinjiang. Nevertheless, right into the last century, the primarily Muslim inhabitants of this province were considered little better than the "barbarian" Uigurs of Xinjiang by central government; the great Muslim revolt of that period, and its participants, were ruthlessly destroyed.

Gansu's geography is remarkable, too – from the great **Yellow River**, dense with silt, surging through the city of **Lanzhou**, to the mountains and deserts of the **Hexi Corridor**, the thousand-kilometre route between mountain ranges that narrows at times to as little as 15km wide. It's the Hexi Corridor that accounts for the curious elongated shape of the province: the Silk Road caravans came down here, the Great Wall was built through here, and today's trains chug through here as well, along the only rail line in western China and the only link through Central Asia between China and the West.

A harsh and barren land, subject to frequent droughts, Gansu has always been a better place for travelling through rather than settling down in. The towns along the Hexi Corridor are mere dots of life in the desert, sustained by irrigation using water from the mountains. Given that agriculture is a barely sustainable activity here, the central government has tried to import a certain amount of industry into the province, particularly in the east. The exploitation of mineral deposits, including oil and coal, has made a tentative beginning. But still the population is relatively small, comprising just twenty million, who continue to display an extraordinary ethnic mix, with Hui, Kazakhs, Mongols and Tibetans all featuring prominently.

Eastern Gansu

West of the border with Shaanxi, the first significant Silk Road city is **Tianshui**, with the spectacular **Maiji Shan** complex just a few kilometres to the southeast. Maiji Shan – literally "Wheatstack Mountain", a name derived from its shape – is the fourth largest Buddhist cave complex in China, after Dunhuang, Datong and Luoyang. Set in stunning wooded hill scenery, the caves are well worth a visit. Tianshui, itself of limited interest to tourists, is the nearest transport hub to the caves, and you will probably need to spend at least one night here. A little way to the west of Tianshui, towards Lanzhou, are some more fascinating Silk Road relics, in and around the towns of **Gangu** and **Wushan**.

Tianshui

TIANSHUI is an enormous industrial city, with two distinct centres, known as **Qincheng** (west side) and **Beidao** (east side), situated some 20km apart. Its main function for tourists is as a base for visiting Maiji Shan (see p.856), though Qincheng also offers a few sights. Whether you choose to stay in Beidao or Qincheng will probably be determined by whether you arrive at the Beidao train station or the Qincheng bus station. If your only interest is a trip to Maiji Shan and back, you should stay in Beidao, from where all the Maiji Shan minibuses depart.

In Qincheng, head west from the main square (at the west end of Minzhu Lu) along Jiefang Lu and you'll reach almost immediately an area of crumbling, traditional architecture with low, upward sweeping roof eaves and heavy tiles now gathering moss. Tiny alleyways lead off in all directions. About fifteen minutes' walk along Jiefang Lu is the Ming-dynasty **Fuxi Miao** which commemorates Fuxi, one of the legendary ancestors of the Chinese people – there is a statue of him in the main hall, clad in leaves. The temple is notable for its beautiful cypress trees; as you enter, you pass a thousand-year-old Chinese scholar tree on the right. Another interesting temple complex, **Yuquan Si**, in the western part of town is in **Yuquanguan Park**, up above Renmin Xi Lu. This is a seven-hundred-year-old active Taoist temple, on a hill about ten minutes' walk northwest of the main square. The temple is surrounded by attractive cypress trees and gives good views over the old city.

Practicalities

All trains stop at the **train station** in Beidao. **Buses**, including services to and from Lanzhou, Linxia, Pingliang and Guyuan (in Ningxia), usually use the long-distance **bus station** in Qincheng. **City transport** between the two centres is swift and efficient, with minibuses between the two stations running 24 hours a day – the run takes about thirty minutes and costs ¥2.5.

Accommodation in **Beidao** is provided by the *Zhengfu Zhaodaisuo* (②) right opposite the train station – not the salubrious-looking place to the right (which doesn't take foreigners), but a dingy place with no English sign to the left. You go through a garage-like entrance and the reception is on the right. There is one other hotel in this area accepting foreigners, the *Longlin Hotel* (☎0938/235594; ③) with comfortable doubles. To reach it, walk due south from the train station, crossing the Wei River and continuing for about twenty-five minutes until you hit a major crossroads – the hotel is right on the junction. Qincheng–Beidao minibuses (or motor-rickshaws) can also drop you here. Considering that Maiji Shan minibuses pass this junction as well, it's by no means a bad location.

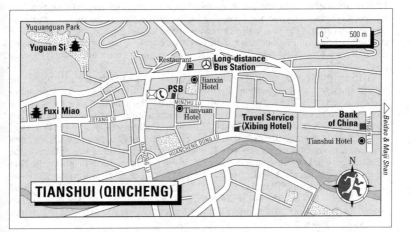

Qincheng has more options. Five minutes' walk west of the bus station and across the road is the *Jianxin* (☎0938/212685; ②), a very cheap and friendly place, with a good restaurant right opposite. Tianshui's most upmarket hotel is also in Qincheng, the *Tianshui* (☎0938/214542; ⑥). From the bus station, walk east, then take the first turning south (as you come out, go left, then right) which will bring you to the main east–west road. From here take bus #1, or any minibus, east and get off at Yingbin Lu. You can also get here on bus #1, or minibuses from Beidao. Another, better-value, place in Qincheng is the smart, new *Tianyuan* (③), on Minzhu Lu. From the bus station, walk west a little way, then take the first lane south which leads after a few minutes to Minzhu Lu. The hotel is just to the west.

The *Bank of China* head office, next to the *Tianshui Hotel*, is closed on Sundays. To make long-distance calls, use the main **post office** on Minzhu Lu where calls still have to be placed through the operator. One useful **travel agent** worth trying in Qincheng, the *China Travel Service of Tianshui* (☎0938/213621), is in the *Xibing Hotel* on Huancheng Dong Lu, facing a small river. There's a very friendly member of staff here with excellent English, which she is delighted to have the chance to practise – she may even be able to act as your guide to the Maiji Shan Caves, for a very reasonable fee (around ¥100).

Maiji Shan

The trip to the Buddhist caves on the mountain of **MAIJI SHAN** is the highlight of eastern Gansu. As is often the case with the Buddhist cave sites in northwest China, the natural setting itself is highly spectacular: although the whole area is very hilly, the sheer, rocky cliffs of Maiji Shan, rising out of the forest, make this one hill a complete anomaly. The centrepiece of the statuary, the giant **sixteen-metre-high Buddha** (complete with birds nesting in its nostril) is visible from far away, hanging high up on the rock in conjunction with two smaller figures. The combination of rickety walkways on the cliff face with the beautiful wooded, mountain scenery opposite makes this an extremely charming site.

The cliffs were apparently split apart by an earthquake in the eighth century and there are in total 194 surviving **caves** on the eastern and western sections, dating from the northern Wei right through to the Qing. The western cliff caves are particularly well preserved, and date mainly from the fourth to the sixth century AD; **cave 133** is considered to be the finest, containing sculptures and engraved stones. You are free to explore on your own, climbing higher and higher up the narrow stairways on the sheer face of the mountain. The caves are all locked though, and you often find yourself peering into half-lit caverns through wire grilles, but for the non-specialist the views are probably adequate – at least some of the art work and statuary shows up clearly.

Visiting the caves from Tianshui, Beidao-side, is straightforward. From the square outside the train station there are frequent **minibuses** – the ride takes 45–60min and costs ¥6 each way, though they usually try to charge foreigners double (according to local maps, bus #5 also goes to the caves from Qincheng; in fact this bus route is now defunct). When you reach Maiji Shan (daily; 8am–6pm), there is a fee of ¥6 per person to enter the mountain area. The minibuses continue for another few hundred metres, after which you have to walk up the hill past the souvenir touts to the ticket office; a ticket without guide costs ¥25. If you require a **guide** to unlock the cave doors and explain the art work, you may be able to find an English-speaker at the site itself, if you ask around. Another option is to arrange this in advance with the *China Travel Service of Tianshui* in the *Xibing Hotel* before you set out (see above). Just before the ticket office, and across a gully, is a cheap but very basic **hotel** (①), which accepts foreigners.

Gangu, Wushan and Pingliang

West of Tianshui, on the road and rail line to Lanzhou, are a couple of little-known but fascinating reminders of the Silk Road era. The attraction at **GANGU**, 65km west of Tianshui, is **Daxiang Shan** (Giant Statue Mountain). It gets its name from the giant statue of a moustached Sakyamuni Buddha which was carved out of the mountain cliff during the Tang dynasty. The statue is over 23 metres tall, and can be reached on foot by a path leading up from the town in about an hour.

From Wushan, 45km farther west from Gangu, you can visit the **Shuilian Dong** (Water Curtain Grottoes), which contain a number of fascinating relics, including the **Lashao Temple** as well as a Thousand Buddha Cave site. This is an extraordinary area, all the more so for being so inaccessible. Digging at the grottoes began during the Sixteen States period (304–439 AD) and continued over the dynasties. The Lashao Temple was built during the Northern Wei (386–534). There is a thirty-metre-high statue of Sakyamuni on the mountain cliff, his feet surrounded by various wild animals including lions and elephants. The grottoes, about 30km north of Wushan, can only be reached along a dried-up river bed – there is as yet no proper road.

All **buses** – and all **trains** except for express (*tekuai*) trains – running between Tianshui and Lanzhou stop at both Gangu and Wushan. It's also possible to visit Gangu as a day trip from Tianshui; minibuses run from the Qincheng bus station in the morning. If you want to visit both Gangu and the grottoes in one day from Tianshui you need to rent a vehicle, which, to handle the rough road from Wushan, needs to be something bigger than a taxi – more like a small minibus. It's a long, tiring day and will cost in the region of ¥500. It might be simpler to stay a night at either Wushan or Gangu, perhaps as a stopover on the way between Tianshui and Lanzhou. Note that access to the Water Curtain Grottoes is dependent on the weather – you won't be able to use the river bed if it has been wet recently.

EASTERN GANSU		
Tianshui	天水	*tiānshuǐ*
Beidao	北道	*běidào*
Fuxi Miao	伏羲庙	*fúxīmiào*
Qincheng	秦城	*qínchéng*
Yuquanguan Park	玉泉观公园	*yùquánguān gōngyuán*
Yuquan Si	玉泉寺	*yùquán sì*
ACCOMMODATION		
Jianxin	建心饭店	*jiànxīn fàndiàn*
Longlin	陇林饭店	*lónglín fàndiàn*
Tianshui	天水宾馆	*tiānshuǐ bīnguǎn*
Tianyuan	天元宾馆	*tiānyuán bīnguǎn*
Zhengfu	政府招待所	*zhèngfǔ zhāodàisuǒ*
Gangu	甘谷	*gāngǔ*
Daxiang Shan	大象山	*dàxiàng shān*
Maiji Shan	麦积山	*màijī shān*
Pingliang	平凉	*píngliáng*
Wushan	武山	*wǔshān*
Lashao Temple	拉稍寺	*lāshāo sì*
Shuilian Dong	水帘洞	*shuǐlián dòng*

Pingliang

About 200km northeast of Tianshui, an eight-hour bus ride, lies the city of **PINGLIANG**. This area is a mountainous and very beautiful part of Gansu Province near to the border with Ningxia, and little known to foreigners. The chief attraction here is **Kongtang Shan**, about 15km north of the city, where a Taoist monastery is perched precariously on the tops of cliffs. It is regarded as the most important Taoist mountain throughout China. Pingliang is only two hours by bus from Guyuan in southern Ningxia (see p.852) and either city can be visited as a day trip from the other.

Lanzhou and around

On the map, **Lanzhou** appears to lie very much in the middle of China – though this is a misleading impression. Culturally and politically it remains remote from the great cities of eastern China, despite being both the provincial capital and the largest industrial centre in the Northwest. Squeezed 1600 metres up into a narrow valley along the mighty Yellow River, it stretches out pencil-thin for nearly 30km. At the head of the Hexi Corridor, it was a vital stronghold along the Silk Road and was the principal crossing point of the river. For centuries it has been a transportation hub, first for caravans, then shallow boats and now rail lines. Not until the Communist era, however, did it become a large population centre as well, in response to the city's burgeoning industry. Now there are nearly three million people in Lanzhou, the vast majority of them Han Chinese. For travellers coming into China from the west this will be the first really major Chinese city you encounter.

Lanzhou is a pleasant place with an excellent **museum**, interesting food markets and busy downtown **shopping** areas. The Yellow River, running thick and chocolaty through the city against a backdrop of hills dim with mist and air pollution, is one of China's classic sights, while the major historical and artistic attraction lies just beyond the city at the **Bingling Si** Buddhist Caves. Nearly all travellers on their way to or from Xinjiang will end up stopping in Lanzhou; it's worth staying at least a couple of days.

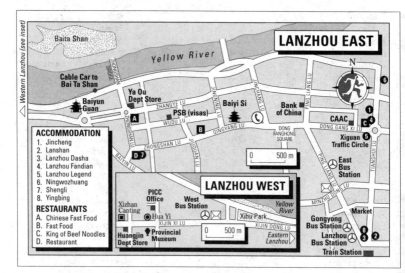

ACCOMMODATION
1. Jincheng
2. Lanshan
3. Lanzhou Dasha
4. Lanzhou Fandian
5. Lanzhou Legend
6. Ningwozhuang
7. Shengli
8. Yingbing

RESTAURANTS
A. Chinese Fast Food
B. Fast Food
C. King of Beef Noodles
D. Restaurant

Orientation, arrival and accommodation

The city is a hugely elongated sprawl from east to west. The modern city centre and most of the hotels and shops are in the east, focused on the Xiguan Traffic Circle and Dongfanghong Square; the oldest part of the town and the most interesting for walking, eating and shopping is roughly in the middle; and the museum and popular *Huaiyi Hotel* are in the west.

Lanzhou's **airport** lies about 70km to the north of the city, at least a two-hour journey, with connections to all major Chinese cities and Dunhuang and Jiayuguan within Gansu Province. The airport buses terminate conveniently in the eastern part of the city, outside the *CAAC* office on Donggang Xi Lu, a few minutes west of the *Lanzhou Hotel*.

Being the main rail hub of northwest China, Lanzhou is an easy place to travel into or out of by train, with direct connections to or from every part of China. Arriving by train, your point of arrival will almost certainly be the main **train station** in the far southeast of the city. There are a number of hotel options in the immediate vicinity of the station, though if you are heading farther afield, the Xiguan Traffic Circle is about 2km due north of here (buses #7, #10 and #34) while western Lanzhou, over a dozen kilometres away, can be reached on buses #1 and #31.

There are several **bus stations** in eastern Lanzhou and one in western Lanzhou. If you are coming on the bus from **Xiahe** you will certainly arrive at the **West bus station** in the western part of town, about 15km from the train station and close to the *Huayi Hotel*. City buses #1 and #31 run east through town from here. Buses from the Hexi Corridor will at the very least run through western Lanzhou; you can request a stop here if you wish. Coming from anywhere else, it is difficult to predict where you will arrive, though the chances are that travellers arriving from the east (Tianshui, Yinchuan, Xi'an) will end up somewhere on Pingliang Lu, within walking distance of the train station.

Accommodation

Most accommodation in Lanzhou is in the vicinity of the train station or in the eastern half of the city, though there is one good option, the *Huaiyi*, in the west.

Huaiyi, Xijin Xi Lu (☎0931/2333051). Formerly the *Friendship Hotel*, this is one of the most pleasant hotels in Lanzhou for budget travellers. Clean, quiet and with 24-hour hot water, it's located in the western part of the city, opposite the museum and just twenty minutes' walk from the West bus station – convenient for Xiahe. If you're arriving by bus from any point in western Gansu (Zhangye or Wuwei) you'll pass in front of the hotel and can ask the driver to let you off. From the train station take bus #1 or trolleybus #31. Foreigners check in at the block at the back of the hotel, a couple of hundred metres behind the front building. There are doubles with good private bathrooms and triple-bed dorms on offer. If you arrive early and the dorms are all full, it's worth waiting around for an hour or two for people to check out. Dorms ②, rooms ⑤.

Jincheng, Tianshui Lu (☎0931/8416638). A very modern place, a little way north of the Xiguan Traffic Circle, 2km due north of the train station. ⑦.

Lanshan, Tianshui Lu (☎0931/8827211 ext 218). Near the station end of Tianshui Lu, the main road directly facing the station. Double rooms and three- and four-bed dorms with fifty percent discount for students. Dorms ②, rooms ③.

Lanzhou Dasha, Tianshui Lu (☎0931/8417210). As you emerge from the train station, you'll see this hotel opposite and slightly to the left. A convenient location, but not a real budget place; the three-bed dorms have their own bathrooms. Dorms ②, rooms ⑤–⑦.

Lanzhou Fandian, Donggang Xi Lu (☎0931/8416321). Right on the Xiguan Traffic Circle. From the train station take bus # 1, #7 or #10 due north for a couple of stops. It's a nice, convenient place with a range of smart doubles and also three-bed dorms. There are a number of travel agents based in this hotel. Dorms ②, rooms ⑤–⑦.

Lanzhou Legend, Panxuan Lu (☎0931/8882876). On the Xiguan Traffic Circle, just south, across the road, from the *Lanzhou Fandian*. This is the plushest hotel in town, of a fully international standard, with doubles starting at ¥780. ⑧.

Ningwozhuang, Tianshui Lu (☎0931/8416221). An older-style, rambling hotel set back from the road in large, quiet gardens, 1km north of the Xiguan Traffic Circle on the east side of Tianshui Lu. ⑦.

Shengli, Zhongshan Lu (☎0931/8465221). This lies right in between the east and west halves of the city, but is handily placed for the downtown eating areas. Note that foreigners can stay only in the east block (*dong lou*) where there are doubles and three-bed dorms. To get here, take trolleybus #31 from the train station (heading west) or from the West bus station (heading east). Dorms ②, rooms ④.

Yingbing, Tianshui Lu (☎0931/8886552). A couple of minutes due north of the train station, on the left-hand side of the road if you're walking from the station. A friendly and quite helpful place offering doubles with bath and three-bed dorms. Dorms ①, rooms ③.

The City

The best place to start a tour of Lanzhou is the main shopping district, roughly in the middle of the city, in the blocks that lie to the north and west of Zhongshan Lu (this street comes south from Zhongshan Bridge, then turns a right angle at the *Shengli Hotel* and continues east). On the one hand the whole area is timeless China with food cooking everywhere, bicycles gliding in slow motion and men with wispy beards and shuffling slippers. On the other, there's a real downtown feel to the place as well with fashion shops, Western music, fast food and smart department stores. Check out the *Ya Ou Department Store*, on the corner of Zhongshan Lu and Zhangye Lu, for the latest word on consumerism in Lanzhou. On the pavement outside here there are lines of plastic chairs where you can sit and drink iced Coke.

Immediately north of this district lies one of the great sights of Lanzhou, the **Yellow River**, already flowing thick and fast although it still has some 1500km to go before it finally reaches the sea at Qingdao. The water of the river is a rich, muddy brown colour, a legacy of the huge quantities of silt it picks up, and the fast flow of the river helps to create a wind corridor through the city, which both moderates the climate and removes some of the worst effects of the pollution. For boating on the river, try the area just west of the majestic Zhongshan Bridge (city side) – there are a few motor boats operating brief viewing trips. For a bird's-eye view, you can take a cable car from here right over the river to the **Baita Park** (White Pagoda Park; daily 7am–7pm; ¥2) on the hills of the far bank. A return ticket costs ¥15 and it's definitely worth the trip if the weather is good. The park contains a number of interesting old buildings, including a seventeen-metre-high white pagoda which dates back to the Ming dynasty (though according to legend a white pagoda was first erected here on the orders of Genghis Khan, to commemorate a Tibetan lama who had pleased him). There are excellent views over the river and the city from the park, and you can get snacks here as well.

On the city side of the river, across the road from the cable-car departure point, is a small Taoist temple, the **Baiyun Guan**. The temple is a thoroughly active institution and if you pop in you can see the monks inside with their characteristic Taoist clothes and hairstyles, performing rites.

Well to the south of here, a few hundred metres south of the terminus of bus #8 (which you can pick up anywhere on Jiuquan Lu in the centre of town) is **Wuquan Park** (daily; 8am–6pm; ¥4) and, south of this, **Lanshan Park**, in the hills that border the city. Wuquan Park is full of mainly Qing pavilions, convoluted stairways twirling up the mountainside interspersed with tea houses, art-exhibition halls and ponds. One of the oldest buildings, the **Jingang Palace**, is Ming and contains a five-metre-high bronze Buddha cast in 1370. It's a nice place to wander with the locals at weekends.

From Wuquan Park, Lanshan Park can be reached by chair lift – it's about twenty minutes to the very top.

Moving east from the central area takes you into the mainly modern part of the city which has few attractions for tourists. One possible exception, a few hundred metres east of Jiuquan Lu (just east of Jingning Lu) on the north side of Qingyang Lu, is the **Baiyi Si** and an accompanying Ming-dynasty pagoda. The temple is interesting more for the poignancy of its location than anything else. With huge construction projects looming up on all sides and a busy securities exchange right next door, the site seems to have been almost completely forgotten about.

The west of the city is an upmarket shopping and residential area strung out along Xijin Xi Lu; from the centre of town take bus #1, #6 or #31. The one sight well worth

---

LANZHOU AND AROUND

Lanzhou	兰州	*lánzhōu*
ARRIVAL		
East bus station	汽车东站	*qìchēdōngzhàn*
Gongyong bus station	公用车站	*gōngyòngchēzhàn*
Lanzhou bus station	兰州汽车站	*lánzhōuqìchēzhàn*
West bus station	汽车西站	*qìchēxīzhàn*
ACCOMMODATION		
Huayi	华宜大酒店	*huáyí dàjiǔdiàn*
Jincheng	金城宾馆	*jīnchéng bīnguǎn*
Lanshan	兰山宾馆	*lánshān bīnguǎn*
Lanzhou Dasha	兰州大厦	*lánzhōu dàshà*
Lanzhou Fandian	兰州饭店	*lánzhōu fàndiàn*
Lanzhou Legend	飞天大酒店	*fēitiān dàjiǔdiàn*
Ningwozhuang	宁卧庄宾馆	*níngwòzhuāng bīnguǎn*
Shengli	胜利宾馆	*shènglì bīnguǎn*
Yingbing	迎宾饭店	*yíngbīn fàndiàn*
THE CITY		
Baita Park	白塔公园	*báitǎ gōngyuán*
Baiyi Si	白衣寺	*báiyī sì*
Baiyun Guan	白云观	*báiyún guān*
Dongfanghong Square	东方红广场	*dōngfānghóng guǎngchǎng*
Lanshan Park	兰山公园	*lánshān gōngyuán*
Gansu Provincial Museum	甘肃省博物馆	*gānsùshěng bówùguǎn*
Wuquan Park	五泉公园	*wǔquán gōngyuán*
Yellow River	黄河	*huánghé*
Xiguan Traffic Circle	西关十字	*xīguān shízì*
AROUND LANZHOU		
Bingling Si Caves	炳灵寺千佛洞	*bǐnglíngsì qiānfódòng*
Bingling Si	炳灵寺	*bǐnglíng sì*
Liujiaxia	刘家峡	*liújiāxiá*
Liujiaxia Reservoir	刘家峡水库	*liújiāxiáshuǐkù*
Yongjing	永靖	*yǒngjìng*

visiting in this area, the **Gansu Provincial Museum** (Mon–Sat 9am–noon & 2.30–5.30pm; ¥25), is located just opposite the *Huaiyi Hotel*. One of the most interesting provincial museums in the country, this is divided between natural resources of Gansu (downstairs) and historical finds (upstairs). Apart from the four-metre-tall **mammoth**, recovered from the Yellow River basin in 1973, the natural resources display is not of enormous interest, but upstairs the display is excellent, with full English explanations. There are some remarkable **ceramics** dating from the Neolithic age as well as a huge collection of **wooden tablets and carvings** from the Han dynasty – priceless sources for studying the politics, culture and economy of the period. The fabulous nine-inch-tall bronze **Flying Horse of Wuwei**, two thousand years old and still with its accompanying procession of horses and chariots, is the highlight, however – note the stylish chariots for top officials with round seats and sunshades. The fourteen-centimetre-tall horse, depicted with one front hoof stepping on the back of a flying swallow, was discovered in a Han-dynasty tomb in Wuwei less than thirty years ago.

Eating and drinking

In the west of the city, **in the vicinity of the Huaiyi Hotel**, you'll find plenty of good food. A pleasant **night market**, full of kebabs and noodles, sets up shop on an alleyway immediately to the east of the hotel, and, about ten minutes' walk west of the hotel, is a clean restaurant called the *Xizhan Canting* specializing in excellent, cheap *baozi* (steamed dumplings); ten *baozi* will leave you full. In the hotel compound itself, in the round building at the front, the speciality is an eat-all-you-like **hotpot** for ¥38 per head – a great meal for a party. Upstairs in the same building the regular Chinese restaurant serves dinner for around ¥25 per head.

The city's best area for eating, however, is in **the streets east of the Shengli Hotel**. Around here practically every house is a restaurant, with cook-it-yourself hotpots the speciality. Next door to the *Shengli*, immediately to the west, is an immaculately clean and bright place with a lively atmosphere and delightful service. There's unfortunately no English (except for the front of the menu where it says "Caesar Rome International Food City"), but you can eat very well here for ¥30 a head. Farther down Zhongshan Lu, east of Jiuquan Lu, is a genuine **fast-food restaurant**. Hamburgers, fries and Coke are all available, as well as Chinese food in plastic trays. Order by pointing to the pictures behind the counter.

At the Xiguan Traffic Circle there's a superb **cake shop** adjacent to the *Lanzhou Legend Hotel*, selling Western delicacies such as pains au chocolat, croissants and chocolate eclairs. Another satisfying fast-food place where you can try a local speciality – beef noodles – is *King of Beef Noodles,* immediately west of the *Lanzhou Hotel*.

Towards the train station, the best place to eat is probably the **night market** on an alley that runs between Tianshui Lu and Pingliang Lu, about ten minutes south of the *Lanzhou Hotel*. Just walk up and down, sampling what you fancy; especially good are the grilled lamb, the *jianbing* (egg pancake stuffed with spicy vegetables) and the spicy hotpot cooked in small earthenware pots. Finally, Lanzhou is famous for its summer **fruit**. Don't leave without trying the melons, watermelons, peaches or grapes.

Listings

Airlines The main *CAAC* office is on Donggang Xi Lu (☎0931/8821964).

Banks and exchange The main *Bank of China* is on Pingliang Lu, a short walk north of Donggang Xi Lu.

Post and telecommunications The Post and Telecommunications Office (Mon–Sat 8am–7pm) stands at the junction of Pingliang Lu and Minzhu Dong Lu. There's also a post office at the West

---

MOVING ON FROM LANZHOU

Buying bus tickets out of the city is complicated by the fact that there are several bus stations, often serving the same cities but charging substantially different prices according to whether or not they differentiate between Chinese and locals. You will also need to show your PICC Travel Insurance Certificate when buying bus tickets in Lanzhou (see box, p.854). You can buy this in the West bus station, or direct from the PICC office on Qingyang Lu.

There is one daily bus to **Xiahe** at 7.30am, from the West bus station (an eight-hour trip). From this station there are also frequent buses to **Linxia**, as well as to **Wuwei**, **Xining** and one early-evening service to **Dunhuang** (about 24hr). Note that foreigners always pay double in this station.

In addition, there are at least three other bus stations you might use in the east of the city. Just a few minutes up Pingliang Lu from the train station, on the left side, is **Lanzhou bus station**. From the street, all you see are a couple of ticket windows. At the time of writing, foreigners could buy cheap local-price tickets here, including **Dunhuang** for ¥83, and a sleeper to **Xi'an** for about ¥100. There were also similarly cheap tickets to **Tianshui**, **Wuwei**, **Xining** and **Yinchuan**.

Don't confuse this station with another station a few minutes farther up the road, Gongyong bus station, which is full of private operators with loud-hailers, and serves all destinations to the west. Buses from here may work out more expensive, but services are more frequent. A third station, the East bus station, is another kilometre north up Pingliang Lu.

Buying train tickets out of Lanzhou can be very fatiguing. It is almost impossible to buy a hard-sleeper ticket at the station. If you queue up, you are unlikely to get anything other than a hard seat without a number - tolerable for trips of only a few hours (for example to Wuwei or Xining), but unbearable for longer journeys such as to Xi'an or Liuyuan. Either go to the station and do a deal with a tout, or approach a travel agency. They can probably get you a ticket with 36 hours' notice, at around ¥30 commission. Expect to pay around ¥260 to Liuyuan (for Dunhuang), ¥171 to Xi'an and ¥363 to Beijing or Ürümqi excluding commission.

---

bus station in the western part of the city, and you can make collect calls at the Telephone and Telegram Office on the corner of Qingyang Lu and Jinchang Lu.

PSB Visas can be extended at an office on Wudu Lu, a couple of hundred metres west of Jiuquan Lu.

Shopping Good things to buy in Lanzhou include army surplus clothes – winter coats, waistcoats, hats and boots are all locally produced, tough and cheap. They come from the local factory at 227 Yanchang Lu, north of the river, the largest such factory in China. You can even visit it if you like and buy direct from them (bus #7 from the train station).

Travel agents There are plenty of travel agencies in and behind the *Lanzhou Hotel* – the *Western Travel Service of Lanzhou Hotel* (☎0931/8416321 ext 638) is recommended. In the *Huaiyi Hotel*, try the *Gansu International Hope Travel Agency* (☎0931/2310637). *CITS* is in the small street behind the *Jincheng Hotel*. These agencies are useful for purchasing train tickets (see box above) and for arranging trips to the Bingling Si Caves.

Bingling Si Caves

The trip out from Lanzhou to the Buddhist caves of **Bingling Si** is one of the best excursions you can make in all of Gansu Province – enough in itself to merit a stay in Lanzhou. Not only does it offer a glimpse of the spectacular **Buddhist cave art** that filtered through to this region along the Silk Road, but it's a powerful introduction to the **Yellow River**.

The caves are carved into a canyon beside the **Liujiaxia Reservoir** on the Yellow River, and can be reached only by boat at certain times of the year (see below). The most convenient way to see the caves is on a pre-booked **one-day trip** from Lanzhou – the whole trip takes up to twelve hours, which includes less than two hours at the caves, but the scenery en route makes it all worthwhile.

From Lanzhou, the first stage of the expedition is a two-hour bus ride through impressively fertile loess fields to the massive **Liujiaxia hydro-electric dam**, a spectacular sight poised above the reservoir and surrounded by colourful rocky mountains. At the dam you board a waiting ferry, which takes three hours to reach the caves. From the ferry, the views are excellent: the land around is busy with fishermen and ferry-boats on the water, and peasants cultivating wheat, sunflowers and rice on the dark, steep banks. During the trip, the ferry enters a tall, hung **gorge**, where the river froths and churns; you'll see sections of the bank being whipped away into the waters. It's said that the Yellow River carries some 35 kilos of silt in every cubic metre of water – hence its constant murkiness and its name.

The ferry docks just below the Bingling Si Caves. Cut into sheer cliff, amid stunning scenery above a tributary of the river, the caves number 183 in all. They are among the earliest significant Buddhist monuments in China – started in the Western Jin and subsequently extended by the Northern Wei, the Tang, Song and Ming. Since they were spared through inaccessibility from the attentions of foreign devils in the nineteenth century and Red Guards in the twentieth, most of the cave sculpture is in good condition, and some impressive restoration work is in progress on the wall paintings. The centrepiece sculpture, approached along a dizzying network of stairs and ramps, is a huge 27-metre seated Buddha, probably carved under the Tang. The art work at Bingling Si reached its peak under the Song and Ming dynasties, and though the wall paintings of this period have been virtually washed away, there remain a considerable number of small and exquisite carvings.

Unfortunately, you'll have less than two hours to look around before the boat leaves – only enough for a cursory look. If you want a detailed guided tour, encompassing all the caves, ask about a private trip at one of the Lanzhou travel services.

Practicalities

Most travel services in Lanzhou can arrange **trips** to the caves (see "Listings", p.863), though if you are on your own you may have to hunt around to find a pre-existing group which you can tag on to. For a maximum car-load of three passengers, an all-inclusive price (car, boat, entry ticket and insurance) usually comes to ¥400–500; the *Gansu International Hope Travel Agency* in the *Huaiyi Hotel* work out their rates at ¥120 per person. There may also be larger (and therefore cheaper) group tours operating out of the *Shengli Hotel* – enquire here for details. Before booking any tour, take heed of the following: the water in the reservoir is only high enough to permit **access** between June and October. Some years, however, the caves remain out of bounds through most of the summer as well, and some tour operators have been known to take people all the way to the reservoir before "discovering" that the water level is too low – no fee refundable. Make sure your travel service gives you information about the situation at the reservoir before you book.

Alternatively, you could consider **travelling independently** to the reservoir on a public bus. Both from the West bus station, and from a special stop outside the *Shengli Hotel*, there are buses to **Yongjing**, which pass the ferry departure point (if you fail to get off at the right place, you'll have to walk back thirty minutes from the bus terminus). From the ferry departure point you can usually charter your own motorboat to the caves, which will cost around ¥500; on the way back you may end up staying the night in Yongjing, if the last public bus back to Lanzhou (around 5pm) leaves without you.

South from Lanzhou

This mountainous and verdant area to the south and southwest of Lanzhou, bordering on Qinghai to the west and Sichuan to the south, is one of enormous scenic beauty, relatively untouched by the scars of industry and overpopulation. The people who live here are not only few in number, but also display a fascinating cultural and ethnic diversity, with a very strong **Hui** and **Tibetan** presence in the towns of **Linxia** and **Xiahe** respectively. Xiahe, in particular, is a delightful place to visit, housing as it does one of the major Lamaist temples in China, and attracting monks and pilgrims from the whole Tibetan world. South of Xiahe it's possible to follow a highly adventurous **route into Sichuan Province**.

From Lanzhou to Xiahe

The road southeast from Lanzhou to Xiahe passes first by Yongjing and Liujiaxia, the jumping-off points for Bingling Si (see p.864) before traversing **Dongxiang Autonomous County**. The Dongxiang minority, numbering nearly two hundred thousand, are Muslims but with Mongol origins. These days, to outsiders at least, they are indistinguishable from the Hui Muslims except for at certain celebrations and festivals when ancient Mongol customs re-emerge. Beyond the pilgrimage centre of Linxia, 60km from Lanzhou, the climb up to Xiahe takes three or four hours (but only two coming down again). The area through which the route passes is potentially fascinating, a zone of cultural overlap between ancient communities of Islamic and Buddhist peoples. A couple of China's lesser-known minorities also live here, the **Baoan** and the **Salar**. The Baoan, who number barely eight thousand, are very similar to the Dongxiang people as they, too, are of Mongolian origins. The Salar live primarily in Xunhua County, in neighboring Qinghai Province, but some of them live here in southern Gansu. They are a Turkic-speaking people, whose origins lie, it is thought, in Samarkand in Central Asia.

Linxia

A three-hour bus journey from Lanzhou, **LINXIA** is a very **Muslim** town, dominated in particular by the Hui people. The town is, unsurprisingly, full of mosques, most of which have been restored since the depredations of the Cultural Revolution. Nearly everybody here seems to wear a white skull cap, and the women additionally wear a square-shaped veil of fine lace, green if they are unmarried and black if they are married. All the large, fancy eye-glasses that old men wear throughout this region are made in Linxia. There's nothing much to see in town; nevertheless, it's an interesting place to stroll around for a few hours if you feel like breaking your journey from Lanzhou to Xiahe.

Linxia's main street runs from north to south through town, called Tuanjie Lu in the north and Jiefang Lu in the south, with a large central square in between the two. The main mosque, the **Nanguan Mosque**, is immediately to the south of the square. Jiefang Lu terminates at a large traffic circle at its southern end. There is no train station in Linxia, though there are **two bus stations**. If you're arriving from the west (Xining or Tongren), you may be deposited at the smaller one in the far northwest of the city (known as the West bus station). In this case you'll have to catch a cycle-rickshaw into town. If you arrive at the main station (the South bus station), which is on Jiefang Nan Lu, a couple of hundred metres south of the Jiefang Lu traffic circle, you'll be able to walk to a **hotel**. The nearest is almost immediately to the north of the station, on the right as you come out – the *Shuiquan* (☎0930/214964; dorms ①, rooms ②–③). It's the cheapest place around, with doubles and three-bed dorms, but they may want to charge you double as a foreigner. A few minutes farther north from here, on the right at the first big roundabout, is the *Longlin* (③). The hotel **restaurant** is quite

SOUTH FROM LANZHOU

Dongxiang Autonomous County	东乡自治县	*dōngxiāng zìzhìxiàn*
Linxia	临夏	*línxià*
Longlin Hotel	龙林饭店	*lónglín fàndiàn*
Nanguan Mosque	南关大寺	*nánguān dàsì*
Shuiquan Hotel	水泉宾馆	*shuǐquán bīnguǎn*
South bus station	汽车南站	*qìchēnánzhàn*
West bus station	汽车西站	*qìchēxīzhàn*
Xiahe	夏河	*xiàhé*
Gongtang Pagoda	贡唐宝塔	*gòngtángbǎo tǎ*
Hongjiao Si	红交寺	*hóngjiāo sì*
Labrang Monastery	拉卜楞寺	*lābóléng sì*
Sangke Grasslands	桑科草原	*sāngkē cǎoyuán*
ACCOMMODATION		
Dasha	大厦宾馆	*dàshà bīnguǎn*
Labrang	拉卜楞宾馆	*lābǔléng bīnguǎn*
Shuijinshan Zhuang	水晶山庄宾馆	*shuǐjīnshānzhuāng bīnguǎn*
White Conch	白海螺宾馆	*báihǎiluó bīnguǎn*
Youyi	友谊宾馆	*yǒuyì bīnguǎn*
Hezuo	合作	*hézuò*
Langmusi	郎木寺	*lángmùsì*
Luqu	碌曲	*lùqǔ*

smart and worth trying. Otherwise, head for the pleasant **night market** centred around the top end of Jiefang Nan Lu (the next roundabout north of the *Longlin Hotel*). You can stuff yourself here on heavy round breads (*bing*) flavoured with curry powder; roast chickens are also available, as well as noodles and soups. On terraces overlooking the central square on the south side are a couple of very pleasant tea houses where you can sit out and enjoy the night air. You can also eat here.

Departing from the main bus station at Linxia, there are frequent buses to Lanzhou and several daily to Xiahe. Buses to Lanzhou all go through Liujiaxia, the stopoff point for Bingling Si. There are also buses to Xining, Tianshui and Wuwei (via Lanzhou). You'll need to show your PICC insurance certificate when buying tickets in Linxia – the **PICC office** is north of the main bus station, beyond the central square – about twenty minutes' walk or one or two yuan in a cycle-rickshaw. The **Bank of China** lies a few minutes north of the *Longlin Hotel*, on the right.

Xiahe and around

A tiny, rural town tucked away three thousand metres up in the remote hills of southern Gansu, right on the edge of the Tibetan plateau, **XIAHE** is an absolutely delightful place to stay a few days. As well as offering glimpses into the life of the **Tibetan people** – living and working in one of the most picturesque Tibetan monasteries you are likely to see in China – Xiahe also offers visitors the rare

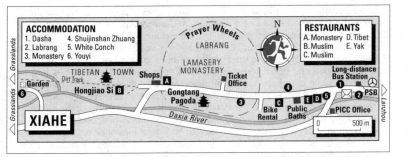

chance to spend some time in open countryside, sited as it is in a sunny, fresh valley surrounded by green hills.

Xiahe is the most important Tibetan monastery town outside Tibet itself, and the **Labrang Monastery** (Labuleng Si) is one of the six major centres of the Gelugpa, or Yellow Hat Sect (of the others, four are in Tibet and one, Ta'er Si, is in Qinghai Province just outside Xining). Tibetans from Tibet itself come here on pilgrimage dressed in traditional costume, and the constant flow of monks in bright purple, yellow and red, alongside semi-nomadic herdsmen wrapped in sheepskins and Hui Muslims with skull caps and wispy beards, makes for an endlessly fascinating scene.

The town is essentially built along a single street that stretches 3–4km along the north bank of the Daxia River, from the bus station in the east, through the Labrang Monastery in the middle, to the old Tibetan town and finally the *Labrang Hotel* in the west. The **eastern end of town,** where the bus station is, is predominantly Hui- and Han-populated. It's also the commercial and administrative part of town, with a couple of banks, a post office and plenty of shops and markets. The shops round here make interesting browsing, with lots of Tibetan religious objects on sale, such as hand-printed sutras, little prayer wheels, bells and jewellery. There's also lots of riding equipment – saddles and bridles – for the nomads who come into town off the nearby grasslands.

Beyond the monastery, at the **western end of town**, is the local Tibetan area. West of the bridge that carries all motorized traffic to the south side of the river, the road becomes a bumpy dirt track with homes built of mud and wood, and goats and cows ambling around. There is one more religious building up here, the **Hongjiao Si**, or Temple of the Red Hat Sect. It's on the right as you walk west from town. Monks of the Red Hat sect are much fewer and live in the shadow of their rich and numerous brethren from the Yellow Hat Sect. Nevertheless, you can recognize them from their dress – their robes are red, rather than purple, and include a large white band.

Labrang Monastery

About 1.5km up from the bus station, the **monastery** area begins. There's no wall separating the town from the monastery – the two communities just merge together and the main road goes right along through the middle of both. The only markers are the long lines of roofed **prayer wheels** stretching out to the right and left of the road – these mark the line of the old pilgrims' route, which traces a complete circle around the monastery. To the south side, in particular, along the north bank of the river, you can now follow the prayer wheels almost to the other end of the monastery – the gaps that still exist along the route are being rapidly filled in. It's a fascinating, if at times mesmerizing, experience to walk along with the pilgrims (clockwise around the monastery), turning each prayer wheel in turn as they go, sending prayers to heaven.

The monastery was founded in 1709 by a monk called E'Ang Zongzhe, who thereby became the first-generation Living Buddha, or **Jiemuyang**. Upon the death of each Jiemuyang, a new one is born, supposedly representing the reincarnation of the previous one. The present Jiemuyang, the sixth incarnation, is third in importance, in the Tibetan Buddhist hierarchy, to the Dalai Lama and Panchen Lama. Although Labrang may seem a peaceful haven today, it has not always been so. In the 1920s ferocious battles took place here between Muslim warlords and Tibetans, with atrocities being committed by both sides. Then in the Cultural Revolution came further disaster, with persecution for the monks and the virtual destruction (and closure) of the monastery. It was not until 1980 that it reopened, and although it is flourishing once again, it is nevertheless a smaller place today than it used to be. For an idea of its original extent, see the painting in the Exhibition Hall, on the wall at the far end from the entrance. There are now around two thousand monks, about half their former number.

The vast majority of the important **monastery buildings** are to the north of the main road. The buildings include six colleges, as well as temple halls, Jiemuyang residences and endless living quarters for the monks themselves. The institutes are of Astronomy, Esoteric Buddhism, Law, Medicine, and Theology (higher and lower) and monks study for degrees at these colleges. There are also schools for dance, music and painting. The **Gongtang Pagoda** (daily 8am–7pm; ¥5) is the only major monastery building to the south of the main road – you pass it when following the prayer wheels. It has recently been restored and it's worth climbing right to the top for a spectacular view over the shining golden roofs of the monastery.

For most non-specialist visitors, however, trying to identify the individual buildings will probably be of secondary importance given the pleasure of simply imbibing the atmosphere created by the monks themselves – whether massing for collective prayers, engaging in religious discussions or larking around like schoolboys (which is actually what many of them really are). There is nothing to stop you, at any time of day or night, from wandering around the entire site by yourself. You may even be allowed to wander into the temples – be sensitive and use your discretion.

On the other hand, given the bewildering wealth of architecture, art and statuary, it is probably a good idea to take a **guided tour** at some stage during your stay in Xiahe. This can be arranged at the ticket office – take the only sizeable turn off the north side of the road within the monastery area (the right if coming from the station). The tours, led by English-speaking monks, cost ¥21.5, and start around 10am and 2pm, more frequently in peak season.

Labrang Monastery is the site of some spectacular **festivals** during the year. As with Chinese festivals, these take place according to the lunar calendar, and fall on different dates of the Gregorian calendar each year. The largest festival, the **Monlam Festival**, takes place three days after the Tibetan new year (late February or early March). The opening of the festival is marked by the unfurling of a huge cloth adorned with a holy painting of the Buddha, measuring twenty metres by thirty, on the south side of the Daxia River. Subsequent days' activities include processions, dances and the lighting of butter lamps. You might see smaller-scale activities of the same type at any season of the year, if you happen to arrive on a special day.

Practicalities

All travellers arrive by **bus**, at the station at the far eastern end of town. The bus station is served by frequent buses from Linxia and Hezuo; there is also one bus a day to and from Lanzhou and Tongren (across the border in Qinghai Province) respectively. For the route to Sichuan, you should take a bus to Hezuo and proceed south from there (see p.870 for more on this route).

There are several **bike rental** places in town, most notably at the *Labrang Hotel* where they cost ¥10 per day. Various restaurants in the station end of town also offer bikes. There is as yet no *Bank of China* in Xiahe, though this situation will probably change soon. In the meantime you **cannot change travellers' cheques** anywhere in town – only cash will do. There are a number of **travel services** in the *Friendship Hotel* (see below).

ACCOMMODATION

The *Labrang* (☎09412/21849; dorms ①, rooms ②–⑤) lies at the far western edge of town, 4km from the bus station, but it's the nicest **hotel** in Xiahe – and one of the nicest budget hotels in China. To reach it from the station take a cycle-rickshaw, which shouldn't cost more than about ¥5, though you'll have to get off and push for one or two stretches. Accommodation ranges from simple three-bed dorms with bath, through plain doubles to beautiful and ornately furnished rooms in Tibetan style. Prices increase at the height of summer, while in winter the hotel may not be open at all.

If you prefer to stay in town, try the *Youyi* (☎09412/21593; ②), across the road from the bus station and a few minutes' walk west. It's a friendly place as well as being very clean and offers doubles with or without bath as well as three- and four-bed dorms. A few minutes farther west, on the north side of the road, you'll come to the old *Dasha* (③), which has grotty doubles with bath. Immediately beyond is the smart, new *White Conch*. At the time of writing this place had not yet opened, but it seems that it will be around ¥200–300 per room. Farther west still (about twenty minutes' walk from the station) on the right-hand side is the *Shuijinshan Zhuang* (☎09412/21223; dorms ②, rooms ④). It has no English sign – look for a new, tiled building with ornate mock-monastery eaves. It's clean and friendly with nice doubles with bath and three-bed dorms. Finally, right in the monastery area itself, is the *Monastery Guesthouse* (①) offering very primitive doubles; there are no showers, but each room has a stove. This might be the place to head for in winter.

EATING AND DRINKING

The influx of tourists has given a huge boost to the Xiahe catering trade in recent years. In the eastern part of town there are **restaurants** with predictable names like the *Yak Restaurant* and the *Tibetan Restaurant*. These two are both on the south side of the main road, about twenty minutes' walk west of the station, and offer Tibetan staples such as *tsampa*, made from yak butter and coarse flour – you add sugar and turn it into a kind of breakfast cereal. For upmarket Chinese food, try the restaurant at the *Shuijinshan Zhuang Hotel*.

At the western end of town, the restaurant at the *Labrang Hotel* itself offers reasonable set dinners for ¥25, though you have to put your name down on a list before 5.30pm. The *Labrang* also has eat-all-you-can breakfasts for ¥16. Walking east along the dirt track from the *Labrang* into the old Tibetan town, the first restaurant on your right – inside a courtyard — is actually a Muslim place. It offers great breakfasts, with yogurt and honey, pancakes, bread and even cream cheese. A little farther to the east (almost opposite the bridge), is the *Monastery Restaurant*, another Muslim place serving some pretty decent yak-meat dishes – a lot of meat for very little money.

Around Xiahe

Even without the monastery, Xiahe would be a delightful place to relax given its rural setting. The hills around the valley offer excellent hiking opportunities, and the views down on to the gleaming roofs of the monastery can be breathtaking. About 15km farther west up the valley are the **Sangke Grasslands** which can be reached by motor-rickshaw (about ¥30 return), or by bicycle. If you're cycling you can follow either the dirt track north of the river, or the sealed road to the south. You'll know when you've arrived – the valley opens out into a vast, grassy pasture, a lovely place to walk in summer. Nomads hang around here offering rides on their horses for ¥25 an hour. You can also stay out here in yurts affiliated to the *Labrang Hotel* – enquire at the hotel reception about these.

The road to Sichuan

South of Xiahe the roads are small and traffic irregular; nevertheless, there is a route you can follow by public buses which leads ultimately to Chengdu in Sichuan Province. It's a rough trip which requires several stopovers in remote towns, but a fascinating one – through one of the most beautiful parts of China. Some of the villages en route, notably Langmusi, are the most authentically Tibetan settlements most travellers are ever likely to see, given that it can be so hard to travel off the beaten track inside Tibet itself. From Xiahe, the first stop is **HEZUO**, about 70km to the southeast. It's a trading post for Tibetan nomads and you'll see some interestingly wild-looking types in the town. If you get here early enough from Xiahe, you might be able to move on to Luqu or Langmusi the same day.

A few buses and minibuses do the two-hour run to **LUQU** every day, another 70km farther south. The countryside around here is beautiful and easily accessible for hiking and a stroll up or down the river is likely to turn up one or two monasteries. In Luqu you can stay at the *Yinghang Zhaodaisuo* (①). There's no English sign, but turn right out of the bus station and it's less than five minutes' walk.

From Luqu it's about 80km on to **LANGMUSI**, which is right on the Gansu–Sichuan border. This is a memorable place to stay, basically comprising a collection of Tibetan monasteries around a valley. There are a couple of very basic guesthouses, where your hosts will come and light fires in your room to keep you warm at night. Everybody in town bathes in a natural lake in summer. You can see many traditional Tibetan practices in this area, including sky burials – the bodies of the dead are left on hill tops for vultures to take to heaven. South from here, in the northern part of Sichuan Province, there are buses on to **Zöigê** and the Songpan Grasslands (see p.812).

The Hexi Corridor

For reasons of simple geography, travellers leaving or entering China to or from Central Asia and the West have always been channelled through this narrow strip of land that runs 1000km northwest of Lanzhou. With the foothills of the Tibetan plateau, in the form of the Qilian Shan range, soaring up to the south, and a merciless combination of waterless desert and mountain to the north, the road known as the **Hexi Corridor** offers the only feasible way through the physical obstacles that crowd in on the traveller west of Lanzhou.

Historically – given the total absence of alternative routes – whoever controlled the corridor could operate a stranglehold on the fabulous riches of the Silk Road trade (see box, p.826). Inevitably the Chinese took an interest from the earliest times, and a certain amount of Great Wall-building was already taking place along the Hexi Corridor under Emperor Qin Shi Huang in the third century BC. Subsequently, the powerful Han dynasty succeeded in incorporating the region into their empire, though the influence of central government remained far from constant for many centuries afterwards, as Tibetans, Uigurs and then Mongols vied for control. Not until the Mongol conquests of the thirteenth century did the corridor finally become a settled part of the Chinese empire, with the Ming consolidating the old Great Wall positions and building its magnificent last fort at **Jiayuguan**.

Two other towns along the corridor, **Wuwei** and **Zhangye**, offer – at the very least – convenient means of breaking the long journey from Lanzhou to Dunhuang, and are well worth visiting in themselves, particularly Wuwei with its substantial historic remains.

Wuwei

Lying approximately halfway between Lanzhou and Zhangye, **WUWEI** is a quiet, relaxing place and definitely worth a brief stopover. As well as some attractive temples, there's a pleasant new town and some quite substantial remains of the old settlement. The town's single most famous object, the Han-dynasty **Flying Horse of Wuwei**, was discovered here in 1969 underneath the Leitai Si. The original is now housed in the Lanzhou Museum (see p.862) but the symbol of the horse, depicted in full gallop and stepping on the back of a swallow, can be seen everywhere in Wuwei.

The interesting part of the city is divided into four quadrants by the main north–south road (Bei Dajie and Nan Dajie) and the east–west road (Dong Dajie and Xi Dajie), with the centre of the city at the crossroads. Wuwei's long-distance bus station is at the bottom of the southwest quadrant. You'll notice the first traces of the **old city** almost as soon as you leave the bus station. Left out of the station and immediately left again along Nan Dajie, you pass between the remains of some massive earth ramparts – the old **city wall**. North from here, take the first road on the right which leads after ten minutes to the **Wen Miao** (daily 8–11.30am & 2.30–5.30pm; ¥20), a really delightful museum in the grounds of a beautiful old temple with large gardens full of oleanders and singing birds. The museum may not grab you for its contents – stone inscriptions and porcelain from the Han dynasty – but the environment is marvellously peaceful.

Ten minutes north of here you reach Dong Dajie; continue into the tangle of narrow old streets farther north to the foot of the **Ancient Bell Tower** (daily 8am–4.30pm; ¥10). You can climb up the tower and inspect the massive bell which is still occasionally used. There are excellent views over the surrounding flat-roofed, mud-built houses, and in the grounds of the bell tower you'll find lots of old men playing *mahjong* or cards and drinking tea under vine trellises and enormous hollyhocks – a rare scene from old China.

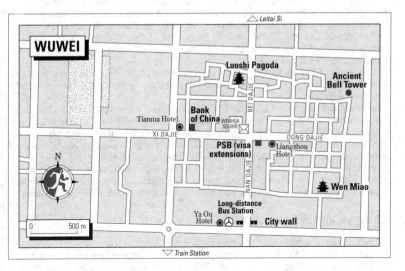

Due west of here, just acros Bei Dajie and into the northwest quadrant of the city, stands the **Luoshi Pagoda**, located right in the grounds of the PSB. The pagoda is unfortunately off-limits, insofar as the PSB staff at the gate tend to stop tourists from entering the premises. You can, however, see at least the top half of the wooden tower from neighbouring streets. South of here, near the corner of Xi Dajie and Bei Dajie, **Wenhua Square** is dominated by a larger-than-life replica of the Flying Horse – it's a lively, pleasant place to sit or stroll, especially in the evening.

Finally, about forty minutes' walk north from the city centre, you'll find the **Leitai Si** (daily, 8am–5pm; ¥18). The original location of this temple, built high up on impressive mud ramparts and surrounded by beautiful countryside, is unfortunately now losing its attraction as the whole area is being swamped by construction, and by the time you read this it may no longer be visible from the road. Nevertheless, the temple remains a pleasantly calm, shady place inside its grounds; and underneath the site, through a separate entrance, you can enter the famous Han-dynasty tomb where the Flying Horse was discovered. There's not much to see – it's a series of very low passageways, with a mock-up of the tomb contents at the back – but the two thousand-year-old brickwork is still in perfect condition and amazingly modern in appearance. You will be accompanied into the tomb by a guide who may speak a little English.

Practicalities

Most travellers arrive by **bus** from Lanzhou or Zhangye. The station is immediately to the south of the old city. For the town centre, come out of the station, turn left and left again, then walk due north for fifteen minutes until you reach the main crossroads. The **train station** is far away to the south; from here take a minibus into the centre for a couple of yuan.

Accommodation in Wuwei for foreigners is fairly scarce. The most convenient place for budget travellers arriving at the bus station is the new, smart *Ya Ou* (☎0935/213778; dorms ①, rooms ②), just a few minutes west of the bus station. The only problem is that it doesn't always take foreigners. The other two possible hotels are not particularly keen on real budget travellers. The *Liangzhou* (☎0935/212450; ②–⑤) on Dong Dajie, a couple of minutes east of the central crossroads, has quite nice doubles with 24-hour hot water and cheaper triples and doubles without private bath. To get into these cheaper rooms you have to be fairly determined, though. Of a slightly higher standard is the *Tianma*, a few blocks west of the *Liangzhou* (☎0935/212355; dorms ②, rooms ⑥–⑦). You can buy a city map here in the hotel shop and, in the north building, there's a travel service.

The **Bank of China**, just to the east of the *Tianma Hotel*, is open Monday to Friday. The **PSB** office that deals with visa extensions is just to the west of the *Liangzhou Hotel* – there's an English sign.

Moving on from Wuwei is probably easiest by **bus**. To Zhangye and Lanzhou there are fairly frequent departures throughout the day. To destinations farther west, there is also a through-bus to Dunhuang. Finally, there's one daily bus to Xining in Qinghai Province, and one bus to Linxia (via Lanzhou) in southern Gansu – the jumping-off point for the Tibetan monastery city of Xiahe. This bus takes about ten hours.

By **train**, Wuwei is served by all trains on the routes connecting Ürümqi and the east. There is also a slow train to Zhongwei (in Ningxia). Try to buy outward tickets from a travel service to avoid long and potentially futile trips out to the train station.

Zhangye and around

A medium-sized town, about 450km northwest of Lanzhou and 150km southeast of Jiayuguan, **ZHANGYE** has always been an important stopover for caravans and travellers on the Silk Road. Indeed, Marco Polo spent a whole year here. Today it's still worth stopping, especially if you have time for a visit to the Buddhist **Mati Si**, 60km south of the town.

During the Ming period, Zhangye was an important garrison town for soldiers guarding the **Great Wall**, and today the road from Wuwei to Zhangye is still a good place from which to view the Wall, visible for a large part of the way as a slightly sad and crumbling line of mud ramparts. Initially it runs to the north of the road, until, quite dramatically, the road suddenly cuts right through a hole in the Wall and continues on the other side.

Although Zhangye is not generally an attractive town, there are a number of places that offer at least a day of sight-seeing. The centre of the town is marked, as in many Chinese towns, by a **Gulou** (Drum Tower) at the crossroads. The tower, built in the Ming dynasty (1507), has two tiers and houses a massive bronze bell. The four streets radiating out from here, Bei Jie, Dong Jie, Nan Jie and Xi Jie, are named after their respective compass points, and most of the sights are in the southwest of town in the vicinity of the *Zhangye Hotel*.

Moving from east to west, the scattering of sights begins with the **Tu Ta** (Earth Tower), a former Buddhist monastery, located just off Nan Jie and now in use as a local Culture Centre (*wenhua guan*), comprising a rather ramshackle collection of flying eaves and a single large stupa 20m in height. Halfway between here and the *Zhangye Hotel* is the city's outstanding sight, the **Dafo Si** (Big Buddha Temple; daily

7.30am–6.30pm; ¥22). Built in 1098 and restored during Qing times, this 34-metre-long Buddha is easily China's largest reclining Buddha and its calm expression and gentle lines make a powerful impression. Immediately behind the Buddha are ten disciples, and standing around in the gloom are a number of slightly grotesque-looking *lohans*

HEXI CORRIDOR

Hexi Corridor	河西走廊	*héxī zǒuláng*
Jiayuguan	嘉裕关	*jiāyùguān*
First Beacon Tower	第一墩	*dìyīdūn*
Fort	城楼	*chénglóu*
Great Wall Museum	长城博物馆	*chángchéng bówùguǎn*
Heishan rock carvings	黑山岩画	*hēishān yánhuà*
Overhanging Wall	悬壁长城	*xuánbì chángchéng*
Qiyi Bingchuan	七一冰川	*qīyī bīngchuān*
Xincheng Dixia Hualang	新城地下画廊	*xīnchéng dìxià huàláng*
ACCOMMODATION		
Changcheng	长城宾馆	*chángchéng bīnguǎn*
Jiaotong	交通宾馆	*jiāotōng bīnguǎn*
Jiayuguan	嘉裕关宾馆	*jiāyùguān bīnguǎn*
Qingnian	青年宾馆	*qīngnián bīnguǎn*
Wumao	物贸宾馆	*wùmào bīnguǎn*
Mati	马蹄	*mǎtí*
Wuwei	武威	*wǔwēi*
Ancient Bell Tower	古钟楼	*gǔzhōnglóu*
Leitai Si	雷台寺	*léitái sì*
Luoshi Pagoda	罗什塔	*luóshí tǎ*
Wen Miao	文庙	*wénmiào*
ACCOMMODATION		
Liangzhou	凉州宾馆	*liángzhōu bīnguǎn*
Tianma	天马宾馆	*tiānmǎ bīnguǎn*
Ya Ou	亚欧宾馆	*yàōu bīnguǎn*
Zhangye	张掖	*zhāngyè*
Dafo Si	大佛寺	*dàfó sì*
Daode Guan	道德关	*dàodé guān*
Ganquan Park	甘泉公园	*gānquán gōngyuán*
Gulou	古楼	*gǔlóu*
Mu Ta	木塔	*mùtǎ*
Tu Ta	土塔	*tǔtǎ*
Xilai Si	西来寺	*xīlái sì*
ACCOMMODATION		
Ganzhou	甘州宾馆	*gānzhōu bīnguǎn*
Jindu	金都宾馆	*jīndū bīnguǎn*
Zhangye	张掖宾馆	*zhāngyè bīnguǎn*

(saintly warriors). The temple is located in a pleasant leafy garden which also houses a fairly humdrum **museum**.

Just a few hundred metres north of the *Zhangye Hotel* looms the 31-metre-tall **Mu Ta** (Wooden Tower), originally built as long ago as the sixth century, before being burnt down and then restored in 1925. Octagonal in shape and home to large numbers of jackdaws, the tower has an unusual location in the grounds of a school – which makes it hard to visit outside the school vacations, though in summer nobody minds you strolling in to take a look. A few hundred metres south of here, and one block to the west of the *Zhangye Hotel*, the **Xilai Si**, a small temple complex, is currently being restored in the Tang–Song style. It is also a centre of active Chinese Buddhism and when you enter you may find a sudden rush of elderly monks coming out to bless you and present you with their name-cards.

Much farther away, about fifteen minutes' walk due east from the Drum Tower on the road to the train station, is the local active Taoist monastery, the **Daode Guan**. It's a small place of Ming origins, containing a tiny garden and some vine trellises, perhaps more interesting for its location than anything else – right in a jumble of narrow lanes behind a building site on the north side of Dong Jie. You may have to scramble over some rubbish dumps to find it. Finally, twenty minutes' walk northwest of the Drum Tower, you'll reach the shady **Ganquan Park**. The lake in the park gets rather dried up, but it's a quiet place to sit around for a couple of hours.

Practicalities

Arriving by **bus**, you can either get off at the easily recognizable Drum Tower on the central roundabout, or carry on to the main bus station in the south of the city. The **train** station is located about 7km away to the northeast; trains are met by waiting minibuses which take you into town for ¥3.

There are a few cheap options for **accommodation**. A couple of minutes south of the Drum Tower is the *Ganzhou* (dorms ①–②, rooms ④), which charges foreigners double, but is still reasonable. Perhaps slightly better value – and more conveniently situated for the sights – is the *Zhangye* (☎0936/21260 ext 400; dorms ②, rooms ④–⑤). Overall, it's quite a pleasant place with rocks, fountains and pagodas in the gardens and it houses the offices of **CITS** (☎0936/212601). To reach the *Zhangye* from the bus station, turn right as you exit the station, then head north for a few minutes up Xianfu Jie; the hotel is on the right. The newest and cleanest place in town is the *Jindu* (☎0936/214184; dorms ①, rooms ②), a couple of minutes east of the Drum Tower on Dong Jie; all rooms and dorms have their own bathrooms.

Eating in Zhangye is not particularly exciting. The *Zhangye Hotel* has a plain, cheap restaurant, while that at the *Jindu* is more upmarket. One quite lively, good-value restaurant worth trying lies just a few minutes to the south of the *Ganzhou Hotel* on Nan Jie.

Mati

The fascinating **Mati Si** – literally Horse-hoof Temple – is located in the tiny Tibetan town of **MATI** in mountains about 60km south of Zhangye. It's a complex of Buddhist caves carved into a cliff face connected by a series of back-breaking passageways, tunnels, balconies and stairways. Once in Mati, finding the cave temples is easy – people will crowd around to show you the way. Apart from the Mati Si, there are other temples and monasteries dotted around the area, all within walking distance. Overall, Mati has an interesting atmosphere, and is full of cheerful Tibetans offering you rides on their horses. The countryside around is an area of cool pine forests, mountains and grasslands.

To visit Mati, you'll need an **Alien Travel Permit** from the Zhangye PSB. The fourth-floor office on Qingnian Xi Jie issues the permit in minutes without fuss. You'll also probably need to stay a couple of nights in Mati – the only bus from Zhangye's main bus station leaves at 3pm and takes three or four hours, while the bus coming back from Mati leaves at 7am. The ride costs around ¥6 each way. You'll find cheap **accommodation** (①–②) in the immediate vicinity of the bus station in Mati.

Moving on from Zhangye is easiest done by **bus** as no trains originate at Zhangye train station – which makes obtaining a ticket with a reservation all the harder. At the long-distance bus station, you may or may not be charged the foreigners' price depending on who serves you; from here there are buses to all parts of Gansu Province, and also to Xining in Qinghai over a spectacular mountain route. In the evening, there are also private bus services from the Drum Tower area, some with sleepers running to Lanzhou. These work out slightly more expensive than the state buses.

Jiayuguan and around

One more cup of wine for our remaining happiness. There will be chilling parting dreams tonight.

Ninth-century poet on a leave-taking at Jiayuguan

To some Chinese the very name of **JIAYUGUAN** is synonymous with sorrow and a ghastly remoteness. The last **fortress** of the Great Wall was built here by the Ming in 1372, from which time the town made its living by supplying the needs of the fortress garrison. This was literally the final defence of the empire, the spot where China ended and beyond which lay a terrifying wilderness. The fort, just outside the town and perfectly preserved, is one of the great sights of northwestern China – there are also a number of other forts and beacons scattered around in the desert outside Jiayuguan.

Apart from the great fort, the city today is a bleak, rather lonely place, laid out in a regular grid pattern, and sliced through diagonally from east to west by the principal Gansu Highway. Its centre is a large traffic circle, overlooked by the *Jiayuguan Hotel* and the post office; Xinhua Lu is the main street leading southeast from here. One of its few attractions is the **Great Wall Museum** (daily 8am–noon & 2.30–6.30pm; ¥20), of which the highlights are the photos of the Wall taken from points right across northern China – places that for the most part lie well away from tourist itineraries. The history of the Wall is traced from Han times right up to the last frenzied spurt of wall building which took place under the Ming, and there are also scale models of sections of wall from different areas and times, showing the materials from which they were built. The museum is on two floors – you may need to ask somebody to open the upstairs for you. It's worth making your way to the top of the museum as there's a great view over the city and surrounding desert from the roof. The museum is due south of the central traffic circle, on the main road, about thirty minutes' walk from the *Jiayuguan Hotel*; alternatively, take bus #1 or any minibus heading to the train station, and get off at the *Gongren Wenhua Gong* (Workers' Culture Palace) – the musuem is just a few minutes' walk south from here.

In the north of the town is an **Entertainment Park** which is a good spot for an evening stroll amid the crowds, giant sculptures, pagodas, pleasure boats and dodgem cars. Head north along Xinhua Bei Lu from the central traffic circle and take the first right along a narrow market street – the park lies at the far end of the street.

Practicalities

Jiayuguan's **train station** is in the far southwest of the city and linked by bus or minibus #1 to the centre. All trains running between Ürümqi and eastern China stop here. The **bus station** has a much more convenient location on the main highway, about a kilometre southwest of the central roundabout. The **airport**, 10km from town, is connected by *CAAC* buses to the **CAAC** office, south of the central traffic circle (Mon–Sat 8.30am–12.30pm & 2.30–6.30pm; ☎09477/226237).

Jiayuguan's *CITS* (☎09477/226983), situated in a downstairs office of the *Jiayuguan Hotel*, can supply train tickets and offers reasonably priced tours – for example, a car carrying four passengers to the fort, the Overhanging Wall, the Heishan rock carvings and the Underground Gallery (see below) will cost about ¥55 per person. They can also arrange a day trip to the July 1st Glacier. There's another travel service upstairs in the same building.

Just around the corner from the bus station, you'll find a couple of very convenient and pleasant **hotels**. One is the *Wumao* (☎09477/227514; dorms ①, rooms ②), immediately to the west of the station across a narrow street, with nice, clean rooms and dorms, all with bath. If you're travelling alone, the chances are you'll get the room to yourself. Very similar conditions prevail at the *Jiaotong* (☎09477/234407; ③), a few minutes' walk east from the station. Otherwise, the best place for budget travellers is probably the *Jiayuguan* (☎09477/226983; dorms ①, rooms ⑥), right on the central roundabout, offering smart doubles and four-bed dorms. The #1 bus from the train sta-

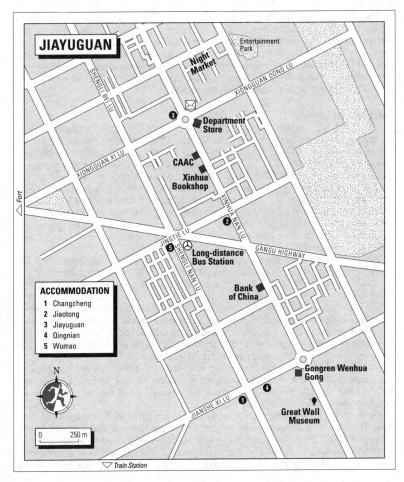

JIAYUGUAN

Entertainment Park

Night Market

XIONGGUAN DONG LU

SHENGLI BEI LU

XIONGGUAN XI LU

❸ Department Store

CAAC

Xinhua Bookshop

XINHUA NAN LU

❷

△ Fort

JINGTIE LU

❺ Long-distance Bus Station

GANSU HIGHWAY

SHENGLI NAN LU

Bank of China

ACCOMMODATION
1 Changcheng
2 Jiaotong
3 Jiayuguan
4 Qingnian
5 Wumao

Gongren Wenhua Gong

N

JIANSHE XI LU

❶ ❹

Great Wall Museum

0   250 m

▽ Train Station

tion stops here. The *Jiayuguan* also does **bike rental**. In the south of the town is the *Qingnian* (☎09477/225833; dorms ②, rooms ④), which has three-bed dorms and faded doubles. To get here from the train station, take bus #1, get off at the Workers' Culture Palace and walk five minutes to the southwest along Jianshe Lu. A few minutes farther to the west, also on Jianshe Lu, is the only really upmarket place in town, the *Changcheng* (☎09477/225277; ⑦–⑧).

For good **food** you need go no farther than the *Jiayuguan Hotel*, which has a new and very pleasant restaurant with a fountain. You can get cheap lunches and dinners here, with cold draught beer. Outdoor food is available at the **night market** north from the *Jiayuguan* and along the road to the Entertainment Park. It's not marvellous but you can get the usual noodles and dumplings. For something smarter, try the upmarket *Fulihua Restaurant* in the *Wumao Hotel*, which has a sophisticated menu, though only in Chinese.

Train tickets out of Jiayuguan are hard to come by – you will almost certainly need the help of a travel service (see above), and may need to resort to soft class if you want a sleeper.

When **buying bus tickets** foreigners are usually charged double, and are asked to show PICC Travel Insurance Certificates. These are sometimes obtainable at the *Jiayuguan Hotel*. You can also buy them at the PICC office on Xinhua Lu, just south of the Gansu Highway. For tourists, the most useful buses to and from Jiayuguan are the frequent connections with Dunhuang. Some services from Jiayuguan, for example the one running between Hami and Jiuquan, are through services only, and you have to flag them down on the highway outside the station.

The Fort and beyond

The **Fort** (Cheng Lou; daily 8am–12.30pm & 2.30–6pm; ¥20) at the Jiayuguan Pass is the outstanding sight in the whole Hexi Corridor. The location, between the permanently snow-capped Qilian Mountains to the north and the curiously black Mazong (Horse's Mane) Mountains to the south, could not be more dramatic – or more strategically valuable. Everything that travels between the deserts of Central Asia and the fertile lands of China – goods, people, armies – has to file through this pass, and for centuries anybody heading west of this point knew that they were leaving the safety and protection of China and entering the unknown world that lay outside. The desolation of the landscape only adds to the melancholy – being forced to leave China altogether was a citizen's worst nightmare, and it was here that the disgraced officials and condemned or fleeing criminals had to make their final, bitter farewells.

Some kind of fort may have occupied this site as early as the Han dynasty, but the surviving building is a Ming construction, completed in 1372, sometimes referred to as the "Impregnable Defile under Heaven" and comprising an outer and an inner wall. The outer wall is over 700m in circumference and about 10m high. At the east and the west of the inner wall stand symbolic gates, the Gate of Enlightenment and the Gate of Conciliation, respectively. Inside each gate are sloping walkways leading up to the top of the wall, enabling horses to climb up and patrol the turrets. In between the Gate of Enlightenment and the outer wall stand a pavilion, a temple and a somewhat haunting open-air theatre which was once used to entertain troops.

The so-called **Overhanging Wall** (daily 8am–6pm; ¥5), about 6km north of the fort, is a section of the Great Wall connecting the fort to the Mazong mountain range, originally built in the sixteenth century and recently restored. From the ramparts there are excellent views of the surrounding land.

It's worth combining your trip to the fort with a trip up to the Overhanging Wall as well. Occasional minibuses leave for the fort from the roundabout outside the *Jiayuguan Hotel* (¥3 one way), but the easiest way if you're with other people is to rent a small **minibus** to take you to both sites (around ¥50 for the whole trip). Alternatively, you could **cycle** – it's around thirty minutes to the fort and another thirty to the

Overhanging Wall. From Jiayuguan, follow the Gansu Highway west from the bus station until you cross the bridge over the rail line. A blue sign pointing right indicates the way to the fort from here. From the Fort to the Overhanging Wall, you go back a little way, then head north along an easy-to-find dirt track to your left, following remnants of the Great Wall as you go. Returning to Jiayuguan from the Overhanging Wall, you can take a direct road into town.

Several other desert attractions around Jiayuguan could also be combined with a trip to the fort and Overhanging Wall. About 6km south of Jiayuguan are the ruins of the **First Beacon Tower**. Built on the Great Wall in the sixteenth century, the long-abandoned tower is now crumbling on a cliff top on the northern bank of the Taolai River at the foot of the Qilian Mountains. The desert also harbours a couple of unusual collections of ancient Chinese art. One is the **Xincheng Dixia Hualang** (Underground Gallery), about 20km east of Jiayuguan. Actually a burial site from the Wei and Jin periods, more than fifteen hundred years ago, the graves are brick-laid and contain paintings depicting contemporary life. Not far beyond the fort, 9km northwest of Jiayuguan, are the **Heishan rock carvings**. These look more like our conception of real cave man's art: on the cliffs of the Heishan mountain are carved more than a hundred pictures of hunting, horse-riding and dancing, all dating back to the Warring States Period (476–221 BC). To visit the First Beacon Tower, and the two art sites in conjunction with a tour of the fort and Overhanging Wall takes a day and costs around ¥250 in a taxi.

Finally, one stupendous but rather inaccessible natural sight is the **Qiyi Bingchuan** (July 1st Glacier), located 4300m up in the Qilian Mountains, 120km from Jiayuguan – remarkably close considering what a hot place Jiayuguan is in the summer. *CITS* can take you there on an expensive and hectic one-day trip, involving a three-hour drive, followed by five hours climbing up and down, and three hours driving back. Reckon on ¥500–1000 for the whole trip, including a guide.

Dunhuang and the Mogao Caves

An oasis town perched right on the outer periphery of old Chinese Turkestan, **DUNHUANG** has always been literally on the edge of the desert – from downtown you can see giant, spectacular **sand dunes** at the bottom of the street. Today, though, increasing numbers of tourists, both from China and abroad, are coming to Dunhuang to view the astonishing art work at the nearby **Mogao Caves**, and in consequence the town has become something of a desert resort with inexpensive hotels, lots of English-language menus in the restaurants and friendly people, who seemed honoured to be living in such a historic town.

Dunhuang itself is nothing more than a few streets – the centre of town is marked by a traffic circle with streets radiating out to the north, east, south and west. On the main street east, Dong Dajie, there's a surprisingly attractive and interesting **souvenir night market** every summer evening, where you can stroll with no pressure to buy. Coins, jade articles, Buddhas, Tibetan bells and horns, scroll paintings and Chinese chops (jade sticks with one end engraved with your signature in Chinese characters) are all on sale. Also on Dong Dajie is the mediocre **Dunhuang Museum**, housing a few of the scrolls left behind after the depredations of the archeologist and adventurer, Sir Aurel Stein (see box, p.884), plus some preserved corpses.

Practicalities

There is no rail line directly to Dunhuang; the nearest **train station** is at Liuyuan, about 130km away; minibuses wait outside the station to carry passengers the two-and-a-half

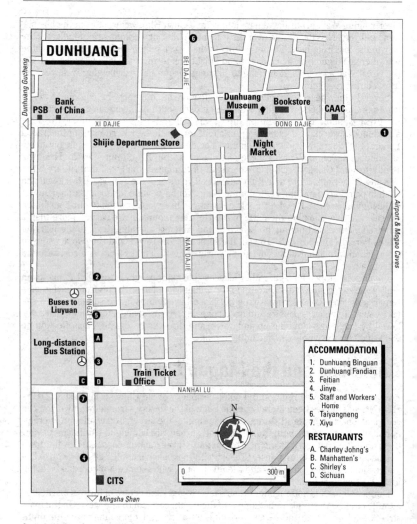

hours to Dunhuang. The **bus station** lies right in the budget hotel area in the south of town on Dingzi Lu, opposite the *Feitian Hotel*. Dunhuang's **airport** is about 13km east of town; the airport bus stops in town at the *CAAC* office (☎09473/22389) near the *Dunhuang Hotel* on Dong Dajie. Flights connect Dunhuang with Xian and Lanzhou daily, and with Beijing thrice weekly.

Accommodation

There's quite a glut of hotel accommodation in Dunhuang, which may go some way to explaining why it is such good value, especially at the lower end of the market – though prices rise in peak season (July and August). The cheaper hotels tend to be in the southeast of town, close to the bus station.

Dunhuang Binguan, Yangguan Dong Lu (☎09473/22415). The longest-established upmarket hotel in Dunhuang, a few blocks east of the main traffic circle. Has a nice lobby with a fountain and a bar, IDD telephone and fax facilities. This is the only place in town where you can change money on Sundays. Dorms ②, rooms ⑦.

Dunhuang Fandian, Dingzi Lu (☎09473/22723). About ten minutes north up the road from the bus station, this place has a rather dingy, dilapidated feel to it. Dorms ①, rooms ④.

Feitian, Dingzi Lu. Directly opposite the bus station, the *Feitian* offers the cheapest beds in town: multi-bed dorms, three-bed dorms and smarter doubles. There's also cheap bicycle rental. Dorms ①, rooms ④–⑤.

Jinye, Dingzi Lu (☎09473/21470). A couple of minutes farther to the south from the *Xiyu Hotel*, and much more upmarket, offering air-conditioned doubles. Credit cards accepted. ⑦.

Staff and Workers' Home, Dingzi Lu (☎09473/22310). From the bus station, cross the road and walk a few minutes to the north. Clean, new and pleasant doubles with bath, and three-bed dorms. Dorms ①, rooms ③–④.

Taiyangneng, Bei Dajie (☎09473/22168). A few minutes due north of the main roundabout, quiet and smart, though in a slightly remote part of town. Air-conditioned doubles and three-bed dorms. Dorms ①, rooms ⑦.

Xiyu, Dingzi Lu (☎09473/23017). Very convenient for the bus station, just one block to the south (turn right when emerging from the station). Very cheap dorms and reasonable doubles with bath. Dorms ①, rooms ③.

Eating and drinking

There are plenty of good places for visitors to **eat** in Dunhuang, especially in the south of town along Dingzi Lu. One block south of the bus station, there are a number of places specializing in cheap Western dishes with English menus, friendly service and tables on the pavement. *Shirley's* is the most popular, but the *Flavour Food Snack Bar* next door produces almost exactly the same fare. Don't come to these places for authentic Chinese food, though – everything here is cooked to suit Western tastes, it's not salty or spicy enough and the meat and vegetables are cut up into big pieces and overcooked. Across the road from *Shirley's* is a rather grubby-looking Sichuan restaurant (Chinese menu only), but the food is authentic and excellent.

A couple of minutes north of the *Feitian Hotel*, on the same side of the road, you'll find *Charley Johng's Café*, whose menu includes a slightly dubious muesli and yogurt, as well as excellent pancakes, banana fritters and chicken curry. The restaurants farther north up Dingzi Lu on the east side of the road from here offer authentic Chinese food, but don't have English menus (and are not used to foreigners).

MOVING ON FROM DUNHUANG

Frequent minibuses leave Dunhuang for the **train station at Liuyuan**, from an alley on Dingzi Lu, opposite the *Dunhuang Fandian*, and the *Dunhuang China International Travel Service* (☎09473/22474), in the south of the town, a few hundred metres south of the *Feitian Hotel*, can help in buying train tickets from Liuyuan. Good English is spoken here. There's also an office where you may be able to buy train tickets yourself – from the *Feitian*, walk south and take the first road left. The ticket office is on the corner of a small road to the left about 100m down.

Buses from Dunhuang run frequently to Jiayuguan (about 8hr) and at least once daily to Lanzhou (24hr) and all points in between. There is also a daily bus to Hami (9hr) in Xinjiang (see p.901). Foreigners intending to take the fifteen-hour bus journey to **Golmud** in Qinghai Province (on the road to Tibet) have to buy special tickets through the Dunhuang branch of Golmud *CITS*, an office located in the bus station. At the time of writing this required paying ¥300, approximately ten times the normal price – and foreigners were not being allowed on to the bus without the special ticket.

DUNHUANG AND AROUND

Dunhuang	敦皇	*dūnhuáng*
Liuyuan	柳园	*liǔyuán*

ACCOMMODATION

Dunhuang Binguan	敦皇宾馆	*dūnhuáng bīnguǎn*
Dunhuang Fandian	敦皇饭店	*dūnhuáng fàndiàn*
Feitian	飞天宾馆	*fēitiān bīnguǎn*
Jinye	金叶宾馆	*jīnyè bīnguǎn*
Staff and Workers' Home	职工人家馆	*zhígōngrénjiāguǎn*
Taiyangneng	太阳能宾馆	*tàiyángnéng bīnguǎn*
Xiyu	西域宾馆	*xīyù bīnguǎn*

AROUND DUNHUANG

Baima Ta	白马塔	*báimǎ tǎ*
Dunhuang Gucheng	敦皇古城	*dūnhuáng gǔchéng*
Mingsha Shan	鸣沙山	*míngshā shān*
Mogao Caves	莫高窟	*mògāokū*
Xi Qianfodong	西千佛洞	*xīqiānfódòng*
Yangguan	阳关	*yángguān*
Yueya Quan	月牙泉	*yuèyá quán*
Yumenguan	玉门关	*yùménguān*

The most atmospheric place to eat in the evening is the excellent **night market** located through an imposing gateway off the south side of Dong Dajie, next to the souvenir market. Inside there are fountains, fairy lights and billiard tables, and you can sit on deck chairs and drink *babao* (eight-treasure tea), full of delicious dried fruits, or have a full meal. Everything is cooked in front of you – just point. On the other side of Dong Dajie is the improbable *Manhattans Café* featuring tuna fish and peanut-butter-and-jelly sandwiches as well as pasta salads, at US prices. The decor is southwest USA American Indian style – try it if you're badly homesick.

Around Dunhuang

A few kilometres to the south of town are the much-touted **Yueya Quan** (Crescent Moon Lake) and **Mingsha Shan** (Singing Sand Dune), the most impressive sand-dune scenery anywhere in China, with dunes 200–300m high. The sands reportedly make a humming noise in windy weather, hence the name. The Crescent Moon Lake is not much to look at, but is curious for being so permanent, despite its location surrounded by shifting sands – it was recorded in history at least two thousand years ago. Various activities take place from the tops of the main dune, such as sand-tobogganing and paragliding. The paragliding is great fun and costs ¥30 – you get to try two or three times if your initial flight isn't successful. Climbing the dune in the first place, however, is incredibly hot, exhausting work; if you use the wooden steps you may have to pay a small fee.

Minibuses from Dunhuang will drop you by a gate and ticket office – foreigners are charged ¥20 to enter. If you object to paying, you can reach the dunes by cutting round the side about 300m back from the gate. In the summer heat the only sensible time to come here is early in the morning around 7.30am, or in the evening. Between

5pm and 6pm minibuses cruise around Dunhuang looking for passengers (¥3 per person). Otherwise you can walk here in about 45 minutes, or cycle in twenty – just head south out of town.

About 20km southwest of the city, right out in the desert, is the **Dunhuang Gucheng** – literally "Dunhuang ancient city". This particular ancient city is actually a film-set less than ten years old; nevertheless, it has become a regular feature on the Dunhuang tourist trail. From a distance it looks impressive with its dramatic backdrop of desert, but the closer you get the more tacky it seems. Inside there are a number of souvenir shops, noodle stands and even yurts to stay in. There are occasional **minibuses** from Dingzi Lu in Dunhuang (¥10 return), usually around lunchtime. You can also cycle here if you can cope with the heat, or else take a taxi for ¥30.

On the way back to Dunhuang, be sure to drop in on the **Baima Ta** (White Horse Dagoba). This attractive, nine-tiered dagoba was built in honour of the horse belonging to the monk Kumarajiva from Kuche (see p.918), which died on this spot in 384 AD. It lies amid corn fields and the remains of the old city walls, about 4km west of town.

A number of other historical sites lie farther away from Dunhuang. One is the **Xi Qianfodong** (Western Thousand Buddha Caves). This is another cave site along the lines of Mogao, but incomparably smaller and less significant. If you are a real Buddhist art buff, talk to a travel service about this place: at the time of writing it was open to groups only, and individuals were being turned away. About ten caves can be viewed, and a taxi ride there and back costs around ¥80.

Finally, there are two Han-dynasty gates, **Yumenguan** and **Yangguan**, which for periods of Chinese history marked the western border of China. They lie to the west of Dunhuang, 80km and 75km away respectively, and were originally joined together by a section of the Great Wall before being abandoned as long ago as the sixth century. Both sites today are impressive for their historic resonance and total desolation as much as for anything else: Yumenguan comprises crumbling ten-metre-high mud walls while Yangguan is little more than a ruined tower. Today, the road to Yangguan is in good condition, but that to Yumenguan is extremely rough – to visit both gates by taxi would take all day and cost over ¥600. One exciting option, however, is to visit the two gates **by camel**. A company based at Yueya Quan (☎09473/23122) offers escorted camel trips out of Dunhuang. To see the two gates, and bits of the Han Great Wall, takes around three days, and in the mild months of the year – early or late summer – this can be an excellent expedition. The cost of your camel, a guide, the guide's camel, and a spare camel, works out at two or three hundred yuan per day; cheaper in a group. The same company also offers camel tours to Kashgar or Xi'an (70 days in either direction).

The Mogao Caves

The **Mogao Caves**, 25km southeast of Dunhuang, are one of the great sites – and archeological discovery stories – of the East. The first known **Buddhist temples** within the boundaries of the Chinese empire, supposedly established in 366 AD by a monk called Lie Zun, they were a centre of culture on the Silk Road right up until the fourteenth century, and today contain religious art works spanning a thousand years of history. Chinese Buddhism radiated out to the whole Han empire from these wild desert cliffs, and with it – gradually adapting to a Chinese context – came the artistic influences of Central Asia, India, Persia and the West.

Of the original thousand or more **caves**, 492 survive in recognizable form, but many are off-limits, either considered no longer of significant value or interest or else containing Tantric murals which the Chinese reckon are too sexually explicit for visitors. Of the thirty main caves open to the public, you are likely to manage only around fifteen in a single day.

THE MOGAO CAVE TREASURES

The story of Mogao's development, then subsequent abandonment and rediscovery, is an intriguing one. Before the arrival of Buddhism from India, the Chinese – Taoist and Confucian – temple tradition had been mainly of buildings in wood, a material well adapted to most Chinese conditions. The idea of cave temples came to China from India, where poverty, lack of building materials and the intense heat had necessitated the development of the form.

The emergence of the complex of cave temples at **Mogao** dominated early Chinese Buddhism, as pilgrims, monks and scholars passing along the Silk Road settled and worked here, translating sutras, or holy texts. Merchants and nobles stopped, too, endowing temples to ensure the success of their caravans or to benefit their souls, as they did in varying degrees all along the Silk Road. Huge numbers of **artists and craftsmen** were employed at Dunhuang, often lying on high scaffoldings in the dim light provided by oil lamps. The workers usually lived in tiny caves in the northern section of Mogao furnished with small brick beds, and were paid a pittance – in a collection of Buddhist scriptures, archeologists have discovered a bill of indenture signed by one sculptor for the sale of his son.

Under the Tang, which saw the establishment of Buddhism throughout the Chinese empire, the monastic community reached its peak, with over a thousand cave temples in operation. Thereafter, however, as the new ocean-going trading links slowly supplanted the Silk Road, Mogao (and Dunhuang) became increasingly provincial. At some point in the fourteenth century the caves were **sealed and abandoned**.

Although Mogao's existence remained known to a few Buddhist scholars, it was only in 1900 that a wandering monk, **Wang Yuan Lu**, stumbled upon them by accident and decided to begin the work of excavation. He at once realized their significance, and made it his life's work to **restore the site**, excavating caves full of sand, touching up the murals, planting trees and gardens and building a guesthouse. This work he undertook with two acolytes and financed through begging expeditions.

The reconstructions might have gone on in relative obscurity were it not for the discovery of a bricked-up hidden chamber (now cave no. 17), which Wang opened to reveal an enormous collection of **manuscripts, sutras and silk and paper paintings** – some a thousand years old and virtually undamaged.

News of the cache soon reached the ears of the Dunhuang authorities, who, having appropriated a fair haul for themselves, decided to re-seal them in the cave on the

Visiting the caves

Getting to the caves from Dunhuang is easy. Simply step on to the street between eight and nine in the morning and you will instantly be accosted by **minibus** drivers. Choose a minibus that is nearly full, as they won't leave until the last seat is occupied. The fare is ¥5 and the trip takes about twenty-five minutes.

The caves are open daily from 8.30am to 11.30am, and from 2.30pm to around 4pm. You are supposed to join an **all-day tour**, which costs ¥80 (discounts possible for students) and which has a morning and an afternoon session, with a long lunch break. The ticket is valid for one whole day only. Make sure that you arrive by around 9.30am at the latest, so that you don't get tagged on to a tour that has already started. You cannot take a **camera** into the caves without an extremely expensive permit, and all bags must be left at an office at the gate (¥2). It is possible to sneak in a compact camera and discreetly take a few shots, but if you are caught, this could result in a large fine. The caves are not lit, to avoid damage to the murals; your guide will have a **flashlight**, but you are strongly advised to bring one of your own as well. You can buy one for about ¥12 outside the caves.

Your guide, who unlocks (and then relocks) the caves as you go along, will decide which caves you visit – there is no set route. If you have specific requests it's up to you

grounds that it would be too expensive to transport them. So it remained for a further seven years, until the arrival in 1907 of the Central Asian explorer and scholar, **Aurel Stein**. Stein, a Hungarian working for the British and the Indian Survey (in other words, a secret agent), had heard rumours of the caves and been offered items for sale. In good Howard Carter tradition, he persuaded Wang to re-open the chamber. This is how Stein later described what he saw:

> *The sight the small room disclosed was one to make my eyes open; heaped up in layers, but without any order, there appeared in the dim light of the priest's little lamp a solid mass of manuscript bundles rising to a height of nearly 10ft and filling, as subsequent measurement showed, close on 500 cubic feet – an unparalleled archeological scoop.*

This was no understatement. Examining the manuscripts, Stein found original sutras brought from India by the temples' founder, Xuan Zang, along with other Buddhist texts written in Sanskrit, Sogdian, Tibetan, Runic-Turkic, Chinese, Uighur and other languages unknown to the scholar. Amid the art finds, hardly less important, were dozens of rare Tang-dynasty paintings on silk and paper – badly crushed but totally untouched by damp.

Eventually Stein, donating the equivalent of £130 to Wang's restoration fund, left Mogao with some seven thousand manuscripts and five hundred paintings. Later in the year a Frenchman, Paul Pelliot, negotiated a similar deal, shipping six thousand manuscripts and many paintings back to Paris. And so, virtually overnight, and before the Beijing authorities could put a stop to it, the British Museum and the Louvre had acquired the core of their Chinese manuscript and painting collections.

Fuelled perhaps by Greek claims on the Elgin marbles, the Chinese are currently pressing for the **return of these missing paintings and manuscripts**. It is hard to dispute the legitimacy of these claims now, though it was only in 1961 that Mogao was declared a National Monument. Had the treasures not been removed, more would almost certainly have been lost in the chaotic years of the twentieth century. A large party of White Russians used the caves as a barracks in 1920, showing their disregard for history by scrawling their names over the frescoes. Fortunately, despite the massive loss in terms of manuscripts and scrolls, the **art work and statuary** at the caves themselves are still fabulously preserved. The cave art was not damaged during the Cultural Revolution – protected, it is said, on a personal order from Premier Zhou Enlai.

to persuade the guide. A lot of people go home after the morning tour, having seen the main highlights, but if you are staying for the afternoon (highly recommended) there are some cheap noodle stands in the car park for lunch. You can also use the break to visit the **Research and Exhibition Centre** at the entrance (see below). For the afternoon tour of the caves you should join the same guide as in the morning, who will know which caves you have already seen. The guides are well-informed, though their English is not always brilliant.

The Research and Exhibition Centre (daily 9am–5pm; ¥15), the impressive modern building opposite the car park, is definitely worth a visit. Paid for by Japanese money, it's worth seeing for the seven replica caves that have been built inside – the big advantage here is that the lights are on, the colours are fresh and you can study the murals close up. The seven caves in replica here are nos. 3, 217, 220, 249, 275, 285 and 419. A further cave is not from Mogao at all, but from the Yulin Caves (no. 25) in nearby Anxi County. Upstairs are a few surviving silk scrolls and manuscripts and there's a film about the Mogao site.

Getting back to Dunhuang isn't difficult. Go to the car park and wait for the next minibus. The last one leaves around 4pm. If you get stuck there's a basic **guesthouse** on the site.

The caves

What makes the caves so interesting is that you can trace the **development of art** over the centuries, from one dynasty to the next. Some grasp of the history of the caves is essential to appreciate them properly, but be warned, restorations and replacements in the modern era have complicated the picture, particularly where statuary is concerned – many of the statues are not original. You may hear your guide blaming the ugly replacements on the Qing dynasty – in other words on the monk Wang Yuan Lu – but some of them are a good deal newer than that. The caves are all clearly labelled with numbers above the doors.

NORTHERN WEI

The earliest caves were hewn out in the fourth and fifth centuries AD during the **Northern Wei** dynasty (386–581). This dynasty was formed by Turkic-speaking people known as the Tobas and as the centuries progressed there was constant friction between the forces of conservatism (who wanted to retain the ancient Toba customs) and those of change (who wanted to adapt Chinese customs).

The Wei caves are relatively small in size, and are often supported in the centre by a large column – a feature imported from India. A statue of the Buddha is usually central, surrounded in tiers on the walls by a **mass of tiny Buddhas** brilliantly painted in black, white, blue, red and green. The statues in fact are made of terracotta: the soft rock inside the caves was not suited to detailed carving, so the craftsmen would first carve a rough outline of the figure, then build it up with clay.

The style of the murals in these caves shows a great deal of **foreign influence**. Faces have long noses and curly hair and women are large-breasted. **Cave 101**, decorated towards the end of the fifth century, provides a good example; the Buddha, enclosed by attendant Bodhisattvas, is essentially a Western figure, recognizably Christ-like, reminiscent of Greek Byzantine frescoes. In **cave 257** the Buddha seems to be dressed in a Roman toga, while the beautiful **cave 428** shows a notably Indian influence in both content (note the peacocks on the ceiling) and style. There are, however, also the beginnings of Chinese influence in the wavy, flower-like angels sometimes seen fluttering above.

Another element in the Wei murals is the high value placed on the ideal of transcending the material world, away from the chaos and war of previous years. The serene, half-smiling face on the Buddha in **cave 259** (the first statue on the right as you enter) is likened by the Chinese to the Mona Lisa.

Murals were designed as a focus of devotional contemplation. But the early days of Buddhism in China inevitably required a **narrative purpose** as well, and the paintings soon move towards a wider subject matter, their story sequences arranged in long horizontal strips. **Cave 135** (early sixth century) illustrates a *jataka* story – concerning a former life of Buddha – in which he gave his own body to feed a starving tigress, unable to succour her cubs. The narrative, read from right to left, is broken up by simple landscapes, a frequently used device. Cave 254 shows the story of Buddha defeating Mara, or Illusion.

Artistic changes, and a shift **towards a Chinese style**, began to appear at the end of the Northern Wei period, around the middle of the sixth century. One of the most strikingly Chinese of the Wei murals is in **cave 120N** and shows, above the devotional niches, a series of battle scenes, interesting for their total lack of perspective. All the figures are drawn as though seen straight on, regardless of their relative positions, a favourite device throughout the history of Chinese painting.

SUI

With the founding of the short-lived but dynamic **Sui dynasty** in 581, Western influences began to decline rapidly. The Chinese empire had been torn apart by civil wars but now there followed a boom in Buddhism, and Buddhist art. In the four decades up to the emergence of the Tang, over seventy caves were carved at Mogao.

Structurally, they dispense with the central column. Artistically, they show the replacement of the bold, slightly crude Wei brushwork with intricate, flowing lines and an increasingly extravagant use of colour that includes gilding and washes of silver. There is a powerful sense of calm, too. In **cave 150**, for example, painted in the last year of the Sui, narrative has been dispensed with altogether in favour of a repeated theme of throned Buddhas and Bodhisattvas. In terms of statuary, the Sui period also shows a change, the figures becoming stiff and inflexible, and dressed in Chinese robes. **Cave 427** contains some characteristic Sui figures – short legs, long bodies (indicating power and divinity) and big, square heads.

TANG

The **Tang-dynasty** artists (618–906), under whom the caves at Mogao reached their artistic zenith, drew both from past traditions and real life. The classic Tang cave has a square floor, tapering roof and a niche for worship set into the back wall. The statuary includes **warriors** – a new theme – and all figures are carefully detailed, the Bodhisattvas above all, with their pleats and folds clinging softly to undulating feminine figures.

For sheer size, their **Buddhas** are the most famous, notably in caves 96 and 130. The astonishing 34-metre-high seated Buddha in **cave 96** – dressed in the traditional dragon robe of the emperor – is thought by some to have been designed deliberately to remind pilgrims of the famous Tang empress Wu Zetian. In **cave 148** there is another huge Buddha, this one reclining as though dead, and surrounded by disciples.

The **Tang paintings** range from huge murals depicting scenes from the sutras — now contained within one composition rather than the earlier cartoon-strip convention – to vivid paintings of individuals, which show a startling new sense of portraiture. Line drawing was also introduced, reaching a high stage of development.

One of the most popular and spectacular Tang mural themes was that of the Visit of the Bodhisattva Manjusri to Vimalakirti. **Cave 1** contains perhaps the greatest expression of this story. Vimalakirti, on the left, is attended by a great host of heavenly beings, eager to hear the discourse of the ailing old king. Above him the plane is tilted to take in a seemingly limitless landscape, with the Buddha surrounded by Bodhisattvas on an island in its midst. Another version can be seen in **cave 51E**, a mural that is also especially notable for the subtle shading of its portraiture which includes a magnificently depicted Central Asian retinue. Other superb Tang murals include a very free, fluid landscape in **cave 70** and, perhaps most developed of all, **cave 139A**'s depiction of the Western Paradise of the Amitabha Buddha. This last is a supremely confident painting, working in elaborate displays of architecture and figures within a style that remains wholly contemplative and calm. The theme is the Buddha's promise of paradise: the souls of the reborn rise from lotus flowers in the foreground, with heavenly scenes enclosing the Buddha above.

THE LATER CAVES

Later work, executed by the **Five Dynasties, Song, and Western Xia** (906–1227), shows different period style, though little real progression from the Tang. Much, in any case, is simply restoration or repainting of existing murals. Song work is perhaps the most interesting, tending towards a heavy richness of colour, and with many of its figures displaying the features of minority races.

During the Mongol **Yuan dynasty** (1260–1368), towards the end of which period Mogao seems to have been abandoned, the standard niche in the back wall of the caves gave way to a central altar, creating fresh and uncluttered space for murals. Subject matter, too, signifies change. Tibetan-style Lamaist (or Tantric) figures were introduced, and occult diagrams (mandalas) became fashionable. The most interesting Yuan art is apparently in **cave 465**, slightly set apart from the main body of grottoes. You might try asking the guides if they will open this up for you, though they will probably only do so for a huge fee. In the fashion of Indian Buddhist painting, the murals include Tantric figures in the ultimate state of enlightenment, graphically represented by the state of sexual union.

QINGHAI

Qinghai Province is for the most part a huge, empty wilderness in the middle of China with a population of just 4.5 million. Geographically and culturally a part of the **Tibetan plateau**, Qinghai has for centuries been a frontier zone, contested between Chinese immigrants and the Tibetans and Muslims who originally dwelt in its pastures and thin snatches of agricultural land. Today, the **minority presence** in Qinghai can still be felt strongly – as well as Tibetans, there are Hui, Salar, Tu, Mongol and Kazakh people all living here.

Only incorporated into the Chinese empire two hundred years ago – and not brought under firm Han control until 1949 when Communist armies defeated those of the Muslim warlord Ma Bufang – the area is still perceived by the Han Chinese as a frontier land for pioneers and prospectors, and, on a more sinister note, a dumping-ground for criminals and political opponents to the regime. The number of inmates held in Qinghai **prison and labour camps**, including those released but who must remain in the province because they cannot regain residency rights in their home-towns, is estimated to reach four hundred thousand – almost one in ten of the population of Qinghai. Of these, a tenth are political prisoners. Several of the prison camps are actually in the outskirts of the capital, Xining, purporting to be ordinary factories.

It is only the eastern part of the province around **Xining** that has a long-established Han presence. With its lush green valleys and plentiful annual rainfall, this is also the only part of Qinghai where sustainable agriculture takes place. To the west and south of here the land rises to a three-thousand-metre plateau which, bitterly cold for half the year, can at best be used as pastureland for cattle and sheep. To the northwest, on the other hand, towards the border with Xinjiang, the land sinks into an arid basin which was good for little until the communist era, when mineral deposits and oil were discovered. Now the area supports extensive mining.

For the traveller, the primary point of interest in Qinghai is the **road into Tibet**, and indeed this remains the only place where foreign tourists can officially cross by land to Lhasa. Qinghai is in many respects itself a part of Tibet, and in addition to the substantial Tibetan minority who live here, the splendid **Ta'er Si**, one of the major Tibetan lamaseries in all China, is located just outside Xining.

The province has other attractions too, chiefly as an unspoilt natural wilderness area. The enormous **Qinghai Hu**, China's biggest lake, in particular, offers opportunities for hiking and bird-spotting. On a more expeditionary level, there are also possibilities for trekking, rafting, hunting and mountaineering. Such activities have to be arranged by local travel agents, who can sometimes manage this at just a few days' notice.

Xining and around

The provincial capital, **XINING**, contains few tourist sights in itself, and is usually regarded as a base from which to explore the nearby Tibetan monastery of Ta'er Si. Nevertheless, as the only sizeable city in Qinghai, Xining is a surprisingly pleasant and interesting place in its own right. Set in a rather extraordinary location, with stark mountains rearing up right behind, and the inhospitable terrain immediately beyond gives the city a cosy, reassuring feel. At a height of 2200 metres, right on the outermost edge of the Tibetan plateau, Xining experiences pleasantly cool weather in summer and bitter cold in winter.

Although definitely a centre of Han population, Xining is also full of minority nationalities, in particular Hui Muslims and rather lost-looking Tibetans. It has quite an ancient history, having been established probably as early as the Han dynasty. It even served as a stopover on a minor southern route of the Silk Road and has been a fairly important trading city for the Han since at least the sixteenth century. Today, connected by fast trains to Lanzhou and other Chinese cities, Xining is a firmly established part of the network of Han China.

The city is bordered by steep hills to the north, along the foot of which runs the Huangshui River. Most of the city lies to the south of the river, though the **train station** lies immediately on the north bank, just across the bridge from the long-distance **bus station**. The centre of Xining is located about 3km to the west of here, along the main east–west streets Dong Dajie and then Xi Dajie, which connects **Da Shizi** (Big Crossroads) with a large traffic circle called **Ximen** a few hundred metres farther west.

Although the overall atmosphere is interesting for the ethnic mix, there are few particular sights to recommend themselves within the city limits. The **Great Mosque**, on Dongguan Dajie, is one of the most attractive mosques in northwest China. It was built in 1380, and encloses a large public square where worshippers can congregate. There is hardly a trace of Arab influence in the architecture – it is purely Chinese in style with flying eaves and colourful painted arches. There is also a **museum**, located in a charming historic building along a small market-lane just south of the *Yongfu Hotel*; at the time of writing, however, it was not open for visits.

To the north of the Huangshui River, a couple of kilometres west of the train station, it is possible to climb the mountain up to the 1400-year-old **Beishan Si** (North Mountain Temple). This is definitely worth the effort. You climb hundreds of steps, then walk along a whole series of walkways and bridges connecting together little caves

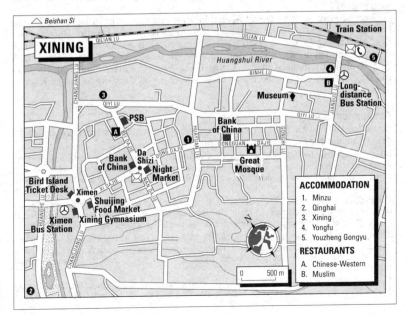

decorated with Taoist designs, often packed with ordinary people engaged in prayer ceremonies. At the very top is a pagoda from where views over the city are quite excellent on a clear day. To reach Qilian Lu at the foot of the mountain, take bus #11 from the train station, or #10 from the town centre just south of Ximen; there is quite an obvious entrance just west of Changjiang Lu.

Perhaps most interesting, however, is simply strolling around the centre of town amid the crowds. Make a point of visiting the **Shuijing Food Market**, a covered market at Shuijing Gang, off Xi Dajie and very close to Ximen. There are more than three thousand fixed stalls down here, offering not only local food, but also specialities from all over the country. Many of the stalls are open until late at night, their stoves blazing in the dark.

Practicalities

Xining's **bus** and **train** stations are located very close together in the eastern part of town on opposite banks of the Huangshui River. There are direct trains to and from most major cities in eastern China, including Lanzhou in Gansu Province (4hr). There's also a twice-daily service west to Golmud, for those heading on to Tibet. Attempting to buy **outward-bound tickets** from the train station is not recommended – any travel service (see below) can arrange tickets for ¥30 commission. The **airport**, 13km from town, has a few scheduled weekly services to and from major Chinese cities.

Most important facilities are located around the large traffic circle, Ximen. The main **Bank of China** (Mon–Fri & Saturday am) is a huge building on Dongguan Dajie near the mosque, though any of the branch offices can also change travellers' cheques – there's one just west of Da Shizi. The main **post office**,where you can also make IDD telephone calls, is on Da Shizi; you enter by climbing the raised pedestrian walkway. You'll find another office for making IDD calls a few minutes east of the train station.

There are two or three **travel agents** in town that may come in handy for buying train or plane tickets, or for organizing trips to more remote parts of Qinghai. The *Qinghai Jiaotong Luxingshe* (☎0971/8149504 ext 2626), based at the front of the long-distance bus station, offers interesting tours to Qinghai Hu (see p.894). Qinghai *CITS* (☎0971/8238701), housed in the *Xining Guest Hotel* (front building), can organize trekking, rafting, mountaineering or other adventure holidays, usually at fairly short notice.

Accommodation

Accommodation in Xining is surprisingly sparse; there is, however, one reasonable budget option, the *Yongfu*, near the train station.

Minzu, Dongda Jie (☎0971/8177951). Just west of Huyuan Jie. Quite a smart, modern place where foreigners are charged double. There's no English sign – it's the big tower a couple of blocks west of the main *Bank of China* building. Buses #1 or #2 from the train station pass by here. Dorms ②, rooms ④.

Qinghai, Huanghe Lu (☎0971/6144888 ext 31). By far the most upmarket place in town, with lots of facilities, far out in the southeast of the city. Take bus #32 from the train station, and ask where to get off. From the bus stop head south towards the vast tower – about ten minutes' walk. ⑦.

Xining Guest Hotel, Qiyi Lu (☎0971/8238701). About 1km north of Da Shizi, this is an ancient, crumbling place with a 1950s atmosphere. The double rooms aren't particularly nice, but the cheap three-bed dorms have their own bathrooms. To get here take bus #9 from the station. Dorms ②, rooms ⑤.

Yongfu, Jianguo Lu (☎0971/8140236). The cheapest option in town, and one of the friendliest, the *Yongfu* is located in a peculiar round building directly across the road from the bus station. From

XINING AND AROUND

Xining	西宁	*xīníng*
Beishan Si	北山寺	*běishān sì*
Da Shizi	大十字	*dàshízì*
Great Mosque	清真大寺	*qīngzhēn dàsì*
Huangshui River	黄水河	*huángshuǐ hé*
Shuijing Food Market	水井巷市场	*shuǐjǐngxiàng shìchǎng*
Ximen	西门	*xīmén*

ACCOMMODATION

Minzu	民族宾馆	*mínzú bīnguǎn*
Qinghai	青海宾馆	*qīnghǎi bīnguǎn*
Xining Guest Hotel	西宁宾馆	*xīníng bīnguǎn*
Yongfu	永富宾馆	*yǒngfú bīnguǎn*
Youzheng Gongyu	邮政公寓	*yóuzhèng gōngyù*

AROUND XINING

Huangzhong	皇中	*huángzhōng*
Ta'er Si	塔尔寺	*tǎěr sì*
Ledu	乐都	*lèdū*
Qutan Si	瞿昙寺	*qútán sì*
Xunhua	循化	*xúnhuà*
Mengda Nature Reserve	孟达自然保护区	*mèngdá zìrán bǎohùqū*

the train station walk ten minutes south straight across the bridge facing you as you exit, and it's on the right (west) side of the street. The reception is on the ground floor, but the hotel begins on the third floor, above a department store and a roller-skating rink. ③.

Youzheng Gongyu, Qilian Lu (☎0971/8140711). Just a couple of hundred metres east of the train station (turn left as you exit), though not particularly good value. Dorms ②, rooms ⑤.

Eating

There are a couple of reasonable **restaurants** round the *Yongfu Hotel*, and the hotel restaurant itself – a tiny place round the back of the building – has a cheap menu. If you want to sit outside, walk around the building to the right from the hotel entrance and there's a Muslim restaurant with a terrace and awnings. For excellent noodles, or a local breakfast of *zasui* soup made with mixed ox and sheep entrails, try the place a couple of minutes to the south down the main road from the *Yongfu*. It's the last building in a little row of shops and has an ornamental mosque-like exterior.

The best places to eat in Xining, though, are the **markets** downtown. The street leading east of Da Shizi fills up with food stalls during the evening and you can walk up and down sampling. The earthenware hotpots – *shaguo* – full of tofu, mushrooms and meat cooked in broth are excellent. You can also get excellent *jiaozi, hundun* soup and other basic dishes prepared on the spot The yoghurt here is good, too. The covered market, Shuijing Gang (see p.890), offers an even wider variety of options. From the main street, walk down through the market, past the shops, to reach the area where you can sit and eat. For something more upmarket, try the Chinese–Western restaurant on Bei Dajie, just north of Da Shizi.

BUS ROUTES OUT OF XINING

There are lots of interesting **bus routes** out of Xining and, at the time of writing, local prices only were being charged, which made all bus **tickets** out of Xining very cheap. In the direction of **Xiahe**, there is a bus to Linxia and another to the monastery town of Tongren, from both of which there are connecting services to Xiahe. There's also a bus to **Zhangye** in Gansu Province, via a spectacular ride north across the mountains. Finally, within Qinghai itself, there are buses to **Golmud** and also to **Lenghu** in the far northwest – from where it is possible, following very little-trodden routes, to travel north to Dunhuang in Gansu Province, or west to Ruoqiang on the Southern Silk Road in Xinjiang. Another equally exciting possibility is a bus southwest to **Maduo**. From here, very close to the source of the Yellow River, you can continue by bus along a very rough route into Sichuan Province.

Ta'er Si and beyond

Lying about 25km southeast from Xining, **Ta'er Si**, known as *Kumbum* in Tibetan, is the most important **monastery** outside Tibet. Although not as attractive as Labrang in Xiahe (see p.867), and rather swamped at weekends by local tourists, Ta'er Si is nevertheless a spectacular introduction to Tibetan culture. Both as the birthplace of Tsongkhapa, the founder of the **Yellow Hat Sect**, and as the former home of the current Dalai Lama, the monastery attracts droves of pilgrims from Tibet, Qinghai and Mongolia, who present a startling picture with their rugged features, huge embroidered coats and bold jewellery.

As well as the monastery itself, there's also the attraction of the **countryside** around. The views stretch away to distant mountains, and you can ramble through hills of wheat, pastures for cattle or horses, and over ridges and passes strewn with wild flowers. Apart from the large numbers of Han Chinese tourists, the people you meet here are mainly Tibetan horsemen, workers in the fields who will offer an ear of roasted barley by way of hospitality, or pilgrims prostrating their way around the monastery walls.

The monastery

The monastery dates from 1560, when building was begun in honour of **Tsongkhapa**, founder of the reformist Yellow Hat Sect of Tibetan Buddhism, who was born on the Ta'er Si estates. Legend tells how, at Tsongkhapa's birth, drops of blood fell from his umbilical cord causing a tree with a thousand leaves to spring up; on each leaf was the face of the Buddha, and there was a Buddha image on the trunk (now preserved in one of the stupas). During his lifetime, Tsongkhapa's significance was subsequently borne out: his two major disciples were to become the two greatest living Buddhas, one the Dalai Lama, the other the Panchen Lama.

Set in the cleft of a valley, the walled complex is an imposing sight. It's an active place of worship for about six hundred monks (ranging in age from ten to eighty) as well as the constant succession of pilgrims. There's plenty to watch: monks in dusty burgundy robes and huge leather boots sitting in temple doorways, collecting wood, drawing water and carrying food to the kitchens. At the entrance to the monastery you buy a single **ticket** for ¥21 in the kiosk to the left. The ticket theoretically gives you access to seven temples, though you can visit more than this if you wish. Just beyond the stupas on the right, there's a primitive old hotel, actually a sixteenth-century **pilgrims' hostel**, wooden and rickety, with an ancient balcony and peeling murals. It is possible to stay here, though it's often full (see below).

The most beautiful of the **temples** is perhaps the **Great Hall of Meditation** (Da Xingtang; temple no. 5 on your ticket), an enormous, very dimly lit prayer hall, colonnaded by dozens of carpeted pillars and hung with long silk tapestries (*thangkas*). Immediately adjacent to this is the **Great Hall of the Golden Roof**, with its gilded tiles, wall paintings of scenes from the Buddha's life and a brilliant silver stupa containing a statue of Tsongkhapa. The grooves on the wooden floor in front of the temple have been worn away by the hands of prostrating monks and pilgrims. This hall, built in 1560, is where the monastery began, on the site of the pipal tree that grew with its Buddha imprints. You will still see pilgrims studying fallen leaves here, apparently searching for the face of the Buddha.

Other interesting temples include the **Lesser Temple of the Golden Roof** (no.1) and the **Hall of Butter Sculpture** (no. 7). The former is dedicated to animals – from the central courtyard you can see stuffed goats, cows and bears on the balcony, wrapped in scarves and flags. The animals are thought to manifest characteristics of certain deities. The Hall of Butter Sculpture contains a display of yak butter sculptures – interesting painted tableaux, depicting Tibetan and Buddhist legends. After touring the temples, you can climb the steep steps visible on one side of the monastery to get a general view over the temples and hills behind.

During the year, five major **festivals** are held at Ta'er Si. All are fixed according to the lunar calendar: In January/February, at the end of the Chinese new year festivities, there's a large ceremony centred around the lighting of yak butter lamps. In April/May is the festival of Bathing Buddha, during which a giant portrait of Buddha is unfurled on a hillside facing the monastery. In July/August the birthday of Tsongkhapa is celebrated, and in September and October there are two more celebrations commemorating the Nirvanas of Sakyamuni and Tsongkhapa respectively.

Practicalities

To reach Ta'er Si from Xining, go to the small Ximen bus station next to the Xining Gymnasium (*Xining Tiyuguan*), just west of Ximen. From here there are frequent **buses and jeeps** to Huangzhong, the small town near Ta'er Si. The ride costs ¥2 or ¥3 and takes just over thirty minutes, through picturesque scenery (in summer) of wheatfields, green hills, woods and meadows of flowering yellow rape seed. On arrival, you may be dropped at the bus station 1km short of the monastery, or you may be taken right up to the complex itself. From the bus station, it's a twenty-minute walk (or take a pony cart for ¥1) uphill past the trinket stalls and rug sellers until you see the row of eight stupas at the monastery entrance. Returning to Xining, there are numerous buses and vehicles departing from the Huangzhong bus station right up to late afternoon.

Most travellers just come up to Ta'er Si for a few hours from Xining. By staying the night, however, you can appreciate the monastery unattended by hordes of day-trippers. **Accommodation** is available at the very cheap and basic *Pilgrim's Hostel* (①). For something slightly smarter, there's also the *Ta'ersi Hotel* (②), a large, newish place facing the monastery across a gully. It's to the left of the monastery entrance, as you arrive.

You can sometimes get **meals** at the *Pilgrim's Hostel*, depending on the vagaries of the cook, otherwise try one of the Muslim restaurants on the road between the town and monastery. These are great value, providing huge, warming bowls of noodles with plenty of vegetables and tea for a few yuan.

Qutan Si

If you feel inspired by Ta'er Si, you might want to visit another Tibetan monastery, **Qutan Si**, around 80km to the east of Xining in Ledu County. The monastery, started in 1387 during the Ming dynasty, was once among the most important Buddhist centres in China and it was maintained and expanded until the seventeenth century. Today, it is still an impressive sight – the temple is most notable for its 51 rooms of murals, exceptionally fine examples of their type, illustrating the life story of Sakyamuni.

You can reach Ledu by direct **bus** or local **train** from Xining. From Ledu you should be able to find cheap minibuses for the seventeen-kilometre ride to Qutan Si; otherwise, take a taxi there and back for about ¥60.

Mengda Nature Reserve

About 200km southeast of Xining lies an area of outstanding natural beauty, centred around **Mengda Heavenly Lake**. This part of the province, Xunhua County, has a wet, mild climate conducive to the prolific growth of trees and vegetation. The woods here are full of wild flowers and inhabited by deer and foxes.

Hardly any foreign tourists come this way, but if you want to try, you can visit it as a stopover on the way between Xining and Linxia in Gansu Province. From both Xining and Linxia, you can take buses to **Guanting** or **Xunhua**, two small towns on either side of the reserve, not more than 30km from it. Xunhua is slightly nearer, but Guanting offers easier access. From either town, hitch with a passing tractor, or take a taxi. **Accommodation** is available at the reserve.

West of Xining

West of Xining, Qinghai for the most part comprises a great emptiness. The land levels out at over 3000m, too high to support any farming, and population centres are almost non-existent – the only people who traditionally have managed to eke out a living in this environment have been nomadic yak-herders. For tourists, the real highlight of the area is the huge and virtually unspoilt **Qinghai Hu**, the size of a small sea, and home to thousands of birds. Beyond here lie a single road and rail line which wend their way slowly to **Golmud**, the only town of any size for hundreds of kilometres around, and an important crossroads for overland travellers, linked by bus not only to Xining, but also to Lhasa in Tibet and Dunhuang on the Silk Road.

Qinghai Hu and around

Situated 150km west of Xining, high up on the Tibetan plateau is the extraordinarily remote **Qinghai Hu**. The lake is vast, occupying an area of more than 4,500 square kilometres and, at 3200m above sea level, its waters are profoundly cold and salty. They are nevertheless teeming with fish and populated by nesting seabirds, particularly at the so-called **Bird Island**, which has long been the main attraction of the lake for visitors.

Apart from a visit to Bird Island – which tends to be a rushed, hectic experience – you can also hike and camp in peaceful solitude around the lake. From the smooth, green, windy shores, grazed by yaks during the brief summer, the blue, icy waters stretch away as far as the eye can see. If you have a tent, and really want a wilderness experience in China, this may be the place to get it. Just take a bus to one of the towns on the southern shore, and then strike off. Don't forget to bring warm clothes and sleeping bags, though.

Alternatively, there is a special tourist site on the southern shore of the lake, the **Qinghai Lake Tourist Centre**, where you can stay and enjoy boating, fishing and horse riding. Again, take any bus running along the southern shore.

If you don't have time to stop here, you can at least admire the view whilst travelling between Golmud and Xining. The train spends some hours running along the northern shore; travelling by bus you will pass the southern shore, and it's well worth scheduling your journey to pass the lake during daylight hours.

Bird Island

This tiny rocky outcrop, situated at the far western side of the lake, is annually nested upon by literally thousands of birds. An immense variety of seasonal birds spend time here – gulls, cormorants, geese, swans and cranes, including the rare black-necked crane. The main **bird-watching season** is from April to July, though the giant swans are best seen from November to February .

If you are not a bird-spotter, you may find the regular day trip to Bird Island a little disappointing. From Xining it's an awfully long way to come just to see a lot of birds nesting on a rock. If you treat the experience as a relaxing day out, however, and concentrate on the general backdrop of blue sky, white clouds, blue water and distant snow-capped mountains, it can turn out perfectly enjoyable.

There are several ways to reach Bird Island; the most common is on a **one-day trip** from Xining. The cheapest way to do this is on the sixty-seater bus that leaves from outside the Xining Gymnasium on either Saturday or Sunday each weekend in summer. You can book a seat at the desk that is set up on the pavement on the corner of Changjiang Lu and Xiguan Dajie the morning of the day before the departure. At 5pm, return to the desk and you will be told whether or not enough people have booked to make the trip viable. If they have, you will then be sold a ticket (¥40). Failing this, you can go with a **private travel service**. The *Qinghai Jiaotong Luxingshe* in Xining (see p.890) runs daily trips to Bird Island in fairly comfortable minibuses. Foreigners are charged ¥130 – food and entrance tickets not included. It's a long trip, leaving at 7am and getting back at around 10pm; up to ten hours of the time is spent driving. On the way up on to the plateau you will probably stop at the Riyue Pass, where there's a Tibetan prayer-flag site and a couple of Chinese towers. One of the highlights is **lunch** – delicious and very cheap fried fish – which you have at a tiny settlement just outside Bird Island.

Visiting Bird Island **independently** is something of a challenge, but it's possible, either as part of a general tour of the lake, or as a stopover between Xining and Golmud. Riding any bus between these two cities, make sure you get off at the right place by the lake – a grubby little Tibetan town called **Heimahe**, about four hours from Xining, which has a shop and a basic hotel. From here a road leads up towards Bird Island and you'll have to hitch a ride from a passing tractor or car. Fifty minutes' drive brings you to the *Bird Island Guesthouse* (②) with clean, but very cold, double rooms with bath. You'll be lucky if there's any hot water, but there's always plenty to eat.

You need to buy a **ticket** (¥22) at the guesthouse to continue the remaining 15km to the two **observation points**. The first of these is actually a beach, which you view from a hide. The second is Bird Island itself, which you observe from the opposite cliff.

WEST OF XINING		
Bird Island	鸟岛	*niǎodǎo*
Chaka Salt Lake	茶卡盐湖	*chákǎ yán hú*
Heimahe	黑马河	*hēimǎhé*
Qinghai Hu	青海湖	*qīnghǎi hú*
Golmud	格尔木	*géěrmù*
Cha Erhan Salt Lake	察尔汗盐湖	*cháěrhàn yán hú*
Golmud Hotel	格尔木宾馆	*géěrmù bīnguǎn*
Kunlun Mountains	昆仑山	*kūnlún shān*
Quanjiafu Jiulou	全家富酒楼	*quánjiāfú jiǔlóu*
Tibet bus station	西藏汽车站	*xīzàng qìchēzhàn*

Chaka Salt Lake

Not far beyond Qinghai Hu is the **Chaka Salt Lake**, which has recently become some-thing of a tourist attraction. It's a potentially beautiful place, with its white gleaming salt crystals forming a perfect mirror-like surface from a distance. At the site, you can ride a small freight train, visit a house of salt, walk on a sixty-kilometre salt bridge – and take a hunk of the stuff home with you afterwards.

At present, the only way to visit Chaka Lake is on a **tour**, usually in conjunction with Qinghai Hu. A hectic two-day visit to these two lakes (sleeping overnight at one of them) is run by the *Qinghai Jiaotong Luxingshe* (see p.890) for ¥600 per person, inclusive of all food, tickets and accommodation. The tour runs only if there are enough people.

Golmud and the road to Tibet

Nearly 3000m up on the plateau, **GOLMUD** is an incredibly isolated city, even by the standards of northwest China. It still has no airport and lies at least sixteen hours away from the nearest sizeable town by the fastest possible means of transport. In spite of this, it still manages to be the second largest city in Qinghai, with a population of around 120,000. This is because it's a city of immigrants – Han Chinese have been moved in here over the years to work the potash plants from which Golmud earns its living. It's hard to imagine that anyone would have come to live in such a cold and arid place otherwise. Geographically, Golmud is located close to the massive **Kunlun Mountains** to the south, and to the **Cai Erhan Salt Lake** to the north. Both are very scenic in parts, though they remain as yet virtually unexplored by foreign tourists.

For travellers, the city is really only interesting as a transit point between Xining in the east, Dunhuang in the north and Lhasa in the south – Golmud is the only place in China from where foreign tourists are officially allowed to cross **by land to Tibet**. For a few intrepid travellers, Golmud can additionally serve as a stopover en route to Ruoqiang on the Southern Silk Road in Xinjiang (see p.921).

Practicalities

Golmud's **train** and **bus** stations sit facing each other, way down in the south of the city. Getting to or from Xining, the easiest way is by train. Leaving Golmud, there are two services, the early afternoon one takes around 19 hours, while the one in the evening takes 23 hours. Buy your tickets in the station; the queues are unusually short here, though for same-day departures you first have to go to a second-floor office, accessible from the platform, to make a reservation. For same-day departures on the fast train to Xining, you can also buy your ticket by queuing up in an office in the front of the *Golmud Hotel*. **Buses** to Xining, surprisingly, are faster than the trains (16hr). There's also an early-morning bus to Dunhuang (15hr) for which you require a "regis-tration" paper (¥20) from Golmud *CITS* in the *Golmud Hotel* to enable you to buy a tick-et at normal price.

The scene as you exit Golmud train station is bleak almost beyond belief: a vast empti-ness, rimmed by distant buildings. It's an ugly forty-minute walk to the town centre; take a minibus (or bus #1) and it'll drop you at the only **hotel**. The *Golmud* (☎0979/412066; dorms ③, rooms ⑥) is not a bad place, comprising two buildings: the dorms are housed in the building on the left and the double rooms on the right. A Western breakfast is supposedly available at the restaurant, but the service is extremely slack.

There is some surprisingly good **food** to be had in town, however. Across the road from the hotel, and a few minutes to the south, is an excellent Sichuan restaurant. You can recognize it from the English words in the window, though there's no English menu – try the old Sichuan favourite, *gongbao jiding*, diced chicken with chillies and peanuts. For Western delicacies, there's an amazingly good menu at the obscurely

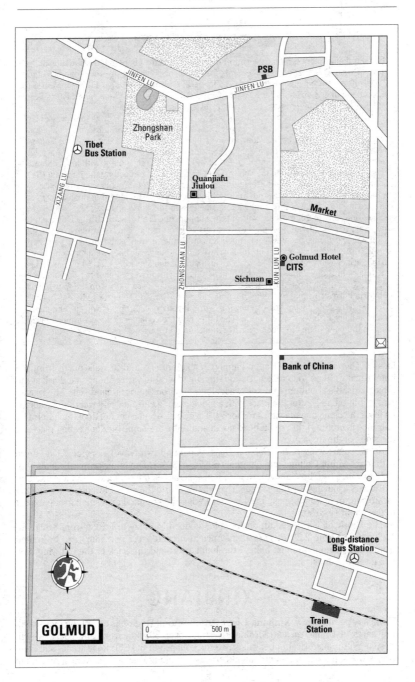

THE ROAD TO TIBET

The regulations concerning travel into **Tibet** are constantly changing: the situation at the time of writing is that all arrangements for Westerners wishing to travel overland into Tibet have to be made through **CITS in Golmud** (☎0979/412764; Mon–Fri 8.30am–noon & 3–6.30pm, Sat 8.30–10.30am & 3–5pm) in the *Golmud Hotel*. There is no other official way of getting a bus ticket or of getting on to the bus.

The deal with *CITS* is that you are buying a **"tour"** to Lhasa; partly as their way of justifying the inflated price of the trip, partly as a means of keeping tabs on independent travellers entering Tibet. The tour involves being picked up in a car from the *Golmud Hotel* and taken to the bus station, before setting off for the 36-hour journey to Lhasa. On arrival you also get a three-day guided tour in Lhasa for your money, without accommodation. However, if – having arrived in Tibet – you are not enticed by the idea of a *CITS* tour, you are perfectly free to forfeit it and set off exploring on your own. The price is ¥1080, or ¥980 if you have a student or teacher's card. Bear in mind that the journey you are paying for is one of the toughest bus journeys in the world anywhere.

The only way to get to Lhasa without the support of *CITS* is by **hitching.** This used to be straightforward, but nowadays drivers carrying foreigners can land themselves in big trouble – so it has become very much a clandestine operation. Basically, if you hang around the Tibet bus station in the northwest of the city, you *may* be approached by a truck driver willing to take you. There's also an English-speaking man who approaches travellers in the *Golmud Hotel*, and matches them with drivers. For this ride you'll still pay ¥500, and you'll run the risk of being caught at police road blocks on the way. In fact, any truck driver willing to risk taking you will usually only do so because he has his own deal with the police – but you can never be sure. If you *are* caught, you will either be fined substantially, or have to pay a bribe. The other point to consider is the desirability of riding in the back of an old truck over five-thousand-metre passes.

---

located *Quanjiafu Jiulou* (Happy Family) restaurant. To find it, walk north from the hotel (turn right as you come out), and then head west towards Zhongshan Park at the crossroads. It's about ten minutes' walk along here, on the right-hand side. The restaurant is immediately after the place with a mock-pagoda entrance and worth the walk for its thick, luscious banana pancakes for ¥4. There's also a market north of the hotel. The entrance is on the right as you head north and there are some outdoor eating places at the sides of the main area.

In the smart wing of the *Golmud Hotel*, you'll find two **travel services**. One deals with tours within Golmud and Qinghai (☎0979/413003). The other primarily deals with trips to Tibet (see box, above), though it also arranges other tours. The most exciting of these is a journey, by four-wheel-drive, all the way to the city of Ruoqiang (see p.921) in Xinjiang over the little-explored western edge of Qinghai. For a small group expect to pay about US$150 each.

The **Bank of China**, south of the hotel, is open Monday to Friday from 8.30am to 12.30pm and from 2.30pm to 6.30pm. Ancient **bicycles** (¥1 per hour) can be rented from a little compound just behind the hotel; go round the back of the old wing, and you'll see the doorway.

XINJIANG

From any point of view, **Xinjiang Uigur Autonomous Region** is one of the most exciting parts of China, an extraordinary terrain, over 3000km from any coast, which, despite all the historical upheavals since the collapse of the Silk Road trade, still comprises the same old oasis settlements strung out along the ancient routes, many still producing the silk and cotton for which they were famed in Roman times (see box, p.826). For travellers, the classic illustration of Xinjiang's remoteness from the rest of China is the extraordinary fact that officially the region's clocks are set to the same time as those in Beijing – in Kashgar, in the far west of the region, this means that in summer the sun rises at 9am or 10am and sets around midnight.

Highlights of Xinjiang might begin with the **Tian Shan** mountain pastures outside Ürümqi, where you can hike in rare solitude and stay beside Heaven Lake with Kazakhs in their yurts; but it is the old **Silk Roads** that will attract most travellers. The most fascinating of the Silk Road oasis cities are **Turpan** and **Kashgar**, both redolent of old Turkestan, and it is now possible to follow not only the Northern Silk Road from Turfan to Kashgar via Aksu and Kuqa, but also the almost forgotten southern route via Khotan. For more intrepid travellers, there's also the possibility of continuing the Silk Road journey out beyond the borders of China itself – not only over the relatively well-established **Karakoram Highway** into Pakistan, but now also over the less well-known routes into Kazakhstan and Kirgyzistan (see p.930). Finally, there exists an exciting if perilous route from Kashgar into western Tibet, a route officially closed to tourists.

Geographically, Xinjiang – literally "New Territories" – occupies an area slightly greater than Western Europe or Alaska, and yet its population is just thirteen million. By far the largest minority in Xinjiang is the Uigur, though there are also some dozen other Central Asian minority populations. Xinjiang is perhaps the least "Chinese" of all parts of the People's Republic, in spite of the fact that the Han population is steadily creeping towards fifty percent of the whole.

The **Uigur** people (pronounced *Weeg-yur*), despite centuries of domination by China, remain ethnically and culturally entirely distinct from the Han Chinese. They are the easternmost branch of the extended family of Turkic peoples who inhabit most of Central Asia and the language they speak is essentially a dialect of Turkish. Although there has been some racial mingling down the centuries, many Uigurs look decidedly un-Chinese – stockily built, bearded, with brown hair and round eyes. For at least a thousand years they have been overwhelmingly Muslim, and religion remains the focus of their identity in the face of relentless Han penetration.

The Uigurs are not in a particularly happy situation. As they are for the most part unable to speak Chinese and therefore unable to attend university or find well-paid work, their prospects for self-improvement inside the People's Republic are generally bleak. Perhaps as a consequence of this, they seem at times to extend their mistrust of Han Chinese to all foreigners – tourists included. Nevertheless, gestures such as drinking tea with them, or trying a few words of their language, will help to break down the barriers and invitations to Uigur homes frequently follow.

The land of Xinjiang is among the least hospitable in all China, covered for the most part by arid **desert and mountain**. Essentially, it can be thought of as two giant basins, both surrounded on all sides by mountains. The range lying between the two basins is the Tian Shan (Heavenly Mountains), which effectively bisects Xinjiang from west to east across the middle. The basin to the north is known as the **Junggar basin**, or Jungaria. The capital of Xinjiang, and only major city, **Ürümqi**, is here, on the very southern edge of the basin, as is the heavily Kazakh town of **Yining**, right up against the border with Kazakhstan. The Junggar basin has been subject to fairly substantial Han settlement over the past forty years, with a degree of industrial and agricultural development. It remains largely grassland, with large state farms in the centre and Kazakh and Mongol herdsmen (still partially nomadic) in the mountain pastures on the fringes. The climate is not particularly hot in summer, and virtually Siberian from October through to March. To the south is the **Tarim basin**, dominated by the scorching Taklamakan desert, where the weather is fiercely hot and dry in summer. This is where the bulk of the Uigur population lives, in strings of oases (Turpan and Kashgar among them) scattered along the old routes of the Silk Road. Some of these oasis cities

---

UIGUR FOOD

Uigur food, unsurprisingly, has far more of a Central Asian than a Chinese flavour. The most basic staple – which often seems to be the only food available – is **laghman**, which comprises a stew of mutton, tomatoes, hot peppers and other vegetables served on rough, handmade noodles. The mutton is often of poor quality and, to delicate Western palates, *laghman* can taste a lot better without meat. For the same spicy sauce but without the noodles and with chicken (served chopped up in its entirety, head, feet and all), try *tohogish* (known in Chinese as *dapan ji*) which is served in smarter restaurants.

In summertime, apart from *laghman*, street vendors also offer endless cold noodle soup dishes, usually very spicy. **Noodles** are far more common than rice, though rice does appear in the saffron-coloured *pilau*, comprising fried rice and hunks of mutton. More familiar to foreigners are the **grilled mutton kebabs** on skewers – it is normal to buy several of them at once, as one skewer does not make much more than a mouthful. They are often eaten with delicious glasses of ice-cold yoghurt (known in Chinese as *suannai*), which are available everywhere in Xinjiang. Oven-baked **breads** are also popular in markets: you'll see bakers apparently plunging their hands into live furnaces, to stick balls of dough on to the brick-lined walls; these are then withdrawn minutes later as bagel-like bread rolls, and *nan* flat breads, or sometimes *permuda* (known in Chinese as *kaobao*), tasty baked dough packets of mutton and onions, which can also be fried – as *samsa* – rather than baked. The steamed version, *manta*, recalls Chinese dumplings or *mantou*.

---

are buried in the desert and long forgotten; others survive on irrigation using water from the various rivers and streams that flow from surrounding mountains. As well as forgotten cities, these sands also cover another buried treasure – **oil**. Chinese estimates reckon that three times the proven US reserves of oil are under the Taklamakan alone.

Some history

The region's history has been coloured by such personalities as Tamerlane, Genghis Khan, Attila the Hun and even Alexander the Great. More often, though, in counterpoint to the great movements of history, Xinjiang has been at the mercy of its isolation and the feudal warring between the rulers of its oasis kingdoms, or **khanates**.

The influence of China has been far from constant. The area – commonly referred to in the West as Eastern (or Chinese) Turkestan until 1949 – first passed under Han control in the second century BC, under Emperor Wu Di. But it was only during the **Tang dynasty** (650–850 AD) that this control amounted to more than a military presence. The Tang period for Xinjiang was something of a golden age, with the oases south of the Tian Shan largely populated by a mysterious but sophisticated Indo-European people, and the culture and Buddhist art of the oases at their zenith. Around the ninth century, however, came a change – the gradual rise to dominance of the **Uigurs**, and their conversion to **Islam**.

Subsequent centuries saw the **conquests of the Mongols** under Genghis Khan and later, from the west, of Tamerlane. Both brought havoc and slaughter in their wake, though during the brief period of Mongol rule (Yuan dynasty 1271–1368) the Silk Road trade was hugely facilitated by the fact that, for the first and only time in history, east and west Asia were under a single government.

After the fall of the Mongols, and the final disappearance of the Silk Road, Xinjiang began to split into khanates and suffered a succession of religious and factional wars. Nonetheless, it was an independence of a kind and Qing **reassertion of Chinese domination** in the eighteenth century was fiercely contested. A century later, in 1862, full-scale **Muslim rebellion** broke out, led by the ruler of Kashgaria, Yakub Beg, armed and supported by the British who were seeking influence in this buffer zone between India and Russia. Ultimately the revolt failed – Beg became a hated tyrant – and the region remained part of the Chinese empire.

At the beginning of the twentieth century, Xinjiang was still a Chinese backwater controlled by a succession of brutal warlords who acted virtually independently of the central government. The last one of these before World War II, **Sheng Shizai**, seemed momentarily to be a reforming force, instituting religious and ethnic freedoms, and establishing trade with the newly emergent Soviet Union. Almost inevitably, however, he ended by abandoning his moderate positions. Slamming the door on the Soviets and on leftist influences within Xinjiang itself in 1940, he began a reign of terror resulting in the deaths of over two hundred thousand Communists, intellectuals, students and Muslim nationalists.

The drive towards the defeat of the Guomindang in 1949 temporarily united the conflicting forces of Muslim nationalism and Chinese communism. After the Communist victory, however, there could be only one result. The principal Muslim Nationalist leaders were quietly murdered, allegedly killed in a plane crash, and the impetus towards a separate state was lost. The last Nationalist leader, a Kazakh named Osman, was executed in 1951.

Since 1949, the Chinese government has made strenuous attempts to stabilize the region by **settling Han Chinese** from the east, into Ürümqi in particular – the number by 1993 was up to six million from just two hundred thousand forty years earlier. The Uigur population of Xinjiang, from being ninety percent of the total in 1949, had slipped to just below fifty percent by 1982, and is probably still slipping, in spite of the minorities' exemption from the One Child Policy. Today, however, the Chinese government is still nervous about Xinjiang, especially given the enormous economic potential of the area, in terms of coal mining, oil exploration and tourism. In recent years there have been outbursts of **Uigur dissent**, most notably in 1992, in the city of Kashgar, when the army and air force were called in to suppress demonstrations, and the city was temporarily closed to foreigners. Bombs, allegedly set by separatists, exploded in Ürümqi in 1992 and Kashgar in 1993. Prior to that, in 1986, there had been protests in response to China's **nuclear tests** at the desert site near Lop Nor, prompted by what seemed to be numerous cases of early death from cancer and a high incidence of deformity in lambs and newborn children. In the meantime the nuclear tests go on, and in the aftermath of the break-up of the Soviet Union, the possibility of a new outbreak of violent nationalism among the Xinjiang Uigurs cannot be ruled out.

Eastern Xinjiang: the road to Turpan

The road from Dunhuang in western Gansu as far as **Hami** and then **Turpan** – the easternmost part of Xinjiang, east of the central area dominated by the Tian Shan – comprises some of the harshest terrain in the whole of China. Geographically an extension of the Tarim basin, little water ever reaches this area of scorching depressions which in summer is the hottest part of the country, and which was dreaded by the Silk Road traders as one of the most hazardous sections of the entire cross-Asia trip. Even today, crossing the area is most memorable for its suffocating heat and monotonous landscapes, though ironically Turpan – despite the heat – can be one of the most relaxing and enjoyable places in all China.

Hami

HAMI today is the eastern gateway to Xinjiang, a rich oasis, in the midst of a seemingly endless desert and famous throughout China for its **melons**, the *Hami gua*. Like Turpan farther to the west, it lies in a depression and is in consequence one of the

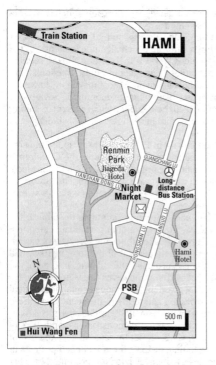

hottest places in China. There's not much here to detain the visitor; nevertheless, it's a pleasant place to stay and a convenient stopping point along the road between Dunhuang and Turpan – it lies more or less midway between the two.

Historically, Hami has always been an important part of the Silk Road, occupying one of the few fertile spots between Gansu Province and Turpan. Xuan Zang, the famous Buddhist pilgrim, nearly died of thirst on his way here, while Marco Polo noted with evident pleasure the locals' habit of not only supplying guests with food and shelter but also allowing them to sleep with their wives.

The small town is centred around the northern end of Zhongshan Lu. The bus station and hotels are in this area, while the train station is farther out in the north of town. There is just one historical site in Hami – the **Hui Wang Fen** (Tombs of the Hami Kings). From 1697 until 1930, Hami was nominally controlled by kings, who for a time had obediently sent tribute to the Qing court, before becoming involved in the Muslim revolts that periodically engulfed Xinjiang. Although the kings ruled until 1930, the city of Hami was virtually destroyed at least twice during these revolts. Today the tomb complex is in the south of the city and comprises a number of domed mausoleums in Islamic style as well as a mosque. To reach it from the centre of town, follow Zhongshan Lu south over the river and right along to the end. It's a forty-minute walk, or you can take bus #1 from Zhongshan Lu south to its terminal and then walk another few minutes on from there in the same direction.

Practicalities

For most travellers, access to Hami is by **bus** from Dunhuang, Turpan or Ürümqi. There are daily buses to and from all three cities (except Sundays), all leaving in the early morning – journey time to Dunhuang and Turpan is approximately eight hours each way, while to Ürümqi it's about eleven hours. There's also a bus link three times a week between Hami and Jiuquan in Gansu Province, which goes through Jiayuguan. From Hami it's also possible to get a bus to the Republic of Outer Mongolia, which lies very close to Hami. This bus runs only very infrequently and you will need a visa to visit Outer Mongolia.

All **trains** running between Lanzhou and Ürümqi also stop at Hami. The train station is linked to the bus station by bus #3 and to Zhongshan Lu by bus #1.

There are various **accommodation** possibilities in the area of the bus station. For something smart and relatively inexpensive, take the side exit of the bus station on to Guangchang Lu and walk west until you come to the first left turn. The shining new *Jiageda* (☎232140; ④) is a few minutes down here, on the far side of the road. In the other direction is the less salubrious but cheaper *Hami* (dorms ①, rooms ③). From the bus station main exit, walk south for about fifteen minutes along Jianguo Lu, or take bus #3 for two stops, then turn left down Yingbing Lu. *CITS* is also located in this hotel. It's sometimes possible to stay in very cheap, basic rooms at guesthouses right at the bus station itself.

For **food**, you need go no farther than the excellent **night market** on Tianshan Dong Lu (south along Jianguo Lu from the bus station, then first right). This is one of the nicest night markets you'll find: extremely friendly, busy and clean, with great kebabs, grilled spicy freshwater fish, noodles and *hundun* soup. You can also get large, deliciously refreshing bowls of yoghurt (*suannai*).

Turpan

The small and economically insignificant town of **Turpan** (Tulufan to the Chinese) has in recent years turned itself into one of the major tourist destinations of Xinjiang. Credit for this must go largely to the local residents, who have not only covered all the main streets and walkways of the town with vine trellises, converting them into delightful shady green tunnels (partly for the benefit of tourists), but have also managed to retain a relatively easy-going manner even in the heady economic climate of modern China. There are still few cars, and donkey carts remain the preferred mode of transport. In summer the weather is reputedly the hottest in China – the **dry heat** is so soporific that there is little call to do anything but sleep or sip cool drinks in outdoor cafés with other tourists. This may not be what you came to China for, but quite a lot of people appreciate it by the time they reach Turpan. To ease the consciences of tourists, there are in addition a number of **ruined cities** and **Buddhist caves** in the countryside around the city, testimony to its past role as an important oasis on the Silk Road route. Bear in mind that Turpan is very much a summer resort; if you come out of season (Nov–Mar), you may find it chilly and rather miserable.

Turpan is an agricultural oasis, famed above all for **grapes**. Today, virtually every household in the town has a hand in the grape business, both in cultivating the vines, and in drying the grapes at the end of the season. Every house has its own ventilated brick barn, usually on the roof, the best spot for catching the hot desiccating winds that sweep through the area. Turpan is located in a depression eighty metres below sea level, which accounts for its extreme climate – well over 40°C in summer, well below freezing in winter.

Today, Turpan is a largely **Uigur-populated** area, and, in Chinese terms, an obscure backwater, but it has not always been so. At the time of the Han dynasty, the Turpan oasis was a crucial point along the Northern Silk Road, and the cities of **Jiaohe**, and later **Gaochang** (both of whose ruins can be visited from Turpan), were important and wealthy centres of power. From the ninth to the thirteenth century, a rich intellectual and artistic culture developed in

Gaochang, resulting from a fusion between the original Indo-European inhabitants and the (pre-Islamic) Uigurs. It was not until the fourteenth century that the Uigurs of Turpan converted to Islam.

The Town

For some travellers, the feature that makes Turpan so relaxing is the absence of sights. The downtown area doesn't amount to much more than two or three quiet streets, protected from the baking summer sun by delightful vine trellises. There is a **museum** (daily 9am–8pm; ¥12) on Gaochang Lu, containing a smallish collection of silk fragments, boots, tools, manuscripts and preserved corpses recovered from the nearby Silk Road sites, including those from the Atsana Graves which you can visit just outside Turpan (see p.907). Other than this, the **bazaars** off Laocheng Lu, a few hundred metres east of Gaochang Lu, are worth a casual look, though they are not comparable to anything in Kashgar. You'll find knives, clothes, hats and boots on sale, while the most distinctively local products include delicious sweet green raisins, as well as walnuts and almonds.

One of the nicest ways to spend an evening after the heat of the day has passed is to **rent a donkey cart** and take a tour of the countryside south of town, a world of dusty tracks, vineyards, wheat fields, shady poplars, running streams and incredibly friendly, smiling people. You are unlikely to encounter many more tranquil rural settings than this in China. It's easy to arrange a tour from any donkey-cart driver around *John's Café*; for a tour lasting an hour or more, two or three people might pay around ¥10–15 each. *John's* also offers **bike rental** for ¥1.5 per hour, which works out slightly cheaper than the hotels' rates.

Practicalities

The only way to arrive in downtown Turpan is by **bus**. Frequent buses run between Ürümqi and Turpan, there's a daily bus service to and from Hami and one three times a week to and from Kashgar. Turpan's **train station** is 35km away at Daheyan – from where it takes at least an hour to get into town by bus. **Getting around town** is best done on foot, by bicycle or by donkey cart, for which you should rarely pay more than ¥1 per journey.

For travel to and from Ürümqi you're better off sticking to the direct **bus**, but for connections with anywhere east of Hami you'll want the **train**. *CITS* (☎0995/521352), in the *Oasis Hotel*, can book your tickets out of Daheyan station for ¥30 commission and will need a couple of days' notice. It is often possible, however, to buy your own train tickets at Daheyan in the station, with sleeper reservations for the same evening if you get there by 6pm. There is no airport at Turpan, but *CITS* can book you **flights** out of Ürümqi for a small commission. Another convenient place to book either train or plane tickets is *John's Information Cafe*.

ACCOMMODATION

There is a **hotel** at the bus station itself, the *Jiaotong,* but tourists get charged double here. Better hotels are located on the north–south Qingnian Lu, two blocks to the east of the bus station – it's a ten-minute walk along Laocheng Lu, or catch a donkey cart. Note that in Turpan, all hotel rooms regardless of price have **air-conditioning** – just make sure that yours is working when you check in.

The *Turpan Guesthouse* (☎0995/522301; dorms ①, rooms ④–⑥), on Qingnian Lu a couple of hundred metres south of the junction with Laocheng Lu, is a popular place with backpackers, offering primitive three-bed dorms and smarter doubles. It's a useful place to be as *John's Information Café* is right opposite, and most of the donkey cart

EASTERN XINJIANG

Hami	哈密	*hāmì*
Hami Hotel	哈密宾馆	*hāmì bīnguǎn*
Hui Wang Fen	回王坟	*huíwángfén*
Jiageda Hotel	加格达宾馆	*jiāgédá bīnguǎn*
Turpan	吐鲁番	*tǔlǔfān*
Daheyan	大河沿	*dàhéyán*
ACCOMMODATION		
Jiaotong	交通宾馆	*jiāotōng bīnguǎn*
Turpan	吐鲁番宾馆	*tǔlǔfān bīnguǎn*
Yiyuan	颐园宾馆	*yíyuán bīnguǎn*
Oasis	绿洲宾馆	*lǜzhōu bīnguǎn*
AROUND TURPAN		
Atsana Graves	阿斯塔娜古墓区	*āsītǎnà gǔmùqū*
Bezeklik Caves	柏孜克里克千佛洞	*bózīkèlìkè qiānfódòng*
Emin Minaret	苏公塔	*sūgōng tǎ*
Flaming Mountains	火焰山	*huǒ yànshān*
Gaochang	高昌	*gāochāng*
Grape Valley	葡萄沟	*pútáogōu*
Jiaohe	交河	*jiāohé*
Karez irrigation site	坎儿井	*kǎnérjǐng*

and minibus drivers hang around here. In the hot summer evenings, there are cheerful displays of local singing and dancing in the gardens round the back, which you can attend (and join in with) for a small entrance fee.

Also on Qingnian Lu, but a couple of minutes north of the junction with Laocheng Lu, on the righthand side, is the *Yiyuan* (☎0995/522170, ext 3201; dorms ①, rooms ③), a small place with no English sign, which has relatively cheap double rooms with private bath and four-bed dorms. Finally, another ten minutes' walk north from the *Yiyuan* is the very pleasant *Oasis* (☎0995/522478; dorms ①, rooms ⑦). It has large grounds, with various facilities including post offices, travel agents, barbers and shops. The only inconvenience here is that the hotel is quite a way from the bus station, which can make a difference in the 45°C heat if you're on foot.

EATING AND DRINKING

John's Information Café is the centre of tourist life in Turpan. "John" is in fact a Chinese entrepreneur who seems to know better than anyone in China how to cater to budget travellers – he also has branches in Kashgar and Ürümqi. The cafés also double as useful travel agencies, though there are rumours that John reports on the activities of travellers to the authorities. If you are planning anything illegal (such as crossing from Kashgar to Tibet), you might be advised not to talk about it here. As for the food, **Western breakfasts**, buttered toast, cheese omelettes, yogurt with honey, and coffee are all available here under the trellises – as well as quite reasonable Chinese dishes. *John's* is also a nice place to try the local **Turpan wine**. The red stuff is sweet and thick like port, but some of the white is very drinkable indeed if you are willing to stretch to about ¥30 a bottle. The outdoor café at the back of the *Turpan Guesthouse* also has an English menu, and is quite a nice place to drink beer, especially in the evenings when you can listen in on the live Uigur singing and dancing performances taking place near-by (see above).

For **Chinese** food there is a whole series of touristy restaurants with English menus, to the west of the main crossroads north of the *Turpan Guesthouse*. All have outdoor tables and chairs under the vines, with reasonable prices and friendly service – though check carefully the prices of what you are ordering. Try *liang ban hong gua*, a delicious cold cucmber salad with garlic and soya sauce. For more upmarket Chinese food, try one of the restaurants in the *Oasis Hotel*, while basic, cheap Uigur staples (see box, p.900)can be picked up in the stalls and cheap resaurants in the west of town on Laocheng Lu, near the bazaar.

Around Turpan

Nearly all visitors to Turpan end up taking the customary **tour** of the historical and natural sights outside the town. The tours are very cheap and quite fun, as much for the chance to get out into the desert as for the sights in themselves, which usually include the two ancient cities of **Gaochang** and **Jiaohe**, the **Emin Minaret**, the **Karez underground irrigation channels**, the **Bezeklik Caves** and **Atsana Graves**. Assuming you can get together a group of five people, a trip to all the above sites will take the best part of a day (with a break for lunch and siesta if you choose) and cost ¥30–50 per person in addition to the entrance tickets totalling at least ¥75 on top – most of the sites ask for ¥10–20 (less if you have a Chinese student card). Sites are open daily, for most of the hours of daylight, around 8am–5pm.You won't have any difficul-ty finding the minibuses – the tourist hotels organize groups, as does *CITS* in the *Oasis Hotel*. The most interesting places are the closest to town, which makes **cycling** a good option if you want to avoid a tour and can stand the heat (see details below). It's perfectly reasonable just to book a half-day tour if you want to only see the minaret, Jiaohe and the irrigation site.

The Emin Minaret, Jiaohe and Karez irrigation site

The most impressive of all the sights around Turpan is the eighteenth-century **Emin Minaret**, just 2km southeast of the city – you can even walk there, by following Jiefang Jie east out of town for about thirty minutes. Slightly bulging and pot-bellied, built of sun-dried brown bricks arranged in differing patterns layer by layer, the minaret tapers its way 40 metres skyward to a rounded tip. The adjacent mosque houses a large, shady space and a lattice-work ceiling held up by wooden supports. From the top of the mosque there's a stupendous view over the green oasis in the foreground and the dis-tant snowy Tian Shan Mountains beyond.

About 9km east of Turpan is the ruined city of **Jiaohe**. Of the two ruined cities in the area, this is the only one that can be reached by bicycle. It's a spectacular, lonely site on top of a plateau carved out by the two halves of a forking river. Although the city of Jiaohe was for large parts of its history under the control of Gaochang (see below), these days the two cities look much the same in size. The site stretches for a couple of kilometres, and the main buildings are signposted in English. As with Gaochang, a Buddhist monastery marks the town centre. Another feature is the presence of ancient wells still containing water. The old buildings comprise little more than crumbling, windswept mud walls the same colour as the desert around them, but nevertheless Jiaohe is an atmospheric place to wander and contemplate – make sure you have at least one hour to explore.

Returning from Jiaohe, minibus drivers usually drop you off at a **Karez irrigation site**. The Karez irrigation system basically taps in on natural underground channels carrying water from source (in this case, glaciers at the base of the Tian Shan mountains) to the point of use. Strategically dug wells then bring water to small surface channels which run around the streets of the town. Many ancient Silk Road cities relied on this system, including those much farther to the west, in areas such as modern Iran: keeping the water underground for as long as possible was essential primarily to reduce evaporation, but also to keep it clean of silt and dust. Throughout Turpan County there are literally hundreds of kilometres of channels, which are still partially in use. In one or two places you can climb down into the tunnels and have a look.

The Bezeklik Caves, Gaochang and Astana Graves

For the other sites, you definitely need a minibus – they are too far to reach by bicycle. The first stop is usually the Bezeklik Caves, but on the way you'll pass the **Flaming Mountains**, made famous in the sixteenth-century Chinese novel *Journey to the West,* a highly embellished version of the story of the Chinese Buddhist Xuan Zang's pilgrimage to India. The novel depicts these sandstone mountains as walls of flame, and it's not hard to see how the story arose, from the red sandstone hillsides, lined and creviced as though flickering with flame in the heat haze.

The **Bezeklik Caves**, however, in a valley among the Flaming Mountains some 50km east of Turpan, are frankly disappointing, offering mere fragments of the former wealth of Buddhist cave art here. The location is beautiful and there is a bizarre, Buddhist fantasy-land under construction on the way into the valley, but most of the murals were cut out and removed to Berlin by Albert Von Le Coq (see p.920) at the beginning of this century. A good deal of them were subsequently destroyed by the allied bombing of Germany in World War II.

South of here lie the ruined city of **Gaochang** and the **Astana Graves**, burial site of the imperial dead of Gaochang. Unfortunately, the graves have had most of their interesting contents removed – little remains here beyond a couple of preserved corpses and some murals. The important relics from the tombs are all in museums in Turpan and Ürümqi. The Gaochang ruins, however, spreading out over a huge area, are somewhat more impressive, although they have suffered both from the ravages of Western archeologists and from the local population, who for centuries have been carting off bits of the city's mud walls to use as soil for their fields. You can walk, or take a donkey cart, from the entrance to the centre of the site, which is marked by a large square building, the remains of a monastery whose outer walls are covered in niches, in each one of which a Buddha was originally seated. Now just a few bare, broken traces of these Buddhas remain. If you have time, the nicest thing you can do in Gaochang is strike off on your own and listen to the hot wind whistling through the mud-brick walls. Although very little can be discerned beyond a jungle of broken walls, many of these are metres high, and certainly extensive enough to give the impression of a substantial settlement.

North of Turpan, and at the western end of the Flaming Mountains, is the so-called **Grape Valley**. There's very little point visiting this place out of season, but from mid-July to August, it's a pleasant little oasis in the middle of a stark desert, covered in shady trellises bulging with fruit (which you have to pay for if you want to eat). This could be included on your minibus tour, or you could reach it on a very hot bicycle ride, but bear in mind that the scenery here is not much different from that of downtown Turpan.

Ürümqi and Tian Chi

ÜRÜMQI is the political, industrial and economic capital of Xinjiang, and by far the largest city in the region, with a population of well over one million, the overwhelming majority of whom are Han Chinese. Its name means "beautiful pastures" – a slightly misleading description these days, even though the skyline to the east is marked by the graceful snowy peaks of the Tian Shan (indeed the city itself is 900m above sea level).

For travellers arriving from western China or Central Asia, this will be the first truly Chinese city on your route, and the first chance to witness the consumer boom that is sweeping the high streets of China, in the shape of smart department stores and designer clothes boutiques. So vital has the city become as China's most westerly industrial outpost that in 1992 it was officially decreed a "port" to enable it to impose the special low rates of tax, normally permitted only in port cities such as Shanghai and Xiamen, as a means of luring in capital; an unusual distinction, to say the least, for a city located 2000km from the nearest sea.

If you're coming from eastern China, however, the city may not seem particularly exciting, given its lack of historical identity. Nevertheless, it does have lively Uigur bazaars, as well as a certain pioneering feel to it – the shiny, new highrise office buildings and hotels downtown seem to suggest a great metropolis, until you notice the barren, scrubby hillsides just around the corner and realize that the whole place has fairly recently been dropped into the desert. Apart from this, the main reason to visit Ürümqi is to arrange a trip to **Tian Chi** (Heaven Lake), four hours east of the city by bus.

Ürümqi does not have a long history. Under the name of Dihua it became the capital of Xinjiang in the late nineteenth century. During the first half of the twentieth century the city was something of a battleground for feuding warlords – in 1916 Governor Yang Zengxin invited all his personal enemies to a dinner party here, and then had their heads cut off one by one during the course of the banquet. Later, shortly before the outbreak of World War II, **Soviet troops** entered the city to help quell a Muslim rebellion; they stayed, in one form or another, until 1960. Ürümqi began to emerge from its extreme backwardness only with the completion of the Lanzhou–Ürümqi **rail line** in 1963. This more than anything helped to integrate the city, economically and psychologically, into the People's Republic. And with the opening of the Ürümqi–Almaty rail line in 1991, the final link in the long-heralded direct route from China through Central Asia to Europe was complete.

Arrival and accommodation

The **train station** is in the southwest of the city, with direct services to and from Beijing, Shanghai, Lanzhou, Xian, Chengdu and Almaty (in Kazakhstan). There's also a local rail line running south to Korla. To or from Turpan, however, you're best off taking the bus.

The main long-distance **bus station** is a few blocks north of the train station, on Heilongjiang Lu. If you're arriving by bus, however, you will not necessarily end up here – Ürümqi has special bus stops for every city in Xinjiang, all located outside their respective regional offices. Kashgar buses, for example, stop near the train station while Turpan minibuses stop at the Erdaoqiao market.

The **airport** is about 15km from the city; access is either by taxi or by the airport bus which stops at the *CAAC* office on Youhao Lu, northwest of the post office. There are flights within the province and to all major Chinese cities, and Ürümqi is also an international airport serving (through various airlines) Almaty, Istanbul, Islamabad, Moscow, Sharjah, Tashkent and Hong Kong. The flight to Islamabad, which at the moment is once-weekly and costs US$300, could be a useful fall-back if the Karakoram Highway is closed.

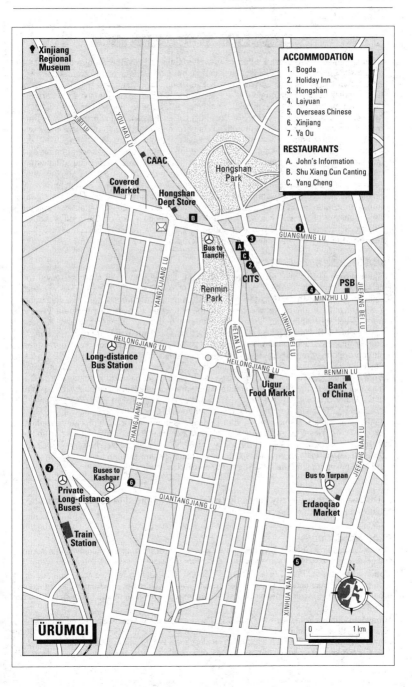

ÜRÜMQI

Xinjiang Regional Museum

XIBEILU

YOU HAO LU

CAAC

Covered Market

Hongshan Dept Store

Hongshan Park

ACCOMMODATION
1. Bogda
2. Holiday Inn
3. Hongshan
4. Laiyuan
5. Overseas Chinese
6. Xinjiang
7. Ya Ou

RESTAURANTS
A. John's Information
B. Shu Xiang Cun Canting
C. Yang Cheng

GUANGMING LU

Bus to Tianchi

CITS

PSB

MINZHU LU

Renmin Park

YANGZIJIANG LU

HETAN LU

XINHUA BEI LU

JIEFANG BEI LU

HEILONGJIANG LU

Long-distance Bus Station

HEILONGJIANG LU

Uigur Food Market

RENMIN LU

Bank of China

CHANGJIANG LU

Buses to Kashgar

Private Long-distance Buses

QIANTANGJIANG LU

JIEFANG NAN LU

Bus to Turpan

Erdaoqiao Market

Train Station

XINHUA NAN LU

N

0   1 km

MOVING ON FROM ÜRÜMQI

Buses connect Ürümqi with all major towns in Xinjiang Province, though lots of buses do not start from the long-distance bus station, but from various points around the town (see map for Kashgar and Turpan buses). This also means that if you board your bus at the long-distance bus station you'll then find yourself driven to the other place where the bulk of the passengers will embark; the only advantage being that you are less likely to be charged a "foreigner's" price. For the short trip to Turpan, you will save a lot of time by picking up your bus or minibus from the Erdaoqiao market, from where there are departures throughout the day. Private buses for many destinations leave from the square outside the train station – of these the most interesting are those running east into Gansu Province, to Liuyuan (the jumping-off point for Dunhuang) and to Lanzhou, which represent a cheap and hassle-free alternative to the trains.

Ürümqi is the starting point for **trains** to most major Chinese cities, including Beijing, Shanghai, Chengdu and Guangzhou – as well as all points in between. The easiest way to buy train tickets out of Ürümqi, is to use the travel agents in the *Hongshan Hotel* – they'll charge about ¥30 commission and usually require two or three days' notice. Buying a ticket by yourself in the station is extremely difficult. For connections to **Kazakhstan** – by bus or train – see below.

ROUTES TO KAZAKHSTAN

The opening of the rail link between China and Kazakhstan in 1990 finally sealed the cross-Asia line that connects the ports of eastern China with those of northwestern Europe – a route that offers the potential of substantial time savings over the trans-Siberian route. In the meantime, however, the link is used by just two **trains** a week in both directions connecting Ürümqi and Almaty, departing on Saturday and Monday nights from both ends. Tickets (sleepers only, from about ¥500) in Ürümqi can be bought one day prior to travel in the International Departure lounge at the north end of the train station building, from 10am–3pm and 5–7pm. **Buses** run daily from Ürümqi long-distance bus station daily for ¥460 and take 24 hours; alternatively, you can pick up a bus from Yining (see p.915) three times a week (Mon, Wed & Sat; ¥250); tickets are sold at a special office inside Yining bus station. There are three **flights** a week between Ürümqi and Almaty; *Kazakh Airlines* in the World Plaza on Beijing Nan Lu (☎0991/3836400) charges US$111, which is considerably less than *CAAC* (¥1600).

After a few years of uncertainty, **visa** regulations now seem to have hardened: nationals of all countries (except CIS) require visas, which can be obtained in Ürümqi from the *Kazakh Airlines* office – for a three-day transit visa you need to show an Uzbeki or Russian visa already in your passport; for tourist visas you need to show "visa support" such as proof of paid hotel bookings or an authorized invitation.

Distances within the city are fairly large, so you will need to use **buses and taxis**. Most taxi rides within the city cost around ¥10.

Accommodation

Bogda, Guangming Lu (☎0991/2824432). Just around the corner from the *Hongshan*, this is a quiet and salubrious place, which sometimes has dormitories available. Dorms ②, rooms ⑥.

Holiday Inn, Xinhua Bei Lu (☎0991/2818788, fax 2817422). Of fully international standard, with a wide range of restaurants, a disco and health club. Even if you're not staying here, foreigners are usually granted the privilege of going up to the lounge on the top floor to watch satellite TV and use the toilets. ⑧.

Hongshan, Xinhua Bei Lu (☎0991/2824973). The principal budget travellers' refuge, offering doubles with bath or a dormitory where you sleep on the carpet – the hot showers are in another building across a car park. The main advantage is its location, close to parks, shops, *John's Café* and the Tian Chi bus stop. It's also full of travel agents' offices, whose reps, mostly language students, will swarm around you whenever you show your face. From the train station, you're best off taking a taxi to get here; otherwise take any bus going north to the main post office – #2 or #52 will do. From the post office it's a fifteen-minute walk east along Guangming Lu. Dorms ①, rooms ④.

Laiyuan (☎0991/2828368). Located on the small lane opposite the *Holiday Inn*, just a few hundred metres down, and offering very plush doubles. ⑧.

Overseas Chinese Hotel, Xinhua Nan Lu (☎0991/2860793). Slightly remote in the south of the city, but has a pleasant, quiet atmosphere, with one old (cheaper) building and one new one. Take bus #7 south down Xinhua Bei Lu. ⑤–⑦.

Xinjiang, corner of Changjiang Lu and Qiantangjiang Lu (☎0991/5852511). Just ten minutes' walk from the train station, this is a lively place full of Pakistani traders. Doubles here range from spartan rooms without bath to pleasant but overpriced with bath. Dorms ②, rooms ④–⑥.

Ya Ou (☎0991/5856699). For travellers arriving by train, this is a very convenient option right in the train station square, to the far left (north) as you come out of the station. Clean modern doubles and three- and four-bed dorms. No English sign. Dorms ②, rooms ⑥.

The City

In the vicinity of the *Hongshan Hotel* are a couple of pleasant parks which are useful for orientation. One is **Renmin Park**, a little to the west of the *Hongshan*, which runs from north to south right through the centre of the city, cooled by various streams and lakes. The other is **Hongshan Park** (Red Mountain Park; ¥10), clearly visible on a hill to the north of the hotel – the entrance is about ten minutes' walk north of here and it's a pleasant place with boating, pavilions and pagodas, and a steep hill to climb. At the top it's cool and shady and you can sit and have a drink, or watch the locals clambering about over the rocks. The view over the city, with desert and snowy mountains in the background, is spectacular; the number of tower cranes will also give a measure of the amount of construction going on in Ürümqi.

The major sight in Ürümqi is the **Xinjiang Regional Museum** (Mon–Sat 9.30am–7pm, Sun 9.30am–5pm; ¥5 downstairs exhibits, ¥15 upstairs) on Xibei Lu. The building itself is an interesting one, with a palpable Russian influence – painted mural reliefs as well as a great, green dome. Unfortunately, given the huge size of the museum, the number of rooms open to display at any one time is limited. The downstairs exhibit focuses on the Silk Road and includes an array of tools, fabrics, coins, jade pieces, pots and pictures. Unfortunately, there are no English labels and the rooms are very gloomy. The upstairs exhibit, on the other hand, does have some English explanations and is much more impressive, including a number of ancient and particularly well-preserved **corpses** retrieved from the dry desert sands, including the so-called "Loulan Beauty", a woman with long blonde-brown hair, allegedly 3800 years old, recovered from the city of Loulan on the Southern Silk Road. The Loulan Beauty, of a distinctly non-Chinese appearance, has been taken to heart by some Uigur nationalists as a symbol of the antiquity (and validity) of their claims for sovereignty over these lands. There are also some antique shops to browse in on the museum site. To reach the museum take bus #7 from Xinhua Bei Lu.

Shopping in Ürümqi can be quite an eye-opener in the crowded, affluent streets just south of Minzhu Lu and west of Jiefang Bei Lu. Fashion boutiques with pseudo-French and Italian names have started springing up – Hong Kong consumerism has reached China's final frontier. For a taste of something with a more local flavour, head south of here, down Jiefang Nan Lu. The shops become steadily more Uigur-orientated, until you reach the Erdaoqiao market, the main **Uigur bazaar** of the city. Here it's the usual dusty jumble of kebabs, melons, clothes and knives, being traded amid jostling donkey carts. The major **mosques** of the city are all located in this area, too, around Jiefang Nan Lu.

Eating and drinking

Right across the road from the *Hongshan Hotel*, on one of the prime sites of the city, *John's Information Café* has recently set up its third branch, following the success of branches in Turpan and Kashgar. In an almost miraculous reincarnation of John's Turpan branch, you can sit outside under the trellises and genuinely forget that you are in the middle of a booming city. Pancakes, apple pie, coffee, toast and omelettes are all available, as well as quite decent Chinese food. On the same side of the street as *John's*, a little farther down towards the *Holiday Inn*, is a place marked in English as the *Yang Cheng Hotel*, which is in fact not a hotel but a cheap restaurant with an English menu. A little further down still, just before the *Holiday Inn*, are some more upmarket **Chinese restaurants**. For air-conditioned luxury, the *Holiday Inn* itself does buffet breakfasts and lunches where you can eat as much as you like for ¥85 and ¥75 repectively. Over the bridge from the *Hongshan Hotel*, on the way to the post office, is the *Shu Xiang Cun Canting* with its name written up in Roman letters. There's no English menu but some English is spoken. The *baozi* are excellent.

If you're looking for **Uigur food**, there are a number of streetside market areas. One central place is on Renmin Lu, just to the west of Xinhua Lu. Another, slightly more wholesome, is the covered market just north of the post office, or try the Erdaoqiao market (take bus #101 heading south down Xinhua Bei Lu).

Listings

Airlines *CAAC*, Youhao Lu (10am–1.30pm, 4–8pm; ☎0991/2817942) is northwest of the post office. Take bus #101 heading west along Guangming Lu. *Aeroflot* (☎0991/2862326) has an office in the *Overseas Chinese Hotel* on Xinhua Nan Lu.

Banks and exchange The *Bank of China* (10am–2pm, 3.30–6.30pm) is at the junction of Renmin Lu and Jiefang Lu.

Bike rental *John's Café* was taking tentative steps towards a bike rental operation at the time of writing.

Bookshops *Xinhua Bookshop* is on Xinhua Bei Lu, on the left side as you head south from the *Holiday Inn*. They stock some English books here.

Cinema There is a cinema (Chinese language only) on Minzhu Lu.

Consulates Kazakhstan maintains a semi-consular presence in Ürümqi, through *Kazakh Airlines* in the World Plaza on Beijing Nan Lu in the north of the city (☎0991/3836400; see box, p.910).

Post and telecommunications The main post office west of the northern end of Renmin Park is one place to make long-distance calls. More simply, however, you can buy and use telephone cards in the lobbies of upmarket hotels (including the *Holiday Inn* and *Hongshan*).

Travel agents There are seemingly dozens of these in the *Hongshan Hotel*. You can take your pick, though the *Heaven Lake International Travel Service* (*CHTS*) in room 219 (☎0991/2816018 ext 219) has some pleasant staff and offers a pretty cheap, all-inclusive package to Lake Tianchi. Ürümqi *CITS* is located in the building immediately south of the *Holiday Inn*.

Tian Chi and Baiyang Gou

Tian Chi means "Heaven Lake" and this unspoilt natural haven 110km east of Ürümqi – the starting point of Vikram Seth's book *From Heaven Lake* – does almost live up to its name, especially for travellers who have spent long in the deserts of northwest China. At the cool, refreshing height of 2000m, the lake is surrounded by grassy meadows, steep, dense pine forests and jagged snow-covered peaks, including the mighty Bogda Feng which soars to over 6000m, and the nicest feature of the area is that you can wander at will. There are no restrictions on accommodation (most people stay in yurts, with the semi-nomadic Kazakh population) and there is virtually limitless hiking. You need only to watch the **weather** – bitterly cold in winter, the lake is really only accessible during the summer months May to September.

The **Kazakhs**, who lead a semi-nomadic herding existence in these hills, are organized into communes, very loosely managed by the State, which in theory owns both their land and animals and lets them out on fifteen or thirty-year "contracts". Their traditional livelihood is from sheep, selling lambs in spring if the winter spares them. But it's a hard, unpredictable business – the State sometimes has to bail them out if the winter is a disastrous one – and revenues come increasingly from tourism. As in Inner Mongolia, the Kazakhs have taken to performing at horse shows, mostly for tourists. The extra income from providing visitors with food and accommodation is also welcome.

There's a small **village** beside the lake, comprising a bus park, some shops and souvenir stands and even a guesthouse. If you have not pre-booked your accommodation (see below), you can simply set off to find yourself a **yurt**. This is a well-established custom, and you'll soon find people eager to cater for you. Most tourists prefer to lodge near the lake, but you can climb right up into the remote valleys of the Tian Shan – for this it's advisable to have a guide and a horse (¥50–100 per day), a service which young Kazakhs at the lakeside are happy to provide. Once up at the snowfields, the valleys are yours. Each is dotted with Kazakh yurts, and there's nearly always somewhere you can spend the night – you'll find yourself directed as soon as you ask. There is no set official rate for board and lodging in a yurt, but the average is around ¥40 per day including meals, which are usually simple affairs of vegetables and noodles. To make your stay more pleasant, it's a good idea to bring a little present for your Kazakh hosts as well – a bottle of *baijiu* rarely goes amiss. If you can come in May – considered the most beautiful time – you may get to try the alcoholic *kumiss*, fermented mare's milk, a rare delicacy. The rest of the year the Kazakhs make do with a kind of tea, with an infusion of dried snow lily and sheep's milk.

Practicalities

Access to the lake is by **bus** from Ürümqi. The bus leaves at 9am from the northern end of Renmin Park, about ten minutes' walk west from the *Hongshan Hotel* – try to buy your ticket the day before, from the bus stop. A day return costs ¥25 and the bus leaves the lakeside at 4pm. If you stay overnight, you have to pay another ¥25 to come back. The hundred-kilometre journey takes around four hours, and the journey from Ürümqi is spectacular, initially through flat desert, then climbing through green meadows, conifer forests and along a wild mountain river.

Communication with the Kazakhs can be problematic. Few speak Chinese, let alone English, which sometimes results in unpleasant misunderstandings – you may find yourself being charged extra for every cup of tea. One way to avoid these anxieties is to join a **pre-booked tour** which will include yurt accommodation as well as transport between Ürümqi and the lake. The best people to do this with seem to be the independent operators who hang around the *Hongshan Hotel* as most are touting their own family yurts. Highly recommended is a certain Mr Rachit who speaks a little English, and who offers two-night tours for ¥100 per person. His two yurts are a couple of kilometres up the lake from the bus park and included in the price are delightful boat rides to and from the yurts. Ürümqi *CITS* offers similar tours, though these are not only twice as expensive, but also less pleasant owing to the proximity of their yurts to the bus park and noisy souvenir stands. The travel agencies in the *Hongshan* might be able to offer even better deals (see p.913).

Baiyang Gou

Seventy-five kilometres south of Ürümqi is another natural paradise, the **Baiyang Gou** (Southern Pastures), located in a spur of the Tian Shan. Basically, it's another green valley with a stream and a waterfall, and a backdrop of fir trees and snowy peaks. The Kazakhs also like to summer here and, accordingly, there are opportunities for tourists to join them. The main difficulty is transport; in summer there *may* be buses running from the north end of Renmin Park in Ürümqi – but normally they leave only if there is sufficient demand.

Yining and the Ili Valley

The pretty **Ili Valley** is centred around the city of **Yining** (known to the Uigurs as Kulja), just 60km east of the border with Kazakhstan, and 400km northwest of Ürümqi. As it is right off the principal Silk Road routes, not many travellers make the detour to get here, but if you have the time, or you're travelling to Kazakhstan, the trip is definitely worthwhile. Ili is one of the three so-called **Kazakh Autonomous Prefectures** within Xinjiang (the other two are Karamay and Altai), which form a block along the northwest frontier. Despite the nominal Kazakh preponderance, however, it is in fact the Uigurs who are the dominant group, and in this city, more than anywhere in Xinjiang, you're likely to encounter open expressions of hostility to Chinese rule. Memories of all too recent atrocities and persecutions still hang heavy in the air – including the forced mass exodus of sixty thousand people, Kazakhs and Uigurs, to the USSR in the early 1960s, an event which has left behind much bitterness.

The **climate** in the whole valley is relatively cool and fresh even at the height of summer, and the views of the Tian Shan mountains from all routes into Yining, especially if you're coming up from Kuqa to the south, are fabulous. Another draw, 180km east of Yining on the road from Ürümqi, is the beautiful **Sayram Lake** (see p.917), where you can find accommodation in Kazakh yurts.

The **road from Kuqa** (see p.918), 400km and 24 hours right over the Tian Shan, is one of the most spectacular in all northwest China. Within an hour of departure, the harsh, rocky landscape of the northern Taklamakan starts giving way to green grass and trees; a couple of hours later the scenery is pure Alpine with dense forests of pine marching up the green slopes, blue skies and the glorious blue waters of **Big Dragon Lake**. Later, the road drifts into a vast grassland that takes hours to cross, the horizon faintly ringed by distant snowy peaks. Scattered over the plain are a few yurts and Kazakh herdsmen on horseback. The weather here can be extremely chilly, even in summer – make sure you have warm clothes for the trip. Finally the bus halts for a meal stop at the small and incredibly remote Mongolian settlement of **Bayanbulak**, before the precipitous descent down the northern side of the mountains begins, the road cutting through giant snow banks which persist well into mid-summer.

The **history** of the Ili Valley is one of intermittent Chinese control. At the time of the Han dynasty, two thousand years ago, the area was occupied by the **Wusun kingdom**. The Wusun people, ancestors of today's Kazakhs, kept diplomatic relations with the Han court and were responsible for introducing them to the horse. By the eighth century, however, a Tang-dynasty army had taken control of the region for China – its value as a staging post for a newly developing branch of the Silk Road was too great a temptation. In the thirteenth and fourteenth centuries, the area was controlled by first Genghis Khan from the east, and then Tamerlane from the west. This east–west tug of war has gone on ever since, with the Qing seizing the area in the eighteenth century, only for the Russians to march in, in 1871, under the cover of Yakub Beg's Xinjiang rebellion (see p.900). There remained a significant Russian presence in one form or another until 1949, and traces of this can still be seen in the architecture of Yining.

Yining

YINING today is a booming frontier city and as such has changed almost unrecognizably from the remote backwater it was just a few years ago. New banks and hotels are zooming up, taxis cruise the streets and young people wear stylish clothes and carry mobile phones. Nevertheless, it's a small, compact place, pleasant for walking, with shady, tree-lined streets and an extraordinary amount of food for sale from street vendors. The centre of town isn't readily obvious – most of the action seems to straddle the length of **Jiefang Lu**, though the old city is centred around **Qingnian Park** to the southeast. The **Uigur bazaars**, just south of Qingnian Park, are well worth exploring, while, over in Renmin Park (¥1) in the west of the city, there's a **museum** (daily; ¥5). However, the building itself – an old Russian place, with plaster reliefs, painted blue and white – is more interesting than its contents, which number a few remains of early settlements in the region (no English labels).

There is no train to Yining. The **bus station** is located in the northwest of the city. Many daily buses run to and from Ürümqi, Kashgar and Kuqa – fierce competition between government and private operators is keeping the prices low and service good. In Yining, you can simply buy your ticket on the pavement outside the front of the station. Another interesting bus service out of Yining is that to Almaty across the border in Kazakhstan, though note that Kazakhstan visas are not available here (see p.910). The only **flights** to Yining are from Ürümqi – Yining's **CAAC** office (☎0999/8022752) is on Jiefang Lu, just around the corner from the *Ili Hotel*, but these tickets are very hard to book at short notice. Try a **travel service** – for example, the conveniently located *Qingnian Travel Service* (building no. 3, room no. 106) in the *Ili Hotel*. Otherwise there's the *Ili International Travel Service* (☎0999/8023535), down on Xinhua Xi Lu (bus #2), where a little English is spoken.

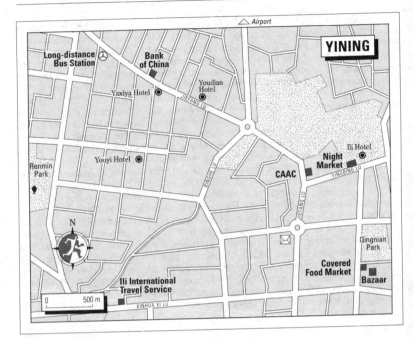

Accommodation

A delightful **place to stay** is the *Ili Hotel* (☎0999/8022794; dorms ②, rooms ③–⑧), an old-fashioned hotel, in huge leafy grounds. There are a number of buildings offering varying degrees of comfort and different prices – the cheaper no. 4 building, for example, offers perfectly respectable, if small, double rooms with bath, as well as three-bed dorms. To reach it from the bus station, take bus #1 heading east for three stops, cross over the road and the hotel is a few minutes' walk east along Yingbing Lu.

The other long-standing hotel in Yining is the *Youyi* (☎0999/8023901; dorms ②, rooms ③–⑥), with cheap doubles and three-bed dorms in the old wing and smarter singles and doubles in the new wing. Overall it's a friendly, pleasant place, though located annoyingly far from any bus route. Leaving the bus station, turn right and walk until you see a sign in English pointing to the hotel. This sign will actually bring you to the back door of the hotel which you can easily miss; it's better to take the next street to the right – the front of the hotel is a fifteen-minute walk along here. On the way, you'll pass another, smaller hotel called the *Yaxiya* (☎0999/8031809; dorms ①, rooms ③). There's no English sign, but you can recognize it from the Greek columns outside. Here you'll find clean and modern doubles and three-bed dorms with bath. Back on the main road, a little farther down from the bus station, is the *Youdian* (☎0999/8023844; dorms ①, rooms ⑤–⑦), offering smart, upmarket double rooms and very cheap dorm beds round at the back.

Eating and drinking

Eating in Yining is fun, with seemingly the whole city turning into an outdoor market in the evening. The *Ili Hotel* has a pleasant Chinese restaurant with a high ceiling (but no English menu), and just outside the hotel, on the right, is a busy **Uigur night-market**. Roast chickens, *samsa* (baked dough packets filled with meat and onions), kebabs and noodles are all available. You can also try the local **beer** here, which is made with honey – the distinctive bottles all have a black rubber cork and cost just ¥1. The street opposite the *Ili*, leading down to Qingnian Park, has lots of **outdoor restaurants**, some of which chalk up dishes and prices in Chinese. Try a *dapanji* (or *tohogish* in Uigur) which basically comprises a whole (or half) chicken cut up on the bone and cooked in a chilli sauce; a whole chicken costs around ¥35. Immediately south of the Qingnian Park is an interesting covered food market. Here you can get goodies from all regions of China, including *baozi*, hotpots and grilled fish. You can also buy the excellent and locally made *kurut* – hard, dry little **cheeses** – from street vendors. Finally, the Ili Valley is famous for its **fruit** – apricots in June, grapes and peaches in July.

Around Yining

Outside the city are one or two places of more specific interest. About 20km south of Yining is the little town of **CHAPUCHA'ER**, the home of the **Xibo** people – a tiny minority, numbering about twenty thousand, who are of Manchu descent despatched to Xinjiang around 1700 AD as warriors to guard and colonize the area. The Xibo still zealously preserve their own language, script and other customs, including a prowess in archery that is of Olympic standard. If you wish to investigate, Chapucha'er is just thirty minutes by bus from Yining's long-distance bus station. From the same bus station, there are also buses to **HUIYUAN**, 30km west of Yining, a small but historic town with a three-storey **drum tower** dating from the last century. Another 20km north of here is the pretty Persian-style **tomb of Telug Timur**, a fourteenth-century Muslim leader, located just outside the small town of **QINGSHUI**. To visit Huiyuan and the tomb of Telug Timur as a combined trip from Yining, rent a car from a travel service – a day with the car will cost about ¥300.

About 180km out of Yining, on the road east to Ürümqi, is **Sayram Lake**. Around 2000m above sea level and decidedly chilly for most of the year, Sayram, with its mountain surroundings and grassy banks, occupies a fantastic location and offers tremendous opportunities for the intrepid to escape the hustle of Chinese cities. Tourism here is still very much at a pioneering stage – there are simple **guesthouses** at the lakeside, otherwise you can try to find accommodation in a Kazakh or Mongol **yurt**.

YINING AND AROUND		
Yining	伊宁	*yīníng*
ACCOMMODATION		
Ili	伊犁宾馆	*yīlí bīnguǎn*
Yaxiya	亚西亚宾馆	*yàxīyà bīnguǎn*
Youdian	邮电宾馆	*yóudiàn bīnguǎn*
Youyi	友谊宾馆	*yǒuyì bīnguǎn*
AROUND YINING		
Chapucha'er	察布查尔	*chápùcháěr*
Huiyuan	惠远	*huìyuǎn*
Sayram Lake	赛里木湖	*sàilǐmù hú*
Ili	伊犁	*yīlí*

If you're hoping to stay in a family yurt, bring a small present, to make dealings friendlier. Access to and from the lake is by bus from Yining or Ürümqi – given the frequency of the buses on this route it should be easy to pick one up from the lake in either direction, if you stand on the road. It's about three hours from Yining, and fifteen hours from Ürümqi.

Ürümqi to Kashgar: The Northern Silk Road

Heading southwest from Ürümqi, the direct route follows an ancient Silk Road trail (see box, p.827) over the Tian Shan mountains and into the Tarim basin, where the road skirts for over a thousand kilometres round the northern rim of the Taklamakan Desert, flanked by snowy peaks. It's largely a barren wilderness, though there are occasional transitions from parched desert to green pasture in the rare places where water from the Tian Shan has found its way down to the plain. The small oasis towns usually comprise brown mud-built houses, perhaps a few vine trellises, and thick muddy water running in trenches beside the streets. The road surface is for the most part in fairly good condition; it may not be a major highway by international standards, but it is still, in the absence of a rail line, the principal land route to Kashgar. The only alternative, in fact – the Southern Silk Road (see p.921) – runs several hundred kilometres to the south of Ürümqi. You can join up with it from here by heading south first to Korla (connected to Ürümqi by rail), and then to Ruoqiang on the southern rim of the Tarim basin.

Kuqa and around

KUQA (pronounced *ku-cheh,* and known to the Chinese as **Kuche**) about one day by bus and 400km to the west of Ürümqi, is an excellent place to break the long journey from Ürümqi to Kashgar. It's a small town with a long history, and a largely Uigur population. The fourth-century linguist and scholar **Kumarajiva**, who came from here, was one of the most famous of all Chinese Buddhists. Having travelled to Kashmir for his education, he later returned to China as a teacher and translator of Buddhist docu-

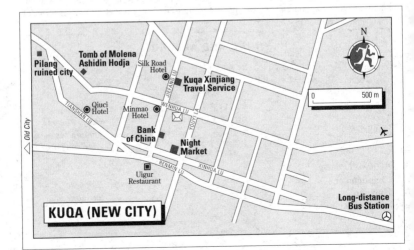

ments from Sanskrit into Chinese. It was in large measure thanks to him that Buddhism came to be so widely understood in China and, by the early Tang, Kuqa was a major **centre of Buddhism** in China. The fantastic wealth of the trade caravans subsidized giant monasteries here, and Xuan Zang, passing through the city in the sixth century, reported the existence of two huge Buddha statues, twenty-seven metres high, guarding its entrances. The city even had its own, Indo-European language. With the arrival of Islam in the ninth century, however, this era finally began to draw to a close, and today only a few traces of Kuqa's glorious past remain.

The City

Kuqa is one of the poorest cities you're likely to visit in China. It is effectively two cities, the old (to the west) and the new (to the east), lying a few kilometres apart. The new city, largely Han-populated, contains all the facilities you'll need – hotels, banks, post offices and the long-distance bus station, while the old city, largely Uigur, is peppered with mosques and bazaars and has a Central Asian atmosphere very different to Chinese towns. To reach the old city, take any bus heading west along Renmin Lu, the main street on which the bus station is located, until you reach a bridge across the river – the old city lies beyond the river.

From the **New City**, a couple of sights are easily accessible. One is the remains of the ruined city of **Pilang**, otherwise known as Qiuci (the old name for Kuqa), though there is nothing really to see beyond a few old rocks. Following Tianshan Lu from the new city, the ruined city is about ten minutes' walk west of the *Qiuci Hotel*. Slightly more interesting is the nearby **Tomb of Molena Ashidin Hodja**, a simple shrine and mosque, in honour of an Arab missionary who came to the city, probably in the thirteenth century. It's on Wenhua Lu, about fifteen minutes' walk west of the *Minmao Hotel*.

The bridge leading to the **Old City** is really where the main area of interest begins. Along the river banks below the bridge, cattle and sheep are traded, and there's also a general **market** here on Fridays – a spectacular display of Uigur colour on a large scale. Beyond the bridge, you can soon lose yourself in the labyrinth of narrow streets and mud-brick houses. Right in the heart of this area, fifteen minutes approximately northeast of the bridge, is the **Kuqa Mosque**, built in 1923. Delightfully neat and compact, with an attractive green-tiled dome, this mosque is of wholly arabesque design, displaying none of the Chinese characteristics of mosques in more eastern parts of the country. Beyond the mosque, on Linqi Lu, is the **museum** (¥15), housing a moderately interesting collection of locally discovered pottery, coins, skeletons and a few frescoes. Opening hours seem to depend on whether the doorman is asleep or

THE NORTHERN SILK ROAD		
Kuqa	库车	*kùchē*
Kizil Thousand Buddha Caves	克孜尔千佛洞	*kèzīěr qiānfódòng*
Pilang	龟兹古城	*qiūcí gǔchéng*
Subashi Ancient City	苏巴什古城	*sūbāshí gǔchéng*
Tomb of Molena Ashidin Hodja	默拉纳额什丁坟	*mòlānà éshídīng fén*
ACCOMMODATION		
Minmao	民贸宾馆	*mínmào bīnguǎn*
Qiuci	龟兹宾馆	*qiūcí bīnguǎn*
Silk Road	丝路宾馆	*sīlù bīnguǎn*

not, probably on account of the infrequency of visitors. To reach it from the bridge, follow the main road through the old city to the end, then turn right and it's a few hundred metres farther on.

Practicalities

There is no rail line to Kuqa. Flights connect the city with Ürümqi and Korla (but not Kashgar) and the **airport** is a very short taxi ride east of the new city. The **bus station** is in the far southeast of the new city, with connections to and from Kashgar, Khotan, Yining, Ürümqi and Turpan, though all of these journeys take between one and one-and-a-half days. For tickets out of Kuqa, and for booking tours of the sites outside the city, it's worth paying a call on the friendly travel agency, the *Kuqa Xinjiang Travel Service* (☎09074/22524), opposite the *Silk Road Hotel* on Jiefang Lu. The lady here speaks some English and is delighted to be of assistance.

There are a couple of **hotels** right outside the bus station, but this is a rather remote corner of the town to stay in. To reach the hotels in the new city, catch a bus from just in front of the station, heading west. Get off at the second stop and take the next road north, Jiefang Lu. Mule carts also operate from the station, or it's around a twenty-minute walk. The *Minmao* (☎09074/22969; ②), on the southwest side of the intersection between Jiefang Lu and Wenhua Lu, is a convenient place to stay. Another fifteen minutes' walk farther north up Jiefang Lu is the *Silk Road Hotel* (☎09074/22901; dorms ①, rooms ②), a big, bright and good-value place set in its own gardens, offering 24-hour hot water and doubles with or without bath, as well four-bed dorms. Finally, the most upmarket accommodation in town is at the secluded *Qiuci* (⑥) on Tianshan Lu, a few minutes west of the new city.

Kuqa is not a great place for **eating**, though one nice place in the new city is the tiled building on the main Renmin Lu, more or less facing the south end of Jiefang Lu. You can sit under an awning with some friendly Uigurs and have a bowl of *laghman* washed down with authentic Uigur tea, with great rough sticks and leaves floating in the cup. A few yards west of here is a man selling delicious baked *kaobao* and *samsa*, dough packets stuffed with meat and vegetables, baked and fried respectively. In the other direction, on Xinhua Lu, a little east of Jiefang Lu, is a busy, smoky **night market** full of the usual kebabs and roast chickens, as well as plenty of fresh fruit in season. For Chinese food, try the restaurant in the *Silk Road Hotel*.

Around Kuqa

Around Kuqa, there is a whole series of ruined cities and Buddhist cave sites – testimony to the fabulous history of the area. Probably the two most significant of these are the **Subashi Ancient City**, 23km north of Kuqa, and the **Kizil Thousand Buddha Caves**, 75km to the west. The Kizil caves, in particular, were a Central Asian treasure trove, a mixture of Hellenistic, Indian and Persian styles with not even a suggestion of Chinese influence.

To visit either of these sites, it's necessary to rent a car, which, from the *Kuqa Xinjiang Travel Service* (see above), will cost around ¥300 to Kizil. Sadly, the site here (daily, 9am–4.30pm; ¥45), consisting of around twenty caves, has suffered the ravages of the German archeologist and art thief, Albert Von Le Coq. At the beginning of the twentieth century, he literally cut out and carried away many of the best frescoes still surviving in the caves, and some are entirely bare. Unless you're a serious student of archeology, you're unlikely to find anything here to compare with the Mogao Caves at Dunhuang in Gansu Province (see p.883). The Subashi Ancient City, on the other hand, abandoned in the twelfth century, still displays fairly extensive ruins and is much closer to Kuqa; you can visit it in a taxi for about ¥100.

The Southern Silk Road

The **Southern Silk Road** splits off from the northern route near Dunhuang in Gansu Province, then skirts the southern rim of the Taklamakan Desert before rejoining the northern road at Kashgar. In modern times this route has fallen into almost total obscurity – lacking any major city and connected by poor roads and minimal transport, it can hardly be compared with its northern counterpart. Of the two branches, however, this route is actually the older and historically more important of the two. The most famous Silk Road travellers used it, including the Chinese Buddhist pilgrims, Fa Xian and Xuan Zang, as well as Marco Polo, and, in the 1930s, the British journalist and adventurer Peter Fleming. The ancient settlements along the way were oases in the desert, kept alive by streams flowing down from the snowy peaks of the Kunlun Shan which constitute the outer rim of the Tibetan plateau to the south.

The option of the southern route opens up the prospect of travelling overland from Turpan to Kashgar one way, and returning another way – effectively circumnavigating the entire Taklamakan Desert. The southern route is not to everyone's taste, in that it chiefly comprises desert interspersed by extremely dusty oasis towns. Nevertheless, it does offer more intrepid travellers the chance to visit an extremely little-known corner of China, meet friendly Uigur people, and also follow up on some of the faint traces that still remain of the oldest Silk Road.

Coming from the east, the route picks up at the city of **RUOQIANG** (*Charkhlik* to the Uigurs), a good 600km south of Ürümqi. Ruoqiang itself is most notable for being the jumping-off point for visits to the ruined city of **Miran** – an intriguing account of one woman's voyage to Miran is documented in Christa Paula's book, *Voyage to Miran*. Northeast of Ruoqiang is **Lop Nor**, a huge, salty marshland which happens to be the site where China's nuclear tests are conducted.

There are several different ways of reaching Ruoqiang; the easiest is by bus via **Korla**, which is linked by both train and bus to the cities of Ürümqi and Turpan. More interesting, though, if you have plenty of time, is to approach on the original

---

THE SOUTHERN SILK ROAD

Korla	库尔勒	*kùěrlè*
Qiemo	且末	*qiěmò*
Ruoqiang	若羌	*ruòqiāng*
Yarkand	莎车	*shāchē*
Yecheng	叶城	*yèchéng*
Yengisar	英吉沙	*yīngjíshā*
Khotan	和田	*hétián*
Carpet factory	地毯厂	*dìtǎnchǎng*
Jade factory	玉器厂	*yùqìchǎng*
Melikawat	米力克瓦特古城	*mǐlìkèwǎtè gǔchéng*
Silk factory	丝厂	*sīchǎng*
ACCOMMODATION		
Baitian Er	白天二宾馆	*báitiānèr bīnguǎn*
Khotan	和田宾馆	*hétián bīnguǎn*
Khotan Shi	和田市宾馆	*hétiánshì bīnguǎn*

Silk Road route from Dunhuang in Gansu (or alternatively from Golmud in Qinghai). For tourists today these routes are still very much at a pioneering stage – there is little if any public transport and the roads are highly unreliable. Nevertheless, it is possible to find jeeps or trucks heading in these directions which you can ride for a fee. Moving west from Ruoqiang towards Kashgar, the route passes through **Qiemo** (Cherchen) and **Khotan** (Hotan) and is served by public buses connecting with Kashgar throughout.

There are reports that another road, cutting right across the middle of the Taklamakan Desert and linking Khotan directly with Korla, is currently under construction. In theory this road would cut travel time between these two cities to as little as twenty-four hours, instead of the current time of several days. It's not yet clear whether foreigners will be allowed to use this road.

Khotan and around

KHOTAN (known in Chinese as **Hetian**) is one of the remotest places in China, and yet for centuries it was famed throughout the country for its **jade**, **carpets and silk**. Even today the highlight of a visit to Khotan is catching a glimpse of ancient silk-making practices. Otherwise, the town is bleak and dusty.

The meagre town centre comprises a couple of blocks to the south and west of the junction between Nuerwake Lu (running east–west) and Gulibake Lu (north–south). The bus station is about 1km to the north of here. Within the city itself there is little to

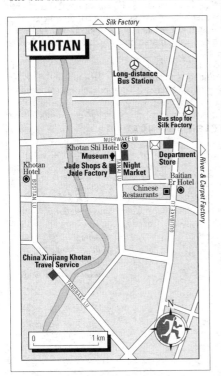

see, though you might consider dropping in on the small **museum** (opening hours irregular; ¥5) which contains a collection of items recovered from the surrounding desert, including fragments of silk, coffee pots, wooden utensils and two mummified bodies. The museum is located on Tanai Lu, just south of where it intersects with Nuerwake Lu (west of Gulibake Lu). Immediately to the south of the museum are some jade shops and the **jade factory** where you can see a few craftsmen at work with small lathes.

About 4km to the east of town, following Nuerwake Lu, is the **river** from which, historically, so much jade has been recovered, and which still yields the odd stone for casual searchers. The town **carpet factory** is just across the river and to the left; you might try dropping in for a visit, particularly if you are interested in making a purchase. Thirty kilometres to the south of town, there is one other sight for Silk Road specialists, the ruined city of **Melikawat**, by the banks of the White Jade River. Today little remains except a few crumbling walls in the desert. This city, formerly

---

SILK PRODUCTION IN KHOTAN

The most interesting thing to do in Khotan is take a short excursion north of the city to discover some of the secrets of modern **silk production**. You can do this through a travel service, or independently if you wish. Take bus #1 from Gulibake Lu, five minutes' walk north of Nuerwake Lu and to the east, where the road is bisected by a small park, right to its last stop. Walk back just a few hundred metres towards town and you'll come to the front entrance of the head office of the **silk factory**. The security man there should understand what you want. If you come during the week (avoid the long lunch break, 1–3pm), the chances are that you will be supplied with an English-speaking factory employee who will gladly show you round, probably for free. You can see the whole process: the initial unpicking of the cocoons, the twisting together of the strands to form a thread (10 strands for each silk thread), the winding of the thread on to reels, and finally the weaving and dying

If you are keen to see the **nurturing of the silk worms** themselves – only possible in the summer months – you'll need to explore some of the nearby country lanes in the vicinity of the factory. From the factory, walk a few hundred metres farther on towards the city, until you come to an area of green trees and vine trellises. If you are able to explain your purpose to people (perhaps a drawing of a silk worm?), they will take you to see their silk worms munching away on rattan trays of fresh, cleaned mulberry leaves in cool, dark sheds. Eventually each worm should spin itself a cocoon of pure silk; each cocoon comprises a single strand of about a kilometre in length. The farmers sell the cocoons to the factory for ¥10 per kilo. The hatching and rearing of silk worms is unreliable work, and for most farmers it's a sideline.

---

an important regional capital on the Silk Road, was abandoned well over a thousand years ago. For a visit to Melikawat, contact a travel service (see below).

Practicalities

Khotan's **airport** is 10km from town, and access is either by taxi, or by the airport bus that meets incoming flights – the only flights in or out of Khotan at present are the daily connections to Ürümqi (¥1000). The **bus station** is in the north of the city. Daily buses connect Khotan with Kashgar, Ürümqi (via the Northern Silk Road route) and Qiemo (the Southern Silk Road). At the time of writing, bus tickets out of Khotan were cheap as the concept of foreigners' prices had not been heard of. To reach Nuerwake Lu from the bus station on foot takes about twenty minutes; turn right as you come out on to the main road. It's probably more sensible to take a cycle-rickshaw, though – they'll charge a foreigner about ¥5 to any hotel.

The *China Xinjiang Khotan Travel Service* (☎09032/222846) on Tangbake Lu is a friendly place, with some English spoken, which can arrange various expensive tours for travellers including interesting four- or five- day jeep-trips to Korla and Dunhuang along the Southern Silk Road, via routes not necessarily covered by public transport. They can also book air tickets to Ürümqi, with onward connections. Their office is rather inconveniently located in the southwest of the city, about fifteen minutes' walk south of the *Khotan Hotel*.

For **accommodation** in town, perhaps the best value is the *Baitian Er* (☎09032/223576; dorms ①, rooms ②) on Gulibake Lu. The sign is in Chinese only and it's about thirty minutes' walk due south from the bus station. The *Khotan Shi* (dorms ①, rooms ⑤), on the intersection of Nuerwake Lu and Tanai Lu, has four-bed dorms with communal bath and doubles with private bath. The upmarket place in town is the *Khotan* (☎09032/223570; ⑥), on Bositan Lu in the west of the city.

Eating in Khotan is not necessarily as dismal as it first looks. There is quite an interesting **night market** on Tanai Lu, just south of Nuerwake Lu. You can get roast chickens, *pulau*, eggs and fish here, as well as the customary kebabs and *laghman*. For **Chinese food**, try the area of Gulibake Lu a little north of, and across the road from, the *Baitian Er Hotel*. Just pull open the curtains in the doorways, and go in; most of the proprietors here are Sichuanese in exile and they know how to cook.

Khotan to Kashgar

On the road to Kashgar, 200km northeast from Khotan, is **YECHANG**, a kind of giant Uigur highway service station, with flashing lights, fires, bubbling cauldrons, overhead awnings and great flanks of mutton hanging from meat hooks. The road divides here, one fork running north towards Kashgar, and the other southwest into Tibet. This **road to Tibet**, although officially closed to foreigners, has always attracted a few dedicated travellers; the route is dangerous, unpredictable, slow, and probably very expensive as well, as you are likely to have to bribe your way through.

Continuing on towards Kashgar, the route passes through **YARKAND**. There are some attractive mosques here and a huge, rustic Sunday market along the same lines as the more famous one in Kashgar. The only **hotel** that accepts foreigners is the *Yarkand* (dorms ①); turn right from the bus station, take the first right and it's a ten-minute walk. The final stretch of road north to Kashgar passes through a bizarre terrain, alternating between stretches of pure desert, and oases of green grass and poplar trees, flourishing on irrigation from mountain streams. En route, 126km from Yarkand, lies the town of **YENGISAR**, which for centuries has been supplying the Uigur people with handcrafted knives. Most of the knives on sale in Xinjiang these days are factory-made, but here at the **Yengisar County Small Knife Factory** a few craftsmen still ply their old skills, inlaying handles with horn or plastic.

Kashgar

A large part of the excitement of **KASHGAR** lies in the experience of reaching it. From eastern China it is fantastically remote: as the crow flies, it's over 4000km from Beijing, of which the thousand plus kilometres from Ürümqi is for the most part sheer desert. As recently as the 1930s, the journey time to and from Beijing ran to a number of months. And yet Kashgar today, an oasis 1200m above sea level, is a remarkably prosperous and pleasant place, despite remaining, in part, an essentially medieval city. Coming from the west, Kashgar is the first point of arrival on the ancient overland routes from Pakistan and Kirgyzistan.

Kashgar, more than any city in Xinjiang, is a bastion of old Chinese Turkestan. The population is nearly ninety percent Muslim, a fact you can hardly fail to notice with the great **Id Kah Mosque** dominating the central square, and the Uigur bazaars and tea shops, the smell of grilled lamb and, above all, the faces of the Turkic people around you. Kashgar's extraordinary **Sunday market**, when half of Central Asia seems to converge on the city, is as exotic to the average Han Chinese as for the foreign tourist.

The history of Kashgar is dominated by its strategic position, first as a critical junction on the Silk Road, and more recently as the meeting point of three empires – **Chinese, Soviet and British**. Both Britain and the Soviet Union maintained consulates in Kashgar until 1949: the British with an eye to their interests across the frontier in India, the Soviets (so everyone assumed) with the long-term intention of absorbing Xinjiang into their Central Asian orbit. The conspiracies of this period are brilliantly evoked in Peter Fleming's *News from Tartary* and Ella Maillart's *Forbidden Journey*. At the time of Fleming's visit, in 1935, the city was in effect run by the Soviets, who had brought their rail line to within two days of Kashgar. During World War II, however, Kashgar swung back under Chinese control; and with the break in Sino-Soviet

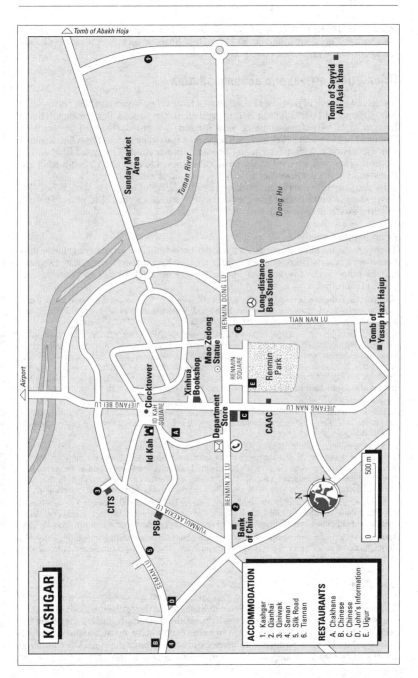

KASHGAR

Tomb of Abakh Hoja

Tomb of Sayyid Ali Asla khan

Sunday Market Area

Tuman River

Dong Hu

Airport

Long-distance Bus Station

TIAN NAN LU

RENMIN DONG LU

Tomb of Yusup Hazi Hajup

Mao Zedong Statue

Xinhua Bookshop

Clocktower

JIEFANG BEI LU

ID KAH SQUARE

Id Kah

Department Store

RENMIN SQUARE

Renmin Park

JIEFANG NAN LU

CAAC

RENMIN XI LU

YUMMULAKEXIA LU

CITS

PSB

SEMAN LU

Bank of China

N

500 m

0

ACCOMMODATION
1. Kashgar
2. Qianhai
3. Qiniwak
4. Seman
5. Silk Road
6. Tiannan

RESTAURANTS
A. Chakhana
B. Chinese
C. Chinese
D. John's Information
E. Uigur

relations in the early 1960s, the Soviet border (and influence) firmly closed. It is only now, with the break-up of the Soviet Union, that Kashgar seems set to resume its status as one of the great travel crossroads of Asia.

Orientation, arrival and accommodation

It's helpful to think of Kashgar as centred on a large cross, with a principal north–south axis, Jiefang Bei Lu and Jiefang Nan Lu, and an east–west axis, Renmin Dong Lu and Renmin Xi Lu. The **long-distance bus station** is a little to the east of centre on Tiannan Lu, just south of Renmin Lu. This station is used by buses connecting Kashgar with most parts of Xinjiang, including Ürümqi, Turpan, Kuqa, Yining and Khotan. The *Qiniwak Hotel,* which serves as the terminal for **buses to and from Tashkurgan** and Pakistan, is in the northwest of the city, a few minutes west of Jiefang Lu.

By air, passengers arrive at the **airport** to the north of town. The airport bus (¥4) drives straight down Jiefang Lu on its way to the terminus at the *CAAC* office. This bus will drop passengers on request.

Accommodation

There are some quite pleasant, inexpensive hotels in Kashgar, catering these days mainly for a rush of Pakistani traders from over the Karakoram Highway. The two most famous hotels – the *Qiniwak* and *Seman* – were once the British and Russian consulates respectively.

Kashgar Guesthouse (☎0998/222368). Well out of town, 3 or 4km east of the centre and in a nice location surrounded by woods, but rather faded and neglected. Access is by bus #10 which runs along Renmin Lu and stops right outside the hotel. ⑦.

Qiniwak (also known as *Chini Bagh* or *Geneva*; ☎0998/225929, fax 223087). This used to be Kashgar's British consulate, and now, under Pakistani management, is one of the best hotels in town. Bus travellers from Pakistan are dropped right outside the front door. If you're arriving on the airport bus, tell the driver and you can be dropped on Jiefang Lu, a few minutes' walk east of the hotel. It's a noisy but cheerful place, popular with Pakistani traders. Singles, doubles and dorms of various sizes with bath in the old wing, and modern, pleasant doubles in the new round tower. Dorms ③, rooms ⑤–⑥.

Qianhai, Renmin Xi Lu (☎0998/222922 ext 7064). A newish, upmarket hotel near the *Bank of China*. You walk through the front building to the one behind – doubles here are modern and air-conditioned but very over-priced. ⑧.

Seman, Seman Lu (☎0998/222129). The most popular place among budget travellers, with the proximity of a number of English-menu restaurants a big attraction. Formerly the Russian consulate, it's a huge, rambling old complex in delightful, secluded gardens located in the west of the city. From the bus station, take a taxi (¥10). All rooms and dorms have their own bathrooms, however, the dorms here can be very noisy owing to a nearby karaoke bar. Dorms ①, rooms ②–⑥.

Silk Road, Seman Lu. A relatively small place halfway between the *Qiniwak* and *Seman* hotels, offering good-value doubles with bath. Its *Oasis Cafe* serves excellent Western breakfasts. Single travellers of either sex may be harassed by the very overt presence of prostitutes in this hotel. ②.

Tiannan. Very convenient, opposite the long-distance bus station, but slightly run-down. Three-bed dorms can cost as little as ¥10 per bed, though staff are reluctant to rent these out to foreigners. Dorms ①, rooms ②–⑤.

The City

There are one or two monuments of note in Kashgar but the main attractions of this city are its ordinary streets – principally the bazaars, the restaurants, the tea shops and the people in them. The streets radiate out from the centre of the original Uigur city which is focused on **Id Kah Square**, with its clock tower and huge mosque. A few hundred metres to the south is the modern, commercial centre of the city, at the junction between Jiefang (Bei and Nan) Lu and Renmin (Xi and Dong) Lu. The main post-liberation monument of Kashgar – the absurdly colossal **statue of Mao Zedong** on Renmin Dong Lu, a towering reminder of the ultimate authority of China over the region – is just to the east of here, opposite Renmin Park. Finally, scattered around the fringes of the city, are a number of **mausoleums** to Uigur heroes of the past – these are best reached by bicycle.

Id Kah Square and around

The main historical sight in central Kashgar is the **Id Kah Mosque**, occupying the western side of Id Kah Square, off Jiefang Bei Lu. Originally built in 1442, it has been restored many times, most recently after the Cultural Revolution. It is one of the biggest mosques, and almost certainly the most active, in the country; you can even hear the call to prayer booming around the city centre, which is a rare sound in China. Although visitors are theoretically allowed in (there is a small entrance fee), nowadays Western tourists are often shooed away by zealous worshippers. The quietest time, when your presence will cause least disturbance, is probably early to mid-morning. Inside are pleasant courtyards and tree-lined gardens where worshippers assemble. Note that visitors of either sex should have their arms and legs fully clothed when entering this (or any other) mosque.

The main Uigur **bazaars** are in the neighbouring streets. The street heading northeast from the square is the main **carpet** area. The best carpets of the region are supposedly from Khotan, a few hundred kilometres to the southeast of Kashgar, but the best bargains in China are to be had in the Kashgar bazaars. You should be able to get a nice felt of rolled coloured wool (1.5m x 2.5m) for less than ¥300. A brightly dyed hand-knotted carpet, approximately 2m x 3m, should be around ¥800. The carpets are relatively rough in quality and have geometric designs only, but the prices are about a third of the equivalent in Turkey. Kashgar **kilims**, produced by nomads, are highly sought after and almost impossible to find locally. None of them seems to reach the open market until they have found their way to Peshawar in northern Pakistan first.

KASHGAR		
Kashgar	喀什	*kāshí*
ACCOMMODATION		
Kashgar Guesthouse	喀什宾馆	*kāshí bīnguǎn*
Qianhai	前海宾馆	*qiánhǎi bīnguǎn*
Qiniwak	其尼巴合宾馆	*qíníbāhé bīnguǎn*
Seman	色满宾馆	*sèmǎn bīnguǎn*
Silk Road	丝绸之路饭店	*sīchóuzhīlù fàndiàn*
Tiannan	天南饭店	*tiānnán fàndiàn*
THE CITY		
Hanoi ancient city	罕诺依古城	*hànnuòyī gǔchéng*
Id Kah Mosque	艾提尕尔清真寺	*àitígǎr qīngzhēnsì*
Id Kah Square	艾提尕尔广场	*àitígǎr guǎngchǎng*
Moor Pagodas	莫尔佛塔	*mùěrfótǎ*
Sunday Market	中西亚市场	*zhōngxīyà shìchǎng*
Tomb of Abakh Hoja	阿巴克和加墓	*ābākèhéjiāmù*
Tomb of Sayyid Ali Asla Khan	赛衣提艾里斯拉ㄢ	*sàiyītíàilìsīlāhànmù*
Tomb of Yusup Hazi Hajup	哈斯哈吉南墓	*hāsīhājínánmù*

The small road leading south from the carpet bazaar (due east of Id Kah Square and parallel to Jiefang Lu) is the big area for Central Asian **hats**. As well as the green and white square-shaped variety, so beloved by Uigur old men, there are prayer caps, skull-caps, furry winter hats and plain workmen's caps. Following this lane south you pass the main bazaar, where all kinds of blacksmiths and carpenters are hard at work in front of their shops, and enter a world of mud-brick walls and pony carts. Items you might come across while exploring the bazaars include **knives** with decorative handles, produced in the neaby city of Yengisar, and **chests** overlaid with brightly coloured tin, purpose-built for carrying special gifts for brides-to-be (insurance against the possible loss of the husband in later years). Locally produced **musical instruments** are also of interest, particularly stringed instruments of inlaid wood, with long slender necks and round bowls. The two-stringed *dutah* is the most common. The *tanber* has an even longer stem and a round bowl shaped like half a gourd, while the *rawupu* has five strings and a snakeskin drum.

To the north of Id Kah Square is a covered **cloth market**, which also includes some of the wildest **Uigur restaurants** – huge wood fires burning in the darkness, vats bubbling, TV sets blaring at an insane volume. In the southern part of the square is the Kashgar **night market**, while to the west – the two roads to the north and south of the Id Kah Mosque – are the bulk of the **Uigur tea shops** and small eating establishments. About a hundred metres down the road leading south from the mosque, on the left-hand side, is the **Chakhana** (tea house). With its upstairs verandah, rickety wooden beams, grimy plaster reliefs on the walls and old men in baggy, oily coats, this place is a filthy but fascinating glimpse into Central Asia of the past.

The outskirts

The historic architecture remaining in Kashgar today chiefly comprises a number of mausoleums to famous Uigur personages of old. The most central of these is the **Tomb of Yusup Hazi Hajup** (daily 8am–5pm; ¥8), the eleventh-century Uigur poet and philosopher. It's about 1.5km south of Renmin Lu, on Tiyu Lu, a small road located between Jiefang Nan Lu and Tiannan Lu. The mausoleum, of handsome blue and white wall tiles, was reconstructed in 1989, though with slightly shoddy workmanship – it's worth dropping by if you are in the vicinity.

To the east of the city lies the **Tomb of Sayyid Ali Asla Khan.** To reach it the best way is to cycle: follow Renmin Lu east, past Dong Hu (East Lake). The lake is a fairly standard Chinese arrangement, with bridges, islands, walkways, pleasure boats and fishing. A few hundred metres after the lake, take the main road right and, after about a kilometre, you'll see a mosque entrance on your right, amid trees. The mausoleum is a rather sad, neglected little construction behind the mosque. More interesting than the mausoleum itself is the graveyard around it, a huge area of mud-built, domed constructions with tiny dark entrances.

The most impressive of all the tombs by far is the **Tomb of Abakh Hoja** (daily 8am–5.30pm; ¥9). To reach it takes about thirty or forty minutes by bike, a pleasant ride through wheat fields and poplar-tree woods. From downtown, head northeast, past the Sunday Market site – there are some fantastic old-style Uigur houses shortly after you cross the river – and the turning for the mausoleum is signposted in English.

The mausoleum itself is actually a large mosque-like building of blue and white tiles with a green dome and tiled minarets. Built in the seventeenth century, it was the resting place for a large number of people – the most famous being Abakh Hoja and his granddaughter Ikparhan (known in Chinese as **Xiang Fei**), who, having led the Uigurs in revolt against Beijing, was subsequently seized and married to the Qing Emperor Qian Long, later being ordered to commit suicide by the emperor's jealous mother. In both commemorating a local heroine and spreading anti-Qing propaganda about the cruelty of the treatment she suffered, the story serves the convenient dual purpose of pleasing both the Uigurs *and* the Han Chinese.

Outside Kashgar and accessible only by car are the **Moor Pagodas** at the **ancient city of Hanoi** on a rough road about 30km east of the city. The pagodas have been worn down to rough stumps about a dozen metres high, though the remains of the ruined Tang city-walls of Hanoi make quite a dramatic scene in what is a virtual desert. To reach this place, you'll need a car from *CITS* or another travel service.

Eating and drinking

Kashgar is full of food. For travellers' perhaps the most convenient places to eat are around the *Seman Hotel*. *John's Information Café* (see Ürümqi, p.912) occupies a prime site just around the corner from the hotel. Their Sino-Western fare includes pancakes, coffee and apple pie as well as standard Chinese dishes. A good dinner with beer will cost around ¥20. Right across the road from the *Seman* are a couple of tourist-friendly Chinese restaurants with outdoor tables and equally good food which are a good deal cheaper than *John's*.

The best place to pick up **Uigur food** is around Id Kah Square. **Street vendors** sell *pilau*, kebabs, cold spicy noodles, *kao bao* and *jiaozi*. *Laghman* is available almost everywhere. In the filthy but picturesque *Chakhana*, southwest of the Id Kah Mosque, a plate of *laghman* costs only ¥3. Other street food worth sampling is the vanilla ice cream, mixed up on the spot in containers encased in lumps of ice, which is delicious if not particularly hygienic. Some slightly smarter – though still pretty chaotic – **Uigur restaurants** with tables and chairs are on the northwestern fringe of Renmin Park.

For **Chinese food**, there's a line of restaurants grouped together at the top of Jiefang Nan Lu, on the west side, just south of Renmin Lu. You can get a really good dinner here, with beer, for under ¥30, though the menus are all in Chinese.

Listings

Airline *CAAC,* Jiefang Nan Lu (daily 10am–1pm & 4–7pm; ☎0998/222113). Daily flights to Ürümqi only; book early in peak season.

Banks and exchange *Bank of China*, Renmin Xi Lu (daily 9.30am–1.30pm & 4–7pm).

Bike rental Bicycles can be rented from *John's Café*, for ¥15 per day, or from outside the entrance to the *Qiniwak Hotel* for ¥1 per hour.

Bookshops *Xinhua Bookshop* is on Jiefang Bei Lu, east side, just north of the intersection with Renmin Lu.

MOVING ON FROM KASHGAR

Foreigners are nearly always charged double when buying tickets from Kashgar's long-distance bus station, and for the **Ürümqi** route are automatically sold tickets for the 36-hour sleeper bus (around ¥380, foreigners' price), although very slow, cheap all-seat buses also exist. To **Turpan**, the direct all-seat bus runs only three times a week, so most tourists take the daily sleeper-bus for Ürümqi, and change at Toksun for the very short connection to Turpan. Heading west, through-tickets for the daily bus to **Sust** in northern Pakistan, via Tashkurgan, can be bought from an office at the *Qiniwak Hotel* for ¥260.

The absurdity of all China setting its clocks to Beijing time is at its most acute in Kashgar. Locally, there is such a thing as unofficial "**Kashgar time**", a couple of hours behind Beijing time. Consequently, when buying bus or plane tickets, you should be absolutely clear about which time is being used.

THE ROAD TO KIRGYZISTAN: THE TORUGUT PASS

The road to **Kirgyzistan** from Kashgar is now open to tourists and travellers, and from Bishkek, the capital of Kirgyzistan, there are convenient rail and road connections to Uzbekistan, Kazakhstan and on into Russia itself.

By the time you read this, there should already be scheduled **buses** in summer from Kashgar over the Torugut Pass to Bishkek, and there may be a new customs post just outside Kashgar, which will certainly make the border crossing far easier and perhaps cheaper – enquire at *John's Café* and *CITS* about the latest developments. For the time being, however, the journey remains a difficult one with various unpredictable factors involved, concerning visas (see below), costs and red tape. What can be said for sure is that it will be expensive.

Travellers who already have visas can **rent a vehicle** directly from Kashgar to take them the 160km to the pass; vehicles do not need special permission to do this journey. It's a four-hour trip along a reasonable road and a taxi will cost around ¥500, for a maximum of three passengers. A large minibus will cost around ¥800. Enquire at *CITS* in Kashgar about the minibus – the brother of one of the employees has done the run for travellers before.

From China to Kirgyzistan, vehicles are not allowed **to cross the border** until after 1pm; coming the other way, you must cross before 1pm. There are noodles shops on the

---

Festivals *Corban* is the traditional festival of the Uigur people, involving activities such as dancing and goat-tussling. It takes place at the end of the Muslim month of Ramadan, and again, exactly two months later, to commemorate the *Hajj*.

Post office Renmin Xi Lu, a short walk west of Jiefang Lu.

PSB On Yunmulakexia Lu, a few minutes' walk southwest of *Qiniwake Hotel* (10.30am–7.30pm).

Telephones Direct dial long-distance calls can be made from an office opposite the post office on Renmin Xi Lu, or from the new wing of the *Qiniwak Hotel*. Both charge by the minute.

Travel agents *CITS* (10am–1.30pm and 3.30–7.30pm; ☎0998/222103 ext 4056)) is in the grounds of the *Qiniwak Hotel;* the staff here are quite friendly and speak English, though *John's InformationCafé.* is more useful for independent, budget travellers.

The Karakoram Highway

For centuries the **Khunjerab Pass**, lying some 400km south of Kashgar, was the key Silk Road crossing point between the Chinese world and the Indian sub-continent – and thence to the whole of the Western world. Today the 4700-metre pass still marks the frontier between China and **Pakistan**, but, while crossing the mountains used to be a highly perilous journey to be undertaken on horse, camel or foot, modern engineering has now blasted a highway right through the pass, opening the route to a seasonal

Chinese side of the pass and lines of waiting trucks. You can also change small amounts of money here, apparently at a better rate than in Kashgar. The weather at the 3750-metre pass is very cold, with snow and hail showers frequent even in midsummer.

The Kirgyzi border post lies a few kilometres farther on from the Chinese post. Your own vehicle will not be permitted to cross this stretch, unless you are coming with a specialist mountaineering organization from Kashgar. This is not a problem, however, because the Chinese border guards will see to it that you are put into passing trucks. You needn't pay for this.

On the Kirgyzi side you may be expected to offer **bribes**: you might try offering US$20 as a starter. If the guards are happy with you, you'll be through in minutes. From here you'll have to hitch to Bishkek, as there is no public transport, and you will be expected to pay for any lifts.

In theory, if you have a **visa** for any CIS country (for example, Kazakhstan, Uzbekistan or Russia) then you should be granted a three-day transit visa through Kirgyzistan at the border. In practice this might mean extra bribes. If you do not have any visa at all, you will not be allowed through the Chinese side. Although it is far easier and cheaper to pick up your visas in Beijing (see p.120), some travellers have managed to organize Kirgyzi visas from Kashgar, by making arrangements direct with travel agencies in Bishkek. One organization that has done this for Western travellers in the past is *Tian Shan Travel* in Bishkek (☎/fax 3312/429825). English is spoken here. Basically, they can arrange for a "guide" to meet you at the border with a group visa. The guide will accompany you to Bishkek, where your passports will be stamped with individual visas. Making this arrangement can take up to three weeks and delays may occur at any time. If you can get together a group of six people in Kashgar – which is often feasible – the cost will work out at approximately US$200 each, taking into account the guide's fee, the bribe for the guards, the cost of the transport to Bishkek and the visa itself. Being allowed **into** China from Kirgyzistan – until recently at least – again requires proof that one is being met on the Chinese side by an authorised agent, such as Kashgar *CITS* (see p.930). With the introduction of regular bus services these awkward restrictions will hopefully be dropped.

stream of trucks and buses. The entire 1300-kilometre route from Kashgar over the mountains to Rawalpindi in northern Pakistan is known as the **Karakoram Highway**). The highway was formally opened in 1982, and foreign tourists have been travelling through in both directions since 1986. The trip is still not without its perils, but it's hard to think of a more exciting route into or out of China.

En route from Kashgar, travellers have to spend a night in **Tashkurgan** on the Chinese side, before crossing over the pass to the Pakistani town of **Sust**. There is also the option of camping out for a night or two by the wintry but beautiful **Lake Karakul**, in the lee of glaciers. The road over the pass is open from the beginning of May until the end of October each year, though it can close without notice when the weather is bad, for days at a time, even in summer. The journey from Kashgar to Rawalpindi/Islamabad, or vice versa, takes a minimum of four days if there are no hold-ups. Most travellers need a **visa to enter Pakistan**, and these are not obtainable locally – get yours in Beijing or Hong Kong.

Lake Karakul

Southwest of Kashgar, the road soon leaves the valley, with its mud-brick buildings and irrigated wheat and rice plantations, behind. Climbing through river gorges strewn with giant boulders, it creeps into a land of treeless, bare dunes of sand and gravel, interspersed with pastures scattered with grazing yaks and camels. The sudden appearence of **Lake Karakul** by the roadside, some 200km out of Kashgar, is dramatic. Right under the feet of the Pamir Mountains and the magnificent 7546-metre Mount Muztagata, whose vast snowy flanks have been split open by colossal glaciers, the waters of the lake are a luminous blue. The opportunities for **hiking** over the surrounding pasture, which blooms green during the brief summer, are virtually limitless, especially if you are equipped with a tent and warm clothing; at 3800m, the weather can be extremely cold even in summer, with snow showers normal well into June. It's possible to walk round the lake in a day, in which case you will almost certainly encounter some friendly Kirgyzi yurt-dwellers on the way – you may well be able to stay with them if you can communicate your meaning (not easy). Otherwise, if you are without your own tent, you can stay at a rather muddy and not particularly enticing tour-group yurt site just off the road, with its own restaurant and local attendants. This costs about ¥40 per head, on the basis of two people in a yurt, plus a rather steep ¥60 per person per day for all meals. The food is good and the local people are friendly. There are very rudimentary washing and toilet facilities, and fresh drinking water is available.

Transport to the lake is simple. From the Kashgar long-distance bus station there is at least one daily **bus** leaving at 8.30 am. From Tashkurgan you can take the Kashgar bus and get off at the lake. Leaving the lake requires slightly more ingenuity – for either direction you will need to flag down the passing buses, which may involve standing assertively in the middle of the road. Check approximate expected times of buses with the local people at the lake. For travellers heading to Pakistan, it is perfectly feasible to travel to Tashkurgan via the lake, and then book yourself on to a bus to Sust from Tashkurgan (contrary to what you may be told in Kashgar).

The stretch of road from Karakul south around Muztagata to Tashkurgan passes just 10km east of the Tadjikistan border. When peaceful times return to Central Asia, the fascinating prospect arises of land routes not only to Tadjikistan, but also to Afghanistan. The borders of both countries lie less than 60km from Tashkurgan.

Tashkurgan

The last town before the border, **TASHKURGAN**, lies 280km southeast of Kashgar, and about 220km north of the Pakistani town of Sust. Its primary importance for travellers is as a staging post between Kashgar and Sust, and all travellers passing through, in either direction, must stay the night here. It's a tiny place, comprising a single main tree-lined street, with the bus station and a couple of budget hotels at the western end. The Chinese customs and immigration are located a few minutes round the corner from the bus station.

The town has a long history and fantastic mountain scenery. The Chinese Buddhist pilgrim and Silk Road traveller Xuan Zang stopped over here in the seventh century, a time when, as now, it was the last outpost of Chinese rule. Today, Tashkurgan has a peculiar atmosphere. The native population is mainly Tadjik, but there are also groups of melancholy Han Chinese, thousands of miles from home, as well as intrepid Pakistanis setting up shop outside their country – plus, incredibly, a minor entertainment industry involving sex and alcohol for Pakistani tourists. Few travellers bother to stop for a day, but you could pleasantly rest up here for 24 hours. If you do stay, there's a vast, black, crumbling, mud-brick **fort**, at least six hundred years old, still standing on the edge of town, which is worth a look. To reach it, walk east from the bus station right to the end of town, then strike off a few hundred metres to the left.

Practicalities

Right next to the bus station is the *Jiaotong* (dorms ①, rooms ③). Water supply – both hot and cold – is highly irregular. A slightly better, and much more friendly, option is the Pakistani-managed *Ice Mountain* (①–②). As you exit the *Jiaotong*, turn right, and walk a hundred metres to the east; it's across the road.

The plentiful **beer** in Tashkurgan often comes as a relief to travellers arriving from Pakistan. For **food**, you can take your pick according to the direction you are coming from. If you're tired of Chinese cooking, try the friendly *Punjabi Frontier*, right opposite the *Jiaotong*, which offers reasonable curries and beer. If you're longing for Chinese cooking, walk east from the *Jiaotong* and there are some Chinese restaurants a couple of hundred metres along. Across the road from these places is a small room with "Fast Food" written above the door curtain. You can get Chinese breakfast here – try a bowl of soupy rice (*xifan*), and fried dough sticks (*youtiao*) – you can always add sugar to the *xifan*, if you like.

The **bank**, **post office** and **PSB office** are together, at the other end of the main street – from the bus station, walk east for about twenty minutes. The immigration point also has a couple of banks where cash and travellers' cheques can be changed at official exchange rates. If arriving from Pakistan, you can easily change your rupees with the locally resident Pakistanis if the banks are closed.

The **entry and exit formalities** for Western tourists are straightforward to the point of being lax. You may or may not be issued with Currency and Valuables Declaration forms – but nobody seems to care what you put on them. If your bus arrives late in the evening, your passports are collected in and formalities take place the next morning. Onward connections, in both directions, will wait until everyone is through customs, so there is no need to worry about being left behind.

Travellers heading to Pakistan do not need to buy onward bus tickets – the ticket from Kashgar covers the whole route right through to Sust. Travellers coming from Pakistan, however, will need to buy a **bus ticket** to Kashgar (¥76) in Tashkurgan. This requires standing in a long and heated queue, but don't worry – sufficient transport will be laid on for however many people need it. If you plan to get off at Lake Karakul (see p.931) en route to Kashgar, you may be asked to pay the full Kashgar fare anyway. The alternative to catching buses is to **hitch a ride** on a truck. These often cruise around town in the evening looking for prospective customers to Kashgar (or Karakul) for the day after. You'll pay, but it'll be cheaper than travelling by bus.

The Khunjerab Pass

Khunjerab means "River of Blood" in the local Tadjik language – whether this refers to the rusty colour of local rivers, or to the long traditions of banditry in these areas, is not quite clear. The trip across the border at the **Khunjerab Pass** is not a totally risk-free affair, even today. You should be aware that if your bus departs in rainy weather, you can almost certainly expect rock slides – and people are killed almost every year by falling rocks on the Karakoram Highway. Your safety will not necessarily be the main consideration when the decision is made as to whether or not buses are permitted to travel.

From Tashkurgan, the road climbs into a vast, bright plain, grazed by yaks and camels, with the mountains, clad in snow mantles hundreds of metres thick, pressing in all around. Emerging on to **the top of the pass**, you're greeted by a clear, silent, wind-swept space of frozen streams, protruding glaciers and glimpses of green pasture under the sunshine. The only creatures that live here are the ginger, chubby Himalayan marmots, a kind of large squirrel or woodchuck, existing, so it is said, off a diet of snow and desert – it's easy to spot them from the bus. At these heights, a lot of travellers experience some form of **altitude sickness**, though most people simply riding up and over the pass will feel little more than a faintly feverish or nauseous sensation.

The journey time between Tashkurgan and the small town of **Sust**, where Pakistani customs and immigration take place, is about seven hours. Travellers in both directions again have to spend a night here, and plentiful accommodation is available. From Sust there are direct daily buses to Gilgit, from where frequent buses cover the sixteen-hour route to **Rawalpindi** and **Islamabad**.

travel details

Trains

Baotou to: Beijing (5 daily; 15hr); Hohhot (6 daily; 3hr); Lanzhou (2 daily; 19hr); Shanghai (daily; 43hr); Yinchuan (3 daily; 9hr);Xi'an (daily; 27hr).

Daheyan (for Turpan) to: Jiayuguan (6 daily; 19hr); Korla (daily; 8hr); Lanzhou (6 daily; 37hr); Liuyuan; 13hr); Ürümqi (6 daily; 3hr); Wuwei (6 daily; 31hr); Zhangye (6 daily; 25hr).

Golmud to: Xining (2 daily; 20hr).

Guyuan to: Zhongwei (daily; 5hr).

Hami to: Beijing (daily; 65hr); Daheyan (6 daily; 7hr); Chengdu (daily; 61hr); Korla (daily; 15hr); Lanzhou (6 daily; 30hr); Shanghai (daily; 66hr); Ürümqi (6 daily; 10hr); Xi'an (daily; 43hr).

Hohhot to: Baotou (6 daily; 3hr); Beijing (6 daily; 12hr); Erlianhot (daily; 12hr); Hailar (daily; 60hr); Shanghai (daily; 40hr); Ulan Batur (daily; 30hr); Xi'an (daily; 24hr).

Jiayuguan to: Beijing (daily; 51hr); Chengdu (daily; 47hr); Daheyan (6 daily; 21hr); Lanzhou (6 daily; 17hr); Liuyuan (6 daily; 6hr); Shanghai (daily; 52hr); Ürümqi (6 daily; 24hr); Wuwei (6 daily; 8hr); Xi'an (daily; 30hr); Zhangye (6 daily; 4hr).

Lanzhou to: Baotou (2 daily; 19hr); Beijing (3 daily; 35hr); Chengdu (daily; 31hr); Daheyan (6 daily; 37hr); Hohhot (2 daily; 22hr); Guangzhou (daily; 53hr); Jiayuguan (6 daily; 17hr); Liuyuan (6 daily; 23hr); Shanghai (2 daily; 36hr); Tianshui (13 daily; 6hr); Ürümqi (6 daily; 40hr); Wuwei (6 daily; 7hr); Xi'an (3 daily; 13hr); Xining (4 daily; 4hr); Yinchuan (daily; 10hr); Zhangye (6 daily; 11hr).

Liuyuan (for Dunhuang) to: Beijing (daily; 58hr); Chengdu (daily; 53hr); Daheyan (6 daily; 13hr); Jiayuguan (6 daily; 6hr); Lanzhou (6 daily; 23hr); Shanghai (daily; 58hr); Ürümqi (6 daily; 18hr); Wuwei (6 daily; 14hr); Xi'an (daily; 35hr); Zhangye (6 daily; 10hr).

Tianshui to: Beijing (3 daily; 29hr); Daheyan (4 daily; 43hr); Jiayuguan (4 daily; 23hr); Guangzhou (daily; 47hr); Lanzhou (13 daily; 6hr); Liuyuan; (4 daily; 29hr); Shanghai (daily; 30hr); Ürümqi (4 daily; 46hr); Wuwei (4 daily; 13hr); Xi'an (3 daily; 7hr); Xining (2 daily; 10hr); Zhangye (4 daily; 17hr).

Ürümqi to: Almaty (daily; 36hr); Beijing (daily; 75hr); Chengdu (daily; 71hr); Daheyan (6 daily; 3hr); Hami (6 daily; 10hr); Jiayuguan (6 daily; 24hr); Korla (daily; 12hr); Lanzhou (6 daily; 40hr); Liuyuan (6 daily; 18hr); Shanghai (daily; 76hr); Xi'an (daily; 53hr); Wuwei (6 daily; 33hr); Zhangye (6 daily; 29hr).

Wuwei to: Beijing (daily; 35hr); Chengdu (daily; 38hr); Jiayuguan (6 daily; 11hr); Lanzhou (6 daily; 7hr); Shanghai (daily; 43hr); Ürümqi (6 daily; 33hr); Xi'an (daily; 53hr); Zhangye (6 daily; 4hr); Zhongwei (daily; 12hr).

Xining to: Beijing (daily; 44hr); Golmud (2 daily; 20hr); Lanzhou (4 daily; 4hr); Shanghai (daily; 40hr); Xi'an (17hr).

Yinchuan to: Baotou (3 daily; 9hr); Beijing (2 daily; 25hr); Hohhot (3 daily; 12hr); Lanzhou (daily; 10hr); Taiyuan (daily; 25hr); Xi'an (daily; 23hr); Zhongwei (2 daily; 3hr).

Zhangye to: Beijing (daily; 39hr); Chengdu (daily; 42hr); Jiayuguan (6 daily; 7hr); Lanzhou (6 daily; 11hr); Shanghai (daily; 47hr); Ürümqi (6 daily; 37hr); Wuwei (6 daily; 4hr); Xi'an (daily; 57hr).

Zhongwei to: Baotou (daily; 11hr); Beijing (daily; 27hr); Guyuan (daily; 5hr); Hohhot (daily; 14hr); Lanzhou (daily; 7hr); Shapotou (daily; 1hr); Yinchuan (2 daily; 3hr); Wuwei (daily; 12hr).

Buses

Baotou (Donghe) to: Beijing (daily; 17hr); Dongsheng (every 30min; 3hr); Hohhot (every 30min; 3hr).

Dongsheng to: Baotou (every 30min; 3hr); Hohhot (3 daily; 5hr); Yulin (daily; 6hr).

Dunhuang to: Golmud (daily; 15hr); Hami (3 weekly; 8hr); Jiayuguan (frequent; 8hr); Lanzhou (daily; 24hr); Liuyuan (frequent; 2hr 30min); Zhangye (daily; 13hr).

Golmud to: Dunhuang (daily; 15hr); Lhasa (daily; 36hr); Xining (3 daily; 16hr).

Guyuan to: Lanzhou (daily; 7hr); Luoyang (daily; 16hr); Pingliang (frequent; 2hr); Sanying (frequent; 1hr); Tianshui (daily; 10hr); Xi'an (2 daily, 10hr); Zhongwei (daily; 6hr).

Hami to: Dunhuang (3 weekly; 8hr); Jiayuguan (3 weekly; 12hr); Turpan (daily; 8hr); Ürümqi (daily; 11hr).

Khotan to: Kashgar (daily; 12hr); Kuqa (daily; 30hr); Qiemo (daily; 12hr); Ürümqi (daily; 48hr).

Hohhot to: Baotou (every 30min; 3hr); Beijing (2 daily; 14hr); Dongsheng (3 daily; 5hr); Erlianhot (8hr); Xilinhot (daily; 12hr), Zhaohe (2 daily; 3hr).

Jiayuguan to: Dunhuang (frequent; 8hr); Hami (3 weekly; 12hr); Lanzhou (5 daily; 16hr); Zhangye (5 daily; 5hr).

Kashgar to: Khotan (daily; 12hr); Kuqa (3 daily; 20hr); Lake Karakul (daily; 6hr); Sust (daily 36hr); Tashkurgan (daily; 8hr); Turpan (3 weekly; 2–3 days); Ürümqi (2 daily; 36hr); Yining (daily; 40hr).

Kuqa to: Kashgar (3 daily; 20hr); Korla (daily; 12hr); Turpan (3 weekly; 24hr); Ürümqi (daily; 24hr); Yining (daily; 24hr).

Lanzhou to: Dunhuang (daily; 24hr); Linxia (frequent, 3hr); Tianshui (daily; 8hr); Wuwei (frequent; 6hr); Xiahe (daily; 8hr); Xi'an (daily; 16hr); Xining (frequent; 6hr); Yinchuan (daily; 14hr); Zhangye (daily; 11hr).

Linxia to: Lanzhou (frequent; 3hr); Tianshui (daily; 9hr); Wuwei (daily; 9hr); Xiahe (4 daily; 5hr); Xining (daily; 11hr).

Liuyuan to: Dunhuang (frequent; 2hr 30min).

Tianshui to: Guyuan (daily; 10hr); Lanzhou (daily; 8hr); Linxia (daily; 9hr); Pingliang (daily; 8hr).

Turpan to: Hami (daily; 8hr); Kashgar (3 weekly; 2–3 days); Kuqa (3 weekly; 24hr); Ürümqi (frequent; 3hr).

Ürümqi to: Almaty (daily; 36hr); Altai (daily; 24hr); Hami (daily; 11hr); Kashgar (2 daily; 36hr); Khotan (daily; 48hr); Liuyuan (daily; 23hr); Lanzhou (daily; 44hr); Turpan (frequent; 3hr); Yining (frequent; 18hr).

Wuwei to: Dunhuang (daily; 18hr); Lanzhou (frequent; 5hr); Linxia (daily; 9hr); Xining (daily; 20hr); Zhangye (frequent; 6hr).

Xiahe to: Hezuo (frequent; 2hr); Lanzhou (daily; 8hr); Linxia (frequent; 4hr); Tongren (daily; 6hr).

Xining to: Golmud (2 daily; 16hr); Lanzhou (frequent; 6hr); Lenghu (daily; 36hr); Linxia (daily; 11hr); Maduo (daily; 24hr); Tongren (3 daily; 8hr); Zhangye (daily; 24hr).

Yinchuan to: Lanzhou (daily; 14hr); Xi'an (several daily; 12hr)

Yining to: Almaty (3 weekly; 24hr); Kashgar (daily; 48hr); Kuqa (daily; 24hr); Ürümqi (frequent; 18hr).

Zhangye to: Dunhuang (daily; 13hr); Jiayuguan (frequent; 5hr); Lanzhou (several daily; 11hr); Wuwei (frequent; 5hr).

Zhongwei to: Guyuan (daily; 6hr); Shapotou (frequent; 1hr); Wuwei (daily; 7hr); Yinchuan (several daily; 4hr).

Planes

Baotou to: Beijing (4 weekly; 1hr 30min); Guangzhou (2 weekly; 4hr 30min); Shanghai (2 weekly; 2hr 50min).

Dunhuang to: Jiayuguan (weekly; 1hr); Lanzhou (weekly; 2hr).

Hailar to: Beijing (weekly; 2hr 30min); Hohhot (2 weekly; 2hr 30min).

Hohhot to: Beijing (2 daily; 1hr); Hailar (2 weekly; 2hr 30min); Guangzhou (5 weekly; 4hr 10min); Shanghai (2 weekly; 2hr 20min); Xilinhot (2 weekly; 1hr 30min).

Jiayuguan to: Dunhuang (weekly; 1hr); Lanzhou (weekly; 1hr 30min).

Kashgar to: Ürümqi (daily; 1hr 20 min).

Khotan to: Ürümqi (3 weekly; 1hr 45min).

Kuqa to: Korla (2 weekly; 1hr 25min); Ürümqi (2 weekly; 1hr 50min).

Lanzhou to: Beijing (2 daily; 2hr 10min); Dunhuang (2 weekly; 2hr); Guangzhou (daily; 3hr); Shanghai (5 weekly; 3hr); Ürümqi (5 weekly; 2hr 45min); Xi'an (daily; 1hr).

Ürümqi to: Altai (2 weekly; 2hr 45min); Almaty (3 weekly; 1hr 20min); Beijing (daily; 3hr 30min); Guangzhou (daily; 4hr 40min); Khotan (3 weekly; 1hr 45min); Islamabad (2 weekly; 2hr 10min); Kashgar (daily; 1hr 20min); Korla (5 weekly; 1hr 25min); Kuqa (2 weekly; 4hr); Lanzhou (5 weekly; 2hr 40min); Moscow (weekly; 6hr 35min); Xi'an (daily; 2hr 45min); Xining (2 weekly; 2hr 20min); Yining (daily; 2hr).

Xining to: Beijing (3 weekly; 2hr 10min); Guangzhou (weekly; 3hr); Shanghai (weekly; 2hr 40min); Ürümqi (weekly; 2hr 25min).

Yinchuan to: Beijing (daily; 2hr); Shanghai (weekly; 3hr 10min); Xi'an (2 daily; 1hr 20min).

Yining to: Ürümqi (daily; 1hr 45min).

CHAPTER FOURTEEN

TIBET

ibet, the "Roof of the World" (*Bod* to Tibetans, *Xizang* to the Chinese), has exerted a pull of almost supernatural proportions over travellers for many centuries. However, it is today a sad, subjugated colony of China. The scenery has a majesty and grandeur that are spellbinding, the religious monuments and practices are overwhelmingly picturesque and moving, and the Tibetan people are welcoming and wonderful, but this is a previously proud and independent nation in thrall to a foreign power: look just a little below the surface and it is all too apparent that Tibet's past has been tragic, its present is painful, and the future looks bleak.

This doesn't mean you should stay away, however. While **tourism** provides legitimacy as well as foreign currency to the Chinese government, many people, the Dalai Lama among them, believe that travellers should visit Tibet to learn all they can of the country and its people. Although the daily bureaucratic irritations for independent visitors can sometimes seem overwhelming, official Chinese policy is to increase the number of tourists, and hence tourist earnings, in Tibet. While the Chinese prefer easily controllable, high-rolling tour parties rather than the less malleable, less lucrative budget travellers, they are, for the moment, prepared to tolerate both.

The isolation of Tibet has long stirred the imagination of the West, yet until the British, under the command of Younghusband, invaded in 1904, only a trickle of bold eccentrics, adventurers and the odd missionary had succeeded in getting close to Lhasa, and then only at serious risk to their lives, for it was firm Tibetan policy to exclude all influence from the outside world. So great was the uncertainty about the geographical nature of the country even 150 years ago that the British in India despatched carefully trained spies, known as *pundits,* to walk the length and breadth of the country, counting their footsteps and mapping as they went. When Younghusband's invasion force finally reached Lhasa they were, perhaps inevitably, disappointed. One journalist accompanying them wrote:

> If one approached within a league of Lhasa, saw the glittering domes of the Potala and turned back without entering the precincts one might still imagine an enchanted city. It was in fact an unsanitary slum. In the pitted streets pools of rainwater and piles of refuse were everywhere: the houses were mean and filthy, the stench pervasive. Pigs and ravens competed for nameless delicacies in open sewers.

Since 1950 Tibet has become much more accessible with approaches eased by plane links with Chengdu and Kathmandu. Today's visitors are perhaps more worldly than to expect a romantic Shangri-la, but there is no doubt that many people are surprised by the heavy military and civilian Chinese presence, the modern apartments and factories alongside traditional Tibetan rural lifestyles and monasteries.

The massive **Tibetan plateau**, at an average height of 4500m above sea level, is guarded on all sides by towering mountain ranges: the Himalaya separates Tibet from India, Nepal and Bhutan to the south, the Karakoram from Pakistan to the west and the Kunlun from Xinjiang to the north. To the east, dividing Tibet from Sichuan and

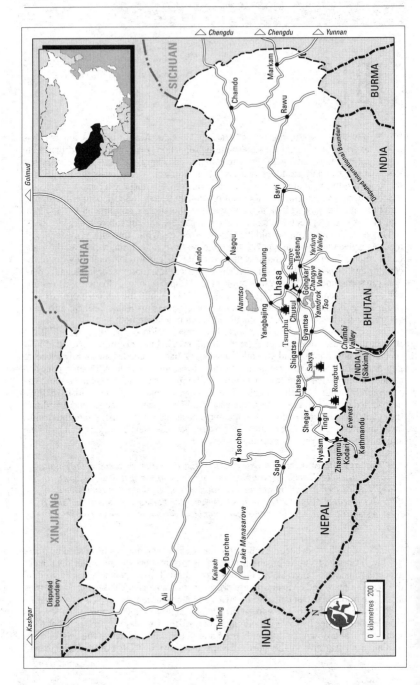

ACCOMMODATION PRICE CODES

All the accommodation in this book has been graded according to the following price codes, which represent the cheapest double room available to foreigners. Most places have a range of rooms, however, and staff will usually offer you the more expensive ones – it's always worth asking if they have anything cheaper. Where the text refers specifically to dorm beds, the price code represents the price per bed. See p.40 for more details.

① less than ¥30   ④ ¥100–150   ⑦ ¥300–500

② ¥30–75   ⑤ ¥150–200   ⑧ ¥500–700

③ ¥75–100   ⑥ ¥200–300   ⑨ ¥700 or more

Yunnan, an extensive series of subsidiary ranges covers almost a thousand kilometres. The plateau is also birthplace to some of the greatest rivers of Asia, with the Yangzi, Mekong, Yellow and Salween rising in the east, and the Indus, Brahmaputra, Sutlej and some feeder rivers of the Ganges in the west near Mount Kailash.

Covering a massive 1.2 million square kilometres, today's **Tibetan Autonomous Region** (TAR) is but a shadow of the former Tibetan lands. The old area, sometimes referred to as Greater Tibet or Ethnographic Tibet, was carved up by the Chinese following their invasion in 1950, when the Amdo and Kham regions were absorbed into Qinghai, Sichuan, Gansu and Yunnan provinces. The TAR consists only of the West and Central (U-Tsang) regions of Greater Tibet and divides into four geographical areas. The northern and largest portion is the almost uninhabited **Chang Tang**, a rocky desert averaging 4000m altitude, where winter temperatures can fall to minus 44°C. South of this is the **mountainous grazing area**, land that cannot support settled agriculture, inhabited by the wide-ranging nomadic people with their herds of yaks, sheep and goats. The **southern valleys**, sandwiched between this nomad area and the **Himalaya** along the southern border, are the most hospitable for human habitation. Not surprisingly, this is the most populated area and where visitors spend the majority of their time, particularly in the extensive valley system of the Tsangpo River (Brahmaputra) and its tributaries.

There has been heavy Han migration into the region since 1950, although it is impossible to know how many Chinese live here now. According to the latest available Chinese figures (1990), there are 2.2 million people in the TAR, 95 percent of them Tibetan, which certainly isn't true; indeed, the Chinese will soon outnumber Tibetans, if they don't already. The situation is most marked in the cities, where the greatest opportunities exist: not only are the numbers of Han increasing all the time, but they are becoming economically dominant too.

It's worth bearing a few things in mind while you're here. Many of the Chinese who have come to Tibet are poor people trying to make a life for themselves and their families – they may have little knowledge or understanding of the wider political implications of their presence here. Equally, life in Tibet has taken its toll on Tibetans, and there have been instances of Tibetans asking for Dalai Lama pictures or asking foreigners to take letters to relatives outside the country and then turning the foreigners in to the security forces to be deported. Be careful whom you trust, but also be aware of the harm you may be doing. Everyday conversations are going to cause no damage, but if you are seen to be asking a lot of politically loaded questions about sensitive issues then not only are you putting yourself at risk but any Tibetans who talk to you could be in danger long after you have left the country.

Tibet offers some of the most awe-inspiring **scenery** in the world, and the sheer scale of the high-altitude valleys, mountains and lakes in which human habitation is but a speck on the landscape is humbling. **Lhasa**, **Shigatse** and **Gyantse** offer the most accessible **monasteries and temples** – the Jokhang, Tashilunpo and the Kumbum respectively – and are also tourist-friendly cities with the biggest range of facilities in the region. The **Potala Palace** in Lhasa remains an enduring image of Tibet in the Western mind and should on no account be missed, and there are plenty of smaller sights in the city to keep anyone busy for several days. Farther afield, the **Yarlung** and **Chongye** valleys to the southeast boast temples and ancient monuments, and the ancient walled monastery of **Samye** is easily combined with these. The tourist corridor between Zhangmu on the Nepalese border and Lhasa is relatively well-trodden these days, although by no means overcrowded, and offers side trips to the huge Mongolian-style monastery at **Sakya** and to **Everest Base Camp**.

Some history

Legend tells how the **earliest Tibetans** came from the union of the ogress, Sinmo, and a monkey, reincarnation of the god Chenresi, on the mountain of Gangpo Ri near Tsetang. Ethnographers, however, think it more likely the Tibetans are descended from the nomadic Ch'iang who roamed eastern Central Asia, to the northwest of China, several thousand years ago. The first Tibetan king, Nyatri Tsenpo, believed to have come to earth via a magical "sky-cord", was the first of a long lineage of 27 kings who ruled in a pre-Buddhist era when the indigenous, shamanistic **Bon religion** held sway throughout the land (see p.814).

Each of the **early kings** held power over a small area and it was not until the time of King Songtsen Gampo, the thirty-third ruler in the dynasty, born in 617 AD, that expansionism began. Songtsen Gampo's twenty-year rule saw the unification of the country and aggressive spread of his empire from Northern India to China. To placate their assertive neighbour, China and Nepal each offered Songtsen Gampo a wife: in 632 he married Princess Bhrikuti (also known as Tritsun) of Nepal and in 641 Princess Wencheng arrived from the Tang court sent by her father, Emperor Taizong. They both brought their Buddhist faith and magnificent statues of the Buddha which are now the centrepieces of Ramoche temple and the Jokhang in Lhasa.

Whilst the geographical boundaries of Tibet always made outside contact difficult, it is apparent that as early as the seventh century there was considerable cultural exchange between Tibet and its neighbours. Pens, ink, silks, jewels and probably tea reached Tibet from China in the seventh century and Tibet for many centuries looked to India for religious teaching.

Songtsen Gampo embraced the **Buddhist faith** and established Buddhist temples throughout the country, although the indigenous Bon faith remained the religion of the ordinary people. Following his death in 650, his descendants strengthened the kingdom politically, and in 763 Tibetan armies even took the Chinese capital Chang'an (modern Xi'an). Trisong Detsen (742–797) was another champion of the new faith who invited two Indian Buddhist teachers to Tibet, Shantarakshita and the charismatic and flamboyant **Padmasambhava**, also known as Guru Rinpoche, who is regarded as responsible for overcoming the resistance of the Bon religion and ensuring the spread of Buddhism within Tibet. Although he is closely associated with the Nyingma school of Buddhism, you'll spot his image somewhere in most temples.

In 838, the infamous **Langdarma** came to the throne, having assassinated his brother. A fervent supporter of Bon, he set about annihilating the Buddhist faith. Temples and monasteries were destroyed, monks forced to flee and the previously unified Tibet broke up into a number of small principalities. A Buddhist revival involving monastery construction, the translation of scriptures into Tibetan and the establishment of several of the schools of Tibetan Buddhism was spearheaded by the arrival of **Atisha** (982–1054), the most famous Indian scholar of the time. Politically the country was not united but the various independent principalities lived largely in harmony and there was little contact with China.

Absorbed in internal events, the Tibetans had largely neglected the outside world where the Muslim surge across India in the twelfth and thirteenth centuries resulted in the destruction of the great Buddhist centres of teaching to which the Tibetans had looked for generations. And to the north and east of Tibet the **Mongol leader**, Genghis Khan, was beginning his assault on China. In 1207 Genghis Khan sent envoys to Tibet demanding submission, which was given without a fight, and the territory was largely ignored until Genghis Khan's grandson, Godan, sent raiding parties deep into the country. Hearing from his troops about the spirituality of the Tibetan lamas, Godan invited the head of the Sakya order, Sakya Pandita, to his court. In exchange for peace, Sakya Pandita again offered Tibetan submission and was created regent of Tibet at the Mongolian court, making the Sakya lamas the effective rulers of Tibet under the patronage of the emperor. This lasted through the generations with Godan's son, **Kublai Khan**, deeply impressed by Sakya Pandita's nephew, Phagpa.

When the Chinese Ming dynasty overcame the Mongols in the fourteenth century, Tibet began a long period of independence which ended in 1642 with the Mongols intervening directly in support of the Fifth Dalai Lama, Lobsang Gyatso, of the **Gelugpa order**.

The Fifth Dalai Lama (1617–1682), often referred to as **"the Great Fifth"**, united the country under Gelugpa rule and within fifteen years, largely neglected by Mongol rulers, he established authority from Kham to Kailash, the first time that one religious and political leader had united and ruled the country. He invited scholars to Tibet, restored and expanded religious institutions and began work on the Potala in Lhasa. One disadvantage of the reincarnation system of succession (in which a new-born child is identified as the next manifestation of the dead lama) is that an unstable period of fifteen or twenty years inevitably follows a death while the next reincarnation grows to adulthood. Initially, the death of the Fifth Dalai Lama in 1682 was concealed by his regent, Sangye Gyatso, who claimed he had entered a period of solitary meditation and meanwhile raised the Sixth Dalai Lama to adulthood.

The following two centuries saw no strong leadership from the Dalai Lamas with repeated incursions by Mongolian factions. The most influential figures in Tibet at this time were the regents and representatives of the Manchu rulers in China, the *ambans*. During the **nineteenth century**, Tibet became increasingly isolationist, fearing Russian plans to expand their empire south and British plans to expand their empire north. Seeing themselves caught in the middle, the Tibetans simply banned foreigners from their land. Tibetan fears appeared justified in 1904 when the British, equally concerned about Russian and Chinese plans, invaded under Younghusband, marching up to Gyantse through the Chumbi Valley and eventually on to Lhasa. However, a series of British Representatives in Lhasa forged good relationships with Tibet and became a window on the outside world. The **Thirteenth Dalai Lama**, Tubten Gyatso (1876–1933), was an insightful and capable leader who realized that Tibet's political position needed urgent clarification, but he had a difficult rule, fleeing into exile twice, and was much occupied with border fighting against the Chinese and tensions with conservatives inside the country. Following his death, the **Fourteenth Dalai Lama** was identified in Amdo in 1938 and was still a young man when world events began to close in on Tibet. The British left India in 1947, withdrawing their Representative from Lhasa. In 1949 the Communists under Mao Zedong created the People's Republic of China and the following year declared their intention "to liberate the oppressed and exploited Tibetans and reunite them with the great motherland". In October 1950, the People's Liberation Army invaded the Kham region of eastern Tibet before proceeding to Lhasa the following year. Under considerable duress, Tibet signed a seventeen-point treaty in 1951, allowing for the "peaceful integration of Tibet".

Initially the Chinese offered goodwill and modernization. Tibet had made little headway into the twentieth century; there were few roads, no electricity, and glass windows, steel girders and concrete were all recent introductions. Hygiene and health care were patchy and lay education was unavailable. While some Tibetans viewed modernization as necessary, the opposition was stiff, as many within the religious hierarchy saw changes within the country and overtures to the outside world as a threat to their influence. Throughout the 1950s an underground resistance operated which flared into a public confrontation in March 1959, fuelled by mounting distrust and hostility, as refugees from eastern Tibet fled to Lhasa and told of the brutality of Chinese rule. In Lhasa the Chinese invited the Dalai Lama to a theatrical performance at the Chinese military base. It was popularly perceived as a ploy to kidnap him, and huge numbers of Tibetans mounted demonstrations and surrounded the Norbulingka where the Dalai Lama was staying. On the night of March 17, the Dalai Lama and his entourage escaped, heading into exile in India where they were later joined (and are still joined today) by tens of thousands of refugees.

Meanwhile the **uprising in Lhasa** was ferociously suppressed – 87,000 people were killed by the Chinese between March 1959 and September 1960. From that point on all pretence of goodwill vanished, and a huge military force moved in, with a Chinese bureaucracy replacing Tibetan institutions. Temples and monasteries were destroyed and Chinese **agricultural policies** proved particularly disastrous. During the years of the Great Leap Forward (1959–60) it is estimated that ten percent of Tibetans starved, and it wasn't until the early 1980s that the food situation in Tibet began to improve. Harrowing accounts tell of parents mixing their own blood with hot water and *tsampa* to feed their children.

In September 1965 the U-Tsang and Western areas of Tibet officially became the **Xizang Autonomous Region** of the People's Republic of China, but more significant was the **Cultural Revolution** (1966–76) during which mass destruction of religious monuments and practices took place under the orders of the Red Guards, some of them young Tibetans. In 1959 there were 2700 monasteries and temples in Tibet; by 1978 there were just eight monasteries and fewer than a thousand monks and nuns in the TAR.

Liberalization followed Mao's death in 1976, leading to a period of relative openness and peace in the early 1980s when monasteries were rebuilt, religion revived and tourism was restored. By the end of the decade, repression was again in place following riots in Lhasa in 1988–9 but in the early 1990s foreigners were allowed back and the current mood seems to be one of apparent openness, with the encouragement of tourism against a background of increased internal control of the Tibetan population. Dissent is ruthlessly quashed and there are currently between six and seven hundred political detainees, more than at any time since 1990. While the true figures will never be known, estimates of three hundred thousand to one million have been given for the number of Tibetans who have perished either directly at the hands of the Chinese or indirectly through starvation and hardship. The International Commission of Jurists in the Hague has held the People's Republic of China to be guilty of genocide.

Meanwhile, the profile of the **Tibetan Government in Exile** based in Dharamsala in northern India, representing 130,000 Tibetan refugees and led by the Dalai Lama, continues to increase. The world community has refused to take a stand for the Tibetans yet the Dalai Lama, earthly incarnation of the god Chenresi, known to the Tibetans as *Gyalwa Rinpoche*, has never faltered from advocating a peaceful solution for Tibet which led to his being awarded the 1989 Nobel Peace Prize.

For the Tibetans who remain here the reality of **life in Tibet** is harsh. China admits that a quarter of the TAR counties cannot feed or clothe themselves, one third of children do not go to school and Tibet's literacy rate is about thirty percent, the lowest in China. Between 1952 and 1994 it is estimated that China has subsidized the TAR to the tune of 35 billion yuan – yet Tibetans are among the poorest people in China and have the lowest life expectancy in the country. As Tibet provides the Chinese with land for their exploding population along with almost untold natural resources, the influx of Han Chinese settlers threatens to swamp the Tibetan population, culture and economy. For more information on Tibet see p.1045.

Tibet Practicalities

The **best time to visit** is April to October, outside the coldest months. June to September are the wettest months when blocked roads and swollen rivers can make travel difficult but the countryside will be at its greenest. However, health considerations should be taken seriously at any time of the year, and even in relatively balmy Lhasa temperatures fall below freezing on a regular basis. In winter, as long as you come fully prepared for the cold (most hotels have no heating) and possible delays due to snow-covered passes, the lack of tourists and the preoccupation of the security forces with staying warm can make for a pleasant trip.

Getting there

Officially you need only a **Chinese visa** to travel to Tibet. However, the authorities control entry into the country by insisting that independent travellers purchase a **"permit"** when they buy travel tickets into the region. You may or may not see this permit and once you are in Tibet nobody is interested in it. **Visa extensions** are a problem in Tibet and best avoided. You can apply for extensions at any PSB but from April 1996 travellers were generally being granted only ten days.

By air
Flights operate daily from **Chengdu** (see p.772 for more details). Expect to pay around ¥2500 including your permit plus ¥50 departure tax at the airport. Flights from **Kathmandu** leave twice weekly (Tues & Sat), but you'll be able to buy an airline ticket in Kathmandu for Lhasa only if you're booked on a tour through a travel agent there (upwards of US$300 for seven days, with flight costs on top). A weekly direct flight from **Beijing** has been timetabled for some time but has yet to materialize.

By land
Overland routes are well established, although they can be physically taxing. From within China, **Golmud to Lhasa** (1160km) is the only officially permitted land route (see p.896). The overland routes from Sichuan (over 2000km from Chengdu to Lhasa), Yunnan (around 2400km from Kunming) and Kashgar (1100km to Ali) are strictly closed to foreigners, although a few intrepid travellers manage to get through. If you're caught by the authorities you may well be imprisoned, fined and/or deported and drivers caught transporting you face at least large fines and maybe more serious trouble.

Overland **from Kathmandu** via Kodari on the Nepal side and Zhangmu on the Tibetan side is a popular option, but travellers are vulnerable to snap policy changes, and also to landslides in summer and snow-blocked passes in winter. Under no circumstances apply for a Chinese visa in Kathmandu if you want to travel independent-

LIVING BUDDHISM

There is little ceremony attached to **visiting Buddhist temples** and they are generally open and welcoming places, although entrance fees are now collected from tourists. Most temples are open in the mornings (9am–noon), when pilgrims do the rounds and usually again after lunch (2 or 3–5pm). Smaller places may well be locked but ask for the caretaker and the chances are you'll be let in. There is no need to remove your shoes, but you should walk clockwise both around the entire complex or building and inside the chapels and you shouldn't eat, drink or smoke inside. It is polite to ask before taking photographs, and the policy on this seems to vary. Small offerings on the altars are welcomed – a few fen or one yuan, or butter for the butter lamps.

The range of **offerings** that devout Tibetans make to their gods is enormous and includes juniper smoke sent skyward in incense burners, prayer flags printed with prayers erected on rooftops and mountains, tiny papers printed with religious images and cast to the wind on bridges and passes (*lungda*), white scarves (*katag*) presented to statues and lamas, butter to keep lamps burning on altars, repetitious *mantras* invoking the gods and the spinning of prayer wheels which have printed prayers rolled up inside. The idea of each is to gain merit in this life and hence affect your *karma*. If you want to take part, watch what other people do and copy them; nobody is at all precious about religion in Tibet. For more on Tibetan Buddhism, see *Contexts*, p.1016.

Giving **alms to beggars** is another way of gaining merit and most large Tibetan temples have a horde of beggars who survive on charity from pilgrims. Whether or not you give money is up to you, but if you do it's wise to give ¥1 or so, roughly the same amount as Tibetans.

Tibetan Buddhism is divided into several **schools** which have different philosophical emphases rather than fundamental differences. The **Nyingma**, the Old Order, traces its origins back to Guru Rinpoche, Padmasambhava, who brought Buddhism to Tibet. The **Kagyupa**, **Sakya** and **Kadampa** all developed during the eleventh-century revival of Buddhism while the now dominant **Gelugpa** (Virtuous School) traces back to Tsongkhapa (1357–1419) and numbers the Dalai Lama and Panchen Lama among its adherents. Virtually all monasteries and temples are aligned to one or other of the schools, but, apart from an abundance of statues of revered lamas of that particular school, you'll spot little difference between the temples. Tibetan people are pretty eclectic and will worship in temples which they feel are particularly sacred and seek blessings from lamas they feel are endowed with special powers regardless of the school they belong to.

GODS AND GODDESSES

Tibetan Buddhism is quite overwhelming with its huge number of **gods and goddesses** and matters are complicated by each deity having different manifestations or forms. For example, there are 21 forms of the favourite goddess Tara and even the most straightforward image has a Sanskrit and Tibetan name. Below are some of the most common you will encounter:

Amitayus (Tsepame) and **Vijaya** (Namgyelma), often placed with White Tara to form the Three Gods of Longevity.

ly to Tibet – the Chinese embassy will not issue these unless you are booked on an organized tour through a Kathmandu travel agent (expect to pay around US$380 for an organized seven-day tour going overland to Lhasa, plus US$190 for the Lhasa–Kathmandu flight). Independent travellers must have their Chinese visa before arrival in Kathmandu. Allow two to three days minimum to reach Lhasa from Zhangmu with no sightseeing on the way. In April 1996, regulations were tightened and Aliens' Travel Permits (see below) for the route to Lhasa (US$30) were being issued only if an organized tour through to the capital was booked with *CITS* in Zhangmu (minimum US$103 per person for a two- or three-day hurtle across the

Avalokiteshvara (Chenresi in Tibetan, and Guanyin in Chinese temples), patron god of Tibet, with many forms, most noticeably with eleven faces and a thousand arms.

Maitreya (Jampa), the Buddha of the Future.

Manjusri (Jampelyang), the God of Wisdom.

Padmasambhava has eight manifestations, most apparent as Guru Rinpoche. You may see him with his consorts, Yeshe Tsogyel and Mandarava.

Sakyamuni, Buddha of the Present.

Tara (Dolma), Goddess of Compassion. Green Tara is associated with protection and White Tara with long life.

FESTIVALS

The Tibetan lunar calendar is used to calculate festival dates and these correspond to different dates on the Western calendar each year.

February/March Driving out of evil spirits (last day of year). Twenth-ninth day of the twelfth lunar month.

Losar, Tibetan New Year. First day of the first lunar month.

Monlam, Great Prayer Festival, Lhasa. Eighth day of the first lunar month.

Butter Lamp Festival – final day of Monlam. Fifteenth day of the first lunar month.

May/June Birth of Buddha. Seventh day of the fourth lunar month.

Saga Dawa (Buddha's Enlightenment). Fifteenth day of the fourth lunar month.

Gyantse Horse Festival. Fifteenth day of the fourth lunar month.

July Tashilunpo Festival, Shigatse. Fifteenth day of the fifth lunar month.

July/August Buddha's First Sermon. Fourth day of the sixth lunar month.

Drepung Festival. Thirtieth day of the sixth lunar month.

August/September Shotun (Yoghurt Festival), Lhasa. First to the seventh day of the seventh lunar month.

Bathing Festival, Lhasa. Twenty-seventh day of the seventh lunar month.

September Damxhung Horse Festival. Thirtieth day of the seventh lunar month.

September/October Harvest Festival. First to the seventh day of the eighth lunar month.

November Lhabab (Buddha's descent from Heaven). Twenty-second day of the ninth lunar month.

November/December Peldon Lhama Festival, Lhasa. Fifteenth day of the tenth lunar month.

region). The best advice is to spend some time in Zhangmu to talk to other travellers, get a feel for the current situation and check out your options. At the time of writing, **cyclists** on this route were managing to persuade the authorities to issue a permit without a tour, but bear in mind that most of the road between Zhangmu and Shigatse is unpaved and very rough. The altitude gain from Kodari to Zhangmu is 530m in about 9km, then 1450m in the 33km to Nyalam followed by a tough 1300m in the 57-kilometre climb to the Lalung Pass at 5050m. Allow around twenty days to cycle from Kathmandu to Lhasa. You'll need camping equipment, food (plus stove) and adequate warm-weather gear. Dogs are a particular hazard near villages.

Getting around

Aliens' Travel Permits are issued by the PSB and give you permission to visit specified places within specified time limits. They cost ¥10 (sometimes plus ¥1 for the form). At the time of writing the few parts of Tibet where you did not need an Aliens' Travel Permit included Lhasa, Shigatse, Zhangmu and Tsetang. For all other areas you need to apply to the PSB in the district capital for a permit. There are some areas where a permit will not be given under any circumstances, such as the highly militarized Chumbi Valley. However, the status of other areas seems to change from one day to the next. Being caught somewhere without a permit can be fairly heavy: travellers have faced big fines, confiscation of passports, been harangued at length and forced to write "confessions". In practice, there are some areas without checkposts on the way and no PSB officers at your destination, for example Namtso Lake, and there's little point in alerting the PSB to the fact you're going.

The **public transport** system in Tibet, such as it is, consists of large public **buses** and the smaller, nippier **minibuses**. For Tibetans these are largely interchangeable, but for foreigners the difference is highly significant. There are, as yet, no problems with foreigners travelling on the public buses, but minibuses come under the label of "private vehicles" and foreigners are banned from travelling on these (although the minibuses that operate within Lhasa itself seem exempt from this ban). This is regardless of the fact that minibuses are often the best, and sometimes the only, public transport between two points. This ban also means foreigners cannot travel in trucks and private cars which effectively rules out hitch-hiking. The zeal with which the PSB enforces this regulation, and hence the willingness of the drivers to take a chance and carry you, changes from month to month. The drivers face huge fines and big trouble if they are caught. The situation with regard to **pilgrim buses** seems even more confused. These are large buses, operating daily to Ganden and Tsurphu monasteries, and while most travellers report few problems, at times of particular tension or zeal by the authorities, drivers may be hesitant about taking you.

Most travellers end up **renting a jeep**, driver and/or guide (this last may be obligatory) for specific trips through one of the many private **tour companies** in Lhasa. All the hotels have agencies and they adorn Beijing Dong Lu and Mentsikhang Lu. You'll need to decide your exact itinerary, get together five people to fill up the jeep, write a contract detailing timings and costs and pay the deposit (usually half the agreed fee) before you go. The tour company should arrange permits and you should check the quote includes the cost of these plus fees, lodging and food for the driver and guide and the cost of fuel, in fact everything except your own food and lodging and the cost of your admission to monasteries. It pays to be precise in your itinerary, so, for example, don't say Rongbuk Monastery if you mean Everest Base Camp. Hopefully you'll have no **problems**, but there have been sufficient misunderstandings between tourists and tour companies that the Tibet Tourism Bureau at 208 Yuan Lin Lu, Lhasa, has a Tour Service Inspection Office which handles complaints about tour companies (☎0891/6333476 or 6334193).

Some **maps** are available in Lhasa. The English-language *China Tibet Tour Map* produced by the Mapping Bureau of the TAR is the best one, a pricey ¥65 at the *Holiday Inn*, although you may get it cheaper elsewhere. The *Yak Hotel* has a dated but detailed handrawn city map (¥3), while the *Lhasa Tour Map* (¥7) is available at the *Xinhua Bookshop*. See *Basics*, p.26, for advice on maps available outside Tibet.

Health

Tibet poses particular health hazards to travellers. Almost every visitor is affected by **altitude** as most of Tibet is over 3000m with plenty of passes over 5000m. For your first two or three days at altitude rest as much as possible and drink plenty of water. A few painkillers should help to relieve any aches and pains and headaches, but more serious problems can develop (see *Basics*, p.23 for more details). Trekkers and anyone travelling long distances in the backs of trucks need to be particularly aware of the dangers of **hypothermia**. Travellers to Tibet should have **rabies immunization** before they travel. The dogs here are very aggressive, bites are common and, if you get bitten, Kathmandu is the nearest place stocking rabies serum. A significant number of travellers to Tibet also suffer from **giardia**, an unpleasant and debilitating intestinal complaint (see p.21), although there is some controversy over whether it is endemic to the region or brought in from outside. The treatment is Tinadozol or Flagyl which is not reliably available in Lhasa; bring a course along if you can.

Accommodation

In most Tibetan towns simple **guesthouses** offer accommodation to foreigners, pilgrims and truck drivers. You can expect dormitory accommodation with bedding, of variable cleanliness, provided. The communal toilets are usually pit latrines and there are few washing facilities, although most places have bowls, and you can expect hot water in vacuum flasks, for drinks and washing, everywhere. Lighting may be by candle. There is a greater choice of accommodation in the main tourist centres of Lhasa, Shigatse, Gyantse, Tsetang and Zhangmu where tourist-class hotels provide comfortable rooms with attached bathrooms and at least some hours of hot water. In the administrative centres of Lhasa and Shigatse these are supplemented by **mid-range hotels**, with rooms of a similar quality but fewer facilities (such as business centres) but generally offering reasonable value for money. If you are trekking, you can camp wherever the fancy takes you, although many trekkers find accommodation in village houses or with nomadic yak-herders. You should not expect them to feed you and should pay ¥15 or so per night.

Lhasa

Situated in a wide, mountain-fringed valley on the north bank of the Kyichu River, **LHASA** (Ground of the Gods), at 4200m, is a sprawling, rapidly expanding, modern Chinese city with a population of around 163,000. An important settlement for well over a thousand years, it was originally called Rasa, but was renamed by King Songtsen Gampo in the seventh century when he moved his capital here from the Yarlung Valley. Following the collapse of the Yarlung dynasty two centuries later, power dispersed among local chieftains and the city lost its pre-eminence. It was not until the seventeenth century, with the installation of the Fifth Dalai Lama as ruler by the Mongolian emperor, Gushri Khan, that Lhasa once again became the seat of government. It continues now as the capital of the TAR and while glorious sites from earlier times are spread throughout the area, it is this third period of growth, following the Chinese invasion, that has given the city its most obvious features – wide boulevards separating tracts of soulless concrete. The Chinese population of Lhasa is highly active economically, with over seven hundred Chinese businesses in Tromzikhang market compared to just three hundred Tibetan.

There are plenty of sights in and around the city to keep most visitors occupied for at least a week; the **Potala**, **Jokhang** and **Barkhor** district are unmissable, and at least one trip to an outlying monastery is a must. It's also worth taking time to see

The **telephone code** for Lhasa is ☎0891

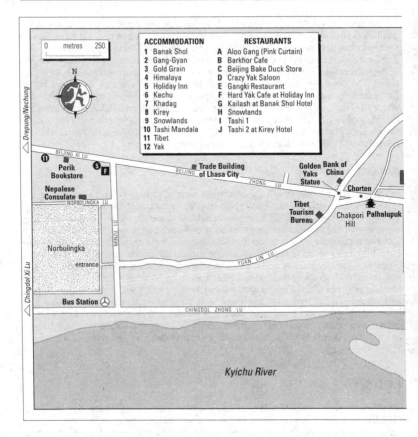

ACCOMMODATION		RESTAURANTS	
1	Banak Shol	A	Aloo Gang (Pink Curtain)
2	Gang-Gyan	B	Barkhor Cafe
3	Gold Grain	C	Beijing Bake Duck Store
4	Himalaya	D	Crazy Yak Saloon
5	Holiday Inn	E	Gangki Restaurant
6	Kechu	F	Hard Yak Cafe at Holiday Inn
7	Khadag	G	Kailash at Banak Shol Hotel
8	Kirey	H	Snowlands
9	Snowlands	I	Tashi 1
10	Tashi Mandala	J	Tashi 2 at Kirey Hotel
11	Tibet		
12	Yak		

some of the smaller, less showy temples and simply to absorb the atmosphere of the "Forbidden City" which large numbers of explorers died in their vain efforts to reach around a hundred years ago.

Offering tourists better **facilities**, with more choice of accommodation, restaurants and shopping than anywhere else in Tibet, Lhasa is the best place to arrange trips to other parts of the region. Whatever the comforts of Lhasa and the complexities of travelling outside, remember that the city is just one face of Tibet and 88 percent of the population live in the countryside.

Orientation, arrival and city transport

The **central areas** of Lhasa are along and between three main roads that run east–west, parallel to and north of the Kyichu River. The most southerly is Chingdrol Lu which changes its name from Chingdol Xi Lu in the west through Chingdol Zhong Lu in the centre to Chingdol Dong Lu in the east. Slightly farther north, Beijing Lu has similar name changes, while Lingkor Bei Lu is the most northerly of the three. Lhasa is at its most sprawling to the west, where there is very little countryside between the outskirts of the city and the monastery of Drepung, 8km away from the centre of town, and north

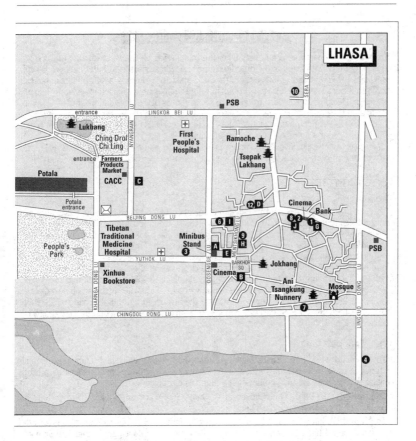

where the city virtually merges into the Sera monastery complex, 4km distant. So far the river has prevented a spread south, while to the east the city peters out within a couple of kilometres as the road towards Ganden deteriorates quickly. The Potala Palace, on Beijing Zhong Lu, is the major landmark visible throughout the city and, together with the Tibetan enclave around the Jokhang temple, known as the Barkhor, forms the centre of interest for most visitors. The Golden Yaks Statue, at the junction of Beijing Zhong Lu and Yuan Lin Lu in the west of the city, erected in 1991 to celebrate the fortieth anniversary of the "liberation" of Tibet, is another useful landmark.

Arriving by air, you'll land at **Lhasa airport** at Gongkhar, a hefty 93km to the southeast of the city. *CACC* buses (¥30) bring you to the *CACC* office on Nyangrain Lu in around two hours. From the office it's about 1km to the Barkhor area and the main concentration of accommodation. Given the altitude it's sensible to hire a cycle-rickshaw (about ¥10) – lugging a bag around on your first day over 4000m is not a good way to acclimatize.

Although a few minibuses and pilgrim buses (notably from Shigatse, Ganden and Tsurphu) ply into the middle of town, usually Barkhor Square, if you come by bus, you'll probably be dropped at the main **bus station** about 3km from town at the junction of Chingdol Zhong Lu and Minzu Lu. From here either take a tractor into town (¥5) or the #2 minibus (¥2) will take you part of the way (see "City transport", p.950).

MOVING ON FROM LHASA

Public bus departures are mostly from the bus station on the western side of town at the junction of Minzu Lu and Chingdol Zhong Lu. It's advisable to buy tickets a day in advance – there's a foreigners' ticket office and staff are generally helpful. Pilgrim buses and minibuses leave from various points but note the possible restrictions on your use of these (p.946). Further details are given in the accounts of the destinations and in "Travel details" at the end of the chapter. The situation in Tibet with regards to transport and regulations is in a constant state of flux. More so than ever, it is essential to talk to other travellers to try to get an up-to-date picture of things.

Lhasa is the best place to **rent transport** and arrange your own itinerary for trips. There are huge numbers of tour operators vying for your business. See "Getting around", p.946.

LEAVING TIBET

Flights

You can buy flight tickets to three destinations at *CACC* in Lhasa or at the ticket agency in the *Tibet Hotel*: Kathmandu (Tues & Sat; ¥1650), Chengdu (daily; ¥1580) and Beijing (Sun involving a change at Chengdu; ¥2690). You'll also have to pay departure tax of ¥75 to Kathmandu or ¥50 into China. Flights leave too early in the morning for same-day public transport from Lhasa. Airport buses leave the *CACC* office in Lhasa in the afternoons (every 30min 2–4.30pm; ¥25). They'll drop you at the *Airport Hotel* (☎6331483; ⑤) and it's difficult to imagine a more miserable place to spend your last night in Tibet – the wallpaper is peeling and the water supply erratic. Far better is the small new guesthouse at the junction of the turning down to the airport and the main road (☎7782109; ③). Alternatively, take an early-morning taxi from Lhasa – five people plus luggage is about ¥350.

Overland

To Golmud (1160km): Buses leave the main bus station daily at 7.30am. There is a choice between luxury buses with reclining seats (¥600) or more basic ones with upright seats (¥400). Student card holders get a fifty percent discount.

To Xining (1937km): Daily buses at 4.30pm (¥608) are advertised "during tourist months" but operate irregularly.

To Nepal: On 2nd, 12th and 22nd day of each month a public bus to Zhangmu is scheduled to leave Lhasa (¥344), but is frequently cancelled. Most people make their own arrangements through **tour companies** in Lhasa, hiring jeep and driver plus guide. Expect to be quoted ¥4500 upwards for six days, seven nights including Rongbuk Monastery. Alternatively, minibuses and jeeps leave Lhasa regularly to collect tour parties at the Nepal border. You have to ask around a bit to arrange transport this way as the companies would rather you took a more expensive tour. They complete the trip in two or three days and it will cost you ¥400–500 per person.

City transport

By far the easiest way to get around the city and its environs is by **minibuses** which have a ¥2 flat fare and run from around 7am to 10pm. Simply flag them down when you want one and pay the conductor before you get off. Cycle-**rickshaws**, a very few **taxis** and, on the outskirts, **tractors** also carry passengers – bargain for the fare before you get in; ¥5 should get you from the bus station to the centre of town on a tractor, or from the Potala to Barkhor Square in a cycle-rickshaw, but you'll pay at least double that in a taxi, if you can find one. **Bike rental** is available at some of the hotels; expect to pay about ¥2 per hour and to leave a deposit, up to ¥100, and sometimes your passport as well. Apart from the altitude there are few problems with cycling in Lhasa; roads are

---

USEFUL MINIBUS ROUTES IN LHASA

#2 West from the small minibus stand opposite the cinema on Yuthok Lu north up Kharnga Dong Lu and then west along the front of the Potala. Some head west on Beijing Zhong Lu and Beijing Xi Lu and then turn south at the *Holiday Inn*, past the Norbulingka, while others follow the old road, Yuan Lin Lu, to the Norbulingka. All pass the bus station and then head west out of the city on Chingdol Xi Lu.

#3 From Beijing Dong Lu either at the junction with Mentsikhang Lu or Dosengge Lu, then loops north at Nyangrain Lu, west along Lingkor Bei Lu, down to the Golden Yaks Statue, then east along Beijing Zhong Lu and Beijing Xi Lu past the *Holiday Inn* and out to Drepung and Nechung monasteries.

#5 From the junction of Beijing Zhong Lu and Nyangrain Lu north to Sera Monastery.

---

wide and while there are no cycle lanes the traffic isn't overwhelming and is controlled by traffic lights and traffic police at the main junctions. There are a few cycle parks outside department stores and the post office, but without the cycle density of other large cities there is less regulation than elsewhere in China.

Accommodation

The choice of **accommodation** in Lhasa is likely to become better as the hotel building boom that has gripped the city comes to fruition, although most of the new ones will be at the top end of the range. When choosing accommodation you'll want to check on the availability of hot water – a cold shower at these temperatures is no fun. The options are essentially between the long-standing budget stalwarts of the *Snowlands, Yak, Banak Shol* or *Kirey* near the Barkhor, the mid-range Chinese hotels at various locations across the city or the top-range duo on the western edges.

Banak Shol, Beijing Dong Lu (☎6323829). Offers basic dorms and a range of rooms with and without bath, and even manages a bit of garden in the courtyard. Beware the rooms at the front which can be noisy. Hot water once a day. The *Kailash* restaurant is conveniently on the premises. Dorms ①, rooms ②–⑤.

Gang-Gyan, Beijing Dong Lu (☎6337666, fax 6335365). A clean, well-furnished, new mid-range hotel, near the Barkhor. Rooms at the back are quieter and there is hot water for two hours each evening. ⑥.

Gold Grain, Yuthok Lu (☎6330357). Close to the Jokhang, this is a convenient new addition to the mid-range options. Hot water 9–11pm. ⑥.

Himalaya, Lingkuo Dong Lu (☎6323775, fax 6332675). Used by tour groups and good value in this price range, but it's rather a hike out in the southeast of the city and no public transport travels down here. There's hot water twice a day and the private bathrooms have showers, not baths. ⑥.

Holiday Inn, Minzu Lu (☎6324509, fax 6334117). This is the most luxurious hotel in Lhasa, with 460 comfortable rooms (20 percent of the hotel rooms open to foreigners in the whole TAR), 24-hour hot water and a range of restaurants, swimming pool (summer only), business centre, in-house doctor and oxygen available. As the only Western and international hotel chain operating in Tibet, it is currently the target of a boycott campaign by Tibet support groups worldwide in objection to the partnership between Holiday Inn Worldwide and the Chinese authorities. ⑧–⑨.

Kechu, Beijing Dong Lu (☎6338824). Centrally located, good-value new addition to the hotel scene. Staff are friendly and the attached bathrooms offer 24-hour hot water. There's a restaurant on site as well as an antiques shop.

Kirey, Beijing Dong Lu (☎6323462). Conveniently close to the Barkhor and with the *Tashi 2* restaurant on the premises. Don't be deterred by the concrete, characterless compound; the rooms are pleasantly furnished and there's hot water once a day. Dorms ①, rooms ②.

Snowlands, Mentsikhang Lu (☎6323687). Well-situated near the Jokhang with a roof terrace to sit out on. The hot water supply is good, but the showers are grungy. Dorms ①, rooms ②.

Tashi Mandala, United New Village Area (☎6326556). Little known, Tibetan-owned hotel tucked away north of Lingkor Bei Lu. Take the first road left off Sera Lu and it's 200m on the left. The area isn't great, but the basic rooms are clean and comfortable. ③.

Tibet, Beijing Xi Lu (☎6334966, fax 6336787). The main competitor to the *Holiday Inn*, this hotel is well west although the #3 minibus passes the door. However, it looks shabby and is poorly organized, lacking the restaurants and swimming pool of its competitor and its business centre offers a more limited service. ⑦–⑨.

Yak, Beijing Dong Lu (☎6323496). Long-time favourite with independent travellers offering a range of options from variable-quality dorms to rooms with attached bathroom, all built around two courtyards. There's a communal area inside a Tibetan tent in one courtyard, but it's far from peaceful as the courtyard doubles as a car park. Hot water is available 11am–7pm in the communal showers. The pungent toilets are a long walk from the most distant rooms. Dorms ①, rooms ④–⑥.

The City

With its mix of ascendant Chinese modernity set side-by-side with shrinking Tibetan traditions, Lhasa is a vibrant and fast-changing city. Construction sites abound, but it is still easy to get around to all the major monuments, many of which are within walking distance of the two central landmarks, the **Potala** and **Jokhang**. Lhasa is a place well used to visitors – pilgrims have flocked here for centuries – and today Westerners blend seamlessly into the itinerant throng that fills the city with a memorable buzz and excitement especially at festival times.

The Potala

Perched atop Marpo Ri (Red Mountain), and named after Riwo Potala in India, holy mountain of the god Chenresi, the **Potala Palace** (Mon–Thurs 9.30am–noon; ¥45) is dazzling both inside and out and an enduring landmark of the city of Lhasa. As you glory in the views from the roof, gaze at the glittering array of gold and jewels and wend your way from chapel to chapel, you'll rub shoulders with excited and awestruck pilgrims from all over ethnic Tibet making offerings at each of the altars. Rising thirteen dramatic storeys and consisting of over a thousand rooms, the palace took a work force of at least seven thousand builders and fifteen hundred artists and craftsmen over fifty years to complete. However, don't tackle it on your first day at altitude, it's a long climb, and even the Tibetans huff and puff on the way up – you'll enjoy it more when you're acclimatized. There's a huge amount to take in on one visit and a second look helps to put it in perspective. The palace's opening hours are a source of major confusion as they seem to change frequently, so check with other travellers before you set off. The policy on photography also varies: some visitors report a hefty ¥50 charge for a permit, others find that only photography inside the chapels is banned. However, there seems to be little problem with taking pictures on the roof or on the balconies outside the chapels with the sunlight slanting down evocatively on to fabulously decorated woodwork.

Built for several purposes, the Potala served as administrative centre, seat of government, monastery, fortress and the home of all the Dalai Lamas from the Fifth to the Fourteenth, although from the end of the eighteenth century, when the Norbulingka was built as the summer palace, they stayed here only in winter. The main mass of the Potala is the **White Palace** (Potrang Karpo), while the central building rising from the centre of this is the **Red Palace** (Potrang Marpo).

The Potala has a long history. King Songtsen Gampo built the first palace on this site in the seventh century, but it was later destroyed by invaders. Today's White Palace (1645–1648) was built during the reign of the Fifth Dalai Lama and he took up residence in 1649, while the Red Palace was completed in 1693. Both survived the Cultural Revolution relatively unscathed; apparently Zhou Enlai ordered their protection.

INTO THE PALACE

The #2 minibus passes the gate in the front wall of the massive compound. You enter here and walk through Shol village, once the red-light district of Lhasa, now lined with souvenir shops and vendors, to the **ticket office** at the foot of the steps up to the Potala.

The steps lead first to the inner courtyard, **Deyang Shar**, of the White Palace, surrounded by monks' rooms and stores with the **Quarters of the Dalai Lama** at its eastern end. The opulently carved and painted Official Reception Hall is dominated by the bulk of the high throne and hung with fabulous brocade and *thangkas* (embroidered or painted religious scrolls) with a small doorway leading into the private quarters of the Fourteenth Dalai Lama next door. There's a small audience chamber, a chapel, a hallway and finally the bedroom with an extremely well-painted mural of Tsongkhapa, founder of the Gelugpa school to which the Dalai Lama belongs, over the bed. On the other side of the Official Reception Hall are the private quarters of the previous Dalai Lamas but these are closed to the public.

Stairs lead from the inner courtyard up into the **Red Palace** and continue straight to the roof for fabulous views across Lhasa. You can then descend a floor at a time to tour the palace, moving clockwise all the way. The first room on the **upper floor** is the **Maitreya Chapel**, its huge number of fabulously ornate statues setting the tone for the remainder of the chapels. It's dominated by a seated statue of Maitreya made at the time of the Eighth Dalai Lama and said to contain the brain of Atisha, the eleventh-century Indian scholar responsible for a Buddhist revival in Tibet (see p.940). On the far left of the Dalai Lama's throne is a statue of the Fifth Dalai Lama commissioned soon after his death and supposedly containing some of his hair.

The Red Palace is the final resting place of the Fifth to Thirteenth Dalai Lamas, except for the Sixth who died on his way to China and is said to be buried near Qinghai Hu (formerly known as Kokonor) in Qinghai Province. However, not all the tombs are open. Although they vary in size, all are jewel-encrusted golden *chortens* (a traditional multi-tiered Tibetan Buddhist monument that usually contains sacred objects) supporting tier upon tier of fantastic engraving; encased deep within are the bodies of the Dalai Lamas preserved in dry salt. You should at least be able to see either the Tomb of the Thirteenth Dalai Lama or Tomb of the Eighth Dalai Lama on the upper floor (see plan, p.954).

Considered as the oldest and holiest shrines in the Potala, the **Lokeshvara Chapel** on the upper floor and the **Practice Chamber of the Dharma King**, directly below on the **upper middle floor**, date back to Songtsen Gampo's original construction, and are the focus of all Potala pilgrims. It's easy to miss the Practice Chamber, entered from a small corridor from the balcony. King Songtsen Gampo supposedly meditated in this dark, dingy room now dominated by statues of the king and his ministers, Tonmi Sambhota and Gawa. At the base of the main pillar is a stove, apparently used by Songtsen Gampo himself.

Although you pass through the lower middle floor, the chapels here are all closed and the remainder of the open rooms are on the **lower floor** leading off the large, many-columned Assembly Hall. The highlight down here is the grand **Chapel of the Dalai Lamas' Tombs**, containing the awesome golden *chorten* of the Fifth Dalai Lama which is three storeys high and consists of 3700kg of gold. To the left and right are smaller *chortens* with the remains of the Tenth and Twelfth Dalai Lamas and the *chortens* on either side of these main ones are believed to contain relics of Buddha himself. Visitors leave the Red Palace by a door behind the altar in the **Chapel of the Holy Born** and the path winds down the west side of the hill to the western gate.

Around the Potala

The area around the Potala offers plenty of smaller but highly enjoyable sights. Opposite the front of the palace, on the south side of Beijing Dong Lu, **People's Park**

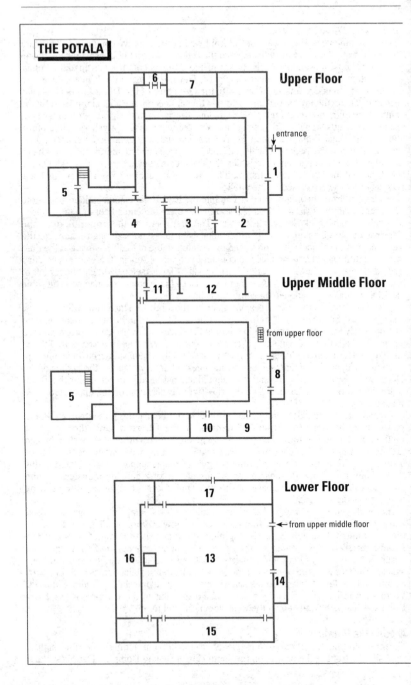

THE POTALA

Upper Floor

Upper Middle Floor

Lower Floor

Potala Key

UPPER FLOOR

1. Maitreya Chapel

2. Chapel of the Three-Dimensional Mandalas Containing three exquisite and unusual three-dimensional *mandalas* (these are usually two-dimensional images created on wall or ceiling) of three gods particularly important in the Gelugpa tradition

3. Chapel Celebrating Victory Over Three Worlds Houses an especially fabulous Chenresi which was commissioned by the Thirteenth Dalai Lama using almost 300kg of precious metal

4. Chapel of Immortal Happiness Amitayus, the God of Long Life, is the main statue with a thousand small versions lining the walls

5. Tomb of the Thirteenth Dalai Lama The chapel is two storeys high and entered at the top level from the upper floor with stairs leading down.

6. Lokeshvara Chapel Awash with statues, the footprints in stone encased on the left are said to have been made by Padmasambhava, Tsongkhapa and Nagarjuna, a second century Indian philosopher

7. Tomb of the Eighth Dalai Lama

UPPER MIDDLE FLOOR

8. Kalachakra Chapel Named after the three-dimensional, gold and copper Kalachakra *mandala*, divine home of the god, which occupies the centre of the room. To the right as you face the *mandala* from the window is a statue of Kalachakra and his consort. On the left on the way out is Padmasambhava on his throne

9. Sakyamuni Chapel Scripture-lined chapel dominated by a figure of Sakyamuni surrounded by the Eight Great Bodhisattvas

10. Amitayus Chapel A room inside a room containing nine statues of the God of Long Life with a White Tara to the far right and a Green Tara to the far left

11. Practice Chamber of the Dharma King

12. Bronze Chapel Entered by a small anteroom containing a large Sakyamuni statue and 276 smaller ones. The main chapel contains over 1500 small Buddha statues

LOWER FLOOR

13. Assembly Hall

14. Chapel of the Stages on the Path to Enlightenment Dominated by a Tsongkhapa statue

15. Knowledge Holder's Chapel Dedicated to Padmasambhava and seven other Indian masters whose statues are lined along the left side of the room with the eight manifestations of Padmasambhava on the right. The central figures are Padmasambhava with his two consorts, Yeshe Tsogyel on the right and Mandarava on the left

16. Chapel of the Dalai Lamas' Tombs

17. Chapel of the Holy Born Equal-sized statues of the Fifth Dalai Lama on the right and Sakyamuni on the left indicate the veneration the Great Fifth inspired. To the left of the door is a small *chorten* containing the remains of the Eleventh Dalai Lama who died in 1855 aged seventeen years.

is a market and recreation area complete with fountain, fighter plane, photographers' stalls and plenty of food sellers. The best place to take a break is the tea house outside the pagoda in the middle of the most northerly pond. The pond is a bit putrid, but the view of the Potala is great.

Farther west along Beijing Dong Lu, the new *chorten* in the middle of the road marks the site of the old West Gate to the city. Due south from here, **Chakpori Hill**, the previous site of the medical college, is now topped by a radio transmitter. For a scenic view of the Potala, take the path that goes in front of the public toilets just south of the *chorten* and climb up the hill; you'll be able to go only as far as a massive tree laden with prayer flags before the guards at the transmitter start shouting.

From just east of the public toilets at the *chorten* a path leads a couple of hundred metres to the fabulously atmospheric **Palhalupuk Temple**, built around an ancient cave. You'll spot the ochre and maroon and far less interesting Neten Temple on the cliff first but Palhalupuk is the smaller, white building below. Entered from an antechapel, the cave, about 5m square, was King Songtsen Gampo's retreat in the seventh century and is lined with rock carvings, many of which date from that time. The most important altar is in front of the huge rock pillar that supports the roof, and the main image is of Sakyamuni flanked by his chief disciples. At the far right-hand corner stands a jewel- and *katag*-bedecked statue of Pelden Lhamo, the fierce protective deity of Tibet, on a tiny altar. The back wall has been left untouched, and it's said that the jewels of Songtsen Gampo's Nepalese wife, Princess Bhrikuti, are hidden behind. They don't get many tourists here and the caretaker and monks are welcoming.

The main area of **rock carvings**, numbering around five thousand, are on the west and southern sides of Chakpori Hill. Back on the road, continue west from the *chorten* along the left fork. Just as you get to the junction with Yuan Lin Lu that leads down from the Golden Yaks Statue a rough track leads off to the left. Follow it beside a stream for a couple of hundred metres and you'll arrive at the start of the rock paintings and carvings, which supposedly represent the visions seen by King Songtsen Gampo during his meditation. The carvers at work here are copying ancient texts and prayers or sacred *mantras* and work partly for alms but also produce work for sale.

Around the other side of the Potala, behind Marpo Ri and entered from the north side of the boating lake or via the entrance at the end of the Farmers Products Market, the park of **Ching Drol Chi Ling** (¥2) has fine views up to the north facade of the Potala and sports a large area of ill-kept trees and a lake formed by the removal of earth during the construction of the palace. On an island in the lake is the small, pleasant **Lukhang**, built by the Sixth Dalai Lama in honour of the *naga* king and for use as a retreat. Legend tells of a pact between the builder of the Potala and the king of the *nagas,* subterranean creatures who resemble dragons – the earth could be used as long as a chapel was built in their honour. The temple is famed for the very old and detailed murals on the middle and top floors, but you'll need a flashlight if you want to study them in detail and the protective wire in front doesn't help. The top-floor pictures showing the stages of human life, the journey of the soul after death and various legends are somewhat esoteric, but the middle-floor murals, depicting the construction of the great monasteries of Sera and Drepung among others, are far more comprehensible.

The Jokhang

The **Jokhang** temple stands in the centre of the only remaining Tibetan enclave in the city – the **Barkhor area** – a maze of cobbled alleyways between Beijing Dong Lu and Chingdol Dong Lu, a kilometre or two east of the Potala. If you're coming from the western side of town the #2 or #3 minibus may come into Barkhor Square if you are lucky or more likely drop you about ten minutes' walk away on Dosengge Lu or Beijing Dong Lu.

From afar the **Jokhang**, sometimes called Tshuglakhang (meaning cathedral), the holiest temple in the Tibetan Buddhist world, is somewhat unprepossessing, but draw close and the air is thick with the veneration and anticipation of the pilgrims. Inside you're in for one of the most unforgettable experiences in Tibet and many visitors end up returning day after day. You should certainly try to come at least twice, once in the morning (9am–12.30pm), when most pilgrims do the rounds and the front entrance and most of the chapels are open, and again in the evening at around 7pm, when the monks are at prayer and you can hear Tibetan **Buddhist chant** in its homeland. You can go to the temple at any time but when the front entrance is closed access is via a side courtyard to the right of the main entrance. From the far side of this courtyard one of several flights of stairs leads up to the **roof** where the views down over Barkhor Square, into the temple courtyard and as far as the Potala in the distance are wonderful and the golden statues even more impressive close to. Other roof staircases are just to the right of the main entrance and in the far southeast corner of the temple itself (see plan, p.958)

King Songtsen Gampo built the Jokhang in the seventh century to house the dowry brought by his Nepalese bride, Princess Bhrikuti, including the statue known as Akshobhya Buddha. This later changed places with the Jowo Sakyamuni statue from Princess Wencheng's dowry that was initially installed in Ramoche temple (see p.961) and which is now regarded as Tibet's most sacred object. The site of the temple was decided by Princess Wencheng after consulting astrological charts, and confirmed by the king following a vision while meditating. However, construction was fraught with problems. Another vision revealed to the king and his queens that beneath the land of Tibet lay a huge, sleeping demoness with her head in the east, feet to the west and heart beneath Lhasa. Only by building monasteries at suitable points to pin her to the earth could construction of the Jokhang succeed. The king embarked on a scheme to construct twelve demon-suppressing temples: four around Lhasa, which included Trandruk (see p.971), to pin her at hips and shoulders, a set of four farther away to pin her at elbows and knees and four even more distant to pin her hands and feet. When these were finished, construction on the Jokhang began.

INSIDE THE TEMPLE

The main entrance to the Jokhang is from **Barkhor Square**, which is to the west of the temple and full of stalls selling prayer flags, white scarves (*katag*) and incense. Two bulbous incense burners in front of the temple send out juniper smoke as an offering to the gods and the two walled enclosures here contain three ancient engraved pillars. The tallest is inscribed with the Tibetan–Chinese agreement of 821 AD and reads: "Tibet and China shall abide by the frontiers of which they are now in occupation. All to the east is the country of Great China; and all to the west is, without question, the country of Great Tibet. Henceforth on neither side shall there be waging of war nor seizing of territory."

In front of the huge temple doors a constant crowd of pilgrims prostrate themselves – you can hear the clack of the wooden protectors on their hands and the hiss as the wood moves along the flagstones when they lie flat on the ground. Head past the giant golden prayer wheel on the left and through the entrance corridor to the open **courtyard**, where ceremonies and their preparations take place. Rows of tiny butter lamps burn on shelves along the far wall and it's a bustling scene as monks make butter statues and dough offerings and tend the lamps. Through another corridor, with small chapels to left and right, you pass into the inner area of the temple. The central section, **Kyilkhor Thil**, houses statues galore, six of them considered particularly important. The most dramatic are the six-metre-high Padmasambhava on the left which dates from 1955 and the half-seated figure of Maitreya, the Buddha of the Future, to the right.

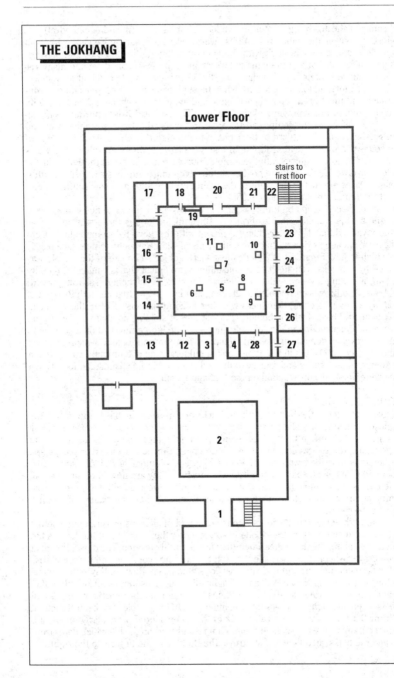

THE JOKHANG

Lower Floor

Jokhang Key

LOWER FLOOR

1. Entrance corridor Lined with huge statues of the four Guardian Kings

2. Open courtyard

3. Nojin Khang Housing male and female wrathful deities

4. Lukhang With images of the *naga* kings who appeared to Songtsen Gampo in a vision and requested that their image was placed in the temple to protect it from water

5. Inner central area The Kyilkhor Thil

6. Padmasambhava statue

7. Chenresi statue Gold and copper with a thousand arms and eleven faces

8. Maitreya statue Buddha of the Future

9. Barzhi Jampa Maitreya statue, named after the family who commissioned it

10. Miwang Jampa Statue named after Miwang Polha who commissioned it in the eighteenth century

11. Padmasambhava statue Small image in a case

12. Chapel of Tsongkhapa and his Eight Disciples Tsongkhapa, seated in the centre, was the founder of the Gelugpa order. His two most famous disciples, Khedrup Je and Gyeltsab Je, are to his right and left

13. Wopame Buddha of Infinite Light. The *chorten* outside the entrance is a replica of a thirteenth-century one that was said to contain relics of King Songtsen Gampo

14. Chapel of the Eight Medicine Buddhas

15. Chapel of Chenresi Second only to the the Jowo Sakyamuni statue in importance, the eleven-headed Chenresi statue is said to have miraculously appeared in Tibet during King Songtsen Gampo's time, and the king and his wives were absorbed into it when they died. Some parts of this statue were smuggled into India by Tibetan refugees and are said to be in Dharamsala

16. Chapel of Maitreya The central image is new but the kneeling Jampelyang, the Bodhisattva of Wisdom, is a restored original

17. Chapel of Tsongkhapa The central image of Tsongkhapa is said to resemble him closely

18. Chapel of the Buddha of Infinite Light The entrance is guarded by the fierce blue Chana Dorje on the left and a form of Hayagriva in red on the right. Pilgrims pray here prior to entering the most sacred chapel next door

19. Seated figures King Songtsen Gampo with Bhrikuti on the left and Princess Wencheng on the right. The smaller figure is Padmasambhava

20. Chapel of Jowo Sakyamuni

21. Chapel of the Protector Maitreya The central statue is a replica of a Maitreya statue called Jampa Chokor which came from Nepal as part of Princess Bhrikuti's dowry. Legend tells that the statue walked the more difficult parts of the journey. The chapel also includes statues of the eight manifestations of Tara, one of the most highly revered deities in Tibet.

22. Chapel of Chenresi (Riding a Lion) The chapel derives its name from the first image to the left of the door, not the largest statue

23. Janzik Chapel New murals of King Songtsen Gampo and his two wives outside

24. Chapel of Maitreya The statue of Maitreya is carried in procession around the Barkhor during the annual Monlam Festival

25 Chapel of the Hidden Jowo The hiding place of the Jowo Sakyamuni statue during the seventh century

26. Chapel of the Seven Mighty Buddhas

27. Chapel of the Nine Forms of Amitayus. Amitayus is usually worshipped to attain long life

28. Chapel of the Dharma Kings Statue of Songtsen Gampo with Trisong Detsen to the left and Ralpachan to the right

Devout pilgrims turn left to move clockwise and enter each chapel in turn to pray and make offerings. They don't hang around, though; stand still to admire the statues and you'll get trampled in the rush. Some of the wooden door frames and columns are original – in particular the door frame of the Chapel of Chenresi and the columns in front of the Chapel of Jowo Sakyamuni were created by Niwari craftsmen from Nepal during the temple's early years. As with all temples in Tibet it's often difficult to know exactly what you are looking at. Some of the statues are original, others were damaged during the Cultural Revolution and have been restored either slightly or extensively, and others are replicas. Whatever their age, all are held in deep reverence by the pilgrims.

It's easy to feel overwhelmed, but if you manage only one chapel it should be the **Chapel of Jowo Sakyamuni** in the middle of the back wall of the temple. The 1.5-metre-high Sakyamuni is depicted at twelve years of age, with a sublimely beautiful golden face. Draped in heavy brocade and jewels, this is the most deeply venerated statue in Tibet. Although the Jokhang was originally built to house the statue, the Jowo Sakyamuni first stood in the temple of Ramoche (see p.961) until rumours of a Tang invasion late in the seventh century led to its removal to a hiding place in the Jokhang. It was later placed in its present position. During the reign of Trisong Detsen, the Bon opponents of Buddhism removed the statue and buried it, but it was found and sent out of Lhasa for safety. The statue was again buried during King Langdarma's attempt to annihilate Buddhism, but eventually returned to the Jokhang where it rests today. Although there is a rumour that the original was destroyed in the eighteenth century by Mongol invaders, neither it nor the chapel was harmed during the Cultural Revolution and the statue is widely regarded as the original. Monks keep the butter lamps topped up while the pilgrims move clockwise around the altar bowing their head to Jowo Sakyamuni's right leg and then his left. A huge number of other statues adorn the chapel, but pale into insignificance beside the centrepiece.

By the time you reach the **upper floor** you'll probably be punch-drunk and there is less of interest up here than down below, although around three-quarters of the chapels are now open after restoration. Of most interest here is the chapel directly above the main entrance in the west wall. This is the **Chapel of Songtsen Gampo**, featuring a large statue of the king flanked by his two queens. Continue up the stairs in the southwest corner of the chapel to one fierce and one peaceful image of **Pelden Lhamo**, who is regarded as the protective deity of Tibet, and is particularly popular with pilgrims.

The Barkhor

Traditionally pilgrims to Lhasa circled the city on two clockwise routes: an outer circuit called the Lingkhor, now vanished under two-lane highways and rebuilding, and the shorter **Barkhor** circuit through the alleyways a short distance from the Jokhang walls. This has survived, a maze of picturesque streets a world away from the rest of Lhasa, now lined with the stalls of an outdoor market selling all manner of goods including saddles and stirrups, Chinese army gear, *thangkas*, jewellery, blankets, cassette tapes, carpets, tin trunks and pictures of lamas to mention a fraction only. The pilgrims, too, are an amazing sight, with statuesque Khampa men with their traditional knives and red-braided hair, decorated with huge chunks of turquoise; Amdo women dripping jewels with their hair in 108 plaits; and old ladies spinning their tiny prayer wheels and intoning *mantras*. The whole Barkhor area is worth exploring – with huge wooden doors set in long white walls leading into hidden courtyards surrounded by traditional stone houses – but try not to miss **Tromzikhang market** to the north of the Jokhang; take the main alleyway into the Barkhor that leads off Beijing Dong Lu just east of Ramoche Lu and it's just down on your left. The two-storey modern building is a bit soulless, but nowhere else in the world can you see (or smell) so much yak butter in one place.

One other sight to seek out here is the **Ani Tsangkung Nunnery** (¥6) to the southeast of the Jokhang – either head west from the main Lhasa mosque, a couple of hundred metres west of Lingkuo Dong Lu or right and then right again into the Barkhor from the next alleyway west of the *Khadag Hotel*. You'll probably need to ask the way (see "Language", p.1059). With over a hundred nuns in residence, several of whom speak good English, there is a lively but devout atmosphere, especially around prayer time at 11am. The main chapel is dominated by a fabulous Chenresi in a glass case. From the back of the chapel, facing the main door, you can head right, round the outside, to visit the long, narrow room containing King Songtsen Gampo's meditation chamber in a pit at the end. Supposedly his meditation here altered the course of the Kyichu River when it looked likely to flood the construction of the Jokhang.

Ramoche

Second only in importance to the Jokhang, the three-storey, solid **Ramoche** (9am-noon; ¥20, plus up to ¥50 per chapel for photographs) was built in the seventh century by Songtsen Gampo's Chinese wife, Princess Wencheng, to house the Jowo Sakyamuni statue that she brought to Tibet. This statue later ended up in the Jokhang and was replaced by the Akshobhya Buddha, a representation of Sakyamuni at the age of eight, brought by Princess Bhrikuti, Songtsen Gampo's Nepalese wife.

The temple, a short walk north of the Barkhor, on Ramoche Lu between Beijing Dong Lu and Lingkor Bei Lu, is believed to have been originally built in Chinese style, has been much renovated over the centuries and was seriously damaged during the Cultural Revolution. The much revered Akshobhya Buddha was broken in two, one part taken to China and narrowly saved from being melted down, while the other was later discovered on a factory scrap heap in Tibet. It's pretty unlikely that the statue in position today is the original.

The main chapels are at the back of the temple with the Four Guardian Kings standing guard at the entrance to the most important shrine, the **Tsangkhang**. The Akshobhya Buddha, sumptuously draped with precious jewels and cloth, sits on a throne and pilgrims walk clockwise pressing their heads to each leg in turn. There are also around a hundred monks in residence here. While this inner sanctum is impressive, at the time of writing, the overall experience of a visit to Ramoche was essentially an expensive trip to a building site. Major renovations are underway, and many statues and altars have been shifted around and draped with huge polythene sheets to protect the treasures. It will be glorious when complete but the date of this is uncertain.

While you're in the area, call in on the tiny **Tsepak Lakhang** to the south of Ramoche. The little entrance is just beside a huge incense burner and you pass along a small alley lined with a row of prayer wheels. There are two small chapels in this hugely popular temple and the 55 friendly monks in residence chant their daily prayers around noon. You can walk the small circuit around the walls of Tsepak Lakhang, where the murals have been newly painted.

Norbulingka

Situated in the west of town, on the route of the #2 minibus, the **Norbulingka** (Jewel Park), the Summer Palace of the Dalai Lamas (Mon–Sat 9.30–noon; ¥17.50), is not in the top league of Lhasa sights, but worth a look if you've time on your hands. However, if you're in Lhasa during the festivals of the Worship of the Buddha (July) or during Shotun, the Yoghurt Festival (Aug/Sept), when crowds flock here for picnics and to see masked dances and traditional opera, you should definitely make the trip out here. The forty-hectare park has been used as a recreation area by the Dalai Lamas since the time of the Seventh incarnation. The first palace to be built was the **Palace of the Eighth Dalai Lama**, the closest to the entrance, constructed towards the end of the eighteenth century and this became the official summer residence to which all Dalai Lamas moved, with due ceremony, on the eighteenth day of the third lunar month. Other buildings open to the public are the **Palace of the Thirteenth Dalai Lama** in the far northwest corner beyond the appalling zoo and, the highlight of the visit, the **New Summer Palace**, built in 1956 by the Fourteenth Dalai Lama. It was from here that he fled Lhasa in 1959. Visitors pass through the audience chamber, via an anteroom to the meditation chamber, on to his bedroom and then into the reception hall dominated by a fabulously carved golden throne, before passing through to the quarters of the Dalai Lama's mother. The Western plumbing and radio sit beside fabulous *thangkas* and religious murals. It's all very sad and amazingly evocative, the forlorn rooms bringing home the reality of exile.

Eating, drinking and entertainment

There is a huge number of **restaurants** in Lhasa, and you could eat in a different place every night for several months. Anyone seriously watching the yuan can get a bowl of nourishing noodles in one of the small places near the Tromzikhang market for ¥3. The **kebab stalls** outside the cinema on Yuthok Lu are also a cheap place to fill up (¥0.5 a skewer), but as they are coated in chilli powder they're very hot – take your own drink. Restaurants in Lhasa generally open fairly late and an early **breakfast** can be hard to find. Opening times are listed below for places where you may want breakfast. All the restaurants reviewed below have English menus.

Aloo Gang (*Pink Curtain*), Dosengge Lu. This friendly place is rather neglected by tourists, but popular with Tibetans and has excellent yak meat (¥20), huge soups (¥8–10) and a few vegetarian options.

Barkhor Café, Barkhor Square. Food (nothing special) and beer are both pricey here, but the draw is the rooftop terrace at the southwest corner of Barkhor Square. Reach the café by the spiral staircase to the right and look down on the evening bustle of the crowds as the setting sun bounces golden rays off the Jokhang roof.

Beijing Bake Duck Store, Nyangrain Lu. As the name suggests, the speciality is Beijing Duck, about ¥30 per person.

Crazy Yak Saloon, Beijing Dong Lu. Pleasant Tibetan furniture and furnishings and the window tables are good for people-watching. The menu is large – yak meat (¥18) is recommended – but the service is erratic and tour groups sometimes take the place over.

Gangki Restaurant, corner of Mentsikhang Lu and Barkhor Square. This rooftop place is good value and has great views of the Jokhang, but is very popular with Tibetans and often extremely busy. Main dishes cost ¥10–30 and Tibetan tea and *tsampa* are also available.

Hard Yak Café, *Holiday Inn*, Minzu Lu. Offering starched linen, Muzak, old magazines and a range of Western food, this place is an expensive haven for the culture-shocked. Expect to pay ¥50–60 for a main meal; the famous Yak Burger (¥55) should be tackled only by the seriously hungry. The banana pancakes (¥30) are highly recommended. Open daily 5am–11pm.

TIBETAN CUISINE

Definitely not among the top cuisines in the world, **Tibetan food** is constrained by what will grow at over 4000m – which is very little. The traditional Tibetan diet consists in large part of **butter tea**, a unique mixture of yak butter, tea and salt, all churned into a blend that most Westerners find largely undrinkable, but which Tibetans consume in huge quantities. Into this brew is stirred **tsampa**, roasted barley flour, to form a dough with the consistency of raw pastry but a not unpleasant nutty flavour. **Yak meat**, yoghurt and cheese (often dried into bite-sized cubes to preserve it) and sometimes a soup of a few vegetables supplement this. Most Tibetan restaurants serve **thukpa** (pronounced tukpa), a noodle soup with a few bits and pieces of whatever is available thrown in and, if you're lucky, you'll find **momos** which are tiny steamed or fried dough-wrapped parcels containing meat or vegetables. A *thri momo* is a solid dough parcel without any filling. The local brew, **chang**, is a sweet, yellow beer made from a mixture of grains.

Kailash, upstairs in the *Banak Shol*, Beijing Dong Lu. Their good-value set breakfast includes eggs, toast, hash browns and tomatoes for ¥15. Also on offer are yak burgers, spaghetti, various vegetarian options and there is even apple pie and custard. Open 9am–10pm.

Snowlands Restaurant, next to the *Snowlands Hotel*, Mentsikhang Lu. Fairly upmarket and moderately priced with a wide range of soups, salads, pizzas, yak steaks and curries prepared by a good Nepalese chef. Main courses for ¥30 and generous set breakfasts from ¥20. Open 9am–10pm.

Tashi 1, corner of Beijing Dong Lu. and Mentsikhang Lu. Along with its sister restaurant, *Tashi 2*, in the *Kirey Hotel*, this restaurant is the mainstay of budget travellers in Lhasa. Both offer the same small and inexpensive menu, including a range of Tibetan *momos* (¥7) and *bobis* (tortillas with sour cream and vegetables or meat), as well as French fries, spaghetti bolognaise, mashed potatoes and fried yak meat. Cheesecake and chocolate cake are excellent. Both restaurants open from 8.30am and start to close down after 10pm.

Entertainment

Traditional Tibetan music, dance and opera seem virtually extinct in Lhasa, unless you happen to be here during a festival. There are occasional shows put on for tourists; ask in your hotel or check for notices in the *Holiday Inn* or *Tibet Hotel*. On the other hand, **discos** and **karaoke bars** are flourishing. It's a lively and expanding scene popular with young Tibetans and Chinese alike and fuelled by lights and even smoke machines. Ask around among younger staff at your hotel or other travellers for the latest hot spot. You can expect PSB or the police to be keeping an eye on things, but they don't seem to be too intrusive. The **cinemas** have some films from the West, but check whether they've been dubbed in Chinese before you bother. Other than that, it's the staple fare of kung fu movies.

Shopping

A major tourist activity in Lhasa is **shopping**. Not only is the stuff on offer so unusual and attractive, but it takes massive self-restraint not to want a souvenir of some sort from the Roof of the World. The main shopping area is the **Barkhor** (see p.960). The vendors on the street outside the *Holiday Inn* have essentially the same range, but in smaller quantities and they start off at higher prices. There are plenty of **department stores**, especially along Yuthok Lu, for everyday requirements.

The search for **postcards** can be frustrating and expensive as sets on offer at the main sights are generally pricey. The sets at the post office are the best value at ¥8 for ten views and ¥13 for a series of traditional and modern Tibetan art cards. The reception of the *Banak Shol Hotel* offers ¥10 and ¥20 sets of the Potala, temples and views. The *Holiday Inn* charges a hefty ¥5 per card for admittedly attractive images of the Tibetan people. You can buy major brands of print **film** (¥13–20) easily enough, although transparency film is more elusive and costly (¥75). Check out the film shops opposite People's Park on Kharnga Dong Lu for the best choice and prices. Processing is also available here; expect to pay about ¥1 per print, although the quality is a bit variable – it's best to ask around among travellers to get a current recommendation.

Books

There are a couple of **bookshops** in town, the *Xinhua Foreign Bookstore* at the western end of Yuthok Lu and the *Perik Bookstore* just east of the *Tibet Hotel*. The only English **novels** available are the ones on the local school syllabus – expect the classics plus *The Thorn Birds*. The lobby shops at the *Holiday Inn* and *Tibet Hotel* and some of the souvenir shops near the Potala sell **picture books** of Tibet. The best on offer is the paperback *Potala Palace* with good pictures of many of the treasures in the Potala that will either be closed when you are there or you'll be too overwhelmed to notice. The hardback glossies, *Tibet* and *Snowland Tibet*, are both pricey and heavy to carry around, but have evocative photographs taken throughout the country. If you're into Buddhist art, take a look at the even glossier and heavier *The Precious True Word Picture Album of the Buddha, Images of Buddhism*.

Carpets

If it's **carpets** you're after you should visit *Khawachen*, 103 Chingdol Xi Lu (Mon–Sat 9am–6.30pm; ☎6333255, fax 6333250), on the route of the #2 minibus. This is a joint American and semi-government organization which offers the best selection of carpets in Lhasa and you can also watch production. Available in muted and attractive traditional designs, plus some with a modern slant, they range from 50cm square (US$25) to 2.7m x 3.6m (US$1280). They can also ship them home for you. The *Lhasa Carpet Factory*, Chingdol Dong Lu (Mon–Fri 9am–1pm & 3.30–6pm, Sat 9am–1pm; ☎6323447), is a bigger operation where you can watch huge carpets being woven, and an extensive range of traditional and modern patterns is available from ¥140 to ¥32,000. Shipping can also be arranged direct. Despite its name, the *Traditional Tibetan Carpet and Rug Factory*, on the left as you approach the ticket office to Norbulingka, is just a small shop, but it has plenty of traditional carpets and also some more unusual contemporary hangings (¥550–1200).

Paintings

Tibetan *thangkas* (religious scrolls) and religious and secular **paintings** would appear to be obvious souvenirs, but many are of poor quality – you'll need to spend some time browsing before you buy. The least expensive *thangkas* – you'll find masses of these in the Barkhor – have a printed religious picture in the middle while the better-quality, and higher-priced ones, have a hand-painted image. Look carefully, though, at the quality of the painting itself; the best ones have finely drawn and highly detailed backgrounds, but the less skilled artists leave larger areas of the canvas blank with less meticulously painted details. The small shops opposite the *Holiday Inn* offer Tibetan paintings, a few of them modern and interesting but all too many are rather uninspiring portraits. The asking prices are high; bargain hard. Look also in the shops in Shol village just inside the Potala gate and the *Holiday Inn* lobby shop (9am–8pm) which has a range of paintings (¥500–2500) and will give you some idea of the top end of the scale. The *Tibet Traditional Art Gallery* next door to Ramoche offers an excellent range of good-quality, hand-painted *thangkas*, but expect prices starting at ¥3000.

Tailors, T-shirts and tents

There are plenty of **tailors** in town, both Chinese and Tibetan, who can make traditional Tibetan or Western dress; look on Beijing Dong Lu west of the *Yak Hotel*. Many have samples made up and you can simply shop around until you find the style and material you want. From first measuring to collecting the finished item usually takes 24 hours. A huge range of materials, from light, summer-weight stuff, to heavier, warmer textiles, are available and, while styles of Western clothes are hardly at the cutting edge of fashion, jackets, skirts and trousers are all available. Price will depend on the material you select but light jackets start around ¥100 and skirts, trousers or a floor-length Tibetan woman's dress (*chuba*) at ¥80.

The best range of **T-shirts** (¥45) is on sale in the T-shirt shop in Shol village, just on the right inside the entrance to the Potala. In various colours and sizes, the motifs include Sakyamuni and Pelden Lhamo as well as more modern images.

Rather like a marquee, **Tibetan tents** are used on religious and ceremonial occasions and are usually white with auspicious symbols appliquéd in blue. The *Tibetan*

Tent Factory is just off the unnamed alley that heads north a couple of hundred metres west of the *Yak Hotel*. Take the right fork just inside the alley and the factory is on the left. Expect to start negotiating at around ¥2500 for a tent and ¥200 for a door curtain; cheaper door curtains of differing qualities are available in the Barkhor.

Listings

Airlines *CACC*, Nyangrain Lu (daily 9am–12.30pm & 3–6.30pm).

Banks and exchange There are several branches of the *Bank of China* around town, but the main one on Lingkor Bei Lu, north of the Golden Yaks Statue (Mon–Fri 9.30am–1pm & 3.30–6pm) is the only place in Tibet for cash advances on credit cards (*Amex, Visa, Mastercard* and *Diners Club* are accepted). The branch on Beijing Dong Lu is conveniently located close to the *Banak Shol* (Mon–Fri 9.30am–6pm, Sat & Sun 11am–3pm). The *Holiday Inn* changes money for guests only and charges commission.

Bike rental *Banak Shol, Yak & Snowlands* hotels; ¥2 per hour plus deposit.

Cinemas Yuthok Lu at the junction with Dosengge Lu and Beijing Dong Lu between the *Banak Shol* and *Kirey* hotels.

Consulates *Nepalese Consulate*, 13 Norbulingka Lu (Mon–Fri 10am–12.30pm; ☎6322881). Next-day service and you'll need one passport photograph. Single-entry fifteen days ¥135, thirty days ¥225; multiple-entry thirty days ¥360, sixty days ¥540, payment can be made in yuan. You can get single-entry visas at Kodari (see p.989), but payment there has to be in US dollars.

TREKKING IN TIBET

For the experienced walker Tibet offers plenty of enticing **trekking** routes. However, you need to be fit, acclimatized, totally self-reliant and prepared to do some research before you go. Once you start trekking you get off the beaten track extremely quickly and there is no infrastructure to support trekkers and no rescue service. Spring (April–June) and autumn (September–November) are the best months to trek. Cold-weather problems such as hypothermia and frostbite should be taken seriously even in these months and whilst trekking is possible at any time in the valleys, high altitudes become virtually impossible in the winter and anyone contemplating trekking at this time should be sure to get local information about the terrain and likely conditions. During the wettest months (June–September), rivers are in flood and crossing can be difficult, even impossible.

Conditions can be severe at any time, so you should come with good-quality **equipment**, although the new *Mount Green Trekking Shop* in Lhasa, just around the corner from *Tashi 1* on Beijing Dong Lu, sells and rents pretty much anything you might need. Export-quality Chinese sleeping bags cost ¥600 to buy (¥20–30 a day to rent), and two- or three-person tents, rucksacks, Karrimats and stoves are ¥30–40 per day to rent.

The popular Ganden to Samye trek (see p.975) has the advantage of both start and finish points being relatively accessible to Lhasa and it takes only three to four days. Also worth considering are treks to the cave hermitage of Drak Yerpa from Lhasa (allow a full day and be prepared to camp), and the five-day trek from Tingri to Everest Base camp via Rongbuk. The more challenging options include the sixteen-day mammoth trek to the Kangshung face of Everest, exploring the valleys east of the mountain, the 24-day circumnavigation of Namtso Lake, including the arduous exploration of the Shang Valley to the southwest, or the great thirty-day circuit (a Tibetan guide is highly recommended) from Lhatse to Lake Dangra up on the Chang Tang plateau.

Whatever you do, you must have adequate **information** on the route before setting off. There are two essential books: *Tibet Handbook: a Pilgrimage Guide* by Victor Chan (Moon) and *Trekking in Tibet* by Gary McCue (Cordee) which is especially good for shorter day treks that anyone can do without all the gear.

Hospital First People's Hospital, Lingkor Bei Lu (Mon–Fri 10am–12.30pm & 4–6pm; emergencies only at weekends). It's better to go in the morning when more staff are available and you'll need to take a Chinese translator. There is no dental treatment available in Lhasa, only extraction. Rabies serum is not available (see "Health", p.946). You could also try the traditional Tibetan Medicine Hospital (*Mentsikhang*), Yuthok Lu (hours as above). Some staff are Tibetan and some Chinese so a translator who speaks both is ideal.

Pharmacies Most are along Yuthok Lu around the junction with Dosengge Lu.

Post office On Beijing Dong Lu, just east of the Potala (daily 9.30am–6.30pm). Poste restante and international customs (Mon–Fri 9.30am–1pm & 3.30–6pm) is the counter facing you on the far left as you enter. Mail should be addressed to Poste Restante, Main Post Office, Lhasa, Tibet, China. Check both the book that lists mail received at the office and ask to see new mail. There's a charge of ¥1.50 per item received.

PSB Lingkor Bei Lu and Beijing Dong Lu (Mon–Fri 9.30am–1pm & 3.30–7pm). Whilst PSB offices should be the place to go for factual information about closed and open areas and permits, the information is rarely reliable and frequently inconsistent from one office to the next.

Telecommunications There's a 24-hour office located next to the post office with direct dialling facilities and fax service. Expect to pay around ¥27 per minute to the US, ¥30 per minute to Europe. Alternatively, the business centre in the *Holiday Inn* (8am–8pm in the tourist season, shorter hours in winter) sends faxes for ¥45–50 per minute and you can have faxes sent there for you, but you'll pay ¥20 per sheet when you collect them. There is no e-mail service.

Around Lhasa

Not only is Lhasa awash with enough sights to keep even the most energetic visitor busy for several days but the major monasteries of **Sera**, **Drepung** and **Ganden** are easily accessible from the city as half-day or day trips. Indeed, Sera and Drepung have virtually been gobbled up in the urban sprawl that now characterizes Lhasa, while the trip to Ganden is a good chance to get out into the countryside. Morning visits to any of them are likely to be in the company of parties of devout pilgrims who'll scurry around the temples making their offerings before heading on to the next target. Follow on behind them and you'll visit all the main buildings – don't worry too much if you aren't sure what you are looking at; most of the pilgrims haven't a clue either. The monasteries are generally peaceful and atmospheric places where nobody minds you ambling at will, and sooner or later you're bound to come across some monks who want to practise their English.

Sera

To reach **Sera Monastery** (Mon–Sat 9am–noon & 2–4pm; ¥15), 4km north of Lhasa, by public transport take a #5 **minibus** from the southern end of Nyangrain Lu or from the small minibus stand opposite the cinema on Yuthok Lu. You'll either be dropped on the road, about 500m outside the white-walled monastery compound or be taken along the track to the entrance. To get back it is better to walk back out to the road. The last minibuses leave just after the end of the debating at about 5pm.

Founded in 1419 by Sakya Yeshe, one of the main disciples of Tsongkhapa, founder of the Gelugpa order, Sera is situated below a hermitage where the great man spent many years in retreat. Spared during the Cultural Revolution, the buildings are in good repair although there is always a fair amount of ongoing building work. All pilgrims proceed on a clockwise circuit visiting the three main **colleges**, Sera Me, Sera Ngag-Pa and Sera Je, and the main assembly hall, Tsokchen. All are constructed with chapels leading off a central hall with more chapels on an upper floor and they are great places to linger and watch the pilgrims rushing about their devotions. However, if you just want to catch the flavour of the most dramatic buildings, head straight up the hill from the main entrance. After a couple of hundred metres you'll reach the **Tsokchen**, built in 1710, Sera's largest building. The hall is supported by over a hundred columns and the main statue of Sakya Yeshe, the founder of the monastery, is between statues of the Fifth and Thirteenth Dalai Lamas. The Sakya Yeshe statue is a reproduction of the original one in Sera Ngag-Pa college. When there were plans to move the original to the Tsokchen, the statue itself said that it wished to stay in the college so a copy was made.

At the top of the path the walled and shady **debating courtyard** is definitely worth a visit at 3.30pm when the monks assemble in small animated groups to practise their highly stylized debating skills involving much posturing, clapping and stamping. They're used to visitors and there seems to be no problem about taking photographs.

To the left of the courtyard, the college of **Sera Je** is the best college to visit if you manage only one. Its spacious assembly hall is hung with fine *thankas*, but the focus for pilgrims here is the Hayagriva Chapel reached via an entrance in the left-hand wall. Hayagriva or Tamdrin, "the Horse-Headed One", is the protective deity of Sera.

If you're feeling energetic, take the path up the hillside, from behind the Tsokchen (follow the telegraph wires) to **Tsongkhapa's Hermitage** (Choding Khang), which is a reconstruction of the original – his meditation cave is a bit farther up. There are splendid views over Lhasa from here.

LIFE IN THE GREAT MONASTERIES

Less than fifty years ago, there were still six great, functioning **Gelugpa monasteries**: Sera, Drepung and Ganden near Lhasa, plus Tashilunpo in Shigatse (see p.981), Labrang (see "Gansu", p.867) and Kumbum (see "Qinghai", p.892). They each operated on a similar system to cope with the huge numbers of monks that were drawn to these major institutions from all over Tibet. In their heyday, Sera and Ganden had five thousand residents each and Drepung (possibly the largest monastery the world has ever known) had between eight and ten thousand.

Each monastery was divided into colleges, **dratsang**, which differed from each other in the type of studies undertaken. Each college was under the management of an abbot (*khenpo*), and a monk responsible for discipline (*ge-kor*). Attached to each college were a number of houses or *khangsten*, where the monks lived during their time at the monastery. Usually these houses catered for students from different geographical regions and admission to the monastery was controlled by the heads of the houses to whom aspirant monks would apply. Each college had its own assembly hall and chapels but there was also a main assembly hall where the entire community could gather.

Not every member of the community spent their time in scholarly pursuits. Communities the size of these took huge amounts of organization and the largest monasteries also maintained large estates. About half the monks might be engaged in academic study while the other half worked at administration, the supervision of the estate work and the day-to-day running of what was essentially a small town.

The most obvious feature of these monasteries **today** is their emptiness; hundreds of monks now rattle around in massive compounds built for thousands. Such has been the fate of religious establishments under the Chinese and the flow of lamas into exile that there are now questions about the quality of the Buddhist education available within the monasteries inside Tibet. Monks and nuns nowadays need to be vetted and receive Chinese government approval before they can join a monastery or convent, and although there are persistent rumours of tourists being informed on by monks it is also apparent that both monks and nuns have been, and continue to be, at the forefront of open political opposition to the Chinese inside Tibet in recent years. The most recent information suggests a crackdown by the Chinese authorities inside the monasteries, with monks being forced into supporting a more "patriotic" Communist Party line.

Drepung and Nechung

Once the largest monastery in the world, **Drepung** (daily 9am–6pm, chapels closed noon–3pm; ¥10, ¥20 if you come on a guided tour) was founded in 1416 by Jamyang Choje, a leading disciple of Tsongkhapa. It was an immediate success and a year after opening there were already two thousand monks in residence and ten thousand by the time of the Fifth Dalai Lama (1617–82). Although it has been sacked three times – in 1618 by the king of Tsang, in 1635 by the Mongols and in the early eighteenth century by the Dzungars – there was relatively little damage during the Cultural Revolution.

To reach Drepung, 8km west of Lhasa, catch the #3 **minibus** on Bejing Dong Lu at the junction with Mentsikhang Lu – just across the road from the *Tashi 1* restaurant. It may drop you on the main road (¥2), leaving you with a thirty-minute walk, or carry on up the hill to the entrance of the massive walled monastery (¥3). Minibuses come back to Lhasa infrequently from the monastery itself, and it's better to walk down the hill to Nechung and then out to the main road to pick up one there.

The easiest way to find your way around is to follow the clockwise pilgrim circuit, although it can be a bit of a hassle, especially on the initial climb from the entrance as the path here seems to be teeming with particularly persistent beggars, many of whom target tourists. Drepung is a huge place and it's easy to attempt to see everything and get overloaded. Make sure you go up on to the **roofs**; the views across the Kyichu Valley are splendid, and it's definitely worth spending a bit of time just wandering the alleyways, courtyards and ancient doorways. But take a stick; Drepung dogs can be fierce.

The pilgrim circuit leads left from the entrance up to the grand and imposing **Ganden Palace**, built in 1530 by the Second Dalai Lama and home to the Dalai Lamas until the Fifth incarnation moved to the Potala. The private quarters of the Dalai Lama are behind the balcony at the top right-hand side of the building, but there's little to see inside.

Continuing clockwise, the next stop is the **Tsokchen**, the main assembly hall and highlight of Drepung, with its entrance via a small door on the left-hand side facing the building. With the roof supported by over 180 solid wooden columns, the size and scale of the hall is awesome and the *thangkas* and brocade hangings add to the incredible ambiance, with dust motes highlighted by the rays of the sun slanting down from the high windows. The main chapel at the rear of the hall is the **Buddha of the Three Ages Chapel** and it's the most impressive in Drepung with statues crammed together in such profusion the mind reels. It would be possible to spend hours here and not identify a fraction of them. The central figures are Sakyamuni with his two main disciples, Shariputra and Maudgalyayana. In addition, there are two upper storeys, both definitely worth a visit. On the next floor up, the **Maitreya Chapel** contains the head and shoulders of a massive statue of Maitreya, at a young age, commissioned by Tsongkhapa himself, while the **Tara Chapel** contains a version of the *Kanjur,* sacred Buddhist scriptures, dating from the time of the Fifth Dalai Lama. In the middle of the volumes, which are loose leaves stored between wooden planks and wrapped in brocade, sits a statue of Prajnaparamita, the Mother of Buddhas; the amulet on her lap is said to contain a tooth of Tsongkhapa's. Of the three chapels on the top floor the highlight is the central **Maitreya Chapel** with a stunning statue of the head of Maitreya, with exquisite gold ornamentation.

Behind the Tsokchen there's a tiny **Manjusri Temple**, obligatory for the pilgrims who make offerings to the image of the Bodhisattva of Wisdom carved out of a large rock. The remainder of the circuit is taken up with the **Ngag-Pa College**, to the northwest of the Tsokchen, and **Loseling, Gomang and Deyang colleges** to the southeast. They all have items of interest – the stuffed goat at the entrance to the Protector Chapel on the upper storey of Loseling, the cosy Deyang, and the wonderful array of statues in the central chapel of Gomang – but don't feel too bad if you've had enough by now. The main steps of the Tsokchen, looking across the huge courtyard in front of the building, are a good place to sit and admire the view and watch the comings and goings of the other visitors..

Nechung

A visit to **Nechung Monastery** (daily 9am–6pm, chapels closed noon–3pm), less than a kilometre southeast of Drepung, and reached by a well-trodden path, can be easily combined with a trip to Drepung, if you have the energy to appreciate both in one day. The monastery was, until 1959, the seat of the **state oracle of Tibet**. By means of complex ritual and chanting, an oracle enters a trance and becomes the mouthpiece of a god. The state oracle is regarded as the voice of Dorje Drakden, the chief minister of Pehar Gyalpo, the main spiritual protector of Tibet, and no important decisions are made by the Dalai Lama or government without reference to him. The original shrine on the site was built in the twelfth century and the Fifth Dalai Lama built the temple later. It was much damaged during the Cultural Revolution, but restoration work is now proceeding quickly. The state oracle fled Tibet in the footsteps of the Dalai Lama in 1959 having questioned Dorje Drakden himself as to what he should do. He died in 1985 in Dharamsala but a successor has been identified there.

The images throughout Nechung are extremely gory – the doors are painted with pictures of human skins and the murals in the courtyard depict various human parts, souls in agony and skulls in a sea of blood. The remains of a tree stump in the left-hand, lower-floor chapel is thought to be the original dwelling place of the god Pehar. Upstairs, the main room is the audience chamber where the Dalai Lama would come to consult the oracle. The inner chapel is dedicated to Tsongkhapa and his statue is between his two main disciples, Gyeltsab Je and Khedrup Je. The statue of Padmasambhava in the only chapel at roof level dates from the early 1980s, but he is gloriously bedecked in old Chinese brocade and it's worth the climb.

Ganden

Situated farther from Lhasa than the other main temples, **Ganden** (daily 9am–noon & 2–4pm; ¥15) is 45km east of Lhasa, the final 6km along a winding track off the Lhasa–Sichuan Highway. It is also the most dramatically situated, high up on the Gokpori Ridge, with excellent views over the surrounding countryside. To get here, take the **pilgrim bus** which leaves Lhasa daily at 7am from the west side of Barkhor Square (¥20; 3–4hr) and returns between noon and 2pm.

Founded by Tsongkhapa himself in 1410 on a site associated with King Songtsen Gampo and his queens, the main hall was not completed until 1417, two years before Tsongkhapa died after announcing his disciple, Gyeltsab Je, as the new leader of the Gelugpa order or **Ganden Tripa**. The appointment is not based on reincarnation but on particular academic qualifications and Ganden is the main seat of the order. Ganden has always been particularly targeted by the Chinese, possibly as the main seat of the Dalai Lama's order, and what you see today is all reconstruction.

While it is possible, as always, to follow the pilgrims through the various buildings on their circuit, the highlight is the imposing **Serdung Lhakhang**, on the left side as you follow the main path north from the car park. This temple contains a huge gold and silver *chorten*. The original contained the body of Tsongkhapa, who was said to have changed into a sixteen-year-old youth when he died. The body was embalmed and placed in the *chorten* and, when the Red Guards broke it open during the Cultural Revolution, they supposedly found the body perfectly preserved, with the hair and fingernails still growing. Only a few pieces of skull survived the destruction and they are in the reconstructed *chorten*. Up the hill and to the right, the **Sertrikhang** houses the golden throne of Tsongkhapa and all later Ganden Tripas; the bag on the throne contains the yellow hat of the present Dalai Lama.

Be sure to allow time to walk the **Ganden kora**, the path around the monastery. The views are startling and it takes about an hour to follow round. There is a basic **guesthouse** (①) at the monastery used mostly by people heading off on the Ganden–Samye trek (see p.975).

Tsetang and around

The town of **Tsetang**, 183km southeast of Lhasa, just south of the Tsangpo River, and the nearby valleys of **Yarlung** and **Chongye** are steeped in ancient history. Legend claims the first Tibetans originated on the slopes of Gongpo Ri to the east of Tsetang and the first king of Tibet descended to the Yarlung Valley upon a sky-cord from the heavens. This king then fathered the first royal dynasty, many members of which are buried in the nearby Chongye Valley and, in the fourth century, the first Buddhist scriptures fell from the sky upon the first king's palace at **Yumbulakhang**. To the west of Tsetang the walled combined village and monastery of **Samye** is not only the most ancient in Tibet, but also a lively and interesting place to spend a day or two.

Tsetang and Samye are easily accessible via a good road and public transport from Lhasa. However, there is no public transport in the Yarlung and Chongye valleys although **getting around** by hitching lifts on tractors is feasible for the Yarlung Valley. Transport out to Chongye is more limited. The best way to explore is to hire a vehicle and driver in Tsetang to take you to Chongye and Yumbulakhang on a day trip. For vehicle rental try the *Tsetang Hotel* first, then the *Gesar Restaurant* opposite – after hard bargaining expect to pay around ¥350 for the day.

Unfortunately, accommodation in Tsetang is not particularly good and the **permit** situation is unclear. You should check in Lhasa whether you currently need a permit for Tsetang. The PSB in Tsetang should issue permits to Yarlung, Chongye, Samye and Lhamo Lhatso but is increasingly refusing to do so unless you are on an organized tour with your own transport and guide. If you want to organize a tour from Lhasa you'll be quoted ¥2000–2500 for a three-day/two-night tour to the Tsetang area.

Tsetang is also the starting point for a trip to **Lhamo Lhatso**, a sacred lake 115km northeast of Tsetang where visions on the surface of the water are believed to contain prophecies. Regents searching for the next incarnations of high lamas come here for clues and Dalai Lamas have traditionally visited for hints about the future. Buses leave the main Tsetang intersection on Monday and Friday for Gyatsa (returning the next day). At Gyatsa you have to walk across the bridge and pick up another ride up to Chokorgye Monastery and then trek for around five hours up to the lake. You should bring your own food and be prepared to camp unless you're intending a long day's walking.

Tsetang

There is little to recommend an extended stay in the town of **TSETANG**, administrative centre of Lhoka Province, a region stretching from the Tsangpo down to the Bhutan border. While it's lively enough, accommodation is a problem and much of the town is in the throes of noisy and unattractive rebuilding although you could spend an interesting few hours exploring the maze-like alleyways of the small Tibetan quarter. However, Tsetang is largely unavoidable as a base for explorations of the area.

Heading south from the main traffic intersection along Naidong Lu, take a narrow left turn through the small, bustling market into the **Tibetan area** of town, a typical jumble of walled compounds swarming with unwelcoming dogs and children scrapping in the dust. The largest monastery and the first you'll come to is **Ganden Chukorlin** (¥5), now bright and gleaming from restoration having been used as a storeroom for many years. It was founded in the mid-eighteenth century on the site of an earlier monastery, and there are good views of the Tibetan quarter from the roof. At the nearby fourteenth-century **Narchu Monastery** (¥5), restoration is less complete, but it's worth stopping by for the three unusual brown-painted Sakyamuni statues on the altar. A little farther up the hill, the **Sanarsensky Nunnery** (¥5) was one of the first nunneries in Tibet. It was founded in the fourteenth century in the Sakya tradition but later became a Gelugpa establishment. It's smaller and less ornate than the other two temples, with just one chapel open at present.

Practicalities

Daily **public buses** leave Lhasa between 7am and 8am from Barkhor Square and run as far as the Samye ferry point (¥23; 4hr). You'll then need to pick up another bus or a minibus for the remaining 33km on to Tsetang (¥15) – it's a bit hit and miss but you shouldn't have to wait more than an hour or so. Alternatively, direct **minibuses** leave the main bus station in Lhasa for Tsetang from 8am onwards (¥35; 3hr), but they may not be willing to take foreigners, although there are currently no checkposts between Lhasa and Tsetang.

Tsetang's **bus station** is about 500m west of the main traffic intersection in town. Turn right at the intersection on to Naidong Lu past the post office and numerous restaurants and you'll come to the grossly over-priced **accommodation** at the *Tsetang Hotel* (☎0893/21899, fax 21688; ⑦). The previous budget mainstays have been demolished in the building frenzy that has gripped the town, but the Chinese-style *Friendship Hotel* (☎0893/21736; ⑤) is worth investigating. It offers double rooms and attached bathroom with warm water for a couple of hours each evening and is about 100m north of the *Tsetang Hotel*, tucked away behind an apartment building. Almost opposite the *Friendship Hotel* is the **PSB** office (Mon–Fri 9am–noon & 3–5pm), a modern, white-tiled building – look for the *Great Bar Umbulha* with smoked-glass windows upstairs. The very basic truck stop accommodation at the bus station is not recommended. Naidong Lu is lined with bars and **restaurants**, but check all prices before you eat or drink.

The Yarlung Valley

Renowned as the seat of the first Tibetan kings, the **Yarlung Valley** is historically important although these days it is the dramatically sited and picturesque **Yumbulakhang,** the first Tibetan palace, that draws visitors to the area. The road from Tsetang, due south along Naidong Lu to Yumbulakhang, is fairly busy and although there's no public transport, it's possible to get a lift without too much trouble.

Trandruk

At the time of writing, the small but extremely significant **Trandruk Monastery** (¥15), 7km south of Tsetang, was undergoing massive reconstruction, although you can still appreciate its grand and imposing structure.

Built in the seventh century during the reign of King Songtsen Gampo, Trandruk is one of the earliest Buddhist temples in Tibet and is one of the Twelve Demon-Suppressing Temples constructed to subdue the demoness believed to lie beneath the country (see p.957) – Trandruk anchors her left shoulder to the earth. Legend tells how the site chosen for Trandruk was covered by a large lake containing a five-headed dragon. King Songtsen Gampo emerged from a period of meditation with such power that he was able to summon a supernatural falcon to defeat the dragon and drink the water of the lake, leaving the earth ready for Trandruk (meaning Falcon-Dragon).

Damaged during the Bon reaction against Buddhism in the ninth century and again by Dzungar invaders in the eighteenth century, the temple's many highly prized religious relics and objects were lost following the Chinese invasion. Its remaining glory is the **Pearl Thangka**, an image of King Songtsen Gampo's wife, Princess Wencheng, as the White Tara, created from thousands of tiny pearls meticulously sewn on to a pink background. This is in the central chapel upstairs, which also houses an original statue of Padmasambhava at the age of eight.

Yumbulakhang

From afar, the fortress temple of **Yumbulakhang**, 12km south of Tsetang, appears dwarfed by the scale of the Yarlung Valley. But once you get close, and make the thirty-minute climb up the spur on which it is perched, the drama of the position and the airiness of the site are apparent. Widely regarded as the work of the first king of Tibet, Nyatri Tsenpo, when he arrived in Yarlung, the original Yumbulakhang would have been over two thousand years old and the oldest building in Tibet when it was almost totally destroyed during the Cultural Revolution. The present building is a 1982 reconstruction in two parts with a small two-storey chapel and an eleven-metre-high tower. The lower floor of the **chapel** is dedicated to the early Tibetan kings; Nyatri Tsenpo is to the left and Songtsen Gampo to the right of the central Buddha statue. The delightful and unusual upper-storey chapel, with Chenresi as the central image, is built on a balcony. Some of the modern murals up here show legendary events in Tibetan history; look out on the left for Nyatri Tsenpo and for the Buddhist scriptures descending from heaven. The energetic can ascend by ladders almost to the top of the tower where King Nyatri Tsenpo supposedly meditated. The deep, slit windows at knee level mean the views aren't that wonderful, however; for the best scenery take a walk up to the ridge behind the temple.

The Chongye Valley

From Tsetang it's a bumpy 27km south along unsealed roads through the attractive **Chongye Valley** to the village of **CHONGYE**, a sleepy little place currently expanding with plenty of new buildings. There are a couple of restaurants and a basic guesthouse here, but you'll need to ask to find it. The target for most visitors, the **Tombs of the Kings**, are around a kilometre farther south from the village. The entire valley is an agricultural development area and the patchwork of fields is interspersed with irrigation work. There's no **public transport** out here from Tsetang and very little traffic, so you'll need to be patient of you're hitching.

Tangboche

On the east side of the valley, about 20km from Tsetang, **Tangboche Monastery** is situated at the base of the hill and somewhat difficult to spot among the village houses. It was founded in the eleventh century and the great Tsongkhapa, founder of the Gelugpa tradition, is thought to have stayed here in the fourteenth century. Take a flashlight so you can really appreciate the most interesting features here – genuine old murals, commissioned in 1915 by the Thirteenth Dalai Lama. They are too numerous to list, but look out in particular for Pelden Lhamo on the left as you enter, and, on the right-hand wall, Padmasambhava, Trisong Detsen and Shantarakshita. The artistry and detail of subject and background make an interesting comparison with some of the more modern painting you'll see in Tibet. A couple of hundred metres up the hill is the **hermitage** where the scholar Atisha spent some time in the eleventh century. It's small and recently renovated and, not surprisingly, dominated by rather lurid images of the Indian master. A much-revered statue of Atisha and a set of texts brought by him from India were lost in the Cultural Revolution.

The Tombs of the Kings

One kilometre south of Chongye, the **Tombs of the Kings** are scattered over a vast area on and around the slopes of Mura Ri. Some are huge, up to 200m in length and 30m high. The body of each king was buried along with statues, precious objects and, some sources suggest, live servants. Some of the greatest kings of the Yarlung dynasty were buried here, although there is disagreement over the precise number of tombs – some sources claim 21, but far fewer are visible and there is uncertainty about which tomb belongs to which king.

For the best view of the entire area climb the largest tomb, **Bangso Marpo** (Red Tomb), belonging to **Songtsen Gampo**, just beside the road that heads south along the valley and easily identifiable by the chapel on the top. Songtsen Gampo, supposedly embalmed and incarcerated in a silver coffin, was entombed with huge numbers of precious gems, gifts from neighbouring countries (India sent a golden suit of armour), his own jewelled robes and objects of religious significance, all of which were looted long ago. The cosy chapel (¥10), originally built in the twelfth century, has central statues of Songtsen Gampo, his wives and principal ministers, Gar and Thonmi Sambhota.

Looking east from this viewpoint, the large tomb straight ahead belongs to Songtsen Gampo's grandson, Mangsong Mangtsen (646–676), who became king at the age of four. The tomb some distance to the left is that of Tri Ralpachan (805–836), and the nearby enclosure contains an ancient pillar, recording the events of his reign, constructed on top of a stone turtle symbolizing the foundation of the universe. Originally every tomb had one of these pillars on top but the others have long since disappeared.

Looking west, the ruins of **Chingwa Tagste Dzong**, perched high on the mountainside, give an idea of the scale of the fortress and capital of the early Yarlung kings before Songtsen Gampo moved to Lhasa. To the left, the monastery of **Riwo Dechen** is visible and a rough road means you can drive to within ten minutes' walk of this now thriving Gelugpa community of around eighty monks. Originally founded in the fifteenth century, it was later expanded by the Seventh Dalai Lama and restored in the mid-1980s. There are three main chapels, the central one dominated by a large Tsongkhapa figure.

Samye

A visit to **SAMYE** on the north bank of the Tsangpo River, is a highlight of Tibet. A unique monastery and walled village rolled into one, it's situated in wonderful scenery and, however you arrive, the journey is splendid. Samye is a popular destination for Tibetan pilgrims, some of whom travel for weeks to get here. You can climb the sacred Hepo Ri to the east of the complex for excellent views (1hr); it was here that Padmasambhava is said to have subdued the local spirits and won them over to Buddhism.

The monastery

Tibet's first monastery, **Samye**, was founded in the eighth century during King Trisong Detsen's reign with the help of the Indian masters Padmasambhava and Shantarakshita whom he had invited to Tibet to help spread the Buddhist faith. The first Tibetan Buddhist monks were ordained here after examination and are referred to as the "Seven Examined Men". Over the years Samye has been associated with several of the schools of Tibetan Buddhism – Padmasambhava's involvement in the founding of the monastery makes it important in the Nyingma school and later it was taken over by the Sakya and Gelugpa traditions. Nowadays, followers of all traditions worship here.

The design of the extensive monastery complex, several hundred metres in diameter, is of a giant **mandala**, a representation of the Buddhist universe, styled after the

Indian temple of Odantapuri in Bihar. The main temple, the **utse**, represents Buddha's palace on the summit of Mount Meru, the mythical mountain at the centre of the Buddhist universe. The four continents in the vast ocean around Mount Meru are represented by the *lingshi* temples, a couple of hundred metres away at the cardinal points, each flanked by two smaller temples, *lingtren*, representing islands in the ocean. The utse is surrounded by four giant *chortens,* each several storeys high, at the corners, and there are *nyima* (Sun) and *dawa* (Moon) temples to the north and south respectively. The whole complex is flanked by a newly renovated enclosing wall topped by 1008 tiny *chortens* with gates at the cardinal points. This sounds hugely ordered, but the reality is far more confusing and fun. Samye has suffered much damage and restoration over the years and today you'll find the temples dotted among houses, barns and animal pens, and onl;y a few of the original 108 buildings on the site remain in their entirety.

THE UTSE

The **utse** (daily 9am–12.30 & 3–5pm; ¥20) is a grand six-storeyed construction and you'll need a couple of hours to see it thoroughly. It is still undergoing renovation and will become even more impressive in the future. Be sure to take a powerful flashlight as there are some good murals tucked away in shadowy corners. The **first floor** is dominated by the grand main assembly hall with fine old *mandalas* on the high ceiling. On either side of the entrance to the main chapel are statues of historical figures associated with the monastery. Those on the left include Shantarakshita, Padmasambhava (said to be a good likeness of him), Trisong Detsen and Songtsen Gampo. The impressive main chapel, **Jowo Khang**, is reached through three tall doorways and is home to a Sakyamuni statue showing Buddha at the age of 38. To the left of the assembly hall is a small temple, **Chenresi Lhakhang**, housing a gorgeous statue of Chenresi with an eye meticulously painted on the palm of each of his thousand hands – if you look at nothing else in Samye, search this out. To the right of the main assembly hall is the **Gonkhang**, a protector chapel, with all the statues heavily and dramatically draped. Most of the deities here were established as the demons of the Bon religion and were adopted by Buddhism as the fierce protectors – the chapel is a dark and eerie place, laden with the fear of centuries.

Although the first floor is the most impressive, the upper storeys are worth a look. The **second floor** is an open roof area, where monks and local people carry out the craft work needed for the temple. The highlight of the **third floor** is the **Quarters of the Dalai Lama**, consisting of a small anteroom, throne room and a bedroom. A securely barred, glass-fronted case in the bedroom is stuffed full of fantastic relics, including Padmasambhava's hair and walking stick, a Tara statue that is reputed to speak and the skull of the Indian master Shantarakshita. among many others. The Tibetan pilgrims take this room very seriously and the crush of bodies may mean you can't linger as long as you would like. From the **fourth floor** up, you'll see only recent, obvious and uncompleted reconstruction, but the views from the balconies are extensive.

THE OTHER BUILDINGS

The surrounding buildings in the complex are in varying stages of renovation. The reconstruction of the four coloured **chortens** is almost complete. Unashamedly modern, they are each slightly different, and visitors seem to love or hate them. There are internal stairs and tiny interior chapels, but generally they are more dramatic from a distance. It's difficult to locate the outer temples accurately and many are still awaiting renovation, some serving as barns and stables, some showing the effects of the Cultural Revolution. The most finely worked murals in Samye are in **Mani Lhakhang**, now a chapel in a house compound in the northwest of the complex, but the occupants are happy for visitors to look around.

THE GANDEN–SAMYE TREK

A popular route to Samye is the three- or four-day **Ganden–Samye trek**. Although popular this route is no less serious and demanding than other treks (see box p.965). The route crosses the mountains that divide the Kyichu Valley from that of the Tsangpo and travels through high mountain passes and alpine pasture to the dry, almost desert-like countryside around Samye. The trek goes by Hebu village and involves camping out or sleeping in caves or nomad encampments, long climbs to the Jooker La and Sukhe La passes and some deep river wading.

There is also an alternative ancient pilgrim route from Dechen Dzong, 21km east of Lhasa, to Samye, which also takes four days and crosses the same mountain range but this time via Changju nomad camp and Gokar La Pass, whose name translates as "white eagle" – apparently they also struggle to get over it. A third option is the four-day trek from the Gyama Valley, Songtsen Gampo's birthplace, via two five-hundred-metre passes.

Practicalities

The Lhasa–Tsetang road runs along the south bank of the Tsangpo and is served by public transport from both points. To reach the monastery, you'll need to cross the river via the **Samye ferry**, 33km from Tsetang and 150km from Lhasa. The crossing (¥3) is highly picturesque and takes an hour or more as the boats wind their way among the sand banks inhabited by Brahmini ducks, grebes and plovers. Ferries leave when full and are more frequent in the morning, but run until mid-afternoon. On the other side, tractors (¥5; 45min) and trucks (¥3; 30min) ply the bumpy 8km to Samye through rolling, deforested sand dunes newly planted here and there with willows. The small, white-painted *chortens* carved out of the hillside about halfway along mark the place where King Trisong Detsen met Padmasambhava when he came to Samye in the eighth century. **Leaving**, a very useful truck departs from the front of the utse each morning at 8am to connect with the ferry and a Lhasa-bound bus on the other side of the river. In addition, the local tractors and trucks run until mid-afternoon, but you may well have to wait at the ferry and on the other side of the river for connections.

The only place to stay at Samye is the **guesthouse** next to the utse, which provides comfortable dorm accommodation (①). The monastery **restaurant** is just north of the utse, but a better option is the newer establishment opposite the east reception office near the east gate. There's no menu in either place; you negotiate based on what they have. There are several small shops in the monastery complex well-stocked with tinned goods, beer, confectionery and even Chinese wine.

At the time of writing, **permits** were needed for Samye but the PSB in Tsetang would issue them only if you had arranged a tour. Travellers arriving in Samye without permits were facing fines up to ¥500 per person, confiscation of passports and being forced to write "confessions". Check the current situation with the PSB and other travellers before setting off.

Tsurphu and Namtso

One of the most rewarding and popular trips is to **Namtso Lake**, around 230km northwest of Lhasa, taking in Tsurphu Monastery and Yangbajing on the way. All these sights can be combined into a two-night/three-day trip in a hired jeep; expect to pay around ¥1800. At the time of writing there were no checkposts on the roads between Lhasa and Namtso, so you should be all right without a permit, but, as always, check the current situation with other travellers in case they've put a checkpost on the way or opened a PSB post at the lake. If you don't have your own transport, Tsurphu and the town of Damxhung are still reachable, although you may find pilgrim bus and minibus drivers are unwilling to risk carrying you. There is only very infrequent transport (every day or two) from Damxhung across to Namtso Qu on the shores of Namtso.

Tsurphu Monastery

Around 70km northeast of Lhasa, it takes two to three hours by jeep to reach **Tsurphu Monastery** – open in the morning from 9am leading up to the blessing (9am–1pm; ¥6) – at a height of 4480m. A pilgrim **bus** leaves Lhasa daily between 7am and 8am (¥20) from the western end of Barkhor Square, returning early afternoon. The final 30km is along a rough track that gradually climbs through tiny hamlets and a patchwork of stony fields to the far end of the Drowolung Valley. The monastery is the seat of the **Karmapa Lama**, the Seventeenth, identified in 1992 at the age of seven years. He is one of the highest incarnate lamas still in Tibet and gives daily blessings to pilgrims at 1pm. Buy a *katag* from one of the traders outside and while horns play and excitement mounts you'll be hustled upstairs (notice the new murals depicting Tsurphu in its former glory on the balcony) to present your scarf and receive a blessing thread. Although there are some dissenters over the authenticity of this boy, both the Chinese authorities and the Tibetan government in exile have recognized him; nevertheless the Chinese have so far refused to allow him to travel outside Tibet, despite invitations from his followers overseas.

Founded in the twelfth century by Dusun Khenyapa, the Karmapa order is a branch of the Kagyupa tradition, where members are known as the **Black Hats** after the Second Karmapa was presented with one by Kublai Khan. Most powerful during the fifteenth century, when they were close to the ruling families of the time, they were eventually eclipsed in 1642 when the Fifth Dalai Lama and the Gelugpa order, aided by the Mongol army, gained the ascendancy. The Karmapa were the first order to institute the system of reincarnated lamas, *tulkus*, a tradition later adopted by the Gelugpa school.

Damaged in the years after the Chinese invasion, Tsurphu is now being reconstructed. The solid **Zhiwa Tratsang** has a splendidly ornate gold roof and houses the main assembly hall, dominated by statues of Sakyamuni and a *chorten* containing the relics of the Sixteenth Karmapa Lama who played a major part in establishing the order overseas and died in Chicago in 1981. The murals depict the successive Karmapa lamas. The festival of **Saga Dawa**, on the full moon of the fourth lunar month, usually in May or June, is especially fine at Tsurphu, as the massive new *thangka*, completed in recent years, is displayed at this time.

A visit to the monastery can be exhausting as it's at a considerably higher altitude than Lhasa. In addition, the clockwise path, the **kora**, climbs steeply up the hill behind the monastery from the left of the temple complex and circles around high above and behind the monastery before descending on the right. The views are great and the truly fit can even clamber to the top of the ridge, but you need to allow two to three hours for the walk.

There's little reason to stay at Tsurphu unless you're trekking in the area, although there is a basic monastery **guesthouse** (①) – you'll need to take your own sleeping bag, food and candles.

Yangbajing hot springs and Damxhung

Don't get carried away by romantic images of these **hot springs** (daily 8am–8pm; ¥10). They flow unspectacularly into a thirty-metre-long concrete pool at the base of **YANGBAJING's** geothermal power station, but they are hot and, at 4270m, are probably the highest swimming pool you'll ever get to swim in. The village is 45km northeast of the Tsurphu turn-off along the main Tibet–Qinghai Highway. It's a scenic road with dramatically striated rock formations clearly visible until the valley narrows into impressive gorges. About a kilometre beyond the village, take a left turn and the pool is 3km farther, on the left, opposite the power station which provides electricity for Lhasa. It's pretty unmissable and ugly as hell with chimneys belching steam.

If you're heading up to Namtso, continue on the main highway past the Yangbajing turning for another 80km to **DAMXHUNG** (4360m), a bleak truck-stop town. The road is good, and the awesome Nyanchen Tanglha mountain range to the north is dramatically topped by the peak of Nyanchen Tanglha itself (7117m). The turning north to Namtso is about halfway through the town where a large concrete bridge crosses the river towards the mountains. Minibuses leave Lhasa from just east of the *Yak Hotel* around 7am each morning (¥30; 3–4hr), and if you need **accommodation** in Damxhung, there are several unmemorable places. The *Tang Shung Shey* (①), opposite the new petrol station at the far end of town, is noisy and basic. In front stands the cavernous, friendly and atmospheric Muslim restaurant, *Ching Jeng*, although there are plenty of Chinese restaurants too.

Namtso

Set at 4700m and frozen over from November to May, **Namtso** (Sky Lake) is 70km long and 30km wide, the second largest saltwater lake in China (only Qinghai Hu, see p.894, is bigger). The scenery comes straight from a dream image of Tibet, with snow-capped mountains towering behind the massive lake and yaks grazing on the plains around nomadic herders' tents.

From Damxhung, the road passes through the Nyanchen Tanglha mountain range at Lhachen La (5150m) and descends to **NAMTSO QU**, the district centre numbering just a couple of houses, at the eastern end of the lake. The target of most visitors is **Tashi Dor Monastery**, considerably farther west (a hefty 42km from Lhachen La), tucked away behind two massive red rocks on a promontory jutting into the lake. There is a more direct route from Damxhung to the monastery over the pass at Kong La, farther south, but these are serious mountains and very easy to get lost in. Make sure you come prepared and know the route before attempting this trek. At Tashi Dor (¥10), a small Nyingma monastery is built around a cave and there's a dirt-floored guesthouse (①) between the monastery and lake. It's a glorious site, but facilities are limited – bring your own food and light. Although some bedding is provided, you'll be more comfortable in your own sleeping bag, and your own stove and fuel would be an advantage. You can walk around the rock at the end of the promontory and also climb to the top for even more startling views. For true devotees, a circuit of the lake takes twenty days, camping on the way.

The old southern road and Gyantse

Heading west from Lhasa, the road divides at the Chusul Bridge and most vehicles follow the paved Friendship Highway along the course of the Yarlung Tsangpo to Shigatse (266km). However, there is an alternative route, the **old southern road** that heads southwest to the shores of **Yamdrok Tso**, before turning west to **Gyantse** and then northwest to Shigatse. This road is longer, 354km from Lhasa to Shigatse, and largely unpaved, but extremely picturesque.

There is no public transport between Lhasa and Gyantse and most people rent jeeps to explore the area or include it on the way to or from the border with Nepal. Allow around six or seven hours' driving time from Lhasa to Gyantse in a good jeep. Day trips to Yamdrok Tso from Lhasa are feasible; you'll start negotiating at about ¥1000 per jeep for these.

Yamdrok Tso and Samding

From Chusul Bridge, on the western outskirts of Lhasa, the southern road climbs steeply up to the Kampa La Pass (4794m) with stunning views of the turquoise waters of the sacred lake, **Yamdrok Tso**, the third largest lake in Tibet. It is said that if it ever dries up then Tibet itself will no longer support life. Yamdrok Tso is currently the site of a controversial hydro-electric scheme started in 1985 which has prompted major concerns about ecological issues and the desecration of the lake. With no external rivers feeding the lake, the most pessimistic projection is that it will be completely drained within twenty years. From the pass, the road descends to Yamtso village before skirting the northern and western shores amid wild scenery dotted with a few tiny hamlets, yaks by the lakeside and small boats on the water.

On the western side of the lake, 57km beyond the Kampa La Pass, the village of **NAKARTSE** is the birthplace of the mother of the Great Fifth Dalai Lama. One kilometre before the village a large board announces the *Hotel Langkari* which turns out to be the local PSB compound and is definitely not expecting guests. There is basic **accommodation** in the village (ask for directions), but there have been instances of midnight awakenings here as the PSB move foreigners on. The village is growing and there are several Chinese **restaurants**. However, the favourite with visitors is the Tibetan restaurant with tables in a tiny courtyard hidden away in the middle of the village where you can eat rice with potato and meat curry (they fish out the meat for vegetarians) under the eyes of the local dogs. Jeep drivers seem to come here instinctively; otherwise look for the tourist vehicles parked outside.

Yamdrok Tso has many picturesque islands and inlets visible from the road, and there's a seven-day circular trek from Nakartse exploring the major promontory into the lake. For those with less time the best expedition is to **Samding Monastery** (¥8), perched on a ridge, 12km by a rough but motorable track from Nakartse. The monastery is the seat of the only female reincarnation in Tibet, Dorje Phagmo, the Thunderbolt Sow, an incarnation of Tara. Legend tells how the reincarnation and her followers magically transformed themselves into pigs at the time of the Dzungar attack in the eighteenth century. The army, arriving at the monastery to find only animals in residence, were amazed when the nuns turned themselves back into humans and the soldiers made offerings instead of destroying the complex. They don't get a lot of visitors up here and you'll be given a friendly welcome.

The climb up from Nakartse to the Karo La Pass (5045m) is long and dramatic with towering peaks on either side as the road heads south and then west towards apparently impenetrable rock faces. From the pass, the road descends gradually, via the mineral mines at Chewang to the broad, fertile and densely farmed Nyang Chu Valley leading to Gyantse.

Gyantse

On the eastern banks of the Nyang Chu at the base of a natural amphitheatre of rocky ridges, **GYANTSE** is an attractive, relaxed town, offering the splendid sights of the **Kumbum** and the old **Dzong**, and, despite the rapidly expanding Chinese section of town, it has retained a pleasant, laid-back air. It lies 263km from Lhasa on the southern route and 90km southeast of Shigatse on a good-quality road.

Little is known about the history of any settlement at Gyantse before the fourteenth century when it emerged as the capital of a small kingdom ruled by a lineage of princes hailing originally from northeast Tibet and claiming descent from the legendary Tibetan folk hero, King Gesar of Ling. They allied themselves to the powerful Sakya order and, owing to its position between Lhasa and Shigatse, with **India** to the south, Gyantse operated as a staging post in the **wool trade** between Tibet and India. By the mid-fifteenth century, the Gyantse Dzong, Pelkor Chode Monastery and the Kumbum had been built, although decline followed as other local families increased their influence.

Gyantse rose to prominence again in 1904 when Younghusband's British expedition, equipped with modern firearms, approached the town via the trade route from Sikkim, routed 1500 Tibetans at Tuna, killing over half of them, and then marched on Gyantse. In July 1904, the British took the Dzong with four casualties while three hundred Tibetans were killed. From here the British marched on to Lhasa. As part of the ensuing agreement between Tibet and Britain, a British Trade Agency was established in Gyantse and as relations between Tibet and the British in India thawed, the trade route from Calcutta up through Sikkim and on to Gyantse became an effective one.

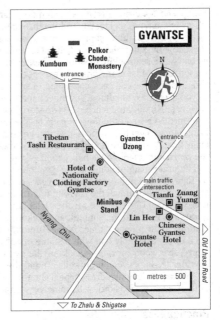

The Town

The best way to get your bearings in Gyantse is to stand at the main traffic intersection at the base of the Dzong. The entrance to the fortress is along the road to the right of the hill, while the road to its left leads to the Kumbum. The road from Shigatse arrives at the intersection to the south, opposite the Dzong, and the old road from Lhasa comes from the southeast.

The original **Gyantse Dzong** (Mon–Sat 7am–7pm; ¥12) dates from the mid-fourteenth century. However, given the extensive damage caused by the British in 1904, today's remains are a lot more recent. Guides will escort you part of the way around the ruins, unlocking the reconstructed buildings on the way, but then you're free to wander at will. Currently visitors are shown the **Meeting Hall**, housing a waxworks tableau, the **Exhibition Hall**, detailing the "Anti-British War" of 1904 in English, and the upper and lower chapels of the **Sampal Norbuling Monastery**. A few of the murals in the upper chapel probably date from the early fifteenth century, but most of the other artefacts are modern. The best views are from the top of the tallest tower in the north of the complex. You'll need to clamber up some very rickety ladders, but the scenery is well worth it.

PELKOR CHODE AND THE GYANTSE KUMBUM

Situated at the northern edge of town, the rather barren monastic compound now containing **Pelkor Chode Monastery** and the glorious **Gyantse Kumbum** (Mon–Sat 9am–noon & 3–5pm; ¥15), famous among scholars of Tibetan art throughout the world, once contained religious colleges and temples belonging to three schools of Tibetan Buddhism: the Gelugpa, Sakya and Bu, a small order, founded by Buton Rinpoche, whose main centre is at Zhalu (see p.980).

Constructed around 1440 by Rabten Kunsang, the Gyantse prince most responsible for the town's fine buildings, the name Kumbum means "a hundred thousand images" which is probably an overestimate, but not by that much. This is a remarkable building, a huge *chorten* crowned with a golden dome and umbrella, with chapels at each level. It's a style unique to Tibetan architecture and, while several such buildings have survived, Gyantse is the best preserved and most accessible. Despite some damage in the 1960s, the building remains largely intact and, although many of the statues have needed extensive renovation, most of the murals are very old – take a flashlight if you want a good look. Most of the chapels, except the very top floors, are now open. The structure has eight levels, each consisting of small chapels, decreasing in number and size as you ascend. With almost seventy chapels on the first four levels alone, there's plenty to see. Highlights include the two-storey chapels at the cardinal points on the first and third levels and the four chapels on the fifth level. The views of the town and surrounding area get better the higher you go and some of the outside stucco work is especially fine. At the sixth level you'll emerge onto an open platform level with the eyes of the *chorten* that look in each direction.

The other main building in the compound is **Pelkor Chode Monastery**, also built by Rabten Kunsang around twenty years earlier than the Kumbum, and used for worship by monks from all the surrounding monasteries. Today in the main assembly hall there are two thrones, one for the Dalai Lama and one for the main Sakya lama. The glitter and gold and the sunlight and flickering butter lamps in the chapels make a fine contrast to the gloom of much of the Kumbum. The main chapel, **Tsangkhang**, is at the back of the assembly hall with a statue of Sakyamuni flanked by deities, amidst some impressive wood carvings – look for the two peacocks perched on a beam. A narrow corridor leads between high walls around the back of this chapel. The second floor of the monastery contains five chapels and the top level just one, **Shalyekhang** (the Peak of the Celestial Mansion), with some very impressive two-metre-wide *mandalas*.

Practicalities

Minibuses operate between the bus station in Shigatse and just south of the main traffic intersection in Gyantse from around 8am to 4pm daily. There are no checkposts between the two towns, but you may still have trouble getting a driver to take you. The fare is ¥18 but most tourists end up paying closer to ¥40 for the two- to three-hour trip.

Accommodation in Gyantse is limited. The *Gyantse Hotel* (☎08019/2222; ⑦), a couple of hundred metres south of the main traffic intersection on the road to Shigatse, is the most comfortable with a spacious lobby and 24-hour hot water. Most independent travellers stay at the opposite extreme, the *Hotel of Nationality Clothing Factory Gyantse* (①), on the left-hand side a couple of hundred metres from the main intersection towards the Kumbum. There are dorms and pit latrines here, but no washing facilities. However, the bedding is quite clean and it's convenient for the sights. The *Chinese Gyantse Hotel* (☎08019/2247; ②), 200m on the right from the main intersection along the old Lhasa road, is best avoided unless they undertake a major renovation.

There are plenty of Chinese **restaurants** in town, clustered to the east of the main traffic intersection along the old Lhasa road. Among them *Tianfu* and *Zuang Yuang* have English menus, but the food is nothing special. Across the road, however, is the real gem, the *Lin Her,* a tiny place with no English sign and only three tables, plus a handwritten English/Chinese menu on the wall. It's very popular with local people so service can be slow, but the food is good, especially the *bao tse* for breakfast. A couple of hundred metres towards the Kumbum, beyond the *Hotel of Nationality Clothing Factory Gyantse*, the *Tibetan Tashi Restaurant* on the left-hand side of the road is fun. They have comfortable sofas, Hindi film-star posters on the wall and basic travellers' food.

Zhalu Monastery

Accessible enough for a day trip from Shigatse or an easy side trip between Gyantse and Shigatse, **Zhalu Monastery** is around 22km from Shigatse, 75km from Gyantse and 4km south of the village of Tsungdu between kilometre markers 18 and 19 on the Gyantse–Shigatse road. Originally built in the eleventh century, Zhalu has a finely colonnaded courtyard decorated with luck symbols, but is most remarkable for the green-glazed tiles that line the roof. It rose to prominence as the seat of the Bu tradition of Tibetan Buddhism founded by Buton Rinchendrub in the fourteenth century. Buton's claim to fame is as the scholar who collected, organized and copied the Tengyur commentaries by hand into a coherent whole, comprising 227 thick volumes in all. However, his original work and pen were destroyed during the Cultural Revolution. Never as numerous as the better-known schools, although there were once about 3500 monks living here, the tradition was influential and Tsongkhapa, among others, was influenced by Buton's teaching. Major renovations are currently underway and chapels have been closed and rearranged. Don't expect too much from the temple itself until the work is complete, but the monks are friendly and the village is a quiet and pleasant place. If you are feeling energetic it's a one- to two-hour walk up in the hills southwest of Zhalu to the hermitage of Riphuk where Atisha is supposed to have meditated. You'll need directions or a guide from Zhalu as you can't see it from the monastery.

About a kilometre north of Zhalu, **Gyankor Lhakhang** dates from 997. Sakya Pandita, who established the relationship between the Mongol Khans and the Sakya hierarchy in the thirteenth century (see p.941) was ordained here as a monk and the stone bowl over which he shaved his head prior to ordination is in the courtyard. Just inside the entrance a conch shell is said to date from the time of Buton Rinchendrub and is believed to be able to sound without human assistance.

Shigatse

Sadly most people use **SHIGATSE**, Tibet's second city, as an overnight stop on the way to or from Lhasa. While one day is long enough to see the two main sights, **Tashilunpo Monastery** and **Shigatse Dzong**, it's worth spending at least an extra night here simply to do everything at a more leisurely pace, take in the market and spend a bit of time absorbing the atmosphere and wandering the attractive, tree-lined streets. Basing yourself here also gives you the opportunity to explore some of the sights along the old southern road to Lhasa (see p.977).

The City

Although the city is fairly spread out, about 2km from end to end, most of the sights and the facilities that you'll need are in or near the north–south corridor around Jiefang Tong Lu and Beijing Bei Lu, extending north along Kesang Ke Lu to the market and Dzong. The main exception is Tashilunpo Monastery which is a bit of a hike west. Shigatse offers an adequate range of accommodation, a variety of shops and some pleasant restaurants, and the dramatic Drolma Ridge rising up on the northern side of town helps you get your bearings easily. The pace of life here is unhurried but there's a buzz provided by the huge numbers of Tibetan pilgrims and foreign visitors, most of whom seem to move on within hours. Stick around for a few days and you'll feel almost local. Although most of the city is modern, you'll find the traditional Tibetan houses concentrated in the area west of the market where you can explore the narrow alleyways running between high whitewashed walls.

Tashilunpo Monastery

Something of a showcase for foreign visitors, the large complex of **Tashilunpo Monastery** (Mon–Sat 9.30am–noon & 3.30–6pm; ¥20) is situated on the western side

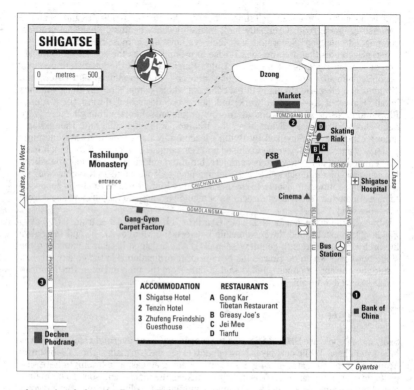

of town just below the Drolma Ridge – the gleaming, golden roofs will lead you in the right direction. The monastery has some of the most fabulous chapels outside Lhasa and it takes several hours to do it justice.

Tashilunpo was founded in 1447 by Gendun Drup, Tsongkhapa's nephew and disciple, who was later recognized as the First Dalai Lama. It rose to prominence in 1642 when the Fifth Dalai Lama declared that Losang Chokyi Gyeltsen, who was his teacher and the abbot of Tashilunpo, was a manifestation of the Amitabha Buddha and the Fourth reincarnation of the Panchen Lama (Great Precious Teacher) in what has proved to be an ill-fated lineage (see box, p.984). The Chinese have consistently sought to use the Panchen Lama in opposition to the Dalai Lama, beginning in 1728 when they gave the Fifth Panchen Lama sovereignty over Western Tibet.

The **temples** and shrines of most interest in Tashilunpo stand in a long line at the northern end of the compound. From the main gate head uphill and left to the **Jamkhang Chenmo**. Several storeys high, this was built by the Ninth Panchen Lama in 1914 and is dominated by a 26-metre gold, brass and copper statue of Maitreya, the Buddha of the Future. Hundreds of small images of Maitreya and Tsongkhapa and his disciples are painted on the walls.

Moving east, the next main building contains the gold and jewel-encrusted **Tomb of the Tenth Panchen Lama**, which was consecrated in 1994 and is reported to have cost US$7.75 million. Near the top is a small window cut into a tiny niche containing his picture. The next building, the **Palace of the Panchen Lamas**, built in the eighteenth century, is closed to the public, but the long building in front houses a series of small, first-floor chapels. The Yulo Drolma Lhakhang, farthest to the right, is worth a look and contains 21 small statues showing each of the 21 manifestations of Tara, the most popular goddess in Tibet.

Continuing east, the **Tomb of the Fourth Panchen Lama**, contains his eleven-metre-high *chorten* with statues of Amitayus, White Tara and Vijaya, the so-called Longevity Triad, in front. His entire body was supposedly interred in the *chorten* in a standing position, together with an ancient manuscript and *thangkas* sent by the second Manchu emperor.

Heading east again the **Kelsang Lhakhang**, the largest, most intricate and confusing building in Tashilunpo, stands in front of the Tomb of the Fifth Panchen Lama. Ongoing renovation is resulting in temporary closures of chapels and the re-routing of tourists, but on no account miss it. The Lhakhang consists of a courtyard, the fifteenth-century assembly hall and a whole maze of small, often interconnecting chapels in the surrounding buildings. The flagged **courtyard** is the setting for all the major temple festivals and the surrounding three-level colonnaded cloisters are covered with murals, many recently renovated. Dominating the **assembly hall** is the huge throne of the Panchen Lama and the hanging *thangkas* depicting all his incarnations. If you've got the energy, it's worth trying to find the **Thongwa Donden Lhakhang**, one of the most sacred chapels in the complex, containing burial *chortens*, including that of the founder of Tashilunpo, the First Dalai Lama, Gendun Drup, as well as early Panchen Lamas and abbots of Tashilunpo.

Spare an hour or so to walk the three-kilometre **kora**, the pilgrim circuit, which follows a clockwise path around the outside walls of the monastery. Turn right on the main road as you exit the monastery and continue around the walls; a stick is useful as some of the dogs are aggressive. The highlight of the walk is the view of the glorious golden roofs from above the top wall. The massive white-painted wall at the top northeast corner is where the forty-metre, giant appliquéed *thangka* is displayed annually at the festival on the fifteenth day of the fifth lunar month (usually in July). At this point, instead of returning downhill to the main road, you can follow the track that continues on around the hillside above the Tibetan part of town and leads eventually to the old Dzong.

Shigatse Dzong and the market

Shigatse Dzong is now a dramatic pile of ruins. It was built in the seventeenth century by Karma Phuntso Namgyel when he was king of the Tsang region and held sway over much of the country, and it's thought that its design was used as the basis for the later construction of the Potala. Initially ruined by the Dzungars in 1717, further damage took place in the 1950s. Unlike at Gyantse, there has been no attempt at rebuilding and the main reason to climb up is for the fantastic views. To get here from town head west along Tomzigang Lu until the paved surface runs out. A little farther along, a motorable track heads up the hill between some houses to a small pass from where you can climb right up to the Dzong.

The **market**, opposite the *Tenzin Hotel*, is worth a browse if you're looking for souvenirs. There's the usual range of jewellery, "antiques" and religious objects, but the scale of the place is a bit easier to manage than the Barkhor in Lhasa. You'll need to brush up on your bargaining skills and patience as the stallholders here are used to hit-and-run tourists so are very pushy and the first asking price is often sky-high.

If you're interested in **carpets**, drop into the *Tibet Gang-Gyen Carpet Factory* (Mon–Fri 9am–1pm & 3–7pm) on Qomolangma Lu, a few minutes from the entrance of Tashilunpo. Carpets are made from ninety percent sheep's wool and ten percent cotton and you can watch the whole process from the winding of the wool through to the weaving and finishing. They have a good range of traditional and modern designs ranging in price from US\$24 up to US\$370, and can also arrange shipping.

THE PANCHEN LAMA CONTROVERSY

The life of the **Tenth Panchen Lama** (1938–89) was a tragic one. Identified at eleven years of age by the Nationalists in 1949 in Xining, without approval from Lhasa, he fell into Communist hands and was for many years the most high-profile collaborator of the People's Republic of China. His stance changed in 1959 when he openly referred to the Dalai Lama as the true ruler of Tibet. In 1961, in Beijing, the Panchen Lama informed Mao of the appalling conditions in Tibet at that time and pleaded for aid, religious freedom and an end to the huge numbers of arrests. Mao assured the Panchen Lama these would be granted, but nothing changed. Instructed to give a speech condemning the Dalai Lama, he refused and was prevented from speaking in public until the 1964 Monlam Great Prayer Festival in Lhasa. With an audience of ten thousand people he again ignored instructions and spoke in the Dalai Lama's support, ending with the words, "Long live the Dalai Lama". He was immediately placed under house arrest and the Chinese instituted a campaign to "Thoroughly Smash the Panchen Reactionary Clique". The Panchen Lama's **trial** in August 1964 lasted seventeen days following which he vanished into Qin Cheng Prison No.1, north of Beijing, for fourteen years, where he was tortured and attempted suicide. He was released in February 1978, following the death of Zhou Enlai two years earlier, and the Chinese used him as evidence that there was a thawing of their hard-line attitude towards Tibet. He never again criticized the Chinese in public and in private he argued that Tibetan culture must survive at all costs, even if it meant giving up claims for independence. Some Tibetans saw this as a sell-out, others worshipped him as a hero when he returned on visits to Tibet. In early 1989, he visited Shigatse for a ceremony marking the restoration of the chapels and tombs in the monastery at Tashilunpo. On the night of January 28, 1989, at the age of fifty, he died, the Chinese say from a heart attack, others claim from the poison of a vengeful China.

The search for the **Eleventh Panchen Lama** was always likely to be fraught. The central issue is whether the Dalai Lama or the Chinese government have the right to determine the identity of the next incarnation – both claim rightful control of the process. Stuck in the middle was the abbot of Tashilunpo, Chadrel Rinpoche, who initially led the search. The search followed the normal pattern with reports of unusual children relayed to the abbot and then checked out by high-ranking monks. On January 25, 1995, the Dalai Lama decided that Gendun Choekyi Nyima, the son of a doctor from Nagchu in Central Tibet, was the reincarnation, but concerned for the child's safety he hesitated about a public announcement. The search committee headed by Chadrel Rinpoche supported the same child.

However, the Chinese decreed that the selection should take place by the drawing of lots from the Golden Urn, an eighteenth-century gold vase, one of a pair used by the Qing emperor Qianlong to resolve disputes in his lands. Chadrel Rinpoche argued against its use. In May, the Dalai Lama, concerned about the delay of an announcement from China, publicly recognized Gendun Choekyi Nyima and the following day Chadrel Rinpoche was arrested while trying to return to Tibet from Beijing. Within days, Gendun Choekyi Nyima and his family were taken from their home by the authorities, put on a plane and disappeared. The Chinese will only admit they are holding them "for protection". Fifty Communist Party officials then moved into Tashilunpo to identify monks still loyal to the Dalai Lama and his choice of Panchen Lama. In July there was open revolt by the monks quelled by riot police and across Tibet the Chinese slowly repressed dissent in the other religious institutions. By the end of 1995 they had re-established enough control to hold the Golden Urn ceremony in the Jokhang in Lhasa where an elderly monk drew out the name of a boy called Gyaincain Norbu. In December he was enthroned at Tashilunpo and taken to Beijing for publicity appearances. Meanwhile, the whereabouts of Gendun Choekyi Nyima and his family are unknown and more than fifty people have been imprisoned in Tibet for maintaining that he is the true incarnation of the Panchen Lama.

Practicalities

Public **buses** run to Shigatse from the Lhasa bus station (¥62). There are also **minibuses** (¥40) from Beijing Dong Lu just east of the *Yak Hotel*, but as there is a checkpost on the Friendship Highway between the two cities, minibus drivers may refuse to carry you. Public buses terminate at the **bus station** on Jiefang Tong Lu, while minibus drivers carrying you illegally are more likely to put you out elsewhere. There are plenty of **tractors** operating as taxis (¥3 for a destination in town) or it's about a twenty-minute walk from the bus station to the *Tenzin Hotel*. Public buses return to **Lhasa** from the bus station daily at 8am and minibuses run between Gyantse and Shigatse until around 4pm. If you are heading **to the border with Nepal**, the furthest west you can get on public transport is the Sakya turn-off on the Friendship Highway, 126km from Shigatse (see p.987 below), although there are unconfirmed rumours of a weekly bus from Shigatse to Lhatse (150km west).

Conveniently situated on Chichinaka Lu, Shigatse's **PSB** (Mon–Fri 9.30am–1pm & 3.30–7pm) is one of the more friendly offices; apply here for permits to Gyantse and west as far as Sakya. The **Bank of China** (daily 9.30am–1pm & 3.30–6pm), just beyond the *Shigatse Hotel*, will cash travellers' cheques but won't give cash advances on credit cards. If you're heading west stock up here on local currency as there are no more facilities until Zhangmu. At the **post office**, on the corner of Beijing Bei Lu and Qomolangma Lu (daily 9.30am–7pm), you can send international letters and faxes, but not parcels. There are also international **telephones** here, but no poste restante service. The Shigatse **hospital** on Jiefang Tong Lu has a first-aid post (10am–12.30pm & 4–6pm) – take a Chinese translator with you.

Accommodation

Although Shigatse is the commercial and political centre of Tsang Province, **accommodation** options are not huge as many of the mid-range Chinese hotels will not accept foreigners. The long-standing travellers' haunt is the *Tenzin Hotel* (☎0892/22018; ①–④), opposite the market, with an increasing range of rooms, erratic showers and an excellent roof terrace for basking in the sunshine. At the other end of the range, the *Shigatse Hotel* (☎0892/22556; ⑦) is the tour group hotel, a bit out of the way on Jiefang Tong Lu, but it's rather cavernous if there aren't plenty of people around. The lobby shop stocks a good range of books and souvenirs. The best mid-range place is the new and comfortable *Zhufeng Friendship Guesthouse* (☎0892/21929; ⑥) on Dechen Phodrang Lu which has 24-hour hot water, although it is a bit out of town.

Eating and drinking

There's no shortage of **restaurants** in Shigatse. The best Chinese ones line Kesang Ke Lu, just in front of the skating rink, and include *Tianfu, Jei Mee* and *Greasy Joe's*, which are small, family affairs with large menus of seafood, meat and vegetable dishes (¥15–30). Slightly farther away, on Tsendu Lu, the *Gong Kar Tibetan Restaurant* has fabulously painted pillars outside and comfortable sofas within. More adventurous carnivores can try yak's heart salad, pig's trotters and ears here, although there are also more mainstream meat and vegetable dishes (¥12–20). A good breakfast bet are the doughnut stalls (*youtiao*), outside the bus station in the early morning.

West to Zhangmu

From Shigatse, the Friendship Highway **west to Zhangmu** on the Nepalese border is partly sealed, but generally rough and quite slow. The only public buses in this direction are the Shigatse–Sakya and the unreliable Lhasa–Zhangmu services, although there are rumours of a service from Shigatse to Lhatse, 24km beyond the Sakya turn-off. From the broad plain around Shigatse, the road gradually climbs to the pass of Tsuo La (4500m) before the steep descent to the Sakya Bridge and the turn-off to Sakya village. If you have time a detour off the Friendship Highway to Sakya is worthwhile; the valleys are picturesque, the villages retain the rhythm of their rural life and **Sakya Monastery** is a dramatic sight, unlike anything you'll encounter elsewhere in Tibet.

Sakya

The small, but rapidly growing village of **SAKYA**, set in the midst of an attractive plain, straddles the small Trum River and is highly significant as the centre of the Sakya school of Tibetan Buddhism. The main reason to visit is to see the remaining monastery, a unique Mongol-style construction dramatically visible from miles away. The village is now a burgeoning Chinese community, full of ugly concrete, but the pleasant pace and atmosphere are still here, with farmers taking their sheep and cattle out to graze in the mornings and herding them home to pens in the village at night.

Sakya Monastery

Experiences of visiting **Sakya Monastery** (Mon–Sat 9am–noon & 4–6pm; ¥20, group visitors ¥30, photographs inside the chapels ¥80) vary considerably. Some people find the monks rude and off-hand, others find them friendly and eager to talk.

Originally there were two monasteries at Sakya, the imposing, Mongol-style structure of the **Southern Monastery** that most visitors come to see today and the **Northern Monastery**, across the river, a more typical monastic complex containing 108 chapels which was completely destroyed during the Cultural Revolution and which has been largely rebuilt as houses. Prior to the Chinese occupation, there were around five hundred monks in the two monasteries; there are now about a hundred. The Northern Monastery was founded in 1073 by Kong Chogyal Pho, a member of the Khon family, whose son, Kunga Nyingpo, did much to establish Sakya as an important religious centre. He married and had four sons; three became monks but the fourth remained a layman and continued the family line. The Sakya order has remained something of a family affair and while the monks take vows of celibacy, the leadership still passes on by the same system of inheritance. One of the early leaders was a grandson of Kunga Nyingpo, known as Sakya Pandita, who started the most illustrious era of the order in the thirteenth century when he journeyed to the court of the Mongol emperor, Godan Khan, and established the Sakya lamas as religious advisers to subsequent emperors and effective rulers of Tibet until their overthrow in 1354 (see p.941). The Southern Monastery was built in the thirteenth century on the orders of Phagpa, nephew of Sakya Pandita. Note the unusual decoration of houses in the area – grey, with white and red vertical stripes; this dates back to a time when it denoted their taxable status within the Sakya principality.

The entrance to the **Southern Monastery** is in its east wall. A massive fortress, there are five main temples in the complex surrounded by a huge wall with turrets at each corner. Starting on the left of the entrance, the tall, spacious chapel on the second floor of the **Puntsok Palace**, the traditional home of one of the two main Sakya lamas who now lives in the USA, is lined with statues – White Tara is nearest to the door and Sakya Pandita farther along the same wall. The *chortens* contain the remains of early Sakya lamas and the figure of Kunga Nyingpo, the founder of the Northern Monastery, shows him as an old man. As you move clockwise around the courtyard, the next chapel is the **Phurkhang**, with statues of Sakyamuni to the left and Manjusri to the right of Sakya Pandita. The whole temple is stuffed with thousands of small statues and editions of sacred texts with murals on the back wall. The **Great Assembly Hall** (facing the entrance to the courtyard), a grand and imposing chapel with walls 3.5 metres thick, has a roof supported by forty solid wooden columns, one of which was said to be a personal gift from Kublai Khan and carried by hand from China. Another was supposedly fetched from India on the back of a tiger, a third brought in the horns of a yak and another is said to weep the black blood of the *naga* water spirit that lived in the tree used for the column. The chapel is overwhelmingly full of brocade hangings, fine statues, butter lamps, thrones, murals and holy books. The grandest statues are of Buddha against a golden, carved background and they contain the remains of previous Sakya lamas. The **Silver Chorten Chapel** houses eleven *chortens* with more in the chapel behind. Completing the circuit, the **Drolma Lhakhang** is on the second floor of the building to the right of the entrance. This is the residence of the other principal Sakya lama, the Sakya Trizin, currently residing in India where he has established his seat in exile in Rajpur. Be sure to take time to walk around the top of the walls for fine views both into the monastery and over the surrounding area.

Practicalities

Situated 149km southwest of Shigatse, Sakya is an easy side trip off the Friendship Highway if you've got your own transport. Public **buses** run to Sakya from Shigatse twice a week (Tues & Sat at 8.30am, but check the latest on this at Shigatse bus station), returning from Sakya at 11am the next morning; it's a surprisingly slow trip, allow six hours or more each way.

On arrival, avoid the miserable **accommodation** at the bus station; turn right out of the bus station entrance and walk straight ahead for 150m to the *Tibetan Hotel* opposite the north wall of the monastery. Only dorms are on offer (①), there is bedding but no sheets, electricity is temperamental and pit latrines are the only facilities. Alternatively, there is basic accommodation on the Friendship Highway at the turn-off for Sakya (①) – there's no sign, ask in the compound there. The best **restaurant** in Sakya, the *Sichuan Flavour Restaurant,* is just west of the hotel entrance, next to a small shop sporting a *Simone Soda and Cigs* sign. This tiny Chinese restaurant has a surprisingly lengthy menu, written in English, with the usual range of meat, vegetable, rice and noodle dishes (¥10–20) and their pancakes make a good breakfast.

The **permit** situation is variable. PSB officers do lurk in the monastery and it's better to try to get a permit if there's any doubt about the current rules. Ask around among other travellers and check at the PSB in Shigatse or Zhangmu.

Sakya to Everest

Just 24km west of Sakya Bridge (there's no checkpost between the two), the truck-stop town of **LHATSE** (4050m) lines the Friendship Highway and has plenty of restaurants and basic accommodation. There's little to detain you unless you're hitching, but most drivers stop here. Another 6km west from Lhatse the road divides: the Friendship Highway continues to the left and the route to the far west of the region heads right. If you're hitching in to Western Tibet walk a couple of kilometres along this right fork until you reach the ferry crossing. All the drivers have to stop and wait for the ferry here.

The continuation of the Friendship Highway is diabolical; allow about four hours in a good jeep, up over the Lhakpa La Pass (5220m) to the checkpost and turn-off to **SHEKAR** (also known as New Tingri). The much-advertised but over-priced *Chomolungma Hotel* (⑥) is a couple of hundred metres towards Shekar off the Friendship Highway. There are no nearby restaurants and meals are charged at a daily rate of ¥230. The village itself is 7km farther on, with the Shekar Chode Monastery on the hillside above. There's basic accommodation (①) in the village, but you'll have to ask, and there's little reason to hang around.

Shekar boasts another checkpost 1km west of the first and some visitors have reported that the guards here are particularly assiduous in confiscating printed material specifically about Tibet from travellers entering the country (books on China which include Tibet seem to be fine). Just 7km west of this checkpost, the small turning to **Rongbuk Monastery** and on up to **Everest Base Camp** is on the south side of the road. It's a long, bumpy and spellbinding 90km to Rongbuk and worth every tortured minute of the three- or four-hour drive along the rough track. About 3km from the turning, the checkpost at Chay will collect entrance fees (¥300 per jeep) for the Everest area.

From Chay the road zigzags, steeply up to the Pang La Pass (5150m), from where the glory of the Everest region is laid out before you – the earlier you go in the day the better the views as it clouds over later. There's a lookout spot with a plan to help you identify individual peaks such as Cho Oyu (8153m), Lhotse (8501m) and Makalu (8463m) as well as the mighty Everest (8848m; Chomolungma in Tibetan, Qomolangma in Chinese). From here the road descends into a network of fertile valleys with small villages in a patchwork of fields. You'll gradually start climbing again and pass through Peruche (19km from Pang La), Passum (10km farther), where there is accommodation just beside the road at the *Passumpembah Teahouse* (①), and Chodzom (another 12km) before the scenery becomes rockier, starker and you eventually reach Rongbuk Monastery, 22km farther on.

The highest monastery in the world, **Rongbuk** (4980m) was founded in 1902 by the Nyingma Lama, Ngawang Tenzin Norbu, although a hardy community of nuns had used meditation huts on the site for about two hundred years before this. With a previous population of over five hundred monks and nuns, there are now around fifty and rebuilding is well advanced. The chapels themselves are of limited interest; Padmasambhava is in pride of place and the new murals are attractive, but the position of the monastery, perched on the side of the Rongbuk Valley leading straight towards the north face of Everest, is stunning. Just to sit outside and watch the play of light on the face of the mountain is the experience of a lifetime. **Everest Base Camp** (5150m) is a farther 8km due south. The road is motorable but it's mostly flat and the walk alongside the river through the boulder-strewn landscape past a small monastery on the cliff is glorious. Base camp is often a bit of a surprise, especially during the climbing seasons (Mar–May & Sept–Oct), when you'll find a colourful tent city festooned with Calor Gas bottles and satellite dishes. It's possible to camp near the monastery where there's also a guesthouse offering dorm **accommodation** (①). Grubby quilts are provided, but you'll be more comfortable with your own sleeping bag. Each room has a stove and pot to boil water (you collect it from up the valley) and the monks will provide fuel (although if you can manage to buy some in the villages on the way this would be insurance against a shortage – a night here without heat would be grim). There's a small monastery shop selling mostly leftovers from mountaineering expeditions – take your own food. Don't be surprised if you suffer with the altitude here. However well you were acclimatized in Lhasa, base camp is around 1300m higher and if you're contemplating a trip here soon after arrival up on the Tibetan plateau, be sensible (see p.946).

To the border

From the Rongbuk and Everest Base Camp turning on the Friendship Highway it's a fast 50km south to **TINGRI** (4342m). The road is good and you should allow about an hour in a jeep. Tingri is a convenient stop before the final day's drive to Zhangmu and has good views south towards Everest. To get the best of these, climb up to the old fort that stands sentinel over the main part of the village. The two **accommodation** options are on the northern side of the main road which runs along north of the village and the most popular, the *Himalaya Hotel* (①), is the farthest east, with dorm accommodation, latrines with view, seats in the sunshine and electricity. The restaurant here has a lively atmosphere, good food and excellent *momos*, but some Tibetan to help you communicate is useful (see *Contexts*, "Language" p.1059).

The road west of Tingri is good quality and lined with ruins of buildings destroyed in an eighteenth-century Gurkha incursion from Nepal. The road climbs gradually for 85km to the double-topped **Lalung La Pass** (5050m) from where the views of the Himalaya are great, especially looking west to the great slab of Shishapangma (8013m). The descent from the pass is steep and startling as the road drops off the edge of the Tibetan plateau and heads down the gorge of the Po Chu River. Vegetation appears and it becomes noticeably warmer as you near Nyalam, around four hours by jeep from Tingri.

Although difficult to spot if you're coming from the north, **Milarepa's Cave** (10km north of Nyalam) is worth a halt – look out for a white *chorten*, to the left of the road on the edge of the gorge. Milarepa (1040–1123) was a much revered Tibetan mystic who led an ascetic, itinerant life living in caves and was loved for his religious songs. The Kagyu order of Tibetan Buddhism was founded by his followers and the impressions in the walls and roof are believed to have been made by Milarepa himself. A temple has been built around the cave and the main statue is of Padmasambhava. Perched on the side of the Matsang Zangpo river gorge, **NYALAM** (3750m) is a small village with several Chinese restaurants and a variety of basic accommodation, although there is little to recommend staying the night here rather than continuing to Zhangmu.

The steep descent through the Himalaya continues on a twisty and dramatic road that winds in and out of the forested mountainsides and feels almost tropical as it descends the 33km to the border town of **ZHANGMU** (2300m). This Chinese-Tibetan-Nepalese hybrid clings gamely to the sheer mountain, a collection of tin shacks, construction sites, wooden huts, shops, brothels and offices. It's a great place with a Wild-West-comes-to-Asia atmosphere, although good-quality **accommodation** is limited. The choice is between the *Zhangmu Hotel* (☎08074/2272; ⑦) at the bottom end of town with no hot water in the private bathrooms, although there's a shower on the top floor of a building opposite, and the *Himalaya Hotel and Lodge* (①), on the right heading down through town, offering clean dorms and great views down the valley. There are no washing facilities, but there's a shower operation just up the hill and putrid latrines across the street. The **PSB** is tucked away in an alley close to the *Zhangmu Hotel*, and *CITS* (daily 9.30am–1pm & 2–6.30pm) is inside the hotel in Room 402. Zhangmu boasts two branches of the **Bank of China** (Mon–Fri 10am–1pm & 3.30–6.30pm, Sat 10am–2pm), one near the border post at the bottom of town and one just above the *Himalaya Hotel and Lodge*. Despite production of exchange certificates they refuse to change Chinese money into either Nepalese or other hard currency, so if you've got excess you'll be forced on to the thriving black market. Follow the music and flashing lights for the nightly disco/hostess/**karaoke bar** in the middle of town, where everyone dances the waltz.

Border formalities

Leaving Tibet, formalities are fairly cursory. The **border posts** (both open daily 9.30am–5pm Chinese time) on the Chinese and Nepalese side, at **Kodari** (1770m), are an extremely steep 9km apart. You can either rent a truck (¥300 for four people), hire a porter (about ¥10 per bag) or carry your own stuff for the ninety-minute walk down (either follow the road or take the short cuts that slice across the zigzags) to the Friendship Bridge where there is another Chinese checkpost before you cross the bridge into Kodari. Don't forget to put your watch back (2hr 30min) when you cross from Tibet into Nepal. The **Nepalese Immigration** post is a couple of hundred metres over the bridge on the left. You can get only single entry visas here and you have to pay in US dollars and produce one passport photograph (see "Lhasa", p.965 for more visa details). From Kodari either take the express bus to Kathmandu or the cheaper local service to Barabise and then change for Kathmandu. Alternatively, there are taxis or you can negotiate for space in a tourist bus that has just dropped its group at the border – bargain hard and you'll end up paying Rp400–500 per person for the four-hour trip.

Western Tibet

Travellers in Lhasa spend huge amounts of time and energy plotting and planning trips to the highlights of **Western Tibet**: Mount Kailash, Lake Manasarovar, and, less popular but just as enticing, the hot springs at Tirthapuri and the remains of the tenth-century Guge kingdom, its capital at Tsaparang and main monastery at Tholing. However, this is no guarantee of reaching any of these destinations.

Regulations regarding trips west change frequently and you shouldn't underestimate the time it will take to set up a trip. Before 1996, tour companies in Lhasa were arranging trips for trucks of travellers, generally quoting around ¥12,000 per truck for a two to three-week return trip. However, in early 1996, regulations were introduced requiring tourists to travel in jeeps (¥15,000–17,500 per jeep). As a jeep carrying more than two people is unable to carry enough fuel for the trip, jeeps often have to be accompanied by trucks (¥22,000 for a jeep and truck). You will need to spend plenty of time talking to people in Lhasa to find out the current situation. Unless you have huge amounts of time and perseverance there is little realistic alternative to going on an organized trip; there is no public transport beyond the Sakya turning and plenty more people give up trying to hitch-hike than make it.

The **southern route passes** through Saga, Dongpa and Horpa, a stunningly picturesque journey, parallel to the Himalaya, but with rivers that become swollen and passes that get blocked by snow. This route is most reliable from May through to the beginning of July, and again in October and November, although luck plays a big part. The distance is around 1400km from Lhasa to Mount Kailash. The alternative **northern route** via Tsochen, Gertse and Gakyi is longer; Lhasa to Ali (Shiquanhe) is over 1700km and then it's another 300km or so southeast to Kailash. It is also less scenic but more reliable and there's more traffic using it. Many tours plan to go on one route and return on the other – expect at least a week travelling time on either.

Mount Kailash and the other sights

Top of most itineraries is **Mount Kailash** (6714m), Gang Rinpoche to the Tibetans, the sacred mountain at the centre of the universe for Buddhists, Hindus and Jains. Access is via **DARCHEN**, where there's a guesthouse used as a base by visiting pilgrims. The 58-kilometre tour around the mountain takes around three days and you might consider hiring a porter and/or yak (from about ¥45 per day each) as it's a tough walk and you need to carry all your gear including a stove, fuel and food. On the first day you should aim to reach Drirapuk Monastery, on the second day you climb over the Dolma La Pass (5636m) to Zutrulpuk Monastery and the third day brings you back to Darchen.

After the exertions of Kailash most tours head south 30km to **Lake Manasarova** (Mapham Yutso), the holiest lake in Asia for Hindus and Tibetan Buddhists alike. For the energetic it's a four-day, ninety-kilometre trek to get around the lake, but plenty of travellers just relax by the lakeside for a day or two.

The third major pilgrimage site in Western Tibet is **Tirthapuri** hot springs which are closely associated with Padmasambhava and situated about 80km northwest of Kailash and accessible by road. Pilgrims immerse themselves in the pools, visit the monastery containing his footprint and the cave that he used, and dig for small pearl-like stones that are believed to have healing properties.

The only remains of the tenth-century kingdom of **Guge**, where Buddhism survived while eclipsed in other parts of Tibet, are the main monastery of **Tholing**, 278km from Ali and the old capital of **Tsaparang**, 26km west of Tholing. Both places are famous for their extensive ruins, some of which are around a thousand years old, and there are many well-preserved murals but it's all even less accessible than Kailash and Manasarovar.

The major town in the area, **ALI** (also known as Shiquanhe) is the largest town for several hundred kilometres and is a modern Chinese-style settlement at the confluence of the Indus and Gar rivers. The only official foreigners' **accommodation** is the overpriced *Ali Hotel* (③–⑥) west of the main crossroads.

travel details

Buses

Gyantse to: Shigatse (frequent minibuses; 2–3hr).

Lhasa to: Damxhung (daily minibus; 3–4hr); Ganden (daily pilgrim bus; 3–4hr); Golmud (daily bus; 30–40hr); Samye ferry crossing (daily bus; 4hr); Shigatse (daily bus; 5–6hr; frequent minibuses; 6–7hr); Tsetang (frequent minibuses; 3hr); Tsurphu (daily pilgrim bus; 2–3hr); Xining (daily bus; 40–50hr); Zhangmu (3 buses monthly; 3–4 days).

Sakya to: Shigatse (2 buses weekly; 6–7hr).

Shigatse to: Gyantse (frequent minibuses; 2–3hr); Lhasa (daily bus; 5–6hr; frequent minibuses; 6–7hr); Sakya (2 buses weekly; 6–7hr).

Tsetang to: Lhasa (frequent minibuses; 3hr).

Planes

Lhasa to: Chengdu (daily; 2hr); Kathmandu (2 weekly; 1hr).

PART THREE

THE
CONTEXTS

HISTORY

As modern archeology gradually confirms ancient records of the country's earliest times, it seems that, however far back you go, China's history is essentially the saga of its dynasties, a succession of warring rulers who ultimately differed only in the degree of their autocracy. Although this generalized view is inevitable in the brief account below, bear in mind that, while the concept of being Chinese has been around for over two thousand years, the closer you look, the less "China" seems to exist as an entity – right from the start, regionalism played an important part in the country's history. And while concentrating on the great events, it's also easy to forget that the lot of those ruled was appalling. The emperors may have lived in splendour while their courts produced talented writers, poets and artisans, but among the peasantry crippling taxes, starvation and early death were the norm, and frequent famine accounted for millions of the rural population. While the Cultural Revolution, ingrained corruption, and brutal clampdowns on political dissidence in Beijing and Tibet may not be a good track record for the People's Republic, it's also true that only since its birth in 1949 – yesterday in China's immense timescale – has even the possibility of a decent quality of life been imaginable for the ordinary citizen.

Chinese legends hold that the creator, **Pan Ku**, was born from the egg of chaos and grew to fill the space between Yin, the earth, and Yang, the heavens. For eighteen thousand years Pan Ku chiselled the earth to its present state with the aid of a dragon, a unicorn, a phoenix and a tortoise. When he died his body became the soil, rivers, and rain, his eyes the sun and moon, while his parasites transformed into human beings. A pantheon of semi-divine rulers known as the **Five Sovereigns** followed, each reigning for a hundred years or more and inventing fire, the calendar, agriculture, silk-breeding and marriage. Later a famous triumvirate included **Yao the Benevolent** who abdicated in favour of **Shu**. Shu toiled in the sun until his skin turned black and then he abdicated in favour of **Yu the Great**, tamer of floods and said to be the founder of China's first dynasty, the **Xia**. The Xia was reputed to have lasted 439 years until their last degenerate and corrupt king was overthrown by the **Shang** dynasty. The Shang was in turn succeeded by the **Zhou**, who ended this legendary era by leaving court histories behind them. Together, the Xia, Shang and Zhou are generally known as the **Three Dynasties**.

As far as archeology is concerned, **homo erectus** remains from Liaoning, Anhui, Beijing and Yunnan provinces indicate that China was already broadly occupied by human ancestors well before modern mankind began to emerge 200,000 years ago. Excavations of more recent Stone-Age sites show that agricultural communities based around the fertile Yellow River and Yangzi basins, such as **Banpo** in Shaanxi and **Homudu** in Zhejiang, were producing pottery and silk by 5000 BC. It was along the Yellow River, too, that solid evidence of the bronze-working Three Dynasties first came to light, with the discovery of a series of large rammed-earth palaces at **Erlitou** near Luoyang, now believed to have been the Xia capital in 2000 BC.

Little is known about the Xia, though their territory apparently encompassed Shanxi, Henan and Hebei. The events of the subsequent Shang dynasty, however, were first documented just before the time of Christ by the historian **Sima Qian**, and his previously discredited accounts have been supported in recent years by a stream of finds. Based over much the same area as their predecessors and lasting from roughly 1750 BC to 1040 BC, Shang society had a king, a class system and a skilled **bronze technology** which permeated beyond the borders into Sichuan and produced the splendid vessels found in today's museums. Excavations on the site of Yin, the Shang capital, have found tombs stuffed with weapons, jade ornaments, traces of silk and sacrificial victims – indicating belief in **ancestor worship** and an afterlife. The Shang also practised divination by studying the pattern of fire cracks through questions incised on tortoiseshell and bone, surviving examples of which provide China's **earliest written records**, covering topics as diverse as rainfall, dreams and ancestral curses.

Around 1040 BC a northern tribe, the **Zhou**, overthrew the Shang, expanded their kingdom west of the Yellow River into Shaanxi and set up a capital at Xi'an. Adopting many Shang customs, the Zhou also introduced the doctrine of the **Mandate of Heaven**: a belief justifying successful rebellion by declaring that heaven grants ruling authority to leaders who are strong and wise, and takes it from those who aren't – still an integral part of the Chinese political perspective. The Zhou consequently styled themselves "Sons of Heaven" and ruled through a hierarchy of vassal lords, whose growing independence led to the gradual dissolution of the Zhou kingdom from around 600 BC. Driven to a new capital at Luoyang, later Zhou rulers exercised only a symbolic role; real power was fought over by some two hundred city states and kingdoms during the four hundred years known as the **Spring and Autumn** and the **Warring States** periods.

This time of violence was also a time of vitality and change. As the feudal system broke down, traditional religion gave way to new ideas based on the writings of Kong Fuzi, or **Confucius**, and also on Taoism and Legalism (see p.1016). As the warring states rubbed up against each other, agriculture and irrigation, trade, transport and diplomacy were all galvanized; iron was first smelted for weapons and tools, and great discoveries made in medicine, astronomy and mathematics. Three hundred years of war and annexation reduced the competitors to seven states, whose territories, collectively known as Zhong Guo, the **Middle Kingdom**, had now expanded west into

Sichuan, south to Hunan and north to the Mongolian border. The fighting came to an end only in the third century BC with the rise of a new dynasty – the **Qin**.

THE QIN DYNASTY

For five hundred years the state of Qin – originally based on modern Shaanxi – had gradually been gobbling up its neighbours. In 221 BC its armies conquered the last pocket of resistance in the Middle Kingdom, east-coast Qi (Shandong), uniting the Chinese as a single centralized state for the first time, and implementing systems of currency and writing that were to last millennia. The rule of China's first emperor, **Qin Shi Huang**, was absolute: ancient literature and historical records were destroyed to wipe out any ideas that conflicted with his own, and peasants were forced off their land to work as labourers on his massive construction projects, which saw thousands of kilometres of roads, canals and an early version of the **Great Wall**, laid down across the new empire. Burning with ambition to rule the entire known world, Huang's armies gradually pushed beyond the Middle Kingdom, expanding Chinese rule, if not absolute control, west and southeast. But, though he introduced the basis of China's enduring legacy of bureaucratic government, Huang's 37-year reign was ultimately too self-centred – still apparent in the massive tomb (guarded by the famous **Terracotta Army**) he had built for himself at his capital, Xi'an. When he died in 210 BC the provinces rose in revolt, and his heirs soon proved to lack the personal authority which had held his empire together. In 206 BC the rebel warlord **Lui Bang** took Xi'an, and founded the **Han dynasty**.

THE HAN DYNASTY

Lasting some four hundred years and larger at its height than contemporary imperial Rome, the Han was the first great empire, one that experienced a flowering of culture and a major impetus to push out frontiers and open them to trade, people and new ideas. In doing so it defined the national identity to such an extent that the main body of the Chinese people still style themselves "**Han Chinese**" after this dynasty.

Liu Bang maintained the Qin model of local government, but to prevent others from repeating his own military takeover, strengthened his position by handing out large chunks of land to his relatives. This secured a period of stability, with effective taxation financing a growing civil service and the building of a huge and cosmopolitan capital, **Chang'an**, at today's Xi'an. Growing revenue also refuelled the expansionist policies of later ruler **Wu Di**. From 135 to 90 BC he extended his lines of defence well into Xinjiang and Yunnan, opening up the Silk Road for trade in tea, spices and silk with India, west Asia and Rome. He used his sons and competent generals to beat off northern tribes, enter Korea, and to subdue and colonize the unruly southern states, including Guangdong and even parts of Vietnam. At home Wu Di stressed the Confucian model for his growing civil service, beginning a two-thousand-year institution of Confucianism in government offices.

But, eventually, the empire's resources and supply lines were stretched to breaking point, while the burden of taxation led to unrest and retrenchment. Gradually the ruling house became decadent and was weakened by power struggles between rival factions of imperial consorts, eunuchs and statesmen, until **Wang Mang**, regent for a child emperor, usurped the rule to found his own brief dynasty in 9 AD. Fifteen years later the **Eastern Han** was re-established from a new capital at Luoyang, where the classical tradition was re-imposed under Emperor **Liu Xiu**, though after his reign the dynasty was again gradually undermined by factional intrigue. Internal strife was later fomented by the **Yellow Turbans**, who drew their following from Taoist cults, while local governments and landowners began to set up as semi-independent rulers, with the country once again splitting into warring states. But by this time two major schools of philosophy and religion had emerged to survive the ensuing chaos. Confucianism's ideology of a centralized universal order had crystallized imperial authority; and **Buddhism**, introduced into the country from India, began to enrich aspects of life and thought, especially in the fine arts and literature, while itself being absorbed and changed by native beliefs.

CREATIVE CHAOS AND DARK AGES – THE THREE KINGDOMS

Nearly four hundred years separate the collapse of the Han in about 220 AD and the return of unity under the Sui in 589. China was under a single government for only about fifty years of that time, though the idea of a unified empire was never forgotten. This was in some ways a dark age, of war, violence and genocide, but it was also a richly formative one and, when the dust had settled, both culturally and economically a very different society had emerged. For much of this time many areas produced a food surplus which could support a rich and leisured ruling class in the cities and the countryside, as well as large armies and burgeoning Buddhist communities. So culture developed, literature flourished, calligraphy and sculpture, especially Buddhist carvings, all enriched by Indian and central Asian elements, reached unsurpassed levels. This was a rich legacy for the Sui and Tang dynasties which followed to inherit and build on.

From 200 AD the three states of **Wei**, **Wu** and **Shu** struggled for supremacy in a protracted and massively complicated war (later immortalized in the saga *Romance of the Three Kingdoms*) that ruined central China and encouraged mass migrations southwards. The following centuries saw China's regionalism becoming entrenched: the **Southern Empire** suffered weak and short-lived dynasties, but nevertheless there was prosperity and economic growth, with the capital at **Nanjing** becoming a thriving trading and cultural centre. Meanwhile, with the borders unprotected, the north was invaded in 386 by the **Tobas**, who established the northern **Wei dynasty** after their aristocracy adopted Chinese manners and customs – a pattern of assimilation that would recur with other invaders. At their first capital, **Datong**, they created a wonderful series of Buddhist carvings, but in 534 their empire fell apart. After grabbing power from his regent in 581, general **Yang Jian** unified the fragmented northern states and then went on to conquer southern China by land and sea, founding the **Sui dynasty**.

THE SUI

The **Sui** get short shrift in historical surveys. Their brief empire was soon eclipsed by their successors, the Tang, but until the dynasty overreached itself on the military front in Korea and burnt out, two of its three emperors could claim considerable achievements. Until his death in 604 Yang Jian himself – Emperor **Wen Di** – was an active ruler who took the best from the past and built on it. He simplified and strengthened the bureaucracy, bought in a new legal code, recentralized civil and military authority and made tax collection more efficient. Near Xi'an his architects designed a new capital, **Da Xing Cheng** (Great Prosperity), with a palace city, a residential quarter of 108 walled compounds, several vast markets and an outer wall over 35km round – quite probably the largest city in the world at that time. After Wen Di's death in 604, **Yang Di** elbowed his elder brother out to become emperor. Yang improved administration, encouraged a revival of Confucian learning and promoted a strong foreign policy. But his engineering works – or rather the forced labour needed to complete them – have left him portrayed as a proverbially "Evil Emperor", principally for ordering the construction of the two-thousand-kilometre **Grand Canal** to transport produce between the rice bowl of the southern Yangzi to his capital at Xi'an. Half the total work force of 5,500,000 died, and Yang Di was assassinated in 618 after popular hatred had inspired a military revolt led by General **Li Yuan**.

MEDIEVAL CHINA: FROM TANG TO SONG

The seventh century marks the beginning of the medieval period of Chinese history. This was the age in which Chinese culture reached its most cosmopolitan and sophisticated peak, a time of experimentation in literature, art, music and agriculture, and one which unified seemingly incompatible elements.

Having changed his name to **Gao Zu**, Li Yuan consolidated his new **Tang dynasty** by spending the rest of his eight-year reign getting rid of all his rivals. Under his son **Tai Zong**, Tang China expanded: the Turks were crushed, the **Tibetans** brought to heel and relations established with Byzantium. China kept open house for traders and travellers of all races and creeds, who settled in the mercantile cities of Yangzhou and Guangzhou, bringing with them their religions, especially **Islam**, and influencing the arts, cookery, fashion and entertainment. China's goods flowed out to India, Persia, the Near East and many other countries, and her language and religion were adopted by Japan and Korea. At home, **Buddhism** remained the all-pervading foreign influence, with Chinese pilgrims travelling widely in India. The best known of these, **Xuan Zang**, was sent off by the emperor in 629 and returned

after sixteen years in India with a mass of Buddhist sutras, adding greatly to China's storehouse of knowledge.

Xi'an's population swelled to over a million and it became one of the world's great cultural centres, heart of a highly centralized and powerful state. A decade after Tai Zong's death in 649, his short-lived son **Gao Zong** and China's only empress, **Wu Chao**, had expanded the Tang empire's direct influence from Korea to Iran, and south into Vietnam. At home, Wu Chao was a great patron of Buddhism, commissioning the famous Longmen carvings outside Luoyang, and she created a civil service selected on merit rather than birth. Her cultured successor, **Xuan Zong**, began well in 712, but his later infatuation with the beautiful concubine **Yang Guifei** led to the collapse of his rule in 756, his flight to Sichuan and Yang's ignominious death at the hands of his mutineering army. Xuan Zong's son, **Su Zong**, enlisted the help of Tibetan and Uigur forces and recaptured Xi'an from the rebels; but though the court was re-established, it had lost its authority, and real power was once again shifting to the provinces.

The following two hundred years saw the country split into regional political and military alliances. From 907 to 960 **Five Dynasties** succeeded each other, all too short-lived to be effective, with the record for brevity going to the Han – a mere seven years. China's northern defences were permanently weakened, while her economic dependence on the south increased and the dispersal of power brought sweeping social changes. The traditional elite whose fortunes were tied to the dynasty gave way to a military and merchant class who bought land to acquire status, plus a professional ruling class selected by examination. In the south the **Ten Kingdoms** (some existing side by side) managed to retain what was left of the Tang civilization, their greater stability and economic prosperity sustaining a relatively high cultural level.

Finally, in 960, a disaffected army in the north put a successful general, **Song Tai Zu**, on the throne. His new ruling house, known as the **Northern Song**, made its capital at **Kaifeng** in the Yellow River basin, well-placed at the head of the Grand Canal for transport to supply its million people with grain from the south. By skilled politicking rather than military might the new dynasty consolidated its authority over surrounding petty kingdoms and re-established civilian primacy. But in 1115, northern China was occupied by the **Jin**, who pushed the imperial court south to **Hangzhou** where, guarded by the Yangzi River, their culture continued to flourish from 1126 as the **Southern Song**. Developments during their 150-year dynasty included gunpowder, the magnetic compass, fine porcelain and moveable type printing. But the Song preoccupation with art and sophistication saw their military might decline and possibly led to them underrating their agressive "barbarian" neighbours, whose own expansionist policies culminated in the thirteenth-century **Mongol Invasion**.

THE YUAN DYNASTY

In fact, Mongolian rule had first penetrated China in the eleventh century, when the Song emperors basically paid tribute to separate Mongolian states to keep their armies from invading. But these individual fiefdoms were unified by **Genghis Khan** in 1206 to form an immensely powerful army, which swiftly began the conquest of northern China. Despite Chinese resistance and dilatory Mongol infighting, by 1278 the **Yuan dynasty** was on the Chinese throne, with **Kublai Khan**, Genghis Khan's grandson, at the head of an empire that stretched way beyond China's borders. From their capital at Khanbalik (modern **Beijing**), the Yuan's emperors' central control boosted China's economy and helped repair five centuries of civil war. The country was also thrown wide open to foreign travellers, traders and missionaries; Arab and Venetians were to be found in many Chinese ports, and a Russian came top of the Imperial Civil Service exam of 1341. The Grand Canal was extended from Beijing to Hangzhou, while in Beijing the **Palace of All Tranquillities** was built inside a new city wall, later known as the **Forbidden City**. Descriptions of much of this were brought back to Europe by **Marco Polo**, who put his impressions of Yuan lifestyle and treasures on paper after living in Beijing for seventeen years and serving in the government of Kublai Khan.

The Yuan retained control over all China only until 1368; although they adopted some Chinese institutions and employed Chinese interpreters and officials as part of their administration, their discriminatory caste system and harsh penal code kept the Chinese well below the Mongols and their allies in the pecking order, and made alien rule deeply unpopular. Ultimately, it was this refusal to assimilate Chinese culture that brought about the Mongols' downfall. Remaining aloof from the general population made them obvious targets for dissent, and after famine and disastrous floods brought a series of rebellions, a monk-turned-bandit leader from the south, **Zhu Yuanzhang**, seized the throne from the last boy emperor of the Yuan in 1368.

THE MING DYNASTY

Zhu Yuanzhang took the name **Hong Wu** and proclaimed himself first emperor of the **Ming dynasty**, with Nanjing as his capital. Zhu's influences on China's history were far-reaching. Aside from his extreme despotism, which saw two appalling purges in which thousands of civil servants and literati died, he also initiated a course of **isolationism** from the outside world which lasted throughout the Ming and Qing eras. Consequently, Chinese culture became inward-looking, and the benefits of trade and connections with foreign powers were lost. Nowhere is this more apparent than in the Ming construction of the current Great Wall, a grandiose but futile attempt to stem the invasion of northern tribes into China, built once military might and diplomacy began to break down in the fifteenth century.

Yet the period also produced fine artistic accomplishments, particularly **porcelain** from the imperial kilns at Jingdezhen, which became famous worldwide. Nor were the Ming rulers entirely isolationist. During the reign of **Yongle**, Zhu's 26th son, the imperial navy (commanded by the Muslim eunuch, Admiral **Zheng He**) ranged right across the Indian Ocean as far as the east coast of Africa on a fact-finding mission. But stagnation set in after Yongle's death in 1424, and the maritime missions were cancelled as being incompatible with Confucian values, which held a strong contempt for foreigners. Thus initiative for world trade and explorations passed into the hands of the Europeans, with the great period of world voyages by Columbus, Magellan and Vasco da Gama. In 1514, **Portuguese** vessels appeared in the Pearl River at the southern port of Guangzhou (Canton), and though they were swiftly expelled from here, Portugal was allowed to colonize nearby **Macao** in 1557.

Though all dealings with foreigners were officially despised by the imperial court, trade flourished, as Chinese merchants and officials were eager to milk the profit from it.

In later years, the Ming produced a succession of less able rulers who allowed power to slip into the hands of the seventy thousand inner court officials where it was used, not to run the empire, but for intriguing amongst the "eunuch bureaucracy". By the early seventeenth century, frontier defences had fallen into decay, and the **Manchu tribes** in the north were already across the Great Wall. A series of peasant and military uprisings against the Ming began in 1627, and when the rebel **Li Zicheng**'s forces managed to break into the capital in 1644, the last Ming emperor fled from his palace and hanged himself – an ignoble end to a three-hundred-year-old dynasty.

1644 TO 1911: THE QING DYNASTY, WAR AND REBELLION

The Manchus weren't slow in turning internal dissent to their advantage. Sweeping down on Beijing, they threw out Li Zicheng's army, claimed the capital as their own and founded the **Qing dynasty**. It took a further twenty years for the Manchus to capture the south of the country, but on its capitulation China was once again under foreign rule. Like the Mongol Yuan dynasty before them, the Qing initially did little to assimilate domestic culture, ruling the people as separate overlords. Manchu became the official language, the Chinese were obliged to wear the Manchu **pigtail** and intermarriage between a Manchu and a Chinese was strictly forbidden. Under the Qing dynasty the distant areas of Inner and Outer Mongolia, Tibet and Turkestan were fully incorporated into the Chinese empire, uniting the Chinese world to a greater extent than during the Tang period.

Soon, however, the Manchus proved themselves susceptible to Chinese culture, and ultimately became deeply influenced by it. Three outstanding Qing emperors also brought an infusion of new blood and vigour to government early on in the dynasty. **Kangxi**, who began his 61-year reign in 1654 at the age of six, was a great patron of the arts, leaving endless scrolls of famous calligraphy and paintings blotted with his seals stating that he had seen them. He assiduously cultivated his image as the Son of Heaven by making royal progresses throughout the country and by his personal style of leadership. He did much to bring the south under control and by 1683 the southern **Rebellion of Three Federations** (military governors) had been savagely put down. His fourth son, the Emperor **Yungzheng** (1678–1735), ruled over what is considered one of the most efficient and least corrupt administrations ever enjoyed by China. This was inherited by **Jian Long** (1711–99) whose reign saw China's frontiers widely extended and the economy stimulated by peace and prosperity. In 1750 the nation was perhaps at its apex, one of the strongest, wealthiest and most powerful countries in the world.

But during the latter half of the eighteenth century, China began to experience growing economic problems. Settled society had produced a **population explosion**, pressing on food resources and causing a land shortage. This in turn saw trouble flaring as migrants from central China tried to settle the country's remoter western provinces, dispossessing the original inhabitants. Meanwhile, expanding European nations were in Asia, looking for financial opportunities. From about 1660, Portuguese traders in Guangzhou had been joined by British merchants shopping for tea, silk and porcelain, and during the eighteenth century the British **East India Company** moved in, eager for a monopoly. But China's rulers, immensely rich and powerful and convinced of their own superiority as they were, had no wish for direct dealings with foreigners. When **Lord Macartney** arrived in 1793 bearing the usual gifts in order to propose a political and trade treaty between King George III and the emperor, he refused to kowtow in submission and his embassy was unsuccessful. The king's "tribute" was accepted but the emperor totally rejected any idea of alliance with one who, according to Chinese ideas, was a subordinate in any case. Macartney was impressed by the vast wealth and power of the Chinese court, but later wrote perceptively that the empire was "like an old crazy first-rate man of war which its officers have contrived to keep afloat to terrify by its appearance and bulk".

THE OPIUM WARS AND THE TAIPING UPRISING

Foiled in their attempts at official negotiations with the Qing court, the East India Company decided to take matters into their own hands and create a clandestine market in China for Western goods. Instead of silver, they began to pay for tea and silk with **opium**, cheaply imported from India. As addicts and demand escalated during the early nineteenth century, China's trade surplus became a deficit, as silver drained out of the country to pay for the drug. The emperor pronounced an ineffectual edict strictly forbidding the trade, then, when this was ignored, suspended the traffic in 1840 by ordering the confiscation and destruction of over twenty thousand chests of opium – the start of the first **Opium War**. After two years of British gunboats shelling coastal ports, the Chinese were forced to sign the **Treaty of Nanjing**, whose humiliating terms included a huge indemnity, the opening up of new ports to foreign trade, and the **cession of Hong Kong**. This was the first in a long series of concessions extracted by Britain and other nations under various **unequal treaties**.

It was a crushing blow for the Chinese, who failed to understand the superiority which alien techniques and organization had secured the Europeans. Furthermore, the country was now confronted with a series of major internal **rebellions** inspired by anti-Manchu feeling and economic hardship – themselves fuelled by rising taxes to pay off China's war indemnity. While serious uprisings occurred in Guizhou and Yunnan, the most widespread was started by the southern Chinese Christian fanatic **Hong Xiuquan**, who, backed by his million strong **Taiping army**, stormed through central China in the 1850s to occupy much of the rich Yangzi Valley. Having captured Nanjing as his "Heavenly Capital", however, Hong's reign was badly weakened by internal dissent; and as the Taipings began to make military forays towards Beijing, the European powers decided to step in, worried that Hong's anti-foreign government might take control of the country. With their support, Qing troops forced the Taipings back to their capital in 1864 and butchered them. Hong Xiuquan committed suicide and the Taiping Uprising was at an end, leaving twenty million people dead and five provinces in ruins.

It was during the uprising that the **Empress Dowager Wu Cixi** first took over the reins of power in China, ruling from behind various emperors from 1861 until 1908. Ignorant, vain and certain that reform would weaken the Qings' grasp of power, she maintained a deep conservatism at a time when China desperately needed to overhaul its antiquated political and economic structure. On the **home front**, profitable mines and industries almost exclusively became owned by foreigners, who channelled their wealth out of the country, and increased Christian missionary activity undermined the traditional concepts on which Chinese society was based. In response, radical advisers persuaded Emperor Guangxu to instigate the **Hundred Days Reform** of 1898, an attempt to modernize agriculture, industry and government institutions. But it was crushed by opposition from the Confucian establishment, backed by Cixi, who imprisoned Guangxu, executed the advisers of reform and repealed their measures.

During this period, China's **colonial empire** was fast disintegrating. France took the former vassal states of Laos, Cambodia and Vietnam in 1883–5; Britain gained Burma; and **Tibet**, which had nominally been under China's control since Tang times, began to assert its independence in direct territorial negotiations with Britain. But perhaps most importantly, in 1894 China sent two thousand troops to support the king of **Korea** when a rebellion broke out. In reply, **Japan** dispatched ten thousand to keep the rebellion going, and within a few months Chinese and Korean forces were beaten. Under the treaty that followed, China was forced to cede the island of **Taiwan**, the Pescadores and the Liaodong Peninsula to Japan. This didn't go down well on the international scene. France, Germany and Russia, fearful of Japan's snowballing power, forced the country to return the Liaodong Peninsula to China. By way of reward the Chinese allowed Russia to build a rail line through Manchuria to their port at Lushun. With the ability to move troops quickly along this line, Russia effectively controlled Manchuria for the next ten years.

THE BOXER REBELLION – THE END OF IMPERIAL CHINA

By the 1890s the whole of China was in chaos. For fifty years, the Qing rulers had done little or nothing to help the common people, spent fortunes on ruinous wars, allowed foreigners to take control of business, and stood idle while the countryside was ravaged by civil strife. A popular organization was all that was needed to realize the support of the peasants, and it came with the **Boxers**, more fully known as the

"Society of Righteous and Harmonious Fists", claiming invulnerability to bullets for all who followed their mystical faith. Their stated aims – "Overthrow the Qing, destroy the foreigner" – were understandably close to the peasants' hearts. After an initial defeat at the hands of her troops in 1899, Cixi's government decided that the Boxer army might in fact make a useful tool, and set them loose to slaughter missionaries, Christian converts and any other foreigner they could lay their hands on. By the summer of 1900 the government had made a wild declaration of war on all foreign powers on its lands, and the Boxers were in Beijing besieging the foreign legation compound. The German and Japanese ministers were murdered, but the British and others managed to hold out until an international relief force arrived on August 14. In the massacre, looting and confusion which followed, during which the Boxers were totally routed, Cixi and the emperor disguised themselves as peasants and fled to Xi'an in a cart, leaving her ministers to negotiate a peace.

Though they feebly clung on for another decade, this was the end of the Qing. As foreign powers took great bites out of the nation's borders, internal movements to dismantle the dynastic system and build a new China proliferated. The most influential of these was the **Tong Meng Hui** society, founded in 1905 in Japan by the exile **Sun Yatsen**, a doctor from a wealthy Guangdong family. Cixi died three years later, and, in 1911, opposition to railway construction by foreigners drew events to a head in Wuchang, Hubei Province, igniting a popular uprising which finally toppled the dynasty. Two thousand years of dynastic succession ended almost quietly, and Sun Yatsen returned to China to take the lead in the provisional **Republican Government** at Nanjing.

FROM REPUBLIC TO COMMUNISM: 1911–1949

Almost immediately the new republic was in trouble. Though a **parliament** was duly elected in 1913, it lacked any real political or military force; in addition, northern China was controlled by the former leader of the Imperial Army, **Yuan Shikai** (who had forced the abdication of the last emperor, **Pu Yi**). Sun Yatsen, faced with a choice between probable civil war and relinquishing his presidency at the head of the newly formed Nationalist People's Party, the **Guomindang**, stepped down. Yuan promptly dismissed the government, forced Sun into renewed exile, and attempted to centralize power – clearly with a view to establishing a new dynasty. But his plans were stalled by his generals, who wanted private fiefdoms of their own, and Yuan's sudden death in 1916 marked the last time in 34 years that China would be united under a single authority. While bickering between Yuan's generals plunged the north into civil war, Sun Yatsen returned yet again, this time to found a southern Guomindang government.

Thus divided, China was unable to stem the increasingly bold territorial incursions made by Japan and other colonial powers as a result of **World War I**. Siding with the Allies, Japan had claimed the German port of Qingdao and all German shipping and industry in the Shangdong Peninsula on the outbreak of war, and in 1915 presented China with **Twenty-One Demands**, many of which Yuan Shikai, under threat of a Japanese invasion, was forced to accept. After the war, hopes that the 1919 **Treaty of Versailles** would end Japanese aggression (as well as the unequal treaties and foreign concessions) were dashed when the Western powers, who had already signed secret pacts with Japan, confirmed Japan's rights in China. This was the last straw. Popular feeling broke out with the **May 4 Movement**, the first in a series of anti-foreign demonstrations and riots over the next few years that had to be broken up by the police.

THE RISE OF THE CHINESE COMMUNIST PARTY

As a reflection of these events, the **Chinese Communist Party** (CCP) formed in Shanghai in 1921, its leadership drawn from two groups who had been active for several years. The first centred around **Li Dazhao**, former librarian at Beijing university, along with the young **Mao Zedong** and **Zhang Gutao**, both students. The second was headed by **Zhou Enlai**, who had organized a Marxist study group in Tianjin. The party was guided by Russian advisers, whose instructions, besides concentrating on the Russian example of an urban proletarian revolution – of dubious value given China's largely rural population – invariably included a measure of Soviet foreign policy. When Moscow asked the CCP to support the Guomindang in its military campaigns against the northern warlords, the reality was that Soviet fear of Japan attacking their eastern lands required a strong China, and they considered the Guomindang the most likely party to achieve this.

While the CCP duly joined the Guomindang, they made unlikely bedfellows, especially after Sun Yatsen died in 1925. He was succeeded by his brother-in-law and military chief **Chiang Kaishek**, an extreme nationalist who had no time for the CCP or its plans to end China's class divisions. Under his leadership, the combined Communist and Guomindang forces, as the National Revolutionary Army (NRA), successfully crushed the rogue warlords on the **Northern Expedition**, but then refused to join Chiang in his new headquarters in Nanchang. Moving on to capture Shanghai on March 21, 1927, Communist elements in the NRA organized a general strike against Chiang, seizing the military arsenal and arming workers. But industry bosses and foreign owners quickly retaliated, financing Chiang to disguise hundreds of thugs as members of the NRA, who then turned on the workers' militia and massacred the Communists, along with anyone else Chiang had decided to eradicate. Around five thousand were murdered; Zhou Enlai escaped only by luck, and Li Dazhao was executed by slow strangulation.

With the army now on his side and much of the original Communist hierarchy summarily executed (including Mao's second wife **Yang Kaihui**), Chiang quickly achieved supremacy and was declared head of a national government in 1928. Under him, the Guomindang became a ruthless military dictatorship, ignoring the wretched state of the people and Japanese encroachments on China's sovereignty in order to subdue all internal opposition by brute force. In this Chiang was aided substantially by Western powers – including the Soviet Union, who never let up on the line that the Communists should maintain their alliance with the GMD. Chiang's domestic power base, however, was small, and, despite attempts at limited social reform, the Party quickly came to represent the interests of a social elite. Those Communists who had escaped Chiang's purges regrouped in remote areas across the country, principally at **Jinggang Shan** in Jiangxi Province, under the leadership of Mao Zedong.

MAO ZEDONG, THE RED ARMY AND THE LONG MARCH

Son of a well-off Hunanese farmer, **Mao** believed social reform lay in the hands of the peasants, a belief hardened by his time as a teacher at the Peasant Training Institute in Guangzhou during the early 1920s. Despite the overthrow of the emperors, peasants still had few rights and no power base. Chronic poverty was rife, caused by oppressive taxation by landlords supported by corrupt government officials, and dissent was crushed by the landlords' private armies. Drawing from Marx's analyses, Mao recognized the parallels between nineteenth-century Europe and twentieth-century China – and that a mass armed rising was the only way the old order could be replaced.

After events in Shanghai, Mao organized the first peasant-worker army in Changsha, in what was later to be called the **Autumn Harvest Uprising**. Moving southeast to the Hunan–Jiangxi border, his troops settled into Jinggang Shan, where they were met by the forces of **Zhu De**, a Guomindang commander from Nanchang who had joined the Communists. Using guerrilla tactics, their combined **Red Army** of peasants, miners and Guomindang deserters achieved unexpected successes against the Nationalist troops sent against them during the early 1930s, until **Li Lisan**, the Communist leader, ordered Mao out of his mountain base to attack the cities. The ensuing open assaults against the vastly superior Guomindang forces were disastrous, and Chiang Kaishek, following up these defeats, mobilized half a million troops and encircled Jinggang Shan with a ring of concrete blockhouses and barbed-wire entanglements.

Forced between choosing to fight or flee, Mao organized 100,000 men, women and children in an epic retreat which became known as the **Long March**: a 9500-kilometre trek on foot across eighteen mountain ranges (five of them snow-capped), 24 rivers and twelve provinces. Starting in October 1934, the journey took a year, with over sixty thousand perishing of cold, hunger or in the innumerable battles that were fought with GMD factions. But by the time they reached safety in **Yan'an** in Shaanxi Province, the Communists had turned a humiliating defeat into an advance towards victory. Along the way, Mao had become undisputed leader of the CCP at the **Zunyi Conference**, severing the Party from its Russian advisers, while thousands of Chinese who had never heard of communism were made aware of their struggles and beliefs. And, despite the death toll, the Long March won the Communists immense respect – an army determined enough to do this could do anything.

JAPANESE INVASION AND THE UNITED FRONT

Meanwhile, Japan had taken over Chinese Manchuria in 1933 and installed Pu Yi (last emperor of the Qing dynasty) as puppet leader. They were obviously preparing to invade eastern China, and Mao wrote to Chiang Kaishek (and to the warlords, bandit leaders and secret societies) advocating an end to civil war and a **United Front** against the threat. Chiang's response was to move his Manchurian armies, under **Zhang Xueliang**, down to finish off the Reds in Shaanxi. Zhang, however, saw an alliance as the only way to evict the Japanese from his homeland, and so secretly entered into an agreement with the Communist forces. On December 12, 1936, Chiang was kidnapped by his own troops in what became known as the **Xi'an Incident** and, with Zhou Enlai as a mediator, reluctantly signed an agreement to the United Front on Christmas Day. Briefly, the parties were united, though both sides knew that the alliance would last only as long as the Japanese threat.

Full-scale war broke out in July 1937 when the Japanese attacked Beijing. The GMD, inadequately armed or trained, were rapidly forced west and south, and at the end of the year the Japanese had taken most of eastern China between Beijing and Guangzhou. With a capital-in-occupation at Nanjing, the Japanese concentrated their efforts on routing the GMD, leaving a vacuum in the north that the Communists quickly filled, establishing what amounted to stable government of a hundred million people across the North China Plain.

The outbreak of war in Europe in September 1939 soon had repercussions in China. Nazi Germany stopped supplying the weaponry the GMD relied on, while with the bombing of Pearl Harbour two years later all military aid from the United States to Japan ceased. With the country's heavy industry in Japanese hands, China's United Front government, having withdrawn to **Chongqing** in Sichuan Province, became dependent on the Americans and British flying in supplies over the Himalayas. But Chiang's true allegiances were never far below the surface, and he failed to distribute the arms among the Red Army, and by 1941 was already ordering his troops to attack Communist forces. The United Front collapsed.

THE END OF THE WAR... AND THE GUOMINDANG

By the time the two atom bombs ended the Japanese empire and World War II in 1945, the Red Army was close on a million strong, with a widespread following throughout the country; Communism in China was established. It wasn't, however, that secure. Predictably, the US sided with Chiang Kaishek and the GMD but, surprisingly, so did the Soviet Union – Stalin believed that with American aid, the GMD would easily destroy the CCP. All the same, **peace negotiations** between the Nationalist and Communist sides were brokered by the US in Chongqing, where Chiang refused to admit the CCP into government, knowing that its policies were uncontrollable while the Red Army still existed. For their part, it was evident to the CCP that without an army, they were nothing. The talks ended in stalemate.

Ironically, it was United States military aid that decided matters in the Communists' favour, when US equipment was captured en masse from GMD troops, providing the Communists with the firepower to continue and build on its victories. Buoyed by a popular support heightened by Chiang's mishandling of the economy, in 1948 the Communists' newly named **People's Liberation Army** (PLA) began a final assault on the GMD, decisively trouncing them that winter at the massive battle of **Huai Hai** in Anhui Province. Demoralized, the Guomindang troops lost the will to fight, and with Shanghai about to fall before the PLA in early 1949, Chiang Kaishek packed the country's entire gold reserves into a plane and took off for **Taiwan** to form the **Republic of China**. Here he would remain until his death in 1975, forlornly waiting to liberate the mainland with the two million troops and refugees who later joined him. Mopping-up operations against mainland pockets of GMD resistance would continue for several years, but in October 1949 Mao was able to proclaim the formation of the **People's Republic of China** in Beijing. The world's most populous nation was now Communist.

THE PEOPLE'S REPUBLIC UNDER MAO: 1949–1976

With the country laid waste by over a century of economical mismanagement and war, massive problems faced the new republic. Though Russia quickly offered its support, the US refused to recognize Mao's government, maintaining that Chiang Kaishek and the Guomindang alone represented the Chinese people. China's road and rail network were mostly destroyed, industrial output had slumped, much of the agricultural areas had been ravaged, and there were no monetary reserves. But the Chinese people, still in awe of their hard-won victory, took to the task of repairing the country with an obsessive energy. By the mid-1950s all industry had been nationalized and output was back at prewar levels, while, for the first time in China's history, land was handed over to the peasants as their own. A million former landlords were executed, while others were enrolled in "**criticism and self-criticism**" classes, a re-education designed to ingrain Marxism and prevent ideologies of elitism or bourgeois deviance from contaminating the revolutionary spirit. People were encouraged to criticize themselves, their past and those around them – for some a traumatic experience and one that broke centuries-old traditions.

With all the difficulties on the home front, the **Korean War** of 1950 was a distraction the government could well have done without. The US had pushed into North Korea and, despite vigorous warnings from Zhou Enlai, had continued through to Chinese territory in what many felt was to be a replay of Japan's invasion. China's hand was forced and, in June, war was declared. Half a million troops steamrollered the Americans back to the 38th parallel and, after much loss of life, forced peace negotiations. As a boost for the morale of the new nation, the incident could not have been better timed. Meanwhile, China's far western borders were seen to be threatened by an uprising in **Tibet**, and Chinese troops were sent in 1951, swiftly occupying the entire country and instituting de facto Chinese rule. Eight years later, a failed coup against the occupation by Tibetan monks saw a massive clampdown on religion, and the flight of the **Dalai Lama** and his followers to Nepal.

THE HUNDRED FLOWERS AND THE GREAT LEAP FORWARD

By 1956 China's economy was healthy, if not burgeoning, but there were signs that the initial euphoria driving the country was slowing. Mao – whose principles held that constant struggle was part of existence, and thus acceptance of the status quo was in itself a bad thing – felt that both government and industry needed to be prodded back into gear. To this end, in 1957 he decided to loosen the restrictions on public expression, in the hope that open criticism would shake up the more complacent bureaucrats and Party officials. Following the slogan "Let a hundred flowers bloom, and a hundred schools of thought contend", intellectuals were encouraged to voice their thoughts and complaints. But the plan backfired badly: instead of picking on inefficient officials as Mao had hoped, the **Hundred Flowers** campaign resulted in blistering attacks on the very Communist system itself. As Mao was never one to take personal criticsm lightly, those who had spoken out swiftly found themselves victims of an **anti-rightist** campaign, confined to jail or undergoing a heavy bout of self-criticism. From this point on, intellectuals as a group – especially those who were involved in running the economy – were mistrusted and constantly scrutinized.

Agriculture and industry were next to receive a shake-up. In August 1958 it was announced that all land held privately by peasant farmers was to be pooled into collective farms, linked together as self-governing **communes**. Five hundred million peasants were to be spread over 24,000 communes, with the aim of turning small-scale farming units into hyper-efficient agricultural areas. Industry was to be fired into activity by the co-option of seasonally employed workers, who would construct heavy industrial plants, dig canals and drain marshes. Propaganda campaigns promised eternal well-being in return for initial hard work and austerity; in one **Great Leap Forward** China would match British industrial output in ten years, and overtake American in fifteen to twenty years. But, from the outset, the Great Leap Forward was a disaster. Having been given their land (and in many cases fought for it) the peasants now found themselves losing it once more, and eagerness to work in huge units was low. Combined with ill-trained commune management, there was an almost immediate slump in agricultural and industrial production. Required to satisfy a stream of ridiculous quotas supplied by Beijing – one campaign required the eradication of all agricultural pests, another that all communes must produce certain quantities of steel, regardless of the availability of raw materials – nobody had time to tend the fields. The 1959 and 1960 harvests both failed and millions starved. As if this wasn't enough, a thaw in US-USSR relations in 1960 saw the Soviet Union stopping all aid to China.

With the economy in tatters, the commune policy was watered down, each peasant given a private house and his own land, and by the mid-1960s the country was back on its feet. Politically, though, the incident had ruined Mao's reputation, and set some members of the Communist Party Central Committee against his policies. The two most outspoken members were **Liu Shaoqi** as Chief of State, and the General Secretary of the Communist Party, **Deng Xiaoping**, who had diffused the effects of commune policy by creating a limited free-market economy among the country's traders. Behind them and their doctrine of material incentives for workers was a large bureaucracy over which Mao held little political sway. Liu and Deng also supported the Minister of Defence, **Peng Dehuai**, in what Mao considered a treasonous move to secure technological and military aid from the Soviet Union, and to free the army from non-military work – a move popular with sections of the army.

THE CULTURAL REVOLUTION

With his policies discredited and feeling that he was losing control of the Party, Mao sought to regain his authority. His most influential supporter was **Lin Biao**, Defence Minister and Vice-Chairman of the Communist Party, who in 1964 formed the **Socialist Education Movement** to destroy the "spontaneous desire to become capitalists" among the peasants. Mao himself widened the movement's aims to include the whole bureaucracy that Liu Shaoqi had founded and, with Lin Biao's help, began orchestrating the youth of China in a campaign against his moderate opponents. Initially this **Great Proletarian Cultural Revolution** seemed a straightforward re-run of the anti-rightist campaign following the Hundred

Flowers fiasco. But in 1966 a student put up a poster at Beijing university, denouncing university administration and supporting the Revolution. Under Mao's guidance Beijing's students organized themselves into a political militia – the **Red Guard**. Within weeks Mao had arranged their removal out of the university and on to the streets.

The enemies of the Red Guard were the **Four Olds**: old ideas, old culture, old customs and old habits. Brandishing copies of the "Quotations of Chairman Mao Zedong" (the famous **Little Red Book**), the Red Guard attacked anything redolent of capitalism, the West or the Soviet Union. Academics were humiliated and assaulted, books were burned, temples and ancient monuments desecrated. Shops selling anything remotely Western were destroyed along with the gardens of the "decadent bourgeoisie". As under the commune system, quotas were set, this time for unearthing and turning in the "Rightists", "Revisionists" and "Capitalist Roaders" corrupting Communist society. Officials who failed to fill their quotas were likely to become the next victims, as were those who failed to destroy property or denounce others enthusiastically enough. With the police and army forbidden to intervene, offenders were paraded through the streets wearing placards carrying humiliating slogans; tens of thousands were ostracized, imprisoned, beaten to death or driven to suicide – and, in one horrendous episode, eaten (see p.680). On August 5 ,1966, Mao proclaimed that reactionaries had reached the highest levels of the CCP. His targets were obvious: Liu Shaoqi was thrown in prison and died there of ill-treatment in 1969; Deng Xiaoping was dismissed from his post and condemned to wait on tables at a Party canteen and turn a lathe at a provincial tractor plant. Peng Dehuai, having been dismissed from his post at the very start of the Cultural Revolution, disappeared, and many other senior officials and army officers were demoted.

Aside from the domestic repercussions, China's standing in the international community sunk to an all-time low during the Cultural Revolution after the Red Guard assaulted members of the British Embassy. As foreign ambassadors were recalled, it was clear that the violence was getting completely out of control, with rival Red Guard factions turning on each other. In August 1967 Mao intervened, ordering the arrest of the most fanatical Red Guard leaders and instructing the surrender of all weapons to the army, but found that the Guard's activities were not easily stopped. After nationwide street fighting broke out in the following spring, order was forcibly restored only when tanks entered the cities and the army stormed the Guard's university strongholds. To clear them out of the way, millions of former Red Guards were rounded up and shipped off into the countryside, ostensibly to reinforce the Communist message amongst the rural community.

THE AFTERMATH: THE FALL OF LIN BIAO

One effect of the Cultural Revolution was the rise of a **personality cult** surrounding Mao Zedong, more a fatalistic acknowledgement of his absolute power over China than a popular seal of approval for his inhuman domestic policies. His very image attained quasi-religious status – in one incident, a soldier spotted a school on fire: his first thought was to save the portrait of Mao in the classrooms and only then start to save those trapped inside. More importantly, the late 1960s also saw Lin Biao, Mao's closest ally during the Cultural Revolution, rise to prominence as Mao's designated successor. But as the chaos of the revolution subsided, the role of the army and Lin, as its chief, were less crucial, and Lin began to feel his power base eroded.

What happened next is conjecture, but Lin may have attempted some form of a **coup** against Mao and organized an assassination attempt. In 1972 it was announced that he had died the previous year when a plane carrying him and his followers had crashed en route to the Soviet Union. The story is plausible but probably fictional; Lin might well have been executed and the tale concocted to underline his treason. What is certain is that with Lin's removal and the uncovering of a plot, Mao needed to broaden his base of support, which he did by rehabilitating some of those who had fallen from grace during the Cultural Revolution. With help from Zhou Enlai, Mao's deputy, **Deng Xiaoping** returned, and as Mao declined in health (he was 80 in 1973), Deng took control of the the day-to-day running of the Communist Party Central Committee.

PING-PONG DIPLOMACY AND THE RISE OF THE RADICALS

The US had continued to support Chiang Kaishek's Guomindang in the postwar period for a straightforward reason. US foreign policy was determined by business and political interests that stood to gain from the collapse of Communism, and so whatever possible was done to stir up paranoia over the chance of a Sino-Soviet pact, despite the split between Khrushchev and Mao in 1960. But in 1964 China exploded its first **atomic bomb**, taking it into the league of nuclear powers not automatically friendly to Washington, and the US began to tread a more pragmatic path. In 1970, envoy Henry Kissinger opened communications between the two countries, cultural and sporting links were formed (a tactic that became known as **ping-pong diplomacy**), and in 1971 the People's Republic became the official representative of the nation called China, invalidating Chiang Kaishek's claims. The following year US President **Richard Nixon** was walking on the Great Wall and holding talks with Mao, trade restrictions were lifted and China began commerce with the West. The "bamboo curtain" had parted, isolationism was over and the damage caused by the Cultural Revolution was slowly being repaired.

This new attitude of realistic reform derived from the moderate wing of the Communist Party, headed by Premier Zhou Enlai and his protégé Deng Xiaoping. Seen as a voice of reason, Zhou's tact had given him a charmed political existence which for fifty years kept him at Mao's side despite policy disagreements – several holy sites such as the carved grottoes at Dazu in Sichuan were apparently saved from the Red Guards at Zhou's direct order. But with Zhou's death early in 1976, the reform movement immediately succumbed to the **Gang of Four**, who, led by Mao's third wife **Jiang Qing**, had become the radical mouthpiece of an increasingly absent Mao. In early April the Chinese commemorate their dead at the **Qing Ming** festival, and the Heroes Monument in Beijing's Tian'anmen Square was filled with wreaths in memory of Zhou. On April 5 radicals removed the wreaths and moderate supporters flooded into the square in protest; a riot broke out and hundreds were attacked and arrested. The obvious scapegoat for what became known as the **Tian'anmen Incident** was Deng Xiaoping, and he was publicly discredited and thrown out of office for a second time.

THE DEATH OF MAO AND RETURN OF DENG XIAOPING

In July 1976 a catastrophic earthquake in the north killed half a million people. The Chinese hold that natural disasters always foreshadow great events, and no-one was too surprised when Mao himself died on September 9. Deprived of their figurehead, and with memories of the Cultural Revolution clear in everyone's mind, his supporters in the Party quickly lost ground to the right. Just a month after Mao's death, Jiang Qing and the other members of the Gang of Four, **Weng Weyuan**, **Wang Hongwen** and **Zhang Chunqiao**, were arrested. Deng returned to the political scene for the third time and was granted a string of positions that included Vice-Chairman of the Communist Party, Vice-Premier and Chief of Staff to the PLA; titles aside, he was now running the country. **Hua Guofeng**, Mao's lookalike and chosen successor, was ousted a couple of years later, and Deng's associates, **Zhao Ziyang** and **Hu Yaobang**, installed as Premier and Party Chairman respectively in his place. The move away from Mao's policies was rapid: in 1978 anti-Maoist dissidents were allowed to display **wall posters** in Beijing and elsewhere, some of which actually criticized Mao by name. Though such public airing of political grievances was later forbidden, by 1980 Deng and the moderates were secure enough to sanction officially a cautious condemnation of Mao's actions. His ubiquitous portraits and statues began to come down, and his cult was gradually undermined.

Yet Mao still had many powerful supporters in the Party, and his public reputation was partially salvaged by the worst of the Cultural Revolution being attributed to the corrupting influence of Jiang Qing and her clique. In 1981 the Gang of Four were brought to trial: though the verdicts were a formality, the sentences were not, for they would be an indication to the people both of the tenor of the new administration, and also how it saw the Cultural Revolution and Mao's part in it. Furthermore, if the death sentence was carried out, Mao's widow might easily become a martyr; if a death sentence was suspended the ability to execute counter-revolutionaries again would be compromised. But the latter course was chosen, and the Gang of Four were given twenty years to reform their ways. All but Wang Hongwen have since died under arrest.

MODERN CHINA: REFORM AND REPRESSION

Under Deng, China has become unrecognizable from the days when Western thought was automatically suspect and the Red Guards enforced ideological purity. Though the Maoist elements are still present, ticking away, say some, to explode when Deng is dead and gone, the new **"open door" policies** of Deng have brought about new social (rather than political) freedoms and massive Westernization, especially in the cities, where Western clothes and music, Japanese motorbikes and fast food are all the rage.

ECONOMIC SUCCESS AND SOCIAL CHANGE

The impetus for such sweeping changes has been economic. Deng's statement, "I don't care whether the cat is black or white as long as it catches mice", illustrates the pragmatic, rather than ideological, approach that he has taken to **economic policy**. In a massive modernization Deng has decentralized production, allowing local and more rational decision-making, based on local conditions. The state has allowed a greater number of goods to be produced and allocated according to market forces, and factories have contracted with each other instead of with the state. In agriculture, the collective economy was replaced and households, after meeting government targets, were allowed to sell their surpluses on the free market. On the coast, **Special Economic Zones (SEZ)** have been set up, where foreign investment is encouraged and Western manufacturing methods, such as the right to fire unsatisfactory workers, are cautiously experimented with.

Deng's economic policies have had a massive impact, and there is no doubt that many Chinese are much better off now than ever before. Annual growth stands at a healthy nine percent, while in certain areas, such as Shenzen, the largest SEZ, it has reached 45 percent, and Chinese economic planners are in the enviable position of trying to slow it down. In the 1970s the "three big buys" – consumer goods that families could realistically aspire to – were a bicycle, a watch and a radio; in the 1980s they were a washing machine, a TV and a refrigerator. Today's young urban mainland Chinese can aspire to the same goals as their counterparts in South Korea and Hong Kong.

But there are **problems**. Not everyone has benefited from the new system. In the country, those who farm unproductive land are probably worse off, and now that the collectives have gone, many of the poorest Chinese no longer have access to education or health care. In the cities, those whose wages are fixed – workers for state-run companies – have suffered badly from inflation, which reached thirty percent in 1989. With the creation of a new class of wealthy entrepreneur, social divisions, between city and country, coast and interior, have widened. One of the more visible results of rising living costs (coupled with increased agricultural mechanization) has been the mass migration of the working class from the country to the cities, where most remain unemployed or are hired by the day as labourers. Short-term gain has become the overriding factor in planning, with the result that the future is mortgaged for present wealth. As success is largely dependent on *guanxi* (connections), the potential for corruption is enormous. To many the price of modernization has become too high – crime and unemployment, formerly seen as Western diseases, have risen dramatically – and the Maoist wing of the Party is understandably displeased.

Perhaps China's biggest problem, however, is its **massive population**, which stood at 1.2 billion in 1992. If China's population continues to rise all the recent economic progress will be wiped out as an expanding population puts an unbearable pressure on resources. The **one child policy**, which began in 1979, has been most successful in the cities, where it is almost impossible for a couple to get away with having a second child. Who is allowed to give birth, as well as when, is controlled by an individual's work unit, and the pressure for an unsanctioned pregnancy to be aborted is high. Couples who have a second child must accept a cut in wages and restricted access to health care and housing. But limiting the size of families has caused much concern; a generation of "little emperors" – spoilt children – is being raised, who will find themselves heavily outnumbered by the elderly when they get to working age. In rural China, thanks to the heavy prejudice towards male children, female infanticide is common, as is the selling of girls as brides in village marketplaces, where there are not enough women to go around.

POLITICAL REPRESSION AND HUMAN RIGHTS

Economic reform has not precipitated political reform, and is really a way of staving it off, with the Party hoping that allowing the populace the right to get rich will halt demands for **political rights**. However, dissatisfaction with corruption, rising inflation, low wages and lack of freedom was vividly expressed in the demonstrations held in **Tian'anmen Square** in 1989. The immediate cause of the gatherings was the death of Hu Yaobang, former Party General Secretary, who had been too liberal for Deng and was dismissed in 1987. An unofficial mourning service in the square soon swelled into a major demonstration, with 150,000 activists holding an impromptu service. Over the next month, the crowds swelled until by mid-May there were nearly a million people around the square. Most were students, but they had now been joined by workers, even cadets from the Party school for cadres. They were aided by Beijing residents, who fed them, and rail workers, who let people wishing to demonstrate travel for free. Students at Beijing's Art Institute constructed the Goddess of Democracy, a statue set up facing Mao's image on Tian'anmen Gate.

The demonstrators demanded **free speech and an end to corruption**. When the Party leadership proved unresponsive, three thousand students went on hunger strike. In May, the demonstrators humiliated the leadership during an official visit by Soviet leader Mikhail Gorbachev to Beijing. Immediately after he left, on May 20, **martial law** was declared, and by the beginning of June, 350,000 troops were massed around Beijing. In the early hours of June 4 they moved in, crushing barriers with tanks and firing into the crowds. There are no reliable figures of the death toll, but the figure is thought to be in the hundreds or possibly thousands. Hospital waiting rooms were piled with corpses and doctors were ordered not to treat casualties.

China's most serious human rights abuses, however, are being perpetrated in **Tibet**, where dissent is ruthlessly suppressed and Tibetan culture is being swamped by Han migration to the region. In 1995, when the exiled Dalai Lama selected a new Panchen Lama following the death of the previous incumbent, the boy he chose was arrested and has become one of the world's youngest political prisoners while the Chinese government have enthroned their own representative (see p.984). Another cause for concern is the Chinese **gulags**, in which up to fourteen million prisoners, an estimated ten percent of them political, are kept in punishing conditions and used as slave labour, a situation that has been highlighted by Harry Wu, the high-profile dissident.

China's human rights record is the biggest obstacle to its desire to achieve i**nternational standing**, though with China's economy set to become the largest in the world some time in the next century, the international community is finding it easy to lose any moral scruples it may have. In 1989, when the Dalai Lama won the Nobel Peace Prize, Western nations were subdued in their congratulations, and in 1995, President Clinton dropped any link between China's human rights abuses and the country's status as most favoured trading nation. China's most recent bid for esteem, the 1995 UN Women's Conference, held in Beijing, was not the unqualified propaganda success the Chinese government had hoped for. Taken by surprise by how radical the women were, the State reacted by keeping the angry delegates in virtual isolation.

TOWARDS THE TWENTY-FIRST CENTURY

Following a clampdown after the Tian'anmen massacre, during which hundreds of liberals were arrested and students made to attend a year of army service and political re-education, China has returned to its course of **controlled liberalization**. A course which, despite the controversies surrounding the current regime, has given the Chinese people one of the most outward-looking and socially minded governments of any time in the last two thousand years.

The future, though, is far from certain. Officially, the 92-year-old **Deng** is retired, and he is no longer thought to be actively involved in decision-making. **Jiang Zemin**, his chosen successor, heads both the government and the Party, but his succession is by no means assured, as his power relies on alliances which may shift with Deng's death. And unless the state can deal effectively with inflation, corruption, increasing regionalism from the prosperous eastern seaboard, rural discontent and the demands of the Chinese people for democratic freedoms, while smoothly managing China's rapid modernization, the government machinery itself will be seriously threatened.

In 1997 China regains control of **Hong Kong** (followed by Macau in 1999). The transition will not be an easy one, and few believe Chinese assurances that the region will retain autonomy under a **"one country, two systems"** concept of Chinese rule. It seems likely that Hong Kong will retain its role as a money-making centre while losing whatever political freedom it had. It will be a move keenly watched by **Taiwan**, where unification with the mainland is also an issue, though the Chinese did not help their cause by firing missiles over the island in 1996 – a failed attempt to influence the result of its first free elections.

China stands ready to be added to the ranks of the "Asian dragons", as a major new world player. Only time will tell whether we are now seeing the last years of a moribund dictatorship about to implode under internal tensions, as so many Chinese dynasties have in the past, or whether (as a Japanese minister recently put it), the twenty-first century belongs to China.

MONUMENTAL CHRONOLOGY

4800 BC	First evidence of **human settlement**.	**Banpo** in the Yellow River basin build Bronze-Age town of **Erlitou** in Henan. Excavation at **Yin** in Anyang reveals rich and developed culture.
21C–16C BC Xia dynasty		
16C–11C BC Shang dynasty		
11C–771 BC Zhou dynasty	The concept of **Mandate from Heaven** introduced.	
770 BC–476 BC Spring and Autumn Period	Kong Fuzi or **Confucius** (c500 BC) teaches a philosophy of adherence to ritual and propriety.	
457 BC–221 BC Warring States		
221 BC–207 BC Qin dynasty	First centralized empire founded by Emperor **Qin Shi Huang**.	The **Great Wall** "completed". **Terracotta Army** guard Qin's tomb.
206 BC–220 BC Han dynasty	**Han emperors** bring stability and great advances in trade. **Confucianism** and **Buddhism** ascendant.	**Han tombs** near Xi'an.
The Three Kingdoms 220–265 Wei 221–263 Shu Han 222–280 Wu	Influence of Buddhist **India** and **Central Asia** enlivens a Dark Age.	
265–420 Jin dynasty	Absorption of northern barbarians into Chinese culture.	
420–581 Southern dynasties and Northern dynasties	Rapid succession of short-lived dynasties brings disunity.	Earliest **Longmen caves** near Luoyang.
581–618 Sui dynasty	Centralization and growth under **Wen Di**.	Extension and strengthening of **Great Wall**; digging of **Grand Canal**.
618–907 Tang dynasty	Arts and literature reach their most developed stage.	**Great Buddha** at Leshan completed.
907–960 Five dynasties	Decline of culture and the northern defences.	**Cliff sculptures** of Dazu.
960–1271 Song dynasties	Consolidation of the lesser kingdoms.	

1271–1368 Yuan dynasty	**Genghis Khan** invades. Under **Kublai Khan** trade with Europe develops. **Marco Polo** opens trade with Venice.	**Forbidden City** built.
1368–1644 Ming dynasty	Isolationist policies end contact with rest of world.	
1644–1911 Qing dynasty	**Manchus** gain control over China and extend its boundaries. Under **Qianlong** (1711–99) culture flourishes.	**Potala Palace** in Lhasa rebuilt by Fifth Dalai Lama. **Summer Palace** in Beijing completed.
Late 18C	**East India Company** monopolizes trade with Britain.	
1839–62	**Opium Wars**. As part of the surrender settlement, Hong Kong is ceded to Britain.	
1851–64	**Taiping Uprising**. Conservative policies of Dowager Empress **Cixi** allow foreign powers to take control of China's industry.	
1899	**Boxer Rebellion**.	
1911 Republic	End of imperial China. **Sun Yatsen** becomes leader of the **Republic**.	
1921	Chinese Communist Party founded in Beijing.	**Peasant Movement Training Institute** built in Guangzhou.
1927	**Chiang Kaishek** orders massacre of Communists in Beijing. **Mao Zedong** organizes first peasant-worker army.	
1932	Japan invades Manchuria.	
1936–41	**United Front**.	
1945	Surrender of Japan. Civil war between Nationalist **Guomindang** and the **People's Liberation Army**.	
1949 Communist takeover	Chiang Kaishek flees to **Taiwan**. **People's Republic** of China supports the North in the **Korean War**.	Much **rebuilding** of cities throughout the 1950s.

1956	The **Hundred Flowers** campaign unsuccessfully attempts liberalizations.	
1958	Agricultural reform in the shape of the **Great Leap Forward** fails. Widespread famine results.	Land organized into **communes**. Heavy **industrial plants** built in rural areas.
1964	China explodes its first atomic weapon.	
1966–8	Red Guards purge anti-Maoist elements in the **Cultural Revolution**.	Much destruction of "ideologically unsound" art and architecture.
1971	People's Republic replaces Taiwan at **United Nations**.	
1972	**President Nixon** visits Beijing.	
1976	The **Tian'anmen Incident** reveals public support for moderate **Deng Xiaoping**. **Mao Zedong dies**, and the **Gang of Four** are arrested shortly afterwards.	
1977	Deng Xiaoping rises to become **Party Chairman**.	
1981	**Trial** of the Gang of Four.	
1980	Beginning of the **Open Door** policy.	
1986	Agreement reached on **Hong Kong**'s return to China in 1997.	
1989	Suppression of the democracy movement in **Tian'anmen Square**.	
1992	Major **cabinet reshuffle** puts Deng's men in power.	
1993	Yuan floated on the world currency market.	
1995	Death of Chen Yun, last of the hardline Maoists in the Politburo.	
1997	Return of **Hong Kong** to the mainland.	

CHINESE BELIEFS: THREE TEACHINGS FLOW INTO ONE

The visitor to modern China will find few obvious indications of the traditional beliefs which underpinned the country's civilization for three thousand years. Certainly, the remains of religious buildings litter the cities and the countryside, yet they appear sadly incongruous amid the furious pace of change all around them. The restored temples – now "cultural relics" with photo booths, concession stands, special foreign tourist shops and cheerful throngs of young Chinese on outings – are garish and evoke few mysteries. This apparent lack of religion is hardly surprising, however: for decades, the old beliefs have been derided by the authorities as superstition, and the oldest and most firmly rooted of them all, Confucianism, has been criticized and repudiated for nearly a century. For any student of Chinese culture one of the most striking aspects of modern China is the degree to which, on the surface at least, the ancient ("feudal") beliefs have been eradicated.

Although this may sound disappointing for travellers seeking the **Tao** ("Way") in China, it should be pointed out that the neglect of the outward forms of religion is by no means a sure indicator of the state of mind of the Chinese people. The **resilience of old ideas** in China, and the ability of the Chinese people to absorb new streams of thought and eventually to dominate them, has been demonstrated again and again over the centuries. The philosophies which unified China and defined the very idea of what it is to be Chinese for millennia are not likely to be forgotten in a mere half century of communism.

The product of the oldest continuous civilization on earth, Chinese religion actually comprises a number of disparate and sometimes contradictory elements. But at the heart of it all, **three basic philosophies** lie intermingled: Confucianism, Taoism and Buddhism. The way in which a harmonious balance has been created among these three is expressed in the often quoted maxim *San Jiao Fa Yi* – "Three Teachings Flow into One".

Both **Confucianism** and **Taoism** are belief systems rooted in the Chinese soil, and they form as much a part of the Chinese collective unconscious as Platonic and Aristotelian thought does in the West. **Buddhism**, though, was a foreign import, brought to China from India along the Silk Road by itinerant monks and missionaries from about the first century AD onwards. As such, it was the first organized religion to penetrate China and enjoyed a glorious, if brief, period of ascendancy under the Tang in the eighth century. Just as the mutual contradictions of Confucianism and Taoism had been accommodated by the Chinese, however, so Buddhism did not long eclipse other beliefs – as it established itself, its tenets were gradually integrated into the existing structure of thought and in turn transformed by them, into something very different from what had originally come out of India. Buddhism may have been the only foreign religion to have left a substantial mark on China, though it was not, incidentally, the only religion to enter China via the Silk Road. Both **Islam** and **Christianity** also trickled into the country this way, and to this day a significant minority of Chinese, numbering possibly in the tens of millions, are Muslims. Unlike most of the rest of Asia, however, China did not yield wholesale to the tide of Islam – the rigid, all-embracing doctrines of the Koran never stood much of a chance with the choosy, flexible Chinese.

Similarly, China may have been periodically dominated by foreign powers, but her belief systems have never been overwhelmed. Instead, conquering invaders such as the Mongolians in the thirteenth and the Manchus in the seventeenth centuries, have found themselves inexorably sinicized. On this strength rests the understandable Chinese **confidence in the ultimate superiority of their beliefs**, a confidence that survived through the lowest periods in Chinese history.

CONFUCIANISM

China's oldest and greatest philosopher, Kong Zi, known in the West by his Latinized name

Confucius, was an obscure and unsuccessful scholar. Born in 551 BC, during the so-called Warring States period, he lived in an age of petty kingdoms where life was blighted by constant war, feuding and social disharmony. Confucius simply saw that society was something that could be improved if individuals behaved properly. Harking back to an earlier, mythic age of peace and social virtues, he preached **adherence to ritual and propriety** as the supreme answer to the horrifying disorder of the world as he found it. During his lifetime he wandered from court to court attempting to teach rulers a better way to rule, though, like his contemporary Socrates far away in Greece, he was largely ignored by men in power. In the centuries after his death, however, Confucianism, as reflected in the **Analects**, a collection of writings on his life and sayings compiled by disciples, became the most influential and fundamental of Chinese philosophies.

Never a religion in the sense of postulating a higher deity, Confucianism is rather a set of **moral and social values** designed to bring the ways of citizens and governments into harmony with each other, and with their ancestors. Through proper training in the scholarly classics and rigid adherence to the rules of propriety, including ancestor-worship, the superior man could attain a level of moral righteousness which would, in turn, assure a stable and righteous social order. As a political theory Confucianism called for the **"wisest sage"**, the one whose moral sense was most refined, to be ruler. With a good ruler, one who practised the virtuous ways of his ancestors and was exemplary in terms of the **five Confucian virtues** (benevolence, righteousness, propriety, wisdom and trustworthiness), the world and society would naturally be in order. Force, the ultimate sanction, would be unnecessary. As Confucius said:

Just as the ruler genuinely desires the good, the people will be good. The virtue of the ruler may be compared to the wind and that of the common people to the grass. The grass under the force of the wind cannot but bend.

Gods play no part in this structure – **man is capable of perfection** in his own right, given a superior ruler whose virtues are mirrored in the behaviour of his subjects. Instead of God,

five hierarchical relationships are the prerequisites for a well-ordered society, and given proper performance of the duties entailed in these, society should be "at ease with itself". The five relationships outline a strict structure of duty and obedience to authority: ruler to ruled; son to father; younger brother to older, wife to husband and, the only equal relationship, friend to friend. The intention is to create order and stability through rule by a moral elite, though in practice adherence to the unbending hierarchy of these relationships as well as to the precepts of filial piety has justified a form of totalitarian rule throughout Chinese history. The supreme virtue of the well-cultivated man and woman was always **obedience**.

From the time of the Han dynasty (206 BC–220 AD) onwards, Confucianism became institutionalized as a **system of government** which was to prevail in China for two thousand years. With it, and with the notion of the scholar-official as the ideal administrator, came the notorious Chinese **bureaucracy**. Men would study half their lives in order to pass the imperial examinations and attain a government commission. These examinations were rigid tests of the scholar's knowledge of the Confucian classics. Right up until the beginning of the twentieth century, power in China was wielded through a bureaucracy steeped in the classics of rites and rituals written five hundred years before Christ.

The Confucian ideal ruler, of course, never quite emerged (the emperor was not expected to sit the exams) and the scholar-officials often deteriorated into corrupt bureaucrats and exploitative landlords. Furthermore, the Confucian ideals of submission to authority would not seem to have much of a shelf-life at the end of the twentieth century. On the other hand, with its emphasis on **community and social cohesion**, Confucianism has played an enormous role in keeping China free of the bigotry and religious fanaticism that have been bringing war to Europe for two thousand years. And today it is clear that Confucius does still have a role to play, not least in his new encarnation as the embodiment of the much trumpeted **"Asian values"**, namely, the non-confrontational (and undemocratic) system of government. On the grass-roots level, too, old practices such as ancestor-worship within the family are making a comeback. Now that the latest foreign religion of Marxism has been thoroughly discredited, it appears that Confucianism is simply reoccupying its rightful position.

TAOISM

The second of the three major teachings which form the roots of Chinese beliefs is **Taoism**. The **Tao** translates literally as the "Way" and, in its purest form, Taoism is the study and pursuit of this ineffable Way, as outlined in the fundamental text, the **Daodejing** (often written as Tao Te Ching) or "The Way of Power". This obscure and mystical text essentially comprises a compilation of the wise sayings of a semi-mythical hermit by the name of **Lao Zi**, who is said to have been a contemporary of Confucius. The Daodejing was not compiled until at least three centuries after his death.

The Tao is never really defined – indeed by its very nature it is undefinable. To the despair of the rationalist, the first lines of the Daodejing read:

The Tao that can be told
is not the eternal Tao.
The name that can be named
is not the eternal name.

In essence, however, it might be thought of as the Way of Nature, the underlying principle and source of all being, the bond which unites man and nature. Its central principle is **Wu Wei**, which can crudely be translated as "no action", though it is probably better understood as 'no action which runs contrary to nature'. Taoism was originally the creed of the recluse. Whereas Confucianism is concerned with repairing social order and social relationships, Taoism is interested in the relationship of the individual with the natural universe. It simply looks at human problems from another, higher plane: having good relations with one's neighbours is of no use if one is not in harmony with nature.

Taoism's second major text is a book of parables written by one ideal practitioner of the Way, **Zhuang Zi**. Like the master Lao Zi, Zhuang Zi is a semi-mythical figure. Acknowledged in his lifetime as a great sage, he rejected all offers of high rank in favour of a life of solitary reflection. His works – allegorical tales which have delighted Chinese readers for centuries – reveal humour as well as perception; in the famous butterfly parable Zhuang Zi examines the many faces of reality:

Once upon a time Zhuang Zi dreamed he was a butterfly. A butterfly flying around and enjoying itself. It did not know it was Zhuang Zi again. We do not know whether it was Zhuang Zi dreaming that he was a butterfly, or a butterfly dreaming he was Zhuang Zi.

As it became part of Chinese culture, Taoism offered a contrast to the stern propriety of Confucianism. In traditional China it was said that the perfect lifestyle was that of a man who was a Confucian during the day – a righteous and firm administrator, upholding the virtues of the gentleman/ruler – and a Taoist after the duties of the day had been fulfilled. The practice of Taoism affirms the virtues of withdrawing from public duties and giving oneself up to a life of **contemplation and meditation**. If Confucianism preaches duty to family and to society, Taoism champions the sublimity of withdrawal, non-committedness and "dropping out". In its affirmation of the irrational and natural sources of life, it has provided Chinese culture with a balance to the rigid social mores of Confucianism. The **art and literature** of China have been greatly enriched by Taoism's notions of contemplation, detachment and freedom from social entanglement, and the Tao has become embedded in the Chinese soul as a doctrine of yielding to the inevitable forces of nature.

BUDDHISM

The Tang dynasty (618–906 AD) was a period of unprecedented openness and prosperity for the Chinese court and it was then that **Buddhism**, originally imported from India through Central Asia around the first century AD, gained acceptance and came for a time to be the dominant religion in China. In the eighth century there were over three hundred thousand Buddhist monks in China, and it was a period which saw the creation of much of the country's **great religious art** – above all the cave shrines at **Luoyang** (Henan), **Datong** (Shanxi) and **Dunhuang** (Gansu), where thousands of carvings of the Buddha and paintings of holy figures attest to the powerful influence of Indian art and religion.

Gradually, though, Buddhism too was submerged into the native belief system. Most schools of Indian Buddhism of the time taught that life on earth was essentially one of suffering, an endless cycle in which people were born, grew old and died, only to be born again in other bodies; the goal was to break out of this cycle by attaining nirvana, which could be done by losing all desire for things of the world. This essentially individualistic doctrine was not likely to appeal the highly regimented Chinese, however, and hence it was that the relatively small **Mahayana School of Buddhism** came to dominate Chinese thinking. The Mahayana taught that perfection for the individual was not possible without perfection for all – and that those who had already attained enlightenment would remain active in the world (as **Bodhisattvas**) to help others along the path. In time Bodhisattvas came to be ascribed miraculous powers, and were prayed to in a manner remarkably similar to that of conventional Confucian ancestor-worship. The mainstream of Chinese Buddhism came to be more about maintaining harmonious relations with Bodhisattvas than about attaining nirvana.

Another entirely new sect of Buddhism also arose in China through contact with Taoism. Known in China as **Chan** (and in Japan as Zen) Buddhism, it offered a less extreme path to enlightenment. For a Chan Buddhist it was not necessary to become a monk or a recluse in order to achieve nirvana – instead this ultimate state of being could be reached through life in accord with, and in contemplation of, the Way.

In short, the Chinese managed to marry Buddhism to their pre-existing belief structures with very little difficulty at all. This was facilitated by the general absence of dogma within Buddhist thought. Like the Chinese, the **Tibetans**, too, found themselves able to adapt the new belief system to their old religion, **Bon**, rather than simply replacing it. Over the centuries, they established their own schools of Buddhism often referred to as Lalaist Buddhism or Lamaism, which differ from the Chinese versions in minor emphases. The now dominant **Gelugpa** (or Yellow Hat) school, of which the

Dalai and Panchen Lamas are members, dates back to the teachings of Tsongkhapa (1357–1419).

POPULAR RELIGION

When Jesuit missionaries first arrived in China in the sixteenth and seventeenth centuries they were astounded and dismayed by the Chinese **flexibility of belief**. One frustrated Jesuit put it : "In China, the educated believe nothing and the uneducated believe everything." For those versed in the classics of Confucianism, Taoism and Buddhism, the normal belief was a healthy and tolerant **scepticism**. For the great majority of illiterate peasants, however, popular religion offered a plethora of ghosts, spirits, gods and ancestors who ruled over a capricious nature and protected humanity. If Christian missionaries handed out rice, perhaps Christ too deserved a place alongside them. In popular Buddhism the hope was to reach the "Pure Land", a kind of heaven for believers ruled over by a female deity known as the Mother Ruler. Popular Taoism shared this feminine deity, but its concerns were rather with the sorcerers, alchemists and martial arts aficionados who sought solutions to the riddle of immortality.

MODERN CHINA

One of the reasons why modern China appears to lack the outward manifestations of her ancient beliefs is that they are not really essential. You will see the traditions more clearly expressed in how the Chinese think and act than in the symbols and rituals of overt worship.

During the twentieth century, confronted by the superior military and technical power of the West, the Chinese have striven to break free from the shackles of superstition. The imperial examinations were abolished at the turn of the century and since then Chinese intellectuals have been searching for a modern yet essentially Chinese philosophy. The **Cultural Revolution** can be seen as the culmination of these efforts to repudiate the past. Hundreds of thousands of temples, ancestral halls and religious objects were defaced and destroyed. Monasteries which had preserved their seclusion for centuries were burnt to the ground and their monks imprisoned. The classics of literature and philosophy – the "residue of the reactionary feudal past" – were burned in huge celebratory bonfires. In 1974, towards the end of the Cultural Revolution, a campaign was launched to "criticize Lin Biao and Confucius", pairing the general with the sage to imply that both were equally reactionary in their opposition to the government.

Yet the very fact that Confucius could still be held up as an object for derision in 1974 reveals the tenacity of **traditional beliefs**. With the Cultural Revolution now long gone, they are once again being accepted as an essential part of the cultural tradition which binds the Chinese people together. The older generation, despite a lifetime of commitment to the Marxist revolution, are comforted and strengthened by their knowledge of the national heritage. The young are rediscovering the classics, the forbidden fruit of their school days. The welcome result is that Chinese temples of all descriptions are prosperous, busy places again, teeming with people who have come to ask for grandchildren or simply for money. The atmosphere may not seem devout or religious, but then perhaps it never did.

ARCHITECTURE

After several weeks in China, it seems that – apart from minor regional variations – one temple looks much like another, even that the differences between a palace, a temple or a substantial private house are negligible, and that there is little sign of historical development. Nor does it take even this long to tire of the cheaply built and disappointingly Westernized appearance of the majority of China's cities. But this overall uniformity in no way reflects China's long architecural heritage; it is rather that several factors have conspired to limit its variety. For a start, little has survived from different periods to emphasize their individual characteristics: early wooden structures were vulnerable to natural disasters, while new dynasties often demolished the work of the old to reinforce their takeover. In addition, war and revolutions – particularly in the past 150 years – have affected every corner of the country, wrecking even domestic architecture in the process.

Compounding these factors, a passion for precedent meant that certain basic rules governing building designs were followed from the earliest times, minimizing the variations which separate the works of different periods. This is not to say that it's impossible to tell a Tang pagoda from a Qing one, but it does mean that a certain **homogeneity** pervades traditional Chinese architecture, making it all the more

exciting on the occasions when you do come across unusually distinctive temples, dwellings or even towns.

FENG SHUI AND BASIC PRINCIPLES

Whatever the scale of a building project, the Chinese consider divination using **feng shui** an essential part of the initial preparations. Literally meaning "wind and water", *feng shui* is a form of **geomancy**, which assesses how buildings must be positioned so as not to disturb the spiritual attributes of the surrounding landscape. This reflects **Taoist cosmology**, which believes that all components of the universe exist in a balance with one another, and therefore the disruption of a single element can cause potentially dangerous alterations to the whole. It's vital, therefore, that sites – whether for peasant homes, the *Hong Kong Bank*'s skyscraper headquarters, entire cities such as Beijing or the underground tomb of the first Qin emperor – are favourably orientated according to points on the compass and protected from local "unlucky directions" by other buildings, walls, hills, mountain ranges, water or even a Terracotta Army. Geomancy further proposes **ideal forms** for particular types of structure, and carefully arranges spaces and components within a building according to time-honoured formulae. As changing any of this risks upsetting the cosmos, there's a strong streak of **conservatism** inherent in all traditional Chinese architecture.

Depending on how heavily their form is governed by geomancy, buildings in China can be very broadly divided into two camps. **Monumental architecture**, such as temples, palaces and city plans, whose designs generally have some religious basis, all follow a similar structural pattern which seldom varies. **Domestic architecture**, however, while still guided by similar principles, also has to serve very practical needs, including the local climate, the ready availability of materials or even political considerations, and it's here you'll find the greatest variety of form.

MONUMENTAL ARCHITECTURE

Chinese monumental architecture is notable for constantly repeating **cosmological themes,** the most central of which can be traced right back to the Bronze Age – though the specific details of feng shui were only formulated during the Song dynasty. Four thousand years ago, **cities** were already laid out in a spiritually favourable **rectangular pattern**, typically facing south on a north–south axis and surrounded by a defensive **wall**. Aside from the business and residential districts, the central (though not necessarily centrally located) focus was a separately walled quarter; this later became the seat of the emperor or his local representative. As the emperor was styled "Son of Heaven", this plan – still apparent in the layout of cities such as Xi'an and Beijing – was a representation of the cosmos, with the ruler at the centre. The same general formula is also echoed in the ground plan of palaces, temples and even large family mansions, complexes of buildings whose organization in many ways represented a microcosm of city life. All these are surrounded by a wall, and all have their own central spiritual focus: a main hall in temples where statues of deities are displayed; a similar building in palaces, where the emper-

or or governor would hold court; or an ancestral shrine in a mansion.

As far as individual buildings themselves are concerned, spiritual considerations also ensured that traditional **temples and palaces** (the two are virtually identical) followed a basic **building structure**, which can be seen in subjects as diverse as two-thousand-year-old pottery models and the halls of Beijing's Ming–Qing Forbidden City. The foundations formed a raised platform of earth, brick or stone according to the building's importance. Columns rested on separate bases with the heads of the columns linked by beams running lengthways and across. Above this, beams of diminishing length were raised one above the other on short posts set on the beam below, creating an interlocking structure which rose to the point of the roof where single posts at the centre supported the roof ridge. The arrangement produced a characteristic **curved roofline** with upcurled eaves, felt to confer good luck. Though scale and space were ultimately limited by a lack of arches, essential in supporting the massive

---

GETTING AROUND A CHINESE TEMPLE

Whether Buddhist or Taoist, **Chinese temples** share the same broad features. Like cities, they generally face south and are surrounded by walls. Gates are sealed by heavy doors, usually guarded by paintings or statues of warrior deities to chase away approaching evil. The doors open on to a courtyard, where further protection is ensured by a **spirit wall** which blocks direct entry; although easy enough for the living to walk around, this foils spirits, who are unable to turn corners. Once inside, you'll find a succession of halls arranged in ornamental courtyards. In case evil influences should manage to get in, the area nearest the entrance contains the least important rooms or buildings, with those of greater significance – living quarters or main temple halls – set deeper inside the complex.

One way to tell Buddhist and Taoist temples apart is by the colour of the **supporting pillars** – Buddhists use bright red, while Taoists favour black. **Animal carvings** are more popular with Taoists, who use decorative good luck and longevity symbols such as bats and cranes; some Taoist halls also have distinctive raised octagonal cupolas sporting the black-and-white *yin-yang* symbol. Most obviously, however, each religion has its own **deities**. Inside the entrance of a **Buddhist**

temple (*si*) you'll be flanked by the Four Heavenly Kings of the Four Directions, and faced by portly **Maitreya**, the Laughing Buddha; there's also likely to be a statue of **Wei Tuo**, the God of Wisdom. The main hall is dominated by three large statues sitting side by side on lotus flowers, representing Buddhas of the past, present and future, while the walls are decorated by often grossly caricatured images of Buddhist saints (*arhats*) – these are sometimes given a separate hall to themselves. Around the back of the Buddhist trinity is a statue of **Guanyin**, the multi-armed, vase-bearing Goddess of Mercy, who again is sometimes given her own room. **Taoist temples** (*miao* or *gong*) are similar, but their halls might be dedicated to any number of mythical and legendary figures. Taoism has its own holy trinity, the **Three Immortals**, who each ride different animals (a crane, tiger and deer) and represent the three levels of the Taoist afterlife. Other figures include the Yellow Emperor, a further Eight Immortals and historical people who were canonized – the *Three Kingdoms* characters **Guan Yu** (the red-faced God of War and Healing) and **Zhuge Liang** are popular choices, as are local heroes. Strangely, statues to Guanyin are often also found in Taoist halls as her help in childbirth makes her universally popular.

walls found in European cathedrals, this structural design was solid enough to allow the use of heavy **ceramic rooftiles**. Introduced in the eighth century, **cantilevered brackets** also allowed the curving eaves to extend well beyond the main pillars and acquire an increasingly decorative value, supplemented by lines of carved animals and figures on the gable ends of the roof.

Development of these features reached a peak of elegance and sophistication during the **Tang and Song eras**, never to be entirely recaptured. Though almost nothing survives intact from this time, later restorations of Tang edifices, such as the temples at Wudang Shan in Hubei Province, or Xi'an's central bell tower, convey something of the period's spirit. Two **regional styles** also developed: **northern** architecture was comparitively restrained and sober, while that from the **south** eventually exaggerated curves and ornamentation to a high degree; Guangdong's Foshan Ancestral Temple is a classic of the latter type. Inside both, however, spaces between the columns were filled by screens providing different combinations of wall, door and latticework, which could be removed or changed to order differently the spaces within. The columns themselves were sometimes carved in stone, or otherwise painted, with different colours denoting specific religions in temples, or the rank of the occupant in palaces. Similarly, **imperial buildings** might be distinguished by four-sided roofs, by higher platforms reached by wide staircases and by special yellow glazed tiles for the roofs. In rare instances, buildings created their own styles without offending *feng shui*; Beijing's circular Temple of Heaven, for example, manages to break with convention by symbolizing the universe in its overall shape.

Pagodas are another important type of monumental structure, originally introduced from India with **Buddhism**. Intended to house saintly relics, they have intrinsically "positive" attributes, are often used to guard cities or buildings from unlucky directions, or are built along rivers to quell (and indicate) dangerous shoals. Their general design in China was probably influenced by the shape of indigenous wooden watch towers, though the earliest surviving example, at Shendong Si in Shandong Province, is stone and more closely resembles the equivalent Indian *stupa*. Most, however, are polygonal, with a central stairway rising through an uneven number of storeys – anything from three to seventeen. Buddhism also gave rise to the extraordinary **cave temples** and grottoes, best preserved in the Northwest at Mogao.

DOMESTIC ARCHITECTURE

In general, the other major group of buildings, **domestic architecture**, shares many of the guiding principles of temple and palace design: curved rooflines are desirable, and larger groups of buildings might also be walled off and include spirit walls or **mirrors**, the latter placed over external doorways to repulse demons. Older homes with these basic features can be found all over the country, but in many cases, practical needs – principally the climate – overrode optimum spiritual designs and created very distinctive **local styles**, which are once again most obvious in a basic north–south divide. **Northern** China's intensely cold winters and hot summers have spawned solidly insulated brick walls, while more stable, subtropical **southern** temperatures encourage the use of open eaves, internal courtyards and wooden lattice screens to allow air to circulate freely.

Rural areas are good places to find some of the more traditional or unusual types of residential architecture; aside from the climate, many of these also reflect local cultures. Striking examples exist in the mountainous border areas between Guizhou and Guangxi provinces, where ethnic **Dong** and **Miao** build large, two- or three-storeyed wooden houses from local cedar. The Dong are further known for their wooden **drum towers** and **wind-and-rain bridges**, which have a spiritual as well as practical function. Another ethnic group building distinctive houses is the **Hakka**, a Han sub-group, whose immense stone circular clan or family mansions – some of which can accommodate hundreds of people – were built for defensive purposes in their Guangdong–Fujian homelands. Extreme adaptation to local conditions can be seen in Shaanxi Province, where **underground homes** have been excavated in prehistoric sedimentary soils deposited by the Yellow River; these are cool in summer and warm in winter.

Traditional **urban architecture** survives, too, though it tends to be less varied. Wood almost invariably formed at least the framework of these buildings, but if fire hasn't claimed them, demolition and replacement by city authorities – either safety-conscious or simply eager to modernize – generally has. Scattered examples of old town houses can still be seen even in large cities such as Beijing, Kunming and Chengdu, however, while the ethnic **Naxi** town of Lijiang in Yunnan sports hundreds of traditional wooden homes, the largest such collection anywhere in China. In the east, the area surrounding Tunxi in Anhui Province contains whole villages built in the immensely inflential seventeenth-century "**Huizhou style**", comprising a two-storeyed house plan built around a courtyard, which epitomized the basic forms of contemporary east-coast provincial architecture.

MODERN ARCHITECTURE

China's **modern architecture** tends to reflect political and economic, rather than ethnic or climatic, considerations. From the mid-nineteenth century onwards, treaty ports were built up in the **European** colonial manner by the foreign merchants, banks, shipping firms and missionaries who conducted their affairs there. Today, the former offices, warehouses and churches – often divided up for Chinese use – still give certain cities a distinctive look. Hankou, part of Wuhan, has a Customs House and whole streets of colonial buildings, as do the former east-coast concessions of Shanghai, Qingdao, Yantai, Shantou, Xiamen and Guangzhou. European-inspired building continued on into the 1930s.

After the **Communist takeover**, there were various attempts to unite Chinese styles with modern materials. When used, this was successful, and many modern rural dwellings still follow traditional designs, simply replacing adobe walls with concrete. But during the 1950s, while Russia was China's ally, a brutally functional **Soviet style** became the urban norm, requiring that everything from factories to hotels be built as identical drab, characterless grey boxes. Since China opened up to the Western world and capitalism in the late 1970s, however, there's been a move towards a more "international" look, as seen in the concrete-and-glass highrises going up across the country. While brighter than the Russian model, these are, in general, hardly any more inspirational or attractive, and are afflicted by a mania for facing new buildings in bathroom tiles. Yet even here there have been attempts to marry the traditional Chinese idiom with current needs, and in a few modern housing estates you'll see apartment buildings surrounded by walled compounds and topped with curled rooftiles.

ART

This very brief survey aims to reflect, and to help you to follow, what you are likely to see most of in Chinese provincial and city museums – and to an extent in situ. Many of the museums have a similar layout and similar contents – some of the exhibits being copies of key discoveries from other areas – but often there is little or no explanation in English. In looking at the art displayed in Chinese museums it should be remembered that while for more than two thousand years an empire with a splendid court produced an incredible wealth of art objects, from the mid-nineteenth century onwards, many of these were acquired – more or less legitimately – or looted, by Westerners. Later, too, some of the great imperial collections were removed by the Nationalists to Taiwan, where they are now in the National Palace Museum.

POTTERY, BRONZES AND SCULPTURE

The earliest Chinese objects date back to the Neolithic farmers of the **Yangshao** culture – well-made **pottery** vessels painted in red, black, brown and white with geometrical designs. You'll notice that the decoration is usually from the shoulders of the pots upwards; this is because what has survived is mostly from graves and was designed to be seen from above when the pots were placed round the

dead. From the same period there are decorated clay heads, perhaps for magic or ritual, and pendants and small ornaments of polished stone or jade, with designs that are sometimes semi-abstract – a simplified sitting bird in polished jade is a very early example of the powerful Chinese tradition of animal sculpture. Rather later is the Neolithic **Longshan** pottery – black, very thin and fine, wheel-turned and often highly polished, with elegantly, sharply defined shapes.

The subsequent era, from some 1500 years BC, is dominated by **Shang and Zhou bronze vessels** used for preparing and serving food and wine, and for ceremonies and sacrifices. There are many distinct shapes, each with its own name and specific usage. One of the most common is the *ding*, a three- or four-legged vessel which harks back to the Neolithic pots used for cooking over open fires. As you'll see from the museums, these bronzes have survived in great numbers. The **Shang** bronze industry appears already fully developed with advanced techniques and designs and no sign of a primitive stage. Casting methods were highly sophisticated, using moulds, while design was firm and assured and decoration often stylized and linear, with both geometric and animal motifs, as well as grinning masks of humans and fabulous beasts. There are some naturalistic animal forms among the vessels, too – fierce tigers, solid elephants and surly-looking rhinoceroses. Other bronze finds include weapons, decorated horse harnesses and sets of bells used in ritual music. Later, under the **Zhou**, the style of the bronzes becomes more varied and rich: some animal vessels are fantastically shaped and extravagantly decorated; others are simplified natural forms; others again seem to be depicting not so much a fierce tiger, for example, as utter ferocity itself. You will also see from the Shang and Zhou small objects – ornaments, ritual pieces and jewellery pendants – with highly simplified but vivid forms of tortoises, salamanders and flying birds. From the end of this period there are also painted clay funeral figures and a few carved wooden figures.

The Shang produced a few small sculptured human figures and animals in marble, but **sculptures** and works in stone begin to be found in great quantities in **Han-dynasty** tombs. The decorated bricks and tiles, the bas reliefs and the terracotta figurines of acrobats, horsemen and ladies-in-waiting placed in the tombs to serve the dead, even the massive stone men and beasts set to guard the Spirit Way leading to the tomb, are all lifelike and reflect concern with everyday activities and material possessions. The scale models of houses with people looking out of the windows and of farmyards with their animals have a spontaneous gaiety and vigour; some of the watchdogs are the most realistic of all. Smaller objects like tiny statuettes and jewellery were also carved, from ivory, jade and wood.

It was the advent of **Buddhism** which encouraged stone carving on a large scale in the round, with mallet and chisel. **Religious sculpture** was introduced from India and in the fourth-century caves at **Datong** (see p.202) and the earlier caves at **Longmen**, near Luoyang (see p.262), the Indian influence is most strongly felt in the stylized Buddhas and attendants. Sometimes of huge size, they have an aloof grace and a rhythmic quality in their flowing robes, but also a smooth, bland and static quality. Not until the **Tang** do you get the full flowering of a native Chinese style, where the figures are rounder, with movement, and the positions, expressions and clothes are more natural and realistic. Some of the best examples are to be seen at **Dunhuang** (see p.879) and in the later caves at Longmen. The **Song** continued to carve religious figures and at **Dazu** in Sichuan (see p.796) you'll find good examples of a highly decorative style which had broadened its subject matter to include animals, ordinary people and scenes of everyday life; the treatment is down to earth, individual, sometimes even comic. The Dazu carvings are very well preserved and you see them painted, as they were meant to be. In later years less statuary was produced until the **Ming** with their taste for massive and impressive tomb sculptures. You can see the best of these in **Nanjing** and **Beijing**.

CERAMICS

In **ceramics** the Chinese tradition is very old. From the Neolithic painted pottery described above onwards, China developed a high level of excellence, based on the availability of high-quality materials. Her pre-eminence was recognized by the fact that for more than four hundred years the English language has used the word "china" to mean fine-quality ceramic

ware. In some of the early wares you can see the influence of shapes derived from bronzes, but soon the rise of regional potteries using different materials, and the development of special types for different uses, led to an enormous variety of shapes, textures and colours. This was noticeable by the **Tang dynasty** when an increase in the production of pottery for daily use was partly stimulated by the spread of tea drinking and by the restriction of the use of copper and bronze to coinage. The Tang also saw major technical advances; the production of true **porcelain** was finally achieved and Tang potters became very skilled in the use of polychrome glazing. You can see evidence of this in the *san cai* (three colour) statuettes of horses and camels, jugglers, traders, polo players, grooms and court ladies, which have come in great numbers from imperial tombs, and which reflect in vivid, often humorous, detail and still brilliant colours so many aspects of the life of the time. It was a cosmopolitan civilization open to foreign influences and this is clearly seen in Tang art.

The **Song** dynasty witnessed a great refinement of ceramic techniques and of regional specialization, many wares being named after the area which produced them. The keynote was simplicity and quiet elegance, both in colour and form. There was a preference for using a **single pure colour** and for incized wares made to look like damask cloth. In the museums you'll see the famous green celadons, the thin white porcelain *Ding* ware and the pale greygreen *Ju* ware reserved for imperial use. The Mongol **Yuan** dynasty, in the early fourteenth century, enriched Chinese tradition with outside influences – notably the introduction of **cobalt blue underglaze**, early examples of the blue and white porcelain which was to become so famous. The **Ming** saw the flowering of great potteries under imperial patronage, especially **Jingdezhen**. Taste moved away from Song simplicity and returned to the liking for vivid colour which the Tang had displayed – deep **red**, **yellow** and **orange** glazes, with a developing taste for pictorial representation. From the seventeeth century, Chinese export wares flowed in great quantity and variety to the West to satisfy a growing demand for chinoiserie, and the efforts of the Chinese artists to follow what they saw as the tastes and techniques of the West produced a style of its own. The early

Qing created delicate enamel wares and *famille rose* and *verte*. So precise were the craftsmen that some porcelain includes the instructions for the pattern in the glaze.

You can visit several potteries such as at **Jingdezhen** in Jiangxi province, where both early wares and modern trends are on display. Five years ago they were turning out thousands of figurines of Mao and Lu Xun sitting in his armchair; now the emphasis is on table lamp bases in the shape of archaic maidens in flowing robes playing the lute, or creased and dimpled Laughing Buddhas.

PAINTING AND CALLIGRAPHY

While China's famous ceramics were produced by nameless craftsmen, with **painting and calligraphy** we enter the realm of the amateur whose name has survived and who was often scholar, official, poet or all three. It has been said that the four great treasures of Chinese painting are the brush, the ink, the inkstone and the paper or silk. The earliest brush found, from about 400 BC, is made out of animal hairs glued to a hollow bamboo tube. Ink was made from pine soot mixed with glue and hardened into a stick which would be rubbed with water on an inkstone made of non-porous, carved and decorated slate. **Silk** was used for painting as early as the third century BC and **paper** was invented by **Cai Lun** in 106 AD. The first known painting on silk was found in a **Han** tomb; records show that there was a great deal of such painting but in 190 AD the vast imperial collection was destroyed in a civil war – the soldiers used the silk to make tents and knapsacks. All we know of Han painting comes from decorated tiles, lacquer, painted pottery and a few painted tombs, enough to show a great sense of movement and energy. There is a scroll in ink and colour on silk attributed to **Gu Kaizhi** about 400 AD and entitled *Admonitions of the Instructress to Court Ladies*, in the British Museum, and we know that the theory of painting was already being discussed, as the treatise *The Six Principles of Painting* dates from about 500 AD.

The **Sui–Tang** period, with a powerful stable empire and a brilliant court, was exactly the place for painting to develop, and a great tradition of figure painting grew up, especially of court subjects – portraits, pictures of the emperor receiving envoys and of court ladies, several of which are to be seen in Beijing.

Although only a few of these survived, the walls of Tang tombs, such as those near Xi'an, are rich in vivid frescoes which provide a realistic portrayal of court life. Wang Wei in the mid-eighth century was an early exponent of monochrome **landscape** painting, but the great flowering of landscape painting came with the **Song dynasty**. An academy was set up under imperial patronage and different schools of painting emerged which analyzed the natural world with great concentration and intensity; their style has set a mark on Chinese landscape painting ever since. There was also lively **figure painting** – a famous horizontal scroll in Beijing showing the Qing Ming River Festival is the epitome of this. The last emperor of the Northern Song, **Hui Zong**, was himself a painter of some note, which indicates the status of painting in China at the time. The Southern Song preferred a more intimate style and such subjects as flowers, birds and still life grew in popularity.

Under the **Mongols** there were many officials who found themselves unwanted or unwilling to serve the alien Yuan dynasty and who preferred to retire and paint. This produced the **"literati" school**, with many painters harking back to the styles of the tenth century. One of the great masters was **Ni Can**. He, among many others, also devoted himself to the ink paintings of bamboo which became important at this time. In this school, of which there are many extant examples, the highest skills of techniques and composition were applied to the simplest of subjects, as also with the paintings of plum flowers. Both of these continued to be employed by painters of the next three or more centuries. From the **Yuan** onwards a tremendous quantity of paintings has survived. Under the **Ming** dynasty there was a great interest in collecting the works of previous ages and a linked willingness by painters to be influenced by tradition. There are plenty of examples of bamboo and plum blossom, and bird and flower paintings being brought to a high decorative pitch, as well as a number of schools of landscape painting firmly rooted in traditional techniques. The arrival of the Manchu **Qing** dynasty did not disrupt the continuity of Chinese painting, but the art became wide open to many influences. It included the Italian **Castiglione** (Lang Shi-ning in Chinese) who specialized in horses, dogs and flowers under imperial patronage, the Four Wangs who re-interpreted Song and Yuan styles in an orthodox manner, and the individualists such as the Eight Eccentrics of Yangzhou and some Buddhist monks who objected to derivative art and sought a more distinctive approach to subject and style. But on the whole, the weight of tradition was powerful enough to maintain the old approach.

CALLIGRAPHY

Calligraphy literally means "beautiful writing" and the use of the brush saw the development of handwriting of various styles crystallizing into a high art form, valued on a par with painting. There are a number of different scripts: the **seal script** is the archaic form found on oracle bones; the **lishu** is the clerical style and was used in inscriptions on stone; while the **kaishu** is the regular style closest to the modern printed form; and *cao shu* cursive, **grass** or **running script**, is the most individual handwritten style. Emperors, poets and scholars over centuries have left examples of their calligraphy cut into stone at beauty spots, on mountains and in grottoes, tombs and temples all over China. You can see some early examples in the caves at Longmen (see p.262). At one stage during the Tang dynasty, calligraphy was so highly thought of that it was the yardstick for the selection of high officials.

OTHER ARTS

Jade and lacquerware have also been constantly in use in China since earliest times. In Chinese eyes, **jade**, in white and shades of green or brown, is the most precious of stones. It was used to make the earliest ritual objects, such as the flat disc **Pi**, symbol of Heaven, which was found in Shang and Zhou graves. Jade was also used as a mark of rank and for ornament, and in its most striking form in the jade burial suits which you will see in the country's museums.

Lacquer is also found as early as the Zhou. Made from the sap of the lac tree, many layers were painted on a wood or cloth base which was then carved and inlaid with gold, silver or tortoiseshell, or often most delicately painted. There are numerous examples of painted lacquer boxes and baskets from the Han and, as with jade, the use of this material has continued ever since.

TRADITIONAL MUSIC

The casual visitor to Beijing or other Chinese cities could be forgiven for thinking that Chinese music consists entirely of Muzak, Richard Clayderman arrangements and schmaltzy Hong Kong pop, blasted out on loudspeakers. But the cities are only a small part of Chinese life, and there's a large gap between urban and rural culture, which has increased since the Communist takeover in 1949. Just as misleading is the gulf between the official, sanitized image of Chinese culture and the realities of traditional life.

The Western clichéd image of Chinese music is caught somewhere between the notions of Confucian nostalgia for the proper Music of the Ancient Sages and the Red Guards brandishing the Little Red Book, destroying all traces of "feudal superstition". However, for such a huge country, a wide variety of styles is only to be expected – and includes **opera**, **folk song**, **narrative singing**, **instrumental** and **ritual music** – so don't be satisfied with the slick urban professional ensembles; any efforts to seek out genuine regional folk traditions will be well rewarded. Traditional music can still be heard during **festivals**, in the local **opera houses** and in **tea houses**, both in villages and towns. You might even run into Chinese musical field workers, who for the last fifteen years have been compiling an exhaustive **Anthology of Chinese Folk Music**, a national project collecting material in each of the provinces.

In towns, **parks** are often a good place to find amateurs getting together to sing and play. In general, the farther you go from the beaten track, the more folk music will come your way. If you're staying a while in one area and want advice on folk activity around county towns, it may be worth going to see cadres at the county **Cultural Centre** (*wenhua guan*), ideally with a Chinese friend. A more informal way is simply to follow your nose, or ears, maybe buttonhole an older person and see if there are any **temple fairs** (*miaohui*), **weddings or funerals** (*hongbai xishi*), **operas** (*xiqu*) or **narrative singing** (*shuochang* or *quyi*) happening in the area. You'll be lucky to hear folk song in action, but narrative singing and opera are more common. For **instrumental music**, shawm-and-percussion bands called "blowers and drummers" (**chuigushou**) often play for ceremonial occasions, performing not only theme tunes from TV, but also lengthy and solemn funerary suites, using circular breathing.

TRADITIONAL INSTRUMENTS

Dizi Transverse flute with membrane

Erhu, **huqin** and **jinghu** Two-stringed bowed fiddles. There are many regional forms of these, including the plaintive *gaohu* used in Cantonese music, and the *jinghu* which is used to accompany Beijing Opera

Guanzi Double-reed oboe

Guqin An introspective plucked zither

Percussion Instruments include drum, clappers, cymbals, gongs and woodblocks

Pipa Pear-shaped plucked lute with four strings

Sanxian Three-stringed banjo

Sheng Free-reed mouth organ

Suona Shawm with flared bell

Yangqin Struck zither

Xiao End-blown flute

Zheng Zither with sixteen or more strings, each with a tuning bridge

It may just be worth visiting the **conservatoires**, too, in the major cities like Beijing, Shanghai, Wuhan, Shenyang, Xi'an, Guangzhou and Chengdu. Some have foreign students who may give you some leads, and the teachers there may point you towards some good music.

ROOTS AND MODERN FORMS

Chinese music dates back millennia – the Tang dynasty was a frequently cited Golden Age – and many traditional forms in the countryside are the product of **gradual accretion** over the last few centuries. Rather like Irish music, Chinese music is heterophonic, with all the musicians playing differently decorated versions of the same melody, and most melodies are basically pentatonic, based on scales of five notes. Percussion plays a major role, both in independent ensembles, and as accompaniment to opera, narrative singing, ritual music and dance. In the towns, some modern forms had their beginnings in the "decadent" early years of this century and the long-delayed meeting of East and West. After the Opium Wars of the mid-nineteenth century, China was continually humiliated at the hands of the imperial powers, and in the turbulent years after 1911, when the last imperial dynasty, the Qing, was overthrown, **Western ideas** became widely popular, at least in the towns.

Musically, some exciting urban forms sprang up, such as new genres of **narrative singing** and the wonderful **Cantonese music** of the 1920s and 1930s. The official Chinese line castigates colonial treaty ports such as Shanghai and Canton (Guangzhou) before 1949 as a place of extreme decadence, and much of their music as "unhealthy" and "pornographic". After the Communist victory of 1949, this kind of music more or less disappeared; indeed, the whole ethos of traditional musical performance was challenged. Anything "feudal" or religious was severely restricted, while Chinese melodies were "cleaned up" with the addition of rudimentary harmonies and bass lines. New **"revolutionary" music**, composed from the 1930s on, was generally march-like and optimistic. During the **Cultural Revolution** (1966–76) musical life effectively ceased, with only eight model operas and ballets permitted on stage.

But rural traditions have always been obstinate, and spurred on by the economic liberalization of the 1980s and 1990s, Chinese traditional and **popular music** has revived, and Western sounds have also entered the scene in a big way. **Chinese pop** dominates the towns, with its bland, escapist lyrics, while musicians such as **Cui Jian**, the first significant and political Chinese rock artist, and the other growing rock groups are popular chiefly with students. Alongside this Western influence, more Chinese aspects have also found their way into rock, for example the interesting fusion of "northwest wind" (*xibei feng*) folk music. There has been some adventurous **film music**, too, notably the soundtrack to *Swan Song*, directed by Zhang Zeming, which focuses on an old Cantonese musician and his son's rejection of the old folk tradition, and Chen Kaige's *Yellow Earth*, which uses traditional music to strong effect.

OPERA AND NARRATIVE SINGING

On the classical Chinese music scene, vocal and dramatic music is dominant. There are several hundred types of regional opera, of which **Beijing Opera**, and the more classical but now rare **Kunqu** are the most widely known. It's a great visual spectacle, and it's also well worth adjusting your ears to the unfamiliar sounds of opera. Listen out, too, for the way the percussion patterns mirror the actions.

You should always be able to find an opera going on somewhere in the country. Even in Beijing you'll see groups of old men meeting in parks or, incongruously, at busy intersections where the old gateways used to be, going through their favourite Beijing Opera excerpts. If you're looking for more music and less acrobatics, seek out the classical Kunqu Opera, performed around Shanghai and also in Beijing. See pp.115–116 and p.350 for details on where to see opera in Beijing and Shanghai.

But every region has its own traditions. **Northern "clapper operas"** (*bangzi xi*) are rustic in flavour, while *pingju* and *huangmei xi* are more modern in style. **Sichuan Opera** has a distinctive female chorus, and you may find ritual masked opera being performed in the countryside iin **Yunnan, Anhui and Guizhou**. **Chaozhou and Fujian** also have beautiful styles of opera, and Fujian, in particular, is home to some wonderful **puppet operas**, the celebrated marionette troupe of Quanzhou being one of the most well known of all. Other good hunting areas are northern Shaanxi and eastern Hebei (around **Tangshan and Laoting**).

Narrative singing often features long classical stories and you may find a tea house full of old people following the story avidly. In Beijing, or especially in **Tianjin**, amateurs sing through traditional **Jingyun dagu** ballads, accompanied by drum and *sanxian* banjo. In **Suzhou**, **pingtan** is a beautiful genre which you may hear in the tea houses there, and **Sichuan** towns also have many tea houses where you're likely to come across narrative singing.

In Beijing you may see **xiangsheng**, a comic dialogue with a know-all and a straight man, though its subtle parodies of traditional opera may elude the outsider.

THE QIN AND OTHER SOLO TRADITIONS

Solo traditions of plucked instruments live on, too, in the conservatoires, with musicians trained as soloists on the pear-shaped **pipa** lute and the **zheng** and **qin** zithers. Of these, the most exalted – and possibly the oldest – is the *qin* (also known as **guqin** – ancient *qin*). This seven-string plucked zither has been a favourite subject of poets and painters for over a thousand years, and it is the most delicate instrument in the Chinese repertoire. It is the most accessible, too, producing expressive slides and ethereal harmonics. In the classic compositions, contemplative melodies give way to dramatic arpeggios in a texture in which silence is as important as sound.

Despite its status, the *qin* is not a well-known instrument outside the conservatoires. Few Chinese have heard its sound, or even heard of the instrument, and there may be only about two hundred *qin* players in the whole of China. I was fortunate enough to hear some of the great elders such as **Zhang Zijian**, **Wu Jinglue** and **Wu Zhaoji**. There is an accomplished middle generation of *qin* players, too, including **Li Xiangting**, **Wu Wen'guang**, **Lin Youren** and **Gong Yi**.

Strangely enough, the art of the *qin* was protected during the Cultural Revolution. Through incongruous personal connections with the notorious Kang Sheng, chief of Mao's secret police, and Yu Huiyong, the leftist composer of the revolutionary opera *Taking Tiger Mountain by Strategy*, the *qin* masters managed to keep working in peace through most of the period. There are many ancient instruments around, too. I've played on a Tang *qin*, over a thousand

years old, and Ming-dynasty instruments (1368–1644) are common.

The *qin* is best heard in informal meetings of aficionados rather than in concert. The **Beijing Qin Association**, led by Li Xiangting of the Central Conservatoire, is very active, and meets on the first Sunday of each month. In Shanghai, Lin Youren, the professor of *guqin* at the conservatoire, will be happy to introduce you to any get-togethers of *qin* enthusiasts in the area. Fortunately, there are some excellent recordings available, too (see box, p.1030).

CEREMONIAL MUSIC

If you are lucky you may come across a **wedding** or **funeral**, where you'll hear the most lively forms of music, especially in more rural areas. Shawm-and-percussion bands, in particular, play wild ceremonial suites. At a funeral in a remote Shanxi village some years back, I saw lay Taoist priests solemnly present offerings to the deities to ensure the path of the deceased to heaven, and then break into a bawdy routine with one of them pretending to smear the snot from the head priest's nose over the face of a straight man who continued playing the **sheng** (the traditional Chinese mouth organ). If you find yourself in a northern village, you may even witness a ritual *sheng-guan* ensemble with oboes, flutes, mouth organs, frames of pitched gongs and percussion. Long and deafening strings of fire-crackers are an inescapable part of much village ceremony, too. Some processions are led by a Western-style brass band with a shawm-and-percussion band behind, competing in volume, oblivious of key.

THE TEMPLES

A little more formally, you could attend a daily **temple ritual** at one of the major Buddhist or Taoist temples on the great religious mountains. Many of these temples have been restored since 1980, particularly in the south of China, where religious practice has been more resilient. Temple building has also been sustained by money from the commercial enterprise of the south and by overseas Chinese who have roots in the region. Temple rituals mainly involve **vocal liturgy** acompanied by ritual percussion, while few now use melodic instruments.

Morning and evening services are held daily (although morning services are usually held

DISCOGRAPHY

Authentic recordings of Chinese instrumental and religious music and opera are only just beginning to match the conservatoire-style recordings of souped-up arrangements that used to dominate the market. The recordings retrieved below should be generally available worldwide.

TRADITIONAL FOLK ANTHOLOGIES

Songs of the Land in China: *Labor Songs and Love Songs* (Wind Records; Taipei); two-CD set. Beautiful archive recordings of folk singing, mostly unaccompanied, from different regions of China, including songs of boatmen, Hua'er songs from the Northwest and songs from northern Shaanxi.

Various *China: Folk Instrumental Traditions* (Archives Internationales de Musique Populaire, Geneva: VDE-Gallo); two-CD set. A varied selection of archive and recent recordings of village ensembles from north and south, including shawm bands, ritual ensembles and silk-and-bamboo.

Various *Chine: Musique Classique* (Ocora, France). A selection of solo pieces featuring the *qin, pipa, sheng, guanzi* (oboe) and *dizi* (flute), played by outstanding instrumentalists of the 1950s.

Various *Musical Travel: China, the 18 Provinces* (Auvidis, Silex, France). Brief but evocative excerpts of a spectrum of sounds, recorded in Beijing, Shanghai, Fujian and Chengdu.

Various *Special Collection of Contemporary Chinese Musicians* (Wind Records, Taipei); two-CD set. Archive recordings of some of the great masters from the 1950s.

REGIONAL TRADITIONS

The Li Family Band *Shawms from Northeast China*; two volumes, "Music of the First Moon" and "The Li Family Band" (Ocora, France). Ear-cleansing shawm-and-percussion music performed for ceremonial.

Sizhu/Silk Bamboo *Chamber Music of South China* (Pan Records, Netherlands). Traditional ensembles from Shanghai, Guangzhou and Xiamen.

Various *China: Chuida Wind & Percussive Instrumental Ensembles* (UNESCO, France). Three traditional ensembles from southern China recorded in 1987, including silk-and-bamboo from Shanghai and ceremonial music for weddings and funerals.

Various *Nan-kouan: Chant Courtois de la Chine du Sud* (Ocora, France); 6 vols. Haunting chamber ballads with a female singer accompanied by end-blown flute and plucked and bowed lutes. Start off with the beautiful first volume, recorded in Paris in 1982.

Various *Rain Dropping on the Banana Tree* (Rounder, Cambridge, Mass.) Reissue of 78s from 1902 to 1930 featuring early masters of Cantonese music and Beijing Opera.

Various *Sizhu zhi xiang and mingqu huicui* (Yunnan Yinxiang Gongsi, China). These two cassettes are authentic Shanghai silk-and-bamboo music. Available, with a bit of luck, in Shanghai.

Various *Xi'an Drums Music* (Hugo, Hong Kong). Majestic wind-and-percussion music performed for funerals and calendrical pilgrimages around Xi'an.

OPERA

Quanzhou Puppet Troupe *China: Ka-lé, Festival of Happiness* (Archives Internationales de Musique Populaire, Geneva, VDE-Gallo). Music from the exquisite puppet operas of southern Fujian.

---

well before temples are open to the public). Try and get to an evening service, even if you have to ask specially. In **Beijing**, temples with fine ritual traditions include the Baiyun Guan, Guangji Si, and Guanghua Si. Southern temples are more lively, though. In **Shanghai**, active temples include the Longhua Si, Yufo Si and Baiyun Guan, and nearby in **Changzhou** the Tianning Si is a major centre of vocal liturgy.

Where **instrumental music** is added, temple music is often quite raucous and earthy, with a strong percussive element, and it is surprisingly accessible, even to ears unaccustomed to Chinese music. The Taoist priests from the Xuanmiao Guan in **Suzhou**, for example, play a wonderful and wide-ranging music, including pieces for silk-and-bamboo instruments, flutes and oboes, some spectacularly long trumpets

Various *An Introduction to Chinese Opera* (Hong Kong Records, Hong Kong). A series of four CDs illustrating different styles, including Beijing, Cantonese, Huangmei and Qinqiang operas.

Various *Opéra du Sichuan: la légende de serpent blanc* (Musique du Monde, France). A double CD of traditional opera from the spicy southwestern province of Sichuan.

Various *The Peony Pavilion: Chinese Classical Opera: Kunqu.* (Auvidis Inedit); two-CD set. Somewhat orchestrated versions of the classical opera.

SOLO INSTRUMENTAL

Li Xiangting *Chine: L'art du Qin* (Ocora, France). Refined meditations on the *qin*. A good and easily available recording.

Lin Shicheng *Chine: L'art du Pipa* (Ocora, France). Classical pieces for the *pipa* played by the senior pipa master.

Various *An Anthology of Chinese and Traditional Folk Music:* a collection of music played on the *guqin* (China Record Co); 8-CD set. A must for serious *qin*-fanatics, reissues of the great masters of the 1950s. May be available in Shanghai or Hong Kong.

Wu Man *Chinese Music for the Pipa* (Nimbus, UK). A fine recording from this brilliant young musician featuring traditional and contemporary works for the solo plucked lute.

TEMPLE MUSIC

Monks of the Zhihua Temple, Beijing *Beijing Zhihua si yinyue* (Wind Records, Hong Kong). These are volumes 8 and 9 from an otherwise dubious series of Chinese ritual music. They feature exquisite ancient music, recorded in 1990, played on double-reed pipes, flutes,

Chinese mouth organs, a frame of pitched gongs and percussion.

Monks of the Zhihua Temple, Beijing *China: Buddhist Music of the Ming Dynasty* (JVC, Japan). Another disc of the Zhihua Temple tradition, in collaboration with musicians from the Central Conservatoire.

Tianjin Buddhist Music Ensemble (Nimbus, UK). Ancient and evocative music with mouth organs, flute, chimes and percussion, but above all some wonderful *guanzi* oboe playing.

Various *Chine: Chant Liturgique Bouddhique* (Ocora, France). Ongoing series of vocal liturgy from Buddhist temples, so far including Quanzhou and Shanghai.

MINORITY PEOPLES

Dayan Ancient Music Association *Naxi Music from Lijiang* (Nimbus, UK). Solemn ceremonial silk-and-bamboo-type ensemble pieces recorded on their 1995 UK tour.

Various *Chine: Xinjiang, the Silk Road* (Playasound, France). A taste of the Turkic vocal and instrumental music of Xinjiang and the western regions of China towards central Asia.

Various *Chinese Turkestan: Uighur Music* (Ocora, France). A two-CD set of classical and popular music traditions from Xinjiang.

Various *A Happy Miao Family* (Pan, Netherlands). The first in a projected series of recordings of minority music in China. Lively recordings of songs and dances from the Miao people of the southwest, with reed organ, lute and tree leaf!

Various *Baishibai: Songs of the Minority Nationalities of Yunnan* (Pan, Netherlands). Field recordings of songs and instrumental music from different tribes in the southwest province.

and a battery of percussion. The Suzhou monks left China for the first time in spring 1994 for a tour of Britain.

COURT MUSIC

In recent years, the rituals of the bygone **imperial courts** have been revived at **Qufu** and a few other towns including **Nanjing**, largely for tourists. While you're in Shandong,

the Taoist music of Tai Shan and the shawm bands of southwestern Shandong (around Heze County) are more authentic.

SILK-AND-BAMBOO

Perhaps the most accessible "folk music" in China, however, is the mellifluous **"silk-and-bamboo" ensembles**. These can be heard at their best on any afternoon, played by old-timers in **Shanghai's tea houses**. The players are all amateur, and turn up for their own pleasure, sitting round a table and taking it in turns to play a set with Chinese fiddles, flutes and banjos. It's a little like an Irish session, only with Chinese tea instead of Guinness. Try and get to a Monday afternoon gathering at the Huxinting Tea House in the Yu Yuan quarter (see p.341), where you can listen to the long unravelling of a piece called "Sanliu", or watch the exhilaration of the dash to the finish of "Street Parade", with its breathless syncopations. Another charming venue for silk-and-bamboo (and other genres) in Shanghai is the Wen Miao, although with a bit of persistence you should be able to find amateur silk-and-bamboo clubs throughout the whole of neighbouring Jiangsu and Zhejiang provinces, especially in **Nanjing** and **Hangzhou**.

This music is also arranged for **professional folk orchestras**. While in China, I attended a "contest" of some forty ensembles from all over the country and throughout Southeast Asia. Most were professional or conservatoire-based and even the groups from the home province of Jiangsu were quite far removed in style from the local folk music. In place of the undemonstrative style of the tea house musicians, they employed Tchaikovsky-esque expressive effects, swaying about on stage, and editing themselves brutally by removing the repeats in case people got bored. The contest wasn't a rewarding listening experience, but it showed just how good and how complex the real tea house music is, with its captivating dovetailing of phrases. And it showed, too, to what extent Chinese music is being bulldozed by half-baked Western romantic misconceptions.

In recent years several traditional genres have found their way into the **concert hall,** though all too often they suffer from the deadening hand of state control. The **Xi'an Conservatoire** has commercialized local ceremonial music, but the real thing is much better and can still be heard at temple festivals in Xi'an itself and in the surrounding area. A more successful exchange has been brought about by the teachers and students of the **Beijing Central Conservatoire**, who have studied the exquisite instrumental music of the Zhihua Temple in Beijing and have even performed it on stage with the temple's former monks.

Another genuine folk music tradition is that of the "Music Association" of **Qujiaying** vil-

lage, one of several hundred **amateur ritual associations** on the otherwise drab plain just south of Beijing. This peasants' music was probably learned in imperial times from monks trained in Beijing and, in an interesting initiative, the village has recently sent six teenagers to study at the Zhihua Temple.

WHERE TO HEAR TRADITIONAL MUSIC

In **Beijing**, apart from the suggestions above, the English-language magazines and the *China Daily* often advertise performances. The *Sanwei Bookstore* also has regular recitals of Chinese music (see p.116).

In **Shaanxi** Province, the capital **Xi'an** has much to offer. Wind-and-percussion ensembles perform the ceremonial music called **Xi'an guyue**, especially during the sixth lunar moon, around July, and the Baxian Gong, in particular, has good ritual music. And if you've seen *Yellow Earth* or *The Story of Qiu Ju*, head for the real thing among the barren loess hills of northern Shaanxi, which are home to fantastic folk-singers, local opera, puppeteers, shawm bands, yang'ge dancing and folk ritual specialists. Aim for counties like Suide, Mizhi and Yulin – and try and get to the Baiyun Guan at Jiaxian high above the Yellow River, ideally for the fourth moon festival, generally around late May.

Sichuan is lively for opera and narrative singing – look out for opera troupes such as the Sichuan Opera Arts Institute or the Sichuan Opera Third Troupe in **Chengdu**. One area where folk festivals often feature folk singing is in the Northwest (**Gansu and Ningxia**), where people congregate to compete in the singing of earthy songs called *Hua'er* – again, at festival times.

Southern Fujian is another fantastic area for folk music, notably Quanzhou and Xiamen. In the haunting **Nanguan** ballads, popular all along the coast of southern Fujian, as in Taiwan across the strait, a female singer is accompanied by an end-blown flute and plucked and bowed lutes. Not only can you hear amateur Nanguan clubs but folk opera and puppetry are often to be heard. Farther south along the coast, **Chaozhou** and the **Hakka** area inland around **Meixian and Dabu** have celebrated string ensembles and ceremonial percussion bands. Temples in the area are also lively, particularly the Kaiyuan Si in Quanzhou, Nanputuo Si in

Xiamen, Guanghua Si in Putian and the Kaiyuan Si in Chaozhou.

Cantonese music is something very different, and from the 1920s fused the local traditional music with sleazy Western elements, notably jazz, played on Chinese instruments, saxophone, violin and xylophone. Musicians like the composer **Lü Wencheng**, the violinist **Yi Zizhong** (who played in London in 1924) and **He Dasha** ("Thicko He") made many wonderful commercial 78s during this period, which richly deserve to be reissued. Today more often heard in modern arrangements, some of the 1930s classics are still great, but around **Guangzhou** you'll more likely find a slick, institutionalized troupe than an amateur band.

Farther afield, folk music should be more accessible among the minority peoples of western China. In **Xinjiang**, try and find **maqam song-and-dance**, popular over a wide area of Central Asia – as ever, better in a folk festival than in an urban concert. In **Urumqi**, there are nightly performances in many of the Uighur restaurants, and in **Kashgar**, the Uighur musical instrument shop in the bazaar is lively, and musicians gather in the main square outside the mosque. Around Tian Chi (Heaven Lake) and Lake Sayrem, and the Ili and Altai regions, **Kazakh and Mongol traditions** can be found, in both organized festivals and spontaneous gatherings.

In **Yunnan**, **Cuihu Park** in Kunming is a convenient place to find peasants from all over the province meeting to sing. The music of the remote but popular town of **Lijiang** has had an extraordinary propagandist in the person of the English-speaking eccentric Xuan Ke. He organizes a group of folk musicians who perform the local Naxi ceremonial music regularly for tourists (see p.739). Throughout the villages of Yunnan there is fantastic music: folk singers, *sheng* mouth-organ players, ritual groups, all performing as part of everyday life.

Stephen Jones

WILDLIFE AND THE ENVIRONMENT

The scale of China's environmental problems makes an ironically appropriate partner for the breadth of its wildlife and natural beauty. It ranks among the most well-endowed countries on earth, and its list of big animals ("megafauna") includes tigers, pandas, elephants and cranes. Yet the country's environmental importance goes far beyond these well-known species, with a massive range of geography and habitats resulting in an extraordinary diversity of plant and animal life. The world's third largest country, China has an elevation differential surpassing all other nations, rising from sea level in the east to the peak of Mount Everest on the border with Nepal. The south shares tropical rainforests with Laos, Vietnam and Burma, while the Da Hinggan Mountains in Inner Mongolia have tundra-type vegetation on top of permafrost. China is also home to East Asia's most important wetlands and Asia's longest river and is the source of two rivers of inestimable importance to hundreds of millions of people in South and Southeast Asia – the Ganges and the Mekong.

Arrayed against this natural beauty and biological importance are a panoply of equally dramatic **problems**. To begin with, China's 1.2 billion souls account for a fifth of the world's

population, but the nation encompasses less than one tenth of the world's arable land. Furthermore, almost the entire population lives in the well-watered eastern half of the country, where virtually every centimetre of farmland has been developed. Indeed, China has very little land of any kind that has not been altered in some way by man. Any attempts at **sustainable development** are complicated by the sheer size of the population relative to available resources, by dramatic growth in the economy and the continuing need to raise living standards for some of Asia's poorest people. Forests and wetlands, grasslands and agricultural fields are stretched beyond the limits of sustainable production. Urban areas face a similar crisis, with air and water widely subjected to intensely unpleasant and destructive **pollution**. Coal dust, factory emissions, vehicle exhaust and wind-blown desert sand give Chinese cities suspended particle and carbon dioxide readings many times the recommended World Health Organization standards – Beijing, Shenyang, Xi'an, Shanghai and Guangzhou are among the top ten most polluted cities in the world. Due to the lack of water treatment in China, more than thirty percent of the nations' rivers are polluted and over ninety percent of water in urban areas is heavily contaminated.

China's development also has a direct impact both on Asia and the rest of the world. Plentiful **coal** resources make it a cheap fuel for generating China's ever-growing power requirements, but will probably create the highest levels of greenhouse gas emissions for any nation early in the twenty-first century. Already, sulphur dioxide produced by coal fires in China causes one-third of the acid rain which falls downwind on South Korea. The **wildlife** of neighbouring countries has also been affected by China's development, with populations often heavily exploited to supply the Chinese market. For example, **tiger bones** from India, Russia and Southeast Asia were sold legally as Chinese medicine until world pressure encouraged the government to outlaw the practice in December 1994. Fish and turtles, however, are still legally imported in huge quantities from Vietnam.

CLIMATE AND GEOGRAPHY

From the top to the bottom of the evolutionary ladder, China contains a large slice of the world's total number of species. Over thirty thousand types of **plants** are found here – a count only exceeded by tropical Brazil and Malaysia – including forty percent of the world's gymnosperms (the class of plants which includes conifers). Less visible, but perhaps equally as important, are China's eight thousand identified species of **fungi** and five thousand identified **bacteria**; while the country also supports thirteen percent of the global total of **mammal and bird species**. These figures are even more remarkable when you consider how many species are **endemic**, existing in China alone: 72 varieties of mammal; 99 varieties of bird (including over half the global species of crane); and some 400 types of aquatic vertebrate. Wolong Nature Reserve in western Sichuan Province contains a total of four thousand vascular plants, including many different species of now domesticated strawberries, apples, plums and pears – most of them local endemics – of huge economic importance all over the world.

This great biological richness derives from China's widely varying environment, and some particular aspects of its geological and climatic history. First of all, China's landmass spans five **climatic zones**: cold-temperate, temperate, warm-temperate, subtropical and tropical. The implications of this are illustrated by the average January temperature in Harbin, the capital of Heilongjiang Province bordering Russia, which is minus 18°C, while the average January temperature in Guangzhou, capital of Guangdong Province bordering Hong Kong, is 13°C. At the same time, **rainfall** is generally plentiful in southern China while scarce in the Northwest.

In Xishuangbanna Dai Autonomous Prefecture, Yunnan Province, Southeast Asia's tropical species make their northernmost stand in China's largest remaining **tropical rainforest**. A line of generally east–west trending mountains forms a climatic barrier at the north of the prefecture, sealing Xishuangbanna from the cooler northern weather. Elephants, gaur (a huge wild cattle species), wild pigs, sambar deer, macaque monkeys, great hornbills, and leopards coexist uneasily with a growing human population. Tigers may also still appear from time to time, cautiously sneaking over the border from Laos or Vietnam. These animals are protected in the five non-contiguous sections of the Xishuangbanna National Nature Reserve. Yet this is also China's most productive **rubber-**

growing area, and massive conversion of natural forests to rubber plantations in the 1970s destroyed much original biodiversity. The provincial government has now outlawed further conversions on state-owned land, though rubber continues to expand into natural forests owned by villages where it is a lucrative cash crop.

FORESTS

China contains a variety of **forest types,** but the country is dominated by subtropical and temperate vegetation. Both the northeast and northwest reaches contain mountains and cold **coniferous forests**. These are characterized by larch, spruce, pine and fir trees, containing over forty species of mammals (including moose and Asiatic black bear) and 120 species of birds. Moist conifer forests can have thickets of bamboo as an understorey, replaced by rhododendrons in higher montane stands of juniper and yew. **Subtropical forests** dominate central and southern China. They support an astounding 146,000 species of flora, as well as the famous giant panda, golden monkey, and South China tiger. **Tropical rainforests** and seasonal rainforests in Yunnan and Hainan Island contain a quarter of China's total number of species on only 0.5 percent of its area, indication again of the fertile diversity of tropical regions.

The extent of **deforestation** over the last half-century has had massive consequences. China is currently the second largest importer of timber in the world. It suffers from dramatically increased desertification in the north and west, faces water shortages over the entire country and has a forestry sector which is dramatically over-employed. Yet, although logging continues at a frightening rate, China's overall forest cover has risen from a low of about eight percent in the early 1970s to the current level of almost fourteen percent. This dramatic increase has been brought about by the **"Green Great Wall" campaign** and associated reforestation efforts, which plan to bring forest cover to seventeen percent of the country by the year 2000. **Tree planting** is currently focused at the upper reaches of major river systems such as the Yangzi, Yellow and Liao rivers, while anti-desertification projects focus on north-central China in Ningxia and Inner Mongolia.

Initial problems with this massive reforestation programme were similar to those which caused the cutting of trees in the first place.

Government policies took too little notice of local conditions and provided inadequate incentives for farmers to care for the trees they planted. While the latter has to a certain extent been solved by allowing farmers to keep the benefit from whatever they plant (for example, they can sell fruit or wood from "their" trees), there is still, at times, the problem of locally inappropriate species being planted. At any rate, while these reforestation programmes are more socially appropriate, the biological value of these replanted forests is far lower than that of the natural forests they are replacing. Replanted forest can provide timber for industrial and household use, but it does not adequately replace the role of natural forests in protecting soil, retaining water or supporting wildlife.

Another fundamental problem faced by China's forest sector has overwhelming implications for conservation: the difficulty of finding **alternative employment** for hundreds of thousands of loggers when the establishment of nature reserves or diminishing forest areas requires that tree cutting be stopped. Nowhere is this more urgent over a broad area than in **giant panda habitat**. Giant pandas require vast quantities of **bamboo**, which grows as an understorey to the moist subtropical forests of mountainous Sichuan, Gansu and Shaanxi provinces. Without an upper storey of trees, bamboo will wither. The logging which has diminished the forest areas of these provinces has shrunk panda habitat as well.

The loggers who cut these trees are generally employed by units of the local government which logs on state-owned land. Nature reserves for the protection of pandas are generally placed on state-owned forest land as well. This direct **conflict in land use** – between logging and nature reserves – provides the crux of the giant panda conservation problem. In certain locations, forestry workers whose forest areas have been converted to giant panda reserves have subsisted for over eighteen months on **government subsidies** of just about ¥100 per month. Even these minimal amounts cannot be continued for ever. The government and international partners are currently seeking longer-term solutions to this problem.

A similar problem hit the national news in China over the summer of 1996. The Yunnan **snub-nosed monkey** (a sub-species of the golden monkey) is endemic to a few isolated forests in the hills of western Yunnan. Some of the monkey's habitat is protected within Baimaxue Shan Nature Reserve, but some extends beyond the boundaries of the reserve into forest that is scheduled for cutting. Deqin County, which became the focus of the issue, relies on timber for 95 percent of its government revenue and thus for the salaries of its employees as well as for its social responsibilities such as schools and health clinics. The original research identifying the range and habitat needs of this species was done between 1991 and 1994 by the Kunming Institute of Zoology and the World Wide Fund for Nature (WWF). A wildlife videographer from Yunnan took special interest in this species and developed a television programme about the research which was broadcast nationally. When word became known that logging activities might threaten some of the monkey's habitat, there was something akin to a national outcry. Students from Beijing University held a candlelit march. Members of a Beijing-based NGO, called Friends of Nature, organized a summer camp to explore the issues in Baimaxue Shan and raise awareness of the problem. The Ministry of Forestry responded with concern and was naturally met with demands for compensation from Deqin County's government. To stop logging would undoubtedly bring economic hardship to the county, already mired in poverty of the most dramatic kind, and with few income options beyond the sale of its one valuable resource. The situation in the winter of 1996 was stable – no cutting was taking place, but no long-term solution had been identified either.

GRASSLANDS AND DESERTS

Together grasslands and deserts make up half of China's total land area. The immense and productive **grasslands** are largely concentrated in Inner Mongolia, Ningxia Autonomous Region, parts of Qinghai and Tibet. The natural wildlife they support includes three extremely rare species on the verge of extinction: Przewalski's horse, the Asiatic wild ass and the Bactrian camel (the ancestor of domesticated camels). Others, including the Tibetan gazelle, are threatened by the influx of gold miners and truck drivers carrying goods to and from Tibet, who poach animals for food and trophies. Millions of domesticated sheep and cows are grazed on the grasslands of Inner Mongolia, leading to severe depletion of the natural carrying capacity and increased threat of desertification. There is often **direct competition** between domestic animals and natural fauna. Herdsmen poison or trap carnivores, and sometimes destroy forests by burning or girdling trees to increase pasture area. The government has recently stepped up efforts to control the conversion of grasslands to pasture, but lacks enforcement and patrol manpower.

Deserts make up one-fifth of China's total territory, largely in the northeast. Arid steppes cover additional area in the Altai, Tian and Kunlun mountains in the far west, an area blocked from the southwestern monsoon by the Tibetan plateau and from the southeastern monsoon by its distance from the sea.

FRESHWATER ECOSYSTEMS

Freshwater ecosystems are of massive importance to China, both in terms of food production and flood control. China contains 25 million hectares of natural **wetlands**, about half of which are rivers and lakes. An additional 36 million hectares are man-made wetlands, including rice paddies and aquaculture ponds. A huge percentage of China's population is dependent on wetland ecosystems for economic production and, somewhat obviously, drinking water.

Seven of the most important **rivers** in the world begin in the highlands of western China. The Yellow River, Yangzi River, Lancang Jiang (Mekong) and the Salween rise in the east of the Qinghai–Tibet plateau. The Indus, Ganges and Brahmaputra rise in the south. Downstream these rivers serve as sources of irrigation and drinking water, modes of transport and centres of cultural and religious importance for probably two billion people in China, India, Pakistan, Bangladesh and throughout Southeast Asia. These rivers rise and gather strength from many of the thousands of freshwater lakes of the region. The black-necked crane breeds in marshland in Tibet and western Sichuan and winters in southeast Tibet, Bhutan, northern Yunnan and by western Guizhou. The bar-headed goose also breeds here.

China's northeast is the focus for much of the country's **freshwater marshes**. Two million hectares on the Sanjiang Plain of Heilongjiang Province are essentially a collection of shallow freshwater lakes and reed-beds where the

Heilongjiang, Sungari and Wusuli rivers come together. Jilin, Liaoning and Inner Mongolia all share these ecosystems. One of the most well-known wildlife areas in this ecosystem is **Zhalong Nature Reserve**, a 2,000-square-kilometre area which was created in 1979 to protect breeding areas for the red-crowned crane. Other crane species which rely on marshes in these provinces for breeding and migration stopovers include the Siberian crane, white-naped crane and common crane. These marshes are also of great value for reed production, the bulk of which is turned into pulp for paper. Waterfowl and reed production can usually coexist, at least at present levels, so this is a useful confluence of conservation and economic uses. Threats to the Sanjiang area stem from large-scale drainage of the wetland and conversion to grain production. The impact of an aid programme from the Japanese government to assist this conversion in the Sanjiang area was being evaluated in the summer of 1996.

China's **freshwater lakes** include the country's best-known wetlands: Jiangxi's Poyang Hu and Hunan's Dongting Hu. These two sites have been nominated by China as "Wetlands of International Importance" under the Ramsar Convention for the wise use of wetlands. The importance of these shallow, seasonally varying lakes on the Yangzi River is multi-faceted, and both are national level nature reserves. **Dongting Hu**, China's second largest freshwater lake, has shrunk by 41 percent since 1949 due to siltation from the Yangzi and reclamation for agriculture. Water pollution from Yueyang City on its banks, overfishing and poaching of waterbirds threaten its fertile wildlife resources. Dongting Hu is essentially a network of small, shallow freshwater lakes and marshes. Four rivers aside from the Yangzi – the Xiangjiang, Zhishui, Yuanjiang and Lishui – contribute their flow, creating annual fluctuations in water levels of almost eighteen metres. Dongting Hu is vitally important for wildlife, including the highly endangered (if not extinct) Yangzi river dolphin and Chinese sturgeon, both of which live in and around Dongting Hu. Birdlife which winters there include the Chinese merganser, the great bustard and four species of cranes.

Poyang Hu is a similar complex of small lakes and marsh areas which also fluctuate seasonally. These fluctuations create its productivity and attractiveness to wintering waterbirds, and have recently added to conservation headaches as well. The entire area of Poyang Hu is submerged under summer floodwaters from the Yangzi, during which time the lake surface area may reach 3,500 square kilometres with a deepest point of only thirty metres. The receding of the water during the autumn exposes land for cultivation. The lowest land supports grass to be grazed by domestic livestock and reed beds which are used for thatch and fodder. These lands also provide food sources for wintering birds. A number of small lakes are left isolated by the receding waters on the peripheries of the main lakes, and are managed for **fish production**. Fish resources are naturally restocked from the main lakes and rivers during the summer floods, then drained to facilitate capture of fish at the end of autumn.

In recent years, however, some of Poyang's larger lakes of great importance to feeding birds have also been drained at the end of autumn. This has left waterfowl with inadequate shallow land on which to feed. Blame has been levelled at local authorities, including the reserve itself, which sought greater fish production at the expense of the fate of the birds. The situation is likely to resolve itself with the interest of the national Ministry of Forestry, parent body for Ramsar sites. In terms of endangered wildlife, the importance of Poyang Hu is hard to overstate. Poyang provides wintering habitat for almost the entire world population of two hundred **Siberian cranes**. Other protected species wintering there include hooded crane, swan goose, Oriental storks, and black storks. As many as five hundred thousand birds may be on Poyang Hu at any one time during the winter months.

SALTWATER LAKES AND COASTAL WETLANDS

About half of China's lakes are **saline** and important breeding grounds for **waterfowl**. Most are concentrated in northwest China on the inland drainage systems of the North Tibetan Plain and in the Zaidan basin. The largest is Qinghai Hu, a 4,426-square-kilometre reserve which attracts thousands of birds each summer, including cormorants, great black-headed gulls, bar-headed geese, and pied avocets. Similarly, the Tarim River basin in Xinjiang supports one of the largest breeding populations of black stork in China. The Ordos plateau

area of Inner Mongolia as well as the Xinjiang's Taolimiao-Alashan Nur (lake) support breeding sites for the highly endangered relict gull. Most of these lakes and marshes fluctuate seasonally and are threatened by increased diversion of water for human use, including household and agricultural uses.

China's **coastline** is approximately 18,000 km long, extending from the Bohai Gulf which freezes in the winter to the tropical waters of the South China Sea. The diversity of wildlife supported by the coast and as many as five thousand offshore islands is remarkable. Coastal wetlands are important as fuel stops for waterfowl on the migratory route between Siberia and Australia. Some species fly directly to China from Australia. Others rely for their survival on the few remaining undisturbed intertidal mudflats along the southern coast. The Saunder's gull breeds exclusively at Chinese coastal wetlands, particularly at the largest remaining site of coastal salt marsh in Yancheng, Jiangsu Province. Chongming Island in the Yangzi River Delta near China's largest city, Shanghai, is vital for migrants heading for Australia. Unfortunately, both Shanghai and Jiangsu are among China's fastest growing regions.

THREATS

As any traveller to China would suspect, **environmental conservation** is by no means assured, as the country rushes to throw off years of economic stagnation by uncontrolled development. Yet when specific habitats vanish, the species they support become extinct too. Currently, China's **endangered flora and fauna** includes a vast proportion of native gymnosperms: the familiar, endemic and dreadfully scarce giant panda; the South China tiger; Yangzi river dolphin; crested ibis; and a host of other plants and animals. Of the above animals, the giant panda is most populous with approximately a thousand individuals left in the wild, while the entire known population of crested ibis – either captive or wild – is perhaps 45. Other highly endangered animals include the snow leopard, which depends on western China for over half its range; the Asian elephant, a resident of Xishuangbanna near Laos and Vietnam; the golden monkey; and migratory species such as the red-crowned crane and black-necked crane.

Wildlife is threatened in China for a vast array of reasons, but most are an outgrowth of common human economic activities. **Intensive cultivation of land** for food production has led to diminishing areas of wildlands and diminishing habitat for wildlife, just as reclamation of wetlands for agriculture, and construction of power stations and water conservancy have diminished the area of freshwater ecosystems. Demand has outstripped growth in supply for virtually all **natural resources**, including timber, animal products and wild plants. **Pollution**, a consequence both of irrational Marxist pricing policies for resources during the early years of the People's Republic and the massive economic growth of the reform period, has damaged habitats and diminished the carrying capacity of water resources. **Wildlife** has diminished because it is not considered a productive use of land, especially when compared with agriculture, energy generation, industrial development and waste disposal.

CONSERVATION

Under these circumstances **conservation** is extremely difficult, though there has been progress made over recent years. In numbers and area covered, China's **nature reserves** have expanded with great speed. From the establishment of Dinghushan Nature Reserve in Guangdong Province in 1956 until 1978 only 34 reserves were created, but since then the numbers have grown exponentially. At present there are over seven hundred nature reserves in the country covering almost six percent of the nation's territory. The Ministry of Forestry is responsible for over five hundred of these, with others being under the National Environmental Protection Agency, the Ministry of Agriculture and the State Oceanic Administration.

These agencies have collaborated with a variety of **external organizations** over the past sixteen years. The first international co-operative conservation programme in China was established by the World Wide Fund for Nature (WWF) and the Ministry of Forestry in 1980, and aimed at giant panda conservation. Since then, the Wildlife Conservation Society, International Crane Foundation and Wetlands International have also supported conservation activities, while the Ford Foundation addresses the interaction of rural development and conservation. The Man and Biosphere Programme of UNESCO counts ten Chinese reserves among its international network, with the Chinese MAB Committee listing a further ninety as part of their domestic projects. A variety of international funding agencies provide technical and financial assistance to China for conservation, including the World Bank, the United Nations Development Programme, and a number of bilateral donors.

While the **government** has shown interest and growing commitment to conservation in recent years, the most encouraging initiatives are those that have taken place in the informal sector among **concerned citizens**. The national campaign to save the Yunnan snub-nosed monkey was the first of its kind in China. It grew from increased awareness among urban people of the unique legacy that China's environment has left them and of the need to strengthen conservation in the face of overwhelming development pressures. Several "non-governmental organizations" now exist and, though few would be recognizable as pressure groups in the Western sense, they indicate the growing space for public debate over the environment. **Environmental television and radio programmes** abound on China's airwaves, responding to, and further fuelling, conservation awareness. Most significantly, younger, technically trained specialists are increasingly taking over responsibility for conservation programmes in nature reserves and at the policy level. While often still subordinate to the poorly considered policies of superiors who have been promoted from the Communist Party or political systems, this younger generation is also developing influence in key areas around the country.

Though the pressures that have led to the degradation of China's environment and wildlife have not abated in recent times – and in fact if anything have increased – the strength of the "opposition" represented by China's conservationists has grown as well. Conservation is a process, and it is difficult to imagine a day when wild resources in China are no longer threatened by a combination of necessity and the desires of its population. There is reason to believe, however, that the increased awareness and commitment of China's citizens and the increased ability of its officials will gradually improve the balance.

Daniel A. Viederman

FILM

Film came early to China. The first moving picture was exhibited in 1896 at a "tea house variety show" in Shanghai, where the country's first cinema would also be built just twelve years later. By the 1930s, modern cinema as we know it today was already playing an important role in the cultural life of Shanghai, though the huge number of resident foreigners ensured a largely Western diet of films – at least eighty percent of them were from Hollywood. Nevertheless, local Chinese films were also starting to be made, mainly by the so-called May Fourth intellectuals (middle-class liberals inspired by the uprising of May 4, 1919), who wanted to turn China into a modern country along Western lines. Naturally, Western stylistic influences on these films were very strong, and early Chinese films have little to do with the highly stylized, formal world of traditional performance arts such as Beijing Opera or puppet shadow theatre. However, early film-showings often employed a traditional style "storyteller" who sat near the screen reading out the titles as they came up, for the benefit of those who could not read the language.

1920–1940: THE SHANGHAI STUDIOS

Of the few important **studios** in Shanghai operating in the 1920s and 1930s, perhaps the most famous was the **Mingxing**, whose films were generally of a left-leaning, anti-imperialist nature quite at odds with the general tenor of Hollywood.

The film *Sister Flower* (1933) tells the story of twin sisters separated at birth, one of whom ends up a city girl living in Shanghai, while the other remains a poor villager. During the course of reuniting the sisters, the film contrasts in some detail the lives of ordinary city-dwellers and peasants. Another film from the same year, *Spring Silk Worm*, an adaptation of a short story written by the well-known contemporary writer Mao Dun, portrays economic decline and hardship in Zhejiang Province outside Shanghai, and implicitly levels the finger of accusation at Japanese imperialism. Finally, *The Goddess* (1934), from the **Lianhua** studio, shows the struggle of a prostitute to have her son educated, against all the prejudices of the age. The improbably glamorous prostitute was played by the woman often referred to as China's own Garbo, the languorous Ruan Lingyu. Despite the liberal pretensions of these films, it was inevitable – given that audiences comprised just a tiny elite of China's total population – that they would later be derided by the Communists as excessively bourgeois.

After the **Japanese occupation** of Shanghai along with other large tracts of China in 1937, "subversive" studios such as the Mingxing and Lianhua were immediately closed, though some of the film-making talent managed to flee into the interior, where work continued. The experience of war undoubtedly put film-makers in closer touch with their potential future audiences, the Chinese masses. China's great wartime epic, **Spring River Flows East** (1947–8) was the cinematic result of this experience. The story spans the whole duration of the anti-Japanese war – and the ensuing civil war – through the lives of a single family, who are themselves torn apart by the conflict. The heroine, living in simple poverty, contrasts with her husband, who has long since abandoned his wife for a decadent urban existence in Shanghai. Traumatized by a decade of war, the Chinese who saw this film appreciated it as an authentic and representative account of the sufferings through which the entire nation had lived. Over three quarters of a million people saw the film at the time of its release, which was a remarkable figure given that the country was still at war.

1940–1980: COMMUNISM AND THE CINEMA

Chinese film-making under the **Communists** is a story which really dates back to 1938, when

Mao Zedong and his fellow Long Marchers finally set up their base in **Yan'an** deep in Shaanxi Province and began to prepare for the seizure of power. There could have been no world farther removed from the glamour of Shanghai than dusty, poverty-stricken Yan'an, full of peasants and simple farmers. This was the ideal location for the film-makers of the future People's Republic to practise their skills. Talent escaping through Japanese lines was soon trickling through in search of employment, among them an obscure actress of high ambitions, one **Jiang Qing**, later to become Mao's wife and self-appointed empress of Chinese culture. One thing that all the leading Communists in Yan'an agreed on was the importance of film as a **centralizing medium**, which could and should be used to unify the culture of the nation after the war had been won.

The immediate consequence of the Communist victory in 1949 was that the showing of foreign films was severely curtailed. Days were numbered for the private Shanghai studios, too, though they still managed to produce a few films in the years immediately after 1949. In 1950, a **Film Guidance committee** was set up, comprising 32 members whose task would be to set standards and, effectively, decide upon all film output for the entire nation. In addition to Mao's wife, Jiang Qing, the members of the committee included Yan'an film-makers as well as May Fourth intellectuals, and the established prewar film-makers drew some confidence from the range of voices represented. By 1953 a unified national system for film production was in place and the first major socialist epic, **Bridge**, appeared in 1949, depicting mass mobilization of workers and peasantry rushing enthusiastically to construct a bridge in record time. Although predictably dull in terms of character and plot, the cast still contained a number of prewar Shanghai actors to divert audiences. The end of the film is marked, for the first time in Chinese cinema, by the entire cast gathering to shout "Long live Chairman Mao!", a scene that was to be re-enacted time and again over the coming years.

A year after *Bridge* one of the very last non-government Shanghai studio films appeared, **The Life of Wu Xun**. This was a huge project that had started years earlier, well before 1949, and, surprisingly, had been allowed to run through to completion despite the change of regime. The subject of the film is the famous nineteenth-century entrepreneur, Wu Xun, who started out life as a beggar and eventually rose to enormous riches, whereupon he set out on his lifetime's ambition to educate the peasantry. Despite the addition of a narrator's voice at the end of the film, pointing out that it was revolution and not education that peasants really needed, the film turned out a disaster for the Shanghai film industry. Mao himself wrote a damning critique of it for idolizing a "Qing landlord", and a full-scale campaign was launched against the legacy of the entire Shanghai film world, studios, actors, critics and audiences alike.

The remains of the May Fourth Movement struggled on. *New Year's Sacrifice*, a film based on a short story from the great prewar intellectual Lu Xun, was released in 1956, though with most of the intelligence and all of the irony taken out. The consolation for the old guard was that newer generations of Chinese film-makers had not yet solved the problem of how to portray life in the contemporary era either. The 1952 screen adaptation of Lao She's short story *Dragon's Beard Ditch*, for example, was supposed to contrast the miserable pre-1949 life of a poor district of Beijing with the happy, prosperous life that was being lived under the Communists. The only problem, as any audience could immediately see, was that the supposedly miserable pre-1949 scenes actually looked a good deal more human and heart-warming than the later ones.

Nevertheless, the Communists did achieve some of their original targets during the **1950s**. The promotion of a universal culture and language was one of them. All characters in all films – from Tibetans to Mongolians to Cantonese – were depicted as speaking in flawless **Mandarin Chinese**. Film production, too, fanned out across China, and was no longer confined to the eastern coastal cities. Above all, there was an explosion in audiences, from around 47 million tickets sold in 1949, to 600 million in 1956, to over 4 billion in 1959. The latter figure should be understood in the context of the madness surrounding the Great Leap Forward, a time of crazed overproduction in all fields, film included. Film studios began sprouting in every town in China, though with a catastrophic loss of quality – a typical studio in Jiangxi Province comprised one man, his bicycle and an antique stills camera. The colossal output of that year included uninspiring titles such as *Loving the Factory as One's Home*.

The conspicuous failure of the Great Leap Forward did, however, bring some short-lived advantages to the film industry. While Mao was forced temporarily into the political sidelines in the late 1950s and early 1960s, the cultural bureaucrats signalled that in addition to "revolutionary realism", a certain degree of **"revolutionary romanticism"** was also to be encouraged. Chinese themes and subjects, as opposed to pure Marxism, were looked upon with more favour. A slight blossoming occurred, with improbable films such as *Lin Zexu* (1959), which covered the life of the great Qing-dynasty official who stood up to the British at the time of the Opium Wars. There was even a tentative branching out into comedy, with the film *What's Eating You?* based on the relatively un-socialist antics of a Suzhou waiter. Unusually, the film featured local dialects, as well as a faintly detectable parody of the "Learn from Lei Feng" campaign, by which the government was seeking to encourage greater sacrifices from individuals by promoting the mythical heroic worker Lei Feng. Generally, films from these years took to depicting so-called "middle" characters, who were neither class heroes nor class villains.

THE CULTURAL REVOLUTION

Unfortunately, this bright period came to a swift end in 1966 with the launching of Mao's Cultural Revolution. Essentially, no interesting work would take place in China for nearly fifteen years, and indeed, no film was produced anywhere in China in the years 1966 to 1970. The few films which did subsequently appear before Mao's death were made under the personal supervision of Jiang Qing, all on the revolutionary model, a kind of ballet with flag waving. Attendance at these dreadful films was virtually **compulsory** for people who did not wish to be denounced for a lack of revolutionary zeal. Ironically, Jiang Qing herself, in the privacy of her home, was a big fan of Hollywood productions.

Recovery from the trauma of the Cultural Revolution was bound to take time, but the years 1979 and 1980 saw a small crop of films attempting for the first time to assess the horror of what the country had just lived through. The best-known of these is **The Legend of Tianyun Mountain**, made in Shanghai in 1980, which featured two men, one of whom had denounced the other for "Rightism" in 1958. The subsequent story is one of guilt, love, emotions and human relationships, all subjects that had been banned during the Cultural Revolution. Understandably, the film was an enormous popular success, though before audiences had time to get too carried away, a subsequent film made in 1981, *Unrequited Love*, was officially criticized for blurring too many issues.

THE 1980s AND BEYOND

In **1984** the Chinese film industry was suddenly brought to international attention for the first time by the arrival of the so-called **"Fifth Generation"** of Chinese film-makers. This was the year that director **Chen Kaige** and his cameraman **Zhang Yimou**, both graduates from the first post-Cultural Revolution class (1982) of the Beijing Film School, made the superb art film **Yellow Earth.** The story of *Yellow Earth* is a minor feature; the interest is in the images and the colours. Still shots predominate, recalling traditional Chinese scroll painting, with giant landscapes framed by hills and the distant Yellow River. The film was not particularly well received in China, either by audiences, who expected something more modern, or by the authorities who expected something more optimistic. Nevertheless, the pattern was now set for a series of increasingly foreign-funded (and foreign-watched) films comprising stunning images of a "traditional" China, irritating the censors at home and delighting audiences abroad.

Chen Kaige's protégé Zhang Yimou was soon stealing a march on his former boss, with his first film **Red Sorghum** in 1987, set in a remote wine-producing village of northern China at the time of the Japanese invasion. This film was not only beautiful, and reassuringly patriotic, but it also introduced the world to **Gong Li**, the actress who was to become China's first international heart-throb. The fact that Gong Li and Zhang Yimou were soon to be lovers added to the general media interest in their work, both in China and abroad. They worked together on a string of hits, including *Judou, The Story of Qiu Ju, Raise the Red Lantern, Shanghai Triads* and *To Live.* None of these could be described as art films in the way that *Yellow Earth* had been, and the potent mix of Gong Li's sexuality with exotic, mysterious locations in 1930s China was clearly targeted at Western rather than Chinese audiences. Chinese like to point out that the figure-hugging Chinese dresses regularly worn by Gong Li are entirely unlike the period costume they purport to represent. For such reasons, "moral" as well as political, Zhang's work continues to suffer censorship in his native country.

One of Zhang's most powerful and – from the point of view of the Chinese authorities – controversial films is **To Live** (1994) which follows the fortunes of a single family from the final, decadent years of the old regime, right through the Communist era to the present day. The various stages of Mao's Communist experiment, from "liberation" to the Great Leap Forward and the Cultural Revolution, are depicted in terms of the disasters they bring upon the family, including the traumatic deaths of both children in needless accidents for which the regime seems to be responsible. The essence of the story is that life cannot be lived to prescription. Its power lies in the fact that it is a very real reflection of the experience of millions of Chinese people. Similarly, Chen Kaige's superb **Farewell My Concubine** (1994) incorporates the whole span of modern Chinese history, and although the main protagonist – a homosexual Chinese opera singer – is hardly typical of modern China, the tears aroused by the film are wept for the country as a whole.

It is interesting that while the authorities still regard Fifth Generation film-makers as subversive (*To Live* has never been screened in China, and *Farewell My Concubine* is shown with cuts), a new, younger Chinese generation, based mainly in Beijing and inevitably dubbed the "Sixth Generation", is criticizing Zhang and Chen for being too bland, for selling out to commercial interests and giving the West a false image of China. They have started producing underground movies, generally shot in black and white, depicting what they consider to be the true story of contemporary China – ugly cities, cold flats, broke and depressed people. One of these, **Beijing Bastards**, has a role for the famous rock singer and rebel **Cui Jian**, who is depicted drinking, swearing and playing the guitar. Unsurprisingly, the Sixth Generation is faring even worse than the Fifth in terms of getting its work screened in China, and is once again having to rely on foreign funds for production.

HONG KONG

Ironically perhaps, the movies which have the least difficulty with the Chinese censors are those produced in **Hong Kong**, the world's third largest movie producer, behind India and the USA. Presumably for commercial reasons, Hong Kong film-makers, despite their profligate output, have avoided awkward political subjects. Indeed, there was little indication that, with their home-grown, high-speed, action-comedy format, they were interested in the rest of the world at all, until the arrival of **John Woo** in 1985, with his film *A Better Tomorrow*, starring the manly Chow Yun Fat alongside a natural counterpart, the effeminate Leslie Cheung. Woo introduced a whole new class of camera dexterity to the genre, and began specializing in mind-boggling special effects of explosions and scenes of reckless violence. His work, and that of the dare-devil stuntman and comic actor, Jackie Chan, have been credited with (or blamed for) inspiring the films of Quentin Tarantino. In 1992, Hong Kong lost Woo to the financial lure of Hollywood but in the meantime Jackie Chan, Chow Yun Fat and Leslie Cheung have become international megastars, particularly in mainland China, where Hong Kong films have taken to outgrossing their Hollywood rivals.

Although the Hong Kong film industry is almost entirely devoted to entertainment rather than "art", there has been interaction with the more earnest mainland directors. Leslie Cheung played the leading role in *Farewell My Concubine*, and actress Gong Li appears regularly in Hong Kong blockbusters. There is, however, only one important Hong Kong director seriously interested in the avant-garde, and his work has led him in a totally different direction from that of his mainland counterparts. **Wong Karwai**, in his extraordinary films **Chungking Express** and **Fallen Angels**, with their blurred motion shots, coffee-bar soundtracks and disjointed plots depicting a disjointed society, is right at the cutting edge of modern film-making. Even without taking into account the Taiwanese director Ang Lee, with his delightful domestic comedies (*The Wedding Banquet* and *Eat, Drink, Man, Woman*), it is hard to dispute that Chinese films are one of the major forces in world cinema and likely to remain so for the foreseeable future.

BOOKS

The following is a personal selection of the books that have proved most useful during the preparation of this guide. Don't expect to find much variety of English-language reading available in China, even in Hong Kong. Translations of some of the great classics of Chinese literature are published in Britain and the US, however; there are also a good many cheap editions published by the Foreign Languages Press (FLP) and Panda Books in Beijing which you'll find in the foreign-language sections of bookshops in China.

Where a title is published by a different publishing house in Britain and America the two are given in that order; o/p signifies out of print.

HISTORY

Jasper Becker *Hungry Ghosts: China's Secret Famine* (John Murray). Meticulously researched, but grimly depressing, account of Mao's ruinous domestic policies of the the 1950s.

Children of the Dragon (Collier Macmillan). A large photo book about the demonstrations and subsequent massacre of 1989. The text, which includes interviews with demonstrators, presents the story of the massacre and its historical context in dramatic fashion, but it is the photographs – bicycles crushed by tanks, soldiers beating up unarmed civilians, piles of corpses – that really get the point across.

Patricia Ebrey *Cambridge Illustrated History of China* (CUP). An up-to-date, easy-going historical overview, excellently illustrated and clearly written.

Peter Fleming *The Siege at Peking* (OUP/Marlboro Books). An account of the events which led up to June 20, 1900, when the foreign legations in Beijing were attacked by the "Boxers" and Chinese imperial troops. The siege, which lasted 55 days, led to a watershed in China's relations with the rest of the world.

Stephen G. Haw *A Traveller's History of China* (Windrush Press/Interlink). This concise overview of the entirety of Chinese history is useful background reading, though the writing is somewhat pedestrian.

Peter Hopkirk *Foreign Devils on the Silk Road* (OUP/Mass UP). The story of the machinations of the various international booty-hunters and archeologists who operated in Eastern Turkestan and the Gobi Desert around the turn of the century. Essential for an appreciation of China's northwest regions.

W. J. F. Jenner *The Tyranny of History: the Roots of China's Crisis* (Penguin). An erudite, scholarly work that goes into great depth examining the state of contemporary China. Full of good insights, but they are used to back up a perhaps too convenient central thesis that China's problems stem from its inability to escape the past.

Kong Demao *In The Mansion of Confucius' Descendants* (Beijing New World Press). This account of life in the Confucius mansion in Qufu by one of Confucius' descendants, though rather turgidly written, provides a rare insider's view of the life of aristocrats in imperial China.

Liang Heng and Judith Shapiro *Son of the Revolution* (Fontana o/p/Random House). Liang Heng grew up with the Cultural Revolution; here he documents those years from the point of view of an ordinary Chinese, caught in the cruelty, madness and euphoria.

Witold Rodzinski *The Walled Kingdom* (Fontana o/p/Free Press o/p). An ambitious history of China, but it's relatively short, with the entire story from Longshan Man to the Twelfth CCP Congress in 1982 compressed into 450 pages. As one of the few available accounts in English written from inside the former Socialist bloc, the Marxist slant will not be to everyone's taste.

Harrison Salisbury *The Long March* (Pan o/p/Mcgraw-Hill) and *The New Emperors*

(Harper Collins/Avon). The first is a comprehensive account by the American China expert, who retraced the route of the actual march in 1983. Access to previously undisclosed archives and interviews with survivors, from Hu Yaobang to the ferryman, throw new light on the march. The second is a highly readable account of the lives of China's two twentieth-century "emperors", Mao Zedong and Deng Xiaoping, which tries to demonstrate that Communist rule in China is no more than an extension of the old imperial Mandate of Heaven.

Edgar Snow *Red Star Over China* (Grove-Atlantic). Definitive first-hand account of the early days of Mao and the Communist "bandits", written in 1936 after Snow, an American journalist, wriggled through the Guomindang blockade and spent months at the Red base in Shaanxi. Compulsive reading.

Jonathan Spence *The Gate of Heavenly Peace* (Penguin), *The Search for Modern China* (Norton) and *God's chinese son*. The first title is a narrative tour de force which traces the history of twentieth-century China through the eyes of the men and women caught up in it – writers, revolutionaries, poets and politicians. One of the best books for getting to grips with China's complex modern history. *The Search for Modern China* is quite hard for a straight-through read, but it's compendious and authoritative and probably the best overall history of China available. *God's chinese son* tells the sensational story of the most terrible civil war in world history, the nineteenth-century Taiping Uprising, focusing on the extraordinary life of its leader, Hong Xiuquan, who saw himself as a modern-day Jesus Christ. Brand-new and highly enjoyable.

Arthur Waldron *The Great Wall of China* (CUP). Despite a promising title, this scholarly book tracing the origins and history of the Wall is more for the academic than the casual reader.

Dick Wilson *The Long March* (Penguin o/p). A well-researched account of this astonishing epic. An important aid to understanding China today, and a powerful story of adventure and revolution in itself.

TIBET

John Avedon *In Exile From the Land of Snows* (Wisdom o/p/HarperCollins). A detailed and moving account of modern Tibetan history, covering both those who remained in the country and those who fled into exile. Required reading for anyone contemplating a trip.

Graham Coleman (ed) *A Handbook of Tibetan Culture: a Guide to Tibetan Centres and Resources Throughout the World* (Rider). The subtitle says it all; the book exhaustively documents cultural organizations, teaching centres and libraries across the globe with a Tibetan focus. It also includes biographies of major Tibetan lamas, brief histories of the major schools of Tibetan Buddhism and an illustrated glossary.

Isabel Hilton *The Search for the Panchen Lama* (Viking). Details the whole sorry story of the search for the Eleventh Panchen Lama which is currently surrounded in controversy.

Peter Hopkirk *Trespassers on the Roof of the World: the Race for Lhasa* (OUP/Kodansha). Around the turn of the century, imperial Britain, with the help of a remarkable band of pundits and wallahs from the Indian Survey, was discreetly charting every nook of the most inaccessible part of the earth, the High Tibetan plateau. Peter Hopkirk has researched his subject thoroughly and come up with a highly readable account of this fascinating backwater of history.

David Snellgrove and Hugh Richardson *A Cultural History of Tibet* (Shambhala). Despite the difficulty of transliteration of Tibetan script this is an excellent and amazingly gripping introduction to early Tibetan history and religion. Especially good on the effects on ordinary people of the great events of history.

Tibet Information Network/Human Rights Watch *Cutting off the Serpent's Head: Tightening Control in Tibet, 1994–1995* (Human Rights Watch). Detailed, wide-ranging and depressing analysis of the most recent Chinese clampdown on dissent and freedom.

For comprehensive information about Tibet, consult **The International Tibet Resource Directory** (International Campaign for Tibet, 1825K St NW, Suite 520, Washington DC 20006; ☎202/785-1515, fax 202/785-4343.

CULTURE AND SOCIETY

Catriona Bass *Inside the Treasure House* (Sphere). An account of a year spent working in Tibet in the mid-1980s. The author eloquently explores the everyday lives of the Tibetans and their relationship with the Han Chinese.

David Bonavia *The Chinese: a Portrait* (Penguin). A highly readable introduction to contemporary China, focusing on the human aspects as a balance to the socio-political trends. Highly recommended.

Buchanan, FitzGerald, and **Ronan** *China* (Crown). A milestone work when published in 1980, and still unequalled in scope as a source of general background information on China's cultural and political heritage.

Fox Butterfield *China: alive in the Bitter Sea* (Random House). With the death of Mao in 1976, the dark ages of the Cultural Revolution came to a close, and China showed a face of enlightenment and steady progress towards the achievement of the "Four Modernizations". Fox Butterfield, *New York Times* correspondent, digs beneath the gleaming surface to catalogue the imperfections.

Mark Elvin and Caroline Blunden *A Cultural Atlas of China* (Facts on File). An invaluable reference tool and one you can dip into for up-to-date and authoritative summaries of history, religions and cultural developments. Plenty of good photographs.

Roger Garside *China after Mao: Coming Alive* (NAL-Dutton). Garside served at the British Embassy in Beijing 1968–1970 and 1976–1979. Here he describes the aftermath of the Cultural Revolution and the downfall of the Gang of Four.

Jacques Gernet *Daily Life in China on the Eve of the Mongol Invasion 1250–1276* (Stanford UP). Based on a variety of Chinese sources, including local gazetteers, letters and anecdotes, this is a fascinating and detailed survey of southern China under the Song, focusing on the capital, Hangzhou, then the largest and richest city in the world. Gernet also deals with the daily lives of a cross-section of society from peasant to leisured gentry, covering everything from cookery to death.

John Gittings *Real China* (Simon & Schuster). A series of essays on rural China giving a very different picture from the descriptions of the economic miracle that most Western commentators have focused on, though lacking in depth. The chapter on cannibalism during the Cultural Revolution is the morbidly fascinating.

Heinrich Harrer *Seven Years In Tibet* (Paladin/Putnam). A classic account of a remarkable journey to reach Lhasa and of the years there prior to the Chinese invasion, when Harrer was tutor to the Fourteenth Dalai Lama. The book has some excellent observations of Tibetan life of the time, and it will be interesting to see how the planned movie turns out (Brad Pitt is due to star).

Khristof and Wudunn *China Wakes* (Nicholas Brealy). Written by two young *New York Times* journalists, this is an extremely well-informed, open-minded and easy-to-read introduction to life in contemporary China.

Jonathan Spence *The Death of Woman Wang* (Penguin). Against the backdrop of a provincial county in Shandong in the seventeenth century, Spence focuses on the lives of ordinary people, set against the grim cycle of floods, crop failures, the attentions of bandits and rapacious tax collectors.

Tiziano Terzani *Behind the Forbidden Door* (Unwin o/p/Holt o/p). In 1980 Terzani was one of the first Western journalists to be allowed to live in China. He was kicked out after four years for the unacceptable honesty of his writing. There is no better evocation of the bad old days of the pre-reform years than this collection of essays on such varied subjects as the rebirth of kung fu, mass executions and the training of crickets.

Thubten Jigme and Colin Turnbull *Tibet, Its History, Religion and People* (Penguin o/p). Co-authored by the brother of the Fourteenth Dalai Lama, this is the best account around of the traditional everyday lives of the Tibetan people.

Zhang Xinxin and Sang Ye *Chinese Lives* (Penguin o/p). This series of first-person narratives from interviews with a broad range of Chinese people is both readable and informative, full of fascinating details of day-to-day existence that you won't read anywhere else.

TRAVEL WRITING

Charles Blackmore *The Worst Desert on Earth* (John Murray). Sergeant-majorly account of an arduous and possibly unique trip across the Taklamakan Desert in northwest China.

Mildred Cable with Francesca French *The Gobi Desert* (Virago). Cable and French were missionaries with the China Inland Mission in the early part of this century. *The Gobi Desert* is a poetic description of their life and travels in Gansu and Xinjiang, without the sanctimonious and patronizing tone adopted by some of their contemporary missionaries.

Peter Fleming *One's Company: a Journey to China* (Penguin) and *News from Tartary* (Abacus). The first is an amusing account of a journey through Russia and Manchuria to China in the 1930s. En route, Peter Fleming, brother to Ian, encounters a wild assortment of Chinese and Japanese officials and the puppet emperor Henry Pu Yi himself. *News from Tartary* records a journey of 3500 miles across the roof of the world to Kashmir in 1935.

Somerset Maugham *On a Chinese Screen* (Mandarin). These are brief, sometimes humorous and often biting sketches of the European missionaries, diplomats and businessmen whom Maugham encountered in China between 1919 and 1921; worth reading for background detail.

Marco Polo *The Travels* (Penguin). Said to have inspired Columbus, *The Travels* is a fantastic read, full of amazing details picked up during his 26 years of wandering in Asia between Venice and the court of Kublai Khan. It's not, however, a coherent history, having been ghost-written by a romantic novelist from notes supplied by Marco Polo.

Vikram Seth *From Heaven Lake: Travels through Sinkiang and Tibet* (Phoenix). A student for two years at Nanjing University, Seth set out in 1982 to return home to Delhi via Tibet and Nepal. This account of how he hitched his way through four provinces, Xinjiang, Gansu, Qinghai and Tibet, is in the best tradition of the early travel books.

Stanley Stewart *Frontiers of Heaven* (Flamingo). The latest in a long line of Silk Road travellers to commit his story to paper, Stewart gives a pleasant but superficial account, for the armchair traveller than the real China buff.

Paul Theroux *Riding the Iron Rooster* (Penguin). Witty and pompous musings about life, travel and travellers in 1980s China – much

of it written from the comfort of a soft-sleeper compartment.

Colin Thubron *Behind the Wall* (Penguin). A thoughtful and superbly poetic description of an extensive journey through China just after it opened up in the early 1980s. This is the single best piece of travel writing to have come out of modern China.

GUIDES AND REFERENCE BOOKS

Stephen Bachelor *The Tibet Guide* (Wisdom). Illustrated with glorious photos, the guide gives a scholarly and detailed account of the main temples and monasteries across Tibet.

Victor Chan *Tibet Handbook: a Pilgrimage Guide* (Moon Publications). A hugely detailed guide to the pilgrimage sites and treks and how to reach them. Absolutely essential if you're considering a trek.

Rodolphe De Schauensee *Birds of China* (OUP). About the only portable book on Chinese birds that could be used as a field guide, though the illustrations are selective and patchy in quality.

Lin Xiang Zhu and Lin Cuifeng *Chinese Gastronomy* (Hsiang Ju Lin & Tsuifeng Lin o/p). A classic work, relatively short on recipes but strong on cooking methods and philosophy. Currently out of print but essential reading for anyone serious about learning the finer details of Chinese cooking.

Kenneth Lo *Chinese Food* (Faber). Good general-purpose cookbook covering a wide range of methods and styles, from Westernised dishes to regional specialities.

Zhao Ji *The Natural History of China* (Collins). A mine of beautiful photographs of rare wildlife, though the text is disappointingly general through obsessively trying to mention as many species as possible.

Pan Ling *In Search of Old Shanghai* (Joint Publishing Company, Hong Kong). If you're planning to stay some time in Shanghai, this guide, written in the early eighties, is an entertaining companion.

Gary McCue *Trekking in Tibet: a Traveller's Guide* (Cordee). Essential reading, together with Chan, above, for anyone planning on trekking during their stay in Tibet. The maps are especially clear and useful, and the day treks provide excellent ideas for anyone wanting to walk, but not too far.

Jessica Rawson *Ancient China: Art and Archaeology* (British Museum Publications). This scholarly introduction to Chinese art from the deputy keeper of Oriental antiquities at the British Museum puts Chinese art in its historical context. Beginning in Neolithic times, it explores the technology and social organization which shaped its development up to the Han dynasty.

Barry Till *In Search of Old Nanjing* (Joint Publishing Company, Hong Kong). Another in the same series as *In Search of Old Shanghai* (see above).

Mary Tregear *Chinese Art* (Thames and Hudson). Authoritative summary of the main strands in Chinese art from Neolithic times, through the Bronze Age and up to the twentieth century. Clearly written and well illustrated.

RELIGION AND PHILOSOPHY

Asiapac Books (Asiapac, Singapore). Published in Singapore but available in Hong Kong and Beijing, this entertaining series of books presents ancient Chinese philosophy in comic-book format, making it accessible without losing its complexity. They are all well written and well drawn. Particularly good is the *Book of Zen*, a collection of stories and parables, and the *Sayings of Confucius*.

Kenneth Chen *Buddhism in China* (Princetown UP). Very helpful for tracing the origin of Buddhist thought in China, the development of its many different schools and the four-way traffic of influence between India, Tibet, Japan and China.

Confucius *The Analects* (Penguin). Good modern translation of this classic text. *The Analects* is a collection of Confucius's teachings focusing on morality and the state.

Lao Zi *Tao Te Ching* (Penguin/Random House). More translated than any other book except the Bible, the *Tao Te Ching* is a collection of mystical thoughts and philosophical speculation that forms the basis of Taoist philosophy.

Arthur Waley, (trans) *Three Ways of Thought in Ancient China* (Unwin). Translated extracts from the writings of three of the early philosophers – Zhuang Zi, Mencius and Han Feizi. A useful introduction.

BIOGRAPHIES AND AUTOBIOGRAPHIES

Anchee Min *Red Azalea* (Indigo/Berkeley). Half-autobiography, half-novel, this beautifully written book is an unusually personal and highly romantic account of surviving the Cultural Revolution.

Ba Jin *Family* (Cheng & Tsul). Born in 1904 into a wealthy Chengdu family, Ba Jin attacks the old family feudal system, chronicles his anarchist phase from age fifteen until 1949 and traces the strong influence worked on him by Russian writers such as Turgenev.

Dalai Lama *Freedom in Exile* (Abacus/HarperCollins).The autobiography of the charismatic and Nobel Prize-winning Fourteenth Dalai Lama from his early years to the early 1990s.

Richard Evans *Deng Xiaoping* (Penguin). The basic handbook to understanding the motives and inspirations behind the most influential man in modern China.

Jung Chang *Wild Swans* (Flamingo/Doubleday). Enormously popular in the West, this family saga covering three generations was unsurprisingly banned in China for its honest account of the horrors of life in turbulent twentieth-century China. It serves as an excellent introduction to modern Chinese history, as well as being a good read.

Naisingoro Pu Yi *From Emperor to Citizen* (FLP, Beijing). The autobiography of the young boy, born into the Qing imperial family and chosen by the Japanese to become the puppet emperor of the state of Manchukuo in 1931.

Nien Cheng *Life and Death in Shanghai* (Flamingo/Penguin). Harrowing personal account of the effects of the Cultural Revolution on this British-educated Chinese woman, denounced as a class enemy in 1966.

Jonathan Spence *Emperor of China: Self Portrait of Kang Xi* (Pimlico/Random House). A magnificent portrait of the longest reigning and greatest emperor of modern China.

Hugh Trevor-Roper *Hermit of Peking: the Hidden Life of Sir Edmund Backhouse* (Eland). Drawn from the voluminous (and often obscene) memoirs of this distinguished scholar and eccentric, who died in 1944. Among his more outrageous claims was that of intimacy with the Dowager Empress.

Marina Warner *The Dragon Empress* (Vintage). Exploration of the life of Cixi, one of only two women rulers of China. Warner lays bare the complex personality of a ruthless woman whose conservatism, passion for power, vanity and greed had such great impact on the events which culminated in the collapse of the imperial ruling house and the founding of the republic.

LITERATURE

TWENTIETH-CENTURY WRITING

Pearl S. Buck *The Good Earth* (Penguin/ Simon & Schuster). The best story from a writer who grew up in China during the early twentieth century, *The Good Earth* follows the fortunes of the peasant Wang Lung from his wedding day to dotage, as he struggles to hold on to his land for his family through a series of political upheavals.

Chen Yuanbin *The Story of Qiuju* (Panda, Beijing). A collection of four tales of which the title story, about a peasant woman pushing for justice after her husband is assaulted by the village chief, was made into a film by award-winning director Zhang Yimou.

Feng Jicai *The Miraculous Pigtail* (Panda, Beijing). For Western readers, Feng Jicai is one of China's most accessible authors – compassionate, humorous, and uncomplicated – though his longer stories tend to sag with rather obvious morals.

Liu Heng *The Obsessed* (Panda, Beijing). Known for his often taboo subject matter – the title story tells of an affair between aunt and nephew in a 1940s village – these three tales are classic Liu Heng.

Lao She *Rickshaw Boy* (FLP, Beijing). One of China's great modern writers, who was driven to suicide during the Cultural Revolution. The story is a haunting account of a young rickshaw puller in pre-1949 Beijing.

Lu Xun *The True Story of Ah Q* (FLP, Beijing). Widely read in China today, Lu Xun is regarded as the father of modern Chinese writing. *Ah Q* is one of his best tales, short, allegorical and cynical, about a simpleton who is swept up in the 1911 revolution.

Mo Yan *The Garlic Ballads* (Penguin). A hard-hitting novel of rural life by one of China's greatest modern writers, this book is banned in China.

Amy Tan *The Joy Luck Club* (Minerva). The moving story of four Chinese mothers and their first-generation daughters, chronicling the life of American Chinese with a perceptive touch.

Various *Seeds of Fire* (Bloodaxe Books). Key writings from the modern protest movement, published just before the 1989 events in Tian'anmen Square. The only English translations available of many of the authors.

Yeshi Tenzin *The Defiant Ones* (Panda, Beijing). Engrossing cultural vignettes, but otherwise a stark tale of a woman's attempted vengeance against her husband's killer in 1930s Tibet, set against a background of brutal feudalism.

Zhang Xianliang *Grass Soup* (Godine). Hellish accounts of the 22 years the author spent in Maoist labour camps, expanded from the cryptic diary entries he was able to make at the time. He survived to write the controversial *Half Man is Woman*.

Zhang Xinxin and Sang Ye *Chinese Profiles* (Panda, Beijing). Immensely entertaining and revealing collection of short interviews with a huge cross-section of the Chinese public – Beijing streetkids, Chongqing hairdressers, a tiger hunter, and more. The book that influenced US writer Studs Terkel.

CLASSICS

Asiapac Books (Asiapac, Singapore). Wonderful series which renders Chinese classics and folk tales into cartoon format. Titles include *Journey to the West*, *I Ching*, *Tales of Laozhai* and *Chinese Eunuchs*.

Cyril Birch, (ed). *Anthology of Chinese Literature from Earliest Times to the Fourteenth Century* (Penguin). This survey spans three thousand years of literature, embracing poetry, philosophy, drama, biography and prose fiction, with interesting variations of translation.

Cao Xueqing and Gao E *Dream of Red Mansions/Story of the Stone* (Penguin/FLP, Beijing). This intricate eighteenth-century tale of manners follows the fortunes of the Jia Clan through the emotionally charged adolescent lives of Jia Baoyu and his two girl cousins, Lin Daiyu and Xue Baochai. The full translation fills five paperbacks, but there's also a much simplified English version available in China.

Luo Guanzhong *Romance of the Three Kingdoms* (Graham Brash/FLP, Beijing). Despite being written 1200 years after the events, this vibrant tale vividly evokes the battles, political schemings and myths surrounding China's turbulent *Three Kingdoms* period. One of the world's great historical novels.

Steven Owen *Anthology of Chinese Literature* (Norton). Unimaginably compendious, this colossal book contains delightfully translated excerpts and analyses from every era of Chinese literature up to 1911. Not a book to carry in your rucksack but great for the bookshelf.

Shi Nai'an and Luo Guanzhong *Outlaws of the Marsh/The Water Margin* (Tynron Press/ FLP, Beijing). A heavy dose of popular legend as a group of Robin Hood-like outlaws take on the government in feudal times. If the full three volume set is too much to plough through, try to find Pearl Buck's snappier abridgement, *All Men are Brothers*, in your library.

Wu Cheng'en *Journey to the West* (FLP, Beijing). Absurd, lively rendering of the Buddhist monk Sanzang's pilgramage to India to collect sacred scriptures, aided by Sandy, Pigsy, and the irrepressible Sun Wu Kong, the monkey king. Arthur Waley's version, *Monkey* (Penguin), retains the tale's spirit while shortening the hundred-chapter opus to paperback length.

LANGUAGE

As the most widely spoken language on earth, Chinese can hardly be overlooked. From the point of view of foreigners, its main distinguishing characteristic is that it is a tonal language. In order to pronounce a word correctly, it is necessary to know not only the sounds of its consonants and vowels but also its correct tone. There are four possible tones in Mandarin Chinese, and every syllable of every word is characterized by one of them, except for a few syllables which are considered toneless. This emphasis on tones does not make Chinese a particularly musical language – English, for example, uses all of the tones of Chinese and many more. The difference is that English uses tone for effects such as exclaiming, questioning, listing, rebuking and so on. In English, to change the tone is to change the mood or the emphasis; in Chinese, to change the tone is to change the word itself.

Despite initial impressions, there is nothing particularly difficult about learning words and expressions with fixed tones, and there is no reason at all why visiting foreign tourists should not make some effort to learn at least the basics. The difference between being able to pronounce correctly a few words of Chinese and being able to speak none at all can mean the difference between a successful trip and a nightmare, given the paucity of English-speakers in China. Anyone considering a visit to the country is highly recommended to study some Chinese before their departure and, above all,

it is worth paying attention to pronunciation and the use of the **pinyin** phonetic system (see below).

What we know as Chinese is, strictly speaking, a series of **dialects** spoken by the dominant ethnic group within China, the Han. Indeed, the term most commonly used by the Chinese themselves to refer to the language is **hanyu** meaning "Han-language", though *zhongyu, zhongwen* and *zhongguohua*, all of which literally mean "Chinese", are frequently used as well. However, not all languages spoken in China are dialects of Chinese. The non-Han peoples such as Uigurs and Tibetans, for example, speak languages which have little or nothing to do with Chinese.

The dialects of *hanyu* are a complicated story in themselves. Some of them are mutually unintelligible and – where the spoken word is concerned – have about as much in common as, say, German and English. The better-known and most distinct minority dialects include those spoken around China's coastal fringes, such as **Shanghainese** (*shanghai hua*), **Fujianese** (*minnan hua*) and **Cantonese** (*guangdong hua*), though even within the areas covered by these dialects you'll find huge local divergences. The most important of all the local dialects, Cantonese, is a language of worldwide significance in itself, being the dialect spoken by the people of Hong Kong and generally among the Chinese communities overseas, particularly those in Southeast Asia.

What enables Chinese from different parts of the country to communicate with each other is **Mandarin Chinese**. Historically based on the language of Han officialdom in the Beijing area, Mandarin has been systematically promoted over the past hundred years to be the official, unifying language of the Chinese people, much as modern French, for example, is based on the original Parisian dialect. It is known in mainland China as **putonghua** – "common language" – and in Taiwan (where it is also the official language) as *guoyu* – "national language". The promotion of Mandarin has led to a situation whereby many Chinese grow up speaking it alongside their local dialect, and can switch freely between the two. As the language of education, government and the media, Mandarin is understood to a greater or lesser extent by the vast majority of Han Chinese, and by many non-Han as well, though there are two caveats to this generalization – first, that knowledge of Mandarin is far more common among the young, the educated and the urban-dwelling, and secondly that many people who understand Mandarin cannot actually speak it. The chances of the average Tibetan peasant being able to speak Mandarin in other words are extremely small. In Hong Kong and Macau, likewise, there has been until recently very little Mandarin spoken though this situation is now changing fast.

Another element tying the various dialects together is the Chinese **script**. No matter how different two dialects may sound when spoken, once they are written down in the form of Chinese characters they become mutually comprehensible again. Leaving aside the complication of traditional versus simplified characters (see below), the different dialects use roughly similar written characters. A sentence of Cantonese, for example, written down beside a sentence of the same meaning in Mandarin, will look broadly similar except for occasional unusual words or structures. Having said this, it should be added that apart from Cantonese it is unusual to see dialects written down at all. Most Chinese people, in fact, associate the written word inextricably with Mandarin.

CHINESE CHARACTERS

Chinese **characters** – pictograms built up of components representing simple concepts such as fire, earth, person, wood – must rank as one of the most extraordinary creations of the Chinese people, and they have had a profound effect on the way the language has developed over the past three thousand years. Every character can be pronounced as a single-syllable sound, but the character itself contains no more than hints as to what its pronunciation should be. Fundamentally, the character stands not for a sound, but for a concept. Because Chinese characters are so immutable and so ancient however, the individual concepts behind many of them, as well as their grammatical function, have become misty and diffuse. To take a random example, a single character *ju* can be a verb meaning "to

lift", "to start" or "to choose", an adjective meaning "whole" and a noun meaning "deed". In a very vague way we might perhaps see the underlying meaning of *ju*, but because of the need for clarity, many of the everyday concepts and objects of modern life are referred to not by single characters but by set combinations of usually two or three characters which, added together, make words. In the case of *ju* above, the addition of *shi* (world) creates a word with the precise meaning "throughout the whole world"; the addition of *mu* (eye) creates a word meaning "look".

SIMPLIFIED AND TRADITIONAL FORMS

The average educated Chinese person knows between five and ten thousand characters (as many as fifty thousand altogether have been recorded, though the majority of these are obsolete), but the learning process is extremely long. Given the difficulty of learning characters, and the negative impact this has had on the general level of literacy, the government of the People's Republic announced, in 1954, that a couple of thousand of the most common characters were to be, quite literally, **simplified**. This drastic measure was not without controversy. Some argued that by interfering with the precise original structure of the characters, vital clues as to their meaning and pronunciation would be lost, making them harder than ever to learn. In the meantime, the simplified characters were also adopted in Singapore, but Hong Kong and Taiwan, as well as the majority of overseas Chinese, continue to use the older, **traditional** forms. Today, ironically, the traditional forms are also making a comeback on the mainland, where they are now seen as sophisticated and smart.

PINYIN

Back in the 1950s it was hoped eventually to replace Chinese characters altogether with a regular alphabet of Roman letters, and to this end the **pinyin** system was devised. Basically pinyin is a precise and exact means of representing all the sounds of Mandarin Chinese. It comprises all the Roman letters of the English alphabet (except for the letter "v"), and the four tones are represented by diacritic marks, or accents, which appear above each syllable. However, there is an added complication that in pinyin the letters do not all have the sounds you would expect, and you'll need to spend an hour or two learning these (see below). You often see pinyin in China, on street signs and shop displays, but only well-educated locals know the system very well. Other dialects of Chinese, such as Cantonese, cannot be written in pinyin.

The old aim of replacing Chinese characters with pinyin was abandoned long ago, but in the meantime pinyin has one very important function, that of helping foreigners to pronounce Chinese words. The Chinese names in this book have been given both in characters and in pinyin; the pronunciation guide below is your first step to making yourself comprehensible. Don't get overly paranoid about your tones: with the help of context, intelligent listeners should be able to work out what you are trying to say. If you're just uttering a single word, however, for example a place name – without a context – you need to hit exactly the right tone, otherwise don't be surprised if nobody understands you. For more information, see the Rough Guide phrasebook, *Mandarin Chinese*.

Occasionally, you will come across systems of rendering Mandarin into Roman letters, which pre-date the pinyin system. The best known of these is the Wade-Giles system, which renders Mao Zedong as Mao Tse-tung and Deng Xiaoping as Teng Hsaio-p'ing. These forms are no longer used in mainland China but you may see them in publications which originate in Taiwan.

GRAMMAR

Chinese **grammar** is delightfully simple. There is no need to conjugate verbs, decline nouns or make adjectives agree – being attached to immutable Chinese characters, Chinese words simply cannot have different "endings". Instead, context and fairly rigid rules about word order are relied on to make those distinctions of time, number and gender, that Indo-European languages are so concerned with. Instead of cumbersome verb tenses, the Chinese make use of words such as "yesterday" or "tomorrow"; instead of plural endings they simply state how many things there are.

For English speakers, Chinese word order is very familiar, and you'll find that by simply stringing words together you'll be producing perfectly grammatical Chinese. Basic sentences follow the subject–verb–object format, and adjectives, as well as all qualifying and describing phrases, precede nouns.

PRONUNCIATION

THE TONES

First or "High" $\bar{a}$ $\bar{e}$ $\bar{\imath}$ $\bar{o}$ $\bar{u}$. In English this tone is used when mimicking robotic or very boring, flat voices.

Second or "Rising" $\check{a}$ $\check{e}$ $\check{\imath}$ $\check{o}$ $\check{u}$. In English, this tone is often used when offering alternatives; the first of the two items has the rising tone. For example *"Black, or white?"*

Third or "Falling-rising" $\acute{a}$ $\acute{e}$ $\acute{\imath}$ $\acute{o}$ $\acute{u}$. Used in English when echoing someone's words with a measure of incredulity. For example, *"John's dead." "De-ad?!"*

Fourth or "Falling" $\grave{a}$ $\grave{e}$ $\grave{\imath}$ $\grave{o}$ $\grave{u}$. Often used in English when counting in a brusque manner – "*One! Two! Three! Four!*".

Toneless A few syllables do not have a tone accent. These are pronounced without emphasis, such as in the English **u**pon.

CONSONANTS

Most consonants are pronounced in a similar way to their English equivalents, with the following exceptions:

c as in ha**ts**

g is hard as in **g**od (except when preceded by "n" when it sounds like sa**ng**)

q as in **ch**eese

x has no direct equivalent in English, but you can make the sound by sliding from an "s" sound to a "sh" sound and stopping midway between the two

z as in su**ds**

zh as in fu**dg**e

VOWELS AND DIPHTHONGS

As in most languages, the vowel sounds are rather harder to quantify than the consonants. The examples below give a rough description of

COMMON WORDS AND PHRASES IN MANDARIN CHINESE

Basics

I	我	wǒ
You (singular)	你	nǐ
He	他	tā
She	她	tā
We	我们	wǒmén
You (plural)	你们	nǐmén
They	他们	tāmén
I want....	我要	wǒ yào....
No, I don't want....	我不要	wǒ bú yào....
Is it possible...?	可不可以.....?	kěbùkěyǐ....?
It is (not) possible	(不)可以	(bù) kěyǐ
Is there any/Have you got any.....?	有没有.....?	yǒu méiyǒu....?
There is/I have	有	yǒu
There isn't/I haven't	没有	méiyǒu
Please help me	请帮我忙	qǐng bāng wǒ máng

Communicating

I don't speak Chinese	我不会说中文	wǒ bú huì shuō zhōngwén
My Chinese is terrible	我的中文很差	wǒ de zhōngwén hěn chà
Can you speak English?	你会说英语吗?	nǐ huì shuō yīngyǔ ma?
Can you get someone who speaks English?	请给我找一个会说英语的人	qǐng gěi wǒ zhǎo yí ge huì shuō yīngyǔ de rén
Please speak slowly	请说地慢一点	qǐng shuōde màn yídiǎn
Please say that again	请再说一遍	qǐng zài shuō yí biàn
I understand	我听得懂	wǒ tīngdedǒng
I don't understand.	我听不懂	wǒ tīngbudǒng
I can't read Chinese characters	我看不懂汉字	wǒ kànbudǒng hànzì
What does this mean?	这是什么意思?	zhè shì shénme yìsi?
How do you pronounce this character?	这个字怎么念?	zhè ge zì zěnme niàn?

Greetings and basic courtesies

Hello/How do you do/How are you?	你好	nǐ hǎo
I'm fine	我很好	wǒ hěn hǎo
Thank you	谢谢	xièxie
Don't mention it/You're welcome	不客气	búkèqi
Sorry to bother you....	麻烦你	máfan nǐ
Sorry/I apologise	对不起	duìbùqǐ
It's not important/No problem	没关系	méi guānxi
Goodbye	再见	zài jiàn

Chitchat

What country are you from?	你是哪个国家的?	nǐ shì nǎ ge guójiā de?
Britain	英国	yīngguó
Ireland	爱尔兰	àiěrlán
America	美国	měiguó
Canada	加拿大	jiānádà
Australia	澳大利亚	àodàlìyà
New Zealand	新西兰	xīnxīlán
China	中国	zhōngguó
Outside China	外国	wàiguó
What's your name?	你叫什么名字?	nǐ jiào shénme míngzi?

My name is...	我叫....	*wǒ jiào...*
Are you married?	你结婚了吗?	*nǐ jiéhūn le ma?*
I am (not) married	我(没有)结婚	*wǒ (méiyǒu) jiéhūn*
Have you got (children)?	你有没有孩子?	*nǐ yǒu méiyǒu háizi?*
Do you like....?	你喜不喜欢.....?	*nǐ xǐ bu xǐhuan....?*
I (don't) like.....	我不喜欢....	*wǒ (bù) xǐhuan...*
What's your job?	你干什么工作?	*nǐ gàn shénme gōngzuò?*
I'm a foreign student	我是留学生	*wǒ shì liúxuéshēng*
I'm a teacher	我是老师	*wǒ shì lǎoshī*
I work in a company	我在一个公司工作	*wǒ zài yí ge gōngsī gōngzuò*
I don't work	我不工作	*wǒ bù gōngzuò*
Clean/dirty	干净/脏	*gānjìng/zāng*
Hot/cold	热/冷	*rè/lěng*
Fast/slow	快/慢	*kuài/màn*
Pretty	漂亮	*piàoliang*
Interesting	有意思	*yǒuyìsi*

Numbers

Zero	零	*líng*
One	一	*yī*
Two	二/两	*èr/liǎng**
Three	三	*sān*
Four	四	*sì*
Five	五	*wǔ*
Six	六	*liù*
Seven	七	*qī*
Eight	八	*bā*
Nine	九	*jiǔ*
Ten	十	*shí*
Eleven	十一	*shíyī*
Twelve	十二	*shíèr*
Twenty	二十	*èrshí*
Twenty-one	二十一	*èrshíyī*
One hundred	一百	*yībǎi*
Two hundred	二百	*èrbǎi*
One thousand	一千	*yīqiān*
Ten thousand	一万	*yīwàn*
One hundred thousand	十万	*shíwàn*
One million	一百万	*yībǎiwàn*
One hundred million	一亿	*yīyì*
One billion	十亿	*shíyì*

*liǎng is used when enumerating, for example "two people" *liǎng ge rén*. *èr* is used when counting.

Time

Now	现在	*xiànzài*
Today	今天	*jīntiān*
(In the) morning	早上	*zǎoshàng*
(In the) afternoon	下午	*xiàwǔ*
(In the) evening	晚上	*wǎnshàng*
Tomorrow	明天	*míngtiān*
The day after tomorrow	后天	*hòutiān*
Yesterday	昨天	*zuótiān*
Week/month/year	星期/月/年	*xīngqī/yuè/nián*
Monday	星期一	*xīngqī yī*
Tuesday	星期二	*xīngqī èr*

Wednesday	星期三	*xīngqī sān*
Thursday	星期四	*xīngqī sì*
Friday	星期五	*xīngqī wǔ*
Saturday	星期六	*xīngqī liù*
Sunday	星期天	*xīngqī tiān*
What's the time?	几点了？	*jǐdiǎn le?*
10 o'clock	十点钟	*shídiǎn zhōng*
10.20	十点二十	*shídiǎn èrshí*
10.30	十点半	*shídiǎn bàn*

Travelling

North	北	*běi*
South	南	*nán*
East	东	*dōng*
West	西	*xī*
Airport	机场	*jīchǎng*
Long-distance bus station	长途汽车站	*chángtú qìchēzhàn*
Train station	火车站	*huǒchēzhàn*
Ferry dock	船码头	*mǎtóu*
Left-luggage office	寄存处	*jìcún chù*
Ticket office	售票处	*shòupiào chù*
Ticket	票	*piào*
Can you buy me a ticket to ... ?	可不可以给我买到.....的	*kěbùkěyǐ gěi wǒ mǎi dào..... de piào?*
I want to go to ...	我想到.....去	*wǒ xiǎng dào.... qù*
I want to leave at (8 o'clock).	我想（八点钟）离开	*wǒ xiǎng (bā diǎn zhōng) líkāi*
When does it leave?	什么时候出发？	*shénme shíhòu chūfā?*
When does it arrive?	什么时候到？	*shénme shíhòu dào?*
How long does it take?	路上得多长时间？	*lùshàng děi duōcháng shíjiān?*

Train

Train	火车	*huǒchē*
Main train station	主要火车站	*zhǔyào huǒchēzhàn*
Hard seat	硬座	*yìngzuò*
Soft seat	软座	*ruǎnzuò*
Hard sleeper	硬卧	*yìngwò*
Soft sleeper	软卧	*ruǎnwò*
Soft-seat waiting room	软卧候车室	*ruǎnwò hòuchēshì*
Upgrade ticket	补票	*bǔpiào*
Platform	站台	*zhàntái*

Getting about town

Map	地图	*dìtú*
Where is.....?	......在哪里？	*....zài nǎlǐ?*
Go straight on	往前走	*wàng qián zǒu*
Turn right	往右拐	*wàng yòu guǎi*
Turn left	往左拐	*wàng zuǒ guǎi*
Taxi	出租车	*chūzū chē*
Please use the meter	请打开记价器	*qǐng dǎkāi jìjiàqì*
Underground/Subway station	地铁站	*dìtiě zhàn*
Rickshaw	三轮车	*sānlún chē*
Bicycle	自行车	*zìxíngchē*
I want to rent a bicycle	我想租自行车	*wǒ xiǎng zū zìxíngchē*
How much is it per hour?	一个小时得多少钱？	*yí gè xiǎoshí děi duōshǎo qián?*

Can I borrow your bicycle?	能不能借你的自行车?	*néng bùnéng jiè nǐ de zìxíngchē?*

Bus

	公共汽车	*gōnggòngqìchē*
Which bus goes to....?	几路车到......去?	*jǐ lù chē dào..... qù?*
Number (10) bus	(十)路车	*(shí) lù chē*
Does this bus go to....?	这车到......去吗?	*zhè chē dào.... qù ma?*
When is the next bus?	下一班车几点开?	*xià yí bān chē jǐ diǎn kāi?*
The first bus	头班车	*tóubān chē*
The last bus	末班车	*mòbān chē*
Please tell me where to get off	请告诉我在哪里下车	*qǐng gàosu wǒ zài nǎlǐ xià chē*

Accommodation

Hotel (upmarket)	宾馆	*bīnguǎn*
Hotel (downmarket)	招待所, 旅馆	*zhāodàisuǒ, lǚguǎn*
Is it possible to stay here?	能不能住在这里?	*néng bù néng zhù zài zhèlǐ?*
Can I have a look at the room?	能不能看一下房间?	*néng bù néng kàn yíxià fángjiān?*
I want the cheapest bed you've got	我要你最便宜的床位	*wǒ yào nǐ zuì piányì de chuángwèi*
Single room	单人间	*dānrén jiān*
Double room	双人间	*shuāngrén jiān*
Three-bed room	三人间	*sānrén jiān*
Dormitory	多人间	*duōrén jiān*
Suite	套房间	*tàofángjiān*
Bed	床位	*chuángwèi*
Passport	护照	*hùzhào*
Deposit	押金	*yājīn*
Key	钥匙	*yàoshi*
When is the hot water on?	什么时候有热水?	*shénme shíhòu yǒu rèshuǐ?*
I want to change my room	我想换一个房间	*wǒ xiǎng huàn yí ge fángjiān*

Shopping, money and banks

How much is it?	这是多少钱?	*zhè shì duōshǎo qián?*
That's too expensive.	太贵了	*tài guì le*
I haven't got any cash.	我没有现金	*wǒ méiyǒu xiànjīn*
Have you got anything cheaper?	有没有便宜一点的?	*yǒu méiyǒu piányì yídiǎn de?*
Do you accept credit cards?	可不可以用信用卡?	*kě bù kěyǐ yòng xìnyòngkǎ?*
¥1 (RMB)	一块(人民币)	*yí kuài (rénmínbì)*
US$1	一块美金	*yí kuài měijīn*
£1	一个英磅	*yí gè yīngbàng*
HK$1	一块港币	*yí kuài gǎngbì*
Change money	换钱	*huàn qián*
Bank of China	中国银行	*zhōngguó yínháng*
Travellers' cheques	旅行支票	*lǚxíngzhīpiào*

Post and telephones

Post office	邮电局	*yóudiànjú*
Envelope	信封	*xìnfēng*
Stamp	邮票	*yóupiào*
Airmail	航空信	*hángkōngxìn*
Surface mail	平信	*píngxìn*
Post restante	邮件侯领处	*yóujiàn hòulǐngchù*
Telephone	电话	*diànhuà*
International telephone call	国际电话	*guójì diànhuà*

Reverse charges/collect call	对方付钱电话	*duìfāngfùqián diànhuà*
Fax	传真	*chuánzhēn*
Telephone card	电话卡	*diànhuàkǎ*
I want to make a telephone call to (Britain).	我想给(英国)打电话	*wǒ xiǎng gěi (yīngguó) dǎ diànhuà*
I want to send a fax to (USA)	我想给(美国)发一个传真	*wǒ xiǎng gěi (měiguó) fā yí gè chuánzhēn*
Can I receive a fax here?	能不能在这里收传真?	*néng bù néng zài zhèlǐ shōu chuánzhēn?*

Health

Hospital	医院	*yīyuàn*
Pharmacy	药店	*yàodiàn*
Medicine	药	*yào*
Chinese medicine	中药	*zhōngyào*
Diarrhoea	腹泻	*fùxiè*
Vomit	呕吐	*ǒutù*
Fever	发烧	*fāshāo*
I'm ill	我生病了	*wǒ shēngbìng le*
I've got flu	我感冒了	*wǒ gǎnmào le*
I'm (not) allergic to....	我对.....(不)过敏	*wǒ duì....(bù) guòmǐn*
Antibiotics	抗生素	*kàngshēngsù*
Quinine	奎宁	*kuíníng*
Condom	避孕套	*bìyùntào*
Mosquito coil	蚊香	*wénxiāng*
Mosquito netting	蚊帐纱	*wénzhàngshā*

the sound of each vowel followed by related-combination sounds.

a usually somewhere between f**a**r and m**a**n

ia as in y**a**k

ua as in s**ua**ve

ian as in y**en**

e usually as in f**u**r

ie as in y**eah**

ue as in the contraction of "you were", **y' were**

er as in b**ar** with a stressed "r"

en is an unstressed sound as at the end of hyph**en**

eng as in s**ung**

i usually as in b**e** or t**ea**

ai as in **eye**

ei as in g**ay**

uai as in **why**

ui as in **way**

Exceptions: in the words *zi, ci, si, ri, zhi, chi* and *shi*, "i" is a short clipped sound like the American military "s**ir**".

o as in b**o**re

uo as in w**o**re

ao as in c**ow**

u usually as in f**oo**l

ou as in sh**ow**

ü as in the German ü (make an "ee" sound and glide slowly into an "oo"; at the mid-point between the two sounds you should hit the ü-sound.

Exceptions: whenever the letter "u" follows j, q, x or y, it is always pronounced ü.

TRAVELLERS' TIBETAN

Although some people involved in the tourist industry are now conversant in several language including English, most Tibetans speak only their native language with perhaps a smattering of Mandarin. Even a few words of Tibetan are not only greeted enthusiastically but are well nigh essential if you're heading off the beaten track or going trekking.

Tibetan belongs to a small group of Tibeto-Burmese languages and has no similarity at all to Mandarin or Hindi. Tibetan script was developed in the seventh century and has thirty consonants and five vowels in its alphabet which are placed either beside, above or below other letters when written down. There are obvious inaccuracies when trying to render this into the Roman alphabet and the situation is further complicated by the many dialects across the region. The Lhasa dialect is given below. Word order is reversed for English speakers with the verb placed at the end. So "This noodle soup is delicious" becomes "tukpa dee shimbo do", literally "noodle soup this delicious is". The only sound you are likely to have trouble with is "ng" at the beginning of words – it is pronounced as in "sa**ng**".

Basic Phrases

Hello	tashi delay
Goodbye, to someone staying	kalay shu
Goodbye, to someone going	kalay pay
Thank you	tuk too jay
Sorry	gonda
Please	coochee
How are you?	kusu debo yinbay? or kam sangbo dugay?
I'm	nga ....
Fine	debo yin
Cold	kya
Hungry	throko- doe
Thirsty	ka gom
Tired	galay ka
I don't understand.	nga ha ko ma-song
What is your name?	kayranggi mingla karay ray?
My name is	ngeye mingla ..... sa
Where are you from?	kayrang kanay ray?
I'm from	nga .... nay yin
Britain	injee
Australia	otaleeya
America	amerika
How old are you?	kayrang lo katsay ray?
I'm	nga lo ...... yin
Where are you going?	kaba drogee yin?
I'm going to	nga ..... la drogee yin
Where is the....?	..... kaba doo?
hospital	menkang
monastery	gompa
temple/chapel	lhakhang
restaurant	sakang
convent	ani gompa
caretaker	konyer
Is there.....?	.... doo gay?
hot water	chu tsa-bo
a candle	yangla

I don't have	nga .... mindoo
Is this OK/ can I do this?	deegee rebay?
It's OK	deegee ray
It's not allowed	deegee maray
Good	yaggo doo
Not good	yaggo mindoo
This is delicious	dee shimbo doo
Do you want .....?	kayrang ..... gobay?
I want tea	nga cha go
I don't want this	dee me-go
What is this?	dee karray ray?
What is that?	day karray ray?
When?	kadoo?
Now	danta
Today	dering
Yesterday	kezang
Tomorrow	sangnyee
Sunday	sa nima
Monday	sa dowa
Tuesday	sa mingma
Wednesday	sa lagba
Thursday	sa purbur
Friday	sa pasang
Saturday	sa pemba
How much is this?	gong kadso ray?

Numbers

1	chee	20	nyi shoo
2	nyee	21	nyi shoo chee
3	soom	etc	
4	zhee	30	soom chew
5	nga	40	shib chew
6	droo	50	ngab chew
7	doon	60	drook chew
8	gyay	70	doon chew
9	goo	80	gyay chew
10	chew	90	goop chew
11	chew chee	100	gya
12	chew nyee	200	nyee gya
etc		etc	
		1000	dong

GLOSSARIES

GENERAL TERMS

Arhat Buddhist saint.

Bei North.

Binguan Hotel – generally a large one, for tourists.

Bodhisattva A follower of Buddhism who has attained enlightenment, but has chosen to stay on earth to teach rather than enter nirvana; Buddhist god or goddess.

Boxers The name given to an anti-foreign organization which originated in Shandong in 1898. Encouraged by the Qing Empress Dowager Cixi, they roamed China attacking Westernized Chinese and foreigners in what became known as the Boxer Rebellion (see p.1001).

CITS China International Travel Service. Tourist organization primarily interested in selling tours, but can also help with obtaining train tickets.

CTS China Travel Service. Tourist organization similar to *CITS*.

Concession Part of a town or city ceded to a foreign power in the nineteenth century.

Cultural Revloution Ten-year period beginning in 1966 and characterized by destruction, persecution and fanatical devotion to Mao (see p.1006).

Dagoba Another name for a stupa.

Dong East.

Dougong Large, carved wooden brackets, a common feature of temple design.

Fandian Restaurant or hotel.

Fen Smallest denomination of Chinese currency – there are one hundred fen to the yuan.

Feng Peak.

Feng shui meaning wind and water, a system of geomancy used to determine the positioning of buildings.

Foreign treaty port A port in which foreigners were permitted to set up residence, for the purpose of trade, under nineteenth-century agreements between China and foreign powers.

Gang of Four Mao's widow and her supporters who were put on trial immediately after Mao's death for their role in the Cultural Revolution, for which they were convenient scapegoats.

Gong Palace.

Grassland Areas of land too high or cold to support anything other than grass, and agriculturally useful only as pastureland for sheep or cattle. Especially in Inner Mongolia, Qinghai and Xinjiang.

Guan Pass.

Guanxi Literally "connections": the reciprocal favours inherent in the process of official appointments and transactions.

Guanyin The ubiquitous Buddhist Goddess of Mercy, who postponed her entry into paradise in order to help ease human misery. Derived from the Indian deity Avalokiteshvara, she is often depicted with up to a thousand arms.

Gulou Drum tower traditionally marking the centre of a town from which a drum was beaten at nightfall and in times of need.

Guomindang (GMD) The Nationalist Peoples' Party. Under Chiang Kaishek, the GMD fought Communist forces for 25 years before being defeated and moving to Taiwan in 1949, where it remains the major political party.

Hai Sea.

Han Chinese The main body of the Chinese people, as distinct from other ethnic groups such as Uigur, Miao, Hui, or Tibetan.

Hu Lake.

Hui Muslims, mainly based in Gansu and Ningxia. Officially a minority, the Hui are, in fact, ethnically indistinguishable from Han Chinese.

Hutong A narrow alleyway.

I Ching The Book of Changes, an ancient handbook for divination that includes some of the fundamental concepts of Chinese thought, such as the duality *yin* and *yang*.

Immortal Taoist saint.

Jiang River.

Jiao (or mao) Ten fen.

Jie Street.

Kang A raised wooden platform in a Chinese home, heated by the stove, on which the residents eat and sleep.

Kazakh A minority, mostly nomadic, in Xinjiang.

Ling Tomb.

Little Red Book A selection of "Quotations from Chairman Mao Zedong", produced in 1966 as a philisophical treatise for Red Guards during the Cultural Revolution.

Long March The Communists' 9500-kilometre tactical retreat in 1934–35 from Guomindang troops advancing on their base in the Jinggan Shan ranges, Jiangxi, to Yan'an in Shaanxi Province.

Lu Street.

Luohan Buddhist disciple.

Mandala Mystic diagram which forms an important part of Buddhist iconography, especially in Tibet.

Men Gate/door.

Miandi Cheap, yellow taxis; the name means bread loaf and is a reference to their boxy shape.

Miao Temple.

Middle Kingdom a literal translation of the Chinese words for China.

Nan South.

PLA The People's Liberation Army, the official name of the Communist military forces since 1949.

PSB Public Security Bureau, the branch of China's police force which deals directly with foreigners.

Pagoda Tower with distinctively tapering structure, often associated with pseudo-science of *feng shui*.

Pailou A freestanding wooden arch or gateway over a street, usually on the approach to a temple or palace.

Pinyin The official system of transliterating Chinese script into Roman characters.

Putonghua Mandarin Chinese; literally "Common Language".

Qianfodong Literally, "Thousand Buddha Cave", the name given to any Buddhist cave site along the Chinese section of the Silk Road.

Qiao Bridge.

RMB Renminbi. Another name for Chinese currency literally meaning "the people's money".

Red Guards The unruly factional forces unleashed by Mao during the Cultural Revolution to find and destroy brutally any "reactionaries" amongst the populace.

Renmin The people.

SEZ Special Economic Zone. A region in which state controls on production have been loosened and Western techniques of economic management are experimented with.

Sakyamuni Name given to future incarnation of Buddha.

Si Temple.

Shan Mountain.

Shui Water.

Spirit wall Wall behind the main gateway to a house, designed to thwart evil spirits, which, it was believed, could move only in straight lines.

Spirit Way The straight road leading to a tomb, lined with guardian figures.

Stele Freestanding stone tablet carved with text.

Stupa Multi-tiered tower associated with Buddhist temples that usually contains sacred objects.

Sutra Buddhist texts, often illustrative doctrines arranged in prayer form.

Ta Tower or pagoda.

Tantrism A strand of Buddhist thinking which emphasises the power of the will over bodily functions.

Taiping Uprising Peasant rebellion against Qing rule during the mid-nineteenth century, which saw over a million troops led by the Christian fanatic Hong Xiuquan establish a capital at Nanjing before their later annihilation at the hands of imperial forces.

Tian Heaven or the sky.

Uigur Substantial minority of Turkic people, living mainly in Xinjiang.

Waiguoren Foreigner.

Xi West.

Yuan China's unit of currency. Also a courtyard or garden (and the name of the Mongol dynasty).

Yurt Round, felt tent used by nomads. Also known as *ger*.

Zhan Station.

Zhao Temple; term used mainly in Inner Mongolia.

Zhong Middle; China is referred to as *zhong guo*, the Middle Kingdom.

Zhonglou Bell tower, usually twinned with a Gulou. The bell it contained was rung at doawn and in emergencies.

Zhou Place or region.

NOTABLE PEOPLE

Chiang Kaishek (1887–1975) Sun Yatsen's brother-in-law and, as leader of the Guomindang from 1925, relentless opponent of the Communist Party.

Cixi (d. 1908) Known as the Empress Dowager and a proud and ruthless autocrat who ruled China for thirty years presiding over the shabby demise of the Qing dynasty.

Deng Xiaoping China's premier since 1977. A veteran political survivor discredited three times during Mao's rule and a controversial leader, popular for his pragmatic policies.

Jiang Qing Mao's wife, a Shanghai movie star who helped orchestrate the Cultural Revolution and was later blamed for its excesses as one of the Gang of Four.

Kangxi (1661–1722) One of the greatest Qing emperors.

Lao She (1898–1966) One of China's greatest twentieth-century writers, persecuted during the Cultural Revolution but rehabilitated after his death. His most famous novel is *The Rickshaw Boy*, which, like most of his work, tells the story of the daily life of the poor in popular language, with an ear for the comic.

Lin Biao From 1968 to 1971 the heir apparent to Mao Zedong and a patron of extreme left-wing factions. Died (or killed) in a mysterious plane crash while attempting to flee China after a power struggle with Mao.

Lu Xun (1881–1936) China's greatest twentieth-century writer and satirist who gave up a promising medical career to write novels with the aim of curing the Chinese spirit from apathy. *The Story of Ah Q* and *Diary of a Madman* are the most influential of his works.

Mao Zedong (1893–1976) The Great Helmsman; poet, genius and despot who led China on its rocky course from 1949 until his death. The present official Chinese line on Mao is that he was seventy percent right and thirty percent wrong.

Puyi The last emperor, who ascended to the throne in 1908 at the age of two. The Qing dynasty collapsed soon afterwards and he was later used as a puppet emperor by the Japanese to legitimize their occupation of Manchuria.

Qianlong (1736–96) Qing emperor under whose reign the Chinese empire reached a zenith of size and prosperity.

Qin Shi Huang (221–210 BC) The first emperor of all China, famous for megalomania and tyranny, and for the Terracotta Army which guards his tomb.

Qu Yuan (340–280 BC) One of China's great poets, whose suicide by drowning is commemorated nationwide by annual dragon-boat races.

Sima Qian (145–85 BC) Having succeeded his father as court astrologer, Sima Qian spent his life compiling the *Historical Records*, the first history of China. After falling from court favour and being castrated as punishment, he consoled himself with the thought that now he could finish his book without distractions.

Su Dongpo (1036–1101) Sichuanese Song-dynasty official and famous poet, also known as Su Shi, whose politics saw him exiled from the court to Hunan and then Hainan Island.

Sun Yatsen (1866–1925) President of the short-lived Chinese Republic and revered by Communists and Guomindang alike for his life-long efforts to unify China and enfranchise the people.

Xuan Zang (602–664) A Tang-dynasty Buddhist monk who made the long trek to India alone in 629, studied under the finest Indian masters for sixteen years, then returned to spend the rest of his life translating the Buddhist classics into Chinese. His travels are the basis for the classic, *Journey to the West*.

Zhou Enlai China's prime minister (or premier) from 1949 to 1976. His memory is much loved in China.

Zhuge Liang (Kongming) The renowned *Three Kingdoms* strategist and governor of the state of Shu (Sichuan) from about 220 AD.

INDEX

The following abbreviations are used throughout this index:

AH Anhui
BJ Beijing
DB Dongbei
FJ Fujian
GD Guangdong
GS Gansu
GX Guangxi
GZ Guizhou
HEB Hebei
HEN Henan
HN Hainan
HUB Hubei
HUN Hunan
IM Inner Mongolia
JS Jiangsu
JX Jiangxi
NX Ningxia
QH Qinghai
SAX Shaanxi
SC Sichuan
SD Shandong
SX Shanxi
TB Tibet
XJ Xinjiang
YN Yunnan
ZJ Zhejiang

direct orders from

		£	US	CAN
Amsterdam	1-85828-086-9	£7.99	US$13.95	CAN$16.99
Andalucia	1-85828-094-X	8.99	14.95	18.99
Australia	1-85828-141-5	12.99	19.95	25.99
Bali	1-85828-134-2	8.99	14.95	19.99
Barcelona	1-85828-221-7	8.99	14.95	19.99
Berlin	1-85828-129-6	8.99	14.95	19.99
Brazil	1-85828-102-4	9.99	15.95	19.99
Britain	1-85828-208-X	12.99	19.95	25.99
Brittany & Normandy	1-85828-224-1	9.99	16.95	22.99
Bulgaria	1-85828-183-0	9.99	16.95	22.99
California	1-85828-181-4	10.99	16.95	22.99
Canada	1-85828-130-X	10.99	14.95	19.99
China	1-85828-225-X	15.99	24.95	32.95
Corsica	1-85828-089-3	8.99	14.95	18.99
Costa Rica	1-85828-136-9	9.99	15.95	21.99
Crete	1-85828-132-6	8.99	14.95	18.99
Cyprus	1-85828-182-2	9.99	16.95	22.99
Czech & Slovak Republics	1-85828-121-0	9.99	16.95	22.99
Egypt	1-85828-188-1	10.99	17.95	23.99
Europe	1-85828-159-8	14.99	19.95	25.99
England	1-85828-160-1	10.99	17.95	23.99
First Time Europe	1-85828-270-5	7.99	9.95	12.99
Florida	1-85828-184-4	10.99	16.95	22.99
France	1-85828-124-5	10.99	16.95	21.99
Germany	1-85828-128-8	11.99	17.95	23.99
Goa	1-85828-156-3	8.99	14.95	19.99
Greece	1-85828-131-8	9.99	16.95	20.99
Greek Islands	1-85828-163-6	8.99	14.95	19.99
Guatemala	1-85828-189-X	10.99	16.95	22.99
Hawaii: Big Island	1-85828-158-X	8.99	12.95	16.99
Hawaii	1-85828-206-3	10.99	16.95	22.99
Holland, Belgium & Luxembourg	1-85828-087-7	9.99	15.95	20.99
Hong Kong	1-85828-187-3	8.99	14.95	19.99
Hungary	1-85828-123-7	8.99	14.95	19.99
India	1-85828-200-4	14.99	23.95	31.99
Ireland	1-85828-179-2	10.99	17.95	23.99
Italy	1-85828-167-9	12.99	19.95	25.99
Kenya	1-85828-192-X	11.99	18.95	24.99
London	1-85828-231-4	9.99	15.95	21.99
Mallorca & Menorca	1-85828-165-2	8.99	14.95	19.99
Malaysia, Singapore & Brunei	1-85828-103-2	9.99	16.95	20.99
Mexico	1-85828-044-3	10.99	16.95	22.99
Morocco	1-85828-040-0	9.99	16.95	21.99
Moscow	1-85828-118-0	8.99	14.95	19.99
Nepal	1-85828-190-3	10.99	17.95	23.99
New York	1-85828-171-7	9.99	15.95	21.99
Pacific Northwest	1-85828-092-3	9.99	14.95	19.99
Paris	1-85828-235-7	8.99	14.95	19.99

In the UK, Rough Guides are available from all good bookstores, but can be obtained from Penguin by contacting: Penguin Direct, Penguin Books Ltd, Bath Road, Harmondsworth, Middlesex UB7 0DA; or telephone the credit line on 0181-899 4036 (9am–5pm) and ask for Penguin Direct. Visa, Access and Amex accepted. Delivery will normally be within 14 working days. Penguin Direct ordering facilities are only available in the UK and the USA. The availability and published prices quoted are correct at the time of going to press but are subject to alteration without prior notice.

around the world

Poland	1-85828-168-7	10.99	17.95	23.99
Portugal	1-85828-180-6	9.99	16.95	22.99
Prague	1-85828-122-9	8.99	14.95	19.99
Provence	1-85828-127-X	9.99	16.95	22.99
Pyrenees	1-85828-093-1	8.99	15.95	19.99
Rhodes & the Dodecanese	1-85828-120-2	8.99	14.95	19.99
Romania	1-85828-097-4	9.99	15.95	21.99
San Francisco	1-85828-185-7	8.99	14.95	19.99
Scandinavia	1-85828-039-7	10.99	16.99	21.99
Scotland	1-85828-166-0	9.99	16.95	22.99
Sicily	1-85828-178-4	9.99	16.95	22.99
Singapore	1-85828-135-0	8.99	14.95	19.99
Spain	1-85828-240-3	11.99	18.95	24.99
St Petersburg	1-85828-133-4	8.99	14.95	19.99
Thailand	1-85828-140-7	10.99	17.95	24.99
Tunisia	1-85828-139-3	10.99	17.95	24.99
Turkey	1-85828-242-X	12.99	19.95	25.99
Tuscany & Umbria	1-85828-243-8	10.99	17.95	23.99
USA	1-85828-161-X	14.99	19.95	25.99
Venice	1-85828-170-9	8.99	14.95	19.99
Vietnam	1-85828-191-1	9.99	15.95	21.99
Wales	1-85828-245-4	10.99	17.95	23.99
Washington DC	1-85828-246-2	8.99	14.95	19.99
West Africa	1-85828-101-6	15.99	24.95	34.99
More Women Travel	1-85828-098-2	9.99	14.95	19.99
Zimbabwe & Botswana	1-85828-186-5	11.99	18.95	24.99
Phrasebooks				
Czech	1-85828-148-2	3.50	5.00	7.00
French	1-85828-144-X	3.50	5.00	7.00
German	1-85828-146-6	3.50	5.00	7.00
Greek	1-85828-145-8	3.50	5.00	7.00
Italian	1-85828-143-1	3.50	5.00	7.00
Mexican	1-85828-176-8	3.50	5.00	7.00
Portuguese	1-85828-175-X	3.50	5.00	7.00
Polish	1-85828-174-1	3.50	5.00	7.00
Spanish	1-85828-147-4	3.50	5.00	7.00
Thai	1-85828-177-6	3.50	5.00	7.00
Turkish	1-85828-173-3	3.50	5.00	7.00
Vietnamese	1-85828-172-5	3.50	5.00	7.00
Reference				
Classical Music	1-85828-113-X	12.99	19.95	25.99
Internet	1-85828-198-9	5.00	8.00	10.00
Jazz	1-85828-137-7	16.99	24.95	34.99
Opera	1-85828-138-5	16.99	24.95	34.99
Reggae	1-85828-247-0	12.99	19.95	25.99
Rock	1-85828-201-2	17.99	26.95	35.00
World Music	1-85828-017-6	16.99	22.95	29.99

In the USA, or for international orders, charge your order by Master Card or Visa (US$15.00 minimum order): call 1-800-253-6476; or send orders, with complete name, address and zip code, and list price, plus $2.00 shipping and handling per order to: Consumer Sales, Penguin USA, PO Box 999 – Dept #17109, Bergenfield, NJ 07621. No COD. Prepay foreign orders by international money order, a cheque drawn on a US bank, or US currency. No postage stamps are accepted. All orders are subject to stock availability at the time they are processed. Refunds will be made for books not available at that time. Please allow a minimum of four weeks for delivery.

Good Vibrations!

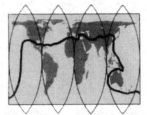